July 29–August 2, 2019
Toronto, ON, Canada

Association for
Computing Machinery

Advancing Computing as a Science & Profession

PODC '19

Proceedings of the 2019 ACM Symposium on
Principles of Distributed Computing

Sponsored by:

ACM SIGACT & ACM SIGOPS

Supported by:

ORACLE, VMWARE, and Uber

Association for
Computing Machinery

Advancing Computing as a Science & Profession

The Association for Computing Machinery
1601 Broadway, 10th Floor
New York, NY 10019-7434

ISBN: 978-1-4503-6670-0 (Digital)

ISBN: 978-1-4503-6217-7 (Print)

Additional copies may be ordered prepaid from:

ACM Order Department
PO Box 30777
New York, NY 10087-0777, USA

Phone: 1-800-342-6626 (USA and Canada)
+1-212-626-0500 (Global)
Fax: +1-212-944-1318
E-mail: acmhelp@acm.org
Hours of Operation: 8:30 am – 4:30 pm ET

PODC 2019 Chairs' Preface

The ACM Symposium on Principles of Distributed Computing (PODC) is the premier international forum on the theory, design, analysis, implementation and application of distributed systems and networks. PODC is sponsored by the ACM Special Interest Group on Algorithms and Computation Theory, SIGACT, and the ACM Special Interest Group in Operating Systems, SIGOPS.

These proceedings contain the papers presented at PODC 2019, the 38th Symposium on Principles of Distributed Computing, held from July 27 to August 2, 2019 in Toronto, Canada. It also includes the citations for two awards jointly sponsored by PODC and the EATCS Symposium on Distributed Computing (DISC), the Edsger W. Dijkstra Prize in Distributed Computing, and the Principles of Distributed Computing Doctoral Dissertation Award.

The 2019 Edsger W. Dijkstra Prize in Distributed Computing will be presented at DISC 2019 in Budapest, Hungary, to Alessandro Panconesi and Aravind Srinivasan for their paper *Randomized Distributed Edge Coloring via an Extension of the Chernoff–Hoeffding Bounds*, which appeared in SIAM Journal on Computing, volume 26, number 2, 1997, pages 350–368.

The 2019 Principles of Distributed Computing Doctoral Dissertation Award was presented to Sepehr Assadi for his dissertation *Combinatorial Optimization on Massive Datasets: Streaming, Distributed, and Massively Parallel Computation*, supervised by Professor Sanjeev Khanna at the University of Pennsylvania.

There were 173 regular papers and 21 brief announcements submitted to the symposium. The program committee accepted 48 papers, each of which has a paper of up to 10 pages in these proceedings. In addition, the committee accepted 19 brief announcements (11 of which were submitted as regular papers). Each brief announcement has a paper of up to 3 pages in these proceedings.

Every submitted paper was read and evaluated by at least three members of the program committee and discussed using HotCRP. The committee was assisted by more than 170 external reviewers. Final decisions were made during a meeting held at the University of Toronto on April 28, 2019, although roughly three quarters of the committee participated via teleconference. Revised and expanded versions of several selected papers will be considered for publication in a special issue of the journal Distributed Computing and in the Journal of ACM.

The Best Paper Award was presented to Yi-Jun Chang and Thatchaphol Saranurak for their paper *Improved Distributed Expander Decomposition and Nearly Optimal Triangle Enumeration.* The Best Student Paper Award was presented to Yi-Jun Chang, Manuela Fischer, and Yufan Zheng for their paper *The Complexity of* $(\Delta + 1)$ *Coloring in Congested Clique, Massively Parallel Computation, and Centralized Local Computation*, coauthored with Mohsen Ghaffari and Jara Uitto, and to Michal Dory and Dean Leitersdorf for their paper *Fast Approximate Shortest Paths in the Congested Clique*, coauthored with Keren Censor-Hillel and Janne Korhonen.

The program included three keynote lectures by Philipp Woelfel (University of Calgary), Ronitt Rubinfeld (MIT and Tel Aviv University), and Ilya Sergey (Yale-NUS College and National University of Singapore).

There were two workshops co-located with PODC, the *7th Workshop on Biological Distributed Algorithms (BDA 2019)* and the *Workshop on Security of Permissionless Systems (SPS 2019).*

There were also four tutorials, *From Classical to Blockchain Consensus: What are the Exact Algorithms?*, by Y. Annie Liu and Scott D. Stoller, *Byzantine Fault Tolerant State Machine Replication in Any Programming Language*, by Ethan Buchman, *Central Control over Distributed Asynchronous Systems: A Tutorial on Software-Defined Networks and Consistent Network Updates*, by Klaus-Tycho Foerster, and *Specifying, Implementing, and Verifying Algorithms for Persistent Memory*, by Wojciech Golab.

We thank the program committee and the external reviewers, who worked hard reviewing papers and providing valuable feedback to the authors. The steering committee provided helpful guidance and the conference committee did a great job with the finances, publicity, tutorials, workshops, proceedings, and local arrangements. Finally, we thank our sponsors, SIGACT and SIGOPS, and our corporate supporters, Oracle, Uber, and VMware.

Faith Ellen
Program Committee Chair
University of Toronto, Canada

Peter Robinson
General Chair
City University of Hong Kong

Table of Co ntents

Session 3

Keynote Lecture 2

Session 4

Session 5

Session 6

Keynote Lecture 3

Session 7

PODC 2019 Organization

General Chair: Peter Robinson (*City University of Hong Kong*)
Program Committee Chair: Faith Ellen (*University of Toronto, Canada*)
Organizing chair: Wojciech Golab (*University of Waterloo, Canada*)
Workshop chair: Avery Miller (*University of Manitoba, Canada*)
Treasurer: Yuval Emek (*Technion, Israel*)
Communication Chair: Christian Konrad (*University of Bristol, UK*)
Proceedings Chair: Thomas Nowak (*Université Paris-Sud, France*)
Publicity: Mark Tuttle (*Amazon, USA*)
Student Travel Grant Coordinator: Sebastian Brandt (*ETH Zurich, Switzerland*)
Steering Committee Chair: Jennifer Welch (*Texas A&M University, USA*)
Steering Committee:
Lorenzo Alvisi (*Cornell University, USA*)
Faith Ellen (*University of Toronto, Canada*)
Yuval Emek (*Technion, Israel*)
Idit Keidar (*Technion, Israel*)
Peter Robinson (*City University of Hong Kong*)
Alexander Schwarzmann (*Augusta University, USA*)

Program Committee:
James Aspnes (*Yale University, USA*)
Hagit Attiya (*Technion, Israel*)
Borzoo Bonakdarpour (*Iowa State University, USA*)
Trevor Brown (*University of Waterloo, Canada*)
Armando Castañeda (*UNAM, Mexico*)
Faith Ellen (*University of Toronto, Canada*)
Panagiota Fatourou (*FORTH and University of Crete, Greece*)
Cyril Gavoille (*LaBRI–University of Bordeaux, France*)
Juan Garay (*Texas A&M University, USA*)
Leszek Gasieniec (*University of Liverpool, UK*)
Rati Gelashvili (*NeuralMagic, USA*)
Maurice Herlihy (*Brown University, USA*)
Valerie King (*University of Victoria, Canada*)
Janne Korhonen (*Aalto University, Finland*)
Fabian Kuhn (*University of Freiburg, Germany*)
Christoph Lenzen (*Max Planck Institut für Informatik, Germany*)
Rotem Oshman (*Tel Aviv University, Israel*)
David Peleg (*Weizmann Institute, Israel*)
Thomas Sauerwald (*Cambridge University, UK*)
Michael L. Scott (*University of Rochester, USA*)
Christian Scheideler (*Paderborn University, Germany*)
Marc Shapiro (*Sorbonne Université–Inria, France*)
Hsin-Hao Su (*Boston College, USA*)
Amitabh Trehan (*Loughborough University, UK*)
Philipp Woelfel (*University of Calgary, Canada*)
Vinod Vaikuntanathan (*MIT, USA*)

External Reviewers:

Gagan Agrawal
Jade Alglave
Dan Alistarh
Saeed Amiri
Karolos Antoniadis
Sepehr Assadi
John Augustine
Chen Avin
Alkida Balliu
Carlos Baquero
Leonid Barenboim
H. Alan Beadle
Ohad Ben-Baruch
Gary Bennett
Béatrice Bérard
Petra Berenbrink
Jan van den Brand
Manuel Bravo
David Budden
Johannes Bund
Christian Cachin
Keren Censor-Hillel
Yi-Jun Chang
Shiri Chechik
Vicent Cholvi
Chi-Ning Chou
Nachshon Cohen
Ran Cohen
Artur Czumaj
Thierry Delisle
Thomas Dickerson
Diego Didona
Klim Efremenko
Michael Elkin
Robert Elsaesser
Yuval Emek
Constantin Enea
Hugues Fauconnier
Michael Feldmann
Manuela Fischer
Orr Fischer
Klaus-Tycho Foerster
Michal Friedman
Matthias Fuegger
George Giakkoupis
Yossi Gilad
Seth Gilbert
Mehrdad Jafari Giv
Wojciech Golab
Thorsten Götte
Spyridoula Gravani
Joseph Halpern
Sara Salem Hamouda
Kenneth Hancock
David Harris
Mohammad Hedayati
Danny Hendler
Kristian Hinnenthal
Juho Hirvonen
Zengfeng Huang
Connor Imes
Joe Izraelevitz
Prasad Jayanti
Stacey Jeffery
Anup Joshi
Tomasz Jurdzinski
Dominik Kaaser
Nikolaos Kallimanis
Eleni Kanellou
Idit Keidar
Seri Khourry
Ralf Klasing
Peter Kling
Christina Kolb
Amos Korman
Eleftherios Kosmas
Dariusz Kowalski
Ajay Kshemkalyani
Petr Kuznetsov
Hung Viet Le
Francois Le Gall
Tuomo Lempiäinen
Stefano Leucci
Reut Levi
Nan Li
Quanquan Liu
Tianren Liu
Darrell Long
Nuno Lopez
Zvi Lotker
Kostas Magoutis
Virendra Marathe
Loris Marchal
Ali Mashreghi
Moti Medina
Uri Meir
Ricardo Mercelin
Andrew Miller
Adam Morrison
William K. Moses Jr.
Achour Mostefaoui
Giorgi Nadiradze
Lars Nagel
Danupon Nanongkai
Ram Prasadh Narayanan
Neha Narula
Yiannis Nikolakopoulos
Dennis Olivetti
Sean Ovens
Sreepathi Pai
Roberto Palmieri
Giorgos Panagiotakos
Gopal Pandurangan
Merav Parter
Boaz Patt-Shamir
Ami Paz
Andrzej Pelc
Sebastiano Peluso
Richard Peng
Matthieu Perrin
Erez Petrank
Gustavo Petri
Maria Potop-Butucaru
Amaury Pouly
Philippe Queinnec
Vijaya Ramachandran
Ling Ren
Isaac Richter
Thibault Rieutord
Noam Rinetzky
Philippe Robert
Peter Robinson
Luís Rodrigues
Paolo Romano
Matthieu Roy
Will Rosenbaum
Eric Ruppert
Joel Rybicki
Jared Saia
Iosif Salem
Raghuvansh Saxena
Philipp Schneider
Michele Scquizzato
Adam Sealfon
Alexander Setzer
William Sigouin
Alexader Spiegelman
Paul Spirakis
Grzegorz Stachowiak
Pierre Sutra
Francois Taiani
Gadi Taubenfeld
Gaël Thomas
Ilyas Toumlilt
Lewis Tseng
Fung Po Tso
Przemysław Uznański
Viktor Vafeiadis
Hoa Vu
Nicole Wein
Jennifer Welch
Haosen Wen
Ben Wiederhake
Xiaodi Wu
Yukiko Yamauchi
Penghui Yao
Maxwell Young
Qi Zhang
Leqi Zhu
Vassilis Zikas
Aleksandar Zlateski

PODC 2019 Sponsors & Supporters

Sponsors:

SIGACT

acm SIGOPS

Sponsors:

ORACLE®

vmware®

Uber

2019 Edsger W. Dijkstra Prize in Distributed Computing

The Edsger W. Dijkstra Prize in Distributed Computing is awarded for outstanding papers on the principles of distributed computing, whose significance and impact on the theory or practice of distributed computing have been evident for at least a decade. It is sponsored jointly by the ACM Symposium on Principles of Distributed Computing (PODC) and the EATCS Symposium on Distributed Computing (DISC). The prize is presented annually, with the presentation taking place alternately at PODC and DISC.

The committee decided to award the 2019 Edsger W. Dijkstra Prize in Distributed Computing to

Alessandro Panconesi and Aravind Srinivasan

for their paper

Randomized Distributed Edge Coloring via an Extension of the Chernoff–Hoeffding Bounds, *SIAM Journal on Computing*, volume 26, number 2, 1997, pages 350–368.

A preliminary version of this paper appeared as "Fast Randomized Algorithms for Distributed Edge Coloring", *Proceedings of the Eleventh Annual ACM Symposium Principles of Distributed Computing (PODC)*, 1992, pages 251–262.

The paper presents a simple synchronous algorithm in which processes at the nodes of an undirected network color its edges so that the edges adjacent to each node have different colors. It is randomized, using $1.6\Delta + O(\log^{1+\delta} n)$ colors and $O(\log n)$ rounds with high probability for any constant $\delta > 0$, where n is the number of nodes and Δ is the maximum degree of the nodes. This was the first nontrivial distributed algorithm for the edge coloring problem and has influenced a great deal of follow-up work. Edge coloring has applications to many other problems in distributed computing such as routing, scheduling, contention resolution, and resource allocation.

In spite of its simplicity, the analysis of their edge coloring algorithm is highly nontrivial. Chernoff–Hoeffding bounds, which assume random variables to be independent, cannot be used. Instead, they develop upper bounds for sums of negatively correlated random variables, for example, which arise when sampling without replacement. More generally, they extend Chernoff–Hoeffding bounds to certain random variables they call λ-correlated. This has directly inspired more specialized concentration inequalities. The new techniques they introduced have also been applied to the analyses of important randomized algorithms in a variety of areas including optimization, machine learning, cryptography, streaming, quantum computing, and mechanism design.

2019 Award Committee:
Lorenzo Alvisi, *Cornell University*
Shlomi Dolev, *Ben Gurion University*
Faith Ellen (chair), *University of Toronto*
Idit Keidar, *Technion*
Fabian Kuhn, *University of Freiburg*
Jukka Suomela, *Aalto University*

2019 Principles of Distributed Computing Doctoral Dissertation Award

The winner of the 2019 Principles of Distributed Computing Doctoral Dissertation Award is

Dr. Sepehr Assadi

for his dissertation

Combinatorial Optimization on Massive Datasets: Streaming, Distributed, and Massively Parallel Computation,

written under the supervision of Prof. Sanjeev Khanna at the University of Pennsylvania.

The thesis resolves a number of long-standing problems in the exciting and still relatively new area of sublinear computation. The area of sublinear computation focuses on design of algorithms that use sublinear space, time, or communication to solve global optimization problems on very large datasets. In addition to addressing a wide range of different problems, comprising graph optimization problems (matching, vertex cover, and connectivity), submodular optimization (set cover and maximum coverage), and resource-constrained optimization (combinatorial auctions and learning), these problems are studied in three different models of computation, namely, streaming algorithms, multiparty communication, and massively parallel computation (MPC). The thesis also reveals interesting relations between these different models, including generic algorithmic and analysis techniques that can be applied in all of them.

For many fundamental optimization problems, the thesis gives asymptotically matching algorithmic and intractability results, completely resolving several long-standing problems. This is accomplished by using a broad spectrum of mathematical methods in very detailed and intricate proofs. In addition to a wide variety of classic techniques, ranging from graph theory, combinatorics, probability, linear algebra and calculus, it also makes heavy use of communication complexity and information theory, for example.

Sepehr's dissertation work has been published in a remarkably large number of top-conference papers. It received multiple best paper awards and multiple special issue invitations, as well as two invitations to the Highlights of Algorithms (HALG) conference. Due to its contributions to the field of distributed computing and all the merits mentioned above, the award committee unanimously selected this thesis as the winner of the 2019 Principles of Distributed Computing Doctoral Dissertation Award.

The award is sponsored jointly by the ACM Symposium on Principles of Distributed Computing (PODC) and the EATCS Symposium on Distributed Computing (DISC). It is presented annually, with the presentation taking place alternately at PODC and DISC. The 2019 award was presented at PODC 2019 in Toronto, Canada.

2019 Award Committee:
Prasad Jayanti, *Dartmouth College*
Nancy A. Lynch, *MIT*
Boaz Patt-Shamir, *Tel Aviv University*
Ulrich Schmid (chair), *TU Wien*

Local Computation Algorithms

Ronitt Rubinfeld
Massachusetts Institute of Technology & Tel Aviv University
Cambridge, MA and Tel Aviv, Israel
ronitt@csail.mit.edu

ABSTRACT

Consider a setting in which inputs to and outputs from a computational problem are so large, that there is not time to read them in their entirety. However, if one is only interested in small parts of the output at any given time, is it really necessary to solve the entire computational problem? Is it even necessary to view the whole input? We survey recent work in the model of "local computation algorithms" which for a given input, supports queries by a user to values of specified bits of a legal output. The goal is to design local computation algorithms in such a way that very little of the input needs to be seen in order to determine the value of any single bit of the output. Though this model describes sequential computations, techniques from local distributed algorithms have been extremely important in designing efficient local computation algorithms.

In this talk, we describe results on a variety of problems for which sublinear time and space local computation algorithms have been developed -- we will give special focus to finding maximal independent sets and sparse spanning graphs.

CCS Concepts/ACM Classifiers

Graph algorithms analysis; Sublinear algorithms; Distributed algorithms; Sparsification and Spanners.

Author Keywords

Sublinear time algorithms; randomized algorithms; approximation algorithms.

ACM ISBN 978-1-4503-6670-0/19/06.
DOI: https://doi.org/10.1145/3293611.3331587

BIOGRAPHY

Ronitt Rubinfeld is a professor of Electrical Engineering and Computer Science at MIT and a professor of Computer Science at Tel-Aviv University.

Her research interests include randomized algorithms and computational complexity. She works in the fields of Property Testing and Sub-linear Time Algorithms, which provide the foundations for measuring the performance of algorithms that analyze data without looking at all of it. Ronitt Rubinfeld was an invited speaker at the International Congress of Mathematicians in 2006 and is an ACM Fellow.

Symmetry Breaking in the Plane: Rendezvous by Robots with Unknown Attributes

Jurek Czyzowicz*
Département d'informatique, Université du Québec en Outaouais
Gatineau, QC, Canada

Leszek Gąsieniec†
Department of Computer Science, University of Liverpool
Liverpool, UK

Ryan Killick‡
School of Computer Science, Carleton University
Ottawa, ON, Canada

Evangelos Kranakis*
School of Computer Science, Carleton University
Ottawa, ON, Canada

ABSTRACT

We study a fundamental question related to the feasibility of deterministic symmetry breaking in the infinite Euclidean plane for two robots that have minimal or no knowledge of the respective capabilities and "measuring instruments" of themselves and each other. Assume that two anonymous mobile robots are placed at different locations at unknown distance d from each other on the infinite Euclidean plane. Each robot knows neither the location of itself nor of the other robot. The robots cannot communicate wirelessly, but have a certain nonzero visibility radius r (with range r unknown to the robots). By rendezvous we mean that they are brought at distance at most r of each other by executing symmetric (identical) mobility algorithms. The robots are moving with unknown and constant but not necessarily identical speeds, their clocks and pedometers may be asymmetric, and their chirality inconsistent.

We demonstrate that rendezvous for two robots is feasible under the studied model iff the robots have either: different speeds; or different clocks; or different orientations but equal chiralities. When the rendezvous is feasible, we provide a universal algorithm which always solves rendezvous despite the fact that the robots have no knowledge of which among their respective parameters may be different.

CCS CONCEPTS

• **Theory of computation → Distributed algorithms.**

KEYWORDS

anonymous, asymmetric clock, chirality, competitive ratio, infinite plane, rendezvous, mobile robot, speed

*Research supported in part by NSERC Discovery grant.
†Research supported in part by the University of Liverpool initiative Networks Sciences and Technologies (NeST)
‡Research supported by the NSERC Canada Graduate Scholarship.

PODC '19, July 29-August 2, 2019, Toronto, ON, Canada

ACM ISBN 978-1-4503-6217-7/19/07...$15.00
https://doi.org/10.1145/3293611.3331608

ACM Reference Format:
Jurek Czyzowicz, Leszek Gąsieniec, Ryan Killick, and Evangelos Kranakis. 2019. Symmetry Breaking in the Plane: Rendezvous by Robots with Unknown Attributes. In *2019 ACM Symposium on Principles of Distributed Computing (PODC '19), July 29-August 2, 2019, Toronto, ON, Canada.* ACM, New York, NY, USA, 10 pages. https://doi.org/10.1145/3293611.3331608

1 INTRODUCTION

Two anonymous robots (represented as points) are placed at unknown but different locations on the infinite Euclidean plane. They can move with constant speeds (which are not guaranteed to be different), their clocks may be asymmetric (they do not run on the same time unit), the distance units they may be able to measure may be different, their orientation and chirality possibly inconsistent, and their initial Euclidean distance unknown to them. To make matters worse, the robots not only cannot communicate wirelessly, but also all of the above parameters, namely moving-speed, clock-speed, distance-unit, orientation, and chirality, are unknown to them. The only ability the robots have is limited visibility so they can see each other only if they are within a given range, albeit this is also unknown to them and its magnitude may not be related in any way to their initial distance.

The question arising in this setting is: can the two robots rendezvous? I.e., can they meet at the same point in the plane? It is not at all obvious that a solution could exist in the general setting described above, where knowledge of their moving-speeds, and the consistency of their clock-speeds, distance-units, orientations, and chiralities cannot be assured. In fact, it might even seem counterintuitive that the problem could be solvable. But if it were, one would want to know what strategies should the robots employ so as to minimize their rendezvous time. Note that the robots operate in the infinite Euclidean plane on which each robot may move with its constant speed. We are interested in symmetric rendezvous so that the robots must execute the same strategy as opposed to the corresponding asymmetric rendezvous problem which may have an optimal solution if one robot waits at its original location while the other is searching for it.

The fundamental problem in the question posed above is related to the feasibility of deterministic rendezvous. More broadly, one is interested to identify the parameters of the given model under which rendezvous is possible to achieve in finite time. Evidently, the overall concern of any strategy is how to break symmetry.

However, unlike traditional ways of symmetry breaking where a robot can make use of *unconcealed* parameters, such as tokens, markers, white-boards, and labels, in our setting we are interested in the possibility of rendezvous under *unknown built-in attributes*, which include parameters important to the operation of the robots, such as moving-speed, clock-speed, distance-unit, orientation, and chirality, which may not have to be revealed by the robots during the execution of the rendezvous algorithm. Our overall objective is to design algorithms that prove the feasibility of rendezvous in such a constrained environment and whenever possible achieve good performance for the time spent by the robots to rendezvous.

In the present paper we show how two robots placed at unknown distance in the Euclidean plane can break symmetry when some of their unknown built-in attributes, including moving-speed, clock-speed, distance-unit, orientation, and chirality are different, and in some instances leading to a universal algorithm which guarantees rendezvous. Furthermore, and contrary to the case of rendezvous for robots with unconcealed parameters studied in the past, knowledge as to which of the parameters is different may be unnecessary and in any case may not even be given as input to the algorithm. Moreover our robots are completely unaware of the value(s) of their individual hidden parameters and do not make use of them in the computations needed to run the algorithm.

When no parameter of our scenario permits to break symmetry, the robots walk indefinitely and the rendezvous never takes place. However, as the robots have no knowledge of their parameters, it is obvious that they can never stop their walks and conclude that the rendezvous is indeed infeasible.

1.1 Model

We consider the symmetric rendezvous problem of two mobile robots $\mathcal{R}$ and $\mathcal{R}'$ modeled as points on the infinite Euclidean plane. The robots are initially located an unknown distance d from each other and each has a non-zero radius of visibility r. The rendezvous problem is solved the first time that the robots see each other, i.e. the first time they are a distance at most r from each other. The robots must employ the same algorithm in order to rendezvous. We assume that robots can store and compute real numbers with arbitrary precision.

We consider a model in which each robot has its own constant speed and in which each is equipped with a clock and compass allowing them to respectively measure their travel time and travel direction. We assume that robots can use their clocks to measure arbitrarily small time intervals. Each robot will consider itself as the origin of its own coordinate system and it will use its clock and compass to fix the distance unit (the product of its speed and local time unit) and orientation of its coordinate axes. We explicitly consider the possibility that the robots have different speeds, clocks, and/or compasses. We study algorithms which progress in a synchronous and continuous time model (i.e. robots are always active) and where robots can be instructed to move to any real position on the plane.

Without loss of generality, we will present our analysis from the viewpoint of the robot $\mathcal{R}$ and thus assume that this robot has maximum unit speed, and that its clock and compass are "correct" in the sense that they agree with some predefined global coordinate system. On the other hand, we set the speed of $\mathcal{R}'$ as $v > 0$; its time unit as $\tau > 0$; its orientation as $\phi \in [0, 2\pi)$; and its chirality as $\chi = \pm 1$. The overall effect of these differences in *reference frames* is that the robots will follow different trajectories despite them using the same algorithm. More specifically, $v \neq 1$ implies the robots have different speeds and will therefore travel different distances in the same unit of time; $\tau \neq 1$ implies that one time unit as measured by the clock of $\mathcal{R}'$ will in fact be τ time units as measured by that of $\mathcal{R}$; $\phi \in [0, 2\pi)$ implies that the coordinate axes of $\mathcal{R}'$ have been rotated (counter-clockwise) by an angle ϕ with respect to those of $\mathcal{R}$; and $\chi = -1$ implies that $\mathcal{R}'$ and $\mathcal{R}$ disagree on the $+y$ direction.

1.2 Related work

Rendezvous problems are well-known in the scientific literature. They are not only of theoretical interest due to the fundamental challenges one encounters to provide adequate mathematical solutions. They are also encountered in numerous applications which include the fields of operations research, search and rescue operations and planning in the mathematical sciences, as well as process synchronization, operating system design, and message sharing in computer science.

The rendezvous problem was first introduced informally in 1976 by Steve Alpern in [2] who later also formulated and formalized the continuous time version of the problem in [1]. A further impetus to the problem was given by the seminal book treatment [3] where rendezvous was viewed as a search-game between two players having the converging goal in that they are aiming to find one another as quickly as possible.

Numerous papers on rendezvous followed, covering several cases depending on various parameters of the model: type of environment (graph or geometric), robot's knowledge about the environment (partial or complete), anonymity of the robot (labeled or not), robot movement mode (synchronous, semi-synchronous or asynchronous), algorithm type (deterministic or randomized), reliability issues related to robot instruments, etc. A survey covering deterministic rendezvous algorithms is presented in [26] while the monograph [23] is dedicated to the ring and torus.

Many papers on rendezvous adopt the discrete model, e.g., where the robots may meet only at graph nodes (e.g., [27]). In the continuous model for graphs, it is possible to consider the agents' meeting in the interior of graph edges (e.g., [16]). However, when the continuous environment is a two-dimensional plane it is necessary to equip robots with devices permitting non-zero visibility, i.e. the rendezvous arises when the robots belong to each other's visibility range (e.g., see [4]).

Our formulation and analysis of rendezvous is based on the continuous time model in which robots are always active. Recent studies in this model include [22, 24] in which the authors focus on distributed local protocols concerning swarms that result in formations like "gathering at one point". In [12] gathering at a point in the plane is analyzed when some of the robots may be faulty. They design algorithms which achieve gathering of all reliable robots within the smallest possible time. In fact, they minimize the competitive ratio, defined as the ratio of the time required to achieve gathering of the reliable robots, to the time required for such gathering to occur under the assumption that the reliable robots were known in advance.

The rendezvous (and its more general version of gathering) problem has also been studied for robots with different speeds [6, 17], inconsistent compasses [8, 20] and chirality or sense of direction [5, 7]. In [19] the authors study the feasibility of gathering by mobile robots that have ϕ-absolute error dynamic compasses, which allows the angle difference between a local coordinate system and the global coordinate system to vary with time in the range of $[0, \phi]$. In [21] a gathering problem is discussed for robots equipped with inaccurate (incorrect) compasses which may point a different direction from other robots' compasses. However, in the studies previously mentioned, these differences were obstacles that needed to be circumvented by the suggested algorithms, rather than used for the benefit of the proposed approach, which is the case of the present paper. To the best of our knowledge, rendezvous in the plane for two robots with unknown attributes in continuous time has never been studied before.

The fundamental issue of the rendezvous problem is *symmetry breaking*, for example by exploiting some specific parameter(s) of the model that permit robots to act differently and not to be trapped in the same relative position to one another (cf. [26]). If there is no such parameter available it may be shown that the rendezvous is infeasible (e.g., [15]). For rendezvous in graph environments, the symmetry may be broken using asymmetry in the graph topology or the robots' positions within it (see [13]). In the case of rendezvous in the two-dimensional plane this is not possible and a symmetry-breaking procedure may exploit, for example, the difference of the robots labels [14, 16] or robot's knowledge of its own position in the Cartesian plane [9]. In all these cases the designer of the rendezvous algorithm needs to know what is this parameter of the studied scenario that permits the symmetry breaking. In the present paper it is shown that the knowledge, which of the parameters of the studied scenario makes the rendezvous possible, is not necessary.

Closely related to our current work is [11] which considers rendezvous of two anonymous robots on an infinite line when their walking speed and time units (which are unknown to the robots) may or may not be the same. The authors introduced the new concept of asymmetric clock and proposed a universal algorithm, so that the robots rendezvous in finite time, in any case when at least one of the parameters is not identical for the two robots.

1.3 Results and outline

The structure and results of the paper are as follows. In Section 2 we consider the problem of search and provide algorithms solving this problem nearly optimally. These algorithms will then form the basis for our rendezvous algorithms. In Section 3 we study the rendezvous problem under the assumption that the robots' time-units are equal. We demonstrate in this setting that rendezvous is always feasible if the robots differ in their speeds, and is only feasible when $v = 1$ if also $\chi = 1$ but $0 < \phi < 2\pi$. When the rendezvous is feasible we provide an algorithm which solves rendezvous in nearly optimal time.

In Section 4 we study the rendezvous problem when the robots' time units differ. In this case we demonstrate that rendezvous is always feasible when $\tau \neq 1$. Moreover, we provide an algorithm which universally solves rendezvous whenever the parameters of the robots are such that rendezvous is feasible. This algorithm does not require the robots to know which of their parameters differ. In Section 5 we conclude with a short discussion.

2 SEARCH

The problem of search is as follows. We have a single robot $\mathcal{R}$ with radius of visibility $r > 0$ which needs to find a stationary target (exit, treasure, etc.) that is initially at an unknown distance d from the robot. This problem was solved in [25] where it was shown that the search time was in $O\left(\log\left(\frac{d}{r}\right)\frac{d^2}{r}\right)$ and that this search time is optimal. We give a slightly different algorithm to the one in [25] which solves the problem in $O\left(\log\left(\frac{d^2}{r}\right)\frac{d^2}{r}\right)$. We will use this search algorithm to build our rendezvous algorithms.

We construct our search algorithm using a number of smaller procedures/algorithms. The first two of these procedures are called `SearchCircle`(δ) and `SearchAnnulus`$(\delta_1, \delta_2, \rho)$. The procedure `SearchCircle`$(\delta)$ takes as input a positive real δ and instructs a robot to move from its initial position to a radius δ, move along the circle of radius δ, and return to its initial position. The procedure `SearchAnnulus`$(\delta_1, \delta_2, \rho)$ takes three positive real parameters δ_1, δ_2, and ρ. It repeatedly calls `SearchCircle`$(\cdot)$ with the end result that all points within the annulus of inner and outer radii δ_1 and δ_2 respectively have been within a distance at most ρ from the robot at some time during the algorithm. These procedures are formally described as Algorithms 1 and 2 respectively.

Algorithm 1 `SearchCircle`(δ)

Input: $\delta > 0$ (real);
Begin:
1: Move along x-axis to radial position δ.
2: Traverse circle with radius δ.
3: Return to initial position.
:End

Algorithm 2 `SearchAnnulus`$(\delta_1, \delta_2, \rho)$

Input: $\delta_1 \geq 0$ (real); $\delta_2 > \delta_1$ (real); $\rho > 0$ (real);
Begin:
1: **for** $i = 0$ to $\left\lceil \frac{\delta_2 - \delta_1}{2\rho} \right\rceil$ **do** `SearchCircle`$(\delta_1 + 2i\rho)$.
:End

The next procedure `Search`(k) takes a positive integer $k \geq 1$ as input and instructs a robot to search the set of $2k - 1$ annuli in such a way that: a) the jth, $0 \leq j \leq 2k - 1$, annulus has inner and outer radii $\delta_{j,k} = 2^{-k+j}$ and $\delta_{j,k+1} = 2^{-k+j+1}$ respectively, and, b) all points of this annulus are approached within a distance of $\rho_{j,k} = 2^{-3k+2j-1}$. The idea is that the robot will search successive annuli of increasing inner and outer radii $\delta_{j,k}$ and $\delta_{j,k+1}$ under the assumption that its visibility radius is $\rho_{j,k}$. The specific values of $\delta_{j,k}$ and $\rho_{j,k}$ are chosen such that the ratio $\delta^2_{j,k}/\rho_{j,k} = 2^{k+1}$. At the end of the algorithm a robot is instructed to wait a rather specific amount of time only in order to simplify algebra later on. This procedure is formally described as Algorithm 3.

Algorithm 3 Search (k)

Input: $k > 0$ (integer);
Begin:
for $j = 0$ to $2k - 1$ **do**
    SearchAnnulus $\left(2^{-k+j}, 2^{-k+j+1}, 2^{-3k+2j-1}\right)$
Wait at initial position for a time $3(\pi + 1)(2^k + 2^{-k})$.
:End

We are now ready to introduce our main search algorithm. This algorithm is formally presented as Algorithm 4. The algorithm repeatedly runs Search (k) until the target is discovered. The idea is that the robot will search regions of the plane in such a way that in each round k a robot spends time proportional to the ratio d^2/r under the assumption that the values of d and r were such that the target was discovered on the round k.

Algorithm 4

Begin:
$k \leftarrow 1$;
repeat
    Perform Search (k);
    $k \leftarrow k + 1$;
until Target found.
:End

We now claim the following:

THEOREM 2.1. *Algorithm 4 solves the search problem in time*

$$T(d, r) < 6(\pi + 1) \log\left(\frac{d^2}{r}\right) \frac{d^2}{r}.$$

We will prove this theorem using a series of lemmas. We begin by demonstrating that the algorithm is correct.

LEMMA 2.2. *Algorithm 4 solves the search problem.*

PROOF. Assume that the target is at distance d and the robot has visibility r. In the round k and sub-round j of Algorithm 3 a robot will search the entire disk of radius at least 2^{-k+j+1} with a granularity of at most $2^{-3k+2j-1}$. The robot must therefore find the target by the end of the round k of Algorithm 4 for which there exists an integer j such that $0 \le j \le 2k - 1$, $2^{-k+j+1} \ge d$, and $2^{-3k+2j-1} \le r$. It is not hard to confirm, for example, that $k = \left\lfloor \log \frac{d^2}{r} \right\rfloor$ and $j = \lfloor \log(d) \rfloor + \left\lfloor \log \frac{d^2}{r} \right\rfloor$ satisfy these constraints. □

We now compute the running times of Algorithms 1 - 4.

LEMMA 2.3. *It takes time:*

- $2(\pi + 1)\delta$ *to complete* SearchCircle (δ).
- $2(\pi + 1)\left(1 + \left\lceil \frac{\delta_2 - \delta_1}{2\rho} \right\rceil\right)\left(\delta_1 + \rho \left\lceil \frac{\delta_2 - \delta_1}{2\rho} \right\rceil\right)$ *to complete* SearchAnnulus $(\delta_1, \delta_2, \rho)$.
- $3(\pi + 1)(k + 1) \cdot 2^{k+1}$ *to complete* Search (k).
- $3(\pi + 1)k \cdot 2^{k+2}$ *to complete the first k rounds of Algorithm 4.*

PROOF. SearchCircle (δ) clearly takes time $2(\pi + 1)\delta$. Let $m = \left\lceil \frac{\delta_2 - \delta_1}{2\rho} \right\rceil$. The time to complete SearchAnnulus $(\delta_1, \delta_2, \rho)$ is then

$$\sum_{i=0}^{m} 2(\pi + 1)(\delta_1 + 2i\rho) = 2(\pi + 1)\left[(m + 1)\delta_1 + \rho(m + 1)m\right]$$
$$= 2(\pi + 1)(1 + m)(\delta_1 + \rho m).$$

Now consider the algorithm Search (k). The time to complete the round j of this algorithm is just the time required to complete SearchAnnulus $\left(\delta_{j,k}, \delta_{j,k+1}, \rho_{j,k}\right)$ where $\delta_{j,k} = 2^{-k+j}$ and $\rho_{j,k} = 2^{-3k+2j-1}$. Observe that $\frac{\delta_{j+1,k} - \delta_{j,k}}{2\rho_{j,k}} = \frac{2^{-k+j+1} - 2^{-k+j}}{2^{-3k+2j}} = 2^{2k-j}$. The time to complete one round of the algorithm is then $2(\pi + 1)\left(1 + 2^{2k-j}\right)\left(2^{-k+j} + 2^{-3k+2j-1} \cdot 2^{2k-j}\right)$ which simplifies to $3(\pi + 1)(2^{j-k} + 2^k)$. Since

$$3(\pi + 1) \sum_{j=0}^{2k-1} (2^{j-k} + 2^k) = 3(\pi + 1)\left[k2^{k+1} + 2^{-k}(2^{2k} - 1)\right]$$

we can conclude that the time required to complete Search (k) is

$$3(\pi + 1)(2^k + 2^{-k}) + 3(\pi + 1)\left[k2^{k+1} + 2^{-k}(2^{2k} - 1)\right]$$
$$= 3(\pi + 1)(k + 1) \cdot 2^{k+1}.$$

Finally, the time to complete the first k rounds of Algorithm 4 is $3(\pi + 1)\sum_{j=1}^{k}(j + 1)2^{j+1} = 3(\pi + 1)k \cdot 2^{k+2}$. □

The next lemma gives a lower bound on the value of $\frac{d^2}{r}$ assuming that the target was found on round k of Algorithm 4:

LEMMA 2.4. *If a robot finds the target on the round k of Algorithm 4 then* $\frac{d^2}{r} \ge 2^{k+1}$.

PROOF. Assume that the target is found on round k and sub-round j, $0 \le j \le 2k - 1$. In this case we know that $d \ge \delta_{j,k} = 2^{-k+j}$ and $r \le \rho_{j,k} = 2^{-3k+2j-1}$. We therefore have that $\frac{d^2}{r} \ge \frac{\delta_{j,k}^2}{\rho_{j,k}} = 2^{k+1}$. □

The proof of Theorem 2.1 is now simple:

PROOF. (Theorem 2.1) By Lemma 2.2 there must exist a round during which the robot finds the target. Assume that the target is found on the round k. Then, by Lemma 2.4, we have $\frac{d^2}{r} \ge 2^{k+1}$ and the time to find the target is upper-bounded by the time to complete the first k rounds of Algorithm 4. Thus, if $T(d, r)$ is the rendezvous time, then by Lemma 2.3 we have that

$$T(d, r) \le 3(\pi + 1)k \cdot 2^{k+2} \le 6(\pi + 1)\left[\log\left(\frac{d^2}{r}\right) - 1\right]\frac{d^2}{r}.$$

□

3 RENDEZVOUS WITH SYMMETRIC CLOCKS

In this section we consider the rendezvous problem when the time units of the two robots are equal, i.e. $\tau = 1$. We will see that this problem is intimately related to search. Indeed, our goal is to demonstrate that the same Algorithm 4 used for search also solves the rendezvous problem (whenever a solution exists).

THEOREM 3.1. *Algorithm 4 solves the rendezvous problem for two robots with equal time units in time*

$$T(d, r, v, \phi, \chi) < \begin{cases} 6(\pi+1)\log\left(\frac{d^2}{\mu r}\right)\frac{d^2}{\mu r}, & \chi = 1 \\ 6(\pi+1)\log\left(\frac{d^2}{(1-v)r}\right)\frac{d^2}{(1-v)r}, & \chi = -1 \end{cases}$$

where $\mu = \sqrt{v^2 - 2v\cos(\phi) + 1}$.

To prove this theorem we will demonstrate that any algorithm which solves rendezvous for two robots with visibility r and initial distance d necessarily generates a corresponding algorithm which solves an instance of the search problem for a single robot with visibility r and initial distance d from an unknown target. The theorem will follow by analyzing the corresponding search algorithm when we use Algorithm 4 as our rendezvous algorithm.

We observe that we can interpret an algorithm for either the search or rendezvous problems as a single parametric trajectory $\vec{S}(t)$ which specifies how the robots should move. In the case of rendezvous things are somewhat complicated by the fact that we have two robots which may not necessarily agree on their *reference frames*, i.e. they may have different speeds, orientations, and/or chiralities. Thus, although only a single trajectory is specified by an algorithm, the two robots will actually follow two different trajectories during the execution of that algorithm – $\mathcal{R}$ will follow the trajectory $\vec{S}(t)$ and $\mathcal{R}'$ will follow a modified trajectory $\vec{S}'(t)$ which depends on the specific values of v, ϕ, and χ. Nevertheless, the single trajectory $\vec{S}(t)$ suffices to completely describe a rendezvous algorithm. In the sequel we will refer to rendezvous and/or search algorithms by the trajectory $\vec{S}(t)$ they correspond to.

In the case of search, an algorithm $\vec{S}(t)$ solves the problem if there exists a time $t \geq 0$ for which $|\vec{S}(t) - \vec{d}| \leq r$ with $\vec{d}$, $|\vec{d}| = d$, a vector pointing from the initial position of the robot to the target. In the case of rendezvous, $\vec{S}(t)$ solves the problem if there exists a time $t \geq 0$ for which $|\vec{S}(t) - \vec{S}'(t) - \vec{d}| \leq r$, where, in this case, $\vec{d}$, $|\vec{d}| = d$, represents a vector pointing from the initial position of $\mathcal{R}$ to that of $\mathcal{R}'$. If we reinterpret the trajectory $\vec{S}_\circ(t) = \vec{S}(t) - \vec{S}'(t)$ as a search algorithm, then it is easy to see that $\vec{S}(t)$ solves rendezvous for a given d and r if (and only if) $\vec{S}_\circ(t)$ solves search for the same d and r. Moreover, if $\vec{S}(t)$ solves rendezvous at the time T, then $\vec{S}_\circ(t)$ solves search at the same time T. Thus, we say that the rendezvous algorithm $\vec{S}(t)$ induces an equivalent search algorithm $\vec{S}(t) - \vec{S}'(t)$. This observation provides our strategy to prove Theorem 3.1 – we show that Algorithm 4, taken as a rendezvous algorithm, induces an equivalent search algorithm which still solves the search problem.

To begin we need to express the trajectory $\vec{S}'(t)$ of the robot $\mathcal{R}'$ in terms of v, ϕ, χ, and $\vec{S}(t)$.

LEMMA 3.2. *Consider a rendezvous algorithm $\vec{S}(t)$. Then the robot $\mathcal{R}$ will follow the trajectory $\vec{S}(t)$ and the robot $\mathcal{R}'$ will follow the trajectory $\vec{S}'(t) + \vec{d}$ where*

$$\vec{S}'(t) = \begin{bmatrix} v\cos(\phi) & -v\chi\sin(\phi) \\ v\sin(\phi) & v\chi\cos(\phi) \end{bmatrix} \vec{S}(t)$$

and $\vec{d}$ points from the initial position of $\mathcal{R}$ to the initial position of $\mathcal{R}'$.

PROOF. If the robots have different chiralities ($\chi = -1$) then they will disagree on the $+y$ direction. This implies that $\mathcal{R}'$ will move along a trajectory that is a reflection about the x-axis of the trajectory followed by $\mathcal{R}$. If the orientation of $\mathcal{R}'$ is ϕ, then its trajectory will be rotated by an angle ϕ with respect to that of $\mathcal{R}$. If the speed of $\mathcal{R}'$ is $v < 1$ then it will travel a smaller distance in the same time interval as compared to v and its trajectory will thus be scaled by a factor of v. Combining all of these transformations together we find that $\vec{S}'(t) = v\begin{bmatrix} \cos(\phi) & -\sin(\phi) \\ \sin(\phi) & \cos(\phi) \end{bmatrix}\begin{bmatrix} 1 & 0 \\ 0 & \chi \end{bmatrix}\vec{S}(t)$. □

Now that we know the trajectory of $\mathcal{R}'$ we can compute the equivalent search trajectory $\vec{S}_\circ(t) = \vec{S}(t) - \vec{S}'(t)$ as

$$\vec{S}_\circ(t) = \vec{S}(t) - \vec{S}'(t) = \begin{bmatrix} 1 - v\cos(\phi) & v\chi\sin(\phi) \\ -v\sin(\phi) & 1 - v\chi\cos(\phi) \end{bmatrix} \vec{S}(t).$$

Let $\mathrm{T}_\circ = \begin{bmatrix} 1 - v\cos(\phi) & v\chi\sin(\phi) \\ -v\sin(\phi) & 1 - v\chi\cos(\phi) \end{bmatrix}$. In the next lemma we rewrite $\mathrm{T}_\circ$ in a more convenient form.

LEMMA 3.3. *The matrix $\mathrm{T}_\circ$ can be factored as $\mathrm{T}_\circ = \Phi\mathrm{T}'_\circ$ where Φ is a rotation matrix, $\mathrm{T}'_\circ = \begin{bmatrix} \mu & \frac{-(1-\chi)v\sin(\phi)}{\mu} \\ 0 & \frac{\chi v^2 - (1+\chi)v\cos(\phi)+1}{\mu} \end{bmatrix}$ and $\mu = \sqrt{v^2 - 2v\cos(\phi) + 1}$.*

PROOF. What we want amounts to a QR-factorization. This is a well known operation and so we just quote the result:

$$\mathrm{T}_\circ = \frac{1}{\mu}\begin{bmatrix} 1 - v\cos(\phi) & v\sin(\phi) \\ -v\sin(\phi) & 1 - v\cos(\phi) \end{bmatrix}\begin{bmatrix} \mu & \frac{-(1-\chi)v\sin(\phi)}{\mu} \\ 0 & \frac{1+\chi v^2-(1+\chi)v\cos(\phi)}{\mu} \end{bmatrix}$$

where we have set $\mu = \sqrt{v^2 - 2v\cos(\phi) + 1}$. It is easy to confirm that $\frac{1}{\mu}\begin{bmatrix} 1 - v\cos(\phi) & v\sin(\phi) \\ -v\sin(\phi) & 1 - v\cos(\phi) \end{bmatrix}$ is an orthogonal matrix with determinant 1. □

Since rotations do not scale distances, the condition $|\mathrm{T}_\circ\vec{S}(t) - \vec{d}| \leq r$ is equivalent to the condition that $|\mathrm{T}'_\circ\vec{S}(t) - \vec{d}| \leq r$. It will be easier to analyze this rotated version of the problem and thus, in the sequel, we will use the following definition for an equivalent search trajectory:

Definition 3.4. The equivalent search trajectory induced by the rendezvous trajectory $\vec{S}(t)$ is the trajectory $\vec{S}_\circ(t)$ where

$$\vec{S}_\circ(t) = \mathrm{T}_\circ\vec{S}(t) = \begin{bmatrix} \mu & \frac{-(1-\chi)v\sin(\phi)}{\mu} \\ 0 & \frac{1+\chi v^2-(1+\chi)v\cos(\phi)}{\mu} \end{bmatrix}\vec{S}(t)$$

and $\mu = \sqrt{v^2 - 2v\cos(\phi) + 1}$.

At this point it will be easier to consider the cases that $\chi = \pm 1$ separately. We begin with the case that $\chi = 1$:

Lemma 3.5. *Algorithm 4 solves rendezvous in time*

$$T(d,r,v,\phi) < 6(\pi+1)\log\left(\frac{d^2}{\mu r}\right)\frac{d^2}{\mu r}$$

where $\mu = \sqrt{v^2 - 2v\cos(\phi) + 1}$.

Proof. We first observe that $\mathbf{T}_\circ$ takes on a particularly simple form when $\chi = 1$. We find that

$$\mathbf{T}_\circ = \begin{bmatrix} \mu & \frac{-(1-\chi)v\sin(\phi)}{\mu} \\ 0 & \frac{1+\chi v^2-(1+\chi)v\cos(\phi)}{\mu} \end{bmatrix} = \begin{bmatrix} \mu & 0 \\ 0 & \mu \end{bmatrix}$$

with the result that $\vec{S}_\circ(t) = \mu\vec{S}(t)$. Thus $\vec{S}_\circ(t)$ is the trajectory of a robot with speed μ performing Algorithm 4. We need to demonstrate that there exists a time $t \geq 0$ for which $|\mu\vec{S}(t) - \vec{d}| \leq r$. Multiplying this inequality by $\frac{1}{\mu}$ gives the equivalent condition $|\vec{S}(t) - \frac{\vec{d}}{\mu}| \leq \frac{r}{\mu}$ and we already know that there exists a time for which this is satisfied when $\vec{S}(t)$ is given by Algorithm 4. We can therefore conclude that Algorithm 4 solves rendezvous. To bound the rendezvous time we can directly use the results of Theorem 2.1 with d and r replaced with $\frac{d}{\mu}$ and $\frac{r}{\mu}$ respectively. □

Now we consider the case that the robots have opposite chiralities. We begin by revisiting what it means for an algorithm to solve the search problem. To this end, assume that we have an algorithm $\vec{S}(t)$ that solves search in time at most T when the robot has visibility r and the target is at a distance d. What this tells us is that all possible positions of the target at distance d from the initial position of the robot can be reached in time at most T. In particular, if the target is located at $\vec{d}$, then there exists a time $0 \leq t \leq T$ for which $|\vec{S}(t) - \vec{d}| \leq r$. Since the distance of closest approach of the robot and the target occurs when the robot is located on the line defined by the unit vector $\hat{d} = \vec{d}/d$, we can conclude that there exists a time $0 \leq t \leq T$ for which the length of the projection of $\vec{S}(t) - \vec{d}$ onto the line defined by $\hat{d} = \vec{d}/d$ is at most r. Thus, if $\vec{S}(t)$ solves search, then there exists a time $0 \leq t \leq T$ for which $(\vec{S}(t) - \vec{d}) \cdot \hat{d} \leq r$. With this observation in hand, we can proceed to prove the following:

Lemma 3.6. *When* $\chi = -1$ *Algorithm 4 solves rendezvous in time*

$$T(d,r,v) < 6(\pi+1)\log\left(\frac{d^2}{(1-v)r}\right)\frac{d^2}{(1-v)r}.$$

Proof. When $\chi = -1$ the matrix $\mathbf{T}_\circ$ simplifies to

$$\mathbf{T}_\circ = \begin{bmatrix} \mu & \frac{-2v\sin(\phi)}{\mu} \\ 0 & \frac{1-v^2}{\mu} \end{bmatrix}.$$

We want to show that there exists a time $t \geq 0$ for which $(\vec{S}_\circ(t) - \vec{d}) \cdot \hat{d} \leq r$ is satisfied. Observe that

$$(\vec{S}_\circ(t) - \vec{d}) \cdot \hat{d} = (\mathbf{T}_\circ\vec{S}(t)) \cdot \hat{d} - d = \vec{S}^T(t)\mathbf{T}_\circ^T\hat{d} - d$$

$$= \vec{S}(t) \cdot (\mathbf{T}_\circ^T\hat{d}) - d = |\mathbf{T}_\circ^T\hat{d}|\left[\vec{S}(t) \cdot \frac{\mathbf{T}_\circ^T\hat{d}}{|\mathbf{T}_\circ^T\hat{d}|} - \frac{d}{|\mathbf{T}_\circ\hat{d}|}\right]$$

$$= |\mathbf{T}_\circ^T\hat{d}|\left[(\vec{S}(t) - \vec{d}') \cdot \hat{d}'\right]$$

where $\hat{d}' = \frac{\mathbf{T}_\circ^T\hat{d}}{|\mathbf{T}_\circ^T\hat{d}|}$ and $\vec{d}' = \frac{d}{|\mathbf{T}_\circ^T\hat{d}|}\hat{d}'$. Thus, the condition that $(\vec{S}_\circ(t) - \vec{d}) \cdot \hat{d} \leq r$ is satisfied for some $t \geq 0$ is equivalent to the condition that $(\vec{S}(t) - \vec{d}') \cdot \hat{d}' \leq r'$ with $r' = \frac{r}{|\mathbf{T}_\circ^T\hat{d}|}$. As we know that Algorithm 4 indeed does satisfy this equality for some $t \geq 0$ we can conclude that Algorithm 4 solves rendezvous. To bound the time of rendezvous we need to replace d and r with $\frac{d}{|\mathbf{T}_\circ^T\hat{d}|}$ and $\frac{r}{|\mathbf{T}_\circ^T\hat{d}|}$ in the bound of Theorem 2.1. To complete the proof we first need to compute the value of $|\mathbf{T}_\circ^T\hat{d}|$ and then maximize the resulting time bound over all possible positions of the target. As we only need to compute the worst case position of $\hat{d}$ in order to bound the rendezvous time, this justifies that we set $\vec{d} = \begin{bmatrix} 0 \\ 1 \end{bmatrix}$ and instead maximize the result over all possible values of ϕ. In this case it is easy to confirm that $|\mathbf{T}_\circ^T\hat{d}| = \frac{1-v^2}{\mu}$. Since the search time scales with $\frac{d^2}{r}$ we want to maximize the quantity $\frac{\mu}{1-v^2}$ with respect to ϕ. This is equivalent to maximizing $\mu = \sqrt{v^2 - 2v\cos(\phi) + 1}$. Clearly, the maximum value of μ is $\sqrt{v^2 + 2v + 1} = 1 + v$. The bound in the lemma then follows from Theorem 2.1 and the fact that $\frac{1+v}{1-v^2} = \frac{1}{1-v}$. □

4 RENDEZVOUS WITH ASYMMETRIC CLOCKS

We now consider rendezvous for the case that the robots have different time units ($\tau \neq 1$). Without loss of generality we will take $\tau < 1$. We will begin with the assumption that the robots have the same speeds ($v = 1$) and then extend our results to cover the case that the speeds of the robots may also be different. Our goal is to demonstrate that rendezvous is always feasible. The main result of this section follows:

Theorem 4.1. *For any fixed* $\tau < 1$ *there exists an algorithm which solves rendezvous in finite time.*

We will prove this theorem constructively and give an algorithm which solves the rendezvous problem in finite time provided that $\tau < 1$. This algorithm will be constructed using the algorithms of Section 2. In the sequel we describe this algorithm and then analyze its running time.

An outline and the idea of our rendezvous algorithm is as follows. The algorithm proceeds in a series of rounds with each round composed of equal length inactive and active phases. In an inactive phase a robot will remain stationary at its initial position. In the active phase of round n a robot will (essentially) perform the first n rounds of Algorithm 4. We observe that this implies that there will be a round n_* of the algorithm for which, say, the robot $\mathcal{R}$ would find $\mathcal{R}'$ if $\mathcal{R}'$ were stationary at its initial position. Moreover, this will be true for every round $n \geq n_*$. We will show that, due to the differing time units of the robots, it will happen that the active and inactive phases of the robots overlap and that the length of the overlap interval grows without bound. Thus, there will exist a round $n \geq n_*$ during which the active and inactive phases of the robots overlap long enough that $\mathcal{R}$ is able to find $\mathcal{R}'$ waiting at its initial location.

Our rendezvous algorithm is formally described as Algorithm 7. In each active phase a robot will run the procedures `SearchAll` (n)

and SearchAllRev (n) which are formally described as Algorithms 5 and 6 respectively. The procedure SearchAll (n) is identical to Algorithm 4 except that it always terminates after n rounds. The procedure SearchAllRev (n) is identical to SearchAll (n) except that it is run in reverse, i.e. it begins on the nth round and ends on the round 1. Figures 1 and 2 illustrate the structure of each round of the algorithm.

Algorithm 5 SearchAll (n)

Input: $n > 0$ (integer);
Begin:
for $k = 1$ to n **do** Perform Search (k).
:End

Algorithm 6 SearchAllRev (n)

Input: $n > 0$ (integer);
Begin:
for $k = n$ to 1 **do** Perform Search (k).
:End

Algorithm 7

Begin:
$n \leftarrow 1$
repeat
    Wait at initial position for a time $2S(n)$.
    Perform SearchAll (n) then SearchAllRev (n).
    $n = n + 1$.
until Rendezvous occurs
:End

We begin our proof of Theorem 4.1 with the following lemma which gives the time at which the inactive and active phases of Algorithm 7 begin.

Lemma 4.2. *The nth inactive phase of Algorithm 7 begins at the time $I(n) = 24(\pi + 1)[(2n - 4) \cdot 2^n + 4]$ and the nth active phase begins at the time $A(n) = 24(\pi + 1)[(3n - 4) \cdot 2^n + 4]$.*

Proof. It is easy to see that each round of Algorithm 7 lasts time $4S(n)$ where $S(n)$ is the time it takes to complete SearchAll (n). Using the results of Lemma 2.3 we have

$$S(n) = 12(\pi + 1)n \cdot 2^n. \tag{1}$$

The beginning of the nth inactive phase is just the total time required to complete the first $n - 1$ rounds of the algorithm. Thus

$$I(n) = 4\sum_{k=1}^{n-1} S(k) = 48(\pi + 1)\sum_{k=1}^{n-1} k2^k = 24(\pi + 1)[(2n - 4)2^n + 4].$$

The nth active phase begins when the nth inactive phase ends. We therefore have $A(n) = I(n) + 2S(n) = 24(\pi + 1)[(3n - 4) \cdot 2^n + 4]$. □

To reiterate, we need to show that the overlap between the active and inactive phases of the robots grows without bound and there will therefore eventually be a round n_* of the algorithm for which $\mathcal{R}$ is able to finish the first (resp. last) k rounds of SearchAll (n_*) (resp. SearchAllRev (n_*)) during an inactive phase of $\mathcal{R}'$ where k is the first round of SearchAll $(\cdot)$ during which $\mathcal{R}$ would find $\mathcal{R}'$ if $\mathcal{R}'$ were stationary at its initial location. Since the robots run both of the procedures SearchAll (n_*) and SearchAllRev (n_*) the inactive and active phases of the robots can overlap in the two ways illustrated in Figure 3. In the next two lemmas we show under what circumstances the robots will find themselves in either of the two situations depicted in Figure 3.

Lemma 4.3. *If $\frac{k}{(k+1+a)2^{a+1}} \leq \tau \leq \frac{3}{2} \cdot \frac{k}{(k+1+a)2^{a+1}}$ and $k \geq 2(a+1)$ for some integer $a \geq 0$ then the kth active phase of $\mathcal{R}$ overlaps with the $(k+1+a)^{th}$ inactive phase of $\mathcal{R}'$ by an amount $\tau \cdot A(k+1+a) - A(k)$.*

Proof. Referring to Figure 3a), one can see that in order for the kth active phase of $\mathcal{R}$ to overlap with the $(k + a)^{th}$ inactive phase of $\mathcal{R}'$ by an amount $\tau \cdot A(k + 1 + a) - A(k)$ we need to satisfy $\tau \cdot I(k+a) \leq A(k) \leq \tau \cdot A(k+a)$. Rearranging these inequalities leads to the equivalent condition $\frac{A(k)}{A(k+1+a)} \leq \tau \leq \frac{A(k)}{I(k+1+a)}$. Thus, in order to prove the lemma we need to demonstrate that $\frac{A(k)}{A(k+1+a)} \leq \frac{k}{(k+1+a)2^{a+1}}$ and $\frac{A(k)}{I(k+1+a)} \geq \frac{3}{2} \cdot \frac{k}{(k+1+a)2^{a+1}}$. Consider the latter inequality first. A simple rearrangement of this inequality yields $(k + 1 + a)2^{a+1}A(k) \leq kA(k + 1 + a)$. Substitution of the expression derived in Lemma 4.2 for $A(k)$ gives

$$(k + 1 + a)2^{a+1}[(3k - 4)2^k + 4] \leq k\{[3(k + 1 + a) - 4]2^{k+1+a} + 4\}.$$

After some manipulation we arrive to the equivalent condition $\frac{a+1}{k} > \frac{1-2^{-a-1}}{2^k-1}$. It is easy to confirm that this inequality is satisfied for all $a \geq 0$ and $k \geq 2(a + 1)$.

Now consider the inequality $\frac{A(k)}{I(k+1+a)} \geq \frac{3}{2} \cdot \frac{k}{(k+1+a)2^{a+1}}$. Rearranging this inequality and substitution of the expressions for $A(k)$ and $I(k)$ from Lemma 4.2 yields

$$2(k+1+a)2^{a+1}[(3k-4)2^k + 4] \leq 3k\{[2(k+1+a) - 4]2^{k+1+a} + 4\}.$$

After some manipulation this reduces to $\frac{k}{a+1} \geq \frac{2}{1+3\frac{1-2^{-a-1}}{2^k-1}}$. It is easy to see that this inequality is also satisfied whenever $a \geq 0$ and $k \geq 2(a + 1)$. □

Lemma 4.4. *If $\frac{2}{3} \cdot \frac{k}{(k+a)2^a} \leq \tau \leq \frac{k}{(k+1+a)2^a}$ and $k \geq 2(a + 1)$ for some integer $a \geq 0$ then the $(k - 1)^{st}$ active phase of $\mathcal{R}$ overlaps with the $(k + a)^{th}$ inactive phase of $\mathcal{R}'$ by an amount $I(k) - \tau \cdot I(k + a)$.*

Proof. Referring to Figure 3b), in order for the $(k - 1)^{st}$ active phase of $\mathcal{R}$ to overlap with the $(k + a)^{th}$ inactive phase of $\mathcal{R}'$ by an amount $I(k) - \tau \cdot I(k+a)$ we need to satisfy $\tau \cdot I(k+a) \leq I(k) \leq \tau \cdot A(k+a)$. Rearranging these inequalities leads to the equivalent condition $\frac{I(k)}{A(k+a)} \leq \tau \leq \frac{I(k)}{I(k+a)}$. Thus, in order to prove the lemma we need to demonstrate that $\frac{I(k)}{A(k+a)} \leq \frac{2}{3}\frac{k}{(k+a)2^a}$ and $\frac{I(k)}{I(k+a)} \geq \frac{k}{(k+1+a)2^a}$. Consider the latter inequality first. Rearrangment and substitution of the expressions for $A(k)$ and $I(k)$ gives

$$3(k + a)2^a[(2k - 4)2^k + 4] \leq 2k\{[3(k + a) - 4]2^{k+a} + 4\}.$$

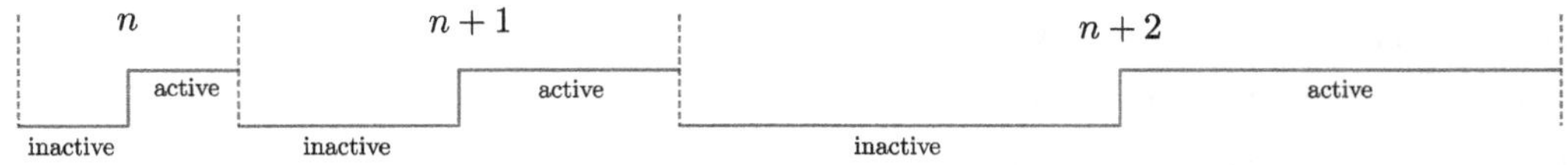

Figure 1: Three rounds of the algorithm.

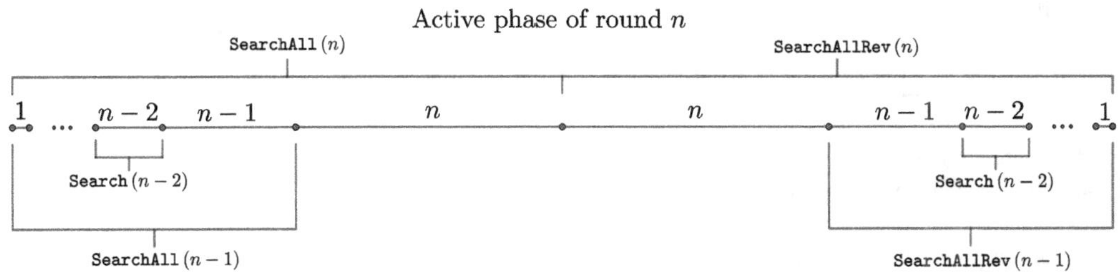

Figure 2: Structure of the active phase of round n**.**

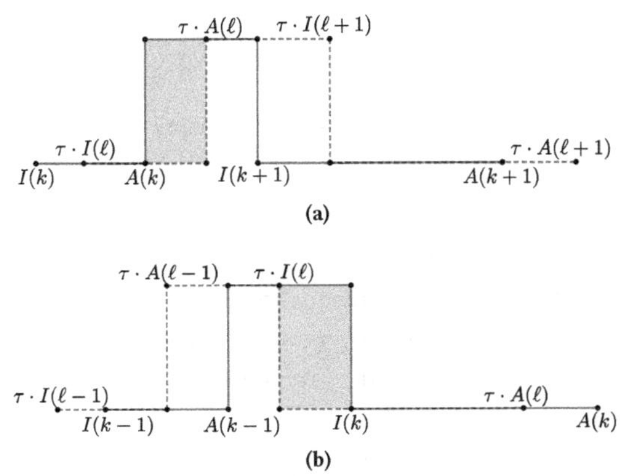

Figure 3: Illustration of how the active phase of $\mathcal{R}$ can overlap with the inactive phase of $\mathcal{R}'$. The intervals of overlap are shaded, the active/inactive phases of $\mathcal{R}$ are indicated by solid lines, and those of $\mathcal{R}'$ are indicated by dashed lines.

After some manipulation we get $3a(2^k - 1) + k(2^k - 3 + 2^{1-a}) \geq 0$. It is easy to confirm that this inequality is satisfied for all $a \geq 0$ and $k \geq 2(a+1)$.

Now consider the inequality $\frac{I(k)}{I(k+a)} \geq \frac{k}{(k+1+a)2^a}$. Rearrangement and substitution of the expression for $I(k)$ yields

$$(k+1+a)2^a[(2k-4)2^k + 4] \leq k\{[2(k+a)-4]2^{k+a} + 4\}.$$

After some manipulation this reduces to $\frac{k}{a+1} \geq \frac{2}{1+\frac{3-2^{-a}}{2^k-1}}$. It is easy to see that this inequality is also satisfied whenever $a \geq 0$ and $k \geq 2(a+1)$. □

In the next two lemmas we determine in which round the robots will rendezvous under the assumption that the conditions of the previous two lemmas are met.

Lemma 4.5. *Assume that $\mathcal{R}$ would find a stationary target located at the initial position of $\mathcal{R}'$ on round n of Algorithm 7. If there exists two integers $a \geq 0$ and $k_0 \geq 2(a+1)$ such that τ satisfies $\frac{k}{(k+1+a)2^{a+1}} \leq \tau \leq \frac{3}{2} \cdot \frac{k}{(k+1+a)2^{a+1}}$ for all rounds $k \geq k_0$ then the robots will rendezvous by the end of the round $k_* = n + \lceil \log\left(\frac{n}{a+1}\right)\rceil$ of Algorithm 7.*

Proof. Assume that integers $a \geq 0$ and $k_0 \geq 2(a+1)$ exist such that τ satisfies the condition of the lemma. This implies that τ must satisfy

$$\frac{1}{2} \cdot 2^{-a} \leq \tau \leq \frac{3}{4} \cdot \frac{k_0}{k_0 + 1 + a} \cdot 2^{-a} \tag{2}$$

since $\frac{k}{k+1+a}$ is increasing with k and $\frac{k}{k+1+a} < 1$.

By Lemma 4.3 the kth active phase of $\mathcal{R}$ overlaps with the $(k+1+a)^{th}$ inactive phase of $\mathcal{R}'$ by an amount $\tau \cdot A(k+1+a) - A(k)$ for all $k \geq k_0$. The robots are guaranteed to rendezvous on or before the first round $k_* \geq k_0$ for which this overlap is larger than $S(n)$. We observe that

$$\begin{aligned}
&\tau A(k+1+a) - A(k) \\
&= 24(\pi+1)\left[\tau[(3(k+1+a)-4)2^{k+1+a} + 4] - (3k-4)2^k - 4\right] \\
&= 24(\pi+1)\left[(3k-4)(\tau 2^{1+a} - 1)2^k + 3\tau(a+1)2^{k+1+a} - 4(1-\tau)\right].
\end{aligned}$$

For τ satisfying (2) we can write

$$\begin{aligned}
\tau \cdot A(k+1+a) - A(k) &\geq 24(\pi+1)\left[3(a+1)2^k - 4\left(1 - \frac{1}{2}2^{-a}\right)\right] \\
&> 24(\pi+1)\left[3(a+1)2^k - 4\right].
\end{aligned}$$

Thus we will have $\tau \cdot A(k+1+a) - A(k) \geq S(n)$ when $24(\pi+1)\left[3(a+1) \cdot 2^k - 4\right] \geq S(n)$. Using the expression (1) for $S(n)$ we can rewrite the above inequality as $3(a+1) \cdot 2^k - 4 \geq \frac{n}{2} \cdot 2^n$ which simplifies to $k \geq \log\left[\frac{1}{3(a+1)}\left(\frac{n}{2} \cdot 2^n + 4\right)\right]$. The robots will therefore rendezvous by the end of the round

$$k_* = \left\lceil \log\left[\frac{1}{3(a+1)}\left(\frac{n}{2} \cdot 2^n + 4\right)\right]\right\rceil < n + \left\lceil \log\left(\frac{n}{a+1}\right)\right\rceil.$$

□

Lemma 4.6. *Assume that $\mathcal{R}$ would find a stationary target located at the initial position of $\mathcal{R}'$ on round n of Algorithm 7. If there exists* *two integers $a \geq 0$ and $k_0 \geq 2(a+1)$ such that τ satisfies $\frac{2}{3} \cdot \frac{k}{(k+a)2^a} \leq \tau \leq \frac{k}{(k+1+a)2^a}$ for all $k \geq k_0$ then the robots will rendezvous by the end of the round $k_* = n + \left\lceil \log(n) + \log\left(1 + \frac{k_0}{a+1}\right)\right\rceil$ of Algorithm 7.*

Proof. Assume that integers $a \geq 0$ and $k_0 \geq 2(a+1)$ exist such that τ satisfies the condition of the lemma. This implies that τ must satisfy

$$\frac{2}{3} \cdot 2^{-a} \leq \tau \leq \frac{k_0}{k_0+1+a} \cdot 2^{-a} \tag{3}$$

since $\frac{k}{k+1+a} < 1$ and is increasing with k.

Assume d and r are chosen such that $\mathcal{R}$ would find a stationary target at the initial position of $\mathcal{R}'$ on round n of Algorithm 7. By Lemma 4.4 the $(k-1)^{st}$ active phase of $\mathcal{R}$ overlaps with the $(k+a)^{th}$ inactive phase of $\mathcal{R}'$ by an amount $I(k)-\tau \cdot I(k+a)$ for all $k \geq k_0$. The robots are guaranteed to rendezvous on or before the first round $k_* \geq k_0$ for which this overlap is larger than $S(n)$. We observe that

$$\begin{aligned} I(k) &- \tau \cdot I(k+a) \\ &= 24(\pi+1)\left[(2k-4)2^k + 4 - \tau[(2(k+a)-4)2^{k+a}+4]\right] \\ &= 24(\pi+1)\left[(2k-4)2^k[1-\tau 2^a] + 4(1-\tau) - 2a\tau 2^{k+a}\right]. \end{aligned}$$

Let $\gamma = \frac{k_0}{k_0+1+a}$. Then, for τ satisfying (3), we can write

$$\begin{aligned} I(k) &- \tau \cdot I(k+a) \\ &\geq 24(\pi+1)\left[(2k-4)2^k(1-\gamma) + 4(1-\gamma 2^{-a}) - 2a\gamma 2^k\right] \\ &> 24(\pi+1)\left[(2k-4)2^k(1-\gamma) - 2a\gamma 2^k\right] \\ &= 48(\pi+1)[(k-2)(1-\gamma) - a\gamma]2^k \end{aligned}$$

Thus we will have $I(k) - \tau \cdot I(k+a) \geq S(n)$ when $[(k-2)(1-\gamma) - a\gamma]2^k \geq \frac{n}{4} \cdot 2^n$. Let $x = (k-2)(1-\gamma) - a\gamma$ such that $k = \frac{x+a\gamma}{1-\gamma} + 2 = \frac{x+(a-2)\gamma+2}{1-\gamma}$. We may write

$$\begin{aligned} [(k-2)(1-\gamma) - a\gamma]2^k &= x \cdot \left(2^{\frac{1}{1-\gamma}}\right)^x \cdot \left(2^{\frac{1}{1-\gamma}}\right)^{(a-2)\gamma+2} \\ &= x \cdot e^{\frac{\ln(2)x}{1-\gamma}} \cdot \left(2^{\frac{1}{1-\gamma}}\right)^{(a-2)\gamma+2}. \end{aligned}$$

Then, in terms of x, we need to satisfy,

$$x \cdot e^{\frac{\ln(2)x}{1-\gamma}} \cdot \left(2^{\frac{1}{1-\gamma}}\right)^{(a-2)\gamma+2} \geq \frac{n}{4} \cdot 2^n$$

or

$$\frac{\ln(2)x}{1-\gamma} \cdot e^{\frac{\ln(2)x}{1-\gamma}} \geq \frac{\ln(2)n}{4(1-\gamma)} \cdot 2^n \cdot \left(2^{\frac{1}{1-\gamma}}\right)^{-(a-2)\gamma-2}.$$

In the case of equality, the above has the form $ze^z = y$ and this has the solution $z = W(y)$ where $W(\cdot)$ is the W-Lambert function [10]. We therefore have that

$$\frac{x\ln(2)}{1-\gamma} = W\left[\frac{\ln(2)n}{4(1-\gamma)} \cdot 2^n \cdot \left(2^{\frac{1}{1-\gamma}}\right)^{-(a-2)\gamma-2}\right].$$

Expressing this again in terms of k we find that k must satisfy

$$k \geq 2 + \frac{a\gamma}{1-\gamma} + \frac{1}{\ln(2)}W\left[\frac{\ln(2)n}{4(1-\gamma)} \cdot 2^n \cdot \left(2^{\frac{1}{1-\gamma}}\right)^{-(a-2)\gamma-2}\right]$$

which implies that

$$k_* = 2 + \left\lceil \frac{a\gamma}{1-\gamma} + \frac{1}{\ln(2)}W\left[\frac{\ln(2)n}{4(1-\gamma)} \cdot 2^n \cdot \left(2^{\frac{1}{1-\gamma}}\right)^{-(a-2)\gamma-2}\right]\right\rceil.$$

Now, $W(x)$ behaves asymptotically as $\ln(x) - \ln(\ln(x))$ [18] and we may therefore simplify this expression to

$$\begin{aligned} k_* &\leq 2 + \left\lceil \frac{a\gamma}{1-\gamma} + \frac{1}{\ln(2)}\ln\left[\frac{\ln(2)n}{4(1-\gamma)} \cdot 2^n \cdot \left(2^{\frac{1}{1-\gamma}}\right)^{-(a-2)\gamma-2}\right]\right\rceil \\ &< n + \left\lceil \frac{1}{\ln 2}\ln\left(\frac{n}{1-\gamma}\right)\right\rceil = n + \left\lceil \log\left(\frac{n}{1-\gamma}\right)\right\rceil. \end{aligned}$$

Finally, rewriting the above in terms of k_0 leads us to the desired result. □

We now determine explicitly an upper bound on the round in which the robots rendezvous.

Lemma 4.7. *Parameterize τ as $\tau = t \cdot 2^{-a}$ for an integer $a \geq 0$ and a real $t \in [\frac{1}{2}, 1)$. Then, if $\frac{1}{2} \leq t \leq \frac{2}{3}$ the robots will rendezvous before the end of the round $k_* = \max\left\{8(a+1),\ n + \left\lceil \log\left(\frac{n}{a+1}\right)\right\rceil\right\}$ and otherwise, for $\frac{2}{3} < t < 1$, the robots will rendezvous before the end of the round $k_* = \max\left\{(a+1)\frac{t}{1-t},\ n + \left\lceil \log\left(\frac{n}{1-t}\right)\right\rceil\right\}$.*

Proof. First note that we may always write τ uniquely as $t \cdot 2^{-a}$ by taking $a = \lfloor -\log(\tau)\rfloor - 1$ and $t = \frac{1}{2}$ if τ is a power of two, and otherwise taking $a = \lfloor -\log(\tau)\rfloor$ and $t = \tau \cdot 2^a$.

First assume that $\frac{1}{2} \leq t \leq \frac{2}{3}$. Then the first part of the lemma will follow from Lemma 4.5 if we can find a k_0 such that $\tau = t \cdot 2^{-a} \leq \frac{3}{4}\frac{k_0}{k_0+1+a} \cdot 2^{-a}$. Solving this inequality we find that k_0 is given by $k_0 \geq 4(a+1)\frac{t}{3-4t}$. For $t \in [\frac{1}{2}, \frac{2}{3}]$ one can easily confirm that k_0 must be at least $8(a+1)$ in order to guarantee that $k_0 \geq 4(a+1)\frac{t}{3-4t}$. Thus, if $n + \left\lceil \log\left(\frac{n}{a+1}\right)\right\rceil \geq 8(a+1)$ the robots will rendezvous before the end of the round $n + \left\lceil \log\left(\frac{n}{a+1}\right)\right\rceil$ otherwise the robots will rendezvous at the end of the round $8(a+1)$.

Now assume that $\frac{2}{3} < \tau < 1$. Then the second part of the lemma will follow from Lemma 4.6 if we can determine a k_0 such that $\tau \leq \frac{k_0}{k_0+1+a} \cdot 2^{-a}$, or, equivalently, $t \leq \frac{k_0}{k_0+1+a}$. Solving this inequality we find that $k_0 = \frac{(a+1)t}{1-t}$. Thus, if $n + \left\lceil \log\left(1 + \frac{k_0}{a+1}\right)\right\rceil \geq \frac{t}{1-t}(a+1)$ the robots will rendezvous before the end of the round $n + \left\lceil \log\left(1 + \frac{k_0}{a+1}\right)\right\rceil = n + \left\lceil \log\left(\frac{1}{1-t}\right)\right\rceil$, and otherwise the robots will rendezvous by the end of the round $(a+1)\frac{t}{1-t}$. □

At this point we can almost prove Theorem 4.1. For now we will prove the following weaker statement:

Lemma 4.8. *For any fixed $\tau < 1$ there exists an algorithm which solves rendezvous in finite time if $v = 1$.*

Proof. Write $\tau = t \cdot 2^{-a}$ where t and a are defined as in the previous lemma. Assume that $\mathcal{R}$ would find a stationary target at the initial position of on round n of Algorithm 7. Then $\frac{d^2}{r} \geq 2^{n+1}$ and also $n \leq \log\left(\frac{d^2}{r}\right) - 1$ (see Lemma 2.4). The robots will rendezvous by the round k_* of Algorithm 7 where k_* is given in Lemma 4.7. The total time to complete k_* rounds is $I(k_*) = 24(\pi+1)[(2k_*-4)2^{k_*}+4]$. Thus, the rendezvous time of the algorithm is $T(d,r,\tau) < 24(\pi+1)[(2k_*-4)2^{k_*}+4]$. We claim that, for any fixed value of $\tau < 1$, this bound is finite. Indeed, observe that k_* is only infinite if $t = 1$.

However, t is strictly smaller than one if $\tau < 1$. We have thus demonstrated that Algorithm 7 solves rendezvous in finite time if $\tau < 1$ and $v = 1$. □

We now extend this result to cover the case that the robots have different speeds. This will conclude the proof of Theorem 4.1.

Proof. (Theorem 4.1) Observe that the speed of a robot does not affect the times at which its active and inactive phases begin and/or end. This implies that everything up to and including Lemma 4.7 applies directly to the case that $v \neq 1$. This already implies that there will be a finite number of rounds until the robots rendezvous. A time bound can be derived in a similar manner to the derivation of the previous lemma. □

We note that we have not needed to consider the chirality and/or orientations of the robots in our analysis due to the fact that our proof relied on one robot finding the other while the other was stationary. Thus Theorem 4.1 applies regardless of the robots' relative orientations and/or chiralities. Moreover, one can use the same techniques of Section 3 to show that Algorithm 7 will also solve the rendezvous problem if the robots have different speeds but equal time units. We can therefore conclude this section with the following theorem:

Theorem 4.9. *Algorithm 7 solves the rendezvous problem in finite time if* $\tau \neq 1$ *or* $v \neq 1$, *or* $\chi = 1$ *and* $0 < \phi < 2\pi$.

5 CONCLUSIONS

In this paper we addressed the fundamental problem of feasibility of deterministic rendezvous in the infinite Euclidean plane for two robots that have minimal or no knowledge of the respective capabilities and "measuring instruments" of themselves and each other. We examined the impact on feasibility of rendezvous that the four parameters of speed, clock, distance, chirality have and presented and analyzed specific algorithms with good performance guarantees on the rendezvous time.

Our approach not only provides a surprising twist to the well-known rendezvous problem on the infinite Euclidean plane, but possibly it also creates interesting avenues for future research. In addition to tightening our bounds, there are several interesting questions that could be considered concerning the rendezvous problem. These include rendezvous for robots that may have alternative capabilities (e.g., variable speed), more general terrains with and without obstacles, and rendezvous in higher dimensional space. In addition, it would be challenging to solve deterministic gathering for multiple robots in this setting of "minimal knowledge".

REFERENCES

[1] S. Alpern. The rendezvous search problem. *SIAM Journal on Control and Optimization*, 33(3):673–683, 1995.

[2] S. Alpern. Hide and seek games, Seminar, Institut für Höhere Studien, Wien, 26 July, 1976.

[3] S. Alpern and S. Gal. *The theory of search games and rendezvous*, volume 55. Kluwer Academic Publishers, 2002.

[4] E. J. Anderson and S. P. Fekete. Two dimensional rendezvous search. *Operations Research*, 49(1):107–118, 2001.

[5] L. Barrière, P. Flocchini, P. Fraigniaud, and N. Santoro. Rendezvous and election of mobile agents: Impact of sense of direction. *Theory Comput. Syst.*, 40(2):143–162, 2007.

[6] S. Bouchard, Y. Dieudonné, A. Pelc, and F. Petit. On deterministic rendezvous at a node of agents with arbitrary velocities. *Inf. Process. Lett.*, 133:39–43, 2018.

[7] Q. Bramas and S. Tixeuil. Wait-free gathering without chirality. In *Structural Information and Communication Complexity - 22nd International Colloquium, SIROCCO 2015, Montserrat, Spain, July 14-16, 2015, Post-Proceedings*, pages 313–327, 2015.

[8] R. Cohen and D. Peleg. Convergence of autonomous mobile robots with inaccurate sensors and movements. In *Annual Symposium on Theoretical Aspects of Computer Science*, pages 549–560. Springer, 2006.

[9] A. Collins, J. Czyzowicz, L. Gasieniec, and A. Labourel. Tell me where I am so I can meet you sooner. In *ICALP*, pages 502–514, 2010.

[10] R. M. Corless, G. H. Gonnet, D. E. G. Hare, D. J. Jeffrey, and D. E. Knuth. On the Lambert W function. *Advances in Computational Mathematics*, 5(1):329–359, Dec 1996.

[11] J. Czyzowicz, R. Killick, and E. Kranakis. Linear rendezvous with asymmetric clocks. In *OPODIS Conference on Principles of Distributed Systems, 17-19 December 2018, Hong Kong*. LIPICS, 2018.

[12] J. Czyzowicz, R. Killick, E. Kranakis, D. Krizanc, and O. Morales Ponce. Gathering in the plane of location-aware robots in the presence of spies. In *SIROCCO 2018, Ma'ale HaHamisha, Israel, June 18-21, 2018, Revised Selected Papers*, pages 361–376, 2018.

[13] J. Czyzowicz, A. Kosowski, and A. Pelc. How to meet when you forget: Log-space rendezvous in arbitrary graphs. *Distributed Computing*, 25:165–178, 2012.

[14] J. Czyzowicz, A. Pelc, and A. Labourel. How to meet asynchronously (almost) everywhere. *ACM Transactions on Algorithms (TALG)*, 8(4):37:1–37:14, 2012.

[15] Y. Dieudonné and A. Pelc. Anonymous meeting in networks. *Algorithmica*, 74:908–946, 2016.

[16] Y. Dieudonné, A. Pelc, and V. Villain. How to meet asynchronously at polynomial cost. *SIAM J. Comput.*, 44(3):844–867, 2015.

[17] O. Feinerman, A. Korman, S. Kutten, and Y. Rodeh. Fast rendezvous on a cycle by agents with different speeds. *Theoretical Computer Science*, 688:77–85, 2017.

[18] A. Hoorfar and M. Hassani. Inequalities on the Lambert W function and hyper-power function. *JIPAM. Journal of Inequalities in Pure & Applied Mathematics [electronic only]*, 9, 01 2008.

[19] T. Izumi, Y. Katayama, N. Inuzuka, and K. Wada. Gathering autonomous mobile robots with dynamic compasses: An optimal result. In *International Symposium on Distributed Computing*, pages 298–312. Springer, 2007.

[20] T. Izumi, S. Souissi, Y. Katayama, N. Inuzuka, X. Défago, K. Wada, and M. Yamashita. The gathering problem for two oblivious robots with unreliable compasses. *SIAM J. Comput.*, 41(1):26–46, 2012.

[21] Y. Katayama, Y. Tomida, H. Imazu, N. Inuzuka, and K. Wada. Dynamic compass models and gathering algorithms for autonomous mobile robots. In *International Colloquium on Structural Information and Communication Complexity*, pages 274–288. Springer, 2007.

[22] P. King and F. M. auf der Heide. Continuous protocols for swarm robotics. In *Proceedings of Moving and Computing, 5-9 June, 2017. La Maddalena, Italy*. Springer, 2017.

[23] E. Kranakis, D. Krizanc, and E. Markou. The mobile agent rendezvous problem in the ring. *Synthesis Lectures on Distributed Computing Theory*, 1(1):1–122, 2010.

[24] S. Li, C. Markarian, F. M. auf der Heide, and P. Podlipyan. A continuous strategy for collisionless gathering. In *International Symposium on Algorithms and Experiments for Sensor Systems, Wireless Networks and Distributed Robotics*, pages 182–197. Springer, 2017.

[25] A. Pelc. Reaching a target in the plane with no information. *Information Processing Letters*, 140:13–17, 2018.

[26] A. Pelc. *Deterministic Rendezvous Algorithms*. In P. Flocchini, G. Prencipe, and N. Santoro, editors, *Distributed Computing by Mobile Entities*, pages 423–454. Springer, 2019.

[27] A. Ta-Shma and U. Zwick. Deterministic rendezvous, treasure hunts, and strongly universal exploration sequences. *ACM Transactions on Algorithms (TALG)*, 10(3):12, 2014.

Composable Computation in Discrete Chemical Reaction Networks

Eric E. Severson*
eseverson@ucdavis.edu
University of California, Davis
Davis, California

David Haley*
drhaley@ucdavis.edu
University of California, Davis
Davis, California

David Doty*
doty@ucdavis.edu
University of California, Davis
Davis, California

ABSTRACT

We study the composability of discrete chemical reaction networks (CRNs) that *stably compute* (i.e., with probability 0 of error) integer-valued functions $f : \mathbb{N}^d \to \mathbb{N}$. We consider *output-oblivious* CRNs in which the output species is never a reactant (input) to any reaction. The class of output-oblivious CRNs is fundamental, appearing in earlier studies of CRN computation, because it is precisely the class of CRNs that can be composed by simply renaming the output of the upstream CRN to match the input of the downstream CRN.

Our main theorem precisely characterizes the functions f stably computable by output-oblivious CRNs with an initial leader. The key necessary condition is that for sufficiently large inputs, f is the minimum of a finite number of nondecreasing *quilt-affine* functions. (An affine function is linear with a constant offset; a *quilt-affine* function is linear with a periodic offset).

CCS CONCEPTS

• **Theory of computation** → *Distributed computing models; Distributed algorithms.*

KEYWORDS

chemical reaction network, population protocol, composable computation, semilinear

ACM Reference Format:

Eric E. Severson, David Haley, and David Doty. 2019. Composable Computation in Discrete Chemical Reaction Networks. In *2019 ACM Symposium on Principles of Distributed Computing (PODC '19), July 29-August 2, 2019, Toronto, ON, Canada.* ACM, New York, NY, USA, 10 pages. https://doi.org/10.1145/3293611.3331615

1 INTRODUCTION

A foundational model of chemistry commonly used in natural sciences is that of chemical reaction networks (CRNs): finite sets of chemical reactions such as $A+B \to A+C$. The model is described as a continuous time, discrete state, Markov process [18]. A configuration of the system is a vector of non-negative integers specifying the molecular counts of the species (e.g., A, B, C), a reaction can occur only when all its reactants are present, and transitions between configurations correspond to reactions (e.g., when the above reaction occurs the count of B is decreased by 1 and the count of C increased by 1). CRNs are widely used to describe natural biochemical systems such as the intricate cellular regulatory networks responsible for the information processing within cells. Looking beyond the *scientific* goal of understanding natural CRNs, to the *engineering* goal of constructing programmable, autonomous smart molecules, artificial CRNs have been implemented using the physical primitive of nucleic-acid strand displacement cascades [8, 11, 22, 23].

Population protocols, a widely-studied model of distributed computing with very limited agents, are a restricted subset of CRNs (those with two reactants and two products in each reaction) that nevertheless capture many of the interesting features of CRNs. The key feature is the inability of agents (molecules) to control their schedule of communication (collisions). The decision problems solvable by population protocols have been studied extensively: they can simulate Turing machines with high probability in polylogarithmic time (with [5] or without [19] an initial leader), whereas requiring probability 0 of error limits the computable predicates to being semilinear [6].

1.1 Function computation

Computation of functions $f : \mathbb{N}^d \to \mathbb{N}$ was discussed briefly in the first population protocols paper [3, Section 3.4], which focused more on Boolean predicate computation, and it was defined formally first for CRNs [10, 15] and later for population protocols [7]. The class of functions stably computable in either model is the same: the semilinear functions [6, 10]. We use the CRN model because it is more natural for describing functions, but our results also apply to the population protocol model.

To represent an input $\mathbf{x} \in \mathbb{N}^d$, we start in a configuration with counts $\mathbf{x}(i)$ of species X_i for each $i \in \{1, \dots, d\}$, and count 1 of a "leader" species L.[1] A function $f : \mathbb{N}^d \to \mathbb{N}$ is *stably computable* by a CRN if a correct and *stable* configuration $\mathbf{O}$ (i.e., on input $\mathbf{x}$ the count of Y is $f(\mathbf{x})$ in all configurations reachable from $\mathbf{O}$) remains reachable no matter what reactions occur.[2]

See Fig. 1 for examples. It is known that a function $f : \mathbb{N}^d \to \mathbb{N}$ is stably computable by a CRN if and only if it is *semilinear*: intuitively, it is a piecewise affine function. (See Definition 2.5.)

*Authors supported by NSF grants 1619343 and 1844976.

PODC '19, July 29-August 2, 2019, Toronto, ON, Canada

ACM ISBN 978-1-4503-6217-7/19/07...$15.00
https://doi.org/10.1145/3293611.3331615

[1] The leader is discussed in Section 1.3. A CRN may ignore its leader, as in Fig. 1.

[2] We use this definition throughout the paper, but we mention here that it is equivalent to two other natural definitions. The first definition is that any fair sequence of reactions *will* take the CRN to such a correct stable configuration, where *fair* means that any configuration that is infinitely often reachable is eventually reached. The second definition is that a correct stable configuration is actually reached with probability 1.

$$\frac{f(x) = 2x}{X \to 2Y} \qquad \frac{f(x_1, x_2) = \min(x_1, x_2)}{X_1 + X_2 \to Y}$$

$$f(x_1, x_2) = \max(x_1, x_2)$$
$$\begin{array}{rcl} X_1 & \to & Z_1 + Y \\ X_2 & \to & Z_2 + Y \\ Z_1 + Z_2 & \to & K \\ K + Y & \to & \emptyset \end{array}$$

Figure 1: Functions stably computed by CRNs. Note max is computed as $x_1 + x_2 - \min(x_1, x_2)$.

1.2 Composability

Note a key difference between the CRNs for min and max in Fig. 1: the former only produces the output species Y, whereas the latter also contains reactions that consume Y. In one possible sequence of reactions for the max CRN, the inputs can be exhausted through the first two reactions before ever executing the last two reactions. In doing so, the count of Y overshoots its correct value of $\max(x_1, x_2)$ before the excess is consumed by the reaction $K + Y \to \emptyset$.

For this reason that the min CRN is more easily composed with a downstream CRN. For example, the function $2 \cdot \min(x_1, x_2)$ is stably computed by the reactions $X_1 + X_2 \to W$ (computing $w = x_1 + x_2$) and $W \to 2Y$ (computing $y = 2w$), renaming the output of the min CRN to match the input of the multiply-by-2 CRN. However, this approach does not work to compute $2 \cdot \max(x_1, x_2)$; changing Y to W in the four-reaction max CRN and adding the reaction $W \to 2Y$ can erroneously result in up to $2(x_1+x_2)$ copies of Y being produced. Intuitively, the multiply-by-2 reaction $W \to 2Y$ competes with the upstream reaction $K + W \to \emptyset$ from the max CRN.

This motivates us to study the class of functions $f : \mathbb{N}^d \to \mathbb{N}$ stably computable by *output-oblivious* CRNs: those in which the output species Y appears only as a product, never as a reactant. We call such a function *obliviously-computable.* Any obliviously-computable function must be nondecreasing, otherwise reactions could incorrectly overproduce output (see Observation 2.1).

Obliviously-computable functions must also be semilinear, so it is reasonable to conjecture that a function is obliviously-computable if and only if it is semilinear and nondecreasing. In fact, this is true for 1D functions $f : \mathbb{N} \to \mathbb{N}$ (see Section 3). However, in higher dimensions, the function $\max : \mathbb{N}^2 \to \mathbb{N}$ is semilinear and nondecreasing, yet not obliviously-computable; its consumption of output turns out to be unavoidable. Assuming there is no leader, this is simple to prove: Since $\max(1, 0) = 1$, starting with one X_1, a Y can be produced. Similarly, a Y can be produced starting with one X_2. Then with one X_1 and one X_2, these reactions can happen in parallel and produce two Y's, too many since $\max(1, 1) = 1$. It is more involved to prove that even with a leader, it remains impossible to obliviously compute max; see Section 4.[3]

1.3 The role of the leader

Our model includes an initial leader, which is essential for our general constructions (see Sections 3 and 6). The class of stably

[3] This result was obtained independently by Chugg, Condon, and Hashemi [12].

$$\frac{f(x) = \min(1, x)}{\begin{array}{c} X \to Y \\ 2Y \to Y \end{array}} \qquad \frac{f(x) = \min(1, x)}{L + X \to Y}$$

Figure 2: $\min(1, x)$ is stably computed by a *leaderless* non-output-oblivious CRN (left), and an output-oblivious CRN with a single leader L (right).

computable functions is identical whether an initial leader is allowed or not [15], as is the class of stably computable predicates [6].

Interestingly, the class of obliviously-computable functions we study is provably larger when an initial leader is allowed. For example, consider the function $f(x) = \min(1, x)$ (see Fig. 2). f is stably computable with or without a leader, but only the construction with a leader is output-oblivious. Without using a leader, f is not obliviously-computable (see Observation 9.1).

Including the leader gives additional power to the model. This gives more power to our CRN constructions, but makes our impossibility results stronger. Fully classifying the obliviously-computable functions in a leaderless model remains an open question.

1.4 Contribution

Our main result, Theorem 5.2, provides a complete characterization of the class of obliviously-computable functions. It builds off a key definition: a *quilt-affine* function is a nondecreasing function that is the sum of a rational linear function and periodic function (formalized as Definition 5.1). For example, functions such as $\lfloor \frac{3x}{2} \rfloor$ are quilt-affine (see Fig. 3a). Such floored division functions are natural to the discrete CRN model ($\lfloor \frac{3x}{2} \rfloor$ is stably computed by reactions $X \to 3Z$, $2Z \to Y$). Fig. 3b shows a higher-dimensional quilt-affine function, with a "bumpy quilt" structure that motivates the name. Quilt-affine functions are also characterized by nonnegative periodic finite differences, a structure key to showing they are obliviously-computable (see Lemma 6.1).

Theorem 5.2 states that a function $f : \mathbb{N}^d \to \mathbb{N}$ is obliviously-computable if and only if

i) [nondecreasing] f is nondecreasing,
ii) [eventually-min] for sufficiently large inputs, f is the minimum of a finite number of quilt-affine functions, and
iii) [recursive] every restriction $f_r : \mathbb{N}^{d-1} \to \mathbb{N}$ obtained by fixing some inputs to a constant value[4] is obliviously-computable (i.e., eventually the minimum of quilt-affine functions).

Condition (ii) characterizes f when all inputs are sufficiently large (greater than some $\mathbf{n} \in \mathbb{N}^d$), whereas condition (iii) characterizes f when some inputs are fixed to smaller values. See Fig. 4a for a representative example of an obliviously-computable $f : \mathbb{N}^2 \to \mathbb{N}$. This pictured function has arbitrary nondecreasing values in the "finite region" where $\mathbf{x} < (4, 4)$, has eventual 1D quilt-affine behavior along the lines $x_1 = 0, 1, 2, 3$ and $x_2 = 0, 1, 2, 3$, and is the minimum of 3 different quilt-affine functions in the "eventual region" where $\mathbf{x} \geq (4, 4)$. This behavior generalizes naturally to higher dimensions.

The most technically sophisticated part of our result is the proof that the eventually-min condition (ii) of Theorem 5.2 is necessary; the main ideas of this proof are outlined in Section 7.1.

[4] Note that Theorem 5.2 defines fixed-input restrictions slightly differently; see Section 5 for an explanation.

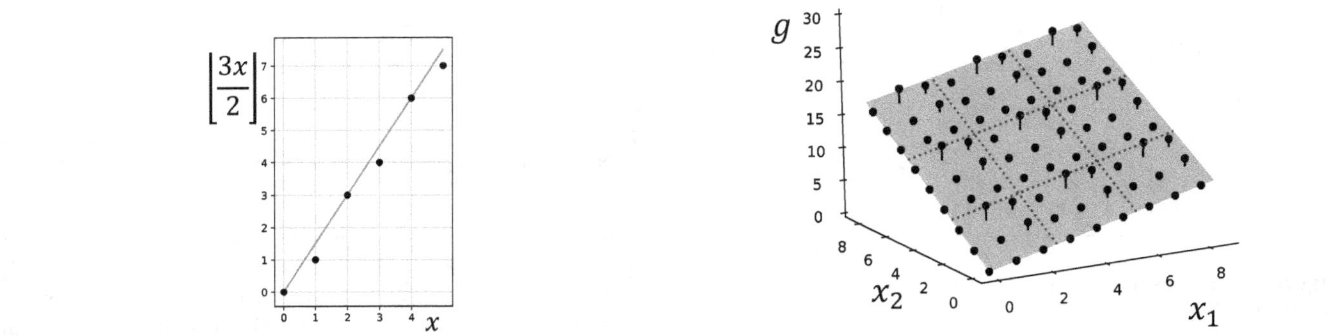

(a) A 1D (single-input) quilt-affine function $\lfloor \frac{3x}{2} \rfloor = \frac{3}{2}x + B(\overline{x} \mod 2)$, where $B(\overline{0}) = 0$ and $B(\overline{1}) = -\frac{1}{2}$.

(b) A 2D quilt-affine function $g(\mathbf{x}) = (1, 2) \cdot \mathbf{x} + B(\overline{\mathbf{x}} \mod 3)$, where $B(\overline{\mathbf{x}}) = 0$ except when $\overline{\mathbf{x}} \in \{\overline{(1, 2)}, \overline{(2, 2)}, \overline{(2, 1)}\}$.

Figure 3: Examples of 1D and 2D quilt-affine functions.

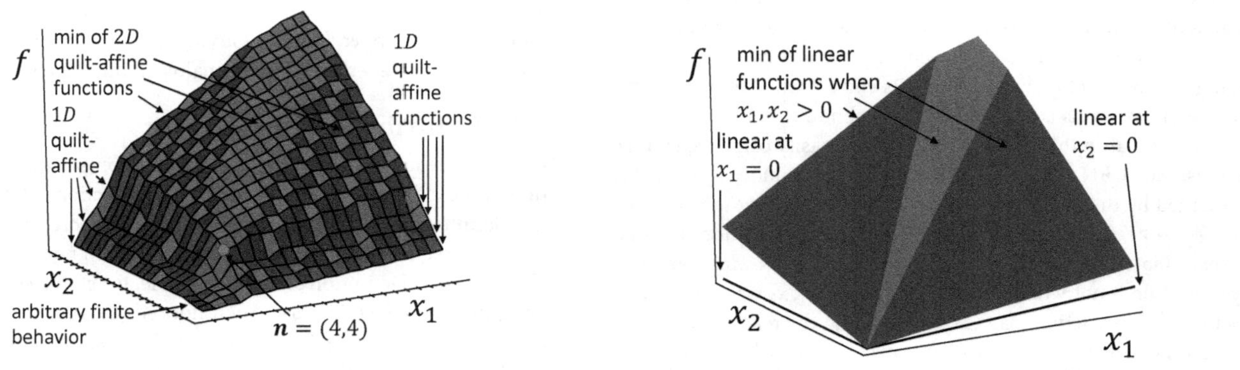

(a) A 2D function satisfying Theorem 5.2.

(b) The scaling limit gives a 2D real-valued obliviously-computable function from [9].

Figure 4: Example discrete and real-valued obliviously-computable functions.

1.5 Related work

Chalk, Kornerup, Reeves, and Soloveichik [9] showed an analogous result in the *continuous* model of CRNs in which species amounts are given by nonnegative real concentrations. A consequence of their characterization is that any obliviously-computable real-valued function is a minimum of linear functions when all inputs are positive. In Theorem 8.2, we demonstrate that the limit of "scalings" of a function $f : \mathbb{N}^d \to \mathbb{N}$ satisfying our main Theorem 5.2 is in fact a function $\hat{f} : \mathbb{R}^d_{\geq 0} \to \mathbb{R}_{\geq 0}$ satisfying the main theorem of [9] (see Fig. 4b). The discrete details lost in the scaling limit constitute precisely the unique challenges of proving Theorem 5.2 that are not handled by [9]. In particular, our function class can contain arbitrary finite behavior and repeated finite irregularities.

Returning to the *discrete* (a.k.a., *stochastic*) CRN model we study, Chugg, Condon, and Hashemi [12] independently investigated the special case of *two-input* functions $f : \mathbb{N}^2 \to \mathbb{N}$ computable by output-oblivious CRNs, obtaining a characterization equivalent to ours when restricted to 2D. Their characterization is phrased much differently, with specially constructed "fissure functions" to describe the function behavior across what we describe as *under-determined regions* (intuitively, thin "1D" regions bounded by parallel lines, where f cannot be described by a unique quilt-affine function, see Section 7). The ideas required to prove the 2D case are sophisticated and far from simple, yet unfortunately, these ideas do not extend straightforwardly to higher dimensions. The planarity of the 2D input space constrains the regions induced by separating hyperplanes (i.e., lines) in a strong way. Furthermore, the fact that there is only one nontrivial integer dimension smaller than 2 implies that the under-determined regions are simpler to reason about than in the case where they can have arbitrary dimension between 1 and d. Finally, even restricted to 2D, a notable aspect of our characterization is expressing f a minimum of quilt-affine functions, which are simple intrinsic building blocks that generalize immediately.

1.6 Other ways of composing computation

In Section 2.3 we show that a for a CRN $\mathcal{C}$ be composable with downstream CRN $\mathcal{D}$ by "concatenation" (renaming $\mathcal{C}$'s output species to match $\mathcal{D}$'s input species and ensuring all other species names are disjoint between $\mathcal{C}$ and $\mathcal{D}$), it is (in a sense) necessary and sufficient for $\mathcal{C}$ to be output-oblivious. There are other ways to compose computations, however.

A common technique (e.g. [17]) is for C to detect when its output has changed and send a *restart* signal to $\mathcal{D}$. However, it is not obvious how to do this with function computation as defined in this paper, where $\mathcal{D}$ changes C's output by consuming it.

Another technique (e.g. [5]) is to set a *termination signal*, which is a sub-CRN that, with high probability, creates a copy of a signal species T, but not before C has converged. T then "activates" the reactions of $\mathcal{D}$, so that $\mathcal{D}$ will not consume the output of C until it is safe to do so. However, this has some positive failure probability. In fact, if we require T to be guaranteed with probability 1 to be produced only after the CRN has converged, only constant functions can be stably computed. Worse yet, in the leaderless case, it is provably impossible to achieve this guarantee even with positive probability [14].

2 PRELIMINARIES

2.1 Notation

$\mathbb{N}$ denotes the set of nonnegative integers. For a set $\mathcal{S}$ (of species), we write $\mathbb{N}^{\mathcal{S}}$ to denote the set of vectors indexed by the elements of $\mathcal{S}$ (equivalently, functions $f : \mathcal{S} \to \mathbb{N}$). Vectors appear in boldface, and we reserve uppercase $\mathbf{A} \in \mathbb{N}^{\mathcal{S}}$ for such vectors indexed by species, and lowercase $\mathbf{a} \in \mathbb{N}^d, \mathbb{Z}^d, \mathbb{Q}^d, \mathbb{R}^d$ for vectors indexed by integers. $\mathbf{A}(S)$ or $\mathbf{a}(i)$ denotes the element indexed by $S \in \mathcal{S}$ or $i \in \{1, \ldots, d\}$. We write $\mathbf{a} \leq \mathbf{b}$ to denote pointwise vector inequality $\mathbf{a}(i) \leq \mathbf{b}(i)$ for all i.

For $p \in \mathbb{N}_+$, $\mathbb{Z}/p\mathbb{Z}$ denotes the additive group of integers modulo p, whose elements are congruence classes. Generalizing to higher dimensions, $\mathbb{Z}^d/p\mathbb{Z}^d$ denotes the additive group of $\mathbb{Z}^d$ modulo p, whose elements are congruence classes. For $\mathbf{x} \in \mathbb{N}^d$ where $d \geq 1$, we write $\overline{\mathbf{x}} \mod p$ to denote the congruence class $\{\mathbf{x} + p\mathbf{z} : \mathbf{z} \in \mathbb{Z}^d\} \in \mathbb{Z}^d/p\mathbb{Z}^d$, also denoted $\overline{\mathbf{x}}$ when p is clear from context.

2.2 Chemical reaction networks

We use the established definitions of stable function computation by (discrete) chemical reaction networks [4, 12]:

A *chemical reaction network* (CRN) $C = (\mathcal{S}, \mathcal{R})$ is defined by a finite set $\mathcal{S}$ of species and a finite set $\mathcal{R}$ of reactions, where a reaction $(\mathbf{R}, \mathbf{P}) \in \mathbb{N}^{\mathcal{S}} \times \mathbb{N}^{\mathcal{S}}$ describes the counts of consumed *reactant* species and produced *product* species.[5] For example, given $\mathcal{S} = \{A, B, C\}$, the reaction $((1, 0, 2), (0, 2, 1))$ would represent $A + 2C \to 2B + C$.

A configuration $\mathbf{C} \in \mathbb{N}^{\mathcal{S}}$ specifies the integer counts of all species. Reaction $(\mathbf{R}, \mathbf{P})$ is *applicable* to $\mathbf{C}$ if $\mathbf{R} \leq \mathbf{C}$, and yields $\mathbf{C}' = \mathbf{C} - \mathbf{R} + \mathbf{P}$, so we write $\mathbf{C} \to \mathbf{C}'$. A configuration $\mathbf{D}$ is *reachable* from $\mathbf{C}$ if there exists a finite sequence of configurations such that $\mathbf{C} \to \mathbf{C}_1 \to \ldots \to \mathbf{C}_n \to \mathbf{D}$; we write $\mathbf{C} \to^* \mathbf{D}$ to denote that $\mathbf{D}$ is reachable from $\mathbf{C}$. Note this reachability relation is additive: if $\mathbf{A} \to^* \mathbf{B}$, then $\mathbf{A} + \mathbf{C} \to^* \mathbf{B} + \mathbf{C}$. This property is key in future proofs to show the reachability of configurations which overproduce output.

To compute a function[6] $f : \mathbb{N}^d \to \mathbb{N}$, the CRN C will include an ordered subset $\{X_1, \ldots, X_d\} \subset \mathcal{S}$ of *input species*, an *output species* Y, and a *leader species* $L \in \mathcal{S}$. (Note that we consider removing the leader in Section 9).

The computation of $f(\mathbf{x})$ will start from an *initial configuration* $\mathbf{I_x}$ encoding the input with $\mathbf{I_x}(X_i) = \mathbf{x}(i)$ for all $i = 1, \ldots, d$, along with a single leader $\mathbf{I_x}(L) = 1$, and count 0 of all other species. A *stable* configuration $\mathbf{C}$ has unchanged output $\mathbf{C}(Y) = \mathbf{D}(Y)$ for any configuration $\mathbf{D}$ reachable from $\mathbf{C}$. The CRN C *stably computes* $f : \mathbb{N}^d \to \mathbb{N}$ if for each initial configuration $\mathbf{I_x}$ encoding any $\mathbf{x} \in \mathbb{N}^d$, and configuration $\mathbf{C}$ reachable from $\mathbf{I_x}$, there is a stable configuration $\mathbf{O}$ reachable from $\mathbf{C}$ with correct output $\mathbf{O}(Y) = f(\mathbf{x})$.

2.3 Composition via output-oblivious CRNs

This section formally defines our notions of "composable computation with CRNs via concatenation of reactions" and "output-oblivious" CRNs that don't consume their output, showing these notions to be essentially equivalent.

A CRN is *output-oblivious* if the output species Y is never a reactant[7]: for any reaction $(\mathbf{R}, \mathbf{P})$, $\mathbf{R}(Y) = 0$. A function $f : \mathbb{N}^d \to \mathbb{N}$ is *obliviously-computable* if f is stably computed by an output-oblivious CRN.

We begin with an easy observation:

Observation 2.1. *An obliviously-computable function $f : \mathbb{N}^d \to \mathbb{N}$ must be nondecreasing.*

Proof. Assume a CRN C (with output species Y) stably computes f, but $f(\mathbf{a}) > f(\mathbf{b})$ for $\mathbf{a} \leq \mathbf{b}$. To stably compute $f(\mathbf{a})$, input configuration $\mathbf{I_a} \to^* \mathbf{O}$ for some configuration with $\mathbf{O}(Y) = f(\mathbf{a})$. However, since $\mathbf{a} \leq \mathbf{b}$, that same sequence of reactions can be applied from the input configuration $\mathbf{I_b} \geq \mathbf{I_a}$. This overproduces Y since $f(\mathbf{a}) > f(\mathbf{b})$. Thus to stably compute $f(\mathbf{b})$, some reaction must consume Y as a reactant, so C cannot be output-oblivious. □

A CRN being output-oblivious was shown in [9] (for *continuous* CRNs) to be equivalent to being "composable via concatenation", meaning renaming the output species of one CRN to match the input of another. This equivalence still holds in our discrete CRN model. This is formalized as Observation 2.2 and Lemma 2.3.

For CRNs C_f stably computing $f : \mathbb{N}^d \to \mathbb{N}$ and C_g stably computing $g : \mathbb{N} \to \mathbb{N}$, define the *concatenated* CRN $C_{g \circ f}$ by combining species and reactions, with C_f's output species as C_g's input species and no other common species, plus a reaction $L \to L^f + L^g$ creating a copy of the leader from each of C_f and C_g.

We first observe that this composition works correctly if the *upstream* CRN C_f is output-oblivious. Intuitively, the reactions from C_g can only affect the reactions from C_f via the common species W, but this output species of C_f is never used as a reactant to stably compute $f(\mathbf{x})$.

Observation 2.2. *If C_f stably computes $f : \mathbb{N}^d \to \mathbb{N}$, C_g stably computes $g : \mathbb{N} \to \mathbb{N}$, and C_f is output-oblivious, then the concatenated CRN $C_{g \circ f}$ stably computes the composition $g \circ f : \mathbb{N}^d \to \mathbb{N}$.*

Note that the downstream CRN C_g need not be output-oblivious, but if two output-oblivious CRNs are composed, then the composition $C_{g \circ f}$ remains output-oblivious. More generally, g can take

[5] We do not limit ourselves to *bimolecular* (two input) reactions, but the higher-order reactions we use can easily be converted to have this form. For example, $3X \to Y$ is equivalent to two reactions $2X \leftrightarrow X_2$ and $X + X_2 \to Y$.

[6] We consider codomain $\mathbb{N}$ without loss of generality, since $f : \mathbb{N}^d \to \mathbb{N}^l$ is stably computable if and only if each output component is stably computable by parallel CRNs.

[7] A more general definition in [12] of *output-monotonic* CRNs just requires no reaction to reduce the count of output species. This can be directly seen to classify the same set of functions, see [21].

any number of inputs from output-oblivious CRNs, which act as modules for arbitrary feedforward composition.

The converse shows that a composable CRN is essentially output-oblivious. If C_f can be correctly composed with any downstream C_g, then C_f must function correctly even if downstream reactions from C_g starve it of the common species W. Thus C_f will still stably compute f if we remove all reactions with output W as a reactant, making it output-oblivious. The proof appears in [21].

Lemma 2.3. *Let C_f stably compute $f : \mathbb{N}^d \to \mathbb{N}$ such that for any C_g stably computing $g : \mathbb{N} \to \mathbb{N}$, the concatenated CRN $C_{g \circ f}$ stably computes the composition $g \circ f : \mathbb{N}^d \to \mathbb{N}$. Then C_f still stably computes f if we remove all reactions using the output species as a reactant, making it output-oblivious.*

2.4 Semilinear functions

The functions stably computable by a CRN were shown in [10], building from work in [4], to be precisely the *semilinear* functions, which are defined based on semilinear sets[8]

Definition 2.4. *A subset $S \subseteq \mathbb{N}^d$ is* semilinear *if S is a finite Boolean combination (union, intersection, complement) of* threshold *sets of the form $\{\mathbf{x} \in \mathbb{N}^d : \mathbf{a} \cdot \mathbf{x} \geq b\}$ for $\mathbf{a} \in \mathbb{Z}^d, b \in \mathbb{Z}$ and* mod *sets of the form $\{\mathbf{x} \in \mathbb{N}^d : \mathbf{a} \cdot \mathbf{x} \equiv b \mod c\}$ for $\mathbf{a} \in \mathbb{Z}^d, b \in \mathbb{Z}, c \in \mathbb{N}_+$.*

A *semilinear function* can be concisely defined as having a semilinear graph, but a more useful equivalent definition comes from Lemma 4.3 of [10][9]:

Definition 2.5 ([10]). *A function $f : \mathbb{N}^d \to \mathbb{N}$ is* semilinear *if f is the finite union of affine partial functions, whose domains are disjoint semilinear subsets of $\mathbb{N}^d$.*

All functions discussed have been semilinear. For example, the function

$$\min(x_1, x_2) = \begin{cases} x_1, & \text{if } x_1 \leq x_2 \\ x_2, & \text{if } x_1 > x_2 \end{cases}$$

is semilinear with affine partial functions on disjoint domains which are defined by a single threshold and thus semilinear.

Similarly, the function

$$\left\lfloor \frac{3x}{2} \right\rfloor = \begin{cases} \frac{3}{2}x, & \text{if } x \text{ is even} \\ \frac{3}{2}x - \frac{1}{2}, & \text{if } x \text{ is odd} \end{cases}$$

is semilinear with affine partial functions on disjoint domains which are defined by parity (a single mod predicate) and thus semilinear. All quilt-affine $f : \mathbb{N}^d \to \mathbb{N}$ are semilinear by the same argument.

Lemma 2.6 ([10]). *A function $f : \mathbb{N}^d \to \mathbb{N}$ is stably computable $\iff$ f is semilinear.*

3 WARM-UP: ONE-DIMENSIONAL CASE

For functions with one-dimensional input, the necessary conditions of being nondecreasing and semilinear are also sufficient.

Theorem 3.1. *$f : \mathbb{N} \to \mathbb{N}$ is obliviously-computable $\iff$ f is semilinear and nondecreasing.*

[8] Semilinear sets have other common equivalent definitions [3]; the above definition is convenient for our proof.

[9] Lemma 4.3 in [10] has domains that are non-disjoint linear sets. We assume the domains are disjoint for convenience, making the domains semilinear sets.

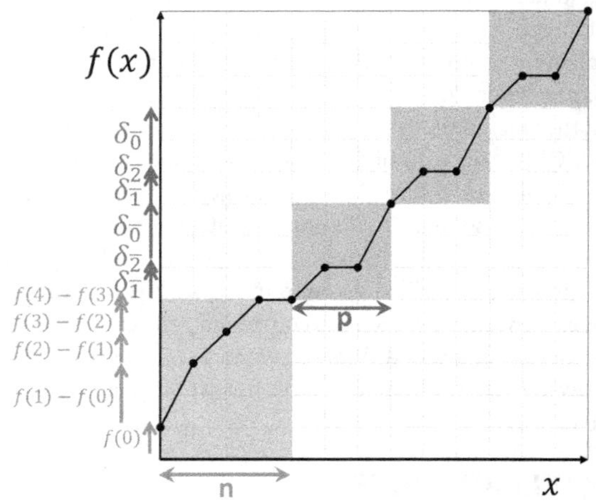

Figure 5: Every semilinear nondecreasing $f : \mathbb{N} \to \mathbb{N}$ is eventually quilt-affine, with periodic finite differences $\delta_{\overline{x}}$.

Intuitively, the proof works as follows. We show semilinear, nondecreasing $f : \mathbb{N} \to \mathbb{N}$ must have the eventually quilt-affine structure in Fig. 5. From this structure, we define a CRN that uses auxiliary leader states to track the value of x (or $\overline{x} \mod p$ once $x \geq n$), while outputting the correct finite differences from adding each input.

Proof. $\Longrightarrow$: Lemma 2.6 and Observation 2.1.

$\Longleftarrow$: If $f : \mathbb{N} \to \mathbb{N}$ is semilinear and nondecreasing, it will eventually be *quilt-affine* (generalized to higher-dimensional functions as Definition 5.1) and thus have periodic finite differences: for some $n \in \mathbb{N}$, period $p \in \mathbb{N}_+$, and finite differences $\delta_{\overline{0}}, \ldots, \delta_{\overline{p-1}} \in \mathbb{N}$, then for all $x \geq n$, $f(x+1) - f(x) = \delta_{(\overline{x} \mod p)}$ (see Fig. 5).

Because f is semilinear, by Definitions 2.4 and 2.5, it can be represented as a disjoint union of affine partial functions, whose domains are semilinear sets, and thus represented as finite Boolean combinations of threshold $\{x \in \mathbb{N} : x \geq a\}$ and mod $\{x \in \mathbb{N} : x \equiv b \mod c\}$ sets. Now take $n \in \mathbb{N}$ greater than all such a and $p = \text{lcm}(c)$ for all such c. Then for all $x \geq n$, f periodically cycles between affine partial functions. Because f is nondecreasing, these periodically-repeated affine partial functions must all have the same slope. This implies f is eventually quilt-affine, with periodic finite differences for all $x \geq n$ as claimed.

The CRN C to stably compute f uses input species X, output species Y, leader L, and species $L_0, \ldots, L_{n-1}, P_{\overline{0}}, \ldots, P_{\overline{p-1}}$ corresponding to auxiliary "states" of the leader, i.e., exactly one of $L, L_0, \ldots, L_{n-1}, P_{\overline{0}}, \ldots, P_{\overline{p-1}}$ is present at any time. Intuitively the leader tracks how many input X it has seen, where the count past n wraps around mod p, and outputs the correct finite differences. The reactions of C are as follows

$$L \to f(0)Y + L_0$$

$$L_i + X \to [f(i+1) - f(i)]Y + L_{i+1} \qquad \text{for all } i = 0, \ldots, n-2$$

$$L_{n-1} + X \to [f(n) - f(n-1)]Y + P_{\overline{n}}$$

$$P_{\overline{a}} + X \to \delta_{\overline{a}}Y + P_{\overline{a+1}} \qquad \text{for all } \overline{a} = \overline{0}, \ldots, \overline{p-1}.$$

□

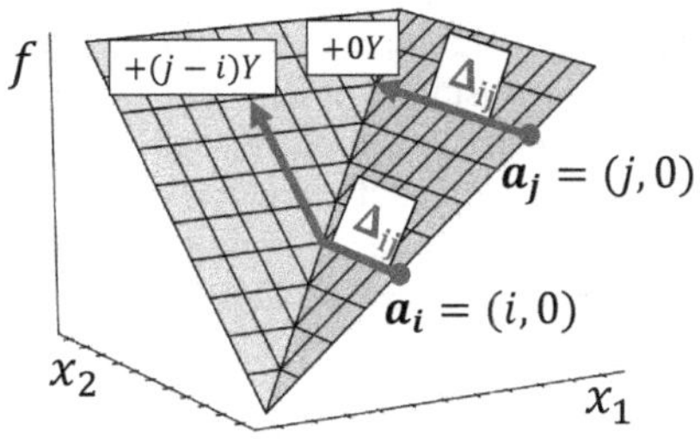

Figure 6: Lemma 4.1 applied to $f = \max(x_1, x_2)$.

In the 1D case, we can also characterize the functions obliviously-computable *without* a leader: they are semilinear and *superadditive*: meaning $f(x) + f(y) \leq f(x + y)$ for all x, y. (Theorem 9.2)

4 IMPOSSIBILITY RESULT

The characterization of obliviously-computable functions as precisely semilinear and nondecreasing from Theorem 3.1 is insufficient in higher dimensions. As an example, consider the function $\max : \mathbb{N}^2 \to \mathbb{N}$, which is both semilinear and nondecreasing. We prove max is not obliviously-computable via a more general lemma:

Lemma 4.1. *Let $f : \mathbb{N}^d \to \mathbb{N}$. If there exists an increasing sequence $(\mathbf{a}_1, \mathbf{a}_2, \ldots) \in \mathbb{N}^d$ such that for all $i < j$ there exists some $\mathbf{\Delta}_{ij} \in \mathbb{N}^d$ with $f(\mathbf{a}_i + \mathbf{\Delta}_{ij}) - f(\mathbf{a}_i) > f(\mathbf{a}_j + \mathbf{\Delta}_{ij}) - f(\mathbf{a}_j)$, then f is not obliviously-computable.*

Before proving Lemma 4.1, we use it to show max is not obliviously-computable.

For $f = \max(x_1, x_2)$, we let $\mathbf{a}_i = (i, 0)$ and $\mathbf{\Delta}_{ij} = (0, j)$, so for $i < j$, $\max(i, j) - \max(i, 0) = j - i > \max(j, j) - \max(j, 0) = 0$ as desired (see Fig. 6). Adding $\mathbf{\Delta}_{ij}$ input after computing $f(\mathbf{a}_i)$ should produce $j - i$ additional output Y. However, adding $\mathbf{\Delta}_{ij}$ input after computing $f(\mathbf{a}_j)$ should not. Lemma 4.1 uses this to show there exists a reaction sequence that overproduces Y, thus max is not obliviously-computable. We now prove Lemma 4.1.

Proof. Assume toward contradiction an output-oblivious CRN $\mathcal{C}$ stably computes f. To stably compute each $f(\mathbf{a}_i)$, the initial configuration $\mathbf{I}_{\mathbf{a}_i} \to^* \mathbf{O}_i$ for some configuration with $\mathbf{O}_i(Y) = f(\mathbf{a}_i)$, giving a sequence of configurations $(\mathbf{O}_i)_{i=1}^{\infty}$. By Dickson's Lemma [13], any sequence of nonnegative integer vectors has a nondecreasing subsequence, so there must be $\mathbf{O}_i \leq \mathbf{O}_j$ for some $i < j$. By assumption there exists $\mathbf{\Delta}_{ij} \in \mathbb{N}^d$ such that

$$f(\mathbf{a}_i + \mathbf{\Delta}_{ij}) - f(\mathbf{a}_i) > f(\mathbf{a}_j + \mathbf{\Delta}_{ij}) - f(\mathbf{a}_j)$$

Now consider the initial configuration $\mathbf{I}_{\mathbf{a}_i+\mathbf{\Delta}_{ij}} \geq \mathbf{I}_{\mathbf{a}_i}$, so define the difference $\mathbf{D} = \mathbf{I}_{\mathbf{a}_i+\mathbf{\Delta}_{ij}} - \mathbf{I}_{\mathbf{a}_i} \in \mathbb{N}^{\mathcal{S}}$. Then the same sequence of reactions $\mathbf{I}_{\mathbf{a}_i} \to^* \mathbf{O}_i$ is applicable to $\mathbf{I}_{\mathbf{a}_i+\mathbf{\Delta}_{ij}}$ reaching configuration $\mathbf{C}_i = \mathbf{O}_i + \mathbf{D}$, with $\mathbf{C}_i(Y) = \mathbf{O}_i(Y) = f(\mathbf{a}_i)$. Then to stably compute $f(\mathbf{a}_i + \mathbf{\Delta}_{ij})$ there must exist a further sequence of reactions α from $\mathbf{C}_i$ that produce an additional $f(\mathbf{a}_i + \mathbf{\Delta}_{ij}) - f(\mathbf{a}_i)$ copies of output Y.

By the same argument, from initial configuration $\mathbf{I}_{\mathbf{a}_j+\mathbf{\Delta}_{ij}}$ the configuration $\mathbf{C}_j = \mathbf{O}_j + \mathbf{D}$ is reachable, with $\mathbf{C}_j(Y) = \mathbf{O}_j(Y) = f(\mathbf{a}_j)$. Then since $\mathbf{O}_i \leq \mathbf{O}_j$, we have $\mathbf{C}_i \leq \mathbf{C}_j$, so the same sequence of reactions α is applicable to $\mathbf{C}_j$, reaching some configuration $\mathbf{C}'_j$ with an additional $f(\mathbf{a}_i + \mathbf{\Delta}_{ij}) - f(\mathbf{a}_i)$ copies of output Y, so

$$\mathbf{C}'_j(Y) = f(\mathbf{a}_j) + f(\mathbf{a}_i + \mathbf{\Delta}_{ij}) - f(\mathbf{a}_i) > f(\mathbf{a}_j + \mathbf{\Delta}_{ij})$$

Then $\mathbf{I}_{\mathbf{a}_j+\mathbf{\Delta}_{ij}} \to^* \mathbf{C}'_j$ overproduces Y, so the output-oblivious CRN $\mathcal{C}$ cannot stably compute $f(\mathbf{a}_j + \mathbf{\Delta}_{ij})$. □

Lemma 4.1 is our main technical tool used to show that a particular semilinear, nondecreasing function is not obliviously-computable, the key challenge in the impossibility direction of Theorem 5.2.

5 MAIN RESULT: FULL-DIMENSIONAL CASE

To formally state our main result, Theorem 5.2, we must first define *quilt-affine* functions as the sum of a linear and periodic function (see Fig. 3b):

Definition 5.1. *A nondecreasing function $g : \mathbb{N}^d \to \mathbb{Z}$ is quilt-affine (with period p) if there exists $\nabla_g \in \mathbb{Q}^d_{\geq 0}$ and $B : \mathbb{Z}^d/p\mathbb{Z}^d \to \mathbb{Q}$ such that $g(\mathbf{x}) = \nabla_g \cdot \mathbf{x} + B(\overline{\mathbf{x}} \mod p)$.*

We call ∇_g the *gradient* of g, and the periodic function B the *periodic offset*. Without loss of generality we have the same period p along all inputs, since p could be the least common multiple of the periods along each input component. Note that $\nabla_g \cdot \mathbf{x}$ and B can each be rational, but the sum $g(x) \in \mathbb{Z}$ will be integer-valued. We allow g to have negative output for technical reasons[10], but in the case that g is quilt-affine with nonnegative output (i.e. $g : \mathbb{N}^d \to \mathbb{N}$), there is a simple output-oblivious CRN construction to stably compute g. The intuitive idea is to use a single leader that reacts with every input species sequentially, tracks the periodic value $\overline{\mathbf{x}} \mod p$, and outputs the correct changes in g (Lemma 6.1).

Our main result has a recursive condition where we fix the input of a function $f : \mathbb{N}^d \to \mathbb{N}$. For each $i = 1, \ldots, d$ and $j \in \mathbb{N}$, define the *fixed-input restriction*[11] $f_{[\mathbf{x}(i)\to j]} : \mathbb{N}^d \to \mathbb{N}$ of f for all $\mathbf{x} \in \mathbb{N}^d$ by $f_{[\mathbf{x}(i)\to j]}(\mathbf{x}) = f(\mathbf{x}(1), \ldots, \mathbf{x}(i-1), j, \mathbf{x}(i+1), \ldots, \mathbf{x}(d))$.

We can now formally state our main result:

Theorem 5.2. *$f : \mathbb{N}^d \to \mathbb{N}$ is obliviously-computable $\iff$*

i) [nondecreasing] f is nondecreasing,
ii) [eventually-min] there exist quilt-affine $g_1, \ldots, g_m : \mathbb{N}^d \to \mathbb{Z}$ and $\mathbf{n} \in \mathbb{N}^d$ such that for all $\mathbf{x} \geq \mathbf{n}$, $f(\mathbf{x}) = \min_k(g_k(\mathbf{x}))$, and
iii) [recursive] all fixed-input restrictions $f_{[\mathbf{x}(i)\to j]}$ are obliviously-computable.

We first prove that these conditions imply f is obliviously-computable via a general CRN construction in Section 6.

The nondecreasing condition (i) is necessary by Observation 2.1. It is immediate to see the recursive condition (iii) is also necessary:

Observation 5.3. *If $f : \mathbb{N}^d \to \mathbb{N}$ is obliviously-computable, then any fixed-input restriction $f_{[\mathbf{x}(i)\to j]} : \mathbb{N}^d \to \mathbb{N}$ is obliviously-computable.*

[10] The quilt-affine functions that describe f for large inputs may be negative on inputs close to the origin.

[11] We define $f_{[\mathbf{x}(i)\to j]}$ to have domain $\mathbb{N}^d$ because it is notationally convenient to have the same domain as f, but $f_{[\mathbf{x}(i)\to j]}$ only has relevant input in $d-1$ of its input components, making condition (iii) recursive.

Proof. Let the output-oblivious CRN C stably compute f. We define the output-oblivious CRN C' to "hardcode" the input $\mathbf{x}(i) = j$ by modifying the reactions of C. Replace all instances of the leader L and input species X_i by L' and X_i' respectively, then add the initial reaction $L \to jX_i' + L'$. It is straightforward to verify that C' stably computes $f_{[\mathbf{x}(i)\to j]}$. □

Then the remaining work (and biggest effort of this paper) is to show the necessity of the eventually-min condition (ii): that every obliviously-computable function can be represented as eventually a minimum of a finite number of quilt-affine functions, which is shown as Theorem 7.1. Its proof relies on f being semilinear, nondecreasing, and not having any "contradiction sequences" to apply Lemma 4.1. Thus the proof of Theorem 7.1 also yields the following alternative characterization to Theorem 5.2:

Theorem 5.4. *$f : \mathbb{N}^d \to \mathbb{N}$ is obliviously-computable $\iff$ f is semilinear, nondecreasing, and has no sequence $(\mathbf{a}_1, \mathbf{a}_2, \ldots)$ meeting the conditions of Lemma 4.1.*

This gives a "negative characterization" identifying behavior obliviously-computable functions must *avoid*, whereas Theorem 5.2, is a "positive characterization" describing the allowable behavior of such functions. We include Theorem 5.4, though it is less descriptive of the function, because it may be useful in other contexts.

6 CONSTRUCTION

First we show that any quilt-affine function with nonnegative range is stably computed by an output-oblivious CRN:

Lemma 6.1. *Every quilt-affine function $g : \mathbb{N}^d \to \mathbb{N}$ is obliviously-computable.*

Proof. Let $g : \mathbb{N}^d \to \mathbb{N}$ be quilt-affine with period p (recalling Definition 5.1). Notice that g has periodic finite differences. For each congruence class $\overline{\mathbf{a}} \in \mathbb{Z}^d/p\mathbb{Z}^d$ and input component $i = 1, \ldots, d$, where $\mathbf{e}_i$ is the ith standard basis vector, define

$$\delta^i_{\overline{\mathbf{a}}} = \nabla_g \cdot \mathbf{e}_i + B(\overline{\mathbf{a} + \mathbf{e}_i} \mod p) - B(\overline{\mathbf{a}} \mod p) \in \mathbb{N}.$$

Observe that for all $\mathbf{x} \in \overline{\mathbf{a}}$, $g(\mathbf{x} + \mathbf{e}_i) - g(\mathbf{x}) = \delta^i_{\overline{\mathbf{a}}}$. We now use these periodic finite differences to construct an output-oblivious CRN C to stably compute g.

The CRN C has input species $X_1, \ldots, X_d$, output species Y, leader species L and p^d additional species $L_{\overline{\mathbf{a}}}$ for each $\overline{\mathbf{a}} \in \mathbb{Z}^d/p\mathbb{Z}^d$ coresponding to auxiliary "states" of the leader. The initial reaction $L \to g(\mathbf{0})Y + L_{\overline{\mathbf{0}}}$ is accompanied by dp^d reactions of the form

$$L_{\overline{\mathbf{a}}} + X_i \to \delta^i_{\overline{\mathbf{a}}} Y + L_{\overline{\mathbf{a}+\mathbf{e}_i}}$$

for each $i = 1, \ldots, d$ and $\overline{\mathbf{a}} \in \mathbb{Z}^d/P\mathbb{Z}^d$. This CRN first creates $g(\mathbf{0})$ output, then sequentially outputs all finite differences, and is easily verified to stably compute g. □

We now prove (in Lemma 6.2) one direction of Theorem 5.2: that conditions (i), (ii), and (iii) imply an output-oblivious CRN can stably compute f. Intuitively, by the eventually-min condition (ii) we compute $f(\mathbf{x})$ for $\mathbf{x} \geq \mathbf{n}$ by composing min and quilt-affine functions. If $\mathbf{x} \not\geq \mathbf{n}$, then $\mathbf{x}(i) = j$ for some input i and $j < \mathbf{n}(i)$. By the recursive condition (iii) we compute $f_{[\mathbf{x}(i)\to j]}(\mathbf{x}) = f(\mathbf{x})$ [12]. The key remaining insight is a trick (similar to a proof in [9]) to compose these pieces using minimum and indicator functions.

The proof of Lemma 6.2 then expresses f as such a minimum of finitely many pieces. We justify that f is obliviously-computable by showing that each piece is obliviously-computable, since by Observation 2.2 obliviously-computable functions are closed under composition.

Lemma 6.2. *If $f : \mathbb{N}^d \to \mathbb{N}$ satisfies the conditions of Theorem 5.2, f is obliviously-computable.*

Proof. Assume $f : \mathbb{N}^d \to \mathbb{N}$ satisfies the conditions of Theorem 5.2. Then by eventually-min condition (ii), there exist quilt-affine $g_1, \ldots, g_m : \mathbb{N}^d \to \mathbb{Z}$ and $\mathbf{n} \in \mathbb{N}^d$ (without loss of generality assume $\mathbf{n} = (n, \ldots, n)$) such that $f(\mathbf{x}) = \min_k(g_k(\mathbf{x}))$ for all $\mathbf{x} \geq \mathbf{n}$.

Let $\mathbf{x} \vee \mathbf{n} = (\max(\mathbf{x}(1), n), \ldots, \max(\mathbf{x}(d), n))$ denote the componentwise max of $\mathbf{x}$ and $\mathbf{n}$. Let $\mathbb{1}_{\{\mathbf{x}(i)>j\}} : \mathbb{N}^d \to \{0, 1\}$ denote the indicator function that is 1 $\iff$ its input $\mathbf{x}$ obeys $\mathbf{x}(i) > j$. Recall $f_{[\mathbf{x}(i)\to j]}$ is the fixed-input restriction setting input $\mathbf{x}(i) = j$. We claim that f can be expressed as

$$f(\mathbf{x}) = \min\Big[f(\mathbf{x} \vee \mathbf{n}), \underbrace{f_{[\mathbf{x}(i)\to j]}(\mathbf{x}) + \mathbb{1}_{\{\mathbf{x}(i)>j\}}(\mathbf{x}) \cdot f(\mathbf{x} \vee \mathbf{n})}_{\substack{i=1,\ldots,d \\ j=0,\ldots,n-1}}\Big]. \quad (1)$$

We first show $f \geq \min[\ldots]$ since for all $\mathbf{x} \in \mathbb{N}^d$, $f(\mathbf{x})$ is achieved by some term. If $\mathbf{x} \geq \mathbf{n}$, then $f(\mathbf{x}) = f(\mathbf{x} \vee \mathbf{n})$. If $\mathbf{x} \not\geq \mathbf{n}$, there must be $\mathbf{x}(i) = j$ for some $i = 1, \ldots, d$ and $j = 0, \ldots, n-1$, so $f(\mathbf{x}) = f_{[\mathbf{x}(i)\to j]}(\mathbf{x}) = f_{[\mathbf{x}(i)\to j]}(\mathbf{x}) + \mathbb{1}_{\{\mathbf{x}(i)>j\}}(\mathbf{x}) \cdot f(\mathbf{x} \vee \mathbf{n})$ since the indicator is 0.

We next show $f \leq \min[\ldots]$ since $f(\mathbf{x}) \leq$ each term for all $\mathbf{x} \in \mathbb{N}^d$. $f(\mathbf{x}) \leq f(\mathbf{x} \vee \mathbf{n})$ since $\mathbf{x} \leq (\mathbf{x} \vee \mathbf{n})$ and f is nondecreasing. When $\mathbb{1}_{\{\mathbf{x}(i)>j\}}(\mathbf{x}) = 1$, we then have $f(\mathbf{x}) \leq f_{[\mathbf{x}(i)\to j]}(\mathbf{x}) + \mathbb{1}_{\{\mathbf{x}(i)>j\}}(\mathbf{x}) \cdot f(\mathbf{x} \vee \mathbf{n})$. If $\mathbb{1}_{\{\mathbf{x}(i)>j\}}(\mathbf{x}) = 0$, then $\mathbf{x}(i) \leq j$ so $f(\mathbf{x}) \leq f_{[\mathbf{x}(i)\to j]}(\mathbf{x})$ since f is nondecreasing. Thus equation 1 holds as claimed.

It remains to show that f is obliviously-computable. From Observation 2.2, output-oblivious CRNs are closed under composition, and equation 1 gives a method to express f as a composition of functions. Thus it suffices to show that each piece is obliviously-computable. Specifically, we show the functions $\min : \mathbb{N}^k \to \mathbb{N}$ (for any k), $f(\mathbf{x} \vee \mathbf{n}) : \mathbb{N}^d \to \mathbb{N}$, $f_{[\mathbf{x}(i)\to j]}(\mathbf{x}) : \mathbb{N}^d \to \mathbb{N}$, and $c(a, b, \mathbf{x}) = a + \mathbb{1}_{\{\mathbf{x}(i)>j\}}(\mathbf{x}) \cdot b : \mathbb{N}^{d+2} \to \mathbb{N}$ are each obliviously-computable. Implicit in the composed CRN to stably compute f as the composition from equation 1 is the "fan out" operation where reactions of the form $X_i \to X_i^1, \ldots, X_i^m$ create multiple copies of species X_i to be used as independent inputs to multiple "modules" in this composition.

$\min : \mathbb{N}^k \to \mathbb{N}$ **is obliviously-computable:**
Consider the CRN with single reaction $X_1, \ldots, X_k \to Y$, the natural generalization of two-input min from Fig. 1.

$f(\mathbf{x} \vee \mathbf{n}) : \mathbb{N}^d \to \mathbb{N}$ **is obliviously-computable:**
By condition (ii), $f(\mathbf{x} \vee \mathbf{n}) = \min_k(g_k(\mathbf{x} \vee \mathbf{n}))$ since $\mathbf{x} \vee \mathbf{n} \geq \mathbf{n}$, so it suffices to show for each quilt-affine $g_k : \mathbb{N}^d \to \mathbb{Z}$ that $g_k(\mathbf{x} \vee \mathbf{n})$ is obliviously-computable.

[12] As a result, this construction is recursive, with an additional input being fixed at each level of the recursion, so the base case is simply a constant function.

By condition (ii), $g_k(\mathbf{x}+\mathbf{n}) \geq f(\mathbf{x}+\mathbf{n}) \geq 0$ since $\mathbf{x}+\mathbf{n} \geq \mathbf{n}$. Then $g_k(\mathbf{x}+\mathbf{n}) : \mathbb{N}^d \to \mathbb{N}$ is still quilt-affine since that property is preserved by translation, but now has guaranteed nonnegative output. Thus by Lemma 6.1, $g_k(\mathbf{x}+\mathbf{n}) : \mathbb{N}^d \to \mathbb{N}$ is obliviously-computable.

Letting $(\mathbf{x}-\mathbf{n})_+ = (\max(\mathbf{x}(1)-n, 0), \ldots, \max(\mathbf{x}(d)-n, 0))$, we then show the function $(\mathbf{x}-\mathbf{n})_+ : \mathbb{N}^d \to \mathbb{N}^d$ is obliviously-computable via the CRN with reactions $(n+1)X_i \to nX_i + Y_i$ for each component $i = 1, \ldots, d$.

Finally, because $\mathbf{x} \vee \mathbf{n} = (\mathbf{x}-\mathbf{n})_+ + \mathbf{n}$, we have shown $g_k(\mathbf{x} \vee \mathbf{n}) = g_k((\mathbf{x}-\mathbf{n})_+ + \mathbf{n})$ is obliviously-computable as the composition of obliviously-computable $g_k(\mathbf{x}+\mathbf{n})$ and $(\mathbf{x}-\mathbf{n})_+$.

$f_{[\mathbf{x}(i)\to j]}(\mathbf{x}) : \mathbb{N}^d \to \mathbb{N}$ **is obliviously-computable:**
This is precisely the assumed recursive condition (iii).

$c(a, b, \mathbf{x}) = a + \mathbb{1}_{\{\mathbf{x}(i)>j\}}(\mathbf{x}) \cdot b : \mathbb{N}^{d+2} \to \mathbb{N}$ **is obliviously-computable:**
Consider the output-oblivious CRN (with input species $A, B, X_1, \ldots, X_d$ and output species Y) with two reactions $A \to Y$ and $(j+1)X_i + B \to (j+1)X_i + Y$. The A is all converted to Y, and $(j+1)$ copies of input species X_i catalyze the conversion of B to Y, which will only happen when $\mathbb{1}_{\{\mathbf{x}(i)>j\}}(\mathbf{x}) = 1$. Thus this stably computes $c(a, b, \mathbf{x})$ as desired. □

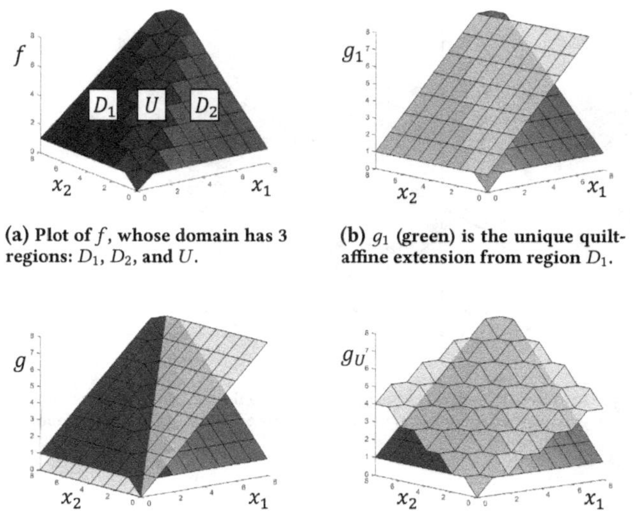

(a) Plot of f, whose domain has 3 regions: D_1, D_2, and U.

(b) g_1 (green) is the unique quilt-affine extension from region D_1.

(c) g (green) is a quilt-affine extension from U, but $g < f$ on D_1.

(d) g_U (green) is a quilt-affine extension from U, and $g_U \geq f$.

Figure 7: **Obliviously-computable f can be expressed as a min of quilt-affine functions.**

7 OUTPUT-OBLIVIOUS IMPLIES EVENTUALLY MIN OF QUILT-AFFINE FUNCTIONS

To complete the proof of Theorem 5.2, it remains to show the necessity of the eventually-min condition (ii):

THEOREM 7.1. *If $f : \mathbb{N}^d \to \mathbb{N}$ is obliviously-computable, then there exist quilt-affine $g_1, \ldots, g_m : \mathbb{N}^d \to \mathbb{Z}$ and $\mathbf{n} \in \mathbb{N}^d$ such that for all $\mathbf{x} \geq \mathbf{n}$, $f(\mathbf{x}) = \min_k(g_k(\mathbf{x}))$.*

For the remainder of Section 7, we fix an obliviously-computable $f : \mathbb{N}^d \to \mathbb{N}$, and Section 7 is devoted to finding $g_1, \ldots, g_m$ and $\mathbf{n}$ satisfying Theorem 7.1.

7.1 Proof outline

Since $f : \mathbb{N}^d \to \mathbb{N}$ is obliviously-computable, f is semilinear (recall Definition 2.5), and we first consider all threshold sets used to define the semilinear domains of the affine partial functions that define f. Each threshold set defines a hyperplane, and we use these hyperplanes to define *regions* (see Fig. 8a and Fig. 8c). We consider regions as subsets of $\mathbb{R}^d_{\geq 0}$, so they are convex polyhedra with useful geometric properties.[13]

The regions partition [14] the points in the domain $\mathbb{N}^d$. To prove Theorem 7.1, for each region R_k we will identify a quilt-affine function g_k (the *extension* of f from region R) such that $g(\mathbf{x}) = f(\mathbf{x})$ for all integer $\mathbf{x} \in R$. To ensure $f = \min_k(g_k)$, we further require that these quilt-affine extensions *eventually dominate* f (each $g_k(\mathbf{x}) \geq f(\mathbf{x})$ for sufficiently large $\mathbf{x}$). Also, because we only care about sufficiently large $\mathbf{x}$, we need only consider *eventual* regions which are unbounded in all inputs (for example regions 3,4, and 5 in Fig. 8a).

As a simple motivating example, consider the semilinear, nondecreasing function

$$f(x_1, x_2) = \begin{cases} x_1 + 1, & \text{if } x_1 < x_2 \text{ (region } D_1) \\ x_2 + 1, & \text{if } x_1 > x_2 \text{ (region } D_2) \\ x_1 & \text{if } x_1 = x_2 \text{ (region } U) \end{cases}$$

As in Definition 2.5, f is piecewise-affine, with semilinear domains that happen to be only defined by threshold sets. These thresholds then partition the domain into three regions: D_1, D_2, and U (see Fig. 7a). For region D_1, there is a unique quilt-affine extension $g_1(x_1, x_2) = x_1 + 1$ (note an affine function is the special case of a quilt-affine function with period 1). Also, g_1 eventually dominates f as desired, since $g_1(\mathbf{x}) \geq f(\mathbf{x})$ for all $\mathbf{x} \in \mathbb{N}^2$ (see Fig. 7b). By symmetry, we have the same for region D_2 and its extension $g_2(x_1, x_2) = x_2 + 1$.

These desirable properties follow from D_1 and D_2 being "wide" regions that we define to be *determined* (formalized later). On the other hand, U is a "narrow" region that is *under-determined.* As a result, there is not a unique quilt-affine extension from U. For example, $g(x_1, x_2) = x_1$ is a quilt-affine extension, however, we do not have $g(\mathbf{x}) \geq f(\mathbf{x})$ for all sufficiently large $\mathbf{x}$ (see Fig. 7c).

In order to identify a quilt-affine extension from U that does eventually dominate f, we will refer to the unique extensions g_1 and g_2 from regions D_1 and D_2, which are *neighbors* of U (formalized later). We can construct a quilt-affine function with a gradient $(\frac{1}{2}, \frac{1}{2})$ that is the average of the gradients $(1, 0)$ of g_1 and $(0, 1)$ of g_2. In particular, we can let $g_U(x_1, x_2) = \lceil \frac{x_1+x_2}{2} \rceil$ (note this is a quilt-affine function with period 2, see Fig. 7d). We then have $f(\mathbf{x}) = \min[g_1(\mathbf{x}), g_2(\mathbf{x}), g_U(\mathbf{x})]$ for all $\mathbf{x} \geq \mathbf{n} = \mathbf{0}$ as guaranteed by Theorem 7.1.

[13] What we consider is a restricted case of a *hyperplane arrangement* [24], with well-studied combinatorial properties.

[14] Without loss of generality, we assume that the hyperplanes do not intersect $\mathbb{N}^d$, so that the partition is well-defined (see Fig. 8a).

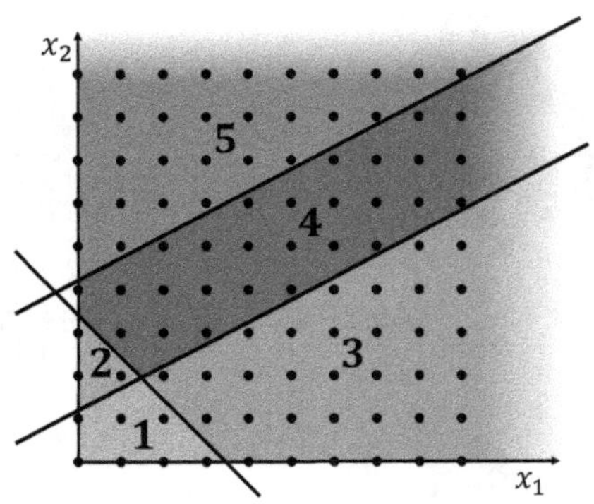

(a) Three threshold hyperplanes creating five regions. Regions 3 and 5 are determined, region 4 is under-determined but still eventual (unbounded in all input).

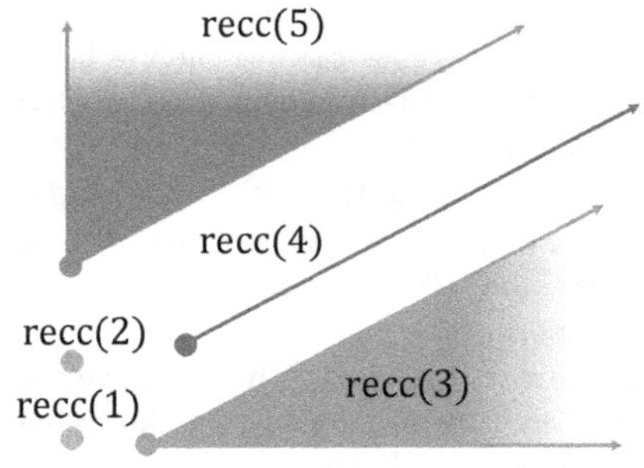

(b) The recession cones of all five regions. For finite regions, recc(1) = recc(2) = $\{\mathbf{0}\}$. Under-determined region 4 has a 1D recession cone, determined regions 3 and 5 have 2D recession cones.

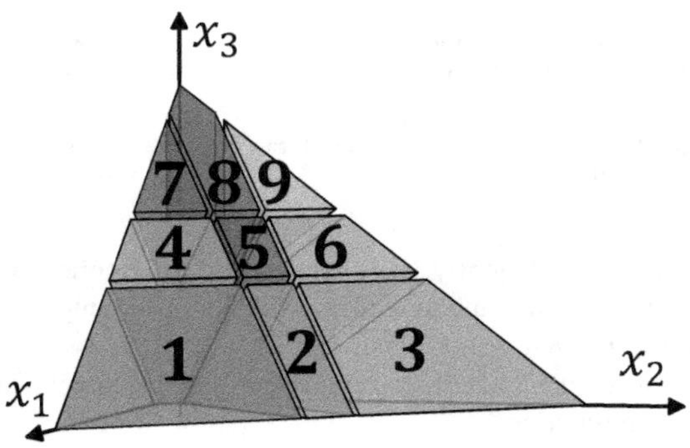

(c) Two pairs of parallel threshold hyperplanes creating nine eventual regions. Regions 1,3,7,9 are determined. Region 5 is under-determined with 1D recession cone. Regions 2,4,6,8 are under-determined with 2D recession cones.

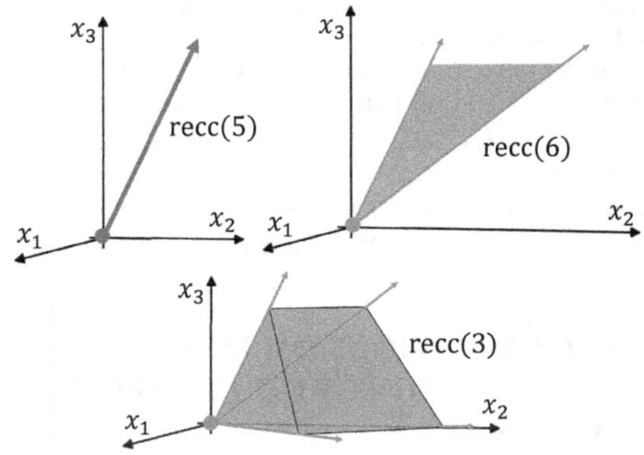

(d) recc(5) $\subseteq$ recc(6) $\subseteq$ recc(3) so region 3 is a determined neighbor of under-determined region 5 and under-determined region 6. Also, region 6 is a neighbor of region 5.

Figure 8: Examples with domains $\mathbb{N}^2$ (top) and $\mathbb{N}^3$ (bottom), with threshold hyperplanes giving regions (left), which are classified by their recession cones (right).

We now describe how we formalize the notion of a *determined region*, *under-determined region*, and *neighbor*, for the general case of domain $\mathbb{N}^d$, where the regions are convex polyhedra in $\mathbb{R}^d$.

To formally define determined regions, we identify the *recession cone* $\text{recc}(R) \subseteq \mathbb{R}^d$ of each region R: the set of vectors along infinite rays in R [20] (see Fig. 8b and Fig. 8d). A determined region D is defined as having a d-dimensional recession cone (see regions 3 and 5 in Fig. 8a and regions 1,3,7,9 in Fig. 8c). For determined regions, we can prove there is a unique quilt-affine extension, which eventually dominates f.

Under-determined regions are then defined as having a recession cone with dimension $< d$ (see regions 1,2,4 in Fig. 8a and regions 2,4,5,6,8 in Fig. 8c). The above arguments do not work for under-determined regions. Instead, identify the *neighbors* of an under-determined region U as regions R with $\text{recc}(U) \subseteq \text{recc}(R)$ (see Fig. 8b and Fig. 8d). We consider the neighbors of U that are determined regions. The possible behavior of f on U is constrained by the unique extensions from these regions, and we can define an extension from U based on an averaging process. Formal definitions and a proof of Theorem 7.1 appear in [21].

8 COMPARISON TO CONTINUOUS CASE

In [9], the authors classified the power of output-oblivious *continuous* CRNs to stably compute real-valued functions $f : \mathbb{R}^d_{\geq 0} \to \mathbb{R}_{\geq 0}$. We can generalize to also consider such functions by introducing the following natural scaling:

Definition 8.1. *For a function* $f : \mathbb{N}^d \to \mathbb{N}$, *the* ∞-scaling $\hat{f} : \mathbb{R}^d_{\geq 0} \to \mathbb{R}_{\geq 0}$ *is given by* $\hat{f}(\mathbf{x}) = \lim_{c \to \infty} \frac{f(\lfloor c\mathbf{x} \rfloor)}{c}$.

Note this limit may not exist for arbitrary $f : \mathbb{N}^d \to \mathbb{N}$, but it will exist for all obliviously-computable f.

The next theorem shows that in this scaling limit, our output-oblivious function class exactly corresponds to the real-valued function class from [9] (see Fig. 4b). The proof appears in [21].

Theorem 8.2. *If* $f : \mathbb{N}^d \to \mathbb{N}$ *is obliviously-computable, then the* ∞-*scaling* $\hat{f} : \mathbb{R}^d_{\geq 0} \to \mathbb{R}_{\geq 0}$ *is obliviously-computable by a continuous CRN. Furthermore, every function obliviously-computable by a continuous CRN is the* ∞-*scaling of some function obliviously-computable by a discrete CRN.*

9 LEADERLESS ONE-DIMENSIONAL CASE

In this section we show a characterization of 1D functions $f : \mathbb{N} \to \mathbb{N}$ that are obliviously-computable *without* a leader. The general case for leaderless oblivious computation in higher dimensions remains open.

Note that the following observation applies to any number of dimensions. We say $f : \mathbb{N}^d \to \mathbb{N}$ is *superadditive* if $f(\mathbf{x}) + f(\mathbf{y}) \leq f(\mathbf{x} + \mathbf{y})$ for all $\mathbf{x}, \mathbf{y} \in \mathbb{N}^d$.

OBSERVATION 9.1. *Every f obliviously-computable by a leaderless CRN is superadditive.*

PROOF. Let C be a leaderless CRN stably computing f. We prove the observation by contrapositive. Suppose f is not superadditive. Then there are $\mathbf{x}, \mathbf{z} \in \mathbb{N}^d$ such that $f(\mathbf{x}) + f(\mathbf{z}) > f(\mathbf{x} + \mathbf{z})$. Recall $\mathbf{I_w}$ is the initial configuration of C representing input $\mathbf{w}$. Let $\alpha_\mathbf{x}$ be a sequence of reactions applied to $\mathbf{I_x}$ to produce $f(\mathbf{x})$ copies of Y, and let $\alpha_\mathbf{z}$ be a sequence of reactions applied to $\mathbf{I_z}$ to produce $f(\mathbf{z})$ copies of Y.

Since C is leaderless, $\mathbf{I_{x+z}} = \mathbf{I_x} + \mathbf{I_z}$. Thus we can apply $\alpha_\mathbf{x}$ to $\mathbf{I_{x+z}}$, followed by $\alpha_\mathbf{z}$, producing $f(\mathbf{x}) + f(\mathbf{z})$ copies of Y. Since this is greater than $f(\mathbf{x} + \mathbf{z})$, to stably compute f, C must have a reaction consuming Y, so it is not output-oblivious. Since C was arbitrary, f cannot be obliviously-computable. □

This added condition of superadditivity gives us the 1D leaderless characterization. The proof appears in [21].

THEOREM 9.2. *For any $f : \mathbb{N} \to \mathbb{N}$, f is obliviously-computable by a leaderless CRN $\iff$ f is semilinear and superadditive.*

10 CONCLUSION

An obvious question is the computational power of output-oblivious CRNs without an initial leader. A leaderlessly-obliviously-computable function must be superadditive, which is a strictly stronger condition than being nondecreasing. The continuous result [9] had the same restriction of superadditivity, so our "scaling limit" reduction to their function class (Theorem 8.2) shows our main function class is already "almost superadditive." We also showed in the 1D case, $f : \mathbb{N} \to \mathbb{N}$ is leaderlessly-obliviously-computable if and only if f is semilinear and superadditive (Theorem 9.2).

Does adding the additional constraint of superaddivity to our full result (Theorem 5.2) classify leaderlessly-obliviously-computable $f : \mathbb{N}^d \to \mathbb{N}$? If this were true, a proof would require modifying our construction (Section 6) to eliminate the leader L. We successfully modified the 1D construction (Theorem 3.1) to remove the leader in proving Theorem 9.2, but it has been difficult to extend the same ideas to our much more complicated general construction.

An initial leader can also help make computation faster [5, 7, 19]. Many recent results in population protocols have shown time upper and lower bounds for computational tasks such as leader election and function/predicate computation [1, 2, 7, 16, 17, 19]. These techniques, however, are not at all designed to handle the constraint of output-obliviousness. It would be interesting to study how this constraint affects the time required for computation.

Acknowledgements. We thank Anne Condon, Cameron Chalk, Niels Kornerup, Wyatt Reeves, and David Soloveichik for discussing their related work with us and contributing early ideas.

REFERENCES

[1] Dan Alistarh, James Aspnes, David Eisenstat, Rati Gelashvili, and Ronald L. Rivest. Time-space trade-offs in molecular computation. In *SODA 2017: Proceedings of the 28th Annual ACM-SIAM Symposium on Discrete Algorithms*, 2017.

[2] Dan Alistarh, James Aspnes, and Rati Gelashvili. Space-optimal majority in population protocols. In *SODA 2018: Proceedings of the Twenty-Ninth Annual ACM-SIAM Symposium on Discrete Algorithms*, pages 2221–2239. SIAM, 2018.

[3] Dana Angluin, James Aspnes, Zoë Diamadi, Michael Fischer, and René Peralta. Computation in networks of passively mobile finite-state sensors. *Distributed Computing*, 18:235–253, 2006. Preliminary version appeared in PODC 2004.

[4] Dana Angluin, James Aspnes, and David Eisenstat. Stably computable predicates are semilinear. In *PODC 2006: Proceedings of the twenty-fifth annual ACM symposium on Principles of distributed computing*, pages 292–299, New York, NY, USA, 2006. ACM Press.

[5] Dana Angluin, James Aspnes, and David Eisenstat. Fast computation by population protocols with a leader. *Distributed Computing*, 21(3):183–199, September 2008. Preliminary version appeared in DISC 2006.

[6] Dana Angluin, James Aspnes, David Eisenstat, and Eric Ruppert. The computational power of population protocols. *Distributed Computing*, 20(4):279–304, 2007.

[7] Amanda Belleville, David Doty, and David Soloveichik. Hardness of computing and approximating predicates and functions with leaderless population protocols. In *ICALP*, volume 80 of *Leibniz International Proceedings in Informatics (LIPIcs)*, pages 141:1–141:14, 2017.

[8] Luca Cardelli. Strand algebras for DNA computing. *Natural Computing*, 10(1):407–428, 2011.

[9] Cameron Chalk, Niels Kornerup, Wyatt Reeves, and David Soloveichik. Composable rate-independent computation in continuous chemical reaction networks. In *Computational Methods in Systems Biology*, 2018.

[10] Ho-Lin Chen, David Doty, and David Soloveichik. Deterministic function computation with chemical reaction networks. *Natural Computing*, 13(4):517–534, 2014. Preliminary version appeared in DNA 2012.

[11] Yuan-Jyue Chen, Neil Dalchau, Niranjan Srinivas, Andrew Phillips, Luca Cardelli, David Soloveichik, and Georg Seelig. Programmable chemical controllers made from DNA. *Nature Nanotechnology*, 8(10):755–762, 2013.

[12] Ben Chugg, Anne Condon, and Hooman Hashemi. Output-oblivious stochastic chemical reaction networks. In *OPODIS 2018: Proceedings of the 22nd International Conference on Principles of Distributed Systems*, 2018.

[13] Leonard E. Dickson. Finiteness of the odd perfect and primitive abundant numbers with n distinct prime factors. *American Journal of Mathematics*, 35(4):413–422, 1913.

[14] David Doty and Mahsa Eftekhari. Efficient size estimation and impossibility of termination in uniform dense population protocols. In *PODC 2019: Proceedings of the 38th ACM Symposium on Principles of Distributed Computing*, 2019. to appear.

[15] David Doty and Monir Hajiaghayi. Leaderless deterministic chemical reaction networks. *Natural Computing*, 14(2):213–223, 2015. Preliminary version appeared in DNA 2013.

[16] David Doty and David Soloveichik. Stable leader election in population protocols requires linear time. *Distributed Computing*, 31(4):257–271, 2018. Special issue of invited papers from DISC 2015.

[17] Leszek Gasieniec and Grzegorz Stachowiak. Fast space optimal leader election in population protocols. In *SODA 2018: Proceedings of the Twenty-Ninth Annual ACM-SIAM Symposium on Discrete Algorithms*, pages 2653–2667, 2018.

[18] Daniel T. Gillespie. Exact stochastic simulation of coupled chemical reactions. *Journal of Physical Chemistry*, 81(25):2340–2361, 1977.

[19] Adrian Kosowski and Przemyslaw Uznanski. Brief announcement: Population protocols are fast. In *PODC 2018: Proceedings of the 2018 ACM Symposium on Principles of Distributed Computing*, pages 475–477. ACM, 2018.

[20] Tyson Rockafeller. *Convex Analysis*, chapter 8. Princeton University Press, 1970.

[21] Eric Severson, David Haley, and David Doty. Composable computation in discrete chemical reaction networks. Technical Report 1602.08032, arXiv, 2019. http://arxiv.org/abs/1903.02637.

[22] David Soloveichik, Georg Seelig, and Erik Winfree. DNA as a universal substrate for chemical kinetics. *Proceedings of the National Academy of Sciences*, 107(12):5393, 2010. Preliminary version appeared in DNA 2008.

[23] Niranjan Srinivas, James Parkin, Georg Seelig, Erik Winfree, and David Soloveichik. Enzyme-free nucleic acid dynamical systems. *Science*, 358(6369):eaal2052, 2017.

[24] Richard Stanley. An introduction to hyperplane arrangments, 2006. URL: http://www.cis.upenn.edu/~cis610/sp06stanley.pdf.

How to Spread a Rumor: Call Your Neighbors or Take a Walk?

George Giakkoupis
Inria, Univ Rennes, CNRS, IRISA
Rennes, France

Frederik Mallmann-Trenn
Massachusetts Institute of Technology
Cambridge, MA, US

Hayk Saribekyan
University of Cambridge
Cambridge, UK

ABSTRACT

We study the problem of randomized information dissemination in networks. We compare the now standard PUSH-PULL protocol, with agent-based alternatives where information is disseminated by a collection of agents performing independent random walks. In the VISIT-EXCHANGE protocol, both nodes and agents store information, and each time an agent visits a node, the two exchange all the information they have. In the MEET-EXCHANGE protocol, only the agents store information, and exchange their information with each agent they meet.

We consider the broadcast time of a single piece of information in an n-node graph for the above three protocols, assuming a linear number of agents that start from the stationary distribution. We observe that there are graphs on which the agent-based protocols are significantly faster than PUSH-PULL, and graphs where the converse is true. We attribute the good performance of agent-based algorithms to their inherently fair bandwidth utilization, and conclude that, in certain settings, agent-based information dissemination, separately or in combination with PUSH-PULL, can significantly improve the broadcast time.

The graphs considered above are highly non-regular. Our main technical result is that on any regular graph of at least logarithmic degree, PUSH-PULL and VISIT-EXCHANGE have the same asymptotic broadcast time. The proof uses a novel coupling argument which relates the random choices of vertices in PUSH-PULL with the random walks in VISIT-EXCHANGE. Further, we show that the broadcast time of MEET-EXCHANGE is asymptotically at least as large as the other two's on all regular graphs, and strictly larger on some regular graphs.

As far as we know, this is the first systematic and thorough comparison of the running times of these very natural information dissemination protocols.

CCS CONCEPTS

• **Computing methodologies** → *Distributed algorithms*; • **Mathematics of computing** → *Stochastic processes.*

KEYWORDS

random walks, information dissemination, rumor spreading

ACM ISBN 978-1-4503-6217-7/19/07...$15.00
https://doi.org/10.1145/3293611.3331622

ACM Reference Format:
George Giakkoupis, Frederik Mallmann-Trenn, and Hayk Saribekyan. 2019. How to Spread a Rumor: Call Your Neighbors or Take a Walk?. In *2019 ACM Symposium on Principles of Distributed Computing (PODC '19), July 29-August 2, 2019, Toronto, ON, Canada.* ACM, New York, NY, USA, 10 pages. https://doi.org/10.1145/3293611.3331622

1 INTRODUCTION

We investigate the problem of spreading information (or rumors) in a distributed network using randomized communication. The archetypal paradigm solution is the so-called, *randomized rumor spreading* protocol, where each informed node samples a random neighbor in each round, and sends the information to it. This is the PUSH version of rumor spreading, introduced by Demers *et al.* in the 80's [14], as a robust and lightweight protocol for distributed maintenance of replicated databases [14, 21].

The PUSH-PULL variant of rumor spreading, popularized by Karp *et al.* in 2000 [27], allows for bidirectional communication: In each round, every node calls a random neighbor and the two nodes exchange all information they have. PUSH-PULL was initially proposed as a way to reduce the message complexity of PUSH on the complete graph [27]. It was subsequently observed that it is significantly faster than PUSH in several families of graphs, including graph models of social networks [11, 16].

The above two protocols have been studied extensively over the past 15 years, and have also found several applications, including data aggregation [7, 28, 31], resource discovery [24], failure detection [35], and even efficient simulation of arbitrary distributed computations [9].

We compare the above well-established protocols for information spreading, with agent-based alternatives that have received almost no attention so far, even though they have very attractive properties, as we will see. These alternative protocols use a collection of agents performing independent random walks to disseminate information. In the VISIT-EXCHANGE protocol, both nodes and agents store information, and each time an agent visits a node, the two exchange all the information they have. In the MEET-EXCHANGE protocol, only the agents store information, and exchange their information with each agent they meet.

Independent parallel random walks have been studied since the late 70s [1], mainly as a way to speed-up cover and hitting times and related graph problems [2, 8, 19, 20]. As far as we know, VISIT-EXCHANGE has not been studied before. For MEET-EXCHANGE there is some limited previous work. It was studied for specific graph families, namely grids [29, 32] and random graphs [13]. Also, general bounds on the broadcast time of MEET-EXCHANGE with respect to the meeting time were shown [15].

In this paper, we restrict our attention to the case where the number of agents in the network is linear in the number of nodes n, and we assume that all agents start from the stationary distribution.

(a) (b) (c) (d) (e)

Figure 1 (a) Star S_n, on which $\mathbb{E}\left[T_{\text{push}}\right] = \Omega(n\log n)$ and all other processes take $O(\log n)$ time w.h.p. (b) Double-star S_n^2, on which $\mathbb{E}\left[T_{\text{ppull}}\right] = \Omega(n)$, and $T_{\text{visitx}}, T_{\text{meetx}} = O(\log n)$ w.h.p. (c) Heavy binary tree B_n (leaves are connected to a clique), on which $T_{\text{push}} = O(\log n)$ w.h.p., $\mathbb{E}[T_{\text{visitx}}] = \Omega(n)$, and, for a leaf source, $T_{\text{meetx}} = O(\log n)$ w.h.p. (d) Siamese heavy binary tree D_n, on which $T_{\text{push}} = O(\log n)$ w.h.p., and $\mathbb{E}[T_{\text{visitx}}], \mathbb{E}[T_{\text{meetx}}] = \Omega(n)$. (e) Cycle-of-stars-of-cliques ($n^{1/3}$ stars, $n^{1/3}$ nodes per clique), on which $\mathbb{E}[T_{\text{visitx}}] = O(n^{2/3})$ and $\mathbb{E}[T_{\text{meetx}}] = \Omega(n^{2/3}\log n)$.

Under the assumption that there is a linear number of agents, the agent-based protocols have similar amount of communication as the rumor spreading protocols, both in terms of the (maximum) total number of messages sent per round, which is linear, and the total number of bits. One can think of the agents simply as tokens passed between nodes, along with the actual information (if there is any). Agents need not be labeled, so each node only needs to send a counter of the number of agents in each message.

The assumption that agents start from the stationary distribution makes sense in a setting where several pieces of information (or rumors) are generated frequently and distributed in parallel over time by the same set of agents, which execute perpetual independent random walks. As discussed later, our results for regular graphs hold also in the case where there is exactly one agent starting from each node.

One distinct advantage of the agent-based protocols is their *locally fair* use of bandwidth, i.e., all edges are used with the same frequency, since the random walks are independent and start from stationarity. Interestingly, the superiority of PUSH-PULL over PUSH is commonly attributed to a similar fairness property: that nodes of larger degree contribute more to the dissemination — except that PUSH-PULL satisfies this property only for *some* graph topologies, and *approximately*, as we will see below. In the agent-based protocols, on the other hand, this property is satisfied in a very precise and exact way.

We will see that this fairness property results in a significant performance advantage of VISIT-EXCHANGE and MEET-EXCHANGE over PUSH and PUSH-PULL in certain families of graphs, on which the first two processes need only logarithmic time to spread an information, whereas the other two need polynomial time.

Contribution. We compare the broadcast times of a single piece of information, originated at an arbitrary node s of an n-node graph $G = (V, E)$, when PUSH (or PUSH-PULL), VISIT-EXCHANGE, and MEET-EXCHANGE are used. In the first three, the broadcast time is the time until all vertices are informed, while in MEET-EXCHANGE it is the time until all *agents* are informed. Also, for MEET-EXCHANGE, we assume that the first agent to visit the source s becomes informed, and from that point on, information is exchanged only between agents.[1] As mentioned before, we assume a linear number of agents, each starting from the stationary distribution.

We observe that in general graphs, the broadcast times of the above protocols are *incomparable*: For any pair of protocols, there are examples of graphs where the first protocol is significantly faster than the other, by a polynomial factor in most cases. The examples we use, depicted in Fig. 1, are fairly simple, mainly trees or superpositions of trees with cliques.

The star graph in Fig. 1(a) is an example where PUSH is known to take $\Omega(n\log n)$ rounds, as the center must contact all leaves. VISIT-EXCHANGE and MEET-EXCHANGE, on the other hand, take only logarithmic time, as roughly half of the walks visit the center in each round, and a constant number visits each leaf on average.

In the star, PUSH-PULL is also (extremely) fast. The next example, the double-star in Fig. 1(b), is a graph where PUSH-PULL (and thus also PUSH) is slow, whereas VISIT-EXCHANGE and MEET-EXCHANGE are still fast. This demonstrates the advantages of the local fairness property we pointed out earlier, and the impact it can have on the broadcast time: Here PUSH-PULL selects the edge between the two stars only with probability $O(1/n)$, which results in an expected broadcast time of $\Omega(n)$. In VISIT-EXCHANGE and MEET-EXCHANGE, on the other hand, the probability that some agent crosses the edge in a round is constant, resulting in a logarithmic broadcast time.

Fig. 1(c) and Fig. 1(d) illustrate examples where rumor spreading protocols have an advantage over agent-based protocols. In both examples PUSH (and thus PUSH-PULL) has logarithmic broadcast time. For VISIT-EXCHANGE, at least linear time is needed: Since almost all the volume of the graph is concentrated on the leaves, it is likely that all agents are on the leaves at time zero, and then it takes linear time before the first walk reaches the root. For MEET-EXCHANGE, we have that it is fast in the first example, as all walks meet quickly in the clique induced by the leaves. However, in the second example, where agents are roughly split between the two induced cliques, the broadcast times of both MEET-EXCHANGE and VISIT-EXCHANGE is $\Omega(n)$.

[1] This is a technicality used to allow for direct comparison between the protocols, and has limited effect on our results.

The above results suggest that in certain settings, agent-based information dissemination, separately or in combination with PUSH-PULL, can significantly improve the broadcast time. We stress that, even though the examples presented may seem contrived, they are intentionally simple to demonstrate the principle reasons that make the protocols perform differently, and we expect that similar result can be observed in a wide range of networks. In particular, we believe that the observations for the double-star example of Fig. 1(b), extend to more general tree-like topologies with high-degree internal nodes.

All examples we have discussed so far, involve highly non-regular graphs. Our main technical result concerns regular graphs, and can be stated somewhat informally as follows. (For the formal, stronger statements see Sect. 4 and 5.)

THEOREM 1. *For any d-regular graph on n vertices, where $d = \Omega(\log n)$, and any source vertex, the broadcast times of PUSH and VISIT-EXCHANGE are asymptotically the same both in expectation and w.h.p.,[2] modulo constant multiplicative factors.*

Recall that PUSH and PUSH-PULL have asymptotically the same broadcast times on regular graphs [23]. Note also that the broadcast times of PUSH and PUSH-PULL on d-regular graphs can vary from logarithmic, e.g., in random d-regular graphs, to polynomial, e.g., in a path of d-cliques where the broadcast time is $\Omega(n)$.

The proof of Theorem 1 uses a novel coupling argument which relates the random choices of vertices in PUSH, with the random walks in VISIT-EXCHANGE. Roughly speaking, for each node u, we consider the list of neighbors that u samples in PUSH, and the list of neighbors to which informed agents move to in their next step after visiting u in VISIT-EXCHANGE. Our coupling just sets the two lists to be identical for each u. Even though the coupling is straightforward, its analysis is not. On the one direction of the proof, showing that the broadcast time of PUSH is dominated by the broadcast time of VISIT-EXCHANGE, the main step is to bound the congestion, i.e., the number of agents encountered along a path, for all possible paths through which information travels. On the reverse direction, we focus only on the fastest path through which information reaches each node in PUSH, and show that an equally fast path exists in VISIT-EXCHANGE. A useful trick we devise, to consider only every other round of VISIT-EXCHANGE in the coupling, simplifies the proof of this second direction. We expect that our proof ideas will be useful in other applications of multiple random walks as well.

In addition to Theorem 1, we observe that the broadcast time of MEET-EXCHANGE is asymptotically at least as large as VISIT-EXCHANGE's on any regular graph of at least logarithmic degree. The idea is that once all agents are informed it takes at most logarithmic time to cover the graph.

It is probably surprising that the converse direction is not true, i.e., there are regular graphs where MEET-EXCHANGE is strictly slower than VISIT-EXCHANGE. Fig. 1(e) presents one such example of a d-regular graph, where $d = n^{1/3}$, for which a logarithmic-factor gap exists between the broadcast times of the two protocols.

[2] By with high probability (w.h.p.) we mean with probability at least $1 - n^{-c}$, with some constant $c > 0$ that can be made arbitrary large, by adjusting the constants in the statement.

Road-map. In Sect. 2, we survey additional related work. In Sect. 3, we provide a formal description of the protocols we study. The first direction of Theorem 1, that PUSH is at least as fast as VISIT-EXCHANGE, is proved in Sect. 4; the other direction is proved in Sect. 5. The result that VISIT-EXCHANGE is at least as fast as MEET-EXCHANGE on regular graphs is provided in Sect. 6. Finally, some open problems are discussed in Sect. 7.

Due to space limitations, several proofs, including the analysis of the broadcast times of the example graphs in Fig. 1, are only available in the full version of the paper.

2 RELATED WORK

The PUSH variant of rumor spreading was first considered in [14]. It was subsequently analyzed on various graphs in [21], where also bounds with the degree and diameter were shown for general graphs. The PUSH-PULL variant was introduced in [27], and was studied initially on the complete graph. More recently, there has been a lot of work on showing that in several settings $O(\log n)$ rounds of rumor spreading suffice w.h.p. to broadcast information [4, 17, 18]. In addition, general bounds in terms of expansion parameters of the graph have been studied extensively, e.g., in [10, 22].

Another line of work compares synchronous and asynchronous versions of rumor spreading, where in the latter each node takes steps at the arrival times of an independent unit-rate Poisson process. In [34], it is shown that the asynchronous version of PUSH has the same broadcast time as standard PUSH on regular graphs. In [3, 23], tight bounds are given for the relation between the broadcast times of synchronous and asynchronous PUSH-PULL.

On the random walk literature, there has been some previous work on models related to MEET-EXCHANGE, motivated mainly by the study of the spread of infectious diseases. The earliest work considering a process equivalent to MEET-EXCHANGE is [15], which studies general graphs. It shows that the broadcast time of MEET-EXCHANGE is at most $O(\log n)$ times larger than the meeting time of two random walks in the graph, and that this upper bound is tight. Later, the authors of [13] studied MEET-EXCHANGE for the case of random regular graphs and $k \leqslant n^{\varepsilon}$ random walks. They showed that the expected broadcast time is $O(n \log k/k)$. In [32], the 2-dimensional grid was studied and a broadcast time of $\tilde{\Theta}(n/\sqrt{k})$ was shown for k random walks. This work was extended to d-dimensional grids in [29], where a tight lower bound up to a poly-logarithmic factor was also shown.

A random process related to MEET-EXCHANGE is the frog model, where only one of the agents is active initially while the remaining agents are inactive. When an inactive agent is hit by an active one, it is activated and starts its own independent random walk. The model has been considered mostly on the infinite grid, where questions about the asymptotic shape of the set of active agents have been studied [25, 33].

Other superficially related processes include coalescing random walks [5, 26], and coalescing branching walks [6, 30]. See also [12] for a survey on multiple random walks.

3 PROTOCOL DESCRIPTIONS

We compare four information spreading protocols. The first two, PUSH and PUSH-PULL, are standard versions of randomized rumor spreading. The other two, VISIT-EXCHANGE and MEET-EXCHANGE, use a system of interacting agents performing independent random walks, and are less standardized. In PUSH and PUSH-PULL, information is communicated between adjacent vertices, whereas in VISIT-EXCHANGE and MEET-EXCHANGE information is passed between an agent and a vertex it visits, or between two agents when their random walks meet. All protocols proceed in a sequence of synchronous rounds. They are applied on a connected undirected graph $G = (V, E)$ with $|V| = n$ vertices, and the information originates from an arbitrary source vertex $s \in V$.

Push. In round zero, vertex s becomes informed. In each round $t \geqslant 1$, every vertex u that was informed in a previous round samples a random neighbor v to send the information to, and if v is not already informed, it becomes informed in this round. We denote by $T_{\text{push}}(G, s)$ the number of rounds before all vertices are informed.

Push-Pull. Similar to PUSH, vertex s is informed in round zero. In each round $t \geqslant 1$, every vertex $u \in V$ (informed or not) samples a random neighbor v to exchange information with, and if exactly one of u and v was informed before round t, then the other vertex becomes informed as well. The number of rounds before all vertices are informed is denoted $T_{\text{ppull}}(G, s)$.

Visit-Exchange. Let A be a set of *agents*. Every agent $g \in A$ performs an independent simple random walk on G, starting from a vertex sampled independently from the stationary distribution (i.e., each vertex v is sampled with probability $\deg(v)/(2|E|)$). In round zero, vertex s becomes informed, and every agent that is on vertex s becomes informed as well. In each subsequent round $t \geqslant 1$, all agents do a single step of their random walk in parallel. If an agent g, which was informed in an earlier round, visits vertex v that is not yet informed, then v becomes informed in this round. If, on the other hand, some not yet informed agent g visits vertex v which was informed either in an earlier round or the current one (by some other informed agent), then g becomes informed. We denote by $T_{\text{visitx}}(G, s)$ the number of rounds before all *vertices* (and thus all agents) are informed.

Meet-Exchange. Similar to VISIT-EXCHANGE, we have a set A of agents that perform independent random walks starting from the stationary distribution. In round zero, all agents that are on vertex s become informed. If there is no agent on s in round zero, then the first agent to visit s after round zero becomes informed (if more than one agents visit s simultaneously, they all get informed). After this point, vertex s does not inform agents visiting it. In each subsequent round t, whenever two agent g, g' meet and exactly one of them was informed in a previous round, the other agent becomes informed as well. We denote by $T_{\text{meetx}}(G, s)$ the number of rounds before all agents are informed. Note that if G is a bipartite graph, then $T_{\text{meetx}}(G, s)$ can be infinite, and, in particular, we have $\mathbb{E}[T_{\text{meetx}}(G, s)] = \infty$. To avoid this complication we will sometimes assume that the random walks of the agents are lazy, i.e., a walk stays put in a round with probability $1/2$. This ensures that $\mathbb{E}[T_{\text{meetx}}(G, s)] < \infty$.

We will collectively refer to $T_{\text{push}}(G, s)$, $T_{\text{ppull}}(G, s)$, $T_{\text{visitx}}(G, s)$, and $T_{\text{meetx}}(G, s)$ as the *broadcast time* of the corresponding protocol. We will sometimes omit graph G and source vertex s in this notation, when they are clear from the context.

4 BOUNDING T_{push} BY T_{visitx} ON REGULAR GRAPHS

In this section, we prove the following theorem, which upper bounds the broadcast time of PUSH in a regular graph by the broadcast time of VISIT-EXCHANGE.

THEOREM 2. *For any constants $\varepsilon, \gamma, \lambda > 0$, there is a constant $c > 0$, such that for any d-regular graph $G = (V, E)$ with $|V| = n$ and $d \geqslant \varepsilon \log n$, and for any source vertex $s \in V$, the broadcast times of PUSH and VISIT-EXCHANGE, with $|A| \leqslant \gamma n$ agents, satisfy*

$$\mathbb{P}\left[T_{\text{push}} \leqslant ck\right] \geqslant \mathbb{P}\left[T_{\text{visitx}} \leqslant k\right] - n^{-\lambda},$$

for any $k \geqslant 0$.

From Theorem 2, it is immediate that if $T_{\text{visitx}} \leqslant T$ w.h.p., then $T_{\text{push}} = O(T)$ w.h.p. Moreover, using Theorem 2 and the known $O(n \log n)$ upper bound on T_{push} which holds w.h.p. [21], one can easily show that $\mathbb{E}\left[\, T_{\text{push}} \,\right] = O(\mathbb{E}[\, T_{\text{visitx}} \,])$.

Proof Overview of Theorem 2. The proof uses the following coupling of processes PUSH and VISIT-EXCHANGE: For each vertex u, let $\langle \pi_u(1), \pi_u(2), \ldots \rangle$ be the sequence of neighbors that u samples in PUSH. Similarly, for VISIT-EXCHANGE, consider all transitions of informed agents from u to neighbor vertices in chronological order (ordering transitions in the same round by, say, agent ID), and let $\langle p_u(1), p_u(2), \ldots \rangle$ be the destination vertices in those transitions. We couple the two processes by setting $\pi_u(i) = p_u(i)$, for all u, i.

The intuition behind this coupling is that in VISIT-EXCHANGE, at most a constant number of agents *in expectation* visits each vertex u in a round (since the graph is regular and $|A| = O(n)$), and thus the same number of agents leaves u per round in expectation. The coupling ensures that for each informed agent that moves from u to a neighbor v, vertex u samples the same neighbor v in PUSH. Thus, if we had a constant upper bound c on the *actual* number (rather than the expected number) of visits to each vertex on each round, then the coupling would immediately yield $T_{\text{push}} \leqslant c \cdot T_{\text{visitx}}$ for the coupled processes. In reality, however, a super-constant number of agents may visit a vertex in a round, and, moreover, the number of visits depends on the past history of the process.

An idea we use to tackle dependencies is to consider a tweaked version of VISIT-EXCHANGE, called T-VISIT-EXCHANGE. The only difference between this process and VISIT-EXCHANGE, is that it arbitrarily removes some agents after each round to ensure that the neighborhood of any vertex contains at most $O(d)$ agents. For $d = \Omega(\log n)$ and $|A| = O(n)$, we have that in the first poly(n) rounds the two processes are identical w.h.p. Therefore, we can consider T-VISIT-EXCHANGE in our proofs. The benefit of that is that since the neighborhood of any vertex u contains $O(d)$ agents in round t, at round $t + 1$ the number of agents that visit u will be bounded by binomial distribution $\text{Bin}(\Theta(d), 1/d)$, *independently of the past.*

To prove the theorem is suffices to show that under our coupling, we have w.h.p. (precisely, with probability at least $1 - n^{-\lambda}$) that if $T_{\text{visitx}} \leqslant k$ then $T_{\text{push}} \leqslant ck$. Further, it suffices to assume that k is at least $\Omega(\log n)$; for $k = o(\log n)$ the theorem follows by showing that $T_{\text{visitx}} = \Omega(\log n)$ w.h.p.

To show that w.h.p. $T_{\text{visitx}} \leqslant k$ implies $T_{\text{push}} \leqslant ck$, we consider all possible paths of length k through which information travels in VISIT-EXCHANGE, and for each path we count the total number of (non-distinct) agents encountered along this path, called the congestion of the path. Formally, we use the notion of a *canonical walk* θ, which is represented by a sequence of vertices $(\theta_0, \theta_1, \ldots, \theta_k)$ starting from $\theta_0 = s$: In each round $1 \leqslant t \leqslant k$, the walk either stays put and $\theta_t = \theta_{t-1}$, or it follows one of the agents g that leave θ_{t-1} in round t, and, in that case, θ_t is the new vertex that g moves to. For any round t, we count the agents that are in θ_t. The sum of these counts, for $0 \leqslant t < k$ is the *congestion* $Q(\theta)$ of the walk.

The congestion of a canonical walk is used to bound the time needed for information to travel along the *same* path in PUSH. Intuitively, larger congestion implies longer travel time for PUSH, for the following reason. Suppose there are m agents in u at some round after it is informed by VISIT-EXCHANGE. The coupled PUSH process, using the same random decisions for the choice of neighbors as VISIT-EXCHANGE, will take m rounds to "go through" them.

To relate the congestion of canonical walks with the time it takes for information to spread in PUSH, we introduce *C-counters*: For each vertex u, we maintain a counter C_u. The counter is initialized in the round t_u in which u becomes informed in VISIT-EXCHANGE. Its initial value is the value of the C-counter of the neighbor from which the first informed agent arrived to u. In each subsequent round $t > t_u$, C_u increases by the number of agents that visited u in round $t-1$. C-counters have the following two properties: If τ_u is the round when u gets informed in PUSH then $\tau_u \leqslant C_u(t_u)$; and for any $t \geqslant t_u$, there is a canonical walk θ of length t such that $C_u(t) = Q(\theta)$. Therefore, to show that w.h.p. $T_{\text{visitx}} \leqslant k$ implies $T_{\text{push}} \leqslant ck$, it suffices to show that the maximum congestion of *all* canonical walks of length k is at most ck w.h.p.

We can bound the congestion of a *single* canonical walk of length k using the property of T-VISIT-EXCHANGE, that the number of agents at a node is bounded by a binomial distribution with constant mean. This results in the desired bound of ck for a single walk with probability at least $1 - a^{-k}$, for some constant $a > 1$. We would like to take a union bound over all canonical walks, which would give the desired result. For this to work, however, we should also bound the total number of canonical walks of length k by at most a^k/n^λ.

We bound the number of canonical walks of length k by introducing a set of *descriptors* for these walks. A descriptor is represented by a matrix, which, together with a given execution of VISIT-EXCHANGE, uniquely defines a walk. Additionally, the set of descriptors suffices to encode all canonical walks, and therefore, it is at least as large as the set of all walks. Thus, we can use a bound on the number of descriptors that can be computed by a simple combinatorial argument involving the number of elements used in the matrix, and the values they can take. A naive construction of descriptors, however, is too wasteful giving us a much larger bound than the a^k/n^λ we need. A key idea here is that the majority of the descriptors represent walks only in executions that happen with low probability. So, we construct a set of *concise descriptors* that can describe all canonical walks in a random execution *w.h.p.* We show that the size of the set of concise descriptors can be bounded by a^k/n^λ, as desired. Next we give the detailed proof.

4.1 Notation and Coupling Description

For each vertex $u \in V$, we denote by τ_u the round when u gets informed in PUSH. By $\pi_u(i)$, for $i \geqslant 1$, we denote the ith vertex that u samples, i.e., the vertex it samples in round $\tau_u + i$. Note that $\pi_u(i)$ gets informed in round $\tau_u + i$, if it is not already informed. In VISIT-EXCHANGE, we denote by t_u the round when vertex u gets informed. For any agent $g \in A$ and $t \geqslant 0$, we denote by $x_g(t)$, the vertex that g visits in round t. Thus, $\{x_g(t)\}_{t\geqslant 0}$ is a random walk on G. Let $Z_u(t)$ be the set of all agents that visit u in round t, i.e.,

$$Z_u(t) = \{g \in A \colon x_g(t) = u\}.$$

Equivalently, $Z_u(t)$ is the set of agents that depart from u in round $t+1$. Consider all visits to u in rounds $t \geqslant t_u$, in chronological order, ordering visits in the same round with respect to a predefined total order over all agents. For each $i \geqslant 1$, consider the agent g that does the ith one of those visits, and let $p_u(i)$ be the vertex that g visits next. Formally, let $X_u = \{(t,g) \colon t \geqslant t_u, x_g(t) = u\}$, and order its elements such that $(t,g) < (t',g')$ if $t < t'$, or $t = t'$ and $g < g'$. If (t,g) is the ith smallest element in X_u, then $p_u(i) = x_g(t+1)$.

Coupling. We couple processes PUSH and VISIT-EXCHANGE by setting $\pi_u(i) = p_u(i)$. Formally, let $\{w_u(i)\}_{u\in V, i\geqslant 1}$, be a collection of independent random variables, where $w_u(i)$ takes a uniformly random value from the set $\Gamma(u)$ of u's neighbors. Then, for every $u \in V$ and $i \geqslant 1$, we set $\pi_u(i) = p_u(i) = w_u(i)$.

4.2 Upper Bound on Agents and Tweaked Visit-Exchange

We will use the next simple bound on the number of agents that visit a given set S of vertices in some round t of VISIT-EXCHANGE. The proof is by a simple Chernoff bound, and relies on the assumption that agents execute independent walks starting from stationarity.

LEMMA 3. *For any $S \subseteq V$, $t \geqslant 0$, and $\beta \geqslant 2e \cdot |A|/n$,*

$$\mathbb{P}\left[\sum_{v\in S} |Z_v(t)| \leqslant \beta \cdot |S|\right] \geqslant 1 - 2^{-\beta|S|}.$$

We remark that the same bound holds also in the case where $|A| = n$, and exactly one walk starts from each vertex. This implies that Theorem 2 holds for that initial setting as well (the rest of the proof does not need any modifications).

In parts of the analysis, we will use a tweaked variant of VISIT-EXCHANGE, called T-VISIT-EXCHANGE, defined as follows. Let

$$\alpha \geqslant 2e \cdot |A|/n \tag{1}$$

be a (sufficiently large) constant to be specified later. If in some round $t \geqslant 0$, there is a vertex $u \in V$ for which the following condition is *not* true:

$$\sum_{v\in\Gamma(u)} |Z_v(t)| \leqslant \alpha \cdot d, \tag{2}$$

then before round $t+1$, we remove a minimal set of agents from the system in such a way that the above condition holds for all vertices u, when counting just the remaining agents.

It is an immediate corollary of Lemma 3 that the modified process is identical to the original one in the first polynomial number of rounds, if constant α is large enough, and $d = \Omega(\log n)$.

Lemma 4. *The probability that no agent is removed in any of the first k rounds of* T-VISIT-EXCHANGE *is at least* $1 - kn \cdot 2^{-\alpha d}$.

Proof. The claim follows by applying Lemma 3, for each $0 \leqslant t < k$ and each pair u, S, where $u \in V$ and $S = \Gamma(u)$, and then combining the results using a union bound. □

We will use the same definitions and notations for both VISIT-EXCHANGE and T-VISIT-EXCHANGE.

4.3 C-Counters

For each $u \in V$, let S_u be the set of neighbors v of u such that v was informed before u in VISIT-EXCHANGE, and some (informed) agent moved from v to u in round t_u, i.e.,

$$S_u = \{v \in \Gamma(u) \colon t_v < t_u,\ Z_v(t_u - 1) \cap Z_u(t_u) \neq \emptyset\}.$$

Thus, S_u contains those neighbors that "informed" u. For each $u \in V$ and $t \geqslant 0$, let

$$C_u(t) = \begin{cases} 0, & \text{if } t < t_u \text{ or } t = t_u = 0; \\ \min_{v \in S_u} C_v(t), & \text{if } t = t_u > 0; \\ C_u(t-1) + |Z_u(t-1)|, & \text{if } t > t_u. \end{cases} \tag{3}$$

That is, C_u is initialized in round t_u to the minimum counter value of the neighbors that informed u (or to zero if $u = s$), and $C_u(t) - C_u(t_u)$ is the number of visits of agents to u from round t_u until round $t - 1$, or equivalently, the number of departures of agents from u in rounds $t_u + 1$ up to t.

Lemma 5. *For any* $u \in V$, $\tau_u \leqslant C_u(t_u)$.

Proof. Consider the following path through which information reaches u in VISIT-EXCHANGE. The path is $(v_0, v_1, \ldots, v_k)$, where $v_0 = s$, $v_k = u$, and for $0 < j \leqslant k$, $v_{j-1} \in S_{v_j}$ and $C_{v_j}(t_{v_j}) = C_{v_{j-1}}(t_{v_j})$. It is easy to verify that such a path exists. In the following, we prove by induction on $0 \leqslant j \leqslant k$ that

$$\tau_{v_j} \leqslant C_{v_j}(t_{v_j}). \tag{4}$$

This holds for $j = 0$, because $v_0 = s$, $t_s = 0$, and $\tau_s = 0 = C_s(0)$. Let $0 < j \leqslant k$, and suppose that $\tau_{v_{j-1}} \leqslant C_{v_{j-1}}(t_{v_{j-1}})$; we will show that $\tau_{v_j} \leqslant C_{v_j}(t_{v_j})$. We have that

$$\begin{aligned} C_{v_j}(t_{v_j}) &= C_{v_{j-1}}(t_{v_j}), \quad \text{by the path property} \\ &= C_{v_{j-1}}(t_{v_{j-1}}) + \sum_{t_{v_{j-1}} \leqslant t < t_{v_j}} |Z_{v_{j-1}}(t)|, \\ &\qquad \text{by recursive application of (3)} \\ &\geqslant \tau_{v_{j-1}} + \sum_{t_{v_{j-1}} \leqslant t < t_{v_j}} |Z_{v_{j-1}}(t)|, \quad \text{by induct. hypothesis.} \end{aligned}$$

Let $\ell = \min\{i \colon p_{v_{j-1}}(i) = v_j\}$, let g be the agent that does the ℓth visit to v_{j-1} since round $t_{v_{j-1}}$, and let r be the round when that visit takes place, thus $x_g(r) = v_{j-1}$ and $x_g(r+1) = v_j$. By the minimality of ℓ, $r + 1$ is the first round when some informed agent moves to v_j from v_{j-1}. Since $v_{j-1} \in S_{v_j}$, it follows that $r + 1 = t_{v_j}$. Then

$$\ell \leqslant \sum_{t_{v_{j-1}} \leqslant t \leqslant r} |Z_{v_{j-1}}(t)| = \sum_{t_{v_{j-1}} \leqslant t < t_{v_j}} |Z_{v_{j-1}}(t)|.$$

Also, from the coupling, $\pi_{v_{j-1}}(\ell) = p_{v_{j-1}}(\ell) = v_j$, which implies

$$\tau_{v_j} \leqslant \tau_{v_{j-1}} + \ell.$$

Combining all the above we obtain $C_{v_j}(t_{v_j}) \geqslant \tau_{v_{j-1}} + \ell \geqslant \tau_{v_j}$, completing the inductive proof of (4). Applying (4) for $j = k$ we obtain $\tau_u \leqslant C_u(t_u)$. □

4.4 Canonical Walks and Congestion

Let $\theta = (\theta_0, \theta_1, \ldots, \theta_k)$ be a walk on G, where $\theta_0 = s$, and $\theta_i \in \Gamma(\theta_{i-1}) \cup \{\theta_{i-1}\}$, for $1 \leqslant i \leqslant k$. We construct θ from VISIT-EXCHANGE as follows. We start from vertex $\theta_0 = s$ in round zero, and in each round $1 \leqslant t \leqslant k$, we either stay put, in which case $\theta_t = \theta_{t-1}$, or we choose one of the agents $g \in Z_{\theta_{i-1}}(t-1)$, which visited θ_{i-1} in the previous round, and move to the same vertex as g in round t, i.e., $\theta_t = x_t(g)$. We call θ a *canonical walk* of length k. A *labeled canonical walk* is a canonical walk that specifies also the agent g_t that the walk follows in each step t, if $\theta_t \neq \theta_{t-1}$. Formally, a labeled canonical walk corresponding to θ is $\eta = (\theta_0, g_1, \theta_1, g_2, \ldots, g_k, \theta_k)$, where $g_t \in Z_{\theta_{t-1}}(t-1) \cap Z_{\theta_t}(t)$ if $\theta_t \neq \theta_{t-1}$, and $g_t = \perp$ if $\theta_t = \theta_{t-1}$. Note that different labeled canonical walks may correspond to the same (unlabeled) canonical walk. We define the *congestion* $Q(\theta)$ of a canonical walk θ as the total number of (non-distinct) agents encountered along the walk, not counting the last step, i.e.,

$$Q(\theta) = \sum_{0 \leqslant t < k} |Z_{\theta_t}(t)|.$$

The congestion of a *labeled* canonical walk is the same as the congestion of the corresponding unlabeled walk. We have the following simple connection between canonical walks and C-counters.

Lemma 6. *For any* $u \in V$ *and* $t \geqslant t_u$, *there is a canonical walk* θ *of length t with* $Q(\theta) = C_u(t)$.

Proof. We consider the same path $(v_0, v_1, \ldots, v_k)$ as in the proof of Lemma 5, where $v_0 = s$, $v_k = u$, and for $0 < j \leqslant k$, $v_{j-1} \in S_{v_j}$ and $C_{v_j}(t_{v_j}) = C_{v_{j-1}}(t_{v_j})$. Consider the canonical walk θ obtained from this path by adding between each pair of consecutive vertices v_{j-1} and v_j, $t_{v_j} - t_{v_{j-1}} - 1$ copies of v_{j-1}, and also appending after v_k a number of $t - t_{v_k}$ copies of v_k. It is then easy to show by induction that $Q(\theta) = C_u(t)$. □

4.5 Concise Descriptors of Canonical Walks

In this section, we bound the number of distinct labeled canonical walks of a given length k. For that, we present a concise description for such walks, and bound the total number of the walks by the total number of different possible descriptions.

We start with a rather wasteful way to describe labeled canonical walks of length k, which we then refine in two steps. Let $\mathcal{A}_k$ denote the set of all $n \times k$ matrices $A_k = [a_{i,j}]$, where $a_{i,j} \in \{0, \ldots, i\}$. Let us fix the first k rounds of VISIT-EXCHANGE, and consider a labeled canonical walk $\eta = (\theta_0 = s, g_1, \theta_1, g_2, \ldots, g_k, \theta_k)$. For each $1 \leqslant t \leqslant k$, let

$$\delta_t = |Z_{\theta_{t-1}}(t-1)|$$

be the number of agents that visit θ_{t-1} in round $t - 1$, and thus also the number of agents that depart from θ_{t-1} in round t. Let $\rho_t = 0$ if $g_t = \perp$, otherwise, ρ_t is equal to the *rank* of g_t in set $Z_{\theta_{t-1}}(t-1)$. We describe walk η by a matrix $A_k \in \mathcal{A}_k$ with the following entries: For each $1 \leqslant t \leqslant k$, if $\delta_t > 0$, then $a_{\delta_t, j} = \rho_t$, for

$j = |\{t' \leqslant t \colon \delta_{t'} = \delta_t\}|$; i.e., value ρ_t is stored in the first unused entry of row $A_k[\delta_t, \cdot]$. At most k of the entries of A_k are specified that way; the remaining entries can have arbitrary values. We call A_k a *non-concise descriptor* of η.

For any realization of VISIT-EXCHANGE, each $A_k \in \mathcal{A}_k$ describes exactly one labeled canonical walk of length k, and any labeled canonical walk of length k has at least one non-concise descriptor $A_k \in \mathcal{A}_k$ (in fact, several ones). The total number of different non-concise descriptors is $|\mathcal{A}_k| = \prod_{1\leqslant i\leqslant n}(i+1)^k$, which is too large for our purposes.

A simple improvement is to use only entries in rows $A_k[i, \cdot]$ for which i is a power of 2 (we assume w.l.o.g. that n is also a power of 2). Roughly speaking, if δ_t is between $2^{\ell-1}$ and 2^ℓ then ρ_t is stored in raw $A_k[2^\ell, \cdot]$. Formally, let b be a large enough constant (to be specified later) that is a power of 2. The matrix $A_k \in \mathcal{A}_k$ we use to describes η has the following entries. For each $1 \leqslant t \leqslant k$:

(1) If $2^{\ell-1} < \delta_t \leqslant 2^\ell$, where $\ell \in \{1+\log b, \dots, \log n\}$, and $|\{t' \leqslant t \colon 2^{\ell-1} < \delta_{t'} \leqslant 2^\ell\}| = j$, then
  (a) if $\rho_t \neq 0$, $a_{2^\ell,j} = \rho_t$;
  (b) if $\rho_t = 0$, $a_{2^\ell,j}$ can take any value in $\{0\} \cup \{\delta_t+1, \dots, 2^\ell\}$;
(2) If $0 \leqslant \delta_t \leqslant b$ and $|\{t' \leqslant t \colon 0 < \delta_{t'} \leqslant b\}| = j$, then
  (a) if $\rho_t \neq 0$, $a_{b,j} = \rho_t$;
  (b) if $\rho_t = 0$, $a_{b,j}$ can take any value in $\{0\} \cup \{\delta_t+1, \dots, b\}$.

The purpose of subcases (b) is to maintain the convenient property that every A_k describes a labeled canonical walk, which would not be the case if we just set $a_{2^\ell,j} = 0$ or $a_{b,j} = 0$, since values greater than δ_t would not correspond to a walk. We call the above A_k a *semi-concise descriptor* of η.

A second modification we make is based on the observation that, in the $\log n$ rows of A_k used in the above scheme, most entries are very unlikely to be actually used. So, for each $i = 2^\ell$, we specify a threshold index $k_i \leqslant k$, such that the first k_i entries in each row $A_k[i, \cdot]$ suffice w.h.p. to describe all labeled canonical walks of length k. Let $\mathcal{B}_k$ be a subset of $\mathcal{A}_k$ defined as follows. Let

$$k_i = b \cdot k/i,$$

and recall that b is a constant power of 2. The set $\mathcal{B}_k$ consists then of all $A_k = [a_{i,j}] \in \mathcal{A}_k$ for which

$$\begin{aligned} a_{i,j} &\in \{0, \dots, i\}, && \text{if } i \in \{2^\ell \colon \log b \leqslant \ell \leqslant \log n\}, \text{ and } j \leqslant k_i; \\ a_{i,j} &= 0, && \text{otherwise.} \end{aligned}$$

A *concise descriptor* of a labeled canonical walk η of length k is any semi-concise descriptor A_k of η that belongs to set $\mathcal{B}_k$.

Next we establish the following upper bound on the number of all possible concise descriptors of length k.

LEMMA 7. $|\mathcal{B}_k| \leqslant (4b)^{2k}$.

PROOF. From the definition of $\mathcal{B}_k$, we have

$$\begin{aligned} |\mathcal{B}_k| &\leqslant \prod_{\log b \leqslant \ell \leqslant \log n} (2^\ell + 1)^{bk/2^\ell} \\ &= \prod_{\log b \leqslant \ell \leqslant \log n} 2^{\ell bk/2^\ell} \cdot \prod_{\log b \leqslant \ell \leqslant \log n} (1 + 2^{-\ell})^{bk/2^\ell} \\ &\leqslant \frac{\prod_{\ell \geqslant 1} 2^{\ell bk/2^\ell}}{\prod_{\ell \leqslant \log b - 1} 2^{\ell bk/2^\ell}} \cdot \prod_{\ell \geqslant \log b} e^{bk/4^\ell} \\ &= \frac{2^{2bk}}{2^{(2(b-\log b-1)k}} \cdot e^{(4/3)k/b} \\ &\leqslant 2^{2(\log b+2)k}, \end{aligned}$$

where in the second-last line we used $\sum_{\ell\geqslant 1} \ell/2^\ell = 2$, $\sum_{\ell \leqslant y} \ell/2^\ell = 2^{-y}(2^{y+1} - y - 2)$, and $\sum_{\ell\geqslant 0} 1/4^\ell = 4/3$; and in the last line we used that $e^{(4/3)} < 4$. □

For any realization of VISIT-EXCHANGE, each $A_k \in \mathcal{B}_k$ is a concise descriptor of some labeled canonical walk of length k. However it is not always the case that a labeled canonical walk of length k has a concise descriptor. The next lemma shows that w.h.p. all labeled canonical walks of length k have concise descriptors for an appropriate choice of constant parameter b. Note that the lemma assumes the T-VISIT-EXCHANGE process.

LEMMA 8. *If $b \geqslant \max\{2\alpha e^2, 64\}$ then, with probability at least $1 - 2^{-bk/4}\log n$, all labeled canonical walks of length k in a random realization of T-VISIT-EXCHANGE have concise descriptors.*

4.6 Proof of Lemma 8

First, we bound the number of steps t in which more than i agents are encountered in a canonical walk of length k.

LEMMA 9. *Fix any $A_k \in \mathcal{A}_k$, and let $\eta = (\theta_0, g_1, \theta_1, g_2, \dots, g_k, \theta_k)$ be the labeled canonical walk in T-VISIT-EXCHANGE that has non-concise (or semi-concise) descriptor A_k. For any $i \geqslant e^2\alpha$ and $\beta \geqslant e^2\alpha$,*

$$\mathbb{P}[|\{t \in \{1, \dots, k\} \colon \delta_t > i\}| \geqslant \beta k/i] \leqslant 2^{-\beta k}.$$

PROOF. Recall that $\delta_t = |Z_{\theta_{t-1}}(t-1)|$ is the number of agents that visit vertex θ_{t-1} in round $t-1$, and thus also the number of agents that depart from θ_{t-1} in round t. We argue that for any $t \geqslant 1$, conditioned on $\delta_1, \dots, \delta_t$, variable δ_{t+1} is stochastically dominated by the binomial variable $\mathrm{Bin}(\alpha d - 1, 1/d) + 1$: From (2), applied for vertex θ_t and round $t-1$, we get

$$\sum_{v \in \Gamma(\theta_t)} |Z_v(t-1)| \leqslant \alpha \cdot d,$$

thus, there are at most αd agents in the neighborhood of θ_t at the beginning of round t. If $g_t = \bot$ (thus $\theta_t = \theta_{t-1}$), then each one of those at most αd agents will visit θ_t in round t independently with probability $1/d$. If $g_t \neq \bot$ (thus $\theta_t \neq \theta_{t-1}$ and $g_t \in Z_{\theta_{t-1}}(t-1) \cap Z_{\theta_t}(t)$), then each of the at most αd agents will visit θ_t in round t independently with probability $1/d$, *except* for agent g_t who visits θ_t with probability 1. In both cases, the number δ_{t+1} of agents that visit θ_t is dominated by $\mathrm{Bin}(\alpha d - 1, 1/d) + 1$. It follows that, for $t > 1$ and $i \geqslant 1$,

$$\begin{aligned} \mathbb{P}[\delta_t > i \mid \delta_1, \dots, \delta_{t-1}] &\leqslant \mathbb{P}[\mathrm{Bin}(\alpha d - 1, 1/d) > i - 1] \\ &\leqslant \mathbb{P}[\mathrm{Bin}(\alpha d, 1/d) \geqslant i] \\ &\leqslant \binom{\alpha d}{i} \cdot \frac{1}{d^i} \leqslant \left(\frac{e\alpha d}{i}\right)^i \cdot \frac{1}{d^i} = \left(\frac{e\alpha}{i}\right)^i. \end{aligned}$$

For the case of $t = 1$, since $|A| \leqslant \alpha n/(2e) < \alpha n$ by (1), we similarly have

$$\mathbb{P}[\delta_1 \geqslant i] \leqslant \mathbb{P}[\mathrm{Bin}(\alpha n, 1/n) \geqslant i] \leqslant \left(\frac{e\alpha}{i}\right)^i.$$

Let $p_i = \left(\frac{e\alpha}{i}\right)^i$. It follows from the above that, for any $\ell \geqslant 1$,

$$\mathbb{P}[|\{t \in \{1,\ldots,k\}\colon \delta_t > i\}| \geqslant \ell] \leqslant \mathbb{P}[\mathrm{Bin}(k,p_i) \geqslant \ell] \leqslant \binom{k}{\ell} \cdot p_i^\ell \leqslant \left(\frac{ekp_i}{\ell}\right)^\ell. \quad (5)$$

For $\ell \geqslant \beta k/i$ and $i \geqslant e^2\alpha$,

$$\begin{aligned}\left(\frac{ekp_i}{\ell}\right)^\ell &\leqslant \left(\frac{ek(e\alpha/i)^i}{\beta k/i}\right)^\ell, && \text{by } p_i = \left(\frac{e\alpha}{i}\right)^i \text{ and } \ell \geqslant \beta k/i\\ &= \left(\frac{e^2\alpha}{\beta}\cdot\left(\frac{e\alpha}{i}\right)^{i-1}\right)^\ell \leqslant \left(\frac{e\alpha}{i}\right)^{(i-1)\ell}, && \text{by } \beta \geqslant e^2\alpha\\ &\leqslant \left(\frac{e\alpha}{i}\right)^{(1-1/i)\beta k}, && \text{by } \ell \geqslant \beta k/i\\ &\leqslant \left(\frac{1}{e}\right)^{(1-1/e^2)\beta k}, && \text{by } i \geqslant e^2\alpha \geqslant e^2\\ &\leqslant 2^{-\beta k}.\end{aligned}$$

Substituting that to (5) completes the proof of Lemma 9. □

We proceed now to the proof of the main lemma. For any $A_k \in \mathcal{A}_k$, and for $\eta = (\theta_0, g_1, \theta_1, g_2, \ldots, \theta_k)$ the labeled canonical walk with semi-concise descriptor A_k, let $\mathcal{E}_{A_k}$ denote the event:

$$|\{t \in \{1,\ldots,k\}\colon 2^{\ell-1} < \delta_t \leqslant 2^\ell\}| \leqslant k_{2^\ell}, \forall \ell \in \{\log b+1,\ldots,\log n\}.$$

Applying Lemma 9, for $i = 2^{\ell-1}$, $\beta = b/2$, and each $\ell \in \{\log b + 1, \ldots, \log n\}$, and then using a union bound, we obtain

$$\mathbb{P}\left[\mathcal{E}_{A_k}\right] \geqslant 1 - 2^{-bk/2}\log n.$$

By Lemma 7 and another union bound,

$$\begin{aligned}\mathbb{P}\left[\bigcap_{A_k\in\mathcal{B}_k}\mathcal{E}_{A_k}\right] &\geqslant 1 - |\mathcal{B}_k|\cdot 2^{-bk/2}\log n\\ &\geqslant 1-(4b)^{2k}\cdot 2^{-bk/2}\log n\\ &\geqslant 1-2^{-bk/4}\log n, \qquad (6)\end{aligned}$$

where the last inequality holds when $b \geqslant 64$. Next we show that event $\bigcap_{A_k\in\mathcal{B}_k}\mathcal{E}_{A_k}$ implies that every labeled canonical walk η has a concise descriptor $A_k \in \mathcal{B}_k$. From this and (6), the lemma follows.

Fix a realization of T-VISIT-EXCHANGE conditioned on the event $\bigcap_{A_k\in\mathcal{B}_k}\mathcal{E}_{A_k}$. Suppose, for contradiction, that there is some labeled canonical walk $\eta' = (\theta'_0, g'_1, \theta'_1, \ldots, g'_k, \theta_k)$ that does *not* have a concise descriptor. Let $\eta = (\theta_0, g_1, \theta_1, \ldots, g_k, \theta_k)$ be a labeled canonical walk that *does* have a concise descriptor $A_k \in \mathcal{B}_k$, and shares a *maximal common prefix* with η'. Consider the first element where η' and η are different. We argue that this element is not a vertex: Suppose, for contradiction, that $(\theta'_0, \ldots, g'_i) = (\theta_0, \ldots, g_i)$ and $\theta'_i \neq \theta_i$, for some $0 \leqslant i \leqslant k$. Then $i \neq 0$, as $\theta'_0 = s = \theta_0$. Moreover, if $i > 0$, then by definition, $(\theta'_0, \ldots, g'_i) = (\theta_0, \ldots, g_i)$ implies $\theta'_i = \theta_i$, contradicting our assumption. Thus, the first element where η' and η are different must be an agent. Suppose $(\theta'_0, g'_1, \ldots, \theta'_{i-1}) = (\theta_0, g_1, \ldots, \theta_{i-1})$ and $g'_i \neq g_i$, for some $1 \leqslant i \leqslant k$. Then, by the maximal prefix assumption, the labeled canonical walk $(\theta_0, \ldots, \theta_{i-1}, g'_i, \theta'_i, \perp, \theta'_i, \perp, \ldots, \perp, \theta'_i)$, which stays at vertex θ'_i in rounds $i+1$ up to k, has no concise descriptor. This can only be true if $|\{t \in \{1,\ldots,i-1\}\colon 2^{\ell-1} < \delta_t \leqslant 2^\ell\}| > k_{2^\ell}$, for some $\ell \in \{\log b+1, \ldots, \log n\}$. But this contradicts event $\mathcal{E}_{A_k}$. Therefore, there exists no labeled canonical walk η' of length k such that η' has no concise descriptor.

4.7 Bound on Congestion

The next lemma gives un upper bound on the congestion of a single canonical walk of length k.

Lemma 10. *Fix any $A_k \in \mathcal{B}_k$, and let η be the labeled canonical walk in T-VISIT-EXCHANGE that has concise descriptor A_k. Then for any $\beta \geqslant 2e\alpha + 1$, $\mathbb{P}[Q(\eta) \leqslant \beta k] \geqslant 1 - 2^{-(\beta-1)k}$.*

Proof. Let $\eta = (\theta_0, g_1, \theta_1, \ldots, g_k, \theta_k)$. Then $Q(\eta) = \sum_{1\leqslant t\leqslant k}\delta_t$, where $\delta_t = |Z_{\theta_{t-1}}(t-1)|$. From the same reasoning as in the proof of Lemma 9, we have that $Q(\eta)$ is stochastically dominated by $k + \sum_{1\leqslant t\leqslant k} B_t$, where $B_1, \ldots, B_k$ are mutually independent binomial random variables, such that $B_1 \sim \mathrm{Bin}(\alpha n, 1/n)$ and, for $t > 1$, $B_t \sim \mathrm{Bin}(\alpha d, 1/d)$. Then $\mathbb{E}[Q(\eta) - k] \leqslant \sum_{1\leqslant t\leqslant k}\mathbb{E}[B_t] = k\alpha$, and

$$\mathbb{P}[Q(\eta) \geqslant \beta k] = \mathbb{P}[Q(\eta) - k \geqslant (\beta-1)k] \leqslant 2^{-(\beta-1)k},$$

where the last inequality follows from a standard Chernoff bound, using that $(\beta-1)k \geqslant 2e\cdot\mathbb{E}[Q(\eta)-k]$. □

4.8 Putting the Pieces Together (Proof of Theorem 2)

We consider first the case where k is at most logarithmic. It is not hard to show that $T_{\text{visitx}} = \Omega(\log n)$ w.h.p., by arguing that some vertices are not visited by any agent (informed or not) during the first logarithmic number of rounds (see the full version of the paper). Thus, there is some constant $\epsilon > 0$ such that if $k \leqslant \epsilon\log n$, $\mathbb{P}[T_{\text{visitx}} \leqslant k] \leqslant n^{-\lambda}$. From this, the theorem's statement follows for $k \leqslant \epsilon\log n$. In the rest of the proof, we assume $k \geqslant \epsilon\log n$.

We have $T_{\text{push}} = \max_{u\in V}\tau_u$, and from Lemma 5,

$$T_{\text{push}} \leqslant \max_{u\in V} C_u(t_u).$$

Since for any fixed realization of VISIT-EXCHANGE and any $u \in V$, $C_u(t)$ is a non-decreasing function of t, and since $t_u \leqslant T_{\text{visitx}}$, it follows

$$T_{\text{push}} \leqslant \max_{u\in V} C_u(T_{\text{visitx}}).$$

By Lemma 6, for any $u \in V$, there is a canonical walk θ of length $t = T_{\text{visitx}}$ with congestion $Q(\theta) = C_u(T_{\text{visitx}})$. Thus, there is also a *labeled* canonical walk η of length T_{visitx} with $Q(\eta) = Q(\theta) = C_u(T_{\text{visitx}})$. It follows

$$T_{\text{push}} \leqslant \max_{\eta\in\mathcal{H}(T_{\text{visitx}})} Q(\eta), \qquad (7)$$

where $\mathcal{H}(t)$ denotes the set of all labeled canonical walks of length t in VISIT-EXCHANGE.

Next we bound $\max_{\eta\in\mathcal{H}(k)} Q(\eta)$. Consider T-VISIT-EXCHANGE, and for any $A_k \in \mathcal{B}_k$, let η_{A_k} be the labeled canonical walk in T-VISIT-EXCHANGE with concise descriptor A_k. From Lemma 10, for any $A_k \in \mathcal{B}_k$ and $\beta \geqslant 2e\alpha + 1$, $\mathbb{P}\left[Q(\eta_{A_k}) \leqslant \beta k\right] \geqslant 1 - 2^{-(\beta-1)k}$. Then

$$\begin{aligned}\mathbb{P}\left[\max_{A_k\in\mathcal{B}_k} Q(\eta_{A_k}) \leqslant \beta k\right] &\geqslant 1 - 2^{-(\beta-1)k}\cdot|\mathcal{B}_k|\\ &\geqslant 1-2^{-(\beta-1)k}\cdot(4b)^{2k},\end{aligned}$$

by Lemma 7. Choosing constant β large enough so that $(\beta-1)/2 \geqslant 2\log(4b)$, yields

$$\mathbb{P}\left[\max_{A_k \in \mathcal{B}_k} Q(\eta_{A_k}) \leqslant \beta k\right] \geqslant 1 - 2^{-(\beta-1)k/2}.$$

From Lemma 8, the probability that all labeled canonical walks of length k have concise descriptors is at least $1 - 2^{-bk/4}\log n$, if $b \geqslant \max\{2\alpha e^2, 64\}$. It follows

$$\mathbb{P}\left[\max_{A_k \in \mathcal{B}_k} Q(\eta_{A_k}) = \max_{\eta \in \mathcal{H}^*(k)} Q(\eta)\right] \geqslant 1 - 2^{-bk/4}\log n,$$

where $\mathcal{H}^*(t)$ is the set of all labeled canonical walks of length t in T-VISIT-EXCHANGE. By Lemma 4, however, VISIT-EXCHANGE and the coupled T-VISIT-EXCHANGE, which use the same random walks, are identical until round k, with probability at least $1 - kn \cdot 2^{-ad}$, thus

$$\mathbb{P}\left[\mathcal{H}(k) = \mathcal{H}^*(k)\right] \geqslant 1 - kn \cdot 2^{-\alpha d}.$$

Combining the last three inequalities above, we obtain

$$\mathbb{P}\left[\max_{\eta \in \mathcal{H}(k)} Q(\eta) \leqslant \beta k\right] \geqslant 1 - 2^{-(\beta-1)k/2} - 2^{-bk/4}\log n - kn \cdot e^{-\alpha d}.$$

Since $k \geqslant \epsilon \log n$ and $d \geqslant \varepsilon \log n$, for any given constant $\lambda > 0$ we can choose constants β, b, α large enough such that

$$\mathbb{P}\left[\max_{\eta \in \mathcal{H}(k)} Q(\eta) \leqslant \beta k\right] \geqslant 1 - n^{-\lambda}. \tag{8}$$

From (7) and (8), we obtain

$$\begin{aligned}
\mathbb{P}\left[T_{\text{push}} \leqslant \beta k\right] &\geqslant \mathbb{P}\left[\max_{\eta \in \mathcal{H}(T_{\text{visitx}})} Q(\eta) \leqslant \beta k\right], \qquad \text{by (7)} \\
&\geqslant \mathbb{P}\left[T_{\text{visitx}} \leqslant k \cap \max_{\eta \in \mathcal{H}(k)} Q(\eta) \leqslant \beta k\right] \\
&\geqslant \mathbb{P}\left[T_{\text{visitx}} \leqslant k\right] - \mathbb{P}\left[\max_{\eta \in \mathcal{H}(k)} Q(\eta) > \beta k\right] \\
&\geqslant \mathbb{P}\left[T_{\text{visitx}} \leqslant k\right] - n^{-\lambda}, \qquad \text{by (8)}.
\end{aligned}$$

This completes the proof of Theorem 2.

5 BOUNDING T_{visitx} BY T_{push} ON REGULAR GRAPHS

The following theorem upper bounds the broadcast time of VISIT-EXCHANGE in a regular graph by the broadcast time of PUSH.

THEOREM 11. *For any constants $\alpha, \beta, \lambda > 0$ with $\alpha \cdot \beta$ sufficiently large, there is a constant $c > 0$, such that for any d-regular graph $G = (V, E)$ with $|V| = n$ and $d \geqslant \beta \log n$, and for any source $s \in V$, the broadcast times of PUSH and VISIT-EXCHANGE, with $|A| \geqslant \alpha n$ agents, satisfy*

$$\mathbb{P}\left[T_{\text{visitx}} \leqslant ck\right] \geqslant \mathbb{P}\left[T_{\text{push}} \leqslant k\right] - n^{-\lambda},$$

for any $k \geqslant 0$.

From Theorem 11, it is immediate that if $T_{\text{push}} \leqslant T$ w.h.p., then $T_{\text{visitx}} = O(T)$ w.h.p., as well. Moreover, using Theorem 11 and the well-known $O(n^2 \log n)$ upper bound w.h.p. on the cover time for a single random walk on a regular graph, which also applies to T_{visitx}, it is easy to show that $\mathbb{E}[T_{\text{visitx}}] = O(\mathbb{E}[T_{\text{push}}])$.

Proof Overview Of Theorem 11. We use a coupling which is similar to that in the proof of the converse result, stated in Theorem 2, but with a twist (which we describe momentarily). Unlike in the proof of Theorem 2, were we essentially consider all possible paths through which information travels, here we focus on the first path by which information reaches each vertex. Let $P = (u_0 = s, u_1, \ldots, u_k = u)$ be such a path for vertex u in PUSH, where each vertex u_i in the path learns the information from u_{i-1}. Let δ_i be the number of rounds it takes for u_{i-1} to sample (and inform) u_i in PUSH. We consider the same path in VISIT-EXCHANGE, and compare δ_i with the number D_i of rounds until some informed agent moves from u_{i-1} to u_i, counting from the round when u_{i-1} becomes informed. Note that $\sum_i \delta_i$ is precisely the round when u is informed in PUSH, while $\sum_i D_i$ is an upper bound on the round when u is informed in VISIT-EXCHANGE.

The coupling we used in Sect. 4 seems suitable for this setup. Recall, in that coupling we let the list of neighbors that a vertex u samples in PUSH, be identical to the list of neighbors that informed agents visit in their next step after visiting u, in VISIT-EXCHANGE. The same intuition applies, namely, that on average each vertex is visited by $|A|/n = \Omega(1)$ agents per round, which suggests that D_i should be close to δ_i. We can even apply a similar trick as in Sect. 4 to avoid some dependencies: In each round, the number of agents in the neighborhood of a vertex is bounded below by $d \cdot |A|/n = \Omega(d)$, w.h.p. This should imply that the number of agents that visit a vertex in a round is bounded below by a geometric distribution with constant expectation. Let $\mathcal{E}$ denote the event that the above $\Omega(d)$ bound holds for all u, for polynomially many rounds.

There is, however, a problem with this proof plan. By fixing path P in advance, to be the first path to inform u in PUSH, we introduce *dependencies from the future.* So, when we analyse D_i and δ_i, we must condition on the event that the i-prefix of the path we have considered so far will indeed be a prefix of the first path to reach u. These kind of dependencies seem hard to deal with.

We use the following neat idea to overcome this problem. We only consider the *odd rounds* of VISIT-EXCHANGE in the coupling, i.e., we match the list of neighbors that a vertex v samples in PUSH (in all rounds), to the list of neighbors that informed agents visit in round $2k+1$ after visiting u in round $2k$, for all $k \geqslant 0$. In even rounds, agents take steps *independently* of the coupled PUSH process.

Under this coupling, we proceed as follows. We condition on the high probability event $\mathcal{E}$ defined earlier (formally, we modify VISIT-EXCHANGE to ensure $\mathcal{E}$ holds). We then fix *all* random choices in PUSH, and thus the information path P to u. For each even round of VISIT-EXCHANGE, we have that vertex u_i in P is visited by at least one agent with constant probability, independently of the past and of the fixed choices in future odd rounds. If indeed some vertex visits u_i in an even round, then in the next round it will visit a vertex dictated by the coupling. This allows us to show that under this coupling, $\sum_i D_i \leqslant c(\sum_i \delta_i + \log n)$, w.h.p. We get rid of the $\log n$ term in the final bound, by using that $T_{\text{push}} = \Omega(\log n)$ w.h.p. The detailed proof can be found in the full version of the paper.

6 BOUNDING T_{visitx} BY T_{meetx} ON REG. GRAPHS

The next theorem bounds the broadcast time of VISIT-EXCHANGE in a regular graph by the broadcast time of MEET-EXCHANGE.

THEOREM 12. *For any constants $\alpha, \beta, \lambda > 0$ with $\alpha \cdot \beta$ sufficiently large, there is a constant $c > 0$, such that for any d-regular graph $G = (V, E)$ with $|V| = n$ and $d \geqslant \beta \ln n$, and for any source $s \in V$, the broadcast times of* VISIT-EXCHANGE *and* MEET-EXCHANGE, *both with $|A| \geqslant \alpha n$ agents, satisfy*

$$\mathbb{P}\left[T_{\text{visitx}} \leqslant k + c \ln n\right] \geqslant \mathbb{P}\left[T_{\text{meetx}} \leqslant k\right] - n^{-\lambda},$$

for any $k \geqslant 0$.

The proof of the theorem shows that once all agents are informed, it takes an additional $O(\log n)$ rounds w.h.p. before each vertex is visited at least once by some agent.

7 OPEN PROBLEMS

This work is the first systematic and thorough comparison of the running times of the standard PUSH and PUSH-PULL rumor spreading protocols with some very natural agent-based alternatives. Several open problems remain. The most obvious question to ask is whether our results for regular graphs hold also when the graph degree is sub-logarithmic. Another question is whether there are graphs where MEET-EXCHANGE is slower than VISIT-EXCHANGE by more than logarithmic factors. In this paper we assumed a linear number of agents. It would be interesting to study the performance of the protocols when a sub-linear number of agents is available.

The main attractive properties of standard rumor spreading protocols are simplicity, scalability, and robustness to failures [21]. Arguably, VISIT-EXCHANGE and MEET-EXCHANGE share the first two properties, but probably not the robustness property. In particular, it seems that faulty nodes or links can result in agents getting lost. It would be interesting to explore fault tolerant variants of these protocols. For example, it seems likely that the protocols could tolerate some number of lost agents, if a *dynamic* set of agents were used, where agents age with time and die, while new agents are born at a proportional rate.

ACKNOWLEDGMENTS

The authors would like to thank Thomas Sauerwald and Nicolás Rivera for helpful discussions. This research was undertaken, in part, thanks to funding from the ANR Project PAMELA (ANR-16-CE23-0016-01), the NSF Award Numbers CCF-1461559, CCF-0939370 and CCF-18107, the Gates Cambridge Scholarship programme, and the ERC grant DYNAMIC MARCH.

REFERENCES

[1] R. Aleliunas, R. M. Karp, R. J. Lipton, L. Lovász, and C. Rackoff. Random walks, universal traversal sequences, and the complexity of maze problems. In *Proc. 20th IEEE Symposium on Foundations of Computer Science, FOCS*, pages 218–223, 1979.

[2] N. Alon, C. Avin, M. Koucký, G. Kozma, Z. Lotker, and M. R. Tuttle. Many random walks are faster than one. *Combinatorics, Probability & Computing*, 20(4):481–502, 2011.

[3] O. Angel, A. Mehrabian, and Y. Peres. The string of diamonds is tight for rumor spreading. In *Proc. Approximation, Randomization, and Combinatorial Optimization. Algorithms and Techniques, APPROX/RANDOM*, pages 26:1–26:9, 2017.

[4] P. Berenbrink, R. Elsässer, and T. Friedetzky. Efficient randomised broadcasting in random regular networks with applications in peer-to-peer systems. *Distributed Computing*, 29(5):317–339, 2016.

[5] P. Berenbrink, G. Giakkoupis, A. Kermarrec, and F. Mallmann-Trenn. Bounds on the voter model in dynamic networks. In *Proc. 43rd International Colloquium on Automata, Languages, and Programming, ICALP*, pages 146:1–146:15, 2016.

[6] P. Berenbrink, G. Giakkoupis, and P. Kling. Tight bounds for coalescing-branching random walks on regular graphs. In *Proc. 29th ACM-SIAM Symposium on Discrete Algorithms, SODA*, pages 1715–1733, 2018.

[7] S. P. Boyd, A. Ghosh, B. Prabhakar, and D. Shah. Randomized gossip algorithms. *IEEE Trans. Information Theory*, 52(6):2508–2530, 2006.

[8] A. Z. Broder, A. R. Karlin, P. Raghavan, and E. Upfal. Trading space for time in undirected s-t connectivity. *SIAM J. Comput.*, 23(2):324–334, 1994.

[9] K. Censor-Hillel, B. Haeupler, J. A. Kelner, and P. Maymounkov. Rumor spreading with no dependence on conductance. *SIAM J. Comput.*, 46(1):58–79, 2017.

[10] F. Chierichetti, G. Giakkoupis, S. Lattanzi, and A. Panconesi. Rumor spreading and conductance. *J. ACM*, 65(4):17:1–17:21, 2018.

[11] F. Chierichetti, S. Lattanzi, and A. Panconesi. Rumor spreading in social networks. *Theor. Comput. Sci.*, 412(24):2602–2610, 2011.

[12] C. Cooper. Random walks, interacting particles, dynamic networks: Randomness can be helpful. In *Proc. Structural Information and Communication Complexity - 18th International Colloquium, SIROCCO*, pages 1–14, 2011.

[13] C. Cooper, A. M. Frieze, and T. Radzik. Multiple random walks in random regular graphs. *SIAM J. Discrete Math.*, 23(4):1738–1761, 2009.

[14] A. J. Demers, D. H. Greene, C. Hauser, W. Irish, J. Larson, S. Shenker, H. E. Sturgis, D. C. Swinehart, and D. B. Terry. Epidemic algorithms for replicated database maintenance. *Operating Systems Review*, 22(1):8–32, 1988.

[15] T. Dimitriou, S. E. Nikoletseas, and P. G. Spirakis. The infection time of graphs. *Discrete Applied Mathematics*, 154(18):2577–2589, 2006.

[16] B. Doerr, M. Fouz, and T. Friedrich. Social networks spread rumors in sublogarithmic time. In *Proc. 43rd ACM Symposium on Theory of Computing, STOC*, pages 21–30, 2011.

[17] B. Doerr, M. Fouz, and T. Friedrich. Social networks spread rumors in sublogarithmic time. In *Proc. 43rd ACM Symposium on Theory of Computing, STOC*, pages 21–30. ACM, 2011.

[18] B. Doerr, T. Friedrich, and T. Sauerwald. Quasirandom rumor spreading. *ACM Trans. Algorithms*, 11(2):9:1–9:35, 2014.

[19] K. Efremenko and O. Reingold. How well do random walks parallelize? In *Proc. Approximation, Randomization, and Combinatorial Optimization. Algorithms and Techniques, 12th International Workshop, APPROX, and 13th International Workshop, RANDOM*, pages 476–489, 2009.

[20] R. Elsässer and T. Sauerwald. Tight bounds for the cover time of multiple random walks. *Theor. Comput. Sci.*, 412(24):2623–2641, 2011.

[21] U. Feige, D. Peleg, P. Raghavan, and E. Upfal. Randomized broadcast in networks. *Random Struct. Algorithms*, 1(4):447–460, 1990.

[22] G. Giakkoupis. Tight bounds for rumor spreading with vertex expansion. In *Proc. 25th ACM-SIAM Symposium on Discrete Algorithms, SODA*, pages 801–815, 2014.

[23] G. Giakkoupis, Y. Nazari, and P. Woelfel. How asynchrony affects rumor spreading time. In *Proc. 35th ACM Symposium on Principles of Distributed Computing, PODC*, pages 185–194, 2016.

[24] M. Harchol-Balter, F. T. Leighton, and D. Lewin. Resource discovery in distributed networks. In *Proc. 18th ACM Symposium on Principles of Distributed Computing, PODC*, pages 229–237, 1999.

[25] J. Hermon. Frogs on trees? *Electron. J. Probab.*, 23, 2018.

[26] V. Kanade, F. Mallmann-Trenn, and T. Sauerwald. On coalescence time in graphs: When is coalescing as fast as meeting? In *Proc. 30th ACM-SIAM Symposium on Discrete Algorithms, SODA*, pages 956–965, 2019.

[27] R. M. Karp, C. Schindelhauer, S. Shenker, and B. Vöcking. Randomized rumor spreading. In *Proc. 41st IEEE Symposium on Foundations of Computer Science, FOCS*, pages 565–574, 2000.

[28] D. Kempe, A. Dobra, and J. Gehrke. Gossip-based computation of aggregate information. In *Proc. 44th IEEE Symposium on Foundations of Computer Science FOCS*, pages 482–491, 2003.

[29] H. Lam, Z. Liu, M. Mitzenmacher, X. Sun, and Y. Wang. Information dissemination via random walks in d-dimensional space. In *Proc. 23rd ACM-SIAM Symposium on Discrete Algorithms, SODA*, pages 1612–1622, 2012.

[30] M. Mitzenmacher, R. Rajaraman, and S. T. Roche. Better bounds for coalescing-branching random walks. *TOPC*, 5(1):2:1–2:23, 2018.

[31] D. Mosk-Aoyama and D. Shah. Fast distributed algorithms for computing separable functions. *IEEE Trans. Information Theory*, 54(7):2997–3007, 2008.

[32] A. Pettarin, A. Pietracaprina, G. Pucci, and E. Upfal. Infectious random walks. *CoRR*, abs/1007.1604, 2010.

[33] S. Y. Popov. Frogs and some other interacting random walks models. In *Proc. Discrete Random Walks, DRW*, pages 277–288, 2003.

[34] T. Sauerwald. On mixing and edge expansion properties in randomized broadcasting. *Algorithmica*, 56(1):51–88, 2010.

[35] R. van Renesse, Y. Minsky, and M. Hayden. A gossip-style failure detection service. In *Proc. IFIP International Conference on Distributed Systems Platforms and Open Distributed Processing*, Middleware '98, pages 55–70, 1998.

Efficient Size Estimation and Impossibility of Termination in Uniform Dense Population Protocols

David Doty*
University of California, Davis
Davis, California
doty@ucdavis.edu

Mahsa Eftekhari*
University of California, Davis
Davis, California
mhseftekhari@ucdavis.edu

ABSTRACT

We study *uniform* population protocols: networks of anonymous agents whose pairwise interactions are chosen at random, where each agent uses an *identical* transition algorithm that does not depend on the population size n. Many existing polylog(n) time protocols for leader election and majority computation are nonuniform: to operate correctly, they require all agents to be initialized with an approximate estimate of n (specifically, the value $\lfloor \log n \rfloor$).

Our first main result is a uniform protocol for calculating $\log(n) \pm O(1)$ with high probability in $O(\log^2 n)$ time and $O(\log^4 n)$ states ($O(\log \log n)$ bits of memory). The protocol is not *terminating*: it does not signal when the estimate is close to the true value of $\log n$. If it could be made terminating with high probability, this would allow composition with protocols requiring a size estimate initially. We do show how our main protocol can be indirectly composed with others in a simple and elegant way, based on *leaderless phase clocks*, demonstrating that those protocols can in fact be made uniform.

However, our second main result implies that the protocol *cannot* be made terminating, a consequence of a much stronger result: a uniform protocol for *any* task requiring more than constant time cannot be terminating even with probability bounded above 0, if infinitely many initial configurations are *dense*: any state present initially occupies $\Omega(n)$ agents. (In particular no leader is allowed.) Crucially, the result holds no matter the memory or time permitted.

CCS CONCEPTS

• **Theory of computation → Distributed algorithms.**

KEYWORDS

population protocols; size estimation; termination

ACM Reference Format:

David Doty and Mahsa Eftekhari. 2019. Efficient Size Estimation and Impossibility of Termination in Uniform Dense Population Protocols. In *2019 ACM Symposium on Principles of Distributed Computing (PODC '19), July 29-August 2, 2019, Toronto, ON, Canada.* ACM, New York, NY, USA, 9 pages. https://doi.org/10.1145/3293611.3331627

*Both authors contributed equally to this research. Authors supported by NSF grants 1619343 and 1844976.

ACM ISBN 978-1-4503-6217-7/19/07...$15.00
https://doi.org/10.1145/3293611.3331627

1 INTRODUCTION

Population protocols [7] are networks that consist of computational entities called *agents* with no control over the schedule of interactions with other agents. In a population of n agents, repeatedly a random pair of agents is chosen to interact, each observing the state of the other agent before updating its own state. They are an appropriate model for electronic computing scenarios such as sensor networks and for "fast-mixing" physical systems such as animal populations [39], gene regulatory networks [18], and chemical reactions [36], the latter increasingly regarded as an implementable "programming language" for molecular engineering, due to recent experimental breakthroughs in DNA nanotechnology [21, 37].

All problems computable with zero error probability by a constant-state population protocol are computable in $O(n)$ time [9, 26]; the benchmark for "efficient" computation is thus sublinear time, ideally polylog(n). For example, the transition $x, q \to y, y$ (starting with at least as many q as the "input" state x) computes $f(x) = 2x$ in expected time $O(\log n)$, whereas $x, x \to y, q$ computes $f(x) = \lfloor x/2 \rfloor$ exponentially slower: expected time $O(n)$ [20].

Although the original model [7] assumed a set of states and transitions that is constant with respect to n, for important distributed computing problems such as leader election [27], majority computation [2], and computation of other functions and predicates [14] no constant-state protocol can stabilize in sublinear time with probability 1.[1] This motivated the study of protocols in which the set of states and transitions grows with n (essentially adding a nonconstant *memory* to each agent). Such protocols achieve leader election and majority computation using $O(\text{polylog}(n))$ time, keeping the number of states "small": typically $O(\text{polylog}(n))$ [2–4, 15, 17], although $O(\log \log n)$ states suffice for leader election [29].

Unfortunately, many of these sublinear-time protocols [2–4, 15, 17] are *nonuniform*: the set of states and transitions are allowed to depend arbitrarily on n (this is not true of all, see for example recent fast, low-memory leader election protocols [29, 30]). This capability is used to initialize each agent with an approximate estimate of n (the value $\lfloor \log n \rfloor$) required by the protocols.

More desirable would be a *uniform* protocol in which each agent's local algorithm for computing the outputs, given the inputs, has no knowledge of n. Such an algorithm may produce outputs longer

[1] A protocol *stabilizes* when it becomes unable to change the output. A protocol *converges* in a given execution when the output stops changing, though it could take longer to subsequently stabilize. Known time lower bounds [2, 14, 27] are on stabilization, not convergence. Recently Kosowski and Uznanski [31] achieved a breakthrough result, showing $O(1)$-state protocols for leader election and all decision problems computable by population protocols (the *semilinear* predicates), converging with high probability in polylog(n) time, and for any $\epsilon > 0$, probability 1 protocols for the same problems converging in $O(n^\epsilon)$ expected time. The latter protocols require $\Omega(n)$ time to stabilize, as would any constant-state protocol due to the cited time lower bounds.

than its inputs, retaining the ability to use a number of states that grows with the population size. A uniform protocol can be deployed into *any* population without knowing in advance the size, or even a rough estimate thereof.

1.1 Contributions

Nonuniform protocols in the literature [2–4, 15, 17] initialize each agent with the value $\lfloor \log n \rfloor$. Hence we study the problem of computing an approximate estimate of $\log n$.

Our first main result, Theorem 3.1, is a uniform protocol, starting from a configuration where all n agents are in an identical state, that with high probability computes $\log n \pm O(1)$ (storing the value in every agent), using $O(\log^2 n)$ time and $O(\log^4 n)$ states. This answers affirmatively open question 5 of [25]. This is done primarily by generating a sequence of geometric random variables,[2] and propagating the maximum to each agent. However, before the maximum reaches all agents they begin computation; thus we use a restart scheme similar to [29] to reset an agent's computation when it updates to a higher estimate of the max.

One might hope to use this protocol as a subroutine to "uniformize" existing nonuniform protocols for leader election and majority [2–4, 15, 17].[3] Suppose the size-estimating protocol could be made terminating, eventually producing a termination "signal" that with high probability does not appear until the size estimate has converged. This would allow composition with other protocols requiring the size estimate. It has been known since the beginning of the population protocol model [7] that termination cannot be guaranteed with probability 1. However, leader-driven protocols can be made terminating with high probability, including simulation of register machines [9] or exact population size counting [32].

Our second main result, Theorem 4.1, shows that this is impossible to do with our leaderless size-estimation protocol and a very wide range of others. This answers negatively open questions 1-3 of [25]. The production of such a terminating signal cannot be delayed, even with probability bounded above 0, by more than $O(1)$ time in any uniform protocol where, for some $\alpha > 0$, infinitely many valid initial configurations are *α-dense*, meaning that each state present is the state of at least αn agents. This holds even for randomized protocols with a nondeterministic transition function. (Because this is an impossibility result, the fact that it holds for both deterministic and randomized protocols makes it stronger than if it held only for deterministic protocols.) Since virtually all nontrivial computation with population protocols requires $\Omega(\log n)$ time[4] (including leader election, and computation of predicates and functions such as majority and $g(x) = 2x$), this implies that no uniform terminating protocol can solve these problems from dense initial configurations.

The hypothesis of density is crucial: with a *leader*, high-probability termination is possible in a uniform protocol [9]. The hypothesis of uniformity is also crucial: if each agent can *initially* store a value $f(n)$, then a termination signal can be delayed until some agent experiences $f(n)$ interactions, an event whose expected time grows unboundedly with n if f grows sufficiently fast. This result uses a density argument similar to that used previously to show time lower bounds, which assume a state set of size $O(1)$ [14, 23, 27] or $\leq \frac{1}{2} \log \log n$ [2]. In contrast, our argument holds for *any* state set size, by showing that a particular subset of states is produced in constant time w.h.p., and using a careful argument to show that this subset necessarily contains the termination signal.

Despite this difficulty in directly composing size estimation with a downstream protocol (or several stages/subprotocols composed in series), we present a general and simple method of composition (via restarting), based on a "leaderless phase clock" using a weaker log population size estimate s (called `logSize2` in the pseudocode in Section 3.2) obtained initially (where $\log n - \log \ln n \leq s \leq 2 \log n$ w.h.p.).[5] Based on s and the expected convergence time of the downstream protocol, each agent once per interaction increments a counter c, from 0 up to $f(s)$, and the first agent to reach $f(s)$ signals the entire population to terminate (or move to the next stage). $f(s)$ is chosen large enough that no agent reaches $f(s)$ before the downstream protocol converges. The entire downstream protocol is reset if the initial size estimate s changes. With the above scheme, agents need to store the variables s, c, and possibly also $f(s)$ (in our case $f(s) = O(s)$ so it need not be stored explicitly, but if $f(s) = \text{poly}(s)$, for example, $f(s)$ may need to be stored separately from s). If the downstream protocol requires $t(n)$ time to converge, then agents also set their threshold $f(s) > t(n)$ (where $f(s)$ is "large" compared to $t(n)$). This requires $O(f(s)^2 \cdot \log n)$ states will be added to the state complexity of the protocol, or $O(\log^2 n)$ if $f(s) = O(\log n)$ (as in our case) since $f(s)$ need not be stored explicitly. To compose multiple downstream stages/subprotocols in series, we also need a way to compute and possibly store the number K of stages (in our case $K = \Theta(\log n)$, also chosen as a constant times s, so K need not be stored explicitly), and we need to store an index indicating which stage we are on. For K stages, this multiplies the state complexity by K if $K = O(\log n)$ and K^2 otherwise (since K must be stored explicitly in the latter case).

1.2 Related work

The work of this paper was inspired by recent work on nonuniform polylog time leader election/majority [2–4, 6, 15, 17, 38]; the fact that those protocols require an approximate size estimate is the direct motivation for seeking a protocol that can compute such an estimate (though unfortunately due to Theorem 4.1, composition of our protocol with these is not totally straightforward).

Some nonuniform protocols crucially rely on an estimate of $\log n$ (e.g. [2–4, 15, 17, 38]) for *correctness*. Other nonuniform protocols are more robust, using the estimate merely to allow the protocol to have a finite number of states. For example, Alistarh and Gelashvili [4] show a $O(\log^3 n)$-time protocol for leader election in which leaders increment a counter on each interaction. The uniform variant of that protocol, with no estimate of $\log n$, is correct with

[2] To our knowledge, this constitutes the first analysis of sums of independent random variables, each of which is a maximum of geometric random variables. Standard Chernoff and other tail bounds generally used for bounded random variables fail in this case. We apply the theory of sub-exponential random variables [35] to obtain strong bounds on the moment-generating function of a maximum of geometric random variables in order to obtain the required Chernoff bounds.

[3] Some protocols for leader election [29, 30] are uniform, but other protocols [2, 4, 15, 17] have the benefit of simplicity and may possibly be easier to reason about and compose with other protocols.

[4] $\Omega(\log n)$ is a lower bound on most interesting computation: by a coupon collector argument, this is the expected time for each agent to have at least one interaction.

[5] The first leaderless phase clock for population protocols was proposed in [3]. Ours is different, based on [38]. Both are nonuniform, relying on an estimate of $\log n$.

probability 1, and the estimate of $\log n$ is used only to bound the counter (hence also the number of states) below $\log n$. Nevertheless, it is not obvious how to modify that protocol to be uniform and have a bounded number of states with high probability.

Self-stabilizing leader election and exact size counting. Cai, Izumi, and Wada [19] (using different terminology) show an impossibility result for uniform population protocols, that no protocol electing a leader can be uniform if it is also required to be *self-stabilizing*: correct with probability 1 from *any* initial configuration. In fact, it must be nonuniform in a very strong way: the *exact* population size must be encoded into each agent. Self-stabilizing exact size computing has also been shown to be possible with a leader [12] in $O(n \log n)$ time and $O(n)$ states for the leader and 2 states for the other agents, all asymptotically optimal parameters in the self-stabilizing setting [10].

Exact size counting. In the less restrictive setting where all agents start from a pre-determined state, Michail [32] proposed a uniform *terminating* protocol (where agents "know" when they have converged) in which a pre-elected leader computes the exact population size n in $O(n \log n)$ time with high probability. Going from the terminating to the less restrictive *converging* criterion (where agents eventually converge on the correct size, but do not know when this occurs), exact size counting is possible in $O(\log n \log \log n)$ time and $O(n^{60})$ states [25], *without* an initial leader.

Approximate size estimation. Alistarh, Aspnes, Eisenstat, Gelashvili, and Rivest [2] show a uniform protocol that in $O(\log n)$ expected time and states converges to an approximation n' of the population size n, computing an integer k such that with high probability $\frac{1}{2}\log n \leq k \leq 9 \log n$, i.e., $\sqrt{n} \leq 2^k \leq n^9$. Each agent generates (an approximation of) a geometric random variable, letting k be their maximum. We use their protocol as the first step of ours. The analysis of [2] is based on synthetic coins with a deterministic transition function, which have bias complicating the analysis. Our randomized model assumes access to perfectly random bits, so a simpler analysis (Corollary 3.7) shows that $\log n - \log \ln n \leq k \leq 2 \log n$ w.h.p. The remainder of our protocol improves this from a constant multiplicative error in approximating $\log n$ to a constant *additive* error. In other words we estimate the population size to within a constant multiplicative factor (instead of a polynomial factor as in [2]), but use $O(\log^2 n)$ time and $O(\log^4 n)$ states.

Berenbrink, Kaaser, and Radzik [16] independently studied the same size estimation problem as ours, obtaining stronger bounds on additive error and number of states: computing the value $\lfloor \log n \rfloor$ or $\lceil \log n \rceil$ (i.e., additive error < 1) with high probability, using $O(\log^2 n)$ time and $O(\log n \log \log n)$ states. They also show a protocol with probability 1 of correctness, using $O(\log^2 n)$ time and $O(\log^2 n \log \log n)$ states.

2 MODEL

To formally define *uniform* computation in population protocols, the agents' transition algorithm is modeled as a 2-tape deterministic Turing machine (TM) with the read only "input tape" as tape 1 (for reading the other agent's state) and read-write "working tape" as tape 2 (for storing this agent's state).[6]

[6] Our model generalizes the original constant-state model [8] by allowing the memory potentially to grow with n; however, constant-state protocols can be implemented with our model. It is worth distinguishing four ways for memory to increase with n: 1) not at all (constant-state), 2) increasing with n but, for each n, bounded by a constant depending on n (most non-uniform protocols), and 3) possibly unbounded but bounded with probability 1 (this paper), 4) unbounded with positive probability.

Our protocol describes a constant number of integer fields comprising each agent's state, which could all be stored in the working tape and separated by a special symbol. An agent's working tape is identical to what it was on the conclusion of the previous interaction. When two agents interact, each copies the content of the other's tape 2 its own tape 1, and then each of their TM states is reset from a halting TM state to the start TM state. The space usage (in bits) s is defined as normal for TMs: the maximum number of tape cells that are written during the computation on the read/write working tape. The number of possible agent states (working tape contents) is then c^s, where s is the maximum space usage of any agent during an execution of the protocol and c is the size of the tape alphabet. For ease of understanding, we will use standard population protocol terminology and not refer explicitly to details of the TM definition except where needed. A *state* $s \in \Lambda$ always refers to the TM working tape content of an agent (leaving out TM state and tape head positions since these are identical in all initial configurations), where Λ is the set of all agent states. A *configuration* $\vec{c} \in \mathbb{N}^\Lambda$ is a vector indexed by a state, where $\vec{c}(s)$ is the *count* of state s in the population. We set the output of our protocol the value stored in a special field labeled "output". Some definitions allow the output to be a function of the fields stored in an agent's memory, without the output itself counting against the memory usage. Our protocol reuses a field for the output that is used prior in the protocol, so our memory usage is the same under either definition.

We furthermore assume that each agent has access to independent uniformly random bits, assumed to be pre-written on a special read-only tape (this allows the TM to be deterministic even though it is computing a nondeterministic relation). This is different from the traditional definition of population protocols, which assumes a deterministic transition function. In our case, we have a transition *relation* $\delta \subseteq \Lambda^4$. Several papers [2, 15] indicate how to use the randomness built into the interaction scheduler to provide nearly uniform random bits to the agents, using various *synthetic coin* techniques, showing that the deterministic model can effectively simulate the randomized model. In the interest of brevity and simplicity of presentation, we will simply assume in the model that each agent has access to a source of uniformly random bits. A variant of our protocol using the sender/receiver choice to simulate uniformly random bits with a deterministic transition function, with the same time, state, and error bounds, is available in [24].

Throughout this paper, n denotes the number of agents in the population. Repeatedly, a pair of agents is selected uniformly at random to interact, where they run the transition algorithm on the pair of states they were in prior to the interaction, and storing the output states for their next interactions. The *time* until some event is measured as the number of interactions until the event occurs, divided by n, also known as parallel time. This represents a natural model of time complexity in which we expect each agent to have $O(1)$ interactions per unit of time, hence across the whole population, $\Theta(n)$ total interactions occur per unit time. All references to "time" in this paper refer to parallel time. An *execution* is a sequence of configurations $\vec{c}_0, \vec{c}_1, \ldots$ such that for all i, applying a transition to $\vec{c}_i$ results in $\vec{c}_{i+1}$. $\log n$ is the base-2 logarithm of n, and $\ln n$ is the base-e logarithm of n.

2.1 Definition of correctness and time

The notion that a protocol's configuration "has the correct answer" is problem-specific. For leader election, it means there is a single leader agent. For predicate computation, it means all agents have the correct Boolean output. In this paper, since our goal is to approximate $\log n$ within additive factor 5.7, we say a configuration is *correct* if the `output` field of each agent is within 5.7 of $\log n$.[7]

The following definitions match those used in the literature, when other notions of "correct" are substituted. Let $\mathcal{E} = (\vec{c}_0, \vec{c}_1, \ldots)$ be an infinite execution. A configuration $\vec{c}$ is *stably correct* if every configuration reachable from $\vec{c}$ is correct.[8] We say $\mathcal{E}$ *converges* at interaction i if $\vec{c}_i$ is not correct and for all $j > i$, $\vec{c}_j$ is correct. We say $\mathcal{E}$ *stabilizes* at interaction i if $\vec{c}_i$ is not stably correct and for all $j > i$, $\vec{c}_j$ is stably correct. A protocol can converge and/or stabilize with probability 1 or a smaller probability. However, if the set of reachable configurations is bounded with probability 1 (which is the case for the protocols discussed in this paper), then for any $p \in [0, 1]$, a protocol converges with probability p if and only if it stabilizes with probability p.[9] For a computational task T equipped with some definition of "correct", we say that a protocol $\mathcal{P}$ *stably computes* T *with probability* p if, with probability p, it stabilizes (equivalently, converges). If p is omitted, it is assumed $p = 1$. However, when measuring time complexity, convergence and stabilization may be much different. We say that $\mathcal{P}$ converges (respectively, stabilizes) in (parallel) time $t(n)$ with probability p if, with probability p, it produces an execution that converges (resp., stabilizes) by interaction i, where $i/n \leq t(n)$. Many protocols converge much faster than they stabilize, such as those that combine a fast, error-prone subprotocol with a slow, error-free protocol, e.g., [9, 20, 31]. However, for the protocol of this paper, convergence and stabilization coincide. We use the term "converge" throughout the paper to refer to this event.

Many papers separately measure high-probability time convergence and expected time to converge. Our protocol has positive probability of error, but we argue that expected time is a meaningful notion only with error probability 0, which is why we do not measure expected time. The only reasonable definition "time until correctness" on a non-converging execution is ∞. So with positive error probability, the expected convergence time is $\mathrm{E}[\text{time}|\text{converges}] + \mathrm{E}[\text{time}|\text{doesn't converge}] = \mathrm{E}[\text{time}|\text{converges}] + \infty = \infty$. One could imagine measuring only $\mathrm{E}[\text{time}|\text{converges}]$. However, conditioning can artificially "speed up" the process.[10]

3 FAST PROTOCOL FOR ESTIMATING $\log n$ WITHIN $O(1)$ ADDITIVE ERROR

In this section we describe a uniform protocol for computing the value of $\log n$ with an additive error, i.e., estimating the population size to within a constant multiplicative factor. We say a population protocol is *leaderless* if all agents start in the same state.

THEOREM 3.1. *There is a uniform leaderless population protocol that converges in time $O(\log^2 n)$ with probability $\geq 1 - 1/n^2$, uses $O(\log^4 n)$ states with probability $\geq 1 - O(\log n)/n$, and stores in each agent an integer k such that $|k - \log n| \leq 5.7$ with probability $\geq 1 - 9/n$.*

We note that the protocol has a positive probability of error. It is open to find a protocol using polylog(n) time/states computing $\log(n) \pm O(1)$ with probability 1.

The protocol is described and its time and state complexity analyzed in Subsection 3.2. Much of the analysis of the approximation involves proving a bound on the moment-generating function of a maximum of geometric random variables, enabling the Chernoff technique can be applied to sums of such variables. This is quite nontrivial; see appendix in [24] .

3.1 Intuition

Alistarh et al. [2] describe a protocol for estimating $\log n$ within a constant multiplicative factor. A $\frac{1}{2}$-geometric random variable is the number of flips needed to get one head when flipping a fair coin. In their protocol, each agent generates an independent geometric random variable $\mathbf{G}_i$, then propagates the maximum $\mathbf{M} = \max_{1 \leq i \leq n} \mathbf{G}_i$ by *epidemic*: transitions of the form $i, j \to j, j$ for $i \leq j$, which in $O(\log n)$ time "infect" all agents with the maximum. It is known that $\mathrm{E}[\mathbf{M}] \approx \log n$ [28], and $\log n - \log \ln n \leq \mathbf{M} \leq 2 \log n$ with probability $\geq 1 - O(1)/n$ (Lemma C.7 [24]).

We take the obvious extension of this approach: do this K times and take an average. The estimated average is within $O(1)$ of $\log n$ so long as $K = \Omega(\log n)$ [24]. One problem to solve first is how to calculate K; after all, $K = \Theta(\log n)$ scales with n, so with a uniform protocol it cannot be encoded into the agents at the start. The agents estimate it using the protocol of [2]. Since that protocol is converging but not terminating (provably it cannot be made terminating by Theorem 4.1), each time an agent updates its value of K, it reinitializes the remainder of its state.

However, a trickier problem remains: a naïve approach to implement "averaging of K numbers" requires storing $K = \Theta(\log n)$ numbers in each agent, each having value $\Theta(\log n)$, implying the number of states is $\Theta((\log n)^{\log n}) = \Theta(n^{\log \log n})$. This is even more

---

[7] We note that our notion of function approximation differs from that of Belleville, Doty, and Soloveichik [14]. They use a *distributed* output convention, where the output of a function $f : \mathbb{N}^d \to \mathbb{N}$ is encoded as the population count of agents in a special output state y. Thus one must examine the entire population to know the output. In our *local* output convention, each agent has a field encoding a value from the function's range. The output is undefined if some agents have different values, and defined to be their common value otherwise. This is similar to how Boolean predicate output with range $\{0, 1\}$ is encoded in population protocols [7].

[8] Belleville, Doty, and Soloveichik [14] also consider function approximation, but define a configuration to be stable if the output cannot change, whereas we allow it to change within a small interval around the correct value. The time lower bound techniques of [14] do not apply to our more relaxed notion of stability.

[9] Let C and S respectively be the set of stabilizing and converging executions. Clearly $S \subseteq C$. Although $S \subsetneq C$ is possible, we argue that $\Pr[C \setminus S] = 0$. Suppose a protocol converges in an execution $(\vec{c}_0, \vec{c}_1, \ldots)$ at interaction i (so $\vec{c}_j$ is correct for all $j > i$). If did not stabilize, then for all $j > i$, some incorrect configuration $\vec{d}_j$ would be reachable from $\vec{c}_j$. Let $p_j > 0$ denote the probability of reaching $\vec{d}_j$ from $\vec{c}_j$. The set of reachable configurations is bounded with probability 1, so $\min_{j>i} p_j$ is well-defined and positive. The probability of never reaching any $\vec{d}_j$ is then 0.

[10] Consider a hypothetical protocol that runs a parallel subprotocol S that completes quickly and, upon completion, somehow prevents the main protocol M from converging. The main protocol, on the other hand, may somehow detect if it completes before S does, and if so, M then shuts S down. Many executions will not converge, but those that do must be very fast in order to converge before S completes. Thus conditioning on convergence "anthropically speeds up" convergence [1]. This is an extreme example that has the property that the probability of correctness is reduced by S, but it nevertheless shows that measuring conditional expected time can be problematic.

than the $O(n^{60})$ sufficient to quickly compute *exactly* n [25]. To overcome this problem, we use a "leaderless phase clock" similar to those of [3, 34, 38], but uniform. Unlike the phase clock used by [3, 34], our leaderless phase clock simply increments a counter on every interaction. This simultaneously gives an elegant way to compose our protocols with downstream protocols requiring the size estimate. Agents count their number of interactions and compare it with a threshold value $\Theta(\log n)$. Whenever their number of interaction passes the threshold they will move to the next round similar to the protocol described above (the population with a leader). The threshold is calculated in the following way. In our protocol, agents start generate a geometric random variable called `logSize2` and propagate the maximum `logSize2` among themselves. After agents agree on the `logSize2` variable, a constant multiple `95.logSize2` is the threshold in their leaderless phase clock. This lets the agents synchronize epochs of the algorithm, each taking $O(\log n)$ time, and prevent the next epoch from starting until the previous has concluded.

The probabilistic clock inside agents might go off very soon at the very beginning of the protocol, but after $O(\log n)$ time all agents will store the maximum generated `logSize2` and their leaderless phase clock will eventually converge to a stable one which goes off after completion of a predefined constant factor of $\log n$; to handle this, each time an agent updates its value of `logSize2`, the remainder of its state is reset and it begins the rest of the protocol anew. Restarting the downstream protocol is a known technique in population protocols also used in [29] to compose two leader elimination subprotocols. The agents then generate K additional geometric random variables in sequence, taking their sum. Upon completing the generation and propagation of the K'th number, the agent divides the sum by K and stores the result in their output field. Composition with a downstream protocol is as simple as letting that protocol be the last phase. However, since our protocol has a positive probability of failure, this would translate to the downstream protocol as well.

The time is $O(\log^2 n)$ by the following rough analysis (details follow). We propagate K numbers one after each other and for each epidemic $O(\log n)$ time is required. Since we set $k = O(\log n)$ then the protocol will take $O(\log^2 n)$ total time to complete.

3.2 Formal specification of protocol

Our protocol uses uniform random bits in multiple places. We assume agents have access to independent uniformly random bits. In the protocol, agents start by dividing in two groups of S and A. A agents are responsible for the most part of the algorithm including generating geometric random variables and propagating their maximums while the S agents only provide memory to store the sum of K maximum geometric random variables. We split the state space such that A agents and S agents are responsible to store different variables. The space multiplexing is a common approach used in population protocols to reduce the space complexity of the protocols [5].

Agents initially have no role (X), and partition into roles via X, X $\rightarrow$ A, S. Since this takes $\Theta(n)$ time to complete, we add transitions A, X $\rightarrow$ A, S and S, X $\rightarrow$ S, A, converging in $O(\log n)$ time, with the price of deviating from $\frac{n}{2}$ for each role. It is proven in [24] this deviation is $O(\sqrt{n \ln n})$, increasing the size estimation error by merely a constant additive factor.[11] All agents start at epoch $= 0$. The A agents generate one geometric random variable (called `logSize2`) and continue by propagating the maximum among the whole population. Since we use this `logSize2` value for all early estimation of $\log n$, each time an agent finds out there was a greater value for the `logSize2` than its own, it will reset all other computations that might have happened.

The maximum `logSize2` amongst the population is a 2 factor estimation of $\log n$. When any agent updates its `logSize2` with a new maximum, it restarts the entire downstream protocol via RESTART. Once the maximum `logSize2` value is generated in the population, it propagates (triggering RESTART) by epidemic in $O(\log n)$ time. The `logSize2` variable could be used to estimate K, which is the number of independent additional geometric random variables each agent will generate. We also use `logSize2` to set the leaderless phase clock inside each agent. In each epoch, the A agents will generate one new geometric random variable and propagate its maximum. They count their number of interactions in each epoch using the `time` variable. At the end of an epoch, when `time` reaches `95.logSize2`, the A agents accumulate the value of the maximum `gr` into the `sum` of a S agent. The A agents increase their `epoch` variable by one and set `time` $= 0$ after either passing the geometric random variable to a S agent or interacting with a S agent in a higher phase. Separately, S agents are responsible to propagate the maximum `sum` and maximum `epoch` among themselves.

In the LOG-SIZE-ESTIMATION protocol, all agents in role A will finally generate $K = 5 \cdot$ `logSize2` geometric random variable and let the S agents to store a sum of maximum one generated for each phase. Once all agents reach epoch $= 5 \cdot$ `logSize2` they set `protocolDone` = TRUE and `output` $= \frac{\text{sum}}{\text{epoch}} + 1$. We use $|A|$, $|S|$ for the cardinality of A and S agents respectively.

COROLLARY 3.2. *In the LOG-SIZE-ESTIMATION protocol the cardinality of agents with* A *role is in the interval of* $\left[\frac{n}{3}, \frac{2n}{3}\right]$ *with probability* $\geq 1 - e^{-n/18}$.

In each epoch, one geometric random variable (in the first epoch `logSize2` and in the subsequent epochs `gr`) is generated and its maximum will be propagated by epidemic among the population. We set the time of each epoch equal to the required time of generating one plus the time for completion of an epidemic. To analyze the time complexity of our protocol, we require the time bounds for completing an epidemic from the paper [9]. The current form is taken from [25]. For all $n \in \mathbb{N}^+$, let $H_n = \sum_{k=1}^{n} \frac{1}{k}$ denote the n'th harmonic number. Note that $\ln n \leq \frac{n-1}{n} H_{n-1} \leq 1 + \ln n$.

LEMMA 3.3 ([9]). *Let T denote the time to complete an epidemic. Then* $\mathrm{E}[T] = \frac{n-1}{n} H_{n-1}$, $\Pr\left[T < \frac{1}{4} \ln n\right] < 2e^{-\sqrt{n}}$, *and for any* $\alpha_u > 0$, $\Pr[T > \alpha_u \ln n] < 4n^{-\alpha_u/4+1}$.

The following corollary describes an epidemic in a subpopulation. This refers to some subset S of the population executing epidemic transitions only among themselves, which slows down the epidemic by only a constant factor if $|S| = \Omega(n)$.

[11] This mechanism of splitting the population approximately in two works for our protocol, because the number of A agents is likely to be so close to $n/2$ that our estimate of $\log n$ is reduced by an additive factor likely to be very close to -1.

Protocol 1 LOG-SIZE-ESTIMATION(rec, sen)

```
▹ initial state of agent:
    role = X,
    time = 0, sum = 0, epoch = 0,
    gr = 1, logSize2 = 1,
    protocolDone = FALSE
PARTITION-INTO-A/S(rec, sen)
if rec.role = A then
    rec.time ← rec.time + 1
    CHECK-IF-TIMER-DONE-AND-INCREMENT-EPOCH(rec)
if sen.role = A then
    sen.time ← sen.time + 1
    CHECK-IF-TIMER-DONE-AND-INCREMENT-EPOCH(sen)
PROPAGATE-MAX-CLOCK-VALUE(rec, sen)
PROPAGATE-INCREMENTED-EPOCH(rec, sen)
if one agent have role = S and one have role = A then
    UPDATE-SUM(rec, sen)
if both agents have role = A then
    PROPAGATE-MAX-G.R.V.(rec, sen)
if sen.protocolDone then
    output ← sum/epoch + 1
```

Subprotocol 2 PARTITION-INTO-A/S(rec, sen)

```
▹ Partition the population in two almost equal size subpopulations.
if sen.role = X, rec.role = X then
    sen.role ← A
    sen.logSize2 ← one geometric random variable
    rec.role ← S
else if sen.role = A, rec.role = X then
    rec.role ← S
else if sen.role = S, rec.role = X then
    rec.role ← A
    rec.logSize2 ← one geometric random variable
```

Subprotocol 3 PROPAGATE-MAX-CLOCK-VALUE(agent1, agent2)

```
▹ Maximum generated geometric variable for logSize2 will be propagated.
if agent1.logSize2 < agent2.logSize2 then
    agent1.logSize2 ← agent2.logSize2
    RESTART(agent1)
else if agent2.logSize2 < agent1.logSize2 then
    agent2.logSize2 ← agent1.logSize2
    RESTART(agent2)
```

Subprotocol 4 RESTART(agent)

```
time ← 0, sum ← 0, epoch ← 0
gr ← one geometric random variable
protocolDone ← FALSE
```

Setting $c = 3$ and $\alpha_u = 24$ in Corollary A.3 of [24] gives the following.

Subprotocol 5 PROPAGATE-MAX-G.R.V.(agent1, agent2)

```
▹ Maximum generated geometric variable for gr will be propagated.
if agent1.epoch = agent2.epoch then
    if agent1.gr < agent2.gr then
        agent1.gr ← agent2.gr
    else if agent2.gr < agent1.gr then
        agent2.gr ← agent1.gr
```

Subprotocol 6 CHECK-IF-TIMER-DONE-AND-INCREMENT-EPOCH(agent)

```
▹ Agents compare their time value to the specified threshold.
if agent.time = 95 × agent.logSize2, agent.protocolDone = FALSE, agent.updatedSUM = TRUE then
    agent.epoch ← agent.epoch + 1
    MOVE-TO-NEXT-G.R.V(agent)
if agent.epoch = 5 × agent.logSize2 then
    agent.protocolDone ← TRUE
```

Subprotocol 7 PROPAGATE-INCREMENTED-EPOCH(agent1, agent2)

```
▹ The maximum epoch will be propagated.
if both agents have role = A then
    if agent1.epoch < agent2.epoch then
        agent1.epoch ← agent2.epoch
        MOVE-TO-NEXT-G.R.V(agent1)
    else if agent2.epoch < agent1.epoch then
        agent2.epoch ← agent1.epoch
        MOVE-TO-NEXT-G.R.V(agent2)
else if both agents have role = S then
    if agent1.epoch < agent2.epoch then
        agent1.epoch ← agent2.epoch
        agent1.sum ← agent2.sum
    else if agent2.epoch < agent1.epoch then
        agent2.epoch ← agent1.epoch
        agent2.sum ← agent1.sum
```

Subprotocol 8 MOVE-TO-NEXT-G.R.V(agent)

```
▹ The agent move to the next epoch:
agent.time ← 0
agent.gr ← one geometric random variable
agent.updatedSUM = FALSE
```

COROLLARY 3.4. *Suppose an epidemic happens among a subpopulation of $n/3$ agents with time* T. *Then* $\Pr[T > 24 \ln n] < 27n^{-3}$.

The next lemma bounds the number of interactions an agent has in a given time, and it is the basis of the leaderless phase clock we use. It is proven in [24]. It follows from a simple Chernoff bound on the number of interactions involving a single agent in a given window of time.

LEMMA 3.5. *Let $C \geq 3$ and $D = 2C + \sqrt{12C}$. In time $C \ln n$, with probability $\geq 1 - 1/n$, each agent has at most $D \ln n$ interactions.*

Subprotocol 9 UPDATE-SUM(agent1, agent2)

```
▷ The agent accumulates the current value of gr in sum:
a ← agent with role = A
s ← agent with role = S
if a.epoch = s.epoch, a.time ≥ 95· a.logSize2, and
a.protocolDone = FALSE then
    s.epoch ← s.epoch + 1
    s.sum ← s.sum+ a.gr
    a.updatedSUM = TRUE
else if a.epoch < s.epoch then
    a.updatedSUM = TRUE
```

COROLLARY 3.6. *Each agent has* $\geq 65 \ln n$ *interactions in time* $24 \ln n$ *with probability* $\leq 1/n$.

By Lemma 3.5 each agent has at most $\left(2 \cdot 24 + \sqrt{12 \cdot 24}\right) \ln n \leq 65 \ln n \leq 94 \log n$ interactions in the time that it takes to generate and propagate maximum of one geometric random variable. Thus, each agent should count up to $94 \log n$ for its leaderless phase clock, to ensure that with high probability none reaches that count until the maximum geometric random variable is known to all agents. However, agents are not aware of any prior approximation of $\log n$. In the LOG-SIZE-ESTIMATION protocol, agents use their `logSize2` variable for this approximation. As mentioned, all the agents in role A start by generating one geometric random variable `logSize2`. The maximum in the population is used as a weak (constant factor) approximation of $\log n$. Their statement and proofs appear in [24].

COROLLARY 3.7. *The* `logSize2` *(*`gr`*) value generated by* GENERATE-CLOCK *(*GENERATE-G.R.V*) is in the interval of* $[\log n - \log \ln n - 2, 2 \log n - 1]$ *with probability at least* $1 - 1/n - e^{-n/18}$.

COROLLARY 3.8. *The number of interactions in each epoch in the* LOG-SIZE-ESTIMATION *is in the interval* $[95 \log n - 95 \log \ln n, 189 \log n]$ *with probability* $\geq 1 - 1/n - e^{-n/18}$.

PROOF. By Corollary 3.6, agents should count up to $96 \ln \leq 139 \log n$ before moving to the next epoch. if we set the threshold of the `time` to $95 \cdot$ `logSize2`, $95 \log n - 95 \log \ln n \geq 93 \log n$ then the `time` variable will be in the interval of $[95 \log n - 95 \log \ln n, 188 \log n + 95]$ with high probability ($188 \log n + 95 \leq 189 \log n$ for $n \geq 2$). □

COROLLARY 3.9. *The number of epochs in the* LOG-SIZE-ESTIMATION *is in the interval* $[5 \log n - 5 \log \ln n, 11 \log n]$ *with probability* $\geq 1 - 1/n - e^{-n/18}$.

PROOF. By Corollary C.10 in [24], to achieve the additive error of 4.7 for our protocol the number of geometric random variables should be $\geq 4 \log n$. By setting the threshold of the number of phases to $5 \times$ `logSize2`, for $n \geq 200$, $5 \log n - 5 \log \ln n \geq 4 \log n$. The number of phases will be in the interval of $[5 \log n - 5 \log \ln n, 10 \log n + 5]$ with high probability ($10 \log n + 5 \leq 11 \log n$ for $n \geq 2$). □

The next Lemma bounds the space complexity of our main protocol by counting the likely range taken by the variables in LOG-SIZE-ESTIMATION. It is proven in [24].

LEMMA 3.10. LOG-SIZE-ESTIMATION *uses* $O(\log^4 n)$ *states with probability* $\geq 1 - O(\log n)/n$.

The next corollary bounds the time complexity of protocol LOG-SIZE-ESTIMATION; the main component of the time complexity is that $\Theta(\log n)$ geometric random variables must be generated and propagated by epidemic among the population, each epidemic taking $\Theta(\log n)$ time. A proof appears in [24].

COROLLARY 3.11. *The* LOG-SIZE-ESTIMATION *protocol converges in* $O(\log^2 n)$ *time with probability at least* $1 - 1/n^2$.

The following result is a Chernoff bound on sums of random variables, each of which is the maximum of independent geometric random variables (with probability of success $\frac{1}{2}$). It is a corollary of a similar Chernoff bound proven in the appendix of [24].

LEMMA 3.12. *Let* $K \geq 4 \log n$ *and* a *be a number in the interval of* $[n/2 - \sqrt{n \ln n}, n/2 + \sqrt{n \ln n}]$. *Let* `sum`$/K$ *be the average of* K $\frac{1}{2}$-*geometric random variables. Then* $\Pr\left[\left|\frac{\texttt{sum}}{K} + 1 - \log n\right| \geq 5.7\right] \leq \frac{6}{n}$.

LEMMA 3.13. *In the* LOG-SIZE-ESTIMATION *protocol, with probability* 1, *all agents converge to the same value* C *in their* `output` *field. Furthermore,* $\Pr[|C - \log n| \geq 5.7] \leq 9/n$.

Termination with a leader and guaranteed size upper bound. Two other results are discussed in more detail in [24]. The first is that we can make the size-estimation protocol terminating with high probability using an initial leader. Intuitively, the leader can be used to trigger an epidemic-based phase clock used to count to $\Omega(\log^2 n)$, enough time for the protocol to probably have converged. The second discusses the possibility of transforming the size estimation, which has a small probability of being much larger *or* much smaller than the actual size, into a *guaranteed upper bound* on the population size.

Reducing the space complexity. In our protocol, we used space multiplexing, a known technique in population protocols that split the state space such that different agents are responsible to store different variables. Although this technique reduces the number of states per agent, we cannot push it further with the current scheme. Our protocol is dependent on *all* agents agreeing on the values of `logSize2` and `epoch` to stay synchronized. Thus, if an agent participates in the protocol it is required to stores the updated value of both `logSize2` and `epoch`.

4 TERMINATION

The concept of termination has been referenced and studied in population protocols [11, 32, 33], but to our knowledge no formal definition exists. We give an abstract definition capturing the behavior of most protocols that "perform a computational task".

Let P be a protocol with a set I of "valid" initial configurations, where each agent's memory has a Boolean field `terminated` set to FALSE in every configuration in I. A configuration $\vec{c}$ of P is *terminated* if at least one agent in $\vec{c}$ has `terminated` = TRUE. (Note the distinction with a *silent* configuration, where no transition can change any agent's state [13].) Let $\kappa > 0$ and $t : \mathbb{N} \to \mathbb{N}$. P is κ-t-*terminating* if, for all $\vec{i} \in I$, with probability $\geq \kappa$, P reaches from $\vec{i}$ to a terminated configuration $\vec{c}$, but takes time $\geq t(n)$ to do so.

This definition leaves totally abstract which particular task (e.g., leader election) is assumed to have terminated. The idea is that if the task will not be complete before time $t(n)$ with high probability, then no agent should set `terminated` = TRUE until time $\geq t(n)$ with high probability. So proving an upper bound on $t(n)$ in the definition of terminating implies that no protocol can be terminating if it requires time $> t(n)$ to converge.

The definition is applicable beyond the narrow goal of terminating a population protocol. It says more generally that a "signal" is produced after some amount of time. This signal may be used to terminate a protocol, move it from one "stage" to another, or it may be some specific Boolean value relevant to a specific protocol, where in any case the value will start FALSE for all agents and eventually be set to TRUE for at least one agent.

Let $\alpha > 0$. We say a configuration $\vec{c}$ is *α-dense* if, for all $s \in \Lambda$, $\vec{c}(s) > 0 \implies \vec{c}(s) \geq \alpha n$. (Recall $n = \|\vec{c}\|$.) In other words, every state present occupies at least fraction α of the population. We say protocol P with valid initial configuration set I is *i.o.-dense* if there exists $\alpha > 0$ such that infinitely many $\vec{i} \in I$ are α-dense. In particular, an i.o.-dense protocol does not always have an initial *leader*: a state present in count 1 in every $\vec{i} \in I$.

The next theorem, our second main result, shows that termination is impossible for uniform i.o.-dense protocols that require more than constant time, no matter the space allowed.

THEOREM 4.1. *Let $\kappa > 0$ and $t : \mathbb{N} \to \mathbb{N}$, and let P be a uniform i.o.-dense population protocol. If P is κ-t-terminating, then $t(n) = O(1)$.*

Let Λ be the (possibly infinite) set of all states of a population protocol. Recall the definition of randomized transitions from Section 2; We now introduce extra notation that will be useful in this Section. We consider a transition *relation* $\Delta \subseteq \Lambda^4$, writing $a, b \to c, d$ to denote that $(a, b, c, d) \in \Delta$ (i.e., if agents in states a and b interact, then one of the possible random outcomes is to change to states c and d). For $\rho \in (0, 1]$, we write $a, b \xrightarrow{\rho} c, d$ to denote that when states a and b interact, with probability ρ they transition to c and d. Say that ρ is the *rate constant* of transition $a, b \xrightarrow{\rho} c, d$. If there exist $a, b \in \Lambda$ and $\rho' \geq \rho$ such that $a, b \xrightarrow{\rho'} c, d$, we write $c \in \text{PROD}_\rho(a, b)$ and $d \in \text{PROD}_\rho(a, b)$. (In other words, $c \in \text{PROD}_\rho(a, b)$ if c is produced with probability at least ρ whenever a and b interact). For any $\Gamma \subseteq \Lambda$ and $\rho \in [0, 1]$, define $\text{PROD}_\rho(\Gamma) = \{s \in \Lambda \mid (\exists a, b \in \Gamma)\ s \in \text{PROD}_\rho(a, b)\}$.

Let $\Lambda^0 \subseteq \Lambda$. For $i \in \mathbb{N}^+$, define $\Lambda^i_\rho = \Lambda^{i-1}_\rho \cup \text{PROD}_\rho(\Lambda^{i-1}_\rho)$. For $m \in \mathbb{N}$, if $s \in \Lambda^m_\rho$, we say s is *m-ρ-producible from* Λ^0. For configuration $\vec{c}$, we say s is *m-ρ-producible from $\vec{c}$* if s is m-ρ-producible from $\Lambda^0 = \{s \in \Lambda \mid \vec{c}(s) > 0\}$, the states present in $\vec{c}$.

Our main technical tool is the following lemma, a variant of the "timer/density lemma" of [23] (see also [2]). The original lemma states that in a protocol with $O(1)$ states, from any sufficiently large α-dense configuration, in $O(1)$ time all states appear with δ-density (for some $0 < \delta < \alpha$). The proof is similar to that of [23], but is retooled to apply to protocols with a non-constant set of states (also to use the discrete-time model of population protocols, instead of the continuous-time model of chemical reaction networks).[12] The key new idea is that, even if a protocol has infinitely many states (of which only finitely many can be produced in finite time), for any subset of states Λ^m_ρ "producible via only m transitions, each having rate constant at least ρ", all states in Λ^m_ρ are produced in constant time with high probability from sufficiently large configurations.

[12] Alistarh et al. [2] also prove a variant applying to protocols with $\omega(1)$ states, but for a different purpose: to show that all states in Λ appear as long as $|\Lambda| \leq \frac{1}{2} \log\log n$. However, beyond that bound, the lemma does not hold [29]. In our case, we are not trying to show that all states in Λ appear, only those in some constant size subset of states, all of which are m-ρ-producible from the initial configuration.

LEMMA 4.2. *Let $\alpha > 0$, $m \in \mathbb{N}^+$, $\rho \in (0, 1]$, and P be a population protocol. Then there are constants $\epsilon, \delta, n_0 > 0$ such that, for all $n \geq n_0$, for all α-dense configurations $\vec{c}$ of P with $n = \|\vec{c}\|$, the following holds. Let Λ^m_ρ be the set of states m-ρ-producible from $\vec{c}$. For $s \in \Lambda$ and $t > 0$, let $C_{t,s}$ be the random variable denoting the count of s at time t, assuming at time 0 the configuration is $\vec{c}$. Then $\Pr\left[(\forall s \in \Lambda^m_\rho)\ C_{1,s} \geq \delta n\right] \geq 1 - 2^{-\epsilon n}$.*

A self-contained proof is in [24]. Intuitively, Lemma 4.2 can be used to prove Theorem 4.1 in the following way. In some "small" population size n_0, the terminal signal appears. The set of states $\Lambda' \subseteq \Lambda$ appearing with the terminal signal is constant size. Lemma 4.2 states that for any constant-size $\Lambda' \subseteq \Lambda$, in all sufficiently large population sizes, all states in Λ' appear in constant time with high probability, so the termination signal appears prematurely in larger populations. This is fairly straightforward for deterministic transition functions, but it requires some care to handle a randomized protocol.

We now use Lemma 4.2 to formally prove Theorem 4.1.

PROOF OF THEOREM 4.1. Assume P is κ-t-terminating; we will show $t(n) = O(1)$. Let $(\vec{c}_i)_{i=1}^\infty$ be an infinite sequence of α-dense initial configurations in I. Dickson's Lemma [22] states that every infinite sequence in $\mathbb{N}^k$ has an infinite nondecreasing subsequence, so assume without loss of generality that $\vec{c}_i \leq \vec{c}_{i+1}$ for all $i \in \mathbb{N}$. Let $\Lambda^0 = \{s \in \Lambda \mid \vec{c}_0(s) > 0\}$ be the set of states present in $\vec{c}_0$.

By hypothesis $\Pr[P \text{ terminates from } \vec{c}_0] \geq \kappa > 0$. Thus there is at least one finite execution $\mathcal{E}$ starting with $\vec{c}_0$ and ending in a terminated configuration. Let $m = |\mathcal{E}|$ be the length of this execution. Let ρ be the minimum rate constant of any transition in $\mathcal{E}$. Then every state appearing in configurations in $\mathcal{E}$ is m-ρ-producible from $\vec{c}_0$, i.e., is in Λ^m_ρ where $\Lambda^0 = \{s \in \Lambda \mid \vec{c}_0(s) > 0\}$ is the set of states present in $\vec{c}_0$.

For any $\ell \geq 1$, since $\vec{c}_0 \leq \vec{c}_\ell$, all states in Λ^m_ρ are m-ρ-producible from $\vec{c}_\ell$ as well. By Lemma 4.2, there are constants $\epsilon, \delta, n_0 > 0$ such that, for all $\ell \in \mathbb{N}$ such that $n = \|\vec{c}_\ell\| \geq n_0$, letting $C_{1,s}$ be the random variable denoting the count of s at time 1, assuming at time 0 the configuration is $\vec{c}_\ell$, $\Pr\left[\left(\forall s \in \Lambda^m_\rho\right)\ C_{1,s} \geq \delta n\right] \geq 1 - 2^{-\epsilon n}$.

However, Λ^m_ρ contains terminated states, so for all $\vec{c}_\ell$ with $\|\vec{c}_\ell\| \geq n_0$, with probability $\geq 1 - 2^{-\epsilon n}$, P terminates within time 1. Since $2^{-\epsilon n} < \kappa$ for sufficiently large n, this implies that if P is κ-t-terminating, then $t(n) \leq 1$ for sufficiently large n. Thus $t(n) = O(1)$. □

Observe how the assumption of uniformity is used in the proof: we take a set of transitions used on the population $\vec{c}_0$ and apply it to a larger population $\vec{c}_\ell$. In a nonuniform protocol, the transitions may not be legal to apply to $\vec{c}_\ell$. As a concrete example, in a nonuniform protocol, an agent increments a counter using transitions such as $c_7, x \to c_8, y$ until the counter exceeds $\log n$, then produces a termination signal t via a transition $c_8, x \to t, y$. The transition

$c_8, x \longrightarrow t, y$ producing this signal is not legal in a population larger than twice n, since the value $\log n$ is at least 1 larger in such a protocol. In this example, the transition of the larger protocol with the same input states simply increments the counter without producing a termination signal: $c_8, x \longrightarrow c_9, y$.

Acknowledgements. We are grateful to Eric Severson for helpful comments and anonymous reviewers for their suggestions, which vastly improved the paper. The second author thanks James Aspnes for discussions that stimulated a key idea used in the main protocol.

REFERENCES

[1] Scott Aaronson. 2006. Computational Complexity and the Anthropic Principle. https://www.scottaaronson.com/talks/anthropic.html.

[2] Dan Alistarh, James Aspnes, David Eisenstat, Rati Gelashvili, and Ronald L Rivest. 2017. Time-space trade-offs in population protocols. In *SODA 2017: Proceedings of the Twenty-Eighth Annual ACM-SIAM Symposium on Discrete Algorithms*. SIAM, 2560–2579.

[3] Dan Alistarh, James Aspnes, and Rati Gelashvili. 2018. Space-optimal majority in population protocols. In *SODA 2018: Proceedings of the Twenty-Ninth Annual ACM-SIAM Symposium on Discrete Algorithms*. SIAM, 2221–2239.

[4] Dan Alistarh and Rati Gelashvili. 2015. Polylogarithmic-Time Leader Election in Population Protocols. In *42nd International Colloquium on Automata, Languages, and Programming (ICALP) (Lecture Notes in Computer Science)*, Vol. 9135. Springer, Berlin, Heidelberg, 479 - 491.

[5] Dan Alistarh and Rati Gelashvili. 2018. Recent Algorithmic Advances in Population Protocols. *SIGACT News* 49, 3 (Oct. 2018), 63–73. https://doi.org/10.1145/3289137.3289150

[6] Dan Alistarh, Rati Gelashvili, and Milan Vojnović. 2015. Fast and Exact Majority in Population Protocols. In *PODC 2015: Proceedings of the 2015 ACM Symposium on Principles of Distributed Computing*. ACM, 47–56.

[7] Dana Angluin, James Aspnes, Zoë Diamadi, Michael J. Fischer, and René Peralta. 2006. Computation in networks of passively mobile finite-state sensors. *Distributed Computing* 18, 4 (March 2006), 235–253.

[8] Dana Angluin, James Aspnes, and David Eisenstat. 2006. Stably computable predicates are semilinear. In *25th annual ACM Symposium on Principles of Distributed Computing (PODC)*. ACM Press, New York, NY, USA, 292–299. https://doi.org/10.1145/1146381.1146425

[9] Dana Angluin, James Aspnes, and David Eisenstat. 2008. Fast computation by population protocols with a leader. *Distributed Computing* 21, 3 (September 2008), 183–199.

[10] James Aspnes, Joffroy Beauquier, Janna Burman, and Devan Sohier. 2017. Time and Space Optimal Counting in Population Protocols. In *20th International Conference on Principles of Distributed Systems (OPODIS 2016)*, Vol. 70. 13:1–13:17.

[11] James Aspnes and Eric Ruppert. 2007. An introduction to population protocols. *Bulletin of the European Association for Theoretical Computer Science* 93 (October 2007), 98–117.

[12] Joffroy Beauquier, Janna Burman, Simon Claviere, and Devan Sohier. 2015. Space-optimal counting in population protocols. In *DISC 2015: International Symposium on Distributed Computing*. Springer, 631–646.

[13] Joffroy Beauquier, Maria Gradinariu, and Colette Johnen. 1999. Memory Space Requirements for Self-stabilizing Leader Election Protocols. In *Proceedings of the 18th Annual ACM Symposium on Principles of Distributed Computing (PODC 1999)*. ACM, 199–207. https://doi.org/10.1145/301308.301358

[14] Amanda Belleville, David Doty, and David Soloveichik. 2017. Hardness of computing and approximating predicates and functions with leaderless population protocols. In *ICALP 2017: 44th International Colloquium on Automata, Languages, and Programming (LIPIcs)*, Vol. 80. 141:1–141:14.

[15] Petra Berenbrink, Dominik Kaaser, Peter Kling, and Lena Otterbach. 2018. Simple and Efficient Leader Election. In *1st Symposium on Simplicity in Algorithms (SOSA 2018)*, Vol. 61. 9:1–9:11.

[16] Petra Berenbrink, Dominik Kaaser, and Tomasz Radzik. 2019. On counting the population size. In *Proceedings of the 38th Annual ACM Symposium on Principles of Distributed Computing (PODC 2019)*. to appear.

[17] Andreas Bilke, Colin Cooper, Robert Elsässer, and Tomasz Radzik. 2017. Brief Announcement: Population protocols for leader election and exact majority with $O(\log^2 n)$ states and $O(\log^2 n)$ convergence time. In *PODC 2017: Proceedings of the ACM Symposium on Principles of Distributed Computing*. ACM, 451–453.

[18] James M Bower and Hamid Bolouri. 2004. *Computational modeling of genetic and biochemical networks*. MIT press.

[19] Shukai Cai, Taisuke Izumi, and Koichi Wada. 2010. Space Complexity of Self-stabilizing Leader Election in Passively-Mobile Anonymous Agents. In *Structural Information and Communication Complexity*, Shay Kutten and Janez Žerovnik (Eds.). Springer Berlin Heidelberg, Berlin, Heidelberg, 113–125.

[20] Ho-Lin Chen, David Doty, and David Soloveichik. 2013. Deterministic Function Computation with Chemical Reaction Networks. *Natural Computing* 13, 4 (2013), 517–534. Special issue of invited papers from DNA 2012.

[21] Yuan-Jyue Chen, Neil Dalchau, Niranjan Srinivas, Andrew Phillips, Luca Cardelli, David Soloveichik, and Georg Seelig. 2013. Programmable chemical controllers made from DNA. *Nature Nanotechnology* 8, 10 (2013), 755–762.

[22] Leonard E. Dickson. 1913. Finiteness of the odd perfect and primitive abundant numbers with n distinct prime factors. *American Journal of Mathematics* 35 (1913), 413–422. Issue 4. https://doi.org/10.2307/2370405

[23] David Doty. 2014. Timing in chemical reaction networks. In *SODA 2014: Proc. of the 25th Annual ACM-SIAM Symp. on Discrete Algorithms*. 772–784.

[24] David Doty and Mahsa Eftekhari. 2018. Efficient size estimation and impossibility of termination in uniform dense population protocols. *CoRR* abs/1808.08913 (2018). arXiv:1808.08913 http://arxiv.org/abs/1808.08913

[25] David Doty, Mahsa Eftekhari, Othon Michail, Paul G. Spirakis, and Michail Theofilatos. 2018. Brief announcement: Exact size counting in uniform population protocols in nearly logarithmic time. In *32nd International Symposium on Distributed Computing (DISC 2018)*. 46:1–46:3.

[26] David Doty and Monir Hajiaghayi. 2015. Leaderless Deterministic Chemical Reaction Networks. *Natural Computing* 14, 2 (2015), 213–223. Preliminary version appeared in DNA 2013.

[27] David Doty and David Soloveichik. 2018. Stable leader election in population protocols requires linear time. *Distributed Computing* 31, 4 (2018), 257–271. Special issue of invited papers from DISC 2015.

[28] Bennett Eisenberg. 2008. On the expectation of the maximum of IID geometric random variables. *Statistics & Probability Letters* 78, 2 (2008), 135 - 143. https://doi.org/10.1016/j.spl.2007.05.011

[29] Leszek Gasieniec and Grzegorz Stachowiak. 2018. Fast Space Optimal Leader Election in Population Protocols. In *SODA 2018: ACM-SIAM Symposium on Discrete Algorithms*. to appear.

[30] Leszek Gasieniec, Grzegorz Stachowiak, and Przemyslaw Uznanski. 2018. *Almost logarithmic-time space optimal leader election in population protocols.* Technical Report. arXiv:1802.06867 http://arxiv.org/abs/1802.06867

[31] Adrian Kosowski and Przemyslaw Uznanski. 2018. Population Protocols Are Fast. *CoRR* abs/1802.06872 (2018). arXiv:1802.06872 http://arxiv.org/abs/1802.06872

[32] Othon Michail. 2015. Terminating Distributed Construction of Shapes and Patterns in a Fair Solution of Automata. In *Proceedings of the 2015 ACM Symposium on Principles of Distributed Computing*. 37–46. Also in *Distributed Computing*, 2017.

[33] Othon Michail, Ioannis Chatzigiannakis, and Paul G Spirakis. 2012. Terminating population protocols via some minimal global knowledge assumptions. In *Stabilization, Safety, and Security of Distributed Systems (SSS)*. Springer, 77–89.

[34] Yves Mocquard, Bruno Sericola, and Emmanuelle Anceaume. 2018. Population protocols with convergence detection. In *2018 IEEE 17th International Symposium on Network Computing and Applications (NCA)*. IEEE, 1–8.

[35] Philippe Rigollet. 2015. Lecture Notes for MIT course 18.S997: High Dimensional Statistics. URL: https://ocw.mit.edu/courses/mathematics/18-s997-high-dimensional-statistics-spring-2015/lecture-notes/.

[36] David Soloveichik, Matthew Cook, Erik Winfree, and Jehoshua Bruck. 2008. Computation with Finite Stochastic Chemical Reaction Networks. *Natural Computing* 7, 4 (2008), 615–633. http://dx.doi.org/10.1007/s11047-008-9067-y

[37] Niranjan Srinivas, James Parkin, Georg Seelig, Erik Winfree, and David Soloveichik. 2017. Enzyme-free nucleic acid dynamical systems. *Science* 358, 6369 (2017), eaal2052.

[38] Yuichi Sudo, Fukuhito Ooshita, Taisuke Izumi, Hirotsugu Kakugawa, and Toshimitsu Masuzawa. 2019. Brief Announcement: Logarithmic Expected-Time Leader Election in Population Protocol Model. In *Proceedings of the 38th Annual ACM Symposium on Principles of Distributed Computing (PODC 2019)*. to appear.

[39] Vito Volterra. 1926. Variazioni e fluttuazioni del numero dâĂŹindividui in specie animali conviventi. *Mem. Acad. Lincei Roma* 2 (1926), 31–113.

On Counting the Population Size

Petra Berenbrink
Universität Hamburg
Hamburg, Germany
petra.berenbrink@uni-hamburg.de

Dominik Kaaser
Universität Hamburg
Hamburg, Germany
dominik.kaaser@uni-hamburg.de

Tomasz Radzik
King's College London
London, UK
tomasz.radzik@kcl.ac.uk

ABSTRACT

We consider the problem of counting the population size in the *population model*. In this model, we are given a distributed system of n identical agents which interact in pairs with the goal to solve a common task. In each time step, the two interacting agents are selected uniformly at random. In this paper, we consider so-called *uniform* protocols, where the actions of two agents upon an interaction may not depend on the population size n. We present two population protocols to count the size of the population: protocol Approximate, which computes with high probability either $\lfloor \log n \rfloor$ or $\lceil \log n \rceil$, and protocol CountExact, which computes the exact population size in optimal $O(n \log n)$ interactions, using $\tilde{O}(n)$ states. Both protocols can also be converted to *stable* protocols that give a correct result with probability 1 by using an additional multiplicative factor of $O(\log n)$ states.

CCS CONCEPTS

• **Theory of computation** → *Distributed algorithms*; • **Mathematics of computing** → *Probabilistic algorithms*.

KEYWORDS

population protocols, population size, counting

ACM Reference Format:

Petra Berenbrink, Dominik Kaaser, and Tomasz Radzik. 2019. On Counting the Population Size. In *2019 ACM Symposium on Principles of Distributed Computing (PODC '19), July 29-August 2, 2019, Toronto, ON, Canada.* ACM, New York, NY, USA, 10 pages. https://doi.org/10.1145/3293611.3331631

1 INTRODUCTION

In this paper we consider the problem of counting the population size in the probabilistic *population model*. The model was introduced in [5] to model distributed systems of resource-limited mobile agents, which interact with each other in order to solve a common task. The computation of a probabilistic *population protocol* can be viewed as a sequence of pairwise interactions of randomly chosen agents. In each interaction, the two participating agents observe each others' states and update their own state according to a transition function common to all agents.

In this setting, we are interested in so-called *uniform* population protocols, where the transition function does not depend on the size of the population, so it can be applied to any population size. In the original definition of population protocols in [5], each agent is a copy of the same finite state machine. Such a protocol is by definition uniform, as its state space has constant size (independent of the size of the population). However, more recent results have shown that many problems can be solved much faster if agents are equipped with a number of states that grows with the population size. For example, a simple protocol with a constant number of states solves the majority problem in expected $O(n^2)$ interactions [17, 20]. On the other hand, a number of protocols have been proposed which solve the majority problem in $O(n \operatorname{polylog} n)$ interactions using $O(\operatorname{polylog} n)$ states [1, 2, 9, 12]. These protocols are all non-uniform since their transition functions refer to values which have to be $\Theta(\log n)$. We note that $\Omega(n \log n)$ interactions are required to reach a positive constant probability that each agent participates in at least one interaction, so $\Omega(n \log n)$ is a lower bound on the number of interactions of a protocol which solves any nontrivial problem.

Turning to the problem of counting the population size, either exactly or approximately, we naturally have to consider population protocol models with growing memory, where lower bounds on the required number of states depend on the desired counting accuracy. The exact counting of the population size requires $\Omega(n)$ states, while estimating the population size up to a constant factor requires $\Omega(\log n)$ states.

There is a simple and uniform protocol for exact population counting, which completes in expected $\Theta(n^2)$ interactions and uses $\Theta(n^2)$ states: the agents start with one token each and keep combining the tokens into bags, propagating at the same time the maximum size of a bag and using that maximum as their current output. The transition function of this protocol does not refer in any way to (any estimate of) the size of the population.

In this paper we are interested in uniform population counting protocols which run in $O(n \operatorname{polylog} n)$ interactions and use a small number of states (relatively to the lower bounds). We present new protocols for exact and approximate population counting, which use a significantly smaller number of states than the previously best protocols shown in [13, 14]. Our protocols have also further desirable properties. Our exact protocol is the first protocol for this problem which completes the computation within asymptotically optimal $O(n \log n)$ interactions. A variant of our approximate protocol is the first $O(\operatorname{polylog} n)$-state, $O(n \operatorname{polylog} n)$-interaction protocol *always* converging to a value which is within a constant factor from the exact size of the population. To give formal statements of the previous results and our new results, we have to introduce first some details of the model and the way the efficiency of population protocols is measures.

PODC '19, July 29-August 2, 2019, Toronto, ON, Canada

ACM ISBN 978-1-4503-6217-7/19/07...$15.00
https://doi.org/10.1145/3293611.3331631

1.1 Computation Model

The computation model is a population of n agents which are capable of performing local computations. A population protocol is specified by a state space Q, an output domain O, a transition function $\delta : Q \times Q \to Q \times Q$, and an output function $\omega : Q \to O$. Each agent has a state $q \in Q$, which is updated during interactions. The current output of an agent in state q is $\omega(q)$. The current *configuration* of the system is the vector from Q^n with the current states of the agents. The computation of a population protocol is a sequence of pairwise interactions of agents. In every time step, a *probabilistic scheduler* selects independently and uniformly at random a pair of agents for interaction, with the first agent called the *initiator* and the second the *responder.* During the interaction the agents update their states by applying the transition function δ. Such an update is denoted by $(x, y) \to (x', y')$, where (x, y) refers to the states of the agents before the interaction and $(x', y') = \delta(x, y)$ to the states after the interaction.

A given problem which we want to solve by population protocols specifies the set of initial (input) configurations, the output domain O, and the desired (output) configurations for given input configurations. For the exact population counting problem, all agents are initially in the same state q_0 and the output domain is the set of positive integers. A desired configuration is when all agents output correctly the (exact) size of the population. In the *leader election* problem, which arises as a sub-problem in many population protocols, including in the protocols for the population counting problem, all agents start with the same initial state and the output domain is $O = \{$ *leader*, *follower* $\}$. A desired configuration is when exactly one agent outputs that it is the leader.

The following two definitions are commonly used to capture important aspects of the time efficiency of population protocols. The *convergence time* T_C of an execution of a protocol is the number of interactions until the system enters a desired configuration and never leaves the set of desired configurations again. The *stabilization time* T_S of an execution of a protocol is the number of interactions until the system enters a desired *stable* configuration, meaning that starting from this configuration no sequence of pairwise interactions can take the system outside of the set of desired configurations. We always have $T_C \le T_S$ for any execution of a protocol, but the stabilization time may be strictly greater than the convergence time. A population protocol is *always correct* (or stable), if for each initial configuration the computation reaches a correct stable configuration with probability 1, or *w.h.p. correct*, if there is a small (of the order of $n^{-\Omega(1)}$), but positive, probability that the system settles with an incorrect output or does not settle at all. We say that a protocol converges (resp. stabilizes) in $T(n)$ time w.h.p. (resp. in expectation), if T_C (resp. T_S) is at most $T(n)$ w.h.p. (resp. in expectation).[1]

The second measure of efficiency of population protocols is the *required number of states.* This is a straightforward notion for simple protocols with constant number of states. For more complex protocols, transition functions are usually described by pseudo-codes, which refer to *variables.* The state space of a protocol which is defined in this way is the Cartesian product of the ranges of the variables. If we consider all possible executions of a uniform protocol, then the ranges of some variables may be very large in terms of n, potentially infinite. We are, however, interested in bounds on the ranges of the variables (and thus bounds on the whole state space) that hold w.h.p.

A population protocol is called *uniform* if the same transition function is used for all population sizes [7]. Uniformity of a protocol is thus a desired property since such protocols can be applied without knowing the size of the population in advance. The original model from [4, 5] is uniform since the number of states of an agent is constant.

1.2 Related Work

It is shown in [4, 5] that with a constant number of states all semilinear predicates (which include, e.g., the majority predicate), can be computed in expected $O(n^2 \log n)$ stabilization time. Recently Kosowski and Uznanski [19] have shown constant-state protocols for computing the semilinear predicates and for electing a leader, which w.h.p. have $O(n \operatorname{polylog} n)$ convergence time. Achieving fast $O(n \operatorname{polylog} n)$ stabilization time for the majority and leader election problems requires a growing state space, as $O(n^{2-\varepsilon})$ stabilization time is not possible with a constant number of states [1, 16].

There are a number of protocols for the majority problem and the leader election problem with $O(n \operatorname{polylog} n)$ stabilization time and $O(\operatorname{polylog} n)$ states [1–3, 9, 12], but they all are non-uniform. The transition functions of these protocols depend on n as they use values $\Omega(\log n)$ or $\Omega(\log\log n)$. For example, each agent may be counting its interactions (which are uniform updates, not dependent on n) and progress to the next phase of the computation when its counter reaches $\log n$ (a non-uniform update).

While the computational power of (uniform) constant-space population protocols is well understood by now, less is known about the power of uniform protocols which allow the state space to grow with the size of population. Doty et al. [14] show a protocol for the exact population counting problem which has $O(n \log n \log\log n)$ stabilization time and uses $O(n^{60})$ states, w.h.p. and in expectation. They also formalize the notion of uniform population protocols, modeling the agents as copies of the same Turing machine, but describe their protocols using pseudo-codes and take the size of the state space as the product of the ranges of the variables.

Doty and Eftekhari [13] consider the problem of estimating the size of population within a constant factor, which they view as the problem of computing $\log n \pm O(1)$. They show a protocol which w.h.p. has $O(n \log^2 n)$ convergence time and uses $O(\log^7 n \log\log n)$ states. Their protocol is not always correct and they left open the question to design a protocol which uses expected $O(n \operatorname{polylog} n)$ interactions and $O(\operatorname{polylog} n)$ states and computes $\log n \pm O(1)$ with probability 1. An earlier work by Alistarh et al. [1] includes a uniform protocol which uses $O(n \log n)$ interactions and $O(\log n)$ states in expectation to compute an integer which w.h.p. is between $c_1 \log n$ and $c_2 \log n$, for some constants $0 < c_1 < 1 < c_2$. This can be viewed as approximating the population size within a polynomial factor.

1.3 Our Results

In this paper we present and analyze two uniform protocols, protocol Approximate for approximating the population size within

[1] *With high probability (w.h.p.)* refers to a probability of at least $1 - n^{-\Omega(1)}$.

constant factors, and protocol CountExact for computing the exact number of agents in the population. Unless stated otherwise we assume that all agents have to output the population size or its approximation. The theorems below summarize the performance of our protocols.

Theorem 1.1. *Protocol* Approximate *is uniform and outputs w.h.p. either $\lfloor \log n \rfloor$ or $\lceil \log n \rceil$.*

(1) *It converges in at most $O(n \log^2 n)$ interactions using $O(\log n \cdot \log\log n)$ states, w.h.p.*
(2) *A variant of the protocol stabilizes in $O(n \log^2 n)$ interactions using at most $O(\log^2 n \cdot \log\log n)$ states, w.h.p.*
(3) *Stabilization can also be achieved w.h.p. in $O(n \log^2 n)$ interactions using $O(\log n \cdot \log\log n)$ states, if not all but only $n - \log n$ agents need to output the result.*

Theorem 1.2. *The protocol* CountExact *is uniform and outputs the exact population size n. It stabilizes in $O(n \log n)$ interactions and uses $\tilde{O}(n)$ states, w.h.p.*[2]

Our protocols improve considerably the time and space bounds of the previous work [13] and [14]. Moreover, our approximate protocol is stable, answering the open question posed in [13], and it calculates a tighter approximation converging to $\lfloor \log n \rfloor$ or $\lceil \log n \rceil$ instead of $\log n \pm 5.7$ shown in [13]. The stabilization time of our exact counting protocol is asymptotically optimal and its number of states is only a polylog n factor away from the lower bound n. We note that in our protocol for exact counting the output value of an agent is a function of the state of this agent, and n is not kept explicitly in the agent's state. This is consistent with the approach in [14].

Our algorithms are based on leader election followed by load balancing phases. A load balancing phase starts with the total load of M tokens in the system and the goal is to relate M to n (the size of the population). If this load balancing phase completes with some agents having zero load, then w.h.p. $M \leq cn$, for a fixed constant $c > 1$. On the other hand, if all agents end up with positive load, then we must have $M \geq n$. To achieve good time and space bounds, we have to carefully control the load balancing phases and integrate them with the process of leader election. To achieve stability both of our protocols use an error detection routine and the leader initializes a process testing if the calculated answer is correct or not.

In Section 2 we discuss the auxiliary protocols which we use in our main protocols. We outline our approximate and exact protocols in Sections 3 and 4, respectively.

2 AUXILIARY PROTOCOLS

In this section we define auxiliary protocols that we will apply in our population counting protocols: one-way epidemics, the junta process, leader election, and phase clocks.

One-Way Epidemics. The goal of one-way epidemics is to spread an information to all members of the population. The state space of the protocol is $\{0, x\}$ for some $x > 0$. Initially at least one agent has the value x, which is then spread to all other agents. The transitions are formally defined as $\delta(u, v) = (\max\{u, v\}, v)$. We will refer to one-way epidemics also as *broadcast*. A natural extension is *maximum broadcast*, where agents do not only spread one possible value x, but instead each agent starts with its own value from the integer interval $[0, x]$. For maximum broadcast, the initiator always adopts the maximum, which is covered by the transition rule above as well. The result on one-way epidemics carries over immediately to maximum broadcast. The following result is well-known, see for example [6].

Lemma 2.1. *Let T_{BC} be the number of interactions required to complete (maximum) broadcast. W.h.p., $T_{BC} = O(n \log n)$.*

Junta Process. The goal of the *junta process* [8, 18] is to mark $\Theta(n^{\varepsilon})$ agents – the *junta*. The state of each agent v in this process is formed by a triplet $(\mathsf{level}_v, \mathsf{active}_v, \mathsf{junta}_v) \in \mathbb{N}_0 \times \{0, 1\}^2$ initially set to $(0, 1, 1)$. The idea of the protocol is as follows. If an active agent v interacts with an active agent on the same level it increases its level, otherwise it sets active_v to 0. Whenever v interacts with an agent on a higher level it sets junta_v to 0. Inactive agents adopt the level of their communication partner if that is higher. The protocol stabilizes when all agents are inactive at the highest level. The *junta* is formed by all agents v that reached the maximum level and have their junta_v bit set to 1. The following lemma is shown in [8], here it is adapted to our setting.

Lemma 2.2. *([8]) Let $\mathsf{level}^* = \max\{\mathsf{level}_v\}$ be the maximal level reached by the junta process. All agents become inactive within $O(n \log n)$ interactions, $\log\log n - 4 \leq \mathsf{level}^* \leq \log\log n + 8$, and the number of agents on the maximal level is $O(\sqrt{n} \cdot \log n)$, w.h.p.*

Phase Clocks. The existence of a non-empty junta of size in $[1, n^{\varepsilon}]$ allows the agents to synchronize themselves via so-called *phase clocks* [6, 18]. The phase clocks allow all agents to divide the time in phases of $\Theta(n \log n)$ interactions each. Each agent v has a state clock_v in $\{0, \ldots, m-1\}$ where m is a constant. Intuitively, these clock states can be seen as the hours on a clock face. The basic idea in every interaction is that the agents always adopt the larger clock state w.r.t. the circular order modulo m. Additionally, in order to keep the clock running, the members of the junta proceed one additional step when they interact with another agent on the same clock state. An agent v enters a new phase in interaction t if clock_v crosses the boundary between $m-1$ and 0. In that case we say the phase clock *ticks*.

For easy access to the phase clocks, we equip each agent v with a variable phase_v of constant size that counts the current phase of an agent modulo some constant. Additionally, each agent v has a flag[3] $\mathsf{firstTick}_v$. This flag is set to 1 whenever the phase_v counter is incremented, and it is set to 0 otherwise.

Let $D_i = [D_i^{\mathsf{start}}, D_i^{\mathsf{end}}]$ be the interval of interactions in Phase i such that the last agent enters Phase i in interaction D_i^{start} and the first agent leaves Phase i in interaction $D_i^{\mathsf{end}} + 1$.

Lemma 2.3 ([18]). *For any constant $c \geq 0$ we can construct a phase clock using $m = m(c) = O(1)$ states such that w.h.p. for all phases $1 \leq i \leq \mathrm{poly}(n)$ we have $cn \log n \leq D_i^{\mathsf{end}} - D_i^{\mathsf{start}} \leq cn \log n + \Theta(n \log n)$.*

[2] We define $\tilde{O}(f(n)) = O(f(n) \cdot \log^{O(1)}(f(n)))$.

[3] Note that for all flags we use FALSE (resp. TRUE) and 0 (resp. 1) interchangeably.

Leader Election. In [18] the authors present a stable and uniform protocol to perform leader election called LEADER_ELECT. It runs in $O(\log n)$ phases of $O(n \log n)$ interactions each.

The process starts with junta election in order to start two nested phase clocks. Agents perform an interaction of the outer phase clock once per phase of the inner phase clock. In the beginning, every agent runs the protocols for the phase clocks, junta election, and leader election in parallel. Whenever an agent encounters another agent on a higher (junta) level, it resets the clocks and the leader election protocol. In that way, all agents eventually run the phase clocks and the leader election process based on the junta on the highest level. The actual leader election process is quite simple: the set of leaders is halved from phase to phase, and the time is measured by the inner phase clock.

For stable leader election the authors of [18] combine their protocol with a slow protocol which is always correct in the following way: the outer phase clock runs only if at least one leader remains in the system. If at some point it counts to m, w.h.p. a total of $\Theta(n \log^2 n)$ interactions have occurred. At this time, all agents override their current leader state from the slow protocol with that of the fast protocol. When the outer phase clock ticks (i.e., it reaches m), at least one leader exists. We equip each agent v with an additional flag leaderDone_v, initially set to FALSE. It is set to TRUE as soon as the outer phase clock ticks.

LEMMA 2.4 ([18]). *The uniform protocol* LEADER_ELECT *elects a unique leader. It stabilizes in $O(n \log^2 n)$ interactions, using $O(\log \log n)$ many states, w.h.p. Furthermore, after at most $O(n \log^2 n)$ interactions all agents v have* leaderDone_v *set to* TRUE *w.h.p., and at that time there is exactly one leader w.h.p.*

Fast Leader Election. In [8] the authors describe a stable leader election protocol that admits a trade-off between the running time and the number of states. When using $\tilde{O}(n)$ states, their protocol stabilizes w.h.p. in $O(n \log n)$ interactions. In the following, we call this protocol FASTLEADERELECTION. The main idea of the protocol is to use $O(\log n)$ random bits to reduce the number of active leaders much faster than in the original protocol from [18].

LEMMA 2.5 ([8]). *The uniform protocol* FASTLEADERELECTION *elects a unique leader. It stabilizes in $O(n \log n)$ interactions, using $\tilde{O}(n)$ many states, w.h.p. Furthermore, after at most $O(n \log n)$ interactions all agents have* leaderDone_u *set to* TRUE *w.h.p.*

3 APPROXIMATE COUNTING

In this section we show Theorem 1.1. In Section 3.1 we assume that a unique leader exists and we present a protocol which calculates $\lfloor \log n \rfloor$ or $\lceil \log n \rceil$ using a load balancing algorithm. In Section 3.2 we analyze the protocol. In Section 3.3 we show how to combine the protocol from Section 3.1 with a leader election protocol. This shows the first part of Theorem 1.1. Finally, in Section 3.4 we show how to build a stable protocol by showing the correctness of our error detection mechanism. This shows the second and the third part of Theorem 1.1.

3.1 Approximating n with a Leader

In this section we assume that a unique leader is given and that all agents are synchronized via the phase clocks. The main idea of our algorithm is to inject an increasing number of tokens into the system and to use a load balancing routine to estimate the number of agents in the system. The process is finished as soon as roughly n tokens are injected into the system. To save on the number of states, the agents do not store the exact number of tokens, they hold but the logarithm of that number.

Every agent v stores two variables $(k_v, \text{searchDone}_v) \in \{-1, 0, 2, \ldots\} \times \{0, 1\}$, initially set to $(-1, 0)$. The variable k_v stores the logarithm of the *load* of agent v, where the special value -1 indicates that the agent is empty. The leader u orchestrates a linear search over $k_u \in \{0, 1, \ldots\}$ to find k_u^* for which $\log n - 1 < k_u^* < \log n + 1$. The variable searchDone_v indicates that the search is finished. The protocol runs in rounds consisting of multiple phases each. At the beginning of round r the leader injects 2^r tokens into the system. The load is then balanced using a *powers-of-two load balancing* process which restricts the load of any agent to a power of two. The search stops when at the end of a round there is an agent v with load larger than 1 ($k_v > 0$). At this time the leader u sets searchDone_u to TRUE and broadcasts the value to all agents using one-way epidemics. Thus when the total number of tokens 2^r becomes large enough so that the load balancing leaves at least one agent with more than one token, then this number 2^r is taken as an approximation of the population size.

In the classical load balancing process (cf. [10]), it is assumed that m indistinguishable tokens are distributed arbitrarily among n agents. At interaction t, the *load vector* $\mathbf{L}(t)$ is defined as $\mathbf{L}(t) = (\ell_1(t), \ldots, \ell_n(t)) \in \mathbb{N}_0^n$, where $\ell_i(t)$ is the number of tokens (load) present at agent i at that interaction. Assume agents u and v balance their loads in interaction $t \geq 1$, then $(\ell_u(t+1), \ell_v(t+1)) = (\lfloor (\ell_u(t) + \ell_v(t))/2 \rfloor, \lceil (\ell_u(t) + \ell_v)/2 \rceil)$. For the powers-of-two load balancing process we define the *logarithmic load vector* $\mathbf{K} = (k_1, \ldots, k_n) \in \{-1, 0, 1, \ldots\}^n$ such that for any agent v we have $\ell_v(t) = 2^{k_v}$ if $k_v \geq 0$ and $\ell_v(t) = 0$ if $k_v = -1$. Assume now that agent u interacts with agent v. A balancing action is only permitted if either u or v is empty (i.e., $k_u = -1$ or $k_v = -1$) and both of them are not the leader. Let k_u' and k_v' be the resulting logarithmic load values. Then

$$(k_u', k_v') = \begin{cases} (k_u - 1, k_u - 1) & \text{if } k_u > 0 \text{ and } k_v = -1 \\ (k_v - 1, k_v - 1) & \text{if } k_u = -1 \text{ and } k_v > 0 \\ (k_u, k_v) & \text{otherwise.} \end{cases} \quad (1)$$

The SEARCH Protocol is defined in Algorithm 1. The protocol runs in rounds of 5 phases. Every agent v uses the variable phase_v to count the number of phases modulo 5 and the flag firstTick_v which is set to TRUE when v initiates the first interaction of a phase (see Section 2). In Phase 1 and Phase 4 the leader is active, in the remaining phases the non-leaders are active.

- Phase 0 and Phase 1 are used for the initialization. Every agent v which is not the leader resets k_v to -1 (Line 11). During the first interaction (u, v) in Phase 1 the leader u transfers 2^{k_u} tokens to v (Line 3).
- In Phase 2, the non-leader agents perform powers-of-two load balancing, as described above (Line 14).
- Phase 3 consists of one-way epidemics where the agents communicate their highest load value (Line 16).

```
Interaction (u, v) in the SEARCH Protocol:
1   if leader_u = TRUE and searchDone_u = FALSE then                ▷ Leader:
2       if phase_u = 1 and firstTick_u = TRUE then                  ▷ Phase 1: load infusion
3           k_v ← k_u
4       if phase_u = 4 and firstTick_u = TRUE then                  ▷ Phase 4: decision
5           if k_v ≤ 0 then
6               k_u ← k_u + 1
7           else
8               searchDone_u ← TRUE
9   if leader_u = FALSE and leader_v = FALSE then                   ▷ Followers:
10      if phase_u = 0 then                                         ▷ Phase 0: initialize
11          k_u ← −1
12      if phase_u = 2 then                                         ▷ Phase 2: load balancing
13          if min { k_u, k_v } = −1 and max { k_u, k_v } > 0 then
14              k_u, k_v ← max { k_u, k_v } − 1
15      if phase_u = 3 then                                         ▷ Phase 3: one-way epidemics
16          k_u, k_v ← max { k_u, k_v }
```

Algorithm 1: The Search Protocol, centerpiece of protocol Approximate

$$s(v) = \Big(\underbrace{\text{phase}_v,\ \text{firstTick}_v,}_{\text{Phase Clocks}}\ \underbrace{\text{leader}_v,}_{\text{Leader Election}}\ \underbrace{k_v,\ \text{searchDone}_v}_{\text{SEARCH Protocol}}\Big)$$
$$S = \{0,\ldots,4\} \times \{0,1\} \times \{0,1\} \times \{-1,0,1,\ldots\} \times \{0,1\}$$

Figure 1: State space of the Search Protocol (Algorithm 1)

- In Phase 4 (Line 5), the leader u decides if the search is finished or not. If the maximum logarithmic load is less than 1 it concludes that the injected logarithmic load was smaller than or equal to $\log n - 1$. The leader u therefore proceeds to the next round and injects twice as many tokens. If the observed maximum logarithmic load is larger than 1, the leader concludes the protocol by setting searchDone_u to TRUE.

The number of agents is now estimated as 2^{k_u}. In the following, the state of an agent v in this algorithm is called $s(v)$. The state space S is the Cartesian product of the domains of the individual variables (phase_v, firstTick_v, leader_v, k_v, searchDone_v). For an overview of the state of agent v in the Search Protocol, see Figure 1. Note that we omit internal states of constant size from auxiliary protocols.

3.2 Analysis of the Search Protocol

Based on the definition in Equation (1) we first show that the powers-of-two load balancing process on n agents balances the load such that the maximum load is at most 1 (i.e., $k_v \le 0$ for all agents v) as long as at most $3/4n$ tokens are injected by the leader. Let $k_v(t)$ be the logarithmic load of agent v at interaction t.

Lemma 3.1. *Assume there exists an agent u with $k_u(0) = \kappa$ and $k_v(0) = -1$ for all $v \neq u$. If $2^\kappa \le 3/4 \cdot n$, then w.h.p. after $t = 16n \log n$ interactions $\max_v \{ k_v(t) \} = 0$.*

The proof of Lemma 3.1 uses the same ideas and shows a similar statement as in Lemmas 2 and 3 in [10] for the classical load balancing process.

In the following, we assume that precisely one agent u is the leader and all agents synchronize themselves via the phase clocks. Based on this assumption we can show the following lemma for the Search Protocol.

Lemma 3.2. *After at most $O(\log n)$ rounds the leader u sets searchDone_u to TRUE, w.h.p. At that time we have w.h.p. that $3/4 \cdot n < 2^{k_u} \le 2^{\lceil \log n \rceil}$.*

Proof. The Search Protocol runs in multiple phases. In the following, we combine every five consecutive phases to a round such that round $r \ge 0$ consists of phases $5r$ to $5r + 4$. For a fixed round r let $k_v(r)$ denote the changing value of variable k of agent v during round r. Assuming that all agents are properly synchronized by the phase clocks (see Lemma 2.3), we can w.h.p. assume that the number of interactions in any round is sufficient for spreading information with one-way epidemics (see Lemma 2.1) and for the powers-of-two load balancing (see Lemma 3.1).

Observe that the leader sets searchDone_u to TRUE in Line 8 of Phase 4 of the Search Protocol. Let v be an agent with maximal load at the beginning of Phase 3. In Phase 3 the agents used one-way epidemics to disseminate the value k_v to all agents. Hence, searchDone_u is set to TRUE in the first round r when an agent v

Interaction (u, v) of protocol APPROXIMATE:
if $\text{level}_v > \text{level}_u$ **then**
  re-initialize states of u for PHASECLOCKS, LEADERELECTION, SEARCHPROTOCOL

JUNTAPROCESS $[(\text{level}_u, \text{junta}_u), (\text{level}_v, \text{junta}_v)]$ ▹ *update auxiliary protocols*
PHASECLOCKS $[(\text{phase}_u, \text{firstTick}_u), (\text{phase}_v, \text{firstTick}_v)]$

if not leaderDone_u **then** ▹ *Stage 1: Leader Election [18]*
  LEADERELECTION $[(\text{leader}_u, \text{leaderDone}_u), (\text{leader}_v, \text{leaderDone}_v)]$

if leaderDone_u **and not** searchDone_u **then** ▹ *Stage 2: Search Stage*
  SEARCHPROTOCOL $[(k_u, \text{searchDone}_u), (k_v, \text{searchDone}_v)]$

if leaderDone_u **and** searchDone_u **then** ▹ *Stage 3: Broadcasting Stage*
  $(\text{searchDone}_v, k_v) \leftarrow (\text{TRUE}, k_u)$

Algorithm 2: Protocol APPROXIMATE

	Junta Process		Phase Clocks		Leader Election		SEARCH Protocol
state of agent v:	$(\text{level}_v, \text{active}_v, \text{junta}_v,$		$\text{clock}_v, \text{phase}_v, \text{firstTick}_v,$		$\text{leader}_v, \text{leaderDone}_v,$		$s(v))$
state space:	$\mathbb{N}_0 \times \{0,1\} \times \{0,1\}$	$\times$	$[m] \times \{0,\ldots,4\} \times \{0,1\}$	$\times$	$\{0,1\} \times \{0,1\}$	$\times$	S

Figure 2: State space of protocol APPROXIMATE (Algorithm 2)

has $k_v(r) > 0$ after the load balancing, meaning agent v has a load of at least two.

To show the lemma we consider 3 cases, depending on the value $k_u(r)$ which corresponds to the load injected by the leader at the beginning of round $r \geq 0$.

Case $2^{k_u(r)} \leq 3/4 \cdot n$: In Phase 1 the leader injects 2^r many tokens. According to Lemma 3.1, w.h.p. at the end of Phase 2 of Round r no agent will have a load larger that one, meaning for all agents v we have $k_v \leq 0$. The maximum value k_v which is communicated via one-way epidemics is at most zero and the leader does not set searchDone_u to TRUE in Phase 4 of Round r. Hence, it injects 2^{r+1} tokens at the beginning of the next round.

Case $3/4 \cdot n < 2^{k_u(r)} < n$: Again, in Phase 1 the leader injects 2^r many tokens. In this case either there exists an agent v with a load larger than one ($k_v > 0$) at the end of Phase 2, or for all agents v we have $k_v \leq 0$. In the latter case we are back to the previous case: the leader does not set searchDone_u to TRUE in Phase 4 of Round r. Hence, it injects 2^{r+1} tokens at the beginning of the next round. If there exists an agent v with $k_v > 0$ the leader sets searchDone_u to TRUE.

Case $n \leq 2^{k_u(r)}$: In Phase 1 the leader injects $2^r \geq n$ many tokens. The agents balance at least n tokens on $n-1$ agents (since the leader does not participate in the load balancing). Hence, at the end of Phase 2 of Round r there exists an agent with a load of at least two, meaning $k_v \geq 1$. The leader sets searchDone_u to TRUE in Phase 4 of Round r.

From the above cases it follows that after at most $\lceil \log n \rceil$ rounds searchDone_u is set to TRUE and then $3/4 \cdot n < 2^{k_u} \leq 2^{\lceil \log n \rceil}$. □

3.3 Combining the SEARCH Protocol with Leader Election

In this section we combine the SEARCH Protocol with the LEADERELECTION protocol from [18]. The combined protocol works as follows. All agents run the JUNTAPROCESS and the PHASECLOCKS protocols in parallel to the LEADERELECTION protocol and, later, the SEARCH Protocol. In the junta process, agents cannot decide whether they have already reached the maximal junta level. Therefore, some agents already perform some interactions of the LEADERELECTION protocol or the SEARCH Protocol at a lower junta level. These agents might be badly synchronized, since the phase clock ticks correctly w.h.p. only on the maximal junta level. We therefore define the following procedure that has already been used in [18]. Whenever an agent u interacts with an agent v in a higher level ($\text{level}_u < \text{level}_v$) all variables for PHASECLOCKS, LEADERELECTION and the SEARCH Protocol are re-initialized. In that way, all agents eventually start the LEADERELECTION protocol and the SEARCH Protocol at the maximal junta level from a clean state.

The combined protocol uses two flags leaderDone_v and searchDone_v for each agent v, initially set to FALSE. The first flag, leaderDone_v, is set once an agent has concluded the leader election protocol (see Section 2). The second flag, searchDone_v, is set by the SEARCH Protocol (see Section 3.1). The two flags leaderDone_v and searchDone_v allow every agent v to distinguish between three stages of the execution of the protocol, the *Leader Election Stage* (1), the *Search Stage* (2), and the *Broadcasting Stage* (3).

In the Leader Election Stage all agents use the protocol from [18] to elect a leader. Recall that the flag leaderDone_u is set to TRUE once the external phase clock ticks (see Section 2). At this time there exists w.h.p. exactly one leader [18]. In the Search Stage, we use the SEARCH Protocol defined in Section 3.1. In the Broadcasting Stage the leader u uses one-way epidemics to inform all other agents of its value k_u. Each agent v uses its value k_v as its output.

We now give the proof of the first part of Theorem 1.1, where we show that protocol APPROXIMATE w.h.p. computes either $\lfloor \log n \rfloor$ or $\lceil \log n \rceil$.

PROOF OF STATEMENT 1 OF THEOREM 1.1. From Lemma 2.2 it follows that after $O(n \log n)$ interactions the junta is elected and all agents are inactive. From that point on no agent in the protocol is ever re-initialized again. Let u be the single leader that according to Lemma 2.4 w.h.p. concludes the leader election protocol. According to Lemma 3.2, the leader u sets searchDone$_u$ to TRUE w.h.p. in $\lfloor \log n \rfloor$ or $\lceil \log n \rceil$ phases of $O(n \log n)$ interactions each, so at that time k_u is either $\lfloor \log n \rfloor$ or $\lceil \log n \rceil$. According to Lemma 2.1, within $O(n \log n)$ further interactions all agents know the value k_u from the leader u. Together, this gives a total number of $O(n \log^2 n)$ interactions, after which w.h.p. all agents know the value k_u from the leader and thus they all output either $\lfloor \log n \rfloor$ or $\lceil \log n \rceil$.

Regarding the required number of states, we observe that level$_v$ from the junta process and k_v from the SEARCH Protocol are the only variables of an agent v that are not of constant size and thus may grow with the population size n. For an overview of the state of agent v, see Figure 2. Note that level$_v$ is bounded w.h.p. by $O(\log \log n)$ according to Lemma 2.2, and k_v is bounded according to Lemma 3.2 w.h.p. by $O(\log n)$. Together this gives that w.h.p. the state space has size $O(\log \log n \cdot \log n)$. This concludes the proof of Statement 1 of Theorem 1.1. □

3.4 The Stable Protocol

In this section we sketch our stable protocol and proofs of Statements 2 and 3 of Theorem 1.1. The details can be found in the full version [11]. The protocol APPROXIMATE is not stable because there is small, but positive, probability that the system never reaches a correct stable configuration (a configuration when all agents output $\lfloor \log n \rfloor$ or $\lceil \log n \rceil$ and cannot change their output whatever future interactions may be). Our stable protocol is a hybrid protocol which combines the protocol APPROXIMATE with a slow *backup* protocol which always finds the correct solution.

The challenge is to design mechanisms which ensure that the combined protocol stabilizes with the output from the backup protocol whenever an *error* occurs within the main protocol. The first error we handle in our stable protocol is concerned with leader election, where it may happen that no agent ever completes the protocol as a leader (so no one ever sets their leaderDone flag to trigger the SEARCH Protocol), or multiple leaders do. To deal with the possibility that no agents ever set the leaderDone flag, all agents run from the very beginning the backup protocol in parallel to their main computation. The initial output is the output from this backup protocol. An agent which sets leaderDone to TRUE, stops at this time the execution of the backup protocol and proceeds with the SEARCH Protocol, which is governed by the leader. At this time the output is switched to the output from the main protocol.

Detecting an error in the SEARCH Protocol is more involved. We develop an ERRORDETECTION protocol which is executed by all agents when they complete their SEARCH Protocol (that is, when they set their searchDone flag). The ERRORDETECTION protocol consists of another load balancing computation. It is a combination of the powers-of-two load balancing used in the SEARCH Protocol, followed by the classical load balancing when the individual loads become less than a fixed constant. Combining these two load balancing computations ensures *precise* load balancing but requires only a constant number of additional states. The total load is set in such a way that, once the load balancing is completed, w.h.p. the load of each agent is at least 3, and no two individual loads differ by more than 2. The agents keep checking these conditions and raise an *error flag* whenever they find out that one of them is violated. The leader u then computes the final output based on its load, which can be shown to be either $\lfloor \log n \rfloor$ or $\lceil \log n \rceil$, or otherwise an error is raised at some point of the computation.

Whenever an agent detects an error, it raises an error flag, which is subsequently adopted by all other agents via one-way epidemics. When an agent sets its error flag, it ignores all its previous computations and executes a new instance of the backup protocol. For example, if multiple agents conclude the leader election stage as leaders, then this error is eventually detected when two leaders interact with each other, resulting in both raising their error flags.

The backup protocol works as follows. Every agent starts with exactly one token. Whenever two agents interact and both have the same amount of tokens, one of them hands its tokens over to the other. The agents do not store the exact number of tokens they hold but the logarithm of that number. Note that, due to the definition of the process, the load of every agent is either 0 or a power of two. After $O(n^2 \log n)$ interactions one agent will store $\lfloor \log n \rfloor$ tokens representing $2^{\lfloor \log n \rfloor}$. For each $0 \le i < \lfloor \log n \rfloor$ there might be one agent storing 2^i tokens (depending on the value of n). The number of states required by this process is $O(\log n)$ if it is sufficient for all but $\log n$ agents to know the approximation for n. Otherwise, the value $\lfloor \log n \rfloor$ has to be sent to every agent via one-way epidemics. In this case there are up to $\log n$ many agents that need $O(\log^2 n)$ many states (exactly those agents which store a value 2^i).

The hybrid protocol constructed in this way stabilizes w.h.p. within $O(n \log^2 n)$ many interactions using $O(\log \log n \cdot \log^2 n)$ many states if all agents have to know the approximation of n, otherwise $O(\log \log n \cdot \log n)$ states are sufficient.

4 COUNTING THE EXACT POPULATION SIZE

In this section we consider the problem of counting the exact population size and present our protocol COUNTEXACT. The main idea is as follows. The protocol first selects a junta using the modified junta process from [8] (see Section 2). It then creates phase clocks and selects a leader using the FASTLEADERELECTION protocol (see Section 2). Again, every agent v has two flags leader$_v$ and leaderDone$_v$ which indicate whether v is a leader and v has completed the leader election protocol, respectively. Recall that the junta uses a variable level$_v$ that stores the maximum level which is reached during the junta election. In [8] it has been shown that in the modified junta process the level reaches w.h.p. a value of $\log \log n \pm c$ for some constant c. Hence, we can use $2^{2^{\text{level}_v}}$ as a first approximation for n. This approximation will be refined in two stages, called APPROXIMATIONSTAGE and REFINEMENTSTAGE, which are described in Section 4.1 and Section 4.2, respectively. The protocol CountExact can be found in Algorithm 3. The output of every agent in the protocol CountExact is defined by the RefinementStage.

4.1 Fast Approximation

In this section we assume that a unique leader has been elected and that all agents are synchronized via the phase clocks. Additionally, we assume that all agents are on the same maximal junta level level* w.r.t. the modified junta process from [8].

The goal of protocol ApproximationStage is to compute $\log n$ up to an additive error of ± 3. (We are not using the protocol from Section 3 because we aim for the $O(n \log n)$ bound on the number of interactions.) The protocol starts with injecting $2^{2^{\text{level}_u - 8}} = n^\eta$ tokens into the system for some $0 < \eta \leq 1$. It alternates between increasing the number of injected tokens by a factor of n^η and load balancing until the total number of tokens M is at least $n/2$. Unfortunately it is possible that M is very close to $n^{1+\eta}$, resulting in a multiplicative error. Hence, the protocol outputs $k_u = \log M - \lfloor \log l_u \rfloor$. In Lemma 4.1 we will show that $\log n - 3 \leq k_u \leq \log n + 3$.

The interactions of the protocol are defined in Algorithm 4. The protocol runs in multiple phases of $O(n \log n)$ interactions each (the phases are determined by the phase clock). Every agent v uses the variables i_v (initialized to 0) as a phase counter and l_v for load balancing. The leader u has an additional variable k_u in which it eventually stores the approximation. In the first phase, every agent v initializes its load l_v to 0 (non-leaders) or to 1 (leader). In the first interaction of every phase, every agent v increases the phase counter i_v and multiplies its load with n^η (see Line 7). During the remainder of the phase, all agents us the classical load balancing process from [10] to balance their tokens. The leader u additionally checks before the multiplication whether it has a load of at least 4 (in which case the total load is at least $2n$ w.h.p.). If this is the case, the leader calculates the approximation k_u as $i_u \cdot \eta - \lfloor \log l_u \rfloor$ and raises the flag ApxDone_u, indicating that the approximation stage has concluded (see Line 5). The flag is then sent to all other agents via one-way epidemics (see Line 9), and the raised flag terminates the process.

Lemma 4.1. *Let u be the leader. After at most $O(n \log n)$ interactions of the Approximation Stage all agents v set ApxDone_v to TRUE w.h.p. At that time, $k_u = \log n \pm 3$ w.h.p. The protocol uses w.h.p. at most $\tilde{O}(n)$ states.*

Proof. First we bound the number of phases until all agents v have ApxDone_v = TRUE. When the leader u sets ApxDone_u to TRUE, all other agents follow via one-way epidemics in the same phase, w.h.p. Therefore it suffices to bound the number of phases until the leader u sets ApxDone_u to TRUE.

Let $\hat{\imath}$ be the first phase in which the leader has a load of at least 4. From load balancing [10] it follows that the total load M at that time is at least $2n$. At the beginning of Phase 1 the leader u has $n^\eta = 2^{2^{\text{level}_v - 8}}$ tokens and all other agents are empty. In the first interaction of Phase $i > 1$ all agents v multiply their load with n^η (see Line 7). Hence, in Phase $i \leq \hat{\imath}$ the total load is $M = n^{i\eta}$, w.h.p. and in Phase $\hat{\imath}$ we have $2n \leq n^{\hat{\imath}\eta} \leq 6 \cdot n^{1+\eta}$ (see [10]). From Lemma 2.2 we obtain that w.h.p. $\log \log n - 4 \leq \text{level}_v$ and therefore $\eta \geq 1/2^{12}$ w.h.p. Since $n^{\hat{\imath}\eta} \leq 6 \cdot n^{1+\eta}$ we get $\hat{\imath} \leq 1/\eta + 1 + o(1)$. Hence the number of phases $\hat{\imath}$ until u sets ApxDone_u to TRUE is bounded by a constant $\hat{\imath} = O(1)$.

We now bound the quality of the approximation k_u. In Phase $\hat{\imath}$, the leader sets its variable k_u to $k_u = \hat{\imath} \cdot 2^{\text{level}_u - 8} - \lfloor \log l_u \rfloor$. From load balancing [10] we get $l_u \leq 2^{\hat{\imath} \cdot 2^{\text{level}_u - 8}}/n + 1.5$ and therefore

$$
\begin{aligned}
k_u &\geq \hat{\imath} \cdot 2^{\text{level}_u - 8} - \log\left(2^{\hat{\imath} \cdot 2^{\text{level}_u - 8}}/n + 1.5\right) \\
&\geq \hat{\imath} \cdot 2^{\text{level}_u - 8} - \log\left(2^{\hat{\imath} \cdot 2^{\text{level}_u - 8}}/n \cdot (1 + 1.5/2)\right) \qquad (2) \\
&= \hat{\imath} \cdot 2^{\text{level}_u - 8} - \log\left(2^{\hat{\imath} \cdot 2^{\text{level}_u - 8}}\right) + \log n - \log 1.75 \\
&\geq \log n - 3 \ ,
\end{aligned}
$$

where (2) holds since $2^{\hat{\imath} \cdot 2^{\text{level}_u - 8}} \geq 2n$. Analogously,

$$
\begin{aligned}
k_u &\leq \hat{\imath} \cdot 2^{\text{level}_u - 8} - \log l_u + 1 \\
&\leq \hat{\imath} \cdot 2^{\text{level}_u - 8} - \log\left(2^{\hat{\imath} \cdot 2^{\text{level}_u - 8}}/n \cdot (1 - 1.5/2)\right) + 1 \\
&\leq \log n + 3 \ .
\end{aligned}
$$

It remains to bound the required number of states. For each agent v, the variables i_v and k_v require w.h.p. at most $O(\log n)$ many states, and the variable l_v stores up to $O(n^\eta) \leq n$ many tokens. □

4.2 Refining the Approximation

As before, we assume that a unique leader has been elected and that all agents are synchronized via the phase clocks. We also assume that the leader holds an approximation of $\log n \pm 3$.

In the Refinement Stage, every agent v holds a variables k_v for the approximation of $\log n$ and a variable l_v that is used for load balancing. The protocol consists of 3 phases. The first phase is used for initialization. The value k_u (the approximation calculated by the leader in the previous stage) is spread among all agents via one-way epidemics (Line 2). In the beginning of the second phase the leader injects $2^8 \cdot 2^{k_u}$ many tokens into the system which are balanced, as before. In the beginning of third phase every agent multiplies its load with 2^{k_u}, and then the load is balanced again. In Lemma 4.2 we show that total number of tokens M is bounded by $2^2 \cdot n^2 \leq M \leq 2^{14} \cdot n^2$. At the end of the phase every agent can compute n as its output function $\omega(v) = \lfloor 2^8 \cdot 2^{2k_v}/l_v \rceil$.[4]

Lemma 4.2. *After at most $O(n \log n)$ interactions of the Refinement Stage, all agents v output $\omega(v) = n$ w.h.p. The protocol uses w.h.p. at most $\tilde{O}(n)$ states.*

Proof. At the end of Phase 0, w.h.p. all agents know k_u from the leader according to one-way epidemics. At the end of Phase 1, w.h.p. $C \cdot 2^{k_u}$ tokens have been balanced such that $l_v = \Theta(1)$ for any agent v. At the end of Phase 2, a total of at least $M \geq 4 \cdot n^2$ tokens have been balanced and every agent v has load $l_v = \lfloor C \cdot 2^{2k_u}/n \rceil \pm 1$ w.h.p.

We now need to show that every agent v can output n using its output function $\omega(v) = \lfloor C 2^{2k_v}/l_v \rceil$, provided that v knows the value $k_v = k_u = \log n \pm 3$ from the leader and the total load M is

[4] The expression $\lfloor x \rceil$ denotes x rounded to the nearest integer, breaking ties arbitrarily.

Interaction (u, v) of protocol CountExact:

if $\mathsf{level}_v > \mathsf{level}_u$ **then**
  re-initialize states of u for PhaseClocks, FastLeaderElection, ApproximationStage, RefinementStage

JuntaProcess $[\mathsf{level}_u, \mathsf{level}_v]$ ▹ *update auxiliary protocols*
PhaseClocks $[(\mathsf{phase}_u, \mathsf{firstTick}_u), (\mathsf{phase}_v, \mathsf{firstTick}_v)]$

if not $\mathsf{leaderDone}_u$ **then** ▹ *Stage 1: Fast Leader Election*
  FastLeaderElection $[(\mathsf{leader}_u, \mathsf{leaderDone}_u), (\mathsf{leader}_v, \mathsf{leaderDone}_v)]$

if $\mathsf{leaderDone}_u$ **and not** $\mathsf{ApxDone}_u$ **then** ▹ *Stage 2: Approximation Stage*
  ApproximationStage $[(k_u, l_u, \mathsf{ApxDone}_u), (k_v, l_v, \mathsf{ApxDone}_v)]$

if $\mathsf{leaderDone}_u$ **and** $\mathsf{ApxDone}_u$ **then** ▹ *Stage 3: Refinement Stage*
  RefinementStage $[(k_u, l_u), (k_v, l_v)]$

Algorithm 3: Protocol CountExact

state of agent u:	(level_u,		phase_u, $\mathsf{firstTick}_u$,		leader_u, $\mathsf{leaderDone}_u$,		i_u, k_u, l_u, $\mathsf{ApxDone}_u$)
	Junta Process		Phase Clock		Leader Election		Approximation and Refinement Stages
state space:	$\mathbb{N}_0$	$\times$	$\mathbb{N}_0 \times \{0,1\}$	$\times$	$\{0,1\} \times \{0,1\}$	$\times$	$\mathbb{N}_0 \times \{-1, 0, 1, \dots\} \times \mathbb{N}_0 \times \{0,1\}$

Figure 3: State space of protocol CountExact (Algorithm 3)

Interaction $[(k_u, l_u, \mathsf{ApxDone}_u), (k_v, l_v, \mathsf{ApxDone}_v)]$ in the ApproximationStage protocol:

if $\mathsf{firstTick}_u = \text{TRUE}$ **then**
  if $\mathsf{leader}_u = \text{TRUE}$ **and** $i_u = 0$ **then** ▹ *initialize first phase*
    $l_u \leftarrow 1$

  if leader_u **and** $l_u \geq 4$ **then** ▹ *found an approximation*
    $\mathsf{ApxDone}_u \leftarrow \text{TRUE}$
    $k_u \leftarrow i_u \cdot 2^{\mathsf{level}_u - 8} - \lfloor \log l_u \rfloor$

  $(i_u, l_u) \leftarrow \left(i_u + 1,\ l_u \cdot 2^{2^{\mathsf{level}_u - 8}}\right)$ ▹ *start new phase: load explosion*

$(l_u, l_v) \leftarrow (\lfloor (l_u + l_v)/2 \rfloor, \lceil (l_u + l_v)/2 \rceil)$ ▹ *classical load balancing*

$\mathsf{ApxDone}_u \leftarrow \max\{\mathsf{ApxDone}_u, \mathsf{ApxDone}_v\}$ ▹ *broadcast* ApxDone

Algorithm 4: CountExact Approximation Stage

Interaction $[(k_u, l_u), (k_v, l_v)]$ in the RefinementStage protocol:

if $\mathsf{phase}_u = 0$ **then** ▹ *initialize agents and broadcast k_u*
  $(k_u, k_v, l_u, l_v) \leftarrow (\max\{k_u, k_v\}, \max\{k_u, k_v\}, 0, 0)$

if $\mathsf{firstTick}_u = \text{TRUE}$ **then**
  if $\mathsf{phase}_u = 1$ **and** $\mathsf{leader}_u = \text{TRUE}$ **then** ▹ *the leader starts with load $2^8 \cdot 2^{k_u}$*
    $l_u \leftarrow 2^8 \cdot 2^{k_u}$

  if $\mathsf{phase}_u = 2$ **then** ▹ *multiply load with 2^{k_u}*
    $l_u \leftarrow l_u \cdot 2^{k_u}$

$(l_u, l_v) \leftarrow (\lfloor (l_u + l_v)/2 \rfloor, \lceil (l_u + l_v)/2 \rceil)$

Algorithm 5: CountExact Refinement Stage

at least $M = C \cdot 2^{2k_u} \geq 4n^2$ tokens. The proof is based on the proof of Lemma 3.8 from [15].

Observe that after the load balancing, w.h.p. $l_v = C \cdot 2^{2k_u}/n + r$ where $r \in [-1.5, 1.5]$ (the error term r covers the remaining discrepancy and the rounding error). Let $\hat{\omega}(v)$ be the output of agent v before the rounding is applied. We derive, analogously to [15],

$$\hat{\omega}(v) = \frac{M}{l_v} = \frac{C \cdot 2^{2k_u}}{C \cdot 2^{2k_u}/n + r} = \frac{C \cdot 2^{2k_u} \cdot n}{C \cdot 2^{2k_u} + rn}$$
$$= \frac{C \cdot 2^{2k_u} \cdot n}{C \cdot 2^{2k_u}\left(1 + \frac{rn}{C \cdot 2^{2k_u}}\right)} = \frac{n}{1 + \frac{rn}{C \cdot 2^{2k_u}}}$$

which gives us, since $r \in [-1.5, 1.5]$

$$\hat{\omega}(v) \geq \frac{n}{1 + \frac{1.5n}{C \cdot 2^{2k_u}}} \overset{(M \geq 4n^2)}{\geq} \frac{n}{1 + \frac{1.5n}{4n^2}}$$
$$= \frac{n}{1 + \frac{1}{3n}} = n - \left(\frac{1}{3} - \frac{1}{3(3n+1)}\right) > n - \frac{1}{2}$$

and
$$\hat{\omega}(v) \leq \frac{n}{1 - \frac{1.5n}{C \cdot 2^{2k_u}}} \overset{(M \geq 4n^2)}{\leq} \frac{n}{1 - \frac{1.5n}{4n^2}}$$
$$= \frac{n}{1 - \frac{1}{3n}} = n + \frac{1}{3} + \frac{1}{3(3n-1)} < n + \frac{1}{2} .$$

Therefore, $\omega(v) = \lfloor \hat{\omega}(v) \rceil = n$. □

4.3 Analysis of CountExact

We now show Theorem 1.2. Due to space limitations, we only show that CountExact calculates the value of n w.h.p. In the full version [11] we show that we can combine the protocol with a slow always-correct backup protocol in order to show stabilization.

Proof. From Lemma 2.2 it follows that after $O(n \log n)$ interactions the junta is elected and all agents are inactive. From that point on no agent in the protocol is ever re-initialized again. Let u be the single leader that w.h.p. concludes the FastLeaderElection protocol according to Lemma 2.5 after at most $O(n \log n)$ interactions. According to Lemma 4.1, the leader u computes $\log n \pm 3$ and sets ApxDone_u to TRUE after at most $O(n \log n)$ further interactions w.h.p. Finally, according to Lemma 4.2, all agents output n after $O(n \log n)$ further interactions. The total number of interactions therefore is $O(n \log n)$. Observe that all protocols require at most $\tilde{O}(n)$ states (see also Figure 3). This concludes the proof. □

In order to argue that CountExact stabilizes, we use the same idea as in Section 3.4, where we combined the protocol for approximate counting with a slow backup protocol which is always correct. Together with an error detection mechanism, this results in a protocol that stabilizes w.h.p. in $O(n \log n)$ interactions such that every agent outputs the exact value n, using $\tilde{O}(n)$ states. Further details can be found in the full version [11].

REFERENCES

[1] Dan Alistarh, James Aspnes, David Eisenstat, Rati Gelashvili, and Ronald L. Rivest. 2017. Time-Space Trade-offs in Population Protocols. In *Proceedings of the Twenty-Eighth Annual ACM-SIAM Symposium on Discrete Algorithms, SODA 2017, Barcelona, Spain, Hotel Porta Fira, January 16-19*, Philip N. Klein (Ed.). SIAM, 2560–2579. https://doi.org/10.1137/1.9781611974782.169

[2] Dan Alistarh, James Aspnes, and Rati Gelashvili. 2018. Space-Optimal Majority in Population Protocols. In *Proceedings of the Twenty-Ninth Annual ACM-SIAM Symposium on Discrete Algorithms, SODA 2018, New Orleans, LA, USA, January 7-10, 2018*, Artur Czumaj (Ed.). SIAM, 2221–2239. https://doi.org/10.1137/1.9781611975031.144

[3] Dan Alistarh, Rati Gelashvili, and Milan Vojnovic. 2015. Fast and Exact Majority in Population Protocols. In *Proceedings of the 2015 ACM Symposium on Principles of Distributed Computing, PODC 2015, Donostia-San Sebastián, Spain, July 21 - 23, 2015*, Chryssis Georgiou and Paul G. Spirakis (Eds.). ACM, 47–56. https://doi.org/10.1145/2767386.2767429

[4] Dana Angluin, James Aspnes, Zoë Diamadi, Michael J. Fischer, and René Peralta. 2004. Computation in networks of passively mobile finite-state sensors. In *Proceedings of the Twenty-Third Annual ACM Symposium on Principles of Distributed Computing, PODC 2004, St. John's, Newfoundland, Canada, July 25-28, 2004*, Soma Chaudhuri and Shay Kutten (Eds.). ACM, 290–299. https://doi.org/10.1145/1011767.1011810

[5] Dana Angluin, James Aspnes, Zoë Diamadi, Michael J. Fischer, and René Peralta. 2006. Computation in networks of passively mobile finite-state sensors. *Distributed Computing* 18, 4 (2006), 235–253. https://doi.org/10.1007/s00446-005-0138-3

[6] Dana Angluin, James Aspnes, and David Eisenstat. 2008. Fast computation by population protocols with a leader. *Distributed Computing* 21, 3 (2008), 183–199. https://doi.org/10.1007/s00446-008-0067-z

[7] Dana Angluin, James Aspnes, David Eisenstat, and Eric Ruppert. 2007. The computational power of population protocols. *Distributed Computing* 20, 4 (2007), 279–304. https://doi.org/10.1007/s00446-007-0040-2

[8] Petra Berenbrink, Robert Elsässer, Tom Friedetzky, Dominik Kaaser, Peter Kling, and Tomasz Radzik. 2018. Majority & Stabilization in Population Protocols. *CoRR* abs/1805.04586 (2018). arXiv:1805.04586 https://arxiv.org/abs/1805.04586

[9] Petra Berenbrink, Robert Elsässer, Tom Friedetzky, Dominik Kaaser, Peter Kling, and Tomasz Radzik. 2018. A Population Protocol for Exact Majority with $O(\log^{5/3} n)$ Stabilization Time and $\Theta(\log n)$ States. In *32nd International Symposium on Distributed Computing, DISC 2018, New Orleans, LA, USA, October 15-19, 2018 (LIPIcs)*, Ulrich Schmid and Josef Widder (Eds.), Vol. 121. Schloss Dagstuhl - Leibniz-Zentrum fuer Informatik, 10:1–10:18. https://doi.org/10.4230/LIPIcs.DISC.2018.10

[10] Petra Berenbrink, Tom Friedetzky, Dominik Kaaser, and Peter Kling. 2019. Tight & Simple Load Balancing. In *Proceedings of the 33rd IEEE International Parallel and Distributed Processing Symposium (IPDPS), Rio de Janeiro, Brazil, 20–24 May 2019*. 718–726. https://doi.org/10.1109/IPDPS.2019.00080

[11] Petra Berenbrink, Dominik Kaaser, and Tomasz Radzik. 2019. On Counting the Population Size. *CoRR* abs/1905.11962 (2019). arXiv:1905.11962 https://arxiv.org/abs/1905.11962

[12] Andreas Bilke, Colin Cooper, Robert Elsässer, and Tomasz Radzik. 2017. Brief Announcement: Population Protocols for Leader Election and Exact Majority with $O(\log^2 n)$ States and $O(\log^2 n)$ Convergence Time. In *Proceedings of the ACM Symposium on Principles of Distributed Computing, PODC 2017, Washington, DC, USA, July 25-27, 2017*, Elad Michael Schiller and Alexander A. Schwarzmann (Eds.). ACM, 451–453. https://doi.org/10.1145/3087801.3087858

[13] David Doty and Mahsa Eftekhari. 2018. Efficient size estimation and impossibility of termination in uniform dense population protocols. *CoRR* abs/1808.08913 (2018). arXiv:1808.08913 https://arxiv.org/abs/1808.08913

[14] David Doty, Mahsa Eftekhari, Othon Michail, Paul G. Spirakis, and Michail Theofilatos. 2018. Brief Announcement: Exact Size Counting in Uniform Population Protocols in Nearly Logarithmic Time. In *32nd International Symposium on Distributed Computing, DISC 2018, New Orleans, LA, USA, October 15-19, 2018*. 46:1–46:3. https://doi.org/10.4230/LIPIcs.DISC.2018.46

[15] David Doty, Mahsa Eftekhari, Othon Michail, Paul G. Spirakis, and Michail Theofilatos. 2018. Exact size counting in uniform population protocols in nearly logarithmic time. *CoRR* abs/1805.04832 (2018). arXiv:1805.04832 https://arxiv.org/abs/1805.04832

[16] David Doty and David Soloveichik. 2018. Stable leader election in population protocols requires linear time. *Distributed Computing* 31, 4 (2018), 257–271. https://doi.org/10.1007/s00446-016-0281-z

[17] Moez Draief and Milan Vojnovic. 2012. Convergence Speed of Binary Interval Consensus. *SIAM J. Control and Optimization* 50, 3 (2012), 1087–1109. https://doi.org/10.1137/110823018

[18] Leszek Gasieniec and Grzegorz Stachowiak. 2018. Fast Space Optimal Leader Election in Population Protocols. In *Proceedings of the Twenty-Ninth Annual ACM-SIAM Symposium on Discrete Algorithms, SODA 2018, New Orleans, LA, USA, January 7-10, 2018*. SIAM, 2653–2667. https://doi.org/10.1137/1.9781611975031.169

[19] Adrian Kosowski and Przemyslaw Uznanski. 2018. Brief Announcement: Population Protocols Are Fast. In *Proceedings of the 2018 ACM Symposium on Principles of Distributed Computing, PODC 2018, Egham, United Kingdom, July 23-27, 2018*. 475–477. https://dl.acm.org/citation.cfm?id=3212788

[20] George B. Mertzios, Sotiris E. Nikoletseas, Christoforos L. Raptopoulos, and Paul G. Spirakis. 2017. Determining majority in networks with local interactions and very small local memory. *Distributed Computing* 30, 1 (2017), 1–16. https://doi.org/10.1007/s00446-016-0277-8

Self-Stabilizing Leader Election

Hsueh-Ping Chen
Department of Electrical Engineering, National Taiwan University
Taipei, Taiwan
r07921034@ntu.edu.tw

Ho-Lin Chen
Department of Electrical Engineering, National Taiwan University
Taipei, Taiwan
holinchen@ntu.edu.tw

ABSTRACT

In this paper, we study the self-stabilizing leader election (SSLE) problem in population protocols. We construct a non-deterministic population protocol that can solve SSLE on directed rings of all sizes. Our algorithm uses a constant number of states and can be converted to a deterministic population protocol on undirected rings using previous techniques [8]. Furthermore, we extend our algorithm to perform SSLE on directed and undirected tori of arbitrary sizes.

CCS CONCEPTS

• **Theory of computation → Distributed algorithms.**

KEYWORDS

leader election, self-stabilizing, population protocols, ring, torus

ACM Reference Format:
Hsueh-Ping Chen and Ho-Lin Chen. 2019. Self-Stabilizing Leader Election. In *2019 ACM Symposium on Principles of Distributed Computing (PODC '19), July 29-August 2, 2019, Toronto, ON, Canada.* ACM, New York, NY, USA, 7 pages. https://doi.org/10.1145/3293611.3331616

1 INTRODUCTION

In distributed systems, many tasks can be solved easily if there exists a special processor, called the leader, to organize the jobs. Thus, electing a leader from a group of processors is an important and basic problem in distributed computing, and has been studied extensively.

Population protocols [4] are an asynchronous and anonymous model of distributed computing, which is used to model systems with simple units such as sensor networks or chemical reaction networks [13, 21]. Generally speaking, in the model of a population protocol, there is a set of agents, which can be viewed as machines with finite states. Each agent is anonymous in the sense that an agent cannot distinguish two agents with the same states. In each time step, a pair of agents are chosen by the scheduler to update their states by doing a pairwise interaction, and the behaviour of the scheduler cannot be predicted. In the beginning, every agent in the system has a starting state, which forms the starting configuration of the system. Then, the agents interact with each other following the interaction rules defined by the protocol. Eventually, the system is expected to converge to some legitimate configurations depending on the problem we discuss. Although a system designer is not allowed to control the scheduler, by adding some fairness conditions, agents can still work together to perform complicated computation [7, 10]. Many tasks have been studied in population protocols, including majority [3, 6], counting [9, 11], and leader election [1, 2, 16].

In [5], population protocols are shown to be able to simulate a register machine with high probability when a unique leader is provided in the initial configuration, which serves as a motivation for study of leader election in population protocols. Some results about the time and space complexity of leader election algorithms can be found in [1, 2, 16].

A distributed algorithm is self-stabilizing [14] if it always converges to the desired result regardless of what the starting configuration of the system is. A self-stabilizing algorithm can recover from any transient failure, which makes the computation reliable. Since distributed systems may suffer from some unexpected errors in practice, we are interested in self-stabilizing leader election (SSLE) algorithms.

SSLE has been studied in many different systems. Itkis and Levin [18] proposed a randomized algorithm that can do SSLE on arbitrary undirected graph with each processor having constant memory space. In their system, a processor can read the content of all its neighbours when doing computation and set a pointer to one of its neighbours. Itkis et al. [19] presented a deterministic algorithm that can do SSLE on rings of prime sizes. In [15], the authors designed a randomized algorithm that can do SSLE on arbitrary undirected graph but their requirement for memory space is $O(\log(n))$ bits, where n is the number of processors.

There also have been some studies for SSLE in population protocols with different underlying topologies. Leader election on a ring is of particular interest due to the traditional token ring LAN. Angluin et al. [8] proposed a population protocol for SSLE on rings of all odd sizes, and left SSLE on rings of all sizes as an open problem. The proposed protocol uses a constant number of states. Fischer et al. [17] introduced an oracle called *eventual detector* $\Omega?$ which can detect whether there is any leader in the ring, and they presented a protocol to solve SSLE on rings of all sizes given the oracle $\Omega?$. On the other hand, Cai et al. [12] showed that under global fairness, it is impossible to solve SSLE on complete graphs using only $n-1$ states, where n is the number of agents.

Our result: The main result of this paper is a non-deterministic population protocol that can solve SSLE on directed rings of all sizes without using any oracle. The protocol uses a constant number

Research supported in part by MOST (Taiwan) grant number 107-2221-E-002-031-MY3.

PODC '19, July 29-August 2, 2019, Toronto, ON, Canada

ACM ISBN 978-1-4503-6217-7/19/07...$15.00
https://doi.org/10.1145/3293611.3331616

of states, and it can be transformed into a deterministic one by applying the result from [8]. Furthermore, the protocol can also work on undirected rings based on a result from the same paper [8]. By presenting this protocol, we solve the open problem proposed by Angluin et al. [8].

In the protocol, we use a special sequence called the *Thue-Morse sequence*, which has been used to detect cycles for the SSLE algorithm on general graphs (in a model different from population protocols) [18]. Although their algorithm cannot directly apply to population protocols, the cube-freeness property of the Thue-Morse sequences still plays an important role in our protocol. We use the sequence to check whether there exists a leader in the ring, which is a key step to do SSLE on a ring. We also generalize our result to SSLE protocols on undirected tori of arbitrary sizes.

The rest of this paper is organized as follows. In section 2, we introduce the definition of population protocols, and also define the SSLE problem formally. In section 3, we describe our main result of solving SSLE on rings. In section 4, we extend the result to tori of arbitrary sizes. In section 5, we give the conclusion of our result, and propose some directions for future research.

2 PRELIMINARIES

In this section, we give the formal definitions of population protocols and self-stabilization, and some of which follow from [8]. Simplified from previous definitions, we define population protocols without inputs, which is sufficient for our results in this paper since we only consider self-stabilizing protocols. The definition of population protocols with inputs can be found in [10].

A population protocol $P(Q, Y, o, \delta)$ consists of four components: the set Q of states, the set Y of outputs, the output function $o : Q \longrightarrow Y$ that maps the state of an agent to its corresponding output, and the transition function $\delta : Q \times Q \longrightarrow \mathcal{P}(Q \times Q) - \{\emptyset\}$, where $\mathcal{P}(Q \times Q)$ denotes the power set of $Q \times Q$. The transition function maps the state pair of the two agents to all the possible state pair of the two agents after an interaction. A population protocol is deterministic when its transition function is deterministic, which becomes $\delta : Q \times Q \longrightarrow Q \times Q$.

A population protocol can be executed on arbitrary communication graphs $G = (V, E)$. Each node $v \in V$ represents an agent, and two agents u, v are allowed to interact with each other if and only if $(u, v) \in E$.

A *configuration* of a population protocol on a graph $G = (V, E)$ is a function $C : V \longrightarrow Q$, that maps each agent to its state, and a *starting configuration* is a configuration that specifies the starting states of all agents in the system. For two configurations C_1, C_2 we define a relation as follows: $C_1 \longrightarrow C_2$ if there exists two agents $u, v \in V$ such that $(C_2(u), C_2(v)) \in \delta(C_1(u), C_1(v))$ and for any other agent $w \notin \{u, v\}, C_1(w) = C_2(w)$. We say that a configuration C' is reachable from a configuration C if $C \overset{*}{\longrightarrow} C'$, where $\overset{*}{\longrightarrow}$ denotes the transitive closure of $\longrightarrow$. A configuration C is called an *output-stable* configuration, if for every C' reachable from C, we have $\forall v \in V, o(C(v)) = o(C'(v))$.

In the system, there exists a scheduler that controls the interactions between agents. At each time step, the scheduler picks a pair of agents $(u, v) \in E$ to take part in an interaction, where we say the edge (u, v) is *activated*. In an interaction where the edge $(u, v) \in E$ is activated, the agent u is called the *initiator* and the agent v is called the *responder*.

An *execution* of a population protocol on a graph given the starting configuration C_0 is an infinite sequence of configurations $C_0, C_1, \ldots$ where $C_i \longrightarrow C_{i+1}$ for $i = 0, 1, 2 \ldots$. We say that the execution satisfies *global fairness* when the following condition holds: if a configuration C appears infinitely often in an execution, then for any configuration C' with $C \longrightarrow C'$, C' must appear infinitely often in the execution. Intuitively, it means that any configuration that is always reachable will eventually be reached.

A population protocol is *self-stabilizing* if for every globally-fair execution of the protocol, it can reach one of the legitimate output-stable configurations from any starting configuration.

For any population protocol to solve the leader election problem, the set of outputs is required to be $\{L, N\}$, where L represents a leader, and N represents a non-leader. We say that an execution $C_0, C_1, \ldots$ of a population protocol on a graph $G = (V, E)$ *selects a leader* if there exists a positive integer t and an agent $v \in V$ such that $i \geq t$ implies $o(C_i(v)) = L$ and $o(C_i(w)) = N$ for any $w \neq v$. A population protocol is said to be a *self-stabilizing* implementation of the leader election problem on a graph if every execution of the protocol on the graph selects a leader no matter what the starting configuration is.

3 SELF-STABILIZING LEADER ELECTION ON RINGS

Angluin *et al.* [8] proposed an open question about whether it is possible to design a population protocol that solves SSLE on rings of arbitrary sizes, using only a constant number of states. In this section, we answer this question by presenting a non-deterministic population protocol, called RingSSLE, which solves SSLE on a directed ring.

RingSSLE uses two sub-protocols, which we introduce in section 3.1 and section 3.2. In section 3.3, we describe RingSSLE and prove its correctness.

3.1 Generate a Cube-free String

In this section, we describe a protocol, called GenThue, which can set the string in a directed ring to be a cube-free string. A string is cube-free if there is no substring of this form "www" ('w' is a string). First, we introduce a famous cube-free string below:

Definition 3.1 (Thue-Morse String [22]). Let $TM_0 = 0$ and $TM_{2^{n+1}} = TM_{2^n}\overline{TM_{2^n}}$, which means that $TM_{2^{n+1}}$ is obtained by concatenating TM_{2^n} and the bitwise complement of TM_{2^n}. Thue-Morse String is defined as TM_∞.

In the protocol GenThue, every agent carries a 0-1 bit (by state field B), and the goal of the protocol is to set the **ring string** to be a prefix of Thue-Morse String. Consider a directed ring $G = (V, E)$ with $|V| = n$, and assume that there exists a special agent L called the leader in the ring. A string $s = s_1s_2 \ldots s_n$ is the **ring string** of G if there exists n distinct nodes $v_1, v_2, \ldots, v_n \in V$ with $v_1 = L$ and $(v_i, v_j) \in E$ for $i = 1, 2, \ldots, n-1$ such that $s_i = v_i.B$ for $i = 1, 2, \ldots, n$.

The state of an agent is represented by a vector (L, B, M, S). $L \in \{0, 1\}$ is an indicator to the leader, $B \in \{0, 1\}$ is the bit of the string we want to construct, and $M \in \{0, 1, 2, 3\}, S \in \{-2, -1, 0, 1, 2, 3\}$ are the remaining state fields for the protocol to construct the string. We summarize the main idea of GENTHUE in Lemma 3.2.

LEMMA 3.2. *The protocol GENTHUE would reach a configuration where the ring string is a prefix of Thue-Morse String from a starting configuration where exactly one agent x with* $x.L = 1, x.B = 0, x.S = 2, x.M = 1$*, and all the other agents* $y \neq x$ *with* $y.L = y.S = y.M = 0$.

PROOF. The design of GENTHUE directly follows from the definition of Thue-Morse String. Starting from a leader, the protocol repeatedly copy the bitwise complement of the current string (state field $M = 2$) to the next section of agents (state field $M = 0$). When a bit (state field B) of an agent is copied, the protocol set its state field $M \leftarrow 1$, and store the bit information in the signal (state field $S \leftarrow 2 - B$), which would propagate along the directed edge to the first unmarked agent (state field $M = 0$). After modifying the bit of the unmarked agent, the protocol set its state field $M \leftarrow 3$, and send a signal (state field $S = -1$) back to copy another bit. When the bitwise complement of the current string has been copied to the next section of agents, one round of the copy process is finished. The protocol starts a new round of copy by sending a signal (state field $S = -2$) and reset agents of the string by setting $M \leftarrow 2$. The above procedure is repeated until the tail of the bit string meets the leader, and the ring string is a prefix of Thue-Morse String. □

Protocol 1 GENTHUE(x,y)

Input: agent x is the initiator, agent y is the responder
if $y.L = 1$ **then** ▷ stop constructing the string
  $x.S \leftarrow 0$
else if $(x.S \in \{1, 2\}) \wedge (y.M = 0)$ **then** ▷ change the bit according to the signal
  $y.B \leftarrow x.S - 1,\ y.M \leftarrow 3,\ y.S \leftarrow -1,\ x.S \leftarrow 0$
else if $(x.S = 3) \wedge (y.M = 0)$ **then**
  $x.S \leftarrow -2$ ▷ a signal to initiate a new round of copy
else if $(x.S > 0) \wedge (y.M \neq 0)$ **then**
  $y.S \leftarrow x.S,\ x.S \leftarrow 0$ ▷ signal propagates
else if $(x.M = 1) \wedge (y.S = -1) \wedge (y.M = 2)$ **then**
  $y.M \leftarrow 1,\ y.S \leftarrow 2 - y.B$ ▷ store the bit information
else if $(x.M = 1) \wedge (y.S = -1) \wedge (y.M = 3)$ **then**
  $y.S \leftarrow 3$ ▷ a round of copy has finished
else if $(x.M \neq 1) \wedge (y.S = -1)$ **then**
  $x.S \leftarrow -1,\ y.S \leftarrow 0$
else if $(x.L = 1) \wedge (y.S = -2)$ **then** ▷ a new round of copy starts
  $x.M \leftarrow 1,\ y.M \leftarrow 2,\ x.S \leftarrow 2 - x.B,\ y.S \leftarrow 0$
else if $y.S = -2$ **then** ▷ signal propagates backward to start a new round of copy
  $x.S \leftarrow -2,\ y.S \leftarrow 0$

3.2 Check Three Strings

In this section, we describe the protocol CHECKTHREE. Starting from a special agent (called the K-agent), the protocol finds the next three K-agents and compares the three strings between each pair of adjacent K-agents. The protocol generates a leader and a barrier when the three strings are identical and do not contain leaders. The four K-agents may overlap if there are less than four K-agents in the whole ring. (For example, if there are only three K-agents in the ring, then the first and fourth K-agents are the same agent.)

The state of an agent is represented by a vector $(L, B, S, M, K, A, C, I, R)$, where (L, B, S, M) are the same as that defined in GENTHUE protocol. The possible values of the other state fields are listed below:

- $K, R \in \{0, 1\}$
- $A = (A_1, A_2, A_3), A_i \in \{0, 1\}$ for $i \in \{1, 2, 3\}$
- $C = (C_1, C_2, C_3), C_i \in \{0, 1\}$ for $i \in \{1, 2, 3\}$
- $I = (I_1, I_2, I_3), I_i \in \{-2, -1, 0, 1, 2, 3, 4, 5\}$ for $i \in \{1, 2, 3\}$

The state field K is used to separate the three strings to be compared. The agents with the state field $K = 1$ are called the K-agents. The agent with $R = 1$ is the barrier. It has no function in the CHECKTHREE protocol and will be explained in section 3.3. The field A_i is set to 1 if and only if the agent is part of the i-th string. Notice that an agent may belong to more than one string if there are less than four K-agents on the ring. The field $C_i = 1$ if the agent is in the i-th string and the bit stored in this agent is identical to the corresponding bits in the other two strings. The fields labeled I_i are used to propagate the information and make the comparisons between different strings.

Starting from the first K-agent, the protocol can recognize three strings between these K-agents by the following way: starting from a K-agent, a signal for initialization $I = (0, 0, -1)$ goes in the opposite direction of the directed edges of the ring. The signal marks all agents between the starting K-agent and the first K-agent it meets as the third string by setting the state field $A_3 \leftarrow 1$, and the signal becomes $I \leftarrow (0, -1, 0)$. Then, it marks agents between the first K-agent and the second K-agent as the second string by setting the state field $A_2 \leftarrow 1$, and the signal becomes $I \leftarrow (-1, 0, 0)$. Finally, the signal marks agents between the second K-agent and the third K-agent as the first string by setting the state field $A_1 \leftarrow 1$. After recognizing the three strings, the initialization for a comparison process is finished, and the protocol starts the comparison process. Note that if the signal for initialization meets a leader, the signal is deleted by setting $I \leftarrow (0, 0, 0)$, which ensures that the three strings are formed by non-leader agents.

The comparison process works as follows: in every round, it marks one bit of the first string by setting the field $C_1 \leftarrow 1$, and then it uses field I to propagate this bit information forward to the second and third strings. If the bit of the second/third string is the same as that of the first string, it marks the bit of the second/third string by setting the field $C_2 \leftarrow 1/C_3 \leftarrow 1$. Then a signal is sent backward to start a new round of comparison. After completing all the comparison, if the three strings are identical, a leader and a barrier is generated.

In the above description, we illustrate how the protocol generates a leader when the three bit-strings (formed by non-leader agents) between four K-agents are identical. When there is only one K-agent in the ring, all four K-agents defined by the protocol will be the same agent and all three sequences being compared are the entire string in the ring. In this case, the comparison process would generate a leader and a barrier since the three strings it compares are identical. This result is formally stated in the following lemma.

LEMMA 3.3. *The protocol* CHECKTHREE *would reach a configuration where there is one agent z with $z.L = z.R = 1$ (a leader and a barrier) from a starting configuration where exactly one agent x with $x.K = 1$, $x.C = (0, 0, 0)$, $x.I = (0, 0, -1)$, $x.L = 0$, and all the other agents y with $y.K = 0$, $y.C = (0, 0, 0)$, $y.I = (0, 0, 0)$, $y.L = 0$.*

Protocol 2 CHECKTHREE(x,y)

```
Input: agent x is the initiator, agent y is the responder
  procedure INIT(p, q, j)                       ▷ p,q are agents, j is the index
    Define r = 𝟙(q.K = 1)
    if (j = 1) ∧ (q.K = 1) then
      q.A_1 ← 1, q.I_1 ← q.B + 1                ▷ the initialization is completed
    else if p.A_{j−r} = 0 then  ▷ avoid two comparison processes working on the same agent
      p.I_{j−r} ← −1, q.A_j ← 1, q.I_j ← 0
  end procedure
  procedure PROPAGATE(p, q, i, j)    ▷ p,q are agents, i,j are indices
    if (q.A_j = 1) ∧ (i > 0) ∧ (j > 0) then ▷ check if the agent is reset (see Section 3.3)
      if p.I ∈ {3, 4} then
        q.I_j ← p.I_i − 2(j − i), p.I_i ← 0
      else if p.I ∈ {1, 2} then
        q.I_j ← p.I_i(1 − j + i), p.I_i ← 0
      else
        q.I_j ← p.I_i, p.I_i ← 0
  end procedure
  Define z = 𝟙((x.K = 0) ∧ (y.K = 1))  ▷ 𝟙 denotes the indicator function
  if Σ_{i=1}^{3} 𝟙(x.I_i ≠ 0) + 𝟙(y.I_i ≠ 0) ≥ 2 then ▷ make sure there is only one signal
    x.I ← y.I ← (0, 0, 0)
  else if Σ_{i=1}^{3} 𝟙(x.I_i ≠ 0) = 1 then
    Define j be the index such that x.I_j ≠ 0
    if (x.I_3 = 5) ∧ (z = 1) then
      y.L ← y.R ← 1, y.B ← 0, y.S ← 2, y.M ← 1
    else if (x.I_3 ∈ {3, 4}) ∧ (z = 1) then
      x.I_3 ← −2
    else if (x.I_j = 5 ∧ y.C_{j+z} = 1) ∨ (x.I_j ∈ {3, 4}) ∨ (x.I_j ∈ {1, 2} ∧ x.C_j = 1) then
      execute PROPAGATE(x, y, j, j + z)
    else if (x.I_j ∈ {1, 2}) ∧ (x.C_j = 0) ∧ (x.B = x.I_i − 1) then
      x.C_j ← 1, x.I_j ← x.I_j + 2
  else if Σ_{i=1}^{3} 𝟙(y.I_i ≠ 0) = 1 then
    Define j be the index such that y.I_j ≠ 0
    if y.I_j = −1 then
      execute INIT(x, y, j)
    else
      if x.C_{j−z} = 1 ∧ j − z = 1 then
        y.C_j ← 1, y.I_j ← (y.B + 3)(1 − z) + 5z
      else
        execute PROPAGATE(y, x, j, j − z)
```

3.3 Main Result

In this section, we introduce a protocol, called RINGSSLE, which can solve SSLE on rings of arbitrary sizes. The two sub-protocols GENTHUE and CHECKTHREE in the previous sections are the building blocks for RINGSSLE.

RINGSSLE has two non-deterministic operations: (1) Arbitrarily reset some state fields of GENTHUE and CHECKTHREE. (2) Start an initialization for a new comparison process of CHECKTHREE (from any K-agent in the ring). The two non-deterministic operations are the key components for RINGSSLE to do SSLE.

The concept for RINGSSLE to do SSLE is the following. First, from any configuration without a leader, the protocol can reset the state fields of all agents to reach a configuration that GENTHUE and CHECKTHREE can work correctly. Then, it starts an initialization for a new comparison process of CHECKTHREE, which can generate a leader and a barrier in the ring by Lemma 3.3. Second, from any configuration with more than one leader, leaders will repeatedly send bullets to kill each other, reducing the number of leaders. When there is only one leader in the ring, a barrier can protect the leader from being killed by itself. Third, when there is exactly one leader in the ring, the sub-protocol GENTHUE can set the ring string to be cube-free by Lemma 3.2, which prevents the sub-protocol CHECKTHREE from generating more leaders.

The state of an agent in RINGSSLE is represented by a vector $(L, B, M, S, K, C, I, A, R, U)$, where $(L, B, M, S, K, C, I, A, R)$ is the same as that defined in the protocols GENTHUE and CHECKTHREE, $R \in \{0, 1\}$ is the barrier that prevents a leader being killed by the bullet, and $U \in \{0, 1\}$ is the bullet that kills leaders.

Protocol 3 RINGSSLE(x,y)

```
Input: agent x is the initiator, agent y is the responder
  Define coin_1, coin_2 as random true-false values generated in this interaction.
  if coin_1 then         ▷ reset some state fields of CHECKTHREE and GENTHUE
    x.K ← x.M ← x.S ← 0, x.C ← x.I ← x.A ← (0, 0, 0)
  if coin_2 then ▷ start an initialization for the comparison process of CHECKTHREE
    x.K ← 1, x.C ← (0, 0, 0), x.I ← (0, 0, −1), y.K ← 0, y.C ← y.I ← y.A ← (0, 0, 0)
  execute GENTHUE(x, y)
  execute CHECKTHREE(x, y)
  if x.L = 1 ∧ y.R ≠ 1 then
    y.U ← 1                                ▷ a leader sends bullets
  if y.R = 1 then
    x.R ← 1, x.U ← 0, y.R ← 0  ▷ barrier moves from y to x, and clears bullet
  else if x.U = 1 then
    y.L ← 0, y.U ← 1, x.U ← 0   ▷ bullet moves from x to y, and kills leader
```

Now, we will show that RINGSSLE does perform SSLE on rings of arbitrary sizes by proving that the system will eventually reach and stay in safe configurations defined below:

Definition 3.4 (safe configuration). A configuration that satisfies the following four conditions is called a *clean configuration*:

(1) For every agent x, $x.M = x.S = x.K = x.U = 0, x.C = x.I = x.A = (0, 0, 0)$.
(2) There is exactly one agent y with $y.L = 1$. (The configuration has exactly one leader.)
(3) There is exactly one agent z with $z.R = 1$. (The configuration has exactly one barrier.)
(4) The ring string is cube-free.

All configurations reachable from a clean configuration are *safe configurations.*

LEMMA 3.5. *Starting from a clean configuration, no leader can be created.*

PROOF. The only way for RINGSSLE to generate a leader is executing sub-protocol CHECKTHREE. We also know that CHECKTHREE can generate a leader under either of the following two situations: (1) When the three bit-strings (formed by non-leader agents) between four K-agents are identical. (2) There is no leader in the ring. In the clean configuration, the ring string is cube-free, and there is one leader in the ring, so CHECKTHREE would not generate a leader if its comparison process works normally.

However, RINGSSLE will non-deterministically reset some state fields of CHECKTHREE or start an initialization for a new comparison process of CHECKTHREE, which seems to have a chance to mess up the comparison process. Here, we claim that CHECKTHREE still wouldn't generate a leader when taking the non-deterministic operations into consideration. The comparison process would work unexpectedly if the following two situations happen: (1) Two comparison processes work on the same agent. (2) Some agent of a comparison process (state fields $A_i = 1$ for $i \in \{1, 2, 3\}$) is reset by the protocol. We argue below that in both situations, the comparison process would not generate a leader.

If the three strings recognized by the new comparison process have an overlap with that of the old comparison process, the new comparison process would not complete its initialization, not to mention to generate a leader. This fact follows from the design of the initialization for a new comparison process. During the initialization, a signal (state field $I_i = -1$ for $i \in \{1, 2, 3\}$) to initiate a new comparison process is sent to mark all agents of the three strings. When this signal meets an agent of an old comparison process (state field $A_i = 1$ where i is the index such that $I_i = -1$), the signal cannot propagate, and the new comparison process would not complete its initialization.

If one agent of a comparison process is reset, the comparison process would be aware of it. This is because when a signal of the comparison process meets an agent whose state fields are reset (state field $A_i = 0$ for $i \in \{1, 2, 3\}$), the signal cannot propagate, which implies no leader can be generated.

By the above argument, we can conclude that RINGSSLE will not generate any leader starting from a safe configuration. □

LEMMA 3.6. *Starting from a clean configuration, the leader in the ring will not be deleted.*

PROOF. A leader is deleted when a bullet agent (state field $U = 1$) reacts with it. In a clean configuration, there is no bullet, and only a leader can produce a bullet. However, there exists a barrier in the clean configuration, which can prevent the leader from being killed by the bullet it produced because of the following design of RINGSSLE. A bullet moves in the clockwise direction starting from the leader and a barrier moves in the counter-clockwise direction, which implies a bullet must encounter a barrier before it can react with the leader. □

LEMMA 3.7. *In the safe configuration, there is exactly one leader.*

PROOF. A safe configuration is reachable from a clean configuration, and there is exactly one leader in the clean configuration. By Lemma 3.5 and Lemma 3.6, starting from a clean configuration, no more leader can be generated and the leader in the ring will not be deleted. Thus, there is exactly on leader in the safe configuration. □

LEMMA 3.8. *For any configuration with no leader, a clean configuration is reachable.*

PROOF. When there is no leader in the ring, RINGSSLE can always generate a leader as described below. First, for every agent, reset the state fields of sub-protocol GENTHUE and CHECKTHREE. Second, select an agent x and set its state field $x.K \leftarrow 1, x.I \leftarrow (0, 0, -1)$. By Lemma 3.3, the sub-protocol CHECKTHREE will generate a leader and a barrier. Then the protocol can make the barrier do a round trip of the ring, which will delete all bullets in the ring if there is any and merge all the barriers in the way. Now, the configuration has exactly one leader, one barrier and no bullets.

When the leader y is generated by CHECKTHREE, its state field for GENTHUE is set ($y.B \leftarrow 0, y.S \leftarrow 2, y.M \leftarrow 1$). By Lemma 3.2, a prefix of Thue-Morse String will be generated in the ring, which meets the cube-freeness requirement of the clean configuration.

Finally, for every agent, RINGSSLE can again reset the state fields of sub-protocol GENTHUE and CHECKTHREE. And the clean configuration is reached. □

LEMMA 3.9. *For any configuration with non-zero leaders, a configuration with no leader or a clean configuration is reachable.*

PROOF. If there is no barrier in the ring, RINGSSLE can make leaders send bullets to kill themselves, and a configuration with no leader is reached. When there are non-zero barriers in the ring, the protocol can make them move into the same agent, which reduces the number of barriers to one. Then, RINGSSLE can make leaders send bullets to kill themselves, and since there is only one barrier in the ring, the number of leaders can be reduced to at most one. If reduced to zero, then a configuration with no leader is reached. If there is one leader left and the configuration is not clean, then a new leader and barrier can be generated. Now, make the two barriers merge into one, and make the new leader send a bullet to kill the old one. As stated in the previous lemma, the protocol can then generate a prefix of Thue-Morse String in the ring and reset the state fields of sub-protocol GENTHUE and CHECKTHREE, which leads to a clean configuration. □

LEMMA 3.10. *For any configuration of RINGSSLE, a clean configuration is reachable.*

PROOF. Lemma 3.8 and lemma 3.9 directly imply this result. □

THEOREM 3.11. *Assuming global fairness, there exists a nondeterministic population protocol using constant number of states which solves SSLE on rings of arbitrary sizes.*

PROOF. By Lemma 3.10, a clean configuration is reachable from any configuration of RINGSSLE. By the assumption of global fairness, a configuration that is infinitely reachable in the execution is reached. Thus, a clean configuration is reached, and by the definition of a safe configuration, the configuration of RINGSSLE would keep being a safe configuration, which implies that the leader election is completed (by lemma 3.7). Since in the description of our protocol, the number of states is independent of the size of the ring, we can conclude that the protocol requires constant number of states for the ring of arbitrary sizes. □

Though our protocol is non-deterministic, it's easy to verify that RINGSSLE satisfies the condition of Theorem 3.5 of [8], which implies there exists a deterministic protocol for SSLE on rings and the number of states used in each agent is still independent of the size of the ring.

In the end, we give a brief discussion about the time complexity of RINGSSLE without the detailed proof. Earlier, our assumption is that the execution of the protocol is globally-fair, but we would prefer considering a probabilistic scheduler here to simplify the analysis of time complexity. At each time step, the probabilistic scheduler uniformly and randomly picks a pair of agents to update their states, and all the possible state transitions are happened with equal probability.

First, we compute the least number of interactions to reach a safe configuration from the worst starting configuration. Let n denote the number of agents in the ring. When there is no leader in the starting configuration and the sequence is cube-free, it takes $O(n^2)$ interactions for the sub-protocol CHECKTHREE to generate a leader. Then, it takes $O(n^2)$ interactions for the sub-protocol GENTHUE to set the ring string to be a prefix of Thue-Morse String. Since all the other detailed procedures of RINGSSLE only take less interactions, the protocol can reach a safe configuration from arbitrary starting configuration using $O(n^2)$ interactions. As the scheduler is uniformly random, the probability that the scheduler follows a predetermined sequences of interactions with length $O(n^2)$ is at least $(1/n)^{O(n^2)}$, which implies that the expected number of steps to reach a safe configuration is upper bounded by $2^{O(n^2 log(n))}$ in the worst case.

RINGSSLE is only a construction for proving that SSLE on rings is computable, whether there exists a more efficient protocol or the expensive time complexity is intrinsic to the task itself is an interesting problem for future research.

4 SELF-STABILIZING LEADER ELECTION ON TORI

4.1 Self-stabilizing leader election on a torus

In this section, we extend our SSLE protocol on rings to an SSLE protocol on tori of arbitrary sizes.

Definition 4.1 (torus). An $m \times n$ torus is a graph $G = (V, E)$, where $V = \{v_{i,j} | 0 \leq i < m \wedge 0 \leq j < n\}$, and $E = \{\{v_{w,x}, v_{y,z}\} | (w = y \wedge z \equiv x + 1 \pmod{n}) \vee (x = z \wedge y \equiv w + 1 \pmod{m})\}$.

We modify the definition of torus orientation from [20] to get the relaxed definition for our purpose to do leader election in population protocol.

Definition 4.2 (relaxed torus orientation). A torus is oriented if it satisfies the following:

(1) Every agent in the torus has a local name, and it also records the local names of its four neighbours, which must be different for an agent to distinguish its neighbours.
(2) Every agent labels its four neighbours as North(N), East(E), South(S) or West(W), and the labels for the four neighbours are different.
(3) For every agent u, let v, w be any two neighbours of u, if u is the only common neighbour of v and w, u should label v and w as opposite directions (N-S or E-W).
(4) For any pair of agents u, v on the same edge, their relative labels should follow the normal sense of orientation (ex: if u labels v as N, then v should label u as S).

For the above relaxed definition of torus orientation, we make sure that the direction N-S and E-W of all agents are globally consistent, but their direction of N and S can be opposite; similarly, E and W can be opposite. The relaxed torus orientation is sufficient for us to do SSLE on torus.

Kekkonen-Moneta [20] proposed an algorithm for self-stabilizing torus orientation under a distributed model different from population protocols, but their algorithm can be adapted to a relaxed torus orientation in population protocol, which we briefly describe below: First, naming each agent such that if the distance of two distinct agents are within four, they should be named by different local names. This can be done by requiring each agent maintaining a tree storing all names of agents within distance four, and agents can communicate with each other to ensure their naming are consistent. Also, when an agent finds there is a distinct agent within distance four having the same name with itself, it can randomly choose a new name from a finite set, and eventually, all agents within distance four have different names.

Besides the naming algorithm, the system also runs the other algorithm simultaneously to check whether the orientation defined by each agent is consistent, which would function correctly after the naming is correct. We demonstrate below how we check the four requirements of Definition 4.2: (1) is correct when the naming algorithm is finished. (2), (3) can be easily checked by an agent observing its own orientation and the naming tree. (4) can be ensured during the pairwise interaction of two agents. By the above description, we can have the following lemma:

LEMMA 4.3. *Under global fairness, there exists a population protocol using constant number of states to solve self-stabilizing relaxed torus orientation.*

Since an $m \times n$ oriented torus contains m (N-S) rings connected in the (E-W) direction, the above lemma allows us to extend our SSLE protocol to tori of arbitrary sizes.

THEOREM 4.4. *Under global fairness, there exists a population protocol using constant number of states which solves SSLE on $m \times n$ torus for arbitrary m, n.*

Proof. By Lemma 4.3, we can do self-stabilizing relaxed torus orientation, and get an oriented torus. A $m \times n$ oriented torus consists of m (N-S) rings and n (E-W) rings. By directly applying RingSsle on all (N-S) rings, we can select n candidates (called L_1) of the leaders in the (N-S) rings. Next, we add a rule to remove L_1 whenever an L_1 agent interact with a non-L_1 neighbour of direction E or W. Thus, L_1 agents will not be removed only when all the n L_1 agents are produced on the same (E-W) ring. In this case, we can simply select a leader of the torus from the n candidates by using RingSsle on this (E-W) ring simultaneously. □

5 CONCLUSION

In this paper, we show that there exists a population protocol that can perform SSLE on directed rings of all sizes, which solves the open problem proposed by Angluin et al. [8]. Furthermore, we extend our algorithm to perform SSLE on directed and undirected tori of arbitrary sizes.

In our protocol, it may take a long time to converge to a safe configuration given the constant reset of the state fields of sub-protocol CheckThree. Designing an efficient SSLE protocol and/or provide a lower bound is an interesting direction of future research. Besides, designing SSLE population protocols using constant states on other classes of graphs is another interesting open problem.

ACKNOWLEDGMENTS

We would like to thank Wing-Kai Hon for pointing us to the Thue-Morse sequence.

REFERENCES

[1] Dan Alistarh, James Aspnes, David Eisenstat, Rati Gelashvili, and Ronald L Rivest. 2017. Time-space trade-offs in population protocols. In *Proceedings of the twenty-eighth annual ACM-SIAM symposium on discrete algorithms*. SIAM, 2560–2579.

[2] Dan Alistarh and Rati Gelashvili. 2015. Polylogarithmic-time leader election in population protocols. In *International Colloquium on Automata, Languages, and Programming*. Springer, 479–491.

[3] Dan Alistarh, Rati Gelashvili, and Milan Vojnović. 2015. Fast and exact majority in population protocols. In *Proceedings of the 2015 ACM Symposium on Principles of Distributed Computing*. ACM, 47–56.

[4] Dana Angluin, James Aspnes, Zoë Diamadi, Michael J Fischer, and René Peralta. 2006. Computation in networks of passively mobile finite-state sensors. *Distributed computing* 18, 4 (2006), 235–253.

[5] Dana Angluin, James Aspnes, and David Eisenstat. 2008. Fast computation by population protocols with a leader. *Distributed Computing* 21, 3 (2008), 183–199.

[6] Dana Angluin, James Aspnes, and David Eisenstat. 2008. A simple population protocol for fast robust approximate majority. *Distributed Computing* 21, 2 (2008), 87–102.

[7] Dana Angluin, James Aspnes, David Eisenstat, and Eric Ruppert. 2007. The computational power of population protocols. *Distributed Computing* 20, 4 (2007), 279–304.

[8] Dana Angluin, James Aspnes, Michael J Fischer, and Hong Jiang. 2008. Self-stabilizing population protocols. *ACM Transactions on Autonomous and Adaptive Systems (TAAS)* 3, 4 (2008), 13.

[9] James Aspnes, Joffroy Beauquier, Janna Burman, and Devan Sohier. 2016. Time and space optimal counting in population protocols. *arXiv preprint arXiv:1611.07238* (2016).

[10] James Aspnes and Eric Ruppert. 2009. An introduction to population protocols. In *Middleware for Network Eccentric and Mobile Applications*. Springer, 97–120.

[11] Joffroy Beauquier, Janna Burman, Simon Clavière, and Devan Sohier. 2015. Space-optimal counting in population protocols. In *International Symposium on Distributed Computing*. Springer, 631–646.

[12] Shukai Cai, Taisuke Izumi, and Koichi Wada. 2012. How to prove impossibility under global fairness: On space complexity of self-stabilizing leader election on a population protocol model. *Theory of Computing Systems* 50, 3 (2012), 433–445.

[13] Ho-Lin Chen, David Doty, and David Soloveichik. 2014. Deterministic function computation with chemical reaction networks. *Natural computing* 13, 4 (2014), 517–534.

[14] Edsger W Dijkstra. 1974. Self-stabilizing Systems in Spite of Distributed Control. *Communications* (1974).

[15] Shlomi Dolev, Amos Israeli, and Shlomo Moran. 1997. Uniform dynamic self-stabilizing leader election. *IEEE Transactions on Parallel and Distributed Systems* 8, 4 (1997), 424–440.

[16] David Doty and David Soloveichik. 2018. Stable leader election in population protocols requires linear time. *Distributed Computing* 31, 4 (2018), 257–271.

[17] Michael Fischer and Hong Jiang. 2006. Self-stabilizing leader election in networks of finite-state anonymous agents. In *International Conference On Principles Of Distributed Systems*. Springer, 395–409.

[18] Gene Itkis and Leonid Levin. 1994. Fast and lean self-stabilizing asynchronous protocols. In *Proceedings of the 35th Annual Symposium on Foundations of Computer Science*. 226–239.

[19] Gene Itkis, Chengdian Lin, and Janos Simon. 1995. Deterministic, constant space, self-stabilizing leader election on uniform rings. In *International Workshop on Distributed Algorithms*. 288–302.

[20] Synnöve Kekkonen-Moneta. 2002. Torus orientation. *Distributed Computing* 15, 1 (2002), 39–48.

[21] David Soloveichik, Matthew Cook, Erik Winfree, and Jehoshua Bruck. 2008. Computation with finite stochastic chemical reaction networks. *Natural Computing* 7, 4 (2008), 615–633.

[22] Axel Thue. 1912. Uber die gegenseitige Lage gleicher Teile gewisser Zeichenreihen. *Kra. Vidensk. Selsk. Skrifer, I. Mat. Nat. Kl.* (1912), 1–67.

Brief Announcement: Logarithmic Expected-Time Leader Election in Population Protocol Model

Yuichi Sudo
y-sudou@ist.osaka-u.ac.jp
Osaka University
Suita, Osaka, Japan

Fukuhito Ooshita
f-oosita@is.naist.jp
Nara Institute of Science and Technology
Ikoma, Nara, Japan

Taisuke Izumi
t-izumi@nitech.ac.jp
Nagoya Institute of Technology
Nagoya, Aichi, Japan

Hirotsugu Kakugawa
kakugawa@rins.ryukoku.ac.jp
Ryukoku University
Otsu, Shiga, Japan

Toshimitsu Masuzawa
masuzawa@ist.osaka-u.ac.jp
Osaka University
Suita, Osaka, Japan

ABSTRACT

In this paper, we present a leader election protocol in the population protocol model that stabilizes within $O(\log n)$ parallel time in expectation with $O(\log n)$ states per agent, where n is the number of agents. Given a rough knowledge m of the population size n such that $m \geq \log_2 n$ and $m = O(\log n)$, this protocol guarantees that exactly one leader is elected and the unique leader is kept forever thereafter.

CCS CONCEPTS

• **Theory of computation → Distributed algorithms.**

KEYWORDS

population protocols, leader election

ACM Reference Format:
Yuichi Sudo, Fukuhito Ooshita, Taisuke Izumi, Hirotsugu Kakugawa, and Toshimitsu Masuzawa. 2019. Brief Announcement: Logarithmic Expected-Time Leader Election in Population Protocol Model. In *2019 ACM Symposium on Principles of Distributed Computing (PODC '19), July 29-August 2, 2019, Toronto, ON, Canada.* ACM, New York, NY, USA, 3 pages. https://doi.org/10.1145/3293611.3331585

1 INTRODUCTION

We consider the *population protocol* (PP) model [5] in this paper. A network called *population* consists of a large number of finite-state automata, called *agents*. Agents make *interactions* (i.e., pair-wise communication) each other by which they update their states. The interactions are opportunistic, that is, they are unpredictable. Agents are strongly anonymous: they do not have identifiers and they cannot distinguish their neighbors with the same states. As with the majority of studies on population protocols, we assume that the network of agents is a complete graph and that the scheduler selects an interacting pair of agents at each step uniformly at random.

In this paper, we focus on leader election problem, which is one of the most fundamental and well studied problems in the PP model. The leader election problem requires that starting from a specific initial configuration, a population reaches a safe configuration in which exactly one leader exists and the population keeps that unique leader thereafter.

There have been many works which study the leader election problem in the PP model (Table 1). Angluin et al. [5] gave the first leader election protocol in 2004, which stabilizes in $O(n)$ parallel time and uses only constant space of each agent, where n is the number of agents and "parallel time" means the number of steps in an execution divided by n. If we stick to constant space, this linear parallel time is optimal; Doty and Soloveichik [8] showed that any constant space protocol requires linear parallel time to elect a unique leader. Alistarh and Gelashvili [3] made a breakthrough in 2015; they achieve poly-logarithmic stabilization time ($O(\log^3 n)$ parallel time) by increasing the number of states from $O(1)$ to only $O(\log^3 n)$. Thereafter, the stabilization time has been improved by many studies [2, 7, 10–12]. Gąsieniec et al. [11] gave a state-of-art protocol that converges in $O(\log n \cdot \log\log n)$ parallel time in expectation with only $O(\log\log n)$ states. Its space complexity is optimal; Alistarh et al. [1] shows that any poly-logarithmic parallel time algorithm requires $\Omega(\log\log n)$ states. Michail et al. [12] gave a protocol with $O(\log n)$ parallel time in expectation but with a linear number of states. Those protocols with non-constant number of states [1–3, 7, 10, 11] are not *uniform*, that is, they require some rough knowledge of n. For example, in the protocol of [10], a $\Theta(\log\log n)$ value must be hard-coded to set the maximum value of one variable (named l in that paper). One can find detailed information about the leader election in the PP model in two survey papers [4, 9].

Our Contribution. In this paper, we present the *first* leader election protocol P_{LL} with logarithmic stabilization time and with a sub-polynomial number of states. Specifically, the proposed protocol P_{LL} stabilizes in $O(\log n)$ parallel time and uses only $O(\log n)$ states per agent. Compared to the state or art protocol [11], P_{LL} achieves shorter (and the fastest in the literature) stabilization time

PODC '19, July 29-August 2, 2019, Toronto, ON, Canada

ACM ISBN 978-1-4503-6217-7/19/07.
https://doi.org/10.1145/3293611.3331585

Table 1: Leader Election Protocols. (Stabilization time is shown in terms of parallel time and in expectation.)

	States	Stabilization Time
[5]	$O(1)$	$O(n)$
[3]	$O(\log^3 n)$	$O(\log^3 n)$
[1]	$O(\log^2 n)$	$O(\log^{5.3} n \cdot \log\log n)$
[7]	$O(\log^2 n)$	$O(\log^2 n)$
[2]	$O(\log n)$	$O(\log^2 n)$
[10]	$O(\log\log n)$	$O(\log^2 n)$
[11]	$O(\log\log n)$	$O(\log n \cdot \log\log n)$
[12]	$O(n)$	$O(\log n)$
This work	$O(\log n)$	$O(\log n)$

but uses larger space of each agent. Compared to [12], P_{LL} achieves drastically small space while maintaining the same stabilization time. The protocol P_{LL} is non-uniform as with the existing non-constant space protocols; it requires a rough knowledge m of n such that $m \geq \log_2 n$ and $m = \Theta(\log n)$.

2 LOGARITHMIC LEADER ELECTION

We give only key ideas of the proposed protocol P_{LL} in this paper due to the lack of space. Each agent v keeps output variable $v.\mathtt{leader} \in \{false, true\}$. An execution of P_{LL} can be regarded as a competition by agents. At the beginning of the execution, every agent has $\mathtt{leader} = true$, that is, all agents are leaders. Throughout the execution, every leader tries to remain a leader and tries to make all other leaders followers so that it becomes the unique leader in the population. The competition consists of three modules *QuickElimination*(), *Tournament*(), and *BackUp*(), which are executed in this order. These three modules guarantees the following properties:

QuickElimination(): An execution of this module takes $O(\log n)$ parallel time in expectation. For any $i \geq 2$, exactly i leaders survive an execution of this module with probability at most 2^{1-i}. The execution never eliminates all leaders, i.e., at least one leader always survives.

Tournament(): An execution of this module takes $O(\log n)$ parallel time in expectation. By an execution of this module, which starts with $i \geq 2$ leaders, the unique leader is elected with probability at least $1 - O(i/\log n)$. This lower bound of probability is independent of an execution of the previous module *QuickElimination*(). The execution never eliminates all leaders, i.e., at least one leader always survives.

BackUp(): An execution of this component elects a unique leader within $O(\log^2 n)$ parallel time in expectation.

From above, it holds that, after executions of *QuickElimination*() and *Tournament*() finish, the number of leaders is exactly one with probability at least $1 - \sum_{i=2}^{n} O\left(\frac{i}{2^{i-1}\log n}\right) = 1 - O(1/\log n)$. Therefore, combined with *BackUp*(), protocol P_{LL} elects a unique leader within $(1 - O(1/\log n)) \cdot \log n + O(1/\log n) \cdot O(\log^2 n) = O(\log n)$ parallel time in expectation.

In the remainder of this paper, we briefly give key ideas to design the three modules satisfying the above guarantees. These ideas are easily implemented with poly-logarithmic number of states per agent, that is, with a constant number of variables with $O(\log\log n)$ bits. Due to the lack of space, we omit from this paper a way to implement these key ideas with $O(\log n)$ states per agent. Moreover, in the following description of the key ideas, we assume a kind of global synchronization, for example, we assume that each agent begins an execution of *Tournament*() after *all* agents finish necessary operations of *QuickElimination*(). We also omit how to implement such synchronization. See the full pre-print paper [13] for those implementations.

2.1 Key Idea for *QuickElimination*()

The goal of this module is to reduce the number of leaders such that, for any $i \geq 2$, the resulting number of leaders is exactly i with probability at most 2^{1-i}. Actually, this module is based on almost the same idea as *the lottery protocol* in [1]. The protocol P_{LL} achieves much faster stabilization time than the lottery protocol thanks to tighter analysis on the number of surviving leaders, which we will see below, and the combination with the other two modules.

First, consider the following game:

- (i) Each agent in V executes a sequence of independent fair coin flips, each of which results in head with probability $1/2$ and tail with probability $1/2$, until it observes tail for the first time,
- (ii) Let s_v be the number of heads that v observes in the above coin flips and let $s_{\max} = \max_{v \in V} s_v$
- (iii) The agents v with $s_v = s_{\max}$ are winners and the other agents are losers.

Let $i \geq 2$ and $j \geq 0$. Consider the situation that exactly i agents observe that their first j coin flips result in head and define $p_{i,j}$ as the probability that all the i agents wins the game in the end starting from this situation. Starting from this situation, if all the i agents observe tail in their $j+1$-st coin flips then exactly i agents win the game with probability 1; if all the i agents observe head in their $j+1$-st coin flips then exactly i agents win with probability $p_{i,j+1}$; Otherwise, the number of winners of the game is less than i with probability 1. Therefore, we have $p_{i,j} = 2^{-i} + 2^{-i} \cdot p_{i,j+1}$. Since we have $p_{i,j} = p_{i,j+1}$ thanks to memoryless property of this game, solving this equality gives $p_{i,j} = 1/(2^i - 1) \leq 2^{1-i}$. Let k_i be the minimum integer j such that exactly i agents observes that all of their first j coin flips result in head. We define $k_n = 0$ for simplicity. Then, for any $i \geq 0$, we have $\Pr(|\{v \in V \mid s_v = s_{\max}\}| = i) = \sum_{j=0}^{\infty} \Pr(k_i = j) \cdot p_{i,j} \leq 2^{1-i} \sum_{j=0}^{\infty} \Pr(k_i = j) \leq 2^{1-i}$.

Module *QuickElimination*() simulates this game in the PP model. Every time an agent v has an interaction, we regard the interaction as the coin flip by v. If v is an initiator at the interaction, we regard the result of the coin flip as head; Otherwise we regard it as tail. The correctness of this simulation comes from the definition of the uniformly random scheduler: at each step, v interacts as an initiator with the same probability as the event that v does as an responder. Strictly speaking, this simple simulation of coin flips does not guarantee independence of coin flips by u and v for any distinct $u, v \in V$. See the full pre-print paper [13] for the mechanism to achieve independent coin flips. Each agent v computes and stores s_v on variable $v.\mathtt{level}_Q$ by counting the number of interactions that it participates in as an initiator until it interacts as a responder for the first time. After every agent v computes s_v on $v.\mathtt{level}_Q$, the maximum value of $\mathtt{level}_Q$, i.e., $s_{\max}$, is propagated from agent to agent via *one-way epidemic* [6], that is, (i) each agent memorizes the largest value of $\mathtt{level}_Q$ it has observed, and (ii) the larger value is propagated to the agent with smaller value at every interaction. It is proven in [6] that all agents obtain the largest value within $O(\log n)$ parallel time with high probability by this simple propagation. If agent v knows $s_v < s_{\max}$, v changes $v.\mathtt{leader}$ from *true* to *false*, that is, v becomes a follower. Thus, when one-way epidemic of $s_{\max}$ finishes, only the agents v satisfying $s_v = s_{\max}$ are leaders. From the above discussion, for any $i \geq 2$, the number of such surviving leaders is exactly i with probability at most 2^{1-i}. On the other hand, there are at least one agent v with $s_v = s_{\max}$, thus this module never eliminates all leaders.

Although we have to define the domain of variable $\mathtt{level}_Q$, a logarithmic number of states is sufficient for $\mathtt{level}_Q$ because each agent v gets more than $c \lg n$ consecutive heads with probability at most n^{-c} for any $c \geq 1$.

2.2 Key Idea for *Tournament*()

Starting from a configuration where the number of leaders is i, the goal of *Tournament*() is to reduce the number of leaders from i to one with probability $1 - O(i/\log n)$. The idea of this component is simple. As with the *QuickElimination*(), we use coin flips in *Tournament*(). Every leader v maintains variable $v.\mathtt{rand}$. Initially, $v.\mathtt{rand} = 0$. Every time it has an interaction, it updates $v.\mathtt{rand}$ by $v.\mathtt{rand} \leftarrow 2v.\mathtt{rand} + j$ where j indicates whether v is a responder in the interaction or not, *i.e.,* $j = 0$ if v is a initiator and $j = 1$ if v is a responder. This operation stops when v encounters $\lceil \log_2 m \rceil = O(\log \log n)$ interactions. Thus, when all the i leaders encounter at least $\lceil \log_2 m \rceil$ interactions, for every leader v, $v.\mathtt{rand}$ is a random variable uniformly chosen from $\{0, 1, \ldots, 2^{\lceil \log_2 m \rceil} - 1\}$. As with *QuickElimination*(), the maximum value rand is propagated to the whole population via one-way epidemic within $O(\log n)$ parallel time with high probability and only leaders with the maximum value remains leaders in the end of *Tournament*().

Let $v_1, v_2, \ldots, v_i$ be the i larders that survive *QuickElimination*(). Let $r_1, r_2, \ldots, r_i$ be the resulting value of $v_i.\mathtt{rand}$ and define $r_{\max}(j) = \max(r_1, r_2, \ldots, r_j)$ for any $j = 1, 2, \ldots, i$. Clearly, the number of leaders at the end of *Tournament*() is exactly one if $r_{j+1} \neq r_{\max}(j)$ holds for all $j = 1, 2, \ldots, i - 1$. By the union bound and from the independence between any two pairs of $r_1, r_2, \ldots, r_i$, this holds with probability at least $1 - \sum_{j=1}^{i-1} 2^{-\lceil \log_2 m \rceil} \geq 1 - i/m = 1 - O(i/\log n)$.

On the other hand, an execution of *Tournament*() never eliminates all leaders since there always at least one leader v_j that satisfies $r_j = r_{\max}(i)$.

2.3 Key Idea for *BackUp*()

The goal of *BackUp*() is to elect a unique leader within $O(\log^2 n)$ parallel time in expectation. We must guarantee this expected time regardless of the number of the agents that survive both *QuickElimination*() and *Tournament*() at the beginning of an execution of *BackUp*(). Every leader v maintains $v.\mathtt{level}_B$. Initially, $v.\mathtt{level}_B = 0$. Every leader v repeats the following procedure until $v.\mathtt{level}_B$ reaches $5m$ or v becomes a follower. First, v makes a coin flip. If the result is head, v increments $v.\mathtt{level}_B$ by one. If the result is tail, v does nothing. Then, v waits for sufficiently long but logarithmic parallel time so that the maximum $\mathtt{level}_B$ propagates to the whole population via one-way epidemic. If it observes larger value in the epidemic, it becomes a follower. Furthermore, if v interacts with another leader with the same level during this period and v is a responder in the interaction, v becomes a follower.

Let j be an arbitrary integer such that $1 \leq j < 5m$. Consider the first time that $\mathtt{level}_B$ of some leader, say v, reaches j. Let $V' \subseteq V$ be the set of leaders at that time. By the definition of the above procedure, every $u \in V'$ other than v satisfies $u.\mathtt{level}_B < j$, and u makes a coin flip at most once with high probability until the maximum value j is propagated from v to u. If the result of the one coin flip is tail, u becomes a follower. Therefore, with probability at least $1/2 - O(n^{-1}) > 1/3$, no less than half of leaders in $V' \setminus v$ becomes followers, that is, the number of leaders decreases to at most $1 + \lfloor |V'|/2 \rfloor$. Thus, we can show that with probability $1 - O(n^{-1})$, exactly one leader survives when all leaders' $\mathtt{level}_B$s reach $5m$ within $O(m \log n)$. Even if multiple leaders survive at that time, a unique leader is elected within the next $O(n)$ parallel time in expectation because when two leaders meet, one of them becomes a follower. Therefore, the total expected parallel time to elect a unique leader is $O(m \log n) + O(n^{-1}) \cdot O(n) = O(\log^2 n)$.

ACKNOWLEDGMENTS

This work was supported by JSPS KAKENHI Grant Numbers 17K19977, 18K18000, 18K11167, and 19K11826 and Japan Science and Technology Agency (JST) SICORP.

REFERENCES

[1] Dan Alistarh, James Aspnes, David Eisenstat, Rati Gelashvili, and Ronald L Rivest. 2017. Time-space trade-offs in population protocols. In *Proceedings of the Twenty-Eighth Annual ACM-SIAM Symposium on Discrete Algorithms*. SIAM, 2560–2579.

[2] Dan Alistarh, James Aspnes, and Rati Gelashvili. 2018. Space-optimal majority in population protocols. In *Proceedings of the Twenty-Ninth Annual ACM-SIAM Symposium on Discrete Algorithms*. SIAM, 2221–2239.

[3] Dan Alistarh and Rati Gelashvili. 2015. Polylogarithmic-time leader election in population protocols. In *Proceedings of the 42nd International Colloquium on Automata, Languages, and Programming*. Springer, 479–491.

[4] Dan Alistarh and Rati Gelashvili. 2018. Recent algorithmic advances in population protocols. *ACM SIGACT News* 49, 3 (2018), 63–73.

[5] D. Angluin, J Aspnes, Z. Diamadi, M.J. Fischer, and R. Peralta. 2006. Computation in networks of passively mobile finite-state sensors. *Distributed Computing* 18, 4 (2006), 235–253.

[6] Dana Angluin, James Aspnes, and David Eisenstat. 2008. Fast computation by population protocols with a leader. *Distributed Computing* 21, 3 (2008), 183–199.

[7] Andreas Bilke, Colin Cooper, Robert Elsässer, and Tomasz Radzik. 2017. Brief Announcement: Population Protocols for Leader Election and Exact Majority with $O(log^2 n)$ States and $O(log^2 n)$ Convergence Time. In *Proceedings of the 38th ACM Symposium on Principles of Distributed Computing*. Springer, 451–453.

[8] David Doty and David Soloveichik. 2018. Stable leader election in population protocols requires linear time. *Distributed Computing* 31, 4 (2018), 257–271.

[9] Robert ElsaŁsser and Tomasz Radzik. 2018. Recent results in population protocols for exact majority and leader election. *Bulletin of EATCS* 3, 126 (2018).

[10] Leszek Gąsieniec and Grzegorz Stachowiak. 2018. Fast space optimal leader election in population protocols. In *Proceedings of the Twenty-Ninth Annual ACM-SIAM Symposium on Discrete Algorithms*. SIAM, 2653–2667.

[11] Leszek Gąsieniec, Grzegorz Stachowiak, and Przemysław Uznański. 2018. Almost logarithmic-time space optimal leader election in population protocols. *arXiv preprint arXiv: 1802.06867* (2018).

[12] Othon Michail, Paul G Spirakis, and Michail Theofilatos. 2018. Simple and Fast Approximate Counting and Leader Election in Populations. In *International Symposium on Stabilizing, Safety, and Security of Distributed Systems*. Springer, 154–169.

[13] Yuichi Sudo, Fukuhito Ooshita, Taisuke Izumi, Hirotsugu Kakugawa, and Toshimitsu Masuzawa. 2018. Logarithmic Expected-Time Leader Election in Population Protocol Model. (2018). arXiv:cs.DC/1812.11309

Brief Announcement: On Site Fidelity and the Price of Ignorance in Swarm Robotic Central Place Foraging Algorithms

Abhinav Aggarwal
University of New Mexico
Albuquerque, NM
abhiag@unm.edu

G. Matthew Fricke
University of New Mexico
Albuquerque, NM
mfricke@unm.edu

Diksha Gupta
University of New Mexico
Albuquerque, NM
dgupta@unm.edu

Melanie E. Moses
University of New Mexico
Albuquerque, NM
melaniem@unm.edu

ABSTRACT

A key factor limiting the performance of central place foraging algorithms is the awareness of the agent(s) about the location of food items around the nest. We study the ratio of how much time an ignorant agent takes relative to an omniscient forager for complete collection of food items in the arena. This effectively quantifies the penalty each algorithm pays for not knowing (or choosing to ignore information gained about) where the resources are located. We model the effect of depletion of food items from the arena on the foraging efficiency over time and analytically verify that returning to the location of the last food item found strongly helps in counteracting this effect. To the best of our knowledge, these results have only been empirically argued so far.

CCS CONCEPTS

• **Computing methodologies → Bio-inspired approaches**; **Distributed algorithms**; Continuous space search;

KEYWORDS

Central Place Foraging, Site Fidelity, Price of Ignorance, Bio-Inspired Computation

ACM Reference Format:
Abhinav Aggarwal, G. Matthew Fricke, Diksha Gupta, and Melanie E. Moses. 2019. Brief Announcement: On Site Fidelity and the Price of Ignorance in Swarm Robotic Central Place Foraging Algorithms. In *2019 ACM Symposium on Principles of Distributed Computing (PODC '19), July 29-August 2, 2019, Toronto, ON, Canada.* ACM, New York, NY, USA, 3 pages. https://doi.org/10.1145/3293611.3331572

1 INTRODUCTION

Foraging of food items around a central location is a well motivated problem in understanding biological systems like ant colonies as well as gaining theoretical insight into distributed collaborative search algorithms. To better understand the effects of overlaps in search trajectories and depletion of food items from the arena, we define the *Price of Ignorance* as a measure of how much time an ignorant agent takes relative to an omniscient forager for complete collection of food items in an arena.

We analyze two algorithms: a deterministic **Distributed Archimedes Spiral Algorithm** (DASA) [4, 7, 12] in which the agents move along interleaved Archimedes spirals [10] around the nest; and a randomized **Ballistic Central Place Foraging Algorithm** (BalCPFA) [15] in which the agents move radially away from the nest until they find a food item or hit the arena boundary. Upon returning to the nest, each agent independently chooses a uniformly random direction for the next ballistic run.

Our analysis shows that preferential foraging around the location of the last found food item (also called *site fidelity*) significantly lowers the foraging time whereas food depletion and large overlaps in search trajectories have an adverse effect. This interplay of exploration vs. exploitation, thus, defines the quality of foraging.

Our Model. We assume a continuous circular arena of radius R around a fixed central location, called the *nest*[1]. This arena consists of F individually collectible food items that are arbitrarily clustered into piles. We assume that each pile is placed independently and uniformly at random in the arena[2]. Our system consists of N agents that move synchronously at a constant unit speed and have a vision radius R_v, *i.e.*, the food item can be detected by any agent that is within a distance of R_v from it. We assume that the agents know R and have unique IDs in $\{1, \ldots, N\}$. However, the locations of the piles and the number of food items in each pile is unknown to the agents. The agents can navigate back to the nest from any location in the arena but cannot remember more than $\Theta(1)$ previously visited locations. We assume that each agent can pick up only one food item at a time and does not communicate with any other agent during the algorithm. We do not model unexpected environmental effects, agent failures, and external noise in this paper.

Site Fidelity. In BalCPFA, we say that an agent employs site fidelity with parameter $p_s \in [0, 1]$ if after returning to the nest with

PODC '19, July 29-August 2, 2019, Toronto, ON, Canada

ACM ISBN 978-1-4503-6217-7/19/07.
https://doi.org/10.1145/3293611.3331572

[1]While most existing work assumes an infinite discrete grid [6, 14], we note that assuming a continuous arena with Euclidean distances only changes the runtime of our algorithms by a factor of $\sqrt{2}$ compared to the Manhattan distance. The assumption of finite arena is biologically motivated since most ant species do not travel very large distances before giving up their search [8, 9].

[2]We compare our model and results with those for the adversarial setting considered in the ANTS model by Feinerman and Korman [6] in Section 3.

a food item, with probability p_s, the agent chooses to return to the location of this item for the next ballistic run. Otherwise, the agent moves along a uniformly random direction.

Omniscient Foraging. Our analysis is relative to an omniscient foraging scenario in which each agent is initially equipped with the exact locations of all food items in the arena and given perfect navigation capabilities to forage these items in the smallest possible time. This ideal algorithm assumes information about the location of the next available food item that no other agent is currently scheduled/planning to collect. The expected number of time steps until the last food item is brought to the nest by some agent is $4\mathrm{RF}/3\mathrm{N}$. This is because each pile is at an expected distance of $2\mathrm{R}/3$ from the nest. Thus, it takes $2(2\mathrm{R}/3) = 4\mathrm{R}/3$ time steps to collect each food item.

The Price of Ignorance. With respect to the ideal foraging described above, we define the price of ignorance, denoted χ, of a given foraging algorithm A as $\chi(A) = 3\mathrm{N}T_A/(4\mathrm{RF})$, where T_A is the number of time steps until some agent brings the last food item to the nest.[3] This metric helps quantify the cost of being oblivious to the (or choosing to ignore any gained) knowledge about the resources and their location in the arena.[4]

2 OVERVIEW OF OUR RESULTS

We now summarize our main results and present an overview of our approach, wherever possible. We refer the reader to the full version of our paper [1] for more details of our proofs .

Cooperative Foraging Speeds up Deterministic Search. We prove that the total time taken by DASA is $O\left(\frac{\mathrm{R}^2}{\mathrm{N}} + \mathrm{R}\left\lceil\frac{\mathrm{F}}{\mathrm{N}}\right\rceil\right)$ and that $\chi(\mathrm{DASA}) < \left\lceil\frac{5}{3\mathrm{R}_v\mathrm{F}} - \frac{\mathrm{N}}{2\mathrm{RF}}\right\rceil \mathrm{R} + \sqrt{2}$. This implies that increasing the number of agents helps reduce the foraging time for DASA. We attribute the improvement in the performance with multiple agents to the fact that the search trajectories are non-overlapping and the location of each food item found helps to continuously eliminate part of the arena for the search that follows (see Figure 1). Additionally, we show that $\chi(\mathrm{DASA}) \geq \left\lceil\frac{\pi}{8\mathrm{R}_v\mathrm{F}} - \frac{9\mathrm{N}}{4\mathrm{RF}}\right\rceil \mathrm{R} + 1$, implying that the bound above is tight up to constant factors.

BalCPFA has a Higher Foraging Time. BalCPFA can be shown to have a higher foraging time compared to DASA, with high probability, using a result about random arc distances on a unit circle by King and Saia [11]. They prove that when M points are placed uniformly at random on the circumference of a unit circle, then the maximum arc distance between any two neighboring points is $\Theta(\log M/M)$ and the minimum distance is $\Theta(1/M^2)$, with probability at least $1 - O(1/M)$.

[3]We refer to this as the time to complete collection for algorithm A. Note that we do not address the problem of protocol termination in this paper and measure the time only until the last food item is collected.

[4]We note that this measure is similar to the notion of *competitiveness* for online algorithms [5], which has been used in the context of foraging in [6]. However, in our application, we do not measure competitiveness with respect to the amount of advice available for the value of N (as in [6]). Rather, from a biological and engineering perspective, we measure competitiveness with respect to the knowledge of the distribution of resources around the nest and in the decision of the foraging algorithm to avoid overlaps in the search trajectories. Additionally, we assume a uniformly random pile placement, which is significantly different from the adversarial setting often for online algorithms.

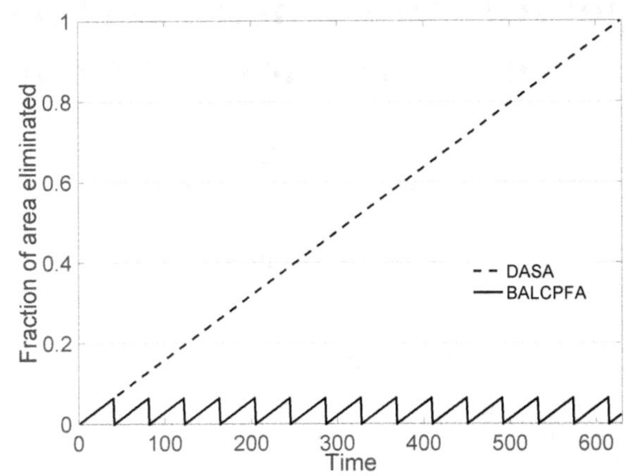

Figure 1: Plot of the fraction of area eliminated by a single agent ($\mathrm{R}_v = 1, \mathrm{R} = 20$) vs. search time while foraging the arena using DASA and BalCPFA.

For a single adversarially placed pile of diameter Δ inside the arena, the number of ballistic runs required to locate this pile is $\Omega(\Delta \log \Delta)$, with high probability. Thus, a total of $\Omega\left(R\left\lceil\frac{\mathrm{F}\Delta\log\Delta}{\mathrm{R}_v\mathrm{N}}\right\rceil\right)$ time steps are needed for complete collection of food items from this pile. Clearly, this is higher than that of DASA.

When the pile is placed uniformly at random instead, we show that when agents do not deploy site fidelity (*i.e.* when $p_s = 0$), it holds that $\chi(\mathrm{BalCPFA}) = \Omega(\lceil\mathrm{R}/\mathrm{R}_v\rceil)$, which, asymptotically, is at least F times higher than the upper bound for DASA. Intuitively, this is because BalCPFA chooses to completely ignore all the information obtained while collecting the first food item while it forages for the second one. Thus, each food item is essentially searched as if it were independently and uniquely placed in the arena, causing large overlaps in the search trajectory (see Figure 1).

Food Depletion has Adverse Effects. If the arena contains multiple piles, the time to complete collection is affected by the rate of depletion of these piles. This is because as these piles become smaller (due to collection of food items in them) and their number decreases, it becomes more challenging for the agents to find the next available food item. To the best of our knowledge, we make the first attempt to model the effect of such a behavior in collaborative foraging and prove that when food depletion is taken into account, one can expect a multiplicative blowup up to $\Omega(M\mathrm{N})$ in the price of ignorance, where M is the number of piles. We model this behavior using a probabilistic recurrence relation and compute the expected foraging time for BalCPFA with depleting piles to obtain our result [1]. Intuitively, while a larger number of agents on one hand collect food items faster (by working in parallel), they also deplete the arena at a faster rate, thus, significantly slowing down locating the remaining food items as time progresses.

Site Fidelity Helps Keep Randomized Foraging Efficient. Our final result proves that deploying site fidelity strongly counteracts the effect of food depletion and helps keep BalCPFA (and thus, other randomized foraging schemes) efficient. This has mostly been empirically argued so far [13] and our result provides one of the first theoretical evidence into this phenomenon. Intuitively, site fidelity is the behavior of the agent in which it chooses to return to the location of the last food item it found. We show that when the agents deploy perfect site fidelity (*i.e.* with $p_s = 1$). the expected price of ignorance of BALCPFA is at most $\left\lceil \frac{\pi}{R_v} - \frac{N}{2FR} \right\rceil R$, which is a significant improvement over the bound obtained above. Note that this does not imply that the agent only moves along one direction indefinitely. When the pile is exhausted, the ballistic run in this direction will go all the way to the arena boundary and return to the nest without any food item in sight. This will cause the agent to move along a random direction for the next ballistic run since site fidelity only applies when a food item is found.

Communication Enhances Foraging Efficiency. We further argue that communication among the agents, and not only working in parallel, can help collect the food items faster. Similar to the approach by Steels [16] using *crumbs* and that by Hecker and Moses [9] using virtual waypoints, we envision a pedagogical scenario with BALCPFA in which agents have a special marker which they can place in the arena at any time. This marker is only visible to the nearby agents and once detected, indicates a desired direction to them. Assuming only a single pile in the arena, when some agent finds a food item in this pile, it places the marker near the nest in the correct direction and all other agents then move along this direction to collect the remaining food items. To further optimize the algorithm, all agents can search the first food item in parallel and the one that finds it first places the marker. The expected distance covered in this marker-based algorithm is $O\left(\frac{R^2}{N} + R\left\lceil\frac{F}{N}\right\rceil\right)$, which closes the gap between the asymptotic performance of BALCPFA and DASA.

Note that this form of communication is different from deploying site fidelity since only one agent returns to the last visited location in the latter. In biological systems, such a communication has been conjectured to happen by laying pheromones that the other agents can pick up and follow [9].

3 DISCUSSION

In this section, we briefly compare our approach to the work by Feinerman and Korman [6] for the ANTS problem. Taking motivation from the distribution resources in the wild [8], we assume a random food placement in the arena in contrast to the adversarial setting considered in [6]. Moreover, in the adversarial case, if the adversary is allowed to place the food items in an online manner, a lower bound of $\Omega\left(R\left\lceil F + \frac{RF}{N}\right\rceil\right)$ can be proved for complete collection of food items in the arena using Yao's minimax principle [17] and the Feinerman-Korman bound in [6]. In our case, however, we show that DASA takes only $O\left(\frac{R^2}{N} + R\left\lceil\frac{F}{N}\right\rceil\right)$ time in expectation for complete collection, which is significantly better than the bound above. Additionally, while only the time to locate the first food item is considered in [6], we study the effect of clustering of food items into piles and the time for complete collection of resources. In fact, it can be shown that when the food items are clustered into a pile of diameter Δ, then even under adversarial placement, there exists a single-agent deterministic foraging strategy which can locate this pile in $\Theta\left(R^2/\Delta\right)$ time steps [2, 3].

From a biological perspective, we provide one of the first analytical insights into naturally observed phenomena of site fidelity [13] and argue in favor of determinism for collaborative foraging. The formal analysis shows that deterministic spirals are best in theory, but simulations and our prior work show that stochastic algorithms can work as well in practice, but with significantly higher variance. Moreover, from a theoretical perspective, our analysis helps quantify the importance of keeping overlaps in search trajectories to a minimum, which is an argument in favor of deterministic search for limited-memory systems (which was also argued empirically by [7, 12, 15]). For stochastic search, our results favor walks with site fidelity as a solution to balancing the effects of spatial sparsity that arises over time (due to depletion).

ACKNOWLEDGMENTS

This work is supported by the NASA MUREP, NNX15AM14A Swarmathon Cooperative Agreement and the James S. McDonnell Foundation, Complex Systems Scholar Award. We also thank Jared Saia, Department of Computer Science, William F. Vining, Moses Biological Computation Lab, University of New Mexico, and David Peleg, Weizmann Institute of Science for their comments and discussions.

REFERENCES

[1] A Aggarwal, D Gupta, W F Vining, G M Fricke, and M E Moses. 2019. Ignorance is Not Bliss: An Analysis of Central-Place Foraging Algorithms. *Manuscript Under Submission. Available at* https://bit.ly/2QcPaX8 (2019).

[2] A Aggarwal and J Saia. 2019. Robustly Finding a Cluster Using the Golden Ratio. *Manuscript Under Submission.* (2019).

[3] A Aggarwal, W F Vining, D Gupta, J Saia, and M E Moses. 2019. A Most Irrational Foraging Algorithm. *Manuscript Under Submission.* (2019).

[4] Ricardo Baeza-Yates and René Schott. 1995. Parallel searching in the plane. *Computational Geometry* 5, 3 (1995), 143–154.

[5] Allan Borodin and Ran El-Yaniv. 2005. *Online computation and competitive analysis.* Cambridge University Press (2005).

[6] Ofer Feinerman and Amos Korman. 2017. The ANTS problem. *Distributed Computing* 30, 3 (2017), 149–168.

[7] G Matthew Fricke, Joshua P Hecker, Antonio D Griego, Linh T Tran, and Melanie E Moses. 2016. A distributed deterministic spiral search algorithm for swarms. In *Intelligent Robots and Systems (IROS), 2016 IEEE/RSJ International Conference on.* IEEE, 4430–4436.

[8] Deborah M Gordon and Alan W Kulig. 1996. Founding, foraging, and fighting: colony size and the spatial distribution of harvester ant nests. *Ecology* 77, 8 (1996), 2393–2409.

[9] Joshua P Hecker and Melanie E Moses. 2015. Beyond pheromones: evolving error-tolerant, flexible, and scalable ant-inspired robot swarms. *Swarm Intelligence* 9, 1 (2015), 43–70.

[10] HC Holland. 1957. The archimedes spiral. *Nature* 179, 4556 (1957), 432.

[11] Valerie King and Jared Saia. 2004. Choosing a random peer. In *Proceedings of the twenty-third annual ACM symposium on Principles of distributed computing.* ACM, 125–130.

[12] Malika Meghjani, Sandeep Manjanna, and Gregory Dudek. 2016. Multi-target rendezvous search. In *Intelligent Robots and Systems (IROS), 2016 IEEE/RSJ International Conference on.* IEEE, 2596–2603.

[13] Danielle P Mersch, Alessandro Crespi, and Laurent Keller. 2013. Tracking individuals shows spatial fidelity is a key regulator of ant social organization. *Science* 340, 6136 (2013), 1090–1093.

[14] Cameron Musco, Hsin-Hao Su, and Nancy Lynch. 2016. Ant-inspired density estimation via random walks. In *Proceedings of the 2016 ACM Symposium on Principles of Distributed Computing.* ACM, 469–478.

[15] Lu Qi, Antonio D. Griego, G. Matthew Fricke, and Melanie E Moses. 2019. Comparing Physical and Simulated Performance of a Deterministic and a Bio-inspired Stochastic Foraging Strategy for Robot Swarms. In *Proceedings of the International Conference on Robotics and Automation (ICRA).* IEEE.

[16] Luc Steels. 1990. Cooperation between distributed agents through self-organisation. In *Intelligent Robots and Systems' 90.'Towards a New Frontier of Applications', Proceedings. IROS'90. IEEE International Workshop on.* IEEE, 8–14.

[17] Andrew Chi-Chin Yao. 1977. Probabilistic computations: Toward a unified measure of complexity. In *18th Annual Symposium on Foundations of Computer Science (sfcs 1977).* IEEE, 222–227.

Improved Distributed Expander Decomposition and Nearly Optimal Triangle Enumeration*

Yi-Jun Chang†
University of Michigan
cyijun@umich.edu

Thatchaphol Saranurak
Toyota Technological Institute at Chicago
saranurak@ttic.edu

ABSTRACT

An (ϵ, ϕ)-expander decomposition of a graph $G = (V, E)$ is a clustering of the vertices $V = V_1 \cup \cdots \cup V_x$ such that (1) each cluster V_i induces subgraph with conductance at least ϕ, and (2) the number of inter-cluster edges is at most $\epsilon|E|$. In this paper, we give an improved distributed expander decomposition, and obtain a nearly optimal distributed triangle enumeration algorithm in the CONGEST model.

Specifically, we construct an (ϵ, ϕ)-expander decomposition with $\phi = (\epsilon/\log n)^{2^{O(k)}}$ in $O(n^{2/k} \cdot \text{poly}(1/\phi, \log n))$ rounds for any $\epsilon \in (0, 1)$ and positive integer k. For example, a $(1/n^{o(1)}, 1/n^{o(1)})$-expander decomposition only requires $O(n^{o(1)})$ rounds to compute, which is optimal up to subpolynomial factors, and a $(0.01, 1/\text{poly} \log n)$-expander decomposition can be computed in $O(n^{\gamma})$ rounds, for any arbitrarily small constant $\gamma > 0$. Previously, the algorithm by Chang, Pettie, and Zhang can construct a $(1/6, 1/\text{poly} \log n)$-expander decomposition using $\tilde{O}(n^{1-\delta})$ rounds for any $\delta > 0$, with a caveat that the algorithm is allowed to throw away a set of edges into an extra part which form a subgraph with arboricity at most n^{δ}. Our algorithm does not have this caveat.

By slightly modifying the distributed algorithm for routing on expanders by Ghaffari, Kuhn and Su [PODC'17], we obtain a triangle enumeration algorithm using $\tilde{O}(n^{1/3})$ rounds. This matches the lower bound by Izumi and Le Gall [PODC'17] and Pandurangan, Robinson and Scquizzato [SPAA'18] of $\tilde{\Omega}(n^{1/3})$ which holds even in the CONGESTED-CLIQUE model. To the best of our knowledge, this provides the first non-trivial example for a distributed problem that has essentially the same complexity (up to a polylogarithmic factor) in both CONGEST and CONGESTED-CLIQUE.

The key technique in our proof is the first distributed approximation algorithm for finding a low conductance cut that is as balanced as possible. Previous distributed sparse cut algorithms do not have this nearly most balanced guarantee.[1]

*The full version of the paper is available at arXiv [7].
†Supported by NSF grants CCF-1514383, CCF-1637546, and CCF-1815316.
[1] Kuhn and Molla [25] previously claimed that their approximate sparse cut algorithm also has the nearly most balanced guarantee, but this claim turns out to be incorrect [8, Footnote 3].

PODC '19, July 29-August 2, 2019, Toronto, ON, Canada

ACM ISBN 978-1-4503-6217-7/19/07...$15.00
https://doi.org/10.1145/3293611.3331618

CCS CONCEPTS

• **Theory of computation → Distributed algorithms.**

KEYWORDS

expander decomposition, low diameter decomposition, triangle enumeration

ACM Reference Format:
Yi-Jun Chang and Thatchaphol Saranurak. 2019. Improved Distributed Expander Decomposition and Nearly Optimal Triangle Enumeration. In *2019 ACM Symposium on Principles of Distributed Computing (PODC '19), July 29-August 2, 2019, Toronto, ON, Canada.* ACM, New York, NY, USA, 8 pages. https://doi.org/10.1145/3293611.3331618

1 INTRODUCTION

In this paper, we consider the task of finding an *expander decomposition* of a distributed network in the CONGEST model of distributed computing. Roughly speaking, an expander decomposition of a graph $G = (V, E)$ is a clustering of the vertices $V = V_1 \cup \cdots \cup V_x$ such that (1) each component V_i induces a high conductance subgraph, and (2) the number of inter-component edges is small. This natural bicriteria optimization problem of finding a good expander decomposition was introduced by Kannan Vempala and Vetta [22], and was further studied in many other subsequent works [3, 31, 32, 34, 37, 41, 43].[2] The expander decomposition has a wide range of applications, and it has been applied to solving linear systems [42], unique games [2, 36, 43], minimum cut [23], and dynamic algorithms [30].

Recently, Chang, Pettie, and Zhang [8] applied this technique to the field of distributed computing, and they showed that a variant of expander decomposition can be computed efficiently in CONGEST. Using this decomposition, they showed that triangle detection and enumeration can be solved in $\tilde{O}(n^{1/2})$ rounds.[3] The previous state-of-the-art bounds for triangle detection and enumeration were $\tilde{O}(n^{2/3})$ and $\tilde{O}(n^{3/4})$, respectively, due to Izumi and Le Gall [19]. Later, Daga et al. [11] exploit this decomposition and obtain the first algorithm for computing edge connectivity of a graph *exactly* using sub-linear number of rounds.

Specifically, the variant of the decomposition in [8] is as follows. If we allow one extra part that induces an n^{δ}-arboricity subgraph[4] in the decomposition, then in $O(n^{1-\delta})$ rounds we can construct

[2] The existence of the expander decomposition is (implicitly) exploited first in the context of property testing [18].
[3] The $\tilde{O}(\cdot)$ notation hides any polylogarithmic factor.
[4] The arboricity of a graph is the minimum number α such that its edge set can be partitioned into α forests.

an expander decomposition in CONGEST such that each component has $1/O(\text{poly}\log n)$ conductance and the number of inter-component edges is at most $|E|/6$.

A major open problem left by the work [8] is to design an efficient distributed algorithm constructing an expander decomposition without the extra low-arboricity part. In this work, we show that this is possible. A consequence of our new expander decomposition algorithm is that triangle enumeration can be solved in $O(n^{1/3}\text{poly}\log n)$ rounds, nearly matching the $\Omega(n^{1/3}/\log n)$ lower bound [19, 33] by a polylogarithmic factor.

The CONGEST *Model.* In the CONGEST model of distributed computing, the underlying distributed network is represented as an undirected graph $G = (V, E)$, where each vertex corresponds to a computational device, and each edge corresponds to a bi-directional communication link. Each vertex v has a distinct $\Theta(\log n)$-bit identifier $\text{ID}(v)$. The computation proceeds according to synchronized *rounds*. In each round, each vertex v can perform unlimited local computation, and may send a distinct $O(\log n)$-bit message to each of its neighbors. Throughout the paper we only consider the randomized variant of CONGEST. Each vertex is allowed to generate unlimited local random bits, but there is no global randomness. We say that an algorithm succeeds *with high probability* (w.h.p.) if its failure probability is at most $1/\text{poly}(n)$.

The CONGESTED-CLIQUE model is a variant of CONGEST that allows all-to-all communication, and the LOCAL model is a variant of CONGEST that allows messages of unbounded length.

Terminology. Before we proceed, we review the graph terminologies related to the expander decomposition. Consider a graph $G = (V, E)$. For a vertex subset S, we write $\text{Vol}(S)$ to denote $\sum_{v \in S} \deg(v)$. Note that by default the degree is with respect to the original graph G. We write $\bar{S} = V \setminus S$, and let $\partial(S) = E(S, \bar{S})$ be the set of edges $e = \{u, v\}$ with $u \in S$ and $v \in \bar{S}$. The *sparsity* or *conductance* of a cut $(S, \bar{S})$ is defined as $\Phi(S) = |\partial(S)|/\min\{\text{Vol}(S), \text{Vol}(\bar{S})\}$. The *conductance* Φ_G of a graph G is the minimum value of $\Phi(S)$ over all vertex subsets S. Define the *balance* $\text{bal}(S)$ of a cut S by $\text{bal}(S) = \min\{\text{Vol}(S), \text{Vol}(\bar{S})\}/\text{Vol}(V)$. We say that S is a *most-balanced* cut of G of conductance at most ϕ if $\text{bal}(S)$ is maximized among all cuts of G with conductance at most ϕ. We have the following relation [20] between the mixing time $\tau_{\text{mix}}(G)$ and conductance Φ_G:

$$\Theta\left(\frac{1}{\Phi_G}\right) \le \tau_{\text{mix}}(G) \le \Theta\left(\frac{\log n}{\Phi_G^2}\right).$$

Let S be a vertex set. Denote $E(S)$ by the set of all edges whose two endpoints are both within S. We write $G[S]$ to denote the subgraph induced by S, and we write $G\{S\}$ to denote the graph resulting from adding $\deg_V(v) - \deg_S(v)$ self loops to each vertex v in $G[S]$. Note that the degree of each vertex $v \in S$ in both G and $G\{S\}$ is identical. As in [39], each self loop of v contributes 1 in the calculation of $\deg(v)$. Observe that we always have

$$\Phi(G\{S\}) \le \Phi(G[S]).$$

Let v be a vertex. Denote $N(v)$ as the set of neighbors of v. We also write $N^k(v) = \{u \in V \mid \text{dist}(u, v) \le k\}$. Note that $N^1(v) = N(v) \cup \{v\}$. These notations $\text{dist}(u, v)$, $N(v)$, and $N^k(v)$ depend on the underlying graph G. When the choice of underlying graph is not clear from the context, we use a subscript to indicate the underlying graph we refer to.

Expander Decomposition. An (ϵ, ϕ)-expander decomposition of a graph $G = (V, E)$ is defined as a partition of the vertex set $V = V_1 \cup \cdots \cup V_x$ satisfying the following conditions.

- For each component V_i, we have $\Phi(G\{V_i\}) \ge \phi$.
- The number of inter-component edges $(|\partial(V_1)| + \cdots + |\partial(V_x)|)/2$ is at most $\epsilon|E|$.

The main contribution of this paper is the following result.

Theorem 1. *Let $\epsilon \in (0, 1)$, and let k be a positive integer. An (ϵ, ϕ)-expander decomposition with $\phi = (\epsilon/\log n)^{2^{O(k)}}$ can be constructed in $O\left(n^{2/k} \cdot \text{poly}(1/\phi, \log n)\right) = O\left(n^{2/k} \cdot \left(\frac{\log n}{\epsilon}\right)^{2^{O(k)}}\right)$ rounds, w.h.p.*

The proof of Theorem 1 is in Section 2. We emphasize that the number of rounds does not depend on the diameter of G. There is a trade-off between the two parameters ϵ and ϕ. For example, an (ϵ, ϕ)-expander decomposition with $\epsilon = 2^{-\log^{1/3} n}$ and $\phi = 2^{-\log^{2/3} n}$ can be constructed in $n^{O(1/\log\log n)}$ rounds by setting $k = O(\log\log n)$ in Theorem 1. If we are allowed to have $\epsilon = 0.01$ and spend $O(n^{0.01})$ rounds, then we can achieve $\phi = 1/O(\text{poly}\log n)$.

Distributed Triangle Finding. Variants of the triangle finding problem have been studied in the literature [1, 5, 8, 12–14, 19, 33]. In the *triangle detection* problem, it is required that at least one vertex must report a triangle if the graph has at least one triangle. In the *triangle enumeration* problem, it is required that each triangle of the graph is reported by at least one vertex. Both of these problems can be solved in $O(1)$ rounds in LOCAL. It is the bandwidth constraint of CONGEST and CONGESTED-CLIQUE that makes these problems non-trivial.

It is important that a triangle $T = \{u, v, w\}$ is allowed to be reported by a vertex $x \notin T$. If it is required that a triangle $T = \{u, v, w\}$ has to be reported by a vertex $x \in T$, then there is an $\Omega(n/\log n)$ lower bound [19] for triangle enumeration, in both CONGEST and CONGESTED-CLIQUE. To achieve a round complexity of $o(n/\log n)$, it is necessary that some triangles T are reported by vertices not in T.

Dolev, Lenzen, and Peled [12] showed that triangle enumeration can be solved deterministically in $O(n^{1/3}/\log n)$ rounds in CONGESTED-CLIQUE. This algorithm is optimal, as it matches the $\Omega(n^{1/3}/\log n)$-round lower bound [19, 33] in CONGESTED-CLIQUE. Interestingly, if we only want to detect one triangle or count the number of triangles, then Censor-Hillel et al. [5] showed that the round complexity in CONGESTED-CLIQUE can be improved to $\tilde{O}(n^{1-(2/\omega)+o(1)}) = o(n^{0.158})$ time [5], where $\omega < 2.373$ is the exponent of the complexity of matrix multiplication [26].

For the CONGEST model, Izumi and Le Gall [19] showed that the triangle detection and enumeration problems can be solved in $\tilde{O}(n^{2/3})$ and $\tilde{O}(n^{3/4})$ time, respectively. These upper bounds were later improved to $\tilde{O}(n^{1/2})$ by Chang, Pettie, and Zhang using a variant of expander decomposition [8].

A consequence of Theorem 1 is that triangle enumeration (and hence detection) can be solved in $\tilde{O}(n^{1/3})$ rounds, almost matching the $\Omega(n^{1/3}/\log n)$ lower bound [19, 33] which holds even in

CONGESTED-CLIQUE. To the best of our knowledge, this provides the first non-trivial example for a distributed problem that has essentially the same complexity (up to a polylogarithmic factor) in both CONGEST and CONGESTED-CLIQUE, i.e., allowing non-local communication links does not help. In contrast, many other graph problems can be solved much more efficiently in CONGESTED-CLIQUE than in CONGEST; see e.g., [17, 21].

Theorem 2. *Triangle enumeration can be solved in $\tilde{O}(n^{1/3})$ rounds in* CONGEST, *w.h.p.*

The proof of Theorem 2 is in Section 3. Note that Theorem 2 immediately implies an algorithm for triangle detection with the same number of rounds. However, while the best known lower bounds [1, 14] for triangle detection can currently exclude only 1-round algorithms. Whether the large gap between upper and lower bounds for this problem can be closed remains an intriguing question.

1.1 Prior Work on Expander Decomposition

In the centralized setting, the first polynomial time algorithm for construction an (ϵ, ϕ)-expander decomposition is by Kannan, Vempala and Vetta [22] where $\epsilon = \tilde{O}(\phi)$. Afterward, Spielman and Teng [40, 41] significantly improved the running time to be near-linear in m, where m is the number of edges. In time $\tilde{O}(m/\text{poly}(\phi))$, they can construct a "weak" $(\text{poly}(\phi, \log n), \phi)$-expander decomposition. Their weak expander only has the following weaker guarantee that each part V_i in the partition of V might not induce an expander, and we only know that V_i is contained in some *unknown* expander. That is, there exists some $W_i \supseteq V_i$ where $\Phi_{G\{W_i\}} \geq \phi$. Although this guarantee suffices for many applications (e.g. [10, 24]), some other applications [9, 30], including the triangle enumeration algorithm of [8], crucially needs the fact that each part in the decomposition induces an expander.

Nanongkai and Saranurak [29] and, independently, Wulff-Nilsen [44] gave a fast algorithm without weakening the guarantee as the one in [40, 41]. In [29], their algorithm finds a $(\phi \log^{O(k)} n, \phi)$-expander decomposition in time $\tilde{O}(m^{1+1/k})$. Although the trade-off is worse in [44], their high-level approaches are in fact the same. They gave the same black-box reduction from constructing an expander decomposition to finding a nearly most balanced sparse cut. The difference only comes from the quality of their nearly most balanced sparse cuts algorithms. Our distributed algorithm will also follow this high-level approach.

Most recently, Saranurak and Wang [37] gave a $(\tilde{O}(\phi), \phi)$-expander decomposition algorithm with running time $\tilde{O}(m/\phi)$. This is optimal up to a polylogarithmic factor when $\phi \geq 1/\text{poly}\log(n)$. We do not use their approach, as their *trimming step* seems to be inherently sequential and very challenging to parallelize or make distributed.

The only previous expander decomposition in the distributed setting is by Chang, Pettie, and Zhang [8]. Their distributed algorithm gave an $(1/6, 1/\text{poly}\log(n))$-expander decomposition with an extra part which is an n^δ-arboricity subgraph in $O(n^{1-\delta})$ rounds in CONGEST. Our distributed algorithm significantly improved upon this work.

1.2 Technical Overview

For convenience, we call a cut with conductance at most ϕ a *ϕ-sparse cut* in this section. To give a high-level idea, the most straightforward algorithm for constructing an expander decomposition of a graph $G = (V, E)$ is as follows. Find a ϕ-sparse cut S. If such a cut S does not exist, then return V as a part in the partition. Otherwise, recurse on both sides $G\{S\}$ and $G\{V - S\}$, and so the edges in $E(S, V - S)$ become inter-cluster edges. To see the correctness, once the recursion stops at $G\{U\}$ for some U, we know that $\Phi_{G\{U\}} \geq \phi$. Also, the total number of inter-cluster edges is at most $O(m\phi \log n)$ because (1) each inter-cluster edge can be charged to edges in the smaller side of some ϕ-sparse cut, and (2) each edge can be in the smaller side of the cut for at most $O(\log n)$ times.

This straightforward approach has two efficiency issues: (1) checking whether a ϕ-sparse cut exists does not admit fast distributed algorithms (and is in fact NP-hard), and (2) a ϕ-sparse cut S can be very unbalanced and hence the recursion depth can be as large as $\Omega(n)$. Thus, even if we ignore time spent on finding cuts, the round complexity due to the recursion depth is too high. At a high-level, all previous algorithms (both centralized and distributed) handle the two issues in the same way up to some extent. First, they instead use *approximate sparse cut algorithms* which either find some ϕ'-sparse cut or certify that there is no ϕ-sparse cut where $\phi' \gg \phi$. Second, they find a cut with some guarantee about the balance of the cut, i.e., the smaller side of the cut should be sufficiently large.

Let us contrast our approach with the only previous distributed expander decomposition algorithm by Chang, Pettie, and Zhang [8]. They gave an approximate sparse cut algorithm such that the smaller side of the cut has $\Omega(n^\delta)$ vertices for some constant $\delta > 0$, so the recursion depth is $O(n^{1-\delta})$. They guarantee this property by "forcing" the graph to have minimum degree at least n^δ, so any ϕ-sparse cut must contain $\Omega(n^\delta)$ vertices (this uses the fact that the graph is simple) To force the graph to have high degree, they keep removing vertices with degree at most n^δ at any step of the algorithms. Throughout the whole algorithm, the removed part form a graph with arboricity at most n^δ. This explains why their decomposition outputs the extra part which induces a low arboricity subgraph. With some other ideas on distributed implementation, they obtained the round complexity of $\tilde{O}(n^{1-\delta})$, roughly matching the recursion depth.

In this paper, we avoid this extra low-arboricity part. The key component is the following. Instead of just guaranteeing that the smaller side of the cut has $\Omega(n^\delta)$ vertices, we give the first efficient distributed algorithm for computing a *nearly most balanced* sparse cut. Suppose there is a ϕ-sparse cut with balance b, then our sparse cut algorithm returns a ϕ'-sparse cut with balance at least $\Omega(b)$, where ϕ' is not much larger than ϕ. Intuitively, given that we can find a nearly most balanced sparse cut efficiently, the recursion depth should be made very small. This intuition can be made formal using the ideas in the centralized setting from Nanongkai and Saranurak [29] and Wulff-Nilsen [44]. Our main technical contribution is two-fold. First, we show the first distributed algorithm for computing a nearly most balanced sparse cut, which is our key algorithmic tool. Second, in order to obtain a fast distributed algorithm, we must modify the centralized approach of [29, 44] on how to construct an expander decomposition. In particular, we need to run a *low diameter decomposition* whenever we encounter a graph with high diameter, as our distributed algorithm for finding a nearly most balanced sparse cut is fast only on graphs with low diameter.

Sparse Cut Computation. At a high level, our distributed nearly most balanced sparse cut algorithm is a distributed implementation of the sequential algorithm of Spielman and Teng [41]. The algorithm of [41] involves $\tilde{O}(m)$ *sequential* iterations of `Nibble` with a random starting vertex on the remaining subgraph. Roughly speaking, the procedure `Nibble` aims at finding a sparse cut by simulating a random walk. The idea is that if the starting vertex v belongs to some sparse cut S, then it is likely that most of the probability mass will be trapped inside S. Chang, Pettie, and Zhang [8] showed that $\tilde{O}(m)$ simultaneous iterations of an approximate version of `Nibble` with a random starting vertex can be implemented efficiently in CONGEST in $O(\text{poly}(1/\phi, \log n))$ rounds, where ϕ is the target conductance. A major difference between this work and [8] is that the expander decomposition algorithm of [8] does not need any requirement about the balance of the cut in their sparse cut computation.

Note that the $\tilde{O}(m)$ *sequential* iterations of `Nibble` in the nearly most balanced sparse cut algorithm of [41] cannot be completely parallelized. For example, it is possible that the union of all $\tilde{O}(m)$ output of `Nibble` equals the entire graph. Nonetheless, we show that this process can be partially parallelized at the cost of worsening the conductance guarantee by a polylogarithmic factor.

Theorem 3 (Nearly most balanced sparse cut). *Given a parameter $\phi = O(1/\log^5 n)$, there is an $O(D \cdot \text{poly}(\log n, 1/\phi))$-round algorithm $\mathcal{A}$ that achieves the following w.h.p.*

- *In case $\Phi(G) \leq \phi$, the algorithm $\mathcal{A}$ is guaranteed to return a cut C with balance $\text{bal}(C) \geq \min\{b/2, 1/48\}$ and conductance $\Phi(C) = O(\phi^{1/3} \log^{5/3} n)$, where b is defined as $b = \text{bal}(S)$, where S is a most-balanced sparse cut of G of conductance at most ϕ.*
- *In case $\Phi(G) > \phi$, the algorithm $\mathcal{A}$ either returns $C = \emptyset$ or returns a cut C with conductance $\Phi(C) = O(\phi^{1/3} \log^{5/3} n)$.*

The proof of Theorem 3 is in the full version of the paper [7]. We note again that this is the first distributed sparse cut algorithm with a nearly most balanced guarantee. The problem of finding a sparse cut the distributed setting has been studied prior to the work of [8]. Given that there is a ϕ-sparse cut and balance b, the algorithm of Das Sarma, Molla, and Pandurangan [38] finds a cut of conductance at most $\tilde{O}(\sqrt{\phi})$ in $\tilde{O}((n+(1/\phi))/b)$ rounds in CONGEST. The round complexity was later improved to $\tilde{O}(D + 1/(b\phi))$ by Kuhn and Molla [25]. These prior works have the following drawbacks: (1) their running time depends on b which can be as small as $O(1/n)$, and (2) their output cuts are not guaranteed to be nearly most balanced (see footnote 1).

Low Diameter Decomposition. The runtime of our distributed sparse cut algorithm (Theorem 3) is proportional to the diameter. To avoid running this algorithm on a high diameter graph, we employ a low diameter decomposition to decompose the current graph into components of small diameter.

The low diameter decomposition algorithm of Miller, Peng, and Xu [28] can already be implemented in CONGEST efficiently. Roughly, their algorithm is to let each vertex v sample $\delta_v \sim \text{Exponential}(\beta)$, $\beta \in (0, 1)$, and then v is assigned to the cluster of u that minimizes $\text{dist}(u, v) - \delta_u$. A similar approach has been applied to construct a *network decomposition* [4, 27].

However, there is one subtle issue that the guarantee that the number of inter-cluster edges is at most $O(\beta|E|)$ only holds *in expectation.* In sequential or parallel computation model, we can simply repeat the procedure for several times and take the best result. In CONGEST, this however takes at least diameter time, which is inefficient when the diameter is large.

We provide a technique that allows us to achieve this guarantee *with high probability* without spending diameter time, so we can ensure that the number of inter-cluster edges is small with high probability in our expander decomposition algorithm.[5]

Intuitively, the main barrier needed to be overcome is the high dependence among the $|E|$ events that an edge $\{u, v\}$ has its endpoints in different clusters. Our strategy is to compute a partition $V = V_D \cup V_S$ in such a way that V_D already induces a low diameter clustering, and the edges incident to V_S satisfy the property that if we run the the low diameter decomposition algorithm of [28], the events that they are inter-cluster have sufficiently small dependence. Then we can use a variant of Chernoff bound with bounded dependence [35] to bound the number of inter-cluster edges with high probability.

Theorem 4 (Low diameter decomposition). *Let $\beta \in (0, 1)$. There is an $O(\text{poly}(\log n, 1/\beta))$-round algorithm $\mathcal{A}$ that finds a partition of the vertex set $V = V_1 \cup \cdots \cup V_x$ satisfying the following conditions w.h.p.*

- *Each component V_i has diameter $O\left(\frac{\log^2 n}{\beta^2}\right)$.*
- *The number of inter-component edges $(|\partial(V_1)| + \cdots + |\partial(V_x)|)/2$ is at most $\beta|E|$.*

Adapting the algorithm of [28] to CONGEST, in $O\left(\frac{\log n}{\beta}\right)$ rounds we can decompose the graph into components of diameter $O\left(\frac{\log n}{\beta}\right)$ such that the number of inter-component edges is $O(\beta|E|)$ *in expectation.* In the full version of the paper [7] we extend this result to obtain a high probability bound and prove Theorem 4.

Triangle Enumeration. Incorporating our expander decomposition algorithm (Theorem 1) with the triangle enumeration algorithm of [8, 15], we immediately obtain an $\tilde{O}(n^{1/3}) \cdot 2^{O(\sqrt{\log n})}$-round algorithm for triangle enumeration. This round complexity can be further improved to $\tilde{O}(n^{1/3})$ by adjusting the routing algorithm of Ghaffari, Kuhn, and Su [15] on graphs of small mixing time. The main observation is their algorithm can be viewed as a distributed data structure with a trade-off between the query time and the pre-processing time. In particular, for any given constant $\epsilon > 0$, it is possible to achieve $O(\text{poly} \log n)$ query time by spending $O(n^{\epsilon})$ time on pre-processing.

[5] We remark that the triangle enumeration algorithm of [8] still works even if the guarantee on the number of inter-cluster edges in the expander decomposition only holds in expectation.

2 EXPANDER DECOMPOSITION

The goal of this section is to prove Theorem 1.

Theorem 1. *Let $\epsilon \in (0,1)$, and let k be a positive integer. An (ϵ, ϕ)-expander decomposition with $\phi = (\epsilon/\log n)^{2^{O(k)}}$ can be constructed in $O\left(n^{2/k} \cdot \text{poly}(1/\phi, \log n)\right) = O\left(n^{2/k} \cdot \left(\frac{\log n}{\epsilon}\right)^{2^{O(k)}}\right)$ rounds, w.h.p.*

For the sake of convenience, we denote

$$h(\theta) = \Theta\left(\theta^{1/3} \log^{5/3} n\right)$$

as an increasing function associated with Theorem 3 such that when we run the nearly most balanced sparse cut algorithm of Theorem 3 with conductance parameter θ, if the output subset C is non-empty, then it has $\Phi(C) \le h(\theta)$. We note that

$$h^{-1}(\theta) = \Theta\left(\theta^3/\log^5 n\right).$$

Let $\epsilon \in (0,1)$ and $k \ge 1$ be the parameters specified in Theorem 1. We define the following parameters that are used in our algorithm.

Nearly Most Balanced Sparse Cut: We define $\phi_0 = O(\epsilon^2/\log^7 n)$ in such a way that when we run the nearly most balanced sparse cut algorithm with this conductance parameter, any non-empty output C must satisfy $\Phi(C) \le h(\phi_0) = \frac{\epsilon/6}{\log\binom{n}{2}}$. For each $1 \le i \le k$, we define $\phi_i = h^{-1}(\phi_{i-1})$.

Low Diameter Decomposition: The parameter $\beta = O(\epsilon^2/\log n)$ for the low diameter decomposition is chosen as follows. Set $d = O((1/\epsilon)\log n)$ as the smallest integer such that $(1 - \epsilon/12)^d \cdot 2\binom{n}{2} < 1$. Then we define $\beta = (\epsilon/3)/d$.

We show that an (ϵ, ϕ)-expander decomposition can be constructed in $O\left(n^{2/k} \cdot \text{poly}(1/\phi, \log n)\right)$ rounds, with conductance parameter $\phi = \phi_k = (\epsilon/\log n)^{2^{O(k)}}$. We will later see that $\phi = \phi_k$ is the smallest conductance parameter we ever use for applying the nearly most balanced sparse cut algorithm.

Algorithm. Our algorithm has two phases. In the algorithm there are three places where we remove edges from the graph, and they are tagged with Remove-j, for $1 \le j \le 3$ for convenience. Whenever we remove an edge $e = \{u, v\}$, we add a self loop at both u and v, and so the degree of a vertex never changes throughout the algorithm. We never remove self loops.

At the end of the algorithm, V is partitioned into connected components $V_1, \ldots, V_x$ induced by the remaining edges. To prove the correctness of the algorithm, we will show that the number of removed edges is at most $\epsilon|E|$, and $\Phi_{G\{V_i\}} \ge \phi$ for each component V_i.

Phase 1.

The input graph is $G = (V, E)$.

(1) Do the low diameter decomposition algorithm (Theorem 4) with parameter β on G. Remove all inter-cluster edges (Remove-1).
(2) For each connected component U of the graph, do the nearly most balanced sparse cut algorithm (Theorem 3) with parameter ϕ_0 on $G\{U\}$. Let C be the output subset.
   (a) If $C = \emptyset$, then the subgraph $G^* = G\{U\}$ quits Phase 1.
   (b) If $C \ne \emptyset$ and $\text{Vol}(C) \le (\epsilon/12)\text{Vol}(U)$, then the subgraph $G^* = G\{U\}$ quits Phase 1 and enters Phase 2.
   (c) Otherwise, remove the cut edges $E(C, U \setminus C)$ (Remove-2), and then we recurse on both sides $G\{C\}$ and $G\{U \setminus C\}$ of the cut.

We emphasize that we do not remove the cut edges in Step 2b of Phase 1.

Lemma 1. *The depth of the recursion of Phase 1 is at most d.*

Proof. Suppose there is still a component U entering the depth $d+1$ of the recursion of Phase 1. Then according to the threshold for $\text{Vol}(C)$ specified in Step 2b, we infer that $\text{Vol}(U) \le (1 - \epsilon/12)^d \text{Vol}(V) < 1$ by our choice of d, which is impossible. □

Phase 2.

The input graph is $G^* = G\{U\}$. Define $\tau \stackrel{\text{def}}{=} ((\epsilon/6) \cdot \text{Vol}(U))^{1/k}$. Define the sequence: $m_1 \stackrel{\text{def}}{=} (\epsilon/6) \cdot \text{Vol}(U)$, and $m_i \stackrel{\text{def}}{=} m_{i-1}/\tau$, for each $1 < i \le k+1$. Initialize $L \leftarrow 1$ and $U' \leftarrow U$. Repeatedly do the following procedure.

- Do the nearly most balanced sparse cut algorithm (Theorem 3) with parameter ϕ_L on $G\{U'\}$. Let C be the output subset. Note that $\Phi_{G\{U'\}}(C) \le \phi_{L-1}$.
  - If $C = \emptyset$, then the subgraph $G\{U'\}$ quits Phase 2.
  - If $C \ne \emptyset$ and $\text{Vol}(C) \le m_L/(2\tau)$, then update $L \leftarrow L+1$.
  - Otherwise, update $U' \leftarrow U' \setminus C$, and remove all edges incident to C (Remove-3).

Intuitively, in Phase 2 we keep calling the nearly most balanced sparse cut algorithm to find a cut C and remove it. If we find a cut C that has volume greater than $m_L/(2\tau)$, then we make a good progress. If $\text{Vol}(C) \le m_L/(2\tau)$, then we learn that the volume of the most balanced sparse cut of conductance at most ϕ_L is at most $2 \cdot m_L/(2\tau) = m_L/\tau = m_{L+1}$ by Theorem 3, and so we move on to the next level by setting $L \leftarrow L+1$.

The maximum possible level L is k. Since by definition $m_k/(2\tau) = 1/2 < 1$, there is no possibility to increase L to $k+1$. Once we reach $L = k$, we will repeatedly run the nearly most balanced sparse cut algorithm until we get $C = \emptyset$ and quit.

When we remove a cut $C \ne \emptyset$ in Phase 2, each $u \in C$ becomes an isolated vertex with $\deg(u)$ self loops, as all edges incident to u have been removed, and so in the final decomposition $V = V_1 \cup \cdots \cup V_x$ we have $V_i = \{u\}$ for some i. We emphasize that we only do the edge removal when $\text{Vol}(C) > m_L/(2\tau)$. Lemma 2 bounds the volume of the cuts found during Phase 2.

Lemma 2. *For each $1 \le i \le k$, define C_i as the union of all subsets C found in Phase 2 when $L \ge i$. Then either $C_i = \emptyset$ or $\text{Vol}(C_i) \le m_i$.*

Proof. We first consider the case of $i = 1$. Observe that the graph $G^* = G\{U\}$ satisfies the property that the most balanced sparse cut of conductance at most ϕ_0 has balance at most $2(\epsilon/12) = \epsilon/6$, since otherwise it does not meet the condition for entering Phase 2. Note that all cuts we find during Phase 2 have conductance at most ϕ_0, and so the union of them C_1 is also a cut of G^* with conductance at most ϕ_0. This implies that $\text{Vol}(C_1) \leq (\epsilon/6)\text{Vol}(U) = m_1$.

The proof for the case of $2 \leq i \leq k$ is exactly the same, as the condition for increasing L is to have $\text{Vol}(C) \leq m_L/(2\tau)$. Let $G' = G\{U'\}$ be the graph considered in the iteration when we increase $L = i - 1$ to $L = i$. The existence of such a cut C of G' implies that the most balanced sparse cut of conductance at most ϕ_{i-1} of G' has volume at most $2\,\text{Vol}(C) \leq m_{i-1}/\tau = m_i$. Similarly, note that all cuts we find when $L \geq i$ have conductance at most ϕ_{i-1}, and so the union of them C_i is also a cut of G' with conductance at most ϕ_{i-1}. This implies that $\text{Vol}(C_i) \leq m_i$. □

Conductance of Remaining Components. For each $u \in V$, there are two possible ways for u to end the algorithm:

- During Phase 1 or Phase 2, the output of the nearly most balanced sparse cut algorithm on the component that u belongs to is $C = \emptyset$. In this case, the component that u belongs to becomes a component V_i in the final decomposition $V = V_1 \cup \cdots \cup V_x$. If ϕ' is the conductance parameter used in the nearly most balanced sparse cut algorithm, then $\Phi(G\{V_i\}) \geq \phi'$. Note that $\phi' \geq \phi_k = \phi$.
- During Phase 2, $u \in C$ for the output C of the nearly most balanced sparse cut algorithm. In this case, u itself becomes a component $V_i = \{u\}$ in the final decomposition $V = V_1 \cup \cdots \cup V_x$. Trivially, we have $\Phi(G\{V_i\}) \geq \phi$.

Therefore, we conclude that each component V_i in the final decomposition $V = V_1 \cup \cdots \cup V_x$ satisfies that $\Phi(G\{V_i\}) \geq \phi$.

Number of Removed Edges. There are three places in the algorithm where we remove edges. We show that, for each $1 \leq j \leq 3$, the number of edges removed due to Remove-j is at most $(\epsilon/3)|E|$, and so the total number of inter-component edges in the final decomposition $V = V_1 \cup \cdots \cup V_x$ is at most $\epsilon|E|$.

(1) By Lemma 1, the depth of recursion of Phase 1 is at most d. For each $i = 1$ to d, the number of edges removed due to the low diameter decomposition algorithm during depth i of the recursion is at most $\beta|E|$. By our choice of β, the number of edges removed due to Remove-1 is at most $d \cdot \beta|E| \leq (\epsilon/3)|E|$.
(2) For each edge $e \in E(C, U \setminus C)$ removed due to the nearly most balanced sparse cut algorithm in Phase 1, we charge the cost of the edge removal to some pairs (v, e) in the following way. If $\text{Vol}(C) < \text{Vol}(U \setminus C)$, for each $v \in C$, and for each edge e incident to v, we charge the amount $|E(C, U \setminus C)|/\text{Vol}(C)$ to (v, e); otherwise, for each $v \in U \setminus C$, and for each edge e incident to v, we charge the amount $|E(C, U \setminus C)|/\text{Vol}(U \setminus C)$ to (v, e). Note that each pair (v, e) is being charged for at most $\log|E|$ times throughout the algorithm, and the amount per charging is at most $h(\phi_0)$. Therefore, the number of edges removed due to Remove-2 is at most $(\log|E|) \cdot h(\phi_0) \cdot 2|E| \leq (\epsilon/3)|E|$ by our choice of ϕ_0.
(3) By Lemma 2, the summation of $\text{Vol}(C)$ over all cuts C in $G^* = G\{U\}$ that are found and removed during Phase 2 due to Remove-3 is at most $m_1 = (\epsilon/6)\text{Vol}(U) \leq (\epsilon/3)|E|$.

Round Complexity. During Phase 1, each vertex participates in at most $d = O((1/\epsilon)\log n)$ times the nearly most balanced sparse cut algorithm and the low diameter decomposition algorithm. By our choice of parameters $\beta = O(\epsilon^2/\log n)$ and $\phi_0 = O(\epsilon^2/\log^7 n)$, the round complexity of both algorithms are $O(\text{poly}(1/\epsilon, \log n))$, as we note that whenever we run the nearly most balanced sparse cut algorithm, the diameter of each connected component is at most $O\left(\frac{\log^2 n}{\beta^2}\right) = O\left(\frac{\log^4 n}{\epsilon^4}\right)$.

For Phase 2, Lemma 2 guarantees that for each $1 \leq i \leq k$ the algorithm can stay $L = i$ for at most 2τ iterations. If we neither increase L nor quit Phase 2 for 2τ iterations, then we have $\text{Vol}(C_L) > m_L$, which is impossible. Therefore, the round complexity for Phase 2 can be upper bounded by

$$2\tau \sum_{i=1}^{k} O(\text{poly}(1/\phi_i, \log n)) \leq O\left(n^{2/k} \cdot \text{poly}(1/\phi, \log n)\right).$$

During Phase 2, it is possible that the graph $G\{U'\}$ be disconnected or has a large diameter, but we are fine since we can use all edges in G^* for communication during a sparse cut computation, and the diameter of G^* is at most $O\left(\frac{\log^2 n}{\beta^2}\right) = O\left(\frac{\log^4 n}{\epsilon^4}\right)$.

3 TRIANGLE ENUMERATION

We show how to derive Theorem 2 by combining Theorem 1 with other known results in [8, 15].

Theorem 2. *Triangle enumeration can be solved in $\tilde{O}(n^{1/3})$ rounds in CONGEST, w.h.p.*

Chang, Pettie, and Zhang [8] showed that given an (ϵ, ϕ)-expander decomposition $V = V_1 \cup \ldots \cup V_x$ with $\epsilon \leq 1/6$, there is an algorithm $\mathcal{A}$ that finds an edge subset $E^* \subseteq E$ with $|E^*| \leq |E|/2$ such that each triangle in G is detected by some vertex during the execution of $\mathcal{A}$, except the triangles whose three edges are all within $|E^*|$. The algorithm $\mathcal{A}$ has to solve $\tilde{O}(n^{1/3})$ times the following routing problem in each $G[V_i]$. Given a set of routing requests where each vertex v is a source or a destination for at most $O(\deg(v))$ messages of $O(\log n)$ bits, the goal is to deliver all messages to their destinations. Ghaffari, Khun, and Su [15] showed that this routing problem can be solved in $2^{O(\sqrt{\log n \log\log n})} \cdot O(\tau_{\text{mix}})$ rounds. This was later improved to $2^{O(\sqrt{\log n})} \cdot O(\tau_{\text{mix}})$ by Ghaffari and Li [16].

Applying our distributed expander decomposition algorithm (Theorem 1), we can find an (ϵ, ϕ)-expander decomposition with $\epsilon \leq 1/6$ and $\phi = 1/O(\text{poly}\log n)$ in $o(n^{1/3})$ rounds by selecting k to be a sufficiently large constant. The mixing time τ_{mix} of each component $G[V_i]$ is at most $O\left(\frac{\log n}{\phi^2}\right) = O(\text{poly}\log n)$. Then we apply the above algorithm $\mathcal{A}$, and it takes $2^{O(\sqrt{\log n})} \cdot O(\tau_{\text{mix}}) = 2^{O(\sqrt{\log n})}$ rounds with the routing algorithm of Ghaffari and Li [16]. After that, we recurse on the edge set E^*, and we are done enumerating all triangles after $O(\log n)$ iterations. This concludes the $O(n^{1/3}) \cdot 2^{O(\sqrt{\log n})}$-round algorithm for triangle enumeration.

To improve the complexity to $\tilde{O}(n^{1/3})$, we make the observation that the routing algorithm of [15] can be seen as a distributed data structure with the following properties.

Parameters: The parameter k is a positive integer that specifies the depth of the hierarchical structure in the routing algorithm. Given k, define β as the number such that $k = \log_\beta m$, where m is the total number of edges.

Pre-processing Time: The algorithm for building the data structure consists of two parts. The round complexity for building the hierarchical structure is $O(k\beta)(\log n)^{O(k)} \cdot O(\tau_{\text{mix}})$ [15, Lemma 3.2]. The round complexity for adding the portals is $O(k\beta^2 \log n) \cdot O(\tau_{\text{mix}})$ [15, Lemma 3.3]

Query Time: After building the data structure, each routing task can be solved in $(\log n)^{O(k)} \cdot O(\tau_{\text{mix}})$ rounds [15, Lemma 3.4].

The parameter k can be chosen as any positive integer. In [15] they used $k = \Theta(\sqrt{\log n / \log\log n})$ to balance the pre-processing time and the query time to show that the routing task can be solved in $2^{O(\sqrt{\log n \log\log n})} \cdot O(\tau_{\text{mix}})$ rounds. This round complexity was later improved to $2^{O(\sqrt{\log n})} \cdot O(\tau_{\text{mix}})$ in [16]. We however note that the algorithm of [16] does not admit a trade-off as above. The main reason is their special treatment of the base layer G_0 of the hierarchical structure. In [16], G_0 is a random graph with degree $2^{O(\sqrt{\log n})}$, and simulating one round in G_0 already costs $2^{O(\sqrt{\log n})}$. τ_{mix} rounds in the original graph G.

In the triangle enumeration algorithm $\mathcal{A}$, we need to query this distributed data structure for $\tilde{O}(n^{1/3})$ times. It is possible to set k to be a large enough constant so that the pre-processing time costs only $o(n^{1/3})$ rounds, while the query time is still $O(\text{poly} \log n)$. This implies that the triangle enumeration problem can be solved in $\tilde{O}(n^{1/3})$ rounds.

4 OPEN PROBLEMS

In this paper, we designed a new expander decomposition algorithm that get rids of the low-arboricity part needed in [8], and this implies that triangle enumeration can solved in $\tilde{O}(n^{1/3})$ rounds, which is optimal up to a polylogarithmic factor.

Many interesting problems are left open. In particular, the current exponent of the polylogarithmic gap between the lower and the upper bounds is enormous. The huge exponent is caused by the inefficient trade-off between the parameters in the (i) hierarchical routing structure and the (ii) expander decomposition algorithm. Improving the current state of the art of (i) and (ii) will lead to an improved upper bound for triangle enumeration, as well as several other problems [11, 15, 16].

We note that the lower bound graph underlying the $\Omega(n^{1/3}/\log n)$ lower bound [19, 33] for triangle enumeration is the Erdős-Rényi random graph $\mathcal{G}(n,p)$ with $p = 1/2$. Hence it does not rule out the possibility of an $n^{(1/3)-\Omega(1)}$-round CONGEST algorithm for the enumeration problem on sparse graphs (i.e. $m = o(n^2)$) or the detection problem. It remains an open problem to find the asymptotically optimal round complexity of these problems in CONGEST. For the case of CONGESTED-CLIQUE, efficient algorithms for these problems are already known: triangle detection can be solved in $\tilde{O}(n^{1-(2/\omega)+o(1)}) = o(n^{0.158})$ time [5], triangle enumeration on m-edge graphs can be solved in $\max\{O(m/n^{5/3}), O(1)\}$ time [6, 33].

We would also like to further investigate the power of the distributed expander decomposition. Can this tool be applied to other distributed problems than triangle detection and enumeration? It has been known that this technique can be applied to give a sublinear-time distributed algorithm for *exact* minimum cut [11]. We expect to see more applications of distributed expander decomposition in the future.

ACKNOWLEDGMENTS

We thank Seth Pettie for very useful discussion.

REFERENCES

[1] Amir Abboud, Keren Censor-Hillel, Seri Khoury, and Christoph Lenzen. 2017. Fooling views: A new lower bound technique for distributed computations under congestion. *arXiv preprint arXiv:1711.01623* (2017).

[2] Sanjeev Arora, Boaz Barak, and David Steurer. 2015. Subexponential Algorithms for Unique Games and Related Problems. *J. ACM* 62, 5, Article 42 (Nov. 2015), 25 pages.

[3] Sanjeev Arora, Satish Rao, and Umesh Vazirani. 2009. Expander Flows, Geometric Embeddings and Graph Partitioning. *J. ACM* 56, 2, Article 5 (April 2009), 37 pages. https://doi.org/10.1145/1502793.1502794

[4] Baruch Awerbuch, Bonnie Berger, Lenore Cowen, and David Peleg. 1994. Low-diameter graph decomposition is in NC. *Random Structures & Algorithms* 5, 3 (1994), 441–452.

[5] Keren Censor-Hillel, Petteri Kaski, Janne H. Korhonen, Christoph Lenzen, Ami Paz, and Jukka Suomela. 2016. Algebraic methods in the congested clique. *Distributed Computing* (2016).

[6] Keren Censor-Hillel, Dean Leitersdorf, and Elia Turner. 2018. Sparse Matrix Multiplication and Triangle Listing in the Congested Clique Model. In *22nd International Conference on Principles of Distributed Systems (OPODIS 2018) (Leibniz International Proceedings in Informatics (LIPIcs))*, Jiannong Cao, Faith Ellen, Luis Rodrigues, and Bernardo Ferreira (Eds.), Vol. 125. Schloss Dagstuhl–Leibniz-Zentrum fuer Informatik, Dagstuhl, Germany, 4:1–4:17. https://doi.org/10.4230/LIPIcs.OPODIS.2018.4

[7] Yi-Jun Chang and Thatchaphol Saranurak. 2019. Improved Distributed Expander Decomposition and Nearly Optimal Triangle Enumeration. *CoRR* abs/1904.08037 (2019). arXiv:1904.08037 http://arxiv.org/abs/1904.08037

[8] Yi-Jun. Chang, Seth Pettie, and Hengjie Zhang. 2019. Distributed Triangle Detection via Expander Decomposition. In *Proceedings of the 30th Annual ACM-SIAM Symposium on Discrete Algorithms (SODA)*. 821–840.

[9] Timothy Chu, Yu Gao, Richard Peng, Sushant Sachdeva, Saurabh Sawlani, and Junxing Wang. 2018. Graph Sparsification, Spectral Sketches, and Faster Resistance Computation, via Short Cycle Decompositions. In *59th IEEE Annual Symposium on Foundations of Computer Science, FOCS 2018, Paris, France, October 7-9, 2018*. 361–372. https://doi.org/10.1109/FOCS.2018.00042

[10] Michael B. Cohen, Jonathan A. Kelner, John Peebles, Richard Peng, Anup B. Rao, Aaron Sidford, and Adrian Vladu. 2017. Almost-linear-time algorithms for Markov chains and new spectral primitives for directed graphs. In *Proceedings of the 49th Annual ACM SIGACT Symposium on Theory of Computing, STOC 2017, Montreal, QC, Canada, June 19-23, 2017*. 410–419. https://doi.org/10.1145/3055399.3055463

[11] Mohit Daga, Monika Henzinger, Danupon Nanongkai, and Thatchaphol Saranurak. 2019. Distributed Edge Connectivity in Sublinear Time. *arXiv preprint arXiv:1904.04341* (2019). To appear at STOC'19.

[12] Danny Dolev, Christoph Lenzen, and Shir Peled. 2012. "Tri, Tri Again": Finding Triangles and Small Subgraphs in a Distributed Setting. In *Proceedings 26th International Symposium on Distributed Computing (DISC)*. 195–209.

[13] Andrew Drucker, Fabian Kuhn, and Rotem Oshman. 2014. On the power of the congested clique model. In *Proceedings 33rd ACM Symposium on Principles of Distributed Computing (PODC)*. 367–376.

[14] Orr Fischer, Tzlil Gonen, Fabian Kuhn, and Rotem Oshman. 2018. Possibilities and Impossibilities for Distributed Subgraph Detection. In *Proceedings of the 30th on Symposium on Parallelism in Algorithms and Architectures (SPAA)*. ACM, New York, NY, USA, 153–162.

[15] Mohsen Ghaffari, Fabian Kuhn, and Hsin-Hao Su. 2017. Distributed MST and Routing in Almost Mixing Time. In *Proceedings 37th ACM Symposium on Principles of Distributed Computing (PODC)*. 131–140.

[16] Mohsen Ghaffari and Jason Li. 2018. New Distributed Algorithms in Almost Mixing Time via Transformations from Parallel Algorithms. In *Proceedings 32nd International Symposium on Distributed Computing (DISC) (Leibniz International Proceedings in Informatics (LIPIcs))*, Ulrich Schmid and Josef Widder (Eds.), Vol. 121. Schloss Dagstuhl–Leibniz-Zentrum fuer Informatik, Dagstuhl, Germany, 31:1–31:16.

[17] Mohsen Ghaffari and Krzysztof Nowicki. 2018. Congested Clique Algorithms for the Minimum Cut Problem. In *Proceedings of the 2018 ACM Symposium on Principles of Distributed Computing (PODC '18)*. ACM, New York, NY, USA, 357–366. https://doi.org/10.1145/3212734.3212750

[18] Oded Goldreich and Dana Ron. 1999. A Sublinear Bipartiteness Tester for Bounded Degree Graphs. *Combinatorica* 19, 3 (01 Mar 1999), 335–373.

[19] Taisuke Izumi and François Le Gall. 2017. Triangle Finding and Listing in CONGEST Networks. In *Proceedings 37th ACM Symposium on Principles of Distributed Computing (PODC)*. 381–389. https://doi.org/10.1145/3087801.3087811

[20] Mark Jerrum and Alistair Sinclair. 1989. Approximating the Permanent. *SIAM J. Comput.* 18, 6 (1989), 1149–1178.

[21] Tomasz Jurdziński and Krzysztof Nowicki. 2018. MST in $O(1)$ Rounds of Congested Clique. In *Proceedings 29th Annual ACM-SIAM Symposium on Discrete Algorithms (SODA)*. 2620–2632.

[22] Ravi Kannan, Santosh Vempala, and Adrian Vetta. 2004. On Clusterings: Good, Bad and Spectral. *J. ACM* 51, 3 (May 2004), 497–515. https://doi.org/10.1145/990308.990313

[23] Ken-Ichi Kawarabayashi and Mikkel Thorup. 2018. Deterministic Edge Connectivity in Near-Linear Time. *J. ACM* 66, 1, Article 4 (Dec. 2018), 4:1–4:50 pages.

[24] Jonathan A. Kelner, Yin Tat Lee, Lorenzo Orecchia, and Aaron Sidford. 2014. An Almost-Linear-Time Algorithm for Approximate Max Flow in Undirected Graphs, and its Multicommodity Generalizations. In *Proceedings of the Twenty-Fifth Annual ACM-SIAM Symposium on Discrete Algorithms, SODA 2014, Portland, Oregon, USA, January 5-7, 2014*. 217–226. https://doi.org/10.1137/1.9781611973402.16

[25] Fabian Kuhn and Anisur Rahaman Molla. 2015. Distributed Sparse Cut Approximation. In *Proceedings 19th International Conference on Principles of Distributed Systems (OPODIS)*. 10:1–10:14.

[26] François Le Gall. 2014. Powers of Tensors and Fast Matrix Multiplication. In *Proceedings of the 39th International Symposium on Symbolic and Algebraic Computation (ISSAC '14)*. ACM, New York, NY, USA, 296–303. https://doi.org/10.1145/2608628.2608664

[27] Nathan Linial and Michael Saks. 1993. Low diameter graph decompositions. *Combinatorica* 13, 4 (01 Dec 1993), 441–454

[28] Gary L. Miller, Richard Peng, and Shen Chen Xu. 2013. Parallel graph decompositions using random shifts. In *Proceedings of the twenty-fifth annual ACM symposium on Parallelism in algorithms and architectures (SPAA)*. ACM, 196–203.

[29] Danupon Nanongkai and Thatchaphol Saranurak. 2017. Dynamic spanning forest with worst-case update time: adaptive, Las Vegas, and $O(n^{1/2-\epsilon})$-time. In *Proceedings of the 49th Annual ACM SIGACT Symposium on Theory of Computing, STOC 2017, Montreal, QC, Canada, June 19-23, 2017*. 1122–1129. https://doi.org/10.1145/3055399.3055447

[30] Danupon Nanongkai, Thatchaphol Saranurak, and Christian Wulff-Nilsen. 2017. Dynamic minimum spanning forest with subpolynomial worst-case update time. In *Proceedings of IEEE 58th Annual Symposium on Foundations of Computer Science (FOCS)*. IEEE, 950–961.

[31] Lorenzo Orecchia and Nisheeth K. Vishnoi. 2011. Towards an SDP-based Approach to Spectral Methods: A Nearly-Linear-Time Algorithm for Graph Partitioning and Decomposition. In *Proceedings of the Twenty-Second Annual ACM-SIAM Symposium on Discrete Algorithms, SODA 2011, San Francisco, California, USA, January 23-25, 2011*. 532–545. https://doi.org/10.1137/1.9781611973082.42

[32] Lorenzo Orecchia and Zeyuan Allen Zhu. 2014. Flow-based Algorithms for Local Graph Clustering. In *Proceedings of the Twenty-fifth Annual ACM-SIAM Symposium on Discrete Algorithms (SODA '14)*. Society for Industrial and Applied Mathematics, Philadelphia, PA, USA, 1267–1286. http://dl.acm.org/citation.cfm?id=2634074.2634168

[33] Gopal Pandurangan, Peter Robinson, and Michele Scquizzato. 2018. On the Distributed Complexity of Large-Scale Graph Computations. In *Proceedings 30th ACM Symposium on Parallelism in Algorithms and Architecture (SPAA)*.

[34] M. Pătraşcu and M. Thorup. 2007. Planning for Fast Connectivity Updates. In *Proceedings 48th IEEE Symposium on Foundations of Computer Science (FOCS)*. 263–271.

[35] Sriram V. Pemmaraju. 2001. Equitable Coloring Extends Chernoff-Hoeffding Bounds. In *Approximation, Randomization, and Combinatorial Optimization: Algorithms and Techniques*, Michel Goemans, Klaus Jansen, José D. P. Rolim, and Luca Trevisan (Eds.). Springer Berlin Heidelberg, Berlin, Heidelberg, 285–296.

[36] Prasad Raghavendra and David Steurer. 2010. Graph Expansion and the Unique Games Conjecture. In *Proceedings 42nd ACM Symposium on Theory of Computing (STOC)*. 755–764.

[37] Thatchaphol Saranurak and Di Wang. 2019. Expander Decomposition and Pruning: Faster, Stronger, and Simpler. In *Proceedings of the 30th Annual ACM-SIAM Symposium on Discrete Algorithms (SODA)*. 2616–2635.

[38] Atish Das Sarma, Anisur Rahaman Molla, and Gopal Pandurangan. 2015. Distributed Computation of Sparse Cuts via Random Walks. In *Proceedings 16th International Conference on Distributed Computing and Networking (ICDCN)*. 6:1–6:10.

[39] Daniel A. Spielman and Nikhil Srivastava. 2008. Graph sparsification by effective resistances. In *Proceedings 40th ACM Symposium on Theory of Computing (STOC)*. 563–568.

[40] Daniel A. Spielman and Shang-Hua Teng. 2011. Spectral Sparsification of Graphs. *SIAM J. Comput.* 40, 4 (2011), 981–1025. https://doi.org/10.1137/08074489X

[41] Daniel A. Spielman and Shang-Hua Teng. 2013. A Local Clustering Algorithm for Massive Graphs and Its Application to Nearly Linear Time Graph Partitioning. *SIAM J. Comput.* 42, 1 (2013), 1–26.

[42] Daniel A. Spielman and Shang-Hua Teng. 2014. Nearly Linear Time Algorithms for Preconditioning and Solving Symmetric, Diagonally Dominant Linear Systems. *SIAM J. Matrix Anal. Appl.* 35, 3 (2014), 835–885.

[43] Luca Trevisan. 2008. Approximation Algorithms for Unique Games. *Theory of Computing* 4, 5 (2008), 111–128.

[44] Christian Wulff-Nilsen. 2017. Fully-dynamic minimum spanning forest with improved worst-case update time. In *Proceedings of the 49th Annual ACM SIGACT Symposium on Theory of Computing, STOC 2017, Montreal, QC, Canada, June 19-23, 2017*. 1130–1143. https://doi.org/10.1145/3055399.3055415

Fast Approximate Shortest Paths in the Congested Clique*

Keren Censor-Hillel
Technion, Department of Computer Science
ckeren@cs.technion.ac.il

Michal Dory
Technion, Department of Computer Science
smichald@cs.technion.ac.il

Janne H. Korhonen
IST Austria
janne.korhonen@ist.ac.at

Dean Leitersdorf
Technion, Department of Computer Science
dean.leitersdorf@gmail.com

ABSTRACT

We design fast *deterministic* algorithms for distance computation in the Congested Clique model. Our key contributions include:

- A $(2+\epsilon)$-approximation for all-pairs shortest paths problem in $O(\log^2 n/\epsilon)$ rounds on unweighted undirected graphs. With a small additional additive factor, this also applies for weighted graphs. This is the first *sub-polynomial* constant-factor approximation for APSP in this model.
- A $(1+\epsilon)$-approximation for multi-source shortest paths problem from $O(\sqrt{n})$ sources in $O(\log^2 n/\epsilon)$ rounds on weighted undirected graphs. This is the first *sub-polynomial* algorithm obtaining this approximation for a set of sources of polynomial size.

Our main techniques are new distance tools that are obtained via improved algorithms for sparse matrix multiplication, which we leverage to construct efficient hopsets and shortest paths. Furthermore, our techniques extend to additional distance problems for which we improve upon the state-of-the-art, including diameter approximation, and an *exact* single-source shortest paths algorithm for weighted undirected graphs in $\tilde{O}(n^{1/6})$ rounds.

CCS CONCEPTS

• **Theory of computation → Distributed algorithms**; *Shortest paths*; *Approximation algorithms analysis.*

KEYWORDS

distributed computing, approximation algorithms, congested clique, all-pairs shortest paths, single-source shortest paths, diameter, matrix multiplication, hopsets

ACM Reference Format:
Keren Censor-Hillel, Michal Dory, Janne H. Korhonen, and Dean Leitersdorf. 2019. Fast Approximate Shortest Paths in the Congested Clique. In *2019 ACM Symposium on Principles of Distributed Computing (PODC '19), July 29-August 2, 2019, Toronto, ON, Canada.* ACM, New York, NY, USA, 10 pages. https://doi.org/10.1145/3293611.3331633

*A full version of this paper [13] is available at https://arxiv.org/abs/1903.05956.

PODC '19, July 29-August 2, 2019, Toronto, ON, Canada

ACM ISBN 978-1-4503-6217-7/19/07...$15.00
https://doi.org/10.1145/3293611.3331633

1 INTRODUCTION

Computing distances in a graph is a fundamental task widely studied in many computational settings. Notable examples are computation of all-pairs shortest paths (APSP), single-source shortest paths (SSSP), and computing specific parameters such as the diameter of a graph. In this work, we study distance computations in the Congested Clique model of distributed computing.

In the Congested Clique model, we have a *fully-connected* communication network of n nodes, where nodes communicate by sending $O(\log n)$-bit messages to each other node in synchronous rounds. The Congested Clique model has been receiving much attention during the past decade or so, due to both its theoretical interest in focusing on congestion alone as a communication resource, and its relation to practical settings that use fully connected overlays [14, 15, 22, 29, 30, 32–34, 37, 41–44, 48, 51–53]. In particular, there have been many recent papers studying distance problems in Congested Clique [8, 14, 15, 25, 37, 43, 49, 53].

1.1 Distance computation in the congested clique

Many state-of-the art results for distance computations in the Congested Clique model exploit the well-known connection between computing distances and matrix multiplication [14, 15, 43]. Specifically, the nth power of the adjacency matrix A of a graph $G = (V, E)$, taken over the *min-plus* or *tropical* semiring (see e.g. [14] for details), correspond to shortest-path distances. Hence, iteratively squaring a matrix $\log n$ times allows computing all the distances in the graph. This approach gives the best known algorithms for APSP in the Congested Clique, including (1) an $\tilde{O}(n^{1/3})$ round algorithm for exact APSP in weighted directed graphs [14], (2) $O(n^{0.158})$ round algorithms for exact APSP in unweighted undirected graphs and $(1+o(1))$-approximate APSP in weighted directed graphs [14], as well as (3) an $O(n^{0.2096})$ round algorithm for exact APSP in directed graphs with constant weights [43]. Additionally, in [15], this connection is used to show an improved APSP algorithm for *sparse* graphs.

For approximating the distances, faster approximations for larger constants can be obtained by computing a k-spanner, which is a sparse graph that preserves distances up to a multiplicative factor of k, and having all nodes learn the entire spanner. Using the Congested Clique spanner constructions of [53], this approach gives a $(2k-1)$-approximation for APSP in $\tilde{O}(n^{1/k})$ rounds, which is still *polynomial* for any constant k.

This raises the following fundamental question:

QUESTION 1. *Can we obtain constant-factor approximations for APSP in* sub-polynomial *time?*

If we restrict our attention to SSSP, sub-polynomial $(1+\epsilon)$-approximation is indeed possible [8, 35]; in particular, the state of the art is a gradient-descent-based algorithm that obtains a $(1+\epsilon)$-approximation in $O(\epsilon^{-3}\text{polylog } n)$ rounds even in the more restricted broadcast version of the CONGESTED CLIQUE model [8]. However, these algorithms from prior work provide distances only from a single source.

1.2 Our Contributions

All-pairs shortest paths. As our first main result, we address the above fundamental question by providing the first *polylogarithmic* constant approximations for APSP in the CONGESTED CLIQUE model. Specifically, we show the following.

THEOREM 1.1. *There is a deterministic $(2+\epsilon)$-approximation algorithm for* unweighted *undirected APSP in the CONGESTED CLIQUE model that takes $O(\frac{\log^2 n}{\epsilon})$ rounds.*

We also obtain a nearly $(2+\epsilon)$-approximation in $O(\frac{\log^2 n}{\epsilon})$ rounds in *weighted* undirected graphs, in the sense that for any distance estimate $d(u,v)$, there is further additive $(1+\epsilon)w_{uv}$ error in the approximation, where w_{uv} is the weight of the heaviest edge on the shortest u-v path.

Our approximation is almost tight for *sub-polynomial* algorithms in the following sense. As noted by [42], a $(2-\epsilon)$-approximate APSP in unweighted undirected graphs is essentially equivalent to fast matrix multiplication, so obtaining a better approximation in complexity below $O(n^{0.158})$ would result in a faster algorithm for matrix multiplication in the CONGESTED CLIQUE. Likewise, a sub-polynomial-time algorithm with *any* approximation ratio for directed graphs would give a faster matrix multiplication algorithm [21], so our results will likely not extend to directed graphs.

Multi-source shortest paths. As our second main result, we show a fast $(1+\epsilon)$-approximation algorithm for the multi-source shortest paths problem (MSSP), which is polylogarithmic as long as the number of sources is $\widetilde{O}(\sqrt{n})$. Specifically, we show the following.

THEOREM 1.2. *There is a deterministic $(1+\epsilon)$-approximation algorithm for the weighted undirected MSSP that takes*

$$O\left(\left(\frac{|S|^{2/3}}{n^{1/3}} + \log n\right) \cdot \frac{\log n}{\epsilon}\right)$$

rounds in the CONGESTED CLIQUE, where S is the set of sources. In particular, the complexity is $O(\frac{\log^2 n}{\epsilon})$ as long as $|S| \leq O(\sqrt{n} \cdot (\log n)^{3/2})$.

This is the first sub-polynomial algorithm that obtains such approximations for a set S of polynomial size. Other advantages of our approach, compared to the previous $(1+\epsilon)$-approximation SSSP algorithm [8], is that it is based on simple combinatorial techniques. In addition, our complexity improves upon the complexity of [8].

Exact SSSP and diameter approximation. In addition to the above, our techniques allow us to obtain a near 3/2-approximation for the diameter in $O(\frac{\log^2 n}{\epsilon})$ rounds, and allows obtaining an $\widetilde{O}(n^{1/6})$-round algorithm for *exact* weighted SSSP, improving the previous $\widetilde{O}(n^{1/3})$-round algorithm [14]. All our algorithms are deterministic.

1.3 Our techniques

The main technical tools we develop for our distance computation algorithms are a new *sparse matrix multiplication* algorithm, extending the recent result of [15], and new deterministic *hopset* construction algorithm for the CONGESTED CLIQUE.

Distance products. We start from the basic idea of using matrix multiplication to compute distances in graphs. Specifically, if A is the weighted adjacency matrix of a graph G, it is well known that distances in G can be computed by iterating the *distance product* $A \star A$, defined as

$$(A \star A)[i,j] = \min_k (A[i,k] + A[k,j]) ,$$

that is, the matrix multiplication over the min-plus semiring.

A simple idea is to apply the recent sparse matrix multiplication algorithm of [15], with running time that depends on the density of the input matrices. In particular, this allows us to multiply two sparse matrices with $O(n^{3/2})$ non-zero entries in $O(1)$ rounds; note that for the distance product, the zero element is ∞. However, using this algorithm for computing distances directly is inefficient, as $A \star A$ can be dense even if A is sparse (e.g. a star graph), and hence iterative squaring is not guaranteed to be efficient. Moreover, our goal is to compute distances in general graphs, not only in sparse graphs. Nevertheless, we show that while using [15] directly may not be efficient, we can use sparse matrix multiplication as a basic building block for distance computation in the CONGESTED CLIQUE.

Our distance tools. The key observation is that many building blocks for distance computation are actually based on computations in sparse graphs or only consider a limited number of nodes. Concrete examples of such tasks include:

- *k-NEAREST problem*: Compute distances for each node to the k closest nodes in the graph.
- *(S,d,k)-SOURCE DETECTION problem*: Given a set of sources S, compute the distances for each node to the k nearest sources using paths of at most d hops.
- *DISTANCE THROUGH SETS problem*: Given a set of nodes S and distances to all nodes in S, compute the distances between all nodes using paths through nodes in S.

For all of these problems, there is a degree of sparsity we can hope to exploit if k or $|S|$ are small enough. For example, the (S,d,k)-SOURCE DETECTION problem, requires the multiplication of a dense adjacency matrix and a possibly sparse matrix, depending on the size of S. However, for any S of polynomial size the algorithm in [15] is polynomial. An interesting property in this problem, though, is that the output matrix is also sparse. If we look at the k-NEAREST problem, both input matrices are sparse, hence we can use the previous sparse matrix multiplication algorithm. However, this does not exploit the sparsity of this problem to the end: in this problem we are interested only in computing the k nearest nodes to each node, hence there is no need to compute the full output matrix. The challenge in this case is that we do not know the identity of the k closest nodes before the computation. To exploit this sparsity we design new matrix multiplication algorithms, that in particular have the ability to sparsify the matrix throughout the computation, and get a complexity that depends only on the size of the output we are interested in.

Sparse matrix multiplication. To compute the above, we design new sparse matrix multiplication algorithms, which differ from [15] by taking into account also the sparsity of the *output matrix*. For matrix M, let ρ_M denote the *density* of M, that is, the average number of non-zero entries on a row. Specifically, for distance product computation $P = ST$, we obtain two variants:

- One variant assumes that the sparsity of the output matrix is known.
- The other *sparsifies* the output matrix on the fly, keeping only the ρ_P smallest entries for each row.

In both of these scenarios, we obtain a running time of

$$O\left(\frac{(\rho_S \rho_T \rho_P)^{1/3}}{n^{2/3}} + 1\right)$$

rounds, improving the running time of the prior sparse matrix multiplication for $\rho_P = o(n)$.

This allows us to obtain faster distance tools, by taking into account the sparsity of the output:

- We can solve the k-NEAREST problem in $O\left(\left(\frac{k}{n^{2/3}} + 1\right) \log k\right)$ rounds.
- We can solve the (S, d, k)-SOURCE DETECTION problem in $O\left(\left(\frac{m^{1/3}k^{2/3}}{n} + 1\right) d\right)$ rounds, where m is the number of edges in the output graph; note that dependence on d becomes linear in order to exploit the sparsity.

In concrete terms, with these output-sensitive distance tools we still get subpolynomial running times even when the parameters are polynomial. For example, we can get the distances to the $\widetilde{O}(n^{2/3})$ closest nodes in $\widetilde{O}(1)$ rounds. Note that though our final results are only for undirected graphs, these distance tools work for directed weighted graphs.

Hopsets. An issue with our (S, d, k)-SOURCE DETECTION algorithm is that in order to exploit the sparsity of the matrices, we must perform d multiplications to learn the distances of all the nodes at hop-distance at most d from S. Hence, to learn the distances of all the nodes from S, we need to do n multiplications, which is no longer efficient. To overcome this challenge, we use *hopsets*, which are a central building block in many distance computations in the distributed setting [23–25, 35, 49]. A (β, ϵ)-hopset H is a sparse graph such that the β-hop distances in $G \cup H$ give $(1 + \epsilon)$-approximations of the distances in G. Since it is enough to look only at β-hop distances in $G \cup H$, using our source detection algorithm together with a hopset allows getting an efficient algorithm for approximating distances, as long as β is small enough.

However, the time complexity of all current hopset constructions depends on the size of the hopset [24, 25, 35], in the following way. The complexity of building a hopset of size $n\rho$ is at least $O(\rho)$. This is a major obstacle for efficient shortest paths algorithms, since based on recent existential results there are no hopsets where both β and ρ are polylogarithmic [1] (see Section 1.4). Nevertheless, we show that our new distance tools allow to build hopsets in a time that *does not* depend on the hopset size. In particular, we show how to implement a variant of the recent hopset construction of Elkin and Neiman [25] in $O(\frac{\log^2 n}{\epsilon})$ rounds. The size of our hopset is $\widetilde{O}(n^{3/2})$, hence constructing it using previous algorithms requires at least $\widetilde{O}(\sqrt{n})$ rounds.

Applying the distance tools. As a direct application of our source detection and hopset algorithms, we obtain a multi-source shortest paths (MSSP) algorithm, allowing to compute $(1 + \epsilon)$-approximate distances to $\widetilde{O}(\sqrt{n})$ sources in polylogarithmic time. Our MSSP algorithm, in turn, forms the basis of a near 3/2-approximation for the diameter, and a $(3 + \epsilon)$-approximation for weighted APSP. To obtain a $(2+\epsilon)$-approximation for unweighted APSP, the high-level idea is to deal separately with paths that contain a high-degree node and paths with only low-degree nodes. A crucial ingredient in the algorithm is showing that in sparser graphs, we can actually compute distances to a larger set of sources S efficiently, which is useful for obtaining a better approximation. Our exact SSSP algorithm uses our algorithm for finding distances to the k-nearest nodes, which allows constructing efficiently the k-shortcut graph described in [23, 49].

1.4 Additional related work

Distance computation in the congested clique. APSP and SSSP are fundamental problems that are studied extensively in various computation models. Apart from the MM-based algorithms in the CONGESTED CLIQUE [14, 15, 43], previous results include also $\widetilde{O}(\sqrt{n})$-round algorithms for exact SSSP and $(2 + o(1))$-approximation for APSP [37, 49], that work in the more restricted *broadcast* CONGESTED CLIQUE model, where nodes send the same message to all the nodes in each round. In this model, it is known that obtaining a $(2-o(1))$-approximation for APSP requires $\widetilde{\Omega}(n)$ rounds [37], which is almost tight. Other distance problems studied in the CONGESTED CLIQUE are construction of hopsets [24, 25, 35] and spanners [53].

Matrix multiplication in the congested clique. As shown by [14], matrix multiplication can be done in CONGESTED CLIQUE in $O(n^{1/3})$ rounds over semirings, and in $O(n^{1-2/\omega})$ rounds over rings, where $\omega < 2.3728639$ is the exponent of the matrix multiplication [28]. For rectangular matrix multiplication, [43] gives faster algorithms. The first sparse matrix multiplication algorithms for CONGESTED CLIQUE were given by [15], as discussed above.

Distance computation in the CONGEST model. The distributed CONGEST model is identical to the CONGESTED CLIQUE model, with the difference that the communication network is identical to the input graph G, and nodes can communicate only with their neighbours in each round. Distance computation is extensively studied in the CONGEST model. The study of *exact* APSP in weighted graphs has been the focus of many recent papers [3, 12, 23, 39], culminating in a near tight $\widetilde{O}(n)$ algorithm [12]. Such results were previously known in unweighted graphs [38, 47, 54] or for approximation algorithms [46, 49]. Approximate and exact algorithms for SSSP are studied in [8, 23, 27, 31, 35, 45, 49]. While near-tight algorithms exist for approximating SSSP [8], there is currently a lot of interest in understanding the complexity of *exact* SSSP and *directed* SSSP [23, 27, 31]. The *source detection* problem is studied in [47], demonstrating the applicability of this tool for many distance problems such as APSP and diameter approximation in unweighted graphs.

An extension for the weighted case is studied in [46]. Algorithms and lower bounds for approximating the diameter are studied in [2, 38, 43, 47, 54].

Distance computation in the sequential setting. Among the rich line of research in the sequential setting, we focus only on the most related to our work. The pioneering work of Aingworth et al. [4], inspired much research on approximate APSP [6, 7, 10, 19, 21] and approximate diameter [5, 10, 17, 55], with the goal of understanding the tradeoffs between the time complexity and approximation ratio. Many of these papers use clustering ideas and hitting set arguments as the basis of their algorithms, and our approximate APSP and diameter algorithms are inspired by such ideas.

Hopsets. Hopsets are a central building block in distance computation and are studied extensively in various computing models [11, 18, 23–25, 35, 36, 49, 56]. The most related to our work are two recent constructions of Elkin and Neiman [25], and Huang and Pettie [40], which are based on the emulators of Thorup and Zwick [57], and are near optimal due to existential results [1]. Specifically, [40] construct (β, ϵ)-hopsets of size $O(n^{1+\frac{1}{2^{k+1}-1}})$ with $\beta = O(k/\epsilon)^k$, where recent existential results show that any construction of (β, ϵ)-hopsets with worst case size $n^{1+\frac{1}{2^k-1}-\delta}$ must have $\beta = \Omega_k((\frac{1}{\epsilon})^k)$, where $k \geq 1$ is an integer and $\delta > 0$. For a detailed discussion of hopsets see the introduction in [24, 25].

1.5 Preliminaries

Notations. Except when specified otherwise, we assume our graphs are undirected with non-negative edge weights. Given a graph $G = (V, E)$ and $u, v \in V$, we denote by $d_G(u, v)$ the distance between u and v in G, and by $d_G^\beta(u, v)$ the length of the shortest path of hop-distance at most β between u and v in G. If G is clear from the context, we use the notation $d(u, v)$ for $d_G(u, v)$.

Routing and sorting. As basic primitives, we use standard routing and sorting algorithms for the CONGESTED CLIQUE model. In the *routing* task, each node holds up to n messages of $O(\log n)$ bits, and we assume that each node is also the recipient of at most n messages. In the *sorting* task, each node has a list of n entries from an ordered set, and we want to sort these entries so that node i receives the ith batch of entries according to the global order of all the input entries. Both of these task can be solved in $O(1)$ rounds [20, 44].

Hitting sets. Let $S_v \subseteq V$ be a set of size at least k. We say that $A \subseteq V$ is a *hitting set* of $\{S_v\}_{v \in V}$ if in each subset S_v there is a node from A. We can construct hitting sets easily by adding each node to A with probability $p = \frac{\log n}{k}$. This gives a hitting set of expected size $O(\frac{n \log n}{k})$, such that w.h.p there is a node from A in each subset S_v. The same parameters are obtained by a recent *deterministic* construction of hitting sets in the CONGESTED CLIQUE [53], which gives the following (see Corollary 17 in [53]).

LEMMA 1.3. *Let $\{S_v \subseteq V\}_{v \in V}$ be a set of subsets of size at least k, such that S_v is known to v. There exists a* deterministic *algorithm in the* CONGESTED CLIQUE *model that constructs a hitting set of size $O(n \log n/k)$ in $O((\log \log n)^3)$ rounds.*

2 SPARSE MATRIX MULTIPLICATION

2.1 Preliminaries

Semirings and matrices. We assume we are operating over a semiring $(R, +, \cdot, 0, 1)$, where 0 is the identity element for addition and 1 is the identity element for multiplication. Note that we do not require the multiplication to be commutative. For the CONGESTED CLIQUE algorithms, we generally assume that the semiring elements can be encoded in messages of $O(\log n)$ bits.

All matrices are assumed to be over the semiring R. For convenience, we identify $[n]$ with the node set V, and use set V to index the matrix entries. For matrix S, we denote the matrix entry at position (v, u) by $S[v, u]$. For sets $U, W \subseteq V$, we denote by $S[U, W]$ by submatrix obtained by taking rows and columns restricted to U and W, respectively.

Matrix multiplication problem. In the *matrix multiplication problem*, we are given two $n \times n$ matrices S and T over semiring R, and the task is to compute the product matrix $P = ST$.

Following [14, 43], we assume for concreteness that in the CONGESTED CLIQUE model, each node receives the row $S[v, V]$ and the column $T[V, v]$ as a local input, and we want to compute the output so that each node locally knows the row $P[v, V]$ of the output matrix.

Matrix densities. For matrix S, we denote by $\text{nz}(S)$ the number of non-zero entries in S. Furthermore, we define the *density* ρ_S as the smallest positive integer satisfying $\text{nz}(S) \leq \rho_S n$.

When discussing the density of a product matrix $P = ST$, we would like to simply consider the density ρ_P; however, for technical reasons, we want to ignore the zero entries that appear due to cancellations. Formally, let $\hat{S}$ be the binary matrix defined as $\hat{S}[i, j] = 1$ if if $S[i, j] \neq 0$, and $\hat{S}[i, j] = 0$ otherwise, and define $\hat{T}$ similarly. Let $\hat{P} = \hat{S}\hat{T}$, where the product is taken over the Boolean semiring. We define the density of the product ST, denoted by $\widehat{\rho}_{ST}$, as the smallest positive integer satisfying $\text{nz}(\hat{P}) \leq \widehat{\rho}_{ST} n$. Note that for most of our applications, we operate over semirings where no cancellations can occur in additions, in which case $\widehat{\rho}_{ST} = \rho_P$.

We also note that while we assume that the input matrices are $n \times n$, we can also use this framework for rectangular matrix multiplications, simply by padding the matrices with zeroes to make them square.

2.2 Output-sensitive sparse matrix multiplication

Our first matrix multiplication result is an output-sensitive variant of sparse matrix multiplication:

THEOREM 2.1. *Matrix multiplication $ST = P$ can be computed deterministically in*

$$O\left(\frac{(\rho_S \rho_T \widehat{\rho}_{ST})^{1/3}}{n^{2/3}} + 1\right)$$

rounds in CONGESTED CLIQUE, *assuming we know $\widehat{\rho}_{ST}$ beforehand.*

We note that for all of our applications, the requirement that we know $\widehat{\rho}_{ST}$ beforehand is satisfied. However, the algorithm can be modified to work without knowledge of $\widehat{\rho}_{ST}$ with the additional cost of multiplicative $O(\log n)$ factor; we simply start with estimate $\widehat{\rho}_{ST} = 2$, restarting the algorithm with doubled estimate if the running time for current estimate is exceeded.

Algorithm overview. Our algorithm follows the basic idea of the classical 3D matrix multiplication algorithm, as presented for CONGESTED CLIQUE by [14], and as adapted for the sparse matrix multiplication by [15]. That is, we want to reduce the matrix multiplication task into n smaller instances of matrix multiplication, and use a single node for each one of these. However, due to the fact that we are working with sparse matrices, we have to make certain considerations in our algorithm:

(1) Whereas the 3D matrix multiplication splits the original multiplication into n products of $n^{2/3} \times n^{2/3}$ matrices, we will split into n rectangular matrix multiplications, where the dimensions depend on the relative sparsities of the input and output matrices.
(2) Unlike in the dense case, we also have to make sure that all of our n products are equally sparse. While this could be achieved using randomization similarly to the triangle detection algorithms of [16, 50], we want to do this deterministically.

We achieve these goals by utilizing a mix of deterministic routing and partitioning techniques. For details, see the full version.

2.3 Matrix multiplication with sparsification

Our second matrix multiplication result is a variant of sparse matrix multiplication where we control the density of the output matrix.

Problem definition. In this section, we assume our semiring

$$(R, +, \cdot, 0, 1)$$

satisfies the following conditions:

(1) there is a total order $<$ on R, and
(2) the addition operation $+$ satisfies $x + y = \min(x, y)$, where min is taken in terms of order $<$.

Let S and T be the input matrices over the semiring R and denote $P = ST$. In the *filtered matrix multiplication problem*, we are given the input matrices S and T along with an output density parameter ρ, and the task is to compute a matrix $\overline{P}$ such that each row of $\overline{P}$ retains ρ smallest entries of P, that is,

(1) either $\overline{P}[v, u] = 0$ or $\overline{P}[v, u] = P[v, u]$,
(2) if row v of P has k non-zero entries, then row v for $\overline{P}$ has $\min(k, \rho)$ non-zero entries, and
(3) if $\overline{P}[v, u] = 0$ and $P[v, u] \neq 0$, then $\max_w \overline{P}[v, w] \leq P[v, u]$.

Filtered matrix multiplication algorithm. Our result for sparsification is the following:

THEOREM 2.2. *Filtered matrix multiplication can be computed in*

$$O\left(\frac{(\rho_S \rho_T \rho)^{1/3}}{n^{2/3}} + 1\right)$$

rounds in the CONGESTED CLIQUE.

The high-level proof idea is largely the same as for Theorem 2.1. The main exception is that we perform two *filtering steps*, one after the computation of the n smaller products, and second after the computation of the output matrix, to remove all but the ρ smallest entries. For details, see the full version.

3 DISTANCE TOOLS

In this section, we use our matrix multiplication algorithms to construct basic distance computation tools that will be used for our final distance computation algorithms. Though we only use the distance tools for undirected graphs, we note that they work also for directed graphs. A more elaborate exposition of this section is given in the full version.

Augmented min-plus semiring. The algorithmic approach for our distance tools is to apply the matrix multiplication algorithms over the min-plus semiring. However, to ensure consistent results in terms of hop distances, a property we require for our distance k-NEAREST and (S, d, k)-SOURCE DETECTION distance tools, we augment the min-plus semiring to keep track of the number of hops.

We define the *augmented min-plus semiring* R to encode paths in distance computations as follows. The elements of R are tuples (w, t), where (1) w is either the weight of an edge or a path, or ∞, and (2) t is a non-negative integer or ∞, representing the number of hops. Let $\prec$ be the lexicographical order on tuples (w, t), and define the addition operator min as the minimum over the total order given by $\prec$. The multiplication operation $+$ is defined as $(w_1, t_1) + (w_2, t_2) = (w_1 + w_2, t_1 + t_2)$. It is easy to verify that $(R, \min, +, (\infty, \infty), (0, 0))$ is a semiring with idempotent addition, that is, $\min(r, r) = r$ for all r. Moreover, the structure satisfies the conditions of Theorem 2.2.

Distance products. We call the product of S and T over the augmented min-plus semiring the *augmented distance product* of S and T, and denote it by $S \star T$. In particular, for a graph $G = (V, E)$, we define the *augmented weight matrix* W by setting

$$W[u, v] = \begin{cases} (0, 0) & \text{if } u = v, \\ (w(u, v), 1) & \text{if there is an edge from } u \text{ to } v, \text{ and} \\ (\infty, \infty) & \text{otherwise.} \end{cases}$$

As with the regular distance product, the dth augmented distance product power W^d gives the distances for all pairs of nodes $u, v \in V$ using paths of at most d hops, as well as the associated number of hops. Moreover, we observe that the augmented distance product gives a consistent ordering in terms of distance from v, in the sense that for two nodes u, w at equal distance from v, the associated value in the distance products is smaller for the one at smaller hop-distance.

k-nearest neighbors. In the k-NEAREST problem, we are given an integer k, and the task is to compute for each node v the set of k nearest nodes and distances to those nodes, breaking ties first by hop distance and then arbitrarily. More formally, we want each node to compute a set $N_k(v)$ of k nodes and distances $d(v, u)$ for all $u \in N_k(v)$, such that the values $W^n[v, u]$ for $u \in N_k(v)$ are the k smallest on row v of W^n in terms of the order $\prec$ on augmented min-sum semiring R.

Note that by the definition of the augmented distance product, all nodes $u \in N_k(v)$ are at most k hops away from v, and all nodes on the shortest path from v to u are also in $N_k(v)$.

Theorem 3.1. *The k-nearest problem can be solved in*

$$O\left(\left(\frac{k}{n^{2/3}}+1\right)\log k\right)$$

rounds in Congested Clique.

Proof sketch. For matrix M, let $\overline{M}$ denote the matrix obtained by discarding all but the k smallest values on each row of M. Starting from $\overline{W}$, we iteratively compute $\overline{W^{2i}} = \overline{\overline{W^i} \star \overline{W^i}}$ for $i = 1, 2, \ldots, \log k$ using Theorem 2.2 with $\rho = k$. The final matrix $\overline{W^k}$ gives the desired set $N_v(k)$ and the associated distances. □

Source detection. In the (S, d, k)-source detection problem, we are given a set of *sources* $S \subseteq V$ and integers k and d, and the task is to compute for each node v the set of k nearest sources within d hops, as well as the distances to those sources using paths of at most d hops.

Theorem 3.2. *It is possible to solve the (S, d, k)-source detection problem in*

$$O\left(\left(\frac{m^{1/3}k^{2/3}}{n}+1\right)d\right)$$

rounds in Congested Clique, where m is the number of edges in the input graph.

Proof sketch. All nodes, including nodes in S, select the k lightest edges to nodes in S, breaking ties arbitrarily. Let W_1 be the augmented weight matrix for the subgraph with these edges; since a total of at most nk edges was selected, we have $\mathrm{nz}(W_1) \le n(k+1)$. We iteratively compute matrices $W_{i+1} = \overline{W \star W_i}$ for $i = 1, 2, \ldots, d-1$ by applying Theorem 2.2 with $\rho_S = m/n$, $\rho_T = k+1$ and $\rho = k+1$. Non-zero elements of W_d give the closest sources. □

Distance through a node set. In the distance through sets problem, we assume that each node v has a set W_v and distance estimates $\delta(v, w)$ and $\delta(w, v)$ for all $w \in W_v$. The task is to compute, for all nodes v, the distance estimates $\min_{w \in W_v \cap W_u}\{\delta(v, w) + \delta(w, u)\}$ for all other nodes $u \in V$.

Theorem 3.3. *It is possible to solve the distance through sets problem in*

$$O\left(\frac{\rho^{2/3}}{n^{1/3}}+1\right)$$

rounds in Congested Clique, where $\rho = \sum_{v \in V} |W_v| / n$.

Proof sketch. We observe that this task corresponds to a single distance product over the standard min-sum semiring, with matrix weights obtained from distance estimates δ. The density of these matrices is ρ, so the claim follows from Theorem 2.1 (or [15]). □

4 HOPSETS

In this section, we describe a construction of hopsets in polylogarithmic time in the Congested Clique model. Given a graph $G = (V, E)$, a (β, ϵ)-hopset $H = (V, E')$ is a graph on the same set of nodes such that the β-hop distances in $G \cup H$ give $(1+\epsilon)$-approximations for the distances in G. Formally, for any pair of nodes $u, v \in V$ it holds that $d_G(u, v) \le d_{G \cup H}(u, v)$ and

$$d_G(u, v) \le d^{\beta}_{G \cup H}(u, v) \le (1+\epsilon) d_G(u, v).$$

Usually the goal is to find a sparse hopset with small β. In our case, we are interested in optimizing both β and the running time for constructing the hopset, but not necessarily the hopset size.

Our construction is based on the recent construction of hopsets in the Congested Clique of Elkin and Neiman [25]. However, the time complexity in [25] depends on β and on the hopset size, and is super-polylogarithmic for any choice of parameters. We show that using our new distance tools we can implement the same construction in polylogarithmic time, regardless of the hopset size, as long as β is polylogarithmic. In particular, we focus on a simple variant with $\widetilde{O}(n^{3/2})$ edges which is enough for all our applications.[1]

4.1 Construction overview

We follow the hopset construction of [25], which is based on the emulators of Thorup and Zwick [57]. A similar construction appears also in [40] without a distributed implementation. We focus only on a simple variant of [25, 40, 57], with slightly different parameters.

Given a graph $G = (V, E)$, let $V = A_0 \supseteq A_1 \supseteq A_2 = \emptyset$, where A_1 is a hitting set of size $O(\sqrt{n})$ of all the sets $N_k(v)$ for $k = O(\sqrt{n}\log n)$. I.e., for any node $v \in V$, there is a node from A_1 among the closest k nodes to v. We can construct A_1 using Lemma 1.3.

For a given subset $A \subseteq V$, we denote by $d_G(v, A)$ the distance from v to the closest node in A. For a node $v \in V$, let $p(v)$ be a node of distance $d_G(v, A_1)$ from v. In general there may be many possible nodes of distance $d_G(v, A_1)$ from v. The node $p(v)$ would be determined by v, as follows. During our algorithm, each node computes the set $N_k(v)$. Since A_1 is a hitting set there is a node from A_1 in the set $N_k(v)$ computed, and v defines $p(v)$ to be the closest such node (breaking ties arbitrarily). For a node $v \in A_0 \setminus A_1$, we define the *bunch*

$$B(v) = \{u \in A_0 : d_G(v, u) < d_G(v, A_1)\} \cup p(v),$$

and for a node $v \in A_1$, we define the bunch $B(v) = A_1$.

The hopset is the set of edges $H = \{\{v, u\} : v \in V, u \in B(v)\}$. We would like to set the length of an edge $\{v, u\}$ to be $d_G(v, u)$. However, we cannot necessarily compute these values. During our algorithm we add exactly all the edges in H to the hopset, but their weights are not necessarily $d_G(v, u)$, but rather an approximation for $d_G(v, u)$.

Claim 1. *The number of edges in H is $O(n^{3/2}\log n)$.*

Proof. For every node in A_1 we add only edges to nodes in A_1, and the size of A_1 is $O(\sqrt{n})$. In addition, for nodes $v \in A_0 \setminus A_1$ we add edges only to nodes closer than $p(v)$. Since A_1 is a hitting set, $p(v)$ is among the closest k nodes to v, which means that we add at most $k = O(\sqrt{n}\log n)$ edges for each node, and $O(n^{3/2}\log n)$ edges in total. □

4.2 Congested clique implementation

Our goal is to build H efficiently in the Congested Clique model. In [25], the authors suggest an iterative algorithm for computing H, where in iteration $1 \le \ell \le \log n$ they compute a 2^{ℓ}-bounded hopset, which approximates the distances between all pairs of nodes that

[1] Using similar ideas, it is possible to implement also the more general hopset from [25]. We leave the details to future work.

have a shortest path between them with at most 2^ℓ edges in G. Given a 2^ℓ-bounded hopset H^ℓ, they show that it is enough to run Bellman-Ford explorations up to hop-distance $O(\beta)$ in the graph $G \cup H^\ell$ to compute a $2^{\ell+1}$-hopset $H^{\ell+1}$. For the stretch analysis to carry on, it is also important to add edges to $H^{\ell+1}$ in a certain order. First, the edges that correspond to bunches of nodes in $A_0 \setminus A_1$ are added, and only then the edges that correspond to bunches of nodes in A_1 are added. They show that the total time complexity for implementing all the Bellman-Ford explorations is proportional to the hopset size. In particular, for our hopset of size $\widetilde{O}(n^{3/2})$, the complexity required is at least $\widetilde{O}(\sqrt{n})$ rounds.

We follow the general approach from [25], with two changes. First, we show that using our distance tools we can compute directly all the bunches of nodes in $A_0 \setminus A_1$, which allows simplifying slightly the algorithm and analysis. The second and more significant difference is that we use our (S, d, k)-algorithm to replace the heavy Bellman-Ford explorations, which results in a polylogarithmic complexity instead of a polynomial one. We next describe the algorithm in detail.

4.2.1 *Algorithm description.*

Computing the bunches. We start by computing the bunches for all the nodes $v \in A_0 \setminus A_1$. This can be done easily using our algorithm for finding the distances to the k-nearest nodes. This follows since $p(v)$ is among the k-nearest nodes to v, hence all the nodes in the bunch of v are among the k-nearest nodes to v. Note that all the nodes $v \in A_0 \setminus A_1$ learn the *exact* distances to all the nodes in their bunch. However, it is not clear how to compute a bunch for a node $v \in A_1$, since v should learn the distances to all the nodes from A_1. Such nodes may be at distance $d = \Omega(n)$ from v, and our (S, d, k)-algorithm depends linearly on the distance d. To overcome this, we follow the approach in [25], and show how to implement it efficiently using our distance tools.

Bounded hopsets. We say that H is a (β, ϵ, t)-hopset if for all $x, y \in G$ it holds that $d_G(x, y) \le d_{G \cup H}(x, y)$, and for all pairs of nodes $x, y \in G$ that have a shortest path between them with at most t hops, i.e., $d_G(x, y) = d^t_G(x, y)$, it holds that

$$d_G(x, y) \le d^\beta_{G \cup H}(x, y) \le (1 + \epsilon) d_G(x, y).$$

Note that the empty set is a $(1, 0, 1)$-hopset, and thus also a $(\beta, \epsilon, 1)$-hopset for any $\beta \ge 1$ and $\epsilon > 0$. The algorithm builds hopsets iteratively, where in iteration ℓ it builds a $(\beta, \epsilon_\ell, 2^\ell)$-hopset H^ℓ, where $(1 + \epsilon_\ell) = (1 + \epsilon)^\ell$ for some $0 < \epsilon < 1/(2 \log n)$. The final hopset H is $H^{\log n}$. Let $H_0 = \{\{u, v\} : u \in A_0 \setminus A_1, v \in B(u)\}$. We already computed the edges H_0 and include them as part of the hopset for all the hopsets H^ℓ.

Building H^ℓ. We define $H^0 = H_0$. To construct H^ℓ for $1 \le \ell \le \log n$ we work as follows. Let $G' = G \cup H^{\ell-1}$. All the nodes in A_1 compute the distances to all the nodes from A_1 at hop-distance at most 4β in the graph G'. We implement it using our (S, d, k')-algorithm with $S = A_1, d = 4\beta, k' = |A_1| = O(\sqrt{n})$. Each node $v \in A_1$, adds to the hopset H^ℓ all the edges $\{v, u\}$ where $u \in A_1$ at hop-distance at most 4β from v in G'. The weight of the edge is the weight that v learned during the (S, d, k)-algorithm. The hopset H^ℓ includes all these edges, as well as all the edges of H_0. Note that if v adds an edge $\{v, u\}$ to the hopset, in the next around it can let u learn about it, so we can assume that both the endpoints know about the edge.

This completes the description of the algorithm. We next analyze the time complexity.

4.2.2 *Complexity.*

Claim 2. *The complexity of the algorithm is $O(\beta \log n)$ rounds.*

Proof. From Lemma 1.3, we can construct deterministically in $O((\log \log n)^3)$ rounds a hitting set A_1 of size $O(\sqrt{n})$ that hits all the sets $N_k(v)$. For the algorithm, each node v should learn the set $N_k(v)$ which is computed using our algorithm for finding the distances to the k-nearest nodes. From Theorem 3.1, this takes

$$O\Big(\Big(\frac{k}{n^{2/3}} + 1\Big) \log k\Big) = O\Big(\Big(\frac{\sqrt{n} \cdot \log n}{n^{2/3}} + 1\Big) \log n\Big) = O(\log n)$$

rounds.

The algorithm for constructing H starts by computing the bunches of nodes $v \in A_0 \setminus A_1$, this only requires each node v to learn the distances to the nodes $N_k(v)$, which was already computed. Next, for $\log n$ iterations, we compute for each node the $O(\sqrt{n})$-nearest nodes from A_1 at hop-distance at most 4β. A_1 is of size $O(\sqrt{n})$, and we are interested in distances to at most $O(\sqrt{n})$ nodes. By Theorem 3.2, each iteration takes

$$O\Big(\Big(\frac{n^{2/3} (\sqrt{n})^{2/3}}{n} + 1\Big) \cdot \beta\Big) = O(\beta)$$

rounds. Overall, all the iterations take $O(\beta \log n)$ rounds. □

In the full version we prove that H^ℓ is indeed a $(\beta, \epsilon_\ell, 2^\ell)$-hopset, the proof follows the proof in [25], and is included in the full version for completeness. Based on these ideas, we get the following.

Theorem 4.1. *Let $0 < \epsilon < 1$. There is a deterministic construction of a (β, ϵ)-hopset with $O(n^{3/2} \log n)$ edges and $\beta = O(\frac{\log n}{\epsilon})$ that takes $O(\frac{\log^2 n}{\epsilon})$ rounds in the Congested Clique model.*

5 APPLICATIONS

5.1 Multi-source shortest paths

As a direct application of our hopsets and source detection algorithms, we get an efficient $(1+\epsilon)$-approximation for the multi-source shortest paths problem (MSSP) with polylogarithmic complexity as long as the number of sources is $\widetilde{O}(\sqrt{n})$.

Theorem 1.2. *There is a deterministic $(1 + \epsilon)$-approximation algorithm for the weighted undirected MSSP that takes*

$$O\left(\left(\frac{|S|^{2/3}}{n^{1/3}} + \log n\right) \cdot \frac{\log n}{\epsilon}\right)$$

rounds in the Congested Clique, where S is the set of sources. In particular, the complexity is $O(\frac{\log^2 n}{\epsilon})$ as long as $|S| \le O(\sqrt{n} \cdot (\log n)^{3/2})$.

Proof. By Theorem 4.1, we can construct a (β, ϵ)-hopset H with $\beta = O(\frac{\log n}{\epsilon})$ in $O(\frac{\log^2 n}{\epsilon})$ rounds. By the definition of hopsets, the β-hop distances in $G \cup H$ give a $(1 + \epsilon)$-approximation to all the distances in G. Hence, to approximate the distances of all the nodes to the set of sources S, we run our (S, d, k)-algorithm in the graph

$G \cup H$ with $d = \beta = O(\frac{\log n}{\epsilon})$ and $k = |S|$. By Theorem 3.2, the complexity is

$$O\left(\left(\frac{n^{2/3}|S|^{2/3}}{n} + 1\right) \cdot \beta\right) = O\left(\left(\frac{|S|^{2/3}}{n^{1/3}} + 1\right) \cdot \frac{\log n}{\epsilon}\right)$$

rounds. The overall complexity is

$$O\left(\left(\frac{|S|^{2/3}}{n^{1/3}} + 1\right) \cdot \frac{\log n}{\epsilon} + \frac{\log^2 n}{\epsilon}\right) = O\left(\left(\frac{|S|^{2/3}}{n^{1/3}} + \log n\right) \cdot \frac{\log n}{\epsilon}\right)$$

rounds. □

5.2 All-pairs shortest paths

As explained, we can get $(1+\epsilon)$-approximate distances from a set of sources S to all the nodes in polylogarithmic time, as long as $|S| = \widetilde{O}(\sqrt{n})$. In this section, we use this to construct algorithms that provide constant approximations for *all* the distances in the graph in *polylogarithmic* time. However, the approximation guarantee increases to $(2+\epsilon)$ for the unweighted case, and at most $(3+\epsilon)$ for the weighted case.

Next, we present our approximation algorithms for the APSP problem. We use the notation $(2+\epsilon, (1+\epsilon)W)$-approximation for an algorithm that for any pair of nodes u, v provides an estimate of the distance between u and v which is at most $(2+\epsilon)d(u,v) + (1+\epsilon)W$ where W is the weight of the heaviest edge in a shortest path between u and v. Note that W is always at most $d(u,v)$, and hence a $(2+\epsilon, (1+\epsilon)W)$-approximation is always better than a $(3+\epsilon')$-approximation (where $\epsilon' = 2\epsilon$).

For simplicity of presentation, we start by sketching a simple $(3+\epsilon)$-approximation for weighted APSP. Then, using a more careful analysis we show that a variant of this algorithm actually obtains a $(2+\epsilon, (1+\epsilon)W)$-approximation. Later, we show an extension of the algorithm that provides a $(2+\epsilon)$-approximation for APSP in unweighted graphs. All our algorithms are deterministic.

A $(3+\epsilon)$-approximation for weighted APSP. Our algorithm starts by computing a hitting set A of size $\widetilde{O}(\sqrt{n})$ that hits all the sets $N_k(v)$ for $k = \widetilde{O}(\sqrt{n})$. We compute for each node $v \in V$, the distances to all the nodes in $N_k(v)$, and we use our MSSP algorithm to compute $(1+\epsilon)$-approximate distances from A to all the nodes. Since $k = \widetilde{O}(\sqrt{n})$ and $|A| = \widetilde{O}(\sqrt{n})$ the complexity is polylogarithmic. To compute an estimate $\delta(u,v)$ of the distance $d(u,v)$, we work as follows. If $v \in N_k(u)$, then u already computed the value $d(u,v)$ and sends it to v. Otherwise, let $p(u) \in N_k(u) \cap A$ be a closest node to u. We estimate $d(u,v)$ with $d(u,p(u)) + d(p(u),v)$. Since $v \notin N_k(u)$, it follows that $d(u,p(u)) \leq d(u,v)$. Hence, using the triangle inequality, we have

$$\begin{aligned} d(u,p(u)) + d(p(u),v) &\leq d(u,p(u)) + d(u,p(u)) + d(u,v) \\ &\leq 3d(u,v). \end{aligned}$$

Since our algorithm computes an $(1+\epsilon)$-approximation for the value $d(v,p(u))$, we get a $(3+\epsilon)$-approximation.

A $(2+\epsilon, (1+\epsilon)W)$-approximation for weighted APSP. We next describe our $(2+\epsilon, (1+\epsilon)W)$-approximation. In our $(3+\epsilon)$-approximation, we used the fact that if $v \notin N_k(u)$, then $d(u,p(u)) \leq d(u,v)$. To obtain a better approximation, we would like to get a better bound on $d(u,p(u))$. If, for example, $d(u,p(u)) \leq \frac{1}{2}d(u,v)$, the same analysis shows a $(2+\epsilon)$-approximation. We show that

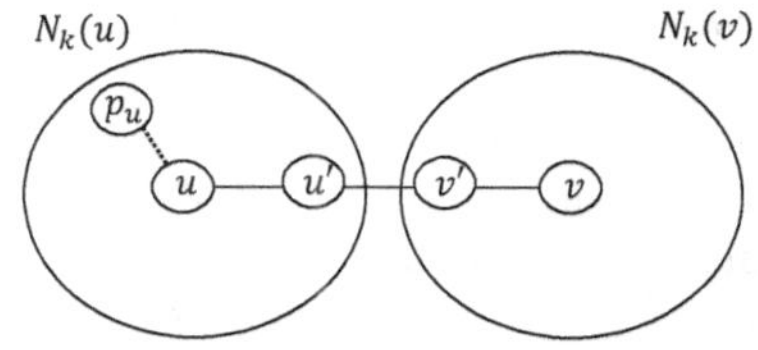

Figure 1: An illustration of the problematic case in the analysis of our $(2+\epsilon, (1+\epsilon)W)$-approximation.

either $\min\{d(u,p(u)), d(v,p(v))\} \leq \frac{1}{2}(d(u,v) + W)$ which proves a $(2+\epsilon, (1+\epsilon)W)$-approximation, or the shortest path between u and v has a node $w \in N_k(u) \cap N_k(v)$. In the latter case, $d(u,w) + d(w,v) = d(u,v)$, and since $|N_k(u)| = |N_k(v)| = \widetilde{O}(\sqrt{n})$ we can use matrix multiplication to compute the distances through all nodes $w \in N_k(u) \cap N_k(v)$, and find the actual distance $d(u,v)$. The complexity of the whole algorithm is $O(\frac{\log^2 n}{\epsilon})$ rounds. Details and proofs appear in the full version.

A $(2+\epsilon)$-approximation for unweighted APSP. In this section, we present the high-level idea of our $(2+\epsilon)$-approximation for unweighted APSP. Details and proofs appear in the full version.

If we look at the analysis of our $(2+\epsilon, (1+\epsilon)W)$-approximation, it turns out that the only case where we do not obtain a $(2+\epsilon)$-approximation is when the shortest path between u and v is composed of a path between u and $u' \in N_k(u) \setminus N_k(v)$, an edge between u' and a node $v' \in N_k(v) \setminus N_k(u)$ and a path between v' and v. See Figure 1 for an illustration.

Note that u knows the distance to u', v knows the distance to v' and both u' and v' know about the edge between them. If we add to the graph all the edges between u and nodes in $N_k(u)$ and between v and nodes in $N_k(v)$, we have a shortest path of length 3 between u and v in the new graph. Intuitively, we would like to use matrix multiplication to learn about this path, but we cannot do this directly since this graph may be dense. In particular, we have no bound on the degrees of u', v'.

To overcome this, we present a new algorithm that takes care separately of shortest paths that include a high-degree node, and shortest paths that have only low-degree nodes, where a node has a high degree if its degree is at least $\widetilde{\Omega}(\sqrt{n})$. This is done as follows. We compute a hitting set A of size $\widetilde{O}(\sqrt{n})$, such that each high-degree node has a neighbour in A. Then, we use the fact that $|A| = \widetilde{O}(\sqrt{n})$, to show that we can compute efficiently $(1+\epsilon)$-approximations of all the shortest paths that go through a node in A. Then, if the shortest path between u and v has a high-degree node, it has a neighbour $w \in A$, and the shortest path from u to v that goes through w already gives a good approximation for the shortest $u-v$ path.

Then, we are left only with paths that do not contain any high-degree node. The graph induced on low-degree nodes is sparse, since the degrees are at most $\widetilde{O}(\sqrt{n})$, and we would like to exploit it. However, although we can multiply two sparse matrices with $\widetilde{O}(n^{3/2})$ elements efficiently, to compute paths of length 3 we need to multiply 3 matrices of this size, which is no longer efficient.

To overcome this, we would like to reduce the degrees further. In particular, we would like to follow the analysis in our $(2+\epsilon,(1+\epsilon)W)$-approximation algorithm, but replace $N_k(v)$ with $N_{k'}(v)$ for $k'<k$ which allows focusing on sparser matrices. The obstacle is that we want to compute a hitting set A' of the sets $\{N_{k'}(v)\}_{v\in V}$, and then use our MSSP algorithm to compute distances to all the nodes in A', but if $k'<k$, we need to compute a larger hitting set A', and our MSSP algorithm is efficient only as long as $|A'|=\widetilde{O}(\sqrt{n})$.

Nevertheless, since our graph is sparse, we show that we can actually compute MSSP from a set A' of size $\widetilde{O}(n^{3/4})$ in polylogarithmic time which allows us to choose $k'=\widetilde{O}(n^{1/4})$. To deal with the problematic case illustrated in Figure 1, we should compute paths of length 3 of the form $\{u,u',v',v\}$ where $u'\in N_{k'}(u)$, $v'\in N_{k'}(v)$ and there is an edge between u' and v'. Since $|N_{k'}(u)|=|N_{k'}(u)|=\widetilde{O}(n^{1/4})$ and u',v' are in the sparse graph and have maximum degree $\widetilde{O}(\sqrt{n})$, we can detect paths of this form efficiently using sparse matrix multiplication, which allows us to show a $(2+\epsilon)$-approximation. The complexity of the algorithm is $O(\frac{\log^2 n}{\epsilon})$ rounds.

5.3 Exact single-source shortest paths

We show that our distance tools allow to get a faster algorithm for exact SSSP in undirected weighted graphs, improving the previous $\widetilde{O}(n^{1/3})$-round algorithm [14]. The algorithm is very simple, and is based on ideas used in [23, 49, 56]. We start by computing the distances to the nodes in $N_k(v)$ for all $v\in V$ using our k-nearest algorithm. Then, we add to the graph all the edges $\{\{u,v\}|u\in V, v\in N_k(u)\}$ with the weights $d(u,v)$ computed by the algorithm, which results in a new graph G'. G' is called the k-shortcut graph or k-shortcut hopset in [23, 49], and it is proved in [49] that the shortest path diameter of G' is $O(n/k)$. I.e., for any pair of nodes u,v there is a shortest path between u and v of hop-distance at most $O(n/k)$ in G'.

LEMMA 5.1. *(Theorem 3.10 in [49]) The shortest path diameter of G' is smaller than $4n/k$.*

Now, to compute SSSP from a certain node we just run the classic Bellman-Ford algorithm [9, 26] in the graph G' which takes $O(n/k)$ rounds in a graph with shortest path diameter $O(n/k)$, even in the more restricted CONGEST model (see e.g., [49]). To optimize the complexity, we choose $k=n^{5/6}$. Now, finding the k-nearest takes $\widetilde{O}(k/n^{2/3})=\widetilde{O}(n^{1/6})$ rounds by Theorem 3.1, and the Bellman-Ford exploration takes $O(n^{1/6})$ rounds, proving the following.

THEOREM 5.2. *There is a deterministic algorithm for exact SSSP in undirected weighted graphs that takes $\widetilde{O}(n^{1/6})$ rounds in the CONGESTED CLIQUE model.*

5.4 Diameter

We show that using our distance tools we can implement efficiently the algorithm of Roditty and Vassilevska Williams for approximating the diameter [55], which is an extension of the algorithm of Aingworth et al. [4]. The algorithm is based on computing BFS trees from $\widetilde{O}(\sqrt{n})$ nodes. This results in a near 3/2-approximation for the diameter in $O(\frac{\log^2 n}{\epsilon})$ rounds. Details and proofs appear in the full version.

6 DISCUSSION

In this paper, we provide new tools for distance computations in the CONGESTED CLIQUE model based on sparse MM. We demonstrate the power of these tools by providing efficient algorithms for many central problems, such as APSP, SSSP, and diameter approximation. We believe that these techniques may be useful for many additional tasks in distance computation in the CONGESTED CLIQUE, and possibly also in additional related models. Many intriguing questions are still open.

First, while we provide constant approximations for many tasks in polylogarithmic time, the complexity of our exact SSSP algorithm is still polynomial. It would be interesting to study whether it is possible to obtain a polylogarithmic algorithm for the exact case. Surprisingly, even for the simple task of computing a BFS tree there is currently no sub-polynomial algorithm in the CONGESTED CLIQUE.

Second, while our MM algorithms work also for the directed case, our hopset construction is only for the undirected case and hence our results are for undirected graphs. Also, as we explain in Section 1.2, obtaining *any* approximation for directed APSP in sub-polynomial time would give a sub-polynomial algorithm for matrix multiplication. It would be interesting to study whether it is possible to provide sub-polynomial algorithms for directed SSSP.

Our unweighted APSP algorithm provides a $(2+\epsilon)$-approximation, whereas in the weighted case there is currently an additional additive term, and a natural question is whether we can get a $(2+\epsilon)$-approximation for weighted APSP in polylogarithmic time as well. Another interesting goal is to obtain *additive* approximations in sub-polynomial time.

ACKNOWLEDGMENTS

We thank Mohsen Ghaffari, Michael Elkin and Merav Parter for fruitful discussions. This project has received funding from the European Union's Horizon 2020 Research And Innovation Program under grant agreement no. 755839. Supported in part by the Israel Science Foundation (grant 1696/14)

REFERENCES

[1] Amir Abboud, Greg Bodwin, and Seth Pettie. 2018. A hierarchy of lower bounds for sublinear additive spanners. *SIAM J. Comput.* 47, 6 (2018), 2203–2236.

[2] Amir Abboud, Keren Censor-Hillel, and Seri Khoury. 2016. Near-linear lower bounds for distributed distance computations, even in sparse networks. In *Proc. DISC 2016*. 29–42.

[3] Udit Agarwal, Vijaya Ramachandran, Valerie King, and Matteo Pontecorvi. 2018. A Deterministic Distributed Algorithm for Exact Weighted All-Pairs Shortest Paths in $\tilde{O}(n^{3/2})$ Rounds. In *Proc. PODC 2018*. 199–205. https://doi.org/10.1145/3212734.3212773

[4] Donald Aingworth, Chandra Chekuri, Piotr Indyk, and Rajeev Motwani. 1999. Fast estimation of diameter and shortest paths (without matrix multiplication). *SIAM J. Comput.* 28, 4 (1999), 1167–1181.

[5] Arturs Backurs, Liam Roditty, Gilad Segal, Virginia Vassilevska Williams, and Nicole Wein. 2018. Towards tight approximation bounds for graph diameter and eccentricities. In *Proc. STOC 2018*. 267–280. https://doi.org/10.1145/3188745.3188950

[6] Surender Baswana, Vishrut Goyal, and Sandeep Sen. 2005. All-pairs nearly 2-approximate shortest-paths in $O(n^2 \text{ polylog } n)$ time. In *Proc. STACS 2005*. 666–679.

[7] Surender Baswana and Telikepalli Kavitha. 2010. Faster algorithms for all-pairs approximate shortest paths in undirected graphs. *SIAM J. Comput.* 39, 7 (2010), 2865–2896.

[8] Ruben Becker, Andreas Karrenbauer, Sebastian Krinninger, and Christoph Lenzen. 2017. Near-Optimal Approximate Shortest Paths and Transshipment in Distributed and Streaming Models. In *Proc. DISC 2017*. https://doi.org/10.4230/

LIPIcs.DISC.2017.7
[9] Richard Bellman. 1958. On a routing problem. *Quarterly of applied mathematics* 16, 1 (1958), 87–90.
[10] Piotr Berman and Shiva Prasad Kasiviswanathan. 2007. Faster approximation of distances in graphs. In *Proc. WADS 2007.* 541–552.
[11] Aaron Bernstein. 2009. Fully Dynamic $(2 + \epsilon)$-Approximate All-Pairs Shortest Paths with Fast Query and Close to Linear Update Time. In *Proc. FOCS 2009.* 693–702. https://doi.org/10.1109/FOCS.2009.16
[12] Aaron Bernstein and Danupon Nanongkai. 2019. Distributed Exact Weighted All-Pairs Shortest Paths in Near-Linear Time In *Proc. STOC 2019.*
[13] Keren Censor-Hillel, Michal Dory, Janne H. Korhonen, and Dean Leitersdorf. 2019. Fast Approximate Shortest Paths in the Congested Clique. arXiv:1903.05956 [cs.DC].
[14] Keren Censor-Hillel, Petteri Kaski, Janne H Korhonen, Christoph Lenzen, Ami Paz, and Jukka Suomela. 2015. Algebraic methods in the congested clique. In *Proc. PODC 2015.* ACM, 143–152.
[15] Keren Censor-Hillel, Dean Leitersdorf, and Elia Turner. 2018. Sparse Matrix Multiplication and Triangle Listing in the Congested Clique Model. In *Proc. OPODIS 2018.* https://doi.org/10.4230/LIPIcs.OPODIS.2018.4
[16] Yi-Jun Chang, Seth Pettie, and Hengjie Zhang. 2018. Distributed Triangle Detection via Expander Decomposition. In *Proc. SODA 2018.* 821–840. https://doi.org/10.1137/1.9781611975482.51
[17] Shiri Chechik, Daniel H Larkin, Liam Roditty, Grant Schoenebeck, Robert E Tarjan, and Virginia Vassilevska Williams. 2014. Better approximation algorithms for the graph diameter. In *Proc. SODA 2014.* 1041–1052.
[18] Edith Cohen. 2000. Polylog-time and near-linear work approximation scheme for undirected shortest paths. *Journal of the ACM (JACM)* 47, 1 (2000), 132–166.
[19] Edith Cohen and Uri Zwick. 2001. All-pairs small-stretch paths. *Journal of Algorithms* 38, 2 (2001), 335–353.
[20] Danny Dolev, Christoph Lenzen, and Shir Peled. 2012. "Tri, Tri again": Finding Triangles and Small Subgraphs in a Distributed Setting. In *Proc. DISC 2012.* 195–209.
[21] Dorit Dor, Shay Halperin, and Uri Zwick. 2000. All-pairs almost shortest paths. *SIAM J. Comput.* 29, 5 (2000), 1740–1759.
[22] Andrew Drucker, Fabian Kuhn, and Rotem Oshman. 2014. On the power of the congested clique model. In *Proc. PODC 2014.* 367–376.
[23] Michael Elkin. 2017. Distributed exact shortest paths in sublinear time. In *Proc. STOC 2017.* ACM, 757–770.
[24] Michael Elkin and Ofer Neiman. 2016. Hopsets with constant hopbound, and applications to approximate shortest paths. In *Proc. FOCS 2016.* 128–137.
[25] Michael Elkin and Ofer Neiman. 2017. Linear-Size Hopsets with Small Hopbound, and Distributed Routing with Low Memory. arXiv:1704.08468 [cs.DS].
[26] Lester R Ford Jr. 1956. *Network flow theory.* Technical Report. RAND CORP SANTA MONICA CA.
[27] Sebastian Forster and Danupon Nanongkai. 2018. A Faster Distributed Single-Source Shortest Paths Algorithm. In *Proc. FOCS 2018.* 686–697. https://doi.org/10.1109/FOCS.2018.00071
[28] François Le Gall. 2014. Powers of Tensors and Fast Matrix Multiplication. In *Proc. ISSAC 2014.* 296–303. https://doi.org/10.1145/2608628.2608664
[29] Mohsen Ghaffari. 2017. Distributed MIS via All-to-All Communication. In *Proc. PODC 2017.* 141–149. https://doi.org/10.1145/3087801.3087830
[30] Mohsen Ghaffari, Themis Gouleakis, Christian Konrad, Slobodan Mitrovic, and Ronitt Rubinfeld. 2018. Improved Massively Parallel Computation Algorithms for MIS, Matching, and Vertex Cover. In *Proc. PODC 2018.* 129–138. https://doi.org/10.1145/3212734.3212743
[31] Mohsen Ghaffari and Jason Li. 2018. Improved distributed algorithms for exact shortest paths. In *Proc. STOC 2018.* 431–444. https://doi.org/10.1145/3188745.3188948
[32] Mohsen Ghaffari and Krzysztof Nowicki. 2018. Congested Clique Algorithms for the Minimum Cut Problem. In *Proc. PODC 2018.* ACM, 357–366.
[33] Mohsen Ghaffari and Merav Parter. 2016. MST in Log-Star Rounds of Congested Clique. In *Proc. PODC 2016.* 19–28. https://doi.org/10.1145/2933057.2933103
[34] James W Hegeman and Sriram V Pemmaraju. 2015. Lessons from the congested clique applied to MapReduce. *Theoretical Computer Science* 608 (2015), 268–281.
[35] Monika Henzinger, Sebastian Krinninger, and Danupon Nanongkai. 2016. A deterministic almost-tight distributed algorithm for approximating single-source shortest paths. In *Proc. STOC 2016.* 489–498. https://doi.org/10.1145/2897518.2897638
[36] Monika Henzinger, Sebastian Krinninger, and Danupon Nanongkai. 2018. Decremental single-source shortest paths on undirected graphs in near-linear total update time. *J. ACM* 65, 6 (2018), 36.
[37] Stephan Holzer and Nathan Pinsker. 2015. Approximation of Distances and Shortest Paths in the Broadcast Congest Clique. In *Proc. OPODIS 2015.* https://doi.org/10.4230/LIPIcs.OPODIS.2015.6
[38] Stephan Holzer and Roger Wattenhofer. 2012. Optimal distributed all pairs shortest paths and applications. In *Proc. PODC 2012.* 355–364.
[39] Chien-Chung Huang, Danupon Nanongkai, and Thatchaphol Saranurak. 2017. Distributed Exact Weighted All-Pairs Shortest Paths in $\tilde{O}(n^{5/4})$ Rounds. In *Proc. FOCS 2017.* 168–179. https://doi.org/10.1109/FOCS.2017.24
[40] Shang-En Huang and Seth Pettie. 2019. Thorup–Zwick emulators are universally optimal hopsets. *Inform. Process. Lett.* 142 (2019), 9–13.
[41] Tomasz Jurdziński and Krzysztof Nowicki. 2018. MST in $O(1)$ rounds of congested clique. In *Proc. SODA 2018.* 2620–2632.
[42] Janne H. Korhonen and Jukka Suomela. 2018. Towards a Complexity Theory for the Congested Clique. In *Proc. SPAA 2018.* 163–172. https://doi.org/10.1145/3210377.3210391
[43] François Le Gall. 2016. Further algebraic algorithms in the congested clique model and applications to graph-theoretic problems. In *Proc. DISC 2016.* 57–70.
[44] Christoph Lenzen. 2013. Optimal deterministic routing and sorting on the congested clique. In *Proc. PODC 2013.* 42–50.
[45] Christoph Lenzen and Boaz Patt-Shamir. 2013. Fast routing table construction using small messages. In *Proc. STOC 2013.* ACM, 381–390.
[46] Christoph Lenzen and Boaz Patt-Shamir. 2015. Fast partial distance estimation and applications. In *Proc. PODC 2015.* ACM, 153–162.
[47] Christoph Lenzen and David Peleg. 2013. Efficient distributed source detection with limited bandwidth. In *Proc. PODC 2013.* 375–382. https://doi.org/10.1145/2484239.2484262
[48] Zvi Lotker, Boaz Patt-Shamir, Elan Pavlov, and David Peleg. 2005. Minimum-weight spanning tree construction in $O(\log \log n)$ communication rounds. *SIAM J. Comput.* 35, 1 (2005), 120–131.
[49] Danupon Nanongkai. 2014. Distributed approximation algorithms for weighted shortest paths. In *Proc. STOC 2014.* ACM, 565–573.
[50] Gopal Pandurangan, Peter Robinson, and Michele Scquizzato. 2018. On the Distributed Complexity of Large-Scale Graph Computations. In *Proc. SPAA 2018.* 405–414. https://doi.org/10.1145/3210377.3210409
[51] Merav Parter. 2018. $(\Delta + 1)$ Coloring in the Congested Clique Model. In *Proc. ICALP 2018.* 160:1–160:14. https://doi.org/10.4230/LIPIcs.ICALP.2018.160
[52] Merav Parter and Hsin-Hao Su. 2018. Randomized $(\Delta + 1)$-Coloring in $O(\log^* \Delta)$ Congested Clique Rounds. In *Proc. DISC 2018.* 39:1–39:18. https://doi.org/10.4230/LIPIcs.DISC.2018.39
[53] Merav Parter and Eylon Yogev. 2018. Congested Clique Algorithms for Graph Spanners. In *Proc. DISC 2018.* 40:1–40:18. https://doi.org/10.4230/LIPIcs.DISC.2018.40
[54] David Peleg, Liam Roditty, and Elad Tal. 2012. Distributed algorithms for network diameter and girth. In *Proc. ICALP 2012.* 660–672.
[55] Liam Roditty and Virginia Vassilevska Williams. 2013. Fast approximation algorithms for the diameter and radius of sparse graphs. In *Proc. STOC 2013.* ACM, 515–524.
[56] Hanmao Shi and Thomas H Spencer. 1999. Time–work tradeoffs of the single-source shortest paths problem. *Journal of algorithms* 30, 1 (1999), 19–32.
[57] Mikkel Thorup and Uri Zwick. 2006. Spanners and emulators with sublinear distance errors. In *Proc. SODA 2006.* 802–809.

Quantum Distributed Algorithm for the All-Pairs Shortest Path Problem in the CONGEST-CLIQUE Model

Taisuke Izumi
Nagoya Institute of Technology
Showa-ku, Nagoya, Aichi, Japan
t-izumi@nitech.ac.jp

François Le Gall
Graduate School of Informatics, Kyoto University
Sakyo-ku, Kyoto, Japan
legall@i.kyoto-u.ac.jp

ABSTRACT

The All-Pairs Shortest Path problem (APSP) is one of the most central problems in distributed computation. In the CONGEST-CLIQUE model, in which n nodes communicate with each other over a fully connected network by exchanging messages of $O(\log n)$ bits in synchronous rounds, the best known general algorithm for APSP uses $\tilde{O}(n^{1/3})$ rounds. Breaking this barrier is a fundamental challenge in distributed graph algorithms. In this paper we investigate for the first time quantum distributed algorithms in the CONGEST-CLIQUE model, where nodes can exchange messages of $O(\log n)$ *quantum* bits, and show that this barrier can be broken: we construct a $\tilde{O}(n^{1/4})$-round quantum distributed algorithm for the APSP over directed graphs with polynomial weights in the CONGEST-CLIQUE model. This speedup in the quantum setting contrasts with the case of the standard CONGEST model, for which Elkin et al. (PODC 2014) showed that quantum communication does not offer significant advantages over classical communication.

Our quantum algorithm is based on a relationship discovered by Vassilevska Williams and Williams (JACM 2018) between the APSP and the detection of negative triangles in a graph. The quantum part of our algorithm exploits the framework for quantum distributed search recently developed by Le Gall and Magniez (PODC 2018). Our main technical contribution is a method showing how to implement multiple quantum searches (one for each edge in the graph) in parallel without introducing congestions.

CCS CONCEPTS

• **Theory of computation** → **Quantum computation theory**; **Graph algorithms analysis**; **Distributed algorithms**.

KEYWORDS

Distributed algorithms; quantum algorithms; all-pairs shortest paths; CONGEST-CLIQUE model

ACM Reference Format:
Taisuke Izumi and François Le Gall. 2019. Quantum Distributed Algorithm for the All-Pairs Shortest Path Problem in the CONGEST-CLIQUE Model. In *2019 ACM Symposium on Principles of Distributed Computing (PODC '19), July 29-August 2, 2019, Toronto, ON, Canada.* ACM, New York, NY, USA, 10 pages. https://doi.org/10.1145/3293611.3331628

PODC '19, July 29-August 2, 2019, Toronto, ON, Canada

ACM ISBN 978-1-4503-6217-7/19/07...$15.00
https://doi.org/10.1145/3293611.3331628

1 INTRODUCTION

Background. The CONGEST-CLIQUE model is a model in distributed computing that has recently been the subject of intensive research [4, 8, 9, 16, 18–21, 25, 29–32, 34, 35]. In this model n nodes communicate with each other over a fully connected network (i.e., a clique) by exchanging messages of $O(\log n)$ bits in synchronous rounds. Compared with the more traditional CONGEST model [36], the CONGEST-CLIQUE model removes the effect of distances between nodes in the computation and thus focuses solely on understanding the role of congestion in distributed computing.

The study of shortest path problems is one of the central topics in the context of distributed graph algorithms. In the CONGEST model, much progress has been done in the past years [1, 2, 4, 10, 12, 15, 21–23, 29, 32]: while for exact computation of the Single-Source Shortest Path problem (SSSP) there is still a small gap between the upper bounds and the lower bounds [12, 37], for the All-Pairs Shortest Path problem (APSP) an algorithm with optimal time complexity (up to possible polylogarithmic factors) has been constructed very recently [2]. In the CONGEST-CLIQUE model, the first non-trivial result attaining sublinear running time was an algorithm by Nanongkai [32], which solves the $(2+\epsilon)$-approximate APSP over undirected weighted graphs within $\tilde{O}(\sqrt{n})$ rounds. This was improved by Censor-Hillel at al. [4], who gave a $\tilde{O}(n^{1/3})$-round exact algorithm for the general APSP (i.e., the APSP over directed graphs with polynomial weights). While faster algorithms based on fast matrix multiplication have been designed for the APSP over graphs with small weights or for approximating the shortest paths [4, 26], the above $\tilde{O}(n^{1/3})$-round is still not only the best known exact algorithm for the general APSP, but also the best known exact algorithm for SSSP in the CONGEST-CLIQUE model.

Quantum distributed computing. The power of distributed network computation in the quantum CONGEST model has been first investigated by Elkin et al. [11]. In this model the nodes can use quantum processing and communicate using quantum bits (qubits): each edge of the network corresponds to a quantum channel (e.g., an optical fiber if qubits are implemented using photons) of bandwidth $O(\log n)$ qubits. Their main conclusion was that for many fundamental problems in distributed computing, including the computation of the s-t shortest path in weighted graphs, quantum communication does not offer significant advantages over classical communication. A significant development recently happened: Le Gall and Magniez [27] constructed a quantum distributed algorithm in the CONGEST model computing the exact diameter within

$\tilde{O}(\sqrt{nD})$ rounds, where D denotes the diameter. Since Frischknecht et al. [13] have shown that any classical algorithm requires $\tilde{\Omega}(n)$ rounds, even in the case $D = O(1)$, this gives a speedup (up to quadratic when the diameter is small). At the core of this quantum algorithm lies a distributed implementation of Grover's seminal quantum algorithm [17]. Grover's algorithm achieves a quadratic speedup over brute-force search for generic search problems in the centralized setting. The algorithm from [27] carefully adapts Grover's algorithm to the distributed CCNGEST model and shows how to combine it with a classical distributed algorithm in a completely black-box way. Due to its versatility, this approach has the potential of accelerating many graph algorithms. A pressing open question is to understand for which problems in distributed computing it can actually help.

Our result. While it is tempting to consider potential quantum acceleration of computing shortest paths using the distributed version of Grover's algorithm, there are several significant obstacles. The distributed quantum diameter algorithm from [27] crucially relies on reducing the computation of the diameter to the search problem of finding a node with the maximum eccentricity, and this strategy does not directly work for shortest path problems. Indeed, as already mentioned, it is known that for s-t shortest paths over weighted graphs, quantum communication cannot offer any significant speedup in the CONGEST model. Even over unweighted graphs, in the CONGEST model it is easy to extend the classical lower bound from [13] to show a $\tilde{\Omega}(n)$-round lower bound for the APSP that holds even in the quantum setting.

In this paper we show that a speedup is possible in the CONGEST-CLIQUE model. Our main result is the following theorem.

Theorem 1.1. *There is a quantum algorithm that solves with high probability the All-Pairs Shortest Path problem over directed graphs with integer weights in* $\{-W, \ldots, W\}$ *using* $\tilde{O}(n^{1/4} \log W)$ *rounds in the CONGEST-CLIQUE model.*

As already mentioned, the best known upper bound for the APSP in the classical CONGEST-CLIQUE is due to Censor-Hillel at al. [4]: for graphs with integer weights in $\{-W, \ldots, W\}$ their upper bound is $\tilde{O}(n^{1/3} \log W)$ rounds. While no nontrivial lower bound is known on the classical complexity of APSP in the CONGEST-CLIQUE model, which is not surprising due to the technical challenges of proving any nontrivial lower bound in this model, the current $\tilde{O}(n^{1/3} \log W)$ bound appears as a significant barrier for classical algorithms. Our quantum algorithm breaks this barrier. This gives strong evidence for the superiority of quantum distributed computing over classical distributed computing in the CONGEST-CLIQUE model as well (unless the barrier can be broken in the classical setting as well — this would in itself be a significant breakthrough). Another interesting observation is that this quantum speedup occurs for a problem (the APSP) for which no quantum speedup can be achieved in the standard CONGEST model, as already mentioned.

Technical overview. The first step of our approach consists in reducing the APSP problem to the problem of detecting *negative triangles* (triangles in which the sum of the weights of the three edges is negative). This reduction is inspired by the recent breakthrough by Vassilevska Williams and Williams [39] in centralized algorithms that revealed the relationship between the APSP and triangle detection, via the computation of the distance product of two matrices. More precisely, our approach reduces the APSP to the problem of identifying all the edges of the graph that are involved in (at least) one negative triangle, under the promise that each edge is involved in at most $O(\log n)$ negative triangles.

In order to solve the latter problem, we would like to design an algorithm running a quadratic number of instances of negative-triangle detection simultaneously, since in the worst case $\Theta(n^2)$ edges involved in negative triangles need to be detected. Due to the fact that the query sequence generated by a single run of the distributed version of Grover's algorithm is a quantum superposition, a naive parallelization would result in high congestion of query messages, causing delays and degradation of the running time. To overcome this difficulty, we develop a novel machinery ensuring that all the parallel runs of the quantum searches are fairly load balanced, which resolves the problem of congestions. This is done by analyzing carefully the error probability of multiple quantum searches and showing that (for the problem considered) ignoring the queries that are not load balanced does not decrease significantly the success probability.

Other related works. As already mentioned, triangle detection and matrix multiplication are closely related to the APSP problem. There are several results considering those problems in the CONGEST or CONGEST-CLIQUE models [4–6, 8, 24, 26, 33]. In the CONGEST-CLIQUE model, in particular, an $\tilde{O}(n^{1/3})$-round algorithm for listing all triangles is proposed by Dolev et al. [8]. This algorithm is combinatorial (i.e., non-algebraic) and thus works for listing negative triangles as well. Combined with our reduction from APSP to negative triangles, this can be used to construct a classical distributed APSP algorithm in the CONGEST-CLIQUE with the same complexity $\tilde{O}(n^{1/3} \log W)$ as the algorithm by Censor-Hillel [4]. While there exist faster algorithms for triangle detection [4, 9, 26], all these faster algorithms are based on an algebraic approach (more precisely, a reduction to matrix multiplication over a ring), and cannot be used to find negative triangles (which corresponds to matrix multiplication over a semiring).

To our knowledge the present work is the first to consider the quantum CONGEST-CLIQUE model. We already mentioned the prior works [11, 27] on the quantum CONGEST model. Besides the vast literature on two-party quantum communication complexity (see, e.g., [3, 7, 40]), there exist a few works that considered other settings in quantum distributed computing. First, exact quantum protocols for leader election in anonymous networks have been developed by Tani et al. [38]. Gavoille et al. [14] then considered quantum distributed computing in the LOCAL model, and showed that for several fundamental problems, allowing quantum communication does not lead to any significant advantage. Very recently Le Gall et al. [28] showed that there nevertheless exist some computational problems for which quantum distributed computing can be much more powerful than classical distributed computing in the LOCAL model.

2 PRELIMINARIES

General notations. Given any positive integer p, we use the notation $[p]$ to represent the set $\{1, 2, \ldots, p\}$. Given a graph $G = (V, E)$ and any two sets $U, U' \subseteq V$, we write $\mathcal{P}(U, U')$ the set of pairs of vertices $\{u, v\}$ with $u \in U$, $v \in U'$ and $u \neq v$. When $U' = U$ we simply write $\mathcal{P}(U) = \mathcal{P}(U, U)$. Finally, for any vertex $v \in V$ we write $\mathcal{N}_G(v)$ the set of neighbors of v.

Quantum CONGEST-CLIQUE model. Recent definitions of the quantum CONGEST model [27] and the quantum LOCAL model [28] are obtained by starting with the corresponding classical model (classical CONGEST model and LOCAL model, respectively) and simply allowing nodes to send quantum information instead of classical information. In this paper we use the same approach to define a natural quantum version of the CONGEST-CLIQUE model.

In the classical CONGEST-CLIQUE model, n nodes communicate with each other over a fully connected network by exchanging messages of $O(\log n)$ bits in synchronous rounds. All links and nodes (corresponding to the edges and vertices of G, respectively) are reliable and suffer no faults. Each node has a distinct identifier. In the quantum CONGEST-CLIQUE model the only difference is that the nodes can exchange quantum information: each message exchanged consists of $O(\log n)$ quantum bits instead of $O(\log n)$ bits in the classical case. In particular, initially the nodes of the network do not share any entanglement.

This paper will describe many classical algorithms and procedures that will be used for pre-processing and post-processing (or even used inside the main quantum part as a subprocedure). We will use many times (sometimes implicitly) the following Lemma by Dolev et al. [8].

Lemma 2.1. *[8] In the CONGEST-CLIQUE model a set of messages in which no node is the source of more than n messages and no node is the destination of more than n messages can be delivered within two rounds if the source and destination of each message is known in advance to all nodes.*

Graph-theoretic problems in the CONGEST-CLIQUE model. When studying graph-theoretic problems such as the APSP problem in the classical or quantum CONGEST-CLIQUE model, the input is a graph $G = (V, E)$ consisting of n nodes, i.e., the number of nodes of the graph is the same as the number of nodes of the communication network. This means that we can assign to each node of the network a distinct label $u \in V$. The input is given as follows: each node with label u of the network receives the row of the adjacency matrix of G corresponding to vertex u of G. The result of the computation is defined similarly: for the APSP the node with label u should output the shortest distance from u to all the other nodes in G. We refer to [4] for details.

3 APSP AND NEGATIVE TRIANGLES

In this section we show how to reduce the APSP to finding all the edges involved in a negative triangle. We first define the latter problem and state the main technical result of this paper (Theorem 3.3). Then we show the computation of the distance product of a matrix reduces to this problem. Finally, we recall the standard reduction from APSP to the computation of the distance product and derive Theorem 1.1 from Theorem 3.3.

Finding the edges in negative triangles. Consider an undirected weighted graph $G = (V, E, f)$ with weight function $f : E \to \mathbb{Z}$. For an edge $\{u, v\} \in E$, we use the notation $f(u, v)$ instead of $f(\{u, v\})$.

Definition 3.1. Given three vertices $u, v, w \in V$, we say that the triple $\{u, v, w\}$ is a negative triangle in G if $\{u, v\}$, $\{u, w\}$ and $\{v, w\}$ are edges and the inequality $f(u, v) + f(u, w) + f(v, w) < 0$ holds.

For any pair $\{u, v\} \in \mathcal{P}(V)$, we use the notation $\Gamma_G(u, v)$ to denote the number of negative triangles involving $\{u, v\}$, i.e.,

$$\Gamma_G(u, v) = |\{w \in V \mid \{u, v, w\} \text{ is a negative triangle in } G\}| .$$

We simply write $\Gamma(u, v)$ when the graph G is clear from the context.

We now define the main problem considered in this paper. This problem, which we denote FindEdges, asks to compute the list of all edges involved in a negative triangle. The formal definition of the problem is as follows.

> FindEdges
>
> Input: an undirected weighted graph $G = (V, E, f)$ distributed among the n nodes of the network (each node u gets $\mathcal{N}_G(u)$)
>
> Output: each node u outputs the list of all pairs $\{u, v\} \in \mathcal{P}(V)$ such that $\Gamma(u, v) > 0$

Let us now consider the version of this problem in which we have the promise $\Gamma(u, v) = O(\log n)$ for all pairs $\{u, v\}$. It will actually be convenient to define a more general problem where there is an additional input $S \subseteq \mathcal{P}(V)$, the promise only holds for the pairs in S and we only require each node to output the edges in S that are involved in a negative triangle. The definition of this version with promise, which we call FindEdgesWithPromise, follows.

> FindEdgesWithPromise
>
> Input: an undirected weighted graph $G = (V, E, f)$ and a set $S \subseteq \mathcal{P}(V)$ distributed among the n nodes of the network (each node u gets $\mathcal{N}_G(u)$ and the list of all pairs in S containing u)
>
> Promise: $\Gamma(u, v) \leq 90 \log n$ for all pairs $\{u, v\} \in S$
>
> Output: each node u outputs the list of all pairs $\{u, v\} \in S$ such that $\Gamma(u, v) > 0$

It is not difficult to show a randomized reduction from solving the problem FindEdges to solving $O(\log n)$ instances of the problem FindEdgesWithPromise. We state this reduction in the following proposition.

Proposition 3.2. *Assume there exists a $T(n)$-round algorithm that solves FindEdgesWithPromise with probability at least $1-\varepsilon$ for some $\varepsilon > 0$. Then there exists a $O(T(n) \log n)$-round algorithm that solves the problem FindEdges with probability at least $1-O((\varepsilon+1/n^3)\log n)$.*

Proof. Let $\mathcal{A}$ denote the $T(n)$-round algorithm for the problem FindEdgesWithPromise. We construct an algorithm for the problem FindEdges as follows.

1. $S \leftarrow \mathcal{P}(V)$; $M \leftarrow \emptyset$; $i \leftarrow 0$.
2. While $60 \cdot 2^i \log n \leq n$ do:

2.1. Sample each edge of G with probability $\sqrt{\frac{60 \cdot 2^i \log n}{n}}$. Let G' be the subgraph of G consisting only of the sampled edges.

2.2. Apply the algorithm $\mathcal{A}$ on input (G', S). Let S' be the output of the algorithm.
2.3. $S \leftarrow S \setminus S'$; $M \leftarrow M \cup S'$; $i \leftarrow i + 1$.
3. Apply the algorithm $\mathcal{A}$ on input (G, S). Let S'' be the output of the algorithm.
4. Output $M \cup S''$.

Let us call Algorithm $\mathcal{B}$ the algorithm we just described. Its round complexity is $O(T(n) \log n)$.

Let us first analyze Algorithm $\mathcal{B}$ under the assumption that Algorithm $\mathcal{A}$ never makes any error. We will prove below by induction the following invariant for the while loop: when testing the exit condition "$60 \cdot 2^i \log n \leq n$" at Step 2 of the while loop for some value i, we have $\Gamma_G(u, v) \leq n/2^i$ for all $\{u, v\} \in S$, and all the pairs $\{u, v\} \in \mathcal{P}(V)$ such that $\Gamma_G(u, v) > n/2^i$ are already contained in M. This shows that at the end of the while loop we have $\Gamma_G(u, v) \leq n/2^c$ for all $\{u, v\} \in S$, and all the pairs $\{u, v\}$ such that $\Gamma_G(u, v) > n/2^c$ are contained in M, where c is the smallest integer such that $60 \cdot 2^c \log n > n$. Since $n/2^c < 90 \log n$, the call to Algorithm $\mathcal{A}$ at Step 3 then finds all the remaining pairs involved in negative triangles and the output at Step 4 is precisely the output of FindEdges.

The loop invariant is obviously satisfied for $i = 0$. Now assume that it is satisfied when $i = k$ for some $k \geq 0$ and let us consider what is happening at Step 2.2. Consider any pair $\{u, v\} \in S$. From the induction hypothesis we have $\Gamma_G(u, v) < n/2^i$. Note that $\mathbb{E}[\Gamma_{G'}(u, v)] = \Gamma_G(u, v) \times \frac{60 \cdot 2^i \log n}{n} \leq 60 \log n$. Chernoff's bound then implies

$$\Pr[\Gamma_{G'}(u, v) > 90 \log n] \leq \exp\left(-\frac{60 \log n}{12}\right) < \frac{1}{n^5},$$

which means that with probability at least $1 - 1/n^3$ the promise required to execute Algorithm $\mathcal{A}$ is satisfied for all $\{u, v\} \in S$. Let us now consider a pair $\{u, v\} \in S$ such that the inequality $\Gamma_G(u, v) > n/2^{i+1}$ holds. We have

$$\begin{aligned}\Pr[\Gamma_{G'}(u, v) = 0] &= \left(1 - \frac{60 \cdot 2^i \log n}{n}\right)^{\Gamma_G(u,v)} \\ &< \exp\left(-\Gamma_G(u, v) \times \frac{60 \cdot 2^i \log n}{n}\right) < \frac{1}{n^{30}}\end{aligned}$$

and thus the pair $\{u, v\}$ is included in the output S' of Algorithm $\mathcal{A}$, and thus removed from S (and added to M) at Step 2.3, with high probability. This proves that the loop invariant is satisfied for $i = k + 1$ as well with probability at least $1 - 1/n^3 - 1/n^{28}$.

We have thus shown that under the assumption that Algorithm $\mathcal{A}$ never makes any error, our algorithm solves FindEdges with probability at least $1 - c/n^3 - c/n^{28}$. Since the error probability of Algorithm $\mathcal{A}$ is at most ε and $\mathcal{A}$ is applied $c + 1$ times, the union bound implies that our algorithm solves the problem FindEdges with probability at least $1 - c/n^3 - c/n^{28} - (c+1)\varepsilon = 1 - O((\varepsilon + 1/n^3) \log n)$. □

The main technical contribution of this paper is the following theorem, which is proved in Section 5.

Theorem 3.3. *There is a $\tilde{O}(n^{1/4})$-round quantum algorithm that solves the problem FindEdgesWithPromise with probability $1 - O(1/n)$ in the CONGEST-CLIQUE model.*

From distance products to negative triangles. We first recall the definition of the distance product of two matrices.

Definition 3.4. Let A and B be two $n \times n$ matrices with entries in $\mathbb{Z} \cup \{-\infty, \infty\}$. The distance product of A and B, denoted $A \star B$, is the $n \times n$ matrix C such that $C[i, j] = \min_{k \in [n]}\{A[i, k] + B[k, j]\}$ for all $(i, j) \in [n] \times [n]$.

Vassilevska Williams and Williams [39] proved a reduction from the computation of the distance product of two $n \times n$ matrices A and B to computing the edges involved in negative triangles in a graph. We state this reduction in the following proposition.

Proposition 3.5. *[39] Assume that there exists a $T(n)$-round algorithm for FindEdges. Then there exists a $O(T(n) \log M)$-round algorithm that computes the distance product of any two $n \times n$ matrices with entries in $\{-M, \ldots, M\} \cup \{-\infty, \infty\}$.*

Sketch of the proof. Let D be an arbitrary symmetric $n \times n$ matrix with integer entries. Consider the undirected tripartite graph $G = (\mathcal{I} \cup \mathcal{J} \cup \mathcal{K}, E, f)$ with $|\mathcal{I}| = |\mathcal{J}| = |\mathcal{K}| = n$ and weight function $f(i, k) = A[i, k]$ for all $(i, k) \in \mathcal{I} \times \mathcal{K}$, $f(j, k) = A[k, j]$ for all $(j, k) \in \mathcal{J} \times \mathcal{K}$ and $f(i, j) = -D[i, j]$ for all $(i, j) \in \mathcal{I} \times \mathcal{J}$. Observe that a triple $\{i, j, k\}$ with $i \in \mathcal{I}$, $j \in \mathcal{J}$ and $k \in \mathcal{K}$ is a negative triangle if and only if

$$A[i, k] + B[k, j] < D[i, j],$$

which implies that the pair $\{i, j\}$ is involved in a negative triangle of G if and only if

$$\min_{k \in [n]}\{A[i, k] + B[k, j]\} < D[i, j]. \tag{1}$$

Thus by finding all the pairs $\{i, j\}$ involved in a negative triangle, we learn for which pairs $\{i, j\}$ the above inequality holds. By starting with the all-zero matrix D and doing binary search (adjusting each time each entry of the matrix D), the distance product can thus be computed by calling $O(\log M)$ times an algorithm for FindEdges. More details can be found in [39]. □

From APSP to distance products and proof of Theorem 1.1. We now recall how the APSP reduces to the computation of the distance product.[1] This is a standard reduction: we refer to, e.g., [41] for a reference in the centralized setting and to [4] for a discussion of the reduction in the CONGEST-CLIQUE model.

Let $G = (V, E, w)$ be a weighted directed graph on n vertices with no self-loop. Assume that the graph has no negative cycle. Let us associate V with the set $[n]$. The graph can be encoded as an $n \times n$ matrix A_G in which

$$A_G[i, j] = \begin{cases} 0 & \text{if } i = j, \\ w(i, j) & \text{if } i \neq j \text{ and } (i, j) \in E, \\ \infty & \text{if } i \neq j \text{ and } (i, j) \notin E, \end{cases}$$

for each $(i, j) \in [n] \times [n]$. It is easy to check that the matrix A_G^n, the n-th power of the matrix A_G with respect to the distance product, contains the distances between all pairs of vertices of G. Moreover, this matrix can be computed using only $O(\log n)$ matrix products. If the weights of the graph are integers in $\{-W, \ldots, W\}$, then all the finite entries of the matrices arising during the computation

[1] Our explanations focus on computing the lengths of the shortest paths. Using standard techniques (see for instance [4]), the approach can be adapted to return the shortest paths as well, at a cost of increasing the complexity only by a polylogarithmic factor.

of A_G^n are between $-nW$ and nW. We summarize this result in the following proposition.

Proposition 3.6. *Assume that there exists a $T(n, M)$-round algorithm that computes the distance product of any two $n \times n$ matrices with entries in $\{-M, \ldots, M\} \cup \{-\infty, \infty\}$. Then there exists a $O(T(n, nW) \log n)$-round algorithm for the APSP with integer weights in $\{-W, \ldots, W\}$.*

Theorem 1.1 then follows from the reductions described in Propositions 3.2, 3.5, 3.6 and from Theorem 3.3. The success probability of the final quantum algorithm is $1 - \tilde{O}((\log W)/n)$, i.e., with probability $1 - \tilde{O}((\log W)/n)$ all the nodes of the network output the correct answer.

4 DISTRIBUTED MULTIPLE QUANTUM SEARCHES

In this section we describe our quantum technique: distributed multiple quantum searches only using typical inputs.

4.1 Distributed quantum search

Here, we explain the basic framework for quantum distributed search developed in [27].

Description of the result. Let X be a finite set and $g\colon X \to \{0, 1\}$ be a Boolean function over X. Let u be an arbitrary node of the network (e.g., an elected leader). Assume that node u can evaluate the function g in r rounds: assume that there exists an r-round classical distributed algorithm C such that node u, when receiving as input $x \in X$, outputs $g(x)$. Now consider the following problem: node u should find one element $x \in X$ such that $g(x) = 1$ (or decide that no such element exists). The trivial strategy is to compute $g(x)$ for each $x \in X$ one by one, which requires $r|X|$ rounds. Le Gall and Magniez [27] showed that there exists a quantum distributed algorithm that solves this problem with high probability in $\tilde{O}(r\sqrt{|X|})$ rounds. While this result is described in [27] for the CONGEST model, it holds for the CONGEST-CLIQUE model as well.

Example. Let us show how the quantum distributed algorithm for the diameter from [27] can be described in this setting. Let $X = V$ be the vertex set of the graph considered. Fix an integer d and define the function $g\colon V \to \{0, 1\}$ as follows: for any vertex $v \in V$ we have $g(v) = 1$ if and only if the eccentricity of vertex v is larger than d. Solving the problem described in the previous paragraph enables us to decide whether the maximum eccentricity of a vertex (i.e., the diameter of the graph) is larger than d, and repeating this process a logarithmic number of times for different values of d (chosen via binary search) enables us to compute the diameter.[2]

Technical details. The quantum distributed algorithm for search is obtained by implementing Grover's well-known quantum search algorithm [17] in the distributed setting. We now explain how this works.

Let us define the two sets $A^0 = \{x \in X \mid g(x) = 0\}$ and $A^1 = X \backslash A^0 = \{x \in X | g(x) = 1\}$ and assume that $|A^1| > 0$. As usual when analyzing Grover's algorithm, we make the convenient assumption $|A^1| < |X|/2$ (otherwise finding a solution is easy). Define the following two quantum states: $|\psi^0\rangle = \frac{1}{\sqrt{|A^0|}} \sum_{x \in A^0} |x\rangle$ and $|\psi^1\rangle = \frac{1}{\sqrt{|A^1|}} \sum_{x \in A^1} |x\rangle$, which are the uniform superpositions over all the elements in A^0 and A^1, respectively. Let $\mathcal{H}$ denote the subspace generated by these two quantum states. Grover's algorithm starts from the quantum state $|\Phi_0\rangle = \frac{1}{\sqrt{|X|}} \sum_{x \in X} |x\rangle$ corresponding to the uniform superposition over all the elements in X. Note that $|\Phi_0\rangle$ belongs to $\mathcal{H}$ and is easy to create. Grover's algorithm then successively applies the unitary operator corresponding to C and then a unitary operator U independent of the function g.[3]

A crucial property is that any state in $\mathcal{H}$ is mapped by UC to a state in $\mathcal{H}$, which means that for any $k \geq 0$ the state of the system after the k-th iteration can be written as $|\Phi_k\rangle = (UC)^k |\Phi_0\rangle = \alpha_k |\psi^0\rangle + \beta_k |\psi^1\rangle$ for some complex numbers α_k and β_k such that $|\alpha_k|^2 + |\beta_k|^2 = 1$. The analysis of Grover's algorithm shows that by choosing k such that $k = O(\sqrt{|X|})$ we can guarantee that $|\beta_k|^2 \approx 1$, which means that measuring the state $|\Phi_k\rangle$ gives an element $x \in A^1$ with high probability. The total round complexity is thus $\tilde{O}(r\sqrt{|X|})$.

Multiple searches. We now describe an easy generalization to multiple searches of the framework presented above. Let X be a finite set and $g_1, \ldots, g_m\colon X \to \{0, 1\}$ be m Boolean functions over X, for some integer $m \geq 1$. For each $i \in [m]$ define the set $A_i^1 = \{x_i \in X \mid g_i(x_i) = 1\}$ and assume for convenience that $|A_i^1| > 0$.[4] Let u be an arbitrary node of the network. Assume now that node u can evaluate the functions $g_1, \ldots, g_m$ simultaneously in r rounds. More precisely, assume that there exists a r-round classical distributed algorithm C_m such that node u, when receiving as input $(x_1, \ldots, x_m) \in X^m$, outputs $(g_1(x_1), \ldots, g_m(x_m))$. Now consider the following problem: node u should find one element in $A_1^1 \times \cdots \times A_m^1$. The framework described above can easily be generalized to this problem by having node u implement in parallel m independent distributed quantum searches. This gives a quantum algorithm solving this problem with high probability in $\tilde{O}(r\sqrt{|X|})$ rounds.

4.2 Multiple searches only using typical inputs

We now show a stronger result for the multiple searches problem introduced in the previous subsection: we construct a quantum algorithm that solves the problem even if the evaluation procedure is correct only on inputs close to typical inputs. The motivation for this assumption on the evaluation procedure is as follows. In a typical application (e.g., the example in Section 4.1), the search domain X represents nodes of the network and evaluation should be delegated to these nodes. In this case, at each evaluation step,

[2] Ref. [27] then observed that in the CONGEST model the function g can be evaluated by computing the eccentricity of the vertex v and sending the information to the node u, which can be done in $O(D)$ rounds, where D denotes the diameter of the graph. Thus the diameter can be computed in $\tilde{O}(\sqrt{n}D)$ rounds. With a few additional improvements it is possible to obtain the better bound $\tilde{O}(\sqrt{nD})$, see [27].

[3] Here the term "unitary operator corresponding to C" means the unitary operator corresponding to the quantum circuit obtained by converting the classical algorithm C into a quantum circuit. We typically denote this unitary operator by the same symbol C, since there is no risk of confusion. The key observation of [27] is that this conversion preserves the complexity: if C is an r-round classical algorithm then the corresponding unitary operator can be implemented in $O(r)$ rounds.

[4] This can easily be enforced by adding dummy solutions. Even if a dummy solution is introduced, if there is a real solution then Grover's algorithm will output it after a few repetitions (since when there are more than one solution Grover's algorithm outputs a random solution).

the node u then needs to send a query to the nodes corresponding to each coordinate of the input $\boldsymbol{x} = (x_1, \ldots, x_m) \in X^m$. Then if $\boldsymbol{x} \in X^m$ is mostly dominated by a single $x \in X$, e.g., $\boldsymbol{x} = (x, x, \ldots, x, x)$, the communication link (u, x) suffers high congestion due to the queries injected by u. In this subsection we show that in some cases such "non-typical" inputs $\boldsymbol{x}$ can be completely ignored, which solves this congestion problem.

Let us first introduce the following notation: for any real number $\beta \geq 0$, let $\Upsilon_\beta(m, X) \subseteq X^m$ denote the set of all $\boldsymbol{x} = (x_1, \ldots, x_m) \in X^m$ such that for each $x \in X$ its frequency in $\boldsymbol{x}$ is at most β (i.e., x appears at most β times in $\boldsymbol{x}$). Note that when $\beta > (1+\delta)m/|X|$ for some large enough $\delta > 0$, the set $\Upsilon_\beta(m, X)$ includes the "typical" elements of X^m, i.e., the elements in which the frequencies of all $x \in X$ are close to the frequencies in an element of X^m chosen uniformly at random.

Suppose that instead of assuming the existence of an r-round algorithm C_m that simultaneously evaluates the functions $g_1, \ldots, g_m$ on X^m, we only assume that we have an r-round classical distributed algorithm $\tilde{C}_m$ in which node u outputs $(g_1(x_1), \ldots, g_m(x_m))$ on an input $(x_1, \ldots, x_m) \in \Upsilon_\beta(m, X)$ but may output an error message (or an arbitrary output) on an input $(x_1, \ldots, x_m) \in X^m \setminus \Upsilon_\beta(m, X)$. Our key result is the following theorem, which shows that the same complexity as in Section 4.1 can be achieved in case β is large enough so that $\tilde{C}_m$ works correctly both on typical elements from X^m and on the solutions of the search problem.

Theorem 4.1. *Assume that $|X| < m/(36 \log m)$. Assume the existence of an evaluation algorithm $\tilde{C}_m$, as just described, for some real number β such that $\beta > 8m/|X|$. Finally, assume that*

$$A_1^1 \times \cdots \times A_m^1 \subseteq \Upsilon_{\beta/2}(m, X).$$

There exists a $\tilde{O}(r\sqrt{|X|})$-round quantum algorithm that outputs an element of $A_1^1 \times \cdots \times A_m^1$ with probability at least $1 - 2/m^2$.

The proof of Theorem 4.1 can be found in the full version of the paper. The basic idea behind the proof is fairly easy to describe. Let Q denote the $\tilde{O}(r\sqrt{|X|})$-round quantum algorithm described in Section 4.1, which uses Algorithm C_m (or more precisely, the quantum operator corresponding to C_m). The initial state of this algorithm is the uniform superposition over all elements of X^m; since β is large enough most of these elements are in $\Upsilon_\beta(m, X)$. The final state is close to the uniform superposition over all elements of $A_1^1 \times \cdots \times A_m^1$; all these elements are also in $\Upsilon_\beta(m, X)$ from the assumption. The algorithm of Theorem 4.1 is exactly the same as Q but uses (the quantum operator corresponding to) $\tilde{C}_m$ instead of (the quantum operator corresponding to) C_m. Using $\tilde{C}_m$ instead of C_m obviously only has a negligible impact at the beginning of computation and at the end of the computation. The main technical difficulty is to show that this has no significant impact at each step of the computation as well. We show this by proving that at any step of the computation the quantum state of the system is close to its projection on the vector space spanned by the basis vectors that are in $\Upsilon_\beta(m, X)$.

5 DETECTING NEGATIVE TRIANGLES

In this section we present a $\tilde{O}(n^{1/4})$-round quantum distributed algorithm that solves the problem FindEdgesWithPromise, which proves Theorem 3.3. Through the section $G = (V, E, f)$ represents the input of FindEdgesWithPromise, i.e., an undirected weighted graph on n vertices that satisfies the promise $\Gamma(u, v) \leq 90 \log n$ for all $\{u, v\} \in S$.

5.1 Overall description of the algorithm

The description of our algorithm will use two partitions of the vertex set V, which we now introduce. For the ease of presentation we assume that the three numbers $n^{1/4}$, $\sqrt{n}$ and $n^{3/4}$ are integers (otherwise we can simply round them to the next integers and slightly adjust the sizes of the sets). The first partition is an arbitrary partition of V into $n^{1/4}$ subsets each containing $n^{3/4}$ elements. We denote $\mathcal{V}$ the collection of subsets making this partition. The second partition is an arbitrary partition of V into $\sqrt{n}$ subsets each containing $\sqrt{n}$ elements. We denote $\mathcal{V}'$ the collection of subsets making this partition. In addition to the labeling scheme described in Section 2, which labels the nodes of the network by elements of V, our algorithm will also use the following two labeling schemes.

Second labeling scheme. Let us write $\mathcal{T} = \mathcal{V} \times \mathcal{V} \times \mathcal{V}'$ and observe that $|\mathcal{T}| = n$. We assign one distinct label from $\mathcal{T}$ to each node of the network. We will simply write "node $(\boldsymbol{u}, \boldsymbol{v}, \boldsymbol{w})$" to refer to the node with label $(\boldsymbol{u}, \boldsymbol{v}, \boldsymbol{w})$, for each triple $(\boldsymbol{u}, \boldsymbol{v}, \boldsymbol{w}) \in \mathcal{T}$. This labeling scheme will be used by the algorithm to decide which node should gather the information of the graph: node $(\boldsymbol{u}, \boldsymbol{v}, \boldsymbol{w})$ will gather the weights of all the edges $\{u, w\} \in \mathcal{P}(\boldsymbol{u}, \boldsymbol{w})$ and $\{w, v\} \in \mathcal{P}(\boldsymbol{w}, \boldsymbol{v})$ of the graph.

Third labeling scheme. We have $|\mathcal{P}(\boldsymbol{u}, \boldsymbol{v})| = \Theta(n^{3/2})$ for each $(\boldsymbol{u}, \boldsymbol{v}) \in \mathcal{V} \times \mathcal{V}$. We will describe below a procedure that partitions the set $\mathcal{P}(\boldsymbol{u}, \boldsymbol{v})$ into $\sqrt{n}$ sets each of size $\tilde{\Theta}(n)$. These sets will be denoted $\Lambda_x(\boldsymbol{u}, \boldsymbol{v})$, for $x \in [\sqrt{n}]$. Our third labeling scheme assigns one distinct label $(\boldsymbol{u}, \boldsymbol{v}, x) \in \mathcal{V} \times \mathcal{V} \times [\sqrt{n}]$ to each node of the network. Again, we will simply write "node $(\boldsymbol{u}, \boldsymbol{v}, x)$" to refer to the node with label $(\boldsymbol{u}, \boldsymbol{v}, x)$, for each triple $(\boldsymbol{u}, \boldsymbol{v}, x) \in \mathcal{V} \times \mathcal{V} \times [\sqrt{n}]$. This labeling scheme will be used by the algorithm to distribute to search for triangles: node $(\boldsymbol{u}, \boldsymbol{v}, x)$ will be in charge of checking the existence of all the triangles involving one edge in the set $\Lambda_x(\boldsymbol{u}, \boldsymbol{v})$.

The partition procedure. We now describe how to construct the sets $\Lambda_x(\boldsymbol{u}, \boldsymbol{v})$. For technical reasons it will be much more convenient to use a covering instead of a partition of $\mathcal{P}(\boldsymbol{u}, \boldsymbol{v})$, i.e., to allow some elements to appear more than once, and to construct the covering randomly rather than deterministically.

Consider the following process. Each node $(\boldsymbol{u}, \boldsymbol{v}, x) \in \mathcal{V} \times \mathcal{V} \times [\sqrt{n}]$ constructs the set $\Lambda_x(\boldsymbol{u}, \boldsymbol{v}) \subseteq \mathcal{P}(\boldsymbol{u}, \boldsymbol{v})$ as follows: starting with the empty set, each pair $\{u, v\} \in \mathcal{P}(\boldsymbol{u}, \boldsymbol{v})$ is added by the node to its set $\Lambda_x(\boldsymbol{u}, \boldsymbol{v})$ with probability $10 \log n/\sqrt{n}$. We say that the set $\Lambda_x(\boldsymbol{u}, \boldsymbol{v})$ is *well-balanced* if the inequality $\left|\{v \in \boldsymbol{v} \mid \{u, v\} \in \Lambda_x(\boldsymbol{u}, \boldsymbol{v})\}\right| \leq 100 \cdot n^{1/4} \log n$ holds for all $u \in \boldsymbol{u}$. The following lemma, which is proved by standard probabilistic arguments, shows that with high probability the sets created by this process are well-balanced and cover all the set $\mathcal{P}(\boldsymbol{u}, \boldsymbol{v})$.

Lemma 5.1. *With probability at least $1 - 2/n$ the following statements hold for all $(\boldsymbol{u}, \boldsymbol{v}) \in \mathcal{V} \times \mathcal{V}$:*

(i) *$\Lambda_x(\boldsymbol{u}, \boldsymbol{v})$ is well-balanced for each $x \in [\sqrt{n}]$;*
(ii) *$\bigcup_{x \in [\sqrt{n}]} \Lambda_x(\boldsymbol{u}, \boldsymbol{v}) = \mathcal{P}(\boldsymbol{u}, \boldsymbol{v})$.*

Proof. Let us fix $(\boldsymbol{u}, \boldsymbol{v}) \in \mathcal{V} \times \mathcal{V}$.

For any $x \in [\sqrt{n}]$ we have

$$\mathbb{E}\left[\left|\{v \in \boldsymbol{v} \mid \{u, v\} \in \Lambda_x(\boldsymbol{u}, \boldsymbol{v})\}\right|\right] = 10n^{1/4} \log n$$

for each $u \in \boldsymbol{u}$. Chernoff's bound and the union bound imply that Condition (i) of the lemma thus holds with probability at least $1 - 1/n^2$.

Let $\{u, v\}$ be an arbitrary pair in $\mathcal{P}(\boldsymbol{u}, \boldsymbol{v})$. For any $x \in [\sqrt{n}]$, this pair is included in $\Lambda_x(\boldsymbol{u}, \boldsymbol{v})$ with probability $10 \log n/\sqrt{n}$. The probability that this pair is not included in any $\Lambda_x(\boldsymbol{u}, \boldsymbol{v})$ is thus

$$\left(1 - \frac{10 \log n}{\sqrt{n}}\right)^{\sqrt{n}} \leq 1/n^4.$$

Condition (ii) of the lemma thus holds with probability at least $1 - 1/n^2$.

The statement of the lemma then follows from the above analyses and the union bound. □

Description and analysis of the algorithm. Our algorithm is called ComputePairs and described in Figure 1. Let us analyze it step by step. Step 1 requires $O(n^{1/4})$ rounds, since $|\mathcal{P}(\boldsymbol{u}, \boldsymbol{w})| = |\mathcal{P}(\boldsymbol{w}, \boldsymbol{v})| = O(n^{5/4})$ hold. Step 2 performs the sampling described in Section 5.1, checks which sampled pairs are in S and loads their weight. Step 2 can be implemented in $O(\log n)$ rounds, since communication occurs only when all the sets $\Lambda_x(\boldsymbol{u}, \boldsymbol{v})$ are well-balanced. Lemma 5.1 implies that with probability at least $1 - 2/n$ the following two statements hold:

(a) Algorithm ComputePairs does not abort at Step 2;
(b) at the end of Step 2, each pair $\{u, v\} \in S$ appears at least once at some node.

Note that when the algorithm does not abort, at the end of Step 2 each node $k = (\boldsymbol{u}, \boldsymbol{v}, x)$ keeps at most $100n \log n$ pairs (since the sets $\Lambda_x(\boldsymbol{u}, \boldsymbol{v})$ are all well-balanced). While the exact number of remaining pairs may naturally depend on the node, in order to simplify the notation we will assume that each node keeps precisely $m = 100n \log n$ pairs.

1. Each node $(\boldsymbol{u}, \boldsymbol{v}, \boldsymbol{w}) \in \mathcal{T}$ loads all the weights $f(u, w)$ and $f(w, v)$ for all $\{u, w\} \in \mathcal{P}(\boldsymbol{u}, \boldsymbol{w})$ and all $\{w, v\} \in \mathcal{P}(\boldsymbol{w}, \boldsymbol{v})$.
2. Each node $k = (\boldsymbol{u}, \boldsymbol{v}, x)$ constructs a random set $\Lambda_x(\boldsymbol{u}, \boldsymbol{v}) \subseteq \mathcal{P}(\boldsymbol{u}, \boldsymbol{v})$ as described in Section 5.1. If the set $\Lambda_x(\boldsymbol{u}, \boldsymbol{v})$ is not well-balanced, then the protocol is aborted. Otherwise, the node $(\boldsymbol{u}, \boldsymbol{v}, x)$ loads the weight $f(u, v)$ of all the pairs $\{u, v\} \in \Lambda_x(\boldsymbol{u}, \boldsymbol{v})$ and also checks which of these pairs are in S. The node $(\boldsymbol{u}, \boldsymbol{v}, x)$ keeps only the pairs in S. Let $\{u_1^k, v_1^k\}, \ldots, \{u_m^k, v_m^k\}$ denote these pairs.
3. Each node $k = (\boldsymbol{u}, \boldsymbol{v}, x)$ executes a search to check, for each $\ell \in [m]$, if there exists some $\boldsymbol{w} \in \mathcal{V}'$ such that there exists $w \in \boldsymbol{w}$ for which (u_ℓ^k, v_ℓ^k, w) is a negative triangle. The node k outputs all the pairs $\{u_\ell^k, v_\ell^k\}$ for which the search is successful.

Figure 1: Algorithm ComputePairs, which computes all $\{u, v\} \in S$ involved in a negative triangle.

Step 3 of Algorithm ComputePairs can easily be implemented in $O(\sqrt{n})$ rounds in the classical setting. In the next subsections we prove the following statement, which shows that a quadratic speedup can be achieved in the quantum setting.

Proposition 5.2. *Step 3 of Algorithm ComputePairs can be implemented by a $\tilde{O}(n^{1/4})$-round quantum algorithm that succeeds with probability at least $1 - O(1/n)$.*

Proposition 5.2 combined with the analysis done in this subsection shows that Algorithm ComputePairs solves the problem FindEdgesWithPromise with probability at least $1 - O(1/n)$ (from the union bound). Its overall complexity is $\tilde{O}(n^{1/4})$. This proves Theorem 3.3.

Overview of the proof of Proposition 5.2. Proposition 5.2 is proved by applying the methodology of Section 4 to perform simultaneous quantum searches over the search space $\mathcal{V}'$. A crucial point of the analysis is to show how to implement the checking procedure in $\tilde{O}(1)$ rounds. Let us discuss below the main difficulties that need to be overcome.

Consider the problem of checking, for some pair $(u_\ell^k, v_\ell^k) \in \boldsymbol{u} \times \boldsymbol{v}$ and some fixed $\boldsymbol{w} \in \mathcal{V}'$, whether there exists $w \in \boldsymbol{w}$ for which (u_ℓ^k, v_ℓ^k, w) is a negative triangle. This can be done easily as follows: node $(\boldsymbol{u}, \boldsymbol{v}, x)$ first sends the pair (u_ℓ^k, v_ℓ^k) and the weight $f(u_\ell^k, v_\ell^k)$ to node $(\boldsymbol{u}, \boldsymbol{v}, \boldsymbol{w})$. Node $(\boldsymbol{u}, \boldsymbol{v}, \boldsymbol{w})$ then checks whether the inequality

$$\min_{w \in \boldsymbol{w}} \{f(u_\ell^k, w) + f(w, v_\ell^k)\} \leq f(u_\ell^k, v_\ell^k)$$

holds, which can be done locally from the information gathered at Step 1 of Algorithm ComputePairs, and sends back this information to node $(\boldsymbol{u}, \boldsymbol{v}, x)$.

For each $(\boldsymbol{u}, \boldsymbol{v}, x) \in \mathcal{V} \times \mathcal{V} \times [\sqrt{n}]$, node $(\boldsymbol{u}, \boldsymbol{v}, x)$ will execute simultaneously m executions of this checking procedure (one for each value of ℓ). Each node $(\boldsymbol{u}, \boldsymbol{v}, \boldsymbol{w})$ can thus receive, in the worst case, $m\sqrt{n} = \tilde{\Theta}(n^{3/2})$ pairs during one call of the checking procedure, which would require $\tilde{\Theta}(\sqrt{n})$ rounds. To reduce the checking cost to $\tilde{O}(1)$ rounds, as needed, we will partition the set $\mathcal{T}$ into classes and use this partition to balance the load of the checking queries in order to avoid congestions.

The partitioning of $\mathcal{T}$ is described in Section 5.2. It will in particular identify the triples of $\mathcal{T}$ containing many edges from S involved in negative triangles. These triples are the main source for the possible congestions in the checking procedure. A simple, but crucial, observation is that there cannot exist many such triples, since the promise of FindEdgesWithPromise guarantees that the total number of negative triangles in the graph is low. This observation is the key idea on which the implementation of the load balancing is based.

5.2 Implementation of Step 3: Dividing the triples into classes

Let us first introduce a crucial definition.

Definition 5.3. For any $(\boldsymbol{u}, \boldsymbol{v}, \boldsymbol{w}) \in \mathcal{T}$, let $\Delta(\boldsymbol{u}, \boldsymbol{v}; \boldsymbol{w})$ be the following quantity:

$$\Delta(\boldsymbol{u}, \boldsymbol{v}; \boldsymbol{w}) = \big\{\{u, v\} \in \mathcal{P}(\boldsymbol{u}, \boldsymbol{v}) \cap S \mid \exists w \in \boldsymbol{w} \text{ such that } \{u, v, w\} \text{ is a negative triangle in } G\big\}.$$

The goal of this subsection is to divide the set of triples $\mathcal{T}$ into classes according to the value of $|\Delta(\boldsymbol{u}, \boldsymbol{v}; \boldsymbol{w})|$. Since we do not know how to compute exactly this value efficiently, we actually need to define the classification based on an approximation of $|\Delta(\boldsymbol{u}, \boldsymbol{v}; \boldsymbol{w})|$ that can be computed efficiently. In Figure 2 we describe a classical algorithm called IdentifyClass that either aborts or assign a non-negative integer $c_{\boldsymbol{uvw}}$ to each node $(\boldsymbol{u}, \boldsymbol{v}, \boldsymbol{w}) \in \mathcal{T}$. Note that the complexity of the algorithm is $O(\log n)$ rounds: Step 1 can obviously be implemented in $20 \log n$ rounds and Step 3 does not require any communication. In the case where the algorithm does not abort, we write $\mathcal{T}_\alpha$ the set of all triples $(\boldsymbol{u}, \boldsymbol{v}, \boldsymbol{w}) \in \mathcal{T}$ such that $c_{\boldsymbol{uvw}} = \alpha$, for each integer $\alpha \geq 0$. This defines a partition of the set $\mathcal{T}$. We now show that with high probability the algorithm does not abort and the partition indeed classifies the triples according to the value of $|\Delta(\boldsymbol{u}, \boldsymbol{v}; \boldsymbol{w})|$.

1. Each node $u \in V$ selects each vertex in $\{v \in V \mid \{u, v\} \in S\}$ with probability $(10 \log n)/n$. Let $\Lambda(u)$ denote the set of selected vertices. If $|\Lambda(u)| > 20 \log n$ for at least one node u, then the algorithm aborts. Otherwise, each node u broadcasts the set $\Lambda(u)$ to all the nodes in V. Let us write $R = \cup_{u \in V} \{\{u, v\} \mid v \in \Lambda(u)\}$.
2. Each node $(\boldsymbol{u}, \boldsymbol{v}, \boldsymbol{w}) \in \mathcal{T}$ locally computes the value
$$d_{\boldsymbol{uvw}} = \Big|\{\{u, v\} \in \mathcal{P}(\boldsymbol{u}, \boldsymbol{v}) \cap R \mid \exists w \in \boldsymbol{w} \text{ s.t. } \{u, v, w\} \text{ is a negative triangle in } G\}\Big|$$
and computes the integer $c_{\boldsymbol{uvw}}$ defined as the smallest $c \geq 0$ such that $d_{\boldsymbol{uvw}} < 10 \cdot 2^c \log n$.

Figure 2: Algorithm IdentifyClass.

Proposition 5.4. *With probability at least $1 - 2/n$, Algorithm IdentifyClass does not abort and the partition $\{\mathcal{T}_\alpha\}_{\alpha \geq 0}$ satisfies the following conditions:*

(i) *for any $(\boldsymbol{u}, \boldsymbol{v}, \boldsymbol{w}) \in \mathcal{T}_0$, the inequality $|\Delta(\boldsymbol{u}, \boldsymbol{v}; \boldsymbol{w})| \leq 2n$ holds;*
(ii) *for any $\alpha > 0$ and any $(\boldsymbol{u}, \boldsymbol{v}, \boldsymbol{w}) \in \mathcal{T}_\alpha$, the inequalities $2^{\alpha-3}n \leq |\Delta(\boldsymbol{u}, \boldsymbol{v}; \boldsymbol{w})| \leq 2^{\alpha+1}n$ hold.*

Proof of Proposition 5.4. Let us first compute the probability that the protocol does not abort. For each node $u \in V$, let X_u be the random variable representing the number of neighbors chosen by u, i.e., $X_u = |\Lambda(u)|$. Observe that
$$\mathbb{E}[X_u] = \frac{10 \log n \times |\{v \in V \mid \{u, v\} \in S\}|}{n} \leq 10 \log n.$$
Chernoff's bound implies the inequality
$$\Pr[X_i \geq 60 \log n] < \frac{1}{n^2}.$$
The probability that the protocol does not abort is thus $1 - 1/n$, from the union bound.

We now consider the probability that Conditions (i) and (ii) hold. Let us consider an arbitrary triple $(\boldsymbol{u}, \boldsymbol{v}, \boldsymbol{w}) \in \mathcal{T}$. The expectation of the random variable $\delta_{\boldsymbol{u},\boldsymbol{v},\boldsymbol{w}}$ is
$$\mathbb{E}[\delta_{\boldsymbol{u},\boldsymbol{v},\boldsymbol{w}}] = \frac{10 \log n \times |\Delta(\boldsymbol{u}, \boldsymbol{v}; \boldsymbol{w})|}{n}.$$

We divide our analysis into three cases.

- The case where $|\Delta(\boldsymbol{u}, \boldsymbol{v}; \boldsymbol{w})| \leq n/6$. Chernoff's bound shows that
$$\Pr[\delta_{\boldsymbol{u},\boldsymbol{v},\boldsymbol{w}} \geq 10 \log n] < 2^{-10 \log n} < \frac{1}{n^2}.$$
Thus $c_{\boldsymbol{uvw}} = 0$ with probability at least $1 - 1/n^2$.
- The case where $|\Delta(\boldsymbol{u}, \boldsymbol{v}; \boldsymbol{w})| > n/6$ and $|\Delta(\boldsymbol{u}, \boldsymbol{v}; \boldsymbol{w})| < 2^{c-3}n$, for some $c \geq 1$. Chernoff's bound implies that
$$\Pr[\delta_{\boldsymbol{u},\boldsymbol{v},\boldsymbol{w}} \geq 10 \cdot 2^{c-1} \log n] < \frac{1}{n^2}.$$
Thus $c_{\boldsymbol{uvw}} \geq c$ with probability at most $1/n^2$.
- Finally, the case $|\Delta(\boldsymbol{u}, \boldsymbol{v}; \boldsymbol{w})| > 2^{c+1}n$ for some $c \geq 0$. Chernoff's bound implies that
$$\Pr[\delta_{\boldsymbol{u},\boldsymbol{v},\boldsymbol{w}} < 10 \cdot 2^c \log n] < \frac{1}{n^2}.$$
Thus $c_{\boldsymbol{uvw}} \leq c$ with probability at most $1/n^2$.

We conclude that the probability that the outputs of all the nodes $(\boldsymbol{u}, \boldsymbol{v}, \boldsymbol{w}) \in \mathcal{T}$ satisfy Conditions (i) and (ii) is at least $1 - 1/n$, from the union bound.

Finally, the union bound again guarantees that the probability that the protocol does not abort and all the nodes $(\boldsymbol{u}, \boldsymbol{v}, \boldsymbol{w}) \in \mathcal{T}$ satisfy Conditions (i) and (ii) is at least $1 - 2/n$. □

5.3 Implementation of Step 3: Details and proof of Proposition 5.2

In this subsection we describe the details of the implementation of Step 3 in Algorithm ComputePairs, which is the only part of the algorithm that uses quantum computation.

The nodes first apply Algorithm IdentifyClass. Proposition 5.4 guarantees that with probability at least $1 - 2/n$ Algorithm IdentifyClass does not abort and the partition $\{\mathcal{T}_\alpha\}_{\alpha \geq 0}$ satisfies the two conditions of the proposition. In all this subsection we will assume that this happens.

Let us write
$$\mathcal{T}_\alpha[\boldsymbol{u}, \boldsymbol{v}] = \{\boldsymbol{w} \in \mathcal{V}' \mid (\boldsymbol{u}, \boldsymbol{v}, \boldsymbol{w}) \in \mathcal{T}_\alpha\}$$
for any $(\boldsymbol{u}, \boldsymbol{v}) \in \mathcal{V} \times \mathcal{V}$ and any $\alpha \geq 0$. We will later use the following two lemmas that are direct consequences of the bounds given in Proposition 5.4.

Lemma 5.5. *With probability at least $1 - 1/n^2$ the inequality*
$$|\Lambda_x(\boldsymbol{u}, \boldsymbol{v}) \cap \Delta(\boldsymbol{u}, \boldsymbol{v}; \boldsymbol{w})| \leq 100 \cdot 2^\alpha \sqrt{n} \log n$$
holds for all $(\boldsymbol{u}, \boldsymbol{v}, x) \in \mathcal{V} \times \mathcal{V} \times [\sqrt{n}]$, all $\alpha \geq 0$ and all $\boldsymbol{w} \in \mathcal{T}_\alpha[\boldsymbol{u}, \boldsymbol{v}]$.

Proof. Let us fix $(\boldsymbol{u}, \boldsymbol{v}) \in \mathcal{V} \times \mathcal{V}$. Consider any $x \in [\sqrt{n}]$, any $\alpha \geq 0$ and any $\boldsymbol{w} \in \mathcal{T}_\alpha[\boldsymbol{u}, \boldsymbol{v}]$. Observe that
$$\mathbb{E}[|\Lambda_x(\boldsymbol{u}, \boldsymbol{v}) \cap \Delta(\boldsymbol{u}, \boldsymbol{v}; \boldsymbol{w})|] \leq 10 \cdot 2^{\alpha+1} \sqrt{n} \log n.$$
Chernoff's bound implies the inequality $|\Lambda_x(\boldsymbol{u}, \boldsymbol{v}) \cap \Delta(\boldsymbol{u}, \boldsymbol{v}; \boldsymbol{w})| \leq 100 \cdot 2^\alpha \sqrt{n} \log n$ holds with probability at most $1/n^5$. The statement of the lemma then follows from the union bound. □

Lemma 5.6. *The following inequality holds for all $\alpha \geq 0$ and all $(\boldsymbol{u}, \boldsymbol{v}) \in \mathcal{V} \times \mathcal{V}$:*
$$|\mathcal{T}_\alpha[\boldsymbol{u}, \boldsymbol{v}]| \leq \frac{720\sqrt{n} \log n}{2^\alpha}.$$

Proof. This is obviously true for $\alpha = 0$. Let us now consider any $\alpha > 0$ and any $(\boldsymbol{u}, \boldsymbol{v}) \in \mathcal{V} \times \mathcal{V}$. Remember that we are assuming that $\Gamma(u, v) \leq 90 \log n$ for all pairs $\{u, v\} \in S$. We thus have

$$\sum_{\boldsymbol{w} \in \mathcal{T}_\alpha[\boldsymbol{u},\boldsymbol{v}]} \Delta(\boldsymbol{u}, \boldsymbol{v}; \boldsymbol{w}) \leq 90n^{3/2} \log n.$$

Combining this upper bound with the lower bound of Statement (ii) of Proposition 5.4 gives the claimed upper bound on $|\mathcal{T}_\alpha[\boldsymbol{u}, \boldsymbol{v}]|$. □

To implement Step 3 of Algorithm ComputePairs, the strategy is to consider each α separately and perform simultaneous quantum searches over $\mathcal{T}_\alpha[\boldsymbol{u}, \boldsymbol{v}]$, as outlined in Figure 3. We first describe in Section 5.3.1 how to implement these quantum searches in $\tilde{O}(n^{1/4})$ rounds for the case $\alpha = 0$, and then in Section 5.3.1 we briefly explain how to achieve the same complexity for the case $\alpha > 0$.

3.1. The nodes apply Algorithm IdentifyClass.
3.2. For each α do:
Each node $k = (\boldsymbol{u}, \boldsymbol{v}, x)$ executes, for each $\ell \in [m]$, a quantum search to check if there exists some $\boldsymbol{w} \in \mathcal{T}_\alpha[\boldsymbol{u}, \boldsymbol{v}]$ such that there exists $w \in \boldsymbol{w}$ for which (u^k_ℓ, v^k_ℓ, w) is a negative triangle. The node k outputs all the pairs $\{u^k_\ell, v^k_\ell\}$ for which the quantum search is successful.

Figure 3: Details of the implementation of Step 3 of Algorithm ComputePairs.

5.3.1 Analysis of Step 3.2 for $\alpha = 0$. In Step 3.2 each node $k = (\boldsymbol{u}, \boldsymbol{v}, x)$ executes m simultaneous quantum searches. In order to describe this process using the framework presented in Section 4, with $X = \mathcal{T}_0[\boldsymbol{u}, \boldsymbol{v}]$ and $m = 100n \log n$, we need to explain the evaluation procedure. Since $\mathcal{T}_0[\boldsymbol{u}, \boldsymbol{v}] \subseteq \mathcal{V}'$, we have $|\mathcal{T}_0[\boldsymbol{u}, \boldsymbol{v}]| \leq \sqrt{n}$. For simplicity (but without loss of generality) we assume below that $|\mathcal{T}_0[\boldsymbol{u}, \boldsymbol{v}]| = \sqrt{n}$. Observe that the evaluation procedure should implement the following test: each node k, when evaluating a list $(\boldsymbol{w}^k_1, \ldots, \boldsymbol{w}^k_m)$ of m elements in $\mathcal{T}_0[\boldsymbol{u}, \boldsymbol{v}]$, should check for each $\ell \in [m]$ whether there exists a vertex $w \in \boldsymbol{w}^k_\ell$ such that $\{u^k_\ell, v^k_\ell, w\}$ is a negative triangle.

Let $L^k_{\boldsymbol{w}} \subseteq \mathcal{P}(\boldsymbol{u}, \boldsymbol{v})$ denote the list consisting of all the pairs $\{u^k_i, v^k_i\}$ such that $\boldsymbol{w}^k_i = \boldsymbol{w}$, for each node $k = (\boldsymbol{u}, \boldsymbol{v}, x)$ and each $\boldsymbol{w} \in \mathcal{T}_0[\boldsymbol{u}, \boldsymbol{v}]$. We make the assumption that $|L^k_{\boldsymbol{w}}| \leq 800\sqrt{n} \log n$ for all $k = (\boldsymbol{u}, \boldsymbol{v}, x)$ and all $\boldsymbol{w} \in \mathcal{T}_0[\boldsymbol{u}, \boldsymbol{v}]$ and describe an evaluation procedure that works under this assumption. The procedure is described in Figure 4.

The procedure of Figure 4 obviously always outputs the correct answers since for each k and each $\ell \in [m]$, Inequality (2) at Step 2 precisely checks if there exists some $w \in \boldsymbol{w}^k_\ell$ such that $\{u^k_\ell, v^k_\ell, w\}$ is a negative triangle (because the pair $\{u^k_\ell, v^k_\ell\}$ is sent to node $(\boldsymbol{u}, \boldsymbol{v}, \boldsymbol{w}^k_\ell)$). We now analyze its complexity. Since each list $L^k_{\boldsymbol{w}}$ contains at most $800\sqrt{n} \log n$ elements, at Step 1 each node $k = (\boldsymbol{u}, \boldsymbol{v}, x)$ sends at most $800\sqrt{n} \log n$ elements to $(\boldsymbol{u}, \boldsymbol{v}, \boldsymbol{w})$ for each $\boldsymbol{w} \in \mathcal{T}_0[\boldsymbol{u}, \boldsymbol{v}]$. Conversely, each node $(\boldsymbol{u}, \boldsymbol{v}, \boldsymbol{w}) \in \mathcal{T}_0$ receives at most $800\sqrt{n} \log n$ elements from $(\boldsymbol{u}, \boldsymbol{v}, x)$ for each $x \in [\sqrt{n}]$. Thus, in the CONGEST-CLIQUE model, Step 1 can be implemented in $O(\log n)$ rounds. Testing whether Inequality (2) holds or not at Step 2 can be done locally using the information collected at Step 1 of Algorithm ComputePairs. Sending back the information at Step 2 can be done with the same complexity as in Step 1. The complexity of the checking procedure is thus $O(\log n)$ rounds.

Input: each node $k = (\boldsymbol{u}, \boldsymbol{v}, x)$ receives a list $(\boldsymbol{w}^k_1, \ldots, \boldsymbol{w}^k_m)$ of m elements from $\mathcal{T}_0[\boldsymbol{u}, \boldsymbol{v}]$
Promise: the inequality $|L^k_{\boldsymbol{w}}| \leq 800\sqrt{n} \log n$ holds for each $k = (\boldsymbol{u}, \boldsymbol{v}, x)$ and each $\boldsymbol{w} \in \mathcal{T}_0[u, v]$
Output: each node $k = (\boldsymbol{u}, \boldsymbol{v}, x)$ decides, for each $\ell \in [m]$, whether there exists $w \in \boldsymbol{w}^k_\ell$ such that $\{u^k_\ell, v^k_\ell, w\}$ is a negative triangle

1. Each node $k = (\boldsymbol{u}, \boldsymbol{v}, x)$ sends the list $L^k_{\boldsymbol{w}}$ to node $(\boldsymbol{u}, \boldsymbol{v}, \boldsymbol{w})$, for each $\boldsymbol{w} \in \mathcal{T}_0[\boldsymbol{u}, \boldsymbol{v}]$. Together to each pair (u, v) sent, its weight $f(u, v)$ is also sent.
2. Each node $(\boldsymbol{u}, \boldsymbol{v}, \boldsymbol{w}) \in \mathcal{T}_0$ checks, for each pair $\{u, v\}$ received at Step 1, whether the inequality
$$\min_{w \in \boldsymbol{w}} \{f(u, w) + f(w, v)\} \leq f(u, v) \tag{2}$$
holds and sends back this information to the node who sent this pair.

Figure 4: Evaluation procedure (in the case $\alpha = 0$) for the quantum searches implemented at Step 3.2 of ComputePairs.

We can apply Theorem 4.1 with $X = \mathcal{T}_0[\boldsymbol{u}, \boldsymbol{v}]$ and $\beta = 800\sqrt{n} \log n$. Lemma 5.5 guarantees that with probability at least $1 - 1/n^2$, the assumptions in the statement of Theorem 4.1 are satisfied. Theorem 4.1 then implies that for $\alpha = 0$ the quantum searches of Step 3.2 of Algorithm ComputePairs can be implemented in $\tilde{O}(n^{1/4})$ rounds and succeed with probability at least $1 - 2/m^2$.

5.3.2 Analysis of Step 3.2 for $\alpha > 0$. The analysis of the complexity of the approach presented in Section 5.3.1 crucially relied on the inequality from Lemma 5.5, which guarantees that $|\Lambda_x(\boldsymbol{u}, \boldsymbol{v}) \cap \Delta(\boldsymbol{u}, \boldsymbol{v}; \boldsymbol{w})| \leq 100 \cdot \sqrt{n} \log n$. For $\alpha > 0$ and $(\boldsymbol{u}, \boldsymbol{v}, \boldsymbol{w}) \in \mathcal{T}_\alpha$, Lemma 5.5 only gives the weaker upper bound

$$|\Lambda_x(\boldsymbol{u}, \boldsymbol{v}) \cap \Delta(\boldsymbol{u}, \boldsymbol{v}; \boldsymbol{w})| \leq 100 \cdot 2^\alpha \sqrt{n} \log n. \tag{3}$$

The upper bound from Lemma 5.6 is the key observation that will make possible to solve this technical issue, as we briefly explain below.

In Section 5.3.1 each node $(\boldsymbol{u}, \boldsymbol{v}, x)$ communicated with node $(\boldsymbol{u}, \boldsymbol{v}, \boldsymbol{w})$ for each $\boldsymbol{w} \in \mathcal{T}_0[\boldsymbol{u}, \boldsymbol{v}]$. We used the upper bound $\mathcal{T}_0[\boldsymbol{u}, \boldsymbol{v}] \leq \sqrt{n}$ in the analysis. In the case $\alpha > 0$ we can use the better upper bound from Lemma 5.6, which reduces the number of destination nodes by (roughly) a factor 2^α. In consequence, we can increase the bandwidth towards these destinations nodes by (roughly) a factor 2^α. (This can be done by duplicating the information owned by the destination nodes.) This is enough to counterbalance the increase by a factor 2^α of the message size due to Inequality (3). We refer to the full version for the complete analysis.

ACKNOWLEDGMENTS

TI was partially supported by JST SICORP and JSPS KAKENHI grants No. 16H02878 and No. 19K11824. FLG was partially supported by JSPS KAKENHI grants No. 15H01677, No. 16H01705, No. 16H05853 and No. 19H04066.

REFERENCES

[1] Ruben Becker, Andreas Karrenbauer, Sebastian Krinninger, and Christoph Lenzen. 2017. Near-Optimal Approximate Shortest Paths and Transshipment in Distributed and Streaming Models. In *Proceedings of the International Symposium on Distributed Computing (DISC)*. 7:1–7:16. https://doi.org/10.4230/LIPIcs.DISC.2017.7

[2] Aaron Bernstein and Danupon Nanongkai. 2019 (to appear). Distributed Exact Weighted All-Pairs Shortest Paths in Near-Linear Time. In *Proceedings of the 51st ACM Symposium on Theory of Computing*. ArXiv:1811.03337.

[3] Anne Broadbent and Alain Tapp. 2008. Can quantum mechanics help distributed computing? *SIGACT News* 39, 3 (2008), 67–76. https://doi.org/10.1145/1412700.1412717

[4] Keren Censor-Hillel, Petteri Kaski, Janne H. Korhonen, Christoph Lenzen, Ami Paz, and Jukka Suomela. 2016. Algebraic Methods in the Congested Clique. *Distributed Computing* (March 2016). https://doi.org/10.1007/s00446-016-0270-2

[5] Yi-Jun Chang, Seth Pettie, and Hengjie Zhang. 2019. Distributed Triangle Detection via Expander Decomposition. In *Proceedings of the ACM-SIAM Symposium on Discrete Algorithms (SODA)*. 821–840. https://doi.org/10.1137/1.9781611975482.51

[6] Yi-Jun Chang and Thatchaphol Saranurak. 2019. Improved Distributed Expander Decomposition and Nearly Optimal Triangle Enumeration. (April 2019). ArXiv:1904.08037.

[7] Vasil S. Denchev and Gopal Pandurangan. 2008. Distributed quantum computing: a new frontier in distributed systems or science fiction? *SIGACT News* 39, 3 (2008), 77–95. https://doi.org/10.1145/1412700.1412718

[8] Danny Dolev, Christoph Lenzen, and Shir Peled. 2012. "Tri, Tri Again": Finding Triangles and Small Subgraphs in a Distributed Setting - (Extended Abstract). In *Proceedings of the International Symposium on Distributed Computing (DISC)*. 195–209. https://doi.org/10.1007/978-3-642-33651-5_14

[9] Andrew Drucker, Fabian Kuhn, and Rotem Oshman. 2014. On the power of the congested clique model. In *Proceedings of the ACM Symposium on Principles of Distributed Computing (PODC)*. 367–376. https://doi.org/10.1145/2611462.2611493

[10] Michael Elkin. 2017. Distributed exact shortest paths in sublinear time. In *Proceedings of the ACM Symposium on Theory of Computing (STOC)*. 757–770. https://doi.org/10.1145/3055399.3055452

[11] Michael Elkin, Hartmut Klauck, Danupon Nanongkai, and Gopal Pandurangan. 2014. Can quantum communication speed up distributed computation?. In *Proceedings of the ACM Symposium on Principles of Distributed Computing (PODC)*. 166–175. https://doi.org/10.1145/2611462.2611488

[12] Sebastian Forster and Danupon Nanongkai. 2018. A Faster Distributed Single-Source Shortest Paths Algorithm. In *Proceedings of the IEEE Symposium on Foundations of Computer Science (FOCS)*. 686–697. https://doi.org/10.1109/FOCS.2018.00071

[13] Silvio Frischknecht, Stephan Holzer, and Roger Wattenhofer. 2012. Networks Cannot Compute Their Diameter in Sublinear Time In *Proceedings of the ACM-SIAM Symposium on Discrete Algorithms (SODA)*. 1150–1162. https://doi.org/10.1137/1.9781611973099.91

[14] Cyril Gavoille, Adrian Kosowski, and Marcin Markiewicz. 2009. What Can Be Observed Locally?. In *Proceedings of the International Symposium on Distributed Computing (DISC)*. 243–257. https://doi.org/10.1007/978-3-642-04355-0_26

[15] Mohsen Ghaffari and Jason Li. 2018. Improved Distributed Algorithms for Exact Shortest Paths. In *Proceedings of the ACM Symposium on Theory of Computing (STOC)*. 431–444. https://doi.org/10.1145/3188745.3188948

[16] Mohsen Ghaffari and Krzysztof Nowicki. 2018. Congested Clique Algorithms for the Minimum Cut Problem. In *Proceedings of the ACM Symposium on Principles of Distributed Computing (PODC)*. 357–366. https://doi.org/10.1145/3212734.3212750

[17] Lov K. Grover. 1996. A Fast Quantum Mechanical Algorithm for Database Search. In *Proceedings of the ACM Symposium on Theory of Computing (STOC)*. 212–219. https://doi.org/10.1145/237814.237866

[18] James W. Hegeman, Gopal Pandurangan, Sriram V. Pemmaraju, Vivek B. Sardeshmukh, and Michele Scquizzato. 2015. Toward Optimal Bounds in the Congested Clique: Graph Connectivity and MST. In *Proceedings of the ACM Symposium on Principles of Distributed Computing (PODC)*. 91–100. https://doi.org/10.1145/2767386.2767434

[19] James W. Hegeman and Sriram V. Pemmaraju. 2014. Lessons from the Congested Clique Applied to MapReduce. In *Proceedings of the International Colloqium on Structural Information and Communication Complexity (SIROCCO)*. 149–164. https://doi.org/10.1007/978-3-319-09620-9_13

[20] James W. Hegeman, Sriram V. Pemmaraju, and Vivek Sardeshmukh. 2014. Near-Constant-Time Distributed Algorithms on a Congested Clique. In *Proceedings of the International Symposium on Distributed Computing (DISC)*. 514–530. https://doi.org/10.1007/978-3-662-45174-8_35

[21] Monika Henzinger, Sebastian Krinninger, and Danupon Nanongkai. 2016. A deterministic almost-tight distributed algorithm for approximating single-source shortest paths. In *Proceedings of the ACM Symposium on Theory of Computing (STOC)*. 489–498. http://arxiv.org/abs/1504.07056

[22] Stephan Holzer and Roger Wattenhofer. 2012. Optimal Distributed All Pairs Shortest Paths and Applications. In *Proceedings of the ACM Symposium on Principles of Distributed Computing (PODC)*. 355–364. https://doi.org/10.1145/2332432.2332504

[23] Chien-Chung Huang, Danupon Nanongkai, and Thatchaphol Saranurak. 2017. Distributed Exact Weighted All-Pairs Shortest Paths in $\tilde{O}(n^{5/4})$ Rounds. In *Proceedings of the IEEE Symposium on Foundations of Computer Science (FOCS)*. 168–179. https://doi.org/10.1109/FOCS.2017.24

[24] Taisuke Izumi and François Le Gall. 2017. Triangle Finding and Listing in CONGEST Networks. In *Proceedings of the ACM Symposium on Principles of Distributed Computing (PODC)*. 381–389. https://doi.org/10.1145/3087801.3087811

[25] Tomasz Jurdziński and Krzysztof Nowicki. 2018. MST in $O(1)$ Rounds of Congested Clique. In *Proceedings of the ACM-SIAM Symposium on Discrete Algorithms (SODA)*. 2620–2632. https://doi.org/10.1137/1.9781611975031.167

[26] François Le Gall. 2016. Further Algebraic Algorithms in the Congested Clique Model and Applications to Graph-Theoretic Problems. In *Proceedings of the International Symposium on Distributed Computing (DISC)*. 57–70. https://doi.org/10.1007/978-3-662-53426-7_5

[27] François Le Gall and Frédéric Magniez. 2018. Sublinear-Time Quantum Computation of the Diameter in CONGEST Networks. In *Proceedings of the ACM Symposium on Principles of Distributed Computing (PODC)*. 337–346. https://doi.org/10.1145/3212734.3212744

[28] François Le Gall, Harumichi Nishimura, and Ansis Rosmanis. 2019. Quantum advantage for the LOCAL model in distributed computing. In *Proceedings of the International Symposium on Theoretical Aspects of Computer Science (STACS)*. 49:1–49:14. https://doi.org/10.4230/LIPIcs.STACS.2019.49 arXiv:1810.10838

[29] Christoph Lenzen and David Peleg. 2013. Efficient Distributed Source Detection with Limited Bandwidth. In *Proceedings of the ACM Symposium on Principles of Distributed Computing (PODC)*. 375–382. https://doi.org/10.1145/2484239.2484262

[30] Christoph Lenzen and Roger Wattenhofer. 2011. Tight bounds for parallel randomized load balancing: extended abstract. In *Proceedings of the ACM Symposium on Theory of Computing (STOC)*. 11–20. https://doi.org/10.1145/1993636.1993639

[31] Zvi Lotker, Elan Pavlov, Boaz Patt-Shamir, and David Peleg. 2003. MST construction in $O(\log \log n)$ communication rounds. In *Proceedings of the Symposium on Parallel Algorithms and Architectures (SPAA)*. 94–100. https://doi.org/10.1145/777412.777428

[32] Danupon Nanongkai. 2014. Distributed Approximation Algorithms for Weighted Shortest Paths. In *Proceedings of the ACM Symposium on Theory of Computing (STOC)*. 565–573. https://doi.org/10.1145/2591796.2591850

[33] Gopal Pandurangan, Peter Robinson, and Michele Scquizzato. 2018. On the Distributed Complexity of Large-Scale Graph Computations. In *Proceedings of the Symposium on Parallel Algorithms and Architectures (SPAA)*. 405–414. https://doi.org/10.1145/3210377.3210409

[34] Merav Parter. 2018. $(\Delta + 1)$-Coloring in the Congested Clique Model. In *Proceedings of the International Colloquium on Automata, Languages and Programming (ICALP)*. 160:1–160:14. https://doi.org/10.4230/LIPIcs.ICALP.2018.160

[35] Boaz Patt-Shamir and Marat Teplitsky. 2011. The round complexity of distributed sorting: extended abstract. In *Proceedings of the ACM Symposium on Principles of Distributed Computing (PODC)*. 249–256. https://doi.org/10.1145/1993806.1993851

[36] David Peleg. 2000. *Distributed computing: a locality-sensitive approach*. Society for Industrial and Applied Mathematics. https://doi.org/10.1137/1.9780898719772

[37] Atish Das Sarma, Stephan Holzer, Liah Kor, Amos Korman, Danupon Nanongkai, Gopal Pandurangan, David Peleg, and Roger Wattenhofer. 2012. Distributed verification and hardness of distributed approximation. *SIAM J. Comput.* 41, 5 (2012), 1235–1265. https://doi.org/10.1137/11085178X

[38] Seiichiro Tani, Hirotada Kobayashi, and Keiji Matsumoto. 2012. Exact Quantum Algorithms for the Leader Election Problem. *ACM Transactions on Computation Theory* 4, 1 (2012), 1:1–1:24. https://doi.org/10.1145/2141938.2141939

[39] Virginia Vassilevska Williams and Ryan Williams. 2018. Subcubic Equivalences Between Path, Matrix, and Triangle Problems. *Journal of the ACM* 65, 5 (2018), 27:1–27:38. https://doi.org/10.1145/3186893

[40] Ronald de Wolf. 2002. Quantum communication and complexity. *Theoretical Computer Science* 287, 1 (2002), 337–353. https://doi.org/10.1016/S0304-3975(02)00377-8

[41] Uri Zwick. 2002. All pairs shortest paths using bridging sets and rectangular matrix multiplication. *Journal of the ACM* 49, 3 (2002), 289–317. https://doi.org/10.1145/567112.567114

Deterministic Distributed Dominating Set Approximation in the CONGEST Model

Janosch Deurer
University of Freiburg
Germany
deurer@cs.uni-freiburg.de

Fabian Kuhn
University of Freiburg
Germany
kuhn@cs.uni-freiburg.de

Yannic Maus*
Technion
Israel
yannic.maus@cs.technion.ac.il

ABSTRACT

We develop deterministic approximation algorithms for the minimum dominating set problem in the CONGEST model with an almost optimal approximation guarantee. For $\varepsilon > 1/\operatorname{poly}\log\Delta$ we obtain two algorithms with approximation factor $(1+\varepsilon)(1+\ln(\Delta+1))$ and with runtimes $2^{O(\sqrt{\log n \log\log n})}$ and $O(\Delta \operatorname{poly}\log\Delta + \operatorname{poly}\log\Delta \log^* n)$, respectively. Further we show how dominating set approximations can be deterministically transformed into a connected dominating set in the CONGEST model while only increasing the approximation guarantee by a constant factor. This results in a deterministic $O(\log\Delta)$-approximation algorithm for the minimum connected dominating set with time complexity $2^{O(\sqrt{\log n \log\log n})}$.

CCS CONCEPTS

• **Distributed algorithms**;

KEYWORDS

dominating set approximation, CONGEST model

ACM Reference Format:

Janosch Deurer, Fabian Kuhn, and Yannic Maus. 2019. Deterministic Distributed Dominating Set Approximation in the CONGEST Model. In *2019 ACM Symposium on Principles of Distributed Computing (PODC'19), July 29–August 2, 2019, Toronto, ON, Canada.* ACM, New York, NY, USA, 11 pages. https://doi.org/10.1145/3293611.3331626

1 INTRODUCTION & RELATED WORK

Given a graph $G = (V, E)$, a dominating set $S \subseteq V$ of G is a set of nodes of G such that any node $u \notin S$ has at least one neighbor $v \in S$. The minimum dominating set (MDS) problem—the objective is to compute a dominating set with minimal cardinality—and the equivalent minimum set cover problem are among the oldest classic combinatorial optimization problems [22–24]. Motivated by potential practical applications (e.g., as a tool for clustering in wireless ad hoc and sensor networks), the minimum dominating set problem has also found attention in a distributed setting. In the last two decades, distributed approximation algorithms for minimum dominating set and closely related problems such as minimum set cover, minimum connected dominating set, or minimum vertex cover have been studied intensively (see, e.g., [10, 12, 16, 21, 26–30]).

It is well known that for graphs with maximum degree Δ, in the standard, sequential setting, the basic greedy algorithm achieves a $\ln(\Delta + 1)$-approximation [22] and that up to lower order terms, this is the best that can be achieved in polynomial time unless P = NP [9]. The first efficient distributed approximation algorithm was given by Jia, Rajaraman, and Suel [21] and it achieves an approximation ratio of $O(\log\Delta)$ in time $O(\log^2 n)$. The algorithm is randomized and it works in the CONGEST model (i.e., with messages of size $O(\log n)$).[1] These bounds were improved by Kuhn, Moscibroda, and Wattenhofer [26], who showed that it is possible to compute an $(1+\varepsilon)(1+\ln(\Delta+1))$-approximation in time $O(\log^2\Delta/\varepsilon^4)$ in the CONGEST model and in time $O(\log n/\varepsilon^2)$ in the LOCAL model. Recently, in [16], Ghaffari, Kuhn, and Maus showed that, in the LOCAL model, at the cost of allowing exponential local computations at the nodes, it is even possible to compute a $(1+o(1))$-approximation in a polylogarithmic number of rounds.

All the above distributed algorithms critically depend on the use of *randomization* for breaking symmetries in an efficient manner. The only existing efficient *deterministic* distributed algorithms for approximating MDS are based on a generic tool known as network decomposition [2, 15, 32, 34]. These algorithms only work in the LOCAL model (i.e., they require large messages) or they only achieve a suboptimal approximation ratio. Concretely, in the LOCAL model, it is possible to compute a $(1+o(1))$-approximation[2] of MDS in time $2^{O(\sqrt{\log n})}$ [16] and in the CONGEST model, an $O(\log^2 n)$-approximation can be computed in time $2^{O(\sqrt{\log n \log\log n})}$ [15]. Note that these deterministic algorithms are exponentially slower than their randomized counterparts. This general behavior is true for many important distributed graph problems such as, e.g., the problems of computing a vertex coloring with $\Delta+1$ or even $O(\Delta)$ colors, the problem of computing a maximal independent set (MIS), or the problem of computing various kinds of (in some sense sparse) decompositions of the network graph into clusters of small diameter [3, 16]. While there are extremely efficient (at most polylogarithmic time) and often very simple randomized algorithms, the best deterministic algorithms are exponentially slower and require $2^{O(\sqrt{\log n})}$. Typically, these deterministic algorithms also abuse the power of the LOCAL model by using network decompositions in a pretty brute-force kind of way: For graphs of small diameter, the algorithms essentially reduce to collecting the whole topology at

*Supported by the European Union's Horizon 2020 Research And Innovation Programme under grant agreement no. 755839.

PODC '19, July 29–August 2, 2019, Toronto, ON, Canada

ACM ISBN 978-1-4503-6217-7/19/07...$15.00
https://doi.org/10.1145/3293611.3331626

[1] For a formal definition of the distributed communication models, we refer to Section 2.

[2] If internal computations at the nodes are restricted to polynomial time, it is possible to obtain a $(1+o(1))\ln(\Delta+1)$-approximation in the same asymptotic time.

a single node—this cannot be done in the CONGEST model—and compute the solution in a centralized way, often through solving NP-complete problems. Whether an exponential gap between the best randomized and deterministic algorithms for these problems is really necessary is considered to be one of the key open questions in the area of distributed graph algorithms [3, 16, 31, 33, 34]. In the context of this more general question, Ghaffari, Harris, and Kuhn recently showed in [14] that also the MDS problem has a key role in this more general question. By using (and extending) a framework developed in [16], they showed the MDS problem is P – SLOCAL complete, meaning: If there is a polylogarithmic-time distributed deterministic algorithm that computes any polylogarithmic approximation for the MDS problem, there are polylogarithmic-time deterministic distributed algorithms for essentially all[3] problems for which there are efficient randomized algorithms.

1.1 Contributions

In the present paper, we give the first deterministic distributed algorithms for the minimum dominating set problem in the CONGEST model, which are efficient in terms of their time complexity and at the same time obtain an essentially optimal approximation ratio. Our first result is based on first computing a network decomposition by an algorithm of [2, 15]. Unlike in the LOCAL model, where partial solutions of clusters of small diameter can be computed in time linear in the cluster diameter by simply collecting the whole cluster topology at one node, in the CONGEST model, we have to be much more careful. Inspired by recent work on other local problems [7, 15], we design a randomized CONGEST algorithm that only requires poly log n-wise independent randomness. Then we use the method of conditional expectations to efficiently derandomize this algorithm. We note that the method of conditional expectations has been quite intensively used in the last couple of years in order to derandomize randomized distributed graph algorithms (see, e.g., [7, 14, 19, 25, 35, 36]).

Theorem 1.1. *For any $\varepsilon > 1/\operatorname{poly}\log\Delta$, there exists a deterministic* CONGEST *algorithm that computes an $(1+\varepsilon)\cdot(1+\ln(\Delta+1))$-approximation for MDS in $2^{O(\sqrt{\log n \log\log n})}$ rounds.*

The above theorem improves a result by Ghaffari and Kuhn in [15], where it was shown that, in the same asymptotic time complexity, it is possible to compute an $O(\log^2 n)$-approximation for the MDS problem. While our algorithm is based on carefully and gradually rounding a given fractional solution to an integer solution (cf. Section 1.2), the algorithm of [15] is based on a relatively direct parallel implementation of the sequential greedy algorithm, where the decision of which nodes to add in each greedy step is achieved by derandomizing a basic distributed hitting set problem.

The time complexity of our algorithm is $2^{O(\sqrt{\log n \log\log n})}$ because this is the best time complexity for deterministically computing a network decomposition of G^2 in the CONGEST model [15] (i.e., a network decomposition, where clusters of the same color are at distance at least 2 from each other). An improved deterministic network decomposition algorithm would directly also lead to an improved deterministic MDS algorithm.[4]

In addition to the algorithm based on network decomposition, we also provide a more local way to derandomize a similar randomized CONGEST algorithm, resulting in a time complexity that mainly depends on the maximum degree Δ of the graph.

Theorem 1.2. *For any $\varepsilon > 1/\operatorname{poly}\log\Delta$, there exists a deterministic* CONGEST *algorithm that computes an $(1+\varepsilon)\cdot(1+\ln(\Delta+1))$-approximation for MDS in $O(\Delta\cdot\operatorname{poly}\log\Delta + \operatorname{poly}\log\Delta\cdot\log^* n)$ rounds.*

We want to emphasize that, except for the algorithm in [15], which provides an $O(\log^2 n)$-approximation, our results are the first deterministic algorithms for MDS in the CONGEST model. By substituting a vertex coloring subroutine in the algorithm of Theorem 1.2 by its LOCAL model counterpart this directly also leads to an improved and slightly more efficient deterministic distributed MDS algorithm in the LOCAL model.

Corollary 1.3. *For any $\varepsilon > 1/\operatorname{poly}\log\Delta$, there exists a deterministic* LOCAL *algorithm that computes an $(1+\varepsilon)\cdot\ln(\Delta+1)$ approximation for MDS in $O(\Delta\cdot\operatorname{poly}\log\Delta + \log^* n)$ rounds.*

In addition to considering the basic dominating set problem, we also provide an algorithm to compute a small connected dominating set (CDS). Here, the objective is to output a dominating set S such that the induced subgraph $G[S]$ is connected. It is well known that a given dominating set S can be extended to a CDS S' of size at most $|S'| < 3|S|$ by connecting the nodes in S through at most $|S|-1$ paths of length at most 3. One computes a spanning tree on the graph induced by the set of nodes in S and with an edge between two nodes in S whenever they are at distance at most 3 in G. In the LOCAL model, one can get a local variant of this construction by replacing the spanning tree with a high girth connected spanning subgraph, which can be computed in logarithmic time. As for example observed by Dubhashi et al. [10], this leads to a randomized polylog-round distributed algorithm with approximation ratio $O(\log\Delta)$. Ghaffari [12] later showed that by using an adapted variant of the linear-size skeleton algorithm of Pettie [38], it is also possible to compute an $O(\log\Delta)$-approximation in polylogarithmic randomized time in the CONGEST model. We show that by using network decomposition, an extended variant of Ghaffari's algorithm can be derandomized to obtain the following result.

Theorem 1.4. *There exists a deterministic* CONGEST *algorithm that computes an $O(\ln\Delta)$ approximation for minimum connected dominating set in $2^{O(\sqrt{\log n \log\log n})}$ rounds.*

As for the basic MDS problem, an improved deterministic network decomposition algorithm would directly also lead to an improved deterministic algorithm for the minimum CDS problem.

[3]This in particular includes all problems where a solution can be locally checked in polylogarithmic time and all problems for which efficient distributed Las Vegas algorithms exist. It also includes many optimization problems such approximating MDS or maximum independent set.

[4]We note that in a recent paper, Ghaffari [13] showed that there is a deterministic CONGEST model algorithm to compute a strong diameter decomposition of G in time $2^{O(\sqrt{\log n})}$. In on-going unpublished work [17], it is even shown that there is a deterministic CONGEST algorithm to compute a weak diameter decomposition of powers of G in time $2^{O(\sqrt{\log n})}$, which has clusters that can be efficiently used in the CONGEST model. As a result, the time complexity of the above theorem can be improved from $2^{O(\sqrt{\log n \log\log n})}$ to $2^{O(\sqrt{\log n})}$.

1.2 Our Algorithms in a Nutshell

The general algorithmic framework: Our algorithms start with a given $1/\operatorname{poly}\Delta$-fractional[5] solution for a fractional dominating set, which can be computed efficiently in the CONGEST model by using the algorithm of [26]. This fractional solution is then gradually and iteratively rounded to an integral solution. To explain a high-level view on the algorithm, let us fix some $\varepsilon = 1/\operatorname{poly}\log\Delta$. The rounding consist of two parts. First, in $O(\log\Delta)$ phases, we roughly double the fractionality of the fractional solution in each phase until we obtain a $1/F$-fractional dominating set for some $F = \operatorname{poly}\log\Delta$. In each of these iterations, the dominating set might increase by a factor $1 + O(\varepsilon/\log\Delta)$ so that over all $O(\log\Delta)$ rounding steps, we only lose a $(1 + O(\varepsilon))$-factor. Once we have a $1/F$-fractional dominating set, we round it into an integral dominating set with a single rounding step. During this step we essentially lose a $\ln(\Delta+1)$ factor in the approximation guarantee. The rounding procedures in both parts are based on the derandomization of simple one-round randomized rounding primitives; derandomizing them in the CONGEST model is one of the main technical contributions of this paper.

Derandomization with network decomposition (runtime as a function of n): In order to implement the approach based on a given network decomposition, we show that the above algorithm can also be implemented if the nodes only have $\operatorname{poly}\log n$-wise independent bits. One can then share a seed of $\operatorname{poly}\log n$ random bits in each cluster of the decomposition, which allows to create sufficiently many $\operatorname{poly}\log n$-wise independent random bits. Finally, one can then use the method of conditional expectation inside each cluster to deterministically determine a seed such that the dominating set is small if we execute the rounding process with that seed.

Derandomization with graph colorings (runtime as a function of Δ): In the original randomized rounding process (with truly independent random bits), nodes at distance at least 3 act independently. By applying the method of conditional expectation, one can derandomize the rounding algorithm as long as the actions of nodes at distance at most 2 are carried out consecutively (see also [14]). If a vertex coloring of the G^2 is given, this leads to an algorithm with a running time that is linear in the number of colors of the given G^2-coloring. This directly leads to an algorithm, with a running time of essentially $O(\Delta^2)$, the maximum degree of G^2. The main challenge in this part of the paper is to substitute one of the Δ factors by a $\operatorname{poly}\log\Delta$ factor. The main idea is to substitute G with its *bipartite representation* B_G, where each node is split into a *constraint node* and a *value node* (see Section 3.3 for more details). To reduce the number of colors we carefully split the constraint nodes of B_G into nodes with much smaller degrees such that it suffices to compute a $O(\Delta\operatorname{poly}\log\Delta)$-coloring of the square of this bipartite graph.

Why do we not just have one iteration of rounding? Our algorithms first double the fractionality for $O(\log\Delta)$ iterations and in the last step, if the fractionality is at least $1/\operatorname{poly}\log\Delta$ rounds to an integral solution in a single iteration. Interestingly, this iterative rounding approach is helpful in both cases, however, for different reasons: When we express the runtime as a function of n we need to round in small steps to make sure that $\operatorname{poly}\log n$-wise independent random bits are sufficient. When we express runtime as a function of Δ, we can only split the constraint nodes of the bipartite representation of the problem into small enough parts and still obtain suffcient concentration in the randomized rounding if we round gradually.

[5] In a *fractional dominating set* each node u is assigned a value $x_u \in [0,1]$ and each node $v \in V$ needs to be covered, that is, the sum $\sum_{u\in N(v)} x_u$ is at least 1 where $N(v)$ denotes the inclusive neighborhood of v. We say that a fractional dominating set solution is λ-fractional if each non-zero fractional value is $\geq \lambda$.

1.3 Outline

Section 2 introduces the model and notation. Section 3 is the technically most involved part of the paper and it is split into four subsections. In Section 3.1 we introduce the abstract randomized rounding primitive, Sections 3.2 and 3.3 are used to derandomize the randomized rounding primitive with the objective to optimize runtime as a function of the number of nodes and the maximum degree, respectively. In Section 4 we show how the computed dominating sets can be transformed into connected dominating sets. Section 3.4 uses instantiations of the rounding primitive and the derandomizations to prove our main result. In Section 5 discuss how our results can be generalized. All missing proofs can be found in the full version [8].

2 MODEL & NOTATION

The LOCAL *Model of Distributed Computing [31, 37].* The graph is abstracted as an n-node network $G = (V, E)$ with maximum degree at most Δ and each node has a unique identifier. Communications happen in synchronous rounds. Per round, each node can send one (unbounded size) message to each of its neighbors. At the end, each node should know its own part of the output, e.g., whether it belongs to a dominating set or not.

The CONGEST *Model [37].* In almost all parts of the paper we use the more restricted CONGEST model which is defined like the LOCAL model with the restriction that messages are of size $O(\log n)$. So messages can fit, e.g., a constant number of node identifiers. The most complicated computations that nodes need to perform in our algorithms are the computations of certain conditional probabilities.

We say that a value in $[0, 1]$ is CONGEST *transmittable* if it is the multiple of $2^{-\iota}$ where ι is the smallest integer such that $2^{-\iota} \leq 1/n^{10}$. During our algorithms we merely require that a value fits into a single message in the CONGEST model and additionally we require that a biased coin that equals 1 with a transmittable probability can be built with polylogarithmically many fair coins.

Graph Notation. Given a graph $G = (V, E)$ we use $N(v)$ to denote the inclusive neighborhood of a node $v \in V$, $\tilde{\Delta} = \max_{v\in V} |N(v)| = \Delta + 1$ for the size of the inclusive neighborhood and Δ for the maximum degree of the graph. We denote the shortest hop distance between two nodes $u, v \in V$ as $d_G(u, v)$. To simplify calculations we assume that $\varepsilon \leq 1$ throughout all results. For our algorithms we need to generalize the notion of a dominating set.

Definition 2.1 (Constraint Fractional Dominating Set). Given a graph $G = (V, E)$ and a function $c : V \to [0, 1]$ assigning constraints and a function $x : V \to [0, 1]$ assigning fractional values, we call (x, c) a *constrained fractional dominating (CFDS)* set if $\forall v \in V$: $\sum_{u\in N(v)} x(u) \geq c(v)$. We furthermore call $\sum_{v\in V} x(v)$ the size of the CFDS. If all constraints equal 1 for all nodes and (x, c) is a constrained fractional dominating set we also call x a *fractional dominating set (FDS)*.

If the fractional values equal 1 or 0 for all nodes and x is a FDS then x is a dominating set (DS) in the classical sense. All of our algorithms start with a fractional dominating set that already is a good approximation but has a bad fractionality. Computing such an initial fractional dominating set can be done by slightly adapting an algorithm from [26].

Lemma 2.2 ([26]). *For any $\varepsilon > 0$ there is a deterministic CONGEST algorithm that computes a $(1+\varepsilon)$-approximation for MDS that is $\varepsilon/(2\Delta)$-fractional and has runtime $O(\varepsilon^{-4}\log^2\Delta)$.*

Proof. First use the algorithm from [26] with $\varepsilon' = \varepsilon/2$ to compute a $(1+\varepsilon)$-approximation for MDS. Then, each node with value $< \varepsilon/(2\Delta)$ sets its value to $\varepsilon/(2\Delta)$. As the size of an optimal dominating can be lower bounded by n/Δ we obtain a $(1+\varepsilon)$ approximation. □

3 DOMINATING SET APPROXIMATION

In this section we provide two deterministic algorithms to approximate the minimum dominating set problem in the CONGEST model. The runtime of the first algorithm (cf. Theorem 1.1) depends on the number of nodes n of the graph and the runtime of the second algorithm (cf. Theorem 1.2) mostly depends on the maximum degree Δ of the graph. Both algorithms rely on deterministic rounding schemes that are obtained through derandomizing instances of a more general abstract randomized rounding process. We use Section 3.1 to define this abstract rounding process, Section 3.2 to derandomize the process while optimizing dependency on n and Section 3.3 to derandomize the process while optimizing the dependency on Δ. In Section 3.4 the rounding schemes are combined to prove our main theorems.

3.1 Abstract Randomized Rounding

The goal of the abstract randomized rounding process is to transform a constraint fractional dominating set into a new CFDS with better fractionality while only slightly increasing its size.

Abstract Randomized Rounding Process: Assume a given (initial) constraint fractional dominating set with values $x(v), v \in V$. Further, each node has a probability $p(v) \geq x(v)$ that might depend on $x(v)$. The rounding process is parameterized by the choice of $p(v)$—we will later essentially consider two variants of the process with different $p(v)$'s. The rounding process consists of two phases and the random variable X_v denotes v's value after the first phase. In the first phase each node v updates its value as follows

$$X_v = \begin{cases} x(v)/p(v), & \text{with probability } p(v) \\ 0, & \text{with probability } 1-p(v). \end{cases}$$

In the second phase of the rounding process all nodes whose constraints are not satisfied join the dominating set, i.e., they set their values to 1.

For node v let E_v be the random variable that equals 1 if node v is uncovered after the first phase of the algorithm and 0 otherwise.

Lemma 3.1. *Let A be an upper bound on the size of the initial constraint fractional dominating set. Then the following statements hold for the abstract randomized rounding process.*

(1) Its output is a constraint fractional dominating set and its fractionality is $\min_{v\in V}\{x(v)/p(v)\}$.
(2) Its output has, in expectation, size $A + \sum_{v\in V}\Pr(E_v = 1)$.

Proof.
(1) The output is a constraint fractional dominating set as all nodes that are uncovered after phase one join the dominating set with value 1 in phase two and constraints can be at most 1. As each node either sets its value to 0, to $x(v)/p(v)$ or to 1 the fractionality can be lower bounded by $\min_{v\in V}\{x(v)/p(v)\}$.
(2) By linearity of expectation the expected size of the dominating set after phase two is upper bounded by $\sum_{v\in V} p(v)\cdot x(v)/p(v) + \sum_{v\in V}\Pr(E_v = 1) = A + \sum_{v\in V}\Pr(E_v = 1)$. □

3.2 Derandomization via Network Decompositions

In this section we derandomize instantiations of the aforementioned abstract randomized rounding process with the help of k-hop network decompositions. [15] shows how these can be computed in the CONGEST model and we restate their definitions and results. We begin with the notion of a cluster graph.

Definition 3.2 (Cluster Graph). Given a graph $G = (V, E)$ and an integer $d \geq 1$ an (N, d)-cluster graph $\mathcal{G} = (\mathcal{V}, \mathcal{E})$ is a graph that is given by a set of clusters $\mathcal{V} = \{C_1, \ldots, C_N\} \in 2^V$ such that

(1) the clusters form a partition of V,
(2) each cluster C_i induces a connected subgraph $G[C_i]$ of G,
(3) each cluster C_i has a leader $\ell(C_i)$ that is known by all nodes of C_i,
(4) inside each cluster, there is a rooted spanning tree $T(C_i)$ of $G[C_i]$ that is rooted at $\ell(C_i)$ and has diameter at most d.

There is an edge $\{C_i, C_j\}$ between two clusters $C_i, C_j \in \mathcal{V}$ if there is edge in G connecting a node in C_i to a node in C_j. The identifier $ID(C_i)$ of a cluster C_i is its leaderâĂŹs ID.

Given a cluster graph $\mathcal{G} = (\mathcal{V}, \mathcal{E})$ of G and an integer $k \geq 1$, we say that two clusters $C, C' \in \mathcal{V}$ are k-separated if for any two nodes u and v of G such that $u \in C$ and $v \in C'$, we have $d_G(u, v) > k$. A strong-diameter k-hop network decomposition of a graph G is then defined as follows.

Definition 3.3 (Network Decomposition). Let $G = (V, E)$ be a graph and let $k \geq 1, d \geq 0$, and $c \geq 1$ be integer parameters. A strong diameter k-hop (d, c)-decomposition of G is a (N, d)-cluster graph $\mathcal{G}$ of G for some integer $N \geq 1$ together with a coloring of the clusters of G with colors $\{1, \ldots, c\}$ such that any two clusters with the same color are k-separated.

[15] shows how to compute k-hop network decompositions in the CONGEST model.

Theorem 3.4 (Theorem 3 in [15]). *Let $G = (V, E)$ be an n-node graph and let $k \geq 1$ be an integer. There is a deterministic CONGEST model algorithm that computes a strong diameter k-hop $(k\cdot f(n), f(n))$-decomposition of G in $k\cdot f(n)$ rounds, where $f(n) = 2^{O(\sqrt{\log n\cdot\log\log n})}$.*

In the proof of our main derandomization lemma we define a process that only needs poly log n-wise independent random bits. A finite set $\mathcal{X}$ of biased coins is *k-wise independent* if any subset $T \subseteq \mathcal{X}$ of size k is independent in the classical sense. We use the following classic result, which is for example proven in [1].

Lemma 3.5. *Let N and k be integers and $p_1, \ldots, p_N \in [0,1]$ multiplies of $2^{-\iota}$ for some $\iota = O(\log N)$. Given a random seed consisting of $K = O(k \log^2 N)$ independent fair coins, one can efficiently and deterministically extract N biased coins with probabilities $p_1, \ldots, p_N$ from the seed and these coins are k-wise independent.*

We can now state our main derandomization lemma with the help of network decompositions.

Lemma 3.6 (Derandomization Lemma I). *There is a determ. CONGEST algorithm that, given*

- *a constraint fractional dominating set of size A with transmittable values $x(v), v \in V$,*
- *a transmittable probability $p(v) \geq x(v)$ for each $v \in V$ and*
- *a sufficiently large parameter $k = \text{poly}\log n$,*

computes a constraint fractional dominating set with fractionality $\min_{v \in V}\{x(v)/p(v)\}$ and size at most $A + \sum_{v \in V} \Pr(E_v = 1) + \frac{1}{n^6}$ where E_v is the event that v is uncovered after the first phase if the abstract randomized rounding process is executed with $x(v)$ and $p(v)$ for $v \in V$ and k-wise independent (biased) coins for the probabilities $p(v)$. The round complexity of the algorithm is $2^{O(\sqrt{\log n \log\log n})}$.

The proof of Lemma 3.6 is based on iterating through the clusters of a network decomposition (of G^2) and creating a random seed of poly log n length inside each cluster. This is sufficient to create poly log n-wise independent bits for all nodes to execute the rounding algorithm. Then the algorithm is derandomized, i.e., bits of the random seeds are fixed deterministically with the method of conditional expectation.

Proof sketch. We show that we can derandomize the aforementioned abstract randomized rounding algorithm in the CONGEST model in $2^{O(\sqrt{\log n \log\log n})}$ rounds. In particular we derandomize the following *'almost equivalent'* randomized process: Deterministically compute a 2-hop (d,c)-network decomposition with $d, c = 2^{O(\sqrt{\log n \log\log n})}$ in $2^{O(\sqrt{\log n \log\log n})}$ rounds (cf. Theorem 3.4). Then iterate through the c color classes. In iteration i each leader of all clusters with color i creates a random seed of length K—the randomness for distinct clusters is independent—and distributes the seed to all members of the cluster. $K = \text{poly}\log n$ is chosen as in Lemma 3.5 such that each node v of the cluster can extract a biased coin (from the random seed) that equals one with probability $p(v)$ and zero otherwise and such that these coin flips are k-wise independent. After all clusters have been processed all nodes execute both phases of the abstract randomized rounding algorithm with their respective random bits. Note that the only randomness used by the algorithm is the generation of the random seeds—one random seed, that is, K random bits, per cluster. Due to linearity of expectation all results of Lemma 3.1 hold despite the limited dependence between coins and thus the process computes a fractional dominating set with fractionality $\min\{x(v)/p(v)\}$ and expected size $A + \sum_{v \in V} \Pr(E_v = 1)$.

To derandomize the above algorithm we use the method of conditional expectation, that is, we fix the random bits in the above algorithm one after another where the expectation (over the randomness of all unset random bits) only increases marginally during each step. There are K random bits per cluster and fixing a single bit takes $O(d)$ rounds—recall that d is the maximum cluster diameter. We will show that random bits of distinct clusters in the same color class can be fixed simultaneously. The full deterministic algorithm has the following steps: 1) compute a 2-hop (d,c)-network decomposition, 2) deterministically determine a random seed for each cluster, 3) deterministically execute the 'randomized algorithm' with these random seeds (using the same network decomposition). The first step needs $2^{O(\sqrt{\log n \log\log n})}$ rounds, the second steps $O(K \cdot c \cdot d) = 2^{O(\sqrt{\log n \log\log n})}$ rounds and the third step can be executed in $O(1)$ rounds.

In the full version [8] we show how the random bits of the random seeds can be fixed. □

We define two algorithms that use the above rounding process (with different choices for $p(v)$) as their main subroutine. Both begin with an initial fractional dominating set with values $x'(v), v \in V$.

One shot rounding. Increase the values of the input fractional dominating set by a factor $\ln \tilde{\Delta}$ and obtain a fractional dominating set where node v has value $x(v) = \min\{1, x'(v) \cdot \ln \tilde{\Delta}\}$. Then execute the randomized rounding process with value $x(v)$ and $p(v) = x(v)$ for all $v \in V$.

Note that the process one shot rounding transforms a fractional dominating set into an integral dominating set.

Factor two rounding. Let $\varepsilon > 0$ and $r = \text{poly}\log n$. Increase the values of the input fractional dominating set by a factor $(1+\varepsilon)$ and obtain a fractional dominating set where node v has value $x(v) = \min\{1, x'(v) \cdot (1+\varepsilon)\}$. Then execute the randomized rounding process with values $x(v)$ for $v \in V$ and

$$p(v) = \begin{cases} \frac{1}{2}, & \text{if } x(v) < 2/r \\ 1, & \text{if } x(v) \geq 2/r . \end{cases}$$

Thus in the factor two rounding nodes with value $x(v) < 2/r$ double their value with probability $1/2$ and otherwise set their value to 0. Nodes with value $x(v) \geq 2/r$ simply keep their value.

Recall that E_v equals 1 if node v is uncovered after the first phase and 0 otherwise. The proofs of the following two crucial lemmas upper bound the probability of $\Pr(E_v = 1)$ and use the following Chernoff type bound for k-wise independent random varibales.

Theorem 3.7 (Theorem 5 in [39]). *Let X be the sum of k-wise independent $[0,\lambda]$-valued random variables with expectation $\mu = E(X)$ and let $\delta \leq 1$. Then we have*

$$Pr(|X - \mu| \geq \delta\mu) \leq e^{-\lfloor \min\{k/2, \delta^2\mu/(3\lambda)\}\rfloor} .$$

Lemma 3.8. *Assume a given $1/F$-fractional dominating set for some integer $F > 0$. Then in the one shot rounding process we have $Pr(E_v = 1) \leq \tilde{\Delta}^{-1}$. The result holds even if the biased coins of the nodes are only k-wise independent for any $k \geq F$.*

Proof. Let $v \in V$ be a node. As the initial dominating set is $1/F$-fractional v is already covered by F nodes of $N(v)$. Let $S \subseteq N(v)$

denote a set of F nodes that cover v. If any $u \in S$ has $x(u) = 1$ node v is covered. Assume that $x(u) < 1$ for all $u \in S$. Then we have $x(u) = \ln\Delta \cdot x'(u)$ for all $u \in S$. Let $Y = \sum_{u\in S} X_u$ and let

$$\mu := \mathbb{E}[Y] = \sum_{u\in S} p(u) \cdot \frac{x(u)}{p(u)} \geq \ln\tilde{\Delta} \sum_{u\in S} x'(u) \geq \ln\tilde{\Delta}\,.$$

Y is the sum of $[0,1]$-valued random variables that are independent as $k \geq F \geq |S|$. We obtain

$$\Pr(v \text{ is uncovered}) \leq \prod_{u\in S}(1-\Pr(X_u = 1)) \leq e^{-\ln\tilde{\Delta}\cdot\sum_{u\in S} x'(v)}$$
$$\leq e^{-\ln\tilde{\Delta}} = \tilde{\Delta}^{-1}\,. \qquad \square$$

Lemma 3.9. *Let $\varepsilon > 0$, $r \geq 256\varepsilon^{-3}\ln\tilde{\Delta}$ and assume a given fractional dominating set. In the factor two rounding process we have $Pr(E_v = 1) \leq \tilde{\Delta}^{-4}$. The result holds even if the biased coins of the nodes are only k-wise independent for some $k \geq 8\ln\tilde{\Delta}$.*

Proof. Recall that $x'(v)$ is the value of node v before the process is executed, $x(v)$ is the value before the randomized rounding is executed and X_v is its value after the first phase. E_v equals 1, if node v is uncovered after the first phase, that is, if $\sum_{u\in N(v)} X_v < 1$.

We say, that a node with $p(v) < 1$ *takes part* in the rounding process and a node with $p(v) = 1$ *does not take part* in the rounding process. Let $F = r$. Fix a node $v \in V$ and let $N^F = \{u \in N^+(v) \mid x(u) \leq 1/F\}$ be the set of its neighbors that take part in the rounding process. Further, let $N^{\overline{F}} = N(v) \setminus N^F$ be the nodes that do not take part in the rounding process. Note that all $u \in N^{\overline{F}}$ have $x(u) \geq 1/F$ and thus either X_u equals 1 or $X_u \geq (1+\varepsilon)x'(u)$. If $X_u = 1$ for some $u \in N^{\overline{F}}$ node v is covered, so without loss of generality we may assume that $X_u \geq (1+\varepsilon)x'(u)$ for all $u \in N^{\overline{F}}$.

Let $S_v = \sum_{u\in N^F} x'(u)$ be the total initial value of the neighbors that take part in the rounding and let $T_v = \sum_{u\in N^{\overline{F}}} x'(u)$ be the total initial value of the neighbors that do not take part in the rounding. As the initial values form a dominating set we have $S_v + T_v \geq 1$. We perform a case distinction depending on the value of S_v.

Case $S_v \leq \frac{\varepsilon}{1+\varepsilon}$: If there is a node $u \in N^{\overline{F}}$ with $X_u = 1$ node v is covered. Otherwise all nodes nodes $u \in N^{\overline{F}}$ have $X_u \geq (1+\varepsilon)x'(u)$ and we have

$$\sum_{u\in N^{\overline{F}}} X_u \geq \sum_{u\in N^{\overline{F}}} (1+\varepsilon)x'(u) \geq (1+\varepsilon)T_v \geq (1+\varepsilon)\cdot(1-S_v) \geq 1\,.$$

Thus in this case v is covered by the nodes in $N^{\overline{F}}$.

Case $S_v > \frac{\varepsilon}{1+\varepsilon}$: If v is uncovered we have

$$1 > \sum_{u\in N(v)} X_u = \sum_{u\in N^{\overline{F}}} X_u + \sum_{u\in N^F} X_u$$
$$\overset{(*)}{\geq} (1+\varepsilon)\cdot(1-S_v) + \sum_{u\in N^F} X_u \geq (1-S_v) + \sum_{u\in N^F} X_u$$

where $(*)$ follows with the same argumentation as in the first case if v is not covered by a single node in $N^{\overline{F}}$. Thus if v is uncovered we have $\sum_{u\in N^F} X_u < S_v$. We next bound the probability of this to happen which yields the claim. Denote $Y = \sum_{u\in N^F} X_u$ and node that Y is the sum of k-wise independent $[0, 2(1+\varepsilon)/F]$ valued random variables as $X_u \leq x(u)/p_u = 2x(u) \leq 2(1+\varepsilon)x'(u) \leq 2(1+\varepsilon)1/F$ for $u \in N^F$. We compute Y's expectation as

$$\mu := \mathbb{E}[Y] = \sum_{u\in N^F} p_u \cdot \frac{x(u)}{p_u} + 0\cdot(1-p(v))$$
$$= \sum_{u\in N^F} (1+\varepsilon)x'(u) = (1+\varepsilon)S_v\,.$$

By Theorem 3.7 we have

$$\Pr(Y < S_v) = \Pr(Y-\mu < S_v - \mu) \leq \Pr(|Y-\mu| \geq \varepsilon S_v)$$
$$= \Pr\left(|Y-\mu| \geq \frac{\varepsilon}{1+\varepsilon}\mu\right)$$
$$\leq e^{-\min\{k/2, \lceil(\frac{\varepsilon}{1+\varepsilon})^2\mu/(3\cdot 2(1+\varepsilon))\cdot F\rceil\}}$$
$$\overset{(*)}{\leq} e^{-\min\{k/2, \varepsilon^3/48\cdot F\}} \overset{(**)}{\leq} \frac{1}{\tilde{\Delta}^4}$$

where $(*)$ holds as $\mu \geq \varepsilon$ and $\varepsilon \leq 1$ and $(**)$ holds due to $k \geq 8\log\tilde{\Delta}$ and $F \geq 256\varepsilon^{-3}\log\tilde{\Delta}$. $\square$

Note that Lemma 3.8 works for all F, but if the fractionality is small we need larger independence. The derandomization lemma (Lemma 3.6) is only efficient if we only need k-wise independence for some $k = \operatorname{poly}\log n$. Lemma 3.9 crucially depends on a small fractionality as, otherwise if only few nodes double their value, there is no concentration around the expectation.

Applying Lemma 3.6 to both processes implies deterministic counterparts whose properties we summarize in the following two lemmas.

Lemma 3.10 (Deterministic One Shot Rounding). *Let $F = \operatorname{poly}\log n$. There is a deterministic* CONGEST *algorithm that, given a $1/F$-fractional dominating set of size A, computes an integral dominating set with size at most $(\ln\tilde{\Delta})\cdot A + \frac{n}{\tilde{\Delta}} + \frac{1}{n^5}$ and has round complexity $2^{O(\sqrt{\log n \log\log n})}$.*

Proof. Apply Lemma 3.6 to the one shot rounding process with $k = F = \operatorname{poly}\log n$ yielding an integral dominating set of size $(\ln\tilde{\Delta})\cdot A + \sum_{v\in V}\Pr(E_v = 1) + n^{-6} + n^{-9} \leq (\ln\tilde{\Delta})\cdot A + \sum_{v\in V}\Pr(E_v = 1) + n^{-5}$ where the n^{-9} occurs as we have to increase each value such that it is transmittable before applying Lemma 3.6. Lemma 3.8 bounds $\Pr(E_v = 1) \leq \tilde{\Delta}^{-1}$ for all $v \in V$ which proves the claim. $\square$

Lemma 3.11 (Deterministic Factor Two Rounding). *Let $\varepsilon > 1/\operatorname{poly}\log n$, $r \geq F = 256\varepsilon^{-3}\ln\tilde{\Delta}$. There is a deterministic* CONGEST *algorithm that, given a $1/r$-fractional dominating set with size A, computes a $2/r$-fractional dominating set with size $(1+\varepsilon)A + \frac{n}{\tilde{\Delta}^4} + \frac{1}{n^5}$ and has round complexity $2^{O(\sqrt{\log n \log\log n})}$.*

Proof. Apply Lemma 3.6 to the one shot rounding process with $k = F = \operatorname{poly}\log n$ yielding an integral dominating set of size $(\ln\tilde{\Delta})\cdot A + \sum_{v\in V}\Pr(E_v = 1) + n^{-6} + n^{-9} \leq (\ln\tilde{\Delta})\cdot A + \sum_{v\in V}\Pr(E_v = 1) + n^{-5}$ where the n^{-9} occurs as we have to increase each value such that it is transmittable before applying Lemma 3.6. Lemma 3.8 bounds $\Pr(E_v = 1) \leq \tilde{\Delta}^{-1}$ for all $v \in V$ which proves the claim. $\square$

3.3 Derandomization via Colorings

In this subsection we present our second derandomization lemma which mainly expressed the runtime as a function of the maximum degree Δ. In its proof we iterate through the color classes of a distance two coloring of a suitable set $S \subseteq V$ of the nodes of a given graph $G = (V, E)$ and at each node we use the method of conditional expectation to locally determine random bits that are sufficient to execute the abstract randomized rounding algorithm such that the computed dominating set is small enough. Here, a coloring of the nodes in S is a *distance two coloring* if $d_G(u, v) > 2$ for any two nodes $u, v \in S$ that have the same color.

LEMMA 3.12 (DERANDOMIZATION LEMMA II). *There is a determ. CONGEST algorithm that, given*

- *a constraint fractional dominating set (x, c) of size A with transmittable values $x(v), v \in V$,*
- *a distance two C-coloring ϕ of $S = \{v \in V \mid p(v) \notin \{0, 1\}\}$ and*
- *transmittable probabilities $p(v) \geq x(v), v \in V$,*

computes a constraint fractional dominating set with fractionality $\min_{v \in V}\{x(v)/p(v)\}$ and size at most $A + \sum_{v \in V} \Pr(E_v = 1) + \frac{1}{n^7}$ where E_v is the event that $v \in V$ is uncovered after the first phase if the abstract randomized rounding process was executed with $x(v)$ and $p(v)$ for $v \in V$. The round complexity of the algorithm is $O(C)$.

The proof of Lemma 3.12 can be found in the full version [8]. It is based on iterating through the color classes of the distance two coloring and fixing random bits with the method of conditional expectation where the objective function is the size of the dominating set after the second phase of the abstract randomized rounding process.

We want to use Lemma 3.12 and the one shot or the two factor rounding process from Section 3.2 to increase the fractionality of a dominating set. However, if we applied Lemma 3.12 to G itself we would inherently have a runtime of $O(\Delta^2)$ rounds as we need $O(\Delta^2)$ colors in a distance two coloring of G. Instead we apply Lemma 3.12 to a graph that we obtain by modifying the so called bipartite representation of G.

Bipartite Representation: The *bipartite representation* B_G of a graph $G = (V, E)$ and a CFDS (x, c) is given through a slight adaption of the *bipartite double cover* of G together with a CFDS $(\tilde{x}, \tilde{c})$. The vertex set of B_G consists of two copies V_L and V_R of V. Two nodes $u \in V_L, u' \in V_R$ are connected in B_G if and only if their counterparts in V are connected in G or if they stem from the same node. The CFDS $(\tilde{x}, \tilde{c})$ of B_G is given through

$$\tilde{x}(v) = \begin{cases} x(v) & v \in V_R \\ 0, & v \in V_L \end{cases} \qquad \tilde{c}(v) = \begin{cases} 0 & v \in V_R \\ c(v), & v \in V_L. \end{cases}$$

This natural identification can be seen as splitting each node $v \in V$ into two nodes, one node in V_L that takes care of the constraint of v and one node in V_R that takes the value of v. The input to the algorithms in the upcoming Lemmas 3.15 and 3.16 is a graph G together with a constraint fractional dominating set (x', c'). First, the algorithms compute the bipartite representation B_G, $(\tilde{x}', \tilde{c}')$. Then they modify B_G and $(\tilde{x}', \tilde{c}')$ to obtain a new bipartite graph $\mathcal{B}$ with a new CFDS (x, c)—the modification consists of the removal of edges, splitting of nodes, changing constraints and so on. The (virtual) graph $\mathcal{B}$ admits a distance two coloring with few colors and at the same time ensures small $\Pr(E_v = 1)$ for all $v \in V(\mathcal{B})$ which is important to obtain a small dominating set in the end. Then we apply Lemma 3.12 to this modified graph $\mathcal{B}$ and a suitable chosen instantiation of the abstract rounding process from Section 3.1—the instantiations are almost identical to the one shot rounding and factor two rounding from Section 3.2. The graph $\mathcal{B}$ and the instantiation of the rounding process are such that we can compute the necessary distance two coloring of nodes in $\mathcal{B}$ with $O(\Delta \operatorname{poly}\log \Delta)$ colors and at the same time we ensure that $\Pr(E_v = 1)$ is small for all nodes of $\mathcal{B}$. Afterwards use the resulting CFDS on $\mathcal{B}$ to construct an FDS on G with the properties of the respective lemma. To make the derandomization work we need the following two resutls.

THEOREM 3.13. *Chernoff Bound [11] Let $\lambda > 0$ and $X = \sum_{i=1}^{n} X_i$ where $X_i, 1 \leq i \leq n$ are independently distributed in $[0, \lambda]$. Then for $\delta > 0$ we have $\Pr(X < (1-\delta)\,\mathbb{E}[X]) \leq e^{-\frac{\delta^2}{2\lambda}\mathbb{E}[X]}$.*

LEMMA 3.14 (BIPARTITE COLORING). *There is a determ. CONGEST algorithm that, given a bipartite graph $B = (V_L \cup V_R, E)$ computes a distance two coloring of V_R with $\Delta_L \cdot \Delta_R$ colors in $O(\Delta_L \cdot \Delta_R + \Delta_L \cdot \log^* n)$ round where Δ_L and Δ_R are the maximum degree of nodes in V_L and V_R, respectively.*

PROOF. Let $G = (V_R, F)$ be the graph on V_R that is obtained by connecting any two nodes in V_R that have a common neighbor in B. The coloring of B is obtained by simulating the CONGEST algorithm from [5] or [4] on G in B. Note that simulating a single round of such an algorithm in B takes $O(\Delta_L)$ rounds. □

LEMMA 3.15 (DETERMINISTIC ONE SHOT ROUNDING). *Let $F > 0$ be an integer. There is a determ. algorithm that, given a graph G with a $1/F$-fractional dominating set of size A, computes an integral dominating set with size at most $\ln \tilde{\Delta} \cdot A + n/\tilde{\Delta} + n^{-6}$ and has round complexity $O(F \cdot \Delta + F \cdot \log^* n)$ in the CONGEST model and round complexity $O(F \cdot \Delta + \log^* n)$ in the LOCAL model.*

PROOF. To apply Lemma 3.12 efficiently we first construct a new (virtual) graph $\mathcal{B}$ that admits a distance two coloring with few colors and at the same time ensures small $\Pr(E_v = 1)$ for all $v \in V(\mathcal{B})$.

Constructing Graph $\mathcal{B}$: Let $x'(v)$ denote the values of the $1/F$-fractional dominating set. First, set $x(v) = \min\{1, \ln \tilde{\Delta} \cdot x'(v)\}$ and set $c(v) = 1$ for all nodes. Note that we actually increase each $x(v)$ such that it is transmittable which increases each value by at most n^{-10} and therefore, summing over all nodes, will give an overall increase to the resulting FDS of at most n^{-9}. Then we build the Bipartite Representation B_G, (x, c) (reuse of notation for the dominating set) of G with (x, c). For every node the fractional value is either 0 or at least $1/F$. Therefore for each node v on the left hand side, there is a set of at most F nodes that cover v. For each node we find such a set. We then remove all edges that connect the node to nodes outside the set. With this we reduce the degree on the left hand side to F.

Instance of the Abstract Rounding Algorithms: Let $p(v) = x(v)$ for all $v \in V(\mathcal{B})$ and consider the abstract randomized rounding process with these values on $\mathcal{B}$.

Bounding $\Pr(E_v = 1)$: For $v \in V(\mathcal{B}$ let E_v be the random variable that is one if v's constraint is violated after the first phase of the abstract randomized rounding process and zero otherwise. If v is on the right hand side of $\mathcal{B}$ its constraint is zero and $\Pr(E_v = 1) = 0$. So let v be a node with $c(v) = 1$. If v has a neighbor u with $x(u) = 1$ then v's constraint is satisfied. Otherwise we have $x(u) \geq \ln\tilde{\Delta} \cdot x'(u)$ for all neighbors of v in $\mathcal{B}$. Thus we can bound the probability that v is uncovered after the first step as follows.

$$\mathbb{P}(E_v) = \prod_{u \in N(v)} (1 - x_u \ln\tilde{\Delta}) \leq \prod_{u \in N(v)} e^{-x_u \ln\tilde{\Delta}}$$
$$= e^{\sum_{u \in N(v)} -x_u \ln\tilde{\Delta}} = e^{-\ln(\tilde{\Delta}) \sum_{u \in N(v)} x_u} \overset{(*)}{\leq} e^{-\ln\tilde{\Delta}} = \frac{1}{\tilde{\Delta}}.$$

The inequality (*) holds since the sum over all $x'(u)$ in the closed neighborhood of v is at least 1 because we used a valid fractional dominating set as an input.

Applying the Derandomization Lemma and Building FDS on G: Using Lemma 3.14 we can color the right hand side nodes V_R with $O(F \cdot \Delta)$ colors in $O(F \cdot \Delta + F \cdot \log^* n)$ rounds. We can then use this coloring together with Lemma 3.12 to generate a dominating set of $\mathcal{B}$ of size

$$\ln\tilde{\Delta} \cdot A + \sum_{v \in V} \Pr(E_v = 1) + \frac{1}{n^8} + \frac{1}{n^9} \leq \ln\tilde{\Delta} \cdot A + \frac{n}{\tilde{\Delta}} + \frac{1}{n^7}.$$

Here the n^{-9} term is due to the rounding of the values to transmittable values that we performed at the beginning. The FDS on $\mathcal{B}$ induces an FDS on G by reverting the bipartite representation where a node sets its value to the maximum of the values of its two copies. The fractionality of the resulting dominating set follows from the fractionality of the abstract randomized rounding algorithm. The result in the LOCAL model follows as the required distance two coloring of V_R can be computed in $O(F \cdot \Delta + \log^* n)$ rounds, e.g., with the algorithm of [5]. □

Lemma 3.16 (Deterministic Factor Two Rounding). *Let $\varepsilon > 0$, $r \geq 256\varepsilon^{-3} \log\tilde{\Delta}$. There is a deterministic CONGEST algorithm that, given a graph G with a $1/r$-fractional dominating set of size A, computes a $\min\{2/r, 1/F\}$-fractional dominating set with size $(1+\varepsilon)A + n/\tilde{\Delta}^4 + n^{-6}$ and has round complexity $O(\varepsilon^{-2}\Delta \cdot \log\Delta + \varepsilon^{-2}\log\Delta \cdot \log^* n)$ in the CONGEST model and round complexity $O(\Delta \cdot \text{poly}\log\Delta + \log^* n)$ in the LOCAL model.*

Proof. The fractionality of the input dominating set is increased if all nodes with value $< 2/r$ double their value with probability 1/2 and set it to 0 otherwise. This can be achieved through an instance of the abstract randomized rounding process and one could use Lemma 3.12 to derandomize this process. However, Lemma 3.12 requires that all nodes that actually take part in the rounding process are distance two colored. Such a coloring of G would have $O(\Delta^2)$ colors and the runtime of the derandomization lemma crucially depends on the number of colors. Thus, we first move to the bipartite representation of G, remove edges and split nodes of this representation and obtain a graph $\mathcal{B}$. Then we derandomize the abstract rounding process on $\mathcal{B}$. The properties of $\mathcal{B}$ ensure 1) that we only need $\Delta\,\text{poly}\log\Delta$ colors in a distance two coloring of the nodes yielding a $\Delta\,\text{poly}\log\Delta$ runtime and 2) that the probability of a node being uncovered in the randomized rounding process is small; the latter is important as the approximation factor of the FDS at the end of derandomization depends on these probabilities.

Constructing Graph $\mathcal{B}$: Let $x'(v)$ denote the value of the input $1/r$-fractional dominating set. Let $x(v) = \min\{1, (1+\varepsilon)x'(v)\}$. We increase each value of x such that it is transmittable, this increases each value by at most $\frac{1}{n^{10}}$ and therefore gives an overall increase to the FDS of at most $\frac{1}{n^9}$. We define the constraints of the graph by $c(v) = 1$, and let $s = 64\varepsilon^{-2}\ln\tilde{\Delta}$. Next, we modify the bipartite Representation B_G of G to obtain a bipartite graph $\mathcal{B} = (U_L \cup U_R, E_{\mathcal{B}})$. Begin with the bipartite representation $B_G = (V_L \cup V_R, E)$ of G. Each node $v \in V_L$ is represented by k nodes $v_1, \ldots, v_k$ in U_L. The edges of v are distributed among these nodes as follows: v_1 is connected to all nodes in U_R that correspond to nodes $u \in V_R$ with $\{v,u\} \in E$ and $x(u) \geq 2/r$. If the number of remaining edges of u is less than s all of them are also given to v_1 (in this case we have $k = 1$). Otherwise the remaining edges of v are split between $v_2, \ldots, v_k$ such that each node gets between s and $2s$ edges. Note that all edges in $\mathcal{B}$ are edges of the original graph and any CONGEST algorithm on $\mathcal{B}$ can be executed without any overhead in the original network graph G. For $v \in U_R$ we set $c(v) = 0$ and for $v \in U_L$ we set the constraints such that they are satisfied by the x' values of their neighbors meaning $c(v) = \max\left\{1, \sum_{u \in N_{\mathcal{B}}(v)} x'(u_G)\right\}$ where u_G is the node that corresponds to u in G . For the fractional values we define $x(v) = 0$ for $v \in U_L$ and $x(v) = x(v_G)$ for $v \in U_R$.

Instance of the Abstract Rounding Algorithms: We define the following instance of the abstract randomized rounding algorithm on $\mathcal{B}$. For $v \in U_L$ we set $p(v) = 1$. For $v \in U_R$ we set

$$p(v) = \begin{cases} \frac{1}{2}, & \text{if } x(v) < 2/r, \\ 1, & \text{if } x(v) \geq 2/r\,. \end{cases} \tag{1}$$

Bounding $\Pr(E_v = 1)$: For $v \in U_L \cup U_R$ let E_v be the random variable that is one if v's constraint is violated after the first phase of the abstract randomized rounding process and zero otherwise. If $v \in U_R$ we clearly have $\Pr(E_v = 1) = 0$ as $c(v) = 0$. For a $v \in U_L$ we have the following cases:

In the first case v is a v_1 type node, meaning all neighbors of v_B are connected to v. If no $u \in N(v)$ has $x(u) < 2/r$ none of the neighbors takes part in the rounding and we have $E_v = 0$ as none of the neighbors change their value and v was covered before the rounding process. Now, assume that v_1 has neighbors $u \in N(v)$ with $x(u) < 2/r$. Let $S = \{u \in N(v) \mid x(u) < 2/r\}$ be the neighbors of v that participate in the rounding process and $T = N(v) \backslash S$. As v is a v_1 type we have $|S| \leq s$ and thus the contribution of participating nodes is at most $\sum_{u \in S} x'(u) \leq \sum_{u \in S} x(u) \leq s \cdot 2/r$. As v is covered before the rounding we obtain that $\sum_{u \in T} x'(u) \geq 1 - 2s/r$. If $x(u) = 1$ for some $u \in T$ we clearly have $E_v = 0$, otherwise we have $x(u) \geq (1+\varepsilon)x'(u)$ and we obtain $\Pr(E_v = 1) = 0$ as

$$\sum_{v \in T} x(u) \geq \sum_{v \in T} (1+\varepsilon)x'(u) \geq (1+\varepsilon)(1 - 2s/r)$$
$$\overset{(*)}{\geq} (1+\varepsilon)\left(1 - \frac{\varepsilon}{1+\varepsilon}\right) = 1\,,$$

where (*) follows because $2s/r \leq \frac{2 \cdot 64\varepsilon^{-2}\ln\Delta}{256\varepsilon^{-3}\ln\Delta} = \frac{\varepsilon}{2} \leq \frac{\varepsilon}{1+\varepsilon}$.

In the second case v is a $v_j, j \geq 2$ type node meaning all neighbors of v have a fractional value of less than $2/r$. Recall that for $u \in N(v)$ the random variable $X_u \in [0, 4/r]$ denotes the value of u after the first phase of the rounding process. Define $X = \sum_{u \in N(v)} X_u$ and note that due to linearity of expectation $\mathbb{E}[X] = c(v)(1+\varepsilon)$. With $\delta = 1 - \frac{1}{1+\varepsilon} = \frac{\varepsilon}{1+\varepsilon}$, $\varepsilon < 1$, $c(v) \geq s/r$, $\lambda = 4/r$ and the Chernoff Bound from Theorem 3.13 we obtain that

$$\begin{aligned}\Pr(E_v = 1) &= \Pr(X < c(v)) = \Pr(X < (1-\delta)\,\mathbb{E}[X]) \\ &\leq e^{-\frac{\delta^2}{2\lambda}\mathbb{E}[X]} = e^{-\frac{\delta^2}{8}\cdot r \cdot c(v)(1+\varepsilon)} \\ &\leq e^{-\frac{\varepsilon^2}{(1+\varepsilon)8}\cdot r\cdot c(v)} = e^{-\frac{\varepsilon^2}{16}\cdot r \cdot c(v)} \\ &\leq e^{-\frac{\varepsilon^2}{16}\cdot s} = \tilde{\Delta}^{-4}.\end{aligned}$$

Applying the Derandomization Lemma and Building FDS on G**:** Note that for all $u \in V_L$ we have $p(u) = 1$ and each $u \in V_L$ is connected to at most $O(s)$ nodes u' in V_R with $p(u') \notin \{0,1\}$. Thus we can use Lemma 3.14 to compute a distance two coloring of $S = \{v \in V_R \mid p(v) \notin \{0,1\}\}$ with $O(s \cdot \Delta) = O(\varepsilon^{-2}\log\Delta\cdot\Delta)$ colors in $O(\varepsilon^{-2}\cdot\log\Delta\cdot\Delta + \varepsilon^{-2}\log\Delta\cdot\log^* n)$.

We now use Lemma 3.12 with graph $\mathcal{B}$, the constraint fractional dominating set (x, c) with transmittable values and the distance two coloring of S to obtain a FDS of $\mathcal{B}$ with size at most

$$\ln\tilde{\Delta}\cdot A + \sum_{v\in V}\Pr(E_v = 1) + \frac{1}{n^8} + \frac{1}{n^9} \leq \ln\tilde{\Delta}\cdot A + \frac{n}{\tilde{\Delta}^4} + \frac{1}{n^7}.$$

Here the n^{-9} term is due to the rounding of the values to transmittable values that we performed at the beginning. The FDS on $\mathcal{B}$ induces an FDS on G by reverting the bipartite representation where a node sets its value to the maximum of the values of its two copies. The fractionality of the resulting dominating set follows from the fractionality of the abstract randomized rounding algorithm. The result in the LOCAL model follows as the required distance two coloring of V_R can be computed in $O(s\cdot\Delta + \log^* n)$ rounds, e.g., with the algorithm of [5]. □

3.4 Proof of Theorem 1.1

We use the deterministic rounding results (Lemmas 3.10, 3.11, 3.15 and 3.16) to prove our main results.

PROOFS OF THEOREM 1.1/THEOREM 1.2/COROLLARY 1.3. Set $\rho = \log(\Delta/\varepsilon)$, $\varepsilon_1 = \min\{\varepsilon/16, 1/4\}$, $\varepsilon_2 = \varepsilon_1/(100\rho)$ and $F = 256\varepsilon^{-3}\log\tilde{\Delta}$. Then the algorithm for all three results consist of three parts.

- **Part I:** Use Lemma 2.2 to build an initial FDS with fractionality $\varepsilon_1/\operatorname{poly}\Delta$ and $(1+\varepsilon_1)$-approximation guarantee,
- **Part II:** iterate (with ε_2) Lemma 3.11 or Lemma 3.16 ρ times to increase the fractionality by a factor two until the fractionality is F and
- **Part III:** use Lemma 3.10 or Lemma 3.15 to round the FDS to an integral one.

In this Lemma 3.11 and Lemma 3.10 are used to prove Theorem 1.1. Lemma 3.16 and Lemma 3.15 are used to prove Theorem 1.2. We begin with a $(1+\varepsilon_1)$ approximation guarantee, roughly loose a $(1+\varepsilon_1/\rho)$ factor in the approximation guarantee in each iteration of second part and roughly a $\ln\tilde{\Delta}$ factor in the third part, which heuristically bounds the approximation guarantee as follows

$$(1+\varepsilon_1)(1+\varepsilon_2/10)(1+\varepsilon_1/(100\rho))^{\rho}\ln\tilde{\Delta} \leq (1+\varepsilon)\ln\tilde{\Delta}.$$

The exact upper bound on the size of the dominating set can be found in the full version [8].

The runtime expressed as a function of n is $\rho\cdot 2^{O(\sqrt{\log\log n})} + 2^{O(\sqrt{\log\log n})} = 2^{O(\sqrt{\log\log n})}$. The runtime mostly expressed as a function of Δ is

$$O(\varepsilon^{-4}\log^2\Delta + \Delta\varepsilon^{-2}\log^2\Delta + \varepsilon^{-2}\log^2\Delta\cdot\log^* n + \Delta\varepsilon^{-3}\log\Delta + \varepsilon^{-3}\log^* n).$$

More details on the runtime can be found in the full version [8]. Corollary 1.3 follows by using the better runtime in the LOCAL model in Lemma 3.16 and Lemma 3.15. □

4 CONNECTED DOMINATING SET

In the following, we discuss how to extend the dominating set algorithm Section 3.2 to obtain a logarithmic approximation of the connected dominating set problem. We first recall how to extend a given dominating set S of a connected graph G to a connected dominating set (CDS) $\bar{S}$ of G. A proof for the following statement for example appears in [10] (see also [18]).

CLAIM 1. *[10, 18] Let $G = (V, E)$ and let $S \subseteq V$ be a dominating set of G. Further, let $G_S = (S, E_S)$ be a graph defined on the nodes in S, where there is an edges $\{u, v\} \in E_S$ for $u, v \in S$ if $d_G(u, v) \leq 3$. Then, G_S is connected if and only if G is connected.*

Algorithm Outline: We can therefore compute a CDS $\bar{S}$ of size at most $3|S|$ by first choosing a spanning tree T_S of G_S and by then replacing each edge of T_S by a path of length at most 3 in G and adding the at most 2 inner nodes of the path to $\bar{S}$. The time to compute a spanning tree in a distributed way is linear in the diameter of the graph. However, we can replace the spanning tree T_S by a slightly larger sparse spanning subgraph that can be computed efficiently in the distributed setting. In the LOCAL model, this is straightforward and has for example be done by Dubhashi et al. in [10]. In the CONGEST model, it is much less straightforward. First, the graph G_S cannot be efficiently simulated because many of the 2 or 3 hop paths might share common node. However, Ghaffari [12] showed that one can efficiently construct a connected subgraph G'_S of G_S, which can be used in the CONGEST model with only constant overhead. A sparse connected subgraph of G'_S can then be computed by using the sparse skeleton construction of Pettie [38]. Note however that the algorithms of [38] and [12] are randomized.

We use the same basic approach as in [12], however we replace the sparse skeleton construction of [38] with a variant of the more basic spanner algorithm of Baswana and Sen [6]. The algorithm of [6] is also randomized, however, recently in [15], Ghaffari and Kuhn gave a derandomization of the algorithm that allows to compute a connected subgraph with $O(n\log^2 n)$ edges of a given n-node graph. If we directly apply this algorithm on G'_S to obtain a CDS of G, we therefore lose an $O(\log^2 n)$ factor in the approximation ratio. In order to avoid this, we first compute a clustering of G'_S in which the network is partitioned into clusters of size $\Omega(\log^2 n)$ and diameter $O(\log^3 n)$. Such a clustering can be computed efficiently (and deterministically) by using a simple ruling set algorithm of [2, 20]. We then show that the deterministic spanner algorithm of [15] can also be applied efficiently on the resulting cluster graph, which then allows to obtain a CDS of size $O(|S|)$.

A detailed discussion of this CDS algorithm, as well as a formal proof of Theorem 1.4 are deferred to the full version [8].

5 CONCLUSIONS

We have efficient deterministic CONGEST model algorithms to compute almost optimal approximate solutions for the minimum dominating set and the minimum connected dominating set problems. To keep things as simple as possible, our algorithms are only given for the standard (unweighted) dominating set problem. However two possible generalizations are worth mentioning. The dominating set problem is a special case of set cover problem, where one is given a collection of finite sets that collectively cover some set of elements X and the objective is to choose a smallest possible number of those set, so that still all elements in X are covered. When considering the set cover problem in a distributed context, it is usually modeled as a graph by defining a node for each set and for each element and by adding an edge between a set and an element node if and only if the respective element is contained in the respective set (see, e.g., [26]). It is not hard to see that our algorithms can also be (almost directly) applied to the more general set cover problem.

Another possible generalization would be to extend our algorithms to also work for the weighted version of the dominating set problem. Here, each node has a weight and the objective is to select a dominating set of minimum total weight. We believe that our rounding method would also work more or less in the same way for the weighted dominating set problem (or for the weighted set cover problem). The part of the algorithm that would require most care are the gradual rounding steps, where we need to reduce the degrees of the constraint nodes in order to obtain efficient algorithms. The partition of a constraint into several lower order constraints seems less clear when weights are involved. We should remark that while we believe that our MDS algorithms can be generalized to also obtain good approximate solutions for the weighted MDS problem, the same is not true for the weighted connected dominating set problem. In [12], Ghaffari shows that the weighted CDS problem has an $\tilde{\Omega}(D + \sqrt{n})$ lower bound in the CONGEST model on graphs with diameter D. The paper also gives a (randomized) CONGEST algorithm that approximates the CDS problem in time $\tilde{O}(D + \sqrt{n})$.

REFERENCES

[1] Noga Alon and Joel H Spencer. 2004. *The probabilistic method.* John Wiley & Sons.

[2] Baruch Awerbuch, Michael Luby, Andrew V. Goldberg, and Serge A Plotkin. 1989. Network Decomposition and Locality in Distributed Computation. In *Proc. 30th Symp. on Found. of Computer Science (FOCS)*. 364–369.

[3] Leonid Barenboim and Michael Elkin. 2013. *Distributed Graph Coloring: Fundamentals and Recent Developments.* Morgan & Claypool Publishers.

[4] Leonid Barenboim, Michael Elkin, and Uri Goldenberg. 2018. Locally-Iterative Distributed $(\Delta + 1)$-Coloring below Szegedy-Vishwanathan Barrier, and Applications to Self-Stabilization and to Restricted-Bandwidth Models. In *Proc. 27th Symp. on Principles of Distributed Computing (PODC)*. 437–446.

[5] Leonid Barenboim, Michael Elkin, and Fabian Kuhn. 2015. Distributed $(\Delta + 1)$-Coloring in Linear (in Δ) Time. *SIAM J. Computing* 43, 1 (2015), 72–95.

[6] Surender Baswana and Sandeep Sen. 2007. A simple and linear time randomized algorithm for computing sparse spanners in weighted graphs. *Random Structures and Algorithms* 30, 4 (2007), 532–563.

[7] Keren Censor-Hillel, Merav Parter, and Gregory Schwartzman. 2017. Derandomizing Local Distributed Algorithms under Bandwidth Restrictions. In *Proc. 31st Symp. on Distributed Computing (DISC)*. 11:1–11:16.

[8] Janosch Deurer, Fabian Kuhn, and Yannic Maus. 2019. Deterministic Distributed Dominating Set Approximation in the CONGEST Model. (2019).

[9] Irit Dinur and David Steurer. 2014. Analytical approach to parallel repetition. In *Proc. 46th ACM Symposium on Theory of Computing (STOC)*. 624–633.

[10] Devdatt Dubhashi, Alessandro Mei, Alessandro Panconesi, Jaikumar Radhakrishnan, and Aravind Srinivasan. 2005. Fast distributed algorithms for (weakly) connected dominating sets and linear-size skeletons. *J. of Computer and System Sciences (JCSS)* 71, 4 (2005), 467–479.

[11] Devdatt P. Dubhashi and Alessandro Panconesi. 2009. *Concentration of Measure for the Analysis of Randomized Algorithms* (1st ed.). Cambridge University Press, New York, NY, USA.

[12] Mohsen Ghaffari. 2014. Near-Optimal Distributed Approximation of Minimum-Weight Connected Dominating Set. In *Proc. 41st Int. Coll. on Automata, Languages, and Programming (ICALP)*. 483–494.

[13] Mohsen Ghaffari. 2019. Distributed Maximal Independent Set using Small Messages. In *Proc. 30th Symp. on Discrete Algorithms (SODA)*. 805–820.

[14] Mohsen Ghaffari, David G. Harris, and Fabian Kuhn. 2018. On Derandomizing Local Distributed Algorithms. In *Proc. 59th Symp. on Foundations of Computer Science (FOCS)*. 662–673.

[15] Mohsen Ghaffari and Fabian Kuhn. 2018. Derandomizing Distributed Algorithms with Small Messages: Spanners and Dominating Set. In *Proc. 32nd Symp. on Distributed Computing (DISC)*. 29:1–29:17.

[16] Mohsen Ghaffari, Fabian Kuhn, and Yannic Maus. 2017. On the complexity of local distributed graph problems. In *Proc. 49th ACM Symp. on Theory of Computing (STOC)*. 784–797.

[17] Mohsen Ghaffari and Julian Portmann. 2019. personal communication.

[18] Sudipto Guha and Samir Khuller. 1998. Approximation Algorithms for Connected Dominating Sets. *Algorithmica* 20, 4 (1998), 374–387.

[19] David G. Harris. 2018. Distributed approximation algorithms for maximum matching in graphs and hypergraphs. *CoRR* abs/1807.07645 (2018). http://arxiv.org/abs/1807.07645

[20] Monika Henzinger, Sebastian Krinninger, and Danupon Nanongkai. 2016. A deterministic almost-tight dis- tributed algorithm for approximating single-source shortest paths. In *Proc. 48th ACM Symp. on Theory of Computing (STOC)*. 489–498.

[21] Lujun Jia, Rajmohan Rajaraman, and Torsten Suel. 2002. An Efficient Distributed Algorithm for Constructing Small Dominating Sets. *Distributed Computing* 15, 4 (2002), 193–205.

[22] David S Johnson. 1974. Approximation Algorithms for Combinatorial Problems. *J. Computer and System Sciences* 9 (1974), 256–278.

[23] David S. Johnson and Michael R Garey. 1979. *Computers and Intractability, A Guide to the Theory of NP-Completeness.* W. H. Freeman and Company.

[24] Richard M. Karp. 1972. Reducibility Among Combinatorial Problems. In *Proc. of a Symposium on the Complexity of Computer Computations.* 85–103.

[25] Ken-ichi Kawarabayashi and Gregory Schwartzman. 2018. Adapting Local Sequential Algorithms to the Distributed Setting. In *Proc. 32nd Symp. on Distributed Computing (DISC)*. 35:1–35:17.

[26] Fabian Kuhn, Thomas Moscibroda, and Roger Wattenhofer. 2006. The Price of Being Near-Sighted. In *Proc. 17th Symp. on Discrete Algorithms (SODA)*. 980–989.

[27] Fabian Kuhn, Thomas Moscibroda, and Roger Wattenhofer. 2016. Local Computation: Lower and Upper Bounds. *J. of the ACM* 63, 2 (2016).

[28] Fabian Kuhn and Roger Wattenhofer. 2005. Constant-Time Distributed Dominating Set Approximation. *Distributed Computing* 17, 4 (2005), 303–310.

[29] Christoph Lenzen, Yvonne-Anne Pignolet, and Roger Wattenhofer. 2013. Distributed minimum dominating set approximations in restricted families of graphs. *Distributed Computing* 26, 2 (2013), 119–137.

[30] Christoph Lenzen and Roger Wattenhofer. 2008. Leveraging Linial's Locality Limit. In *Proc. 22nd Symp. on Distributed Computing (DISC)*. 394–407.

[31] Nati Linial. 1992. Locality in Distributed Graph Algorithms. *SIAM J. Comput.* 21, 1 (1992), 193–201.

[32] Nati Linial and Michael Saks. 1993. Low Diameter Graph Decompositions. *Combinatorica* 13, 4 (1993), 441–454.

[33] Yannic Maus. 2018. *The power of locality: exploring the limits of randomness in distributed computing.* Ph.D. Dissertation. University of Freiburg, Freiburg im Breisgau, Germany. https://freidok.uni-freiburg.de/data/16780

[34] Alessandro Panconesi and Aravind Srinivasan. 1995. On the Complexity of Distributed Network Decomposition. *Journal of Algorithms* 20, 2 (1995), 581–592.

[35] Merav Parter. 2018. (Delta+1) Coloring in the Congested Clique Model. In *Proc. 45th Int. Coll. on Automata, Languages, and Programming (ICALP)*. 160:1–160:14.

[36] Merav Parter and Eylon Yogev. 2018. Congested Clique Algorithms for Graph Spanners. In *Proc. 32nd Symp. on Distributed Computing (DISC)*. 40:1–40:18.

[37] David Peleg. 2000. *Distributed Computing: A Locality-Sensitive Approach.* SIAM.

[38] Seth Pettie. 2010. Distributed algorithms for ultrasparse spanners and linear size skeletons. *Distributed Computing* 22, 3 (2010), 147–166.

[39] Jeanette P. Schmidt, Alan Siegel, and Aravind Srinivasan. 1995. Chernoff-Hoeffding Bounds for Applications with Limited Independence. *SIAM J. Discrete Math.* 8, 2 (1995), 223–250.

Brief Announcement: Optimal Distributed Covering Algorithms

Ran Ben-Basat*
Harvard University
ran@seas.harvard.edu

Guy Even
Tel Aviv University
guy@eng.tau.ac.il

Ken-ichi Kawarabayashi†
National Institute of Informatics
k_keniti@nii.ac.jp

Gregory Schwartzman‡
National Institute of Informatics
greg@nii.ac.jp

Abstract

We present a time-optimal deterministic distributed algorithm for approximating a minimum weight vertex cover in hypergraphs of rank f. This problem is equivalent to the Minimum Weight Set Cover problem in which the frequency of every element is bounded by f. The approximation factor of our algorithm is $(f+\varepsilon)$. Let Δ denote the maximum degree in the hypergraph. Our algorithm runs in the CONGEST model and requires $O(\log\Delta/\log\log\Delta)$ rounds, for constants $\varepsilon \in (0,1]$ and $f \in \mathbb{N}^+$. This is the first distributed algorithm for this problem whose running time does not depend on the vertex weights nor the number of vertices. Thus adding another member to the exclusive family of *provably optimal* distributed algorithms.

For constant values of f and ε, our algorithm improves over the $(f+\varepsilon)$-approximation algorithm of [16] whose running time is $O(\log\Delta + \log W)$, where W is the ratio between the largest and smallest vertex weights in the graph. Our algorithm also achieves an f-approximation for the problem in $O(f\log n)$ rounds, improving over the classical result of [13] that achieves a running time of $O(f\log^2 n)$. Finally, for weighted vertex cover ($f = 2$) our algorithm achieves a *deterministic* running time of $O(\log n)$, matching the *randomized* previously best result of [14].

We also show that integer covering-programs can be reduced to the Minimum Weight Set Cover problem in the distributed setting. This allows us to achieve an $(f+\varepsilon)$-approximate integral solution in $O\left((1+f/\log n)\cdot\left(\frac{\log\Delta}{\log\log\Delta} + (f\cdot\log M)^{1.01}\cdot\log\varepsilon^{-1}\cdot(\log\Delta)^{0.01}\right)\right)$ rounds, where f bounds the number of variables in a constraint, Δ bounds the number of constraints a variable appears in, and $M = \max\{1, \lceil 1/a_{\min}\rceil\}$, where a_{min} is the smallest normalized constraint coefficient. This significantly improves over the results of [16] for the integral case, which achieves the same guarantees in $O\left(\varepsilon^{-4}\cdot f^4\cdot\log f\cdot\log(M\cdot\Delta)\right)$ rounds.

ACM Reference Format:
Ran Ben-Basat, Guy Even, Ken-ichi Kawarabayashi, and Gregory Schwartzman. 2019. Brief Announcement: Optimal Distributed Covering Algorithms. In *2019 ACM Symposium on Principles of Distributed Computing (PODC '19), July 29-August 2, 2019, Toronto, ON, Canada.* ACM, New York, NY, USA, 3 pages. https://doi.org/10.1145/3293611.3331577

*Supported by the Zuckerman Institute, the Technion Hiroshi Fujiwara Cyber Security Research center, and the Israel Cyber Directorate.
†Supported by JST ERATO Kawarabayashi Large Graph Project JPMJER1201 and by JSPS Kakenhi JP18H05291.
‡Supported by JSPS Kakenhi Grant Number JP19K20216 and JP18H05291.

ACM ISBN 978-1-4503-6217-7/19/07.
https://doi.org/10.1145/3293611.3331577

1 Introduction

In the Minimum Weight Vertex Cover (MWVC) problem, we are given an undirected graph $G = (V, E)$ with vertex weights $w : V \to \{1, \ldots, W\}$, for $W = n^{O(1)}$. The goal is to find a minimum weight *cover* $U \subseteq V$ such that $\forall e \in E : e \cap U \neq \emptyset$. This problem is one of the classical NP-hard problems presented in [12].

In this paper, we consider the Minimum Weight Hypergraph Vertex Cover (MWHVC) problem, a generalization of the MWVC problem to *hypergraphs* of rank f. In a hypergraph, $G = (V, E)$, each edge is a nonempty subset of the vertices. A hypergraph is of rank f if the size of every hyperedge is bounded by f. The MWVC problem naturally extends to MWHVC using the above definition. Note that MWHVC is equivalent to the Minimum Weight Set Cover problem with element frequencies bounded by f.

We consider the MWHVC problem in the distributed setting, where the communication network is a bipartite graph $H(E \cup V, \{\{e, v\} \mid v \in e\})$. We refer to the network vertices as *nodes* and network edges as *links*. The nodes of the network are the hypergraph vertices on one side and hyperedges on the other side. There is a network link between vertex $v \in V$ and hyperedge $e \in E$ iff $v \in e$. The computation is performed in synchronous rounds, where messages are sent between neighbors in the communication network. As for message size, we consider the CONGEST model where message sizes are bounded to $O(\log|V|)$. This is more restrictive than the LOCAL model where message sizes are unbounded.

1.1 Related work

We survey the state-of-the art results for MWHVC. We also focus on the specific case of Minimum Vertex Cover, which received significant attention in the literature. A list of results for vertex cover appear in Table 1 for graphs and in Table 2 for hypergraphs.

Vertex Cover. Denoting by Δ the maximum vertex degree in a graph G, any distributed constant-factor approximation algorithm requires $\Omega(\log\Delta/\log\log\Delta)$ rounds to terminate, even for unweighted graphs and $f = 2$ [17] in the LOCAL model. The lower bound was matched by [3] with a $(2+\varepsilon)$-approximation algorithm (BCS algorithm) with optimal round complexity in the CONGEST model for every $\varepsilon = \Omega(\log\log\Delta/\log\Delta)$. In [14] an $O(\log n)$-round 2-approximation randomized algorithm for weighted graphs in the CONGEST model is given. We note that [14] was the first to achieve this running time with no dependence on W, the maximum weight of the nodes.

Hypergraph Vertex Cover. For constant values of f, Astrand et al. [2] present an f-approximation algorithm for anonymous networks whose running time is $O(\Delta^2 + \Delta \cdot \log^* W)$ (where W is the ratio between the largest and smallest weights in the graph). Khuller et al. [13] provide a solution that runs in $O(f \log 1/\varepsilon \cdot \log n)$ rounds in the CONGEST model for any $\varepsilon > 0$ and achieves an $(f + \varepsilon)$-approximation. Setting $\varepsilon = 1/W$ (recall that $W = poly(n)$) results in a f-approximation in $O(f \log^2 n)$-rounds. For constant ε and f values, Kuhn et al. [15, 16] present an $(f + \varepsilon)$-approximation algorithm that terminates in $O(\log \Delta + \log W)$ rounds.

For the Minimum Cardinality Vertex Cover in Hypergraphs Problem, the lower bound was recently matched by [7] with an $(f + \varepsilon)$-approximation algorithm in the CONGEST model. The round complexity in [7] is $O\left(f/\varepsilon \cdot \frac{\log(f\cdot\Delta)}{\log\log(f\cdot\Delta)}\right)$, which is optimal for constant f and ε. The algorithm in [7] and its analysis is a deterministic version of the MIS algorithm of [8].

1.2 Our contributions

In this paper, we present a deterministic distributed $(f + \varepsilon)$-approximation algorithm for minimum weight vertex cover in f-rank hypergraphs, which completes in

$$O\left(f \cdot \log(f/\varepsilon) + \frac{\log \Delta}{\log\log \Delta} + \min\left\{\log \Delta, f \cdot \log(f/\varepsilon) \cdot (\log \Delta)^{0.001}\right\}\right)$$

rounds in the CONGEST model. For any constants $\varepsilon \in (0, 1)$ and $f \in \mathbb{N}^+$ this implies a running time of $O(\log \Delta/\log\log \Delta)$, which is optimal according to [17].This is the first distributed algorithm for this problem whose round complexity does not depend on the node weights nor the number of vertices.

Our algorithm is one of a handful of distributed algorithms for *local* problems which are *provably optimal* [3, 4, 7, 9]. We also achieve a *deterministic* f-approximation for the problem in $O(f \log n)$ rounds. This improves over the best known result for hypergraphs $O(f \log^2 n)$ [13] and matches the *randomized* results for weighted vertex cover of $O(\log n)$-rounds [14].

We also show that general covering Integer Linear Programs (ILPs) can be reduced to MWHVC in the distributed setting. That is, LP constraints can be translated into hyperedges such that a cover for the hyperedges satisfies all covering constraints. This allows us to achieve an $(f + \varepsilon)$-approximate *integral* solution in $O\left((1 + f/\log n) \cdot \left(\frac{\log \Delta}{\log\log \Delta} + (f \cdot \log M)^{1.01} \cdot \log \varepsilon^{-1} \cdot (\log \Delta)^{0.01}\right)\right)$ rounds, where f bounds the number of variables in a constraint, Δ bounds the number of constraints a variable appears in, and $M = \max\{1, \lceil 1/a_{\min} \rceil\}$, where $a_{\min}$ smallest normalized constraint coefficient. This significantly improves over the results of [16] for the integral case, which combined with rounding achieves the same guarantees in $O\left(\varepsilon^{-4} \cdot f^4 \cdot \log f \cdot \log(M \cdot \Delta)\right)$ rounds. Note that the results of [16] also include a $(1+\varepsilon)$-approximation for the fractional case, while our result only allows for an integral solution. We also note that plugging $\varepsilon = 1/nWM$ into our algorithm, achieves an f-approximation for ILPs in polylogarithmic time, a similar result cannot be achieved using [16].

1.3 Tools and techniques

The Primal-Dual schema. The Primal-Dual approach introduces, for every hyperedge $e \in E$, a dual variable denoted by $\delta(e)$. The dual edge packing constraints are $\forall v \in V, \sum_{v \in e} \delta(e) \le w(v)$. If for some $\beta \in [0, 1)$ it holds that $\sum_{v \in e} \delta(e) \ge (1 - \beta) \cdot w(v)$, we say the v is β-tight. Let $\beta = \varepsilon/(f + \varepsilon)$. For every feasible dual solution, the weight of the set of β-tight vertices is at most $(f + \varepsilon)$ times the weight of an optimal (fractional) solution. The algorithm terminates when the set of β-tight edges constitutes a vertex cover.

det.	weighted	approximation	time	algorithm
yes	no	3	$O(\Delta)$	[19]
yes	no	2	$O(\Delta^2)$	[1]
yes	yes	2	$O(1)$ for $\Delta \le 3$	[1]
yes	yes	2	$O(\Delta + \log^* n)$	[18]
yes	yes	2	$O(\Delta + \log^* W)$	[2]
yes	yes	2	$O(\log^2 n)$	[13]
yes	yes	2	$O(\log n \log \Delta/\log^2 \log \Delta)$	[6]
no	yes	2	$O(\log n)$	[10, 14]
yes	**yes**	**2**	$\mathbf{O(\log n)}$	**This work**
yes	yes	$2+\varepsilon$	$O(\varepsilon^{-4} \log(W \cdot \Delta))$	[11, 16]
yes	yes	$2+\varepsilon$	$O(\log \varepsilon^{-1} \log n)$	[13]
yes	yes	$2+\varepsilon$	$O(\varepsilon^{-1} \log \Delta/\log\log \Delta)$	[3, 7]
yes	yes	$2+\varepsilon$	$O\left(\frac{\log \Delta}{\log\log \Delta} + \frac{\log \varepsilon^{-1} \log \Delta}{\log^2 \log \Delta}\right)$	[6]
yes	**yes**	$\mathbf{2+\varepsilon}$	$O\left(\frac{\log \Delta}{\log\log \Delta} + \log \varepsilon^{-1} \cdot (\log \Delta)^{0.001}\right)$	**This work**

Table 1: Running times for Weighted Vertex Cover.

weighted	approximation	time	algorithm
yes	f	$O\left(f^2\Delta^2 + f\Delta \log^* W\right)$	[2]
yes	f	$O\left(f \log^2 n\right)$	[13]
yes	$\mathbf{f}$	$\mathbf{O(f \log n)}$	**This work**
no	$f+\varepsilon$	$O\left(\varepsilon^{-1} \cdot f \cdot \frac{\log(f\Delta)}{\log\log(f\Delta)}\right)$	[7]
yes	$f+\varepsilon$	$O(f \cdot \log(f/\varepsilon) \cdot \log n)$	[13]
yes	$f+\varepsilon$	$O\left(\varepsilon^{-4} \cdot f^4 \cdot \log f \cdot \log(W \cdot \Delta)\right)$	[16]
yes	$\mathbf{f+\varepsilon}$	$O\left(f \cdot \log(f/\varepsilon) \cdot (\log \Delta)^{0.001} + \frac{\log \Delta}{\log\log \Delta}\right)$	**This work**

Table 2: Running times are stated for deterministic MWHVC.

The challenge. When designing a Primal-Dual distributed algorithms, the main challenge is in controlling the rate at which we increase the dual variables. On the one hand, we must grow them rapidly to reduce the number of communication rounds. On the other hand, we may not violate the edge packing constraints. This is tricky in the distributed environments as we have to coordinate between nodes. For example, the result of [3] does not generalize to hypergraphs, as hyperedges require the coordination of more than two nodes in order to increment edge variables.

Our Algorithm. The algorithm proceeds in iterations, each of which requires a constant number of communication rounds. We initialize the dual variables in a "safe" way so that feasibility is guaranteed. We refer to the additive increase of the dual variable $\delta(e)$ as deal$(e)/2$. Similarly to [6], we use *levels* to measure the progress made by a vertex. Whenever the level of a vertex increases, it sends a message about it to all incident edges, which multiply (decrease) their deals by 0.5. Intuitively, the level of a vertex equals the logarithm of its uncovered portion. Formally, we define the level of a vertex v as $\ell(v) \triangleq \left\lfloor \log \frac{w(v)}{w(v) - \sum_{e \ni v} \delta(e)} \right\rfloor$. That is, the initial level of v is 0 and it is increased as the dual variables of the edges incident to v grow. The level of a vertex never reaches $z \triangleq \lceil \log \beta^{-1} \rceil$ as this implies that it is β-tight and entered the cover. Loosely speaking, the algorithm increases the increments deal(e) exponentially (multiplication by α) provided that no vertex $v \in e$ is $(0.5^{\ell(v)}/\alpha)$-tight with respect to the deals of the previous iteration. Here, $\alpha \ge 2$ is a positive parameter that we determine later. The analysis builds on two observations: (1) The number of times that deal(e) is multiplied by α is bounded by $\log_\alpha \Delta$. (2) The number of iterations in which deal(e) is not multiplied by α is bounded by $O(f \cdot z \cdot \alpha)$. Loosely speaking, each such iteration means that for at least one vertex $v \in e$ the sum of deals is at least an $1/(2\alpha)$-fraction of its slack. Therefore, after at most $O(\alpha)$ such iterations that vertex will level up. Since there are z levels per vertex and f vertices in e, we have that the number of such iterations is at most $O(f \cdot z \cdot \alpha)$. Hence the total number of iterations is bounded by $O(\log_\alpha \Delta + f \cdot z \cdot \alpha)$. Next, we show distributed reductions that allow us to compute an $(f + \varepsilon)$-approximation for general covering integer linear programs (ILPs). To that end, we first show that any Zero-One covering program (where all variables are binary) can be translated into a set cover instance in which the vertex degree is bounded by 2^f times the bound on the number of constraints each ILP variable appears in. We then generalize to arbitrary covering ILPs by replacing each variable with multiple vertices in the hypergraph, such that the value associated with the ILP variable will be the weighted sum of the vertices in the cover. We provide full problem definitions in the full version [5].

2 Distributed Approximation of MWHVC

Input: The input is a hypergraph $G = (V, E)$ with non-negative vertex weights $w : V \longrightarrow \mathbb{N}^+$ and an approximation ratio parameter $\varepsilon \in (0, 1]$. We denote the number of vertices by n, the rank of G by f (i.e., each hyperedge contains at most f vertices), and the maximum degree of G by Δ. **Output:** A vertex cover $C \subseteq V$. Namely, for every hyperedge $e \in E$, the intersection $e \cap C$ is not empty. The set C is maintained locally in the sense that every vertex v knows whether it belongs to C or not.

Communication Network The communication network $N(E \cup V, \{\{e, v\} \mid v \in e\})$ is a bipartite graph. There are two types of nodes in the network: *servers* and *clients*. The set of servers is V (the vertex set of G) and the set of clients is E (the hyperedges in G). There is a link (v, e) from server $v \in V$ to a client $e \in E$ if $v \in e$. Note that the degree of the clients is bounded by f and the degree of the servers is bounded by Δ. Parameters and Variables: (1) The approximation factor parameter is $\varepsilon \in (0, 1]$. The parameter β is defined by $\beta \triangleq \varepsilon/(f + \varepsilon)$, where f is the rank of the hypergraph. (2) Each vertex v is assigned a level $\ell(v)$ which is a nonnegative integer. (3) We denote the dual variables at the end of iteration i by $\delta_i(e)$ (see [5] for a description of the dual edge packing linear program). The amount by which $\delta_i(e)$ is increased in iteration i is denoted by $\text{deal}_i(e)$. Namely, $\delta_i(e) = \sum_{j \le i} \text{deal}_j(e)/2$. (4) The parameter $\alpha > 1$ determines the factor by which deals are multiplied. We determine its value in the the full version [5].

Notation (1) We say that an edge e is *covered* by C if $e \cap C \neq \emptyset$. (2) Let $E(v) \triangleq \{e \in E \mid v \in e\}$ denote the set of hyperedges that contain v. (3) For every vertex v, the algorithm maintains a subset $E'(v) \subseteq E(v)$ that consists of the uncovered hyperedges in $E(v)$ (i.e., $E'(v) = \{e \in E(v) \mid e \cap C = \emptyset\}$).

2.1 Algorithm MWHVC

(1) Initialization. Set $C \leftarrow \emptyset$. For every vertex v, set level $\ell(v) \leftarrow 0$ and uncovered edges $E'(v) \leftarrow E(v)$.
(2) Iteration $i = 0$. Every edge e collects the weight $w(v)$ and degree $|E(v)|$ from every vertex $v \in e$, and sets: $\text{deal}(e) = 0.5 \cdot \min_{v \in e}\{w(v)/|E(v)|\}$. The value $\text{deal}(e)$ is sent to every $v \in e$. The dual variable is set to $\delta(e) \leftarrow \text{deal}(e)$.
(3) For $i = 1$ to ∞ do:
   (a) Check β-tightness. For every $v \notin C$, if $\sum_{e \in E(v)} \delta(e) \geq (1 - \beta)w(v)$, then v joins the cover C, sends a message to every $e \in E'(v)$ that e is covered, and vertex v terminates.
   (b) For every uncovered edge e, if e receives a message that it is covered, then it tells all its vertices that e is covered and terminates.
   (c) For every vertex $v \notin C$, if it receives a message from e that e is covered, then $E'(v) \leftarrow E'(v) \setminus \{e\}$. If $E'(v) = \emptyset$, then v terminates (without joining the cover).
   (d) Increment levels and scale deals.
   For every active (that has not terminated) vertex:
   While $\sum_{e \in E(v)} \delta(e) > w(v)(1 - 0.5^{\ell(v)+1})$ do
      (i) $\ell(v) \leftarrow \ell(v) + 1$
      (ii) For every $e \in E'(v)$: $\text{deal}(e) \leftarrow 0.5 \cdot \text{deal}(e)$
   (e) For every active vertex, if $\sum_{e \in E'(v)} \text{deal}(e) \leq \frac{1}{\alpha} \cdot 0.5^{\ell(v)+1} \cdot w(v)$, then send the message "raise" to every $e \in E'(v)$; otherwise, send the message "stuck" to every $e \in E'(v)$.
   (f) For every uncovered edge e, if *all* incoming messages are "raise" $\text{deal}(e) \leftarrow \alpha \cdot \text{deal}(e)$. Send $\text{deal}(e)$ to every $v \in e$, who updates $\delta(e) \leftarrow \delta(e) + \text{deal}(e)/2$.

Termination. Every vertex v terminates when either $v \in C$ or every edge $e \in E(v)$ is covered (i.e., $E'(v) = \emptyset$). Every edge e terminates when it is covered (i.e., $e \cap C \neq \emptyset$). The algorithm terminates when all the vertices and edges have terminated. The analysis and extension to integer linear programs appear in the full version [5].

References

[1] M. Astrand, P. Floréen, V. Polishchuk, J. Rybicki, J. Suomela, and J. Uitto. [n. d.]. A Local 2-Approximation Algorithm for the Vertex Cover Problem, DISC 2009.
[2] M. Astrand and J. Suomela. 2010. Fast distributed approximation algorithms for vertex cover and set cover in anonymous networks. In *SPAA*.
[3] R. Bar-Yehuda, K. Censor-Hillel, and G. Schwartzman. 2017. A Distributed $(2 + \varepsilon)$-Approximation for Vertex Cover in $O(\log \Delta / \varepsilon \log \log \Delta)$ Rounds. *J. ACM* (2017).
[4] R. Bar-Yehuda, K. Hillel, M. Ghaffari, and G. Schwartzman. 2017. Distributed Approximation of Maximum Independent Set and Maximum Matching. In *PODC*.
[5] R. Ben-Basat, G. Even, K. Kawarabayashi, and G. Schwartzman. 2019. Optimal Distributed Covering Algorithms. abs/1902.09377 (2019).
[6] R. Ben-Basat, G. Even, K.-i. Kawarabayashi, and G. Schwartzman. 2018. A Deterministic Distributed 2-Approximation for Weighted Vertex Cover in $O(\log n \log \Delta/\log^2 \log \Delta)$ Rounds. In *SIROCCO*.
[7] Guy Even, Mohsen Ghaffari, and Moti Medina. 2018. Distributed Set Cover Approximation: Primal-Dual with Optimal Locality. In *DISC*.
[8] Mohsen Ghaffari. 2016. An improved distributed algorithm for maximal independent set. In *SODA*.
[9] Mohsen Ghaffari and Hsin-Hao Su. 2017. Distributed Degree Splitting, Edge Coloring, and Orientations. In *SODA*.
[10] Fabrizio Grandoni, Jochen Könemann, and Alessandro Panconesi. 2008. Distributed weighted vertex cover via maximal matchings. *TALG* (2008).
[11] Dorit S. Hochbaum. 1982. Approximation Algorithms for the Set Covering and Vertex Cover Problems. *SIAM J. Comput.* 11, 3 (1982), 555–556. https://doi.org/10.1137/0211045
[12] Richard M. Karp. 1972. Reducibility Among Combinatorial Problems. In *Complexity of Computer Computations*.
[13] Samir Khuller, Uzi Vishkin, and Neal E. Young. 1994. A Primal-Dual Parallel Approximation Technique Applied to Weighted Set and Vertex Covers. *J. Algorithms* 17, 2 (1994), 280–289. https://doi.org/10.1006/jagm.1994.1036
[14] C. Koufogiannakis and N. E. Young. 2011. Distributed algorithms for covering, packing and maximum weighted matching. *Distributed Computing* (2011).
[15] Fabian Kuhn. 2005. *The price of locality: exploring the complexity of distributed coordination primitives*. Ph.D. Dissertation. ETH Zurich.
[16] Fabian Kuhn, Thomas Moscibroda, and Roger Wattenhofer. 2006. The price of being near-sighted. In *SODA*.
[17] Fabian Kuhn, Thomas Moscibroda, and Roger Wattenhofer. 2016. Local Computation: Lower and Upper Bounds. *J. ACM* 63, 2 (2016), 17:1–17:44.
[18] Alessandro Panconesi and Romeo Rizzi. 2001. Some simple distributed algorithms for sparse networks. *Distributed Computing* 14, 2 (2001), 97–100.
[19] Valentin Polishchuk and Jukka Suomela. 2009. A simple local 3-approximation algorithm for vertex cover. *Inf. Process. Lett.* 109, 12 (2009), 642–645.

Secure Distributed Computing Made (Nearly) Optimal

Merav Parter
merav.parter@weizmann.ac.il
Weizmann Institute

Eylon Yogev
eylony@gmail.com
Technion

ABSTRACT

In this paper, we study *secure* distributed algorithms that are nearly *optimal*, with respect to running time, for the given input graph G. Roughly speaking, an algorithm is *secure* if the nodes learn only their final output while gaining no information on the input (or output) of other nodes.

A graph theoretic framework for secure distributed computation was recently introduced by the authors (SODA 2019). This framework is quite general and it is based on a new combinatorial structure called *private neighborhood trees*: a collection of n trees $T(u_1), \ldots, T(u_n)$ such that each tree $T(u_i)$ spans the neighbors of u_i without going through u_i. Intuitively, each tree $T(u_i)$ allows all neighbors of u_i to exchange a *secret* that is hidden from u_i. The efficiency of the framework depends on two key parameters of these trees: their depth and the amount of overlap. In a (d, c)-private neighborhood trees each tree $T(u_i)$ has depth $O(\mathsf{d})$ and each edge $e \in G$ appears in at most $O(\mathsf{c})$ different trees. An *existentially* optimal construction of private neighborhood trees with $\mathsf{d} = O(\Delta \cdot D)$ and $\mathsf{c} = \widetilde{O}(D)$ was[1] presented therein. We make two key contributions:

Universally Optimal Private Trees: We show a combinatorial construction of nearly (universally) optimal (d, c)-private neighborhood trees with $\mathsf{d} + \mathsf{c} = \widetilde{O}(\mathsf{OPT}(G))$ for any input graph G. Perhaps surprisingly, we show that $\mathsf{OPT}(G)$ is equal to the best depth possible for these trees even without the congestion constraint. We also present efficient distributed constructions of these private trees.

Optimal Secure Computation: Using the optimal constructions above, we get a secure compiler for distributed algorithms where the overhead for each round is $\widetilde{O}(\mathsf{poly}(\Delta) \cdot \mathsf{OPT}(G))$. As our second key contribution, we design an optimal compiler with an overhead of merely $\widetilde{O}(\mathsf{OPT}(G))$ per round for a class of "simple" algorithms. This class includes many standard distributed algorithms such as Luby-MIS, the standard logarithmic-round algorithms for matching and $\Delta + 1$-coloring, as well as the computation of aggregate functions.

[1]Throughout, $\widetilde{O}(\cdot)$ hides poly-logarithmic terms in the number of vertices.

PODC '19, July 29–August 2, 2019, Toronto, ON, Canada

ACM ISBN 978-1-4503-6217-7/19/07...$15.00
https://doi.org/10.1145/3293611.3331620

CCS CONCEPTS

• **Theory of computation** → **Graph algorithms analysis**; *Design and analysis of algorithms*; *Parallel algorithms*; *Distributed algorithms*.

KEYWORDS

distributed algorithms, multi-party computation, private neighborhood trees, secure computation

ACM Reference Format:

Merav Parter and Eylon Yogev. 2019. Secure Distributed Computing Made (Nearly) Optimal. In *2019 ACM Symposium on Principles of Distributed Computing (PODC'19), July 29–August 2, 2019, Toronto, ON, Canada.* ACM, New York, NY, USA, 10 pages. https://doi.org/10.1145/3293611.3331620

1 INTRODUCTION

Motivation and Background. A common principle underlying all distributed graph algorithms (regardless of the model specification) is that the input of the algorithm is given in a *distributed format*, and consequently the goal of each vertex is to compute its *own* part of the output, e.g., whether it is a member of a computed maximal independent set, its incident edges in the minimum spanning tree, or its chosen edge for a maximal matching solution. An inherent property of almost all distributed algorithms is that throughout their execution the nodes get to learn not only their final output but rather gain quite a lot of information on the input or output of (potentially) many other vertices in the network. This leakage of information raises serious concerns in settings where that computation involves private data of the users such as sensitive medical or financial information.

Recently, Parter and Yogev [18] introduced a graph-theoretic framework for secure distributed algorithms in the CONGEST model. Their main result is a secure compiler that can take any (non-secure) *natural*[2] distributed algorithm and transform it into one that is secure. The price of security comes as an overhead in the number of rounds. For an n-vertex graph of diameter D and max-degree Δ if the original (non-secure) algorithm works in r rounds then the secure compiled algorithm works in $r' = \widetilde{O}(r \cdot D \cdot \mathsf{poly}(\Delta))$ rounds. For bounded degree graphs, this overhead is *existentially* optimal as the $\Omega(D)$ factor can be shown to be necessary. The goal of this work is to optimize the price of security by designing *universally* optimal compilers[3] even for graphs with a large maximum degree or diameter. As will be shown later on, this universal optimality approach might yield an improvement of $\Omega(n)$-factor in the round complexity of the secure algorithms on n-vertex graphs. Beyond speeding up computation, those constructions are potentially resilient against much stronger adversaries, e.g., that collide with many users in the graphs, provided that they are sufficiently distant.

[2]By natural we mean distributed algorithms in which the local computation of every vertex is polynomial.

[3]That do the best possible for the input graph G.

Before delving into details, we start by a high-level explanation of our security notion.

What is a Secure Distributed Algorithm? Let $\mathcal{A}$ be a (non-secure) distributed algorithm. Roughly speaking, we say that a distributed algorithm $\mathcal{A}'$ *securely* simulates $\mathcal{A}$ if (1) they have the same output for every node (or the same output distribution if the algorithm is randomized) and (2) each node learns "nothing more" than its final output. This notion of security is known as "perfect privacy" and it provides information-theoretic guarantees on the privacy. This is formalized by the existence of an (unbounded) simulator. See [18] for a more elaborate discussion on the meaning of such a simulator.

The simulation provides security against a *semi-honest* adversary that is trying to learn as much as possible by the execution of the algorithm[4]. The security notion of [18] also does not allow the adversary to collude with other nodes in the network, as we will see later, in this work we can relax this restriction to some extent. Finally, the topology of the graph G is *not* considered private and is not protected by the security notion. Only the private inputs of the nodes and the randomness chosen during the execution are private and not revealed to other entities. The precise details of this definition appear in Definition 1.

How to Exchange Secrets in a Graph? The compiler of [18] is a bit technical and involves tools from the cryptographic world. However, the key challenge is purely graph theoretic, which we describe here. Using cryptographic protocols for secure multiparty computation (MPC), the task of designing an efficient and secure compiler boils down into a clean distributed problem:

> For each node u in the graph, the neighbors of u are required to exchange a random string R_u that is *hidden* from u. This should be done of all nodes u simultaneously.

This secret (shared random bits) in each neighborhood enables the compiler to securely simulate a single round of the original distributed algorithm. Note that all these secrets (inside each neighborhood) must be exchanged simultaneously while respecting the bandwidth limitations of the edges to keep the number of rounds small. A naïve solution where these messages are sent on an arbitrary small depth tree $T(u)$ in $G \setminus \{u\}$ that span the neighbors of u, for every node u, might result in overloading some edges with $\Omega(n)$ messages (i.e., when a given edge appears in many such trees). Hence, it is desirable to have trees $T(u) \subseteq G \setminus \{u\}$ with a minimal amount of overlap possible while still enjoying a small depth. These objectives are captured by *private-neighborhood trees.*

Private Neighborhood Trees. Private neighborhood trees is a combinatorial object that allows the simultaneous private communication within each neighborhood. It consists of n trees $T(u_1), \ldots, T(u_n)$ in the graph G such that each tree $T(u_i)$ spans the neighbors of u_i without going through u_i. In a (d, c)-private neighborhood trees, each tree $T(u_i)$ has depth $O(\mathsf{d})$ and each edge $e \in G$ appears in at most $O(\mathsf{c})$ different trees. The motivation for such a definition is that using the random delay approach [10, 15] it is possible to exchange all the secrets in each neighborhood $\Gamma(u_i)$ in $\widetilde{O}(\mathsf{d} + \mathsf{c} \cdot R)$ rounds, where R is the length of the largest secret. An *existentially* optimal construction of private neighborhood trees was provided in [18] with parameters $\mathsf{d} = \widetilde{O}(\Delta \cdot D)$ and $\mathsf{c} = \widetilde{O}(D)$.

Given a (d, c)-private neighborhood trees in a distributed manner[5], the compiler can securely simulate a single round in $\mathsf{poly}(\Delta)(\mathsf{d}+\mathsf{c})$ rounds. Plugging in $\mathsf{d} = \widetilde{O}(\Delta \cdot D)$ and $\mathsf{c} = \widetilde{O}(D)$ the compiler translates an r-round non-secure algorithm to an equivalent secure algorithm with $r' = \widetilde{O}(r \cdot D \cdot \mathsf{poly}(\Delta))$ rounds. Our goal in this paper is to reduce both the $(\mathsf{d} + \mathsf{c})$ factor and the $\mathsf{poly}(\Delta)$ factor.

Relation to Secure Multiparty Computation. Secure Multiparty Computation (MPC) is an area in cryptography that studies secure protocols. In this setting, there are n entities with private inputs $x_1, \ldots, x_n$ that wish to jointly compute a function $f(x_1, \ldots, x_n) = y$ where each party learns y but "nothing more". There has been tremendous amount of work on MPC protocols, and there are even general results that show how to construct a secure MPC protocol with perfect privacy for any function f [5, 6, 11, 23]. The problem is that these protocols do not quite fit our distributed setting, i.e., the CONGEST model. First, most of the MPC protocols assume that every two nodes in the network have a private channel, i.e., the graph is a clique. Second, and more importantly, they are more concerned with other complexity measures, rather than the locality of the function. The MPC work that do support general graph topologies usually adapt the secure protocol that works in a clique into a protocol that works on any graph. We, on the other hand, take the somewhat dual approach: we start with a non-secure algorithm that computes the function on a *general* graph, and transforms it into a secure one.

Our Contribution

In this paper, we revisit the construction of private trees in [18] for the sake of constructing optimal secure compilers. We seek for the stronger notion of optimality – universal optimality introduced by Garay, Kutten, and Peleg [9] where the proposed algorithm solves the problem optimally on every instance. We then build upon these optimized trees and construct a new optimized compiler that obtains the optimal overhead (up to log-factors) for a large class of *simple* graph algorithms.

Universally Optimal Private Trees. Our first main result is a construction of private neighborhood trees with (nearly) universally optimal bounds. We introduce a new diameter measure of the graph which we call the *private diameter* of the graph. The *private diameter* of u_i denoted by $\mathsf{PrivateDiam}(u_i, G) = \max_{x,y \in \Gamma(u_i)} \mathsf{dist}(x, y, G \setminus \{u_i\})$ is the maximum distance between u_i's neighbors in $G \setminus \{u_i\}$, where $\Gamma(u_i)$ are the neighbors of u_i in G. The private diameter of G is then defined by $\mathsf{PrivateDiam}(G) = \max_{u_i \in V} \mathsf{PrivateDiam}(u_i, G)$.

Letting $\mathsf{OPT_T}(G)$ be the minimum $\mathsf{d}+\mathsf{c}$ over all (d, c) private trees for G. Since the depth of any tree $T(u_i)$ is at least $\mathsf{PrivateDiam}(u_i, G)$, we get that $\mathsf{OPT_T}(G) \geq \mathsf{PrivateDiam}(G)$. Quite surprisingly, our constructions also show that $\mathsf{OPT_T}(G) = \widetilde{O}(\mathsf{PrivateDiam}(G))$ (i.e., the congestion constraint does not increase the cost of the optimal trees). While there are graphs with $\mathsf{PrivateDiam}(G) = \Omega(\Delta \cdot D)$, in many graphs it might be much smaller (even a constant), see Fig. 1 for an example. We prove the following:

[4] This is also known as an honest but curios adversary, that is honest enough to follows the protocol but tries to get as much information out of it on the other nodes in the graph.

[5] where each vertex knows its parent in each of the trees it belongs to.

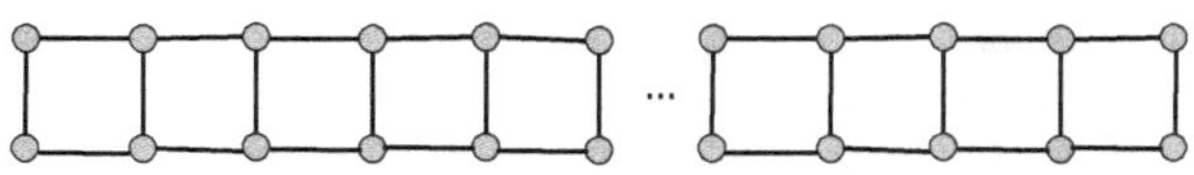

Figure 1: An example where the diameter of the graph is $\Theta(n)$ but the private diameter is $O(1)$.

THEOREM 1. *For every biconnected*[6][7] *graph G, one can compute* (d, c) *private neighborhood trees* $\mathcal{T} = \{T(u_1), \ldots, T(u_n)\}$ *with* $\mathsf{d}, \mathsf{c} = \widetilde{O}(\mathsf{PrivateDiam}(G)) = \widetilde{O}(\mathsf{OPT_T}(G))$. *In addition, each tree* $T(u_i)$ *has depth* $\widetilde{O}(\mathsf{PrivateDiam}(u_i, G))$. *These trees can be computed in* $O(n + \Delta \cdot \mathsf{OPT_T}(G))$ *rounds of pre-processing, where* Δ *is the maximum degree.*

We also have a more efficient distributed construction although with sub-optimal bounds.

THEOREM 2. *For every biconnected n-vertex graph G, one can construct a* (d, c) *private trees collection in r rounds, where* $r, \mathsf{d}, \mathsf{c} = 2^{O(\sqrt{\log n})} \cdot \widetilde{O}(\mathsf{OPT_T})$.

An Optimized Secure Compiler. To use the private trees in the context of the secure compiler, the latter should be constructed once, in a pre-processing step, and can be used for any future application of the secure compiler. Using the instance optimal version of the private neighborhood trees, we get a secure compiler for distributed algorithms where the overhead for each round is $\mathsf{poly}(\Delta, \log n) \cdot \mathsf{OPT_T}(G)$. This is (nearly) universally optimal for bounded degree graphs. Our next goal is to get an optimal compiler even for graphs with large degrees.

Towards this end, we identify a collection of properties and denote a distributed algorithm that satisfies all these properties as "simple". These properties are restrictive enough to allow us to create an efficient version of the secure compiler with minimal overhead on the one hand, and on the other hand, are expressive enough to capture a collection of classical distributed algorithms. Our simple algorithms refer to distributed algorithms in which the local computation performed by a single node can be expressed by a symmetric read-once formula, i.e., a tree. This enables us to match this tree with the private tree used by the compiler. That is, the topology of circuit for the local computation is actually a tree that matches the topology of the graph in a way that lets us distribute the computation of the circuit via the nodes of the graph. Informally, we get the following theorem:

THEOREM 3. *Let G be a n-vertex graph with maximum degree* Δ. *Let* $\mathcal{A}$ *be a "simple" distributed algorithm, that runs on G in r rounds. Then,* $\mathcal{A}$ *can be transformed to an equivalent algorithm* $\mathcal{A}'$ *with perfect privacy which runs in* $\widetilde{O}(r \cdot \mathsf{OPT_T})$ *rounds, using* $\widetilde{O}(n + \mathsf{OPT_T} \cdot \Delta)$ *rounds of pre-processing.*

Implications for Classical Distributed Algorithms. Using our optimized compiler, we can obtain an optimal overhead of $\widetilde{O}(\mathsf{OPT_T})$ for many simple algorithms such as Luby-MIS [16], standard algorithms for maximal matching and 2Δ-coloring [3], and the computation of simple aggregate functions in the network (e.g., MIN, MAX and SUM). For instance, we can now compute the average salaries of all nodes in D-diameter graphs in $\widetilde{O}(D \cdot \mathsf{OPT_T})$ rounds, where nodes learn nothing on the individual salaries except for the final result.

[6] A graph is biconnected if a removal of any *vertex* does not disconnect the graph.
[7] The requirement for the graph to be biconnected has been shown in [18] to be essential.

Remark 1: A Stronger Adversary. Our universally-optimal structures have an additional benefit, beyond the round complexity. They allow to protect against a much stronger adversary, for some graphs. Recall that $\mathsf{PrivateDiam}(G)$ is the private diameter of the graph (which can be considerably smaller than $\mathsf{Diam}(G)$). Then our compiler is resilient against an adversary that takes over potentially many nodes in the graph as long as these nodes are $\widetilde{\Omega}(\mathsf{PrivateDiam}(G))$ distance apart. In [18], the depth of the private trees is $\Omega(\mathsf{Diam}(G))$ and hence an analog statement could not be applicable.

Remark 2: Computationally-Based Solutions. If one assumes computational assumptions such as public-key encryption, then it is possible to design a secure compiler with an overhead of $O(\lambda)$ per round, where λ is the "security parameter" of the encryption scheme. The value of λ might depend on the specific context, but it is usually much larger than $\log n$. In contrast, in this paper as in [18], the security notion is information-theoretic, thus does not depend on any computational assumptions.

Remark 3: Distributed Constructions. The key contribution in this paper is in providing optimal secure compilers given that the graph theoretic infrastructures of private trees have been computed in a pre-processing step. The main algorithm for private trees provided in the main paper naturally extends to the distributed setting given an efficient distributed construction of cycle covers. The latter has been studied in earlier works [19, 20]. For completeness, all the distributed implementations are in the full version.

2 PRELIMINARIES AND MODEL

Graph Notations. For $u, v \in G$, let $\mathrm{dist}(u, v, G)$ be the length (in edges) of the shortest $u - v$ path in G. For every integer $i \geq 1$, let $\Gamma_i(u, G) = \{v : \mathrm{dist}_G(u, v) \leq i\}$. When $i = 1$, we simply write $\Gamma(u, G)$. For a subset of vertices $S_i \subseteq V(G)$, let $G[S_i]$ be the induced subgraph on S_i. For a subgraph G', and vertex pair $u, v \in V(G')$, let $\pi(u, v, G')$ be the unique short-path between u and v in G', breaking ties in a consistent manner.

2.1 Distributed Algorithms

We use the standard CONGEST model [21], where the execution proceeds in synchronous rounds and in each round, each node can send a message of size $O(\log n)$ to each of its neighbors. Each node holds a processor with a unique and arbitrary ID of $O(\log n)$ bits.

A Distributed Algorithm. Consider an n-vertex graph G with maximal degree Δ. We model a distributed algorithm A that works in r rounds as describing r functions $f_1, \ldots, f_r$ as follows. Let u be a node in the graph with input x_u and neighbors $v_1, \ldots, v_\Delta$. At any round i, the memory of a node u consists of a state, denoted by σ_i and Δ messages $m_{v_1 \to u} \ldots, m_{v_\Delta \to u}$ that were received in the previous round.

Initially, we set σ_0 to contain only the input x_u of u and its ID and initialize all messages to $\perp$. At round i the node u updates its state to σ_{i+1} according to its previous state σ_i and the message from the previous round, and prepares Δ messages to send $m_{u\to v_1},\ldots,m_{u\to v_\Delta}$. To ease notation (and without loss of generality) we assume that each state contains the ID of the node u, thus, we can focus on a single update function f_i for every round i that works for all nodes. The function f_i gets the state σ_i and messages $m_{v_1\to u}\ldots,m_{v_\Delta\to u}$, and randomness s_i and outputs the next state and outgoing message:

$$(\sigma_i,m_{u\to v_1},\ldots,m_{u\to v_\Delta})\leftarrow f(\sigma_{i-1},m_{v_1\to u},\ldots,m_{v_\Delta\to u},s_i).$$

At the end of the r rounds, each node u has a state σ_r and a final output of the algorithm. Without loss of generality, we assume that σ_r is the final output of the algorithm (we can always modify f_r accordingly).

For an algorithm $\mathcal{A}$, graph G, input $X=\{x_v\}_{v\in G}$ we denote by $\mathcal{A}_u(G,X)$ the random variable of the output of node u while performing algorithm $\mathcal{A}$ on the graph G with inputs X (recall that $\mathcal{A}$ might be randomized and thus the output is a random variable and not a value). Denote by $\mathcal{A}(G,X)=\{\mathcal{A}_u(G,X)\}_{u\in G}$ the collection of outputs (in some canonical ordering). Let $\mathsf{View}_u^{\mathcal{A}}(G,X)$ be a random variable from the viewpoint of u when running of the algorithm $\mathcal{A}$. This includes messages sent to u, its memory and the random coins used during all rounds of the algorithm.

Secure Distributed Computation. Let $\mathcal{A}$ be a distributed algorithm. Informally, we say that $\mathcal{A}'$ simulates $\mathcal{A}$ in a secure manner if when running the algorithm $\mathcal{A}'$ every node u learns its final output in $\mathcal{A}$ but "nothing more". This notion is captured by the existence of a simulator and is defined below.

Definition 1 (Perfect Privacy). *Let $\mathcal{A}$ be a distributed (possibly randomized) algorithm, that works in r rounds. We say that an algorithm $\mathcal{A}'$ simulates $\mathcal{A}$ with perfect privacy if for every graph G and every $u\in G$, it holds that:*

(1) ***Correctness:*** *For every input $X=\{x_v\}_{v\in V}$: $\mathcal{A}(G,X)\equiv\mathcal{A}'(G,X)$*[8]*.*
(2) ***Perfect Privacy:*** *There exists a randomized algorithm (simulator) Sim such that for every input $X=\{x_v\}_{v\in V}$ it holds that $\mathsf{View}_u^{\mathcal{A}'}(G,X)\equiv\mathsf{Sim}(G,x_u,\mathcal{A}_u(G,X))$.*

2.2 Cryptography with Perfect Privacy

One of the main cryptographic tools we use is a specific protocol for secure multiparty computation that has perfect privacy. Feige, Kilian and Naor [8] suggested a model where two players having inputs x and y wish to compute a function $f(x,y)$ in a secure manner. They achieve this by each sending a single message to a third party that is able to compute the output of the function f from these messages but learn nothing else about the inputs x and y. For the protocol to work, the two parties need to share private randomness that is not known to the third party. This model was later generalized to multi-players and is called the Private Simultaneous Messages Model [12], which we formally describe next.

[8]We use the sign $\equiv$ to take into account the setting where the output of the algorithm is a distribution.

Definition 2 (The PSM model). *Let $f\colon(\{0,1\}^m)^k\to\{0,1\}^m$ be a k variant function. A PSM protocol for f consists of a pair of algorithms $(\mathsf{PSM.Enc},\mathsf{PSM.Dec})$ where $\mathsf{PSM.Enc}\colon\{0,1\}^m\times\{0,1\}^r\to\{0,1\}^t$ and $\mathsf{PSM.Dec}\colon(\{0,1\}^t)^k\to\{0,1\}^m$ such that*

- *For any $X=(x_1,\ldots,x_k)$ it holds that: $\Pr_{R\in\{0,1\}^r}[\mathsf{PSM.Dec}(\mathsf{PSM.Enc}(x_1,R),\ldots,\mathsf{PSM.Enc}(x_k,R))=f(x_1,\ldots,x_k)]=1$.*
- *There exists a randomized algorithm (simulator) Sim such that for $X=x_1,\ldots,x_k$ and for R sampled from $\{0,1\}^r$, it holds that $\{\mathsf{PSM.Enc}(x_i,R)\}_{i\in[k]}\equiv\mathsf{Sim}(f(x_1,\ldots,x_k))$.*

The communication complexity of the PSM protocol is the encoding length t and the randomness complexity of the protocol is defined to be $|R|=r$.

Theorem 4 (Follows from [12]). *For every function $f:(\{0,1\}^m)^k\to\{0,1\}^\ell$ that is computable by an $s=s(m,k)$-space TM there is an efficient perfectly secure PSM protocol whose communication complexity and randomness complexity are $O(km\ell\cdot 2^{2s})$.*

3 UNIVERSALLY OPTIMAL CYCLE COVERS

A key structure underlying the construction of private trees is *low-congestion cycle covers* [19].

Definition 3 (Low-Congestion Cycle Cover). *For a bridgeless*[9] *graph $G=(V,E)$, a (d,c)-cycle cover C of G is a collection of cycles that cover all edges of G such that each cycle $C\in C$ is of length at most $O(\mathsf{d})$ and each edge appears in at most $O(\mathsf{c})$ cycles in C. That is, for every $e\in E$ it holds that $1\le|\{C\in C\mid e\in C\}|\le O(\mathsf{c})$.*

Parter and Yogev [19] showed that every bridgeless graph with diameter D has a (d,c)-cycle cover with $\mathsf{d}=\widetilde{O}(D)$ and $\mathsf{c}=\widetilde{O}(1)$. This is *existentially* optimal (up to $\mathrm{polylog}(n)$ factors) where a matching lower bound example is the cycle graph. Using t-neighborhood covers[10] [2], [19] also showed that this existentially optimal construction can be converted into a universally optimal one. For every edge $e\in E(G)$, let $C(e)$ be the shortest cycle in G that contains e (breaking ties arbitrarily).

Lemma 1. *[19] Given a bridgeless graph $G=(V,E)$, one can compute a cycle cover such that (1) each edge e is covered by a cycle of length $\widetilde{O}(|C_e|)$, and (2) each edge appears on $\widetilde{O}(1)$ cycles.*

From Cycle Covers to Private Trees. In [18], a general algorithm for computing (d,c)-private trees given a $(\mathsf{d}',\mathsf{c}')$ cycle covers was provided.

Lemma 2 (Private Trees via Cycle Covers). *[18] Let G be a biconnected graph with maximum degree Δ. Given a (d,c) cycle cover for G, one can compute a $(\mathsf{d}',\mathsf{c}')$ private trees where $\mathsf{d}'=\Delta\cdot\mathsf{d}$ and $\mathsf{c}'=O(\mathsf{d}\cdot\mathsf{c}\log\Delta)$.*

Proof Sketch: The construction computes low-congestion cycle cover in some auxiliary graph in $O(\log\Delta)$ phases. Initially, each node u holds an empty forest $F_0(u)$ consisting only of u's neighbors. The algorithm is based on a standard forest growing procedure

[9]A graph is bridgeless if a removal of any edge does not disconnect the graph.
[10]The *t-neighborhood cover* [1] of the graph G is a collection of clusters in the graph with small overlap, such that for every vertex there exists a cluster which contains its entire t-neighborhood.

(i.e., Borůvka style). In each phase, the algorithm computes a low-congestion cycle cover on some transformed graph G', such that by adding the cycles that pass through u to the forest, the number of connected components get reduced by roughly a half. Repeating this process for $O(\log \Delta)$ iterations results in one connected component, namely, the output private tree $T(u)$ for the node u.

The Challenges and Limitation of the Approach from [18]. Combining Lemma 2 with Lemma 1 immediately yields a Δ-approximation for private trees: i.e., (d, c) private trees with $\mathsf{d} = O(\Delta \cdot \mathsf{OPT_T})$ and $\mathsf{c} = \widetilde{O}(\mathsf{OPT_T})$. The loss of Δ-factor is unavoidable in the standard forest growing procedure. Specifically, in the forest growing procedure of [18], given the current forest $F_i(u)$ in phase i, the algorithm connects *some* representative vertices from different components in $F_i(u)$ in order to reduce the number of connected components by half. Importantly, this algorithm cannot choose these representatives in a clever way in order to control the growth of the diameter of the output tree, possibly leading to an increase of Δ-factor in the final diameter.

The key contribution of this paper is in providing a machinery that gives us the power for choosing the representatives smartly. Instead of connecting components arbitrarily (as in the standard Borůvka algorithm), our algorithm connects only the *centers* of the components. In each of the $O(\log \Delta)$ phases of the forest growing procedure, the algorithm is required to solve the following task: given n subsets of neighbors $R(u) \subseteq \Gamma(u)$ for each vertex u (corresponding to the centers of the components), the goal is to match the nodes in each $R(u)$ into pairs and to connect them by paths which are (1) private - do not go through their common neighbor u, (2) short and (3) of small overlap. This problem is formalized as the *private routing problem*, which can be observed as an extension of the classic routing disjoint matching problem from [21] to the secure setting, and might be of independent interest.

4 NEARLY OPTIMAL PRIVATE NEIGHBORHOOD TREES

For a biconnected graph $G = (V = \{u_1, \ldots, u_n\}, E)$, a (d, c)-private tree collection is a collection of trees denoted by $\mathcal{T} = \{T(u_1), \ldots, T(u_n)\}$, where for every $i \in \{1, \ldots n\}$ we have: (i) $\Gamma(u_i, G) \subseteq T(u_i)$ and $u_i \notin T(u_i)$, (ii) $\mathsf{Depth}(T(u_i)) = O(\mathsf{d})$, and (iii) every edge $e \in E(G)$ appears in $O(\mathsf{c})$ trees.

Recall that the private diameter of a vertex $u \in G$, denoted by $\mathsf{PrivateDiam}(u, G)$, is the maximum distance between u's neighbor in $G \setminus \{u\}$. Moreover, $\mathsf{PrivateDiam}(G)$ is the maximum private diameter over all vertices in the graph. Clearly, in every set of private trees $\mathcal{T} = \{T(u_i), u_i \in V\}$, $\mathsf{Depth}(T(u_i)) \geq \mathsf{PrivateDiam}(u_i, G)$, and thus any set of (d, c) private trees must satisfy that $\mathsf{d} \geq \mathsf{PrivateDiam}(G)$. Perhaps surprisingly, we will show in this section that $\mathsf{OPT_T}(G) = \widetilde{O}(\mathsf{PrivateDiam}(G))$. While there are graphs for which the private diameter is $\Omega(\Delta \cdot D)$, in many graphs it might be much smaller (e.g., Fig. 1).

The main contribution of this section is showing the existence (and the efficient construction) of (d, c) private trees $\mathcal{T}$ with $\mathsf{d} + \mathsf{c} = \widetilde{O}(\mathsf{PrivateDiam}(G))$. Note that the depth of the trees $\widetilde{O}(\mathsf{PrivateDiam}(G))$ is the best possible even without the congestion constraint. We, therefore, interchange $\mathsf{PrivateDiam}(G)$ and $\mathsf{OPT_T}(G)$ (when we can ignore the $O(\log n)$ factor). Furthermore, the trees can be nearly optimal with respect to each node u_i where $\mathsf{Depth}(T(u_i)) = \widetilde{O}(\mathsf{PrivateDiam}(u_i, G))$. The algorithm will be based on the following slight modification of the optimal cycle cover algorithm of [19], see the full version for the proof.

Recall that for an edge e, C_e is the shortest cycle in G that contains e. For a subset of edges E', define $\mathsf{OPT}(E', G) = \max_{e \in E'} |C_e|$.

THEOREM 5. *There is an algorithm* OptimalSubsetCover, *that for any n-vertex graph $G = (V, E)$ and additional edge set E' (that is disjoint from E, and on the vertex set V) computes a collection of cycle C in the graph $G' = (V, E \cup E')$ such that: (1) each edge $e' \in E'$ is covered by exactly one cycle[11]; (2) each $e \in E$ participates in at most $\widetilde{O}(1)$ cycles. (3) each cycle $C \in C$ is of length at most $\widetilde{O}(\mathsf{OPT}(E', G))$; and (4) each cycle $C \in C$ is used to cover at most $O(\log n)$ edges of E', i.e., $|C \cap E'| = O(\log n)$.*

Alg. OptimalSubsetCover can be made a distributed algorithm following [19, 20], as explained in the full version.

4.1 Private Routing with Low-Congestion

In the *Private Routing* Problem, one is given a collection of subsets of neighbors $R(u_1), \ldots, R(u_n)$ where $R(u_i) \subseteq \Gamma(u_i)$ for every i. For simplicity, we assume that each $|R(u_i)|$ is even. The goal is to compute a matching $\mathsf{m}^*_{u_i} : R(u_i) \rightarrow R(u_i)$ between pairs in each $R(u_i)$ along with a path P_{x,y,u_i} connecting each matched pair $x, y \in R(u_i)$. Let $\mathcal{P}$ be the collection of the computed P_{x,y,u_i} paths (i.e., for all $R(u_1), \ldots, R(u_n)$). This path collection should satisfy:

(PR1) [Privacy] $P_{x,y,u_i} \subseteq G \setminus \{u_i\}$ for every $P_{x,y,u_i} \in \mathcal{P}$.

(PR2) [Dilation] $|P_{x,y,u_i}| = \widetilde{O}(\mathsf{OPT_T})$ for every[12] $P_{x,y,u_i} \in \mathcal{P}$.

(PR3) [Congestion] Every edge $e \in G$ appears on at most $\widetilde{O}(\mathsf{OPT_T})$ paths of $\mathcal{P}$.

Recall that $\mathsf{OPT_T} = \widetilde{O}(\mathsf{PrivateDiam}(G))$ and hence for every u, and every $x, y \in \Gamma(u)$, there is an x-y path in $G \setminus \{u\}$ of length $\widetilde{O}(\mathsf{OPT_T})$. In other words, the goal is to match (a given subset) of 2-hop neighbors $x, y \in \Gamma(u)$ for every u, and to connect the matched pairs by short *private* paths, i.e., that do not go through their common neighbor u. Since it is desirable to send information on all these paths simultaneously, we require in addition that each edge appears on a small number of paths (i.e., that the paths will be almost edge disjoint). A high-level description of Algorithm PrivateRouting is given next. The complete distributed implementation is in the full version of the paper.

High-Level Description of Algorithm PrivateRouting. The starting point for computing the low congestion private paths is a careful choice of the matching. Observe that without this freedom, it might be impossible to compute such paths that satisfy all the desired requirements. The key challenge is in finding the "right" matching. Our algorithm takes the following strategy: *"Pick an arbitrary matching, and fix it later".* Indeed, the algorithm first matches the vertices in each set $R(u)$ into pairs arbitrarily, and then based on the computed paths, might reorganize the matching. The surprising property of the algorithm is that in case that it fails to find good

[11] Note that C should not cover all edges in G, only the external edges E'.

[12] We observe that it is possible adapt the construction to get that $|P_{x,y,u_i}| = O(\log n \cdot \mathsf{dist}(x, y, G \setminus \{u_i\}))$ at the cost of increasing the congestion by a factor of $O(\log n)$.

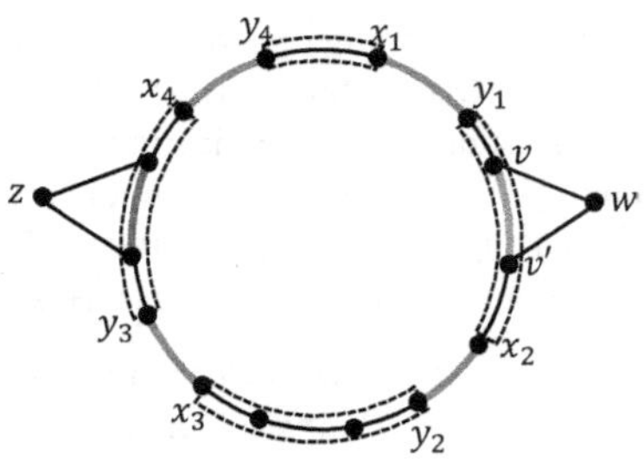

Figure 2: Illustration of a cycle C generated by PrivateRouting. Red edges correspond to type-u edges, green edges correspond to type-w edges and blue edge to a type-z edge. The dashed black boxes represent the cycle segments between the newly matched pairs of the type-u edges.

paths for the given matching, the certificate for this failure gives us a hint about the right matching. The originally matched pairs are represented as virtual edges added to the graph. We call a virtual edge between a matched pair $x, y \in R(u)$, a type-u virtual edge. The next step is to connect the matched pairs x, y by short paths while avoiding their common neighbor u.

Sampling Subgraphs. The first naïve approach to connect the endpoints of the virtual edges is by applying a cycle cover algorithm to cover these edges. Clearly, this approach might fail miserably as the cycle cover algorithm might cover all virtual edges (x, y) for $x, y \in R(u)$ but taking the edges (x, u) and (u, y), which violates property (PR1).

The key idea is to compute a small number of sampled subgraphs, such that each subgraph contains only a sub-sample of the vertices in G, and to apply a cycle cover algorithm in each of these subgraphs. The set of sampled subgraphs should satisfy that for each $x, y \in R(u)$, there will be some subgraph G_i that does not contain u but includes at least one short x-y path. We will then obtain the desired private x-y path by computing a cycle cover in G_i.

Specifically, the algorithm employs a sampling procedure (borrowed from fault tolerant design [7, 22]) that consists of several iterations or *experiments*. In each experiment j, it samples a subset of vertices V_j by adding each vertex $v \in V$ into V_j independently with probability $(1 - 1/\mathsf{OPT_T})$, letting $G_j = G[V_j]$. Overall, we will have $\widetilde{O}(\mathsf{OPT_T})$ experiments. Since $\text{dist}(x, y, G \setminus \{u\}) \leq \mathsf{PrivateDiam}(G) = \widetilde{O}(\mathsf{OPT_T})$, w.h.p, we guarantee that for each virtual type-u edge $e' = (x, y)$, there is a subgraph G_j such that: (i) the entire shortest x-y path in $G \setminus \{u\}$ is in G_j, and (ii) the forbidden vertex u is not in V_j. When both events (i) and (ii) hold for a virtual edge e' in the graph G_j, we say that e' is *successful* in the jth experiment. Zooming into the jth experiment, let $\widetilde{E}_j$ be the virtual edges that are successful at that experiment. Next, the virtual edges $\widetilde{E}_j$ are covered by cycles by employing Alg. OptimalSubsetCover (from the cycle cover variant of Theorem 5) on G_j, taking E' to be $\widetilde{E}_j$, and $\mathsf{OPT}' = \mathsf{OPT_T}$. The output is a cycle cover C_j for the edges $\widetilde{E}_j$.

New Matching via Cycle Cover. Ideally, we would like to connect each matched pair $(x, y) \in \widetilde{E}_j$ for $x, y \in R(u)$ via the cycle segment of $C \in C_j$ that covers that virtual edge (x, y). However, since C is computed in $G_j \cup \widetilde{E}_j$, it might contain other virtual edges. The main concern is when the cycle segment between x and y contains other virtual edges of type u, see Fig. 2. This is a problem as replacing these virtual edges with their corresponding 2-length paths in G introduces u into the x-y path which defeats the all purpose of the computation. We now use our freedom to re-match the pairs in each $R(u)$ according to the structure of the cycle C. For each cycle $C \in C_j$, consider the set U of vertices u with some type-u virtual edge on C. For every $u \in U$, we consider all the type-u edges on C and re-match the endpoints of these edges, in a way that the cycle segments between the newly matched pairs are free of any other type-u edges. The cycle segments between the newly matched pairs might still contain type-w edges for some other $w \neq u \in U$. This is easy to take care of, as all type-w edges (x', y') can be safely replaced by their 2-length path $x' - w - y'$ in G (safe in the sense that the resulting path does not go through u). As a result, the cycle segment between a newly matched pair in $R(u)$ is translated into a path in G that is (i) short (as replacing the virtual edges increases the length by factor 2), (ii) avoids the forbidden vertex u, and (iii) has small-overlap due to the properties of the cycle cover of Theorem 5. See Figure 3 in for pseudocode of the algorithm. The analysis appears in the full version of the paper.

Description of Algorithm PrivateRouting

Input: Sets $R(u) \subseteq \Gamma(u)$ for every $u \in G$.
Output:
(i) Matching $\mathsf{m}_u^* : R(u) \longrightarrow R(u)$.
(ii) Path collection $\mathcal{P}$ which connects each matched pair and satisfies (PR1-PR3).

Run:

(1) Compute an arbitrary matching $\mathsf{m}_u : R(u) \longrightarrow R(u)$.
(2) Connect each matched pair $(x, \mathsf{m}_u(x))$ in $R(u)$ by a virtual edge (of type-u).
(3) For $j = 1$ to $\ell = c \cdot \log n \cdot \mathsf{OPT_T}$ do:
  (a) Sample each vertex $v \in V$ to V_j with probability
  $$1 - 1/(\mathsf{OPT_T} + 1).$$
  (b) Let $G_j = G[V_j]$ and $\widetilde{E}_j$ be the set of successful virtual edges.
  (c) $C_j \leftarrow \mathsf{OptimalSubsetCover}(G_j, \widetilde{E}_j)$.
  (d) For every $C \in C_j$ do:
    (i) Re-match the type-u endpoints on C for every u.
    (ii) Translate the cycle segments between matched pairs to simple G-paths.
    (iii) Add these paths to $\mathcal{P}$ and omit matched pairs from $R(u)$ for every u.

Figure 3: The description of Algorithm PrivateRouting.

Challenges for the Distributed Implementation. The main challenge is in performing the $\widetilde{O}(\mathsf{OPT_T})$ experiments simultaneously[13]. Towards this goal, the procedure employed on each independent experiment should not only be *round* efficient, but also efficient with respect to the total number of *messages* passed through each

[13]That is, without increasing the runtime by a factor of $\widetilde{O}(\mathsf{OPT_T})$.

particular edge. In the full version, we show that each such experiment can run in $r(\mathsf{OPT_T})$ rounds while passing only $\widetilde{O}(1)$ messages on each edge, where $r(\cdot)$ is the round complexity of computing $(\widetilde{O}(\mathsf{OPT_C}), \widetilde{O}(1))$ cycle covers. Hence, using the random delay approach, the collection of $\widetilde{O}(\mathsf{OPT_T})$ experiments can be simulated simultaneously within $\widetilde{O}(r \cdot \mathsf{OPT_T})$ rounds.

4.2 Constructing Private Trees with Nearly Optimal Bounds

We first note that combining the optimal construction of cycle covers from [19] with the private tree construction of [18] results in a (d, c)-private trees with $\mathsf{d} = \widetilde{O}(\mathsf{OPT_T} \cdot \Delta)$ and $\mathsf{c} = \widetilde{O}(\mathsf{OPT_T})$. Hence, structures that are optimal up to a dependency in Δ. The goal of this section is to eliminate this dependency in Δ, and obtain a nearly optimal bound of $\mathsf{d} = \widetilde{O}(\mathsf{OPT_T})$. Algorithm ApproxPrivateTrees consists of $\ell = O(\log \Delta)$ phases. The trees are computed in à la Borůvka's style [17] with key modifications to control the depth of the output trees. Initially, the algorithm considers the trivial empty forest $\mathcal{F}_0(u)$ for every $u \in V$, containing the neighbors of u, each in an isolated component. In each phase, every component is identified with a rooted tree that span the vertices in the component, the root of this tree is called the *center* of the component. In each phase i, the number of connected components in the forest $\mathcal{F}_i(u)$ for every u, will be reduced by a factor of 2, and the depth of each component will get increased by an additive term of $\widetilde{O}(\mathsf{OPT_T})$. To control the depth of the output tree, our algorithm connects only the centers of the components. (In the standard Borůvka algorithm, the components are connected via arbitrarily chosen representative.) Connecting the centers is done by employing Algorithm PrivateRouting, and adding the output low-congestion paths between centers to the forests. Indeed, the main contribution of Algorithm PrivateRouting is that it allows us to decide which vertices should be connected in each component, and that freedom allows us to enjoy an improved depth bound.

Specifically, in each phase $i \geq 1$, we are given a forest collection $\mathcal{F}_{i-1} = \{F_{i-1}(u_1), \ldots, F_{i-1}(u_n)\}$. Each forest consists of a collection of rooted trees $F_{i-1}(u_j) = \{T_{i-1,1}(u_j), \ldots, T_{i-1,k}(u_j)\}$. Consider node u_j and let $r_1, \ldots, r_k$ be roots of the trees in $F_{i-1}(u_j)$. All these roots are neighbors of u_j are denoted as centers. For every u_j, let $R(u_j) = \{r_1, \ldots, r_k\}$ be the set of centers of the components in the forest $F_{i-1}(u_j)$. For ease of description assume that all the $R(u_j)$ sets have an even size. To reduce the number of connected components in $F_{i-1}(u_j)$, the algorithm uses Alg. PrivateRouting to compute low-congestion short paths between pairs of centers in $R(u_j)$. The output of the algorithm is a matching $\mathsf{m}^*_{u_j} : R(u_j) \to R(u_j)$ for the vertices in $R(u_j)$ for every $u_j \in V$ and a set of corresponding paths $\mathcal{P}$. The paths between matched pairs in $R(u_j)$ are then added to the forest $F_i(u_j)$. As a result, the two components C_x, C_y of each matched pair $r_x, r_y \in R(u_j)$ are merged into one component $C_{k'}$ in $F_i(u_j)$. The center of each newly merged component is the vertex of higher ID among the two centers $r_x, r_y \in R(u_j)$. After $O(\log \Delta)$ phases, each forest contains a single rooted tree of depth $\widetilde{O}(\mathsf{OPT_T})$, this is the output private neighborhood trees $\mathcal{T}$. In the distribute implementation, at the end of the algorithm, each vertex learns its parent in each of the private trees it participates in (see full version for details).

5 A SECURE COMPILER FOR SIMPLE ALGORITHMS

We give a high-level overview of our secure compiler for "simple" distributed algorithms, where the definition of simple is explained next. The overhead of the compiler is a factor of $\widetilde{O}(\mathsf{OPT_T})$ per round. The compiler is an improved version of the secure compiler presented in [18]. Specifically, the compiler of [18] works by securely computing the local function gate-by-gate while incurring an overhead of the number of gates in the round complexity. In our case, we avoid this overhead by computing the gates of the circuit *layer-by-layer*. In general, this might not lead to any improvement in the round complexity, as computing a single layer might already be too costly. The key observation is that for a sufficiently "simple" circuit, one can compute a single layer in *parallel* in an efficient manner, as described next.

Simple Algorithms. A distributed algorithm $\mathcal{A}$ is called *simple* if it satisfies the following: (1) broadcast: in each round a node sends the same message to all neighbors, (2) small state: each node has a local state of polylog(n) bits, and (3) simple local computation: the local computation function performed by each node can be expressed as a *balanced symmetric read-once formula.*

DEFINITION 4 (BALANCED SYMMETRIC READ-ONCE FORMULA). *A k variate formula over a field $\mathbb{F}$ with a set $\mathcal{B}$ of gates is a binary tree whose leaves are labeled with input variables $x_1, \ldots, x_k$ or field elements and whose internal nodes (gates) are labeled with the operations in $\mathcal{B}$. If each variable is labeled at most once, then we say that the formula is* read-once. *It is symmetric if the function is oblivious to the ordering of the inputs. It is also* balanced *if the tree has depth at most $O(\log k)$.*

The local computation function f of a distributed algorithm refers to the algorithm that each node runs in each round in order to update its local state according to the messages received. That is, $\sigma_u^{i+1} = f_{\sigma_u^i}(m_1, \ldots, m_\Delta)$ where σ_u^i is the local state of node u at round i, and $m_1, \ldots, m_\Delta$ are the messages that u received at that round.

While in general, such a formula is a relatively weak model of computation, in our setting we allow the gates to be quite powerful. The reason is that in our case the variables of the formula are allowed to be over a finite field $\mathbb{F}$ where $\log |\mathbb{F}| = \text{polylog}(n)$, and the gates of the formula can be any (2-variate) function that is computable in logarithmic space. Moreover, we let the state of the node be hardwired in the gate. This makes the class of simple algorithms powerful enough to capture many of the existing distributed algorithms. We next show how these properties of simple algorithms can be leveraged to yield an optimal compiler.

Secure Simulation of a Single Round. We start by a explaining how to securely compile a single round of the non-secure (simple) algorithm. This already captures the main technical challenges and the modifications of our compiler in comparison to that of [18]. The full details of the compiler are given in the full version of the paper.

The compiler is based on a cryptographic primitive called a PSM protocol (see Definition 2), which is a protocol that enables a node u to securely compute a function f of its neighbors as long as the neighbors hold a private random string (i.e., the node u does not know the string). The neighbors exchange this random string via the private neighborhood trees, which has an (almost) optimal diameter and congestion. Thus, the only other complexity left to optimize is the size of the messages sent in the PSM protocol. By Theorem 4, the communication complexity of the protocol is exponential in the space required to compute f, and linear in the input size and output size of f. Thus, in order to efficiently and securely compute f, the protocol of [18] computes the function gate-by-gate, such that the space needed to compute a single gate is negligible. This results in a blowup of a factor of $s = |f|$ (the number of gates in the circuit that computes f) in the number of rounds of the compiler.

We want to avoid this overhead of s in our the compiler, by taking advantage of the properties of simple algorithms. Recall that the communication of the PSM depends on the output length and input length of f. Since we assumed that the state is small we have that the input length is small. Moreover, since we assumed that the algorithm is broadcast, the output of the function (which in general might include Δ messages) is only the new state of u. Thus, the communication complexity (and randomness complexity) of the protocol is bounded by $O(\log n)$ (which is negligible in our context). Finally, instead of computing f gate-by-gate we use the formula of f to compute each gate in each level in *parallel.* Since the formula is balanced it has only $O(\log \Delta)$ levels.

Suppose we have a simple one-round algorithm $\mathcal{A}$, and let f be its local function. That is, f gets as input Δ messages, $m_1, \ldots, m_\Delta$ from the neighbors of a node u, and outputs the final output y for the node u. The function f has hardwired the initial state of u, which contains its ID, any randomness required for the computation (i.e., a random coloring in a coloring algorithm) and possibly some initial input.

To efficiently compute all gates of one level i in parallel (and in a secure manner), we need to map the incoming gates of level i into neighbors of u such that the secure communication of all level i gates will be done along a collection of edge-disjoint paths. W.l.o.g. we assume that the incoming degree of each gate in the formula tree is 2. Let T_u be the private-tree of u. Focus on level i and let $g_1, \ldots, g_k$ be the gates on this level. For each g_j, let $g_{j,1}, g_{j,2}$ be the incoming gates of g_j. We then map each of the level $(i-1)$ gates $g_{1,1}, g_{1,2}, \ldots, g_{k,1}, g_{k,2}$ to a distinct neighbor of u. I.e., we define a function $L_i\colon \{g_{1,1}, g_{1,2}, \ldots, g_{k,1}, g_{k,2}\} \to \Gamma(u)$. To compute this mapping we use the TreeEdgeDisjointPath algorithm describe next.

Algorithm TreeEdgeDisjointPath solves the following problem ([13], and Lemma 4.3.2 [21]): given a rooted tree T and a set of $2k$ marked nodes $M \subseteq V(T)$ for $k \leq n/2$, the goal is to find (by a distributed algorithm) a matching of these vertices $\langle w_i, w_j \rangle$ into pairs such that the tree paths $\pi(w_i, w_j, T)$ connecting the matched pairs are *edge-disjoint.*

The mapping satisfies that the private-tree paths $\pi_j = \pi(L(g_{j,1}), L(g_{j,2}), T_u)$ for every $j \in \{1, \ldots, k\}$ are *edge-disjoint.* This allows u's neighbors $L(g_{j,1})$ and $L(g_{j,2})$ that are mapped to inputs $g_{j,1}$ and $g_{j,2}$ of each gate g_j to exchange a secret on a short path, that does not contain u. As all these paths $\pi_1, \ldots, \pi_k$ are edge disjoint, this can be done indeed in parallel for all gates in level i. Once all these pairs of neighbors $L(g_{j,1})$ and $L(g_{j,2})$ are equipped with the shared private randomness, we can apply the PSM protocol on the edges $(u, L(g_{j,1}))$ and $(u, L(g_{j,1}))$. Again, all these PSM's can be done in parallel as they send information along disjoint set edges. Overall, exchanging the secret of $O(\log n)$ bits along the edge-disjoint π_j paths takes $\widetilde{O}(\mathsf{OPT_T})$ rounds for a single node u (as the depth of T_u is $\widetilde{O}(\mathsf{OPT_T})$). In addition, recall that each edge $e \in T_u$ appears on $\widetilde{O}(\mathsf{OPT_T})$ other trees T_v. Therefore using the random delay approach, one can exchange the secrets for the PSMs of the i-level gates for all the vertices in parallel within $\widetilde{O}(\mathsf{OPT_T})$ rounds. An illustration of the first iteration of the labeling algorithm is given in Figure 5. The precise algorithm is given in Figure 4.

The algorithm FormulaLabeling(f, T_u, u)

1. Let $v_1, \ldots, v_\Delta$ be the neighbors of u by increasing order of IDs.
2. Mark all the neighbors of u.
3. For $i = 1, \ldots, \mathsf{Depth}(T_u)$ do:
   (a) Run TreeEdgeDisjointPath algorithm on the private tree T_u with the marked nodes to get a matching $m_i(v) = v'$ of the nodes with disjoint paths $P_i(v, v') = \pi(v, v', T_u)$.
   (b) Each neighbor v sends its matched node v' to u.
   (c) For each matched pair $(v, m_i(v))$, **unmark** the node with the larger ID.
4. The label function L_i is defined as follows:
   (a) The root gate is assigned the label v_1.
   (b) A gate at level i with label v label its left child with v and its right child with $m_i(v)$ and assigns both the corresponding path $P_i(v, m_i(v))$.

Figure 4: Algorithm for labeling the gates of a formula f with nodes of $\Gamma(u)$ based in the private tree T_u.

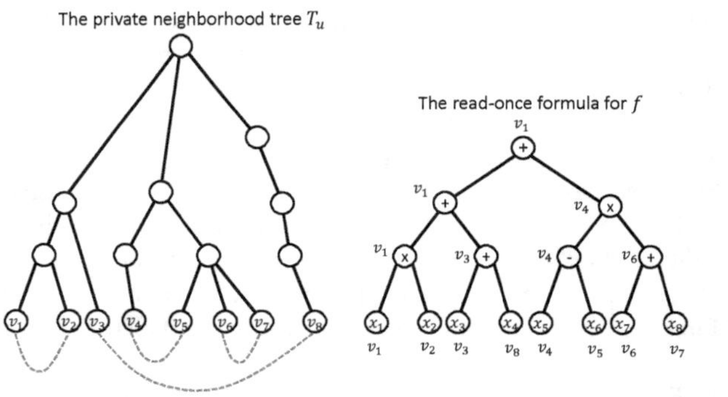

Figure 5: An example of an execution of the FormulaLabeling **algorithm. On the right side, is the formula for f on variables $x_1, \ldots, x_8$. Next to each gate g in level i of the formula shown in the labeled vertex $L_i(g)$ that the algorithm has assigned. On the left side shown is the private neighborhood tree T_u of a node u with neighbors $v_1, \ldots, v_8$. The red lines are the matched neighbors in the first iteration.**

This approach still has an issue to be handled. We cannot simply compute g_w as the output solution would reveal partial computation which might hold more information than the final output of the formula. This is the same issue that arises when compiling a distributed algorithm with many rounds: the intermediate states of the nodes might reveal more information than the final output. The compiler of [18] already handles this by augmenting the local function to work on "encrypted data" (this is known as a "one-time-pad" encryption) and homomorphically computing the function under the encryption. In the end, only the key for the last state is revealed so that nodes learn their final state which consists only of the final output. We use the same techniques and thus do not elaborate in this high-level overview. The full details are given in the full version of the paper.

5.1 Which Algorithms are Simple?

We have seen that the definition of a simple algorithm is restrictive enough to allow the design of very efficient secure compilers. We now show that the family of simple algorithms is expressive enough to capture many of the known distributed algorithms.

Recall that simple algorithms are broadcast algorithms with small local states and have simple local computation functions (balanced symmetric read-once formula). Thus, some of the standard algorithms such as Luby-MIS, Matching, the standard algorithm for 2Δ-Coloring and computing aggregate functions fall directly under the definition of a simple algorithm.

A more challenging example is that of the $\Delta + 1$ coloring algorithm by [4]. This algorithm has $O(\log n)$ rounds, where in each round the node u with constant probability $1/2$ stays the same and with probability $1/2$ picks a color uniformly at random from a list of all the available colors, i.e., colors not yet assigned to its colored neighbors. While this algorithm is broadcast (a node sends only its color), and has a small state, it is less immediate to verify if its local computation function can be expressed as a read-once formula. The main task in this function (besides other small computations) is to choose a random color from the domain of available colors (i.e., colors that are not chosen by any neighbor that already fixed its color). We show how to slightly modify the (non-secure) $\Delta + 1$ coloring algorithm such that it is expressible by a read-once formula and thus can be captured by our compiler.

Modification of the $\Delta+1$ algorithm by [4]. The new algorithm will simulate a single round of the [4] using $\log \Delta$ rounds. These rounds will have no communication, their entire purpose is to split the local computations into small steps, where each step can be expressed as a read-once formula such that the final algorithm is simple. The new algorithm will have a $\log \Delta$ overhead in the number of rounds which is negligible in our context.

Let the colors be $1, \ldots, \Delta + 1$ and assume for simplicity of this presentation that neighbors have all different colors and that $\Delta + 1$ is a power of 2 (this captures the main ideas).

In the first round, we split the colors into two equal parts by lexicographic order $1, \ldots, (\Delta + 1)/2$ and $(\Delta + 1)/2 + 1, \ldots, \Delta + 1$. Then, we write a read-once formula that counts how many available colors are in the first half, denoted by x_1, and how many in the second half, denoted x_2. Each gate in the formula will simply check if the input color is in the first half or not and we sum up these values. Then, we choose to go to the first half with probability $p = x_1/(x_1 + x_2)$, and to the second half with probability $1 - p$. We continue this recursively until we have sampled an available color. We note that of $\Delta + 1$ is not a power of two then one can simply divide to two parts that are not equal, and adjust the probabilities accordingly.

We observe that in this method we choose a uniform available color. Moreover, the local function for a single round of this modified algorithm is a balanced symmetric read-once formula. Thus the modified algorithm is indeed simple.

The general case (where not all colors are different) requires more care, and in particular the algorithm will not choose a uniform color from the set of available colors, but the distribution will be random enough for the analysis to work. Since not all colors are different, we cannot count the number of available colors in a particular part. Instead, we can only count the number of neighbors with a color in this part. Note that difference between the size of the part and the number of neighbors with a color within it is not the number of available colors since several neighbors might choose the same color. However, we still run the same algorithm that computes the probabilities by the difference – as if all the colors are distinct. The precise algorithm is given in Figure 6.

Description of modified Algorithm for $\Delta + 1$-coloring
Input: a (number of active neighbors), b (number of non-active neighbors)
Algorithm:

(1) Set $i = 0, j = \Delta + 1$.
(2) For $k = 1 \ldots \log(\Delta + 1)$ do:
  (a) If $i = j$ then output i.
  (b) Let $t = (i + j)/2$ and let $\ell = t - i + 1$ (i.e., the length of the segments $[i, t]$ and $[t, j]$).
  (c) Let x be the number of non-active neighbors with color $c \in [i, t]$, and let $x' = \max\{\ell - x, 0\}$.
  (d) Let y be the number of non-active neighbors with color $c \in [t + 1, j]$, and let $y' = \max\{\ell - y, 0\}$.
  (e) With probability $p = \frac{x'}{x'+y'}$ set $j = t$, and with probability $(1 - p)$ set $i = t$.

Figure 6: The description of Algorithm PrivateRouting.

Fix some available color c, and recall that a is the number of active neighbors, and b is the number of non-active neighbors. We observe that for the analysis in [4] to work it suffices to show that the probability of choosing c is at most $1/(a + 1)$.

To choose the color c, the algorithm needs to choose the range containing c in each iteration. Each time, this happens with some probability p_i where p_i depends only on i, j, x, y in the current iteration. That is, it depends on how many non-active neighbors have a fixed color in the range $[i, t]$ and $[t, j]$ and does *not* depend on how they are spread out within the range. Thus, in each iteration, we apply a sequence of changes to the colors of the non-active neighbors such that at the end all the colors are different and each change might only decrease the value of the p_i's.

Suppose, w.l.o.g., that $c \in [i, t]$. If $y \geq \ell$ (there are more non-active neighbors then possible colors), then we can simply ignore some of the neighbors such that $y = \ell$, since in both cases the probability of choosing the range $[j, t]$ is zero. On the other hand, if $x \geq \ell$ then we have that the probability of choosing $[i, t]$ is zero, and thus the probability of choosing the color c is zero, and we are done (since we only need to show that the probability is smaller than $1/(a+1)$). Thus, we have $x, y < \ell$.

Now, we can change the colors of the non-active neighbors in $[t, j]$ such that they are all distinct and within the range $[t, j]$, since this will not change the probability p_i. This continues, for all iterations until all colors are distinct (or we have stopped since the probability is zero). In the end, we have that the distribution is uniform over the number of available colors which is at least $a + 1$ (it might be larger if we have ignored some of the neighbors). Thus, the probability of choosing c is at most $1/(a+1)$.

The modifications we performed to the $\Delta + 1$-coloring serve mainly as an example for the potential expressive power of simple algorithms. We believe that this class of simple algorithm is quite wide, and captures many other classical algorithms.

ACKNOWLEDGMENTS

Merav Parter is supported in part by grants from the Israel Science Foundation (no. 2084/18) and Minerva No. 713238. Eylon Yogev is supported by the European Union's Horizon 2020 research and innovation program under grant agreement No. 742754.

REFERENCES

[1] Baruch Awerbuch, Bonnie Berger, Lenore Cowen, and David Peleg. 1996. Fast distributed network decompositions and covers. *J. Parallel and Distrib. Comput.* 39, 2 (1996), 105–114.

[2] Baruch Awerbuch, Bonnie Berger, Lenore Cowen, and David Peleg. 1998. Near-linear time construction of sparse neighborhood covers. *SIAM J. Comput.* 28, 1 (1998), 263–277.

[3] Leonid Barenboim and Michael Elkin. 2013. Distributed graph coloring: Fundamentals and recent developments. *Synthesis Lectures on Distributed Computing Theory* 4, 1 (2013), 1–171.

[4] Leonid Barenboim and Michael Elkin. 2013. *Distributed Graph Coloring: Fundamentals and Recent Developments.* Morgan & Claypool Publishers. https://doi.org/10.2200/S00520ED1V01Y201307DCT011

[5] Michael Ben-Or, Shafi Goldwasser, and Avi Wigderson. 1988. Completeness Theorems for Non-Cryptographic Fault-Tolerant Distributed Computation (Extended Abstract). In *Proceedings of the 20th Annual ACM Symposium on Theory of Computing, May 2-4, 1988, Chicago, Illinois, USA.* 1–10.

[6] David Chaum, Claude Crépeau, and Ivan Damgård. 1988. Multiparty Unconditionally Secure Protocols (Extended Abstract). In *Proceedings of the 20th Annual ACM Symposium on Theory of Computing, May 2-4, 1988, Chicago, Illinois, USA.* 11–19.

[7] Michael Dinitz and Robert Krauthgamer. 2011. Fault-tolerant spanners: better and simpler. In *Proceedings of the 30th annual ACM SIGACT-SIGOPS symposium on Principles of distributed computing.* ACM, 169–178.

[8] Uriel Feige, Joe Kilian, and Moni Naor. 1994. A minimal model for secure computation (extended abstract). In *STOC.*

[9] Juan A Garay, Shay Kutten, and David Peleg. 1998. A sublinear time distributed algorithm for minimum-weight spanning trees. *SIAM J. Comput.* 27, 1 (1998), 302–316. https://doi.org/10.1137/S0097539794261118

[10] Mohsen Ghaffari. 2015. Near-Optimal Scheduling of Distributed Algorithms. In *Proceedings of the 2015 ACM Symposium on Principles of Distributed Computing, PODC.* 3–12.

[11] Oded Goldreich, Silvio Micali, and Avi Wigderson. 1987. How to Play any Mental Game or A Completeness Theorem for Protocols with Honest Majority. In *Proceedings of the 19th Annual ACM Symposium on Theory of Computing, 1987, New York, New York, USA.* 218–229.

[12] Yuval Ishai and Eyal Kushilevitz. 1997. Private Simultaneous Messages Protocols with Applications. In *Fifth Israel Symposium on Theory of Computing and Systems, ISTCS 1997, Ramat-Gan, Israel, June 17-19, 1997, Proceedings.* 174–184.

[13] Philip Klein and R Ravi. 1995. A nearly best-possible approximation algorithm for node-weighted Steiner trees. *Journal of Algorithms* 19, 1 (1995), 104–115.

[14] Eyal Kushilevitz, Yehuda Lindell, and Tal Rabin. 2010. Information-Theoretically Secure Protocols and Security under Composition. *SIAM J. Comput.* 39, 5 (2010), 2090–2112.

[15] Frank Thomson Leighton, Bruce M Maggs, and Satish B Rao. 1994. Packet routing and job-shop scheduling in o(congestion+ dilation) steps. *Combinatorica* 14, 2 (1994), 167–186.

[16] Michael Luby. 1986. A simple parallel algorithm for the maximal independent set problem. *SIAM journal on computing* 15, 4 (1986), 1036–1053.

[17] Jaroslav Nesetril, Eva Milková, and Helena Nesetrilová. 2001. Otakar Borůvka on minimum spanning tree problem Translation of both the 1926 papers, comments, history. *Discrete Mathematics* 233, 1-3 (2001), 3–36. https://doi.org/10.1016/S0012-365X(00)00224-7

[18] Merav Parter and Eylon Yogev. 2019. Distributed Algorithms Made Secure: A Graph Theoretic Approach. In *Proceedings of the Thirtieth Annual ACM-SIAM Symposium on Discrete Algorithms, SODA 2019, San Diego, California, USA, January 6-9, 2019.* 1693–1710.

[19] Merav Parter and Eylon Yogev. 2019. Low Congestion Cycle Covers and Their Applications. In *Proceedings of the Thirtieth Annual ACM-SIAM Symposium on Discrete Algorithms, SODA 2019, San Diego, California, USA, January 6-9, 2019.* 1673–1692.

[20] Merav Parter and Eylon Yogev. 2019. Optimal Short Cycle Decomposition in Almost Linear Time. In *Automata, Languages and Programming: 31st International Colloquium, ICALP.*

[21] David Peleg. 2000. *Distributed Computing: A Locality-sensitive Approach.* SIAM.

[22] Oren Weimann and Raphael Yuster. 2010. Replacement paths via fast matrix multiplication. In *Foundations of Computer Science (FOCS), 2010 51st Annual IEEE Symposium on.* IEEE, 655–662.

[23] Andrew Chi-Chih Yao. 1982. Protocols for Secure Computations (Extended Abstract). In *23rd Annual Symposium on Foundations of Computer Science, Chicago, Illinois, USA, 3-5 November 1982.* 160–164.

With Great Speed Come Small Buffers: Space-Bandwidth Tradeoffs for Routing

Avery Miller*
avery.miller@umanitoba.ca
Department of Computer Science
University of Manitoba
Winnipeg, Manitoba, Canada

Boaz Patt-Shamir†
boaz@tau.ac.il
School of Electrical Engineering
Tel Aviv University
Tel Aviv, Israel

Will Rosenbaum
will.rosenbaum@gmail.com
Max Planck Institute for Informatics
Saarbrücken, Germany

ABSTRACT

We consider the Adversarial Queuing Theory (AQT) model, where packet arrivals are subject to a maximum average rate $0 \leq \rho \leq 1$ and burstiness $\sigma \geq 0$. In this model, we analyze the size of buffers required to avoid overflows in the basic case of a path. Our main results characterize the space required by the average rate and the number of distinct destinations: we show that $O(\ell d^{1/\ell} + \sigma)$ space suffice, where d is the number of distinct destinations and $\ell = \lfloor 1/\rho \rfloor$; and we show that $\Omega(\frac{1}{\ell} d^{1/\ell} + \sigma)$ space is necessary. For directed trees, we describe an algorithm whose buffer space requirement is at most $1 + d' + \sigma$ where d' is the maximum number of destinations on any root-leaf path.

CCS CONCEPTS

• **Theory of computation → Routing and network design problems**; • **Networks** → *Network control algorithms*; *Packet-switching networks*.

KEYWORDS

packet networks; adversarial queuing theory; packet forwarding; buffer overflow; multiple destinations directed paths; directed trees

ACM Reference Format:

Avery Miller, Boaz Patt-Shamir, and Will Rosenbaum. 2019. With Great Speed Come Small Buffers: Space-Bandwidth Tradeoffs for Routing. In *2019 ACM Symposium on Principles of Distributed Computing (PODC'19), July 29–August 2, 2019, Toronto, ON, Canada.* ACM, New York, NY, USA, 10 pages. https://doi.org/10.1145/3293611.3331614

1 INTRODUCTION

Background. Routing, be it physical (cars, trains, air traffic) or virtual (data packets, voice call circuits, multicasts) has long been recognized as a critical component of any system that allows for interaction and communication. The introduction of packet networks and store-and-forward routing as the basic technique of the Internet (when it was still called DARPANET [11]) brought to the forefront an interesting parameter, namely the buffer space at nodes.

Buffers are, in some sense, the universal glue that connects different components of a system smoothly. Intuitively, buffers allow each part of a system to run at its own pace. This is necessary even in tightly synchronized systems, because local processing speed depends on local resources and local load, which are rarely uniform across the system. Obviously, buffers cannot make up for prolonged gaps between the rates of demand and capacity, but they help in overcoming short bursts by smoothing the demand over time. This partial decoupling of input and output makes buffer control and analysis a tricky issue. Andrews et al. [3] give strong results regarding the required buffer space and maximal latency, but assuming that all packets are available at start, and ignoring initial storage.

Typically, buffers are simple and easy to use so long as the load is light. However, problems arise once loads increase and buffers are filled: packet discards due to full buffers are usually viewed as a failure.[1] From the theoretical viewpoint (possibly because packet drops greatly complicate stochastic analysis à la queuing-theory), the issue of dropped packets was largely ignored by analytic studies in the Theory of Networks. The introduction of competitive analysis allowed for investigating the issue from the throughput viewpoint [13], gaining new insights into the problem (see, e.g., the survey [12]). But by and large, the positive results concerned a single device (a switch or a router), and results for even slightly more complex systems were mostly negative [14], in the sense that in the examined cases, the competitive ratio of any algorithm could be unacceptably large for practical applications.

A different approach was advocated by Adversarial Queuing Theory (AQT), introduced in [6]. AQT considers the scenario in which each packet has a predetermined route, and forwarding is *greedy*. That is, if there is a packet buffered for a link e at time t, then some packet will be forwarded over e at time t. A *scheduling policy* is a rule which selects which packet each buffer forwards in each round. Classical AQT addresses the following qualitative question: Which scheduling policies ensure that all buffer occupancies are bounded irrespective of the duration of execution?

*Supported in part by the Natural Sciences and Engineering Research Council of Canada (NSERC), Discovery Grant RGPIN-2017-05936.
†Supported in part by the Israel Science Foundation grant No.1444/14.

PODC '19, July 29–August 2, 2019, Toronto, ON, Canada

ACM ISBN 978-1-4503-6217-7/19/07...$15.00
https://doi.org/10.1145/3293611.3331614

[1]TCP, the Internet's prevalent transport protocol, is an exception in this respect. TCP in fact forces periodic packet drops, as a part of its ongoing quest to grab free bandwidth. Since no explicit information about utilization is assumed, the protocol keeps increasing demand until an indication of a packet drop is received.

To have a meaningful answer for the above question, one must somehow restrict the demand presented by new packets. The criterion used by AQT (adopting ideas of Cruz [8]) is, roughly, that the set of routes associated with packets that appear together ("injected by the adversary") at any step is edge-disjoint. This ensures that the raw bandwidth required by packets does not exceed the available bandwidth. (In fact, overlap is allowed, but not more than some $\sigma \geq 0$; a second parameter, $0 \leq \rho \leq 1$ bounds the maximum rate in which any edge is requested. See Def. 2.1.)

AQT was fruitful in identifying strengths and weaknesses of different (greedy) scheduling policies (e.g., [5]). However, the theory was limited in two important respects. First, restricting forwarding policies to be greedy turned out to be a serious handicap in terms of efficiency [2]. Secondly, the qualitative-only view of the required buffer space (either bounded or infinite) is quite coarse. For example, some protocols may be stable, but with space requirement which is exponential in the number of nodes. Notable exceptions to this state of affairs are the work of Adler and Rosén on DAGs [1] and the work by Rosén and Scalosub on lines [20]. The relative simplicity of the topologies in these studies is not coincidental. The difficulty of understanding maximum buffer size *quantitatively* drove research to examine simple cases first: even the case of a line turned out to be subtle (see [10] for a recent result).

Recent progress: Single-destination trees. Recently, several studies have addressed the problem of quantifying the required buffer size under a (ρ, σ)-restricted packet injections, but without the requirement that the forwarding protocol must be greedy, and with an eye on *locality*. In [16], it was shown that in the case of a single-destination tree, a centralized algorithm can route any instance using $O(\rho + \sigma)$ buffer space at every node. In [9] and [18] it is shown that $\Theta(\rho \log n + \sigma)$ buffer space are necessary and sufficient for protocols with constant locality. That result was later extended in [19] to show that $\Theta\left(\rho \left\lceil \frac{\log n}{r} \right\rceil + \sigma\right)$ is necessary and sufficient for protocols with locality r. An interesting consequence of this result is that $O(\log n)$ locality is sufficient to perform as well as the best (offline) strategy.

Our results: Multiple destinations. In [18] it was shown that on a line, $\Omega(d)$ space is necessary to avoid overflows if there are d distinct destinations, and if the average injection rate satisfies $\rho > 1/2$. In this paper we show that the latter condition was no accident: On one hand, we show that if the average rate satisfies $\frac{1}{\ell+1} < \rho \leq \frac{1}{\ell}$ for some integer ℓ, then there is a centralized online algorithm which routes all packets using buffer space $O(\ell d^{1/\ell} + \sigma)$ and on the other hand, we prove a lower bound of $\Omega(\frac{1}{\ell} d^{1/\ell} + \sigma)$ buffer space required by any (offline) algorithm, for any integer $\ell > 1/\rho$. In particular, this result means that if $\rho \leq \frac{1}{\log d}$, $O(\log d)$ buffer space suffices. In addition, for the directed tree topology, we prove that buffers of size $1 + d' + \sigma$ are sufficient, where d' is an upper bound on the number of destinations along any leaf-root path.

Implications and open problems. One way to interpret our positive result is the following: Suppose that in a given line system, some buffer space suffices to avoid packet drops. If the system is modified so that the number of destinations is increased by a factor $\alpha > 1$ without changing the overall offered load per link, overflows can be avoided by either increasing the buffer sizes by factor α, or by increasing both buffer space and link bandwidths by an $O(\log \alpha)$ factor. This result corresponds nicely to previous results such as online virtual circuit admission control [4, 7] exhibiting $O(\log n)$ competitiveness when demands are at most $O(1/\log n)$ of the capacity.

Great challenges remain open on our way to fully understand the general case. These include finding a decentralized (local) algorithm for the multi-destination case, and extending the restricted topologies we consider to general topologies. Regarding the former, we expect the OED algorithm [9, 18] to be useful as it was for algorithms of parameterized locality [19]. Regarding the latter, we note that the case of a union of trees is also important, due to the fact that this topology is the output of many routing algorithms.

Paper organization. We present the algorithm gradually, from the simplest to the most general case: In Sec. 3 we present algorithms for any utilization parameter ρ, and also extend them to directed trees. The algorithm is then generalized in Sec. 4 to be hierarchical, with $\left\lfloor \frac{1}{\rho} \right\rfloor$ hierarchy levels. The lower bound is presented in Sec. 5. Sec. 2 formalizes the model and defines some concepts and notation.

Due to lack of space, some arguments are omitted. Full details appear in [17].

2 PRELIMINARIES

Given a positive integer n, we use the notation $\langle n \rangle = \{0, \ldots, n-1\}$. We model a network as a directed graph $G = (V, E)$, where packets flow along the direction of edges. For the most part, in this paper we restrict attention to the case where G is a path, and take $V = \langle n \rangle$, $E = \{(i, i+1) : 0 \leq i < n-1\}$. We view this path horizontally with nodes $0, \ldots, n-1$ in increasing order from left to right.

An execution of an algorithm proceeds in synchronous rounds. Each round consists of two steps: an ***injection step***, during which new packets arrive, and a ***forwarding step***, during which the algorithm performs computations and forwards packets. In this paper we assume that in each round, at most one packet can be forwarded over each link. When we refer to a state at round t, we compute the state *after* the injection step, but *before* the forwarding step. We denote the time in round t immediately after the forwarding step by $t+$. For example, $L^t(v)$ denotes the state of the buffer at v after packets are injected and before forwarding; and $L^{t+}(v)$ denotes the state after forwarding, but before round $t+1$ packets arrive. A buffer containing m packets stores them in an array in positions $1, \ldots, m$.

A node may partition its buffer into several parts, which we refer to as ***pseudo-buffers***. We use the notation $L^t_k(v)$ and $L^t_{j,k}(v)$ to denote pseudo-buffers, where j and k are parameters described below. We make no assumptions about the priority assigned to packets within a single (pseudo)-buffer, but for concreteness it is convenient to assume that all (pseudo)-buffers use Last-In, First-Out (LIFO) priority.

Throughout an execution, packets arrive in the network, controlled by an adversary. An ***adversary*** or ***injection pattern*** is a set A of packets. A packet P is represented by a triple $P = (t, i_P, w_P)$ where $t \in \mathbb{N}$ is the injection round of P, $i_P \in V$ is P's injection site, and $w_P \in V$ is P's destination. We denote the unique path from i_P to w_P by $\text{Path}(i_P, w_P)$.

We say that P's path ***contains*** a buffer v if $v \in \text{Path}(i_P, w_P)$. For an adversary A, a set of rounds T, and a buffer v, we denote the number of packets injected during T whose trajectories contain v by $N_T(v)$. That is,

$$N_T(v) = |\{(t, i_P, w_P) \in A \,:\, v \in \text{Path}(i_P, w_P) \text{ and } t \in T\}|.$$

DEFINITION 2.1. *For any $\rho \in \mathbf{R}^+$, $\sigma \in \mathbf{N}$, and adversary A, we say that A is **(ρ, σ)-bounded** if for all buffers v and intervals of time T, we have $N_T(v) \leq \rho\,|T| + \sigma$.*

Intuitively, an adversary A is (ρ, σ)-bounded if the average rate of packets needing to cross any particular edge i is at most ρ. This average may not be exceeded by more than σ packets when taken over any contiguous interval of time. The term σ thus bounds the "burstiness" of A.

The term "excess" gives a measure of how much of the adversary's burst budget has been expended.

DEFINITION 2.2. *Fix an adversary A, rate ρ, round t, and buffer $v \in V$. The **excess** of v at time t, denoted $\xi^t(v)$, is given by*

$$\xi^t(v) = \max_{s \leq t}(\{N_{[s,t]}(v) - \rho(t - s + 1)\} \cup \{0\}). \tag{1}$$

The following lemma, which applies to graphs of any topology, gives two basic properties of excess.

LEMMA 2.3. *Suppose A is (ρ, σ)-bounded. Then for all rounds t and buffers $v \in V$, we have*

(1) $\xi^t(v) \leq \sigma$, and

(2) $N_{\{t\}}(v) \leq \xi^t(v) - \xi^{t-1}(v) + \rho$.

PROOF. The first claim follows from the definition of (ρ, σ) bound: For all $T = [s, t]$ we have $N_T(v) \leq \rho\,|T| + \sigma$, hence $N_T(v) - \rho\,|T| \leq \sigma$. For the second claim, suppose ν packets are injected in round t whose trajectories contain v, and let $T' = [s, t - 1]$ be an interval achieving the maximum in the definition of $\xi^{t-1}(v)$. Then we have

$$\begin{aligned}\xi^t(v) &\geq N_{[s,t]}(v) - \rho(t - s + 1)\\ &= N_{[s,t-1]}(v) + \nu - \rho((t - 1) - s + 1) - \rho\\ &\geq \xi^{t-1}(v) + \nu - \rho\end{aligned}$$

Rearranging this expression gives $\nu \leq \xi^t(v) - \xi^{t-1}(v) + \rho$, as desired. □

In what follows, we sometimes consider algorithms that only accept packets every few rounds. Specifically, for some fixed ℓ and every $k \in \mathbf{N}$, the algorithm treats all packets injected at times $t = (k - 1)\ell, (k - 1)\ell + 1, \ldots, k\ell - 1$ as being injected at time $k\ell$. The algorithm performs forwarding steps in each round $k\ell, k\ell + 1, \ldots, (k+1)\ell - 1$ ignoring packets that are injected in these rounds, as they will be considered as injected in round $(k + 1)\ell$, etc.

DEFINITION 2.4. *Let A be an adversary and ℓ a positive integer. The **ℓ-reduction** of A, denoted A_ℓ is the injection pattern defined by*

$$A_\ell = \{(\lfloor t/\ell \rfloor + 1, i_P, w_P) \,:\, (t, i_P, w_P) \in A\}.$$

The following lemma characterizes A_ℓ using the parameters of A.

LEMMA 2.5. *Suppose A is (ρ, σ) bounded and ℓ a positive integer. Then A_ℓ is $(\ell \cdot \rho, \sigma)$ bounded.*

PROOF. Fix an interval of time $T = [s, t]$ and buffer $v \in V$. From the definition of A_ℓ, we have

$$\begin{aligned}N_T(v) &= |\{(u, i_P, w_P) \in A \,:\, \ell \cdot (s - 1) \leq u \leq \ell \cdot t - 1\}|\\ &\leq \rho \cdot \ell(t - s + 1) + \sigma.\end{aligned}$$

The inequality holds because A is (ρ, σ)-bounded. Therefore, A_ℓ is $(\ell \cdot \rho, \sigma)$-bounded, as desired. □

3 THE BASIC ALGORITHMS

In this section, we describe a simple algorithm that requires buffers of size $O(d + \sigma)$ for all rates $\rho \leq 1$ and d destinations. By Thm. 5.1, this space requirement is optimal for rates ρ satisfying $1/2 < \rho \leq 1$. We break the algorithm description into two parts. We first consider the case where all packets have a common destination: Algorithm "Peak-to-Sink" (PTS) achieves the best possible buffer space of $O(1 + \sigma)$ packets. We then reduce the case of multiple destinations to single destinations in Algorithm "Parallel Peak-to-Sink" (PPTS). Finally we extend the result to directed trees.

Implementation convention. In order to determine which buffers forward packets in round t, a buffer $L^t(v)$ can be ***active*** or ***inactive***. In each round, all buffers are initially inactive. During the forwarding step, our algorithms select buffers to activate, then all active buffers simultaneously forward. We denote the family of activated buffers by $\mathcal{A}$.

3.1 Peak to Sink (PTS) forwarding

Assume first that all packets $P \in A$ have a common destination w, which we take to be $w = n - 1$ without loss of generality. Consider a configuration L^t. We say that a buffer $i \in \langle n \rangle$ is ***bad*** if $|L^t(i)| \geq 2$. We say that a packet P in a buffer i is ***bad*** if it is stored in a position $p \geq 2$ in $L^t(i)$. Algorithm PTS (Alg. 1) is simple: if i is the left-most bad buffer, then all non-empty buffers $i' \geq i$ forward. PTS requires the minimal possible buffer space, as we claim next.

Algorithm 1 PTS(w) (do each round)

```
1: i ← min{i' : |L^t(i')| ≥ 2}
2: 𝒜 ← [i, w − 1]
3: forward from all buffers in 𝒜
```

PROPOSITION 3.1. *Suppose A is a (ρ, σ)-bounded adversary with $\rho \leq 1$ and all packets $P \in A$ have destination w. Then the maximum buffer size is at most $\sigma + 2$.*

PROOF. For each time t, let $B^t(w - 1)$ denote the number of bad packets in the network after the t-th injection step. That is

$$B^t(w - 1) = \sum_{i \in \langle n \rangle} \max\{|L^t(i)| - 1, 0\}.$$

Similarly, let $B^{t+}(w - 1)$ be the number of bad packets after the t-th forwarding step. We will argue by induction that for all t

$$B^t(w - 1) \leq \xi^t(w - 1) + 1 \quad \text{and} \quad B^{t+}(w - 1) \leq \xi^t(w - 1). \tag{2}$$

Since the maximum load of any buffer can be at most $B^t(w - 1) + 1$, and $\xi^t(w - 1) \leq \sigma$ by Lemma 2.3, the proposition follows.

For the base case, $t = 0$, (2) trivially holds as all quantities are zero. For the inductive step, suppose (2) holds for round $t - 1$. Let $\nu(t)$

denote the number of new packets injected during the t-th injection step. By part 2 of Lemma 2.3, $\nu(t) \leq \xi_{w-1}(t) - \xi_{w-1}(t-1) + 1$. Therefore

$$\begin{aligned} B^t(w-1) &\leq B^{t-1}(w-1) + \nu(t) \\ &\leq \xi^t(w-1) + (\xi^t(w-1) - \xi^{t-1}(w-1) + 1) \\ &= \xi^t(w-1) + 1\,. \end{aligned}$$

Thus the first expression in (2) holds, as desired. To show the second expression also holds, it suffices to show that if $B^t(w-1) \geq 1$, then $B^{t+}(w-1) = B^t(w-1) - 1$. To this end, let L^{t+} denote the configuration after forwarding. Let i be the left-most buffer for which $\left|L^t(i)\right| \geq 2$. Since i forwards, but $i-1$ does not, we have $L^{t+}(i) = L^t(i) - 1 \geq 1$. Since every non-empty $i' > i$ forwards, and no i' receives more than one packet from $i'-1$, we have for all $i' > i$

$$\left|L^{t+}(i')\right| \leq \max\left\{1, \left|L^t(i')\right|\right\}\,.$$

Therefore, we compute

$$\begin{aligned} B^{t+}(w-1) &= (\left|L^{t+}(i)\right| - 1) + \sum_{i'>i} \max\left\{\left|L^{t+}(i')\right| - 1, 0\right\} \\ &\leq L^t(i) - 2 + \sum_{i'>i} \max\left\{\left|L^t(i')\right| - 1, 0\right\} \\ &= B^t(w-1) - 1, \end{aligned}$$

as desired. □

3.2 Parallel Peak to Sink (PPTS) forwarding

Assume now that there are d destinations $W = \{w_0, w_1, \ldots, w_{d-1}\}$, where $w_0 < w_1 < \cdots < w_{d-1}$. The idea of the algorithm is for each $w \in W$ to treat all packets with destination w as an instance of the single destination algorithm. Capacity constraints preclude us from performing all d instances in parallel every round, so PPTS chooses an appropriate maximal set of (pseudo)-buffers that can simultaneously forward.

To describe PPTS formally, we view each buffer i as a collection of d pseudo-buffers, where the k-th pseudo-buffer in i stores packets destined for w_k.[2] We denote the contents of i's k-th pseudo-buffer by

$$L_k^t(i) = \left\{P \in L^t(i) \text{ and } P \text{ has destination } w_k\right\}.$$

For any destination w_k, we refer to pseudo-buffers $L_k(i)$ as ***k*-pseudo-buffers**. We say that a pseudo-buffer $L_k^t(i)$ is **bad** at time t if $\left|L_k^t(i)\right| \geq 2$. In this case we call $L^t(i)$ ***bad for k***. We call a packet P in a k-pseudo-buffer ***k*-bad** if it is stored in a position $p \geq 2$ in $L_k^t(i)$.

PPTS (Alg. 2) works as follows. Starting from the right-most destination, w_{d-1}, the algorithm searches for the left-most bad $(d-1)$-pseudo-buffer, if any. If a bad $(d-1)$-pseudo-buffer $L_{d-1}^t(i_{d-1})$ is found, all $(d-1)$-pseudo-buffers in the range $[i_{d-1}, w_{d-1} - 1]$ are activated. The algorithm then searches for bad $d-2$ pseudo-buffers. Suppose $L_{d-2}^t(i_{d-2})$ is the left-most $(d-2)$-pseudo-buffer. If $i_{d-2} < i_{d-1}$, then all $(d-2)$-pseudo-buffers in the interval $[i_{d-2}, i_{d-1} - 1]$ are activated; otherwise, no $(d-2)$-pseudo-buffers are activated. This process is continued for destinations $w_{d-3}, w_{d-4}, \ldots, w_0$, where an interval of k-pseudo-buffers is activated only if a k-bad pseudo-buffer is encountered to the left of all pseudo-buffers activated thus far. By construction, the intervals activated for each destination are disjoint, so forwarding can be implemented without violating capacity constraints.

Algorithm 2 PPTS(I, W) (do each round)

```
W = {w_0 < w_1 < ··· < w_{d-1}}                          {destinations}
i ← w_d, 𝒜 ← ∅
for k ← d − 1 downto 0 do
    if there exists i' < i such that i' is bad for w_k then
        i_k ← min {i' : L_k(i') is bad}
        𝒜 ← 𝒜 ∪ {L_k(i) : i ∈ [i_k, i − 1]}
        i ← i_k
    end if
end for
each nonempty L_k(i) ∈ 𝒜 forwards
```

We note that algorithm PPTS need not be told the set of destinations W to which an adversary A injects in advance. Instead, we can assume that all nodes $i \in [1, n-1]$ are potential destinations, giving rise to n pseudo-buffers per node. However, if an adversary only injects packets with d distinct destinations, then at most d pseudo-buffers in any given buffer will be non-empty.

Our analysis shows that for any (ρ, σ)-bounded adversary A, PPTS maintains the following invariant: For each buffer i, the number of bad packets that must cross i, i.e., the number of bad packets in buffers $i' \leq i$ with destinations $w_k > i$, is at most one plus the excess $\xi^t(i) + 1 \leq \sigma + 1$. In particular, every buffer $L(i)$ contains at most $1 + \sigma + d$ packets, as it can contain at most d packets that are not bad. The following proposition states the key property of PPTS.

Proposition 3.2. *Let A be any (ρ, σ)-bounded adversary such that all packets have destinations in W with $d = |W|$. Then the maximum buffer usage of PPTS is at most $1 + d + \sigma$.*

To facilitate the proof of Prop. 3.2, we introduce the concept of "badness," along with some new notation.

Definition 3.3. *Let $i \in \langle n \rangle$ be a buffer, and w_k a destination such that $w_k > i$. Given t, we denote the number of k-bad packets in i at time t by $\beta_k^t(i)$. Formally, $\beta_k^t(i) = \max\{0, |L_k^t(i)| - 1\}$. The* ***k*-badness** *of i, denoted $B_k^t(i)$, is the total number of bad packets in buffers $i' \leq i$ with destination w_k. That is, $B_k^t(i) = \sum_{i' \leq i} \beta_k^t(i')$. The* **badness** *of i, denoted $B^t(i)$, is the total number of bad packets in buffers $i' \leq i$ with destinations $w > i$. Thus, $B^t(i) = \sum_{k: w_k > i} B_k^i(t)$.*

We stress that $B_k^t(i)$ and $B^t(i)$ count also badness of packets upstream from i. In the proof of Prop. 3.2, we use the following key lemma.

Lemma 3.4. *Let L be a configuration of $\langle n \rangle$ with destinations $W = \{w_0 < w_1 < \cdots < w_{d-1}\}$. Suppose that for some $k \in \langle d \rangle$, $I_k = [a_k, b_k] \subseteq \langle n \rangle$ is an interval such that $|L_k(a_k)| \geq 2$ and $b_k < w_k$. Let L^+ be the configuration obtained by forwarding only from nonempty k-pseudo-buffers in I_k. For $i \in \langle n \rangle$ let $B_k(i)$ and $B_k^+(i)$ be the k-badness of i before and after forwarding, respectively.*

[2] This is known in practice as "virtual output queuing" (e.g., [15]).

Similarly, $B(i)$ and $B^+(i)$ denote the badness of i before and after forwarding. Then

$$B_k^+(i) \le \begin{cases} B_k(i) - 1 & \text{if } i \in I_k \\ B_k(i) & \text{if } i \notin I_k \,, \end{cases}$$

and similarly,

$$B^+(i) \le \begin{cases} B(i) - 1 & \text{if } i \in I_k \\ B(i) & \text{if } i \notin I_k \,. \end{cases}$$

Proof. First observe that since only k-packets are forwarded, so only k-loads—hence k-badness—changes after forwarding. Thus, the second claim follows immediately from the first.

For a buffer i, let $\beta_k(i)$ and $\beta_k^+(i)$ denote the number of k-bad packets stored in i before and after forwarding, respectively. We consider 4 cases separately:

- $i < a_k$ or $i > b_k + 1$. In this case, i neither sends nor receives a packet so that $\beta_k^+(i) = \beta_k(i)$.
- $i = a_k$. In this case, $L_k(a_k) \ge 2$. Since a_k sends but does not receive a packet, we have $\beta_k^+(a_k) = \beta_k(a_k) - 1$.
- $a_k + 1 \le i \le b_k$. Observe that i receives at most one packet, and if $L_k(i) \ge 1$, i forwards one packet. Thus $L_k^+(i) \le \max\{L_k(i), 1\}$, hence $\beta_k^+(i) \le \beta_k(i)$.
- $i = b_k + 1$. In this case, i receives at most one packet, hence $\beta_k^+(i) \le \beta_k(i) + 1$.

The lemma follows from the four cases above, using the definitions of $B_k(i)$ and $B_k^+(i)$. □

Proof of Proposition 3.2. For each round $t > 0$ we, use $t+$ to denote the time after the forwarding step of round t. For example, $B^{t+}(i)$ is the badness of i *after* the t-th forwarding step (whereas $B^t(i)$ is the badness after the injection step, before forwarding). We will show that for all rounds t and buffers $i \in \langle n \rangle$, we have

$$B^t(i) \le \xi^t(i) + 1 \quad \text{and} \quad B^{t+}(i) \le \xi^t(i). \tag{3}$$

To see that the proposition follows from (3), we compute

$$\begin{aligned} |L^t(i)| &= \sum_{k \in \langle d \rangle} |L_k^t(i)| \le \sum_{k \in \langle d \rangle} (1 + \beta_k^t(i)) \le d + \sum_{k \in \langle d \rangle} \beta_k^t(i) \\ &\le d + \sum_{k \in \langle d \rangle} B_k^t(i) = d + B^t(i)\,. \end{aligned}$$

Therefore, from (3), we obtain $|L^t(i)| \le d + 1 + \xi^t(i)$. By Claim 1 of Lemma 2.3, $\xi^t(i) \le \sigma$, so that $L^t(i) \le d + 1 + \sigma$, as desired.

In order to prove (3), we argue by induction on t. The proof for $t = 0$ is trivial, as no packets have yet been injected. Suppose that (3) holds for every $i \in \langle n \rangle$ at time $t - 1$. Let $N_{\{t\}}(i)$ denote the number of packets injected in round t whose paths contain i. We compute

$$\begin{aligned} B^t(i) &\le B^{(t-1)+}(i) + N_{\{t\}}(i) \\ &\le \xi^{t-1}(i) + N_{\{t\}}(i) && \text{(inductive hypothesis)} \\ &\le \xi^{t-1}(i) + (\xi^t(i) - \xi^{t-1}(i) + 1) && \text{(Lemma 2.3)} \\ &= \xi^t(i) + 1\,. \end{aligned}$$

Therefore, the first equation of (3) holds.

To prove the second equation in (3), it suffices to show that if $B^t(i) > 0$, then after the t-th forwarding step we have $B^{t+}(i) = B^t(i) - 1$. For each $k \in \langle d \rangle$, let I_k be the (possibly empty) interval of k-pseudo-buffers activated in Line 6 of PPTS. We have the following.

Claim 1. *Let $\iota \in \langle n \rangle$. If $B^t(\iota) > 0$, then there exists $\kappa \in \langle d \rangle$ such that $\iota \in I_\kappa$.*

Proof of Claim 1. Let κ be the maximum index such that $B_\kappa^t(\iota) > 0$. Thus, for all $k > \kappa$, there is no k-bad packet in any buffer $i \le \iota$. Therefore, in the corresponding iteration $k = \kappa$ of PPTS, we have $i_k \le \iota$ in Line 5. Since i is only ever assigned to a buffer containing a bad packet (Line 7 of PPTS), during the k-th iteration we must have had $\iota < i$ in Line 6 when $I_k = [i_k, i-1]$ is activated. Thus, $\iota \in I_k$, as desired. □

Finally, suppose i satisfies $B^t(i) > 0$. Applying the claim, let $I_k = [a_k, b_k]$ be the activated interval containing i. Further, by the definition of $i_k (= a_k)$ in Line 5 of PPTS, we have $\beta_k^t(a_k) > 0$. Therefore, by Lemma 3.4, we have $B_k^{t+}(i) \le B_k^t(i) - 1$. For all $k' \ne k$, Lemma 3.4 gives $B_{k'}^{t+}(i) \le B_{k'}^t(i)$. Summing over all destinations gives

$$\begin{aligned} B^{t+}(i) &= \sum_{k' \in \langle d \rangle} B_{k'}^{t+}(i) = B_k^{t+}(i) + \sum_{k' \ne k} B_{k'}^{t+}(i) \\ &\le B_k^t(i) - 1 + \sum_{k' \ne k} B_{k'}^t(i) \le B^t(i) - 1, \end{aligned}$$

as desired. □

3.3 Extension to Trees

In the full version [17], we explain how to extend both PTS and PPTS to the case of directed trees. We assume that all edges are directed toward the root, and that packets follow directed paths. In this setting we prove the following.

Proposition 3.5. *Let A be any (ρ, σ)-bounded adversary such that all packets have destinations in W. Then the maximum buffer usage of PPTS is at most $1 + d' + \sigma$, where d' is the maximum number of destinations in any leaf-root path.*

4 HIERARCHICAL ALGORITHM

In this section, we describe Algorithm HPTS (Hierarchical Peak-to-Sink), that achieves significantly better performance than PPTS in the case where the rate of the adversary satisfies $\rho \le 1/2$. The algorithm description is parametrized by the number of ***levels*** in the construction, denoted $\ell \in \mathbb{N}$. In the case $\ell = 1$, HPTS reduces to PPTS. In the general case, we obtain the following result. For the remainder of the section, we assume that ρ and ℓ satisfy $\rho \cdot \ell \le 1$.

Theorem 4.1. *There exists an algorithm, HPTS, such that for every positive integer ℓ and (ρ, σ)-bounded adversary A such that $\rho \cdot \ell \le 1$, the space requirement of HPTS is at most $\ell n^{1/\ell} + \sigma + 1$.*

4.1 Network Partition

Our algorithm is based on a hierarchical partition of the line. For simplicity, we assume that $n = m^\ell$ for some integers m and ℓ. We consider the base-m representation of buffer indices. That is, given $i \in \langle n \rangle$ we write the string $i = i_{\ell-1} i_{\ell-2} \cdots i_0$, where $i_j \in \langle m \rangle$ for $j = 0, \ldots \ell - 1$ and $i = \sum_{j=0}^{\ell-1} i_j m^j$. We refer to i_j as the j-th *digit*, or the digit in the j-th *position*, of i.

Using this convention, for $j \in \langle \ell \rangle$ and $r \in \langle m^{\ell-j-1} \rangle$, define the intervals $I_{j,r}$ by

$$I_{j,r} = \left\{ rm^{j+1} + k \,:\, 0 \le k < m^{j+1} \right\} .$$

Intuitively, the interval $I_{j,r}$ consists of all m^{j+1} nodes whose most significant $\ell - j - 1$ digits have value r. For each fixed j, the set of intervals $\mathcal{I}_j = \{I_{j,r} : r \in \langle m^{\ell-j-1} \rangle\}$ forms a partition of $\langle n \rangle$. We call $\mathcal{I}_j$ the ***level-j*** partition, and refer to each $I_{j,r} \in \mathcal{I}_j$ as a ***level-j*** interval. For each $j > 0$, each level-j interval contains exactly m level-$(j-1)$ subintervals. We denote the union of the partitions by $\mathcal{I} = \mathcal{I}_0 \cup \mathcal{I}_1 \cup \cdots \cup \mathcal{I}_{\ell-1}$.

The idea of HPTS is to run an independent instance of PPTS in each interval of $\mathcal{I}$, allowing each interval of level j to have exactly m (intermediate) destinations: one for each left endpoint of a subinterval of level $j-1$. Intermediate destinations are chosen so as to "correct" the index of a packet's location to the index of its final destination, digit by digit: position j of the index is corrected at level j. Formally, we have the following.

Definition 4.2. *Let $i, w \in \langle n \rangle$. Assume that $i < w$ and that the largest position (in base-m notation) in which i and w differ is j. Then the* **intermediate destination of i to w** *is $x(i, w) = \lfloor w/m^j \rfloor m^j$. The route $[i, x(i, w)]$ is called a* **segment**, *and its* **level**, *denoted $\mathrm{lv}(i, w)$, is j.*

A packet P with destination w residing in a buffer $L(i)$, **crosses i at level** *$\mathrm{lv}(i, P) = \mathrm{lv}(i, w)$. If $j = \mathrm{lv}(i, P)$, we define P's* **level-j intermediate destination** *to be $w_{P,j} = x(i, w)$.*

If the largest position in which i and w differ is j, then the segment from i to $x(i, w)$ is contained in a level-j interval I_j. If $j \ge 1$, then for all $j' \le j$, $x(i, w)$ is the left endpoint of some level-j' interval. If a packet is injected into buffer i with destination w, we can think of its trajectory $[i, w]$ as being partitioned into segments $[i, x(i, w) - 1], [x(i, w), x(x(i, w), w) - 1], \ldots$, where the level of these segments is strictly decreasing. Further, with the possible exception of the initial segment, the left endpoints of all segments are left endpoints of intervals $I \in \mathcal{I}$.

When P is stored in a buffer i, we think of P as virtually residing in the subinterval I_j at level $j = \mathrm{lv}(i, P)$ containing i. When P is forwarded to its next intermediate destination, $w_{P,j} = x(i, w)$, its virtual location moves to the corresponding interval at level $j' = \mathrm{lv}(w_{P,j}, P)$. We emphasize that the *virtual* location of each packet P in a buffer i (i.e., level and intermediate destination) is a function of i and P's destination. Thus, i can compute the virtual location of each packet it stores locally. Figure 1 illustrates the virtual motion packets through the network. Formally, the HPTS algorithm implements the virtual packet movement by partitioning each buffer into pseudo-buffers, as defined below.

Definition 4.3. *Let $t \in \mathbb{N}$, $i \in \langle n \rangle$, $j \in \langle \ell \rangle$ and $k \in \langle m \rangle$. Let $I_j(i)$ be the level-j interval containing i. Let $W_j(i) = \{w_0 < \cdots < w_{m-1}\}$ denote the left endpoints of the level-$(j-1)$ intervals contained in $I_j(i)$. We define the* **(j, k)-pseudo-buffer** *of i at time t, denoted $L^t_{j,k}(i)$, to contain all packets in $L^t(i)$ whose current segment level is j and whose next intermediate destination is w_k.*

Since $j \in \langle \ell \rangle$ and $k \in \langle m \rangle$, each buffer $L^t(i)$ is partitioned into $\ell m = \ell n^{1/\ell}$ pseudo-buffers. As in our description of the PPTS algorithm, we define a notion of badness for packets, pseudo-buffers, and buffers.

Definition 4.4. *Let $t \in \mathbb{N}$, $i \in \langle n \rangle$, $j \in \langle \ell \rangle$, and $k \in \langle m \rangle$. We say that the (j, k)-pseudo-buffer $L^t_{j,k}(i)$ is* **bad** *at time t if $|L^t_{j,k}(i)| \ge 2$. A packet in $L^t_{j,k}(i)$ is called* **bad** *if its position in $L^t_{j,k}(i)$ is at least 2. The number of bad packets in $L^t_{j,k}(i)$ is $\beta^t_{j,k}(i) = \max\left\{ |L^t_{j,k}(i)| - 1, 0 \right\}$.*

In the definition below, note that the badness of a node accounts also for bad packets in other (upstream) nodes.

Definition 4.5. *Let $i \in \langle n \rangle$, $j \in \langle \ell \rangle$, $k \in \langle m \rangle$ and let $I = [a, b]$ be a level-j interval containing i. The* **(j, k)-badness** *of a node i at time t, denoted $B^t_{j,k}(i)$, is defined by $B^t_{j,k}(i) = \sum_{i'=a}^{i} \beta^t_{j,k}(i')$. That is, $B^t_{j,k}(i)$ is the number of bad packets in buffers $i' \in I$ with $i' \le i$ whose segment level at i is j and whose level j intermediate destination is w_k. The* **level-j badness** *of i is $B^t_j(i) = \sum_{k \in \langle m \rangle} B^t_{j,k}(i)$, and the* **badness** *of i is $B^t(i) = \sum_{j \in \langle \ell \rangle} B^t_j(i)$.*

4.2 Algorithm description

The idea of Algorithm HPTS (Alg. 3) is as follows. Let us refer to a sequence of rounds $t, t+1, \ldots, t+\ell-1$ with $t \equiv 0 \pmod{\ell}$ as a ***phase***. That is, the φ-th phase consists of rounds $(\varphi-1)\ell, \ldots, \varphi\ell - 1$. We assume that all packets injected during a phase φ are only accepted during the first round of phase $\varphi + 1$ (Lines 3–5). This results in A_ℓ, i.e., the ℓ-reduction of A (cf. Def. 2.4).

Due to capacity constraints, not all pseudo-buffers can simultaneously forward packets, so HPTS employs *time-division multiplexing*: At any time t, only the level-$(\ell - 1 - \lambda)$ intervals are activated in Lines 7–9, where $\lambda \equiv t \pmod{\ell}$. In other words, levels are activated in decreasing order as a phase progresses. Since same-level intervals are edge-disjoint, all intervals in $\mathcal{I}_{\ell-1-\lambda}$ can be active in parallel.

We note that the family of buffers activated by Algorithm 4 is identical to the activation pattern in an iteration of PPTS in which (1) only level-j packets are considered, and (2) the destination of each packet is taken to be its level-j intermediate destination. The difference between HPTS and PPTS is in Lines 10–12 of Alg. 3: Activating buffers in one level may cause the activation of buffers in lower levels. This is done to anticipate when a packet reaches an intermediate destination and switches level—and interval instance—where it may become bad in the new instance. Activating the new instance just before a new packet arrives to a bad position is sufficient to avoid an increase of badness for any buffer in a given round. Formally, we define the notion of pre-badness as follows.

Definition 4.6. *Suppose $L^t_{j,k}(i)$ is activated and let $P \in L^t_{j,k}(i)$ be the packet sent by $L^t_{j,k}(i)$. Suppose that P's level-j intermediate destination is $i+1$ (i.e., P is about to make the last hop in its level-j segment), where it will be associated with pseudo-buffer $L_{j',k}(i+1)$ with $j' < j$. We say that the packet P is* **pre-bad** *if $|L^t_{j',k}(i+1)| \ge 1$. In this case, we also call the buffer $i+1$* **pre-bad for P at level j'**.

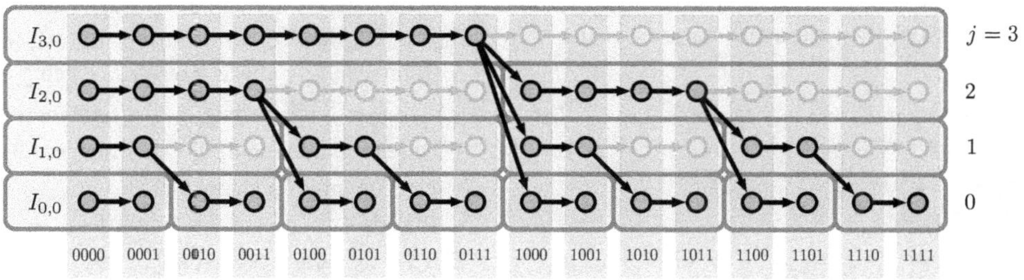

Figure 1: *The network with $n = 16$, $m = 2$, and $\ell = 4$. Each column represents a single buffer, and each row represents a level. The horizontal boxes indicate divisions between intervals in $\mathcal{I}$. Given a packet P injected into i with destination w, the virtual trajectory of P is given by the unique path from a pseudo-buffer in i to a level-0 pseudo-buffer in $w - 1$.*

Algorithm 3 HPTS(n, ℓ, t) (do each round)

1: $\mathcal{A} \leftarrow \varnothing$ {active pseudo-buffers}
2: $\lambda \leftarrow t \bmod \ell$
3: **if** $\lambda = 0$ **then**
4: accept round $(t - \ell)$-,..., $(t - 1)$-injections
5: **end if**
6: $\hat{j} \leftarrow \ell - 1 - \lambda$ {level to activate this round}
7: **for all** $r \in \langle m^{\lambda} \rangle$ **do**
8: $\mathcal{A} \leftarrow$ FormPaths($I_{\hat{j},r}, \hat{j}$)
9: **end for**
10: **for** $j = \hat{j} - 1$ **downto** 0 **do**
11: $\mathcal{A} \leftarrow$ ActivatePreBad($\mathcal{A}, j$)
12: **end for**
13: each nonempty $L_{j,k}(i) \in \mathcal{A}$ forwards a packet

Algorithm 4 FormPaths(I, j)

1: Let $W = \{w_0 < w_1 < \cdots < w_{m-1}\}$ be the intermediate destinations in I
2: $\mathcal{A} \leftarrow \varnothing$; $i' \leftarrow w_{m-1}$
3: **for** $k \leftarrow m - 1$ **downto** 0 **do**
4: **if** there exists $i < i'$ such that i is *bad* for w_k **then**
5: $i_k \leftarrow \min \left\{ i'' : |L^t_{j,k}(i'')| \geq 2 \right\}$
6: $\mathcal{A} \leftarrow \mathcal{A} \cup \left\{ L^t_{j,k}(i) \mid i \in [i_k, \min\{i' - 1, w_k - 1\}] \right\}$
7: $i' \leftarrow i_k$
8: **end if**
9: **end for**
10: **return** $\mathcal{A}$

Algorithm 5 ActivatePreBad($\mathcal{A}, j$)

1: **for all** $r \in \langle m^{\ell - j - 1} \rangle$ **do**
2: $I = [a, b] \leftarrow I_{j,r}$
3: **if** $\exists P$ pre-bad for a at level j and a is inactive **then**
4: $k \leftarrow$ index s.t. $w_k = w_{P,j}$
5: $w \leftarrow \max \{ i \in I : i \leq w_k$ and $[a, i]$ is inactive$\}$
6: $\mathcal{A} \leftarrow \mathcal{A} \cup \left\{ L^t_{j,k}(i) : i \in [a, w] \right\}$
7: **end if**
8: **end for**
9: **return** $\mathcal{A}$

4.3 Algorithm analysis

Our strategy in the analysis of HPTS is to bound the badness of each buffer i by σ at the end of each phase (just as our analysis of PPTS bounds the badness of each buffer at the end of each round). Since each buffer contains $\ell \cdot m = \ell \cdot n^{1/\ell}$ pseudo-buffers, each buffer can contain at most $\ell \cdot n^{1/\ell}$ non-bad packets. Thus Theorem 4.1 follows from giving an appropriate bound on the badness of each buffer. The basic argument is the same as our analysis of PPTS: apply Lemma 2.3 to show that the increase in badness of a buffer is at most one more than the increase in excess of the buffer, then show that forwarding reduces the badness of the buffer by at least one (if it is positive). First, we show that the forwarding in Line 13 of HPTS is feasible.

Lemma 4.7. *Consider the set $\mathcal{A}$ of active pseudo-buffers immediately before Line 13 of HPTS. Then $\mathcal{A}$ is* feasible, *i.e., for each $i \in \langle n \rangle$, there is at most one active pseudo-buffer $L^t_{j,k}(i) \in \mathcal{A}$.*

Proof. Consider the state of $\mathcal{A}$ following the calls to FormPaths in Lines 7–9. For any fixed $\hat{j} \in \langle \ell \rangle$, the intervals $I_{\hat{j},r}$ are disjoint, and in each interval $I_{\hat{j},r}$, the level-$\hat{j}$ pseudo-buffers are activated in the same pattern as a call to PPTS. Thus the feasibility of $\mathcal{A}$ after Line 9 follows from the observation that the activation pattern for PPTS is feasible. $\mathcal{A}$ remains feasible after each call to ActivatePreBad, because only previously inactive buffers are activated in Line 5. □

Lemma 4.8 asserts that if a node has positive badness at the beginning of a phase, its badness strictly decreases during the phase. Thus, it is analogous to the analysis of PTS and PPTS. Thm. 4.1 follows from an argument analogous to the proofs of Prop. 3.1 and Prop. 3.2.

Lemma 4.8. *Let $t = (\varphi - 1)\ell$ so that the φ-th phase consists of rounds $t, t + 1, \ldots, t + \ell - 1$. Assume that no new packets arrive during rounds $t + 1, t + 2, \ldots, t + \ell - 1$. Then the HPTS algorithm guarantees that for all $i \in \langle n \rangle$, $B^{(t+\ell-1)+}(i) \leq \max\left\{B^t(i) - 1, 0\right\}$.*

The proof of Lemma 4.8 follows from two claims. First, in each round of a phase, the badness of each node is non-increasing. Second, if $B^t(i) > 0$, then $B(i)$ strictly decreases during some round of the phase. Essentially, we show that if $B_{\hat{j}}(i) > 0$ in some round of the phase, then either $B(i)$ decreases, or a bad packet (for i) at level $\hat{j}$ is replaced with a bad packet at some level $j > \hat{j}$ (that was pre-bad before forwarding). Since levels are activated in decreasing order over the course of a phase, $B(i)$ strictly decreases in some round of the phase.

Claim 2. *Let $t = (\varphi - 1)\ell$ and $s = t + \lambda$ for some $\lambda \in \langle \ell \rangle$. Let $\hat{j} = \ell - 1 - \lambda$. Then for all $i \in \langle n \rangle$ the following hold:*

(1) For all $j > \hat{j}$, $B_j^{s+}(i) = B_j^s(i)$.
(2) $B_{\hat{j}}^{s+}(i) \leq \max\{0, B_{\hat{j}}^s(i) - 1\}$.
(3) $B^{s+}(i) \leq B^s(i)$.

Proof. Item (1) holds because HPTS can only activate buffers at levels $j' \leq \hat{j}$ in round $t + \lambda$ and no packet ever moves from level j' to j with $j > j'$. Thus, for $j > \hat{j}$, states of level-j pseudo buffers are unchanged after forwarding. For Item (2), observe that for each interval $I \in \mathcal{I}_{\hat{j}}$ the paths activated in I are precisely the same pseudo-buffers as are activated by PPTS (where the intermediate destinations play the role of destinations in the PPTS algorithm). Thus, Item (2) follows from Lemma 3.4.

In order to prove that Item (3) holds, we carefully argue that packets arriving at intermediate destinations do not cause too much badness at levels $j < \hat{j}$. Before proceeding to the proof, we first make some useful observations about how our algorithm activates paths to deal with such pre-bad packets. Consider a level-j segment A added to $\mathcal{A}$ in a call to ActivatePreBad, and let $I_j = [a_j, b_j] \in \mathcal{I}$ be the level-j interval containing A. Thus $A = [a_j, i_j]$ for some $i_j < b_j$. Let P be the unique pre-bad packet for a_j, and let k be the index such that $w_{P,j}$ is I_j's k-th destination. Observe that one of the following events occurred:

(a) $i_j = w_{P,j} - 1$ and activating A creates a new pre-bad packet P' in buffer $L_{j,k}^s(i_j)$.
(b) $i_j = w_{P,j} - 1$ but activating A does not create another pre-bad packet.
(c) $i_j < w_{P,j} - 1$ and every $i \in I_j$ with $i > i_j$ is active at level $\hat{j}$.[3]

From items (a)–(c) above, each pre-bad P created in the call to FormPaths induces a (possibly empty) sequence $A_1, A_2, \ldots$ of consecutive segments at decreasing levels, where each segment A_{i+1} is activated because event (a) occurred in the activation of A_i. Conversely, every pre-bad packet P' at a level $j < \hat{j}$ is induced from a unique pre-bad packet P at level $\hat{j}$.

To prove Item (3) of the claim, let $i \in I_j$ for some $j < \hat{j}$. We consider three (exhaustive) cases separately.

Case 1: $i \in A_\alpha$ where A_α is the unique activated segment containing i.
Case 2: i is active at level $\hat{j}$, and an active segment $A_\alpha \subseteq I_j$ terminates as in case (c) above (necessarily with $i_j < i$).
Case 3: i is not active.

In Case 1, suppose the segment A_α is at level j. First observe that for $j' \neq j$, we have $B_{j'}^{s+}(i) = B_{j'}^s(i)$ because no buffer $i' \leq i$ at level j' containing packets with intermediate destination $w \geq i$ is active. As for the level-j badness of i, we have $B_j^{s+}(i) \leq B_j^s(i)$. To see this, let $I_j = [a_j, b_j]$ be the level-j interval containing i, so that a_j receives a pre-bad packet P during forwarding. Let k be the index such that $w_{P,j}$ is I_j's k-th intermediate destination. If $\left|L_{j,k}^s(a_j)\right| \geq 2$, then forwarding A_α strictly decreases $B_{j,k}(i)$ by Lemma 3.4, while $B_j(i)$ increases by one as a result of P being forwarded. Similarly, if $\left|L_{j,k}^s(a_j)\right| = 1$, forwarding A_α does not increase $B_{j,k}(i)$. In this case, P being forwarded to a_j does not increase $B_j(i)$, because $L_{j,k}^s(a_j)$'s sole occupant is forwarded.

In Case 2, for all $j' \neq \hat{j}, j$, we have $B_{j'}^{s+}(i) = B_{j'}^s(i)$. Also, $B_{\hat{j}}^{s+}(i) \leq B_{\hat{j}}^s(i) - 1$ by Lemma 3.4. We argue that $B_j^{s+}(i) \leq B_j^s(i) + 1$. To see this first consider the case where $\left|L_{j,k}(a_j)\right| \geq 2$. In this case, $\beta_{j,k}^{s+}(a_j) = \beta_{j,k}^s(a_j)$ because a_j forwards one bad packet, and receives one bad packet. For $i' \in [a_j + 1, i_j]$, $\beta_{j,k}(i')$ does not increase because each non-empty $L_{j,k}(i')$ forwards. Finally $\beta_{j,k}(i_j + 1)$ increases by at most one as a result of $i_j + 1$ receiving a level-j packet, but sending none. Since no other level-j pseudo-buffers forward, in this case, $B_j^{s+}(i) \leq B_j^s(i) + 1$. If $\left|L_{j,k}(i)\right| = 1$, then forwarding P does not create a bad packet, but forwarding A_α could create a single new bad packet (in buffer $i_j + 1$), so the same conclusion holds.

Finally for Case 3, no packet that is pre-bad for any level j has a path crossing i at level j (otherwise Cases 1 or 2 would have occurred). Therefore, forwarding pre-bad packets will not increase $B_j(i)$ for any $j < \hat{j}$, i.e., $B_j^{s+}(i) \leq B_j^s(i)$ for all such j. Further, by Items (1) and (2) of the Claim, we have $B_j^{s+}(i) \leq B_j^s(i)$ for all $j \geq \hat{j}$. □

Proof of Lemma 4.8. Since we assume no injections are made in rounds $t+1, t+2, \ldots, t+\ell-1$, we have $B^{s+1}(i) = B^{s+}(i)$ for all $s = t, t+1, \ldots, t+\ell-2$. Applying Item (3) of Claim 2 iteratively for $t, t+1, \ldots, t+\ell-1$, we find that $B^{(t+\ell-1)+}(i) \leq B^t(i)$. Thus, it suffices to show that if $B^t(i) \geq 1$, there is some round $s = t + \lambda$ for $\lambda \in \langle \ell \rangle$ such that $B^{s+}(i) < B^s(i)$. Let $\hat{j} = \ell - 1 - \lambda$. By Claim 2, in each round s such that $B^s(i) > 0$, either $B^{s+}(i) \leq B^s(i) - 1$, or

$$B_0^{s+}(i) + B_1^{s+}(i) + \cdots + B_{\hat{j}-1}^{s+}(i) = B_0^s(i) + B_1^s(i) + \cdots + B_{\hat{j}-1}^s(i) + 1.$$

That is, either the badness of i decreases, or the level-j badness of i for some $j < \hat{j}$ increases. Consider the largest $\lambda \in \langle \ell \rangle$ such that $B_{\hat{j}}^{t+\lambda}(i) > 0$ where $\hat{j} = \ell - 1 - \lambda$. Then the level-$j$ badness of i did not increase in round $t + \lambda$ for any $j < \hat{j}$, hence, by Claim 2, we have $B^{s+}(i) < B^s(i)$, as desired. □

Proof of Theorem 4.1. Let A be a (ρ, σ)-bounded adversary such that $\rho \cdot \ell \leq 1$, and let A_ℓ be the ℓ-reduction of A (Definition 2.4). For each φ, let $t(\varphi) = (\varphi - 1) \cdot \ell$ denote the beginning of the φ-th phase, and let $t(\varphi+)$ denote the time at the end of phase φ—that is, after the forwarding step of round $t(\varphi) + \ell - 1$.

We claim that for each φ and buffer $i \in \langle n \rangle$, we have $B^{t(\varphi)}(i) \leq \xi^{t(\varphi)}(i) + 1$ and $B^{t(\varphi+)}(i) \leq \max\left\{B^{t(\varphi)}(i) - 1, 0\right\}$. The argument follows by induction. For the base case, both inequalities hold trivially, as no packets have been accepted. For the inductive step, suppose the equations above hold for phase $\varphi - 1$. By Lemmas 2.3 and 2.5, the number of new packets arriving whose paths contain i during phase $\varphi - 1$ satisfies

$$N_{[t(\varphi-1), t(\varphi)-1]}(i) \leq \xi^{t(\varphi)}(i) - \xi^{t(\varphi-1)}(i) + \ell \cdot \rho.$$

[3] The second conclusion holds because intervals activated in FormPaths always terminate at intermediate destinations for level $\hat{j}$. Since $j < \hat{j}$, I_j is contained in the interval between consecutive intermediate level-$\hat{j}$ intermediate destinations, if some $i \in I_j$ is active at level $\hat{j}$, all buffers $i' \in I_j$ with $i' \geq i$ are active at level $\hat{j}$.

Therefore, by the inductive hypothesis, we have

$$B^{t(\varphi)}(i) \le B^{t((\varphi-1)+)}(i) + N_{[t(\varphi-1),t(\varphi)-1]}(i) \le \xi^{t(\varphi)}(i) + \ell \cdot \rho \le \xi^{t(\varphi)}(i) + 1\,,$$

and the inequality $B^{t(\varphi+)}(i) \le \max\{0, B^{t(\varphi)}(i) - 1\}$ follows from Lemma 4.8. □

5 LOWER BOUND

We now show that the upper bound achieved by HPTS is optimal, up to a factor of $O(\rho^{-2})$. We only sketch the argument here. Full details appear in [17].

THEOREM 5.1. *For any $\rho > 1/(\ell+1)$, there exists a $(\rho, 1)$-bounded adversary such that for all forwarding protocols, the buffer requirement is $\Omega\left(\frac{(\ell+1)\rho-1}{2\ell} n^{1/\ell}\right)$.*

Assume that n is of the form $n = (\ell+1)m^\ell$ for some $m, \ell \in \mathbb{N}$, $\ell \ge 2$. We define an injection pattern $\mathcal{A}$ consisting of m^ℓ phases each of length m. During each phase, $\mathcal{A}$ injects packets with $\ell+1$ non-overlapping routes, for a total of $\rho m(\ell+1)$ packets. The rightmost injection site, denoted $F(t)$, decreases by some predetermined amount at the end of each phase, and routes for the next phase are adjusted correspondingly. The routes are constructed such that by the time *any* packet reaches its destination, it must be to the right of the current value of $F(t)$. Thm. 5.1 follows by establishing the following dichotomy: when $F(t)$ is decreased at the end of each phase, either the average load of the interval $[F(t+1), F(t)]$ is $\Omega(m)$, or the average load behind $F(t+1)$ increased during the round. Thus, we show that at the end of the execution, either some interval $[F(t+1), F(t)]$ had a large average load at the end of some phase, or the average load in $[0, F(t)]$ is sufficiently large.

We express each round number $t \ge 0$ in as its base-m representation $t_\ell t_{\ell-1} \cdots t_0$ where $t = \sum_{i=0}^{\ell} t_i m^i$ with each $t_i \in \langle m \rangle$. For each round $t \ge 0$, the phase containing t is called the **$t_\ell \cdots t_1$-phase.** Equivalently, the $t_\ell \cdots t_1$-phase consists of the m rounds starting with $\sum_{k=1}^{\ell} t_k m^k$.

In each $t_\ell \cdots t_1$-phase, the packet injection sites are defined based on the values of $t_\ell, \ldots, t_1$ as follows. For each $t_\ell \cdots t_1$-phase, and $i \in [\ell]$ we define the i-th site

$$v_i(t_\ell \cdots t_1) = \sum_{k=i}^{\ell} \left((k+1)m^k - (t_k+1)km^{k-1}\right)\,.$$

The Injection Pattern. During the $t_\ell \cdots t_1$-phase, A injects packets as follows:

- inject ρm packets into buffer $v_1(t_\ell \cdots t_1)$ with destination n;
- for each $k = 2, \ldots, \ell$, inject ρm packets into buffer $v_k(t_\ell \cdots t_1)$ with destination $v_{k-1}(t_\ell \cdots t_1)$;
- inject ρm packets into buffer 0 with destination $v_\ell(t_\ell \cdots t_1)$.

We define the ***type*** of a packet by its injection site: for each $k \in \{1, \ldots, \ell\}$, packets injected at buffer $v_k(t_\ell \cdots t_1)$ are ***type-k*** packets and those injected at buffer 0 are ***type-(ℓ + 1)*** packets.

For any round t, we denote $F(t) = v_1(t_\ell \cdots t_1)$. That is, $F(t)$ is the site of all injections of type-1 packets (which coincides with destination of all injected type-2 packets) during the $t_\ell \cdots t_1$-phase.

For any packet P, let $P(t)$ denote the buffer in which packet P is stored in round t. We assign each packet a status depending on the relative values of $P(t)$ and $F(t)$: we say that P is ***fresh*** in round t if $P(t) \le F(t)$. Otherwise, if $P(t) > F(t)$, then P is ***stale.*** Note that a packet is fresh when it is injected in a round t, since $P(t)$ is either 0 or $v_1(t_\ell \cdots t_1) = F(t)$. We say that P ***becomes stale at the end of round t*** if P is fresh in round t and is stale in round $t+1$. For any $t_\ell \in \{0, \ldots, m-1\}$, let $f(t_\ell)$ denote the number of fresh packets in the network at the beginning of the $t_\ell 0 \cdots 0$-phase. The following lemma gives conditions under which a packet can become stale.

LEMMA 5.2. *A packet P can only become stale at the end of a round t if either (1) $P(t) = F(t)$ and P is forwarded in round t; or (2) $F(t+1) < F(t)$ and $P(t+1) \in [F(t+1)+1, F(t)]$.*

As packets can become stale for different reasons, we say that a packet is ***α-stale*** if it became stale due to condition 1 of Lemma 5.2, and P is ***β-stale*** if it became stale due to condition 2. The following lemma shows that no packet reaches its destination while it is fresh. The idea is that, in the time it takes for a packet to reach its destination, $F(t)$ moves to the left of the packet's destination.

LEMMA 5.3. *If P has reached its destination in round t', then P is stale in round t'.*

We now give a lower bound on the number of fresh packets in the network at any given time. To do so, we give an upper bound on the number of packets that go stale in each $(t_\ell \cdots t_1)$-phase.

LEMMA 5.4. *Over any interval of $\tau \ge 0$ rounds, the number of packets that become α-stale is at most τ. Let $t \in \langle m^\ell \rangle$. If t is not the last round of the $t_\ell \cdots t_1$-phase, then no packets become β-stale at the end of round t. If t is the last round of the $t_\ell \cdots t_1$-phase, and k is the smallest integer in $\langle \ell \rangle$ such that $t_{k+1} < m-1$, then the number of packets that become β-stale at the end of round t is $L^{t+1}\left(\left[v_1(t_\ell \cdots t_1) - \frac{m(m^k-1)}{m-1}\,,\ v_1(t_\ell \cdots t_1)\right]\right)$.*

LEMMA 5.5. *Consider any fixed $t'_\ell \in \{0, \ldots, m-2\}$. At least one of the following scenarios occurs:*

(1) There exists a $k \in \{0, \ldots, \ell-1\}$ such that $t_{k+1} < m-1$ and at least $((\ell+1)\rho - 1)m^{k+1}/2\ell$ packets become β-stale at the end of the $t'_\ell t_{\ell-1} \cdots t_{k+1}(m-1) \cdots (m-1)$-phase.
(2) $f(t'_\ell + 1) \ge f(t'_\ell) + ((\ell+1)\rho - 1)m^\ell/2$.

PROOF OF THM. 5.1. We proceed by case analysis. First, suppose that the first scenario of Lemma 5.5 is satisfied, i.e., there exists a $t_\ell \in \{0, \ldots, m-2\}$ and an $k \in \{0, \ldots, \ell-1\}$ such that $t_{k+1} < m-1$ and at least $((\ell+1)\rho-1)m^{k+1}/2\ell$ packets become β-stale at the end of the $t_\ell \cdots t_{k+1}(m-1) \cdots (m-1)$-phase. Then, by Lemma 5.4, $L^{t+1}([v_1(t_\ell \cdots t_1) - m(m^k-1)/(m-1), v_1(t_\ell \cdots t_1)]) \ge ((\ell+1)\rho - 1)m^{k+1}/2k$. As $[v_1(t_\ell \cdots t_1) - m(m^k-1)/(m-1), v_1(t_\ell \cdots t_1)]$ consists of $O(m^k)$ buffers, the average load of a buffer in this range is at least $\Omega(((\ell+1)\rho-1)m/2\ell)$. Hence, there is at least one buffer with load at least $\Omega(((\ell+1)\rho-1)m/2\ell)$, giving the desired conclusion.

Otherwise, suppose that the first scenario from Lemma 5.5 is never satisfied in any $t_\ell \cdots t_1$-phase with $t_\ell \in \{0, \ldots, m-2\}$. Then, by Lemma 5.5, the second scenario occurs for every $t_\ell \in \{0, \ldots, m-2\}$. Therefore, $f(m-1) \ge (m-1)((\ell+1)\rho-1)m^\ell/2$. By Lemma 5.3, the total load over all buffers in the first round

t of the $(m-1)0\cdots0$-phase is bounded below by the number of fresh packets, i.e., $L^t([n]) \geq f(m-1) \geq (m-1)((\ell+1)\rho-1)m^\ell/2$. Therefore, the average load in the network in round t is at least $(m-1)((\ell+1)\rho-1)m^\ell/2n = (m-1)((\ell+1)\rho-1)m^\ell/2(\ell+1)m^\ell = (m-1)((\ell+1)\rho-1)/2(\ell+1) \in \Omega\left(\frac{(\ell+1)\rho-1}{2\ell}n^{1/\ell}\right)$, and the conclusion of the theorem follows. □

REFERENCES

[1] Micah Adler and Adi Rosén. 2002. Tight Bounds for the Performance of Longest-in-System on DAGs. In *STACS 2002: 19th Annual Symposium on Theoretical Aspects of Computer Science*, Helmut Alt and Afonso Ferreira (Eds.). Springer Berlin Heidelberg, Berlin, Heidelberg, 88–99. https://doi.org/10.1007/3-540-45841-7_6

[2] William Aiello, Rafail Ostrovsky, Eyal Kushilevitz, and Adi Rosén. 2003. Dynamic Routing on Networks with Fixed-size Buffers. In *Proc. 14th Ann. ACM-SIAM Symp. on Discrete Algorithms (SODA '03)*. SIAM, Philadelphia, PA, USA, 771–780. http://dl.acm.org/citation.cfm?id=644108.644236

[3] Matthew Andrews, Antonio Fernández, Mor Harchol-Balter, Frank Thomson Leighton, and Lisa Zhang. 2000. General Dynamic Routing with Per-Packet Delay Guarantees of O(Distance + 1/Session Rate). *SIAM J. Comput.* 30, 5 (2000), 1594–1623. https://doi.org/10.1137/S009753979935061X

[4] Baruch Awerbuch, Yossi Azar, and Serge A. Plotkin. 1993. Throughput-Competitive On-Line Routing. In *34th Annual Symposium on Foundations of Computer Science, Palo Alto, California, USA, 3-5 November 1993*. IEEE Computer Society, 32–40. https://doi.org/10.1109/SFCS.1993.366884

[5] Rajat Bhattacharjee, Ashish Goel, and Zvi Lotker. 2004. Instability of FIFO at Arbitrarily Low Rates in the Adversarial Queueing Model. *SIAM J. Comput.* 34, 2 (2004), 318–332. https://doi.org/10.1137/S0097539703426805

[6] Allan Borodin, Jon Kleinberg, Prabhakar Raghavan, Madhu Sudan, and David P. Williamson. 2001. Adversarial Queuing Theory. *J. ACM* 48, 1 (Jan. 2001), 13–38. https://doi.org/10.1145/363647.363659

[7] Niv Buchbinder and Joseph Naor. 2009. The Design of Competitive Online Algorithms via a Primal-Dual Approach. *Foundations and Trends in Theoretical Computer Science* 3, 2-3 (2009), 93–263. https://doi.org/10.1561/0400000024

[8] R. L. Cruz. 1991. A calculus for network delay, part I: Network elements in isolation. *IEEE Transactions on Information Theory* 37, 1 (January 1991), 114–131. https://doi.org/10.1109/18.61109

[9] Stefan Dobrev, Manuel Lafond, Lata Narayanan, and Jaroslav Opatrny. 2017. Optimal Local Buffer Management for Information Gathering with Adversarial Traffic. In *Proceedings of the 29th ACM Symposium on Parallelism in Algorithms and Architectures, SPAA 2017, Washington DC, USA, July 24-26, 2017*. ACM, 265–274. https://doi.org/10.1145/3087556.3087577

[10] Guy Even, Moti Medina, and Adi Rosén. 2016. A Constant Approximation Algorithm for Scheduling Packets on Line Networks. In *24th Annual European Symposium on Algorithms (ESA 2016) (Leibniz International Proceedings in Informatics (LIPIcs))*, Piotr Sankowski and Christos Zaroliagis (Eds.), Vol. 57. Schloss Dagstuhl–Leibniz-Zentrum fuer Informatik, Dagstuhl, Germany, 40:1–40:16. https://doi.org/10.4230/LIPIcs.ESA.2016.40

[11] L. Fratta, M. Gerla, and L. Kleinrock. 1973. The flow deviation method: An approach to store-and-forward communication network design. *Networks* 3, 2 (1973), 97–133. https://doi.org/10.1002/net.3230030202 arXiv:https://onlinelibrary.wiley.com/doi/pdf/10.1002/net.3230030202

[12] Michael H. Goldwasser. 2010. A Survey of Buffer Management Policies for Packet Switches. *SIGACT News* 41, 1 (March 2010), 100–128. https://doi.org/10.1145/1753171.1753195

[13] Alexander Kesselman, Zvi Lotker, Yishay Mansour, Boaz Patt-Shamir, Baruch Schieber, and Maxim Sviridenko. 2004. Buffer Overflow Management in QoS Switches. *SIAM J. Comput.* 33, 3 (2004), 563–583. https://doi.org/10.1137/S0097539701399666 arXiv:http://dx.doi.org/10.1137/S0097539701399666

[14] Alexander Kesselman, Yishay Mansour, Zvi Lotker, and Boaz Patt-Shamir. 2003. Buffer overflows of merging streams. In *SPAA 2003: Proceedings of the Fifteenth Annual ACM Symposium on Parallelism in Algorithms and Architectures, June 7-9, 2003, San Diego, California, USA (part of FCRC 2003)*, Arnold L. Rosenberg and Friedhelm Meyer auf der Heide (Eds.). ACM, 244–245. https://doi.org/10.1145/777412.777452

[15] Nick McKeown, Martin Izzard, Adisak Mekkittikul, William Ellersick, and Mark Horowitz. 1997. Tiny Tera: a packet switch core. *IEEE Micro* 17, 1 (1997), 26–33. https://doi.org/10.1109/40.566194

[16] Avery Miller and Boaz Patt-Shamir. 2016. Buffer Size for Routing Limited-Rate Adversarial Traffic. In *DISC 2016: Proceedings of the 30th International Symposium on Distributed Computing, Paris, France, September 27-29, 2016*. Springer, 328–341. https://doi.org/10.1007/978-3-662-53426-7_24

[17] Avery Miller, Boaz Patt-Shamir, and Will Rosenbaum. 2019. With Great Speed Come Small Buffers: Space-Bandwidth Tradeoffs for Routing. arXiv:arXiv:1902.08069

[18] Boaz Patt-Shamir and Will Rosenbaum. 2017. The Space Requirement of Local Forwarding on Acyclic Networks. In *PODC 2017: Proceedings of the ACM Symposium on Principles of Distributed Computing, Washington, DC, USA, July 25-27, 2017*, Elad Michael Schiller and Alexander A. Schwarzmann (Eds.). ACM, 13–22. https://doi.org/10.1145/3087801.3087803

[19] Boaz Patt-Shamir and Will Rosenbaum. 2019. Space-Optimal Nearly-Local Forwarding on Trees. In *INFOCOM 2019: Proc. 2019 IEEE Conference on Computer Communications, Paris, France, April 29 – May 2, 2019*. To appear.

[20] Adi Rosén and Gabriel Scalosub. 2011. Rate vs. Buffer Size–Greedy Information Gathering on the Line. *ACM Trans. Algorithms* 7, 3 (2011), 32:1–32:22. https://doi.org/10.1145/1978782.1978787

Plain SINR is Enough!

Magnús M. Halldórsson
ICE-TCS, Department of Computer Science,
Reykjavik University
Reykjavik, Iceland
mmh@ru.is

Tigran Tonoyan
ICE-TCS, Department of Computer Science,
Reykjavik University
Reykjavik, Iceland
ttonoyan@gmail.com

ABSTRACT

We develop randomized distributed algorithms for many of the most fundamental communication problems in the wireless SINR model, including (multi-message) broadcast, local broadcast, coloring, MIS, and aggregation. The complexity of the algorithms is optimal up to polylogarithmic preprocessing time. It shows – contrary to expectation – that the plain vanilla SINR model is just as powerful and fast (modulo the preprocessing) as various extensions studied, including power control, carrier sense, collision detection, free acknowledgements, and GPS location. A key component of the algorithms is an efficient simulation of Congest algorithms on a constant-density SINR backbone.

CCS CONCEPTS

• **Networks → Ad hoc networks; Network control algorithms;** • **Theory of computation → Distributed algorithms.**

KEYWORDS

wireless network, distributed algorithm, plain SINR

ACM Reference Format:
Magnús M. Halldórsson and Tigran Tonoyan. 2019. Plain SINR is Enough!. In *2019 ACM Symposium on Principles of Distributed Computing (PODC '19), July 29-August 2, 2019, Toronto, ON, Canada.* ACM, New York, NY, USA, 10 pages. https://doi.org/10.1145/3293611.3331602

1 INTRODUCTION

Research on distributed algorithms has generally three major thrusts:

- Develop algorithms for fundamental communication tasks that are optimal in the context of the model in question,
- Determine the value of natural extensions to the model, or additional primitives, and
- Compare and relate the model to other natural models.

We address and make significant progress on all of these in the context of wireless networking, specifically with respect to the *SINR model*.

ACM ISBN 978-1-4503-6217-7/19/07...$15.00
https://doi.org/10.1145/3293611.3331602

In wireless networking, we have n transceivers located in space that have no prior information about the other nodes. They communicate by transmitting over a shared channel, which has the downside of causing interference for other nearby transmissions. There are two major families of models of wireless networking, that differ on impact of interference and what constitutes a successful transmission. In the *radio network model* (RN), communication and interference follows a given graph. Transmission from a node v to a node w succeeds if they are neighbors and no other neighbor of w is transmitting. In the *SINR model*, nodes are embedded on the Euclidean plane and the strength of a transmission decreases with the distance traveled. A transmission succeeds if the strength of the signal at the receiver exceeds by a given factor the sum of the signal strengths of the concurrent interfering transmissions. Fading channels (like the SINR model) differ crucially in two ways from the graph-based models (like RN). On one hand, they capture the cumulative interference of transmissions outside the immediate neighborhood, which makes the design of protocols more challenging. On the other hand, the model is "scale-free", with transmissions succeeding between sufficiently close-by nodes in spite of significant interference, which has the potential of leading to more efficient algorithms. While all of these abstract models are by nature idealized, the aim of studying them is to understand the impact of different features of the complicated space of communication patterns.

Various extensions have been proposed and studied, especially for the SINR model. With *collision detection*, nodes can determine whether a transmission was made but failed due to conflicting transmissions. This may be achieved using *carrier sense*, which allows nodes to measure the strength of received signals and/or the signal-to-noise ratio of the strongest signal. This can be used to *infer distances* of transmitting nodes. With GPS signals, the nodes may even determine their *position* in space. And *power control* can be used both to make inferences about distances, as well as to improve the efficiency of the communication. The *weak devices* model assumes that signal is never received at distances close to the communication range, thus avoiding global effect of interference in some extent. Finally, *prior knowledge* about the network, or the structure of the nearby nodes, can sometimes be leveraged. Some of these features have been shown to lead to faster algorithms, but little has been known if they are provably stronger.

Some of the most fundamental problems in multi-hop wireless networks are:

- *(Multi-Message) Broadcast (MMB)*: forward a message (collection of k messages) from its source(s) to all the nodes.
- *Local Broadcast (LBcast)*: transmit a message from each node to all of its neighbors.

- *Aggregation*: compute a compressible function of values at the nodes.
- *Maximal Independent Set (MIS)*: select an independent subset of nodes that dominate all the others.
- *$O(\Delta)$-coloring*: assign the nodes colors proportional to the size of the largest neighborhood.

Problem	*Our result*	*Lower Bound*
MMB	$D + k + \tilde{O}(\log^2 n)$	$D + k + \log n$
LBcast	$\Delta + \tilde{O}(\log^2 n)$	$\Delta + \log n$
Aggregation	$D + \log \Lambda \cdot \tilde{O}(\log n)$	$D + \log n$
MIS	$\tilde{O}(\log^2 n)$	$\log n$
Coloring	$\log \Lambda \cdot \tilde{O}(\log n)$ $\Delta + \tilde{O}(\log^2 n)$	$\log n$

Table 1: Order-of-growth runtime of our algorithms. D,Δ,Λ and n denote the diameter, maximum degree, max-to-min distance ratio, and total number of nodes in the instance, respectively (see Sec. 2).

1.1 Our Results

We address the problems above in the PLAINSINR model, which refers to the SINR model without any extension. Our results, listed in Table 1, are universally optimal (i.e., for every instance, and compared with lower bounds even in the extensions of SINR), modulo a polylogarithmic additive term and constant multiplicative factors. Moreover, for all problems except LBcast and single-message broadcast, we give the *first ever* explicit results that hold in PLAINSINR. For LBcast, we eliminate the multiplicative log-factor known in PLAINSINR, and essentially match what was known for some SINR extensions (see the Related Work). In the bounds in Table 1, $\tilde{O}$ hides $O(\log \log n)$ factors. Observe also that the geometric parameter Λ is polynomial in n in any reasonable instance.

Simulations of higher-level models allow for an effective way to sidestep the issue of designing algorithms for the lower-level fading-channel models. We give a simulation of the broadcast-CONGEST model in PLAINSINR with an overhead factor of $O(\Delta \log \Delta)$, where Δ is the maximum neighborhood density. This is an adaptation of a recent result of Censor-Hillel et al. [4] for a noisy version of RN. Aside from its general utility, we crucially depend on this simulation for the MMB and LBcast algorithms.

Our results also lead to some interesting contrasts between the core wireless models: RN and PLAINSINR. LBcast is known to require a multiplicative logarithmic factor in RN [10], which we now know is not needed in PLAINSINR. The best algorithms for global broadcast in RN without collision detection run in asymptotically $D \log n$ time, while it is not known if this is necessary when preprocessing is allowed. Perhaps the most surprising result is the polylogarithmic round algorithm for coloring. Previous algorithms were at least linear in the neighborhood size Δ (even under the assumption that $\Lambda = poly(n)$). In fact, $\Omega(\Delta)$ is a lower bound for coloring in any graph-based wireless model: in order for the nodes to learn their color, Δ slots are necessary, even in a clique graph. The same holds for Aggregation: In any graph, Δ time slots are always necessary, while in PLAINSINR the dependence on Δ is only logarithmic. We have thus uncovered a property of the fading channel that can lead to dramatic speedups over the more classical models.

Techniques. Our results rely heavily on the availability of a *backbone*, which has recently been shown to be efficiently computable [15]. A backbone is a constant-degree subgraph that functions as a connected dominating set allowing for optimal throughput (modulo constants). The backbone solves the hardest part in designing distributed algorithms in the SINR model: avoiding *weak links*. Nodes that are almost unit distance apart may be able to communicate sporadically but the link connecting them is so susceptible to interference that it should not be relied on. Some previous work has sidestepped the issue by essentially forbidding such weak forms of communication (e.g., [6, 20, 26]).

Our algorithms are structured in three phases, where the data transport is first loaded onto the backbone, then across the backbone, and finally off the backbone to the non-backbone nodes. The otherwise challenging middle phase is made near trivial with our CONGEST simulation applied to the backbone. The other two phases are local and after coloring the clusters defined by the backbone nodes, we can utilize known single-hop algorithms for these tasks. Thus, a by-product of this work is a mechanism to extend single-hop algorithms to work in a multi-hop setting.

1.2 Related Work

The recent result on backbone construction [15] is the starting point of our work. It is used there in straightforward manner to achieve global broadcast in $O(D) + \tilde{O}(\log^2 n)$ steps, whereas the previous best bound was $O(D \log n + \log^2 n)$ [18] (see also [5, 12]). Better results are known with location information [17, 19], power control [25], or carrier sense [23], with the latter two running in $O(D + \log n)$ rounds. MMB has been addressed in [16] and [25]. The former uses location information of nodes to devise a deterministic algorithm with runtime $O(D + k + \Delta poly \log(n))$, while the latter uses power control to give $O(D + k + \log^2 n)$[1] round algorithm. Both papers use the weak devices assumption.

The best result for LBcast in PLAINSINR model is $O(\Delta \log n)$ [11] when Δ is known and $O(\Delta \log n + \log^2 n)$ [14, 24] for unknown Δ. This can be improved to $O(\Delta + \log^2 n)$ when additionally assuming that acknowledgements are free [14], to $O(\Delta + \log n \cdot \log \log n)$ when Δ is additionally known [2], and to $O(\Delta + \log n)$ with carrier sensing [27].

There are several algorithms for node coloring in the SINR model that run in $O(\Delta \log n)$ [6, 8] or $O(\Delta \log n + \log^2 n)$ [26] rounds. The papers [8, 26] compute a $\Delta + 1$-coloring (assuming Δ is known), while [6] computes $O(\Delta)$-coloring. They all assume the weak devices model. No explicit algorithm has been given for MIS, which again has to do with the difficulty of avoiding weak links. It was achieved in $O(\log^2 n)$ steps with power control [26]. *Constant-density dominating set (CDDS)*, which is a relaxed variant of a MIS, was constructed in $\tilde{O}(\log^2 n)$ steps in PLAINSINR model in [15]. Using carrier sense, CDDS can be constructed in $O(\log n)$ steps [23]. A

[1] There is an additional assumption in [25], that the diameter of the network with communication radius R is proportional to the diameter w.r.t. a smaller communication radius δR, for a small constant $\delta \in (0, 1)$.

distributional variant of CDDS (which yields a logarithmic-density dominating set) was obtained in PLAINSINR in $O(\log^2 n)$ steps [18].

Aggregation can be achieved in a single-hop setting in $O(\log \Lambda)$ steps after $O(\log \Lambda \log n \log^* n)$ preprocessing [13]. The only results in multi-hop settings use additional features, both power control and distance measurements [3], running in $O(D + \log n)$ steps after polylogarithmic (in Λ and n) preprocessing.

The optimal complexity for LBcast in RN is $\Delta \cdot \tilde{\Theta}(\log n)$ [10]. For global broadcast, a $O(D \log n + \log^2 n)$ algorithm, with an essentially matching lower bound holds in the *non-spontaneous* case [21, 22], even when allowing collision detection. With preprocessing *and* collision detection, $O(D + polylog(n))$ can be achieved [9], but if only preprocessing is allowed but no collision detection, the best lower bound seems to be $\Omega(D + \log^2 n)$ [1].

2 MODELS AND STRUCTURES

Let V denote the input set of n wireless nodes, represented as distinct points in the Euclidean plane. The transmission power of all nodes is set to a static value P. The *r-disk* of a node $v \in V$ is a closed disk of radius r centered at v. We only consider disks centered at nodes. The *maximum degree* Δ_S of a set S of nodes (or simply Δ, if S is clear from the context) is the maximum number of nodes of S in a single 1-disk. The *ϵ-diameter* (or simply diameter) D_ϵ of a set S of nodes is the diameter of the graph over S where two nodes are adjacent if and only if their distance is at most $1 - \epsilon$.

2.1 Backbone

A *δ-core* of network V, for $\delta \in (0, 1)$, is a subset $U \subseteq V$ of nodes such that: a) U is a *δ-dominating set*: every δ-disk contains at least one node of U, b) U is *sparse*, of degree $\delta^{-O(1)}$, and c) Every node $v \in V$ knows its unique *dominator*, i.e., a node $u \in U$ in the δ-disk of v. The set of nodes with a common dominator u is called a *cluster*.

A *reliable δ-communication graph* over a set U of nodes, for $\delta \in (0, 1)$, is a simple graph $G = (U, E)$, such that: a) Nodes in U at distance at most $1 - \delta$ are adjacent, b) Nodes know their neighbors, and c) There is a constant $c > 0$, such that for any assignment of transmission probabilities $\{p_v\}$ to nodes $v \in U$ with the property that the total probability mass in every 1-disk B is at most $\sum_{v \in B \cap U} p_v \le c\delta$, it holds that if every node $v \in U$ transmits independently w.p.[2] p_v, then the transmission of each node w is received by all its neighbors in G w.p. $\Omega(p_w)$.

An *ϵ-backbone* of network V, for a parameter $\epsilon > 0$, consists of an ϵ-core U together with a reliable ϵ-communication graph on U.

2.2 PLAINSINR model

According to the *physical* or *SINR* model of communication, if the nodes of a subset U transmit simultaneously, the transmission of a node $u \in U$ is successfully received by a *listening* node v, iff $\frac{P}{d(u,v)^\alpha} > \beta \cdot (N + I_v)$, where d denotes the (Euclidean) distance, $\alpha > 2$ is the *path-loss* constant, $\beta > 1$ is the *reception threshold*, $N > 0$ is the *ambient noise*, and $I_v = \sum_{w \in U \setminus \{u\}} \frac{P}{d(w,v)^\alpha}$ is the *interference* on node v by nodes in $U \setminus \{u\}$. Note that $d_{max} = (P/(\beta N))^{1/\alpha}$ is the maximum distance at which communication between two nodes is possible, in the absence of interference. We scale the distances so that $d_{max} = 1$, which implies that $P = \beta N$.

We refer to the above model as PLAINSINR model to emphasize that it excludes any extra features or primitives such as power control, carrier sensing, knowledge of geoposition, channel coding techniques or weak devices assumption.

Assumptions. We assume *spontaneous* mode of operation, where the nodes simultaneously start executing a protocol at a pre-specified time. The computations are performed in synchronous rounds. Nodes have unique IDs, and know the SINR parameters α, β, N. They also know the precision parameter ϵ and a polynomial upper-bound on n.

THEOREM 2.1 ([15]). *There is a PLAINSINR randomized algorithm that for every constant $\epsilon \in (0, 1/3]$, computes an ϵ-backbone in $\ell = \tilde{O}(\log^2 n)$ rounds, w.h.p.*

3 CONGEST ALGORITHMS OVER THE BACKBONE

An algorithm using a backbone to perform certain computation can be seen as a combination of two logical parts: Local computation within individual clusters, and computation over the backbone communication graph. In this section, we address the first part in isolation. To this end, we use the method developed in [4] to simulate any CONGEST algorithm over the communication graph using the probabilistic communication of the backbone. We simulate broadcast-CONGEST algorithms, which can in turn be used to simulate any CONGEST algorithm, by increasing the runtime by a Δ_b factor, where $\Delta_b = O(1)$ is the maximum degree of the communication graph. In broadcast-CONGEST, nodes communicate in synchronous rounds, and in each round, every node can send a single packet of size $O(\log n)$ to all its neighbors. We will refer to the algorithm to be simulated as the *original algorithm*, while to the simulation algorithm as *simulation*.

Our algorithm is based on the ideas of [4, Thm. 3] but is slightly faster than the algorithm there.[3] We consider the following general communication model, where there is a single *transmit* operation, with the following properties: *if all neighbors of node v transmit in a given round, then v receives the message of any given neighbor independently with probability (at least) c/Δ_b, for a constant $c > 0$, and the receptions in different rounds are independent across all nodes.* This model can be implemented over a backbone in PLAINSINR, as well as in the *noisy radio network model* of [4].

The simulation setup is as follows. Every node v holds messages $m_v(i)$, $i \le r_v$, where r_v is the current round number, initialized to 1. The data $m_v(i)$ includes the message node v needs to send to its neighbors in round i of the original algorithm, and is a function of the set of $m_w(j)$, for all $j \le i - 1$ and all neighbors w. Note that $m_v(1)$ is the initial value of node v, and $m_v(j) = \perp$ if node v had no message to send in round j of the original algorithm (i.e., in the simulation, v always sends some message for every round). Hence, the goal of node v with current round number r is to receive values $m_w(j)$ for all $j \le i - 1$ and all nodes $w \in N(v)$, in order to be

[2] We use w.p. and w.h.p. for "with probability" and "with high probability" (namely, w.p. $1 - n^{-c}$, for a constant $c \ge 1$), respectively.

[3] The runtime claimed in [4, Thm. 3] actually coincides with the one we claim, but we believe there should be an extra $\log \Delta_b$ factor there, which can be seen by examining Algs. 5 and 6.

able to increment r_v and construct the message $m_v(r_v+1)$, where $N(v)$ denotes the neighborhood of v in the communication graph. Additionally, v maintains a binary variable ready_v, initialized to 0, which is set to 1 when v has received messages $m_w(r_v)$ from each $w \in N(v)$ and indicates that it is ready to move to the next round.

Algorithm 1 SIMULATION(node v)

```
r_v ← 1, ready_v ← 0, m_v(r_v) ← input value
r_w ← 0, ready^r_w ← 0, ∀w ∈ N(v), r ≥ 1
while original algorithm not completed do
    transmit (m_v(r_v), ready_v)
    if received (m_w(r), x) then
        ready^r_w ← x, r_w ← r
    end if
    if r_w ≥ r_v for each w ∈ N(v) then
        ready_v ← 1
    end if
    if ready^{r_v}_w = 1 for each w ∈ N(v) then
        r_v ← r_v + 1, ready_v ← 0, construct m_v(r_v)
    end if
end while
```

It is easy to see that Alg. 1 correctly simulates the operation of the original algorithm. Next, we bound the runtime of simulation.

THEOREM 3.1. *If the original algorithm terminates in $T = poly(n)$ time, then the simulation terminates in time $O((T+\log n)\Delta_b \log \Delta_b) = O(T+\log n)$, w.h.p. in n.*

PROOF. We partition the runtime of the simulation into contiguous blocks of $c\Delta_b \log n \log \Delta_b$ rounds, for an appropriate constant $c > 0$. For each $i \geq 1$, assuming that at the beginning of the ith block $r_v \geq (i-1)\log n$ holds for every node v, we show that by the end of the block, each node v has $r_v \geq i \cdot \log n$ w.p. at least $1 - 1/(Tn)$. This is sufficient for the proof, since using a simple induction and the union bound, we can see that the simulation will terminate by the end of block $T/\log n + 1$ w.h.p., and will have spent at most $(T/\log n+1)\cdot O(\Delta_b \log n \log \Delta_b) = O((T+\log n)\Delta_b \log \Delta_b)$ time.

Thus, we focus on a block for which the inductive assumption holds. Moreover, we consider w.l.o.g. the first block. Let $T_{v,x}$ denote the first simulation round when a node v sets $r_v = x$, for $x > 1$. Let further $R_{v,x}$ denote the first simulation round when $r_v = x$ and $\text{ready}_v = 1$. Suppose that at some time during the simulation, we have $r_w \geq x-1$ and $\text{ready}_w = 1$, for each neighbor $w \in N(v)$ of a node v. Then, v sets $r_v = x$ (if it has not done that by that time) as soon as it receives a message from each neighbor. This observation implies that

$$T_{v,x} \leq \max_{w \in N(v)} R_{w,x-1} + C_{v,x}, \tag{1}$$

where $C_{v,x}$ is a random variable that bounds the time needed for v to receive a message from each neighbor. Next, let us bound $R_{v,x}$. Observe that starting from a time when $r_w = x$, for all $w \in N(v)$, node v sets $\text{ready}_v = 1$ as soon as it receives a new message from each neighbor. Therefore, we have $R_{v,x} \leq \max_{w\in N(v)} T_{v,x} + C'_{v,x}$, where $C'_{v,x}$ has the same distribution as $C_{v,x}$. Plugging this in (1), we obtain the recursion

$$\begin{aligned} T_{v,x} &\leq \max_{u \in N^2(w)} (T_{u,x-1} + C'_{u,x-1}) + C_{v,x} \\ &\leq \max_{w_1,w_2,\dots,w_x} \sum_{i=1}^{x} (C_{w_i,x_i} + C'_{w_i,x_i}) \\ &\leq 2 \cdot \max_{w_1,w_2,\dots,w_x} \sum_{i=1}^{x} C_{w_i,x_i} \end{aligned}$$

where $N^2(v)$ is the 2-hop neighborhood of node v, $x_i = x - i + 1$ and the maximum is taken over all tuples $w_1, w_2, \dots, w_x$ (called *blaming chains* in [4]) with $w_1 = v$ and $w_{i+1} \in N^2(w_i)$, for all $i \leq x-1$. The last inequality holds because $C_{v,x}$ and $C'_{v,x}$ are identically distributed.

We would like to bound $T_{v,t}$ with $t = \log n$. Let us first bound the sum $L = \sum_{i=1}^{t} C_{w_i,x_i}$ corresponding to a fixed tuple $w_1,\dots,w_t$. Note that the variables C_{w_i,x_i} are independent, as we consider the corresponding events *separated in time.* $C_{w,x}$ is a Coupon Collector type r.v. that bounds the time until node w receives a message (corresponding to a coupon in the Coupon Collector's Problem) from every neighbor. Assuming that w has collected messages from $\Delta_b - i$ neighbors, the probability that it receives a message from the remaining i neighbors in a simulation round is at least $c'i/\Delta_b$, for a constant $c' > 0$. Therefore, $C_{w,x}$ can be seen as a sum $\sum_{i=1}^{\Delta_b} g_{w,x,i}$ of geometric r.v. $g_{w,x,i}$ with parameters $c'i/\Delta_b$, implying:

$$L = \sum_{i=1}^{t} C_{w_i,x_i} = \sum_{i=1}^{t}\sum_{j=1}^{\Delta_b} g_{w_i,x_i,j} = \sum_{j=1}^{\Delta_b}\sum_{i=1}^{t} g_{w_i,x_i,j} \,.$$

Note that the inner sum $L_j = \sum_{i=1}^{t} g_{w_i,x_i,j}$ is a sum of i.i.d. geometric r.v. with parameter $p_j = c'j/\Delta_b$. The sum $L = \sum_j L_j$ can further be regrouped into $L = \sum_{l=0}^{\log \Delta_b} SL_l$, where $SL_l = \sum_{j=2^l}^{2^{l+1}-1} L_j$. Note that SL_l is probabilistically dominated by a sum of $s = 2^l t$ i.i.d. geometric r.v.s with parameter $q_l = c'2^l/\Delta_b$.

Let us focus on SL_l with a fixed value l. We can assume for simplicity that $SL_l = \sum_{j=1}^{s} g_j$, where g_j are i.i.d. geometric with parameter q_l. Since g_j are independent, their sum can be considered as the time it takes to flip a coin with probability of heads q_l until flipping s heads. Thus, for an integer $k \geq 1$ we have $\mathbb{P}[SL_l > k \cdot s] \leq \mathbb{P}[Bin(ks, q_l) < s]$, where $Bin(n,p)$ is the number of successes in n independent trials with success probability p. A standard Chernoff bound gives,

$$\mathbb{P}[SL_l > k \cdot s] \leq \mathbb{P}[Bin(ks, q_l) < s] \leq \exp\left(-\left(1 - \frac{1}{kq_l}\right)^2 \frac{ksq_l}{2}\right)$$

for every $k > 1/q_l$. For choosing k consider two cases.

Case $l \geq \log\log \Delta_b$: Let $k = 13c''/q_l$ for a constant $c'' \geq \max\{\log_n^T, 1\}$, to obtain that $SL_l \leq ks = 13c''\Delta_b t$ w.p. at least $1 - \exp(-6c''s) \geq 1 - \exp(-6c''t \log \Delta_b)$, using $s \geq t \log \Delta_b$.

Case $l < \log\log \Delta_b$: Let $k = 13c'' \log \Delta_b/(2^l q_l)$. Then w.p. at least $1 - \exp(-6c''t \log \Delta_b)$,

$$SL_l \leq sk \leq 2^l t \cdot 13c'' \log \Delta_b/(2^l q_l) = \frac{13c''}{c'2^l} \Delta_b \log \Delta_b t \,.$$

By the union bound, w.p. $1-\exp(-6c''t\log\Delta_b)\log\Delta_b$ the bounds above hold for all l, in which case we have:

$$\begin{aligned} L &= \sum_{l=0}^{\log\log\Delta_b} SL_l + \sum_{l=\log\log\Delta_b}^{\log\Delta_b} SL_l \\ &< \frac{13c''}{c'}\Delta_b\log\Delta_b t\cdot\sum_{l=0}^{\log\log\Delta_b} 2^{-l} + 13c''\Delta_b t\log\Delta_b \\ &< \frac{39c''}{c'}\Delta_b\log\Delta_b t\,. \end{aligned}$$

It remains to apply the union bound over all possible tuples in order to bound $T_{v,\log n}$. There are at most $\Delta_b^{2\log n+2}\le\exp(3\log n\log\Delta_b)$ many such tuples, hence we have, as required,

$$\begin{aligned} &\mathbb{P}\left[T_{v,\log n} > \frac{39c''}{c'}\Delta_b\log\Delta_b t\right] \\ &\quad< \exp(3\log n\log\Delta_b)\cdot\exp(-6c''\log n\log\Delta_b)\log\Delta_b\,. \end{aligned}$$

The latter is at most $1-\frac{1}{Tn^2}$, implying that w.p. $1-\frac{1}{Tn}$, by the end of the block of $O(\Delta_b\log\Delta_b\log n)$ simulation rounds, every node v will have $r_v\ge\log n$. □

4 LOCAL PRIMITIVES

The goal of *local primitives* is to communicate data between backbone nodes and their clusters. In what follows, we will assume that *we are given an ϵ-backbone with $\epsilon\le d_0$*, where d_0 is a distance satisfying Prop. 4.1, which can be found (in some form) in every other paper on the SINR model.

Proposition 4.1. *Let U be the set of nodes that transmit in a given time slot, and let $u\in U$. Assume that: a) Every 1/3-disk contains at most a constant number c of nodes from U, and b) The 1/3-disk of v contains no other node from U. There is a distance $1/3 > d_0 > 0$, depending only on parameters α, β and c, such that all nodes in the d_0-disk of node v receive v's message.*

4.1 Coloring Schedule

For all primitives, we use a schedule of the backbone nodes consisting of a vertex coloring of the communication graph with colors from $[1,2,\ldots,c]$, where c is a constant (depending on the parameter ϵ). Such a coloring can be computed in $O(\log n)$ rounds and is assumed to be given. By *coloring schedule* of the backbone we will refer to the process of activating backbone nodes of color i in ith *phase*, where i cycles from 1 to c in a round robin fashion, and a phase is a fixed number of consequent rounds (depending on the application.)

4.2 Download

In the *Download* primitive, each backbone node v has a number m_v of messages and the goal is to broadcast them to all nodes in its cluster. The algorithm consists of backbone nodes transmitting their messages one by one, according to the coloring schedule. Node v terminates the algorithm when it has sent all its messages. Prop. 4.1 implies that every transmission of a backbone node is received *deterministically*, since in every round, only backbone nodes of the same color can transmit simultaneously.

Proposition 4.2. *Each backbone node v completes Download in m_v rounds.*

4.3 Upload

Upload is the inverse operation of Download: Each node in the network has a number of messages, and the goal is for each node to send its messages to its dominator in the backbone.

Let us first consider the special case of the problem, *single-hop data collection*, where every pair of nodes is within distance $1-\epsilon$ and there is a single dominator.

Single-hop data collection. This variant can be addressed using a local broadcast algorithm of [14, Sec. 5] that runs in $O(\Delta+\log^2 n)$ rounds in a (multi-hop) network with unknown max degree Δ (we present an alternative simple implementation in Appendix A.) In order to make progress, nodes that successfully transmit a message to their neighbors (in the $(1-\epsilon)$)-disk) need to bow out. This is achieved in [14] by either carrier sensing or by letting nodes wait long enough to be confident they succeeded. In our setting, since only the dominator needs to receive the messages, we can use a third option: the dominator acknowledges the messages it receives. This can be implemented, e.g., by partitioning the rounds into even and odd, and running the original algorithm of [14] in even rounds, while reserving the odd rounds for the dominator to acknowledge the last message it has received (it can receive only a single message per round). Note that transmissions of the dominator always succeed, since it is the only node transmitting. It is also straightforward to show that the algorithm works even when each node can have *more than one message.* Moreover, some messages can be *duplicated* across several nodes, i.e., multiple nodes trying to broadcast the same message. It follows from [14, Lemma 10] that each time *a message* is transmitted, it is heard by the dominator with constant probability, and hence leaves the contention in the following round (this clearly holds for duplicated messages as well). With this in hand, the bound in [14, Lemma 5] becomes $O((k+\log n)/\log n)$ instead of $O((N_x+\log n)/\log n)$, and we obtain the following result by repeating the rest of the original proof almost verbatim.

Proposition 4.3. *There is a randomized algorithm for single-hop data collection, where $k=poly(n)$ messages are sent to the leader in $O(k+\log^2 n)$ rounds, w.h.p.*

The multi-hop case. The result above can be extended to implement the Upload primitive on the backbone. We use a coloring schedule with phase length $f\in[1,O(\log^2 n)]$, i.e., time is split into phases of length f. All clusters of color i run the algorithm for single-hop data collection in parallel in (and only in) phases with number $t=i \mod c+1$. Thus, we can assume each color class runs the algorithm in parallel, but in isolation from other classes. Note that the algorithm of [14] is designed for the multi-hop setting, so the only thing that needs to be argued here is that every (ack) message of each dominator is received by its cluster nodes[4]. This follows from the choice of the parameter ϵ of the backbone, the coloring of the backbone nodes, and Prop. 4.1. The total runtime is then $O(c\cdot k+f)=O(k+\log^2 n)$.

[4]It is not hard to show that probabilistic reception of the ack messages (with constant probability) also suffices.

Proposition 4.4. *There is a randomized algorithm for Upload, where every backbone node receives all k messages from its cluster within $O(k + \log^2 n)$ rounds, w.h.p.*

4.4 Local Aggregation

A *Local Aggregation Tree* for a cluster is a tree structure over the set of cluster nodes which allows, among other things, aggregating values of cluster nodes into the dominator (e.g., computing the max value).

Distances between the nodes can be partitioned into classes, where class $i \geq 0$ contains distances between 2^{-i-1} and 2^{-i} (assuming max distance is 1). We assume the nodes have an upper bound Π on the number of distance classes. It is easy to see that $\Pi = O(\log \Lambda)$, where Λ is the max to min distance ratio. As argued by Fineman et al. [7], $\Pi = O(\log n)$ in most reasonable networks.

The single-hop case. An aggregation tree for a single-hop network is constructed in [13] in $O(\Pi \log n \log^* n)$ rounds, and has the following properties [13, Thm. 4]:

(1) The tree has height $h = O(\Pi)$. A node of the network may represent tree vertices along a root-leaf subpath, but incomparable tree vertices are represented by distinct network nodes.
(2) The tree edges/links between level-i and level-$(i+1)$ vertices are scheduled in $O(1)$ slots, for $i = 0, 1, \ldots, h-2$. In particular, data can be aggregated from the leaves (i.e., all nodes) to the root in $O(h)$ rounds. Moreover, the schedule is *bi-directional*, that is, every link can transmit in either parent-to-child or the reverse direction.

The tree is constructed level-by-level, starting from the leaves (see [13, Sec. 6.3]). The key property of the SINR model that underlies this construction is the following [13, Lemma 1]:

Proposition 4.5. *Let U be the set of nodes that transmit in a given time slot, and let $u \in U$. Let d denote the minimum pairwise distance in U. For any constant $1 \leq b \leq (1-\epsilon)/d$, there is a constant $a > 1$ s.t. if the $a \cdot d$-disk of u contains no nodes from U then every node in the $b \cdot d$-disk of u receives the transmission of u.*

Consider the construction of a level $\ell - 1$, given the set U of level-ℓ nodes with minimum pairwise distance d. First, using a simple randomized algorithm, we construct a graph H over U, s.t. for a constant $a \geq 1$, H has an edge for every pair of nodes in U within distance ad, and the maximum degree of H is bounded by a constant, w.h.p. (the proof is based on Prop. 4.5.) The graph H is vertex-colored using a constant number of colors. Nodes transmit according to the time-schedule induced by the coloring, and the edges along which the transmissions did not succeed (in either direction) are removed from H. Finally, an MIS M of H is computed, and M becomes the level $\ell - 1$, where a vertex v in U that is not in M chooses an arbitrary neighbor in M as its parent. The schedule of the edges between the two levels is derived from the coloring schedule above. Now, the key observation is that even after the edge-removal phase, every pair of nodes within distance bd is still adjacent in H, where constant b can be chosen between 1 and $(1-\epsilon)/d$, by appropriately choosing constant a, by Prop. 4.5. Hence, the minimum distance between level-$(\ell-1)$ nodes is at least bd, and an inductive argument shows that the tree will have $O(\Pi)$ levels.

The multi-hop case. The construction above is adapted to our setting as follows. The construction is performed by using the coloring schedule of the backbone, where each color class operates in isolation. For a color class, the algorithm above is run in parallel by all clusters. This scheduling can be done because the nodes know (an upper bound on) the runtime of the single-hop algorithm. The first key observation is that Prop. 4.5 holds in this setting as well (with an identical proof), where U is the set of transmitting nodes in the whole network (rather than a single cluster). Hence, the construction of graph H and its properties hold, except that the distance d now is the minimum pairwise distance for the level-ℓ nodes across all clusters (in the same color class). The coloring and MIS algorithms are also straightforwardly extended to our setting[5].

Proposition 4.6. *There is a randomized algorithm that constructs an aggregation tree with properties 1 and 2 above in each cluster in $O(\Pi \log n \log^* n)$ rounds, w.h.p.*

5 OPTIMAL ALGORITHMS

5.1 Local Broadcast

Recall that in LBcast, the goal is for each node to transmit a message to all nodes in its $(1-\delta)$-disk, for a constant $\delta > 0$. A backbone can be used to perform randomized LBcast in $O(\Delta) + \tilde{O}(\log^2 n)$ rounds (including backbone construction), w.h.p., for any constant $\delta \in (0, 1/3)$. We do not assume the nodes have an estimate of Δ. This improves the current best runtime of $O(\Delta \log n + \log^2 n)$ [14] for this setting, and the current best runtime of $O(\Delta \log n)$ [11] with the (approximate) knowledge of Δ. Since $\Omega(\Delta)$ is a lower bound, this result is tight up to constant factors and the additive poly-logarithmic term.

Given an ϵ-backbone with $\epsilon < \min(d_0, \delta/2)$, the algorithm simply consists of three phases: *Upload, Forward, Download.* In the first phase, the Upload primitive is used for each node to transmit its message to its dominator. In the second phase, the dominator forwards the messages it has received to its neighbors in the backbone, simulating a simple single-round Congest algorithm for LBcast (Thm. 3.1). In the third phase, each backbone node uses the Download primitive to send the messages it has received in the Forward phase to its cluster. It easily follows from the construction of the backbone that every node correctly performs LBcast. The runtime of the algorithm directly follows from Prop. 4.4, Thm. 3.1 and Prop. 4.2.

Proposition 5.1. *There is a randomized algorithm that performs Local Broadcast in $O(\Delta) + \tilde{O}(\log^2 n)$ rounds, w.h.p.*

Note that the algorithm above assumes that the backbone nodes have enough buffer space to hold all messages they receive in the Upload phase. This can be avoided by partitioning the running time of each phase into sub-phases of, e.g., $O(\log n)$ rounds, and running the phases in an interleaved fashion.

[5] [13] adapts known Congest algorithms for bounded degree graphs, where each Congest round is simulated with $O(\log n)$ SINR rounds.

5.2 Multi-Message Broadcast

In the MMB problem, there are k messages $m_1, m_2, \ldots, m_k$ originating at not necessarily distinct nodes, that need to be broadcast over the network. Consider first the problem in the broadcast-Congest model over a communication graph of diameter D.

Consider the following simple algorithm: each node v maintains a FIFO queue of messages m_i, initialized by the messages v originates, and in every round v transmits the message in the head of the queue to its neighbors (and evicts it from the queue). Upon receiving a message m_i, node v appends it to the queue if and only if m_i has not been in the queue of v before.

Proposition 5.2. *Every message m created in a round r is received by a node at distance d from its originator by round $r + d + t$, where t is the number of messages that were created before r and were still in the queue of at least one node at round r. In particular, the algorithm delivers every message to all nodes within $D + k$ rounds from its creation.*

For MMB in a SINR network with a backbone, we simply use the Upload primitive to send the messages to the backbone nodes, which then use the simulation of the MMB algorithm above (via Thm. 3.1) to disseminate the messages over the backbone, followed (or interleaved, as in LBcast) by the Download primitive, to deliver the messages to the respective clusters.

Proposition 5.3. *There is a randomized Multi-message Broadcast algorithm, where each of the k messages reaches every node in $O(D_\epsilon + k + \log^2 n)$ time, after $\ell = \tilde{O}(\log^2 n)$ preprocessing time, w.h.p.*

5.3 Aggregation

In the *Aggregation* problem, each node v has a value m_v, and the goal is to compute an aggregation function of values m_v at a global sink node. Aggregation can be easily solved by combining the Local Aggregation primitive with a simulation of a simple Congest algorithm (via Thm. 3.1) to aggregate the data at, e.g., the minimum ID backbone node. Having constructed the backbone (in $\ell = \tilde{O}(\log^2 n)$ rounds) and the Local Aggregation Trees (in $O(\Pi \log n \log^* n)$ rounds), Aggregation can be performed in $O(D_\epsilon + \Pi + \log n)$ time, where $O(\Pi)$ is the time to aggregate the data at the corresponding backbone nodes (recall that each Local Aggregation Tree has height $O(\Pi)$ and each level has a transmission schedule of $O(1)$ rounds), and $O(D_\epsilon + \log n)$ is the time to aggregate over the backbone.

Proposition 5.4. *There is a randomized Aggregation algorithm with runtime $O(D_\epsilon + \Pi + \log n)$, after $\tilde{O}(\log n) \cdot (\Pi + \log n)$ preprocessing time, w.h.p.*

5.4 Coloring

Our local primitives can be used to compute a $O(\Delta)$-coloring of the network nodes, where nodes within distance $1 - \delta$ have distinct colors, for a constant $\delta > 0$. We present two algorithms. Assume we have an ϵ-backbone with $\epsilon \le \delta/2$. In both algorithms, the main task is to *enumerate* the nodes of each cluster with m nodes with labels from 1 to m. With this at hand, the final color of a node with label i that is dominated by a backbone node with color j (in the backbone coloring) is given by the pair (i, j). Clearly, this coloring uses $O(\Delta)$ colors. Consider nodes u, v within distance $1 - 2\epsilon \ge 1 - \delta$. If they are in the same cluster, then the first component of their color is different. Otherwise, by the coloring of the backbone, their dominators must have different colors in the backbone coloring. Hence, in either case, u and v are differently colored.

Thus, the main question is how to enumerate the nodes in each cluster. The first algorithm uses the Upload and Download primitives. Using the Upload primitive, the nodes send their IDs to their dominator, the dominator assigns the labels and announces the labels via the Download primitive. Each of the primitives takes $O(\Delta + \log^2 n)$ rounds.

Proposition 5.5. *There is a randomized algorithm that computes a $O(\Delta)$-coloring in $O(\Delta + \log^2 n)$ rounds, after $\tilde{O}(\log^2 n)$ preprocessing time, w.h.p.*

This result improves state of the art algorithms in two ways: first, we avoid the weak devices assumption, i.e., that nodes at distance at least $1 - \delta$ cannot communicate (even without other concurrent transmissions). Second, we improve the best previous runtime $O(\Delta \log n)$ for networks with max degree $\omega(\log n)$.

Our second algorithm uses the Local Aggregation primitive. It has been noted in [13, Sec. 7.2] that the Local Aggregation Tree of height h can be used to enumerate the m nodes participating in the tree with numbers from 1 to m in $O(h) = O(\Pi)$ rounds. With the observations above, this gives us a coloring algorithm.

Proposition 5.6. *There is a randomized algorithm that computes a $O(\Delta)$-coloring in $O(\Pi)$ rounds, after $\tilde{O}(\log n) \cdot (\Pi + \log n)$ preprocessing time, w.h.p.*

To our knowledge, this is the first coloring algorithm with runtime based on the geometric parameter Π. As it was noted above, for most practical networks, $\Pi = O(\log n)$, in which case the last algorithm would be much faster in a non-sparse network than algorithms with runtime linear in Δ.

5.5 Maximal Independent Set

A logical definition of an MIS in an SINR network would be: the distances between the MIS nodes are larger than $1-\delta$ (for a constant δ), while every other node has an MIS node within distance $1 - \delta$. This, however, seems to require precise distance measurement abilities, which may not be available. Instead, we can construct an MIS in the following sense, which seems to be a reasonable substitute for the more strict definition above[6]: set M is an MIS if
1. (Independence) The pairwise distance between nodes in M is more than $1 - \delta$,
2. (Coverage) If all nodes in M transmit with a small enough constant probability $p > 0$, then every node $u \notin M$ receives a message with a constant probability $p' > 0$.

Assume we have an ϵ-backbone with $\epsilon \le \delta/2$. Initially, all nodes are *uncovered* and the set M of current MIS nodes is empty. To construct the MIS, we discover uncovered nodes and join their dominators to M. In order to avoid joining nodes that are within distance $1-\delta$ from each other, we do this according to the backbone coloring schedule, i.e., in c phases, where c is the number of backbone colors. In each phase i (of $O(\log^2 n)$ rounds), only uncovered nodes with cluster of color i are considered.

[6]This definition stems from the interpretation of MIS as independent dominating set.

In order to find uncovered nodes, we use a procedure FindUncovered: for $a \log n$ rounds, where a is a constant parameter, each node in the backbone transmits with a constant probability p, and each node $v \notin M$ counts the number t of messages it receives from nodes in M of the current color class. If $t \geq \log n$, then v becomes *covered*. We can choose c and p so that if there is a node $u \in M$ within distance $1-\epsilon$ then v receives $\log n$ messages w.h.p. Moreover, if a node becomes covered then the Coverage property holds for it (see Appendix B for details).

Next, we have a procedure NotifyDominator that allows each backbone node to learn if there is an uncovered node in its cluster. This is implemented by uncovered nodes executing the Upload primitive, where each cluster has (at most) a *single duplicated message* (i.e., all nodes trying to send the same message, as defined in Sec. 4.3) to send to the dominator, so each dominator learns about the existence of uncovered nodes in $O(\log^2 n)$ rounds (due to Prop. 4.4), and terminates the execution if it does not receive a message in $O(\log^2 n)$ rounds.

The final algorithm is as follows. Let M denote the MIS at the current stage, initially $M = \emptyset$. For each i, let C_i denote the set of clusters whose dominator has color i and is not in M. The algorithm runs in phases $i = 1, 2, \ldots, c$, where in phase i, the nodes execute FindUncovered, followed by nodes in C_i executing NotifyDominator, and each dominator that has an uncovered node in its cluster joins M.

It remains to show that at the end of the algorithm, M is an MIS. Note that as soon as the Coverage property is satisfied for a node at some point in the algorithm, it will be satisfied in the final solution too. Thus, the Coverage property holds. In order to see the Independence property, note that it trivially holds at the beginning, and let us show that it is maintained when a new node joins M. Note that every new node u is a dominator of an uncovered node v. Before adding u, since v was uncovered, its distance from the closest node $w \in M$ was larger than $1 - \epsilon$, which implies that the distance between u and w is more than $1 - 2\epsilon \geq 1 - \delta$. Hence, including u in M does not violate Independence. Also, if there are multiple dominators added to M in the same phase, they are at distance at least $1 - \epsilon > 1 - \delta$ from each other, since they belong the same color class. Thus, Independence holds for the final M.

Proposition 5.7. *There is a randomized algorithm that computes an MIS in $O(\log^2 n)$ rounds, after $\tilde{O}(\log^2 n)$ preprocessing time, w.h.p.*

6 CONCLUSIONS

We have shown that optimal time complexity bounds can be obtained for the most fundamental problems in the barebones SINR model, after polylogarithmic preprocessing. It would be interesting to explore various extensions, such as model relaxations (e.g., *ad hoc* SINR [5]), dynamic settings, and unreliable networks.

ACKNOWLEDGMENTS

This work was supported by grants nos. 152679-05 and 174484-05 from the Icelandic Research Fund.

REFERENCES

[1] Noga Alon, Amotz Bar-Noy, Nathan Linial, and David Peleg. 1991. A Lower Bound for Radio Broadcast. *J. Comput. Syst. Sci.* 43, 2 (1991), 290–298. https://doi.org/10.1016/0022-0000(91)90015-W

[2] Leonid Barenboim and David Peleg. 2015. Nearly Optimal Local Broadcasting in the SINR Model with Feedback. In *SIROCCO*. 164–178.

[3] Marijke H. L. Bodlaender, Magnús M. Halldórsson, and Pradipta Mitra. 2013. Connectivity and aggregation in multihop wireless networks. In *PODC '13*. 355–364.

[4] Keren Censor-Hillel, Bernhard Haeupler, D. Ellis Hershkowitz, and Goran Zuzic. 2018. Erasure Correction for Noisy Radio Networks. *CoRR* abs/1805.04165 (2018). http://arxiv.org/abs/1805.04165

[5] Sebastian Daum, Seth Gilbert, Fabian Kuhn, and Calvin C. Newport. 2013. Broadcast in the Ad Hoc SINR Model. In *DISC'13*. 358–372.

[6] Bilel Derbel and El-Ghazali Talbi. 2010. Radio Network Distributed Algorithms in the Unknown Neighborhood Model. In *ICDCN*. 155–166.

[7] Jeremy T. Fineman, Seth Gilbert, Fabian Kuhn, and Calvin C. Newport. 2016. Contention Resolution on a Fading Channel. In *DISC'16*. 155–164.

[8] Fabian Fuchs and Roman Prutkin. 2015. Simple Distributed $\Delta + 1$ Coloring in the SINR Model. In *SIROCCO'15*. 149–163.

[9] Mohsen Ghaffari, Bernhard Haeupler, and Majid Khabbazian. 2013. Randomized broadcast in radio networks with collision detection. In *PODC'13*. 325–334.

[10] Mohsen Ghaffari, Bernhard Haeupler, Nancy A. Lynch, and Calvin C. Newport. 2012. Bounds on Contention Management in Radio Networks. In *DISC*. 223–237.

[11] Olga Goussevskaia, Thomas Moscibroda, and Roger Wattenhofer. 2008. Local broadcasting in the physical interference model. In *DIALM-POMC*. 35–44.

[12] Magnús M. Halldórsson, Stephan Holzer, and Nancy A. Lynch. 2015. A Local Broadcast Layer for the SINR Network Model. In *PODC*. 129–138.

[13] Magnús M. Halldórsson, Fabian Kuhn, Nancy A. Lynch, and Calvin Newport. 2017. An Efficient Communication Abstraction for Dense Wireless Networks. In *DISC*. 25:1–25:16.

[14] Magnús M. Halldórsson and Pradipta Mitra. 2012. Towards tight bounds for local broadcasting. In *FOMC*. 2.

[15] Magnús M. Halldórsson and Tigran Tonoyan. 2018. Leveraging Indirect Signaling for Topology Inference and Fast Broadcast. In *PODC'18*. 85–93.

[16] Tomasz Jurdzinski and Dariusz R. Kowalski. 2012. Distributed Backbone Structure for Algorithms in the SINR Model of Wireless Networks. In *DISC'12*. 106–120.

[17] Tomasz Jurdzinski, Dariusz R. Kowalski, Michal Rozanski, and Grzegorz Stachowiak. 2013. Distributed Randomized Broadcasting in Wireless Networks under the SINR Model. In *DISC'13*. 373–387.

[18] Tomasz Jurdzinski, Dariusz R. Kowalski, Michal Rozanski, and Grzegorz Stachowiak. 2014. On the impact of geometry on ad hoc communication in wireless networks. In *PODC'14*. 357–366.

[19] Tomasz Jurdzinski, Dariusz R. Kowalski, and Grzegorz Stachowiak. 2013. Distributed Deterministic Broadcasting in Uniform-Power Ad Hoc Wireless Networks. In *FCT'13*. 195–209.

[20] Tomasz Jurdzinski, Dariusz R. Kowalski, and Grzegorz Stachowiak. 2013. Distributed Deterministic Broadcasting in Wireless Networks of Weak Devices. In *ICALP'13*. 632–644.

[21] Eyal Kushilevitz and Yishay Mansour. 1998. An $\Omega(D \log(N/D))$ lower bound for broadcast in radio networks. *SIAM J. Comput.* 27, 3 (1998), 702–712. https://doi.org/10.1137/S0097539794279109

[22] Calvin C. Newport. 2014. Radio Network Lower Bounds Made Easy. In *DISC*. 258–272.

[23] Christian Scheideler, Andréa W. Richa, and Paolo Santi. 2008. An O(log n) dominating set protocol for wireless ad-hoc networks under the physical interference model. In *MobiHoc*. 91–100.

[24] Dongxiao Yu, Qiang-Sheng Hua, Yuexuan Wang, and Francis C. M. Lau. 2012. An $O(\log n)$ Distributed Approximation Algorithm for Local Broadcasting in Unstructured Wireless Networks. In *DCOSS'12*. 132–139.

[25] Dongxiao Yu, Qiang-Sheng Hua, Yuexuan Wang, Haisheng Tan, and Francis C. M. Lau. 2016. Distributed multiple-message broadcast in wireless ad hoc networks under the SINR model. *Theor. Comput. Sci.* 610 (2016), 182–191.

[26] Dongxiao Yu, Yuexuan Wang, Qiang-Sheng Hua, and Francis C. M. Lau. 2014. Distributed $(\Delta+1)$-coloring in the physical model. *Theor. Comput. Sci.* 553 (2014), 37–56.

[27] Dongxiao Yu, Yuexuan Wang, Tigran Tonoyan, and Magnús M. Halldórsson. 2017. Dynamic Adaptation in Wireless Networks Under Comprehensive Interference via Carrier Sense. In *IPDPS'17*. 337–346.

A IMPLEMENTATION OF THE UPLOAD PRIMITIVE

Algorithm 2 Upload(v,t)

```
if (nothing to transmit) then
    p_v ← 0, Halt
end if
if (t = 0 (mod T)) then
    if (σ_v > M) then
        p_v ← max{p_v/2, p_min}
    else
        p_v ← min{2p_v, p_max}
    end if
    σ_v ← 0
end if
With probability p_v, transmit
if (transmitted or received) then
    σ_v ← σ_v + 1
end if
```

Due to the discussion in Sec. 4, we can focus on a single cluster and assume the dominator only listens (does not transmit), and *whenever it receives a message, that message (and its duplicates) stops being transmitted any further.*

Let $\zeta, \delta \in (0, 1)$ be constants satisfying Prop. A.1 and denote $T = \frac{8}{\delta\zeta}\log n$, $M = \log n$. Node v maintains probability $p_v \le p_{max} = 1$ and a counter σ_v. Nodes start running the algorithm at round $t = 0$, with $p_v = p_{min} = \frac{\delta}{3n}$ and $\sigma_v = 0$. A *control phase* is an interval $[t, t + T]$ of rounds with $t = 0(\text{mod } T)$. Nodes maintain their probabilities constant during a control phase. A control phase is *idle for node* v if $\sigma_v \le M$ at the end of it, and is *busy*, otherwise. An *epoch* is a sequence of $\gamma \log n$ control phases, where $\gamma = \frac{12}{\zeta} + 4\log\frac{3}{\delta}$. An epoch is *idle for node* v if at least 3/4-th of its phases are idle for v, and is *busy*, otherwise. We denote by P_t the sum of transmission probabilities, i.e., *the contention*, in a cluster. We say *contention is bounded* in round t if $P_t < \delta$ holds for every cluster.

The first claim of the following proposition is a well-known (and simple) fact (see, e.g. [14, Lemma 10]). The remaining claims follow by applying a standard Chernoff bound.

Proposition A.1. *There are constants $\delta, \zeta > 0$ satisfying the following. Assume contention is bounded in every round. If a node v transmits, all nodes in v's cluster receive its message w.p. ζ. If a message is transmitted $\frac{3}{\zeta}\log n$ times, the dominator receives it w.h.p. Moreover, from every $\frac{3}{\zeta}\log n$ transmissions in a cluster, the dominator receives at least $\log n$ messages, w.h.p.*

Lemma A.2. *Assume contention is bounded during a control phase, and $P_t > \delta/2$ for a fixed cluster C. Then it is a busy phase for all nodes in C, w.h.p.*

Proof. By Prop. A.1, the probability that a node transmits and all nodes in C receive the message is at least $\zeta\delta/2$ in every round t of the control phase. The expected number of rounds when this happens is $T \cdot \frac{\delta\zeta}{2} = 4\log n$, so standard Chernoff bound implies that it happens at least $M = \log n$ times w.h.p., i.e. it is a busy phase for all nodes in C. □

Proposition A.3. *Contention is always bounded, w.h.p.*

Proof. At start, we have $P_t < np_{min} = \delta/3$. Consider the contention in C just before a phase. If $P_t < \delta/2$ for all clusters, then $P_t < 2 \cdot (\delta/2) = \delta$ after the phase. Hence, assume that $P_t < \delta$ for all clusters, but $P_t > \delta/2$ for some cluster C. Lemma A.2 implies that it is a busy phase for all nodes in C, and hence the probabilities in C are not increased after the phase, i.e. $P_t(u) < \delta/2$, w.h.p. The claim follows by induction over the phases, combined with the union bound over the clusters and phases. □

Lemma A.4. *Node v successfully sends a message to its dominator during an idle epoch, w.h.p.*

Proof. Node v doubles its probability after an idle phase and halves it after a busy phase. Since the fraction of busy phases is at most 1/4 and the minimum probability is $p_{min} = \delta/(3n)$, a simple counting argument shows that v has $p_v = p_{max} = 1$ in at least $\frac{\gamma}{4}\log n - \log\frac{3n}{\delta} \ge \frac{3}{\zeta}\log n$ phases. The claim then follows from Props. A.1 and A.3. □

Theorem A.5. *The dominator of a cluster receives all k messages from its cluster in $O(k + \log^2 n)$ rounds, w.h.p.*

Proof. Consider a message that a node v is trying to transmit. Consider a busy epoch for node v. In each busy phase, v receives at least $M = \log n$ messages, so there is a total of $\frac{\gamma}{4}\log^2 n$ messages transmitted in v's cluster during a busy epoch. By Prop. A.1, the dominator receives $\Omega(\log^2 n)$ of those transmissions, w.h.p. Hence the number of messages decreases by $\Omega(\log^2 n)$ in every busy epoch, implying that the number of busy epochs is bounded by $O(k/\log^2 n + 1)$, after which there will be an idle epoch, where by Lemma A.4, v's message will be received by the dominator. Since this holds for every message, the claim follows. □

B IMPLEMENTATION OF FINDUNCOVERED

Given an intermediate solution M, the algorithm FindUncovered is as follows. Let $a > 0$ and $p \in (0, 1)$ be constants, to be determined later. Denote $T = a\log n$ and $N = \log n$. For T rounds, the nodes in the backbone (including M) transmit in each round w.p. p. Each node $u \notin M$ maintains a counter σ_u, initialized to 0, and increments σ_u each time it receives a message from a node $v \in M$. At the end of T rounds, u is *covered* if $\sigma_v \ge N$ and *uncovered*, otherwise.

Below is the property we need to prove.

Proposition B.1. *(i) If a node $u \notin M$ is within distance $1 - \epsilon$ from a node $v \in M$ then u is covered, and (ii) If a node $u \notin M$ is covered then in the final solution M_{final}, if all nodes in M_{final} transmit w.p. p, u receives a message w.p. $p' = \Omega(1)$.*

Let $\Delta = O(1)$ denote the maximum degree of the backbone. We use two known results. The first lemma is a basic fact proved, e.g., in [11, Lemma 4.1]. The second one follows from the SINR definition and the triangle inequality.

Lemma B.2. *In every round, the expected interference on a node u from nodes outside of u's 2-disk is bounded by $c_1\Delta pP/\beta$, where $c_1 > 0$ is a constant determined by the value of α.*

Lemma B.3. *Assume a node v transmits and a listening node u is in the $(1-\epsilon)$-disk of v. If the interference on v is less than $\frac{P}{\beta} \cdot ((1-\epsilon)^{-\alpha} - 1)$ then u successfully receives the transmission.*

Consider a node $u \notin M$ and assume there is a node $v \in M$ within distance $1-\epsilon$ from u. In order for u to receive a message from v, it is enough that no other node transmits in the 2-disk B of v, and the interference at v from nodes outside of B is bounded as in Lemma B.3. Using Lemma B.2 with Markov's inequality, we see that in every round, with probability at least 1/2, the interference at v from nodes outside of B is bounded by $2c_1 \Delta pP/\beta$. *We choose* $p < \frac{(1-\epsilon)^{-\alpha}-1}{2c_1\Delta}$, which fulfils the requirements of Lemma B.3. On the other hand, the probability that in a given round, v is the unique node transmitting in B is at least $p \cdot (1-p)^{c_2}$, where $c_2 = c'\Delta$ is a bound on the number of nodes in B, and c' is an absolute constant. Thus, in every round, node u receives a message from v w.p. at least $p_r = p \cdot (1-p)^{c_2}/2 = \Omega(1)$. In expectation, at least $p_r T = p_r a \log n$ messages are received during FindUncovered. *We choose* $a = 3/p_r$. Then, by Chernoff's bound, at least $N = \log n$ messages are received w.h.p., and u is covered.

Now, suppose a node u receives at least N messages during the algorithm and determines it is covered. Let p' denote the probability that u receives a message from M in a round. If $p' < p_r/5$ then u receives at most $Tp_r/5 = (3/5)\log n$ messages in expectation, so it receives less than N messages w.h.p. Therefore, if a node is covered, it receives messages from M w.p. at least $p_r/5$.

Efficient Multiparty Interactive Coding for Insertions, Deletions, and Substitutions

[Extended Abstract]*

Ran Gelles†
Bar-Ilan University
ran.gelles@biu.ac.il

Yael Tauman Kalai
Microsoft Research & MIT
yael@microsoft.com

Govind Ramnarayan‡
MIT
govind@mit.edu

ABSTRACT

In the field of interactive coding, two or more parties wish to carry out a distributed computation over a communication network that may be noisy. The ultimate goal is to develop efficient coding schemes that can tolerate a high level of noise while increasing the communication by only a constant factor (i.e., constant rate).

In this work we consider synchronous communication networks over an arbitrary topology, in the powerful adversarial insertion-deletion noise model. Namely, the noisy channel may adversarially alter the content of any transmitted symbol, as well as completely remove a transmitted symbol or inject a new symbol into the channel.

We provide efficient, constant rate schemes that successfully conduct any computation with high probability as long as the adversary corrupts at most $\frac{\varepsilon}{m}$ fraction of the total communication, where m is the number of links in the network and ε is a small constant. This scheme assumes an *oblivious* adversary which is independent of the parties' inputs and randomness. We can remove this assumption and resist a worst-case adversary at the price of being resilient to $\frac{\varepsilon}{m \log m}$ errors.

While previous work considered the insertion-deletion noise model in the two-party setting, to the best of our knowledge, our scheme is the first multiparty scheme that is resilient to insertions and deletions. Furthermore, our scheme is the first *computationally efficient* scheme in the multiparty setting that is resilient to *adversarial* noise.

CCS CONCEPTS

• **Theory of computation** → **Interactive computation**; **Error-correcting codes**; *Distributed algorithms*.

KEYWORDS

interactive coding, distributed algorithms, error correcting codes

*See [16] for a longer version of this work.

†Supported in part by the Israel Science Foundation (ISF) through grant No. 1078/17.
‡Supported in part by NSF award CCF 1665252 and NSF award DMS-1737944.

PODC '19, July 29–August 2, 2019, Toronto, ON, Canada

ACM ISBN 978-1-4503-6217-7/19/07...$15.00
https://doi.org/10.1145/3293611.3331621

ACM Reference Format:
Ran Gelles, Yael Tauman Kalai, and Govind Ramnarayan. 2019. Efficient Multiparty Interactive Coding for Insertions, Deletions, and Substitutions: [Extended Abstract]. In *2019 ACM Symposium on Principles of Distributed Computing (PODC'19), July 29–August 2, 2019, Toronto, ON, Canada.* ACM, New York, NY, USA, 10 pages. https://doi.org/10.1145/3293611.3331621

1 INTRODUCTION

In his pioneering work, Schulman [28, 29] introduced and studied the problem of how to perform an interactive two-party computation over a noisy communication channel. In [27], Rajagopalan and Schulman extended the two-party case and considered a network of n parties that wish to compute some function of their private inputs by communicating over an arbitrary[1] *noisy* network. The work of [27] shows that if each channel is the binary symmetric channel[2] (BSC_ε), then one can obtain a *coding scheme* that takes any protocol Π that assumes noiseless communication, and converts it into a resilient protocol that computes the same task over the noisy network.

The coding scheme in [27] defies noise by adding redundancy. The amount of added redundancy is usually measured with respect to the noiseless setting—the *rate* of the coding scheme is the communication of the noiseless protocol divided by the communication of the noise-resilient one. The rate assumes values between zero and one, and ideally is bounded away from zero, commonly known as *constant* or *positive* rate. The rate may vary according to the network in consideration, for instance, the rate in [27] behaves as $1/O(\log(d+1))$ where d is the maximal degree in the network. Hence, for networks where the maximal degree is non-constant, the rate approaches zero as the network size increases.

The next major step for multiparty coding schemes was provided by Jain, Kalai, and Lewko [24] and by Hoza and Schulman [23]. In these works the noise is no longer assumed to be stochastic but instead is adversarial. That is, they consider worst-case noise where the only limit is the number of bits flipped by the adversary. They showed that as long as the adversary flips at most ε/m-fraction of the total communication, a coding scheme with a constant rate can be achieved, where ε is some small constant, and m is the number of communication links in the network.[3]

While both these works consider adversarial errors, they consider different communication models. The work [23] assumes that every party sends a single bit to all its neighbors in each round;

[1]By "arbitrary" we mean that the topology of the network can be an arbitrary graph $G = (V, E)$ where each node is a party and each edge is a communication channel connecting the parties associated with these nodes.
[2]That is, a channel that flips every bit with some constant probability $\varepsilon \in (0, 1/2)$.
[3][24] obtained this result for the specific star network, whereas [23] generalized this result to a network with arbitrary topology.

scheme	topology	noise level	noise type	rate	efficient
RS94 [27]	arbitrary		BSC_ε	$1/O(\log(d+1))$	No
ABEGH16 [3]	clique		BSC_ε	$\Theta(1)$	Yes
HS16 [23]	arbitrary	$O(1/m)$	substitution	$\Theta(1)$	No
HS16 [23]	arbitrary	$O(1/n)$	substitution	$1/O(m\log(n)/n)$	No
JKL15 [24]	star	$O(1/m)$	substitution	$\Theta(1)$	No
Algorithm A	arbitrary	$O(1/m)$	*oblivious* insertions and deletions	$\Theta(1)$	Yes
Algorithm B	arbitrary	$O(1/(m\log m))$	insertions and deletions	$\Theta(1)$	Yes

Table 1: Interactive coding schemes in the multiparty setting. The first four are in the *fully-utilized* model, while JKL15 [24] and all algorithms in this paper are in the non-fully-utilized model.

this model is sometimes called *fully utilized*, and is commonly considered in multiparty interactive coding [3, 8, 23, 27]. On the other hand, the work in [24] uses a relaxed communication setting, in which parties may or may not speak in a given round; this setting is very common for distributed computations, and is relatively less studied in previous work on interactive coding. Furthermore, in [24] the *underlying* protocol is not assumed to be fully utilized; instead this work uses the (weaker) assumption that the order of speaking in the underlying protocol is known, and is independent of the parties' inputs. Naturally, one can convert any protocol in the non-fully-utilized model to a fully-utilized protocol by forcing all parties to speak at every round, and then applying an interactive coding scheme to the fully-utilized protocol. However, the conversion to a fully-utilized protocol may cause the communication complexity to increase by a factor of up to m, greatly harming the rate of the coding scheme.

1.1 Our Contributions and Comparison to Previous Work

We design coding schemes for adversarial noise in the same communication model as [24]; namely, where parties may or not speak in a given round, and the underlying protocol is only assumed to have a fixed speaking order. One of the most interesting aspects of our work is that our coding schemes are *computationally efficient*, unlike either [24] or [23].[4]

Also, we consider a stronger type of noise, *insertions and deletions*, albeit in the synchronous setting. This type of noise may completely remove a transmission (so that the receiver is not aware that a bit was sent to him), or inject new transmissions (so that the receiver receives a bit while the sender didn't send anything). Insertion and deletion noise is more general, and considered to be more difficult, than bit-flips. Indeed, a bit flip (a *substitution noise*) can be simulated by a deletion followed by an insertion. We note that insertions and deletions are trivially correctable in the fully utilized communication model; indeed, each party expects to hear a message from each of its neighbors in each round, so a deletion reduces to an erasure. By contrast, in the non-fully-utilized setting, insertions and deletions seem non-trivial to correct. Indeed, as first noted by Hoza [22], it seems *crucial* to allow insertion and deletion errors in the non-fully-utilized setting to make the problem non-trivial. To see this, consider a party that speaks once every two rounds—on an even round to communicate the bit '0' and on an odd round to communicate '1'. In fact, this communication is completely resilient to noise that only flips bits since only the timing of the transmission matters.

Finally, our coding scheme works on arbitrary topologies, in contrast to [24], which only applies to the star graphs. As mentioned above, in the fully utilized model, [23] also handles arbitrary graphs.

Our first coding scheme (Algorithm A) achieves a constant rate, and is resilient to ε/m-fraction of adversarial insertion, deletion, and substitution noise.[5] This scheme assumes a limited type of noise, i.e., an *oblivious adversary* whose corruptions are predetermined and are independent of parties' inputs and randomness. In our second coding scheme (Algorithm B), we remove the restriction of the obliviousness of the adversary, at the price of being resilient to $\varepsilon/(m\log m)$-fraction of errors. See Table 1 for a comparison of our new results (Algorithm A and Algorithm B) with the state of the art.

1.2 Future Directions

Before describing our results and techniques in further detail, we stop to highlight promising directions for future work. While we consider error rates of at most $O(1/m)$ in this paper, this is not the optimal noise rate for multiparty interactive coding in general. Indeed, Hoza and Schulman [23] further improve their noise resilience to $\Omega(1/n)$, where n is the number of parties, at the expense of reducing the rate to $1/O(m\log(n)/n)$, which is no longer constant. It is an interesting open question whether there exists a constant-rate coding scheme with noise resilience $\Omega(1/n)$, in any communication model. Furthermore, we note that our noise resilience to non-oblivious adversaries is $O(1/m\log(m))$, as opposed to the $\Omega(1/m)$ noise resilience in [23] and [24]; this seems to be inherent to our approach, designed to yield computational efficiency. We discuss this barrier further in Section 3.

Even though our noise-resilient protocol increases the communication complexity by only a constant factor, it may blow up the *number of rounds* of communication by more than a constant factor. In our model, unlike the fully utilized model, the communication complexity does not determine the round complexity. Specifically, in our model an interactive protocol with communication complexity CC may consist of CC$/m$ rounds (in the case that the network if fully utilized) or may consist of CC rounds (in the case where

[4]These coding schemes utilized a combinatorial object known a *tree code*, for which no efficient construction is known.

[5]We assume that each insertion, deletion, or substitution counts as a single corruption.

the communication is very sparse). Simulating either one of these interactive protocols with the algorithms in this paper will take $\Theta(\mathrm{CC})$ rounds. It is an interesting question as to whether one can extend our results to simultaneously achieve constant blowup in rounds.

2 MAIN RESULTS

We give efficient interactive coding schemes with constant rate for arbitrary synchronous networks (not necessarily fully-utilized) that suffer from a certain fraction of insertion, deletion and substitution noise. Our result is two-fold. First, we assume that the adversary is oblivious, i.e., the noise is predetermined and is independent of the randomness used by the parties.

Theorem 2.1 (oblivious noise, informal). *Let $G = (V, E)$ be an arbitrary synchronous network with $n = |V|$ nodes and $m = |E|$ links. For any noiseless protocol Π over G with a predetermined order of speaking, and for any sufficiently small constant ε, there exists an efficient coding scheme that simulates Π over a noisy network G. The simulated protocol is robust to adversarial insertion, deletion, and substitution noise, assuming at most ε/m-fraction of the communication is corrupted. The simulated protocol communicates $O(\mathrm{CC}(\Pi))$ bits, and succeeds with probability at least $1 - \exp(-\mathrm{CC}(\Pi)/m)$, assuming the noise is oblivious.*

As an intermediate step towards proving Theorem 2.1, we first prove the result assuming that the parties pre-share a common random string (to which the adversary is oblivious). Then we show how to remove this assumption without any loss in parameters. We give more details in Section 4.

Next, we remove the restriction that the noise is oblivious. Namely, we consider adversaries that may adaptively decide which transmissions to corrupt according to the observed transcript, as well as the parties inputs (however, the noise is unaware of any private coin-tossing a party may perform later in the protocol). In this case we still obtain an efficient coding scheme with a constant rate, albeit, with slightly smaller noise resilience.

Theorem 2.2 (non-oblivious noise, informal). *Let $G = (V, E)$ be an arbitrary synchronous network with $n = |V|$ nodes and $m = |E|$ links. For any noiseless protocol Π over G with a predetermined order of speaking, and for any sufficiently small constant ε, there exists an efficient coding scheme that simulates Π over a noisy network G. The simulated protocol is robust to adversarial insertion, deletion, and substituition noise, assuming at most $(\varepsilon/m \log m)$-fraction of the communication is corrupted. The simulated protocol communicates $O(\mathrm{CC}(\Pi))$ bits, and succeeds with probability at least $1 - \exp(-\mathrm{CC}(\Pi)/m)$.*

3 THE CODING SCHEME

3.1 The multiparty interactive-communication model

Before proceeding to describe our coding scheme, we elaborate on our communication model. The communication model works in synchronous rounds as follows. At each round, any subset of parties may decide to speak. Each link is allowed to transmit at most one symbol per round in each direction from a constant-sized alphabet Σ. We will assume throughout this paper that $\Sigma = \{0, 1\}$ (both in the noiseless and noisy settings), however, our results extend to a larger alphabet as well. At each round, a party is allowed to send multiple (possibly different) symbols over multiple links. A *transmission* over a certain link at a certain round is the event of a party sending a message on this link at that round (if both parties send messages these are two separate transmissions).

We re-emphasize that, contrary to most previous work, our communication model is not fully-utilized and does not demand all parties to speak at each round on every communication channel connected to them; in fact we don't demand a certain party to speak at all at any given round.

3.2 Towards a robust simulation: Key ideas

In this section we motivate the elements of our coding scheme at a high level. The basic idea towards constructing a multiparty coding scheme is to have each pair of parties perform a two-party coding scheme [23, 24, 27]. However, merely correcting errors in a pairwise manner is insufficient, since if a pair of parties found an inconsistency and backtracked, this may cause new inconsistencies (in particular, between these parties and their other neighbors). In [24], this problem was solved by assuming there is one party who is connected to all parties (i.e., the star topology). This party has a global view on the progress of the simulation in the *entire network*, and hence can function as the "conductor of the orchestra."

In our setting, no such central party exists and consequently no party knows the state of the simulation in the entire network. Instead, each party only sees its local neighborhood, and needs to propagate its "status" to the entire network in a completely decentralized manner.

We mention that Hoza and Schulman [23] also considered an arbitrary topology, but they consider the fully-utilized model. Correcting errors efficiently in the non-fully-utilized model seems to be trickier, since errors may remain unnoticed longer just due to the fact that parties may communicate very rarely. We elaborate on this towards the end of this section.

In order to keep our simulation *efficient*, as opposed to previous works in the multiparty setting which used the (inefficient) tree-code approach, we use the rewind-if-error approach [5, 14, 20, 25, 28] (see also [13]). Namely, each two neighboring parties send a hash of their simulated pairwise transcripts, and if the hashes do not match, then an error is detected, and the two parties initiate a "meeting-points" mechanism [20, 28] in order to find a previous point where their transcripts agree. Since we want a constant-rate coding scheme with error rate up to $\Omega(1/m)$, our goal is to ensure that any corruption only causes the network to waste $O(m)$ communication. Indeed, if the parties need K communication to correct a single error, then constant-rate coding implies a maximal noise level of $1/K$. If the noise level is higher, the communication required to correct the errors is already too high to preserve a constant-rate coding. Therefore, to tolerate error rate $\Omega(1/m)$, in our coding schemes the parties will have to detect errors by communicating at most $O(1)$ bits per check, so that the consistency-checking costs $O(m)$ communication overall. In hindsight, this will restrict the parties to use hash functions with *constant-sized outputs*.

Let us now describe a preliminary attempt at a coding scheme. The coding scheme will have many *iterations*, where each iteration will consist of the following. First, every pair of parties will send each other hashes of their simulated pairwise transcripts. If these match, they continue simulating with each other for a small number of rounds; else, they use the meeting points mechanism to find a common "meeting" point where both their partial transcripts agree and rewind their partial transcript back to that point. Until they have done so, they refuse to simulate with any other party. The parties continue repeating these two steps (1. Send Hashes / Do Meeting Points and 2. Simulate / Stay Silent) until they finish simulating the underlying protocol. Each step will take a fixed number of rounds, and since we are in the synchronous model, the parties will always be able to tell which part currently is being carried out.

This naive coding scheme has a clear but important flaw, which was alluded to at the beginning of this subsection. Namely, once a party u decides to rewind due to an error on the link (u, v), this has an effect on the simulation of u with its other neighbors. In order to ensure correctness of the overall simulation, u must rewind the simulation with each and every one of its neighbors that may be affected.

It is tempting to rewind u's neighborhood by having u immediately truncate its simulated transcript for each adjacent link (u, w), to the same place it rewound the link (u, v). After such a truncation, a discrepancy would appear on the link (u, w) since w did not change its simulated transaction, and the meeting points mechanism would resolve any such resulting discrepancy in the next iteration. In particular, an error on the link (u, v) would cause u and v to perform meeting points and rewind their transcript to a consistent point. Then, in the next iteration, u will be inconsistent with its other neighbors and will initiate meeting points with all its other neighbors, resulting in them rewinding their transcripts accordingly. In the following iteration, any neighbor w of u would find an inconsistency with any other party in its *own* neighborhood, initiate meeting points with them, and so on until the entire network has rewound.

While the entire network eventually rewinds in this scheme, the number of iterations this takes is proportional to the diameter of the network. Recall that to ensure constant rate, we need to correct any error with at most $O(m)$ communication (with high probability), which in our case means just $O(1)$ iterations. So this naive approach could *not* achieve constant rate.

Worse still, even if we augmented the consistency check step so that news propagates through the entire network in just a single iteration, this approach would still fail with high probability. The consistency checking involves exchanging hashes of transcripts and verifying whether they match. *Hash collisions* are a major problem here; a hash collision will cause parties u and v to believe that their transcripts are consistent, when really they are not. This can cause u and v to continue simulating when they should not, wasting communication on an incorrect simulation that will have to be rewound later. Since we are restricted to use constant-sized hashes to keep the rate constant, hash collisions occur with constant probability in each exchange. Note that at least $n-1$ hash exchanges are required to inform all n parties that an error have occurred. The probability that none of these hash exchanges suffers a collision is negligible, hence, many parties will not be informed of the error and will not rewind their transcript.

What saves us here is that u does not need to initiate a meeting points protocol to tell w to rewind—u can tell w to rewind *directly*. The meeting points protocol is designed to find a point where the transcripts of u and w are consistent, when neither u nor w has any idea where that point may be. But in the above case, u is confident that w should rewind, and should simply inform w that it should rewind.

To summarize the above ideas, each iteration in our coding scheme consists of the following phases: 1. Consistency Check, 2. Simulate / Stay Silent, and 3. Rewind request (if necessary). As before, each of these phases takes a fixed number of rounds, so the parties are always in sync with regards to which phase they are in.

Some care needs to be taken with the Rewind phase. Specifically, u may not be able to instantly communicate to its neighbor w how far it wants w to rewind. For instance, u may have rewound a very large number of rounds, and even telling its neighbor how many rounds to rewind would require a large amount of communication; this cannot be communicated in the fixed number of rounds that the rewind phase contains. Instead, u should be satisfied with just telling w to rewind a small amount at a time, spanning the rewind process over several consecutive iterations.

We stress that in the multiparty setting, hash collisions are very expensive (that is, they cause the parties to waste a lot of communication), and so the parties should try to minimize the potential number of hash collisions. For instance, in the above process of rewinding w, party u keeps sending hashes according to the partially rewound transcript. This would make the link (u, w) look "consistent" to the two parties, since both truncated the same amount of chunks each time. This prevents u and w from initiating a meeting points protocol on an inconsistent link, thus reducing the potential of more hash collisions, due to the fact that when the link is consistent, no hash collision can occur. This is one of the key conceptual observations behind our work.

There is one final issue that is specific to the non-fully-utilized model. Recall that in the non-fully-utilized model, communication may be sparse. For concreteness, assume the following sparse protocol over the *line* (i.e., a path graph, where party $i \in \{1, 2, \ldots, n-1\}$ is connected to party $i+1$). In this example protocol, party 1 communicates back-and-forth with party 2 for n rounds while other parties remain silent, then party 2 communicates with party 3 for n rounds while other parties remain silent, and so on, until the communication reaches parties $n-1$ and n, and bounces back towards party 1. The communication that occurs in any set of n rounds of this underlying protocol is n, since only a single party is speaking in any given round. An iteration of our coding scheme would give the parties n rounds to simulate, after which they perform a single consistency check.

However, when *simulating* the underlying protocol in our coding scheme, the parties may not all be in agreement about which round they are simulating. For example, parties 1, 2, and 3 could think they are simulating round 1 (where parties 1 and 2 talk a lot), while party 4, 5, and 6 think they are simulating round $3n+1$ (where parties 4 and 5 talk a lot), and generally parties $3i+1, 3i+2$, and $3i+3$ think they are simulating round $i \cdot n+1$. In this case, there will be $\Omega(n^2)$ communication in just one iteration of our coding scheme (in $O(n)$ rounds). This is potentially disastrous. Not only might this lead to the rate of the coding scheme being super-constant, but also the adversary would have the budget to place $\Omega(\varepsilon n)$ additional errors, and may be able to use these errors to derail any attempts of getting the simulation back on track.

To avoid this issue altogether, we introduce a "flag-passing" phase in which each party informs the entire *network* whether all seems correct and the simulation should continue, or if it sees an inconsistency and the network should idle while this is fixed. This fixes the issue above, since party 3 will realize that there is an inconsistency between its transcripts with parties 2 and 4, and will notify the network to avoid simulation.

Putting it all together, our resilient protocol consists of repeatedly executing the following four phases in order: (i) consistency check, (ii) flag passing, (iii) simulation, and (iv) rewind. The coding scheme cycles through these four phases in a fixed manner, where each phase takes a fixed amount of rounds to avoid ambiguity. We now describe these phases in thorough detail.

3.3 The Basic Coding Scheme

Before we describe our scheme, let us elaborate on why we need to assume that in the underlying (noiseless) protocol Π, the speaking order of the parties does not depend on the parties' inputs or communication so far. This (limiting) assumption is crucial to keep our coding scheme with a constant rate despite $\Theta(1/m)$ fraction of noise. To see that, consider the simulation phase, and assume that it consists of a fixed number of rounds, say, K rounds. Now, the communication in each phase may be between K and Km bits. On one hand, the communication cannot be too small: the other phases take $\Theta(m)$ communication, hence we need $K = \Omega(m)$ to keep the rate constant. On the other hand, the communication cannot be too large. Assume $K = m$ and the communication is m^2. This means that a single error would rewind the protocol by causing the retransmission of another m^2 bits. As mentioned above, wasting $\omega(m)$ bits per error would prevent us from reaching $\Theta(1/m)$ resilience.

Our solution to the above conundrum is to maintain a fixed amount of *communication* in each simulation phase. We will define a *chunk* as a set of consecutive rounds that consists of $\Theta(m)$ communication in our underlying protocol Π; note that different chunks may have different number of rounds, but they all have the same amount of bit transmissions. In order to split the underlying protocol into chunks, its communication must be known at the beginning of the coding scheme—it must be fixed and independent of inputs and noise.

While for Algorithm A (the oblivious-noise case) we need each chunk to contain $\Theta(m)$ bits of communication, in Algorithm B (the non-oblivious case) we will actually need it to be $\Theta(m\log(m))$. Planning ahead, we will set the amount of communication in a chunk via the parameter K, and require that the communication in any chunk will be between $4K$ and $5K$. We assume for now that $K = m$, and later (in Algorithm B) increase it to $K = m\log m$. We let $|\Pi|$ denote the number of chunks in Π.

We now summarize the different phases and provide pseudo-code.

(i) **Consistency check:** Each time the parties enter the "consistency check" phase they do a *single* iteration of the meeting-points mechanism [20], which consists of sending two hashes. If the hashes mismatch, they send the next two hash values (of some prefixes of the transcript, as instructed by the meeting-points mechanism) *next time they enter the consistency check phase.* In each iteration the hash functions are seeded with fresh randomness, assumed to be shared between the two parties.

(ii) **Flag passing:** Each party starts by generating a "flag" (i.e., a stop/continue bit) based on its state after the Consistency Check phase: if it experienced a hash mismatch with a neighbor, or has two neighbors with whom it has simulated up to different chunks in the underlying protocol, the flag is "stop," and otherwise it is "continue." It passes this flag along a fixed spanning tree $\mathcal{T}$ of G. Namely, each party receives flags from each of its children in $\mathcal{T}$. If one of the flags is stop, or if the party sees inconsistency with one of its neighbors, it sends a stop flag to its parent in the tree. Otherwise, it sends its parent the continue flag. After this phase ends and the root of $\mathcal{T}$ receives all the flags, the root propagates the computed flag in the opposite direction back to the leaves.

(iii) **Simulation:** In this phase, the parties "execute" the next chunk of Π, sending and receiving messages as dictated by the protocol Π. This phase *always* takes $5K$ rounds, which is the maximal number of rounds required to simulate $5K$ transmissions of Π. The simulation of a specific chunk may take fewer rounds; in this case, the phase still takes $5K$ rounds where all the parties remain silent after the chunk's simulation has completed until $5K$ rounds have passed. We note that some parties may be aware that the simulation so far contains errors that were not corrected yet, based on the previous phases. In the simulation phase, these parties will send a dummy message $\perp$ to their neighbors to indicate they are not simulating. Similarly, a party will refuse to simulate if its flag (obtained in the previous phase) is "stop".

(iv) **Rewind:** If the partial transcript between u and v consists of k chunks, then u will send a "rewind" message to any neighbor z for which the partial transcript between u and z contains more than k chunks. Once a party u sends a rewind message to a neighbor z, party z will truncate one chunk of the transcript that corresponds to the link (u, z), and might then want to send rewind messages to its own neighbors, who may then want to send even more rewinds. The phase takes n rounds altogether. This ensures that this cascade of rewinds has enough time to go through the entire network. Note, however, that each link rewinds only a *single chunk* per rewind phase; if the inconsistency is larger the rewind process spans along several rewind phases (in consecutive iterations).

The formal coding scheme, assuming oblivious noise and a common shared randomness is depicted as Algorithms 1–3 below. The meeting points procedure is given in Algorithm 4. These serve as our base coding scheme. We obtain Theorems 2.1 and 2.2 by introducing small modifications to this base scheme, which we now describe.

3.4 Modifications for Algorithms A and B

To get Algorithms A and B from our basic scheme, we need two steps. First, we need to remove the common random string while

Algorithm 1 A noise-resilient simulation of Π (for party u)

Let $T_{u,v}$ denote the partial, pairwise transcript between u and v *according to* u, and let $|T_{u,v}|$ denote the number of *chunks* simulated so far in $T_{u,v}$.

1: InitializeState()

2: **for** $i = 1$ to $100|\Pi|$ **do**
3:   **for all** $v \in N(u)$ in parallel **do** ▷ **meeting points**
4:     $status_{u,v} \leftarrow$ MeetingPoints$(u, v, S_{i,u,v})$
5:   $minChunk \leftarrow \min_{v \in N(u)} |T_{u,v}|$
6:   **if** exists v such that $status_{u,v}$ = "meeting points" **then**
7:     $status_u \leftarrow 0$
8:   **else if** exists v such that $|T_{u,v}| > minChunk$ **then**
9:     $status_u \leftarrow 0$
10:   **else**
11:     $status_u \leftarrow 1$

12:   $netCorrect_u \leftarrow$ FlagPassing$(u, status_u)$ ▷ **flag passing**

13:   **if** $netCorrect_u = 1$ **then** ▷ **simulation**
14:     Listen for one round.
15:     Simulate chunk $|T_{u,v}| + 1$ with each party $v \in N(u)$ from whom we have not received $\perp$ at the first round. The simulation is based on the partial transcript $T_{u,w}$ for each $w \in N(u)$, as well as the input to u.
16:     If the above step took less than $5K$ rounds, wait until $5K$ rounds have passed
17:     **if** received no $\perp$'s in Line 14 in this iteration **then**
18:       $minChunk \leftarrow minChunk + 1$
19:   **else**
20:     Send a single $\perp$ to each neighbor, and wait $5K$ rounds.

21:   **for** round $r = 1$ to n **do** ▷ **rewind**
22:     **for all** $v \in N(u)$ in parallel **do**
23:       **if** $status_{u,v} \neq$ "meeting points" and $alreadyRewound_{u,v} = 0$ **then**
24:         **if** $|T_{u,v}| > minChunk$ **then**
25:           Send a rewind message to v and truncate $T_{u,v}$ by one chunk
26:           $alreadyRewound_{u,v} \leftarrow 1$
27:       **if** a rewind message is received from v **then**
28:         **if** $status_{u,v} \neq$ "meeting points" and $alreadyRewound_{u,v} = 0$ **then**
29:           Truncate $T_{u,v}$ by one chunk
30:           $alreadyRewound_{u,v} \leftarrow 1$

Algorithm 2 InitializeState()

$K \leftarrow m$
for all neighbors $v \in N(u)$ **do**
  Initialize $T_{u,v} = \emptyset$
  Initialize $k_{u,v}, E_{u,v}, mpc1_{u,v}, mpc2_{u,v} \leftarrow 0$
  $status_{u,v} \leftarrow$ "simulate"
  $alreadyRewound_{u,v} \leftarrow 0$
  $S_{u,v} := (S_{i,u,v})_{i \in [100|\Pi|]} \overset{\text{unif}}{\leftarrow} \left(\{0,1\}^{\Theta(|\Pi|K)}\right)^{100|\Pi|}$
(These are uniform bits of randomness assumed to be pre-shared between u and v.)
$status_u \leftarrow 1.$
$netCorrect_u \leftarrow 1$

Algorithm 3 FlagPassing(u, $status$)

Let $\rho \in V$ be a specific node known by all the parties. Let $\mathcal{T}$ be a spanning tree generated by a breadth-first-search starting from ρ. Denote the depth of $\mathcal{T}$ as $d(\mathcal{T})$, where the depth of a single vertex is 1. Finally, let the *level* of a vertex be defined as $\ell(v) := \ell(u) + 1$, where u is the parent of v in $\mathcal{T}$, and $\ell(\rho) = 1$.

$netCorrect \leftarrow status$
if u is a leaf in $\mathcal{T}$ **then**
  Send $netCorrect$ to parent vertex in $\mathcal{T}$.
  Sleep for $\ell(u) - 1$ rounds.
else
  Sleep for $d(\mathcal{T}) - \ell(u)$ rounds. Ignore any messages received in these rounds.
  Receive $b_1, \ldots, b_k$, one symbol from each child in $\mathcal{T}$.
  $netCorrect \leftarrow \bigwedge_{i=1}^{k} b_i \wedge status$
  if $u \neq \rho$ **then**
    Send $netCorrect$ to parent.
    Sleep for $\ell(u) - 1$ rounds. Ignore any messages received in these rounds.
if $u = \rho$ **then**
  Send $netCorrect$ to children.
else
  Sleep for $\ell(u) - 1$ rounds. Ignore any messages received in these rounds.
  Receive b from parent.
  $netCorrect \leftarrow b \wedge status$
  if u is not a leaf in $\mathcal{T}$ **then**
    Send $netCorrect$ to children.
    Sleep for $d(\mathcal{T}) - \ell(u)$ rounds. Ignore any messages received in these rounds.
return $netCorrect$

keeping an oblivious adversary, which gets us Algorithm A. Then, we make the protocol resilient to non-oblivious adversaries to get Algorithm B.

The basic idea for removing the common random string is adopted from previous work [5, 17, 20]: simply have each pair of parties sample this string and send it across their shared link. However, this random string is very long, and sending it will increase the communication complexity by a quadratic factor. Therefore, instead, the parties communicate a short random string S which serves as a seed that generates a longer δ-biased string. This is done via a well-known technique by Naor and Naor [26], or Alon et al. [4]. This δ-biased randomness is used instead of the shared randomness

Algorithm 4 **MeetingPoints**(u,v, $S_{i,u,v}$, K)

Method called by u, with $v \in N(u)$. $S_{i,u,v} \in \{0,1\}^{\Theta(|\Pi|K)}$ is a large random seed to be split up and used for hashing. $\Pi \leftarrow$ protocol to be simulated.
$h \leftarrow$ inner product hash family w/ input length[6] $\Theta(|\Pi|K)$, $p = 2^{-\Theta(K/m)}$ sufficiently small, $o = \Theta(K/m)$, $s = |S_{i,u,v}|/10$.
$(S_1, S_2, \dots, S_{10}) \leftarrow S_{i,u,v}$. $S_{i,u,v}$ is split into ten seeds. Wlog we assume that $S_1, \dots, S_5$ are for the hashes it sends, and $S_6, \dots, S_{10}$ are for the hashes it uses for comparisons (so v is using $S_6, \dots S_{10}$ for the hashes it sends, and $S_1, \dots, S_5$ for comparisons, respectively).
$k \leftarrow k + 1$
$\widetilde{k} \leftarrow 2^{\lfloor \log k \rfloor}$. Let c be the largest integer such that $c\widetilde{k} \le |T_{u,v}|$.
$T_1 \leftarrow T_{u,v}[1 : c\widetilde{k}]$, $T_2 \leftarrow T_{u,v}[1 : (c-1)\widetilde{k}]$
Send $(h_{S_1}(k), h_{S_2}(T_1), h_{S_3}(T_1), h_{S_4}(T_2), h_{S_5}(T_2))$ to neighbor v.
$(H_k, H^{(1)}_{T_1}, H^{(1)}_{T_2}, H^{(2)}_{T_1}, H^{(2)}_{T_2}) \leftarrow$
  $(h_{S_6}(k), h_{S_7}(T_1), h_{S_8}(T_2), h_{S_9}(T_1), h_{S_{10}}(T_2))$
Receive $(H'_k, H^{(1)'}_{T_1}, H^{(2)'}_{T_1}, H^{(1)'}_{T_2}, H^{(2)'}_{T_2})$ from our neighbor v.
if $H_k \neq H'_k$ **then**
  $E \leftarrow E + 1$
if $k = 1, E = 0$, and $H^{(1)}_{T_1} = H^{(1)'}_{T_1}$ **then**
  $k \leftarrow 0$
  $status \leftarrow$ "simulate" **return** $status$
if $H^{(1)}_{T_1} = H^{(1)'}_{T_1}$ or $H^{(2)}_{T_1} = H^{(1)'}_{T_2}$ **then**
  $mpc1 \leftarrow mpc1 + 1$
else if $H^{(1)}_{T_2} = H^{(2)'}_{T_1}$ or $H^{(2)}_{T_2} = H^{(2)'}_{T_2}$ **then**
  $mpc2 \leftarrow mpc2 + 1$
if $2E \ge k$ **then**
  $k \leftarrow 0, E \leftarrow 0, mpc1 \leftarrow 0, mpc2 \leftarrow 0$
  $status \leftarrow$ "meeting points"
else if $k = \widetilde{k}$ **then**
  if $mpc1 > 0.4k$ **then**
    $T \leftarrow T_1$
    $k \leftarrow 0, E \leftarrow 0$
  else if $mpc2 > 0.4k$ **then**
    $T \leftarrow T_2$
    $k \leftarrow 0, E \leftarrow 0$
  $mpc1 \leftarrow 0, mpc2 \leftarrow 0$
  $status \leftarrow$ "meeting points"
else
  $status \leftarrow$ "meeting points"
return $status$

in Algorithm 1, and this yields Algorithm A. Specifically, Algorithm A uses Algorithm 5 for InitializeState(), which in turn uses Algorithm 6 to share the δ-biased randomness.

To get Algorithm B from Algorithm A, all we need to do is change the chunk size K to be $m\log(m)$ instead of m. Specifically, Algorithm B uses Algorithm 7 for InitializeState(). We provide an overview of the analysis of Algorithms A and B in Section 4.

Algorithm 5 InitializeState() (for simulation without assuming a CRS)

$K \leftarrow m$
for all neighbors $v \in N(u)$ in parallel **do**
  Initialize $T_{u,v} = \emptyset$
  Initialize $k_{u,v}, E_{u,v}, mpc1_{u,v}, mpc2_{u,v} \leftarrow 0$
  $status_{u,v} \leftarrow$ "simulate"
  $alreadyRewound_{u,v} \leftarrow 0$
  $\delta := 2^{-\Theta(|\Pi|K/m)}$
  $S := (S_{i,u,v})_{i \in [100|\Pi|]} \leftarrow$ RandomnessExchange(u, v, δ, K)
$status_u \leftarrow 1$.
$netCorrect_u \leftarrow 1$

Algorithm 6 RandomnessExchange(u, v, δ, K)

input: u calling party, $v \in N(u)$. $\delta > 0$ is a parameter that specifies the bias we desire from our random string.

Fix an arbitrary total order on the vertices in V (common for all instantiations of this procedure).
$\ell \leftarrow \Theta(|\Pi|K) \cdot 100|\Pi|$,
$r \leftarrow \Theta(\log(1/\delta) + \log(\ell))$, large enough to generate a string of length at least ℓ and bias at most δ.
$C \leftarrow$ error correcting code with block length $\Theta(r)$, constant rate and constant distance.
if $u < v$ in the ordering **then**
  Sample a uniformly random string $L \in \{0,1\}^r$
  Send $C(L)$ to v
else
  Receive W from v
  $L \leftarrow C^{-1}(W)$, the decoding of W with respect to the code C.
$S_{u,v} \leftarrow \left(\{0,1\}^{\Theta(|\Pi|K)}\right)^{100|\Pi|}$ gets the δ-biased string of length ℓ generated from L.
Output $S_{u,v}$.

Algorithm 7 InitializeState() for nonoblivious noise

$K \leftarrow m\log(m)$
for all neighbors $v \in N(u)$ in parallel **do**
  Initialize $T_{u,v} = \emptyset$
  Initialize $k_{u,v}, E_{u,v}, mpc1_{u,v}, mpc2_{u,v} \leftarrow 0$
  $status_{u,v} \leftarrow$ "simulate"
  $alreadyRewound_{u,v} \leftarrow 0$
  $\delta := 2^{-\Theta(|\Pi|K/m)}$
  $S := (S_{i,u,v})_{i \in [100|\Pi|]} \leftarrow$ RandomnessExchange(u, v, δ, K)
$status_u \leftarrow 1$.
$netCorrect_u \leftarrow 1$

4 ANALYSIS

A main hurdle is analyzing the correctness of the scheme and its probability of success. Similar to previous work, our analysis utilizes a potential argument that measures the progress of the simulation. The progress is measured in two parts. The first part is the progress of simulating the partial transcript of each individual link. This part is similar to the two-party case [20]. The second is the "global" progress which considers the progress of the simulation in the entire network. Each part entails its own potential function; this 'divide-and-conquer' approach greatly simplifies the analysis.

By defining a potential function in this manner, we can show that the parties make significant progress towards simulating the noiseless protocol correctly in each iteration as long as the adversary does not commit too many errors and there are not too many hash collisions. Ensuring that these bad events do not occur is the main technical difficulty of the analysis.

The first difficulty is to bound the number of errors the adversary can commit, and this arises from the fact our communication model is not fully-utilized. Namely, recall that the adversary's error budget is proportional to the communication of the parties. Knowing this, the adversary may try to insert errors that will cause the parties get out of sync, and as a result speak all simultaneously, which in turn gives the adversary more budget for errors. To rule this out, we show that the communication in any iteration of our coding scheme is proportional to $O(m(1+\ell))$, where ℓ is the number of errors or hash collisions that have occurred in that iteration. Recalling that an iteration of our coding scheme simulates a chunk consisting of m bits of communication, this lets us prove that the communication overall in our coding scheme is $O(\mathrm{CC}(\Pi))$ with high probability over the hashes. This analysis crucially relies on the flag-passing step, where parties keep silent whenever they suspect an error has occurred, rather than continue in the simulation.

The second difficulty relates to bounding the number of hash collisions when the collision probability is a constant. We note that in the two-party coding scheme of [20] hash collisions also occur with constant probability. Just like in that work, we want to bound the number of hash collisions that occur, even when the parties do not use a CRS and the adversary is non-oblivious. However, we encounter significant obstacles when extending the same approach to the multiparty setting, which stem from the fact that we are dealing with a non-fully-utilized multiparty protocol, which gives the adversary more flexibility in their attacks.

Our analysis is performed in three steps. We begin by assuming the parties share a common random string (CRS), and assume that the noise is independent of this CRS. The random string is used as seeds to the hash functions. Since the CRS is independent of the noise, we can bound (with high probability) the number of hash collisions throughout the coding scheme. This in turn bounds the increase in the total communication attributed to hash collisions, by a constant factor. This part of the analysis is similar to the analysis done in previous works, e.g., [20].

The next step is removing the CRS. We replace the CRS with a δ-biased string, and argue that the number of hash collisions does not increase by much, assuming the adversary is oblivious to the δ-biased string. The final step is considering the case where the adversary is non-oblivious. Here we union-bound over all the possible oblivious attacks, yet, even here we must address an obstacle that does not show up in the two-party setting. Let us expand on the last two steps of our analysis.

4.1 Removing the Common Random String

As mentioned earlier, the idea for removing the common random string is to have each pair of parties agree on a short random string, and use this as a seed to generate a longer δ-biased string that they use for randomness in the protocol. The key intuition as to why δ-biased randomness suffices is that hashing with a δ-biased seed behaves "close" to hashing with a truly uniform seed; this idea dates back to the papers of Naor and Naor [26] and Alon et al. [4]. However, this holds only when the input to the hash function is independent of the δ-biased seed. Unfortunately, in our setting, the input to the hash function may depend on the δ-biased seed: indeed, the parties hash their partial transcripts in each meeting points phase, and these partial transcripts *do* depend on seed, since they are a function of the output of previous hashes, e.g., on whether or not hash collisions occurred in previous rounds.

We circumvent this issue by showing that a given pattern of hash collisions determines the (partial) transcripts throughout the protocol. Once the transcripts are fixed, the hashes output behave similarly to the case of uniform randomness, up to a statistical difference of at most δ. Therefore, if δ is small enough, we can prove robustness for all possible fixed patterns of hash collisions. Then, we can union bound over all the possible patterns of hash collisions, which bounds the failure probability for the δ-biased case by the failure of the uniform case plus an error term that depends on δ and the cardinality of the different hash patterns. One cannot take δ to be too small, since generating the δ-biased string requires communicating $\approx O(m\log(1/\delta))$ bits, hence the smaller δ gets, the more communication we need. Luckily, we can set δ to be sufficiently small so that the probability of failure is still exponentially small even after the union bound, while keeping a constant rate in the communication.

Finally, we note that sharing the seeds for δ-biased randomness requires communication, so the adversary may try to corrupt this communication and mess up the "shared" randomness for some pair of parties. Just like in the work of [20], we handle this by encoding the seed using an error correcting code with sufficiently large distance. However, in the non-fully-utilized setting, an adversary might try to corrupt the randomness exchange in the hopes that the increased communication in the rest of the protocol will pay for their errors. We address this similarly to how we bound the communication for Algorithm 1 (the basic coding scheme). Namely, we show that corrupting the randomness requires so many errors that the adversary can only do so by exceeding their budget.

4.2 Dealing with a non-oblivious adversary

Finally, we consider the case where the adversary is non-oblivious. We would like to follow the approach of [20] and simply union bound over all the possible oblivious attacks. Unfortunately, as opposed to the two-party case of [20], knowledge of the hash seeds gives the adversary too many options for attacks, and the proof fails spectacularly.

To see why this is, fix an edge (u, v) in the network, and suppose for simplicity that we use truly random functions for our hashes. Since we use constant length hash outputs and the adversary knows the random seeds ahead of time, with constant probability over the random seed, the adversary can corrupt the simulation on the link (u, v) such that a hash collision is guaranteed in the next meeting points phase. In this case, the parties will continue to simulate (incorrectly). But there is no guarantee that it will be caught in the next phase either; if the adversary was fortunate, perhaps he was able to make an error that causes hash collisions in *two consecutive meeting points phases*. Generalizing this reasoning, with probability $1/m$, the adversary forces hash collisions on the link (u, v) for $\Theta(\log m)$ consecutive phases, leading to $\Theta(m \log m)$ wasted communication. Since there are m links for the adversary to choose from when making his error, with high probability there exists a link on which such an attack is possible. Therefore, he can create $\Theta(m \log m)$ wasted communication with just a single error.

To overcome this issue, we increase the length of the hash output, so it is no longer constant but rather $\Theta(\log m)$. Then the hash collision probability drops to $1/\text{poly}(m)$, and the union bound yields the desired outcome. However, the length of each hash increased from a constant to $\Theta(\log m)$, and the rate of the coding scheme is no longer constant. To fix this, we simulate the protocol in larger chunks. That is, instead of sending a hash every $\Theta(m)$ bits of communication of Π, parties exchange hashes of length $\Theta(\log m)$ every $\Theta(m \log m)$ bits of simulation, thus increasing the overall communication by just a constant factor.

5 RELATED WORK

As mentioned above, interactive coding was initiated by Schulman [28, 29]. Over the last several years there has been tremendous amount of work on interactive coding schemes in the two-party setting (e.g., [6, 7, 10, 14, 18, 19]), and in the multi-party setting (detailed below). We refer the reader to [13] for a survey on the field (and to references therein).

Coding schemes for insertions and deletions in the two-party setting were first constructed by Braverman, Gelles, Mao, and Ostrovsky [9]. As was noted above, in the model where in each round each party sends a single bit (which is the model used by most previous works, including [9]), insertions and deletions are only meaningful in the *asynchronous* model, as otherwise, such an error model is equivalent to the erasure model. However, the asynchronous model seems to be incompatible with insertions and deletions, since a single deletion can cause a "deadlock", where both parties wait to the next incoming message. Braverman et al. suggested a model where any deletion is followed by an insertion, thus the protocol never "halts" due to noise. However, the noise may delete a certain message and then inject a spoofed "reply" to the original sender. Then, one party believes that the protocol has progressed by one step, while the other party is completely oblivious to this. This type of noise was called *synchronization attack* as it brings the parties out of synch.

Braverman et al. [9] constructed a coding scheme for insertions and deletions in this model with constant communication rate, and resilience to constant fraction of noise. Later, Sherstov and Wu [30] showed that a very similar scheme can actually resist an *optimal* noise level. Both these schemes are computationally inefficient. Haeupler, Shahrasbi, and Vitercik [21] constructed an efficient scheme that is resilient to (a small) constant fraction of insertions and deletions. Furthermore, they constructed a scheme where the communication rate approaches 1 as the noise level approaches 0. Efremenko, Haramaty, and Kalai [12] considered the *synchronous* setting, where parties can send messages of arbitrary length in each round, and the adversary may insert and delete bits in the content of each message. They construct an efficient coding scheme with constant communication rate, and constant blowup in the round complexity, that is resilient to a constant fraction of noise. All the above schemes consider only the two-party setting.

In the multiparty setting, Rajagopalan and Schulman [27] constructed a coding scheme for stochastic noise that achieves a rate of $1/O(\log(d+1))$ for networks with maximal degree d. This implies a constant rate coding scheme for graphs with constant degree. Alon et al. [3] showed that if the topology is a clique, or a dense d-regular graph, then constant rate coding is also possible. Yet, Braverman, Efremenko, Gelles, and Haeupler [8] proved that a constant rate is impossible if the topology is a star. All the above works assume a synchronous fully-utilized network. Gelles and Kalai [15] showed that constant rate coding schemes are impossible also on graphs with constant degree, such as a cycle, assuming a synchronous, yet not fully-utilized model.

The case of adversarial noise in the multiparty setting was first considered by Jain, Kalai, and Lewko [24], who constructed a constant-rate coding scheme over an asynchronous star network that is resilient to $O(1/n)$ fraction of noise. Hoza and Schulman [23] considered synchronous networks with arbitrary topology and constructed a constant rate coding scheme that is resilient to $O(1/m)$ noise. Via routing and scheduling techniques, they show how to resist a fraction of $O(1/n)$-noise, while reducing the rate to $1/O(m \log(n)/n)$. Both these schemes use tree-codes, and therefore are computationally inefficient.

Aggarwal, Dani, Hayes, and Saia [1] constructed an efficient synchronous coding scheme, assuming the parties have shared randomness that is unknown to the adversary. They consider a somewhat different communication model than the above, where the length of the protocol is not predetermined and may vary with the noise (similar to the two-party adaptive notion of [2]). Their coding scheme is resilient to an arbitrary (and *a priori* unknown) amount of bit-flips (as long as the noise-pattern is predetermined and independent of parties shared randomness), and has a rate of $1/O(\log(nCC(\Pi)))$.

Censor-Hillel, Gelles, and Haeupler [11] constructed asynchronous schemes, where the parties do not know the topology of the network (an assumption that is very common in the distributed computation community). Their scheme is resilient to $O(1/n)$ noise and has a rate of $1/O(n \log^2 n)$.

REFERENCES

[1] Abhinav Aggarwal, Varsha Dani, Thomas P. Hayes, and Jared Saia. 2017. Distributed Computing with Channel Noise. Cryptology ePrint Archive, Report 2017/710. https://eprint.iacr.org/2017/710.

[2] Shweta Agrawal, Ran Gelles, and Amit Sahai. 2016. Adaptive Protocols for Interactive Communication. In *2016 IEEE International Symposium on Information Theory (ISIT)*. 595–599. https://doi.org/10.1109/ISIT.2016.7541368

[3] Noga Alon, Mark Braverman, Klim Efremenko, Ran Gelles, and Bernhard Haeupler. 2016. Reliable Communication over Highly Connected Noisy Networks. In *Proceedings of the 2016 ACM Symposium on Principles of Distributed Computing (PODC '16)*. 165–173. https://doi.org/10.1145/2933057.2933085

[4] Noga Alon, Oded Goldreich, Johan Håstad, and René Peralta. 1992. Simple Constructions of Almost k-wise Independent Random Variables. *Random Structures & Algorithms* 3, 3 (1992), 289–304. https://doi.org/10.1002/rsa.3240030308

[5] Zvika Brakerski and Yael Tauman Kalai. 2012. Efficient Interactive Coding against Adversarial Noise. *Proceedings of the IEEE Symposium on Foundations of Computer Science* (2012), 160–166.
[6] Zvika Brakerski, Yael T. Kalai, and Moni Naor. 2014. Fast Interactive Coding Against Adversarial Noise. *J. ACM* 61, 6, Article 35 (Dec. 2014), 30 pages. https://doi.org/10.1145/2661628
[7] M. Braverman and K. Efremenko. 2017. List and Unique Coding for Interactive Communication in the Presence of Adversarial Noise. *SIAM J. Comput.* 46, 1 (2017), 388–428. https://doi.org/10.1137/141002001
[8] Mark Braverman, Klim Efremenko, Ran Gelles, and Bernhard Haeupler. 2017. Constant-Rate Coding for Multiparty Interactive Communication Is Impossible. *J. ACM* 65, 1, Article 4 (Dec. 2017), 41 pages. https://doi.org/10.1145/3050218
[9] M. Braverman, R. Gelles, J. Mao, and R. Ostrovsky. 2017. Coding for Interactive Communication Correcting Insertions and Deletions. *IEEE Transactions on Information Theory* 63, 10 (Oct 2017), 6256–6270. https://doi.org/10.1109/TIT.2017.2734881
[10] M. Braverman and A. Rao. 2014. Toward Coding for Maximum Errors in Interactive Communication. *Information Theory, IEEE Transactions on* 60, 11 (Nov 2014), 7248–7255. https://doi.org/10.1109/TIT.2014.2353994
[11] Keren Censor-Hillel, Ran Gelles, and Bernhard Haeupler. 2018. Making Asynchronous Distributed Computations Robust to Channel Noise. In *9th Innovations in Theoretical Computer Science Conference (ITCS 2018) (Leibniz International Proceedings in Informatics (LIPIcs))*, Anna R. Karlin (Ed.), Vol. 94. Schloss Dagstuhl–Leibniz-Zentrum fuer Informatik, Dagstuhl, Germany, 50:1–50:20. https://doi.org/10.4230/LIPIcs.ITCS.2018.50
[12] Klim Efremenko, Elad Haramaty, and Yael Kalai. 2018. Interactive Coding with Constant Round and Communication Blowup. *Electronic Colloquium on Computational Complexity (ECCC)* 25 (2018), 54. https://eccc.weizmann.ac.il/report/2018/054
[13] Ran Gelles. 2017. Coding for Interactive Communication: A Survey. *Foundations and Trends® in Theoretical Computer Science* 13, 1–2 (2017), 1–157. https://doi.org/10.1561/0400000079
[14] R. Gelles, B. Haeupler, G. Kol, N. Ron-Zewi, and A. Wigderson. 2018. Explicit Capacity Approaching Coding for Interactive Communication. *IEEE Transactions on Information Theory* 64, 10 (Oct 2018), 6546–6560. https://doi.org/10.1109/TIT.2018.2829764
[15] R. Gelles and Y. T. Kalai. 2019. Constant-Rate Interactive Coding Is Impossible, Even in Constant-Degree Networks. *IEEE Transactions on Information Theory* 65, 6 (June 2019), 3812–3829. https://doi.org/10.1109/TIT.2019.2904576
[16] Ran Gelles, Yael Tauman Kalai, and Govind Ramnarayan. 2019. Efficient Multiparty Interactive Coding for Insertions, Deletions and Substitutions. *CoRR preprint* arXiv:1901.09863 (2019). http://arxiv.org/abs/1901.09863
[17] Ran Gelles, Ankur Moitra, and Amit Sahai. 2011. Efficient and Explicit Coding for Interactive Communication. In *Proceeding of the IEEE Symposium on Foundations of Computer Science (FOCS '11)*. 768–777. https://doi.org/10.1109/FOCS.2011.51
[18] Ran Gelles, Ankur Moitra, and Amit Sahai. 2014. Efficient Coding for Interactive Communication. *Information Theory, IEEE Transactions on* 60, 3 (March 2014), 1899–1913. https://doi.org/10.1109/TIT.2013.2294186
[19] Mohsen Ghaffari and Bernhard Haeupler. 2014. Optimal Error Rates for Interactive Coding II: Efficiency and List Decoding. In *Proceedings of the IEEE Symposium on Foundations of Computer Science (FOCS '14)*. 394–403. https://doi.org/10.1109/FOCS.2014.49
[20] Bernhard Haeupler. 2014. Interactive Channel Capacity Revisited. In *Proceedings of the IEEE Symposium on Foundations of Computer Science (FOCS '14)*. 226–235. https://doi.org/10.1109/FOCS.2014.32
[21] Bernhard Haeupler, Amirbehshad Shahrasbi, and Ellen Vitercik. 2017. Synchronization Strings: Channel Simulations and Interactive Coding for Insertions and Deletions. *CoRR preprint* arXiv:1707.04233 (2017). http://arxiv.org/abs/1707.04233
[22] William M. Hoza. 2015. Private communication.
[23] William M. Hoza and Leonard J. Schulman. 2016. The Adversarial Noise Threshold for Distributed Protocols. In *Proceedings of the Twenty-Seventh Annual ACM-SIAM Symposium on Discrete Algorithms*. 240–258. https://doi.org/10.1137/1.9781611974331.ch18
[24] Abhishek Jain, Yael Tauman Kalai, and Allison Lewko. 2015. Interactive Coding for Multiparty Protocols. In *Proceedings of the 6th Conference on Innovations in Theoretical Computer Science, ITCS '15*. 1–10. https://doi.org/10.1145/2688073.2688109
[25] Gillat Kol and Ran Raz. 2013. Interactive channel capacity. In *STOC '13: Proceedings of the 45th annual ACM Symposium on theory of computing*. 715–724. https://doi.org/10.1145/2488608.2488699
[26] Joseph Naor and Moni Naor. 1993. Small-Bias Probability Spaces: Efficient Constructions and Applications. *SIAM J. Comput* 22 (1993), 838–856.
[27] Sridhar Rajagopalan and Leonard Schulman. 1994. A coding theorem for distributed computation. In *STOC '94: Proceedings of the twenty-sixth annual ACM symposium on Theory of computing*. 790–799. https://doi.org/10.1145/195058.195462
[28] Leonard J. Schulman. 1992. Communication on noisy channels: a coding theorem for computation. *Foundations of Computer Science, Annual IEEE Symposium on* (1992), 724–733. https://doi.org/10.1109/SFCS.1992.267778
[29] Leonard J. Schulman. 1996. Coding for interactive communication. *IEEE Transactions on Information Theory* 42, 6 (1996), 1745–1756. https://doi.org/10.1109/18.556671
[30] Alexander A. Sherstov and Pei Wu. 2017. Optimal Interactive Coding for Insertions, Deletions, and Substitutions. In *2017 IEEE 58th Annual Symposium on Foundations of Computer Science (FOCS)*. 240–251. https://doi.org/10.1109/FOCS.2017.30

Brief Announcement: Multiparty Interactive Communication with Private Channels

Abhinav Aggarwal
abhiag@unm.edu
University of New Mexico
Albuquerque, NM

Varsha Dani
varsha@unm.edu
University of New Mexico
Albuquerque, NM

Thomas P. Hayes
hayes@cs.unm.edu
University of New Mexico
Albuquerque, NM

Jared saia
saia@cs.unm.edu
University of New Mexico
Albuquerque, NM

ABSTRACT

A group of n players wants to run a distributed protocol $\mathcal{P}$ over a network where communication occurs via private point-to-point channels. Can we efficiently simulate $\mathcal{P}$ in the presence of an adversary who knows $\mathcal{P}$ and is able to maliciously flip bits on the channels? We show that this is possible, even when L, the number of bits sent in $\mathcal{P}$, the average message size α in $\mathcal{P}$, and T, the number of bits flipped by the adversary are not known in advance. In particular, we show how to create a robust version of $\mathcal{P}$, $\mathcal{P}'$ such that 1) $\mathcal{P}'$ fails with probability at most δ, for any $\delta > 0$; and 2) $\mathcal{P}'$ sends $O(L(1 + (1/\alpha)\log(nL/\delta)) + T)$ bits. We note that if α is $\Omega(\log(nL/\delta))$, then $\mathcal{P}'$ sends only $O(L + T)$ bits, and is therefore within a constant factor of optimal. Critically, our result requires that $\mathcal{P}$ runs correctly in an asynchronous network and our protocol $\mathcal{P}'$ must run in a synchronous network.

CCS CONCEPTS

• **Theory of computation** → **Distributed algorithms**; • **Security and privacy** → *Distributed systems security*;

KEYWORDS

Interactive Communication, Private Channels, Resource Competitive Analysis

ACM Reference Format:
Abhinav Aggarwal, Varsha Dani, Thomas P. Hayes, and Jared saia. 2019. Brief Announcement: Multiparty Interactive Communication with Private Channels. In *2019 ACM Symposium on Principles of Distributed Computing (PODC '19), July 29-August 2, 2019, Toronto, ON, Canada.* ACM, New York, NY, USA, 3 pages. https://doi.org/10.1145/3293611.3331571

1 INTRODUCTION

How can we compute in the presence of noise? The problem of interactive communication formalizes this problem [2, 9, 10]. In this problem, n players are in a network connected by point-to-point binary symmetric channels, and we want to simulate a distributed protocol $\mathcal{P}$, even when an adversary can flip bits on any of the channels at any time. Our goal is to create a new protocol $\mathcal{P}'$ that correctly simulates $\mathcal{P}$ even in the presence of such adversarial bit flipping, and does so while minimizing the number of bits sent.

Under certain special conditions on $\mathcal{P}$, it is already known how to create a $\mathcal{P}'$ with a multiplicative blowup in bits sent that is $O(\log n)$ [9], or even $O(1)$ for certain network topologies [2, 6, 7]. However, the conditions on $\mathcal{P}$ are strong: it must be a protocol that sends exactly 1 bit over every channel in every time step. Unfortunately, in a complete network, where the average number of messages sent per round in $\mathcal{P}$ is only $\tilde{O}(n)$, the multiplicative blowup can become $\tilde{\Omega}(n)$.

A naive idea is to run the 2-player algorithm of Dani et al. [5] over each communication channel. Unfortunately, this fails. In particular, the protocol of [5] assumes that a player sends a bit on the channel in each time step[1]. However, in the multiparty problem, there may be many time steps where, for many channels, neither player on the channel sends a bit. This can happen because delay due to noise on one channel is holding up the protocol on all other channels, or simply because both players connected by a channel are waiting for messages from other players before using that channel.

In this paper, we take a first step toward designing an algorithm with costs that scale well for any network topology. In particular, if an adversary flips T bits, then our algorithm sends $\tilde{O}(L + T)$ bits, where L is the number of bits sent in $\mathcal{P}$. Here the $\tilde{O}$ notation hides a logarithmic term in n, L and δ; if the desired δ is polynomially (or even sub-polynomially) small in n, then the $\tilde{O}$ notation hides a logarithmic (polylogarithmic) term just in n and L. Moreover, if the average message size in $\mathcal{P}$ is $\Omega(\log(nL/\delta))$, then $\mathcal{P}'$ sends only $O(L + T)$ bits which is within a constant factor of optimal. Importantly, our algorithm requires no *a priori* knowledge of T or L.

There exist many examples of asynchronous algorithms known for common problems that need to be solved in noisy networks. Our result allows using any asynchronous algorithm to design a new synchronous algorithm that is robust to channel noise. This new algorithm sends significantly fewer bits compared to prior work, which sends $\Omega(nL)$ bits [2, 3, 6, 9]. Additionally, when $T = \tilde{O}(L)$, the new algorithm sends only $\tilde{O}(L)$ bits.

[1]A time step is defined as the amount of time that it takes to send one bit over a channel.

ACM ISBN 978-1-4503-6217-7/19/07.
https://doi.org/10.1145/3293611.3331571

Model Details: To obtain our result, we make two key simplifying assumptions over [2, 3, 6, 9]. First, as in [5], we assume all channels are private, but otherwise make no cryptographic assumptions. Second, we assume that $\mathcal{P}$ is asynchronous: it runs correctly even with arbitrary message delays. As in previous work, $\mathcal{P}'$ is assumed to run in a synchronous network.

In each time step, a bit value is set for every channel. This is the value received by any player listening on the channel. In any contiguous sequence of time steps where no player sends a bit, the adversary sets the bits, and pays a cost of 1 for each time it changes the value. As in prior work [2, 9], we assume that all players know the value n but may not know the values L, T and α. In the case where we want an error probability that is polynomially small in n, we require that all players know a desired error probability δ.

We make use of two key ideas from [5]. First, we use *Algebraic Manipulation Detection (AMD) Codes* [4]. These codes enable detection of any bit flips in a code word with probability of error that is exponentially small in the number of bits added to the message word.[2] Second, similarly to [5], we use error-correcting encoding of AMD code words to ensure that when we have to resend a message, our costs are linear in the number of bits flipped by the adversary.

How is our model different? Our work is not directly comparable to most past results because we do not quantify our results in terms of the fraction of messages that are corrupted, and more importantly, we assume that communication takes place over private channels. The stronger assumption of private channels means that up to a $1/\log(nL)$ fraction of message bits can be corrupted, and our algorithm is still likely to succeed with a cost overhead that is only $O(\log(nL))$. In our setting, the adversarial strategy of trying to cut off all communications to and from a single player requires corruption of much more than a $1/n$ fraction of bits. This is true since our protocol can detect the noise, and then increase the fraction of the total communication involving the beleaguered player. Finally, to the best of our knowledge, all prior work on Interactive Communication assumes players know L in advance. We are able to remove this assumption of a priori knowledge of L.

2 ALGORITHM OVERVIEW

Our algorithm proceeds in rounds, each of which consists of the following steps.[3]

(1) If u has a message for v, it initiates a message exchange by asking v for a key.
(2) Upon receipt of this key, u sends the message along with the key.
(3) v terminates the message exchange upon successful authentication and retrieval of the message.
(4) u terminates the message exchange upon hearing silence from v.

This goes on until all the messages in $\mathcal{P}$ have been communicated to the intended recipients.

[2]We note that this error probability is smaller than what can be achieved via digital signatures [8].

[3]For convenience, our presentation assumes two bidirectional channels between each pair of (neighboring) players, one for each player to initiate a round with the other. We can simulate these two channels by multiplexing over a single channel, at the cost of a factor 2 increase in the number of time steps.

Rounds. For each message m in $\mathcal{P}$ that needs to be sent from some player u to his neighbor v, we communicate m through a sequence of exchanges between players u, referred to as *Alice*, and v, referred to as *Bob*, in $\mathcal{P}'$ using Algorithms 1 and 2, respectively. The sequence of time steps corresponding to steps 1-4 of the algorithm overview constitute what we call a *round*. Thus, each round of $\mathcal{P}$ consists of exactly four *words*, one for each of the steps 1-4. The length of each word in round r is denoted w_r. This depends on the round number r and is therefore a function of the current time step, which can be computed independently by each player using the global clock. We make w_r gradually increase with r (the exact dependence will be provided shortly).

Since each message in $\mathcal{P}$ is just a single bit, it takes exactly one round to be communicated in $\mathcal{P}'$, if no successful corruption happens, and more otherwise. If a round for some message m is corrupted, we attempt resending m in the subsequent round, which provides higher security due to a larger word length.

At the beginning of each round, Bob must listen for a key request during the first w_r time steps. If no valid request is received, he idles until the start of the next round. Thus Bob is active in every round. For her part, Alice only participates in a round if, in $\mathcal{P}$, she has a message to send to Bob.

Parity Bit. Observe that Alice and Bob may have different views on whether a particular round was successful. If Bob encounters two rounds that contain the same message, with no silent round in between, he needs to distinguish between whether Alice is resending the message or whether Alice's next message happens to be the same as the previous one. To disambiguate these cases, Alice appends a bit b to each message m that she sends to Bob, where b is the parity of the index of m.

Word Generation. Both Alice and Bob generate their words for round r using a function $\mathcal{E}_r(x, k)$, described below, which returns the encoding of the word's content x using the key k based on the security settings for round r. Here x may be the message m from $\mathcal{P}$, a special keyword used by Alice to request Bob's key, or Bob's key for the round. The key k, for round r, is a string of length $2\left\lceil \log \frac{4n\pi r}{\sqrt{\delta}} \right\rceil$ bits. This key length, and other corresponding encoding parameters, are chosen to ensure the failure events for our algorithm occur within the given error tolerance, δ (see [1] for more details).

In Alice's first call to $\mathcal{E}$, the key k is a random string. In Bob's call, k is the key he received from Alice in the previous word, but x is a random string of the appropriate length. In Alice's second call, k is the key she received from Bob in the previous word. Alice and Bob generate fresh random keys for each round in which they desire to send a message.

The function $\mathcal{E}_r(x, k)$ is formally defined as follows. The function uses a key k of length $\kappa_r = 2\left\lceil \log \frac{4n\pi r}{\sqrt{\delta}} \right\rceil$ bits and appends it to the content x. Then, it encodes this concatenated string of bits with an AMD code using $\eta_r = \frac{\delta}{2n^2\pi^2 r^2}$. Then, it encodes this AMD codeword with a (1/3)-error-correcting code. Finally, it pads $38\left\lceil \log \frac{2n\pi r}{\sqrt{\delta}} \right\rceil$ random bits to the ECC codeword. These random bits are added to ensure that players are unlikely to confuse words with silence and that the adversary is unlikely to flip bits of a word

Algorithm 1: Sender's algorithm.

1. Generate a random session key k_A.
2. Request a session key k_B from the recipient. Include k_A in the message;
3. If silence is heard, wait for $2w_r$ time steps and proceed to the next round;
4. Else, decode the message and check if k_A is correctly reproduced. If so, append the message m with k_B and send it across.
5. Proceed to the next message if silence is heard, else resend the message.

Algorithm 2: Receiver's algorithm.

1. Generate a random session key k_B
2. If a valid key request is heard, send k_B. Echo k_A in the message.
3. If silence is heard, wait for $3w_r$ time steps and proceed to the next round;
4. Else, decode the message and check if k_B is correctly reproduced. If so, extract the message m and stay silent. Else, send noise for w_r time steps.

to forge silence. As a result, the word length for round r is given as $w_r = O\left(\log \frac{nr}{\delta}\right)$.

Similar to $\mathscr{E}_r(x,k)$, we define a decoding function which returns either a pair (x',k') such that $\mathscr{E}_r(x',k') = m$ or returns $(\perp,\perp)$, if no such (x',k') exists. It begins by stripping off the padding at the end of m to obtain a shorter string m'. Then it decodes the error correction, computing $m'' = \texttt{ecDec}(m')$. If $\texttt{IsCodeword}(m'',\eta_r)$, then $\mathscr{D}$ outputs $\texttt{amdDec}(m'',\eta)$, otherwise it returns $(\perp,\perp)$.

Failure Events. There are certain events which may cause our algorithm to fail. More specifically, it is possible that the adversary (1) converts one AMD codeword to another, so that the decoded content is different from the content intended; (2) converts a non-silence word into silence; and (3) correctly guesses some player's key and uses it to communicate bits that are not in $\mathcal{P}$. We bound the probability of these failure events by the error tolerance, δ.

3 OVERVIEW OF OUR RESULTS

Our main result is summarized in the following theorem.

THEOREM 3.1. *Let $\mathcal{P}$ be an asynchronous protocol for $n \geq 2$ players that sends a total of L bits. Let α be the average message length in $\mathcal{P}$. Let $\delta > 0$. Then we can create a synchronous protocol $\mathcal{P}'$ such that for any number T of adversarial bit flips, $\mathcal{P}'$ succeeds with probability at least $1-\delta$ and sends $O\left(L\left(1+\frac{1}{\alpha}\log\left(\frac{nL}{\delta}\right)\right)+T\right)$ bits. The total latency of $\mathcal{P}'$ is $O\left(\max_p\left\{\Lambda_p\left(1+\frac{1}{\alpha}\log\left(\frac{n(L+T)}{\delta}\right)\right)+T_p\right\}\right)$ where p ranges over all communication paths in the asynchronous simulation of $\mathcal{P}$, Λ_p is the latency of p, and T_p is the total number of bits flipped by the adversary on channels in p.*

To compare our result with other work, we compute the coding rate of our algorithm. Recall that the coding rate of an interactive communication algorithm is the number of bits sent in $\mathcal{P}'$ divided by the number of bits sent in $\mathcal{P}$. In our work we do not assume that the noise rate is known in advance, but only require that the adversary flip a finite number of bits. Thus, we compute the coding rate as a function of the *a posteriori* noise rate. Such a comparison is only meaningful when the adversary's total budget is less than L, the length of $\mathcal{P}$, so for this section we will assume that $T < L$.

Let L' denote the length of $\mathcal{P}'$. Theorem 3.1 states that our algorithm achieves $L' \leq CL\left(1+\frac{1}{\alpha}\log\left(\frac{nL}{\delta}\right)\right)+CT$ for some constant C, where δ is the permissible failure probability for the algorithm and α is the average message length in $\mathcal{P}$. Furthermore, since $T < L$ this translates to the absolute upper bound $L' \leq CL\left(2+\frac{1}{\alpha}\log\left(\frac{nL}{\delta}\right)\right)$. Let $\varepsilon = T/L'$ be the *a posteriori* noise rate. Then $T = \varepsilon L'$. Making this substitution for T in the inequality above and dividing by L, we get $\frac{L'}{L} \leq 2C + \frac{C}{\alpha}\left[\log(nL/\delta) + \log\left(1+\varepsilon\left(2C+\frac{C\log(2nL/\delta)}{\alpha}\right)\right)\right]$. Finally, using $\log(1+x) \leq x$ on the second logarithm in this expression, we get $\frac{L'}{L} \leq \left(2C+\frac{C\log(2nL/\delta)}{\alpha}\right)\left(1+\frac{\varepsilon C}{\alpha}\right)$.

To summarize, for the worst case where $\alpha = 1$, the above shows that we achieve a coding rate that increases linearly with the noise rate ε and with the logarithm of nL/δ. In particular, the coding rate is $O((1+\varepsilon)\log(nL/\delta))$. For arbitrary α, we achieve a coding rate of $O((1+\varepsilon/\alpha)\log(nL/\delta)/\alpha)$.

ACKNOWLEDGMENTS

This work is supported by the National Science Foundation grants CNS 1816250, CCF 1320994, CNS 1318880 and CCF 1613772.

REFERENCES

[1] Abhinav Aggarwal, Varsha Dani, Thomas P. Hayes, and Jared Saia. 2018. Multiparty Interactive Communication with Private Channels. (2018). https://goo.gl/JZqPWe

[2] Noga Alon, Mark Braverman, Klim Efremenko, Ran Gelles, and Bernhard Haeupler. 2016. Reliable Communication Over Highly Connected Noisy Networks. In *Proceedings of the ACM Symposium on Principles of Distributed Computing (PODC)*. ACM, 165–173.

[3] Keren Censor-Hillel, Ran Gelles, and Bernhard Haeupler. 2018. Making Asynchronous Distributed Computations Robust to Channel Noise. In *9th Innovations in Theoretical Computer Science Conference, ITCS 2018, January 11-14, 2018, Cambridge, MA, USA*. 50:1–50:20.

[4] Ronald Cramer, Yevgeniy Dodis, Serge Fehr, Carles Padró, and Daniel Wichs. 2008. Detection of Algebraic Manipulation with Applications to Robust Secret Sharing and Fuzzy Extractors. In *Advances in Cryptology–EUROCRYPT 2008*. Springer, 471–488.

[5] Varsha Dani, Thomas P. Hayes, Mahnush Movahedi, Jared Saia, and Maxwell Young. 2018. Interactive Communication with Unknown Noise Rate. *Information and Computation* (2018).

[6] William M Hoza and Leonard J Schulman. 2016. The adversarial noise threshold for distributed protocols. In *Proceedings of the twenty-seventh annual ACM-SIAM symposium on Discrete algorithms*. SIAM, 240–258.

[7] Abhishek Jain, Yael Tauman Kalai, and Allison Bishop Lewko. 2015. Interactive coding for multiparty protocols. In *Proceedings of the 2015 Conference on Innovations in Theoretical Computer Science*. ACM, 1–10.

[8] Jonathan Katz and Yehuda Lindell. 2014. *Introduction to modern cryptography*. CRC press.

[9] Sridhar Rajagopalan and Leonard Schulman. 1994. A Coding Theorem for Distributed Computation. In *Proceedings of ACM Symposium on Theory of computing (STOC)*. ACM, 790–799.

[10] Leonard J. Schulman. 1996. Coding for Interactive Communication. *IEEE Transactions on Information Theory* 42, 6 (1996), 1745–1756.

Brief Announcement: Coded State Machine - Scaling State Machine Execution under Byzantine Faults

Songze Li
University of Southern California
songzeli@usc.edu

Saeid Sahraei
University of Southern California
ss_805@usc.edu

Mingchao Yu
University of Southern California
mingchay@usc.edu

Salman Avestimehr
University of Southern California
avestimehr@ee.usc.edu

Sreeram Kannan
University of Washington
ksreeram@ee.washington.edu

Pramod Viswanath
University of Illinois at Urbana-Champaign
pramodv@illinois.edu

ABSTRACT

We introduce Coded State Machine (CSM), an information-theoretic framework to securely and efficiently execute multiple state machines on Byzantine nodes. The standard method of solving this problem is using State Machine Replication, which achieves high security at the cost of low efficiency. CSM simultaneously achieves the optimal linear scaling in storage, throughput, and security with increasing network size. The storage is scaled via the design of Lagrange coded states and coded input commands that require the same storage size as their origins. The computational efficiency is scaled using a novel delegation algorithm, called INTERMIX, which is an information-theoretically verifiable matrix-vector multiplication algorithm of independent interest.

KEYWORDS

state machine execution, Byzantine faults, security, computational efficiency, information theory, verifiable computing

ACM Reference Format:
Songze Li, Saeid Sahraei, Mingchao Yu, Salman Avestimehr, Sreeram Kannan, and Pramod Viswanath. 2019. Brief Announcement: Coded State Machine - Scaling State Machine Execution under Byzantine Faults. In *2019 ACM Symposium on Principles of Distributed Computing (PODC '19), July 29-August 2, 2019, Toronto, ON, Canada.* ACM, New York, NY, USA, 3 pages. https://doi.org/10.1145/3293611.3331573

1 INTRODUCTION

We consider the problem of securely implementing K independent and identical state machines over a network of $N \geq K$ untrusted compute nodes, some of which are subject to Byzantine faults. For such a system, there are three critical performance metrics: 1) security β, defined as the maximum number of malicious nodes that can be tolerated; 2) storage efficiency γ, defined as the total number of state machines that can be supported given that each node has a storage size of a single state; and 3) throughput λ, defined as the total number of input commands processed per unit time. Information theoretically, all three metrics scale at most linearly with the network size N.

The canonical approach to deal with faulty nodes/processors is state machine replication (SMR) (see, e.g., [1, 5, 12, 13]). For *full replication*, all K state machines are replicated at all N nodes. This achieves a security of $\beta_{\text{full}} = \frac{N}{2}$, but a storage efficiency of $\gamma_{\text{full}} = 1$, and a throughout of $\lambda_{\text{full}} = \frac{1}{c(f)}$, where $c(f)$ is the computational complexity of the state transition function f. Alternatively, for *partial replication*, distinct state machines are replicated at a different disjoint subset of $q = N/K$ nodes. Partial replication improves the storage efficiency and throughout to $\gamma_{\text{partial}} = K$ and $\lambda_{\text{partial}} = \frac{K}{c(f)}$, which scale linearly with N by letting $K = \Theta(N)$. However, the security drops to $\beta_{\text{partial}} = \frac{q}{2}$. A key theoretical question in this context is whether this tradeoff between efficiency and security is fundamental or can be circumvented by careful algorithm design.

Table 1: Performance comparison of proposed CSM with SMR and information-theoretic limits in synchronous networks. Here $0 \leq \mu < \frac{1}{2}$ is some constant that denotes the fraction of malicious nodes. The state transition function f is an arbitrary multivariate polynomial with constant degree d. $c(f)$ and c(coding) are the computational complexities of f and the coding operations per node in CSM respectively.

	Security	Storage efficiency	Throughput
Full Replication	$\frac{N}{2}$	1	$\frac{1}{c(f)}$
Partial Replication	$\frac{N}{2K}$	K	$\frac{K}{c(f)}$
Information-Theoretic Limit	$\frac{N}{2}$	N	$\frac{N}{c(f)}$
Coded State Machine (CSM)	μN	$(1-2\mu)N/d+1-1/d$	$\frac{(1-2\mu)N/d+1-1/d}{c(f)+c(\text{coding})}$

Our Contributions. We propose "Coded State Machine" (CSM), which *simultaneously* achieves linear scaling for both storage efficiency and security, for both synchronous and partially synchronous networks (see Table 1). CSM also achieves an almost linear scaling for throughput under synchronous networks through the development of an interactive matrix-vector multiplication verification protocol named INTERMIX (specifically, INTERMIX helps to reduce the coding complexity per node c(coding) in Table 1 to $O(\log^2 N \log\log N)$).

Related Works. Conventional SMR research focuses on designing optimal protocols for the consensus phase (where the nodes aim to agree on a log of input commands submitted by clients) that tolerate the maximum number of faulty processors [5, 8, 13, 14, 19].

PODC '19, July 29-August 2, 2019, Toronto, ON, Canada

ACM ISBN 978-1-4503-6217-7/19/07.
https://doi.org/10.1145/3293611.3331573

Concepts from coding theory have been utilized earlier to provide fault tolerance to state machine execution. Fused state machine is proposed in [2], where given n primary finite state machines, f fusion replicas are constructed to correct up to $\frac{f}{2}$ Byzantine faults, using closed partition lattice [15] of the reachable product state of the primary machines. Compared with CSM, while the fused state machine also achieves security scaling, the storage size at each replica increases with n, as opposed to a constant storage size in CSM. When the state machine operations are write and read, erasure codes have been exploited to minimize the storage costs given the coexistence of multiple versions of the data object, while ensuring that a reader can decode an atomically consistent version [3, 4, 11, 22].

The coding design of CSM is inspired by recent developments in *coded computing* [7, 16–18, 21, 23, 24], which leverage tools from coding theory to inject computation redundancy in order to improve latency, security, and privacy. In particular, as similarly done in Lagrange Coded Computing [23] to create coded data batches, CSM creates and processes coded states/commands using the Lagrange polynomial. However, in contrast to one-shot computation on static data in [23], the requirement of dynamically updating the local coded state that is compatible with the upcoming state transition poses new challenges in the design of CSM.

Compared to the existing verifiable matrix-vector multiplication schemes [9, 10, 20, 25], INTERMIX has two advantages. First, it is information-theoretically secure, i.e., no computational limitation assumptions are made on the nodes. Second, INTERMIX enables almost every node in the network (with the exception of a constant number of auditors) to verify the correctness of the results in constant time. In contrast, in the existing schemes the complexity of the verifier is at least linear in the size of the output.

2 MODEL

We consider operating K independent state machines with the same state transition function f on $N \geq K$ unreliable nodes. At round t, each machine k has state $S_k(t)$, and executes an input command $X_k(t)$ by computing $(S_k(t+1), Y_k(t)) = f(S_k(t), X_k(t))$, where $Y_k(t)$ is the output, and $S_k(t+1)$ is the state in next round.

Each state machine maintains a group of clients who continuously and concurrently submit their commands to be processed by broadcasting them to all nodes. For the communication between the nodes, we study two settings:

Synchronous network, with a fixed and *known* upper bound on the communication latency between any pair of nodes.

Partially synchronous network, with unbounded communication delay until an *unknown* global stabilization time (GST), after which the network becomes synchronous.

At round t, each node i locally stores some (possibly coded) data $Z_i(t)$, which is generated from the states $S_1(t), \ldots, S_K(t)$.

Consensus Phase. For each t, all network nodes run some consensus protocol, via exchanging messages, to reach an agreement on a set of input commands $X_1(t), \ldots, X_K(t)$ to process (the consensus setting is standard in the literature, e.g., [6]).

Execution Phase. Each node i computes some intermediate result from its stored data $Z_i(t)$, and the commands $X_1(t), \ldots, X_K(t)$ agreed in the consensus phase, and communicates it to other nodes. Using the local computation result, and the results received from others, each node i recovers the state transition functions for a subset of machines, returns the recovered outputs to the intended clients, and updates its local storage to $Z_i(t+1)$.

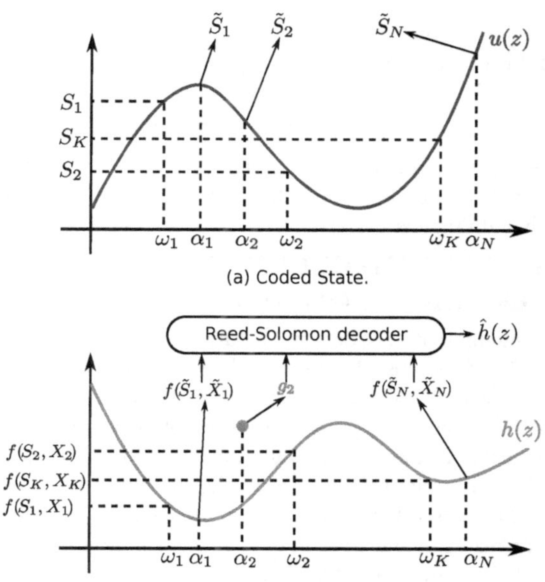

Figure 1: Illustration of Coded State Machine. (a) Coded State: node i stores a coded state $\tilde{S}_i$. (b) Coded Execution: node i computes an intermediate result $f(\tilde{S}_i, \tilde{X}_i)$, which is given to a Reed-Solomon decoder to recover output results.

Network nodes may be subject to *authenticated Byzantine faults*. That is, a faulty node can exhibit arbitrary behaviors that deviate from the above described protocol, but message impersonation is easily detectable.

We evaluate a state machine computation scheme P using the following performance metrics (defined in Section 1): security (β_P), storage efficiency (γ_P), and throughput (λ_P). Here we focus on the regime where computation latency is dominated by operations in the execution phase.

3 CODED STATE MACHINE ALGORITHM

CSM consists of two components: *Coded State* and *Coded Execution*.

Coded State. CSM views a (possibly coded) state variable as evaluating a polynomial $u(z)$ at a point. As illustrated in Figure 1(a), having specified $u(z)$ using the uncoded states $S_1, \ldots, S_K$ via Lagrange interpolation at distinct points $\omega_1, \ldots, \omega_K$, CSM generates N coded states $\tilde{S}_1, \ldots, \tilde{S}_N$, by evaluating $u(z)$ at distinct points $\alpha_1, \ldots, \alpha_N$, and stores $\tilde{S}_i$ at node i. Since each coded state has the same size as an uncoded state, the CSM scheme has a storage efficiency of $\gamma_{\text{CSM}} = K$.

Coded Execution. The consensus phase is performed the same as conventional SMR. In the execution phase, each node i generates a coded command $\tilde{X}_i$ from the agreed commands $X_1, \ldots, X_K$ as done for the state encoding, and directly feeds $\tilde{S}_i$ and $\tilde{X}_i$ into the state transition function f. For any multivariate polynomial f, $f(\tilde{S}_i, \tilde{X}_i)$ can be viewed as evaluating a composite polynomial h of higher degree at the point α_i (see Figure 1(b)). From the intermediate computation results $h(\alpha_1), \ldots, h(\alpha_N)$, a subset of which may be erroneous, CSM exploits efficient noisy interpolation techniques like Reed-Solomon decoding to recover h, and evaluates it at ω_k to obtain the output $f(S_k, X_k) = h(\omega_k)$, for all $k = 1, \ldots, K$. When μ fraction of the nodes are malicious, CSM can securely support up to $K = \frac{(1-2\mu)N-1}{d} + 1$ machines in a synchronous network, and up to $K = \frac{(1-3\mu)N-1}{d} + 1$ machines in a partially synchronous network.

Using CSM, both the storage efficiency and the security improves linearly with the network size N.

4 SCALING THROUGHPUT VIA DELEGATED VERIFIABLE COMPUTING

The throughput of CSM does not naturally scale with the network size N. This is because that the encoding and decoding, performed separately at each node, incur computational complexities that scale with N. Observing that polynomial interpolation and multi-point polynomial evaluation, as the building blocks of the CSM coding, are special matrix multiplications, we develop an information-theoretic protocol named INTERMIX that securely delegate the multiplication of a matrix A and a vector X to a single worker node, where efficient algorithms can be applied to reduce overall complexity.

As the first step of INTERMIX, a worker and a constant number of auditors are chosen randomly from the N nodes. Each auditor repeats the computation of $Y = AX$ and compares it with the result returned by the worker. As detailed in Algorithm 1, an (honest) auditor who detects a fraud will interactively enforce the worker to produce an inconsistent result which can be checked in constant time by the remaining nodes.

Algorithm 1 Algorithm run by an honest auditor

Input: $A, X, \hat{Y}$.
Output: One bit indicating whether the auditing process has succeeded or failed. A string ζ that localizes the failure.

if $\hat{Y} = Y$ **then**
  Return True.
end if
Choose i such that $\hat{Y}_i \neq Y_i$. Set $\zeta = [i]$.
Set $j = 1$, $A^{(1)} = A_i$, $X^{(1)} = X$, $\hat{Y}^{(1)} = \hat{Y}_i$, $s = \text{length}(A^{(1)})$.
while $(s > 1)$ **do**
  Let $A^{(j,1)} = A^{(j)}_{1:\lfloor s/2 \rfloor}$, $A^{(j,2)} = A^{(j)}_{\lfloor s/2 \rfloor+1:s}$, $X^{(j,1)} = X^{(j)}_{1:\lfloor s/2 \rfloor}$, $X^{(j,2)} = X^{(j)}_{\lfloor s/2 \rfloor+1:s}$.
  Request $Y^{(j,1)} = A^{(j,1)}X^{(j,1)}$ and $Y^{(j,2)} = A^{(j,2)}X^{(j,2)}$ from the worker. Receive $\hat{Y}^{(j,1)}, \hat{Y}^{(j,2)}$.
  if $\hat{Y}^{(j,1)} + \hat{Y}^{(j,2)} \neq \hat{Y}^{(j)}$ **then**
    Return (False, ζ).
  else
    Choose $\ell \in \{1, 2\}$ such that $\hat{Y}^{(j,\ell)} \neq Y^{(j,\ell)}$. Let $s = \text{length}(Y^{(j,\ell)})$ and $\zeta = [\zeta, \ell]$.
    Let $Y^{(j+1)} = Y^{(j,\ell)}$, $\hat{Y}^{(j+1)} = \hat{Y}^{(j,\ell)}$, $A^{(j+1)} = A^{(j,\ell)}$ and $X^{(j+1)} = X^{(j,\ell)}$. Increment j.
  end if
end while
Return (False, ζ).

Using INTERMIX, the coding complexity at each node reduces to $O(N \log^2 N \log\log N)$, enabling CSM to achieve throughput $\lambda_{\text{CSM}} = \Theta\left(\frac{N}{\log^2 N \log\log N}\right)$, which scales almost linearly with N.

ACKNOWLEDGMENTS

This work is supported by Defense Advanced Research Projects Agency under Contract No. HR001117C0053, NSF grants CCF-1703575, CCF-1763673, and CCF-1705007, ONR award No. N00014-16-1-2189, ARO awards W911NF1810400 and W911NF1810332, Distributed Technologies Research, and SNSF grant 178309. The views, opinions, and/or findings expressed are those of the author(s) and should not be interpreted as representing the official views or policies of the Department of Defense or the U.S. Government.

REFERENCES

[1] Peter A Alsberg and John D Day. 1976. A principle for resilient sharing of distributed resources. In *Proceedings of the 2nd international conference on Software engineering*. IEEE Computer Society Press, 562–570.
[2] Bharath Balasubramanian and Vijay K Garg. 2014. Fault tolerance in distributed systems using fused state machines. *Distributed computing* 27, 4 (2014), 287–311.
[3] Christian Cachin and Stefano Tessaro. 2006. Optimal resilience for erasure-coded Byzantine distributed storage. In *IEEE DSN'06*. 115–124.
[4] Viveck R Cadambe, Zhiying Wang, and Nancy Lynch. 2016. Information-theoretic lower bounds on the storage cost of shared memory emulation. In *Proceedings of the 2016 ACM Symposium on Principles of Distributed Computing*. ACM, 305–313.
[5] Miguel Castro and Barbara Liskov. 2002. Practical Byzantine fault tolerance and proactive recovery. *ACM TOCS* 20, 4 (2002), 398–461.
[6] Danny Dolev, Cynthia Dwork, and Larry Stockmeyer. 1987. On the minimal synchronism needed for distributed consensus. *JACM* 34, 1 (1987), 77–97.
[7] Sanghamitra Dutta, Viveck Cadambe, and Pulkit Grover. 2016. Short-dot: Computing large linear transforms distributedly using coded short dot products. In *NIPS*. 2100–2108.
[8] Cynthia Dwork, Nancy Lynch, and Larry Stockmeyer. 1988. Consensus in the presence of partial synchrony. *JACM* 35, 2 (1988), 288–323.
[9] Kaoutar Elkhiyaoui, Melek Önen, Monir Azraoui, and Refik Molva. 2016. Efficient techniques for publicly verifiable delegation of computation. In *ASIA CCS*.
[10] Dario Fiore and Rosario Gennaro. 2012. Publicly verifiable delegation of large polynomials and matrix computations, with applications. In *Proceedings of the 2012 ACM conference on Computer and communications security*. ACM, 501–512.
[11] James Hendricks, Gregory R Ganger, and Michael K Reiter. 2007. Low-overhead byzantine fault-tolerant storage. In *ACM SIGOPS Operating Systems Review*, Vol. 41. ACM, 73–86.
[12] Leslie Lamport. 1978. The implementation of reliable distributed multiprocess systems. *Computer networks* 2, 2 (1978), 95–114.
[13] Leslie Lamport. 1998. The part-time parliament. *ACM TOCS* 16, 2 (1998), 133–169.
[14] Leslie Lamport, Robert Shostak, and Marshall Pease. 1982. The Byzantine generals problem. *ACM TOPLAS* 4, 3 (1982), 382–401.
[15] David Lee and Mihalis Yannakakis. 2002. Closed partition lattice and machine decomposition. *IEEE Trans. Comput.* 51, 2 (2002), 216–228.
[16] Kangwook Lee, Maximilian Lam, Ramtin Pedarsani, Dimitris Papailiopoulos, and Kannan Ramchandran. 2018. Speeding up distributed machine learning using codes. *IEEE Transactions on Information Theory* 64, 3 (2018), 1514–1529.
[17] Songze Li, Mohammad Ali Maddah-Ali, and A Salman Avestimehr. 2016. A Unified Coding Framework for Distributed Computing with Straggling Servers. *IEEE Workshop on Network Coding and Applications* (Sept. 2016).
[18] S. Li, M. A. Maddah-Ali, Q. Yu, and A. S. Avestimehr. 2018. A Fundamental Tradeoff Between Computation and Communication in Distributed Computing. *IEEE Transactions on Information Theory* 64, 1 (Jan. 2018).
[19] Brian M Oki and Barbara H Liskov. 1988. Viewstamped replication: A new primary copy method to support highly-available distributed systems. In *Proceedings of the seventh annual ACM Symposium on Principles of distributed computing*. 8–17.
[20] Saeid Sahraei and A Salman Avestimehr. 2019. INTERPOL: Information Theoretically Verifiable Polynomial Evaluation. *arXiv preprint arXiv:1901.03379* (2019).
[21] Rashish Tandon, Qi Lei, Alexandros G. Dimakis, and Nikos Karampatziakis. 2017. Gradient Coding: Avoiding Stragglers in Distributed Learning. In *Proceedings of the 34th International Conference on Machine Learning*. 3368–3376.
[22] Zhiying Wang and Viveck R Cadambe. 2018. Multi-Version Coding-An Information-Theoretic Perspective of Consistent Distributed Storage. *IEEE Transactions on Information Theory* 64, 6 (2018), 4540–4561.
[23] Qian Yu, Songze Li, Netanel Raviv, Seyed Mohammadreza Mousavi Kalan, Mahdi Soltanolkotabi, and A Salman Avestimehr. 2019. Lagrange Coded Computing: Optimal Design for Resiliency, Security, and Privacy. In *AISTATS*.
[24] Qian Yu, Mohammad Ali Maddah-Ali, and A Salman Avestimehr. 2017. Polynomial Codes: an Optimal Design for High-Dimensional Coded Matrix Multiplication. In *NIPS*. 4406–4416.
[25] Yihua Zhang and Marina Blanton. 2014. Efficient secure and verifiable outsourcing of matrix multiplications. In *International Conference on Information Security*. Springer, 158–178.

Brief Announcement: On Termination of a Flooding Process

Walter Hussak
Amitabh Trehan
W.Hussak@lboro.ac.uk
A.Trehan@lboro.ac.uk
Computer Science, Loughborough University
Loughborough, Leicestershire, U.K.

ABSTRACT

Flooding is a fundamental distributed algorithms technique. Consider the following flooding process, for simplicity, in a synchronous message passing network: A distinguished node begins the flooding process by sending the (same) message to all its neighbours in the first round. In subsequent rounds, every node receiving the message relays a copy of the message further to all those, and only those, nodes it did not receive the message from in the previous round. However, the nodes do not remember if they've taken part in the flooding before and therefore will repeat the process every time they get a message. In other words, they execute an *amnesiac* flooding process with memory only of the present round. The flooding process terminates in a particular round when no edge in the network carries the message in that, and, hence, subsequent, rounds. We call this process *Amnesiac Flooding (AF)*.

In this work, the main question we address is whether *AF* will terminate on an arbitrary network (graph) and in what time? We show that, indeed, *AF* terminates on any arbitrary graph. Further, *AF* terminates in at most D rounds in bipartite graphs and at most $2D + 1$ rounds in non-bipartite graphs - in this brief announcement, we show this for the bipartite case only.

We also show that in a natural asynchronous variant of *AF*, an adversary can always ensure non-termination.

CCS CONCEPTS

• **Mathematics of computing → Graph algorithms**; Combinatorial algorithms; • **Networks → Network algorithms**; *Network protocol design*; • **Theory of computation → Graph algorithms analysis**; *Concurrent algorithms*; • **Computing methodologies → Distributed algorithms**; • **Information systems** → Social networks;

KEYWORDS

Flooding, Memory, Termination, Bipartiteness, Synchrony

ACM Reference Format:
Walter Hussak and Amitabh Trehan. 2019. Brief Announcement: On Termination of a Flooding Process. In *2019 ACM Symposium on Principles of Distributed Computing (PODC '19), July 29-August 2, 2019, Toronto, ON, Canada.* ACM, New York, NY, USA, 3 pages. https://doi.org/10.1145/3293611.3331586

ACM ISBN 978-1-4503-6217-7/19/07.
https://doi.org/10.1145/3293611.3331586

1 INTRODUCTION

Flooding is among the most basic of distributed algorithms. To quote Apnes [1]: *Flooding is about the simplest of all distributed algorithms. It's dumb and expensive, but easy to implement, and gives you both a broadcast mechanism and a way to build rooted spanning trees.* Often flooding is implemented with a flag that is set when the message is seen for the first time to ensure termination and with other mechanisms to detect termination of the process (see e.g. [2]). We are interested in a variant of flooding which does not explicitly use such a flag or even keep a memory of having seen the message before. A node only sends the message to the complement of its neighbours from whom it has just received the message and subsequently forgets about that activity. In a way, the node behaves like an aggressive social media (say, *WhatsApp*) user that has a compulsion to forward every message but does not want to annoy those who have just sent it the message it's forwarding. This idea of avoiding the most recently chosen node(s) has been used before in distributed protocols e.g. in social networks [3] and broadcasting [4] but we are not aware of this fundamental variant of flooding having been studied before.

1.1 Model and Problem Definitions:

Let $G(V, E)$ be the graph representing a network where the vertices represent the nodes of the network and edges represent the connections between the nodes. Consider the following process in a synchronous network where the computation proceeds in synchronous rounds where each round consists of every node receiving messages from all its neighbours, doing local computation and sending messages to all (or some of) its neighbours. No messages are lost in transit.

Definition 1.1. **Amnesiac Flooding (AF):** A distinguished node, say ℓ, sends a message (say, M) to all its neighbours in round 1. In subsequent rounds, every node receiving M forwards a copy of M to every, and only those, nodes it did not receive the message from in that round.

Note that this is an 'amnesiac' process i.e. nodes do not retain memory of having received or sent the message in the previous rounds. We say that *AF terminates* when no message (i.e. a copy of M) is being sent over any edge in the network. The question is whether, *for any finite graph G over n nodes, beginning from any arbitrary node, will AF always terminate?* In this work, we prove that this is indeed true i.e. this flooding process will terminate for every G. We prove that *AF* terminates in at most D rounds on a bipartite graph, where D is the diameter of the graph. We also prove (in the full paper) that the termination time on any arbitrary graph is, in fact, $O(D)$ too (but strictly larger than D in non-bipartite graphs).

We believe that we pose an interesting theoretical question. We believe our results may have applications in designing amnesiac/low-memory algorithms, in topology detection (e.g. to detect/test non-bipartiteness of graphs), analysing social media and natural flooding processes, among others. We also show that in a natural asynchronous variant of *AF*, an adversary can always ensure non-termination and pose a number of interesting questions.

1.2 Some illustrative examples:

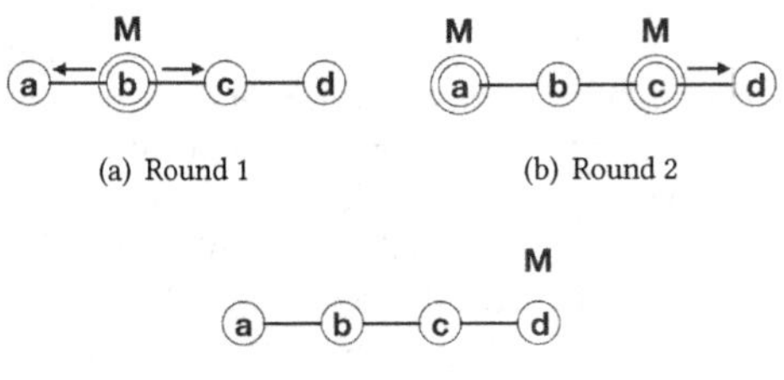

(a) Round 1 (b) Round 2

(c) Round 3

Figure 1: Amnesiac Flooding over a line network beginning with node b in 2 (< diameter = 3) rounds. Circled nodes are sending M in that round.

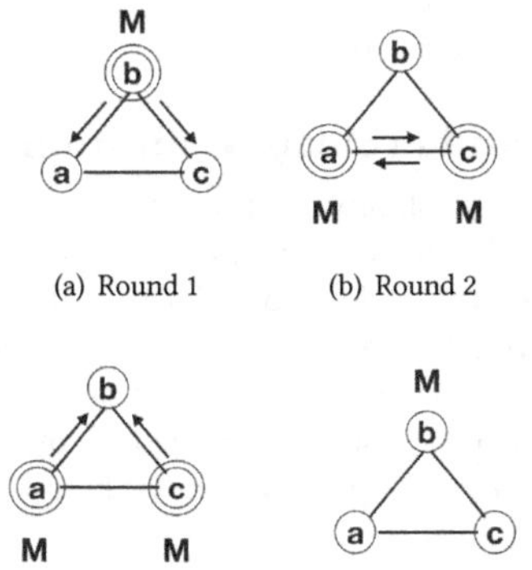

(a) Round 1 (b) Round 2

(c) Round 3 (d) Round 4

Figure 2: *AF* over a Triangle (Odd Cycle/Clique) network beginning with node b. Both node a and c send M to each other in round 2 and to b in round 3. Also, this is an odd (# nodes) cycle and termination takes $2D + 1$ time (D= diameter = 1).

Figure 1 shows *AF* over a line graph. The process begins with the node b and terminates at the ends of the graph and takes only 2 rounds, which is less than the diameter of the graph. Note that a line is an example of a bipartite graph. The triangle graph is another interesting illustrative example (Figure 5) – here, termination takes 3 rounds, whereas, the diameter is only 1. Note that the triangle is also the smallest clique and the smallest non-trivial cycle with odd number of nodes (an important topology for us). The even cycle is another interesting topology but here termination will happen in D rounds (as expected according to our bipartite graphs result). Of course, a graph can have far more complicated topology with cyclic and acyclic subgraphs. For lack of space, we do not discuss more indiividual topologies in detail.

2 TERMINATION IN BIPARTITE GRAPHS

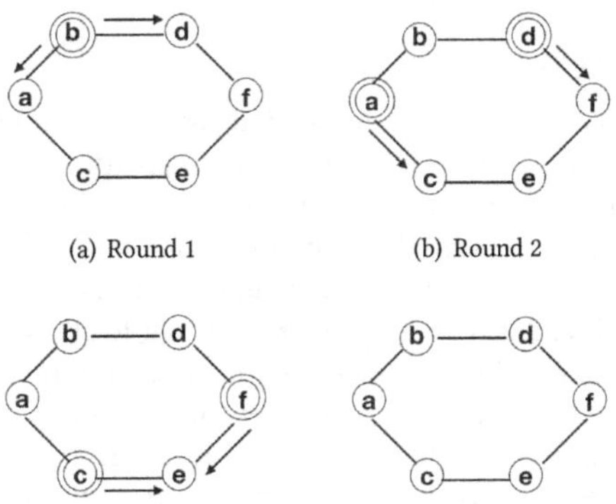

(a) Round 1 (b) Round 2

(c) Round 3 (d) Round 4

Figure 3: Termination in a bipartite graph (an even cycle) in diameter $D = 3$ time.

First, we show that *AF* terminates on a bipartite graph and, in fact, terminates, in the least time possible visiting each node exactly once and terminating in time equal to the eccentricity of the originating node. Figure 1 shows termination in a simple bipartite graph i.e. in a line. It is easy to see that *AF* terminates in 2 rounds which is the maximum distance from node b to any other node in the graph. Consider a more sophisticated example in Figure 3 - that of a cycle with six nodes. Here, *AF* from any originating node will terminate in diameter (=3) rounds. Since the eccentricity of nodes is upper bounded by the graph diameter, *AF* terminates in at most diameter rounds. Consider a connected bipartite graph. The following holds.

LEMMA 2.1. *In a connected bipartite graph B, Amnesiac flooding terminates in rounds = e(a), where e(a) is the eccentricity of the vertex a in graph B, where a is the node originating the process.*

Proof It is straightforward to see that amnesiac flooding executes a parallel BFS traversal from node a, which is the originating process. Nodes at a distance i from a receive the message at the same time in round i. All and only the nodes at distance $i + 1$ will now receive the message in round $i + 1$ since all the edges from distance-$(i - 1)$ nodes to distance-i nodes have been used and nodes at distance i do not share any edge since this is a bipartite graph.

The process terminates at the leaves of the BFS tree which have a maximum depth of $e(a)$.

■

Since the maximum eccentricity in a graph is its diameter, this corollary follows:

COROLLARY 2.2. *In a connected bipartite graph, the process terminates by round D, where D is the diameter of the graph.*

3 TERMINATION IN SYNCHRONOUS NETWORKS

The following theorem gives a proof of termination in general for synchronous networks. Note that Figure 3 illustrates *AF* in a triangle which is the smallest non-bipartite graph, showing termination, and in $2D + 1$ synchronous rounds where $D = 1$ is the diameter.

THEOREM 3.1. *Given a finite graph G, Amnesiac Flooding (AF) from a single source will terminate in a finite number of rounds.*

Proof
Let G be the network graph. We define *round-sets* $R_0, R_1, \ldots$ as:

R_0 *is the singleton containing the initial origin node,*
R_i *is the set of nodes which receive a message at round i* $(i \geq 1)$.

Define $\mathcal{R}$ to be the set of finite sequences of consecutive round-sets of the form:

$$\underline{R} = R_s, \ldots, R_{s+d} \quad \text{where } s \geq 0,\ d > 0, \text{ and } R_s \cap R_{s+d} \neq \emptyset\,. \quad (1)$$

In (1), s is the *start-point* $s(\underline{R})$ and d is the *duration* $d(\underline{R})$ of $\underline{R}$. Note that, a node $x \in G$ belonging to R_s and R_{s+d} may also belong to other R_i in (1). Consider the subset $\mathcal{R}^e$ of sequences in $\mathcal{R}$ where d is even.

LEMMA 3.2. *AF is non-terminating only if* $\mathcal{R}^e$ *is non-empty.*

Proof Since G is finite, some node $x \in G$ must occur in infinitely many round-sets R_i. If R_{i_1}, R_{i_2} and R_{i_3} are the first three round-sets that x occurs in, then the duration between R_{i_1} and R_{i_2}, R_{i_2} and R_{i_3}, or R_{i_1} and R_{i_3} will be even. ■

To prove termination, it suffices to prove that $\mathcal{R}^e$ is empty as follows from Lemma 3.2. We assume that $\mathcal{R}^e$ is non-empty and derive a contradiction. Let $\mathcal{R}^e_{md}$ be the subset of $\mathcal{R}^e$ comprising sequences of minimum (even) duration md, i.e.

$$\mathcal{R}^e_{md} = \{\underline{R} \in \mathcal{R}^e \mid \forall\, \underline{R}' \in \mathcal{R}^e.\ d(\underline{R}') \geq d(\underline{R}) = md\} \quad (2)$$

Clearly, if $\mathcal{R}^e$ is non-empty then so is $\mathcal{R}^e_{md}$. Let $\underline{R}^* \in \mathcal{R}^e_{md}$ be the sequence with earliest start-point ms, i.e.

$$\underline{R}^* = R_{ms}, \ldots, R_{ms+md} \quad (3)$$

where

$$\forall\, \underline{R}' \in \mathcal{R}^e_{md}\,.\ s(\underline{R}') \geq s(\underline{R}^*) = ms \quad (4)$$

By (1), there exists $x \in R_{ms} \cap R_{ms+md}$. Choose a node y which sends a message to x in round $ms + md$ (y must exist since $md > 0$). As y is a neighbour of x, either y sends a message to x in round ms or x sends a message to y in round $ms + 1$. Each of these cases leads to a contradiction:
Case (i): x receives a message from node y in round ms (Figure 4(a)) or *Case (ii): x sends a message to y in round ms* + 1 (Figure 4(b))

For lack of space, we give an informal sketch for the rest of the proof. Refer to Figure 4(a) for case (i). Notice that node y has M in both rounds R_{ms-1} and $R_{ms+md-1}$. However, this is a contradiction since it shows a $\underline{R}^*$ with an earlier starting point than ms. Now, consider case (ii) referring to Figure 4(b). Notice from the figure that node y has M in both R_{ms+1} and $R_{ms+md-1}$ - this shows a $\underline{R}^*$ with a shorter duration $md - 2$. Again, this is a contradiction by our assumptions on $\underline{R}^*$.

■

(a) Node x receives M from node y in round ms

(b) Node x sends M to node y in round $ms + 1$

Figure 4: Termination in an arbitrary graph: two cases for a shortest even length sequence

We also show the following in the full paper:

THEOREM 3.3. *In a connected non-bipartite graph, the process terminates by round 2D + 1, where D is the diameter of the graph.*

4 ASYNCHRONOUS AMNESIAC FLOODING

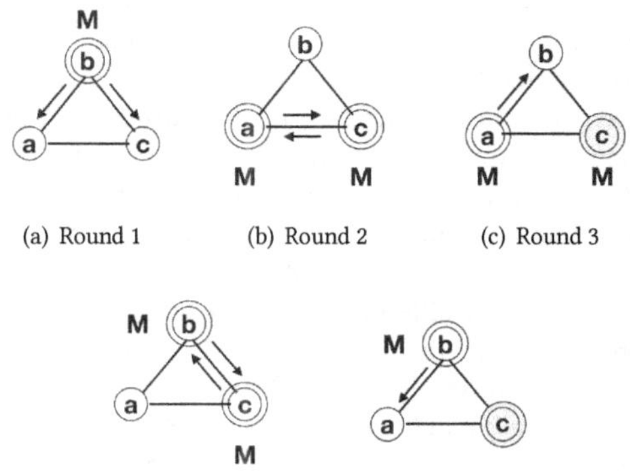

(a) Round 1 (b) Round 2 (c) Round 3

(d) Round 4 (e) Round 5

Figure 5: Asynchronous *AF* over a Triangle. Both node *a* and *c* send *M* to each other in round 2. In round 3, *a* sends *M* to *b* but the adversary makes *c* holds the message for one round (shaded node). In the next round, we have a round analogous to round 2 and so on.

Non-termination in an adversarial asynchronous setting: Informally, consider an asynchronous setting where a scheduling adversary can adaptively choose the delay on every message edge i.e. which round to forward a message on. Consider round 3 in the triangle in Figure 5. The adversary delays M at node c but a continues and sends to b. In round 4, node b and c both send M so that the beginning of the next round is now identical to round 2. This process can now continue *ad infinitum*.

REFERENCES

[1] James Aspnes. 2019. Flooding. http://www.cs.yale.edu/homes/aspnes/pinewiki/Flooding.html
[2] Hagit Attiya and Jennifer Welch. 2004. *Distributed Computing: Fundamentals, Simulations and Advanced Topics.* John Wiley & Sons.
[3] Benjamin Doerr, Mahmoud Fouz, and Tobias Friedrich. 2011. Social Networks Spread Rumors in Sublogarithmic Time. *Electronic Notes in Discrete Mathematics* 38 (2011), 303 – 308. The Sixth European Conference on Combinatorics, Graph Theory and Applications, EuroComb 2011.
[4] Robert Elsässer and Thomas Sauerwald. 2008. The Power of Memory in Randomized Broadcasting. In *Proceedings of the Nineteenth Annual ACM-SIAM Symposium on Discrete Algorithms (SODA '08).* SIAM, Philadelphia, PA, USA, 218–227.

Towards a Theory of Randomized Shared Memory Algorithms

Philipp Woelfel
woelfel@ucalgary.ca
University of Calgary
Calgary, Canada

ABSTRACT

Randomization has become an invaluable tool to overcome some of the problems associated with asynchrony and faultiness. Allowing processors to use random bits helps to break symmetry, and to reduce the likelihood of undesirable schedules. As a consequence, randomized techniques can lead to simpler and more efficient algorithms, and sometimes to solutions of otherwise unsolvable computational problems. However, the design and the analysis of randomized shared memory algorithms remains challenging. This talk will give an overview of recent progress towards developing a theory of randomized shared memory algorithms.

For many years, *linearizability* [6] has been the gold standard of distributed correctness conditions, and the corner stone of modular programming. In deterministic algorithms, implemented linearizable methods can be assumed to be atomic. But when processes can make random choices, the situation is not the same: Probability distributions of outcomes of algorithms using linearizable methods may be very different from those using equivalent atomic operations [4]. In general, modular algorithm design is much more difficult for randomized algorithms than for deterministic ones. The first part of the talk will present a correctness condition [2, 5] that is suitable for randomized algorithms in certain settings, and will explain why in other settings no such correctness condition exists [3] and what we can do about that.

To this date, almost all randomized shared memory algorithms are Las Vegas, meaning they permit no error. Monte Carlo algorithms, which allow errors to occur with small probability, have been studied thoroughly for sequential systems. But in the shared memory world such algorithms have been neglected. The second part of this talk will discuss recent attempts to devise Monte Carlo algorithms for fundamental shared memory problems (e.g., [1]). It will also present some general techniques, that have proved useful in the design of concurrent randomized algorithms.

CCS CONCEPTS

• **Theory of computation → Probabilistic computation; Concurrent algorithms; Distributed computing models.**

KEYWORDS

Randomized algorithms, shared memory, concurrency, strong linearizability, correctness condition, mutual exclusion, Monte Carlo

PODC '19, July 29-August 2, 2019, Toronto, ON, Canada

ACM ISBN 978-1-4503-6217-7/19/07.
https://doi.org/10.1145/3293611.3338838

ACM Reference Format:
Philipp Woelfel. 2019. Towards a Theory of Randomized Shared Memory Algorithms. In *2019 ACM Symposium on Principles of Distributed Computing (PODC '19), July 29-August 2, 2019, Toronto, ON, Canada.* ACM, New York, NY, USA, 1 page. https://doi.org/10.1145/3293611.3338838

BIOGRAPHY

Philipp Woelfel is Canada Research Chair in Randomized and Distributed Algorithms in the Department of Computer Science at the University of Calgary. He received the dissertation award of the University of Dortmund, Germany, for his Ph.D. in 2003. Before joining the University of Calgary, he worked as a postdoctoral fellow at the University of Toronto, funded by the "Emmy Noether" excellence program of the German Research Foundation. In 2014, he received a prestigious NSERC Discovery Accelerator Supplement for his research program on randomized shared memory algorithms. His research has focused on complexity theory, randomized algorithms, and the theory of distributed computing.

ACKNOWLEDGEMENTS

The author acknowledges the support of the Natural Sciences and Engineering Research Council of Canada (NSERC). This research was undertaken, in part, thanks to funding from the Canada Research Chairs program.

REFERENCES

[1] James Aspnes, Bernhard Haeupler, Alexander Tong, and Philipp Woelfel. Allocate-on-use space complexity of shared-memory algorithms. In *Proc. of 32nd DISC*, pages 8:1–8:17, 2018.
[2] Oksana Denysyuk and Philipp Woelfel. Wait-freedom is harder than lock-freedom under strong linearizability. In *Proc. of 29th DISC*, pages 60–74, 2015.
[3] Oksana Denysyuk and Philipp Woelfel. Are shared objects composable under an oblivious adversary? In *Proc. of 35th PODC*, pages 335–344, 2016.
[4] Wojciech Golab, Lisa Higham, and Philipp Woelfel. Linearizable implementations do not suffice for randomized distributed computation. In *Proc. of 43rd ACM STOC*, pages 373–382, 2011.
[5] Maryam Helmi, Lisa Higham, and Philipp Woelfel. Strongly linearizable implementations: possibilities and impossibilities. In *Proc. of 31st PODC*, pages 385–394, 2012.
[6] Maurice Herlihy and Jeannette Wing. Linearizability: A correctness condition for concurrent objects. *ACM Trans. Program. Lang. Syst.*, 12(3):463–492, 1990.

Optimal Memory-Anonymous Symmetric Deadlock-Free Mutual Exclusion

Zahra Aghazadeh
zaghazad@ucalgary.ca
University of Calgary
Calgary, Canada

Damien Imbs
damien.imbs@lis-lab.fr
LIS, Université d'Aix-Marseille,
CNRS, Université de Toulon
Marseille, France

Michel Raynal
michel.raynal@irisa.fr
IRISA, Université de Rennes &
Hong Kong Polytechnic University
Rennes, France

Gadi Taubenfeld
tgadi@idc.ac.il
The Interdisciplinary Center
Herzliya, Israel

Philipp Woelfel
woelfel@ucalgary.ca
University of Calgary
Calgary, Canada

ABSTRACT

The notion of an anonymous shared memory, introduced by Taubenfeld in PODC 2017, considers that processes use different names for the same memory location. As an example, a location name A used by a process p and a location name $B \neq A$ used by another process q can correspond to the very same memory location X, and similarly for the names B used by p and A used by q which may (or may not) correspond to the same memory location $Y \neq X$. In this context, the PODC paper presented a 2-process symmetric deadlock-free mutual exclusion (mutex) algorithm and a necessary condition on the size m of the anonymous memory for the existence of such an n-process algorithm. This condition states that m must be belongs to $M(n) \setminus \{1\}$ where $M(n) = \{m : \forall \ell : 1 < \ell \leq n : \gcd(\ell, m) = 1\}$. *Symmetric* means here that, process identities define a specific data type which allows a process to check only if two identities are equal or not.

The present paper presents two optimal deadlock-free symmetric mutual exclusion algorithms for n-process systems where communication is through m registers. The first algorithm, which considers anonymous read/write registers, works for any m which is $\geq n$ and belongs to the set $M(n)$. It follows that this condition on m is both necessary and sufficient for symmetric deadlock-free mutual exclusion in this anonymity context, and this algorithm is optimal with respect to m. The second algorithm, which considers anonymous read/modify/write atomic registers, works for any $m \in M(n)$, which is shown to be necessary and sufficient for anonymous read/modify/write registers. It follows that, when $m > 1$, $m \in M(n)$ is a tight characterization of the size of the anonymous shared memory needed to solve deadlock-free mutex, be the registers read/write or read/modify/write.

ACM ISBN 978-1-4503-6217-7/19/07...$15.00
https://doi.org/10.1145/3293611.3331594

CCS CONCEPTS

• **Theory of computation → Distributed computing models; Shared memory algorithms; Distributed algorithms.**

KEYWORDS

anonymous shared memory, asynchronous system, atomic register, computability, deadlock-freedom, mutual exclusion, read-modify-write register, read-write register

ACM Reference Format:
Zahra Aghazadeh, Damien Imbs, Michel Raynal, Gadi Taubenfeld, and Philipp Woelfel. 2019. Optimal Memory-Anonymous Symmetric Deadlock-Free Mutual Exclusion. In *2019 ACM Symposium on Principles of Distributed Computing (PODC '19), July 29-August 2, 2019, Toronto, ON, Canada.* ACM, New York, NY, USA, 10 pages. https://doi.org/10.1145/3293611.3331594

1 INTRODUCTION

1.1 Memory Anonymity

While the notion of *memory-anonymity* has been implicitly used in some works in the early eighties (e.g., [16]), it was explicitly captured as a concept and investigated only very recently in [21][1]. More precisely, this paper considers the explicit case where "there is no a priori agreement between processes on the names of shared memory locations", and presents possibility/impossibility results in such systems.

Considering a shared memory defined as an array $R[1..m]$ of m memory locations (registers), memory-anonymity means that, while the same location identifier $R[x]$ always denotes the same memory location for a process p, it does not necessarily denote the same memory location for two different processes p and q. This means that there is an adversary that may initially give different global names to different processes for the same memory locations. In other words, the adversary associates a permutation on the set of memory indices $\{1, \ldots, m\}$ with each process p, and p uses them to access the memory locations. This is illustrated in Table 1, which considers two processes p and q and a shared memory comprising three registers (as an example the register known as $R[2]$ by p and the register known as $R[3]$ for q are the very same register, which actually is $R[1]$ from an external omniscient observer point of view).

[1] See [18] for an introductory survey to process anonymity and memory anonymity.

names for an external observer	location names for process p	location names for process q
$R[1]$	$R[2]$	$R[3]$
$R[2]$	$R[3]$	$R[1]$
$R[3]$	$R[1]$	$R[2]$
permutation	2, 3, 1	3, 1, 2

Table 1: Example of an anonymous memory model

1.2 Related Work and Motivation

Related work. The memory-anonymous mutual exclusion problem was introduced by Taubenfeld in [21], where are presented the first results on mutual exclusion in read/write memory-anonymous systems. More precisely, are presented

- a symmetric deadlock-free algorithm for two processes (the notion of "symmetric" is related to the use of process identifiers, and will be defined in Section 2.3);
- a theorem stating that there is no deadlock-free algorithm if the number of processes is not known; and
- a necessary condition stating that any deadlock-free symmetric mutex algorithm for n processes, which uses $m \geq 2$ read/write registers, requires that m belongs to the set $M(n) = \{m : \forall \ell : 1 < \ell \leq n : \gcd(\ell, m) = 1\}$ (i.e., ℓ and m are relatively prime). Let us observe that $M(n)$ is infinite (among other values, it contains an infinite number of prime numbers).

A common technique employed by shared memory algorithms that aims at minimizing the number of read/write registers, is that a process keeps writing its ID (and possibly additional information) to different registers, until sufficiently many registers store the information written by that process. Sufficiently many registers means that, even if all other processes write at the same time (possibly to different registers), they cannot obliterate too much information. This idea is used, e.g., by obstruction-free algorithms for space efficient test-and-set objects [7, 8] (which can be viewed as one-time mutual exclusion primitives). Our mutual exclusion algorithms also require a process to "win" sufficiently many registers by writing its ID to them. However, this serves another purpose, in addition to ensuring that not too much information can get obliterated by overwrites: Once all $m \in M(n)$ registers have been written, not every process's ID can appear equally often, which allows breaking ties. The main algorithmic idea is to let processes "remove" themselves from registers, if the tie-breaking mechanism favors other processes. This has to be done carefully to ensure that different processes, which may view different system configurations, do not all back off at the same time.

Motivation. This work has two primary motivations. The first is related to the basics of computing, namely, computability and complexity lower/upper bounds. Increasing our knowledge of what can (or cannot) be done in the context of an anonymous memory, and providing associated necessary and sufficient conditions, helps us determine the weakest possible system assumptions under which fundamental problems, such as mutual exclusion, can be solved. The second one is more application-oriented. It appears that the concept of an anonymous memory allows epigenetic cell modification to be modeled from a computing point of view [19]. Hence, anonymous shared memories could be useful in biologically inspired distributed systems [14, 15]. If this is the case, mastering mutex in such an adversarial context could be of primary importance.

1.3 Content of the Paper

As announced, this paper is on deadlock-free mutual exclusion in an n-process system ($n \geq 2$), where the processes communicate by accessing a shared memory composed of m anonymous registers (hence there are no other non-anonymous registers).

Preliminary definitions. Two types of registers are considered, giving rise to two communication models.

- A read/write (RW) register is an atomic register that provides the processes with a read operation and a write operation [12]. In the RW communication model, all registers are RW registers.
- A read/modify/write (RMW) register is an atomic register that provides the processes with a read operation, a write operation, and an additional read/modify/write operation [10]. Such an operation allows a process to atomically read a register, and, based on the value read, compute a new value that is assigned to the register. One of the most prominent read/modify/write operations is compare&swap(). When a process invokes R.compare&swap(x, *old*, *new*), where $R[x]$ is an anonymous register, it reads the value of the register locally known as $R[x]$, say v, and assigns it the value *new* if and only if *new* $= v$. In that case the operation returns `true`, and otherwise it returns `false`. In the RMW communication model, all the registers are RMW registers.

Results presented in the paper.

- RW anonymous communication model. A deadlock-free mutex algorithm for this model is presented, which assumes the necessary condition stated above, namely, $m \in M(n)$. As the condition $m \geq n$ is necessary to solve mutex in an RW non-anonymous system [3], it remains necessary in an anonymous system. The very existence of the proposed algorithm shows that the predicate $m \in M(n) \wedge m \geq n$ (which is equivalent to $m \in M(n) \wedge m \neq 1$) is a tight characterization of the values of m that permit a deadlock-free mutex algorithm in RW anonymous systems. In this sense, the proposed algorithm is space optimal.
- RMW anonymous communication model. A deadlock-free mutex algorithm for this model is presented, which requires $m \in M(n)$. As, in this communication model, $m \geq n$ is not a previously known necessary requirement to solve deadlock-free mutex in a non-anonymous system, we cannot conclude from the existence of the previous algorithm that $m \in M(n)$ is a tight characterization of the values of m which allow deadlock-free mutex algorithm in RMW anonymous systems.

  To address this issue, the paper presents a proof that $m \in M(n)$ is actually a necessary and sufficient condition for deadlock-free mutex in RMW anonymous systems. Let us observe that when the whole memory is composed of a single register (case $m = 1$), the fact that it is anonymous or not is irrelevant as when they access the shared memory, the processes access the very same register. (Said differently, when $m = 1$, the adversary defining the addressing permutations has no power, and consequently the notion of non-anonymous/anonymous register disappears.)

Hence, eliminating the pathological case $m = 1$, deadlock-free mutex for both the RW model and the RMW model can be solved if and only if $m \in M(n)$. The corresponding algorithms differ in their algorithmic design, and in the fact that, to enter the critical section, the algorithm for the RW model requires a process to read its identity from all m anonymous registers, while the algorithm for the RMW model requires it to read its identity from a majority of the anonymous registers only. Hence, while requiring the same computability assumption (namely $m \in M(n)$ assuming $m \neq 1$), these algorithms differ from a complexity point of view (measured as the number of registers that have to contain the same process identity to allow this process to enter the critical section).

1.4 Roadmap

This paper is composed of 7 sections. Section 2 introduces the computational model and provides some technical definitions. Section 3 presents an n-process symmetric deadlock-free mutex algorithm for the anonymous RW communication model. Section 4 proves its correctness. Section 5 presents an n-process symmetric deadlock-free mutex algorithm for the anonymous RMW communication model. Section 6.1 proves its correctness, while Section 6.2 proves a space lower bound which shows that the algorithm is space optimal. Finally, Section 7 concludes the paper. It is important to notice that both algorithms have a first class noteworthy property, namely, their simplicity.

2 SYSTEM MODEL, SYMMETRIC ALGORITHM, AND MUTUAL EXCLUSION

2.1 Processes and Anonymous Registers

The system is composed of n asynchronous processes $p_1, ..., p_n$ with identifiers from a set $\mathcal{P}$. "Asynchronous" means that each process proceeds in its own speed, which can vary with time and always remains unknown to the processes.

When considering a process p_i, i is its index, which is used only to distinguish processes from an external point of view. A process p_i knows its own identity, denoted id_i, but never knows its index i. No two processes have the same identity. Each process knows the number n of processes in the system, and all processes know a common symbol $\perp \notin \mathcal{P}$, which is interpreted as a default identity (hence, when it reads an anonymous register, a process can distinguish a process identity from $\perp$).

2.2 Anonymous Registers

RW communication model. Processes communicate through a shared anonymous memory, represented by an array $R[1..m]$. It is important to stress that the size m of the shared memory is imposed by the system model, and is not under the control of the programmer. The entire memory is anonymous. Consequently the only means for processes to communicate is by accessing $R[1..m]$. Each register can be accessed by two operations, denoted write and read. As already indicated, memory-anonymity means that, for each process p_i, there is a permutation $f_i()$ over the set $\{1, \ldots, m\}$ such that, when p_i uses address $R[x]$, it actually accesses $R[f_i(x)]$. Anonymity means that no permutation f_i is known by any process; each f_i is defined by an adversary.

- When a process p_i invokes R.write(x, v) it writes value v in the atomic read/write register $R[f_i(x)]$,
- When a process p_i invokes R.read(x) it obtains the value currently saved in the register locally denoted $R[f_i(x)]$.

To simplify the presentation of the first algorithm, we also assume that process p_i can use an operation R.snapshot() to obtain the value of array $\left[R[f_i(1)], \ldots, [R[f_i(m)]\right]$ as if the read of all its entries were instantaneous (i.e., produced at a single point of the time line during the operation [10, 12]). We require that the operation snapshot() satisfies the following progress guarantee (slightly modified from [9]):

> Any invocation of R.snapshot() by a process p_i terminates within a finite number of p_i's steps, given that no process invokes write() during its execution. (1)

The memory-anonymous snapshot() operation is a simple extension of the classical snapshot() introduced in [1, 2]. All its executions are linearizable [10]. The operation R.snapshot() can be implemented with the well-known "double scan" technique (as used in [1]), where each process p_i is provided with an additional local sequence number sn_i, which it uses to identify all its write invocations (namely, when it invokes R.write(x, v), p_i actually issues the following sequence of statements "$sn_i \leftarrow sn_i + 1$; $R[x] \leftarrow (v, id_i, sn_i)$". As no two processes have the same identity, each invocation of R.write() is unambiguously identified.[2] To not overload the presentation, the sequence numbers associated with the write operations (and used in the "double scan" inside the snapshot operations) are left implicit in the rest of the paper[3].

RMW anonymous communication model. This is the RW model where, in addition to the operations R.read(x) and R.write(x, v), a process can also invoke an additional operation denoted R.compare&swap$(x, -, -)$ defined in Section 1.3. (The deadlock-free mutex algorithm described in Section 5 does not use the operation R.snapshot().)

[2] The proof of the operations R.write(), R.read(), and R.snapshot() terminate and are linearizable is the same as the one in [1]. As far as the proof for R.snapshot() is concerned, this comes from the observation that, in the algorithm described in [1], the order in which a process scans the array $R[1..m]$ is irrelevant. The important point is that, after it sequentially scanned twice the array $R[1..m]$, a process compares the corresponding entries of the two copies of $R[1..m]$ it has obtained. In our case, for any x, the first read of $R[x]$ and a second read of $R[x]$ by the same process are on the very same memory location, from which follows that the process correctly compares the corresponding entries of the two copies it has obtained to see if $R[1..m]$ changed between the two consecutive scans.

[3] Defining each register as a record which has two fields (a value field and a sequence number field) with global (non-anonymous) names is done only for convenience. The two values in these fields can be encoded as a single value, removing the need for using more than one field.

2.3 Symmetric Algorithm

The notion of a *symmetric algorithm* dates back to the eighties [6, 11]. Here, as in [21], a *symmetric algorithm* is an algorithm in which there is no way for two processes to distinguish one from the other.

This means that the process identities are defined by a specific data type, which allows to compare two identities for equality only. Hence process identities are not convertible to other data types, such as integers to know (the odd/even notion is meaningless for this data type). This type is similar to the Boolean data type in the sense that while Boolean values can be compared, there no odd/even notion for Boolean values).

Let us notice that the previous notion of symmetry can be seen as a weak notion of process anonymity in the sense it is not possible to define a ranking function on processes that could be exploited to solve mutual exclusion.

2.4 Initial Values

Moreover, in order for the initial values not to be used to destroy anonymity (which could favor a given process), all registers are initialized to the same value, namely the default value $\bot$.

2.5 Mutual Exclusion

Mutual exclusion is the oldest and one of the most important synchronization problems. Formalized by E. W. Dijkstra in the mid-sixties [4], it consists in building what is called a lock (or mutex) object, defined by two operations, denoted lock() and unlock(). (Recent textbooks including mutual exclusion and variants of it are [17, 20].)

The invocation of these operations by a process p_i always follows the following pattern: "lock(); *critical section*; unlock()", where "critical section" is any sequence of code. A process that is not in the critical section and has no pending lock() or unlock() invocation, is said to be in the *remainder section*. An infinite execution is *fair*, if every process that has a pending lock() or unlock() invocation, either finishes its operation or executes infinitely many steps. The mutex object satisfying the deadlock-freedom progress condition is defined by the following two properties.

- Mutual exclusion: No two processes are simultaneously in their critical section.
- Deadlock-freedom: If a process p_i has a pending lock() or unlock() invocation and no process is in the critical section, then some process p_j (possibly $p_j \neq p_i$) eventually finishes its lock() or unlock() operation, provided the execution is fair.

3 ANONYMOUS RW MODEL: SYMMETRIC DEADLOCK-FREE MUTUAL EXCLUSION

This section presents Algorithm 1, that is a symmetric (with respect to equality) deadlock-free mutex algorithm suited to the RW memory-anonymous communication model. As indicated in the introduction, as this algorithm works for the necessary condition $(m > 1) \wedge (m \in M(n))$, its existence proves that this condition is also sufficient.

3.1 Representation of the Lock Object

Shared memory. Let m be such that $m > 1$ and $m \in M(n)$. The shared memory is composed of a memory-anonymous array $R[1..m]$, as defined in Section 2.1.

For any $x \in \{1, \ldots, m\}$, the initial value of a register $R[x]$ is $\bot$. If $R[x] \neq \bot$, it contains the identity of the last process that wrote in this register. Given any execution and any of its configuration C, we use the following terminology (intuitively, a *configuration* is a consistent global state –local state of each process and value of each anonymous register– See [13] for a formal definition):

- "process p_i owns $R[x]$", if $R[x] = id_i$;
- "register $R[x]$ is owned" if $R[x] \neq \bot$;
- "R is full" if all its entries are owned;
- "R is empty" if none of its entries are owned.

Local memory. Each process p_i manages two local variables: an integer denoted cnt_i, and a local array denoted $view_i[1..m]$. The aim of $view_i[1..m]$ is to contain the value of R obtained by p_i from its last invocation of R.snapshot(). To prevent confusion, the shared array $R[1..m]$ is denoted with an uppercase letter, while the local variables are denoted with lowercase letters. As already indicated, the local sequence number associated with each write operation of a process p_i is left implicit.

3.2 Algorithm 1

Underlying principles. The core of Algorithm 1 consists in managing a competition among the processes until all the entries of $R[1..m]$ contain the same process identity, the corresponding process being the winner.

When a process invokes unlock(), or when it concludes while competing that it will not be the winner, it resets the entries of $R[1..m]$ containing its identity to $\bot$ (their initial value).

Hence, the core of the algorithm lies in the definition of predicates that direct a process to either withdraw from the competition or continue competing. To this end, a process p_i checks whether its local view $view_i$ (obtained from the invocation of R.snapshot()) is full (line 5), and if so, whether p_i owns less than the average of all registers present in the competition (line 9).

Detailed description of the algorithm. Operation unlock() is a simple invocation of an internal operation called shrink() (line 12). With a shrink() invocation, a process p_i removes itself from the array by considering its latest view, $view_i$. More specifically, for each index $x \in \{1, \ldots m\}$ with $view_i[x] = id_i$, process p_i first reads $R[x]$, and if $R[x]$ still equals id_i, it writes $\bot$ into $R[x]$ (line 2).

The core of the algorithm is the code of the operation lock(). When a process p_i invokes this operation, it enters a "repeat-until" loop from which it can only exit when it obtains a snapshot of the anonymous shared memory $R[1..m]$, according to which p_i owns all entries (lines 3-11).

Hence, process p_i repeatedly invokes R.snapshot() (line 4) until it sees only the default value $\bot$ in the array $view_i$ obtained from R.snapshot() (which means that, from its local point of view, there is no competition), or it is present in this array (which means it is already competing). Then, when it stops looping, p_i checks whether $view_i$ is full (line 5) to know if it should continue writing (line 6) or if it should consider withdrawing from the competition (lines 7-9).

```
m > 1 and m ∈ {m such that ∀ ℓ ∈ {2, ..., n} : gcd(ℓ, m) = 1}
R[1..m]: array of anonymous RW atomic registers, each initialized to ⊥
p_i: process executing this code; id_i is its identity
view_i: process p_i's local array of size m (with global scope)
-----------------------------------------------------------------
operation owned() is
(1)  return (|{x ∈ {1, ..., m} : view_i[x] = id_i}|). % # of registers owned by p_i %
-----------------------------------------------------------------
operation shrink() is
(2)  for each x such that view_i[x] = id_i do if (R.read(x) = id_i) then R.write(x, ⊥) end if end for.
-----------------------------------------------------------------
operation lock() is
(3)  repeat
(4)     repeat view_i ← R.snapshot() until owned() > 0 ∨ ∀ x ∈ {1, ..., m} : view_i[x] = ⊥ end repeat;
        % This point is reached only if either p_i is present (at least one entry of R contains id_i) or no one is %
(5)     if (∃ x ∈ {1, ..., m} : view_i[x] = ⊥)
(6)        then R.write(x, id_i)
(7)        else  % view_i is full %
(8)              let cnt_i = |{view_i[1], ..., view_i[m]}|; % number of current competitors %
(9)              if (owned() < m/cnt_i) then shrink() end if
                   % p_i owns fewer registers than the average ⇒ p_i withdraws from the competition %
(10)    end if
(11) until ∀ x ∈ {1, ..., m} : view_i[x] = id_i end repeat.
-----------------------------------------------------------------
operation unlock() is
(12) shrink().
```

Figure 1: (Algorithm 1) RW memory-anonymous deadlock-free mutex (n-process system, $n \geq 2$, code for p_i)

If $view_i$ is full, processes are engaged in a competition. If its identity appears in fewer than the average number of owned registers, process p_i withdraws from the competition by invoking the operation shrink() (lines 7-9), which suppresses its identity from the anonymous RW memory $R[1..m]$. After finishing its shrink() invocation, a process re-enters the repeat-until loop at line 4. The fact that $m \in M(n)$ guarantees that not all processes that appear in R when it is full, own the same number of registers, so at least one process will withdraw. If a process owns at least the average number of registers when its view is full, it re-enters the repeat-until loop and invokes the operation snapshot() again at line 4.

If $view_i$ is not full and p_i owns at least one register, it continues competing. To this end, before re-entering the repeat-until loop, p_i chooses an entry of $R[1..m]$ equal to $\bot$ and writes its identifier id_i in this register (lines 5-6).

To summarize, during a lock() operation, a process p_i decides its future steps based on its latest view of the anonymous memory as follows:

(1) If p_i owns all registers, it enters the critical section (line 11).
(2) If p_i owns no register, and the view is not empty, then it waits (by repeatedly taking snapshots) until it obtained an empty view (line 4).
(3) If the view is full, and cnt_i different processes own some registers, and p_i owns fewer than m/cnt_i registers, then it removes itself from all registers it owns by calling shrink() (line 9).
(4) If the view is not full, there is at least one register that is not owned, and p_i writes its identity id_i into any not owned register (line 6).

4 ANONYMOUS RW MODEL: PROOF OF ALGORITHM 1 AND TIGHT SPACE LOWER BOUND

4.1 RW Memory-Anonymous Model: Proof of Algorithm 1

Let us remember that the anonymous RW array $R[1..m]$ is the only object that the processes can use to communicate. The notions of "time", "first" and "last" used in the proofs are well-defined, as all write() and read() operations are atomic. As stated in Section 2.1, the proof assumes that operation snapshot() (which can be implemented from atomic read/write operations) is linearizable and satisfies the progress condition 1. The proof assumes $n \geq 2$, as otherwise mutual exclusion is trivial. Moreover, let us remember that m is assumed to be greater than 1 and belong to the set $M(n) = \{m : \forall \ell : 1 < \ell \leq n : \gcd(\ell, m) = 1\}$, from which it follows that $m > n$.

Let E be an arbitrary infinite execution E, $L(E)$ an execution where all snapshot() operations occur atomically at their linearization points (i.e., $L(E)$ is a linearization of all operations on R in E).

Theorem 1. *Algorithm 1 satisfies mutual exclusion.*

Proof Consider history $L(E)$. Let us suppose by contradiction that two processes are inside their critical section at the same time, and assume that p_i is the first of them to take its last snapshot before entering its critical section. More precisely, suppose process p_i's lock() invocation terminates (and thus p_i enters the critical section) following some iteration of the outer repeat-until loop in lock(). Then due to the predicate of line 11, p_i owns all registers of R at the point of p_i's snapshot() (line 4) in its last iteration. Therefore, in the same iteration the predicate of line 5 and the predicate of lines 9 are false, and the predicate of lines 11 is true. Hence, the snapshot() in line 4 at the beginning of the iteration is p_i's last access to the RW anonymous memory before its lock() operation terminates. We therefore say a *process enters the critical section* at the point when it is taking a snapshot in line 4 while owning all registers.

Now suppose p_i enters the critical section at some point t. Let t' be the point when p_i executes its first shared memory operation in its subsequent unlock() invocation, if there is such an invocation, and otherwise $t' = \infty$. Let us consider the following claim:

Claim 1. *Throughout $[t, t']$, the value of the anonymous memory returned by all the invocations of* snapshot() *contains the identity of p_i.*

It follows from this claim that at no point in $[t, t']$ a process other than p_i can observe itself as owning all registers. Also, as assumed at the beginning of the proof, process p_i is the *first* to take its last snapshot before entering its critical section. Thus no other process, except p_i, can be in the critical section throughout $[t, t']$, which contradicts the assumption that p_i is not alone in the critical section.

Proof of the claim. For the purpose of a contradiction, let us assume that Claim 1 is not true. Because all m registers are owned by p_i at time t and $m > n$, by the pigeonhole principle, at least one process has issued more than one write that changed the value of a register from the identity of p_i to another value. Let p_j be the first process to do so. Hence, process p_j took a snapshot at some point $T_s \in [t, t']$ in line 4 at the beginning of the iteration of the outer repeat-until loop in which it executes its second R.write() in line 5, that changes the value of a register from the identity of p_i to another value.

Process p_i is the only process that can write its own identity, it owns all the registers at time t, and it does not execute any write operation in $[t, t']$. Then, in the snapshot taken at $T_s \in [t, t']$ by p_j, the second register overwritten by p_j contains p_i's identity, and is not chosen at line 5. A contradiction which completes the proof of the claim and the theorem. $\Box_{Theorem\ 1}$

Theorem 2. *Algorithm 1 is deadlock-free.*

The remainder of this section is devoted to the proof of this theorem. For the purpose of contradiction let us assume that E is an infinite fair execution, and that after some point t^* no invocation of lock() or unlock() terminate, even though at least one process has a pending lock() or unlock() operation and no process is in the critical section. Since unlock() is wait-free [9] (see also the Claim 2 below) we may assume w.l.o.g. that no invocation of unlock() is pending at any point after t^*.

Definitions.

- A process is *shrinking* if it is poised to read or write in a shrink() operation.
- A process is *large* if it owns at least 2 registers.

Claim 2. *In any execution, each invocation of* shrink() *by a process p_i terminates within a finite number of p_i's steps, and when it does, process p_i owns no register.*

Proof Process p_i executes at most m iterations of the for-loop in shrink(), and in each iteration it executes the wait-free operations write() and read(), so shrink() terminates after a finite number of p_i's steps. Before calling shrink(), process p_i calls snapshot() to obtain $view_i$ (line 6), and it does not write to the RW anonymous memory $R[1..m]$ between that snapshot() and its subsequent call of shrink(). In the for-loop in the operation shrink(), process p_i writes $\perp$ into all registers $R[x]$, $x \in \{1, \ldots, m\}$, such that $view_i[x] = id_i$. Since no other process writes the value id_i to any register $R[x]$, no register contains id_i anymore when p_i terminates its shrink() operation. $\Box_{Claim\ 2}$

Claim 3. *If a process owns a register, then it is not in the remainder section (i.e., it has a pending* lock() *or* unlock() *invocation, or it is in the critical section).*

Proof A process p_i can only begin to own a register $R[x]$, $x \in \{1, \ldots, m\}$, by writing id_i into $R[x]$, that can only happen in line 12 of the operation lock(). When p_i enters the remainder section, it has not written to any register of R since its latest shrink() invocation in the operation unlock() terminated, so the statement follows from the Claim 2. $\Box_{Claim\ 3}$

In the following, for any given time $t \geq t^*$, we say that p_i is *competing* if p_i has a pending lock() operation at t and the last snapshot taken by p_i before t satisfies the condition at line 4 (i.e. p_i is not stuck in the inner loop).

Claim 4. *At any point $t \geq t^*$, there is a competing process p_i whose last* snapshot() *invocation does not cause it to invoke* shrink() *at line 9.*

Proof If at least one competing process p_i obtains a view that is not full, the condition at line 5 is satisfied, and thus this view does not cause p_i to invoke shrink(). We can then consider that all competing processes have obtained a full view in their last snapshot.

Let p_i be the process that owns the most registers in the last snapshot taken before t (if more than one process satisfy this condition, p_i can be chosen arbitrarily among them). If p_i took this snapshot, it wouldn't cause it to invoke shrink() (p_i owns more than the average, condition at line 9). Let us then consider that p_i didn't take this last snapshot before t, but took one previously at time $t' < t$. Process p_i is the only one which can write its own identity, and its last view was full, causing it not to write (condition at line 4). At time t', p_i then owns at least as many registers as in the last snapshot taken before t. Furthermore, any competing process in the last snapshot taken before t is also competing at time t' (otherwise it would be stuck in the inner loop at line 4). Thus, the view taken by p_i at time t' does not satisfy the condition at line 9, and does not cause p_i to invoke shrink(). $\Box_{Claim\ 4}$

Claim 5. *At any point $t \geq t^*$, if there is more than one competing process, at least one of them will invoke* shrink().

Proof Suppose not. Note that the only point at which a process can write $\perp$ is during the shrink() operation. If at least one competing process obtains a view that is not full, it will invoke R.write(). This will happen again until no register has the value $\perp$ and all competing processes obtain full views in their last snapshot, preventing them from writing. We can then consider w.l.o.g. that, at time t, all competing processes have stopped writing and have obtained the same view. Let cnt be the number of these competing processes.

Because $1 < cnt \leq n$ and $\forall \ell : 1 < \ell \leq n : \gcd(\ell, m) = 1$, at least one competing process owns less registers than m/cnt, causing it to call shrink(); a contradiction which proves the claim. $\Box_{Claim\ 5}$

Proof of Theorem 2.
By Claim 4, at any point $t \geq t^*$, there is a competing process whose last snapshot() invocation does not cause it to invoke shrink(). By Claim 2, any shrink() operation terminates, and causes the invoking process to be stuck in the inner loop at line 4, causing it to stop competing after its next snapshot() invocation. This implies that at least one competing process never calls shrink() after point t^*.

By assumption, no process is in the critical section, and no unlock() operation is pending. By Claim 3, if a process owns a register, then it is not in the remainder section. The only processes that own registers are then the ones that are competing.

By Claim 5, if there is more than one competing process, at least one of them invokes shrink(), causing it to stop competing. There is then eventually a single competing process that owns all the registers, a contradiction with the original assumption that after some point t^*, no invocation of lock() or unlock() terminates, even though at least one process has a pending lock() or unlock() operation and no process is in the critical section. $\Box_{Theorem\ 2}$

4.2 Anonymous RW Model: Tight Space Bound

Given $M(n) = \{m : \forall \ell : 1 < \ell \leq n : \gcd(\ell, m) = 1\}$, it is shown in [21] that $m \in M(n)$ is a necessary condition for any algorithm solving symmetric deadlock-free mutex in an anonymous memory composed of m read/write registers. As already indicated, as $m \geq n$ is a necessary condition for any algorithm solving deadlock-free mutex in a non-anonymous system, it remains necessary in a read/write anonymous system. This translates as follows: $m \in M(n) \setminus \{1\}$ is a necessary condition for deadlock-free mutex in an anonymous memory composed of m read/write registers.

As Algorithm 1 solves deadlock-free mutex under this condition, it follows that $m \in M(n) \setminus \{1\}$ is a necessary and sufficient condition.

5 ANONYMOUS RMW MODEL: SYMMETRIC DEADLOCK-FREE MUTUAL EXCLUSION

This section presents an algorithm implementing a deadlock-free mutex lock object in an n-process read/modify/write (RMW) memory-anonymous system. As the previous algorithm, the algorithm presented below is particularly simple.

5.1 Representation of the Lock Object

The shared anonymous memory is made up of m RMW atomic registers, denoted $R[1..m]$ where $m \in \{1\} \cup \{m : \forall \ell : 1 < \ell \leq n : \gcd(\ell, m) = 1\}$ (let us notice that this set includes the value 1).

In Algorithm 2, a process uses three local variables, denoted $most\_present_i$, $owned_i$, and $view_i$ (which has the same meaning as in Algorithm 1).

5.2 Algorithm 2

When a process p_i invokes lock(), it enters a repeat loop from which it will exit when it will obtain a view $view_i[1..m]$ in which its own identity appears in a majority of registers (line 12).

Process p_i first invokes the RMW operation compare&swap() on all registers in order to write its identity in all the registers whose current value is the default value $\perp$ (line 2). Then, it reads (asynchronously) the whole anonymous memory and saves it in $view_i[1..m]$ (line 3). From this non-atomic view of the shared memory, p_i computes the occurrence number of the most present value ($most\_present_i$, line 4) and the occurrence number of its own identity ($owned_i$, line 5).

- If $owned_i \geq most\_present_i$, p_i proceeds to the next iteration of the repeat-until loop if $owned_i \leq m/2$, and enters the critical section if $owned_i > m/2$.
- If $owned_i < most\_present_i$, p_i resigns from the competition. To this end, it first writes $\perp$ in all entries that, from its local point of view, contain its identity (line 7), and then waits until it sees that all the anonymous registers contain the default value $\perp$ (lines 8-10).

When a process p_i invokes unlock(), it simply resets to $\perp$ all the registers that contain its identity id_i (line 13).

6 ANONYMOUS RMW MODEL: PROOF OF ALGORITHM 2 AND TIGHT SPACE LOWER BOUND

6.1 Proof of Algorithm 2

Theorem 3. *Algorithm 2 satisfies mutual exclusion.*

Proof Assume that a process p_i is in its critical section, while some other process, say process p_j, is executing the operation lock(). Before p_i entered its critical section the exit predicate of line 12, namely, $owned_i > m/2$ must be evaluated to true. This means that, before p_i entered its critical section, it succeeded to change more than $m/2$ RMW anonymous registers from $\perp$ to its identifier id_i. As long as process p_i does not set these RMW registers back to $\perp$, process p_j cannot succeed in changing more than $m/2$ registers from $\perp$ to id_j. Thus, process p_j will not be able to enter its critical section while p_i is in its critical section. $\Box_{Theorem\ 3}$

Theorem 4. *Algorithm 2 is deadlock-free.*

Proof We show that if a process is trying to enter its critical section, then some process eventually enters its critical section.

In the first for loop (line 2) each process scans the m RMW anonymous registers trying to set those that are $\perp$ to its identifier. If the process is running alone, it will clearly succeed to set them all to its identifier and will enter its critical section.

```
m ∈ {m such that ∀ ℓ ∈ {2, ..., n} : gcd(ℓ, m) = 1}
R[1..m]: array of anonymous RMW atomic registers, each initialized to ⊥
p_i: process executing this code; id_i is its identity
view_i: process p_i's local array of size m (with global scope)
-----------------------------------------------------------------
operation owned() is return (|{x ∈ {1, ..., m} : view_i[x] = id_i}|). % # of registers owned by p_i %
-----------------------------------------------------------------
operation lock() is
(1)  repeat
(2)    for each x ∈ {1, ..., m} do R.compare&swap(x, ⊥, id_i) end for;
(3)    for each x ∈ {1, ..., m} do view_i[x] ← R.read(x) end for;
(4)    most_present_i ← maximum number of times the same non-⊥ value appears in view_i;
(5)    owned_i ← owned();
(6)    if owned_i < most_present_i then
(7)      for each x ∈ {1, ..., m} do if (view_i[x] = id_i) then R.write(x, ⊥) end if end for;
(8)      repeat
(9)        for each x ∈ {1, ..., m} do view_i[x] ← R.read(x) end for
(10)     until ∀ x ∈ {1, ..., m} : view_i[x] = ⊥ end repeat
(11)   end if
(12) until owned_i > m/2 end repeat.
-----------------------------------------------------------------
operation unlock() is
(13) for each x ∈ {1, ..., m} do R.compare&swap(x, id_i, ⊥) end for.
```

Figure 2: (Algorithm 2) RMW mem.-anonymous deadlock-free mutex (n-process system, $n \geq 2$, code for p_i)

When there is contention (i.e., several processes are in their entry codes) since $\forall\, x \in \{1, ..., n\} : m$ and x are relatively prime, at least one of the processes p_k must find that less than $most\_present_k$ of the RMW registers are set to its identifier. It follows from lines 6-7 that p_k gives up the competition, and waits in the inner repeat loop (lines 8-10). This enables at least one other process p_j, for which $most\_present_j$ of the RMW registers are set to its identifier, to proceed. Repeating this argument, eventually one of the processes will find that its identifier appears in more than $m/2$ of the RMW registers and will enter its critical section.

Finally, as in its exit code (line 13), a process sets to $\perp$ all the registers containing its identifier. This enables a possibly waiting process to continue. Thus, it is not possible for all the processes to simultaneously remain forever in the operation lock(). $\square_{Theorem\ 4}$

6.2 Anonymous RMW Model: Tight Space Lower Bound

Theorem 5. *There is an n-process symmetric deadlock-free mutual exclusion algorithm using $m \geq 1$ anonymous RMW registers only if $m \in M(n) = \{m : \forall\, \ell : 1 < \ell \leq n : \gcd(\ell, m) = 1\}$.*

Proof Let us assume to the contrary, namely, there is a symmetric deadlock-free mutual exclusion algorithm for n processes using $m \geq 1$ anonymous RMW registers such that for some positive integer $1 < \ell \leq n$, m and ℓ are not relatively prime. This means that there is a number $1 < \ell \leq m$ such that ℓ divides m.

Let us arrange the m RMW registers on a ring with m nodes where each register is placed on a different node. Then, let us pick ℓ processes. For simplicity let us call these processes $p_0, ..., p_{\ell-1}$. To each one of the ℓ processes, we assign an initial RMW register (namely, the first register that the process accesses) such that for every two processes p_i and $p_{i+1\ (mod\ \ell)}$, the distance between their initial registers is exactly m/ℓ when walking on the ring in a clockwise direction. Here we use the assumption that ℓ divides m.

The lack of global names, allows us to assign for each process an initial RMW register and an ordering of the registers which determines how the process scans the registers.

An execution in which the ℓ processes are running in *lock steps*, is an execution where we let each process take one step (in the order $p_0, ..., p_{\ell-1}$), and then let each process take another step, and so on. For process p_i and integer k, let $order(p_i, k)$ denotes the kth new register that p_i accesses during an execution where the ℓ processes are running in lock steps, and assume that we arrange that $order(p_i, k)$ is the register whose its distance from p_i's initial registers is exactly $(k-1)$, when walking on the ring in a clockwise direction.

We notice that $order(p_i, 1)$ is p_i's initial register, $order(p_i, 2)$ is the next new register that p_i accesses and so on. That is, p_i does not access $order(p_i, k+1)$ before accessing $order(p_i, k)$ at least once, but for every $j \leq k$, p_i may access $order(p_i, j)$ several times before accessing $order(p_i, k+1)$ for the first time.

With this arrangement of RMW registers, we run the ℓ processes in lock steps. Since only comparisons for equality are allowed, and all registers are initialized to a the same value –which (to preserve anonymity) is not a process identity– processes that take the same number of steps will be at the same state, and thus it is not possible to break symmetry. It follows that either all the processes will enter

Registers	RW anonymous	RMW anonymous
Sufficient condition	This paper (Algorithm 1)	This paper (Algorithm 2)
Necessary condition	[21][4]	This paper (Theorem 5)

Table 2: A global picture for n-process anonymous mutex ($n \geq 2$)

their critical sections at the same time, violating mutual exclusion, or no process will ever enter its critical section, violating deadlock-freedom. A contradiction. □$_{Theorem\ 5}$

7 CONCLUSION

"Anonymous shared memory" means there is no a priori agreement among the processes on the names of the shared registers. Moreover, "symmetric algorithm" means that the process identities define a specific data type with no internal structure (such as a total order) and no relation with other data type (hence an identity cannot be compared with an integer). Identities can only be read, written, and compared with equality.

Considering two types of anonymous registers (the atomic read/write (RW) registers and the atomic read/modify/write (RMW) registers) this paper presented several results on symmetric mutual exclusion algorithms, summarized in Table 2. These algorithms differ in their design principles and their costs (measured as the number of registers which must contain the identity of a process to allow it to enter the critical section).

The symmetric deadlock-free mutex algorithm built on top of an anonymous memory made up of m atomic RW registers works for $m \in M(n) \setminus \{1\}$, where $M(n) = \{m : \forall \ell : 1 < \ell \leq n : \gcd(\ell, m) = 1\}$, while the algorithm for m atomic RMW registers works for $m \in M(n)$. The necessity of the first condition was proved in [21], while the necessity of the second condition was proved in this paper. The existence of the algorithms presented in the paper proves these conditions are also sufficient.

Let us remark that a system composed of a single anonymous register is no really anonymous. Hence, if we eliminate the "pathological" case $m = 1$, the condition $m \in M(n)$ is a necessary and sufficient for symmetric deadlock-free mutex in both the read/write and the read/modify/write anonymous register models. This shows a fundamental computability difference separating the "memory anonymity" adversary (which operates before the execution and is consequently *static*) and the "process crash" adversary (which operates during the execution and is consequently *dynamic*), for which read/write and read/modify/write registers (provided with an operation such as compare&swap) are located at the two extremes of the synchronization power hierarchy as defined in [9]. (Let us remind that mutex can be solved neither in the read/write nor in the read/modify/write non-anonymous register models in the presence of process crashes.) Last but not least, a noteworthy property of the two algorithms that have been presented lies in their simplicity.

[4]Notice that the lower bound for the RW model from [21], follows immediately from our stronger lower bound for the RMW model present in this paper.

ACKNOWLEDGMENTS

Zahra Aghazadeh and Philipp Woelfel were partially supported by the Canada Research Chairs program and by the Discovery Grants program of the Natural Sciences and Engineering Research Council of Canada (NSERC). Michel Raynal was partially supported by the French ANR project 16-CE40-0023-03 DESCARTES devoted to layered and modular structures in distributed computing.

The authors want to thank the referees for their constructive comments.

REFERENCES

[1] Afek Y., Attiya H., Dolev D., Gafni E., Merritt M. and Shavit N., Atomic snapshots of shared memory. *Journal of the ACM*, 40(4):873-890 (1993)

[2] Anderson J., Multi-writer composite registers. *Distributed Computing*, 7(4):175-195 (1994)

[3] Burns J. E. and Lynch N. A., Bounds on shared memory for mutual exclusion. *Information and Computation*, 107(2):171-184 (1993)

[4] Dijkstra E .W., Solution of a problem in concurrent programming control. *Communications of the ACM*, 8(9):569 (1965)

[5] Fischer M. J., Lynch N. A., and Paterson M. S., Impossibility of distributed consensus with one faulty process. *Journal of the ACM*, 32(2):374-382 (1985)

[6] Garg V.K. and Ghosh J., Symmetry in spite of hierarchy. *Proc. 10th Int'l Conference on Distributed Computing Systems (ICDCS'90)*, IEEE Computer Press, pp. 4-11 (1990)

[7] Giakkoupis G., Helmi M., Higham L., and Woelfel P., An O(sqrt n) space bound for obstruction-free leader election. *Proc. 27th Int'l Symposium Distributed Computing (DISC'13)*, Springer, LNCS 8205, pp. 46-60 (2013)

[8] Giakkoupis G., and Woelfel P., Randomized abortable mutual exclusion with constant amortized RMR complexity on the CC Model. *Proc. 36th ACM Symposium on Principles of Distributed Computing (PODC'17)*, ACM Press, pp. 221-229 (2017)

[9] Herlihy M.P., Wait-free synchronization. *ACM Transactions on Programming Languages and Systems*, 13(1):124-149 (1991)

[10] Herlihy M.P. and Wing J.M., Linearizability: a correctness condition for concurrent objects. *ACM Transactions on Programming Languages and Systems*,12(3):463-492, (1990)

[11] Johnson R.E., and Schneider F.B., Symmetry and similarity in distributed systems. *Proc.4th ACM Symposium on Principles of Distributed Computing (PODC'85)*, pp. 13-22, ACM Press (1985)

[12] Lamport L., On interprocess communication, Part I: basic formalism. *Distributed Computing*, 1(2):77-85 (1986)

[13] Loui M. and Abu-Amara H., Memory requirements for agreement among unreliable asynchronous processes. *Advances in Computing Research*, 4:163-183, JAI Press (1987)

[14] Navlakha S. and Bar-Joseph Z., Algorithms in nature: the convergence of systems biology and computational thinking. *Molecular systems biology*, 7(546):1-11 (2011)

[15] Navlakha S. and Bar-Joseph Z., Distributed information processing in biological and computational systems. *Communications of the ACM*, 58(1):94-102 (2015)

[16] Rabin M., The choice coordination problem. *Acta Informatica*, 17(2):121-134 (1982)

[17] Raynal M., *Concurrent programming: algorithms, principles and foundations*. Springer, 515 pages, ISBN 978-3-642-32026-2 (2013)

[18] Raynal M. and Cao J., Anonymity in distributed read/write systems: an introductory survey. *Proc. 6th Int'l Conference on Networked Systems (NETYS'18)*, Springer LNCS, 17 pages (2018)

[19] Rashid S., Taubenfeld G., and Bar-Joseph Z., Genome wide epigenetic modifications as a shared memory consensus. *6th Workshop on Biological Distributed Algorithms (BDA'18)*, London (2018)

[20] Taubenfeld G., *Synchronization algorithms and concurrent programming*. Pearson Education/Prentice Hall, 423 pages, ISBN 0-131-97259-6 (2006)

[21] Taubenfeld G., Coordination without prior agreement. *Proc. 36th ACM Symposium on Principles of Distributed Computing (PODC'17)*, ACM Press, pp. 325-334 (2017)

Constant Amortized RMR Abortable Mutex for CC and DSM

Prasad Jayanti*
ప్రసాద్ జయంతి
प्रसाद् जयन्ति
prasad.jayanti@dartmouth.edu
Dartmouth College

Siddhartha Jayanti†
సిద్ధార్థ జయంతి
सिद्धार्थ जयन्ति
jayanti@mit.edu
MIT

ABSTRACT

The Abortable mutual exclusion problem, proposed by Scott and Scherer in response to the needs in real time systems and databases, is a variant of mutual exclusion that allows processes to abort from their attempt to acquire the lock. Worst-case constant remote memory reference (RMR) algorithms for mutual exclusion using hardware instructions such as Fetch&Add or Fetch&Store have long existed for both Cache Coherent (CC) and Distributed Shared Memory (DSM) multiprocessors, but no such algorithms are known for abortable mutual exclusion. Even relaxing the worst-case requirement to amortized, algorithms are only known for the CC model.

In this paper, we improve this state-of-the-art by designing a deterministic algorithm that uses Fetch&Store (FAS) to achieve amortized $O(1)$ RMR in both the CC and DSM models. Our algorithm supports Fast Abort (a process aborts within six steps of receiving the abort signal), and has the following additional desirable properties: it supports an arbitrary number of processes of arbitrary names, requires only $O(1)$ space per process, and satisfies a novel fairness condition that we call "Airline FCFS". Our algorithm is short and practical with fewer than a dozen lines of code.

CCS CONCEPTS

• Theory of computation → Concurrency; Data structures design and analysis; Shared memory algorithms; Concurrent algorithms; • Software and its engineering → Mutual exclusion; Concurrency control; *Distributed memory.*

KEYWORDS

mutual exclusion, abortable, mutex, amortized, fast abort, constant RMR, AFCFS, CC, DSM

ACM Reference Format:

Prasad Jayanti and Siddhartha Jayanti. 2019. Constant Amortized RMR Abortable Mutex for CC and DSM. In *2019 ACM Symposium on Principles of Distributed Computing (PODC '19), July 29-August 2, 2019, Toronto, ON, Canada.* ACM, New York, NY, USA, 10 pages. https://doi.org/10.1145/3293611.3331592

*I am grateful to the Frank Family and Dartmouth College for their support through the James Frank Family Professorship.

†I am grateful to the Department of Defense (DoD) for their support through the National Defense Science & Engineering Graduate Fellowship (NDSEG) Program.

PODC '19, July 29-August 2, 2019, Toronto, ON, Canada

ACM ISBN 978-1-4503-6217-7/19/07...$15.00
https://doi.org/10.1145/3293611.3331592

1 INTRODUCTION

The *Mutual exclusion problem*, proposed by Dijkstra, is an abstraction of a *lock* that is owned by at most one process at any time [7]. The *abortable* mutual exclusion problem, proposed by Scott and Scherer [21] in response to the needs in real time systems and databases, is the variant that allows processes to abort from their attempt to acquire the lock. Worst-case constant remote memory reference (RMR) algorithms for mutual exclusion using hardware instructions such as Fetch&Add or Fetch&Store have long existed for both Cache Coherent (CC) and Distributed Shared Memory (DSM) multiprocessors [2, 3, 5, 8, 11, 17, 18], but no such algorithms are known for abortable mutual exclusion. Even relaxing the worst-case requirement to amortized, algorithms are only known for the CC model—Lee's deterministic algorithm [16] and Giakkoupis and Woelfel's randomized algorithm [9]. In this paper, we improve this state-of-the-art by designing a deterministic algorithm that uses Fetch&Store (FAS) to achieve amortized constant RMR in both the CC and DSM models. A further highlight of our algorithm is that a process can abort in $O(1)$ steps in the worst-case, a property that neither Lee's nor Giakkoupis and Woelfel's algorithm has. In the rest of this section, we specify the problem, the RMR complexity metric, and describe our contribution in the context of prior research.

1.1 Specification of Abortable Mutual Exclusion

In the abortable mutual exclusion problem, each process is modeled by five sections of code—Remainder, Try, Critical, Exit, and Abort sections. A process stays in the Remainder section when it does not need the lock and, once it wants the lock, it executes the Try section concurrently with others that are also competing for the lock. Anytime a process is outside the Remainder section, the environment can send an "abort" signal to the process (how the environment sends this signal to a process does not concern us). From the Try section, a process jumps either to the Critical Section (CS) or to the Abort section, with the proviso that a process may jump to the Abort section only if it receives the "abort" signal from the environment while in the Try section. While in the CS, a process has exclusive ownership of the lock. When it no longer needs the lock, the process gives it up by executing the Exit section to completion and then moving back to the Remainder section. If a process enters the Abort section from the Try section, upon completing the Abort section the process moves back to the Remainder section.

The *abortable mutual exclusion problem* consists of designing the code for the Try, Exit, and Abort sections so that the following properties are satisfied [12].

- Mutual Exclusion: At most one process is in the CS at any time.
- Bounded Exit: There is a bound b such that each process in the Exit section completes that section in at most b of its own steps.
- Bounded Abort: There is a bound b such that, once a process receives the abort signal from the environment, it will enter the CS or the Remainder section in at most b of its own steps. We call this bound b the *abort-time.*
- Starvation-Freedom: Under the assumption that no process stays in the CS forever and no process stops taking steps while in the Try, Exit, or Abort sections, if a process in the Try section does not abort, it subsequently enters the CS.

We now state another desirable property that has never been proposed or investigated earlier. In any application, the environment sends the abort signal to a process only when there is some urgent task that the environment needs the process to attend to. In such a situation, we would want the process to "quickly" abort from its attempt to acquire the lock. Accordingly, we define *abort-time* as the worst-case number of steps that a process takes between receiving an abort signal and subsequently entering the CS or the Remainder section. So, we would like the abort time to be a constant independent of the number of processes:

- Fast Abort: The abort-time is an absolute constant.

Next, we define a novel fairness property called *Airline First Come First Served* (AFCFS), which is a natural relaxation of the standard First Come First Served (FCFS) property for the abortable setting. For intuition, imagine you are waiting to check-in in a long airline queue. You will not mind if someone who was ahead of you but left for the restroom (i.e. aborted) comes back to their old position in the queue. However, you will not allow a newcomer to take a position ahead of you in the queue. Before formalizing this property below, recall that FCFS for standard mutual exclusion (i.e. without the abort feature) is formalized using either the notion of a bounded Doorway [14], or more directly by the following condition: there is a bound b such that if a process p_1 performs b steps of the Try section before a process p_2 enters the Try section, then p_2 does not enter the CS before p_1.

Turning our attention back to the abortable problem, we say a process begins a *passage* when it first enters the Try section or when it first enters the Try section after the end of its previous passage, and the passage ends when the process completes the Exit section. Note that a process can abort arbitrarily many times within each of its passages. Let π_1 be a passage of p_1 and π_2 a passage of p_2. We say that π_1 *b-precedes* π_2 if p_1 executes b steps $s_1, s_2, \ldots, s_b$ of the Try section in π_1 before the start of π_2 and p_1 does not abort in π_1 after step s_1.

- Airline First Come First Served (AFCFS): There is a bound b such that if a passage π_1 by process p_1 b-precedes a passage π_2 by process p_2, then p_2 does not enter the CS in π_2 before p_1 enters the CS in π_1.

Note that if no aborts are ever performed, then AFCFS coincides identically with standard FCFS.

1.2 RMR Complexity

In a *cache-coherent* (CC) machine each process has a cache. A read operation by a process p on a shared variable X fetches a copy of X from shared memory to p's cache, if a copy is not already present. Any non-read operation on X by any process invalidates copies of X at all caches. An operation on X by p counts as a *remote memory reference* (RMR) if either the operation is not a read or X's copy is not in p's cache. In a *distributed shared memory* (DSM) machine, instead of caches, shared memory is partitioned, with one partition residing at each process, and each shared variable resides in exactly one partition. Any operation (read or non-read) by a process on a shared variable X is counted as an RMR if X is not in p's partition.

The *worst-case RMR complexity* of an algorithm is the maximum number of RMRs incurred by a process between the times of leaving and subsequently re-entering the Remainder section. The *amortized RMR complexity* of an algorithm is the maximum value of x/y, where x is the total number of RMRs performed by all processes and y is the total number of times the Try section was entered by any process. In general, the RMR complexity is function of n, which is the maximum number of processes that execute the algorithm.

1.3 The Impact of Synchronization Primitives on RMR Complexity

The RMR complexity of the mutual exclusion problem is well known to depend on the synchronization primitives available for use in algorithms. A long standing lower bound due to Cypher [6], and an even stronger lower bound due to Attiya, Hendler, and Woelfel [4] establish that constant RMR complexity is unachievable even for standard mutual exclusion using read, write, and Compare&Swap (CAS). In fact, sub-logarithmic deterministic RMR complexity is unachievable even with amortization using only read, write, and CAS [4]. On the other hand, it has long been known that standard mutual exclusion has constant RMR algorithms using non-conditional primitives, such as Fetch&Add (F&A) [2, 3] or Fetch&Store (FAS) [5, 8, 11, 17, 18] (the constant bound holds only on CC machines for some of these algorithms, and for both CC and DSM machines for the others). Thus, FAS or F&A can be more effective than CAS when solving mutual exclusion and related problems. The algorithm in this paper uses FAS.

There is another sense in which FAS and F&A are stronger than CAS: unlike FAS() and F&A, CAS admits a deterministic $O(1)$ RMR implementation using read and write operations [10]. Consequently, any algorithm A that uses read, write, and CAS can be transformed into an algorithm A' that uses only read and write by replacing each instance of CAS in A with its implementation via reads and writes. The resulting algorithm A' would have the same asymptotic RMR complexity as A, and may appear to solve the same problem as A does. However, the latter is not always the case because the CAS implementation via reads and writes is blocking. As a result, if A is a mutual exclusion algorithm that uses CAS in the Exit section, A' may not satisfy the Bounded Exit property even if A does. If A is an *abortable* mutual exclusion algorithm that uses CAS in its Try section, A' no longer solves the problem because the CAS implementation via reads and writes is not abortable.

1.4 Our Contribution

We investigate whether $O(1)$ RMR complexity is feasible for *abortable* mutual exclusion in the CC and DSM models. If the goal is $O(1)$ *worst case* complexity, the problem has been and continues to be open. On the other hand, for $O(1)$ *amortized* complexity, there has been some progress, albeit only for the CC model. In light of the lower bound described above, it follows that any algorithm that aspires for $O(1)$ amortized RMR complexity must either use synchronization primitives other than CAS or use randomization. The former approach was taken by Lee [16], and the latter by Giakkoupis and Woelfel [9]. Lee's algorithm (the second one in his thesis [16]) is deterministic and uses FAS and CAS, but its amortized RMR complexity bound is unproven. Giakkoupis and Woelfel's algorithm, uses CAS and randomization, but has expected $O(1)$ amortized RMR complexity only against an oblivious scheduler. Their algorithm uses infinite arrays but they also sketch how to keep the memory use bounded to a polynomial (of unknown constant degree).

For the DSM model, there are no algorithms using common synchronization primitives of even sub-logarithmic amortized complexity, let alone $O(1)$. In fact, only two algorithms of bounded RMR complexity are known: Jayanti's algorithm [12] and the first algorithm in Lee's thesis [16], both of which have logarithmic worst-case RMR complexity.

In this paper, we design a deterministic algorithm that uses FAS[1] and guarantees $O(1)$ amortized RMR complexity for both the CC and DSM models. Our algorithm supports Fast Abort: a process aborts within 6 steps of receiving the abort signal. The algorithms of Lee and Giakkoupis and Woelfel do not have the fast abort property, making ours the first to support Fast Abort and have $O(1)$ amortized RMR complexity in either model. (To the familiar reader, Lee's algorithm does not satisfy fast abort because an aborting process p may find as many as $\Theta(n)$ aborted nodes ahead of its node. In this case, p removes each of these nodes from the wait-queue, taking $\Theta(n)$ steps, before aborting.)

Our algorithm has the following additional desirable properties: It satisfies AFCFS, requires only $O(1)$ space per active or aborted process, and supports an arbitrary number of processes of arbitrary names. It is also short and practical with fewer than a dozen lines of code.

Our algorithm is inspired by a long line of research on *queue locks*, especially of the MCS variety [18], where waiting processes are organized as a linked list. The MCS lock uses both FAS and CAS, and does not satisfy Bounded Exit. Craig refines this algorithm to use only FAS and bound the exit section [5]. These locks use only $O(1)$ space per active process and support an arbitrary number of processes which Lee's algorithm as well as ours inherit. The second algorithm in Lee's Thesis [16] builds on Craig's algorithm to implement the abort feature on CC machines. Lee's clever insight is that an aborting process could leave its node in the queue and try to reclaim that position the next time it attempts to capture the lock (thereby realizing AFCFS). Our algorithm builds on Lee's with two further insights. The first concerns what actions a process takes upon receiving the abort signal. In Lee's algorithm, an aborting process—even as it leaves its own node in the queue—kicks out all contiguous aborted nodes in front of it. In contrast, our algorithm kicks out at most one node. This idea makes the proof of starvation freedom more complex, but is crucial to achieving Fast Abort. Second, our algorithm incorporates the requisite indirection to ensure constant RMR complexity even on DSM machines. This indirection is algorithmically subtle because, even though it "falsely" wakes waiting processes multiple times, neither correctness nor the constant amortized bound is broken. We prove mutual exclusion through invariants, and starvation-freedom and complexity analysis through potential functions.

[1] The Fetch&Store (FAS) instruction behaves as follows: FAS(X, v) changes shared variable X's value to v and returns X's previous value.

1.5 Prior Research

We list previous algorithms for abortable mutual exclusion and their properties in Table 1. Scott and Scherer were the first to formulate the abortable mutual exclusion problem [21], but their algorithm and Scott's subsequent algorithm [20] have unbounded RMR complexity. Jayanti presents the first algorithm of bounded RMR complexity [12]. His algorithm uses CAS and has $O(\log n)$ RMR complexity which is optimal by the aforementioned lower bound [4]. Giakkoupis and Woelfel gave a CAS-based randomized abortable lock of $O(1)$ expected amortized RMR complexity [9], which contrasts positively with the lower bound [4] that deterministic sub-logarithmic complexity is infeasible even with amortization. Another CAS-based algorithm by Woelfel and Pareek [19] uses randomization yet again to beat the lower bound and attain a sub-logarithmic, albeit non-constant, expected RMR complexity.

Lee's dissertation has four FAS based deterministic algorithms with worst-case RMR complexities of $\Theta(\log n)$, $\Theta(n)$, $\Theta(n^2)$, and $\Theta(n^2)$ [16]. The second algorithm has $O(1)$ *amortized* RMR complexity and satisfies AFCFS, although neither of these facts is proved by him. Alon and Morrison [1] design a deterministic Fetch&Add based algorithm with sub-logarithmic, but non-constant RMR complexity.

Of the above, only two algorithms have bounded RMR complexity in the DSM model—Jayanti's [12] and Lee's first algorithm [16].

2 AN AMORTIZED $O(1)$ RMR ALGORITHM FOR CC AND DSM

In this section, we present our abortable mutual exclusion algorithm (or simply, abortable lock) that has $O(1)$ amortized RMR complexity for both the CC and DSM models. To help the reader understand the algorithm, below we first present the high level ideas and only later point the reader to the actual algorithm and our line-by-line commentary of the algorithm.

2.1 Intuitive Description of the Main Ideas and Their Representation

Our algorithm is essentially a queue lock: in the Try section, as processes wait to acquire the lock, they wait in a queue. When a process enters the Try section, it adds itself to the end of the queue. The process that is at the front of this queue is the one that enters the

Algorithm	Primitive	RMRs	WC / Amrt	Det.	Space	DSM	Fairness	Fast Abort
Scott et al. [21]	FAS, CAS	∞	WC	✓	∞	✓		
Scott CLH-NB [20]	FAS, CAS	∞	WC	✓	∞	✓		
Scott MCS-NB [20]	FAS, CAS	∞	WC	✓	∞	✓		
Jayanti [12]	CAS	$\Theta(\log n)$	WC	✓	$\Theta(n)$	✓	FCFS	
Lee Alg 1 [16]	None	$\Theta(\log n)$	WC	✓	$\Theta(n \log n)$	✓		
Lee Alg 2 [16]	FAS, CAS	$\Theta(n)/\Theta(1)$	WC/Amrt	✓	$\Theta(n)$		AFCFS	
Lee Alg 3 [16]	FAS	$\Theta(n^2)$	WC	✓	∞		FCFS	
Lee Alg 4 [15, 16]	FAS	$\Theta(n^2)$	WC	✓	$\Theta(n^2)$		FCFS	
Woelfel et al. [19]	CAS	$O(\frac{\log n}{\log \log n})$	WC		$\Theta(n)$			
Giakkoupis et al. [9]	CAS	$\Theta(1)$	Amrt		∞			
Alon et al. [1]	F&A, CAS	$O(\frac{\log n}{\log \log n})$	WC	✓	$O(n^2)$			
This Paper	FAS	$\Theta(1)$	Amrt	✓	$\Theta(n)$	✓	AFCFS	✓

Table 1: Summary of abortable locks. The columns describe: RMR complexity; whether the complexity is worst case (WC) or amortized (Amrt); whether the algorithm is Deterministic (Det.) or randomized; space complexity; whether the RMR bound holds for the DSM model; what fairness condition (if any) the algorithm satisfies; and whether the algorithm supports Fast Abort.

CS. When a process leaves the CS, it removes itself from the queue, and lets the next process, which is now at the front of the queue, enter the CS. In our informal description and in the statement of our invariant, we let Q denote this abstract "process-queue", $k \geq 0$ denote the number of processes in Q, and $q_1, q_2, \ldots, q_k$ denote the sequence of processes in Q, where q_1 is the front process and q_k is the tail process.

This abstract process-queue Q is represented in the algorithm by a list of nodes. A node is simply a single word of shared memory. If a set P consisting of n processes participate in the algorithm (some of which are in the Remainder section and the others active in Try, Critical, Exit, or Abort sections), then the algorithm employs a total of $n + 1$ nodes, of which n nodes are owned by the n processes and the remaining node is not owned by any process. Thus, at any point, each process owns one node and different processes own different nodes. However, the node that a process owns and the node that is not owned by any process change with time. In the algorithm, each process p has a local variable $mynode_p$ that holds the address of the node that p owns. We let N denote the set of addresses of the $n + 1$ nodes.

Turning our attention back to the abstract process-queue Q of length k, it is represented in the algorithm by a list of $k + 1$ nodes whose addresses we denote by $a_0, a_1, \ldots, a_k$, where $a_1, a_2, \ldots, a_k$ are the addresses of the nodes owned by $q_1, q_2, \ldots, q_k$, respectively, and a_0 is the address of the node that is not owned by any process. Thus, for all $i \in [1, k]$, $a_i = mynode_{q_i}$. We call the list $a_0, a_1, \ldots, a_k$ the "node-queue", which closely corresponds to but is distinct from the process-queue Q. We say q_{i+1} is q_i's *successor process* and q_{i-1} is q_i's *predecessor process*. Similarly, we call a_{i+1} is q_i's *successor node* and a_{i-1} is q_i's *predecessor node*. Process q_k has no successor node, but q_1 has a_0 as its predecessor node. Henceforth, we simply use the terms successor and predecessor, and let it be inferred from the context whether we are referring to the process or to the node.

In the algorithm, each process p has another local variable $pred_p$ through which p remembers the address of its predecessor node. In particular, for all $i \in [1, k]$, $pred_{q_i} = a_{i-1}$. There is also a shared variable TAIL, which holds a_k, the address of the last node in the node-queue. When a process p enters the Try section, it performs a FAS(TAIL, $mynode_p$) and stores the return value in $pred_p$ so as to both add itself to the end of the queue and simultaneously remember its predecessor.

The node a_0 is the only node that may contain a special value denoted `token`. Once a process p enters the Try section and adds itself to the queue, it checks if its predecessor node contains `token`. If it does, p knows it is q_1 and enters the CS. Otherwise, p busy-waits until its predecessor will inform p that p's turn to the enter the CS has come up. In the algorithm, there is a shared variable called GO_p for this purpose—it is on this variable that p busywaits. For p's predecessor to later inform p that it may enter the CS, the predecessor needs to know the address of GO_p, so p deposits GO_p's address in its predecessor node before busywaiting.

The final high level idea concerns how a process aborts. When a process q_i in the Try section wishes to abort, it leaves its node a_i intact, but marks the node as "aborted" by writing the address of its predecessor node into its node, i.e., by writing a_{i-1} into $*a_i$. By doing this writing with a FAS, q_i simultaneously learns the address of $\text{GO}_{q_{i+1}}$, where its successor busy-waits, and wakes up the successor. The successor q_{i+1} then reads its predecessor node a_i, where it sees the address a_{i-1} and infers that q_i has aborted, so splices out a_i from the queue by writing `nil` in $*a_i$, and henceforth regarding a_{i-1} as its predecessor.

Suppose that after q_i aborted, it decides to invoke the Try section in a bid to acquire the lock. Since it is possible that its node is not yet spliced out of the queue by its successor, q_i tries to reclaim its old spot in the queue by simply switching the value in its node from a_{i-1} to `nil`; a similar idea was employed by Lee [16]. If in the process, it notices that it was already spliced out, the process adds its node to the end of the queue as in the normal course. Otherwise, it has happily reclaimed its old spot in queue.

2.2 The algorithm and line-by-line commentary

Having elaborately described the main ideas and how they are represented and implemented by the local and shared variables, we refer the reader to the precise algorithm (Algorithm 1) and informally explain how it works by going over the code of an arbitrary process p line by line. A note about our convention on how lines are numbered: in a single step of the execution, a process performs an operation on a single shared variable, but can perform any number of local actions. Therefore, in the figure, we numbered only those lines where an operation is performed on a *shared* variable.

Being at Line 1 amounts to being in the Remainder section. At Line 1, p is unsure whether it had aborted its previous attempt, but if it had aborted, p knows that it would have left $pred_p$ in its node. So, to reclaim its old spot in the queue (in the event that it aborted its previous attempt and its node has not yet been spliced out of the queue by its successor), p performs a FAS on its node (Line 1). If the FAS returns $pred_p$, p is sure it has reclaimed its old spot in the queue and proceeds to Line 3. Otherwise, p realizes that either it didn't abort its previous attempt or its aborted node has since been spliced out, so p appends its node afresh to the queue and records its predecessor node in $pred_p$ (Line 2). Once in the queue, p performs a FAS on its predecessor node to simultaneously inform the predecessor of the address of its busy-wait variable and learn the value v_p in the predecessor node (Line 3). If v_p is `token`, p infers that it is q_1, the front process in the wait-queue, so it terminates the Try section and proceeds to the CS. If v_p is non-`nil` and not the address of p's busy-wait variable, then it must be the case that the predecessor aborted and v_p has the address of the predecessor's predecessor. In this case, p knows that it spliced its predecessor out of the queue, and updates its predecessor (this shortens the queue by one node, which is crucial to proving starvation-freedom). Having updated its predecessor, p proceeds to Line 6 to check what is in store at this new predecessor. In the remaining case (when v_p is either `nil` or the address of its busy-wait variable), p understands it has no option but to wait until woken by its predecessor. So, it busy-waits (Line 4) and, once woken by its predecessor, resets $\textsc{go}_p$ to prepare it for the any busy-wait in the future (Line 5), and then moves on to inspect the predecessor node (Line 6) to determine why the predecessor woke it up.

Once p leaves the CS, it deposits the token in its node to signal its successor that it may enter the CS (Line 7). If the FAS operation at Line 7 returns a non-`nil` value, p knows that the value must be the address where the successor is busy-waiting. So, p wakes up its successor (Line 8). Importantly, the moment p deposits `token` in its node at Line 7, that node becomes the new a_0, the token holding node that does not belong to any process, and p grabs its predecessor node (the old a_0) as its own node

Before describing the Abort section, we note that in our algorithm, after p receives the abort signal from the environment, it is allowed to jump to the Abort section only after performing Line 3, or any iteration of Line 4, or Line 5, or Line 6. In particular, if the abort signal comes from the environment when p is at Line 3, it is required to execute Line 3 and all local actions associated with Line 3 before jumping to the Abort section. Furthermore, if the abort signal comes while p is looping at Line 4, p does not have to wait until the wait-till loop terminates before jumping to the Abort section; it can jump to the Abort section immediately (i.e., regardless of whether $\textsc{go}_p$ is true or false).

At the start of the Abort section, p erases the address of its busy-wait variable from its predecessor node because p is on the way out and no longer wants to be woken by the predecessor (Line 9). However, if p observes the token in the predecessor node, p knows that it has the permission enter the CS now. However, since p wishes to abort, it will sidestep CS and proceed directly to the Exit section (and complete its abort by executing the Exit section and returning to the Remainder from there). Another possibility is that $v_p \neq \&\textsc{go}_p$, which means that p's predecessor aborted, in which case p updates its predecessor to v_p, which holds p's predecessor's predecessor. At this point, p marks its node as aborted by writing in it p's predecessor (Line 10). A non-nil return value would be the address where p's successor is busy-waiting, so p informs the successor of its departure by setting the successor's busy-wait variable (Line 11).

3 PROOF OF CORRECTNESS

We state the invariant of Algorithm 1 in Figure 1. Below we claim the correctness of this invariant—the proof is in the full version of the paper [13].

THEOREM 3.1. *The statement I in Figure 1, which is the conjunction of $I_1, I_2, \ldots, I_{12}$ is an invariant of Algorithm 1. Furthermore, the quantities k, A, and Q in the invariant I are unique.*

COROLLARY 3.2. *Algorithm 1 satisfies mutual exclusion.*

PROOF. I_{10} states that only process q_1 can be in the critical section. □

THEOREM 3.3. *Algorithm 1 satisfies AFCFS where the doorway constitutes Lines 1 and 2 of the Try Section.*

PROOF. In order to show this property, we prove the following stronger statement by induction: *if process $p = q_i$ in the queue and process $p' = q_j$ in the queue with $j > i$, then p started its passage before p' finished its doorway.* This statement is true initially since Q is empty. The statement continues to hold inductively whenever any process leaves Q from any position. Thus, we are left with the case where a new process p enters Q. Since this case occurs only if p executes Line 2, and thereby just finishes the doorway, it is clear that every other process in Q has started its passage before p finished its doorway in its current passage. Now in conjuction with our inductive statement, we observe that by I_{10}, only the first process in Q, q_1 , can be in the CS; that finishes the proof. □

3.1 Proof of starvation freedom

To prove starvation freedom, we define a distance function δ that maps each process p in the Try section to a positive integer $\delta(p)$ that represents how far away p is from entering the CS. By our definition of δ, the minimum value possible for $\delta(p)$ is 1, and it is attained exactly when p is in the CS. To show that p will eventually enter the CS if it does not abort, we prove that if $\delta(p) > 1$, there is

Algorithm 1 : Abortabale Mutual Exclusion Algorithm with Amortized $O(1)$ RMR Complexity.

Shared Variables

SENTINEL: a node, initially token
TAIL: holds a node address, initially &SENTINEL
When a process p joins the protocol it allocates memory for:
  NODE_p: holds nil, token, or an address in shared memory, initially nil
  GO_p: boolean, initially *false*. (In DSM GO_p is in p's partition of shared memory)

Local Variables

For each process p:
  $mynode_p$: holds the address of a NODE, initially $\&\text{NODE}_p$
  $pred_p$: holds the address of a NODE, initially $\&\text{NODE}_p$
  v_p: holds nil, token or an address in shared memory, arbitrarily initialized

```
    Section Try(p)
1:  if FAS(*mynode_p, nil) ≠ pred_p then
2:      pred_p ← FAS(TAIL, mynode_p)
3:  v_p ← FAS(*pred_p, &GO_p)
    while v_p ≠ token do {
        if v_p ∉ {nil, &GO_p} then
            pred_p ← v_p
        else {
4:          wait till GO_p = true
5:          GO_p ← false
        }
6:      v_p ← FAS(*pred_p, &GO_p)
    }
```

```
    Section Exit(p)
7:  v_p ← FAS(*mynode_p, token)
    mynode_p ← pred_p
    if v_p ≠ nil then
8:      *v_p ← true

    Section Abort(p)
9:  v_p ← FAS(*pred_p, nil)
    if v_p = token then
        goto Exit (line 7)
    else {
        if v_p ∉ {nil, &GO_p} then
            pred_p ← v_p
10:     if (v_p ← FAS(*mynode_p, pred_p)) ≠ nil then
11:         *v_p ← true
    }
```

a nonempty set $\Psi(p)$ of "promoter" processes in the Try, Exit, or Abort sections such that (i) if a process from $\Psi(p)$ takes the next step, $\delta(p)$ decreases, and (ii) if a process not in $\Psi(p)$ takes the next step, $\delta(p)$ does not increase and the promoters set $\Psi(p)$ remains unchanged. Since a process from $\Psi(p)$ must eventually take a step, $\delta(p)$ is guaranteed to eventually decrease. By repeatedly applying this argument, we see that $\delta(p)$ eventually attains the minimum value of 1, at which point p enters the CS.

Our distance function δ is based on a carefully crafted auxiliary function f that maps each process $r \in Q$ to a decimal digit, based on r's program counter PC_r and the value of its GO_r variable, as follows.

$$f(r) = \begin{cases} 3 & \text{if } PC_r = 1 \\ 2 & \text{if } PC_r = 3 \\ 8 & \text{if } PC_r = 4 \wedge \text{GO}_r = \mathit{true} \\ 9 & \text{if } PC_r = 4 \wedge \text{GO}_r = \mathit{false} \\ 7 & \text{if } PC_r = 5 \\ 2 & \text{if } PC_r = 6 \\ 1 & \text{if } PC_r = 7 \\ 6 & \text{if } PC_r = 9 \\ 5 & \text{if } PC_r = 10 \end{cases} \tag{1}$$

Since a process in Q cannot be at Lines 2 or 8 (by I_6), we didn't specify $f(r)$ for $PC_r \in \{2, 8\}$. For a process p in the Try section, we are now ready to define p's distance from CS $\delta(p)$, and p's promoters set $\Psi(p)$.

Definition 3.4 (Distance function δ and Promoters set Ψ). Let p be a process in the Try section or CS (i.e., $PC_p \in \{3, 4, 5, 6, 7\}$). It follows from I_8 that $p \in Q$. Let $i \geq 1$ be p's position in Q (i.e., $p = q_i$), and let $m = \min\{j \mid 1 \leq j \leq i, PC_{q_j} \neq 1\}$. (Since $PC_{q_i} \in \{3, 4, 5, 6, 7\}$, m is well defined.) Then:

- p's distance from CS, $\delta(p)$, is defined as the i-digit decimal number $d_1 d_2 \ldots d_i$, where each digit d_j, for $1 \leq j \leq i$, is specified as follows:

$$d_j = \begin{cases} f(q_j) = 3 & \text{if } j < m \\ f(q_m) & \text{if } j = m \\ 0 & \text{if } j > m \end{cases}$$

  For example, if $i = 4$, $m = 3$, and $PC_{q_3} = 5$, then $\delta_p = 3370$.
- p's set of promoters, $\Psi(p)$, is defined by

$$\Psi(p) = \begin{cases} \{r \in P \mid PC_r \in \{8, 11\} \wedge v_r = \&\text{GO}_{q_m}\} & \text{if } PC_{q_m} = 4 \wedge \text{GO}_{q_m} = \mathit{false} \\ \{q_m\} & \text{otherwise} \end{cases}$$

The next lemma follows easily from the definition of $\delta(p)$.

Lemma 3.5. *For any process $p \in Q$ in the Try section or CS, $\delta(p) \geq 1$, and $\delta(p) = 1$ if and only if p is in the CS.*

The values of $\delta(p)$, $\Psi(p)$, and PC_p can change from one configuration to the next. So, in contexts such as the next lemma where we need to refer to these values in more than one configuration, we add a configuration C as an extra parameter and denote these values as $\delta(p, C)$, $\Psi(p, C)$, and $PC_p(C)$.

Lemma 3.6. *Suppose that a process $p \in Q$ is in the Try section in a configuration C (i.e., $PC_p(C) \in \{3, 4, 5, 6\}$) and some process π (possibly the same as p) takes a step from C. Let C' denote the configuration immediately immediately after π's step.*

(1) *If $\pi \in \Psi(p, C)$, then $\delta(p, C') < \delta(p, C)$.*
(2) *If $\pi \notin \Psi(p, C)$, then either $\delta(p, C') < \delta(p, C)$ or $(\delta(p, C') = \delta(p, C) \wedge \Psi(p, C') = \Psi(p, C))$.*

Lemma 3.6, which is used in the next theorem, is proved in Appendix B.

Theorem 3.7 (Starvation Freedom). *If a process $p \in Q$ is in the Try section (i.e., $PC_p \in \{3, 4, 5, 6\}$) and does not abort, it eventually enters the CS.*

Proof. Let C be a configuration where $PC_p \in \{3, 4, 5, 6\}$. Since p is not in the CS in C, , it follows from Lemma 3.5 that $\delta(p) > 1$ in C. By Lemma 3.6, as processes take steps from C, $\delta(p)$ never increases. It cannot remain the same forever because some process in $\Psi(p, C)$ eventually takes a step, causing $\delta(p)$ to decrease (by Lemma 3.6). Thus, $\delta(p)$ keeps decreasing as the execution progresses, until eventually hitting the minimum possible value of 1, at which point p is in the CS (by Lemma 3.5). □

4 COMPLEXITY ANALYSIS

In this section we analyze the space and RMR complexities of Algorithm 1.

Theorem 4.1. *Algorithm 1 has a $O(n)$ space complexity, where n is the total number of processes that join the protocol.*

Proof. The algorithm simply needs a constant number of local and shared variables per process, plus one sentinel node. □

We now wish to show that a process p performs only an amortized constant number of RMRs per attempt in Algorithm 1 in both the CC and DSM cost models. We analyze complexity by the potential method, by defining two different potential functions Φ_{CC} and Φ_{DSM}.

We start by motivating the definition of Φ_{DSM}, the simpler of the functions. Since we are proving a constant bound, we must show that each iteration of p's while-loop (lines 4, 5, and 6) is paid for by some other action. Since, GO_p is in p's partition of memory, lines 4 and 5 have no cost in the DSM model, so we focus on line 6. The two ways that p can get to line 6 are: (1) GO_p becomes *true* when p is busy-waiting on line 4, and (2) a FAS on either line 3 or 6 successfully removes an aborted node from the linked list. So, we charge the executions of line 6 to processes that write *true* to GO_p or abort a node by writing $pred_p$ in $*mynode_p$. This gives rise to the definition:

$$\Phi_{DSM} = \sum_{p \in P} \mathbb{1}_{\{\text{GO}_p = true\}} + \mathbb{1}_{\{PC_p = 6\}} + \mathbb{1}_{\{*mynode_p = pred_p\}}$$

In this definition $\mathbb{1}_{\{prop\}}$ is an indicator—it equals one if *prop* is *true* and zero otherwise. Note that Φ_{DSM} is a *proper potential function*, since it is zero in the initial configuration and always non-negative. We now state a lemma (proved in Appendix C) that bounds the amortized cost in the DSM model of line ℓ, $\alpha_{DSM}(\ell)$, for each $\ell \in [1, 11]$.

Lemma 4.2. *$\alpha_{DSM}(\ell) \leq 1$ for lines $\ell \in [1, 3] \cup \{7, 9\}$, $\alpha_{DSM}(\ell) \leq 2$ for lines $\ell \in \{8, 10, 11\}$, and $\alpha_{DSM}(\ell) \leq 0$ for $\ell \in [4, 6]$.*

The CC model is more complicated to analyze than the DSM model since: (1) line 4 can now have a real cost if GO_p is not in p's cache, and (2) line 5 always has a real cost, since it is a write operation, and causes GO_p to become uncached. To deal with (1), we define $notcached(p)$ to be the predicate that GO_p is not in p's cache, and add the indicator $\mathbb{1}_{\{notcached(p)\}}$ to Φ_{CC}. To deal with (2), we simply multiply the weight of the indicator that $\text{GO}_p = true$, to pay for the additional costs incurred on line 5. This results in the definition:

$$\Phi_{CC} = \sum_{p \in P} (3 \times \mathbb{1}_{\{\text{GO}_p = true\}} + \mathbb{1}_{\{PC_p = 6\}} + \mathbb{1}_{\{*mynode_p = pred_p\}} + \mathbb{1}_{\{notcached(p)\}})$$

At the cost of charging one unit to a process that is newly joining the protocol, we think of GO_p as initially residing in p's cache; so, Φ_{CC} is also a proper potential function. We define $\alpha_{CC}(\ell)$ as the amortized cost in the CC model of line ℓ of Algorithm 1, and state a lemma analgous to Lemma 4.2 for the CC model (proof in Appendix C).

Lemma 4.3. *$\alpha_{CC}(\ell)$ is bounded by a constant for all $\ell \in [1, 11] - [4, 6]$, and $\alpha_{CC}(\ell) \leq 0$ for $\ell \in [4, 6]$.*

Theorem 4.4. *Algorithm 1 has an $O(1)$ amortized RMR complexity for abortable mutual exclusion with starvation freedom and AFCFS in both the CC and DSM models. Furthermore, Algorithm 1 has a worst-case $O(1)$ RMR complexity for the Exit Section, uses only $O(n)$ space, and satisfies Fast Abort in both the CC and DSM models.*

Proof. In both the CC and DSM models, all the lines (4, 5, and 6) that appear in the while-loop of Algorithm 1 have zero amortized cost, and the remaining lines have constant amortized cost by Lemma 4.3 and 4.2. Since lines that are not in the loop are executed at most once per attempt, the amortized cost of an attempt is $O(1)$ in both the CC and DSM models.

The Exit Section has only two shared memory instructions, and thus has worst-case $O(1)$ RMR complexity in both models. Regardless of when the environment sends an abort signal to process p, process p can reach either the Exit or Abort section within three shared memory instructions, and either of these sections takes at most three more shared memory instructions. So, aborting happens within six shared instructions, and is thereby the algorithm satisfies Fast Abort. □

There is an integer $k \geq 0$, and a sequence $A = a_0, \ldots, a_k$ of $k+1$ addresses of distinct nodes and a sequence $Q = q_1, \ldots, q_k$ of k distinct processes such that

I_1) $\textsc{tail} = a_k$

I_2) $\forall i \in [1,k],\ mynode_{q_i} = a_i$

I_3) $\forall i \in [1,k],\ pred_{q_i} = a_{i-1}$

I_4) $N = \{a_0\} \cup \{mynode_p \mid p \in P\}$

I_5) $\forall p \in P,\ pred_p \in N$

I_6) $\forall p \in P,\ PC_p \in \{2,8\} \implies p \notin Q$

$\forall p \in P,\ PC_p = 2 \implies *mynode_p = \texttt{nil}$

$\forall p \in P,\ PC_p = 8 \implies *mynode_p \in \{\texttt{nil}, \&\textsc{go}_p\}$

I_7) If $k \geq 1$, then:

$PC_{q_k} \in \{3,4,5,6,7,9,10\} \implies *mynode_{q_k} = \texttt{nil}$

$PC_{q_k} \in \{1,11\} \implies *mynode_{q_k} = pred_{q_k}$

If $k \geq 2$, then for all $q_i \in \{q_1, \ldots, q_{k-1}\}$:

$PC_{q_i} \in \{3,4,5,6,7,9,10\} \implies *mynode_p \in \{\texttt{nil}, \&\textsc{go}_{q_{i+1}}\}$

$PC_{q_i} \in \{1,11\} \implies *mynode_{q_i} = pred_{q_i}$

I_8) $\forall p \in P,\ p \notin Q \implies (PC_p \in \{1,2,8,11\} \wedge *mynode_p \neq pred_p)$

I_9) If $(k = 0 \vee PC_{q_1} \neq 7)$ then $*a_0 = \texttt{token}$, else $*a_0 \in \{\texttt{nil}, \textsc{go}_{q_1}\}$

I_{10}) $\forall p \in P,\ p \neq q_1 \implies PC_p \neq 7$

I_{11}) $(PC_{q_1} = 4 \wedge \textsc{go}_{q_1} = \mathit{false}) \implies \exists p \in P,\ (PC_p = 8 \wedge v_p = \&\textsc{go}_{q_1})$

$\forall i \in [2,k],\ ((PC_{q_i} = 4 \wedge \textsc{go}_{q_i} = \mathit{false}) \implies$

$((*a_{i-1} = \&\textsc{go}_{q_i}) \vee ((*a_{i-1} = pred_{q_{i-1}}) \wedge (PC_{q_{i-1}} = 11) \wedge (v_{q_{i-1}} = \&\textsc{go}_{q_i}))))$

$\forall p \in P, PC_p \in \{8,11\} \implies v_p \in \{\&\textsc{go}_p \mid p \in P\}$

I_{12}) $\forall p \in P,\ PC_p = 5 \implies \textsc{go}_p = \mathit{true}$

Note: by I_4, the queue of node addresses starts with the unique node address a_0 that is no process p's $mynode_p$ and by I_1 ends with TAIL. This together with I_2 and I_3, implies that k, A, and Q are uniquely defined.

Figure 1: Invariant $I = \bigwedge_{j=1}^{14} I_j$ is the main invariant of Algorithm 1.

ACKNOWLEDGMENTS

We thank the PODC reviewers and Philipp Woelfel for some helpful comments.

REFERENCES

[1] Adam Alon and Adam Morrison. 2018. Deterministic Abortable Mutual Exclusion with Sublogarithmic Adaptive RMR Complexity. In *Proceedings of the 37th ACM Symposium on Principles of Distributed Computing (PODC '18)*. http://www.cs.tau.ac.il/~mad/publications/podc2018-mutex.pdf

[2] James H. Anderson and Yong-Jik Kim. 2003. Local-spin Mutual Exclusion Using Fetch-and-\phi Primitives. In *23rd International Conference on Distributed Computing Systems (ICDCS 2003), 19-22 May 2003, Providence, RI, USA*. 538. https://doi.org/10.1109/ICDCS.2003.1203505

[3] T. E. Anderson. 1990. The performance of spin lock alternatives for shared-money multiprocessors. *IEEE Transactions on Parallel and Distributed Systems* 1, 1 (Jan 1990), 6–16. https://doi.org/10.1109/71.80120

[4] Hagit Attiya, Danny Hendler, and Philipp Woelfel. 2008. Tight RMR Lower Bounds for Mutual Exclusion and Other Problems. In *Proceedings of the Fortieth Annual ACM Symposium on Theory of Computing (STOC '08)*. ACM, New York, NY, USA, 217–226. https://doi.org/10.1145/1374376.1374410

[5] Travis S. Craig. 1993. *Building FIFO and Priority-Queuing Spin Locks from Atomic Swap*. Technical Report. Dept. of Computer Science, Univ. of Washington.

[6] Robert Cypher. 1995. The Communication Requirements of Mutual Exclusion. In *Proceedings of the Seventh Annual ACM Symposium on Parallel Algorithms and Architectures (SPAA '95)*. ACM, New York, NY, USA, 147–156. https://doi.org/10.1145/215399.215434

[7] E. W. Dijkstra. 1965. Solution of a Problem in Concurrent Programming Control. *Commun. ACM* 8, 9 (Sept. 1965), 569–. https://doi.org/10.1145/365559.365617

[8] R. Dvir and G. Taubenfeld. 2017. Mutual exclusion algorithms with constant RMR complexity and wait-free exit code. (2017).

[9] George Giakkoupis and Philipp Woelfel. 2017. Randomized Abortable Mutual Exclusion with Constant Amortized RMR Complexity on the CC Model. In *Proceedings of the ACM Symposium on Principles of Distributed Computing (PODC '17)*. ACM, New York, NY, USA, 221–229. https://doi.org/10.1145/3087801.3087837

[10] Wojciech Golab, Vassos Hadzilacos, Danny Hendler, and Philipp Woelfel. 2007. Constant-RMR Implementations of CAS and Other Synchronization Primitives Using Read and Write Operations. In *Proceedings of the Twenty-sixth Annual ACM Symposium on Principles of Distributed Computing (PODC '07)*. ACM, New York, NY, USA, 3–12. https://doi.org/10.1145/1281100.1281105

[11] G. Graunke and S. Thakkar. 1990. Synchronization algorithms for shared-memory multiprocessors. *IEEE Computers* 23, 6 (June 1990), 60–69. https://doi.org/10.1109/2.55501

[12] Prasad Jayanti. 2003. Adaptive and Efficient Abortable Mutual Exclusion. In *Proceedings of the Twenty-second Annual Symposium on Principles of Distributed Computing (PODC '03)*. ACM, New York, NY, USA, 295–304. https://doi.org/10.1145/872035.872079

[13] Prasad Jayanti and Siddhartha V. Jayanti. 2018. Constant Amortized RMR Complexity Deterministic Abortable Mutual Exclusion Algorithm for CC and DSM Models. *CoRR* abs/1809.04561 (2018). arXiv:1809.04561 http://arxiv.org/abs/1809.04561

[14] Leslie Lamport. 1974. A New Solution of Dijkstra's Concurrent Programming Problem. *Commun. ACM* 17, 8 (Aug. 1974), 453–455. https://doi.org/10.1145/361082.361093

[15] Hyonho Lee. 2010. Fast Local-spin Abortable Mutual Exclusion with Bounded Space. In *Proceedings of the 14th International Conference on Principles of Distributed Systems (OPODIS'10)*. Springer-Verlag, Berlin, Heidelberg, 364–379. http://dl.acm.org/citation.cfm?id=1940234.1940271

[16] Hyonho Lee. 2011. *Local-spin Abortable Mutual Exclusion*. Ph.D. Dissertation. University of Toronto.

[17] Peter S. Magnusson, Anders Landin, and Erik Hagersten. 1994. Queue Locks on Cache Coherent Multiprocessors. In *Proceedings of the 8th International Symposium on Parallel Processing, Cancún, Mexico, April 1994*. 165–171. https://doi.org/10.1109/IPPS.1994.288305

[18] John M. Mellor-Crummey and Michael L. Scott. 1991. Algorithms for Scalable Synchronization on Shared-memory Multiprocessors. *ACM Trans. Comput. Syst.* 9, 1 (Feb. 1991), 21–65. https://doi.org/10.1145/103727.103729

[19] Abhijeet Pareek and Philipp Woelfel. 2012. RMR-Efficient Randomized Abortable Mutual Exclusion. *CoRR* abs/1208.1723 (2012). arXiv:1208.1723 http://arxiv.org/abs/1208.1723

[20] Michael L. Scott. 2002. Non-blocking timeout in scalable queue-based spin locks. In *Proceedings of the Twenty-First Annual ACM Symposium on Principles of Distributed Computing, PODC 2002, Monterey, California, USA, July 21-24, 2002.* 31–40. https://doi.org/10.1145/571825.571830

[21] Michael L. Scott and William N. Scherer III. 2001. Scalable queue-based spin locks with timeout. In *Proceedings of the 2001 ACM SIGPLAN Symposium on Principles and Practice of Parallel Programming (PPOPP'01), Snowbird, Utah, USA, June 18-20, 2001.* 44–52. https://doi.org/10.1145/379539.379566

A PROOF OF STARVATION FREEDOM LEMMA

LEMMA 3.6. *Suppose that a process $p \in Q$ is in the Try section in a configuration C (i.e., $PC_p(C) \in \{3,4,5,6\}$) and some process π (possibly the same as p) takes a step from C. Let C' denote the configuration immediately immediately after π's step.*

(1) *If $\pi \in \Psi(p, C)$, then $\delta(p, C') < \delta(p, C)$.*
(2) *If $\pi \notin \Psi(p, C)$, then either $\delta(p, C') < \delta(p, C)$ or $(\delta(p, C') = \delta(p, C) \wedge \Psi(p, C') = \Psi(p, C))$.*

PROOF. Since $PC_p(C) \in \{3,4,5,6\}$, it follows from I_8 that $p \in Q(C)$. Let $p = q_i(C)$, and $\delta(p, C)$ be the i-digit decimal number $d_1 d_2 \ldots d_i$, where the digits d_j are as defined above. Let $m = \min\{j \mid 1 \le j \le i,\ PC_{q_j}(C) \ne 1\}$.

We prove Part (1) of the lemma in two cases:

- Suppose that $PC_{q_m}(C) = 4 \wedge \text{GO}_{q_m}(C) = \textit{false}$. Then, since $\pi \in \Psi(C)$, it follows that $PC_\pi(C) \in \{8, 11\} \wedge v_\pi(C) = \&\text{GO}_{q_m}$. Therefore, π's step writes *true* in GO_{q_m}, making $f(q_m, C') = 8$ (note that $f(q_m, C)$ was 9). Thus, the mth digit is less in $\delta(p, C')$ than in $\delta(p, C)$, while the other digits of $\delta(p)$ remain unchanged from C to C'. Therefore, $\delta(p, C') < \delta(p, C)$.
- Suppose that it is not the case that $PC_{q_m}(C) = 4 \wedge \text{GO}_{q_m}(C) = \textit{false}$. Since $\pi \in \Psi(C)$, it follows that $\pi = q_m$.
  Suppose that $m = 1$ and $PC_{q_m}(C) \in \{3, 6\}$. Then, it follows from I_9 that q_1's step causes it jump to Line 7. So, the first digit of $\delta(p)$ changes from $f(q_1)$ in C (which is 2) to $f(q_1)$ in C' (which is 1); therefore, $\delta(p, C') < \delta(p, C)$.
  Suppose that $m > 1$ and $PC_{q_m}(C) \in \{3, 6\}$. Since $PC_{q_{m-1}} = 1$, it follows from the second part of I_7 that $*mynode_{q_{m-1}} = pred_{q_{m-1}}$. Therefore, q_m's step shortens the queue by one, causing p's position in Q to change from i in C to $i-1$ in C'. Thus, $\delta(p, C')$ has one fewer digit than $\delta(p, C)$. Therefore, $\delta(p, C') < \delta(p, C)$.
  Suppose that $PC_{q_m}(C) = 7$. Then, m must be 1 (by I_{10}) and q_1's step causes $q_1(C)$ to be no longer in Q in C', thereby causing p's position in Q to change from i in C to $i-1$ in C'. Thus, $\delta(p, C')$ has one fewer digit than $\delta(p, C)$. Therefore, $\delta(p, C') < \delta(p, C)$.
  If $PC_{q_m}(C)$ is anything else (i.e., $PC_{q_m}(C) \in \{4, 5, 7, 9, 10, 11\}$), the function f is so defined that because of the changed value of q_m's program counter, $f(q_m)$ is less in C' than in C. Thus, the mth digit of $\delta(p, C')$ is less than the mth digit of $\delta(p, C)$ (while all other digits of $\delta(p, C')$ are respectively the same as those of $\delta(p, C)$). Therefore, $\delta(p, C') < \delta(p, C)$.

For the proof of Part (2) of the lemma, we consider the same two cases.

- Suppose that $PC_{q_m}(C) = 4 \wedge \text{GO}_{q_m}(C) = \textit{false}$, and $\pi \notin \Psi(C)$.
  If $\pi = q_m$, q_m's step will not change the configuration (i.e., $C' = C$); therefore, $\delta(p, C') = \delta(p, C)$ and $\Psi(p, C') = \Psi(p, C)$.
  If $\pi = q_j$ for some $j < m$, then q_j's PC changes from 1 to 3. So, by the definition of f, the jth digit of $\delta(p)$ changes from 3 in C to 2 in C', while all more significant digits of $\delta(p, C')$ are respectively the same as those of $\delta(p, C)$. Therefore, $\delta(p, C') < \delta(p, C)$.
  If π is different from all of $q_1, q_2, \ldots, q_m$, then $\delta(p, C') = \delta(p, C)$ and $\Psi(p, C') = \Psi(p, C)$.
- Suppose that it is not the case that $PC_{q_m}(C) = 4 \wedge \text{GO}_{q_m}(C) = \textit{false}$, and $\pi \notin \Psi(C)$. Then $\pi \ne q_m$. If $\pi = q_j$ for some $j < m$, then q_j's PC changes from 1 to 3 and, as just argued, $\delta(p, C') < \delta(p, C)$. If π is different from all of $q_1, q_2, \ldots, q_m$, then $\delta(p, C') = \delta(p, C)$ and $\Psi(p, C') = \Psi(p, C)$.

□

B PROOF OF AMORTIZED LINE COSTS

LEMMA 4.2. *$\alpha_{DSM}(\ell) \le 1$ for lines $\ell \in [1,3] \cup \{7,9\}$, $\alpha_{DSM}(\ell) \le 2$ for lines $\ell \in \{8, 10, 11\}$, and $\alpha_{DSM}(\ell) \le 0$ for $\ell \in [4, 6]$.*

PROOF. We will prove the invariant by induction on steps of the multiprocessor system. In particular, we consider what happens when a process π executes its next step.

line 1: The real cost of the line is zero or one depending on whether $*mynode_p$ is in π's partition. This line can only decrease the potential (by decreasing the indicator $\mathbb{1}_{\{*mynode_p = pred_p\}}$). So, amortized cost is $\alpha_{DSM}(1) \le 1$.

line 2: The real cost of the line is one due to the FAS, and the potential function is unchanged. So, $\alpha_{DSM}(2) = 1$.

lines 3,7, and 9: The real cost of the line is zero or one depending on whether the FAS is on a node in π's partition. This line can only decrease the potential (by decreasing the indicator $\mathbb{1}_{\{*mynode_p = pred_p\}}$). So, $\alpha_{DSM}(3)$, $\alpha_{DSM}(7)$, $\alpha_{DSM}(9) \le 1$.

line 4: The real cost of this line is zero since GO_p is in p's partition. The potential change is also zero. So, $\alpha_{DSM}(4) = 0$.

line 5: The real cost of this line is zero since GO_p is in p's partition. When this line is executed, $\mathbb{1}_{\{\text{GO}_\pi = true\}}$ indicator must decrease by one due to I_{12} and $\mathbb{1}_{\{PC_\pi = 6\}}$ must increase by one. So, the potential change is zero. So, $\alpha_{DSM}(5) = 0$.

line 6: The real cost of the line is zero or one depending on whether $*pred_p$ is in π's partition. Here we have two cases. If $*pred_\pi = mynode_p$ for some process p and $*mynode_p = pred_p$, then we use the indicator $\mathbb{1}_{\{*mynode_p = pred_p\}}$ to pay for the real cost (since PC_π will become 6 again). Otherwise, PC_π will end up at some other line, and we pay for the real cost using the potential drop caused by the indicator $\mathbb{1}_{\{PC_\pi = 6\}}$. So, in either case the amortized cost of this line is $\alpha_{DSM}(6) \le 0$.

line 8, and 11: The real cost of the line is zero or one depending on whether $*v_\pi$ is in π's partition. The potential change

is at most one, since at most one indicator $\mathbb{1}_{\{\text{GO}_\pi = true\}}$ can go high. So, $\alpha_{DSM}(8), \alpha_{DSM}(11) \leq 2$.
line 10: The real cost of the line is zero or one depending on whether the FAS is on a node in π's partition. The potential can go up by at most one since $*mynode_\pi = pred_\pi$ after the line. So, $\alpha_{DSM}(10) \leq 2$.

□

Lemma 4.3. *$\alpha_{CC}(\ell)$ is bounded by a constant for all $\ell \in [1, 11] - [4, 6]$, and $\alpha_{CC}(\ell) \leq 0$ for $\ell \in [4, 6]$.*

Proof. We will prove the invariant by induction on steps of the multiprocessor system. In particular, we consider what happens when a process π executes its next step.

line 1: The real cost of the line is one due to the FAS. The change in potential is non-positive. So, amortized cost is $\alpha(1) \leq 1$.
line 2: The real cost of the line is one due to the FAS, The change in the potential is zero. So, the amortized cost is $\alpha(2) = 1$.
lines 3, 7, and 9: The real cost of this line is one due to the FAS. The change in potential is once again non-positive. So, the amortized cost is $\alpha_{CC}(3), \alpha_{CC}(7), \alpha_{CC}(11) \leq 1$.
line 4: There are two cases for this line: either GO_π is in π's cache, or not. If GO_π is cached, then both the real and amortized costs are zero. If GO_π is not cached, then the real cost is one, but is cancelled out by the drop in potential caused by the fact that GO_π becomes cached. So, the amortized cost of this line is $\alpha_{CC}(4) \leq 0$.
line 5: The real cost of this line is one due to the writing of *false*. Additionally, GO_π becomes uncached (if it was previously cached), thereby causing a one unit potential increase; and PC_π becomes 6, causing the corresponding indicator to become one. However, by I_{12}, there is a three unit potential drop due to GO_π becoming *false*. So, the amortized cost of this line is $\alpha_{CC}(5) = 0$.
line 6: The real cost of the line is one due to the FAS. Here we have two cases. If $*pred_\pi = mynode_p$ for some process p, and $*mynode_p = pred_p$, then we use the indicator $\mathbb{1}_{\{*mynode_p = pred_p\}}$ to pay for the real cost (since PC_π will become 6 again). Otherwise, PC_π will end up at some other line, and we pay for the real cost using the potential drop caused by the indicator $\mathbb{1}_{\{PC_\pi = 6\}}$. So, in either case the amortized cost of this line is $\alpha_{CC}(6) \leq 0$.
lines 8 and 11: The real cost of this line is one for the write operation. Since $*v_\pi$ is a GO-variable (by I_{11}) being set to *true*, this line can cause a potential increase of three units. So, the amortized cost of this line is $\alpha_{CC}(8), \alpha_{CC}(11) \leq 4$.
line 10: The real cost of the line is one due to the FAS. Since $*mynode_\pi$ becomes $pred_\pi$ due to this line, there is a possible potential increase of one unit. So, the amortized cost of this line is $\alpha_{CC}(10) \leq 2$.

□

A Recoverable Mutex Algorithm with Sub-logarithmic RMR on Both CC and DSM

Prasad Jayanti[*]
prasad@cs.dartmouth.edu
Dartmouth College
Hanover, NH

Siddhartha Jayanti[†]
jayanti@mit.edu
Massachusetts Institute of Technology
Cambridge, MA

Anup Joshi[‡]
anupj@cs.dartmouth.edu
Dartmouth College
Hanover, NH

ABSTRACT

In light of recent advances in non-volatile main memory technology, Golab and Ramaraju reformulated the traditional mutex problem into the novel *Recoverable Mutual Exclusion* (RME) problem. In the best known solution for RME, due to Golab and Hendler from PODC 2017, a process incurs at most $O(\frac{\log n}{\log \log n})$ remote memory references (RMRs) per passage on a system with n processes, where a passage is an interval from when a process enters the Try section to when it subsequently returns to Remainder. Their algorithm, however, guarantees this bound only for cache-coherent (CC) multiprocessors, leaving open the question of whether a similar bound is possible for distributed shared memory (DSM) multiprocessors.

We answer this question affirmatively by designing an algorithm for a system with n processes, such that, it satisfies the same complexity bound as Golab and Hendler's for both CC and DSM multiprocessors. Our algorithm has some additional advantages over Golab and Hendler's: (i) its Exit section is wait-free, (ii) it uses only the Fetch-and-Store instruction, and (iii) on a CC machine our algorithm needs each process to have a cache of only $O(1)$ words, while their algorithm needs a cache of size that is a function of n.

CCS CONCEPTS

• **Theory of computation** → **Shared memory algorithms**; • **Software and its engineering** → *Mutual exclusion*; • **Computer systems organization** → Reliability.

KEYWORDS

concurrent algorithm, synchronization, mutual exclusion, recoverable algorithm, fault tolerance, non-volatile main memory, shared memory, multi-core algorithms

[*]Prasad Jayanti is grateful to the Frank family and Dartmouth College for their support through James Frank Family Professorship of Computer Science.
[†]Siddhartha Jayanti was supported by the Department of Defense (DoD) through the National Defense Science & Engineering Graduate Fellowship (NDSEG) Program, the NSF awards CCF-1617730 and IIS-1741137, a Simons Investigator Award, a Google Faculty Research Award, and an MIT-IBM Watson AI Lab research grant.
[‡]Anup Joshi is grateful for the support from Dartmouth College.

ACM ISBN 978-1-4503-6217-7/19/07...$15.00
https://doi.org/10.1145/3293611.3331634

ACM Reference Format:
Prasad Jayanti, Siddhartha Jayanti, and Anup Joshi. 2019. A Recoverable Mutex Algorithm with Sub-logarithmic RMR on Both CC and DSM. In *2019 ACM Symposium on Principles of Distributed Computing (PODC '19), July 29-August 2, 2019, Toronto, ON, Canada.* ACM, New York, NY, USA, 10 pages. https://doi.org/10.1145/3293611.3331634

1 INTRODUCTION

In light of recent advances in non-volatile main memory technology, Golab and Ramaraju reformulated the traditional mutex problem into the novel *Recoverable Mutual Exclusion* (RME) problem. The best known algorithm for RME, due to Golab and Hendler [5], has sub-logarithmic remote memory reference (RMR) complexity for Cache-Coherent (CC) multiprocessors, but unbounded RMR complexity for Distributed Shared Memory (DSM) multiprocessors. In this paper, we present an algorithm that ensures the same sublogarithmic bound as theirs for both CC and DSM multiprocessors, besides possessing some additional desirable properties. In the rest of this section, we describe the model, the RME problem, the complexity measure, and then describe this paper's contribution in the context of prior work.

1.1 The Model

The advent of *Non-Volatile Main Memory* (NVMM) [15][16][17] — memory whose contents remain intact despite process crashes — has led to a new and natural model of a multiprocessor and spurred research on the design of algorithms for this model. In this model, asynchronous processes communicate by applying operations on shared variables stored in an NVMM. A process may crash from time to time. When a process π crashes, all of π's registers lose their contents: specifically, π's program counter is reset to point to a default location ℓ in π's program, and all other registers of π are reset to $\perp$; however, the shared variables stored in the NVMM are unaffected by a crash and retain their values. A crashed process π eventually restarts, executing the program beginning from the instruction at the default location ℓ, regardless of where in the program π might have previously crashed.

When designing algorithms for this model, informally the goal is to ensure that when a crashed process restarts, it reconstructs the lost state by consulting the shared variables in NVMM. To appreciate that this goal can be challenging, suppose that a process π crashes when it is just about to perform an operation such as $r \leftarrow$ FAS$(X, 5)$, which fetches the value of the shared variable X into π's register r and then stores 5 in X. If a different process π' performs FAS$(X, 10)$ and then π restarts, π cannot distinguish whether it crashed immediately before or immediately after executing its FAS instruction.

1.2 Recoverable Mutual Exclusion (RME)

In the Recoverable Mutual Exclusion (RME) problem, there are n asynchronous processes, where each process repeatedly cycles through four sections of code—Remainder, Try, Critical, and Exit sections. An *algorithm* (for RME) specifies the code for the Try and Exit sections of each process. Any process can execute a *normal step* or a *crash step* at any time. In a normal step of a process π, π executes the instruction pointed by its program counter PC_π. We assume that if π executes a normal step when in Remainder, π moves to Try; and if π executes a normal step when in CS, π moves to Exit. A crash step models the crash of a process and can occur regardless of which section of code the process is in. A crash step of π sets π's program counter to point to its Remainder section and sets all other registers of π to $\perp$.

A *run* of an algorithm is an infinite sequence of steps. We assume every run satisfies the following conditions: (i) if a process is in Try, Critical, or Exit sections, it later executes a (normal or crash) step, and (ii) if a process enters Remainder because of a crash step, it later executes a (normal or crash) step.

1.2.1 Passage and Super-passage Complexity. In a CC machine each process has a cache. A read operation by a process π on a shared variable X fetches a copy of X from shared memory to π's cache, if a copy is not already present. Any non-read operation on X by any process invalidates copies of X at all caches. An operation on X by π counts as a *remote memory reference* (RMR) if either the operation is not a read or X's copy is not in π's cache. When a process crashes, we assume that its cache contents are lost. In a DSM machine, instead of caches, shared memory is partitioned, with one partition residing at each process, and each shared variable resides in exactly one partition. Any operation (read or non-read) by a process on a shared variable X is counted as an RMR if X is not in π's partition.

A *passage* of a process π in a run starts when π enters Try (from Remainder) and ends at the earliest later time when π returns to Remainder (either because π crashes or because π completes Exit and moves back to Remainder).

A *super-passage* of a process π in a run starts when π either enters Try for the first time in the run or when π enters Try for the first time after the previous super-passage has ended, and it ends when π returns to Remainder by completing the Exit section.

The *passage complexity* (respectively, *super-passage complexity*) of an RME algorithm is the worst-case number of RMRs that a process incurs in a passage (respectively, in a super-passage).

1.2.2 Problem statement. An algorithm *solves* the RME problem if all of the following conditions are met in every run of the algorithm (Conditions P1, P3', P4 are from Golab and Ramaraju [7], and P2, P5, P6 are from Jayanti and Joshi [10]):

- P1 Mutual Exclusion: *At most one process is in the CS at any point.*
- P2 Wait-Free Exit: *There is a bound b such that, if a process π is in the Exit section, and executes steps without crashing, π completes the Exit section in at most b of its steps.*
- P3' Weak-Starvation Freedom [7]: *If the total number of crashes in the run is finite and a process is in the Try section, then it later enters the CS.*
  Note, an algorithm that allows the following scenario to occur satisfies this property. A process π never crashes in a run, however, another process π' has infinite number of super-passages in that run and crashes finite number of times in every super-passage. Thus, π' has infinite number of crashes in that run. Furthermore, in the same run π never enters the CS due to the crashes by other processes, but all other processes enter and exit the CS in each of their super-passages. Hence, π is blocked in spite of never crashing. To prevent such a scenario, we desire that our algorithm satisfies a stronger property as described below.
- P3 Starvation Freedom: *If every process crashes only a finite number of times in each of its super-passages in a run, then every process enters the CS in each of its super-passages in that run.*
- P4 Critical Section Reentry (CSR) [7]: *If a process π crashes while in the CS, then no other process enters the CS during the interval from π's crash to the point in the run when π next reenters the CS.*
- P5 Wait-Free Critical Section Reentry (Wait-Free CSR) [10]: Given that the CSR property above mandates that after a process π's crash in the CS no other process may enter the CS until π reenters the CS, it makes sense to insist that no process should be able to obstruct π from reentering the CS. Specifically:
  There is a bound b such that, if a process crashes while in the CS, it reenters the CS before completing b consecutive steps without crashing.
  (As observed in [10], Wait-Free CSR, together with Mutual Exclusion, implies CSR.)
- P6 Wait-Free Recovery to Exit [10]: *There is a bound b such that if a process crashes while in the Exit section, then the process enters either the CS or the Exit section before completing b consecutive steps without crashing.*
  (We note that properties P5 and P6 together imply the "Well-formedness" property of [10].)

Note, the model used by Golab and Ramaraju [7] included an additional "Recover" section that was executed whenever a process begun a passage. The main purpose of this section was to recover the internal structure of the algorithm, if the process entered that section after restarting from a crash. Thereby, they proposed a property called "Bounded Recovery" which stipulated that a process should be able to complete the Recover section in a bounded number of its own steps, if no process (including that process itself) was concurrently executing the Recover section immediately following a crash. Comparing this with our model we note the absence of such a "Recover" section in our model, with all the recovery happening in the Try section. Hence, in our model, a process executes the Try section whenever it begins a passage. Also, regardless of the state of any other process, it moves to CS or Exit in a bounded number of its own steps if it crashed in either of those two sections (this follows from properties P5 and P6). However, it is possible that a process might crash in the Try section and would have to wait for other recovering processes before performing its own recovery.

Hence, according to our model, a process may have to wait twice in the Try section itself, i.e., once to perform any essential recovery following a crash and once prior to entering the CS, as compared to Golab and Ramaraju's model [7], where it may wait in the Recover section once and then in the Try section.

1.3 Our contribution

The passage complexity of an RME algorithm can, in general, depend on n, the maximum number of processes the algorithm is designed for. The ideal of course would be to design an algorithm whose complexity is independent of n, but is this ideal achievable? It is well known that, for the traditional mutual exclusion problem, the answer is yes: MCS and many other algorithms that use FAS and CAS instructions have $O(1)$ passage complexity [3][4][13]. For the RME problem too, algorithms of $O(1)$ passage complexity are possible, but they use esoteric instructions not supported on real machines, such as Fetch-And-Store-And-Store (FASAS) and Double Word CAS, which manipulate two shared variables in a single atomic action [5][8]. The more interesting question, however, is how well can we solve RME using only operations supported by real machines.

With their tournament based algorithm, Golab and Ramaraju showed that $O(\log n)$ passage complexity is possible using only read and write operations [7]. In fact, in light of Attiya et al's lower bound result [2], this logarithmic bound is the best that one can achieve even with the additional support of comparison-based operations such as CAS. However in PODC '17, by using FAS along with CAS, Golab and Hendler [5] succeeded in breaching this logarithmic barrier for CC machines: their algorithm has $O(\frac{\log n}{\log\log n})$ passage complexity for CC machines, but unbounded passage complexity for DSM machines. In this paper we close this gap with the design of an algorithm that achieves the same sub-logarithmic complexity bound as theirs for *both* CC and DSM machines. Some additional advantages of our algorithm over Golab and Hendler's are:

(1) Our algorithm satisfies the Wait-Free Exit property.
(2) On a CC machine, Golab and Hendler's algorithm [5] requires a cache of size that is a function of n words at each process, but our algorithm needs a cache of only $O(1)$ words. (We explain the reason in the next subsection.)
(3) Our algorithm needs only the FAS instruction (whereas Golab and Hendler's [5] needs both FAS and CAS).
(4) Our algorithm eliminates the race conditions present in Golab and Hendler's algorithm [5] that cause processes to starve.[1] (We have described these issues in detail in Appendix A of the full version of this paper [9].)

1.4 Comparison to Golab and Hendler [5]: Similarities and differences

Golab and Hendler [5] derived their sublogarithmic RMR RME algorithm in the following two steps, of which the first step is the intellectual workhorse:

- The first step is the design of an RME algorithm, henceforth referred to as GH, of $O(n)$ passage complexity and $O(1+fn)$ super-passage complexity, where f is the number of times that a process crashes in the super-passage. The exciting implication of this result is that, in the common case where a process does not fail in a super-passage, the process incurs only $O(1)$ RMRs in the super-passage.
- The second step is the design of an RME algorithm where the n processes compete by working their way up on a tournament tree. This tree has n leaves and each of the tree nodes is implemented by an instance of GH in which $\log n/\log\log n$ processes compete. (thus, the degree of each node is $\log n/\log\log n$, which makes the height of the tree to be $O(\log n/\log\log n)$). The resulting algorithm has the desired $O(\frac{\log n}{\log\log n})$ passage complexity and $O((1+f)\frac{\log n}{\log\log n})$ super-passage complexity.

The GH algorithm is designed by converting the standard MCS algorithm [13] into a recoverable algorithm. As we now explain, this conversion is challenging because MCS uses the FAS instruction to insert a new node at the end of a queue. The queue has one node for each process waiting to enter the CS, and a shared variable Tail points to the last node in the queue. When a process π enters the Try section, it inserts its node x into the queue by performing FAS(Tail, x). The FAS instruction stores the pointer to x in Tail and returns Tail's previous value *prev* to π in a single atomic action. The value in *prev* is vital because it points to x's predecessor in the queue. Suppose that π now crashes, thereby losing the *prev* pointer. Further suppose that a few more processes enter the Try section and insert their nodes behind π's node x. If π now restarts, it cannot distinguish whether it crashed just before performing the FAS instruction or just after performing it. In the former case, π will have to perform FAS to insert its node, but in the latter case it would be disastrous for π to perform FAS since x was already inserted into the queue. Yet, there appears no easy way for π to distinguish which of the scenarios it is in. Notice further that, like π, many other processes might have failed just before or after their FAS, causing the queue to be disconnected into several fragments. All of these failed processes, upon restarting, have to go through the contents of the shared memory to recognize whether they are in the queue or not and, if they are in, piece together their fragment with other fragments without introducing circularity or other blemishes in the queue. Since concurrent "repairing" by multiple recovering processes can lead to races, Golab and Hendler make the recovering processes go through an RME algorithm RLock so that at most one recovering process is doing the repair at any time. This RLock does not have to be too efficient since it is executed by only a failing process, which can afford to perform $O(n)$ RMRs. Thus, this RLock can be implemented using one of the known RME algorithms. However, while a process is trying to repair, correct processes can be constantly changing the queue, thereby making the repair task even more challenging.

The broad outline of our algorithm is the same as what we have described above for GH, but our algorithm differs substantially in important technical details, as we explain below.

- In GH a recovering process raises a fail flag only after confirming that there is evidence that its FAS was successful.

[1] We communicated the issues described in Appendix A of the full version of this paper [9] with the authors of [5] who acknowledged the bugs and after a few weeks informed us that they were able to fix them.

This check causes GH to deadlock (see Scenario 1 in Appendix A of the full version of this paper [9]). Our algorithm eliminates this check.

- Since the shared memory can be constantly changing while a repairing process π is scanning the memory to compute the disjointed fragments (so as to connect π's fragment to another fragment), the precise order in which the memory contents are scanned can be crucial to algorithm's correctness. In fact, we found a race condition in GH that can lead to fragments being incorrectly pieced together: two different nodes can end up with the same predecessor, leading to all processes starving from some point on (see Scenario 2 in Appendix A of the full version of this paper [9]).
- When a repairing process explores from each node x, GH does a "deep" exploration, meaning that the process visits x's predecessor x_1, x_1's predecessor x_2, x_2's predecessor x_3, and so on until the chain is exhausted. Our algorithm instead does a shallow exploration: it simply visits x's predecessor and stops there. The deep exploration of GH from each of the n nodes leads to $O(n^2)$ local computation steps per passage and requires each process to have a large cache of $O(n)$ words in order to ensure the desired $O(n)$ passage-RMR-complexity. When we consider the sublogarithmic RMR RME algorithm by Golab and Hendler [5], which is implemented using instances of GH on which $\log n/\log\log n$ processes compete, every instance would still need a cache of size $O(\frac{\log n}{\log\log n})$. With our shallow exploration, we reduce the number of local steps per passage to $O(n)$ and the RMR complexity of $O(n)$ is achieved with a cache size of only $O(1)$ words.
- How an exiting process hands off the ownership of CS to the next waiting process is done differently in our algorithm so as to ensure a wait-free Exit section and eliminate the need for the CAS instruction. The design of the Exit section in our algorithm is motivated from Craig's algorithm [3] for mutual exclusion.

1.5 Related research

Beyond the works that we discussed above, Golab and Hendler [6] presented an algorithm at last year's PODC that has the ideal $O(1)$ passage complexity, but this result applies to a different model of system-wide crashes, where a crash means that *all* processes in the system *simultaneously* crash. Ramaraju [14] and Jayanti and Joshi [10] design RME algorithms that also satisfy the FCFS property [12]. These algorithms have $O(n)$ and $O(\log n)$ passage complexity, respectively. Recently, Jayanti and Joshi [11] designed an RME algorithm that has the abort capability. Attiya, Ben-Baruch, and Hendler present linearizable implementations of recoverable objects [1].

2 A SIGNAL OBJECT

Our main algorithm, presented in the next section, relies on a "Signal" object, which we specify and implement in this section. The Signal object is specified in Figure 1, which includes a description of two procedures — `set` and `wait` — through which the object is accessed.

2.1 An implementation of Signal Object

It is trivial to implement this object on a CC machine using a boolean variable Bit, initialized to `0`. To execute `set()`, a process writes 1 in Bit, and to execute `wait()`, a process simply loops until Bit has 1. With this implementation, both operations incur just $O(1)$ RMRs on a CC machine. Realizing $O(1)$ RMR complexity on a DSM machine is less trivial, especially because the identity of the process executing `wait()` is unknown to the process executing `set()`. Figure 2 describes our DSM implementation $\mathcal{X}$ of a Signal object X, which assumes that no two processes execute the `wait()` operation concurrently on the Signal object. Our implementation provides two procedures: $\mathcal{X}$.`set()` and $\mathcal{X}$.`wait()`. Process π executes $\mathcal{X}$.`set()` to perform X.`set()` and $\mathcal{X}$.`wait()` to perform X.`wait()`. Our implementation ensures that a call to $\mathcal{X}$.`set()` and $\mathcal{X}$.`wait()` incur only $O(1)$ RMR.

When π invokes $\mathcal{X}$.`set()`, at Line **1** it records for future $\mathcal{X}$.`wait()` calls that X.State = 1, hence those calls can return without waiting. Thereafter, π finds out if any process is already waiting for X.State to be set to 1. It does so by checking if any waiting process has supplied the address of its own local-spin variable to π on which it is waiting (Lines **2**-**3**). If π finds that a process is waiting (i.e., $addr_\pi \neq$ NIL), then it writes *true* into that process's spin-variable to wake it up from the wait loop (Line **4**).

When a process π' invokes $\mathcal{X}$.`wait()`, at Line **5** it creates a new local-spin variable that it hosts in its own memory partition (Line **5**). It initializes that variable for waiting (Line **6**) and notifies the object about its address (Line **7**) so that the caller of $\mathcal{X}$.`wait()` can wake π' up as described above. Then π' checks if Bit == 1 (Line **8**), in which case X.State = 1 already and π' can return without waiting. Otherwise, π' waits for $*go_{\pi'}$ to turn *true* (Line **9**).

Theorem 2.1. *$\mathcal{X}$.`set()` and $\mathcal{X}$.`wait()` described in Figure 2 implement a Signal object X (specified in Figure 1). Specifically, the implementation satisfies the following properties provided no two executions of $\mathcal{X}$.`wait()` are concurrent: (i) $\mathcal{X}$.`set()` is linearizable, i.e., there is a point in each execution of $\mathcal{X}$.`set()` when it appears to atomically set $\mathcal{X}$.State to 1, (ii) A process completes $\mathcal{X}$.`set()` in a bounded number of its own steps, (iii) When $\mathcal{X}$.`wait()` returns, $\mathcal{X}$.State is 1, (iv) Once $\mathcal{X}$.State becomes 1, any execution of $\mathcal{X}$.`wait()` by a process π completes in a bounded number of π's steps, (v) each execution of $\mathcal{X}$.`set()` and $\mathcal{X}$.`wait()` incurs $O(1)$ RMRs.*

3 A k-PORT RME ALGORITHM

In this section we present a k-port RME algorithm, similar to the one by Golab and Hendler [5]. This algorithm is later used as a building block in getting the sub-logarithmic RMR RME algorithm in Section 4. Like in [5], the algorithm has *k ports*, that allow upto k different processes out of the n processes in the system to use the lock concurrently. The correctness of the algorithm relies on

X.State $\in \{1, 0\}$, initially `0`.

- X.`set()` sets X.State to 1.
- X.`wait()` is a blocking operation that does not return until X.State is 1.

Figure 1: Specification of a Signal object X.

Shared variables (stored in NVMM)

BIT ∈ {1,0}, initially 0.

GOADDR is a **reference to a boolean**, initially NIL.

```
procedure X.set()
    BIT ← 1
    addr_π ← GOADDR
    if addr_π ≠ NIL then
        *addr_π ← true

procedure X.wait()
    go_π ← new Boolean
    *go_π ← false
    GOADDR ← go_π
    if BIT == 0 then
        wait till *go_π == true
```

Figure 2: Implementation of a Signal object specified in Figure 1. Code shown for a process π.

the assumption that there are no two concurrent passages on any port. The algorithm ensures that a process incurs $O(1)$ RMRs when it does not crash in its super-passage, but incurs $O(fk)$ RMRs if it crashes $f \geq 1$ times during its super-passage.

The k-port RME algorithm is presented in Figures 3-4. We assume that all shared variables are stored in the NVMM, and process local variables (subscripted by process name, which is π in the code) are stored in respective processor registers. We assume that the CS is an idempotent block of code, which allows a process to re-execute it from start even if the process crashes in the middle of the CS. As mentioned above, we assume that if a process uses a particular port during its super-passage in a run then no other process will use the same port during that super-passage. A process decides which port to use for a super-passage inside the Remainder section itself before starting with the super-passage, and the Remainder section ensures that the process does not change the port during that super-passage in case the process witnesses a crash. Hence, the algorithm presented in Figures 3-4 is designed for use by a process π on port p.

3.1 Crucial components of the algorithm and their purpose

We describe the crucial components that our algorithm relies on as follows, their usage will be clear in the algorithm description.

QNode: Our algorithm uses a queue structure as in the MCS lock [13] and QNode is the node type used in such a queue. However, we modify the node structure in the following ways to suit our needs. A node has three fields: PRED, NONNIL_SIGNAL, and CS_SIGNAL. The PRED field stores a reference to the node used by the predecessor of a process. It is also used as a checkpoint in the algorithm, hence, it may store one of the values in {NIL, &CRASH, &INCS, &EXIT}. NONNIL_SIGNAL and CS_SIGNAL are instances of Signal object described in Section 2. NONNIL_SIGNAL is used by repairing processes to wait on the owner of the node and CS_SIGNAL is used by a successor process to wait on the owner of the node before entering the CS.

RLOCK: The RLOCK is used by a crashed process to partially repair the broken queue. The RLOCK is itself a recoverable mutual exclusion algorithm, and we require that it satisfy the following constraints: (a) it should have $O(k)$ RMR complexity, and (b) it satisfy the Starvation freedom property (P3 in Section 1.2) in order for our algorithm to satisfy the Starvation freedom property. Golab and Ramaraju's [7] extension of Yang and Anderson's [18] read-write based algorithm is one such algorithm that satisfies these constraints (see Section 3.2 in [7] for more details), therefore we use it in our algorithm.

TAIL: This shared variable, like in the MCS algorithm [13], stores the address of the last node in the queue. However, the queue might be broken into several fragments during an execution due to simultaneous crashes by different active processes. In such case, TAIL points to the last node in one of those fragments.

NODE[p]: This is a reference to a QNode that is used by some process on port p to complete a super-passage. In essence NODE[p] binds a process π to the port p through the QNode π uses for its super-passage.

SPECIALNODE, CRASH, INCS, and EXIT: These are reserved QNode instances stored in NVMM. If the queue is empty and a process is recovering from a prior crash, then SPECIALNODE is used in recovery to start a new queue. We describe the use of this node later in the description of the algorithm. In the event of a crash, we use the value of the PRED pointer to determine the subsequent recovery procedure. Hence, CRASH, INCS, and EXIT act as a checkpoint in the algorithm and are pointed to by the PRED pointer of a process' QNode.

3.2 Informal description

The symbol & is the usual "address of" operator, prefixed to a shared object to obtain the address of that shared object. The symbol "." (dot) dereferences a pointer and accesses a field from the record pointed to by that pointer. When invoked on a path σ in a graph, the functions `start`(σ) and `end`(σ) return the start and end vertices of the path σ. We assume that a process π is in the Remainder section when PC_π = **10** and is in the CS when PC_π = **25**.

As discussed above, we modify the node structure in the following way to suit our needs. The node of a process π has, apart from a PRED pointer, two instances of a Signal object: CS_SIGNAL and NONNIL_SIGNAL. π's successor process will use the CS_SIGNAL instance from π's node to wait on π before entering the CS. The NONNIL_SIGNAL instance is used by any repairing process to wait till π sets the PRED pointer of its node to a value other than NIL. Every node has a unique instance of these Signal objects. We ensure that the call to CS_SIGNAL.`wait`() happens from a single predecessor and the call to NONNIL_SIGNAL.`wait`() is made in a mutually exclusive manner, thus ensuring that no two executions of `wait`() are concurrent on the same object instance.

Crash-free super-passage. We first describe how π would execute the Try and Exit section in the absence of a crash as follows. When a process π wants to enter the CS through port p from the Remainder section, it starts executing the Try section. At Line **10** it checks

Types

QNode = **record**{Pred : **reference to** QNode, NonNil_Signal : Signal object, CS_Signal : Signal object } **end record**

Shared objects (stored in NVMM)

Crash, InCS, and Exit are distinct QNode instances, such that,
Crash.Pred = &Crash, InCS.Pred = &InCS, and Exit.Pred = &Exit.

SpecialNode is a QNode instance, such that, SpecialNode.Pred = &Exit,
SpecialNode.NonNil_Signal.State = 1, and SpecialNode.CS_Signal.State = 1.

RLock is a k-ported starvation-free RME algorithm that incurs $O(k)$ RMR per passage on CC and DSM machines
(e.g. the arbitration tree RME algorithm from Section 3.2 of [7]).

Shared variables (stored in NVMM)

Tail is a **reference to** a QNode, initially &SpecialNode.

Node is an **array**$[0 \ldots k-1]$ of **reference to** QNode. Initially, $\forall i$, Node$[i]$ = NIL.

```
    Try Section
10. if Node[p] = NIL then
11.     mynode_π ← new QNode
12.     Node[p] ← mynode_π
13.     mypred_π ← FAS(Tail, mynode_π)
14.     mynode_π.Pred ← mypred_π
15.     mynode_π.NonNil_Signal.set()
16. else
17.     mynode_π ← Node[p]
18.     if mynode_π.Pred = NIL then mynode_π.Pred ← &Crash
19.     mypred_π ← mynode_π.Pred
20.     if mypred_π = &InCS then go to Critical Section else if mypred_π = &Exit then go to Line 26
21.     mynode_π.NonNil_Signal.set()
22.     Execute RLock
23. mypred_π.CS_Signal.wait()
24. mynode_π.Pred ← &InCS

    Exit Section
25. mynode_π.Pred ← &Exit
26. mynode_π.CS_Signal.set()
27. Node[p] ← NIL
```

Figure 3: k-ported n-process RME algorithm for CC and DSM machines. Code shown for a process π that uses port $p \in \{0, \ldots, k-1\}$. (Code continued in Figure 4.)

if its previous passage ended in a crash. Our algorithm maintains an invariant that Node$[p]$ = NIL, if that is not the case. Since we are considering a crash-free super-passage, at this point π finds Node$[p]$ = NIL. It then executes Line **11** which allocates a new QNode for π in the NVMM, such that the Pred pointer holds NIL, and the objects CS_Signal and NonNil_Signal have State = 0 (i.e., their initial values). At Line **12** π stores a reference to this new node in Node$[p]$ so that it can continue to reuse this node in the current super-passage in case of a crash. π then links itself to the queue by swapping $mynode_\pi$ into Tail (Line **13**) and stores the previous value of Tail (copied in $mypred_\pi$) into $mynode_\pi$.Pred (Line **14**). The value of $mypred_\pi$, from Line **13** onwards, is an address of π's predecessor's node. At Line **15** π announces that it has completed inserting itself in the queue by setting $mynode_\pi$.NonNil_Signal to 1 (we explain later why this announcement is important). π then proceeds to Line **23** where it waits for $mypred_\pi$.CS_Signal.State to become 1. If the owner of the node pointed by $mypred_\pi$ has already left the CS, then $mypred_\pi$.CS_Signal.State is 1; otherwise, π has to wait for a signal from its predecessor (see description of Signal object in previous section). Once π comes out of the call to $mypred_\pi$.CS_Signal.wait(), it makes a note in $mynode_\pi$.Pred that it has ownership of the CS (Line **24**). π then proceeds to the CS. When π completes the CS, it first makes a note to itself that it no longer needs the CS by writing &Exit in $mynode_\pi$.Pred (Line **25**). It then wakes up any successor process that might be waiting on π to enter the CS (Line **26**). π then writes NIL into Node$[p]$ at Line **27**, which signifies that the super-passage has completed.

Recovery from a crash. We now explain how the algorithm performs recovery, if a crash is encountered anywhere outside the Remainder section. When π begins a passage after the previous passage ended in a crash, π starts by checking Node$[p]$ at Line **10**. If it has the value NIL, then π crashed before it put itself in the queue, hence it treats the situation as if π didn't crash in the previous passage and continues as described above. Otherwise, π moves to Line **17** where it recovers the node it was using in the previous passage. If π crashed while putting itself in the queue (i.e., right before executing Lines **13** or **14**), it treats the crash as if it performed the FAS at Line **13** and crashed immediately. Hence, it makes a

Critical Section of RLock

28. **if** $mypred_\pi \neq$ &CRASH **then go to** Exit Section of RLock
29. $tail_\pi \leftarrow$ TAIL; $V_\pi \leftarrow \phi$; $E_\pi \leftarrow \phi$; $tailpath_\pi \leftarrow$ NIL; $headpath_\pi \leftarrow$ NIL
30. **for** $i_\pi \leftarrow 0$ **to** $k-1$
31. $cur_\pi \leftarrow$ NODE$[i_\pi]$
32.   **if** $cur_\pi =$ NIL **then continue**
33. cur_π.NONNIL_SIGNAL.wait()
34. $curpred_\pi \leftarrow cur_\pi$.PRED
35.   **if** $curpred_\pi \in$ {&CRASH, &INCS, &EXIT} **then** $V_\pi \leftarrow V_\pi \cup \{cur_\pi\}$
36.   **else** $V_\pi \leftarrow V_\pi \cup \{cur_\pi, curpred_\pi\}$; $E_\pi \leftarrow E_\pi \cup \{(cur_\pi, curpred_\pi)\}$
37. Compute the set $Paths_\pi$ of maximal paths in the graph (V_π, E_π)
38. Let $mypath_\pi$ be the unique path in $Paths_\pi$ that contains $mynode_\pi$
39. **if** $tail_\pi \in V_\pi$ **then** let $tailpath_\pi$ be the unique path in $Paths_\pi$ that contains $tail_\pi$
40. **for each** $\sigma_\pi \in Paths_\pi$
41.   **if** end(σ_π).PRED $\in$ {&INCS, &EXIT} **then**
42.   **if** start(σ_π).PRED $\neq$ &EXIT **then**
43. $headpath_\pi \leftarrow \sigma_\pi$
44. **if** $tailpath_\pi =$ NIL $\vee$ end$(tailpath_\pi)$.PRED $\in$ {&INCS, &EXIT} **then**
45. $mypred_\pi \leftarrow$ **FAS**(TAIL, start$(mypath_\pi)$)
46. **else if** $headpath_\pi \neq$ NIL **then** $mypred_\pi \leftarrow$ start$(headpath_\pi)$ **else** $mypred_\pi \leftarrow$ &SPECIALNODE
47. $mynode_\pi$.PRED $\leftarrow mypred_\pi$

Figure 4: (Code continued from Figure 3.) k-ported n-process recoverable mutual exclusion algorithm for CC and DSM machines. Code shown for a process π that uses port $p \in \{0, \ldots, k-1\}$. Vertex names in V_π are node references, hence the "." symbol dereferences the address and accesses the members of the node. The functions start(σ) and end(σ) used at Lines 41, 42, 44-46 return the start and end vertices of the path σ.

note to itself that it crashed by writing &CRASH in $mynode_\pi$.PRED (Line **18**). It then reads the value of $mynode_\pi$.PRED into $mypred_\pi$ (Line **19**). At Line **20** π first checks if it crashed while in the CS, in which case it moves to the CS. Otherwise, it checks if it already completed executing the CS in current super-passage and crashed while executing the Exit section. In that case π goes to the Exit section and starts executing at Line **26**. If π reached Line **21**, it is clear that it crashed before entering the CS in the previous passage. In that case repairing the queue might be needed if π didn't set $mynode_\pi$.PRED to point to a predecessor node. In any case, π announces that $mynode_\pi$.PRED no longer has the value NIL (because it either has a value pointing to a predecessor node or it was set to &CRASH at Line **18**) by setting $mynode_\pi$.NONNIL_SIGNAL.STATE to 1. π then goes on to capture RLock so that it gets exclusive access to repair the queue, if it is broken at its node.

High level view of repairing the queue after a crash. Before diving into the code commentary of the CS of RLock, where π repairs the queue broken at its end, we describe how the repairing happens at a high level. Please refer to Figure 5 for a visual illustration of our description below. π uses the RLock to repair the queue, if it crashed around the FAS operation (Lines **13-14**) in the Try section. A crash by a process on Lines **13-14** can give rise to the following scenarios: (i) the queue is not affected by the crash (crash at Line **13** or at Line **14** but the queue was already broken), (ii) the queue is broken due to the crash (crash at Line **14**). Therefore consider the following configuration. Process π_1, π_3, and π_5 have crashed at Line **14**. Process π_2, π_4, and π_6 are executing the procedure wait() at Line **23**, such that, π_2's predecessor is π_1, π_4's predecessor is π_3, and π_6's predecessor is π_5. Process π_7 and π_8 have crashed at Line **13**. We describe the repair by each of these crashed processes as follows.

Each of the crashed processes executes the RLock and waits for its turn to repair the queue in a mutually exclusive manner. Assume that the repair is performed by the processes in the order: $(\pi_1, \pi_7, \pi_5, \pi_8, \pi_3)$. When π_1 performs the repair, it first scans the NODE array and notices that the queue is broken at process π_3 and π_5's nodes (it notices that by reading &CRASH in the PRED pointer of the process nodes). NODE array also gives an illusion to π_1 that queue is broken at π_7 and π_8's node although these processes didn't perform a FAS prior to their crash. π_1 also notices that no node has a predecessor node whose PRED pointer is set to &INCS or &EXIT, hence, no process is in the CS or is poised to enter it. Therefore π_1 sets its own node's predecessor to be SPECIALNODE (from Figure 3, SPECIALNODE.PRED = &EXIT). Note, no other crashed process will set their own node's PRED pointer to point to SPECIALNODE simultaneously because repair operation is performed in a mutually exclusive manner by π_1. Also, the PRED pointer of each node has a non-NIL value (otherwise, π_1 waits till it sees a non-NIL value before doing the actual repair). This way π_1 completes the repair operation on the queue and is now poised to enter the CS, which it does enter upon returning to the Try section.

When π_7 (crashed at Line **13**) performs the repair, it first scans the NODE array and notices that the queue is broken at process π_3, π_5, π_7, and π_8's nodes. Since it notices that no process points to π_2, it sets the PRED pointer of its own node to point to π_2's node. Thereby π_7 finishes the repair by placing itself in the queue, without ever performing the FAS. It then gives up its control over RLock to return to Line **23** in Try section.

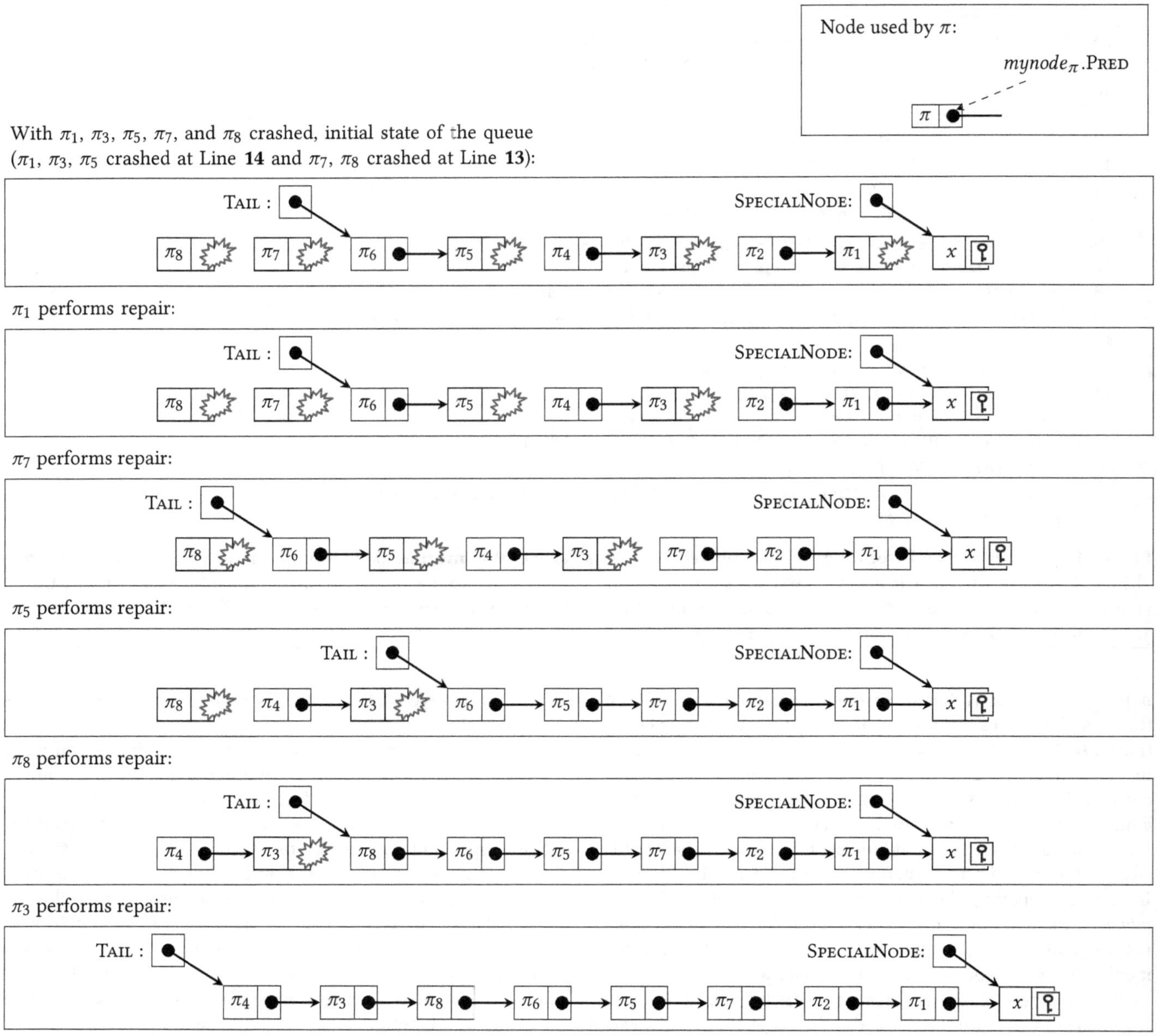

Figure 5: Queue states after repair is performed by different processes in a sequence. Explosion symbol in place of a PRED pointer on a node denotes the said process has crashed without updating the PRED pointer of its node.

When π_5 (crashed at Line **14**) performs the repair, it follows an approach similar to that of π_7's. It sees that the queue is broken at process π_3, π_5, and π_8. It then notices that no process points to π_7 and therefore sets the PRED pointer of its own node to point to π_7's node. This way π_5 and π_6 are now attached to the queue in a way that there is a path from their node to a node containing the address &EXIT. Also, TAIL points to π_6's node, so it appears as if the queue is unbroken if a traversal was done starting at the TAIL pointer.

Now that a traversal from TAIL would lead to a node used by a process that is in Critical section (π_1 in this case), the queue is partially in place. In order to fix the remaining broken fragments the queue might need to be broken somehow to fit the remaining fragments. However, π_3 and π_8 can do the repair from here on without affecting the existing structure of the queue. π_8 can put itself in the queue by performing the FAS operation on the TAIL with its own node. Whereas π_3 first identifies the fragment its node is part of, and thereby all the nodes that are part of its fragment. It then performs a FAS one more time on TAIL with the last node in its own fragment (i.e., π_4's node) and sets the PRED pointer of its own node to the previous value of TAIL that is returned by the

FAS (address of π_8's node). This ends the repair operation for π_3 and thereby the repair for all the process.

Informal description of CS of RLOCK. We proceed to give a description of the CS of RLOCK that does the above mentioned repair. At Line **28** π checks if it was already in the queue before its last crash (such a situation may occur either when π crashes after executing the CS of RLOCK to completion but before executing the Exit section of RLOCK, or when π crashes in the Try after performing Line **14**). If so, it notices that there is no need for repair, hence, it goes to the Exit section of RLOCK. Otherwise, at Line **29** π reads the reference to the node pointed to by TAIL into the variable $tail_\pi$ and initializes other variables used during the repair procedure. Thereafter π constructs a graph that models the queue structure. To this purpose, it reads each node pointed to by the NODE array in order to construct the graph (Lines **30-36**). The graph is constructed as follows. First a cell from the NODE array is read into cur_π (i.e., NODE$[i_\pi]$) at Line **31** and checked if it is a node of some process (Line **32**). If NODE$[i_\pi]$ = NIL, π moves on to the next cell in the array. Otherwise, at Line **33** π waits till NODE$[i_\pi]$.PRED assumes a non-NIL value (i.e., wait for the owner of that node to have executed either Line **15** or **21**). Once cur_π's PRED pointer has a non-NIL value, that value is read into $curpred_\pi$ (Line **34**). There are now two possibilities: (i) the PRED pointer points to one of &CRASH, &INCS, or &EXIT, or (ii) the PRED pointer points to another node. The purpose of waiting for cur_π.NONNIL_SIGNAL.STATE to become 1 is simple: we want to be sure which of the above two cases is true about cur_π. In the first case only cur_π is added as a vertex to the graph (the name of that vertex is the value of cur_π). In the second case cur_π and $curpred_\pi$ are added as vertices and a directed edge $(cur_\pi, curpred_\pi)$ is added to the graph (we consider this as a simple graph, so repeated addition of a vertex counts as adding it once). This process is repeated until all cells from the NODE array are read. Once all the nodes are read from the cells of NODE array, including nodes not yet in the queue (π_7 and π_8 in the above example), we have the graph (V_π, E_π) that models the broken queue structure such that each maximal path in the graph models a broken queue fragment. Note, such a graph is a directed acyclic graph. At Line **37** set $Paths_\pi$ of maximal paths in the graph (V_π, E_π) is created and at Line **38** a path $mypath_\pi$ is picked from $Paths_\pi$ such that $mynode_\pi$ appears in it. At Line **39** a path $tailpath_\pi$ containing the node $tail_\pi$ is picked from $Paths_\pi$, if $tail_\pi$ appears in the graph. In Lines **40-43** we try to find a path in the graph such that its start vertex belongs to a process that has not finished the critical section but a traversal on that path leads to a node holding one of the addresses &INCS or &EXIT (i.e., it leads to a node in or out of CS). If such a path is found, $headpath_\pi$ is set to point to that path, otherwise, $headpath_\pi$ remains NIL. In Line **44** we first check if the queue is already partially repaired (e.g., if the repair was being performed by π_8 or π_3 in the example above). If so, at Line **45** the fragment containing $mynode_\pi$ is inserted into the queue by performing a FAS on TAIL with the last node in that fragment (i.e., `start`($mypath_\pi$) would give the address of last node appearing in $mynode_\pi$'s fragment). We store the previous value of TAIL into $mypred_\pi$ so that we can update $mynode_\pi$.PRED later. Otherwise, π needs to connect its own fragment to the queue. To this purpose it needs to be ensured that the queue is not broken at its head and some active process is poised to enter or is in the Critical section. Line **46** does this by checking if Lines **40-43** found a path in the graph such that its start vertex belongs to a process that has not finished the Critical section but a traversal on that path leads to a node out of CS (i.e., is $headpath_\pi \neq$ NIL). If $headpath_\pi \neq$ NIL, then π's predecessor is set to be the start node on the path $headpath_\pi$ (π_7, π_5 in the example above). Otherwise, the queue is broken at its head, therefore, at Line **46**, π's predecessor is set to be SPECIALNODE (π_1 in example above). At Line **47**, π has the correct address to its predecessor node in $mypred_\pi$ (as noted in Lines **44-46**) which is written into $mynode_\pi$.PRED. This completes the CS of RLOCK and the repair of π's fragment. π then proceeds back to Line **23** after completing the Exit section of RLOCK.

Correctness. The correctness properties of the algorithm are captured in the following theorem.

THEOREM 3.1. *The algorithm in Figures 3-4 solves the RME problem for k ports on CC and DSM machines and satisfies properties P1-P6 described in Section 1.2. It has an RMR complexity of $O(1)$ for a process that does not crash during its passage, and $O(fk)$ for a process that crashes $f \geq 1$ times during its super-passage.*

4 $O((1 + f) \log n / \log \log n)$ RMRS ALGORITHM

To obtain a sub-logarithmic RMR complexity algorithm on both CC and DSM machines, we use the arbitration tree technique as used by Golab and Hendler (described in Section 5 in [5]). In this technique a tree is constructed in such a way that it has a height of $\Theta(k)$ and degree of k, where $k = \lceil \log n / \log \log n \rceil$, and n leaves. Each internal node in such a tree is an instance of the k port RME lock described in Section 3. Each process is bound to a leaf node of the tree. To enter the CS a process traverses the path from its leaf node up to the root node by executing the Try sections of the RME locks it encounters on the way. Hence, as the process traverses the path by accessing a node from its jth child, the process uses the jth port to access the RME lock on that node. When it is time to give up its ownership of the CS, the process traverses the same path in the reverse order and executes the Exit sections of the locks it encounters on the way. Hence, from the above and Theorem 3.1, the following theorem follows.

THEOREM 4.1. *The arbitration tree algorithm solves the RME problem for n processes on CC and DSM machines and satisfies properties P1-P6 described in Section 1.2. It has an RMR complexity of $O((1+f) \log n / \log \log n)$ per super-passage for a process that crashes $f \geq 0$ times during its super-passage.*

REFERENCES

[1] Hagit Attiya, Ohad Ben-Baruch, and Danny Hendler. 2018. Nesting-Safe Recoverable Linearizability: Modular Constructions for Non-Volatile Memory. In *Proceedings of the 2018 ACM Symposium on Principles of Distributed Computing*. ACM, 7–16.

[2] Hagit Attiya, Danny Hendler, and Philipp Woelfel. 2008. Tight RMR Lower Bounds for Mutual Exclusion and Other Problems. In *Proc. of the Fortieth ACM Symposium on Theory of Computing (STOC '08)*. ACM, New York, NY, USA, 217–226.

[3] Travis S. Craig. 1993. *Building FIFO and Priority-Queuing Spin Locks from Atomic Swap*. Technical Report TR-93-02-02. Department of Computer Science, University of Washington.

[4] Rotem Dvir and Gadi Taubenfeld. 2017. Mutual exclusion algorithms with constant RMR complexity and wait-free exit code. In *Proceedings of The 21st International Conference on Principles of Distributed Systems (OPODIS 2017)*.

[5] Wojciech Golab and Danny Hendler. 2017. Recoverable Mutual Exclusion in Sub-logarithmic Time. In *Proceedings of the ACM Symposium on Principles of Distributed Computing (PODC '17)*. ACM, New York, NY, USA, 211–220.

[6] Wojciech Golab and Danny Hendler. 2018. Recoverable Mutual Exclusion Under System-Wide Failures. In *Proceedings of the 2018 ACM Symposium on Principles of Distributed Computing (PODC '18)*. ACM, New York, NY, USA, 17–26.

[7] Wojciech Golab and Aditya Ramaraju. 2016. Recoverable Mutual Exclusion: [Extended Abstract]. In *Proceedings of the 2016 ACM Symposium on Principles of Distributed Computing (PODC '16)*. ACM, New York, NY, USA, 65–74.

[8] Prasad Jayanti, Siddhartha Jayanti, and Anup Joshi. 2018. Optimal Recoverable Mutual Exclusion using only FASAS. In *The 6th Edition of The International Conference on Networked Systems (NETYS 2018)*.

[9] Prasad Jayanti, Siddhartha V. Jayanti, and Anup Joshi. 2019. A Recoverable Mutex Algorithm with Sub-logarithmic RMR on Both CC and DSM. *CoRR* abs/1904.02124 (2019). arXiv:1904.02124 http://arxiv.org/abs/1904.02124

[10] Prasad Jayanti and Anup Joshi. 2017. Recoverable FCFS mutual exclusion with wait-free recovery. In *31st International Symposium on Distributed Computing (DISC 2017)*. 30:1–30:15.

[11] Prasad Jayanti and Anup Joshi. 2019. Recoverable Mutual Exclusion with Abortability. In *Accepted for publication in NETYS' 19*.

[12] Leslie Lamport. 1974. A New Solution of Dijkstra's Concurrent Programming Problem. *Commun. ACM* 17, 8 (Aug. 1974), 453–455.

[13] John M. Mellor-Crummey and Michael L. Scott. 1991. Algorithms for Scalable Synchronization on Shared-memory Multiprocessors. *ACM Trans. Comput. Syst.* 9, 1 (Feb. 1991), 21–65.

[14] Aditya Ramaraju. 2015. *RGLock: Recoverable mutual exclusion for non-volatile main memory systems*. Master's thesis. University of Waterloo. https://uwspace.uwaterloo.ca/handle/10012/9473

[15] Simone Raoux, Geoffrey W Burr, Matthew J Breitwisch, Charles T Rettner, Yi-Chou Chen, Robert M Shelby, Martin Salinga, Daniel Krebs, Shih-Hung Chen, Hsiang-Lan Lung, et al. 2008. Phase-change random access memory: A scalable technology. *IBM Journal of Research and Development* 52, 4/5 (2008), 465.

[16] Dmitri B Strukov, Gregory S Snider, Duncan R Stewart, and R Stanley Williams. 2008. The missing memristor found. *nature* 453, 7191 (2008), 80.

[17] Saied Tehrani, Jon M Slaughter, Mark Deherrera, Brad N Engel, Nicholas D Rizzo, Jonn Salter, Mark Durlam, Renu W Dave, Jason Janesky, Brian Butcher, et al. 2003. Magnetoresistive random access memory using magnetic tunnel junctions. *Proc. IEEE* 91, 5 (2003), 703–714.

[18] Jae-Heon Yang and Jams H. Anderson. 1995. A fast, scalable mutual exclusion algorithm. *Distributed Computing* 9, 1 (1995), 51–60.

Randomized Concurrent Set Union and Generalized Wake-Up

Siddhartha Jayanti*
సిద్ధార్థ జయంతి
jayanti@mit.edu
MIT

Robert E. Tarjan†
prof.tarjan@gmail.com
Princeton University
Intertrust Technologies

Enric Boix-Adserà‡
eboix@mit.edu
MIT

ABSTRACT

We consider the disjoint set union problem in the asynchronous shared memory multiprocessor computation model. We design a randomized algorithm that performs at most $O(\log n)$ work per operation (with high probability), and performs at most $O(m \cdot (\alpha(n, m/(np)) + \log(np/m + 1))$ total work in expectation for a problem instance with m operations on n elements solved by p processes. Our algorithm is the first to have work bounds that grow sublinearly with p against an adversarial scheduler.

We use Jayanti's Wake Up problem and our newly defined *Generalized Wake Up* problem to prove several lower bounds on concurrent set union. We show an $\Omega(\log \min\{n, p\})$ expected work lower bound on the cost of any single operation on a set union algorithm. This shows that our single-operation upper bound is optimal across all algorithms when $p = n^{\Omega(1)}$. Furthermore, we identify a class of "symmetric algorithms" that captures the complexities of all the known algorithms for the disjoint set union problem, and prove an $\Omega(m \cdot (\alpha(n, m/(np)) + \log(np/m + 1)))$ expected total work lower bound on algorithms of this class, thereby showing that our algorithm has optimal total work complexity for this class. Finally, we prove that any randomized algorithm, symmetric or not, cannot breach an $\Omega(m \cdot (\alpha(n, m/n) + \log\log(np/m + 1)))$ expected total work lower bound.

CCS CONCEPTS

• **Theory of computation → Concurrent algorithms; Data structures design and analysis; Shared memory algorithms.**

KEYWORDS

disjoint set union, union find, concurrent, asynchronous, data structure, linearizable, wait free, lower bound, Jayanti's wake up

*I am grateful to the Department of Defense (DoD) for their support through the National Defense Science & Engineering Graduate Fellowship (NDSEG) Program.
†Paritally supported by an innovation research grant from Princeton University and a gift from Microsoft.
‡Supported by a MIT Lemelson Engineering Presidential Fellowship.

PODC '19, July 29-August 2, 2019, Toronto, ON, Canada

ACM ISBN 978-1-4503-6217-7/19/07...$15.00
https://doi.org/10.1145/3293611.3331593

ACM Reference Format:
Siddhartha Jayanti, Robert E. Tarjan, and Enric Boix-Adserà. 2019. Randomized Concurrent Set Union and Generalized Wake-Up. In *2019 ACM Symposium on Principles of Distributed Computing (PODC '19), July 29-August 2, 2019, Toronto, ON, Canada.* ACM, New York, NY, USA, 10 pages. https://doi.org/10.1145/3293611.3331593

1 INTRODUCTION

As data sets get bigger and bigger, it becomes more and more important to harness the potential of parallelism to solve computational problems—even linear time is too slow. In the late twentieth century, many beautiful and efficient algorithms were developed in the PRAM (parallel random access machine) model, which assumes a memory shared among many synchronized processors. In practice, however, synchronization is expensive or may not be possible. A weaker model that has attracted much attention in the distributed systems community is the APRAM (asynchronous parallel random access machine) model, in which a common memory is shared among many unsynchronized processors. In the most general version of this model, any processor can be arbitrarily slow compared to any other.

Obtaining efficiency bounds in the asynchronous model is extremely challenging: the use of locks, for example, seems to make it impossible to guarantee efficiency, since one process could set a lock and then go to sleep indefinitely, blocking progress by any other process that needs access to the same resource. To overcome this problem, systems researchers have invented synchronization primitives that do not use locks, notably CAS (compare and swap) [11], transactional memory [12], and others. These primitives allow at least the possibility of obtaining good efficiency bounds for asynchronous concurrent algorithms. Yet, except for "embarrassingly parallel" computations, this possibility is almost unrealized. Obtaining concurrent algorithms with only small per-operation overheads in the number of processes is a major research goal in distributed data structures. However, efficient algorithms for objects as simple as counters require clever ideas in the face of asynchrony [6, 16], and the exact complexities of data structures as fundamental as stacks, queues, and priority queues remain unknown.

An important problem in data structures that could benefit from an efficient concurrent algorithm is disjoint *set union*, also known as the *union-find* problem. The simplest version of this problem requires maintaining a collection of disjoint sets, each containing a unique element called its representative, under three operations:

- FIND(x): return the representative of the set containing element x.
- SAMESET(x, y): return true if x and y are currently in the same set and false otherwise.

- UNITE(x, y): if elements x and y are in different sets, unite these sets into a single set and designate some element in the new set to be its representative; otherwise, do nothing.

Initially, each element x is in a singleton set whose representative is x. The implementation is free to choose the representative of each new set produced by a unite.

Applications of disjoint set union include storage allocation in compilers [19], finding minimum spanning trees using Kruskal's algorithm [18], maintaining the connected components of an undirected graph under edge additions, testing percolation [21], finding loops and dominators in flow graphs [7], and finding strong components in directed graphs. Some of these applications are generally performed on immense graphs, notably finding connected components and finding strong components [3, 4, 21]. In particular, model checking requires finding strong components in huge, implicitly defined directed graphs [3, 4]. There are sequential linear-time strong components algorithms [22], but the model-checking application could potentially benefit from an even faster algorithm. The sequential algorithms use depth-first search [22], which apparently cannot be efficiently parallelized [20]. If one had an efficient concurrent disjoint set union algorithm one could use it in combination with breadth-first search to potentially speed up model checking. This application, described to the second author by Leslie Lamport, was the original motivation for our work.

The classical sequential algorithm for the disjoint set union problem is the compressed tree data structure [23, 24]. With appropriate tree linking and path compaction rules, m operations on sets containing a total of n elements take $O(m \cdot \alpha(n, m/n))$ time [23, 24], where α is a functional inverse of Ackermann's function, defined in Section 3. Three linking rules that suffice are linking by size [23], linking by rank [24], and linking by random index [10]; three compaction rules that suffice are compression [23], splitting [24], and halving [24]. The set union algorithm obtained by combining any of these linking and compaction rules has asymptotically optimal amortized time complexity for the sequential problem; this was proved by Fredman and Saks [8].

There have been two significant works on the concurrent set union problem. While both works have significant ideas that have propelled our work, they contain flaws that reveal the subtlety of the problem and the difficulty in analyzing even simple tree data structure manipulations in a concurrent shared memory system.

The goal of designing a concurrent set union algorithm is to prove an amortized per-operation work bound that is as close to the sequential work bound as possible. The amortized work bounds for all the algorithms we discuss in this paper are of the form $O(\alpha(n, \cdot)+\Delta(p))$. Here, the *inverse-Ackerman term*, $\alpha(n, \cdot)$, is nearly equal to the $\alpha(n, \frac{m}{n})$ term that is optimal for the sequential case. The extra additive term $\Delta(p)$ is called the *concurrency overhead*, since it represents the extra work per operation that is needed by the data structure in order to support concurrent access by the p processes. Since the inverse-Ackermann term is almost constant, a single process running an optimal sequential set union algorithm can do $\Theta(1/\alpha(n, \frac{m}{n})) \approx \Theta(1)$ operations in a unit of time. In the concurrent case, the work complexity of the data structure is approximately proportional to $\Delta(p)$ if we ignore inverse-Ackermann terms. Thus, if p processes are using the data structure together, and we consider the ideal case where they each run at approximately the same speed as a single uniprocessor, they can perform about $\Theta(p/\Delta(p))$ operations in unit time. So, we define $p/\Delta(p)$ as the *speed-up* of a concurrent algorithm, and hope to use algorithms where $\Delta(p)$ is at most polylogarithmic to get near-linear speed-ups that facilitate the possibility of fast parallel algorithms. (For some algorithms the function $\Delta(\cdot)$ can also depend on m and n for technical reasons; we have simply omitted these parameters here to emphasize the semantic meaning of the term.)

Anderson and Woll were the first to define and attempt the concurrent version of the set union problem [1]. They set up a framework to facilitate turning compressed tree sequential algorithms into concurrent algorithms, and developed a concurrent solution to the set union problem that combines linking by rank with a concurrent version of path halving. In their problem formulation, they note that many applications of the set union data structure benefit from having a SAMESET(x, y) operation that returns whether x and y are in the same set. A highlight of their work was a succinct algorithm that reduces SAMESET to FIND while cleverly avoiding possible errors due to concurrency. Both Jayanti and Tarjan's algorithm (discussed next) and our present work use Anderson and Woll's original SAMESET algorithm, whose pseudo-code is in Appendix A. The amortized and worst-case work complexities of SAMESET are identical to those of UNITE in the case of each of the algorithms. Anderson and Woll claimed an amortized $\Theta(\alpha(m, 1)+p)$ work bound, corresponding to a linear concurrency overhead of $\Delta(p) = p$. Unfortunately, the proof of their upper bound is incomplete, since they try to reduce to the sequential algorithm's proof without accounting for interference among different processes doing halving on intersecting paths. Their analysis describes in detail how their algorithm can create equal rank chains of length $\Omega(p)$, and thus how their algorithm can require $\Omega(np)$ work to do $n - 1$ unite operations. Thus in the worst case their algorithm gives no speed-up. This sparked further research into the problem.

While Anderson and Woll attempted to parallelize the deterministic compressed trees algorithm that links by rank and does compaction by path halving, Jayanti and Tarjan instead chose to work on linking by random index and compaction by splitting [17]. The change in linking method is key to their work. In their algorithm, the n nodes of the set union object are given randomized indices, i.e. a random permutation of the natural numbers from 1 through n, in the preprocessing phase. They assume that the adversary does not know this random permutation. They use the simple linking rule that links a node of a smaller index under a node of a larger index. Jayanti and Tarjan do not analyze their algorithm under an adversarial scheduler. Rather, they define a particular type of scheduler that guarantees that the linearization order of set union operations performed by the processes is independent of the schedule. Unfortunately, even an oblivious scheduler, or more simply a scheduler that gives processes turns in rounds, does not necessarily satisfy this property. They claimed a work bound of $O(m \cdot (\alpha(n, m/(np)) + \log(np/m + 1)))$ if the schedule is of the correct type, which would reduce $\Delta(p)$ to $\log(p)$ for this class of schedules. Unfortunately their attempt to account for interference during concurrent splits has a subtle error. Correcting it results in the slightly worse bound of $O(m(\alpha(n, m/(np^2)) + \log(np^2/m + 1)))$, that still gives $\Delta(p) = \log(p)$. We believe this bound is tight for their algorithm. If the scheduler is adversarial, however, there are sequences of $O(n)$ operations that take $\Omega(np^{1/2})$ expected work, making the speed-up for this algorithm at best the square root of the number of processes.

In this paper, we develop the first algorithm for union-find that provably gives speed-up under adversarial scheduling. In fact, our algorithm gives near-linear speed-up. An initial hope would be to design an algorithm with no concurrency overhead (i.e. $\Delta(p) \equiv 0$). However, we prove that this is impossible by giving many shared memory step complexity lower bounds for the set union problem. A main contribution of our paper is a proof that $\Delta(p) = \Omega(\log\log \frac{np}{m})$. Furthermore, we give compelling evidence that an even stronger lower bound may hold for the problem, by showing that there is an $\Omega(\log \min\{n,p\} + \log(n)/\log\log(n))$ lower bound on worst-case work complexity, and for the large class of *symmetric algorithms*—a class that includes all known set union algorithms and techniques to parallelize sequential algorithms a stronger $\Omega(\alpha(n, m/(np)) + \log(np/m+1))$ lower bound on amortized work complexity. Thus, the goal is to design an algorithm with $\Delta(p) = \log(np/m)$. A highlight of our paper is the design and analysis of a randomized symmetric algorithm that has an expected work complexity of $\Theta(\alpha(n, m/(np)) + \log(np/m+1))$, matching the lower bound. Furthermore, with high probability the worst-case work complexity of a single set union operation for the algorithm is $O(\log n)$, which is optimal if $p = n^{\varepsilon}$ for any constant ε and at most a factor of $\log\log(n)$ away from optimality regardless of p. A sequential algorithm of Blum shows that set union operations can be done in at most $O(\log(n)/\log\log(n))$ if $p = 1$ [5].

Our lower bound proofs introduce a novel technique, which we call the *generalized wake-up technique*, for proving lower bounds on the *amortized* complexities of operations on linearizable data types that are built from primitive variables supporting read, write, and compare-and-swap (CAS). Our technique is developed by generalizing *Jayanti's wake-up problem*, and extending his lower bound analysis to our generalized version of the problem [15]. As we show in the paper, our technique is general and gives amortized lower bounds on the complexities of several other data types along with set union. In particular, we also obtain the following two results:

(1) Define an r-relaxed counter as a fetch-and-increment object whose "fetch" returns a value that is within an additive r of the correct counter value. Then m operations on a $((1-\varepsilon)p/2)$-relaxed counter take $\Omega(m \log p)$ steps in the worst case.

Remark: Our lower bound shows that Ellen and Woelfel's implementation of fetch-and-increment [6] and Jayanti's implementation of a counter [16] have optimal amortized step complexity. Furthermore, the $\Omega(\log p)$ overhead for counting in an asynchronous system holds even for randomized algorithms, and even if the counter needs to be only approximately accurate.

(2) Define an r-relaxed priority queue as an object that returns one of the top r items in priority order. For $r > 1$, this is a relaxation of the standard priority queue–which corresponds to the 1-relaxed priority queue. Then m *deleteMin* operations on a $((1-\varepsilon)p)$-relaxed priority queue take $\Omega(m \log p)$ steps in the worst case. We also prove analagous results for the r-relaxed stack and r-relaxed queue objects.

The remainder of our paper consists of four sections and the appendices. Section 2 contains a description of the shared-memory model. Section 3 motivates and defines the generalized wake up problem, and proves our lower bounds. Section 4 presents our algorithm for the set union problem. We end with some remarks and open problems in Section 5.

2 CONCURRENCY MODEL

We consider the shared memory asynchronous multiprocessor model of computing with p processes $P = \pi_1, \ldots, \pi_p$ that run concurrently. We assume that each process π_i has access to both a (small) private memory and the collective shared memory. We assume that the size of shared memory words is $O(\log n)$ bits, where n is the number of nodes in the data structure. Asynchronicity is modeled by an adversarial scheduler. We call a process *active* if it is currently executing instructions. At each time step t of the asynchronous system, the scheduler gets to adversarially pick which active process it would like to allocate the next step to. This decision can be based on the current state of shared memory, process program counters, and past randomness, but not on future randomness. The resultant time indexed sequence σ of which process got to execute at which time steps is called the *schedule*. The *history* of a process π_i up to time t is the entire sequence of operations performed by π_i and return values received by π_i up to time t. In particular, if the history of a particular process π_i is the same if t_1 steps of algorithm A are executed under schedule σ_1 or if t_2 steps of algorithm A are executed under schedule σ_2, then the two scenarios are *indistinguishable* to π_i. The notion of indistinguishability is key to impossibility results.

To provide synchronization of writes to shared memory, we use the atomic compare and swap primitive CAS(x, a, b). Given the address x of a word in shared memory and two values a and b, the CAS operation tests whether word x holds value a; if so, it stores value b in word x (overwriting a) and returns true; if not, it returns false. In general, we allow values written to shared memory via a regular write or CAS operation to include random bits. We use \$ to symbolize a random bit in our pseudo-code.

We are interested in concurrent algorithms for set union that are *linearizable* [13] and *bounded wait-free* [11, 13]. To be linearizable means that (i) the outcome of a concurrent execution is the same as if each set operation were executed instantaneously at some distinct time (its *linearization point*) during its actual execution and (ii) the sequential execution sequence given by the linearization points is correct; that is, all find operations produce answers that are correct at their linearization points. The linearization points define a total order of the operations, called the *linearization order*. To be bounded wait-free means that every operation finishes in a bounded number of its own steps.

We measure the efficiency of algorithms using two different but very related metrics. The *work complexity*, or simply *work*, done by a concurrent algorithm is the total number of primitive instructions done by all processes to complete all operations. The *step complexity* is defined almost identically, but only counts *shared memory* instructions. The *amortized work* of an algorithm is its total work divided by the total number of operations started across all processes. The *amortized step complexity* is defined analogously. Since the work complexity is always bounded below by the step complexity, upper bounds on work complexities and lower bounds on step complexities are the strongest results. When analyzing our algorithms, we will use the convention that m is the number of operations, n is the number of nodes, and p is the number of processes. In general, we assume that $m \geq n/2$—every node is part of some operation, and $m \geq p$—there is at least one operation per process.

We call an algorithm *symmetric* if it satisfies the following three properties: (1) data structure operations have the same code for all processes, i.e. the code does not depend on process IDs; (2) all random bits used by a process are written directly to shared memory via a write or CAS; (3) the algorithm does not use the (true/false) return values of CAS operations. This class of algorithms is of particular interest to us, since it captures the complexity of all known algorithms for the set union problem in the following sense. The algorithms of Anderson and Woll and Jayanti and Tarjan superficially break from (3) by using the return value of the CAS operation in the link step; however, it is straightforward to verify that simply removing the return value of the CAS (i.e., making all CAS operations return false even if they succeed), affects neither correctness nor any work complexity bounds for their algorithms. Our algorithm presented in Section 4 is symmetric as presented.

3 LOWER BOUNDS

In this section we prove three step complexity lower bounds on the set union object: a worst-case operation step complexity bound that holds for all algorithms; an amortized operation step complexity bound that holds for *symmetric* algorithms; and a weaker amortized operation step complexity bound that holds for *all* algorithms. In subsequent sections, we will design and analyze a symmetric algorithm that matches the first two lower bounds.

Our proofs depend on the previous results of Jayanti [15] and Fredman and Saks [8]. We briefly recapitulate these results below.

3.1 Preliminaries

In the asynchronous scheduling model, no process knows when it and other processes will be given their first step. *Jayanti's wake-up* problem [15], requires one of the p processes to discover that all processes have been given at least one step. Formally, the problem is to give code for the p processes such that the following conditions are met:

1. (termination) Each process π_i returns either false or true in a bounded number of its own steps.
2. (truthfulness) No process π_i returns a true before all processes have taken at least one step.
3. (non-triviality) At least one process must return true.

Theorem 3.1 (Jayanti's Theorem: Theorem 6.1 in [15]). *Let $\mathcal{A}$ be a randomized algorithm that solves Jayanti's wake-up for the processes in set P of size $p = |P|$. Then, there is a schedule σ, such that the processes of P executing $\mathcal{A}$ under schedule σ results in some process performing $\Omega(\log p)$ steps in expectation.*

Fredman and Saks show a tight cell probe lower bound on the deterministic complexity of the sequential set-union problem. Their theorem extends to randomized algorithms to yield the following theorem.

Theorem 3.2 ([8]). *Let $\mathcal{A}$ be any deterministic or randomized algorithm that solves the sequential set-union problem for n nodes. (1) The expected amortized work complexity of $m \geq n$ operations is $\Omega(\alpha(n, m/n))$, and (2) the expected worst-case work complexity of a single operation is $\Omega(\log(n)/\log\log(n))$.*

3.2 Concurrent Set Union Lower Bounds from Jayanti's Wake Up

We solve Jayanti's wake up via set union to get a lower bound on the complexity of a single operation.

Lemma 3.3. *Algorithm 1 solves the wake-up problem for k processes using a disjoint set union instance with $k+1$ nodes, where each process executes one* Unite *and two* Find *operations.*

Proof. Let $q_1, \ldots, q_k$ be the k processes and let the nodes be labelled $0, \ldots, k$. The algorithm below correctly solves wake-up because:

Algorithm 1 : q_j's code in wake-up solution.

```
procedure WakeUp
    Unite(j − 1, j); x ← Find(0); y ← Find(p); return x = y
```

(i) the last process to complete Unite finds that the representatives of nodes 0 and k are the same and thus returns true, and (ii) no process returns true before all processes have linearized their Unite operations, since no representative of k can be the same as any representative of 0 until all of the nodes are in the same set. □

Theorem 3.4. *Let $\mathcal{A}$ be any linearizable wait-free algorithm for the set union problem on n nodes with p processes. he expected work complexity of a single operation with $\mathcal{A}$ is $\Omega(\log\min\{n,p\}+\log(n)/\log\log(n))$.*

Proof. Instantiate Lemma 3.3 with $k = \min\{n-1, p\}$. The most expensive of the three set union operations of the process that performs the most work in the adversarial schedule of Theorem 3.1 must do $\Omega(\log\min\{n,p\})$ expected work. Combining this with the worst-case lower bound from Theorem 3.2 yields the theorem. □

We extend the worst-case lower bound to an amortized lower bound for symmetric algorithms. The key ideas in this extension are the use of a shadowing schedule and a combinatorial argument.

Lemma 3.5. *Let $\mathcal{A}$ be any symmetric linearizable wait-free algorithm for the set-union problem on n nodes and p processes. The amortized work of m operations is at least $\Omega(\log(np/m+1))$ in expectation.*

Proof. Divide the n nodes into $g = \frac{m}{p}$ groups of size $k+1$, where $k = \frac{np}{8m}$ (disregard any additional nodes); label the groups $G_1, \ldots, G_g$. Note that $m \geq p$ and $m \geq \frac{n}{2}$, so $k \leq \frac{p}{4}$. We divide $\frac{p}{2}$ processes into two sets $A = \{q_1, \ldots, q_k\}$ and $B = \{q_{k+1}, \ldots, q_{p/2}\}$. Note that $|B| \geq \frac{p}{4}$ and $|A \cup B| = \frac{p}{2}$.

Consider running the wake-up algorithm of Lemma 3.3 on the k processes in A using the $k+1$ nodes in G_1. By Theorem 3.1 there is a schedule σ_1 in which some process q_i performs $\Omega(\log k)$ steps. Assign to each process in B the same sequence of three set union operations as what q_i performs, and define schedule σ_1' to be the schedule σ_1, with the processes of B interleaved to run in lockstep with q_i. In this schedule, the processes $q_1, \ldots, q_{p/2}$ perform $\Omega(p \log k)$ work to do $\frac{3}{2}p$ set union operations. Repeating this procedure on each group G_j produces schedules σ_j', each of which performs $\Omega(p \log k)$ work. Therefore, in the concatenated schedule of $\sigma_1'\sigma_2' \cdots \sigma_g'$, the processes $q_1, \ldots, q_{p/2}$ perform a total of $\Omega(gp \log(k+1)) = \Omega(m \cdot \log(np/m+1))$ work to do a total of $gp = m$ operations. □

The lower bound from Lemma 3.5 becomes trivial when $m \geq np$. The next lemma shows that the amortized work complexity is still lower bounded by an inverse-Ackermann term.

Lemma 3.6. *Let $\mathcal{A}$ be any symmetric linearizable wait-free algorithm for the set-union problem on n nodes and p processes. The amortized work of $m \geq n$ operations is at least $\Omega(\alpha(n, m/(np))$ in expectation.*

Proof. The main idea of the proof is to use a shadowing schedule on the result of Theorem 3.2. We break the proof into two cases, $m > np$ and $n \leq m \leq np$.

Case $m > np$: In this case, we let $M = m/p$. Since $M > n$, Theorem 3.2 yields a sequence of M operations that can be performed on a single process resulting in $\Omega(M \cdot \alpha(n, M/n)) = \Omega(\frac{m}{p} \cdot \alpha(n, m/(np)))$ work. Simply give each of the p processes this same sequence of operations. Running the processes in a lock-step schedule as in Lemma 3.5 will make each of them do the same amount of work since the algorithm is symmetric. So, the total work is $\Omega(m \cdot \alpha(n, m/(np)))$.

Case $n \leq m \leq np$: In this case, $m/(np)$ is just a constant between 0 and 1, so it suffices to show a sequence of m operations that requires $\Omega(m \cdot \alpha(n, c))$ for any constant c, since all of these values are within constant factors of each other. So, let $p' \geq 1$ be a number of processes such that $n(p'+1) > m > np'$. Repeating the argument from the $m > np$ case using only p' processes instead of all p yields a lower bound of $\Omega(m \cdot \alpha(n, m/(np'))) = \Omega(m \cdot \alpha(n, c))$ where $c \approx 1$. □

Theorem 3.7. *Let $\mathcal{A}$ be any symmetric linearizable wait-free algorithm for the set-union problem on n nodes and p processes. The amortized work of m operations is at least $\Omega(\alpha(n, m/(np)) + \log(np/m + 1))$ in expectation.*

Proof. Combining the lower bound results of Lemmas 3.5 and 3.6 yields the theorem. □

The lower bound of Theorem 3.7 is tight, as we will show by designing a symmetric algorithm whose work complexity matches the step complexity lower bound. However, it still leaves open the question of whether there is a fundamental barrier to eliminating concurrency overhead for non-symmetric algorithms. We will now develop a new technique, called the generalized wake up technique, for showing amortized lower bounds that will imply an $\Omega(\log\log \frac{np}{m})$ lower bound on the amortized complexity of shared memory set union operations.

3.3 Generalized Wake Up

To motivate generalized wake up, we consider the reduction in Algorithm 1 again. We were able to get a *worst case* lower bound on the step complexity of set union using the reduction, since Jayanti's theorem showed a non-trivial lower bound on the *step complexity of a single process* in any solution to his wake up problem. If however, we could show a non-trivial lower bound on the *total step complexity* (over all processes) for a solution to Jayanti's wake-up, then we could get an *amortized* lower bound on the step complexity of set union using the same reduction. Unfortunately, this is not possible since Jayanti's wake-up problem can be solved in $O(p)$ total work. But we dig deeper into the proof idea of Jayanti's Theorem to reveal that generalizing the wake-up problem can lead to a different problem that is strong enough to show powerful amortized lower bounds. We give an informal description of this proof method below.

Consider the setting where the processes in the set P are running a randomized algorithm $\mathcal{A}$ that uses variables in the set V. At any point of time, we can define a *knowledge set* for each process π_i. The knowledge set of π_i at time t is the set of processes that π_i can infer are awake, i.e. have taken at least one step, based on its history–its sequence of operations on shared memory and the values it received in return. Similarly, we can define a knowledge set for each variable $x \in V$. The knowledge set of x is the set of processes that a process could infer is awake if it reads x. Since a process can return true only after it is sure that every other process is awake, the process that returns 1 must have a knowledge set of size p before it returns. Jayanti proves his theorem by constructing a special schedule σ^* and a sequence of *"knowledge"* functions parametrized by round r: $K_r : (P \cup V) \to 2^P$, and shows that:

(1) According to σ^*, each process that is yet to return takes exactly one step in each round r.
(2) $|K_r(\Psi)|$ is an upper bound on the knowledge set of entity $\Psi \in (P \cup V)$ after round r.
(3) $|K_r(\Psi)| \leq 4^r$ for any round r.

By the last inequality, Jayanti shows that when the algorithm $\mathcal{A}$ is run under schedule σ^*, there must be at least one process that does not return until round $r = \log_4 p$.

In order to get the correct generalization of the wake-up problem, we interpret the above schema in the following way.

Observation 3.1. *The step complexity lower bound for wake-up comes about because a single process must reveal that it has a large knowledge set.*

Therefore, in order to get a stronger lower bound, we define a generalization of wake-up that forces *multiple* processes to reveal that they have large knowledge sets. Thus motivated, we define the generalized wake-up problem below.

The *Generalized Wake-Up (GWU)* family of problems for p processes is parametrized by a monotonically non-increasing sequence $s_1, \ldots, s_p$ of values between 1 and p. The problem $GWU(s_1, \ldots, s_p)$ is to design an algorithm for the p processes such that each process π_i returns an integer in the range $[1, p]$ (a lower bound on the the number of processes it knows to have woken up), that satisfies the following conditions:

(1) (termination) Each process π_i must return a value in the range $[1, p]$.
(2) (truthfulness) If π_i returns k at time t, then at least k processes are awake.
(3) (non-triviality) At least k processes must return a value greater than s_k.

Informally, generalized wake-up specifies a sequence of values, and the algorithm must ensure that the processes demonstrate *at least* as much knowledge as the sequence requests.

Observe that Jayanti's wake-up problem is the instance $GWU(p, 1, 1, \ldots, 1)$. Also, note that there is no algorithm with bounded step complexity for instances of generalized wake-up where $s_i > p - i + 1$, since the scheduler can wait for an unbounded amount of time before letting the $(p - i)th$ process wake up. So, we call the instance $GWU(p, p-1, p-2, \ldots, 1)$ the *Strong Wake-Up (SWU)* problem, and in general require that the sequence s be majorized by the sequence of descending numbers from p.

The following is our main theorem about Generalized Wake-Up; a formal proof of this theorem will appear in the full version of this paper due to space constraints in the abstract.

THEOREM 3.8. *Let $\mathcal{A}$ be a randomized algorithm that solves the problem $GWU(s_1, \ldots, s_p)$ for processes $\pi_1, \ldots, \pi_p$. There is an asynchronous schedule σ such that when algorithm $\mathcal{A}$ is run under schedule σ, the total number of steps performed by all the processes is $\Omega\left(p + \sum_{i=1}^{p}(\log s_i)\right)$.*

While it relies on a simple observation, Theorem 3.8 yields powerful amortized lower bounds for some data structures. In the next section, we prove an such a lower bound for set union. Please see Appendix B for more results.

3.4 Concurrent Set Union Lower Bound from Generalized Wake Up

In order to prove an amortized lower bound on set union operations complexities, we find a set union instance that is weak enough to be solvable by set union but also strong enough to be provably hard by Theorem 3.8. The key therefore is to design a set union based algorithm that ensures that many processes gain knowledge of many other processes being awake even in the presence of an adversary that will schedule the processes in a way that minimizes process knowledges given any fixed algorithm. Our high-level idea for forcing processes to gain knowledge is to leverage path lengths in graphs. We start with an empty graph on the vertex set V, and a fixed set $E \subseteq V \times V$ of edges to be added (generally not including all possible edges). A process p can dynamically "add the edge $(u, v) \in E$" to the graph by performing $\textsc{Unite}(u, v)$. After some processes have added some edges, there is a resultant graph $H = (V, F)$, where $F \subseteq E$ is the set of edges that have already been added to the graph. A process p' can "check if vertices u' and v' are connected" in the resultant graph H by performing $\textsc{SameSet}(u', v')$. We observe that if $\textsc{SameSet}(u', v')$ is true, then at least $\delta(u', v')$ edges must have been added to the graph, where δ is the shortest path length function on the original graph $G = (V, E)$. In particular, if each process is somehow restricted to add at most one edge in our algorithm, then a process that sees that $\textsc{SameSet}(u', v')$ is true learns that at least $\delta(u', v')$ processes are awake. On the other hand, if $\textsc{SameSet}(u', v')$ is false, no wake-up knowledge is gained. So, in order to get an amortized bound, we must design a procedure to ensure that many processes will get non-trivial wake-up information, so that we can leverage the generalized wake-up lower bound.

We will see as the proof unfolds that ensuring many $\textsc{SameSet}$ operations return true amounts to picking a highly connected graph G. However, the length of the shortest paths become smaller as connectivity goes up. For instance, in the best connected graph—the complete graph—all shortest paths are of length one, and thus even when $\textsc{SameSet}$ operations return true, very little wake-up information is gained. This inherent trade-off between connectivity and long paths makes the graph we pick pivotal to the proof. We formalize the notion of graph connectivity that we will require:

Definition 3.9. The edge expansion constant $h(G)$ of a graph $G = (V, E)$ is defined as

$$h(G) \triangleq \min_{\substack{S \subset V \\ |S| \le |V|/2}} \frac{|E_{out}(S)|}{|S|},$$

where $E_{out}(S)$ is the set of edges that have one vertex in S and one in $V - S$.

The edge expansion constant measures the connectivity of a graph—the higher the constant, the more connected the graph is. Sparse graphs with a high edge expansion constant are called *expanders*, and are known to have many applications in computer science [14]. The following result implied by Friedman [9] states that good expanders exist for any number of vertices. These are the graphs that we will use in our proof:

LEMMA 3.10 (BY FRIEDMAN [9]). *For every large-enough n, there is a 4-regular expander graph $\mathcal{G}_n = (V, E)$ with $|V| = n$, $|E| = 2n$, and $h(\mathcal{G}_n) > 0.2$.*

Moreover, all subgraphs of an expander with sufficiently many edges have large connected components:

LEMMA 3.11. *Let $a = 0.95 < 1$ and $b = 0.5 > 0$. Then for large enough n, if $H = (V, F)$ is a subgraph of $\mathcal{G}_n = (V, E)$ with $|F| \ge a|E|$, then the largest connected component of H has size at least $b|V|$.*

PROOF. Assume by contradiction that all connected components $C_1, \ldots, C_\ell$ of H have size less than $|V|/2$. Then, by definition of $h(\cdot)$, there are at least $h(\mathcal{G}_n) \cdot |C_i|$ edges of E between C_i and $V - C_i$. Thus,

$$|E| - |F| \ge \frac{1}{2}\sum_{i=1}^{\ell} |E_{out}(C_i)| \ge \frac{1}{2}\sum_{i=1}^{\ell} h(G)|C_i| = \frac{h(G)|V|}{2} = \frac{h(G)|E|}{4}.$$

So $|F| \le |E|(1 - h(G)/4) < 0.95|E|$. □

We will now show how to solve a non-trivially hard instance of generalized wake up via set union operations. For any integer $t > 0$ and large enough n so that $\mathcal{G}_n$ has the properties of Lemma 3.10 and Lemma 3.11, let $p = 2n^3 t$ and $m = 2p$. We describe an algorithm on p processes that performs m operations of concurrent disjoint set union on n nodes.

Work with $\mathcal{G}_n = (V, E)$. Define a *process type* to be a triple $(e = (u, v), x, y)$ where $e \in E$ and $u, v, x, y \in V$. Since $|E| = 2|V| = 2n$, there are a total of $2n^3 = p/t$ process types, so we can create t processes of each type. The process of type $((u, v), x, y)$ performs the steps in Algorithm 2. (Note that $\delta(x, y)$ is a constant known to the process ahead of time.)

Algorithm 2 A reduction to generalized wake-up

```
procedure GWU(((u, v), x, y))
    UNITE(u, v)
    return max(δ(x, y) × SAMESET(x, y), 1)
```

Order the processes as $\pi_1, \ldots, \pi_p$ based on the linearization points of completing the UNITE operation on line 2. We denote the type of π_i by $T(\pi_i) = (e_i = (u_i, v_i), x_i, y_i)$. Let $I = [1, \ell]$, be the indices of the first ℓ processes to linearize their UNITE operations; and define $H = (V, F)$ where $F = \bigcup_{i \in I}\{e_i\}$ is the set of edges. The constant ℓ will be defined by the schedule to be the smallest constant that ensures a "large" connected component in H by Lemma 3.11. In particular, pick ℓ to be the minimum number such that $|F| \geq a|E|$. Let C be the set of vertices in the largest connected component of H. Let $P \triangleq \{\pi_i : e_i \notin F\}$ be the set of processes whose UNITE operation in Algorithm 2 will not attempt to add an edge in F. Finally, let a, b be the constants from Lemma 3.11.

We will now prove a series of short lemmas that have the following informal meanings:

(1) The largest connected component in $H = (V, F)$, i.e. C, contains a constant fraction of the vertices in V. Furthermore, the processes in P which will attempt to unite edges not in F, is at least a constant fraction of the total number of processes.
(2) If x and y are random vertices in V, then with constant probability they will be in the connected component C and the distance between them will be $\Omega(\log n)$.
(3) The first two lemmas imply that a constant fraction of the processes will return a value that is $\Omega(\log n)$.
(4) Theorem 3.8 then implies the $\Omega(\log \log n)$ lower bound.

LEMMA 3.12. *$|C| \geq bn = \Omega(n)$ and $|P| \geq (1 - a)p - p/|E| = \Omega(p)$.*

PROOF. $|C| \geq b|V| = bn$ by Lemma 3.11, since $|F| \geq a|E|$.

Since there are $p/|E|$ processes that are trying to perform a union involving the vertices of any given edge in G, $|P| \geq (|E| - \lceil a|E| \rceil) \cdot \frac{p}{|E|} \geq p(1 - a) - p/|E|$. □

LEMMA 3.13. *Let (x, y) be a random pair of vertices from V.*

$$\mathbb{P}(x, y \in C \text{ and } \delta(x, y) > (1/2)\log_4 n) \geq b^2(1 - 2/(b\sqrt{n})).$$

PROOF. $\mathbb{P}(x, y \in C) \geq b^2$ because $|C| \geq b|V|$ by Lemma 3.12. And $\mathbb{P}(\delta(x, y) > (1/2)\log_4 n \mid x, y \in C) > 1 - 2/(b\sqrt{n})$, since by the 4-regularity of $\mathcal{G}_n$, the radius $r > 1$ neighborhood of vertex x has size at most $2 \cdot 4^r$. So, the $r = (1/2)\log_4 n$ neighborhood of x has at most $2\sqrt{n}$ vertices. □

LEMMA 3.14. *A constant fraction of the processes return a value that is $\Omega(\log n)$.*

PROOF. All the processes $\pi_i \in P$ for which $x_i, y_i \in C$ and $\delta(x_i, y_i) \geq (1/2)\log_d n$, return at least $(1/2)\log_d n = \Omega(\log n) = \Omega(\log p)$, since $i > \ell$ by the definition of P. By Lemma 3.13, the fraction of such processes returning $\Omega(\log n)$ is at least $b^2(1 - 2/b\sqrt{n})$. So the total number of such processes is at least $|P|b^2(1 - 2/b\sqrt{n}) \geq \Omega(p)$, by Lemma 3.12. □

LEMMA 3.15. *Algorithm 2 solves $GWU(s_1, \ldots, s_p)$ where $s_1 = s_2 = \cdots = s_\kappa = \Omega(\log n)$, $s_{\kappa+1} = \cdots = s_p = 1$ and $\kappa = \Omega(p)$.*

PROOF. We argue each of the generalized wake up conditions. Termination follows by wait-freedom of the Union Find data structure. Truthfulness follows since every process adds at most a single edge to the graph through its unite operation on line 2, so a successful SAMESET(x, y) operation indicates that at least $\min(1, \delta(x, y))$ processes have woken up. And non-triviality follows by Lemma 3.14. □

We now translate the lower bound from Lemma 3.15 into a lower bound parametrized by the number of operations m, the number of processes p, and the size of the set union object n, through a combinatorial argument.

THEOREM 3.16. *Consider any randomized algorithm for p-process shared memory set union on an instance with n nodes. Let $m > n$ and $m > 2p$. Then, there is a sequence of m set union operations on the p processes and n nodes that takes $\Omega(m \log\log(np/m))$ shared memory steps.*

PROOF. Divide the n nodes into groups of size $s = \lfloor 2np/m \rfloor$. Have $g = \lfloor m/2p \rfloor$ groups $V_1, \ldots, V_g$, ignoring extra nodes.

For each group V_i, do not use all the nodes in the group, but only use $s' = \Theta(s^{1/3}) = O(p^{1/3})$ of the nodes, so that we can choose t so that $p' \triangleq 2(s')^3 t = \Omega(p)$ and $p' \leq p$, and can run Algorithm 2 on p' processes, where there are t processes of each type. By Lemma 3.15 and the GWU lower bound (Theorem 3.8), running Algorithm 2 with these parameters takes $\Omega(p' \log\log s') = \Omega(p \log\log(np/m))$ shared memory operations in the worst case.

We therefore run Algorithm 2 as above for each group of nodes, in a series of g rounds, letting all operations from the previous round complete before starting the next one. The total worst-case cost is $\Omega(gp \log\log(np/m)) = \Omega(m \log\log(np/m))$, the total number of processes used is $\leq p$, the total number of nodes used is at most n, and the total number of set union operations invoked is at most $2p' \cdot g \leq 2p \cdot m/(2p) = m$. □

In the remainder of the paper, we describe our randomized algorithm for set union.

4 OUR CONCURRENT ALGORITHM

Our concurrent set union algorithms use the same structure as the best sequential algorithms: a *compressed forest*. This forest contains one rooted tree per set, whose nodes are the elements of the set and whose root is the set representative. We assume that the nodes have indices 1 through n and thus can be compared via '<'. Each node x has a field $x.p$ to store the address of a *parent* node, a field $x.r$ to store a non-zero integer *rank*, and a field $x.b$ to store a single *root-bit* signifying whether or not x is the root of its tree. Initially, $x.p = x$, $x.r = 0$, and $x.b = 1$. The rank is never more than n, and thus needs only $\lceil \log n \rceil$ bits to represent. In fact, the rank is at most $O(\log n)$ and thus only needs $O(\log \log n$ bits with high probability. So, we will assume that all three fields are written down in a single word in memory in the form of a triple $x.f = [x.p, x.r, x.b]$. The memory words are of size $2\lceil \log n \rceil + 1 = O(\log n)$ in this representation. Alternatively, we could have written the algorithm using structs that contain three different words for the three different fields of each node (as in [1]), and obtained the same expected space and work bounds. We picked this formulation because it leads to a concise implementation that is clearer to the reader.

A note about our representation: If the root-bit $x.b$ is set to 1, x is a root and thus our implementation disregards the value of the parent field $x.p$. Notably, our representation is different from the classic representation, where the parent field $x.p = x$ for a root node x. This fact is crucial to understanding the pseudo-code.

Concurrency significantly complicates the implementation of the set operations. One complication is that processes can interfere with each other by trying to update the same field at the same time, requiring our algorithms to be robust to such interference. Consider doing unites concurrently. The pseudo code for unite and link is presented in Algorithm 3. In the pseudo-code, \$ represents a random bit, i.e. a *Bernoulli*$(1/2)$. The implementation of the FIND(x) procedure used in the code is discussed in the next subsection.

To do UNITE(x, y), we start as in the sequential case by finding the roots u and v of the trees containing x and y, respectively (Line 2). If $u = v$, then x and y are already in the same set and no work needs to be done (Line 3). Otherwise, x and y are in different trees, so we can try to link u and v by doing a CAS to make v the parent of u or vice-versa (Line 4). We mark the LINK on Line 4 and subsequent linearization points with an asterisk in the code. (Further explanation of the pivotal LINK procedure is in the next paragraph.) But we must allow for the possibility of the CAS failing. The CAS can fail, for example if it tries to make v the parent of u but in the meantime some other process makes another node the parent of u. Notably, it even fails if the other process does the exact same CAS and makes v the parent of u. A solution that works in either case is to simply continue walking up the tree from the present u and v (Line 5), until the paths intersect or another attempt at linking is necessary. This method was first proposed by Anderson and Woll [1] and was subsequently used by Jayanti and Tarjan [17].

A key novelty in our algorithm is our linking rule, which we call *randomized linking by rank*. In the classic *linking by rank* heuristic [24], each node x has an associated *rank* field $x.r$, that is an approximation of the height of x in its tree; so, initially all ranks are zero. When two roots u and v are to be linked, the node of larger rank *wins*, i.e. it becomes the parent of the other node. If the two nodes have equal rank, then the winner is chosen arbitrarily, but its rank is incremented by one to reflect its (possible) increase in height. Anderson and Woll implemented a parallelization of this heuristic, but were unable to get a good work bound [1].

Linking by rank is easy to execute concurrently when the ranks of the nodes u and v in question are different; one simply needs to change the parent of the smaller ranked node. However, when the nodes are of equal rank, *two* changes have to take place: the parent of one node must be updated, while the rank of *the other* must also be updated. Making these two changes atomically seems impossible, since the two fields to be changed belong to different nodes, and neither the write nor the CAS primitive can modify two fields in a single step.

Anderson and Woll's implementation handles the equal rank case by always updating the parent pointer first, and rank field second. This implementation allows one process to modify $u_1.p$ to u_2, and another to modify $u_2.p$ to u_3 etc. where all of the u_i have the same rank. If all p processes partake in such a sequence of links, the *equal rank chain* can grow to length $\Omega(p)$. These equal rank chains cause their algorithms to have linear concurrency overhead.

A natural alternative strategy would update the rank before the parent. Unfortunately, this can lead to ranks becoming too large and no longer serving as good proxies for height; which in turn breaks down the efficiency guarantees of linking by rank. Preliminary calculations suggest that this method also leads to concurrency overheads that are at least linear in p. Our key insight lies here: while updating parent first or rank first each lead to an algorithm with linear concurrency overhead, we show that picking between the two randomly and either only updating the parent or only incrementing the rank yields an algorithm with at most logarithmic concurrency overhead.

Algorithm 3 : Pseudo-code to unite x and y.

```
1: procedure UNITE(x, y)
2:     u ← FIND(x); v ← FIND(y)
3:     while u ≠ v* do
4:         LINK(u, v)*
5:         u ← FIND(u); v ← FIND(v)
6: procedure LINK(u, v)
7:     [u_p, r, u_b] ← u.f
8:     [v_p, s, v_b] ← v.f
9:     if r < s then CAS(u.f, [u_p, r, 1], [v, r, 0])*
10:    else if s < r then CAS(v.f, [v_p, s, 1], [u, s, 0])*
11:    else
12:        if u < v then CAS(u.f, [u_p, r, 1], [v, r + 1, $])*
13:        else CAS(v.f, [v_p, s, 1], [u, s + 1, $])*
```

An explanation of our Linking heuristic: Link initally reads the fields of u and v (Lines 7-8). If u's rank, r, is less than v's rank, s, it attempts to change u's parent to v, and u's root-bit to 0 ("not a root"), while leaving the rank unchanged (Line 9). If v's rank, s, is less than u's rank, r, a symmetric change is attempted (Line 10). The implementation is subtle in the case where $r = s$: if $u < v$ (check on Line 12 succeeds), the algorithm tries to update u's parent to v *and* increment u's rank, and also set u's root-bit randomly (Line 12). The previous statement deviates from our intuitive description of the algorithm, so we now explain why the algorithm tries to change *both* the parent and rank fields. If the update succeeds and the root-bit, $u.b$, gets set to 1, then u continues to be a root, and thus the parent field is disregarded by the algorithm, so it does not matter that it was updated to v. On the other hand, if the update succeeds and root-bit gets set to 0, then u is no longer a root, and the rank field is thenceforth disregarded by the algorithm, so it does not matter that it was incremented to $r + 1$. Line 13 acts symmetrically in the case that $u.r = v.r$ and $v < u$ as opposed to $u < v$.

4.1 The Find Procedure

We present two different implementations of FIND(x): *naïve* and *two-try splitting* in Algorithm 4. The first procedure, Naïve find simply uses an auxiliary variable u (Line 2) that walks up the parent pointers in the tree (Line 4) until it reaches a root (Line 3). FIND(x) returns this node as the representative (Line 5). The linearization point of this procedure is the time at which u is discovered to be a root. The sequence of nodes traversed by u is the *find sequence.*

Algorithm 4 : Find algorithms respectively: naïve and two-try splitting

```
1:  procedure FIND(x)
2:      u ← x
3:      while not u.b* do
4:          u ← u.p
5:      return u
6:  procedure FIND(x)
7:      u ← x;
8:      while not u.b* do
9:          [v, r, u_b] ← u.f; [w, s, v_b] ← v.f*
10:         if v_b then return v
11:         CAS(u.f, [v, u.r, 0], [w, u.r, 0])
12:         [v, r, u_b] ← u.f; [w, s, v_b] ← v.f*
13:         if v_b then return v
14:         CAS(u.f, [v, u.r, 0], [w, u.r, 0])
15:         u ← v
16:     return u
```

Subsequent finds can be made more efficient if the parents of nodes on the find sequence are updated to be closer to the root. Such changes are said to *compact* the tree. *Splitting* is a classical compaction rule that was discovered by Tarjan and van Leeuwen [24], and used by Jayanti and Tarjan in their concurrent algorithm [17]. Rather than using the auxiliary variable u to simply walk up the find sequence, splitting calculates u's parent v and v's parent w, and tries to *improve* u's position in the tree by changing u's parent to w through a CAS. Find with splitting moves up the find sequence in this way until it has reached a root to return.

Work complexity bounds for splitting are derived through a potential argument. In the argument, a process performing a find operation gains potential each time it successfully *improves* a node's parent pointer to one closer to the root. Thus, it is important to account for the number of successful improvements in an execution of find in order to calculate the potential difference caused by the find. In the sequential case, all attempts to improve the tree succeed. In the concurrent case however, attempts at improvement can fail if another *interfering* process successfully changes u's parent between the time the original process reads u's parent and attempts its CAS. Jayanti and Tarjan miss some cases of this interference in their complexity analysis. Their bounds increase when interference is properly handled.

In order to overcome this issue, we develop the novel two-try splitting algorithm that tries to improve each node u on the find sequence twice. Although both attempts to improve u may fail in two-try splitting, our analysis shows how the potential decrease caused by interfering processes can be redistributed to account for the work done by all the processes in question if two attempts are made. Unfortunately, the same argument does not hold for the simpler one-try splitting.

An explanation of the two-try splitting find pseudo-code: Find uses an auxiliary variable u to walk up the tree (Line 7). If u is not a root (Line 8), its parent v, and $v.p = w$ are read (Line 9). If v is a root, Find has succeeded and can return v (Line 10); otherwise, an improvement is attempted on Line 11. A successful CAS on Line 11 changes only u's parent, and does not modify the other fields. After a second attempt to improve the same node u (Lines 12-14), u is updated to its parent v in order to keep walking up the tree (Line 15). Finally, if u becomes the root (Line 8), it is returned on Line 16. The linearization point of the procedure is the time when the root-bit of the returned node is read, since that is time at which the returned node is surely the root of the tree.

4.2 Main Theorem

We now state the main amortized upper bound result about our set union algorithm. We defer the proof of this theorem to the full version of this paper due to the page limit on this extended abstract.

THEOREM 4.1. *Given a union-find instance with n nodes on a shared memory asynchronous multiprocessor with p processes:*

(1) *The expected total work of the set union algorithm over m total unite and find operations is* $\Theta(m \cdot (\alpha(n, m/(np)) + \log(1 + np/m)))$.
(2) *This total work bound is optimal up to constant factors in the family of symmetric algorithms in the parameter regime* $m = \Omega(n)$ *and* $m = \Omega(p)$ *since it matches the lower bound from Theorem 3.7.*
(3) *The worst-case work for a single operation is* $\Theta(\log n)$ *in expectation and with probability at least* $1 - 1/n^c$ *for any* $c > 0$.
(4) *This worst-case per-operation work bound is optimal in expectation across all algorithms (including symmetric and non-symmetric) in the parameter regime where* $p = n^{\Omega(1)}$ *since it matches the lower bound from Theorem 3.4.*

5 REMARKS

We have designed the first concurrent set union algorithm that has sublinear concurrency overhead against an adversarial scheduler, thereby resolving a 28 year old open question from [1]. The concurrency overhead of our algorithm is at most $\Delta(p) = \log p$. Therefore, the speed-up of our algorithm is the near-linear $p/\log p$. Our algorithm has optimal amortized work in the class of symmetric algorithms, which captures the complexities of all known algorithms for the concurrent set union problem. This is shown by our tight lower bound on the expected amortized work complexities of algorithms in this class. We have also presented the generalized wake up technique and have used to to show that linear speed-up cannot be achieved for set union. We hope that the new techniques introduced in this paper can be extended to better understand concurrency overheads and produce more efficient concurrent data structures.

ACKNOWLEDGMENTS

We thank Prasad Jayanti for helpful discussions, and Philipp Woelfel and the PODC reviewers for helpful comments. We also thank the AlgoPARC workshop (funded by NSF grant CCF-1745331) where part of our research was conducted.

REFERENCES

[1] Richard J. Anderson and Heather Woll. 1991. Wait-free Parallel Algorithms for the Union-Find Problem. In *Proceedings of the 23rd Annual ACM Symposium on Theory of Computing, May 5-8, 1991, New Orleans, Louisiana, USA.* 370–380. https://doi.org/10.1145/103418.103458

[2] Richard J. Anderson and Heather Woll. 1991. Wait-free Parallel Algorithms for the Union-Find Problem. In *Proceedings of the 23rd Annual ACM Symposium on Theory of Computing, May 5-8, 1991, New Orleans, Louisiana, USA.* 370–380. https://doi.org/10.1145/103418.103458

[3] Vincent Bloemen. 2015. *On-The-Fly Parallel Decomposition of Strongly Connected Components.* Master's thesis. University of Twente.

[4] Vincent Bloemen, Alfons Laarman, and Jaco van de Pol. 2016. Multi-Core On-The-Fly SCC Decomposition. In *Proceedings of the 21st ACM SIGPLAN symposium on Principles and practice of parallel programming (PPoPP '16).* to appear.

[5] Norbert Blum. 1985. On the single-operation worst-case time complexity of the disjoint set union problem. In *Annual Symposium on Theoretical Aspects of Computer Science (STACS 1985).*

[6] Faith Ellen and Philipp Woelfel. 2013. An Optimal Implementation of Fetch-and-Increment. In *Proceedings of the 27th International Symposium on Distributed Computing - Volume 8205 (DISC 2013).* Springer-Verlag New York, Inc., New York, NY, USA, 284–298. https://doi.org/10.1007/978-3-642-41527-2_20

[7] Wojciech Fraczak, Loukas Georgiadis, Andrew Miller, and Robert Endre Tarjan. 2014. Corrections to "Finding dominators via disjoint set union" [J. Discrete Algorithms 23 (2013) 2-20]. *J. Discrete Algorithms* 26 (2014), 106–110. https://doi.org/10.1016/j.jda.2014.01.002

[8] Michael L. Fredman and Michael E. Saks. 1989. The Cell Probe Complexity of Dynamic Data Structures. In *Proceedings of the 21st Annual ACM Symposium on Theory of Computing, May 14-17, 1989, Seattle, Washigton, USA.* 345–354. https://doi.org/10.1145/73007.73040

[9] Joel Friedman. 2003. A proof of alon's second eigenvalue conjecture. In *Proceedings of the thirty-fifth annual ACM symposium on Theory of computing.* ACM, 720–724.

[10] Ashish Goel, Sanjeev Khanna, Daniel H. Larkin, and Robert Endre Tarjan. 2014. Disjoint Set Union with Randomized Linking. In *Proceedings of the Twenty-Fifth Annual ACM-SIAM Symposium on Discrete Algorithms, SODA 2014, Portland, Oregon, USA, January 5-7, 2014.* 1005–1017. https://doi.org/10.1137/1.9781611973402.75

[11] Maurice Herlihy. 1991. Wait-free Synchronization. *ACM Trans. Program. Lang. Syst.* 13, 1 (Jan. 1991), 124–149. https://doi.org/10.1145/114005.102808

[12] Maurice Herlihy and J. Eliot B. Moss. 1993. Transactional Memory: Architectural Support for Lock-free Data Structures. *SIGARCH Comput. Archit. News* 21, 2 (May 1993), 289–300. https://doi.org/10.1145/173682.165164

[13] Maurice P. Herlihy and Jeannette M. Wing. 1990. Linearizability: A Correctness Condition for Concurrent Objects. *ACM Trans. Program. Lang. Syst.* 12, 3 (July 1990), 463–492. https://doi.org/10.1145/78969.78972

[14] Shlomo Hoory, Nathan Linial, and Avi Wigderson. 2006. Expander graphs and their applications. *Bull. Amer. Math. Soc.* 43, 4 (2006), 439–561.

[15] Prasad Jayanti. 1998. A Time Complexity Lower Bound for Randomized Implementations of Some Shared Objects. In *Proceedings of the Seventeenth Annual ACM Symposium on Principles of Distributed Computing (PODC '98).* ACM, New York, NY, USA, 201–210. https://doi.org/10.1145/277697.277735

[16] Prasad Jayanti. 2002. F-arrays: Implementation and Applications. In *Proceedings of the Twenty-first Annual Symposium on Principles of Distributed Computing (PODC '02).* ACM, New York, NY, USA, 270–279. https://doi.org/10.1145/571825.571875

[17] Siddhartha V. Jayanti and Robert E. Tarjan. 2016. A Randomized Concurrent Algorithm for Disjoint Set Union. In *Proceedings of the 2016 ACM Symposium on Principles of Distributed Computing (PODC '16).* ACM, New York, NY, USA, 75–82. https://doi.org/10.1145/2933057.2933108

[18] Joseph B. Kruskal. 1956. On the Shortest Spanning Subtree of a Graph and the Traveling Salesman Problem. *Proc. Amer. Math. Soc.* 7, 1 (Feb. 1956), 48–50. http://www.jstor.org/stable/2033241

[19] Chris Lattner and Vikram Adve. 2002. Automatic Pool Allocation for Disjoint Data Structures. *SIGPLAN Not.* 38, 2 supplement (June 2002), 13–24. https://doi.org/10.1145/773039.773041

[20] John Reif. 1985. Depth First Search is Inherently Sequential. *Information Processing Letters 20* 1, 2 (1985), 229–234.

[21] Robert Sedgewick and Kevin Wayne. 2011. *Algorithms, 4th Edition.* Addison-Wesley. I–XII, 1–955 pages.

[22] Robert Tarjan. 1972. Depth first search and linear graph algorithms. *SIAM JOURNAL ON COMPUTING* 1, 2 (1972).

[23] Robert Endre Tarjan. 1975. Efficiency of a Good But Not Linear Set Union Algorithm. *J. ACM* 22, 2 (April 1975), 215–225. https://doi.org/10.1145/321879.321884

[24] Robert E. Tarjan and Jan van Leeuwen. 1984. Worst-case Analysis of Set Union Algorithms. *J. ACM* 31, 2 (March 1984), 245–281. https://doi.org/10.1145/62.2160

A SAME SET PSEUDO-CODE

Algorithm 5 : Test whether x and y are in the same set.

```
1: procedure SameSet(x, y)
2:     u ← Find(x); v ← Find(y)*
3:     while u ≠ v* do
4:         if u.b = 1 then return false
5:         u ← Find(u); v ← Find(v)
6:     return true
```

The pseudo-code is an adaptation of Anderson and Woll's same set algorithm [2]. The procedure starts by finding the roots of x and y's respective trees (Line 2). If the roots are the same (Line 3), then x and y are in the same set and thus true is returned (Line 6). However if they are not the same, then there are two possibilities:

Case 1: Some other process has performed a successful UNITE and thus u is no longer a root (check on Line 4). In this case, the algorithm simply tries again, but starts its finds at the higher nodes u and v (Lines 5).

Case 2: The first root to be discovered, namely u, is still a root (check on Line 4). In this case, it can safely be concluded that the root of y's tree was not u at the linearization point of the FIND(y) on Line 2, since u was a root from the time of FIND(x) to Line 4, and v was a (different) root at the time of FIND(y). So, the algorithm returns false on Line 4.

B OTHER AMORTIZED LOWER BOUNDS

We give amortized lower bounds for counters and ordered collections in this section. We define the data structures and simply state the results that can be shown via reduction to generalized wake up. Due to space constraints in the extended abstract we omit proofs. An r-approx-counter is an r-additive approximation of a counter.

THEOREM B.1 (COUNTERS).

(1) *Let $\mathcal{A}$ be any linearizable randomized algorithm for fetch-and-inc. For every $m \geq p$, there is a sequence of m operations and a schedule that forces $\mathcal{A}$ to take $\Omega(m \log p)$ steps to perform the operations.*

(2) *Let $\mathcal{A}$ be any linearizable randomized algorithm for a $p(1-\varepsilon)/2$-approx-counter, where $\varepsilon > 0$ is a constant. For every $m \geq 2p$, there is a sequence of m operations and a schedule that forces $\mathcal{A}$ to take $\Omega(m \log p)$ steps to perform the operations.*

Remark. *Theorem B.1 shows the step complexity optimality of two algorithms: (1) Ellen and Woelfel's linearizable wait-free* fetch-and-increment *construction in [6], and (2) Jayanti's counter in [16].*

THEOREM B.2. *Let $\mathcal{A}$ be any linearizable randomized algorithm for an r-relaxed Queue, r-relaxed Stack, or r-relaxed Priority Queue for $r = (1-\varepsilon)p$, where $\varepsilon > 0$ is a constant. For every $m \geq p$, there is a set of m REMOVE operations and a schedule that forces $\mathcal{A}$ to take $\Omega(m \log p)$ steps to perform the operations.*

Strongly Linearizable Implementations of Snapshots and Other Types*

Sean Ovens
sgovens@ucalgary.ca
University of Calgary
Calgary, Canada

Philipp Woelfel
woelfel@ucalgary.ca
University of Calgary
Calgary, Canada

ABSTRACT

Linearizability is the gold standard of correctness conditions for shared memory algorithms, and historically has been considered the practical equivalent of atomicity. However, it has been shown [16] that replacing atomic objects with linearizable implementations can affect the probability distribution of execution outcomes in randomized algorithms. Thus, linearizable objects are not always suitable replacements for atomic objects. A stricter correctness condition called strong linearizability has been developed and shown to be appropriate for randomized algorithms in a strong adaptive adversary model [16].

We devise several new lock-free strongly linearizable implementations from atomic registers. In particular, we give the first strongly linearizable lock-free snapshot implementation that uses bounded space. This improves on the unbounded space solution of Denysyuk and Woelfel [14]. As a building block, our algorithm uses a lock-free strongly linearizable ABA-detecting register. We obtain this object by modifying the wait-free linearizable ABA-detecting register of Aghazadeh and Woelfel [5], which, as we show, is not strongly linearizable.

Aspnes and Herlihy [8] identified a wide class of types that have wait-free linearizable implementations. These types require that any pair of operations either commute, or one overwrites the other. Aspnes and Herlihy gave a general wait-free linearizable implementation of such types, employing an atomic snapshot object. We show that this implementation is strongly linearizable, proving that all types in this class have a lock-free strongly linearizable implementation from atomic registers.

KEYWORDS

distributed algorithms; shared memory; strong linearizability; snapshots; ABA; lock-freedom

*We acknowledge the support of the Natural Sciences and Engineering Research Council of Canada (NSERC). This research was undertaken, in part, thanks to funding from the Canada Research Chairs program.

PODC '19, July 29-August 2, 2019, Toronto, ON, Canada

ACM ISBN 978-1-4503-6217-7/19/07...$15.00
https://doi.org/10.1145/3293611.3331632

ACM Reference Format:
Sean Ovens and Philipp Woelfel. 2019. Strongly Linearizable Implementations of Snapshots and Other Types. In *2019 ACM Symposium on Principles of Distributed Computing (PODC '19), July 29-August 2, 2019, Toronto, ON, Canada.* ACM, New York, NY, USA, 10 pages. https://doi.org/10.1145/3293611.3331632

1 INTRODUCTION

Correctness and linearizability are often equated in distributed algorithm design. Informally, linearizable objects that are accessed concurrently by multiple processes behave the same way they would in a sequential execution. That is, overlapping operations performed on a linearizable object still take effect in a predictable, linear fashion, without violating the sequential specification of the underlying type. Linearizable objects are frequently considered "effectively" atomic, since they seem to behave exactly like atomic objects, whose operations take effect instantaneously upon invocation.

While linearizability adequately guarantees correct behaviour for deterministic implementations, it has been shown that the same is not true for randomized algorithms [16]. The probability distribution over outcomes of a randomized algorithm that uses only atomic objects can change when these atomic objects are replaced with linearizable implementations. To deal with this impasse, Golab, Higham, and Woelfel [16] defined the notion of strong linearizability. Strongly linearizable implementations are not only linearizable, but they also exhibit the "prefix-preservation" property. This extra condition ensures that the linearization order of operations does not change retroactively. As a result, strongly linearizable implementations are resilient against strong adaptive adversaries, which have the power to schedule processes with the knowledge of the entire system state, including all previous random choices (coin flips) made by processes. That is, replacing atomic objects with strongly linearizable ones in a randomized algorithm does not change the probability distribution of the algorithm's outcome, assuming a strong adaptive adversary. More generally speaking, strongly linearizabile implementations preserve hyperproperties of their atomic counterparts [10]. For the purpose of randomized algorithm design, it is therefore desirable to design strongly linearizable implementations, or to prove their non-existence.

Unless otherwise noted we assume the standard asynchronous shared memory system, where n processes with unique IDs in $\{1, \ldots, n\}$ communicate through atomic read and write operations on shared (multi-reader multi-writer) registers. Until now, work on strong linearizability has focused almost entirely on this model. But it is also known that standard wait-free universal constructions, e.g., Herlihy's [18], using n-process consensus objects are strongly linearizable [16], while any wait-free strongly linearizable implementation of a queue or a stack requires n-process consensus objects [9].

Helmi, Higham and Woelfel [17] have shown that essentially no non-trivial object has a deterministic wait-free strongly linearizable implementation from *single-writer* registers. The authors also gave a wait-free strongly linearizable implementation of bounded max-registers from unrestricted (multi-writer) registers [6]. Their algorithm trivially extends to a lock-free strongly linearizable unbounded max-register implementation, using an infinite number of registers. Denysyuk and Woelfel [14] showed that several types, such as counters and single-writer snapshots (defined below), have lock-free strongly linearizable implementations. However, since the algorithm of Denysyuk and Woelfel relies on an unbounded max-register implementation [17], it also requires an unbounded number of registers. The algorithm inherently requires infinite space, because a so-called version number must increase with each state change of the implemented object.

Indeed, until now, there was no strongly linearizable implementation of a non-trivial type known, which supported an infinite number of state changes but required only bounded space. In this paper we devise a lock-free strongly linearizable snapshot object that uses only bounded space. As a building block we also devise a lock-free bounded space implementation of an ABA-detecting register (definition below). Finally, we show that a wide class of types [8] have lock-free strongly linearizable implementations (from an unbounded number of registers).

The snapshot type [2] is fundamental for distributed algorithm design and research [1, 3, 8, 13, 15, 19]. A single-writer snapshot object maintains a vector of n values from a given domain D, and supports two operations, *update* and *scan*. Operation *update*(x), $x \in D$, by process p changes the p-th element in the vector to x, and a *scan* operation returns the entire vector. Thus, the *scan* operation of a snapshot object allows any process to obtain a consistent view of multiple shared memory cells.

Several wait-free linearizable implementations of single-writer snapshot objects from registers are known [2, 7, 11, 12, 22], but it is impossible to have an implementation that achieves strong linearizability in addition to wait-freedom [14]. As mentioned above, Denysyuk and Woelfel [17] sacrificed wait-freedom for lock-freedom to obtain a strongly linearizable implementation using an unbounded number of registers. We give the first such implementation that needs only bounded space.

THEOREM 1. *There is a lock-free strongly linearizable implementation of a snapshot object from* $O(n)$ *registers of size* $O(\log n + \log |D|)$.

The *amortized* step complexity of our implementation is $O(n^3)$. (An object has amortized step complexity k if all processes combined execute at most $k \cdot \ell$ steps in any execution that comprises ℓ operation invocations.) Our algorithm uses as base objects a linearizable snapshot object S, so the step complexity heavily depends on the implementation of S. But in the absence of contention, each *update* and *scan* operation of the strongly linearizable snapshot needs only a constant number of operations on S in addition to a constant number of register accesses.

To assist in the design of the above implementation, we also design a lock-free strongly linearizable ABA-detecting register based on an existing linearizable implementation [5]. An ABA-detecting register supports *write* and *read* operations. A *write*(x) operation writes the value $x \in D$, and a *read* operation returns the latest written value together with a Boolean flag. This flag indicates whether there has been a *write* operation since the previous *read* by the same process. ABA-detecting registers are used to combat the ABA problem, which occurs when two *read* operations with interleaving *write* operations return the same value; this situation prevents the reading process from reacting to any changes that might have occurred in the object. This type was defined by Aghazdeh and Woelfel [5], who also gave a wait-free linearizable implementation from $O(n)$ bounded registers. We show that their algorithm is not strongly linearizable, and modify it to achieve strong linearizability, but sacrifice wait-freedom for lock-freedom.

THEOREM 2. *There is a lock-free strongly linearizable implementation of an ABA-detecting register from* $O(n)$ *registers, each of size* $O(\log n + \log |D|)$.

The amortized step complexity of our implementation is $O(n)$. Moreover, each *write* needs only $O(1)$ steps, and each *read* has constant step complexity in the absence of contention.

Aspnes and Herlihy [8] defined a large class of types with wait-free linearizable implementations. Any two operations on an object of such a type must either commute (meaning the system configuration obtained after both operations have been executed consecutively is independent of the order of the two operations), or one operation overwrites the other (meaning that the system configuration obtained after the overwriting operation has been performed is not affected by whether or not the other operation is executed immediately before it). In this paper we refer to such types as *simple* types. (Anderson and Moir [23] referred to those types as *resilient*, but their definition is slightly different from the one in [8].) Aspnes and Herlihy [8] describe a general wait-free construction of any simple type, which makes use of a snapshot object. We show that if this snapshot object is atomic, then Aspnes and Herlihy's algorithm is strongly linearizable. Combining this with Theorem 1 yields:

THEOREM 3. *Any simple type has a lock-free strongly linearizable implementation from registers.*

Aspnes and Herlihy introduce the notion of *linearization graphs*, which are directed acyclic graphs whose nodes are operations (we will define these structures more formally in Section 5). A linearization function is defined using topological orderings of these linearization graphs. However, since operations may be written to the "middle" of a linearization graph (i.e. an operation might have outgoing edges immediately as it is written to the graph), this linearization function is not prefix-preserving. Hence, even though we do not modify the algorithm, the proof of strong linearizability is involved.

2 PRELIMINARIES

We consider an asynchronous shared memory system with n processes, each of which has a unique identifier in $\{1, \dots, n\}$. More precisely, processes communicate by performing operations on shared objects. An operation *op* consists of an *invocation event*, denoted *inv*(*op*), and possibly a *response event*, denoted *rsp*(*op*). Processes perform operations sequentially. A type is defined by a *sequential specification*, which is the set of allowable sequences of operations on any object of that type. A *transcript* is a sequence of *steps*, each of which is either an invocation event or a response event of some operation. If T and U are transcripts, we use $T \circ U$ to denote the *concatenation* of T and U.

A *projection* of a transcript T onto an object O, denoted $T|O$, is the sequence of steps in T that are performed on O. Similarly, a projection of a transcript T onto a process p, denoted $T|p$, is the sequence of invocation and response events by process p. An operation op is *pending* in some transcript T if T contains its invocation but no matching response. If an operation $op \in T$ is not pending in T, then it is *complete*. A transcript T is *complete* if, for every operation $op \in T$, op is complete. Otherwise, T is *incomplete*. An operation op is *atomic* in a transcript T if $inv(op)$ is immediately followed by $rsp(op)$ in T. A transcript T is *well-formed* if, for every process p and any complete operation $op \in T$ by p, $T = T_1 \circ inv(op) \circ T_2 \circ rsp(op) \circ T_3$, and $T_2|p$ is complete. Throughout this paper, we assume all transcripts are well-formed.

An object O is *atomic* if every operation in any transcript on O is atomic. We say an object O is *implemented* if each operation invocation on O is associated with a *method*, which is a sequence of operation invocations. A process p that executes an operation on an implemented object O, such that $inv(op)$ is associated with a method M, sequentially executes each invocation step described by M. During the execution of this method, other processes may also take steps, which interleave with the steps taken by p.

Operation op_1 *happens before* operation op_2 in transcript T, or $op_1 \xrightarrow{T} op_2$, if and only if $rsp(op_1)$ occurs before $inv(op_2)$ in T. Operations $op_1, op_2 \in T$, for some transcript T, are *concurrent* if op_1 does not happen before op_2, and op_2 does not happen before op_1.

A *history* is a transcript such that, for every process p, every operation in $H|p$ is atomic. A *completion* of a history H is a complete history H' that is constructed from H by either removing or appending a response to each incomplete operation in H. A *sequential history* is a history that contains no concurrent operations. A sequential history S consisting of steps on an object O of type $\mathscr{T}$ is *valid* if and only if S is in the sequential specification of $\mathscr{T}$. If T is a transcript, the *interpreted history* $\Gamma(T)$ can be constructed by removing, for every process p, every step that appears after $inv(op)$ and not after $rsp(op)$, for any operation $op \in T$ with process identifier p. Intuitively, $\Gamma(T)$ consists of all "high-level" steps that exist in T. If $\mathcal{T}$ is a set of transcripts, then $\Gamma(\mathcal{T}) = \{\Gamma(T) : T \in \mathcal{T}\}$.

Linearizability was originally defined by Herlihy and Wing [21]. The following definition is taken from the textbook by Herlihy and Shavit [20]: a history H is *linearizable* if it has a completion H' such that there is a sequential history S with the following properties:

- All operations in H' are present in S, with identical invocations and responses;
- the sequential history S is valid; and
- the happens-before order of operations in S extends the happens-before order of operations in H'.

We call a sequential history S that satisfies the above properties a *linearization* of H. An implementation of an object is linearizable if every history in the set of possible histories on the object is linearizable. That is, if O is some object and $\mathcal{H}$ is the set of possible histories on O, then O is linearizable if and only if for all $H \in \mathcal{H}$, H is linearizable. If $\mathcal{H}$ is a set of histories, and f is a function such that, for every $H \in \mathcal{H}$, $f(H)$ is a linearization of H, then f is called a *linearization function* for the set $\mathcal{H}$.

We often refer to the *time* at which particular steps are executed; this simply refers to the step's position in a transcript. That is, if e is a step in a transcript T, then $time_T(e) = t$ if the t-th element of T is e. Where T is clear from context, we simply write $time(e) = t$. If e is a step that is not present in a transcript T, then let $time_T(e) = \infty$. If op is a complete operation whose implementation contains an atomic operation invocation on line x, we use op^x to denote the (atomic) operation invoked by the final call to line x performed by op. If am is an atomic operation in a transcript T, then we use $time(am)$ as a shorthand for $time(rsp(am))$. For the sake of brevity, if am is an atomic operation in a transcript T, then we say am *happens* at $time(am)$

Another characterization of linearizability relies on the notion of *linearization points*. A linearization point is a point in time between the invocation and response of an operation op at which op "appears" to take effect. In any transcript of a linearizable implementation, each operation can be assigned a linearization point, such that the sequential history that results from ordering each operation by these points is valid. Throughout this paper, we will use $pt(op)$ to reference the linearization point of an operation op.

The *prefix closure* of a set of transcripts $\mathcal{T}$, denoted $close(\mathcal{T})$, is the set of all transcripts S such that there exists a transcript T such that $S \circ T \in \mathcal{T}$. A *strong linearization function* f for a set of transcripts $\mathcal{T}$ has the following properties [16]:

- The function f is a linearization function for $\Gamma(close(\mathcal{T}))$.
- For any two transcripts $S, T \in \mathcal{T}$ such that S is a prefix of T, $f(S)$ is a prefix of $f(T)$. That is, f is *prefix-preserving*.

An implementation O of a type $\mathscr{T}$ is called *strongly linearizable* if and only if the set of all transcripts on instances of O has a strong linearization function.

An implementation of a type is *wait-free* if each operation terminates within a finite number of the calling process' steps. It is *lock-free* if some operation terminates provided that some process takes sufficiently many steps.

3 A STRONGLY LINEARIZABLE ABA-DETECTING REGISTER

An ABA-detecting register [5] is a type that stores a single value R from some domain D, and supports the operations $DWrite_q(x)$ for $x \in D$, and $DRead_q()$ with the following sequential specification: Initially, $R = \bot \in D$, and a $DWrite_q(x)$ operation changes the value of R to x. A $DRead_q()$ operation returns a pair $(x, a) \in D \times \{true, false\}$, where x is the value of R, and a is $true$ if and only if q performed an earlier $DRead_q()$ operation, and a $DWrite_p$ was performed by some process p since q's last $DRead_q()$.

3.1 A Linearizable ABA-Detecting Register

Aghazadeh and Woelfel [5] presented a wait-free linearizable ABA-detecting register, which is included here as Algorithm 1 for reference. For a detailed description of the algorithm and a proof of its linearizability, see [4, 5]. This algorithm works by associating each write with a process identifier and a sequence number. Processes are also responsible for "announcing" the sequence numbers they read into a global array of single-writer registers. That is, if process

p reads process identifier q and sequence number s, then it writes the pair (q, s) to the p-th entry of the announcement array A; a writer does not use a sequence number if it is paired with their process identifier in this announcement array. A writer also does not use any sequence number that is present in a local queue, called *usedQ* in Algorithm 1, which contains $n + 1$ values. This queue stores the previous $n + 1$ sequence numbers chosen by the writing process, and it initially contains $n + 1$ elements valued $\perp$. Finally, if a write occurs during a read operation, the reader sets a local flag. This flag is used to delegate the task of acknowledging the modification to the reading process' next read operation.

Algorithm 1: Lin. ABA-detecting register [5]

```
shared:
   register X = (⊥, ⊥, ⊥)
   register A[0 ... n − 1] = ((⊥, ⊥), ..., (⊥, ⊥))
local (to each process):
   Boolean b = False
   Queue usedQ[n + 1] = (⊥, ..., ⊥)
   Set na = {}
   Integer c = 0

Function DWrite_p(x):
1     s ← GetSeq()
2     X.Write(x, p, s)
Function GetSeq_p():
3     (r, s_r) ← A[c].Read()
4     if r = p then na ← (na \ {(c, i) | i ∈ ℕ}) ∪ (c, s_r)
5     else na ← na \ {(c, i) | i ∈ ℕ}
6     c ← (c + 1) mod n
7     choose an s ∈ ({0, ..., 2n + 1} \ ({i | (j, i) ∈ na} ∪ usedQ))
8     usedQ.enq(s)
9     usedQ.deq()
10    return s
Function DRead_q():
11    (x, p, s) ← X.Read()
12    (r, s_r) ← A[q].Read()
13    A[q].Write(p, s)
14    (x', p', s') ← X.Read()
15    if (p, s) = (r, s_r) then ret ← (x, b)
16    else ret ← (x, True)
17    if (x, p, s) = (x', p', s') then b ← False
18    else b ← True
19    return ret
```

Observation 4. *The ABA-detecting register in Algorithm 1 is not strongly linearizable.*

Algorithm 1 is not strongly linearizable because the point at which a *DRead* operation takes effect depends on whether or not a *DWrite* operation executes line 2 between lines 11 and 14 of the *DRead*; that is, if a process sets its b flag during a *DRead* operation, then it must linearize on line 11, since the following read will detect any *DWrite* operations that occur between lines 11 and 14. Conversely, if a process does not set its b flag during a *DRead* operation, then this operation is responsible for detecting any *DWrite* operations that occur between lines 11 and 14, and it must therefore linearize on line 14. This behaviour allows a scheduler to insert a *DRead* operation in front of *DWrite* operations that have already taken effect. We give a formal proof of Observation 4 in the full version of this paper.

3.2 Making the Algorithm Strongly Linearizable

Algorithm 1 can be modified in order to make the implementation strongly linearizable. Our modification to the *DRead* method of the linearizable ABA-detecting register is provided in Algorithm 2. The *GetSeq* and *DWrite* methods are the same as in [4]. Our strategy is to "stretch" *DRead* operations until a period of quiescence is observed by the reading process. Our new *DRead* operation executes the same sequence of reads as in Algorithm 1. However, each *DRead* is now responsible for acknowledging all concurrent *DWrite* operations, rather than delegating this task to the next *DRead* by the same process. Processes no longer maintain a local flag b; instead, each *DRead* operation begins by initializing a flag called *changed* to *false* on line 20, before starting a repeat-until loop. During an iteration of the repeat-until loop by a *DRead* operation, a process p that notices a difference in the values read from X on line 22 and line 25, or that $A[p]$ does not contain the same value as X, sets *changed* to *true* on line 27 before repeating its sequence of reads. A process p performing a *DRead* operation also announces the process identifier/sequence number pair read from X on line 22 to $A[p]$ on line 24. As before, the purpose of this announcement is to prevent *DWrite* operations from choosing sequence numbers that have been observed recently. When p sees that its sequence of reads all return the same value, it can safely return this value along with the *changed* flag. In that case, p's return value is consistent with the state of the ABA-detecting register at the point of p's last shared memory operation, i.e., when it reads X for the last time. Hence, each *DRead* method may now always be linearized at the time of its final read operation. Similarly, *DWrite* operations linearize at their final shared memory operation, which is when they write to X. It is easy to see that if all operations can linearize with their final shared memory operation, the corresponding linearization function is prefix-preserving, and thus the object is strongly linearizable.

Algorithm 2: *DRead* of a Strongly Linearizable ABA-Detecting Register

```
Function DRead_q():
20    changed = false
21    repeat
22       (x, p, s) ← X.Read()
23       (r, s_r) ← A[q].Read()
24       A[q].Write(p, s)
25       (x', p', s') ← X.Read()
26       if (p, s) ≠ (r, s_r) or (x, p, s) ≠ (x', p', s') then
27          changed ← true
28    until (p, s) = (r, s_r) and (x, p, s) = (x', p', s')
29    return (x', changed)
```

We now outline an argument that Algorithm 2 is strongly linearizable. Complete proofs of correctness are provided in the full version of this paper.

For any operation op in a transcript T on an instance of the implementation in Algorithm 2, let $pt(op)$ be defined as follows:

Q-1 If op is a *DRead* operation, then let $pt(op) = time(op^{25})$.

Q-2 If op is a $DWrite$ operation, then let $pt(op) = time(op^{2})$.

If $pt(op) \neq \infty$ for some operation op, then we say *op linearizes* at $pt(op)$. If T is a transcript on some instance of the object implementation in Algorithm 2, then we claim H is a linearization of T, where H is a sequential history composed of operations in $\Gamma(T)$ ordered by their corresponding pt values. That is, if op_i and op_j are operations in $\Gamma(T)$ and $pt(op_i) < pt(op_j)$, then $op_i \xrightarrow{H} op_j$. Also, for any operation $op \in \Gamma(T)$ such that $pt(op) = \infty$, omit op from H. Let f be a function that maps every transcript on Algorithm 2 to a sequential history as described above (the existence of such a function is trivial).

The following three lemmas are stated here without proof:

Lemma 5. *If an $X.Write(x, p, s)$ operation happens at time t, then there exists a $DWrite_p(x)$ operation dw by p such that $pt(dw) = t$.*

Lemma 6. *Let dr be a complete $DRead_q()$ operation performed by process q, and suppose at least one $DWrite$ dw linearizes after $time(dr^{22})$ and before q invokes any other DRead() operation following dr. Let p be the process executing dw, and s the sequence number associated with dw. Then*

(a) $A[q] \neq (p, s)$ at $time(dr^{23})$; and

(b) $pt(dw) \notin [time(dr^{22}), time(dr^{25})]$.

Lemma 7. *Let dr be a complete $DRead_p()$ operation that returns (val, a) for some $val \in D$, $val \neq \bot$, and some $a \in \{true, false\}$. Then there is some $DWrite$ operation that linearizes prior to $pt(dr)$. If dw is a $DWrite_q(x)$ operation, such that no $DWrite$ operation linearizes in $(pt(dw), pt(dr)]$, then $x = val$.*

We now show that ordering operations in T by their respective pt values results in a valid sequential history. We accomplish this by showing that, for any complete *DRead* operation dr by process p, the second component of the tuple returned by dr is $True$ if and only if some $DWrite$ operation linearizes before $pt(dr)$, but after dr', where dr' is the *DRead* operation by p that is performed immediately before dr.

Lemma 8. *Let dr_1, dr_2 be two complete DRead operations in T by process q, with $dr_1 \xrightarrow{T} dr_2$, where dr_1 is the latest DRead operation performed by q that precedes dr_2. Suppose dr_2 returns (val, a) for some value val and $a \in \{True, False\}$. Then $a = true$ if and only if some $DWrite$ operation linearizes in the interval $(pt(dr_1), pt(dr_2))$.*

Proof. First, suppose $a = True$. Then q executes line 27 during dr_2. Since the if condition on line 26 is satisfied if and only if the loop-guard on line 28 is false, q must execute line 27 on the first iteration of the repeat-until loop on line 21 during dr_2. Let (x, p, s) and (x', p', s') be the tuples returned by the X.*Read*() operations xr and xr' performed during the first iteration of the loop on line 22 and line 25, respectively. Also let (r, s_r) be the pair returned by the $A[q]$.*Read*() operation ar performed during the first iteration of the loop on line 23. Since dr_1 and dr_2 are performed in sequence, xr, xr', and ar all happen after $pt(dr_1)$. Additionally, since $pt(dr_2) = time(dr_2^{25})$ (i.e. dr_2 linearizes at its *final* execution of line 25), and dr_2 performs the repeat-until loop on line 21 more than once,

$$xr, xr', \text{and } ar \text{ all happen in } (pt(dr_1), pt(dr_2)). \quad (1)$$

By the condition on line 26, there are two cases:

(i) Suppose $(x, p, s) \neq (x', p', s')$. Since xr' returns (x', p', s'), there exists an $X.Write(x', p', s')$ in $(time(xr), time(xr'))$. Hence, by (1) and Lemma 5 there exists a $DWrite_{p'}(x')$ operation that linearizes in $(pt(dr_1), pt(dr_2))$.

(ii) Suppose $(p, s) \neq (r, s_r)$. Assume that dr_1 writes (p_1, s_1) to $A[q]$ in its final call to line 24. By the loop-guard on line 28,

$$dr_1^{25} \text{ returns } (x_1, p_1, s_1). \quad (2)$$

Since q performs dr_2 immediately after dr_1, and q is the only process that can write to $A[q]$, $(r, s_r) = (p_1, s_1)$. But since $(p, s) \neq (r, s_r)$ by assumption, $(x, p, s) \neq (x_1, p_1, s_1)$. Due to (2), there must be an $X.Write(x, p, s)$ operation that happens in $(time(dr_1^{25}), time(xr))$. By Lemma 5, there exists a $DWrite$ operation that linearizes in $(time(dr_1^{25}), time(xr))$, and by (1), this $DWrite$ linearizes in $(pt(dr_1), pt(dr_2))$.

Now suppose $a = False$. Assume, for the sake of a contradiction, that some $DWrite$ linearizes in $(pt(dr_1), pt(dr_2))$. Let dw be the $DWrite$ operation that linearizes at the latest time in this interval. Suppose dw is a $DWrite_{p_1}(x_1)$ by process p_1 with associated sequence number s_1. Due to Lemma 6 (b), we know that no $DWrite$ can linearize in the interval $[time(dr_2^{22}), time(dr_2^{25})]$. Thus,

$$dw \text{ linearizes in } (time(dr_1^{25}), time(dr_2^{22})). \quad (3)$$

Since dw is the final $DWrite$ operation that linearizes prior to dr_2^{25},

$$X = (x_1, p_1, s_1) \text{ throughout } [pt(dw), pt(dr_2)]. \quad (4)$$

If dr_2 performs the repeat-until loop on line 21 more than once, then since the loop-guard on line 38 is true if and only if the condition line 26 is true, q sets *changed* to $True$ during dr_2, which is a contradiction. Hence, dr_2 must perform only one iteration of the repeat-until loop. By (3) and (4), the X.*Read*() operation dr_2^{22} must return (x_1, p_1, s_1). Also, q reads (p_1, s_1) from $A[q]$ during dr_2^{23}, as otherwise the loop would repeat by the loop-guard on line 38. Hence, the last write to $A[q]$ prior to dr_2^{23} must have been an $A[q].Write(p_1, s_1)$ operation. Since q only performs one iteration of the repeat-until loop during dr_2, and thus does not write anything to $A[q]$ prior to dr_2^{23} while executing dr_2, q must have written (p_1, s_1) to $A[q]$ in the final iteration of the repeat-until loop of dr_1 (i.e. during dr_1^{24}). Since the repeat-until loop of dr_1 also terminated after that write, q must have read (p_1, s_1) from $A[q]$ during dr_1^{23}. This, along with (3), contradicts Lemma 6 (a). □

Together, Lemma 7 and Lemma 8 imply that Algorithm 2 is linearizable. In the full version of this paper, we provide a (straightforward) argument that the linearization function f is prefix-preserving. Thus, we obtain the following:

Theorem 9. *The implementation represented by Algorithm 2 is strongly linearizable.*

It is easy to see that each $DWrite_q$ performs only two shared memory steps (a read of $A[q]$ and a write to X). Hence, the implementation of $DWrite$ is wait-free. However, a $DRead_q$ by a process q may not terminate if it gets "interrupted" by infinitely many $DWrite$ operations. But note that in each iteration of the repeat-until loop process q writes the same pair (p, s) to $A[q]$ in line 24 that it previously read in line 22 from the second and third component of X. Hence, if q executes sufficiently many steps while X does not change, then q will eventually read the same pair from X in line 22, from $A[q]$ in line 23, and from X again in line 25. After that, q's $DRead$ terminates. Thus, in any transcript in which q takes sufficiently many steps, either its $DRead$ terminates, or a $DWrite$ terminates. This proves that Algorithm 2 is lock-free.

A more precise analysis yields the following result.

THEOREM 10. *(a) Each DWrite() performs at most two shared memory operations; and*

(b) for any transcript that contains r DRead and w DWrite invocations, the total number of steps devoted to DRead operations is $O(\min\{r, n\} \cdot w + r)$.

In particular, the implementation is lock-free and has amortized step complexity $O(n)$.

Theorems 9 and 10 yield Theorem 2.

4 A STRONGLY LINEARIZABLE SNAPSHOT

A *(single-writer) snapshot* [2] is a type that stores a vector $S \in D^n$, where D is some domain, and supports the operations $update_q(x)$ and $scan_q()$. Operation $update_q(x)$ replaces the q-th element of the vector with value x and operation $scan_q()$ returns the vector.

We use brackets to denote individual entries in vectors and snapshot objects. More precisely, if $X = (x_1, \ldots, x_k)$, then $X[p] = x_p$ for each $p \in \{1, \ldots, k\}$.

4.1 Unbounded Implementation

Denysyuk and Woelfel [14] define a general lock-free construction for *versioned* objects, which each store a version number. A versioned object has an atomic update operation, which increases the object's version number every time it is invoked. A versioned object also supports a read operation, which returns the state of the object along with its version number. The simple lock-free linearizable snapshot algorithm based on clean double collects from [2] can be transformed into a versioned snapshot object easily, by adding a sequence number field to each component that is incremented with each update of the component. The version number of the entire object may be obtained by calculating the sum of the sequence numbers of every component.

The strongly linearizable construction of a versioned object uses a strongly linearizable bounded max-register described by Helmi, Higham, and Woelfel [17]. Denysyuk and Woelfel augment the max-register implementation such that it stores a pair (x, y). The augmented max-register supports a *maxRead*() operation, which returns the pair (x, y), and a $maxWrite(x', y')$ operation, which replaces the stored pair (x, y) with (x', y') provided that $x' > x$.

Denysyuk and Woelfel's construction uses a single instance of a versioned object S of type $\mathcal{T}$, along with a single instance of an augmented max-register R. A strongly linearizable object S' of type $\mathcal{T}$ is obtained as follows: to perform an $S'.update(x)$ operation, a process executes an $S.update(x)$ operation, reads S to obtain the pair (y, v), and finally performs an $R.maxWrite(v, y)$ operation (note that v represents the version number of the object). To execute an $S'.read()$ operation, a process performs an $R.maxRead()$ operation to obtain the pair (v, y), and returns the value y.

The fact that this algorithm is strongly linearizable follows from a simple argument. Let up be some $S'.update(x)$ operation. Suppose that S' has version number v immediately after up performs its $S.update(x)$ operation. Then up may be linearized as soon as some $R.maxWrite(v', y)$ operation, with $v' \geq v$, linearizes. If multiple $S'.update$ operations linearize at the same step, then these operations may be ordered by the times at which their atomic $S.update$ operations responded. An $S'.read()$ operation may be linearized as soon as its $R.maxRead()$ operation linearizes. Since each operation on S' can be linearized at the same step as an operation on R, then S' is strongly linearizable because R is strongly linearizable.

As mentioned previously, the construction uses an implementation of a *bounded* max-register, which means that the version number of the strongly linearizable object is bounded. Hence, without further modification, the algorithm only supports a finite number of update operations on the constructed object. Helmi, Higham, and Woelfel's [17] max-register implementation becomes unbounded with a simple modification, but this modification requires an unbounded number of registers.

4.2 Bounded Implementation

Our strongly linearizable snapshot object uses any lock-free or wait-free linearizable implementation of a snapshot object. To achieve a strongly linearizable snapshot object that uses bounded space, we must ensure that the underlying linearizable snapshot implementation also uses only bounded space. For the sake of concreteness, we use an implementation by Attiya and Rachman [12], which is wait-free and linearizable. The bounded implementation presented in [12] uses $O(n^3)$ registers of size $O(\log n + \log |D|)$ to represent views of the snapshot object (where D is the set of values that may be stored by a component), plus $O(n^5)$ registers of size $O(\log n)$ to manage sequence numbers. This implementation therefore has space complexity $O(n^3(\log n + \log |D|) + n^5 \log n)$. The algorithm performs $O(n \log n)$ operations on MRSW registers during any *scan* or *update* operation. Let S be an instance of this bounded wait-free linearizable snapshot object implementation. Our algorithm also uses a shared atomic ABA-detecting register R. The snapshot object S is used to hold the contents of the strongly linearizable snapshot object, while the ABA-detecting register R contains a vector of size n that represents the state of S at some previous point in time. Since strong linearizability is a composable property [10, 16], we can replace the atomic ABA-detecting register R with our strongly linearizable one from Section 3.

In order to clearly distinguish between operations on the linearizable snapshot object S and the implemented strongly linearizable snapshot, we call the operations on the latter one *SLupdate* and *SLscan*. Pseudocode for our implementation is presented in Algorithm 3.

The *SLupdate* operation is nearly identical to the update operation of the unbounded implementation: to perform an $SLupdate_p(x)$ operation, for some $x \in D$, a process p first performs an $S.update_p(x)$

Algorithm 3: Strongly Linearizable Snapshot Object

```
shared:
    linearizable snapshot object S
    atomic ABA-detecting register R

Function SLupdate_p(x):
30      S.update_p(x)
31      s ← S.scan()
32      R.DWrite_p(s)
Function SLscan_p():
33      repeat
34          (s1, c1) ← R.DRead_p()
35          ℓ ← S.scan()
36          (s2, c2) ← R.DRead_p()
37          if !(s1 = ℓ = s2) then R.DWrite_p(ℓ)
38      until (s1 = ℓ = s2) and !c2
39      return s2
```

operation on line 30. Process p then performs an $S.scan()$ operation on line 31, and finally writes the result of this call to R on line 32.

An $SLscan_p()$ operation, for some process p, is "stretched" until a period of time is observed during which the underlying objects S and R are not modified. The method works by repeatedly performing an $R.DRead_p()$ operation on line 34, then an $S.scan()$ operation on line 35, and finally another $R.DRead_p()$ operation on line 36. Process p continues to perform this sequence of operations until the same vector is returned by all of these calls. Whenever p observes that the contents of R and S are inconsistent, p helps pending *SLupdate* operations by writing the previously-taken snapshot of S to R on line 37 before resuming its main loop. When p observes that the $S.scan()$ operation and the two $R.DRead_p()$ operations return the same vector, p makes sure that R was not changed between its most recent pair of $R.DRead_p()$ operations by checking the boolean flag returned by the second *DRead* on line 38; if this flag is false, then p returns the value that was returned by its final *DRead*.

Both *SLscan* and *SLupdate* operations work to stabilize the contents of S and R. The underlying snapshot object S always contains the most recent state of the object, and operations write the state of S that they observed most recently to R (on both line 32 for *SLupdate* operations and line 37 for *SLscan* operations). A pending $SLupdate_p(x)$ operation by process p can be linearized as soon as some concurrent *SLscan* operation returns a vector that contains x in its p-th entry. The key is that we choose a linearization point for this *SLupdate* operation at which the p-th component of S contains x and the value of $R[p]$ is x. We choose to linearize *SLscan* operations on their final execution of line 36. Our choice of linearization points results in a strong linearization function because *SLscan* operations always linearize at their final shared memory step, and when an *SLscan* operation linearizes, it is already determined which *SLupdate* operations are caused to linearize by this *SLscan* operation.

We now outline an argument that Algorithm 3 is strongly linearizable. Complete proofs of correctness are provided in the full version of this paper.

Since S is a non-atomic implementation of a snapshot object, its value at any particular step of a transcript is not well-defined. Hence, we introduce the notion of an *interpreted value*, which simplifies our arguments. Let T be a transcript on an instance of Algorithm 3. Let pt_S be a function that maps operations in $\Gamma(T|S)$ to linearization points in T. That is, $pt_S(op_i) < pt_S(op_j)$ implies that op_i takes effect before op_j in T. Assume that if $pt_S(op_i) = pt_S(op_j)$, op_i is an *update* operation, and op_j is a *scan* operation, then op_i takes effect before op_j in T.Then the interpreted value of $S[p]$ at step t of T is x if there exists an $update_p(x)$ operation up by p such that $pt_S(up) \le t$, and there is no $update_p(x')$ operation up' by p such that $pt_S(up) < pt_S(up') \le t$.

For any operation op in a transcript T on some instance of the implementation provided in Algorithm 3, we define $pt(op)$ as follows:

R-1 Suppose op is some *SLscan* operation. Then $pt(op)$ is the time at which the final shared memory step is performed by op. That is, $pt(op) = time(op^{36})$.

R-2 Suppose op is some $SLupdate_p(x)$ operation for some $x \in D$. If T contains an *SLscan* operation sc such that $pt(sc) \neq \infty$, $time(inv(op)) < pt(sc)$, and sc returns a vector whose p-th entry contains x, then let sc_0 be such an *SLscan* operation with the lowest possible pt value. Let $t = pt(sc_0)$ if sc_0 exists, or $t = \infty$ otherwise. Then $pt(op) = min(t, time(op^{32}))$.

If $pt(op) \neq \infty$ for some operation op, then we say op *linearizes* at $pt(op)$. If T is a transcript on some instance of the object implementation in Algorithm 3, then we claim H is a linearization of T, where H is a sequential history composed of operations in $\Gamma(T)$ ordered by their corresponding pt values. That is, if op_i and op_j are operations in $\Gamma(T)$ performed by processes p and q respectively, and $pt(op_i) < pt(op_j)$, then $op_i \xrightarrow{H} op_j$. If $pt(op_i) = pt(op_j)$, then $op_i \xrightarrow{H} op_j$ if either op_j is an *SLscan* operation and op_i is an *SLupdate* operation, or both operations are of the same type and $p < q$. Also, for any operation $op \in \Gamma(T)$ such that $pt(op) = \infty$, omit op from H. Let f be a function that maps every transcript on Algorithm 3 to a sequential history as described above (the existence of such a function is trivial).

The following four lemmas are stated here without proof:

Lemma 11. *For any complete SLscan or SLupdate operation op in T, $pt(op) \in [time(inv(op)), time(rsp(op))]$.*

Lemma 12. *Let sc be some $SLscan_p()$ operation by some process p such that $pt(sc) \neq \infty$. Then no R.DWrite operation occurs in the interval $[time(sc^{34}), time(sc^{36})]$.*

Lemma 13. *Let up be some complete $SLupdate_p(x)$ operation, for some process p and some $x \in D$. Then the interpreted value of $S[p]$ induced by pt_S is x and $R[p] = x$ at $pt(up)$.*

Lemma 14. *Let sc be some complete $SLscan_q()$ operation in T by process q, which returns $(x_1, x_2, \ldots, x_n)$. Then $x_p \neq \bot$ if and only if there exists some $SLupdate_p(x_p)$ operation up in T, for some $x_p \in D$, such that $pt(up) \le pt(sc)$.*

We now show that ordering operations in T by their respective pt values results in a valid sequential history. We accomplish this by showing that, for any complete *SLscan* operation sc, each component of the vector returned by sc contains the value written by the *SLupdate* operation that linearized most recently (relative to $pt(sc)$).

LEMMA 15. *Let sc be some complete* $SLscan_q()$ *operation in* T *by process* q *that returns* $(x_1, x_2, \ldots, x_n)$, *and suppose* $x_p \neq \bot$ *for some process* p. *Then there is some* $SLupdate_p(x_p)$ *operation* up_{x_p} *such that* $pt(up_{x_p}) \leq pt(sc)$, *and there is no* $SLupdate_p(x)$ *operation* up_x *such that* $pt(up_{x_p}) < pt(up_x) \leq pt(sc)$, *for any* $x \in D$.

PROOF. Let up_{x_p} be the last $SLupdate_p(x_p)$ operation by p that linearizes at or before $pt(sc)$ (Lemma 14 guarantees that such an operation exists). To derive a contradiction, suppose that some $SLupdate_p(x)$ operation with $x \neq x_p$ exists, which linearizes in the interval $\big(pt(up_{x_p}), pt(sc)\big]$. Let up_x be the latest such operation. So,

$$pt(up_{x_p}) < pt(up_x) \leq pt(sc). \tag{5}$$

By Lemma 13,

$$\text{the interpreted value of } S[p] \text{ is } x \text{ at } pt(up_x), \text{ and} \tag{6}$$

$$R[p] = x \text{ at } pt(up_x). \tag{7}$$

Let sc_ℓ be the final *S.scan()* operation performed by sc. By the definition of pt_S and the implementation of Algorithm 3,

$$time(sc^{34}) < pt_S(sc_\ell) < time(sc^{36}). \tag{8}$$

There are two cases:

(i) Operation up_x linearizes after sc_ℓ. That is,

$$pt(up_x) > pt_S(sc_\ell). \tag{9}$$

By R-1,

$$pt(sc) = time(sc^{36}). \tag{10}$$

By (5), (8), (9) and (10),

$$time(sc^{34}) < pt(up_x) < time(sc^{36}). \tag{11}$$

By (7), there is an $R.DWrite(X)$ operation dw, with $X[p] = x_p$, such that

$$pt(up_x) < time(dw) < time(sc^{36}). \tag{12}$$

But by (11) and (12), $time(dw) \in \big(time(sc^{34}), time(sc^{36})\big)$, which contradicts Lemma 12.

(ii) Operation up_x linearizes not after sc_ℓ. That is,

$$pt(up_x) \leq pt_S(sc_\ell). \tag{13}$$

Due to (6) and (13), there must be an $S.update_p(x_p)$ operation that linearizes after $pt(up_x)$, but not after $pt_S(sc_\ell)$. Let up'_{x_p} be the $SLupdate_p(x_p)$ operation by p that performs this $S.update_p(x_p)$ operation. Then by R-2, $pt(up'_{x_p}) \leq pt(sc)$, which, combined with (5), contradicts the assumption that up_{x_p} is the final $SLupdate_p(x_p)$ operation to linearize not after $pt(sc)$.

□

Together, Lemma 11 and Lemma 15 imply that Algorithm 3 is linearizable. In the full version of this paper, we provide a (straightforward) argument that the linearization function f is prefix-preserving. Thus, we obtain the following:

THEOREM 16. *The implementation represented by Algorithm 3 is strongly linearizable.*

In the full version of this paper, we also provide an amortized analysis of the complexity of our implementation. The result is expressed in terms of the number of operations on the snapshot object S and the ABA-detecting register R.

THEOREM 17. *(a) Each SLupdate() performs at most one S.update(), one S.scan(), and one R.DWrite() operation.*

(b) For any transcript that contains u SLupdate and s SLscan invocations, the total number of operation invocations on S and R during SLscan() operations is $O(s + n^3 u)$.

In particular, the implementation is lock-free provided that S and R are.

As mentioned previously, we can use any lock-free or wait-free linearizable snapshot implementation for S. Instead of an atomic ABA-detecting register R, we can use the lock-free strongly linearizable one from Section 3. Thus, Theorems 2, 16, and 17 yield Theorem 1.

5 GENERAL CONSTRUCTION

Aspnes and Herlihy [8] defined the large class of *simple* types, and demonstrated that any type in this class has a wait-free linearizable implementation from atomic multi-reader multi-writer registers. Simple types require that any pair of operations either commute, or one overwrites the other (see below for a formal definition). Algorithm 4 depicts Aspnes and Herlihy's general wait-free linearizable implementation of an arbitrary simple type $\mathcal{T}$. Processes communicate only through an atomic snapshot object, *root* (which can be replaced with a wait-free linearizable implementation from registers). The algorithm supports a single operation *execute(invoc)* that takes an invocation event *invoc* as an argument. Consider a sequential history $S = e_{h_1} \circ e_{h_2} \circ \ldots \circ e_{h_k}$, such that e_{h_i} is an $execute(inv(h_i))$ operation and h_i is an operation on $\mathcal{T}$ for any $i \in \{1, \ldots, k\}$. Then S is valid if and only if $H = h_1 \circ h_2 \circ \ldots \circ h_k$ is in the sequential specification of $\mathcal{T}$. Aspnes and Herlihy proved that Algorithm 4 is linearizable w.r.t. this sequential specification. We prove that it is in fact strongly linearizable, and thus it remains strongly linearizable if *root* is a strongly linearizable snapshot object. Thus, using our lock-free snapshot implementation from Section 4 for *root* yields Theorem 3.

An operation op on an object O is *total* if, for every sequential history H on O, there exists a response $rsp(op)$ such that $H \circ inv(op) \circ rsp(op)$ is valid. The following definitions are due to Aspnes and Herlihy [8]: Two sequential histories H and H' are *equivalent* if, for any sequential history S, $H \circ S$ is valid if and only if $H' \circ S$ is valid. Invocations $inv(op_1)$ and $inv(op_2)$ *commute* if, for all sequential histories H, $H \circ op_1 \circ op_2$ and $H \circ op_2 \circ op_1$ are valid and equivalent, provided $H \circ op_1$ and $H \circ op_2$ are valid. Invocation $inv(op_2)$ *overwrites* $inv(op_1)$ if, for all sequential histories H, $H \circ op_1 \circ op_2$ is valid and equivalent to $H \circ op_2$, provided $H \circ op_1$ and $H \circ op_2$ are valid. As a shorthand, we say an operation op_1 commutes with (resp. overwrites) an operation op_2 if $inv(op_1)$ commutes with (resp. overwrites) $inv(op_2)$. These properties allow us to describe the class of *simple* types.

Definition 18. *Let $\mathscr{T}$ be a type that supports a set of total operations O. Then $\mathscr{T}$ is* simple *if, for every pair of operations $op_1, op_2 \in O$, either op_1 and op_2 commute, or one overwrites the other.*

A *precedence graph* $G = (V, E)$ of a history H is a directed graph whose vertices are operations, such that for any $op_1, op_2 \in H$ there is a directed path from op_1 to op_2 in G if and only if $op_1 \xrightarrow{H} op_2$. Notice that the happens-before relation is the transitive closure of G. An operation op_1 by process p *dominates* an operation op_2 by process q if either op_1 overwrites op_2 but not vice versa, or both operations overwrite each other and $p > q$. A *linearization graph, lingraph(G)*, is constructed by adding directed edges to the precedence graph G as follows: First, an arbitrary topological order $(op_1, \ldots, op_k)$ of G is fixed. Then all pairs (i, j), $1 \leq i < j \leq k$, are considered in lexicographical order, and if one of the two operations in $\{op_i, op_j\}$ dominates the other, an edge is added from the dominated operation to the dominating one, provided that edge does not close a cycle. A precise description of the construction of a linearization graph is provided in the *lingraph* method of Algorithm 4.

Algorithm 4 maintains a partial representation of a precedence graph in a shared snapshot object called *root*. Each entry of the *root* variable contains a reference to an instance of type *node*, which has three fields: *invocation*, *response*, and *preceding*. The *invocation* and *response* fields contain a matching invocation and response event, respectively. We refer collectively to the *invocation* and *response* fields of a node x as the *operation* stored by x. The *preceding* field is an array containing n references to nodes. For a node x, $x.preceding[i]$ contains either $\bot$ or a pointer to a node y. The algorithm maintains the invariant that if $x.preceding[i] = y \neq \bot$, then the response event stored in $y.response$ occurred before the invocation event stored in $x.invocation$. This way, *root* represents a precedence graph $G = (V, E)$, as follows: An operation *op* is in V if and only if a *root.update(x)* operation has been executed for a node x that stores *op*, and the predecessors of *op* are the operations stored in the nodes pointed to by $x.preceding[1], \ldots, x.preceding[n]$.

Consider a transcript of *execute* operations, which each take as an argument some invocation event of a simple type $\mathscr{T}$. Let e_h be an *execute(inv(h))* by process p, for some operation h. Process p begins e_h by performing a *root.scan()* operation on line 49. This *root.scan()* operation returns a vector *view* of references to nodes. In line 50 process p computes a precedence graph G using a straightforward graph search, starting with the nodes stored in *view*. It then calculates a sequential history H on line 51 by topologically sorting a linearization graph *lingraph(G)*. That history is a linearization of the transcript that ended with p's *root.scan()*. Now p constructs a new node x that stores the invocation event $inv(h)$ and a response event $rsp(h)$ such that $H \circ inv(h) \circ rsp(h)$ is valid (lines 52-54). The existence of the response $rsp(h)$ is guaranteed by the fact that operations on a simple type are total. Note that the node referenced by $view[q]$ is the most recent node written to *root* by process q prior to the *root.scan()* operation performed by e_h. For every process $q \in \{1, \ldots, n\}$, p stores $view[q]$ in $x.preceding[q]$ on line 55. Finally, p writes the address of the constructed node to the snapshot object on line 56.

We proceed by first outlining an argument for the linearizability, and then for the strong linearizability of Algorithm 4. On line 51, an operation ensures that it calculates a valid response with respect

Algorithm 4: Implementation of a Simple Type [8]

```
struct node :
    invocation event, invocation
    response event, response
    pointers to nodes, preceding[1...n]
shared
    atomic snapshot object root = (null, ..., null)

Function lingraph(G):
40  Let op_1, ..., op_k be a topological sort of G
41  L ← G
42  for i ∈ {1, ..., k − 1} do
43      for j ∈ {i + 1, ..., k} do
44          if op_i dominates op_j and adding (op_j, op_i) to L
              does not complete a cycle then
45              Add (op_j, op_i) to L
46          if op_j dominates op_i and adding (op_i, op_j) to L
              does not complete a cycle then
47              Add (op_i, op_j) to L
48  return L

Function execute_p(invoc):
49  view ← root.scan()
50  G ← precedence graph constructed from view
51  H ← topological sort of lingraph(G)
52  initialize a new node e ← {⊥, ⊥, ⊥}
53  e.invocation ← invoc
54  e.response ← resp s.t. H ∘ invoc ∘ resp is valid
55  for i ∈ {1, ..., n} do e.preceding[i] ← view[i]
56  root.update_p(address of e)
57  return e.response
```

to the sequential history H constructed on line 51. Then assuming that H is valid, the algorithm is correct as long as writing out a node constructed by a pending *execute* operation does not invalidate the response of some concurrent *execute* operation. Suppose e_{h_1} is an *execute(inv(h_1))* operation, e_{h_2} is an *execute(inv(h_2))* operation, and e_{h_1} and e_{h_2} are concurrent. Since the simulated object is simple, either h_1 and h_2 commute, or one overwrites the other. If h_1 and h_2 commute, then it does not matter which operation is written to *root* first, since their responses are valid in either case. If h_2 overwrites h_1 and h_1 is written to the precedence graph first, then the response eventually calculated by e_{h_2} for h_2 is still valid, since h_1 is overwritten by h_2. If h_2 overwrites h_1 and h_2 is written to *root* first, then since e_{h_1} and e_{h_2} are concurrent, h_1 still calculates a valid response, because h_2 is not in the precedence graph constructed by e_{h_1} on line 50. It follows that the precedence graph represented by *root* remains linearizable after any pending *execute* operation writes its node to *root*.

We now provide a brief argument that the algorithm is strongly linearizable; the full proof is lengthy and technical, and has been omitted due to space restrictions. After a process performs the *root.scan*() operation on line 49, the response of simulated operation is entirely determined, since it is chosen based on the contents of the precedence graph constructed from *view* on line 50. If, during some *execute*(*inv*(h_1)) operation e_{h_1}, an *execute*(*inv*(h_2)) operation e_{h_2} writes its constructed node to *root*, and h_2 dominates h_1, then e_{h_1} may be linearized immediately before e_{h_2}, since h_1 no longer has any effect on the responses calculated by subsequent *execute* operations. Hence, operations may only linearize when some node is written to *root* on line 56, and it is entirely determined which operations linearize as a particular node is written to the graph (i.e. all concurrent operations that are dominated by the operation stored by the written node).

6 DISCUSSION

We have provided a lock-free strongly linearizable implementation of a snapshot object using atomic multi-reader multi-writer registers as base objects. We used this implementation to demonstrate that any simple object also has a lock-free strongly linearizable implementation from atomic multi-reader multi-writer registers. It is as yet unknown whether the existence of a lock-free strongly linearizable implementation of an object from registers implies that the object is simple. Additionally, we have not yet explored the characteristics of objects that enable wait-free strongly linearizable implementations from registers.

The class of simple types seems to be a large subset of the set of types that have wait-free linearizable implementations. In fact, we are not aware of any natural or useful type that has a wait-free linearizable implementation but is not simple. This is one of the reasons that leads us to conjecture that any type that has a wait-free linearizable implementation from atomic registers, also has strongly linearizable implementations with the following properties: (1) lock-free from atomic registers; and (2) wait-free from atomic single-writer snapshot objects. (Note that the second conjecture implies the first one.)

Anderson and Moir [23] define a class of *readable* objects, which support a single operation that returns the entire state of the object, along with a set of update operations that do not return anything and may modify the state of the object. Anderson and Moir claim that a "resiliency condition" is necessary and sufficient for the existence of a wait-free implementation of an object from registers. This condition is similar to Aspnes and Herlihy's definition of simple types, and Anderson and Moir claim that the sufficiency of the resiliency condition follows from the general construction in [8]. However, the resiliency condition is dynamic in the sense that, after a particular history two invocations may commute, while after another history these same two invocations may no longer commute, while instead one overwrites the other. Hence, while all simple objects satisfy Anderson and Moir's resiliency condition, it is not true that all objects which satisfy the resiliency condition are simple. Therefore, Anderson and Moir's claim that a readable object has a wait-free implementation from registers if the object satisfies the resiliency condition remains unproven. Note that if Anderson and Moir's claim was true, combined with our results this would imply that a readable object has a lock-free strongly linearizable implementation from atomic multi-reader multi-writer registers if and only if it satisfies the resiliency condition.

REFERENCES

[1] Karl Abrahamson. On achieving consensus using a shared memory. In *Proceedings of the Seventh Annual ACM Symposium on Principles of Distributed Computing*, PODC '88, pages 291–302, New York, NY, USA, 1988. ACM. URL: http://doi.acm.org/10.1145/62546.62594, doi:10.1145/62546.62594.

[2] Yehuda Afek, Hagit Attiya, Danny Dolev, Eli Gafni, Michael Merritt, and Nir Shavit. Atomic snapshots of shared memory. In *Journal of the Association for Computing Machinery*, pages 873–890, 1993.

[3] Yehuda Afek and Eytan Weisberger. The instancy of snapshots and commuting objects. *Journal of Algorithms*, 30(1):68–105, 1999.

[4] Zahra Aghazadeh. *Efficient Shared Memory Algorithms for Bounding Space*. PhD thesis, University of Calgary, 2018.

[5] Zahra Aghazadeh and Philipp Woelfel. On the time and space complexity of ABA prevention and detection. In *Proceedings of the 2015 ACM Symposium on Principles of Distributed Computing*, pages 193–202, 2015.

[6] James Aspnes, Hagit Attiya, and Keren Censor. Max registers, counters, and monotone circuits. In *Proceedings of the 28th Annual ACM Symposium on Principles of Distributed Computing, PODC 2009, Calgary, Alberta, Canada, August 10-12, 2009*, pages 36–45, 2009. URL: https://doi.org/10.1145/1582716.1582728, doi:10.1145/1582716.1582728.

[7] James Aspnes and Keren Censor-Hillel. Atomic snapshots in o (log 3 n) steps using randomized helping. In *International Symposium on Distributed Computing*, pages 254–268. Springer, 2013.

[8] James Aspnes and Maurice Herliny. Wait-free data structures in the asynchronous PRAM model. In *Proceedings of the 1990 ACM Symposium on Parallel algorithms and architectures*, pages 340–349, 1990.

[9] Hagit Attiya, Armando Castañeda, and Danny Hendler. Nontrivial and universal helping for wait-free queues and stacks. *J. Parallel Distrib. Comput.*, 121:1–14, 2018. URL: https://doi.org/10.1016/j.jpdc.2018.06.004, doi:10.1016/j.jpdc.2018.06.004.

[10] Hagit Attiya and Constantin Enea. Putting strong linearizability in context: Preserving hyperproperties in programs that use concurrent objects. Manuscript, May 2019.

[11] Hagit Attiya, Maurice Herlihy, and Ophir Rachman. Atomic snapshots using lattice agreement. *Distributed Computing*, 8(3):121–132, 1995.

[12] Hagit Attiya and Ophir Rachman. Atomic snapshots in o (n log n) operations. *SIAM Journal on Computing*, 27(2):319–340, 1998.

[13] Elizabeth Borowsky and Eli Gafni. Immediate atomic snapshots and fast renaming. In *Proceedings of the twelfth annual ACM symposium on Principles of distributed computing*, pages 41–51. ACM, 1993.

[14] Oksana Denysyuk and Philipp Woelfel. Wait-freedom is harder than lock-freedom under strong linearizability. In *International Symposium on Distributed Computing*, pages 60–74, 2015.

[15] Rainer Gawlick, Nancy Lynch, and Nir Shavit. Concurrent timestamping made simple. In *Theory of Computing and Systems*, pages 171–183. Springer, 1992.

[16] Wojciech Golab, Lisa Higham, and Philipp Woelfel. Linearizable implementations do not suffice for randomized distributed computation. In *Proceedings of the 2011 ACM symposium on Theory of Computing*, pages 373–382, 2011.

[17] Maryam Helmi, Lisa Higham, and Philipp Woelfel. Strongly linearizable implementations: possibilities and impossibilities. In *Proceedings of the 2012 ACM symposium on Principles of Distributed Computing*, pages 385–394, 2012.

[18] Maurice Herlihy. Wait-free synchronization. *ACM Transactions on Programming Languages and Systems (TOPLAS)*, 13(1):124–149, 1991. doi:10.1145/114005.102808.

[19] Maurice Herlihy and Nir Shavit. The asynchronous computability theorem for t-resilient tasks. In *STOC*, volume 93, pages 111–120, 1993.

[20] Maurice Herlihy and Nir Shavit. *The Art of Multiprocessor Programming*. Morgan Kaufmann, 2012.

[21] Maurice Herlihy and Jeannette Wing. Linearizability: a correctness condition for concurrent objects. *ACM Transactions on Programming Languages and Systems (TOPLAS)*, 12(3):463–492, 1990. doi:10.1145/78969.78972.

[22] Michiko Inoue, Toshimitsu Masuzawa, Wei Chen, and Nobuki Tokura. Linear-time snapshot using multi-writer multi-reader registers. In *International Workshop on Distributed Algorithms*, pages 130–140. Springer, 1994.

[23] Anderson James and Moir Mark. Towards a necessary and sufficient condition for wait-free synchonization. In *Proceedings of the 1993 International Workshop on Distributed Algorithms*, 1993.

Brief Announcement: Fast Concurrent Data Sketches

Arik Rinberg
arikrinberg@campus.technion.ac.il
Technion

Alexander Spiegelman
spiegelmans@vmware.com
VMware Research

Edward Bortnikov
ebortnik@verizonmedia.com
Yahoo Research

Eshcar Hillel
eshcar@verizonmedia.com
Yahoo Research

Idit Keidar
idish@ee.technion.ac.il
Technion

Hadar Serviansky
hadar.serviansky@weizmann.ac.il
Weizmann Institute

ABSTRACT

Data sketches are approximate succinct summaries of long data streams. They are widely used for processing massive amounts of data and answering statistical queries about it. Existing libraries producing sketches are very fast, but do not allow parallelism for creating sketches using multiple threads or querying them while they are being built. We present a generic approach to parallelising data sketches efficiently and allowing them to be queried in real time, while bounding the error that such parallelism introduces. Utilising relaxed semantics and the notion of strong linearisability we prove our algorithm's correctness and analyse the error it induces in two specific sketches. Our implementation achieves high scalability while keeping the error small. We have contributed one of our concurrent sketches to the open-source data sketches library.

CCS CONCEPTS

• **Theory of computation** → *Parallel algorithms*; • **Computer systems organization** → *Parallel architectures*; Real-time systems.

KEYWORDS

concurrency, synchronization, persistence, design, analysis of distributed algorithms

ACM Reference Format:

Arik Rinberg, Alexander Spiegelman, Edward Bortnikov, Eshcar Hillel, Idit Keidar, and Hadar Serviansky. 2019. Brief Announcement: Fast Concurrent Data Sketches. In *2019 ACM Symposium on Principles of Distributed Computing (PODC '19), July 29–August 2, 2019, Toronto, ON, Canada.* ACM, New York, NY, USA, 2 pages. https://doi.org/10.1145/3293611.3331567

1 INTRODUCTION

Data sketching algorithms, or *sketches* for short [6], have become an indispensable tool for high-speed computations over massive datasets in recent years. Their applications include a variety of analytics and machine learning use cases, e.g., data aggregation [2, 4], graph mining [5], anomaly (e.g., intrusion) detection [20], real-time data analytics [8], and online classification [16].

Sketches are designed for *stream* settings in which each data item is only processed once. A sketch data structure is essentially a succinct (sublinear) summary of a stream that approximates a specific query (unique element count, quantile values, etc.). The approximation is typically very accurate – the error drops fast with the number of processed elements [6].

Practical implementations of sketch algorithms have recently emerged in toolkits [19] and data analytics platforms (e.g., PowerDrill [12], Druid [8], Hillview [17], and Presto [1]). However, these implementations are not thread-safe, allowing neither parallel data ingestion nor concurrent queries and updates; concurrent use is prone to exceptions and gross estimation errors. Applications using these libraries are therefore required to explicitly protect all sketch API calls by locks [9, 13].

In our full paper [15], we present a generic approach to parallelising data sketches efficiently, while bounding the error that such a parallelisation might introduce. Our goal is to enable simultaneous queries and updates to a sketch from an arbitrary number of threads. Our solution is carefully designed to do so without slowing down operations as a result of synchronisation. This is particularly challenging because sketch libraries are extremely fast, often processing tens of millions of updates per second.

We capitalise on the well-known sketch *mergeability* property [6], which enables computing a sketch over a stream by merging sketches over substreams. Previous works have exploited this property for distributed stream processing (e.g., [7, 12]), devising solutions with a sequential bottleneck at the merge phase and where queries cannot be served before all updates complete. In contrast, our method is based on shared memory, with parallel updates of small thread-local sketches, and continuous background propagation of local results to a common, queryable sketch.

We instantiate our generic algorithm with two popular sketches from the open-source Java DataSketches library [19]: (1) a KMV Θ sketch [4], which estimates the number of unique elements in a stream; and (2) a Quantiles sketch [2] estimating the stream element with a given rank. Our design is generic and applicable to additional sketches. Figure 1 compares the ingestion throughput of our concurrent Θ sketch to that of a lock-protected sequential sketch, on multi-core hardware. As expected, the trivial solution does not scale whereas our algorithm scales linearly.

Concurrency induces an error, and one of the main challenges we address is analysing this additional error. To begin with, we need to specify a correctness criterion for the concurrent sketch. We do so using a flavour of *relaxed consistency* due to Henzinger et al. [11] that allows operations to "overtake" some other operations. Thus, a query may return a result that reflects all but a bounded number of the updates that precede it. While relaxed semantics were previously used for deterministic data structures like stacks [11]

PODC '19, July 29–August 2, 2019, Toronto, ON, Canada

ACM ISBN 978-1-4503-6217-7/19/07.
https://doi.org/10.1145/3293611.3331567

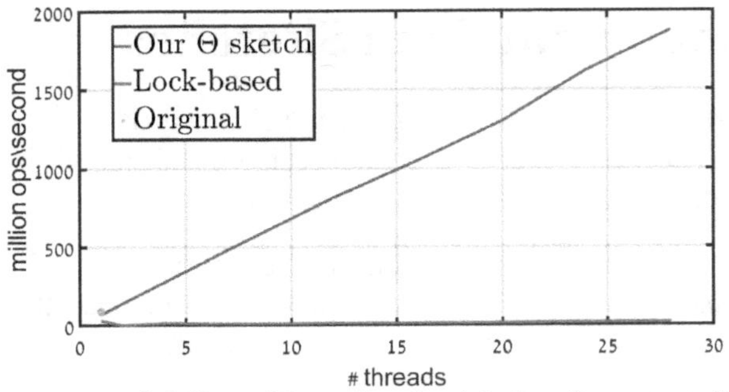

Figure 1: Scalability of DataSketches' Θ sketch protected by a lock vs. our concurrent implementation.

and priority queues [3, 14], we believe that they are a natural fit for data sketches. This is because sketches are typically used to summarise streams that arise from multiple real-world sources and are collected over a network with variable delays, and so even if the sketch ensures strict semantics, queries might miss some real-world events that occur before them. Additionally, sketches are inherently approximate. Relaxing their semantics therefore "makes sense", as long as it does not excessively increase the expected error.

But this raises a new difficulty: relaxed consistency is defined wrt a deterministic specification, whereas sketches are randomised. We therefore first de-randomise the sketch's behaviour by delegating the random coin flips to an oracle. We can then relax the resulting sequential specification. Next, because our concurrent sketch is used within randomised algorithms, it is not enough to prove its linearisability. Rather, we prove that our generic concurrent algorithm instantiated with sequential sketch S satisfies *strong linearisability* [10] wrt a relaxed sequential specification of the de-randomised S.

We then analyse the error of the two relaxed sketches under random coin flips, with an adversarial scheduler that may delay operations in a way that maximises the error. We show that our concurrent Θ sketch's error is coarsely bounded by twice that of the corresponding sequential sketch. The error of the concurrent Quantiles sketch approaches that of the sequential one as the stream size tends to infinity.

Main contribution. In summary, our full paper [15] this paper tackles an important practical problem, offers a general efficient solution for it, and rigorously analyses this solution. While the paper makes use of many known techniques, it combines them in a novel way; we are not aware of any previous application of relaxed consistency to randomised statistical algorithms. The main technical challenges we address are (1) proving the relaxed consistency of a high-performance generic algorithm that supports real-time queries concurrently with updates; and (2) analysing the error induced by this relaxation. We have contributed our parallel Θ sketch implementation to the DataSketches library [18].

REFERENCES

[1] 2018. HyperLogLog in Presto: A significantly faster way to handle cardinality estimation. https://code.fb.com/data-infrastructure/hyperloglog/.

[2] Pankaj K. Agarwal, Graham Cormode, Zengfeng Huang, Jeff Phillips, Zhewei Wei, and Ke Yi. 2012. Mergeable Summaries. In *Proceedings of the 31st ACM SIGMOD-SIGACT-SIGAI Symposium on Principles of Database Systems (PODS '12)*. ACM, New York, NY, USA, 23–34. https://doi.org/10.1145/2213556.2213562

[3] Dan Alistarh, Justin Kopinsky, Jerry Li, and Nir Shavit. 2015. The SprayList: A Scalable Relaxed Priority Queue. *SIGPLAN Not.* 50, 8 (Jan. 2015), 11–20. https://doi.org/10.1145/2858788.2688523

[4] Ziv Bar-Yossef, T. S. Jayram, Ravi Kumar, D. Sivakumar, and Luca Trevisan. 2002. Counting Distinct Elements in a Data Stream. In *Randomization and Approximation Techniques in Computer Science*, Jos'e D. P. Rolim and Salil Vadhan (Eds.). Springer Berlin Heidelberg, Berlin, Heidelberg, 1–10.

[5] Edith Cohen. 2014. All-distances Sketches, Revisited: HIP Estimators for Massive Graphs Analysis. In *Proceedings of the 33rd ACM SIGMOD-SIGACT-SIGART Symposium on Principles of Database Systems (PODS '14)*. ACM, New York, NY, USA, 88–99. https://doi.org/10.1145/2594538.2594546

[6] Graham Cormode. 2017. Data Sketching. *Queue* 15, 2, Article 60 (April 2017), 19 pages. https://doi.org/10.1145/3084693.3104030

[7] Graham Cormode, S Muthukrishnan, and Ke Yi. 2011. Algorithms for distributed functional monitoring. *ACM Transactions on Algorithms (TALG)* 7, 2 (2011), 21.

[8] Druid. [n. d.]. How We Scaled HyperLogLog: Three Real-World Optimizations. http://druid.io/blog/2014/02/18/hyperloglog-optimizations-for-real-world-systems.html.

[9] Github. [n. d.]. ArrayIndexOutOfBoundsException during serialization. https://github.com/DataSketches/sketches-core/issues/178#issuecomment-365673204..

[10] Wojciech Golab, Lisa Higham, and Philipp Woelfel. 2011. Linearizable implementations do not suffice for randomized distributed computation. In *Proceedings of the forty-third annual ACM symposium on Theory of computing*. ACM, 373–382.

[11] Thomas A Henzinger, Christoph M Kirsch, Hannes Payer, Ali Sezgin, and Ana Sokolova. 2013. Quantitative relaxation of concurrent data structures. In *ACM SIGPLAN Notices*, Vol. 48. ACM, 317–328.

[12] Stefan Heule, Marc Nunkesser, and Alex Hall. 2013. HyperLogLog in Practice: Algorithmic Engineering of a State of The Art Cardinality Estimation Algorithm. In *Proceedings of the EDBT 2013 Conference*. Genoa, Italy.

[13] Lee Rhodes. [n. d.]. SketchesArgumentException: Key not found and no empty slot in table. https://groups.google.com/d/msg/sketches-user/S1PEAneLmhk/dI8RbN6iBAAJ..

[14] Hamza Rihani, Peter Sanders, and Roman Dementiev. 2014. Multiqueues: Simpler, faster, and better relaxed concurrent priority queues. *arXiv preprint arXiv:1411.1209* (2014).

[15] Arik Rinberg, Alexander Spiegelman, Edward Bortnikov, Eshcar Hillel, Idit Keidar, and Hadar Serviansky. 2019. Fast Concurrent Data Sketches. *arXiv preprint arXiv:1902.10995* (2019).

[16] Kai Sheng Tai, Vatsal Sharan, Peter Bailis, and Gregory Valiant. 2018. Sketching Linear Classifiers over Data Streams. In *Proceedings of the 2018 International Conference on Management of Data (SIGMOD '18)*. ACM, New York, NY, USA, 757–772. https://doi.org/10.1145/3183713.3196930

[17] VMware. [n. d.]. Hillview: A Big Data Spreadsheet. https://github.com/vmware/hillview.

[18] Yahoo. [n. d.]. DataSketches: Concurrent Theta Sketch Implementation. https://github.com/DataSketches/sketches-core/blob/master/src/main/java/com/yahoo/sketches/theta/ConcurrentDirectQuickSelectSketch.java.

[19] Yahoo! [n. d.]. DataSketches: sketches library from Yahoo! https://datasketches.github.io/.

[20] Tong Yang, Jie Jiang, Peng Liu, Qun Huang, Junzhi Gong, Yang Zhou, Rui Miao, Xiaoming Li, and Steve Uhlig. 2018. Elastic Sketch: Adaptive and Fast Network-wide Measurements. In *Proceedings of the 2018 Conference of the ACM Special Interest Group on Data Communication (SIGCOMM '18)*. ACM, New York, NY, USA, 561–575. https://doi.org/10.1145/3230543.3230544

Brief Announcement: Self-Stabilizing Snapshot Objects for Asynchronous Failure-Prone Networked Systems

Chryssis Georgiou
Department of Computer Science, University of Cyprus, Cyprus.
chryssis@cs.ucy.ac.cy

Oskar Lundström
Department of Computer Science and Engineering, Chalmers University of Technology, Sweden
osklunds@student.chalmers.se

Elad M. Schiller
Department of Computer Science and Engineering, Chalmers University of Technology, Sweden
elad@chalmers.se

ACM Reference Format:
Chryssis Georgiou, Oskar Lundström, and Elad M. Schiller. 2019. Brief Announcement: Self-Stabilizing Snapshot Objects for Asynchronous Failure-Prone Networked Systems. In *2019 ACM Symposium on Principles of Distributed Computing (PODC '19), July 29-August 2, 2019, Toronto, ON, Canada.* ACM, New York, NY, USA, 3 pages. https://doi.org/10.1145/3293611.3331584

Context and contribution. A *snapshot object* simulates the behavior of an array of single-writer/multi-reader shared registers that can be read atomically. Delporte-Gallet *et al.* [1] proposed two fault-tolerant algorithms for snapshot objects in asynchronous crash-prone message-passing systems. Their first algorithm is *non-blocking*; it allows snapshot operations to terminate once all write operations had ceased. It uses $O(n)$ messages of $O(n \cdot v)$ bits, where n is the number of nodes and v is the number of bits it takes to represent the object. Their second algorithm allows snapshot operations to *always terminate* independently of write operations. It incurs $O(n^2)$ messages. The fault model of Delporte-Gallet *et al.* [1] considers node failures (crashes). We aim at the design of even more robust snapshot objects. We do so through the lenses of *self-stabilization*—a very strong notion of fault-tolerance. In addition to Delporte-Gallet *et al.*'s fault model, a self-stabilizing algorithm can recover after the occurrence of *transient faults*; these faults represent arbitrary violations of the assumptions according to which the system was designed to operate (as long as the code stays intact). In particular, in this work, we propose self-stabilizing variations of Delporte-Gallet *et al.*'s non-blocking algorithm and always-terminating algorithm. Our algorithms have similar communication costs to the ones by Delporte-Gallet *et al.* [1] and $O(1)$ recovery time (in terms of asynchronous cycles) from transient faults. The main differences are that our proposal considers repeated gossiping of $O(v)$ bits messages and deals with bounded space, which is a prerequisite for self-stabilization. Due to the page limit, omitted details and proofs appear in [3], together with an explanation on how to extend our solutions to reconfigurable ones.

Task description. We consider an asynchronous system consisting of a set $\mathcal{P}$ of n failure-prone nodes. Their interaction is based on the emulation of Single-Writer/Multi-Reader (SWMR) shared registers for message-passing systems. Snapshot objects can read the entire array of system registers. The system lets each node to update its own register via write() operations and retrieve the value of all shared registers via snapshot() operations. Note that these snapshot operations occur concurrently to the write operations that individual nodes perform. However, we study the task of atomic snapshot objects that are linearizable. I.e., the operations write() and snapshot() appear as if they have been executed instantaneously, one after the other (in other words, they appear to preserve real-time ordering). To the best of our knowledge, we are the first to propose a self-stabilizing algorithm for snapshot objects in message-passing systems that are prone to node failures.

Delporte-Gallet *et al.*'s non-blocking snapshot, which is non-self-stabilizing. This solution by Delporte-Gallet *et al.* [1, Algorithm 1] allows all write operations to terminate regardless of the invocation patterns of the other write or snapshot operations (as long as the invoking nodes do not fail during the operation). However, for the case of snapshot operations, termination is guaranteed only if eventually the system execution reaches a period in which there are no concurrent write operations. Algorithm 1 represents [1, Algorithm 1] if the reader ignores the boxed code lines.

Local variables. Node p_i stores the array *reg* (line 2), such that the k-th entry stores the most recent information about node p_k's object and *reg*$[i]$ stores p_i's actual object value. Every entry is a pair of the form (v, ts), where the field v is an object value and ts is an unbounded integer that stores the object index (timestamp). Algorithm 1 defines also the relation $\preceq$ that compares (v, ts) and (v', ts') according to the write operation indices (line 1). Moreover, p_i maintains an index for the snapshot operations, i.e., *ssn*.

The write(v) *operation.* Algorithm 1's write(v) operation appears in lines 6 to 7 (client-side) and lines 8 to 14 (server-side). The client-side operation write(v) stores the pair (v, ts) in *reg*$[i]$ (line 6), where p_i is the calling node and ts is a unique operation index. The primitive broadcast sends to all the nodes in $\mathcal{P}$ the message WRITE about p_i's local perception of *reg*'s value. Upon the arrival of a WRITE message to p_i from p_j (line 16), the server-side code is ran. Node p_i updates *reg* according to the timestamps of the arriving values (line 17). Then, p_i replies to p_j with the message WRITEack (line 19), which includes p_i's local perception of the system shared registers. Getting back to the client-side, node p_i repeatedly broadcasts the message WRITE to all nodes until it receives replies from a majority of them (line 7). Once that happens, it uses the arriving values for keeping *reg* up-to-date (line 7).

PODC '19, July 29-August 2, 2019, Toronto, ON, Canada

ACM ISBN 978-1-4503-6217-7/19/07.
https://doi.org/10.1145/3293611.3331584

Algorithm 1: Self-stabilizing algorithm for non-blocking snapshot object; code for p_i. The boxed code lines mark our additions to Delporte-Gallet *et al.* [1, Algorithm 1].

1 **Definitions of** $\preceq$: For values x and x' as well as integers t and t': $(x,t) \preceq (x',t') \iff t \le t'$; For arrays tab and tab' of $(value, integer)$: $tab \preceq tab' \iff \forall i \in [1,\ldots,n] : tab[i] \preceq tab'[i]$; Also, $a \prec b \equiv a \preceq b \wedge a \neq b$;

2 **Local initialization:** $ssn \leftarrow 0; ts \leftarrow 0; reg \leftarrow [\bot,\ldots,\bot]$;

3 **macro** merge(Rec) {
 $ts \leftarrow \max(\{ts, reg[i].ts\} \cup \{r[i].ts \mid r \in Rec\})$; **for** $k \in \{1,\ldots,n\}$ **do**
 $reg[k] \leftarrow \max(\{reg[k]\} \cup \{r[k] \mid r \in Rec\})$ };

4 **macro** broadcast(m) {**for** $p_k \in \mathcal{P}$ **send** m **to** p_k;};

5 **do forever** { $ts \leftarrow \max\{ts, reg[i].ts\}$;
 for $k \in \{1,\ldots,n\} : k \neq i$ **do** send GOSSIP($reg[k]$) to p_k };

6 **operation** write(v) { $ts \leftarrow ts + 1; reg[i] \leftarrow (v, ts)$;

7 **repeat** broadcast WRITE(reg) **until** WRITEack($regJ \succeq reg$) *received from a majority;* merge(Rec) **where** *Rec is the set of reg arrays received at line 7*};

8 **operation** snapshot() **begin**

9 **repeat**

10 **let** $prev := reg$; $ssn \leftarrow ssn + 1$;

11 **repeat** broadcast SNAPack(reg, ssn) **until** SNAPack($\bullet, ssnJ = ssn$) *received from a majority*;

12 merge(Rec) **where** Rec is the set of reg arrays received at line 11;

13 **until** $prev = reg$;

14 **return**(reg);

15 **upon** message GOSSIP($regJ$) **arrival from** p_j
 $reg[i] \leftarrow \max\{reg[i], regJ\}; ts \leftarrow \max\{ts, reg[i].ts\}$;}

16 **upon** message WRITE($regJ$) **arrival from** p_j **begin**

17 **for** $k \in \mathcal{P}$ **do** $reg[k] \leftarrow \max_{\preceq}(reg[k], regJ[k])$**send** WRITEack($reg$) **to** p_j;

18 **upon** message SNAPack($regJ, ssn$) **arrival from** p_j **begin**

19 **for** $k \in \mathcal{P}$ **do** $reg[k] \leftarrow \max_{\preceq}\{reg[k], regJ[k]\}$; **send** SNAPack($reg, ssn$) to p_j;

The snapshot(v) *operation.* Algorithm 1's snapshot() operation appears in lines 8 to 14 (client-side) and lines 18 to 19 (server-side). Recall that Delporte-Gallet *et al.* [1, Algorithm 1] is non-blocking with respect to the snapshot operations as long as are no concurrent write operations. Thus, the client-side is written in the form of a repeat-until loop. Node p_i tries to query the system for the most recent value of the shared registrars. The success of such attempts depends on the above assumption. Therefore, before each such broadcast, p_i copies reg's value to $prev$ (line 10) and exits the repeat-until loop only when the updated value of reg indicates that there are no concurrent write operations. Figure 1 depicts an execution of the non-self-stabilizing algorithm [1]. It illustrates a write operation that is followed by a snapshot operation and then a second write.

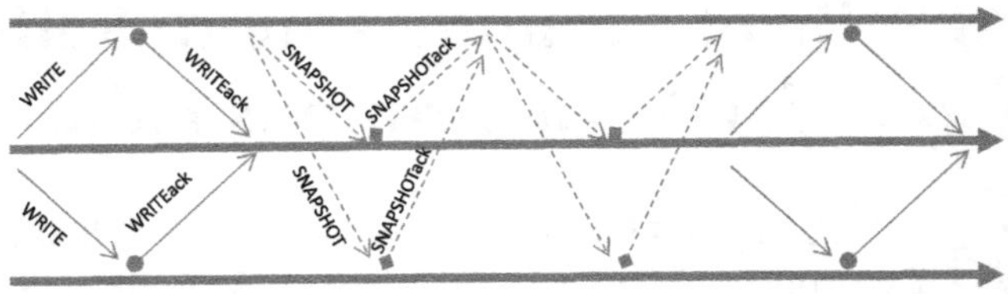

Figure 1: An example of Algorithm 1's execution. The drawing illustrates a case of a terminating snapshot operation (dashed lines) that occurs between two write operations (solid lines). The acknowledgments of these messages are arrows that start with circles and squares, respectively.

Unbounded Self-stabilizing Non-blocking Snapshot. We propose Algorithm 1 as an extension of Delporte-Gallet *et al.* [1, Algorithm 1]. The boxed code lines mark our additions. Our description refers to the values of variable X at node p_i as X_i, i.e., the variable name with a subscript that indicates the node identifier. Algorithm 1 considers the case in which any of p_i's operation indices, ssn_i and ts_i, is smaller than some other ssn or ts value, say, ssn_m $reg_i[i].ts$, $reg_j[i].ts$ or $reg_m[i].ts$, where X_m appears in the X field of some on transit message. For the case of corrupted ssn values, p_i's client-side simply ignores arriving messages with ssn values that do not match ssn_i (line 11). For the sake of clarity of our proposal, the do-forever loop removes any stored snapshot replies that their ssn fields are not equal to ssn_i. For the case of corrupted ts values, p_i's loop makes sure that ts_i is not smaller than $reg_i[i].ts$ (line 5) before gossiping to every node $p_j \in \mathcal{P}$ its local copy of the shared register (line 5). Also, upon the arrival of such gossip messages, Algorithm 1 merges the arriving information with the local one (line 15). Moreover, when replies from write or snapshot messages arrive to p_i, it merges the arriving ts value with the one in ts_i (line 3).

Lemmas 1.1 and 1.2 demonstrate the required properties for self-stabilization and use the term *asynchronous cycles* of a fair execution R, which is the shortest prefix of R in which every non-failing node p_i performs a completed iteration of p_i's do forever loop, all messages p_i sent during that iteration were delivered, and all of the iteration's requests were replied.

Lemma 1.1 (Convergence). *Let R be a fair and unbounded execution of Algorithm 1. Within $O(1)$ asynchronous cycles, the system reaches a state $c \in R$ in which the value of ts_i is greater than or equal to any p_i's timestamp value. Moreover, suppose that node p_i takes a step immediately after c that includes the execution of line 6. Then in c it holds that $ts_i = reg_i[i].ts = reg_j[i].ts$ as well as for every messages $m \in channel_{i,j}, channel_{j,i}$ that is in transit from p_i to p_j or p_j to p_i it holds that $m.reg[i].ts = ts_i$. Moreover, ssn_i is not smaller than any p_i's snapshot sequence number.*

Proof Sketch. The proof regarding p_i's timestamp is followed by arguments (1) to (3). (1) *The values installed in ts_i, $reg_i[i].ts$, $reg_j[i].ts$, $reg_i[i]$ and $reg_j[i]$ are non-decreasing.* This is true, because the values of the ts and reg fields are never decremented during R. (2) *Within $O(1)$ asynchronous cycles, $ts_i \geq reg_i[i].ts$.* This is true, because p_i executes line 5 at least once in every asynchronous cycle. (3) Within $O(1)$ asynchronous cycles, $reg_i[i].ts \geq$

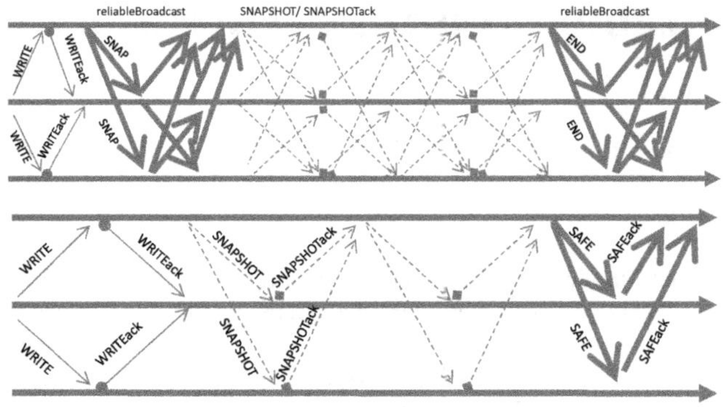

Figure 2: [1, Algorithm 2]'s run for the case of Figure 1 uppers in the upper drawing. The lower drawing depicts an example execution of the proposed self-stabilizing solution.

$reg_m[i].ts$ and $reg_i[i].ts \geq regJ[i].ts$ whenever p_j raises the events WRITE($regJ$) or SNAPack($regJ, ssn$), where m' is a message on transit from p_j to p_k and denote $reg_{m'}$ as values of the reg filed in m', and $p_i, p_j, p_k \in \mathcal{P}$ are non-failing nodes (and $i = k$ possibly holds). Moreover, $reg_j[i].ts \geq reg_{m'}[i].ts$ and $reg_i[i].ts \geq regJ[i].ts$ whenever p_k raises GOSSIP($regJ$), WRITEack($regJ$) or SNAPack($regJ$, •). The proof here considers the way that nodes exchange messages in R. The proof regarding p_i's snapshot index is by arguments similar to (1) to (3). ■

Lemma 1.2 (Closure). *Let R be an execution of Algorithm 1 that starts in system state c in which the timestamps and snapshot sequence numbers have converged (cf. Lemmas 1.1). Execution R is correct with respect to the task of emulating snapshot objects.*

Proof Sketch. The proof is by reduction of Algorithm 1 to [1, Algorithm 1]. This is indeed possible because Algorithm 1 only adds gossip messages and code lines that assert Lemma 1.1's invariants, which hold throughout R. Also, the added code does not affect the system state due to the assumption about c. ■

Delporte-Gallet *et al.*'s always-terminating snapshot, which is non-self-stabilizing. Delporte-Gallet *et al.* [1, Algorithm 2] guarantee termination for any invocation pattern of write and snapshot operations, as long as the invoking nodes do not fail during these operations. Delporte-Gallet *et al.* [1, Algorithm 2] use a job-stealing scheme for allowing rapid termination of individual snapshots. Node $p_i \in \mathcal{P}$ starts each snapshot by queueing this new task at all nodes $p_j \in \mathcal{P}$. Once p_j receives p_i's new task and when that task reaches the queue front, p_j starts a joint processing the snapshot task in a way that makes sure that no write operation can stand in the way of this snapshot. Specifically, Delporte-Gallet *et al.* guarantee termination of snapshots via the interleaving of writes and snapshots. Note that [1, Algorithm 2] processes one snapshot task at a time and uses reliable broadcasts for disseminating the snapshot tasks and their results, cf. Figure 2's upper drawings.

Unbounded self-stabilizing always-terminating snapshot. We propose a self-stabilizing variation of Delporte-Gallet *et al.* [1, Algorithm 2]. Our self-stabilizing solution has some constraints. *E.g.*, it must have a clear bound on the number of pending snapshot tasks. Our solution assumes that the system needs, for each node, to cater for at most one pending snapshot task. In addition to improved fault-tolerance, our solution advances the state of the art by aiming at reducing the number of messages needed for snapshot operations. [1, Algorithm 1] uses $O(n)$ messages per snapshot operation whereas [1, Algorithm 2] uses $O(n^2)$ messages. Our solution can defer snapshot tasks until either (i) at least one node was able to observe at least δ concurrent writes, where δ is an input parameter, or (ii) there are no concurrent writes, which might interfere with the termination of snapshots. The tunable parameter δ balances between the latency (with respect to snapshot operations) and communication costs. *I.e.*, if δ is a very high value, our solution guarantees termination in a way that resembles [1, Algorithm 1], which uses $O(n)$ messages per snapshot operation, and for the case of $\delta = 0$, our solution behaves in a way that resembles [1, Algorithm 2], which uses $O(n^2)$ messages per snapshot. Our solution aims to further improve communication costs by piggybacking the snapshot results. Another improvement is that the proposed algorithm avoids using a reliable broadcast mechanism, which Delporte-Gallet *et al.* use, and instead, a simpler mechanism for safe registers. Figure 2's lower drawing depicts an example of an execution of the proposed algorithm in which a write operation is followed by a snapshot operation. Note that fewer messages are considered when comparing to Figure 1's example.

A Bounded Variation on the Proposed Solutions. There is a technique for transforming a self-stabilizing atomic register algorithm that uses unbounded operation indices into one with bounded indices [2]. Once p_i notices an index that is at least MAXINT $= 2^{64} - 1$, it disables new operations and starts gossiping of the maximal indices (while merging the arriving information with the local one). Once all nodes share the same maximal indices, the procedure uses a consensus-based global reset procedure for replacing, per operation type, the highest index with its initial value, 0, while keeping the values of all shared registers unchanged. After the end of the global reset procedure, all operations are enabled.

Discussion. We showed how to transform a couple of non-self-stabilizing algorithms of Delporte-Gallet *et al.* [1] into ones that can recover after the occurrence of transient faults. This requires some non-trivial considerations that are imperative for self-stabilizing systems, such as the explicit use of bounded memory and the reoccurring clean-up of stale information. Interestingly, these considerations are not restrictive for the case of Delporte-Gallet *et al.* [1]. One future direction emanating from this work is to consider the $O(n)$ gap in the number of messages when designing future applications. For example, one might prefer the use of repeated snapshots (using the proposed solution) over a replicated state machine, which always costs $O(n^2)$ messages per state transition.

REFERENCES

[1] Carole Delporte-Gallet, Hugues Fauconnier, Sergio Rajsbaum, and Michel Raynal. 2018. Implementing Snapshot Objects on Top of Crash-Prone Asynchronous Message-Passing Systems. *IEEE Trans. Parallel Distrib. Syst.* 29, 9 (2018), 2033–2045.

[2] Shlomi Dolev, Thomas Petig, and Elad Michael Schiller. 2018. Self-Stabilizing and Private Distributed Shared Atomic Memory in Seldomly Fair Message Passing Networks. *CoRR* abs/1806.03498 (2018). arXiv:1806.03498 http://arxiv.org/abs/1806.03498

[3] Chryssis Georgiou, Oskar Lundström, and Elad Michael Schiller. 2019. Self-Stabilizing Snapshot Objects for Asynchronous Failure-Prone Networked Systems. *CoRR* (2019).

Brief Announcement: The Recoverable Consensus Hierarchy

Wojciech Golab*
University of Waterloo, Department of Electrical and Computer Engineering
Waterloo, Ontario, Canada
wgolab@uwaterloo.ca

ABSTRACT

Herlihy's consensus hierarchy ranks the power of various synchronization primitives for solving consensus in a model where asynchronous processes communicate through shared memory, and may fail by halting. This paper revisits the consensus hierarchy in a model with crash-recovery failures, where the specification of consensus, called *recoverable consensus* in this paper, is weakened by allowing non-terminating executions when a process fails infinitely often. Two variations of this model are considered: with independent process failures, and with simultaneous (i.e., system-wide) process failures. We prove two fundamental results: (i) Test-And-Set is at level 2 of the recoverable consensus hierarchy if failures are simultaneous, and similarly for any primitive at level 2 of the traditional consensus hierarchy; and (ii) Test-And-Set drops to level 1 of the hierarchy if failures are independent, unless the number of such failures is bounded. To our knowledge, this is the first separation between the simultaneous and independent crash-recovery failure models with respect to the computability of consensus.

CCS CONCEPTS

• **Theory of computation → Shared memory algorithms.**

KEYWORDS

concurrency; shared memory; consensus; fault tolerance; theory

ACM Reference Format:

Wojciech Golab. 2019. Brief Announcement: The Recoverable Consensus Hierarchy. In *2019 ACM Symposium on Principles of Distributed Computing (PODC'19), July 29–August 2, 2019, Toronto, ON, Canada.* ACM, New York, NY, USA, 3 pages. https://doi.org/10.1145/3293611.3331574

1 INTRODUCTION

Herlihy's consensus hierarchy [4] ranks the power of synchronization primitives for solving consensus – a problem where processes agree on a decision chosen from a set of proposed values. The position of a primitive P in the hierarchy is defined by its *consensus number* – the largest n such that P used in conjunction with read/write registers solves n-process consensus in the asynchronous shared memory model with permanent crash failures. Test-And-Set (TAS) is at level two of this hierarchy as it can be used to solve 2-process (but not 3-process) consensus: a TAS object is initialized to 0, each process then announces its proposal in a shared read/write register, executes a TAS operation, returns its own proposal if it wins, and returns the proposal of the other process if it loses. Motivated by the possibility of recovering program state from non-volatile main memory (NVRAM) after a failure, we revisit the consensus hierarchy in a *crash-recovery* model where a failure merely resets the private variables of a process (including its program counter) to their initial values, and preserves the state of shared variables.

Building on the results of Berryhill, Golab, and Tripunitara [2], who proved that consensus remains sufficiently powerful to implement any shared object type for any number of processes in the crash-recovery failure model, we consider solutions of the *recoverable consensus* (RC) problem. RC is a natural adaptation of consensus to crash-recovery failures that relaxes wait-freedom by allowing non-terminating executions in cases where failures occur infinitely often. The correctness properties of RC are defined as follows:

(1) *Agreement:* distinct processes never output different decisions.
(2) *Validity:* each decision returned is the proposal value of some process.
(3) *Recoverable wait-freedom:* each time a process executes its algorithm from the beginning, it either returns a decision after a finite number of its own steps, or crashes.

The *recoverable consensus hierarchy* is the analog of the traditional consensus hierarchy for the RC problem in the crash-recovery model, and defines (recoverable) consensus numbers for a variety of shared object types and synchronization primitives. We establish two fundamental results with respect to the position of TAS in this new hierarchy: (i) TAS is at level 2 if failures are simultaneous, and similarly for any primitive at level 2 of the traditional consensus hierarchy; and (ii) TAS drops to level 1 if failures are independent, unless the number of such failures is bounded. Intuitively, our result captures the observation that when failures are simultaneous, a process recovers with more information regarding the states of other processes than when failures are independent. To our knowledge, this is the first separation between the simultaneous and independent crash-recovery failure models with respect to the computability of consensus.

2 RESULTS FOR SIMULTANEOUS FAILURES

This section presents a technique for transforming any 2-process conventional consensus algorithm into a 2-process RC algorithm that tolerates arbitrarily many simultaneous crash-recovery failures. The transformation is presented in detail in Figure 1. It uses

*Author supported in part by an Ontario Early Researcher Award, and by a Google Faculty Research Award.

PODC '19, July 29–August 2, 2019, Toronto, ON, Canada

ACM ISBN 978-1-4503-6217-7/19/07...$15.00
https://doi.org/10.1145/3293611.3331574

```
Shared variables:
  • P[1..2]: array of proposal values, init ⊥
  • C: conventional wait-free 2-process consensus object
  • D: decision, init ⊥
Private variables:
  • other: process ID
  • d: decided value
Procedure Decide(v: proposal value) for proc. p_i, i ∈ 1..2
1  if i = 1 then other := 2 else other := 1
2  if P[i] = ⊥ ∧ P[other] = ⊥ then
3  |  P[i] := v
4  |  d := C.Decide(v)
5  |  D := d
6  |  return d
7  else if D ≠ ⊥ then
8  |  return D
9  else if P[i] ≠ ⊥ ∧ P[other] = ⊥ then
10 |  return P[i]
11 else if P[i] = ⊥ ∧ P[other] ≠ ⊥ then
12 |  return P[other]
13 else // P[i] ≠ ⊥ ∧ P[other] ≠ ⊥
14 |  return P[1]
```

Figure 1: Transformation from 2-process conventional consensus to 2-process recoverable consensus.

a shared array $P[1..2]$ to announce proposals, a conventional 2-process consensus algorithm C to reach agreement in some scenarios (e.g., failure-free executions), and a shared variable D to record the decision value computed using C.

Starting from the initial state where both elements of $P[1..2]$ are initialized to $\perp$, process p_i records its proposal, executes C, and records the outcome in D (lines 2–6). Assuming that some process completes line 5, recovery from a failure is achieved easily by returning the value saved in D (lines 7–8). However, recovery from a failure prior to line 5 is more difficult because if the failure occurred while some process p_i was at line 4 then the algorithm must guarantee that p_i does not access C incorrectly (i.e., by resuming the interrupted execution of C.**Decide** from the beginning). Recovery in this scenario is accomplished by case analysis. If a failure occurs before any process has completed line 3, then the execution path on recovery is identical to the failure-free path since $P[1..2]$ and C remain in their initial states. On the other hand, if some process did complete line 3, then the algorithm terminates after a bounded number of read operations, without updating shared memory. If exactly one element of $P[1..2]$ is $\perp$ (lines 9–12) then the algorithm returns the unique recorded proposal. Finally, if both elements of $P[1..2]$ are non-$\perp$, then the algorithm makes an arbitrary but deterministic choice among these two proposal values and returns the chosen one (lines 13–14).

The correctness properties of the algorithm are captured in Theorem 2.1, whose detailed proof appears in [3].

Theorem 2.1. *The algorithm shown in Figure 1 satisfies agreement, validity, and recoverable wait-freedom.*

Because the non-recoverable consensus algorithm C can be implemented in a wait-free manner using TAS, as explained in Section 1, Theorem 2.1 implies that TAS is at level 2 (or higher) of the RC hierarchy if failures are simultaneous.

3 RESULTS FOR INDEPENDENT FAILURES

3.1 Solution for Finitely Many Failures

This section presents a technique for transforming any n-process conventional consensus algorithm into an n-process recoverable consensus algorithm that tolerates up to a (predefined) number f of independent crash-recovery failures. The transformation is presented in detail in Figure 2, and uses $f + 1$ instances of the conventional consensus algorithm denoted by the array $C[0..f]$. To a first approximation, the transformation works by having each process p_i access the $f + 1$ consensus algorithms in a for loop at line 15 until the **Decide** procedure is executed to completion without failing. The array $R[1..n]$ is used at line 16 and line 17 to determine which consensus algorithm in the array $C[0..f]$ will be accessed in the next iteration by each process, and hence to avoid unsafe access to these base objects. Assuming that there are at most f failures, this strategy ensures that p_i eventually computes a decision because the total number of iterations required is at most $f + 1$. The main technical challenge lies in ensuring agreement in cases when processes compute decisions in different iterations, using distinct instances of the conventional consensus algorithm. This is accomplished by a pair mechanisms working in synergy.

In the first mechanism, a process p_i that is executing iteration k of the outer for loop checks at lines 18–20 whether a decision was reached in a lower-numbered iteration using $C[k']$ for some $k' < k$, and recorded in $D[k']$ at line 22, before p_i proceeds to execute the consensus algorithm $C[k]$ at line 21. If $D[k']$ holds such a decision value then p_i adopts this value in lieu of its own proposal at line 20. This statement is inside the inner for loop and may be executed multiple times in one iteration of the outer for loop, in which case p_i adopts the decision value corresponding to the largest possible k'. This mechanism alone is not sufficient, however, since a race can occur between a process that is about to write $D[k-1]$ and a process that is about to access $C[k]$.

The second mechanism deals with the above race condition at lines 23–26 by inspecting the elements of array $R[1..n]$ belonging to other processes. If p_i finds some element $R[z]$, $z \neq i$, holding an integer larger than $R[i]$, then p_z is at least one iteration ahead of p_i. In this case p_i "forgets" the decision it computed earlier at line 21 by resetting the private variable d at line 26, and continues to the next iteration of the for loop; the conditional statement at line 27 bypasses the return statement at line 28. If p_i does not find such a process p_z, then p_i reaches line 28, where it returns the decision it computed in the current iteration of the outer for loop. The two mechanisms combined ensure agreement despite the possibility that the consensus algorithms $C[0..f]$ may not all reach the same decision.

The correctness properties of the algorithm are captured in Theorem 3.1, whose detailed proof appears in [3].

Shared variables:

- $R[1..n]$: **array** of read/write register, **init** 0
- $C[0..f]$: **array** of conventional wait-free n-process consensus objects
- $D[0..f]$: **array** of read/write register, **init** $\perp$

Private variables:

- k, k': integers, uninitialized
- d: decision value, uninitialized

Procedure Decide(v: proposal value) for proc. p_i, $i \in 1..n$

```
for k in 0..f do
    if R[i] = k then
        R[i] := k + 1
        // check for a decision in a
           lower-numbered iteration
        for k' ∈ 0..(k − 1) do
            if D[k'] ≠ ⊥ then
                v := D[k']
        d := C[k].Decide(v)
        D[k] := d
        // check for a collision with a
           higher-numbered iteration
        if k < f then
            for z ∈ 1..n, z ≠ i do
                if R[z] > R[i] then
                    d := ⊥
        // return decision if known
        if d ≠ ⊥ then
            return d
```

Figure 2: Transformation from n-process conventional consensus to n-process recoverable consensus ($\leq f$ failures).

Theorem 3.1. *The algorithm shown in Figure 2 satisfies agreement, validity, and recoverable wait-freedom in every execution with at most f failures.*

3.2 Impossibility Result for Test-And-Set

Any impossibility result for solving consensus in the conventional asynchronous model with halting failures (or without failures) applies also to solving RC in the asynchronous model with crash-recovery failures. This is because any execution that is possible in the conventional model is also admissible in the crash-recovery model, and because a violation of wait-freedom in such an execution implies a violation of recoverable wait-freedom as well. Thus, the position of a primitive in the RC hierarchy cannot be higher than its position in the traditional consensus hierarchy [4]. In particular, TAS can be no higher than at level 2 in the RC hierarchy, and so the analysis from Section 2 implies that TAS is precisely at level 2 for simultaneous failures. In this section, we extend and complete the latter result by settling the position of TAS in the RC hierarchy for independent crash-recovery failures.

Theorem 3.2. *The 2-process RC problem cannot be solved using readable Test-And-Set objects and read/write registers if failures are independent.*

Proof sketch. We suppose for contradiction that such a solution does exist. The proof uses a valency argument inspired by Herlihy's [4] and adapted to work in the crash-recovery model.[1] A restricted subset of executions is considered where only one designated process p_1 may crash, and only in states satisfying two criteria: (i) p_1's previous step was the first TAS operation by p_1 on some TAS object; and (ii) the same TAS object has been accessed by p_2 as well. Following the standard argument, processes p_1 and p_2 take steps until a bivalent state s is reached where every enabled step is a decision step (i.e., leads to a univalent state). Recoverable wait-freedom ensures that this construction terminates eventually, as otherwise p_1 crashes infinitely often, in which case p_2 is stuck forever without crashing because each crash by p_1 is associated with a distinct step by p_2. Moreover, p_1 and p_2 are enabled to take decision steps leading to a v_1-valent and v_2-valent state, respectively, for some $v_1 \neq v_2$. These decision steps must be TAS operations on the same shared object that is in its initial state of 0, which implies that p_1 has not yet applied a TAS to this object. If p_1 takes its decision step followed by p_2, and then p_1 crashes, we arrive at a v_1-valent state s_1. Similarly, if p_2 takes its decision step followed by p_1, and then p_1 crashes, we arrive at a v_2-valent state s_2. The states s_1 and s_2 are indistinguishable to p_1, and a contradiction is then reached following the standard argument since $v_1 \neq v_2$. □

The extended version of this paper [3] uses an alternative form of the above proof to relate the number of TAS objects used by a recoverable consensus algorithm to the maximum number of failures it can tolerate:

Theorem 3.3. *For any integer $f > 0$, there is no algorithm that uses at most f readable Test-And-Set objects and any number of read/write registers, and solves 2-process recoverable consensus in executions with up to f independent failures.*

Theorem 3.3 implies that the transformation shown in Figure 2 is optimal as it can be instantiated to use $f+1$ TAS-based conventional 2-process consensus objects to solve 2-process recoverable consensus in executions with up to f independent failures.

REFERENCES

[1] Hagit Attiya, Ohad Ben-Baruch, and Danny Hendler. Nesting-safe recoverable linearizability: Modular constructions for non-volatile memory. In *Proc. of the 2018 ACM Symposium on Principles of Distributed Computing (PODC)*, pages 7–16, 2018.

[2] Ryan Berryhill, Wojciech Golab, and Mahesh Tripunitara. Robust shared objects for non-volatile main memory. In *Proc. of the 19th International Conference on Principles of Distributed Systems (OPODIS)*, pages 20:1–20:17, 2016.

[3] Wojciech Golab. Recoverable consensus in shared memory. *CoRR*, 2018. URL https://arxiv.org/abs/1804.10597.

[4] Maurice Herlihy. Wait-free synchronization. *ACM Transactions on Programming Languages and Systems*, 13(1):124–149, 1991.

[1] Attiya, Ben-Baruch, and Hendler developed a similar proof technique in parallel with our work, in the context of *Nesting-Safe Recoverable Linearizability* [1]. They use a more specialized notion of valency that captures the possible outputs of an algorithm in *failure-free* execution fragments. A state that is univalent in their analysis can be either univalent or bivalent according to our definition.

Brief Announcement: How Fast Reads Affect Multi-Valued Register Simulations

Soma Chaudhuri
Iowa State University
chaudhur@iastate.edu

Reginald Frank
Texas A&M University
reginaldfrank77@tamu.edu

Jennifer L. Welch
Texas A&M University
welch@cse.tamu.edu

ABSTRACT

We consider the problem of simulating a k-valued register in a wait-free manner using binary registers as building blocks, where $k > 2$. We show that for any simulation using atomic binary base registers to simulate a safe k-valued register in which the read algorithm takes the optimal number of steps ($\log_2 k$), the write algorithm must take at least $\log_2 k$ steps in the worst case. *A fortiori*, the same lower bound applies when the simulated register should be regular. Previously known algorithms show that both these lower bounds are tight. We also show that in order to simulate an atomic k-valued register for two readers, the optimal number of steps for the read algorithm must be strictly larger than $\log_2 k$.

CCS CONCEPTS

• **Theory of Computation → Concurrency.**

KEYWORDS

register simulations, wait-freedom

ACM Reference Format:

Soma Chaudhuri, Reginald Frank, and Jennifer L. Welch. 2019. Brief Announcement: How Fast Reads Affect Multi-Valued Register Simulations. In *2019 ACM Symposium on Principles of Distributed Computing (PODC '19), July 29-August 2, 2019, Toronto, ON, Canada.* ACM, New York, NY, USA, 3 pages. https://doi.org/10.1145/3293611.3331580

1 INTRODUCTION

We consider the problem of how to use a collection of shared read-write registers with certain properties to simulate a shared read-write register with stronger properties in a wait-free manner. Each simulated read or write operation can access some of the building block, or "base", registers. In a *wait-free* simulation, each simulated operation terminates in a finite number of steps by the invoking process, regardless of the behavior of the other processes, which may be arbitrarily fast, or arbitrarily slow, or even crash. Lamport formalized the notions of safe, regular, and atomic registers, proposed a formal model, and provided numerous algorithms for simulating certain kinds of registers out of other kinds [6].

Simulating a k-valued register using binary base registers, where $k > 2$, has been studied in, e.g., [3, 4, 6, 8], while generalizations for simulating large registers out of small registers appear in [1, 2, 7].

ACM ISBN 978-1-4503-6217-7/19/07.
https://doi.org/10.1145/3293611.3331580

Regardless of the consistency conditions of the simulated register and the base registers, the number of steps taken by the simulated read must be at least $\log_2 k$ [4]. However, little work has been done in exploring tradeoff results in the optimal number of base registers or the optimal number of steps taken by the simulated write when the simulated read is limited to $\log_2 k$ steps. The only previous work we are aware of is an asymptotic result that, for the regular case, if the simulated read takes $O(\log k)$ steps, then the simulated write must take $\Omega(\log k)$ steps [5].

In this paper we consider what happens when the simulated read is limited to $\log_2 k$ steps. In the safe and regular cases, we show that this restriction results in a lower bound of $\log_2 k$ on the number of steps that the simulated write must take. These lower bounds are tight due to algorithms in [6] for the safe case and [4] for the regular case. In the atomic case we show that, if there are at least two readers, no such algorithm is possible, thus giving a lower bound of $1 + \log_2 k$ on the number of steps by the simulated read. This bound is not tight as the best known upper bound is $1 + 2 \cdot \log_2 k$ [5].

2 MODEL AND DEFINITIONS

The goal is to simulate a k-valued register $\mathbb{X}$, with value set V, $|V| = k > 2$, that supports n readers and one writer. We assume k is a power of 2. When the i-th reader invokes a READ on $\mathbb{X}$, a read process, denoted RP_i, $1 \leq i \leq n$, performs some computation and eventually outputs a RETURN with a value in V to the reader. Similarly, when the writer invokes a WRITE with a value in V on $\mathbb{X}$, the write process, denoted WP, performs some computation and eventually outputs an ACK to the writer. The read and write processes communicate with other through a finite set $\mathbb{B}$ of atomic base registers, each with a binary value set. Since the base registers are atomic, we model the read and write operations on them as occurring instantaneously. The values appearing in the RETURNS should satisfy one of the following consistency conditions [6]: *safety* (each simulated read that does not overlap a simulated write must return the value of the latest preceding simulated write), *regularity* (each simulated read must return the value of an overlapping simulated write or of the latest preceding simulated write), or *atomicity* (it should appear as if each simulated operation takes place instantaneously at some point between its invocation and response). Furthermore, as long as any particular process keeps taking steps, it should provide responses to the invocations on $\mathbb{X}$ no matter how the other processes are scheduled.

All bounds are worst-case.

3 SAFE AND REGULAR: STEP LOWER BOUND FOR WRITE WHEN READ IS FAST

An easy extension to a result in [4] shows:

Theorem 3.1. *For any wait-free simulation of a safe k-valued register using atomic binary registers, the number of steps in the simulated read is at least $\log_2 k$.*

The main result of the section is next.

Theorem 3.2. *For any wait-free simulation of a safe k-valued register using atomic binary registers, if the simulated read uses at most $\log_2 k$ reads, then the simulated write uses at least $\log_2 k$ writes.*

Proof. Let $\mathbb{A}$ be any such simulation and V be the value set of the simulated register, $|V| = k$.

For each i, $1 \leq i \leq n$, we recursively define the *decision tree* of read process RP_i, denoted T_i, as follows. The purpose is to capture which base registers are read during the first simulated read that RP_i executes in any execution. Each vertex in T_i is labeled with either a base register or a value in V. The basis step defines the root of T_i as a vertex labeled with the first base register read in the first simulated read performed by RP_i. For the inductive step, let x be a vertex in T_i labeled with register r. If the code tells RP_i to read base register s next after reading 0 (resp., 1) from r, then give x a vertex as its left (resp., right) child labeled with s. If the code tells RP_i to do Return(v) next after reading 0 (resp., 1) from r, then give x a vertex as its left (resp., right) child labeled with v. Continue until all leaves of T_i are labeled with values.

For each $v \in V$ and each i, $1 \leq i \leq n$, define σ_v^i as the execution of $\mathbb{A}$ in which a simulated write of v is performed by WP followed by a simulated read by RP_i. By correctness (i.e., safety) of $\mathbb{A}$, the simulated read must return v.

Lemma 3.3. *For each i, $1 \leq i \leq n$, T_i is a complete binary tree with exactly k leaves in which every leaf is at depth $\log_2 k$ and every root-to-leaf path π corresponds to the sequence of base registers read during the simulated read in σ_v^i, where v is is the label of the leaf in π.*

Proof. Fix i, $1 \leq i \leq n$. The existence of σ_v^i for each $v \in V$ implies that T_i must have at least k leaves. By the assumption that the step complexity of the simulated read is at most $\log_2 k$, every root-to-leaf path in T_i has at most $\log_2 k$ internal vertices. Since T_i is a binary tree, basic facts from graph theory imply that T_i has exactly k leaves and each leaf is at depth exactly $\log_2 k$. Thus the root-to-leaf path π ending at the leaf labeled v corresponds to the sequence of base registers read during the simulated read in σ_v^i. □

Note that the first simulated read by each RP_i is invisible, i.e., contains no writes to base registers, since it must have $\log_2 k$ reads in it and we assume that the step complexity is at most $\log_2 k$.

Lemma 3.4. *Let π be any root-to-leaf path in T_i, for any i, $1 \leq i \leq n$. Then every internal node on π has a unique register label.*

Proof. Fix i, $1 \leq i \leq n$. Suppose in contradiction some root-to-leaf path π has two occurrences of the register label r, say at distances a and b from the root, with $a < b$. The tree vertex representing the b-th read in π has two children, since T_i is complete by Lemma 3.3, one of which is on π. Let π' be a root-to-leaf path in T_i that is the same as π through the b-th read but then diverges. By Lemma 3.3, π corresponds to execution σ_v^i for some $v \in V$ and π' corresponds to execution $\sigma_{v'}^i$ for some $v' \in V$ with $v' \neq v$.

However, it is not possible for σ_v^i and $\sigma_{v'}^i$ to read different values from r at the b-th read since the only process that is taking steps during the simulated reads is RP_i: even if RP_i writes to r during the simulated read, it will write the same value in σ_v^i as in $\sigma_{v'}^i$, as nothing differs in those two executions until reaching the b-th read. □

Now we can finish the proof of the theorem. Without loss of generality, assume that the initial value of every base register is 0. Consider the rightmost root-to-leaf path in the decision tree T_1. By Lemma 3.3, in the corresponding execution σ_v^1, the reader RP_1 reads 1 from a base register $\log_2 k$ times during the simulated read. By Lemma 3.4, none of the base registers read during the simulated read is a repeat. Thus during the simulated write in σ_v^1, the writer WP writes 1 to the each of the $\log_2 k$ base registers that are read during the simulated read. □

Since regularity is stronger than safety, we have the following corollary to the preceding theorem:

Corollary 3.5. *For any wait-free simulation of a regular k-valued register using atomic binary registers, if the simulated read uses at most $\log_2 k$ reads, then the simulated write uses at least $\log_2 k$ writes.*

4 ATOMIC: STEP LOWER BOUND FOR READ

Now we consider the atomic case. We show that when there are two read processes, then it is impossible to simulate a k-valued register if the simulated read takes only $\log_2 k$ steps. The key to the proof is showing that, if the simulated read takes only $\log_2 k$ steps, then the first simulated read by each of the read processes must start by reading the same binary register first. We use the concept of decision tree and Lemmas 3.3 and 3.4 from inside the proof of Theorem 3.1.

Theorem 4.1. *No wait-free simulation of an atomic k-valued register using atomic binary registers can have a simulated read that takes at most $\log_2 k$ steps, assuming there are at least two readers.*

Proof. Assume in contradiction there is such a simulation $\mathbb{A}$, with readers RP_1 and RP_2. We already observed that their first simulated reads are invisible (contain no writes to base registers). Let T_i be the decision tree of the first simulated read by RP_i, $i = 1, 2$.

Lemma 4.2. *T_1 and T_2 have the same root register.*

Proof. Suppose in contradiction the root r_1 of T_1 is not equal to the root r_2 of T_2. Let z be a value whose root-to-leaf path in T_2 does not include r_1. Such a value must exist since r_1 is not the root of T_2. Without loss of generality, suppose z appears in the right half of the leaf level of T_1. Let a be a value that appears in the left half of the leaf level of T_1.

Consider an execution e consisting of two simulated writes, $W_0(a)$ followed by $W_1(z)$. After W_0, r_1 must equal 0, as it's possible that RP_1's first simulated read is immediately after W_0, in which case it must return a and thus must see 0 in r_1. A similar argument shows that after W_1, r_1 must equal 1. Thus W_1 must contain a write of 1 to r_1.

Consider adding two simulated reads to e to make execution e': immediately after the first write of 1 to r_1 in W_1, insert RP_1's first simulated read R_1, immediately followed by RP_2's first simulated read R_2. By regularity, R_1 must return either a or z and since R_1 observes 1 in r_1, it must return z. Then by atomicity, R_2 must return z as well.

Consider execution e'' which is obtained from e' by moving R_1 to appear immediately before the first write of 1 to r_1 in W_1 and moving R_2 to appear immediately before R_1. The only difference in the registers during the execution of R_2 in e'' versus e' is the value of r_1. But r_1 does not lie on the root-to-leaf path in T_2 leading to z, and thus R_2 will behave the same in e'' as it does in e' and return z.

Consider the occurrence of R_1 in e''. By atomicity, R_1 must return z, but R_1 reads 0 in r_1 and thus cannot return z, a contradiction. □

By Lemma 4.2, T_1 and T_2 have the same root, call it register r. Let a and b be two "sibling" values that are in the left half of the leaf level of T_1, with a to the left of b, and z be a value that is in the right half of the leaf level of T_1. Since T_1 and T_2 have the same root r, a and b are also in the left half of the leaf level of T_2 and z is also in the right half of the leaf level of T_2. Let x be the register that is the parent of a and b in T_1.

Consider an execution e consisting of three simulated writes: $W_0(a)$ followed by $W_1(z)$, followed by $W_2(b)$. We make the following observations:

- After W_0 finishes, $r = x = 0$. The reason is that it is possible that RP_1 does its first simulatd read between W_0 and W_1, which must return a by safety and thus T_1 must have $r = x = 0$.
- After W_1 finishes, $r = 1$. The reason is that it is possible that RP_1 does its first simulated read between W_1 and W_2, which must return z by safety and thus T_1 must have $r = 1$. So during W_1 there must be at least one write of 1 to r.
- After W_2 finishes, $r = 0$ and $x = 1$. The reason is that it is possible that RP_1 does its first simulated read after W_2, which must return b by safety and thus T_1 must have $r = 0$ and $x = 1$. So during W_2 there must be at least one write of 0 to r during W_2. Also, there must be at least one write of 1 to x in the interval between the beginning of W_1 and the end of W_2.

The rest of the proof has two cases, depending on whether the first write of 1 to x between the beginning of W_1 and the end of W_2 occurs before or after the first write of 0 to r in W_2; if before, we will show that atomicity is violated; if after, that regularity is violated.

Case 1: The first write of 1 to x occurs before the first write of 0 to r in W_2.

Now consider another execution e_1 in which we add a simulated read R_1 by RP_1 and a simulated read R_2 by RP_2 to execution e. Since simulated reads are invisible, their existence does not affect the behavior of the simulated writes in e.

Suppose R_1 starts after W_0 ends and reads r through the parent of x in T_1 before W_1 begins. Then R_1 reads x immediately after the first write of 1 to x (which occurs in either W_1 or W_2), and thus sees $x = 1$. So R_1 returns b, as indicated by its decision tree T_1.

Now suppose R_2 starts after R_1 ends and reads r before W_2's first write of 0 to r, and thus sees $r = 1$. By definition of atomicity, the only legal value that R_2 can return is b, but by the structure of its decision tree T_2 it will not return b, since it read 1 from r. Contradiction.

Case 2: The first write of 1 to x occurs after the first write of 0 to r in W_2.

Now consider another execution e_2 in which we add a simulated read R_1 by RP_1 to execution e. As in Case 1, since simulated reads are invisible, its existence does not affect the behavior of the simulated writes in e.

Suppose R_1 starts and reads r immediately after the first write of 0 to r in W_2, seeing $r = 0$, and then R_1 completes all its reads before the first write of 1 to x in W_2. The structure of the decision tree T_1 implies that R_1 cannot return z, since R_1 read 0 in r, and R_1 cannot return b, since R_1 read 0 in x. But b and z are the only valid return values that satisfy atomicity (or even regularity for that matter). Contradiction. □

The same impossibility holds with only one read process assuming that its first two simulated reads start by reading the same binary register.

5 CONCLUSION

We have shown how having a fast read algorithm affects the speed of the write algorithm when simulating a safe or regular k-valued register and that the read algorithm must be slower in the atomic case than in the safe and regular cases. Open questions include getting rid of the need for two readers to show the $1 + \log_2 k$ lower bound on the read algorithm step complexity in the atomic case. More generally, we would like to close the gap between the upper bound of $1 + 2 \cdot \log_2 k$ on this measure due to [5] and the lower bound.

ACKNOWLEDGMENTS

This work was supported in part by NSF grant 1816922.

REFERENCES

[1] Zahra Aghazadeh, Wojciech M. Golab, and Philipp Woelfel. Making objects writable. In *ACM Symposium on Principles of Distributed Computing*, pages 385–395, 2014.
[2] Alon Berger, Idit Keidar, and Alexander Spiegelman. Integrated bounds for disintegrated storage. In *32nd International Symposium on Distributed Computing*, pages 11:1–11:18, 2018.
[3] Soma Chaudhuri, Martha J. Kosa, and Jennifer L. Welch. One-write algorithms for multivalued regular and atomic registers. *Acta Inf.*, 37(3):161–192, 2000.
[4] Soma Chaudhuri and Jennifer L. Welch. Bounds on the costs of multivalued register implementations. *SIAM J. Comput.*, 23(2):335–354, 1994.
[5] Tian Ze Chen and Yuanhao Wei. Step optimal implementations of large single-writer registers. In *20th International Conference on Principles of Distributed Systems (OPODIS)*, pages 32:1–32:16, 2016.
[6] Leslie Lamport. On interprocess communication. Part II: Algorithms. *Distributed Computing*, 1(2):86–101, 1986.
[7] Gary L. Peterson. Concurrent reading while writing. *ACM Trans. Program. Lang. Syst.*, 5(1):46–55, 1983.
[8] K. Vidyasankar. Converting Lamport's regular register to atomic register. *Inf. Process. Lett.*, 28(6):287–290, 1988.

Topological Characterization of Consensus under General Message Adversaries

Dedicated to the 2018 Dijkstra Prize winners Bowen Alpern and Fred B. Schneider

Thomas Nowak*
Université Paris-Sud
Orsay, France
thomas.nowak@lri.fr

Ulrich Schmid
TU Wien
Vienna, Austria
s@ecs.tuwien.ac.at

Kyrill Winkler†
TU Wien
Vienna, Austria
kwinkler@ecs.tuwien.ac.at

ABSTRACT

In this paper, we provide a rigorous characterization of consensus solvability in synchronous directed dynamic networks controlled by an arbitrary message adversary using point-set topology: We extend the approach introduced by Alpern and Schneider in 1985 by introducing two novel topologies on the space of infinite executions: the process-view topology, induced by a distance function that relies on the local view of a given process in an execution, and the minimum topology, which is induced by a distance function that focuses on the local view of the process that is the last to distinguish two executions. We establish some simple but powerful topological results, which not only lead to a topological explanation of bivalence arguments, but also provide necessary and sufficient topological conditions on the admissible graph sequences of a message adversary for solving consensus. In particular, we characterize consensus solvability in terms of connectivity of the set of admissible graph sequences. For non-compact message adversaries, which are not limit-closed in the sense that there is a convergent sequence of graph sequences whose limit is not permitted, this requires the exclusion of all "fair" and "unfair" limit sequences that coincide with the forever bivalent runs constructed in bivalence proofs. For both compact and non-compact message adversaries, we also provide tailored characterizations of consensus solvability, i.e., tight conditions for impossibility and existence of algorithms, based on the broadcastability of the connected components of the set of admissible graph sequences.

CCS CONCEPTS

• **Theory of computation → Distributed algorithms**;

KEYWORDS

Topological characterization; point-set topology; consensus; dynamic networks; message adversaries

*Thomas Nowak has been supported by the Université Paris-Saclay project DEPEC MODE.

†Kyrill Winkler has been supported by the Austrian Science Fund (FWF) under project ADynNet (P28182) and RiSE/SHiNE (S11405).

PODC '19, July 29-August 2, 2019, Toronto, ON, Canada

ACM ISBN 978-1-4503-6217-7/19/07.
https://doi.org/10.1145/3293611.3331624

ACM Reference Format:
Thomas Nowak, Ulrich Schmid, and Kyrill Winkler. 2019. Topological Characterization of Consensus under General Message Adversaries: Dedicated to the 2018 Dijkstra Prize winners Bowen Alpern and Fred B. Schneider. In *2019 ACM Symposium on Principles of Distributed Computing (PODC '19), July 29-August 2, 2019, Toronto, ON, Canada.* ACM, New York, NY, USA, 10 pages. https://doi.org/10.1145/3293611.3331624

1 INTRODUCTION

We provide a complete characterization of consensus solvability in synchronous directed dynamic networks, controlled by a general message adversary, using a novel approach based on point-set topology as introduced by Alpern and Schneider [2]. Dynamic networks (see [14] for an overview) consist of a set of n fault-free processes that execute in communication-closed lock-step rounds. In every round, a directed communication graph (determined by the message adversary) defines which messages are delivered and which are lost. A *message adversary* (MA) [1] is thus just a set of infinite sequences of communication graphs.

Assuming that every process starts with some input value, the goal of a consensus algorithm is to irrevocably compute a common output value at every process eventually. A natural question to ask in this context is to describe the properties of the message adversaries that make deterministic consensus solvable. Until now, combinatorial methods were employed successfully to answer this question for certain classes of message adversaries [8, 9, 22, 24], but, to the best of our knowledge, there has been no success in finding a characterization for the general message adversary notion outlined above. Inspired by the 2018 Dijkstra Prize winning paper by Alpern and Schneider [2], our approach is thus based on point set topology.

Related work. In their celebrated paper [22], Santoro and Widmayer provided the first comprehensive characterization of consensus solvability in synchronous distributed systems prone to communication errors. Using bivalence arguments [10], they proved that consensus is impossible if up to $n-1$ messages may be lost (by the same process) in each round. In [23], Schmid et al. showed that consensus can even be solved when a quadratic number of messages is lost per round, provided these losses do not isolate the processes. These approaches were generalized by the HO model by Charron-Bost and Schiper [7], which has been extended to also cover corrupted communication in [4].

All the above communication failure models (without corrupted messages) can also be expressed in terms of *oblivious* message adversaries [8], whose sequences are determined by all combinations

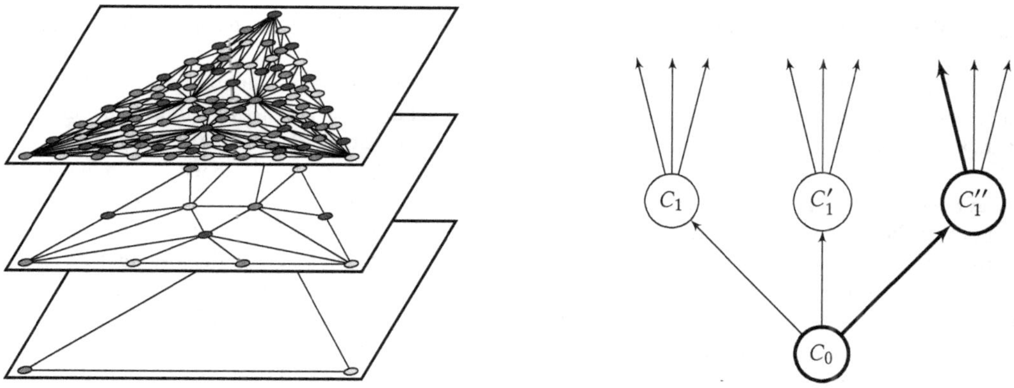

Figure 1: Comparison of the combinatorial topology approach and the point-set topology approach: The combinatorial topology approach (left) studies sequences of increasingly refined spaces in which the objects of interest are simplices (corresponding to configurations). The point-set topology approach (right) studies a single space in which the objects of interest are executions (i.e., infinite sequences of configurations).

of a *set* of possible communication graphs. For example, for $n = 2$ processes (the lossy link scenario), the result of [22] implies that if the message adversary may choose from the set of communication graphs $\{\leftarrow, \leftrightarrow, \rightarrow\}$ (where, e.g., $\rightarrow$ represents successful communication from process 1 to process 2), consensus is impossible.

The above results were substantially refined by Coulouma, Godard and Peters in [8]. The authors identified a property of an equivalence relation defined on the set of communication graphs, which exactly captures consensus solvability in the oblivious setting. A universal consensus algorithm was also given, which, e.g., allows to solve consensus when the set of possible graphs for $n = 2$ consists of $\{\leftarrow, \rightarrow\}$.

The situation is considerably more complex for non-oblivious message adversaries, where the set of possible graphs may change over time. In sharp contrast to oblivious message adversaries, it need not be the case that the set of graph sequences is limit-closed, i.e., the model does not need to be compact, cf. [15]. For example, eventually stabilizing message adversaries like the *vertex-stable source component* (VSSC) message adversaries described in [6, 24] guarantee that some rounds with "good" communication graphs (a VSSC, which allows a consensus algorithm to terminate) occur eventually. However, limits of these sequences, in which the VSSC would never appear, are of course not in the message adversary.

For the special case of $n = 2$, Fevat and Godard [9] provided a complete characterization of consensus solvability for non-oblivious message adversaries as well: Using a bivalence argument, they showed that certain graph sequences (a "fair sequence" or a special pair of "unfair sequences") must not be in the message adversary to render consensus solvable, and provided a universal algorithm for this case. However, a complete characterization of consensus solvability for arbitrary system sizes did not exist until now.

Regarding topological methods, one has to distinguish point-set topology, as introduced in [2], and combinatorial topology, as used for proving theorems characterizing solvable tasks in wait-free asynchronous shared memory systems with process crashes[1] [13] or under fair adversaries [15], for example. Combinatorial topology studies the topology of the reachable states of admissible executions, captured by simplicial complexes as shown in Figure 1 (left), and has been developed into a widely applicable tool for the analysis of distributed systems [12].

By contrast, the primary objects of point-set topology are infinite executions, as shown in Figure 1 (right), where closed and dense sets precisely characterize safety and liveness properties, respectively. Apart from early work of one of the authors on characterizing consensus solvability in standard compact models [19], and a topological study of the strongly dependent decision problem [5], which both use the classic common prefix metric [2], the only distributed computing work we are aware of that utilizes point-set topology is [16]. In this paper, Lubitch and Moran introduced a construction for schedulers that lead to compact submodels of classic non-compact distributed computing models (like up to t crash failures). Whereas this greatly simplifies impossibility proofs, it does not lead to a precise characterization of solvability in non-compact models, however. Note that, in a similar spirit, [15] allows to reason, in the setting of combinatorial topology, about non-compact models by considering equivalent affine tasks that are compact.

Main contributions. We provide a complete[2] characterization of consensus solvability under compact and non-compact message adversaries, for an arbitrary number of processes. Rather than utilizing classic distributed computing techniques, we developed a novel modeling and analysis approach based on point-set topology. We had to add several new topological ideas to the setting of [2], as detailed below, which at the end provided us with a very powerful "toolbox" that, for example, allowed us to provide a topological explanation of bivalence [10] and bipotence [17] proofs. As our approach can be adapted to different distributed computing models, we believe that it could be of independent interest.

(i) We define two new topologies on the execution space, which allow to reason about sequences of local views of a certain process, rather than about configuration sequences. If this process is a fixed

[1] Note that message adversaries do not fall into this category of models.

[2] Lacking space did not allow us to also include the proofs, which can be found in the full version [20] of our paper.

one (p), the resulting $\{p\}$*-view topology* is induced by a pseudo-metric $d_{\{p\}}(\alpha, \beta)$ based on the common prefix of p's local views in the executions α, β. Alternatively, this process can be the last one to notice a difference between executions, which gives rise to the *minimum topology* induced by the pseudo-semi-metric $d_{\min}(\alpha, \beta) = \min_{p\in[n]} d_{\{p\}}(\alpha, \beta)$.

(ii) Since the set of possible views is not necessarily finite, the product topologies built on the execution space are not compact *a priori.* Fortunately, the space of sequences of process-time graphs [3], which are finite, comes to our rescue: Since the local transition function τ, which maps sequences of admissible process-time graphs to the corresponding admissible executions Γ, is continuous, the resulting product subspaces *are* compact.

(iii) We show that consensus can be modeled as a continuous decision function Δ, which maps an admissible execution to its unique decision value. In conjunction with the above results, this allows us to prove that consensus is solvable if and only if all the decision sets, i.e., the pre-images $\Gamma_v = \Delta^{-1}[\{v\}]$ resp. $PS_v = \tau^{-1}\big[\Delta^{-1}[\{v\}]\big]$ for every decision value v, are separated in our topologies. We also provide a universal consensus algorithm, which relies on this separation. Moreover, we show that separability is equivalent to broadcastability of the connected components (in the sense that there is a process that is heard by all processes in every sequence in a connected component).

(iv) Using some properties of the pseudo-metric $d_{\{p\}}$, we provide a topological definition of fair and unfair sequences [9]. They turn out to be the limits of two infinite sequences of executions lying in two different decision sets, which have distance 0, and happen to coincide with the forever bivalent/bipotent executions constructed in bivalence proofs. We show that a message adversary must not include such fair and unfair sequences for consensus to be solvable.

(v) We use our generic results to give a complete characterization of consensus solvability for both compact and non-compact message adversaries. For the former (like [8, 22, 23]), we introduce a simple ε-approximation of a decision set, which is equivalent to the set of the $(\log \frac{1}{\varepsilon})$-prefixes of the sequences contained therein. We prove that consensus can be solved, using our universal algorithm, if and only if the ε-approximations are broadcastable for some ε. For non-compact message adversaries (like [6, 9, 24]), the ε-approximation does not work, so one needs to apply our universal algorithm based on the connected components directly.

Paper organization. In Section 2 and 3, we define the elements of the spaces that are endowed with our new topologies in Section 4. Section 5 introduces the consensus problem in topological terms and provides our abstract characterization result (Theorem 5.5, which also provides a universal algorithm). We refine our characterization according to the properties of the minimum topology (Theorem 5.11) and the process-view topology (Corollary 5.18). Section 6 is devoted to the application of our generic results to compact (Theorem 6.6) and non-compact (Theorem 6.7) message adversaries. Some conclusions in Section 7 round off our paper.

2 SYSTEM MODEL

We consider deterministic algorithms for a synchronous directed dynamic network consisting of n processes with unique identifiers taken from $[n] = \{1, \ldots, n\}$.

A *communication graph* is any directed graph $G = ([n], E)$, $E \subseteq [n] \times [n]$ with node set $[n]$. A *message adversary* (MA) is a set of infinite sequences of communication graphs. Graph sequences in this set are called *admissible* under the message adversary.

An algorithm $\mathcal{A}$, an initial configuration C^0 of $\mathcal{A}$, and a graph sequence $\mathbf{G} = (G^t)_{t\geq 1}$ uniquely determine an *execution* in a round-by-round fashion: During round t, every process p updates its previous local state C_p^{t-1} to its new state C_p^t in a deterministic way according to $\mathcal{A}$, based on the messages it received during round t. Rounds advance synchronously in a send–receive–compute order. Messages in round t are delivered according to communication graph G^t: Process q receives process p's message in round t if and only if (p, q) is an edge of G^t.

An algorithm is defined by the local transition function and a set of initial states for every process. Since we are only interested in consensus algorithms, we stipulate that processes have an initial state for every initial value v of the finite input domain $\mathcal{V}_I$. Note carefully that we assume that a process running $\mathcal{A}$ does not know n a priori, and cannot always infer n from the messages it receives in an execution either. By contrast, the message adversary need not be oblivious w.r.t. the algorithm, i.e., it may know $\mathcal{A}$ and choose its graph sequences accordingly.

A *configuration* is a tuple $(C_1, \ldots, C_n)$ of process states. Whenever $\mathcal{A}$ is clear from the context, we denote its set of possible configurations by C. C^ω denotes the set of all infinite sequences of configurations, $\Gamma \subseteq C^\omega$ is the set of admissible executions resulting from admissible graph sequences. Executions are represented by Greek letters $\alpha, \beta, \ldots$.

3 PROCESS-TIME GRAPHS

We will consider *process-time graphs* [3], which are useful for reasoning about the *causal past* of a process in a given round, and which will play a crucial role in our topological framework.

For every graph sequence $\mathbf{G} = (G^t)_{t\geq 1}$ and every assignment of initial values $x \in \mathcal{V}_I^n$ to the n processes, we inductively construct the following sequence of process-time graphs PT^t:

- The process-time graph PT^0 at time 0 contains the nodes $(p, 0, x_p)$ for all processes $p \in [n]$, with input value $x_p \in \mathcal{V}_I$, and no edges.
- The process-time graph PT^1 at time 1 contains the nodes $(p, 0, x_p)$ and $(p, 1)$ for all processes $p \in [n]$. It contains an edge from $(p, 0, x_p)$ to $(q, 1)$ if and only if $(p, q) \in G^1$.
- For $t \geq 2$, the process-time graph PT^t at time t contains the nodes of PT^{t-1} and the nodes (p, t) for all processes $p \in [n]$. It contains an edge from $(p, t-1)$ to (q, t) if and only if $(p, q) \in G^t$.

Figure 2 contains an example of a process-time graph at time 2.

Let $\mathcal{PT}^t$ be the set of all possible process-time graphs at time $t \geq 0$, which is finite for any $t \geq 0$. Furthermore, let $\mathcal{PT}^\omega = \mathcal{PT}^0 \times \mathcal{PT}^1 \times \ldots$ be the set of all infinite sequences of possible process-time graphs.[3]

Given an input domain $\mathcal{V}_I$, every message adversary uniquely corresponds to a subset PS of $\mathcal{PT}^\omega$ generated by the graph sequences admissible under the message adversary.

[3]Please note that we slightly abuse the notation $\mathcal{PT}^\omega$ here, which normally represents $\mathcal{PT} \times \mathcal{PT} \times \ldots$.

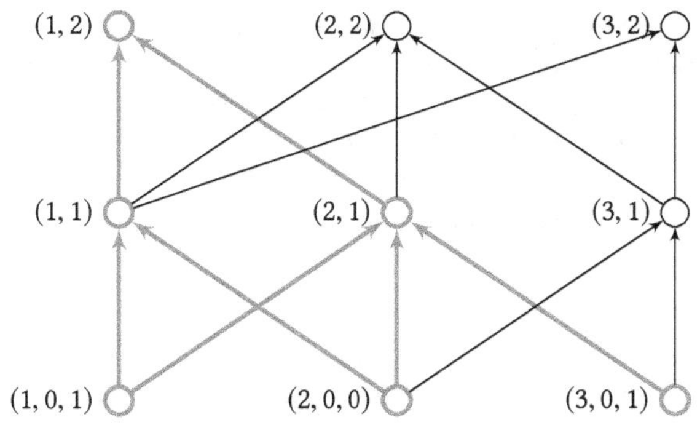

Figure 2: Example of a process-time graph PT^2 at time $t = 2$ with $n = 3$ processes and initial values $x = (1, 0, 1)$. Process 1's view $V_{\{1\}}(PT^2)$ is highlighted in bold green.

Note that process-time graphs are *independent* of the particular algorithm used, but do depend on the input values. For conciseness, we will use the term process-time graphs for the elements of $\mathcal{PT}^\omega$ as well. We will denote elements of $\mathcal{PT}^\omega$ by Roman letters $a, b, \ldots$ (or sometimes $PT, PT', \ldots$).

4 TOPOLOGICAL STRUCTURE

In this section, we will endow the various sets introduced in Section 2 and 3 with suitable topologies. We first recall briefly the basic topological notions that are needed for our exposition. For a more thorough introduction, however, the reader is advised to refer to a textbook [18].

A topology for a set X is a family $\mathcal{T}$ of subsets of X such that $\emptyset \in \mathcal{T}$, $X \in \mathcal{T}$, and $\mathcal{T}$ contains all arbitrary unions as well as all finite intersections of its members. We call X endowed with $\mathcal{T}$, often written as $(X, \mathcal{T})$, a (topological) space and the members of $\mathcal{T}$ open sets. The complement of an open set is called closed and sets that are both open and closed, such as $\emptyset$ and X itself, are called clopen. A metric on X is a function $d : X \times X \to \mathbb{R}_+$ such that for all $x, y, z \in X$ we have $d(x, y) = 0$ if and only if $x = y$, $d(x, y) = d(y, x)$, and $d(x, z) \le d(x, y) + d(y, z)$. The topology induced by a metric d is the collection of sets U such that for each $u \in U$, there is an ε-ball $B_\varepsilon(u) = \{v \mid d(u, v) < \varepsilon\}$ with $\varepsilon > 0$ and $u \in B_\varepsilon(u) \subseteq U$.

A function from space X to space Y is continuous if the pre-image of every open set in Y is open in X. Given a space $(X, \mathcal{T})$, $Y \subseteq X$ is called a subspace of X if Y is equipped with the subspace topology $\{Y \cap U \mid U \in \mathcal{T}\}$. Given $A \subseteq X$, the closure of A is the intersection of all closed sets containing A. For a space X, if $A \subseteq X$, we call x a limit point of A if it belongs to the closure of $A \setminus \{x\}$. It can be shown that the closure of A is the union of A with all limit points of A. A space X is called compact if every union of open sets that covers X contains a finite union of open sets that covers X. Note that our topologies are also sequentially compact, which ensures that every infinite sequence of elements has a convergent subsequence.

In previous work on point-set topology [19], the set of configurations C of some fixed algorithm $\mathcal{A}$ was endowed with the discrete topology, induced by the discrete metric $d_{\max}(C, D) = 1$ if $C \neq D$ and 0 otherwise (for configurations $C, D \in C$)[4] Moreover, C^ω was endowed with the corresponding product topology[5], which happens to be induced by the *common prefix metric*

$$d_{\max}(\alpha, \beta) = 2^{-\inf\{t \ge 0 \mid \alpha^t \neq \beta^t\}} \ . \tag{1}$$

Our generalization will focus on the local views of the processes, which are obtained by suitable projection functions: For a tuple $x = (x_1, \ldots, x_n)$ and any $\emptyset \neq P = \{p_1, \ldots, p_k\} \subseteq [n]$, the P-projection function is defined as $\pi_P(x) = (x_{p_1}, \ldots, x_{p_k})$ where $p_1 \le \cdots \le p_k$. Similarly, for any infinite sequence $\theta = (\theta^0, \theta^1, \ldots)$ and any $t \ge 0$, the t-projection function is defined as $\pi^t(\theta) = \theta^t$.

The views of a fixed non-empty subset of the processes in a configuration can be defined as follows:

Definition 4.1 (Views). For any configuration $C \in C$, the view of the processes in $\emptyset \neq P \subseteq [n]$ is $V_P(C) = \pi_P(C)$. The set of all possible P-views is defined as $\text{Views}_P = \{V_P(C) \mid C \in C\}$.

4.1 Process-View Topologies

We will now introduce a topology on the set C of configurations that relies on the corresponding set of views Views_P of a set of processes P.

Definition 4.2 (P-view topology for configurations). Let $P \subseteq [n]$ be a nonempty set of processes. The *P-view topology* $\mathcal{T}_P^C$ on C is defined as the topology induced by the subbasis $\{V_P^{-1}[V] \mid V \subseteq \text{Views}_P\}$, i.e., is the arbitrary union of finite intersections of the elements $V_P^{-1}[V]$ for an arbitrary set $V \subseteq \text{Views}_P$.

The topology $\mathcal{T}_P^C$ is induced by the pseudo-metric[6]

$$d_P(C, D) = \begin{cases} 0 & \text{if } V_P(C) = V_P(D) \\ 1 & \text{else .} \end{cases}$$

Note that the topology $\mathcal{T}_P^C$ is much coarser than the discrete topology on C, as it does not distinguish the local states of processes outside of P.

The corresponding product topology on the set C^ω of sequences of configurations, also denoted *P-view topology*, can be defined as follows: The P-view topology $\mathcal{T}_P^{C^\omega}$ on C^ω is defined as the topology induced by the subbasis $\{(\pi^t)^{-1}[U] \mid t \ge 0, U \in \mathcal{T}_P^C\}$, i.e., is an arbitrary union of finite intersections of the elements $(\pi^t)^{-1}[U]$, where U is an arbitrary open set in $\mathcal{T}_P^C$.

We will show that the P-view topology is induced by the following pseudo-metric on C^ω:

$$d_P(\alpha, \beta) = 2^{-\inf\{t \ge 0 \mid V_P(\alpha^t) \neq V_P(\beta^t)\}}.$$

We call this the *P-pseudo-metric* on C^ω. Figure 3 shows an example for different sets P.

It follows immediately from the definition that, if $\alpha, \beta \in C^\omega$ satisfy $d_P(\alpha, \beta) < 2^{-t}$, then the processes in P have the same view of the first t configurations in α and β. Moreover, the P-pseudo-metric satisfies the following properties:

[4]The notation $d_{\max}$ stems from the fact that it is equal to the maximum of the P-pseudo-metrics defined in the next subsection.

[5]The product topology on a product $\Pi_{\iota \in I} X_\iota$ of topological spaces is defined as the coarsest topology such that all projections $\pi_i : \Pi_{\iota \in I} X_\iota \to X_i$ are continuous.

[6]A pseudo-metric has the same properties as a metric, except that it lacks definiteness, i.e., we can have $d(x, y) = 0$ for $x \neq y$.

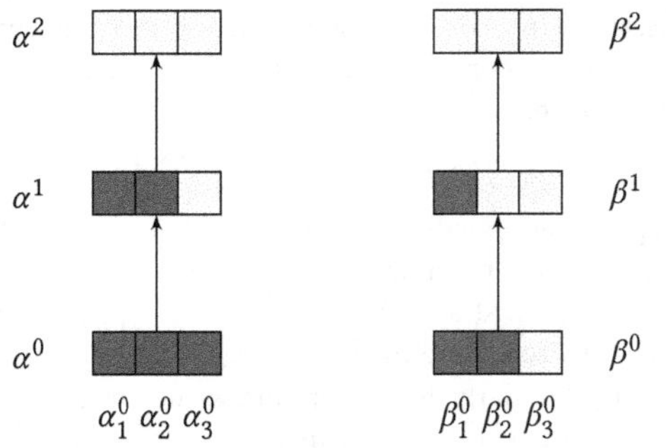

Figure 3: Comparison of the P-view, minimum, and common prefix topologies. The first three configurations of each of the two executions α and β with three processes and two different possible local states (dark blue and light yellow) are depicted. We have $d_{\max}(\alpha,\beta) = d_{\{3\}}(\alpha,\beta) = 1$, $d_{\{2\}}(\alpha,\beta) = 1/2$, and $d_{\min}(\alpha,\beta) = d_{\{1\}}(\alpha,\beta) = 1/4$.

Theorem 4.3 Properties of P-pseudo-metric. *The P-pseudo-metric $d_P(\alpha,\beta)$ on C^ω satisfies*

$$\begin{aligned} d_P(\alpha,\beta) &= d_P(\beta,\alpha) && \text{(symmetry)},\\ d_P(\alpha,\gamma) &\le d_P(\alpha,\beta) + d_P(\beta,\gamma) && \text{(triangle inequality)},\\ d_P(\alpha,\beta) &\le d_Q(\alpha,\beta) && \text{(monotonicity for } P \subseteq Q),\\ d_{[n]}(\alpha,\beta) &= d_{\max}(\alpha,\beta) && \text{(common prefix metric)}. \end{aligned}$$

Despite of the lack of definiteness, most properties of metric spaces, including compactness, hold also in pseudo-metric spaces [11]. What is obviously lost is the uniqueness of the limit of a convergent sequence of executions, however: if $\alpha_k \to \hat{\alpha}$ and $d_P(\hat{\alpha},\hat{\beta}) = 0$, then $\alpha_k \to \hat{\beta}$ as well.

Theorem 4.4 P-view topology induced by P-pseudo-metric. *The P-view topology $\mathcal{T}_P^{C^\omega}$ on C^ω is induced by the P-pseudo-metric.*

We could use exactly the same machinery as above for endowing the set $\mathcal{G}$ of communication graphs and the set $\mathcal{G}^\omega$ of sequences of graph sequences, like C and C^ω, with an analogous P-view topology. It turns out, however, that this does not lead to a transition function that is continuous w.r.t. the P-pseudo-metric for all algorithms.

Fortunately, however, the P-view projection function $V_P(\cdot)$ is also meaningful for any process-time graph PT^t: It just represents the causal past of the processes in P at the end of round t, i.e., the sub-graph induced by all process-time nodes (q,t') that have a path to node (p,t) for some $p \in P$ in the process-time graph PT^t.

Moreover, we can define a P-view topology on $\mathcal{PT}^\omega$, analogous to that on C^ω. The same is true for the proof of the correspondence Theorem 4.4, which hence also holds here.

In sharp contrast to the set of configurations C, however, the set of process-time graphs $\mathcal{PT}^t$ is finite for any time t since $\mathcal{V}_I^n \times \mathcal{G}^t$ is finite. Tychonoff's theorem[7] hence implies compactness of the P-view topology on $\mathcal{PT}^\omega$, which is not necessarily the case for C^ω.

[7] Tychonoff's theorem states that any product of compact spaces is compact (with respect to the product topology).

Since the algorithms take decisions based on local states only, we can define the *transition function* $\tau : \mathcal{PT}^\omega \to C^\omega$ that provides $C^t = \tau(PT^t)$ for every $t \ge 0$, i.e., maps process-time graphs to the corresponding configurations. The following Lemma 4.5 shows that τ is continuous w.r.t. the P-pseudo-metric.

Lemma 4.5 Continuity of τ w.r.t. d_P. *Let $P \subseteq [n]$. The transition function $\tau : \mathcal{PT}^\omega \to C^\omega$ is continuous when both $\mathcal{PT}^\omega$ and C^ω are endowed with d_P.*

Since the image of a compact space under a continuous function is compact, it hence follows that the set $\tau[\mathcal{PT}^\omega] \subseteq C^\omega$ of admissible executions is a compact subspace of $(C^\omega, \mathcal{T}_P^{C^\omega})$.

The common structure of $\mathcal{PT}^\omega$ and its image under the transition function τ, implied by the continuity of τ, allows us to reason in either of these spaces. We will usually reason in $\mathcal{PT}^\omega$ or in its subspace PS. Note also that any sequence $a \in \mathcal{PT}^\omega$ or $\gamma \in \tau[\mathcal{PT}^\omega]$ can also be identified by specifying a vector $x \in \mathcal{V}_I^n$ of input values and a graph sequence $\mathbf{G} \in \mathcal{G}^\omega$ that leads to a and hence γ.

4.2 Minimum Topology

For our characterization of consensus solvability, we endow the set C^ω of configuration sequences and the set of process-time graphs $\mathcal{PT}^\omega$ with a slightly different but related topology, induced by the distance function

$$d_{\min}(\alpha,\beta) = \min_{p\in[n]} d_{\{p\}}(\alpha,\beta), \tag{2}$$

which reflects the common prefix length of the process p that is the *last* one to distinguish its q-view in α and β.

Note carefully, however, that $d_{\min}$ only satisfies symmetry and nonnegativity but not the triangle inequality, i.e., is only a *pseudo-semi-metric*: There may be sequences with $d_{\{p\}}(\alpha,\beta) = 0$ and $d_{\{q\}}(\beta,\gamma) = 0$ but $d_{\{q\}}(\alpha,\gamma) > 0$ for all $q \in [n]$. Hence, the topology $\mathcal{T}_{\min}^{C^\omega}$ on C^ω induced by $d_{\min}$ lacks many of the properties of (pseudo-)metric spaces, but will turn out to be already sufficient for the characterization of the possibility/impossibility of consensus (see Theorem 5.4). Alternatively, however, one can also consider all individual pseudo-metric spaces induced by $d_{\{p\}}$, $p \in [n]$, separately and compute the minimum afterwards.

Pseudo-semi-metrics induce a topology just like (pseudo)-metrics. In fact, a much more general result holds:

Lemma 4.6 Pseudo-semi-metrics induce topologies. *Let X be a nonempty set and $d : X \times X \to \mathbb{R}$ be a function. Define $\mathcal{T} \subseteq 2^X$ by setting $U \in \mathcal{T}$ if and only if for all $x \in U$ there exists some $\varepsilon > 0$ such that*

$$B_\varepsilon(x) = \{y \in X \mid d(x,y) < \varepsilon\} \subseteq U \ .$$

Then $\mathcal{T}$ is a topology on X.

Denote by $\mathcal{T}_{\min}^C$ the topology on the set C of configurations induced by

$$d_{\min}(C,D) = \min_{p\in[n]} d_{\{p\}}(C,D) \ .$$

Then the function $d_{\min}$ defined on C^ω induces the product topology $\mathcal{T}_{\min}^{C^\omega}$, where every copy of C is endowed with $\mathcal{T}_{\min}^C$:

Lemma 4.7 Pseudo-semi-metric for product topologies. *Let X be a nonempty set and let $d : X \times X \to \{0,1\}$ be a function. Then* *the product topology of X^ω, where every copy of X is endowed by the topology $\mathcal{T}^\omega$ induced by d, is induced by*

$$d^\omega : X^\omega \times X^\omega \to \mathbb{R} \quad , \quad d^\omega(\alpha,\beta) = 2^{-\inf\{t\geq 0 | d(\alpha^t,\beta^t)>0\}} \ .$$

Specializing to $X = C$ and $d = d_{\min}$, we get:

Lemma 4.8 Minimum topology in terms of process-view topologies. *We have*

$$d^\omega(\alpha,\beta) = \min_{p\in[n]} d_{\{p\}}(\alpha,\beta) = d_{\min}(\alpha,\beta)$$

for all $\alpha,\beta \in C^\omega$.

Like for $\mathcal{T}_P^{\mathcal{PT}^\omega}$, we get from Tychonoff's theorem and the finiteness, and hence compactness, of every $\mathcal{PT}^t$ that $(\mathcal{PT}^\omega, \mathcal{T}_{\min}^{\mathcal{PT}^\omega})$ is compact.

We finally show that the function $\tau : \mathcal{PT}^\omega \to C^\omega$ is continuous also for the distance $d_{\min}$.

Lemma 4.9 Continuity of τ w.r.t. $d_{\min}$. *The local transition function $\tau : \mathcal{PT}^\omega \to C^\omega$ is continuous when $\mathcal{PT}^\omega$ and C^ω are endowed with $d_{\min}$.*

Like for the P-view topologies, the continuity of τ also implies the compactness of $\tau[\mathcal{PT}^\omega]$ in the minimum-topology.

5 CONSENSUS

In this section, we will develop a topological condition for consensus under message adversaries. Unlike in [19], where the admissible graph sequences needed to be compact in the space induced by the common prefix metric, this is usually not the case here: The set of admissible graph sequences need not be limit-closed in general, see Section 6.2.

We will consider the consensus problem, which is defined as follows:

Definition 5.1 (Consensus). Every process $p \in [n]$ has an input value $x_p \in \mathcal{V}_I$, taken from a finite input domain $\mathcal{V}_I$, which is set in the initial state, and an output value $y_p \in \mathcal{V}_O \cup \{\perp\}$, with a finite output domain $\mathcal{V}_O \supseteq \mathcal{V}_I$, initially $y_p = \perp$. In every admissible execution, a correct consensus algorithms $\mathcal{A}$ must ensure the following properties:

- (T) Eventually, every p must decide, i.e., change to $y_p \neq \perp$, exactly once (termination).
- (A) If p and q have decided, then $y_p = y_q$ (agreement).
- (V) If $x_p = v$ for all $p \in [n]$, then v is the only possible decision value (validity).

Note that our framework can be easily adapted to different validity conditions, like strong validity, where every decision value must satisfy $y_p = x_q$ for some $q \in [n]$.

If we endow the set $\mathcal{V}_O$ with the discrete topology, it turns out that consensus can be described by a continuous map from the set of admissible executions, endowed with any P-view topology or the minimum topology, to $\mathcal{V}_O$.

Lemma 5.2 Continuity of consensus. *Let $\Gamma \subseteq C^\omega$ be the set of admissible executions of some consensus algorithm $\mathcal{A}$. Define the map $\Delta : \Gamma \to \mathcal{V}_I$ such that $\Delta(\gamma)$ is the common decision value of algorithm $\mathcal{A}$ in γ. Then, Δ is continuous, both with respect to any P-view topology and the minimum topology.*

In the following definition, we introduce the sets of process-time graphs and executions that lead to a given decision value:

Definition 5.3 (Decision sets). For every output value $v \in \mathcal{V}_O$, let $PS(v) = \tau^{-1}[\Delta^{-1}[\{v\}]] \subseteq PS$ and $\Gamma(v) = \Delta^{-1}[\{v\}]$ be the set of admissible process-time graph sequences and admissible executions that lead to a common decision value v, respectively.

We need a few more basic topological terms: A set in a topological space is *clopen*, if it is both closed and open. A topological space is *disconnected*, if it contains a nontrivial clopen set, which means that it it can be partitioned into two disjoint open sets. It is *connected*, if it is not disconnected.

With these preparations, we can already provide a topological consensus impossibility result:

Theorem 5.4 Consensus impossibility. *If an algorithm solves consensus, then all of its decision sets $\Gamma(v) = \Delta^{-1}[\{v\}]$, $v \in \mathcal{V}_O$, and $PS(v) = \tau^{-1}[\Delta^{-1}[\{v\}]]$ are clopen in the subspace topology of Γ and PS, respectively, both w.r.t. any d_P and $d_{\min}$.*

In particular, consensus is impossible if the set Γ of admissible executions or the set PS of admissible process-time graphs is connected.

5.1 Characterization in the Minimum Topology

We call a process-time graph z_v, for $v \in \mathcal{V}_O$, v-valent, if it starts from an initial configuration where all processes $p \in [n]$ have the same input value $x_p(z_v) = v$. Let PS_{z_v} denote the connected component of PS that contains the v-valent $z_v \in PS$. In the minimum topology $\mathcal{T}_{\min}^{\mathcal{PT}^\omega}$, we get the following characterization of consensus solvability:

Theorem 5.5 Consensus characterization. *Consensus is solvable with a message adversary generating the set of admissible process-time graph sequences PS if and only if there exists a partition of PS into sets $PS(v)$, $v \in \mathcal{V}_O$ such that the following holds:*

1. *Every $PS(v)$ is open in PS with respect to the minimum topology.*
2. *Every admissible v-valent $z_v \in PS$ satisfies $z_v \in PS(v)$.*

Proof. ($\Rightarrow$): Define $PS(v) = (\Delta \circ \tau)^{-1}[\{v\}] \subseteq PS$ using the functions τ and Δ defined by an algorithm that solves consensus. This is clearly a partition of PS by the termination and validity property of consensus. The validity condition of the algorithm also implies property (2). It thus remains to show openness of the $PS(v)$, which follows from the continuity of $\Delta \circ \tau : PS \to \mathcal{V}_O$, as every singleton $\{v\}$ is open (and closed) in the discrete topology.

($\Leftarrow$): We construct an algorithm as follows. Each process's state contains a variable V whose value is equal to the projection of process-time graphs onto its own view. State updates happen in such a way that process p's variable at the end of round t in the execution with process-time graph a is equal to $V = \pi_{\{p\}}(a^t)$. Process p decides value v in round t if the ball of radius $\varepsilon = 2^{-t}$ around the set of sequences of process-time graphs $\pi_{\{p\}}^{-1}[\{V\}]$ compatible with its locally recorded view V is contained in $PS(v)$, i.e., if

$$\left\{b \in PS \mid \pi_{\{p\}}(b^t) = V\right\} \subseteq PS(v) \ .$$

We first show termination of the resulting algorithm. Let $a \in PS$ and let $v \in \mathcal{V}_O$ such that $a \in PS(v)$. Since $PS(v)$ is open w.r.t. $d_{\min}$, there exists some $\varepsilon > 0$ such that

$$\{b \in PS \mid d_{\min}(b, a) < \varepsilon\} \subseteq PS(v) \ .$$

Let $t \geq 0$ such that $2^{-t} \leq \varepsilon$. We hence have

$$\{b \in PS \mid d_{\min}(b, a) < 2^{-t}\} \subseteq \{b \in PS \mid d_{\min}(b, a) < \varepsilon\} \subseteq PS(v) \ .$$

By Lemma 4.8, we have

$$\{b \in PS \mid d_{\{p\}}(b, a) < 2^{-t}\} \subseteq \{b \in PS \mid d_{\min}(b, a) < 2^{-t}\} \subseteq PS(v)$$

for every process $p \in [n]$. By the definition of the distance $d_{\{p\}}$, we have

$$\{b \in PS \mid d_{\{p\}}(b, a) < 2^{-t}\} = \{b \in PS \mid \pi_{\{p\}}(b^t) = \pi_{\{p\}}(a^t)\} \ .$$

Since, by construction, process p's variable V at the end of round t is equal to $\pi_{\{p\}}(a^t)$, this shows that process p decides in or before round t.

To show agreement, assume by contradiction that there exists some $a \in PS$ such that process p_1 decides v_1 in round t_1 and process p_2 decides v_2 in round t_2 in execution $\tau(a)$ with $q_1 \neq q_2$. By the definition of the algorithm, we have

$$\{b \in PS \mid \pi_{\{p_1\}}(b^{t_1}) = \pi_{\{p_1\}}(a^{t_1})\} \subseteq PS(v_1)$$

and

$$\{b \in PS \mid \pi_{\{p_2\}}(b^{t_2}) = \pi_{\{p_2\}}(a^{t_2})\} \subseteq PS(v_2) \ .$$

In particular, $a \in PS(v_1)$ and $a \in PS(v_2)$, a contradiction to the fact that the $PS(v)$ form a partition of PS.

Validity is an immediate consequence of property (2). □

This characterization gives rise to the following meta-procedure for determining whether consensus is solvable and constructing an algorithm if it is, which will be instantiated for some examples in Section 6. It requires knowledge of the connected components of the space PS with respect to the minimum topology:

(1) Initially, start with an empty set $PS(v)$ for every value $v \in \mathcal{V}_O$.
(2) Add to $PS(v)$ every connected component PS_{z_v} of every v-valent $z_v \in PS$.
(3) Add every remaining connected component of PS to an arbitrarily chosen set $PS(v)$ (i.e., decide on default value v).
(4) If the sets $PS(v)$ are pairwise disjoint, then consensus is solvable. In this case, the sets $PS(v)$ determine a consensus algorithm via the universal construction in the proof of Theorem 5.5. If the $PS(v)$ are not pairwise disjoint, then consensus is not solvable.

In particular, this meta-procedure gives rise to the following succinct characterization of consensus solvability.

Corollary 5.6. *Consensus is solvable with a message adversary MA generating the set of admissible process-time graph sequences PS if and only if none of its connected components with respect to the minimum topology contains z_v and z_w, $v, w \neq v \in \mathcal{V}_O$ that are v-valent and w-valent, respectively.*

We will now develop another characterization of consensus solvability, with rests on broadcastability of the PS_{z_v}.

Definition 5.7 (Diameter of a set). For $A \subseteq \mathcal{PT}^{\omega}$ and P' denoting either $P \subseteq [n]$ or min, define A's diameter as $d_{P'}(A) = \sup\{d_{P'}(a, b) \mid a, b \in A\}$.

Definition 5.8 (Broadcastability). We call a subset $A \subseteq PS$ of admissible process-time graphs *broadcastable* by the broadcaster $p \in [n]$, if for every $a \in A$ there is some round $T(a) < \infty$ where every process $q \in [n]$ knows p's input value $x_p(a)$ in a, i.e., $(p, 0, x_p(a))$ is in $V_{\{q\}}(a^{T(a)})$.

We will now prove the essential fact that *connected* broadcastable sets have a diameter strictly smaller than 1:

Theorem 5.9 Diameter of broadcastable connected sets. *If a connected set $A \subseteq PS$ of admissible process-time graph sequences is broadcastable by some process p, then $d_{\min}(A) \leq d_{\{p\}}(A) \leq 1/2$, i.e., p's input value $x_p(a)$ is the same for all $a \in A$.*

Corollary 5.10 follows immediately from Theorem 5.9:

Corollary 5.10 Diameter of broadcastable PS_{z_v}. *If PS_{z_v} for a v-valent $z_v \in PS$ is broadcastable for p, then $d_{\min}(PS_{z_v}) \leq d_{\{p\}}(PS_{z_v}) \leq 1/2$ since p's input value $x_p(a) = v$ is the same for all $a \in PS_{z_v}$.*

We can now prove the following necessary and sufficient condition for solving consensus based on broadcastability:

Theorem 5.11 Consensus characterization via broadcastability. *A message adversary allows to solve consensus if and only if it guarantees that the connected components of the set PS of admissible processes-time graphs are broadcastable for some process.*

5.2 Characterization in the P-View Topologies

It is possible to shed some additional light on the consensus characterization given in Theorem 5.5, by exploiting the fact that d_P (unlike $d_{\min}$) is a pseudo-metric: Since most of the convenient properties of metric spaces, including sequential compactness, also hold in pseudo-metric spaces, we can further explore the border of the decision sets $PS(v)$. It will turn out in Corollary 5.18 that consensus is impossible if and only if certain limit points in the P-view topology $\mathcal{T}_P^{\mathcal{PT}^{\omega}}$ are admissible.

For a given consensus algorithm, we again consider the set of all admissible process-time graph sequences PS resp. the corresponding set of admissible executions Γ. We endow PS with the subspace topology generated by $\mathcal{PT}^{\omega} \cap PS$ resp. Γ with the subspace topology[8] generated by $C^{\omega} \cap \Gamma$, both in the P-view topology. Recall that PS and Γ are not closed in general, hence not compact, even though $\mathcal{PT}^{\omega}$ resp. $\tau(\mathcal{PT}^{\omega})$ are compact.

Definition 5.12 (Distance of sets). For $A, B \subseteq \mathcal{PT}^{\omega}$, let $d_P(A, B) = \inf\{d_P(a, b) \mid a \in A, b \in B\}$.

In [19, Theorem 4.3], the following theorem has been proved:

Theorem 5.13 Compact set distance condition. *Let $A \subseteq \mathcal{PT}^{\omega}$ be closed and $B \subseteq \mathcal{PT}^{\omega}$ be compact with respect to the $[n]$-view topology. If $A \cap B = \emptyset$, then $d_{[n]}(A, B) > 0$.*

[8] Whenever we state a topological property w.r.t. the subspace topology, we will refer to Γ (resp. PS), otherwise to C^{ω} (resp. $\mathcal{PT}^{\omega}$).

We prove the following result, which also holds when A, B are not closed/compact. Note that it also implies Theorem 5.13 as a simple corollary for any P-view topology: Corollary 5.15 shows that it also holds in the minimum topology.

Theorem 5.14 General set distance condition. *Let $P \subseteq [n]$ with $P \neq \emptyset$. Let A, B be arbitrary subsets of $\mathcal{PT}^{\omega}$. Then, $d_P(A, B) = 0$ if and only if there are infinite sequences $(a_k) \in A^{\omega}$ and $(b_k) \in B^{\omega}$ of process-time graphs as well as $\hat{a}, \hat{b} \in \mathcal{PT}^{\omega}$ with $a_k \to \hat{a}$ and $b_k \to \hat{b}$ with respect to the P-view topology and $d_P(\hat{a}, \hat{b}) = 0$.*

The representation $d_{\min} = \min_{p\in[n]} d_{\{p\}}$ from (2) allows us to extend this result from the P-topologies to the minimum topology:

Corollary 5.15. *Let $P \subseteq [n]$ with $P \neq \emptyset$. Let A, B be arbitrary subsets of $\mathcal{PT}^{\omega}$. Then, $d_{\min}(A, B) = 0$ if and only if there are infinite sequences $(a_k) \in A^{\omega}$ and $(b_k) \in B^{\omega}$ of process-time graph sequences as well as $\hat{a}, \hat{b} \in \mathcal{PT}^{\omega}$ with $a_k \to \hat{a}$ and $b_k \to \hat{b}$ with respect to the minimum topology and $d_{\min}(\hat{a}, \hat{b}) = 0$.*

The above Theorem 5.14 allows us to distinguish 3 main cases that cause $d_P(A, B) = 0$: (i) If $\hat{a} \in A \cap B \neq \emptyset$, one can choose the sequences defined by $a_k = b_k = \hat{a} = \hat{b}, k \geq 1$. (ii) If $A \cap B = \emptyset$ and $\hat{a} = \hat{b}$, there is a "fair sequence" as the common limit. (iii) If $A \cap B = \emptyset$ and $\hat{a} \neq \hat{b}$, there is a pair of "unfair sequences" acting as limits, which have distance 0 (and are hence also common w.r.t. the pseudo-metric d_P). We note, however, that due to the non-uniqueness of the limits in our pseudo-metric, (iii) are actually two instances of (ii). We kept the distinction for compatibility with the existing results [9, 21] for $n = 2$.

Definition 5.16 (Fair and unfair process-time graph sequences). Consider two process-time graph sequences $r, r' \in \mathcal{PT}^{\omega}$ of some consensus algorithm with partitions $PS(v)$, $v \in \mathcal{V}_O$, in the P'-topology with $P' = \{p\}, p \in [n]$, or $P' = \min$:

- r is called *fair*, if for some $v, w \neq v \in \mathcal{V}_O$ there are convergent sequences $(a_k) \in PS(v)$ and $(b_k) \in PS(w)$ with $a_k \to r$ and $b_k \to r$ with respect to $\mathcal{T}_{P'}^{\mathcal{PT}^{\omega}}$.
- r, r' are called a pair of *unfair* sequences, if for some $v, w \neq v \in \mathcal{V}_O$ there are convergent sequences $(a_k) \in PS(v)$ with $a_k \to r$ and $(b_k) \in PS(w)$ with $b_k \to r'$ and $d_{P'}(r, r') = 0$ with respect to $\mathcal{T}_{P'}^{\mathcal{PT}^{\omega}}$.

An illustration is shown in Figure 5.

The above findings go nicely with the alternative characterization of consensus solvability given in Corollary 5.18, which results from applying the following Lemma 5.17 from [18] to Theorem 5.5.

Lemma 5.17 Separation lemma [18, Lemma 23.12]. *If Y is a subspace of X, a separation of Y is a pair of disjoint nonempty sets A and B whose union is Y, neither of which contains a limit point of the other. The space Y is connected if and only if there exists no separation of Y.*

Corollary 5.18 Separation-based characterization. *Consensus is solvable with a message adversary MA generating the set of admissible process-time graph sequences PS if and only if there exists a partition of PS into sets $PS(v), v \in \mathcal{V}_O$ such that the following holds:*

1. *No $PS(v)$ contains a limit point of any other $PS(w)$ w.r.t. the minimum topology in $\mathcal{PT}^{\omega}$.*
2. *Every v-valent admissible sequence z_v satisfies $z_v \in PS(v)$.*

We hence immediately obtain:

Corollary 5.19 Fair/unfair consensus impossibility. *The set of admissible process-time graphs PS of a consensus algorithm $\mathcal{A}$ with partitions $PS(v)$, $v \in \mathcal{V}_O$, does not contain any fair process-time graph sequence r or any pair r, r' of unfair process-time graph sequences.*

6 APPLICATIONS

In this section, we will apply our various topological characterizations of consensus solvability to particular classes of examples. We start in Section 6.1 with the broad class of message adversaries that have been shown, or can be shown, to make consensus impossible by means of bivalence proofs. We the proceed with a complete characterization of consensus solvability the class of compact message adversaries in Section 6.2. A characterization for the class of non-compact message adversaries will be provided in Section 6.3.

6.1 Bivalence-based Impossibilities

Our topological results shed some new light on the now standard technique of bivalence-based impossibility proofs introduced in the celebrated FLP paper [10], which have been generalized in [17] and used in many different contexts: Our results reveal that the forever bivalent executions constructed inductively in bivalence proofs such as [22, 23] and [6, 24] are just the common limit of two infinite sequence of executions $\alpha_0, \alpha_1, \ldots$ all contained in, say, $\Gamma(0)$ and $\beta_0, \beta_1, \ldots$ all contained in $\Gamma(1)$ that have a common limit $\alpha_k \to \hat{\alpha}$ and $\beta_k \to \hat{\beta}$ in some $\{p\}$-view topology with $d_{\{p\}}(\hat{\alpha}, \hat{\beta}) = 0$.

More specifically, what is common to these proofs is that one shows that, for any consensus algorithm, there is an admissible forever bivalent run. This is usually done inductively, by showing that there is a bivalent initial configuration and that, given a bivalent configuration C^{t-1} at the end of round $t-1$, there is a 1-round extension leading to a bivalent configuration C^t at the end of round t. By definition, bivalence of C^t means that there are two admissible executions α_t with decision value 0 and β_t with decision value 1 starting out from C^t, i.e., having a common prefix that leads to C^t. Consequently, their distance, in any $\{p\}$-view topology, satisfies $d_{\{p\}}(\alpha_t, \beta_t) < 2^{-t}$. Note that this is also true for the more general concept of a bipotent configuration C^t, as introduced in [17].

By construction, the $(t-1)$-prefix of α_t and α_{t-1} are the same, for all t, which implies that they converge to a limit $\hat{\alpha}$ (and analogously for $\hat{\beta}$), see Figure 5 for an illustration. Therefore, these executions match Definition 5.16, and Corollary 5.19 implies that the stipulated consensus algorithm cannot be correct. Concrete examples are the lossy link impossibility [22], i.e., the impossibility of consensus under an oblivious message adversary for $n = 2$ that may choose any graph out of the set $\{\leftarrow, \leftrightarrow, \rightarrow\}$, and the impossibility of solving consensus with vertex-stable source components with insufficient stability interval [6, 24]. In the case of the oblivious lossy link message adversary using the reduced set $\{\leftarrow, \rightarrow\}$ considered in [8], consensus is solvable and there is no forever bivalent run. Indeed, there exists a consensus algorithm, such that all configurations reached after the first round are already univalent.

6.2 Compact Message Adversaries

In this section, we consider message adversaries (like oblivious ones [8, 22]) that are limit-closed, in the sense that every convergent sequence of process-time graphs $a_0, a_1, \ldots$ with $a_i \in PS$ for every i has a limit $\hat{a} \in PS$. An illustration is shown in Fig. 4, where the blue dots represent the a_i's and $\times$ the limit point $\hat{a}$ at the boundary.

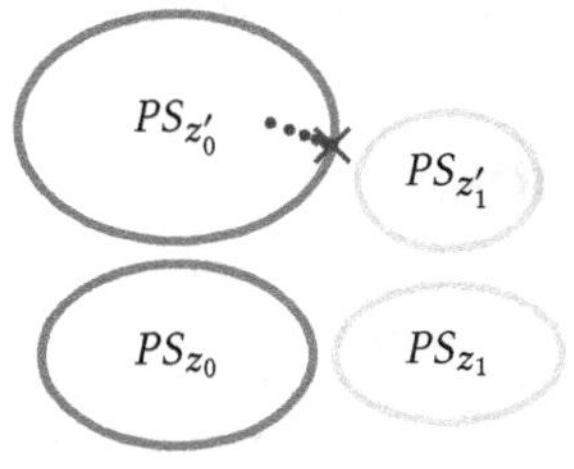

Figure 4: Examples of two connected components of the decision sets $PS(0) = PS_{z_0} \cup PS_{z'_0}$ and $PS(1) = PS_{z_1} \cup PS_{z'_1}$ for a compact message adversary. They are closed in $\mathcal{PT}^{\omega}$, hence contain all their limit points (marked by $\times$) and have a distance > 0 by Theorem 5.13.

In this case, the set of admissible process-time graph sequences PS is closed and hence a compact subspace both in any P-view topology and in the minimum topology. Moreover, we obtain:

Corollary 6.1 Decision sets for compact MAs are compact. *For every correct consensus algorithm for a compact message adversary and every $v \in \mathcal{V}_O$, $PS(v)$ is closed in PS and compact, and $d_{\{p\}}(PS(v), PS(w)) > 0$ for any $v, w \neq v \in \mathcal{V}_O$ and $p \in [n]$, and hence also $d_{\min}(PS(v), PS(w)) > 0$.*

Moreover, there are only finitely many different connected components PS_x, $x \in PS$, which are all compact, and for every x, y with $PS_x \neq PS_y$, it holds that $d_{\{p\}}(PS_x, PS_y) > 0$ and hence also $d_{\min}(PS_x, PS_y) > 0$.

We now make the abstract characterization of Theorem 5.5 and our meta-procedure more operational, by introducing the ε-approximation of the connected component PS_z that contains a process-time graph $z \in PS$, typically for some $\varepsilon = 2^{-t}$, $t \geq 0$. It is constructed iteratively, using finitely many iterations (since the number of different possible t-prefixes satisfies $|\mathcal{PT}^t| < \infty$) of the following algorithm:

Definition 6.2 (ε-approximations). Let $z \in PS$ be an admissible process-time graph. In the minimum topology, we iteratively define PS_z^ε, for $\varepsilon > 0$, as follows: $PS_z^\varepsilon[0] = \{z\}$; for $\ell > 0$, $PS_z^\varepsilon[\ell] = \bigcup_{a \in PS_z^\varepsilon[\ell-1]}(B_\varepsilon(a) \cap PS)$; and $PS_z^\varepsilon = PS_z^\varepsilon[m]$ where $m < \infty$ is such that $PS_z^\varepsilon[m] = PS_z^\varepsilon[m+1]$. For $v \in \mathcal{V}_O$, the ε-approximation $PS^\varepsilon(v)$ is defined as $PS^\varepsilon(v) = \bigcup_{z_v \in PS} PS_{z_v}^\varepsilon$, where every z_v denotes a v-valent process-time graph.

Lemma 6.3 Properties of ε-approximation. *For every $\varepsilon > 0$, every $v, w \in \mathcal{V}_O$, every $z \in PS$, v-valent z_v, and every w-valent z_w, the ε-approximations have the following properties:*

(i) *For a compact message adversary, there are only finitely many different PS_z^ε, $z \in PS$.*
(ii) *For every $0 < \varepsilon' \leq \varepsilon$, it holds that $PS_{z_v}^{\varepsilon'} \subseteq PS_{z_v}^{\varepsilon}$.*
(iii) *$PS_{z_v}^\varepsilon \cap PS_{z_w}^\varepsilon \neq \emptyset$ implies $PS_{z_v}^\varepsilon = PS_{z_w}^\varepsilon$.*
(iv) *$PS_z \subseteq PS_z^\varepsilon$.*

We now show that PS_x^ε and PS_y^ε for sequences x and y with $PS_x \neq PS_y$ have a distance > 0, provided ε is sufficiently small:

Lemma 6.4 Separation of ε-approximations for compact MAs. *For a compact message adversary that allows to solve consensus, let $x \in PS$ and $y \in PS$ be such that $PS_x \neq PS_y$. Then, there is some $\varepsilon > 0$ such that, for any $0 < \varepsilon' \leq \varepsilon$, it holds that $d_{\min}(PS_x^{\varepsilon'}, PS_y^{\varepsilon'}) > 0$.*

We immediately get the following corollary, which allows us to reformulate Theorem 5.11 as given in Theorem 6.6.

Corollary 6.5 Matching ε-approximation. *For a compact message adversary, if $\varepsilon > 0$ is chosen in accordance with Lemma 6.4, then $PS_z^\varepsilon = PS_z$ for every $z \in PS$.*

Theorem 6.6 Consensus characterization for compact MAs. *A compact message adversary allows to solve consensus if and only if there is some $\varepsilon > 0$ such that every v-valent $PS_{z_v}^\varepsilon$, $v \in \mathcal{V}_O$, is broadcastable for some process.*

Note carefully that if consensus is solvable, then, for every $0 < \varepsilon' \leq \varepsilon$, the universal algorithm from Theorem 5.5 with $PS(v) = PS^{\varepsilon'}(v) \cup PS \setminus \bigcup_{w \neq v \in \mathcal{V}_O} PS^{\varepsilon'}(w)$ for some arbitrary value $v \in \mathcal{V}_O$, and $PS(w) = PS^{\varepsilon'}(w)$ for the remaining $w \in \mathcal{V}_O$, can be used.

We conclude this section with noting that checking the broadcastability of $PS_{z_v}^\varepsilon$ can be done by checking broadcastability only in *finite* prefixes. More specifically, like the decision function Δ of consensus, the function $T(a)$ that gives the round by which every process in $a \in PS$ has $(p, 0, x_p(a))$ of the broadcaster p in its view is locally constant for a sufficiently small neighborhood, namely, $B_{2^{-T(a)}}(a)$, and hence continuous. Since $PS_{z_v} = PS_{z_v}^\varepsilon$ is compact, $T(a)$ is in fact uniformly continuous and hence attains its maximum $\hat{T}$ in $PS_{z_v}^\varepsilon$. It hence suffices to check broadcastability in the t-prefixes of $PS_{z_v}^\varepsilon$ for $t = \max\{\lfloor \log_2(1/\varepsilon) \rfloor, \hat{T}\}$ in Theorem 6.6.

6.3 Non-compact Message Adversaries

In this section, we finally consider message adversaries that are not limit-closed, like the ones of [9, 21, 24]. Unfortunately, we cannot use the ε-approximations according to Definition 6.2 for non-compact message adversaries. Even if ε is made arbitrarily small, Lemma 6.4 does not hold. An illustration is shown in Fig. 5. Hence, adding a ball $B_\varepsilon(a)$ in the iterative construction of PS_z^ε, where $d_{\min}(a, r) < \varepsilon$ for some forbidden limit sequence r, inevitably lets the construction grow into some $PS_{z'}^\varepsilon$, where z' has a different valence than z. Whereas this could be avoided by adapting ε when coming close to r, the resulting approximation does not provide any advantage over directly using the connected components.

Actually, this is in accordance with the existing solutions for non-compact message adversaries we are aware of, albeit they typically use their complement, namely, excluded sequences. For example, the binary consensus algorithms for $n = 2$ given in [9, 21] assume that the algorithm knows a fair or a pair of unfair sequences a priori, which effectively partition the sequence space into two connected components.[9] The $(D + 1)$-VSRC message adversary of [24] even excludes all sequences without a root component that is vertex-stable for at least $D + 1$ rounds, where D is the dynamic diameter

[9] Note that there are uncountably many choices for separating $PS(0)$ and $PS(1)$ here.

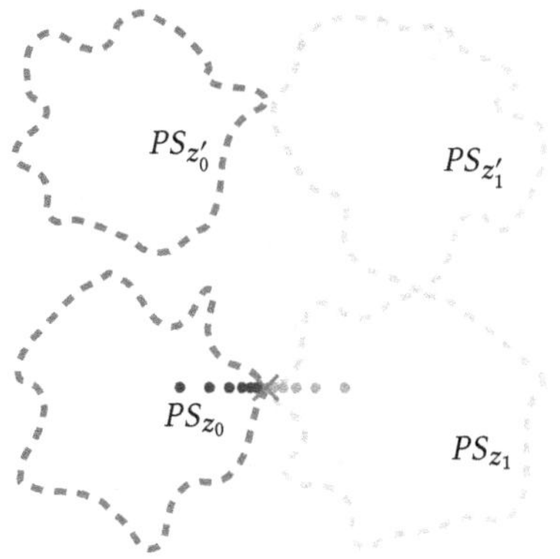

Figure 5: Examples of two connected components of the decision sets $PS(0) = PS_{z_0} \cup PS_{z'_0}$ and $PS(1) = PS_{z_1} \cup PS_{z'_1}$ for a non-compact message adversary. They are not closed in $\mathcal{PT}^\omega$ and may have distance 0; common limit points (like for PS_{z_0} and PS_{z_1}, marked by $\times$) must hence be excluded by Corollary 5.18.

that ensures broadcastability by all root members, which renders the remaining connected components broadcastable.

We restate the following necessary and sufficient condition for solving consensus with a non-compact message adversary from Theorem 5.11:

THEOREM 6.7 CONSENSUS CHARACTERIZATION FOR NON-COMPACT MAS. *A non-compact message adversary allows to solve consensus if and only if every v-valent PS_{z_v}, $v \in \mathcal{V}_O$, is broadcastable for some process.*

We will finally prove that the set of to be excluded limit sequences for any decision set $PS(v)$ is compact for a message adversary that allows to solve consensus:

LEMMA 6.8 COMPACTNESS OF EXCLUDED SEQUENCES. *Let $PS(v)$, $v \in \mathcal{V}_O$, be any decision set of a correct consensus algorithm for an arbitrary message adversary, $\overline{PS}(v)$ be its closure in $\mathcal{PT}^\omega$ and $Int(PS)(v)$ its interior. Then, $\hat{PS}(v) = \overline{PS}(v) - Int(PS)(v)$, which is the set of to be excluded limit points, is compact.*

7 CONCLUSIONS

We provided a complete topological characterization of the solvability of consensus in synchronous directed dynamic networks of arbitrary size controlled by a general message adversary: Consensus can only be solved when the space of admissible process-time graph sequences can be partitioned into at least two non-empty sets that are both closed and open in specific topologies. This requires exclusion of certain fair and unfair limit sequences, which limit broadcastability and happen to coincide with the forever bivalent executions constructed in bivalence and bipotence proofs.

Part of our future work will be devoted to a generalization of our topological framework to other distributed computing models and, most importantly, to other decision problems. Another very interesting area of future research is to study the homology of non-compact message adversaries, i.e., the topological structure of the space of admissible executions using combinatorial topology.

REFERENCES

[1] Yehuda Afek and Eli Gafni. 2013. Asynchrony from Synchrony. In *Distributed Computing and Networking*, Davide Frey, Michel Raynal, Saswati Sarkar, Rudrapatna K. Shyamasundar, and Prasun Sinha (Eds.). Lecture Notes in Computer Science, Vol. 7730. Springer Berlin Heidelberg, 225–239. https://doi.org/10.1007/978-3-642-35668-1_16

[2] Bowen Alpern and Fred B. Schneider. 1985. Defining Liveness. *Inform. Process. Lett.* 21, 4 (1985), 181–185.

[3] Ido Ben-Zvi and Yoram Moses. 2014. Beyond Lamport's Happened-before: On Time Bounds and the Ordering of Events in Distributed Systems. *J. ACM* 61, 2, Article 13 (April 2014), 26 pages. https://doi.org/10.1145/2542181

[4] Martin Biely, Bernadette Charron-Bost, Antoine Gaillard, Martin Hutle, André Schiper, and Josef Widder. 2007. Tolerating Corrupted Communication. In *Proceedings of the 26th ACM Symposium on Principles of Distributed Computing (PODC'07)*. ACM, Portland, OR, USA, 244–253. http://www.vmars.tuwien.ac.at/php/pserver/extern/docdetail.php?DID=2240&viewmode=paper&year=2007

[5] Martin Biely and Peter Robinson. 2019. On the hardness of the strongly dependent decision problem. In *Proceedings of the 20th International Conference on Distributed Computing and Networking, ICDCN 2019, Bangalore, India, January 04-07, 2019*. 120–123. https://doi.org/10.1145/3288599.3288614

[6] Martin Biely, Peter Robinson, Ulrich Schmid, Manfred Schwarz, and Kyrill Winkler. 2018. Gracefully degrading consensus and k-set agreement in directed dynamic networks. *Theoretical Computer Science* 726 (2018), 41–77. https://doi.org/10.1016/j.tcs.2018.02.019

[7] Bernadette Charron-Bost and André Schiper. 2009. The Heard-Of model: computing in distributed systems with benign faults. *Distributed Computing* 22, 1 (April 2009), 49–71. https://doi.org/10.1007/s00446-009-0084-6

[8] Étienne Coulouma, Emmanuel Godard, and Joseph G. Peters. 2015. A characterization of oblivious message adversaries for which Consensus is solvable. *Theor. Comput. Sci.* 584 (2015), 80–90. https://doi.org/10.1016/j.tcs.2015.01.024

[9] Tristan Fevat and Emmanuel Godard. 2011. Minimal Obstructions for the Coordinated Attack Problem and Beyond. In *25th IEEE International Symposium on Parallel and Distributed Processing, IPDPS 2011, Anchorage, Alaska, USA, 16-20 May, 2011 - Conference Proceedings*. 1001–1011. https://doi.org/10.1109/IPDPS.2011.96

[10] Michael J. Fischer, Nancy A. Lynch, and M. S. Paterson. 1985. Impossibility of Distributed Consensus with one Faulty Process. *J. ACM* 32, 2 (April 1985), 374–382.

[11] Ronald C. Freiwald. 2014. *An Introduction to Set Theory and Topology*. Washington University in St. Louis. https://doi.org/10.7936/K7D798QH

[12] Maurice Herlihy, Dmitry N. Kozlov, and Sergio Rajsbaum. 2013. *Distributed Computing Through Combinatorial Topology*. Morgan Kaufmann. https://store.elsevier.com/product.jsp?isbn=9780124045781

[13] Maurice Herlihy and Nir Shavit. 1999. The Topological Structure of Asynchronous Computability. *J. ACM* 46, 6 (Nov. 1999), 858–923. https://doi.org/10.1145/331524.331529

[14] F. Kuhn and R. Oshman. 2011. Dynamic networks: Models and algorithms. *SIGACT News* 42(1) (2011), 82–96.

[15] Petr Kuznetsov, Thibault Rieutord, and Yuan He. 2018. An Asynchronous Computability Theorem for Fair Adversaries. In *Proceedings of the 2018 ACM Symposium on Principles of Distributed Computing, PODC 2018, Egham, United Kingdom, July 23-27, 2018*. 387–396. https://dl.acm.org/citation.cfm?id=3212765

[16] Ronit Lubitch and Shlomo Moran. 1995. Closed Schedulers: A Novel Technique for Analyzing Asynchronous Protocols. *Distrib. Comput.* 8, 4 (June 1995), 203–210. https://doi.org/10.1007/BF02242738

[17] Yoram Moses and Sergio Rajsbaum. 2002. A Layered Analysis of Consensus. *SIAM J. Comput.* 31, 4 (2002), 989–1021.

[18] James Munkres. 2000. *Topology (2nd Edition)*. Pearson.

[19] Thomas Nowak. 2010. *Topology in Distributed Computing*. Master Thesis. Embedded Computing Systems Group, Technische Universität Wien.

[20] Thomas Nowak, Ulrich Schmid, and Kyrill Winkler. 2019. Topological Characterization of Consensus under General Message Adversaries. *arXiv:1905.09590* (May 2019). https://arxiv.org/abs/1905.09590 (appeared in Proc. PODC'19).

[21] Daniel Pfleger. 2018. *Knowledge and Communication Complexity*. Master's thesis. Technische Universität Wien, Institut für Computer Engineering, Treitlstr. 3/2/182-2, 1040 Vienna, Austria. http://publik.tuwien.ac.at/files/publik_273447.pdf

[22] Nicola Santoro and Peter Widmayer. 1989. Time is not a healer. In *Proc. 6th Annual Symposium on Theor. Aspects of Computer Science (STACS'89) (LNCS 349)*. Springer-Verlag, Paderborn, Germany, 304–313.

[23] Ulrich Schmid, Bettina Weiss, and Idit Keidar. 2009. Impossibility Results and Lower Bounds for Consensus under Link Failures. *SIAM J. Comput.* 38, 5 (2009), 1912–1951. https://doi.org/10.1137/S009753970443999X

[24] Kyrill Winkler, Manfred Schwarz, and Ulrich Schmid. 2019. Consensus in Directed Dynamic Networks with Short-Lived Stability. *Distributed Computing* (2019). https://doi.org/10.1007/s00446-019-00348-0

Can Distributed Uniformity Testing Be Local?

Uri Meir
Tel-Aviv University
Tel-Aviv, Israel
urimeir@mail.tau.ac.il

Dor Minzer*
Institute for Advanced Study
Princeton, NJ, USA
minzer.dor@gmail.com

Rotem Oshman†
Tel-Aviv University
Tel-Aviv, Israel
roshman@tau.ac.il

ABSTRACT

In the distributed uniformity testing problem, k servers draw samples from some unknown distribution, and the goal is to determine whether the unknown distribution is uniform or whether it is ε-*far* from uniform, where ε is a proximity parameter. Each server decides whether to accept or reject, and these decisions are sent to a referee, who makes a final decision based on the servers' local decisions. Uniformity testing is a particularly useful building-block, because it is complete for the problem of testing identity to any fixed distribution.

It was recently shown that distributing the task of uniformity testing allows each server to draw fewer samples than are needed in the centralized case, but so far the number of samples required for distributed uniformity testing has not been well understood. In this paper we settle this question, and also investigate the cost of using *local decision rules*, such as rejecting iff at least one server wants to reject (the usual decision rule used in local distributed decision). To answer these questions, we develop a new Fourier-based technique for proving lower bounds on the sample complexity of distribution testing, which lends itself particularly well to the distributed case.

Using our technique, we tightly characterize the number of samples required for uniformity testing when the referee can apply any decision function to the servers' local decisions. We also show that if the network rejects whenever one server wants to reject, then the cost of uniformity testing is much higher, and in fact we do not gain compared to the centralized case unless the number of servers is exponential in $\Omega(1/\varepsilon)$. Finally, we apply our lower bound technique to the case where the referee applies a *threshold* decision rule, and also generalize a lower bound from [1] for learning an unknown input distribution.

CCS CONCEPTS

• **Theory of computation** → *Distributed algorithms*;

KEYWORDS

distributed computing, uniformity testing, boolean analysis

ACM Reference Format:
Uri Meir, Dor Minzer, and Rotem Oshman. 2019. Can Distributed Uniformity Testing Be Local?. In *2019 ACM Symposium on Principles of Distributed Computing (PODC '19), July 29-August 2, 2019, Toronto, ON, Canada.* ACM, New York, NY, USA, 10 pages. https://doi.org/10.1145/3293611.3331613

1 INTRODUCTION

In the distribution testing problem, we are given samples from some unknown distribution μ, and we want to test whether μ satisfies some desired property $\mathcal{P}$, or whether μ is *far* from satisfying the property. The central question is how many samples are needed to distinguish these two cases with high confidence.

This question has been extensively studied in the centralized setting, where one tester examines all the samples and outputs an answer (e.g., [2, 6, 10, 11, 13] and many others). Recently, distribution testing has also been considered in the distributed setting, where it is also useful (e.g, [1, 7]). For example, suppose we have a sensor network whose sensors take measurements of their environment, and must raise an alarm if the measurements deviate significantly from normal; or a distributed algorithm designed under the assumption that its input distribution satisfies some property $\mathcal{P}$, but to make the system more robust, we want to *verify* that $\mathcal{P}$ is satisfied before running the algorithm. In such cases, we would like to deploy a distributed tester for $\mathcal{P}$, where every network node draws as few samples as possible, and the network together decides whether $\mathcal{P}$ is satisfied or is far from being satisfied. Note that an algorithm that has success probability $1 - \delta$ under a distribution μ also has success probability $1 - \delta - \varepsilon$ under any distribution that is ε-close to μ, so for many setting, it is enough to distinguish whether $\mathcal{P}$ is satisfied or far from satisfied.

Uniformity testing. In this paper we focus on the problem of *uniformity testing*: distinguishing the case where the input distribution μ is the uniform distribution U_n on a fixed domain $\{1, \dots, n\}$, from the case where μ is far from uniform in ℓ_1 distance:

$$\|\mu - U_n\|_1 = \sum_{i=1}^{n} \left|\mu(i) - \frac{1}{n}\right| \geqslant \varepsilon,$$

where ε is a proximity parameter. Uniformity testing is particularly important, because the problem of testing equality to any fixed distribution reduces to it; furthermore, uniformity testing is a special case of many other problems, such as independence testing and closeness testing, and lower bounds on uniformity testing imply lower bounds on these other problems as well. It is known that centralized uniformity testing requires $\Theta(\sqrt{n}/\varepsilon^2)$ samples [16]. Our focus in this paper is on lower bounds for distributed uniformity

*Supported partially by NSF grant CCF-1412958 and Rothschild Fellowship.
†Rotem Oshman and Uri Meir are partially supported by Israeli Center of Research Excellence in Algorithms (ICORE). This work was done in part while the authors were visiting the Simons Institute for the Theory of Computing.

ACM ISBN 978-1-4503-6217-7/19/07...$15.00
https://doi.org/10.1145/3293611.3331613

testing. (Note that some applications require $\varepsilon = o(1)$, so understanding the dependence on ε is important: in general, if X is a random variable whose maximum possible value is M, and μ, η are distributions with $\|\mu - \eta\|_1 = \varepsilon$, then $\mathbb{E}_\mu[X] \leqslant \mathbb{E}_\eta[X] + M \cdot \varepsilon/2$.)

What is a distributed tester? It is trivial to simply take the centralized uniformity tester and "make it distributed" by having one node draw $\Theta(\sqrt{n}/\varepsilon^2)$ samples and run the centralized tester. Our question is: can we use the power of distributed computing to develop a distributed tester where the *individual sample complexity* of each node is significantly smaller than $\Theta(\sqrt{n}/\varepsilon^2)$?

Ideally, a distributed tester should behave as a *local decision algorithm*: each node examines its own input and makes a decision; if some node "raises an alarm" by rejecting, then the whole network rejects, and may need to take some action; otherwise, the network accepts, and no action is necessary. This local-decision model, and variants that allow a few communication rounds (e.g., [8, 9]), are often used in settings where we want to perform some "sanity check" of the state of the network – e.g., *proof labeling schemes* [15]. However, previous work on distributed property testing has also allowed for more general decision rules, where the decision of the network is any function of the individual decisions of the nodes (not necessarily their AND). This has allowed for the development of testers that use fewer samples, but it comes at the cost of *locality* – instead of each node raising an alarm independently of the other nodes, we now need to collect the nodes' decisions and apply some (possibly complex) function to them. So far, it has been unclear whether locality comes at an extra cost, or whether any distributed tester can be made local without using more samples.

Distributed uniformity testing. In [7], two uniformity testers are developed: for a network of k nodes, the first tester uses the standard AND decision rule (the network rejects if at least one node rejects), and has a sample complexity of $O(\sqrt{n}/(k^{\Theta(\varepsilon^2)}\varepsilon^2))$ at each node. This tester only improves on the centralized tester when the number of nodes is *exponential* in $1/\varepsilon^2$. For this reason, [7] also develops a tester which uses a threshold rule, where the network rejects if at least some *fraction* of nodes reject; the threshold-based tester has a much better sample complexity, $O(\sqrt{n/k}/\varepsilon^2)$. Still, the tester does not achieve "perfect parallelism", in the sense that the number of samples each node must draw is larger than a $(1/k)$-fraction of the centralized sample complexity.

In contrast, [1] focuses exclusively on the case where each node has a single sample. Each node sends ℓ bits to a *referee*, who then outputs the answer (this corresponds to allowing the network to use an arbitrary decision rule). It is shown in [1] that in the single-sample setting, the number of nodes must be $\Theta(n/\varepsilon^2)$. We note that the decision rule used in [1] is "global", in the sense that when the input distribution is ε-far from uniform, no subset of $o(n)$ nodes can figure out that it should be rejected.

Our goal in this paper is to answer the following questions:

(1) What is the sample complexity of distributed uniformity testing with *any* decision rule, as a function of the universe size n, the number of nodes k, and the promixity parameter ε?
(2) Can we make distributed uniformity testing efficient *and* local, or does insisting on the AND decision rule come at the cost of requiring more samples? What about intermediate levels of locality, such as checking if a *few* nodes want to reject?

Initial steps towards answering the first question were made in [1, 7], but the picture remained far from clear (see Section 1.1). As for the second question, to our knowledge, the cost of using local decision rules has so far not been considered.[1]

Our techniques. In the world of centralized distribution testing, lower bounds are usually proven by showing directly that if the number of samples q is too small, then q samples "look the same" whether or not the property $\mathcal{P}$ is satisfied. Such arguments do not apply in our setting, because even though each node has only a small number of samples, together the nodes have many more samples than are needed to test $\mathcal{P}$. Thus, the samples themselves *do* provide the answer. Instead, we must show that by sending only a single bit (its decision whether to accept or reject), a node cannot *provide much useful information* about its samples. We use techniques from the world of Boolean analysis, and study the Fourier spectrum of the nodes' messages; this allows us to quantify the "difference" in a node's message when it is fed samples from the uniform distribution, compared to samples from a distribution that is ε-far from uniform.

To quantify the cost of using a local decision rule, we argue that the AND-rule or a threshold-rule with a small threshold "force" the nodes to give highly-biased bits, which have a very high probability of being 1. Using analytical techniques, we analyze the behavior of such functions, and show that, essentially, they provide even less information about the samples. Therefore, *more* samples are required. Our proof uses the *level inequalities*, developed in [14] with the motivation of studying distributed coin flipping.

The reader is not assumed to have any prior knowledge of Fourier analysis; we review the necessary concepts in Section 2 below.

Contributions. For an arbitrary decision rule, when $k = O(n)$, we are able to show that the tester of [7] is tight:

Theorem 1.1 (Informal). *For any decision rule $f : \{0,1\}^k \to \{0,1\}$, if $k \leqslant n/\varepsilon^2$, then the individual sample complexity of ε-uniformity testing using the f-rule is $\Omega(\sqrt{n/k}/\varepsilon^2)$.*

We also show that the AND decision rule is much more expensive, and if we insist on using it, we do not gain much compared to the centralized tester, unless $k = 2^{\Omega(1/\varepsilon)}$:

Theorem 1.2. *There exists a constant $c > 0$ such that for every $\varepsilon > 0$, if $k \leqslant 2^{c/\varepsilon}$, then the individual sample complexity of ε-uniformity testing using the AND-rule is $\Omega(\sqrt{n}/(\log(k)^2\varepsilon^2))$.*

For the range $k \approx 2^{c/\varepsilon}$, this lower bound is equivalent to having a bound of the form $\tilde{\Omega}(\sqrt{n}/(k^{\tilde{\Theta}(\varepsilon)}\varepsilon^2))$, leaving open a possible quadratic improvement in the exponent of k (from $\Omega(\varepsilon)$ to $\Omega(\varepsilon^2)$) compared to the tester of [7]. We remark that in the setting of [1], where each node has only one sample, it is *impossible* to solve uniformity testing using the AND decision rule, no matter how many nodes we have. We refer the reader to the full version for a proof.

Next we consider the T-*threshold* decision rule, where we reject if at least T nodes decide to reject. This rule was shown in [7]

[1]There is an example in the literature of a problem, "at most one marked node", which is trivial for randomized local decision algorithms with a certain success probability, but if we insist that the success probability be "too high", the problem becomes very hard [9]. This already shows that using the AND decision rule has an inherent cost.

to yield a tester which is sample-optimal, in light of Theorem 1.1 above. We show:

Theorem 1.3. *There exists $c > 0$ such that the following holds. Fix $n, \varepsilon > 0$, and let $k \leqslant \sqrt{n}$. For any threshold $T > 0$, if $T < c/(\varepsilon^2 \log^2(k/\varepsilon))$, then the individual sample cost of ε-uniformity testing using the T-threshold rule is $\Omega\left(\sqrt{n}/(T\log(k/\varepsilon)^2 \cdot \varepsilon^2)\right)$.*

We see that we need to take either $T = \tilde{\Omega}(1/\varepsilon^2)$, or T that grows with k, in order to start gaining significantly compared to the centralized case. Again, this leaves open a possible quadratic improvement, because in [7], the threshold used was $T = \Theta(1/\varepsilon^4)$.

Finally, we address the question of *learning a distribution*, which was studied in [1]. We extend the trade-off shown in [1] to any number of samples, and show:

Theorem 1.4. *There exists $\delta > 0$, such that any q-query protocol on the distributed network that computes a δ-approximation to an unknown input distribution must have $k = \Omega(n^2/q^2)$ nodes.*

Although we have so far assumed that each node sends a single bit (its decision whether to accept or reject), our results generalize to any number $\ell \geqslant 1$ of bits: the lower bounds decay as $2^{-\Theta(\ell)}$. We do not yet know whether this behavior is tight.

1.1 Related Work

The study of distribution testing began in [10, 13], where the uniformity testing problem was considered implicitly, as part of a property tester for the expansion of a graph. In [10, 13] it is shown that for constant ε, uniformity testing requires $\Theta(\sqrt{n})$ samples. The dependence on ε was characterized exactly in [16], which showed that $\Theta(\sqrt{n}/\varepsilon^2)$ samples are needed. Uniformity testing was shown to be complete for testing equality between an unknown input distribution to a known distribution in [6, 11]. We refer to [3, 12] for more background on distribution testing.

Distributed property testing for distributions was independently introduced by [1, 7], each taking a different perspective. In [1], it is assumed that each node receives exactly one sample from the unknown distribution, and the question is how many nodes are needed; it is shown that if each node can send ℓ bits to a referee, then $\Theta(n/(2^{\ell/2}\varepsilon^2))$ nodes are sufficient and necessary. Moreover, for the problem of *learning* an ε-approximation to the input distribution, [1] gives upper and lower bounds of $\Theta(n^2/(2^{\ell}\varepsilon^2))$. Our techniques recover the lower bounds of [1], and generalize them to the case where nodes receive more queries. Although we study a single player's message using very different techniques from [1], when it comes to *combining* the messages, our lower bounds for an arbitrary decision rule use the standard technique used in [1].

In [7], each node receives $q \geqslant 1$ queries, and several settings are studied: the simultaneous communication model, the CONGEST network model, and the LOCAL network model. The most directly relevant results from [7] are the testers we mentioned above: using the AND decision rule, [7] shows that $q = O(\sqrt{n}/(k^{\Theta(\varepsilon^2)}\varepsilon^2))$ samples are sufficient at each node, and using a threshold decision rule, $q = O(\sqrt{n/k}/\varepsilon^2)$ samples suffice. It is also shown in [7] that if we use the AND rule, an anonymous tester requires $\Omega(\sqrt{n/k})$ samples at each node, when the promixity parameter ε is a sufficiently small constant. Our new lower bounds show that in fact, $\Omega(\sqrt{n/k}/\varepsilon^2)$ samples are necessary for *any* decision rule and any tester, assuming that $k = O(n)$, and we derive much stronger bounds for the AND rule and the threshold rule.

2 PRELIMINARIES

Distributed property testing for distributions. We have k nodes (also called *players* in prior work), who each receive q iid samples from an unknown distribution μ supported on a universe of size n. The goal is to distinguish whether μ satisfies some property $\mathcal{P}$ of distributions, or whether μ is ε far from satisfying $\mathcal{P}$, in the sense that for any distribution η that *does* satisfy $\mathcal{P}$ we have $\|\mu - \varepsilon\|_1 > \varepsilon$. Here, $\|\cdot\|_1$ denotes the ℓ_1-norm, $\|v\|_1 = \sum_i |v_i|$.

Each of the k nodes sends a bit x_i to a *referee*, who then applies some decision function $f : \{0,1\}^k \to \{0,1\}$ and outputs $f(x_1, \ldots, x_k)$. We require that if μ satisfies the property $\mathcal{P}$ then $f(x_1, \ldots, x_k) = 1$ w.p. at least 2/3, but if μ is ε-far from satisfying $\mathcal{P}$, then $f(x_1, \ldots, x_k) = 0$ w.p. at least 2/3. Our goal in this paper is to prove lower bounds on the number q of samples required by each player, as a function of the universe size n, the proximity parameter ε, and the number of players k.

We say that the referee *uses the AND decision rule* if we set $f(x_1, \ldots, x_k) = \bigwedge_i x_i$, and the *threshold decision rule* with threshold t if $f(x_1, \ldots, x_k) = 1$ exactly when $\sum_i x_i \geqslant k - t$.

Fourier analysis. Consider the vector space of real-valued functions from the boolean cube $f \colon \{-1,1\}^n \to \mathbb{R}$, with the inner product

$$\langle f, g \rangle \stackrel{def}{=} \mathop{\mathbb{E}}_{x \in \{-1,1\}^n} [f(x) \cdot g(x)].$$

Here and throughout the paper, unless we say otherwise, expectations are taken with respect to the uniform distribution, and we omit the distribution from the subscript. This inner product also induces the ℓ_2-norm over the space of real-valued functions:[2]

$$\|f\|_2 = \sqrt{\langle f, f \rangle} = \sqrt{\mathop{\mathbb{E}}_{x}\left[f(x)^2\right]}.$$

The *Fourier basis* of the vector space of functions $f \colon \{-1,1\}^n \to \mathbb{R}$ is the set of *character functions*, $\{\chi_S : \{-1,1\}^n \to \{-1,1\}\}_{S \subseteq [n]}$, where each χ_S is given by

$$\chi_S(x) := \prod_{i \in S} x_i.$$

(We adopt the convention that if $S = \emptyset$, then $\prod_{i \in S} x_i = 1$.)

The set of character functions forms an orthonormal basis under the inner product defined above. Any function $f \colon \{-1,1\}^n \to \mathbb{R}$ can be written as a linear combination of characters,

$$f(x) = \sum_{S \subseteq [n]} \widehat{f}(S) \cdot \chi_S(x).$$

This is called the *Fourier transform of f*. Because $\{\chi_S\}_{S \subseteq [n]}$ is an *orthonormal* basis, the coefficients $\widehat{f}(S)$ have a particularly simple form: $\widehat{f}(S) = \langle f, \chi_S \rangle$.

Two particularly useful properties of the Fourier transform are the following. First, the inner product of two functions can be written in terms of their Fourier coefficients:

[2] We use here the *expectation* form, which is simply the usual ℓ_2-norm but divided by the domain size.

Fact 2.1 (Plancherel/Parseval). *For any $f, g\colon \{-1,1\}^n \to \mathbb{R}$, we have $\langle f, g\rangle = \sum_{S\subseteq[n]} \widehat{f}(S)\cdot\widehat{g}(S)$. In particular, when $f = g$, we have $\|f\|_2^2 = \sum_{S\subseteq[n]} \widehat{f}(S)^2$.*

Next, let us view the function $f\colon \{-1,1\}^n \to \mathbb{R}$ as a random variable, which is sampled by choosing a uniformly random $x \in \{-1,1\}^n$ and computing $f(x)$. Now consider the *expectation* of this random variable, denoted $\mu(f) = \mathbb{E}_x[f(x)]$, and its *variance*,

$$\mathrm{var}(f) = \mathop{\mathbb{E}}_x\left[f(x)^2\right] - \mathop{\mathbb{E}}_x[f(x)]^2.$$

These can be expressed in terms of the Fourier coefficients of f:

Fact 2.2. *For any $f\colon \{-1,1\}^n \to \mathbb{R}$ we have $\mu(f) = \widehat{f}(\emptyset)$ and $\mathrm{var}(f) = \sum_{S\neq\emptyset} \widehat{f}(S)^2$.*

Notation. In our lower bound, we work with a family of distributions, $\{\nu_z\}_{z\in\mathcal{Z}}$ (for some universe $\mathcal{Z}$). We use the notation $\mathbb{E}_z[\nu_z]$ to denote the distribution obtained by sampling a uniformly random $z \in \mathcal{Z}$ and applying ν_z; that is, $\mathbb{E}_z[\nu_z](\omega) = (1/|\mathcal{Z}|)\sum_z \nu_z(\omega)$ for any element ω in the domain.

We use the notation $\mu(f)$ to indicate the expected value of a Boolean function f over the uniform distribution, and we also sometimes abuse notation by using μ to denote the uniform distribution itself. (This has a good reason: for a Boolean function f, if we think of f as the indicator for some event, then indeed $\mu(f)$ is both the probability of the event and the expected value of f under the uniform distribution.)

3 THE HARD DISTRIBUTIONS

Our proof uses a family of distributions introduced in [16] to show the lower bound of $\Omega(\sqrt{n}/\varepsilon^2)$ on centralized uniformity testing. However, in order to use the machinery of Boolean analysis, we would like to view them as distributions on the vertices of the Boolean cube (while in [16] and others, typically the domain of the distribution is thought of as $\{1,\ldots,n\}$). To this end, we think of our universe as $n = 2^{\ell+1}$, *two copies* of the Boolean cube $\{-1,1\}^\ell$, where the last bit is used to match each vertex from the "left" cube to a vertex from the "right". We represent the elements of the universe as pairs (x, s), where $x \in \{-1,1\}^\ell$ and $s \in \{-1,+1\}$. Thus, the element $(x,+1)$ (from the left cube) is "matched" to $(x,-1)$ (from the right).

The uniform distribution on $2^{\ell+1}$ assigns equal weight to all vertices. We construct a distribution that is ε-far from uniform by perturbing the vertices of the left cube, adding $+\varepsilon/n$ or $-\varepsilon/n$ weight to each one, and compensate by making the opposite adjustments on the right cube (so that the resulting object is still a distribution, i.e., the weights sum to 1). In other words, if we decide to add ε/n weight to $(x,+1)$, then we compensate by removing ε/n weight from $(x,-1)$, and vice-versa.

Formally, let $z\colon \{-1,1\}^\ell \to \{-1,1\}$ be a "perturbation vector" deciding whether to add or remove weight from each $x \in \{-1,1\}^\ell$ on the left cube. For each such z, we define the distribution ν_z, supported on $\{-1,1\}^\ell \times \{-1,1\}$:

$$\nu_z(x,s) = \frac{1 + s\cdot z(x)\cdot\varepsilon}{n}.$$

The distribution resulting from drawing q independent samples from ν_z is denoted by ν_z^q, and is given by

$$\nu_z^q(x_1,s_1,\ldots,x_q,s_q) = \prod_{i=1}^q \frac{1+s_i z(x_i)\varepsilon}{n}.$$

The distribution ν_z^q has a particularly nice representation in terms of the characters $\{\chi_S\}_{S\subseteq[q]}$:

Claim 3.1. $\nu_z^q(x_1,s_1,\ldots,x_q,s_q) = \frac{1}{n^q}\sum_{S\subseteq[q]} \varepsilon^{|S|}\chi_S(s)\prod_{j\in S} z(x_j)$.

Proof. Expanding the definition, we see that

$$\prod_{i=1}^q \frac{1+s_i z(x_i)\varepsilon}{n} = \frac{1}{n^q}\prod_{i=1}^q (1+s_i z(x_i)\varepsilon)$$
$$= \frac{1}{n^q}\sum_{S\subseteq[q]}\prod_{i\in S} s_i z(x_i)\varepsilon = \frac{1}{n^q}\sum_{S\subseteq[q]} \varepsilon^{|S|}\chi_S(s)\prod_{i\in S} z(x_i).$$

□

For convenience, we write $\nu_z^q(x,s) = \nu_z^q(x_1,\ldots,x_q,s_1,\ldots,s_q)$ instead of $\nu_z^q(x_1,s_1,\ldots,x_q,s_q)$ (i.e., we "collect" all the x_is and the s_is).

Informal discussion. Let us make a few remarks that may be help understand why the familiy $\{\nu_z^q\}_z$ for a random z is supposed to be hard to distinguish from a uniform distribution. First, we observe that for any $(x,s) \in \{-1,1\}^{\ell+1}$, the expected mass of $\nu_z(x,s)$ is

$$\mathop{\mathbb{E}}_z[\nu_z(x,s)] = \frac{1}{n} + \frac{1}{n}\varepsilon s\mathop{\mathbb{E}}_z[z(x)] = \frac{1}{n},$$

so the average of the distributions ν_z is precisely the uniform distribution. What happens when we take q independent samples, i.e., consider ν_z^q? It is no longer true that the average probability of any specific observation of q samples is equal to its probability under the uniform measure — this is what allows uniformity testers to work; specifically, we can distinguish the uniform distribution from an ε-far distribution by *counting collisions* [10, 13, 16]. The Fourier transform provides a convenient tool to measure the difference between the mixture $\mathbb{E}_z[\nu_z]$ and the uniform distribution. It also allows us to make explicit the fact that a tester only gains information by counting collisions, that is, looking for samples that repeat themselves.

For any distribution $\eta : \{-1,1\}^m \to \mathbb{R}$, the distribution η^q of q iid samples from η can be viewed as a non-negative function, $\eta^q\colon \{-1,1\}^{m\cdot q} \to \mathbb{R}^+$, and thus we can consider its Fourier transform, $\eta^q = \sum_{S\subseteq[m\cdot q]} \widehat{\eta^q}(S)\chi_S$. Applying Fact 2.2, we see that the coefficient of the empty character is

$$\widehat{\eta^q}(\emptyset) = \mathop{\mathbb{E}}_{w\in\{-1,1\}^{m\cdot q}}\left[\eta^q(w)\right] = \frac{1}{2^{m\cdot q}}\sum_w \eta^q(w) = \frac{1}{2^{m\cdot q}},$$

regardless of which distribution η we take. For the *uniform* distribution, the other Fourier coefficients are zero (that is, $\mu^q = \widehat{\mu^q}(\emptyset)\cdot\chi_\emptyset = 1/2^{m\cdot q}$). Therefore, the *difference* between η^q and the uniform distribution is given by all the non-empty coefficients. A hard distribution should be "well-spread" over many Fourier coefficients, so that we cannot distinguish it by approximating some particularly heavy coefficient of the distribution; we want the non-zero coefficients to be small and rare.

This property holds for the distributions ν_z^q: fixing x, we get using Claim 3.1 that $\nu_z^q(x,s)$ has the Fourier transform

$$g_x(s) = \frac{1}{n^q} \sum_{T \subseteq [q]} b_x(T) \varepsilon^{|T|} \chi_T(s),$$

where $b_x(T) = \mathbb{E}_z \left[\prod_{i \in T} z(x_i)\right] \in \{0,1\}$.

If $x = (x_1, \ldots, x_q)$ has no "collision" with respect to T, that is, if $x_i \neq x_j$ for all $i \neq j \in T$, then $b_x(T) = 0$: we choose the signs $z(x_i) \in \{-1,1\}$ independently at random, so we get cancelation. In fact, to get cancelation, it suffices to have *at least one* value $y \in \{-1,1\}^\ell$ that appears *an odd number of times* in the multiset $\{x_i\}_{i \in T}$. On the other hand, suppose the multiset $\{x_i\}_{i \in T}$ is "perfectly paired up", with every $y \in \{-1,1\}^\ell$ appearing an even number of times (possibly zero). Then

$$b_x(T) = \mathbb{E}_z \left[\prod_{y \in \{-1,1\}^\ell} z(y)^2 \right] = 1.$$

We see that the only non-zero Fourier coefficients correspond to "bad pairs" (x, T) where the multiset $\{x_i\}_{i \in T}$ is "perfectly paired up". In our proof, we show that for a small number of samples q, such bad pairs are rare, and therefore the spectrum of our distribution is very similar to that of the uniform distribution, where all non-empty characters are 0.

4 VIEWING THE PLAYERS' BEHAVIOR AS A BOOLEAN FUNCTION

The behavior of each of our k players can be modeled as a Boolean function, $G : \{-1,1\}^{(\ell+1)q} \to \{0,1\}$, which tells the player what bit to send upon seeing a set of q samples, $S \in \{-1,1\}^{(\ell+1)q}$. Define:

- $\nu_z(G) = \mathbb{E}_{S \sim \nu_z^q}[G(S)] = \Pr_{S \sim \nu_z^q}[G(S) = 1]$: the probability the player sends 1 when the input distribution is ν_z.
- $\mu(G) = \mathbb{E}_{S \sim \mu^q}[G(S)] = \Pr_{S \sim \mu^q}[G(S) = 1]$: the probability the player sends 1 when the input distribution is uniform (μ). More explicitly,

$$\mu(G) = \frac{1}{n^q} \sum_{x,s} G(x,s).$$

We are interested in bounding the typical difference between the behaviour of a player on the uniform distribution and on ν_z,

$$\nu_z(G) - \mu(G). \tag{1}$$

We want to show that for a "typical" z, the probability of sending 1 is very close to the probability under the uniform distribution. When all players behave this way, the referee cannot distinguish whether the distribution is uniform or far from uniform.

For notational convenience, as we did above, we write $G(x,s)$ instead of $G(x_1, s_1, \ldots, x_q, s_q)$ for the output of a player when receiving $(x_1, s_1), \ldots, (x_q, s_q)$ as queries (where $x = (x_1, \ldots, x_q)$, $s = (s_1, \ldots, s_q)$). The following lemma expresses the difference in behaviour of G under ν_z and μ using Fourier coefficients, and will be used several times in our proofs. Just as we did above, we *fix* x, and study the behavior of the function $G_x(s) = G(x,s)$.

Lemma 4.1. *Let $G\colon \{-1,1\}^{(\ell+1)q} \to \{0,1\}$, and consider the function $G_x\colon \{-1,1\}^q \to \{0,1\}$ defined by $G_x(s) = G(x,s)$. Then*

$$\nu_z(G) - \mu(G) = \frac{2^q}{n^q} \sum_{S \neq \emptyset} \sum_x \varepsilon^{|S|} \prod_{j \in S} z(x_j) \widehat{G}_x(S).$$

The proof is a simple calculation (using Claim 3.1), and it is deferred to the full version.

Consider the term $\prod_{j \in S} z(x_j) \widehat{G}_x(S)$ appearing in the sum; since the $z(x_j)$s are chosen iid from $\{-1,1\}$, when we take the expectation over z, we will again get the type of "odd cancelation" that we pointed out above, and only the "evenly paired up" summands will survive. This is key to our proof.

4.1 The Main Lemmas

Our lower bounds rely on the following lemmas, which bound the difference we see in a player's behavior when fed uniform samples compared for samples from ν_z, for a random z.

The lower bound against referees that can use any decision rule (Theorem 1.1) relies on the following:

Lemma 4.2. *Let $q \leqslant \frac{\sqrt{n}}{20\varepsilon^2}$, $G\colon \{-1,1\}^{(\ell+1)q} \to \{0,1\}$. Then*

$$\mathbb{E}_z\left[|\mu_z(G) - \mu(G)|^2\right] \leqslant \left(20\frac{q^2\varepsilon^4}{n} + \frac{q\varepsilon^2}{n}\right) \mathrm{var}(G).$$

Here, $\mathrm{var}(G) = \mathbb{E}_{x,s}\left[G(x,s)^2\right] - \mathbb{E}_{x,s}[G(x,s)]^2$ denotes the variance of G, as explained in Section 2.

The lower bound against the AND decision rule (Theorem 1.2) uses the following bound, which improves on Lemma 4.2 when the bit G is highly-biased — that is, when its variance is low:

Lemma 4.3. *Let $m \in \mathbb{N}$. Suppose $q \leqslant \min\left(\frac{\sqrt{n}}{40m^2\varepsilon^2}, \frac{\sqrt{n}}{(40m^2\varepsilon^2)^{m+1}}\right)$. Then*

$$\left|\mathbb{E}_z[\mu_z(G)] - \mu(G)\right| \leqslant \left(\frac{q}{\sqrt{n}} + \left(\frac{q}{\sqrt{n}}\right)^{1/(2m+2)}\right) 40m^2\varepsilon^2 \mathrm{var}(G)^{\frac{2m+1}{2m+2}}.$$

Finally, for the lower bound against thresholds (Theorem 1.3), we need the following lemma, which essentially interpolates between the two previous lemmas, and gives a better bound when G has medium variance.

Lemma 4.4. *There exists a constant $C > 0$, such that the following holds. Let $m \in \mathbb{N}$, and assume $q \leqslant \min\left(\frac{\sqrt{n}}{((40m)^2\varepsilon^2)^{m+1}}, \frac{\sqrt{n}}{(40m)^2\varepsilon^2}\right)$. Then*

$$\mathbb{E}_z\left[|\nu_z(G) - \mu(G)|^2\right] \leqslant \frac{2\varepsilon^2 q}{n}\mathrm{var}(G) + C\left(\frac{q}{\sqrt{n}} + \frac{q^{1/(m+1)}}{\sqrt{n}^{1/(m+1)}}\right) m^2\varepsilon^2 \mathrm{var}(G)^{2-1/(m+1)}.$$

In Section 5 we prove a somewhat weaker version of Lemma 4.2, to illustrate the main ideas behind our approach. We also give the proof of Lemma 4.3 . The proofs of Lemma 4.2 and Lemma 4.4 use similar ideas and appear in the full version of the paper. Then, in Section 6, we show how these lemmas can be used in order to prove our distributed lower bounds (Theorem 1.1, Theorem 1.2 and Theorem 1.3).

5 A SIMPLIFIED LEMMA

We prove the following weaker version of Lemma 4.2:

Lemma 5.1. *Let* $q \leqslant \frac{\sqrt{n}}{4\varepsilon^2}$, $G\colon \{-1,1\}^{(\ell+1)q} \to \{0,1\}$. *Then*

$$\left|\mathop{\mathbb{E}}_{z}[v_z(G)] - \mu(G)\right| \leqslant \frac{4q\varepsilon^2}{\sqrt{n}}\sqrt{\mathrm{var}(G)}.$$

Proof. We begin by writing out the expression inside the absolute value using Lemma 4.1:

$$\mathop{\mathbb{E}}_{z}[v_z(G)] - \mu(G) = \frac{2^q}{n^q}\sum_{S\neq\emptyset}\sum_{x}\varepsilon^{|S|}\mathop{\mathbb{E}}_{z}\left[\prod_{j\in S} z(x_j)\right]\widehat{G_x}(S). \quad (2)$$

For each $S \subseteq [q]$ and $x = x_1, \ldots, x_q$, we are interested in the multiset $\{x_j\}_{j\in S}$ of points that appear in x in indices covered by S. Observe that if there exists a point $a \in \{-1,1\}^\ell$ that appears an odd number of times in $\{x_j\}_{j\in S}$, then the contribution of x to (2) is zero (the "odd cancelation" we pointed out before): to see this, let $R = \{j \in S \mid x_j = a\} \subseteq S$ be all the places in S where a appears in x. Because the coordinates of z are independent, we can write

$$\mathop{\mathbb{E}}_{z}\left[\prod_{j\in S} z(x_j)\right] = \mathop{\mathbb{E}}_{z(a)}\left[z(a)^{|R|}\right]\cdot \mathop{\mathbb{E}}_{z(\{-1,1\}^\ell\setminus\{a\})}\left[\prod_{j\in S\setminus R} z(x_j)\right],$$

but $\mathbb{E}_{z(a)}\left[z(a)^{|R|}\right] = 0$, since $|R|$ is odd and $z(a)$ takes the values 1 or -1 with equal probability.

Hence, for a summand to make a non-zero contribution to (2), every point $a \in \{-1,1\}^\ell$ must appear an *even* number of times in the multi-set $x_S := \{x_j\}_{j\in S}$. We refer to this property as an "evenly covered" multi-set x_S. Let

$$X_S = \left\{x \in (\{-1,1\}^\ell)^q \mid x_S \text{ is evenly covered}\right\}.$$

What happens when x_S *is* evenly covered? Inside the product $\prod_{j\in S} z(x_j)$, every value $z(a) \in \{-1,1\}$ for $a \in \{-1,1\}^\ell$ appears an even number of times, so the product is 1. Thus, (2) simplifies to

$$\mathop{\mathbb{E}}_{z}[v_z(G)] - \mu(G) = \frac{2^q}{n^q}\sum_{S\neq\emptyset}\sum_{x\in X_S}\varepsilon^{|S|}\widehat{G_x}(S). \quad (3)$$

Our goal now is to bound the absolute value of (3), by showing that for a given set S, the set X_S of x's that are evenly covered by S is typically very small.

Proposition 5.2. *The following holds:*

(1) $|X_S|$ depends only on $|S|$, and is 0 when $|S|$ is odd.
(2) $|X_S| \leqslant (|S|-1)!!(n/2)^{q-|S|/2}$.

Note that here, the notation $N!!$ is the double-factorial, the product of all integers from 1 to N that have the same parity as N.

Proof. The number of x's that are evenly covered by S depends only on $|S|$ by symmetry. Furthermore, if $|S|$ is odd, then *no* x can be evenly covered by S (some point must appear an odd number of times in x_S).

Now assume that $\{S\}$ is even, and let us bound $|X_S|$. Observe that the following process can produce all points in X_S: write $2r = |S|$, $S = \{j_1, \ldots, j_{2r}\}$. Pick a matching on S, and for each matched pair (j_{i_1}, j_{i_2}) choose a common value, $x_{j_{i_1}} = x_{j_{i_2}} \in \{-1,1\}^\ell$. For $i \notin S$, pick $x_i \in \{-1,1\}^\ell$ arbitrarily.

This process generates all the points in X_S, but it over-counts, since some points can be generated in more than one way. Still, the size of X_S is upper-bounded by the number of outputs the process can produce, which is $(2r-1)!!(2^\ell)^{r+(q-2r)} = (2r-1)!!(n/2)^{q-r}$. □

Since $|X_S|$ depends only on $|S|$, we sometimes write $|X_{2r}|$ instead of $|X_S|$ when $|S| = 2r$. Partitioning the summation in (3) by the size of S, we get

$$(3) = \frac{2^q}{n^q}\left|\sum_{r=1}^{q/2}\varepsilon^{2r}\sum_{S:|S|=2r}\sum_{x\in X_S}\widehat{G_x}(S)\right|. \quad (4)$$

The inner sum is upper-bounded using the following claim.

Proposition 5.3. *For any* $1 \leqslant r \leqslant q/2$, *we have*

$$\left|\sum_{S:|S|=2r}\sum_{x\in X_S}\widehat{G_x}(S)\right| \leqslant q^r\left(\frac{n}{2}\right)^{q-r/2}\sqrt{\mathrm{var}(G)}$$

Proof. We essentially argue that (a) for each S, there are not many $x \in X_S$ (by Proposition 5.2); and (b) for each x, the sum of the Fourier coefficients $\widehat{G_x}(S)$ is bounded (using Fact 2.2). Formally, applying Cauchy-Schwartz, we get

$$\begin{aligned}\left|\sum_{S:|S|=2r}\sum_{x\in X_S}\widehat{G_x}(S)\right| &\leqslant \sqrt{\sum_{S:|S|=2r}\sum_{x\in X_S}1^2}\sqrt{\sum_{S,x\in X_S}\widehat{G_x}(S)^2}\\ &= \sqrt{\binom{q}{2r}|X_{2r}|}\sqrt{\sum_{S,x\in X_S}\widehat{G_x}(S)^2}.\end{aligned}$$

Using Proposition 5.2 to bound $|X_{2r}|$, and the fact that $\binom{q}{2r} \leqslant \frac{q^{2r}}{(2r)!}$, the first term is upper-bounded by

$$\sqrt{\binom{q}{2r}|X_{2r}|} \leqslant \sqrt{\frac{q^{2r}}{(2r)!}}\cdot\sqrt{(2r-1)!!}\cdot(n/2)^{(q-r)/2} \leqslant q^r(n/2)^{(q-r)/2}.$$

The second term is upper bounded by the square root of

$$\begin{aligned}\sum_{S\neq\emptyset, x\in X_S}\widehat{G_x}(S)^2 &\leqslant \sum_{x}\sum_{S\neq\emptyset}\widehat{G_x}(S)^2 = \sum_{x}\mathrm{var}(G_x) \quad \text{(By Fact 2.2)}\\ &= \left(\frac{n}{2}\right)^q\left(\mathop{\mathbb{E}}_{x}\left[\mathop{\mathbb{E}}_{s}[G_x(s)^2]\right] - \mathop{\mathbb{E}}_{x}\left[\mathop{\mathbb{E}}_{s}[G_x(s)]^2\right]\right)\\ &\leqslant \left(\frac{n}{2}\right)^q\left(\mathop{\mathbb{E}}_{x,s}[G_x(s)^2] - \mathop{\mathbb{E}}_{x,s}[G_x(s)]^2\right)\\ &= \left(\frac{n}{2}\right)^q\mathrm{var}(G),\end{aligned}$$

where the last inequality uses Jensen's inequality.

The claimed bound follows by combining the two upper bounds. □

Plugging Proposition 5.3 into (4), we see that

$$(4) \leqslant \sum_{r=1}^{q/2}\left(\frac{2}{n}\right)^{r/2}\varepsilon^{2r}q^r\sqrt{\mathrm{var}(G)} \leqslant \sqrt{\mathrm{var}(G)}\sum_{r=1}^{\infty}\left(\frac{2q\varepsilon^2}{\sqrt{n}}\right)^r.$$

Since $q \leqslant \frac{\sqrt{n}}{4\varepsilon^2}$, the last infinite series is dominated by twice its first summand, finishing the proof. □

5.1 Proof of Lemma 4.3

The proof of Lemma 4.3 uses the same technique of Lemma 5.1 as well as the following additional ingredients.

Level inequalities. Let $f\colon \{-1,1\}^n \to \{0,1\}$. Since the sum of squares of fourier coefficients of a function is $\mu(f)$, its weight on any given Fourier level is upper bounded by μ. The famous KKL lemma, due to Khan, Kalai and Linial [14], gives an improved bound for the weight that lies on low levels whenever the average of the function $\mu(f)$ is small.

Lemma 5.4 ([14]). *Let $f\colon \{-1,1\}^n \to \{-1,1\}$ be a function whose average is μ, $1 \leqslant r \leqslant n$, and $\delta > 0$. Then*

$$\sum_{|S|\leqslant r} \widehat{f}^2(S) \leqslant \delta^{-r}\mu^{\frac{2}{1+\delta}}.$$

A moment estimation. For $x \in \{-1,1\}^{(\ell+1)q}$, let

$$a_r(x) = \left|\{S \mid |S| = 2r, \{x_j\}_S \text{ is evenly covered}\}\right|.$$

By interchanging the order of summation,

$$\sum_x a_r(x) = \binom{q}{2r}|X_{2r}|.$$

Switching to expectation notations and using the upper bounds on binomial coefficient and $|X_{2r}|$ from 3.1, we get

$$\mathop{\mathbb{E}}_x[a_r(x)] \leqslant \left(\frac{q^2}{n}\right)^r.$$

This estimate has been used in the proof of Lemma 5.1. For Lemma 4.3 we require more detailed information on $a_r(x)$ in the form of higher moments. Letting $1_{E(x,S)}$ be the indicator of the event x_S is evenly covered, we have the identity

$$a_r(x) = \sum_{|S|=2r} 1_{E(x,S)},$$

and since we understand the dependencies among $1_{E(x,S)}$ quite well, we may prove good bounds on higher moments of $a_r(x)$.

Lemma 5.5. *Let $m, r \in \mathbb{N}$.*

(1) If $q \geqslant \sqrt{\frac{n}{2}}$, then

$$\mathop{\mathbb{E}}_x\left[a_r(x)^m\right] \leqslant (4m)^{2mr}\left(\frac{q}{\sqrt{n/2}}\right)^{2mr}.$$

(2) If $q < \sqrt{\frac{n}{2}}$, then

$$\mathop{\mathbb{E}}_x\left[a_r(x)^m\right] \leqslant (4m)^{2mr}\left(\frac{q}{\sqrt{n/2}}\right)^{2r}.$$

Proof. Expanding out the definition of $a_r(x)$ as the sum of indicators, we have

$$\mathop{\mathbb{E}}_x\left[a_r(x)^m\right] = \mathop{\mathbb{E}}_x\left[\sum_{S_1,\ldots,S_m} 1_{E(x,S_1)}\cdots 1_{E(x,S_m)}\right]$$
$$= \sum_{j=2r}^{\min(2mr,q)} \sum_{|J|=j} \sum_{S_1\cup\ldots\cup S_m=J} \mathop{\mathbb{E}}_x\left[1_{E(x,S_1)}\cdots 1_{E(x,S_m)}\right].$$

Denote $J = S_1\cup\ldots\cup S_m$. Note that whenever $1_{E(S_1,x)}\cdots 1_{E(S_m,x)} = 1$, each element in the multi-set $\{x_j\}_{j\in J}$ must appear at least twice (otherwise, for some S_i, this element appears only once in x_{S_i}, preventing it from being evenly covered). We denote this event by $B(x,J)$, letting $j = |J|$, and noting that $2r \leqslant j \leqslant 2mr$. We can now write (potentially adding zeroes for convenience, since for $2mr \geqslant i > q$, we have $\binom{q}{i} = 0$)

$$\mathop{\mathbb{E}}_x\left[a_r(x)^m\right] \leqslant \sum_{j=2r}^{2mr}\binom{q}{j}\binom{j}{2r}^m \Pr_x[B(J,x)].$$

We again follow a process in order to bound the probability of the event $B(x,J)$: fix J. Observing the multi-set x_J of j elements: we choose half of them to be the leaders, then give those leaders a "free" value, and restrict the rest to only have values that were assigned to some leader. We note that any x that fulfills $B(x,J)$ is outputted by this process. Indeed: the multi-set x_J can have at most $\lfloor j/2\rfloor$ distinct elements. Putting them aside, the rest must have values that were already chosen. Counting outputs of the process, we have the bound:

$$\Pr_x[B(J,x)] \leqslant \frac{\binom{j}{\lfloor j/2\rfloor} n^{\lfloor j/2\rfloor}\lceil j/2\rceil^{\lfloor j/2\rfloor}}{n^j}.$$

Simplifying, this is at most $(2j)^{j/2}n^{-j/2}$, and thus

$$\mathop{\mathbb{E}}_x\left[a_r(x)^m\right] \leqslant \sum_{j=2r}^{2mr}\frac{q^j}{j!}\left(\frac{ej}{2r}\right)^{2mr}(2j)^{j/2}n^{-j/2}$$
$$\leqslant \sum_{j=2r}^{2mr}\left(\frac{ej}{2r}\right)^{2mr} q^j\left(\frac{2}{n}\right)^{j/2}.$$

Bounding the first term in the sum using $j \leqslant 2mr$, we get that

$$\mathop{\mathbb{E}}_x\left[a_r(x)^m\right] \leqslant (em)^{2mr}\sum_{j=2r}^{2mr}\left(q\sqrt{\frac{2}{n}}\right)^j.$$

If $q \geqslant \sqrt{n/2}$, the above sum is dominated by $2mr$ times the summand for $j = 2mr$, and we get the desired upper bound. Else, $q < \sqrt{n/2}$ and the above sum is dominated by $2mr$ times the summand for $j = 2r$, and we get the desired upper bound. □

Proof of Lemma 4.3. As in the proof of Lemma 5.1, we have that the difference is equal to

$$\frac{2^q}{n^q}\left|\sum_{r=1}^{q/2}\varepsilon^{2r}\sum_{|S|=2r}\sum_{x\in X_S}\widehat{G}_x(S)\right|, \tag{5}$$

We now use the fact that the function is biased. We will apply Holder's inequality, leveraging our stronger bounds from Lemma 5.4 and Lemma 5.5. Fix level r. Using Cauchy-Schwarz (for the summation over S), we have that:

$$\left|\sum_{x,\,|S|=2r} 1_{E(x,S)}\widehat{G}_x(S)\right| \leqslant \sum_x\sqrt{a_r(x)}\sqrt{\sum_{|S|=2r}\widehat{G}_x(S)^2}. \tag{6}$$

Let $\delta = \frac{1}{2m+1}$, and fix an x. Note that $G_x, 1-G_x$ have the same weight on level $2r$, so let us assume without loss of generality that

$\mu(G_x) \leqslant \frac{1}{2}$ (otherwise we apply the following argument on $1 - G_x$). Applying Lemma 5.4, the weight on level $2r$ of G_x is at most:

$$\sum_{|S|=2r} \widehat{G}_x(S)^2 \leqslant \delta^{-2r}\mu(G_x)^{\frac{2}{1+\delta}} \leqslant 2\delta^{-2r}\mathrm{var}(G_x)^{\frac{2}{1+\delta}},$$

In the second inequality we used the fact that $\mu(G_x) \leqslant \frac{1}{2}$, thus $\mathrm{var}(G_x) = \mu(G_x)(1 - \mu(G_x)) \geqslant \frac{1}{2}\mu(G_x)$. (which is also applied to either G_x or $1 - G_x$).

Hence, plugging this in we have that 6 is at most:

$$\delta^{-r}\sum_x \sqrt{a_r(x)} \cdot \mathrm{var}(G_x)^{\frac{1}{1+\delta}}. \tag{7}$$

We now apply Holder's inequality with powers $\frac{1+\delta}{\delta}, 1+\delta$ to get the above sum is at most

$$\delta^{-r}\left(\sum_x a_r(x)^{(1+\delta)/(2\delta)}\right)^{\frac{\delta}{1+\delta}}\left(\sum_x \mathrm{var}(G_x)\right)^{\frac{1}{1+\delta}}.$$

Turning the last sum into expectation and using Jensen's inequality we have

$$\sum_x \mathrm{var}(G_x) = \left(\frac{n}{2}\right)^q \mathop{\mathbb{E}}_x[\mathrm{var}(G_x)] \leqslant \left(\frac{n}{2}\right)^q \cdot \mathrm{var}(G).$$

Plugging this back into (6), turning the other sum into expectation, and using $\delta = (2m+1)^{-1}$, we conclude:

$$\left|\sum_{\substack{x,S\\|S|=2r}} 1_E\widehat{G}_x(S)\right| \leqslant (2m+1)^r\left(\frac{n}{2}\right)^q \mathrm{var}(G)^{\frac{2m+1}{2m+2}}\left(\mathop{\mathbb{E}}_x a_r(x)^{m+1}\right)^{\frac{1}{2m+2}}. \tag{8}$$

To upper bound this and finish the proof, we wish to apply Lemma 5.5 and for that we have to consider the two cases $q \geqslant \sqrt{n/2}$ and $q < \sqrt{n/2}$ separately.

Case $q < \sqrt{n/2}$. In this case, applying Lemma 5.5 we see that

$$\mathop{\mathbb{E}}_x\left[a_r(x)^{m+1}\right] \leqslant (5(m+1))^{2(m+1)r}\left(\frac{q}{\sqrt{n/2}}\right)^{2r},$$

so by (8) we get that

$$\left|\sum_{\substack{x,S\\|S|=2r}} 1_{E(x,S)}\widehat{G}_x(S)\right| \leqslant (20m^2)^r\left(\frac{n}{2}\right)^q \mathrm{var}(G)^{\frac{2m+1}{2m+2}}\left(\frac{q}{\sqrt{n/2}}\right)^{\frac{r}{m+1}}.$$

Summing over values of r, we get

$$(5) \leqslant \mathrm{var}(G)^{1-1/(2m+2)}\sum_{r=1}^{q/2}\left(\frac{20m^2q^{1/(m+1)}\varepsilon^2}{\sqrt{n}^{1/(m+1)}}\right)^r.$$

Using $q \leqslant \frac{\sqrt{n}}{(40m^2\varepsilon^2)^{m+1}}$, the sum is upper bounded by twice the summand for $r = 1$, so overall we get that

$$(5) \leqslant 40m^2\varepsilon^2\left(\frac{q}{\sqrt{n}}\right)^{1/(2m+2)}\mathrm{var}(G)^{1-1/(2m+2)}.$$

Case $q \geqslant \sqrt{n/2}$. As before, applying Lemma 5.5 to (8) we get

$$\left|\sum_{x,|S|=2r} 1_{E(x,S)}\widehat{G}_x(S)\right| \leqslant (20m^2)^r\left(\frac{n}{2}\right)^q \mathrm{var}(G)^{\frac{2m+1}{2m+2}}\left(\frac{q}{\sqrt{n/2}}\right)^r$$

Therefore,

$$(5) \leqslant \mathrm{var}(G)^{1-1/(2m)}\sum_{r=1}^{q/2}\left(\frac{20m^2\varepsilon^2 q}{\sqrt{n}}\right)^r.$$

Using $q \leqslant \frac{\sqrt{n}}{40m^2\varepsilon^2}$, the sum is upper bounded by twice the summand for $r = 1$, and so

$$(5) \leqslant 40m^2\varepsilon^2\frac{q}{\sqrt{n}}\mathrm{var}(G)^{1-1/(2m+2)}.$$

□

6 APPLYING THE LEMMAS

In this section, we show how to use our analysis from previous sections to prove lower bounds for computational tasks in the distributed computing model. A similar approach was taken in [1] for the case $q = 1$, i.e.,t each player receives a single query.

6.1 Uniformity Testing Lower Bounds

In this section, we use Lemma 4.2 with standard tools from information theory to prove a lower bound on the individual sample complexity of uniformity testing.

Theorem 6.1. *There exists $C > 0$, such that the individual sample complexity q of uniformity testing in a k-player protocol, in which each player outputs r-bits is at least $\frac{C}{\varepsilon^2}\min\left(\frac{\sqrt{n}}{\sqrt{k}}, \frac{n}{k}\right)$.*

Remark. We note that the lower bound holds even when the players have shared randomness. When each player has one sample ($q = 1$), this theorem recovers the lower bound $k = \Omega(\frac{n}{\varepsilon^2})$ of [1].

We prove that for any fixing of the random coins, if q is too small, the protocol fails to distinguish uniform from ε-far from uniform with sufficiently high probability. This implies Theorem 6.1 for randomized protocols.

Thus, fix the randomness of the protocol, and denote the message that player j sends to the referee by $G_j : \{-1,1\}^{(\ell+1)q} \to \{0,1\}$. Denote the decision function of the referee by $R : \{0,1\}^k \to \{0,1\}$, and consider the following distributions:

- $\mu_{G_1,\ldots,G_k}$: the joint distribution of the bits the players send when they are fed samples from the *uniform* distribution,
- $\nu^z_{G_1,\ldots,G_k}$: the joint distribution of the bits the players send when they are fed samples from ν_z.

Upon receiving messages drawn from $\mu_{G_1,\ldots,G_k}$, the referee should *accept* with high probability (the input distribution is uniform); upon receiving messages drawn from $\nu^z_{G_1,\ldots,G_k}$, the referee should *reject* with high probability (the input distribution is far from uniform). Therefore, these two distributions need to be "very different" from each other, as this difference is all that allows the referee to make the correct decision.

There are many ways to measure the difference between two distributions; here we will use the *KL divergence*,

$$\mathrm{D}(P \,|||\, Q) = \sum_{\omega \in \Omega} P(\omega) \log \frac{P(\omega)}{Q(\omega)}.$$

The reason we use KL divergence is that it is additive:

Fact 6.2 (Additivity of KL divergence). *If X, Y are independent under two distributions $P_{X,Y}$ and $Q_{X,Y}$, then*

$$\mathrm{D}(P_{X,Y} \,|||\, Q_{X,Y}) = \mathrm{D}(P_X \,|||\, Q_X) + \mathrm{D}(P_Y \,|||\, Q_Y),$$

where P_X, P_Y (resp. Q_X, Q_Y) are the marginal distributions of X, Y under P (resp. Q).

In our case, for any fixed z, the players' samples are independent from each other under ν_z; this means their bits $G_1, \ldots, G_k$ are also independent. Similarly, when the samples are from the uniform distribution, the players are independent. Therefore, for any z,

$$\mathrm{D}\left(\nu^z_{G_1,\ldots,G_k} \,|||\, \mu_{G_1,\ldots,G_k}\right) = \sum_{j=1}^{k} \mathrm{D}\left(\nu^z_{G_j} \,|||\, \mu_{G_j}\right). \tag{9}$$

Proof of Theorem 6.1. First, we bound from below the expected divergence $\mathbb{E}_z\left[\mathrm{D}\left(\nu^z_{G_j} \,|||\, \mu_{G_j}\right)\right]$ required for the referee to succeed.

To succeed with probability $1-\delta$, we need to have

$$\mathop{\mathbb{E}}_z \mathrm{D}\left(\nu^z_{G_1,\ldots,G_k} \,|||\, \mu_{G_1,\ldots,G_k}\right) = \sum_{j=1}^{k} \mathop{\mathbb{E}}_z \mathrm{D}\left(\nu^z_{G_j} \,|||\, \mu_{G_j}\right) > \frac{1}{10}\log\frac{1}{\delta}.$$

Thus, the average player needs to have average divergence

$$\mathop{\mathbb{E}}_z\left[\mathrm{D}\left(\nu^z_{G_j} \,|||\, \mu_{G_j}\right)\right] \geqslant \frac{1}{10k}\log\frac{1}{\delta} \tag{10}$$

between the bit they send on uniform input and the bit they send when the input is ε-far from uniform.

Next, using Lemma 4.2, we bound the divergence from above, in terms of the number of samples each player has, and the number of players. We use a well-known relationship between the KL divergence and another measure of distance, called *ξ-squared divergence*:

Fact 6.3. *[4] For any $\alpha, \beta \in (0,1)$, let $\mathrm{B}(\alpha)$, $\mathrm{B}(\beta)$ be Bernoulli random variables with parameters α, β. Then*

$$\mathrm{D}(\mathrm{B}(\alpha) \,|||\, \mathrm{B}(\beta)) \leqslant \frac{(\alpha-\beta)^2}{\mathrm{var}(\mathrm{B}(\beta)) \ln 2}.$$

Using this fact, for every j since player j has q samples, we have

$$\mathop{\mathbb{E}}_z\left[\mathrm{D}\left(\nu^z_{G_j} \,|||\, \mu_{G_j}\right)\right] \leqslant \frac{1}{\ln 2}\mathop{\mathbb{E}}_z\left[\frac{(\mu_z(G_j) - \mu(G_j))^2}{\mathrm{var}(G_j)}\right] \tag{11}$$

$$\leqslant \frac{1}{\ln 2}\left(20\frac{q^2\varepsilon^4}{n} + \frac{q\varepsilon^2}{n}\right). \tag{12}$$

In the last inequality we used Lemma 5.1, assuming $q \leqslant \frac{\sqrt{n}}{20\varepsilon^2}$ (since otherwise we are already done).

Combining (10) and (12), we get that

$$\max\left(\frac{q^2\varepsilon^4}{n}, \frac{q\varepsilon^2}{n}\right) \geqslant \Omega\left(\frac{\log(1/\delta)}{k}\right), \tag{13}$$

and rearranging establishes the claimed lower bound on q. □

6.2 Extensions of Theorem 6.1

Lower bound for longer answers. One may generalize the proof of Theorem 6.1 to the case each player message consists of r-bit answer. We model by a function $G_i \colon \{-1,1\}^{(\ell+1)q} \to \{0,1\}^r$.

Theorem 6.4. *There exists $C > 0$, such that the individual sample complexity of uniformity testing in a k-player protocol, in which each player outputs r-bits is at least $\frac{C}{\varepsilon^2}\min\left(\frac{\sqrt{n}}{\sqrt{2^r k}}, \frac{n}{2^r k}\right)$.*

The proof is similar to the proof of Theorem 6.1, and thus omitted.

Asymmetric-cost model. The question of uniformity testing in the LOCAL model has been reduced in [7] to the simultaneous case, however the reduction pointed towards a generalized setting, in which the players have a fixed amount of time, τ, and each player i samples at its own sampling rate T_i, collecting $q_i = T_i \cdot \tau$ samples. In [7], an algorithm for this more generalized settings was shown with time $\tau = O\left(\frac{\sqrt{n}}{\varepsilon^2 \cdot \|T\|_2}\right)$, where $\|T\|_2 = \sqrt{T_1^2 + \ldots + T_k^2}$.

Our proof shows that, assuming that $q_i \geqslant 1/(20\varepsilon^2)$ for all i (no player is "too slow"), this time complexity is in fact best possible (up to constant factors). Indeed, repeating the proof of Theorem 6.1 we have:

$$\Omega(\log(1/\delta)) \leqslant \sum_{j=1}^{k} \mathop{\mathbb{E}}_z\left[\mathrm{D}\left(\nu^z_{G_j} \,|||\, \mu_{G_j}\right)\right] \leqslant \sum_{j=1}^{k} \frac{2q_i^2\varepsilon^4}{n} = \frac{2\tau^2\varepsilon^4}{n}\|T\|_2^2,$$

and after re-arranging and fixing $\delta = 1/3$, we obtain the tight lower bound of $\tau = \Omega\left(\frac{\sqrt{n}}{\varepsilon^2 \cdot \|T\|_2}\right)$. [3]

Remark. Inequality (13) can also recover known lower bounds for the centralized setting. For $k = 1$, we get a lower bound for the centralized model with error probability δ, matching the bound from [5]. We can also consider asymmetric error probabilities: let δ_1 be the probability that the protocol rejects the uniform distribution, and let δ_0 be the probability that the protocol accepts an ε-far from uniform distribution. Then we can replace the term $\log(1/\delta)$ by $\mathrm{D}(\mathrm{B}(\delta_1) \,|||\, \mathrm{B}(1-\delta_0))$. This shows that the highly biased tester of [7] is optimal in its sample complexity.

From a slightly different angle, it is natural to ask how many players are needed to test uniformity where q is thought of as fixed (as in [1]). For $q \leqslant 1/\varepsilon^2$, inequality (13) implies that $k \geqslant n/(q\varepsilon^2)$ players are needed (generalizing the case where $q = 1$). For $q \geqslant 1/\varepsilon^2$, we get the bound $k \geqslant \frac{n}{q^2\varepsilon^4}$, which is tight by the collision-based distributed tester of [7].

6.3 Distributed Uniformity Testing with the AND Rule

In this section we show how to use Lemmas 5.1, 4.3 to prove lower bounds for uniformity testing of distributions in a simple distributed computing model. In this model, given messages $b_1, \ldots, b_k$ from the k players, the decision of the referee is $b_1 \wedge \ldots \wedge b_k$.

Remark. Using the AND rule, it is easy to show that $q > 1$ is necessary for uniformity testing to be testable in the distributed model at all (a proof appears in the full version).

[3] Note that if $T_i = 1$ for all i, then we are back to the symmetric case, and indeed we get the same bound since $\|T\|_2 = \sqrt{k}$.

Theorem 6.5. *There exists $c > 0$ such that the following holds. If $k \leqslant 2^{c/\varepsilon}$ then any k-player's protocol for solving uniformity testing must use at least $\Omega\left(\frac{\sqrt{n}}{\log(k)^2\varepsilon^2}\right)$ queries.*

Proof. Let d be large enough constant. For any $\varepsilon \geqslant 1/d^2$, we have that $1/\varepsilon$ and k are both bounded by a constant, and in particular we only demand to show $q = \Omega(\sqrt{n})$, which is evident from Theorem 6.1. We therefore may assume that $\varepsilon \leqslant 1/d^2$.

We now show that if $k \leqslant 2^{1/(d\cdot\varepsilon)}$, and $q \leqslant \frac{\sqrt{n}}{8d\log(k)^2\varepsilon^2}$, then no distributed protocol succeeds in distinguishing the uniform distribution and randomly chosen ν_z. We note that in this regime of parameters, the conditions of Lemma 4.3 hold for $m = \log(k)$, and we will apply it this way.

Let $G_i(x)$ be the message player i sends to the referee upon receiving queries x, and denote the probability it says 1 when x is sampled according to the uniform distribution by $1 - \xi_i$. Since D accepts the uniform distribution, $\mathcal{U}$, with probability $\geqslant \frac{2}{3}$, we know that

$$e^{-\sum_{i=1}^{k}\xi_i} \geqslant \prod_{i=1}^{k}(1-\xi_i) = \Pr\left[\text{Referee accepts } \mathcal{U}\right] \geqslant \frac{2}{3},$$

i.e. $\sum_{i=1}^{k}\xi_i \leqslant \ln(3/2)$.

Choose $m = \log(k)$ and apply Lemma 4.3 for each i, to get that

$$\mathop{\mathbb{E}}_{z}\left[\mu_z(G_i)\right] \geqslant 1 - \xi_i - 40m^2\varepsilon^2\xi_i^{\frac{2m+1}{2m+2}}\left(q/\sqrt{n} + (q/\sqrt{n})^{1/(2m+2)}\right).$$

We note that by the assumption on q,

$$q/\sqrt{n} \leqslant \frac{1}{d\log(k)^2\varepsilon^2}$$

and subsequently

$$(q/\sqrt{n})^{1/(2m+2)} = O(\varepsilon^{-1/(1+\log k)}).$$

So we get that

$$\mathop{\mathbb{E}}_{z}\left[\mu_z(G_i)\right] \geqslant 1 - \xi_i - O\left(\frac{1}{d}\right)\xi_i^{\frac{2m+1}{2m+2}} + O(\varepsilon^2\log^2 k\varepsilon^{\frac{-1}{1+\log k}})\xi_i^{\frac{2m+1}{2m+2}}.$$

Elementary calculus shows that for $1 \leqslant k \leqslant 2^{1/(d\cdot\varepsilon)}$, the maximum of $\varepsilon^2 \cdot \log^2 k \cdot \varepsilon^{-1/(1+\log k)}$ is obtained at one of the endpoints, and using $\varepsilon \leqslant 1/d^2$ we see that this maximum is at most $O(\frac{1}{d})$. Therefore,

$$\mathop{\mathbb{E}}_{z}\left[\mu_z(G_i)\right] \geqslant 1 - \xi_i - O\left(\frac{1}{d}\right)\xi_i^{\frac{2m+1}{2m+2}}.$$

Denote by $E_i(z)$ the event that (x_i, s_i) was sampled according to ν_z and $G_i(x_i, s_i) = 1$. Then

$$\Pr_{z,x_i,s_i}\left[E_i(z)\right] = \mathop{\mathbb{E}}_{z}\left[\mu_z(G_i)\right] \geqslant 1 - \xi_i - O\left(\frac{1}{d}\right)\xi_i^{\frac{2m+1}{2m+2}},$$

and thus by considering the complement events and using the Union Bound, we get that:

$$\Pr_z\left[\cap_{i=1}^{k}E_i(z)\right] = 1 - \Pr_z\left[\cup_{i=1}^{k}\overline{E_i(z)}\right]$$
$$\geqslant 1 - \sum_{i=1}^{k}\Pr_z\left[\overline{E_i(z)}\right] \geqslant 1 - \sum_{i=1}^{k}\xi_i - O\left(\frac{1}{d}\right)\sum_{i=1}^{k}\xi_i^{\frac{2m+1}{2m+2}}.$$

The sum of the ξ_i is at most $\ln(3/2) \leqslant \frac{1}{2}$. By Holder's inequality, the sum of the second term is:

$$\sum_{i=1}^{k}\xi_i^{\frac{2m+1}{2m+2}} \leqslant k^{1/(2m+2)}\left(\sum_{i=1}^{k}\xi_i\right)^{\frac{2m+1}{2m+2}} \leqslant k^{1/(2m+2)} = O(1),$$

where we used $m = \log(k)$.

Collecting these estimates with the previous inequality, we conclude that

$$\Pr_z\left[\cap_{i=1}^{k}E_i(z)\right] \geqslant \frac{1}{2} - O(1/d).$$

Choosing sufficiently large constant d, the last probability is larger than $1/3$, and thus the protocol would accept with probability greater than $1/3$. This means that all events $E_i(z)$ holds with probability $1/3$, in which case the referee would accept. Stated otherwise, the protocol accepts an ε-far from uniform distribution with probability $> \frac{1}{3}$, and thus fails. □

REFERENCES

[1] Jayadev Acharya, Clément L. Canonne, and Himanshu Tyagi. 2018. Distributed Simulation and Distributed Inference. *CoRR* abs/1804.06952 (2018).

[2] Tugkan Batu, Lance Fortnow, Ronitt Rubinfeld, Warren D. Smith, and Patrick White. 2000. Testing that distributions are close. In *41st Annual Symposium on Foundations of Computer Science, FOCS 2000*. 259–269.

[3] Clément L. Canonne. 2015. A Survey on Distribution Testing: Your Data is Big. But is it Blue? *Electronic Colloquium on Computational Complexity (ECCC)* 22 (2015), 63.

[4] Thomas M. Cover and Joy A. Thomas. 2006. *Elements of Information Theory (Wiley Series in Telecommunications and Signal Processing)*. Wiley-Interscience, New York, NY, USA.

[5] Ilias Diakonikolas, Themis Gouleakis, John Peebles, and Eric Price. 2018. Sample-Optimal Identity Testing with High Probability. In *45th International Colloquium on Automata, Languages, and Programming, ICALP 2018*. 41:1–41:14.

[6] Ilias Diakonikolas and Daniel M. Kane. 2016. A New Approach for Testing Properties of Discrete Distributions. In *IEEE 57th Annual Symposium on Foundations of Computer Science, FOCS 2016*. 685–694.

[7] Orr Fischer, Uri Meir, and Rotem Oshman. 2018. Distributed Uniformity Testing. In *Proceedings of the 2018 ACM Symposium on Principles of Distributed Computing, PODC 2018*. 455–464.

[8] Pierre Fraigniaud, Mika Göös, Amos Korman, and Jukka Suomela. 2013. What Can Be Decided Locally Without Identifiers?. In *Proceedings of the 2013 ACM Symposium on Principles of Distributed Computing (PODC '13)*. 157–165.

[9] Pierre Fraigniaud, Amos Korman, and David Peleg. 2011. Local Distributed Decision. *2011 IEEE 52nd Annual Symposium on Foundations of Computer Science* (2011), 708–717.

[10] Goldreich and Ron. 2002. Property Testing in Bounded Degree Graphs. *Algorithmica* 32, 2 (01 Feb 2002), 302–343.

[11] Oded Goldreich. 2016. The uniform distribution is complete with respect to testing identity to a fixed distribution. *Electronic Colloquium on Computational Complexity (ECCC)* 23 (2016), 15.

[12] Oded Goldreich. 2017. *Introduction to Property Testing*. Cambridge University Press.

[13] Oded Goldreich and Dana Ron. 2000. On Testing Expansion in Bounded-Degree Graphs. *Electronic Colloquium on Computational Complexity (ECCC)* 7, 20 (2000).

[14] J. Kahn, G. Kalai, and N. Linial. 1988. The influence of variables on Boolean functions. In *[Proceedings 1988] 29th Annual Symposium on Foundations of Computer Science*. 68–80.

[15] Amos Korman, Shay Kutten, and David Peleg. 2010. Proof Labeling Schemes. *Distrib. Comput.* 22, 4 (2010), 215–233.

[16] L. Paninski. 2008. A Coincidence-Based Test for Uniformity Given Very Sparsely Sampled Discrete Data. *IEEE Transactions on Information Theory* 54, 10 (2008), 4750–4755.

Hardness of Distributed Optimization*

Nir Bacrach
Technion, Israel
bachrach.nir@gmail.com

Keren Censor-Hillel
Technion, Israel
ckeren@cs.technion.ac.il

Michal Dory
Technion, Israel
smichald@cs.technion.ac.il

Yuval Efron
Technion, Israel
efronyuv@gmail.com

Dean Leitersdorf
Technion, Israel
dean.leitersdorf@gmail.com

Ami Paz
CNRS & Université de Paris, France
amipaz@irif.fr

ABSTRACT

This paper studies lower bounds for fundamental optimization problems in the CONGEST model. We show that solving problems *exactly* in this model can be a hard task, by providing $\tilde{\Omega}(n^2)$ lower bounds for cornerstone problems, such as minimum dominating set (MDS), Hamiltonian path, Steiner tree and max-cut. These are almost tight, since all of these problems can be solved optimally in $O(n^2)$ rounds. Moreover, we show that even in bounded-degree graphs and even in simple graphs with maximum degree 5 and logarithmic diameter, it holds that various tasks, such as finding a maximum independent set (MaxIS) or a minimum vertex cover, are still difficult, requiring a near-tight number of $\tilde{\Omega}(n)$ rounds.

Furthermore, we show that in some cases even *approximations* are difficult, by providing an $\tilde{\Omega}(n^2)$ lower bound for a $(7/8 + \epsilon)$-approximation for MaxIS, and a nearly-linear lower bound for an $O(\log n)$-approximation for the k-MDS problem for any constant $k \geq 2$, as well as for several variants of the Steiner tree problem.

Our lower bounds are based on a rich variety of constructions that leverage novel observations, and reductions among problems that are specialized for the CONGEST model. However, for several additional approximation problems, as well as for exact computation of some central problems in P, such as maximum matching and max flow, we show that such constructions *cannot* be designed, by which we exemplify some limitations of this framework.

KEYWORDS

distributed computing, optimization problems, approximation algorithms, congest, communication complexity

ACM Reference Format:

Nir Bacrach, Keren Censor-Hillel, Michal Dory, Yuval Efron, Dean Leitersdorf, and Ami Paz. 2019. Hardness of Distributed Optimization. In *2019 ACM Symposium on Principles of Distributed Computing (PODC '19), July 29-August 2, 2019, Toronto, ON, Canada.* ACM, New York, NY, USA, 10 pages. https://doi.org/10.1145/3293611.3331597

*A full version of this paper is available on arXiv [2]

ACM ISBN 978-1-4503-6217-7/19/07...$15.00
https://doi.org/10.1145/3293611.3331597

1 INTRODUCTION

Optimization problems are cornerstone problems in computer science, for which finding exact and approximate solutions is extensively studied in various computational settings. Since optimization problems are fundamental for a variety of computational tasks, mapping trade-offs between their time complexity and approximation ratio is a holy-grail, especially for those that are NP-hard.

Distributed settings share this necessity of resolving the complexity of exact and approximate solutions for optimization problems, and a rich landscape of complexities is constantly being explored. However, distributed settings exhibit very different behavior, compared with their sequential counterpart, in terms of what is efficiently solvable and what is hard. Here, we focus on the CONGEST model in which n vertices communicate synchronously over the underlying network graph, using an $O(\log n)$-bit bandwidth [33]. Since the local computation of vertices is not polynomially bounded, hardness results in the sequential setting do not translate to hardness results in the distributed one. In particular, any natural graph problem can be solved in the CONGEST model in $O(m)$ rounds, m being the number of edges, by letting the vertices learn the whole graph. For some problems, such as MaxIS and finding the chromatic number [7], this naïve solution is known to be nearly-tight, whereas for other problems more efficient solutions exist. On the other hand, there do exist problems with a polynomial sequential complexity, which require $\tilde{\Omega}(m)$ rounds in the CONGEST model, such as deciding whether the graph contains a cycle of a certain length and weight [7].

In the sequential setting, finding an exact solution for some problems, such as minimum dominating set (MDS) or a maximum independent set (MaxIS), is known to be NP-hard [22]. In such cases, it is sometimes possible to obtain efficient approximations, such as an $O(\log \Delta)$-approximation for MDS, where Δ is the maximum degree in the graph [37]. However, in some cases, even obtaining an approximation is hard. For MDS, any approximation better than logarithmic is hard to obtain [29]. MaxIS does not admit even an $O(n^{1-\epsilon})$ approximation [18]. In the CONGEST model, there are polylogarithmic $O(\log \Delta)$-approximations for MDS [21, 25, 26], and it is also known that obtaining such an approximation requires at least a polylogarithmic time. More specifically, there are lower bounds of $\Omega(\sqrt{\log n/\log\log n})$ and $\Omega(\log \Delta/\log\log \Delta)$ [25]. However, currently nothing else is known with respect to better approximations or exact solutions. For the MaxIS problem, there are efficent $(\Delta+1)/2$ and 0.529Δ approximations for the unweighted and weighted cases, respectively [5]. However, the complexity of achieving any better approximations is not known. Solving it *exactly* requires $\tilde{\Omega}(n^2)$

rounds [7]. In the closely related LOCAL model, where the size of messages is not bounded, $(1+\epsilon)$-approximations for both problems can be obtained in polylogarithmic time [16].

The curious aspect of the huge gaps that are present in our current understanding of various optimization and approximation complexities in the CONGEST model is that *we do not have any hardness conjectures to blame these gaps on.* This raises the natural question: can we obtain better approximations efficiently in the CONGEST model?

For problems in P, in many cornerstone cases, such as min cut, max flow and maximum matching, we have efficient $(1+\epsilon)$-approximations [15, 28, 30], but the complexity of *exact* computation is still open. Many additional questions are open with respect to various optimization problems.

The contributions of this paper are three-fold, providing (i) novel techniques for nearly-tight lower bounds for exact optimizations, (ii) advanced approaches for nearly-tight lower bounds for approximations, and (iii) new methods for showing limitations of the main lower-bound framework.

1.1 Our contributions, the challenges, and our techniques

Lower bounds for exact computation. We show that in many cases, solving problems *exactly* in the CONGEST model is hard, by providing many new $\tilde{\Omega}(n^2)$ lower bounds for fundamental optimization problems, such as MDS, max-cut, Hamiltonian path, Steiner tree and minimum 2-edge-connected spanning subgraph (2-ECSS). Such results were previously known only for the minimum vertex cover (MVC), MaxIS and minimum chromatic number problems [7]. Our results are inspired by [7], but combine many new technical ingredients. In particular, one of the key components in our lower bounds are reductions between problems. After having a lower bound for MDS, a cleverly designed reduction allows us to build a new lower bound construction for Hamiltonian path. These constructions serve as a basis for our constructions for the Steiner tree and minimum 2-ECSS. We emphasize that we *cannot* directly use known reductions from the sequential setting, but rather we must create reductions that do not blow up the number of vertices or the size of the cut.

To demonstrate the challenge, we now give more details about the general framework. We use the well-known framework of reductions from 2-party communication complexity, as originated in [34] and used in many additional works, e.g., [1, 6, 10, 13, 14, 35]. In communication complexity, two players, Alice and Bob, receive private input strings and their goal is to solve some problem related to their inputs, for example, decide whether their inputs are disjoint, by communicating the minimum number of bits possible. To show a lower bound for the CONGEST model, the high-level idea is to create a graph that satisfies some required property, for example, have an MDS of a certain size iff the input strings satisfy some property. If a fast algorithm in the CONGEST exists, Alice and Bob can simulate it and solve the communication problem. Then, lower bounds from communication complexity translate to lower bounds in the CONGEST model. The exact lower bound we can show depends on certain parameters such as the size of the graph, the size of the inputs and the size of the cut between the parts of the graph that the players simulate. An attempt to use the known reduction from MVC to MDS together with the $\tilde{\Omega}(n^2)$ lower bound for MVC from [7] faces a complication: This reduction requires adding a new vertex for each edge in the original graph, which blows up the size of the graph with respect to the inputs, and allows showing only a nearly-linear lower bound. For similar reasons, known reductions from MVC to Hamiltonian cycle and Steiner tree cannot show any super-linear lower bound. Nevertheless, we show that in some cases reductions can be a powerful tool in providing new $\tilde{\Omega}(n^2)$ bounds, but they need to be designed carefully in order to preserve certain parameters of the graph, such as the number of vertices and the size of the cut between the two players.

A succinct summary of our results in this section is the following.

- We show an $\tilde{\Omega}(n^2)$ lower bound for solving MDS, weighted max-cut, Hamiltonian path and cycle, minimum Steiner tree, and unweighted 2-ECSS on general graphs. For unweighted max-cut, we show an $\tilde{O}(n)$ algorithm for computing a $(1-\epsilon)$-approximation for max-cut in general graphs, for all $\epsilon > 0$.

Lower bounds in bounded-degree graphs. In many cases, the graph over which one needs to solve a certain problem is not a worst-case instance, but rather is drawn from a specific graph family that does allow efficient solutions. For example, while we show that finding a Hamiltonian path requires $\tilde{\Omega}(n^2)$ rounds in the worst case, in random graphs $G_{n,p}$, there exist fast algorithms, with the exact complexity depending on the probability p [9, 17, 36]. When we focus on bounded-degree graphs, there exist efficient *constant* approximations for many optimization problems, such as MaxIS and MDS, whereas in general graphs such results are currently not known in the CONGEST model. We show that when it comes to *exact* computation, even in bounded-degree graphs many problems are still difficult. Specifically, to solve MaxIS or MVC in bounded-degree graphs one would need $\tilde{\Omega}(n)$ rounds, and this holds even in graphs with logarithmic diameter and maximum degree 5. A similar result is shown for MDS. This is nearly-optimal, since all these problems can be solved in $O(m) = O(n)$ rounds in these graphs. Our lower bound here is again based on reductions, but this time not necessarily between graph problems. To show a lower bound for MaxIS we use a sequence of reductions between MaxIS and max 2SAT instances. Replacing a graph by a CNF formula ϕ is useful since it allows us to use the power of expander graphs and replace ϕ by a new equivalent CNF formula ϕ' where each variable appears only a constant number of times. This reduction is inspired by [11, 32] and is the main ingredient that allows us eventually to convert our graph to a bounded-degree graph. Once we have a lower bound for MaxIS, a lower bound for MVC and MDS is obtained using standard reductions between the problems.

A succinct summary of our results in this section is the following.

- We show an $\tilde{\Omega}(n)$ lower bound for solving MVC, MDS, MaxIS, and weighted 2-spanner on bounded-degree graphs.

Hardness of approximation. While solving problems *exactly* seems to be a difficult task, one can hope to find fast and efficient approximation algorithms. In the CONGEST model, currently the best efficient approximation algorithms known for many problems achieve the same approximation factors as the best approximations known for polynomial sequential algorithms. An intriguing question is whether better approximations can be obtained efficiently. As a first step towards answering this question, we show that in some cases even just *approximating* the optimal solution is hard.

The challenge in showing such a lower bound is that we need to create a *gap*. It is no longer enough that the graph satisfies some predicate iff the inputs are, for example, disjoint, but rather we want that the size of the optimal solution would *change dramatically* according to the inputs. Creating gaps is also crucial in showing inapproxiambility results in the sequential setting, a prime example for this is the PCP theorem which is a key tool for creating such gaps. In the distributed setting, we may need a more direct approach. Several approaches to create such gaps are shown in previous work. In weighted problems, sometimes we can use the weights to create a gap, as done in the constructions of Das Sarma et al. [35]. In some cases, the construction itself allows showing a gap. For example, if the chromatic number of a graph is either at most $3c$ or at least $4c$ depending on the inputs, it shows a lower bound for a $(4/3-\epsilon)$-approximation [7]. Similar ideas are used in lower bounds for approximating the diameter [1, 14, 19, 20]. Another option is to reduce from a problem in communication complexity that already embeds a gap in it, such as the *gap disjointness* problem [6], or to design a specific construction that produces a gap, as done in the lower bound for directed k-spanners [6].

We add two new techniques to this toolbox, namely, we show that *error-correcting codes* and *probabilistic methods* are useful for creating gaps also in the CONGEST model. Based on these, we show that obtaining a $(7/8+\epsilon)$-approximation for MaxIS requires $\tilde{\Omega}(n^2)$ rounds. Although MaxIS may be very difficult to approximate, we later prove that our framework is incapable of showing any lower bound for approximation better than 1/2. For other problems, however, we are able to show a lower bound for a stronger approximation. Specifically, we show a near-linear lower bound for obtaining an $O(\log n)$-approximation for the k-MDS problem for $k \geq 2$, and for several variants of the Steiner tree problem. Here, k-MDS is the problem of finding in a given vertex weighted graph $G=(V,E,w)$, a minimum weight set $S \subseteq V$ such that for all $v \in V$, either $v \in S$, or $d(v,S) \leq k$. We also show such a result for MDS, but with some restrictions on the algorithm. For general algorithms, we show that we cannot use the Alice-Bob framework to show any hardness result for approximation above 2. This simply follows from the fact that if each one of Alice and Bob solves the problem optimally on its part, the union of the solutions gives a 2-approximation. Our results demonstrate a clear separation between the CONGEST and LOCAL models, since in the latter there are efficient $(1+\epsilon)$-approximations for MaxIS and k-MDS [16].[1] Such a separation for a *local approximation problem*, a problem whose approximate solution does not require diameter many rounds when the message size is unbounded, was previously known only for approximating spanners [6].

A succinct summary of our results in this section is the following.

- We show an $\tilde{\Omega}(n^2)$ and an $\tilde{\Omega}(n)$ lower bounds for computing a $(\frac{7}{8}+\epsilon)$-approximation for MaxIS and a $(\frac{5}{6}+\epsilon)$-approximation for MaxIS, respectively, for any constant $\epsilon > 0$. We also show a nearly-linear lower bound for computing an $O(\log n)$-approximation for weighted k-MDS for all $k \geq 2$. We show similar results also for several variants of the Steiner tree problem. In addition, we show such results for weighted MDS, assuming some restrictions on the algorithm.

Limitations. Finally, we study the limitations of this general lower bound framework. While it is capable of providing many near-quadratic lower bounds for *exact and approximate* computations, we show that sometimes it is limited in showing hardness of approximation. In addition, we prove impossibility of using this framework for providing lower bounds for exact computation for several central problems in P, such as maximum matching, max flow, min s-t cut and weighted s-t distance. Interestingly, we also show it cannot provide strong lower bounds for several *verification* problems, which stands in sharp contrast to known lower bounds for these problems [35]. This implies that using a fixed cut as in our paper, is provably weaker than allowing a changing cut as in [35].

One tool for showing such results is providing a protocol that allows Alice and Bob solve the problem by communicating only a small number of bits. Such ideas are used in showing the limitation of this framework for obtaining any lower bound for triangle detection [12], any super-linear lower bound for weighted APSP [7] (recently proven to have a linear solution [4]), and any lower bound larger than $\Omega(\sqrt{n})$ for detecting 4-cliques [10].

We push this idea further, showing that a *non-deterministic* protocol for Alice and Bob, which may be much easier to establish, can imply the limitations of the technique. We also show how to obtain such protocols using a connection to *proof labeling schemes* (PLS).

1.2 Preliminaries

We denote by $[n]$ the set $\{0,\ldots,n-1\}$. To prove lower bounds on the number of rounds necessary in order to solve a distributed problem in the CONGEST model, we use reductions from two-party communication complexity problems. In what follows, we give the required definitions and the main reduction mechanism.

1.3 Communication complexity

In the two-party communication complexity setting [27], there is a function $f:\{0,1\}^K \times \{0,1\}^K \to \{\text{TRUE}, \text{FALSE}\}$, and two players, Alice and Bob, who are given two input strings, $x,y \in \{0,1\}^K$, respectively, and need to compute $f(x,y)$ by exchanging bits according to some protocol π. The *communication complexity* $CC(\pi)$ of π is the maximal number of bits Alice and Bob exchange in π, taken over all possible pairs of K-bit strings (x,y).

For our lower bounds, we consider deterministic and randomized protocols. To show limitations of obtaining lower bounds we also consider nondeterministic protocols. In a randomized protocol, Alice and Bob can generate truly random bits of their own, and the final output of Alice and Bob needs to be correct (according to f) with probability at least 2/3 over the random bits generated by both players.

The *deterministic communication complexity* $CC(f)$ of f is the minimum $CC(\pi)$, taken over all deterministic protocols π for computing f. The *randomized communication complexity* $CC^R(f)$ is defined analogously.

The main communication complexity problem that we use for our lower bounds is *set disjointness*, DISJ_K, which is defined as

[1] The algorithm for k-MDS follows from the known algorithm for MDS, since in the LOCAL model we can simulate an MDS algorithm in the graph G^k.

$\text{DISJ}_K(x, y) = \text{FALSE}$ if and only if there is an index $i \in \{0, \ldots, K-1\}$ such that $x_i = y_i = 1$. It is known that $CC(\text{DISJ}_K) = \Theta(K)$ and $CC^R(\text{DISJ}_K) = \Theta(K)$ [27, Example 3.22]. The latter holds even if Alice and Bob are allowed to generate shared random bits.

1.4 Family of lower bound graphs

To formalize the reductions, we use the following definition which is taken from [7].

Definition 1.1. *Family of Lower Bound Graphs*
Given integers K and n, a Boolean function $f : \{0,1\}^K \times \{0,1\}^K \to \{\text{TRUE}, \text{FALSE}\}$ and some Boolean graph property or predicate denoted P, a set of graphs $\left\{G_{x,y} = (V, E_{x,y}) \mid x, y \in \{0,1\}^K\right\}$ is called a family of lower bound graphs *with respect to f and P if the following hold:*

1. *The set of vertices V is the same for all the graphs in the family, and we denote by V_A, V_B a fixed partition of the vertices.*
2. *Given $x, y \in \{0,1\}^K$, the only part of the graph which is allowed to be dependent on x (by adding edges or weights, no adding vertices) is $G[V_A]$.*
3. *Given $x, y \in \{0,1\}^K$, the only part of the graph which is allowed to be dependent on y (by adding edges or weights, no adding vertices) is $G[V_B]$.*
4. *$G_{x,y}$ satisfies P if and only if $f(x, y) = \text{TRUE}$.*

The set of edges $E(V_A, V_B)$ is denoted by E_{cut}, and is the same for all graphs in the family.

We use the following theorem whose proof can be found in [7].

Theorem 1.1. *Fix a function $f : \{0,1\}^K \times \{0,1\}^K \to \{\text{TRUE}, \text{FALSE}\}$ and a predicate P. If there exists a family of lower bound graphs $\{G_{x,y}\}$ w.r.t. f and P then any deterministic algorithm for deciding P in the* CONGEST *model takes $\Omega(CC(f)/(|E_{cut}| \log n))$ rounds, and every randomized algorithm for deciding P in the* CONGEST *model takes $\Omega(CC^R(f)/(|E_{cut}| \log n))$ rounds.*

2 NEAR QUADRATIC EXACT LOWER BOUNDS

2.1 Minimum dominating set

Our construction for an $\Omega(n^2/\log^2 n)$ lower bound for MDS is inspired by the construction for vertex cover from [7]. As explained, we cannot use known reductions as they induce weak parameters. Since MDS is a very basic problem, showing a lower bound for it allows us to later show lower bounds for additional problems such as Steiner Tree and Hamiltonian cycle.

We build a family of graphs $G_{x,y}$ with respect to $f = \text{DISJ}_{k^2}$, where k is a power of 2, and the predicate P that says that the graph $G_{x,y}$ contains a dominating set of size $4 \log k + 2$.

The fixed graph construction: Start with a fixed graph G (see Figure 1), consisting of four sets (*rows*) of k vertices each (*row vertices*), denoted $A_1 = \{a_1^i \mid 0 \le i \le k-1\}$, $A_2 = \{a_2^i \mid 0 \le i \le k-1\}$, $B_1 = \{b_1^i \mid 0 \le i \le k-1\}$, $B_2 = \{b_2^i \mid 0 \le i \le k-1\}$. For each set $S \in \{A_1, A_2, B_1, B_2\}$ and $\ell \in \{1, 2\}$ add three sets of vertices $T_S = \{t_S^h \mid 0 \le h \le \log k - 1\}$, $F_S = \{f_S^h \mid 0 \le h \le \log k - 1\}$ and $U_S = \{u_S^h \mid 0 \le h \le \log k - 1\}$; we refer to these vertices as *bit-gadget vertices*. For each $0 \le h \le \log k - 1$ and each $\ell \in \{1, 2\}$, connect the 6-cycle $(f_{A_\ell}^h, t_{A_\ell}^h, u_{A_\ell}^h, f_{B_\ell}^h, t_{B_\ell}^h, u_{B_\ell}^h)$. The cycles are connected to A_1, A_2, B_1, B_2 by their binary representation: Given a row vertex $s_\ell^i \in S$, i.e., $s \in \{a, b\}$, $\ell \in \{1, 2\}$, $i \in [k]$, let i_h denote the h-th bit in the binary representation of i. Connect s_ℓ^i to the set $\text{bin}(s_\ell^i) \subset (F_S \cup T_S)$, defined as $\text{bin}(s_\ell^i) = \{f_S^h \mid i_h = 0\} \cup \{t_S^h \mid i_h = 1\}$. Similarly, define $\overline{\text{bin}}(s_\ell^i) = \{f_S^h \mid i_h = 1\} \cup \{t_S^j \mid i_h = 0\}$. Let V_A be the set of nodes indexed with a or A, and $V_B = V \setminus V_A$.

Constructing $G_{x,y}$ from G given $x, y \in \{0,1\}^{k^2}$: Index x and y by pairs (i, j), for $0 \le i, j \le k-1$. For each pair (i, j), add the edge $\{a_1^i, a_2^j\}$ iff $x_{i,j} = 1$, and add the edge $\{b_1^i, b_2^j\}$ iff $y_{i,j} = 1$.

Lemma 2.1. *$G_{x,y}$ has a dominating set of size $4 \log k + 2$ if and only if $\text{DISJ}_{k^2}(x, y) = \text{FALSE}$.*

The proof sketch is as follows: If $\text{DISJ}_{k^2}(x, y) = \text{FALSE}$, then there is a pair (i, j) s.t. $x_{i,j} = y_{i,j} = 1$, i.e., the edges $\{a_1^i, a_2^j\}, \{b_1^i, b_2^j\}$ are both in $G_{x,y}$. One can verify that the following set of $4 \log k + 2$ vertices is a dominating set: a_1^i, b_1^i, and all the vertices in $\overline{\text{bin}}(a_1^i), \overline{\text{bin}}(a_2^j), \overline{\text{bin}}(b_1^i), \overline{\text{bin}}(b_2^j)$. For the other direction, we show that any dominating set D of size $4 \log k + 2$ does not intersect one of the pairs $\{f_{A_\ell}^h, f_{B_\ell}^h\}$ or $\{t_{A_\ell}^h, t_{B_\ell}^h\}$ from each 6-cycle. Hence, there are 4 row vertices $\{a_1^i, b_1^i, a_2^j, b_2^j\}$, such that for each vertex v of them, $\text{bin}(v)$ does not intersect D. Thus, each of these vertices must either be in D or have a neighbor in it. But, only two row vertices can be in D, so it must be the case that both edges $\{a_1^i, a_2^j\}$ and $\{b_1^i, b_2^j\}$ exist in $G_{x,y}$, and one vertex of each edge is in D. These edges exist only if $x_{(i,j)} = y_{(i,j)} = 1$, and the inputs are not disjoint. The lower bound for MDS is now a simple corollary of Theorem 1.1 and Lemma 2.1.

Additional results: Relying on our MDS construction, we show $\tilde{\Omega}(n^2)$ lower bounds for the Steiner tree problem and for the Hamiltonian path problem (see Section 2.2). While there are standard reductions to both problems also from MVC, using them together with the $\tilde{\Omega}(n^2)$ lower bound from [7] can only show a near-linear lower bound. Roughly speaking, this follows since for each edge in the lower bound graph for MVC we must add at least one vertex, which blows up the number of vertices with respect to the inputs. In MDS, we cover *vertices* and not *edges* which allows showing an $\tilde{\Omega}(n^2)$ lower bound.

Max Cut: Using a similar construction as for MDS, we show that any exact algorithm for the weighted case requires $\Omega(n^2/\log^2 n)$ rounds. The key technical hurdle is that inserting an edge into a graph according to x, y (imagine for now the MDS graph) *may not change the value of the maximum cut*, e.g., if it connects two vertices on its same side. The novelty of our construction is in circumventing the above by adding weights to all edges, and adding some (small) constant number of new vertices, among them two vertices N_A and N_B, connected to all $A_1 \cup A_2$ and $B_1 \cup B_2$ vertices, respectively. The role of N_A, N_B is the following. As in the MDS construction, we add an edge of weight 1 between a_1^i and a_2^j iff $x_{i,j} = 0$, and similarly for y. The crux of our construction is that for each row vertex, say a_1^i, the weight of its edge to N_A is equal to the number of vertices in A_2 to which a_1^i is *not* connected. Thus, the sum of weights of edges going from a_1^i to vertices in $A_2 \cup \{N_A\}$ is exactly k. Intuitively, if we now add another edge from a_1^i to some a_2^j that is on the same side of a given cut, and if a_1^i and N_A are not on the same side, then

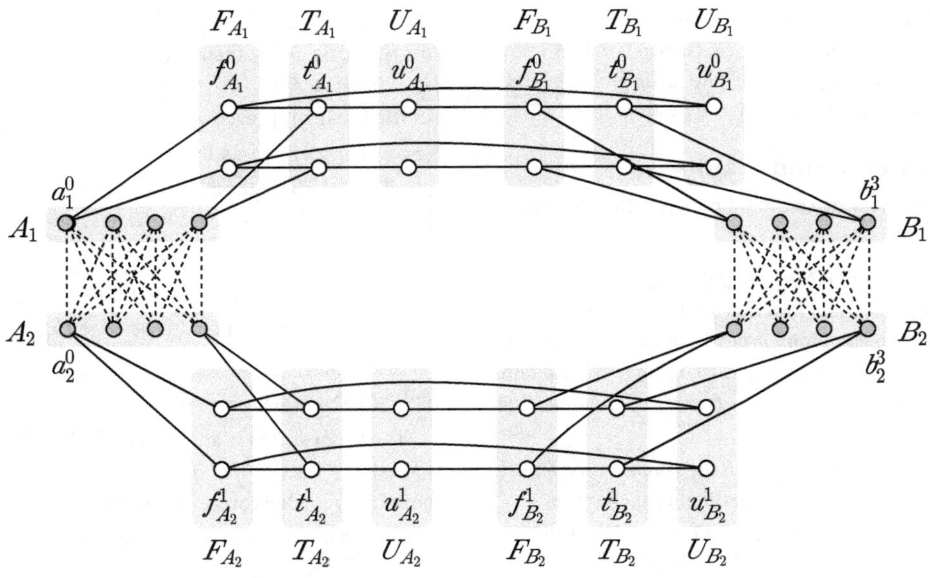

Figure 1: The lower bound construction for MDS, with $k = 4$.

the value of the cut now decreases by 1. We give weights to the remaining edges, such that some heavy-weighted edges force any max-cut to take both t^h_S vertices or both f^h_S vertices from every row h to the same side of the cut. Combining the above ingredients gives that in order for the maximum cut to retain its weight, the inputs strings x, y must not be disjoint, which is what allows us to obtain our lower bound. We also show that for the unweighted case, the $(1-\epsilon)$-approximation algorithm of [38] can be implemented in the CONGEST model within $\tilde{O}(n)$ rounds.

2.2 Hamiltonian path

We reduce the lower bound construction for MDS into a lower bound construction for the existence of a directed Hamiltonian path. While the latter is not an optimization problem, it is known to be NP-hard, e.g., through a reduction from minimum vertex cover [22]. A lower bound of $\tilde{\Omega}(\sqrt{n}+D)$ is known for the *verification* version of the problem [35] (see Section 5.2), and Hamiltonian paths can be found efficiently in random graphs [9, 17, 36]. However, in general graphs we show an $\tilde{\Omega}(n^2)$ lower bound.

Imagine traversing our lower bound graph for MDS in search for a Hamiltonian path, to which we add *start* and *end* vertices, where the path begins and ends, respectively. We need the existence of such a path to determine if the input strings x, y are disjoint, so our approach is to traverse the bit-gadget vertices and the row vertices such that after a certain prefix, it remains to use a single edge from A_1 to A_2 followed by a single edge from B_1 to B_2 in order to reach *end*. The crux is to guarantee that these two edges have corresponding indexes. Since row vertices in different sides are not connected, we add a special vertex that is reachable from all A_2 vertices, leading to another special vertex that is connected to all B_1 vertices, which adds a single edge to E_{cut}.

The key challenge is guaranteeing that we can use the two edges iff they have the same indexes, implying that we need the prefix of the path to exclude exactly such 4 vertices. The second challenge is that there are more row vertices than bit-gadget vertices, so we cannot simply walk back and forth between these two types of vertices without reaching the bit-gadget vertices multiple times.

Our high-level approach for addressing these two issues is as follows (see Figure 2). For each row vertex in $S \in \{A_1, A_2, B_1, B_2\}$ and each of its corresponding $2\log k$ bit-gadget vertices, we plug in a *gadget* of constant size that replaces the bit-gadget vertices altogether. Further, we traverse the gadgets in an order that corresponds to some choice of TRUE and FALSE for each index of row vertices. The latter is what promises that we reach *end* iff we use a single edge from A_1 to A_2 and a single edge from B_1 to B_2 with corresponding indexes. However, since the number of gadget-vertices is proportional to $2\log k$ times the number of row vertices k, we now face an opposite problem: there are more gadget vertices than row vertices, and the latter play a role in multiple gadgets. Moreover, if we chose to traverse the gadgets that correspond to, say, a TRUE choice for some index, we still need to visit the gadget vertices of the FALSE choice and we need to do so without visiting its respective row vertex. The power of the gadget is that it is designed to allow us to choose whether the path *visits* the row vertex of that gadget, or *skips* it and continues to the next gadget. This has two main strengths: First, it nullifies the issue that is caused by having row vertices appear in multiple gadgets. Second, it allows us to traverse all the gadget vertices that do not correspond to the TRUE / FALSE choices that we make. This eventually allows us to obtain our desired claim, that a directed Hamiltonian path exists if and only if $\text{DISJ}_K(x, y) = \text{FALSE}$ for an appropriate K that allows a near-quadratic lower bound.

Additional results: This lower bound extends to Hamiltonian cycle, to the undirected variants, and to minimum 2-edge connected spanning subgraph.

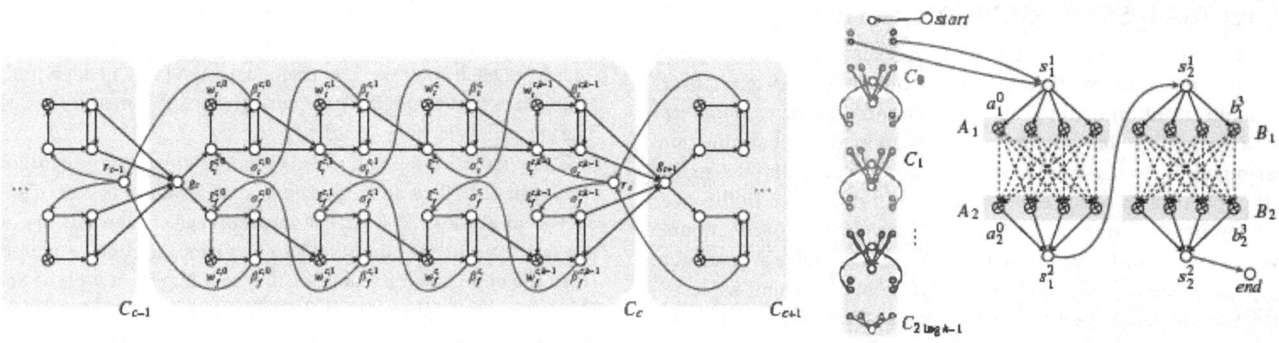

Figure 2: The lower bound construction for Hamiltonian path, with $k = 4$. Left: the internal topology of each box C_i. Right: the connections between the boxes and themselves and to the rest of the graph.

3 LOWER BOUNDS FOR BOUNDED-DEGREE GRAPHS

Here we show that the fundamental problems MaxIS, MVC and MDS remain difficult even in bounded-degree graphs, requiring a near-tight $\tilde{\Omega}(n)$ number of rounds for a family of graphs with constant degree and logarithmic diameter. All the above problems admit efficient constant approximations in bounded-degree graphs, whereas in general graphs currently there are no efficient constant approximations for MaxIS and MDS in the CONGEST model. We show a lower bound for MaxIS, and the other lower bounds are obtained by standard reductions. Let $\alpha(G)$ be the size of a maximum independent set in G. For a CNF formula ϕ, let $f(\phi)$ be the maximum number of clauses that can be satisfied in ϕ. An assignment is *maximal* is it satisfies $f(\phi)$ clauses.

Our construction is based on a series of (non-distributed) reductions between MaxIS and max 2SAT instances. These reductions are applied on a family of lower bound graphs for MaxIS to obtain a new family of lower bound graphs for MaxIS which have bounded degrees. First, we replace our graph G with a CNF formula ϕ, where $f(\phi)$ is determined by $\alpha(G)$. Working with ϕ instead of G allows us to use the power of expander graphs and replace ϕ by a new equivalent CNF formula ϕ' where each variable appears only a constant number of times. Finally, ϕ' is replaced by a bounded-degree graph G' such that $\alpha(G')$ is determined by $\alpha(G)$. The first and last reductions are based on standard ideas, whereas the second one is inspired by [11, 32] and is the main ingredient that allows us eventually to convert our graph to a bounded-degree graph. We next give the high-level approach of the reductions.

The reductions. To convert a graph $G = (V, E)$ to a CNF formula ϕ, we have a variable x_v and a clause x_v for each vertex. Additionally, for each edge $e = \{u, v\}$, we add the clause $(\neg x_u \vee \neg x_v)$. Intuitively, this guarantees that we do not take both u and v to the independent set. The formula ϕ is the conjunction of all the clauses. It is easy to show that a MaxIS, I, gives an assignment that satisfies $\alpha(G) + |E|$ clauses, by setting all the variables x_v for $v \in I$ to TRUE. This satisfies all the edge clauses and exactly $\alpha(G)$ variable clauses, based on which, we have $f(\phi) = \alpha(G) + |E|$.

The second reduction converts ϕ to a formula ϕ', in which each variable appears a constant number of times. Here, we describe the high-level idea of a slightly simpler variant of our reduction. First, replace each variable x_v that appears d_v times in ϕ, by d_v new variables $\{x_v^i\}_{i=1}^{d_v}$, each appearing in exactly one clause. For example, the clause $(\neg x_u \vee \neg x_v) \in \phi$ is replaced by a corresponding clause $(\neg x_u^i \vee \neg x_v^j) \in \phi'$ for some i, j. Currently, each variable really appears in one clause, but there are no dependencies between the different variables $\{x_v^i\}_{i=1}^{d_v}$. To guarantee that all of them receive the same value we add additional clauses using an expander graph. For simplicity, assume that we have a *bounded-degree* graph H with d_v vertices, such that in each cut $(S, \bar{S})$, the number of edges that cross the cut is larger than $\min\{|S|, |\bar{S}|\}$. H is an *expander* graph.[2] We identify each variable from $\{x_v^i\}_{i=1}^{d_v}$ with one vertex in H, and for each edge $\{x_v^i, x_v^j\}$ in H, we add to ϕ' two additional clauses that are equivalent to the condition $x_v^i = x_v^j$. These new clauses are called the *expender clauses.* We do this for each variable, and show that there is always a maximal assignment that gives the same value to all the variables $\{x_v^i\}_{i=1}^{d_v}$. The intuition is that if we have a maximal assignment π that does not satisfy the above, we can look at the cut $(S, \bar{S})$ between variables that receive TRUE and variables that receive FALSE. Assume w.l.o.g that S is the smaller side of the cut. If we change the assignment to the variables in S, we get a new assignment π' where all the expander clauses are satisfied. In particular, for each edge that crosses that cut there is a clause that is satisfied by π' but not by π. In addition, for each variable in S there may be additional clause that was satisfied by π but not by π'. By the expander properties, the number of edges that cross the cut is larger than $\min\{|S|, |\bar{S}|\}$, which shows that the number of satisfied clauses may only increase. Based on these ideas, we show that $f(\phi')$ is determined by $f(\phi)$.

The last reduction from ϕ' to a bounded-degree graph G' is based on standard ideas. Using the above reductions, we show how to convert a family of lower bound graphs for MaxIS from [7] to a family graphs with logarithmic diameter and maximum degree 5, by having Alice and Bob simulate the reductions locally based on their inputs. We then use known reductions to obtain $\tilde{\Omega}(n)$ lower bounds in bounded-degree graphs also for the MVC, MDS and minimum 2-spanner problems.

[2] We use a slightly different graph that allows getting a construction with smaller maximum degree.

4 HARDNESS OF APPROXIMATION

In this section, we show that in some cases it is difficult not only to solve a problem *exactly*, but even to obtain an approximation. The main intuition behind our constructions is that we *enhance the bit-gadget*. The bit-gadget is a key component in obtaining our near-quadratic lower bounds for *exact* computation. However, in all these constructions there is only a slight difference in the size of the optimal solutions according to the disjointness of the inputs. One of the reasons for this is that our row vertices have a vertex for any possible binary representation. Hence, in particular, we have vertices with almost identical binary representations, which limits the potential lower bounds we can show. To overcome this, one approach could be to leave only a subset of the row vertices that satisfy additional suitable properties, for example, a set of vertices in which any two have very different binary representations. Both of our constructions, one for MaxIS and one for k-MDS and additional problems, rely on this idea and develop it.

4.1 MaxIS

Our construction for MaxIS is inspired by the construction from [7], which shows an $\tilde{\Omega}(n^2)$ lower bound for the *exact* case. This construction is similar to our MDS construction, and in particular has the same *row* vertices and *bit-gadget* vertices. A slight difference is that in [7], the bit-gadget vertices are connected by 4-cycles and not by 6-cycles, and in each row the row vertices are connected by a clique. The inputs x, y affect the graph in a way similar to the one in [7]: For all pairs (i, j), we add the edge $\{a_1^i, a_2^j\}$ if and only if $x_{i,j} = 0$, and we add the edge $\{b_1^i, b_2^j\}$ if and only if $y_{i,j} = 0$.

If the inputs are not disjoint, a MaxIS can be obtained by choosing either the 2 TRUE vertices or the 2 FALSE vertices from each cycle and one vertex from each row whose binary representation is the complement of these choices. An obstacle in using this construction to show a hardness of approximation result, is that even if the inputs are disjoint, we can construct a MaxIS with almost the same size by taking 2 vertices from each one of the cycles and only 3 row vertices, instead of 4. To overcome this, we can change the weights of row vertices, to be roughly $\Theta(\log k)$, which motivates taking 4 of them to the MaxIS. However, this is still insufficient, because we may be able to take 4 vertices such that the vertices in the sides of Alice and Bob do not have the *exact same* binary representation, but have *similar* binary representations, so that we can take 2 vertices from *almost* all the cycles and obtain a MaxIS of a similar size.

The code-gadget. We propose a construction in which even the slightest change in the input strings has a large impact on the size of the MaxIS in the graph, while maintaining a small cut in order to obtain the nearly quadratic lower bound. *Error correcting codes*, and more specifically, *Reed-Solomon* (RS) codes allow us to do just that. By representing each of the row vertices with a codeword from a RS code, we make sure that the representations of different row vertices in each row differ significantly. Denoting $t = \log k$, we use a Reed-Solomon code C of length $\ell + t$ and distance $\ell + 1$ over a field of size q, and choose $\ell = \Theta(\log^2 n)$ s.t. ℓ also satisfies $\ell + t + 1 = q$. The idea of the construction is to replace the bit gadget of each set of row vertices $S \in \{A_1, A_2, B_1, B_2\}$ with a new *code gadget* that has $\ell + t$ rows, according to the code length, where each row has q vertices that represent the elements of the field. Each row vertex corresponds to a *codeword*. Now, each row vertex is connected to all the vertices in its appropriate code gadget, apart from the $\ell + t$ (one from each row) vertices that correspond to its codeword. This guarantees that two different row vertices differ in at least ℓ places. The row vertices have weight ℓ.

The correctness proof is based on showing that according to the inputs of Alice and Bob the size of a MaxIS is either at least $8\ell + 4t$ or at most $7\ell + 4t$. The intuition is as follows. If the inputs are not disjoint we can take 4 row vertices and $4(\ell + t)$ vertices from the code gadget which results in a MaxIS of weight $8\ell + 4t$. Otherwise, we either take only 3 row vertices which reduces the size of the MaxIS by ℓ or we take 4 row vertices but not with matching representations in Alice and Bob sides, which results in at least ℓ additional vertices in the code gadget that we cannot add to the MaxIS. Based on this, we show an $\tilde{\Omega}(n^2)$ lower bound for a $(7/8 + \epsilon)$-approximation.

Additional results: To improve the approximation ratio in our hardness result, we show also an $\tilde{\Omega}(n)$ lower bound for a $(5/6 + \epsilon)$-approximation. Additionally, we extend both the hardness results to the *unweighted* case, by replacing each row vertex with an independent set of ℓ vertices.

4.2 2-MDS

The 2-MDS problem requires finding a minimum weight set of vertices, such that each vertex is either in the set or is at distance at most two from it. Our 2-MDS construction uses a collection C of sets $S_1, S_2, \ldots, S_T$ of the universe $U = \{1, \ldots, \ell\}$, with the following property. For any choice of r sets from $S_1, S_2, \ldots, S_T, \overline{S_1}, \overline{S_2}, \ldots, \overline{S_T}$ that does not contains a set S_i and its complement $\overline{S_i}$, there is at least one element in U that is not covered, i.e., does not appear in any of the r sets. We call this property of C the *r-covering property*. Collections with this property can be constructed using the *probabilistic method* and are used [29, 31] to show the inapproximability of set cover in different models. We use different parameters T, ℓ to get different time-approximation tradeoffs. In general, constructions of such sets exist where T is exponential in ℓ, and r is logarithmic in ℓ. In particular, we choose $r = c \log \ell$ for a constant $c < 1$. We next explain how this property is useful for showing a lower bound for 2-MDS.

We have a vertex for each of the sets $S_i, \overline{S_i}$. For each element $j \in U$, we have two vertices a_j and b_j, connected by an edge. Each set S_i is connected to a vertex a_j iff $j \in S_i$. Similarly, the set $\overline{S_i}$ is connected to a vertex b_j iff $j \in \overline{S_i}$, or equivalently iff $j \notin S_i$. The weights of the vertices $S_i, \overline{S_i}$ are determined by inputs x, y, such that their weight is either 1 or $\alpha > r$, if the corresponding input bit is 1 or 0, respectively. All the vertices a_j, b_j have weight α, and there is an additional vertex R of weight 0 at distance 2 from the vertices $S_i, \overline{S_i}$.

Based on the r-covering property of the collection C, the size of a 2-MDS is determined by the inputs of Alice and Bob, as follows. If x, y are not disjoint, there is an index i where both the vertices S_i and $\overline{S_i}$ have weight 1. Since any element $j \in U$ is either in S_i or in $\overline{S_i}$, adding both of these vertices to the 2-MDS, covers all the vertices a_j, b_j. The rest of the vertices are covered by the vertex R of weight 0, which results in a 2-MDS of weight 2. If, however, the inputs are disjoint, from the r-covering property we must

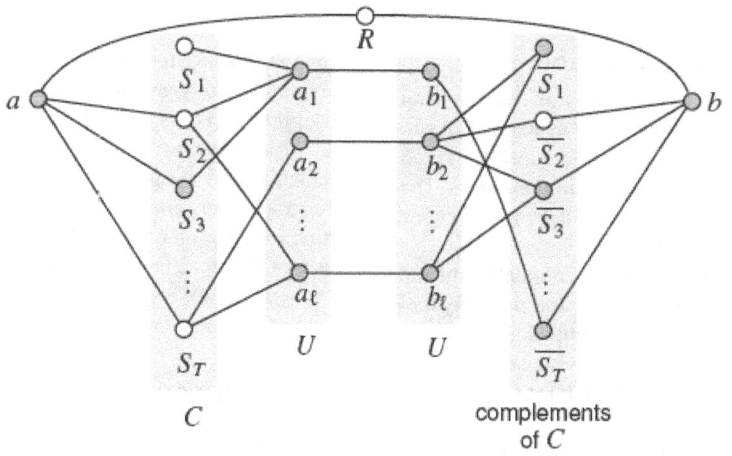

Figure 3: The lower bound construction for 2-MDS. Gray vertices have weight α; the vertices $S_i, \overline{S_i}$ may have weight 1 or α depending on the strings x, y.

add at least r set-vertices of weight 1 to cover all the elements, or add a heavy vertex of weight α to the 2-MDS; in both cases the weight of the resulting 2-MDS is at least $r = c \log \ell$. Choosing different parameters for T, ℓ we show an $\Omega(n^{1-\epsilon} / \log n)$ lower bound for an $O(\epsilon \log n)$-approximation, and an $\widetilde{\Omega}(n)$ lower bound for an $O(\log \log n)$-approximation.

Additional results: Based on this construction we show similar results also for the k-MDS problem for $k \geq 2$, for the directed Steiner tree problem, and for the node weighted Steiner tree problem. We also show a similar result for MDS in a restricted class of algorithms we call *local aggregate* algorithms. The main idea is to replace the sets of vertices $\{a_j\}_{j=1}^{\ell}, \{b_j\}_{j=1}^{\ell}$ by just one set $\{1, ..., \ell\}$. This in turn increases significantly the size of the cut, but since the number of vertices in the new set is small, we show that Alice and Bob can simulate a local aggregate algorithm in this graph by exchanging only $O(\ell \log n)$ bits per round, which allows us to show a lower bound. The new set of vertices is not in any of the sides, but is simulated together by Alice and Bob, based on the facts that all the edges connected to it are known either to Alice or to Bob, and that the algorithm is a local aggregate algorithm. For general algorithms, we show in Section 5 that we cannot use this framework to show lower bound for MDS for any approximation above 2.

5 LIMITATIONS OF THEOREM 1.1

We have seen that Theorem 1.1 is useful in proving many near-quadratic lower bounds, both for exact and for approximate computations. In this section, we show that for some problems, Theorem 1.1 is somewhat limited. These problems include, e.g., maximum matching and max-flow, which are in P. To prove this, we use a known approach for showing limitations, and equip it with new machinery.

5.1 Limitations of approximations

Bounded-degree graphs: In Section 3, we showed that solving *unweighted* MaxIS, MVC and MDS *exactly* in bounded-degree graphs requires $\widetilde{\Omega}(n)$ rounds. A natural question is whether these problems are also difficult to approximate. We do not answer this question, but we prove that the current framework is incapable of showing such lower bounds. Specifically, we show that Theorem 1.1 cannot give a lower bound stronger than $\Omega(1/\epsilon)$ for a $(1+\epsilon)$-approximation. We illustrate the simple proof idea through MVC. Consider a lower bound graph construction w.r.t. a function f and a predicate that implies a $(1 + \epsilon)$-approximation for unweighted MVC. It could be that the number of edges in the cut between Alice and Bob satisfies $|E_{cut}| \leq \epsilon m/2\Delta$. Then, if Alice and Bob solve MVC optimally only on their parts of the graph and then add all the vertices that touch the cut, they get a $(1 + \epsilon)$-approximation. Otherwise, $\epsilon m/2\Delta \leq |E_{cut}|$, hence $m \leq 2\Delta|E_{cut}|/\epsilon$. Note that Alice and Bob can solve the problem optimally by learning all m edges of the graph, which requires exchanging $O(|E_{cut}| \log n/\epsilon)$ bits, since Δ is constant. Hence, in that time they can solve the corresponding communication complexity problem f. Since the lower bound implied by Theorem 1.1 is of the form $\Omega(CC(f)/|E_{cut}| \cdot \log n)$, it implies that we cannot show a lower bound stronger than $\Omega(1/\epsilon)$.

General graphs: Using a similar argument, we show a limitation for *unweighted* max-cut in general graphs. We also provide a result for the weighted case based on [23]. With respect to *weighted* MDS and MaxIS, simple arguments show that we cannot prove any $\Omega(1)$ lower bound for a 2-approximation or a 1/2-approximation, respectively. These are very far from the current best approximations known in the CONGEST model. We show two results for MVC. First, this framework cannot prove any $\Omega(1)$ lower bound for a 3/2-approximation for *weighted* MVC. Second, it cannot prove any $\Omega(n/\epsilon)$ lower bound for a $(1 + \epsilon)$-approximation for *unweighted* MVC. In particular, it cannot show any *super-linear* lower bound for a constant approximation. The first result is obtained by providing a simple protocol: Alice and Bob solve MVC optimally on their sides of the graph and take to the solution the minimum of them, and then the other player adds additional vertices to cover the remaining uncovered edges in its side and in the cut. Since the minimum of the solutions costs at most $OPT/2$, and the additional added edges cost at most OPT, this provides a 3/2-approximation. The proof of the second result is inspired by [3].

5.2 Limitations of exact computation

In this section, we prove limitations of the framework in providing lower bounds for several central problems in P as maximum cardinality matching (MCM), max flow, min (s, t)-cut and weighted (s, t)-distance. We also consider several verification problems. The main tools we introduce are connections to *non-deterministic* complexity, and to *proof labeling schemes* (PLS).

Specifically, we prove that having an efficient nondeterministic protocol that allows Alice and Bob to verify a graph property and an efficient nondeterministic protocol for the complementary property, proves a limitation of this framework in giving certain lower bounds on the communication complexity of deterministically (or randomly) deciding this property.

First, we give a limitation for obtaining a lower bound for Max (s, t)-flow using this framework. If the function that is used is DISJ or EQ then this limitation holds for any super-constant lower bound. For a general function f, even if it has both nondeterministic and co-nondeterministic complexities asymptotically smaller than K, then no lower bound larger than $\sqrt{K}$ can be obtained.

For simplicity, while our full result addresses all functions f, we consider here only lower bounds using $f = \text{DISJ}_K$, for which the nondeterministic communication complexity asymptotically equals its deterministic one. Let P be the predicate of having an (s, t)-flow of size at least k, for some k. Assume a lower bound is proven by a family $\{G_{x,y}\}$ of lower bound graphs w.r.t. f and P, or w.r.t. $\neg f$ and P. We show nondeterministic algorithms that allow Alice and Bob, given their parts in $G_{x,y}$, to verify both claims: The graph $G_{x,y}$ has a flow of size k, and the graph does not have such a flow. In the first protocol, Alice and Bob exchange the flow on the cut edges, while the second protocol describes an (s, t)-cut with capacity smaller than k. In both protocols, the players exchange $O(|E_{cut}| \log n)$ bits. By the definition of a family of lower bound graphs, our protocols imply that Alice and Bob have nondeterministic protocols *both* for f and for $\neg f$, both using $O(|E_{cut}| \log n)$ bits. Since for $f = \text{DISJ}$ it holds that $CC(f)$ equals to the non-deterministic complexity of f or $\neg f$, we have that $CC(f) = O(|E_{cut}| \log n)$. Thus, a lower bound achieved using Theorem 1.1 is $\Omega(CC(f)/|E_{cut}| \cdot \log n)$, which is no larger than a constant.

While for the max-flow problem we construct nondeterministic protocols, for many other problems we can leverage known results about *proof labeling schemes* (PLS) [24]. Roughly speaking, a PLS is a mechanism that nondeterministically assigns small labels to vertices, such that vertices can exchange labels with their neighbors, and then decide if some graph predicate holds. For example, a PLS for the predicate that a graph is bipartite assigns a 0 or 1 label to each vertex, and each vertex verifies that none of its neighbors have the same label as its own. We show that the existence of logarithmic-size PLS for P and for $\neg P$ immediately implies nondeterministic protocols for Alice and Bob for deciding P and $\neg P$ on a family of lower bound graphs, which exchange $O(|E_{cut}| \log n)$ bits. A similar argument as for max-flow then shows that a super-constant lower bound cannot be proven using DISJ, and gives a limit on the possible lower bounds using a general function f.

We use this idea to prove the impossibility of this framework in proving a lower bound for many problems. The first problem is maximum cardinality matching, where we use a PLS from [8] for the non-existence of a matching of a certain size, and give a simple PLS for proving its existence. We then present PLSs for the weighted (s, t)-distance problem.

We then move to a set of verification problems, discussed in [35], which includes, e.g., connectivity of a subgraph, bipartitness of a subgraph, and verifying a given Hamiltonian cycle or a given spanning tree. For all these problems, [35] give tight lower bounds by using DISJ and a family of lower bound graphs with a dynamically-changing cut. We shows that no such lower bounds are attainable using the framework in which the cut is fixed and f is DISJ.

6 DISCUSSION

In this paper, we provide many near-quadratic lower bounds for exact computation, as well as some hardness of approximation results. However, we also show the limitations of these lower bound techniques when it comes to approximations and to exact computation of some central problems in P. For example, while we show a near-quadratic lower bound for a $(7/8 + \epsilon)$ approximation to MaxIS, we show that the same approach cannot say anything about a $1/2$-approximation, although this problem may be much more difficult to approximate. When it comes to exact computation of problems in P, such as maximum matching and max flow, we show that the lower bound techniques are limited, at least if we use reductions from standard problems in communication complexity, such as disjointness or equality. It would be interesting to study whether different techniques or reductions from non-standard communication complexity problems can provide such lower bounds.

It is intriguing to note that apart from the $(1\text{-}\epsilon)$-approximation for max-cut, the other optimization problems addressed in this paper do not admit any non-trivial algorithms that obtain an approximation factor that is NP-hard to obtain in the sequential setting. There is currently no common ground to blame for the big gaps in terms of the approximation factors that one can obtain in the CONGEST model within any sub-quadratic complexity. Understanding this hardness is a major open research direction in this model.

ACKNOWLEDGMENTS

We would like to thank Seri Khoury and Eyal Kushilevitz for many valuable discussions. This project has received funding from the European Union's Horizon 2020 Research And Innovation Program under grant agreement no.755839. Supported in part by the Binational Science Foundation (grant 2015803). Supported in part by the Israel Science Foundation (grant 1696/14). Ami Paz is supported by the Fondation Sciences Mathématiques de Paris (FSMP).

REFERENCES

[1] Amir Abboud, Keren Censor-Hillel, and Seri Khoury. 2016. Near-Linear Lower Bounds for Distributed Distance Computations, Even in Sparse Networks. In *30th International Symposium on Distributed Computing, DISC.* 29–42.

[2] Nir Bachrach, Keren Censor-Hillel, Michal Dory, Yuval Efron, Dean Leitersdorf, and Ami Paz. 2019. Hardness of Distributed Optimization. *CoRR* abs/11905.10284 (2019). arXiv:1905.10284 http://arxiv.org/abs/1905.10284

[3] Ran Ben-Basat, Ken-ichi Kawarabayashi, and Gregory Schwartzman. 2018. Parameterized Distributed Algorithms. *CoRR* abs/1807.04900 (2018). arXiv:1807.04900 http://arxiv.org/abs/1807.04900

[4] Aaron Bernstein and Danupon Nanongkai. 2018. Distributed Exact Weighted All-Pairs Shortest Paths in Near-Linear Time. *CoRR* abs/1811.03337 (2018). arXiv:1811.03337 http://arxiv.org/abs/1811.03337 To appear in STOC 2019.

[5] Ravi B. Boppana, Magnús M. Halldórsson, and Dror Rawitz. 2018. Simple and Local Independent Set Approximation. In *Structural Information and Communication Complexity - 25th International Colloquium, SIROCCO*. 88–101. https://doi.org/10.1007/978-3-030-01325-7_12

[6] Keren Censor-Hillel and Michal Dory. 2018. Distributed Spanner Approximation. In *Proceedings of the 2018 ACM Symposium on Principles of Distributed Computing, PODC*. 139–148. https://doi.org/10.1145/3212734.3212758

[7] Keren Censor-Hillel, Seri Khoury, and Ami Paz. 2017. Quadratic and Near-Quadratic Lower Bounds for the CONGEST Model. In *31st International Symposium on Distributed Computing, DISC*. 10:1–10:16. https://doi.org/10.4230/LIPIcs.DISC.2017.10

[8] Keren Censor-Hillel, Ami Paz, and Mor Perry. 2017. Approximate Proof-Labeling Schemes. In *Structural Information and Communication Complexity - 24th International Colloquium, SIROCCO*. 71–89. https://doi.org/10.1007/978-3-319-72050-0_5

[9] Soumyottam Chatterjee, Reza Fathi, Gopal Pandurangan, and Nguyen Dinh Pham. 2018. Fast and Efficient Distributed Computation of Hamiltonian Cycles in Random Graphs. In *38th IEEE International Conference on Distributed Computing Systems, ICDCS*. 764–774. https://doi.org/10.1109/ICDCS.2018.00079

[10] Artur Czumaj and Christian Konrad. 2018. Detecting Cliques in CONGEST Networks. In *32nd International Symposium on Distributed Computing, DISC*. 16:1–16:15. https://doi.org/10.4230/LIPIcs.DISC.2018.16

[11] Erik Demaine. 2014. Lecture 10 in Algorithmic Lower Bounds. https://ocw.mit.edu/courses/electrical-engineering-and-computer-science/6-890-algorithmic-lower-bounds-fun-with-hardness-proofs-fall-2014/lecture-notes/MIT6_890F14_Lec10.pdf.

[12] Andrew Drucker, Fabian Kuhn, and Rotem Oshman. 2014. On the power of the congested clique model. In *Proceedings of the 33rd ACM Symposium on Principles of Distributed Computing, PODC*. 367–376.

[13] Orr Fischer, Tzlil Gonen, Fabian Kuhn, and Rotem Oshman. 2018. Possibilities and Impossibilities for Distributed Subgraph Detection. In *Proceedings of the 30th on Symposium on Parallelism in Algorithms and Architectures, SPAA*. 153–162. https://doi.org/10.1145/3210377.3210401

[14] Silvio Frischknecht, Stephan Holzer, and Roger Wattenhofer. 2012. Networks cannot compute their diameter in sublinear time. In *23rd Annual ACM-SIAM Symposium on Discrete Algorithms, SODA*. 1150–1162. http://portal.acm.org/citation.cfm?id=2095207&CFID=63838676&CFTOKEN=79617016

[15] Mohsen Ghaffari, Andreas Karrenbauer, Fabian Kuhn, Christoph Lenzen, and Boaz Patt-Shamir. 2018. Near-Optimal Distributed Maximum Flow. *SIAM J. Comput.* 47, 6 (2018), 2078–2117. https://doi.org/10.1137/17M113277X

[16] Mohsen Ghaffari, Fabian Kuhn, and Yannic Maus. 2017. On the complexity of local distributed graph problems. In *49th Annual ACM SIGACT Symposium on Theory of Computing, STOC*. ACM, 784–797.

[17] Mohsen Ghaffari and Jason Li. 2018. New Distributed Algorithms in Almost Mixing Time via Transformations from Parallel Algorithms. In *32nd International Symposium on Distributed Computing, DISC*. 31:1–31:16. https://doi.org/10.4230/LIPIcs.DISC.2018.31

[18] Johan Håstad. 1996. Clique is Hard to Approximate Within $(n^{1-\epsilon})$. In *37th Annual Symposium on Foundations of Computer Science, FOCS*. 627–636. https://doi.org/10.1109/SFCS.1996.548522

[19] Stephan Holzer and Nathan Pinsker. 2015. Approximation of Distances and Shortest Paths in the Broadcast Congest Clique. In *Proceedings of the 19th International Conference on Principles of Distributed Systems, OPODIS*. 6:1–6:16.

[20] Stephan Holzer and Roger Wattenhofer. 2012. Optimal distributed all pairs shortest paths and applications. In *Proceedings of the 2012 ACM symposium on Principles of distributed computing, PODC*. ACM, 355–364.

[21] Lujun Jia, Rajmohan Rajaraman, and Torsten Suel. 2002. An efficient distributed algorithm for constructing small dominating sets. *Distributed Computing* 15, 4 (2002), 193–205.

[22] Richard M. Karp. 2010. Reducibility Among Combinatorial Problems. In *50 Years of Integer Programming 1958-2008 - From the Early Years to the State-of-the-Art*. Springer, 219–241. https://doi.org/10.1007/978-3-540-68279-0_8

[23] Dmitry Kogan and Robert Krauthgamer. 2015. Sketching cuts in graphs and hypergraphs. In *Proceedings of the 2015 Conference on Innovations in Theoretical Computer Science*. ACM, 367–376.

[24] Amos Korman, Shay Kutten, and David Peleg. 2010. Proof labeling schemes. *Distributed Computing* 22, 4 (2010), 215–233. https://doi.org/10.1007/s00446-010-0095-3

[25] Fabian Kuhn, Thomas Moscibroda, and Roger Wattenhofer. 2016. Local Computation: Lower and Upper Bounds. *J. ACM* 63, 2 (2016), 17:1–17:44. https://doi.org/10.1145/2742012

[26] Fabian Kuhn and Roger Wattenhofer. 2005. Constant-time distributed dominating set approximation. *Distributed Computing* 17, 4 (2005), 303–310.

[27] Eyal Kushilevitz and Noam Nisan. 1997. *Communication Complexity*. Cambridge University Press, New York, NY, USA.

[28] Zvi Lotker, Boaz Patt-Shamir, and Seth Pettie. 2015. Improved Distributed Approximate Matching. *J. ACM* 62, 5 (2015), 38:1–38:17.

[29] Carsten Lund and Mihalis Yannakakis. 1994. On the hardness of approximating minimization problems. *Journal of the ACM (JACM)* 41, 5 (1994), 960–981.

[30] Danupon Nanongkai and Hsin-Hao Su. 2014. Almost-Tight Distributed Minimum Cut Algorithms. In *Distributed Computing - 28th International Symposium, DISC*. 439–453. https://doi.org/10.1007/978-3-662-45174-8_30

[31] Noam Nisan. 2002. The communication complexity of approximate set packing and covering. In *International Colloquium on Automata, Languages, and Programming, ICALP*. Springer, 868–875.

[32] Christos H Papadimitriou and Mihalis Yannakakis. 1991. Optimization, approximation, and complexity classes. *Journal of computer and system sciences* 43, 3 (1991), 425–440.

[33] David Peleg. 2000. *Distributed Computing: A Locality-Sensitive Approach*. Society for Industrial and Applied Mathematics.

[34] David Peleg and Vitaly Rubinovich. 2000. A Near-Tight Lower Bound on the Time Complexity of Distributed Minimum-Weight Spanning Tree Construction. *SIAM J. Comput.* 30, 5 (2000), 1427–1442. https://doi.org/10.1137/S0097539700369740

[35] Atish Das Sarma, Stephan Holzer, Liah Kor, Amos Korman, Danupon Nanongkai, Gopal Pandurangan, David Peleg, and Roger Wattenhofer. 2012. Distributed Verification and Hardness of Distributed Approximation. *SIAM J. Comput.* 41, 5 (2012), 1235–1265. https://doi.org/10.1137/11085178X

[36] Volker Turau. 2018. A Distributed Algorithm for Finding Hamiltonian Cycles in Random Graphs in $O(\log n)$ Time. In *Structural Information and Communication Complexity - 25th International Colloquium, SIROCCO*. 72–87. https://doi.org/10.1007/978-3-030-01325-7_11

[37] Vijay V. Vazirani. 2001. *Approximation algorithms*. Springer. http://www.springer.com/computer/theoretical+computer+science/book/978-3-540-65367-7

[38] Mariano Zelke. 2009. *Algorithms for streaming graphs*. Ph.D. Dissertation. Martin Luther University of Halle-Wittenberg, Saxony-Anhalt, Germany. http://edoc.hu-berlin.de/dissertationen/zelke-mariano-2009-02-18/PDF/zelke.pdf

Broadcast Congested Clique: Planted Cliques and Pseudorandom Generators*

Lijie Chen
EECS, MIT
Cambridge, MA
wjmzbmr@gmail.com

Ofer Grossman
EECS, MIT
Cambridge, MA
ofer.grossman@gmail.com

ABSTRACT

We develop techniques to prove lower bounds for the BCAST($\log n$) Broadcast Congested Clique model (a distributed message passing model where in each round, each processor can broadcast an $O(\log n)$-sized message to all other processors). Our techniques are built to prove bounds for natural input distributions. So far, all lower bounds for problems in the model relied on constructing specifically tailored graph families for the specific problem at hand, resulting in lower bounds for artificially constructed inputs, instead of natural input distributions.

One of our results is a lower bound for the directed planted clique problem. In this problem, an input graph is either a random directed graph (each directed edge is included with probability 1/2), or a random graph with a planted clique of size k. That is, k randomly chosen vertices have all of the edges between them included, and all other edges in the graph appear with probability 1/2. The goal is to determine whether a clique exists. We show that when $k = O(n^{1/4-\varepsilon})$, this problem requires a number of rounds polynomial in n.

Additionally, we construct a pseudo-random generator which fools the Broadcast Congested Clique. This allows us to show that every k round randomized algorithm in which each processor uses up to n random bits can be efficiently transformed into an $O(k)$-round randomized algorithm in which each processor uses only up to $O(k \log n)$ random bits, while maintaining a high success probability. The pseudo-random generator is simple to describe, computationally very cheap, and its seed size is optimal up to constant factors. However, the analysis is quite involved, and is based on the new technique for proving lower bounds in the model.

The technique also allows us to prove the first average case lower bound for the Broadcast Congested Clique, as well as an average-case time hierarchy. We hope our technique will lead to more lower bounds for problems such as triangle counting, APSP, MST, diameter, and more, for natural input distributions.

CCS CONCEPTS

• **Theory of computation → Distributed algorithms.**

*The full version of this paper can be found in https://arxiv.org/abs/1905.07780.

PODC '19, July 29-August 2, 2019, Toronto, ON, Canada

ACM ISBN 978-1-4503-6217-7/19/07...$15.00
https://doi.org/10.1145/3293611.3331599

KEYWORDS

broadcast congested clique; multi-party communication complexity; planted clique; pseudo-random generators

ACM Reference Format:

Lijie Chen and Ofer Grossman. 2019. Broadcast Congested Clique: Planted Cliques and Pseudorandom Generators. In *2019 ACM Symposium on Principles of Distributed Computing (PODC '19), July 29-August 2, 2019, Toronto, ON, Canada.* ACM, New York, NY, USA, 8 pages. https://doi.org/10.1145/3293611.3331599

1 INTRODUCTION

Recently there has been a surge of lower bound results in the CONGEST, and Broadcast Congested Clique models ([11, 16, 25, 31] to list a few, though there are many more). In general, these results take the following approach: a specific carefully chosen family of graphs is constructed, and the vertices are partitioned into two parts (or, in some rare cases, three parts), and a reduction from classical two-party communication complexity is used.

A main downside of this approach is that it merely proves worst case lower bounds. For all we know, for more natural input distributions (instead of the artificially constructed graph families used for these communication complexity reductions), many problems which are worst-case hard may become easy. One of our main goals in this paper is to develop techniques that prove lower bounds for more natural input distributions.

The distributed model we consider is the Broadcast Congested Clique model (BCAST(1))[1]. In this model, there are n processors, each with unlimited local computational power. Computation proceeds in rounds, and in each round each processor broadcasts a single bit[2] to all other processors (within a single round, a processor must broadcast the same bit to all other processors).

Our results include a lower bound for the planted clique problem. Additionally, we show how to use our techniques to construct a pseudo-random generator that fools the Broadcast Congested Clique model. This is the first pseudo-random generator which fools a distributed message passing model. As simple corollaries, we obtain an average-case lower bound for the model, and an average-case time hierarchy for the model.

[1]Note that every lower bound for BCAST(1) can be extended to a lower bound for BCAST($\log n$) with only a $\log n$ factor loss in the number of rounds

[2]It is standard to use messages of size $O(\log n)$, but for our purposes it is more natural to consider single-bit messages. All of our results generalize to the setting of logarithmic sized messages.

1.1 Our Approach

How to deal with distributions. Consider the (directed) planted clique problem[3]. In this problem, the input is a directed graph which is either a random graph (each directed edge is included with probability $1/2$), or a random graph where k of the vertices are chosen at random and all edges within this set of k vertices are included (these k vertices are called the planted clique). The goal is to distinguish between these two distributions (or, one can consider the search version of the problem, in which a graph with a planted clique is given, and the goal is to find the clique). For now, one can think of k as approximately $n^{1/4}$.

When trying to prove a lower bound for the problem, one's first approach may be to try reducing to two-party communication complexity: split the vertices into two parts, and argue that a lot of information must pass between the parts. This approach will not work for the problem, since no matter how the graph is split up, at least one of the parts will be able to detect the presence of the clique, since at least one of the parts must have many of the clique's vertices.

One's next approach may be the following: show that for any Congested Clique algorithm, after t rounds, the distribution of transcripts of the Congested Clique algorithm (the "transcript" is the history of the algorithm; that is, the "transcript" is a list of all messages sent so far as well as who sent which message and when the message was sent) if the input were uniform is close to the distribution of transcripts if the input had a planted clique. To prove this, one may take an inductive approach: show that if the transcripts were similar for $t-1$ rounds, the next round can distinguish between the distributions with only low probability. In this round, all vertices are broadcasting, so one may try to use another approach: show that each vertex reveals little information about whether the graph has a planted clique or not, and therefore, the whole round reveals little information about whether there is a clique. This way, we would only need to analyze a single broadcast at a time, a much simpler task than considering a whole round at once.

There is an issue, however. The problem is that the inputs of different nodes may not be independent. Therefore, it is possible that while each processor's broadcast on its own will not reveal substantial information about whether the graph contains a clique, when we consider many processors' broadcasted bits the information revealed may be more than the sum of the information of the individual broadcasts.

To get around this, we instead split the planted clique distributions into a sum of many distributions, such that for each of these distributions, all processors' inputs are independent. Specifically, we can write the planted clique distribution as a sum over all possible cliques C of a random graph with a clique planted at C. Notice that after fixing C, each vertex's input is independent of all other vertices' inputs. Now, when considering whether an algorithm distinguishes between a random graph with a clique at C and a truly random graph, we can consider each node's output on its own, instead of trying to deal with all nodes at the same time. This is one of our main high level ideas: splitting the distribution into many distributions where in each one, different vertices' inputs are independent. This greatly simplifies the analysis by letting us avoid having to deal with many messages at once, and is what makes proving the lower bounds possible.

Statistical Inequalities. The idea of partitioning a distribution into distributions with independent vertex inputs makes proving the lower bounds possible, but there is still lots of technical work to do. Specifically, we now have a bunch of distributions, and we need to show that any algorithm can distinguish only few of those distributions from uniform. At the high level, the idea to do this is to show that for any algorithm, for almost all cliques, when a vertex broadcasts a bit, the probability of that bit being broadcast with the clique vs without the clique is similar. This is basically a problem about Boolean functions: if we let f be the function which takes in the node's input, and outputs what the node will broadcast, we wish to show that for almost all cliques C, when f's input is uniform, the output distribution is similar to the distribution when f's input is chosen with a planted clique at C. The inequalities we show are at the high level similar to this, but many more technical issues arise. For example, since we have to prove a multi-round lower bound, we have to condition on what a node broadcasted in previous rounds, so instead of proving the statistical inequalities for total functions, we instead have to prove the inequalities for functions definitionned on only part of $\{0,1\}^n$. These inequalities are not true for all partial functions, but we manage to prove that they are true for all functions which are definitionned on a large enough subset. So then, there is another challenge of proving that with high probability, after conditioning on a transcript, the set of possible inputs to a node is large.

1.2 Our Results

Lower bounds for the planted clique problem. One of the problems we consider is the (directed) planted clique problem. In this problem, the input is a directed graph which is either a random graph (each directed edge is included with probability $1/2$), or a random graph where k of the vertices are chosen and all edges within this set of k vertices are added. The goal is to distinguish between these two distributions (or, one can consider the search version of the problem, in which a graph with a planted clique is given, and the goal is to find the clique). Because a random graph contains cliques of size $\Theta(\log n)$, the problem makes sense for larger values of k. Once k goes substantially above $\sqrt{n}$, it is possible to find the clique by considering the vertices with highest degree. Hence, the interesting values of k are between approximately $\log n$ and $\sqrt{n}$.

In the classical (non-distributed) setting, the planted clique problem is very well studied. There exists a spectral algorithm solving the problem when $k = O(\sqrt{n})$, and it remains a major open problem in complexity theory to understand whether the problem is hard when k is smaller.

It has been shown that proving lower bounds in the unicast CONGESTED-CLIQUE[4] would imply some strong circuit lower

[3]Note that in the broadcast congested clique model, as opposed to the CONGEST or unicast congested clique model, it is not possible to reduce from directed to undirected in one round.

[4]In the unicast model, in each round each processor can send one bit to each other processor without the requirement that the same bit is broadcast to all other processors; that is, within a single round a processor may choose to send the message "1" to some processors, and "0" to others.

bounds [16], so finding lower bounds for the problem in this setting is quite a challenge. Finding upper bounds for planted clique in the unicast CONGESTED-CLIQUE model is an interesting problem, but it seems difficult - maybe impossible - to improve upon simple sampling-based algorithms for the problem. The next model one can look at is the broadcast CONGESTED-CLIQUE model, which is the model we consider. Specifically, we prove that for cliques of size $O(n^{1/4-\varepsilon})$, the planted clique problem requires polynomially many rounds:

Theorem 1.1 (Planted Clique lower bound). *When $k = n^{1/4-\varepsilon}$ for a constant ε, no $n^{o(1)}$ round BCAST(1) protocol Π can distinguish between $\mathcal{A}_{\text{rand}}$ and $\mathcal{A}_k$ with advantage*[5] $\Omega(1)$.

Pseudo-random generators for distributed computation: Historically, pseudo-random generators were used to fool adversaries modeled as Turing Machines or Circuits. One of our main contributions is constructing the first pseudo-random generator which fools a distributed message passing setting. That is, we show how within the BCAST(1) Congested Clique model, the processors can each sample a small random seed, and end with each processor having a longer string than it started with, such that these longer strings *look random* to the system. That is, no low-round BCAST(1) protocol can distinguish between these pseudo-random strings and truly uniformly random strings within few rounds (except with some low probability). Thus, any algorithm can use a pseudo-random string instead of true randomness, thereby saving random bits.

Pseudo-random generators have been used to derandomize specific problems in message passing models, for example in [39]. Our construction is the first pseudo-random generator which fools *all* low-round algorithms in the BCASTmodel (as opposed to just fooling a specific algorithm).

Definition 1.2 (BCAST(1) pseudo-random generator). A (k, m, n, ℓ) BCAST(1) pseudo-random generator (PRG) is an n-processor BCAST(1) protocol Π such that:

- At the beginning every processor independently gets k private uniform and independent random bits as input.
- After participating in protocol Π, each processor outputs m bits (these bits are not broadcasted: they are the node's pseudo-random bits).
- The joint distribution of all processors' output bits cannot be distinguished (with better than $\frac{1}{n}$ probability[6]) from a truly uniform random distribution by any ℓ round BCAST(1) protocol. Specifically, the statistical distance between the distribution of the protocol's transcript when using a pseudo-random generator and the distribution of the transcript when using true randomness is small.

Theorem 1.3. *For all $m = O(n)$ and $k = \Omega(\log n)$, there exists an $(O(k), m, n, \Theta(k))$ BCAST(1) PRG that can be constructed within $O(k)$ rounds. In particular, the PRG works as follows*

- *Each processor gets $k + k \cdot \frac{(m-k)}{n} = O(k)$ private random bits.*
- *Then in $O\left(\frac{m-k}{n} \cdot k\right) = O(k)$ rounds, all processors broadcast their last $k \cdot \frac{(m-k)}{n}$ random bits. And they use that to construct a random matrix $M \in \{0,1\}^{k \times (m-k)}$.*
- *Each processor's output is simply the concatenation of its first k random bits x and $x^T M$.*

That is, with k random bits per processor as a seed, for every constant c, within $O(k)$ rounds we can turn them into cn pseudo-random bits per processor which require $\Omega(k)$ rounds to be distinguished from random.

So, for example, within $O(\log^2(n))$ round (In the BCAST($\log n$) model, $O(\log n)$ rounds would suffice), one can construct a pseudo-random generator which is indistinguishable from random for any $\log^2 n$-round algorithm, except with low probability (the seed size for each processor would be $O(\log^2 n)$, while the size of the pseudo-random string is $\Theta(n)$).

The PRG is very simple to describe (we describe it here with seed size $2k$): first each processor shares k random bits to create k public random elements from $\mathbb{F}_2^n$ (i.e., k random n-bit vectors). Then, each processor uses its remaining k random bits to pick a random linear combination of those vectors (which requires k bits to sample), and the result of this linear combination is the node's pseudo-random bits. So, essentially the pseudo-random generator is a distribution of low-rank matrices (which is very close to the uniform distribution matrices of rank up to k). Although the description and construction of the PRG are simple, and the seed size is tight up to a constant factor, the analysis is quite technical and involves new techniques. We remark that the pseudo-random generator has the additional nice property that it is computationally cheap; the only operations done by the processors is computing dot products of vectors over $\mathbb{F}_2$.

Efficiently saving random bits. It is possible to show that in the broadcast congested clique there is a randomized-deterministic separation (by reductions from two-player communication complexity for equality). That is, there are certain problems with faster randomized algorithms than the best possible deterministic algorithms. So, there is no hope for a general derandomization theorem. However, one can ask: in general, what is the fewest number of random bits needed to efficiently solve problems in the Broadcast Congested Clique model? Using a technique of Newman [38] from communication complexity, it is possible to show that for any protocol with output size k per processor, $O(k)$ random bits per processor is enough (see the full version of this paper). The main downside of Newman's technique is that it is computationally inefficient: it holds in the case where all the processors have unbounded computational power, and is not a practical tool for saving random bits.

In this work, we ask the following question: In the Broadcast Congested Clique with *computationally bounded (polynomial time)* processors, how many random bits are needed to perform general randomized computation? We can use our pseudo-random generator to show that every k-round algorithm where $k = \Omega(\log n)$ in which every processor uses up to $O(n)$ random bits can be transformed into an $O(k)$-round algorithm in which every processor uses up to k random bits (that is, we can show that each processor needs to use at most 1 random bit per round, while only increasing

[5] An algorithm distinguishing between two distributions D_1 and D_2 with advantage ε is an algorithm A which, when given a random sample s which with probability 1/2 is drawn from D_1 and probability 1/2 is drawn from D_2, then A can successfully guess from which distribution s was drawn with probability $1/2 + \varepsilon$.

[6] All of our constructions in the paper can achieve arbitrarily low inverse polynomial probability.

the run-time by a constant factor). Furthermore, this transformation is efficient. That is, if in the original algorithm all processors work in polynomial time, they also work in polynomial time in the new algorithm (in fact, there is only an *additive* overhead of $O(kn)$ computation time for each processor. This overhead is the time required to compute the pseudo-random bits from the seed).

Stated in the setting of BCAST($\log n$), where messages are of size $O(\log n)$ instead of 1, we show that every k round randomized algorithm using up to n random bits per processor can be transformed into an $O(k)$ round algorithm using up to $O(k \log n)$ random bits per processor.

First BCAST(1) Average Case Lower Bound and Hierarchy: As a simple corollary of our PRG construction, we prove a BCAST(1) average case lower bound, which is the first average case lower bound proven in the model. Specifically, we show that when each processor receives a row of a sample from a certain close-to-uniform distribution of $n \times n$ matrices of rank $n-1$, this cannot be distinguished from each processor receiving n uniformly random bits. We show that this implies that determining whether an input has rank n or not is hard (it takes $\Omega(n)$ rounds), even when the input is chosen uniformly at random:

THEOREM 1.4. *Let n be a large enough integer and $F_{\text{full-rank}} : \{0,1\}^{n\times n} \to \{0,1\}$ be the indicator function which indicates whether the given matrix has full rank. Suppose there are n processors, and the i-th processor is given the i-th row of the input matrix. For all $n/20$-round BCAST(1) protocols and all processors i in it, i cannot compute F correctly with probability better than 0.99 when the input is a uniformly chosen random matrix from $\{0,1\}^{n\times n}$.*

We also obtain an average-case time hierarchy theorem for the model:

THEOREM 1.5. *For any $\omega(\log n) \le k \le n$, there is a function F such that a k-round BCAST(1) protocol can compute exactly, while any $k/20$-round BCAST(1) protocols cannot compute F correctly with probability 0.99 over the uniform distribution.*

1.3 Toy Example: One Round Lower Bound for Planted Clique

As a toy example to illustrate our proof framework, in the following we prove that the planted clique problem is hard for one-round BCAST(1) protocols when $k = o(n^{1/4})$. We begin with some notations.

Notations. Let $\mathcal{U}_m$ denote the uniform distribution on $\{0,1\}^m$. For a function $f : \{0,1\}^* \to \{0,1\}^*$ and a distribution $\mathcal{D}$ on $\{0,1\}^*$, we use $f(\mathcal{D})$ to denote the distribution of the output of f when the input is drawn from $\mathcal{D}$. For two distributions $\mathcal{D}_1$ and $\mathcal{D}_2$, we use $\|\mathcal{D}_1 - \mathcal{D}_2\| = \frac{1}{2}\sum_{x\in\{0,1\}^*} |\mathcal{D}_1(x) - \mathcal{D}_2(x)|$ to denote their statistical distance (where $\mathcal{D}(x)$ is the probability that a sample from $\mathcal{D}$ equals x).

Let $\mathcal{A}^n_{\text{rand}}$ be the distribution on $\{0,1\}^{n\times n}$ such that for a sample A from $\mathcal{A}^n_{\text{rand}}$, for all $i \ne j$, $A_{i,j}$ is an independent uniform random bit in $\{0,1\}$, and $A_{i,i}$ is always 0 for all i. Let C be a subset of $[n]$. We use $\mathcal{A}^n_C$ to denote the conditional distribution of $\mathcal{A}^n_{\text{rand}}$ on the event that for all $i,j \in C$ and $i \ne j$, $A_{i,j} = 1$ (that is, C is a clique). We also use $\mathcal{A}^n_k$ to be the mixed distribution of $\mathcal{A}^n_C$'s when C is a uniform random subset of $[n]$ of size k. When the meaning is clear, we often drop the superscripts of the aforementioned distributions for simplicity.

So, to summarize, $\mathcal{A}^n_{\text{rand}}$ is the uniform distribution over a random directed graph, $\mathcal{A}^n_C$ is the distribution where the vertices of C are in a clique, and the rest of the edges are uniformly random, and $\mathcal{A}^n_k$ is the distribution where a random k vertices are chosen to be a clique, and the rest of the edges are chosen uniformly at random.

By Yao's principle [41], we can assume all processors are deterministic as we are trying to prove a lower bound for distinguishing two input distributions. Processor i can then be definitionned by a function $f_i : \{0,1\}^n \times \{0,1\}^* \to \{0,1\}$, such that $f_i(z,p)$ is the bit that processor i outputs when it gets the input z and transcript p.[7] We use $f_i^{|p}$ to denote the function $f_i(\cdot,p)$ for simplicity. If transcript p is incompatible with processor i having input z, then we set $f_i(z,p)$ arbitrarily.

Given a BCAST(1) protocol Π and an input distribution $\mathcal{D}$, we use $\mathcal{P}(\Pi,\mathcal{D})$ to denote the distribution of the transcripts of the protocol Π running on a input drawn from $\mathcal{D}$ (that is, given a matrix A which is drawn from the distribution $\mathcal{D}$, the processor i gets the i-th row of A, and all processors act according to the protocol Π).

In this section we prove the following theorem.

THEOREM 1.6. *Let n be the number of processors and k be an integer. For any one round BCAST(1) protocol Π, we have*

$$\|\mathcal{P}(\Pi,\mathcal{A}_{\text{rand}}) - \mathcal{P}(\Pi,\mathcal{A}_k)\| \le O\left(\frac{k^2}{\sqrt{n}}\right).$$

That is, for any one-round protocol, the distribution of transcripts when run on a uniformly random input is statistically close to the distribution on an input with a planted clique. As a simple corollary, we immediately have:

COROLLARY 1.7. *When $k = o(n^{1/4})$, no one-round BCAST(1) protocol Π can distinguish between $\mathcal{A}_{\text{rand}}$ and $\mathcal{A}_k$ with advantage $\Omega(1)$ (that is, any protocol which accepts on $\mathcal{A}_{\text{rand}}$ with probability p, must accept on $\mathcal{A}_k$ with probability $p \pm o(1)$).*

That is, there is no way to solve the planted clique problem for cliques of size $o(n^{1/4})$ within one round of the Broadcast Congested Clique.

Let $\mathcal{S}^T_k$ be the uniform distribution on all size-k subsets of T. To prove Theorem 1.6, we need the following technical lemma, whose proof is deferred to the end of this section. In this lemma $f(x)$ represents the bit broadcasted by a processor, and x represents the input to the processor. The lemma states that when picking a random clique C of size k, then any function f behaves similarly when the input is sampled from the uniform distribution vs. when the input is sampled from the uniform distribution with a clique planted on C. Basically, this means that for almost all possible cliques, f does not substantially help distinguish between the clique existing, or the input being uniform.

[7] In a zero-round protocol, the processor's f_i does not take in an input p, since there is no transcript yet, just an input. However, in our proof, we assume that the processors broadcast their messages sequentially (that is, first the first processor speaks, then the second, and so on). In this stronger model, all but one of the processors do see a transcript before they broadcast their first bit.

Lemma 1.8. *Let n, k be integers such that $k \le n^{1/4}$, and $\mathcal{U}_n^C$ be the uniform distribution on $\{x : x \in \{0,1\}^n, x_i = 1 \text{ for all } i \in C\}$. For all function $f : \{0,1\}^n \to \{0,1\}$, we have*

$$\mathop{\mathbb{E}}_{C\sim S_k^{[n]}} \left\| f(\mathcal{U}_n) - f(\mathcal{U}_n^C) \right\| \le O\left(\frac{k}{\sqrt{n}}\right).$$

We also need the following lemma to bound the increase of the statistical distance when a processor speaks.

Lemma 1.9. *Let X and Y be two sets, $\mathcal{D}$ and $\mathcal{D}'$ be two distributions on $X \times Y$. Let $\mathcal{D}_{|X}$ and $\mathcal{D}'_{|X}$ be the respective marginal distribution of $\mathcal{D}$ and $\mathcal{D}'$ on set X. For $a \in X$, we use $\mathcal{D}_{X=a}$ and $\mathcal{D}'_{X=a}$ to denote the respective conditional distribution of $\mathcal{D}$ and $\mathcal{D}'$ on Y conditioning on $X = a$.*[8] *We have*

$$\|\mathcal{D} - \mathcal{D}'\| \le \|\mathcal{D}_{|X} - \mathcal{D}'_{|X}\| + \mathop{\mathbb{E}}_{a\sim\mathcal{D}_{|X}} \|\mathcal{D}_{X=a} - \mathcal{D}'_{X=a}\|.$$

Proof. We first define an auxiliary distribution $\mathcal{D}_{\text{aux}}$ as follows: for $(a, b) \in X \times Y$, if $\mathcal{D}'_{|X}(a) > 0$, (we use $\mathcal{D}'_{|X}(a)$ to denote the probability that a sample from $\mathcal{D}'_{|X}$ equal a).

$$\mathcal{D}^{\text{aux}}(a, b) := \mathcal{D}'(a, b) \cdot \frac{\mathcal{D}_{|X}(a)}{\mathcal{D}'_{|X}(a)}.$$

Otherwise, we set $\mathcal{D}^{\text{aux}}(a, b) := \frac{1}{|Y|} \cdot \mathcal{D}_{|X}(a)$. It is easy to verify that $\mathcal{D}^{\text{aux}}_{|X} = \mathcal{D}_{|X}$ and for all a $\mathcal{D}^{\text{aux}}_{X=a} = \mathcal{D}'_{X=a}$, and therefore it is a distribution.

Now, it is easy to see that

$$\|\mathcal{D}^{\text{aux}} - \mathcal{D}'\| = \|\mathcal{D}_{|X} - \mathcal{D}'_{|X}\|.$$

Moreover, we have

$$\|\mathcal{D}^{\text{aux}} - \mathcal{D}\| = \mathop{\mathbb{E}}_{a\sim\mathcal{D}_{|X}} \|\mathcal{D}_{X=a} - \mathcal{D}'_{X=a}\|.$$

Putting everything together, we have

$$\begin{aligned}\|\mathcal{D} - \mathcal{D}'\| &\le \|\mathcal{D}^{\text{aux}} - \mathcal{D}'\| + \|\mathcal{D}^{\text{aux}} - \mathcal{D}\|. \\ &\le \|\mathcal{D}_{|X} - \mathcal{D}'_{|X}\| + \mathop{\mathbb{E}}_{a\sim\mathcal{D}_{|X}} \|\mathcal{D}_{X=a} - \mathcal{D}'_{X=a}\|.\end{aligned}$$

□

Now we are ready to prove Theorem 1.6.

Proof of Theorem 1.6. Instead of viewing the algorithm as a single round algorithm, we will prove a slightly stronger lower bound. Consider the model where we have n turns. On the tth turn, processor t gets to send a single bit. This model is stronger than one round of the BCAST(1) model, since it allows the later processors to condition their outputs on earlier the processors' messages. Hence, our lower bound implies a lower bound for the BCAST(1) model as well.

Let $\mathcal{P}^{(t)}_{\text{rand}}$ and $\mathcal{P}^{(t)}_C$ be the distributions of the transcript of the first t turns when the input is drawn from $\mathcal{A}_{\text{rand}}$ or $\mathcal{A}_C$, respectively. Note that to prove the theorem, it suffices to show that $\mathcal{P}^{(n)}_{\text{rand}}$ is close to most $\mathcal{P}^{(n)}_C$. For this purpose, we are going to prove the following inequality holds for any $t \le n$:

$$\mathop{\mathbb{E}}_{C\sim S_k^{[n]}} \left\| \mathcal{P}^{(t)}_{\text{rand}} - \mathcal{P}^{(t)}_C \right\| \le t \cdot c_1 \cdot \frac{k^2}{n} \cdot \frac{1}{\sqrt{n}}, \tag{1}$$

where c_1 is a large enough universal constant. This inequality states that when picking a clique at random, the distribution of transcripts is similar to the distribution of transcripts when the input is chosen uniformly at random. It is easy to see that plugging in $t = n$, (1) implies the theorem.

We prove the inequality above inductively. Clearly, (1) holds when $t = 0$. So it suffices to show that when it holds for $t - 1$, it also holds for t.

Let $\mathcal{D}_t$ and $\mathcal{D}^C_t$ be the input distributions to processor t in $\mathcal{A}_{\text{rand}}$ and $\mathcal{A}_C$, respectively. For a fixed $C \subsetneq [n]$, by Lemma 1.9, we have:

$$\left\| \mathcal{P}^{(t)}_{\text{rand}} - \mathcal{P}^{(t)}_C \right\| \le \left\| \mathcal{P}^{(t-1)}_{\text{rand}} - \mathcal{P}^{(t-1)}_C \right\| + \mathop{\mathbb{E}}_{p\sim\mathcal{P}^{(t-1)}_{\text{rand}}} \left\| f_t^{|p}(\mathcal{D}_t) - f_t^{|p}(\mathcal{D}^C_t) \right\|. \tag{2}$$

We think of $\|\mathcal{P}^{(t)}_{\text{rand}} - \mathcal{P}^{(t)}_C\|$ as the amount of evidence the transcript is giving us about whether the distribution is uniform or if it has C as a clique. (If this value were 0, that would mean the transcript gives us no evidence. If the value were 1, that would mean we have "full" evidence and could distinguish between the two with no error given the transcript). So, with this interpretation, the inequality above is basically stating that the amount of evidence we have after round t is the sum of the evidence from all rounds up to $t - 1$, plus the extra evidence we get from the broadcast of the processor in round t.

By definitionnition, $\mathcal{D}_t$ is the uniform distribution on the set $\{x : x \in \{0,1\}^n, x_t = 0\}$. And $\mathcal{D}^C_t = \mathcal{D}_t$ if $t \notin C$, and is the uniform distribution on the set $\{x : x \in \{0,1\}^n, x_t = 0, x_j = 1 \text{ for all } j \in C \setminus \{t\}\}$ otherwise.

We care not about the probability of distinguishing a particular clique existing, but about whether any clique exists, so we take the expected value over all possible cliques of both sides of (2) gives:

$$\begin{aligned}&\mathop{\mathbb{E}}_{C\sim S_k^{[n]}} \left\| \mathcal{P}^{(t)}_{\text{rand}} - \mathcal{P}^{(t)}_C \right\| \\ &\le \mathop{\mathbb{E}}_{C\sim S_k^{[n]}} \left\| \mathcal{P}^{(t-1)}_{\text{rand}} - \mathcal{P}^{(t-1)}_C \right\| + \mathop{\mathbb{E}}_{p\sim\mathcal{P}^{(t-1)}_{\text{rand}}} \mathop{\mathbb{E}}_{C\sim S_k^{[n]}} \left\| f_t^{|p}(\mathcal{D}_t) - f_t^{|p}(\mathcal{D}^C_t) \right\|\end{aligned} \tag{3}$$

We can bound $\mathbb{E}_{C\sim S_k^{[n]}} \left\| \mathcal{P}^{(t-1)}_{\text{rand}} - \mathcal{P}^{(t-1)}_C \right\|$ by the inductive hypothesis, so it suffices to bound $\mathbb{E}_{p\sim\mathcal{P}^{(t-1)}_{\text{rand}}} \mathbb{E}_{C\sim S_k^{[n]}} \left\| f_t^{|p}(\mathcal{D}_t) - f_t^{|p}(\mathcal{D}^C_t) \right\|$. For $p \sim \mathcal{P}^{(t-1)}_{\text{rand}}$, there are two cases:

- When $t \notin C$, which happens with probability $1 - \frac{k}{n}$, we have

  $$\left\| f_t^{|p}(\mathcal{D}_t) - f_t^{|p}(\mathcal{D}^C_t) \right\| = 0,$$

  as $\mathcal{D}^C_t = \mathcal{D}_t$. That is, since t is not in C, what t says gives us no information about whether C is a clique (whether there is a clique or not does not affect the input of t, and therefore does not affect their message).

[8]For simplicity, we let $\mathcal{D}_{X=a}$ be the uniform distribution on Y if $\Pr_{(x,y)\sim\mathcal{D}}[x = a] = 0$.

- When $t \in C$, which happens with probability $\frac{k}{n}$, by Lemma 1.8, we have

$$\mathop{\mathbb{E}}_{C' \sim \mathcal{S}_{k-1}^{[n]\setminus\{t\}}} \left\| f_t^{|P}(\mathcal{D}_t) - f_t^{|P}(\mathcal{D}_t^{C'\cup\{t\}}) \right\| \le O\left(\frac{k}{\sqrt{n}}\right).$$

That is, when t is in C, while t might give information about whether C is a clique, there are many cliques that may include t, and the inequality states that t cannot give too much information about many of cliques (the expected amount of information revealed about a randomly chosen clique of size k containing t is bounded by $O\left(\frac{k}{\sqrt{n}}\right)$).

So, now we have bounded how much evidence the t-th processor reveals when broadcasting. We know that when the clique is chosen randomly, with probability $1 - k/n$ no information is revealed, and with probability k/n at most $O(k/\sqrt{n})$ information is revealed in expectation. Combining these facts gives:

$$\mathop{\mathbb{E}}_{p \sim \mathcal{P}_{\text{rand}}^{(t-1)}} \mathop{\mathbb{E}}_{C \sim \mathcal{S}_k} \left\| f_t^{|P}(\mathcal{D}_t) - f_t^{|P}(\mathcal{D}_t^C) \right\| \le \frac{k}{n} \cdot O\left(\frac{k}{\sqrt{n}}\right),$$

which, plugging into (3) and using the inductive hypothesis proves inequality (1) for t. □

1.3.1 Proof of Lemma 1.8. We need the following lemma first, whose proof is based on tools from information theory, and is deferred to the end of this subsection.

Lemma 1.10. *Let n be an integer, and $\mathcal{U}_n^{[i]}$ be the uniform distribution on $\{x : x \in \{0,1\}^n, x_i = 1\}$. For all function $f : \{0,1\}^n \to \{0,1\}$, we have*

$$\mathop{\mathbb{E}}_{i \leftarrow [n]} \left\| f(\mathcal{U}) - f(\mathcal{U}^{[i]}) \right\| \le O\left(\frac{1}{\sqrt{n}}\right).$$

That is, if we consider a function f, suppose that on a uniform distribution, the probability it outputs 1 is p. Then, if we pick a random index and set it to 1, we still expect that if we randomly pick the rest of the coordinates, the output will be 1 with probability approximately p.

Now we are ready to prove Lemma 1.8 (restated below).

Reminder of Lemma 1.8 *Let n, k be integers such that $k \le n^{1/4}$, and $\mathcal{U}_n^C$ be the uniform distribution on $\{x : x \in \{0,1\}^n, x_i = 1 \text{ for all } i \in C\}$. For all function $f : \{0,1\}^n \to \{0,1\}$, we have*

$$\mathop{\mathbb{E}}_{C \sim \mathcal{S}_k^{[n]}} \left\| f(\mathcal{U}_n) - f(\mathcal{U}_n^C) \right\| \le O\left(\frac{k}{\sqrt{n}}\right).$$

The idea of the proof is that each bit we set to 1, by Lemma 1.10, will change the expected output of f by $O\left(\frac{1}{\sqrt{n}}\right)$. Hence, if we set k of those bits to 1, that will change the expected outcome by $O\left(\frac{1}{\sqrt{n}}\right)$ at most k times, for a total of $O\left(\frac{k}{\sqrt{n}}\right)$. A formal proof is included below:

Proof of Lemma 1.8. Instead of choosing C from $\mathcal{S}_k^{[n]}$, we choose an ordered k-tuple of $a = (a_1, a_2, \ldots, a_k)$ of k distinct elements in $[n]$ uniformly at random. Let the distribution be $\mathcal{T}_k^{[n]}$.

We have

$$\mathop{\mathbb{E}}_{C \sim \mathcal{S}_k^{[n]}} \left\| f(\mathcal{U}_n) - f(\mathcal{U}_n^C) \right\| \tag{4}$$

$$= \mathop{\mathbb{E}}_{a \sim \mathcal{T}_k^{[n]}} \left\| f(\mathcal{U}_n) - f(\mathcal{U}_n^{\{a_i\}_{i=1}^k}) \right\|$$

$$\le \sum_{\ell=1}^{k} \mathop{\mathbb{E}}_{a \sim \mathcal{T}_\ell^{[n]}} \left\| f(\mathcal{U}_n^{\{a_i\}_{i=1}^{\ell-1}}) - f(\mathcal{U}_n^{\{a_i\}_{i=1}^{\ell}}) \right\|$$

$$\le \sum_{\ell=0}^{k-1} \mathop{\mathbb{E}}_{a \sim \mathcal{T}_\ell^{[n]}} \mathop{\mathbb{E}}_{j \leftarrow [n] \setminus \{a_i\}_{i=1}^{\ell}} \left\| f(\mathcal{U}_n^{\{a_i\}_{i=1}^{\ell}}) - f(\mathcal{U}_n^{\{a_i\}_{i=1}^{\ell} \cup \{j\}}) \right\|. \tag{5}$$

Now we are to bound the right side of (5) for each $0 \le \ell \le k-1$ separately. Applying Lemma 1.10 on the restriction of f such that all bits in $\{a_i\}$ are set to 1, we have

$$\mathop{\mathbb{E}}_{j \leftarrow [n] \setminus \{a_i\}_{i=1}^{\ell}} \left\| f(\mathcal{U}_n^{\{a_i\}_{i=1}^{\ell}}) - f(\mathcal{U}_n^{\{a_i\}_{i=1}^{\ell} \cup \{j\}}) \right\| \le O\left(\frac{1}{\sqrt{n-\ell}}\right).$$

Plugging the above in (5) and noting that $k \le n^{1/4}$ completes the proof. □

The proof of Lemma 1.10 makes use several tools from information theory, we first introduce them here.

Preliminaries on Information Theory. Let X, Y be random variables in the same probability space Ω. The entropy of X, denoted by $H(X)$, is defined as $H(X) := \Pr_{a \sim X} \log \frac{1}{\Pr[X=a]}$. The conditional entropy of X given Y, denoted as $H(X|Y)$, is defined as $H(X|Y) := \mathbb{E}_{y \sim Y} H(X|Y=y)$.

The mutual information between X and Y, denoted by $I(X;Y)$, is defined as $I(X;Y) := H(X) - H(X|Y) = H(Y) - H(Y|X) = H(X) + H(Y) - H(X,Y)$.

For two distributions $\mathcal{P}$ and $\mathcal{Q}$ on the same set S, their Kullback-Leibler (KL) divergence is defined as

$$D(\mathcal{P}||\mathcal{Q}) := \sum_{s \in S} \mathcal{P}(s) \cdot \log \frac{\mathcal{P}(s)}{\mathcal{Q}(s)}.$$

KL divergence is related to mutual information in the following way.

Fact 1.

$$I(X;Y) := \mathop{\mathbb{E}}_{x \sim X} D(Y|X = x||Y),$$

Lemma 1.11 (Pinsker's Inequality). *For two distributions $\mathcal{D}_1$ and $\mathcal{D}_2$, we have*

$$\|\mathcal{D}_1 - \mathcal{D}_2\| \le \sqrt{\frac{1}{2} \cdot D(\mathcal{D}_1||\mathcal{D}_2)}.$$

Now we are ready to prove Lemma 1.10.

Proof of Lemma 1.10. Throughout the proof we will assume X is a random variable drawn uniformly from $\{0,1\}^n$. For $i \in [n]$, let X_i be the random variable of the i-th bit of X.

We have

$$I(X_i; f(X)) = H(X_i) - H(X_i|f(X)) = 1 - H(X_i|f(X)).$$

And by the sub-additivity of conditional entropy, we have

$$\sum_{i=1}^{n} H(X_i | f(X)) \geq H(X | f(X)) \geq n - 1.$$

Therefore,

$$\sum_{i=1}^{n} I(X_i; f(X)) \leq n - (n-1) \leq 1.$$

or equivalently,

$$\mathop{\mathbb{E}}_{i \leftarrow [n]} I(X_i; f(X)) \leq \frac{1}{n}.$$

Note that by Fact 1,

$$I(X_i; f(X)) := \mathop{\mathbb{E}}_{x \sim X_i} D(f(X)_{X_i = x} || f(X)).$$

Taking expected values over i of both sides and using

$$\mathop{\mathbb{E}}_{i \leftarrow [n]} I(X_i; f(X)) \leq \frac{1}{n}$$

gives

$$\mathop{\mathbb{E}}_{i \leftarrow [n]} I(X_i; f(X)) = \mathop{\mathbb{E}}_{i \leftarrow [n]} \mathop{\mathbb{E}}_{x \sim X_i} D(f(X)_{X_i = x} || f(X)) \leq \frac{1}{n}.$$

By Pinsker's inequality (Lemma 1.11) and the fact that $\sqrt{x}$ is a concave function, we have

$$\mathop{\mathbb{E}}_{i \leftarrow [n]} \mathop{\mathbb{E}}_{x \sim X_i} || f(X)_{X_i = x} - f(X) || \leq \sqrt{\frac{1}{n}},$$

and

$$\mathop{\mathbb{E}}_{i \leftarrow [n]} \frac{1}{2} \cdot || f(X)_{X_i = 1} - f(X) || \leq \sqrt{\frac{1}{n}}.$$

Note that by definitionnition, $f(X)_{X_i = 1}$ is distributed identically to $f(\mathcal{U}^{[i]})$, which completes the proof. □

1.4 Related Work

BCAST(1) Congested Clique: The specific distributed model we investigate is the Broadcast Congested Clique. In this model, there are n processors, and computation proceeds in rounds. In each round, each processor broadcasts a short message to all other processors. It has recently been studied in [3, 4, 8, 9, 12, 16, 21, 24, 25, 29, 30, 35, 37], among others. It has been used to study other areas in computer science such as streaming algorithms [1] and mechanism design [15].

Complexity Theoretic approaches in Distributed Computing: Recently, more complexity theoretic approaches and results have been made in the congested clique and distributed computation in general, for example in [10, 20, 23, 32].

Pseudo-randomness and Distributed Computing: In [5], the authors construct a pseudo-random generator which creates additional shared random bits in a distributed system. Specifically, the authors work in a setting where every pair of processors can privately communicate with each other (whereas we work in the broadcast model), and some of the processors may be adversarially faulty. They show how to use few shared random bits, and unlimited private random bits to efficiently compute more shared random bits. In our setting, we are saving on private random bits flipped (when all processors are non-faulty, it is easy to turn a private random bit into a public random bit – simply broadcast it).

In [27], the authors construct pseudo-randomness for a different distributed system, in which the network has a topology. Their main application is constructing pseudo-randomness that fools all low-space computation.

In [36], a different setting than ours is considered, in which the processors are computationally bounded, and a cryptographic pseudo-random function is being evaluated.

In [39], a pseudo-random generator that fools DNFs is used to deterministically construct spanners in the congested clique. In that work, the pseudo-random generator is used for the specific problem considered, as opposed to being a pseudo-random generator which fools all algorithms in the model.

Pseudo-randomness in the context of complexity theory has been very widely studied. See Vadhan's survey [40].

In [22], the authors introduce general methods for derandomizing algorithms in the LOCAL model to obtain better deterministic algorithms.

Planted Clique: The planted clique problem (or hidden clique problem) was introduced in [28] and [33]. The best known classical algorithm [13, 17] can find the hidden clique when its size is $k = \Omega(\sqrt{n})$ in near linear-time. For $k \ll \sqrt{n}$, the naïve algorithm (looking for a clique of size $10 \log n$ with brute force, and then extending that clique to the whole clique) can solve it in $n^{O(\log n)}$ time, and the problem is conjectured to be not solvable in polynomial time. However, since it is an average-case problem, it is unlikely that the hardness of this problem can be derived from standard complexity assumptions such as $\mathsf{P} \neq \mathsf{NP}$ [6, 19]. Therefore, much work has been put into trying to show limitations for certain classes of algorithm on this problem [2, 14, 18, 26, 34], or showing tight hardness for closely-related worst-case problems under standard assumptions [7].

Distributed Clique lower bounds: There is some literature on lower bounds for finding cliques in the congested clique model [16], as well as the standard CONGEST model [11]. These lower bounds hold in the worst case, and have no direct implications about the hardness of the planted clique problem.

ACKNOWLEDGMENTS

The first author is supported by NSF CCF-1741615. The second author is supported by the Fannie and John Hertz Foundation Fellowship, an NSF Graduate Research Fellowship, NSF CNS-1413920, DARPA 491512803, Sloan 996698, and MIT/IBM W1771646. This work was done in part while the authors were visiting the Simons Institute for the Theory of Computing.

We would like to thank Shafi Goldwasser, Yang Liu, and Merav Parter for helpful discussions. Many thanks to Sidhanth Mohanty for very fruitful discussions about the planted clique problem.

Thanks to anonymous reviewers for many useful comments.

REFERENCES

[1] Noga Alon, Yossi Matias, and Mario Szegedy. 1999. The Space Complexity of Approximating the Frequency Moments. *J. Comput. Syst. Sci.* 58, 1 (1999), 137–147. https://doi.org/10.1006/jcss.1997.1545

[2] Boaz Barak, Samuel B. Hopkins, Jonathan A. Kelner, Pravesh Kothari, Ankur Moitra, and Aaron Potechin. 2016. A Nearly Tight Sum-of-Squares Lower Bound for the Planted Clique Problem. In *IEEE 57th Annual Symposium on Foundations*

of Computer Science, FOCS 2016, 9-11 October 2016, Hyatt Regency, New Brunswick, New Jersey, USA. 428–437. https://doi.org/10.1109/FOCS.2016.53
[3] Florent Becker, Antonio Fernández Anta, Ivan Rapaport, and Eric Rémila. 2015. Brief Announcement: A Hierarchy of Congested Clique Models, from Broadcast to Unicast. In *Proceedings of the 2015 ACM Symposium on Principles of Distributed Computing, PODC 2015, Donostia-San Sebastián, Spain, July 21 - 23, 2015*. 167–169. https://doi.org/10.1145/2767386.2767447
[4] Florent Becker, Pedro Montealegre, Ivan Rapaport, and Ioan Todinca. 2018. The Impact of Locality on the Detection of Cycles in the Broadcast Congested Clique Model. In *Latin American Symposium on Theoretical Informatics*. Springer, 134–145.
[5] Mihir Bellare, Juan A. Garay, and Tal Rabin. 1996. Distributed Pseudo-Random Bit Generators - A New Way to Speed-Up Shared Coin Tossing. In *Proceedings of the Fifteenth Annual ACM Symposium on Principles of Distributed Computing, Philadelphia, Pennsylvania, USA, May 23-26, 1996*. 191–200. https://doi.org/10.1145/248052.248090
[6] Andrej Bogdanov and Luca Trevisan. 2006. On Worst-Case to Average-Case Reductions for NP Problems. *SIAM J. Comput.* 36, 4 (2006), 1119–1159. https://doi.org/10.1137/S0097539705446974
[7] Mark Braverman, Young Kun-Ko, Aviad Rubinstein, and Omri Weinstein. 2017. ETH Hardness for Densest-k-Subgraph with Perfect Completeness. In *Proceedings of the Twenty-Eighth Annual ACM-SIAM Symposium on Discrete Algorithms, SODA 2017, Barcelona, Spain, Hotel Porta Fira, January 16-19*. 1326–1341. https://doi.org/10.1137/1.9781611974782.86
[8] Keren Censor-Hillel, Petteri Kaski, Janne H. Korhonen, Christoph Lenzen, Ami Paz, and Jukka Suomela. 2015. Algebraic Methods in the Congested Clique. In *Proceedings of the 2015 ACM Symposium on Principles of Distributed Computing, PODC 2015, Donostia-San Sebastián, Spain, July 21 - 23, 2015*. 143–152. https://doi.org/10.1145/2767386.2767414
[9] Keren Censor-Hillel, Merav Parter, and Gregory Schwartzman. 2016. Derandomizing local distributed algorithms under bandwidth restrictions. *arXiv preprint arXiv:1608.01689* (2016).
[10] Yi-Jun Chang and Seth Pettie. 2017. A Time Hierarchy Theorem for the LOCAL Model. In *58th IEEE Annual Symposium on Foundations of Computer Science, FOCS 2017, Berkeley, CA, USA, October 15-17, 2017*. 156–167. https://doi.org/10.1109/FOCS.2017.23
[11] Artur Czumaj and Christian Konrad. 2018. Detecting cliques in CONGEST networks. *arXiv preprint arXiv:1807.01070* (2018).
[12] Pablo Moisset de Espanés, Ivan Rapaport, Daniel Remenik, and Javiera Urrutia. 2016. Robust reconstruction of Barabási-Albert networks in the broadcast congested clique model. *Networks* 67, 1 (2016), 82–91. https://doi.org/10.1002/net.21662
[13] Yael Dekel, Ori Gurel-Gurevich, and Yuval Peres. 2014. Finding Hidden Cliques in Linear Time with High Probability. *Combinatorics, Probability & Computing* 23, 1 (2014), 29–49. https://doi.org/10.1017/S096354831300045X
[14] Yash Deshpande and Andrea Montanari. 2015. Improved Sum-of-Squares Lower Bounds for Hidden Clique and Hidden Submatrix Problems. In *Proceedings of The 28th Conference on Learning Theory, COLT 2015, Paris, France, July 3-6, 2015*. 523–562.
[15] Shahar Dobzinski, Noam Nisan, and Sigal Oren. 2014. Economic efficiency requires interaction. In *Symposium on Theory of Computing, STOC 2014, New York, NY, USA, May 31 - June 03, 2014*. 233–242. https://doi.org/10.1145/2591796.2591815
[16] Andrew Drucker, Fabian Kuhn, and Rotem Oshman. 2014. On the power of the congested clique model. In *ACM Symposium on Principles of Distributed Computing, PODC '14, Paris, France, July 15-18, 2014*. 367–376. https://doi.org/10.1145/2611462.2611493
[17] Uriel Feige and Robert Krauthgamer. 2000. Finding and certifying a large hidden clique in a semirandom graph. *Random Struct. Algorithms* 16, 2 (2000), 195–208.
[18] Uriel Feige and Robert Krauthgamer. 2003. The Probable Value of the Lovász–Schrijver Relaxations for Maximum Independent Set. *SIAM J. Comput.* 32, 2 (2003), 345–370. https://doi.org/10.1137/S009753970240118X
[19] Joan Feigenbaum and Lance Fortnow. 1993. Random-Self-Reducibility of Complete Sets. *SIAM J. Comput.* 22, 5 (1993), 994–1005. https://doi.org/10.1137/0222061
[20] Pierre Fraigniaud, Amos Korman, and David Peleg. 2013. Towards a complexity theory for local distributed computing. *J. ACM* 60, 5 (2013), 35:1–35:26. https://doi.org/10.1145/2499228
[21] François Le Gall. 2016. Further Algebraic Algorithms in the Congested Clique Model and Applications to Graph-Theoretic Problems. In *Distributed Computing - 30th International Symposium, DISC 2016, Paris, France, September 27-29, 2016. Proceedings*. 57–70. https://doi.org/10.1007/978-3-662-53426-7_5
[22] Mohsen Ghaffari, David G. Harris, and Fabian Kuhn. 2018. On Derandomizing Local Distributed Algorithms. In *FOCS, to appear.*
[23] Mohsen Ghaffari, Fabian Kuhn, and Yannic Maus. 2017. On the complexity of local distributed graph problems. In *Proceedings of the 49th Annual ACM SIGACT Symposium on Theory of Computing, STOC 2017, Montreal, QC, Canada, June 19-23, 2017*. 784–797. https://doi.org/10.1145/3055399.3055471
[24] Ofer Grossman, Bernhard Haeupler, and Sidhanth Mohanty. 2018. Algorithms for Noisy Broadcast with Erasures. In *LIPIcs-Leibniz International Proceedings in Informatics*, Vol. 107. Schloss Dagstuhl-Leibniz-Zentrum fuer Informatik.
[25] Stephan Holzer and Nathan Pinsker. 2015. Approximation of Distances and Shortest Paths in the Broadcast Congest Clique. In *19th International Conference on Principles of Distributed Systems, OPODIS 2015, December 14-17, 2015, Rennes, France*. 6:1–6:16. https://doi.org/10.4230/LIPIcs.OPODIS.2015.6
[26] Samuel B Hopkins, Pravesh Kothari, Aaron Henry Potechin, Prasad Raghavendra, and Tselil Schramm. 2018. On the integrality gap of degree-4 sum of squares for planted clique. *ACM Transactions on Algorithms (TALG)* 14, 3 (2018), 28.
[27] Russell Impagliazzo, Noam Nisan, and Avi Wigderson. 1994. Pseudorandomness for network algorithms. In *Proceedings of the twenty-sixth annual ACM symposium on Theory of computing*. ACM, 356–364.
[28] Mark Jerrum. 1992. Large Cliques Elude the Metropolis Process. *Random Struct. Algorithms* 3, 4 (1992), 347–360. https://doi.org/10.1002/rsa.3240030402
[29] Tomasz Jurdzínski and Krzysztof Nowicki. 2017. Brief Announcement: On Connectivity in the Broadcast Congested Clique. In *LIPIcs-Leibniz International Proceedings in Informatics*, Vol. 91. Schloss Dagstuhl-Leibniz-Zentrum fuer Informatik.
[30] Tomasz Jurdzinski and Krzysztof Nowicki. 2017. MSF and connectivity in limited variants of the congested clique. *arXiv preprint arXiv:1703.02743* (2017).
[31] Janne H Korhonen and Joel Rybicki. 2017. Deterministic subgraph detection in broadcast CONGEST. *arXiv preprint arXiv:1705.10195* (2017).
[32] Janne H Korhonen and Jukka Suomela. 2017. Towards a complexity theory for the congested clique. *arXiv preprint arXiv:1705.03284* (2017).
[33] Ludek Kucera. 1995. Expected Complexity of Graph Partitioning Problems. *Discrete Applied Mathematics* 57, 2-3 (1995), 193–212. https://doi.org/10.1016/0166-218X(94)00103-K
[34] Raghu Meka, Aaron Potechin, and Avi Wigderson. 2015. Sum-of-squares Lower Bounds for Planted Clique. In *Proceedings of the Forty-Seventh Annual ACM on Symposium on Theory of Computing, STOC 2015, Portland, OR, USA, June 14-17, 2015*. 87–96. https://doi.org/10.1145/2746539.2746600
[35] Pedro Montealegre and Ioan Todinca. 2016. Deterministic graph connectivity in the broadcast congested clique. *arXiv preprint arXiv:1602.04095* (2016).
[36] Moni Naor, Benny Pinkas, and Omer Reingold. 1999. Distributed Pseudo-random Functions and KDCs. In *Advances in Cryptology - EUROCRYPT '99, International Conference on the Theory and Application of Cryptographic Techniques, Prague, Czech Republic, May 2-6, 1999, Proceeding*. 327–346. https://doi.org/10.1007/3-540-48910-X_23
[37] Jelani Nelson and Huacheng Yu. 2018. Optimal Lower Bounds for Distributed and Streaming Spanning Forest Computation. *arXiv preprint arXiv:1807.05135* (2018).
[38] Ilan Newman. 1991. Private vs. common random bits in communication complexity. *Information processing letters* 39, 2 (1991), 67–71.
[39] Merav Parter and Eylon Yogev. 2018. Congested Clique Algorithms for Graph Spanners. *CoRR* abs/1805.05404 (2018). arXiv:1805.05404
[40] Salil P Vadhan. 2012. Pseudorandomness. *Foundations and Trends® in Theoretical Computer Science* 7, 1–3 (2012), 1–336.
[41] Andrew Chi-Chih Yao. 1977. Probabilistic Computations: Toward a Unified Measure of Complexity (Extended Abstract). In *18th Annual Symposium on Foundations of Computer Science, Providence, Rhode Island, USA, 31 October - 1 November 1977*. 222–227. https://doi.org/10.1109/SFCS.1977.24

Brief Announcement: Connectivity Lower Bounds in Broadcast Congested Clique

Shreyas Pai
Department of Computer Science
The University of Iowa
Iowa City, IA
shreyas-pai@uiowa.edu

Sriram V. Pemmaraju
Department of Computer Science
The University of Iowa
Iowa City, IA
sriram-pemmaraju@uiowa.edu

Abstract

We prove three new lower bounds for graph connectivity in the 1-bit broadcast congested clique model, BCC(1). First, in the KT-0 version of BCC(1), in which nodes are aware of neighbors only through port numbers, we show an $\Omega(\log n)$ round lower bound for Connectivity even for constant-error randomized Monte Carlo algorithms. The deterministic version of this result can be obtained via the well-known "edge-crossing" argument, but, the randomized version of this result requires establishing new combinatorial results regarding the indistinguishability graph induced by inputs. In our second result, we show that the $\Omega(\log n)$ lower bound result extends to the KT-1 version of the BCC(1) model, in which nodes are aware of IDs of all neighbors, though our proof works only for deterministic algorithms. Since nodes know IDs of their neighbors in the KT-1 model, it is no longer possible to play "edge-crossing" tricks; instead we present a reduction from the 2-party communication complexity problem Partition in which Alice and Bob are given two set partitions on $[n]$ and are required to determine if the join of these two set partitions equals the trivial one-part set partition. While our KT-1 Connectivity lower bound holds only for deterministic algorithms, in our third result we extend this $\Omega(\log n)$ KT-1 lower bound to constant-error Monte Carlo algorithms for the closely related ConnectedComponents problem. We use information-theoretic techniques to obtain this result. All our results hold for the seemingly easy special case of Connectivity in which an algorithm has to distinguish an instance with one cycle from an instance with multiple cycles. Our results showcase three rather different lower bound techniques and lay the groundwork for further improvements in lower bounds for Connectivity in the BCC(1) model.

CCS Concepts

• **Theory of computation** → *Communication complexity; Distributed algorithms.*

Keywords

broadcast congested clique; communication complexity; connectivity; information theory; lower bounds; set partition

PODC '19, July 29-August 2, 2019, Toronto, ON, Canada

ACM ISBN 978-1-4503-6217-7/19/07.
https://doi.org/10.1145/3293611.3331569

ACM Reference Format:
Shreyas Pai and Sriram V. Pemmaraju. 2019. Brief Announcement: Connectivity Lower Bounds in Broadcast Congested Clique. In *2019 ACM Symposium on Principles of Distributed Computing (PODC '19), July 29-August 2, 2019, Toronto, ON, Canada.* ACM, New York, NY, USA, 3 pages. https://doi.org/10.1145/3293611.3331569

1 Introduction

We are given an n-node, completely connected *communication network* in which each node can broadcast at most b bits in each round. These n nodes and a subset of the edges of the communication network form the *input graph*. The question we ask is this: how many rounds of communication does it take to determine if the input graph is connected? This is the well known Connectivity problem in the *b-bit Broadcast Congested Clique*, i.e., the BCC(b) model.

A series of recent rapid improvements [9, 11, 14] have shown that Connectivity and in fact *minimum spanning tree (MST)*, can be solved in $O(1)$ rounds w.h.p.[1] in the *b-bit Congested Clique* model, CC(b), when $b = \log n$. The CC(b) model allows each node to send a possibly different b-bit message to each of the other $n-1$ nodes in the network, in each round. In contrast, the fastest known algorithm for Connectivity in the BCC($\log n$) model, due to Jurdziński and Nowicki [13], is deterministic and it runs in $O\left(\frac{\log n}{\log\log n}\right)$ rounds. This contrast between BCC(b) and CC(b) is not surprising, given how much larger the overall bandwidth in CC(b) is compared to BCC(b). Becker et al. [3] show that the *pair-wise set disjointness* problem can be solved in $O(1)$ rounds in CC(1), but needs $\Omega(n)$ rounds in BCC(1). But, despite the fact that Connectivity is such a fundamental problem, no non-trivial lower bound is known for Connectivity in BCC(1). In fact, prior to this paper, we could not even rule out an $O(1)$-round Connectivity algorithm in BCC(1).

Lower bound arguments in "congested" distributed computing models typically use a "bottleneck" technique [4–8, 12]. At a high level, this technique consists of showing that there is a low bandwidth cut in the communication network across which a high volume of information has to flow in order to solve the given problem. The lower bound on information flow is usually obtained via 2-party communication complexity lower bounds [16]. Not surprisingly, the "bottleneck" technique does not work in the CC(b) model because any cut with $\Theta(n)$ vertices in each part, has a high bandwidth of $\Theta(n^2 \cdot b)$ bits. In fact, a result of Drucker et al. [7], showing that circuits can be simulated efficiently in the Congested Clique model,

[1]We use "w.h.p." as short for "with high probability" which refers to the probability that is at least $1 - 1/n^c$ for $c \geq 1$.

indicates that no technique we currently know of can prove nontrivial lower bounds in the CC(b) model. However, as further shown by [7], "bottlenecks" are possible for some problems in the weaker BCC(b) model. In this model, every cut has bandwidth $O(n \cdot b)$ and for example Drucker et al. [7] provide a reduction showing that for the problem of detecting the presence of a K_4 in the input graph there is a cut across which $\Omega(n^2)$ information has to flow. This leads to an $\Omega(n/b)$ lower bound for K_4-detection in the BCC(b).

All known lower bounds [7, 12] in the BCC($\log n$) model have this general structure and these techniques work for problems such as fixed subgraph detection, all pairs shortest paths, diameter computation, etc., that are relatively difficult, requiring polynomially many rounds to solve. For "simpler" problems such as CONNECTIVITY and MST, we need lower bound techniques that allow us to prove polylogarithmic lower bounds. Specifically, since CONNECTIVITY can be solved in BCC(b) for any $b \geq 1$ in just $O(\text{poly}(\log n))$ rounds, the best we can expect is to show the existence of a cut across which $\Omega(n \cdot \text{poly}(\log n))$ volume of information needs to flow. In fact, the connected components of a subgraph can be represented in $O(n \log n)$ bits and this is all that needs to communicated across a cut to solve CONNECTIVITY. Thus the best lower bound we can expect for CONNECTIVITY via this technique is an $\Omega(\log n/b)$. However, even this was unknown prior to this paper and one contribution of this paper is an $\Omega(\log n/b)$ lower bound for CONNECTIVITY using the "bottleneck" technique.
The reader is encouraged to refer to the full version of this paper available on arxiv [19] for all proofs and other technical details.

2 Our Contributions

We consider the CONNECTIVITY problem and the closely related CONNECTEDCOMPONENTS problem in the BCC(1) model. In the latter problem, each node needs to output the label of the connected component it belongs to. We work in the BCC(1) model because it allows us to isolate barriers due to different levels of initial local knowledge (e.g., knowing IDs of neighbors vs not knowing IDs). This is also without loss of generality because a t-round lower bound in BCC(1) immediately translates to a t/b-round lower bound in BCC(b). We consider two natural versions of the BCC(1) model, that we call KT-0 and KT-1 (using notation from [1]). In the KT-0 ("Knowledge Till 0 hops") version, nodes are unaware of IDs of other nodes in the network and the $n-1$ communication ports at each node are arbitrarily numbered 1 through $n-1$. In the KT-1 ("Knowledge Till 1 hop") version, nodes know all n IDs in the network and the $n-1$ communication ports at each node are respectively labeled with the IDs of the nodes at the other end of the port. Note that if the bandwidth $b = \Omega(\log n)$, then there is essentially no distinction between the KT-0 and KT-1 versions since each node in the KT-0 version can send its ID to neighbors in constant rounds and then nodes would have as much knowledge as they initially do in the KT-1 version. But the difference in initial knowledge plays a critical role when $b = o(\log n)$ and in fact our best results in these two models use completely different techniques. We present three main lower bound results in this paper, derived using very different techniques.

2.1 Randomized KT-0 Lower Bounds

In the KT-0 version of BCC(1) we show an $\Omega(\log n)$ round lower bound for CONNECTIVITY even for constant-error randomized Monte Carlo algorithms. In fact, the lower bound is shown for the seemingly simpler "one cycle vs two cycles" problem in which the input graph is either a single cycle or consists of two disjoint cycles and the algorithm has to distinguish between these two possibilities. We use a well-known *indistinguishability* argument involving "edge crossing" [2, 15, 20] for this result, but the main novelty here is how this argument deals with the possibility that the algorithm can err on a constant fraction of the input instances. In a standard edge crossing argument one shows that for a particular YES instance (i.e., a connected or "one-cycle" instance) G, many of the NO instances $G(e, e')$ obtained by crossing pairs of edges e and e' in G cannot be distinguished even after some t rounds of a BCC(1) algorithm. But for a randomized lower bound in BCC(1), it is not enough to consider a single YES instance. Instead, we use the bipartite *indistinguishability graph* induced by all YES and NO instances and show that this satisfies a polygamous version of Hall's Theorem. This allows us to show the existence of a large generalized matching in the indistinguishability graph, which in turn shows that every $o(\log n)$ round constant-error Monte Carlo algorithm can be fooled into making more errors than it is allowed. The precise result we prove is the following. Here the TWOCYCLE problem refers to the problem, mentioned earlier, of distinguishing between two n-vertex graph types: a single cycle or two disconnected cycles each of length at least 3. The lower bound is for public coin randomized Monte Carlo algorithms with 2-sided error ϵ.

THEOREM 2.1. *For a sufficiently small constant $0 < \epsilon \leq 1/2$, the ϵ-error randomized round complexity of the TWOCYCLE problem in the KT-0 model is bounded below by $\Omega(\log n)$.*

2.2 Deterministic KT-1 Lower Bounds

We then show that the above lower bound result extends to the KT-1 version of the BCC(1) model, though our proof only works for deterministic algorithms. In KT-1, because of knowledge of IDs of neighbors, it is no longer possible to perform "edge crossing" tricks. But we are able to successfully use the "bottleneck" technique and show that there is a cut for the CONNECTIVITY problem across which $\Omega(n \log n)$ bits need to flow. We prove this result by presenting a reduction from the 2-party communication complexity problem PARTITION [10]. In the PARTITION problem, we have a ground set $[n]$ and Alice and Bob respectively are given two set partitions P_A and P_B of $[n]$. The goal is to output 1 iff $P_A \vee P_B = 1$ where $P_A \vee P_B$ (read as "P_A join P_B") is the finest partition P such that both P_A and P_B are refinements of P [2] and 1 is the trivial partition consisting of the single set $[n]$. For example, if $P_A = (1, 2)(3, 4)(5)$, $P_B = (1, 2, 4)(3)(5)$, and $P_C = (1, 2, 4)(3, 5)$ then $P_A \vee P_B = (1, 2, 3, 4)(5)$ and $P_A \vee P_C = (1, 2, 3, 4, 5)$. We then use the fact that the deterministic communication complexity of PARTITION is $\Omega(n \log n)$ to obtain our result. Again, this time using a linear-algebraic argument, we show our result for a seemingly simple special case of CONNECTIVITY: "one cycle vs multiple cycles."

[2]Given two set partitions P and P' of $[n]$, P is said to be a *refinement* of P' if for every part $S \in P$, there is a part $S' \in P'$ such that $S \subseteq S'$. For example the partition (1, 2)(3, 4)(5) is a refinement of (1, 2)(3, 4, 5).

As far as we know, randomized communication complexity of PARTITION is a long-standing unresolved problem. Showing a lower bound on the randomized communication complexity of PARTITION will immediately lead to a KT-1 lower bound for randomized CONNECTIVITY algorithms, via our reduction. The precise result we show in the following. Here the MULTICYCLE problem refers to the problem of distinguishing between input that is a single cycle versus input that consists of multiple cycles, each of length at least 4.

THEOREM 2.2. *The round complexity of any deterministic algorithm that solves the MULTICYCLE problem in the KT-1 model is* $\Omega(\log n)$.

Along the way to proving this result, we show the following new 2-party communication complexity result. Here TWOPARTITION refers to the special case of the PARTITION problem in which every part of the given set partitions has size exactly 2.

THEOREM 2.3. *The communication complexity of any 2-party deterministic protocol that solves TWOPARTITION is* $\Omega(n \log n)$.

2.3 Randomized KT-1 Lower Bounds for CONNECTEDCOMPONENTS

Our final result arises from our attempt to obtain a KT-1 lower bound even for constant-error Monte Carlo algorithms. We consider a version of the PARTITION problem, called PARTITIONCOMP, in which Alice and Bob are required to output the join of their respective input partitions P_A and P_B instead of just determining if $P_A \vee P_B = \mathbf{1}$. We use an information-theoretic argument to show that the mutual information of any algorithm, even a constant-error Monte Carlo algorithm, that solves this version of PARTITION is $\Omega(n \log n)$. This leads to an $\Omega(\log n)$-round lower bound for CONNECTEDCOMPONENTS in the KT-1 version of BCC(1), even for constant-error randomized Monte Carlo algorithms. The precise result we show in the following.

THEOREM 2.4. *For any constant* $0 < \epsilon < 1$, *the round complexity of an* ϵ*-error randomized Monte Carlo algorithm that solves the CONNECTEDCOMPONENTS problem in the KT-1 version of the BCC(1) model is* $\Omega(\log n)$.

3 Conclusion

We prove in this paper the first non-trivial lower bounds for CONNECTIVITY in the BCC(1) model. The fact that our lower bounds hold even in the KT-1 model implies that the difficulty of the problem does not arise just from lack of knowledge of IDs of other nodes. The fact that our lower bounds hold for extremely sparse (i.e., 2-regular) graphs, suggests that there might be room to get stronger lower bounds by considering dense input graphs. In fact, using a deterministic sketching technique [17, 18], it is possible to obtain a deterministic $O(\log n)$-round BCC(1) algorithm for CONNECTIVITY for graphs with arboricity bounded by a constant. This implies that our lower bounds are tight for uniformly sparse graphs.

References

[1] Baruch Awerbuch, Oded Goldreich, David Peleg, and Ronen Vainish. 1990. A Trade-Off Between Information and Communication in Broadcast Protocols. *J. ACM* 37, 2 (1990), 238–256. https://doi.org/10.1145/77600.77618

[2] Mor Baruch, Pierre Fraigniaud, and Boaz Patt-Shamir. 2015. Randomized Proof-Labeling Schemes. In *Proceedings of the 2015 ACM Symposium on Principles of Distributed Computing, PODC 2015, Donostia-San Sebastián, Spain, July 21 - 23, 2015.* 315–324. https://doi.org/10.1145/2767386.2767421

[3] Florent Becker, Antonio Fernández Anta, Ivan Rapaport, and Eric Rémila. 2016. The Effect of Range and Bandwidth on the Round Complexity in the Congested Clique Model. In *Computing and Combinatorics - 22nd International Conference, COCOON 2016, Ho Chi Minh City, Vietnam, August 2-4, 2016, Proceedings.* 182–193. https://doi.org/10.1007/978-3-319-42634-1_15

[4] Keren Censor-Hillel, Seri Khoury, and Ami Paz. 2017. Quadratic and Near-Quadratic Lower Bounds for the CONGEST Model. In *31st International Symposium on Distributed Computing, DISC 2017, October 16-20, 2017, Vienna, Austria.* 10:1–10:16. https://doi.org/10.4230/LIPIcs.DISC.2017.10

[5] Artur Czumaj and Christian Konrad. 2018. Detecting cliques in CONGEST networks, In 32nd International Symposium on Distributed Computing (DISC 2018). *Leibniz International Proceedings in Informatics (LIPIcs).* http://wrap.warwick.ac.uk/106950/

[6] Atish Das Sarma, Stephan Holzer, Liah Kor, Amos Korman, Danupon Nanongkai, Gopal Pandurangan, David Peleg, and Roger Wattenhofer. 2011. Distributed Verification and Hardness of Distributed Approximation. In *Proceedings of the Forty-third Annual ACM Symposium on Theory of Computing (STOC '11).* ACM, New York, NY, USA, 363–372. https://doi.org/10.1145/1993636.1993686

[7] Andrew Drucker, Fabian Kuhn, and Rotem Oshman. 2014. On the Power of the Congested Clique Model. In *Proceedings of the 2014 ACM Symposium on Principles of Distributed Computing (PODC '14).* ACM, New York, NY, USA, 367–376. https://doi.org/10.1145/2611462.2611493

[8] Orr Fischer, Tzlil Gonen, Fabian Kuhn, and Rotem Oshman. 2018. Possibilities and Impossibilities for Distributed Subgraph Detection. In *Proceedings of the 30th on Symposium on Parallelism in Algorithms and Architectures, SPAA 2018, Vienna, Austria, July 16-18, 2018.* 153–162. https://doi.org/10.1145/3210377.3210401

[9] Mohsen Ghaffari and Merav Parter. 2016. MST in Log-Star Rounds of Congested Clique. In *Proceedings of the 2016 ACM Symposium on Principles of Distributed Computing, PODC 2016, Chicago, IL, USA, July 25-28, 2016.* 19–28. https://doi.org/10.1145/2933057.2933103

[10] András Hajnal, Wolfgang Maass, and György Turán. 1988. On the Communication Complexity of Graph Properties. In *Proceedings of the 20th Annual ACM Symposium on Theory of Computing, May 2-4, 1988, Chicago, Illinois, USA.* 186–191. https://doi.org/10.1145/62212.62228

[11] James W. Hegeman, Gopal Pandurangan, Sriram V. Pemmaraju, Vivek B. Sardeshmukh, and Michele Scquizzato. 2015. Toward Optimal Bounds in the Congested Clique: Graph Connectivity and MST. In *Proceedings of the 2015 ACM Symposium on Principles of Distributed Computing (PODC '15).* ACM, New York, NY, USA, 91–100. https://doi.org/10.1145/2767386.2767434

[12] Stephan Holzer and Nathan Pinsker. 2015. Approximation of Distances and Shortest Paths in the Broadcast Congest Clique. In *19th International Conference on Principles of Distributed Systems, OPODIS 2015, December 14-17, 2015, Rennes, France.* 6:1–6:16. https://doi.org/10.4230/LIPIcs.OPODIS.2015.6

[13] Tomasz Jurdzinski and Krzysztof Nowicki. 2017. Brief Announcement: On Connectivity in the Broadcast Congested Clique. In *31st International Symposium on Distributed Computing, DISC 2017, October 16-20, 2017, Vienna, Austria.* 54:1–54:4. https://doi.org/10.4230/LIPIcs.DISC.2017.54

[14] Tomasz Jurdziński and Krzysztof Nowicki. 2018. MST in O(1) Rounds of Congested Clique. In *Proceedings of the Twenty-Ninth Annual ACM-SIAM Symposium on Discrete Algorithms (SODA '18).* Society for Industrial and Applied Mathematics, Philadelphia, PA, USA, 2620–2632. http://dl.acm.org/citation.cfm?id=3174304.3175472

[15] Amos Korman, Shay Kutten, and David Peleg. 2010. Proof labeling schemes. *Distributed Computing* 22, 4 (2010), 215–233. https://doi.org/10.1007/s00446-010-0095-3

[16] Eyal Kushilevitz and Noam Nisan. 1997. *Communication Complexity.* Cambridge University Press, New York, NY, USA.

[17] Pedro Montealegre and Ioan Todinca. 2016. Brief Announcement: Deterministic Graph Connectivity in the Broadcast Congested Clique. In *Proceedings of the 2016 ACM Symposium on Principles of Distributed Computing (PODC '16).* ACM, New York, NY, USA, 245–247. https://doi.org/10.1145/2933057.2933066

[18] Pedro Montealegre and Ioan Todinca. 2016. Deterministic graph connectivity in the broadcast congested clique. *CoRR* abs/1602.04095 (2016). http://arxiv.org/abs/1602.04095

[19] Shreyas Pai and Sriram V. Pemmaraju. 2019. Connectivity Lower Bounds in Broadcast Congested Clique. arXiv:cs.DC/1905.09016

[20] Boaz Patt-Shamir and Mor Perry. 2017. Proof-Labeling Schemes: Broadcast, Unicast and in Between. In *Stabilization, Safety, and Security of Distributed Systems - 19th International Symposium, SSS 2017, Boston, MA, USA, November 5-8, 2017, Proceedings.* 1–17. https://doi.org/10.1007/978-3-319-69084-1_1

Brief Announcement: Does Preprocessing Help under Congestion?

Klaus-Tycho Foerster
klaus-tycho.foerster@univie.ac.at
Faculty of Computer Science, University of Vienna
Vienna, Austria

Janne H. Korhonen
janne.korhonen@ist.ac.at
IST Austria
Klosterneuburg, Austria

Joel Rybicki*
joel.rybicki@ist.ac.at
IST Austria
Klosterneuburg, Austria

Stefan Schmid
stefan_schmid@univie.ac.at
Faculty of Computer Science, University of Vienna
Vienna, Austria

ABSTRACT

This paper investigates the power of preprocessing in the CONGEST model. Schmid and Suomela (ACM HotSDN 2013) introduced the SUPPORTED CONGEST model to study the application of distributed algorithms in Software-Defined Networks (SDNs). In this paper, we show that a large class of lower bounds in the CONGEST model still hold in the SUPPORTED model, highlighting the robustness of these bounds. This also raises the question how much does preprocessing help in the CONGEST model.

CCS CONCEPTS

• **Theory of computation → Distributed computing models; Distributed algorithms;** • **Networks → Network algorithms.**

KEYWORDS

graph algorithms, congest model, preprocessing, software defined networking, lower bounds, supported model

ACM Reference Format:

Klaus-Tycho Foerster, Janne H. Korhonen, Joel Rybicki, and Stefan Schmid. 2019. Brief Announcement: Does Preprocessing Help under Congestion?. In *2019 ACM Symposium on Principles of Distributed Computing (PODC '19), July 29-August 2, 2019, Toronto, ON, Canada.* ACM, New York, NY, USA, 3 pages. https://doi.org/10.1145/3293611.3331581

1 INTRODUCTION

Common models of distributed computation typically consider scenarios where the computation always starts from *scratch*, i.e., in an *unknown* communication topology. However, in many practical scenarios, the communication topology does not change as frequently as the problem input. For example, the distributed algorithm may always be run in networks whose topology is known in advance, but the input instance may vary. In such cases, it is natural to *support* distributed algorithms by allowing preprocessing of the underlying network topology [11].

With this in mind, Schmid and Suomela [11] proposed two SUPPORTED models of distributed computation to enhance distributed algorithms with the power of preprocessing: SUPPORTED LOCAL and SUPPORTED CONGEST.

Subsequently, Korhonen and Rybicki considered subgraph detection problems [8] in the SUPPORTED CONGEST model, whereas Foerster et al. [6] investigated the power of the SUPPORTED LOCAL model. In this paper, we focus on SUPPORTED CONGEST.

Contribution. We observe that many lower bounds in the standard CONGEST model still hold under such preprocessing. Given that intuitively preprocessing seems to be very powerful, this may come as a surprise. This raises the question of how much preprocessing actually helps in the CONGEST model. Indeed, it may be either that the power of preprocessing is very limited or that the current lower bounds for non-supported CONGEST are not tight. In the light of this, we propose the following challenge: *is there a separation between supported and non-supported models?* If the answer is no, then there may be a way to easily simulate preprocessing, and thus, simplify algorithm design in the CONGEST model. In the converse case, preprocessing may offer a practical way to accelerate current distributed algorithms.

Model. In the SUPPORTED CONGEST model, the communication topology is an undirected graph $H = (V, E)$ and each node has a unique identifier of size $O(\log n)$ bits. The logical state is given by an undirected subgraph, i.e., the *input* graph $G \subseteq H$, which inherits the identifiers in H. The computation proceeds in two steps: First, in the preprocessing phase, the nodes may compute any function on $f(H)$ and store the result locally. In the second phase, the nodes are tasked to solve a problem instance on the input graph G in the CONGEST model. To this end, the edges of H may be used for communication and additionally the local outputs of the preprocessing. Note that the congested clique [9] model is a special case of the SUPPORTED model: the support H is simply a clique. In addition, one may also restrict the communication of the SUPPORTED model to just the input graph G after preprocessing; this model is called the *passive* SUPPORTED model.

*This project has received funding from the European Union's Horizon 2020 research and innovation programme under the Marie Skłodowska-Curie grant agreement No 754411.

PODC '19, July 29-August 2, 2019, Toronto, ON, Canada

ACM ISBN 978-1-4503-6217-7/19/07.
https://doi.org/10.1145/3293611.3331581

Lower bound	Problem
$\Omega(n^{1/2}/\log n)$	4-cycle [4], $2k$-cycle [8], Girth ($(2-\varepsilon)$-apx.) [7]
$\Omega(n/\log n)$	$(2k+1)$-cycle [4], APSP, Diameter ($(3/2-\varepsilon)$-apx.) [7]
$\Omega(n/(\log n)^2)$	Diameter on sparse graphs [1]
$\Omega(n/(\log n)^3)$	Diameter and radius ($(3/2-\varepsilon)$-apx.), eccentricities ($(5/3-\varepsilon)$-apx.), all on sparse graphs [1]
$\Omega(n^{2-1/k}/(k\log n))$	Subgraph detection (for any k) [5]
$\Omega(n^2/(\log n)^2)$	Min. vertex cover, max. independent set, chrom. number ($(4/3-\varepsilon)$-apx.), weighted 8-cycle [3]
$\Omega(n^2)$	Identical subgraphs (deterministic only) [3]

Table 1: Lower bounds that transfer from the CONGEST **to the** SUPPORTED CONGEST **model.**

2 LOWER BOUNDS FOR THE SUPPORTED CONGEST MODEL

We show that CONGEST lower bounds obtained using the now standard *family of lower bound graphs* construction [2] easily translate to the SUPPORTED model. To this end, we adapt here the proof of Abboud et al. [2]. Using existing constructions for families of lower bound graphs then immediately give the lower bounds shown in Table 1. We note that this technique does not directly cover the lower bounds of Das Sarma et al. [10], though we believe they can be similarly translated.

Two-party communication complexity. Let $f\colon \{0,1\}^{2k} \to \{0,1\}$ be a Boolean function. In the two-party communication game on f, there are two players who receive a private k-bit string x_0 and x_1 as input, and the task is to have at least one of the players compute $f(x) = f(x_0, x_1)$. The *deterministic communication complexity* $\mathrm{CC}(f)$ of a function f is the maximum number of bits the two players need to exchange in the worst case (over all deterministic protocols and input strings) in order to compute $f(x_0, x_1)$. Similarly, the *randomised communication complexity* $\mathrm{RCC}(f)$ is the worst-case complexity of protocols, which compute f with probability at least $2/3$ on all inputs.

Definition 2.1. Let $f_n\colon \{0,1\}^{2k(n)} \to \{0,1\}$ and $C\colon \mathbb{N} \to \mathbb{N}$ be functions and Π a graph predicate. Suppose that there exists a constant n_0 such that for all $n > n_0$ and $x_0, x_1 \in \{0,1\}^{k(n)}$ there exists a (weighted) graph $G(n, x_0, x_1)$ satisfying the following properties:

(1) $G(n, x_0, x_1)$ satisfies Π if and only if $f_n(x_0, x_1) = 1$,
(2) $G(n, x_0, x_1) = (V_0 \cup V_1, E_0 \cup E_1 \cup S)$, where
  - V_0 and V_1 are disjoint and $|V_0 \cup V_1| = n$,
  - $E_i \subseteq V_i \times V_i$ for $i \in \{0,1\}$,
  - $S \subseteq V_0 \times V_1$ is a cut and has size at least $C(n)$, and
  - the (weighted) subgraph $G_i = (V_i, E_i)$ only depends on i, n and x_i, i.e., $G_i = G_i(n, x_i)$.

If $\mathcal{G}(n) = \{G(n,x) : x \in \{0,1\}^{2k(n)}\}$, then $\mathcal{F} = (\mathcal{G}(n))_{n>n_0}$ is a *family of lower bound graphs.*

Theorem 2.2. *Let $\mathcal{F}$ be a family of lower bound graphs. Any algorithm deciding Π on a graph family $\mathcal{H}$ containing $\bigcup \mathcal{G}(n)$ for all $n > n_0$ in the passive or active* SUPPORTED CONGEST *model with bandwidth $b(n)$ needs*

$$\Omega\left(\frac{\mathrm{CC}(f_n)}{C(n)b(n)}\right) \quad \text{and} \quad \Omega\left(\frac{\mathrm{RCC}(f_n)}{C(n)b(n)}\right)$$

deterministic and randomised rounds, respectively.

Proof. Suppose $\mathcal{A}$ is an algorithm that decides Π on the graph family $\mathcal{H}$ in $T(n)$ communication rounds. We now construct a two-player protocol π that computes $f_n(x_0, x_1)$ by simulating $\mathcal{A}$. Let $x_0, x_1 \in \{0,1\}^{k(n)}$ be the input, $G = G(n, x_0, x_1)$, and $H = \bigcup \mathcal{G}(n)$.

Given its input x_i, player i can locally construct the subgraph $G_i(n, x_i) \subset G(n, x_0, x_1)$. Note that given $G_i(x_i)$, the support graph H does not reveal any information about E_{1-i} or x_{1-i} to player i, since for any $y \in \{0,1\}^{k(n)}$ we have $G_{1-i}(y) \subseteq H[V_{1-i}]$. Simulating any messages sent between vertices of $G_i(n,x)$ can be done without any communication with player $1-i$. Any messages from V_i to V_{1-i} must go across the cut S and are communicated by player i to player $1-i$. As in each round each player communicates at most $b(n)$ bits over any edge in S, the total amount of bits communicated during the course of T rounds is at most $2b(n)|S(x)|T(n) \geq 2b(n)C(n)T(n)$, which must be at least $\mathrm{CC}(f_n)$ for deterministic algorithms and $\mathrm{RCC}(f_n)$ for randomised algorithms. Thus, the claim follows by observing that $\frac{\mathrm{CC}(f_n)}{2b(n)C(n)} \leq T(n)$ and $\frac{\mathrm{RCC}(f_n)}{2b(n)C(n)} \leq T(n)$. □

3 TOWARDS NEW ALGORITHMIC OPPORTUNITIES?

We saw in Section 2 that many lower bounds from the CONGEST model translate directly to the SUPPORTED CONGEST model, even though intuitively, the SUPPORTED model may seem significantly more powerful. This raises the question if the SUPPORTED model is actually a stronger model in a meaningful sense or if the prior lower bounds were so strong that they easily transferred.

First separation results. Prior work on the SUPPORTED LOCAL model [6] already pointed out that computing an upper bound on the network size separates the LOCAL ($\Omega(D)$ rounds) and the SUPPORTED LOCAL model (0 rounds). Analogous results hold if the support graph is promised to have certain (monotone) properties that apply to all its subgraphs, e.g., being k-colorable. These results directly carry over to the SUPPORTED CONGEST model, providing a 0 vs $\Omega(D)$ round separation, even in an identifier-independent setting. On the other hand, in the SUPPORTED LOCAL model, all problems can be solved trivially in diameter time, but can the SUPPORTED CONGEST go further? Observe that the naïve problem of collecting all identifiers does not provide an $\Omega(n^2)$ separation in the SUPPORTED CONGEST model, as the problem may only depend on the input graph, which may omit nodes present in the support graph. Notwithstanding, we can alter the problem s.t. each node has to e.g. output two sets I_0, I_1 of identifiers with $|I_0| = |I_1|$, where I_1 contains a superset of all identifiers in G and none of the identifiers in I_0 appear in G.

Open questions and possibilities. While the separation results for restricted graph classes can be directly used to accelerate many specialized algorithms (e.g., coloring when the support graph has a small chromatic number), we leave it as an open question how the SUPPORTED model can be leveraged outside the case of collecting identifiers and providing upper bounds on the graph size, even though the latter is sometimes needed as an input for some algorithms. We believe that exciting possibilities arise, no matter the outcome to this open question. For example, if the CONGEST model could simulate the SUPPORTED model with negligible overhead beyond the previously mentioned exceptions, the SUPPORTED model could greatly simplify algorithm design by incorporating preprocessing. On the other hand, even a strong separation could lead to significantly faster algorithms in neighboring research areas, e.g. for Software Defined Networks [11].

REFERENCES

[1] Amir Abboud, Keren Censor-Hillel, and Seri Khoury. 2016. Near-Linear Lower Bounds for Distributed Distance Computations, Even in Sparse Networks. In *Proc. 30th International Symposium on Distributed Computing (DISC 2016)*. 29–42. https://doi.org/10.1007/978-3-662-53426-7_3

[2] Amir Abboud, Keren Censor-Hillel, Seri Khoury, and Ami Paz. 2019. Smaller Cuts, Higher Lower Bounds. http://arxiv.org/abs/1901.01630 arxiv:1901.01630 [cs.DC].

[3] Keren Censor-Hillel, Seri Khoury, and Ami Paz. 2017. Quadratic and Near-Quadratic Lower Bounds for the CONGEST Model. In *Proc. 31st International Symposium on Distributed Computing (DISC 2017)*. https://doi.org/10.4230/LIPIcs.DISC.2017.10

[4] Andrew Drucker, Fabian Kuhn, and Rotem Oshman. 2014. On the power of the congested clique model. In *Proc. Symposium on Principles of Distributed Computing (PODC 2014)*. 367–376. https://doi.org/10.1145/2611462.2611493

[5] Orr Fischer, Tzlil Gonen, Fabian Kuhn, and Rotem Oshman. 2018. Possibilities and Impossibilities for Distributed Subgraph Detection. In *Proc. 30th Symposium on Parallelism in Algorithms and Architectures (SPAA 2018)*. 153–162. https://doi.org/10.1145/3210377.3210401

[6] Klaus-Tycho Foerster, Juho Hirvonen, Stefan Schmid, and Jukka Suomela. 2019. On the Power of Preprocessing in Decentralized Network Optimization. In *Proc. 39th IEEE International Conference on Computer Communications (INFOCOM 2019)*. https://arxiv.org/pdf/1812.00854v1.pdf

[7] Silvio Frischknecht, Stephan Holzer, and Roger Wattenhofer. 2012. Networks cannot compute their diameter in sublinear time. In *Proc. 23rd ACM-SIAM Symposium on Discrete Algorithms (SODA 2012)*. 1150–1162. https://doi.org/10.1137/1.9781611973099.91

[8] Janne H. Korhonen and Joel Rybicki. 2017. Deterministic Subgraph Detection in Broadcast CONGEST. In *Proc. 21st International Conference on Principles of Distributed Systems (OPODIS 2017)*. https://doi.org/10.4230/LIPIcs.OPODIS.2017.4

[9] Zvi Lotker, Elan Pavlov, Boaz Patt-Shamir, and David Peleg. 2003. MST construction in $O(\log \log n)$ communication rounds. In *Proc. 15th ACM Symposium on Parallelism in Algorithms and Architectures (SPAA 2003)*. 94–100. https://doi.org/10.1145/777412.777428

[10] Atish Das Sarma, Stephan Holzer, Liah Kor, Amos Korman, Danupon Nanongkai, Gopal Pandurangan, David Peleg, and Roger Wattenhofer. 2012. Distributed Verification and Hardness of Distributed Approximation. *SIAM J. Comput.* 41, 5 (2012), 1235–1265. https://doi.org/10.1137/11085178X

[11] Stefan Schmid and Jukka Suomela. 2013. Exploiting locality in distributed SDN control. In *Proc. 2nd ACM SIGCOMM Workshop on Hot Topics in Software Defined Networking (HotSDN 2013)*. 121–126. https://doi.org/10.1145/2491185.2491198

The Distributed Complexity of Locally Checkable Problems on Paths is Decidable

Alkida Balliu
alkida.balliu@aalto.fi
Aalto University

Sebastian Brandt
brandts@ethz.ch
ETH Zurich

Yi-Jun Chang
cyijun@umich.edu
University of Michigan

Dennis Olivetti
dennis.olivetti@aalto.fi
Aalto University

Mikaël Rabie
mikael.rabie@irif.fr
Aalto University and
IRIF, University of Paris

Jukka Suomela
jukka.suomela@aalto.fi
Aalto University

ABSTRACT

Consider a computer network that consists of a path with n nodes. The nodes are labeled with inputs from a constant-sized set, and the task is to find output labels from a constant-sized set subject to some local constraints—more formally, we have an LCL (locally checkable labeling) problem. How many communication rounds are needed (in the standard LOCAL model of computing) to solve this problem?

It is well known that the answer is always either $O(1)$ rounds, or $\Theta(\log^* n)$ rounds, or $\Theta(n)$ rounds. In this work we show that this question is *decidable* (albeit PSPACE-hard): we present an algorithm that, given any LCL problem defined on a path, outputs the distributed computational complexity of this problem and the corresponding asymptotically optimal algorithm.

CCS CONCEPTS

• **Theory of computation → Distributed computing models**; *Complexity classes*; *Distributed algorithms*.

KEYWORDS

distributed computing, complexity, decidability

ACM Reference Format:
Alkida Balliu, Sebastian Brandt, Yi-Jun Chang, Dennis Olivetti, Mikaël Rabie, and Jukka Suomela. 2019. The Distributed Complexity of Locally Checkable Problems on Paths is Decidable. In *2019 ACM Symposium on Principles of Distributed Computing (PODC '19), July 29-August 2, 2019, Toronto, ON, Canada.* ACM, New York, NY, USA, 10 pages. https://doi.org/10.1145/3293611.3331606

1 INTRODUCTION

To what extent is it possible to *automate* the design of algorithms and the study of computational complexity? While algorithm synthesis problems are typically undecidable, there are areas of theoretical computer science in which we can make use of computational techniques in algorithm design—at least in principle, and sometimes also in practice. One such area is the theory of *distributed computing*; see [4, 6, 8, 10, 11, 17, 19, 26] for examples of recent success stories. In this work we bring yet another piece of good news:

> Consider this setting: there is a computer network that consists of a path with n nodes, the nodes are labeled with inputs from a constant-sized set, and the task is to find output labels from a constant-sized set subject to some local constraints. We show that for any given set of local constraints, *it is decidable* to tell what is the asymptotically optimal number of communication rounds needed to solve this problem (as a function of n, for the worst-case input).

Background: **LCL***s and the* **LOCAL** *Model.* We focus on what are known as LCL (*locally checkable labeling*) problems [22] in the LOCAL model of distributed computing [20, 24]. We define the setting formally in Section 2, but in essence we look at the following question:

- We are given an unknown input graph of maximum degree $\Delta = O(1)$; the nodes are labeled with *input labels* from a constant-size set Σ_{in}, and the nodes also have unique identifiers from a polynomially-sized set.
- The task is to label the nodes with *output labels* from a constant-size set Σ_{out}, subject to some *local* constraints $\mathcal{P}$; a labeling is globally feasible if it is locally feasible in all radius-r neighborhoods for some $r = O(1)$.
- Each node has to produce its own output label based on the information that it sees in its own radius-$T(n)$ neighborhoods for some function T.

Here the local constraints $\mathcal{P}$ define an LCL problem. The rule that the nodes apply to determine their output labels is called a *distributed algorithm* in the LOCAL model, and function $T(n)$ is the *running time* of the algorithm—here $T(n)$ determines how *far* a node has to see in order to choose its own part of the solution, or equivalently, how many *communication rounds* are needed for each node to gather the relevant information if we view the input graph as a communication network.

In this setting, the case of $T(n) = \Theta(n)$ is trivial, as all nodes can see the entire input. The key question is to determine which problems $\mathcal{P}$ can be solved in sublinear time—here are some examples:

PODC '19, July 29-August 2, 2019, Toronto, ON, Canada

ACM ISBN 978-1-4503-6217-7/19/07...$15.00
https://doi.org/10.1145/3293611.3331606

- Vertex coloring with $\Delta + 1$ colors: can be solved in time $O(\log^* n)$ [9, 16] and this is tight [20, 21].
- Vertex coloring with Δ colors, for $\Delta > 2$: can be solved in polylogarithmic time [23] and requires at least logarithmic time [7] for deterministic algorithms.

While the study of this setting was initiated already in the seminal work by Naor and Stockmeyer in 1995 [22], our understanding of these questions has rapidly advanced in the past three years [2, 3, 5, 7, 8, 12–15, 25]. The big surprises have been these:

- There are LCL problems with infinitely many different time complexities—for example, we can construct LCL problems with a time complexity exactly $\Theta(n^\alpha)$ for any rational number $0 < \alpha \leq 1$.
- Nevertheless, there are also wide gaps in the complexity landscape: for example, no LCL problem has a (deterministic) computational complexity that is between $\omega(\log^* n)$ and $o(\log n)$.

However, what is perhaps most relevant for us is the following observation: if we look at the case of $\Delta = 2$ (paths and cycles), then the time complexity of any LCL problem is either $O(1)$, $\Theta(\log^* n)$, or $\Theta(n)$, and the same holds for both deterministic and randomized algorithms [6, 8, 22].

Decidability of **LCL** *Time Complexities.* For a fixed Δ, any LCL problem has a trivial finite representation: simply enumerate all feasible radius-r local neighborhoods. Hence it makes sense to ask whether, given an LCL problem, it is possible to determine its time complexity. The following results are known by prior work:

- If the input graph is an *unlabeled path or cycle*, the time complexity is decidable [6, 22].
- If the input graph is a *grid or toroidal grid*, the time complexity is undecidable [22]. However, there are also some good news: in unlabeled toroidal grids, the time complexity falls in one of the classes $O(1)$, $\Theta(\log^* n)$, or $\Theta(n)$, it is trivial to tell if the time complexity is $O(1)$, and it is semi-decidable to tell if it is $\Theta(\log^* n)$ [6].
- In the case of trees, there are infinitely many different time complexities, but there is a gap between $\omega(\log n)$ and $n^{o(1)}$, and it is decidable to tell on which side of the gap a given problem lies [8].

Somewhat surprisingly, the seemingly simple case of *labeled paths or cycles* has remained open all the way since the 1995 paper by Naor and Stockmeyer [22], which defined LCLs with inputs but analyzed decidability questions only in the case of unlabeled graphs.

We initially expected that the question of paths with input labels is a mere technicality and the interesting open questions are related to much broader graph families, such as rooted trees, trees, and bounded-treewidth graphs. However, it turned out that the *main obstacle for understanding decidability in any such graph family seems to lie in the fact that the structure of the graph can be used to encode arbitrary input labels*, hence it is necessary to first understand how the input labels influence decidability—and it turns out that this makes all the difference in the case of paths.

In this work we show that the time complexity of a given LCL problem on *labeled paths or cycles* is decidable. However, we also show that decidability is far from trivial: the problem is PSPACE-hard, as LCL problems on labeled paths are expressive enough to capture linear bounded automata (Turing machines with bounded tapes).

Full Version. Due to space constraints, this version is missing some proofs and other details. The full version can be found here [1].

2 MODEL

The **LOCAL** *Model.* The model of computation we consider in this work is the LOCAL model of distributed computing [20, 24]. In the LOCAL model, each node of the input graph is considered as a computational entity that can communicate with the neighboring nodes in order to solve some given graph problem. Computation is divided into synchronous rounds, where in each round each node first sends messages of arbitrary size to its neighbors, then receives the messages sent by its neighbors, and finally performs some local computation of arbitrary complexity. Each node is equipped with a globally unique identifier (ID) which is simply a bit string of length $O(\log n)$, where n denotes the number of nodes of the input graph. In the beginning of the computation, each node is aware of its own ID, the number of nodes and the maximum degree Δ of the input graph, and potentially some additional problem-specific input. Each node has to decide at some point that it terminates, upon which it returns a local output and does not take part in any further computation; the problem is solved correctly if the local outputs of all nodes together constitute a global output that satisfies the output constraints of the given problem.

Each node executes the same algorithm; the running time of the distributed algorithm is the number of rounds until the last node terminates. It is well known that, due to the unbounded message sizes, an algorithm with runtime $T(n)$ can be equivalently described as a function from the set of all possible radius-$T(n)$ neighborhoods to the set of allowed outputs. In other words, we can assume that in a $T(n)$-round algorithm, each node first gathers the topology of and the input labels contained in its radius-$T(n)$ neighborhood, and then decides on its output based solely on the collected information.

Locally Checkable Labelings. The class of problems we consider is *locally checkable labeling* (LCL) problems [22]. LCL problems are defined on graphs of bounded degree, i.e., we will assume that $\Delta = O(1)$. Formally, an LCL problem is given by a finite input label set Σ_{in}, a finite output label set Σ_{out}, an integer r, and a finite set C of graphs where every node is labeled with a pair $(\ell_{\text{in}}, \ell_{\text{out}}) \in \Sigma_{\text{in}} \times \Sigma_{\text{out}}$ and one node is marked (as the center). Each node of the input graph is assigned an input label from Σ_{in} before the computation begins, and the global output of a distributed algorithm is correct if the radius-r neighborhood of each node v, including the input labels given to the contained nodes and the output labels returned by the contained nodes, is isomorphic to an element of C where v corresponds to the node marked as the center.

In the case of directed paths as our class of input graphs, we are interested in identifying the simplest possible form of LCL problems. For this purpose, we define β*-normalized* LCLs; these are problems for which the input is just binary, and the size of the set of output labels is β. Moreover, the solution can be checked at each node v by just inspecting the input and output of v, and, separately, the output

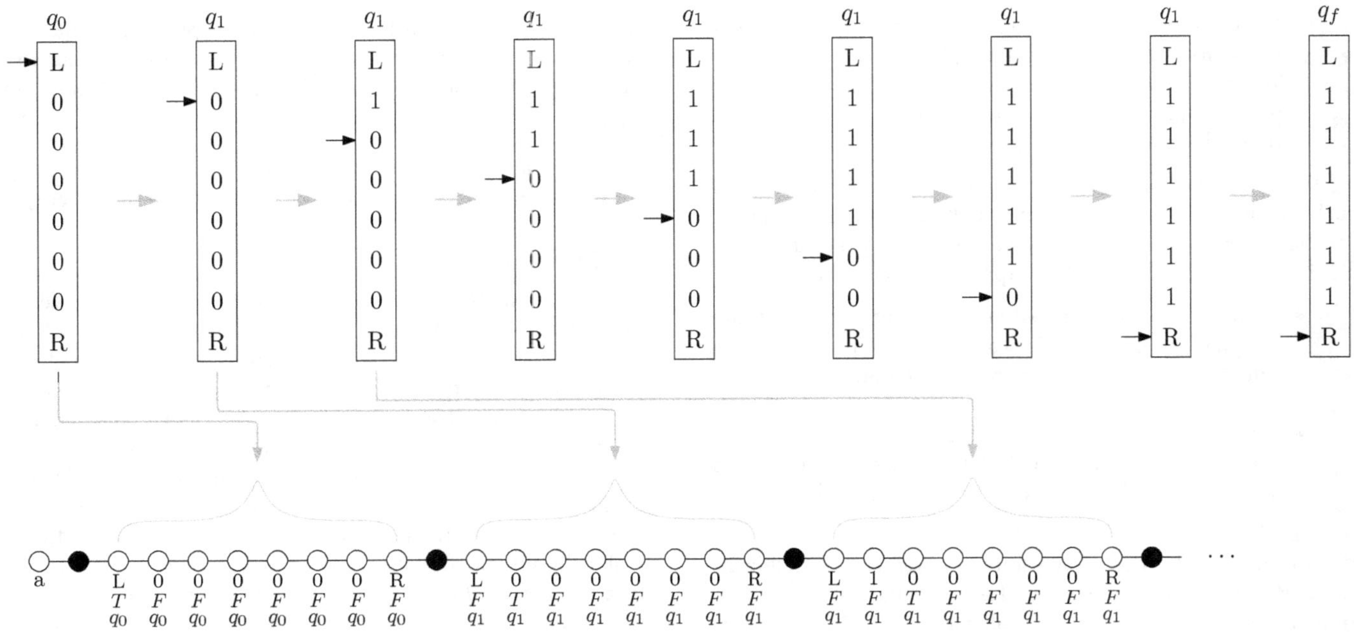

Figure 1: Illustration of a correct encoding of the execution of an LBA on a path; black nodes act as separators between the encoding of two consecutive steps of the LBA; in the example, the LBA executes a unary counter.

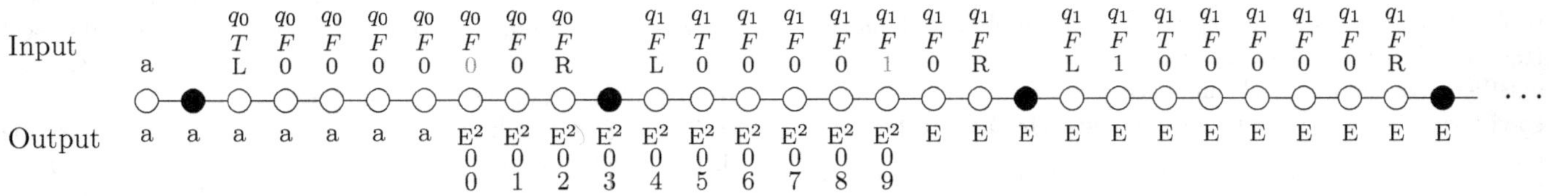

Figure 2: Illustration of an incorrect encoding of the execution of an LBA on a path; in the example, the tape of the LBA is wrongly copied (the inputs in red are different, while they should be the same). The error output E^2 encodes the distance of $B+1$ between the two nodes, and the input wrongly copied.

of v and the output of its predecessor. More formally, a *β-normalized* LCL problem is given by finite input and output label sets Σ_{in}, Σ_{out} satisfying $|\Sigma_{\text{in}}| = 2$, $|\Sigma_{\text{out}}| = \beta$, a finite set $C_{\text{in-out}}$ of pairs $(\ell_{\text{in}}, \ell_{\text{out}}) \in \Sigma_{\text{in}} \times \Sigma_{\text{out}}$ and a finite set $C_{\text{out-out}}$ of pairs $(\ell_{\text{out}}, \ell'_{\text{out}}) \in \Sigma_{\text{out}} \times \Sigma_{\text{out}}$. The global output of a distributed algorithm for the β-normalized LCL problem is correct if the following hold:

- For each node v, we have $(\text{Input}(v), \text{Output}(v)) \in C_{\text{in-out}}$, where $\text{Input}(v)$ denotes the input label of v, and $\text{Output}(v)$ the output label of v.
- For each node v that has a predecessor, we have $(\text{Output}(v), \text{Output}(u)) \in C_{\text{out-out}}$, where u is the predecessor of v, and $\text{Output}(v)$, $\text{Output}(u)$ are the output labels of v and u, respectively.

It is straightforward to check that a β-normalized LCL problem is indeed a special case of an LCL problem where $r = 1$.

3 HARDNESS

In this section we study the hardness of determining the distributed complexity of LCLs on paths and cycles with input labels. More precisely, we start by proving the existence of a family Π of LCL problems for consistently globally oriented paths, such that, given an LCL problem in Π, it is PSPACE-hard to decide if its distributed complexity is $O(1)$ or $\Theta(n)$. The main result is summarised in the following theorem.

THEOREM 1. *It is PSPACE-hard to distinguish whether a given* LCL *problem $\mathcal{P}$ with input labels can be solved in $O(1)$ time or needs $\Omega(n)$ time on globally oriented path graphs.*

The high level idea of the proof of Theorem 1 is as follows. We would like to encode the execution of Turing machines as LCLs on consistently oriented paths, and then define some LCL for which the complexity depends on the running time of the machine. This is fairly easy on oriented grids, for example, where we can use one dimension of the grid as a tape, and the other dimension as time. One may try to do the same on paths, by projecting everything on a single dimension, concatenating the tape state of each step. Unfortunately, the obtained encoding is not locally checkable, since the length of the tape may be non-constant. Hence, in order to guarantee the local checkability, we should consider Turing machines having a tape of size at most B, where B is a constant with respect to the number of nodes in the path where we want to encode its

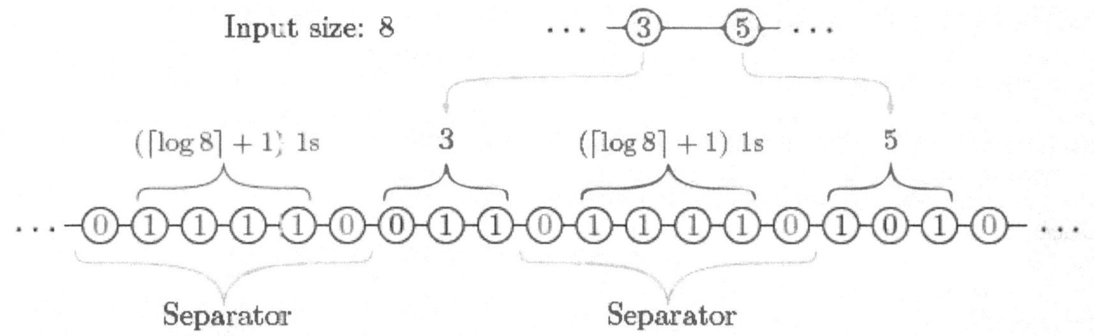

Figure 3: Illustration of the normalization of an LCL.

execution. For this purpose, we consider Linear Bounded Automata (LBA) [18, p. 225]. An LBA is a Turing machine that has a tape of size upper bounded by some B. We show that, if B is constant with respect to the number of nodes in the path, we can then encode the execution of an LBA M_B as an LCL for directed paths. Moreover, we show that by seeing this encoding as a two party game between a *prover* and a *disprover*, we can encode the execution of M_B using labels of constant size that do not depend on B, even in the case in which the LCL checkability radius is 1. If the execution of M_B is not correctly encoded in the input of the LCL, then we can disprove its correctness using output labels of size $O(B)$. Moreover, we ensure that, if the execution of M_B is correctly encoded in the input of the LCL, it is not possible to produce a correct proof of non-correctness. Then, in order to obtain an LCL with a distributed complexity that depends on the execution time of M_B, we encode some secret input at the first node of the path. We require then that all nodes involved in a correct encoding must produce the same secret as output. Figure 1 shows an example of an LBA that executes a unary counter, and its encoding as input to nodes on a path. In this instance, all nodes must produce the symbol a as output. Figure 2 shows an example of the wrong input (the tape has been copied incorrectly between two consecutive steps of the LBA). In this case, nodes are allowed to produce a chain of errors. Different types of errors will be handled using different types of error labels. In the example, all nodes that produce the error chain, output E^2, indicating an error of type 2. We will show that we need $O(B)$ symbols to handle all possible errors (including the case in which the input tape is too long, way more than B). Also, it is necessary that all error chains that we allow as outputs must be locally checkable.

Another interesting problem is to identify, for an LCL that can be distributedly solved in constant time, how big this constant can be. In particular, we first focus on identifying the simplest possible description of an LCL, and then, we provide a lower bound on the complexity of a constant time LCL, as a function of the size of the LCL description. For this purpose, we consider β-normalized LCLs, i.e., problems for which the input labeling is just binary and there are β possible output labels. Also, the verifier for these LCLs is the simplest possible: it can only check if the output of a node is correct w.r.t. its input, and separately, if the output of a node is correct w.r.t. the output of its predecessor. Therefore, we show how to convert an LCL to a β-normalized one by encoding the input in binary (Figure 3 shows an example), and obtain the following result.

Theorem 2. *There are β-normalized* LCLs *that can be solved in constant time but the distributed time complexity is* $2^{\Omega(\beta)}$.

All results we described so far apply to globally oriented paths. Nevertheless, we show that the ideas and techniques can be generalized to work on undirected paths and cycles as well, obtaining essentially the same results. Finally, we will show how to lift these results to trees *without* input labels, proving the following theorem.

Theorem 3. *It is PSPACE-hard to distinguish whether a given* LCL *problem $\mathcal{P}$ without input labels can be solved in $O(1)$ time or needs $\Omega(n)$ time on trees with degree $\Delta = 3$.*

4 DECIDABILITY

In this section, we show that the two gaps $\omega(1)$—$o(\log^* n)$ and $\omega(\log^* n)$—$o(n)$ for LCL problems *with input labels* on paths and cycles are decidable. More specifically, given a specification of an LCL problem $\mathcal{P}$, there is an algorithm that outputs a description of an asymptotically optimal deterministic LOCAL algorithm for $\mathcal{P}$, as well as its time complexity.

We will prove the statements for the case of cycles, but the analogous results for cycles and paths follows as a simple corollary, as we can encode constraints related to degree-1 nodes as constraints related to nodes adjacent to a special input label. Furthermore, having a promise that the input is a path does not change the time complexity of an LCL problem: if a problem can be solved in time $T = o(n)$ in labeled paths, the same algorithm will solve it also in time $T = o(n)$ in labeled cycles.

The proof of Theorem 4 is in Section 4.2; the proof of Theorem 5 is in Section 4.5.

Theorem 4. *For any* LCL *problem $\mathcal{P}$ on cycle graphs, its deterministic* LOCAL *complexity is either $\Omega(n)$ or $O(\log^* n)$. Moreover, there is an algorithm that decides whether $\mathcal{P}$ has complexity $\Omega(n)$ or $O(\log^* n)$ on cycle graphs; for the case the complexity is $O(\log^* n)$, the algorithm outputs a description of an $O(\log^* n)$-round deterministic* LOCAL *algorithm that solves $\mathcal{P}$.*

Theorem 5. *For any* LCL *problem $\mathcal{P}$ on cycle graphs, its deterministic* LOCAL *complexity is either $\Omega(\log^* n)$ or $O(1)$. Moreover, there is an algorithm that decides whether $\mathcal{P}$ has complexity $\Omega(\log^* n)$ or $O(1)$ on cycle graphs; for the case the complexity is $O(1)$, the algorithm outputs a description of an $O(1)$-round deterministic* LOCAL *algorithm that solves $\mathcal{P}$.*

For convenience, in this section, a directed path P with input labels is alternatively described as a string in Σ_{in}^k, where $k > 0$ is the number of nodes in P. Similarly, an output labeling $\mathcal{L}$ of P is alternatively described as a string in Σ_{out}^k. In subsequent discussion, we freely switch between the graph-theoretic notation and the string notation. Given an output labeling $\mathcal{L}$ of P, we say that $\mathcal{L}$ is *locally consistent* at v if the input and output labeling assigned to $N^r(v)$ is acceptable for v. Note that $N^r(v)$ refers to the radius-r neighborhood of v. Given two integers $a \le b$, the notation $[a, b]$ represents the set of all integers $\{a, a+1, \ldots, b\}$. Given a string w, denote w^R as the reverse of w.

4.1 Pumping Lemmas for Paths

Let $P = (s, \ldots, t)$ be a directed path, where each node has an input label from Σ_{in}. The *tripartition* of the nodes $\xi(P) = (D_1, D_2, D_3)$ is defined as follows:

$$D_1 = N^{r-1}(s) \cup N^{r-1}(t),$$
$$D_2 = \left(N^{2r-1}(s) \cup N^{2r-1}(t)\right) \setminus D_1,$$
$$D_3 = P \setminus (D_1 \cup D_2).$$

See Figure 4 for an illustration. More specifically, suppose $P = (u_1, \ldots, u_k)$, and let $i \in [1, k]$. Then we have:

- $u_i \in D_1$ if and only if $i \in [1, r] \cup [k - r + 1, k]$.
- $u_i \in D_2$ if and only if $i \in [r + 1, 2r] \cup [k - 2r + 1, k - r]$.
- $u_i \in D_3$ if and only if $i \notin [1, 2r] \cup [k - 2r + 1, k]$.

Let $\mathcal{L}\colon D_1 \cup D_2 \to \Sigma_{\text{out}}$ assign output labels to $D_1 \cup D_2$. We say that $\mathcal{L}$ is *extendible* w.r.t. P if there exists a complete labeling $\mathcal{L}_\diamond$ of P such that $\mathcal{L}_\diamond$ agrees with $\mathcal{L}$ on $D_1 \cup D_2$, and $\mathcal{L}_\diamond$ is locally consistent at all nodes in $D_2 \cup D_3$.

An Equivalence Class. We define an equivalence class $\overset{\star}{\sim}$ for the directed paths (i.e., the set of all non-empty strings in Σ_{in}^*), as follows.

Consider two directed paths $P = (u_1, \ldots, u_x)$ and $P' = (v_1, \ldots, v_y)$, and let $\xi(P) = (D_1, D_2, D_3)$ and $\xi(P') = (D_1', D_2', D_3')$. Consider the following natural 1-to-1 correspondence $\phi\colon (D_1 \cup D_2) \to (D_1' \cup D_2')$ defined as $\phi(u_i) = v_i$ and $\phi(u_{x-i+1}) = v_{y-i+1}$ for each $i \in [1, 2r]$. The 1-to-1 correspondence is well-defined so long as (i) $x = y$ or (ii) $x \ge 4r$ and $y \ge 4r$. We have $P \overset{\star}{\sim} P'$ if and only if the following two statements are met:

- **Isomorphism:** The 1-to-1 correspondence ϕ is well-defined, and for each $u_i \in D_1 \cup D_2$, the input label of u_i is identical to the input label of $\phi(u_i)$.
- **Extendibility:** Let $\mathcal{L}$ be *any* assignment of output labels to nodes in $D_1 \cup D_2$, and let $\mathcal{L}'$ be the corresponding output labeling of $D_1' \cup D_2'$ under ϕ. Then $\mathcal{L}$ is extendible w.r.t. P if and only if $\mathcal{L}'$ is extendible w.r.t. P'.

Note that for the special case of $x \le 4r$, we have $P \overset{\star}{\sim} P'$ if and only if P is identical to P'.

Define $\text{Type}(P)$ as the equivalence class of P w.r.t. $\overset{\star}{\sim}$. The following lemma is analogous to [8, Theorem 3] in a specialized setting.

One useful consequence of this lemma is that if we start with a path or a cycle G with a legal labeling, after replacing its subpath P with another one P' having the same type as P, then it is always possible to assign output labeling to P' to get a legal labeling without changing the already-assigned output labels of nodes outside of P'.

Lemma 6. *Let G be a path graph or a cycle graph where all nodes have input labels from Σ_{in}. Let P be a directed subpath of G, and let P' be another directed path such that $\text{Type}(P') = \text{Type}(P)$. Let $\mathcal{L}_\diamond$ any complete labeling of G such that $\mathcal{L}_\diamond$ is locally consistent at all nodes in P. Let $G' = \text{Replace}(G, P, P')$ be the graph resulting from replacing P with P' in G. Then there exists a complete labeling $\mathcal{L}_\diamond'$ of G' such that the following two conditions are met.*

1. *For each $v \in V(G) \setminus V(P)$ and its corresponding $v' \in V(G') \setminus V(P')$, we have $\mathcal{L}_\diamond(v) = \mathcal{L}_\diamond'(v')$. Moreover, if $\mathcal{L}_\diamond$ is locally consistent at $v \in V(G) \setminus V(P)$, then $\mathcal{L}_\diamond'$ is locally consistent at v'.*
2. *$\mathcal{L}_\diamond'$ is locally consistent at all nodes in P'.*

The following lemma is analogous to [8, Theorem 4] in a specialized setting. We only use this lemma in Section 4.1.

Lemma 7. *Let $P = (v_1, \ldots, v_k)$, and let $P' = (v_1, \ldots, v_{k-1})$. Let the input label of v_k be α. Then $\text{Type}(P)$ is a function of α and $\text{Type}(P')$.*

The number of types can be upper bounded as follows.

Lemma 8. *The number of equivalence classes of $\overset{\star}{\sim}$ (i.e., types) is at most $|\Sigma_{\text{in}}|^{4r} 2^{|\Sigma_{\text{out}}|^{4r}}$.*

Proof. Let P be a directed path, and let $\xi(P) = (D_1, D_2, D_3)$. Then $\text{Type}(P)$ is determined by the following information.

- The input labels in $D_1 \cup D_2$. Note that there are at most $|\Sigma_{\text{in}}|^{4r}$ possible input labeling of $D_1 \cup D_2$.
- A length-x binary string indicating the extendibility of each possible output labeling of $D_1 \cup D_2$, where $x = |\Sigma_{\text{out}}|^{4r}$.

Therefore, there are at most $|\Sigma_{\text{in}}|^{4r} 2^{|\Sigma_{\text{out}}|^{4r}}$ equivalence classes of $\overset{\star}{\sim}$. □

Define ℓ_{pump} as the total number of types. Observe that Lemma 7 implies that $\text{Type}(P)$ can be computed by a finite automaton whose number of states is the total number of types, which is a constant independent of P. Thus, we have the following two *pumping lemmas* which allow us to extend the length of a given directed path P while preserving the type of P. The following two lemmas follow from the standard pumping lemma for regular language.

Lemma 9. *Let $P \in \Sigma_{\text{in}}^k$ with $k \ge \ell_{\text{pump}}$. Then P can be decomposed into three substrings $P = x \circ y \circ z$ such that (i) $|xy| \le \ell_{\text{pump}}$, (ii) $|y| \ge 1$, and (iii) for each non-negative integer i, $\text{Type}(x \circ y^i \circ z) = \text{Type}(P)$.*

Lemma 10. *For each $w \in \Sigma_{\text{in}}^{>0}$, there exist two positive integers a and b such that $a + b \le \ell_{\text{pump}}$, and $\text{Type}(w^{ai+b})$ is invariant for each non-negative integer i.*

4.2 The $\omega(\log^* n)$—$o(n)$ Gap

In this section we show that the $\omega(\log^* n)$—$o(n)$ gap is decidable. More specifically, we show that an LCL problem $\mathcal{P}$ can be solved

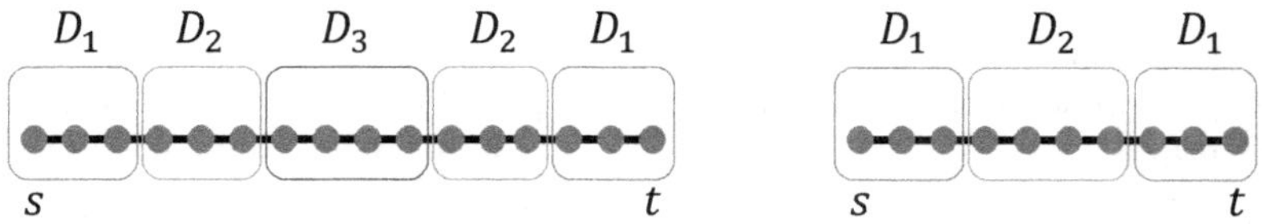

Figure 4: Illustration of the tripartition $\xi(P) = (D_1, D_2, D_3)$ with $r = 3$.

in $O(\log^* n)$ rounds if and only if there exists a *feasible function*, which is defined as follows.

Input: A directed path $P = w_1 \circ S \circ w_2$, where $|w_1| \in [\ell_{\text{pump}}, \ell_{\text{pump}}+1]$, $|w_2| \in [\ell_{\text{pump}}, \ell_{\text{pump}}+1]$, and $|S| = 2r$. The decomposition $P = w_1 \circ S \circ w_2$ is considered part of the input.

Output: A string $\mathcal{L} \in \Sigma_{\text{out}}^{2r}$ that represents the output labeling of S.

Requirement: Any such function f is said to be *feasible* if the following requirement is met for any paths S_1, S_2 and w_a, w_b, w_c, w_d such that $\{|w_a|, |w_b|, |w_c|, |w_d|\} \subseteq [\ell_{\text{pump}}, \ell_{\text{pump}}+1]$ and $|S_1| = |S_2| = 2r$. Let $P = w_a \circ S_1 \circ w_b \circ w_c \circ S_2 \circ w_d$, and consider the following assignment of output labels to $S_1 \cup S_2$.

- Either label S_1 by $f(w_a \circ S_1 \circ w_b)$ or label S_1^R by $f(w_b^R \circ S_1^R \circ w_a^R)$.
- Either label S_2 by $f(w_c \circ S_2 \circ w_d)$ or label S_2^R by $f(w_d^R \circ S_2^R \circ w_c^R)$.

It is required that given such a partial labeling of P, the middle part $w_b \circ w_c$ can be assigned output labels in such a way that the labeling of (i) the last r nodes of S_1, (ii) all nodes in $w_b \circ w_c$, and (iii) the first r nodes of S_2 are locally consistent.

The following lemma is a straightforward consequence of the well-known $O(\log^* n)$-round MIS algorithm on cycles.

Lemma 11. *Let G be a cycle graph of n nodes, and let $s \leq k$ be two constant integers such that $n \geq (s+k)^2$. Then in $O(\log^* n)$ rounds we can compute a decomposition $V = A \cup B$ such that each connected component of A has size s, and each connected component of B has size within $[k, k+1]$.*

Lemma 12. *If a feasible function f exists, then there is an $O(\log^* n)$-round deterministic* LOCAL *algorithm for $\mathcal{P}$ on cycles.*

Proof. Given that the number of nodes n is at least some large enough constant, in $O(\log^* n)$ rounds we can compute a decomposition $V = A \cup B$ such that each connected component of A has size $2r$, and each connected component of B has size within $[2\ell_{\text{pump}}, 2\ell_{\text{pump}}+1]$. This can be done using Lemma 11 with $s = 2r$ and $k = 2\ell_{\text{pump}}$. We further decompose each connected component P of B into two paths $P = P_1 \circ P_2$ in such a way that the size of both P_1 and P_2 are within the range $[\ell_{\text{pump}}, \ell_{\text{pump}}+1]$. We write $\mathscr{P}$ to denote the set of all these paths.

Let S be a connected component of A, and let w_1 and w_2 be its two neighboring paths in $\mathscr{P}$ so that $(w_1 \circ S \circ w_2)$ is a subpath of the underlying graph G. The output labels of S are assigned either by labeling S with $f(w_1 \circ S \circ w_2)$ or by labeling S^R with $f(w_2^R \circ S^R \circ w_1^R)$. At this moment, all components of A have been assigned output labels using f. By the feasibility of f, each connected component of B is able to label itself output labels in such a way that the labeling of all nodes are locally consistent. □

Lemma 13. *If there is an $o(n)$-round deterministic* LOCAL *algorithm for $\mathcal{P}$ on cycles, then a feasible function f exists.*

Proof. Fix s to be some sufficiently large number, and fix $n = 8(s + \ell_{\text{pump}}) + 2(2r)$. We select s to be large enough so that the runtime of $\mathcal{A}$ is smaller than $0.1s$. For any given directed path w with $|w| \in [\ell_{\text{pump}}, \ell_{\text{pump}}+1]$, we fix w^+ as the result of applying the pumping lemma (Lemma 9) on w so that the following two conditions are met: (i) $|w^+| \in [s, s+\ell_{\text{pump}}]$ and (ii) $\text{Type}(w) = \text{Type}(w^+)$.

Constructing a Feasible Function f by Simulating $\mathcal{A}$. The function $f(w_1 \circ S \circ w_2)$ is constructed by simulating a given $o(n)$-round deterministic LOCAL algorithm for $\mathcal{P}$. The output labeling given by $f(w_1 \circ S \circ w_2)$ is exactly the result of simulating $\mathcal{A}$ on the path $P = w_1^+ \circ S \circ w_2^+$ while assuming the number of nodes of the underlying graph is n. Remember that the round complexity of $\mathcal{A}$ is $o(n)$ on n-node graphs. By setting s to be large enough, the runtime of $\mathcal{A}$ can be made smaller than $0.1s$. Thus, the calculation of $f(w_1 \circ S \circ w_2)$ only depends on the IDs and the input labels of (i) the last $0.1s$ nodes in w_1^+, (ii) all nodes in S, and (iii) the first $0.1s$ nodes in w_2^+. In the calculation of $f(w_1 \circ S \circ w_2)$, the IDs of the nodes that participate in the simulation of $\mathcal{A}$ are chosen arbitrarily so long as they are distinct.

Feasibility of f. Now we verify that the function f constructed above is feasible. Consider any choices of paths S_1, S_2 and w_a, w_b, w_c, w_d such that $\{|w_a|, |w_b|, |w_c|, |w_d|\} \subseteq [\ell_{\text{pump}}, \ell_{\text{pump}}+1]$ and $|S_1| = |S_2| = 2r$. Define $P = w_a \circ S_1 \circ w_b \circ w_c \circ S_2 \circ w_d$, and let G be the cycle graph formed by connecting the two ends of the path P. To show that f is feasible, we need to consider the following four ways of assigning output labels to $S_1 \cup S_2$.

(1) Label S_1 by $f(w_a \circ S_1 \circ w_b)$; label S_2 by $f(w_c \circ S_2 \circ w_d)$.
(2) Label S_1 by $f(w_a \circ S_1 \circ w_b)$; label S_2^R by $f(w_d^R \circ S_2^R \circ w_c^R)$.
(3) Label S_1^R by $f(w_b^R \circ S_1^R \circ w_a^R)$; label S_2 by $f(w_c \circ S_2 \circ w_d)$.
(4) Label S_1^R by $f(w_b^R \circ S_1^R \circ w_a^R)$; label S_2^R by $f(w_d^R \circ S_2^R \circ w_c^R)$.

For each of the above four partial labelings of P, we need to show that the middle part $w_b \circ w_c$ can still be assigned output labels in such a way that the labeling of (i) the last r nodes of S_1, (ii) all nodes in $w_b \circ w_c$, and (iii) the first r nodes of S_2 are locally consistent.

Proof of the First Case. In what follows, we focus on the first case, i.e., the partial labeling is given by labeling S_1 by $f(w_a \circ S_1 \circ w_b)$ and labeling S_2 by $f(w_c \circ S_2 \circ w_d)$; the proof for the other three cases are analogous. In this case, we define $P' = w_a^+ \circ S_1 \circ w_b^+ \circ w_c^+ \circ S_2 \circ w_d^+$, and let G' be the cycle graph formed by connecting the two ends of P'. Note that the number of nodes in G' is at most $8(s+\ell_{\text{pump}})+2(2r) = n$. All we need to do is to find an output labeling $\mathcal{L}$ of G such that the following conditions are satisfied.

(a) The output labels of S_1 is given by $f(w_a \circ S_1 \circ w_b)$.
(b) The output labels of S_2 is given by $f(w_c \circ S_2 \circ w_d)$.
(c) The labeling of (i) the last r nodes of S_1, (ii) all nodes in $w_b \circ w_c$, and (iii) the first r nodes of S_2 are locally consistent.

We first generate an output labeling $\mathcal{L}'$ of G' by executing $\mathcal{A}$ on G' under the following ID assignment. The IDs of (i) the last $0.1s$ nodes in w_a^+, (ii) all nodes in S_1, and (iii) the first $0.1s$ nodes in w_b^+ are chosen as the ones used in the definition of $f(w_a \circ S_1 \circ w_b)$. Similarly, the IDs of (i) the last $0.1s$ nodes in w_c^+, (ii) all nodes in S_2, and (iii) the first $0.1s$ nodes in w_d^+ are chosen as the ones used in the definition of $f(w_c \circ S_2 \circ w_d)$. The IDs of the rest of the nodes are chosen arbitrarily so long as when we run $\mathcal{A}$ on G', no node sees two nodes with the same ID. Due to the way we define f, the output labeling $\mathcal{L}'$ of the subpath S_1 is exactly given by $f(w_a \circ S_1 \circ w_b)$, and the output labeling $\mathcal{L}'$ of S_2 is exactly $f(w_c \circ S_2 \circ w_d)$. Due to the correctness of $\mathcal{A}$, $\mathcal{L}'$ is a legal labeling.

We transform the output labeling $\mathcal{L}'$ of G' to a desired output labeling $\mathcal{L}$ of G. Remember that G is the result of replacing the four subpaths w^+ of G' by w, and we have $\text{Type}(w^+) = \text{Type}(w)$. In view of Lemma 6, there is a legal labeling $\mathcal{L}$ of G such that all nodes in S_1 and S_2 are labeled the same as in G'. Therefore, the labeling $\mathcal{L}$ satisfies the above three conditions (a), (b), and (c).

The Other Cases. We briefly discuss how we modify the proof to deal with the other three cases. For example, consider the second case, where the partial labeling is given by labeling S_1 by $f(w_a \circ S_1 \circ w_b)$ and labeling S_2^R by $f(w_d^R \circ S_2^R \circ w_c^R)$. In this case, the path P' is defined as

$$P' = w_a^+ \circ S_1 \circ w_b^+ \circ \left((w_c^R)^+\right)^R \circ S_2^R \circ \left((w_d^R)^+\right)^R.$$

During the ID assignment of G', the IDs of (i) the last $0.1s$ nodes in w_c^+, (ii) all nodes in S_2, and (iii) the first $0.1s$ nodes in w_d^+ are now chosen as the ones used in the definition of $f(w_d^R \circ S_2^R \circ w_c^R)$. Using such an ID assignment, the output labeling $\mathcal{L}'$ of S_2^R as the result of executing $\mathcal{A}$ on G' will be exactly the same as the output labeling given by $f(w_d^R \circ S_2^R \circ w_c^R)$. The rest of the proof is the same. □

Theorem 4 follows from the above two lemmas. The decidability result is due to the simple observation that whether a feasible function exists is decidable.

4.3 Partitioning a Cycle

In the following sections, we prove the decidability result associated with the $\omega(1)$–$o(\log^* n)$ gap. In this proof, we also define a feasible function, prove its decidability, and show the existence given an $o(\log^* n)$-time algorithm. The main challenge here is that an MIS cannot be computed in $O(1)$ time. To solve this issue, we decompose a cycle into paths with unrepetitive patterns and paths with repetitive patterns. For paths with unrepetitive patterns, we are able to compute a sufficiently well-spaced MIS in $O(1)$ time by making use of the irregularity of the input patterns.

Section 4.3 considers an $O(1)$-round algorithm that partitions a cycle into some short paths and some paths that have a repeated input pattern. Section 4.4 defines a *feasible function* whose existence characterizes the $O(1)$-round solvable LCL problems. In Section 4.5, we prove Theorem 5.

Partitioning an Undirected Cycle into Directed Paths. Let G be a cycle graph. An orientation of a node v is an assignment to one of its neighbor, this can be specified using port-numbering. An orientation of the nodes in G is called *ℓ-orientation* if the following condition is met. If $|V(G)| \le \ell$, then all nodes in G are oriented to the same direction. If $|V(G)| > \ell$, then each node $v \in V(G)$ belongs to a path P such that (i) all nodes in P are oriented to the same direction, and (ii) the number of nodes in P is at least ℓ. In $O(1)$ rounds we can compute an ℓ-orientation of G for any constant ℓ.

Lemma 14 ([8]). *Let G be a cycle graph. Let ℓ be a constant. There is a deterministic* LOCAL *algorithm that computes an ℓ-orientation of G in $O(1)$ rounds.*

In this section, we will use a generalization of an ℓ-orientation that satisfies an additional requirement that the input labels of each directed path P in the decomposition with $|V(P)| > 2\ell_{\text{width}}$ (where $2\ell_{\text{width}}$ is a threshold) must form a periodic string (whose period length is at most ℓ_{pattern}).

A string $w \in \Sigma_{\text{in}}^*$ is called *primitive* if w cannot be written as x^i for some $x \in \Sigma_{\text{in}}^*$ and $i \ge 2$. Let G be a cycle graph or a path graph where each node $v \in V(G)$ has an input label from Σ_{in}. We define an *$(\ell_{\text{width}}, \ell_{\text{count}}, \ell_{\text{pattern}})$-partition* as a partition of G into a set of connected subgraphs $\mathscr{P}$ meeting the following criteria. We assume $|V(G)| > 2\ell_{\text{width}}$ and $\ell_{\text{pattern}} \ge \ell_{\text{width}}$.

Direction and Minimum Length: For each $P \in \mathscr{P}$, the nodes in P are oriented to the same direction, and $|V(P)| \ge \ell_{\text{width}}$.
Short Paths: Define $\mathscr{P}_{\text{short}}$ as the subset of $\mathscr{P}$ that contains paths having at most $2\ell_{\text{width}}$ nodes. For each $P = (v_1, \ldots, v_k) \in \mathscr{P}_{\text{short}}$, each node v_i in P knows its rank i.
Long Paths: Define $\mathscr{P}_{\text{long}} = \mathscr{P} \setminus \mathscr{P}_{\text{short}}$. Then the input labeling of the nodes in P is of the form w^k for some primitive string $w \in \Sigma_{\text{in}}^*$ such that $|w| \le \ell_{\text{pattern}}$ and $k \ge \ell_{\text{count}}$. Moreover, each node v in P knows the string w.

Note that $\mathscr{P}$ may contain a cycle. This is possible only when G is a cycle where the input labeling is a repetition (at least ℓ_{count} times) of a primitive string $w \in \Sigma_{\text{in}}^*$ of length at most ℓ_{pattern}. In this case, we must have $\mathscr{P} = \mathscr{P}_{\text{long}} = \{G\}$. Otherwise, $\mathscr{P}$ contains only paths.

The goal of this section is to show that an $(\ell_{\text{width}}, \ell_{\text{count}}, \ell_{\text{pattern}})$-partition can be found in $O(1)$ rounds.

We first show that an $(\ell_{\text{width}}, \ell_{\text{count}}, \ell_{\text{pattern}})$-partition can be found in $O(1)$ rounds for the case G is *directed*. That is, all nodes in G are initially oriented to the same direction, and we are allowed to re-orient the nodes.

Lemma 15. *Let G be a directed cycle or a directed path where each node $v \in V(G)$ has an input label from Σ_{in}, and $|V(G)| > 2\ell_{\text{width}}$. Let $\ell_{\text{width}}, \ell_{\text{count}}, \ell_{\text{pattern}}$ be three constants such that $\ell_{\text{pattern}} \ge \ell_{\text{width}}$. There is a deterministic* LOCAL *algorithm that computes an $(\ell_{\text{width}}, \ell_{\text{count}}, \ell_{\text{pattern}})$-partition in $O(1)$ rounds*

Combining Lemma 15 and Lemma 14, we are able to construct an $(\ell_{\text{width}}, \ell_{\text{count}}, \ell_{\text{pattern}})$-partition in $O(1)$ rounds for undirected graphs.

Lemma 16. *Let G be a cycle or a path where each node $v \in V(G)$ has an input label from Σ_{in}, and $|V(G)| > 2\ell_{\text{width}}$. Let $\ell_{\text{width}}, \ell_{\text{count}}$, and ℓ_{pattern} be three constants such that $\ell_{\text{pattern}} \geq \ell_{\text{width}}$. There is a deterministic LOCAL algorithm that computes an $(\ell_{\text{width}}, \ell_{\text{count}}, \ell_{\text{pattern}})$-partition in $O(1)$ rounds*

Proof. The algorithm is as follows. Compute an ℓ-orientation of G by Lemma 14 in $O(1)$ rounds with $\ell = 2\ell_{\text{width}} + 1$. For each maximal-length connected subgraph P where each constituent node is oriented to the same direction, find an $(\ell_{\text{width}}, \ell_{\text{count}}, \ell_{\text{pattern}})$-partition of P in $O(1)$ rounds by Lemma 15. □

4.4 Feasible Function

The goal of this section is to define a *feasible function* whose existence characterizes the $O(1)$-round solvable LCL problems. With respect to an LCL problem $\mathcal{P}$ and a function f which takes a string $w \in \Sigma_{\text{in}}^k$ with $1 \leq k \leq \ell_{\text{pump}}$ as input, and returns a string $f(w) \in \Sigma_{\text{out}}^k$, we define some partially or completely labeled path graphs which are used in the definition of a feasible function.

Completely Labeled Graph $\mathcal{G}_{w,z}$: Let $w \in \Sigma_{\text{in}}^*$ be any string of length at least 1 and at most ℓ_{pump} Let z be any non-negative integer. Define $\mathcal{G}_{w,z} = (G_{w,z}, \mathcal{L})$ as follows. The graph $G_{w,z}$ is a path of the form $w^r \circ w^z \circ w^r$. The labeling $\mathcal{L}$ is a complete labeling of the form $f(w)^{z+2r}$. Define $\mathsf{Mid}(G_{w,z})$ as the middle subpath w^z of $G_{w,z}$.

Partially Labeled Graph $\mathcal{G}_{w_1,w_2,S}$: Let $w_1, w_2 \in \Sigma_{\text{in}}^*$ be any two strings of length at least 1 and at most ℓ_{pump}. Let $S \in \Sigma_{\text{in}}^*$ be any string (can be empty). Define $\mathcal{G}_{w_1,w_2,S} = (G_{w_1,w_2,S}, \mathcal{L})$ as follows. The path graph $G_{w_1,w_2,S}$ is of the form $w_1^{\ell_{\text{pump}}+2r} \circ S \circ w_2^{\ell_{\text{pump}}+2r}$. The labeling $\mathcal{L}$ is a partial labeling of $G_{w_1,w_2,S}$ which fixes the output labels of the first $2r|w_1|$ and the last $2r|w_2|$ nodes by $f(w_1)^{2r}$ and $f(w_2)^{2r}$, respectively. Define $\mathsf{Mid}(G_{w_1,w_2,S})$ as the middle subpath $w_1^{\ell_{\text{pump}}+r} \circ S \circ w_2^{\ell_{\text{pump}}+r}$ of $G_{w_1,w_2,S}$.

Feasible Function: We call f a *feasible function* if the following conditions are met: (i) For each $\mathcal{G}_{w,z} = (G_{w,z}, \mathcal{L})$, the complete labeling $\mathcal{L}$ is locally consistent at all nodes in $\mathsf{Mid}(G_{w,z})$. (ii) Each partially labeled graph $\mathcal{G}_{w_1,w_2,S}$ admits a complete labeling $\mathcal{L}_\diamond$ that is locally consistent at all nodes in $\mathsf{Mid}(\mathcal{G}_{w_1,w_2,S})$.

Lemma 17. *Given an LCL problem $\mathcal{P}$ on cycle graphs. It is decidable whether there is a feasible function.*

Proof. Note that it is not immediate from its definition as to whether a feasible function exists is decidable, since there appears to be *infinitely* many graphs $\mathcal{G}_{w,z}$ and $\mathcal{G}_{w_1,w_2,S}$ needed to be examined. However, the following simple observations show that it suffices to check only a constant number of these graphs.

- If the complete labeling $\mathcal{L}$ of $\mathcal{G}_{w,1} = (G_{w,1}, \mathcal{L})$ is locally consistent at all nodes in $\mathsf{Mid}(G_{w,1})$, then for all $z \geq 1$, the complete labeling $\mathcal{L}$ of $\mathcal{G}_{w,z} = (G_{w,z}, \mathcal{L})$ is also locally consistent at all nodes in $\mathsf{Mid}(G_{w,z})$.
- If $\mathcal{G}_{w_1,w_2,S}$ admits a complete labeling $\mathcal{L}_\diamond$ that is locally consistent at all nodes in $\mathsf{Mid}(\mathcal{G}_{w_1,w_2,S})$, then for each S' such that $\mathsf{Type}(S) = \mathsf{Type}(S')$, the partially labeled graph $\mathcal{G}_{w_1,w_2,S'}$ also admits a complete labeling $\mathcal{L}_\diamond$ that is locally consistent at all nodes in $\mathsf{Mid}(\mathcal{G}_{w_1,w_2,S'})$. This is due to Lemma 6.

Therefore, to decide whether a function f is feasible, we only need to check all possible $\mathcal{G}_{w,z}$ and $\mathcal{G}_{w_1,w_2,S}$. For each w we only need to consider the graph $\mathcal{G}_{w,z}$ with $z = 1$. For each w_1 and w_2, we do not need to go over all S; we only need to consider (i) the empty string $S = \emptyset$, and (ii) for each type τ, a string $S \in \Sigma_{\text{in}}^*$ such that $\mathsf{Type}(S) = \tau$. By Lemma 9, for each type τ, there exists $P \in \Sigma_{\text{in}}^x$ with $x \leq \ell_{\text{pump}}$ such that $\mathsf{Type}(P) = \tau$. Therefore, a string S with $\mathsf{Type}(S) = \tau$ can be found in bounded amount of time; also note that the number of types is bounded; see Lemma 8. □

For the rest of this section, we show that as long as the deterministic LOCAL complexity of $\mathcal{P}$ is $o(\log^* n)$ on cycle graphs, there exists a feasible function f. In Lemma 18 we show how to extract a function f from a given $o(\log^* n)$-round deterministic LOCAL algorithm $\mathcal{A}$, and then in Lemma 19 we prove that such a function f is feasible. Intuitively, Lemma 18 shows that there exists an ID-assignment such that when we run $\mathcal{A}$ on a subpath whose input labeling is a repetition of a length-k pattern w, the output labeling is also a repetition of a length-k pattern w'. The function f will be defined as $f(w) = w'$.

Lemma 18. *Let $\mathcal{A}$ be any deterministic LOCAL algorithm that solves $\mathcal{P}$ in $t(n) = o(\log^* n)$ rounds. Then there is a number n' and function f which takes a string $w \in \Sigma_{\text{in}}^k$ with $1 \leq k \leq \ell_{\text{pump}}$ as input, and returns a string $f(w) \in \Sigma_{\text{out}}^k$ meeting the following condition. For any $P = w^i \circ w^{2r+1} \circ w^i$ such that $|w^i| \geq t(n')$ and $1 \leq |w| \leq \ell_{\text{pump}}$, there is an assignment of distinct $\Theta(\log n')$-bit IDs to the nodes in P such that the following is true. Simulating $\mathcal{A}$ on P while assuming that the total number of nodes in the underlying graph is n' yields the output labeling $f(w)^{2r+1}$ for the middle subpath w^{2r+1}.*

Proof. In this proof we assume that there is no such a number n'. Then we claim that using $\mathcal{A}$ it is possible to obtain a deterministic LOCAL algorithm for MIS on an n-node directed cycle G *without input labeling*, in $O(t(n)) + O(1) = o(\log^* n)$ rounds. This contradicts the well-known $\Omega(\log^* n)$ lower bound for MIS [20].

Let G be an n-node directed cycle without input labeling. The MIS algorithm on G is described as follows. Let $w \in \Sigma_{\text{in}}^k$ with $1 \leq k \leq \ell_{\text{pump}}$ be chosen such that for any function f, the string $f(w) \in \Sigma_{\text{out}}^k$ does not satisfy the conditions stated in the lemma for the number $n' = nk$. Define G' as the graph resulting from replacing each node $v \in V(G)$ with a path w. We can simulate the imaginary graph G' in the communication network G by letting each node $v \in V(G)$ simulate a path w.

We execute the algorithm $\mathcal{A}$ on G' while assuming that the total number of nodes is n'. The execution takes $t(n') = O(t(n))$ rounds. For each node $v \in V(G)$, define the color of v as the sequence of the output labels of the path w^{2r} simulated by the node v and the $2r - 1$ nodes following v in the directed cycle G. This gives us a proper $O(1)$-coloring, since otherwise there must exist a subpath $P = w^{2r+1}$ of G' such that the output labeling of P is of the form

y^{2r+1} for some y, contradicting our choice of w. Using the standard procedure of computing an MIS from a coloring, with extra $O(1)$ rounds, an MIS of G can be obtained.

Note that there is a subtle issue about how we set the IDs of nodes in $V(G')$. The following method is guaranteed to output distinct IDs. Let $v \in V(G)$, and let $u_1, \ldots, u_k$ be the nodes in $V(G')$ simulated by v. Then we may use $\mathrm{ID}(u_i) = k \cdot \mathrm{ID}(v) + i$. □

Lemma 19. *Suppose that the deterministic* LOCAL *complexity of* $\mathcal{P}$ *is* $o(\log^* n)$ *on cycle graphs. Then there exists a feasible function* f.

Proof. Let $\mathcal{A}$ be any deterministic LOCAL algorithm that solves $\mathcal{P}$ in $t(n) = o(\log^* n)$ rounds. Let n' and f be chosen to meet the conditions in Lemma 18 for $\mathcal{A}$. The goal of the proof is to show that f is a feasible function. According to the conditions specified in Lemma 18 for the function f, we already know that the complete labeling $\mathcal{L}$ of each $\mathcal{G}_{w,z} = (G_{w,z}, \mathcal{L})$ is locally consistent at all nodes in $\mathsf{Mid}(G_{w,z})$. Therefore, all we need to do is the following. For each partially labeled graph $\mathcal{G}_{w_1,w_2,S}$, find a complete labeling $\mathcal{L}_\diamond$ that is locally consistent at all nodes in $\mathsf{Mid}(\mathcal{G}_{w_1,w_2,S})$.

Given the three parameters w_1, w_2, and S, define G as the cycle resulting from linking the two ends of the path $w_1^{\ell_{\text{pump}}} \circ w_1^{2r+1} \circ w_1^{\ell_{\text{pump}}} \circ S \circ w_2^{\ell_{\text{pump}}} \circ w_2^{2r+1} \circ w_2^{\ell_{\text{pump}}}$. Define $\mathcal{L}$ as the partial labeling of G which fixes the output labeling of the two subpaths w_1^{2r+1} and w_2^{2r+1} by $f(w_1)^{2r+1}$ and $f(w_2)^{2r+1}$, respectively. We write P_1^{mid} and P_2^{mid} to denote the two subpaths w_1^{2r+1} and w_2^{2r+1}, respectively.

In what follows, we show that the partially labeled graph $\mathcal{G} = (G, \mathcal{L})$ admits a legal labeling $\mathcal{L}_\diamond$. Since $\mathcal{G}_{w_1,w_2,S}$ is a subgraph of $\mathcal{G} = (G, \mathcal{L})$, such a legal labeling $\mathcal{L}_\diamond$ is also a complete labeling of $\mathcal{G}_{w_1,w_2,S}$ that is locally consistent at all nodes in $\mathsf{Mid}(\mathcal{G}_{w_1,w_2,S})$.

For the rest of the proof, we show the existence of $\mathcal{L}_\diamond$. This will be established by applying a pumping lemma. Define the graph G' as the result of the following operations on G.

- Replace the two subpaths $w_1^{\ell_{\text{pump}}}$ by w_1^x, where the number x is chosen such that $x|w_1| \geq 2t(n') + r$, and $\mathrm{Type}(w_1^{\ell_{\text{pump}}}) = \mathrm{Type}(w_1^x)$.
- Replace the two subpaths $w_2^{\ell_{\text{pump}}}$ by w_2^y, where the number y is chosen such that $y|w_2| \geq 2t(n') + r$, and $\mathrm{Type}(w_2^{\ell_{\text{pump}}}) = \mathrm{Type}(w_2^y)$.

The existence of the numbers x and y above is guaranteed by Lemma 10. The IDs of nodes in G' are assigned as follows. For $i = 1, 2$, select the IDs of the nodes in $\bigcup_{v \in P_i^{\text{mid}}} N^{t(n')}(v)$ in such a way that the output labeling of P_i^{mid} resulting from executing $\mathcal{A}$ on G' while assuming that the total number of nodes is n' is $f(w_i)^{2r+1}$. The existence of such an ID assignment is guaranteed by Lemma 18. For all remaining nodes in G', select their IDs in such a way that all nodes in $N^{r+t(n')}(v)$ receive distinct IDs, for each $v \in V(G')$. This ensures that the outcome of executing $\mathcal{A}$ on G' while assuming that the total number of nodes is n' is a legal labeling.

Let $\mathcal{L}'_\diamond$ be the legal labeling of G' resulting from executing $\mathcal{A}$ with the above IDs while pretending that the total number of nodes is n'. Note that $\mathcal{L}'_\diamond$ must label P_1^{mid} and P_2^{mid} by $f(w_1)^{2r+1}$ and $f(w_2)^{2r+1}$, respectively. A desired legal labeling $\mathcal{L}_\diamond$ of $\mathcal{G}$ can be obtained from the legal labeling $\mathcal{L}'_\diamond$ of G' by applying Lemma 6, as we have $\mathrm{Type}(w_1^{\ell_{\text{pump}}}) = \mathrm{Type}(w_1^x)$ and $\mathrm{Type}(w_2^{\ell_{\text{pump}}}) = \mathrm{Type}(w_2^y)$. □

4.5 The $\omega(1)$–$o(\log^* n)$ Gap

In this section we prove that it is decidable whether a given LCL problem $\mathcal{P}$ has complexity $\Omega(\log^* n)$ or $O(1)$ on cycle graphs.

Lemma 20. *Let* f *be any feasible function. Let* G *be any cycle graph. Let* $\mathscr{P}$ *be any set of disjoint subgraphs in* G *such that the input labeling of each* $P \in \mathscr{P}$ *is of the form* w^x *such that* $x \geq 2\ell_{\text{pump}} + 2r$, *and* $w \in \Sigma_{\text{in}}^k$ *is a string with* $1 \leq k \leq \ell_{\text{pump}}$. *For each* $P \in \mathscr{P}$, *define the subgraph* P' *as follows. If* P *is a cycle, define* $P' = P$. *If* P *is a path, write* $P = w^{\ell_{\text{pump}}} \circ w^i \circ w^{\ell_{\text{pump}}}$, *and define* P' *as the middle subpath* w^i. *Let* $\mathcal{L}$ *be a partial labeling of* G *defined as follows. For each* $P = w^x \in \mathscr{P}$, *fix the output labels of each subpath* w *of* P' *by* $f(w)$. *Then* $\mathcal{G} = (G, \mathcal{L})$ *admits a legal labeling* $\mathcal{L}_\diamond$.

Proof. Define V_1 as the set of all nodes such that $v \in V_1$ if v belongs to the middle subpath w^j of some path $P = w^{\ell_{\text{pump}}} \circ w^r \circ w^j \circ w^r \circ w^{\ell_{\text{pump}}} \in \mathscr{P}$. By the definition of feasible function, $\mathcal{L}$ is already locally consistent at all nodes in V_1. Thus, all we need to do is to construct a complete labeling $\mathcal{L}_\diamond$ of $\mathcal{G} = (G, \mathcal{L})$, and argue that $\mathcal{L}_\diamond$ is locally consistent at all nodes in $V_2 = V(G) \setminus V_1$.

There are two easy special cases. If $\mathscr{P} = \emptyset$, then no output label of any node in G is fixed, and so $\mathcal{G}$ trivially admits a legal labeling. If $\mathscr{P}$ contains a cycle, then $\mathscr{P} = \{G\}$, and hence $\mathcal{L}$ is already a legal labeling as $V_1 = V(G)$.

In subsequent discussion, we restrict ourselves to the case $\mathscr{P}$ is non-empty and contains only paths. The output labeling $\mathcal{L}_\diamond$ is constructed as follows. Define $\mathscr{P}_{\text{unlabeled}}$ as the maximal-length subpaths of G that are not assigned any output labels by $\mathcal{L}$. A path $P \in \mathscr{P}_{\text{unlabeled}}$ must be of the form $w_1^{\ell_{\text{pump}}} \circ S \circ w_2^{\ell_{\text{pump}}}$, where $w_1, w_2 \in \Sigma_{\text{in}}^*$ are two strings of length at least 1 and at most ℓ_{pump}, and $S \in \Sigma_{\text{in}}^*$ can be any string (including the empty string). Given $P \in \mathscr{P}_{\text{unlabeled}}$, we make the following definitions.

- Define P^+ as the subpath of G that includes P and the $r|w_1|$ nodes preceding P, and the $r|w_2|$ nodes following P in the graph G. Note that the set V_2 is exactly the union of nodes in P^+ for all $P \in \mathscr{P}_{\text{unlabeled}}$.
- Define P^{++} as the subpath of G that includes P and the $2r|w_1|$ nodes preceding P, and the $2r|w_2|$ nodes following P in the graph G. The path P^{++} must be of the form $w_1^{\ell_{\text{pump}}+2r} \circ S \circ w_2^{\ell_{\text{pump}}+2r}$, and the labeling $\mathcal{L}$ already fixes the output labels of the first $2r|w_1|$ and the last $2r|w_2|$ nodes of P^{++} by $f(w_1)^{2r}$ and $f(w_2)^{2r}$, respectively.

Observe that the path $P^{++} = w_1^{\ell_{\text{pump}}+2r} \circ S \circ w_2^{\ell_{\text{pump}}+2r}$ together with the labeling $\mathcal{L}$ is exactly the partially labeled graph $\mathcal{G}_{w_1,w_2,S}$. We assign the output labels to the nodes in P by the labeling $\mathcal{L}_\diamond$ guaranteed in the definition of feasible function. It is ensured that the labeling of all nodes within P^+ are locally consistent. By doing so for each $P \in \mathscr{P}_{\text{unlabeled}}$, we obtain a desired complete labeling that is locally consistent at all nodes in V_2. □

Lemma 21. *Suppose that there is a feasible function* f *for the* LCL *problem* $\mathcal{P}$. *Then there is an* $O(1)$*-round deterministic* LOCAL *algorithm* $\mathcal{A}$ *on cycle graphs.*

Proof. The first step of the algorithm $\mathcal{A}$ is to compute an $(\ell_{\text{width}}, \ell_{\text{count}}, \ell_{\text{pattern}})$-partition in $O(1)$ rounds by Lemma 16. We set $\ell_{\text{count}} = 2\ell_{\text{pump}} + 2r$ and $\ell_{\text{width}} = \ell_{\text{pattern}} = \ell_{\text{pump}}$. We assume $|V(G)| > 2\ell_{\text{width}}$. Recall that an $(\ell_{\text{width}}, \ell_{\text{count}}, \ell_{\text{pattern}})$-partition decomposes the cycle G into two sets of disjoint subgraphs $\mathscr{P}_{\text{short}}$ and $\mathscr{P}_{\text{long}}$.

Define G' as the graph resulting from applying the following operations on G. For each $P \in \mathscr{P}_{\text{short}}$, replace the path P by the path $P^* = x \circ y^i \circ z$ such that $i = \ell_{\text{count}}$, $1 \le |y| \le \ell_{\text{pattern}}$, and the type of P^* is the same as the type of P. The path P^* is obtained via Lemma 9. Note that each path $P \in \mathscr{P}_{\text{short}}$ has at least $\ell_{\text{width}} = \ell_{\text{pump}}$ nodes and at most $2\ell_{\text{width}} = 2\ell_{\text{pump}}$ nodes. Define $\mathscr{P}^*$ as the set of all P^* such that $P \in \mathscr{P}_{\text{short}}$. The graph G' is simulated in the communication graph G by electing a leader for each path $P \in \mathscr{P}_{\text{short}}$ to simulate P^*.

Calculate a partial labeling $\mathcal{L}'$ of G' using the feasible function f as follows. Recall $\ell_{\text{count}} = 2\ell_{\text{pump}} + 2r$. For each $P^* = x \circ y^{\ell_{\text{pump}}} \circ y^{2r} \circ y^{\ell_{\text{pump}}} \circ z \in \mathscr{P}^*$, label the middle subpath y^{2r} by the function f. For each $P = w^{\ell_{\text{pump}}} \circ w^i \circ w^{\ell_{\text{pump}}} \in \mathscr{P}_{\text{long}}$, label the middle subpath w^i by $f(w)^i$. Even though a path $P \in \mathscr{P}_{\text{long}}$ can have $\omega(1)$ nodes, this step can be done locally in $O(1)$ rounds due to the following property of $(\ell_{\text{width}}, \ell_{\text{count}}, \ell_{\text{pattern}})$-partition. All nodes in a path $P \in \mathscr{P}_{\text{long}}$ agree with the same direction and know the primitive string w.

By Lemma 20, the remaining unlabeled nodes in G' can be labeled to yield a legal labeling of G'. This can be done in $O(1)$ rounds since the connected components formed by unlabeled nodes have at most $O(1)$ nodes. Given any valid labeling of G', a legal labeling of G can be obtained by applying Lemma 6 in $O(1)$ rounds. Remember that $\text{Type}(P) = \text{Type}(P^*)$ for each $P \in \mathscr{P}_{\text{short}}$, and G' is exactly the result of replacing each $P \in \mathscr{P}_{\text{short}}$ by P^*. □

Combining Lemma 17, Lemma 19, and Lemma 21, we have proved Theorem 5. That is, for any LCL problem $\mathcal{P}$ on cycle graphs, its deterministic LOCAL complexity is either $\Omega(\log^* n)$ or $O(1)$. Moreover, there is an algorithm that decides whether $\mathcal{P}$ has complexity $\Omega(\log^* n)$ or $O(1)$ on cycle graphs; for the case the complexity is $O(1)$, the algorithm outputs a description of an $O(1)$-round deterministic LOCAL algorithm that solves $\mathcal{P}$.

ACKNOWLEDGMENTS

Many thanks to Laurent Feuilloley, Juho Hirvonen, Janne H. Korhonen, Christoph Lenzen, Yannic Maus, and Seth Pettie for discussions, and to anonymous reviewers for their helpful comments on previous versions of this work. This work was supported in part by the Academy of Finland, Grant 285721, and NSF grants CCF-1514383, CCF-1637546, and CCF-1815316.

REFERENCES

[1] Alkida Balliu, Sebastian Brandt, Yi-Jun Chang, Dennis Olivetti, Mikaël Rabie, and Jukka Suomela. 2018. The distributed complexity of locally checkable problems on paths is decidable. *arXiv preprint arXiv:1811.01672* (2018).

[2] Alkida Balliu, Sebastian Brandt, Dennis Olivetti, and Jukka Suomela. 2018. Almost global problems in the LOCAL model. In *Proc. 32nd International Symposium on Distributed Computing (DISC 2018) (Leibniz International Proceedings in Informatics (LIPIcs))*. Schloss DagstuhlâĂŞLeibniz-Zentrum für Informatik. https://doi.org/10.4230/LIPIcs.DISC.2018.9

[3] Alkida Balliu, Juho Hirvonen, Janne H Korhonen, Tuomo Lempiäinen, Dennis Olivetti, and Jukka Suomela. 2018. New classes of distributed time complexity. In *Proc. 50th ACM Symposium on Theory of Computing (STOC 2018)*. ACM Press, 1307–1318. https://doi.org/10.1145/3188745.3188860

[4] Roderick Bloem, Nicolas Braud-Santoni, and Swen Jacobs. 2016. Synthesis of Self-Stabilising and Byzantine-Resilient Distributed Systems. In *Proc. International Conference on Computer Aided Verification (CAV 2016)*. Springer, 157–176. https://doi.org/10.1007/978-3-319-41528-4_9

[5] Sebastian Brandt, Orr Fischer, Juho Hirvonen, Barbara Keller, Tuomo Lempiäinen, Joel Rybicki, Jukka Suomela, and Jara Uitto. 2016. A lower bound for the distributed Lovász local lemma. In *Proc. 48th ACM Symposium on Theory of Computing (STOC 2016)*. ACM Press, 479–488. https://doi.org/10.1145/2897518.2897570

[6] Sebastian Brandt, Juho Hirvonen, Janne H Korhonen, Tuomo Lempiäinen, Patric R J Östergård, Christopher Purcell, Joel Rybicki, Jukka Suomela, and Przemysław Uznański. 2017. LCL problems on grids. In *Proc. 36th ACM Symposium on Principles of Distributed Computing (PODC 2017)*. ACM Press, 101–110. https://doi.org/10.1145/3087801.3087833

[7] Yi-Jun Chang, Tsvi Kopelowitz, and Seth Pettie. 2016. An Exponential Separation between Randomized and Deterministic Complexity in the LOCAL Model. In *Proc. 57th IEEE Symposium on Foundations of Computer Science (FOCS 2016)*. IEEE, 615–624. https://doi.org/10.1109/FOCS.2016.72

[8] Yi-Jun Chang and Seth Pettie. 2017. A Time Hierarchy Theorem for the LOCAL Model. In *Proc. 58th IEEE Symposium on Foundations of Computer Science (FOCS 2017)*. IEEE, 156–167. https://doi.org/10.1109/FOCS.2017.23

[9] Richard Cole and Uzi Vishkin. 1986. Deterministic coin tossing with applications to optimal parallel list ranking. *Information and Control* 70, 1 (1986), 32–53. https://doi.org/10.1016/S0019-9958(86)80023-7

[10] Danny Dolev, Keijo Heljanko, Matti Järvisalo, Janne H Korhonen, Christoph Lenzen, Joel Rybicki, Jukka Suomela, and Siert Wieringa. 2016. Synchronous counting and computational algorithm design. *J. Comput. System Sci.* 82, 2 (2016), 310–332. https://doi.org/10.1016/j.jcss.2015.09.002

[11] Fathiyeh Faghih and Borzoo Bonakdarpour. 2015. SMT-Based Synthesis of Distributed Self-Stabilizing Systems. *ACM Transactions on Autonomous and Adaptive Systems* 10, 3 (2015), 1–26. https://doi.org/10.1145/2767133

[12] Manuela Fischer and Mohsen Ghaffari. 2017. Sublogarithmic Distributed Algorithms for Lovász Local Lemma, and the Complexity Hierarchy. In *Proc. 31st International Symposium on Distributed Computing (DISC 2017)*. 18:1–18:16. https://doi.org/10.4230/LIPIcs.DISC.2017.18

[13] Mohsen Ghaffari, David G Harris, and Fabian Kuhn. 2018. On Derandomizing Local Distributed Algorithms. In *Proc. 59th IEEE Symposium on Foundations of Computer Science (FOCS 2018)*. https://doi.org/10.1109/FOCS.2018.00069 arXiv:1711.02194

[14] Mohsen Ghaffari, Juho Hirvonen, Fabian Kuhn, and Yannic Maus. 2018. Improved Distributed Δ-Coloring. In *Proc. 37th ACM Symposium on Principles of Distributed Computing (PODC 2018)*. ACM, 427–436. https://doi.org/10.1145/3212734.3212764

[15] Mohsen Ghaffari and Hsin-Hao Su. 2017. Distributed Degree Splitting, Edge Coloring, and Orientations. In *Proc. 28th ACM-SIAM Symposium on Discrete Algorithms (SODA 2017)*. Society for Industrial and Applied Mathematics, 2505–2523. https://doi.org/10.1137/1.9781611974782.166

[16] Andrew V. Goldberg, Serge A. Plotkin, and Gregory E. Shannon. 1988. Parallel Symmetry-Breaking in Sparse Graphs. *SIAM Journal on Discrete Mathematics* 1, 4 (1988), 434–446. https://doi.org/10.1137/0401044

[17] Juho Hirvonen, Joel Rybicki, Stefan Schmid, and Jukka Suomela. 2017. Large cuts with local algorithms on triangle-free graphs. *Electronic Journal of Combinatorics* 24, 4 (2017). http://www.combinatorics.org/ojs/index.php/eljc/article/view/v24i4p21

[18] John E Hopcroft and Jeffrey D Ullman. 1979. *Introduction to Automata Theory, Languages and Computation.* Addison-Wesley.

[19] Alex Klinkhamer. 2016. *On the Limits and Practice of Automatically Designing Self-Stabilization.* Doctoral thesis. Michigan Technological University. https://digitalcommons.mtu.edu/etdr/90

[20] Nathan Linial. 1992. Locality in Distributed Graph Algorithms. *SIAM J. Comput.* 21, 1 (1992), 193–201. https://doi.org/10.1137/0221015

[21] Moni Naor. 1991. A lower bound on probabilistic algorithms for distributive ring coloring. *SIAM Journal on Discrete Mathematics* 4, 3 (1991), 409–412. https://doi.org/10.1137/0404036

[22] Moni Naor and Larry Stockmeyer. 1995. What Can be Computed Locally? *SIAM J. Comput.* 24, 6 (1995), 1259–1277. https://doi.org/10.1137/S0097539793254571

[23] Alessandro Panconesi and Aravind Srinivasan. 1995. The local nature of Δ-coloring and its algorithmic applications. *Combinatorica* 15, 2 (1995), 255–280. https://doi.org/10.1007/BF01200759

[24] David Peleg. 2000. *Distributed Computing: A Locality-Sensitive Approach.* Society for Industrial and Applied Mathematics. https://doi.org/10.1137/1.9780898719772

[25] Seth Pettie. 2018. Automatically Speeding Up LOCAL Graph Algorithms. In *7th Workshop on Advances in Distributed Graph Algorithms (ADGA 2018)*. http://adga.hiit.fi/2018/Seth.pdf

[26] Joel Rybicki and Jukka Suomela. 2015. Exact bounds for distributed graph colouring. In *Proc. 22nd International Colloquium on Structural Information and Communication Complexity (SIROCCO 2015) (Lecture Notes in Computer Science)*, Vol. 9439. Springer, 46–60. https://doi.org/10.1007/978-3-319-25258-2_4

Hardness of Exact Distance Queries in Sparse Graphs Through Hub Labeling

Adrian Kosowski*
IRIF and Inria
Paris, France
adrian.kosowski@inria.fr

Przemysław Uznański†
Institute of Computer Science,
University of Wrocław
Wrocław, Poland
puznanski@cs.uni.wroc.pl

Laurent Viennot*
IRIF and Inria
Paris, France
laurent.viennot@inria.fr

ABSTRACT

A *distance labeling scheme* is an assignment of bit-labels to the vertices of an undirected, unweighted graph such that the distance between any pair of vertices can be decoded solely from their labels. An important class of distance labeling schemes is that of *hub labelings*, where a node $v \in G$ stores its distance to the so-called hubs $S_v \subseteq V$, chosen so that for any $u, v \in V$ there is $w \in S_u \cap S_v$ belonging to some shortest uv path. Notice that for most existing graph classes, the best distance labelling constructions existing use at some point a hub labeling scheme at least as a key building block.

Our interest lies in hub labelings of sparse graphs, i.e., those with $|E(G)| = O(n)$, for which we show a lowerbound of $\frac{n}{2^{O(\sqrt{\log n})}}$ for the average size of the hubsets. Additionally, we show a hub-labeling construction for sparse graphs of average size $O(\frac{n}{\mathrm{RS}(n)^c})$ for some $0 < c < 1$, where $\mathrm{RS}(n)$ is the so-called Ruzsa-Szemerédi function, linked to structure of induced matchings in dense graphs. This implies that further improving the lower bound on hub labeling size to $\frac{n}{2^{(\log n)^{o(1)}}}$ would require a breakthrough in the study of lower bounds on $\mathrm{RS}(n)$, which have resisted substantial improvement in the last 70 years.

For general distance labeling of sparse graphs, we show a lowerbound of $\frac{1}{2^{\Theta(\sqrt{\log n})}}\textsc{SumIndex}(n)$, where $\textsc{SumIndex}(n)$ is the communication complexity of the Sum-Index problem over Z_n. Our results suggest that the best achievable hub-label size and distance-label size in sparse graphs may be $\Theta(\frac{n}{2^{(\log n)^c}})$ for some $0 < c < 1$.

CCS CONCEPTS

• **Theory of computation** → *Design and analysis of algorithms; Data structures design and analysis; Distributed algorithms.*

KEYWORDS

Hub labeling; Distance labeling; Lower bound; Ruzsa-Szemerédi function

ACM Reference Format:
Adrian Kosowski, Przemysław Uznański, and Laurent Viennot. 2019. Hardness of Exact Distance Queries in Sparse Graphs Through Hub Labeling. In *2019 ACM Symposium on Principles of Distributed Computing (PODC '19), July 29-August 2, 2019, Toronto, ON, Canada.* ACM, New York, NY, USA, 8 pages. https://doi.org/10.1145/3293611.3331625

1 INTRODUCTION

Hub labeling schemes are a popular way of distributed encoding shortest path structure for easy retrieval. Given a graph $G = (V, E)$ (across this paper we assume, unless stated otherwise, that G is undirected and unweighted, with $|V| = n$ and $|E| = m$), we store with each vertex $v \in V(G)$ the so-called hubset $S_v \subseteq V(G)$ together with shortest path distances between v and its hubs. The distance query uv is resolved by returning

$$\min_{w \in S(u) \cap S(v)} \mathrm{dist}(u, w) + \mathrm{dist}(w, v).$$

This framework was introduced in [18] under the name of 2-hop covers, further explored by [4]) (as landmark labelings) and [3]. The computed distance between all pairs of nodes u and v is exact if set $S(u) \cap S(v)$ contains at least one node on some shortest $u - v$ path. This property of the family of sets $(S(u) : u \in V)$ is known as *shortest path cover.*

Hub labeling schemes are a special case of the more general *distance labeling* schemes, in which the task is the assignment of a binary string $\mathsf{label}(u)$ to each node $u \in V$, so that the graph distance between u and v is uniquely determined by the pair of labels: $\mathsf{label}(u)$ and $\mathsf{label}(v)$, using a decoding function specified as part of the distance labeling. A central question in the distributed computing literature consists in identifying, for a given graph class, the optimal size of a distance labeling, expressed in terms on a bound on the average or maximum size of the labels used, taken over all nodes of a graph, for graphs belonging to the considered graph class.

In general graphs, the distance labeling problem was first investigated by Graham and Pollak [27], who provided the first labeling scheme with labels of size $O(n)$. A subsequent line of research contributed to reducing the *decoding time*, with results of [23, 40] and finally [8] presented a scheme with labels of size $\frac{\log_2 3}{2} n + o(n)$ and $O(1)$ decoding time. This result is asymptotically tight: by a

*Supported by Irif CNRS laboratory and ANR projects DESCARTES (ANR-16-CE40-0023) and DISTANCIA (ANR-17-CE40-0015).
†Supported by Polish National Science Centre grant 2016/22/E/ST6/00499.

ACM ISBN 978-1-4503-6217-7/19/07...$15.00
https://doi.org/10.1145/3293611.3331625

simple counting argument, the label size of a node has to be at least $\frac{1}{2}n - O(1)$, regardless of decoding time [23].

By contrast, when considering classes of *sparse graphs* (where $m = O(n)$), no similar asymptotically tight bounds on distance label size are known. The first sublinear-space distance labeling schemes were proposed only recently: [7] and later [24] presented a hub labeling scheme with hubs of size $O(\frac{n}{\log n} \log \log n)$ and $O(\frac{n}{\log n})$, respectively. Interpreted in terms of distance labeling schemes, these works provide $O(\frac{n}{\log n} (\log \log n)^2)$ and $O(\frac{n}{\log n} \log \log n)$ bits per label respectively, through some careful encoding of distances to vertices of hubsets. This leaves a substantial gap with respect to the best known lower bound of $\Omega(\sqrt{n})$ for the bit size of distance labels and of hub labeling schemes per node, given in [23].

The objective of this paper is to help understand the source of hardness of distance labeling in sparse graphs. We show a basic obstacle on the path to the construction of better distance labelings: a lower bound of $\frac{n}{2^{O(\sqrt{\log n})}}$ on the hub set size in hub labeling. As we discuss further on in the related work section, this is an issue as all currently known approaches to distance labeling rely inherently (possibly implicitly) on the construction of some form of hub labels. More rigorously, we succeed in tying-in the distance label size to two long-standing open questions: one from combinatorics on the value of the so-called Ruzsa-Szemerédi function RS(n) on graphs, one from communication complexity on the bit complexity SumIndex(n) of a basic 3-party communication problem known as Sum-Index.

We remark that our results can perhaps help to shed further light on the question of designing (centralized) distance oracles for sparse graphs. A natural objective, so far unachieved in general, would be to obtain for n-node sparse graphs a spectrum of data structures, using space S and resolving exact distance queries in time T, with a time-space tradeoff of $ST = \tilde{O}(n^2)$. This tradeoff is trivially achieved at its endpoints ($S = \tilde{O}(n)$, $S = \tilde{O}(n^2)$), but the existence of such oracles appears open, e.g., for $S = \tilde{O}(n^{3/2})$ and $T = O(n^{1/2})$ (cf. [19, 38]). Our result precludes the existence of such a centralized oracle relying on an application of hub labeling.

1.1 Related work

Distance labelings vs. Hub labelings. It is noteworthy that for most existing graph classes, the best known distance labelling constructions are based on hub labeling schemes, either explicitly or as a key building block. Such constructions usually involve some form of compression and/or encoding of all distances (from a vertex to its hubs), to avoid $\log n$ overhead when going from hubsets to binary labels (see e.g. [24]).

For example, for the case of arbitrary graphs, a distance labeling may be constructed as follows: an additive approximation scheme for hub-labeling is constructed, that is for each pair uv, there is $w \in S(u) \cap S(v)$ such that either w or some neighbor $x \in N(w)$ is on shortest uv path. This guarantees that the absolute error of estimation is either 0, 1 or 2. Constructing such (small) approximate hub-set and complementing it with explicit correction tables (which require $\frac{\log_2 3}{2} n$ bits per vertex) suffices. Many more ingredients and insights are required to achieve constant decoding time as described in [8], which goes beyond the scope of this overview.

Distance labeling of sparse graphs and sub-classes. Constructions for distance labeling in sparse graphs were considered in the previously mentioned papers [7] and [24]. Both of them use hubsets as the underlying technique. The first of these constructions relies on the observation that, by selecting randomly a hubset S of size $O(\frac{n}{D} \log D)$ and assigning $S \subseteq S(u)$ for any u, one already covers almost all pairs of vertices which are at distance D to each other, except at most a $1/D$ fraction of these pairs. Selecting $D = \Theta(\log n)$ and storing vertices closer than D as hubs explicitly leads to desired hubset sizes (however, a careful approach is required when dealing with large degree vertices which may appear in a sparse graph, guaranteed only to have constant average degree). Second work shaves $\log \log n$ term by derandomizing the construction.

For the class of trees, the constructions of [34] and [9] are based on selection of central vertices as hubs, and proceeding recursively on obtained subtrees. In terms of bit size, those constructions give $\Theta(\log^2 n)$ bits per label (which is asymptotically optimal due to lowerbound of [23]), which corresponds to $\log n$ hubs per vertex. The construction of [22] through very careful assignment of pieces of information thorough the construction achieves $\frac{1}{4} \log^2 n + o(\log^2 n)$ bits per label, which is optimal up to lower order terms due to the lowerbound of [9].

For planar graphs, the main technical ingredient is an existence of small size separators. Specifically, in any planar graph there is a $S \subseteq V$ such that $|S| = O(\sqrt{n})$ and S separates V into V_1 and V_2 that are balanced (up to a factor 2) in sizes. Taking advantage of this, [23] described $O(\sqrt{n})$ hub labeling and $O(\sqrt{n} \log n)$ bits distance labeling schemes, by applying the separation recursively. They also present $\Omega(\sqrt[3]{n})$ lower bound (for both hub and distance labeling schemes). The distance labeling size was later improved in [25] to $O(\sqrt{n})$, through better encoding of distances from vertex to its hub (and thus avoiding $\log n$ overhead).

Lower bounds. The aforementioned lowerbounds on size of distance labels and/or hubsets for sparse graphs, and especially for planar graphs, follow a particular line of thought, which can be called a *counting argument.* One can construct a family of graphs $\mathcal{F}$ on n vertices within the considered graph class, with a preselected subset of vertices $V' \subseteq V$, such that knowing $|V'|^2$ pairwise distances in graph G is enough to identify the graph $G \in \mathcal{F}$. One can reason then that the total length of the $|V'|$ labels in some graph in $\mathcal{F}$ needs to be at least $\log_2 |\mathcal{F}|$, thus giving a lowerbound of $\frac{1}{|V'|} \log_2 |\mathcal{F}|$ bits per label (the same reasoning applies to hub-labeling schemes as well). This reasoning has one fundamental limitation, in that it is unable to separate *a distributed data structure* from *a centralized* one. For example, it is believed that unweighted planar graphs do in fact admit $\Omega(\sqrt{n})$ lowerbound for size of distance labels (as is the case for weighted planar graphs). Current lower bound construction of [23] uses counting technique construction with $|V'| = \Theta(n^{1/3})$ and $\log_2 |\mathcal{F}| = \Theta(n^{2/3})$. This cannot be improved with counting technique: [1] shows that planar graphs do in fact admit *distance oracles* which take in total $O(\min |V'|^2, \sqrt{n}|V'|)$ bits to encode all $|V'|^2$ pairwise distances, which is $O(\min |V'|, \sqrt{n/|V'|})$ bits per vertex and is maximized when $|V'| = n^{1/3}$ (one needs to argue that counting technique is not able to separate distance oracles from distance labelings, which is the case). This motivates the search for alternative techniques when proving lower bounds.

Hub labeling in practice. We remark that the hub-based method of distance computation is efficient for many real-world networks (even in centralised scenarios, as a distance oracle) for at least two reasons. First of all, for transportation-type networks it is possible to show bounds on the sizes of sets S, which follow from the network structure. Notably, Abraham et al. [2] introduce the notion of highway dimension h of a network, which is presumed to be a small constant e.g. for road networks, and show that an appropriate cover of all shortest paths in the graph can be achieved using sets S of size $\widetilde{O}(h)$. Moreover, the order in which elements of sets $S(u)$ and $S(v)$ is browsed when performing the minimum operation is relevant, and in some schemes, the operation can be interrupted once it is certain that the minimum has been found, before probing all elements of the set. This is the principle of numerous heuristics for the exact shortest-path problem, such as contraction hierarchies and algorithms with arc flags [13, 32].

1.2 Overview of our results and proof techniques

In this work we first show a lower bound on the size of hub labelings in sparse graphs. Note that in the regimes of both distance labeling and hub labeling, the state-of-the-art results for sparse graphs were leaving a huge gap: while upper bounds are of the form $O(n/\log n)$ at best (ignoring poly-loglog terms), the lower bounds are $\Omega(\sqrt{n})$. We close this gap for hub labeling with the following result.

Theorem 1.1. *Graphs of max-degree* 3 *require average hub size to be at least* $\frac{n}{2^{\Theta(\sqrt{\log n})}}$, *where n is the number of vertices.*

(See Section 2 for a detailed proof.)

This result is complemented by an upper bound on hub set size, given by Theorem 1.4.

Our technical contributions are obtained by using the following observations as a starting point. First, let us fix $D = n^{o(1)}$ to be a threshold value, such that we consider distances up to D as small, and large otherwise. Simply using random hubsets of size roughly n/D we can cover all uv pairs with uv-distance being at least D. We therefore see immediately that only small distances are crucial (regardless of whether we are constructing a hard instance for a lowerbound, or small hubsets).

Next, we observe that in the regime of small distances, we can afford to fix our attention to *monotone* hubsets, where we require that for any u, if $x \in S(u)$, then all vertices on some chosen shortest ux path belong to $S(u)$ as well. It trivially follows that minimal *monotone* hubset covering all small distances is withing a factor of D in size from minimal arbitrary hubset. Monotone hubsets have a following advantage in analysis: for uv connected by an *unique* shortest path, for any x belonging to such path, either u or v has to "pay" for hub x, that is $x \in S(u)$ or $x \in S(v)$. Thus, looking for hard instances, it is advantageous to consider the following: fix $u \in V$, and consider set $S'(u) = \{h : \text{dist}(u, h) = \text{dist}(h, v) = D/2\}$ where $v \in V$ iterates over vertices such that $\text{dist}(u, v) = D$. If we ensure that $S'(u)$ need to be almost-linear in size (on average), since $\sum |S'(u)|$ is within a D factor from total size of hubsets, we have our desired hard instance for hubset covering.

Induced matchings in dense graphs. It turns out that the connection between structure of shortest paths and induced matchings is at the heart of the hardness of the hub labeling problem in sparse graphs. This connection as such has already been noted in the literature (cf. [16]); here, we provide a brief exposition from a perspective most relevant to our study. Let us first recall the terminology.

Definition 1.2. *We say that $M \subseteq E(G)$ is an induced matching of G if (i) it is a matching and (ii) there is a set of vertices $V' \subseteq V(G)$ such that M is a subgraph of G induced by V'.*

The connection between induced matchings and the shortest path structure follows from considering the bipartite graph $G' = (V, V, E')$, where $(u, v) \in E$ iff u and v are at distance at most D in G, for some fixed threshold value D. Now consider a quadruple of vertices u, v, u', v' such that $(u, v) \in G'$ and $(u', v') \in G'$, $\text{dist}(u, v) = \text{dist}(u', v') \leq D$. Take now some hub candidate $h \in V$ and some integers a, b such that $a + b = \text{dist}(u, v)$. If h is on the unique shortest uv path and $h \in S(u) \cap S(v)$ and $\text{dist}(u, h) = a$, $\text{dist}(h, v) = b$, we can mark it by selecting uv as an edge in some subgraph $M_h \subseteq E'$. We do the same for $u'v'$ and every other pair of vertices, adding edges to M_h if h is a hub on shortest path located at distance a from one endpoint and b from other. It is now an easy observation that e.g. $\text{dist}(u, v') \leq a + b$, and if the distance is indeed $a + b$, pair u, v' is already covered by hub h. Since $h \in S(u)$ and $h \in S(v')$ was already amortized by paying for edges uv and $u'v'$ in M_h, there is no need for adding edge uv', and we can ensure that M_h is indeed an induced matching (repeating the reasoning for $u'v$ pair).

We are thus interested in structure of (linear in n) induced matchings in (potentially dense) graphs. Specifically, when looking for hubset constructions, it is advantageous for us to have an upper bound on number of induced matchings graph can be edge partitioned into. Similarly, when looking for a lowerbound construction, we are interested in an explicit construction of dense graphs edge partitioned into large induced matchings, and moreover in having such graphs realisable as a structure of unique shortest paths. The first of these questions has been studied extensively in the combinatorics literature.

The Ruzsa-Szemerédi function $\text{RS}(n)$ is a graph-theoretic function, defined as follows.

Definition 1.3. *An undirected, unweighted graph G on n vertices whose edges can be partitioned into at most n induced matchings is called a Ruzsa-Szemerédi graph.*[1] *Then $\text{RS}(n)$ is the largest value such that every Ruzsa-Szemerédi graph has at most $n^2/\text{RS}(n)$ edges.*

The study of values of $\text{RS}(n)$ was initiated by [37] who showed that $\text{RS}(n) = \omega(1)$. Current bounds state that

$$2^{\Omega(\log^* n)} \leq \text{RS}(n) \leq 2^{O(\sqrt{\log n})}$$

due to results of [21] and [14] (see [20] for current best upperbound up to lower-order terms). $\text{RS}(n)$ finds applications in algorithms and complexity theory, e.g. communication over a shared channel [15], PCP Theorem [29], property testing [6] and streaming algorithms [26, 30, 31]. We note that another work to exploit the connections between $\text{RS}(n)$ and the structure of shortest paths in graphs was [16], although this was done for the different (distantly related)

[1] In the literature there exists term of (r, t)-Ruzsa-Szemerédi graph, where edges are partitioned into t induced matchings of size r. We follow the convention of [16] and drop the indices.

problem of constructing *distance preservers*. Whereas the lite-motif of noting connections between sets of shortest paths and induced matchings is inherent to both [16] and our work, the combinatorial arguments used in the respective constructions are significantly different.

Using a number of combinatorial insights and properties of the hub labeling problem, we show the following result.

Theorem 1.4. *Any graph $G = (V, E)$ on n vertices and $O(n)$ edges admits a hub labeling $\{S_v\}$ of average size $\frac{1}{n}\sum_v |S(v)| = O(\frac{n}{\mathsf{RS}(n)^{1/c}})$ for some constant $c \leq 7$.*

(See Section 4 for a detailed proof.)

This result can be read twofold. First, it hints at the possibility that there are hub labeling schemes for sparse graphs with average hub size $O(\frac{n}{2^{\log^c n}})$ for some $0 < c < 1$, if one is to believe that the true value of $\mathsf{RS}(n)$ is on the side of the currently best upperbound. Secondly, it gives a (conditional) lowerbound on our lowerbound technique: one cannot hope to significantly improve the bound from Theorem 1.1 without strengthening existing bounds on value of $\mathsf{RS}(n)$, which is a hard open problem.

The connection between induced matchings and the structure of shortest paths leads us to the missing ingredient necessary for proving Theorem 1.1. Namely, in hard instances we are looking for, in addition to already discussed structure, we need the structure of shortest paths to realize some form of Ruzsa-Szemerédi structure, that is admit edge partion into preferably $O(n/\mathsf{RS}(n))$ induced matchings of n edges. Luckily, related ideas for such constructions were explored by [5]. The construction presented there involves graph with vertex set $[C]^d$ for some constants C, d, and interpreting vertices as d-dimensional vectors, the rule for connecting with edge $\vec{x}$ and $\vec{y}$ iff $|\|\vec{x} - \vec{y}\|_2^2 - \mu| \leq n$ for some chosen constant μ. We tweak the construction by using $[C]^d \times [\ell]$ as our vertex set, interpreted as ℓ d-dimensional layers, and connecting with an edge only between neighbouring layers (edges go always between i-th and $(i+1)$-th layer for some i). We fix ℓ to be a small value being in the order of *diameter* of the graph in the original construction - thus there is an equivalence between paths in the original graph of length ℓ and path in the new graph from first to last layer. Finally, we simplify the predicate deciding the existence of an edge (edges connect $\vec{x}$ and $\vec{y}$ if they differ in at most one coordinate), and ensure the uniqueness of a shortest paths by introducing weights over the edges of the graph.

Distance labelings and and the Sum-Index problem. Our graph family used in the proof of Theorem 1.1 has a very regular structure. Namely, one can distinguish three (large) layers of vertices $A, B, C \subset V$, such that each layer is labeled with vectors from a high-dimensional integer grid, and the following property holds: for $u_{\vec{x}} \in A$ and $w_{\vec{z}} \in C$, the unique shortest path intersects B in a single vertex that is precisely $v_{(\vec{x}+\vec{z})/2} \in B$. It is tempting to construct a family of (sparse) graphs, where shortest path length from vertices in A to vertices in C is sensitive to existence (or removal) of vertices in B. We can imagine this scenario as a game, where two players, one residing on A side, and one residing on C side of the graph, are evaluating in coordination a $A \times C \to \{0, 1\}$ function. To our advantage, such a problem has been widely considered in *communication complexity* in the 1990's.

Definition 1.5 (Sum-Index Problem). *Let $S = S_0 S_1 \ldots S_{n-1} \in \{0,1\}^n$. Alice holds S and $a \in [0, n-1]$. Bob holds S and $b \in [0, n-1]$. They both simultaneously send a messages M_a and M_b to a referee, whose goal is to compute $f(M_a, M_b) = S_{(a+b) \bmod n}$.*

This problem has been first stated explicitly in [35], as a single-bit-output "extract" of a $\{0,1\}^n \times [n] \to \{0,1\}^n$ shift function: $\mathrm{shift}_k(x) = y$, where $y_i = x_{(i+k) \bmod n}$. Analysis of shift is closely connected to a program of proving highly non-trivial lowerbounds in circuit complexity, c.f. [28] for a precise reduction. Informally, the goal is to prove super-linear lowerbounds on the size of circuits for some function $\{0,1\}^n \to \{0,1\}^n$, and shift was considered a strong candidate. However, the result of [35] and later [10] have shown that such direction is unfeasible (at least with shift), by showing existence of sub-linear communication complexity protocols for evaluation of Sum-Index. Those results were called "unexpected" upperbounds, and the best construction up-to-date is due to [10] with $\textsc{SumIndex}(n) = O(\frac{n \log^{0.25} n}{2^{\sqrt{\log n}}})$ bits complexity, where $\textsc{SumIndex}(n)$ denotes the exact bit complexity of the problem. It is also known that $\textsc{SumIndex}(n) = \Omega(\sqrt{n})$, cf. [11, 12, 33, 36], and the precise complexity is still a major open problem. We prove the following reduction.

Theorem 1.6. *Distance labeling in graphs on n vertices and max-degree 3 requires at least $\frac{1}{2^{\Theta(\sqrt{\log n})}}\textsc{SumIndex}(n)$ bits per vertex.*

(See Section 3 for a detailed proof.)

We note that our linkage between distance labeling size and communication complexity lowerbounds appears to be the first advancement of the techniques in the area going beyond the graph-counting technique of [23], and actually using distribution of information as a source of hardness in labeling schemes (although links between communication complexity and related to ours topic of compact routing have been investigated in [39]). One might hope that, with the advancement of communication complexity bounds, this approach will eventually result in non-trivial *unconditional* lowerbounds for distance labelings.

2 LOWER BOUND ON HUB LABELING

This section is devoted to the proof of the following theorem.

Theorem 2.1. *For any positive integers $\ell \in \mathbb{N}$ (the* number of levels*) and $b \in \mathbb{N}$ (the* side length parameter*) there exists a graph $G_{b,\ell}$ such that:*

(i) $|V(G_{b,\ell})| = 2^{b\ell} \cdot 2^{\Theta(b + \log \ell)}$ *(number of nodes).*
(ii) $\Delta(G_{b,\ell}) = 3$ *(maximum degree).*
(iii) *any hub labeling $\{S_v\}$ of $G_{b,\ell}$ satisfies:* $\frac{1}{|V(G_{b,\ell})|}\sum_{v \in V(G_{b,\ell})} |S_v| \geq 2^{b\ell} \cdot 2^{-\Theta(b+\ell)}$ *(average size of hub sets).*

Proof. In order to construct $G_{b,\ell}$, we more conveniently describe a weighted graph with non-uniform length edges, $H_{b,\ell} = (V, E, w)$ with integer edge weights appropriately chosen from the range $w(e) \in [1, (3\ell + 1) \cdot 2^{2b}]$,[2] for all $e \in E$.

In following we set $s = 2^b$ (the *side length*). We define vertex set of $H_{b,\ell}$ as $V = \bigcup_{r=0}^{2\ell} V_i$, where each *level* V_i, $i \in [0, 2\ell]$, satisfies

[2]Throughout the text, we use the integer range notation $[a, b] \equiv \{a, a+1, \ldots, b\}$ and $[a, b) \equiv [a, b-1]$, for $a, b \in \mathbb{N}$.

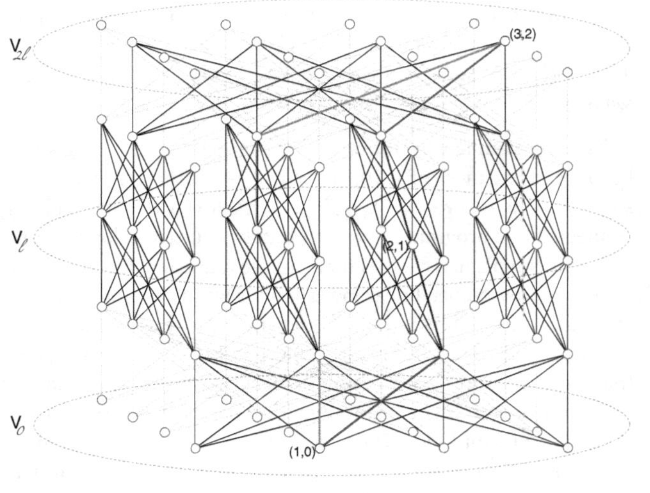

Figure 1: Graph $H_{b,\ell}$ with $b = 2$ and $\ell = 2$ ($s = 4$). Some edges are drawn in light gray for better readability. The blue path is the only shortest path from $v_{0,(1,0)}$ to $v_{4,(3,2)}$. It passes through $v_{2,(2,1)}$ (which is a point of symmetry for the path) and has length $4A + 4$. The red path has length $4A + 8$.

$|V_i| = s^\ell$ and is identified with a set of ℓ-dimensional vectors, $V_i = \{v_{i,\vec{j}} : \vec{j} \in [0, s-1]^\ell\}$.

The edges of $H_{b,\ell}$ are given so that we put an edge between $v_{i,\vec{j}}$ and $v_{i+1,\vec{j}'}$ when $\vec{j}$ and $\vec{j}'$ differ at most on one coordinate c: that is $j_k = j'_k$ for all $k \neq c$, where $c = i + 1$ for $i < \ell$ and $c = 2\ell - i$ for $i \geq \ell$. The weight of of such an edge is then given as $w(\{v_{i,\vec{j}}, v_{i+1,\vec{j}'}\}) = A + (j_c - j'_c)^2$ where $A = 3\ell s^2$. Note that each node $v_{i,\vec{j}}$ has exactly $s = 2^b$ neighbors in V_{i+1} (if $i < 2\ell$) and s neighbors in V_{i-1} (if $i > 0$). See Figure 1 for an illustration.

We convert $H_{b,\ell}$ into $G_{b,\ell}$ as follows.

- We associate each vertex v of $H_{b,\ell}$ with two disjoint perfectly balanced binary trees T_v^{in} and T_v^{out} in $G_{b,\ell}$, both roots being linked to v. Each tree has s leaves and depth $\log_2 s = b$. If $v \in V_i$, then leaves of T_v^{in} are labeled as v_u^{in}, with $u \in V_{i-1}$, $\{u, v\} \in E(H_{b,\ell})$ (T_v^{in} is omitted when $i = 0$), and leaves of T_v^{out} are labeled as v_u^{out}, with $u \in V_{i+1}$, $\{v, u\} \in E(H_{b,\ell})$ (T_v^{out} is omitted when $i = 2\ell$).
- We associate each edge $e = \{u, v\}$ of $H_{b,\ell}$, $u \in V_i, v \in V_{i+1}$ of length $w(e)$ to a path of length $w(e)-2b+-2$ with $w(e)-2b-3$ auxiliary vertices in $G_{b,\ell}$, starting at u_v^{out} and ending at v_u^{in}. Note that the path length satisfies $w(e) - 2b + -2 \geq 3\ell s^2 - 2b - 2 > 0$ for $\ell \geq 1$ and $b \geq 1$, and that using T_u^{out} and T_v^{in}, we obtain a path of length $w(\{u, v\})$ in $G_{b,\ell}$ for each edge $\{u, v\} \in E(H_{b,\ell})$.

We have $|V(G_{b,\ell})| \leq |V(H_{b,\ell})| \cdot 4s + \sum_{e \in E(H_{b,\ell})} w(e) \leq 4s \cdot s^\ell \cdot (2\ell + 1) + (3\ell + 1)s^2 \cdot s^\ell \cdot 2\ell \cdot s$, so the claims (i) and (ii) follow directly from the construction. To show claim (iii), we first observe that the following property holds.

Lemma 2.2. *Let $\vec{x}, \vec{z} \in [0, s-1]^\ell$ be such that for all $k \in [1, \ell]$, $z_k - x_k$ is even. Then there exists a unique shortest path in $H_{b,\ell}$ (and consequently also in $G_{b,\ell}$) between vertices $v_{0,\vec{x}}$ and $v_{2\ell,\vec{z}}$. Moreover, this shortest path passes through vertex $v_{\ell,(\vec{x}+\vec{z})/2}$.*

We defer the proof of the Lemma 2.2.

Now, let $\{S_v\}$ be any fixed hub labeling of $G_{b,\ell}$. Fix arbitrarily shortest path trees T_v rooted at each vertex v of $G_{b,\ell}$, and let S_v^* be the vertex set of the minimal subtree of T_v rooted at v which contains all vertices of S_v. We obviously have:

$$|S_v^*| \leq \text{diam}(G_{b,\ell}) \cdot |S_v| \leq (3\ell + 1)s^2 \cdot 4\ell \cdot |S_v|. \qquad (1)$$

Thus, the sets S_v and S_v^* are of equivalent size up to lower-order terms, and from now on, we focus on showing a lower bound on $\sum_{v \in V} S_v^*$.

Consider all triplets $(\vec{x}, \vec{y}, \vec{z})$ such that $\vec{x}, \vec{y}, \vec{z} \in [0, s-1]^\ell$ and that $\vec{y} = (\vec{x} + \vec{z})/2$. There is $s^\ell \cdot (s/2)^\ell$ such triplets. Denote $x = v_{0,\vec{x}}$, $y = v_{\ell,\vec{y}}$ and $z = v_{2\ell,\vec{z}}$, then by Lemma 2.2 y lies on the unique shortest xz path, thus $y \in S_x^*$ or $y \in S_z^*$. Since $\vec{z} = 2\vec{x} - \vec{y}$, we have that value of $\vec{z}$ is uniquely determined by fixing $\vec{x}$ and $\vec{y}$, and similarly by $\vec{x} = 2\vec{z} - \vec{y}$, value of $\vec{x}$ is uniquely determined by fixing $\vec{y}$ and $\vec{z}$. Thus in each triplet $(\vec{x}, \vec{y}, \vec{z})$, vertex y contributes by 1 to the size of S_x^* or S_z^*. Thus $\sum_{v \in V} S_v^* \geq (s^\ell)^2 \cdot 2^{-\ell}$, and taking into account Eq. (1), claim (iii) follows. □

Proof of Lemma 2.2. Finally, we prove the Lemma 2.2. We first consider the weighted graph $H_{b,\ell}$ only. Intuitively, we show that the unique shortest path in $H_{b,\ell}$ has the following structure: it climbs from level 0 to level ℓ on its first ℓ edges, reaching vertex $v_{\ell,\vec{y}}$, and then climbs next ℓ edges to level 2ℓ; the portions of the path from $v_{0,\vec{x}}$ to $v_{\ell,\vec{y}}$ and from $v_{\ell,\vec{y}}$ to $v_{2\ell,\vec{z}}$ have a point symmetry with respect to $v_{\ell,\vec{y}}$.

Let $d(v_{0,\vec{x}}, v_{2\ell,\vec{z}})$ denote the weighted distance between the pair of nodes considered in the Lemma.

Consider any path $P_{\vec{x},\vec{z}} = (v_{\vec{x}} \equiv v_{0,\vec{j}^0}, v_{1,\vec{j}^1}, \ldots, v_{2\ell-1,\vec{j}^{2\ell-1}}, v_{2\ell,\vec{j}^{2\ell}} \equiv v_{\vec{z}})$ in $H_{b,\ell}$ on 2ℓ edges. Denote $\delta_i = j_i^i - j_i^{i-1}$ and for $i \in [1, \ell]$ and $\delta_i = j_{2\ell-i+1}^i - j_{2\ell-i+1}^{i-1}$ for $i \in [\ell + 1, 2\ell]$.

The following properties hold:

- The weighted length of any such $P_{\vec{x},\vec{z}}$ is:
$$\sum_{i=1}^{2\ell} \left(A + \delta_i^2\right) \leq 2\ell A + 2\ell s^2 < (2\ell + 1)A.$$
- All $v_{0,\vec{x}} v_{2\ell,\vec{z}}$ paths in $H_{b,\ell}$ have at least 2ℓ edges.
- Any $v_{0,\vec{x}} v_{2\ell,\vec{z}}$ path in $H_{b,\ell}$ with at least $2\ell + 1$ edges has weighted length at least $(2\ell + 1)A$, which is greater than that of $P_{\vec{x},\vec{z}}$.
- $P_{\vec{x},\vec{z}}$ satisfies $\delta_i + \delta_{2\ell+1-i} = z_i - x_i$. It thus follows that the total length $\sum_{i=1}^{\ell} \left(2A + \delta_i^2 + \delta_{2\ell+1-i}^2\right)$ is minimized when $\delta_i = \delta_{2\ell+1-i} = \frac{1}{2}(z_i - x_i)$, realized by an unique $v_{0,\vec{x}} v_{2\ell,\vec{z}}$ path having point symmetry at $v_{\ell,\vec{y}}$.

This finishes the proof for $H_{b,\ell}$. To complete the proof for $G_{b,\ell}$ we observe that for any $u \in V_i$ and $v \in V_j$ with $i < j$, we have $\text{dist}_{G_{b,\ell}}(u, v) = \text{dist}_{H_{b,\ell}}(u, v)$. This comes from the construction of $G_{b,\ell}$ for $j = i + 1$ and from the fact that any $V_{i'}$ with $i < i' < j$ is a vertex cut in $G_{b,\ell}$ separating u and v for $j > i + 1$: any shortest path Q from u to v in $G_{b,\ell}$ must pass through $j - i - 1$ vertices in $V_{i+1} \cup \cdots \cup V_{j-1}$ corresponding to a path P in $G_{b,\ell}$ such that $|Q| = w(P)$. The shortest path from $v_{0,\vec{x}}$ to $v_{2\ell,\vec{z}}$ in $G_{b,\ell}$ is thus unique and passes through $v_{\ell,(\vec{x}+\vec{z})/2}$ similarly as the shortest path in $H_{b,\ell}$, which concludes the proof. □

Setting both $b = \ell = \sqrt{\log N}$ for some appropriately chosen $N = n/2^{\Theta(\sqrt{\log n})}$ in Theorem 2.1 we finally obtain the main result of the Section.

Theorem 1.1. *Graphs of max-degree 3 require average hub size to be at least* $\frac{n}{2^{\Theta(\sqrt{\log n})}}$, *where n is the number of vertices.*

3 LOWER BOUND FOR DISTANCE LABELING

We now show that distance labeling in sparse graphs is no easier than solving Sum-Index. We essentially use the graph construction from Theorem 1.1, and the the fact that the distance between nodes $v_{0,\vec{x}}$ and $v_{2\ell,\vec{z}}$ is sensitive to the presence (or absence) in the graph of the node $v_{\ell,(\vec{x}+\vec{z})/2}$.

Theorem 1.6. *Distance labeling in graphs on n vertices and max-degree 3 requires at least* $\frac{1}{2^{\Theta(\sqrt{\log n})}}$ *SumIndex(n) bits per vertex.*

Proof. Let S be the binary vector of length m from Sum-Index Problem, with m to be determined later. We describe the strategies of Alice and Bob of constructing the messages M_a and M_b respectively. Consider graph $G_{b,\ell}$ from Theorem 2.1. We construct $G'_{b,\ell}$ by removing some vertices from layer V_ℓ (together with all adjacent edges) from $G_{b,\ell}$. We denote the choice of whether to include or remove particular vertex $v_{\ell,\vec{x}}$ as $W(\vec{x})$, and we defer how we decide those to later part of the proof.

Observation 3.1. *Let $\vec{x}$ and $\vec{z}$ be as in Lemma 2.2, that is for any $k \in [1,\ell]$ $z_k - x_k$ is even. Then $W((\vec{x}+\vec{z})/2)$ can be decoded based only on $\vec{x},\vec{z}$ and the length of the shortest path between $v_{0,\vec{x}}$ and $v_{2\ell,\vec{z}}$ in $G'_{b,\ell}$.*

We also note that G' has $2^{b\ell} \cdot 2^{\Theta(b+\lg \ell)}$ vertices and maximum degree of 3.

Recall we denoted $s = 2^b$ the side-length of a layer in G (or G'). We fix $m = (s/2)^\ell$. For a vector $\vec{x} \in [s]^\ell$ we denote $\text{repr}(\vec{x}) = \left(\sum_i x_i \cdot (s/2)^i\right) \bmod m$ as the integer value coming from treating coordinates of $\vec{x}$ as digits in $(s/2)$-ary representation. Observe that while repr() is a bijection between $[0, s/2-1]^\ell$ and $[0,(s/2)^\ell - 1]$, this is not the case for the whole space $[0, s-1]^\ell$ (in fact every value is in the image of 2^ℓ vectors). We fix the predicate $W(\vec{x})$ as: $W(\vec{x}) \equiv [S_{\text{repr}(\vec{x})} = 1]$.

The protocol for Alice is as follow:

(1) Alice constructs graph $G'_{b,\ell}$ based on binary word $S \in \{0,1\}^m$.
(2) Alice constructs a *distance labeling* for $G'_{b,\ell}$.
(3) Alice finds unique $\vec{x} \in [0, s/2-1]^\ell$ such that $\text{repr}(\vec{x}) = a$ (based on the $(s/2)$-ary representation of a).
(4) Alice sends to the referee the label of vertex $v_{0,2\vec{x}}$ together with integer a.

Bob proceeds analogously, representing b as vector $\vec{z}$, constructing the same distance labeling of $G'_{b,\ell}$ as Alice and sending the label of $v_{2\ell,2\vec{z}}$ with integer b. The referee is then able to compute distance between Alice's and Bob's vertices, reconstructs vectors $\vec{x}$ and $\vec{z}$, and by the Observation 3.1 knows the bit $S_{\text{repr}(\vec{x}+\vec{z})} = S_{(a+b) \bmod m}$, which follows from $\text{repr}(\vec{x}+\vec{z}) = (\text{repr}(\vec{x}) + \text{repr}(\vec{z})) \bmod m = (a+b) \bmod m$.

We thus reach the conclusion that distance labeling of sparse graph with $2^{b\ell} \cdot 2^{\Theta(b+\log \ell)}$ requires at least $\text{SumIndex}(2^{(b-1)\ell}) - b\ell$ bits per label. Fixing $b = \ell = \sqrt{\log N}$ for some $N = \frac{n}{2^{\Theta(\sqrt{\log n})}}$ finishes the proof. □

4 UPPER BOUND

In this section we show how to take advantage of a structure of induced matchings in dense graphs to construct hubsets. We start by considering a case of graphs of constant maxdegree.

Theorem 4.1. *Any graph $G = (V,E)$ on n vertices and maxdegree $\Delta = O(1)$ admits a hub labeling $\{S_v\}$ of total size $\sum_v |S_v| = O(\frac{n^2}{\text{RS}(n)^{1/c}})$ for some constant $c \le 7$.*

Proof. Let D be a parameter $1 \le D \le \text{RS}(n)$ to be fixed later. For any pair of vertices u, v we denote H_{uv} the set of all valid hubs for this pair, that is $H_{uv} \equiv \{x : \text{dist}(u,x) + \text{dist}(x,v) = \text{dist}(u,v)\}$.

We start by formulating the following property for a set $S \subseteq V$: $(*)$ for two vertices u, v such that $|H_{uv}| \ge D$, we have $S \cap H_{uv} \ne \emptyset$. There exists a set S such that $|S| = O(\frac{n}{D}\log D)$ and $(*)$ is satisfied for all pairs uv except $\frac{n^2}{D}$ many. Existence of such set can proven by probabilistic method (c.f. [17]). Indeed, pick such set uniformly at random with $|S| = \frac{n}{D}\ln D$. Any pair u, v with at least D hubs is *not covered* with probability at most $(1 - D/n)^{|S|} \le 1/D$, thus the expected number of uncovered pairs is at most n^2/D, and there is a selection of S with at most that many pairs not covered. From now on we focus on such S, and we denote by $\{Q_v\}$ a family of sets such that if a pair uv is not covered by S and satisfies $H_{uv} \ge D$, then we put $v \in Q_u$. By the property of S, we have $\sum_{v\in V} |Q_v| \le n^2/D$.

We now color all vertices of G with D^3 colors, so that for each $v \in V$, the color $c_v \in [1, D^3]$ is assigned independently and uniformly at random. Consider the following event: for a pair u, v, each vertex from H_{uv} is assigned a different color. If $|H_{uv}| \le D$, then such an event happens with probability at least $1 - 1/D$, and the opposite event with probability at most $1/D$. If we define sets $\{R_u\} = \{v :$ there are $x, y \in H_{u,v}$ such that $c_x = c_y\}$, then by simple computation of expected value, there is a choice of colors c_v such that $\sum_v |R_v| \le n^2/D$. Thus we can afford for each v to store as hubs R_v, the vertices where coloring of potential hubs failed to assign unique colors.

We now deal with u, v such that $|H_{uv}| \le D$ and H_{uv} was properly colored using different colors. First, we iterate through $a, b \ge 0$ such that $1 \le a + b \le D$ and iterate $h \in V$. Consider bipartite graph $(V, V, E^h_{a,b})$, $E^h_{a,b} \subseteq V \times V$. For u, v we put $(u,v) \in E^h_{a,b}$ if the following conditions hold: (i) $|H_{uv}| \le D$, (ii) each vertex of H_{uv} was colored using distinct color, (iii) $h \in H_{uv}$, $\text{dist}(u,h) = a$ and $\text{dist}(h,v) = b$. We now use the following Lemma, with proof provided later:

Lemma 4.2. *Construct $\{F_v\}$ as follow: a, b iterate so that $1 \le a+b \le D$ and h iterate over V, and consider some minimum vertex cover (V_1, V_2), $V_1, V_2 \subseteq V$ of $(V, V, E^h_{a,b})$. If $v \in V_1 \cup V_2$, we put h into F_v. We then have $\sum_v |F_v| = O(D^5 \frac{n^2}{\text{RS}(n)})$.*

For $X \subseteq V$, let $N(X) = \{v : \exists_{x \in X} \text{dist}(v, x) \leq 1\}$ denote neighborhood. We observe, that for any two vertices u, v, one of the following holds:

(1) If $H_{uv} \geq D$, then either there exists $h \in S$ such that $h \in H_{uv}$ is a hub for u, v, or $v \in Q_u$ is a hub for u, v.
(2) If $H_{uv} \leq D$ and there is a color conflict in H_{uv}, then $v \in R_u$ is a hub for u, v.
(3) If $H_{uv} \leq D$ and there is no color conflict in H_{uv}, then for any $h \in H_{uv}$, there are $a = \text{dist}(u, h)$ and $b = \text{dist}(h, v)$ such that $(u, v) \in E^h_{a,b}$. Thus at least one of u, v is in the corresponding vertex cover, and so $h \in F_u$ or $h \in F_v$. Since this holds for any $h \in H_{uv}$, and w.l.o.g. $u \in F_u$, $v \in F_v$, by induction along a uv-shortest path there is an edge $(x, y) \in E$ such that $x \in F_u$ and $y \in F_v$ and $x, y \in H_{uv}$, guaranteeing that $N(F_u) \cap N(F_v) \neq \emptyset$.

We then set each vertex hubset $H_v = S \cup Q_v \cup R_v \cup N(F_v)$. A bound on size follows $\sum_v |H_v| \leq n \cdot |S| + \sum_v |Q_v| + \sum_v |R_v| + (\Delta + 1) \sum_v |F_v| \leq O(\frac{n^2}{D} \log D) + O(\frac{n^2}{D}) + O(D^5 \frac{n^2}{\text{RS}(n)})$ using Lemma 4.2. Setting $D = \text{RS}(n)^{1/6}$ completes the proof.

□

Proof of Lemma 4.2. Fix values a, b and h and vertex cover $VC^h_{a,b}$ used in that iteration. By relation between maximum matching and minimum vertex cover, any maximal matching $MM^h_{a,b} \subseteq E^h_{a,b}$ satisfies $|VC^h_{a,b}| \leq 2|MM^h_{a,b}|$. For each color c, consider bipartite graph $G^c_{a,b} = \bigcup_{h: c_h = c} MM^h_{a,b}$. We now show that $MM^h_{a,b}$ is in fact an induced matching in $G^c_{a,b}$. It is enough to show the following: for any two distinct $(u_1, v_1), (u_2, v_2) \in MM^h_{a,b}$, we have $(u_1, v_2) \notin G^c_{a,b}$ and $(u_2, v_1) \notin G^c_{a,b}$. Assume otherwise, that $(u_1, v_2) \in MM^{h'}_{a,b}$ for some $h' \neq h$ (we know we can exclude $(u_1, v_2) \in MM^h_{a,b}$ due to $MM^h_{a,b}$ being a matching). We know that $\text{dist}(u_1, h) = a$ and $\text{dist}(h, v_2) = b$, and each vertex of $H_{u_1 v_2}$ was colored using a different color, thus either $\text{dist}(u_1, v_2) < a+b$ or $c_{h'} \neq c_h$, a contradiction.

This shows that $G^c_{a,b}$ is a Ruzsa-Szemerédi graph (on $2n$ vertices), with edge partition into induced matchings $MM^h_{a,b}$ for $h : c_h = c$. It thus follows that $|G^c_{a,b}| \leq \frac{(2n)^2}{\text{RS}(2n)} = O(\frac{n^2}{\text{RS}(n)})$.[3] We then obtain the following bound:

$$\begin{aligned}\sum_{v \in V} |F_v| &\leq \sum_{1 \leq a+b \leq D} \sum_{h \in V} |VC^h_{a,b}| \\ &\leq \sum_{1 \leq a+b \leq D} \sum_{h \in V} 2|MM^h_{a,b}| \\ &\leq \sum_{1 \leq a+b \leq D} \sum_{c \in [1, D^3]} 2|G^c_{a,b}| \\ &= O(D^5 \frac{n^2}{\text{RS}(n)}).\end{aligned}$$

□

Note that the construction used in proof of Theorem 4.1 generalizes to edges with $\{0, 1\}$ weights since any path length $c \leq D$ still decomposes in at most D sums $c = a + b$ of two path lengths.

[3]It is straightforward to show $\text{RS}(2n) = \Theta(\text{RS}(n))$.

We now note that if G is a graph of constant *average degree*, that is $m/n = O(1)$, then we can reduce construction of hub labeling to constant *max degree* case as follow. First, we construct G' by subdividing any vertex $v \in V(G)$ of degree $\deg(v)$ into $\lceil \frac{\deg(v)}{\lceil m/n \rceil} \rceil$ vertices of degree at most $2 + \lceil m/n \rceil$, using a path with weight-0 auxiliary edges for linking them (treating all the non-auxiliary edges as weight-1 edges). We have then $|E(G')| = O(m)$ and $|V(G')| = O(m)$. We note that for any $v' \in V(G')$ there is $v \in V(G)$ that originated v', and for any $v \in V(G)$ we can pick one $v' \in V(G')$ as a representative of v in G'. Having constructed hub labeling for G', denote it $\{H'_v\}$, we construct a hubset of $v \in V(G)$ by taking hubset of its representative in G' and projecting back each selected hub in G' to its original vertex in G. We thus have reached our main result on the side of upper bounds.

Theorem 1.4. *Any graph $G = (V, E)$ on n vertices and $O(n)$ edges admits a hub labeling $\{S_v\}$ of average size $\frac{1}{n} \sum_v |S(v)| = O(\frac{n}{\text{RS}(n)^{1/c}})$ for some constant $c \leq 7$.*

REFERENCES

[1] A. Abboud, P. Gawrychowski, S. Mozes, and O. Weimann. Near-optimal compression for the planar graph metric. In *SODA*, pages 530–549, 2018.
[2] I. Abraham, D. Delling, A. Fiat, A. V. Goldberg, and R. F. Werneck. Highway dimension and provably efficient shortest path algorithms. *J. ACM*, 63(5):41:1–41:26, 2016.
[3] I. Abraham, D. Delling, A. V. Goldberg, and R. F. Werneck. Hierarchical hub labelings for shortest paths. In *ESA*, pages 24–35, 2012.
[4] I. Abraham and C. Gavoille. On approximate distance labels and routing schemes with affine stretch. In *DISC*, pages 404–415, 2011.
[5] N. Alon, A. Moitra, and B. Sudakov. Nearly complete graphs decomposable into large induced matchings and their applications. In *STOC*, pages 1079–1090, 2012.
[6] N. Alon and A. Shapira. Testing subgraphs in directed graphs. *J. Comput. Syst. Sci.*, 69(3):354–382, 2004.
[7] S. Alstrup, S. Dahlgaard, M. B. T. Knudsen, and E. Porat. Sublinear distance labeling. In *ESA*, pages 5:1–5:15, 2016.
[8] S. Alstrup, C. Gavoille, E. B. Halvorsen, and H. Petersen. Simpler, faster and shorter labels for distances in graphs. In *SODA*, pages 338–350, 2016.
[9] S. Alstrup, I. L. Gørtz, E. B. Halvorsen, and E. Porat. Distance labeling schemes for trees. In *ICALP*, pages 132:1–132:16, 2016.
[10] A. Ambainis. Upper bounds on multiparty communication complexity of shifts. In *STACS*, pages 631–642, 1996.
[11] L. Babai, A. Gál, P. G. Kimmel, and S. V. Lokam. Communication complexity of simultaneous messages. *SIAM J. Comput.*, 33(1):137–166, 2003.
[12] L. Babai, P. G. Kimmel, and S. V. Lokam. Simultaneous messages vs. communication. In *STACS*, pages 361–372, 1995.
[13] R. Bauer and D. Delling. SHARC: Fast and robust unidirectional routing. *J. Exp. Algorithmics*, 14:4:2.4–4:2.29, Jan. 2010.
[14] F. A. Behrend. On sets of integers which contain no three terms in arithmetical progression. *Proceedings of the National Academy of Sciences of the United States of America*, 32(12):331, 1946.
[15] Y. Birk, N. Linial, and R. Meshulam. On the uniform-traffic capacity of single-hop interconnections employing shared directional multichannels. *IEEE Trans. Information Theory*, 39(1):186–191, 1993.
[16] G. Bodwin. Linear size distance preservers. In *SODA*, pages 600–615, 2017.
[17] B. Bollobás, D. Coppersmith, and M. Elkin. Sparse distance preservers and additive spanners. *SIAM Journal on Discrete Mathematics*, 19(4):1029–1055, 2005.
[18] E. Cohen, E. Halperin, H. Kaplan, and U. Zwick. Reachability and distance queries via 2-hop labels. *SIAM J. Comput.*, 32(5):1338–1355, May 2003.
[19] H. Cohen and E. Porat. On the hardness of distance oracle for sparse graph. *CoRR*, abs/1006.1117, 2010.
[20] M. Elkin. An improved construction of progression-free sets. In *SODA*, pages 886–905, 2010.
[21] J. Fox. A new proof of the graph removal lemma. *Annals of Mathematics*, pages 561–579, 2011.
[22] O. Freedman, P. Gawrychowski, P. K. Nicholson, and O. Weimann. Optimal distance labeling schemes for trees. In *PODC*, pages 185–194, 2017.
[23] C. Gavoille, D. Peleg, S. Pérennes, and R. Raz. Distance labeling in graphs. *J. Algorithms*, 53(1):85–112, Oct. 2004.
[24] P. Gawrychowski, A. Kosowski, and P. Uznański. Sublinear-space distance labeling using hubs. In *DISC*, pages 230–242, 2016.

[25] P. Gawrychowski and P. Uznański. A note on distance labeling in planar graphs. *CoRR*, abs/1611.06529, 2016.

[26] A. Goel, M. Kapralov, and S. Khanna. On the communication and streaming complexity of maximum bipartite matching. In *SODA*, pages 468–485, 2012.

[27] R. Graham and H. Pollak. On embedding graphs in squashed cubes. In Y. Alavi, D. Lick, and A. White, editors, *Graph Theory and Applications*, volume 303 of *Lecture Notes in Mathematics*, pages 99–110. Springer Berlin Heidelberg, 1972.

[28] J. Håstad and M. Goldmann. On the power of small-depth threshold circuits. *Computational Complexity*, 1:113–129, 1991.

[29] J. Håstad and A. Wigderson. Simple analysis of graph tests for linearity and PCP. *Random Struct. Algorithms*, 22(2):139–160, 2003.

[30] M. Kapralov. Better bounds for matchings in the streaming model. In *SODA*, pages 1679–1697, 2013.

[31] C. Konrad. Maximum matching in turnstile streams. In *ESA*, pages 840–852, 2015.

[32] E. Köhler, R. H. Möhring, and H. Schilling. Fast point-to-point shortest path computations with arc-flags. In *9th DIMACS Implementation Challenge*, 2006.

[33] N. Nisan and A. Wigderson. Rounds in communication complexity revisited. *SIAM J. Comput.*, 22(1):211–219, 1993.

[34] D. Peleg. Proximity-preserving labeling schemes. *Journal of Graph Theory*, 33(3):167–176, 2000.

[35] P. Pudlák. Unexpected upper bounds on the complexity of some communication games. In *ICALP*, pages 1–10, 1994.

[36] P. Pudlák, V. Rödl, and J. Sgall. Boolean circuits, tensor ranks, and communication complexity. *SIAM J. Comput.*, 26(3):605–633, 1997.

[37] I. Z. Ruzsa and E. Szemerédi. Triple systems with no six points carrying three triangles. *Combinatorics (Keszthely, 1976), Coll. Math. Soc. J. Bolyai*, 18:939–945, 1978.

[38] C. Sommer, E. Verbin, and W. Yu. Distance oracles for sparse graphs. In *FOCS*, pages 703–712, 2009.

[39] A. D. Twigg. Compact forbidden-set routing. Technical report, University of Cambridge, Computer Laboratory, 2006.

[40] O. Weimann and D. Peleg. A note on exact distance labeling. *Inf. Process. Lett.*, 111(14):671–673, 2011.

On the Complexity of Distributed Splitting Problems

Philipp Bamberger
University of Freiburg, Germany
philipp.bamberger@cs.uni-freiburg.de

Mohsen Ghaffari
ETH Zürich, Switzerland
ghaffari@inf.ethz.ch

Fabian Kuhn
University of Freiburg, Germany
kuhn@cs.uni-freiburg.de

Yannic Maus*
Technion, Israel
yannic.maus@cs.technion.ac.il

Jara Uitto
ETH Zürich/University of Freiburg
jara.uitto@inf.ethz.ch

ABSTRACT

One of the fundamental open problems in the area of distributed graph algorithms is whether randomization is needed for efficient symmetry breaking. While there are poly log n-time randomized algorithms for all the classic symmetry breaking problems, for many of them, the best deterministic algorithms are almost exponentially slower. The following basic local splitting problem, which is known as *weak splitting*, takes a central role in this context: Each node of a graph $G = (V, E)$ has to be colored red or blue such that each node of sufficiently large degree has at least one neighbor of each color. Ghaffari, Kuhn, and Maus [STOC '17] showed that this seemingly simple problem is complete w.r.t. the above fundamental open question in the following sense: If there is an efficient poly log n-time determinstic distributed algorithm for weak splitting, then there is such an algorithm for all locally checkable graph problems for which an efficient randomized algorithm exists. We investigate the distributed complexity of weak splitting and some closely related problems and we in particular obtain the following results:

- We obtain efficient algorithms for special cases of weak splitting in nearly regular graphs. We show that if $\delta = \Omega(\log n)$ and Δ are the minimum and maximum degrees of G, weak splitting can be solved deterministically in time $O(\frac{\Delta}{\delta} \cdot \text{poly}(\log n))$. Further, if $\delta = \Omega(\log \log n)$ and $\Delta \leq 2^{\varepsilon\delta}$, the time complexity is $O(\frac{\Delta}{\delta} \cdot \text{poly}(\log \log n))$.
- We prove that the following two related problems are also complete in the same sense: (I) Color the nodes of a graph with $C \leq$ poly log n colors such that each node with a sufficiently large polylogarithmic degree has at least $2 \log n$ different colors among its neighbors, and (II) Color the nodes with a large constant number of colors so that for each node of a sufficiently large at least logarithmic degree $d(v)$, the number of neighbors of each color is at most $(1 - \varepsilon)d(v)$ for some constant $\varepsilon > 0$.

*Supported by the European Union's Horizon 2020 Research And Innovation Programme under grant agreement no. 755839.

ACM ISBN 978-1-4503-6217-7/19/07...$15.00
https://doi.org/10.1145/3293611.3331630

KEYWORDS

distributed graph algorithms, weak splitting, LOCAL Model, distributed symmetry breaking, randomness

ACM Reference Format:
Philipp Bamberger, Mohsen Ghaffari, Fabian Kuhn, Yannic Maus, and Jara Uitto. 2019. On the Complexity of Distributed Splitting Problems. In *2019 ACM Symposium on Principles of Distributed Computing (PODC '19), July 29-August 2, 2019, Toronto, ON, Canada.* ACM, New York, NY, USA, 10 pages. https://doi.org/10.1145/3293611.3331630

1 INTRODUCTION

In this paper, we investigate the distributed complexity of the *splitting* problem and its variants in the LOCAL model.[1] This problem is an important distributed symmetry breaking problem; to set the stage, let us start with an overview of the *splitting* problem and its significance.

1.1 The Splitting Problem and its Significance

Splitting can be seen as a basic algorithmic tool to develop distributed divide-and-conquer algorithms for graph problems. Let us introduce it by using the well-studied vertex coloring problem as a toy example. Consider an n-node graph $G = (V, E)$ with maximum degree Δ. Our objective is to color V using as few colors as possible so that no two neighbors receive the same color. The best known deterministic distributed algorithm which is efficient—i.e., runs in poly log n rounds— computes a $\Delta \cdot 2^{O(\frac{\log \Delta}{\log \log \Delta})}$ coloring [2]. Naturally, we would like to do much better; ideally $O(\Delta)$ or even just $\Delta + 1$ colors, see, e.g., Open Problem 11.3 in the book by Barenboim and Elkin [3].

Let us define the splitting problem to be dividing the nodes of the graph into two groups, say red and blue, such that the number of neighbors of each node in each group is at most $\frac{\Delta}{2}(1 + \varepsilon)$ for some small value ε.[2] If we had access to an efficient deterministic algorithm for splitting whenever $\Delta = \Omega(\log n/\varepsilon^2)$, by repeated applications of it, we could partition the graph into $\frac{\Delta}{K}$ induced subgraphs, for $K \in$ poly log n, each with maximum degree at most $K(1 + \varepsilon)^{\log \Delta}$. Thus, setting $\varepsilon = o(1/\log \Delta)$, each subgraph would

[1] The LOCAL model [20, 22] is a standard synchronous message passing model on graphs, where in every round, each node can send an arbitrarily large message to each of its neighbors.

[2] Something weaker would suffice for this special application; it would be enough if each node has at most $\frac{\Delta}{2}(1 + \varepsilon)$ neighbors in its own color. This is a form of defective coloring, and it is a weaker requirement than splitting. But let us use the convenient context of the coloring problem to motivate the stronger problem of splitting.

have degree $(1 + o(1))K$. Since we have efficient distributed algorithms for coloring graphs of maximum degree d using $d + 1$ colors in $\tilde{O}(\sqrt{d}) + O(\log^* n)$ rounds [12], we would immediately get a $\Delta(1 + o(1))$-coloring for the whole graph in poly log n rounds deterministically. This would be a breakthrough for the distributed coloring problem would resolve a long-standing open problem.

Of course, the catch is that we do not know an efficient deterministic method for constructing such a splitting. We emphasize that it is a matter of efficient construction and not a matter of existence. It is not hard to see that such a split always exists for $\Delta = \Omega(\log n/\varepsilon^2)$, which is the regime where we need splitting, and in a randomized way it can be constructed (w.h.p.) by independently coloring each node red or blue uniformly at random. This nicely highlights the significance of splitting for distributed graph coloring: While there is a trivial randomized distributed algorithm for splitting that does not even require the nodes to communicate, an efficient deterministic algorithm would lead to major progress on the deterministic distributed coloring problem.

It is worth noting that the natural edge variant of the splitting problem is proved to be extremely instrumental for the variant of the coloring problem where we want to color the edges. Edge splitting (also known as degree splitting) can be defined as coloring all edges red or blue such that each node has at most $\frac{\Delta}{2}(1 + \varepsilon)$ edges in each color. Ghaffari and Su [19] provided a poly log n-round algorithm for edge-splitting, which led to the first efficient deterministic distributed $2\Delta(1 + o(1))$-edge-coloring algorithm, thus partially resolving Open Problem 11.4 of [3]. A significantly more efficient edge splitting algorithm was later provided in [16]. The most classic variant of the distributed edge coloring problem asks for a solution with $2\Delta - 1$ colors as this is the number of colors obtained by a simple sequential greedy algorithm. The first efficient (poly log n time) deterministic distributed algorithms for the $(2\Delta - 1)$-edge coloring problem were obtained recently [11, 14]. These results were achieved by solving a generalization of the edge splitting problem in low-rank hypergraphs. Even more progress was achieved later and currently the best known efficient deterministic edge coloring algorithm—which is also based on solving edge splitting on the network graph and on some related low-rank hypergraphs—provides a $(1 + o(1))\Delta$-edge coloring [18], whenever $\Delta = \Omega(\log n)$, thus almost matching the Vizing bound for the number of colors [6, Section 17.2].

Unfortunately, the splitting problem for vertices turned out to be much harder. Perhaps fortunately, it is also far more significant than just its relation to the coloring problem. It is tightly connected to the fundamental and long-standing open question of whether randomization is necessary for efficient distributed symmetry breaking. Currently, for many problems (such as $(\Delta + 1)$-coloring or computing a maximal independent set (MIS)), there is an exponential gap between the best randomized algorithm and the best deterministic algorithms and whether poly log n-time deterministic algorithms for these problems exist is considered to be one of the main open problems in the area of local distributed graph algorithms [3]. Due to results of Ghaffari et al. [17], we now know the splitting problem is complete with respect to this question in the following sense. If one can find a poly log n-time deterministic distributed algorithm for splitting, then one can derandomize any poly log n-time randomized distributed algorithm for *any* locally checkable problem into a poly log n-time deterministic distributed algorithm for that problem. The simple splitting problem (which has a trivial 0-round randomized algorithm) therefore exactly captures the complete power of randomization for obtaining poly log n-time algorithms for local distributed graph problems.

In fact, Ghaffari et al.[17] showed that a much more relaxed version of the splitting problem is already complete: It is enough to ensure that each node with degree at least $\Omega(\log n)$ has at least one neighbor in each color. They call this the *weak splitting* problem and they showed that if one can find a poly log n-time deterministic distributed algorithm for weak splitting, that also implies that one can derandomize any poly log n-time randomized distributed algorithm for *any* locally checkable problem into a poly log n-time deterministic distributed algorithm for that problem. Notice that weak splitting would not be sufficient for the method described above for the coloring problem. The proof of Ghaffari et al.[17] for using weak splitting goes a very different route, it uses weak splitting to build a certain network decomposition, and [14] shows how to use such network decompositions to derandomize randomized algorithms for any locally checkable problem.

To summarize, weak splitting—which might even look deceivingly simple—is all that we need so that we can obtain deterministic poly log n-time algorithms for locally checkable graph problems and thus to answer many of the outstanding open questions regarding efficient deterministic local graph algorithms. In this paper, we show some partial progress on our understanding of the weak splitting problem, and we also show that even some very relaxed variants of it can be proven to be complete (in the same completeness sense as weak splitting).

1.2 Our Contributions

Algorithmic Results/Deterministic: Our algorithmic contribution is a new weak splitting algorithm that is efficient in nearly regular graphs. Let Δ and δ denote the maximum and minimum degrees of the given graph. If $\delta = \Omega(\log n)$, we give a deterministic algorithm that solves weak splitting in $O(\frac{\Delta}{\delta}$ poly log $n)$ rounds. Hence, for all graphs that are somewhat regular and satisfy $\frac{\Delta}{\delta} \leq$ poly log n, we obtain a deterministic poly log n-time weak splitting algorithm. To state the result more formally, and to open way for our other results, let us phrase the splitting problem in a more general format.

We first introduce some notation and terminology. Let us consider a bipartite graph $B = (U \cup V, E)$ where we view nodes of U as *constraint nodes* and nodes of V as *variable nodes*. Equivalently, we can think of U as vertices of a hypergraph and V as the hyperedges of it. Throughout the paper, when using a bipartite graph $B = (U \cup V, E)$, we refer to U as the left side, V as the right side, and we use δ_B and Δ_B to denote the minimum and maximum degree of nodes in U and we use r_B to denote the maximum degree of nodes in V, where r_B stands for the rank of the corresponding hypergraph, i.e., the maximum number of vertices in a hyperedge. We omit the subscripts if the corresponding graph is clear from the context. Weak splitting can then formally be defined as follows:

Definition 1.1 (Weak Splitting). Let $B = (U \cup V, E)$ be a bipartite graph. A weak splitting of B is a 2-coloring of the nodes in V such that every node in U has at least one neighbor of each color.

Notice that the splitting problem on general graphs $G = (V_G, E_G)$ discussed above can be phrased as such a bipartite/hypergraph problem: for each node $v \in V_G$, make two copies of it, one for $v_L \in U$ and one for $v_R \in V$. For each edge $\{u, v\} \in E_G$, we connect v_L to u_R and v_R to u_L. Distinguishing these left U and right V sides allows us to distinguish between the constraints and the variables of the problem, and facilitates our discussions in several places. We prove the following.

Theorem 1.1. *There is a deterministic distributed algorithm that in any n-node bipartite graph $B = (U \cup V, E)$ in which the minimum degree of the nodes in U is $\delta \geq 2 \log n$, solves the weak splitting problem in $O(\frac{r}{\delta} \cdot \text{poly} \log n)$ rounds.*

In addition, in Theorem 2.7, we show that if $\delta \geq 6r$, the above problem can even be solved in poly log n time without any additional requirement on δ (i.e., without requiring that $\delta = \Omega(\log n)$). However, this result can not be applied to general graphs as converting a graph to a bipartite graph as described above will always yield a bipartite graph with $\delta \leq r$.

Further, in the full version [1], we prove that if the bipartite graph B has girth at least 10, the requirement on δ can be improved to $\delta = \Omega(\sqrt{\log n})$.

The above results provide only a partial progress on our understanding of the weak splitting problem and they certainly fall short of the ultimate goal of enabling us to derandomize any poly log n-round randomized algorithm for any locally checkable problem to a poly log n-round deterministic algorithm for it. If we could strengthen the above result in one of two directions, that would be a breakthrough: (A) If we could extend this weak splitting to all graphs, we would get the aforementioned desired derandomization algorithm, thus resolving many classic open problems of distributed graph algorithms, including the first three in the Open Problems section of the book of Barenboim and Elkin [3]; (B) Alternatively, if we could change this weak splitting algorithm for nearly regular graphs to a splitting algorithm for nearly regular graphs, then we would obtain a $\Delta(1 + o(1))$-coloring algorithm in poly log n rounds, hence resolving Open Problem 11.3 of [3]. We think that the partial progress that this paper provides may still be a concrete step in approaching these ultimate goals.

Algorithmic Results/Randomized: In addition, we study randomized algorithms for the weak splitting problem. The randomized complexity of the problem might be interesting in the context of the recent interest in understanding the complexity landscape of randomized sublogarithmic-time distributed graph algorithms. In [9], Chang and Pettie show that for any locally checkable labeling (LCL) problem[3] for which a randomized algorithm with running time $o(\log_\Delta n)$ exists, this algorithm can be sped up to run in the time for solving generic instances of problems where the existence of a solution follows from a polynomially relaxed version of the Lovász Local Lemma (LLL). The best known generic randomized algorithm for such LLL problems on bounded-degree graphs—and in fact also for graphs with poly log log n degrees—is $2^{O(\sqrt{\log^{\varepsilon} \log n})}$ [10, 14], for any constant $\varepsilon > 0$. Moreover, it is conjectured in [9] that this complexity should be poly log log n or even $O(\log \log n)$. The weak splitting problem—and also the splitting problem more generally—is a particularly simple and seemingly well-behaved problem that falls into this class of LLL problems and it would therefore be interesting to understand whether at least weak splitting can be solved in time poly log log n in bounded-degree graphs or in graphs with degrees at most poly log log n. We make some partial progress and prove that this is at least true for bipartite graphs $B = (U \cup V, E)$, where the minimum degree δ in U is at least $\Omega(\log \log n)$.

Theorem 1.2. *Consider an arbitrary n-node bipartite graph $B = (U \cup V, E)$ where the minimum degree in U is $\delta \geq c \log(r \log n)$ for a sufficiently large constant $c > 1$. Then, there is a randomized distributed algorithm that in $O(\frac{r}{\delta} \cdot \text{poly}(\log(r \log n)))$ rounds solves the weak splitting problem on B.*

Similar to the case of deterministic algorithms, we show that slightly stronger results hold for special cases also for randomized algorithms. As long as $\delta \geq 6r$, the problem can be solved in time poly log log n (Theorem 2.7) and if the bipartite graph has girth at least 10, the problem can be solved in time $O(\frac{r}{\delta} \cdot \text{poly} \log \log n)$ even if we only require that $\delta = \Omega(\sqrt{\log \log n})$ (see [1]).

Hardness Results: To strengthen our understanding of the splitting problem, we also investigate it from the (conditional) hardness side. Our goal here is to identify weaker and alternative forms of splitting, which are still complete in the above sense. Let us first briefly introduce the necessary formal background. Let P-LOCAL and P-RLOCAL be the classes of poly log(n)-*locally checkable*[4] graph problems that can be solved by poly log(n)-time deterministic and poly log(n)-time randomized LOCAL algorithms, respectively. We say that a graph problem $\mathcal{P}$ is P-RLOCAL-*complete* if it is in the class P-RLOCAL and if a poly log(n)-time deterministic LOCAL algorithm for $\mathcal{P}$ would imply that P-LOCAL = P-RLOCAL. In [17], Ghaffari, Kuhn, and Maus show that the weak splitting problem on bipartite graphs $B = (U \cup V, E)$ is P-RLOCAL-complete even if the minimum degree in U is at least polylogarithmic in n.[5] We define the following two multicolor variants of the splitting problem, which are much more relaxed, and we show that they are still complete. As splitting, both problems are defined on a bipartite graph $B = (U \cup V, E)$.

Definition 1.2 ((C, λ)-Multicolor Splitting). Given a bipartite graph $B = (U \cup V, E)$ and parameters $C \geq 2$ and $\lambda \geq 2/C$, a (C, λ)-*multicolor splitting* of B is a coloring of the nodes in V with C colors such that each $u \in U$ of degree has at most $\lceil \lambda \cdot \deg(u) \rceil$ neighbors of each color.

Definition 1.3 (C-Weak Multicolor Splitting). Given a bipartite Graph $B = (U \cup V, E)$, a C-*weak multicolor splitting* of B is a coloring

[3]LCL problems [21] are graph problems, where the output of every node is a label from a bounded alphabet and the validity of a solution can be checked a deterministic constant-time distributed algorithm.

[4]A graph problem is called d-locally checkable if given a solution, there is a deterministic d-round LOCAL algorithm in which every node outputs "yes" if and only if the given solution if a valid solution for the given problem [13]. LCL problems are a special important case of $O(1)$-locally checkable problems.

[5]To be precise, in [17], completeness was not shown w.r.t. to P-RLOCAL, but w.r.t. a class P-SLOCAL of efficient deterministic *sequential* local algorithms. However, as shown in [14], for poly log(n)-locally checkable problems, these two classes coincide.

of the nodes in V with $C \geq 2\log n$ colors such that each node $u \in U$ of degree $\deg(u) \geq 2(\log n + 1)\ln n$ sees at least $2\log n$ different colors.

We note that here (and throughout the rest of the paper), we use $\log x$ to refer to $\log_2 x$ and we use $\ln x$ to refer to the natural logarithm. In Theorem 3.2, we show that the C-weak multicolor splitting problem is P-RLOCAL-complete for any $C \leq \text{poly}\log n$, even if the minimum degree of nodes in U is $\log^c n$ for an arbitrary constant $c \geq 2$. Further, in Theorem 3.3, we prove that (C, λ)-multicolor splitting is P-RLOCAL-complete as long as the minimum degree of nodes in U is at least $\alpha \ln^2 n$ for a sufficiently large constant and as long as $C \leq \text{poly}\log n$ and $\lambda \leq C^{-\varepsilon}$ for some constant $\varepsilon > 0$.

Parameter Preserving Hardness Results: The hardness results mentioned above, and also those of [17], provide reductions from graph or hypergraph problems where the degrees might become very large, up to n, even if the degree in the original graph was somewhat small. Our last contribution is to provide some degree preserving reductions from the problems of maximal independent set and $\Delta(1 + o(1))$-coloring to the splitting problem. In Section 4, we show that if the latter can be solved in time $T_{n,\Delta}$ in graphs of degree Δ and n nodes, then the former problems can also be solved in $\text{poly}(\log n) \cdot T_{n,\Delta}$. Hence, for instance, an algorithm with complexity $\Delta^{1-\varepsilon}\,\text{poly}(\log n)$ for the splitting problem, for any constant $\varepsilon > 0$, would yield an MIS algorithm with complexity $\Delta^{1-\varepsilon}\,\text{poly}(\log n)$, which would be better than all known algorithms whenever $\Delta \in (\text{poly}(\log n), 2^{O(\sqrt{\log n})})$.

2 ALGORITHMS FOR WEAK SPLITTING

We next describe our deterministic and randomized algorithms for the weak splitting problem.

2.1 Basic Det. Weak Splitting Algorithm

If the minimum degree δ of the nodes on the left hand side is at least $2\log n$, a union bound shows that the following simple randomized algorithm solves the weak splitting problem w.h.p.

Color each node on the right side red/blue with probability 1/2 each.

Using the derandomization results from [14] this can be derandomized given a suitable coloring of the input graph. The formal result is as follows.

Lemma 2.1. *There is a deterministic algorithm to compute a weak splitting in time $O(\Delta \cdot r)$ if $\delta \geq 2\log n$.*

Proof. Let $B = (U \cup V, E)$ be an instance of the weak splitting problem with minimum degree $\delta \geq 2\log n$ on the left hand side. In the aforementioned randomized algorithm the probability that $u \in U$ has a monochromatic neighborhood is

$$\Pr(\text{all neighbors red}) + \Pr(\text{all neighbors blue}) \leq \frac{2}{2^{\delta}} \leq \frac{2}{n^2}.$$

With a union bound over all nodes in U we obtain that the probability that there is a node with a monochromatic neighborhood is at most $2/n < 1$ and a node can check whether it has a monochromatic neighborhood by looking at its 1-hop neighborhood. Hence, by [14, Theorem III.1], this randomized 0-round algorithm with checking radius 1 can be derandomized into an SLOCAL(2)-algorithm. By [15, Proposition 3.2] this can be transformed into an $O(C)$ LOCAL algorithm if a C-coloring of B^2, i.e., the graph that one obtains from B by additionally connected any two nodes in distance at most two to each other, is given. As the maximum degree of B^2 is Δr we can compute the necessary coloring with $O(\Delta r)$ colors and in $O(\Delta r + \log^* n)$ rounds, e.g., with the algorithm from [4]. Thus the total runtime can be bounded as $O(\Delta r + \log^* n) = O(\Delta r)$ as $\Delta \geq \delta \geq 2\log n$. □

2.2 Deterministic Degree-Rank Reduction

By first modifying the input graph—we arbitrarily remove edges until every node on the left hand side has degree $2\log n$— and then applying Lemma 2.1 graph we obtain the following result.

Lemma 2.2. *There is a deterministic algorithm to compute a weak splitting in time $O(r \cdot \log n)$ if $\delta \geq 2\log n$.*

Proof. Let $B = (U \cup V, E)$ be an instance of the weak splitting problem with minimum degree $\delta \geq 2\log n$ on the left hand side. If $\delta > 2\log n$, each node in U deletes an arbitrary set of its incident edges such that at least $\delta' = \lceil 2\log n \rceil$ remain. By Lemma 2.1, we can compute a weak splitting on the resulting graph H in $O(\delta' \cdot r) = O(r \cdot \log n)$ rounds. The computed coloring of the right hand side of H immediately induces a weak splitting of the original graph B as the weak splitting property is conserved under adding edges to a graph. □

In the algorithm in Lemma 2.2, we deleted edges of high degree nodes in U arbitrarily. The idea of our main deterministic weak splitting algorithm is to do this deletion more thoughtfully such that we are guaranteed that also the rank shrinks to a sufficient extent.

Definition 2.1. Given an undirected (multi-)graph $G = (V, E)$, a *directed degree splitting* of G with discrepancy $\kappa : \mathbb{N} \to \mathbb{R}$ is an orientation of the edges of G such that for every node $v \in V$, the absolute value of the difference between the number of its incident incoming and its incident outgoing edges is at most $\kappa(\deg_G(v))$.

In [16] it was shown that directed degree splittings can be computed efficiently.

Theorem 2.3 (Theorem 1 in [16]). *For every $\varepsilon > 0$, there is a deterministic $O(\varepsilon^{-1} \cdot \log \varepsilon^{-1} \cdot (\log\log \varepsilon^{-1})^{1.71} \cdot \log n)$ round distributed algorithm for directed degree splitting such that the discrepancy at each node v of degree $d(v)$ is at most $\varepsilon \cdot d(v) + 2$. The randomized runtime of the same result is $O(\varepsilon^{-1} \cdot \log \varepsilon^{-1} \cdot (\log\log \varepsilon^{-1})^{1.71} \cdot \log\log n)$*

Note that the randomized runtime of the theorem is not stated in [16] but follows by substituting each deterministic $O(\log n)$-round sinkless orientation algorithm in their proofs with the randomized $O(\log\log n)$-round sinkless orientation algorithm from [19]. To ease presentation, we omit the log log term and upper bound the runtime of the directed degree splitting algorithm by $O(\varepsilon^{-1} \cdot (\log \varepsilon^{-1})^{1.1} \cdot \log n)$ whenever we apply Theorem 2.3. We now iteratively use the degree splitting algorithm from Theorem 2.3 to reduce the degrees on the left hand side and the rank on the right hand side at the same time.

Degree-Rank Reduction I: Given a bipartite graph $B = (U \cup V, E)$ and parameters ε and k, compute a directed degree splitting on B with discrepancy at most $\varepsilon \cdot d(v) + 2$ for each $v \in U \cup V$. Now that all edges are oriented, delete all edges from B that are directed from a node in V towards a node in U. Repeat this process on the residual graph. Stop after k iterations.

We can lower bound the degree on the left hand side and upper bound the 'rank' on the right hand side after k iterations of the algorithm as follows.

Lemma 2.4. *Let B be a bipartite graph with minimum degree δ and rank r and let δ_k (r_k) be the minimum degree (rank) of the graph obtained after k iterations of the Degree-Rank Reduction Algorithm on B with some $0 < \varepsilon < 1/3$. Then*

$$\delta_k > \left(\frac{1-\varepsilon}{2}\right)^k \delta - 2 \qquad \text{and} \qquad r_k < \left(\frac{1+\varepsilon}{2}\right)^k r + 3\,.$$

Proof. In each iteration only incoming edges to nodes in V survive. If a node has δ_i edges before iteration i it has at least $\frac{1-\varepsilon}{2}\delta_i - 1$ incoming edges in the directed splitting computed in iteration i. Thus a simple induction shows that after k iterations the minimum degree of nodes in V can be lower bounded by

$$\delta_k \geq \left(\frac{1-\varepsilon}{2}\right)^k \delta - \sum_{i=0}^{k-1}\left(\frac{1-\varepsilon}{2}\right)^i .$$

This implies the first claim as $\sum_{i=0}^{k-1}\left(\frac{1-\varepsilon}{2}\right)^i \leq \sum_{i=0}^{k-1}\left(\frac{1}{2}\right)^i < 2$.

Similar to the first claim one can show by induction that the maximum degree on the right hand side can be upper bounded by

$$r_k \leq \left(\frac{1+\varepsilon}{2}\right)^k r + \sum_{i=0}^{k-1}\left(\frac{1+\varepsilon}{2}\right)^i .$$

This implies the second claim as

$$\sum_{i=0}^{k-1}\left(\frac{1+\varepsilon}{2}\right)^i < \sum_{i=0}^{\infty}\left(\frac{1+\varepsilon}{2}\right)^i = \left(1-\frac{1+\varepsilon}{2}\right)^{-1} < 3 \quad \text{for } \varepsilon < 1/3\,.$$

□

We can now prove Theorem 1.1, our main deterministic splitting result. The following is a more precise version of Theorem 1.1.

Theorem 2.5. *There is a deterministic distributed algorithm that, given a weak splitting instance $B = (U \cup V, E)$ with $\delta \geq 2\log n$, computes a weak splitting in time*

$$O\left(\frac{r}{\delta}\cdot\log^2 n + \log^3 n\,(\log\log n)^{1.1}\right).$$

Proof. Let $B = (U \cup V, E)$ a weak splitting instance. If $\delta \leq 48\log n$, the algorithm from Lemma 2.2 gives an $O(r \cdot \log n) = O(r/\delta \cdot \log^2 n)$ algorithm. Thus for the rest of the proof we assume that $\delta > 48\log n$. Let $\varepsilon = \min\{1/k, 1/3\}$ and $k := \lfloor \log\left(\frac{\delta}{12\log n}\right)\rfloor$. Let $\bar{B}$ denote the bipartite graph that we obtain after k iterations of the degree-rank reduction algorithm with accuracy ε. Due to Lemma 2.4 the maximum rank of $\bar{B}$ can be upper bounded as

$$r_{\bar{B}} < \left(\frac{1+1/k}{2}\right)^k r + 3 \leq \left(\frac{e^{1/k}}{2}\right)^k r + 3 = \frac{e}{2^k}\cdot r + 3$$
$$\leq 24e \cdot \frac{r}{\delta}\log n + 3$$

and the minimum degree of the nodes on the left hand side can be lower bounded by

$$\delta_{\bar{B}} \overset{(*)}{>} \left(\frac{1-1/k}{2}\right)^k \cdot \delta - 2 \geq \frac{1}{4}\cdot 2^{-k}\cdot\delta - 2 \geq 12\log n - 2$$
$$\overset{(n\geq 4)}{\geq} 2\log n\,.$$

At $(*)$ we used that $\delta > 48\log n$ implies that we have more than two iterations of the splitting algorithm, i.e., $k > 2$ which implies $(1-1/k)^k \geq 1/4$. Now, we use Lemma 2.2 to compute a weak splitting on $\bar{B}$ that is also a weak splitting on the original graph B. The runtime of computing a weak splitting on $\bar{B}$ is $O(r_{\bar{B}} \cdot \log n) = O(r/\delta \cdot \log^2 n)$. The runtime of each of the $k = O(\log n)$ execution of the degree-rank reduction algorithm is $O(\varepsilon^{-1}\cdot(\log\varepsilon^{-1})^{1.1}\cdot\log n)$ (cf. Theorem 2.3). Due to $\varepsilon^{-1} = \lfloor\log\left(\frac{\delta}{12\log n}\right)\rfloor$ the time complexity of all iterations can be bounded by $O\left(\log^2 n(\log\log n)^{1.1}\right)$ and the runtime of the algorithm is $O(r/\delta\cdot\log^2 n + \log^3 n(\log\log n)^{1.1})$. □

2.3 An Efficient Det. Algorithm when $\delta \geq 6r$

The splitting algorithm that we use in the degree-rank reduction I in Section 2.2 has an inaccuracy on both sides of the bipartite graph; in particular, a node on the right hand side that has 2 or less edges remaining might loose all of its incident edges in one iteration. To solve the weak splitting problem efficiently for $\delta \geq 6r$ we define a degree-rank reduction algorithm that always obtains discrepancy one or zero on the right hand side of the bipartite graph.

Degree-Rank Reduction II: Given a bipartite graph $B = (U \cup V, E)$ and an *accuracy parameter* ε we define one iteration of the degree-rank reduction II as follows: Each $v \in V$ groups its $d := \deg(v)$ neighbors $u_1, \ldots, u_d \in N_B(v)$ into pairs $(u_1, u_2), (u_3, u_4), \ldots$ (if d is odd, u_d remains unpaired). Then we define a multigraph G with vertex set U. G contains an edge $e = \{u_i, u_{i+1}\}$ for any of these pairs and we say that v is the *corresponding node* for edge e. Note that there can be multiple edges between two nodes in G with distinct corresponding nodes. Now, we compute a directed degree splitting on G with discrepancy at most $\varepsilon\cdot\deg_G(u) + 2$ for each $u \in U$. We obtain a residual graph $B' \subseteq B$ through removing edges from B as follows: For any edge $e = \{u, \bar{u}\}$ of G let v_e be the corresponding node for e. If e is directed from u to $\bar{u}$, delete the edge $\{\bar{u}, v_e\}$ from B; if e is directed from $\bar{u}$ to u, delete the edge $\{u, v_e\}$ from B. All other edges of B remain and are edges of the residual graph B'. If we consider several iterations of the degree-rank reduction we always repeat the process on the residual bipartite graph.

The crucial property of the above algorithm is that the rank of the bipartite graph can never go below one as any node on the right hand side keeps at least one out of two neighbors and if it has only one neighbor left it also keeps that one.

Lemma 2.6. *Let B be a bipartite graph with rank r and let r_k be the minimum degree (rank) of the graph obtained after k iterations of the Degree-Rank Reduction II Algorithm on B applied with an arbitrary accuracy parameter ε. Then we have $r_{\lceil\log r\rceil} = 1$.*

PROOF. First, we perform an induction over the number of iterations and show that

$$r_k < \frac{1}{2^k}r + \sum_{i=1}^{k}\frac{1}{2^i} \tag{1}$$

holds. For $k = 0$ the hypothesis (1) simplifies to $r < r + 1$ and is trivially satisfied.
Induction Step: Assume the that (1) holds for k. As a node on the right hand side never looses more than half of its edges in one iteration of rank-reduction II we have $r_{k+1} = \lceil \frac{r_k}{2} \rceil$. As r_k is an integer we obtain

$$r_{k+1} \le \frac{r_k}{2} + \frac{1}{2} \overset{\text{I.H.}}{<} \frac{1}{2^{k+1}}r + \sum_{i=2}^{k+1}\frac{1}{2^i} + \frac{1}{2} = \frac{1}{2^{k+1}}r + \sum_{i=1}^{k+1}\frac{1}{2^i}.$$

With $\sum_{i=1}^{k} \frac{1}{2^i} < 1$ we obtain $r_k < \frac{1}{2^k}r + 1$ for any k and in particular $r_{\lceil \log r \rceil} < 2$. Hence we obtain $r_{\lceil \log r \rceil} = 1$ as $r_{\lceil \log r \rceil}$ is an integer and cannot be smaller than 1. □

The following theorem is obtained by using the degree-rank reduction II for $\lceil \log r \rceil$ iterations until the rank r of the remaining graph is 1. With the condition $\delta \ge 6r$, one can then show that the minimum degree of the left-side nodes is still at least 2 and we have thus reduced the problem to a trivial weak splitting instance.

THEOREM 2.7. *If $\delta \ge 6r$, we can solve the weak splitting problem deterministically in* polylog n *rounds and randomized in* polyloglog n *rounds.*

PROOF. If $\delta \ge 2\log n$ we can solve the problem deterministically with the algorithm from Theorem 2.5 in time complexity $O(\log^2 n + \log^3 n(\log\log n)^{1.1})$. Thus assume that $\delta < 2\log n$. Set $\varepsilon = 1/(10\Delta) = 1/(20\delta)$ (see the comment at the beginning of Section 2.4 which states that it is sufficient to solve weak splitting with almost regular degrees on the left hand side to solve it for all degrees) and execute $k = \lceil \log r \rceil$ iterations of degree-rank reduction II. We now want to lower bound the minimum degree after these k iterations. As $\varepsilon \cdot d(u) < 1$ for all nodes $u \in U$ and $\deg_G(u) \le \deg_B(u)$ we obtain that the discrepancy of the computed splitting in degree-rank reduction is at most 1 if the degree of u is odd and 2 if the degree of u is even. Thus a node $u \in U$ with initial degree δ has degree at least $\delta/2 - 1$ after one iteration of the algorithm. If $r \le 2$ we only need one iteration and obtain that the minimum degree after this iteration is at least $\delta/2 - 1 \ge 2$. For $r > 2$ an induction over the number of iterations shows that the minimum degree in iteration $\lceil \log r \rceil$ is strictly larger than $\delta \cdot 2^{-\lceil \log r \rceil} - 2$. As we have $2^{\lceil \log r \rceil} \le 2r - 2$ for $r > 2$ we obtain that the minimum degree after $k = \lceil \log r \rceil$ iterations is strictly larger than

$$\frac{\delta}{2^{-\lceil \log r \rceil}} - 2 \ge \frac{\delta}{2r-2} - 2 \overset{(\delta \ge 6r)}{\ge} \frac{\delta}{\frac{\delta}{3} - 2} - 2$$
$$= \frac{3}{1 - \frac{6}{\delta}} - 2 \overset{(\delta \ge 6r \ge 12)}{=} 1,$$

i.e., the mininmum degree is at least 2. Thus in all cases the resulting graph has rank 1 and minimum degree at least 2. Thus, every node in U can choose one of its neighbor to be colored red and one of its neighbors to be colored blue. The obtained coloring is a weak splitting of B. The deterministic runtime of the algorithm with $\delta < 2\log n$ is $O(k \cdot \varepsilon^{-1} \cdot (\log \varepsilon^{-1})^{1.1} \cdot \log n) = O(\log^3 n \log^{1.1} \log n)$ due to the deterministic runtime of Theorem 2.3.

The proof of the polylog log n randomized algorithm is along similar lines. If $\delta \ge 2\log n$ the zero round randomized algorithm that we explain at the beginning of Section 2.1 solves the problem. If $\delta, r \le 2\log n$ but $\delta \ge c\log\log n$ for a sufficiently large constant c we use Theorem 1.2 to solve the problem in $\frac{r}{\delta}$ polyloglog n = polyloglog n rounds—note that $\delta \ge c\log\log n$ implies that $\delta \ge c'\log(r\log n)$ holds for a slightly smaller constant c if $r \le \delta \le 2\log n$. If $\delta < c\log\log n$ we use the degree-reduction II as in the deterministic case. The runtime bound follows with ε^{-1} = polyloglog n and the randomized runtime in Theorem 2.3. □

2.4 A Rand. Algorithm for Weak Splitting

For proving Theorem 1.2 we assume *almost uniform* degrees on the left hand side, i.e., $\delta > \Delta/2$. This is sufficient because we can split each node $u \in U$ with $\deg(u) > 2\delta$ into $\lfloor \deg(u)/\delta \rfloor$ virtual nodes with degree at least δ and less than 2δ and compute a weak splitting on this graph, which directly induces a weak splitting on the original graph. The algorithm of Theorem 1.2 is based on the infamous graph shattering technique that consists of two parts: In the first part, we use a random process to fix the colors of some nodes in V such that the probability that a node in U is *unsatisfied*, i.e., does not have a red and blue neighbor, is $1/\text{poly}\,\Delta$. The residual graph consisting of the unsatisfied nodes on the left side and the uncolored nodes on the right side will have small connected components, say size poly$(\log n)$, such that we can efficiently compute a weak splitting with the deterministic algorithm from Theorem 2.5. For more information on the shattering technique consult, e.g., [5]. More formally we use the following theorem to bound the size of the unsolved components after the first part.

THEOREM 2.8 (THEOREM V.1 IN [14]). *Suppose a random process in which given a graph G, each node v survives to a residual graph H with probability at most $(e\Delta)^{-4c}$ and this bound holds even for adversarial choices of the random bits outside the c-neighborhood of v. Then w.h.p. each connected component of H has size $O(\Delta^{2c}\log n)$.*

Our shattering algorithm works as follows:

Shattering Algorithm: *Coloring phase:* Each node in V colors itself red with probability $1/4$, blue with probability $1/4$ and remains uncolored otherwise. *Uncoloring phase:* Any $u \in U$ that has more than $3/4$ colored neighbors in V uncolors all of its neighbors.

After the execution of the shattering algorithm, a node $u \in U$ is *satisfied* if it has at least one red and at least one blue neighbor, otherwise it is *unsatisfied*.

LEMMA 2.9. *If $\Delta \ge c\log r$ for a sufficiently large constant c, the probability for a node $u \in U$ to be unsatisfied after the execution of the shattering algorithm is at most $e^{-\eta\Delta}$ for some $\eta > 0$. In particular, the probability for u to be unsatisfied is at most $(e\Delta r)^{-8}$.*

PROOF. If a node $u \in U$ is unsatisfied, one of the following events occurs after the coloring phase:

(1) $A_1(u)$ = less than $1/4$ of its neighbors are colored
(2) $A_2(u)$ = more than $3/4$ of its neighbors are colored

(3) $A_3(u)$ = between $1/4$ and $3/4$ of its neighbors are colored and the colored neighbors are all red or all blue
(4) $A_4(u)$ = there is a node $\bar{u} \in U$ two hops from u which has less than $1/4$ or more than $3/4$ of its neighbors colored (in which case $\bar{u}$ uncolors a common neighbor and thus possibly destroys u's satisfaction)

Next, we bound the probability of the events $A_1(u), A_2(u), A_3(u)$ and $A_4(u)$. Let $d := \deg(u)$ and $v_1, \ldots, v_d \in V$ be u's neighbors. For every $i \in \{1, \ldots, d\}$ introduce a random variable X_i with $X_i = 1$ if v_i is colored and $X_i = 0$ otherwise. Let $X := \sum_{i=1}^{d} X_i$. With Chernoff bounds and $\delta \geq \Delta/2$ we obtain

$$\Pr(A_1(u)) = \Pr\left(X < \frac{1}{4}d\right) \leq e^{-\frac{d}{16}} \leq e^{-\frac{\Delta}{32}}$$

$$\Pr(A_2(u)) \leq \Pr\left(X > \frac{3}{4}d\right) \leq e^{-\frac{d}{16}} \leq e^{-\frac{\Delta}{32}}$$

With a union bound over u's 2-hop neighborhood $N^2(u)$ we get

$$\Pr(A_1(u) \vee A_2(u) \vee A_4(u)) \leq \sum_{u' \in N^2(u)} \Pr(A_1(u') \cup A_2(u')) \leq 2e^{-\frac{\Delta}{32}}\Delta r$$

For A_3, given that at least $1/4$ of u's neighbors are colored, we have $X \geq d/4$. Thus the probability that all colored neighbors are red (blue resp.) is at most $2^{-X} \leq 2^{-\frac{d}{4}}$. Hence, $\Pr(A_3) \leq 2 \cdot 2^{-\frac{d}{4}} \leq 2 \cdot 2^{-\frac{\Delta}{8}}$. Thus we obtain

$$\Pr(u \text{ is unsatisfied}) \leq \Pr(A_1 \vee A_2 \vee A_3 \vee A_4) \leq 2e^{-\frac{\Delta}{32}}\Delta r + 2 \cdot 2^{-\frac{\Delta}{8}}.$$

With a sufficiently large constant c in $\Delta \geq c \log r$ we obtain an $\eta > 0$ such that $\Pr(u \text{ is unsatisfied}) \leq e^{-\eta\Delta} \leq (e\Delta r)^{-8}$. □

Based on Theorem 2.8 and Lemma 2.9, we can now prove Theorem 1.2, our main randomized weak splitting result. Theorem 2.8 and Lemma 2.9 together can be used to show that after running the above shattering algorithm, the remaining problem is a weak splitting instance on components on poly log n size. On these components, we can use our deterministic algorithm (Theorem 1.1) to solve the problem in poly log log n time.

Proof of Theorem 1.2. Let $B = (U \cup V, E)$ be a bipartite graph. If $\delta > 2\log n$, the trivial 0-round algorithm (color each node in V red/blue with probability $1/2$) computes a weak splitting w.h.p.: The probability of $u \in U$ to have a monochromatic neighborhood is at most $2 \cdot 2^{-\deg(u)} \leq 2 \cdot n^{-2}$. With a union bound over the nodes in U we get that the failure probability of the algorithm is less than $2/n$. So in the following we assume $\delta \leq 2\log n$. Our algorithm first executes the shattering algorithm on B. The residual graph H is the graph induced by the unsatisfied nodes in U and the uncolored nodes in V after the shattering. Then we use the deterministic weak splitting algorithm from Theorem 2.5 on the connected components of H. Let n_H be the maximum size of a connected component of H. We need to show that $\delta_H \geq 2\log n_H$ (to use the algorithm from Theorem 2.5) and $n_H = \text{poly}(r, \log n)$ (to achieve the stated runtime).

Upper Bounding n_H: Let G be the graph on the node set U obtained by inserting an edge between two nodes in U if they have a common neighbor in B. We have $\Delta_G \leq \Delta_B \cdot r_B$ (in the following let $\Delta = \Delta_B$ and $r = r_B$). To use Theorem 2.8 on G we define a randomized process on G that is equivalent to the shattering algorithm: Each node $v \in V$ is assigned to its neighbor $u \in U$ with the smallest id. Then the behaviour of v, that is, picking a random color, informing neighbors about the color choice and potentially uncoloring itself is simulated by u. All other definitions remain the same, in particular, a node $u \in U$ is satisfied if there are $v', v'' \in V$ that are simulated by nodes $u', u'' \in U$ and v' is colored red and v'' is colored blue. Thus, the process is a random process on G in which a node $u \in V(G)$ is unsatisfied with probability at most $(e\Delta r)^{-8}$, even if random bits at nodes in distance larger than 2 in G are drawn adversarially. With Theorem 2.8 it follows that after the shattering, w.h.p., each connected component of the residual graph $H' \subseteq G$ induced by the unsatisfied nodes in G has size $n_{H'} = O(\Delta^4 r^4 \log n)$. As each node of G has at most $\Delta = O(\log n)$ neighbors we can bound the size of the connected components of unsatisfied nodes in U and uncolored nodes in V as $n_H \leq n_{H'} \cdot \Delta = O(r^4 \log^6 n)$, w.h.p.

Lower Bounding δ_H: Due to the uncoloring phase of the shattering algorithm, each node has at least $1/4$ of its neighbors uncolored after the shattering. It follows that $\delta_H \geq \delta/4$. If we choose the constant c in $\delta \geq c\log(r\log n)$ large enough, we get $\delta_H \geq 2\log n_H$.

Solving Small Connected Components/Runtime: Due to $\delta_H \geq 2\log n_H$ we can apply the deterministic algorithm from Theorem 2.5 on the unsolved connected components of H. The splitting algorithm including the uncoloring runs in $O(1)$ rounds. The application of Theorem 2.5 on the small components has runtime

$$O(r_H/\delta_H \cdot \log^2 n_H + \log^3 n_H (\log\log n_H)^{1.1}) = O\left(\frac{r}{\delta}\log^2(r\log n) + \log^3(r\log n)(\log\log(r\log n))^{1.1}\right),$$

where we used $n_H = \text{poly}(r, \log n)$, $R_H \leq R$ and $\delta_H \geq \delta/4$. □

2.5 Lower Bound for Weak Splitting

We conclude this section by giving a simple lower bound that shows that the weak splitting problem requires $\Omega(\log_\Delta \log n)$ time randomized and $\Omega(\log_\Delta n)$ time deterministically even on instances of rank $r = 2$. The proof is based on a reduction from the sinkless orientation problem and the main steps of the reduction are depicted in Figure 1. Given a graph G on which we want to compute a sinkless orientation, we build a bipartite graph B with right-hand side degree at most 2 such that a weak splitting solution directly gives a sinkless orientation G. The lower bounds then follows from the sinkless orientation lower bounds in [7, 8].

Theorem 2.10. *There is no randomized distributed algorithm for solving the weak splitting problem in bipartite graphs with maximum degree Δ, even if the rank is as small as 2 in $o(\log_\Delta \log n)$ rounds.*

Proof. We show how to reduce the sinkless orientation problem for graphs with minimum degree at least 5 to the weak splitting problem. The statement then follows as there is an $\Omega(\log_\Delta \log n)$ lower bound for sinkless orientation (in regular graphs) from [7].

For an illustration of the following process, we refer to Figure 1. We are given a graph $G = (V, E)$ with minimum degree $\delta_G \geq 5$ on which we want to compute a sinkless orientation by reduction to a

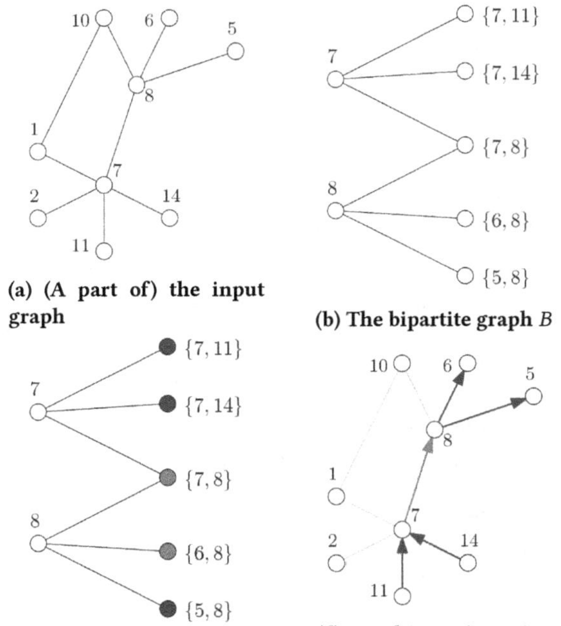

(a) (A part of) the input graph

(b) The bipartite graph B

(c) A weak splitting

(d) Resulting orientation

Figure 1: Figure (b) illustrates the neighborhoods of nodes 7 and 8 in the bipartite graph B. The graph B has rank at most 2, since the nodes on the right correspond to edges that have at most 2 endpoints. Figure (c) shows a possible outcome of a weak splitting. Since the edge $\{7, 8\}$ is red, it gets directed from smaller to larger. Since 8 has also a blue neighbor, at least one of its edges will get directed outwards.

weak splitting instance. For this purpose, we define a bipartite graph B (i.e., a weak splitting instance) between the nodes and edges of G in the following way: There is a left-hand-side node in B for every node $v \in V$ of G and there is a right-hand side node in B for every edge $e \in E$ of G. We connect each left-hand-side node $u \in V$ to the right-hand-side nodes corresponding to some of u's edges in G: if at least half of u's neighbors in G have a larger ID than u, we connect u to every $e = \{u, v\} \in E$ for which $\mathrm{ID}(v) > \mathrm{ID}(u)$. Otherwise, i.e., if more than half of u's neighbors have a smaller IDs than u, we connect u to every $e = \{u, v\} \in E$ for which $\mathrm{ID}(v) < \mathrm{ID}(u)$. The resulting bipartite graph has rank at most 2 and degree at least $\lceil \delta_G/2 \rceil \geq 3$, which is sufficient for the weak splitting problem on B to be solvable. A weak splitting solution on B is a red/blue coloring of the right-hand-side nodes of B and thus of the edges E of G. Either (if at least half of u's neighbors have a larger ID) u gets both a red and a blue edge to a larger ID neighbor, or (if at more than half of u's neighbors have a smaller ID), u gets both a red and a blue edge to a lower ID neighbor. We therefore directly obtain a sinkless orientation of G by orienting the edges $e \in E$ as follows. If an edge $e \in E$ is colored red, it gets directed from the node with smaller ID towards the node with higher ID, and if e is colored blue, it is directed the other way around.

For the number of nodes in B, denoted by n_B, we have $n_B = |V| + |E|$ and for the degrees we have $\Delta_B \leq \Delta_G$. Thus, if one could solve a weak splitting in $o(\log_{\Delta_B} \log n_B)$ rounds, one could also compute a sinkless orientation in time $o(\log_{\Delta_G} \log n_G)$. □

Corollary 2.11. *There does not exist a deterministic distributed algorithm solving the weak splitting problem in bipartite graphs in $o(\log_\Delta n)$ rounds.*

Proof. If there was a $o(\log_\Delta n)$ deterministic algorithm for weak splitting, it could be transformed to run in $O(\log^* n - \log^* \Delta + 1)$ rounds ([8]), violating the lower bound from Theorem 2.10. □

3 COMPLETENESS OF WEAK SPLITTING VARIANTS

In this section, we prove that the (C, λ)-multicolor splitting and the C-weak multicolor splitting problems that were introduced in Section 1.2 are P-RLOCAL-complete. That is, if a poly $\log n$-time deterministic LOCAL algorithm for one of the two problems exists, then such an algorithm exists for all problems in P-RLOCAL and thus in particular for problems such as $(\Delta + 1)$-coloring or MIS. In the two proofs, we use the SLOCAL model, which was introduced in [17]. The SLOCAL model can be seen as a sequential version of the LOCAL model. In a SLOCAL(t)-algorithm, the nodes of a given graph G are processed in an arbitrary sequential order. Each node is assumed to have some local memory, which initially just contains its unique ID and any possible input to the problem we need to solve. When a node is processed, it can read the current state of its t-hop neighborhood and based on this information, it can store its output and possibly additional information in its local memory. Before proving the completeness of the two new problems, we give a slightly more precise P-RLOCAL-completeness result than the one proved in [17].

Lemma 3.1. *For bipartite graphs $B = (U \cup V, E)$ where all nodes $u \in U$ have degree $\deg(u) \geq 2 \log n$, the weak splitting problem has a deterministic* SLOCAL(2)*-algorithm and it is* P-RLOCAL*-complete.*

Proof. It follows directly from the proof of [17, Theorem 1.8] that the given weak splitting problem is P-RLOCAL-hard. It remains to show that the problem is in P-RLOCAL. Consider the 0-round randomized algorithm where each node in V picks color red or blue uniformly at random. The probability that a node only sees one color is at most $2(1/2)^{2\log n} = 2/n^2$. Since the validity of a weak splitting solution can be checked in a single round deterministically, it now follows directly from [14, Theorem III.1] that the above weak splitting solution has a deterministic SLOCAL(2) algorithm. In [17], it is shown that such an algorithm can be turned in to randomized LOCAL model with poly $\log n$ time complexity. □

Theorem 3.2. *For bipartite graphs $B = (U \cup V, E)$ where all nodes in $u \in U$ have degree $\deg(u) \geq (2 \log n + 1) \ln^c n$ for some constant $c \geq 1$, the weak multicolor splitting problem is* P-RLOCAL*-complete for any $C \leq$ polylog n.*

Proof. We first show that for the given parameters, the problem is in P-RLOCAL. Consider the randomized process where every node in V chooses one of the first $\lceil 2 \log n \rceil$ colors independently and uniform at random. For each node $u \in U$ and each color x

(among the $\lceil 2\log n \rceil$ colors), the probability that no neighbor of u chooses color x is

$$\left(1 - \frac{1}{\lceil 2\log n \rceil}\right)^{\deg(u)} \overset{(c>1)}{<} \left(1 - \frac{1}{2\log n + 1}\right)^{(2\log n+1)\ln n} < \frac{1}{n}.$$

As the number of nodes in U is less than n, it follows the expected number of nodes in U that see less than $2\log n$ different colors is less than 1. As the above random process can be implemented in the LOCAL model in 0 rounds (i.e., without communication) and since the correctness of a weak multicolor splitting solution can be locally checked in a single round, it follows by [14, Theorem III.1] that the above random process can be derandomized into a deterministic SLOCAL(2) algorithm that solves the given weak multicolor splitting problem. It is shown in [17] that such an algorithm can be turned into a poly $\log n$-time randomized LOCAL algorithm and we can therefore conclude that the given weak multicolor splitting problem is in P-RLOCAL.

To prove the hardness of the problem, we reduce the weak splitting problem to the weak multicolor splitting problem in polylog n rounds. Assume that we are given a bipartite graph $B = (U \cup V, E)$ where all nodes in $u \in U$ have degree $\deg(u) \geq (2\log n - 1)\ln^c n$ for some constant $c \geq 1$ on which we want to solve weak splitting. By Lemma 3.1, we know that weak splitting on bipartite graphs with those parameters is P-RLOCAL-complete. In order to solve weak splitting on B, we first solve the weak multicolor splitting with C colors on B. Each node $u \in U$ is then guaranteed to have at least $2\log n$ (and thus also at least $\lceil 2\log n \rceil$) different colors among its neighbors. For $u \in U$, let $S(u) \subseteq R$ be a set of $\lceil 2\log n \rceil$ neighbors of u such that all nodes in $S(u)$ have different colors. We transform the graph B into a graph B' by only keeping the $\lceil 2\log n \rceil$ edges for each $u \in U$ that connect u to its neighbors in $S(u)$. A valid weak splitting solution on B' is also a valid weak splitting solution on B and we can therefore solve weak splitting on B' instead of B. Since for each node $u \in U$, all its neighbors in B' have different colors, any two nodes $v, w \in V$ at distance 2 in B' have different colors. The given coloring is therefore a proper partial C-coloring of the graph B'^2 in which each node in V has a color. By using the method on [14, Proposition III.2], this coloring can be used to run an SLOCAL(2)-algorithm on B' in $O(C)$ rounds in the LOCAL model as long as this SLOCAL algorithm only needs to assign output values to the nodes in V (i.e., to the colored nodes). By Lemma 3.1, the weak splitting problem on B' has such an SLOCAL(2)-algorithm and given the C-coloring the nodes in V, we can therefore compute a weak splitting of B' in $O(C) = O(\text{poly}\log n)$ rounds deterministically in the LOCAL model. □

Theorem 3.3. *Let the number of colors $C \in \mathbb{N}$ be such that $C \geq 2$ and $C \leq \text{poly}\log n$ and assume that $\lambda \geq \min\left\{0.95, \frac{3}{C-1}\right\}$. Then, for bipartite graphs $H = (L \cup R, E)$ where all nodes in $u \in L$ have degree $\deg(u) \geq \frac{\alpha}{\lambda} \cdot \ln^c(n)$ for a sufficiently large constant $\alpha > 0$ and some constant $c \geq 1$, (C, λ)-multicolor splitting is in* P-RLOCAL *and it is* P-RLOCAL*-complete if $\lambda \leq C^{-\varepsilon}$ for some constant $\varepsilon > 0$ and if each node in L has degree at least $\beta \ln^2 n$ for a sufficiently large constant $\beta > 0$.*

Proof Sketch. *(A detailed proof can be found in [1])* We use a reduction from weak multicolor splitting. The basic idea is to iteratively apply (C, λ)-multicolor splitting for i steps until we (essentially) get at (C^i, λ^i)-multicolor splitting. If we choose i such that $\lambda^i \leq 1/(2\log n)$, each left-side node necessarily sees $2\log n$ different colors and we thus have computed a weak multicolor splitting. □

4 FASTER SPLITTINGS IMPLY FASTER COLORING AND MIS ALGORITHMS

In this section, we explain how to reduce the coloring problem and the MIS problem to the splitting problem on (a subgraph of) the same network. Hence, this reduction for instance does not increase the maximum degree of the network.

4.1 Vertex Coloring

The Uniform Splitting Problem. Let $G = (V, E)$ be a graph with maximum degree Δ and minimum degree $\delta \geq \Delta/2$ and let $\varepsilon > 0$. In the splitting problem, the task is to divide the nodes in V into two disjoint sets $R, B \subseteq V$. The goal is that for each node v, the degree of the graphs induced by R and B is at most $(1/2 + \varepsilon)d_G(v)$ and at least $(1/2 - \varepsilon)d_G(v)$. In the *uniform* splitting problem, the input graph has a minimum degree of $\delta \geq \Delta/2$.

Remark. Consider the following slight modification of the uniform splitting problem. Instead of demanding an almost Δ-regular graph, we may focus on general graphs and impose no restrictions on nodes of degree less than $\delta = \Delta/2$. It is clear that the uniform splitting problem is not easier than the modification. For a reduction from the modification to the original problem, consider a graph G and add the following virtual gadgets to every node v with $\deg(v) < \delta$. Construct a δ-clique and add (virtual) edges from $\delta - \deg(v)$ nodes to v. The degree of v becomes δ and the degrees of the virtual nodes are at most δ. Then we can run a uniform splitting algorithm on the virtual graph and obtain a solution to the modified problem. The naïve approach yields a graph of size $O(n \cdot \Delta)$, but the size can easily be reduced to $O(n)$.

Lemma 4.1. *Let $\mathcal{A}$ be an algorithm for the uniform splitting problem and let $T_{USP}(n, \varepsilon)$ be its runtime. Then there is a $(1+o(1))\Delta$-vertex-coloring algorithm with runtime $O(\log n \cdot T_{USP}(n, \varepsilon) + \text{poly}(\log n))$.*

Proof. Suppose that $\Delta = \omega(\log\log n)$. Otherwise, we can directly run a $(\Delta + 1)$ coloring algorithm in $O(\log\log n) = O(\log n \cdot T_{USP}(n, \varepsilon)))$ time [12]. Set $\varepsilon = 1/\log^2 n$. We apply algorithm $\mathcal{A}$ recursively $r = \log\Delta - \log\log n$ times until the maximum degree drops to $\Delta^* = \text{poly}\log n$. This takes $O(r \cdot T_{USP}(n, \varepsilon)) = O(\log\Delta \cdot T_{USP}(n, \varepsilon))$ time.

We obtain 2^r subgraphs with maximum degree $\Delta^* = 2^{-r} \cdot (1 + \varepsilon)^r \cdot \Delta$. Now, we color the subgraphs in with disjoint color palettes, in poly$(\log n)$ time, using the algorithm of [12]. Notice that $2^r = o(\Delta)$. In total, the number of colors we require is

$$\begin{aligned} 2^r \cdot (\Delta^* + 1) &= 2^r \cdot 2^{-r} \cdot (1+\varepsilon)^r \cdot \Delta + 2^r = (1+\varepsilon)^r \cdot \Delta + o(\Delta) \\ &\leq e^{\varepsilon \cdot r} \cdot \Delta + o(\Delta) = e^{r/\log^2 n} \cdot \Delta + o(\Delta) \\ &= e^{1/\Omega(\log n)} \cdot \Delta + o(1) = \Delta + o(\Delta) + o(\Delta) \\ &= (1 + o(1))\Delta \end{aligned}$$

□

4.2 Maximal Independent Set

Lemma 4.2. *Let $T_{SP}(n, \varepsilon)$ be the runtime of a non-uniform strong splitting algorithm. Then there is an MIS algorithm with runtime $O(\log^4 n \cdot \log^2 \Delta \cdot T_{SP}(n, \varepsilon) + \text{poly}(\log n))$.*

The MIS Algorithm. Our MIS algorithm is divided into $O(\log \Delta)$ steps, where in each step we reduce the maximum degree by a factor of 2. Each of these steps consist of $O(\text{poly} \log n)$ iterations of eliminating high degree nodes, where in each iteration, we reduce the number of high degree nodes by a polylogarithmic factor. Once the maximum degree is polylogarithmic, we can execute an MIS algorithm with runtime linear in the maximum degree on the remaining graph [4].

Heavy Node Elimination. Consider a graph with maximum degree Δ. We call a node v *heavy*, if $\deg(v) \geq \Delta/2$. Let G' be the graph induced by the heavy nodes and their neighbors.

We create a variable node for every node in G' and a constraint node for each active node. We connect the constraint node of a node v to the variable nodes that correspond to the neighbors of v in G'. Then we use the splitting algorithm with $\varepsilon = 1/\log^2 n$ to color the variable nodes red and blue. All nodes whose variable node is blue become passive. In addition, every node with fewer than $\log n$ red neighbors becomes passive. The splitting step is repeated $2 \log \Delta - \log\log n - 1$ times to obtain a graph G^* where all nodes have at most $\Delta \cdot (1/2 + \varepsilon)^{\log \Delta - \log\log n - 1} < 4 \log n$ active neighbors and similarly, each heavy node has more than $\log n$ active neighbors.

We compute an MIS in G^* and remove all the MIS nodes and their neighbors from the (original) graph. This process is iterated until the set of heavy nodes is empty.

Lemma 4.3. *Let $G = (V, E)$ be a graph with maximum degree Δ. Let $I \subseteq V$ be a maximal independent set. Then $|I| \geq |V|/(\Delta + 1)$.*

Proof. Consider the following process: Every node in the MIS gives one dollar to itself and its neighbors. In total, at most $\ell = (\Delta + 1) \cdot |I|$ dollars are distributed.

By definition of an MIS, every node gets at least one dollar. Hence, $\ell \geq n$ and furthermore

$$(\Delta + 1) \cdot |I| = \ell \geq n \iff |I| \geq \frac{n}{\Delta + 1}$$ □

Lemma 4.4. *Let I be an MIS on G^*. Then at least $\Omega(|V_H|/\log^3 n)$ heavy nodes are covered by I.*

Proof. Let A be the graph induced by the active nodes. By the design of our algorithm, every active node has degree at most $4 \log n$. We make the following observations.

(1) At least $|A|/(5 \log n)$ nodes are selected to I. This follows by Lemma 4.3.
(2) Every active node is either heavy or has at least one heavy neighbor. This is true by definition of G'.

Combining the observations with the maximum degree of A, we get that at least $|A|/(4 \log n \cdot 5 \log n) = |A|/(20 \log^2 n)$ heavy nodes are neighbored by a node in I. Furthermore, combining the observations with the fact the every heavy node has at most $4 \log n$ active neighbors, we get that $|V_H| \leq |A| \cdot 4 \log n$. Putting all of the above together, we have that at least

$$\frac{|A|}{20 \log^2 n} \geq \frac{|V_H|}{4 \log n} \cdot \frac{1}{20 \log^2 n} = \frac{|V_H|}{80 \log^3 n}$$

heavy nodes have a neighbor in I. □

Proof of Lemma 4.2. In every iteration of the heavy node elimination method, we perform at most $O(\log \Delta)$ degree splittings. Furthermore, by Lemma 4.4 and by observing that always at least one heavy node is eliminated, after $O(\log^4 n)$ repetitions, all the heavy nodes are eliminated. Our algorithm consists of $O(\log \Delta)$ executions of the heavy node eliminating, plus some $\text{poly}(\log n)$ time to handle the resulting graphs with $\text{poly}(\log n)$ degrees, hence resulting in a total runtime of $O(\log^4 n \cdot \log^2 \Delta \cdot T_{SP}(n, \varepsilon) + \text{poly}(\log n))$. □

REFERENCES

[1] Philipp Bamberger, Mohsen Ghaffari, Fabian Kuhn, Yannic Maus, and Jara Uitto. 2019. On the Complexity of Distributed Splitting Problems. arXiv:1905.11573
[2] Leonid Barenboim and Michael Elkin. 2011. Deterministic Distributed Vertex Coloring in Polylogarithmic Time. *J. ACM* 58, 5 (2011), 23:1–23:25.
[3] Leonid Barenboim and Michael Elkin. 2013. *Distributed Graph Coloring: Fundamentals and Recent Developments.* Morgan & Claypool Publishers.
[4] Leonid Barenboim, Michael Elkin, and Fabian Kuhn. 2014. Distributed (Δ+1)-Coloring in Linear (in Δ) Time. *SIAM J. Comput.* 43, 1 (2014), 72–95.
[5] Leonid Barenboim, Michael Elkin, Seth Pettie, and Johannes Schneider. 2016. The Locality of Distributed Symmetry Breaking. *J. ACM* 63, 3 (2016), 20:1–20:45.
[6] John Adrian Bondy, Uppaluri Siva Ramachandra Murty, et al. 1976. *Graph theory with applications.* Vol. 290. Citeseer.
[7] Sebastian Brandt, Orr Fischer, Juho Hirvonen, Barbara Keller, Tuomo Lempiäinen, Joel Rybicki, Jukka Suomela, and Jara Uitto. 2016. A lower bound for the distributed Lovász local lemma. In *Proc. 48th Symp. on Theory of Computing (STOC).* 479–488.
[8] Yi-Jun Chang, Tsvi Kopelowitz, and Seth Pettie. 2016. An Exponential Separation between Randomized and Deterministic Complexity in the LOCAL Model. In *57th IEEE Symp. on Foundations of Computer Science (FOCS).* 615–624.
[9] Yi-Jun Chang and Seth Pettie. 2017. A Time Hierarchy Theorem for the LOCAL Model. In *Proc. 58th IEEE Symp. on Foundations of Computer Science (FOCS).* 156–167.
[10] Manuela Fischer and Mohsen Ghaffari. 2017. Sublogarithmic Distributed Algorithms for Lovász Local lemma, and the complexity hierarchy. In *Proc. 31st Symp. on Distributed Computing (DISC).* 18:1–18:16.
[11] Manuela Fischer, Mohsen Ghaffari, and Fabian Kuhn. 2017. Deterministic Distributed Edge-Coloring via Hypergraph Maximal Matching. In *Proc. 58th IEEE Symp. on Foundations of Computer Science (FOCS).*
[12] Pierre Fraigniaud, Marc Heinrich, and Adrian Kosowski. 2016. Local Conflict Coloring. In *Proc. 57th IEEE Symp. on Foundations of Computer Science (FOCS).*
[13] Pierre Fraigniaud, Amos Korman, and David Peleg. 2013. Towards a complexity theory for local distributed computing. *J. ACM* 60, 5 (2013), 35.
[14] Mohsen Ghaffari, David G. Harris, and Fabian Kuhn. 2016. On Derandomizing Local Distributed Algorithms. In *Proc. 59th Symp. on Foundations of Computer Science (FOCS).* 662–673.
[15] Mohsen Ghaffari, David G. Harris, and Fabian Kuhn. 2017. On Derandomizing Local Distributed Algorithms. *CoRR* abs/1711.02194 (2017). arXiv:1711.02194 http://arxiv.org/abs/1711.02194
[16] Mohsen Ghaffari, Juho Hirvonen, Fabian Kuhn, Yannic Maus, Jukka Suomela, and Jara Uitto. 2017. Improved Distributed Degree Splitting and Edge Coloring. In *Proc. 31st Symp. on Distributed Computing (DISC).* 19:1–19:15.
[17] Mohsen Ghaffari, Fabian Kuhn, and Yannic Maus. 2017. On the complexity of local distributed graph problems. In *Proc. 49th Symp. on Theory of Computing (STOC).* 784–797.
[18] Mohsen Ghaffari, Fabian Kuhn, Yannic Maus, and Jara Uitto. 2018. Deterministic distributed edge-coloring with fewer colors. In *Proceedings of the 50th Annual ACM SIGACT Symposium on Theory of Computing.* ACM, 418–430.
[19] Mohsen Ghaffari and Hsin-Hao Su. 2017. Distributed Degree Splitting, Edge Coloring, and Orientations. In *Proc. 28th ACM-SIAM Symp. on Discrete Algorithms (SODA).* 2505–2523.
[20] Nathan Linial. 1992. Locality in Distributed Graph Algorithms. *SIAM J. Comput.* 21, 1 (1992), 193–201.
[21] Moni Naor and Larry Stockmeyer. 1995. What Can Be Computed Locally? *SIAM J. Comput.* 24, 6 (1995), 1259–1277.
[22] David Peleg. 2000. *Distributed Computing: A Locality-Sensitive Approach.* SIAM.

On the Use of Randomness in Local Distributed Graph Algorithms*

Mohsen Ghaffari
ghaffari@inf.ethz.ch
ETH Zurich
8092 Zurich, Switzerland

Fabian Kuhn
kuhn@cs.uni-freiburg.de
University of Freiburg
79110 Freiburg, Germany

ABSTRACT

We attempt to better understand randomization in local distributed graph algorithms by exploring how randomness is used and what we can gain from it:

- We first ask the question of how much randomness is needed to obtain efficient randomized algorithms. We show that for *all* locally checkable problems with poly log n-time randomized algorithms, there are such algorithms even if either (I) there is a only a single (private) independent random bit in each poly log n-neighborhood of the graph, (II) the (private) bits of randomness of different nodes are only poly log n-wise independent, or (III) there are only poly log n bits of global shared randomness (and no private randomness).
- Second, we study how much we can improve the error probability of randomized algorithms. For all locally checkable problems with poly log n-time randomized algorithms, we show that there are such algorithms that succeed with probability $1-n^{-2^{\varepsilon(\log\log n)^2}}$ and more generally T-round algorithms, for $T \geq$ polylog n, with success probability $1 - n^{-2^{\varepsilon \log^2 T}}$. We also show that poly log n-time randomized algorithms with success probability $1 - 2^{-2^{\log^{\varepsilon} n}}$ for some $\varepsilon > 0$ can be derandomized to poly log n-time deterministic algorithms.

Both of the directions mentioned above, reducing the amount of randomness and improving the success probability, can be seen as partial derandomization of existing randomized algorithms. In all the above cases, we also show that any significant improvement of our results would lead to a major breakthrough, as it would imply significantly more efficient deterministic distributed algorithms for a wide class of problems.

CCS CONCEPTS

• **Theory of computation → Distributed algorithms.**

KEYWORDS

distributed symmetry breaking, randomness, shared randomness, LOCAL model, CONGEST model

ACM Reference Format:
Mohsen Ghaffari and Fabian Kuhn. 2019. On the Use of Randomness in Local Distributed Graph Algorithms. In *2019 ACM Symposium on Principles of Distributed Computing (PODC '19), July 29-August 2, 2019, Toronto, ON, Canada.* ACM, New York, NY, USA, 10 pages. https://doi.org/10.1145/3293611.3331610

1 INTRODUCTION

The gap between the complexity of randomized and deterministic distributed algorithms for local graph problems is one of the foundational, deep, and long-standing questions in distributed algorithms. A well-known special case is the question of Linial from 1987 [22, 23] about the Maximal Independent Set (MIS) problem: While we have known randomized MIS algorithms that work in $O(\log n)$ rounds of the LOCAL model—i.e., synchronous message passing rounds—since the celebrated work of Luby [25] and Alon, Babai, and Itai [1], Linial's question for obtaining a *deterministic* algorithm that computes an MIS in poly log n rounds still remains open. There is an abundance of similar questions about other concrete graph problems, several of which remain open. See e.g., the first five problems[1] in the open problems chapter of the book by Barenboim and Elkin [7]. More generally, we can ask whether

$$\text{P-LOCAL} \stackrel{?}{=} \text{P-RLOCAL}$$

Here, P-LOCAL denotes the family of *locally checkable problems*[2] that can be solved by deterministic algorithms in poly log n rounds in n-node graphs and P-RLOCAL denotes the family of *locally checkable problems* that can be solved by randomized algorithms in poly log n rounds, with success probability $1 - 1/n$. Both of these are with respect to the LOCAL model. One may view the above question as an analog of the well known P vs. BPP question in centralized computational complexity, i.e., (deterministic) polynomial-time vs. bounded-error probabilistic polynomial-time [3, Chapter 7]. However, as we will see below, the questions are inherently very different.

In this paper, we try to shed more light on this fundamental question by taking a step back and asking *"what is the randomness used in these randomized distributed graph algorithms?"* That is, (A) how much randomness is needed, and (B) how strong are the probabilistic guarantees that randomized algorithms can provide? Both of these questions can be used as means for interpolating

*Full version of the paper available at https://arxiv.org/abs/1906.00482

[1]Though, the last two of these are no longer open [13, 17].

[2]To make the question more widely applicable, we use a relaxed version of local checkability, where the local checking radius can be up to polylogarithmic in n. For a precise definition, we refer to Section 2.

ACM ISBN 978-1-4503-6217-7/19/07...$15.00
https://doi.org/10.1145/3293611.3331610

between randomized and deterministic algorithms: Randomized algorithms, under the standard definition, can use an unbounded number of independent random bits at different nodes and they guarantee success with probability $1-1/n$. Deterministic algorithms use no randomness and they always guarantee success (which is at least as strong as guaranteeing success with probability 1).

Before delving into our answers to these questions, let us review some of the recent work centered on the gap between deterministic and randomized algorithms.

1.1 An Overview of the Recent Developments

Over the past decade, there has been a number of beautiful developments, which are related to the aforementioned deterministic versus randomized question. We give a brief overview here.[3]

The Shattering Method and its Necessity: One of the influential developments of the past decade for local distributed graph problems was the introduction and wide usage of the shattering method. The methodis inspired by Beck's algorithmic version of the Lovász Local Lemma (LLL) [9] and was first introduced in the distributed setting in [8]. In a rough sense, the method leads to randomized algorithms with two phases: a first efficient randomized phase that typically works in time that only depends on local graph parameters such as the maximum degree Δ and leaves a graph made of only small, typically $\text{poly}\log n$-size components; and a second phase that solves each of these connected components separately, all in parallel, using deterministic algorithms. The dependency on n in randomized algorithms is brought down to the deterministic complexity for networks of size $N = \text{poly}\log n$. For instance, for MIS, we know an $O(\log \Delta) + 2^{O(\sqrt{\log\log n})}$-round randomized algorithm with success probability $1 - 1/n$ [15], and the second complexity term here mirrors the $2^{O(\sqrt{\log n})}$ complexity of the best known deterministic MIS algorithm [28]. We run deterministic algorithms in the second phase, because the usual error probability bound of randomized algorithms, which is $1/\text{poly}(N)$ for N-node instances, is not sufficient to union bound over all components. Here, the issue is more about the *success probability*, rather than the bits of randomness. Chang et al. [11] showed that the randomized complexity of any locally checkable problem on n-node networks (with success probability $1 - 1/n$) is at least its deterministic complexity on graphs with $\sqrt{\log n}$ nodes. This underlines the importance of understanding the complexity of deterministic algorithms, even if eventually we only care about randomized algorithms.

Exponential Separations in the Landscape of Lower Complexities: Another significant recent development was the emergence of provable exponential separations between randomized and deterministic algorithms, though in a complexity regime below $O(\log n)$. Brandt et al. [10] showed a lower bound of $\Omega(\log\log n)$ on the round complexity of computing a sinkless orientation in constant-degree graphs, which also implied a similar lower bound for Δ-coloring trees of degree $\Delta = O(1)$. Chang et al. [11] extended these to $\Omega(\log n)$ lower bounds for deterministic algorithms. They also exhibited an $O(\log\log n)$ round randomized algorithm and an $O(\log n)$ round deterministic algorithm for Δ-coloring trees, hence proving that these complexities are tight and they have an exponential separation. Ghaffari and Su [20] showed that the original problem of sinkless orientation (which is a special case of the LLL) also exhibits the same exponential separation, by providing a $\Theta(\log\log n)$-round randomized and a $\Theta(\log n)$-round deterministic algorithm. We emphasize that this exponential separation is between complexities in $O(\log n)$. To the best of our understanding, this separation has no bearing on the P-LOCAL vs. P-RLOCAL question or particular cases of it such as Linial's MIS question.

A Complexity-Theoretic Study and Derandomization: As a step toward studying deterministic vs. randomized complexities, Ghaffari et al. [19] introduced the sequential SLOCAL model: here a sequential algorithm processes vertices in an arbitrary order $v_1, v_2, \dots, v_n$, each time deciding about the output of the vertex v_i that is being processed—e.g., its color in the coloring problem—by reading the current information available within a small r-hop neighborhood of v_i, including the related topology, and then recording the result (and potentially the gathered information) in the node v_i. See [19] for the precise definitions. The parameter r is the locality of such an SLOCAL algorithm. The model provides a generalization of sequential greedy processes for problems such as MIS and $\Delta + 1$ coloring, which both can be solved with locality 1 in the SLOCAL model. The model may seem too powerful at first sight, given that it allows sequential processing, but it is no more powerful than adding randomization to the LOCAL model: It was shown in [19] that any (randomized or deterministic) SLOCAL algorithm with locality $\text{poly}\log n$ for any locally checkable problem can be transformed to a $\text{poly}\log n$-round randomized LOCAL algorithm. Given this, Ghaffari et al. [19] studied the question of P-SLOCAL vs. P-LOCAL: whether any locally checkable problem that admits a deterministic SLOCAL algorithm with locality $\text{poly}\log n$ can be solved using a $\text{poly}\log n$-round deterministic LOCAL algorithm. A number of problems were shown to be complete with respect to P-SLOCAL [17, 19], in the following sense: they admit deterministic SLOCAL algorithms with locality $\text{poly}\log n$ and if one can provide a $\text{poly}\log n$-round deterministic LOCAL for any of them, one has proven that P-SLOCAL = P-LOCAL. Complete problems include network decompositions, splitting [19], and certain locally verifiable versions of approximating dominating set or set cover [17].

The work of [19] investigated *a part* of the question of randomized vs. deterministic by examining P-SLOCAL vs. P-LOCAL. A different work of Ghaffari et al. [17] showed that this actually *fully* captures the issue, by proving that P-RLOCAL = P-SLOCAL. That is, any $\text{poly}\log n$-round randomized LOCAL algorithm that solves a locally checkable problem with high probability can be derandomized into a deterministic SLOCAL algorithm for the same problem with locality $\text{poly}\log n$. Hence, the question P-SLOCAL vs. P-LOCAL is equivalent to P-RLOCAL vs. P-LOCAL and the aforementioned problems are complete also with respect to P-RLOCAL. All of those problems admit $\text{poly}\log n$-round randomized LOCAL algorithms, and any $\text{poly}\log n$-round deterministic LOCAL algorithm for any of them would imply that P-RLOCAL = P-LOCAL. Given what is known about these complete problems, and particularly network decomposition [28], the best known derandomization is that any $\text{poly}\log n$-round randomized algorithm for *any* locally

[3]This is certainly not exhaustive and it probably does not do justice to all the recent progress. We discuss only the cases that are most directly related to the current paper, in our understanding.

checkable problem can be derandomized to a $2^{O(\sqrt{\log n})}$-round deterministic algorithm [17].

As a side remark, it is worth noting that the complexity-theoretic view mentioned above and some of the algorithmic and derandomization tools developed around it have already had concrete algorithmic applications: In particular, [13, 17] resolved a couple of the open questions regarding deterministic vs. randomized distributed algorithm for particular graph problems, including Open Problems 11.4, 11.5 and 11.10 of the book of Barenboim and Elkin [7].

1.2 Our Contributions

As mentioned above, we try to shed more light on the P-RLOCAL vs. P-LOCAL problem by asking two questions about randomized distributed graph algorithms: (A) "how much" randomness do they need for their efficiency, to solve in particular the above complete problems—e.g., network decompositions with poly log n parameters—in poly log n-rounds? (B) And what kind of a bound can we prove on their error probability, given some limit on the time complexity. In each direction, we provide results that are in some sense the strongest that we one can achieve, barring a major breakthrough. More concretely, if one achieves a considerably stronger result, that would either prove P-SLOCAL = P-LOCAL or at least provide a much faster deterministic algorithm for all problems in P-RLOCAL, including MIS, $(\Delta + 1)$-coloring, and network decomposition with poly log n parameters.

Before diving to the answers, let us make something concrete. In much of the discussions in this paper, instead of talking about all possible randomized algorithms for all problems, we will focus directly on problems that are now known to be complete with respect to the P-RLOCAL vs. P-LOCAL question, in the sense mentioned above. In particular, much of our focus will be on network decompositions as introduced in [5]. A network decomposition of $G = (V, E)$ with α colors and diameter β—often abbreviated as an (α, β) network decomposition—is a partitionong of V into α disjoint sets $V_1, \ldots, V_\alpha$ such that for each $i \in \{1, \ldots, \alpha\}$, each connected component of the induced subgraph $G[V_i]$ has diameter at most β (see Section 2 for a formal definition). In the following, when referring to a network decomposition with poly log n parameters, we mean that α = poly log n and β = poly log n. It is known that every n-node network admits an $(O(\log n), O(\log n))$ network decomposition and that such a decomposition can be computed in $O(\log^2 n)$ rounds of the LOCAL model using randomized algorithms, with success probability $1 - 1/n$ [24]. The best known deterministic algorithm to compute a network decomposition with poly log n (or even weaker) parameters is exponentially slower and requires $2^{O(\sqrt{\log n})}$ rounds [4, 28]. We ask how much randomness is needed to compute network decompositions with poly log n parameters (or some other related questions such as splitting) or what kind of a probabilistic guarantees can randomized algorithms provide in a given amount of time, for these problems. Given the aformentioned completeness results, we know that these concrete questions capture the role of randomness for all locally checkable problems: For instance, if we can construct a network decomposition with poly log n parameters in poly log n time using a certain "amount of randomness", then the same is true for any problem in P-RLOCAL (using the same amount of randomness).

1.2.1 Direction 1 — How much randomness is needed? We formalize the question about the amount of randomness in three ways: (A) the number of bits in each "local neighborhood", (B) the independence of the bits in different nodes, and (C) the number of bits shared in the whole network. We next discuss these cases separately.

(A) First, we note that the standard definition for randomized algorithms allows each node to have unbounded amount of randomness. Usual algorithms use only poly log n bits per node [24]. We show in Theorems 3.1 and 3.7 that even much less suffices: even if for each node there is just one bit of randomness somewhere within its poly log n hops, and these bits are independent of each other, then we can still compute all P-RLOCAL problems in poly log n. We also give an algorithm that, in such a setting, builds a network decomposition with poly log n parameters, in poly log n rounds of the CONGEST model, with probability $1 - 1/\text{poly}(n)$. Recall that the CONGEST model is a variant of the LOCAL model where the message sizes are limited to $O(\log n)$ bits, in contrast to the LOCAL model which allows unbounded message sizes.

Two comments are in order. First, this one bit per poly log n-hop neighborhood is in some sense the least that we need to assume. Otherwise, there can be large poly log n-hop neighborhoods where there is no randomness, and hence poly log n-time algorithms that work in those areas are actually providing a deterministic algorithm. Second, our theoretical result might have some message for practical settings when thinking outside the realm of the worst-case analysis. Probably, in many networking settings, it is reasonable to assume that one can "extract" one bit of randomness out of various network properties (topology, identifiers, etc.) in each poly log n neighborhood. In a very informal sense, our result implies that there are probably reasonable ways of building efficient "deterministic" algorithms (with only 1 bit of pseudo-randomness per poly log n-hop neighborhood), such that breaking these algorithms requires very carefully built input networks[4].

(B) Second, we investigate the independence between the random bits. Standard algorithms assume the bits of different nodes to be fully independent. In Theorem 3.5, we show that poly log n-wise independence suffices for computing a network decomposition with poly log n parameters in poly log n rounds.Hence, any problem in P-RLOCAL can be solved in poly log n rounds, even if the random bits of different nodes are only poly log n-wise independent.

(C) Third, as a result of (B), we can also bound the total number of random bits required in the whole network. Standard models of randomized algorithms implicitly assume a total of at least $\Omega(n)$ bits, i.e., at least one bit per node. We show that just poly log n shared random bits suffice. For the local splitting problem shown to be complete in [19], we prove in Lemma 3.4 that just $O(\log n)$ bits of shared randomness suffices. This concretely shows that the P-RLOCAL vs. P-LOCAL question is very different from its well-known centralized P vs. BPP analog (polynomial-time vs. bounded-error probabilistic polynomial time) [3, 30]. Note that for this centralized question, any probabilistic algorithm with $O(\log n)$ bits of randomness can be derandomized trivially in polynomial time, by checking all the

[4]There is much to be investigated here. What kind of randomness extraction is possible, under different network assumptions? Also, can we formalize the sufficiency of such randomness against a computationally bounded adversary who builds the input graph, perhaps using some cryptographic assumptions?

$2^{O(\log n)} = n^{O(1)}$ possibilities for the $O(\log n)$ bits of randomness. Our result about splitting shows that even problems that are solvable efficiently with $O(\log n)$ bits of randomness can be hard with respect to P-RLOCAL vs. P-LOCAL. Furthermore, we note that this bound of $O(\log n)$ bits is asymptotically the least that we can assume, unless we come up with a deterministic algorithm[5].

We also show that something similar can be said about more standard graph problems, for instance network decomposition. The result of the item (B) discussed above, combined with standard constructions for k-wise independent bits [2], shows that poly log n bits of shared randomness build network decompositions with poly log n parameters, in poly log n rounds of the LOCAL model. We show such a result also for the much more stringent CONGEST model, using a very different method: In Theorem 3.6, we show that we can build network decompositions with poly log n parameters, in poly log n rounds of the CONGEST model, using only poly log n bits of shared randomness (and no private randomness).

1.2.2 Direction 2 — Error Probability vs. Round Complexity. Usually, the study of distributed graph algorithms has focused only on two regimes of error probabilities: an error probability of 0, for deterministic algorithms, and an error probability of $1/\operatorname{poly}(n)$, for randomized algorithms. In a number of places where we need deterministic algorithms, the main property that we require from the algorithms is that the error probability is 0 or close to 0 and not how many random bits we use. Our second direction is to explore the trade-off between error probability and running time. Concretely, how small can we make the error probability in a certain time budget? Moreover, at what point is the error probability small enough so that we can derandomize the algorithm completely?

For any $T \geq \log^c n$, where c is a sufficiently large constant, we give a randomized algorithm that succeeds with probability at least $1 - 2^{-2^{\varepsilon \log^2 T}} = 1 - n^{-2^{\varepsilon \log^2 T}}$ for some constant $\varepsilon > 0$ and that computes a network decomposition with cluster diameter T and T cluster colors in T rounds of the CONGEST model (see Theorem 4.2). For instance, for $T = \operatorname{polylog} n$, this results in an error probability of $n^{-2^{\varepsilon \log^2 \log n}}$, which is much stronger than the $n^{-\Theta(1)}$ error probability bound of standard randomized algorithms. In Theorem 4.3, we also show that the result of Theorem 4.2 is nearly the best error probability that one can guarantee, unless we improve the deterministic complexity of network decompositions. Concretely, any randomized algorithm with round complexity T—even in the LOCAL-model—that has success probability at least $1 - 2^{2^{\varepsilon \log^{\beta} T}}$ for any constant $\varepsilon > 0$ and any constant $\beta > 2$ would imply a deterministic network decomposition with poly log n parameters in $2^{O(\log^{1/\beta} n)} \ll 2^{O(\sqrt{\log n})}$ rounds, thus significantly improving on the long-standing bounds of Panconesi and Srinivasan [28]. Similarly, in Theorem 4.6, we show that any randomized poly log n-round algorithm with success probability better than $1 - 2^{-2^{\log^{\varepsilon} n}}$, for an arbitrary constant $\varepsilon > 0$, would imply a poly log n-round network decomposition with poly log n parameters, thus proving that P-RLOCAL = P-LOCAL. Previously, the best known such derandomization result was that any randomized algorithms with a much stronger success probability of $1 - 2^{-\Theta(n^2)}$ can be derandomized (via a union bound over all $2^{\Theta(n^2)}$ many possibilities for n-node graphs). This was implicit in Theorem 3 of [11].

2 MODEL AND PRELIMINARIES

Communication Model: We work with two closely related models of distributed computing, LOCAL and CONGEST: The communication network is abstracted as an n-node graph $G = (V, E)$, with one processor on each node $v \in V$ which has a unique identifier. We typically assume that the identifiers are represented by $\Theta(\log n)$ bits. Communication happens in synchronous rounds, where per round each node can send one message to each neighbor. In the LOCAL model, message sizes can be unbounded. In the CONGEST model, each message can have $O(\log n)$ bits. At the beginning, the processors/nodes do not know the topology of the network, except for potentially knowing some global parameters (as we shall discuss next). At the end, each processor should know its own part of the output, e.g., its color in the vertex coloring problem.

Uniform and Non-Uniform Algorithms: In most cases, we assume that the nodes of a distributed algorithm initially know the number of nodes n or an upper bound on n.x We call such an algorithm a *non-uniform* distributed algorithm and we call an algorithm where the nodes initially do not know anything about n a *uniform* algorithm. We formally model the knowledge of n as follows. In a non-uniform distributed algorithm, all nodes are given n as input. We say that a non-uniform algorithm $\mathcal{A}$ solves a distributed graph problem $\mathcal{P}$ in time $T(n)$ if $\mathcal{A}$ solves $\mathcal{P}$ in time at most $T(n)$ on all graph with at most n nodes. If the correctness of a solution to a graph problem $\mathcal{P}$ depends on the number of nodes n, we use the notation $\mathcal{P}(n)$ to make this clear. A solution to problem $\mathcal{P}(n)$ that satisfies the requirements for graphs with at most n nodes. If we for example compute an $(O(\log n), O(\log n))$-decomposition of a graph $G = (V, E)$ with at most n nodes, the cluster diameter and number of cluster colors can depend logarithmically on n rather than just on the actual number of nodes $|V|$. The error probability of a non-uniform algorithm is defined as follows.

Definition 2.1 (Error Probability). We say that a (non-uniform) distributed algorithm $\mathcal{A}$ solves a given distributed graph problem $\mathcal{P}$ on n-node graphs with error probability $\delta(n)$ in time $T(n)$ if the following holds. When given n as an input, $\mathcal{A}$ computes a correct solution to $\mathcal{P}$ with probability at least $1 - \delta(n)$ on all graphs G with at most n nodes.

The definition implies that a randomized algorithm has to succeed with probability $1 - \delta(n)$ even if the actual graph has fewer than n nodes. If $\delta(n) \leq 1/n^c$ for a constant $c > 1$ that can be chosen sufficiently large, we say that algorithm $\mathcal{A}$ solves the problem $\mathcal{P}$ with high probability (w.h.p.).

Local Checkability: As mentioned, we study distributed graph problems where the validity of a solution is locally checkable [14]. Roughly, a graph problem $\mathcal{P}$ is said to be d-locally checkable if given a solution to $\mathcal{P}$, there exists a deterministic d-round algorithm $\mathcal{A}_C$ in the LOCAL model such that every node outputs "yes" if and only

[5]An algorithm with $b < \log n$ bits of randomness is a uniformly random choice among $2^b < n$ possible deterministic algorithms. Each deterministic algorithm either succeeds or fails. Hence, the highest probability that is not 1 would be at most $1-1/2^b < 1-1/n$. Thus, if the probability is at least $1 - 1/n$, it is equal to 1.

if the given solution is a valid solution to $\mathcal{P}$. The class of problems we consider contains the well-known class of locally checkable labeling (LCL) problems[6], however, we use a much looser definition of local checkability, where in particular the checking radius can depend on n and which is formally defined as follows.

Definition 2.2 (Local Checkability). Let $\mathcal{P}$ be a distributed graph problem. We say that $\mathcal{P}$ is $d(n)$*-locally checkable* for a function $d(n)$ if there exists a deterministic non-uniform distributed algorithm $\mathcal{A}_C$, which is given n as input an which has the following properties. Given a graph $G = (V, E)$ of size $|V| \leq n$ and values x_v for $v \in V$, $\mathcal{A}_C$ has round complexity at most $d(n)$ and it checks whether $\{x_v : v \in V\}$ is a correct solution for $\mathcal{P}$. After running $\mathcal{A}_C$, each node outputs "yes" or "no" such that all nodes output "yes" if and only if $\{x_v : v \in V\}$ is a correct solution for $\mathcal{P}$. We say that $\mathcal{P}$ is *strictly* $d(n)$*-locally checkable* if the round complexity is $d(|V|)$, i.e., if the checking radius only depends on the actual number of nodes and not on the upper bound n.

Note that any LCL problem and more generally any problem that is $O(1)$-locally checkable is also strictly locally checkable.

Network Decomposition: As discussed, the complexity of computing a network decomposition is at the core of understanding the role of randomization in local distributed graph algorithms: Given a network decomposition with poly$(\log n)$ parameters for a sufficiently large (polylogarithmic) power G^r of the network graph G, any randomized poly$(\log n)$-time algorithm for a poly$(\log n)$-locally checkable problem can be derandomized to a deterministic poly$(\log n)$-time algorithm [17, 19]. We slightly adapt the definition of a network decomposition from the one introduced in [5, 24] to make it more directly useful in the CONGEST model. Given a graph $G = (V, E)$, a strong $(d(n), c(n))$-decomposition of G is partition of V into clusters $C_1, \ldots, C_p$ together with a subtree T_i of G and a color $\gamma_i \in \{1, \ldots, c(n)\}$ for each cluster C_i. The tree T_i of cluster C_i contains all nodes of C_i (i.e., T_i spans the cluster C_i). Each tree T_i has diameter at most $d(n)$ (which implies that each cluster has weak diameter at most $d(n)$) and the colors of the clusters are chosen such that clusters that are connected by an edge of G are assigned different colors. We say that a decomposition has *congestion* $\kappa \geq 1$ if each node is containted in at most κ clusters of each color.[7] Usually, in the literature, the trees spanning the clusters are not given as part of the definition and instead of explicitly specifying the congestion of a decomposition, the literature distinguishes between strong and weak diameter decompositions. The decompositions of the above definition have weak diameter $d(n)$. In a strong diameter decomposition, the tree T_i of each cluster C_i consists exactly of the nodes in C_i such that each node participates only in the tree of its cluster. A strong diameter decomposition is therefore a special case of a decompositions with congestion 1.

3 RANDOMNESS AS A SCARCE RESOURCE

In this section, we view randomness as a resource and use this perspective to interpolate between standard randomized algorithms and deterministic algorithms. Deterministic distributed algorithms do not use any randomness. Randomized distributed algorithms, in the standard definitions, can use an unbounded number of bits of randomness in each node of the network, where all the bits (in the same node and also across the whole network) are assumed to be independent of each other. As mentioned before, for many of the classic problems in distributed graph algorithms, the known randomized algorithms are considerably more time-efficient compared to their deterministic counterparts. Our goal in this section is to investigate this gap, by viewing the bits of randomness as a scarce resource and asking "how much" of it is really needed for "efficiency". We next discuss how we make these two phrases of how much and efficiency more concrete.

Regarding "efficiency", our concrete objective is to be able to solve the classic local problems in distributed graph algorithms (e.g., network decompositions, maximal independent set, and $\Delta + 1$ coloring) in time polylogarithmic in n, given the limited randomness that we have. Recall that this polylogarithmic time is usually construed as a first-order definition of efficiency [6] and it is achievable using randomized algorithms with unbounded randomness per node. Regarding "how much" randomness, we formalize the question and study it in three different ways:

- **(A)** What if instead of each node having access to its own (unbounded) source of random bits, we only have some few bits of randomness in the whole network but such that each node can reach at least one of them? Concretely, we assume that some nodes $S \subseteq V$ of the network hold some bits of randomness (which are independent of each other), each holding just a single bit, and for each node $v \in V$, there is at least one node $s \in S$ within distance h hops of v. In order so that just accessing this bit of randomness is time-efficient, we will assume that $h = \text{poly}\log n$.
- **(B)** What if the bits of the randomness in the network are correlated and have only some limited independence, e.g., they that k-wise independent for $k = \text{poly}\log n$?
- **(C)** What if instead of each node having its own independent bits, which amounts to $\Omega(n)$ bits in the whole network, we have only k bits of global shared randomness?

We discuss these directions separately, (A) in Section 3.1 and (B) and (C) in Section 3.2.

3.1 One Bit of Private Randomness in Each Polylogarithmic Neighborhood

In this subsection, we work under the assumption that there is one bit of randomness within poly $\log n$ distance of each node, and we show that this amount suffices for building network decompositions with poly $\log n$ colors and radius. Therefore, this amount of randomness suffices to have a poly $\log n$-round LOCAL model algorithm for any (locally checkable) problem that can be solved in poly $\log n$ rounds of the LOCAL model using unbounded randomness. We provide a construction of network decomposition in the CONGEST model, with the hope that this construction can be useful also in settings where we care about having small messages.

[6]LCL problems are graph problems where the output of each node is a label from a constant-size alphabet and where the correctness of a solution can be checked with a constant-time LOCAL algorithm [27].

[7]For efficient usage in CONGEST, one could require that each edge is only used by a few clusters per color.

THEOREM 3.1. *Suppose that nodes $S \subseteq V$ of the network hold some independent bits of randomness, each holding just a single bit, and for each node $v \in V$, there is at least one node $s \in S$ within distance h hops of v, where $h = \text{poly} \log n$. Then, there is a $\text{poly} \log n$-time distributed algorithm in the* CONGEST *model that, using only these bits as its source of randomness, constructs a $(O(\log n), h \, \text{poly} \log n)$-network decomposition of the the graph with congestion* 1.

The proof of Theorem 3.1 directly follows from the statements of the following Lemmas 3.2 and 3.3. Note that an undesirable property of Theorem 3.1 is that h appears in the diameter of the network decomposition. In Theorem 3.7, we explain how to fix that issue, using some of the methods that we will discuss in the next subsection. Before stating the two lemmas to prove Theorem 3.1, we first recall the notion of ruling sets and the known deterministic algorithms for them.

Ruling Sets: We need the notion of ruling sets as introduced in [5] in some of our algorithms. Given a graph $G = (V, E)$, a subset $U \subseteq V$ of the nodes of G, and two parameters $\alpha, \beta \geq 1$, a (α, β)-ruling set of G w.r.t. U is a subset $S \subseteq U$ of the nodes in U such that for all $x, y \in S$, $d_G(x, y) \geq \alpha$ and for all $x \in U$, there exists a $y \in S$ such that $d_G(x, y) \leq \beta$. For any $\alpha \geq 2$, a $(\alpha, \alpha \log n)$-ruling set of G w.r.t. S can be computed deterministically in time $O(\alpha \cdot \log n)$ in time $O(\alpha \cdot \log n)$ in the CONGEST model [5, 21].

Now, we are ready to provide the lemmas that prove Theorem 3.1. The proofs appear in the full version [18].

LEMMA 3.2. *Suppose that nodes $S \subseteq V$ of the network hold some independent bits of randomness, each holding just a single bit, and for each node $v \in V$, there is at least one node $s \in S$ within distance h hops of v, where $h = \text{poly} \log n$. Then, there is an $O(hk \log n)$-round deterministic algorithm in the* CONGEST *model that partitions the nodes into disjoint clusters, each inducing a connected subgraph with diameter $O(kh \log n)$, with the following property: Each cluster is either (A) isolated — meaning that it has no neighboring cluster — or (B) its center holds k bits of randomness, which are independent of each other and independent of the bits held by other cluster centers.*

LEMMA 3.3. *Suppose that we are given a partitioning of the nodes into disjoint clusters, each inducing a connected subgraph with diameter $O(h \log^3 n)$, with the following property: Each cluster is either (A) isolated — meaning that it has no neighboring cluster — or (B) its center holds $C \log^2 n$ bits of randomness, which are independent of each other and independent of the bits held by other cluster centers. Then, there is a $h \cdot \text{poly} \log n$-time distributed algorithm in the* CONGEST *model that, using only these bits as its source of randomness, constructs a $(O(\log n), h \, \text{poly} \log n)$-network decomposition of the the graph with congestion* 1.

3.2 Shared Randomness and Private Randomness with Limited Independece

We now ask how many bits of globally shared randomness are sufficient for efficiency (when there is no private randomness). Another way of viewing the question is asking how much randomness is needed, in total, over the whole network. Standard randomized algorithms use $\Omega(n)$ bits, e.g., at least one bit per node. The arguments of the previous section can be used to lower this somewhat but it might still be $\tilde{\Omega}(n)$ bits in some networks. But in fact, much less suffices, merely $\text{poly} \log n$ bits. Incidentally, when showing this, we will also prove that in the standard model where each node has some private randomness, say e.g., $\text{poly} \log n$ bits, we do not need these bits to be fully independent and it suffices if the bits in the whole network are only $\text{poly} \log n$-wise independent.

First, we investigate these questions in the LOCAL model. We explain that with just $O(\log n)$ bits of shared randomness, we can solve the splitting problem introduced by Ghaffari et al.[19]. This is a problem that nicely captures the power of randomness as it can be solved using randomized algorithms in zero rounds, and it was shown[19] that if one can solve it in $\text{poly} \log n$ rounds deterministically, then we can derandomize all $\text{poly} \log n$-round randomized algorithms for any locally checkable problem. In particular, [19] gives a reduction that solves network decomposition using $\text{poly} \log n$ iterations of splitting, and this implies $\text{poly} \log n$ bits of shared randomness suffice for network decomposition, in the LOCAL model. Then, we also show that similar ideas can be used to prove that $\text{poly} \log n$-wise independence among the private bits of randomness in the network suffices for network decomposition in the CONGEST model. Finally, we turn our attention to the CONGEST model and show a more explicit algorithm (instead of reductions) that builds network decompositions in $\text{poly} \log n$ rounds using $\text{poly} \log n$ bits of shared randomness.

Splitting in zero rounds, using $O(\log n)$ bits of shared randomness: Ghaffari et al.[19] defined a certain problem called *splitting*, which can be solved using randomized algorithms in zero rounds with high probability, and showed that if one can solve this problem in $\text{poly} \log n$ rounds deterministically, then one can derandomize all $\text{poly} \log n$-round randomized algorithms for any locally checkable problem. We show that $O(\log n)$ bits of shared randomness suffice for solving this problem in zero rounds, with high probability. In the splitting problem, we are given a bipartite graph $H = (U, V, E)$ where each node in U has at least $\Omega(\log^c n)$ neighbors in V and we should color each node of V red or blue so that each node of U has at least one neighbor in each color. Here, c can be set to be a desirably large constant $c \geq 1$.

LEMMA 3.4. *There is a randomized algorithm that using $O(\log n)$ bits of shared randomness solves the splitting problem, in zero rounds, with probability at least $1 - 1/n$.*

PROOF. Notice that coloring each node of U randomly red or blue satisfies this constraint, with high probability (by applying a Chernoff bound on the neighborhood of each node in U and then a union bound over all nodes in U).

There are two well-known arguments for showing that a small amount of shared randomness suffices for this problem. First, thanks to the variant of Chernoff that holds for p-wise independent random variables [29], we can see that $O(\log n)$-wise independence suffices for this argument. Moreover, we can build $\text{poly}(n)$ bits that are p-wise independent, by using merely $O(p \log n)$ bits that are fully independent, using standard constructions, see e.g., [2]. This means $O(p \log n) = O(\log^2 n)$ bits of shared randomness suffice for splitting. Second, a result of Naor and Naor[26] can be used to show that even $O(\log n)$ bits suffice. They give a construction of p-wise ε-bias spaces. Very roughly speaking, these are spaces that are approximately k-wise independent; see their paper for the definition, and also for the concentration inequalities that can be derived for such random variables. In their section 6.1, they show that a sample space of size $n^{O(1)}$ suffices for getting a coloring where each node has at least one neighbors in each color[8]. This $n^{O(1)}$ size space means $O(\log n)$ bits of shared randomness suffice to sample from this space. □

Network decomposition in LOCAL *using* poly log *n-wise independent bits:* There are known randomized construction of network decomposition with poly log n parameters in poly log n rounds of the LOCAL model[12, 24]. These all assume that the random bits of different nodes are fully independent of each other. We show that limited independence suffices. Concretely, it is enough if each node has poly log n bits of randomness and over the whole network these bits are poly log n-wise independent. Notice that this also allows us to say that we can build such a network decomposition with only poly log n bits of shared randomness. The reason is that by standard constructions of k-wise independent random bits[2], we need only $O(k \log n)$ fully independent random bits to be able to produce poly(n) random bits that are k-wise independent. Hence, if there are poly log n bits of shared randomness, we can construct poly(n) many bits of randomness out of them which are poly log n-wise independent, using a deterministic procedure. These bits can be shared among the nodes, e.g., just by identifiers. Hence, we then have a setting where each node poly(n) bits of randomness and the bits over the whole network are poly log n-wise independent. By what we will show below, this allows us to build a network decomposition with poly log n parameters in poly log n rounds of the LOCAL model.

Theorem 3.5. *There is a distributed algorithm that builds a network decomposition with* poly log n *parameters in* poly log n *rounds of the* LOCAL *model, assuming each node has* poly log n *bits of randomness and over the whole network these bits are* poly log n*-wise independent.*

An idea similar to above can be used to show that poly log n bits of shared randomness suffice for network decomposition, thanks to standard constructions of k-wise independent random bits. The following theorem given an even stronger result, by showing that such a construction can be performed even in the CONGEST model (using a very different method, and by making use of a randomized construction of Elkin and Neiman[12].)

Theorem 3.6. *There is a distributed algorithm for constructing an* $\big(O(\log n), O(\log^2 n)\big)$*-network decomposition with congestion 1, in* poly log n *rounds in the* CONGEST *model, using only* poly log n *bits of shared randomness (and no private randomness).*

Proof. The construction works in $O(\log n)$ phases, where per phase each node gets clustered with at least a constant probability, and remains for the next phases otherwise. We describe the process for one phase, which will define non-adjacent clusters, each with radius $O(\log^2 n)$, such that each node is clustered with at least a constant probability. Repeating this process for $O(\log n)$ phases gives us the desired network decomposition, with high probability. The point for us is to describe how we perform one phase in poly log n rounds of the CONGEST model and using only poly log n bits of shared randomness. We first describe a construction assuming fully independent random bits and then argue why it can be performed using only poly log n bits.

Construction for One Phase: The construction for one phase consists of $p = \Theta(\log n)$ epoch, indexed by $i = 1, 2, ..., p$. For epoch i, we define a base radius $R_i := (p - i) \cdot c \log n$ for a sufficiently large constant $c \geq 10$. At the beginning of an epoch, each node that is still available decides to be a center with probability $O(2^i \cdot \log n)/n$. Each node u that decides to be a center then chooses a random variable X_u according to a geometric distribution with parameter 1/2. That is, $Pr[X_u = Z] = 2^{-Z}$ for any integer $Z \geq 1$. Notice that with high probability, for each center u, we have $X_u \leq c \log n$. The intuitive way of interpreting these random variables is that the cluster of center u will grow up to a distance of at most $R_i + X_u$, from its center u. We say the cluster of u can reach node v if $(R_i + X_u) \geq d_G(u, v)$. The actual clusters are defined as follows: Each node v selects a center u for which $(R_i + X_u) - d_G(u, v) \geq 0$ and who maximizes $(R_i + X_u) - d_G(u, v)$. For v, let m_1 and m_2 be the the two largest values $R_i - (X_u + d_G(u, v))$ among cluster center whose cluster reaches v. If there is no second cluster, define $m_2 = 0$. If v received from at least one cluster center, then v will be removed in this phase, and either *clustered* or *set aside*, according to the following criterion: If $m_1 - m_2 > 1$, then v joins the cluster of its center u; otherwise, it is set aside and it remains unclustered for the whole duration of this phase (it will be brought back in the next phases, to get clustered then). If no cluster reaches v in this epoch, then v continues to the next epoch.

Correctness: The fact that the carved clusters are non-adjacent and each has strong diameter at most $O(\log^2 n)$ are similar to the case discussed before, for the construction in Lemma 3.3; the argument is the same as [12, Lemma 4]. We can also show that each node v has probability 1/2 to be clustered, in each phase. Consider the first epoch in which node v is reached by some cluster. Similar to Lemma 3.3, and as shown in [12, Claim 6], we see that conditioned on v being reached by some cluster, the probability that it has $m_1 - m_2 > 1$ is at least a constant. If v is reached in this epoch but it has $m_1 - m_2 \in \{1, 0\}$, then it is set aside and it remains for the next phases. Given the fact that the probability of being chosen as a centered grows as $\frac{2^i \log n}{n}$ with epoch number i, in some epoch, some center's cluster reaches v; because at the very latest, in the last epoch, v itself (if remaining) becomes a center with probability 1 and its ball reaches itself. Thus, in each phase, v gets clustered with at least a constant probability. Therefore, in $O(\log n)$ phases, node v gets clustered with high probability.

Randomness: We now discuss how to use a limited amount of randomness for the above algorithm. We use a source of $\Theta(\log^2 n)$-wise independent random bits for nodes deciding whether they are sampled or not, for each epoch. Randomness in different epochs and different phases are independent. Moreover, we use another (independent) source of $\Theta(\log^2 n)$-wise independent random bits

[8]Their phrasing is different. They talk about a problem called set balancing, in the context of discrepancy theory. But the problems are the same and when we assume that the minimum degree is at least d, their construction in section 6.1 suffices to get a discrepancy of $O(d^{1/2+\delta} \cdot \sqrt{\log n})$ between the two colors, for any constant $\delta > 0$. Setting $\delta = 0.1$ and $c \geq 1 + 4\delta = 1.4$ in the definition of the splitting problem ensures that $d^{1/2+\delta} \cdot \sqrt{\log n} = o(d)$.

for each sampled center u determining their random radii X_u. We next argue why this suffices.

Notice that the radius R_i decreases by $c \log n$ in each epoch, and the random values X_u for the centers are always upper bounded by $c \log n$, with high probability. We can use this to conclude that in each epoch, w.h.p., each node v can only be reached by at most $O(\log n)$ different centers. The reason is as follows: If there are more than $C \log n$ centers that can reach v in the current epoch i, for a sufficiently large C, it means that the number of nodes in distance R_{i-1} of v is at least $\frac{Cn}{2 \cdot 2^i}$, with high probability (using Chernoff for sum of variables that are $(\log n)$–wise independent). That means, in epoch $i-1$ where the sampling probability was $\frac{\log n \cdot 2^{i-1}}{n}$, with high probability, at least one of these nodes should have been sampled to be a center (again, using Chernoff for sum of variables that are $(\log n)$–wise independent). That means at least one center would have reached v in the previous epoch, which means v would have been removed for this epoch. Thus, we conclude that in each epoch, at most $O(\log n)$ sampled centers can reach v.

Now, we come to analyzing the random radii, and the probability of a node v being clustered in the the first epoch in which a cluster reaches it. Notice that thanks to the property discussed above, there are only $O(\log n)$ sampled centers that can reach v. Hence, the event of whether v is clustered or not depends only on the random radii of these $O(\log n)$ cluster centers. But that is an event that is determined by $O(\log^2 n)$ bits of randomness, $O(\log n)$-bits per cluster center. Given $\Theta(\log^2 n)$-wise independence of the bits used for defining radii, this space is the same as when the randomness is fully independent. Hence, the analysis explained above applies and shows that v is clustered in this epoch with probability at least a constant. Since different phases have independent randomness, we can conclude that v gets clustered in some phase, with high probability. □

Theorem 3.7. *Suppose that nodes $S \subsetneq V$ of the network hold some independent bits of randomness, each holding just a single bit, and for each node $v \in V$, there is at least one node $s \in S$ within distance h hops of v, where $h = \text{poly} \log n$. There is a distributed algorithm that works in $h \,\text{poly} \log n$ rounds of the CONGEST model and constructs a strong-diameter network decomposition with $O(\log n)$ colors and $O(\log^2 n)$ radius.*

Proof Sketch. We perform the bit gathering of Lemma 3.2 so that each cluster center has $O(\log^4 n)$ bits. Then, we share this randomness to all the nodes of the cluster. We then apply the network decomposition explained in the previous section, using these $O(\log^4 n)$ bits. Notice that in each cluster, the bits of randomness are independent and they can be viewed as shared randomness. In different clusters, we have bits that are fully independent of each other. This allows us to run the construction of Section 3.2, in a direct way, and obtain a strong-diameter network decomposition with $O(\log n)$ colors and $O(\log^2 n)$ radius. □

4 TIME VS. ERROR PROBABILITY TRADE-OFFS

In this second part, we investigate the success probability randomized local distributed graph algorithms. In particular, we are interested in understanding the trade-off between the time complexity of a randomized algorithm and its success probability. Given a time budget, what is the best achievable error probability and at what point is it even possible to completely derandomize and obtain a deterministic algorithm? We first state a basic (and known) such derandomization lemma.

Lemma 4.1 (Implicit in [11]). *Assume that we are given a non-uniform randomized distributed algorithm $\mathcal{A}$ that is given n as input and solves a given distributed graph problem $\mathcal{P}$ on node graphs of size at most n with probability at least $1 - 2^{-n^2}$ in time $T(n)$. Then, there also exists a deterministic algorithm $\mathcal{A}'$ that solves $\mathcal{P}$ on graphs of size at most n in time $T(n)$. If $\mathcal{A}$ works in the CONGEST model, $\mathcal{A}'$ also works in the CONGEST model.*

We are usually interested in success probabilities of the form $1 - 1/n^c$ for some constant c. By increasing the running time by a factor $\tau > 1$, one can often improve the error probability by a factor that is exponentially small in τ. This leads to error probabilities that are at best exponentially small in the running time. As a first contribution of this section, the following theorem shows that by using the graph shattering technique (cf. the respective discussion in Section 1), we can boost the success probability when computing a network decomposition significantly beyond this. By the reductions in [17, 19], we then also immediately get the same improvement in the success probability for all poly$(\log n)$-locally checkable graph problems that have poly$(\log n)$-time randomized distributed algorithms with only polynomially small error probability.

Theorem 4.2. *Let $T(n) \geq \log^c n$ for a sufficiently large constant $c > 0$. There is a randomized CONGEST algorithm that computes a $\big(T(n), T(n)\big)$-decomposition with congestion 1 and a randomized LOCAL algorithm to compute a strong diameter $\big(O(\log n), O(\log n)\big)$-decomposition in time $T(n)$ with success probability at least $1 - n^{-2^{\varepsilon \cdot \log^2 T(n)}}$ for some constant $\varepsilon > 0$.*

Proof. For convenience, we only prove that the time complexities of the resulting CONGEST and LOCAL algorithms is $T(n) \cdot \text{poly} \log n$. Note that by applying this weaker statement for an appropriately chosen smaller value of $T(n)$ and by choosing the constants c and ε appropriately, the claim of the theorem then follows.

The algorithm consists of 2 main steps. First, we apply a standard randomized polylog-time network decomposition algorithm $\mathcal{A}$ that succeeds w.h.p. The success probability of $\mathcal{A}$ is not as high as we need it to be, however, we show that after running $\mathcal{A}$, the number of sufficiently separated remaining nodes is small with the "right" success probability. This allows to compute a decomposition on the remaining nodes by using adeterministic network decomposition algorithm.

For the first step, we apply the randomized decomposition algorithm of Elkin and Neiman [12], which computes a strong diameter $\big(O(\log n), O(\log n)\big)$-decomposition in time $O(\log^2 n)$ in the CONGEST model (and thus in particular a decomposition with congestion 1). The parameters in the algorithm of [12] such that it succeeds with probability at least $1 - 1/n^2$. In the following, assume that the algorithm is run in this way. In particular, this also implies that for every node $v \in V$, the probability at v is in a cluster after running the algorithm is at leat $1 - 1/n^2$.

For a subset $S \subseteq V$, we say that S is d-separated if any two nodes in S are at distance at least d in G. Let $t(n) = O(\log^2 n)$ be the running time of the algorithm of [12]. Further, let $\bar{V} \subseteq V$ be the set of nodes that are not inside a cluster after running the algorithm. Note that the output of a node $u \in V$ can only depend on the random bits of nodes within distance at most $t(n)$ of u. Hence, the outputs of a set S of nodes at pairwise distance at least $2t(n) + 1$ are independent. In particular, the events that the nodes in S are in $\bar{V}$ are independent. Let $S \subseteq V$ therefore be such a $(2t(n)+1)$-separated set of nodes. The probability that all nodes in S are in $\bar{V}$ is at most $1/n^{2|S|}$. For any $K \geq 1$, the probability that $\bar{V}$ contains a $(2t(n)+1)$-separated set S of size at least K is thus at most $\binom{n}{K} \cdot 1/n^{2K} \leq 1/n^K$. We choose the value K such that this probability is upper bounded by the failure probability required by the lemma statement, i.e., we choose K such that $n^K \geq n^{2^{\varepsilon \cdot \log^2 T(n)}}$ and we can thus choose $K = 2^{\varepsilon \cdot \log^2 T(n)}$ for an appropriate constant $\varepsilon > 0$.

Our goal is to reduce the remaining problem to deterministically computing a network decomposition on a graph of size at most K. As a first step, we compute a $(2t(n) + 1)$-separated subset $S \subseteq \bar{V}$ of remaining nodes. This can be done by computing a $\big(2t(n)+1, O(t(n)\log n)\big)$-ruling set S w.r.t. $\bar{V}$. Note that because S is a $(2t(n)+1)$-separated set of nodes, with probability at least $1-1/n^K$, its size is at most K. For the rest of the proof, we therefore assume that S is of size at most K. Because S is a $\big(2t(n) + 1, O(t(n)\log n)\big)$-ruling set w.r.t. $\bar{V}$, each remaining node $u \in \bar{V}$ has at least one node in S within distance $O(t(n)\log n)$ in G. By starting parallel BFS explorations from each node $v \in S$, we can therefore build a cluster C_v of radius at most $O(t(n)\log n)$ around each node $v \in S$ such that each node $u \in \bar{V}$ is contained in the cluster of its closest node in S (ties broken arbitrarily). For each cluster C_v, we obtain a spanning tree of depth $O(t(n)\log n)$ and the trees of different clusters are vertex-disjoint. We note that the trees might contain nodes of $V \setminus \bar{V}$. We define the cluster graph G_C as the graph defined on the set of clusters C_v for $v \in S$, where two clusters C_u and C_v are neighbors whenever there are nodes $x \in C_u \cap \bar{V}$ and $y \in C_v \cap \bar{V}$ that are neighbors in G. In [16], it is possible to compute a strong-diameter $\big(2^{O(\sqrt{\log K})}, 2^{O(\sqrt{\log K})}\big)$-decomposition of such a cluster graph in time $2^{O(\sqrt{\log K})}$ times the maximum cluster radius. Note that since the clusters a vertex-disjoint, a strong-diameter decomposition of G_C leads to a decomposition with congestion 1 for the remaining nodes $\bar{V}$ on G. By our choice of $K = 2^{\varepsilon \cdot \log^2 T(n)}$, we have $2^{c\sqrt{\log K}} = T^{\sqrt{\varepsilon} \cdot c}$ and the CONGEST model part of the claim of the lemma thus follows by choosing the constant $\varepsilon > 0$ sufficiently small. The claim about the LOCAL model then follows in the LOCAL model any $(d(n), c(n))$-decomposition can be turned into an $(O(\log n), O(\log n))$-decomposition in time $O(d(n) \cdot c(n) \cdot \log^2 n)$ [4, 19]. □

The following theorem shows that the error probability bound of Theorem 4.2 is essentially tight, in the following sense. A stronger bound would be a major breakthrough and directly imply a significant improvement over the 25-year old and currently best deterministic network decomposition algorithm [28], which has a time complexity of $2^{O(\sqrt{\log n})}$. The following theorem also shows that the approach of the above algorithm is best possible. A better deterministic network decomposition algorithm resulting from a better error probability bound would directly also allow to improve the above algorithm to achieve this same error probability bound. In order to work for general locally checkable problems (such that in particular network decomposition is included), the following theorem is stated in an rather technical way. We discuss what it means for specific problems below.

THEOREM 4.3. *Let $\mathcal{P}(n)$ be a distributed graph problem, where the solution might depend on n. Assume that there is non-uniform randomized distributed algorithm that given n as input solves $\mathcal{P}(n)$ in time $T(n)$ with probability at least $1 - 2^{2^{\varepsilon \log^{\beta} T(n)}}$ for some constant $\varepsilon > 0$ and some $\beta > 2$. Then, there is a deterministic distributed algorithm that solves $\mathcal{P}(N)$ in time $2^{O(\log^{1/\beta} n)}$, where N is chosen such that $T(N) = 2^{c \cdot \log^{1/\beta} n}$ for some constant $c > 0$.*

If the problem $\mathcal{P}(n)$ is strictly $d(n)$-locally checkable for some function $d(n)$, the deterministic algorithm solves $\mathcal{P}(n)$ rather than $\mathcal{P}(N)$. Further, if the randomized algorithm works in the CONGEST *model, the deterministic algorithm also works in the* CONGEST *model.*

PROOF. We apply a technique that was first used by Chang, Kopelowitz, and Pettie in [11]. The basic idea is to "lie" to the algorithm about the number of nodes and pretend that the graph has size $N \gg n$ rather than n in order to boost the success probability of the algorithm to value that is sufficiently clost to 1 in order to apply Lemma 4.1.

Assume that we are given a graph G with n nodes on which we have to solve $\mathcal{P}(n)$. The nodes of G cannot distinguish the graph G from a graph G' with N nodes, which contains G as one of its connected components. A randomized algorithm that is given n as input and solves $\mathcal{P}(n)$ on G in time $T(n)$ with probability at least $1 - \delta(n)$ can therefore also be used to solve $\mathcal{P}(N)$ on G' (and thus also on G) in time $T(N)$ with probability at least $1 - \delta(N)$. If we choose N such that $\delta(N) \leq 2^{-n^2}$ by Lemma 4.1, the resulting algorithm can be derandomized when applied on G.

We thus have to choose the size N of the "virtual" graph G' such that $2^{\varepsilon \log^{\beta} T(N)} \geq n^2$. This implies that $\log T(N) \geq \left(\frac{2}{\varepsilon}\right)^{1/\beta} \log^{1/\beta} n$, which is satisfied for $T(N) = 2^{c \cdot \log^{1/\beta} n}$ for some constant $c > 0$. We therefore get a deterministic algorithm for $\mathcal{P}(N)$ with time complexity $2^{O(\log^{1/\beta} n)}$, where N is chosen such that $T(N) = 2^{c \cdot \log^{1/\beta} N}$. If the randomized algorithm works in the CONGEST model, the deterministic algorithms also works in the CONGEST model.

If the problem $\mathcal{P}(n)$ is strictly $d(n)$-locally checkable for some function $d(n)$, the checking algorithm cannot distinguish between the graphs G and the component isomorphic to G in G'. A valid solution to $\mathcal{P}(N)$ on a graph of size N is therefore also a valid solution to $\mathcal{P}(n')$ for each connected component of G of size n'. □

As the above theorem is stated for general graph problems $\mathcal{P}(n)$ and general time complexities $T(n)$ (which both can depend on n in various ways), it is interesting to discuss what the theorem implies for specific choices of $T(n)$ and for concrete graph problems. We first consider the case of randomized algorithms that have running times that are between poly$(\log n)$ and $2^{O(\sqrt{\log n})}$. That is, we consider running times that are between the best randomized (in the classic sense) and deterministic time complexities for network decomposition and many other important problems. The following corollary follows immediately from Theorem 4.3.

Corollary 4.4. *Let $\alpha > \beta > 2$ be two constants, let $\mathcal{P}(n)$ be a distributed graph problem, and assume that there is non-uniform randomized distributed algorithm that given n as input solves $\mathcal{P}(n)$ in time $2^{O(\log^{1/\alpha} n)}$ with probability at least $1 - 2^{2^{\varepsilon \log^{\beta/\alpha} n}}$ for some constant $\varepsilon > 0$. Then, there is a deterministic distributed algorithm that solves $\mathcal{P}(N)$ in time $2^{O(\log^{1/\beta} n)}$, where N is chosen such that $\log N = \Theta(\log^{\alpha/\beta} n)$ for some constant $c > 0$.*

If the problem $\mathcal{P}(n)$ is strictly $d(n)$-locally checkable for some function $d(n)$, the deterministic algorithm solves $\mathcal{P}(n)$ rather than $\mathcal{P}(N)$. Further, if the randomized algorithm works in the CONGEST *model, the deterministic algorithm also works in the* CONGEST *model.*

Note that if the parameters $\mathcal{P}(n)$ only depend polylogarithmically on n, the parameters of $\mathcal{P}(N)$ also depend polylogarithmically on n. For example if $\mathcal{P}(n)$ is the problem of computing an $\big(O(\log n), O(\log n)\big)$-network decomposition, then $\mathcal{P}(N)$ refers to the problem of computing an $\big(O(\log^{\alpha/\beta} n), O(\log^{\alpha/\beta} n)\big)$-network decomposition. Further, if $\mathcal{P}$ is an LCL problem (e.g., MIS or $(\Delta+1)$-coloring), $\mathcal{P}$ is strictly $O(1)$-locally checkable. Hence, for this important and widely studied class of problems, the stronger versions of Theorem 4.3 and Corollary 4.4 hold, i.e., in both cases we get a deterministic $2^{O(\log^{1/\beta} n)}$-time algorithm that solves $\mathcal{P}$ in its original form. The following corollary shows that the same (and actually something slightly stronger) also holds for the network decomposition problem in the LOCAL model.

Corollary 4.5. *Assume that there is non-uniform randomized distributed algorithm that given n as input computes a $(T(n), T(n))$-decomposition in time $T(n)$ with probability at least $1 - 2^{2^{\varepsilon \log^{\beta} T(n)}}$ for some constant $\varepsilon > 0$ and some $\beta > 2$. Then, there exists a deterministic $2^{O(\log^{1/\beta} n)}$-round algorithm to compute a $\big(O(\log n), O(\log n)\big)$-decomposition in the* LOCAL *model.*

The next theorem bounds the error probability that is needed to derandomize a polylogarithmic-time randomized algorithm to a polylogarithmic-time deterministic algorithm. As this result is most interesting for strictly locally checkable graph problems, we only state it for this case.

Theorem 4.6. *Let $\mathcal{P}$ be a strictly $d(n)$-locally checkable graph problem for some function $d(n)$ or let $\mathcal{P}$ be the problem of computing a network decomposition with $\text{poly}(\log n)$ parameters. Further assume that there is randomized non-uniform distributed algorithm that solves $\mathcal{P}$ in $\text{poly}(\log n)$ time with probability at least $1 - 2^{-2^{\log^{\varepsilon} n}}$ for some constants $\varepsilon > 0$. Then, there is a deterministic distributed $\text{poly}\log n$-time algorithm for $\mathcal{P}$.*

Remark: One could of course get similar results for other time complexity bounds. In the same way as in Theorem 4.6, it can for example be shown that if we have a randomized quasi-polylogarithmic time algorithm with success probability $1 - 2^{-2^{2^{(\log\log n)^{\varepsilon}}}}$ for some constant $\varepsilon > 0$, we can derandomize it to a quasi-polylogarithmic deterministic algorithm for the same problem. By quasi-polylogarithmic running time, we mean a running time of the form $2^{(\log\log n)^{c}}$ for some constant $c > 0$.

REFERENCES

[1] Noga Alon, László Babai, and Alon Itai. 1986. A Fast and Simple Randomized Parallel Algorithm for the Maximal Independent Set Problem. *Journal of Algorithms* 7, 4 (1986), 567–583.

[2] Noga Alon and Joel Spencer. 2004. *The probabilistic method.* John Wiley & Sons.

[3] Sanjeev Arora and Boaz Barak. 2009. *Computational complexity: a modern approach.* Cambridge University Press.

[4] Baruch Awerbuch, Bonnie Berger, Lenore Cowen, and David Peleg. 1996. Fast Network Decompositions and Covers. *J. of Parallel and Distributed Computing* 39, 2 (1996), 105–114.

[5] Baruch Awerbuch, Andrew V. Goldberg, Michael Luby, and Serge A. Plotkin. 1989. Network Decomposition and Locality in Distributed Computation. In *Proc. 30th IEEE Symp. on Foundations of Computer Science (FOCS).* 364–369.

[6] Leonid Barenboim. 2012. On the Locality of Some NP-Complete Problems. In *Proc. 39th Coll. on Automata, Languages, and Programming (ICALP).* 403–415.

[7] Leonid Barenboim and Michael Elkin. 2013. *Distributed Graph Coloring: Fundamentals and Recent Developments.* Morgan & Claypool Publishers.

[8] Leonid Barenboim, Michael Elkin, Seth Pettie, and Johannes Schneider. 2016. The Locality of Distributed Symmetry Breaking. *J. ACM* 63, 3 (2016), 20:1–20:45.

[9] József Beck. 1991. An algorithmic approach to the Lovász local lemma. I. *Random Structures & Algorithms* 2, 4 (1991), 343–365.

[10] Sebastian Brandt, Orr Fischer, Juho Hirvonen, Barbara Keller, Tuomo Lempiäinen, Joel Rybicki, Jukka Suomela, and Jara Uitto. 2016. A lower bound for the distributed Lovász local lemma. In *Proc. 48th ACM Symp. on Theory of Computing (STOC).* 479–488.

[11] Yi-Jun Chang, Tsvi Kopelowitz, and Seth Pettie. 2016. An Exponential Separation Between Randomized and Deterministic Complexity in the LOCAL Model. In *Proc. 57th IEEE Symp. on Foundations of Computer Science (FOCS).*

[12] Michael Elkin and Ofer Neiman. 2016. Distributed Strong Diameter Network Decomposition. In *Proc. 35th ACM Symp. on Principles of Distributed Computing (PODC).* 211–216.

[13] Manuela Fischer, Mohsen Ghaffari, and Fabian Kuhn. 2017. Deterministic Distributed Edge-Coloring via Hypergraph Maximal Matching. In *Proc. 58th IEEE Symp. on Foundations of Computer Science (FOCS).*

[14] Pierre Fraigniaud, Amos Korman, and David Peleg. 2013. Towards a complexity theory for local distributed computing. *J. ACM* 60, 5 (2013), 35.

[15] Mohsen Ghaffari. 2016. An improved distributed algorithm for maximal independent set. In *Proc. 27th ACM-SIAM Symp. on Discrete Algorithms (SODA).* 270–277.

[16] Mohsen Ghaffari. 2019. Distributed Maximal Independent Set using Small Messages. In *Proc. 30th Symp. on Discrete Algorithms (SODA).* 805–820.

[17] Mohsen Ghaffari, David G Harris, and Fabian Kuhn. 2018. On derandomizing local distributed algorithms. In *2018 IEEE 59th Annual Symposium on Foundations of Computer Science (FOCS).* IEEE, 662–673.

[18] Mohsen Ghaffari and Fabian Kuhn. 2019. On the Use of Randomness in Local Distributed Graph Algorithms. *arXiv preprint arXiv:1906.00482* (2019).

[19] Mohsen Ghaffari, Fabian Kuhn, and Yannic Maus. 2017. On the Complexity of Local Distributed Graph Problems. In *Proc. 49th ACM Symp. on Theory of Computing (STOC).* 784–797.

[20] Mohsen Ghaffari and Hsin-Hao Su. 2017. Distributed Degree Splitting, Edge Coloring, and Orientations. In *Proc. 28th ACM-SIAM Symp. on Discrete Algorithms (SODA).* 2505–2523.

[21] Monika Henzinger, Sebastian Krinninger, and Danupon Nanongkai. 2016. A deterministic almost-tight dis- tributed algorithm for approximating single-source shortest paths. In *Proc. 48th ACM Symp. on Theory of Computing (STOC).* 489–498.

[22] Nathan Linial. 1987. Distributive graph algorithms – Global solutions from local data. In *Proc. 28th IEEE Symp. on Foundations of Computer Science (FOCS).* 331–335.

[23] Nathan Linial. 1992. Locality in Distributed Graph Algorithms. *SIAM J. Comput.* 21, 1 (1992), 193–201.

[24] Nathan Linial and Michael Saks. 1993. Low Diameter Graph Decompositions. *Combinatorica* 13, 4 (1993), 441–454.

[25] Michael Luby. 1986. A Simple Parallel Algorithm for the Maximal Independent Set Problem. *SIAM J. Comput.* 15 (1986), 1036–1053.

[26] Joseph Naor and Moni Naor. 1993. Small-bias probability spaces: Efficient constructions and applications. *SIAM journal on computing* 22, 4 (1993), 838–856.

[27] Moni Naor and Larry J. Stockmeyer. 1995. What Can Be Computed Locally? *SIAM J. Comput.* 24, 6 (1995), 1259–1277.

[28] Alessandro Panconesi and Aravind Srinivasan. 1995. On the Complexity of Distributed Network Decomposition. *Journal of Algorithms* 20, 2 (1995), 581–592.

[29] Jeanette P Schmidt, Alan Siegel, and Aravind Srinivasan. 1995. Chernoff–Hoeffding bounds for applications with limited independence. *SIAM Journal on Discrete Mathematics* 8, 2 (1995), 223–250.

[30] Michael Sipser. 2006. *Introduction to the Theory of Computation.* Vol. 2. Thomson Course Technology Boston.

Brief Announcement: Message Reduction in the LOCAL Model is a Free Lunch

Shimon Bitton
sbitton@technion.ac.il
Technion - Israel Institute of Technology
Haifa, Israel

Yuval Emek
yemek@technion.ac.il
Technion - Israel Institute of Technology
Haifa, Israel

Taisuke Izumi
t-izumi@nitech.ac.jp
Nagoya Institute of Technology
Nagoya, Aichi, Japan

Shay Kutten
kutten@ie.technion.ac.il
Technion - Israel Institute of Technology
Haifa, Israel

ABSTRACT

A new *spanner* construction algorithm is presented, working under the *LOCAL model* assuming unique edge IDs. Given an n-node communication graph, a spanner with a constant stretch and $\tilde{O}(n^{1+c})$ edges (for any small constant $c > 0$) is constructed efficiently — i.e., in a constant number of rounds and a message complexity of $\tilde{O}(n^{1+2c})$ whp.

One of the many known applications of spanners is for reducing the number of messages of various algorithms. However, usually, one still needs to pay the cost of constructing the spanner. Due to the efficiency of the spanner construction here, we show that every t-round LOCAL algorithm can be transformed into a randomized one with the *same* asymptotic time complexity and $O(t^2 n^{1+O(1/\log t)})$ message complexity. All previous message-reduction schemes for LOCAL algorithms incur either an $O(\log n)$-multiplicative or an $O(\text{polylog}(n))$-additive blow-up of the round complexity.

CCS CONCEPTS

• **Theory of computation → Sparsification and spanners; Distributed algorithms.**

KEYWORDS

datasets, neural networks, gaze detection, text tagging

ACM Reference Format:
Shimon Bitton, Yuval Emek, Taisuke Izumi, and Shay Kutten. 2019. Brief Announcement: Message Reduction in the LOCAL Model is a Free Lunch. In *2019 ACM Symposium on Principles of Distributed Computing (PODC '19), July 29–August 2, 2019, Toronto, ON, Canada.* ACM, New York, NY, USA, 3 pages. https://doi.org/10.1145/3293611.3331582

1 INTRODUCTION

What is the minimum number of messages that must be sent by *distributed graph algorithms* for solving a certain task? Is there a tradeoff between the message and time complexities of such algorithms? How do the message complexity bounds depend on the exact model assumptions? These questions are among the most fundamental ones in distributed computing with a vast body of literature dedicated to their resolution.

A graph-theoretic concept that plays a key role in this regard is that of *spanners*. Introduced by Peleg and Ullman [8], an α-*spanner*, or a spanner with *stretch* bound α, of a connected graph $G = (V, E)$ is a (spanning) subgraph $H = (V, S)$ of G where the distance between any two vertices is at most α times their distance in G.[1] More general spanners are also considered, in particular, in (α, β)-*spanners*, the spanner distance between any two nodes is at most α times their distance in G plus an additive β-term, are also often considered (e.g., [5]).

Sparse spanners are known to provide the means to save on message complexity without a significant increase in the round complexity. This can be done via several classic techniques that share the following general approach: Given a communication graph $G = (V, E)$ and a distributed task $\mathcal{T}$ that should be solved in G, (1) construct an α-spanner $H = (V, S)$ of G; and (2) simulate $\mathcal{T}$ on G by communicating only over the edges of H. The crux of this approach is that if α and $|S|$ are 'small', then stage (2) typically incurs 'good' round and message bounds, respectively. In particular, the message complexity of this stage is determined by $|S|$, irrespective of the number $|E|$ of edges in the original graph G. Looking at the stage (1) approaches, however, a common thread among distributed spanner-construction algorithms are that they all send $\Omega(|E|)$ messages when running on graph $G = (V, E)$. Therefore, accounting for the messages sent during the 'preprocessing stage' of constructing the spanner H (stage (1)), the 'overall' message complexity of the algorithms resulting from the aforementioned spanner-based techniques include a seemingly inherent $\Omega(|E|)$ term. That is, the following question is at the core of spanner-based message reduction schemes: Can one avoid the (at least linear) dependence on $|E|$ in the construction of a good spanner without significantly increasing its round complexity? Despites a vast number of literatures on the distributed spanner constructionnone of them directly addresses this question.

On the positive side, an application of the result by Censor-Hillel et al.[3] or Haeupler[6] (presented there for a different model) solves

PODC '19, July 29–August 2, 2019, Toronto, ON, Canada

ACM ISBN 978-1-4503-6217-7/19/07...$15.00
https://doi.org/10.1145/3293611.3331582

[1] An equivalent definition requires that it admits a path of length at most α between any two node adjacent in G.

this question partially. Given a LOCAL algorithm with time t_1 and message complexity m_1, they derive a GOSSIP algorithm whose time complexity t is either $t = O(t_1 \log n)$ or $t = t_1 + O(polylog(n))$ and the message complexity is $m = nt_1$.[2] For algorithms with a large t_1, these simulations indeed reduce the number of messages at a negligible cost in terms of time. However, the main interest in local algorithms for the LOCAL model lies in the polylog, or even the sublog time complexity land. For such algorithms, using those schemes can increase the time complexity significantly. In particular, applying the simulations of [3, 6] to an algorithm for constructing a spanner, would yield an algorithm that is significantly less efficient than the one presented here.

1.1 Definitions and Results

Throughout, we consider a communication network represented by a connected unweighted undirected graph $G = (V, E)$ and denote $n = |V|$. The nodes of G participate in a distributed algorithm under the (fully synchronous) *LOCAL model* [7] with the following two model assumptions: (i) the nodes know an $O(1)$-approximate upper bound on $\log n$ (equivalently, a poly(n)-approximate upper bound of n) at all times ; and (ii) the graph admits *unique edge IDs* so that the ID of an edge is known to both its endpoints at all times.[3] Other than that, the nodes have no a priori knowledge of G's topology. Our main technical contribution is a new algorithm for constructing sparse spanners, called Sampler, whose guarantees are cast in the following Theorem.

Theorem 1.1. *Fix integer parameters $1 \leq k \leq \log\log n$ and $0 \leq h \leq \log n$. Algorithm* Sampler *constructs an edge set $S \subseteq E$ of size $|S| \leq \tilde{O}(n^{1+1/(2^{k+1}-1)})$ such that $H = (V, S)$ is a $O(3^k)$-spanner of G whp.*[4] [5] *The round complexity of* Sampler *is $O(3^k h)$ and its message complexity is $\tilde{O}(n^{1+1/(2^{k+1}-1)+(1/h)})$ whp.*

Utilizing the technique of implementing t-local broadcast on top of our spanner construction with parameters satisfying $1/(2^{k+1} - 1) = 1/h = c$ for any small constant $1 > c > 0$, we obtain a message-reduction scheme which reduces the message complexity of any t-round LOCAL algorithm to $\tilde{O}(tn^{1+2c})$ while keeping the $O(t)$-round running time. In addition, if the running time t is super-constant, we can improve the message reduction even further by the following two-stage algorithm: (1) Using the spanner constructed by Sampler to reduce the messages of some known LOCAL algorithm to construct an even sparser spanner; (2)(2) using the spanner constructed in stage (1) to reduce the messages of other algorithms. For example, we can use the spanner-construction algorithm of Derbel et al.[4] (which constructs a $(3, O(3^k))$-spanner H with $\tilde{O}(3^k n^{1+1/O(k)})$ edges within $O(3^k)$ rounds). By a careful parameter tuning, we show that the message complexity of any t-round LOCAL algorithm is reduced to $\tilde{O}(tn^{1+O(1/(\log t))})$ with no sacrifice of asymptotic time complexity. The performance of our message-reduction schemes are precisely stated by the following theorem:

Theorem 1.2. *Every distributed task solvable by a t-round LOCAL algorithm can be solved with any one of the following pairs of time and message complexities:*

- *$\tilde{O}(tn^{1+2/(2^{\gamma+1}-1)})$ message complexity and $O(3^\gamma t + 6^\gamma)$ round complexity for any $1 \leq \gamma \leq \log\log n$,*
- *$\tilde{O}(t^2 n^{1+1/O(\log n)})$ message complexity and $O(t)$ round complexity.*

1.2 Techniques Overview

Algorithm Sampler employs *hierarchical node sampling*, where a sampled node u in level j of the hierarchy forms the *center* of a cluster that includes (some of) its non-sampled neighbors v. An edge connecting u and v is added to the spanner. The clusters are then contracted into the nodes of the next level $j + 1$. Also added to the spanner are all incident edges of every non-center node that has no adjacent center.

This hierarchical node sampling is used also in the distributed spanner construction of Baswana and Sen [2] and similar recursive clustering techniques were used in other papers as well. Common to all these papers is that the centers in each level communicate directly with *all* their neighbors to facilitate the cluster forming task.[6] As this leads inherently to $\Omega(|E|)$ messages, we are forced to follow a different approach, also based on (a different) sampling process.

The first thing to notice in this regard is that it is enough for a non-center node v to find a *single* center u in its neighborhood, so perhaps there is no need for the center nodes to announce their status to *all* their neighbors? Indeed, we invoke an *edge sampling* process in the non-center nodes v that identifies a subset of v's incident edges over which *query* messages are sent. Our analysis shows that (1) the number of query messages is small whp; (2) if v does have an adjacent center, then the edge sampling process finds such a center whp; and (3) if v does not have an adjacent center, then v's degree is small; in this case, all its incident edges are queried and join the spanner whp.

However, this edge sampling idea by itself does not suffice: Note that the graph (in some level of the hierarchical construction) is constructed via cluster contraction (into a single node) in lower levels of the hierarchy. Hence thise graph it typically exhibits edge multiplicities (even if the original communication graph is simple). This means that some neighbors w of v may have many more (parallel) (w, v)-edges than others. Informally, this can bias the probabilities for finding additional neighbors in the edge sampling process. The key idea in resolving this issue is to run the edge sampling process (in each level) in a carefully designed *iterative* fashion. Intuitively, the first iterations in each level "peels off" the neighbors to which a large fraction of v's incident edges lead. This increases the probability of finding one of the rest of the neighbors in later iterations. Note that once v found a neighbor u, node v can identify all v's edges leading to u (and so "peel them off" from the

[2]Essentially, the GOSSIP model differ from the LOCAL one, by limiting a node to a message only to one neighbor in each round.

[3]Alternatively, the algorithm can run under the rather common KT_1 model variant [1], where the nodes are associated with unique IDs and each node knows the ID of the other endpoint of each one of its incident edges. Unique edge IDs can be simulated under KT_1.

[4]Here, an event occurs *with high probability*, abbreviated by *whp*, if the probability that it does not occur is at most n^{-c} for an arbitrarily large constant c.

[5]The asymptotic notation $\tilde{O}(\cdot)$ may hide $\log^{O(1)} n$ factors.

[6]Some of these papers consider weighted communication graphs and as such, have to deal with other issues that are spared in the current paper.

next iterations), by having u the report to v the IDs of all the edges touching u.

2 CONSTRUCTING A $O(3^k)$-SPANNER

Consider some undirected graph $G = (V, E)$, which is not necessarily simple, namely, the edge set E may include edge multiplicities (a.k.a. *parallel* edges). Given disjoint node subsets $U, U' \subseteq V$, let $E(U)$ denote the subset of edges with (exactly) one endpoint in U and let $E(U, U') = E(U) \cap E(U')$ denote the subset of edges with one endpoint in U and the other in U'.

Let $C = \{C_1, \ldots, C_\ell\}$ be a collection of non-empty pairwise disjoint node subsets referred to as *clusters* of G.[7] The *cluster graph* (cf. [7]) induced by C on G, denoted by $G(C)$, is the undirected graph whose nodes are identified with the clusters in C, and the edges connecting nodes C_i and C_j, $1 \le i \ne j \le \ell$, correspond to the edges crossing between clusters C_i and C_j in G, that is, the edges in $E(C_i, C_j)$. Observe that $G(C)$ may include edge multiplicities even if G is a simple graph.

In the following argument, let $\delta = 1/(2^{k+1} - 1)$ and $\epsilon = 1/h$ for short. Denote the simple graph input to the algorithm by $G_0 = (V_0, E_0)$. Algorithm `Sampler` generates a sequence $G_1, \ldots, G_k$ of graphs, where $G_j = (V_j, E_j)$. Let n_j and m_j be the numbers of nodes and edges in G_j respectively, $N_j(v)$ be the set of neighbors in G_j of node $v \in V_j$, and $E_j(v, u)$ be the set of edges connecting v to u in G_j. The process is executed in an iterative fashion, where in each iteration $j = 0, \ldots, k$, the algorithm constructs a collection $C \subset 2^{V_j}$ of pairwise disjoint clusters and an edge set $F \subseteq E_j$ that is added to the spanner edge set S (as an exception, in the final iteration of $j = k$, only F is constructed but the cluster collection C is not created). The graph G_{j+1} is then defined to be the cluster graph $G_j(C)$ induced by C on G_j. The construction of C and F is handled by procedure `Cluster`$_j$ that is described soon. To avoid confusion, in what follows, we fix $n = n_0 = |V_0|$.

Procedure `Cluster`$_j$*:* On input graph G_j ($0 \le j \le k$), this procedure constructs the cluster collection $C \subset 2^{V_j}$ and edge set $F = \cup_{v \in V_j} F_v$ ($F_v \subseteq E_j$) to be added to the spanner edges. The procedureconsists of two steps. In the first step, each node v tries to identify $\min\{c \exp_n(2^j\delta) \log n, |N_j(v)|\}$ neighbors by an iterative random-edge sampling process[8], where c is a sufficiently large constant to guarantee high success probability of the algorithm. For this process, v maintains a set $X_v \subseteq E_j(\{v\})$ of the edges that have not been explored yet. Initially, X_v is set to $X_v = E_j(\{v\})$; the content of X_v is then gradually eliminated by running $2/\epsilon = 2h$ *trials*. In every trial, each node $v \in V_j$ chooses $c^2 \exp_n(2^j\delta + \epsilon) \log^3 n$ edges from X_v independently and uniformly at random (possibly choosing the same edge twice or more). Each chosen edge is said to be a *query* edge. For a neighbor $u \in N_j(v)$ such that $E_j(\{v\}, \{u\})$ contains a query edge, we say that u is *queried* by v. For each queried node $u \in N_j(v)$, v adds one arbitrary query edge $e \in E_j(\{u\}, \{v\})$ to the edge set F_v, and eliminates all the edges in $E_j(\{u\}, \{v\})$ from X_v. Then the procedure advances to the next trial unless $|F_v| \ge c \exp_n(2^j\delta) \log n$ holds or X_v is emptied. Let $\hat{N}_j(v) \subseteq N_j(v)$ be the set of the nodes queried by v after finishing $2h$ trials. A node $v \in V_j$ is called *light* if $\hat{N}_j(v) = N_j(v)$ holds, or called *heavy* if $|N_j(v)| > |\hat{N}_j(v)| \ge c \exp_n(2^j\delta) \log n$. It is proved later that every node becomes either light or heavy whp.

In the second step, the algorithm creates (only if $j < k$) the vertex set V_{j+1} by clustering the nodes in V_j. The algorithm marks each node $v \in V_j$ as a *center* w.p. $p_j = \exp_n(-2^j\delta)$. Each node v having a center u contained in $\hat{N}_j(v)$ is merged into u (if two or more centers are contained, an arbitrary one is chosen). A merged cluster corresponds to a node in G_{j+1}. As a result, letting $C \subset 2^{V_j}$ be the clusters inducing the cluster graph G_{j+1}, each cluster $C = C(u) \in C$ contains exactly one center $u \in V_j$ and some subset of $N_j(u)$. The node which is not merged into any center is said to be an *unclustered* node. Due to some technical reason, all the nodes in G_k are defined to be unclustered. It is shown that every heavy node is merged into some center whp., and that every node in G_k is light. Thus, every unclustered node is light. By definition, every light node has a connection to each neighbors and thus every node in G_k, corresponding to a small-diameter cluster in G, establishes the "inter-cluster" edges connecting itself with all neighbors.

The distributed implementation of Algorithm `Sampler` relies on the observation that procedures `Cluster`$_j$ would have been naturally distributed if the nodes in $V_0, V_1, \ldots, V_k$ could have performed local computations and exchanged messages over their incident edges in $G_0, G_1, \ldots, G_k$, respectively So the main problem is how local actions in graph G_j, $1 \le j \le k$, are simulated in the actual communication graph G. It is not difficult to check that spanner edges in construction necessarily include a spanning tree of each cluster. In the distributed implementation, the local actions of node v in G_j are simulated by all the nodes (of G) in the corresponding cluster via a constant number of broadcast-convergecast sessions over the tree which spans the cluster. Spending $O(3^j)$ rounds suffices to simulate one round in G_j, Then the total running time of `Sampler` is bounded by $O(3^k h)$ rounds.

ACKNOWLEDGMENTS

This work was supported in part by JST SICORP and KAKENHI No.16H02878 and 19K11824,

REFERENCES

[1] Baruch Awerbuch, Oded Goldreich, Ronen Vainish, and David Peleg. 1990. A trade-off between information and communication in broadcast protocols. *Journal of the ACM (JACM)* 37, 2 (1990), 238–256.

[2] Surender Baswana and Sandeep Sen. 2007. A simple and linear time randomized algorithm for computing sparse spanners in weighted graphs. *Random Structures & Algorithms* 30, 4 (2007), 532–563.

[3] Keren Censor-Hillel, Bernhard Haeupler, Jonathan Kelner, and Petar Maymounkov. 2012. Global Computation in a Poorly Connected World: Fast Rumor Spreading with No Dependence on Conductance. In *Proceedings of the Forty-fourth Annual ACM Symposium on Theory of Computing (STOC)*. 961–970.

[4] Bilel Derbel, Cyril Gavoille, David Peleg, and Laurent Viennot. 2009. Local Computation of Nearly Additive Spanners. In *Proceedings of 23rd International Symposium on Distributed Computing (DISC)*. 176–190.

[5] Michael Elkin and David Peleg. 2004. $(1+\epsilon, \beta)$-Spanner Constructions for General Graphs. *SIAM J. Comput.* 33, 3 (2004), 608–631.

[6] Bernhard Haeupler. 2015. Simple, Fast and Deterministic Gossip and Rumor Spreading. *J. ACM* 62, 6 (Dec. 2015), 47:1–47:18.

[7] David Peleg. 2000. *Distributed Computing: A Locality-sensitive Approach*. Society for Industrial and Applied Mathematics, Philadelphia, PA, USA.

[8] David Peleg and Jeffrey D. Ullman. 1989. An Optimal Synchronizer for the Hypercube. *SIAM J. Comput.* 18, 4 (1989), 740–747.

[7]Notice that the union of the clusters is not required to be the whole node set V. Each cluster here will be a connected component.

[8]For ease of writing long exponents, define $\exp_a(x) = a^x$.

Brief Announcement: P-SLOCAL-Completeness of Maximum Independent Set Approximation

Yannic Maus*
yannic.maus@cs.technion.ac.il
Department of Computer Science, Technion
Haifa, Israel

ABSTRACT

We prove that the maximum independent set approximation problem with polylogarithmic approximation factor is P-SLOCAL-complete.

CCS CONCEPTS

• **Theory of computation → Distributed algorithms**; *Distributed computing models.*

KEYWORDS

SLOCAL, maximum independent set, P-SLOCAL-completeness, conflict-free multicoloring

ACM Reference Format:
Yannic Maus. 2019. Brief Announcement: P-SLOCAL-Completeness of Maximum Independent Set Approximation. In *2019 ACM Symposium on Principles of Distributed Computing (PODC '19), July 29-August 2, 2019, Toronto, ON, Canada.* ACM, New York, NY, USA, 3 pages. https://doi.org/10.1145/3293611.3331578

1 INTRODUCTION

To formally present our results we recall the model of computation.

The LOCAL *Model of distributed computing [6].* A graph is abstracted as an n-node network $G = (V, E)$ with maximum degree Δ. Communications happen in synchronous rounds. Per round, each node can send one (unbounded size) message to each of its neighbors. At the end, each node should know its own part of the output, e.g., whether it belongs to an independent set or its own color in a vertex coloring. Typically, an algorithm in the LOCAL model is considered *fast* or *efficient* if its time complexity is polylogarithmic in the number of nodes n.

The maximal independent set problem (MIS)[1] and the $(\Delta + 1)$-vertex coloring problem have fast randomized algorithms [7] and exponentially slower deterministic algorithms [1]. The question whether the MIS problem has a polylogarithmic time deterministic algorithm dates back to Linial's seminal paper [6] and is still considered to be one of the most important open questions of the area [2, 8]. With the objective to shed some light on *the role of randomness* in solving problems like MIS or vertex coloring efficiently Ghaffari, Kuhn and Maus [5] defined a sequential variant of the LOCAL model, the SLOCAL model. In an SLOCAL algorithm with complexity (or locality) r the nodes of the network graph are processed in an arbitrary order. When a node v is processed it can see the current state of all nodes in its r-hop neighborhood (including all topological information of this neighborhood) and its output can be an arbitrary function of this neighborhood. Additionally, it can store information that can be read by later nodes as part of v' state. The maximal independent set problem admits an SLOCAL algorithm with locality $r = 1$ by iterating through the nodes in an arbitrary order and joining the independent set if none of the already processed neighbors is already contained in the set. An SLOCAL algorithm with constant locality is not known for the maximum independent set problem. Then, [5] defines the class P-SLOCAL, i.e., the class of problems that can be solved with polylogarithmic complexity in the SLOCAL model. Besides MIS and vertex-coloring the class contains many other classic and related problems. In particular, it contains all problems that can be solved efficiently by randomized algorithms in the LOCAL model as long as a solution of the problem can be verified efficiently [4]. Most important for our results is the notion of P-SLOCAL-completeness: A problem is P-SLOCAL-*complete* if it is contained in the class P-SLOCAL and if it is P-SLOCAL-*hard*, that is, any other problem in the class can be efficiently reduced to it via a local reduction.[2] If any P-SLOCAL-complete problem can be solved efficiently by a deterministic algorithm in the LOCAL model all problems in the class P-SLOCAL can be solved efficiently by deterministic algorithms; this includes the MIS and vertex coloring problem.

Among few others the following are P-SLOCAL-complete problems: $(\text{poly}\log n, \text{poly}\log n)$-network decompositions, (weak) local splittings [5], approximations of dominating set and distributed set cover [4]. However, it would be most interesting if the MIS or the vertex coloring problem were shown to be complete [8]. We cannot show either one but we show that computing sufficiently good approximations for the maximum independent set problem is complete.

Theorem 1.1. *Polylogarithmic maximum independent set approximation is* P-SLOCAL*-complete.*

The proof of Theorem 1.1 is through a reduction from the conflict-free multicoloring problem, one of the first problems known to

*Supported by the European Union's Horizon 2020 Research And Innovation Programme under grant agreement no. 755839.

[1]An *MIS* of a graph $G = (V, E)$ is an inclusion maximal independent set $M \subseteq V$. A *maximum independent set (MaxIS)* is an independent set with maximum cardinality; this cardinality is denoted by the *independence number* $\alpha(G)$. A λ-approximation of a maximum independent set is an independent set of size at least $\alpha(G)/\lambda$.

[2]For the formal definitions of reductions, the model and the complexity class we refer to [5]. For this work it is sufficient to think of a reduction from problem $\mathcal{B}$ to problem $\mathcal{A}$ as a LOCAL algorithm that uses an algorithm for problem $\mathcal{A}$ to solve problem $\mathcal{B}$ while only incurring a polylogartihmic overhead.

PODC '19, July 29-August 2, 2019, Toronto, ON, Canada

ACM ISBN 978-1-4503-6217-7/19/07.
https://doi.org/10.1145/3293611.3331578

be P-SLOCAL-complete [5]. The objective of the conflict-free k-coloring problem is to compute a vertex coloring $f : V \to \{1, \dots, k\}$ of a hypergraph $H = (V, E)$ such that for each edge $e \in E$ there exists a node $v \in e$ with a unique color, that is, there is no $u \neq v$ with $u \in e$ and $f(u) = f(v)$. We call an edge with this property *happy* in coloring f—in proofs we consider colorings in which only some edges are happy. In the conflict-free multicoloring problem each node is allowed to have more than one color and all other requirements are the same. For a given constant $0 < \varepsilon \leq 1$ we call a hypergraph $H = (V, E)$ *almost uniform* if there is an arbitrary k such that for all edges $e \in E$ we have $k \leq |e| \leq (1 + \varepsilon)k$.

THEOREM 1.2 ([5]). *Conflict-free multicoloring with* poly log n *colors in almost uniform hypergraphs with* poly n *hyperedges is* P-SLOCAL*-complete.*

The unpublished work [3] uses the MaxIS to solve conflict-free coloring on so called *interval hypergraphs.* To show the P-SLOCAL-hardness of MaxIS approximations we adapt their techniques and reduce the conflict-free multicoloring problem to the problem of computing MaxIS approximations.

2 COMPLETENESS OF MAXIMUM INDEPENDENT SET APPROXIMATION

We define the *conflict graph* G_k of conflictfree k coloring a hypergraph H: The vertex set $V(G_k)$ consists of all triples (e, v, c), $e \in E(H), v \in e, 1 \leq c \leq k$. The edge set $E(G_k)$ is

$$E_{vertex} = \{\{(e, v, c), (g, v, d)\} \mid v \in V(H), 1 \leq c \neq d \leq k\} \cup$$
$$E_{edge} = \{\{(e, v, c), (e, u, d)\} \mid e \in E(H),\ u, v \in e,\ 1 \leq c, d \leq k\} \cup$$
$$E_{color} = \Big\{\{(e, v, c), (g, u, c)\} \mid e, g \in E(H),\ 1 \leq c \leq k,\ \{u, v\} \subseteq e \text{ or } \{u, v\} \subseteq g, \Big\}.$$

We explain how any independent set of G_k naturally corresponds to a partial vertex coloring of the hypergraph H and vice versa: Given an independent set I of G_k define the partial vertex coloring:

$$f : V \to \{1, \dots, k\} \cup \{\perp\},$$
$$f_I(v) = \begin{cases} c, & \exists e \text{ such that } (e, v, c) \in I, \\ \perp, & \text{otherwise} . \end{cases} \tag{1}$$

Vice versa, given a conflictfree coloring f of H with k colors we construct an independent set of G_k as follows: For each edge e we add a single node (e, v, c)—breaking ties arbitrarily—to the independent set I_f where $v \in e$, $f(v) = c$ and there is no $u \neq v$ with $u \in e$ and $f(u) = c$. More formally, we prove the following statement about the correspondence.

LEMMA 2.1. *Let $k > 0$, H be a hypergraph and G_k the conflict graph of conflictfree k-coloring H.*

a) Any conflict-free k-coloring f of H induces a maximum independent set I_f of the conflict graph G_k. The size of this maximum independent set is $m = |E(H)|$.

b) For any independent set $I \subseteq V(G_k)$ the induced coloring f_I is well defined and at least $|I|$ edges of H are happy in f_I.

PROOF. *Proof of a):* We first show by a proof of contradiction that I_f is an independent set. So, let $\mathfrak{v}_1 = (e, v, c)$ and $\mathfrak{v}_2 = (g, u, d)$ be two nodes in I_f and assume that they are connected by an edge $h \in E(G_k)$. We perform a case distinction depending on whether $h \in E_{vertex}$, $h \in E_{edge}$ or $h \in E_{color}$ and deduce a contradiction in all three cases.

$h \in E_{vertex}$: This means that $v = u$ and also that $c \neq d$. However, this would mean that edge e added node $\mathfrak{v}_1$ to I_f because v is the unique node with color c in coloring f and edge g added $\mathfrak{v}_2$ to I_f because v is the unique node with color d in coloring f, a contradiction to v having only one color in f.

$h \in E_{edge}$: This means that $e = g$, i.e., edge e added $\mathfrak{v}_1$ and $\mathfrak{v}_1$ to the independent set I_f. However, each edge only adds one node to the independent set I_f, a contradiction.

$h \in E_{color}$: This means that $c = d$, i.e., the nodes in the independent set are $\mathfrak{v}_1 = (e, v, c)$ and $\mathfrak{v}_2 = (g, u, c)$, and $\mathfrak{v}_1$ is added to I_f by edge e and $\mathfrak{v}_2$ is added to I_f by edge g. Furthermore, $\{v, u\} \subseteq e$ or $(\{v, u\} \subseteq g$ holds. Without loss of generality assume that $\{v, u\} \subseteq e$ holds. Edge g added $\mathfrak{v}_2$ to the independent set I_f because u is the only node among the nodes in edge g with color c. Edge e added $\mathfrak{v}_1$ to the independent set I_f because v is the only node among the nodes in edge e with color c in f, a contradiction as $u \in e$ and u also has color c in f.

I_f is a maximum independent set: As f is a conflictfree coloring each edge e adds one node of the form $(e, \star, \star)$ to the independent set. A node cannot be added to the independent by two distinct edges. Thus $|I_f| \geq m = |E(H)|$. Further, any independent set of G_k has at most m nodes as any node of the form $(e, \star, \star)$ in the independent set forbids any other node of that form in the independent set due to the definition of E_{edge}.

Proof of b): We first show that the color assignment in Equation (1) is well defined, that is, for each node u there is at most one c such that $(\star, u, c) \in I$. For contradiction, assume that there are two nodes $\mathfrak{v}_1$ of type $(\star, v, c)$ and $\mathfrak{v}_2$ of type $(\star, v, d)$ with $c \neq d$ in the independent set I. By E_{vertex} there is an edge in G_k between $\mathfrak{v}_1$ and $\mathfrak{v}_2$, a contradiction to both nodes being in I.

At least $|I|$ edges are happy in f_I: Let $\mathfrak{v} = (e, v, c) \in I$ be a node of the independent set. We prove that edge e is happy: Node v is colored with color c in f_I; assume that there is a further node $u \in e, u \neq v$ that is colored with color c. By the definition of f_I this means that there is some node $\mathfrak{v}' = (g, u, c)$ in the independent set. As $\{u, v\} \subseteq e$ the nodes $\mathfrak{v}$ and $\mathfrak{v}'$ are connected in G_k due to the definition of E_{color}, a contradiction. Thus for each node $(e, \star, \star) \in I$ the edge e is happy. Further, for each happy edge e there is at most one node $(e, \star, \star) \in I$ due to the definition of E_{edge}. Thus the number of happy edges equals the size of the independent set I. □

The conflict graph G_k can be efficiently simulated in H in the LOCAL model. The iterative computation of maximum independent set approximations in suitably chosen conflict graphs combined with Lemma 2.1 are sufficient to prove the hardness in Theorem 1.1.

PROOF OF THEOREM 1.1. The containment was proven in [5, Theorem 7.1].

To prove the hardness we reduce from the P-SLOCAL-complete conflictfree multicoloring problem (Theorem 1.2). Assume that we can compute λ-approximations for MaxIS and let H be a hypergraph with $m =$ poly n edges as in Theorem 1.2. First note, that the graphs used for the hardness in the proof of Theorem 1.2 all admit a conflictfree k-coloring where each node only has a single color and $k = \text{poly}\log n$; fix this k and let $\rho = \lambda \cdot \ln m + 1$. In the reduction we use phases $1, \ldots, \rho$ and in each phase we color some of the vertices in V using a distinct palette of size k for each phase; after each phase we remove all happy edges from the graph. We continue with describing the phases in more detail. For $i = 1, \ldots, \rho$ let $H_i = (V, E_i)$ denote the hypergraph in phase i where $H_1 = H = (V, E)$ is the original graph. In phase i we use the hypergraph $H_i = (V, E_i)$ to build the conflict graph G_k^i. G_k^i has polynomially many nodes and edges and can be simulated locally. Then we compute an independent set $\mathcal{I}^i$ of G_k^i that is a λ-approximation for MaxIS. Each node $v \in V(H)$ that has some $(v, \star, c) \in \mathcal{I}^i$ colors itself with color c (using a distinct palette of size k for each phase); all other nodes remain uncolored in this phase. The algorithm continues with the next phase.

We continue with analyzing the number of edges of the hypergraph that become happy, that is, are removed per phase. G_k^i has an independent set of size $|E_i|$ because of Lemma 2.1, a) and as H and also $H_i \subseteq H$ admit a conflictfree k-coloring . As $\mathcal{I}^i$ is a λ-approximation for MaxIS we obtain $|\mathcal{I}^i| \geq \frac{|E_i|}{\lambda}$. Due to Lemma 2.1, b) there is a distinct happy edge in E_i for each node in $\mathcal{I}^i$. Thus $|E_{i+1}| \leq |E_i| - |\mathcal{I}^i| \leq (1 - 1/\lambda)|E_i|$. Thus after ρ phases we have $||E_{\rho+1}| \leq (1-1/\lambda)^\rho |E| \leq e^{\frac{\rho}{\lambda}} m < 1$, i.e., all edges of the initial hypergraph H are happy and removed. Thus the obtained multicoloring is conflictfree and the total number of colors is $k \cdot \rho = \text{poly}\log n$. □

It remains open whether the MIS or the $(\Delta + 1)$ vertex coloring problem are P-SLOCAL-complete.

REFERENCES

[1] Baruch Awerbuch, Andrew V. Goldberg, Michael Luby, and Serge A. Plotkin. 1989. Network Decomposition and Locality in Distributed Computation. In *Proc. 30th Symp. on Found. of Computer Science (FOCS)*. 364–369.

[2] Leonid Barenboim and Michael Elkin. 2013. *Distributed Graph Coloring: Fundamentals and Recent Developments*. Morgan & Claypool Publishers.

[3] S. M. Dhannya and N. S. Narayanaswamy. 2018. Conflict-Free Colouring using Maximum Independent Set and Minimum Colouring. *arXiv e-prints* (2018), arXiv:1812.01459. arXiv:cs.DS/1812.01459

[4] Mohsen Ghaffari, David G. Harris, and Fabian Kuhn. 2018. On Derandomizing Local Distributed Algorithms. In *59th IEEE Annual Symposium on Foundations of Computer Science, FOCS 2018, Paris, France, October 7-9, 2018*. 662–673. DOI: https://doi.org/10.1109/FOCS.2018.00069

[5] Mohsen Ghaffari, Fabian Kuhn, and Yannic Maus. 2017. On the complexity of local distributed graph problems. ACM, 784–797.

[6] Nati Linial. 1992. Locality in Distributed Graph Algorithms. *SIAM J. Comput.* 21, 1 (1992), 193–201.

[7] Michael Luby. 1986. A Simple Parallel Algorithm for the Maximal Independent Set Problem. *SIAM J. Comput.* 15 (1986), 1036–1053.

[8] Yannic Maus. 2018. *The power of locality: exploring the limits of randomness in distributed computing*. Ph.D. Dissertation. University of Freiburg, Freiburg im Breisgau, Germany. https://freidok.uni-freiburg.de/data/16780

Engineering Distributed Systems that We Can Trust (and Also Run)

Ilya Sergey
Yale-NUS College and National University of Singapore
Singapore
ilya.sergey@yale-nus.edu.sg

ABSTRACT

The interest in formal methods and verification of correctness-critical distributed systems is on the rise in the past few years. But what are the gains from proving statements about software in full mathematical rigour? Do they justify the high cost of verification? And how far can we extend our trust in formal methods when talking about realistic distributed systems and their client programs?

This talk is in three parts. First, I will provide an overview of the state of the art in machine-assisted reasoning about distributed consensus protocols, their implementations, and applications. Next, I will discuss the trade-offs that have to be made in order to enable mechanised proofs about runnable systems code, as well as implications of the assumptions made to describe the real-world execution environments. Lastly, I will focus on the ongoing work propelled by the programming languages community towards engineering modular proofs about distributed protocols—a way to build correct-by-construction composite systems from verified reusable components.

CCS Concepts/ACM Classifiers

Theory of computation, Logic and verification; Software and its engineering, Distributed programming languages

Author Keywords

Verification; Formal Methods; Distributed Systems; Proofs; Modularity

BIOGRAPHY

Ilya Sergey is an Associate Professor at Yale-NUS College and at the School of Computing of the National University of Singapore. He was previously a faculty at University College London and a postdoctoral researcher at IMDEA Software Institute. He holds a PhD in Computer Science from KU Leuven. Before joining academia he worked as a software engineer at JetBrains. He does research in programming language theory, including, but not limited to types, semantics, software verification, and program synthesis. Lately, he has been mostly focusing on developing sound and scalable methodologies for building provably correct concurrent and distributed systems. Dr. Sergey is a recipient of a 2017 Google Faculty Award and the AITO Dahl-Nygaard Junior Prize 2019 for his contributions to the development and application of programming language techniques to various problems across the programming spectrum, covering object-oriented, functional, distributed, and concurrent programming. He has also designed and co-developed Scilla, a programming language for safe and secure smart contracts, used by Zilliqa, a Singapore blockchain start-up.

PODC '19, July 29–August 2, 2019, Toronto, ON, Canada.

ACM ISBN 978-1-4503-6670-0/19/06.
DOI: https://doi.org/10.1145/3293611.3338839

The Consensus Number of a Cryptocurrency

Rachid Guerraoui
rachid.guerraoui@epfl.ch
EPFL
Lausanne, Switzerland

Petr Kuznetsov
petr.kuznetsov@telecom-paristech.fr
LTCI, Télécom Paris, IP Paris
Paris, France

Matteo Monti
matteo.monti@epfl.ch
EPFL
Lausanne, Switzerland

Matej Pavlovič
matej.pavlovic@epfl.ch
EPFL
Lausanne, Switzerland

Dragos-Adrian Seredinschi*
dragos-adrian.seredinschi@epfl.ch
EPFL
Lausanne, Switzerland

ABSTRACT

Many blockchain-based algorithms, such as Bitcoin, implement a decentralized *asset transfer system*, often referred to as a *cryptocurrency*. As stated in the original paper by Nakamoto, at the heart of these systems lies the problem of preventing *double-spending*; this is usually solved by achieving *consensus* on the order of transfers among the participants. By treating the asset transfer problem as a *concurrent object* and determining its *consensus number*, we show that consensus is not necessary to prevent double-spending.

We first consider the problem as defined by Nakamoto, where only a single process—the account owner—can withdraw from each account. Safety and liveness need to be ensured for correct account owners, whereas misbehaving account owners might be unable to perform transfers. We show that the consensus number of an asset transfer object is 1. We then consider a more general k*-shared* asset transfer object where up to k processes can atomically withdraw from the same account, and show that this object has consensus number k.

We first establish these these results in the context of shared memory with benign faults, in order to properly understand the level of difficulty of the asset transfer problem. Then, we translate our result in the more practically relevant message passing setting with Byzantine players. We describe an asynchronous Byzantine fault-tolerant asset transfer implementation that is both simpler and more efficient than state-of-the-art consensus-based solutions. Our results are applicable to both the permissioned (private) and permissionless (public) setting, as normally their differentiation is hidden by the abstractions on top of which our algorithms are based.

CCS CONCEPTS

• **Theory of computation → Distributed algorithms.**

KEYWORDS

distributed computing, distributed asset transfer, blockchain, consensus

ACM Reference Format:
Rachid Guerraoui, Petr Kuznetsov, Matteo Monti, Matej Pavlovič, and Dragos-Adrian Seredinschi. 2019. The Consensus Number of a Cryptocurrency. In *2019 ACM Symposium on Principles of Distributed Computing (PODC'19), July 29–August 2, 2019, Toronto, ON, Canada.* ACM, New York, NY, USA, 10 pages. https://doi.org/10.1145/3293611.3331589

1 INTRODUCTION

The Bitcoin protocol, introduced in 2008 by Satoshi Nakamoto, implements a *cryptocurrency*: an electronic decentralized asset transfer system [39]. Since then, many alternatives to Bitcoin came to prominence. These include major cryptocurrencies such as Ethereum [48] or Ripple [41], as well as systems sparked from research or industry efforts such as Bitcoin-NG [18], Algorand [22], ByzCoin [33], Stellar [38], Hyperledger [4], Corda [27], or Solida [2]. Each alternative brings novel approaches to implementing decentralized transfers, and sometimes offers a more general interface (known as smart contracts [44]) than the original protocol proposed by Nakamoto. They improve over Bitcoin in various aspects, such as performance, energy-efficiency, or security.

A common theme in these protocols, whether they are for basic transfers [34] or smart contracts [48], is that they seek to implement a *blockchain*—a distributed ledger where all the transfers in the system are totally ordered. Achieving total order among multiple inputs (e.g., transfers) is fundamentally a hard task, equivalent to solving *consensus* [26, 28]. Consensus [19], a central problem in distributed computing, is known for its notorious difficulty. It has no deterministic solution in asynchronous systems if just a single participant can fail [19]. Partially synchronous consensus algorithms are tricky to implement correctly [1, 12, 15] and face tough trade-offs between performance, security, and energy-efficiency [5, 8, 24, 47]. Not surprisingly, the consensus module is a major bottleneck in blockchain-based protocols [27, 43, 47].

A closer look at Nakamoto's original paper reveals, however, that the major issue in implementing a decentralized asset transfer system (i.e., a cryptocurrency) is preventing *double-spending*, i.e., spending the same money more than once [39]. Bitcoin and numerous follow-up systems typically assume that total order—and thus consensus—is vital to preventing double-spending [20].

*This work has been supported in part by the European ERC Grant 339539 - AOC.

PODC '19, July 29–August 2, 2019, Toronto, ON, Canada

ACM ISBN 978-1-4503-6217-7/19/07...$15.00
https://doi.org/10.1145/3293611.3331589

There seems to be a common belief, indeed, that a consensus algorithm is essential for implementing decentralized asset transfers [9, 24, 32, 39].

We show that this belief is false by casting the asset transfer problem as a *sequential object type* and determining that it has *consensus number* 1 in Herlihy's hierarchy [28].[1]

The intuition is the following. An asset transfer object maintains a set of accounts. Each account is associated with an *owner* process that is the only one allowed to issue transfers withdrawing from this account. Every process can however read the balance of any account.

The main insight here is that relating accounts to unique owners obviates the need for consensus. It is the owner that decides on the order of transfers from its own account, without the need to agree with any other process—thus the consensus number 1. Other processes only validate the owner's decisions, ensuring that causal relations across accounts are respected. We describe a simple asset transfer implementation using atomic-snapshot memory [3]. A withdrawal from an account is validated by relating the withdrawn amount with the incoming transfers found in the memory snapshot. Intuitively, as at most one withdrawal can be active on a given account at a time, it is safe to declare the validated operation as successful and post it in the snapshot memory.

We then present a natural generalization of our result to the setting in which multiple processes are allowed to withdraw from the same account. A k*-shared* asset-transfer object allows up to k processes to execute outgoing transfers from the same account. We prove that such an object has consensus number k and thus allows for implementing *state machine replication* (now often referred to as *smart contracts*) among the k involved processes using k-consensus objects [31]. We show that k-shared asset transfer has consensus number k by reducing it to k-consensus (known to have consensus number k) and reducing k-consensus to asset transfer.

Having established the relative ease of the asset transfer problem using the shared memory model, we present a real practical solution to this problem in the setting of Byzantine fault-prone processes communicating via message passing, arguably better suited for realistically deployable distributed systems. We describe an asset transfer implementation that does not resort to consensus. Instead, the implementation relies on a *secure broadcast* primitive that ensures uniform reliable delivery with only weak ordering guarantees [36, 37], circumventing hurdles imposed by consensus. In the k-shared case, discussed in detail in the full version of this paper [23], our results imply that to execute some form of *smart contract* involving k users, consensus is only needed among these k nodes and not among all nodes in the system. In particular, should these k nodes be faulty, the rest of the accounts will not be affected.

To summarize, we argue that treating the asset transfer problem as a concurrent data structure and measuring its hardness through the lense of distributed computing help understand it and devise better solutions to it.

The rest of this paper is organized as follows. We first give the formal definition of the shared memory model and the asset transfer object type (Section 2). Then, we show that it has consensus number 1 (Section 3). Next, we generalize our result by proving that a k-shared asset transfer object has consensus number k (Section 4). Finally, we describe the implications of our results in the message passing model with Byzantine faults (Section 5) and discuss related work (Section 6).

[1]The consensus number of an object type is the maximal number of processes that can solve consensus using only read-write shared memory and arbitrarily many objects of this type.

2 SHARED MEMORY MODEL AND ASSET-TRANSFER OBJECT TYPE

We now present the shared memory model (Section 2.1) and precisely define the problem of asset-transfer as a sequential object type (Section 2.2).

2.1 Definitions

Processes. We assume a set Π of N asynchronous processes that communicate by invoking atomic operations on shared memory objects. Processes are sequential—we assume that a process never invokes a new operation before obtaining a response from a previous one.

Object types. A sequential object type is defined as a tuple $T = (Q, q_0, O, R, \Delta)$, where Q is a set of states, $q_0 \in Q$ is an initial state, O is a set of operations, R is a set of responses and $\Delta \subseteq Q \times \Pi \times O \times Q \times R$ is a relation that associates a state, a process identifier and an operation to a set of possible new states and corresponding responses. We assume that Δ is total on the first three elements.

A *history* is a sequence of invocations and responses, each invocation or response associated with a process identifier. A *sequential history* is a history that starts with an invocation and in which every invocation is immediately followed with a response associated with the same process. A sequential history is *legal* if its invocations and responses respect the relation Δ for some sequence of state assignments.

Implementations. An *implementation* of an object type T is a distributed algorithm that, for each process and invoked operation, prescribes the actions that the process needs to take to perform it. An *execution* of an implementation is a sequence of *events*: invocations and responses of operations or atomic accesses to shared abstractions. The sequence of events at every process must respect the algorithm assigned to it.

Failures. Processes are subject to *crash* failures (we consider more general Byzantine failures in the next section). A process may halt prematurely, in which case we say that the process is *crashed*. A process is called *faulty* if it crashes during the execution. A process is *correct* if it is not faulty. All algorithms we present in the shared memory model are *wait-free*—every correct process eventually returns from each operation it invokes, regardless of an arbitrary number of other processes crashing or concurrently invoking operations.

Linearizability. For each pattern of operation invocations, the execution produces a *history*, i.e., a sequence of distinct invocations and responses, labelled with process identifiers and unique sequence numbers.

A projection of a history H to process p, denoted $H|p$ is the subsequence of elements of H labelled with p. An invocation o by a process p is *incomplete* in H if it is not followed by a response in $H|p$. A history is *complete* if it has no incomplete invocations.

A *completion* of H is a history $\bar{H}$ that is identical to H except that every incomplete invocation in H is either removed or *completed* by inserting a matching response somewhere after it.

An invocation o_1 *precedes* an invocation o_2 in H, denoted $o_1 <_H o_2$, if o_1 is complete and the corresponding response r_1 precedes o_2 in H. Note that $<_H$ stipulates a partial order on invocations in H. A *linearizable* implementation (also said an *atomic object*) of type T ensures that for every history H it produces, there exists a completion $\bar{H}$ and a legal sequential history S such that (1) for all processes p, $\bar{H}|p = S|p$ and (2) $<_H \subseteq <_S$.

Consensus number. The problem of *consensus* consists for a set of processes to *propose* values and *decide* on the proposed values so that no two processes decide on defferent values and every correct process decides. The *consensus number* of a type T is the maximal number of processes that can solve consensus using atomic objects of type T and read-write registers.

2.2 The asset transfer object type

Let $\mathcal{A}$ be a set of *accounts* and $\mu : \mathcal{A} \rightarrow 2^{\Pi}$ be an "owner" map that associates each account with a set of processes that are, intuitively, allowed to debit the account. We define the asset-transfer object type associated with $\mathcal{A}$ and μ as a tuple (Q, q_0, O, R, Δ), where:

- The set of states Q is the set of all possible maps $q : \mathcal{A} \rightarrow \mathbb{N}$. Intuitively, each state of the object assigns each account its *balance*.
- The initialization map $q_0 : \mathcal{A} \rightarrow \mathbb{N}$ assigns the initial balance to each account.
- Operations and responses of the type are defined as $O = \{transfer(a, b, x) : a, b \in \mathcal{A}, x \in \mathbb{N}\} \cup \{read(a) : a \in \mathcal{A}\}$ and $R = \{true, false\} \cup \mathbb{N}$.
- Δ is the set of valid state transitions. For a state $q \in Q$, a process $p \in \Pi$, an operation $o \in O$, a response $r \in R$ and a new state $q' \in Q$, the tuple $(q, p, o, q', r) \in \Delta$ if and only if one of the following conditions is satisfied:
  - $o = transfer(a, b, x) \land p \in \mu(a) \land q(a) \geq x \land q'(a) = q(a) - x \land q'(b) = q(b) + x \land \forall c \in \mathcal{A} \setminus \{a, b\} : q'(c) = q(c)$ (all other accounts unchanged) $\land\ r = true$;
  - $o = transfer(a, b, x) \land (p \notin \mu(a) \lor q(a) < x) \land q' = q \land r = false$;
  - $o = read(a) \land q = q' \land r = q(a)$.

In other words, operation *transfer*(a, b, x) invoked by process p *succeeds* if and only if p is the owner of the source account a and account a has enough balance, and if it does, x is transferred from a to the destination account b. A *transfer*(a, b, x) operation is called *outgoing* for a and *incoming* for b; respectively, the x units are called *outgoing* for a and *incoming* for b. A transfer is *successful* if its corresponding response is *true* and *failed* if its corresponding response is *false*. Operation *read*(a) simply returns the balance of a and leaves the account balances untouched.

As in Nakamoto's original paper [39] we assume for the moment that an asset-transfer object has at most one owner per account: $\forall a \in \mathcal{A} : |\mu(a)| \leq 1$. Later we lift this assumption and consider more general k-shared asset-transfer objects with arbitrary owner maps μ (Section 4). For the sake of simplicity, we also restrict ourselves to transfers with a single source account and a single destination account. However, our definition (and implementation) of the asset-transfer object type can trivially be extended to support transfers with multiple source accounts (all owned by the same sequential process) and multiple destination accounts.

3 ASSET TRANSFER HAS CONSENSUS NUMBER 1

In this section, we show that the asset-transfer type can be wait-free implemented using only read-write registers in a shared memory system with crash failures. Thus, the type has consensus number 1 [28].

Consider an asset-transfer object associated with a set of accounts $\mathcal{A}$ and an ownership map μ where $\forall a \in \mathcal{A}, |\mu(a)| \leq 1$. Our implementation is described in Figure 1. Every process p is associated with a distinct location in an atomic snapshot object [3] storing the set of all successful *transfer* operations executed by p so far. Since each account is owned by at most one process, all outgoing transfers for an account appear in a single location of the atomic snapshot (associated with the owner process). This principle bears a similarity to the implementation of a counter object.

Recall that the atomic snapshot (AS) memory is represented as a vector of N shared variables that can be accessed with two atomic operations: *update* and *snapshot*. An *update* operation modifies the value at a given position of the vector and a *snapshot* returns the state of the whole vector. We implement the *read* and *transfer* operations as follows.

- To read the balance of an account a, the process simply takes a snapshot S and returns the initial balance plus the sum of incoming amounts minus the sum of all outgoing amounts. We denote this number by *balance*(a, S). As we argue below, the result is guaranteed to be non-negative, i.e., the operation is correct with respect to the type specification.
- To perform *transfer*(a, b, x), a process p, the owner of a, takes a snapshot S and computes *balance*(a, S). If the amount to be transferred does not exceed *balance*(a, S), we add the transfer operation to the set of p's operations in the snapshot

```
Shared variables:
  AS, atomic snapshot, initially {⊥}^N

Local variables:
  ops_p ⊆ A × A × N, initially ∅

Upon transfer(a, b, x)
  S = AS.snapshot()
  if p ∉ μ(a) ∨ balance(a, S) < x then
    return false
  ops_p = ops_p ∪ {(a, b, x)}
  AS.update(ops_p)
  return true

Upon read(a)
  S = AS.snapshot()
  return balance(a, S)
```

Figure 1: Wait-free implementation of asset-transfer: code for process p

object via an *update* operation and return *true*. Otherwise, the operation returns *false*.

THEOREM 1. *The asset-transfer object type has a wait-free implementation in the read-write shared memory model.*

PROOF. Fix an execution E of the algorithm in Figure 1. Atomic snapshots can be wait-free implemented in the read-write shared memory model [3]. As every operation only involves a finite number of atomic snapshot accesses, every process completes each of the operations it invokes in a finite number of its own steps.

Let *Ops* be the set of:

- All invocations of *transfer* or *read* in E that returned, and
- All invocations of *transfer* in E that completed the *update* operation (line 5).

Let H be the history of E. We define a completion of H and, for each $o \in Ops$, we define a linearization point as follows:

- If o is a *read* operation, it linearizes at the linearization point of the *snapshot* operation in line 7.
- If o is a *transfer* operation that returns *false*, it linearizes at the linearization point of the *snapshot* operation in line 1.
- If o is a *transfer* operation that completed the *update* operation, it linearizes at the linearization point of the *update* operation in line 5. If o is incomplete in H, we complete it with response *true*.

Let $\bar{H}$ be the resulting complete history and let L be the sequence of complete invocations of $\bar{H}$ in the order of their linearization points in E. Note that, by the way we linearize invocations, the linearization of a prefix of E is a prefix of L.

Now we show that L is legal and, thus, H is linearizable. We proceed by induction, starting with the empty (trivially legal) prefix of L. Let L_ℓ be the legal prefix of the first ℓ invocations and *op* be the $(\ell + 1)$st operation of L. Let *op* be invoked by process p. The following cases are possible:

- *op* is a *read*(a): the snapshot taken at the linearization point of *op* contains all successful transfers concerning a in L_ℓ. By the induction hypothesis, the resulting balance is non-negative.
- *op* is a failed *transfer*(a, b, x): the snapshot taken at the linearization point of *op* contains all successful transfers concerning a in L_ℓ. By the induction hypothesis, the resulting balance is non-negative.
- *op* is a successful *transfer*(a, b, x): by the algorithm, before the linearization point of *op*, process p took a snapshot. Let L_k, $k \leq \ell$, be the prefix of L_ℓ that only contain operations linearized before the point in time when the snapshot was taken by p.

  We observe that L_k includes a *subset* of all incoming transfers on a and *all* outgoing transfers on a in L_ℓ. Indeed, as p is the owner of a and only the owner of a can perform outgoing transfers on a, all outgoing transfers in L_ℓ were linearized before the moment p took the snapshot within *op*. Thus, *balance*(a, L_k) $\leq$ *balance*(a, L_ℓ).[2]

  By the algorithm, as *op* = *transfer*(a, b, x) succeeds, we have *balance*(a, L_k) $\geq x$. Thus, *balance*(a, L_ℓ) $\geq x$ and the resulting balance in $L_{\ell+1}$ is non-negative.

Thus, H is linearizable. □

[2] Analogously to *balance*(a, S) that computes the balance for account a based on the transfers contained in snapshot S, *balance*(a, L), if L is a sequence of operations, computes the balance of account a based on all transfers in L.

```
Shared variables:
  R[i], i ∈ 1, ..., k, k registers, initially R[i] = ⊥, ∀i
  AT, k-shared asset-transfer object containing:
      - an account a with initial balance 2k
        owned by processes 1, ..., k
      - some account s

Upon propose(v):
1   R[p].write(v)
2   AT.transfer(a, s, 2k − p))
3   return R[AT.read(a)].read()
```

Figure 2: Wait-free implementation of consensus among k processes using a k-shared asset-transfer object. Code for process $p \in \{1, \ldots, k\}$.

COROLLARY 1. *The asset-transfer object type has consensus number* 1.

4 k-SHARED ASSET TRANSFER HAS CONSENSUS NUMBER k

We now consider the case with an arbitrary owner map μ. We show that an asset-transfer object's consensus number is the maximal number of processes sharing an account. More precisely, the consensus number of an asset-transfer object is $\max_{a \in \mathcal{A}} |\mu(a)|$.

We say that an asset-transfer object, defined on a set of accounts $\mathcal{A}$ with an ownership map μ, is *k-shared* iff $\max_{a \in \mathcal{A}} |\mu(a)| = k$. In other words, the object is k-shared if μ allows at least one account to be owned by k processes, and no account is owned by more than k processes.

We show that the consensus number of any k-shared asset-transfer object is k, which generalizes our result in Corollary 1. We first show that such an object has consensus number *at least* k by implementing consensus for k processes using only registers and an instance of k-shared asset-transfer. We then show that k-shared asset-transfer has consensus number *at most* k by reducing it to k-consensus, an object known to have consensus number k [31].

LEMMA 1. *Consensus has a wait-free implementation for k processes in the read-write shared memory model equipped with a single k-shared asset-transfer object.*

PROOF. We now provide a wait-free algorithm that solves consensus among k processes using only registers and an instance of k-shared asset-transfer. The algorithm is described in Figure 2. Intuitively, k processes use one shared account a to elect one of them whose input value will be decided. Before a process p accesses the shared account, p announces its input in a register (line 1). Process p then tries to perform a transfer from account a to another account. The amount withdrawn this way from account a is chosen specifically such that:

(1) only one transfer operation can ever succeed, and
(2) if the transfer succeeds, the remaining balance on a will uniquely identify process p.

To satisfy the above conditions, we initialize the balance of account a to $2k$ and have each process $p \in \{1, \ldots, k\}$ transfer $2k-p$ (line 2). Note that transfer operations invoked by distinct processes $p, q \in \{1, \ldots, k\}$ have arguments $2k-p$ and $2k-q$, and $2k-p+2k-q \geq 2k-k+2k-(k-1) = 2k+1$. The initial balance of a is only $2k$ and no incoming transfers are ever executed. Therefore, the first transfer operation to be applied to the object succeeds (no transfer tries to withdraw more then $2k$) and the remaining operations will have to fail due to insufficient balance.

When p reaches line 3, at least one transfer must have succeeded:

(1) either p's transfer succeeded, or
(2) p's transfer failed due to insufficient balance, in which case some other process must have previously succeeded.

Let q be the process whose transfer succeeded. Thus, the balance of account a is $2k - (2k-q) = q$. Since q performed a transfer operation, by the algorithm, q must have previously written its proposal to the register $R[q]$. Regardless of whether $p = q$ or $p \neq q$, reading the balance of account a returns q and p decides the value of $R[q]$. □

To prove that k-shared asset-transfer has consensus number at most k, we reduce k-shared asset-transfer to k-consensus. A k-consensus object exports a single operation *propose* that, the first k times it is invoked, returns the argument of the first invocation. All subsequent invocations return $\perp$. Given that k-consensus is known to have consensus number exactly k [31], a wait-free algorithm implementing k-shared asset-transfer using only registers and k-consensus objects implies that the consensus number of k-shared asset-transfer is not more than k.

The algorithm reducing k-shared asset-transfer to k-consensus is given in Figure 3. Before presenting a formal correctness argument, we first informally explain the intuition of the algorithm. In our reduction, we associate a series of k-consensus objects with every account a. Up to k owners of a use the k-consensus objects to agree on the order of outgoing transfers for a.

We maintain the state of the implemented k-shared asset-transfer object using an atomic snapshot object *AS*. Every process p uses a distinct entry of *AS* to store a set *hist*. *hist* is a subset of all completed outgoing transfers from accounts that p owns (and thus is allowed to debit). For example, if p is the owner of accounts d and e, p's *hist* contains outgoing transfers from d and e. Each element in the *hist* set is represented as $((a, b, x, s, r), \mathit{result})$, where a, b, and x are the respective source account, destination account, and the amount transferred, s is the originator of the transfer, and r is the *round* in which the transfer was invoked by the originator. The value of $\mathit{result} \in \{\texttt{success}, \texttt{failure}\}$ indicates whether the transfer succeeds or fails. A transfer becomes "visible" when any process inserts it in its corresponding entry of *AS*.

To read the balance of account a, a process takes a snapshot of *AS*, and then sums the initial balance $q_0(a)$ and amounts of all successful incoming transfers, and subtracts the amounts of successful outgoing transfers found in *AS*. We say that a successful transfer tx is in a snapshot *AS* (denoted by $(tx, \texttt{success}) \in AS$) if there exists an entry e in *AS* such that $(tx, \texttt{success}) \in AS[e]$.

To execute a transfer o outgoing from account a, a process p first announces o in a register R_a that can be written by p and read by

```
Shared variables:
  AS, atomic snapshot object
  for each a ∈ 𝒜:
    R_a[i], i ∈ Π, registers, initially [⊥, ..., ⊥]
    kC_a[i], i ≥ 0, list of instances of k-consensus objects

Local variables:
    hist: a set of completed trasfers, initially empty
  for each a ∈ 𝒜:
    committed_a, initially ∅
    round_a, initially 0

Upon transfer(a, b, x):
  if p ∉ μ(a) then
    return false
  tx = (a, b, x, p, round_a)
  R_a[p].write(tx)
  collected = collect(a) \ committed_a
  while tx ∈ collected do
    req = the oldest transfer in collected
    prop = proposal(req, AS.snapshot())
    decision = kC_a[round_a].propose(prop)
    hist = hist ∪ {decision}
    AS.update(hist)
    committed_a = committed_a ∪ {t : decision = (t, *)}
    collected = collected \ committed_a
    round_a = round_a + 1
  if (tx, success) ∈ hist then
    return true
  else
    return false

Upon read(a):
  return balance(a, AS.snapshot())

collect(a):
  collected = ∅
  for all i = Π do
    if R_a[i].read() ≠ ⊥ then
      collected = collected ∪ {R_a[i].read()}
  return collected

proposal((a, b, q, x), snapshot):
  if balance(a, snapshot) ≥ x then
    prop = ((a, b, q, x), success)
  else
    prop = ((a, b, q, x), failure)
  return prop

balance(a, snapshot):
  incoming = {tx : tx = (*, a, *, *, *) ∧ (tx, success) ∈ snapshot}
  outgoing = {tx : tx = (a, *, *, *, *) ∧ (tx, success) ∈ snapshot}
  return q_0(a) + (Σ_{(*, a, x, *, *)∈incoming} x) − (Σ_{(a, *, x, *, *)∈outgoing} x)
```

Figure 3: Wait-free implementation of a k-shared asset-transfer object using k-consensus objects. Code for process p.

any other process. This enables a "helping" mechanism needed to ensure wait-freedom to the owners of a [28].

Next, p collects the transfers proposed by other owners and tries to agree on the order of the collected transfers and their results using a series of k-consensus objects. For each account, the agreement on the order of transfer-result pairs proceeds in rounds. Each round is associated with a k-consensus object which p invokes with a proposal chosen from the set of collected transfers. Since each process, in each round, only invokes the k-consensus object once, no k-consensus object is invoked more than k times and thus each invocation returns a value (and not $\perp$).

A transfer-result pair as a proposal for the next instance of k-consensus is chosen as follows. Process p picks the "oldest" collected but not yet committed operation (based on the round number $round_a$ attached to the transfer operation when a process announces it; ties are broken using process IDs). Then p takes a snapshot of *AS* and checks whether account a has sufficient balance according to the state represented by the snapshot, and equips the transfer with a corresponding `success` / `failure` flag. The resulting transfer-result pair constitutes p's proposal for the next instance of k-consensus. The currently executed transfer by process p returns as soon as it is decided by a k-consensus object, the flag of the decided value (*success*/*failure*) indicating the transfer's response (*true*/*false*).

Lemma 2. *The k-shared asset-transfer object type has a wait-free implementation in the read-write shared memory model equipped with k-consensus objects.*

Proof. We essentially follow the footpath of the proof of Theorem 1. Fix an execution E of the algorithm in Figure 3. Let H be the history of E.

To perform a transfer o on an account a, p *registers* it in $R_a[p]$ (line 4) and then proceeds through a series of k-consensus objects, each time collecting R_a to learn about the transfers concurrently proposed by other owners of a. Recall that each k-consensus object is wait-free. Suppose, by contradiction, that o is registered in R_a but is never decided by any instance of k-consensus. Eventually, however, o becomes the request with the lowest round number in R_a and, thus, some instance of k-consensus will be only accessed with o as a proposed value (line 9). By validity of k-consensus, this instance will return o and, thus, p will be able to complete o.

Let *Ops* be the set of all complete operations and all *transfer* operations o such that some process completed the update operation (line 11) in E with an argument including o (the atomic snapshot and k-consensus operation has been linearized). Intuitively, we include in *Ops* all operations that *took effect*, either by returning a response to the user or by affecting other operations. Recall that every such *transfer* operation was agreed upon in an instance of k-consensus, let it be kC^o. Therefore, for every such *transfer* operation o, we can identify the process q^o whose proposal has been decided in that instance.

We now determine a completion of H and, for each $o \in Ops$, we define a linearization point as follows:

- If o is a *read* operation, it linearizes at the linearization point of the snapshot operation (line 19).
- If o is a *transfer* operation that returns *false*, it linearizes at the linearization point of the snapshot operation (line 8) performed by q^o just before it invoked kC^o.*propose*().
- If o is a *transfer* operation that some process included in the update operation (line 11), it linearizes at the linearization point of the *first* update operation in H (line 11) that includes o. Furthermore, if o is incomplete in H, we complete it with response *true*.

Let $\bar{H}$ be the resulting complete history and let L be the sequence of complete operations of $\bar{H}$ in the order of their linearization points in E. Note that, by the way we linearize operations, the linearization of a prefix of E is a prefix of L. Also, by construction, the linearization point of an operation belongs to its interval.

Now we show that L is legal and, thus, H is linearizable. We proceed by induction, starting with the empty (trivially legal) prefix of L. Let L_ℓ be the legal prefix of the first ℓ operation and *op* be the $(\ell + 1)$st operation of L. Let *op* be invoked by process p. The following cases are possible:

- *op* is a *read*(a): the snapshot taken at *op*'s linearization point contains all successful transfers concerning a in L_ℓ. By the induction hypothesis, the resulting balance is non-negative.
- *op* is a failed *transfer*(a, b, x): the snapshot taken at the linearization point of *op* contains all successful transfers concerning a in L_ℓ. By the induction hypothesis, the balance corresponding to this snapshot non-negative. By the algorithm, the balance is less than x.
- *op* is a successful *transfer*(a, b, x). Let L_s, $s \leq \ell$, be the prefix of L_ℓ that only contains operations linearized before the moment of time when q^o has taken the snapshot just before accessing kC^o.
  As before accessing kC^o, q went through all preceding k-consensus objects associated with a and put the decided values in *AS*, L_s must include *all* outgoing *transfer* operations for a. Furthermore, L_s includes a *subset* of all incoming transfers on a. Thus, $balance(a, L_k) \leq balance(a, L_\ell)$.
  By the algorithm, as $op = transfer(a, b, x)$ succeeds, we have $balance(a, L_k) \geq x$. Thus, $balance(a, L_\ell) \geq x$ and the resulting balance in $L_{\ell+1}$ is non-negative.

Thus, H is linearizable. □

Theorem 2. *A k-shared asset-transfer object has consensus number k.*

Proof. It follows directly from Lemma 1 that k-shared asset-transfer has consensus number at least k. Moreover, it follows from Lemma 2 that k-shared asset-transfer has consensus number at most k. Thus, the consensus number of k-shared asset-transfer is exactly k. □

5 ASSET TRANSFER IN MESSAGE PASSING

We established our theoretical results in a shared memory system with crash failures, proving that consensus is not necessary for implementing an asset transfer system. Moreover, a natural generalization of such a system where up to k processes have access to atomic operations on the same account has consensus number k. These results help us understand the level of difficulty of certain problems in the domain of cryptocurrencies. To achieve a practical impact, however, we need an algorithm deployable as a distributed system in a realistic setting. Arguably, such a setting is one where processes (some of which are potentially malicious) communicate by exchanging messages.

In this section we overview an extension of our results to the message passing system with Byzantine failures. Instead of consensus, we rely on a *secure broadcast* primitive that provides reliable delivery with weak (weaker than FIFO) ordering guarantees [37]. Using secure broadcast, processes announce their transfers to the rest of the system. We establish *dependencies* among these transfers that induce a partial order. Using a method similar to (a weak form of) vector clocks [30], we make sure that each process applies the transfers respecting this dependency-induced partial order. In a nutshell, a transfer only depends on all previous transfers outgoing from the same account, and on a subset of transfers incoming to that account. Each transfer operation corresponds to one invocation of secure broadcast by the corresponding account's owner. The message being broadcast carries, in addition to the transfer itself, references to the transfer's dependencies.

As secure broadcast only provides liveness if the sender is correct, faulty processes might not be able to perform any transfers. However, due to secure broadcast's delivery properties, the correct processes will always have a consistent view of the system state.

Every transfer operation only entails a single invocation of secure broadcast and our algorithm does not send any additional messages. Our algorithm inherits the complexity from the underlying secure broadcast implementation, and there is plenty of such algorithms optimizing complexity metrics for various settings [10, 11, 21, 26, 36, 37, 46]. In practice, as shown by a preliminary deployment based on a naive quadratic secure broadcast implementation [10] in a medium-sized system (up to 100 processes), our solution outperforms a consensus-based one by $1.5x$ to $6x$ in throughput and by up to $2x$ in latency.

The implementation can be further extended to solve the k-*shared* asset transfer problem. As we showed in Section 4, agreement among a subset of the processes is necessary in such case. We associate each account (owned by up to k processes) with a Byzantine-fault tolerant state machine replication (BFT) service executed by the owners [13] of that account. The BFT service assigns sequence numbers to transfers which the processes then submit to an extended version of the above-mentioned transfer protocol. As long as the replicated state machine is safe and live, we guarantee that every invoked transfer operation eventually returns. If an account becomes compromised (i.e., the safety or liveness of the BFT is violated), only the corresponding account might lose liveness. In other words, outgoing transfers from the compromised account may not return, while safety and liveness of transfers from "healthy" accounts are always guaranteed. For more details see the extended version of this paper [23].

In the rest of this section, we give details on the Byzantine message passing model, adapt our asset-transfer object accordingly (Sec. 5.1) and present its broadcast-based implementation (Sec. 5.2).

5.1 Byzantine Message Passing Model

A process is Byzantine if it deviates from the algorithm it is assigned, either by halting prematurely, in which case we say that the process is *crashed*, or performing actions that are not prescribed by its algorithm, in which case we say that the process is *malicious*. Malicious processes can perform arbitrary actions, except for ones that involve subverting cryptographic primitives (e.g. inverting secure hash functions). A process is called *faulty* if it is either crashed or malicious. A process is *correct* if it is not faulty and *benign* if it is not malicious. Note that every correct process is benign, but not necessarily vice versa.

We only require that the transfer system behaves correctly towards *benign* processes, regardless of the behavior of Byzantine ones. Informally, we want to require that no benign process can be a victim of a double-spending attack, i.e., every execution appears to benign processes as a correct sequential execution, respecting the original execution's real-time ordering [28].

For the sake of efficiency, in our algorithm, we slightly relax the last requirement—while still preventing double-spending. We require that *successful transfer* operations invoked by benign processes constitute a legal sequential history that preserves the real-time order. A *read* or a failed *transfer* operation invoked by a benign process p can be "outdated"—it can be based on a stale state of p's balance. Informally, one can view the system requirements as *linearizability* [29] for successful transfers and *sequential consistency* [6] for failed transfers and reads. One can argue that this relaxation incurs little impact on the system's utility, since all incoming transfers are eventually applied. As progress (liveness) guarantees, we require that every operation invoked by a correct process eventually completes.

Definition 1. *Let E be any execution of an implementation and H be the corresponding history. Let $ops(H)$ denote the set of operations in H that were executed by correct processes in E. An asset-transfer object in message passing guarantees that each invocation issued by a correct process is followed by a matching response in H, and that there exists $\bar{H}$, a completion of H, such that:*

1. *Let $\bar{H}^t$ denote the sub-history of successful transfers of $\bar{H}$ performed by correct processes and $<^t_{\bar{H}}$ be the subset of $<_{\bar{H}}$ restricted to operations in $\bar{H}^t$. Then there exists a legal sequential history S such that (a) for every correct process p, $\bar{H}^t|p = S|p$ and (b) $<^t_{\bar{H}} \subseteq <_S$.*
2. *For every correct process p, there exists a legal sequential history S_p such that:*
   - *$ops(\bar{H}) \subseteq ops(S_p)$, and*
   - *$S_p|p = \bar{H}|p$.*

Notice that property (2) implies that every update in H that affects the account of a correct process p is eventually included in p's "local" history and, therefore, will reflect reads and transfer operations subsequently performed by p.

5.2 Asset Transfer Implementation in Message Passing

Instead of consensus, we rely on a secure broadcast primitive that is strictly weaker than consensus and has a fully asynchronous implementation. It provides uniform reliable delivery despite Byzantine faults and so-called *source order* among delivered messages. The source order property, being even weaker than FIFO, guarantees that messages from the same source are delivered in the same order by all correct processes. More precisely, the secure broadcast primitive we use in our implementation has the following properties [37]:

- **Integrity:** A benign process delivers a message m from a process p at most once and, if p is benign, only if p previously broadcast m.
- **Agreement:** If processes p and q are correct and p delivers m, then q delivers m.
- **Validity:** If a correct process p broadcasts m, then p delivers m.
- **Source order:** If p and q are benign and both deliver m from r and m' from r, then they do so in the same order.

Operation. To perform a transfer tx, a process p securely broadcasts a message with the transfer details: the arguments of the *transfer* operation (see Section 2.2) and some metadata. The metadata includes a per-process *sequence number* of tx and references to the *dependencies* of tx. The dependencies are transfers incoming to p that must be known to any process before applying tx. These dependencies impose a causal relation between transfers that must be respected when transfers are being applied. For example, suppose that process p makes a transfer tx to process q and q, after observing tx, performs another transfer tx' to process r. q's broadcast message will contain tx', a local sequence number, and a reference to tx. Any process (not only r) will only evaluate the validity of tx' after having applied tx. This approach is similar to using vector clocks for implementing causal order among events [30].

To ensure the authenticity of operations—so that no process is able to debit another process's account—we assume that processes sign all their messages before broadcasting them. In practice, similar to Bitcoin and other transfer systems, every process possesses a public-private key pair that allows only p to securely initiate transfers from its corresponding account. For simplicity of presentation, we omit this mechanism in the algorithm pseudocode.

Figure 4 describes the full algorithm implementing asset-transfer in a Byzantine-prone message passing system. Each process p maintains, for each process q, an integer *seq*$[q]$ reflecting the number of transfers which process q initiated and which process p has validated and applied. Process p also maintains, for every process q, an integer *rec*$[q]$ reflecting the number of transfers process q has initiated and process p has delivered (but not necessarily applied).

Additionally, there is also a list *hist*$[q]$ of transfers which *involve* process q. We say that a transfer operation involves a process q if that transfer is either outgoing or incoming on the account of q. Each process p maintains as well a local variable *deps*. This is a set of transfers *incoming* for p that p has applied since the last successful *outgoing* transfer. Finally, the set *toValidate* contains delivered transfers that are pending validation (i.e., have been delivered, but not yet validated).

To perform a *transfer* operation, process p first checks the balance of its own account, and if the balance is insufficient, returns *false* (line 3). Otherwise, process p broadcasts a message with this operation via the secure broadcast primitive (line 4). This message includes the three basic arguments of a *transfer* operation as well as *seq*$[p]+1$ and dependencies *deps*. Each correct process in the system eventually delivers this message via secure broadcast (line 8). Note that, given the assumption of no process executing more than one concurrent transfer, every process waits for delivery of its own

```
Local variables:
seq[ ], initially seq[q] = 0, ∀q {Number of validated transfers outgoing from q}
rec[ ], initially rec[q] = 0, ∀q {Number of delivered transfers from q}
hist[ ], initially hist[q] = ∅, ∀q {Set of validated transfers involving q}
deps, initially ∅ {Set of last incoming transfers for account of local process p}
toValidate, initially ∅ {Set of delivered (but not validated) transfers}

1  operation transfer(a, b, x) where μ(a) = {p}
2    if balance(a, hist[p] ∪ deps) < x then
3      return false
4    broadcast([(a, b, x, seq[p] + 1), deps])
5    deps = ∅

6  operation read(a)
7    return balance(a, hist[a] ∪ deps)

8  upon deliver(q, m)
9    let m be [(q, d, y, s), h]
10   if s = rec[q] + 1 then
11     rec[q] = rec[q] + 1
12     toValidate = toValidate ∪ {(q, m)}

13 upon (q, [t, h]) ∈ toValidate ∧ Valid(q, t, h)
14   let t be (q, d, y, s)
15   hist[q] := hist[q] ∪ h ∪ {t}
16     seq[q] = s
17     if d = p then
18       deps = deps ∪ (q, d, y, s)
19     if q = p then
20       return true

21 function Valid(q, t, h)
22   let t be (c, d, y, s)
23   return (q = c)
24          and (s = seq[q] + 1)
25          and (balance(c, hist[q]) ≥ y)
26          and (∀(a, b, x, r) ∈ h : (a, b, x, r) ∈ hist[a])

27 function balance(a, h)
28   return sum of incoming minus outgoing transfers for account a in h
```

Figure 4: Consensusless transfer system based on secure broadcast. Code for every process p.

message before initiating another broadcast. This effectively turns the source order property of secure broadcast into FIFO order. Upon delivery, process p checks this message for well-formedness (lines 9 and 10), and then adds it to the set of messages pending validation. We explain the validation procedure later.

Once a transfer passes validation (the predicate in line 13 is satisfied), process p applies this transfer on the local state. Applying a transfer means that process p adds this transfer and its dependencies to the history of the outgoing (line 15) account. If the transfer is incoming for local process p, it is also added to *deps*, the set of current dependencies for p (line 18). If the transfer is outgoing for p, i.e., it is the currently pending *transfer* operation invoked by p, then the response *true* is returned (line 20).

To perform a *read*(a) operation for account a, process p simply computes the balance of this account based on the local history *hist*$[a]$ (line 28).

Before applying a transfer *op* from some process q, process p validates *op* via the *Valid* function (lines 21–26). To be valid, *op* must satisfy four conditions. The first condition is that process q (the issuer of transfer *op*) must be the owner of the outgoing account for *op* (line 23). Second, any preceding transfers that process q issued must have been validated (line 24). Third, the balance of account q must not drop below zero (line 25). Finally, the reported dependencies of *op* (encoded in h of line 26) must have been validated and exist in $hist[q]$.

Lemma 3. *In any infinite execution of the algorithm (Figure 4), every operation performed by a correct process eventually completes.*

Proof. A transfer operation that fails or a read operation invoked by a correct process returns immediately (lines 3 and 7, respectively).

Consider a transfer operation T invoked by a correct process p that *succeeds* (i.e., passes the check in line 2), so p broadcasts a message with the transfer details using secure broadcast (line 4). By the validity property of secure broadcast, p eventually delivers the message (via the secure broadcast callback, line 8) and adds it to the *toValidate* set. By the algorithm, this message includes a set *deps* of operations (called h, line 9) that involve p's account. This set includes transfers that process p delivered and validated after issuing the prior successful outgoing transfer (or since system initialization if there is no such transfer) but before issuing T (lines 4 and 5).

As process p is correct, it operates on its own account, respects the sequence numbers, and issues a transfer only if it has enough balance on the account. Thus, when it is delivered by p, T must satisfy the first three conditions of the *Valid* predicate (lines 23–25). Moreover, by the algorithm, all dependencies (labeled h in function *Valid*) included in T are in the history $hist[p]$ and, thus the fourth validation condition (line 26) also holds.

Thus, p eventually validates T and completes the operation by returning *true* in line 20. □

Theorem 3. *The algorithm in Figure 4 implements an asset-transfer object type.*

Proof. Fix an execution E of the algorithm, let H be the corresponding history.

Let $\mathcal{V}$ denote the set of all messages that were delivered (line 8) and validated (line 23) at correct processes in E. Every message $m = [(q, d, y, s), h] \in \mathcal{V}$ is put in $hist[q]$ (line 15). We define an order $\leq \subseteq \mathcal{V} \times \mathcal{V}$ as follows. For $m = [(q, d, y, s), h] \in \mathcal{V}$ and $m' = [(r, d', y', s'), h'] \in \mathcal{V}$, we have $m \leq m'$ if and only if one of the following conditions holds:

- $q = r$ and $s < s'$,
- $(r, d', y', s') \in h$, or
- there exists $m'' \in \mathcal{V}$ such that $m \leq m''$ and $m'' \leq m'$.

By the source order property of secure broadcast (see Section 5.2), correct processes p and r deliver messages from any process q in the same order. By the algorithm in Figure 4, a message from q with a sequence number i is added by a correct process to *toValidate* set only if the previous message from q added to *toValidate* had sequence number $i - 1$ (line 10). Furthermore, a message $m = [(q, d, y, s), h]$ is validated at a correct process only if all messages in h have been previously validated (line 26). Therefore, $\leq$ is acyclic and thus can be extended to a total order.

Let S be the sequential history constructed from any such total order on messages in $\mathcal{V}$ in which every message $m = [(q, d, y, s), h]$ is replaced with the invocation-response pair *transfer*(q, d, y); *true*.

By construction, every operation *transfer*(q, d, y) in S is preceded by a sequence of transfers that ensure that the balance of q does not drop below y (line 25). In particular, S includes all outgoing transfers from the account of q performed previously by q itself. Additionally S may order some *incoming* transfer to q that did not appear at $hist[q]$ before the corresponding (q, d, y, s) has been added to it. But these "unaccounted" operations may only increase the balance of q and, thus, it is indeed legal to return *true*.

By construction, for each correct process p, S respects the order of successful transfers issued by p. Thus, the subsequence of successful transfers in H "looks" linearizable to the correct processes: H, restricted to successful transfers witnessed by the correct processes, is consistent with a legal sequential history S.

Let p be a correct process in E. Now let $\mathcal{V}_p$ denote the set of all messages that were delivered (line 8) and validated (line 23) at p in E. Let $\leq_p$ be the subset of $\leq$ restricted to the elements in $\mathcal{V}_p$. Obviously, $\leq_p$ is cycle-free and we can again extend it to a total order. Let S_p be the sequential history build in the same way as S above. Similarly, we can see that S_p is legal and, by construction, consistent with the local history of *all* operations of p (including reads and failed transfers).

By Lemma 3, every operation invoked by a correct process eventually completes. Thus, E indeed satisfies the properties of an asset-transfer object type. □

6 RELATED WORK

Many systems address the problem of asset transfers, be they for a permissioned (private, with a trusted external access control mechanism) [4, 27, 32] or permissionless (public, prone to Sybil attacks) setting [2, 16, 22, 34, 39, 45]. Decentralized systems for the public setting are open to the world. To prevent malicious parties from overtaking the system, these systems rely on Sybil-proof techniques, e.g., proof-of-work [39], or proof-of-stake [7]. The above-mentioned solutions, whether for the permissionless or the permissioned environment, seek to solve consensus. They must inevitably rely on synchrony assumptions or randomization. By sidestepping consensus, we can provide a deterministic and asynchronous implementation.

It is worth noting that many of those solutions allow for more than just transfers, and support richer operations on the system state—so-called smart contracts. Our paper focuses on the original asset transfer problem, as defined by Nakamoto [39], and we do not address smart contracts, for certain forms of which consensus is indeed necessary. However, our approach allows for arbitrary operations, if those operations affect groups of the participants that can solve consensus among themselves. Potential safety or liveness violations of those operations (in case this group gets compromised) are confined to the group and do not affect the rest of the system.

In the blockchain ecosystem, a lot of work has been devoted to avoid a totally ordered chain of transfers. The idea is to replace the totally ordered linear structure of a blockchain with that of a directed acyclic graph (DAG) for structuring the transfers in the system. Notable systems in this spirit include Byteball [14], Vegvisir [32], Corda [27], Nano [35], or the GHOST protocol [42]. Even if these systems use a DAG to replace the classic blockchain, they still employ consensus.

We can also use a DAG to characterize the relation between transfers, but we do not resort to solving consensus to build the DAG, nor do we use the DAG to solve consensus. More precisely, we can regard each account as having an individual history. Each such history is managed by the corresponding account owner without depending on a global view of the system. Histories are loosely coupled through a causality relation established by dependencies among transfers.

The important insight that an asynchronous broadcast-style abstraction suffices for transfers appears in the literature as early as 2002, due to Pedone and Schiper [40]. Duan et. al. [17] introduce efficient Byzantine fault-tolerant protocols for storage and also build on this insight. So does recent work by Gupta [25] on financial transfers which seems closest to ours; the proposed algorithm is based on similar principles as some implementations of secure broadcast [36, 37]. To the best of our knowledge, however, we are the first to formally define the asset transfer problem as a shared object type, study its consensus number, and propose algorithms building on top of standard abstractions that are amenable to a real deployment in cryptocurrencies.

REFERENCES

[1] Ittai Abraham, Guy Gueta, Dahlia Malkhi, Lorenzo Alvisi, Rama Kotla, and Jean-Philippe Martin. 2017. Revisiting Fast Practical Byzantine Fault Tolerance. *arXiv preprint arXiv:1712.01367* (2017). https://arxiv.org/abs/1712.01367

[2] Ittai Abraham, Dahlia Malkhi, Kartik Nayak, Ling Ren, and Alexander Spiegelman. 2016. Solida: A Blockchain Protocol Based on Reconfigurable Byzantine Consensus. *CoRR* abs/1612.02916 (2016). http://arxiv.org/abs/1612.02916

[3] Yehuda Afek, Hagit Attiya, Danny Dolev, Eli Gafni, Michael Merritt, and Nir Shavit. 1993. Atomic Snapshots of Shared Memory. 40, 4 (1993), 873–890.

[4] Elli Androulaki, Artem Barger, Vita Bortnikov, Christian Cachin, Konstantinos Christidis, Angelo De Caro, David Enyeart, Christopher Ferris, Gennady Laventman, Yacov Manevich, Srinivasan Muralidharan, Chet Murthy, Binh Nguyen, Manish Sethi, Gari Singh, Keith Smith, Alessandro Sorniotti, Chrysoula Stathakopoulou, Marko Vukolic, Sharon Weed Cocco, and Jason Yellick. 2018. Hyperledger fabric: a distributed operating system for permissioned blockchains. In *EuroSys*.

[5] Karolos Antoniadis, Rachid Guerraoui, Dahlia Malkhi, and Dragos-Adrian Seredinschi. 2018. State Machine Replication is More Expensive Than Consensus. In *DISC*.

[6] Hagit Attiya and Jennifer L. Welch. 1994. Sequential consistency versus linearizability. *ACM TOCS* 12, 2 (1994), 91–122.

[7] Iddo Bentov, Ariel Gabizon, and Alex Mizrahi. 2016. Cryptocurrencies without proof of work. In *International Conference on Financial Cryptography and Data Security*. Springer, 142–157.

[8] Piotr Berman, Juan A. Garay, and Kenneth J. Perry. 1989. Towards Optimal Distributed Consensus. In *FOCS*.

[9] Joseph Bonneau, Andrew Miller, Jeremy Clark, Arvind Narayanan, Joshua A. Kroll, and Edward W. Felten. 2015. SoK: Research Perspectives and Challenges for Bitcoin and Cryptocurrencies. In *IEEE S&P*.

[10] Gabriel Bracha and Sam Toueg. 1985. Asynchronous Consensus and Broadcast Protocols. *JACM* 32, 4 (1985).

[11] Christian Cachin, Klaus Kursawe, Frank Petzold, and Victor Shoup. 2001. Secure and efficient asynchronous broadcast protocols. In *Annual International Cryptology Conference*. Springer, 524–541.

[12] Christian Cachin and Marko Vukolić. 2017. Blockchains consensus protocols in the wild. *arXiv preprint arXiv:1707.01873* (2017).

[13] Miguel Castro and Barbara Liskov. 1999. Practical Byzantine Fault Tolerance. In *OSDI (OSDI '99)*. 173–186.

[14] Anton Churyumov. 2016. Byteball: A decentralized system for storage and transfer of value. *https://byteball.org/Byteball.pdf* (2016).

[15] Allen Clement, Edmund L Wong, Lorenzo Alvisi, Michael Dahlin, and Mirco Marchetti. 2009. Making Byzantine Fault Tolerant Systems Tolerate Byzantine Faults. In *NSDI*.

[16] Christian Decker, Jochen Seidel, and Roger Wattenhofer. 2016. Bitcoin meets strong consistency. In *Proceedings of the 17th International Conference on Distributed Computing and Networking*. 13.

[17] Sisi Duan, Michael K. Reiter, and Haibin Zhang. 2018. BEAT: Asynchronous BFT Made Practical. In *CCS*.

[18] Ittay Eyal, Adem Efe Gencer, Emin Gün Sirer, and Robbert Van Renesse. 2016. Bitcoin-NG: A Scalable Blockchain Protocol. In *NSDI*.

[19] Michael J. Fischer, Nancy A. Lynch, and Michael S. Paterson. 1985. Impossibility of Distributed Consensus with one Faulty Process. 32, 2 (April 1985), 374–382.

[20] Juan Garay, Aggelos Kiayias, and Nikos Leonardos. 2015. The Bitcoin Backbone Protocol: Analysis and Applications. In *Advances in Cryptology - EUROCRYPT 2015*.

[21] Juan A Garay, Jonathan Katz, Ranjit Kumaresan, and Hong-Sheng Zhou. 2011. Adaptively Secure Broadcast, Revisited. In *PODC*. Citeseer, 179–186.

[22] Yossi Gilad, Rotem Hemo, Silvio Micali, Georgios Vlachos, and Nickolai Zeldovich. 2017. Algorand: Scaling byzantine agreements for cryptocurrencies. In *SOSP*.

[23] Rachid Guerraoui, Petr Kuznetsov, Matteo Monti, Matej Pavlovic, and Dragos-Adrian Seredinschi. 2019. The Consensus Number of a Cryptocurrency (Extended Version). *EPFL Infoscience* (2019).

[24] Rachid Guerraoui, Matej Pavlovic, and Dragos-Adrian Seredinschi. 2018. Blockchain Protocols: The Adversary is in the Details. In *Symposium on Foundations and Applications of Blockchain*.

[25] Saurabh Gupta. 2016. *A Non-Consensus Based Decentralized Financial Transaction Processing Model with Support for Efficient Auditing*. Master's thesis. Arizona State University, USA.

[26] Vassos Hadzilacos and Sam Toueg. 1993. Fault-tolerant broadcasts and related problems. In *Distributed Systems*, Sape J. Mullender (Ed.). Addison-Wesley, Chapter 5, 97–145.

[27] Mike Hearn. 2016. Corda: A distributed ledger. *Corda Technical White Paper* (2016).

[28] Maurice Herlihy. 1991. Wait-free synchronization. 13, 1 (1991), 123–149.

[29] Maurice P Herlihy and Jeannette M Wing. 1990. Linearizability: A correctness condition for concurrent objects. *ACM Transactions on Programming Languages and Systems (TOPLAS)* 12, 3 (1990).

[30] Colin J. Fidge. 1988. Timestamps in message-passing systems that preserve partial ordering. In *Proceedings of the 11th Australian Computer Science Conference*.

[31] Prasad Jayanti and Sam Toueg. 1992. Some results on the impossibility, universability and decidability of consensus. In *International Workshop on Distributed Algorithms (LNCS)*, Vol. 647. Springer Verlag.

[32] Kolbeinn Karlsson, Weitao Jiang, Stephen Wicker, Danny Adams, Edwin Ma, Robbert van Renesse, and Hakim Weatherspoon. 2018. Vegvisir: A Partition-Tolerant Blockchain for the Internet-of-Things. In *ICDCS*.

[33] Eleftherios Kokoris Kogias, Philipp Jovanovic, Nicolas Gailly, Ismail Khoffi, Linus Gasser, and Bryan Ford. 2016. Enhancing bitcoin security and performance with strong consistency via collective signing. In *USENIX Security*.

[34] Eleftherios Kokoris-Kogias, Philipp Jovanovic, Linus Gasser, Nicolas Gailly, Ewa Syta, and Bryan Ford. 2018. Omniledger: A secure, scale-out, decentralized ledger via sharding. In *IEEE S&P*.

[35] Colin LeMahieu. 2018. Nano: A feeless distributed cryptocurrency network. *Nano [Online resource]: https://nano. org/en/whitepaper (accessed 18.01. 2019)* (2018).

[36] Dahlia Malkhi, Michael Merritt, and Ohad Rodeh. 1997. Secure Reliable Multicast Protocols in a WAN. In *ICDCS*.

[37] Dahlia Malkhi and Michael K. Reiter. 1997. A High-Throughput Secure Reliable Multicast Protocol. *Journal of Computer Security* 5, 2 (1997), 113–128. https://doi.org/10.3233/JCS-1997-5203

[38] David Mazieres. 2015. The stellar consensus protocol: A federated model for internet-level consensus. *Stellar Development Foundation* (2015).

[39] Satoshi Nakamoto. 2008. Bitcoin: A Peer-to-Peer Electronic Cash System. (2008).

[40] Fernando Pedone and André Schiper. 2002. Handling message semantics with generic broadcast protocols. *Distributed Computing* 15, 2 (2002), 97–107.

[41] Philip Rapoport, Roman Leal, Patrick Griffin, and Wellington Sculley. 2014. The Ripple Protocol. (2014).

[42] Yonatan Sompolinsky and Aviv Zohar. 2013. Accelerating Bitcoin's transaction processing: fast money grows on trees, not chains. *IACR Cryptology ePrint Archive, 2013:881* (2013).

[43] Joao Sousa, Alysson Bessani, and Marko Vukolic. 2018. A byzantine fault-tolerant ordering service for the hyperledger fabric blockchain platform. In *DSN*.

[44] Nick Szabo. 1997. Formalizing and securing relationships on public networks. *First Monday* 2, 9 (1997).

[45] Team-Rocket. 2018. Snowflake to Avalanche: A Novel Metastable Consensus Protocol Family for Cryptocurrencies. *White Paper* (2018). Revision: 05/16/2018 21:51:26 UTC.

[46] Sam Toueg. 1984. Randomized Byzantine Agreements. In *PODC*. 163–178.

[47] Marko Vukolić. 2015. The Quest for Scalable Blockchain Fabric: Proof-of-work vs. BFT Replication. In *International Workshop on Open Problems in Network Security*. Springer, 112–125.

[48] Gavin Wood. 2015. Ethereum: A secure decentralized generalized transaction ledger. White paper. (2015).

Communication Complexity of Byzantine Agreement, Revisited

Ittai Abraham
VMware Research

T-H. Hubert Chan
The University of Hong Kong

Danny Dolev
The Hebrew University of Jerusalem

Kartik Nayak
VMware Research

Rafael Pass
Cornell Tech

Ling Ren
VMware Research

Elaine Shi
Cornell University

ABSTRACT

As Byzantine Agreement (BA) protocols find application in large-scale decentralized cryptocurrencies, an increasingly important problem is to design BA protocols with improved communication complexity. A few existing works have shown how to achieve sub-quadratic BA under an *adaptive* adversary. Intriguingly, they all make a common relaxation about the adaptivity of the attacker, that is, if an honest node sends a message and then gets corrupted in some round, the adversary *cannot erase the message that was already sent* — henceforth we say that such an adversary cannot perform "after-the-fact removal". By contrast, many (super-)quadratic BA protocols in the literature can tolerate after-the-fact removal. In this paper, we first prove that disallowing after-the-fact removal is necessary for achieving subquadratic-communication BA.

Next, we show a new subquadratic binary BA construction (of course, assuming no after-the-fact removal) that achieves near-optimal resilience and expected constant rounds under standard cryptographic assumptions and a public-key infrastructure (PKI). In comparison, all known subquadratic protocols make additional strong assumptions such as random oracles or the ability of honest nodes to erase secrets from memory, and even with these strong assumptions, no prior work can achieve the above properties. Lastly, we show that some setup assumption is necessary for achieving subquadratic multicast-based BA.

ACM Reference Format:
Ittai Abraham, T-H. Hubert Chan, Danny Dolev, Kartik Nayak, Rafael Pass, Ling Ren, and Elaine Shi. 2019. Communication Complexity of Byzantine Agreement, Revisited. In *2019 ACM Symposium on Principles of Distributed Computing (PODC '19), July 29-August 2, 2019, Toronto, ON, Canada.* ACM, New York, NY, USA, 10 pages. https://doi.org/10.1145/3293611.3331629

1 INTRODUCTION

Byzantine agreement (BA) [24] is a central abstraction in distributed systems. Typical BA protocols [5, 11, 12] require all players to send messages to all other players, and thus, n-player BA requires at least n^2 communication complexity. Such protocols are thus not well suited for *large-scale distributed systems* such as decentralized cryptocurrencies [26]. A fundamental problem is to design BA protocols with improved communication complexity.

In fact, in a model with *static* corruption, this is relatively easy. For example, suppose there are at most $f < (\frac{1}{2} - \epsilon)n$ corrupt nodes where ϵ is a positive constant; further, assume there is a trusted common random string (CRS) that is chosen independently of the adversary's (static) corruption choices. Then, we can use the CRS to select a κ-sized committee of players. Various elegant works have investigated how to weaken or remove the trusted set-up assumptions required for committee election and retain subquadratic communication [6, 22]. Once a committee is selected, we can run any BA protocol among the committee, and let the committee members may send their outputs to all "non-committee" players who could then output the majority bit. This protocol works as long as there is an honest majority on the committee. Thus, the error probability is bounded by $\exp(-\Omega(\kappa))$ due to a standard Chernoff bound.

Such a committee-based approach, however, fails if we consider an *adaptive attacker.* Such an attacker can simply observe what nodes are on the committee, then corrupt them, and thereby control the entire committee! A natural and long-standing open question is thus whether subquadratic communication is possible w.r.t. an adaptive attacker:

> *Does there exist a BA protocol with subquadratic communication complexity that resists adaptive corruption of players?*

This question has been partially answered in a few prior works. First, a breakthrough work by King and Saia [21] presented a BA protocol with communication complexity $O(n^{1.5})$. More recent works studied practical constructions motivated by cryptocurrency applications: notably the celebrated Nakamoto consensus [17, 26] can reach agreement in subquadratic communication assuming idealized proof-of-work. Subsequently, several so-called "proof-of-stake" constructions [7, 9] also showed how to realize BA with subquadratic communication. All of the above works tolerate adaptive corruptions.

What is both intriguing and unsatisfying is that all these works happen to make a common relaxing assumption about the adaptivity of the adversary, namely, if adversary adaptively corrupts an honest node i who has just sent a message m in round r, the adversary is unable to erase the honest message m sent in round r. Henceforth we say that such an adversary is incapable of *after-the-fact removal.* In comparison, many natural $\Omega(n^2)$-communication BA protocols [1, 11, 20] can be proven secure even if the adversary is capable of after-the-fact removal – henceforth referred to as a *strongly adaptive* adversary. That is, if an honest node i sends a message m in round r, a strongly adaptive adversary (e.g., who

PODC '19, July 29-August 2, 2019, Toronto, ON, Canada

ACM ISBN 978-1-4503-6217-7/19/07...$15.00
https://doi.org/10.1145/3293611.3331629

controls the egress routers of many nodes) can observe m and then decide to corrupt i and erase the message m that node i has just sent in round r. This mismatch in model naturally raises the following question:

Is disallowing after-the-fact removal necessary for achieving subquadratic-communication BA?

Main result 1: disallowing "after-the-fact" removal is necessary. Our first contribution is a new lower bound showing that any (possibly randomized) BA protocol must incur at least $\Omega(f^2)$ communication in expectation in the presence of a strongly adaptive adversary where f denotes the number of corrupt nodes. The proof of our lower bound is inspired by the work of Dolev and Reischuk [10], who showed that any *deterministic* BA protocol must incur $\Omega(f^2)$ communication even against a *static* adversary. We remark our lower bound (as well as Dolev-Reischuk) holds in a very strong sense: even when making common (possibly very strong) assumptions such as proof-of-work and random oracles, and even under a more constrained *omission* adversary who is only allowed to omit messages sent from and to corrupt nodes, but does not deviate from the protocol otherwise.

Theorem 1 (Impossibility of BA with subquadratic communication w.r.t. a strongly adaptive adversary). *Any (possibly randomized) BA protocol must in expectation incur at least $\Omega(f^2)$ communication in the presence of a strongly adaptive adversary capable of performing after-the-fact removal, where f denotes the number of corrupt nodes.*

Main result 2: near-optimal subquadratic BA with minimal assumptions. On the upper bound front, we present a subquadratic BA protocol that, besides the necessary "no after-the-fact removal" assumption, relies only on standard cryptographic and setup assumptions. Our protocol achieves near-optimal resilience and expected constant rounds.

Our results improve upon existing works in two major aspects. Firstly, besides "no after-the-fact removal", all existing subquadratic protocols make very strong *additional* assumptions, such as random oracles [7, 9] or proof-of-work [26]. In particular, some works [7, 21] assume the ability of honest nodes to securely erase secrets from memory and that adaptive corruption cannot take place between when an honest node sends a message and when it erases secrets from memory. Such a model is referred to as the "erasure model" in the cryptography literature and as "ephemeral keys" in Chen and Micali [7]. To avoid confusing the term with "after-the-fact message removal", we rename it the *memory-erasure model* in this paper. Secondly, and more importantly, even with those strong assumptions, existing protocols do not achieve the above properties (cf. Section 1.1).

The multicast model. In a large-scale peer-to-peer network, it is usually much cheaper for a node to multicast the same message to everyone, than to unicast n different messages (of the same length) to n different nodes — even though the two have identical communication complexity in the standard pair-wise model. Indeed, all known consensus protocols deployed in a decentralized environment (e.g. Bitcoin, Ethereum) work in the multicast fashion. Since our protocols are motivated by these large-scale peer-to-peer networks, we design our protocols to be multicast-based.

A multicast-based protocol is said to have *multicast complexity* C if the total number of messages multicast by all honest players is upper bounded by C. Clearly, a protocol with multicast complexity C has communication complexity nC. Thus, to achieve subquadratic communication complexity, we need to design a protocol in which only a sublinear (in n) number of players multicast.

Theorem 2. *Assuming standard cryptographic assumptions and a public-key infrastructure (PKI), for any constant $0 < \epsilon < 1/2$, there exists a synchronous BA protocol with expected $O(\kappa)$ multicast complexity, expected $O(1)$ round complexity, and $\exp(-\Omega(\kappa))$ error probability that tolerates $f < (1-\epsilon)n/2$ adaptively corrupted players out of n players in total.*

Our construction requires a random verifiable function (VRF) that is secure against an adaptive adversary. Here, adaptive security means security under *selective opening* of corrupt nodes' secret keys, which is a different notion of adaptivity from in some prior works [4, 18]. Most previously known VRF constructions [4, 18, 25] do not provide security under an adaptive adversary. Chen and Micali [7] use random oracles (RO) and unique signatures to construct an adaptively secure VRF. In the full version of this paper, we will show how to instantiate an adaptively secure VRF from standard cryptographic assumptions such as bilinear groups.

Main result 3: on the necessity of setup assumptions. In light of the above Theorem 2, we additionally investigate whether the remaining setup PKI assumption is necessary. We show that if one insists on a multicast-based protocol, indeed some form of setup assumption is necessary for achieving sublinear multicast complexity. Specifically, we show that without any setup assumption, i.e., under the plain authenticated channels model, a (possibly randomized) protocol that solves BA with C multicast complexity with probability $p > 5/6$ can tolerate no more than C adaptive corruptions.

Theorem 3 (Impossibility of sublinear multicast BA without setup assumptions). *In a plain authenticated channel model without setup assumptions, no protocol can solve BA using C multicast complexity with probability $p > 5/6$ under C adaptive corruptions.*

We remark that this lower bound also applies more generally to protocols in which few nodes (i.e., less than C nodes) speak (multicast-style protocols are a special case). Also note that there exist protocols with subquadratic communication and no setup assumptions that rely on many nodes to speak [21].

Organization. The rest of the paper is organized as follows. Section 1.1 reviews related work. Section 2 presents the model and definitions of BA. Section 3 proves Theorem 1. Section 4 and 5 construct an adaptively secure BA protocol to prove Theorem 2. Section 6 proves Theorem 3.

1.1 Related Work

Dolev and Reischuk [10] proved that quadratic communication is necessary for any deterministic BA protocol. Inspired by their work, we show a similar communication complexity lower bound for randomized protocols, but now additionally assuming that the adversary is strongly adaptive.

A number of works explored randomized BA protocols [3, 27] to achieve expected constant round complexity [1, 13, 20] even under a strongly adaptive adversary. A line of works [8, 16, 19] focused on a simulation-based stronger notion of adaptive security for Byzantine Broadcast. These works have at least quadratic communication complexity.

King and Saia first observed that BA can be solved with subquadratic communication complexity if a small probability of error is allowed [21]. More recently Nakamoto-style protocols, based on either proof-of-work [26] or proof-of-stake [7, 9] also showed how to realize BA with subquadratic communication. Compared to our protocol in Section 5, these existing works make other strong assumptions, and even with those strong assumptions, cannot simultaneously achieve near-optimal resilience and expected constant rounds. Nakamoto consensus [26] assumes idealized proofs-of-work. Proof-of-stake protocols assume random oracles [7, 9]. King-Saia [21] and Chen-Micali [7] assume memory-erasure. Nakamoto-style protocols [9, 26] and King-Saia [21] cannot achieve expected constant rounds. Chen-Micali [7] have sub-optimal tolerance of $f < (\frac{1}{3} - \epsilon)n$.

2 MODEL AND DEFINITION

Communication model. We assume that network is synchronous and the protocol proceeds in rounds. Every message sent by an honest node is guaranteed to be received by an honest recipient at the beginning of the next round. We measure communication complexity by the number of messages sent by honest nodes. Our protocols in Section 4 and 5 use multicasts only, that is, whenever an honest node sends a message, it sends that message to all nodes including itself. We say a protocol has multicast complexity C if the total number of multicasts by honest nodes is bounded by C.

Adversary model. Prior to the protocol execution, each node generates its public/private key pair honestly and sends its public key to all other nodes. The adversary is denoted $\mathcal{A}$. $\mathcal{A}$ can *adaptively* corrupt nodes any time during the protocol execution after the trusted setup. The total number of corrupt nodes at the end of the execution is at most f. At any time in the protocol, nodes that remain honest so far are referred to as *so-far-honest* nodes and nodes that remain honest till the end of the protocol are referred to as *forever-honest* nodes. All nodes that have been corrupt are under the control of $\mathcal{A}$, i.e., the messages they receive are forwarded to $\mathcal{A}$, and $\mathcal{A}$ controls what messages they will send in each round once they become corrupt. We assume that when a so-far-honest node i multicasts a message m, it can immediately become corrupt in the same round and be made to send one or more messages in the same round. However, the message m that was already multicast before i became corrupt *cannot be retracted* — it will be received by all so-far-honest nodes at the beginning of the next round. In other words, the adversary is adaptive but not strongly adaptive (i.e., incapable of after-the-fact removal).

Agreement vs. broadcast. (Binary) Byzantine Agreement is typically studied in two forms. In the *broadcast version*, also called *Byzantine broadcast*, there is a *designated sender* (or simply *sender*) known to all nodes. Prior to protocol start, the sender receives an input $b \in \{0, 1\}$. A protocol solves Byzantine broadcast with probability p if it achieves the following properties with probability at least p.

- *Termination.* Every forever-honest node i outputs a bit b'_i.
- *Consistency.* If two forever-honest nodes output b'_i and b'_j respectively, then $b'_i = b'_j$.
- *Validity.* If the sender is forever-honest and the sender's input is b, then all forever-honest nodes output b.

In the *agreement version*, sometimes referred to as Byzantine "consensus" in the literature, there is no designated sender. Instead, each node i receives an input bit $b_i \in \{0, 1\}$. A protocol solves Byzantine agreement (BA) with probability p if it achieves the following properties with probability at least p.

- *Termination* and *Consistency* same as Byzantine broadcast.
- *Validity.* If all forever-honest nodes receive the same input bit b, then all forever-honest nodes output b.

With synchrony and PKI, the *agreement* version (where everyone receives input) can tolerate up to minority corruption [15] while the broadcast version can tolerate up to $n - 1$ corruptions [11, 24]. Under minority-corruption, the two versions are equivalent from a feasibility perspective, i.e., we can construct one from the other. Moreover, one direction of the reduction preserves communication complexity. Specifically, given an adaptively secure BA protocol (agreement version), one can construct an adaptively secure Byzantine Broadcast protocol by first having the designated sender multicasting its input to everyone, and then having everyone invoke the BA protocol. This way, if the BA protocol has subquadratic communication complexity (resp. sublinear multicast complexity), so does the resulting Byzantine Broadcast protocol. For this reason, we state all our upper bounds for BA and state all our lower bounds for Byzantine Broadcast — this makes both our upper- and lower-bounds stronger.

3 COMMUNICATION LOWER BOUND UNDER A STRONGLY ADAPTIVE ADVERSARY

In this section, we prove that any (possibly randomized) BA protocol must in expectation incur at least $\Omega(f^2)$ communication in the presence of a strongly adaptive adversary capable of performing after-the-fact removal. For the reasons mentioned in Section 2, we prove our lower bound for Byzantine Broadcast (which immediately applies to BA). Our proof strategy builds on the classic Dolev-Reischuk lower bound [10, Theorem 2], which shows that in every deterministic Byzantine Broadcast protocol honest nodes need to send at least $\Omega(f^2)$ messages.

Warmup: the Dolev-Reischuk lower bound. We first explain the Dolev-Reischuk proof at a high level. Observe that for a deterministic protocol, an execution is completely determined by the input (of the designated sender) and the adversary's strategy. Consider the following adversary $\mathcal{A}$: $\mathcal{A}$ corrupts a set V of $f/2$ nodes that does not include the designated sender. Let U denote the set of remaining nodes. All parties in V behave like honest nodes, except that (i) they ignore the first $f/2$ messages sent to them, and (ii) they do not send messages to each other. Suppose the honest designated sender has input 0. For validity to hold, all honest nodes must output 0.

If at most $(f/2)^2$ messages are sent to V in the above execution, then there exists a node $p \in V$ that receives at most $f/2$ messages. Now, define another adversary $\mathcal{A}'$ almost identically as $\mathcal{A}$ except that: (i) $\mathcal{A}'$ does not corrupt p, (ii) $\mathcal{A}'$ corrupts all nodes in U that send p messages (possibly including the designated sender), prevents them from sending any messages to p, but behaves honestly to other nodes. Since p receives at most $f/2$ messages under $\mathcal{A}$, $\mathcal{A}'$ corrupts at most f nodes.

Observe that honest nodes in U receive identical messages from all other nodes in the two executions. So these nodes still output 0 under $\mathcal{A}'$. However, p does not receive any message but has to output some value. If this value is 1, consistency is violated. If p outputs 0 when receiving no messages, we can let the sender send 1 under $\mathcal{A}$ and derive a consistency violation under $\mathcal{A}'$ following a symmetric argument.

Our lower bound. We now extend the above proof to randomized protocols. In a randomized protocol, there are two sources of randomness that need to be considered carefully. On one hand, honest nodes can use randomization to their advantage. On the other hand, an adaptive adversary can also leverage randomness. Indeed our lower bound uses a randomized adversarial strategy. In addition, our lower bound crucially relies on the adversary being *strongly adaptive* – the adversary can observe that a message is sent by an honest node h to any other party in a given round r, decide to adaptively corrupt h, and then remove messages sent by h in round r. We prove the following theorem — here we say that a protocol solves Byzantine Broadcast with probability q iff for any non-uniform p.p.t. strongly adaptive adversary, with probability q, every honest node outputs a bit at the end of the protocol, and consistency and validity are satisfied.

Theorem 4. *If a protocol solves Byzantine Broadcast with $\frac{3}{4}+\epsilon$ probability against a strongly adaptive adversary, then in expectation, honest nodes collectively need to send at least $(\epsilon f)^2$ messages.*

Proof. For the sake of contradiction, suppose that a protocol solves Byzantine Broadcast against a strongly adaptive adversary with $\frac{3}{4}+\epsilon$ probability using less than $(\epsilon f)^2$ expected messages. This means, regardless of what the adversary does, the protocol errs (i.e., violate either consistency, validity or termination) with no more than $\frac{1}{4}-\epsilon$ probability. We will construct an adversary that makes the protocol err with a probability larger than the above.

Without loss of generality, assume that there exist $\lceil n/2 \rceil$ nodes that output 0 with at most 1/2 probability if they receive no messages. (Otherwise, then there must exist $\lceil n/2 \rceil$ nodes that output 1 with at most 1/2 probability if they receive no messages, and the entire proof follows from a symmetric argument.) Let V be a set of $f/2$ such nodes not containing the designated sender. Note that these nodes may output 1 or they may simply not terminate if they receive no messages. (We can always find such a V because $f/2 < \lceil n/2 \rceil$). Let U denote the remaining nodes. Let the designated sender send 0.

Next, consider the following adversary $\mathcal{A}$ that corrupts V and makes nodes in V behave honestly except that:

(1) Nodes in V do not send messages to each other.
(2) Each node in V *ignores* (i.e., pretends that it does not receive) the first $f/2$ messages sent to it by nodes in U.

For a protocol to have an expected message complexity of $(\epsilon f)^2$, honest nodes collectively need to send fewer than that many messages in expectation *regardless of* the adversary's strategy. Let z be a random variable denoting the number of messages sent by honest nodes to V. We have $E[z] < (\epsilon f)^2$. Let X_1 be the event that $z \le \frac{\epsilon}{2}f^2$. By Markov's inequality, $\Pr[z > \frac{1}{2\epsilon}E[z]] < 2\epsilon$. Thus, $\Pr[z \le \frac{\epsilon}{2}f^2] \ge \Pr[z \le \frac{1}{2\epsilon}E[z]] > 1-2\epsilon$.

Let X_2 be the event that among the first $\frac{\epsilon}{2}f^2$ messages, a node p picked uniformly at random from V by the adversary receives at most $f/2$ messages. Observe that among the first $\frac{\epsilon}{2}f^2 = 2\epsilon|V|(f/2)$ messages, there exist at most $2\epsilon|V|$ nodes that receive more than $f/2$ of those. Since p has been picked uniformly at random from V, $\Pr[X_2] \ge 1-2\epsilon$. Thus, we have that

$$\begin{aligned}\Pr[X_1 \cap X_2] &= \Pr[X_1] + \Pr[X_2] - \Pr[X_1 \cup X_2] \\ &> (1-2\epsilon) + (1-2\epsilon) - 1 = 1-4\epsilon.\end{aligned}$$

Now, define another adversary $\mathcal{A}'$ almost identically as $\mathcal{A}$ except that:

(1) $\mathcal{A}'$ picks a node $p \in V$ uniformly at random and corrupts everyone else in V except p.
(2) $\mathcal{A}'$ blocks the first $f/2$ attempts that nodes in U send p messages. In other words, whenever some node $s \in U$ attempts to send a message to p in a round, if this is within the first $f/2$ attempts that nodes in U send p messages, $\mathcal{A}'$ immediately corrupts s (unless s is already corrupted) and removes the message s sends p in that round. Corrupted nodes in U behave honestly otherwise. (In particular, after the first $f/2$ messages from U to p have been blocked, corrupted nodes behave honestly to p as well.)

Observe that $X_1 \cap X_2$ denotes the event that under adversary $\mathcal{A}$, the total number of messages sent by honest nodes to V is less than $\frac{\epsilon}{2}f^2$ and among those, the randomly picked node p has received at most $f/2$ messages. In this case, p receives no message at all under adversary $\mathcal{A}'$. By the definition of V, p outputs 0 with at most 1/2 probability if it receives no messages. Let Y_1 be the event that p does *not* output 0 under $\mathcal{A}'$. Recall that Y_1 includes the event that p outputs 1 as well as the event that p does not terminate. We have $\Pr[Y_1] \ge \Pr[Y_1 | X_1 \cap X_2] \cdot \Pr[X_1 \cap X_2] > \frac{1}{2}(1-4\epsilon)$.

Meanwhile, we argue that honest nodes in U cannot distinguish $\mathcal{A}$ and $\mathcal{A}'$. This is because the only difference between the two scenarios is that, under $\mathcal{A}$, the first $f/2$ messages from U to p are intentionally ignored by a corrupt node p, and under $\mathcal{A}'$, the first $f/2$ messages from U to an honest p are blocked by $\mathcal{A}'$ using after-the-fact removal. Thus, honest nodes in U receive identical messages under $\mathcal{A}$ and $\mathcal{A}'$ and cannot distinguish the two adversaries. Under $\mathcal{A}$, they need to output 0 to preserve validity. Recall that the protocol solves Byzantine broadcast with at least $\frac{3}{4}+\epsilon$ probability. Thus, with at least the above probability, all honest nodes in U output 0 under $\mathcal{A}$. Let Y_2 be the event that all honest nodes in U output 0 under $\mathcal{A}'$. Since they cannot distinguish $\mathcal{A}$ and $\mathcal{A}'$, $\Pr[Y_2] \ge \frac{3}{4}+\epsilon$.

If Y_1 and Y_2 both occur, then the protocol errs under $\mathcal{A}'$: either consistency or termination is violated. We have

$$\Pr[Y_1 \cap Y_2] = \Pr[Y_1] + \Pr[Y_2] - \Pr[Y_1 \cup Y_2]$$
$$> \frac{1}{2}(1 - 4\epsilon) + (\frac{3}{4} - \epsilon) - 1 = \frac{1}{4} - \epsilon.$$

This contradicts the hypothesis that the protocol solves Byzantine broadcast with $\frac{3}{4} + \epsilon$ probability. □

4 SUBQUADRATIC BA: $f < (1/3 - \epsilon)n$

This section presents the main ingredients for achieving subquadratic BA. In this section, we opt for conceptual simplicity over other desired properties. In particular, the protocol in this section tolerates only $\frac{1}{3} - \epsilon$ fraction of adaptive corruptions, and completes in $O(\kappa)$ rounds. In the next section, we will show how to improve the resilience to $\frac{1}{2} - \epsilon$ and round complexity to expected $O(1)$.

4.1 Warmup: A Simple Quadratic BA Tolerating 1/3 Corruptions

We first describe an extremely simple quadratic BA protocol, inspired by the Phase-King paradigm [2], that tolerates less than 1/3 corruptions. The protocol proceeds in κ iterations $r = 1, 2, \ldots \kappa$, and every iteration consists of two rounds. For the time being, assume a random leader election oracle that elects and announces a random leader at the beginning of every iteration. At initialization, every node i sets b_i to its input bit, and sets its "sticky flag" $F = 1$ (think of the sticky flag as indicating whether to "stick" to the bit in the previous iteration). Each iteration r now proceeds as follows where all messages are signed, and only messages with valid signatures are processed:

(1) The leader of iteration r flips a random coin b and <u>multicasts</u> $(\texttt{Propose}, r, b)$. Every node i sets $b_i^* := b_i$ if $F = 1$ or if it has not heard a valid proposal from the current iteration's leader. Else, it sets $b_i^* := b$ where b is the proposal heard from the current iteration's leader (if proposals for both $b = 0$ and $b = 1$ have been observed, choose an arbitrary bit).
(2) Every node i <u>multicasts</u> $(\texttt{Vote}, r, b_i^*)$. If at least $\frac{2n}{3}$ votes from distinct nodes have been received and vouch for the same b^*, set $b_i := b^*$ and $F := 1$; else, set $F := 0$.

At the end of the last iteration, each node outputs the bit that it last voted for.

In short, in every iteration, every node either switches to the leader's proposal (if any has been observed) or it sticks to its previous "belief" b_i. This simple protocol works because of the following observations. Henceforth, we refer to a collection of $\frac{2n}{3}$ votes from distinct nodes for the same iteration and the same b as a *certificate* for b.

- *Consistency within an iteration.* Suppose that in iteration r, honest node i observes a certificate for b from a set of nodes denoted S, and honest node j observes a certificate for b' from a set S'. By a standard quorum intersection argument, $S \cap S'$ must contain at least one forever-honest node Since honest nodes vote uniquely, it must be that $b = b'$.
- *A good iteration exists.* Next, suppose that in some iteration r the leader is honest. We say that this leader chooses a lucky bit b^* iff in iteration $r - 1$, no honest node has seen a certificate for $1 - b^*$. This means, in iteration r, every honest node either sticks with b^* or switches to the leader's proposal of b^*. Clearly, an honest leader chooses a lucky b^* with probability at least 1/2. Except with $\exp(-\Omega(\kappa))$ probability, an honest-leader iteration with a lucky choice exists.
- *Persistence of honest choice after a good iteration.* Now, as soon as we reach an iteration (denoted r) with an honest leader and its choice of bit b^* is lucky, then all honest nodes will vote for b^* in iteration r. Thus all honest nodes will hear certificates for b^* in iteration r; therefore, they will all stick to b^* in iteration $r + 1$. By induction, in all future iterations they will stick to b^*.
- *Validity.* If all honest nodes receive the same bit b^* as input then due to the same argument as above the bit b^* will always stick around in all iterations.

4.2 Subquadratic Communication through Vote-Specific Eligibility

The above simple protocol requires in expectation linear number of multicast messages (in each round every node multicasts a message). We now consider how to improve the multicast complexity of the warmup protocol. We will also remove the idealized leader election oracle in the process.

Background on VRFs. We rely on a verifiable random function (VRF) [25]. A trusted setup phase is used to generate a public-key infrastructure (PKI): each node $i \in [n]$ obtains a VRF secret key sk_i, and its corresponding public key pk_i. A VRF evaluation on the message μ denoted $(\rho, \pi) \leftarrow \mathsf{VRF}_{\mathsf{sk}_i}(\mu)$ generates a deterministic pseudorandom value ρ and a proof π such that ρ is computationally indistinguishable from random without the secret key sk_i, and with pk_i everyone can verify from the proof π that ρ is evaluated correctly. We use VRF^1 to denote the first output (i.e., ρ above) of the VRF.

Strawman: the Chen-Micali approach. We first describe the paradigm of Chen and Micali [7] but we explain it in the context of our warmup protocol. Imagine that now not everyone is required to vote in a round r. Instead, we use the function $\mathsf{VRF}^1_{\mathsf{sk}_i}(\texttt{Vote}, r) < D$ to determine whether i is eligible to vote in round r where D is a difficulty parameter appropriately chosen such that, in expectation, κ many nodes would be chosen to vote in each round. When node i sends a $\texttt{Vote}$ message, it attaches the VRF's evaluation outcome as well as the proof such that every node can verify its eligibility using its public key pk_i. Correspondingly, when we tally votes, the original threshold $\frac{2n}{3}$ should be changed to $\frac{2\kappa}{3}$, i.e, two-thirds of the expected committee size.

Evaluating the VRF requires knowing the node's secret key. Thus, only the node itself knows at what rounds it is eligible to vote. This may seem to solve the problem because the adversary cannot predict in advance who will be sending messages in every round The problem with this is that once an adaptive adversary $\mathcal{A}$ notices that some player i was eligible to vote for b in round r (because i just sent a valid vote for b), $\mathcal{A}$ can corrupt i immediately and make i vote for $1 - b$ in the same round!

To tackle this precise issue, Chen and Micali [7] relies on the memory-erasure model (referred to as ephemeral keys in their paper) and a *forward-secure* signing scheme. Informally, in a forward secure signing scheme, in the beginning, a node has a key that can sign any messages from any round; after signing a message for round t, the node updates its key to one that can henceforth sign only messages for round $t+1$ or higher, and the round-t secret key should be immediately erased at this point. This way, even if the attacker instantly corrupts a node, it cannot cast another vote in the same round.

Our key insight: bit-specific eligibility. Our key insight is to make the eligibility bit-specific. To elaborate, the committee eligible to vote for b in round r is chosen *independently* from the committee eligible to vote on $1-b$ in the same round. Concretely, node i is eligible to send a Vote message for the bit $b \in \{0,1\}$ in round r iff $\mathsf{VRF}^1_{\mathsf{sk}_i}(\mathsf{Vote}, r, b) < D$, where D is the aforementioned difficulty parameter.

What does this achieve? Suppose that the attacker sees some node i votes for the bit b in round r. Although the attacker can now immediately corrupt i, the fact that i was allowed to vote for b in round r does not make i any more likely to be eligible to vote for $1-b$ in the same round. Thus, corrupting i is no more useful to the adversary than corrupting any other node.

Finally, since we already make use of the VRF, as a by-product we can remove the idealized leader election oracle in the warmup protocol: a node i is eligible for making a proposal in iteration r iff $\mathsf{VRF}^1_{\mathsf{sk}_i}(\mathsf{Propose}, r, b) < D_0$ where D_0 is a separate difficult parameter explained below. Naturally, the node attaches the VRF evaluation outcome and proof with its proposal so that others can verify its eligibility.

Difficulty parameters. The two difficulty parameters D and D_0 need to be specified differently. Recall that D is used to elect a committee in each round for sending Vote messages; and D_0 is used for leader election.

(1) D should be set such that each committee is κ-sized in expectation; whereas
(2) D_0 should be set such that every node has a $\frac{1}{2n}$ probability to be eligible to propose.

Since we are interested in making communication scale better with n, we assume $n = \omega(\kappa)$ and $n > \kappa$; otherwise, one should simply use the quadratic protocol.

Putting it together. More formally, we use the phrase "node i *conditionally multicasts* a message (T, r, b)" to mean that node i checks if it is eligible to vote for b in iteration r and if so, it multicasts $(\mathsf{T}, r, b, i, \pi)$, where $\mathsf{T} \in \{\mathsf{Propose}, \mathsf{Vote}\}$ stands for the type of the message and π is a proof proving that i indeed is eligible (note that π includes both the pseudorandom evaluation result and the proof output by the VRF). Now, our new committee-sampling based subquadratic protocol is almost identical to the warmup protocol except for the following changes:

- every occurrence of multicast is now replaced with "conditionally multicast";
- the threshold of certificates (i.e., number of votes for a bit to stick) is now $\frac{2\kappa}{3}$; and
- upon receiving every message, a node checks the proof to verify the sender's eligibility to send that message.

4.3 Proof Sketch

To help our analysis, we shall abstract away the cryptography needed for eligibility election, and instead think of eligibility election as making queries to a trusted party called $\mathcal{F}_{\text{mine}}$. We call an attempt for node i to check its eligibility to send either a Propose or Vote message a *mining* attempt for a Propose or Vote message (inspired by Bitcoin's terminology where miners "mine" blocks). Specifically, if a node i wants to check its eligibility for sending (T, r, b) where $\mathsf{T} \in \{\mathsf{Propose}, \mathsf{Vote}\}$, it calls $\mathcal{F}_{\text{mine}}.\mathsf{mine}(\mathsf{T}, r, b)$, and $\mathcal{F}_{\text{mine}}$ shall flip a random coin with appropriate probability to determine whether this "mining" attempt is successful. If successful, $\mathcal{F}_{\text{mine}}.\mathsf{verify}((\mathsf{T}, r, b), i)$ can vouch to any node of the successful attempt – this is used in place of verifying the VRF proof. If a so-far-honest node makes a mining attempt for some (T, r, b), it is called an *honest mining attempt* (even if the node immediately becomes corrupt afterwards in the same round). Else, if an already corrupt node makes a mining attempt, it is called a *corrupt mining attempt*.

We now explain why our new protocol works by following similar arguments as the underlying BA — but now we must additionally analyze the stochastic process induced by eligibility election.

Consistency within an iteration. We first argue why "consistency within an iteration" still holds with the new protocol. There are at most $(\frac{1}{3}-\epsilon)n$ corrupt nodes, each of which might try to mine for two votes (one for each bit) in every iteration r. On the other hand, each so-far-honest node will try to mine for only one vote in each iteration. Therefore, in iteration r, the total number of mining attempts (honest and corrupt) for Vote messages is at most $2(\frac{1}{3}-\epsilon)n + (\frac{2}{3}+\epsilon)n = (\frac{4}{3}-\epsilon)n$, each of which is **independently** successful with probability $\frac{\kappa}{n}$. Hence, if there are $\frac{2\kappa}{3}$ votes for each of the bits 0 and 1, this means there are at least in total $\frac{4\kappa}{3}$ successful mining attempts, which happens with $\exp(-\Omega(\kappa))$ probability, by the Chernoff bound. Therefore, except with $\exp(-\Omega(\kappa))$ probability, if any node sees $\frac{2\kappa}{3}$ votes for some bit b, then no other node sees $\frac{2\kappa}{3}$ votes for a different bit b'.

A good iteration exists. We now argue why "a good iteration exists" in our new protocol. Here, for an iteration r to be good, the following must hold: 1) a *single* so-far-honest node successfully mines a Propose message, and no already corrupt node successfully mines a Propose message; and 2) if some honest nodes want to stick to a bit b^* in iteration r, the leader's random coin must agree with b^*. (Note that if multiple so-far-honest nodes successfully mine Propose messages, this iteration is not a good iteration). Every so-far-honest node makes only one Propose mining attempt per iteration. Every already corrupt node can make two Propose mining attempts in an iteration, one for each bit. Since our Propose mining difficulty parameter D_0 is set such that each attempt succeeds with $\frac{1}{2n}$ probability, in every iteration, with $\Theta(1)$ probability, a single honest Propose mining attempt is successful and no corrupt Propose mining attempt is successful. Since our protocol consists of κ iterations, a good iteration exists except with $\exp(-\Omega(\kappa))$ probability,

Remainder of the proof. Finally, "persistence of honest choice after a good iteration" and "validity" hold in a relatively straightforward fashion by applying the standard Chernoff bound.

Remark. We stress that for the above argument to hold, it is important that the eligibility be tied to the bit being proposed/voted. Had it not been the case, the adversary could observe whenever an honest node sends (T, r, b), and immediately corrupt the node in the same round and make it send $(\mathsf{T}, r, 1-b)$ too. If T is Vote, whenever there are $\frac{2\kappa}{3}$ votes for b in iteration r, by corrupting all these nodes that are eligible to vote, the adversary can construct $\frac{2\kappa}{3}$ votes for $1-b$, and thus "consistency within an iteration" does not hold. If T is Propose, whenever there is a so-far-honest leader in iteration r, by corrupting this leader, the adversary gets a corrupt leader, and thus no good iteration would exist.

5 SUBQUADRATIC BA: $f < (1/2 - \epsilon)n$

In this section, we present our synchronous BA protocol that achieves expected subquadratic communication complexity (expected sublinear multicast complexity) and expected constant round complexity, and tolerates $f < (\frac{1}{2} - \epsilon)n$ adaptive corruptions. Our starting point is Abraham et al. [1], a synchronous quadratic BA protocol tolerating $f < n/2$ corruptions. We explain Abraham et al. at a high level and then apply the techniques introduced in the previous section to achieve subquadratic communication complexity.

5.1 Warmup: Quadratic BA Tolerating 1/2 Corruptions

Our description below assumes $n = 2f + 1$ nodes in total. The protocol runs in iterations $r = 1, 2, \ldots$ Each iteration has four synchronous rounds called Status, Propose, Vote, and Commit, respectively. Messages sent at the beginning of a round will be received before next round. All messages are signed. Henceforth, a collection of $f+1$ (signed) iteration-r Vote messages for the same bit $b \in \{0, 1\}$ from distinct nodes is said to be an *iteration-r certificate* for b. For the time being, assume a random leader election oracle that elects a random leader L_r at the beginning of every iteration r.

Below is the protocol for an iteration $r \geq 2$. The protocol for the very first iteration $r = 1$ skips the Status and Propose rounds.

(1) Status. Every node multicasts a Status message of the form $(\mathsf{Status}, r, b, C)$ containing the highest certified bit b it has seen so far as well as the corresponding certificate C.

(2) Propose. The leader L_r chooses a bit b with a highest certificate denoted C breaking ties arbitrarily. The leader multicasts $(\mathsf{Propose}, r, b)$. To unify the presentation, we say that a bit b without any certificate has an iteration-0 certificate and it is treated as the lowest ranked certificate.

(3) Vote. For the very first iteration $r = 1$, a node votes for its input bit b by multicasting $(\mathsf{Vote}, r = 1, b)$.
For all iterations $r \geq 2$, if a validly signed $(\mathsf{Propose}, r, b)$ message has been received from L_r with a certificate C for b, and if the node has not observed a *strictly* higher certificate for $1-b$, it multicasts an iteration-r Vote message for b of the form (Vote, r, b) with the leader's proposal attached. Importantly, if the node has observed a certificate for the opposite bit $1-b$ from the same iteration as C, it *will* vote for b.

(4) Commit. If a node has received $f+1$ iteration-r signed votes for the same bit b from distinct nodes (which form an iteration-r certificate C for b) and no iteration-r vote for $1-b$, it multicasts an iteration-r Commit message for b of the form (Commit, r, b) with the certificate C attached.

★ (This step is not part of the iteration and can be executed at any time.) If a node has received $f+1$ Commit messages for the same b from the same iteration from distinct nodes, it multicasts a termination message of the form $(\mathsf{Terminate}, b)$ with the $f+1$ Commit messages attached. The node then outputs b and terminates. This last message will make all other nodes multicast Terminate, output b and terminate in the next round.

Consistency. The protocol achieves consistency due to the following key property. *If an honest node outputs a bit b in iteration r, then no certificate for 1 − b can be formed in iteration r and all subsequent iterations.* We explain why this property holds below.

An honest node outputs b in iteration r, only if it has observed $f+1$ iteration-r Commit messages (from distinct nodes) for b. One of these must have been sent by an honest node henceforth indexed by i^*. For an iteration-r certificate for $1-b$ to exist, an honest node must have multicast a vote for $1-b$. But in that case, i^* would have received this conflicting vote i and thus would not have sent the commit message for b. We have reached a contradiction. Thus, we can rule out any iteration-r certificate for $1-b$.

Furthermore, by the end of iteration r, all nodes will receive from node i^* an iteration-r certificate for b. Since no iteration-r certificate for $1-b$ exists, no honest node votes for $1-b$ in iteration $r+1$; hence, no iteration-$(r+1)$ certificate for $1-b$ can come into existence; hence no honest node votes for $1-b$ in iteration $r+2$, and so on ...... The preference for a higher certificate ensures consistency for all subsequent iterations following a simple induction.

Validity. Recall that the very iteration skips Status and Propose and directly starts with Vote. If all honest nodes have the same input bit b, then they all vote for b in the first iteration. By the end of the first iteration, every honest node has an iteration-1 certificate for b and no iteration-1 certificate for $1-b$ exists. Validity then follows from consistency.

Expected constant round complexity. Once an iteration has an honest leader, it will sign a unique proposal for the bit b with the highest certificate reported by honest nodes. Then, all honest nodes send Vote and Commit messages for b, output and terminate in that iteration. Since leaders are selected at random, in expectation, an honest leader emerges in two iterations.

5.2 Subquadratic Communication through Vote-Specific Eligibility

The above simple protocol requires quadratic communication (in each round every node multicasts a message). We now improve the communication complexity to subquadratic and we will also remove the idealized leader election oracle in the process.

We now use the vote-specific eligibility to determine for each iteration, who is eligible for sending Status Propose, Vote and Commit messages for 0 and 1, respectively. To keep the presentation simple, we abstract away the cryptographic primitives for eligibility election and model it as an ideal functionality $\mathcal{F}_{\text{mine}}$. As before, we call an attempt for node i to check eligibility to send a message a *mining* attempt. Concretely, node i is eligible to send a (T, r, b)

where T is Status, Vote, or Commit, iff

$$\mathcal{F}_{\text{mine}}.\texttt{mine}(i, \texttt{T}, r, b) < D,$$

node i is eligible to send (Terminate, b) iff

$$\mathcal{F}_{\text{mine}}.\texttt{mine}(i, \texttt{Terminate}, b) < D,$$

and node i is eligible to send (Propose, r, b) iff

$$\mathcal{F}_{\text{mine}}.\texttt{mine}(i, \texttt{Propose}, r, b) < D_0.$$

D and D_0 are appropriate *difficulty* parameters such each mining attempt for Status/Vote/Commit/Terminate has a κ/n probability to be successful and each mining attempt for leader proposal has a $1/2n$ probability to be successful. As before, we assume $n = \omega(\kappa)$ and $n > \kappa$; otherwise, one should simply use the quadratic protocol.

We use the phrase "node i *conditionally multicasts* a message" to mean that node i checks with $\mathcal{F}_{\text{mine}}$ if it is eligible to send that message and only multicasts the message if it is. Now, the committee-sampling based subquadratic protocol is almost identical to the warmup protocol except for the following changes:

- every occurrence of multicast is now replaced with "conditionally multicast";
- every occurrence of $f + 1$ Vote or Commit messages is now replaced with $\kappa/2$ messages of that type; and
- upon receiving a message of the form $(i, \texttt{m})$ (including messages attached with other messages), a node invokes $\mathcal{F}_{\text{mine}}.\texttt{verify}(i, \texttt{m})$ to verify node i's eligibility to send that message. Note that m can be of the form $(\texttt{T}, r, b)$ where $\texttt{T} \in \{\texttt{Status}, \texttt{Propose}, \texttt{Vote}, \texttt{Commit}\}$ or of the form $(\texttt{Terminate}, b)$.

5.3 Proof

We prove our new protocol works in this subsection. The proofs mostly follow the sketch in Section 5.1 — except that we now need to analyze the stochastic process induced by eligibility.

To prove consistency and validity, we first establish two lemmas, Lemma 5 and 6, to show that each bad event we care about happens with $\exp(-\Omega(\kappa))$ probability. We will then show there are at most poly(κ) such bad events that we need to take a union bound over, so the overall error probability is still exponentially small in κ. Recall that $n > \kappa$ and that the adversary can make at most $(1/2 - \epsilon)n$ adaptive corruptions where $0 < \epsilon < 1/2$ is a constant.

Lemma 5. *Except for* $\exp(-\Omega(\kappa))$ *probability, if* $\epsilon n/2$ *honest nodes have terminated, all honest nodes terminate in the next round.*

Proof. Each of those $\epsilon n/2$ nodes has a κ/n probability to be eligible to send Terminate. The probability that none of them is eligible is $(1 - \kappa/n)^{\epsilon n/2} < \exp(-\epsilon\kappa/2) = \exp(-\Omega(\kappa))$. Note that the adversary can fully control in what order honest nodes terminate, but it cannot predict which honest nodes are eligible to send Terminate. Thus, it cannot bias the above probability. Except for this exponentially small probability, a Terminate message sent by an honest eligible node makes all honest nodes terminate in the next round. □

Lemma 6. *Except for* $\exp(-\Omega(\kappa))$ *probability, For any* Status/Vote/Commit *message for bit* b *in iteration* r, *(i) less than* $\kappa/2$ *already-corrupt nodes are eligible to send it, and (ii) either* $\epsilon n/2$ *honest nodes have terminated, or at least* $\kappa/2$ *so-far-honest not-yet-terminated nodes are eligible to send it.*

Proof. For (i), observe that there are at most $(\frac{1}{2} - \epsilon)n$ already-corrupt nodes at any time. By our choice of D, in expectation, at most $(\frac{1}{2} - \epsilon)\kappa$ already-corrupt nodes are eligible to send the said message. A simple Chernoff bound completes the proof.

For (ii), if the "either" part is not true, then there are at least $(\frac{1}{2} + \frac{\epsilon}{2})n$ so-far-honest nodes that have not terminated. By our choice of D, in expectation, at least $(\frac{1}{2} + \frac{\epsilon}{2})\kappa$ of them are eligible to send the said message. A simple Chernoff bound completes the proof. □

Theorem 7 (Consistency). *Except for* $\exp(-\Omega(\kappa))$ *probability, if an honest node outputs a bit* b *in iteration* r, *then no certificate for* $1 - b$ *can be formed in iteration* r *and all subsequent iterations.*

Proof. An honest node outputs b in iteration r, only if it has observed $\kappa/2$ Commit messages for b. By Lemma 6, except for $\exp(-\Omega(\kappa))$ probability, one of the Commit messages was sent by a so-far-honest node henceforth indexed by i^*. Similarly, for an iteration-r certificate for $1 - b$ to exist, except for $\exp(-\Omega(\kappa))$ probability, a so-far-honest node has multicast a vote for $1 - b$. But in that case, i^* would have received this conflicting vote and thus, still being honest by then, would not have sent the Commit message for b. We have reached a contradiction. Thus, no iteration-r certificate for $1 - b$ exists except for $\exp(-\Omega(\kappa))$ probability.

Furthermore, by the beginning of iteration $r + 1$, all so-far nodes will receive from node i^* an iteration-r certificate for b. The lack of iteration-r certificate for $1 - b$ together with the preference to higher certificate ensures that no honest node will vote for $1 - b$ in iteration $r + 1$. To form a certificate for $1 - b$ in a subsequent iteration, all $\kappa/2$ votes have to come from already-corrupt nodes, which happens with $\exp(-\Omega(\kappa))$ probability by Lemma 6. □

Theorem 8 (Validity). *Except for* $\exp(-\Omega(\kappa))$ *probability, if all honest nodes have the same input bit* b, *then all nodes will output* b.

Proof. Straightforward from Lemma 6: in the first iteration, except for the said probability, there will be sufficient honest nodes to send $(\texttt{Vote}, r = 1, b)$, and there will not be sufficient corrupt nodes to vote for $1 - b$. Validity then follows from consistency. □

We then turn to analyze round complexity and communication/multicast complexity.

We say an iteration r is a good iteration if a *single* so-far-honest node successfully mines a Propose message, and no already corrupt node successfully mines a Propose message. (Note that if multiple so-far-honest nodes successfully mine Propose messages, this iteration is not a good iteration).

Lemma 9. *Every iteration independently has a probability at least* $\frac{1}{2e}$ *to be a good iteration.*

Proof. In any fixed iteration r, there are $2n$ total attempts to propose (every node can attempt to propose 0 or 1). The probability that exactly one of these attempts succeeds is $\binom{2n}{1}\frac{1}{2n}(1 - \frac{1}{2n})^{2n-1}$. It is not hard to show (using derivatives) that the above expression decreases as n increases and is greater than $1/e$. With at least 1/2 probability, this successful propose attempt comes from a so-far-honest node. Thus, every iteration independently has at least $\frac{1}{2e}$ probability to be a good iteration. □

THEOREM 10 (EFFICIENCY). *In expectation, all honest nodes terminate in $O(1)$ rounds and collectively send $O(n\kappa)$ messages (i.e., $O(\kappa)$ multicasts).*

PROOF. By Lemma 9, with at least $\frac{1}{2e}$ probability, a single so-far-honest node is elected leader in an iteration. After this honest leader multicasts a unique proposal, all honest nodes will output and terminate in three rounds, unless there are insufficient eligible honest nodes to send `Vote` or `Commit` messages. Each of the above bad event happens with $\exp(-\Omega(\kappa))$ probability by Lemma 6. Thus, in each iteration, there is a $\frac{1}{2e} - \exp(-\Omega(\kappa)) = \Theta(1)$ probability that all nodes terminate. The expected constant round complexity thus follows in a straightforward fashion. In each round, in expectation, at most κ so-far-honest nodes multicast messages. The expected $O(n\kappa)$ communication complexity thus follows. □

COROLLARY 11 (EFFICIENCY). *Except for $\exp(-\Omega(\kappa))$ probability, all honest nodes terminate in $O(\kappa)$ rounds and collectively send $O(n\kappa^2)$ messages (i.e., $O(\kappa^2)$ multicasts).*

PROOF. The probability that none of consecutive κ iterations is good is $(1 - \frac{1}{2e})^\kappa = \exp(-\Omega(\kappa))$. □

THEOREM 12. *For any constant $0 < \epsilon < 1/2$, the protocol in this section solves Byzantine agreement with $1 - \exp(-\Omega(\kappa))$ probability, terminates in expected $O(1)$ rounds, and achieves expected $O(\kappa)$ multicast complexity.*

PROOF. Follows from Theorem 7, 8, and 10. □

6 NECESSITY OF SETUP ASSUMPTIONS FOR SUBLINEAR MULTICAST COMPLEXITY

In this section, we show that some form of setup assumption is needed for multicast-based subquadratic BA. Specifically, with plain authenticated channels, we show the impossibility of sublinear multicast-complexity BA. In this model, a message carries the true identity of the sender, i.e., the communication channel authenticates the sender, but no other setup is available.

As mentioned in Section 2, proving the lower bound for Byzantine broadcast makes it stronger (and applicable to BA). Thus, we restate the lower bound (i.e., Theorem 3) for Byzantine broadcast below.

THEOREM 13. *In a plain authenticated channel model without setup assumptions, no protocol can solve Byzantine broadcast with C multicast complexity with probability $p > 5/6$ under C adaptive corruptions.*

Although the lower bound is stated for multicast-based protocols, the same bound applies to a more general class of protocols in which at most C nodes send messages with $p > 5/6$ probability. In addition, the lower bound holds even when assuming the existence of a random oracle or a memory-erasure model.

Our proof is inspired by the classical techniques for proving consensus lower bounds in the authenticated channel model [14, 23, 24]; however, we extend known techniques in novel manners,

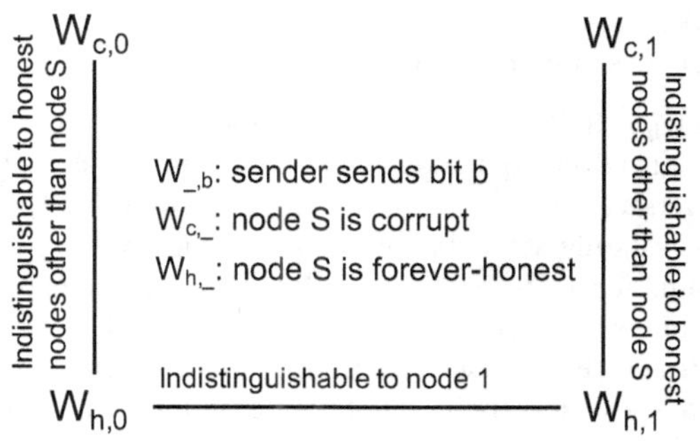

Figure 1: Relationships between different worlds in the sublinear multicast complexity without setup assumptions.

particularly in the way we rely on the ability to make adaptive corruptions to complete the proof.

PROOF. Suppose for the sake of contradiction that there exists a protocol that solves Byzantine broadcast using C multicast complexity with probability $p > 5/6$, in the authenticated channel model without any trusted setup, and tolerating C adaptive corruptions.

We focus on a special node S that is not the designated sender. We consider four worlds: $W_{c,0}$, $W_{c,1}$, $W_{h,0}$, and $W_{h,1}$. In world $W_{c,*}$, node S is corrupt whereas in world $W_{h,*}$, node S is forever-honest. The designated sender sends bit b in world $W_{*,b}$.

The high-level structure of the proof is depicted in Figure 1. First, since the designated sender is honest in $W_{c,b}$, with probability $p > 5/6$, honest nodes output b in $W_{c,b}$ to preserve validity. Next, we will show that world $W_{c,b}$ and world $W_{h,b}$ are indistinguishable to nodes that are forever-honest in both. Hence, with probability $p > 5/6$, these forever-honest nodes output 0 in $W_{h,0}$ and 1 in $W_{h,1}$. Lastly, we will show that with a constant probability, an honest node S cannot distinguish between $W_{h,0}$ and $W_{h,1}$, leading to a consistency violation with probability $> 1 - p$ in one of the two worlds. Note that the designated sender may be corrupted in $W_{h,b}$, so we need to show a violation of consistency, not validity.

World $W_{c,b}$: In $W_{c,b}$, node S is (statically) corrupt. All other nodes (including the designated sender) are honest and execute the protocol as specified. The corrupt node S simulates an execution in the $W_{c,1-b}$ world in its head for up to C multicasts. To elaborate, for every round, in addition to receiving messages from honest nodes in $W_{c,b}$, the corrupt node S simulates the receipt of messages multicast by all other nodes in world $W_{c,1-b}$, until C multicasts have occurred in the simulated execution. The corrupt node S treats the received messages (from both the real world $W_{c,b}$ and the simulated world $W_{c,1-b}$) as if they are from the same execution. It then sends multicast messages as instructed by an honest execution of the protocol. When node S multicasts a message in the real execution, its messages arrive in both the real as well as the simulated execution. We note that a simulation of $W_{h,1-b}$ by node S is possible only due to the non-existence of a trusted setup.

Observe that in world $W_{c,b}$, only node S is corrupted and the designated sender is honest. Hence, by the validity guarantee of the

Byzantine broadcast protocol, we have: With probability $p > 5/6$, honest nodes in $W_{c,b}$ output b.

World $W_{h,b}$: In $W_{h,b}$, all nodes are honest at the start of the protocol and the adversary makes adaptive corruptions along the way. The adversary simulates a protocol execution in world $W_{h,1-b}$ in its head. Specifically, at the start of each round, the adversary simulates this round for all nodes *except node* S in $W_{h,1-b}$ in its head, and checks to see which nodes will send a message in this round of the simulated execution. Whenever a node j in the simulated execution wants to speak, if there have not been C multicast messages from nodes other than node S in this execution, the adversary adaptively corrupts node j (unless it is already corrupt) in world $W_{h,b}$. If node S multicasts messages in the real execution, its messages arrive in both the real as well as the simulated execution.

In a round, a corrupt node j does the following. It sends all messages as instructed for node j by the protocol. In addition, it sends the messages node j in $W_{h,1-b}$ would have sent to node S in this round; note that these messages are sent to node S only and not to anyone else.

Indistinguishability between worlds $W_{h,b}$ and $W_{c,b}$ for forever-honest nodes. The corrupt node S in $W_{c,b}$ behaves exactly like the honest node S in $W_{h,b}$. Corrupt nodes in $W_{h,b}$ behave honestly towards forever-honest nodes other than node S. Therefore, the views of the nodes that are forever-honest in both $W_{h,b}$ and $W_{c,b}$ are identically distributed. Let Y denote the event that these forever-honest nodes output b in $W_{h,b}$. Based on the indistinguishability and the aforementioned validity guarantee in $W_{c,b}$, we have $\Pr[Y] \geq p > 5/6$.

Indistinguishability between worlds $W_{h,b}$ and $W_{h,1-b}$ for node S. Observe that in both worlds, the honest node S receives all the messages in that world (through the honest protocol execution) and messages from the first up to C nodes in the other world (through messages sent by adaptively corrupted nodes that would be sending honest messages in the simulated world). Thus, given that the honest and the simulated execution both have C multicast complexity, the view of node S in worlds $W_{h,b}$ and $W_{h,1-b}$ is identically distributed.

More formally, let A_r and A_s denote the events that the real and simulated executions respectively have C multicast complexity. Recall that the protocol satisfies consistency, validity and termination, and has C multicast complexity with probability p. Thus, $\Pr[A_r] \geq p$, $\Pr[A_s] \geq p$, and $\Pr[A_r \cap A_s] \geq \Pr[A_r] + \Pr[A_s] - 1 \geq 2p - 1$.

Let X denote the event that node S does not output 1. Given that the view of node S is identically distributed when the honest and the simulated executions both have C multicast complexity, without loss of generality, we have $\Pr[X|A_r \cap A_s] \geq 1/2$, and

$$\Pr[X] \geq \Pr[X \cap A_r \cap A_s] = \Pr[X|A_r \cap A_s] \cdot \Pr[A_r \cap A_s] \geq \frac{1}{2}(2p-1) > 1/3.$$

Consistency violation in $W_{h,1}$. The probability that consistency of Byzantine broadcast is violated is given by

$$\Pr[\text{consistency violation}] \geq \Pr[X \cap Y] > 1/3 + 5/6 - 1 = 1/6.$$

This contradicts the supposition that the protocol solves Byzantine broadcast with > 5/6 probability. □

Acknowledgement. This work is partially supported by The Federmann Cyber Security Center in conjunction with the Israel National Cyber Directorate.

REFERENCES

[1] Ittai Abraham, Srinivas Devadas, Danny Dolev, Kartik Nayak, and Ling Ren. 2019. Synchronous byzantine agreement with expected $O(1)$ rounds, expected $O(n^2)$ communication, and optimal resilience. In *Financial Crypto.*

[2] Hagit Attiya and Jennifer Welch. 2004. *Distributed Computing: Fundamentals, Simulations and Advanced Topics.* John Wiley & Sons, Inc., USA.

[3] Michael Ben-Or. 1983. Another Advantage of Free Choice (Extended Abstract): Completely Asynchronous Agreement Protocols. In *PODC.*

[4] Nir Bitansky. 2017. Verifiable Random Functions from Non-interactive Witness-Indistinguishable Proofs. In *Theory of Cryptography.* 567–594.

[5] Miguel Castro and Barbara Liskov. 1999. Practical Byzantine Fault Tolerance. In *OSDI.*

[6] Nishanth Chandran, Wutichai Chongchitmate, Juan A. Garay, Shafi Goldwasser, Rafail Ostrovsky, and Vassilis Zikas. 2015. The Hidden Graph Model: Communication Locality and Optimal Resiliency with Adaptive Faults. In *ITCS.*

[7] Jing Chen and Silvio Micali. 2016. ALGORAND: The Efficient and Democratic Ledger. https://arxiv.org/abs/1607.01341.

[8] Ran Cohen, Sandro Coretti, Juan Garay, and Vassilis Zikas. 2016. Probabilistic Termination and Composability of Cryptographic Protocols. In *the 36th Annual International Cryptology Conference on Advances in Cryptology — CRYPTO 2016.* Springer, 240–269.

[9] Bernardo Machado David, Peter Gazi, Aggelos Kiayias, and Alexander Russell. 2018. Ouroboros Praos: An Adaptively-Secure, Semi-synchronous Proof-of-Stake Blockchain. In *Eurocrypt.*

[10] Danny Dolev and Rüdiger Reischuk. 1985. Bounds on Information Exchange for Byzantine Agreement. *J. ACM* 32, 1 (Jan. 1985), 191–204.

[11] Danny Dolev and H. Raymond Strong. 1983. Authenticated Algorithms for Byzantine Agreement. *Siam Journal on Computing - SIAMCOMP* 12, 4 (1983), 656–666.

[12] Cynthia Dwork, Nancy Lynch, and Larry Stockmeyer. 1988. Consensus in the Presence of Partial Synchrony. *J. ACM* (1988).

[13] Paul Feldman and Silvio Micali. 1988. Optimal algorithms for Byzantine agreement. In *Proceedings of the twentieth annual ACM symposium on Theory of computing.* ACM, 148–161.

[14] Michael J. Fischer, Nancy A. Lynch, and Michael Merritt. 1985. Easy Impossibility Proofs for Distributed Consensus Problems. In *PODC.*

[15] Matthias Fitzi. 2002. *Generalized communication and security models in Byzantine agreement.* Ph.D. Dissertation. ETH Zurich.

[16] Juan A. Garay, Jonathan Katz, Ranjit Kumaresan, and Hong-Sheng Zhou. 2011. Adaptively Secure Broadcast, Revisited. In *Proceedings of the 30th Annual ACM SIGACT-SIGOPS Symposium on Principles of Distributed Computing (PODC '11).* ACM, New York, NY, USA, 179–186.

[17] Juan A. Garay, Aggelos Kiayias, and Nikos Leonardos. 2015. The Bitcoin Backbone Protocol: Analysis and Applications. In *Eurocrypt.*

[18] Rishab Goyal, Susan Hohenberger, Venkata Koppula, and Brent Waters. 2017. A Generic Approach to Constructing and Proving Verifiable Random Functions. In *TCC*, Vol. 10678. Springer, 537–566.

[19] Martin Hirt and Vassilis Zikas. 2010. Adaptively Secure Broadcast. In *EUROCRYPT*, Vol. 6110. Springer, 466–485.

[20] Jonathan Katz and Chiu-Yuen Koo. 2009. On Expected Constant-round Protocols for Byzantine Agreement. *J. Comput. Syst. Sci.* 75, 2 (Feb. 2009), 91–112.

[21] Valerie King and Jared Saia. 2011. Breaking the $O(N^2)$ Bit Barrier: Scalable Byzantine Agreement with an Adaptive Adversary. *J. ACM* 58, 4 (July 2011), 18:1–18:24.

[22] Valerie King, Jared Saia, Vishal Sanwalani, and Erik Vee. 2006. Scalable Leader Election. In *SODA.*

[23] Leslie Lamport. 1983. The Weak Byzantine Generals Problem. *J. ACM* 30, 3 (1983), 668–676.

[24] Leslie Lamport, Robert Shostak, and Marshall Pease. 1982. The Byzantine Generals Problem. *ACM Trans. Program. Lang. Syst.* 4, 3 (July 1982), 382–401.

[25] Silvio Micali, Salil Vadhan, and Michael Rabin. 1999. Verifiable Random Functions. In *FOCS.*

[26] Satoshi Nakamoto. 2008. Bitcoin: A peer-to-peer electronic cash system. (2008).

[27] Michael O. Rabin. 1983. Randomized Byzantine Generals. In *Proceedings of the 24th Annual Symposium on Foundations of Computer Science.* IEEE, 403–409.

Exact Byzantine Consensus on Undirected Graphs under *Local Broadcast* Model *

Muhammad Samir Khan
mskhan6@illinois.edu
University of Illinois at Urbana-Champaign

Syed Shalan Naqvi
naqvi5@illinois.edu
University of Illinois at Urbana-Champaign

Nitin H. Vaidya
nitin.vaidya@georgetown.edu
Georgetown University

ABSTRACT

This paper considers the Byzantine consensus problem for nodes with binary inputs. The nodes are interconnected by a network represented as an undirected graph, and the system is assumed to be synchronous. Under the classical point-to-point communication model, it is well-known that the following two conditions are both necessary and sufficient to achieve Byzantine consensus among n nodes in the presence of up to f Byzantine faulty nodes: $n \geq 3f + 1$ and vertex connectivity at least $2f + 1$. In the classical point-to-point communication model, it is possible for a faulty node to *equivocate*, i.e., transmit conflicting information to different neighbors. Such equivocation is possible because messages sent by a node to one of its neighbors are *not overheard* by other neighbors.

This paper considers the *local broadcast* model. In contrast to the point-to-point communication model, in the local broadcast model, messages sent by a node are received identically by *all of its neighbors*. Thus, under the local broadcast model, attempts by a node to send conflicting information can be detected by its neighbors. Under this model, we show that the following two conditions are both necessary and sufficient for Byzantine consensus: vertex connectivity at least $\lfloor 3f/2 \rfloor + 1$ and minimum node degree at least $2f$. Observe that the local broadcast model results in a lower requirement for connectivity and the number of nodes n, as compared to the point-to-point communication model.

We extend the above results to a *hybrid model* that allows some of the Byzantine faulty nodes to equivocate. The hybrid model bridges the gap between the point-to-point and local broadcast models, and helps to precisely characterize the trade-off between equivocation and network requirements.

CCS CONCEPTS

• **Theory of computation → Distributed algorithms.**

KEYWORDS

complexity and impossibility results for distributed computing, fault-tolerance, reliability, self-organization, self-stabilization

ACM Reference Format:
Muhammad Samir Khan, Syed Shalan Naqvi, and Nitin H. Vaidya. 2019. Exact Byzantine Consensus on Undirected Graphs under *Local Broadcast* Model . In *2019 ACM Symposium on Principles of Distributed Computing (PODC '19), July 29-August 2, 2019, Toronto, ON, Canada.* ACM, New York, NY, USA, 10 pages. https://doi.org/10.1145/3293611.3331619

1 INTRODUCTION

This paper considers Byzantine consensus for nodes with binary inputs. The nodes are interconnected by a communication network represented as an undirected graph, and the system is assumed to be synchronous. Under the classical point-to-point communication model, it is well-known [7] that the following two conditions are both necessary and sufficient to achieve Byzantine consensus among n nodes in the presence of up to f Byzantine faulty nodes: $n \geq 3f + 1$ and vertex connectivity at least $2f + 1$. In the classical point-to-point communication model, it is possible for a faulty node to *equivocate* [4], i.e., transmit conflicting information to different neighbors. Such equivocation is possible because messages sent by a node to one of its neighbors are *not overheard* by other neighbors.

In contrast, in the *local broadcast* model [3, 15] considered in this paper, a message sent by any node is received identically by *all of its neighbors* in the communication network. Thus, under the local broadcast model, attempts by a node to equivocate (i.e., send conflicting information to its neighbors) can be detected by its neighbors.

This paper obtains tight necessary and sufficient conditions on the underlying communication network to be able to achieve Byzantine consensus under the *local broadcast* model. As summarized in Section 2, although there has been significant work [1, 3, 5, 6, 9–12, 15, 16, 19, 23, 25–27, 29, 33] that uses either the local broadcast model or other models that restrict equivocation, tight necessary and sufficient conditions for Byzantine consensus under the local broadcast model have not been obtained previously. In particular, this paper makes the following contributions, some of which have been documented elsewhere [13, 14, 21, 22] as well:

1) **Necessary and sufficient condition:** In Sections 4 and 5, we establish that, under the *local broadcast* model, to achieve Byzantine consensus, it is necessary and sufficient for the communication graph to have vertex connectivity at least $\lfloor 3f/2 \rfloor + 1$ and minimum degree at least $2f$. Observe that the local broadcast model results in a lower connectivity requirement as compared to the $(2f + 1)$-connectivity required under the point-to-point communication model.

*This research is supported in part by the National Science Foundation awards 1409416 and 1733872, and Toyota InfoTechnology Center. Any opinions, findings, and conclusions or recommendations expressed here are those of the authors and do not necessarily reflect the views of the funding agencies or the U.S. government.

PODC '19, July 29-August 2, 2019, Toronto, ON, Canada

ACM ISBN 978-1-4503-6217-7/19/07...$15.00
https://doi.org/10.1145/3293611.3331619

2) **Efficient algorithm:** We constructively prove the sufficiency of the tight condition stated above by presenting an algorithm that achieves Byzantine consensus. This algorithm, however, is not efficient. For the case when vertex connectivity is at least $2f$, we have a more efficient algorithm. Due to lack of space, the algorithm is presented in the full version of the paper [13]. In Section 5.3, we present a tool used in the algorithm which exploits the $2f$-connectivity. Note that for $f = 1, 2$, the tight condition presented above implies vertex connectivity of 2 and 4, respectively (i.e., connectivity equal to $2f$ when $f = 1, 2$).
3) **Hybrid model:** In Section 6, we extend the above necessary and sufficient condition to a *hybrid model* wherein at most $t \leq f$ faulty nodes may have the ability to equivocate to their neighbors (i.e., the ability to send messages to each neighbor without being overheard by the other neighbors), while the remaining faulty nodes are restricted to local broadcast (i.e., their messages will be received identically by all the neighbors). The point-to-point communication model and the local broadcast model are both obtained as special cases of the hybrid model when $t = f$ and $t = 0$, respectively. Thus, the hybrid model provides a bridge between those two models and helps to precisely characterize the trade-off between equivocation and network requirements.

2 RELATED WORK

There is a large body of work on Byzantine fault-tolerant algorithms [2, 7, 17, 20, 24]. Here we focus primarily on related work that imposes constraints on a faulty node's ability to equivocate.

Rabin and Ben-Or [26] considered a global broadcast model and showed that $n \geq 2f + 1$ is both sufficient and necessary for consensus in a synchronous system. The local broadcast model considered in our work reduces to the global broadcast model when the network is a complete graph. The necessary and sufficient conditions obtained in this paper are (not surprisingly) equivalent to $n \geq 2f + 1$ when the network is a complete graph. Clement et. al. [5] also considered non-equivocation in a *complete* graph under asynchronous communication. Our work obtains results for arbitrary *incomplete* graphs with synchronous communication.

The goal of a Byzantine broadcast algorithm is to allow a single source node to deliver its message reliably to all the other nodes. Prior work has explored such algorithms under the local broadcast model [3, 15, 16]. However, the results for Byzantine *broadcast* do not provide insights into the network requirements for Byzantine *consensus* problem considered in this paper.

There has been significant work on other similar models, sometimes called "partial broadcast". To motivate these models, consider a network consisting of several Ethernet channels, with a subset of nodes S_i being connected to channel i. Then, transmission by any node in S_i on channel i will be received by all the nodes in channel i. Each node may be connected to several different such channels. An Ethernet channel to which h nodes are connected may be viewed as an h-hyperedge in a communication network represented by a hypergraph. Fitzi and Maurer [9] considered a network in which every subset of three nodes form a hyperedge, in addition to every subset of two nodes also forming a hyperedge (i.e., a complete (2,3)-uniform hypergraph). Ravikant et. al. [27] also considered a (2,3)-uniform hypergraph, but with only a subset of 3-hyperedges being present. Jaffe et. al. [12] gave asymptotically tight bounds for the number of 3-hyperedges required in such graphs. Amitanand et. al. [1] considered a complete network wherein, for each faulty node k, the remaining nodes are partitioned such that transmission by the faulty node k to any node is received identically by all the nodes in its partition. One key difference from our work is that we consider incomplete networks, whereas [1] assumes that each node can communicate directly with all the other nodes. Amitanand et. al. [1] considered an adversary structure that characterizes the set of nodes that may be simultaneously faulty, instead of using a threshold on the number of faults. Other work [6, 10, 11, 33] has explored the trade-off between reliability and privacy on partial broadcast networks.

Some prior work has explored a *restricted* class of iterative algorithms that achieve *approximate* Byzantine consensus under the local broadcast model [18, 35]. In particular, this class of algorithms is iterative in nature, with a state variable at each node being updated in each iteration as a linear interpolation of the states of selected neighbors. Due to the restriction on the algorithm behavior, the network requirements exceed the necessary and sufficient conditions shown in this paper. Additionally, these restricted algorithm structures yield only approximate consensus in finite time. Li et. al. [19] extended this line of work to a network consisting of 3-hyperedges and 2-hyperedges. Vaidya et. al. [28, 31, 32] have investigated the iterative algorithm structure in the point-to-point communication model.

3 SYSTEM MODEL AND NOTATION

We consider a synchronous system. The communication network interconnecting n nodes is represented by an undirected graph $G = (V, E)$. Every node in the system knows graph G. Each node u is represented by vertex $u \in V$. We will use the terms *node* and *vertex* interchangeably. Two nodes u and v are *neighbors* if and only if $uv \in E$ is an edge of G. For a set $S \subseteq V$, node u is said to be a neighbor of set S if $u \notin S$ and there exists $v \in S$ such that $uv \in E$.

Each edge uv represents a FIFO link between the two nodes u and v. When a message m sent by node u is received by node v, node v knows that m was sent by node u. In Sections 4 and 5, we assume the *local broadcast* model wherein a message sent by a node u is received identically and correctly by each node v such that $uv \in E$ (i.e., by each neighbor of u). A *hybrid* model is considered later in Section 6.

A *Byzantine* faulty node may exhibit arbitrary behavior. We consider the *Byzantine consensus problem* assuming that each node has a binary input. The goal is for each node to output a binary value, satisfying the following conditions, in the presence of at most $f < n$ Byzantine faulty nodes.

1) **Agreement:** All non-faulty nodes must output the same value.
2) **Validity:** The output of each non-faulty node must be the input of some non-faulty node.
3) **Termination:** All non-faulty nodes must decide on their output in finite time.

Paths in graph G**:** A path is a sequence of nodes such that any two adjacent nodes in the sequence are neighbors in the graph.

- For $u, v \in V$, a uv-path P_{uv} is a path between nodes u and v. u and v are *endpoints* of path P_{uv}. Any node in path P_{uv} that is not an endpoint is said to be an *internal* node of P_{uv}. All uv-paths have u and v as endpoints, by definition. Two uv-paths are *node-disjoint* if they do not have any internal nodes in common.

- For $U \subset V$ and a node $v \notin U$, a Uv-path is a uv-path for some node $u \in U$. All Uv-paths have v as one endpoint. Two Uv-paths are *node-disjoint* if they do not have any nodes in common except endpoint v. In particular, although two node-disjoint Uv-paths have endpoint v in common, the other endpoints are distinct for the two paths.

Fault-free paths: A path is said to *exclude* a set of nodes $X \subseteq V$ if no internal node of the path belongs to X; however, its endpoints may potentially belong to X. A path is said to be *fault-free* if none of its internal nodes are faulty. In other words, a path is fault-free if it excludes the set of faulty nodes. Note that a fault-free path may have a faulty node as an endpoint.

Degree and Connectivity: The *degree* of a node u is the number of u's neighbors (i.e., the number of edges incident to u). Minimum degree of G is the minimum over the degree of all the vertices in G. A graph G is k-connected if $n > k$ and removal of less than k nodes does not disconnect G. By Menger's Theorem [34] a graph G is k-connected if and only if for any two nodes $u, v \in V$ there exist k node disjoint uv-paths. Another standard result [34] for k-connected graphs is that if G is k-connected, then for any node v and a set of at least k nodes U there exist k node-disjoint Uv-paths.

4 NECESSARY CONDITIONS UNDER LOCAL BROADCAST

Theorem 4.1 below states the necessary conditions for Byzantine consensus under the local broadcast model. Section 5 presents a Byzantine consensus algorithm and constructively proves that the necessary conditions are also sufficient.

THEOREM 4.1. *If there exists a Byzantine consensus algorithm under the local broadcast model on graph G tolerating at most f Byzantine faulty nodes, then both the following conditions must be true: (i) G has minimum degree at least $2f$, and (ii) G is $(\lfloor 3f/2 \rfloor + 1)$-connected.*

Appendix A presents a proof of Theorem 4.1. Necessity of conditions (i) and (ii) in the theorem is proved separately in Lemmas A.1 and A.2, respectively. We use a state machine based approach [2, 7, 8] to prove Lemmas A.1 and A.2.

It should be easy to see that a complete graph consisting of $2f + 1$ nodes satisfies the necessary conditions in Theorem 4.1 for any f. Figure 1 presents other examples of graphs that satisfy the necessary conditions. Figure 1(a) shows a cycle consisting of 5 nodes. For this graph, the minimum degree is 2, and the graph is 2-connected. Thus, the cycle satisfies the conditions in Theorem 4.1 for $f = 1$. The graph in Figure 1(b) satisfies the necessary conditions when $f = 2$.

Section 5 below proves that the above necessary conditions are also sufficient. Before proceeding to Section 5, let us consider the 5-node cycle in Figure 1(a) to build some intuition on why these conditions may be sufficient. Since $f = 1$, we do not have $2f + 1$ node-disjoint paths between every pair of nodes in the cycle in Figure 1(a). Despite lower connectivity, we can show a useful property. In particular, suppose that node 1 attempts to send a message M to node 4, by transmitting it along two node-disjoint paths 1-2-3-4 and

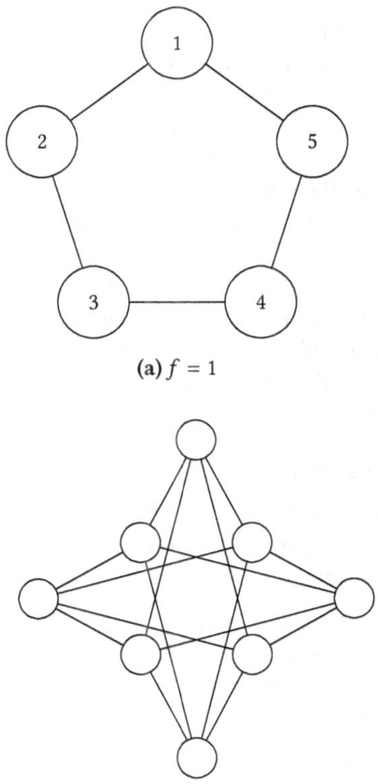

(a) $f = 1$

(b) $f = 2$

Figure 1: Graphs satisfying conditions in Theorem 4.1

1-5-4, respectively. That is, node 1 will send the message to nodes 2 and 5 (its neighbors) in a single transmission – local broadcast model allows node 1 to send its message to all its neighbors simultaneously. The neighbors 2 and 5 will then forward the message and subsequently, node 3 will forward the message received from node 2. Due to the local broadcast model, all neighbors of each node will receive its transmissions. Consider two cases:

- Case (i): The internal nodes (namely, 2, 3 and 5) on the two paths behave correctly: In this case, node 4 receives identical copies of the message along the two disjoint paths. Because $f = 1$, node 4 can be certain that it has correctly received the message that was transmitted by node 1 (when $f = 1$, internal nodes on at most one disjoint path may be faulty).
- Case (ii): Node 3 is faulty, and tampers the message received from node 2 before forwarding it to node 4: In this case, node 4 will not receive two identical copies of the message along the two disjoint paths. Therefore, node 4 cannot determine the message sent by node 1. However, in this case, node 2 is non-faulty. Node 2 correctly forwards message M received from node 1 to node 3, and then observes that node 3 is forwarding a tampered message to node 4, not the correct message M. Node 2 can observe the faulty behavior of node 3 due to the local broadcast property – when node 3 sends the tampered message to node 4, node 2 receives it too, because node 2 is a neighbor of node 3.
Node 2 can now notify node 1 that node 3 is faulty. Of course, on receiving this notification, node 1 cannot be certain whether

node 3 is indeed faulty, or node 2 is faulty and it is incorrectly accusing node 3 of misbehavior. However, node 1 can be certain that one of nodes 2 and 3 must be faulty. Because $f = 1$, node 1 can then infer that the path 4-5-1 is fault-free. Thus, any messages received by node 1 from node 4 along the path 4-5-1 could not be tampered by the internal node on this path, namely, node 5. This allows node 1 to now receive messages transmitted by node 4 reliably.

The example above can be generalized to derive a similar capability for reliable communication in at least one direction between each pair of nodes. Although the algorithm presented next does not seem to explicitly utilize this property, it implicitly relies on such a behavior.

5 BYZANTINE CONSENSUS ALGORITHM UNDER LOCAL BROADCAST

Theorem 5.1 below states that the necessary conditions in Theorem 4.1 are also sufficient.

THEOREM 5.1. *Under the local broadcast model, Byzantine consensus tolerating at most f Byzantine faulty nodes is achievable on graph G if both the following conditions are true: (i) G has minimum degree at least $2f$, and (ii) G is $(\lfloor 3f/2 \rfloor + 1)$-connected.*

We prove correctness of Theorem 5.1 constructively by providing a Byzantine consensus algorithm (in Section 5.1) and showing its correctness (in Section 5.2).

5.1 Proposed Algorithm

Assume that graph G satisfies the properties stated in Theorem 5.1. That is, G has minimum degree at least $2f$ and is $(\lfloor 3f/2 \rfloor + 1)$-connected. Pseudo-code for the proposed algorithm is presented below. To understand the description presented next, it will help the reader to read the corresponding steps in Algorithm 1 below.

Initialization: Each node $v \in V$ maintains a local state variable named γ_v, which is initialized to equal node v's binary input.

Phases of the algorithm: Recall that we assume a synchronous system. The execution of the algorithm is divided into many *phases*, each phase corresponding to a distinct subset of nodes F, such that F contains at most f nodes. Each iteration of the For loop in Algorithm 1 corresponds to one phase of the algorithm. The set F chosen in each phase is a *candidate* for the actual set of faults; however, set F in only one of the phases will exactly equal the actual set of faulty nodes in the given execution. This is similar to the Byzantine consensus algorithm for directed graphs under the point-to-point communication model by Tseng and Vaidya [30]. However, the rest of the algorithm proceeds differently since we consider the local broadcast model.

Step (a): At the beginning of each phase, each node v attempts to communicate its current value of γ_v via "flooding", as described soon. Any message transmitted during flooding has the form (b, Π), where $b \in \{0, 1\}$ and Π is a path. Flooding proceeds in synchronous rounds, with each node possibly forwarding messages received in the previous round, following the rules presented below. Flooding will end after n rounds, as should be clear from the following description.

To initiate flooding of its γ_v value, node v transmits message $(\gamma_v, \perp)$ to its neighbors, where $\perp$ represents an empty path. Each node in the network similarly initiates flooding of its own γ value in step (a). If v is faulty and does not initiate flooding, then non-faulty neighbors of v replace the missing message with the default message of $(1, \perp)$. Therefore, we can assume that a value is indeed flooded by each node, even if it is faulty. When node v receives from a neighbor u a message (b, Π), where $b \in \{0, 1\}$ and Π is a path, it takes the following steps sequentially. In the following, Π - u denotes a path obtained by concatenating identifier u to path Π.

(i) If path Π - u does not exist in graph G, then node v discards the message (b, Π). Recall that each node knows graph G, and the message (b, Π) was received by node v from node u.

(ii) Else if, in the current phase, node v has previously received from u another message containing path Π (i.e., a message of the form (b', Π)), then node v discards the message (b, Π).

(iii) Else if path Π already includes node v's identifier, node v discards the message (b, Π).

(iv) Else node v is said to have received value b along path Π - u and node v forwards message $(b, \Pi$ - $u)$ to its neighbors. Recall that v received message (b, Π) from neighbor u.

Rules (i) and (ii) above are designed to prevent a faulty node from sending spurious messages. Recall that, under the local broadcast model, all neighbors of any node receive all its transmissions. Thus, rule (ii) above essentially prevents a faulty node from successfully delivering mismatching messages to its neighbors (i.e., this prevents equivocation). Rule (iii) ensures that flooding will terminate after n rounds.

Rule (ii) above crucially also ensures the following useful property due to the local broadcast model: even if node u is Byzantine faulty, but paths P_{uv} and P_{uw} are fault-free, then nodes v and w will receive identical value in the message from u forwarded along paths P_{uv} and P_{uw}, respectively. Recall that a path is fault-free if none of the internal nodes on the path are faulty.

Step (b): Recall that a path is said to exclude set F if none of its *internal* nodes are in F. For each $u \in V$, node v chooses an arbitrary uv-path P_{uv} that excludes F. It can be shown (Lemma 5.4) that such a path always exists under the conditions in Theorem 5.1. For the purpose of step (b), node v is deemed to have received its own γ_v along path P_{vv} (containing only node v). Node v computes sets Z_v and $N_v = V - Z_v$, as shown in the pseudo-code.

Step (c): This step specifies the rules for updating value γ_v. γ_v is not necessarily updated in each phase.

Output: After all the phases (i.e., all iterations of the For loop) are completed, the value of γ_v is chosen as the output of node v.

The proof of correctness of Algorithm 1 is presented in Section 5.2. As we discussed earlier when describing the flooding mechanism, the faulty nodes are effectively limited to delivering a unique value on all fault-free paths (i.e., paths that do not have faulty nodes as internal nodes). If this unique value corresponding to a faulty node is 0, we will say that the faulty node flooded value 0; else we will say that the node flooded value 1.

Let Z be the set of nodes that flooded 0 in step (a) and let $N = V - Z$ be the set of the remaining nodes that flooded 1. Recall from the description of flooding above, that even a faulty node effectively floods one value, and one value only, in step (a) of each phase. Note that either Z or N may possibly be empty, but not both. In step (b), each non-faulty node v obtains its own estimates Z_v and N_v of Z and V, respectively. If the set F in the current phase does not contain all the faulty nodes, then these estimates can be incorrect. However, at least in one phase, F will contain all the faulty nodes and, in that phase, as shown later, it is guaranteed that $Z = Z_v$ and $N = N_v$. This observation is important for the correctness of the algorithm, as seen later.

As shown later, step (c) is designed to ensure that the fault-free nodes will reach consensus in a phase in which F contains all the faulty nodes. In each phase, step (c) also ensures the invariant that γ_v, at any non-faulty node v, at the end of the phase is equal to γ_u, for some non-faulty node u, at the start of that phase.

Algorithm 1: Proposed algorithm for Byzantine consensus under the local broadcast model: Steps performed by node v are shown here.

Each node v has a binary input value in $\{0, 1\}$ and maintains a binary state $\gamma_v \in \{0, 1\}$.

Initialization: $\gamma_v :=$ input value of node v

For *each* $F \subseteq V$ *such that* $|F| \leq f$ **do**

Step (a): Flood value γ_v. (The steps taken to achieve flooding are described in the text preceding Algorithm 1 pseudo-code.)

Step (b): For each node $u \in V$, identify a single uv-path P_{uv} that excludes F. Let,

$$Z_v := \{u \in V \mid v \text{ received value 0 from } u \text{ along } P_{uv} \text{ in step (a) }\},$$

$$N_v := V - Z_v.$$

Step (c): Define sets A_v and B_v as follows.

Case 1: If $|Z_v \cap F| \leq \lfloor f/2 \rfloor$ and $|N_v| > f$, then $A_v := N_v$ and $B_v := Z_v$.

Case 2: If $|Z_v \cap F| \leq \lfloor f/2 \rfloor$ and $|N_v| \leq f$, then $A_v := Z_v$ and $B_v := N_v$.

Case 3: If $|Z_v \cap F| > \lfloor f/2 \rfloor$ and $|Z_v| > f$, then $A_v := Z_v$ and $B_v := N_v$.

Case 4: If $|Z_v \cap F| > \lfloor f/2 \rfloor$ and $|Z_v| \leq f$, then $A_v := N_v$ and $B_v := Z_v$.

If $v \in B_v$ and v receives value $\delta \in \{0, 1\}$ along any $f + 1$ node-disjoint $A_v v$-paths that exclude F in step (a), then $\gamma_v := \delta$.

end

Output γ_v.

5.2 Proof of Correctness of Algorithm 1

In this section, we assume that graph G satisfies the conditions stated in Theorem 5.1, even if this is not always stated explicitly below. Appendix B presents the proofs of the lemmas in this section.

The proof of correctness relies on two key lemmas, Lemma 5.2 and 5.3. We will present additional results and discuss the intuition behind the proofs of these lemmas subsequently. Formal proofs are presented in Appendix B. Recall that the algorithm execution is divided into *phases*, each phase corresponding to a different choice of F, where $|F| \leq f$. For convenience of presentation, we will refer to γ_v as the "state of node v". Recall that state γ_v of node v may possibly be modified in step (c) in each phase.

LEMMA 5.2. *For a non-faulty node v, its state γ_v at the end of any given phase equals the state of some non-faulty node at the start of that phase.*

LEMMA 5.3. *Consider a phase of Algorithm 1 wherein all the faulty nodes are contained in set F corresponding to that phase. At the end of this phase, every pair of non-faulty nodes $u, v \in V$ have identical state, i.e., $\gamma_u = \gamma_v$.*

As shown next, these two lemmas imply correctness of Algorithm 1, thus proving Theorem 5.1.

Proof of Theorem 5.1: Algorithm 1 terminates in finite time because the number of phases is finite, and flooding in each phase completes in finite time. Thus, the algorithm satisfies the *termination* condition.

Since there are at most f faulty nodes in any given execution, there exists at least one phase in which set F will contain all the faulty nodes. Then, from Lemma 5.3, we have that all non-faulty nodes have the same state at the end of this phase. Lemma 5.2 implies that the state of the non-faulty nodes will remain unchanged after any subsequent phases. Therefore, all non-faulty nodes will have the same state at the end of the algorithm and their output will be identical. This proves that the algorithm satisfies the *agreement* condition.

At the start of phase 1, the state of each non-faulty node equals its own input. Now, applying Lemma 5.2 inductively implies that the state of a non-faulty node always equals the *input* of some non-faulty node. This, in turn, implies that the algorithm satisfies the *validity* condition. Thus, we have proved correctness of Algorithm 1 under the conditions stated in Theorem 5.1. □

The proofs of Lemmas 5.2 and 5.3, stated above, rely on two other lemmas, presented next. The reader may skip the rest of this section without a loss of continuity. Lemma 5.4 below implies that path P_{uv} used in step (b) of the algorithm indeed exists.

LEMMA 5.4. *For any choice of set F in the algorithm, and any two nodes $u, v \in V$, there exists a uv-path that excludes F.*

Proof: Recall that a path is said to exclude F if none of the *internal* nodes in the path belong to F. Since G is $(\lfloor 3f/2 \rfloor + 1)$-connected, by Menger's Theorem, there are at least $\lfloor 3f/2 \rfloor + 1$ node-disjoint paths between any two nodes u, v. For any $f \geq 0$, we have $\lfloor 3f/2 \rfloor + 1 \geq f + 1$. Thus, there are at least $f + 1$ node-disjoint uv-paths, of which at least one path must exclude F, since $|F| \leq f$. □

The next lemma states that the choice of sets A_v and B_v in step (c) ensures that the node-disjoint paths used in that step indeed exist.

LEMMA 5.5. *For any non-faulty node v, and any given phase with the corresponding set F, in step (c), if $v \in B_v$, then there exist $f + 1$ node-disjoint $A_v v$-paths that exclude F.*

The formal proof of the above lemma is presented in Appendix B. Observe that there are four distinct cases in step (c) for determining sets A_v and B_v. The proof of the above claim in cases 1 and 3 in step (c) follows from $(\lfloor 3f/2 \rfloor + 1)$-connectivity of graph G, while the proof in cases 2 and 4 follows from the fact that the minimum degree of G is at least $2f$.

In step (c), observe that if node v modifies its state γ_v, then it must have received identical value along $f + 1$ node-disjoint $A_v v$ paths. So, at least one of these path must not only be fault-free, but also have non-faulty endpoints. The proof of Lemma 5.2 in Appendix B relies on this observation.

Now consider Lemma 5.3. The correctness of this lemma relies on the local broadcast property and rule (ii) used in flooding. Suppose that set F in a certain phase contains all the faulty nodes. Since the paths used in step (b) of the algorithm exclude set F, these paths are fault-free (i.e., none of their internal nodes are faulty). Then, the earlier discussion of flooding implies that any two non-faulty nodes u, v will obtain $Z_u = Z_v$ and $N_u = N_v$ in step (b) of this phase. By a similar argument, all the paths used in step (c) of this phase are also fault-free, and any two non-faulty nodes will end step (c) of this phase with an identical state. A complete proof of Lemma 5.3 is presented in Appendix B.

5.3 An Efficient Algorithm

The number of phases in Algorithm 1 is exponential in f, since there exists one phase corresponding to each choice of set F such that $|F| \le f$. When the communication graph G is $2f$-connected, we have developed an efficient algorithm that requires $O(n)$ time. Although in general $2f$-connectivity is a stronger requirement on graph G as compared to the requirement in Theorem 5.1, observe that when $f = 1, 2$ these two requirements are equivalent.

Theorem 5.6. *Under the local broadcast model, Byzantine consensus tolerating at most f Byzantine faulty nodes is achievable on graph G in $O(n)$ synchronous rounds if G is $2f$-connected.*

We prove Theorem 5.6 constructively by giving an efficient algorithm. Due to lack of space, the efficient algorithm is presented in the full version of the paper [13]. Using the example in Figure 1(a), we now illustrate a tool used in that algorithm, which exploits the $2f$-connectivity. The graph in Figure 1(a) is 2-connected, i.e., $2f$-connected for $f = 1$. Similar to our algorithm in the previous section, suppose that node 1 floods value b, which is propagated to node 4 along path 1-2-3-4. When node 2 forwards the value to node 3, all of node 2's neighbors hear the forwarded message. Similarly, when node 3 forwards the message to node 4, all of node 3's neighbors hear the forwarded message.

Suppose now that we ask each node to additionally "report" on its neighbors by flooding any messages heard/received in the above propagation from node 1 to node 5. Then the message forwarded by node 4, as overheard by node 3, will be flooded by node 3. Since the graph G is $2f$-connected, node 4 has at least $2f$ neighbors, each of which will take similar steps. Now consider two cases:

- Node 3 is faulty: Since node 3 is faulty, there are at most $f - 1$ other faulty nodes. In this case, $2f$-connectivity implies that there are at least $f + 1$ node-disjoint fault-free paths from neighbors of node 3 to node 1. Thus, node 1 can receive $f + 1$ identical and correct reports of all messages transmitted by node 3. Therefore, node 1 can correctly determine the message forwarded by node 3. In general, each node can correctly learn messages transmitted by any faulty node, when the connectivity is $2f$.
- Node 3 is non-faulty: In this case, it is possible that node 1 does not receive identical reports about node 3's messages on $f + 1$ node-disjoint paths. This inability to receive $f + 1$ identical reports, however, allows node 1 to infer that node 3 must be non-faulty.

In summary, as illustrated above, each node can observe all messages sent by any faulty node. Also, each node can either observe all messages sent by another non-faulty node, or learn that it is non-faulty. In some instances, these observations help non-faulty nodes identify the faulty nodes accurately. Our algorithm in [13] relies on this property to improve the time complexity.

6 HYBRID MODEL

In this section we consider a hybrid model. The hybrid model is designed to help explore the gap between the network requirements for Byzantine consensus under the point-to-point communication model and the local broadcast model. Under the hybrid model, up to $f < n$ nodes may be Byzantine faulty. The faulty nodes are of two types:

- Equivocating faulty nodes: At most $t \le f$ of the faulty nodes may equivocate, that is, they are not restricted to perform local broadcast. If u is an equivocating faulty node and has neighbors v and w, then node u may send message M_v to node v without node w receiving M_v, and similarly send message M_w to node w without node v receiving M_w. Thus, equivocating faulty nodes can behave similar to the faulty nodes under the point-to-point communication model.
- Non-equivocating faulty nodes: Any faulty node that is not an equivocating faulty node is said to be a non-equivocating faulty node. A non-equivocating faulty node conforms to the local broadcast model. Thus, if node u is a non-equivocating faulty node, and has neighbors v and w, then any message M transmitted by node u will be received identically by v and w both.

Observe that when $t = 0$, the hybrid model reduces to the local broadcast model, since all the faulty nodes are restricted to perform local broadcast. On the other hand, when $t = f$, the hybrid model reduces to the classical point-to-point communication model because all the faulty nodes can equivocate. The following theorem extends results from Sections 4 and 5 to the hybrid model.

Theorem 6.1. *Under the hybrid model, Byzantine consensus tolerating at most f Byzantine faulty nodes, of which at most t are equivocating faulty nodes, is achievable on graph G if and only if all the following conditions are true:*

(i) G is $(\lfloor 3(f-t)/2 \rfloor + 2t + 1)$-connected,

(ii) if $t = 0$, then G has minimum degree at least $2f$, and

(iii) if $t > 0$, then every set of nodes S, such that $0 < |S| \le t$, has at least $2f + 1$ neighbors.

Observe that when $t = 0$, condition (ii) lower bounds the number of neighbor of each vertex. On the other hand, when $t > 0$, condition (iii) lower bounds the number of neighbors of each subset of nodes of size at most t. Recall that neighbors of S are nodes outside of S that have an edge to some node in S. Theorem 6.1 is proved in the full version of the paper [13]. Consider three cases:

- When $t = 0$, as noted earlier, the hybrid model reduces to the local broadcast model. In this case, condition (iii) imposes no restrictions, and conditions (i) and (ii) reduce to the graph requirements in Theorems 4.1 and 5.1.
- When $t = f$, the hybrid model reduces to the point-to-point communication model. In this case, condition (ii) imposes no restrictions, condition (i) requires G to be $(2f + 1)$-connected, and condition (iii) implies $n \geq 3f + 1$.
- When $0 < t < f$, the above theorem provides insights into the trade-off between equivocation and network requirements.

The necessity and sufficiency of the conditions in Theorem 6.1 is proved using similar techniques as the proofs of Theorems 4.1 and 5.1, respectively. The proof of Theorem 6.1 appears in [13]. To prove sufficiency, Algorithm 1 is modified to obtain an algorithm for the hybrid model – the modified algorithm is presented in [13].

7 SUMMARY

In this work, we investigated Byzantine Consensus under the local broadcast model. We showed that $(\lfloor 3f/2 \rfloor + 1)$-connectivity and minimum degree at least $2f$ are together necessary and sufficient conditions to achieve Byzantine consensus in the presence of at most f Byzantine faults under the local broadcast model. The sufficiency proof is constructive. However, the algorithm presented requires exponential synchronous rounds. For a stronger network condition of $2f$-connectivity, an efficient algorithm achieves consensus in linear number of rounds. We leave finding an efficient algorithm for the tight condition for future work.

We also considered a hybrid model where some faulty nodes may equivocate but other faulty nodes are restricted to local broadcast. We presented necessary and sufficient conditions for this model, which provide insights into the trade-off between equivocation and network requirements.

REFERENCES

[1] S. Amitanand, I. Sanketh, K. Srinathant, V. Vinod, and C. Pandu Rangan. 2003. Distributed Consensus in the Presence of Sectional Faults. In *Proceedings of the Twenty-second Annual Symposium on Principles of Distributed Computing (PODC '03)*. ACM, New York, NY, USA, 202–210. https://doi.org/10.1145/872035.872065

[2] Hagit Attiya and Jennifer Welch. 2004. *Distributed Computing: Fundamentals, Simulations and Advanced Topics.* John Wiley & Sons, Inc., USA.

[3] Vartika Bhandari and Nitin H. Vaidya. 2005. On Reliable Broadcast in a Radio Network. In *Proceedings of the Twenty-fourth Annual ACM Symposium on Principles of Distributed Computing (PODC '05)*. ACM, New York, NY, USA, 138–147. https://doi.org/10.1145/1073814.1073841

[4] Byung-Gon Chun, Petros Maniatis, Scott Shenker, and John Kubiatowicz. 2007. Attested Append-only Memory: Making Adversaries Stick to Their Word. *SIGOPS Oper. Syst. Rev.* 41, 6 (Oct. 2007), 189–204. https://doi.org/10.1145/1323293.1294280

[5] Allen Clement, Flavio Junqueira, Aniket Kate, and Rodrigo Rodrigues. 2012. On the (Limited) Power of Non-equivocation. In *Proceedings of the 2012 ACM Symposium on Principles of Distributed Computing (PODC '12)*. ACM, New York, NY, USA, 301–308. https://doi.org/10.1145/2332432.2332490

[6] Jeffrey Considine, Matthias Fitzi, Matthew Franklin, Leonid A. Levin, Ueli Maurer, and David Metcalf. 2005. Byzantine Agreement Given Partial Broadcast. *Journal of Cryptology* 18, 3 (01 Jul 2005), 191–217. https://doi.org/10.1007/s00145-005-0308-x

[7] Danny Dolev. 1982. The Byzantine generals strike again. *Journal of Algorithms* 3, 1 (1982), 14 – 30. https://doi.org/10.1016/0196-6774(82)90004-9

[8] Michael J. Fischer, Nancy A. Lynch, and Michael Merritt. 1986. Easy impossibility proofs for distributed consensus problems. *Distributed Computing* 1, 1 (01 Mar 1986), 26–39. https://doi.org/10.1007/BF01843568

[9] Mattias Fitzi and Ueli Maurer. 2000. From Partial Consistency to Global Broadcast. In *Proceedings of the Thirty-second Annual ACM Symposium on Theory of Computing (STOC '00)*. ACM, New York, NY, USA, 494–503. https://doi.org/10.1145/335305.335363

[10] Matthew Franklin and Rebecca N. Wright. 2000. Secure Communication in Minimal Connectivity Models. *Journal of Cryptology* 13, 1 (01 Jan 2000), 9–30. https://doi.org/10.1007/s001459910002

[11] M. Franklin and M. Yung. 2004. Secure Hypergraphs: Privacy from Partial Broadcast. *SIAM Journal on Discrete Mathematics* 18, 3 (2004), 437–450. https://doi.org/10.1137/S0895480198335215 arXiv:https://doi.org/10.1137/S0895480198335215

[12] Alexander Jaffe, Thomas Moscibroda, and Siddhartha Sen. 2012. On the Price of Equivocation in Byzantine Agreement. In *Proceedings of the 2012 ACM Symposium on Principles of Distributed Computing (PODC '12)*. ACM, New York, NY, USA, 309–318. https://doi.org/10.1145/2332432.2332491

[13] Muhammad Samir Khan, Syed Shalan Naqvi, and Nitin H. Vaidya. 2019. Exact Byzantine Consensus on Undirected Graphs under Local Broadcast Model. *CoRR* abs/1903.11677 (2019). arXiv:1903.11677 http://arxiv.org/abs/1903.11677

[14] Muhammad Samir Khan and Nitin H. Vaidya. 2019. Byzantine Consensus under Local Broadcast Model: Tight Sufficient Condition. *CoRR* abs/1901.03804 (2019). arXiv:1901.03804 http://arxiv.org/abs/1901.03804

[15] Chiu-Yuen Koo. 2004. Broadcast in Radio Networks Tolerating Byzantine Adversarial Behavior. In *Proceedings of the Twenty-third Annual ACM Symposium on Principles of Distributed Computing (PODC '04)*. ACM, New York, NY, USA, 275–282. https://doi.org/10.1145/1011767.1011807

[16] Chiu-Yuen Koo, Vartika Bhandari, Jonathan Katz, and Nitin H. Vaidya. 2006. Reliable Broadcast in Radio Networks: The Bounded Collision Case. In *Proceedings of the Twenty-fifth Annual ACM Symposium on Principles of Distributed Computing (PODC '06)*. ACM, New York, NY, USA, 258–264. https://doi.org/10.1145/1146381.1146420

[17] Leslie Lamport, Robert Shostak, and Marshall Pease. 1982. The Byzantine Generals Problem. *ACM Trans. Program. Lang. Syst.* 4, 3 (July 1982), 382–401. https://doi.org/10.1145/357172.357176

[18] H. J. LeBlanc, H. Zhang, X. Koutsoukos, and S. Sundaram. 2013. Resilient Asymptotic Consensus in Robust Networks. *IEEE Journal on Selected Areas in Communications* 31, 4 (April 2013), 766–781. https://doi.org/10.1109/JSAC.2013.130413

[19] C. Li, M. Hurfin, Y. Wang, and L. Yu. 2016. Towards a Restrained Use of Non-Equivocation for Achieving Iterative Approximate Byzantine Consensus. In *2016 IEEE International Parallel and Distributed Processing Symposium (IPDPS)*. 710–719. https://doi.org/10.1109/IPDPS.2016.62

[20] Nancy A. Lynch. 1996. *Distributed Algorithms.* Morgan Kaufmann Publishers Inc., San Francisco, CA, USA.

[21] Syed Shalan Naqvi. 2018. *Exact Byzantine consensus under local-broadcast channels (Advisor: Nitin Vaidya).* Master's thesis. University of Illinois at Urbana-Champaign.

[22] Syed Shalan Naqvi, Muhammad Samir Khan, and Nitin H. Vaidya. 2018. Exact Byzantine Consensus Under Local-Broadcast Model. *CoRR* abs/1811.08535 (2018). arXiv:1811.08535 http://arxiv.org/abs/1811.08535

[23] Aris Pagourtzis, Giorgos Panagiotakos, and Dimitris Sakavalas. 2017. Reliable broadcast with respect to topology knowledge. *Distributed Computing* 30, 2 (01 Apr 2017), 87–102. https://doi.org/10.1007/s00446-016-0279-6

[24] M. Pease, R. Shostak, and L. Lamport. 1980. Reaching Agreement in the Presence of Faults. *J. ACM* 27, 2 (April 1980), 228–234. https://doi.org/10.1145/322186.322188

[25] Andrzej Pelc and David Peleg. 2005. Broadcasting with Locally Bounded Byzantine Faults. *Inf. Process. Lett.* 93, 3 (Feb. 2005), 109–115. https://doi.org/10.1016/j.ipl.2004.10.007

[26] T. Rabin and M. Ben-Or. 1989. Verifiable Secret Sharing and Multiparty Protocols with Honest Majority. In *Proceedings of the Twenty-first Annual ACM Symposium on Theory of Computing (STOC '89)*. ACM, New York, NY, USA, 73–85. https://doi.org/10.1145/73007.73014

[27] D. V. S. Ravikant, V. Muthuramakrishnan, V. Srikanth, K. Srinathan, and C. Pandu Rangan. 2004. On Byzantine Agreement over (2,3)-Uniform Hypergraphs. In *Distributed Computing*, Rachid Guerraoui (Ed.). Springer Berlin Heidelberg, Berlin, Heidelberg, 450–464.

[28] Lewis Tseng and Nitin Vaidya. 2013. Iterative Approximate Byzantine Consensus under a Generalized Fault Model. In *Distributed Computing and Networking*, Davide Frey, Michel Raynal, Saswati Sarkar, Rudrapatna K. Shyamasundar, and Prasun Sinha (Eds.). Springer Berlin Heidelberg, Berlin, Heidelberg, 72–86.

[29] Lewis Tseng, Nitin Vaidya, and Vartika Bhandari. 2015. Broadcast using certified propagation algorithm in presence of Byzantine faults. *Inform. Process. Lett.* 115, 4 (2015), 512 – 514. https://doi.org/10.1016/j.ipl.2014.11.010

[30] Lewis Tseng and Nitin H. Vaidya. 2012. Exact Byzantine Consensus in Directed Graphs. *CoRR* abs/1208.5075 (2012). arXiv:1208.5075 http://arxiv.org/abs/1208.5075

[31] Nitin H. Vaidya. 2014. Iterative Byzantine Vector Consensus in Incomplete Graphs. In *Distributed Computing and Networking*, Mainak Chatterjee, Jian-nong Cao, Kishore Kothapalli, and Sergio Rajsbaum (Eds.). Springer Berlin Heidelberg, Berlin, Heidelberg, 14–28.

[32] Nitin H. Vaidya, Lewis Tseng, and Guanfeng Liang. 2012. Iterative Approximate Byzantine Consensus in Arbitrary Directed Graphs. In *Proceedings of the 2012*

ACM Symposium on Principles of Distributed Computing (PODC '12). ACM, New York, NY, USA, 365–374. https://doi.org/10.1145/2332432.2332505

[33] Yongge Wang and Yvo Desmedt. 2001. Secure Communication in Multicast Channels: The Answer to Franklin and Wright's Question. *Journal of Cryptology* 14, 2 (01 Mar 2001), 121–135. https://doi.org/10.1007/s00145-001-0002-y

[34] Douglas Brent West et al. 2001. *Introduction to graph theory*. Vol. 2. Prentice hall.

[35] H. Zhang and S. Sundaram. 2012. Robustness of information diffusion algorithms to locally bounded adversaries. In *2012 American Control Conference (ACC)*. 5855–5861. https://doi.org/10.1109/ACC.2012.6315661

A PROOFS OF SECTION 4

In the appendices, with a slight abuse of terminology, we allow a *partition* of a set to have empty parts. That is, $(Z_1, \ldots, Z_k)$ is a partition of a set Y if $\bigcup_{i=1}^{k} Z_i = Y$ and $Z_i \cap Z_j = \emptyset$ for all $i \neq j$, but some Z_i's can be possibly empty.

A Byzantine Consensus algorithm $\mathcal{A}$ outlines a procedure $\mathcal{A}_u$ for each node $u \in V$ that describes state transitions of u. In each synchronous round, each node optionally sends messages to its neighbors, receives messages from the neighbors, and then updates its state. The new state of u depends entirely on u's previous state and the messages received by u from its neighbors. The state of u determines the messages sent by u.

Lemma A.1. *If there exists a Byzantine consensus algorithm under the local broadcast model on a graph G tolerating at most f Byzantine faulty nodes, then G has minimum degree at least $2f$.*

Proof: When $f = 0$, the lemma does not impose any restrictions on G. So we assume that $f > 0$. It is easy to show that, when $n > 1$, each node must have at least one neighbor to be able to achieve consensus. So in the rest of the proof we assume that the degree of each node in G is at least 1. Suppose for the sake of contradiction that there exists a node z in G of degree less than $2f$ and there exists an algorithm $\mathcal{A}$ that solves Byzantine consensus under the local broadcast model on G. Then there exists a partition (F^1, F^2) of the neighborhood of z such that $|F^1| < f$ and $|F^2| \leq f$. Let $W = V - (F^1 \cup F^2 \cup \{z\})$ be the set of remaining nodes. Note that some of these sets can be possibly empty. However, since $n > f > 0$ and z has degree at least 1, we select these sets so that F^2 is necessarily non-empty. Recall that $\mathcal{A}$ outlines a procedure $\mathcal{A}_u$ for each node u that describes u's state transitions in each round.

We first create a network $\mathcal{G}$ to model behavior of nodes in G in three different executions E_1, E_2, and E_3, which we will describe later. Figure 2 depicts $\mathcal{G}$. The network $\mathcal{G}$ has some directed edges, the behavior of which will be explained later. We denote a directed edge from u to v as $\overrightarrow{uv}$. $\mathcal{G}$ consists of two copies of each node in W and a single copy of the remaining nodes. We denote the two sets of copies of W as W_0 and W_1. For each node $u \in W$, we denote by u_0 and u_1 the two copies of u in W_0 and W_1 respectively. For each edge $uv \in E(G)$, we create edges in $\mathcal{G}$ as follows:

1) If $u, v \in W$, then there are two edges u_0v_0 and u_1v_1 in $\mathcal{G}$. These edges are not shown in Figure 2.
2) If $u, v \in V - W$, then there is a single edge uv in $\mathcal{G}$. Some of these edges are also not shown in Figure 2.
3) If $u \in F^1$ and $v \in W$, then there are two edges uv_0 and $\overrightarrow{uv_1}$ in $\mathcal{G}$. In Figure 2, these edges are illustrated by a single undirected edge between sets F^1 and W_0, and a single directed edge from F^1 to W_1.
4) If $u \in F^2$ and $v \in W$, then there are two edges $\overrightarrow{uv_0}$ and uv_1 in $\mathcal{G}$. In Figure 2, these edges are illustrated by a single directed edge from F^2 to W_0, and a single undirected edge between sets F^2 and W_1.

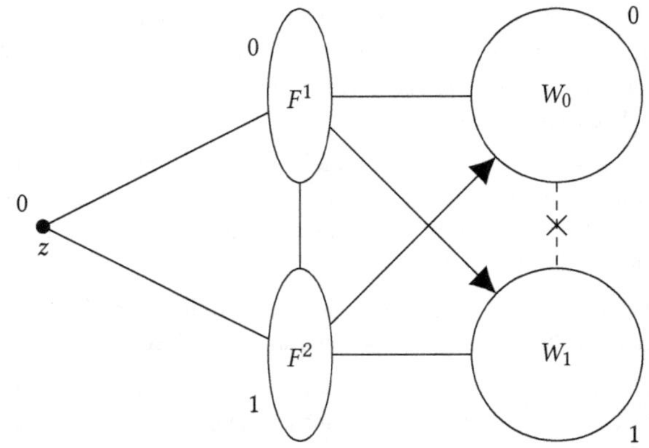

Figure 2: Network $\mathcal{G}$ to model executions E_1, E_2, and E_3. The edges in $\mathcal{G}$ are described in the text. Edges within the sets are not shown while edges between sets/nodes are depicted as single edges. The crossed dotted line between W_0 and W_1 emphasizes that there are no edges between W_0 and W_1. The numbers adjacent to the sets/nodes are the corresponding inputs in execution $\mathcal{E}$. Table 1 illustrates which nodes in $\mathcal{E}$ model the corresponding nodes in E_1, E_2, and E_3.

		(Sets of) nodes in network $\mathcal{G}$			
		z	F^1	F^2	W
Executions on G	E_1	z	F^1	F^2	W_0
	E_2	z	F^1	F^2	W_1
	E_3	z	F^1	F^2	W_1

Table 1: This table illustrates which nodes in execution $\mathcal{E}$ on network $\mathcal{G}$ (Figure 2) model the corresponding nodes in the three executions E_1, E_2, and E_3 on graph G for proof of Lemma A.1. The entries in red indicate faulty nodes in E_1, E_2, and E_3.

Note that there are no edges between W_0 and W_1. This is emphasized in Figure 2 by drawing a cross on a dotted line between W_0 and W_1.

All message transmissions in $\mathcal{G}$ are via local broadcast, as follows. When a node u in $\mathcal{G}$ transmits a message, the following nodes receive this message identically: each node with whom u has an undirected edge and each node to whom there is an edge directed away from u. Note that a directed edge $e = \overrightarrow{uv}$ behaves differently for u and v. All messages sent by u are received by v. No message sent by v is received by u. Observe that with this behavior of directed edges, the structure of $\mathcal{G}$ ensures the following property. For each edge uv in the original graph G, each copy of u receives messages from exactly one copy of v in $\mathcal{G}$. This allows us to create an algorithm for $\mathcal{G}$ corresponding to $\mathcal{A}$ as follows. For each node

$u \in G$, if $\mathcal{G}$ has one copy of u, then u runs $\mathcal{A}_u$. Otherwise there are two copies u_0 and u_1 of u. Both u_0 and u_1 run $\mathcal{A}_u$.

Consider an execution $\mathcal{E}$ of the above algorithm on $\mathcal{G}$ as follows. Each node in $W_0 \cup F^1 \cup \{z\}$ has input 0 and the remaining nodes have input 1. Observe that it is not guaranteed that nodes in $\mathcal{G}$ will decide on the same value or that the algorithm will terminate. We will show that the algorithm does indeed terminate but nodes do not reach agreement in $\mathcal{G}$, which will be useful in deriving the desired contradiction. We use $\mathcal{E}$ to describe three executions E_1, E_2, and E_3 of $\mathcal{A}$ on the original graph G as follows (see also Table 1).

E_1: F^2 is the set of faulty nodes. In each round, a faulty node broadcasts the same messages as the corresponding node in $\mathcal{G}$ in execution $\mathcal{E}$ in the same round. All non-faulty nodes have input 0. Note that the behavior of non-faulty nodes in $F^1 \cup \{z\}$ and W is modelled by the corresponding (copies of) nodes in $F^1 \cup \{z\}$ and W_0, respectively, in $\mathcal{E}$. Since $\mathcal{A}$ solves Byzantine consensus on G, nodes in $W \cup F^1 \cup \{z\}$ decide on output 0 (by validity) in finite time.

E_2: F^1 is the set of faulty nodes. In each round, a faulty node broadcasts the same messages as the corresponding node in $\mathcal{G}$ in execution $\mathcal{E}$ in the same round. z has input 0 and all the remaining non-faulty nodes have input 1. Note that the behavior of non-faulty nodes in $F^2 \cup \{z\}$ and W is modelled by the corresponding (copies of) nodes in $F^2 \cup \{z\}$ and W_1, respectively, in $\mathcal{E}$. The output of the non-faulty nodes will be described later.

E_3: $F^1 \cup \{z\}$ is the set of faulty nodes. In each round, a faulty node broadcasts the same messages as the corresponding node in $\mathcal{G}$ in execution $\mathcal{E}$ in the same round. All non-faulty nodes have input 1. Note that the behavior of non-faulty nodes in F^2 and W is modelled by the corresponding (copies of) nodes in F^2 and W_1, respectively, in $\mathcal{E}$. Since $\mathcal{A}$ solves Byzantine consensus on G, nodes in $W \cup F^2$ decide on output 1 (by validity) in finite time.

Due to the output of nodes in $W \cup F^1 \cup \{z\}$ in E_1, the nodes in $W_0 \cup F^1 \cup \{z\}$ output 0 in $\mathcal{E}$. Similarly, due to the output of nodes in $W \cup F^2$ in E_3, the nodes in $W_1 \cup F^2$ output 1 in $\mathcal{E}$. It follows that in E_2, nodes in W and F^2, as modeled by W_1 and F^2 in $\mathcal{E}$, output 1 while z outputs 0. Recall that, by construction, F^2 is non-empty. This violates agreement, a contradiction. □

Lemma A.2. *If there exists a Byzantine consensus algorithm under the local broadcast model on a graph G tolerating at most f Byzantine faulty nodes, then G is* $(\lfloor 3f/2 \rfloor + 1)$*-connected.*

Proof: Suppose for the sake of contradiction that G is not $(\lfloor 3f/2 \rfloor + 1)$-connected and there exists an algorithm $\mathcal{A}$ that solves Byzantine consensus under the local broadcast model on G. Then there exists a vertex cut C of G of size at most $\lfloor 3f/2 \rfloor$ with a partition (A, B, C) of V such that A and B (both non-empty) are disconnected in $G - C$ (so there is no edge between a node in A and a node in B). Since $|C| \le \lfloor 3f/2 \rfloor$, there exists a partition (C^1, C^2, C^3) of C such that $|C^1|, |C^2| \le \lfloor f/2 \rfloor$ and $|C^3| \le \lceil f/2 \rceil$. Recall that $\mathcal{A}$ outlines a procedure $\mathcal{A}_u$ for each node u that describes u's state transitions in each round.

Similar to the proof of Lemma A.1, we first create a network $\mathcal{G}$ to model behavior of nodes in G in three different executions E_1, E_2, and E_3, which we will describe later. $\mathcal{G}$ consists of two copies of each node in A and B, and a single copy of the remaining nodes. Figure 3 depicts $\mathcal{G}$. The edges in $\mathcal{G}$ can be deduced from Figure 3 along the lines of the proof of Lemma A.1. However, edges within C are not shown in Figure 3. They are copied exactly from G. As in proof of Lemma A.1, the structure of $\mathcal{G}$ ensures that, for each edge uv in the original graph G, each copy of u receives messages from exactly one copy of v in $\mathcal{G}$. This allows us to create an algorithm for $\mathcal{G}$ corresponding to $\mathcal{A}$ as follows. For each node $u \in G$, if $\mathcal{G}$ has one copy of u then u runs $\mathcal{A}_u$. Otherwise there are two copies u_0 and u_1 of u. Both u_0 and u_1 run $\mathcal{A}_u$.

Consider an execution $\mathcal{E}$ of the above algorithm on $\mathcal{G}$ as follows. Each node in A_0, B_0, and C^1 has input 0 and the remaining nodes have input 1. As in proof of Lemma A.1, we will show that the algorithm does indeed terminate but nodes do not reach agreement in $\mathcal{G}$, which will be useful in deriving the desired contradiction. We use $\mathcal{E}$ to describe three executions E_1, E_2, and E_3 of $\mathcal{A}$ on the original graph G as follows.

E_1: $C^2 \cup C^3$ is the set of faulty nodes. In each round, a faulty node in $C^2 \cup C^3$ broadcasts the same messages as the corresponding node in $\mathcal{G}$ in execution $\mathcal{E}$ in the same round. All non-faulty nodes have input 0. Note that the behavior of non-faulty nodes in A, B, and C^1 is modelled by the corresponding (copies of) nodes in A_0, B_0, and C^1, respectively, in $\mathcal{E}$. Since $\mathcal{A}$ solves

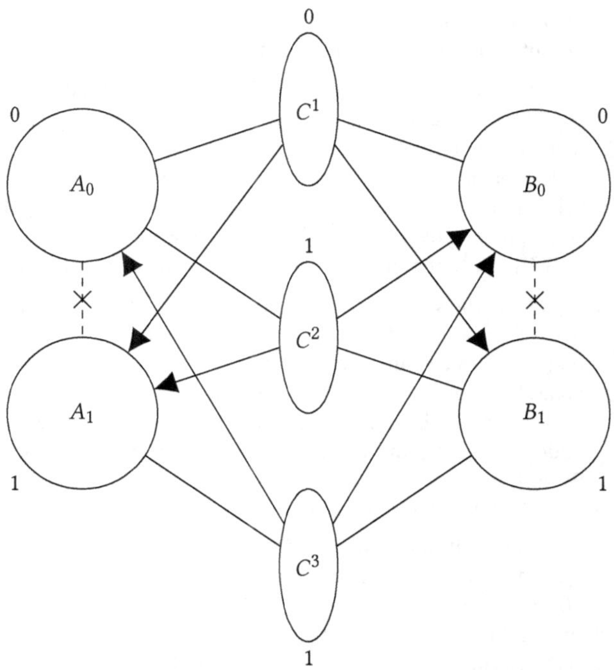

Figure 3: Network $\mathcal{G}$ to model executions E_1, E_2, and E_3. Edges within the sets are not shown while edges between sets/nodes are depicted as single edges. The crossed dotted lines emphasize that there are no edges between the corresponding sets. The numbers adjacent to the sets/nodes are the corresponding inputs in execution $\mathcal{E}$. To reduce clutter, edges within C are not shown.

Byzantine consensus on G, nodes in A, B, and C^1 decide on output 0 (by validity) in finite time.

E_2: $C^1 \cup C^3$ is the set of faulty nodes. In each round, a faulty node in $C^1 \cup C^3$ broadcasts the same messages as the corresponding node in $\mathcal{G}$ in execution $\mathcal{E}$ in the same round. A has input 0 and all the remaining non-faulty nodes have input 1. Note that the behavior of non-faulty nodes in A, B, and C^2 is modelled by the corresponding (copies of) nodes in A_0, B_1, and C^2, respectively, in $\mathcal{E}$. The output of the non-faulty nodes will be described later.

E_3: $C^1 \cup C^2$ is the set of faulty nodes. In each round, a faulty node in $C^1 \cup C^2$ broadcasts the same messages as the corresponding node in $\mathcal{G}$ in execution $\mathcal{E}$ in the same round. All non-faulty nodes have input 1. Note that the behavior of non-faulty nodes in A, B, and C^3 is modelled by the corresponding (copies of) nodes in A_1, B_1, and C^3, respectively, in $\mathcal{E}$. Since $\mathcal{A}$ solves Byzantine consensus on G, nodes in A, B, and C^3 decide on output 1 (by validity) in finite time.

Due to the output of nodes in A, B, and C^1 in E_1, the nodes in A_0, B_0, and C^1 output 0 in $\mathcal{E}$. Similarly, due to the output of nodes in A, B, and C^3 in E_3, the nodes in A_1, B_1, and C^3 output 1 in $\mathcal{E}$. It follows that in E_2, nodes in A, as modeled by A_0 in $\mathcal{E}$, output 0 while nodes in B, as modeled by B_1, output 1. Recall that, by construction, both A and B are non-empty. This violates agreement, which is a contradiction. □

Proof of Theorem 4.1: Directly from Lemmas A.1 and A.2. □

B PROOFS OF SECTION 5

In this section, we assume that the graph G satisfies the conditions in Theorem 5. The following observation follows from the rules used for flooding.

Observation B.1. *For any phase of Algorithm 1, in step (a) for any two nodes $u, v \in V$ (possibly faulty), if v receives value b along a fault-free uv-path then u broadcast the value b to its neighbors during flooding.*

Recall that, if a faulty node does not initiate flooding, then for the purpose of the above observation, its behavior is equivalent to it flooding the value 1. We now give proofs of Lemmas 5.5, 5.2, and 5.3.

Proof of Lemma 5.5: Fix a phase of the algorithm and the corresponding set F. Consider an arbitrary non-faulty node v such that $v \in B_v$ in step (c). There are 4 cases to consider, corresponding to the 4 cases in step (c).

Case 1: $|Z_v \cap F| \leq \lfloor f/2 \rfloor$ and $|N_v| > f$. Then $A_v := N_v$ and $B_v := Z_v$. Therefore there exist at least $f+1$ nodes in A_v. Node v selects $f+1$ nodes A'_v from A_v by choosing all nodes from $A_v \cap F$ and the rest arbitrarily from $A_v - F$. Define $B'_v := B_v \cap (F - v)$. Now, $|B'_v| \leq |B_v \cap F| = |Z_v \cap F| \leq \lfloor f/2 \rfloor$ by assumption of case 1. Since G is $(\lfloor 3f/2 \rfloor + 1)$-connected, $G - B'_v$ is at least $(f+1)$-connected and there exist $f+1$ node-disjoint $A'_v v$-paths in $G - B'_v$. Furthermore, since all the nodes in $A_v \cap F$ are endpoints in these paths and $F = (A_v \cap F) \cup (B_v \cap F)$, we have that these paths exclude[1] F.

Case 2: $|Z_v \cap F| \leq \lfloor f/2 \rfloor$ and $|N_v| \leq f$. Then $A_v := Z_v$ and $B_v := N_v$. Note that when $f = 0$, this case is not possible since $v \in B_v$ and so $B_v = N_v$ must be non-empty. Since the degree of v is at least $2f$ and there are at most f nodes in B_v (including v), we have that v has at least $f+1$ neighbors in A_v. There are therefore $f+1$ node-disjoint $A_v v$-paths that have no internal nodes and hence exclude F.

Case 3: $|Z_v \cap F| > \lfloor f/2 \rfloor$ and $|Z_v| > f$. Then $A_v := Z_v$ and $B_v := N_v$. We have that

$$|N_v \cap F| = |F| - |Z_v \cap F| \leq f - \lfloor f/2 \rfloor - 1 \leq \lfloor f/2 \rfloor .$$

So this case is the same as Case 1 with the roles of Z_v and N_v swapped.

Case 4: $|Z_v \cap F| > \lfloor f/2 \rfloor$ and $|Z_v| \leq f$. Then $A_v := N_v$ and $B_v := Z_v$. From the analysis in Case 3, we have that $|N_v \cap F| \leq \lfloor f/2 \rfloor$. So this case is the same as Case 2 with the roles of Z_v and N_v swapped.

In all four cases we have that there do exist $f+1$ node-disjoint $A_v v$-paths that exclude F. □

Proof of Lemma 5.2: Fix a phase of the algorithm and the corresponding set F. For any node u, we denote the state at the beginning of the phase by γ_u^{start} and the state at the end of the phase by γ_u^{end}. Consider an arbitrary non-faulty node v, and the sets A_v and B_v in step (c). If $\gamma_v^{\text{start}} = \gamma_v^{\text{end}}$, then the claim is trivially true. So suppose $v \in B_v$ and v receives identical value along $f+1$ node-disjoint $A_v v$-paths that exclude F in step (a). Since the number of faulty nodes is at most f, thus at least one of these paths is both fault-free and has a non-faulty endpoint (other than v), say u. By Observation B.1, it follows that whatever value is received by v along this path in step (a) is the value flooded by u. Therefore, $\gamma_v^{\text{end}} = \gamma_u^{\text{start}}$, where u is a non-faulty node, as required. □

Proof of Lemma 5.3: Fix a phase of the algorithm and the corresponding set F such that all faulty nodes are contained in F. Let Z be the set of nodes that flooded 0 in step (a) of the phase and let N be the set of nodes that flooded 1 in step (a). We first show that for any non-faulty node v, $Z_v = Z$ and $N_v = N$. Consider an arbitrary node $w \in Z$ (resp. $w \in N$) that flooded 0 (resp. 1) in step (a) of this phase. Observe that P_{wv} identified in step (b) of the phase excludes F and is fault-free. Therefore, by Observation B.1, v receives 0 (resp. 1) along P_{wv} and correctly puts w in the set Z_v (resp. N_v), as required.

It follows that for any two non-faulty nodes u and v, we have that $Z_u = Z_v = Z$ and $N_u = N_v = N$. Thus $A_u = A_v$ and $B_u = B_v$. Let $A := A_u$ and $B := B_u$. First note that A is always non-empty as follows. If B is empty, then $A = V$ is non-empty. If B is non-empty, then let $w \in B$ be a node in B. By Lemma 5.5, there exist $f+1$ node-disjoint Aw-paths, which implies that $|A| \geq f+1$. Now all nodes in A flooded identical value in step (a), say α. If $u \in A$, then u's state is α at the beginning of the phase and stays unchanged in step (c). Therefore, at the end of the phase $\gamma_u = \alpha$. If $u \in B$, then observe that the $f+1$ node-disjoint Au-paths identified by u in step (c) are all fault-free. By Observation B.1, it follows that u receives α identically along these $f+1$ paths and so, at the end of the phase, $\gamma_u = \alpha$. Similarly for v, we have that $\gamma_v = \alpha$, as required. □

[1]Recall that a path that excludes X does not have nodes from X as internal nodes; however, nodes from X may be the endpoints of the path.

Asymptotically Optimal Validated Asynchronous Byzantine Agreement

Ittai Abraham
VMware Research

Dahlia Malkhi
VMware Research

Alexander Spiegelman
VMware Research

ABSTRACT

We provide a new protocol for Validated Asynchronous Byzantine Agreement in the authenticated setting. Validated (multi-valued) Asynchronous Byzantine Agreement is a key building block in constructing Atomic Broadcast and fault-tolerant state machine replication in the asynchronous setting Our protocol has optimal resilience of $f < n/3$ Byzantine failures and asymptotically optimal expected $O(1)$ running time to reach agreement. Honest parties in our protocol send only an expected $O(n^2)$ messages where each message contains a value and a constant number of signatures. Hence our total expected communication is $O(n^2)$ words. The best previous result of Cachin et al. from 2001 solves Validated Byzantine Agreement with optimal resilience and $O(1)$ expected time but with $O(n^3)$ expected word communication. Our work addresses an open question of Cachin et al. from 2001 and improves the expected word communication from $O(n^3)$ to asymptotically optimal $O(n^2)$.

CCS CONCEPTS

• **Theory of computation → Distributed algorithms**; • **Security and privacy →** *Cryptography*.

KEYWORDS

byzantine agreement, optimal protocol, asynchronous, validated

ACM Reference Format:

Ittai Abraham, Dahlia Malkhi, and Alexander Spiegelman. 2019. Asymptotically Optimal Validated Asynchronous Byzantine Agreement. In *2019 ACM Symposium on Principles of Distributed Computing (PODC '19), July 29-August 2, 2019, Toronto, ON, Canada.* ACM, New York, NY, USA, 10 pages. https://doi.org/10.1145/3293611.3331612

1 INTRODUCTION

Byzantine agreement is a fundamental problem in computer science introduced by Pease, Shostak and Lamport [31] in 1980. In Byzantine Agreement there are n parties each of which has an input value, at most $f < n$ are corrupted (i.e., controlled by an adversary), and the goal of the honest parties is to decide on a unique value. Many models with various assumptions have been proposed in the literature.

Renewed interest in Byzantine Agreement follows from the need to implement Atomic Broadcast and fault tolerant state machine replication in the asynchronous setting [12, 16, 27]. In this model, Cachin et al. [10] defined the problems of Atomic Broadcast and Validated Asynchronous Byzantine Agreement (VABA) to guarantee a decision on some party's input, provided it satisfies a globally verifiable *external validity* condition. They show how to solve VABA in the *authenticated* setting, namely there is a trusted setup phase and security depends on computational hardness assumptions and the random oracle model. Their solution achieves optimal resilience $n = 3f + 1$, asymptotically optimal time $O(1)$, and $O(n^3)$ expected word communication. Improving the expected word communication for VABA in this model from $O(n^3)$ to the $O(n^2)$ is an open problem stated in [10] and has been open for almost 20 years.

This paper presents the first VABA solution with optimal resilience, asymptotically optimal time whose expected word communication is $O(n^2)$, thus closing this gap. More precisely, we prove the following theorem:

THEOREM 1. *There exists a protocol among n parties that solves VABA in the authenticated setting and is secure against an adaptive adversary that controls up to $f < n/3$ parties, with expected $O(n^2)$ word communication and expected constant running time.*

Complexity Measures. Bracha [9] shows that even strictly weaker primitives than Asynchronous Byzantine agreement can only be solved when the number of parties n is larger than $3f$ where f is the maximum number of parties the adversary can corrupt. We therefore say that a solution has *optimal resilience* if it solves Byzantine agreement for $n = 3f + 1$. A theorem of Fischer, Lynch and Paterson [19] states that any protocol solving Asynchronous Agreement must have a non-terminating execution even in the face of a single (benign) failure. Ben-Or [7] shows that randomization can be used to make such non-terminating executions become events with probability 0. Feldman and Micali [18] show that Asynchronous Byzantine Agreement can be solved with optimal resilience $n = 3f + 1$ and with an expected $O(1)$ asynchronous running time (where running time is the maximum duration as defined by Canetti and Rabin [13] and is essentially the number of steps when the protocol is embedded into a lock-step timing model). We therefore say that a solution has *asymptotically optimal time* if it solves Byzantine agreement using an expected $O(1)$ running time. We show in the full paper [2] that a recent lower bound of Abraham et al. [1] implies that any protocol solving Asynchronous Byzantine Agreement against an adaptive adversary (and without a constant error probability) must have the honest parties send expected $\Omega(n^2)$ messages. We therefore say that a solution has *asymptotically optimal word communication* if it solves Byzantine agreement using an expected $O(n^2)$ messages and each message contains just a single *word* where we assume a word contains a constant number of signatures and domain values.

PODC '19, July 29-August 2, 2019, Toronto, ON, Canada

ACM ISBN 978-1-4503-6217-7/19/07...$15.00
https://doi.org/10.1145/3293611.3331612

Multi-valued Agreement. A simplified version of the agreement problem is the *binary agreement problem* in which the inputs of the parties are restricted to the set $\{0, 1\}$. A fundamental work by Cachin, Kursawe, and Shoup [11] was the first to give an optimal algorithm in terms of time, resilience, and word communication in the random oracle model, which they formalized to fit the distributed settings. In particular, the algorithm withstands up to $f < n/3$ Byzantine failures, runs in constant expected number of asynchronous views (rounds), and the expected communication cost is $O(n^2)$ messages of the size of one or two RSA signatures [33]. A more recent work by Mostéfaoui et al. [28] shows how to achieve optimality without any cryptographic assumptions besides the existence of a common random coin[1].

As for the multi-valued Byzantine agreement, the original problem specification due to Lamport et al. [31] was motivated by the following setting: Four computers in control of a space-shuttle cockpit need to reach agreement on a sensor reading, despite one being potentially faulty. The problem was captured via the following condition:

Definition 1 (Weak validity [15]). *If all honest parties propose a value v, then every honest party that terminates decides v.*

Note that while the Weak Validity condition is well defined, it says nothing about a situation in which parties propose different values, allowing them to (1) return some default value $\bot$ that indicates that no agreement was reached or (2) agree on a value proposed by a corrupted party. Mostéfaoui et al. [29] consider a slightly stronger property in which only a value proposed by an honest party or $\bot$ are allowed to be returned [2]. However, honest parties may still decide $\bot$ if they initially disagree. In particular, it is not clear how this slightly stronger validity property can be used to solve Atomic Broadcast [10].

Cachin et al. formulated in [10] a problem specification that captures the practical settings where parties propose updates to a replicated state. Agreement is formed on a sequence of updates, hence a non-default decision is needed in order to make progress. To prevent updates from rogue parties, the model is extended with an *External Validity* predicate as follows:

Definition 2 (External validity). *If an honest party decides on a value v, then v is externally valid.*

Mostéfaoui et al. presented in [29] a signature-free deterministic reduction from their binary agreement protocol [28] that solves asynchronous Byzantine Agreement with Weak validity. It has optimal resilience and asymptotically optimal time and word communication. Unfortunately, BA with Weak validity only does not solve Atomic Broadcast or State Machine Replication (SMR).

Cachin et al. gave in [10] a reduction from their binary agreement algorithm [11] to VABA and also showed how to use it in order to implement an atomic broadcast. Their VABA protocol provides external validity, has optimal resilience, asymptotically optimal time, and expected message complexity $O(n^3)$. That paper explicitly mentions the open problem of improving the expected word communication from $O(n^3)$ to $O(n^2)$.

Our Contribution. The main contribution of this paper is solving this open question. Just like [10], our protocol solves Asynchronous Byzantine agreement with external validity (VABA), has optimal resilience and asymptotically optimal time. Improving on [10], our expected word communication is also asymptotically optimal. In particular, honest parties send a total expected $O(n^2)$ messages, which is optimal and each message is roughly the size of one or two threshold signatures.

Our protocol is secure against an adaptive adversary. This follows from using adaptively secure threshold signatures of Libert et al. [25] and adaptively secure common coin protocol of Loss and Moran [26]. Cachin et al. [10] note that their binary protocol [11] and their Validated protocol [10] also immediately generalize to be secure against adaptive adversaries by using the primitives above.

Techniques and Challenges. At a high level, the main conceptual contribution of this paper is a new approach for solving Byzantine agreement in the *asynchronous model* by using view-change based techniques that were traditionally used only in the *partially synchronous model* [14, 17, 24]. Traditionally, all view-change based protocols depend on some timeout mechanism. To adopt view-change based protocols to full asynchronous models and obtain optimal word communication against an adaptive adversary our work needs to overcome three core challenges (1) remove timeouts (2) provide safety and liveness against an an adaptive adversary and (3) reduce communication to a minimum.

Unlike previous constructions (e.g., [10, 27]), our protocol does not go through a randomized binary agreement black-box. Instead, much like Katz and Koo's Synchronous Byzantine agreement protocol [22], in each view, we run n parallel leader-based threads and then use a random leader election primitive to decide which leader is elected in hindsight. To adopt this idea to the asynchronous model each leader-based thread is a separate instance of the leader-based paradigm of [14] that uses view-change to replace leaders safely in asynchronous settings.

The idea of letting n parties concurrently broadcast their values and then using a leader election to determine which value should be further considered was first introduced in [8]. However, while in [8] they use this value as an input to a Byzantine agreement instance, we use a view-change mechanism to determine if this value can be safely decided or should it be adopted to the following views otherwise. By opening the black box agreement protocols used by both [10] and [8] we are able to reduce the communication complexity to a minimum. Just like [22], not all honest parties in our protocol reach agreement in the same view. To guarantee safety between different views we use a view-change protocol that guarantees that new leaders can propose only safe values. To guarantee liveness between different views, instead of using a timeout, the trigger is the knowledge that $n - f$ leader-based threads have made sufficient progress inside their protocol.

On the one hand, to obtain $O(n^2)$ word communication per view, we need each of the n leader-based protocols to use just $O(n)$ words and we need the global view change protocol to use just $O(n^2)$ words. On the other hand, to guarantee progress we must guarantee that our view change protocol will allow progress even in

[1]while the construction of [28] requires only $O(n^2)$ bits given a common coin, the word communication of the resulting binary Byzantine Agreement protocol is dominated by the common random coin protocol that requires threshold signatures and $O(n^2)$ word communication.

[2]Note that this property is much weaker than the one required for strong consensus [20, 30] since parties are allowed to return $\bot$.

asynchronous settings. To balance between frugal communication and liveness we adopt a four step leader-based protocol that is inspired by an approach taken in the partial synchronous model by Yin et al. [34].

To obtain the optimal $O(1)$ expected time against an adaptive adversary, the next challenge is to guarantee that when the first honest party enters the leader election phase, there is a constant fraction of potential leaders such that if one of them is elected then all honest parties will decide in constant time. By electing the leader after many leaders have completed their work we limit the adaptive power of the adversary. Moreover, if the elected leader did not complete its broadcast, we need a mechanism to allow parties to abandon the elected leader's broadcast before running the global view-change protocol.

Cryptography vs Full information. In this paper we assume an environment with a trusted setup providing authenticated but asynchronous communication channels, and a computationally bounded adversary that cannot read the private state of non-faulty parties.

It is natural to ask if similar results can be obtained in the *full information model* where the adversary is computationally unbounded and can see the state of all parties. Recent years has seen major advances in this model. Kapron et al. [21] solve ABA with just $O(n^2)$ bits against a static full information adversary that controls less than $n/6$ parties. King and Saia [23] solve ABA against a dynamic full information adversary that controls less than $n/500$. Bar Joseph and Ben Or [4] show that there is a fundamental gap between the full information model and the cryptographic model. They prove that any randomized solution against an adaptive full information fail-stop adversary that controls a constant fraction of the parties must take at least $\Omega(\sqrt{n/\log n})$ rounds in the synchronous model. By using cryptographic assumptions we overcome this lower bound and obtain the asymptotically optimal $O(1)$ expected rounds and $O(n^2)$ word communication in the asynchronous model. We are not aware of any lower bound for obtaining $O(n^2)$ bits against a dynamic full information adversary with optimal resilience in the asynchronous model.

2 MODEL

In order to reason about distributed algorithms in cryptographic settings we adopt the model defined in [10, 11]. We consider an asynchronous message passing system consisting of a set Π of n parties, an adaptive adversary, and a trusted dealer. The adversary may control up to $f < n/3$ parties during an execution. An adaptive adversary is not restricted to choose which parties to corrupt at the beginning of an execution, but is free to corrupt (up to f) parties on the fly. Note that once a party is corrupted, it remains corrupted, and we call it *faulty*. A party that is never corrupted in an execution is called *honest*. To be able to use the threshold signature from [25] and the coin tossing from [26] we assume the cryptographic random oracle model. In addition, as in [6], we treat a hash function like a random oracle.

We assume an initial setup before every execution in which the trusted dealer generates the initial states of all parties, and we assume that the adversary cannot obtain the states of honest parties at any time during an execution.

Computation. Following [10, 11], we use standard modern cryptographic assumptions and definitions. We model the computations made by all system components as probabilistic Turing machines, and bound the number of computational basic steps allowed by the adversary by a polynomial in a *security parameter k*. A function $\epsilon(k)$ is *negligible* in k if for all $c > 0$ there exists a k_0 s.t. $\epsilon(k) < 1/k^c$ for all $k > k_0$. A computational problem is called *infeasible* if any polynomial time probabilistic algorithm solves it only with negligible probability. Note that by the definition of infeasible problems, the probability to solve at least one such problem out of a polynomial in k number of problems is negligible. Intuitively, this means that for any protocol P that uses a polynomial in k number of infeasible problems, if P is correct provided that the adversary does not solve one of its infeasible problems, then the protocol is correct except with negligible probability. We assume that the number of parties n is bounded by a polynomial in k.

Communication. We assume asynchronous links controlled by the adversary, that is, the adversary can see all messages and decide when and what messages to deliver. In order to fit the communication model with the computational assumptions, we restrict the adversary to perform no more than a polynomial in k number of computation steps between the time a message m from an honest party p_i is sent to an honest party p_j and the time m is delivered by p_j[3]. In addition, for simplicity, we assume that messages are *authenticated* in a sense that if an honest party p_i receives a message m indicating that m was sent by an honest party p_j, then m was indeed generated by p_j and sent to p_i at some prior time. This assumption is reasonable since it can be easily implemented with standard symmetric-key cryptographic techniques [5] in our model.

Termination. Note that the traditional definition of the liveness property in distributed system, which requires that all correct (honest) parties *eventually* terminate provided that all messages between correct (honest) parties eventually arrive, does not make sense in this model. This is because the traditional definition allows the following:

- Unbounded delivery time between honest parties, which potentially gives the adversary unbounded time to solve infeasible problems.
- Unbounded runs that potentially may consist of an unbounded number of infeasible problems, and thus the probability that the adversary manages to solve one is not negligible.

Following Cachin et al. [10, 11], we address the first concern by restricting the number of computation steps the adversary makes during message transmission among honest parties. So as long as the total number of messages in the protocol is polynomial in k, the error probability remains negligible. To deal with the second concern, we do not use a standard liveness property in this paper, but instead we reason about the total number of messages required for all honest parties to terminate. We adopt the following definition from [10, 11]:

Definition 3 (Uniformly Bounded Statistic). *Let X be a random variable. We say that X is probabilistically uniformly bounded*

[3]Note that although this restriction gives some upper bound on the communication in terms of the adversary local speed, the model is still asynchronous since speeds of different parties are completely unrelated.

if there exist a fixed polynomial $T(k)$ and a fixed negligible functions $\delta(l)$ and $\epsilon(k)$ such that for all $l, k \geq 0$,

$$Pr[X > lT(k)] \leq \delta(l) + \epsilon(k)$$

With the above definition Cachin et al. [10, 11] define a progress property that makes sense in the cryptographic settings:

- *Efficiency: The number of messages generated by the honest parties is probabilistically uniformly bounded*

The efficiency property implies that the probability of the adversary to solve an infeasible problem is negligible, which makes it possible to reason about the correctness of the primitives' properties. However, note that this property can be trivially satisfied by a protocol that never terminates but also never sends any messages. Therefore, in order for a primitive to be meaningful in this model, Cachin et al. [10, 11] require another property:

- *Termination*[4]: If all messages sent by honest parties have been delivered, then all honest parties terminated.

In this paper we consider both efficiency and termination properties as defined in [10, 11]. However, note that when considering an adaptive adversary, it is also possible to define a slightly weaker termination property:

- *Weak termination*: If all messages sent by parties before they were corrupted have been delivered, then all honest parties terminated.

Note that while any protocol that satisfies termination satisfies weak termination as well, a lower bound for termination does not apply for weak termination. Indeed our lower bound (see full paper [2]) is for protocols that obtain the termination property. We leave the study of lower bounds for protocols with weak termination as an open question.

Complexity. We use the following standard complexity notions (see for example Cannetti and Rabin [13]). We measure the expected *word communication* of our protocol as the maximum over all inputs and applicable adversaries of the expected total number of *words* sent by honest parties where expectation is taken over the random inputs of the players and of the adversary. We assume a finite domain $\mathcal{V}$ of valid values for the Byzantine agreement problem, and say that a word can contain a constant number of signatures (see Section and domain values 2.1). We measure the expected *running time* of our protocol as the maximum over all inputs and applicable adversaries of the expected *duration* where expectation is taken over the random inputs of the players and of the adversary. The duration of an execution is the total time until all honest players have terminated divided by the longest delay of a message in this execution. Essentially the duration of an execution is the number of steps taken if this execution is re-run in lock-step model where each message takes exactly one time step.

Following Cachin et al. [10] (see Lemma 1 therein), in order to show that our view-based protocol runs in an expected constant running time and has expected $O(n^2)$ word communication, it is enough to show that:

- every view consists of $R(k) = O(n^2)$ messages that consist of one word, and
- the total number of messages is probabilistically uniformly bounded by R.

2.1 Cryptographic abstractions

The main focus of this paper is on a novel distributed algorithm, which uses cryptographic tools as black-boxes. To this end, we present our protocol assuming the existence of two cryptographic abstractions:

- **Threshold signatures scheme.** We assume that each party p_i has a private function *share-sign*$_i$, and we assume 3 public functions: *share-validate, threshold-sign,* and *threshold-validate*. Informally, given $n-f$ validated shares, the function *threshold-sign* returns a valid threshold signature.
- **Threshold coin-tossing.** We assume that each party p_i has a private function *coin-share*$_i$, and we assume 2 public functions: *coin-share-validate* and *coin-toss*. Informally, given $f+1$ validated coin shares, the function *coin-toss* returns a unique and pseudorandom number from the range $[1, \ldots, n]$.

The for formal definitions and implementation details can be found in the full paper [2].

2.2 Validated asynchronous byzantine agreement (VABA)

In this paper we follow Cachin et al. [10] and define a (multi-valued) Byzantine agreement with an external validity function we call *EX-VABA-VAL*. The purpose of this function is to determine whether a value is externally valid for agreement, and the validity property of the VABA requires parties to decide only on externally valid values. To rule out trivial solutions in which parties always decide on some pre-defined externally valid value, we could try to add a requirement that only a value that was actually proposed by some party (honest or not) can be decided. However, since byzantine parties can propose one value and act as if they proposed a different value, this requirement seems to be impossible to achieve. Instead, we add another property to the VABA problem defined in [10], which we call *quality*. The *quality* property bounds the probability that the decision value was proposed by an honest party. Note that every probability that is grater than zero rules out trivial solutions, however, to capture the "fairness" of the decision value we require this probability to be $1/2$ [5]. We conjecture that higher probability is impossible to achieve in our model. The formal definition of the VABA protocol is given below.

Definition 4 (Validated Byzantine Agreement). *A protocol solves validated Byzantine agreement if it satisfies the following properties except with negligible probability:*

- *Validity: If an honest party decides an a value v, then* EX-VABA-VAL(v) = *true*.
- *Quality: The probability of choosing a value that was proposed by an honest party is at least $1/2$.*
- *Agreement: All honest parties that terminate decide on the same value.*

[4]Called liveness in [11], but we find this name confusing since it is not a liveness [3] property.

[5]Note that although they do not explicitly define it, the protocol of Cachin et al. [10, 11] already obtains this Quality property.

- *Termination: If all honest parties start with externally valid values and all messages sent among honest parties have been delivered, then all honest parties decide.*
- *Efficiency: The number of messages generated by the honest parties is probabilistically uniformly bounded.*

3 ASYMPTOTICALLY OPTIMAL VABA PROTOCOL

In this section we give a protocol for asynchronous byzantine agreement, secure against an adaptive adversary that controls up to $f < n/3$ parties, with expected word communication $O(n^2)$ and expected running time $O(1)$. We present a modular implementation, which consists of three sub protocols: a simple two-round broadcast primitive we call *Provable-Broadcast*, a simple *Leader-Election* protocol, and another primitive, we call *Proposal-Promotion*, which is built on top of 4 sequential instances of Provable-Broadcast. In Section 3.1, we give an overview of the protocols, and in Section 3.2 we present detailed pseudocode and description.

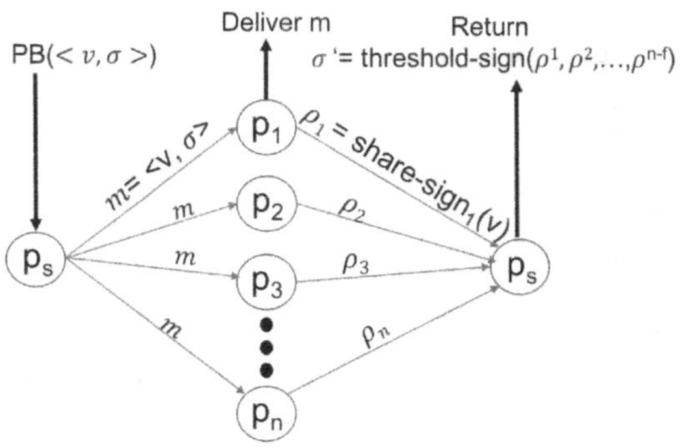

Figure 1: Provable-Broadcast illustration. The message external validation by all parties is omitted. When a party receives a value v and a proof σ from the sender, it first uses σ to externally validate v, and only then deliver, sign, and send its share v back to the sender.

3.1 Our VABA protocol overview

Provable-Broadcast. The Provable-Broadcast is a simple two-round broadcast that adds an external validity to the basic echo multicast protocol from [10, 32]. In the first round, the sender sends a message, that contains a value and a proof for external validity, to all parties. In the second round, each party first validates, with an external validation function (which implements a logic of the protocol that is implemented on top of the broadcast), that the message is valid. Then, it (1) delivers the message (value and proof), (2) threshold-signs it, and (3) sends the signed share back to the sender. When the sender gets $n - f$ properly signed shares, it combines them into one threshold signature and returns it. An illustration of the Provable-Broadcast protocol appears in Figure 1. Informally, the provability property of this simple broadcast satisfies the following: (1) An honest sender returns a threshold signature which he can later use to prove that at least $f + 1$ honest parties delivered the message; and (2) a faulty sender cannot produce two such proofs for two different messages. This proof is later used by the sender for external validity in other parts of the VABA protocol.

Proposal-Promotion. As we explain below, the VABA protocol works in a view-based manner, where in each view the parties participate in n concurrent Proposal-Promotion sub-protocols. Each party i is acting as the leader of the ith Proposal-Promotion invocation and tries to promote its proposal by distributing them to all other parties. The distribution inside a Proposal-Promotion sub-protocol consists of 4 sequential steps, each of which invokes an instances of a Provable-Broadcast. An illustration of the sub-protocol appears in Figure 2. All parties participating in an instance of a Proposal-Promotion maintain 3 local variables: **key**, **lock**, and **commit**. The **key** variable stores the message (value and proof) delivered in the second step (second instance of the Provable-Broadcast), the **lock** variable stores the message delivered in the third step, and the **commit** variable stores the message delivered in the fourth step. For clarity, we refer to these delivery events as **key** delivery, **lock** delivery, and **commit** delivery, respectively.

A leader (the initiating party) of a Proposal-Promotion invocation that successfully completes gets a proof of its completeness, which is the threshold signature output of the last Provable-Broadcast instance therein. As for the external validity of the Provable-Broadcast steps inside a Proposal-Promotion, we distinguish between the first instance and the last 3. For the first instance (first step) the leader provides a proof *key* that the proposed value (the one to be promoted) is safe for the current view of the VABA protocol. (More details on this below). For each of the other 3 instances, the leader provides the threshold signature output of the preceding Provable-Broadcast instance, which is a proof of its successful completion. Informally, the provability property together with the external validity of Provable-Broadcast guarantee the following:

- All values delivered by honest parties in the **key**, **lock**, and **commit** deliveries are (1) equal and (2) satisfy the safety logic of the higher level VABA protocol for this view.
- A valid completeness proof indicates that at least $f + 1$ honest parties delivered **commit**. In addition, if an honest party delivered **commit**, then at least $f + 1$ honest parties previously delivered **lock**, and if an honest party delivered **lock**, then at least $f + 1$ honest parties previously delivered **key**.

Leader-Election. The Leader-Election primitive is a simple one-round protocol that uses the cryptographic threshold coin-tossing abstraction to elect a unique leader [6] among the parties for each view. In every view R, each party p_i uses $coin\text{-}share_i(R)$ to produce a share ρ_i and sends it to all other parties. When a party gets $f + 1$ proper shares for view R it uses the function *coin-toss* to compute the leader of view R. Informally, the main properties are that (1) all honest parties agree on the leader, (2) the adversary cannot predict who is the leader unless one honest party participates, and (3) every party has an equal probability to became the leader of every view.

[6]Note that every instance of a Proposal-Promotion has a unique leader, but here we choose among them one unique leader for each view.

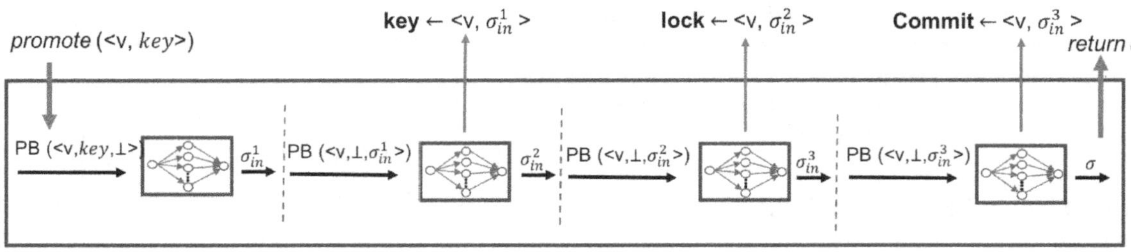

Figure 2: Illustration of the 4 steps of a Proposal-Promotion sub protocol.

Putting everything together into the VABA protocol. The Proposal-Promotion and the Leader-Election sub-protocols are used as building blocks for our VABA protocol. The protocol works in a view-based manner, where each view consists of three phases: *Leader-nomination, Leader-election*, and *View-change*. In the *Leader-nomination Phase*, each party promotes its proposal value via the Proposal-Promotion sub-protocol. Parties wait to learn that $n - f$ instances of Proposal-Promotion, initiated by different parties, have *completed* by getting $n - f$ such proofs. (Recall that the *promote* function returns a proof of completion that indicates that at least $f + 1$ honest parties delivered **commit** in that instance). Then, in the *Leader-election Phase*, parties choose a unique leader uniformly at random, via the Leader-Election primitive. Finally, in the *View-change Phase*, parties learn what happened in the elected leader's Proposal-Promotion protocol and update their local state accordingly. This is done by an all-to-all communication, where each party sends to all other parties the **key**, **lock**, and **commit** it delivered (if any) in the Proposal-Promotion sub-protocol initiated by the chosen leader. If they learn that some party delivered **commit**($\langle v, \sigma\rangle$) (where σ is a valid proof for v to be committed), they can decide v. Otherwise, they need to carefully adopt a value, (by analysing what **key** and **lock** were delivered), and continue to the next view.

The local state of each party includes two essential variables *LOCK* and *KEY*, which are updated at the end of each round (based on the received view-change messages) and used by the first instance of the Provable-Broadcast in every Proposal-Promotion to determine whether the promoted value is externally valid. Informally, the *KEY* variable stores a view number *view*, a value v and a proof σ s.t. (1) a **key** = $\langle v, \sigma\rangle$ was received in the *View-change* phase of *view*, (2) σ is a proof for v's delivery in the second instance of the Provable-Broadcast in the Proposal-Promotion of *view*, and (3) *view* is the highest view that satisfies (1) and (2). The *LOCK* variable stores a view number that corresponds to the highest view in which a view-change message with a valid **lock** (contains $\langle v, \sigma\rangle$ s.t. σ is a proof for v's delivery in the third instance of the Provable-Broadcast in the Proposal-Promotion of *view*) was received. Informally, the external validity function in the first instance of the Provable-Broadcast of each Proposal-Promotion checks that the promoted value is attached to a valid key that was obtained in view that is at least large as the the view of the local variable *LOCK*. An high-level illustration appears in Figure 3, and more details are given in the description below.

Our protocol guarantees that at least $n - f$ Proposal-Promotion instances complete in the broadcast phase before a leader is elected. If the elected leader has completed its Proposal-Promotion (implying that at least $f + 1$ honest parties delivered a **commit**) then even an adaptive adversary cannot prevent progress. Otherwise, the view-change phase ensures that agreement is not violated even if a bad leader is elected. Since the probability to choose a leader that completed its Proposal-Promotion is constant, the number of views in the protocol is constant in expectation. More concretely, the probability to choose a completed broadcast is greater than 2/3, and thus the number of views in expectation is less than 3/2.

Communication complexity. Each of the **key**, **lock**, and **commit** variables stores one value and one threshold signature. Therefore, the total word complexity of the View-change phase is $O(n^2)$. The word complexity of a single instance of Proposal-Promotion is $O(n)$, which leads to total $O(n^2)$ word complexity of the Leader-nomination phase. Since the Leader-election phase has a single round all-to-all communication with messages of size 1 word, we get that all to all, our VABA protocol has an optimal $O(n^2)$ word complexity in expectation.

3.2 Detailed VABA protocol description

In this section we give a detailed description of our VABA protocol. A formal proof and a complexity analysis appear in the full paper [2]. For better readability we use the top down approach. We first present the VABA protocol and then describe the sub-protocols it uses. The formal definition of the properties as well as the pseudocode of the simple Leader-election primitive are deferred to Appendix B. As defined in the model, there is an external function, called *EX-VABA-VAL*(v), which checks if v is a valid value for the byzantine agreement. An instance of the high-level VABA protocol is identified with a parameter *id*. Every instance of every sub-protocol is identified with a parameter *ID*, which extends *id*. For example, the *ID* of p_i's Proposal-Promotion in view $view$ is $\langle id, i, view\rangle$, and the *ID* of the second instance of the Provable-Broadcast therein is $\langle\langle id, i, view\rangle, 2\rangle$.

Local variables. We start by presenting the local variables parties maintain (see Algorithm 1). All parties maintain two cross-view variables, *LOCK* and *KEY*:

- The *LOCK* variable stores the highest view number for which the party ever received a view-change message that includes a **lock** that was delivered in the Proposal-Promotion of the chosen leader of this view.
- The *KEY* variable stores the 3-tuple: view, proof and value, derived from the maximum view for which the party ever

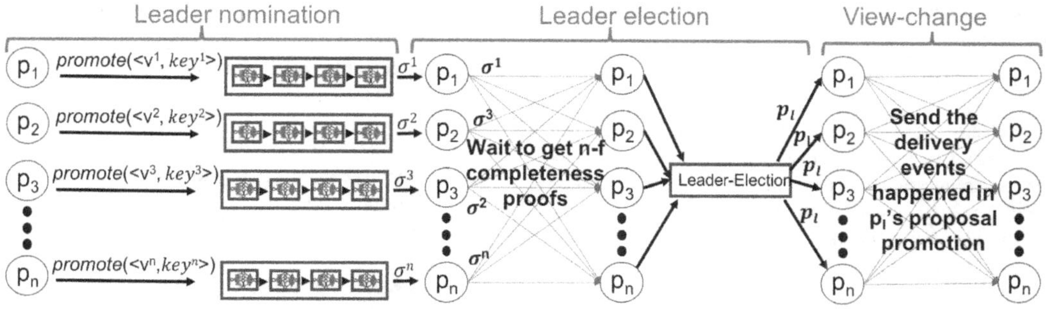

Figure 3: An illustration of a single view in the VABA protocol. Blue thin arrows represent messages and black thick arrows represent invocations and responds of sub-protocols.

received a view-change message that includes a **key** (composing of value and proof) that was delivered in the Proposal-Promotion of the chosen leader of this view.

In addition, all parties maintain per-view variables: For a view *view*, each party stores the elected leader of this view in *Leader*[*view*], and few variables, *PPdone*[*view*], *PPskip*[*view*], *skip*[*view*], which are used to make sure that at least $n - f$ parties completed their Proposal-Promotion before some honest party moves to the leader election phase.

Algorithm 1 Local variables initialization for party p_i.

$LOCK \leftarrow 0$
$KEY \leftarrow \langle 0, v_i, \bot \rangle$ with selectors *view, value, proof* ▷ v_i is p_i's input
for every $view \geq 1$, **initialize**:
  $Leader[view] \leftarrow \bot$
  $PPdone[view] \leftarrow 0$
  $PPskip[view] \leftarrow \{\}$
  $skip[view] \leftarrow false$

The pseudocode of the top VABA protocol appears in algorithms 2 and 3. We next describe the phases in each view:

Leader nomination phase. Each party promotes, using a Proposal-Promotion sub-protocol, the value and *key* it has adopted from the previous views, as determined in the View-Change Phase (explained below); at view 1, a party promotes its input and an empty key. Parties participate in *n* concurrent Proposal-Promotions, and each party sends a DONE notification about the completion of its own Proposal-Promotion carrying its output for proof. When a party receives $n-f$ such notifications, it sends a signature share on a SKIP-SHARE message. For termination, each party waits to obtain (directly or indirectly) a combined threshold SKIP signature, forwards it to others, and moves to the Leader-election phase (even if its Proposal-Promotion has not completed due to *abandon* invocation of other parties).

Leader election phase. Once a party enters the Leader-election Phase, it abandons all the Proposal-Promotion instances (more details on *abandon* is given below). The parties elect a leader via the leader election primitive and continue to the next phase as if only the chosen leader's Proposal-Promotion ever occurred. From now on, we refer to the Proposal-Promotion of the leader of a view *view*

Algorithm 2 Validated asynchronous byzantine agreement with identification *id*: protocol for party p_i.

$view \leftarrow 1$
while true **do**
  $ID \leftarrow \langle id, i, view \rangle$ ▷ Leader nomination phase
  $key \leftarrow \langle KEY.view, KEY.proof \rangle$
  $\sigma \leftarrow$ promote($ID, \langle KEY.value, key \rangle$)
  wait for *promote* to return or $skip[view]$ to become *true*
  if $skip[view] = false$ **then**
    send "*id*, DONE, *view*, *KEY.value*, σ" to all parties
  wait until $skip[view] = true$
  ▷ Leader election phase
  for all k=1,...,n **do**
    $abandon(\langle id, k, view \rangle)$ ▷ abandon Proposal-Promotion with $ID = \langle id, k, view \rangle$
  $Leader[view] \leftarrow elect(\langle id, view \rangle)$
  ▷ View-change phase
  $ID_{leader} = \langle id, Leader[view], view \rangle$
  send "*id*, VIEW-CHANGE, *view*, $getKey(ID_{leader})$, $getLock(ID_{leader})$, $getCommit(ID_{leader})$" to all parties
  wait for VIEW-CHANGE messages from $n - f$ different parties
  $view \leftarrow view + 1$

as the Proposal-Promotion of view *view*, and refer to its delivery events as the deliveries of view *view*.

View-change phase. In the View-change Phase of every view, parties report their delivery events (value and proof) of this view (delivery in the chosen leader's Proposal-Promotion) to all other parties. Each party waits to collect $n-f$ reports. Recall that Proposal-Promotion provides the following guarantees: If some honest party delivers a **commit**, then $f + 1$ honest parties deliver **lock**, hence all honest parties recieve this **lock** in the view-change exchange. Similarly, if some honest party delivers a **lock**, then $f + 1$ honest parties deliver a **key**, hence all honest parties receive this **key**.

Once a party has collected $n - f$ view-change messages, it processes them as follows. If it receives a **commit** with a value *v*, it decides *v*. Otherwise, if it receives a **lock**, it increases its *LOCK* variable to the current view. Last, if it receives a **key**, it updates its *KEY* variable to store the current view and the received **key**. If it

Algorithm 3 Validated asynchronous byzantine agreement with identification *id*: messages.

```
upon receiving "id, DONE, view, v, σ" from party p_k for the first time do
    if threshold-validate(⟨⟨⟨id, k, view⟩, 4⟩, v⟩, σ) then
        PPdone[view] ← PPdone[view] + 1
        if "SKIP-SHARE" message was not sent yet in view view then
            if PPdone[view] = n − f then
                ρ ← sigh-share(⟨id, SKIP, view⟩)
                send "id, SKIP-SHARE, view, ρ" to all parties

upon receiving "id, SKIP-SHARE, view, ρ" from party p_k for the first time in view view do
    if share-validate(⟨id, SKIP, view⟩, k, ρ) then
        PPskip[view] ← PPskip[view] ∪ {ρ}
        if |PPskip[view]| = n − f then
            σ ← threshold-sign(PPskip[view])
            send "id, SKIP, view, σ" to all parties

upon receiving "id, SKIP, view, σ" do
    if threshold-validate(⟨id, SKIP, view⟩, σ) = true then
        skip[view] ← true
        if "SKIP" message was not sent yet in view view then
            send "id, SKIP, view, σ" to all parties

upon receiving "id, VIEW-CHANGE, view, ⟨v2, σ2⟩, ⟨v3, σ3⟩, ⟨v4, σ4⟩" do
    leader ← Leader[view]
    if v4 ≠ ⊥ then
        if threshold-validate(⟨⟨⟨id, leader, view⟩, 3⟩, v4⟩, σ4) then
            decide v4
    if v3 ≠ ⊥ ∧ view > lock then
        if threshold-validate(⟨⟨⟨id, leader, view⟩, 2⟩, v3⟩, σ3) then
            LOCK ← view
    if v2 ≠ ⊥ ∧ view > key.view then
        if threshold-validate(⟨⟨⟨id, leader, view⟩, 1⟩, v2⟩, σ2) then
            KEY ← ⟨view, v2, σ2⟩
```

did not reach a decision, a party adopts the value v of its (up-to-date) *KEY* variable and moves to the next view, where it *promotes* v together with *KEY* as proof for the external validation function (*EX-PB-VAL*) of the Provable-Broadcast.

As mentioned above, a party participates in a Proposal-Promotion only if the message $m = \langle v, \langle \mathcal{R}, \sigma_{\mathbf{key}} \rangle \rangle$ (note that $\langle \mathcal{R}, v, \sigma_{\mathbf{key}} \rangle =$ *KEY*) passes the external validation test. The external validation *EX-PB-VAL* includes a crucial *key-locking mechanism* (see Algorithm 5, lines 18 to 28). In particular, in view $j > 1$, a party checks that the $\sigma_{\mathbf{key}}$ is valid for v and $\mathcal{R}$ (meaning that $\sigma_{\mathbf{key}}$ is a proof that **key**($\langle v, \sigma_{\mathbf{key}} \rangle$) could have been deliverd by an honest party in the Proposal-Promotion of view $\mathcal{R}$), and that the view $\mathcal{R}$ is at least as large as the *LOCK* variable. We prove in the full paper [2] that the key-locking mechanism together with the fact that parties abandon all broadcasts before sending the view-change messages guarantee agreement and satisfy progress. Here we give some intuition for the proof:

- Lock Safety: If some party has a proof for **commit** delivery in view $\mathcal{R}$, then at least $f+1$ honest parties previously delivered **lock** and thus locked ($lock = \mathcal{R}$) in view $\mathcal{R}$.

Algorithm 4 Provable-Broadcast with identification *ID*: Protocol for the sender

```
Local variables initialization:
    S = {}

upon PB(ID,⟨v, σ⟩) invocation do
    send "ID, SEND, ⟨v, σ⟩" to all parties
    wait until |S| = n − f
    return threshold-sign(S)

upon receiving "ID, ACK, ρ_k" form party p_k for the first time do
    if share-validate(⟨ID, v⟩, k, ρ_k) = true then
        S ← S ∪ {ρ_k}
```

- Key Safety: If some party has a proof for **commit** delivery with a value v in view $\mathcal{R}$, then it is not possible for a party to have a valid **key** that contains a value other than v in view higher than or equal to $\mathcal{R}$.
- Key Progress: If some party p_i is locked in view $\mathcal{R}$, then at least $f+1$ honest parties delivered a **key** in $\mathcal{R}$ before sending the view-change messages of view $\mathcal{R}$, and thus all honest parties will have a *KEY* with view at least $\mathcal{R}$. Meaning that all honest parties will have a key to "unlock" p_i in the next view.

We now continue to the detailed description of the VABA sub-protocols:

Provable-Broadcast. In addition to what is mention in the overview above, Provable-Broadcast also exposes a *PB-abandon(ID)* API, which parties invoke to explicitly stop their participation in the Provable-Broadcast protocol associated with identification *ID* – no message is delivered and no signed share is sent after *PB-abandon(ID)* is invoked. A Provable-Broadcast of a message $m = \langle v, \sigma \rangle$ with identification *ID* is denoted *PB(ID,m)*. The external validation function used by the Provable-Broadcast is denoted by *EX-PB-VAL(ID,* $\langle v, \sigma \rangle$*)*. This function has access to the local variables of the high-level VABA protocol. For better readability, the formal definition of the properties satisfied by Provable-Broadcast is deferred to Appendix A. The pseudocode of the sub-protocol and the *EX-PB-VAL((ID,* $\langle v, \sigma \rangle$*))* function appear in Algorithms 4 and 5. The *EX-PB-VAL((ID,* $\langle v, \sigma \rangle$*))* function implements an important logic of the VABA protocol. The proof σ consists of two proofs $\langle view, \sigma_{key} \rangle$ and σ_{in}. If *ID* is an identification of a first Provable-Broadcast instance of some Proposal-Promotion sub-protocol, then $\langle view, \sigma_{key} \rangle$ is passed to function called *check-key* to check if v is a safe proposal for the current view by verifying that (1) σ_{key} is a valid **key** from view *view* and (2) *view* is not smaller than *LOCK*. Otherwise, *EX-PB-VAL* checks that σ_{in} is a valid output of the preceding instance of Provable-Broadcast by verifying that it is the correct threshold signature.

Proposal-Promotion. Besides the *promote* function mentioned in the overview, Proposal-Promotion also has an *abandon* function that invokes *PB-abandon* on all 4 instances of Provable-Broadcast therein. In addition, it also exposes *getKey*, *getLock*, and *getCommit* API for the VABA protocol to be able to get the delivered **key**, **lock**, and **commit**, respectively. For clarity and readability we do not

Algorithm 5 Provable-Broadcast with identification ID: Protocol for a party p_i

```
Local variables initialization:
    stop ← false

upon receiving "ID, SEND, ⟨v, σ⟩" from the sender do
                              ▷ parse ID as ⟨⟨id, k, j⟩, l⟩; P_k is the sender
    if stop = false ∧ EX-PB-VAL(ID,⟨v, σ⟩) = true then
        stop ← true
        ρ_i ← share-sign_i(⟨ID, v⟩)
        deliver ⟨v, σ⟩
        send "ID, ACK, ρ_i" to the sender

upon PB-abandon(ID) do
    stop ← true

procedure EX-PB-VAL(ID, ⟨v, σ⟩)
    parse ID as ⟨ID̅, step⟩      ▷ ID̅ is the identification of the higher
                                  level Proposal-Promotion; step is the
                                  Provable-Broadcast instance therein
    parse σ as ⟨key, σ_in⟩
    if step = 1 then       ▷ first instance of PB in a Proposal-Promotion
        if check-key(v,key) then
            return true
    if step > 1 ∧ threshold-validate(⟨⟨ID̅, step − 1⟩, v⟩, σ_in) then
        return true
    return false

procedure CHECK-KEY(v, key)
    if EX-VABA-VAL(v) = false then   ▷ external VABA validity check
        return false
    parse key as ⟨view, ρ⟩
    if view ≠ 1 then                        ▷ need to validate the key
        if threshold-validate(⟨⟨⟨id, Leader[view], view⟩, 1⟩, v⟩, ρ)
           = false then
            return false
    if view ≥ LOCK then
        return true
    else
        return false   ▷ the key was obtained in a view that is smaller
                         than the view on which LOCK is locked
```

define formal properties for the Proposal-Promotion sub-protocol. Instead, we use it for exposition modularity and prove the VABA protocol by using the Provable-Broadcast properties directly. The pseudocode of Proposal-Promotion appears in Algorithms 7 and 6.

4 DISCUSSION

Our protocol addresses an open problem introduced by Cachin et al. [10] and reduces the expected word communication from $O(n^3)$ to $O(n^2)$ against an asynchronous adaptive adversary. We also show that in the standard definition of an asynchronous adaptive adversary this expected word communication is asymptotically optimal for any protocol that obtains the standard definition of termination (liveness) as defined [10, 11]. An interesting open question is related to protocols that obtain weak termination in the adaptive setting: is there a $\Omega(n^2)$ lower bound against an adaptive adversary that is required to deliver all messages sent by parties before they are corrupted? or does there exist a protocol with near linear expected word communication under this weak termination property?

Algorithm 6 Proposal-Promotion with identification ID: Protocol for all parties.

```
Local variables initialization:
    key = lock = commit = ⟨⊥, ⊥⟩

upon delivery(⟨ID, step⟩, ⟨v, ⟨key, σ_in⟩⟩) do
    if step = 2 then
        key ← ⟨v, σ_in⟩
    if step = 3 then
        lock ← ⟨v, σ_in⟩
    if step = 4 then
        commit ← ⟨v, σ_in⟩

upon abandon(ID) do
    for step = 1, . . . , 4 do
        PB-abandon(⟨ID, step⟩)

Upon getKey(ID) return key
Upon getLock(ID) return lock
Upon getCommit(ID) return commit
```

Algorithm 7 Proposal-Promotion with identification ID: Protocol for a sender.

```
upon promote(ID,⟨v, key⟩) invocation do
    σ_in ← ⊥
    for step = 1, .., 4 do
        σ_in ← PB(⟨ID, step⟩, ⟨v, ⟨key, σ_in⟩⟩)
    return σ_in
```

ACKNOWLEDGEMENTS

We thank Christian Cachin and the anonymous reviewers for their high quality feedback.

REFERENCES

[1] Ittai Abraham, Srinivas Devadas, Danny Dolev, Kartik Nayak, and Ling Ren. Synchronous byzantine agreement with expected $O(1)$ rounds, expected $O(n^2)$ communication, and optimal resilience. Cryptology ePrint Archive, 2018.
[2] Ittai Abraham, Dahlia Malkhi, and Alexander Spiegelman. Asymptotically optimal validated asynchronous byzantine agreement. *arXiv preprint*, 2018.
[3] Bowen Alpern and Fred B Schneider. Defining liveness. Technical report, 1985.
[4] Ziv Bar-Joseph and Michael Ben-Or. A tight lower bound for randomized synchronous consensus. In *PODC*, volume 98, pages 193–199, 1998.
[5] Mihir Bellare, Ran Canetti, and Hugo Krawczyk. A modular approach to the design and analysis of authentication and key exchange protocols (extended abstract). In *Proceedings of the Thirtieth Annual ACM Symposium on Theory of Computing*, STOC '98, pages 419–428, New York, NY, USA, 1998. ACM.
[6] Mihir Bellare and Phillip Rogaway. Random oracles are practical: A paradigm for designing efficient protocols. In *Proceedings of the 1st ACM conference on Computer and communications security*, pages 62–73. ACM, 1993.
[7] Michael Ben-Or. Another advantage of free choice (extended abstract): Completely asynchronous agreement protocols. In *Proceedings of the Second Annual ACM Symposium on Principles of Distributed Computing*, PODC '83, 1983.
[8] Michael Ben-Or and Ran El-Yaniv. Resilient-optimal interactive consistency in constant time. *Distributed Computing*, 16(4):249–262, 2003.
[9] Gabriel Bracha. Asynchronous byzantine agreement protocols. *Inf. Comput.*, 75(2):130–143, November 1987.

[10] Christian Cachin, Klaus Kursawe, Frank Petzold, and Victor Shoup. Secure and efficient asynchronous broadcast protocols. In *Advances in Cryptology*, 2001.
[11] Christian Cachin, Klaus Kursawe, and Victor Shoup. Random oracles in constantinople: Practical asynchronous byzantine agreement using cryptography. *Journal of Cryptology*, 18, 2000.
[12] Christian Cachin and Marko Vukolic. Blockchain consensus protocols in the wild (keynote talk). In Andréa W. Richa, editor, *31st International Symposium on Distributed Computing, DISC 2017, October 16-20, 2017, Vienna, Austria*, 2017.
[13] Ran Canetti and Tal Rabin. Fast asynchronous byzantine agreement with optimal resilience. In *Proceedings of the Twenty-fifth Annual ACM Symposium on Theory of Computing*, STOC '93, pages 42–51, New York, NY, USA, 1993. ACM.
[14] Miguel Castro, Barbara Liskov, et al. Practical byzantine fault tolerance. In *OSDI*, volume 99, pages 173–186, 1999.
[15] Danny Dolev and H. Raymond Strong. Authenticated algorithms for byzantine agreement. *SIAM Journal on Computing*, 12(4):656–666, 1983.
[16] Sisi Duan, Michael K. Reiter, and Haibin Zhang. BEAT: asynchronous BFT made practical. In *Proceedings of the 2018 ACM SIGSAC Conference on Computer and Communications Security, CCS 2018, Toronto, ON, Canada*, 2018.
[17] Cynthia Dwork, Nancy Lynch, and Larry Stockmeyer. Consensus in the presence of partial synchrony. *Journal of the ACM (JACM)*, 35(2):288–323, 1988.
[18] Paul Feldman and Silvio Micali. Optimal algorithms for byzantine agreement. In *Proceedings of the Twentieth Annual ACM Symposium on Theory of Computing*, STOC '88, pages 148–161, New York, NY, USA, 1988. ACM.
[19] Michael J. Fischer, Nancy A. Lynch, and Michael S. Paterson. Impossibility of distributed consensus with one faulty process. *J. ACM*, 32(2):374–382, April 1985.
[20] Matthias Fitzi and Juan A Garay. Efficient player-optimal protocols for strong and differential consensus. In *Proceedings of the twenty-second annual symposium on Principles of distributed computing*, pages 211–220. ACM, 2003.
[21] Bruce M Kapron, David Kempe, Valerie King, Jared Saia, and Vishal Sanwalani. Fast asynchronous byzantine agreement and leader election with full information. *ACM Transactions on Algorithms (TALG)*, 6(4):68, 2010.
[22] Jonathan Katz and Chiu-Yuen Koo. On expected constant-round protocols for byzantine agreement. *J. Comput. Syst. Sci.*, 75(2):91–112, 2009.
[23] Valerie King and Jared Saia. Byzantine agreement in polynomial expected time. In *Proceedings of the forty-fifth annual ACM symposium on Theory of computing*, pages 401–410. ACM, 2013.
[24] Leslie Lamport. The part-time parliament. *ACM Trans. Comput. Syst.*, 1998.
[25] Benoît Libert, Marc Joye, and Moti Yung. Born and raised distributively: Fully distributed non-interactive adaptively-secure threshold signatures with short shares. *Theor. Comput. Sci.*, 645:1–24, 2016.
[26] Julian Loss and Tal Moran. Combining asynchronous and synchronous byzantine agreement: The best of both worlds. Cryptology ePrint Archive, Report 2018/235, 2018. https://eprint.iacr.org/2018/235.
[27] Andrew Miller, Yu Xia, Kyle Croman, Elaine Shi, and Dawn Song. The honey badger of BFT protocols. In *Proceedings of the 2016 ACM SIGSAC Conference on Computer and Communications Security*, CCS '16, New York, NY, USA, 2016.
[28] Achour Mostéfaoui, Hamouma Moumen, and Michel Raynal. Signature-free asynchronous binary byzantine consensus with $t < n/3$, $O(n^2)$ messages, and $o(1)$ expected time. *Journal of the ACM (JACM)*, 62(4):31, 2015.
[29] Achour Mostéfaoui and Michel Raynal. Signature-free asynchronous byzantine systems: from multivalued to binary consensus with $t < n/3$, $O(n^2)$ messages, and constant time. *Acta Informatica*, 54, 2017.
[30] Gil Neiger. Distributed consensus revisited. *Information processing letters*, 49(4):195–201, 1994.
[31] M. Pease, R. Shostak, and L. Lamport. Reaching agreement in the presence of faults. *J. ACM*, 27(2):228–234, April 1980.
[32] Michael K Reiter. Secure agreement protocols: Reliable and atomic group multicast in rampart. In *Proceedings of the 2nd ACM Conference on Computer and Communications Security*, pages 68–80. ACM, 1994.
[33] Victor Shoup. Practical threshold signatures. In *International Conference on the Theory and Applications of Cryptographic Techniques*. Springer, 2000.
[34] Maofan Yin, Dahlia Malkhi, Michael K. Reiter, Guy Golan Gueta, and Ittai Abraham. HotStuff: BFT consensus in the lens of blockchain. *PODC*, 2019.

Appendix A PROVABLE-BROADCAST PROPERTIES

Provable-Broadcast with identification ID satisfies the following properties except with negligible probability:

- **PB-Integrity:** An honest party delivers a message at most once.
- **PB-Validity:** If an honest party p_i delivers m, then *EX-PB-VAL*$_i(id, m) = true$.
- **PB-Abandon-ability:** An honest party does not deliver any message after it invokes *PB-abandon*(ID).
- **PB-Provability:** For all v, v', if the sender can produce strings σ, σ' s.t. *threshold-validate*$(\langle id, v\rangle, \sigma) = true$ and *threshold-validate*$(\langle id, v'\rangle, \sigma') = true$, then (1) $v = v'$ and (2) $f + 1$ honest parties delivered a message m s.t. $m.v = v$.
- **PB-Termination:** If the sender is honest, no honest party invokes *PB-abandon*(ID), all messages among honest parties arrive, and the message m that is being broadcast is externally valid, then (1) all honest parties deliver m, and (2) *PB*(ID,m) returns (to the sender) σ, which satisfies *threshold-validate*$(\langle ID, m.v\rangle, \sigma) = true$.

Note that an Provable-Broadcast does not guarantee any agreement property, however, when several instances are combined together (e.g., Proposal-Promotion) strong and useful properties can be guaranteed.

Appendix B LEADER-ELECTION: PROPERTIES AND PSEUDOCODE

The Leader-Election primitive provides one operation to elect a unique party (called a leader) among the parties. An instance of a leader election primitive is identified via an identification *ID*, and exposes an operation *elect*(*ID*) to all parties, which returns a party $p \in \Pi$. Formal definitions are given below and the pseudocode appears in Algorithm 8.

A protocol for leader election associated with id *id* satisfies the following properties except with negligible probability.

- **Termination:** If $f + 1$ honest parties invoke *elect*(), and all messages among honest parties arrive, then all invocations by honest parties return.
- **Agreement:** All invocations of *elect*(*id*) by honest parties return the same party.
- **Validity:** If an invocation of *elect*(*id*) by an honest party returns, it returns a party p with probability $1/|\Pi|$ for every $p \in \Pi$.
- **Unpredictability:** The probability of the adversary to predict the returned value of *elect*(*id*) invocation by an honest party before it returns is at most $1/|\Pi| + \epsilon(k)$, where $\epsilon(k)$ is a negligible function.

Algorithm 8 Leader election. Protocol for party p_i

```
Local variables initialization:
Σ ← {}

upon elect(id) do
    ρ_i ← coin-share_i(ID)
    send "SHARE, ID, ρ_i" to all parties
    wait until |Σ| = f + 1
    return coin-toss(ID, Σ)

upon receiving "SHARE, ID, ρ_j" from p_j for the first time do
    if coin-share-validate(id, j, ρ_j) = true then
        Σ ← Σ ∪ {ρ_j}
```

HotStuff: BFT Consensus with Linearity and Responsiveness

Maofan Yin
Cornell University
VMware Research

Dahlia Malkhi
VMware Research

Michael K. Reiter
UNC-Chapel Hill
VMware Research

Guy Golan Gueta
VMware Research

Ittai Abraham
VMware Research

ABSTRACT

We present HotStuff, a leader-based Byzantine fault-tolerant replication protocol for the partially synchronous model. Once network communication becomes synchronous, HotStuff enables a correct leader to drive the protocol to consensus at the pace of actual (vs. maximum) network delay—a property called *responsiveness*—and with communication complexity that is linear in the number of replicas. To our knowledge, HotStuff is the first partially synchronous BFT replication protocol exhibiting these combined properties. Its simplicity enables it to be further pipelined and simplified into a practical, concise protocol for building large-scale replication services.

CCS CONCEPTS

• Software and its engineering → Software fault tolerance; • Security and privacy → Distributed systems security.

KEYWORDS

Byzantine fault tolerance; consensus; responsiveness; scalability; blockchain

ACM Reference Format:
Maofan Yin, Dahlia Malkhi, Michael K. Reiter, Guy Golan Gueta, and Ittai Abraham. 2019. HotStuff: BFT Consensus with Linearity and Responsiveness. In *2019 ACM Symposium on Principles of Distributed Computing (PODC '19), July 29-August 2, 2019, Toronto, ON, Canada.* ACM, New York, NY, USA, 10 pages. https://doi.org/10.1145/3293611.3331591

1 INTRODUCTION

Byzantine fault tolerance (BFT) refers to the ability of a computing system to endure arbitrary (i.e., Byzantine) failures of its components while taking actions critical to the system's operation. In the context of state machine replication (SMR) [35, 47], the system as a whole provides a replicated service whose state is mirrored across n deterministic replicas. A BFT SMR protocol is used to ensure that non-faulty replicas agree on an order of execution for client-initiated service commands, despite the efforts of f Byzantine replicas. This, in turn, ensures that the $n - f$ non-faulty replicas will run commands identically and so produce the same response for each command. As is common, we are concerned here with the partially synchronous communication model [25], whereby a known bound Δ on message transmission holds after some unknown *global stabilization time* (GST). In this model, $n \geq 3f + 1$ is required for non-faulty replicas to agree on the same commands in the same order (e.g., [12]) and progress can be ensured deterministically only after GST [27].

When BFT SMR protocols were originally conceived, a typical target system size was $n = 4$ or $n = 7$, deployed on a local-area network. However, the renewed interest in Byzantine fault-tolerance brought about by its application to blockchains now demands solutions that can scale to much larger n. In contrast to *permissionless* blockchains such as the one that supports Bitcoin, for example, so-called *permissioned* blockchains involve a fixed set of replicas that collectively maintain an ordered ledger of commands or, in other words, that support SMR. Despite their permissioned nature, numbers of replicas in the hundreds or even thousands are envisioned (e.g., [30, 42]). Additionally, their deployment to wide-area networks requires setting Δ to accommodate higher variability in communication delays.

The scaling challenge. Since the introduction of PBFT [20], the first practical BFT replication solution in the partial synchrony model, numerous BFT solutions were built around its core two-phase paradigm. The practical aspect is that a stable leader can drive a consensus decision in just two rounds of message exchanges. The first phase guarantees proposal uniqueness through the formation of a quorum certificate (QC) consisting of $(n - f)$ votes. The second phase guarantees that the next leader can convince replicas to vote for a safe proposal.

The algorithm for a new leader to collect information and propose it to replicas—called a *view-change*—is the epicenter of replication. Unfortunately, view-change based on the two-phase paradigm is far from simple [38], is bug-prone [4], and incurs a significant communication penalty for even moderate system sizes. It requires the new leader to relay information from $(n - f)$ replicas, each reporting its own highest known QC. Even counting just authenticators (digital signatures or message authentication codes), conveying a new proposal has a communication footprint of $O(n^3)$ authenticators in PBFT, and variants that combine multiple authenticators into one via threshold digital signatures (e.g., [18, 30]) still send $O(n^2)$ authenticators. The total number of authenticators transmitted if $O(n)$ view-changes occur before a single consensus decision is reached is $O(n^4)$ in PBFT, and even with threshold signatures is $O(n^3)$. This scaling challenge plagues not only PBFT, but many other protocols developed since then, e.g., Prime [9], Zyzzyva [34], Upright [22], BFT-SMaRt [13], 700BFT [11], and SBFT [30].

HotStuff revolves around a three-phase core, allowing a new leader to simply pick the highest QC it knows of. It introduces a second phase that allows replicas to "change their mind" after voting in the phase, without requiring a leader proof at all. This alleviates the above complexity, and at the same time considerably simplifies the leader replacement protocol. Last, having (almost)

PODC '19, July 29-August 2, 2019, Toronto, ON, Canada

ACM ISBN 978-1-4503-6217-7/19/07.
https://doi.org/10.1145/3293611.3331591

canonized all the phases, it is very easy to pipeline HotStuff, and to frequently rotate leaders.

To our knowledge, only BFT protocols in the blockchain arena like Tendermint [15, 16] and Casper [17] follow such a simple leader regime. However, these systems are built around a synchronous core, wherein proposals are made in pre-determined intervals that must accommodate the worst-case time it takes to propagate messages over a wide-area peer-to-peer gossip network. In doing so, they forego a hallmark of most practical BFT SMR solutions (including those listed above), namely *optimistic responsiveness* [42]. Informally, *responsiveness* requires that a non-faulty leader, once designated, can drive the protocol to consensus in time depending only on the *actual* message delays, independent of any known upper bound on message transmission delays [10]. More appropriate for our model is *optimistic responsiveness*, which requires responsiveness only in beneficial (and hopefully common) circumstances—here, after GST is reached. Optimistic or not, responsiveness is precluded with designs such as Tendermint/Casper. The crux of the difficulty is that there may exist an honest replica that has the highest QC, but the leader does not know about it. One can build scenarios where this prevents progress ad infinitum (see Section 4.4 for a detailed liveless scenario). Indeed, failing to incorporate necessary delays at crucial protocol steps can result in losing liveness outright, as has been reported in several existing deployments, e.g., see [2, 3, 19].

Our contributions. To our knowledge, we present the first BFT SMR protocol, called HotStuff, to achieve the following two properties:

- **Linear View Change**: After GST, any correct leader, once designated, sends only $O(n)$ authenticators to drive a consensus decision. This includes the case where a leader is replaced. Consequently, communication costs to reach consensus after GST is $O(n^2)$ authenticators in the worst case of cascading leader failures.
- **Optimistic Responsiveness**: After GST, any correct leader, once designated, needs to wait just for the first $n - f$ responses to guarantee that it can create a proposal that will make progress. This includes the case where a leader is replaced.

Another feature of HotStuff is that the costs for a new leader to drive the protocol to consensus is no greater than that for the current leader. As such, HotStuff supports frequent succession of leaders, which has been argued is useful in blockchain contexts for ensuring chain quality [28].

HotStuff achieves these properties by adding another phase to each view, a small price to latency in return for considerably simplifying the leader replacement protocol. This exchange incurs only the actual network delays, which are typically far smaller than Δ in practice. As such, we expect this added latency to be much smaller than that incurred by previous protocols that forgo responsiveness to achieve linear view-change. Furthermore, throughput is not affected due to the efficient pipeline we introduce in Section 5.

HotStuff has the additional benefit of being remarkably simple. Safety is specified via voting and commit rules over graphs of nodes. The mechanisms needed to achieve liveness are encapsulated within a *Pacemaker*, cleanly separated from the mechanisms needed for safety (Section 6).

2 RELATED WORK

Reaching consensus in face of Byzantine failures was formulated as the Byzantine Generals Problem by Lamport et al. [37], who also coined the term "Byzantine failures". The first synchronous solution was given by Pease et al. [43], and later improved by Dolev and Strong [24]. The improved protocol has $O(n^3)$ communication complexity, which was shown optimal by Dolev and Reischuk [23]. A leader-based synchronous protocol that uses randomness was given by Katz and Koo [32], showing an expected constant-round solution with $(n-1)/2$ resilience.

Meanwhile, in the asynchronous settings, Fischer et al. [27] showed that the problem is unsolvable deterministically in asynchronous setting in face of a single failure. Furthermore, an $(n-1)/3$ resilience bound for any asynchronous solution was proven by Ben-Or [12]. Two approaches were devised to circumvent the impossibility. One relies on randomness, initially shown by Ben-Or [12], using independently random coin flips by processes until they happen to converge to consensus. Later works used cryptographic methods to share an unpredictable coin and drive complexities down to constant expected rounds, and $O(n^3)$ communication [18].

The second approach relies on partial synchrony, first shown by Dwork, Lynch, and Stockmeyer (DLS) [25]. This protocol preserves safety during asynchronous periods, and after the system becomes synchronous, DLS guarantees termination. Once synchrony is maintained, DLS incurs $O(n^4)$ total communication and $O(n)$ rounds per decision.

State machine replication relies on consensus at its core to order client requests so that correct replicas execute them in this order. The recurring need for consensus in SMR led Lamport to devise Paxos [36], a protocol that operates an efficient pipeline in which a stable leader drives decisions with linear communication and one round-trip. A similar emphasis led Castro and Liskov [20, 21] to develop an efficient leader-based Byzantine SMR protocol named PBFT, whose stable leader requires $O(n^2)$ communication and two round-trips per decision, and the leader replacement protocol incurs $O(n^3)$ communication. PBFT has been deployed in several systems, including BFT-SMaRt [13]. Kotla et al. introduced an optimistic linear path into PBFT in a protocol named Zyzzyva [34], which was utilized in several systems, e.g., Upright [22] and Byzcoin [33]. The optimistic path has linear complexity, while the leader replacement protocol remains $O(n^3)$. Abraham et al. [4] later exposed a safety violation in Zyzzyva, and presented fixes [5, 30]. On the other hand, to also reduce the complexity of the protocol itself, Song et al. proposed Bosco [49], a simple one-step protocol with low latency on the optimistic path, requiring $5f + 1$ replicas. SBFT [30] introduces an $O(n^2)$ communication view-change protocol that supports a stable leader protocol with optimistically linear, one round-trip decisions. It reduces the communication complexity by harnessing two methods: a collector-based communication paradigm by Reiter [45], and signature combining via threshold cryptography on protocol votes by Cachin et al. [18].

A leader-based Byzantine SMR protocol that employs randomization was presented by Ramasamy et al. [44], and a leaderless

Protocol	Authenticator complexity: Correct leader	Leader failure (view-change)	f leader failures	Responsiveness
DLS [25]	$O(n^4)$	$O(n^4)$	$O(n^4)$	
PBFT [20]	$O(n^2)$	$O(n^3)$	$O(fn^3)$	✓
SBFT [30]	$O(n)$	$O(n^2)$	$O(fn^2)$	✓
Tendermint [15] / Casper [17]	$O(n^2)$	$O(n^2)$	$O(fn^2)$	
Tendermint* / Casper*	$O(n)$	$O(n)$	$O(fn)$	
HotStuff	$O(n)$	$O(n)$	$O(fn)$	✓

*Signatures can be combined using threshold signatures, though this optimization is not mentioned in their original works.

Table 1: Performance of selected protocols after GST.

variant named HoneyBadgerBFT was developed by Miller et al. [39]. At their core, these randomized Byzantine solutions employ randomized asynchronous Byzantine consensus, whose best known communication complexity was $O(n^3)$ (see above), amortizing the cost via batching. However, most recently, based on the idea in this HotStuff paper, a parallel submission to PODC'19 [8] further improves the communication complexity to $O(n^2)$.

Bitcoin's core is a protocol known as Nakamoto Consensus [40], a synchronous protocol with only probabilistic safety guarantee and no finality (see analysis in [6, 28, 41]). It operates in a *permissionless* model where participants are unknown, and resilience is kept via Proof-of-Work. As described above, recent blockchain solutions hybridize Proof-of-Work solutions with classical BFT solutions in various ways [7, 17, 26, 29, 31, 33, 42]. The need to address rotating leaders in these hybrid solutions and others provide the motivation behind HotStuff.

3 MODEL

We consider a system consisting of a fixed set of $n = 3f + 1$ *replicas*, indexed by $i \in [n]$ where $[n] = \{1, \ldots, n\}$. A set $F \subset [n]$ of up to $f = |F|$ replicas are Byzantine faulty, and the remaining ones are correct. We will often refer to the Byzantine replicas as being coordinated by an *adversary*, which learns all internal state held by these replicas (including their cryptographic keys, see below).

Network communication is point-to-point, authenticated and reliable: one correct replica receives a message from another correct replica if and only if the latter sent that message to the former. When we refer to a "broadcast", it involves the broadcaster, if correct, sending the same point-to-point messages to all replicas, including itself. We adopt the *partial synchrony model* of Dwork et al. [25], where there is a known bound Δ and an unknown Global Stabilization Time (GST), such that after GST, all transmissions between two correct replicas arrive within time Δ. Our protocol will ensure safety always, and will guarantee progress within a bounded duration after GST. (Guaranteeing progress before GST is impossible [27].) In practice, our protocol will guarantee progress if the system remains stable (i.e., if messages arrive within Δ time) for sufficiently long after GST, though assuming that it does so forever simplifies discussion.

Cryptographic primitives. HotStuff makes use of threshold signatures [14, 18, 48]. In a (k, n)-threshold signature scheme, there is a single public key held by all replicas, and each of the n replicas holds a distinct private key. The i-th replica can use its private key to contribute a *partial signature* $\rho_i \leftarrow tsign_i(m)$ on message m. Partial signatures $\{\rho_i\}_{i \in I}$, where $|I| = k$ and each $\rho_i \leftarrow tsign_i(m)$, can be used to produce a digital signature $\sigma \leftarrow tcombine(m, \{\rho_i\}_{i \in I})$ on m. Any other replica can verify the signature using the public key and the function $tverify$. We require that if $\rho_i \leftarrow tsign_i(m)$ for each $i \in I$, $|I| = k$, and if $\sigma \leftarrow tcombine(m, \{\rho_i\}_{i \in I})$, then $tverify(m, \sigma)$ returns true. However, given oracle access to oracles $\{tsign_i(\cdot)\}_{i \in [n] \setminus F}$, an adversary who queries $tsign_i(m)$ on strictly fewer than $k - f$ of these oracles has negligible probability of producing a signature σ for the message m (i.e., such that $tverify(m, \sigma)$ returns true). Throughout this paper, we use a threshold of $k = 2f + 1$. Again, we will typically leave invocations of $tverify$ implicit in our protocol descriptions.

We also require a cryptographic hash function h (also called a *message digest* function), which maps an arbitrary-length input to a fixed-length output. The hash function must be *collision resistant* [46], which informally requires that the probability of an adversary producing inputs m and m' such that $h(m) = h(m')$ is negligible. As such, $h(m)$ can serve as an identifier for a unique input m in the protocol.

Complexity measure. The complexity measure we care about is *authenticator complexity*, which specifically is the sum, over all replicas $i \in [n]$, of the number of authenticators received by replica i in the protocol to reach a consensus decision after GST. (Again, before GST, a consensus decision might not be reached at all in the worst case [27].) Here, an *authenticator* is either a partial signature or a signature. Authenticator complexity is a useful measure of communication complexity for several reasons. First, like bit complexity and unlike message complexity, it hides unnecessary details about the transmission topology. For example, n messages carrying one authenticator count the same as one message carrying n authenticators. Second, authenticator complexity is better suited than bit complexity for capturing costs in protocols like ours that reach consensus repeatedly, where each consensus decision (or each view proposed on the way to that consensus decision) is identified by a monotonically increasing counter. That is, because such a counter increases indefinitely, the bit complexity of a protocol that sends such a counter cannot be bounded. Third, since in practice, cryptographic operations to produce or verify digital signatures and to produce or combine partial signatures are typically the most computationally intensive operations in protocols that use them, the authenticator complexity provides insight into the computational burden of the protocol, as well.

4 BASIC HOTSTUFF

HotStuff solves the State Machine Replication (SMR) problem. At the core of SMR is a protocol for deciding on a growing log of *command* requests by clients. A group of state-machine replicas apply commands in sequence order consistently. A client sends a command request to all replicas, and waits for responses from $(f + 1)$ of them. For the most part, we omit the client from the discussion, and defer to the standard literature for issues regarding numbering and de-duplication of client requests.

The Basic HotStuff solution is presented in Algorithm 2. The protocol works in a succession of *views* numbered with monotonically increasing view numbers. Each *viewNumber* has a unique dedicated leader known to all. Each replica stores a *tree* of pending commands as its local data structure. Each tree *node* contains a proposed command (or a batch of them), metadata associated with the protocol, and a *parent* link. The *branch* led by a given node is the path from the node all the way to the tree root by visiting parent links. During the protocol, a monotonically growing branch becomes *committed*. To become committed, the leader of a particular view proposing the branch must collect votes from a quorum of $(n-f)$ replicas in three phases, PREPARE, PRE-COMMIT, and COMMIT.

A key ingredient in the protocol is a collection of $(n - f)$ votes over a leader proposal, referred to as a *quorum certificate* (or "QC" in short). The QC is associated with a particular node and a view number. The *tcombine* utility employs a threshold signature scheme to generate a representation of $(n - f)$ signed votes as a single authenticator.

Below we give an operational description of the protocol logic by phases, followed by a precise specification in Algorithm 2, and conclude the section with safety, liveness, and complexity arguments.

4.1 Phases

PREPARE phase. The protocol for a new leader starts by collecting NEW-VIEW messages from $(n - f)$ replicas. The NEW-VIEW message is sent by a replica as it transitions into *viewNumber* (including the first view) and carries the highest *prepareQC* that the replica received ($\perp$ if none), as described below.

The leader processes these messages in order to select a branch that has the highest preceding view in which a *prepareQC* was formed. The leader selects the *prepareQC* with the highest view, denoted *highQC*, among the NEW-VIEW messages. Because *highQC* is the highest among $(n - f)$ replicas, no higher view could have reached a commit decision. The branch led by *highQC.node* is therefore safe.

Collecting NEW-VIEW messages to select a safe branch may be omitted by an incumbent leader, who may simply select its own highest *prepareQC* as *highQC*. We defer this optimization to Section 6 and only describe a single, unified leader protocol in this section. Note that, different from PBFT-like protocols, including this step in the leader protocol is straightforward, and it incurs the same, linear overhead as all the other phases of the protocol, regardless of the situation.

The leader uses the CREATELEAF method to extend the tail of *highQC.node* with a new proposal. The method creates a new leaf node as a child and embeds a digest of the parent in the child node. The leader then sends the new node in a PREPARE message to all other replicas. The proposal carries *highQC* for safety justification.

Upon receiving the PREPARE message for the current view from the leader, replica r uses the SAFENODE predicate to determine whether to accept it. If it is accepted, the replica sends a PREPARE vote with a partial signature (produced by $tsign_r$) for the proposal to the leader.

SAFENODE predicate. The SAFENODE predicate is a core ingredient of the protocol. It examines a proposal message m carrying a QC justification *m.justify*, and determines whether *m.node* is safe to accept. The safety rule to accept a proposal is the branch of *m.node* extends from the currently locked node *lockedQC.node*. On the other hand, the liveness rule is the replica will accept m if *m.justify* has a higher view than the current *lockedQC*. The predicate is true as long as either one of two rules holds.

PRE-COMMIT phase. When the leader receives $(n - f)$ PREPARE votes for the current proposal *curProposal*, it combines them into a *prepareQC*. The leader broadcasts *prepareQC* in PRE-COMMIT messages. A replica responds to the leader with PRE-COMMIT vote having a signed digest of the proposal.

COMMIT phase. The COMMIT phase is similar to PRE-COMMIT phase. When the leader receives $(n - f)$ PRE-COMMIT votes, it combines them into a *precommitQC* and broadcasts it in COMMIT messages; replicas respond to it with a COMMIT vote. Importantly, a replica becomes *locked* on the *precommitQC* at this point by setting its *lockedQC* to *precommitQC* (Line 25 of Algorithm 2). This is crucial to guard the safety of the proposal in case it becomes a consensus decision.

DECIDE phase. When the leader receives $(n-f)$ COMMIT votes, it combines them into a *commitQC*. Once the leader has assembled a *commitQC*, it sends it in a DECIDE message to all other replicas. Upon receiving a DECIDE message, a replica considers the proposal embodied in the *commitQC* a committed decision, and executes the commands in the committed branch. The replica increments *viewNumber* and starts the next view.

NEXTVIEW interrupt. In all phases, a replica waits for a message at view *viewNumber* for a timeout period, determined by an auxiliary NEXTVIEW(*viewNumber*) utility. If NEXTVIEW(*viewNumber*) interrupts waiting, the replica also increments *viewNumber* and starts the next view.

4.2 Data Structures

Messages. A message m in the protocol has a fixed set of fields that are populated using the MSG() utility shown in Algorithm 1. m is automatically stamped with *curView*, the sender's current view number. Each message has a type $m.type \in$ {NEW-VIEW, PREPARE, PRE-COMMIT, COMMIT, DECIDE}. *m.node* contains a proposed node (the leaf node of a proposed branch). There is an optional field *m.justify*. The leader always uses this field to carry the QC for the different phases. Replicas use it in NEW-VIEW messages to carry the highest *prepareQC*. Each message sent in a replica role contains a partial signature *m.partialSig* by the sender over the tuple $\langle m.type, m.viewNumber, m.node\rangle$, which is added in the VOTEMSG() utility.

Quorum certificates. A Quorum Certificate (QC) over a tuple $\langle type, viewNumber, node\rangle$ is a data type that combines a collection of signatures for the same tuple signed by $(n - f)$ replicas. Given a QC *qc*, we use *qc.type*, *qc.viewNumber*, *qc.node* to refer to the matching fields of the original tuple.

Tree and branches. Each command is wrapped in a node that additionally contains a parent link which could be a hash digest of the parent node. We omit the implementation details from the pseudocode. During the protocol, a replica delivers a message only after the branch led by the node is already in its local tree. In practice, a recipient who falls behind can catch up by fetching missing nodes from other replicas. For brevity, these details are also omitted from the pseudocode. Two branches are *conflicting* if neither one is an extension of the other. Two nodes are conflicting if the branches led by them are conflicting.

Bookkeeping variables. A replica uses additional local variables for bookkeeping the protocol state: (i) a $viewNumber$, initially 1 and incremented either by finishing a decision or by a NEXTVIEW interrupt; (ii) a locked quorum certificate $lockedQC$, initially $\bot$, storing the highest QC for which a replica voted COMMIT; and (iii) a $prepareQC$, initially $\bot$, storing the highest QC for which a replica voted PRE-COMMIT. Additionally, in order to incrementally execute a committed log of commands, the replica maintains the highest node whose branch has been executed. This is omitted below for brevity.

4.3 Protocol Specification

The protocol given in Algorithm 2 is described as an iterated view-by-view loop. In each view, a replica performs phases in succession based on its role, described as a succession of "**as**" blocks. A replica can have more than one role. For example, a leader is also a (normal) replica. Execution of **as** blocks across roles can be proceeded concurrently. The execution of each **as** block is atomic. A NEXTVIEW interrupt aborts all operations in any **as** block, and jumps to the "Finally" block.

Algorithm 1 Utilities (for replica r).

```
function Msg(type, node, qc)
    m.type ← type
    m.viewNumber ← curView
    m.node ← node
    m.justify ← qc
    return m
function voteMsg(type, node, qc)
    m ← Msg(type, node, qc)
    m.partialSig ← tsign_r(⟨m.type, m.viewNumber, m.node⟩)
    return m
procedure createLeaf(parent, cmd)
    b.parent ← parent
    b.cmd ← cmd
    return b
function QC(V)
    qc.type ← m.type : m ∈ V
    qc.viewNumber ← m.viewNumber : m ∈ V
    qc.node ← m.node : m ∈ V
    qc.sig ← tcombine(⟨qc.type, qc.viewNumber, qc.node⟩,
                      {m.partialSig | m ∈ V})
    return qc
function matchingMsg(m, t, v)
    return (m.type = t) ∧ (m.viewNumber = v)
function matchingQC(qc, t, v)
    return (qc.type = t) ∧ (qc.viewNumber = v)
function safeNode(node, qc)
    return (node extends from lockedQC.node) ∨     // safety rule
    (qc.viewNumber > lockedQC.viewNumber)          // liveness rule
```

Algorithm 2 Basic HotStuff protocol (for replica r).

```
for curView ← 1, 2, 3, ... do
  ▷ prepare phase
    as a leader  // r = leader(curView)
    // we assume special new-view messages from view 0
        wait for (n − f) new-view messages:
            M ← {m | matchingMsg(m, new-view, curView−1)}
        highQC ← ( arg max_{m∈M} {m.justify.viewNumber} ).justify
        curProposal ← createLeaf(highQC.node,
                                 client's command)
        broadcast Msg(prepare, curProposal, highQC)
    as a replica
        wait for message m from leader(curView)
            m : matchingMsg(m, prepare, curView)
        if m.node extends from m.justify.node ∧
                safeNode(m.node, m.justify) then
            send voteMsg(prepare, m.node, ⊥) to leader(curView)

  ▷ pre-commit phase
    as a leader
        wait for (n − f) votes:
            V ← {v | matchingMsg(v, prepare, curView)}
        prepareQC ← QC(V)
        broadcast Msg(pre-commit, ⊥, prepareQC)
    as a replica
        wait for message m from leader(curView)
            m : matchingQC(m.justify, prepare, curView)
        prepareQC ← m.justify
        send to leader(curView)
            voteMsg(pre-commit, m.justify.node, ⊥)
  ▷ commit phase
    as a leader
        wait for (n − f) votes:
            V ← {v | matchingMsg(v, pre-commit, curView)}
        precommitQC ← QC(V)
        broadcast Msg(commit, ⊥, precommitQC)
    as a replica
        wait for message m from leader(curView)
            m : matchingQC(m.justify, pre-commit, curView)
        lockedQC ← m.justify
        send to leader(curView)
            voteMsg(commit, m.justify.node, ⊥)
  ▷ decide phase
    as a leader
        wait for (n − f) votes:
            V ← {v | matchingMsg(v, commit, curView)}
        commitQC ← QC(V)
        broadcast Msg(decide, ⊥, commitQC)
    as a replica
        wait for message m from leader(curView)
            m : matchingQC(m.justify, commit, curView)
        execute new commands through m.justify.node,
        respond to clients
  ▷ Finally
    nextView interrupt: goto this line if nextView(curView) is
    called during "wait for" in any phase
    send Msg(new-view, ⊥, prepareQC) to leader(curView + 1)
```

4.4 Safety, Liveness, and Complexity

Safety. We first define a quorum certificate qc to be *valid* if $tverify(\langle qc.type, qc.viewNumber, qc.node\rangle, qc.sig)$ is true.

Lemma 1. *For any valid qc_1, qc_2 in which $qc_1.type = qc_2.type$ and $qc_1.node$ conflicts with $qc_2.node$, we have $qc_1.viewNumber \neq qc_2.viewNumber$.*

Proof. To show a contradiction, suppose $qc_1.viewNumber = qc_2.viewNumber = v$. Because a valid QC can be formed only with $n - f = 2f + 1$ votes (i.e., partial signatures) for it, there must be a correct replica who voted twice in the same phase of v. This is impossible because the pseudocode allows voting only once for each phase in each view. □

Theorem 2. *If w and b are conflicting nodes, then they cannot be both committed, each by a correct replica.*

Proof. We prove this important theorem by contradiction. Let qc_1 denote a valid *commitQC* (i.e., $qc_1.type$ = COMMIT) such that $qc_1.node = w$, and qc_2 denote a valid *commitQC* such that $qc_2.node = b$. Denote $v_1 = qc_1.viewNumber$ and $v_2 = qc_2.viewNumber$. By Lemma 1, $v_1 \neq v_2$. W.l.o.g. assume $v_1 < v_2$.

We will now denote by v_s the lowest view higher than v_1 for which there is a valid *prepareQC*, qc_s (i.e., $qc_s.type$ = PREPARE) where $qc_s.viewNumber = v_s$, and $qc_s.node$ conflicts with w. Formally, we define the following predicate for any *prepareQC*:

$$E(prepareQC) := (v_1 < prepareQC.viewNumber \leq v_2) \wedge (prepareQC.node \text{ conflicts with } w).$$

We can now set the *first* switching point qc_s:

$$qc_s := \underset{prepareQC}{\arg\min} \left\{ \begin{array}{c} prepareQC.viewNumber \mid \\ prepareQC \text{ is valid} \wedge E(prepareQC) \end{array} \right\}.$$

Note that, by assumption such a qc_s must exist; for example, qc_s could be the *prepareQC* formed in view v_2.

Of the correct replicas that sent a partial result $tsign_r(\langle qc_1.type, qc_1.viewNumber, qc_1.node\rangle)$, let r be the first that contributed $tsign_r(\langle qc_s.type, qc_s.viewNumber, qc_s.node\rangle)$; such an r must exist since otherwise, one of $qc_1.sig$ and $qc_s.sig$ could not have been created. During view v_1, replica r updates its lock *lockedQC* to a *precommitQC* on w at Line 25 of Algorithm 2. Due to the minimality of v_s, the lock that replica r has on w is not changed before qc_s is formed. Otherwise r must have seen some other *prepareQC* with lower view because Line 17 comes before Line 25, contradicting to the minimality. Now consider the invocation of SAFENODE in the PREPARE phase of view v_s by replica r, with a message m carrying $m.node = qc_s.node$. By assumption, $m.node$ conflicts with $lockedQC.node$, and so the disjunct at Line 26 of Algorithm 1 is false. Moreover, $m.justify.viewNumber > v_1$ would violate the minimality of v_s, and so the disjunct in Line 27 of Algorithm 1 is also false. Thus, SAFENODE must return false and r cannot cast a PREPARE vote on the conflicting branch in view v_s, a contradiction. □

Liveness. There are two functions left undefined in the previous section: LEADER and NEXTVIEW. Their definition will *not* affect safety of the protocol, though they do matter to liveness. Before giving candidate definitions for them, we first show that after GST, there is a bounded duration T_f such that if all correct replicas remain in view v during T_f and the leader for view v is correct, then a decision is reached. Below, we say that qc_1 and qc_2 *match* if qc_1 and qc_2 are valid, $qc_1.node = qc_2.node$, and $qc_1.viewNumber = qc_2.viewNumber$.

Lemma 3. *If a correct replica is locked such that lockedQC = precommitQC, then at least $f + 1$ correct replicas voted for some prepareQC matching lockedQC.*

Proof. Suppose replica r is locked on *precommitQC*. Then, $(n-f)$ votes were cast for the matching *prepareQC* in the PREPARE phase (Line 10 of Algorithm 2), out of which at least $f + 1$ were from correct replicas. □

Theorem 4. *After GST, there exists a bounded time period T_f such that if all correct replicas remain in view v during T_f and the leader for view v is correct, then a decision is reached.*

Proof. Starting in a new view, the leader collects $(n - f)$ NEW-VIEW messages and calculates its *highQC* before broadcasting a PREPARE messsage. Suppose among all replicas (including the leader itself), the highest kept lock is $lockedQC = precommitQC^*$. By Lemma 3, we know there are at least $f+1$ correct replicas that voted for a $prepareQC^*$ matching $precommitQC^*$, and have already sent them to the leader in their NEW-VIEW messages. Thus, the leader must learn a matching $prepareQC^*$ in at least one of these NEW-VIEW messages and use it as *highQC* in its PREPARE message. By the assumption, all correct replicas are synchronized in their view and the leader is non-faulty. Therefore, all correct replicas will vote in the PREPARE phase, since in SAFENODE, the condition on Line 27 of Algorithm 1 is satisfied (even if the *node* in the message conflicts with a replica's stale $lockedQC.node$, and so Line 26 is not). Then, after the leader assembles a valid *prepareQC* for this view, all replicas will vote in all the following phases, leading to a new decision. After GST, the duration T_f for these phases to complete is of bounded length.

The protocol is Optimistically Responsive because there is no explicit "wait-for-Δ" step, and the logical disjunction in SAFENODE is used to override a stale lock with the help of the three-phase paradigm. □

We now provide simple constructions for LEADER and NEXTVIEW that suffice to ensure that after GST, eventually a view will be reached in which the leader is correct and all correct replicas remain in this view for T_f time. It suffices for LEADER to return some deterministic mapping from view number to a replica, eventually rotating through all replicas. A possible solution for NEXTVIEW is to utilize an exponential back-off mechanism that maintains a timeout interval. Then a timer is set upon entering each view. When the timer goes off without making any decision, the replica doubles the interval and calls NEXTVIEW to advance the view. Since the interval is doubled at each time, the waiting intervals of all correct replicas will eventually have at least T_f overlap in common, during which the leader could drive a decision.

Livelessness with two-phases. We now briefly demonstrate an infinite non-deciding scenario for a "two-phase" HotStuff. This explains the necessity for introducing a synchronous delay in Casper and Tendermint, and hence for abandoning (Optimistic) Responsiveness.

In the two-phase HotStuff variant, we omit the PRE-COMMIT phase and proceed directly to COMMIT. A replica becomes locked when it votes on a *prepareQC*. Suppose, in view v, a leader proposes b. It completes the PREPARE phase, and some replica r_v votes for the *prepareQC*, say qc, such that $qc.node = b$. Hence, r_v becomes locked on qc. An asynchronous network scheduling causes the rest of the replicas to move to view $v + 1$ without receiving qc.

We now repeat ad infinitum the following single-view transcript. We start view $v + 1$ with only r_v holding the highest *prepareQC* (i.e. qc) in the system. The new leader l collects new-view messages from $2f + 1$ replicas excluding r_v. The highest *prepareQC* among these, qc', has view $v - 1$ and $b' = qc'.node$ conflicts with b. l then proposes b'' which extends b', to which $2f$ honest replicas respond with a vote, but r_v rejects it because it is locked on qc, b'' conflicts with b and qc' is lower than qc. Eventaully, $2f$ replicas give up and move to the next view. Just then, a faulty replica responds to l's proposal, l then puts together a $prepareQC(v + 1, b'')$ and one replica, say r_{v+1} votes for it and becomes locked on it.

Complexity. In each phase of HotStuff, only the leader broadcasts to all replicas while the replicas respond to the sender once with a partial signature to certify the vote. In the leader's message, the QC consists of a proof of $(n - f)$ votes collected previously, which can be encoded by a single threshold signature. In a replica's response, the partial signature from that replica is the only authenticator. Therefore, in each phase, there are $O(n)$ authenticators received in total. As there is a constant number of phases, the overall complexity per view is $O(n)$.

5 CHAINED HOTSTUFF

It takes three phases for a Basic HotStuff leader to commit a proposal. These phases are not doing "useful" work except collecting votes from replicas, and they are all very similar. In Chained HotStuff, we improve the Basic HotStuff protocol utility while at the same time considerably simplifying it. The idea is to change the view on *every* PREPARE *phase*, so each proposal has its own view. This reduces the number of message types and allows for pipelining of decisions. A similar approach for message type reduction was suggested in Casper [1].

More specifically, in Chained HotStuff the votes over a PREPARE phase are collected in a view by the leader into a *genericQC*. Then the *genericQC* is relayed to the leader of the next view, essentially delegating responsibility for the next phase, which would have been PRE-COMMIT, to the next leader. However, the next leader does not actually carry a PRE-COMMIT phase, but instead initiates a new PREPARE phase and adds its own proposal. This PREPARE phase for view $v + 1$ simultaneously serves as the PRE-COMMIT phase for view v. The PREPARE phase for view $v + 2$ simultaneously serves as the PRE-COMMIT phase for view $v + 1$ and as the COMMIT phase for view v. This is possible because all the phases have identical structure.

The pipeline of Basic HotStuff protocol phases embedded in a chain of Chained HotStuff proposals is depicted in Figure 1. Views v_1, v_2, v_3 of Chained HotStuff serve as the PREPARE, PRE-COMMIT, and COMMIT Basic HotStuff phases for cmd_1 proposed in v_1. This command becomes committed by the end of v_4. Views v_2, v_3, v_4 serve as the three Basic HotStuff phases for cmd_2 proposed in v_2, and it becomes committed by the end of v_5. Additional proposals generated in these phases continue the pipeline similarly, and are denoted by dashed boxes. In Figure 1, a single arrow denotes the $b.parent$ field for a node b, and a double arrow denotes $b.justify.node$.

Hence, there are only two types of messages in Chained HotStuff, a NEW-VIEW message and generic-phase GENERIC message. The GENERIC QC functions in all logically pipelined phases. We next explain the mechanisms in the pipeline to take care of locking and committing, which occur only in the COMMIT and DECIDE phases of Basic HotStuff.

Dummy nodes. The *genericQC* used by a leader in some view *viewNumber* may not directly reference the proposal of the preceding view ($viewNumber - 1$). The reason is that the leader of a preceding view fails to obtain a QC, either because there are conflicting proposals, or due to a benign crash. To simplify the tree structure, CREATELEAF extends $genericQC.node$ with blank nodes up to the height (the number of parent links on a node's branch) of the proposing view, so view-numbers are equated with node heights. As a result, the QC embedded in a node b may not refer to its parent, i.e., $b.justify.node$ may not equal $b.parent$ (the last node in Figure 2).

One-Chain, Two-Chain, and Three-Chain. When a node b^* carries a QC that refers to a direct parent, i.e., $b^*.justify.node = b^*.parent$, we say that it forms a *One-Chain*. Denote by $b'' = b^*.justify.node$. Node b^* forms a *Two-Chain*, if in addition to forming a One-Chain, $b''.justify.node = b''.parent$. It forms a *Three-Chain*, if b'' forms a Two-Chain.

Looking at chain $b = b'.justify.node$, $b' = b''.justify.node$, $b'' = b^*.justify.node$, ancestry gaps might occur at any one of the nodes. These situations are similar to a leader of Basic HotStuff failing to complete any one of three phases, and getting interrupted to the next view by NEXTVIEW.

If b^* forms a One-Chain, the PREPARE phase of b'' has succeeded. Hence, when a replica votes for b^*, it should remember $genericQC \leftarrow b^*.justify$. We remark that it is safe to update *genericQC* even when a One-Chain is not direct, so long as it is higher than the current *genericQC*. In the implementation code described in Section 6, we indeed update *genericQC* in this case.

If b^* forms a Two-Chain, then the PRE-COMMIT phase of b' has succeeded. The replica should therefore update $lockedQC \leftarrow b''.justify$. Again, we remark that the lock can be updated even when a Two-Chain is not direct—safety will not break—and indeed, this is given in the implementation code in Section 6.

Finally, if b^* forms a Three-Chain, the COMMIT phase of b has succeeded, and b becomes a committed decision.

Algorithm 3 shows the pseudocode for Chained HotStuff. The proof of safety given by [50] is similar to the one for Basic HotStuff. We require the QC in a valid node refers to its ancestor. For brevity, we assume the constraint always holds and omit checking in the code.

Algorithm 3 Chained HotStuff protocol.

```
procedure CREATELEAF(parent, cmd, qc)
    b.parent ← branch extending with blanks from parent to height
      curView; b.cmd ← cmd; b.justify ← qc; return b

for curView ← 1, 2, 3, . . . do
  ▷ GENERIC phase
  as a leader  // r = LEADER(curView)
      wait for (n − f) NEW-VIEW messages:
          M ← {m | MATCHINGMSG(m, NEW-VIEW, curView−1)}
          // M includes the previous leader NEW-VIEW message, if received
```

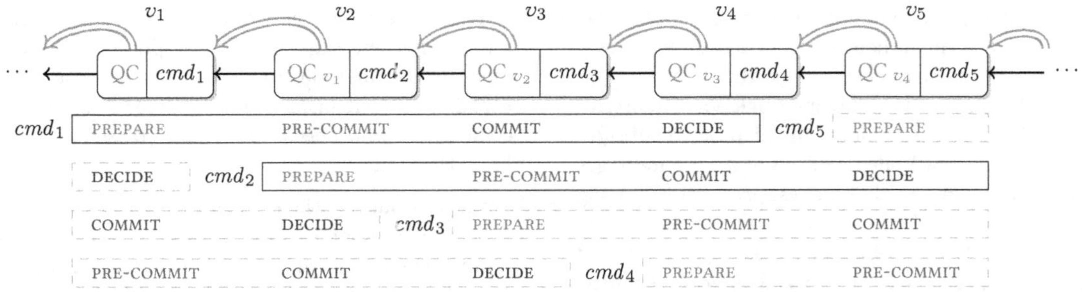

Figure 1: Chained HotStuff is a pipelined Basic HotStuff where a QC can serve in different phases simultaneously.

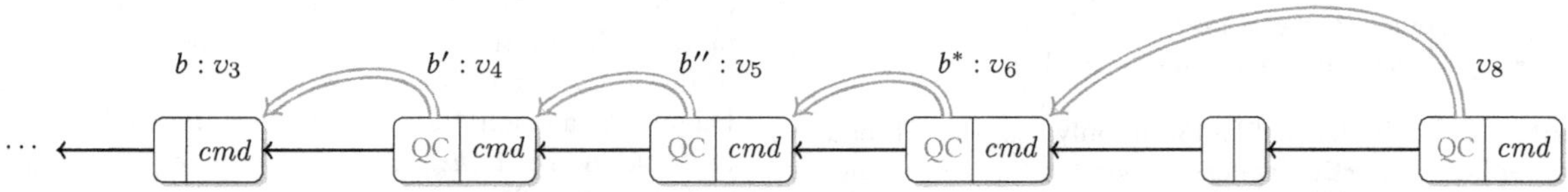

Figure 2: The nodes at views v_4, v_5, v_6 form a Three-Chain. The node at view v_8 does not make a valid One-Chain in Chained HotStuff (but it is a valid One-Chain after relaxation in the algorithm of Section 6).

```
        // while waiting in previous view
6:      genericQC ← (argmax_{m∈M} {m.justify.viewNumber}).justify
7:      curProposal ← CREATELEAF(genericQC.node,
                            client's command, genericQC)
        // PREPARE phase (leader-half)
8:      broadcast MSG(GENERIC, curProposal, ⊥)
9:    as a replica
10:     wait for message m from LEADER(curView)
            m : MATCHINGMSG(m, GENERIC, curView)
11:     b* ← m.node; b″ ← b*.justify.node;
        b′ ← b″.justify.node; b ← b′.justify.node
12:     if SAFENODE(b*, b*.justify) then
13:         send VOTEMSG(GENERIC, b*, ⊥) to LEADER(curView)
        // start PRE-COMMIT phase on b*'s parent
14:     if b*.parent = b″ then
15:         genericQC ← b*.justify
        // start COMMIT phase on b*'s grandparent
16:     if (b*.parent = b″) ∧ (b″.parent = b′) then
17:         lockedQC ← b″.justify
        // start DECIDE phase on b*'s great-grandparent
18:     if (b*.parent = b″) ∧ (b″.parent = b′) ∧
            (b′.parent = b) then
19:         execute new commands through b, respond to clients
20:   as a leader  // PRE-COMMIT phase (leader-half)
21:     wait for (n − f) votes:
            V ← {v | MATCHINGMSG(v, GENERIC, curView)}
22:     genericQC ← QC(V)
      // for liveness, the message here counts as (n − f) at Line 5
23:   as the next leader
24:     wait for message m from LEADER(curView)
            m : MATCHINGMSG(m, NEW-VIEW, curView)
  ▷ Finally
25:   NEXTVIEW interrupt: goto this line if NEXTVIEW(curView) is
      called during "wait for" in any phase
26:   send MSG(NEW-VIEW, ⊥, genericQC) to LEADER(curView + 1)
```

6 IMPLEMENTATION

HotStuff is a practical protocol for building efficient SMR systems. Because of its simplicity, we can easily turn Algorithm 3 into an event-driven-style specification that is almost like the code skeleton for a prototype implementation.

As shown in Algorithm 4, the code is further simplified and generalized by extracting the liveness mechanism from the body into a module named *Pacemaker*. Instead of the next leader always waiting for a $genericQC$ at the end of the GENERIC phase before starting its reign, this logic is delegated to the Pacemaker. A stable leader can skip this step and streamline proposals across multiple heights. Additionally, we relax the direct parent constraint for maintaining the highest $genericQC$ and $lockedQC$, while still preserving the requirement that the QC in a valid node always refers to its ancestor. The proof of correctness is similar to Chained HotStuff and we also defer it to the appendix of [50].

Data structures. Each replica u keeps track of the following main state variables:

$V[\cdot]$	mapping from a node to its votes.
$vheight$	height of last voted node.
b_{lock}	locked node (similar to $lockedQC$).
b_{exec}	last executed node.
qc_{high}	highest known QC (similar to $genericQC$) kept by a Pacemaker.
b_{leaf}	leaf node kept by a Pacemaker.

It also keeps a constant b_0, the same genesis node known by all correct replicas. To bootstrap, b_0 contains a hard-coded QC for itself, $b_{lock}, b_{exec}, b_{leaf}$ are all initialized to b_0, and qc_{high} contains the QC for b_0.

Pacemaker. A Pacemaker is a mechanism that guarantees progress after GST. It achieves this through two ingredients.

The first one is "synchronization", bringing all correct replicas, and a unique leader, into a common height for a sufficiently long period. The usual synchronization mechanism in the literature [15, 20, 25] is for replicas to increase the count of Δ's they spend at larger heights, until progress is being made. A common way to deterministically elect a leader is to use a rotating leader scheme in which all correct replicas keep a predefined leader schedule and rotate to the next one when the leader is demoted.

Second, a Pacemaker needs to provide the leader with a way to choose a proposal that will be supported by correct replicas. As shown in Algorithm 5, after a view change, in ONRECEIVENEWVIEW, the new leader collects NEW-VIEW messages sent by replicas through ONNEXTSYNCVIEW to discover the highest QC to satisfy the second part of the condition in ONRECEIVEPROPOSAL for liveness (Line 18 of Algorithm 4). During the same view, however, the incumbent leader will chain the new node to the end of the leaf last proposed by itself, where no NEW-VIEW message is needed. Based on some application-specific heuristics (to wait until the previously proposed node gets a QC, for example), the current leader invokes ONBEAT to propose a new node carrying the command to be executed.

It is worth noting that even if a bad Pacemaker invokes ONPROPOSE arbitrarily, or selects a parent and a QC capriciously, and against any scheduling delays, safety is always guaranteed. Therefore, safety guaranteed by Algorithm 4 alone is entirely decoupled from liveness by any potential instantiation of Algorithm 5.

Algorithm 4 Event-driven HotStuff (for replica *u*).

```
1: procedure CREATELEAF(parent, cmd, qc, height)
2:     b.parent ← parent; b.cmd ← cmd;
3:     b.justify ← qc; b.height ← height; return b
4: procedure UPDATE(b*)
5:     b'' ← b*.justify.node; b' ← b''.justify.node
6:     b ← b'.justify.node
       // PRE-COMMIT phase on b''
7:     UPDATEQCHIGH(b*.justify)
8:     if b'.height > b_lock.height then
9:         b_lock ← b'  // COMMIT phase on b'
10:    if (b''.parent = b') ∧ (b'.parent = b) then
11:        ONCOMMIT(b)
12:        b_exec ← b  // DECIDE phase on b
13: procedure ONCOMMIT(b)
14:    if b_exec.height < b.height then
15:        ONCOMMIT(b.parent); EXECUTE(b.cmd)
16: procedure ONRECEIVEPROPOSAL(MSG_v(GENERIC, b_new, ⊥))
17:    if b_new.height > vheight ∧ (b_new extends b_lock ∨
18:      b_new.justify.node.height > b_lock.height) then
19:        vheight ← b_new.height
20:        SEND(GETLEADER(), VOTEMSG_u(GENERIC, b_new, ⊥))
21:    UPDATE(b_new)
22: procedure ONRECEIVEVOTE(m = VOTEMSG_v(GENERIC, b, ⊥))
23:    if ∃⟨v, σ'⟩ ∈ V[b] then return  // avoid duplicates
24:    V[b] ← V[b] ∪ {⟨v, m.partialSig⟩}  // collect votes
25:    if |V[b]| ≥ n − f then
26:        qc ← QC({σ | ⟨v', σ⟩ ∈ V[b]})
27:        UPDATEQCHIGH(qc)
28: function ONPROPOSE(b_leaf, cmd, qc_high)
29:    b_new ← CREATELEAF(b_leaf, cmd, qc_high, b_leaf.height + 1)
       // send to all replicas, including u itself
30:    BROADCAST(MSG_u(GENERIC, b_new, ⊥))
31:    return b_new
```

Algorithm 5 Code skeleton for a Pacemaker (for replica *u*).

```
// We assume Pacemaker in all correct replicas will have synchronized
leadership after GST.
function GETLEADER  // ... specified by the application
procedure UPDATEQCHIGH(qc'_high)
    if qc'_high.node.height > qc_high.node.height then
        qc_high ← qc'_high
        b_leaf ← qc_high.node
procedure ONBEAT(cmd)
    if u = GETLEADER() then
        b_leaf ← ONPROPOSE(b_leaf, cmd, qc_high)
procedure ONNEXTSYNCVIEW
    send MSG(NEW-VIEW, ⊥, qc_high) to GETLEADER()
procedure ONRECEIVENEWVIEW(MSG(NEW-VIEW, ⊥, qc'_high))
    UPDATEQCHIGH(qc'_high)
```

Algorithm 6 UPDATE replacement for two-phase HotStuff.

```
procedure UPDATE(b*)
    b' ← b*.justify.node ; b ← b'.justify.node
    UPDATEQCHIGH(b*.justify)
    if b'.height > b_lock.height then b_lock ← b'
    if (b'.parent = b) then ONCOMMIT(b); b_exec ← b
```

Two-phase HotStuff variant. To further demonstrate the flexibility of the HotStuff framework, Algorithm 6 shows the two-phase variant of HotStuff. Only the UPDATE procedure is affected, a Two-Chain is required for reaching a commit decision, and a One-Chain determines the lock. As discussed above (Section 4.4), this two-phase variant loses Optimistic Responsiveness, and is similar to Tendermint/Casper. The benefit is fewer phases, while liveness may be addressed by incorporating in Pacemaker a wait based on maximum network delay.

Evaluation. Due to the space limitation, we defer our evaluation results to the longer paper [50]. There, we compare our implementation to BFT-SMaRt [13], a state-of-the-art implementation based on a two-phase PBFT variant. We show that even though three-phase HotStuff has an additional phase for its responsiveness and uses digital signatures universally (where BFT-SMaRt only uses MACs for votes), it still achieves similar latency, while being able to outperform BFT-SMaRt in throughput. It also scales better than BFT-SMaRt.

ACKNOWLEDGMENTS

We are thankful to Mathieu Baudet, Avery Ching, George Danezis, François Garillot, Zekun Li, Ben Maurer, Kartik Nayak, Dmitri Perelman, and Ling Ren, for many deep discussions of HotStuff, and to Mathieu Baudet for exposing a subtle error in a previous version posted to the ArXiv of this manuscript.

REFERENCES

[1] 2017. Casper FFG with One Message Type, and Simpler Fork Choice Rule. https://ethresear.ch/t/casper-ffg-with-one-message-type-and-simpler-fork-choice-rule/103. (2017).

[2] 2018. Istanbul BFT's Design Cannot Successfully Tolerate Fail-Stop Failures. https://github.com/jpmorganchase/quorum/issues/305. (2018).

[3] 2018. A Livelock Bug in the Presence of Byzantine Validator. https://github.com/tendermint/tendermint/issues/1047. (2018).

[4] Ittai Abraham, Guy Gueta, Dahlia Malkhi, Lorenzo Alvisi, Ramakrishna Kotla, and Jean-Philippe Martin. 2017. Revisiting Fast Practical Byzantine Fault Tolerance. *CoRR* abs/1712.01367 (2017). arXiv:1712.01367

[5] Ittai Abraham, Guy Gueta, Dahlia Malkhi, and Jean-Philippe Martin. 2018. Revisiting Fast Practical Byzantine Fault Tolerance: Thelma, Velma, and Zelma. *CoRR* abs/1801.10022 (2018). arXiv:1801.10022

[6] Ittai Abraham and Dahlia Malkhi. 2017. The Blockchain Consensus Layer and BFT. *Bulletin of the EATCS* 123 (2017).

[7] Ittai Abraham, Dahlia Malkhi, Kartik Nayak, Ling Ren, and Alexander Spiegelman. 2017. Solida: A Blockchain Protocol Based on Reconfigurable Byzantine Consensus. In *21st International Conference on Principles of Distributed Systems, OPODIS 2017, Lisbon, Portugal, December 18-20, 2017.* 25:1–25:19. https://doi.org/10.4230/LIPIcs.OPODIS.2017.25

[8] Ittai Abraham, Dahlia Malkhi, and Alexander Spiegelman. 2019. Validated Asynchronous Byzantine Agreement with Optimal Resilience and Asymptotically Optimal Time and Word Communication. In *Proceedings of the 2019 ACM Symposium on Principles of Distributed Computing, PODC 2019, Toronto, ON, Canada, July 29-August 2, 2019.*

[9] Yair Amir, Brian A. Coan, Jonathan Kirsch, and John Lane. 2011. Prime: Byzantine Replication under Attack. *IEEE Trans. Dependable Sec. Comput.* 8, 4 (2011), 564–577. https://doi.org/10.1109/TDSC.2010.70

[10] Hagit Attiya, Cynthia Dwork, Nancy A. Lynch, and Larry J. Stockmeyer. 1994. Bounds on the Time to Reach Agreement in the Presence of Timing Uncertainty. *J. ACM* 41, 1 (1994), 122–152. https://doi.org/10.1145/174644.174649

[11] Pierre-Louis Aublin, Rachid Guerraoui, Nikola Knezevic, Vivien Quéma, and Marko Vukolic. 2015. The Next 700 BFT Protocols. *ACM Trans. Comput. Syst.* 32, 4 (2015), 12:1–12:45. https://doi.org/10.1145/2658994

[12] Michael Ben-Or. 1983. Another Advantage of Free Choice: Completely Asynchronous Agreement Protocols (Extended Abstract). In *Proceedings of the Second Annual ACM SIGACT-SIGOPS Symposium on Principles of Distributed Computing, Montreal, Quebec, Canada, August 17-19, 1983.* 27–30. https://doi.org/10.1145/800221.806707

[13] Alysson Neves Bessani, João Sousa, and Eduardo Adílio Pelinson Alchieri. 2014. State Machine Replication for the Masses with BFT-SMART. In *44th Annual IEEE/IFIP International Conference on Dependable Systems and Networks, DSN 2014, Atlanta, GA, USA, June 23-26, 2014.* 355–362. https://doi.org/10.1109/DSN.2014.43

[14] Dan Boneh, Ben Lynn, and Hovav Shacham. 2004. Short Signatures from the Weil Pairing. *J. Cryptology* 17, 4 (2004), 297–319. https://doi.org/10.1007/s00145-004-0314-9

[15] Ethan Buchman. 2016. *Tendermint: Byzantine fault tolerance in the age of blockchains.* Ph.D. Dissertation.

[16] Ethan Buchman, Jae Kwon, and Zarko Milosevic. 2018. The Latest Gossip on BFT Consensus. *CoRR* abs/1807.04938 (2018). arXiv:1807.04938

[17] Vitalik Buterin and Virgil Griffith. 2017. Casper the Friendly Finality Gadget. *CoRR* abs/1710.09437 (2017). arXiv:1710.09437

[18] Christian Cachin, Klaus Kursawe, and Victor Shoup. 2005. Random Oracles in Constantinople: Practical Asynchronous Byzantine Agreement Using Cryptography. *J. Cryptology* 18, 3 (2005), 219–246. https://doi.org/10.1007/s00145-005-0318-0

[19] Christian Cachin and Marko Vukolic. 2017. Blockchain Consensus Protocols in the Wild. *CoRR* abs/1707.01873 (2017). arXiv:1707.01873

[20] Miguel Castro and Barbara Liskov. 1999. Practical Byzantine Fault Tolerance. In *Proceedings of the Third USENIX Symposium on Operating Systems Design and Implementation (OSDI), New Orleans, Louisiana, USA, February 22-25, 1999.* 173–186. https://dl.acm.org/citation.cfm?id=296824

[21] Miguel Castro and Barbara Liskov. 2002. Practical Byzantine Fault Tolerance and Proactive Recovery. *ACM Trans. Comput. Syst.* 20, 4 (2002), 398–461. https://doi.org/10.1145/571637.571640

[22] Allen Clement, Manos Kapritsos, Sangmin Lee, Yang Wang, Lorenzo Alvisi, Michael Dahlin, and Taylor Riche. 2009. Upright cluster services. In *Proceedings of the 22nd ACM Symposium on Operating Systems Principles 2009, SOSP 2009, Big Sky, Montana, USA, October 11-14, 2009.* 277–290. https://doi.org/10.1145/1629575.1629602

[23] Danny Dolev and Rüdiger Reischuk. 1985. Bounds on Information Exchange for Byzantine Agreement. *J. ACM* 32, 1 (1985), 191–204. https://doi.org/10.1145/2455.214112

[24] Danny Dolev and H. Raymond Strong. 1982. Polynomial Algorithms for Multiple Processor Agreement. In *Proceedings of the 14th Annual ACM Symposium on Theory of Computing, May 5-7, 1982, San Francisco, California, USA.* 401–407. https://doi.org/10.1145/800070.802215

[25] Cynthia Dwork, Nancy A. Lynch, and Larry J. Stockmeyer. 1988. Consensus in the Presence of Partial Synchrony. *J. ACM* 35, 2 (1988), 288–323. https://doi.org/10.1145/42282.42283

[26] Ittay Eyal, Adem Efe Gencer, Emin Gün Sirer, and Robbert van Renesse. 2016. Bitcoin-NG: A Scalable Blockchain Protocol. In *13th USENIX Symposium on Networked Systems Design and Implementation, NSDI 2016, Santa Clara, CA, USA, March 16-18, 2016.* 45–59.

[27] Michael J. Fischer, Nancy A. Lynch, and Mike Paterson. 1985. Impossibility of Distributed Consensus with One Faulty Process. *J. ACM* 32, 2 (1985), 374–382. https://doi.org/10.1145/3149.214121

[28] Juan A. Garay, Aggelos Kiayias, and Nikos Leonardos. 2015. The Bitcoin Backbone Protocol: Analysis and Applications. In *Advances in Cryptology - EUROCRYPT 2015 - 34th Annual International Conference on the Theory and Applications of Cryptographic Techniques, Sofia, Bulgaria, April 26-30, 2015, Proceedings, Part II.* 281–310. https://doi.org/10.1007/978-3-662-46803-6_10

[29] Yossi Gilad, Rotem Hemo, Silvio Micali, Georgios Vlachos, and Nickolai Zeldovich. 2017. Algorand: Scaling Byzantine Agreements for Cryptocurrencies. In *Proceedings of the 26th Symposium on Operating Systems Principles, Shanghai, China, October 28-31, 2017.* 51–68. https://doi.org/10.1145/3132747.3132757

[30] Guy Golan-Gueta, Ittai Abraham, Shelly Grossman, Dahlia Malkhi, Benny Pinkas, Michael K. Reiter, Dragos-Adrian Seredinschi, Orr Tamir, and Alin Tomescu. 2018. SBFT: a Scalable Decentralized Trust Infrastructure for Blockchains. *CoRR* abs/1804.01626 (2018). arXiv:1804.01626

[31] Timo Hanke, Mahnush Movahedi, and Dominic Williams. 2018. DFINITY Technology Overview Series, Consensus System. *CoRR* abs/1805.04548 (2018). arXiv:1805.04548

[32] Jonathan Katz and Chiu-Yuen Koo. 2009. On Expected Constant-Round Protocols for Byzantine Agreement. *J. Comput. Syst. Sci.* 75, 2 (2009), 91–112. https://doi.org/10.1016/j.jcss.2008.08.001

[33] Eleftherios Kokoris-Kogias, Philipp Jovanovic, Nicolas Gailly, Ismail Khoffi, Linus Gasser, and Bryan Ford. 2016. Enhancing Bitcoin Security and Performance with Strong Consistency via Collective Signing. *CoRR* abs/1602.06997 (2016).

[34] Ramakrishna Kotla, Lorenzo Alvisi, Michael Dahlin, Allen Clement, and Edmund L. Wong. 2009. Zyzzyva: Speculative Byzantine Fault Tolerance. *ACM Trans. Comput. Syst.* 27, 4 (2009), 7:1–7:39. https://doi.org/10.1145/1658357.1658358

[35] Leslie Lamport. 1978. Time, Clocks, and the Ordering of Events in a Distributed System. *Commun. ACM* 21, 7 (1978), 558–565. https://doi.org/10.1145/359545.359563

[36] Leslie Lamport. 1998. The Part-Time Parliament. *ACM Trans. Comput. Syst.* 16, 2 (1998), 133–169. https://doi.org/10.1145/279227.279229

[37] Leslie Lamport, Robert E. Shostak, and Marshall C. Pease. 1982. The Byzantine Generals Problem. *ACM Trans. Program. Lang. Syst.* 4, 3 (1982), 382–401. https://doi.org/10.1145/357172.357176

[38] James Mickens. 2014. The Saddest Moment. *;login:* 39, 3 (2014). https://www.usenix.org/publications/login/june14/mickens

[39] Andrew Miller, Yu Xia, Kyle Croman, Elaine Shi, and Dawn Song. 2016. The Honey Badger of BFT Protocols. In *Proceedings of the 2016 ACM SIGSAC Conference on Computer and Communications Security, Vienna, Austria, October 24-28, 2016.* 31–42. https://doi.org/10.1145/2976749.2978399

[40] Satoshi Nakamoto. 2008. Bitcoin: A Peer-to-Peer Electronic Cash System. https://bitcoin.org/bitcoin.pdf. (2008).

[41] Rafael Pass, Lior Seeman, and Abhi Shelat. 2017. Analysis of the Blockchain Protocol in Asynchronous Networks. In *Advances in Cryptology - EUROCRYPT 2017 - 36th Annual International Conference on the Theory and Applications of Cryptographic Techniques, Paris, France, April 30 - May 4, 2017, Proceedings, Part II.* 643–673. https://doi.org/10.1007/978-3-319-56614-6_22

[42] Rafael Pass and Elaine Shi. 2018. Thunderella: Blockchains with Optimistic Instant Confirmation. In *Advances in Cryptology - EUROCRYPT 2018 - 37th Annual International Conference on the Theory and Applications of Cryptographic Techniques, Tel Aviv, Israel, April 29 - May 3, 2018 Proceedings, Part II.* 3–33. https://doi.org/10.1007/978-3-319-78375-8_1

[43] Marshall C. Pease, Robert E. Shostak, and Leslie Lamport. 1980. Reaching Agreement in the Presence of Faults. *J. ACM* 27, 2 (1980), 228–234. https://doi.org/10.1145/322186.322188

[44] HariGovind V. Ramasamy and Christian Cachin. 2005. Parsimonious Asynchronous Byzantine-Fault-Tolerant Atomic Broadcast. In *Principles of Distributed Systems, 9th International Conference, OPODIS 2005, Pisa, Italy, December 12-14, 2005, Revised Selected Papers.* 88–102. https://doi.org/10.1007/11795490_9

[45] Michael K. Reiter. 1994. The Rampart Toolkit for Building High-Integrity Services. In *Theory and Practice in Distributed Systems, International Workshop, Dagstuhl Castle, Germany, September 5-9, 1994, Selected Papers.* 99–110. https://doi.org/10.1007/3-540-60042-6_7

[46] Phillip Rogaway and Thomas Shrimpton. 2004. Cryptographic Hash-Function Basics: Definitions, Implications, and Separations for Preimage Resistance, Second-Preimage Resistance, and Collision Resistance. In *Fast Software Encryption, 11th International Workshop, FSE 2004, Delhi, India, February 5-7, 2004, Revised Papers (Lecture Notes in Computer Science)*, Bimal K. Roy and Willi Meier (Eds.), Vol. 3017. Springer, 371–388. https://doi.org/10.1007/978-3-540-25937-4_24

[47] Fred B. Schneider. 1990. Implementing Fault-Tolerant Services Using the State Machine Approach: A Tutorial. *ACM Comput. Surv.* 22, 4 (1990), 299–319. https://doi.org/10.1145/98163.98167

[48] Victor Shoup. 2000. Practical Threshold Signatures. In *Advances in Cryptology - EUROCRYPT 2000, International Conference on the Theory and Application of Cryptographic Techniques, Bruges, Belgium, May 14-18, 2000, Proceeding.* 207–220. https://doi.org/10.1007/3-540-45539-6_15

[49] Yee Jiun Song and Robbert van Renesse. 2008. Bosco: One-Step Byzantine Asynchronous Consensus. In *Distributed Computing, 22nd International Symposium, DISC 2008, Arcachon, France, September 22-24, 2008. Proceedings.* 438–450. https://doi.org/10.1007/978-3-540-87779-0_30

[50] Maofan Yin, Dahlia Malkhi, Michael K. Reiter, Guy Golan Gueta, and Ittai Abraham. 2018. HotStuff: BFT Consensus in the Lens of Blockchain. *CoRR* abs/1803.05069 (2018). arXiv:1803.05069

Fault Tolerant Gradient Clock Synchronization*

Johannes Bund
Max Planck Institute for Informatics
Saarbrücken, Germany
jbund@mpi-inf.mpg.de

Christoph Lenzen
Max Planck Institute for Informatics
Saarbrücken, Germany
clenzen@mpi-inf.mpg.de

Will Rosenbaum
Max Planck Institute for Informatics
Saarbrücken, Germany
wrosenba@mpi-inf.mpg.de

ABSTRACT

Synchronizing clocks in distributed systems is well-understood, both in terms of fault-tolerance in fully connected systems, and the optimal achievable local skew in general fault-free networks. However, so far nothing non-trivial is known about the local skew that can be achieved in non-fully-connected topologies even under a single Byzantine fault. In this work, we show that asymptotically optimal local skew can be achieved in the presence of Byzantine faults.

Our approach combines the Lynch-Welch algorithm [19] for synchronizing a clique of n nodes with up to $f < n/3$ Byzantine faults, and the gradient clock synchronization (GCS) algorithm by Lenzen et al. [15] in order to render the latter resilient to faults. This is not possible on general graphs, so we augment an arbitrary input graph $\mathcal{G}$ by replacing each node with a fully connected cluster of $3f + 1$ copies, and execute an instance of the Lynch-Welch algorithm within each cluster. We interpret the clusters as supernodes executing the GCS algorithm on $\mathcal{G}$, where each node in the cluster maintains an estimate of the logical clock of its supernode. By also fully connecting clusters corresponding to neighbors in $\mathcal{G}$, supernodes maintain estimates of neighboring clusters' logical clocks. We achieve asymptotically optimal local skew, assuming that no cluster contains more than f faulty nodes. This construction yields factors of $O(f)$ and $O(f^2)$ overheads in terms of nodes and edges, respectively. Since tolerating f faulty neighbors trivially requires degrees larger than f, these overheads are asymptotically optimal.

CCS CONCEPTS

• **Theory of computation** → **Distributed algorithms**; • **Computer systems organization** → **Dependable and fault-tolerant systems and networks**; • **Networks** → *Network algorithms*.

KEYWORDS

clock synchronization, gradient clock synchronization, fault tolerance, local skew

ACM Reference Format:
Johannes Bund, Christoph Lenzen, and Will Rosenbaum. 2019. Fault Tolerant Gradient Clock Synchronization. In *2019 ACM Symposium on Principles of Distributed Computing (PODC '19), July 29-August 2, 2019, Toronto, ON, Canada.* ACM, New York, NY, USA, 9 pages. https://doi.org/10.1145/3293611.3331637

*This project has received funding from the European Research Council (ERC) under the European Union's Horizon 2020 research and innovation programme (grant agreement 716562).

ACM ISBN 978-1-4503-6217-7/19/07.
https://doi.org/10.1145/3293611.3331637

1 INTRODUCTION AND RELATED WORK

Synchronizing clocks across distributed systems is a fundamental task. Clock synchronization may be used for coordination, e.g. in a time division multiple access scheme to a shared resource such as a wireless channel. Clock synchronization also plays a crucial role in (distributed) measurements by enabling a system to correctly correlate data, and it can form the basis of a decentralized system clock for a System-on-Chip or Network-on-Chip.

Gradient clock synchronization (GCS) algorithms aim to minimize the *local skew*, i.e., the worst-case phase difference between the logical clocks computed by neighbors in a network graph. While the *global skew* — the worst-case skew between any pair of clocks in the network — is linear in the network diameter D [1],[1] a bound of $\Theta(\log_b D)$ on the local skew was established in [15]. Here, the base is $b = \mu/\rho$, where $1 + \mu$ is the maximum factor by which a node speeds up its logical clocks relative to its hardware clock. The bound of $\Theta(\log_b D)$ is tight, subject to the constraints that (i) the nodes' hardware clocks always run at rates between 1 and $1 + \rho$, (ii) nodes' logical clocks always run at rates between 1 and $(1+\rho)(1+\mu)$, and (iii) $\mu/\rho = 1 + \Omega(1)$.

The problem of minimizing the local skew is well-studied. Under worst-case assumptions (on hardware clock rates, message delays, etc), small bounds on the local skew can be achieved with logical clocks whose parameters (e.g., maximum and minimum rates) are only slightly worse than the parameters of the underlying hardware clocks. Results in the same vein hold for dynamic graphs [10, 11]. The results for dynamic networks immediately imply analogous results for networks with crash faults. From the perspective of the remaining system, a node crashing is equivalent to removing all of its incident links. The algorithm achieving small local skew is inherently self-stabilizing, provided one ensures that excessive global skews are detected and reduced, e.g., by a reset procedure.

Unfortunately, the GCS algorithm utterly fails in face of non-benign faults. Even a single node that refuses to adjust its logical clock rate would invalidate any non-trivial bound on skews. Given that distributed systems of sufficient size invariably tend to violate (overly optimistic) specifications [21], this raises the following question.

Can small local skew be achieved despite Byzantine faults?

[1]Throughout this paper, we assume that all parameters like delays and delay uncertainties on links are uniform, so that D refers to the hop diameter of the network. However, prior results generalize to heterogeneous settings in a natural way. In such instances, the hop diameter is replaced by the weighted diameter of the graph where each link has weight equal to its delay uncertainty.

When posing this question, obviously we need to restrict attention to skews between non-faulty nodes only. Nonetheless, the answer is trivially "no" in general: a node with exactly two neighbors, one of which is Byzantine, cannot reliably decide which neighbor's clock it should follow. More generally, a node with up to f faulty neighbors must have at least $2f + 1$ neighbors to avoid trivial impossibility of synchronization. A more careful argument shows that, without cryptographic assumptions, $n > 3f$ is necessary even if the network is a clique [4, 14]. In the case of a clique, the Lynch-Welch algorithm [19] achieves asymptotically optimal skew for any n and f satisfying $n > 3f$.

The Lynch-Welch algorithm, like other fault-tolerant clock synchronization algorithms designed for cliques, can be extended to networks of larger diameter in a straightforward way.[2] The idea is to set up a central cluster running the algorithm and synchronize "slave" clusters of nodes to the central cluster. That is, slave clusters simply "echo" the clock pulses generated by the central cluster. Clusters farther away from the central cluster echo the messages of slave clusters, and so on, resulting in a tree structure with each tree node corresponding to a cluster of nodes. So long as in each cluster less than one third of the nodes is faulty, subsequent groups can synchronize both to their parent cluster in the tree and among themselves, using the same technique based on approximate agreement [7] that lies at the heart of the Lynch-Welch algorithm.

If clusters have uniform size of $3f + 1$ and nodes fail independently with probability p, then the probability that more than f nodes in a cluster are faulty is

$$\sum_{i=f+1}^{3f+1} \binom{3f+1}{i} p^i (1-p)^{3f+1-i} \leq \binom{3f+1}{f+1} p^{f+1} \leq (3ep)^{f+1} . \quad (1)$$

Thus, if the *distribution* of faults across the system is benign, even small choices of f can improve reliability dramatically, without causing impractically large degrees. For $f \in \Theta(\log n)$, the system as a whole operates correctly with high probability even for a constant failure probability p of individual nodes.

The simplistic approach of synchronizing clusters to a central cluster succeeds in the sense that it achieves asymptotically optimal global skew in a sparse network (assuming that at most f nodes fail in each cluster). However, it does not offer a non-trivial bound on the local skew. Setting $f = 0$, the algorithm specializes to a simple master-slave synchronization algorithm on (fault-free) tree topologies. If a clock pulse propagates through a line network with the global skew equally distributed over the line, this will "compress" the full global skew onto a single edge, cf. [17]. In contrast, GCS algorithms need to take into account whether neighbors are lagging behind when deciding how to adjust their logical clocks. More sophisticated strategies are needed for a fault-tolerant GCS algorithm!

1.1 Our contribution

We present a simple and general transformation that takes an arbitrary network $\mathcal{G}$ and yields a larger network on which we can achieve fault-tolerant GCS with asymptotically optimal local skew.

[2]We are not aware of this being explicitly shown, but [5] discusses the approach in a synchronous setting and the argument transfers to the "semi-synchronous" model we consider without issue.

The basic idea is simple enough: each node is replaced by a (fully connected) cluster of $3f + 1$ nodes and each edge is replaced by a complete bipartite graph between the respective clusters. We then use the Lynch-Welch algorithm [19] to synchronize within clusters, and simulate the (non-fault-tolerant) GCS algorithm from [15] on virtual clocks defined for the clusters.

Our approach is simplified by employing the two algorithms (almost) as black boxes. This is made possible by leveraging the worst-case assumptions on clock rates the Lynch-Welch algorithm can handle: Our algorithm treats the speed adjustments made by the concurrently running GCS algorithm as changes in "hardware" clock speeds. Thus we fully exploit the analysis of the Lynch-Welch algorithm without having to prove statements again from scratch. Similarly, the GCS algorithm from [15] can be phrased such that each node acts solely on estimates of real time differences between events (which any node gets from its hardware clock) and estimates of neighboring logical clocks. We exploit the latter by having nodes use their own logical clocks in the Lynch-Welch algorithm as stand-in for the (virtual) cluster clocks, which they can never know precisely.

The main obstacle to this approach is that using both algorithms as black boxes results in the problem with the "additional" (amortized) clock drift induced by the Lynch-Welch algorithm's corrections to nodes' clocks. This additional drift is proportional to the (intra-cluster) synchronization quality divided by the length of the resynchronization interval. The synchronization quality is proportional to the difference between maximum and minimum clock rate times the length of the resynchronization interval. This means that a naive analysis would require that the clock drift the GCS algorithm needs to combat is at least as large as the increase in clock speed the GCS algorithm is willing to use to do so. In other words, fast-running clocks would need to be able to outrun other fast-running clocks, leaving the GCS algorithm with no way of reducing skews at all.

We resolve this circularity in the naive implementation by exploiting the convergence properties of the Lynch-Welch algorithm in combination with the flexibility of the GCS algorithm. The GCS algorithm allows for slack between conditions under which logical clocks *must* run fast or slow, and *triggers* that indicate when a node actually switches from fast to slow mode, or vice versa. This slack enables an implementation despite the fact that clock values of neighbors are never known exactly. We also use this slack to buy some time for responding to critical skews. By the time a cluster is required to be in, say, fast mode, *all* (correct) nodes in the cluster will have satisfied the fast trigger for some time. The period of time between when the fast triggers are unanimously satisfied and when the node is required to run fast is sufficiently long that the Lynch-Welch algorithm converges to a smaller skew within the cluster. Thus, when the cluster is required to run fast, the Lynch-Welch corrections are significantly smaller than the worst-case bounds for non-unanimous clusters. This behavior allows us to bound the amortized clock rates of individual nodes in clusters satisfying the fast or slow conditions, thereby showing that fast clusters indeed run faster than slow clusters. The gap is sufficiently large that we can apply the analysis of the GCS algorithm as a black box. Specifically, we show the following.

THEOREM 1.1. *Let $\mathcal{G} = (C, \mathcal{E})$ be an arbitrary network. Let $G = (V, E)$ be the augmented graph formed by replacing each node in $\mathcal{G}$ with a clique of $k \geq 3f + 1$ nodes, and fully connecting such cliques if they correspond to neighbors in $\mathcal{G}$. Suppose messages in G are subject to maximum delay d, delay uncertainty U, and hardware clock drifts are at most ρ, where ρ is sufficiently small.[3] Suppose further that within each cluster corresponding to a node in $\mathcal{G}$, at most f of the nodes are faulty. Then there exists an algorithm that computes logical clocks $L_v(t)$ for each correct node $v \in V \setminus F$ such that (i) for each $v \in V \setminus F$, L_v increases at rates between 1 and $1 + O(\rho)$ and (ii) for all $\{v, w\} \in E$ with $v, w \in V \setminus F$, and for all $t \in \mathbb{R}^+$, we have*

$$|L_v(t) - L_w(t)| = O((\rho \cdot d + U) \log D),$$

where D is the network diameter.

1.2 Paper Organization

We discuss further related work in Section 2. We formalize our computational model in Section 3. Section 4 provides a description of the intra-cluster synchronization portion of our algorithm, ClusterSync, and states our main technical lemmas. Section 5 contains a description of the inter-cluster synchronization portion of our algorithm, InterclusterSync, and provides a proof of our main result, Theorem 1.1. Due to space restrictions, we do not provide proofs of the technical lemmas leading to the proof of Theorem 1.1. Technical details are provided in the full version of this paper, which is available online [2].

2 FURTHER RELATED WORK

Srikanth and Toueg [22] introduced a basic synchronization algorithm that can cope with Byzantine faults. In a fully connected network, the Srikanth-Toueg algorithm maintains synchronization among the nodes by a propose-and-pull mechanism: Nodes propose to resynchronize either after a local timeout, or upon having received at least $f + 1$ proposals. The nodes then resynchronize after receiving at least $n - f$ proposals. This procedure achieves asymptotically optimal [18] skew of $O(d)$ despite $f < 3n$ Byzantine faults in the case where there is no guaranteed *lower* bound on the communication delay. The Lynch-Welch algorithm [19] improves the skew to $O(U + (\vartheta - 1)d)$ under the additional assumption that message delay is at least $d - U$ time. The skew $O(U + (\vartheta - 1)d)$ is asymptotically optimal, and is strictly better than the $O(d)$ skew attained by the Srikanth and Toueg algorithm when there is some a priori lower bound on the minimum message delay.[4] The Lynch-Welch algorithm achieves synchronization by simulating synchronous rounds, each of which is used to perform an approximate agreement [7] step on when the round should have started and adjusting clocks accordingly.

Either the Srikanth-Toueg or the Lynch-Welch algorithm could be employed in our construction, where we chose Lynch-Welch for its better skew. Both algorithms also share the characteristic that, in their basic variants, logical clocks "jump" to implement phase corrections. This discontinuous behavior is incompatible with the requirement that logical clocks satisfy lower and upper bounds on their rates in a GCS algorithm. This issue is easily addressed by amortizing clock adjustments over sufficient periods of time [13]. The amortization process requires that we adjust the "round length" of these algorithms, but this change has no asymptotic impact on skews.

A series of works considers synchronization algorithms that are simultaneously resilient to $f < n/3$ Byzantine faults and self-stabilizing [3, 6, 8, 9, 16]. That is, synchronization is re-established despite the (ongoing) interference from Byzantine faulty nodes after transient faults cease. Dolev and Welch [8] proposed the problem, proving that it can actually be solved. However, their algorithm has exponential stabilization time, i.e., $2^{\Omega(f)}d$ time may pass after transient faults cease before the logical clocks meet the synchronization and progress requirements. The stabilization time was improved to polynomial [3], then linear [6], and finally (randomized) logarithmic [16]. The latter construction transforms any synchronous R-round consensus algorithm into a solution to the problem that stabilizes in $O(R \log n)$ time and sends $O(M \log n)$ bits over each link in $\Theta(d)$ time, where M is the message size of the consensus algorithm. If the consensus algorithm is randomized, the transformation works the same way, but the stabilization time bound holds with high probability (instead of deterministically). Beside the smallest known stabilization time, this transformation also yields the best known trade-offs between stabilization time and amount of communication. All of these algorithms have in common that they achieve $O(d)$ skew, as they rely on the propose-and-pull mechanic underlying the Srikanth-Toueg algorithm. However, such algorithms can be used to make the Lynch-Welch algorithm self-stabilizing, by utilizing the inaccurate (and typically also infrequent) synchronization events to "jump-start" the simulation of synchronous approximate agreement rounds upon which the Lynch-Welch algorithm is based [9]. The result is a routine that combines the extreme resilience of the self-stabilizing routine, with the asymptotically optimal skew of the Lynch-Welch algorithm.

To date, GCS has been studied in fault-free networks only. The problem was introduced by Fan and Lynch [20], alongside a surprising lower bound of $\Omega(\log D / \log \log D)$ on the local skew. The first non-trivial upper bound of $O(\sqrt{D})$ on the local skew is due to Locher and Wattenhofer [17]. In the algorithm of [17], nodes try to catch up with the maximum logical clock value among their neighbors, but under the constraint that they never run faster than their hardware clock rate when there is a neighbor whose clock lags $\Theta(\sqrt{D})$ or more behind. As the global skew is bounded by $O(D)$, at most $O(\sqrt{D})$ consecutive nodes can be "blocked" from catching up. Thus an individual node is not prevented from speeding up for more than $\Theta(\sqrt{D})$ time. This gives rise to the bound on the skew. Subsequently, the tight bound of $\Theta(\log D)$ on the local skew was established in [15]. The GCS algorithm in [15] can be seen as switching between the "catching up" and "blocking" strategy depending on the amount of local skew witnessed by a node. Specifically, each node compares the largest $s \in \mathbb{N}_0$ such that some neighbor's clock is at least $s\kappa$ ahead to the largest $s' \in \mathbb{N}_0$ such that some neighbor's clock is at least $s'\kappa$ behind, for some suitably chosen κ. One can then show that the length of paths with sufficient skew to "block" nodes from catching up decreases exponentially with s, which yields the stated bound.

[3] In our initial analysis, we do not derive explicit bounds on ρ for which our claims hold.

[4] The optimality follows from [18], together with a simple indistinguishability argument for the $(\vartheta - 1)d$ term.

The algorithmic approach of the GCS algorithm [15] turns out to be quite robust and flexible. The GCS algorithm generalizes to networks in which edges $e = \{v, w\}$ have weights ϵ_e indicating the accuracy with which v and w can estimate each other's clock values, by simply choosing κ proportional to ϵ_e. The generalization to heterogeneous networks was described by Kuhn and Oshman in [12], who also introduced the description of the GCS algorithm in terms of the fast and slow conditions we use in our exposition (see Section 5). The GCS algorithm is also "almost" self-stabilizing, in the sense that it will re-establish its local skew bound from any state in $O(\mathcal{S}/\mu)$ time, provided that a global skew bound of $\mathcal{S}$ is satisfied. As logical clocks must not run more than factor $1 + \mu$ faster than hardware clocks, this time bound is optimal so long as we impose this restriction on the maximum rate of logical clocks. Moreover, the stabilization property can be leveraged to allow for dynamic topologies. That is, edges may appear and disappear in a worst-case fashion, yet the algorithm maintains its skew bounds on all paths that consist only of edges that have been present for $\Omega(\mathcal{S}/\mu)$ time. Adding a mechanism to carefully "activate" the consideration of newly arriving edges level by level (i.e., for increasing values of s) in a well-timed fashion, the algorithm guarantees the claimed skew bounds with no further modification [10, 11]. In addition, choosing $\mu = \Theta(1)$ and using that the algorithm achieves $\mathcal{S} = O(D)$, where D is the (weighted, dynamic) diameter of the graph, we see that the algorithm stabilizes new edges in $O(D)$ time. Again, this bound is worst-case optimal [11]. The dynamic version of the algorithm in particular shows that crash failures can be tolerated, as repeatedly checking liveness of nodes (which is implicit, as estimating clock values necessitates communication) enables the mapping of crash failures. Live nodes can then "delete" all incident links to the crashed node.

In this work, we provide the first (non-trivial) GCS algorithm resilient to non-benign faults. As it is based on the same algorithmic concept and a generic construction, we anticipate that all of the results mentioned in the preceding discussion can be carried over, even though we confine ourselves to the static setting in this paper.

3 COMPUTATIONAL MODEL

3.1 Network

Let $\mathcal{G} = (\mathcal{C}, \mathcal{E})$ be an arbitrary graph. We consider a network $G = (V, E)$ constructed from $\mathcal{G}$ in the following way. We identify each $C \in \mathcal{C}$ with a set of k nodes $C = \{v_1, v_2, \ldots, v_k\}$. We refer to the sets $C \in \mathcal{C}$ as ***clusters***. For distinct clusters $B, C \in \mathcal{C}$, the corresponding sets of nodes in V are disjoint, i.e., $V = \bigcup_{C \in \mathcal{C}} C$. The edge set E contains two different "types" of edges defined as follows:

cluster edges: for each $C \in \mathcal{C}$ and $v, w \in C$, we have $(v, w) \in E$;

intercluster edges: for each $(B, C) \in \mathcal{E}$, $v \in B$ and $w \in C$ we have $(v, w) \in E$.

We assume that each vertex $v \in V$ knows the identities of its neighbors, as well as the identity of the cluster to which each neighbor belongs.

3.2 Communication and computation

Nodes in the network communicate by sending content-less messages, known as *pulses*, to their neighbors. When a (correct) node broadcasts a pulse, all of its neighbors receive the pulse after some delay, which is itself subject to some uncertainty. We denote the maximal message delay by d, and the uncertainty by U. Thus a pulse sent by v at Newtonian time p_v is received by each of v's neighbors at a time $t \in [p_v + d - U, p_v + d]$.

3.3 Timing and clocks

We assume that the entire network inhabits an inertial reference frame, and the parameter $t \in \mathbb{R}$ denotes an absolute, Newtonian time. The network operates in a semi-synchronous model, where each node $v \in V$ has an associated hardware clock. Hardware clocks are prone to some uncertainty, which we model by a variable rate of v's clock that may change over time. Formally, for each v there is a locally integrable function $h_v : \mathbb{R} \to \mathbb{R}$ satisfying $1 \le h_v(t) \le 1+\rho$ for all $t \in \mathbb{R}$. Here $\rho > 0$ is (an upper bound on) v's ***hardware clock drift***.[5] In our algorithm, nodes use their hardware clocks exclusively to measure time differences, so we may assume without loss of generality that the hardware clocks are initialized to 0 at time 0. Accordingly, the hardware clock of v at time t is defined by $H_v(t) = \int_0^t h_v(\tau)\, d\tau$. Each node v accesses $H_v(t)$ directly, enabling it to estimate the time that passed between local events.

While h_v determines the (unknown) rate of v's hardware clock, our algorithm controls its logical clock by adjusting the logical clock rate relative to the hardware clock. Specifically, the algorithm controls two parameters: $\delta_v(t) \in \mathbb{R}_{\ge 0}$, and $\gamma_v(t) \in \{0, 1\}$. The parameter $\delta_v(t)$ is adjusted by the intra-cluster synchronization algorithm in order to maintain synchronization within each cluster in accordance with the Lynch-Welch algorithm (see Section 4). The parameter $\gamma_v(t)$ indicates whether or not a node runs in "fast mode" in accordance with the inter-cluster algorithm simulating the GCS algorithm between clusters (see Section 5). The logical clock value $L_v(t)$ is computed to be

$$L_v(t) = \int_0^t (1 + \varphi \cdot \delta_v(\tau))(1 + \mu \cdot \gamma_v(\tau)) h_v(\tau)\, d\tau. \quad (2)$$

The parameters φ and μ are constants whose values will be determined later on, where we already fix that $0 < \varphi < 1$ and $\mu > 0$.

It is convenient to assume that L_v is differentiable in our analysis, even though δ_v, γ_v, and h_v may be discontinuous. However, as L_v is Lipschitz continuous, it can be approximated arbitrarily well by a differentiable function for which the derivative satisfies the desired bounds, so this assumption is without loss of generality.

3.4 Faults

We assume that the network G contains a fixed subset $F \subsetneq V$ of ***faulty*** processes. The nodes $v \in F$ are fully Byzantine: we make no assumptions whatsoever about their behavior; in particular, they are not required to communicate by broadcast. We assume that the number of faulty nodes *within each cluster* is bounded by a parameter f, i.e., $\max_C |F \cap C| \le f$, and we require that $k \ge 3f + 1$.

[5] Our notation differs from some previous work in that our clock drift is always positive—hardware clocks *always* run fast. This is done without loss of generality, as one can rescale time to model drifts that are both positive and negative. However, assuming one-sided drifts reduces notational clutter in our analysis.

Recall that Inequality (1) relates this deterministic requirement to a setting in which nodes fail uniformly and independently at random with probability p; in this case, one can tolerate a value of p up to roughly $n^{-1/f}$. In contrast, an adversarial placement of faults would necessitate degrees larger than the total number of faults.

3.5 Initialization

Our analysis requires that at time 0 none of the skew bounds of our algorithm are violated. To achieve this, the following two options for initializing the system come to mind:

- We perform an initial flooding to trigger node initialization, where we (formally) extend the hardware and logical clock functions of nodes to include the interval between the starting time of the flooding and their initialization in a manner consistent with the model. To maintain tight bounds on the initial skew in a fault-tolerant way, this can e.g. be done as described in the introduction (without fixing communication to a tree). Note that, depending on the precise model assumptions, the source cluster(s) of such a flooding operation may need to perform an "internal" approximate agreement step to synchronize their outgoing messages to other clusters, or even run consensus to determine when to initiate the procedure.
- If the above method is not applicable, after initialization we can first wait until the clusters have stabilized to small internal skews by running the Lynch-Welch algorithm based on (an arbitrarily loose, but known) bound on their internal skew at initialization (cf. [9]). We then treat all inter-cluster edges as newly inserted in the dynamic graph model considered in [11], which ensures stabilization to optimal skews within $O(\mathcal{S}/\mu)$ time assuming that the global skew is bounded by $\mathcal{S}$. To ensure fault-tolerance, adjacent clusters run consensus on when to add an edge $e \in \mathcal{E}$, i.e., we avoid inconsistent opinions among correct nodes whether an edge is currently "considered" by the algorithm or not.

Neither of the above solutions offers significant novelty, but the involved technicalities would significantly complicate the description and analysis of our algorithm. Accordingly, in the interest of simplicity and readability, we assume that all nodes wake up almost simultaneously, and initialize their logical clocks at time 0.

4 CLUSTER ALGORITHM

In this section, we only consider nodes and edges within a fixed cluster $C \in \mathcal{C}$. Within C, the logical clocks maintain synchronization by using a variant of the Lynch-Welch algorithm [19] similar to the one described by Khanchandani and Lenzen [9]. Following the description in [9], the cluster algorithm proceeds in rounds. During each round, each (correct) node pulses once at a prespecified logical time. Once a node records the relative times of its neighbors' pulses, it computes an adjustment to its logical clock using an "approximate agreement" step as in the Lynch-Welch algorithm (cf. [7]). The clock adjustment is then made by setting $\delta_v(t)$ in Equation (2) to an appropriate (non-negative) value for the remainder of the round. The length of each round is inductively defined, where the initial round's length depends on (an upper bound on) the initial clock skew in the cluster.

4.1 Algorithm description

Each round $r \in \mathbb{N}$ consists of three phases, of logical durations $\tau_1(r)$, $\tau_2(r)$, and $\tau_3(r)$, respectively; the total round length is $T(r) = \tau_1(r) + \tau_2(r) + \tau_3(r)$. The phases play the following roles.

Phase 1. This phase is sufficiently long for all non-faulty nodes within a cluster to have transitioned to round r by the end of phase 1. Each node sends a pulse at the end of phase 1.

Phase 2. During this phase, each node waits to receive pulses from its neighbors. Phase 2 is sufficiently long that by the end of this phase, each node will have received pulses from all of its (correct) neighbors within its cluster. At the end of the phase, each node v computes an adjustment $\Delta_v(r)$ to its own logical clock.

Phase 3. During this final phase, v implements the clock adjustment computed at the end of phase 2 by setting δ_v to an appropriate value for the duration of the phase.

During phases 1 and 2, each node sets $\delta_v = 1$. We give pseudo-code for ClusterSync in Algorithm 1. The algorithm uses the following notation. For each round r and nodes $v, w \in C$:

- $t_v(r)$ is the Newtonian time at which v begins round r;
- $p_v(r)$ is the Newtonian time at which v sends its pulse in round r;
- $t_{wv}(r)$ is the Newtonian time at which v receives the pulse w sent in (w's) round r.

In cases where v or w is faulty, the values above may not be well-defined. In such cases, we can assign their values arbitrarily. While the notation above is convenient for describing the algorithm, we emphasize that nodes cannot access the values $t_v(r)$, etc., directly. Instead, v stores, for example, $L_v(t_{wv}(r))$, the logical time at which it receives w's round r pulse.

Algorithm 1: ClusterSync($v, \tau_1, \tau_2, \tau_3$)

$L_v \leftarrow 0$;
foreach *round* $r \in \mathbb{N}$ **do**
  $\delta_v \leftarrow 1$;
  start listening for messages;
  at-time $L_v(t_v(r)) + \tau_1(r)$ **do**
    broadcast clock pulse;
  at-time $L_v(t_v(r)) + \tau_1(r) + \tau_2(r)$ **do**
    $S_v \leftarrow \emptyset$; // multiset, ordered ascendingly
    foreach *node* $w \in C_v$ **do**
      $\tau_{wv} \leftarrow L_v(t_{wv}(r)) - L_v(t_{vv}(r))$;
      $S_v \leftarrow S_v \cup \{\tau_{wv}\}$;
    $\Delta_v(r) \leftarrow \frac{S_v^{f+1} + S_v^{n-f}}{2}$; // S_v^i is the i-th element of S_v
    $\delta_v \leftarrow 1 - \left(1 + \frac{1}{\varphi}\right) \frac{\Delta_v(r)}{\tau_3(r) + \Delta_v(r)}$;
  at-time $L_v(t_v(r)) + \tau_1(r) + \tau_2(r) + \tau_3(r)$ **do**
    end round r;

We define the ***nominal rate*** of node v as

$$h_v^{\mathrm{nom}}(t) = (1 + \varphi)(1 + \mu \cdot \gamma_v(t)) h_v(t). \quad (3)$$

The ***nominal length*** or ***nominal duration*** of an interval $[t, t']$ is defined to be $\int_t^{t'} h_v^{\text{nom}}(\tau)\, d\tau$.

The following lemma shows that ClusterSync simulates an execution of the Lynch-Welch algorithm (cf. [9]), where the nominal clock in ClusterSync plays the role of the hardware clock in the Lynch-Welch algorithm.

Lemma 4.1. *Fix a non-faulty node $v \in C \setminus F$ and a round $r \in \mathbb{N}$. Then the nominal length of round r for v is $T(r) + \Delta_v(r)$, where $T(r) = \tau_1(r) + \tau_2(r) + \tau_3(r)$ is the logical length of round r. That is, $\int_{t_v(r)}^{t_v(r+1)} h_v^{\text{nom}}(\tau)\, d\tau = T(r) + \Delta_v(r)$.*

Lemma 4.1 shows that Algorithm 1 achieves the same effect at the end of the round as the variant of the Lynch-Welch algorithm given in [9]. In [9], L_v is discontinuously adjusted by $-\Delta_v(r)$ at the end of Phase 2, and increases at the nominal rate at all other times. The advantage of our formulation of Algorithm 1 is that $L_v(t)$ is continuous and increases at a rate that can be kept close to the nominal rate by choosing $\tau_3(r)$ sufficiently large. This is essential for the GCS inter-cluster algorithm and its analysis, as the analysis of GCS assumes clock rates are bounded from above and below.

4.2 Analysis

In the full version of the paper [2], we employ the analysis from [9] with the adjustments necessary for our variant of the algorithm. We define the following parameters:

$$\begin{aligned} \vartheta_g &= (1+\rho)(1+\mu) \\ \xi_g &= (\vartheta_g - 1)(1+\varphi) \\ \alpha_g &= \frac{1}{1-\xi_g}\left(\frac{2\vartheta_g^2 + 5\vartheta_g - 5}{2(\vartheta_g+1)} + \xi_g \cdot (1 + 1/\varphi)\right) \\ \beta_g &= \frac{1}{1-\xi_g}(3\vartheta_g - 1 + \xi_g/\varphi)\cdot U + \frac{\xi_g}{1-\xi_g} d \\ e_g^\infty &= \frac{\beta_g}{1-\alpha_g}. \end{aligned} \tag{4}$$

Suppose $\alpha_g < 1$ (which is possible for sufficiently small ρ and suitable choices of μ and φ). Then the analysis in the full version implies the following bound on skew within clusters, for suitable choices of τ_1, τ_2, and τ_3. To simplify the presentation, we assume that clusters are initialized to have small skew. Our analysis is sufficient to deal with the general case, but assuming a nice initialization condition allows us to eliminate the dependence of the τ_i on the round r.

In what follows, we define $\mathbf{p}(r)$ to be the multiset of (Newtonian) times at which the non-faulty nodes in a cluster make their round r pulses. That is,

$$\mathbf{p}(r) = \{p_v(r) \mid v \in C \setminus F\}.$$

We define the ***pulse width*** of round r, denoted $\|\mathbf{p}(r)\|$, to be the difference between maximum and minimum times in $\mathbf{p}(r)$:

$$\|\mathbf{p}(r)\| = \max \mathbf{p}(r) - \min \mathbf{p}(r).$$

Since every node produces its round r pulse at the same logical time — namely $L_v(p_v(r)) = T(0) + T(1) + \cdots + T(r-1) + \tau_1(r)$ — bounds on the pulse width $\|\mathbf{p}(r)\|$ together with bounds on $T(r)$ and logical clock rates imply corresponding bounds on the cluster skew in round r. Our analysis in the full version yields the following bound on cluster skew.

Proposition 4.2. *Suppose logical clocks are initialized so as to ensure $\|\mathbf{p}(0)\| \le e_g^\infty$, and parameters are chosen such that $\alpha_g < 1$ in Equation (4). Then for all $r \in \mathbb{N}$ take*

$$\begin{aligned} \tau_1(r) &= \tau_1 = \vartheta_g \cdot e_g^\infty \\ \tau_2(r) &= \tau_2 = \vartheta_g \cdot (e_g^\infty + d) \\ \tau_3(r) &= \tau_3 = \vartheta_g \cdot \frac{1}{\varphi} \cdot (e_g^\infty + U). \end{aligned} \tag{5}$$

Suppose $\rho > 0$ is sufficiently small. Then for suitable choices of μ and φ, for all $t \in \mathbb{R}^+$ and non-faulty nodes $v, w \in C \setminus F$, we have

$$|L_v(t) - L_w(t)| \le 6e_g^\infty.$$

In accordance with the conclusion of Proposition 4.2, we define

$$\mathcal{L} = 6e_g^\infty. \tag{6}$$

By the proposition, $\mathcal{L}$ is an upper bound on the skew between any pair of nodes within the same cluster throughout an execution. We note that $\mathcal{L} = O(\rho \cdot d + U)$, which asymptotically matches the best possible bound for fault tolerant clock synchronization in a fully connected network.

4.3 Cluster clocks and estimates

Here we define the notion of a "cluster clock" which is a function of the logical clocks of correct nodes in the cluster. In Section 5 we describe an algorithm such that the cluster clocks simulate an execution of the GCS algorithm from [11, 15]. Our main result then follows from the analysis of the GCS algorithm, and Corollary 4.5 below, which shows that logical clocks within each cluster approximate the cluster clock.

Definition 4.3. *Fix a cluster C. For each time t define $L_C^+(t)$ and $L_C^-(t)$ to be the maximum and minimum values (respectively) of logical clock values of non-faulty clocks in C at time t. That is, $L_C^+(t) = \max\{L_v(t) \mid v \in C \setminus F\}$ and $L_C^-(t) = \min\{L_v(t) \mid v \in C \setminus F\}$. We define C's **cluster clock** L_C by the formula $L_C(t) = (L_C^+(t) + L_C^-(t))/2$.*

At several points, we will appeal to the following result about cluster clocks:

Observation 4.4. *Suppose that over some interval $[t', t]$ the logical clock of each $v \in C \setminus F$ increases at a rate at most ϑ. Then we have $L_C(t) - L_C(t') \le \vartheta \cdot (t - t')$. Indeed, if each clock individually satisfies some upper (lower) bound on its rate, then in particular the rates of $L_C^+(t)$ and $L_C^-(t)$ satisfy the same bound, hence so does $L_C(t)$. Symmetrically, if all logical clock rates are at least ϑ, then we have $L_C(t) - L_C(t') \ge \vartheta \cdot (t - t')$.*

Suppose C is a cluster and w a node adjacent to C (i.e., $w \in B$ where $(B, C) \in \mathcal{E}$). Then w computes an estimate $\widetilde{L}_C^w(t)$ of $L_C(t)$ as follows. The node w listens to the pulses of nodes in C and simulates the ClusterSync algorithm, without sending pulses itself. Then w takes $\widetilde{L}_C^w(t)$ to be the logical clock value computed in its simulation of ClusterSync. Applying the analysis of ClusterSync (unchanged!) to w's estimate $\widetilde{L}_C^w(t)$, we obtain the following guarantee.

Corollary 4.5. *Let C be a cluster and w a node adjacent to C. Suppose $\mathcal{L}$ is as in (6). Then for all $v \in C \setminus F$ and times t we have $|\widetilde{L}_C^w(t) - L_v(t)| \le \mathcal{L}$. Thus for all t we have $|\widetilde{L}_C^w(t) - L_C(t)| \le \mathcal{L}/2$.*

4.4 Bounds for unanimous clusters

In this section we state bounds on the amortized rates of cluster clocks when all correct nodes are running in fast or slow modes. We say that a cluster C is ***unanimous at time*** t if either (1) for all $v \in C \setminus F$, $\gamma_v(t) = 1$ or (2) for all $v \in C \setminus F$, $\gamma_v(t) = 0$. In the former case, we call C ***(unanimously) fast***, and in the latter case C is ***(unanimously) slow***. For a round $r \in \mathbb{N}$, we say that C is (unanimously) fast (resp. slow) in round r if every $v \in C \setminus F$ is in fast mode (resp. slow mode) for all $t \in [t_v(r), t_v(r+1)]$.

In order to implement the GCS algorithm for cluster clocks, we must show that unanimously fast clusters can "catch up" to unanimously slow clusters. This is true for individual nominal clocks: if v is in fast mode and w is in slow mode, then $h_v^{\text{nom}}(t)/h_w^{\text{nom}}(t) \geq (1+\mu)/(1+\rho) = 1 + \Omega(\mu - \rho)$. So as long as $\mu \gg \rho$, a fast node can always catch up to a slow node.

The story for clusters is, unfortunately, more complicated. Suppose C is (unanimously) fast for an entire round r. Even though the individual *nominal* clocks in $C \setminus F$ all run at rates at least $(1+\varphi)(1+\mu)$, the amortized rate of L_C may be significantly slower because of the adjustment made to the logical clocks in the Lynch-Welch step. Specifically, this adjustment could be as large as $e_g^\infty \sim \mu T(r)$. Thus, the amortized rate of L_C over round r could be as small as $(1+\varphi)(1+\mu - e_g^\infty/T(r)) \sim (1+\varphi)$. Thus, the logical clock of a cluster in fast mode may increase *slower* than a cluster in slow mode!

To address this potential problem, observe that if a cluster is unanimous, then the nominal clocks for $v \in V$ satisfy $\zeta \leq h_v^{\text{nom}} \leq \zeta \cdot \vartheta_u$, where $\vartheta_u = 1 + \rho$ and $\zeta = 1 + \varphi$ or $(1+\varphi)(1+\mu)$ depending on whether the cluster is unanimously slow or fast. Thus, the nominal clock drift between nodes is at most ρ, rather than $(1+\rho)(1+\mu) - 1$. This smaller hardware clock drift allows the cluster synchronization algorithm to converge to a smaller skew. In particular, ClusterSync achieves skews of size εe_g^∞ for an arbitrarily small $\varepsilon > 0$ for suitable choices of parameters, assuming that the cluster is unanimous for sufficiently many rounds. Thus, we ensure that the amortized rate of L_C when C is unanimously fast is at least $(1+\varphi)(1+7\mu/8)$. Similarly, we show that any cluster in slow mode increases at an amortized rate between $(1+\varphi)(1-\mu/8)$ and $(1+\varphi)(1+\mu/8)$, assuming it has been in slow mode for sufficiently long.

We denote the steady state error for a unanimous execution (in which all nodes are unanimously fast or slow in all rounds) to be e_u^∞. We derive explicit bounds on e_u^∞ in the full version [2]. The following lemma shows that by choosing appropriate values of μ and φ, we can ensure that e_u^∞ is significantly smaller than e_g^∞. To make the dependence on ρ in all expressions explicit, we define parameters c_1 and c_2 and take

$$\varphi = \rho/c_1 \quad \text{and} \quad \mu = c_2 \cdot \rho.$$

Lemma 4.6. *Let $\varphi = \rho/c_1$ and $\mu = c_2 \cdot \rho$, and define τ_1, τ_2, and τ_3 by (5). Suppose logical clocks are initialized so as to ensure $\|\mathbf{p}(0)\| \leq e_g^\infty$, and parameters are chosen such that $\alpha_g < 1$ in Equation (4). Then there exist constants c_1, c_2, and k with $k \geq 1$ such that for all sufficiently small $\rho > 0$ the following hold:*

(1) *If C is unanimously fast for rounds $r-k, r-k+1, \ldots, r$ then for all $v \in C \setminus F$ we have*

$$(1+\varphi)\left(1+\frac{7}{8}\mu\right) \leq \frac{L_v(t_v(r+1)) - L_v(t_v(r))}{t_v(r+1) - t_v(r)}.$$

(2) *If C is unanimously slow for rounds $r-k, r-k+1, \ldots, r$, then for all $v \in C \setminus F$ we have*

$$(1+\varphi)\left(1-\frac{1}{8}\mu\right) \leq \frac{L_v(t_v(r+1)) - L_v(t_v(r))}{t_v(r+1) - t_v(r)} \leq (1+\varphi)\left(1+\frac{1}{8}\mu\right).$$

If additionally C is unanimously fast (resp. slow) in round $r+1$, then the cluster clock $L_C(t)$ satisfies conclusion 1 (resp. 2) above.

5 INTER-CLUSTER ALGORITHM

In this section we describe an algorithm that synchronizes clocks between adjacent clusters. The algorithm simulates an execution of the gradient clock synchronization (GCS) algorithm [11, 15], where each cluster plays the role of a single node in the GCS algorithm. Specifically, our algorithm ensures that the cluster clocks L_C (Definition 4.3) faithfully simulate an execution of the GCS algorithm, in a sense made precise below. While L_C is only defined implicitly from the logical clocks of individual nodes within a cluster, Proposition 4.2 and Corollary 4.5 ensure that every node maintains good estimates of its own and neighboring cluster clocks. In our algorithm, each node individually simulates the GCS algorithm. We then apply Lemma 4.6 to argue that when the behavior of nodes within a cluster is unanimous, the corresponding cluster clocks behave as required by the GCS algorithm.

5.1 Fast and slow conditions and triggers

Let κ be a parameter (to be chosen later), and let C be a cluster. We denote the set of neighboring clusters of C by N_C. The following definitions give conditions under which the cluster C should be in fast mode or slow mode in order to implement the GCS algorithm.

Definition 5.1. *We say that C satisfies the **fast condition** (FC) at time t if there exists $s \in \mathbb{N}$ such that the following conditions hold:*

- *FC-1 There exists $A \in N_C$ such that $L_A(t) - L_C(t) \geq 2s\kappa$.*
- *FC-2 For all $B \in N_C$, $L_C(t) - L_B(t) \leq 2s\kappa$.*

Definition 5.2. *We say that C satisfies the **slow condition** (SC) at time t if there exists $s \in \mathbb{N}$ such that the following two conditions hold:*

- *SC-1 There exists $A \in N_C$ such that $L_C(t) - L_A(t) \geq (2s-1)\kappa$.*
- *SC-2 For all $B \in N_C$, $L_B(t) - L_C(t) \leq (2s-1)\kappa$.*

In order to implement the GCS algorithm, we must guarantee that if a cluster satisfies the fast (resp. slow) condition, then the cluster is unanimously fast (resp. slow). Further, in order to maintain the guarantees on *amortized* rates of cluster clocks of Lemma 4.6, our implementation of the fast and slow conditions should guarantee that clusters remain unanimously fast or slow for several rounds before any round in which the respective (fast or slow) condition is satisfied. To this end, for each $v \in C$ and $B \in N_C$, v maintains an estimate $\tilde{L}_B^v$ of L_B (see Corollary 4.5 and preceding discussion). In order to implement the fast and slow conditions, we define the following triggers. The parameter δ will be chosen later.

Definition 5.3. *We say that $v \in C$ satisfies the **fast trigger** (FT) at time t if there exists $s \in \mathbb{N}$ such that the following two conditions hold:*

- *FT-1 There exists $A \in N_C$ such that $\tilde{L}_A^v(t) - L_v(t) \geq 2s\kappa - \delta$.*
- *FT-2 For all $B \in N_C$, $L_v(t) - \tilde{L}_B^v(t) \leq 2s\kappa + \delta$.*

Definition 5.4. *We say that $v \in C$ satisfies the* **slow trigger** *(ST) at time t if there exists $s \in \mathbb{N}$ the following two conditions hold:*

- *ST-1 There exists $A \in N_C$ such that $L_v(t) - \widetilde{L}_A^v(t) \geq (2s-1)\kappa - \delta$.*
- *ST-2 For all $B \in N_C$, $\widetilde{L}_B^v(t) - L_v(t) \leq (2s-1)\kappa + \delta$.*

The following lemma shows that for all $\delta < 2\kappa$ the triggers above cannot both be simultaneously satisfied. In particular, taking $\delta = 0$, the following lemma implies that the fast and slow *conditions* are also mutually exclusive.

Lemma 5.5 ([12]). *The conditions FT and ST are mutually exclusive. That is, if C satisfies FT, then C does not satisfy ST, and vice versa.*

Algorithm 2: InterclusterSync(v, κ, δ, T)

```
foreach round r ∈ ℕ do
    at-time L_v(t_v(r)) do
        if v satisfies FT then
            γ_v ← 1;
        else if v satisfies ST then
            γ_v ← 0;
```

With the fast and slow triggers defined, we describe the intercluster algorithm, InterclusterSync (Algorithm 2). InterclusterSync differs from other descriptions of the GCS algorithm [11, 12, 15] in that it can only switch from fast to slow mode, or vice versa, at predetermined discrete times. For the analysis of the GCS algorithm, we require that the fast (resp. slow) trigger implements the fast (resp. slow) condition in the sense that whenever the condition is satisfied, the corresponding trigger is also satisfied. For *clusters* we require more: Even if a cluster is unanimously fast or slow, we cannot immediately infer sufficiently tight bounds on the rate of L_C. Instead, we must apply Lemma 4.6. In particular, we must wait until $k = O(1)$ unanimous rounds have elapsed until we can guarantee sufficiently tight bounds on the rate of L_C to apply the GCS algorithm analysis as a black box. The following definition describes sufficient conditions under which InterclusterSync guarantees that a node has been in fast (resp. slow) mode "sufficiently long" whenever the fast (resp. slow) condition is satisfied.

Definition 5.6. *Let $T : \mathbb{N} \to \mathbb{R}$ be a sequence of round lengths, C a cluster, and $v \in C$. For every $r \in \mathbb{N}$, let $t_v(r)$ denote the time at which v begins round r in an execution of the* ClusterSync *algorithm. Let k be a constant such that the conclusion of Lemma 4.6 is satisfied. For any time t, let $r_t = \max\{r \mid t_v(r) \leq t\}$. We say that an execution of* InterclusterSync *is* ***faithful for*** *v if the following conditions hold:*

- *For all $t \in \mathbb{R}^+$ such that C satisfies FC at time t, v satisfies FT at all $t' \in [t_v(r_t - k - 1), t_v(r_t)]$.*
- *For all $t \in \mathbb{R}^+$ such that C satisfies SC at time t, v satisfies ST at all $t' \in [t_v(r_t - k - 1), t_v(r_t)]$.*

We say that the execution is ***faithful for*** *C if it is faithful for every node $v \in C \setminus F$.*

Applying Definition 5.6 we obtain the following consequence of Lemma 4.6:

Corollary 5.7. *Suppose X is a faithful execution for C. Then for every $t \in \mathbb{R}$ the following holds. If C satisfies FC at time t then*

$$(1+\varphi)\left(1+\frac{7}{8}\mu\right) \leq \frac{L_v(t_v(r_t+1)) - L_v(t_v(r_t))}{t_v(r_t+1) - t_v(r_t)}.$$

If C satisfies SC at time t then

$$(1+\varphi)\left(1-\frac{1}{8}\mu\right) \leq \frac{L_v(t_v(r_t+1) - L_v(t_v(r_t))}{t_v(r_t+1) - t_v(r_t)} \leq (1+\varphi)\left(1+\frac{1}{8}\mu\right)$$

We will show that Corollary 5.7 is strong enough that we can apply the analysis of the GCS algorithm as a black box to bound skew between adjacent clusters. In the remainder of this section, we will give sufficient conditions—in particular, choices of the parameters κ and δ—under which every execution is guaranteed to be faithful. We fix k to be a constant such that the conclusion of Lemma 4.6 is satisfied.

Lemma 5.8. *Suppose the hypotheses of Proposition 4.2 are satisfied, and that k is sufficiently large that the conclusion of Lemma 4.6 holds. Let $\delta = (k+5)\mathcal{L}$ and $\kappa = 3\delta$. Then for every cluster $C \in \mathcal{C}$, every execution X is faithful for C.*

5.2 InterclusterSync simulates GCS

We now show that a faithful execution X of InterclusterSync on the (physical) network G *simulates* an execution $\overline{X}$ of the GCS algorithm on the network $\mathcal{G}$ in a sense made precise below. As a result, we can apply the analysis of the GCS algorithm to $\overline{X}$ to derive bounds on the local skew between adjacent cluster clocks in X. Before defining simulation formally, we recall the axioms required by the GCS algorithm.

Definition 5.9. *Suppose $\mathcal{G} = (\mathcal{C}, \mathcal{E})$ is a network, and each $C \in \mathcal{C}$ computes a logical clock $L_C : \mathbb{R} \to \mathbb{R}$. We say that the logical clocks satisfy the* **GCS axioms** *if there exist constants $\rho, \mu > 0$ such that the following hold for all times $t \in \mathbb{R}$ and nodes $C \in \mathcal{C}$:*

(A1) $1 \leq \frac{d}{dt}L_v(t) \leq (1+\rho)(1+\mu)$.
(A2) *If C satisfies SC at time t, then* $\frac{d}{dt}L_v(t) \leq 1+\rho$.
(A3) *If C satisfies FC at time t then* $1+\mu \leq \frac{d}{dt}L_v(t)$
(A4) $\mu/\rho > 1$.

Any execution of any algorithm satisfying these axioms is said to ***implement GCS****.*

Theorem 5.10 ([11, 12]). *Suppose an algorithm A implements GCS and the global skew is bounded by $\mathcal{S}$. Then for all $(B, C) \in \mathcal{E}$ and sufficiently large t we have $|L_B(t) - L_C(t)| = O(\kappa \log_{\mu/\rho} \mathcal{S})$.*

In general, an execution of our algorithm does not satisfy the GCS axioms for the values of ρ and μ as specified in the previous sections. However, for suitable choices of these parameters, we can find different parameters $\overline{\rho}, \overline{\mu}$ for which our logical clocks do satisfy the GCS axioms. In the appendix, we prove the following.

Proposition 5.11. *Suppose X is a faithful execution of* InterclusterSync *on G. Then the cluster clocks $\{L_C \mid C \in \mathcal{C}\}$ satisfy the GCS axioms for $\overline{\rho} = (1+\varphi)(1+(1/4)\mu) - 1$ and $\overline{\mu} = (1+\varphi)(1+(7/8)\mu) - 1$.*

5.3 Derivation of main result

So far, we have neglected the global skew $\mathcal{S}$. We can bound $\mathcal{S} = O(D)$, where D is the network diameter as follows. Each node v maintains an (under)-estimate M_v of the maximum logical clock value of any node in the network. If L_v is not too far behind M_v, and v does not satisfy FT-1 for any s, then v defaults to slow mode, even if ST is not satisfied. This behavior ensures that if $L_v(t)$ is the maximal logical clock in the network, then v runs in slow mode. On the other hand, if L_v is significantly behind M_v ($M_v(t)-L_v(t) \geq c \cdot D$ for some suitable constant c) and v does not satisfy ST-1 for any s, then v defaults to fast mode. This behavior ensures that if the global skew is large, the slowest node runs in fast mode. Together, the two additional triggers described above ensure that the global skew satisfies $\mathcal{S} = O(D)$. We provide details in the full version [2].

We now have all the pieces in place to prove our main result, Theorem 1.1. We assume the parameters ρ, d, and U are given with ρ sufficiently small, and choose suitable values of μ and φ such that the conclusions of all required lemmas hold.

Proof of Theorem 1.1. Let $v, w \in V \setminus F$ with $\{v, w\} \in E$. We first consider the case where $v, w \in C$ for some cluster C. Then by Lemma 4.2, we have $|L_v(t) - L_w(t)| \leq \mathcal{L}$ for all t, where $\mathcal{L} = 6\beta_g/(1-\alpha_g) = O(\rho \cdot d + U)$.

Now consider the case where $v \in B$ and $w \in C$ with $(B, C) \in \mathcal{E}$. By Proposition 5.11, InterclusterSync implements the GCS algorithm on $\mathcal{G}$ for cluster clocks L_C, with $\overline{\rho} = (1+\varphi)(1+(1/4)\mu) - 1$ and $\overline{\mu} = (1+\varphi)(1+(7/8)\mu) - 1$. Since $\varphi = \rho/c_1$ and $\mu = c_2 \cdot \rho$ for some absolute constants c_1 and c_2, there exists an absolute constant $c > 0$ such that

$$\frac{\overline{\mu}}{\overline{\rho}} = 1 + c + O(\rho).$$

Thus $\overline{\mu}/\overline{\rho} \geq 1 + c/2$ for sufficiently small ρ. By Theorem 5.10, we therefore have

$$|L_B(t) - L_C(t)| = O(\kappa \log_{\overline{\mu}/\overline{\rho}} \mathcal{S}) = O(\mathcal{L} \log D).$$

We then bound

$$\begin{aligned}|L_v(t) - L_w(t)| &\leq |L_v(t) - L_B(t)| + |L_B(t) - L_C(t)| \\ &\quad + |L_C(t) - L_w(t)| \\ &\leq \frac{1}{2}\mathcal{L} + O(\mathcal{L}\log D) + \frac{1}{2}\mathcal{L} \\ &= O(\mathcal{L}\log D),\end{aligned}$$

which gives the desired conclusion. □

REFERENCES

[1] Saâd Biaz and Jennifer Lundelius Welch. 2001. Closed Form Bounds for Clock Synchronization Under Simple Uncertainty Assumptions. *Inform. Process. Lett.* 80, 3 (2001), 151–157.

[2] Johannes Bund, Christoph Lenzen, and Will Rosenbaum. 2019. Fault Tolerant Gradient Clock Synchronization. arXiv:1902.08042

[3] Ariel Daliot, Danny Dolev, and Hanna Parnas. 2003. Self-stabilizing Pulse Synchronization Inspired by Biological Pacemaker Networks. In *Proc. 6th International Symposium on Self-Stabilizing Systems (SSS 2003)*. 32–48.

[4] Danny Dolev, Joe Halpern, and H. Raymond Strong. 1984. On the Possibility and Impossibility of Achieving Clock Synchronization. In *Proc. 16th Symposium on Theory of Computing (STOC)*. 504–511.

[5] Danny Dolev, Keijo Heljanko, Matti Järvisalo, Janne H. Korhonen, Christoph Lenzen, Joel Rybicki, Jukka Suomela, and Siert Wieringa. 2016. Synchronous Counting and Computational Algorithm Design. *J. Comput. Syst. Sci.* 82, 2 (2016), 310–332.

[6] Danny Dolev and Ezra N. Hoch. 2007. Byzantine Self-stabilizing Pulse in a Bounded-delay Model. In *Proc. 9th International Symposium on Stabilization, Safety, and Security of Distributed Systems (SSS 2007)*. 234–252.

[7] Danny Dolev, Nancy A. Lynch, Shlomit S. Pinter, Eugene W. Stark, and William E. Weihl. 1986. Reaching Approximate Agreement in the Presence of Faults. *J. ACM* 33 (1986), 499–516. Issue 3.

[8] S. Dolev and J. L. Welch. 2004. Self-Stabilizing Clock Synchronization in the Presence of Byzantine Faults. *J. ACM* 51, 5 (2004), 780–799.

[9] Pankaj Khanchandani and Christoph Lenzen. 2018. Self-Stabilizing Byzantine Clock Synchronization with Optimal Precision. *Theory of Computing Systems* (2018).

[10] Fabian Kuhn, Christoph Lenzen, Thomas Locher, and Rotem Oshman. 2010. Optimal Gradient Clock Synchronization in Dynamic Networks. In *Proc. 29th ACM Symposium on Principles of Distributed Computing (PODC)*.

[11] Fabian Kuhn, Christoph Lenzen, Thomas Locher, and Rotem Oshman. 2018. Optimal Gradient Clock Synchronization in Dynamic Networks. *CoRR* abs/1005.2894 (2018).

[12] Fabian Kuhn and Rotem Oshman. 2009. Gradient Clock Synchronization Using Reference Broadcasts. In *Principles of Distributed Systems*, Tarek Abdelzaher, Michel Raynal, and Nicola Santoro (Eds.). Springer Berlin Heidelberg, Berlin, Heidelberg, 204–218.

[13] Leslie Lamport and P. M. Melliar-Smith. 1985. Synchronizing Clocks in the Presence of Faults. *J. ACM* 32, 1 (1985), 52–78.

[14] Christoph Lenzen. 2018. Fault-Tolerant Clock Synchronization. Lecture notes.

[15] Christoph Lenzen, Thomas Locher, and Roger Wattenhofer. 2010. Tight Bounds for Clock Synchronization. *J. ACM* 57, 2 (2010), 1–42.

[16] Christoph Lenzen and Joel Rybicki. 2017. Self-Stabilising Byzantine Clock Synchronisation is Almost as Easy as Consensus. In *Proc. 31st Symposium on Distributed Computing (DISC)*. 32:1–32:15.

[17] Thomas Locher and Roger Wattenhofer. 2006. Oblivious Gradient Clock Synchronization. In *20th Symposium on Distributed Computing (DISC)*.

[18] Jennifer Lundelius and Nancy Lynch. 1984. An Upper and Lower Bound for Clock Synchronization. *Information and Control* 62, 2–3 (1984), 190–204.

[19] Jennifer Lundelius Welch and Nancy A. Lynch. 1988. A New Fault-Tolerant Algorithm for Clock Synchronization. *Information and Computation* 77, 1 (1988), 1–36.

[20] Nancy Lynch and Rui Fan. 2004. Gradient Clock Synchronization. In *Proc. 23rd Symposium on Principles of Distributed Computing (PODC)*.

[21] Arnon Rotem-Gal-Oz. [n. d.]. http://www.rgoarchitects.com/Files/fallacies.pdf.

[22] T. K. Srikanth and Sam Toueg. 1987. Optimal Clock Synchronization. *J. ACM* 34, 3 (1987), 626–645.

Brief Announcement: Bootstrapping Public Blockchains Without A Trusted Setup

Abhinav Aggarwal
University of New Mexico
Albuquerque, NM 87131
abhiag@unm.edu

Mahnush Movahedi
Dfinity
Palo Alto, CA
mahenush@gmail.com

Jared Saia
University of New Mexico
Albuquerque, NM 87131
saia@cs.unm.edu

Mahdi Zamani
Visa Research
Palo Alto, CA
mzamani@visa.com

ABSTRACT

We propose a protocol that allows the participants of a permissionless decentralized system to agree on a set of identities in the presence of a computationally-bounded Byzantine adversary. Our protocol guarantees that the fraction of identities belonging to the adversary in the set of identities is at most equal to the total computational hash power of the adversary.

We significantly improve on the existing state-of-the-art in the following four ways. First, our algorithm runs in expected $O(1)$ rounds, in contrast to previous results which require $O\left(\frac{\log n}{\log\log n}\right)$ rounds, where n is the number of initial nodes in the system. Second, we require each node to solve just one computational puzzle, whereas previous algorithms require $O\left(\frac{\log n}{\log\log n}\right)$ puzzles per node. Third, our algorithm sends only $O(n)$ bits per node in expectation, whereas previous algorithms send $O\left(n\frac{\log^2 n}{\log\log n}\right)$ bits in expectation. Finally, in contrast to past results, our algorithm handles dynamic joining and leaving of nodes.

CCS CONCEPTS

•**Security and privacy → Distributed systems security;**

KEYWORDS

Proof-of-Work, Sybil Attack, View Reconciliation, Blockchains

ACM Reference format:
Abhinav Aggarwal, Mahnush Movahedi, Jared Saia, and Mahdi Zamani. 2019. Brief Announcement: Bootstrapping Public Blockchains Without A Trusted Setup. In *Proceedings of 2019 ACM Symposium on Principles of Distributed Computing, (PODC '19), July 29-August 2, 2019, Toronto, ON, Canada.* ACM, New York, NY, USA, 3 pages.
https:doi.org/10.1145/3293611.3331570

ACM ISBN 978-1-4503-6217-7/19/07.
https://doi.org/10.1145/3293611.3331570

1 INTRODUCTION

Blockchain protocols rely on an agreement mechanism to ensure that their participants collectively decide on the next block of transactions. Current protocols require some trusted initial setup to defend against *Sybil attacks* [6], where an adversary maliciously influences the collective decisions of the system by generating a large number of fake identities. One technique is to use a genesis block [16], which ensures that all nodes begin *proof-of-work* [11], or *PoW*, puzzles at the same time [13]. Another technique is to assume a public-key infrastructure (PKI) [15, 18], which provides authenticated communication.

In this paper, we consider an adversary controlling $f < 1/2$ fraction of the computational power in the network. We ask: *Can we efficiently enable agreement on a set of identities against this adversary, without any trusted setup?* In particular, can we ensure that the participants agree on a set of identities, where the fraction of adversarially controlled identities in this set is at most f?

Aspnes et al. [4] first formally addressed this problem using PoW puzzles, but with no genesis block. Subsequent work [3, 13, 14, 17] improved efficiency and robustness of this initial solution. The current state-of-the-art, by Hou et al. [14] solves this problem in $O\left(\frac{\log n}{\log\log n}\right)$ rounds, where in each round, every honest node needs to send $\Theta(n\log n)$ bits and solves one computational puzzle. We improve this result as follows.

Theorem 1.1 (Informal). *Our algorithm ensures that n participants agree on a set of identities such that the fraction of identities in this set controlled by an adversary is at most equal to its computational hash power. Moreover, (1) each node solves a computational puzzle only once; (2) the protocol runs in $O(1)$ rounds with high probability; (3) a total of only $O(n)$ bits per node, in expectation, are sent; and (4) a linear amount of dynamic joins and leaves from the system is allowed with only $O(n)$ additional messages per node.*

Our Model. We assume a synchronous network of n nodes $P_1, ..., P_n$, where n is initially unknown. All messages are exchanged using a diffuse primitive, which enables a message to be sent to all other nodes. Without loss of generality, we assume that all honest nodes have the same computational power. Additionally, we assume a Byzantine adversary who controls up to an $f < 1/2$ fraction of the total computational power. We assume that the adversarially controlled nodes may deviate from the protocol in any arbitrary

Node P_i (with set S_i and $n_i \leftarrow 2^{\lceil \log |S_i| \rceil}$) does the following:

(1) **(Committee Election)** Arrange all solutions $s_j = H(h_j|pk_j|C_j)$ into buckets of size $\frac{1}{n_i}$, so that s_j falls into the kth bucket $b_{i,k}$ iff $s_j \in \left(\frac{k-1}{n_i}, \frac{k}{n_i}\right]$. Let $B_{i,k}$ denote the set of solutions that fall into bucket $b_{i,k}$. Let $\ell_{i,k} = \arg\min_j\{s_j \in B_{i,k}\}$ be the public key of the node with the smallest solution in the kth bucket and $\text{CView}_i = \bigcup_{k=1}^{c\lceil \log n_i \rceil}\{\ell_{i,k}\}$.

(2) **(Byzantine agreement)** If $pk_i \in \text{CView}_i$, run the Byzantine agreement algorithm of Abraham et al. [1] using input S_i with other members in CView_i. Diffuse the output set to the entire network.

(3) **(Final Output)** If $pk_i \notin \text{CView}_i$, output the set obtained using a majority filtering from the sets of the nodes in CView_i.

Figure 1: Our View-Reconciliation Protocol

manner. We do not rely on any trusted setup or secure broadcast channel, but we assume the existence of a random oracle hash function [11, 14]. We finally assume up to an $\epsilon < 1/6$ fraction of the nodes can join or leave after the bootstrapping is complete.

Rounds. Our algorithm proceeds in *rounds*, in which a node can perform the following three steps: (1) receive messages from other nodes; (2) perform some local computation; and (3) send messages to other nodes. Following past work [14], we assume all local computation except solving puzzles is instantaneous.

1.1 Solution Overview

Our protocol consists of two phases. In the first phase, all nodes perform an initial diffusion of computational puzzles, similar to the protocol of Aspnes et al. [4]. In the second phase, we propose a novel solution to the view-reconciliation problem [14] in order to resolve inconsistencies among the views of the honest nodes.

Phase I (Sybil Defense). The first phase proceeds as follows: (1) Each honest node P_i locally generates a random public/private key pair (pk_i, sk_i) along with a random challenge string $c_i \in \{0,1\}^\kappa$, where κ is the security parameter. This challenge is then diffused to the network. (2) Let C_i denote the set of challenges that P_i receives from other nodes, and H be a random oracle hash function known to all the nodes. P_i attempts to solve a PoW puzzle by computing a nonce $h_i \in \{0,1\}^\kappa$ such that $H(h_i|pk_i|C_i) < d$, where d is the PoW difficulty parameter (determined similar to [14]). Once a valid solution is obtained, P_i diffuses the tuple (h_i, pk_i, C_i) to the network. (3) For every tuple (h_j, pk_j, C_j) received, P_i checks if the PoW was computed correctly with respect to h_j, pk_j, d, and that $c_i \in C_j$. If so, P_i includes pk_j in its local identity set S_i and sets $n_i = 2^{\lceil \log |S_i| \rceil}$ as its estimate of the number of unique identities.

The above algorithm ensures that the local identity sets of honest nodes will contain all honest identities and at most f fraction of the identities from the adversary. However, it is possible for these sets to be inconsistent in the identities they contain. Hence, in the second phase, we need to ensure that the honest nodes agree on a single, common set of participants in the system.

Phase II (View Reconciliation). We now describe our view reconciliation algorithm through which honest nodes can agree on exactly the same set of identities. The main steps of this phase are described in Figure 1.

(Step 1) Committee Election. Note that the PoW solutions obtained so far have sufficient randomness [5] to locally select a random committee without any communication among the nodes. Thus, we can perform a probabilistic committee election to achieve Byzantine agreement on the set of identities. We run agreement among only $O(\log n)$ identities to limit the number of bits exchanged during this phase.

Our committee election protocol proceeds as follows. Each node P_i splits its local set S_i into n_i *buckets*, where the identity with the smallest solution in each bucket is then chosen as the representative of that bucket. The set of the first $c\lceil \log n_i \rceil$ bucket representatives constitute P_i's local view CView_i of what it considers as the committee. Since the adversary can send messages to a strict subset of the nodes, it is possible that $n_i \neq n_j$ and $\text{CView}_i \neq \text{CView}_j$, for some honest node $P_{j \neq i}$.

Our algorithm ensures that with probability at least $1 - O\left(\frac{\log^3 n}{n}\right)$, the views of the committee members can differ only in the membership of the adversarial nodes and contain a sufficiently-large core of honest identities. This is sufficient to run Byzantine agreement among these nodes [9, 10].

Moreover, the solutions computed by the adversary must fall uniformly at random into the buckets of the honest nodes. This is because for an honest node to accept a solution s, the corresponding puzzle must have included the honest node's challenge string from Phase *I*. Thus, the adversary could not have precomputed a solution to the puzzle and hence, s is uniformly random in its range (by the random oracle assumption).

(Step 2) Byzantine agreement. The agreement on the set of honest identities in the local CViews at the end of Step 1 allows for the use of Byzantine agreement protocol by Abraham et al. [1] as a subroutine executed by the committee members to decide on the final set of identities. This protocol is able to handle the selective message sending by the adversary and allows the committee members to agree on the membership in the system.

Since the committee size is $O(\log n)$, in expectation, only $O(\log^3 n)$ bits per committee member are sent for the view-reconciliation. Additionally, since each honest node is equally likely to be in the committee, this bandwidth cost is load balanced in expectation.

(Step 3) Diffusing the Final Output. Once the committee members have reached an agreement on a final set of identities, they diffuse this solution to the network. Each node then takes the set received from a majority of nodes in the committee as their final output.

1.2 Handling Non-Simultaneous Joins and Linear Churn

In a permissionless setting, nodes may join or leave the system at various times. Moreover, the initial n nodes that run the protocol may join the system at different times. To handle this type of non-simultaneous start for the Phase I of our algorithm, we use a parameter `offset` (for the maximum number of rounds between any two honest joins) to synchronize the initial nodes, similar to the approach by [14].

Additionally, it is now possible that once the view reconciliation algorithm terminates, some new nodes join the system and some existing ones depart. We assume that an adversary schedules these joins and departures at the beginning of the protocol and that each honest node informs the whole system of its departure when it leaves the system. Other aspects of our model are similar to that of prior work [12].

We handle at most an $\epsilon < 1/6$ fraction of new joins/departures in each round (after the bootstrap) by making each node that joins the system solve an entrance puzzle generated by the current committee. Only identities with valid solutions are admitted by the committee and their IDs are diffused to the entire network. When the system size changes sufficiently (as detected by the committee), a system-wide puzzle is issued and based on the solutions, a new committee is elected in a manner similar to Step 1 of Figure 1. Thus, at most $O(n)$ messages are exchanged per node, until the new committee is elected and with high probability, the system always maintains an honest majority and a consistent set of identities at any time.

2 CONCLUSION AND FUTURE WORK

We have described a protocol that allows a set of nodes to agree on a set of identities for each other such that the number of Sybil identities is minimized. Compared to past work, our algorithm is efficient in terms of its simplicity, bandwidth and number of solutions to PoW puzzles required by the nodes. In expectation, we terminate in a constant number of rounds, require each honest node to solve only one computational puzzle and send only $O(n)$ bits per node.

Some interesting problems for future work are as follows. (1) Is there a lower bound on the number of bits required for view reconciliation for permissionless systems? (2) What happens if the adversary performs adaptive or sporadic corruption of nodes? We suspect that handling this case is non-trivial in that simply replacing the Byzantine agreement protocol with a version that is robust to sporadic participation will not suffice. Finally, (3) although it has been shown that PoW based schemes cannot be used for asynchronous networks [2], is it possible to establish a trusted setup in such systems?

ACKNOWLEDGMENTS

This work is supported by the National Science Foundation grants CNS 1816250, CCF 1320994 and CNS 1318880. We also thank Dr. Loi Luu from Kyber Network for his insightful comments and discussions during the early phases of this work.

REFERENCES

[1] I. Abraham, S. Devadas, K. Nayak, and L. Ren. *Efficient Synchronous Byzantine Agreement.* In ArXiv preprint arXiv:1704.02397 (2017).

[2] R. Pass and E. Shi. *Rethinking Large-Scale Consensus.* In IEEE 30th Computer Security Foundations Symposium (CSF). IEEE, 2017.

[3] M. Andrychowicz and S. Dziembowski. *PoW-Based Distributed Cryptography with No Trusted Setup,* In Annual Cryptology Conference (CRYPTO). Springer, Berlin, Heidelberg, 2015.

[4] J. Aspnes, C. Jackson, and A. Krishnamurthy. *Exposing Computationally-Challenged Byzantine Impostors.* Yale University Technical Report, 2005.

[5] J. Bonneau, J. Clark, and S. Goldfeder. *On Bitcoin as a Public Randomness Source.* IACR Cryptology ePrint Archive, 2015:1015, 2015.

[6] J. R. Douceur. *The Sybil Attack.* In Int'l Workshop on Peer-to-Peer Systems, 2002.

[7] N. Lynch. *Distributed Algorithms.* Elsevier, 1996.

[8] L. Lamport, R. Shostak and M. Pease. *The Byzantine generals problem.* ACM Transactions on Programming Languages and Systems (TOPLAS) 4.3 (1982): 382-401.

[9] U. Feige. *Noncryptographic selection protocols.* 40th Annual Symposium on Foundations of Computer Science (Cat. No. 99CB37039). IEEE, 1999.

[10] V. King and J. Saia. *Breaking the $O(n^2)$ bit barrier: scalable byzantine agreement with an adaptive adversary.* Journal of the ACM (JACM) 58.4 (2011): 18.

[11] C. Dwork and M. Naor. *Pricing via Processing or Combatting Junk Mail.* In Annual International Cryptology Conference (CRYPTO). Springer, Berlin, Heidelberg, 1992.

[12] D. Gupta and J. Saia and M. Young. *Peace Through Superior Puzzling: An Asymmetric Sybil Defense.* In 33rd IEEE International Parallel and Distributed Processing Symposium (IPDPS). 2019.

[13] J. A. Garay, A. Kiayias, N. Leonardos, and G. Panagiotakos. *Bootstrapping the Blockchain, with Applications to Agreement and Fast PKI Setup.* In IACR International Workshop on Public Key Cryptography. Springer, Cham, 2018.

[14] R. Hou, I. Jahja, L. Luu, P. Saxena, and H. Yu. *Randomized View Reconciliation in Permissionless Distributed Systems.* In IEEE INFOCOM 2018-IEEE Conference on Computer Communications. IEEE, 2018.

[15] K. Jae. *Tendermint: Agreement Without Mining.* May 2014. https://allquantor.at/blockchainbib/pdf/buchman2016tendermint.pdf

[16] S. Nakamoto. *Bitcoin: A Peer-to-Peer Electronic Cash System.* 2008.

[17] J. Katz, A. Miller, E. Shi. *Pseudonymous Broadcast and Secure Computation from Cryptographic Puzzles.* IACR Cryptology ePrint Archive, 2014:857, 2014.

[18] D. Dolev and H.R. Strong. *Authenticated algorithms for Byzantine agreement.* SIAM Journal on Computing 12.4 (1983): 656-666.

Hardness of Minimal Symmetry Breaking in Distributed Computing

Alkida Balliu
alkida.balliu@aalto.fi
Aalto University

Juho Hirvonen
juho.hirvonen@aalto.fi
Aalto University

Dennis Olivetti
dennis.olivetti@aalto.fi
Aalto University

Jukka Suomela
jukka.suomela@aalto.fi
Aalto University

ABSTRACT

A graph is *weakly 2-colored* if the nodes are labeled with colors black and white such that each black node is adjacent to at least one white node and vice versa. In this work we study the distributed computational complexity of weak 2-coloring in the standard LOCAL model of distributed computing, and how it is related to the distributed computational complexity of other graph problems.

First, we show that weak 2-coloring is a *minimal* distributed symmetry-breaking problem for regular even-degree trees and high-girth graphs: if there is any non-trivial *locally checkable labeling problem* that is solvable in $o(\log^* n)$ rounds with a distributed graph algorithm in the middle of a regular even-degree tree, then weak 2-coloring is also solvable in $o(\log^* n)$ rounds there.

Second, we prove a *tight lower bound* of $\Omega(\log^* n)$ for the distributed computational complexity of weak 2-coloring in regular trees; previously only a lower bound of $\Omega(\log \log^* n)$ was known. By minimality, the same lower bound holds for any non-trivial locally checkable problem inside regular even-degree trees.

CCS CONCEPTS

• **Theory of computation → Distributed computing models**; **Complexity classes**.

KEYWORDS

Distributed complexity theory, graph algorithms, locally checkable labelings, LOCAL model

ACM Reference Format:
Alkida Balliu, Juho Hirvonen, Dennis Olivetti, and Jukka Suomela. 2019. Hardness of Minimal Symmetry Breaking in Distributed Computing. In *2019 ACM Symposium on Principles of Distributed Computing (PODC '19), July 29-August 2, 2019, Toronto, ON, Canada.* ACM, New York, NY, USA, 10 pages. https://doi.org/10.1145/3293611.3331605

ACM ISBN 978-1-4503-6217-7/19/07...$15.00
https://doi.org/10.1145/3293611.3331605

1 INTRODUCTION

In this work, we show that distributed symmetry-breaking problems in regular trees are either solvable in $O(1)$ rounds or they require $\Omega(\log^* n)$ rounds, and this is tight. This is an exponential improvement over the previous bound of $\Omega(\log \log^* n)$ rounds.

Symmetry breaking in distributed graph algorithms. Local symmetry breaking is a fundamental primitive in computer networks. As a simple example, consider the task of 3-vertex coloring an n-cycle: the topology of the computer network is a cycle with n nodes (computers) and n edges (communication links), and each computer has to output a value from the set $\{1, 2, 3\}$ such that adjacent computers output different values.

If all nodes are identical and run the same deterministic algorithm, this is impossible: if all nodes start in the same state, they will send the same messages to their neighbors, they will receive the same messages from their neighbors, and switch to the same new state, ad infinitum – and in 3-coloring adjacent nodes have to reach distinct states. Hence we will need to assume that the nodes have e.g. *unique identifiers* from a poly(n)-sized set, or they have access to a source of *random bits*.

With unique identifiers we can solve any graph problem trivially in $T = O(n)$ communication rounds, not only in cycles but more generally in any connected graph: all nodes can gather full information on the entire graph, solve the problem locally by brute force, and output their own part of the solution. We are interested in *fast* distributed algorithms: each node should produce its own part of the output after some $T = o(n)$ communication rounds. It is good to note that here time (number of communication rounds) and distance (shortest-path distance in the input graph) are, in essence, equivalent: in T rounds all nodes can gather full information on their T-round neighborhood, and nothing beyond that.

Distributed symmetry breaking in cycles is nowadays completely understood [6, 9, 20]. For example, the task of 3-coloring is solvable in time $T = \Theta(\log^* n)$ and this is tight; this holds for deterministic algorithms that use unique identifiers, as well as for randomized algorithms that work with high probability. We can also give a much stronger statement: Consider *any* problem P in which the task is to label the cycle with values from some constant-size set X, subject to some local constraints. Then P falls in one of the following classes:

(1) *trivial:* it is solvable in $O(1)$ rounds,
(2) *local:* its computational complexity is $\Theta(\log^* n)$ rounds,

(3) *global:* we need $\Theta(n)$ rounds just to check if a feasible solution exists.

Examples of problems of type (2) include vertex coloring with $k \geq 3$ colors, edge coloring with $k \geq 3$ colors, maximal independent set, and maximal matching. Examples of problems of type (3) include vertex or edge coloring with 2 colors.

However, once we switch from cycles to regular higher-degree graphs, we have a much more diverse landscape of computational complexity. The main gap of our current knowledge is in the low end of the complexity spectrum: we do not know if there are any problem of the above form that would require $\omega(1)$ rounds but that would be solvable in $o(\log^* n)$ rounds e.g. in regular high-girth graphs or regular trees [9].

Prior work on distributed computational complexity. Formally, the model of computing that we study here is known as the LOCAL model of distributed computing [18, 22]: the same graph plays the dual role of being both the unknown input graph and the structure of the computer network, the nodes correspond to computers, the edges correspond to communication links, the nodes are labeled with unique identifiers from a poly(n)-sized set, computation proceeds in synchronous communication rounds, and the complexity measure that we care about is the number of rounds until all nodes have stopped and announced their local outputs. In particular, local computation is free and the message size is unbounded.

In the past three years, there has been a long sequence of papers [1, 2, 5, 8, 9, 11–15, 23] that have studied the computational complexity landscape of graph problems in the LOCAL model. The primary goal has been to understand so-called LCL problems, or *locally checkable labeling* problems. In brief, these are problems in which the task is to label nodes with values from a constant-sized set, subject to local constraints. Informally, this is a natural distributed analogue of the class NP: all LCL problems are such that, given a feasible solution, it is easy to *verify* in a distributed manner. Now given an LCL problem P, what can we say about its computational complexity in the LOCAL model?

Surprisingly, the answer is that we can say quite a lot, even though the family of LCL problems is very diverse. For example, if we focus on bounded-degree graphs, we can prove *gap results*: there is no LCL problem whose deterministic or randomized distributed complexity falls between $\omega(1)$ and $o(\log \log^* n)$ rounds, and there is no problem whose deterministic distributed complexity falls between $\omega(\log^* n)$ and $o(\log n)$ rounds.

Challenges below the log-star threshold. In the case of bounded-degree graphs, there are LCL problems with complexities such as $\Theta(\log \log^* n)$ and $\Theta(\sqrt{\log^* n})$ [2]. However, all known problems in this region are highly artificial, and the worst-case input graphs have a rather peculiar structure, with lots of short cycles.

No *natural* LCL problems in this region are known, and neither are there any known LCL problems that would have a computational complexity between $\omega(1)$ and $o(\log^* n)$ e.g. in bounded-degree *trees* or regular *high-girth graphs.* This is an open question identified by Chang and Pettie [9]: do any such LCL problems exist at all?

The main reason that this question has remained open is related to the limitations of the current proof techniques. The proof technique introduced by Naor and Stockmeyer [20] is based on the following idea: if there is an algorithm A that solves an LCL problem P such that each node only sees $o(\log^* n)$ other nodes in its radius-T neighborhood, then using the hypergraph version of Ramsey's theorem we can construct another algorithm A' that solves the same problem P in the same running time in an *order-invariant* manner: A' does not use the numerical values of the identifiers but only their relative order.

If we apply this idea to a cycle, we can set $T = o(\log^* n)$. Then each node in A makes its own decision based on the identifiers of $o(\log^* n)$ other nodes, and hence we can turn A into order-invariant A'. And now A' cannot solve any non-trivial LCL problem (consider the case in which the nodes are placed in an increasing order along the cycle; most of the nodes have then isomorphic radius-T neighborhoods w.r.t. such a total order).

However, if we try to apply this idea to e.g. 4-regular trees, we must have $T = o(\log \log^* n)$ in order to guarantee that radius-T neighborhoods contain only $o(\log^* n)$ nodes. The technique does not say anything about e.g. algorithms that would have a running time of $T = O(\sqrt{\log^* n})$. Some ad-hoc extensions of the proof technique exist for the case of d-dimensional grids [9], but nothing of that sort is known about trees.

Focus on homogeneous LCL*s.* LCLs are a broad family of problems. At one extreme, we have got symmetry-breaking problems such as 3-coloring of a cycle: the nodes have isomorphic local neighborhoods, yet they need to produce different outputs. At the other extreme, we have got problems in which nontrivial instances are exactly those in which symmetry has already been broken: for example, typical load balancing problems are trivial if the load is already uniformly distributed, and nontrivial only if there are differences in the load.

We focus in this work only on symmetry-breaking problems. In essence, we look at LCL problems that are nontrivial inside a regular even-degree tree (or regular even-degree high-girth graph), and trivial in all other cases. We formalize the notion of *homogeneous* LCLs in Section 3.2. In brief, the idea is that we can turn any given LCL problem P into a homogeneous LCL problem P' such that, to solve P', for each local neighborhood it is enough to either solve P or find an irregularity in the input graph (for example, a short cycle or a low-degree node). Problem P' is well-defined in any input graph, but the worst-case instances will be regular balanced trees.

It is easy to see that any homogeneous LCL is solvable in $O(\log n)$ rounds by brute force, and by prior work we know there are several examples of homogeneous LCLs with deterministic complexities $\Theta(\log n)$ [5, 8, 15, 21], $\Theta(\log^* n)$ [10, 16, 18], and $\Theta(1)$ [20]. There is also a gap between $o(\log n)$ and $\omega(\log^* n)$ [8], and another gap between $o(\log \log^* n)$ and $\omega(1)$ [9, 20]. However, nothing is currently known about the region between $o(\log^* n)$ and $\Omega(\log \log^* n)$.

Contribution. We show that there are no homogeneous LCLs with complexity between $o(\log^* n)$ and $\Omega(\log \log^* n)$. Together with prior work [7–9, 20], we have now a complete characterization of homogeneous LCLs: each such problem falls in one of the classes listed in Table 1, and all of the classes are nonempty.

Table 1: All possible distributed time complexities of homogeneous LCLs; see the full version [3] for details.

Deterministic	Randomized	Example
$\Theta(\log n)$	$\Theta(\log n)$	2-coloring
$\Theta(\log n)$	$\Theta(\log \log n)$	sinkless orientation
$\Theta(\log^* n)$	$\Theta(\log^* n)$	weak 2-coloring, even-degrees
$\Theta(1)$	$\Theta(1)$	weak 2-coloring, odd-degrees

In this work we focus on the proof of the gap between $o(\log^* n)$ and $\Omega(\log \log^* n)$, as everything else follows from prior work; we give an overview of the other gap results in the full version [3].

Approach, part 1: identifying a minimal problem. In complexity theory, the concept of *complete* problems has played a fundamental role. In this work we introduce the complementary concept of *minimal* problems. Informally:

- P is X-complete: if we can solve P efficiently, we can solve any $Q \in X$ efficiently.
- P is X-minimal: if we can solve some $Q \in X$ efficiently, we can solve P efficiently.

Let LogStar be the class of homogeneous LCLs with time complexity $O(\log^* n)$ and $\Omega(\log \log^* n)$. In this work we:

- identify a problem P that is LogStar-minimal,
- prove a lower bound of $\Omega(\log^* n)$ for the time complexity of problem P.

Hence all problems in class LogStar will require $\Theta(\log^* n)$ rounds.

It turns out that the following problem is LogStar-minimal: *weak 2-coloring in even-degree graphs.* In a weak 2-coloring, the task is to label the nodes with colors 1 and 2 such that each node with label 1 is adjacent to at least one node with label 2 and vice versa. This is the problem studied in the seminal work by Naor and Stockmeyer [20] – they showed that weak 2-coloring is solvable in $O(1)$ rounds in *odd-degree* graphs. We prove a lower bound of $\Omega(\log^* n)$ rounds for *even-degree* graphs.

The claim is trivial in the case of degree 2 (i.e., cycles); this follows from the standard Ramsey-theoretic argument and also more directly from Linial's [18] lower bound. The interesting cases are degrees $4, 6, \ldots$, where one may think that, since it is necessary to break symmetry with just one neighbor, the problem becomes *easier* as the degree increases. Note that, while for the standard $\Delta + 1$ coloring problem we can prove a lower bound of $\Omega(\log^* n)$ on graphs of higher degree by reduction from the 2-regular case, an algorithm for finding a weak 2-coloring in e.g. 4-regular graphs does *not* imply an algorithm for solving the same problem in 2-regular graphs.

We prove that weak 2-coloring in regular trees of any even constant degree requires $\Omega(\log^* n)$ rounds, even for a randomized algorithm, and even if identifiers are exactly in $\{1, \ldots, n\}$.

Approach, part 2: lower bound for weak 2-coloring. Our proof technique is based on a *speedup simulation argument*: On a high level, the idea is to show that given an algorithm A_0 that solves problem P_0 in time T, we can construct another algorithm A_1 that solves problem P_1 in time $T - 1$, and eventually an algorithm A_T that solves problem P_T in time 0. This is a contradiction, as P_T is a nontrivial problem that cannot be solved in 0 rounds. Hence P_0 cannot be solved in T rounds, either.

In prior work, there have been two main types of such arguments. The first flavor is what Linial [18] and Naor [19] used (see also [17]). Here in each iteration we have the same problem—vertex coloring—but with different parameters. Here is an informal version of the main idea:

- Assume that algorithm A finds a c-vertex coloring in time T. Then we can construct algorithm A' that finds a 2^c-vertex coloring in time $T - 1$.

The second flavor is what Brandt et al. [5] used. Here we have two different problems—in their case so-called sinkless orientation and sinkless coloring—and we alternate between them. Here is an informal version of the main idea:

- Assume that algorithm A finds a sinkless orientation in time T. Then we can construct algorithm A' that finds a sinkless coloring in time T.
- Assume that algorithm A' finds a sinkless coloring in time T. Then we can construct algorithm A'' that finds a sinkless orientation in time $T - 1$.

Here sinkless orientation is an *edge-based problem*, in which the task is to label each edge, while sinkless coloring is a *node-based problem*, in which the task is to label each node. By alternating between edge-based and node-based perspectives (and also edge-centric and node-centric models of distributed computing), we can turn any algorithm that finds a sinkless orientation into a faster algorithm that solves the same problem (we only lose in the success probability here).

In this work we combine the above two ideas. We alternate between a node-based and an edge-based problem, similar to what Brand et al. [5] did. However, we replace a single node-based problem with a family of node-based problems P_i, in the spirit of Linial [18] and Naor [19], and similarly we replace a single edge-based problem with a family of edge-based problems Q_i:

- Assume that algorithm A solves Q_i in time T. Then we can construct algorithm A' that solves P_i in time T.
- Assume that algorithm A' solves P_i in time T. Then we can construct algorithm A'' that solves Q_{i+1} in time $T - 1$.

Iterating this process, we get a 0-time algorithm for solving a nontrivial problem P_T (with a sufficiently high success probability), which will be a contradiction.

In our case the node-based problem P_i will be weak coloring with $f(i)$ colors, for a suitable choice of function $f(i)$. One of the main challenges is identifying a suitable edge-based problem Q_i so that the recursion works; a somewhat unusual variant of non-proper edge coloring will do the trick.

Open questions for future work. The main question left open is to extend the result from homogeneous LCLs to arbitrary LCLs on trees or high-girth graphs. We conjecture that the same gap between $o(\log^* n)$ and $\omega(1)$ holds also in that case.

2 MODEL AND DEFINITIONS

We consider simple, undirected and connected graphs $G = (V, E)$. We denote by $n = |V|$ the size of the graph. The *distance* between two nodes u and v, $\mathrm{dist}(u, v)$, is the number of edges on the shortest path between u and v. A *labeling* of a graph G is a mapping $\ell\colon V \longrightarrow \Sigma$. If we consider a labeled graph (G, ℓ), the *t-radius neighborhood* of a node v, $B_t(v)$, is a pair (G', ℓ'), where G' is the subgraph of G induced by all nodes at distance at most t from v, and ℓ' is the labeling function ℓ restricted to the nodes of G'. The t-radius neighborhood of an edge is the union of the t-radius neighborhoods of its endpoints.

2.1 The LOCAL model

We consider the standard LOCAL model of distributed computing [18, 22]. A distributed network is represented as a graph $G = (V, E)$, where each node $v \in V$ represents a computational entity, and an edge $e \in E$ represents a communication link between two entities. Each node $v \in V$ runs the same algorithm $\mathcal{A}$. An algorithm is randomized if, on each node, it can access a private sequence of unbiased random bits, otherwise it is deterministic. The sequence of random bits can be seen as a labeling of the nodes, mapping a node to its own sequence of bits. The maximum degree of G is bounded by some constant Δ, and this parameter is known to $\mathcal{A}$. Also, $\mathcal{A}$ knows the size of the network $n = |V|$. Nodes may be provided with identifiers in $\{1, \dots, n^c\}$, where $c \geq 1$ is a constant known to the algorithm. If the algorithm is not provided with identifiers, then $\mathcal{A}$ is said to be *anonymous*. Unless specified, we assume nodes to have identifiers. While in the standard LOCAL model nodes may be provided with some additional input, for our purpose we assume that nodes do not have any.

Initially, each node $v \in V$ knows just its degree, the size of the network n and the maximum degree Δ. Then, the computation proceeds in synchronous rounds. At each round, each node $v \in V$ does the following:

- sends a (possibly different) message to each of its neighbors,
- receives the messages sent by the neighbors,
- performs some local computation.

After each round, a node may decide to halt and produce an output. We do not impose any constraint on the size of the messages exchanged by the nodes. Also, we do not impose constraints on the local computational power. The only parameter we are interested to analyze is the number of rounds required to solve a task. The running time of an algorithm is the number of rounds required until all nodes have stopped. Since there are no constraints on the bandwidth nor on the amount of local computation, we can see a T-round algorithm $\mathcal{A}$ as a mapping from radius-T neighborhoods to valid outputs.

2.2 Locally checkable labelings

Locally checkable labellings (LCLs) were introduced by Naor and Stockmeyer [20]. These graph problems are described by a constant-size set of possible input labels Σ_{in}, a constant-size set of possible output labels Σ_{out}, and a set of local constraints C. Given an LCL $P = (\Sigma_{\mathrm{in}}, \Sigma_{\mathrm{out}}, C)$, each node $v \in V$ is labeled with some input from Σ_{in}, and the goal is to label all nodes with some output from Σ_{out}, such that each r-radius neighborhood of the graph satisfies the constraints C. Here $r = O(1)$ is called the *radius* of the LCL. We assume that the input graphs have maximum degree at most $\Delta = O(1)$. Since Δ and r are constants, the local constraints can be described as a finite set of valid r-radius input-output labeled neighborhoods. In this work, we consider LCLs in which nodes have no input, that is, $\Sigma_{\mathrm{in}} = \{\bot\}$.

An example of LCL is $(\Delta + 1)$-coloring. In this case, $\Sigma_{\mathrm{in}} = \{\bot\}$, $\Sigma_{\mathrm{out}} = \{1, \dots, \Delta + 1\}$, $r = 1$, and the local constraints impose that a node of color $c \in \Sigma_{\mathrm{out}}$ cannot be adjacent to another node of the same color c.

Let $\mathsf{DLOCAL}(T)$ and $\mathsf{RLOCAL}(T)$ be the classes of LCLs that can be solved in the LOCAL model in time T using a deterministic and a randomized algorithm, respectively.

3 MINIMAL SYMMETRY BREAKING

Our plan is to show that, in a certain formal sense, weak colorings form a family of minimal symmetry breaking problems. We start with the observation that given a distance-k weak c-coloring, for any constant k and c, it is possible to compute a weak 2-coloring in constant time. It then follows that if we consider any LCL P that is nontrivial inside regular even-degree trees, a solution for P also gives a solution for weak 2-coloring.

3.1 Weak colorings are constant-time reducible to each other

Formally we consider the following family of weak colorings.

Definition 1. For $c, k = O(1)$, a labeling $\varphi\colon V \longrightarrow [c]$ is a distance-k weak c-coloring if for every node v, there exists u with $\mathrm{dist}(v, u) \leq k$ and $\varphi(v) \neq \varphi(u)$. A distance-1 weak c-coloring is also called a weak c-coloring.

Lemma 2. *Given a distance-k weak c-coloring, for $k, c = O(1)$, it is possible to compute a weak 2-coloring in time $O(1)$.*

Proof. First we compute a weak $2c$-coloring as follows. Let φ denote the initial distance-k weak c-coloring. Each node v finds the closest node u such that u has a different color $\varphi(u) \neq \varphi(v)$ from v. Break ties by choosing one of the nodes with the smallest such color. Then v outputs the color $\varphi'(v) = (\varphi(v), \mathrm{dist}(u, v) \bmod 2)$. The number of colors in φ' is $2c$, and φ' can be computed in k rounds.

For node v, if there is a neighbor u such that $\varphi(v) \neq \varphi(u)$, then $\varphi'(v) \neq \varphi'(u)$ since the first elements are the old colors. Now assume that this was not the case and consider w, a neighbor of v on the path to u, the closest node with a different color from v. Now u must be the closest node of different color to w, since if there was a $u' \neq u$ with $\mathrm{dist}(w, u') < \mathrm{dist}(w, u)$ and $\varphi(w) \neq \varphi(u')$, then u' would be the closest node to v with a different color as well. Since $\mathrm{dist}(v, u) = \mathrm{dist}(w, u) + 1$ we have that $\varphi'(v) \neq \varphi'(w)$.

The last step is to reduce the number of colors from $2c$ to 2, and here we can directly apply the algorithm by Naor and Stockmeyer [20]. First use the standard Cole–Vishkin color reduction algorithm [4, 10, 16] to go from $2c$ colors to 3 colors in time $O(\log^* c)$: each node picks one of its neighbors with a different color, and the color reduction algorithm is run on the resulting oriented pseudoforest [24, Section 5.2]. This reduces the number of colors to 3. Finally, we use the 3-coloring to greedily find a maximal independent set in the pseudoforest and interpret this as a weak 2-coloring in the natural way. □

3.2 Minimality of weak colorings

We start by defining a *pointer problem* P^*, which we will later use to formalize the concept of *homogeneous* LCLs. Assume that $\Delta \in \{4, 6, \dots\}$. In problem P^*, each node v outputs a natural number $0 \le d(v) < \Delta$ and a possibly empty *pointer* $p(v)$ that points to one of its neighbors. We say that a node v is P^**-happy* if all of the following holds:

(1) If $\deg(v) = \Delta$, then $p(v) = u$, where u is one of the neighbors of v.
(2) If $\deg(v) < \Delta$, then $p(v) = \bot$ and $d(v) = \deg(v)$.
(3) If $p(v) = u$, then $d(v) = d(u)$ (pointer chains are labeled consistently).
(4) If $p(v) = u$, then $p(u) \neq v$ (pointer chains do not backtrack).
(5) If $p(v) = u$, then $p(u) \neq \bot$ or $\deg(u) = d(v)$ (pointer chains terminate at correct degree).

We have a feasible solution for P^* if all nodes are P^*-happy. Note that P^*-happiness can be verified locally in 1 round. If we encode the pointers as port numbers, we will have constantly many possible output labels for any constant Δ, and hence P^* is an LCL problem.

The definition of P^* implies that there is a chain of pointers starting from each node v of degree Δ, consistently labeled with some $d < \Delta$, and that chain can only end in a node of degree $d < \Delta$, or there is a cycle in the pointer chain.

We call nodes of degree less than Δ and cycles of nodes of degree Δ *irregularities.* We are interested in the closest irregularity to a given node. The distance $\operatorname{dist}(v, C)$ to a cycle C is defined as $\min_{u \in C}\{\operatorname{dist}(v, u)\} + \ell(C)$, where $\ell(C)$ is $|C|/2$ for even cycles and $\lfloor |C|/2 \rfloor + 1$ for odd cycles. This ensures that if a node does not have any irregularities within distance r, then its r-neighborhood is a regular tree.

The following lemma states that the 1-neighborhood of each node within distance r to an irregularity can be feasibly labeled according to P^* in time $O(r)$; for a proof, see the full version [3].

Lemma 3. *Let G be a graph of maximum degree Δ. Problem P^* can be solved in the 1-neighborhood of all nodes with irregularities within distance r in time $O(r)$.*

Lemma 3 yields an upper bound of $O(\log n)$ for P^*, as there is always an irregularity at such a distance. In the full version [3] we prove a matching lower bound, which gives the following theorem:

Theorem 4. *The distributed time complexity of P^* is $\Theta(\log_\Delta n)$.*

Homogeneous LCLs. In a homogeneous LCL, we will need to solve some problem P in those parts of the graph in which we do not have any irregularities, but we do not care about the correctness in the neighborhoods in which we have irregularities. We formalize this idea by constructing a homogeneous version P_H of P, in which any node can always fall back to solving the pointer problem P^*. Hence whenever a node sees any irregularities nearby, it can simply choose to construct a pointer chain pointing to an irregularity.

Recall that we assumed that $\Delta \in \{4, 6, \dots\}$. Given an LCL P with maximum degree Δ, we form a Δ*-homogeneous* LCL $P_H = (P, P^*)$, in which the labeling ℓ_H is a pair (ℓ_P, ℓ_{P^*}), where we also allow $\ell_{P^*}(v)$ to be empty. At each node v the verifier for P_H accepts if and only if one of the following is true:

(1) v has a nonempty P^*-label and v is P^*-happy, or
(2) v has an empty P^*-label and verifier for P accepts.

In particular, if an algorithm starts solving P^* in some neighborhood, the pointer chains it creates cannot terminate without meeting an irregularity.

Classification of homogeneous LCLs. Our aim is to characterize completely the computational complexity of homogeneous LCLs. In the following sections we study the complexity of weak 2-coloring and prove a lower bound of $\Omega(\log^* n)$ for it. Using the minimality of weak 2-coloring together with the previous work on the complexity theory of LCL problems (see the full version [3] for details), we will then obtain the following theorem:

Theorem 5. *A Δ-homogeneous* LCL *$P_H = (P, P^*)$ can have the following complexities.*

(1) *$O(1)$ deterministic and randomized,*
(2) *$\Theta(\log^* n)$ deterministic and randomized,*
(3) *$\Theta(\log n)$ deterministic and $\Theta(\log \log n)$ randomized, or*
(4) *$\Theta(\log n)$ deterministic and randomized.*

4 LOWER BOUND FOR WEAK 2-COLORING: OVERVIEW

In Sections 5–7 we will give a lower bound of $\Omega(\log^* n)$ for weak 2-coloring. Specifically, we will prove the following theorem that holds even if the input graph is promised to be a regular tree of any even constant degree, also for randomized algorithms, even if a globally consistent orientation is provided, and even if nodes are provided with identifiers exactly in $\{1, \dots, n\}$.

Theorem 6. *Solving weak 2-coloring on trees of any even constant degree with global success probability at least $\frac{1}{2}$ requires $\Omega(\log^* n)$ communication rounds.*

We will first consider the case in which the tree is 4-regular. In Section 5 we will prove a simulation result, informally stating that given an algorithm that can compute a weak c-coloring in t rounds, we can find a weak c'-coloring in $t-1$ rounds, with bounded growth in error probability and palette size. Then, in Section 6, we show how to use the simulation result to prove our main theorem for the case of 4-regular trees. These proofs are heavily based on the ideas presented by Naor [19].

Finally, in Section 7, we will show how our results can be generalized to any regular tree of constant degree, completing the proof of Theorem 6.

5 SPEEDUP SIMULATION IN 4-REGULAR TREES

In this section we show that, given an algorithm for weak c-coloring on 4-regular oriented trees, we can speed it up and obtain a weak coloring algorithm that is one round faster but uses a larger palette and has a larger local failure probability. The size of the new palette is doubly exponential in c, and the new algorithm has a failure probability that is polynomial in the failure probability of the original algorithm.

Setting: consistently oriented trees. We assume that nodes do not have unique identifiers, but have access to random bits. Nodes are assumed to know n, the size of the input graph. We also assume that the edges are oriented in a consistent manner, that is, a labeling in $\{U, D, L, R\}$, representing the directions *up*, *down*, *left*, and *right*, satisfying that if the edge $\{u, v\}$ is labeled R for u, then it is labeled L for v, and that if the edge is labeled U for u, then it is labeled D for v.

Since the graph topology is always assumed to be a 4-regular tree, t-round algorithm A is a function that maps each t-neighborhood $B_t(v)$ to an output. The output $A(v)$ only depends on the random bit assignment to the neighborhood. An algorithm A fails locally with probability at most p if, for each node v, $\Pr[\,\forall u \in N(v), A(u) = A(v)\,] \leq p$.

Intermediate problem: weak edge coloring. We will not directly show how to convert a t-round algorithm to a $(t-1)$-round algorithm. Instead, we define an intermediate problem that requires to produce an edge coloring such that for each node, either the edges labeled U and D have different colors, or the edges labeled L and R have different colors. If the number of allowed colors is c, we refer to this problem as *weak edge c-coloring*. For this problem we construct an algorithm in a different, edge-based, model of computation: edges are computing entities, and two edges can communicate if they are incident to the same node. A t-round edge algorithm A' is a function that maps t-edge neighborhoods $B_t(\{u, v\}) = B_t(u) \cup B_t(v)$, labeled with random bits, to the outputs. Notice that, even if it is an edge-based model of computation, random bits are still given to the nodes. Since the topology is assumed to be a 4-regular tree, the output $A'(e)$ only depends on the type of the edge e and the random bits. We say that an edge algorithm A' fails locally around node v with probability at most p if $\Pr[A'(e_U(v)) = A'(e_D(v)) \text{ and } A'(e_L(v)) = A'(e_R(v))] \leq p$, where $e_x(v)$ is the edge incident to v labeled x.

We show how to convert a t-round node based algorithm into a $(t-1)$-round edge based algorithm in Lemma 7. Then, we show how to convert a $(t-1)$-round edge algorithm into a $(t-1)$-round node algorithm in Lemma 8.

Lemma 7 (First speedup lemma). *Let A be a t-round weak c-coloring algorithm with local failure probability at most p. Then there exists a $(t-1)$-round edge based algorithm A' for weak edge 2^{2c}-coloring with local failure probability $p' \leq 5p^{1/5} \cdot c^{4/5}$.*

Lemma 8 (Second speedup lemma). *Let A be a t-round weak edge c-coloring algorithm with local failure probability at most p. Then there exists a t-round algorithm A' for weak 2^{4c}-coloring with local failure probability $p' \leq 4p^{1/4} \cdot c^{3/4}$.*

5.1 First speedup lemma

Proof of Lemma 7. We will construct the edge based algorithm A' using a simulation of A. The $(t-1)$-neighborhood of an edge $e = (v, u)$, $B_{t-1}(e)$, almost fixes the t-radius neighborhoods of nodes u and v. The part that is still not fixed, for nodes u and v, is the random assignments of nodes in $B_t(v) \setminus B_{t-1}(e)$ and in $B_t(u) \setminus B_{t-1}(e)$. Note that these two sets are disjoint, since the topology is assumed to be a tree.

The high level idea of the simulation is the following. Edge e knows a part of the radius-t neighborhood of nodes u and v, and it can complete these partial views to full t-radius views in all possible ways. Each time it can simulate the original algorithm A and see what color this algorithm would have assigned to the nodes. Thus, for each color c and endpoint v, the edge e knows the frequency with which the algorithm gives color c to node v. This procedure gives $2c$ frequencies (c for each endpoint). We can then apply a threshold function, obtaining a bit string of length $2c$, that we will show to be a weak edge 2^{2c}-coloring.

Thus, algorithm A' does the following. Each edge e starts by gathering $B_{t-1}(e)$, and then goes over all random bit assignments in $B_t(v) \setminus B_{t-1}(e)$ and in $B_t(u) \setminus B_{t-1}(e)$, simulates A on $B_t(v)$ and $B_t(u)$, and computes the frequency of each color $i \in [c]$ appearing as the output of v and u, respectively. Let $f \in [0, 1]$ be a parameter to be decided later. We say that a color is *frequent* for v given $B_{t-1}(e)$, if it is the output of $A(v)$ with probability at least f.

Let us fix an orientation for the nodes u and v: edge e is either $e_U(v)$ or $e_R(v)$ for v, while e is either $e_D(u)$ or $e_L(u)$ for u. The output of A' is a bit vector of length $2c$: for the first c bits, the bit i is 1 if and only if the color i is frequent for v. For the next c bits, bit $c+i$ is 1 if and only if color i is frequent for u. Given an edge $e = (v, u)$, the output $A'(e)$ is also seen as the pair $(A'(v, e), A'(u, e))$ that consists of the sets of frequent colors $A'(v, e)$ of v and $A'(u, e)$ of u.

We will show that, for most of the random bit assignments, a local failure of algorithm A' will also imply a local failure of the original algorithm A with a smaller probability. We say that the assignment of random bits to $B_t(v)$ is *good* if, for each edge e incident to v, we have that $A(v)$, the true output of A, is contained in $A'(v, e)$. Since there are at most c colors, the probability of having $A(v) \notin A'(v, e)$ is bounded by cf. By taking a union bound over the edges of v, we have that $\Pr[B_t(v) \text{ is good}] \geq 1 - 4cf$.

Now assume that A' fails locally in a good neighborhood $B_t(v)$. Let $e_x = e_x(v)$. Denote the partial outputs of edges e_R, e_L, e_U, and e_D corresponding to node v by X, Y, Z, and W, respectively. See Figure 1 for an illustration. Since by assumption A' does not break symmetry neither horizontally nor vertically, we must have that $A'(e_R) = A'(e_L) = (X, Y)$ and that $A'(e_U) = A'(e_D) = (Z, W)$. Since the random bit assignment was good, we have that $A(v) \in X \cap Y \cap Z \cap W$.

We have only fixed the random bits in $B_t(v)$. Since $A(v)$ is a frequent color for each neighbor of v over their respective edges, this implies that for each neighbor u, $\Pr[A(u) = A(v) \mid B_t(v)] \geq f$, and that, since these events are independent, all neighbors of v output $A(v)$ with probability at least f^4. Now if A' fails locally with probability p', we get that

$$\begin{aligned}
p &= \Pr[A \text{ fails locally}] \\
&\geq \Pr[A' \text{ fails locally in a good neighborhood}] \cdot f^4 \\
&\geq (1 - \Pr[A' \text{ does not fail}] - \Pr[\text{neighborhood is not good}]) \cdot f^4 \\
&\geq (p' - 4cf) \cdot f^4.
\end{aligned}$$

To maximize this probability we set $f = p'/(5c)$. This implies that $p \geq (p' - 4cf)f^4 = (p'/5)^5 c^{-4}$, and conversely that $p' \leq 5p^{1/5} \cdot c^{4/5}$. □

5.2 Second speedup lemma

Proof of Lemma 8. We prove the statement for a $(t-1)$-round algorithm. We will again construct A' by a simulation of A and

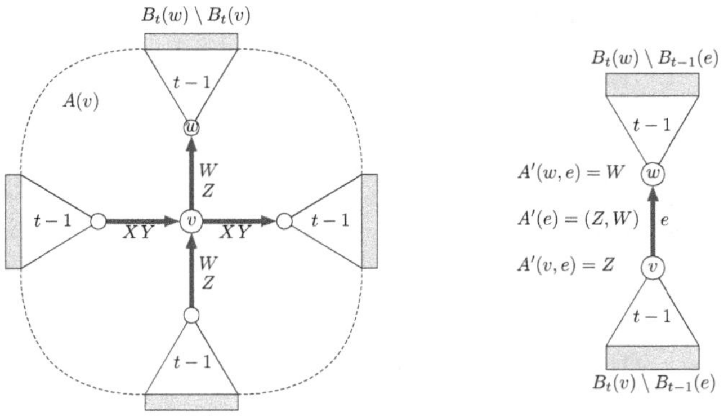

Figure 1: First speedup lemma: simulation of A based on $(t-1)$-edge neighborhoods. On the left: the output of node v is determined by the random bit assignment in its t-neighborhood. Given $B_t(v)$, the outputs of its neighbors are independent of each other. Assignment to $B_t(v)$ is good, if $A(v) \in X, Y, Z$, and W. On the right: the outputs of edges are constructed as simulations of A at the endpoints v and w. A color i is included in the set $A'(w,e) = W$ if w outputs $A(w) = i$ with probability $\geq f$ given $B_{t-1}(e)$. Given $B_{t-1}(e)$, the outputs of v and w are independent. Simulation A' fails at v if horizontal and vertical edges produce the same pairs of labels. In a good neighborhood this implies that A also fails with probability at least f^4.

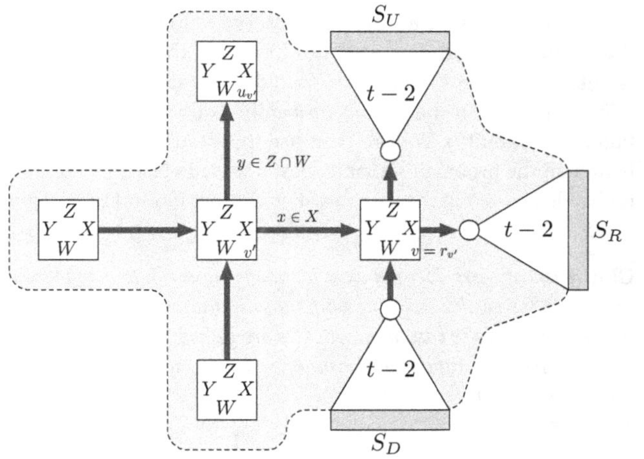

Figure 2: Second speedup lemma: bounding the local failure probability of A based on A'. The neighborhood of node v' is good if for its right and up edges e and e', the outputs $A(e) = x$ and $A(e') = y$ of those edges are in sets generated by the simulations in their endpoints: $x \in X$ and $y \in Z, W$. The simulation A' fails at v' if all neighbors of v' also output the same 4-tuple (X, Y, Z, W). This implies that, since the outputs of the edges incident to v are independent given the $(t-1)$-neighborhood of v, the original algorithm A fails around v with probability at least f^3.

show that the local failure probability of A' is bounded by the local failure probability of A.

The algorithm A' is constructed as follows. Given the random bits assigned to $B_{t-1}(v)$, node v simulates A on each of its incident edges. For each edge e, node v outputs a bit vector of length c: the i-th bit is 1 if and only if $\Pr[A(e) = i \mid B_{t-1}(v)] \geq f$. Denote the vector of the edge e by $A'_e(v)$. We say that the edge color i is frequent for edge e at node v if $A'_e(v)$ contains a 1 in position i. The output $A'(v)$ is then defined as the ordered 4-tuple consisting of the outputs of the right, left, up, and down edges of v at v. Clearly, the output of A' can take 2^{4c} different values.

Now we bound the probability that the output of A' is not a weak coloring. We will show that, if the algorithm A' fails on some node v', then A fails on a neighbor v of v' with some probability.

Let $r_{v'}$ and $u_{v'}$ denote the right and up neighbors of some node v', respectively (see Figure 2). The t-neighborhood of node v' is good if the following holds. For $(v', r_{v'})$ the output $A((v', r_{v'})) = x$ is frequent at node v', and the output $A((v', u_{v'})) = y$ is frequent at v' and $u_{v'}$. For an arbitrary edge e, the probability that $A(e)$ is not a frequent color of e at its endpoint is, by definition, at most cf. By a union bound, the t-neighborhood of a node is good with probability at least $1 - 3cf$.

Now consider arbitrary nodes v, v' such that $v = r_{v'}$, and assume that the t-neighborhood around a node v' is good, but that A' fails at v'. Denote the output $A'(v')$ of v' by (X, Y, Z, W). The failure of A' implies that A' outputs (X, Y, Z, W) for each neighboring node of v' as well (including v). Since the neighborhood of v' is good, we have that $x = A((v', v)) \in X$ and that $y = A((v', u_{v'})) \in Z \cap W$. Now consider v: given $B_{t-1}(v) \subseteq B_t(v')$, the outputs of its incident edges in A, not counting (v', v), depend only on the random bit assignment in $B_t(v) \setminus B_t(v')$ (the regions S_U, S_R, S_D in Figure 2), and the outputs are independent of each other given $B_{t-1}(v)$. Since $A((v', v)) = x$ and since we have that $x \in X$ and $y \in Z \cap W$, with probability at least f^3 the algorithm A outputs x on the right edge of v, and y on both the up and down edges of v, meaning that A fails around node v.

Let p' denote the local failure probability of A'. Then the local failure probability p of A is lower bounded by $p \geq (p' - 3cf) \cdot f^3$. Again, we maximize this by setting $f = p'/(4c)$. We get that $p \geq (p' - 3cp'/(4c))(p'/(4c))^3 = (p'/4)^4 \cdot c^{-3}$. Conversely we have that $p' \leq 4p^{1/4} \cdot c^{3/4}$. □

6 LOWER BOUND IN 4-REGULAR TREES

In this section we show how Lemmas 7 and 8 imply a lower bound of $\Omega(\log^* n)$ for weak 2-coloring. Note that, in the context of distributed complexity theory, it is usually required to obtain local high probability of success when $O(\log n)$-bit identifiers are given. In this section we prove a stronger statement, that is, at least $\frac{1}{2}\log^* n - 4$ rounds are required to obtain global success probability of at least $\frac{1}{2}$, when identifiers from 1 to n are given. However, in order to prove Theorem 5, only Claim 11 and Claim 12 are required.

Lemma 9. *Any randomized weak 2-coloring algorithm for 4-regular trees, with a running time less than $t = \frac{1}{2}\log^* n - b - 3$ rounds, produces a legal weak 2-coloring with probability at most*

$$\left(1 - \frac{1}{\log^{(2b)} n}\right)^{n^{\frac{1}{3(2t+1)}}} + \frac{1}{2n^{1/3}}.$$

In order to prove the lemma we proceed as follows. We consider the setting in which nodes do not have IDs, that is, the network is anonymous (as in Lemmas 7 and 8). In this setting we prove a lower bound on the failure probability of a single node (local failure probability). We can then use this result to prove a lower bound on the probability that at least one node fails (global failure probability), even in the case in which distinct IDs in $\{1,\ldots,n\}$ are given.

Claim 10. *If there does not exist an anonymous randomized t-round algorithm for weak 2-coloring with a local failure probability at most p, then, even in the case in which IDs are given, there does not exist a randomized t-round algorithm for weak 2-coloring with a global success probability at least*

$$(1-p)^{n^{\frac{1}{3(2t+1)}}} + \frac{1}{2n^{1/3}}.$$

Proof. Consider a node v in a 4-regular tree of n nodes, satisfying that $B_k(v)$, for $k = \log_3 \frac{n^{1/3}+1}{2}$, does not contain any leaf of the tree. Now $B_k(v)$ is a ball containing exactly $n^{\frac{1}{3}}$ nodes. Since the execution of a t-round algorithm on node v depends only on nodes at distance at most t from v, then if two nodes u and v are at distance at least $2t+1$, we can assume that their executions are independent. In particular, the events of nodes u and v failing are independent.

In order to compute a lower bound on the global failure probability, we start by computing a lower bound on the number of independent executions in $B_k(v)$, that is, on the number of nodes that could fail independently. We give a lower bound on the number of nodes having pairwise distance at least $2t+1$ with the following process. Let $m(u,x)$ be the node reached by starting from u and moving $2t+1$ times to the edge labeled x, where $x \in \{L,R,U,D\}$. Consider the set I of nodes at distance exactly 7 from v. The size of I is $4\cdot 3^6$. Start from each node $u \in I$ and consider the 3 nodes $m(u,x)$ where $x = \{L,R,U,D\} \setminus \{\ell\}$, and ℓ is the label of the edge incident to u on the shortest path between u and v. Let S be the set of these nodes. Repeat this process from nodes in S and add the new reached nodes to S. At each time we add 3 new nodes for each node added at the previous step, each one at distance at least $2t+1$ from all the other nodes. The nodes added to S at step $i \geq 1$ are at distance $7 + i(2t+1)$ from v. Thus we can repeat the process for $k' = \lfloor \frac{k-7}{2t+1} \rfloor - 1$ steps and obtain a set of nodes S that are pairwise at distance at least $2t+1$, and their ball is fully contained in $B_k(v)$, meaning that in t rounds they do not see nodes not contained in $B_k(v)$. The size of S is

$$\begin{aligned}4\cdot 3^6 \cdot \left(\sum_{i=1}^{k'} 3^i\right) &= 4\cdot\frac{3^7}{2}\left(3^{k'}-1\right) \geq 2\cdot 3^7\cdot 3^{k'-1} \geq 2\cdot 3^{7+\frac{k-7}{2t+1}-3}\\ &= 2\cdot 3^{4-\frac{7}{2t+1}}\cdot\left(\frac{n^{1/3}+1}{2}\right)^{\frac{1}{2t+1}} \geq 3^{4-\frac{7}{2t+1}}\cdot n^{\frac{1}{3(2t+1)}}\\ &\geq n^{\frac{1}{3(2t+1)}},\end{aligned}$$

assuming that $t \geq 1$. This implies that the number of independent executions of nodes in $B_k(v)$ is at least $n^{\frac{1}{3(2t+1)}}$. Thus, since for an algorithm to succeed it is required that at least all nodes in $B_k(v)$ succeed, and that requires that at least all nodes in S succeed, the probability that the (anonymous) algorithm succeeds is at most

$$(1-p)^{n^{\frac{1}{3(2t+1)}}}.$$

We now want to compute an upper bound on the global success probability of a randomized algorithm running on nodes labeled with distinct IDs from $\{1,\ldots,n\}$. Our speedup result is shown for anonymous randomized algorithms. Such algorithms can use randomness to generate unique identifiers with high probability. We bound the success probability of any algorithm in the randomized LOCAL model by comparing it to a model where the identifiers are random but always globally unique. Such an assignment is at least as good as the worst-case assignment of unique identifiers.

Let X be the event that the algorithm succeeds, let Y the event that a random ID assignment is correct, let X' be the event that the algorithm succeeds for all nodes contained in $B_k(v)$ and let Y' be the event that a random ID assignment is correct (meaning that it is globally unique) in $B_k(v)$. The global success probability is at most the success probability of the algorithm running in an instance where IDs have been assigned randomly and correctly. Thus, we can upper bound the global success probability as $\Pr[X|Y] \leq \Pr[X'|Y'] \leq \Pr[X'] + \Pr[\bar{Y}']$. Intuitively, $Pr[X|Y]$ is the global success probability of an algorithm running on nodes labeled with randomly assigned distinct IDs, while $\Pr[X'|Y']$ is the probability that no node fails in $B_k(v)$, given that nodes of $B_k(v)$ have randomly assigned distinct IDs. Then, $\Pr[X']$ is the probability that all nodes of $B_k(v)$ succeed for an algorithm running on an anonymous network, and $\Pr[\bar{Y}']$ is the probability that a random ID assignment is not correct for nodes in $B_k(v)$. We will use, as upper bound for $Pr[X']$, the previously computed probability that all nodes of the set S succeed.

By assigning random IDs in $\{1,\ldots,n\}$ to the nodes of $B_k(v)$, the probability that at least a pair of nodes chooses the same ID is at most

$$\binom{n^{1/3}}{2}\frac{1}{n} < \frac{1}{2n^{1/3}}.$$

Thus, if an algorithm locally fails with probability at least p, then the global success probability is at most

$$Pr[X|Y] \leq Pr[X'] + Pr[\bar{Y}'] \leq (1-p)^{n^{\frac{1}{3(2t+1)}}} + \frac{1}{2n^{1/3}},$$

even if the IDs are provided. □

Claim 11. *Suppose that any 0-round weak-c_0 coloring algorithm locally fails with probability at least p_0. Then, any t-time weak 2-coloring algorithm locally fails with probability at least $(\frac{p_0}{5c_0})^{5^{2t+1}}$.*

Proof. Lemma 7 and 8 imply that if there exists a t-round algorithm that produces a weak c_t coloring with local failure probability at most p_t, then there exists a $(t-1)$-round algorithm that produces a weak $c_{t-1} = 2^{4\hat{c}_{t-1}}$ coloring, where $\hat{c}_{t-1} = 2^{2c_t}$, such that the failure probability is at most p_{t-1}, where $p_{t-1} = 4\hat{p}_{t-1}^{1/4}\cdot\hat{c}_t^{3/4}$ and $\hat{p}_{t-1} = 5p_t^{1/5}\cdot c_t^{4/5}$. Thus, by starting with a small value of p_t and applying the two lemmas recursively, we obtain a small value for p_0. If the obtained value of p_0 is smaller than the assumed minimum, we obtain a contradiction for p_t. This implies that we can compute a lower bound for p_t as a function of p_0 and c_0. We can define p_t as a function of p_{t-1} as follows: $p_t = (\hat{p}_{t-1}/5)^5/c_t^4$, where $\hat{p}_{t-1} = (p_{t-1}/4)^4/\hat{c}_t^3$, $c_{t-1} = 2^{4\hat{c}_{t-1}}$, and $\hat{c}_{t-1} = 2^{2c_t}$. It is now possible to define a new recurrence that we can use to give a lower bound for p_t:

$$p_t \geq \tilde{p}_{2t+1}, \text{with } \tilde{p}_{i+1} = \frac{(\tilde{p}_i/5)^5}{\tilde{c}_{i+1}^4}, \tilde{c}_i = 2^{2\tilde{c}_{i+1}}, \tilde{c}_1 = c_0, \text{and } \tilde{p}_1 = p_0.$$

A lower bound for $\tilde{p}_{i+1}$ can be given by noting that $\tilde{c}_1 \geq \tilde{c}_i$, for all i. Thus,

$$\tilde{p}_{i+1} = \frac{(\tilde{p}_i/5)^5}{\tilde{c}_{i+1}^4} \geq \frac{(\tilde{p}_i/5)^5}{\tilde{c}_1^4} \geq \left(\frac{\tilde{p}_i}{5\tilde{c}_1}\right)^5.$$

We prove the following by induction on i:

$$\tilde{p}_{i+1} \geq \frac{(\tilde{p}_1)^{5^{i+1}}}{(5\tilde{c}_1)^{\sum_{j=1}^{i} 5^j}} \geq \left(\frac{\tilde{p}_1}{5\tilde{c}_1}\right)^{5^{i+1}}.$$

For $i = 0$ the claim trivially holds. By inductive hypothesis,

$$\tilde{p}_{i+1} \geq \frac{(\tilde{p}_1)^{5^{i+1}}}{(5\tilde{c}_1)^{\sum_{j=1}^{i} 5^j}}.$$

Thus, $\tilde{p}_{i+2}$ can be lower bounded as follows:

$$\tilde{p}_{i+2} \geq \left(\frac{\tilde{p}_{i+1}}{5\tilde{c}_1}\right)^5 \geq \left(\frac{(\tilde{p}_1)^{5^{i+1}}}{(5\tilde{c}_1)^{\sum_{j=1}^{i} 5^j}}\right)^5 /(5\tilde{c}_1)^5 = \frac{(\tilde{p}_1)^{5^{i+2}}}{(5\tilde{c}_1)^{\sum_{j=1}^{i+1} 5^j}}.$$

Finally, we obtain a lower bound for p_t:

$$p_t \geq \tilde{p}_{2t+1} \geq \left(\frac{\tilde{p}_1}{5\tilde{c}_1}\right)^{5^{2t+1}} = \left(\frac{p_0}{5c_0}\right)^{5^{2t+1}}. \qquad \square$$

Claim 12. *Any* $(\frac{1}{2}\log^* n - b - 3)$*-round weak 2-coloring algorithm fails locally with probability at least* $\frac{1}{\log^{(2b)} n}$*, where* $b \geq 1$.

Proof. Since a 0-round algorithm has no information about its neighbors, the random output based on the uniform distribution minimizes the failure probability, that is, the probability that a node has the same color of all its neighbors. Thus, $p_0 \geq \frac{1}{c_0^4}$. Let us fix $t = \frac{1}{2}\log^* n - b - 3$. We can apply Claim 11, obtaining that the local failure probability of a t-round weak 2-coloring algorithm must be at least

$$\left(\frac{p_0}{5c_0}\right)^{5^{2t+1}} \geq \left(\frac{1}{5c_0^5}\right)^{5^{2t+1}} \geq \left(\frac{1}{5c_0}\right)^{5^{2t+2}}.$$

A t-round algorithm must produce a weak 2-coloring, thus $c_t = 2$. Also, by definition,

$$c_0 \leq 2^{4 \cdot 2^{\cdot^{\cdot^{4 \cdot 2^{4c_t}}}}},$$

where the number of terms "4·2" in the tower is $2t-1 = \log^* n - 2b - 7$. In order to compute a lower bound on the failure probability p_t, we start by giving an upper bound for c_0. It is easy to see that

$$\log^{(x)} c_0 \leq 6 \cdot 2^{4 \cdot 2^{\cdot^{\cdot^{4 \cdot 2^{4c_t}}}}},$$

where the number of terms "$4 \cdot 2$" in the tower is $\log^* n - 2b - 7 - x$, implying that $\log^{(\log^* n - 2b - 5)} c_0 \leq 6$. By taking the logarithm on both sides for 3 additional times, we get that $\log^{(\log^* n - 2b - 2)} c_0 \leq 1$. By definition, $\log^{(\log^* n - 1)} n > 1$. This is equivalent to taking the logarithm $(2b + 1)$ times, and then applying the logarithm again for $(\log^* n - 2b - 2)$ times on the result. Thus, we have that $\log^{(\log^* n - 2b - 2)} \log^{(2b+1)} n > 1$. We can finally obtain a bound on c_0 as a function of n, since the above constraints imply that $c_0 \leq \log^{(2b+1)} n$.

We can now lower bound p_t by

$$\left(\frac{1}{5\log^{(2b+1)} n}\right)^{5^{2t+2}}.$$

By taking the inverse of each side we get that

$$\frac{1}{p_t} \leq (5\log^{(2b+1)} n)^{5^{2t+2}},$$

and by taking the logarithm of each side we obtain that

$$\log\left(\frac{1}{p_t}\right) \leq 5^{2t+2}(\log 5 + \log\log^{(2b+1)} n) = 5^{2t+2}(\log 5 + \log^{(2b+2)} n).$$

For large enough n, this is at most $5^{2t+2}(2\log^{(2b+2)} n)$, which, since $t = O(\log^* n)$, can be upper bounded by $\log^{(2b+1)} n$. Thus, we get that $p_t \geq \frac{1}{\log^{(2b)} n}$. $\square$

Now Lemma 9 follows from Claim 10 and Claim 12. We can apply it to prove Theorem 13.

Theorem 13. *Solving weak 2-coloring with global success probability at least* $\frac{1}{2}$ *requires* $\Omega(\log^* n)$ *rounds.*

Proof. Let $t = \frac{1}{2}\log^* n - 4$. Applying Lemma 9 with $b = 1$, we get that the global success probability is at most

$$\left(1 - \frac{1}{\log\log n}\right)^{n^{1/(3(2t+1))}} + \frac{1}{2n^{1/3}} \leq e^{-\frac{n^{1/(3(2t+1))}}{\log\log n}} + \frac{1}{2n^{1/3}}.$$

First, note that, for large enough n, we have that $\frac{1}{2n^{1/3}} < \frac{1}{4}$. In order to prove that the other addendum is also at most $\frac{1}{4}$, we prove that

$$\frac{n^{1/(3(2t+1))}}{\log\log n} > 2.$$

The above follows by noting that, since $t = O(\log^* n)$, for large enough n,

$$\frac{\log n}{3(2t+1)} - \log\log\log n > 1. \qquad \square$$

7 GENERALIZING THE LOWER BOUND BEYOND 4-REGULAR TREES

In this section we will describe how to adapt the presented techniques in order to prove an $\Omega(\log^* n)$ lower bound for weak 2-coloring any Δ-regular oriented tree, for any constant even $\Delta = 2k$. We start by describing how to adapt the speedup result of Section 5.

In Section 5, we assumed to have a consistent orientation on the two directions, horizontal and vertical. We now assume to have a consistent orientation among each of the k dimensions. The new weak edge c-coloring problem is defined as follows. For each node v, there must exist one dimension $d \in \{1, \ldots, k\}$, such that the edges of dimension d incident to v are labeled with two different colors in $\{1, \ldots, c\}$. It is easy to see that for $k = 2$ we obtain the original problem.

Then, using similar techniques of Section 5, it is possible to prove the following.

Lemma 14 (First generalized speedup lemma). *Let A be a t-round weak c-coloring algorithm with local failure probability $\leq p$. Then there exists a $(t-1)$-round edge based algorithm A' for weak edge 2^{2c}-coloring with local failure probability $p' \leq (\Delta+1)p^{1/(\Delta+1)} \cdot c^{1-1/(\Delta+1)}$.*

To prove this lemma we can define the new coloring in the same way it has been defined in the $\Delta = 4$ case (by computing the color probability of each endpoint of an edge). Then, we can prove that if the new algorithm fails with probability p', then the old algorithm must fail with probability $p \geq (p' - \Delta cf) \cdot f^{\Delta}$.

Lemma 15 (Second generalized speedup lemma). *Let A be a t-round weak edge c-coloring algorithm with local failure probability $\leq p$. Then there exists a t-round algorithm A' for weak $2^{\Delta c}$-coloring with local failure probability $p' \leq \Delta p^{1/\Delta} \cdot c^{1-1/\Delta}$.*

To prove this lemma we can define the new coloring in a similar way it has been defined in the $\Delta = 4$ case. Since now a node has Δ incident edges, we obtaining a bit string of length Δc, that is a $2^{\Delta c}$ coloring. Then, we can argue that the neighborhood of a node v' is good with probability at least $1 - (\Delta - 1)cf$, and that the same neighborhood will be bad for a specific neighbor v of v' with probability $f^{\Delta-1}$, obtaining that if the new algorithm fails with probability p', then the old algorithm must fail with probability $p \geq (p' - (\Delta-1)cf) \cdot f^{\Delta-1}$. This time, the choice of f that maximizes the failure probability is $f = \frac{p'}{\Delta c}$. We get that

$$p \geq \left(\frac{p'}{\Delta}\right)^{\Delta} \cdot \frac{1}{c^{\Delta-1}}.$$

Once we have these lemmas, we can use similar techniques of Section 6 to prove a lower bound for the global failure probability. First, the exact statement of Claim 10 can be proved for any constant Δ, by setting

$$k = \log_{\Delta-1}\left((n^{1/3} - 1)\frac{\Delta - 2}{\Delta} + 1\right).$$

Then, we can prove a generalized version of Claim 11 by following exactly the same reasoning.

Claim 16. *If any 0-round weak-c_0 coloring algorithm fails locally with probability at least p_0, then any t-round weak 2-coloring algorithm fails locally with probability at least $\left(p_0/((\Delta+1)c_0)\right)^{(\Delta+1)^{2t+1}}$.*

Then, using similar techniques to Claim 12, we can prove that there exists some constant b that depends on Δ, such that any $(\frac{1}{2}\log^* n - b)$-round weak 2-coloring algorithm locally fails with probability at least $\frac{1}{\log\log n}$. Finally, we can prove the following theorem, using the same ideas of Theorem 13.

Theorem 6. *Solving weak 2-coloring on trees of any even constant degree with global success probability at least $\frac{1}{2}$ requires $\Omega(\log^* n)$ communication rounds.*

ACKNOWLEDGMENTS

We would like to thank Sebastian Brandt for discussions related to weak 2-coloring, Tuomo Lempiäinen for discussions related to the concept of minimality, and anonymous reviewers for their helpful comments on previous versions of this work. This work was supported in part by the Academy of Finland, Grants 285721 and 314888.

REFERENCES

[1] Alkida Balliu, Sebastian Brandt, Dennis Olivetti, and Jukka Suomela. 2018. Almost global problems in the LOCAL model. In *Proc. 32nd International Symposium on Distributed Computing (DISC 2018) (Leibniz International Proceedings in Informatics (LIPIcs))*. Schloss Dagstuhl-Leibniz-Zentrum für Informatik.

[2] Alkida Balliu, Juho Hirvonen, Janne H Korhonen, Tuomo Lempiäinen, Dennis Olivetti, and Jukka Suomela. 2018. New classes of distributed time complexity. In *Proc. 50th ACM Symposium on Theory of Computing (STOC 2018)*. ACM Press, 1307–1318.

[3] Alkida Balliu, Juho Hirvonen, Dennis Olivetti, and Jukka Suomela. 2018. Hardness of minimal symmetry breaking in distributed computing. arXiv:1811.01643 http://arxiv.org/abs/1811.01643

[4] Leonid Barenboim and Michael Elkin. 2013. *Distributed Graph Coloring: Fundamentals and Recent Developments*. Vol. 4.

[5] Sebastian Brandt, Orr Fischer, Juho Hirvonen, Barbara Keller, Tuomo Lempiäinen, Joel Rybicki, Jukka Suomela, and Jara Uitto. 2016. A lower bound for the distributed Lovász local lemma. In *Proc. 48th ACM Symposium on Theory of Computing (STOC 2016)*. ACM Press, 479–488.

[6] Sebastian Brandt, Juho Hirvonen, Janne H Korhonen, Tuomo Lempiäinen, Patric R J Östergård, Christopher Purcell, Joel Rybicki, Jukka Suomela, and Przemysław Uznański. 2017. LCL problems on grids. In *Proc. 36th ACM Symposium on Principles of Distributed Computing (PODC 2017)*. ACM Press, 101–110.

[7] Yi-Jun Chang, Qizheng He, Wenzheng Li, Seth Pettie, and Jara Uitto. 2018. The Complexity of Distributed Edge Coloring with Small Palettes. In *Proc. 29th ACM-SIAM Symposium on Discrete Algorithms (SODA 2018)*. Society for Industrial and Applied Mathematics, 2633–2652.

[8] Yi-Jun Chang, Tsvi Kopelowitz, and Seth Pettie. 2016. An Exponential Separation between Randomized and Deterministic Complexity in the LOCAL Model. In *Proc. 57th IEEE Symposium on Foundations of Computer Science (FOCS 2016)*. IEEE, 615–624.

[9] Yi-Jun Chang and Seth Pettie. 2017. A Time Hierarchy Theorem for the LOCAL Model. In *Proc. 58th IEEE Symposium on Foundations of Computer Science (FOCS 2017)*. IEEE, 156–167.

[10] Richard Cole and Uzi Vishkin. 1986. Deterministic coin tossing with applications to optimal parallel list ranking. *Information and Control* 70, 1 (1986), 32–53.

[11] Manuela Fischer and Mohsen Ghaffari. 2017. Sublogarithmic Distributed Algorithms for Lovász Local Lemma, and the Complexity Hierarchy. In *Proc. 31st International Symposium on Distributed Computing (DISC 2017)*. 18:1–18:16.

[12] Mohsen Ghaffari, David G Harris, and Fabian Kuhn. 2018. On Derandomizing Local Distributed Algorithms. In *Proc. 59th IEEE Symposium on Foundations of Computer Science (FOCS 2018)*. arXiv:1711.02194

[13] Mohsen Ghaffari, Juho Hirvonen, Fabian Kuhn, and Yannic Maus. 2018. Improved Distributed Δ-Coloring. In *Proc. 37th ACM Symposium on Principles of Distributed Computing (PODC 2018)*. ACM, 427–436.

[14] Mohsen Ghaffari, Fabian Kuhn, and Yannic Maus. 2017. On the complexity of local distributed graph problems. In *Proc. 49th ACM SIGACT Symposium on Theory of Computing (STOC 2017)*. ACM Press, 784–797.

[15] Mohsen Ghaffari and Hsin-Hao Su. 2017. Distributed Degree Splitting, Edge Coloring, and Orientations. In *Proc. 28th ACM-SIAM Symposium on Discrete Algorithms (SODA 2017)*. Society for Industrial and Applied Mathematics, 2505–2523.

[16] Andrew V. Goldberg, Serge A. Plotkin, and Gregory E. Shannon. 1988. Parallel Symmetry-Breaking in Sparse Graphs. *SIAM Journal on Discrete Mathematics* 1, 4 (1988), 434–446.

[17] Juhana Laurinharju and Jukka Suomela. 2014. Brief announcement: Linial's lower bound made easy. In *Proc. 33rd ACM SIGACT-SIGOPS Symposium on Principles of Distributed Computing (PODC 2014)*. ACM Press, 377–378.

[18] Nathan Linial. 1992. Locality in Distributed Graph Algorithms. *SIAM J. Comput.* 21, 1 (1992), 193–201.

[19] Moni Naor. 1991. A lower bound on probabilistic algorithms for distributive ring coloring. *SIAM Journal on Discrete Mathematics* 4, 3 (1991), 409–412.

[20] Moni Naor and Larry Stockmeyer. 1995. What Can be Computed Locally? *SIAM J. Comput.* 24, 6 (1995), 1259–1277.

[21] Alessandro Panconesi and Aravind Srinivasan. 1995. The local nature of Δ-coloring and its algorithmic applications. *Combinatorica* 15, 2 (1995), 255–280.

[22] David Peleg. 2000. *Distributed Computing: A Locality-Sensitive Approach*. Society for Industrial and Applied Mathematics.

[23] Seth Pettie. 2018. Automatically Speeding Up LOCAL Graph Algorithms. In *7th Workshop on Advances in Distributed Graph Algorithms (ADGA 2018)*. http://adga.hiit.fi/2018/Seth.pdf

[24] Joel Rybicki. 2011. *Exact bounds for distributed graph colouring*. Master's thesis. University of Helsinki. http://hdl.handle.net/10138/26560

An Automatic Speedup Theorem for Distributed Problems

Sebastian Brandt
brandts@ethz.ch
ETH Zürich
Switzerland

ABSTRACT

Recently, Brandt et al. [STOC'16] proved a lower bound for the distributed Lovász Local Lemma, which has been conjectured to be tight for sufficiently relaxed LLL criteria by Chang and Pettie [FOCS'17]. At the heart of their result lies a speedup technique that, for graphs of girth at least $2t + 2$, transforms any t-round algorithm for one specific LLL problem into a $(t - 1)$-round algorithm for the same problem. We substantially improve on this technique by showing that such a speedup exists for *any* locally checkable problem Π, with the difference that the problem Π_1 the inferred $(t-1)$-round algorithm solves is not (necessarily) the same problem as Π. Our speedup is *automatic* in the sense that there is a fixed procedure that transforms a description for Π into a description for Π_1 and *reversible* in the sense that any $(t - 1)$-round algorithm for Π_1 can be transformed into a t-round algorithm for Π. In particular, for any locally checkable problem Π with exact deterministic time complexity $T(n, \Delta) \leq t$ on graphs with n nodes, maximum node degree Δ, and girth at least $2t + 2$, there is a sequence of problems $\Pi_1, \Pi_2, \ldots$ with time complexities $T(n, \Delta) - 1, T(n, \Delta) - 2, \ldots$, that can be inferred from Π.

As a first application of our generalized speedup, we solve a long-standing open problem of Naor and Stockmeyer [STOC'93]: we show that weak 2-coloring in odd-degree graphs cannot be solved in $o(\log^* \Delta)$ rounds, thereby providing a matching lower bound to their upper bound.

CCS CONCEPTS

• **Distributed algorithms**;

KEYWORDS

distributed graph algorithms, locally checkable problems, weak coloring

ACM Reference Format:
Sebastian Brandt. 2019. An Automatic Speedup Theorem for Distributed Problems. In *2019 ACM Symposium on Principles of Distributed Computing (PODC'19), July 29–August 2, 2019, Toronto, ON, Canada.* ACM, New York, NY, USA, 10 pages. https://doi.org/10.1145/3293611.3331611

ACM ISBN 978-1-4503-6217-7/19/07...$15.00
https://doi.org/10.1145/3293611.3331611

1 INTRODUCTION

In this work, we study the question of determining the time complexity of distributed graph problems from the perspective of *round elimination*. More concretely, we ask: Given a problem Π, can we find another problem Π' which can be solved in exactly one round less? Is it perhaps even possible to infer such a problem Π' from Π in an automated fashion, so that we can obtain a sequence of problems with decreasing complexities until we end up with a problem that can be solved in 0 rounds? We will show that, given certain (reasonable) conditions, the answer to both questions is yes. As a concrete evidence of the power of this automatic speedup, we resolve the complexity of odd-degree weak 2-coloring, an open question asked by Naor and Stockmeyer in 1993 [22].

Model. Our distributed model of computation is a variant of the well-known LOCAL model [20, 23], a synchronous message passing model where the nodes of a given input graph G are processors that have the task to collaboratively solve some graph problem on G. The essential difference between our model and the LOCAL model is that in our case nodes are not equipped with unique identifiers, but (potentially) have some other symmetry breaking information available. The class of problems we consider are *locally checkable* problems, i.e., problems where the global validity of a solution can be checked locally by the nodes in constant time. More precisely, for some constant r, each node has a set of acceptable output configurations for its radius-r neighborhood, and a global solution is considered valid if and only if the output configuration of each node's radius-r neighborhood is acceptable. Our speedup results are about the *deterministic* time complexity of locally checkable problems; however, there exist known techniques to lift the obtained bounds to both the randomized and the deterministic LOCAL model. We will elaborate on these techniques in Section 2.2.

Full Version. Due to space constraints, this version of our work is missing many details, such as helpful intuition, technical lemmas, proofs, and the like. The full version of the paper is available at https://arxiv.org/abs/1902.09958.

1.1 Our Contributions

Our main contributions are twofold: 1) We present a speedup theorem that generalizes the speedup technique of Brandt et al. [9]: In that work, the authors obtain a lower bound for the distributed Lovász Local Lemma by developing a round elimination technique for a problem called sinkless orientation. We show that such a speedup exists for arbitrary locally checkable problems. In particular, we provide a method that takes the description of a problem Π as input and outputs the description of a problem Π' that can be solved one round faster but not any faster than that. This facilitates exciting new approaches for obtaining time complexity lower (and upper) bounds. 2) We show that our speedup technique is a powerful tool by using it to prove a tight lower bound for weak 2-coloring in odd-degree graphs, answering the long-standing open question by Naor and Stockmeyer.

Speedup Results. We provide an automatic procedure that transforms any given locally checkable problem Π into a (locally checkable) problem Π_1 such that, informally speaking, the following holds.

THEOREM 4.1 (INFORMAL). *Let Π be a locally checkable problem and Π_1 the problem obtained by applying our speedup transformation. On graphs of girth at least $2t + 2$, the following two statements are equivalent:*

(1) There is an algorithm solving Π in time t.
(2) There is an algorithm solving Π_1 in time $t - 1$.

If Π has an exact deterministic time complexity $T(n, \Delta) \leq t$ on graphs with n nodes, maximum node degree Δ, and girth at least $2t + 2$, then applying this speedup iteratively yields a sequence of problems $\Pi_1, \Pi_2, \ldots$ with time complexities $T(n, \Delta) - 1, T(n, \Delta) - 2, \ldots$. Now determining the time complexity of just a single Π_i in the sequence will automatically determine the time complexities of all other Π_j, and, most importantly, of our initial problem Π. We will give a detailed explanation how to apply this technique to infer bounds for the complexity of a problem in Section 2.1, but let us first consider a concrete application. We remark that, apart from the following application, our speedup theorem also semi-automatically reproduces previously known techniques, such as the sinkless orientation speedup [9] and color reduction on rings (leading to the $O(\log^* n)$ upper bound for 3-coloring a ring [14, 18]), as we will see in Section 4.4 (and Section 4.5 in the full version). Moreover, building on our speedup technique, Balliu et al. [2] very recently proved new lower bounds for maximal matching and maximal independent set, in both the deterministic and the randomized setting.

Odd-Degree Weak 2-Coloring. Weak k-coloring is the problem of coloring the nodes of a given input graph with k colors such that each node (of degree at least 1) has *at least one* neighbor with a different color. In their seminal work [22], Naor and Stockmeyer proved that in graphs where each node has odd degree, a weak 2-coloring can be found in time $O(\log^* \Delta)$. As one of their three open questions they asked whether this bound can be improved. While the question seemed simple enough, surprisingly no progress has been made over the past 25 years, indicating that the available lower bound techniques might not be sufficient for showing that the upper bound is tight. Using our speedup results, we close this gap by showing the following theorem.

THEOREM 5.2. *There is no $o(\log^* \Delta)$-time algorithm solving weak 2-coloring in odd-degree graphs.*

Given the speedup framework, the main technical ingredient in our proof is a generalization of weak 2-coloring to a problem we call *superweak k-coloring* that has the following two nice properties:

(1) If we set Π to be superweak k-coloring, then the problem Π_1 obtained by applying our speedup is at least as hard as superweak k'-coloring, for some $k' > k$.
(2) Relaxing Π_1 to superweak k'-coloring (and then continuing to apply the speedup technique) is sufficiently *tight*, in the sense that we essentially still need $\Omega(\log^* \Delta)$ speedup steps until we obtain a 0-round solvable problem.

More concretely, a rough proof outline goes as follows. Relax weak 2-coloring to superweak 2-coloring, apply our speedup, relax the obtained problem to superweak k-coloring for some $k > 2$, apply our speedup, relax to superweak k'-coloring for some $k' > k$, etc. Then, show that any problem obtained after $o(\log^* \Delta)$ steps of speedup and relaxation is still not solvable in 0 rounds. Our speedup results then immediately imply that there is no $o(\log^* \Delta)$-algorithm for weak 2-coloring.

1.2 Related Work

Follow-up Work. In a recent breakthrough, Balliu et al. [2] used our speedup technique to show that, both for maximal matching and maximal independent set, there is no randomized algorithm with runtime $o(\Delta + \log \log n / \log \log \log n)$ and no deterministic algorithm with runtime $o(\Delta + \log n / \log \log n)$. As documented in [2, Section 3.7], apart from the speedup provided by Theorem 4.1, the authors also apply both of our simplification techniques (see Section 2.1) to achieve their lower bounds.

Further Related Work. The first occurrence of the round elimination speedup technique we extend to any locally checkable problem was seen in [9], where the authors show that such a speedup works for the problem of (Δ-regular) sinkless orientation, resulting in a randomized lower bound of $\Omega(\log \log n)$ that also applies to the (constructive symmetric) distributed Lovász Local Lemma (LLL) and Δ-coloring. In [12], Chang et al. proved that this result can be extended to a deterministic lower bound of $\Omega(\log_\Delta n)$, which is tight (for sinkless orientation) due to a matching upper bound by Ghaffari and Su [17], who also gave a matching upper bound for the deterministic case. Chang and Pettie [13] conjectured that the (randomized) lower bound for the distributed LLL is tight for sufficiently relaxed LLL criteria; despite a recent improvement of the upper bound by Ghaffari et al. [16], this conjecture is still open. In [11], Chang et al. simplified the randomized speedup technique of [9] and showed that the sinkless orientation lower bounds also imply an $\Omega(\log_\Delta n)$ deterministic and an $\Omega(\log_\Delta \log n)$ randomized lower bound for $(2\Delta - 2)$-edge coloring.

Weak k-coloring on odd-degree graphs was introduced by Naor and Stockmeyer [22] as an example of a non-trivial problem that can be solved in constant time *on graphs of bounded degree.* As they show, the odd-degree condition is a necessary requirement; there are graph classes where nodes are allowed to have even degrees for which no constant-time weak coloring algorithm exists. Very recently, Balliu et al. [5] refined our knowledge in this regard by proving a tight lower bound of $\Omega(\log^* n)$ for weak 2-coloring on regular trees. While, from a theory perspective, weak coloring is interesting as "a problem with minimal symmetry breaking requirements" [19, p.139], a more concrete application exists in the form of certain resource allocation problems [22]. Naor and Stockmeyer provided an $O(\log^* \Delta)$-algorithm for odd-degree weak 2-coloring, which was subsequently simplified and adapted to the dynamic setting by Mayer et al. [21]. While progress has been made for other relaxations of the standard node coloring problem, such as defective [6, 19] or arbdefective [7] coloring, the question by Naor and Stockmeyer whether their bound can be improved has remained open until now.

Naor and Stockmeyer's work also initiated, together with [20], the line of research on local algorithms, and introduced the concept of *locally checkable labeling* (LCL) problems. This class of problems has been subject to many investigations, resulting in an almost complete understanding of the respective complexity landscape very recently [3, 4, 9, 10, 12, 13, 15, 16]. We remark that, while our speedup applies to LCL problems, it is not restricted to them: in particular, we do not require the considered graphs to be of constant degree.

2 TECHNICAL OVERVIEW

In this section, we will outline how to apply the speedup technique to obtain new bounds, including further helpful techniques for the application of the speedup. Moreover, we will give an overview of the available techniques to extend bounds achieved from our speedup (in our model) to the LOCAL model and to randomized complexities.

2.1 How to Apply the Speedup Results

The most natural application of our speedup technique is to prove a lower bound for some given problem Π. The roadmap is as follows. Starting with Π, we apply our speedup theorem iteratively, resulting in a problem sequence $\Pi, \Pi_1, \Pi_2, \ldots$, where each problem can be solved exactly one round faster than the previous one. Given the mentioned conditions, our speedup works until we reach a problem that can be solved in 0 rounds; hence, in theory, the only thing we have to do is to look at our sequence $\Pi, \Pi_1, \Pi_2, \ldots$ and to determine which is the first problem in this sequence that is solvable in 0 rounds (usually depending on our parameters n and/or Δ). If Π_t is the first problem solvable in 0 rounds, the problem Π we are interested in has time complexity t. However, since Theorem 4.1 requires girth at least $2t + 2$, only the *lower* bound of t holds for general graphs.

While 0-round solvable problems have a simple characterization, there is a catch: in general, the description of an inferred problem Π_i is much more complex than the description of the original problem. In fact, dealing with this explosion in complexity is one of the main challenges in applying our speedup. To this end, we provide two simplification techniques.

Relaxation. After inferring a new problem Π_{i+1} from Π_i via the speedup, we can try to find a relaxed version of Π_{i+1} (i.e., a problem that is provably not harder than Π_{i+1}) that has a much simpler description, and use this problem as the starting point for the next speedup step. Alternating between relaxation and speedup, we continue this process until we reach a problem Π_t that is solvable in 0 rounds. Then t is a *lower bound* for the time complexity of our initial problem Π. Of course, we can also stop before we reach a 0-round solvable problem, and the respective index of the problem is also a lower bound.

If, informally speaking, we relax the problems obtained after each speedup step too much, the lower bound we obtain in the end might be asymptotically worse than the correct (tight) bound, or no improvement on existing bounds at all, so finding the right relaxation is a challenging problem. Moreover, in order to avoid having to find "good" relaxations for many very different problems, it is desirable to find relaxed problems that are *similar* (perhaps with different parameters of some kind) to *previous* problems in the problem sequence. The above outline captures exactly what we do in our lower bound for weak 2-coloring.

We remark that a dual version of the relaxation technique exists, where we obtain upper bounds on high-girth graphs by making problems harder instead of relaxing them. We will see a concrete example for this dual technique when we consider color reduction on rings as a special case of our speedup in Section 4.5 (in the full version).

Description Simplification. As the second tool in our toolbox for managing the increasing description complexity, we provide a "maximality constraint" that can be applied twice per speedup step in order to decrease the set of allowed outputs and thereby simplify the problem. Despite its simplicity, this technique can significantly reduce the description complexity of a problem, as we will see in Section 4.5. As we show in Theorem 4.3, this simplification comes at no cost, keeping the complexity of the problem under consideration as it is.

2.2 How to Lift Bounds to the LOCAL Model.

A requirement for our speedup result is that the class of input graphs satisfies a property that we call t-independence. Informally, a graph class is t-independent if the following holds: If any node[1] v that has gathered all information in its radius-$(t-1)$ neighborhood extends its view by one hop along some edge, then the new information v obtains does not affect what information v might see if it extends its view by one hop along any other edge. In particular, if the nodes are equipped with globally unique identifiers, then t-independence does not hold: if a node sees some ID in the extended view along some edge, it knows that this ID cannot be in any of the extended views along the other edges, due to our girth condition. While almost every other kind of symmetry breaking information commonly used, such as node colorings, edge colorings, edge orientations, or combinations thereof, satisfy t-independence, extending bounds obtained by our speedup technique to the setting with unique IDs, i.e., the LOCAL model, requires additional techniques. Note that *upper* bounds obtained by our technique immediately apply to the LOCAL model (as basically every other symmetry breaking information can be inferred from unique IDs), hence we will focus on lower bounds in the following.

Method I: Randomization. As demonstrated in [2, 9], by explicitly incorporating error probabilities into the speedup steps, lower bounds in our setting can be lifted to the randomized LOCAL model (which essentially guarantees t-independence since no unique IDs are required). The obtained bounds are weaker than the original bounds from our setting, which is to be expected considering that allowing randomization can only lower the complexity of a problem. In a second step, the randomized bounds can then be lifted to the (deterministic) LOCAL model, by exploiting gaps in the complexity

[1] If we want to be a bit more precise, the same also has to hold for any edge, where for simplicity, we also consider edges as computational entities.

landscape of so-called LCL problems [12], or by explicitly showing that the existence of a deterministic algorithm of some complexity would imply the existence of a randomized algorithm that violates the randomized lower bound [2]. The available evidence [2, 12] suggests that this detour via the randomized complexity does not weaken the deterministic bound: in both cases, the bound in our setting is identical to the bound in the LOCAL model. This is not too surprising since the uniqueness of IDs might simply not be enough to change the complexity of a problem (as compared to, say, a setting with non-unique IDs); however, a proof for this is not known and would be a valuable step forward.

Method II: Order-Invariant Algorithms. A second technique to lift bounds to the LOCAL model comes into play when we are interested in time complexities as a function of the maximum node degree Δ of the input graph. By a result of Naor and Stockmeyer [22], if there is a constant-time algorithm solving a locally checkable problem in the LOCAL model, then there is also an order-invariant algorithm with the same runtime, where order-invariant indicates that any node only uses the *relative* IDs, i.e., the order of the IDs it sees, but not the actual ID values, in order to determine its output. Hence, if there is an algorithm solving a locally checkable problem with runtime independent of n, then we can essentially restrict attention to order-invariant algorithms. We provide an extension of our speedup result (Theorem 4.4) that shows that for order-invariant algorithms our speedup holds also in the case of unique IDs, i.e., in the LOCAL model. We will make use of this extension when we prove our lower bound for weak 2-coloring (in the LOCAL model).

3 PRELIMINARIES

Graphs. We denote the set of nodes of a graph G by $V(G)$ and the set of edges by $E(G)$, and we set $n := |V(G)|$. We write $d(v)$ for the degree of a node v and denote the maximum node degree of a graph by Δ. The *girth* of a graph is the length of the smallest cycle.

An important component in designing and proving our speedup is the idea to split the output of a node into parts that *belong* to incident edges. As the basis for a convenient representation of such a split output, define $B(G)$ as the set of all pairs (v, e) where $e \in E(G)$ and $v \in V(G)$ is an endpoint of e. Finally, for a graph class $\mathcal{G}$, we denote the subclass of $\mathcal{G}$ consisting of the contained graphs with n nodes and maximum degree Δ by $\mathcal{G}_{n,\Delta}$, for all non-negative integers n, Δ. Similarly, the subclass of graphs with maximum degree Δ is denoted by $\mathcal{G}_\Delta$.

Input-Labeled Graphs. Commonly, locally checkable problems are defined by allowed configurations of output labels and a specification of the given inputs and the considered graph class. We will strictly separate between the outputs on one side (which will define what we call a problem) and the inputs and the graph class on the other side (which will be given by input-labeled graphs).

For the definition of input-labeled graphs, we will also use the set $B(G)$ defined above, which allows for a convenient way to encode, e.g., edge orientations. Furthermore, we will not restrict attention to graphs with bounded degree or to bounded input label sets; instead we will use the following more complicated, but also more general definition, which allows, e.g., to define graph classes of unbounded degree with an input edge coloring (which requires $\Omega(\Delta)$ labels), or unique IDs (which come from a set that is a function of n).

Let Σ be a (possibly infinite) set of input labels and $\iota : \mathbb{N}^2 \to 2^\Sigma$ a function such that $\Sigma_{n,\Delta} := \iota(n, \Delta)$ is a *finite* subset of Σ, for all $(n, \Delta) \in \mathbb{N}^2$. A Σ-input-labeled graph is a pair (G, φ_G), where G is a graph and φ_G is a function $\varphi_G : B(G) \to \Sigma_{n,\Delta}$, where n and Δ are the number of nodes and the maximum degree of G, respectively. We will usually omit the function φ_G and simply denote the Σ-input-labeled graph by G. We extend the notion of being Σ-input-labeled to graph classes and say that a graph class $\mathcal{G}$ is Σ-input-labeled if each graph in $\mathcal{G}$ is Σ-input-labeled.

Problems. The speedup results we present apply to all locally checkable problems; however, formally, we will only consider problems where the validity of a global output essentially[2] can be checked on edges, i.e., there is a set of acceptable output configurations for the two endpoints of an edge, and the global output is correct if and only if the configuration for each edge is acceptable. Restriction to these problems does not lose generality for our purposes: by requiring that each node outputs the computed output labels (and the topology[3]) of its whole radius-r neighborhood for some suitably large constant r, any locally checkable problem can be transformed into an edge-checkable[2] problem with the same asymptotic time complexity.

Formally, for the scope of this paper, a problem Π is defined by

(1) a (possibly infinite) set O of output labels,
(2) a function $f : \mathbb{N} \to 2^O$ such that $f(\Delta)$ is a *finite* subset of O, for all $\Delta \in \mathbb{N}$,
(3) a function g that maps each $\Delta \in \mathbb{N}$ to a set of 2-element multisets where both elements are taken from $f(\Delta)$, and
(4) a function h that maps each $\Delta \in \mathbb{N}$ to a set of multisets with at most Δ elements, all taken from $f(\Delta)$.

The specification of f ensures that problems that require the set of output labels to depend on Δ, such as $(\Delta + 1)$-coloring, are included in our problem definition. The sets $g(\Delta)$ and $h(\Delta)$ formalize which output configurations are allowed on an edge $e = \{u, v\}$ (i.e., at $(u, e) \in B(G)$ and $(v, e) \in B(G)$), resp. at a node v (i.e., at $(v, e_1), \ldots, (v, e_{d(v)})$, where $e_1, \ldots, e_{d(v)}$ are the edges incident to v). For instance, the problem of $(\Delta+1)$-coloring can be described by setting $O := \mathbb{N}^+$, $f(\Delta) := \{1, \ldots, \Delta + 1\}$, $g(\Delta) := \{\{c_1, c_2\} \mid c_1, c_2 \in f(\Delta), c_1 \neq c_2\}$, $h(\Delta) := \{\{c_1, \ldots, c_i\} \mid 0 \leq i \leq \Delta, c_1 = \cdots = c_i\}$.

Combining problems and input-labeled graphs, we define a *realized problem* as a pair $(\Pi, \mathcal{G})$, where Π is a problem and $\mathcal{G}$ a Σ-input-labeled graph class. We say that an algorithm $\mathcal{A}$ solves a realized problem $(\Pi, \mathcal{G})$ (or, equivalently, that $\mathcal{A}$ solves Π on $\mathcal{G}$) if, for any Δ and any graph $G \in \mathcal{G}_\Delta$, $\mathcal{A}$ assigns an output $o_{v,e} \in f(\Delta)$ to each pair $(v, e) \in B(G)$ such that, for each edge $e = \{u, v\} \in E(G)$, the multiset $\{o_{u,e}, o_{v,e}\}$ is contained in $g(\Delta)$, and for each node $v \in V(G)$, the multiset $\{o_{v,e_1}, \ldots, o_{v,e_{d(v)}}\}$ is contained in $h(\Delta)$.

[2]Due to our particular way of splitting the output of a node into partial outputs for each incident edge, our formal definition of a problem will contain acceptable configurations for both edges and nodes; a more precise term for edge-checkability would thus be node-and-edge-checkability.

[3]Note that in general graphs where nodes do not have unique identifiers, the information a node obtains in t rounds may not be enough to determine the exact topology of the subgraph induced by all nodes in distance at most t; however, since we will only consider radius-t neighborhoods in graphs that have girth at least $2t + 2$, the subgraph topology in each radius-t neighborhood is a tree which implies that each node can determine the exact topology of its radius-t neighborhood.

Model. Since we defined inputs to be part of the considered graph class, we can use a very weak model of computation, which is why we formally choose the port numbering model [1] as our model of computation. In the port numbering model, each node v of the input graph $G \in \mathcal{G}$ has $d(v)$ many ports $1, \ldots, d(v)$ which correspond to the edges incident to v; the two endpoints of an edge may have different ports corresponding to the connecting edge. Each node can communicate with its neighbors by sending messages along the connecting edges. Computation proceeds in synchronous rounds where in each round each node first sends arbitrarily large messages to its neighbors and then, upon receiving the messages sent by its neighbors, performs some arbitrarily complex local computation. Each node executes the same algorithm and has to terminate at some point, upon which it outputs its local part of the global solution (e.g., if the task is to find a proper node coloring, each node outputs its own color). The runtime of such a distributed algorithm is the number of rounds until the last node terminates. In the beginning of the computation, each node v is aware of the parameters n and Δ and sees the input label assigned to $(v, e) \in B(G)$ for all incident edges e, i.e., one input label per port. When terminating, a node v assigns an output label from $f(\Delta)$ to each (v, e). We are interested in the *worst-case* runtime of a distributed algorithm, i.e., for worst-case input-labeled graphs with worst-case assignments of port numbers to edges.

A distributed algorithm is correct if the output labels assigned to the elements in $B(G)$ satisfy the constraints encoded in $g(\Delta)$ and $h(\Delta)$ at each edge, resp. node. More precisely, we say that a distributed algorithm solves a realized problem $(\Pi, \mathcal{G})$ if the above is true for each graph $G \in \mathcal{G}$ (where $f(\Delta), g(\Delta), h(\Delta)$ are defined by Π). In this work, we formally only consider deterministic algorithms; the implications for randomized algorithms have been discussed in Section 2.2.

t-Independence. As mentioned in Section 2.2, our speedup results require a property called t-independence. This property essentially only exists in graph classes with sufficiently high girth which is the reason why we restrict attention to these classes of graphs. We defer the formal (quite cumbersome) definition of t-independence to the full version; the important intuitive characterization to keep in mind is the following: If the considered graph class contains globally unique IDs as inputs, t-independence is not satisfied; if the graph class instead only contains node colorings, edge colorings, edge orientations, or combinations thereof as input, t-independence is satisfied.

4 THE SPEEDUP THEOREM

In this section, we will present our speedup results and apply them to several problems (see full version for all considered problems). We start by defining our automatic speedup that produces a sequence of problems with decreasing runtimes, and subsequently prove our main theorem (Section 4.1). In Section 4.2, we introduce an important simplification technique that reduces the complexity of the descriptions of the problems in our sequence (by transforming the problems) and show that this technique is compatible with the main theorem. Then we prove that the main theorem can be extended to settings with unique IDs if we restrict attention to order-invariant algorithms (Section 4.3). In Section 4.4 and (and Section 4.5 in the full version), we will see how to obtain two known results by applying our speedup, confirming the viability and generality of the speedup technique. Finally, in Section 4.5, we will examine the effect of our speedup on weak 2-coloring, giving some intuition for the generalization of weak 2-coloring that is essential for our lower bound proof in Section 5.

4.1 The Theorem

Our speedup consists of two steps: First we transform Π into an intermediate problem $\Pi_{1/2}$, then we transform $\Pi_{1/2}$ into the problem Π_1 that can be solved one round faster than Π.

Deriving Problems. Let Π be a problem, and let O be the set of output labels and f, g, h the functions used to define Π. We define the problem $\Pi_{1/2}$ by specifying the set $O_{1/2}$ of output labels and the three required functions $f_{1/2}, g_{1/2}$, and $h_{1/2}$ as follows.

We set $O_{1/2} := 2^O$ and $f_{1/2}(\Delta) := 2^{f(\Delta)}$, and we define $g_{1/2}(\Delta)$ as the set of all multisets $\{Y, Z\}$, where $Y, Z \in f_{1/2}(\Delta)$, with the following property:

(1) For any $y \in Y, z \in Z$, the multiset $\{y, z\}$ is contained in $g(\Delta)$.

We define $h_{1/2}(\Delta)$ as the set of all multisets $\{Y_1, \ldots, Y_i\}$, where $i \leq \Delta$ and $Y_1, \ldots, Y_i \in f_{1/2}(\Delta)$, with the following property:

(2) There exist elements $y_1 \in Y_1, \ldots, y_i \in Y_i$ such that the multiset $\{y_1, \ldots, y_i\}$ is contained in $h(\Delta)$.

Similarly to how we derived $\Pi_{1/2}$ from Π, we will now derive Π_1 from $\Pi_{1/2}$. More precisely, Π_1 is defined as follows. We set $O_1 := 2^{O_{1/2}}$ and $f_1(\Delta) := 2^{f_{1/2}(\Delta)}$, and we define $g_1(\Delta)$ as the set of all multisets $\{Y, Z\}$, where $Y, Z \in f_1(\Delta)$, with the following property:

(3) There exist elements $y \in Y, z \in Z$ such that the multiset $\{y, z\}$ is contained in $g_{1/2}(\Delta)$.

We define $h_1(\Delta)$ as the set of all multisets $\{Y_1, \ldots, Y_i\}$, where $i \leq \Delta$ and $Y_1, \ldots, Y_i \in f_1(\Delta)$, with the following property:

(4) For any $y_1 \in Y_1, \ldots, y_i \in Y_i$, the multiset $\{y_1, \ldots, y_i\}$ is contained in $h_{1/2}(\Delta)$.

For an illustration of the definitions, we refer to the concrete examples in Sections 4.4 and 4.5. In the same way as we derived $\Pi_{1/2}$ and Π_1 from Π, we can derive problems $\Pi_{3/2}$ and Π_2 from Π_1. In general, set $\Pi_0 := \Pi$, and for any positive integer k, define recursively $\Pi_{k+1/2} := (\Pi_k)_{1/2}$ and $\Pi_{k+1} := (\Pi_k)_1$.

Theorem 4.1. *Consider some arbitrary problem Π and the derived problem Π_1. Let $\mathcal{G}_{n,\Delta}$ be a Σ-input-labeled graph class consisting of n-node graphs with maximum degree Δ. Assume that $\mathcal{G}_{n,\Delta}$ is t-independent for some positive integer t and contains only graphs of girth at least $2t + 2$. Then, the following two statements are equivalent:*

(1) There is an algorithm solving $(\Pi, \mathcal{G}_{n,\Delta})$ in time t.
(2) There is an algorithm solving $(\Pi_1, \mathcal{G}_{n,\Delta})$ in time $t - 1$.

Theorem 4.1 provides an explicit version of our speedup guarantees for graph classes $\mathcal{G}_{n,\Delta}$. We formulate the implications for general graph classes in the following corollary of Theorem 4.1.

Corollary 4.2. *Consider some arbitrary problem Π, and let $\mathcal{G}$ be a Σ-input-labeled graph class and $T : \mathbb{N} \times \mathbb{N} \to \mathbb{N}^+$ some function. If, for all $n, \Delta \in \mathbb{N}$, it holds that $\mathcal{G}_{n,\Delta}$ is $T(n, \Delta)$-independent and* *contains only graphs of girth at least $2T(n, \Delta) + 2$, then the following two statements are equivalent:*

(1) *There is an algorithm solving $(\Pi, \mathcal{G})$ in time $T(n, \Delta)$.*
(2) *There is an algorithm solving $(\Pi_1, \mathcal{G})$ in time $T(n, \Delta) - 1$.*

Note that Theorem 4.1 and Corollary 4.2 do not contradict the existence of known gaps [12, 13, 22] in the time complexity landscape of LCL problems since the problem obtained after applying our speedup a non-constant number of times is not necessarily an LCL problem anymore (but is still locally checkable).

4.2 Simplification via Maximality

Simplified Problems. We obtain the simplified version $\Pi'_{1/2}$ of $\Pi_{1/2}$ by replacing Property 1 in the description of $\Pi_{1/2}$ by the following extension:

(5) For any $y \in Y, z \in Z$, the multiset $\{y, z\}$ is contained in $g(\Delta)$ and the sets Y and Z are maximal with this property, i.e., for any $Y' \supsetneq Y$, the multiset $\{Y', Z\}$ does not satisfy Property 1, and for any $Z' \supsetneq Z$, the multiset $\{Y, Z'\}$ does not satisfy Property 1.

Analogously, we obtain the simplified version of Π_1 by replacing Property 4 by the following extension:

(6) For any $y_1 \in Y_1, \ldots, y_i \in Y_i$, the multiset $\{y_1, \ldots, y_i\}$ is contained in $h_{1/2}(\Delta)$ and the sets $Y_1, \ldots, Y_i$ are maximal with this property, i.e., for any $1 \leq j \leq i$, it holds that, for any $Y'_j \supsetneq Y_j$, the multiset $\{Y_1, \ldots, Y_{j-1}, Y'_j, Y_{j+1}, \ldots, Y_i\}$ does not satisfy Property 4.

However, just performing the latter replacement as it is will result in a (simplified) problem that is derived from $\Pi_{1/2}$, not from $\Pi'_{1/2}$. Hence, we define Π'_1 by not only performing the above replacement, but also replacing $g_{1/2}$ by $g'_{1/2}$ in Property 3, where $g'_{1/2}$ is the analogue to $g_{1/2}$ in $\Pi'_{1/2}$ (and actually the only part in which the definitions of $\Pi_{1/2}$ and $\Pi'_{1/2}$ differ). Now, similarly to above we can define simplified problems recursively for any positive k by setting $\Pi'_{k+1/2} := (\Pi'_k)'_{1/2}$ and $\Pi'_{k+1} := (\Pi'_k)'_1$.

THEOREM 4.3. *If we augment the conditions of Theorem 4.1 by the requirement that the inputs for the graphs from $\mathcal{G}_{n,\Delta}$ contain an orientation for each edge, then the following two statements are equivalent:*

(1) *There is an algorithm solving $(\Pi, \mathcal{G}_{n,\Delta})$ in time t.*
(2) *There is an algorithm solving $(\Pi'_1, \mathcal{G}_{n,\Delta})$ in time $t - 1$.*

4.3 Order-Invariant Algorithms

THEOREM 4.4. *Consider some arbitrary problem Π and the derived problems Π_1 and Π'_1. Let $\mathcal{G}_{n,\Delta}$ be a Σ-input-labeled graph class consisting of n-node graphs with maximum degree Δ. Assume that $\mathcal{G}_{n,\Delta}$ is t-independent for some positive integer t and contains only graphs of girth at least $2t + 2$. Let $S \subseteq \mathbb{N}^+$ be a finite set of identifiers satisfying $|S| \geq 4\Delta^{2t}$. Let $\mathcal{G}'_{n,\Delta}$ be the class consisting of all (input-labeled) graphs obtained by taking a graph from $\mathcal{G}_{n,\Delta}$ and assigning unique identifiers from S to the nodes of the graph. Then, the following statements are equivalent:*

(1) *There is an order-invariant algorithm solving $(\Pi, \mathcal{G}'_{n,\Delta})$ in time t.*
(2) *There is an order-invariant algorithm solving $(\Pi_1, \mathcal{G}'_{n,\Delta})$ in time $t - 1$.*
(3) *There is an order-invariant algorithm solving $(\Pi'_1, \mathcal{G}'_{n,\Delta})$ in time $t - 1$.*

4.4 Warm-up: Sinkless Coloring and Sinkless Orientation

In this section, we will apply our speedup technique to the problem of sinkless orientation. As we will see, our technique gives a deterministic version of the randomized speedup for sinkless orientation presented in [9], showing that our speedup in some sense encompasses known techniques for concrete problems as special cases. In particular, the duality between sinkless orientation and sinkless coloring which is essential for the lower bound proof in [9] is automatically produced by our speedup.

The problem of sinkless coloring (as it is given in [9]) is defined as follows: Given a Δ-regular edge Δ-colored graph, each node has to output an orientation for each incident edge such that the two endpoints of an edge agree on the orientation of the edge and each node has at least one outgoing edge.

While our speedup does not require the edge coloring, we will add edge orientations to the input in order to be able to apply our simplification technique. Note that adding edge orientations or some other symmetry breaking information as input is *required* in the deterministic case since the random bits used to break symmetry in the randomized case are not available and the edge coloring alone is not sufficient for breaking symmetry.

While it is possible to set our initial problem Π to be sinkless orientation (in which case the derived problem $\Pi_{1/2}$ is also sinkless orientation, roughly speaking because the output for sinkless orientation describes an *edge* property), it is more natural to choose Π to be the dual problem called sinkless coloring (since for this problem the output describes a *node* property). Sinkless coloring is defined as follows: Given a Δ-regular edge Δ-colored graph, each node has to output one of the edge colors such that at least one of the two endpoints of any edge outputs a different color than the color of the edge.

Due to our choice of having one output per element of $B(G)$, not per node, there is a simple (and canonical) way to encode this problem in our setting, even without an input edge coloring. Define Π as follows (where an output of 1 at (v, e) indicates that v chooses the color of e). Set

$$\begin{aligned} f(\Delta) &:= O := \{0, 1\} \ , \\ g(\Delta) &:= \{\{0, 0\}, \{0, 1\}\} \ , \\ h(\Delta) &:= \{\{0, \ldots, 0, 1\}\} \ , \end{aligned}$$

where the only element of $h(\Delta)$ is a multiset with Δ elements. Applying our speedup transformation, we obtain for the derived problem $\Pi_{1/2}$

$$\begin{aligned} f_{1/2}(\Delta) &= O_{1/2} = \{ \ \{\}, \quad \{0\}, \quad \{1\}, \quad \{0, 1\} \ \} \ , \\ g_{1/2}(\Delta) &= \{ \ \{\{0\}, \{0\}\}, \quad \{\{0\}, \{1\}\}, \quad \{\{0\}, \{0, 1\}\} \ \} \ , \\ h_{1/2}(\Delta) &= \{\{Y_1, \ldots, Y_\Delta\} \mid Y_i \in f_{1/2}(\Delta) \text{ for all } 1 \leq i \leq \Delta, \\ &\qquad 1 \in Y_1, 0 \in Y_j \text{ for all } 2 \leq j \leq \Delta\} \ . \end{aligned}$$

Applying our simplification technique, we see that the only element of $g_{1/2}(\Delta)$ that is maximal is $\{\{0\}\{0,1\}\}$. Hence, we obtain for $\Pi'_{1/2}$

$$f_{1/2}(\Delta) = O_{1/2} = \{ \ \{0\}, \ \ \{0,1\} \ \ \} ,$$
$$g_{1/2}(\Delta) = \{ \ \ \{\{0\},\{0,1\}\} \ \ \} ,$$
$$h_{1/2}(\Delta) = \{\{Y_1,\dots,Y_\Delta\} \mid Y_i \in f_{1/2}(\Delta) \text{ for all } 1 \le i \le \Delta, \ Y_1 = \{0,1\}\} .$$

Writing 0 for $\{0\}$ and 1 for $\{0,1\}$, we can describe $\Pi'_{1/2}$ equivalently by

$$f_{1/2}(\Delta) = O_{1/2} := \{0,1\} ,$$
$$g_{1/2}(\Delta) = \{\{0,1\}\} ,$$
$$h_{1/2}(\Delta) = \{\{Y_1,\dots,Y_\Delta\} \mid Y_i \in \{0,1\} \text{ for all } 1 \le i \le \Delta, Y_1 = 1\} .$$

This specification describes exactly the problem of sinkless orientation, where an output of 1 at (v,e) indicates that v orients e away from itself, and an output of 0 at (v,e) that v orients e towards itself. Now, deriving $\Pi_{1/2}$ leads to the problem Π_1 specified by

$$f_1(\Delta) = O_1 = \{ \ \ \{\}, \ \ \{0\}, \ \ \{1\}, \ \ \{0,1\} \ \ \} ,$$
$$g_1(\Delta) = \{\{Y,Z\} \mid Y,Z \in f_1(\Delta), 0 \in Y, 1 \in Z\} ,$$
$$h_1(\Delta) = \{\{Y_1,\dots,Y_\Delta\} \mid Y_i \in f_1(\Delta) \setminus \{\emptyset\} \text{ for all } 1 \le i \le \Delta, \ Y_1 = \{1\}\}$$

Observing that $h_1(\Delta)$ contains only one maximal element, namely $\{\{1\},\{0,1\},\dots,\{0,1\}\}$, we see that Π'_1 is given by

$$f_1(\Delta) = O_1 = \{ \ \ \{1\}, \ \ \{0,1\} \ \ \} ,$$
$$g_1(\Delta) = \{ \ \ \{\{0,1\},\{1\}\}, \ \ \{\{0,1\},\{0,1\}\} \ \ \} ,$$
$$h_1(\Delta) = \{ \ \ \{\{1\},\{0,1\},\dots,\{0,1\}\} \ \ \} .$$

Writing 0 for $\{0,1\}$ and 1 for $\{1\}$, we see that we are back at sinkless coloring, i.e., $\Pi_1 = \Pi$.

Applying Theorem 4.3 iteratively, we see that the existence of a t-independent graph class $G_{n,\Delta}$ of girth at least $2t+2$ implies that any t-round algorithm for sinkless coloring can be transformed into a 0-round algorithm for sinkless coloring. Since the latter does not exist, whereas, for any $\Delta \ge 3$, such high-girth t-independent graph classes exist for some $t \in \Omega(\log n)$ (as can be shown using [8, Chapter III, Theorem 1.4′], or, in the case of an input edge-coloring, [9, Lemma 9]), we obtain an $\Omega(\log n)$ lower bound for sinkless coloring, and therefore also for sinkless orientation, for each $\Delta \ge 3$.

4.5 Weak 2-coloring

The goal of this section is to give an intuition for the generalization of weak 2-coloring we use to prove our lower bound in Section 5. Recall that, in order to apply our speedup technique iteratively without having to look at each problem in the produced problem sequence individually, we would like to start with a problem Π for which applying our speedup technique results in some problem that can be relaxed to a problem that is *very similar* to Π. Ideally, the relaxed problem is the same as Π except for that some parameters in the problem description are different. Also, our initial problem Π should be similar to the problem we want to prove a lower bound for, i.e., weak 2-coloring; the simplest case would be that Π is a relaxation of weak 2-coloring so that lower bounds for Π immediately apply to weak 2-coloring.

In order to obtain some intuition for the effects of our speedup on problems that are similar to weak 2-coloring, the obvious approach is to apply the speedup to weak 2-coloring itself, which we do in the following. Recall that in the weak 2-coloring (resp. weak k-coloring) problem, each node has to output a color from, say, the set $\{1,2\}$ (resp. $\{1,\dots,k\}$), such that there is at least one neighbor with a different color (or the node has no neighbors). Note that this formulation of the problem is not even edge-checkable; before we can apply our speedup we first have to bring weak 2-coloring in a form that adheres to our definition of a problem.

Problem Π. Consider the following problem Π: Each node has to output a color from $\{1,2\}$ and a pointer to an adjacent node. The output is correct if each node v points to a node that has a different color than v. Formally, we can describe Π by setting

$$f(\Delta) := O := \{1,2\} \times \{\rightarrow, \bullet\} ,$$
$$g(\Delta) := \{\{(y,y'),(z,z')\} \mid y,z \in \{1,2\}, y',z' \in \{\rightarrow,\bullet\}, \ y \ne z \vee y' = \bullet = z'\} ,$$
$$h(\Delta) := \{\{(y_1,y'_1),\dots,(y_\Delta,y'_\Delta)\} \mid y_1,\dots,y_\Delta \in \{1,2\}, \ y_1 = \dots = y_\Delta, y'_1 = \rightarrow, y'_2 = \dots = y'_\Delta = \bullet\} .$$

Note that, in the formal description, we use the fact that we are only interested in Δ-regular graphs since we will prove our lower bound in Section 5 already for this class of graphs.

Clearly, Π satisfies our definition of a problem; furthermore, we argue that if there is an algorithm solving weak 2-coloring, then it can be transformed into an algorithm for Π that requires only one additional round. This is easy to see: each node can learn the color of each adjacent node (according to the algorithm for weak 2-coloring) in this additional round and then point to a node of different color. We call Π the *pointer version* of weak 2-coloring; however, in this section we will simply refer to Π as weak 2-coloring (as it is essentially the same problem).

Problem $\Pi'_{1/2}$. In the following, we derive problem $\Pi'_{1/2}$ from Π. According to the process of deriving $\Pi'_{1/2}$, described in Sections 4.1 and 4.2, we obtain $f_{1/2}(\Delta) = O_{1/2} = 2^{\{1,2\}\times\{\rightarrow,\bullet\}}$. Furthermore, $h_{1/2}(\Delta)$ consists of all multisets $\{Y_1,\dots,Y_\Delta\}$ such that A) each Y_j is a subset of $\{1,2\}\times\{\rightarrow,\bullet\}$, and B) there is some $c \in \{1,2\}$ such that $(c,\rightarrow) \in Y_1$ and $(c,\bullet) \in Y_i$ for all $2 \le i \le \Delta$. The most interesting part of the definition of $\Pi'_{1/2}$ is $g_{1/2}(\Delta)$ as Property 5 comes into play here. Observe that for each multiset $\{Y,Z\}$ contained in $g_{1/2}(\Delta)$, it holds that if $(c,\rightarrow) \in Y$, then both $(c,\rightarrow)$ and $(c,\bullet)$ are not contained in Z. Taking the maximality constraint of Property 5 into account, we obtain that $g_{1/2}(\Delta)$ contains exactly the multisets $\{Y,Z\}$ where

$$Y = \{(1,\rightarrow),(1,\bullet),(2,\rightarrow),(2,\bullet)\}, \qquad Z = \{\}, \text{ or}$$
$$Y = \{(1,\rightarrow),(1,\bullet)\}, \qquad Z = \{(2,\rightarrow),(2,\bullet)\}, \text{ or}$$
$$Y = \{(1,\rightarrow),(1,\bullet),(2,\bullet)\}, \qquad Z = \{(2,\bullet)\}, \text{ or}$$
$$Y = \{(2,\rightarrow),(2,\bullet),(1,\bullet)\}, \qquad Z = \{(1,\bullet)\}, \text{ or}$$
$$Y = \{(1,\bullet),(2,\bullet)\}, \qquad Z = \{(1,\bullet),(2,\bullet)\}.$$

Note that the definition of $g_{1/2}(\Delta)$ allows for one of Y and Z being empty; however, our function $h_{1/2}(\Delta)$ ensures that an empty set cannot be chosen as output, thereby ruling out the first listed row as a possibility for outputs Y,Z on some edge. Hence, as we can see from the description of $g_{1/2}(\Delta)$, there are only 7 outputs that can be used by any correct algorithm for $\Pi'_{1/2}$. This indicates that there may be a simpler, or more accessible, (equivalent) description of $\Pi'_{1/2}$, and indeed there (arguably) is, as given in the following.

An Equivalent Description. We start by setting $f_{1/2}(\Delta) := O_{1/2} := \{01, 02, 10, 11, 12, 20, 21\}$, i.e., the set of allowed outputs is the set of all trit[4] sequences of length 2 excluding the two sequences 00 and 22. For any trit sequence $a = a_1 \dots a_k$ of length k, any $0 \leq i \leq 2$, and any $1 \leq j \leq k$, we say that *a has an i at position j* if $a_j = i$. Define $h_{1/2}(\Delta)$ to consist of all multisets of cardinality Δ of trit sequences from $f_{1/2}(\Delta)$ such that there is an index $1 \leq j \leq 2$ such that (at least) one of the trit sequences in the multiset has a 2 at position j and none of the trit sequences has a 0 at position j. Furthermore, define $g_{1/2}(\Delta)$ to be the set of multisets $\{a, a'\}$ of trit sequences from $f_{1/2}(\Delta)$ such that the tritwise addition of a and a' yields the trit sequence 22. For instance, the multiset $\{02, 11, \dots, 11, 12, 21\}$ of cardinality Δ is an element of $h_{1/2}(\Delta)$ (pick $j = 2$), and the multiset $\{01, 21\}$ is an element of $g_{1/2}(\Delta)$.

Why is this an equivalent description for $\Pi'_{1/2}$? Consider mapping the set of the "usable" 7 outputs in the initial description to our new output set $O_{1/2}$. More specifically, map each output Y to the trit sequence $a_1 a_2$ that satisfies that a_j is equal to the number of elements from $\{(j, \rightarrow), (j, \bullet)\}$ contained in Y. For instance, $Y = \{(2, \rightarrow), (2, \bullet), (1, \bullet)\}$ is mapped to the trit sequence 12, whereas $Y = \{(1, \rightarrow), (1, \bullet)\}$ is mapped to 20. Clearly, this mapping is a bijection. Note that if Y is mapped to a trit sequence $a_1 a_2$ satisfying $a_j = 1$ for some $1 \leq j \leq 2$, then $(j, \bullet)$ is contained in Y, whereas $(j, \rightarrow)$ is not. Using this observation, it is straightforward to check that the two functions $h_{1/2}(\Delta)$ in the two descriptions are equivalent. In order to see that the same holds for $g_{1/2}(\Delta)$, it is sufficient to observe that in the initial description of $\Pi'_{1/2}$, for each multiset (Y, Z) contained in $g_{1/2}(\Delta)$, the set $Y \cup Z$ contains exactly two elements where the first entry is 1, and exactly two elements, where the first entry is 2. Hence, our two definitions describe the same problem. We will use the second, arguably simpler description of $\Pi'_{1/2}$ for the next step on our agenda, i.e., for the task of deriving Π'_1 from $\Pi'_{1/2}$.

Problem Π'_1. According to the derivation process for Π'_1, we obtain $f_1(\Delta) = O_1 = 2^{O_{1/2}}$. Furthermore, $g_1(\Delta)$ consists of all multisets $\{W, X\}$ such that A) $W, X \subseteq \{01, 02, 10, 11, 12, 20, 21\}$, and B) there exist elements $w \in W, x \in X$ such that the tritwise sum of w and x is 22. Finally, $h_1(\Delta)$ consists of all multisets $\{W_1, \dots, W_\Delta\}$ of sets $W_i \subseteq \{01, 02, 10, 11, 12, 20, 21\}$ such that A) for any $w_1 \in W_1, \dots, w_\Delta \in W_\Delta$, there is an index $1 \leq j \leq 2$ such that (at least) one w_i has a 2 at position j and none of the w_i has a 0 at position j, and B) the multiset is maximal with Property A), i.e., if we add a new element from $\{01, 02, 10, 11, 12, 20, 21\}$ to some arbitrary W_i in the multiset, then the multiset does not satisfy Property A) anymore.

While the description of $g_1(\Delta)$ provides a good intuition for which 2-element multisets are actually contained in $g_1(\Delta)$, the maximality condition for $h_1(\Delta)$ makes it harder to see the same for $h_1(\Delta)$. In fact, $h_1(\Delta)$ is an excellent example for the power of the simplification technique introduced in Section 4.2: with some work, it is possible to show that $h_1(\Delta)$ actually contains only 9 elements (or fewer if Δ is very small)! As the goal of this section is merely to provide intuition for our lower bound approach in Section 5, we will only highlight the important observations that can be made by examining those 9 elements.

Problem Π^*_1. As outlined in the beginning of this section, we would like to relax Π'_1 to a problem Π^*_1 that is similar to weak coloring and has a simpler description. A very natural idea is to try to relax Π'_1 to weak 9-coloring as follows. Map each of the 9 elements of $h_1(\Delta)$ to a different color and then show that any algorithm $\mathcal{A}$ for Π'_1 also solves weak 9-coloring in the following way: Each node v executes $\mathcal{A}$ to determine the outputs at all (v, e), then checks which element of $h_1(\Delta)$ the outputs constitute together, and finally outputs the color corresponding to the element of $h_1(\Delta)$ at each (v, e). On top of that, each node (somehow) infers from its output according to $\mathcal{A}$ an adjacent node it can safely point to (i.e. an adjacent node that must have a different color).

While for most of the 9 elements in $h_1(\Delta)$ this approach can be made to work[5], there is one element in $h_1(\Delta)$ that some node v and *all* its neighbors might "output" (if we gather all partial outputs of the respective node according to algorithm $\mathcal{A}$). In other words, the envisioned solution of $\mathcal{A}$ for weak 9-coloring can make v and all its neighbors output the same color, which makes it impossible for v to output a correct pointer. However, this particular element of $h_1(\Delta)$ (recall that such an element is a multiset of cardinality Δ) has a very special form: we can write it as $Q = \{Q_1, Q_2, Q_3, Q_4, \dots, Q_4\}$, where $\{Q_1, Q_3\}$ and $\{Q_2, Q_3\}$ are the only two elements of $g_1(\Delta)$ that involve Q_1 or Q_2 (i.e., if the outputs of two adjacent nodes u, v according to $\mathcal{A}$ both correspond to Q and the output at (u, e) is Q_1 or Q_2, then the output at (v, e) must be Q_3, where $e = \{u, v\}$).

This leads to the idea of modifying our weak 9-coloring problem slightly: Instead of having to output one pointer that has to point to a differently colored node, a node v can also choose to output two pointers and one "inverse pointer" (at three different (v, e)), where a (non-inverse) pointer has to point to a differently colored node or to an inverse pointer. For this modified problem, any node v has a simple way to infer a correct output if its output according to $\mathcal{A}$ corresponds to Q: node v simply outputs a pointer at the two (v, e) where $\mathcal{A}$ outputs Q_1 or Q_2, and an inverse pointer at the one (v, e) where $\mathcal{A}$ outputs Q_3.

As it turns out, this particular property of Q is not an isolated case but *characteristic* for problems Π'_1 that are derived from the problems we generalize weak 2-coloring to. More precisely, for any such Π'_1 and any Q in the corresponding $h_1(\Delta)$, we can essentially write Q as $\{Q_1, \dots Q_i, Q'_1, \dots, Q'_j, Q''_1, \dots, Q''_\ell\}$ such that 1) $i > j$, and 2) if two nodes u, v connected by an edge e both output Q, and u outputs some element from $\{Q_1, \dots Q_i\}$ at (u, e), then v has to output some element from $\{Q'_1, \dots, Q'_j\}$ at (v, e) (by the definition of the corresponding $g_1(\Delta)$). This insight suggests the generalization of weak 2-coloring that we present in Section 5.

[4] A trit is the ternary analogue of a bit.

[5] In fact, using several speedup-related tricks, it is possible to relax Π'_1 to to weak 11-coloring; however, these tricks seem to apply only for our very specific case of Π being weak 2-coloring and do not generalize to weak k-coloring or similar problems.

5 A TIGHT LOWER BOUND FOR ODD-DEGREE WEAK 2-COLORING

This section is devoted to proving a lower bound for weak 2-coloring on odd-degree graphs that matches the upper bound presented by Naor and Stockmeyer [22]. In Section 5.1, we will introduce the problem of superweak k-coloring, which is a generalization of weak 2-coloring, and prove a speedup lemma (Lemma 5.1) for this new problem via a series of technical lemmas (see full version). More precisely, we show that we can save one round in the runtime if we increase the parameter k in the problem definition exponentially (a constant number of times). Subsequently, in Section 5.2, we will use the speedup lemma to prove our lower bound, i.e., we prove that there is no algorithm solving weak 2-coloring in time $o(\log^* \Delta)$ in odd-degree graphs in the setting used by Naor and Stockmeyer [22] (which differs from the LOCAL model by assuming *unbounded* IDs), or in the LOCAL model [20, 23].

5.1 A Speedup Lemma for Superweak k-Coloring

Superweak k-Coloring. Let $k \geq 2$ be some integer. We define the problem of superweak k-coloring as follows (using the insights obtained in Section 4.5). Each node has to output a color from $\{1, \dots, k\}$ and a number of pointers to adjacent nodes. There are two kinds of pointers, *demanding* pointers and *accepting* pointers. A node is not allowed to point to the same neighbor with two pointers; furthermore, the number of demanding pointers a node uses must be strictly greater than the number of accepting pointers it uses (the latter can be 0). The number of accepting pointers a node is allowed to use is bounded from above by k. The output is correct if for each demanding pointer from a node v to a node u, the two nodes have different colors or u has an accepting pointer pointing to v.

Lemma 5.1. *Let $k \geq 2$, and fix some $\Delta \geq 2^{4^k+1}$. Let $\mathcal{G}_{n,\Delta}$ be a Σ-input-labeled graph class such that every contained graph has n nodes, is Δ-regular and the given input includes an orientation for each edge. Assume that $\mathcal{G}_{n,\Delta}$ is t-independent for some positive integer t and contains only graphs of girth at least $2t + 2$. Let $S \subseteq \mathbb{N}^+$ be a finite set of identifiers satisfying $|S| \geq 4\Delta^{2t}$. Let $\mathcal{G}'_{n,\Delta}$ be the class consisting of all (input-labeled) graphs obtained by taking a graph from $\mathcal{G}_{n,\Delta}$ and assigning unique identifiers from S as inputs to the nodes of the graph. Set $k' := 2^{2^{5^k}}$. If there is an order-invariant algorithm solving superweak k-coloring on $\mathcal{G}'_{n,\Delta}$ in time t, then there is also an order-invariant algorithm solving superweak k'-coloring on $\mathcal{G}'_{n,\Delta}$ in time $t - 1$.*

5.2 Proving the Lower Bound

Building on the above speedup lemma, we are finally able to prove the desired lower bound.

Theorem 5.2. *There is no $o(\log^* \Delta)$-time algorithm solving weak 2-coloring in odd-degree graphs.*

Proof. Assume for a contradiction that such an $o(\log^* \Delta)$-time algorithm $\mathcal{A}$ exists, and, for each odd $\Delta \in \mathbb{N}$, let $T(\Delta) \in o(\log^* \Delta)$ denote the (worst-case) runtime of $\mathcal{A}$ on Δ-regular graphs. We can assume w.l.o.g. that $T(\Delta) \geq 1$ for all $\Delta \in \mathbb{N}$ (by choosing our algorithm $\mathcal{A}$ suitably). Fix $\Delta > 16$ to be an odd positive integer such that $1 \leq T(\Delta) \leq (\log^* \Delta - 7)/5$ (such a Δ must exist since $T(\Delta) \in o(\log^* \Delta)$).

Let $\mathcal{G}_{n,\Delta}$ be the (Σ-input-labeled) graph class consisting of all Δ-regular graphs with n nodes, girth at least $2(T(\Delta) + 1) + 2$, and arbitrary edge orientations as inputs, where n is a sufficiently large even constant (in particular, the ID space, which depends on n, has to be of cardinality at least $4\Delta^{2T(\Delta)+2}$ since we want to apply Lemma 5.1). Let $\mathcal{G}'_{n,\Delta}$ be the class consisting of all graphs obtained by taking a graph from $\mathcal{G}_{n,\Delta}$ and assigning unique $O(\log n)$-bit IDs as inputs to the nodes of the graph. Let $\mathcal{G}''_{n,\Delta}$ be the graph class obtained from $\mathcal{G}'_{n,\Delta}$ by removing the edge orientations from the input (as those are not part of the LOCAL model). We will show that our lower bound already holds on $\mathcal{G}''_{n,\Delta}$. Note that the three defined graph classes are all non-empty as assured, e.g., by [8, Chapter III, Theorem 1.4′].

Since, by assumption, $\mathcal{A}$ solves weak 2-coloring on $\mathcal{G}''_{n,\Delta}$ in time $T(\Delta) \leq (\log^* \Delta - 8)/5$, and since Δ is a fixed constant, there must also be an *order-invariant* algorithm doing the same, by [22, Theorem 3.3] (or, more precisely, by the proof thereof). Hence, in the following assume that $\mathcal{A}$ is order-invariant. Clearly, our order-invariant algorithm $\mathcal{A}$ also solves weak 2-coloring on $\mathcal{G}'_{n,\Delta}$ in time $T(\Delta) \leq (\log^* \Delta - 8)/5$, by simply ignoring the additional input information. As argued in Section 4.5, any algorithm that solves weak 2-coloring can be transformed into an algorithm that solves the pointer version of weak 2-coloring and requires at most one additional round. It is straightforward to check that this transformation also preserves order-invariance; for simplicity, denote the algorithm obtained after the transformation also by $\mathcal{A}$. Moreover, any algorithm that solves the pointer version of weak 2-coloring also solves superweak 2-coloring, by the definition of the latter. Hence, it follows that $\mathcal{A}$ solves superweak 2-coloring on $\mathcal{G}'_{n,\Delta}$ in time $T(\Delta) + 1 \leq (\log^* \Delta - 3)/5$.

Observe that the definition of our graph class $\mathcal{G}_{n,\Delta}$ ensures that $\mathcal{G}_{n,\Delta}$ is $(\leq T(\Delta) + 1)$-independent. Hence we can use Lemma 5.1 to repeatedly speed $\mathcal{A}$ up until we obtain an algorithm that solves superweak k'-coloring for some large k' in 0 rounds. Set $k_0 := 2$, and define recursively $k_{i+1} := F(F(F(F(F(k_i)))))$, where $F(x) := 2^x$. Since $k_{i+1} \geq 2^{2^{5^{k_i}}}$ for all i and any algorithm for superweak j-coloring also solves superweak j'-coloring if $j' \geq j$, we see that $T(\Delta) + 1$ applications of Lemma 5.1 result in a 0-round algorithm $\mathcal{A}^*$ that solves superweak k^*-coloring on $\mathcal{G}'_{n,\Delta}$, where $k^* \leq k_{T(\Delta)+1} \leq \log \Delta$. Note that $k_i \leq \log\log\log\log \Delta$ for all $i \leq T(\Delta)$, which implies that the condition $\Delta \geq 2^{4^k+1}$ in Lemma 5.1 is satisfied in each application of the lemma. In the following we argue that such a 0-round algorithm cannot exist.

Consider a node v in some graph from $\mathcal{G}'_{n,\Delta}$, and assume that v has only incoming edges at the first $(\Delta - 1)/2$ ports and only outgoing edges at the remaining $(\Delta + 1)/2$ ports. Let ID_1 and ID_2 be two IDs such that v would output the same color according to $\mathcal{A}^*$ if it has either of the two IDs as input. Such two IDs must exist by the pigeonhole principle. Now assume that v is given ID_1 as input, and let $e = \{u, v\}$ be some edge incident to v such that v outputs $\rightarrow$ at (v, e) according to $\mathcal{A}^*$. Assume that u has the same constraint on the incoming and outgoing edges as v (which is possible due to our choice of $\mathcal{G}'_{n,\Delta}$) and let ID_2 be the input ID for u, which implies that u outputs the same color as v. Moreover, since $k^* \leq \log \Delta \leq (\Delta - 3)/2$ (due to $\Delta > 16$), there are at least one edge e_{in} incoming at u and one edge e_{out} outgoing at u such that u outputs $\multimap$ neither at (u, e_{in}) nor at (u, e_{out}) (since u has at most k^* pointers $\multimap$ available). Clearly, there exists a port numbering at u such that $e_{\mathrm{in}} = e$ or $e_{\mathrm{out}} = e$. In this case, u and v output the same color, v outputs $\longrightarrow$ at (v, e), and u does not output $\multimap$ at (u, e), which yields an incorrect output for superweak k^*-coloring at e. Hence, there is no $o(\log^* \Delta)$-time algorithm as described in the theorem statement. □

6 CONCLUSION

In this work, we developed a new technique for determining (or at least bounding) the time complexity of a given distributed problem, based on the idea of automatically transforming the problem into a problem that can be solved exactly one round faster. We proved the viability of the technique by showing that it can be used for reproducing known results in a (semi-)automatic fashion and that it is powerful enough to facilitate answering a long-standing open question that has resisted proof attempts for 25 years. Given that the technique can be applied to any locally checkable problem, we expect many other problems to be solved by this technique. A first confirmation has already been given by the follow-up work of Balliu et al. [2], where the authors use our speedup technique to prove lower bounds for maximal matching and maximal independent set.

One main difficulty in applying our speedup technique lies in the fact that the complexity of the problem description increases substantially in each speedup step. We provided a simplification technique (maximization) and outlined two general approaches (relaxation for a lower bound, making a problem harder for an upper bound) that mitigate this problem. Are there other techniques for reducing the description complexity? Is there a good way to determine which parts of the description of a derived problem are important and which can be discarded? Is finding the correct lower bound only a matter of finding the right relaxation (and to which degree can this be automated)? Answering these questions would be an important step forward in establishing the presented speedup as a main technique for determining the time complexity of locally checkable problems.

REFERENCES

[1] Dana Angluin. 1980. Local and Global Properties in Networks of Processors (Extended Abstract). In *Proceedings of the 12th Annual ACM Symposium on Theory of Computing, April 28-30, 1980, Los Angeles, California, USA*. 82–93. https://doi.org/10.1145/800141.804655

[2] Alkida Balliu, Sebastian Brandt, Juho Hirvonen, Dennis Olivetti, Mikaël Rabie, and Jukka Suomela. 2019. Lower bounds for maximal matchings and maximal independent sets. *CoRR* abs/1901.02441 (2019). arXiv:1901.02441 http://arxiv.org/abs/1901.02441

[3] Alkida Balliu, Sebastian Brandt, Dennis Olivetti, and Jukka Suomela. 2018. Almost Global Problems in the LOCAL Model. In *32nd International Symposium on Distributed Computing, DISC 2018, New Orleans, LA, USA, October 15-19, 2018*. 9:1–9:16. https://doi.org/10.4230/LIPIcs.DISC.2018.9

[4] Alkida Balliu, Juho Hirvonen, Janne H. Korhonen, Tuomo Lempiäinen, Dennis Olivetti, and Jukka Suomela. 2018. New classes of distributed time complexity. In *Proceedings of the 50th Annual ACM SIGACT Symposium on Theory of Computing, STOC 2018, Los Angeles, CA, USA, June 25-29, 2018*. 1307–1318. https://doi.org/10.1145/3188745.3188860

[5] Alkida Balliu, Juho Hirvonen, Dennis Olivetti, and Jukka Suomela. 2018. Hardness of minimal symmetry breaking in distributed computing. *CoRR* abs/1811.01643 (2018). arXiv:1811.01643 http://arxiv.org/abs/1811.01643

[6] Leonid Barenboim and Michael Elkin. 2009. Distributed (delta+1)-coloring in linear (in delta) time. In *Proceedings of the 41st Annual ACM Symposium on Theory of Computing, STOC 2009, Bethesda, MD, USA, May 31 - June 2, 2009*. 111–120. https://doi.org/10.1145/1536414.1536432

[7] Leonid Barenboim and Michael Elkin. 2010. Deterministic distributed vertex coloring in polylogarithmic time. In *Proceedings of the 29th Annual ACM Symposium on Principles of Distributed Computing, PODC 2010, Zurich, Switzerland, July 25-28, 2010*. 410–419. https://doi.org/10.1145/1835698.1835797

[8] Béla Bollobás. 1978. *Extremal Graph Theory*. 437 pages.

[9] Sebastian Brandt, Orr Fischer, Juho Hirvonen, Barbara Keller, Tuomo Lempiäinen, Joel Rybicki, Jukka Suomela, and Jara Uitto. 2016. A lower bound for the distributed Lovász local lemma. In *Proceedings of the 48th Annual ACM Symposium on Theory of Computing (STOC)*. 479–488. https://doi.org/10.1145/2897518.2897570

[10] Sebastian Brandt, Juho Hirvonen, Janne H. Korhonen, Tuomo Lempiäinen, Patric R. J. Östergård, Christopher Purcell, Joel Rybicki, Jukka Suomela, and Przemyslaw Uznanski. 2017. LCL Problems on Grids. In *Proceedings of the ACM Symposium on Principles of Distributed Computing, PODC 2017, Washington, DC, USA, July 25-27, 2017*. 101–110. https://doi.org/10.1145/3087801.3087833

[11] Yi-Jun Chang, Qizheng He, Wenzheng Li, Seth Pettie, and Jara Uitto. 2018. The Complexity of Distributed Edge Coloring with Small Palettes. In *Proceedings of the Twenty-Ninth Annual ACM-SIAM Symposium on Discrete Algorithms, SODA 2018, New Orleans, LA, USA, January 7-10, 2018*. 2633–2652. https://doi.org/10.1137/1.9781611975031.168

[12] Yi-Jun Chang, Tsvi Kopelowitz, and Seth Pettie. 2016. An Exponential Separation between Randomized and Deterministic Complexity in the LOCAL Model. In *Proceedings of the 57th Annual Symposium on Foundations of Computer Science (FOCS)*. 615–624. https://doi.org/10.1109/FOCS.2016.72

[13] Yi-Jun Chang and Seth Pettie. 2017. A Time Hierarchy Theorem for the LOCAL Model. In *58th IEEE Annual Symposium on Foundations of Computer Science, FOCS 2017, Berkeley, CA, USA, October 15-17, 2017*. 156–167. https://doi.org/10.1109/FOCS.2017.23

[14] Richard Cole and Uzi Vishkin. 1986. Deterministic coin tossing and accelerating cascades: micro and macro techniques for designing parallel algorithms. In *Proceedings of the 18th Annual ACM Symposium on Theory of Computing, May 28-30, 1986, Berkeley, California, USA*. 206–219. https://doi.org/10.1145/12130.12151

[15] Manuela Fischer and Mohsen Ghaffari. 2017. Sublogarithmic Distributed Algorithms for Lovász Local Lemma, and the Complexity Hierarchy. In *31st International Symposium on Distributed Computing, DISC 2017, October 16-20, 2017, Vienna, Austria*. 18:1–18:16. https://doi.org/10.4230/LIPIcs.DISC.2017.18

[16] Mohsen Ghaffari, David G. Harris, and Fabian Kuhn. 2018. On Derandomizing Local Distributed Algorithms. In *59th IEEE Annual Symposium on Foundations of Computer Science, FOCS 2018, Paris, France, October 7-9, 2018*. 662–673. https://doi.org/10.1109/FOCS.2018.00069

[17] Mohsen Ghaffari and Hsin-Hao Su. 2017. Distributed Degree Splitting, Edge Coloring, and Orientations. In *Proceedings of the Twenty-Eighth Annual ACM-SIAM Symposium on Discrete Algorithms, SODA 2017, Barcelona, Spain, Hotel Porta Fira, January 16-19*. 2505–2523. https://doi.org/10.1137/1.9781611974782.166

[18] Andrew V. Goldberg, Serge A. Plotkin, and Gregory E. Shannon. 1987. Parallel Symmetry-Breaking in Sparse Graphs. In *Proceedings of the 19th Annual ACM Symposium on Theory of Computing, 1987, New York, New York, USA*. 315–324. https://doi.org/10.1145/28395.28429

[19] Fabian Kuhn. 2009. Weak graph colorings: distributed algorithms and applications. In *SPAA 2009: Proceedings of the 21st Annual ACM Symposium on Parallelism in Algorithms and Architectures, Calgary, Alberta, Canada, August 11-13, 2009*. 138–144. https://doi.org/10.1145/1583991.1584032

[20] Nathan Linial. 1992. Locality in Distributed Graph Algorithms. *SIAM J. Comput.* 21, 1 (1992), 193–201. https://doi.org/10.1137/0221015

[21] Alain J. Mayer, Moni Naor, and Larry J. Stockmeyer. 1995. Local Computations on Static and Dynamic Graphs (Preliminary Version). In *Third Israel Symposium on Theory of Computing and Systems, ISTCS 1995, Tel Aviv, Israel, January 4-6, 1995, Proceedings*. 268–278. https://doi.org/10.1109/ISTCS.1995.377023

[22] Moni Naor and Larry J. Stockmeyer. 1993. What can be computed locally?. In *Proceedings of the Twenty-Fifth Annual ACM Symposium on Theory of Computing, May 16-18, 1993, San Diego, CA, USA*. 184–193. https://doi.org/10.1145/167088.167149

[23] David Peleg. 2000. *Distributed Computing: A Locality-Sensitive Approach*. Society for Industrial and Applied Mathematics. https://doi.org/10.1137/1.9780898719772

7 ACKNOWLEDGMENTS

I would like to thank Alkida Balliu, Dennis Olivetti, and Jukka Suomela for insghtful discussions about weak coloring.

A Sharp Threshold Phenomenon for the Distributed Complexity of the Lovász Local Lemma

Sebastian Brandt
ETH Zürich
Switzerland
brandts@ethz.ch

Yannic Maus*
Technion
Israel
yannic.maus@cs.technion.ac.il

Jara Uitto†
ETH Zürich and U. of Freiburg
Switzerland/Germany
jara.uitto@inf.ethz.ch

ABSTRACT

The *Lovász Local Lemma (LLL)* says that, given a set of bad events that depend on the values of some random variables and where each event happens with probability at most p and depends on at most d other events, there is an assignment of the variables that avoids all bad events if the *LLL criterion* $ep(d+1) < 1$ is satisfied. Nowadays, in the area of distributed graph algorithms it has also become a powerful framework for developing—mostly randomized—algorithms. A classic result by Moser and Tardos yields an $O(\log^2 n)$ algorithm for the distributed Lovász Local Lemma [JACM'10] if $ep(d+1) < 1$ is satisfied. Given a *stronger* criterion, i.e., demanding a smaller error probability, it is conceivable that we can find better algorithms. Indeed, for example Chung, Pettie and Su [PODC'14] gave an $O(\log_{epd^2} n)$ algorithm under the $epd^2 < 1$ criterion. Going further, Ghaffari, Harris and Kuhn introduced an $2^{O(\sqrt{\log\log n})}$ time algorithm given $d^8 p = O(1)$ [FOCS'18]. On the negative side, Brandt et al. and Chang et al. showed that we cannot go below $\Omega(\log\log n)$ (randomized) [STOC'16] and $\Omega(\log n)$ (deterministic) [FOCS'16], respectively, under the criterion $p \leq 2^{-d}$. Furthermore, there is a lower bound of $\Omega(\log^* n)$ that holds for *any* criterion.

In this paper, we study the dependency of the distributed complexity of the LLL problem on the chosen LLL criterion. We show that for the fundamental case of each random variable of the considered LLL instance being associated with an *edge* of the input graph, that is, each random variable influences at most two events, a sharp threshold phenomenon occurs at $p = 2^{-d}$: we provide a simple deterministic (!) algorithm that matches the $\Omega(\log^* n)$ lower bound in bounded degree graphs, if $p < 2^{-d}$, whereas for $p \geq 2^{-d}$, the $\Omega(\log\log n)$ randomized and the $\Omega(\log n)$ deterministic lower bounds hold.

In many applications variables affect more than two events; our main contribution is to extend our algorithm to the case where random variables influence at most three different bad events. We show that, surprisingly, the sharp threshold occurs at the exact same spot, providing evidence for our conjecture that this phenomenon always occurs at $p = 2^{-d}$, independent of the number r of events that are affected by a variable. Almost all steps of the proof framework we provide for the case $r = 3$ extend directly to the case of arbitrary r; consequently, our approach serves as a step towards characterizing the complexity of the LLL under different exponential criteria.

CCS CONCEPTS

• **Distributed algorithms**;

KEYWORDS

Lovász Local Lemma, Distributed Graph Algorithms

ACM Reference Format:

Sebastian Brandt, Yannic Maus, and Jara Uitto. 2019. A Sharp Threshold Phenomenon for the Distributed Complexity of the Lovász Local Lemma. In *2019 ACM Symposium on Principles of Distributed Computing (PODC'19), July 29–August 2, 2019, Toronto, ON, Canada.* ACM, New York, NY, USA, 10 pages. https://doi.org/10.1145/3293611.3331636

1 INTRODUCTION

The probabilistic method is a standard tool for proving the existence of combinatorial objects satisfying a set of properties $\mathcal{P}$. It states that if the probability that a randomly chosen object—where objects are chosen from an appropriate class of objects—satisfies all properties in $\mathcal{P}$ is larger than zero then there exists an object that satisfies all properties in $\mathcal{P}$. One can characterize the properties in $\mathcal{P}$ through a set of "bad events" $\mathcal{E}_1, \ldots, \mathcal{E}_n$ over some random variables. Then, showing the existence of an object is the same as showing that the probability that no bad event happens is strictly positive, i.e., there is an assignment of the variables such that none of the bad events occur. Suppose that we can bound the probability $\Pr[\mathcal{E}_i] < 1/n$ for each event $\mathcal{E}_i$. Then, we can use the well-known *union bound* and obtain that $\Pr[\cap \bar{\mathcal{E}}_i] > 0$. The downside of the union bound is that it is *global* in the sense that the bound we require gets more demanding with the number of events. The celebrated Lovász Local Lemma (LLL) [10] can be seen as a *local* version of the union bound. Let d be the maximum number of other events that any event $\mathcal{E}_i$ depends on and let p be an upper bound on the probability that event $\mathcal{E}_i$ occurs.[1] Then, the lemma states that if the local *LLL criterion* $ep(d+1) < 1$ is satisfied, then the probability of avoiding all bad events is strictly positive and due to the probabilistic method there is also an assignment to the variables avoiding all bad events. Notice that unlike in the union-bound approach, the criterion does not depend on the number n of bad events.

*Supported by the European Union's Horizon 2020 grant no. 755839
†Supported by ERC grant no. 336495 (ACDC)

PODC '19, July 29–August 2, 2019, Toronto, ON, Canada

ACM ISBN 978-1-4503-6217-7/19/07...$15.00
https://doi.org/10.1145/3293611.3331636

[1] In the *symmetric* version of LLL, one assumes that p is the same for all events $\mathcal{E}_i$.

In its original form, the proof of the lemma is existential and does not provide an efficient algorithm for finding an assignment of the variables that avoids the bad events. For 15 years, finding such a method eluded the research community. After the first constructive proof and an algorithm for the lemma by Beck [3], a lot of work was dedicated to improving the algorithms for LLL [1, 9, 19, 21, 23]. In 2010, Moser and Tardos [20] provided a beautiful solution to the problem using a simple algorithm that iteratively (re-)samples all the random variables associated with some bad event that occurred. Their work was particularly good news for the distributed community; the approach is easy to parallelize.

Distributed LLL. Let $V = \{\mathcal{E}_1, \ldots, \mathcal{E}_n\}$ be a finite set of (bad) events that depend on a set of random variables with a discrete finite range. The *dependency graph* of an LLL instance is a graph where V is the node set and two nodes are connected by an edge if the corresponding events depend on a common variable. In the *distributed LLL*, the dependency graph corresponds to a communication network and the model of computing is the standard distributed message passing model on graphs, the LOCAL model: The nodes communicate in synchronous rounds and in every round, each node can send one (unbounded size) message to each of its neighbors and perform (unbounded) local computations. In the end of the computation, each node has to know the assignment to the variables that influence its own event and agree on the assignment with its neighbors (that share the variables). An LLL instance is solved if the nodes have jointly computed an assignment that avoids all bad events. The complexity measure is the number of rounds.

Criteria vs. Time. It is natural to assume that if we strengthen the LLL criterion $ep(d + 1) < 1$, i.e., the bad events are less likely to happen, we can find better algorithms. From previous work we know, that if $p \geq 2^{-d}$, one cannot hope to obtain a better runtime than $\Omega(\log\log n)$ [5] randomized and $\Omega(\log n)$ deterministic [6]. It is known that $\Omega(\log^* n)$ cannot be beaten under *any* LLL criterion that is a function of d [8]. Central questions in the field are how close can we get to these bounds and under which criteria.

Our Contributions. Our first contribution is a simple and natural deterministic algorithm that solves the LLL problem in time $O(d + \log^* n)$ under the exponential criterion $p < 2^{-d}$. Our algorithm works under the assumption that each random variable affects at most two bad events. For constant degree graphs, our algorithm is optimal in two ways. First, it matches the $\Omega(\log^* n)$ lower bound and second, the $O(\log^* n)$ runtime which we obtain is unachievable for any criterion that is weaker than $p < 2^{-d}$. In particular, crossing the threshold $p = 2^{-d}$ introduces a fundamental phase shift in the complexity landscape of LLL. For randomized algorithms, the complexity drops from $\Omega(\log\log n)$ to $O(\log^* n)$ and for deterministic, the drop is from $\Omega(\log n)$ to $O(\log^* n)$.

Let us explain our first result in more detail: Since every variable affects at most two events, one can assume that the variables are located on the edges of the dependency graph. Our algorithm iterates over these edges and deterministically fixes the random variables shared by the endpoints of the edge. The order of the edges can be adversarial. In particular, the assigned values are never changed once they are fixed. We show that independent of the execution history, we can always find an assignment for the variables on an edge that increases the (conditional) probabilities of the corresponding bad events to occur by a factor of at most 2 per edge that we consider. Since there are at most d edges incident on any event, at the end of this process, the probability of any bad event is at most $p \cdot 2^d < 1$. As all random variables in the probability space are fixed, there is no randomness left and hence, the probability must be 0.

Theorem 1.1. *Consider an LLL instance with the criterion $p < 2^{-d}$ and where every random variable affects at most 2 bad events. There is a* sequential *and* local *deterministic process that computes an assignment to the variables that avoids all bad events.*

The algorithm of Theorem 1.1 is *local* in the sense that it can be run in parallel with the help of a suitable edge-coloring of the dependency graph. The edge-coloring can be computed, e.g., with the algorithm from [22], which implies the following corollary.

Corollary 1.2. *Consider an LLL instance with the criterion $p < 2^{-d}$ and where every random variable affects at most 2 bad events. There is an $O(d + \log^* n)$ round deterministic distributed algorithm that solves the LLL problem.*

Beyond Two Events per Variable. In many distributed problems, the output of a node may affect many of its neighbors. Hence, it is natural to study the LLL setting where the random variables influence more than two events. Our core question is:

> *If r is an upper bound on the number of events that any variable affects, what is the weakest LLL criterion that allows us to solve the problem deterministically in $O(\text{poly}(d) + \log^* n)$ time?*

Our algorithms for the case of $r = 2$ generalize in a straightforward way. However, this comes with a cost. First, every time our algorithm fixes an assignment for a random variable, the probabilities of the affected events to occur may increase by a factor of r. Furthermore, every event may depend on $\binom{d}{r-1}$ different variables[2]. Hence, the criterion we need is $p < r^{-\binom{d}{r-1}}$. Our second question is whether this criterion is inherent to the case of larger r.

Our main contribution is to answer the aforementioned questions for the case that r is 3. Furthermore, most parts of our proof—but unfortunately not all—generalize to all $r > 3$. If each variable affects at most three events and $p < 2^{-d}$ we provide a sequential process that iterates over the random variables and assigns values to them deterministically; the assigned values are never changed once they are fixed. Just as in the case $r = 2$, this process can be run in parallel and as a corollary, we obtain a distributed algorithm with the same asymptotic runtime as for $r = 2$. Surprisingly, we do not need any compromise in the LLL criterion.

> *There is a sharp threshold phenomenon for the distributed complexity of the Lovász Local Lemma at $p = 2^{-d}$ if variables can affect at most three events. The phase shift is from $\Omega(\log n)$ deterministic and $\Omega(\log\log n)$ randomized time above the threshold to $O(\text{poly}\, d + \log^* n)$ strictly below the threshold. The threshold is the same as in the case where each variable affects at most two events.*

[2] In principle, the number of variables could be larger. However, it is straightforward to reformulate the instance in a way that combines variables affecting the same r events.

Formally we prove the following statements for the case $r = 3$.

THEOREM 1.3. *Consider an LLL instance with the criterion* $p2^d < 1$ *and where every random variable affects at most* 3 *bad events. There is a* sequential *and* local *deterministic process that computes an assignment to the variables that avoids all bad events.*

Here the process is *local* in the sense that the choice of the value for a random variable only depends on the 1-hop neighborhood of the variable in the dependency graph. Thus, we can fix variables in parallel as long as we do not simultaneously fix variables that influence the same event. We obtain our desired runtime by first 2-hop coloring[3] the graph with $O(d^2)$ colors. Then, we iterate through the color classes and fix *all* the random variables of the nodes in the current color class. Using the algorithm by Fraigniaud, Heinrich and Kosowski, the coloring can be found in $\widetilde{O}(d) + \log^* n$ time [12].

COROLLARY 1.4. *Consider an LLL instance with the criterion* $p < 2^{-d}$ *and where every random variable affects at most* 3 *bad events. There is an* $O(d^2 + \log^* n)$ *round deterministic distributed algorithm that solves the LLL problem.*

This deterministic algorithm improves on the previously best randomized algorithm which has a runtime of $\omega(\text{poly} \log \log n)$ [14] (see related work section for more details). In a recent breakthrough, Ghaffari, Harris, and Kuhn gave a general derandomization method for LOCAL algorithms that requires, per node, a small *global* failure probability, i.e., small as a function of n. Put into this frame, our result is a first step towards a general derandomization method under a *local* bound on the failure probability. Notice that even the very strong criterion $p < 2^{-d}$ is much less demanding than $p < 1/n$ in the case of low degree graphs. Generalizing it to weaker criteria and random variables that affect arbitrarily many events would be a major breakthrough.

Applications. In the sinkless orientation problem, the goal is to assign an orientation to each edge such that no node forms a sink. It is the prime example of a problem that is just very slightly above the "exponential threshold" for which our derandomization works. In fact the failure probability for each node is exactly at the threshold 2^{-d} if each edge is oriented randomly and the problem also served for proving the randomized $\Omega(\log \log n)$ lower bound [5] and deterministic $\Omega(\log n)$ [6] lower bound for LLL in the regime $p \geq 2^{-d}$. It has been studied vividly since its first appearance, see e.g. [5, 6], and has also become an important subroutine for solving classic problems such as edge coloring [15, 17], and hence, studying its relaxations is a canonical step for future work. A natural extension to this problem is to consider orientations in *hypergraphs*, where each edge is allowed to contain more than two nodes. A hyperedge is assigned an orientation towards one of its nodes, i.e., exactly one node is chosen as the head of the hyperedge and the rest are chosen as tails. For example, the following setting falls into our regime: Consider hypergraphs of rank 3, i.e., the maximum number of nodes per edge is 3. Node v is a sink if it is the head of all of its hyperedges. The goal is to compute 3 orientations of the edges such that each node v is not a sink in at least two of the orientations. For the parameters to work out, the degree of the dependency graph must be at least 7.

Another problem that is slightly above the exponential threshold is the weak splitting problem [16] which is defined as follows. You are given a bipartite graph $B = (V \cup U, E)$ with the objective to color the nodes in U with two colors such that each node in V has at least one neighbor in U of each color. The seemingly simple problem has recently gotten a lot of attention because it is P-SLOCAL-complete, that is, an efficient, i.e., poly $\log n$ rounds, deterministic algorithm for the problem would imply an efficient deterministic algorithm for many classic problems such at MIS and $\Delta + 1$-vertex coloring. Interpreting the vertices in U as variables—the maximum degree of nodes in U corresponds to our parameter r, i.e., how many events share a variable— makes it a canonical problem that fits the LLL framework with very weak guarantees. However, the standard case of weak splitting with 2 colors and the requirement that every node sees at least 1 neighbor of each color is slightly above the "exponential threshold". Hence, it does not fall into the regime that we can solve with the results in this work. As a matter of fact, there is a $\Omega(\log n)$ lower bound for the problem [2] which is proven through a reduction from the sinkless orientation problem.

By weakening the conditions of the weak splitting problem a tiny bit, the problem also fits into our framework and we immediately acquire new algorithms. As an example, consider the weak splitting with $r \leq 3$, where r is the maximum degree of U, using 16 colors and requiring every node to see at least 2 colors. Notice that a natural interpretation of this setting is a hypergraph edge-coloring, where the nodes of U correspond to rank r hyperedges. These type of weak variants have also been studied in the aforementioned submission [2], however, with the objective to show that they are P-SLOCAL-complete when r can be of arbitrary size. Even though the runtime of our algorithms is polynomial in the maximum degree and thus, mostly efficient for very small degrees, we believe that derandomizing weak splitting variants might pave the way to new ideas, also for solving the original problem. Variants of the weak splitting have also appeared under the name of frugal edge coloring, e.g., in [18, Definition 2.5].

Techniques and Generalization. Now, we discuss which parts of our approach generalize to the case where $r > 3$, and which do not. For $r = 3$, we show that, informally speaking, there is a way to fix the random variables such that no node is unlucky too often. The rough intuition is that if the probability of bad event $\mathcal{E}_v$ has increased a lot, it must have neighboring bad events whose probability is (relatively) low. Hence, when the next random variable affecting these events is to be fixed, there is a way to make sure that the probability of $\mathcal{E}_v$ does not increase much (or even decreases) since incurring a large increase for the probabilities of the neighboring events is acceptable. We show this by careful bookkeeping during the execution of our algorithm. The main technical challenge is to show that each time we fix a random variable, there is a good choice, i.e., a choice that ensures that certain values we keep track of never grow too much. In the end, these values bound the increase of the probabilities of the individual bad events, The proof is very technical, but ultimately, we reduce existence of a good choice for each random variable to the convexity of a certain function.

[3] A proper coloring of a graph is a 2-hop coloring if nodes in distance at most two do not have the same color.

For the case of $r = 3$, we were able to express this function as a relatively clean closed expression. For the case of $r > 3$, finding such an expression and using this knowledge to show that the assoiciated function is convex is the only challenge in obtaining full generality. All the other parts of our method generalize to higher ranks. We believe that the approach is viable to higher r, but needs new analytic insights that are posed as a direction for future work.

CONJECTURE 1.5. *Consider an LLL instance with the criterion $p < 2^{-d}$ and where every random variable affects at most r bad events. For any r, there is a distributed algorithm that solves the LLL problem with criterion $p < 2^{-d}$ in time $O(d^2 + \log^* n)$.*

REMARK. *If we tighten the LLL criterion in Conjecture 1.5 to $p < 2^{-\Omega(d^2 \cdot \log d)}$, we can use the deterministic algorithm by Fischer and Ghaffari [11] to solve the LLL in time $O(d^2 + \log^* n)$ in the following way. First, in time $\widetilde{O}(d) + \log^* n$, we compute a 2-hop coloring of the dependency graph with $O(d^2)$ colors and treat this coloring as a $(O(d^2), 0)$-network decomposition. Then, using this network decomposition with the algorithm by Fischer and Ghaffari, we obtain an LLL algorithm with runtime $O(d^2 + \log^* n)$.*

Related Work. A straightforward distributed implementation of the resampling framework of Moser and Tardos [20] yields an $O(\log^2 n)$ algorithm for the distributed LLL problem under the $ep(d + 1) < 1$ criterion. Recently, Chung et al. [8] designed an algorithm with runtime $O(\log n \cdot \log^2 d)$ which was then improved to $O(\log n \cdot \log d)$ by Ghaffari [13]. The runtime landscape changes if we make the LLL criterion stronger, i.e., make the bad events less likely to happen. Under the $epd^2 < 1$ criterion, Chung et al. [8] gave an $O(\log_{1/epd^2} n)$ time algorithm for LLL. For an even stronger polynomial criterion of $epd^{32} < 1$ and assuming that $d = O(\log^{1.5} \log n)$, Fischer and Ghaffari gave a $2^{O(\sqrt{\log\log n})}$ time algorithm [11]. The state-of-the-art under the polynomial criteria, is a $\exp^{(i)} O((\log^{(i+1)} n)^{0.5}) = 2^{o(\sqrt{\log\log n})} \ll \text{poly}(\log n)$ [14][4] round algorithm for any i under the $d^8 p = O(1)$ criterion.

In a recent breakthrough, Chang and Pettie [7] underlined the general importance of the LLL problem for distributed randomized algorithms. They showed that in constant degree graphs, LLL is "complete" for problems solvable in sublogarithmic time in the following sense: Any algorithm that has a runtime of $o(\log n)$ can be automatically turned into a new algorithm that runs in time $O(T_{\text{LLL}})$, where T_{LLL} stands for the randomized complexity of solving the LLL problem under *any* polynomial criterion. The authors make the following conjecture.

CONJECTURE 1.6 ([7]). *Assume that $d \geq 2$. There exists a sufficiently large constant c such that the distributed LLL problem can be solved in $O(\log\log n)$ time on bounded degree graphs, under the symmetric LLL criterion $p < d^{-c}$.*

One aspect of their conjecture is to find a threshold criterion that allows for $O(\log\log n)$ time algorithms. We show that in the exponential end of the spectrum, this threshold can be achieved and even broken without using any randomization. This picture highlights another interesting question for future work: What bounds can we achieve for LLL criteria between exponential and polynomial?

All the related work that we surveyed so far are for randomized algorithms and there are very few deterministic results for the distributed LLL problem. A $\lambda \cdot n^{1/\lambda} \cdot 2^{\sqrt{\log n}}$ time algorithm under the criterion $p(ed)^\lambda < 1$ is known [11] and the state-of-the-art runtime of $\exp^{(i)} O((\log^{(i)} n)^{0.5})$ is by Ghaffari, Harris and Kuhn [14].

[4]Here $\exp^{(i)}$ stands for a power tower of height i and $\log^{(i)}$ stands for a logarithm iterated i times.

2 WARM-UP: WHEN VARIABLES AFFECT AT MOST TWO EVENTS

In this section, we discuss our results for the setting where each random variable affects at most two events. In other words, each random variable of the given LLL instance belongs to one edge in the dependency graph. Note that we can assume that there is *exactly* one variable per edge: the definition of the dependency graph ensures in this setting that there is at least one variable per edge, and if an edge is associated with more than one random variable we can encode these random variables in one new random variable. We start by proving the following statement.

THEOREM 1.1. *Consider an LLL instance with the criterion $p < 2^{-d}$ and where every random variable affects at most 2 bad events. There is a* sequential *and* local *deterministic process that computes an assignment to the variables that avoids all bad events.*

PROOF. Our sequential process does not depend on the order in which we fix the random variables; in fact our algorithm still works if an (even adaptive) adversary chooses the order in which we have to fix the random variables. Let X be a random variable chosen by this adversary, let $e = \{u, v\}$ be the edge associated with X, let $\mathcal{E}_u$ and $\mathcal{E}_v$ be the two bad events associated with u and v, and let $X_1, \ldots X_z$ be the random variables that are affecting at least one of $\mathcal{E}_u, \mathcal{E}_v$ and have already been fixed, say, to values $x_1, \ldots, x_z$. Let $p_1, \ldots, p_k$ denote the probabilities with which X assumes the k possible values $y_1, \ldots, y_k$, respectively.

We claim that there exists a value y_i for X such that, by fixing $X = y_i$, the increase for the probability that $\mathcal{E}_u$ occurs and the increase for the probability that $\mathcal{E}_v$ occurs add up to at most 2. Introduce the term $\theta = \bigwedge_{i=1}^{z}(X_i = x_i)$; then, in other words, we want to show that there exists a value y_i for X such that

$$\frac{\Pr[\mathcal{E}_u \mid \theta, X = y_i]}{\Pr[\mathcal{E}_u \mid \theta]} + \frac{\Pr[\mathcal{E}_v \mid \theta, X = y_i]}{\Pr[\mathcal{E}_v \mid \theta]} \leq 2 .$$

Suppose our claim is false. Then we have

$$\begin{aligned} 2 &= \sum_{i=1}^{k} p_i \cdot 2 \\ &< \sum_{i=1}^{k} \left(p_i \cdot \left(\frac{\Pr[\mathcal{E}_u \mid \theta, X = y_i]}{\Pr[\mathcal{E}_u \mid \theta]} + \frac{\Pr[\mathcal{E}_v \mid \theta, X = y_i]}{\Pr[\mathcal{E}_v \mid \theta]} \right) \right) \\ &= \frac{\sum_{i=1}^{k} (p_i \cdot \Pr[\mathcal{E}_u \mid \theta, X = y_i])}{\Pr[\mathcal{E}_u \mid \theta]} + \frac{\sum_{i=1}^{k} (p_i \cdot \Pr[\mathcal{E}_v \mid \theta, X = y_i])}{\Pr[\mathcal{E}_v \mid \theta]} \\ &= \frac{\Pr[\mathcal{E}_u \mid \theta]}{\Pr[\mathcal{E}_u \mid \theta]} + \frac{\Pr[\mathcal{E}_v \mid \theta]}{\Pr[\mathcal{E}_v \mid \theta]} = 2 , \end{aligned}$$

yielding a contradiction. Hence, the claim is true; in particular, we can choose a value for our random variable X such that the probability that $\mathcal{E}_u$ occurs increases by a factor of at most 2 and the same holds for $\mathcal{E}_v$. Imagine that we choose a value with this property for each random variable. Then, after all random variables are fixed, the total increase for the probability of a bad event $\mathcal{E}_v$ to occur is upper-bounded by $2^{\deg(v)} \leq 2^d$ because each random variable associated with an edge incident to v supplies an increase of at most 2 and all other random variables do not change the probability of $\mathcal{E}_v$ to occur. Since, in the beginning, $\Pr[\mathcal{E}_v] < 2^{-d}$, the probability of $\mathcal{E}$ to occur after fixing all random variables in the described way is strictly smaller than 1 and must therefore be 0. Hence, none of the bad events occurs. □

Proof of Corollary 1.2. As the variables in the proof of Theorem 1.1 can be fixed simultaneously if they do not influence the same event, we can parallelize the algorithm with an edge-coloring of the dependency graph—recall that there is one variable on each of the edges of the dependency graph. An $O(d)$-edge-coloring of the dependency graph can be computed in $O(d + \log^* n)$ rounds and then we can iterate through the color classes in $O(d)$ rounds and fix all variables. □

3 AN ALGORITHM FOR $r = 3$

In this section we show our main result, a sequential and local process to fix the variables of an LLL with exponential criterion $p < 2^{-d}$ where each variable affects at most three events. We use Sections 3.1 to 3.3 for its proof. In Section 3.4, we show how this leads to an $O(d^2 + \log^* n)$ distributed algorithm for the LLL problem. Before outlining our proof, we introduce some necessary notation.

Let $H = (V, F)$ be the hypergraph defined on the same node set as the dependency graph, where, for each variable in the LLL instance, we have one hyperedge connecting exactly the nodes from V that depend on the variable. The *rank* of a hypergraph is the cardinality of the largest hyperedge. In this section, we focus on the case that H has rank at most 3, that is, any variable influences at most three events. If a hyperedge has cardinality k, then we call the associated random variable a *rank* k variable.

Throughout this section, we will assume that all considered random variables are of rank *exactly* 3. This does not lose generality, due to the following observation: If the random variable Y under consideration is of rank 2, then we can simply extend Y to a rank 3 random variable by adding a virtual third affected bad event, where each choice for the value of Y does not change the probability of the new bad event to occur.

3.1 Proof Outline

We will show that it is possible to fix values for the random variables in a completely arbitrary order. Moreover, the value a random variable is fixed to only depends on the current state of the radius-1 neighborhood of the random variable. While it is not obvious at all that fixing random variables in the local way and arbitrary order described above is possible, we show that this is indeed the case, by designing a property which we call P^* such that

1) for each input graph (including already fixed random variables) that satisfies P^*, and each random variable that has not been fixed yet, there is a value for the random variable such that fixing the random variable to this value will preserve P^*, and
2) after all random variables are fixed (by subsequently choosing values as promised by 1)), the P^* guarantees that none of the bad events occurs.

The most challenging part of our work is to come up with such a property and to prove that it satisfies 1) and 2).

We continue with describing property P^* more detailed. During the process of fixing the random variables, we keep track, for each event, how favorable or unfavorable the decisions made so far were. This is done in a peculiar way: On each edge $e = \{u, v\}$ of the dependency graph we maintain two non-negative values e_u and e_v with $e_u + e_v \leq 2$, that is, we have one value for each endpoint. Initially all of these values are set to 1. Apart from the sum being at most 2, these values measure the favorability and unfavorability of previous decisions in the following way: For each node v, the probability of the associated bad event to occur—in the probability space spanned by all still unfixed variables—is always upper-bounded by p times the product of the values written on the incident edges on the side of v, that is, the probability of the bad event at v is always upper bounded by $p \cdot \Pi_{v \in e} e_v$. At the start, this is trivially satisfied as this product equals 1. We say *property* P^* holds at some point during our algorithm if the values on the edges are such that the aforementioned conditions hold. We will soon give some intuition on why we can always find these values for the edges when fixing a variable, but let us first show that 2) holds: At the end of the process, when all variables are fixed, we obtain that this product is at most 2^d as there are at most d incident edges in the dependency graph and each value on an edge can be at most 2. When all random variables are fixed, then, for each bad event, the probability that it occurs is at most $p \cdot \Pi_{v \in e} e_v \leq p \cdot 2^d < 1$, which implies that none of the bad events occurs and 2) holds.

While this explains why it is desirable to define P^* in the aforementioned way (in particular, why the "bookkeeping" is performed on the edges of the dependency graph), it is far from clear why, when fixing a random variable, a value for the variable as promised in 1) exists.

To shed some light on the intuitive reason for this existence, recall the case where variables affect at most two events, and assume that we want to fix variable X on edge $e = \{u, v\}$. A choice for X is *good* if the induced increases of the probabilities that the bad events $\mathcal{E}_u$ and $\mathcal{E}_v$ occur are representable on the single edge e between u and v in the dependency graph. For $r = 2$, *representable* means that the sum of the increases is at most 2. In Section 2, we formally show that such a choice always exists, mostly due to linearity of expectation. For $r = 3$, let $\{u, v, w\}$ share a hyperedge on which we want to fix a variable Y. Again, we want to show that there is a choice for Y such that the increases of the probabilities that the events $\mathcal{E}_u, \mathcal{E}_v$ and $\mathcal{E}_w$ occur can be represented on the three edges between u, v and w in the dependency graph. However, in contrast to rank 2, the condition on whether a triple (a, b, c) of increases can be represented is much more delicate and relies on nonlinear relations between the values a, b and c. Thus, for rank 3 we cannot deduce the existence of a good choice immediately from the linearity of expectation.

To better understand our approach for rank 3, let us look at the case of rank 2 from a slightly different point of view, where we do not encode different random variables corresponding to the same edge in one new random variable, but instead allow those random variables to be processed individually. As explained in Section 2 and elaborated upon above, it is always possible to find a value for the random variable corresponding to some edge of the dependency graph such that, for the two endpoints, the increases in the probabilities that the respective bad events occur add up to at most 2. As it turns out, an even stronger existential statement of this kind is true: If we have to fix several random variables that all correspond to the same edge, we can do so sequentially, each time ensuring that the so-far obtained *total* increases for the probabilities of the affected two events add up to at most 2. In other words, for any two given non-negative values s, t with $s + t \leq 2$, we can find a value for any given random variable in a way that ensures that s times the induced probability increase of the first affected bad event plus t times the induced probability increase of the seconded affected bad event is at most 2. This statement can be seen as a weighted version of the original statement from Section 2, and, as we will see, both carry over to the case $r = 3$. We next define property P^* formally.

Definition 3.1 (Property P^*). Let G be the dependency graph of an LLL instance with bad events $\mathcal{E}_1, \ldots, \mathcal{E}_n$, variables $X_1, \ldots, X_m$ and assume that some of the random variables, say, $X_1, \ldots, X_z$, have already been fixed to values $x_1, \ldots, x_z$, respectively. Let φ be a function that maps each pair $(e, v) \in E \times V$, where v is an endpoint of e, to a value $\varphi_e^v \in [0, 2]$. We say that (G, φ) satisfies *property P^** if

(1) $\varphi_e^v + \varphi_e^u \leq 2$ for all $e = \{u, v\} \in E$, and
(2) $\Pr[\mathcal{E}_v \mid X_1 = x_1, \ldots, X_z = x_z] \leq p \cdot \prod_{e \ni v} \varphi_e^v$ for all $v \in V$.

The main technical ingredient for proving our main result is the following lemma.

Lemma 3.2 (Variable Fixing Lemma). *Let $X_1, \ldots, X_z$ be the random variables that have been fixed so far and X an arbitrary random variable that has not been fixed yet. Assume that (G, φ) satisfies P^*. Then there is a value x that X can assume and a function $\psi : \{(e, v) \in E \times V \mid v \in e\} \longrightarrow [0, 2]$ such that (G, ψ) satisfies P^*. Moreover, if u is a node not contained in the hyperedge in H associated with X, then for any edge $e = \{u, w\} \in E$ we have $\psi_e^u = \varphi_e^u$ and $\psi_e^w = \varphi_e^w$.*

We postpone the proof of Lemma 3.2 to Section 3.3 and first show that using Lemma 3.2 proving our main theorem is straightforward.

Theorem 1.3. *Consider an LLL instance with the criterion $p2^d < 1$ and where every random variable affects at most 3 bad events. There is a* sequential *and* local *deterministic process that computes an assignment to the variables that avoids all bad events.*

Proof. In the proof of Theorem 1.1, we could essentially fix each random variable without using any other information than which values were assigned to the adjacent already fixed random variables. In the current proof, during the process of fixing the random variables, we will also maintain a function $\varphi : \{(e, v) \in E \times V \mid v \in e\} \longrightarrow [0, 2]$ such that, at all times, (G, φ) satisfies property P^*. Define $B := \{(e, v) \in E \times V \mid v \in e\}$. In the beginning, before fixing any random variable, we set $\varphi_e^v := 1$, for all $(e, v) \in B$, thereby ensuring that (G, φ) indeed satisfies property P^*.

Now Lemma 3.2 asserts that there is a value for any adversarially chosen random variable and an update to our function φ such that after assigning this value and updating φ accordingly, (G, φ) still satisfies property P^*. Let all random variables be fixed according to this scheme. Then, after fixing the random variables, property P^* ensures that the probability of some specific bad event $\mathcal{E}_v$ to occur is upper-bounded by

$$p \cdot \prod_{e \ni v} \varphi_e^v < 2^{-d} \cdot \prod_{e \ni v} 2 \leq 1 .$$

Hence, for each bad event, the probability that it occurs is 0. □

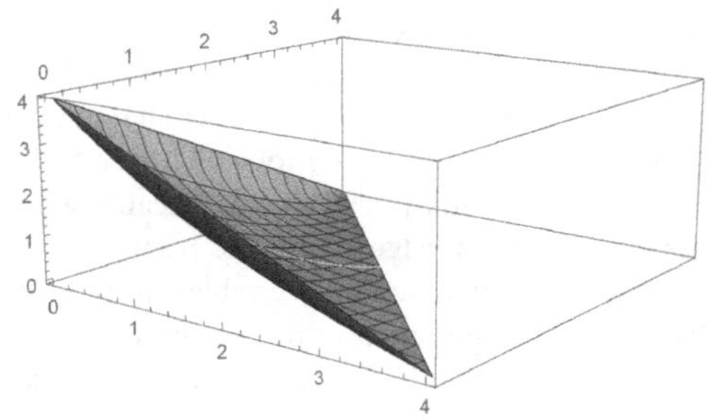

Figure 1: The set S_{rep} of representable triples consists of all points in the first octant that are below the orange shaded surface. The reader might use the plot to convince himself of the fact that the set is incurved, that is, if two points $s, s' \in \mathbb{R}^3_{\geq 0}$ are not in S_{rep} then also the line connecting them does not intersect with the set S_{rep}.

3.2 Representable Triples

The first subproperty of property P^* naturally gives rise to the notion of a very useful class of objects which we call representable triples.

Definition 3.3 (Representable triples). A triple $(a, b, c) \in \mathbb{R}^3_{\geq 0}$ is called *representable* if there are values $a_1, a_2, b_1, b_3, c_2, c_3 \in [0, 2]$ such that $a_1 \cdot a_2 = a$, $b_1 \cdot b_3 = b$, $c_2 \cdot c_3 = c$, $a_1 + b_1 \leq 2$, $a_2 + c_2 \leq 2$, and $b_3 + c_3 \leq 2$. Let $S_{\text{rep}} = \{(a, b, c) \in \mathbb{R}^3_{\geq 0} \mid (a, b, c) \text{ is representable}\}$ denote the set of all representable triples.

See Figure 2 for an illustration of a representable triple and Figure 1 for an illustration of the set S_{rep}. Note that in any representable triple (a, b, c) we have $a, b, c \leq 4$. Before we can shed light on how we will use representable triples to obtain the desired result, we need to define another concept that is closely related to convexity.

Definition 3.4 (incurved). We say that a set $S \subseteq \mathbb{R}^3_{\geq 0}$ is *incurved* if there are no $q \in [0, 1]$, $s, s' \in \mathbb{R}^3_{\geq 0} \setminus S$ such that $q \cdot s + (1 - q) \cdot s' \in S$.

Now we are set to give a high-level overview of our approach to prove Lemma 3.2. The "representable triples" from Section 3.2 formalize both the situation at the beginning of the variable fixing performed in Lemma 3.2 and the desired outcome, or more precisely, the part of the situation (resp. outcome) corresponding to subproperty (1) of property P^*: before fixing the variable in question, the

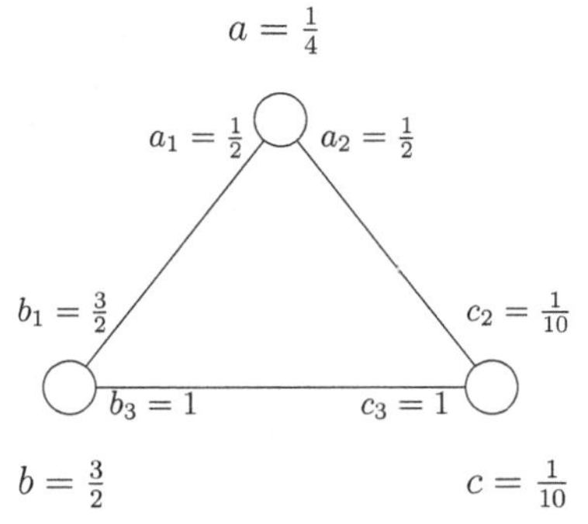

Figure 2: A quick calculation verifies that since $a_1 + b_1 \leq 2$, $a_2 + c_2 \leq 2$, and $b_3 + c_3 \leq 2$, the illustrated triple $(a, b, c) = \left(\frac{1}{4}, \frac{3}{2}, \frac{1}{10}\right)$ is representable.

values given by φ add up to at most 2 on each edge, hence the corresponding triple is representable, and Lemma 3.2 assures that the same holds for the values given by ψ after the fixing. The situation before the fixing is worst-case if the respective representable triple lies on the surface bounding the set of all representable triples and if we can find a new representable triple (as the desired outcome, together with a suitable value for the random variable), then we can also find one that lies on this surface. Hence, we can reduce our considerations to this surface. It turns out that the question whether there exists a suitable value for the random variable to be fixed in Lemma 3.2 depends on the shape of this surface: if there is no such suitable value, then the function describing the surface is not convex. However, Lemma 3.5 and Lemma 3.6 show that this function is convex, thereby ensuring that a suitable value exists, which essentially proves Lemma 3.2. For technical reasons, we use the concept of incurvedness (instead of the closely related convexity) for the proof of the relation between the existence of a suitable value for the random variable and the shape of the surface (Lemma 3.9), and show that the convexity of the surface-describing function implies the incurvedness of the set S_{rep} that is bounded by the function (Lemma 3.7). We encourage the reader to consult the plot given in Figure 1 to convince her- or himself that S_{rep} is incurved.

Lemma 3.5. (Proof Deferred to the Appendix) *For $f(a,b) := 4 + 1/2 \cdot (ab - 2a - 2b - \sqrt{ab(4-a)(4-b)})$ we obtain*

$$S_{\text{rep}} = \{(a,b,c) \subseteq \mathbb{R}^3_{\geq 0} \mid a + b \leq 4, c \leq f(a,b)\}\ .$$

Lemma 3.6. (Proof deferred to the Appendix) *The function $f(a,b) := 4 + 1/2 \cdot (ab - 2a - 2b - \sqrt{ab(4-a)(4-b)})$ is convex on $\{(a,b) \in \mathbb{R}^2_{\geq 0} \mid a + b \leq 4\}$.*

The characterization of S_{rep} given in Lemma 3.5 together with the convexity of $f(a,b)$ from Lemma 3.6 imply that S_{rep} is incurved. The formal proof of this statement is given by Lemma 3.7. Note that Lemma 3.5 and Lemma 3.6 are not crucial to our general approach if one can find a different proof to show that S_{rep} is incurved.

Lemma 3.7. *S_{rep} is incurved.*

Proof. Suppose for a contradiction that there are $q \in [0,1]$, $s, s' \in \mathbb{R}^3_{\geq 0} \setminus S_{\text{rep}}$ with $q \cdot s + (1-q) \cdot s' \in S_{\text{rep}}$. Let $s = (a,b,c)$, $s' = (a',b',c')$ and set $(a_q, b_q, c_q) := q \cdot s + (1-q) \cdot s'$. We consider three cases, depending on the values of a, b and a', b'.

(1) <u>$a + b \leq 4$ and $a' + b' \leq 4$.</u> Consider the two triples (a,b,γ) and (a',b',γ'), where $\gamma = f(a,b)$ and $\gamma' = f(a',b')$. By Lemma 3.5, we have $(a,b,\gamma), (a',b',\gamma') \in S_{\text{rep}}$, and since $s, s' \notin S_{\text{rep}}$, we have $c > \gamma$ and $c' > \gamma'$, which implies that $q \cdot c + (1-q) \cdot c' > q \cdot \gamma + (1-q) \cdot \gamma'$. By Lemma 3.6, we know that $q \cdot \gamma + (1-q) \cdot \gamma' \geq f(q \cdot a + (1-q) \cdot a', q \cdot b + (1-q) \cdot b')$, hence we have $q \cdot c + (1-q) \cdot c' > f(q \cdot a + (1-q) \cdot a', q \cdot b + (1-q) \cdot b')$. In other words, if we set $(a_q, b_q, c_q) := q \cdot s + (1-q) \cdot s'$, then $c_q > f(a_q, b_q)$, which implies $(a_q, b_q, c_q) \notin S_{\text{rep}}$, by Lemma 3.5, and we obtain a contradiction.

(2) <u>$a + b > 4$ and $a' + b' > 4$.</u> In this case, we see that, for any $q \in [0,1]$, we have $a_q + b_q > 4$, which implies $(a_q, b_q, c_q) \notin S_{\text{rep}}$, by Lemma 3.5, and, again, we obtain a contradiction.

(3) <u>$a + b \leq 4$ and $a' + b' > 4$ or vice versa.</u> W.l.o.g., we can assume that $a + b \leq 4$ and $a' + b' > 4$. Let $r \in [0,1]$ be the uniquely defined value such that, for the triple $s_r := (a_r, b_r, c_r) := r \cdot s + (1-r) \cdot s'$, we have $a_r + b_r = 4$. Observe that if $q \leq r$, we can write (a_q, b_q, c_q) as $q' \cdot s + (1-q') \cdot s_r$, for some $q' \in [0,1]$, by setting $q' := 1 - (1-q)/(1-r)$ (or $q' := 0$ if $r = 1$). But then we obtain a contradiction by applying the argumentation in Case 1 for the triples s and s_r. Hence, we know that $q > r$. Similarly to before, we can write (a_q, b_q, c_q) as $q' \cdot s_r + (1-q') \cdot s'$, for some $q' \in [0,1)$. In particular, we have $q' \neq 1$ which together with $a_r + b_r = 4$ and $a' + b' > 4$ implies that $a_q + b_q = q' \cdot (a_r + b_r) + (1-q') \cdot (a' + b') > 4$. By Lemma 3.5, $(a_q, b_q, c_q) \notin S_{\text{rep}}$, yielding a contradiction. □

3.3 Proof of the Variable Fixing Lemma (Lemma 3.2)

Consider the random variable X we are about to fix in Lemma 3.2, and assume that it affects the three events located at the nodes u, v, w which then are connected in the dependency graph by the edges $e = \{u,v\}$, $e' = \{u,w\}$, and $e'' = \{v,w\}$. Recall that our input graph G together with the function φ satisfies P^*. Let the discrete distribution of X be given by the set $\{y_1, \ldots, y_k\}$ of possible values for X and corresponding positive probabilities $p_1, \ldots, p_k$ with which those values occur. For each possible value y of X we are interested in the increases (or decreases) of the probabilities of our bad events due to fixing $X = y$. For each value y and each $t \in \{u, v, w\}$, define

$$\text{Inc}(t,y) := \frac{\Pr[\mathcal{E}_t \mid X_1 = x_1, \ldots, X_z = x_z, X = y]}{\Pr[\mathcal{E}_t \mid X_1 = x_1, \ldots, X_z = x_z]}\ .$$

If $\Pr[\mathcal{E}_t \mid X_1 = x_1, \ldots, X_z = x_z] = 0$, set $\text{Inc}(v,y) = 0$.

Now if we can find a value y for X and values $\psi^u_e, \psi^v_e, \psi^u_{e'}, \psi^w_{e'}, \psi^v_{e''}, \psi^w_{e''} \in [0,2]$ with $\psi^u_e + \psi^v_e \leq 2$, $\psi^u_{e'} + \psi^w_{e'} \leq 2$, $\psi^v_{e''} + \psi^w_{e''} \leq 2$, such that

$$\psi^u_e \psi^u_{e'} \geq \text{Inc}(u,y) \cdot \varphi^u_e \varphi^u_{e'}\ ,$$
$$\psi^v_e \psi^v_{e''} \geq \text{Inc}(v,y) \cdot \varphi^v_e \varphi^v_{e''}\ , \text{ and}$$
$$\psi^w_{e'} \psi^w_{e''} \geq \text{Inc}(w,y) \cdot \varphi^w_{e'} \varphi^w_{e''}\ ,$$

then we can prove Lemma 3.2 by identifying ψ and φ on $\{(e''', v) \in E \times V \mid v \in e''', e''' \notin \{e, e', e''\}\}$. In order to find such a value y, we will need the definition of an evil value.

Definition 3.8 (evil value). Let $S_{\text{rep}} \subseteq \mathbb{R}^3_{\geq 0}$ denote the set of all representable triples, and fix some $(a, b, c) \in S_{\text{rep}}$. We call a value y of a rank 3 random variable X (a, b, c)*-evil* if there exists no $(a', b', c') \in S_{\text{rep}}$ such that

$$a' \geq \text{Inc}(u, y) \cdot a \ ,$$
$$b' \geq \text{Inc}(v, y) \cdot b \ , \text{ and}$$
$$c' \geq \text{Inc}(w, y) \cdot c \ .$$

In particular, if y is (a, b, c)-evil, then the triple $(\text{Inc}(u, y) \cdot a, \text{Inc}(v, y) \cdot b, \text{Inc}(w, y) \cdot c)$ is not contained in S_{rep}. We prove the following.

LEMMA 3.9. *If there exist a rank 3 random variable X and a triple $(a, b, c) \in S_{\text{rep}}$ such that all possible values y for X are (a, b, c)-evil, then S_{rep} is not incurved.*

PROOF. Let X and (a, b, c) be as described above. Let $\{y_1, \ldots, y_k\}$ be the set of possible values for X, occurring with positive probabilities $p_1, \ldots, p_k$. Let $\mathcal{E}_u, \mathcal{E}_v, \mathcal{E}_w$ denote the bad events affected by X, and let u, v, w denote the associated nodes in the dependency graph, respectively. For $x \in \{u, v, w\}$, we denote by $\Pr[\mathcal{E}_x]$ the probability of bad event $\mathcal{E}_x$ to occur conditioned on the values the already fixed random variables have been assigned. By the definition of $\text{Inc}(\cdot, \cdot)$, we have, for any $x \in \{u, v, w\}$,

$$\sum_{i=1}^{k} (p_i \cdot \text{Inc}(x, y_i)) = \sum_{i=1}^{k} \frac{p_i \cdot \Pr[\mathcal{E}_x \mid X = y_i]}{\Pr[\mathcal{E}_x]} = \frac{\Pr[\mathcal{E}_x]}{\Pr[\mathcal{E}_x]} = 1 \ .$$

For $1 \leq i \leq k$, consider the triples $s_i \in \mathbb{R}^3_{\geq 0}$ defined by $s_i := (\text{Inc}(u, y_i) \cdot a, \text{Inc}(v, y_i) \cdot b, \text{Inc}(w, y_i) \cdot c)$. Since y_i is (a, b, c)-evil for each $1 \leq i \leq k$, we see that no s_i is contained in S_{rep}. Moreover, by our above observations, we have

$$\sum_{i=1}^{k} (p_i \cdot s_i) = \left(\sum_{i=1}^{k} (p_i \cdot \text{Inc}(u, y_i) \cdot a), \sum_{i=1}^{k} (p_i \cdot \text{Inc}(v, y_i) \cdot b), \right.$$
$$\left. \sum_{i=1}^{k} (p_i \cdot \text{Inc}(w, y_i) \cdot c) \right) = (a, b, c) \ .$$

Hence, $\sum_{i=1}^{k} (p_i \cdot s_i) \in S_{\text{rep}}$. Consider the sequence $(t_1, \ldots, t_k)$ of triples defined by $t_1 := s_1$ and

$$t_j := \frac{\sum_{i=1}^{j-1} p_i}{\sum_{i=1}^{j} p_i} \cdot t_{j-1} + \frac{p_j}{\sum_{i=1}^{j} p_i} \cdot s_j \ ,$$

for all $2 \leq j \leq k$. Let j^* be the smallest index such that $t_{j^*} \in S_{\text{rep}}$. A straighforward induction shows that

$$t_j = \sum_{i=1}^{j} \left(\frac{p_i}{\sum_{i'=1}^{j} p_{i'}} \cdot s_i \right) .$$

Hence, we know that such a j^* exists since $t_k = \sum_{i=1}^{k} (p_i \cdot s_i) \in S_{\text{rep}}$ as shown above. Moreover, since $t_1 = s_1 \notin S_{\text{rep}}$, we see that $j^* \geq 2$. Thus, due to the choice of j^*, by setting $s := t_{j^*-1} \notin S_{\text{rep}}$, $s' := s_{j^*} \notin S_{\text{rep}}$, and

$$q := \frac{\sum_{i=1}^{j^*-1} p_i}{\sum_{i=1}^{j^*} p_i} \ ,$$

we obtain the desired s, s', q since $q \cdot s + (1 - q) \cdot s' = t_{j^*} \in S_{\text{rep}}$. Note that all t_j are elements of $\mathbb{R}^3_{\geq 0}$ as they are weighted averages of elements in $\mathbb{R}^3_{\geq 0}$, by the characterization of the t_j given above. □

PROOF OF LEMMA 3.2. Recall our setting and observation immediately before Definition 3.8. By combining Lemma 3.7 and Lemma 3.9, we see that for the random variable X and the representable triple $(a, b, c) := (\varphi^u_e \varphi^u_{e'}, \varphi^v_e \varphi^v_{e''}, \varphi^w_{e'} \varphi^w_{e''})$, there exist a value y for X and a representable triple (a', b', c') such that

$$a' \geq \text{Inc}(u, y) \cdot a \ , \ b' \geq \text{Inc}(v, y) \cdot b \ , \text{ and}$$
$$c' \geq \text{Inc}(w, y) \cdot c \ .$$

Since (a', b', c') is representable, there exist values $\psi^u_e, \psi^v_e, \psi^u_{e'}, \psi^w_{e'}, \psi^v_{e''}, \psi^w_{e''} \in [0, 2]$ with $\psi^u_e + \psi^v_e \leq 2$, $\psi^u_{e'} + \psi^w_{e'} \leq 2$, $\psi^v_{e''} + \psi^w_{e''} \leq 2$ and $a' = \psi^u_e \psi^u_{e'}$, $b' = \psi^v_e \psi^v_{e''}$, $c' = \psi^w_{e'} \psi^w_{e''}$. Hence,

$$\psi^u_e \psi^u_{e'} \geq \text{Inc}(u, y) \cdot \varphi^u_e \varphi^u_{e'} \ ,$$
$$\psi^v_e \psi^v_{e''} \geq \text{Inc}(v, y) \cdot \varphi^v_e \varphi^v_{e''} \ , \text{ and}$$
$$\psi^w_{e'} \psi^w_{e''} \geq \text{Inc}(w, y) \cdot \varphi^w_{e'} \varphi^w_{e''} \ ,$$

which implies that, for the function ψ completed by identifying ψ and φ on $\{(e''', v) \in E \times V \mid v \in e''', e''' \notin \{e, e', e''\}\}$, the pair (G, ψ) satisfies property P^*. Lemma 3.2 follows. □

3.4 Proof of the Main Corollary

COROLLARY 1.4. *Consider an LLL instance with the criterion $p < 2^{-d}$ and where every random variable affects at most 3 bad events. There is an $O(d^2 + \log^* n)$ round deterministic distributed algorithm that solves the LLL problem.*

PROOF. We begin by finding a 2-hop vertex-coloring of the dependency graph with $O(d^2)$ colors. This can be done in $\widetilde{O}(d + \log^* n)$ time [12]. Then, we iterate through the color classes and every node of a color class fixes, one by one but in a single communication round, *all* of its variables that are not fixed yet. We make two observations. First, since we are iterating through a 2-hop-coloring, no two nodes ever fix variables that share an event. Put otherwise, variables incident on events within at least 3 hops from each other cannot share an event. Second, we are effectively fixing the random variables according to *some* order on the variables. Since Theorem 1.3 works for *any* order and due to the local nature of the fixing and bookkeeping in the proof of Theorem 1.3, our process correctly solves the LLL instance. Putting the above together, we obtain an $O(d^2 + \log^* n)$ time algorithm for the LLL problem. □

ACKNOWLEDGEMENTS

We thank Mohsen Ghaffari for bringing the considered problem to our attention, together with providing the solution for rank 2.

REFERENCES

[1] Noga Alon. 1991. A Parallel Algorithmic Version of the Local Lemma. *Random Structures & Algorithms* 2, 4 (1991), 367–378.

[2] Philipp Bamberger, Mohsen Ghaffari, Fabian Kuhn, Yannic Maus, and Jara Uitto. 2019. On the Complexity of Distributed Splitting Problems. In *the Proceedings of the ACM Symposium on Principles of Distributed Computing (PODC)*. ACM.

[3] József Beck. 1991. An Algorithmic Approach to the Lovász Local Lemma. *Random Structures & Algorithms* 2, 4 (1991), 343–365.

[4] Stephen Boyd and Lieven Vandenberghe. 2004. *Convex Optimization*. Cambridge University Press. https://doi.org/10.1017/CBO9780511804441

[5] Sebastian Brandt, Orr Fischer, Juho Hirvonen, Barbara Keller, Tuomo Lempiäinen, Joel Rybicki, Jukka Suomela, and Jara Uitto. 2016. A Lower Bound for the Distributed Lovász Local Lemma. In *the Proceedings of the ACM-SIAM Symposium on Discrete Algorithms (SODA)*.

[6] Yi-Jun Chang, Tsvi Kopelowitz, and Seth Pettie. 2016. An Exponential Separation between Randomized and Deterministic Complexity in the LOCAL Model. In *the Proceedings of the Symposium on Foundations of Computer Science (FOCS)*. 615–624.

[7] Yi-Jun Chang and Seth Pettie. 2017. A Time Hierarchy Theorem for the LOCAL Model. In *the Proceedings of the Symposium on Foundations of Computer Science (FOCS)*. 156–167. https://doi.org/10.1109/FOCS.2017.23

[8] Kai-Min Chung, Seth Pettie, and Hsin-Hao Su. 2017. Distributed Algorithms for the Lovász Local Lemma and Graph Coloring. *Distributed Computing* 30, 4 (2017), 261–280. https://doi.org/10.1007/s00446-016-0287-6

[9] Artur Czumaj and Christian Scheideler. 2000. Coloring Non-uniform Hypergraphs: A New Algorithmic Approach to the General Lovász Local Lemma. In *the Proceedings of the ACM-SIAM Symposium on Discrete Algorithms (SODA)*. 30–39.

[10] Paul Erdös and László Lovász. 1974. Problems and Results on 3-chromatic Hypergraphs and some Related Questions. *Colloquia Mathematica Societatis János Bolyai* (1974), 609–627.

[11] Manuela Fischer and Mohsen Ghaffari. 2017. Sublogarithmic Distributed Algorithms for Lovász Local Lemma, and the Complexity Hierarchy. In *the Proceedings of the 31st International Symposium on Distributed Computing (DISC)*. 18:1–18:16. https://doi.org/10.4230/LIPIcs.DISC.2017.18

[12] Pierre Fraigniaud, Marc Heinrich, and Adrian Kosowski. 2016. Local Conflict Coloring. In *the Proceedings of the Symposium on Foundations of Computer Science (FOCS)*. 625–634.

[13] Mohsen Ghaffari. 2016. An Improved Distributed Algorithm for Maximal Independent Set. In *the Proceedings of the ACM-SIAM Symposium on Discrete Algorithms (SODA)*. 270–277.

[14] Mohsen Ghaffari, David G. Harris, and Fabian Kuhn. 2018. On Derandomizing Local Distributed Algorithms. In *the Proceedings of the Symposium on Foundations of Computer Science (FOCS)*. 662–673.

[15] Mohsen Ghaffari, Juho Hirvonen, Fabian Kuhn, Yannic Maus, Jukka Suomela, and Jara Uitto. 2017. Improved Distributed Degree Splitting and Edge Coloring. 19:1–19:15.

[16] Mohsen Ghaffari, Fabian Kuhn, and Yannic Maus. 2017. On the complexity of local distributed graph problems. In *the Proceedings of the ACM-SIAM Symposium on Discrete Algorithms (SODA)*. ACM, 784–797.

[17] Mohsen Ghaffari and Hsin-Hao Su. 2017. Distributed Degree Splitting, Edge Coloring, and Orientations. In *Proc. 28th ACM-SIAM Symp. on Discrete Algorithms (SODA)*.

[18] David G. Harris. 2018. Distributed approximation algorithms for maximum matching in graphs and hypergraphs. *CoRR* abs/1807.07645 (2018). arXiv:1807.07645 http://arxiv.org/abs/1807.07645

[19] Michael Molloy and Bruce Reed. 1998. Further Algorithmic Aspects of the Local Lemma. In *the Proceedings of the ACM-SIAM Symposium on Discrete Algorithms (SODA)*. 524–529.

[20] Robin A. Moser and Gábor Tardos. 2010. A Constructive Proof of the General Lovász Local Lemma. *J. ACM* (2010), 11:1–11:15.

[21] János Pach and Gábor Tardos. 2009. Conflict-free Colourings of Graphs and Hypergraphs. *Combinatorics Probability and Computing* 18, 5 (2009).

[22] Alessandro Panconesi and Romeo Rizzi. 2001. Some Simple Distributed Algorithms for Sparse Networks. *Distributed Computing* 14, 2 (2001), 97–100.

[23] Aravind Srinivasan. 2008. Improved Algorithmic Versions of the Lovász Local Lemma. In *the Proceedings of the ACM-SIAM Symposium on Discrete Algorithms (SODA)*. 611–620.

A DEFERRED PROOFS

Proof of Lemma 3.5. Let $T := \{(a,b,c) \subseteq \mathbb{R}^3_{\geq 0} \mid a+b \leq 4, c \leq f(a,b)\}$ We first show that any representable (a,b,c) is in T. If (a,b,c) is representable there are $a_1, a_2, b_1, b_3, c_2, c_3 \in [0,2]$ with $a_1+b_1 \leq 2, a_2+c_2 \leq 2, b_3+c_3 \leq 2, a = a_1a_2, b = b_1b_3$ and $c = c_2c_3$. Thus we obtain $a+b = a_1a_2+b_1b_3 \leq 2a_1+2b_1 \leq 2a_1+2(2-a_1) = 4$. We now show that the maximal c for which (a,b,c) is representable for given $a,b \in [0,4]$ with $a+b \leq 4$ equals $f(a,b)$. Note that this implies that any $0 \leq c \leq f(a,b)$ is also representable. We consider several cases for a and b where the only non trivial case is $a,b \neq 0$.

- Case $a = b = 0$: We can choose $a_1 = a_2 = b_2 = b_3 = 0$ and $c_2 = c_3 = 2$, i.e, $(a,b,4)$ is representable and we also have $f(0,0) = 4$.
- Case $a = 0, b \neq 0$: We can choose $a_1 = a_2 = 0$ and $b_1 = c_2 = 2$. Then we obtain $c \leq c_2c_3 = 2c_3 \leq 2(2-b_3) = 2(2-b/2) = 4-b$ and we also have $f(0,b) = 4-b$.
- Case $a \neq 0, b = 0$: The proof of this case is analogous to the case $a = 0, b \neq 0$.
- Case $a,b \neq 0$. First note that $a,b \neq 0$ implies $a,b \neq 4$ because $a+b \leq 4$. For fixed $a,b \notin \{0,4\}$ we vary the value of a_1 to see which values of c can be represented. We denote this varying value of a_1 by x. As $2 \geq a_2 = a/x$ we obtain $x \geq a/2$ and due to $2 \geq b_3 = b/(2-x)$ we obtain $x \geq 2 - b/2$. Thus we obtain that $c \leq c_2c_3 \leq (2-a_2)(2-b_3) \leq \left(2 - \frac{a}{x}\right)\left(2 - \frac{b}{2-x}\right) =: c(x)$ and $a/2 \leq x \leq 2 - b/2$. To find the maximal value of c we compute the derivative $\frac{d}{dx}c(x)$ as

$$\frac{d}{dx}c(x) = \frac{2((a-b)x^2 - a(4-b)x + a(4-b))}{(x-2)^2x^2} .$$

Thus we have $\frac{d}{dx}c(x) = 0$ if and only if $(a-b)x^2 + (ab-4a)x + 4a - ab = 0$.

Case $a = b \neq 0$: The equality is satisfied for $x = 1$, that is, $c \leq c(1) = (2-a)^2 = f(a,a)$.

Case $a \neq b, a, b \neq 0$: Let $p = \frac{a(4-b)}{(a-b)}$. Then we get $\frac{d}{dx}c(x) = 0$ if and only if $x^2 - px + p = 0$ which is satisfied for

$$x_{1,2} = \frac{p}{2} \pm \sqrt{\frac{p^2-4p}{4}} = \frac{a(4-b) \pm \sqrt{ab(4-a)(4-b)}}{2(a-b)} .$$

The value $x_2 = \frac{p}{2} + \sqrt{\frac{p^2-4p}{4}}$ is outside of the range $[a/2, 2-b/2]$ as for $b > a$ it is negative and for $a > b > 0$ it is larger than $2 - b/2$. Plugging $x_1 = \frac{p}{2} - \sqrt{\frac{p^2-4p}{4}}$ into $c(\cdot)$ yields

$$\begin{aligned}
c(x_1) &= \left(2 - \frac{a}{x_1}\right)\left(2 - \frac{b}{2-x_1}\right) \\
&= \left(2 - \frac{2a(a-b)}{a(4-b) - \sqrt{ab(4-a)(4-b)}}\right) \\
&\quad \cdot \left(2 - \frac{2b(a-b)}{-(4-a)b + \sqrt{ab(4-a)(4-b)}}\right) \\
&= 4 \cdot \frac{a(4-a) - \sqrt{ab(4-a)(4-b)}}{a(4-b) - \sqrt{ab(4-a)(4-b)}} \\
&\quad \cdot \frac{b(4-b) - \sqrt{ab(4-a)(4-b)}}{b(4-a) - \sqrt{ab(4-a)(4-b)}}
\end{aligned}$$

Factoring $\sqrt{ab(4-a)(4-b)} \neq 0$ out of the four terms yields

$$\begin{aligned}
& 4 \cdot \frac{\frac{\sqrt{a(4-a)}}{\sqrt{b(4-b)}} - 1}{\frac{\sqrt{a(4-b)}}{\sqrt{b(4-a)}} - 1} \cdot \frac{\frac{\sqrt{b(4-b)}}{\sqrt{a(4-a)}} - 1}{\frac{\sqrt{b(4-a)}}{\sqrt{a(4-b)}} - 1} \\
&= 4 \cdot \frac{\frac{\sqrt{a(4-a)} - \sqrt{b(4-b)}}{\sqrt{b(4-b)}}}{\frac{\sqrt{a(4-b)} - \sqrt{b(4-a)}}{\sqrt{b(4-a)}}} \cdot \frac{\frac{\sqrt{b(4-b)} - \sqrt{a(4-a)}}{\sqrt{a(4-a)}}}{\frac{\sqrt{b(4-a)} - \sqrt{a(4-b)}}{\sqrt{a(4-b)}}} \\
&= 4 \cdot \left(\frac{\sqrt{a(4-a)} - \sqrt{b(4-b)}}{\sqrt{a(4-b)} - \sqrt{b(4-a)}}\right)^2
\end{aligned}$$

and multiplying nominator and denominator with $\sqrt{a(4-b)}+\sqrt{b(4-a)} \neq 0$ yields

$$4 \cdot \left(\frac{(a-b)\sqrt{(4-a)(4-b)} - (a-b)\sqrt{ab}}{4(a-b)} \right)^2 = \left(\frac{\sqrt{(4-a)(4-b)} - \sqrt{ab}}{2} \right)^2 = 4 + \frac{1}{2} \cdot (ab - 2a - 2b - \sqrt{ab(4-a)(4-b)}) .$$

As $x \in [a/2, 2-b/2]$ and we have $c(a/2) = c(2-b/2) = 0$ the maximum possible value for c for a given $a, b \in [0,4]$ with $a, b \neq 0$ and $a + b \leq 4$ is $c(x_1) = f(a,b)$. This concludes the case $a, b \neq 0$.

Summarizing all cases we have shown that any representable (a,b,c) is contained in the set T. For the converse direction let $(a,b,c) \in T$, that is, $a, b, c \in [0,4]$, $a + b \leq 4$ and $c \leq f(a,b)$. The previous proof has shown that $(a,b,f(a,b))$ is representable by letting $a_1 = x_1, a_2 = a/a_1, b_1 = 2-a_1, b_3 = b/b_2, c_2 = 2-a_2$ and $c_3 = 2-b_3$. As $c \leq f(a,b)$ we can also represent (a,b,c) by decreasing c_2 (or c_3) without violating the constraints. □

Proof of Lemma 3.6. Set $U := \{(a,b) \in \mathbb{R}^2_{\geq 0} \mid a + b \leq 4\}$ and $U' := \{(a,b) \in \mathbb{R}^2_{>0} \mid a + b < 4\}$. Since $f(a,b)$ is continuous on U, it is sufficient to show convexity of $f(a,b)$ on the open domain U', which in turn can be showed by proving that at every point $x \in U'$, the Hessian $\nabla^2 f(x)$ of f is positive semi-definite (cf., e.g., [4, Section 3.1.4]). We will prove the slightly stronger statement that $\nabla^2 f(x)$ is positive definite, which, by Sylvester's criterion, is equivalent to the statement that all leading principal minors of $\nabla^2 f(x)$ are positive. In other words, we will prove our lemma by showing that $\frac{\partial^2 f(x)}{\partial a^2} > 0$ and $\frac{\partial^2 f(x)}{\partial a^2} \cdot \frac{\partial^2 f(x)}{\partial b^2} - \frac{\partial^2 f(x)}{\partial a \partial b} \cdot \frac{\partial^2 f(x)}{\partial a \partial b} > 0$ for all $x \in U'$. To this end, we first calculate the four involved terms for $x = (a,b) \in U'$. We have

$$\frac{\partial f(a,b)}{\partial a} = \frac{1}{2} \cdot \left(b - 2 - \frac{b(4-b)(4-2a)}{2\sqrt{ab(4-a)(4-b)}} \right) ,$$

which implies

$$\frac{\partial^2 f(a,b)}{\partial a^2} = \frac{1}{2} \cdot - \frac{-4b(4-b)\sqrt{ab(4-a)(4-b)}}{4ab(4-a)(4-b)} - \frac{1}{2} \cdot \frac{\frac{2b(4-b)(4-2a)b(4-b)(4-2a)}{2\sqrt{ab(4-a)(4-b)}}}{4ab(4-a)(4-b)} = \frac{1}{2} \cdot \left(\sqrt{\frac{b(4-b)}{a(4-a)}} + \frac{(2-a)^2}{a(4-a)} \cdot \sqrt{\frac{b(4-b)}{a(4-a)}} \right) = \frac{2}{a(4-a)} \cdot \sqrt{\frac{b(4-b)}{a(4-a)}}$$

$$\frac{\partial f(a,b)}{\partial a \partial b} = \frac{1}{2} \cdot \left(1 - \frac{2(4-2b)(4-2a)\sqrt{ab(4-a)(4-b)}}{4ab(4-a)(4-b)} - \frac{\frac{2b(4-b)(4-2a)a(4-a)(4-2b)}{2\sqrt{ab(4-a)(4-b)}}}{4ab(4-a)(4-b)} \right) = \frac{1}{2} \cdot \left(1 - \frac{2(2-b)(2-a)}{\sqrt{ab(4-a)(4-b)}} + \frac{(2-a)(2-b)}{\sqrt{ab(4-a)(4-b)}} \right) = \frac{1}{2} - \frac{(2-a)(2-b)}{2\sqrt{ab(4-a)(4-b)}} .$$

Since our function $f(a,b)$ is symmetric in a and b, we also have

$$\frac{\partial^2 f(a,b)}{\partial b^2} = \frac{2}{b(4-b)} \cdot \sqrt{\frac{a(4-a)}{b(4-b)}} \text{ and } \frac{\partial f(a,b)}{\partial b \partial a} = \frac{1}{2} - \frac{(2-a)(2-b)}{2\sqrt{ab(4-a)(4-b)}} .$$

Hence, we obtain

$$\frac{\partial^2 f(a,b)}{\partial a^2} = \frac{2}{a(4-a)} \cdot \sqrt{\frac{b(4-b)}{a(4-a)}} > 0$$

$$\begin{aligned} &\frac{\partial^2 f(a,b)}{\partial a^2} \cdot \frac{\partial^2 f(a,b)}{\partial b^2} - \frac{\partial^2 f(a,b)}{\partial a \partial b} \cdot \frac{\partial^2 f(a,b)}{\partial a \partial b} \\ &= \frac{2}{a(4-a)} \cdot \sqrt{\frac{b(4-b)}{a(4-a)}} \cdot \frac{2}{b(4-b)} \cdot \sqrt{\frac{a(4-a)}{b(4-b)}} - \left(\frac{1}{2} - \frac{(2-a)(2-b)}{2\sqrt{ab(4-a)(4-b)}} \right)^2 \\ &= \frac{4}{ab(4-a)(4-b)} - \frac{1}{4} + \frac{(2-a)(2-b)}{2\sqrt{ab(4-a)(4-b)}} - \frac{(2-a)^2(2-b)^2}{4ab(4-a)(4-b)} \\ &= \frac{16 - ab(4-a)(4-b) + 2(2-a)(2-b)\sqrt{ab(4-a)(4-b)}}{4ab(4-a)(4-b)} - \frac{(a^2-4a+4)(b^2-4b+4)}{4ab(4-a)(4-b)} \\ &= \frac{-2a^2b^2 + 8a^2b + 8ab^2 - 4a^2 - 4b^2 - 32ab + 16a}{4ab(4-a)(4-b)} + \frac{16b + (2ab - 4a - 4b + 8)\sqrt{ab(4-a)(4-b)}}{4ab(4-a)(4-b)} \\ &= \frac{16 - (4 + ab - 2a - 2b - \sqrt{ab(4-a)(4-b)})^2}{4ab(4-a)(4-b)} \\ &= \frac{16 - \left(\frac{1}{2} \cdot \left(\sqrt{(4-a)(4-b)} - \sqrt{ab} \right)^2 - 4 \right)^2}{4ab(4-a)(4-b)} > 0 , \end{aligned}$$

for all $(a,b) \in U'$. Here, the last inequality follows from the fact that, for all $(a,b) \in U'$, we have $0 < \left(\sqrt{(4-a)(4-b)} - \sqrt{ab} \right)^2 < 16$ since $0 < a < 4-b$, $0 < b < 4-a$, and $(4-a)(4-b) < 16$. As argued above, it follows that $f(a,b) := 4 + 1/2 \cdot (ab - 2a - 2b - \sqrt{ab(4-a)(4-b)})$ is convex on U. □

Reconfigurable Atomic Transaction Commit

Manuel Bravo
IMDEA Software Institute

Alexey Gotsman
IMDEA Software Institute

ABSTRACT

Modern data stores achieve scalability by partitioning data into shards and fault-tolerance by replicating each shard across several servers. A key component of such systems is a Transaction Certification Service (TCS), which atomically commits a transaction spanning multiple shards. Existing TCS protocols require $2f + 1$ crash-stop replicas per shard to tolerate f failures. In this paper we present atomic commit protocols that require only $f + 1$ replicas and reconfigure the system upon failures using an external reconfiguration service. We furthermore rigorously prove that these protocols correctly implement a recently proposed TCS specification. We present protocols in two different models—the standard asynchronous message-passing model and a model with Remote Direct Memory Access (RDMA), which allows a machine to access the memory of another machine over the network without involving the latter's CPU. Our protocols are inspired by a recent FARM system for RDMA-based transaction processing. Our work codifies the core ideas of FARM as distributed TCS protocols, rigorously proves them correct and highlights the trade-offs required by the use of RDMA.

CCS CONCEPTS

• **Theory of computation** → **Distributed algorithms**; *Distributed computing models*;

KEYWORDS

Atomic commit, vertical Paxos, RDMA.

ACM Reference Format:
Manuel Bravo and Alexey Gotsman. 2019. Reconfigurable Atomic Transaction Commit. In *2019 ACM Symposium on Principles of Distributed Computing (PODC '19), July 29-August 2, 2019, Toronto, ON, Canada.* ACM, New York, NY, USA, 10 pages. https://doi.org/10.1145/3293611.3331590

1 INTRODUCTION

Modern data stores are often required to manage massive amounts of data while providing stringent transactional guarantees to their users. They achieve scalability by partitioning data into independently managed *shards* (aka *partitions*) and fault-tolerance by replicating each shard across a set of servers [7, 11, 23]. Such data stores often use optimistic concurrency control [27], where a transaction is first executed speculatively, and the results (e.g., read and write sets) are then *certified* to determine whether the transaction can commit or must abort because of a conflict with concurrent transactions. The certification is implemented by a *Transaction Certification Service (TCS)*, which accepts a stream of transactions and outputs decisions based on a given *certification function*, defining the concurrency-control check for the desired isolation level. TCS is the most challenging part of transaction processing in systems with the above architecture, since it requires solving a distributed agreement problem among the replicated shards participating in the transaction. This agreement problem has been recently formalized as the *multi-shot commit problem* [6], generalizing the classical *atomic commit problem* [10] to more faithfully reflect the requirements of modern transaction processing systems (we review the new problem statement in §2).

Most existing solutions to the TCS problem require replicating each shard among $2f + 1$ replicas to tolerate f crash-stop failures within each shard [7, 11, 16, 28], which allows using a replication protocol such as Paxos [17]. This is expensive: if transaction data are written to all replicas of the shard, only $f+1$ replicas are needed for the data to survive failures. Since, in this case even a single replica failure will block transaction processing, to recover we need to *reconfigure* the system, i.e., change its membership to replace failed replicas with fresh ones. Unfortunately, processes concurrently deciding to reconfigure the system need to be able to agree on the next configuration; this reduces to solving consensus, which again requires $2f + 1$ replicas [18]. The way out of this conundrum is to use a separate *configuration service* with $2f + 1$ replicas to perform consensus on the configuration. In this way, we use $2f + 1$ replicas only to store the small amount of information about the configuration and $f+1$ replicas to store the actual data. This *vertical approach* [19], which layers replication on top of a configuration service, has been used by a number of practical systems [1, 5, 9]. It is particularly suitable for deployment in local-area networks, where the configuration service can be reached quickly.

In this paper we propose the first rigorously proven protocols for implementing a TCS in a vertical system, with $f + 1$ replicas per shard and an external configuration service. We present protocols in two different models—the standard asynchronous message-passing model (§3) and a model with Remote Direct Memory Access (RDMA), which allows a machine to access the memory of another machine over the network without involving the latter's CPU (§5). Our protocols are parametric in the isolation level provided, and we prove that they correctly implement the TCS specification from the multi-shot commit problem [6] (§4).

Our work complements and takes its inspiration from a recent FARM system [9, 24]—a transaction processing system that achieves impressive scalability and availability by exploiting RDMA and the vertical approach. FARM currently forms the core of a graph database used to serve some of search queries in Microsoft Bing. It is a complex system that includes a number of optimizations, both specific to RDMA and not. FARM's design was presented without a rigorous proof of correctness, and it did not highlight which features

PODC '19, July 29-August 2, 2019, Toronto, ON, Canada

ACM ISBN 978-1-4503-6217-7/19/07...$15.00
https://doi.org/10.1145/3293611.3331590

are motivated by the use of RDMA and which are inherent to the vertical approach. Our work provides a theoretical complement to FARM: we codify its core ideas as distributed transaction commit protocols and rigorously prove them correct with respect to the TCS specification. By basing our protocols on a principled footing, we are also able to provide better fault-tolerance guarantees than FARM. Finally, by presenting two related protocols using message passing and RDMA, we determine the trade-offs required by the use of RDMA.

In more detail, a straightforward way to implement TCS is using the classical *two-phase commit (2PC)* protocol [12]. Since 2PC is not fault-tolerant, we can make each shard simulate a reliable process in 2PC using a replication protocol such as Paxos [7, 11]. This vanilla approach requires every 2PC action to be replicated using Paxos, which results in a high latency (7 message delays to learn a decision on a transaction [22]) and a high load on Paxos leaders. To improve on this, our protocol combines 2PC and Vertical Paxos [19] into one coherent protocol, thereby minimizing the latency and load on Paxos leaders. Upon a failure inside a shard, we use the reconfiguration service to replace the failed replicas, as in Vertical Paxos. This reconfiguration interacts nontrivially with the 2PC part of the protocol: e.g., reconfiguration may lead to losing undecided transactions that affected 2PC computations of decisions on other transactions—a behavior that we nevertheless show to be correct. Finally, we show that the price of exploiting RDMA to efficiently write transaction data to replicas is that reconfiguration has to be performed globally, instead of per-shard: when reconfiguring a shard, we have to ensure that the whole system is aware of the configuration before activating it.

2 TRANSACTION CERTIFICATION SERVICE

Service interface and certification functions. A *Transaction Certification Service (TCS)* is meant to be used in the context of transactional processing systems with optimistic concurrency control [27], where transactions are first executed speculatively, and the results are submitted for certification to the TCS. We start by reviewing its specification proposed in [6]. Clients invoke the TCS using requests of the form $\mathtt{certify}(t, l)$, where $t \in \mathcal{T}$ is a unique transaction identifier and $l \in \mathcal{L}$ is the transaction payload, which carries the results of the optimistic execution of the transaction (e.g., read and write sets). Responses of the service are of the form $\mathtt{decide}(t, d)$, where $d \in \mathcal{D} = \{\textsc{abort}, \textsc{commit}\}$. A TCS is specified using a *certification function* $f : 2^{\mathcal{L}} \times \mathcal{L} \to \mathcal{D}$, which encapsulates the concurrency-control policy for the desired isolation level. The result $f(L, l)$ is the decision for the transaction with payload l given the set of payloads L of the previously committed transactions. We require f to be *distributive* in the following sense:

$$\forall L_1, L_2, l.\ f(L_1 \cup L_2, l) = f(L_1, l) \sqcap f(L_2, l), \quad (1)$$

where $\sqcap$ is such that $\textsc{commit} \sqcap \textsc{commit} = \textsc{commit}$ and $d \sqcap \textsc{abort} = \textsc{abort}$ for any d. This requirement is justified by the fact that common definitions of $f(L, l)$ check l for conflicts against each transaction in L separately.

As an example, consider a transactional system managing *objects* from Obj with values from Val, where transactions can execute reads and writes on the objects. The objects are associated with a totally ordered set Ver of *versions*. Then the payload of a transaction t is a triple $\langle R, W, V_c \rangle$. Here the *read set* $R \subseteq \mathrm{Obj} \times \mathrm{Ver}$ is the set of objects with their versions that t read, which contains one version per object. The *write set* $W \subseteq \mathrm{Obj} \times \mathrm{Val}$ is the set of objects with their values that t wrote, which contains one value per object. We require that any object written has also been read: $\forall (x, \_) \in W.\, (x, \_) \in R$. Finally, the *commit version* $V_c \in \mathrm{Ver}$ is the version to be assigned to the writes of t. We require this version to be higher than any of the versions read: $\forall (\_, v) \in R.\, V_c > v$. Given this domain of transactions, the following certification function encapsulates the classical concurrency-control policy for serializability [27]: $f(L, \langle R, W, V_c \rangle) = \textsc{commit}$ iff none of the versions in R have been overwritten by a transaction in L, i.e.,

$$\forall x, v.\, (x, v) \in R \implies (\forall (\_, W', V_c') \in L.\, (x, \_) \in W' \implies V_c' \le v). \quad (2)$$

TCS specification. We represent TCS executions using *histories*—sequences of $\mathtt{certify}$ and $\mathtt{decide}$ actions such that every transaction appears at most once in $\mathtt{certify}$, and each $\mathtt{decide}$ is a response to exactly one preceding $\mathtt{certify}$. For a history h we let $\mathrm{act}(h)$ be the set of actions in h. For actions $a, a' \in \mathrm{act}(h)$, we write $a \prec_h a'$ when a occurs before a' in h. A history h is *complete* if every $\mathtt{certify}$ action in it has a matching $\mathtt{decide}$ action. A complete history is *sequential* if it consists of pairs of $\mathtt{certify}$ and matching $\mathtt{decide}$ actions. A transaction t *commits* in a history h if h contains $\mathtt{decide}(t, \textsc{commit})$. We denote by $\mathrm{committed}(h)$ the projection of h to actions corresponding to the transactions that are committed in h. For a complete history h, a *linearization* ℓ of h [14] is a sequential history such that h and ℓ contain the same actions and

$$\forall t, t'.\, \mathtt{decide}(t, \_) \prec_h \mathtt{certify}(t', \_) \implies \mathtt{decide}(t, \_) \prec_\ell \mathtt{certify}(t', \_).$$

A complete sequential history h is *legal* with respect to a certification function f, if its decisions are computed according to f:

$$\forall t, l, d.\, \mathtt{certify}(t, l), \mathtt{decide}(t, d) \in \mathrm{act}(h) \implies d = f(\{l' \mid \mathtt{certify}(t', l') \in \mathrm{act}(h) \land \mathtt{decide}(t', \textsc{commit}) \prec_h \mathtt{decide}(t, d)\}, l).$$

A history h is *correct* with respect to f if $h \mid \mathrm{committed}(h)$ has a legal linearization. A TCS implementation is *correct* with respect to f if so are all its histories.

A TCS implementation satisfying the above specification can be readily used in a transaction processing system. For example, consider the domain of transactions defined earlier. A typical system based on optimistic concurrency control will ensure that transactions submitted for certification only read versions written by previously committed transactions. A history produced by such a system that is correct with respect to certification function (2) is also serializable [6]. Hence, a TCS correct with respect to this certification function can indeed be used to implement serializability.

Shard-local certification functions. We are interested in TCS implementations in systems where the data are partitioned into shards from a set $\mathcal{S}$. In such systems TCS is usually implemented using a variant of the classical *two-phase commit protocol (2PC)* [12].

In this protocol each shard s receiving a transaction for certification first *prepares* it, i.e., performs a local concurrency-control check and accordingly votes to commit or abort the transaction. The votes on the transaction by different shards are aggregated, and the final decision is then distributed to all shards: the transaction can commit only if all votes are commit. When a shard s votes on a transaction, it does not have information about all transactions in the system, but only those that concern it. Hence, the votes are computed using not the global certification function f, but *shard-local certification functions* [6], which check for conflicts only on objects managed by the shard and correspondingly take as parameters only the parts of the transaction payloads relevant to the shard: for a payload l we denote this by $l \mid s$. For example, let Obj_s be the set of objects managed by a shard s. For a payload $l = \langle R, W, V_c \rangle$ of the form given above, we let $l \mid s = \langle R^s, W^s, V_c \rangle$, where $R^s = \{(x, \_) \in R \mid x \in \mathrm{Obj}_s\}$ and $W^s = \{(x, \_) \in W \mid x \in \mathrm{Obj}_s\}$. There are two shard-local functions, $f_s : 2^{\mathcal{L}} \times \mathcal{L} \to \mathcal{D}$ and $g_s : 2^{\mathcal{L}} \times \mathcal{L} \to \mathcal{D}$. As its first argument f_s takes the set of shard-relevant payloads of transactions that previously committed at the shard, and g_s the set of such payloads for transactions that have been prepared to commit. As their second argument, the functions take the part of the payload of the transaction being certified relevant to the shard. We require that these functions are distributive, similarly to (1).

For example, the shard-local certification functions for serializability are defined as follows: $f_s(L, \langle R, W, V_c \rangle) = \text{COMMIT}$ iff

$$\forall x \in \mathrm{Obj}_s.\, \forall v.\, (x, v) \in R \implies (\forall \langle \_, W', V_c' \rangle \in L.\, (x, \_) \in W' \implies V_c' \le v),$$

and $g_s(L, \langle R, W, V_c \rangle) = \text{COMMIT}$ iff

$$\forall x \in \mathrm{Obj}_s.\, \forall v.\, ((x, \_) \in R \implies (\forall \langle \_, W', \_ \rangle \in L.\, (x, \_) \notin W')) \land ((x, \_) \in W \implies (\forall \langle R', \_, \_ \rangle \in L.\, (x, \_) \notin R')).$$

The function f_s certifies a transaction t against previously committed transactions similarly to the certification function (2) for serializability, but taking into account only the objects managed by the shard s. The function g_s certifies t against transactions prepared to commit, and its check is stricter than that of f_s. In our example, the function g_s aborts a transaction t if: *(i)* it read an object written by a transaction t' prepared to commit; or *(ii)* it writes to an object read by a transaction t' prepared to commit. This reflects the behaviour of typical implementations, which upon preparing a transaction acquire read locks on its read set and write locks on its write set, and abort the transaction if the locks cannot be acquired.

For a sharded TCS implementation to be correct, shard-local functions have to *match* the global certification function, i.e., perform similar conflict checks. We formalize the required conditions as follows. Assume a function $\mathrm{shards} : \mathcal{T} \to 2^{\mathcal{S}}$ that determines the shards that need to certify a transaction with a given identifier, which are usually the shards storing the data the transaction accesses. We also assume a distinguished *empty* payload $\varepsilon \in \mathcal{L}$ such that $\forall s, L.\, f_s(L, \varepsilon) = \text{COMMIT}$. For example, for a payload $l = \langle R, W, \_ \rangle$ of the form given above, $l = \varepsilon$ is such that $R = \emptyset$ and $W = \emptyset$. We require that for a transaction $t \in \mathcal{T}$ with payload $l \in \mathcal{L}$, for each shard $s \notin \mathrm{shards}(t)$, we have $l \mid s = \varepsilon$. We further lift the $\mid$ operator to sets of payloads: for any $L \subseteq \mathcal{L}$ we let $(L \mid s) = \{(l \mid s) \mid l \in L\}$. Then we require that global and local certification functions match as follows:

$$\forall l \in \mathcal{L}.\, \forall L \subseteq \mathcal{L}.\, f(L, l) = \text{COMMIT} \iff \forall s \in \mathcal{S}.\, f_s((L \mid s), (l \mid s)) = \text{COMMIT}. \quad (3)$$

Finally, for each shard $s \in \mathcal{S}$, the two functions f_s and g_s are required to be related to each other as follows [6]:

$$\forall l \in \mathcal{L}.\, L \subseteq \mathcal{L}.\, g_s(L, l) = \text{COMMIT} \implies f_s(L, l) = \text{COMMIT}; \quad (4)$$

$$\forall l, l' \in \mathcal{L}.\, g_s(\{l\}, l') = \text{COMMIT} \implies f_s(\{l'\}, l) = \text{COMMIT}. \quad (5)$$

Property (4) requires the conflict check performed by g_s to be no weaker than the one performed by f_s. Property (5) requires a form of commutativity: if a transaction with payload l' is allowed to commit after a still-pending transaction with payload l, then the latter would be allowed to commit after the former.

3 ATOMIC COMMIT PROTOCOL

System model. We consider an asynchronous message-passing system consisting of a set of processes $\mathcal{P}$ which may fail by crashing, i.e., permanently stopping execution. We assume that processes are connected by reliable FIFO channels: messages are delivered in FIFO order, and messages between non-faulty processes are guaranteed to be eventually delivered. A function $\mathrm{client} : \mathcal{T} \to \mathcal{P}$ determines the client process that issued a given transaction.

Each shard $s \in \mathcal{S}$ is managed by a group of *replica* processes, whose membership can change over time. For simplicity, we assume that the groups of replica processes managing different shards are disjoint. Each shard moves through a sequence of *configurations*, determining its membership. *Reconfiguration* is the process of changing the configuration of a shard. In our protocols reconfiguration is initiated by a replica when it suspects another replica of failing: for simplicity we do not expose it in the TCS interface. Every member of a shard in a given configuration is either the *leader* of the shard or a *follower*. A configuration of a shard s is then a tuple $\langle e, M, p_l \rangle$ where e is the *epoch* identifying the configuration, $M \in 2^{\mathcal{P}}$ is the set of processes that manage s at e, and $p_l \in M$ is the leader of s at e.

Configurations are stored in an external *configuration service (CS)*, which for simplicity we assume to be a reliable process. In practice, this service may be implemented using Paxos-like replication over $2f + 1$ processes out of which at most f can fail (as done in systems such as Zookeeper [15]). The configuration service stores the configurations of all shards and provides three operations. An operation `compare_and_swap`$(s, e, \langle e', M, p_l \rangle)$ succeeds if the epoch of the last stored configuration of s is e; in this case it stores the provided configuration with a higher epoch $e' > e$. Operations `get_last`(s) and `get`(s, e) respectively return the last configuration of s and the configuration of s associated with a given epoch e.

Protocol preliminaries. We give the pseudocode of our protocol in Figure 1, illustrate its message flow in Figure 2 and summarize the key invariants used in its proof of correctness in Figure 3. The protocol weaves together the two-phase commit protocol across shards [12] and a Vertical Paxos-based reconfiguration protocol within each shard [19]. At any given time, a process participates in a single configuration of the shard it belongs to. The process stores the information about this configuration as well as those of other shards in several arrays: configuration epochs are stored in an array epoch $\in \mathcal{S} \to \mathbb{N}$, the current members in members $\in \mathcal{S} \to 2^{\mathcal{P}}$, and the current leader in leader $\in \mathcal{S} \to \mathcal{P}$. The entries for the shard the process belongs to give the configuration the process is in; the other entries maintain information about the configurations of the other shards. A status variable at a process records whether it is a LEADER, a FOLLOWER or is in a special RECONFIGURING state used during reconfiguration. Each process keeps track of the status of transactions in an array phase, whose entries initially store START. The transaction status changes to PREPARED when the shard determines its vote and to DECIDED when a final decision on the transaction is reached.

Failure-free case. A client submits a transaction for certification by calling the `certify` function at any replica process, which will serve as the *coordinator* of the transaction (line 1). The function takes as arguments the transaction's identifier and its payload. The transaction coordinator first sends a PREPARE message to the leaders of the relevant shards, which includes the payload part for each shard (line 3). The leader of a shard arranges all transactions it receives into a total *certification order*, which the leader stores in an array txn $\in \mathbb{N} \to \mathcal{T}$; a next $\in \mathbb{Z}$ variable points to the last filled slot in the array. When the leader receives a PREPARE message for a transaction for the first time (line 8), it appends the transaction to the certification order, stores the transaction's payload in an array payload $\in \mathbb{N} \to \mathcal{L}$, and sets the transaction's phase to PREPARED. It then computes a vote on the transaction and stores it in an array vote $\in \mathbb{N} \to \{\text{COMMIT}, \text{ABORT}\}$ (line 12). The vote is computed using the shard-local certification functions f_{s_0} and g_{s_0} to check for conflicts against transactions that have been previously committed or prepared to commit; the results are combined using the $\sqcap$ operator, so that the transaction can commit only if both functions say so. We defer the description of the cases when the leader has previously received the transaction in the PREPARE message (line 6) and when the payload in the message is an undefined value $\perp$ (line 14).

Our protocol next replicates the leader's decision and the transaction payload at the followers. Instead of having the leader to do this directly, the protocol delegates this task to the coordinator of the transaction. This design is used by practical systems, such as Corfu [1] and FARM [9], since it minimizes the load on the leaders, which are the main potential performance bottleneck. Instead, the network-intensive task of persisting transactions at multiple followers is spread among a number of different transaction coordinators. As we explain in the following, this optimization interacts in a nontrivial way with transaction certification. In more detail, after preparing a transaction the leader sends a PREPARE_ACK message to the coordinator of the transaction, which carries the leader's epoch, the transaction identifier, its position in the certification order, the payload, and the vote (line 20). Upon receiving the PREPARE_ACK message (line 18), the coordinator forwards the data from the PREPARE_ACK message to the followers in an ACCEPT message.

A process handles an ACCEPT message only if it participates in the corresponding epoch (line 22). The process stores the transaction identifier, its payload and vote, and advances the transaction's phase to PREPARED. It then sends an ACCEPT_ACK message to the coordinator of the transaction, confirming that the process has accepted the transaction and the vote. The certification order at a follower is always a prefix with zero or more holes of the certification order at the leader of the epoch the follower is in, as formalized by Invariant 1 (Figure 3). The holes in the prefix arise from the lack of FIFO ordering in the communication between the leader of a given epoch and its followers, as the ACCEPT message for a given transaction is sent to the followers by the coordinator of the transaction and not directly by the leader.

The coordinator of a transaction t acts once it receives ACCEPT_ACK messages for t from every follower of its shards $s \in \text{shards}(t)$ (line 26); it determines this using the configuration information it stores for every shard. The coordinator computes the final decision on t using the $\sqcap$ operator on the votes of each involved shard: the transaction can commit if all votes are commit. The coordinator then sends the final decision in DECISION messages to the client and to each of the relevant shards. When a process receives a decision for a transaction (line 30), it stores the decision and advances the transaction's phase to DECIDED. In a realistic implementation, at this point the process would also upcall into the transaction processing system running at its server, to inform it about the decision and allow it to apply the transaction's writes to the database if the decision is to commit.

In the absence of failures, our protocol allows the client to learn a decision on a transaction in 5 message delays, instead of 7 required by vanilla protocols that use Paxos as a black-box [7, 11]. We can further reduce this to 4 by co-locating the client with the transaction coordinator. The protocol also minimizes the load on Paxos leaders, which are the main potential bottleneck: each involved leader only has to receive one PREPARE and one DECISION message, and send one PREPARE_ACK message.

Reconfiguration. When a failure is suspected in a shard s, any process can initiate a reconfiguration of the shard to replace failed replicas. Reconfiguration is done only in the affected shard, without disrupting others. It aims to preserve Invariant 2, which is key in proving the correctness of the protocol. This assumes that all followers in s at an epoch e have received ACCEPT(e, k, t, l, d) and responded to it with ACCEPT_ACK; in this case we say that the transaction t has been *accepted* at shard s. The invariant guarantees that the accepted transaction t will persist in epochs higher than e; this is used to prove that the protocol computes a unique decision on each transaction. The invariant also guarantees that the entries preceding t in the certification order in epochs higher than e may only contain the votes that the leader of s at epoch e took into account when computing the vote d on t (some of these votes may be missing due to the lack of FIFO order in the communication between the leader and its followers). This property is necessary to guarantee that the protocol computes decisions according to a single global certification order, as required by the TCS specification.

To ensure Invariant 2, a process performing reconfiguration first *probes* previous configurations to determine which processes are still alive and to find a process whose state contains all transactions previously accepted at the shard, which will serve the new leader. The new leader then transfers its state to the members of the new configuration, thereby *initializing* them. A variable initialized $\in \{\text{TRUE}, \text{FALSE}\}$ at a process records whether it has

```
1  function certify(t, l)
2      forall s ∈ shards(t) do
3          send PREPARE(t, (l | s)) to leader[s];

4  when received PREPARE(t, l) from p_j
5      pre: status = LEADER;
6      if ∃k. t = txn[k] then
7          send PREPARE_ACK(epoch[s_0], s_0, k, txn[k],
                   payload[k], vote[k]) to p_j
8      else
9          next ← next + 1;
10         (txn, phase)[next] ← (t, PREPARED);
11         if l ≠ ⊥ then
12             vote[next] ← f_{s_0}(L_1, l) ⊓ g_{s_0}(L_2, l);
13             payload[next] ← l;
14         else
15             vote[next] ← ABORT;
16             payload[next] ← ε;
17         send PREPARE_ACK(epoch[s_0], s_0, next, t,
                   payload[next], vote[next]) to p_j;

18 when received PREPARE_ACK(e, s, k, t, l, d)
19     pre: epoch[s] = e;
20     send ACCEPT(e, k, t, l, d) to members[s] \ leader[s];

21 when received ACCEPT(e, k, t, l, d) from p_j
22     pre: status = FOLLOWER ∧ epoch[s_0] = e;
23     if phase[k] = START then
24         (txn, payload, vote, phase)[next] ← (t, l, d, PREPARED);
25     send ACCEPT_ACK(s_0, e, k, t, d) to p_j;

26 when for every s ∈ shards(t) received an
   ACCEPT_ACK(s, epoch[s], k_s, t, d_s) from every
   p_j ∈ members[s] \ leader[s]
27     send DECISION(t, ⨅_{s∈shards(t)} d_s) to client(t);
28     forall s ∈ shards(t) do
29         send DECISION(epoch[s], k_s, ⨅_{s∈shards(t)} d_s)
               to members[s];

30 when received DECISION(e, k, d)
31     pre: status ∈ {LEADER, FOLLOWER} ∧ epoch[s_0] ≥ e;
32     (dec, phase)[k] ← (d, DECIDED);

33 function reconfigure(s)
34     pre: probing = FALSE;
35     probing ← TRUE;
36     ⟨probed_epoch, probed_members, _⟩ ← get_last(s) at CS;
37     recon_epoch ← probed_epoch + 1;
38     recon_shard ← s;
39     send PROBE(recon_epoch) to probed_members;

40 when received PROBE(e) from p_j
41     pre: e ≥ new_epoch;
42     status = RECONFIGURING;
43     new_epoch ← e;
44     send PROBE_ACK(initialized, e, s_0) to p_j;

45 when received PROBE_ACK(TRUE, recon_epoch,
                   recon_shard) from p_j
46     pre: probing = TRUE;
47     probing ← FALSE;
48     M ← compute_membership();
49     var r ← compare_and_swap(recon_shard,
           recon_epoch − 1, ⟨recon_epoch, M, p_j⟩) at CS;
50     if r then send NEW_CONFIG(recon_epoch, M) to p_j;

51 non-deterministically when received
   PROBE_ACK(FALSE, recon_epoch, recon_shard) from
   p_j ∈ probed_members and no
   PROBE_ACK(TRUE, recon_epoch, recon_shard)
52     pre: probing = TRUE;
53     probed_epoch ← probed_epoch − 1;
54     probed_members ← get(recon_shard,
                   probed_epoch) at CS;
55     send PROBE(recon_epoch) to probed_members;

56 when received NEW_CONFIG(new_epoch, M) from p_j
57     status = LEADER;
58     (epoch, members, leader)[s_0] ← (e, M, p_i);
59     next ← max{k | phase[k] ≠ START};
60     send NEW_STATE(new_epoch, M, txn, payload, vote,
                   dec, phase) to M \ p_i;

61 when received NEW_STATE(e, M, txn, payload, vote,
                   dec, phase) from p_j
62     pre: e ≥ new_epoch;
63     initialized ← TRUE;
64     status = FOLLOWER;
65     (epoch, members, leader)[s_0] ← (e, M, p_j);
66     (txn, payload, vote, dec, phase) ←
           (txn, payload, vote, dec, phase);

67 when received CONFIG_CHANGE(s, e, M, p_l) from CS
68     pre: epoch[s] < e ∧ s ≠ s_0;
69     (epoch, members, leader)[s] ← (e, M, p_l);

70 function retry(k)
71     pre: phase[k] = PREPARED;
72     forall s ∈ shards(txn[k]) do
73         send PREPARE(txn[k], ⊥) to leader[s];
```

Figure 1: Atomic commit protocol at a process p_i in a shard s_0. At line 12 we let $L_1 = \{\text{payload}[k] \mid k < \text{next} \wedge \text{phase}[k] = \text{DECIDED} \wedge \text{dec}[k] = \text{COMMIT}\}$; $L_2 = \{\text{payload}[k] \mid k < \text{next} \wedge \text{phase}[k] = \text{PREPARED} \wedge \text{vote}[k] = \text{COMMIT}\}$.

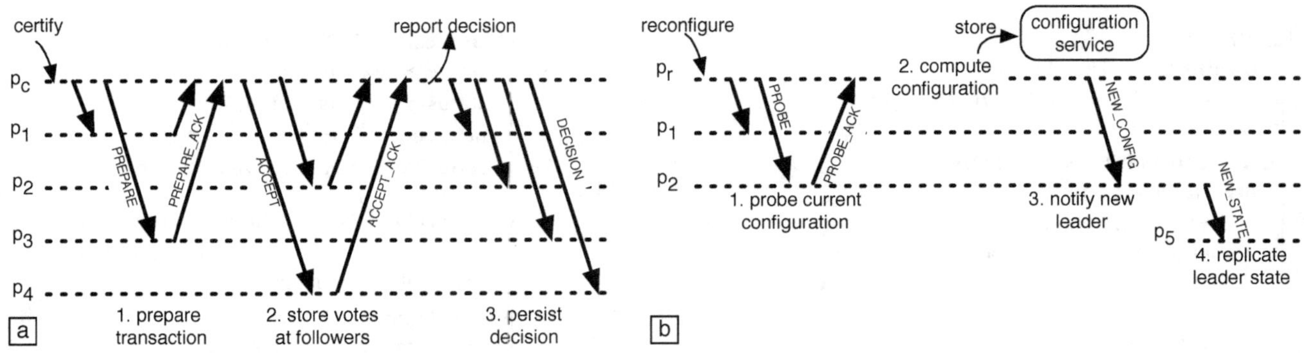

Figure 2: Illustrations of the behavior of the atomic commit protocol during (a) failure-free operation; (b) reconfiguration. In both cases p_1 is the initial leader of shard s_1 and p_2 its follower; p_3 is the leader of shard s_2 and p_4 its follower. In (b), after the reconfiguration of s_1, process p_2 becomes the leader of s_1 and a fresh process p_5 becomes its follower.

1. If a process p_i receives ACCEPT(e, k, t, l, d) and replies with ACCEPT_ACK, then after this and while epoch$[s] = e$ at p_i, we have $\mathsf{txn}\rfloor_k \prec txn\rfloor_k$, $\mathsf{vote}\rfloor_k \prec vote\rfloor_k$ and $\mathsf{payload}\rfloor_k \prec payload\rfloor_k$, where *txn*, *vote* and *payload* were the values of the arrays txn, vote and payload at the leader of s at e when it sent the corresponding message PREPARE_ACK(e, s, k, t, l, d).
2. Assume that all followers in s at e received ACCEPT(e, k, t, l, d) and responded to it with ACCEPT_ACK, and at the time the leader of s at e sent the corresponding message PREPARE_ACK(e, s, k, t, l, d) it had $\mathsf{txn}\rfloor_k = txn$, $\mathsf{vote}\rfloor_k = vote$ and $\mathsf{payload}\rfloor_k = payload$. Whenever at a process in s we have epoch$[s] = e' > e$, we also have $\mathsf{txn}\rfloor_k \prec txn$, $\mathsf{vote}\rfloor_k \prec vote$ and $\mathsf{payload}\rfloor_k \prec payload$.
3. After a process receives PROBE(e) and replies with PROBE_ACK$(_, e, s)$, it will never send ACCEPT_ACK$(s, e', _, _, _)$ with $e' < e$.
4. (a) For any messages DECISION$(_, k, d_1)$ and DECISION$(_, k, d_2)$ sent to processes in the same shard, we have $d_1 = d_2$.
   (b) For any messages DECISION(t, d_1) and DECISION(t, d_2) sent, we have $d_1 = d_2$.
5. Assume that all followers in s at e received ACCEPT(e, k, t, l, d) and replied with ACCEPT_ACK. Let the process p_i be a member of s at e' such that $e' < e$. If p_i is not a member of s at e then p_i cannot be member of s at any $e'' > e$.

Figure 3: Key invariants of the atomic commit protocol. Given a sequence α, we let $\mathsf{length}(\alpha) = \max\{k \mid \alpha[k] \neq \bot\}$ and let $\alpha\rfloor_k$ be the prefix of α of length k. Given a second sequence β, we let $\beta \prec \alpha$ if $\mathsf{length}(\alpha) = \mathsf{length}(\beta) \land (\forall k \leq \mathsf{length}(\beta).\ \beta[k] \neq \bot \implies \beta[k] = \alpha[k])$.

ever been initialized. Our protocol guarantees that a shard can become *operational*, i.e., start accepting transactions, only after all its members have been initialized.

The probing phase is complicated by the fact that there may be a series of failed reconfiguration attempts, where the new leader fails before initializing all its followers. Hence, probing requires traversing epochs from the current one down, skipping epochs that are not operational. Probing selects as the new leader the first initialized process it encounters during this traversal; we can show that this process is guaranteed to know about all transactions accepted at the shard, and thus making it the new leader will preserve Invariant 2 (§4).

In more detail, a process p_r initiates a reconfiguration of a shard s by calling `reconfigure(s)` (line 33). The process picks an epoch number recon_epoch higher than the epoch of s stored in the configuration service and then starts the probing phase, as marked by the flag probing. The process p_r keeps track of the shard being reconfigured in recon_shard, the epoch being probed in probed_epoch and the membership of this epoch in probed_members. The process initializes these variables when it first reads the current configuration from the configuration service (line 36). It then sends a PROBE message to the members of the current configuration, asking them to join the new epoch recon_epoch. Upon receiving a PROBE(e) message (line 40), a process first checks that the proposed epoch is equal or higher than the highest epoch it has ever been asked to join, which the process stores in new_epoch (we always have epoch$[s] \leq$ new_epoch at a process in s). In this case, the process sets new_epoch to e and changes its status to RECONFIGURING, which causes it to stop transaction processing. It then replies to p_r with a PROBE_ACK message, which indicates whether it has been previously initialized or not. If p_r finds a process that has previously been initialized, and hence can serve as the new leader, p_r ends probing (line 45). If p_r does not find such a process in the epoch probed_epoch and receives at least one reply PROBE_ACK from a process that has not been initialized (line 51), p_r can conclude that the epoch probed_epoch is not operational and will never become such, because it has convinced at least one of its members to join the new epoch; this is formalized by Invariant 3. In this case p_r starts probing the preceding epoch. Since no transactions could have been accepted at the epoch probed_epoch, picking a new leader from an earlier epoch will not lose any accepted transactions and thus will not violate Invariant 2.

Once the probing finds a new leader p_j for the shard s (line 45), the process p_r computes the membership of the new configuration using a function `compute_membership` (line 48). We do not prescribe a particular implementation of this function, except that the new membership must contain the new leader p_j and may only contain the processes that replied to probing or fresh processes. The latter can be added to reach the desired level of fault tolerance. Once the new configuration is computed, p_r attempts to store it in the configuration service using a compare-and-swap operation. This succeeds only if the current epoch is still the epoch from which p_r started probing, which means that no concurrent reconfiguration occurred while p_r was probing. In this case, p_r sends a NEW_CONFIG message with the new configuration to the new leader of s.

When the new leader of s receives the NEW_CONFIG message (line 56), it sets next to the length of its sequence of transactions, epoch[s] to the new epoch and status to LEADER, which allows it to start processing new transactions. It then sends a NEW_STATE message to its followers, containing its state. Upon receiving this message (line 61), a process overwrites its state with the one provided, changes its status to FOLLOWER, and sets initialized to TRUE. As part of the state update, the process also updates its epoch epoch[s_0] to the new one. Hence, the process will not accept transactions from the new leader until it receives the NEW_STATE message.

When a new configuration of a shard s is persisted in the configuration service, the service sends it in a CONFIG_CHANGE message to the members of shards other than s. A process updates the locally stored configuration upon receiving this message (line 67).

Coordinator recovery. If a process that accepted a transaction t does not receive the final decision on it, this may be because the coordinator of t has failed. In this case the process may decide to become a new coordinator by executing a `retry` function (line 70). For this, the process just sends a PREPARE(t, $\perp$) message to the leaders of the shards of t, carrying a special undefined value $\perp$ as the payload. If a leader receiving PREPARE(t, $\perp$) has already certified t, it re-sends the corresponding PREPARE_ACK message to the new coordinator, including the transaction payload and vote (line 6). Otherwise, if the leader does not have the payload of t, it prepares the transaction as aborted and with an empty payload ε (line 15). In either case, the new coordinator will finish processing the transaction as usual. The above case when the transaction is aborted because the leader of a shard does not know its payload may arise when the old coordinator crashed in between sending PREPARE messages to different shards. Note that if the old coordinator was suspected spuriously and will try later to submit the transaction to a shard where it was aborted, it will just get a PREPARE_ACK message with an ABORT vote.

Our protocol allows any number of processes to become coordinators of a transaction at the same time. Nevertheless, the protocol ensures that they will all reach the same decision, even in case of reconfigurations. We formalize this by Invariant 4: part (a) ensures an agreement on the decision on the k-th transaction in the certification order at a given shard; part (b) ensures a system-wide agreement on the decision on a given transaction t. The latter part establishes that the protocol computes a unique decision on each transaction. Invariant 4 is proved as a corollary of Invariant 2.

Losing undecided transactions. Recall that our protocol uses the optimization that delegates persisting transactions at followers to coordinators [1, 9]. We now highlight how this optimization interacts with transaction certification. Because of the optimization, transactions prepared by a leader of a shard s can be persisted at followers out of order. For example, t_2 may follow t_1 in the certification order at the leader, but may be persisted at followers first. If now the leader of s and the coordinator of t_1 crashes before t_1 is persisted at followers, t_1 will be lost forever, something that is allowed by Invariant 2 (due to the use of $\prec$). In this case we lose a transaction t_1 on the basis of which the vote on the transaction t_2 was computed (e.g., the payload l_1 of t_1 was in L_2 when the vote on t_2 was computed at line 12). This does not violate correctness, since the vote on t_2 makes sense also in the context excluding t_1: due to distributivity of certification functions (§2), if t_2 was allowed to commit in the presence of t_1 ($f_s(\{l_1\}, l_2)$ = COMMIT), it can also commit in its absence ($f_s(\emptyset, l_2)$ = COMMIT). Note that in this case a decision on t_1 could not have been exposed to the client: otherwise t_1 could not get lost due to Invariant 2. Also note that, since we assume the transaction execution component produces payloads with read-sets containing only values written by committed transactions (§2), in the above case t_2 could not have read a value written by t_1.

4 CORRECTNESS

The next theorem states the safety of our protocol, showing that it implements the TCS specification.

THEOREM 4.1. *A transaction certification service implemented using the protocol in Figure 1 is correct with respect to a certification function f matching the shard-local certification functions f_s and g_s.*

We defer the proof to [4] and only sketch the proof of the key Invariant 2. This relies on auxiliary Invariant 5, which we prove first.

Proof sketch for Invariant 5. We prove the invariant by induction on e''. Assume that the invariant holds for all $e'' < e^*$. We now show it for $e'' = e^*$. The members of s at e^* are computed at line 48 by a reconfiguring process p_r using the `compute_membership` function, which returns either fresh processes or processes that responded to p_r's probing. Since p_i was a member of s at $e' < e^*$, it is not fresh; then by assumptions on `compute_membership` p_i must have received PROBE(e^*) from p_r and replied with PROBE_ACK(_, e^*, s). The process p_r starts probing at epoch $e^* - 1$ and ends it upon receiving a PROBE_ACK(TRUE, e^*, s) message. By the induction hypothesis, p_i is not a member of s at any epoch from $e^* - 1$ down to $e + 1$. Hence, if the probing stops before reaching e, then p_i will not be a member of s at e^*, as required. Assume now that the probing reaches e. By Invariant 3, each follower in s at e must have sent ACCEPT_ACK(s, e, t) before receiving PROBE(e^*). Then any member of s at e receiving PROBE(e^*) will have initialized = TRUE. Hence, if any member of s at e replies with PROBE_ACK(*initialized*, e^*, s), we have that *initialized* = TRUE. Since the process p_r will not move to the preceding epoch until at least one process replies with PROBE_ACK, this means that the probing can never go beyond e. Since the process p_i is not a member of e, it cannot be included as a member of s in e^*, as required. □

Proof sketch for Invariant 2. We prove the invariant by induction on e'. Assume that the invariant holds for all $e' < e''$. We now show it for $e' = e''$ by induction on the length of the protocol execution. We only consider the most interesting transition in line 56, when a process p_i becomes a leader of s at an epoch e''. We show that after this transition at p_i we have $\text{txn}\rfloor_k \prec txn$, $\text{vote}\rfloor_k \prec vote$ and $\text{payload}\rfloor_k \prec payload$.

Since p_i was chosen as the leader of s at e'', this process replied with PROBE_ACK(TRUE, e'', s) to a PROBE(e''). Therefore, p_i was a member of s at an epoch $e^* < e''$ that was being probed. Probing ends when at least one process sends a PROBE_ACK(TRUE, e'', s). From Invariant 3 and the assumption that all followers in e replied with ACCEPT_ACK to ACCEPT(e, k, t, l, d), we can conclude that probing could no have gone further than e. Hence, $e \leq e^* < e''$.

Let e_0 be the value of epoch[s] at p_i right before the transition at line 56. We have $e_0 \geq e$, as otherwise p_i would not be a member of s at e and by Invariant 5 could not be picked as the leader of s at e''. It is also easy to show that $e_0 < e''$. Hence, $e \leq e_0 < e''$.

If $e < e_0$, then by the induction hypothesis, we have $\mathsf{txn}\rfloor_k \prec txn$, $\mathsf{vote}\rfloor_k \prec vote$ and $\mathsf{payload}\rfloor_k \prec payload$ right after the transition in line 56, as required. Assume now that $e_0 = e$. If p_i was the leader of s at e, then we trivially have $\mathsf{txn}\rfloor_k \prec txn$, $\mathsf{vote}\rfloor_k \prec vote$ and $\mathsf{payload}\rfloor_k \prec payload$ right after the transition in line 56, as required. Otherwise, by Invariant 3, p_i must have received ACCEPT(e, k, t, l, d) and responded to it with ACCEPT_ACK(s, e, t) before the transition in line 56. Then the required follows from Invariant 1. □

We next state liveness properties of our protocol (we again defer proofs to [4]). The reconfiguration procedure in the protocol will get stuck if it cannot find an initialized process, which may happen if enough processes crash, so that all shard data is lost. We now state conditions under which this cannot happen. We associate two events with each configuration e of a shard s: *introduction* and *activation*. Introduction indicates that the configuration comes into existence and is triggered when the configuration is successfully persisted in the configuration service (line 49). Activation indicates that the configuration becomes operational and is triggered when all the followers of the configuration have processed the NEW_STATE messages sent by its leader (line 61).

Once a configuration has been activated, we say that it is *active*. We define its *lifetime* as the time interval between its introduction and when a succeeding configuration becomes active. Note that not every introduced configuration necessarily becomes active, since its leader may never complete the data transfer to the followers. To ensure our protocol is live we make the following assumption, similar to the ones made by other protocols with changing membership [3, 26].

Assumption 1. *At least one member in each configuration is non-faulty throughout the lifetime of a configuration.*

The following two theorems show that, under this assumption, a single reconfiguration makes progress.

Theorem 4.2. *If a process p_r attempts to reconfigure a shard s and no other process attempts to reconfigure s simultaneously, then if p_r is non-faulty for long enough, it will eventually introduce a new configuration.*

Theorem 4.3. *If a configuration of a shard s is introduced by a process p_r, then it will eventually be activated, provided no process attempts to reconfigure s simultaneously, and p_r and all the members of the configuration are non-faulty for long enough.*

Finally, the following theorem shows that in the absence of failures or reconfigurations, transaction certification makes progress.

Theorem 4.4. *Assume that the current configuration of each shard is active, all processes are aware of the current configuration of each shard, and no reconfiguration is in progress. If a transaction is submitted for certification, then it will eventually be decided, provided no reconfiguration is attempted and all the processes belonging to the current configuration of each shard are non-faulty for long enough.*

5 EXPLOITING RDMA

We now present a variant of our protocol that uses Remote Direct Memory Access (RDMA), which follows the design of the FARM system [9, 24]. By comparing this protocol with that of §3 we highlight the trade-offs required by the use of RDMA. Due to space constraints, we defer the pseudocode of our protocol to [4] and describe the required changes in the protocol of §3 only informally.

We assume the same system model as in §2, except that processes can communicate using RDMA. This allows a machine to access the memory of another machine over the network without involving the latter's CPU, thus lowering latency. Like FARM, our protocol uses RDMA to implement a primitive for point-to-point communication between processes with the following interface. The primitive allows a sender process to reliably send a message m to a receiver process p_j (**send-rdma**(m, p_j)) by remotely writing into a specific memory region of p_j. The sender then gets an acknowledgement when the message reaches the receiver's memory (**ack-rdma**(m, p_j)), sent by the receiver's network interface card (NIC) without interrupting its CPU. The receiver is notified at a later point that a new message is available (**deliver-rdma**(m, p_j)). Hence, the guarantee provided by **ack-rdma**(m, p_j) is that the receiver will eventually deliver the message m, even if the sender crashes, since the message is already in the receiver's memory. The operation **open**(p_i) grants p_i access to a region of the caller's memory, and **close**(p_i) revokes it. Once the latter operation completes, p_i cannot send any message to the caller using **send-rdma**. Finally, we assume that the communication primitive includes another operation: **flush**. This operation blocks the caller until it has delivered all messages addressed to it that have been acknowledged by its NIC through an **ack-rdma**.

To implement the above primitive, the receiver usually keeps a circular buffer in memory for each process that may send it a message [8, 21]. The operation **send-rdma**(m, p_j) issued by a process p_i appends a message to the corresponding buffer at the receiver using RDMA writes. Receivers periodically pull messages from the buffers and deliver them to the application via **deliver-rdma**. If a buffer at a process p_j gets full, the associated sender process will not be able to send a message to p_j until the latter pulls some messages.

Following FARM, we use the above RDMA-based communication primitive in our protocol to persists votes and decisions (steps 2 and 3 of Figure 2a). This requires the following changes to the protocol in Figure 1. First, ACCEPT and DECISION messages are sent using **send-rdma** instead of **send** (lines 20 and 29). Second, the followers do not send explicit ACCEPT_ACK messages to transaction coordinators (line 25); instead, the latter act once they receive an RDMA acknowledgement **ack-rdma**. This makes the checks at lines 22 and 31 redundant, as followers cannot reject ACCEPT or DECISION messages under any circumstance. The practical rationale for these changes is that persisting a transaction t at followers using

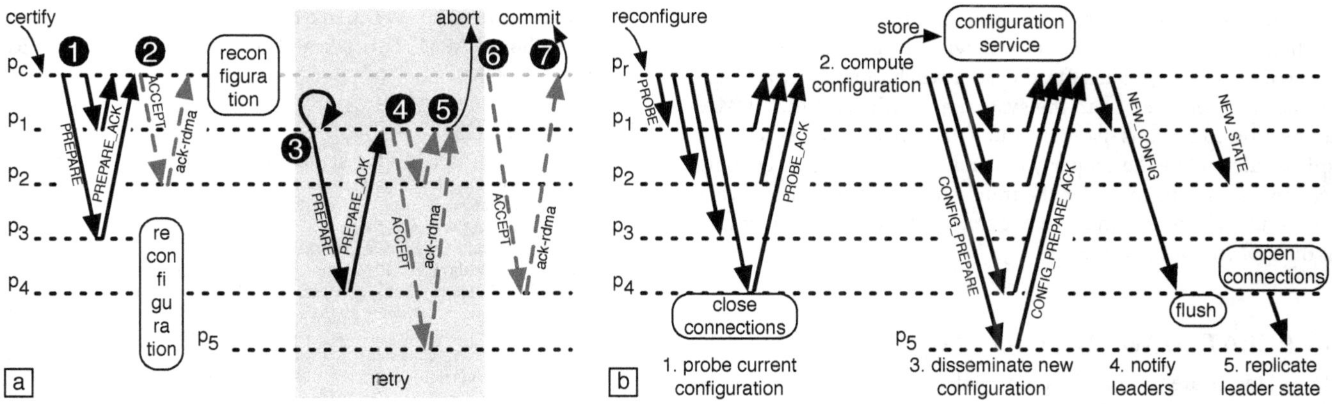

Figure 4: Illustrations of (a) a counter-example showing the need to change the reconfiguration protocol when using RDMA; (b) the changed reconfiguration protocol. Red dashed lines denote RDMA operations. In both cases p_1 is the leader of shard s_1 and p_2 its follower; p_3 is the initial leader of shard s_2 and p_4 its follower. After the reconfiguration of s_2, process p_4 is the new leader and a fresh process p_5 is its follower.

RDMA minimizes the time during which the transaction is prepared at leaders, which requires them to vote abort on all transactions conflicting with t (via the certification function g_s, §2); this results in lower abort rates [2, 9]. Transaction processing at followers (e.g., adding them to the local copy of the certification order, line 21) is done off the critical path of certification.

Unfortunately, the above changes to the failure-free path of the protocol do not preserve correctness without changes to reconfiguration, as illustrated by an example execution in Figure 4a. In this execution, two shards s_1 and s_2 are involved in the certification of a transaction t, coordinated by a process p_c from a third shard. The transaction is prepared to commit at the leaders p_1 and p_3 of both shards (step ❶), and the COMMIT vote from the leader of s_1 (p_1) is persisted at the follower p_2 using RDMA (step ❷). Before the coordinator p_c persists the vote from the leader p_3 of s_2 at the follower p_4, the leader p_3 is suspected of failure and a reconfiguration is triggered at shard s_2. This promotes the follower p_4 to a new leader and brings online a fresh follower p_5. Next, the leader p_1 of s_1 suspects the coordinator p_c of failure and triggers a reconfiguration to remove it. Once p_c is removed from its shard, p_1 retries the processing of t (step ❸, line 70 in Figure 1). The new leader p_4 of s_2 does not know about t, so this results in the transaction being aborted, because its payload at shard s_2 is thought to be lost (steps ❹ and ❺). But now the coordinator p_c, who did not actually fail and still believes s_2 is in the old configuration, finishes its processing by persisting the COMMIT vote of the old leader p_3 of s_2 at the old follower p_4, which is now the new leader of s_2 (step ❻). Since this is done via RDMA, p_4 cannot reject the vote and, thus, p_c commits the transaction (step ❼). This violates safety, as two contradictory results have been externalized. The protocol in §3 is not subject to this problem, because in that protocol the new leader p_4 of the shard s_2 would reject the ACCEPT message due to the failure of the check at line 22.

To make the RDMA-based protocol correct, we need to change the reconfiguration protocol so that *the whole system* participates in reconfiguration instead of just the affected shard. Figure 4b illustrates the message flow of the redesigned reconfiguration protocol. Processes now maintain a single epoch variable instead of a vector. The data structures maintained by the external configuration service and its interface are adjusted accordingly. Like in our previous commit protocol, the process p_r performing reconfiguration first probes previous configurations by sending PROBE messages. However, p_r now probes *all* shards. A process receiving PROBE handles it as before (line 40), but additionally closes all incoming RDMA connections using **close**, which guarantees that the process accepts no more transactions at its previous epoch. This is needed because, due to communication via RDMA, the protocol cannot longer leverage the safety check at line 22. The logic of the reconfiguring process is also changed: after this process computes the new configuration and stores it in the configuration service (line 49), the process sends a new CONFIG_PREPARE message to *all* processes in the configuration. Upon receiving CONFIG_PREPARE, a process updates its locally stored configuration and replies with a CONFIG_PREPARE_ACK message. This ensures that the whole system is aware of the new configuration before it is activated. Only after this does the reconfiguring process send a NEW_CONFIG message to the leaders of the new configuration. Upon receiving NEW_CONFIG (line 56), a leader p_l first calls **flush**. This guarantees that all the messages that have been acknowledged as having reached p_l's memory will be replicated to followers in NEW_STATE messages; this is necessary since transaction coordinators may have already externalized decisions taken based on these acknowledgements. Finally, processes open RDMA connections to all other processes in the configuration using **open**: a leader after sending NEW_STATE to its followers, and followers upon receiving NEW_STATE (line 61).

The new protocol guarantees that: (*) if a process receives an ACCEPT message for a transaction t while at epoch e, then the leader that prepared t was at epoch e when it prepared this transaction. This property is key in proving the correctness of the protocol, as it provides the same guarantees as the removed guard in line 22, which we could not leverage due to the use of RDMA. The property (*) holds because: *(i)* at any time, a process only maintain RDMA connections to the members of its current epoch; and *(ii)* before persisting a vote at a follower, the coordinator of a transaction checks that the transaction was prepared in its current epoch (line 19).

We now show how the revised reconfiguration protocol prevents the bug in Figure 4a. In this protocol, when p_c attempts to persist the COMMIT vote at p_4 (step ❻), the latter will be already aware that p_c has been removed from the system and will close the RDMA connection to it. Thus, p_c will be unable to persist the vote at p_4 (this would violate the property (*)) and will never gather enough acknowledgements to decide the transaction. Hence, no contradictory results will be externalized. We state and prove the correctness of the RDMA-based protocol in [4].

6 RELATED WORK AND DISCUSSION

Our protocols are inspired by the recent FARM system for transaction processing, which also uses $f + 1$ replicas per shard and deals with failures using reconfiguration [9, 24]. FARM was presented as a complete database system with a number of optimizations, including the use of RDMA. In contrast, our work distills the core ideas of FARM into protocols solving the well-defined transaction certification problem, parametric in the isolation level provided and rigorously proven correct. This allows us to simplify some aspects of the FARM design. In particular, FARM has a more complex way of determining the state of the new leader upon a reconfiguration, which merges the states from all surviving replicas of the previous configuration. In contrast, our protocols take the state of any single initialized replica. Our reconfiguration protocols also provide better fault-tolerance guarantees on a par with those of existing ones [3, 26]. This is because, like Vertical Paxos I [19], our protocols look through a sequence of configurations to find the new leader, whereas FARM only considers the previous configuration. Hence, FARM reconfiguration can get stuck even when there exists a non-faulty replica with the necessary data. Finally, by presenting two related protocols using message passing and RDMA, we are able to identify the price of exploiting RDMA—having to reconfigure the whole system instead of a single shard.

There have been a number of protocols for solving the atomic commit problem, which requires reaching a decision on a single transaction [10, 12, 13, 25]. In contrast to these works, our protocol solves the more general problem of implementing a Transaction Certification Service, which requires reaching decisions on a stream of transactions. This problem more faithfully reflects the requirements of modern transaction processing systems [6].

Our protocol weaves together two-phase commit (2PC) [12] and Vertical Paxos [19], instead of using Paxos replication as a black box. This is similar to several existing sharded systems for transaction processing, which integrate protocols for distribution and replication [6, 16, 22, 28]. However, these systems considered a static set of $2f + 1$ processes per shard, whereas we assume $f + 1$ processes and allow the system to be reconfigured. Achieving this correctly is nontrivial and requires a subtle interplay between the reconfigurable replication mechanism and cross-shard coordination. For example, as we explained in §3, on failures our protocol may lose information about transactions that influenced votes on other transactions, but this does not violate correctness. As is well-known [20], using $f + 1$ instead of $2f + 1$ replicas results in somewhat weaker availability guarantees: upon a single failure, our protocols have to stop processing transactions while the system is reconfigured.

Acknowledgments. We thank Dushyanth Narayanan for discussions about FARM. This research was supported by an ERC grant RACCOON.

REFERENCES

[1] M. Balakrishnan, D. Malkhi, V. Prabhakaran, T. Wobber, M. Wei, and J. D. Davis. Corfu: A shared log design for flash clusters. In *Conference on Networked Systems Design and Implementation (NSDI)*, 2012.

[2] C. Binnig, A. Crotty, A. Galakatos, T. Kraska, and E. Zamanian. The end of slow networks: It's time for a redesign. *PVLDB*, 9(7), 2016.

[3] K. Birman, D. Malkhi, and R. V. Renesse. Virtually synchronous methodology for building dynamic reliable services. In K. Birman, editor, *Guide to Reliable Distributed Systems - Building High-Assurance Applications and Cloud-Hosted Services*, Texts in Computer Science, chapter 22. Springer, 2012.

[4] M. Bravo and A. Gotsman. Reconfigurable atomic transaction commit (extended version). *arXiv CoRR*, 1906.01365, 2019. Available from `https://arxiv.org/abs/1906.01365`.

[5] F. Chang et al. Bigtable: A distributed storage system for structured data. In *Symposium on Operating Systems Design and Implementation (OSDI)*, 2006.

[6] G. Chockler and A. Gotsman. Multi-shot distributed transaction commit. In *Symposium on Distributed Computing (DISC)*, 2018.

[7] J. C. Corbett et al. Spanner: Google's globally-distributed database. In *Symposium on Operating Systems Design and Implementation (OSDI)*, 2012.

[8] A. Dragojević, D. Narayanan, O. Hodson, and M. Castro. FaRM: Fast remote memory. In *Conference on Networked Systems Design and Implementation (NSDI)*, 2014.

[9] A. Dragojević, D. Narayanan, E. B. Nightingale, M. Renzelmann, A. Shamis, A. Badam, and M. Castro. No compromises: Distributed transactions with consistency, availability, and performance. In *Symposium on Operating Systems Principles (SOSP)*, 2015.

[10] C. Dwork and D. Skeen. The inherent cost of nonblocking commitment. In *Symposium on Principles of Distributed Computing (PODC)*, 1983.

[11] L. Glendenning, I. Beschastnikh, A. Krishnamurthy, and T. Anderson. Scalable consistency in Scatter. In *Symposium on Operating Systems Principles (SOSP)*, 2011.

[12] J. Gray. Notes on data base operating systems. In *Operating Systems, An Advanced Course*, 1978.

[13] V. Hadzilacos. On the relationship between the atomic commitment and consensus problems. In *Asilomar Workshop on Fault-Tolerant Distributed Computing*, 1990.

[14] M. P. Herlihy and J. M. Wing. Linearizability: A correctness condition for concurrent objects. *ACM Trans. Program. Lang. Syst.*, 12(3), 1990.

[15] P. Hunt, M. Konar, F. P. Junqueira, and B. Reed. Zookeeper: Wait-free coordination for internet-scale systems. In *USENIX Annual Technical Conference (USENIX ATC)*, 2010.

[16] T. Kraska, G. Pang, M. J. Franklin, S. Madden, and A. Fekete. MDCC: Multi-data center consistency. In *European Conference on Computer Systems (EuroSys)*, 2013.

[17] L. Lamport. The part-time parliament. *ACM Trans. Comput. Syst.*, 16(2), 1998.

[18] L. Lamport. Lower bounds for asynchronous consensus. *Distributed Computing*, 19(2), 2006.

[19] L. Lamport, D. Malkhi, and L. Zhou. Vertical Paxos and primary-backup replication. In *Symposium on Principles of Distributed Computing (PODC)*, 2009.

[20] L. Lamport and M. Massa. Cheap Paxos. In *International Conference on Dependable Systems and Networks (DSN)*, 2004.

[21] J. Liu, J. Wu, and D. K. Panda. High performance RDMA-based MPI implementation over InfiniBand. *Int. J. Parallel Program.*, 32(3), 2004.

[22] H. Mahmoud, F. Nawab, A. Pucher, D. Agrawal, and A. El Abbadi. Low-latency multi-datacenter databases using replicated commit. *Proc. VLDB Endow.*, 6(9), 2013.

[23] M. Saeida Ardekani, P. Sutra, and M. Shapiro. G-DUR: A middleware for assembling, analyzing, and improving transactional protocols. In *International Middleware Conference (Middleware)*, 2014.

[24] A. Shamis, M. Renzelmann, S. Novakovic, G. Chatzopoulos, A. Dragojević, D. Narayanan, and M. Castro. Fast general distributed transactions with opacity. In *International Conference on Management of Data (SIGMOD)*, 2019. To appear.

[25] D. Skeen. Nonblocking commit protocols. In *Conference on Management of Data (SIGMOD)*, 1981.

[26] A. Spiegelman, I. Keidar, and D. Malkhi. Dynamic reconfiguration: Abstraction and optimal asynchronous solution. In *Symposium on Distributed Computing (DISC)*, 2017.

[27] G. Weikum and G. Vossen. *Transactional Information Systems: Theory, Algorithms, and the Practice of Concurrency Control and Recovery*. Morgan Kaufmann Publishers Inc., 2001.

[28] I. Zhang, N. K. Sharma, A. Szekeres, A. Krishnamurthy, and D. R. K. Ports. Building consistent transactions with inconsistent replication. In *Symposium on Operating Systems Principles (SOSP)*, 2015.

The Impact of RDMA on Agreement

Marcos K. Aguilera
VMware
maguilera@vmware.com

Naama Ben-David
CMU
nbendavi@cs.cmu.edu

Rachid Guerraoui
EPFL
rachid.guerraoui@epfl.ch

Virendra Marathe
Oracle
virendra.marathe@oracle.com

Igor Zablotchi
EPFL
igor.zablotchi@epfl.ch

ABSTRACT

Remote Direct Memory Access (RDMA) is becoming widely available in data centers. This technology allows a process to directly read and write the memory of a remote host, with a mechanism to control access permissions. In this paper, we study the fundamental power of these capabilities. We consider the well-known problem of achieving consensus despite failures, and find that RDMA can improve the inherent trade-off in distributed computing between failure resilience and performance. Specifically, we show that RDMA allows algorithms that simultaneously achieve high resilience and high performance, while traditional algorithms had to choose one or another. With Byzantine failures, we give an algorithm that only requires $n \geq 2f_P + 1$ processes (where f_P is the maximum number of faulty processes) and decides in two (network) delays in common executions. With crash failures, we give an algorithm that only requires $n \geq f_P + 1$ processes and also decides in two delays. Both algorithms tolerate a minority of memory failures inherent to RDMA, and they provide safety in asynchronous systems and liveness with standard additional assumptions.

ACM Reference Format:
Marcos K. Aguilera, Naama Ben-David, Rachid Guerraoui, Virendra Marathe, and Igor Zablotchi. 2019. The Impact of RDMA on Agreement. In *2019 ACM Symposium on Principles of Distributed Computing (PODC '19), July 29-August 2, 2019, Toronto, ON, Canada.* ACM, New York, NY, USA, 10 pages. https://doi.org/10.1145/3293611.3331601

1 INTRODUCTION

In recent years, a technology known as Remote Direct Memory Access (RDMA) has made its way into data centers, earning a spotlight in distributed systems research. RDMA provides the traditional send/receive communication primitives, but also allows a process to directly read/write remote memory. Research work shows that RDMA leads to some new and exciting distributed algorithms [3, 10, 25, 31, 45, 49].

RDMA provides a different interface from previous communication mechanisms, as it combines message-passing with shared-memory [3]. Furthermore, to safeguard the remote memory, RDMA provides *protection* mechanisms to grant and revoke access for reading and writing data. This mechanism is fine grained: an application can choose subsets of remote memory called *regions* to protect; it can choose whether a region can be read, written, or both; and it can choose individual processes to be given access, where different processes can have different accesses. Furthermore, protections are *dynamic*: they can be changed by the application over time. In this paper, we lay the groundwork for a theoretical understanding of these RDMA capabilities, and we show that they lead to distributed algorithms that are inherently more powerful than before.

While RDMA brings additional power, it also introduces some challenges. With RDMA, the remote memories are subject to failures that cause them to become unresponsive. This behavior differs from traditional shared memory, which is often assumed to be reliable[1]. In this paper, we show that the additional power of RDMA more than compensates for these challenges.

Our main contribution is to show that RDMA improves on the fundamental trade-off in distributed systems between failure resilience and performance—specifically, we show how a consensus protocol can use RDMA to achieve *both* high resilience and high performance, while traditional algorithms had to choose one or another. We illustrate this on the fundamental problem of achieving consensus and capture the above RDMA capabilities as an M&M model [3], in which processes can use both message-passing and shared-memory. We consider asynchronous systems and require safety in all executions and liveness under standard additional assumptions (e.g., partial synchrony). We measure resiliency by the number of failures an algorithm tolerates, and performance by the number of (network) delays in common-case executions. Failure resilience and performance depend on whether processes fail by crashing or by being Byzantine, so we consider both.

With Byzantine failures, we consider the consensus problem called weak Byzantine agreement, defined by Lamport [37]. We give an algorithm that (a) requires only $n \geq 2f_P + 1$ processes (where f_P is the maximum number of faulty processes) and (b) decides in two delays in the common case. With crash failures, we give the first algorithm for consensus that requires only $n \geq f_P + 1$ processes and decides in two delays in the common case. With both Byzantine or crash failures, our algorithms can also tolerate crashes of memory—only $m \geq 2f_M + 1$ memories are required, where f_M is the maximum number of faulty memories. Furthermore, with crash failures, we improve resilience further, to tolerate crashes of a minority of the combined set of memories and processes.

[1]There are a few studies of failure-prone memory, as we discuss in related work.

PODC '19, July 29-August 2, 2019, Toronto, ON, Canada

ACM ISBN 978-1-4503-6217-7/19/07...$15.00
https://doi.org/10.1145/3293611.3331601

Our algorithms appear to violate known impossibility results: it is known that with message-passing, Byzantine agreement requires $n \geq 3f_P + 1$ even if the system is synchronous [44], while consensus with crash failures require $n \geq 2f_P + 1$ if the system is partially synchronous [27]. There is no contradiction: our algorithms rely on the power of RDMA, not available in other systems.

RDMA's power comes from two features: (1) simultaneous access to message-passing and shared-memory, and (2) dynamic permissions. Intuitively, shared-memory helps resilience, message-passing helps performance, and dynamic permissions help both.

To see how shared-memory helps resilience, consider the Disk Paxos algorithm [29], which uses shared-memory (disks) but no messages. Disk Paxos requires only $n \geq f_P + 1$ processes, matching the resilience of our algorithm. However, Disk Paxos is not as fast: it takes at least four delays. In fact, we show that no shared-memory consensus algorithm can decide in two delays (Section 6).

To see how message-passing helps performance, consider the Fast Paxos algorithm [39], which uses message-passing and no shared-memory. Fast Paxos decides in only two delays in common executions, but it requires $n \geq 2f_P + 1$ processes.

Of course, the challenge is achieving both high resilience and good performance in a single algorithm. This is where RDMA's dynamic permissions shine. Clearly, dynamic permissions improve resilience against Byzantine failures, by preventing a Byzantine process from overwriting memory and making it useless. More surprising, perhaps, is that dynamic permissions help performance, by providing an uncontended instantaneous guarantee: if each process revokes the write permission of other processes before writing to a register, then a process that writes successfully knows that it executed uncontended, without having to take additional steps (e.g., to read the register). We use this technique in our algorithms for both Byzantine and crash failures.

In summary, our contributions are as follows:

- We consider distributed systems with RDMA, and we propose a model that captures some of its key properties while accounting for failures of processes and memories, with support of dynamic permissions.
- We show that the shared-memory part of our RDMA improves resilience: our Byzantine agreement algorithm requires only $n \geq 2f_P + 1$ processes.
- We show that the shared-memory by itself does not permit consensus algorithms that decide in two steps in common executions.
- We show that with dynamic permissions, we can improve the performance of our Byzantine Agreement algorithm, to decide in two steps in common executions.
- We give similar results for the case of crash failures: decision in two steps while requiring only $n \geq f_P + 1$ processes.
- Our algorithms can tolerate the failure of memories, up to a minority of them.

The rest of the paper is organized as follows. Section 2 gives an overview of related work. In Section 3 we formally define the RDMA-compliant M&M model that we use in the rest of the paper, and specify the agreement problems that we solve. We then proceed to present the main contributions of the paper. Section 4 presents our fast and resilient Byzantine agreement algorithm. In Section 5 we consider the special case of crash-only failures, and show an improvement of the algorithm and tolerance bounds for this setting. In Section 6 we briefly outline a lower bound that shows that the dynamic permissions of RDMA are necessary for achieving our results. Finally, in Section 7 we discuss the semantics of RDMA in practice, and how our model reflects these features.

Due to space limitations, most proofs have been omitted from this version, and appear in the full version of this paper [4].

2 RELATED WORK

RDMA. Many high-performance systems were recently proposed using RDMA, such as distributed key-value stores [25, 31], communication primitives [25, 32], and shared address spaces across clusters [25]. Kaminsky *et al.* [33] provides guidelines for designing systems using RDMA. RDMA has also been applied to solve consensus [10, 45, 49]. Our model shares similarities with DARE [45] and APUS [49], which modify queue-pair state at run time to prevent or allow access to memory regions, similar to our dynamic permissions. These systems perform better than TCP/IP-based solutions, by exploiting better raw performance of RDMA, without changing the fundamental communication complexity or failure-resilience of the consensus protocol. Similarly, Rüsch *et al.* [46] use RDMA as a replacement for TCP/IP in existing BFT protocols.

M&M. Message-and-memory (M&M) refers to a broad class of models that combine message-passing with shared-memory, introduced by Aguilera et al. in [3]. In that work, Aguilera et al. consider M&M models without memory permissions and failures, and show that such models lead to algorithms that are more robust to failures and asynchrony. In particular, they give a consensus algorithm that tolerates more crash failures than message-passing systems, but is more scalable than shared-memory systems, as well as a leader election algorithm that reduces the synchrony requirements. In this paper, our goal is to understand how memory permissions and failures in RDMA impact agreement.

Byzantine Fault Tolerance. Lamport, Shostak and Pease [40, 44] show that Byzantine agreement can be solved in synchronous systems iff $n \geq 3f_P + 1$. With unforgeable signatures, Byzantine agreement can be solved iff $n \geq 2f_P + 1$. In asynchronous systems subject to failures, consensus cannot be solved [28]. However, this result is circumvented by making additional assumptions for liveness, such as randomization [11] or partial synchrony [18, 27]. Many Byzantine agreement algorithms focus on safety and implicitly use the additional assumptions for liveness. Even with signatures, asynchronous Byzantine agreement can be solved only if $n \geq 3f_P + 1$ [16].

It is well known that the resilience of Byzantine agreement varies depending on various model assumptions like synchrony, signatures, equivocation, and the exact variant of the problem to be solved. A system that has non-equivocation is one that can prevent a Byzantine process from sending different values to different processes. Table 1 summarizes some known results that are relevant to this paper.

Our Byzantine agreement results share similarities with results for shared memory. Malkhi *et al.* [41] and Alon *et al.* [5] show bounds on the resilience of strong and weak consensus in a model with reliable memory but Byzantine processes. They also provide consensus protocols, using read-write registers enhanced with

Work	Synchrony	Signatures	Non-Equiv	Strong Validity	Resiliency
[40]	✓	✓	✗	✓	$2f+1$
[40]	✓	✗	✗	✓	$3f+1$
[5, 41]	✗	✓	✓	✓	$3f+1$
[21]	✗	✓	✗	✗	$3f+1$
[21]	✗	✗	✓	✗	$3f+1$
[21]	✗	✓	✓	✗	$2f+1$
This paper	✗	✓	✗ (RDMA)	✗	$2f+1$

Table 1: Known fault tolerance results for Byzantine agreement.

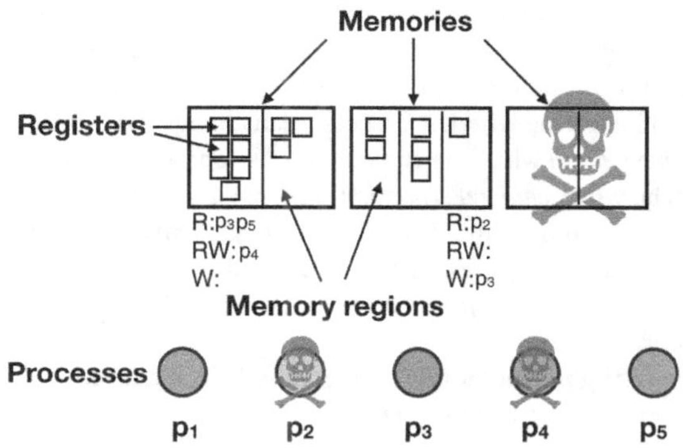

Figure 1: Our model with processes and memories, which may both fail. Processes can send messages to each other or access registers in the memories. Registers in a memory are grouped into memory regions that may overlap, but in our algorithms they do not. Each region has a permission indicating what processes can read, write, and read-write the registers in the region (shown for two regions).

sticky bits (write-once memory) and access control lists not unlike our permissions. Bessani *et al.* [12] propose an alternative to sticky bits and access control lists through Policy-Enforced Augmented Tuple Spaces. All these works handle Byzantine failures with powerful objects rather than registers. Bouzid *et al.* [14] show that $3f_P+1$ processes are necessary for strong Byzantine agreement with read-write registers.

Some prior work solves Byzantine agreement with $2f_P+1$ processes using specialized trusted components that Byzantine processes cannot control [19, 20, 22, 23, 34, 48]. Some schemes decide in two delays but require a large trusted component: a coordinator [19], reliable broadcast [23], or message ordering [34]. For us, permission checking in RDMA is a trusted component of sorts, but it is small and readily available.

At a high-level, our improved Byzantine fault tolerance is achieved by preventing equivocation by Byzantine processes, thereby effectively translating each Byzantine failure into a crash failure. Such translations from one type of failure into a less serious one have appeared extensively in the literature [9, 16, 21, 43]. Early work [9, 43] shows how to translate a crash tolerant algorithm into a Byzantine tolerant algorithm in the synchronous setting. Bracha [15] presents a similar translation for the asynchronous setting, in which $n \geq 3f_P + 1$ processes are required to tolerate f_P Byzantine failures. Bracha's translation relies on the definition and implementation of a *reliable broadcast* primitive; in this paper we define and implement a similar, but weaker, broadcast primitive that can tolerate more failures due to the capabilities of RDMA.

Faulty memory. Afek *et al.* [2] and Jayanti *et al.* [30] study the problem of masking the benign failures of shared memory or objects. We use their ideas of replicating data across memories. Abraham *et al.* [1] considers honest processes but malicious memory.

Common-case executions. Many systems and algorithms tolerate adversarial scheduling but optimize for common-case executions without failures, asynchrony, contention, etc (e.g., [13, 24, 26, 35, 36, 39, 42]). None of these match both the resilience and performance of our algorithms. Some algorithms decide in one delay but require $n \geq 5f_P + 1$ for Byzantine failures [47] or $n \geq 3f_P + 1$ for crash failures [17, 24].

3 MODEL AND PRELIMINARIES

We consider a message-and-memory (M&M) model, which allows processes to use both message-passing and shared-memory [3]. The system has n processes $P = \{p_1, \ldots, p_n\}$ and m (shared) *memories* $M = \{\mu_1, \ldots, \mu_m\}$. Processes communicate by accessing memories or sending messages. Throughout the paper, memory refers to the shared memories, not the local state of processes.

The system is asynchronous in that it can experience arbitrary delays. We expect algorithms to satisfy the safety properties of the problems we consider, under this asynchronous system. For liveness, we require additional standard assumptions, such as partial synchrony, randomization, or failure detection.

Memory permissions. Each memory consists of a set of *registers*. To control access, an algorithm groups those registers into a set of (possibly overlapping) *memory regions*, and then defines permissions for those memory regions. Formally, a memory region *mr* of a memory μ is a subset of the registers of μ. We often refer to *mr* without specifying the memory μ explicitly. Each memory region *mr* has a *permission*, which consists of three disjoint sets of processes R_{mr}, W_{mr}, RW_{mr} indicating whether each process can read, write, or read-write the registers in the region. We say that *p has read permission on mr* if $p \in R_{mr}$ or $p \in RW_{mr}$; we say that *p has write permission on mr* if $p \in W_{mr}$ or $p \in RW_{mr}$. In the special case when $R_{mr} = P \setminus \{p\}$, $W_{mr} = \emptyset$, $RW_{mr} = \{p\}$, we say that *mr* is a Single-Writer Multi-Reader (SWMR) region—registers in *mr* correspond to the traditional notion of SWMR registers. Note that a register may belong to several regions, and a process may have access to the register on one region but not another—this models the existing RDMA behavior. Intuitively, when reading or writing data, a process specifies the region and the register, and the system uses the region to determine if access is allowed (we make this precise below).

Permission change. An algorithm indicates an initial permission for each memory region *mr*. Subsequently, the algorithm may wish to change the permission of *mr* during execution. For that, processes can invoke an operation *changePermission*(*mr*, *new_perm*), where *new_perm* is a triple (R, W, RW). This operation returns no results and it is intended to modify R_{mr}, W_{mr}, RW_{mr} to R, W, RW.

To tolerate Byzantine processes, an algorithm can restrict processes from changing permissions. For that, the algorithm specifies a function *legalChange(p, mr, old_perm, new_perm)* which returns a boolean indicating whether process p can change the permission of *mr* to *new_perm* when the current permissions are *old_perm*. More precisely, when *changePermission* is invoked, the system evaluates *legalChange* to determine whether *changePermission* takes effect or becomes a no-op. When *legalChange* always returns false, we say that the *permissions are static*; otherwise, the *permissions are dynamic*.

Accessing memories. Processes access the memories via operations *write*(mr, r, v) and *read*(mr, r) for memory region mr, register r, and value v. A *write*(mr, r, v) by process p changes register r to v and returns *ack* if $r \in mr$ and p has write permission on mr; otherwise, the operation returns *nak*. A *read*(mr, r) by process p returns the last value successfully written to r if $r \in mr$ and p has read permission on mr; otherwise, the operation returns *nak*. In our algorithms, a register belongs to exactly one region, so we omit the mr parameter from write and read operations.

Sending messages. Processes can also communicate by sending messages over a set of directed links. We assume messages are unique. If there is a link from process p to process q, then p can send messages to q. Links satisfy two properties: *integrity* and *no-loss*. Given two correct processes p and q, integrity requires that a message m be received by q from p at most once and only if m was previously sent by p to q. No-loss requires that a message m sent from p to q be eventually received by q. In our algorithms, we typically assume a fully connected network so that every pair of correct processes can communicate. We also consider the special case when there are no links (see below).

Executions and steps. An execution is as a sequence of process steps. In each step, a process does the following, according to its local state: (1) sends a message or invokes an operation on a memory (read, write, or changePermission), (2) tries to receive a message or a response from an outstanding operation, and (3) changes local state. We require a process to have at most one outstanding operation on each memory.

Failures. A memory m may fail by crashing, which causes subsequent operations on its registers to hang without returning a response. Because the system is asynchronous, a process cannot differentiate a crashed memory from a slow one. We assume there is an upper bound f_M on the maximum number of memories that may crash. Processes may fail by crashing or becoming Byzantine. If a process crashes, it stops taking steps forever. If a process becomes Byzantine, it can deviate arbitrarily from the algorithm. However, that process cannot operate on memories without the required permission. We assume there is an upper bound f_P on the maximum number of processes that may be faulty. Where the context is clear, we omit the P and M subscripts from the number of failures, f.

Signatures. Our algorithms assume unforgeable signatures: there are primitives *sign*(v) and *sValid*(p, v) which, respectively, signs a value v and determines if v is signed by process p.

Messages and disks. The model defined above includes two common models as special cases. In the *message-passing* model, there are no memories ($m = 0$), so processes can communicate only by sending messages. In the *disk* model [29], there are no links, so processes can communicate only via memories; moreover, each memory has a single region which always permits all processes to read and write all registers.

Consensus

In the consensus problem, processes propose an initial value and must make an irrevocable decision on a value. With crash failures, we require the following properties:

- **Uniform Agreement.** If processes p and q decide v_p and v_q, then $v_p = v_q$.
- **Validity.** If some process decides v, then v is the initial value proposed by some process.
- **Termination.** Eventually all correct processes decide.

We expect Agreement and Validity to hold in an asynchronous system, while Termination requires standard additional assumptions (partial synchrony, randomization, failure detection, etc). With Byzantine failures, we change these definitions so the problem can be solved. We consider weak Byzantine agreement [37], with the following properties:

- **Agreement.** If correct processes p and q decide v_p and v_q, then $v_p = v_q$.
- **Validity.** With no faulty processes, if some process decides v, then v is the input of some process.
- **Termination.** Eventually all correct processes decide.

Complexity of algorithms. We are interested in the performance of algorithms in *common-case executions*, when the system is synchronous and there are no failures. In those cases, we measure performance using the notion of *delays*, which extends message-delays to our model. Under this metric, computations are instantaneous, each message takes one delay, and each memory operation takes two delays. Intuitively, a delay represents the time incurred by the network to transmit a message; a memory operation takes two delays because its hardware implementation requires a round trip. We say that a consensus protocol is k-*deciding* if, in common-case executions, some process decides in k delays.

4 BYZANTINE FAILURES

We now consider Byzantine failures and give a 2-deciding algorithm for weak Byzantine agreement with $n \geq 2f_P + 1$ processes and $m \geq 2f_M + 1$ memories. The algorithm consists of the composition of two sub-algorithms: a slow one that always works, and a fast one that gives up under hard conditions.

The first sub-algorithm, called *Robust Backup*, is developed in two steps. We first implement a primitive called *non-equivocating broadcast*, which prevents Byzantine processes from sending different values to different processes. Then, we use the framework of Clement *et al.* [21] combined with this primitive to convert a message-passing consensus algorithm that tolerates crash failures into a consensus algorithm that tolerates Byzantine failures. This yields Robust Backup.[2] It uses only static permissions and assumes memories are split into SWMR regions. Therefore, this sub-algorithm works in the traditional shared-memory model with SWMR registers, and it may be of independent interest.

[2] The attentive reader may wonder why at this point we have not achieved a 2-deciding algorithm already: if we apply Clement *et al.* [21] to a 2-deciding crash-tolerant algorithm (such as Fast Paxos [13]), will the result not be a 2-deciding Byzantine-tolerant algorithm? The answer is no, because Clement *et al.* needs non-equivocated broadcast, which incurs at least 6 delays.

The second sub-algorithm is called *Cheap Quorum*. It uses dynamic permissions to decide in two delays using one signature in common executions. However, the sub-algorithm gives up if the system is not synchronous or there are Byzantine failures.

Finally, we combine both sub-algorithms using ideas from the Abstract framework of Aublin et al. [8]. More precisely, we start by running Cheap Quorum; if it aborts, we run Robust Backup. There is a subtlety: for this idea to work, Robust Backup must decide on a value v if Cheap Quorum decided v previously. To do that, Robust Backup decides on a *preferred value* if at least $f+1$ processes have this value as input. To do so, we use the classic crash-tolerant Paxos algorithm (run under the Robust Backup algorithm to ensure Byzantine tolerance) but with an initial set-up phase that ensures this safe decision. We call the protocol *Preferential Paxos*.

Algorithm 2: Non-Equivocating Broadcast

```
SWMR slots[n,M,n]; initialized to ⊥. slots[p] is array of SWMR(p) registers.

Code for process p to broadcast (k,m)
  write(slots[p,j,p], sign((k,m)));

Code for process p
  Last[n] is local array with last k delivered from each process
  while true {
    for q in Π {
      try_deliver(q); } }

  try_deliver(q) {
    k = Last[q]
    val = (key,msg) = read(slots[q,k,q]);
    if (val == ⊥ || !sValid(p, val) || key≠k)
      return; //q hasn't written anything or is Byzantine. Will retry later.
    Write(slots[p,k,q], val);
    for i in Π {
      otherV = (otherK, otherM) = read(slots[i,k,q]);
      if (otherV ≠ val && otherV ≠ ⊥ && sValid(q, otherV) && otherK == key)
        return;  } //q is Byzantine; no delivery.
    deliver(k,msg, q)
    Last[q] += 1 }
```

4.1 The Robust Backup Sub-Algorithm

We develop Robust Backup using the construction by Clement *et al.* [21], which we now explain. Clement *et al.* show how to transform a message-passing algorithm $\mathcal{A}$ that tolerates f_P crash failures into a message-passing algorithm that tolerates f_P Byzantine failures in a system where $n \geq 2f_P + 1$ processes, assuming unforgeable signatures and a non-equivocation mechanism. They do so by implementing trusted message-passing primitives, *T-send* and *T-receive*, using non-equivocation and signature verification on every message. Processes include their full history with each message, and then verify locally whether a received message is consistent with the protocol. This restricts Byzantine behavior to crash failures.

To apply this construction in our model, we show that our model can implement non-equivocation and message passing. We first show that shared-memory with SWMR registers (and no memory failures) can implement these primitives, and then show how our model can implement shared-memory with SWMR registers.

Consider a shared-memory system. While Clement *et al.* receive and verify a message separately, we combine the two steps into one primitive called *non-equivocating broadcast*.

Definition 1. Non-equivocating broadcast *is defined in terms of two primitives, broadcast(k, m) and deliver(k, m, q). When a process p invokes broadcast(k, m) we say that p* broadcasts (k, m). *When a process p invokes deliver(k, m, q) we say that p* delivers (k, m) from q. *Each correct process p must invoke broadcast(k, ∗) with k one higher than p's previous invocation (and first invocation with k=1). The following holds:*

1. *If a correct process p broadcasts (k, m), then all correct processes eventually deliver (k, m) from p.*
2. *If p and q are correct processes, p delivers (k, m) from r, and q delivers (k, m′) from r, then m=m′.*
3. *If a correct process delivers (k, m) from p, p must have broadcast (k, m).*

A correct implementation of non-equivocating broadcast replaces the send and receive primitives with broadcast and deliver respectively in Clement *et al.*'s implementation of T-send and T-receive.

We now show how to implement non-equivocating broadcast in shared-memory. The idea of the algorithm is that before delivering a message (k, m) from q, each process p checks that no other process saw a different value from q. More specifically, each process p has n memory slots per sequence number, that only p can write to, but all processes can read from. These slots are initialized to $\perp$, and p uses them to write the values that it has seen. To broadcast its k-th message, p simply writes a signed version of the message in slot (k, p) of its memory. To deliver a message m from process q with sequence number k, process p does three things: (1) p reads slot (q, k) from q's memory. If p reads $\perp$ from q's (k, q) slot, then q has not yet sent any message with sequence number k; p retries at a later time. If p reads a value that is not signed by q, it also restarts, pretending that it did not see any value. (2) Otherwise, if p read some signed value m from q's (k, q) slot, p writes m into slot (k, q) in its own memory, and (3) p reads slot (k, q) in every other process's memory. If, for every other process r, p reads either m or $\perp$ in (k, q) in r's memory, then p delivers q's message. Otherwise, since other processes cannot forge q's signature, this means that q has tried to equivocate, as some other process saw a different value when it read from q. p handles this case by ignoring the value from q.

Lemma 4.1. *Non-equivocating broadcast is implementable in shared-memory with SWMR regular registers.*

The result of Clement et al. [21] and Lemma 4.1 immediately imply the following result.

Theorem 4.2. *There exists an algorithm for weak Byzantine agreement in a shared-memory system with SWMR regular registers, signatures, and up to* f_P *process crashes where* $n \geq 2f_P + 1$.

In particular, we can implement weak Byzantine agreement by taking any correct consensus algorithm $\mathcal{A}$ for the classic crash-only message passing model, and replacing all its sends and receives by non-equivocating broadcast and deliver (respectively) that also attach a process's entire execution history to each message. We call this method of communication *trusted sends and receives*, or simply T-send and T-receive primitives. Clement et al. [21] show that implementing such T-send and T-receive primitives with non-equivocation and signatures yields a Byzantine-tolerant replacement for classic sends and receives. In the full version of this paper, we present a pseudocode for T-send and T-receive with non-equivocating broadcast.

Non-equivocation in our model. To convert the above algorithm to our model, where memory may fail, we use the ideas in [2, 7, 30] to implement failure-free SWMR regular registers from the fail-prone memory, and then run weak Byzantine agreement using those regular registers. To implement an SWMR register, a process writes or reads all memories, and waits for a majority to respond. When reading, if p sees exactly one distinct non-$\perp$ value v across the memories, it returns v; otherwise, it returns $\perp$.

Definition 2. *Let $\mathcal{A}$ be a message-passing algorithm.* Robust Backup($\mathcal{A}$) *is the algorithm $\mathcal{A}$ in which all send and receive operations are replaced by T-send and T-receive operations (respectively) implemented with non-equivocating broadcast.*

From the result of Clement et al. [21], Lemma 4.1, and the above handling of memory failures, it is easy to see that with $\mathcal{A}$ being a correct consensus algorithm for the crash-only setting, Robust Backup($\mathcal{A}$) solves weak Byzantine agreement with the desired fault tolerance in our dynamic permission M&M model. This is summarized in the follow theorem.

Theorem 4.3. *There exists an algorithm for Weak Byzantine Agreement in a message-and-memory model with up to f_P Byzantine processes and f_M memory crashes, where $n \geq 2f_P + 1$ and $m \geq 2f_M + 1$.*

4.2 The Cheap Quorum Sub-Algorithm

We now give an algorithm that decides in two delays in common executions in which the system is synchronous and there are no failures. It requires only one signature for a fast decision, whereas the best prior algorithm requires $6f_P + 2$ signatures and $n \geq 3f_P + 1$ [8]. Our algorithm, called Cheap Quorum, is not in itself a complete consensus algorithm; it may abort in some executions. If Cheap Quorum aborts, it outputs an *abort value*, which is used to initialize the Robust Backup so that their composition preserves weak Byzantine agreement. This composition is inspired by the Abstract framework of Aublin *et al.* [8].

The algorithm has a special process ℓ, say $\ell = p_1$, which serves both as a *leader* and a *follower*. Other processes act only as *followers*. The memory is partitioned into $n + 1$ regions denoted *Region*[p] for each $p \in \Pi$, plus an extra one for p_1, *Region*[ℓ] in which it proposes a value. Initially, *Region*[p] is a regular SWMR region where p is the writer. Unlike in Algorithm 2, some of the permissions are dynamic; processes may remove p_1's write permission to *Region*[ℓ] (i.e., the *legalChange* function returns false to any permission change requests, except for ones revoking p_1's permission to write on *Region*[ℓ]).

Processes initially execute under a *normal* mode in common-case executions, but may switch to *panic* mode if they intend to abort, as in [8]. The pseudo-code of the normal mode is in Algorithm 3.

Algorithm 3: Cheap Quorum normal operation—code for process p

```
Leader code
propose(v) {
    sign(v);
    status = Value[ℓ].write(v);
    if (status == nak) Panic_mode();
    else decide(v); }

Follower code
propose(w){
    do {v = read(Value[ℓ]);
        for all q ∈ Π do pan[q] = read(Panic[q]);
    } until (v ≠ ⊥ || pan[q] == true for some q || timeout);
    if (v ≠ ⊥ && sValid(p1,v)) {
        sign(v);
        write(Value[p],v);
        do {for all q ∈ Π do val[q] = read(Value[q]);
            if |{q : val[q] == v}| ≥ n then {
                Proof[p].write(sign(val[1..n]));
                for all q ∈ Π do prf[q] = read(Proof[q]);
                if |{q : verifyProof(prf[q]) == true}| ≥ n {
                  ↪ decide(v); exit; } }
            for all q ∈ Π do pan[q] = read(Panic[q]);
        } until (pan[q] == true for some q || timeout); }
    Panic_mode();}
```

Algorithm 4: Cheap Quorum panic mode—code for process p

```
panic_mode(){
    Panic[p] = true;
    changePermission(Region[ℓ], R: Π, W: {}, RW: {});
       ↪   // remove write permission
    v = read(Value[p]);
    prf = read(Proof[p]);
    if (v ≠⊥){  Abort with ⟨v, prf⟩; return; }
    LVal = read(Value[ℓ]);
    if (LVal ≠⊥) {Abort with ⟨LVal, ⊥⟩; return;}
    Abort with ⟨myInput, ⊥⟩; }
```

Region[p] contains three registers *Value*[p], *Panic*[p], *Proof*[p] initially set to $\perp$, *false*, $\perp$. To propose v, the leader p_1 signs v and writes it to *Value*[ℓ]. If the write is successful (it may fail because its write permission was removed), then p_1 decides v; otherwise p_1 calls *Panic_mode*(). Note that all processes, including p_1, continue their execution after deciding. However, p_1 never decides again if it decided as the leader. A follower q checks if p_1 wrote to *Value*[ℓ] and, if so, whether the value is properly signed. If so, q signs v, writes it to *Value*[q], and waits for other processes to write the same value to *Value*[$*$]. If q sees $2f + 1$ copies of v signed by different processes, q assembles these copies in a *unanimity proof*, which it signs and writes to *Proof*[q]. q then waits for $2f + 1$ unanimity proofs for v to appear in *Proof*[$*$], and checks that they are valid, in which case q decides v. This waiting continues until a timeout expires[3], at which time q calls *Panic_mode*(). In *Panic_mode*(), a process p sets *Panic*[p] to *true* to tell other processes it is panicking; other processes periodically check to see if they should panic too. p then removes write permission from *Region*[ℓ], and decides on a value to abort: either *Value*[p] if it is non-$\perp$, *Value*[ℓ] if it is non-$\perp$,

[3]The timeout is chosen to be an upper bound on the communication, processing and computation delays in the common case.

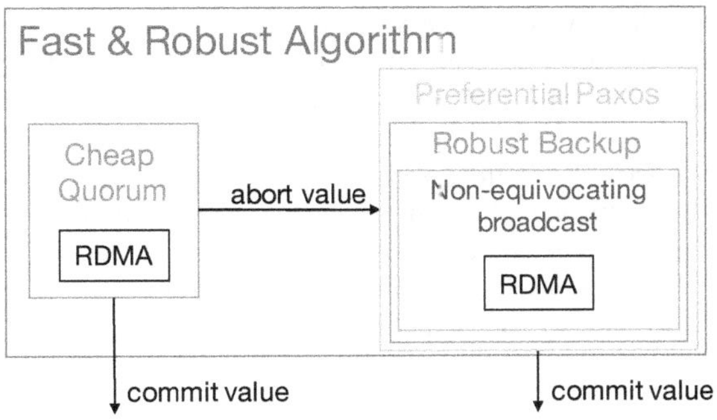

Figure 5: Interactions of the components of the Fast & Robust Algorithm.

or p's input value. If p has a unanimity proof in *Proof*[p], it adds it to the abort value.

In the full version of this paper [4], we prove the correctness of Cheap Quorum, and in particular we show the following two important agreement properties:

LEMMA 4.4 (CHEAP QUORUM DECISION AGREEMENT). *Let p and q be correct processes. If p decides v_1 while q decides v_2, then $v_1 = v_2$.*

LEMMA 4.5 (CHEAP QUORUM ABORT AGREEMENT). *Let p and q be correct processes (possibly identical). If p decides v in Cheap Quorum while q aborts from Cheap Quorum, then v will be q's abort value. Furthermore, if p is a follower, q's abort proof is a correct unanimity proof.*

The above construction assumes a fail-free memory with regular registers, but we can extend it to tolerate memory failures using the approach of Section 4.1, noting that each register has a single writer process.

4.3 Putting it Together: the Fast & Robust Algorithm

The final algorithm, called Fast & Robust, combines Cheap Quorum (§4.2) and Robust Backup (§4.1), as we now explain. Recall that Robust Backup is parameterized by a message-passing consensus algorithm $\mathcal{A}$ that tolerates crash-failures. $\mathcal{A}$ can be any such algorithm (e.g., Paxos).

Roughly, in Fast & Robust, we run Cheap Quorum and, if it aborts, we use a process's abort value as its input value to Robust Backup. However, we must carefully glue the two algorithms together to ensure that if some correct process decided v in Cheap Quorum, then v is the only value that can be decided in Robust Backup.

For this purpose, we propose a simple wrapper for Robust Backup, called *Preferential Paxos*. Preferential Paxos first runs a set-up phase, in which processes may adopt new values, and then runs Robust Backup with the new values. More specifically, there are some *preferred* input values $v_1 \dots v_k$, ordered by priority. We guarantee that every process adopts one of the top $f + 1$ priority inputs. In particular, this means that if a majority of processes get the highest priority value, v_1, as input, then v_1 is guaranteed to be the decision value. The set-up phase is simple; all processes send each other their input values. Each process p waits to receive $n - f$ such messages, and adopts the value with the highest priority that it sees. This is the value that p uses as its input to Paxos. The pseudocode for Preferential Paxos is given in the full version of our paper [4], where we also prove the following lemma about Preferential Paxos:

LEMMA 4.6 (PREFERENTIAL PAXOS PRIORITY DECISION). *Preferential Paxos implements weak Byzantine agreement with $n \geq 2f_P + 1$ processes. Furthermore, let $v_1, \dots, v_n$ be the input values of an instance C of Preferential Paxos, ordered by priority. The decision value of correct processes is always one of $v_1, \dots, v_{f+1}$.*

We can now describe Fast & Robust in detail. We start executing Cheap Quorum. If Cheap Quorum aborts, we execute Preferential Paxos, with each process receiving its abort value from Cheap Quorum as its input value to Preferential Paxos. We define the priorities of inputs to Preferential Paxos as follows.

DEFINITION 3 (INPUT PRIORITIES FOR PREFERENTIAL PAXOS). *The input values for Preferential Paxos as it is used in Fast & Robust are split into three sets (here, p_1 is the leader of Cheap Quorum):*

- $T = \{v \mid v \text{ contains a correct unanimity proof}\}$
- $M = \{v \mid v \notin T \wedge v \text{ contains the signature of } p_1\}$
- $B = \{v \mid v \notin T \wedge v \notin M\}$

The priority order of the input values is such that for all values $v_T \in T$, $v_M \in M$, and $v_B \in B$, $priority(v_T) > priority(v_M) > priority(v_B)$.

Figure 5 shows how the various algorithms presented in this section come together to form the Fast & Robust algorithm. In the full version, we show that Fast & Robust is correct, with the following key lemma:

LEMMA 4.7 (COMPOSITION LEMMA). *If some correct process decides a value v in Cheap Quorum before an abort, then v is the only value that can be decided in Preferential Paxos with priorities as defined in Definition 3.*

THEOREM 4.8. *There exists a 2-deciding algorithm for Weak Byzantine Agreement in a message-and-memory model with up to f_P Byzantine processes and f_M memory crashes, where $n \geq 2f_P + 1$ and $m \geq 2f_M + 1$.*

5 CRASH FAILURES

We now restrict ourselves to crash failures of processes and memories. Clearly, we can use the algorithms of Section 4 in this setting, to obtain a 2-deciding consensus algorithm with $n \geq 2f_P + 1$ and $m \geq 2f_M + 1$. However, this is overkill since those algorithms use sophisticated mechanisms (signatures, non-equivocation) to guard against Byzantine behavior. With only crash failures, we now show it is possible to retain the efficiency of a 2-deciding algorithm while improving resiliency. In Section 5.1, we first give a 2-deciding algorithm that allows the crash of all but one process ($n \geq f_P + 1$) and a minority of memories ($m \geq 2f_M + 1$). In Section 5.2, we improve resilience further by giving a 2-deciding algorithm that tolerates crashes of a minority of the combined set of memories and processes.

5.1 Protected Memory Paxos

Our starting point is the Disk Paxos algorithm [29], which works in a system with processes and memories where $n \geq f_P + 1$ and $m \geq$

Algorithm 6: Protected Memory Paxos—code for process p

```
Regions: for i=1..m, Region[i] is all of memory i,
                   with initial permission (R:
                         ↪ Π - {p₁}, W: ∅, RW: {p₁} )
Registers: for i=1..m, p ∈Π,
           slot[i,p]: tuple (minProp,accProp, value)
                ↪ in Region[i] // in memory i
Ω: failure detector that returns current leader

propose(v) {
  repeat forever {
    wait until Ω == p; // wait to become leader
    propNr = choose number higher than any proposal
        ↪ numbers seen before;
    if (p ≠ p₁){
      pfor i=1..m {  // for each memory i
          changePermission(Region[i], R:{Π-{p}},W:
              ↪ ∅, RW:{p}); //get write perm
          write1Success[i] = write(slot[i,p], {
              ↪ propNr, ⊥, ⊥})
          for all q ∈Π do localInfo[i,q] = read(
              ↪ slot[i,q]) }
      wait for completion of m - f_M iterations of
          ↪ pfor loop
      if (!write1Success[i] for some i) then
          ↪ continue;
      if (localInfo[i,q].minProp > propNr for some
          ↪ i,q) continue;
      if (localInfo[i,q].value = ⊥ for all i,q)
          ↪ myValue = v
      else myValue = localInfo[i,q].value where i,q
          ↪ maximizes localInfo[i,q].accProp }
    pfor i=1..m do write2Success[i] = write(slot[i,p
        ↪ ], {propNr, propNr, myValue})
    wait for completion of m - f_M iterations of pfor
        ↪ loop
    if !write2Success[j] for some j then continue;
    decide myValue  }}
```

$2f_M + 1$. This is our resiliency goal, but Disk Paxos takes four delays in common executes. Our new algorithm, called Protected Memory Paxos, removes two delays; it retains the structure of Disk Paxos but uses permissions to skip steps. Initially some fixed leader $\ell = np_1$ has exclusive write permission to all memories; if another process becomes leader, it takes the exclusive permission. Having exclusive permission permits a leader ℓ to optimize execution, because ℓ can do two things simultaneously: (1) write its consensus proposal and (2) determine whether another leader took over. Specifically, if ℓ succeeds in (1), it knows no leader ℓ' took over because ℓ' would have taken the permission. Thus ℓ avoids the last read in Disk Paxos, saving two delays. Of course, care must be taken to implement this without violating safety.

The pseudocode of Protected Memory Paxos is in Algorithm 6. Each memory has one memory region, and at any time exactly one process can write to a region. Each memory i holds a register $slot[i,p]$ for each process p. Intuitively, $slot[i,p]$ is intended for p to write, but p may not have write permission to do that if it is not the leader—in that case, no process writes $slot[i,p]$.

When a process p becomes leader, it executes a special phase (the first leader p_1 can skip this phase), where p acquires exclusive write permission for a majority of memories, writes a new proposal number in its slot in a majority of memories, and then reads all slots in a majority of memories. If any of p's writes fail or p finds a proposal with a higher proposal number, then p gives up. Otherwise, p adopts the value with highest proposal number. In the next phase, p writes its value to its slot in a majority of memories. If a write fails, p gives up (then the current leader restarts the algorithm). If p succeeds, this is where we optimize time: p can simply decide, whereas Disk Paxos must read the memories again.

The code ensures that some correct process eventually decides, but it is easy to extend it so all correct processes decide [18]. Also, the code shows one instance of consensus, with p_1 as initial leader. With many consensus instances, the leader terminates one instance and becomes the default leader in the next.

Theorem 5.1. *Consider a message-and-memory model with up to f_P process crashes and f_M memory crashes, where $n \geq f_P + 1$ and $m \geq 2f_M + 1$. There exists a 2-deciding algorithm for consensus.*

5.2 Aligned Paxos

We now further enhance the failure resilience. We show that memories and processes are equivalent *agents*, in that it suffices for a majority of the agents (processes and memories together) to remain alive to solve consensus. Our new algorithm, *Aligned Paxos*, achieves this resiliency. To do so, the algorithm relies on the ability to use both the messages and the memories in our model; permissions are not needed. The key idea is to align a message-passing algorithm and a memory-based algorithm to use any majority of agents. We align Paxos [38] and Protected Memory Paxos so that their decisions are coordinated. More specifically, Protected Memory Paxos and Paxos have two phases. To align these algorithms, we factor out their differences and replace their steps with an abstraction that is implemented differently for each algorithm. The result is our *Aligned Paxos* algorithm, which has two phases, each with three steps: *communicate, hear back*, and *analyze*. Each step treats processes and memories separately, and translates the results of operations on different agents to a common language. We implement the steps using their analogues in Paxos and Protected Memory Paxos[4]. The pseudocode of Aligned Paxos is given in the full version of our paper [4].

6 DYNAMIC PERMISSIONS ARE NECESSARY FOR EFFICIENT CONSENSUS

In §5.1, we showed how dynamic permissions can improve the performance of Disk Paxos. Are dynamic permissions necessary? We prove that with shared memory (or disks) alone, one cannot achieve 2-deciding consensus, even if the memory never fails, it has static permissions, processes may only fail by crashing, and the system is partially synchronous in the sense that eventually there is a known upper bound on the time it takes a correct process to take a step [27]. This result applies a fortiori to the Disk Paxos model [29].

Theorem 6.1. *Consider a partially synchronous shared-memory model with registers, where registers can have arbitrary static permissions, memory never fails, and at most one processes may fail by crashing. No consensus algorithm is 2-deciding.*

[4]We believe other implementations are possible. For example, replacing the Protected Memory Paxos implementation for memories with the Disk Paxos implementation yields an algorithm that does not use permissions.

Proof. Assume by contradiction that A is an algorithm in the stated model that is 2-deciding. That is, there is some execution E of A in which some process p decides a value v with 2 delays. We denote by R and W the set of objects which p reads and writes in E respectively. Note that since p decides in 2 delays in E, R and W must be disjoint, by the definition of operation delay and the fact that a process has at most one outstanding operation per object. Furthermore, p must issue all of its read and writes without waiting for the response of any operation.

Consider an execution E' in which p reads from the same set R of objects and writes the same values as in E to the same set W of objects. All of the read operations that p issues return by some time t_0, but the write operations of p are delayed for a long time. Another process p' begins its proposal of a value $v' \neq v$ after t_0. Since no process other than p' writes to any objects, E' is indistinguishable to p' from an execution in which it runs alone. Since A is a correct consensus algorithm that terminates if there is no contention, p' must eventually decide value v'. Let t' be the time at which p' decides. All of p's write operations terminate and are linearized in E' after time t'. Execution E' is indistinguishable to p from execution E, in which it ran alone. Therefore, p decides $v \neq v'$, violating agreement. □

Theorem 6.1, together with the Fast Paxos algorithm of Lamport [39], shows that an atomic read-write shared memory model is strictly weaker than the message passing model in its ability to solve consensus quickly. This result may be of independent interest, since often the classic shared memory and message passing models are seen as equivalent, because of the seminal computational equivalence result of Attiya, Bar-Noy, and Dolev [7]. Interestingly, it is known that shared memory can tolerante more failures when solving consensus (with randomization or partial synchrony) [6, 16], and therefore it seems that perhaps shared memory is strictly stronger than message passing for solving consensus. However, our result shows that there are aspects in which message passing is stronger than shared memory. In particular, message passing can solve consensus faster than shared memory in well-behaved executions.

7 RDMA IN PRACTICE

Our model is meant to reflect capabilities of RDMA, while providing a clean abstraction to reason about. We now give an overview of how RDMA works, and how features of our model can be implemented using RDMA.

RDMA enables a remote process to access local memory directly through the network interface card (NIC), without involving the CPU. For a piece of local memory to be accessible to a remote process p, the CPU has to *register* that memory region and associate it with the appropriate connection (called *Queue Pair*) for p. The association of a registered memory region and a queue pair is done indirectly through a *protection domain*: both memory regions and queue pairs are associated with a protection domain, and a queue pair q can be used to access a memory region r if q and r and in the same protection domain. The CPU must also specify what access level (read, write, read-write) is allowed to the memory region in each protection domain. A local memory area can thus be registered and associated with several queue pairs, with the same or different access levels, by associating it with one or more protection domains. Each RDMA connection can be used by the remote server to access registered memory regions using a unique region-specific key created as a part of the registration process.

As highlighted by previous work [45], failures of the CPU, NIC and DRAM can be seen as independent (e.g., arbitrary delays, too many bit errors, failed ECC checks, respectively). For instance, *zombie servers* in which the CPU is blocked but RDMA requests can still be served account for roughly half of all failures [45]. This motivates our choice to treat processes and memory separately in our model. In practice, if a CPU fails permanently, the memory will also become unreachable through RDMA eventually; however, in such cases memory may remain available long enough for ongoing operations to complete. Also, in practical settings it is possible for full-system crashes to occur (e.g., machine restarts), which correspond to a process and a memory failing at the same time—this is allowed by our model.

Memory regions in our model correspond to RDMA memory regions. Static permissions can be implemented by making the appropriate memory region registration before the execution of the algorithm; these permissions then persist during execution without CPU involvement. Dynamic permissions require the host CPU to change the access levels; this should be done in the OS kernel: the kernel creates regions and controls their permissions, and then shares memory with user-space processes. In this way, Byzantine processes cannot change permissions illegally. The assumption is that the kernel is not Byzantine. Alternatively, future hardware support similar to SGX could even allow parts of the kernel to be Byzantine.

Using RDMA, a process p can grant permissions to a remote process q by registering memory regions with the appropriate access permissions (read, write, or read/write) and sending the corresponding key to q. p can revoke permissions dynamically by simply deregistering the memory region.

For our non-equivocation algorithm, each process can register the two dimensional array of values in read-only mode with a protection domain. All the queue pairs used by that process are also created in the context of the same protection domain. Additionally, the process can preserve write access permission to its row via another registration of just that row with the protection domain, thus enabling single-writer multiple-reader access. Thereafter the non-equivocation algorithm can be implemented trivially by using RDMA reads and writes by all processes. Non-equivocation with unreliable memories is similarly straightforward since failure of the memory ensures that no process will be able to access the memory.

For Cheap Quorum, the static memory region registrations are straightforward as above. To revoke the leader's write permission, it suffices for a region's host process to deregister the memory region. Panic messages can be relayed using RDMA message sends.

In our crash-only consensus algorithm, we leverage the capability of registering overlapping memory regions in a protection domain. As in above algorithms, each process uses one protection domain for RDMA accesses. Queue pairs for connections to all other processes are associated with this protection domain. The process' entire slot array is registered with the protection domain in read-only mode. In addition, the same slot array can be dynamically registered (and deregistered) in write mode based on incoming write permission requests: A proposer requests write permission using an RDMA message send. In response, the acceptor first deregisters write permission for the immediate previous proposer. The acceptor thereafter registers the slot array in write mode and responds to the proposer with the new key associated with the newly registered slot array. Reads of the slot array are performed by the proposer using RDMA reads. Subsequent second phase RDMA write of the value can be performed on the slot array as long as the proposer continues to have write permission to the slot array. The RDMA write fails if the acceptor granted write permission to another proposer in the meantime.

Acknowledgements. We wish to thank the anonymous reviewers for their helpful comments on improving the paper. This work has been supported in part by the European Research Council (ERC) Grant 339539 (AOC), and a Microsoft PhD Fellowship.

REFERENCES

- [1] Ittai Abraham, Gregory Chockler, Idit Keidar, and Dahlia Malkhi. Byzantine disk paxos: optimal resilience with byzantine shared memory. *Distributed computing (DIST)*, 18(5):387–408, 2006.
- [2] Yehuda Afek, David S. Greenberg, Michael Merritt, and Gadi Taubenfeld. Computing with faulty shared memory. In *ACM Symposium on Principles of Distributed Computing (PODC)*, pages 47–58, August 1992.
- [3] Marcos K Aguilera, Naama Ben-David, Irina Calciu, Rachid Guerraoui, Erez Petrank, and Sam Toueg. Passing messages while sharing memory. In *ACM Symposium on Principles of Distributed Computing (PODC)*, pages 51–60. ACM, 2018.
- [4] Marcos K. Aguilera, Naama Ben-David, Rachid Guerraoui, Virendra Marathe, and Igor Zablotchi. The Impact of RDMA on Agreement. *ArXiv preprint arXiv:1905.12143*, 2019.
- [5] Noga Alon, Michael Merritt, Omer Reingold, Gadi Taubenfeld, and Rebecca N Wright. Tight bounds for shared memory systems accessed by byzantine processes. *Distributed computing (DIST)*, 18(2):99–109, 2005.
- [6] James Aspnes and Maurice Herlihy. Fast randomized consensus using shared memory. *Journal of algorithms*, 11(3):441–461, 1990.
- [7] Hagit Attiya, Amotz Bar-Noy, and Danny Dolev. Sharing memory robustly in message-passing systems. *Journal of the ACM (JACM)*, 42(1):124–142, 1995.
- [8] Pierre-Louis Aublin, Rachid Guerraoui, Nikola Knežević, Vivien Quéma, and Marko Vukolić. The next 700 BFT protocols. *ACM Transactions on Computer Systems (TOCS)*, 32(4):12, 2015.
- [9] Rida Bazzi and Gil Neiger. Optimally simulating crash failures in a byzantine environment. In *International Workshop on Distributed Algorithms (WDAG)*, pages 108–128. Springer, 1991.
- [10] Jonathan Behrens, Ken Birman, Sagar Jha, Matthew Milano, Edward Tremel, Eugene Bagdasaryan, Theo Gkountouvas, Weijia Song, and Robbert Van Renesse. Derecho: Group communication at the speed of light. Technical report, Technical Report. Cornell University, 2016.
- [11] Michael Ben-Or. Another advantage of free choice (extended abstract): Completely asynchronous agreement protocols. In *ACM Symposium on Principles of Distributed Computing (PODC)*, pages 27–30. ACM, 1983.
- [12] Alysson Neves Bessani, Miguel Correia, Joni da Silva Fraga, and Lau Cheuk Lung. Sharing memory between byzantine processes using policy-enforced tuple spaces. *IEEE Transactions on Parallel and Distributed Systems*, 20(3):419–432, 2009.
- [13] Romain Boichat, Partha Dutta, Svend Frolund, and Rachid Guerraoui. Reconstructing paxos. *SIGACT News*, 34(2):42–57, March 2003.
- [14] Zohir Bouzid, Damien Imbs, and Michel Raynal. A necessary condition for byzantine k-set agreement. *Information Processing Letters*, 116(12):757–759, 2016.
- [15] Gabriel Bracha. Asynchronous byzantine agreement protocols. *Information and Computation*, 75(2):130–143, 1987.
- [16] Gabriel Bracha and Sam Toueg. Asynchronous consensus and broadcast protocols. *Journal of the ACM (JACM)*, 32(4):824–840, 1985.
- [17] Francisco Brasileiro, Fabíola Greve, Achour Mostéfaoui, and Michel Raynal. Consensus in one communication step. In *International Conference on Parallel Computing Technologies*, pages 42–50. Springer, 2001.
- [18] Tushar Deepak Chandra and Sam Toueg. Unreliable failure detectors for reliable distributed systems. *Journal of the ACM (JACM)*, 43(2):225–267, 1996.
- [19] Byung-Gon Chun, Petros Maniatis, and Scott Shenker. Diverse replication for single-machine byzantine-fault tolerance. In *USENIX Annual Technical Conference (ATC)*, pages 287–292, 2008.
- [20] Byung-Gon Chun, Petros Maniatis, Scott Shenker, and John Kubiatowicz. Attested append-only memory: making adversaries stick to their word. In *ACM Symposium on Operating Systems Principles (SOSP)*, pages 189–204, 2007.
- [21] Allen Clement, Flavio Junqueira, Aniket Kate, and Rodrigo Rodrigues. On the (limited) power of non-equivocation. In *ACM Symposium on Principles of Distributed Computing (PODC)*, pages 301–308. ACM, 2012.
- [22] Miguel Correia, Nuno Ferreira Neves, and Paulo Veríssimo. How to tolerate half less one byzantine nodes in practical distributed systems. In *International Symposium on Reliable Distributed Systems (SRDS)*, pages 174–183, 2004.
- [23] Miguel Correia, Giuliana S Veronese, and Lau Cheuk Lung. Asynchronous byzantine consensus with 2f+ 1 processes. In *ACM symposium on applied computing (SAC)*, pages 475–480. ACM, 2010.
- [24] Dan Dobre and Neeraj Suri. One-step consensus with zero-degradation. In *International Conference on Dependable Systems and Networks (DSN)*, pages 137–146. IEEE Computer Society, 2006.
- [25] Aleksandar Dragojević, Dushyanth Narayanan, Miguel Castro, and Orion Hodson. FaRM: Fast remote memory. In *USENIX Symposium on Networked Systems Design and Implementation (NSDI)*, pages 401–414, 2014.
- [26] Partha Dutta, Rachid Guerraoui, and Leslie Lamport. How fast can eventual synchrony lead to consensus? In *International Conference on Dependable Systems and Networks (DSN)*, pages 22–27. IEEE, 2005.
- [27] Cynthia Dwork, Nancy Lynch, and Larry Stockmeyer. Consensus in the presence of partial synchrony. *Journal of the ACM (JACM)*, 35(2):288–323, 1988.
- [28] Michael J Fischer, Nancy A Lynch, and Michael S Paterson. Impossibility of distributed consensus with one faulty process. *Journal of the ACM (JACM)*, 1985.
- [29] Eli Gafni and Leslie Lamport. Disk paxos. *Distributed computing (DIST)*, 16(1):1–20, 2003.
- [30] Prasad Jayanti, Tushar Deepak Chandra, and Sam Toueg. Fault-tolerant wait-free shared objects. *Journal of the ACM (JACM)*, 45(3):451–500, May 1998.
- [31] Anuj Kalia, Michael Kaminsky, and David G Andersen. Using RDMA efficiently for key-value services. *ACM SIGCOMM Computer Communication Review*, 44(4):295–306, 2015.
- [32] Anuj Kalia, Michael Kaminsky, and David G Andersen. FaSST: Fast, scalable and simple distributed transactions with two-sided (RDMA) datagram RPCs. In *USENIX Symposium on Operating System Design and Implementation (OSDI)*, volume 16, pages 185–201, 2016.
- [33] Anuj Kalia Michael Kaminsky and David G Andersen. Design guidelines for high performance RDMA systems. In *USENIX Annual Technical Conference (ATC)*, page 437, 2016.
- [34] Rüdiger Kapitza, Johannes Behl, Christian Cachin, Tobias Distler, Simon Kuhnle, Seyed Vahid Mohammadi, Wolfgang Schröder-Preikschat, and Klaus Stengel. Cheapbft: resource-efficient byzantine fault tolerance. In *European Conference on Computer Systems (EuroSys)*, pages 295–308, 2012.
- [35] Idit Keidar and Sergio Rajsbaum. On the cost of fault-tolerant consensus when there are no faults: preliminary version. *ACM SIGACT News*, 32(2):45–63, 2001.
- [36] Klaus Kursawe. Optimistic byzantine agreement. In *International Symposium on Reliable Distributed Systems (SRDS)*, pages 262–267, October 2002.
- [37] Leslie Lamport. The weak byzantine generals problem. *Journal of the ACM (JACM)*, 30(3):668–676, July 1983.
- [38] Leslie Lamport. The part-time parliament. *ACM Transactions on Computer Systems (TOCS)*, 16(2):133–169, 1998.
- [39] Leslie Lamport. Fast paxos. *Distributed computing (DIST)*, 19(2):79–103, 2006.
- [40] Leslie Lamport, Robert Shostak, and Marshall Pease. The byzantine generals problem. *ACM Transactions on Programming Languages and Systems (TOPLAS)*, 4(3):382–401, 1982.
- [41] Dahlia Malkhi, Michael Merritt, Michael K Reiter, and Gadi Taubenfeld. Objects shared by byzantine processes. *Distributed computing (DIST)*, 16(1):37–48, 2003.
- [42] Jean-Philippe Martin and Lorenzo Alvisi. Fast byzantine consensus. *IEEE Transactions on Dependable and Secure Computing (TDSC)*, 3(3):202–215, July 2006.
- [43] Gil Neiger and Sam Toueg. Automatically increasing the fault-tolerance of distributed algorithms. *Journal of Algorithms*, 11(3):374–419, 1990.
- [44] Marshall Pease, Robert Shostak, and Leslie Lamport. Reaching agreement in the presence of faults. *Journal of the ACM (JACM)*, 27(2):228–234, 1980.
- [45] Marius Poke and Torsten Hoefler. DARE: High-performance state machine replication on RDMA networks. In *Symposium on High-Performance Parallel and Distributed Computing (HPDC)*, pages 107–118. ACM, 2015.
- [46] Signe Rüsch, Ines Messadi, and Rüdiger Kapitza. Towards low-latency byzantine agreement protocols using RDMA. In *IEEE/IFIP International Conference on Dependable Systems and Networks Workshops (DSN-W)*, pages 146–151. IEEE, 2018.
- [47] Yee Jiun Song and Robbert van Renesse. Bosco: One-step byzantine asynchronous consensus. In *International Symposium on Distributed Computing (DISC)*, pages 438–450, September 2008.
- [48] Giuliana Santos Veronese, Miguel Correia, Alysson Neves Bessani, Lau Cheuk Lung, and Paulo Veríssimo. Efficient byzantine fault-tolerance. *IEEE Trans. Computers*, 62(1):16–30, 2013.
- [49] Cheng Wang, Jianyu Jiang, Xusheng Chen, Ning Yi, and Heming Cui. APUS: Fast and scalable paxos on RDMA. In *Symposium on Cloud Computing (SoCC)*, pages 94–107. ACM, 2017.

Brief Announcement: Hyaline: Fast and Transparent Lock-Free Memory Reclamation

Ruslan Nikolaev
Virginia Tech, USA
rnikola@vt.edu

Binoy Ravindran
Virginia Tech, USA
binoy@vt.edu

ABSTRACT

We present a new lock-free safe memory reclamation algorithm, Hyaline, which is fast, scalable, and transparent to the underlying data structures. Hyaline easily handles virtually unbounded number of threads that can be created and deleted dynamically, while retaining $O(1)$ reclamation cost. We also extend Hyaline to avoid situations where stalled threads prevent others from reclaiming newly allocated objects, a common problem with epoch-based reclamation. Our evaluation reveals that Hyaline's throughput is high – it steadily outperformed other reclamation schemes by > 10% in one test and yielded even higher gains in oversubscribed scenarios.

CCS CONCEPTS

• **Theory of computation** → **Concurrent algorithms**.

KEYWORDS

lock-free; memory reclamation; concurrent data structures

ACM Reference Format:
Ruslan Nikolaev and Binoy Ravindran. 2019. Brief Announcement: Hyaline: Fast and Transparent Lock-Free Memory Reclamation. In *2019 ACM Symposium on Principles of Distributed Computing (PODC '19), July 29–August 2, 2019, Toronto, ON, Canada.* ACM, New York, NY, USA, 3 pages. https://doi.org/10.1145/3293611.3331575

1 INTRODUCTION

One of the most fundamental problems for lock-free data structures that use dynamic memory allocation is that memory blocks need to be safely deallocated. Safe memory reclamation (SMR) techniques are typically needed for unmanaged (C/C++) code. Many existing approaches for SMR originate from or improve upon epoch-based reclamation (EBR) [4, 5] and hazard pointers (HP) [6]. EBR provides a simple API but lacks protection against stalled threads that can prevent timely reclamation and lead to memory exhaustion. HP does not suffer from this problem, but is harder to use and slower in practice. (SMR schemes that defend against stalled threads are called *robust* [1, 10].) Furthermore, some algorithms [1, 2] rely on special OS abstractions, making it difficult to use them in certain cases, such as within OS kernels or platform-independent code.

We present Hyaline, a new algorithm that is not based on EBR or HP directly, has very low overhead, and scales well. Unlike most SMR algorithms, which typically reserve per-thread entries, Hyaline supports virtually unbounded number of threads using a small number of *slots*. Moreover, Hyaline bounds the cost of reclamation to $\approx O(1)$ per operation, irrespective of the total number of threads.

In oversubscribed scenarios, Hyaline particularly shines due to its unique asynchronous block tracking mechanism (we saw more than 30% gain over other algorithms). Threads do not need to periodically check if block(s) can be safely freed. Instead, tracking is reminiscent of reference counting, but Hyaline avoids the prohibitive cost of classical reference counting [9].

Hyaline is well suited for preemptive environments where the number of threads substantially exceeds the number of cores and can change dynamically such as in OS kernels and server applications. Unlike many other techniques, in Hyaline, threads that delete blocks (nodes) are not necessarily those that end up freeing them. This results in better *transparency*, as threads are "off the hook" as soon as they complete data structure operations. Unlike in EBR or HP, Hyaline's threads can immediately be recycled or destroyed without worrying about the fate of their previously deleted blocks.

2 OVERALL DESIGN

In Hyaline, programs explicitly *retire* objects and ensure that retired objects are not reachable from subsequent operations on the data structures. Each operation on the data structures must be enclosed between *enter* and *leave* calls. Hyaline's use of reference counters is triggered only when handling retired nodes.

We first present Hyaline's simpler version that manipulates just a single *retirement list*. Hyaline's key idea is that all threads participate in the tracking of retired nodes between *enter* and *leave* in this global list even if they are not actively retiring any nodes themselves. A special `Head` tuple is associated with this list. The `HPtr` field of this tuple is a pointer to the beginning of the list, and the `HRef` field counts the number of active threads. When each thread *enters*, it atomically increments the `HRef` field to indicate that a new thread has arrived. At the same time, the thread records a snapshot value of `HPtr` into a special per-thread `Handle` variable.

Each node for a data structure incorporates a special header which contains `Next` and `NRef` fields. `Next` is a pointer to the next node in the list, and `NRef` of every non-Head node counts threads that can still access this node. For the very first node, `HRef` itself serves this purpose. When retiring a new node, its `NRef` is set to 0. After appending the node, the current thread atomically adds the snapshot value of `HRef` to the `NRef` field of the predecessor node (`Head` no longer points to the predecessor node).

When a thread *leaves*, it decrements `HRef`. At the same time, it retrieves the `HPtr` pointer and traverses a sublist of nodes from `HPtr` to `Handle` that were retired since it *entered*. While traversing, the thread decrements `NRef` counters for every non-Head node.

ACM ISBN 978-1-4503-6217-7/19/07.
https://doi.org/10.1145/3293611.3331575

```
forall head_t Head ∈ Heads[k] do                                   // Initialization
    Head.HRef = 0, Head.HPtr = Null;
handle_t enter(int slot)
    Last = FAA(&Heads[slot], { .HRef=1, .HPtr=0 });
    return Last.HPtr;                                              // Returns a handle
void leave(int slot, handle_t handle)
    do                                                 // Decrement HRef and fetch Next
        Head = Heads[slot];
        Curr = Head.HPtr;
        if ( Curr ≠ handle )
            Next = Curr->Next;
        New.HPtr = Curr;
        if ( Head.HRef = 1 ) New.HPtr = Null;
        New.HRef = Head.HRef - 1;
    while not CAS(&Heads[slot], Head, New);
    if ( Head.HRef = 1 and Curr ≠ Null )                           // Treat Curr as
        adjust(Curr, Adjs);                                // if it were a predecessor
    if ( Curr ≠ handle )                                           // Non-empty list
        traverse(Next, handle);
handle_t trim(int slot, handle_t handle)
    Head = Heads[slot];                                            // Do not alter head
    Curr = Head.HPtr;
    if ( Curr ≠ handle )                                           // Non-empty list
        traverse(Curr->Next, handle);
    return Curr;                                                   // Returns a new handle
```

```
void retire(batch_t *batch)
    doAdj = False, Empty = 0, Inserts = 0;
    batch->NRefNode()->NRef = 0;
    forall int slot ∈ 0..k-1 do
        do                                                 // Add the batch to this slot
            Head = Heads[slot];
            if ( Head.HRef = 0 )                                          // REF #1#
                doAdj = True, Empty += Adjs;
                continue with the next slot;
            New.HPtr = batch->NextNode();
            New.HRef = Head.HRef;
            New.HPtr->Next = Head.HPtr;
        while not CAS(&Heads[slot], Head, New);
        adjust(Head.HPtr, Adjs + Head.HRef);                              // REF #2#
    if ( doAdj ) adjust(batch->FirstNode(), Empty);                       // REF #3#
void adjust(node_t *node, int val)
    Ref = node->NRefNode;
    if ( FAA(&Ref->NRef, val) = -val ) free_batch(Ref->First);
void traverse(node_t *next, handle_t handle)
    do                                            // Traverse the retirement sublist
        Curr = next;
        if ( Curr = Null ) break;
        next = Curr->Next;
        Ref = Curr->NRefNode;
        if ( FAA(&Ref->NRef, -1) = 1 ) free_batch(Ref->First);
    while Curr ≠ handle;
```

Figure 1: Hyaline for double-width CAS.

```
handle_t enter(int slot)
    Heads[slot] = { .HRef=1, .HPtr=Null };
    return Null;                                                   // Returns a handle
// Replace #2# in retire() with: Inserts++
```

```
void leave(int slot, handle_t handle)
    Head = SWAP(&Heads[slot], { .HRef=0, .HPtr=Null });
    if ( Head.HPtr ≠ Null ) traverse(Head.HPtr, handle);
// Replace #3#: adjust(batch->FirstNode(), Inserts)
```

Figure 2: Hyaline-1 for single-width CAS.

```
int AllocEra = 0;                                                  // Initialization
thread int AllocCounter = 0;
forall int Access ∈ Accesses[k] do Access = 0;
forall signed int Ack ∈ Acks[k] do Ack = 0;
node_t *deref(int slot, node_t **ptr_node)
    Access = Accesses[slot];
    while True do
        node_t * Node = (*ptr_node);
        Alloc = AllocEra;
        if ( Access = Alloc ) return Node;
        Access = touch(slot, Alloc);
void retire(batch_t *batch)
    // Replace #1# in retire() with:
    Access = Accesses[slot];
    Min = batch->MinBirth();
    if ( Head.HRef = 0 or Access < Min ) ...;
    FAA(&Acks[slot], Head.HRef);                                   // Skip in Hyaline-1S
```

```
void init_node(node_t *node)
    if ( AllocCounter++ mod Freq = 0 ) FAA(&AllocEra, 1);
    node->BirthEra = AllocEra;                                // Shares space with Next
int touch(int slot, int era)
    do                               // Hyaline-1S: touch is ordinary memory write
        Access = Accesses[slot];
        if ( Access ≥ era ) return Access;
    while not CAS(&Accesses[slot], Access, era);
    return era
// Changes below are for Hyaline-S, not Hyaline-1S
handle_t enter(int *slot)
    while Acks[*slot] ≥ Threshold do
        *slot = (*slot + 1) mod k;                            // Try out all k slots
void traverse(int slot, node_t *next, handle_t handle)
    Counter = 0;
    do Counter++ ... while ...;
    FAA(&Acks[slot], −Counter);
```

Figure 3: Hyaline-S: dealing with stalled threads.

To alleviate contention due to *retire*, threads retire nodes in batches and keep a single reference counter per batch rather than individual node. To alleviate contention due to *enter* and *leave*, we introduce the concept of *slots*, which a thread chooses randomly. Each slot has its own Head, and thus, we end up with multiple retirement lists. When a batch is retired, it is added to every slot that has its HRef $\neq 0$ (i.e., slots with active threads). Since slots may end up with non-identical order of batches, we require the number of nodes in batches to be strictly greater than the number of slots. Each node in a batch keeps the Next pointer for the corresponding slot's list, and a dedicated node keeps the per-batch NRef counter instead. All nodes in the batch are linked together, and each node has an extra pointer to the node with NRef. Thus, each node keeps three variables irrespective of batch sizes and total number of slots.

We generalize the idea of NRef adjustments to accommodate Hyaline's multiple-list version. When adjusting a predecessor in slot *i*, we add $Adjs + HRef_i$ rather than just $HRef_i$, where *Adjs* is a special constant which prevents the adjustment for the predecessor to complete until all slots are handled. Assuming that the number of slots, *k*, is a power of 2, and the maximum representable unsigned integer value is $2^N - 1$, we calculate: $Adjs = \left\lfloor \frac{2^N - 1}{k} \right\rfloor + 1$.

Hyaline-1 for Single-width CAS. If every thread allocates its own unique slot, we can squeeze HRef into a single bit and merge it with HPtr. This approach simplifies *enter* and *leave*, and adjustments. Instead of adjusting predecessors and empty slots, we count the number of slots a batch is added to. After adding the batch to the last slot, `NRef` of the batch is adjusted by this counter.

3 ALGORITHM DESCRIPTIONS

In Figure 1, we present pseudocode. (Hyaline-1 in Figure 2 replaces *enter* and *leave* with simpler equivalents.) Hyaline requires double-width CAS but can also be implemented with LL/SC; see [7] for details. Correctness arguments are given in [7]. *enter* atomically increments `HRef` while fetching the current pointer in a given slot. *retire* inserts a batch to all slots. *leave* decrements `HRef` and dereferences preceding nodes in the *traverse* helper method. An optional *trim* operation (we do not use it in Section 4) is equivalent to *leave* followed by *enter*, but avoids the unwanted alteration of `Head`.

To deal with stalled threads in Hyaline, we create Hyaline-S (Figure 3) by partially adopting the idea from hazard eras (HE) [8] and interval-based reclamation (IBR) [10] to record *birth eras* when allocating memory. However, we do not use retire eras and also support multiple threads per each slot. Our API is similar to 2GE-IBR [10]: all pointer dereferences must be wrapped in *deref*. The eras are 64-bit numbers which are assumed to never overflow in practice. When nodes are allocated, *init_node* initializes their birth eras with the era clock value. Threads must share per-slot eras, and the maximum era needs to be set (when dereferencing) using the *touch* helper function. *retire* uses the minimum birth era across all nodes in a batch, and skips slots with stale eras.

Since threads share per-slot eras in Hyaline-S, *enter* avoids slots occupied by stalled threads by using `Ack` values. To retain robustness, we adaptively change the number of slots; see [7].

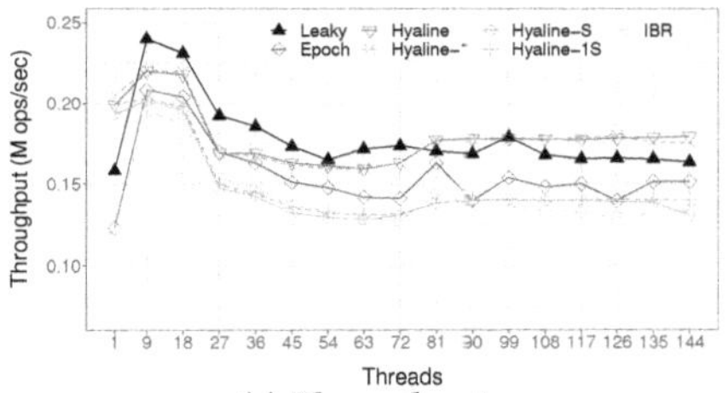

(a) Throughput

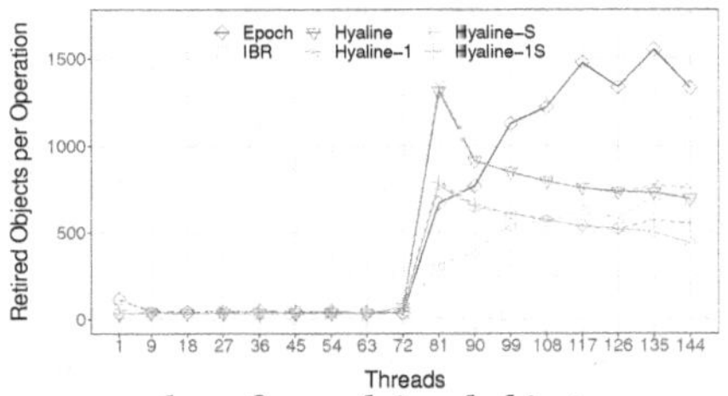

(b) Average number of unreclaimed objects per operation

Figure 4: Bonsai Tree (50% *insert*, 50% *delete*).

4 EVALUATION

We extended the test framework of [10] to support Hyaline. We present results for Bonsai Tree [3] under write-intensive workload (50% *insert*, 50% *delete*). For more results, see [7]. We ran our tests for up to 144 threads on a 72-core machine consisting of four Intel Xeon E7-8880 v3 2.30 GHz (45MB L3 cache) CPUs with hyper-threading disabled and 128GB of RAM. Threads are pinned in order, socket by socket. We use jemalloc and clang 6.0 with `-O3`. For each data point, the experiment starts by prefilling the data structure with 50,000 elements and runs 10 seconds (5 times). Each thread then randomly performs the aforementioned operations. The key used in each operation is randomly chosen from the range of 0 to 100,000 with equal probability.

We compare all Hyaline variants against a variant [10] of EBR and 2GE-IBR. The benchmark parameters [10] for these algorithms already appear to be optimized for high throughput. We also present **Leaky** which does not perform any memory reclamation. For Hyaline(-S), we cap the number of slots, k, at 128 (rounded number of cores). We use batches of at least 64 nodes and at most $k + 1$.

Throughput (Figure 4a) decreases for all schemes as we approach 18 per-CPU cores. Hyaline has the best performance and steadily outperforms Epoch by ≈10%. IBR, Hyaline-S, and Hyaline-1S have similar performance; it is worse than their non-robust counterparts due to a substantial number of pointer dereferences. The number of unreclaimed objects in Figure 4b for Hyaline and Hyaline-S is generally smaller than that of Epoch and IBR, respectively.

5 CONCLUSION

We presented Hyaline, a new algorithm for memory reclamation which has a number of advantages: great performance and scalability, easy integration with underlying data structures, and handling of stalled threads (in Hyaline-(1)S). All Hyaline schemes are transparent and suitable for environments where threads are created, recycled, and deleted dynamically: threads are "off-the-hook" as soon as they *leave* and need not check retirement lists afterwards.

We thank the anonymous reviewers for their valuable feedback. We also thank Mohamed Mohamedin for helping with experiments for an early version of the algorithm. This work is supported in part by AFOSR under grants FA9550-15-1-0098 and FA9550-16-1-0371.

Complete details of the algorithms, analysis, and experimental results are available in [7]. We provide code for all Hyaline variants at https://github.com/rusnikola/lfsmr.

REFERENCES

[1] Oana Balmau, Rachid Guerraoui, Maurice Herlihy, and Igor Zablotchi. 2016. Fast and Robust Memory Reclamation for Concurrent Data Structures. In *The 28th ACM Symp. on Parallelism in Algorithms and Architectures (SPAA '16)*. 349–359.

[2] Trevor Alexander Brown. 2015. Reclaiming Memory for Lock-Free Data Structures: There Has to Be a Better Way. In *Proceedings of the 2015 ACM Symposium on Principles of Distributed Computing (PODC '15)*. 261–270.

[3] Austin T. Clements, M. Frans Kaashoek, and Nickolai Zeldovich. 2012. Scalable Address Spaces Using RCU Balanced Trees. In *The 17th Inter. Confer. on Architectural Support for Programming Languages and OS (ASPLOS XVII)*. 199–210.

[4] Keir Fraser. 2004. *Practical Lock-freedom (Ph.D. dissert.)*. University of Cambridge.

[5] Thomas E. Hart, Paul E. McKenney, Angela Demke Brown, and Jonathan Walpole. 2007. Performance of memory reclamation for lockless synchronization. *J. Parallel and Distrib. Comput.* 67, 12 (2007), 1270 – 1285.

[6] Maged M. Michael. 2004. Hazard pointers: safe memory reclamation for lock-free objects. *IEEE Trans. on Parallel and Distributed Systems* 15, 6 (June 2004), 491–504.

[7] Ruslan Nikolaev and Binoy Ravindran. 2019. Hyaline: Fast and Transparent Lock-Free Memory Reclamation (full paper, arXiv). http://arxiv.org/abs/1905.07903.

[8] Pedro Ramalhete and Andreia Correia. 2017. Brief Announcement: Hazard Eras - Non-Blocking Memory Reclamation. In *Proceedings of the 29th ACM Symposium on Parallelism in Algorithms and Architectures (SPAA '17)*. 367–369.

[9] John D. Valois. 1995. Lock-free Linked Lists Using Compare-and-swap. In *The 14th ACM Symposium on Principles of Distributed Computing (PODC '95)*. 214–222.

[10] Haosen Wen, Joseph Izraelevitz, Wentao Cai, H. Alan Beadle, and Michael L. Scott. 2018. Interval-based Memory Reclamation. In *Proceedings of the 23rd ACM Symposium on Principles and Practice of Parallel Programming (PPoPP '18)*. 1–13.

Brief Announcement: Layering Data Structures over Skip Graphs for Increased NUMA Locality

Samuel Thomas
Hammurabi Mendes
sathomas@davidson.edu
hamendes@davidson.edu
Davidson College
Davidson, NC, USA

ABSTRACT

We present a lock-free, linearizable, and NUMA-aware data structure that implements sets, maps, and priority queue abstract data types (ADTs), based on using thread-local, sequential maps that are used to "jump" to suitable positions in a lock-free, linearizable variant of a skip graph. Our skip graph is suitably constrained in height and subjected to a data partition scheme that reduces contention and increases NUMA locality. We developed an additional skip graph variant, which we call sparse skip graph, that causes our thread-local maps as well as our shared structure to become more sparse. Compared to using regular skip graphs, sparse skip graphs show increased performance in workloads dominated by "insert" or "remove" operations, and comparable performance in workloads dominated by "contains" operations.

CCS CONCEPTS

• **Computing methodologies → Concurrent algorithms**; • **Software and its engineering → Concurrency control**.

KEYWORDS

synchronization, skip graphs, NUMA, lock-freedom, locality

ACM Reference Format:
Samuel Thomas and Hammurabi Mendes. 2019. Brief Announcement: Layering Data Structures over Skip Graphs for Increased NUMA Locality . In *2019 ACM Symposium on Principles of Distributed Computing (PODC '19), July 29-August 2, 2019, Toronto, ON, Canada.* ACM, New York, NY, USA, 3 pages. https://doi.org/10.1145/3293611.3331576

1 OUR APPROACH

We implemented a lock-free, linearizable, and NUMA-aware data structure that implements a set, map, and priority queue abstract data types (ADTs), based on using thread-local, sequential maps *layered* on top of a lock-free, linearizable variant of a *skip graph* [1, 3]. Our *layered structure* is composed of multiple *local structures*, all thread-local, sequential, navigable maps, and a single *shared structure*, a skip graph, operated concurrently by all threads. A skip graph is comprised of multiple skip lists that increasingly share lower levels (see more details below).

We distinguish between *local nodes* or *shared nodes* depending on which structure they belong to. Each local structure's job is to map elements inserted by their owning thread to shared nodes in the skip graph. Inserting an element e adds a shared node s to the skip graph, and creates a mapping $e \longrightarrow$ s in the local structure. A removal of element e will (i) *logically delete* the shared node s in the skip graph, (ii) cause a physical cleanup in the shared structure and (iii) cause the thread that contains the mapping $e \longrightarrow$ s in its local structure to physically cleanup that association upon detection. Steps (ii) and (iii) can happen in any order.

The skip graph and its partitioning. Our skip graph contains multiple singly-linked lists at different levels (Fig. 1). Starting from level zero, each level i contains 2^i lists. All elements belong to the level-0 list, labeled as "λ", the empty string. The level-0 list is partitioned into two level-1 lists, labeled "0" and "1". Each level-1 list is further partitioned into two level-2 lists: the level-1 list labeled "0" (resp. "1") is partitioned in two level-2 lists, labeled "00" and "01" (resp. "10" and "11"). The partitioning of elements is *not* done in a probabilistic way as in the original skip graph: we have a *partitioning scheme* that assigns threads to levels.

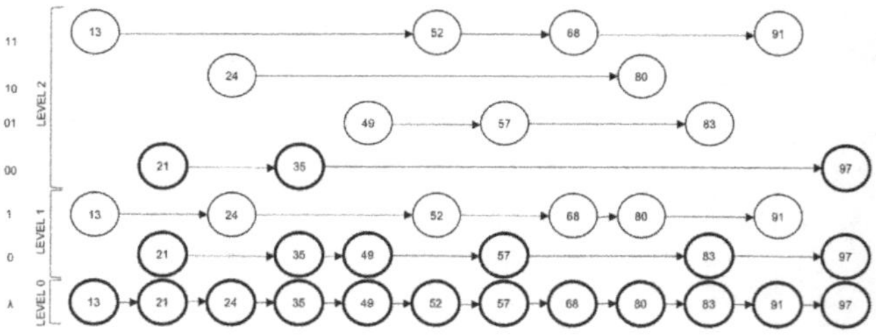

Figure 1: A skip graph is a collection of skip lists sharing their bottom levels. We partition our dataset suitably so that we increase NUMA locality and reduce contention.

We consider a system of T threads $\{t_1 \ldots t_T\}$. The skip graph's maximum level is $\text{MaxLevel} = \lceil \log(T) \rceil - 1$. A low MaxLevel like this does not guarantee logarithmic searches on a skip graph standing by itself, but our local structures compensate this fact by "jumping" to positions in the skip graph near where data structure operations take place. This "jump" happens *without any contention*, as each thread's local structure is private. Each thread T_i will have a *membership vector* M_i, a sequence of MaxLevel bits,

PODC '19, July 29-August 2, 2019, Toronto, ON, Canada

ACM ISBN 978-1-4503-6217-7/19/07.
https://doi.org/10.1145/3293611.3331576

whose suffixes indicate on which *unique* shared skip lists the particular thread can operate. This essentially makes all insertions from a single thread to happen in a unique skip list within the skip graph, denoted by L_i, and called the *associated skip list* of thread T_i. As an example, consider the skip graph with $\text{MaxLevel} = 2$ of Fig. 1. Each thread will have a 2-bit membership vector. If, say, T_i has M_i = "10", then T_i will always insert or remove in the skip list $L_i = (\lambda, 0, 10)$. With this scheme, we have at most two threads operating in each of the top-level shared linked lists, and at most $T/2^i$ threads operating in any particular level-i list. Note that the original definition of skip graphs assumes a membership vector *per element*, while in our approach all elements inserted by a single thread share the *thread*'s membership vector. Membership vectors can be generated as simply as taking the binary suffix of appropriate length of each thread ID, or *according to physical NUMA characteristics* of the machine.

We define *local* memory accesses as those operating in memory initially allocated by the current thread (under first-touch NUMA policy), and *remote* accesses simply as those that are non-local. Note that we adopt a conservative notion of local, as data initially allocated by two different threads could be located within the same NUMA node. Nevertheless, our approach, implemented in ~10K lines of C++14, operate up to 23% faster than a highly-optimized lock-free skip list, an optimized version of that in [6] (our fastest contender), with up to 70% of reduction on the number of remote synchronized reads, and up to a 3.21 times increase in CAS locality – that is, the ratio of local over remote CAS instructions – for 32 threads. In addition, we implemented another skip graph variant, called *sparse skip graph*. Using sparse skip graphs as our shared structure causes our local structures to be made more sparse, as we discuss later in page 2. Compared to using regular skip graphs, sparse skip graphs show increased performance in workloads dominated by "insert" or "remove" operations, and comparable performance in workloads dominated by "contains" operations. We discuss the details in our full paper (available in [7]). Essentially, the overhead of the sparse index (i.e. the increased number of node traversals on searches) is compensated by more efficient insertions and removals if the underlying skip graph is also more sparse. Our technique assumes a homogeneous workload among threads, yet we can imagine adaptations of our mechanism, such as searching using another thread's local structure, or using some form of delegation/helping mechanism to handle heterogeneous workloads.

A relevant previous work that also relies on using "indexes" to improve access locality on "shared structures" is NUMASK [4], a modified skip list that uses its higher levels as a hierarchical index to the bottom-level list. We differ from [4] as our shared structure consists of a multi-level skip graph, aiming (i) to avoid that traversals navigate back and forth across NUMA nodes, increasing locality; and (ii) to reduce contention with a careful partitioning scheme that creates areas within the shared structure where only subsets of threads operate. A similar separation of thread-local views and shared parts has been discussed in [2], although their approach is more akin to combining [5], as they merge local views into the global structure from time to time.

Sparse Skip Graphs. As noted before, we developed a second shared data structure, which we call *sparse skip graph*. This data structure is a skip graph where elements are present in level i *of any shared skip list* with expectation $1/2^i$, just like in a regular skip list. The sparse skip graph is still a set of skip lists sharing their bottom levels, although the levels become more and more sparse just like in a skip list. For instance, in Fig. 1, each of the level-1 lists "0" and "1" would partition only 50% of the elements of "λ", which would be selected at 50% chance independently. So, "0" and "1" would each have about 25% of the elements in "λ". Similarly, the level-2 lists "00" and "01" would partition only 50% of the elements of "0", each selected at 50% chance, independently. So, lists "00" and "01" would each have about 6.25% of the elements in "λ". Note that elements are present in level i *of a particular linked list* with expectation $1/4^i$. Importantly, in our technique, only elements that reach the top level are added to the local structures. Therefore, sparse skip graphs also cause the local structures to become more sparse. This is crucial because the local structures, besides pointing to shared nodes nearby the target destinations, should also point to maximum-level nodes from which we can start an efficient search. Hence, using sparse skip graphs gives two immediate advantages: (i) the local structures are smaller; and (ii) the insertion and removal in the shared structure requires changes in less than MaxLevel levels. The tradeoff is that the starting point given by the local structures is not as close to the requested element compared to regular skip graphs. Our preprint [7] has a complete discussion on linearizability, both for skip graphs and for sparse skip graphs.

2 EVALUATION

We conduct experiments in a system with 2 (NUMA) sockets, 16 Intel Xeon E5-2620 cores (32 hardware threads), each running at 2.0-2.5GHz (varies due to TurboBoosting), and 128GB of memory. The tool `numactl --hardware` reports relative intra-node distances of 10 and inter-node distances of 21. The system is running Ubuntu 18.04 LTS with kernel version 4.15.0-43. We use `clang++ 6.0`, passing the `-std=c++14 -O3` build flags. We run over 4700 tests, spanning 12.4 hours. We run experiments for 10s of CPU time *per thread*, reporting the total number of operations per millisecond, averaged from 5 runs. We run insert-remove-contains mixes of 60-30-10, 30-60-10, and 20-20-60. The numbers denote the percentage of each operation. Insert and contains operations are done with keys chosen uniformly at random from the element space. Removals are done with keys chosen uniformly at random from either (i) the element space; or (ii) the elements previously inserted by the current thread. Each time, a thread chooses either strategy (i) or (ii) with chance 50%. Threads run batches of 10 operations in order to amortize `clock_gettime()`, the *only* system call in the measured interval. The data structures are always preloaded with 20% of their maximum capacity before any measurements. Threads are pinned to each CPU, and we fill a socket before adding threads to another socket. We use `libnuma` on Linux to have each thread *preallocate* 3GB of private memory, under a first-touch NUMA memory policy. We preallocate memory in order to avoid intra-socket delays for operations in the local structure, and we never free it as we do not want to mistakenly account for the performance of the memory allocator. The actual method by which we report the ratio of local vs. total memory accesses is by *manual code instrumentation*.

1 - Remote read-syncs and CASes. Experiments in [7] showed that the absolute number of CAS and read-syncs per operation is highly reduced in our approach in comparison to the skip lists. CASes are reduced only about 7%, but read-syncs are reduced by half with 32 threads, considering our sparse skip graphs. We attribute this to *the impact of our local structure indexing, with the maps*, that indeed jumps to nearby locations. Our experiments also reveal a higher success rate of CASes in the layered approach, with up to 99.4% of successes vs. 95.7% in the skip lists for the 30-60-10. We attribute this to our *partitioning scheme*, designed to accomplish this goal as well as to increase NUMA locality.

2 - Indexing efficiency. Another experiment (see [7]) shows how a layered structure with a non-sparse skip graph has a 76% reduction in the number of traversed shared nodes compared to a regular, non-NUMA, concurrent skip list, on 32 threads, particularly for non-sparse skip graphs. Sparse skip graphs imply more sparse local structure indexing, as less shared nodes reach the topmost level and get included in the local structures. Our result shows that even though the initial point of the search is not as optimized as in the non-sparse skip graph, the number of traversed nodes per search operation is still about half of what we have in a traditional skip list. We also see a test showing our local structure indexing a simple linked list, meant to isolate the performance benefits of skip graphs. With 32 threads, in a workload dominated by contains (so fewer insertions), the number of traversed nodes per search of this indexed linked list can go over 50% higher than in a skip list, whereas in our structures they are at most 50% of the value in a skip list. See [7] for a full set of diagrams.

3 - NUMA locality. Our experiments in [7] also show that the *ratio* of local over total memory accesses is much improved in our approach. For CASes, with 32 threads, a non-sparse skip graph has 81.3% of its operations local (i.e., traversing elements inserted by the operating thread), while this percentage for a sparse skip graph is 40.7%, and for a skip list only 25.3%. For read-sync operations, 60% of them are local in the non-sparse skip graph, 17.4% in the sparse skip graph, but only 2.2% in a skip list (see [7]).

4 - General performance and design by experimentation. As discussed in [7], we noticed that when we use padding to align individual pointers of the `next` array into distinct cache lines, we not only increase memory usage dramatically, but also *hurt* performance (~ 30% slowdown). This makes sense as our algorithms typically perform read-syncs or CAS instructions across all levels of a node's successor pointers. We also tried to physically delete immediately after its logical deletion, noticing a ~ 10% slowdown even at relatively low contention. We attribute this to missing the chance of using the "hot" cache lines. We do introduce padding in the `head` of the skip graph, as threads only access specific indexes. Figure 2 shows the performance of a contains-heavy scenario in operations/msec. The structures tested are: `map_{sg/ssg}`, C++ maps over skip graphs (resp. sparse skip graphs); `sl_{sg/ssg}`, the same but with a skip list used as the local structure; a lock-based skip list; a concurrent skip graph and a skip list without our layering technique; Finally, `indexed_list` is the approach of merely layering the local structures on top of a shared linked list. We use this test to demonstrate the benefit of skip graphs and our partitioning scheme. We also show insert-heavy and remove-heavy workloads in [7], and *we perform even better in those workloads.*

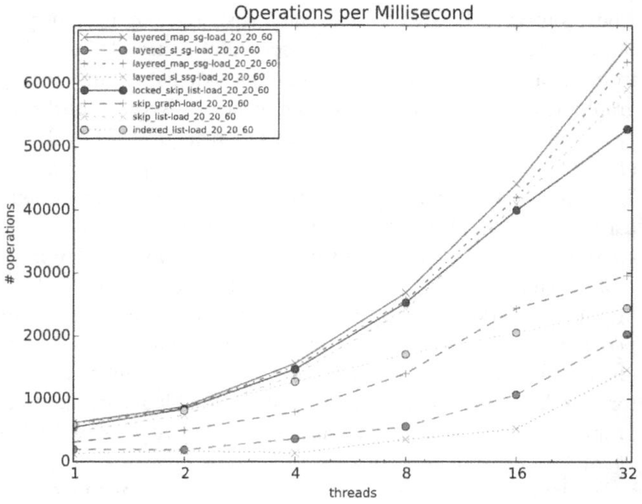

Figure 2: Average ops/msec, 20-20-60

3 CONCLUSION

We presented a technique based on layering local, sequential data structures over skip graphs variants aiming at increasing NUMA locality. At a high level, our design consists of a carefully designed and partitioned shared structure, well-integrated with sequential local structures, operating without contention. Together, these data structures promote increased NUMA locality, as verified by experimentation. Compared to skip lists, our experiments show (i) a much higher ratio of memory reference locality (up to 3.21 times); (ii) better performance for our approach (up to 23%) even though some variants require more synchronization per operation than others; (iii) a slight increase in cache performance (hit ratio), particularly for the sparse skip graphs; (iv) a strong reduction on the number of remote synchronized reads (up to 70%). As future work, we are interested in exploring our structural advantages in the design of exact and relaxed priority queues (see in [7]).

REFERENCES

[1] Nicholas J. A, Dunagan Michael, B. Jones, and Stefan Saroiu. Skipnet: A scalable overlay network with practical locality properties. In *Proceedings of USENIX Symposium on Internet Technologies and Systems*, 2003.

[2] Deepthi Akkoorath, José Brandão, Annette Bieniusa, and Carlos Baquero. Global-local view: Scalable consistency for concurrent data types. In Marco Aldinucci, Luca Padovani, and Massimo Torquati, editors, *Euro-Par 2018: Parallel Processing*, pages 492–504, Cham, 2018. Springer International Publishing.

[3] James Aspnes and Gauri Shah. Skip graphs. *ACM Transactions on Algorithms*, 3(4), November 2007.

[4] Henry Daly, Ahmed Hassan, Michael F. Spear, and Roberto Palmieri. NUMASK: High Performance Scalable Skip List for NUMA. In Ulrich Schmid and Josef Widder, editors, *32nd International Symposium on Distributed Computing (DISC 2018)*, volume 121 of *Leibniz International Proceedings in Informatics (LIPIcs)*, pages 18:1–18:19, Dagstuhl, Germany, 2018. Schloss Dagstuhl–Leibniz-Zentrum fuer Informatik.

[5] Panagiota Fatourou and Nikolaos D. Kallimanis. Revisiting the combining synchronization technique. In *Proceedings of the 17th ACM SIGPLAN Symposium on Principles and Practice of Parallel Programming*, PPoPP '12, pages 257–266, New York, NY, USA, 2012. ACM.

[6] M. Herlihy and N. Shavit. *The Art of Multiprocessor Programming*. Morgan Kaufmann, 2008.

[7] Samuel Thomas and Hammurabi Mendes. Layering data structures over skip graphs for increased NUMA locality. *CoRR*, abs/1902.06891, 2019.

Partially Replicated Causally Consistent Shared Memory: Lower Bounds and An Algorithm *

Zhuolun Xiang
University of Illinois at Urbana-Champaign
xiangzl@illinois.edu

Nitin H. Vaidya
Georgetown University
nitin.vaidya@georgetown.edu

ABSTRACT

The focus of this paper is on causal consistency in a *partially replicated* distributed shared memory (DSM) system that provides the abstraction of shared read/write registers. Maintaining causal consistency in distributed shared memory systems has received significant attention in the past, mostly on *full replication* wherein each replica stores a copy of all the registers in the shared memory. To ensure causal consistency, all causally preceding updates must be performed before an update is performed at any given replica. Therefore, some mechanism for tracking causal dependencies is required, such as vector timestamps with the number of vector elements being equal to the number of replicas in the context of full replication. In this paper, we investigate causal consistency in *partially replicated systems*, wherein each replica may store only a subset of the shared registers. Building on the past work, this paper makes three key contributions:

- We present a necessary condition on the metadata (which we refer as a *timestamp*) that must be maintained by each replica to be able to track causality accurately. The necessary condition identifies a set of directed edges in a *share graph* that a replica's timestamp must keep track of.
- We present an algorithm for achieving causal consistency using a timestamp that matches the above necessary condition, thus showing that the condition is necessary and sufficient.
- We define a measurement of timestamp space size and present a lower bound (in bits) on the size of the timestamps. The lower bound matches our algorithm in several special cases.

CCS CONCEPTS

• **Theory of computation → Shared memory algorithms.**

KEYWORDS

distributed shared memory; causal consistency; tight conditions; lower bounds

*A brief announcement summarizing the results appeared at PODC 2018 [38]. This research is supported in part by National Science Foundation award 1409416, and Toyota InfoTechnology Center. Any opinions, findings, and conclusions or recommendations expressed here are those of the authors and do not necessarily reflect the views of the funding agencies or the U.S. government.

PODC '19, July 29-August 2, 2019, Toronto, ON, Canada

ACM ISBN 978-1-4503-6217-7/19/07...$15.00
https://doi.org/10.1145/3293611.3331600

ACM Reference Format:
Zhuolun Xiang and Nitin H. Vaidya. 2019. Partially Replicated Causally Consistent Shared Memory: Lower Bounds and An Algorithm . In *2019 ACM Symposium on Principles of Distributed Computing (PODC '19), July 29-August 2, 2019, Toronto, ON, Canada.* ACM, New York, NY, USA, 10 pages. https://doi.org/10.1145/3293611.3331600

1 INTRODUCTION

Distributed shared memory systems maintain multiple replicas of the shared memory locations, which we refer to as shared registers. In recent years, the *causal consistency* model for the shared memory has received significant attention due to its emerging applications, such as social networking. Intuitively, causal consistency ensures that before an update is applied to a shared register, all the causally preceding updates must be applied at the same replica. This paper mainly focuses on the architecture illustrated in Figure 1a, which we refer to as the *peer-to-peer* architecture. Each peer has a *client* that issues read/write operations to the shared memory and a *replica* that helps implement the shared memory abstraction. We focus on the case when each replica is *partial* and may store a copy of just a subset of the shared registers. *Full replication* is obtained as a special case when each replica stores a copy of each shared register.

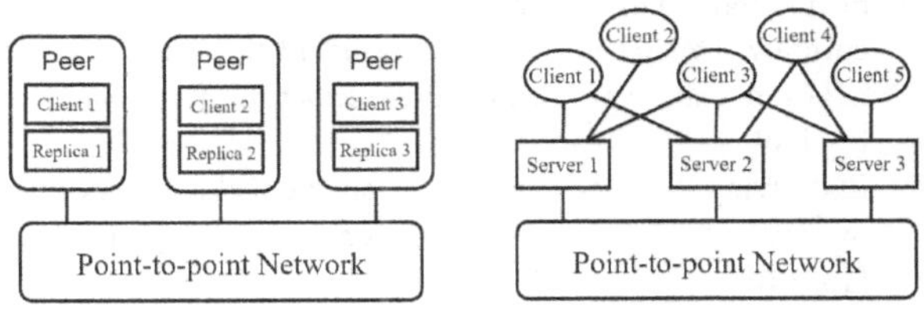

(a) Peer-to-peer architecture **(b) Client-server architecture**

We primarily present the results for the peer-to-peer architecture. The results can be extended to the client-server architecture in Figure 1b where each client may be accessing replicas stored at an arbitrary subset of the servers, as briefly discussed in Section 5.

In the context of *full replication*, several causally consistent shared memory systems have been designed, including Lazy Replication [22], COPS [24], GentleRain [12], Orbe [11], SwiftCloud [39], Occult [27], and Causalspartan [35]. Recently, there is also growing interest in *partial replication* due to the potential storage efficiencies that can be attained [2, 4, 6, 7, 9, 16, 17, 19, 25, 27]. For *full replication*, it suffices to use a vector timestamp [8, 14, 26] of length equal to the number of replicas [22] to achieve causal consistency.

Several researchers have observed that *partial replication* requires larger amount of metadata to track causal dependencies [2, 9, 16, 24]. For partial replication, in general, the timestamp (or metadata) overhead is expected to be larger than that for full replication in order to avoid *false dependencies* as will be explained below. One straightforward method to implement partial replication is by adding "virtual registers" at each replica to simulate full replication. The virtual registers do not store actual data and cannot be accessed by clients. Then solutions for full replication such as vector clocks can be easily adapted for partial replication. However, there are several issues: (1) Every update message with metadata will be sent to all replicas in full replication, which is not necessary for partial replication. This may result in high bandwidth usage. (2) Simulating full replication introduces unnecessary dependencies (which we call *false dependencies*) among the update messages. For instance, if update u_x on register x depends on update u_y on register y, i.e. u_x can only be applied after u_y is applied, then on any replica who received u_x first will wait for the receipt of u_y, even if register y is virtual and not stored locally. However, there is no reason for such delay, since the virtual register y will not be accessed by any client from this replica, and thus u_x can be applied without the receipt of u_y. Therefore this simulation approach may result in stale versions.

Partial replication yields a trade-off between the flexibility of replication, number of false dependencies on update messages, and overhead of the metadata for tracking causality. A goal of our work is to characterize this trade-off. Intuitively, in our solution, each replica maintains an *edge-indexed vector timestamp* which keeps counters for a subset of edges in a *"share graph"* that characterizes how registers are shared among the replicas. We show that our timestamp is optimal in the sense that the subset of share graph edges tracked is necessary for correctness (Theorem 1). Also, there is no false dependency introduced in our solution. Our main contributions are as follows:

- We present a necessary condition on the metadata that must be maintained by each replica to be able to track causality accurately. The necessary condition identifies a set of directed edges in a share graph that a replica's timestamp must keep track of.
  In deriving the necessary condition, we make improvements over results presented in prior work of Hélary and Milani [16, 30].
- We present an algorithm for achieving causal consistency using a timestamp that matches the above necessary condition, thus showing that the condition is necessary and sufficient.
- We define a measurement of timestamp space size and present a lower bound (in bits) on the size of the timestamps. The lower bound matches our algorithm in several special cases.

2 PRELIMINARIES

We assume an asynchronous system, and the replicas communicate using reliable point-to-point message-passing channels. The communication channels are not necessarily FIFO. In Sections 2 through 4, we assume the peer-to-peer architecture in Figure 1a. Each peer contains a client and a replica. There are R peers, and hence there are R replicas. The replicas are numbered 1 through R. Replica i stores copies of a subset of shared registers named X_i. With full replication, $X_i = X_j$ for all replicas i, j. With partial replication, it is possible that $X_i \neq X_j$ for $i \neq j$. We define $X_{ij} = X_i \cap X_j$, the set of registers stored at replicas i and j both. For instance,in partial replication with four replicas, we may have $X_1 = \{x\}$, $X_2 = \{x, y\}$, $X_3 = \{y, z\}$, and $X_4 = \{z\}$, where x, y, z are registers. In this case, $X_{23} = \{y\}$ and $X_{14} = \emptyset$. In practice, set X_r for replica r may change dynamically, however, we consider the *static* case in this paper and leave the *dynamic* case for future work.

Hélary and Milani [16] introduced the notion of a *share graph* to represent a partially replicated system. Similar notions of *graph of groups* are introduced in causal multicast literature as well [5]. We will use the share graph when obtaining results for the *peer-to-peer* architecture in Section 3 and 4. To extend these results to the *client-server* architecture, in Section 5, we will introduce an *augmented* version of the share graph.

Definition 1 (**Share Graph [16]**). *We denote e_{ij} as a directed edge from i to j. Share graph is defined as a directed graph $G = (V, E)$, where $V = \{1, 2, \cdots, R\}$, and vertex $i \in V$ represents replica i. There exist directed edges e_{ij} and e_{ji} in E if and only if $X_{ij} \neq \emptyset$.*

As such, if $e_{ij} \in E$ then $e_{ji} \in E$, and G may be defined as an undirected graph as originally defined in [16]. However, as seen later, it is convenient to represent the sharing using directed edges.

X_{ij} will be referred to as the label of edges e_{ij} and e_{ji}. In this paper, we assume that *each replica has the knowledge of the share graph including the labels on each edge.*

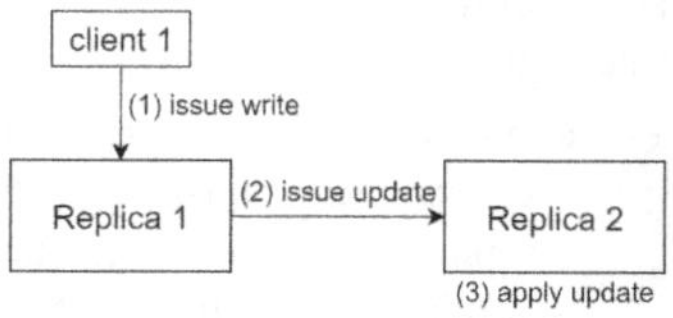

Figure 2: Illustration

Recall that each peer contains a client and a replica, and the client can issue *read* or *write* operations on a shared register stored at the local replica. Define *read*(x) to be a read operation on register x, and *write*(x, v) to be a write operation on register x that writes value v. When performing *read*(x) or *write*(x, v) operation on register $x \in X_i$, client i sends a request to replica i, and awaits the replica's response. The response to a write operation is an acknowledgement, and the response to a read operation is a returned value. Define update to be a tuple of the form *update*(i, T, x, v), where i is the sender of the update, T is the timestamp attached with the update, x is the register being updated and v is the value. As illustrated in Figure 2, upon receiving *write* operations from the client, the replica will *issue updates* to some other replicas, i.e., sending *update*(i, T, x, v) to other replicas who also replicate x in order to update their registers. Upon receiving *update*(i, T, x, v) from other replica, the replica can decide when to *apply the update*, i.e., write the new value v into the register x. An *execution* is defined to be a sequence of clients' read/write operations and replicas' operations in issuing/applying updates. With our definition of replica-centric causal consistency in the next section, we will often construct executions by declaring the replicas' operations on updates without explicitly mentioning the clients' operations.

2.1 Replica-centric Causal Consistency

In this section, we will use the notions of *issuing an update* and *applying an update* mentioned above. A client i may only read/write registers in X_i. Thus, replica i may only issue updates to registers in X_i. For convenience, each *write* operation on a given register is assumed to write a unique value.

In past work, several variations of causal consistency have been explored. One of the commonly used definitions of causal consistency is defined from clients' viewpoint, which we refer to as *client-centric causal consistency* below.

Definition 2 (Happened-before relation $\longrightarrow$ for operations [23]). *Let o_1, o_2 be two operations of the client. o_1 happened-before o_2, denoted as $o_1 \longrightarrow o_2$, if and only if at least one the following conditions is true: (1) Both o_1 and o_2 are performed by the same client, and o_1 occurs before o_2. (2) o_1 is a write operation, and o_2 is a read operation that returns the value written by o_1. (3) There exists an operation o_3 such that $o_1 \longrightarrow o_3$ and $o_3 \longrightarrow o_2$.*

Client-centric causal consistency is defined based on the relation $\longrightarrow$ for operations above.

Definition 3 (Client-centric Causal Consistency). *Client-centric causal consistency is achieved if the following two properties are satisfied:*

- **Safety:** *If a read operation o_3 on some register x returns the value written by write operation o_1 on register x, then there* must not exist *another write operation o_2 on register x such that $o_1 \longrightarrow o_2 \longrightarrow o_3$.*
- **Liveness:** *For a write operation o_1 by some client that writes value v in register x, all replicas that store copies of register x should be updated with the value v within a finite time.*

The causal consistency model addressed in our work is inspired by replicated shared memory systems such as Lazy Replication [22]. We refer to this model as the *replica-centric* causal consistency model. We define the *happened-before* relation [23] between updates as follows.

Definition 4 (Happened-before relation $\hookrightarrow$ for updates). *Given updates u_1 and u_2, $u_1 \hookrightarrow u_2$ if and only if at least one of the following conditions is true:*

(1) u_1 is applied at a replica on any of its register sometime before the same replica issues u_2 on any of its register.
(2) There exists an update u_3 such that $u_1 \hookrightarrow u_3$ and $u_3 \hookrightarrow u_2$.

Intuitively, relation $\hookrightarrow$ is analogous to the happened-before relation between events in the context of causal multicast. That is, an update issued by replica i is considered causally dependent on any updates that were previously applied at that replica, regardless of whether the previously updated registers were read by the client or not.

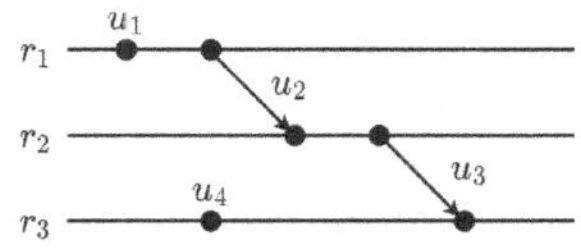

Figure 3: Relation $\hookrightarrow$

We give an example of relation $\hookrightarrow$ in Figure 3. In this example, there are 3 replicas r_1, r_2, r_3, where r_1 issues updates u_1 and u_2, r_2 issues update u_3 and r_3 issues update u_4. u_1 is applied at r_1, u_2 is applied at r_1, r_2, u_3 is applied at r_2, r_3 and u_4 is applied at r_3. In the figure, the send event of arrow with label u_2 depicts when update u_2 is issued at r_1, and the receive event of that arrow depicts the time when r_2 applies update u_2. By condition (1) of the $\hookrightarrow$ definition, we have $u_1 \hookrightarrow u_2$ and $u_2 \hookrightarrow u_3$, and by condition (2) we have $u_1 \hookrightarrow u_3$. Also, u_1 and u_4 are concurrent, i.e. $u_1 \not\hookrightarrow u_4$ and $u_4 \not\hookrightarrow u_1$. Similarly, u_2 and u_4 are concurrent.

Definition 5 (Replica-centric Causal consistency). *Replica-centric causal consistency is achieved if the following two properties are satisfied:*

- **Safety:** *If an update u_1 for register $x \in X_i$ has been applied at a replica i, then there* must not exist *update u_2 for some register in X_i such that (i) $u_2 \hookrightarrow u_1$, and (ii) replica i has not yet applied u_2.*
- **Liveness:**[1] *Any update u issued by a replica i for a register $x \in X_i$ should be applied at each replica j such that $x \in X_j$ within a finite time after all dependencies of u have been applied at j, i.e., all u' for some register $y \in X_j$ such that $u' \hookrightarrow u$ have been applied.*

For three reasons, we consider the replica-centric causal consistency in this paper. (i) First, the necessary conditions presented in Section 3.1 and 4 for the replica-centric causal consistency also applies to the client-centric causal consistency, because the proof construction in this paper can be adapted for client-centric causal consistency by the client reading all registers in its replica before issuing any write operation. (ii) Second, the algorithms for replica-centric causal consistency also implement the client-centric causal consistency, but with possible false dependencies. (iii) Third, in practice, maintaining the replica-centric causal consistency is efficient in metadata size, since it only uses a single timestamp per replica (as compared to, for instance, a timestamp per register per replica for the client-centric causal consistency). Many practical systems, including Lazy Replication [22], ChainReaction [1] and SwiftCloud [39], in fact, conform to the replica-centric view.

Relation with Causal Group Multicast. As we mentioned earlier, the definition of replica-centric causal consistency is analogous to the requirement for causal group multicast [5], where the messages need to be delivered to the processes in a causal order. The following correspondence can be obtained. Replicas sharing the same register x correspond to processes belonging to the same multicast group G_x. Any update to register x by replica i results in a multicast to group G_x by replica i. In the case of partial replication, our algorithm later in section 3.2 can essentially be viewed as causal group multicast with *overlapping groups* [5, 20, 32], where each process may belong to multiple groups (determined by how they share registers) and the multicast within a group is only received by members in that group. Hence our results below in Section 3.1 and 3.2 also apply to causal multicast with overlapping groups. For the sake of the consistency of presentation, we state our results in the context of distributed shared memory. Related work on causal group multicast and the comparison with our work are discussed in Section 6.

> In this paper, we consider algorithms that implement causal consistency by storing and attaching metadata (timestamps) with update messages, where the metadata is some encoding of the information about the execution history. When to apply a received update at a replica is determined only using the replica's local metadata and the metadata attached with the update.

[1] Note that our definition of Liveness implies no false dependencies.

3 TIMESTAMPS FOR REPLICA-CENTRIC CAUSAL CONSISTENCY

In this section, we consider partially replicated shared memory systems, which satisfy the replica-centric causal consistency model in Section 2.1 using an algorithm under the assumptions mentioned in Section 2. In particular, we identify a necessary and sufficient condition on the timestamp τ_i maintained by each replica i. Intuitively, our condition identifies a subset of directed edges in the share graph that are *necessary and sufficient* to "keep track" of for each replica in order to achieve replica-centric causal consistency.

For a replica i, and directed edge e_{jk} (from j to k) in the share graph, Definition 6 defines an (i, e_{jk})-loop as illustrated in Figure 4. We will use $-$ to denote the set difference, i.e., $A - B = \{x \in A \mid x \notin B\}$. After introducing the definition below, we provide intuition behind the definition.

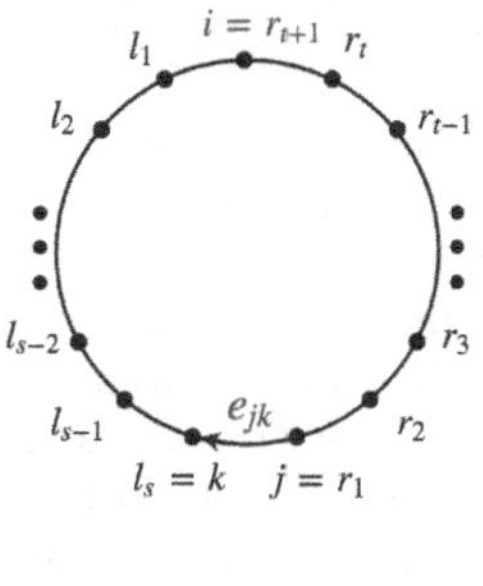

Figure 4: (i, e_{jk})-loop

Definition 6 (**(i, e_{jk})-loop**). *Given replica i and edge e_{jk} ($j \neq i \neq k$) in share graph G, consider a simple loop of the form $(i, l_1, l_2, \cdots, l_s = k, j = r_1, r_2, \cdots, r_t, i)$, where $s \geq 1$ and $t \geq 1$. Define $i = r_{t+1}$. The simple loop is said to be an (i, e_{jk})-loop provided that:*

(i) $X_{jk} - \left(\cup_{1 \leq p \leq s-1} X_{l_p}\right) \neq \emptyset$,

(ii) $X_{jr_2} - \left(\cup_{1 \leq p \leq s-1} X_{l_p}\right) \neq \emptyset$, and

(iii) for $2 \leq q \leq t$, $X_{r_q r_{q+1}} - \left(\cup_{1 \leq p \leq s} X_{l_p}\right) \neq \emptyset$.

As shown later, when there exists an (i, e_{jk})-loop, replica i needs to keep information regarding updates on edge e_{jk} in order to achieve causal consistency.

Intuition: This discussion refers to Figure 4. The definition of (i, e_{jk})-loop will be used to characterize the timestamp used by replica i in our algorithm. As we will show later in the proof of Theorem 1, the timestamp at replica i must reflect information regarding updates on edge e_{jk} if an (i, e_{jk})-loop exists. Consider the following execution. Let u be an update issued by replica j which is sent to replica k (i.e., an update on edge e_{jk}) since replica k stores the register that u is updating. Also suppose that there is a sequence of causally dependent updates propagated along the path $(j, r_2, \cdots, i, \cdots, l_{s-1}, k)$. Denote the update from l_{s-1} to k as u', so that we have $u \hookrightarrow u'$. Then the timestamps attached with u' should contain enough information about the $u \hookrightarrow u'$ relation for replica k to apply these two updates in the correct order, or postpone the application of u' if u' is received before u. Thus, it is necessary for replicas such as replica i to "keep track of" causally preceding updates that have taken place on edge e_{jk}. This allows replica i to propagate the dependency information to other replicas in the above loop that need it (particularly, replica l_1 to l_s). If condition (i) is not true, update u will also be sent to some replica l_p where $1 \leq p \leq s - 1$, since all registers shared by j, k are also shared by j and some replica l_p. Similarly, if condition (ii) or (iii) is not true, the updates along the path $(j, r_2, ..., i)$ will also be sent to some replica l_p. Since the timestamps of these updates sent to some l_p may contain the information about $u \hookrightarrow u'$, it is not necessary for replica i to "keep track of" the causality for updates on edge e_{jk}. On the other hand, when all three conditions are true, replica i has to maintain such information to ensure causal consistency. For more details, the reader may refer to the proofs for the necessary and sufficient condition in later sections.

Example: Figure 5a shows a share graph for a system of 4 replicas. Suppose that $X_1 = \{a, y, w\}$, $X_2 = \{b, x, y\}$, $X_3 = \{c, x, z\}$ and $X_4 = \{d, y, z, w\}$. The label on edges between replicas i and j in Figure 5a corresponds to the registers in X_{ij}. For instance, $X_{34} = \{z\}$. By Definition 6, $(1, 4, 3, 2)$ is *not* a $(1, e_{34})$-loop since $X_{21} - X_4 = \emptyset$ which violates condition (iii). Similarly, $(1, 4, 3, 2)$ is *not* a $(1, e_{23})$-loop due to a similar reason. On the other hand, $(1, 2, 3, 4)$ is a $(1, e_{43})$-loop. Due to the existence of register w in X_{14}, $X_{14} - X_2 \neq \emptyset$, and the reader can easily check that all three conditions in Definition 6 are satisfied. Similarly, $(1, 2, 3, 4)$ is a $(1, e_{32})$-loop.

To help present the necessary condition in Section 3.1, we now define a *timestamp graph*. Intuitively, timestamp graph G_i consists of directed edges that are *necessary and sufficient* for replica i to keep track of in its timestamp, as we will show later in Section 3.1 and 3.2.

Definition 7 (**Timestamp graph G_i of replica i**). *Given share graph $G = (V, E)$, timestamp graph of replica i is defined as a directed graph $G_i = (V_i, E_i)$, where*

$$E_i = \{e_{ij} \mid e_{ij} \in E\} \cup \{e_{ji} \mid e_{ji} \in E\} \cup \{e_{jk} \mid \exists\, (i, e_{jk})\text{-loop in } G,\ j \neq i \neq k,\ e_{jk} \in E\}$$
$$V_i = \{u, v \mid e_{uv} \in E_i\}$$

Thus, E_i consists of all directed edges incident at i, and each edge $e_{jk} \in E$ such that an (i, e_{jk})-loop exists. Consider the share graph example in Figure 5(a) again. Figure 5(b) shows the *timestamp graph* for replica 1. Observe that the edge e_{43} is in G_1 but e_{34} is not in G_1, due to the fact that $(1, 2, 3, 4)$ is a $(1, e_{43})$-loop but $(1, 4, 3, 2)$ is *not* a $(1, e_{34})$-loop, as we explained earlier for the example of (i, e_{jk})-loop. By the example above and the definition of timestamp graph, we make the following three observations:

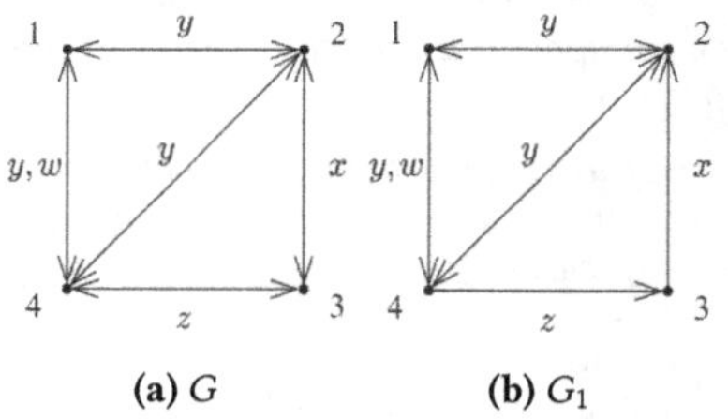

Figure 5

1. Timestamp graphs may be different from the share graph. 2. Different replicas may have different timestamp graphs. 3. Edges in the timestamp graph are not necessarily bidirectional.

3.1 A Necessary Condition for Timestamps

As briefly stated in Section 2, each replica maintains a timestamp. To achieve replica-centric causal consistency, the timestamp must contain enough information. In this section, we obtain a necessary condition on the timestamps. In particular, Theorem 1 below shows that, if e_{jk} is in the timestamp graph of replica i, then it is necessary for replica i to "keep track of" updates performed by replica j to registers in X_{jk}. To present the result formally, we introduce some additional terminology.

Definition 8 (**Causal past and Causal dependency graph [29]**). *Causal dependency graph $\mathcal{R}$ of a replica that has applied updates in set U consists of vertices in $S = U \cup \{u' \mid u \in U,\ u' \hookrightarrow u\}$ and directed edges in $\{(u_1, u_2) \mid u_1 \hookrightarrow u_2 \text{ and } u_1, u_2 \in S\}$. Set S is referred as the* causal past *of the replica [29].*

Theorem 1 will use the following terminology:

- We define relation for causal dependency graph $\mathcal{R}_0, \mathcal{R}_1$ of replica i as follows: $\mathcal{R}_0 < \mathcal{R}_1$ if there exists an execution in which replica i's causal dependency graph equals $\mathcal{R}_0$ at some point of time, and $\mathcal{R}_1$ subsequently.
- Two causal dependency graphs with vertex sets S_1 and S_2 are said to differ only in updates on e_{jk} if and only if (i) all the updates in $(S_1 - S_2) \cup (S_2 - S_1)$ are issued by replica j for registers in X_{jk} and (ii) the edges between any vertices in $S_1 \cap S_2$ are identical in both the causal dependency graphs.
- We will say that replica i with causal dependency graph $\mathcal{R}_0$ is *oblivious* to updates on e_{jk}, if the replica's timestamp is identical for every pair of causal dependency graphs $\mathcal{R}_1$ and $\mathcal{R}_2$ such that (i) $\mathcal{R}_0 < \mathcal{R}_1$ and $\mathcal{R}_0 < \mathcal{R}_2$, and (ii) $\mathcal{R}_1$ and $\mathcal{R}_2$ differ only in updates to X_{jk}.

Intuitively, a replica that is oblivious to updates on e_{jk} does not keep track of updates to registers in X_{jk} by replica j.

Theorem 1. *Consider a partially replicated shared memory system that implements replica-centric causal consistency. Any replica i must not be oblivious to update on any edge $e \in E_i$, where E_i is the edge set in the timestamp graph of replica i.*

The proof of Theorem 1 is provided in Appendix A. Intuitively, the theorem states that replica i's timestamp needs to be dependent on the updates performed on edge e_{jk} for each $e_{jk} \in E_i$. For instance, a vector timestamp whose elements are indexed by edges in E_i, and count updates performed on the corresponding edges, satisfies the requirements in Theorem 1. Indeed, in Section 3.2 we present an algorithm that uses precisely such a timestamp, proving that the necessary condition in Theorem 1 is sufficient as well. Later in Section 4 we obtain a lower bound on the size of the timestamps in the unit of bits. The necessary condition of Theorem 1 does not provide a measure of the size of the timestamps, whereas Theorem 2 provides lower bound on the size.

3.2 Sufficiency of Tracking Edges in Timestamp Graph

We propose an algorithm for implementing causally consistent shared memory in this section. The algorithm is for peer-to-peer architecture where each client only issues operations to one corresponding replica. Recall that $G_i = (V_i, E_i)$ is the timestamp graph of replica i.

Timestamps: Each replica i maintains an *edge-indexed* vector timestamp τ_i that is indexed by the edges in E_i. For edge $e_{jk} \in E_i$, $\tau_i[e_{jk}]$ is an integer, initialized to 0.

Client's Algorithm:

(1) Upon *read* operation on register x: send $read(x)$ to the replica, wait for the value returned by the replica.

(2) Upon *write* operation on register x with value v: send $write(x, v)$ to the replica, wait for the acknowledgement from the replica.

Replica's Algorithm:

(1) Upon receiving a $read(x)$ request from the client: replica i responds with the value of the local copy of register x.

(2) Upon receiving a $write(x, v)$ request from the client: replica i performs the following operations atomically:

(a) write v into the local copy of register x,

(b) for each $e_{jk} \in E_i$, update timestamp τ_i as

$$\tau_i[e_{jk}] := \begin{cases} \tau_i[e_{jk}] + 1, & \text{if } j = i \text{ and } x \in X_{ik}, \\ \tau_i[e_{jk}], & \text{otherwise} \end{cases}$$

(c) send $update(i, \tau_i, x, v)$ message to each other replica $k \in V$ such that $x \in X_k$,

(d) return *ack* to the client.

(3) Upon receiving a message $update(k, \tau_k, x, v)$ from replica k:
replica i adds $update(k, \tau_k, x, v)$ to a local data structure named $pending_i$.

(4) For any $update(k, \tau_k, x, v) \in pending_i$, when $\tau_i[e_{ki}] = \tau_k[e_{ki}] - 1$ and $\tau_i[e_{ji}] \geq \tau_k[e_{ji}]$ for each $e_{ji} \in E_i \cap E_k$, $i \neq j \neq k$, replica i performs the following operations atomically:

(a) writes value v to its local copy of register x,

(b) for each $e \in E_i$, updates timestamp τ_i as

$$\tau_i[e] := \begin{cases} \max(\tau_i[e], \tau_k[e]), & \text{for each } e \in E_i \cap E_k, \\ \tau_i[e], & \text{for each edge } e \in E_i - E_k \end{cases}$$

(c) removes $update(k, \tau_k, x, v)$ from $pending_i$.

The proof for the correctness of the algorithm is provided in the full version [37]. Note that the timestamp used by the algorithm implies replica i is not oblivious to update on any edge $e_{jk} \in E_i$, indicating the necessary condition in Theorem 1 is also sufficient.

Intuition for correctness: Our algorithm is similar to standard causal multicast algorithms [5]. The novelty of our algorithm lies in the *edge-indexed* vector timestamp, which contains a counter for each edge in the timestamp graph of the replica. Intuitively, keeping track of edges incident at i ensures FIFO delivery of update messages to/from i, and keeping track of the other edges in E_i guarantees that causal dependencies are carried when a chain of causally dependent update messages are propagated along a cycle. Although maintaining counters for all the edges in cycles for the second part is sufficient, it is not always necessary – our (i, e_{jk})-loop characterizes precisely which subset of edges in the cycle is necessary and sufficient for maintaining causal consistency.

Optimizations: We briefly discuss some mechanisms to reduce the timestamp size (details in the full version [37]). (1) *Timestamp Compression:* We observe that, in our algorithm, the different elements of the vector τ_i at replica i are not necessarily independent.

For instance, suppose that $e_{j1}, e_{j2}, e_{j3}, e_{j4} \in E_i$ for some $j \neq i$, with $X_{j1} = \{x\}$, $X_{j2} = \{y\}$, $X_{j3} = \{z\}$ and $X_{j4} = \{x, y, z\}$. Observe that the number of updates performed to registers corresponding to these four edges is *not independent*. Thus, it is possible to compress the timestamp to reduce its space requirement. (2) *Allowing False Dependencies:* A false dependency occurs when the application of an update u_1 is delayed at some replica, waiting for some update u_2 to be applied, even though $u_2 \not\hookrightarrow u_1$. We can introduce a "dummy" copy of some register at replicas to change the share graph and thus reduce the timestamp size possibly, but at the cost of extra update messages. (3) *Restricting Inter-Replica Communication Patterns:* It is known that restricted communication graphs can allow dependency tracking with a lower overhead [7, 21, 28] in the message-passing context. A similar observation applies in the case of partial replication too.

3.3 Relation to previous results

Our results make an improvement over previous results [16] regarding the timestamp size. Hélary and Milani [16] identify a larger set of edges (compared to E_i) that replica i needs to "track", however their result, although sufficient, does not always yield the necessary set of edges to track. Note that Hélary and Milani's results [16] consider the client-centric causal consistency. As mentioned when introducing the replica-centric causal consistency, our necessary conditions presented in Section 3.1 and 4 applies to their settings. The definition of the minimal x-hoop in [16, 30] states the following.

Definition 9 (Hoop [16, 30]). *Given a register x and two replicas r_a and r_b in $C(x)$ where $C(x)$ is the set of the replicas that stores x, we say that there is a x-hoop between r_a and r_b, if there exists a path ($r_a = r_0, r_1, ..., r_k = r_b$) in the share graph G such that: i) $r_h \notin C(x)$ ($1 \leq h \leq k-1$) and ii) each consecutive pair (r_{h-1}, r_h) shares a register x_h such that $x_h \neq x$ ($1 \leq h \leq k$)*

Definition 10 (Minimal Hoop [16, 30]). *An x-hoop ($r_a = r_0, r_1, ..., r_k = r_b$) is said to be minimal, if and only if i) each edge of the hoop can be labelled with a different register and ii) none of the edge label is shared by replica r_a and r_b.*

The following result in [16, 30] intended to be a tight condition for achieving causal consistency.

Lemma 1 ([16, 30]). *A replica has to transmit some information about a register x if and only if the replica stores x or belongs to a "minimal x-hoop"*

As we show with an example now, the condition in Lemma 1 from [16, 30] is not, in fact, tight [31].

Consider the share graph in Figure 6 (we omit the direction of each edge in the figure for brevity). In the figure, the label on edges e_{uv}, e_{vu} shows set X_{uv}. The share graph consists of replicas $i, a_1, a_2, k, j, b_1, b_2$. Replicas j and k share register x, replicas b_1, b_2, a_1 share register y, and replicas b_2, a_1, a_2 share register z. Labels on other edges are unique and distinct from x, y, z.

The loop ($j, b_1, b_2, i, a_1, a_2, k$) is considered a "minimal x-hoop" by Definition 10 from [16, 30] because (i) the label on each edge in the loop is distinct, (ii) none of the edge labels is shared by replica j and replica k. The result in Hélary and Milani [16, 30] implies that replica i must transmit (or keep) information about updates to register x by replicas j, k. However, it can be shown that presence of the two edges labeled y (and the manner they are situated) makes it unnecessary for replica i to be aware of updates to register x issued by replica j.

For instance, consider the execution where there is an update by replica j on x and then a sequence of causally dependent updates propagating along the hoop $j, b_1, b_2, i, a_1, a_2, k$ on registers t, y, q, p, z, s respectively. Since the update by replica i on register p is also causally dependent on the update issued by replica b_1 on register y, replica a_1 will apply the update on y before the update on p. Since the update on y already record the dependency of the update on x, there is no need for replica i to be aware of updates to x issued by replica j. More details can be found in the correctness proof of the algorithm. Similarly, replica i does not need to transmit information regarding updates to x issued by replica k. Our necessary condition (Theorem 1) does not require replica i to keep track of these updates.

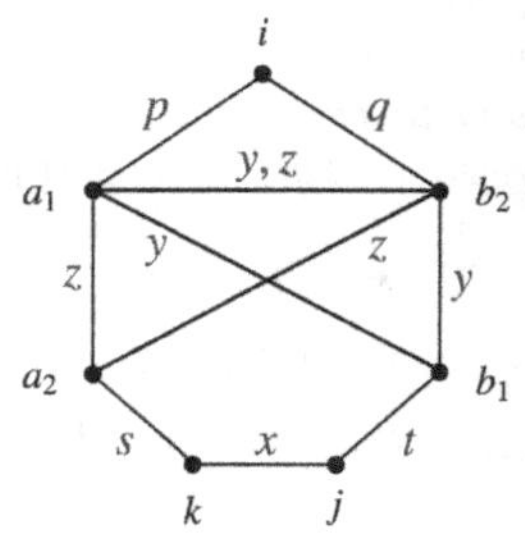

Figure 6: Example

In general, our definition of the timestamp graph (Definition 7) identifies a necessary and sufficient set of edges for each replica which is a subset of the edge set identified in [16].

4 LOWER BOUND ON TIMESTAMP SIZE

Section 3.1 obtained a necessary condition on the timestamps assigned to the replica. In this section, we obtain a lower bound (in bits) on the size of the timestamps. From the definition of the causal dependency graph it should be apparent that two different causal dependency graphs may possibly correspond to the same *causal past* (i.e., set S in Definition 8). In order to derive the lower bound, we impose the following constraint[2].

Constraint 1. *For any replica i, its timestamp at any given time is a function of its causal past at that time.*

Definition 11. **Timestamp space size $\sigma^i(m)$ of replica i under Constraint 1:** *Consider the set of executions $\mathcal{E}$ in which each replica issues up to m updates. The timestamp space size of replica i under Constraint 1, denoted as $\sigma^i(m)$, is the minimum number of distinct timestamps that replica i must assign over all the executions in $\mathcal{E}$.*

Note that replica i may not use all the distinct $\sigma^i(m)$ timestamps in the same execution. However, over all possible executions, replica i will need to use at least $\sigma^i(m)$ distinct timestamps.

Let S be a causal past, which is a set of updates as per Definition 8. Recall that $G = (V, E)$ denotes the share graph. For $e_{jk} \in E$, let $S|_{e_{jk}}$ denote the set of updates in S that are issued by replica j on registers in X_{jk}. For $e_{jk} \notin E$, define $S|_{e_{jk}} = \emptyset$ for convenience.

Definition 12 (Conflict). *Given share graph $G = (V, E)$, and two possible causal pasts S_1, S_2 of replica i from executions in $\mathcal{E}$, we say that S_1 and S_2 conflict if following conditions hold:*

[2] Note that our proposed algorithm in Section 3.2 actually satisfies this constraint.

(1) $\forall e \in E, S_1|_e \neq \emptyset \neq S_2|_e$, *and*
(2) $\exists e \in E$ *such that* $S_1|_e \subset S_2|_e$, *where*
  (a) $e = e_{ij}$ *or*
  (b) $e = e_{ji}$ *or*
  (c) $\exists$ *a simple loop* $(i, l_1, \cdots, l_s, r_1, \cdots, r_t, i = r_{t+1}) \in G$ *where* $e = e_{r_1 l_s}$ *such that*
    (1) $S_1|_{e_{r_p l_q}} = S_2|_{e_{r_p l_q}}$ *for* $1 \leq p \leq t+1, 1 \leq q \leq s$ *and* $e_{r_p l_q} \neq e_{r_1 l_s}$, *and*
    (2) $S_x|_{e_{r_p r_{p+1}}} - \bigcup_{1 \leq q \leq s} S_x|_{e_{r_p l_q}} \neq \emptyset$ *for* $1 \leq p \leq t$ *and* $x = 1, 2$

Explanation: Condition (1) means that both causal pasts S_1, S_2 have at least one update on every edge in the share graph, which allows us to construct executions where some replica i's causal past can equal to S_1 or S_2. More specifically, using this property we can construct executions where the updates in S_1 (or S_2) are issued and propagated via a spanning tree rooted at replica i in the share graph, thus leading to causal past S_1 (or S_2) in replica i. Condition (2) means that the set of updates in S_1 on some edge is a strict subset of those in S_2 on the same edge. As we will show in the proof, the set difference above ensures that replica must distinguish S_1 from S_2, otherwise causal consistency may be violated. Three kinds of edges are listed in the definition (see Figure 7), (a) outgoing edges of replica i, (b) incoming edges of replica i, and (c) edges $e_{r_1 l_s}$ that are in a loop which satisfies two conditions stated in the definition: (1) the set of updates on any "chord edges" in the loop except $e_{r_1 l_s}$ are identical for S_1 and S_2, and (2) for both causal pasts S_1 and S_2, for replica r_p in $r_1, ..., r_t$, there exists some update sent to r_{p+1} that is not sent to any of $l_1, ..., l_s$. All conditions above will be used in the proof of Lemma 2.

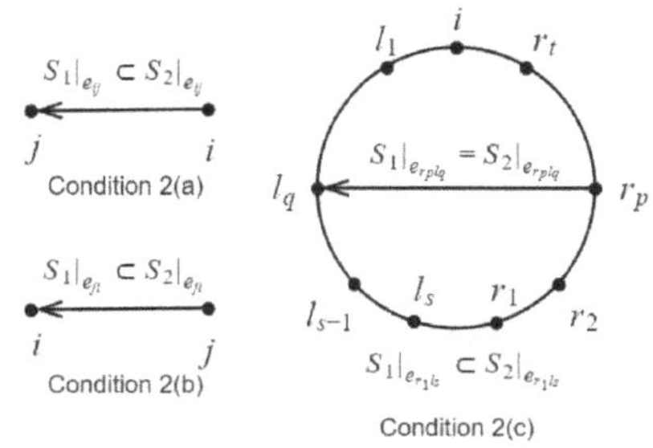

Figure 7: Condition 2 of Definition 12

Lemma 2. *Consider two possible causal pasts* S_1, S_2 *of replica* i. *If* S_1 *and* S_2 *conflict, then distinct timestamps must be assigned to them for ensuring the safety and liveness properties in Definition 5.*

Proof Sketch. The proof is presented in the full version [37]. Here we give some intuition of the proof. First we create two executions $\mathcal{E}_1$ and $\mathcal{E}_2$, after which replica i has causal past S_1 and S_2 respectively. The executions need to be created carefully such that they can be extended later to derive a contradiction as follows. If S_1 and S_2 conflict, but are assigned with the same timestamp, then replica i cannot distinguish whether it has causal past S_1 in $\mathcal{E}_1$ or S_2 in $\mathcal{E}_2$. Note that S_1 and S_2 differs in updates on some edge e. Suppose the difference is the update set U and $e = e_{jk}$. Then we can carefully extended the executions $\mathcal{E}_1$ and $\mathcal{E}_2$ such that replica k with identical local timestamps T_k receives an update u also with identical timestamps t_u in both extensions, and in one extension u is causally dependent on updates in U while in another it is not. Then replica k cannot distinguish between the two executions, and hence may violate either safety or liveness for causal consistency. □

Once we know all the pairs of conflicting causal pasts of a replica, we can easily derive the lower bound for the timestamp space size of that replica. For replica i, we define a *conflict graph* H_i with vertex set equal to the set of all possible causal pasts of replica i. An edge is added between any two causal pasts of replica i that conflict. Then, the *chromatic number* for the conflict graph is a lower bound on timestamp space size. Therefore, we have the following theorem.

Theorem 2. *Consider a partially replicated shared memory system that implements replica-centric causal consistency using an algorithm under Constraint 1. Let* $\chi(H_i)$ *denote the chromatic number of conflict graph* H_i. *Then,* $\sigma^i(m) \geq \chi(H_i)$ *for any replica* i.

Implication: Although our result does not explicitly imply a closed-form lower bound for the timestamp sizes, it can be shown that in several cases the lower bound has closed form and is tight.

- For instance, if the share graph is a tree, the timestamp lower bound is $2N_i \log m$ bits for replica i, where N_i is the number of i's neighbors in the share graph and m is the maximum number of updates that i will issue in the execution.
- When the share graph is a cycle of n replicas, the timestamp size for each replica has lower bound $2n \log m$ bits. Note that the timestamp sizes are tight in the above examples, since our algorithm will use timestamps of these sizes.
- In the case of *full replication* where the share graph is a clique and each edge shares identical set of registers, the above theorem implies the lower bound of the timestamp space size to be m^R where R is the total number of replicas. This lower bound is also tight, because the traditional vector timestamps satisfy this bound (similar to the timestamps used by Lazy Replication [22] when applied to the *peer-to-peer* architecture in Figure 1a).

One may relate the m^R lower bound for *full replication* to the classic lower bound on the vector clock size obtained by Charron-Bost [8] for determining happened-before relation in a message passing system. Although two bounds equal for full replication, however, it is not true in general for partial replication. *Timestamps for deciding happened-before relation between events cannot be directly used for maintaining causal consistency and vice versa.* One reason is that to achieve causal consistency, the timestamps should reflect information about whether there is any causally dependent update missing, but not false dependencies. Another reason is that the happened-before relation may have to be determined between any two events, while to achieve causal consistency, only for updates received by the same replica we need to determine the happened-before relation. As a result, our previous necessary and sufficient condition on the timestamps from Section 3.1 and 3.2 implies that the vector clock should have size equal to the number of edges in the timestamp graph (Definition 7), which may be larger than, smaller than or equal to n depending on the share graph.

5 EXTENDING RESULTS TO THE CLIENT-SERVER ARCHITECTURE

The results presented for the peer-to-peer architecture in Section 3 can be extended to the client-server architecture. The system model of client-server architecture is illustrated in Figure 1b. There are C clients numbered 1 through C. Each client i is associated with an arbitrary subset of replicas R_i. Client i is restricted to perform read/write operations on registers in $\cup_{r \in R_i} X_r$.

Several natural extensions of the previous definitions are introduced in the full version [37] to obtain the results for the client-server architecture: (a) The algorithm is extended by taking into account the fact that a client may propagate dependencies across two replicas. In particular, in the client-server architecture, a client also needs to maintain a timestamp locally, and the timestamp will be included with the request to the replicas. (b) The share graph is augmented as shown below with additional edges that capture the causal dependencies propagation across the replicas due to the client accessing multiple replicas. (c) The definitions of (i, e_{jk})-loop and timestamp graph can then be suitably modified to apply to the client-server architecture.

Below we only present the definition of augmented share graph. Full details of the modifications for the client-server architecture can be found in the full version [37]. Recall that E is the set of edges in the share graph defined previously in Section 2.

Definition 13 (**Augmented Share Graph**). *Augmented share graph $\widehat{G}$ consists of vertices in $V = \{1, \cdots, R\}$ and directed edges in $\widehat{E} = E \cup \{e_{jk} \mid \exists$ client c such that $j, k \in R_c\}$.*

For replica j, k such that $X_{jk} = \emptyset$, there is no edge in E. However, if there exists client c such that $j, k \in R_c$, then directed edges between j and k exist in $\widehat{E}$.

Using the augmented share graph, we can obtain a necessary condition similar to Theorem 1, and an algorithm similar to that in Section 3.2, showing that the condition is also sufficient for achieving causal consistency in the client-server architecture.

6 RELATED WORK

Some of the relevant work is already discussed in Section 1, therefore, it is not included here.

Causal group communication: Several protocols [5, 20, 32] have been proposed for implementing causal group multicast with overlapping groups, and a simulation-based evaluation on causal group multicast is presented in [18]. Kshemkalyani [20] studied a causal group multicast protocol wherein each message M is piggybacked with metadata consisting of the list of messages that happened-before M and their corresponding destinations. They investigated the necessary and sufficient conditions on the destination information tracked in this piggybacked metadata. As a result, their algorithm can remove redundant information in the metadata at run-time. However, compared to our work, their result assumes a particular structure of the metadata, and the conditions do not express how the overlapping groups (or how replicas share registers in the context of shared memory) affect the size of the metadata. To the best of our knowledge, lower bound for metadata size required for causality tracking with *overlapping* multicast groups is not previously obtained.

Algorithms for message passing: The prior work on timestamps for capturing causality in message-passing is relevant here, in particular, several approaches for reducing timestamp size by exploiting communication topology information [21, 28, 34]. Charron-Bost proved the minimum size of the vector clock is the number of the processes in the message passing system in order to capture causality [8]. Lower bounds on non-structured timestamps for capturing causal dependencies between events have been studied previously [29], but the results do not directly apply to our problem setting. First, the events that satisfy happened-before relation in the message passing system may be false dependencies in our partial replication setting, if the event (or update) is sent to some different replica. Second, maintaining causal consistency only concerns the causality of the updates received by the same replica, not any pair of events as in message passing system in the previous works.

Algorithms for causal consistency: Hélary and Milani identified the difficulty of efficient implementation under causal consistency for partial replication [16, 30]. As discussed earlier, our work improves on the results of Hélary and Milani. Milani has systematically studied mechanisms to implement causal consistency, and presented a propagation-based protocol for partial replication [3]. Raynal [33] and Birman [5] studied protocols for implementing partially replicated causal objects, with an architecture similar to that in Figure 1a, but the size of the metadata is $O(mn)$ in general, where n is the number of replicas and m is the number of objects. Shen et al. [36] proposed two algorithms, *Full-Track* and *Opt-Track*, to achieve causal consistency for partial replication under relation $\rightarrow_{co}$ proposed by Milani [3]. Based on the previous work [20], their algorithm *Full-Track* carries metadata of size $O(n^2)$ and *Opt-Track* carries metadata of optimal size assuming a particular metadata structure. Kshemkalyani and Hsu's work on approximate causal consistency sacrifices accuracy of causal consistencies to reduce the meta-data [17, 19].

In a somewhat different line of research, concurrent timestamp systems for shared memory, which enable processes to order operations using bounded timestamps have been explored [10, 13, 15]; the problem addressed in our work is distinct from this prior work.

7 SUMMARY

This paper investigates partially replicated causally consistent shared memory systems. We present a tight necessary and sufficient condition on the replica timestamp and a lower bound on the size of the timestamps for implementing replica-centric causal consistency in a partially replicated system.

REFERENCES

[1] Sérgio Almeida, João Leitão, and Luís Rodrigues. 2013. ChainReaction: a causal+ consistent datastore based on chain replication. In *Proceedings of the 8th ACM European Conference on Computer Systems*. ACM, 85–98.

[2] Peter Bailis, Alan Fekete, Ali Ghodsi, Joseph M Hellerstein, and Ion Stoica. 2012. The potential dangers of causal consistency and an explicit solution. In *Proceedings of the Third ACM Symposium on Cloud Computing*. ACM, 22.

[3] R. Baldoni, A. Milani, and S. T. Piergiovanni. 2006. Optimal propagation-based protocols implementing causal memories. *Distributed Computing* 18 (2006), 461–474.

[4] Nalini Belaramani, Mike Dahlin, Lei Gao, Amol Nayate, Arun Venkataramani, Praveen Yalagandula, and Jiandan Zheng. 2006. PRACTI replication. In *Proceedings of the 3rd conference on Networked Systems Design & Implementation-Volume 3*. USENIX Association, 5–5.

[5] K. Birman, A. Schiper, and P. Stephenson. 1991. Lightweight causal and atomic group multicast. *ACM Transactions on Computer Systems (TOCS)* 9, 3 (1991), 272–314.

[6] Manuel Bravo, Luís Rodrigues, and Peter Van Roy. 2015. Towards a scalable, distributed metadata service for causal consistency under partial geo-replication. In *Proceedings of the Doctoral Symposium of the 16th International Middleware Conference*. ACM, 5.

[7] Manuel Bravo, Luís Rodrigues, and Peter Van Roy. 2017. Saturn: a distributed metadata service for causal consistency. In *Proceedings of the Twelfth European Conference on Computer Systems*. ACM, 111–126.
[8] Bernadette Charron-Bost. 1991. Concerning the size of logical clocks in distributed systems. *Inform. Process. Lett.* 39, 1 (1991), 11–16.
[9] Tyler Crain and Marc Shapiro. 2015. Designing a causally consistent protocol for geo-distributed partial replication. In *Proceedings of the First Workshop on Principles and Practice of Consistency for Distributed Data*. ACM, 6.
[10] Danny Dolev and Nir Shavit. 1997. Bounded concurrent time-stamping. *SIAM J. Comput.* 26, 2 (1997), 418–455.
[11] Jiaqing Du, Sameh Elnikety, Amitabha Roy, and Willy Zwaenepoel. 2013. Orbe: Scalable causal consistency using dependency matrices and physical clocks. In *Proceedings of the 4th annual Symposium on Cloud Computing*. ACM, 11.
[12] Jiaqing Du, Călin Iorgulescu, Amitabha Roy, and Willy Zwaenepoel. 2014. Gentlerain: Cheap and scalable causal consistency with physical clocks. In *Proceedings of the ACM Symposium on Cloud Computing*. ACM, 1–13.
[13] Cynthia Dwork and Orli Waarts. 1992. Simple and efficient bounded concurrent timestamping or bounded concurrent timestamp systems are comprehensible!. In *Proceedings of the twenty-fourth annual ACM symposium on Theory of computing*. ACM, 655–666.
[14] C. J. Fidge. 1987. Timestamps in message-passing systems that preserve the partial ordering. In *11th Australian Computer Science Conference*.
[15] S. Haldar and P. Vitányi. 2002. Bounded concurrent timestamp systems using vector clocks. *Journal of the ACM (JACM)* 49 1 (2002), 101–126.
[16] Jean-Michel Hélary and Alessia Milani. 2006. About the efficiency of partial replication to implement distributed shared memory. In *2006 International Conference on Parallel Processing (ICPP'06)*. IEEE, 263–270.
[17] T. Hsu and A. Kshemkalyani. 2016. Performance of Approximate Causal Consistency for Partially Replicated Systems. In *Proceedings of the Third International Workshop on Adaptive Resource Management and Scheduling for Cloud Computing*. ACM, 7–13.
[18] Michael H Kalantar and Kenneth P Birman. 1999. Causally ordered multicast: the conservative approach. In *Proceedings. 19th IEEE International Conference on Distributed Computing Systems (Cat. No. 99CB37003)*. IEEE, 36–44.
[19] Ajay D Kshemkalyani and Ta-yuan Hsu. 2015. Approximate causal consistency for partially replicated geo-replicated cloud storage. In *Proceedings of the Fifth International Workshop on Network-Aware Data Management*. ACM, 3.
[20] Ajay D Kshemkalyani and Mukesh Singhal. 1998. Necessary and sufficient conditions on information for causal message ordering and their optimal implementation. *Distributed Computing* 11, 2 (1998), 91–111.
[21] Sandeep S Kulkarni and Nitin H Vaidya. 2017. Effectiveness of Delaying Timestamp Computation. In *Proceedings of the ACM Symposium on Principles of Distributed Computing*. ACM, 263–272.
[22] R. Ladin, B. Liskov, L. Shrira, and S. Ghemawat. 1992. Providing High Availability Using Lazy Replication. *ACM Trans. Comput. Syst.* 10 (1992), 360–391.
[23] Leslie Lamport. 1978. Time, clocks, and the ordering of events in a distributed system. *Commun. ACM* 21, 7 (1978), 558–565.
[24] Wyatt Lloyd, Michael J Freedman, Michael Kaminsky, and David G Andersen. 2011. Don't settle for eventual: scalable causal consistency for wide-area storage with COPS. In *Proceedings of the Twenty-Third ACM Symposium on Operating Systems Principles*. ACM, 401–416.
[25] Tariq Mahmood, Shankaranarayanan Puzhavakath Narayanan, Sanjay Rao, TN Vijaykumar, and Mithuna Thottethodi. 2016. Achieving causal consistency under partial replication for geo-distributed cloud storage. (2016).
[26] F. Mattern. 1988. Virtual Time and Global States of Distributed Systems. In *Workshop on Parallel and Distributed Algorithms*.
[27] Syed Akbar Mehdi, Cody Littley, Natacha Crooks, Lorenzo Alvisi, Nathan Bronson, and Wyatt Lloyd. 2017. I can't believe it s not causal! scalable causal consistency with no slowdown cascades. In *Proceedings of the 14th USENIX Conference on Networked Systems Design and Implementation*. USENIX Association, 453–468.
[28] Sigurd Meldal, Sriram Sankar, and James Vera. 1991. Exploiting locality in maintaining potential causality. In *Proceedings of the tenth annual ACM symposium on Principles of distributed computing*. ACM, 231–239.
[29] G. Melideo. 2001. *Tracking Causality in Distributed Computations*. Ph.D. Dissertation.
[30] A. Milani. 2006. *Causal Consistency in Static and Dynamic Distributed Systems*. Ph.D. Dissertation. Università di Roma.
[31] Alessia Milani. 2019. personal communication.
[32] Achour Mostefaoui and Michel Raynal. 1993. Causal multicasts in overlapping groups: Towards a low cost approach. In *Distributed Computing Systems, 1993., Proceedings of the Fourth Workshop on Future Trends of*. IEEE, 136–142.
[33] Michel Raynal and Mustaque Ahamad. 1998. Exploiting write semantics in implementing partially replicated causal objects. In *Proceedings of the Sixth Euromicro Workshop on Parallel and Distributed Processing-PDP'98-*. IEEE, 157–163.
[34] Luis ET Rodrigues and Paulo Verissimo. 1995. Causal separators for large-scale multicast communication. In *Proceedings of 15th International Conference on Distributed Computing Systems*. IEEE, 83–91.
[35] Mohammad Roohitavaf, Murat Demirbas, and Sandeep Kulkarni. 2017. Causalspartan: Causal consistency for distributed data stores using hybrid logical clocks. In *2017 IEEE 36th Symposium on Reliable Distributed Systems (SRDS)*. IEEE, 184–193.
[36] Min Shen, Ajay D Kshemkalyani, and Ta-Yuan Hsu. 2015. Causal consistency for geo-replicated cloud storage under partial replication. In *2015 IEEE International Parallel and Distributed Processing Symposium Workshop*. IEEE, 509–518.
[37] Zhuolun Xiang and Nitin H Vaidya. 2017. Lower bounds and algorithm for partially replicated causally consistent shared memory. *arXiv preprint arXiv:1703.05424* (2017).
[38] Zhuolun Xiang and Nitin H Vaidya. 2018. Brief Announcement: Partially Replicated Causally Consistent Shared Memory. In *Proceedings of the 2018 ACM Symposium on Principles of Distributed Computing*. ACM, 273–275.
[39] Marek Zawirski, Nuno Preguiça, Sérgio Duarte, Annette Bieniusa, Valter Balegas, and Marc Shapiro. 2015. Write fast, read in the past: Causal consistency for client-side applications. In *Proceedings of the 16th Annual Middleware Conference*. ACM, 75–87.

ACKNOWLEDGEMENTS

The authors thank Alessia Milani for her feedback. The authors also thank the anonymous reviewers for the in-depth review and helpful suggestions.

Appendix

A PROOF OF THEOREM 1

We prove Theorem 1 by showing that either safety or liveness property in Definition 5 will be violated if replica i is oblivious to update on any edge $e_{jk} \in E_i$. Consider an execution $\mathcal{E}$ in which all issued updates have been applied at the relevant replicas, and replica i's causal dependency graph is $\mathcal{R}$. This can happen since the system satisfies liveness property of the replica-centric causal consistency and all updates are applied within a finite time. We will now extend the execution to show contradictions. *In the following extended executions, suppose any other message that is not explicitly mentioned is delayed indefinitely.* This is possible since the system is asynchronous. From Definition 7 of edge set E_i, there are three possible types of edges in E_i, as in the following three cases.

Case 1: $e = e_{ij} \in E_i$:

Let $\mathcal{E}_1$ be an extended execution where replica i issues update u_1 on edge e_{ij} (i.e., for a register in X_{ij}) after $\mathcal{E}$. Suppose that the causal dependency graph of i after issuing u_1 is $\mathcal{R}_1$. Let $\mathcal{E}_2$ be an extended execution where replica i issues update u_2 on edge e_{ij} after $\mathcal{E}_1$, and let $\mathcal{R}_2$ be the causal dependency graph of i after issuing u_2.

Since $\mathcal{R}_1$ and $\mathcal{R}_2$ only differ in update u_2 on edge $e = e_{ij}$, and replica i is oblivious to update on e_{ij}, the timestamp attached to u_1, u_2 that sent to j will be identical. Thus, replica j cannot determine the correct order in which to these two updates were sent (recall that the channel is not FIFO). Thus, causal consistency cannot be assured.

Case 2: $e = e_{ji} \in E_i$:

Let $\mathcal{E}_1$ be an extended execution where replica j issues update u_1 on edge e_{ji} (i.e., for a register in X_{ij}) after $\mathcal{E}$, but u_1 is not yet applied at replica i. Let the causal dependency graph of i before applying u_1 be $\mathcal{R}_1$. Let $\mathcal{E}_2$ be an extended execution where replica j issues update u_2 on edge e_{ji} after $\mathcal{E}_1$, and suppose that u_1 is applied at replica i but not u_2. Let the new causal dependency graph of i be $\mathcal{R}_2$.

Since $\mathcal{R}_1$ and $\mathcal{R}_2$ only differ in updates on edge $e = e_{ji}$, and replica i is oblivious to update on e_{ji}, replica i has identical timestamps after applying u_1 and before. Thus, when replica i receives update u_2, it cannot differentiate between the following two cases: (i) i has already received and applied update u_1, and thus, it can now apply update u_2. (ii) i has not yet received update u_1, so it must wait for that update message before applying u_2. If replica i applies u_2 when u_2 arrives (i.e., without waiting for another update message), but the situation is as in (ii), then safety requirement of causal consistency is violated. On the other hand, if replica i decides to wait, but the situation is as in (i), then another update may never be received from j, and liveness requirement of causal consistency is violated.

Case 3: $e = e_{jk} \in E_i$ **and there exists an** (i, e_{jk})**-loop** $(i, l_1, \cdots, l_s = k, j = r_1, \cdots, r_t, i)$:

By the definition of the (i, e_{jk})-loop, we have

(i) $X_{jk} - \left(\cup_{1 \le p \le s-1} X_{l_p}\right) \ne \emptyset$,

(ii) $X_{jr_2} - \left(\cup_{1 \le p \le s-1} X_{l_p}\right) \ne \emptyset$, and

(iii) for $2 \le q \le t$, $X_{r_q r_{q+1}} - \left(\cup_{1 \le p \le s} X_{l_p}\right) \ne \emptyset$.

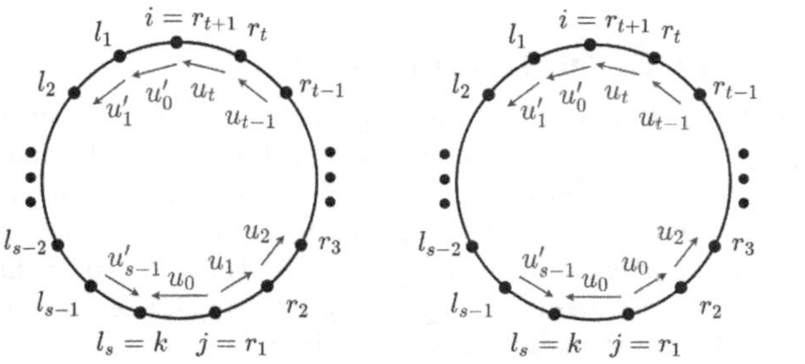

(a) Illustration for Case 3.1 (b) Illustration for Case 3.2

Figure 8: Examples of Timestamp Graphs

Case 3.1: $X_{jr_2} - \left(\cup_{1 \le p \le s} X_{l_p}\right) \ne \emptyset$, that is, X_{jr_2} has a register w_1 that is not shared by any of replicas in $l_1, \cdots, l_s$.

Consider the following extension of $\mathcal{E}$ as the execution $\mathcal{E}_1$, as illustrated in Figure 8a.

- Initially, replica $r_1 = j$ issues an update u_0 on edge e_{jk} on register w_0, where $w_0 \in X_{jk} - \left(\cup_{1 \le p \le s-1} X_{l_p}\right)$, i.e. not shared by any replicas in $l_1, \cdots, l_{s-1}$. Such w_0 exists since $X_{jk} - \left(\cup_{1 \le p \le s-1} X_{l_p}\right) \ne \emptyset$. Thus, u_0 is sent to l_s but not any of $l_1, \cdots, l_{s-1}$.
- Replica $r_1 = j$ then issues update u_1 on edge $e_{r_1 r_2}$ on register $w_1 \in X_{jr_2} - \left(\cup_{1 \le p \le s} X_{l_p}\right)$, i.e. w_1 is not shared by any replicas in $l_1, \cdots, l_s$. Thus, u_1 is sent to r_2 but not any of $l_1, \cdots, l_s$. The corresponding update message is next received by r_2.
- For $p = 2$ to t: r_p receives an update message from r_{p-1} and applies the update. The update can be applied since all its causal dependencies have been applied. Then r_p issues an update on edge $e_{r_p r_{p+1}}$ on a register w_p that is not shared by any of $l_1, \cdots l_s$. Such w_p exists since for $2 \le q \le t$, $X_{r_q r_{q+1}} - \left(\cup_{1 \le p \le s} X_{l_p}\right) \ne \emptyset$. Let us call this update u_p. Thus, we have constructed a sequence of updates so far such that $u_0 \hookrightarrow u_1 \hookrightarrow u_2 \hookrightarrow \cdots \hookrightarrow u_t$, where $r_{t+1} = i$.
- Subsequently, i issues an update u'_0 on edge e_{il_1}. l_1 receives the update message, applies the update, and then issues an update u'_1 on edge $e_{l_1 l_2}$. The update can be applied since all its causal dependencies have been applied. Continuing in this manner, we build a sequence of updates such that $u'_0 \hookrightarrow u'_1 \hookrightarrow \cdots \hookrightarrow u'_{s-1}$, where update u'_p in this chain is issued by replica l_p on edge $e_{l_p l_{p+1}}$.
- Combining the two sequences of updates, we obtain the following sequence, $u_0 \hookrightarrow u_1 \hookrightarrow u_2 \hookrightarrow \cdots \hookrightarrow u_t \hookrightarrow u'_0 \hookrightarrow u'_1 \hookrightarrow u'_2 \hookrightarrow \cdots \hookrightarrow u'_{s-1}$.

Now consider an alternate extension of $\mathcal{E}$ as the execution $\mathcal{E}_2$ in which replica j does not initially perform update u_0, but the remaining sequence of updates above are performed. The timestamp of replica i when issuing update u'_0 will be identical in both executions, because the causal dependency graphs at i when issuing update u'_0 only differ by updates on edge e_{jk}.

By induction, we can easily show that the timestamp attached to the update u'_{s-1} received by l_s from l_{s-1} will be identical in both executions. In performing the induction, we make use of the assumption that any other message that is not explicitly mentioned in the above executions is delayed indefinitely, including those on edges in $\{e_{r_x l_y} | r_x l_y \ne r_1 l_s\}$. In the first execution $u_0 \hookrightarrow u'_{s-1}$, but this is not the case in the second execution. If the update message from r_1 to l_s is not delivered before l_s receives the update from l_{s-1}, then replica l_s cannot determine whether it should wait for an update from r_1 or not, and either safety or liveness condition may be violated.

Case 3.2: $X_{jr_2} - \left(\cup_{1 \le p \le s} X_{l_p}\right) = \emptyset$. Since by condition (ii), $X_{jr_2} - \left(\cup_{1 \le p \le s-1} X_{l_p}\right) \ne \emptyset$, $\exists w_1 \in X_{jr_2} \cap X_{jl_s} - \left(\cup_{1 \le p \le s-1} X_{l_p}\right)$, that is, X_{jr_2} has a register w_1 that is shared by l_s but not any of replicas in $l_1, \cdots, l_{s-1}$.

We build two extensions of $\mathcal{E}$, similar to Case 3.1. Figure 8b illustrates this case.

For the first execution, replica $r_1 = j$ issues an update u_0 on the register w_1. Since w_1 is also shared by r_2, u_0 will be also sent and delivered to r_2. Also, note that u_0 is sent to k, r_2 but not any of $l_1, \cdots, l_{s-1}$. Unlike Case 3.1, no other update is performed on edge $e_{r_1 r_2}$. The remaining sequence of updates is identical to Case 3.1. This results in the following happened-before relation.

$u_0 \hookrightarrow u_2 \hookrightarrow u_3 \hookrightarrow \cdots \hookrightarrow u_t \hookrightarrow u'_0 \hookrightarrow u'_1 \hookrightarrow \cdots \hookrightarrow u'_{s-1}$

For the second execution, replica r_1 does not issue update u_0, but the remaining sequence of updates are performed.

By similar argument as in Case 3.1, the timestamp attached to the update u'_{s-1} will be identical in both executions, and replica l_s cannot determine whether it should wait for an update from r_1 or not, and either safety or liveness condition may be violated.

Vorpal: Vector Clock Ordering For Large Persistent Memory Systems

Kunal Korgaonkar
kkorgaon@eng.ucsd.edu
UC San Diego

Joseph Izraelevitz
jizraelevitz@eng.ucsd.edu
UC San Diego

Jishen Zhao
jzhao@eng.ucsd.edu
UC San Diego

Steven Swanson
swanson@eng.ucsd.edu
UC San Diego

ABSTRACT

In systems with non-volatile main memories (NVMMs), programmers must carefully control the order in which writes become persistent. Otherwise, what will remain in persistence after a crash may be unusable upon recovery. Prior art has already explored semantic models for specifying this persist order, but most enforcement algorithms for the order are not scalable to large server machines because they assume that the machine contains only one or two memory controllers. In this paper, we describe a collection of provably-correct algorithms for enforcing the persist-order across writes, generated at many different cores, and persisted across numerous different memory controllers. Relative to existing solutions, our algorithms improve performance by 48% by reducing both traffic and serialization overheads.

ACM Reference Format:
Kunal Korgaonkar, Joseph Izraelevitz, Jishen Zhao, and Steven Swanson. 2019. Vorpal: Vector Clock Ordering For Large Persistent Memory Systems. In *2019 ACM Symposium on Principles of Distributed Computing (PODC '19), July 29-August 2, 2019, Toronto, ON, Canada.* ACM, New York, NY, USA, 10 pages. https://doi.org/10.1145/3293611.3331598

1 INTRODUCTION

Non-volatile main memories (NVMMs), such as phase-change memory (PCM) [46], resistive RAM (ReRAM) [38], and 3D Xpoint [31], are likely to bring profound changes to many aspects of computer systems. Like DRAM, these devices are *byte-addressable*, and programs interact with them using the traditional load/store (read-/write) interface. Unlike DRAM, but like disk, these devices are *non-volatile* — their contents are guaranteed to survive a power outage. As such, NVMMs are poised to provide a medium for fast, durable storage. Given their non-volatile property, NVMM are also referred to as *persistent* memories.

Unfortunately, from the perspective of durable storage, NVMMs are somewhat undermined by the fact that processor caches and registers lose their contents on power failure. Consequently, barring additional effort, data in NVMMs is likely to be unusable after a power failure because processor caches and registers lose their contents on power failure — what will survive in NVMM is that data that was not held within the cache hierarchy at the time of failure. As a consequence, NVMMs require programs to carefully control the order in which their writes reach persistent memory. A failure in the middle of a linked-list insertion, for example, may lead to a post-crash dangling reference, if the "next" pointer of the predecessor node is written into persistent memory while the pointed (inserted) node itself remains in a cache.

To give programmers a tool to manage the order of writes to persistent memory, modern ISAs provide a *memory persistency model*, which is a set of instructions that control the order in which writes to NVMM become persistent, such that they will be visible after a power failure [35]. The memory persistency model is specified in conjunction with of the similar, yet, different, *memory consistency model*, which describes the order in which concurrent threads' updates become visible to each other. These models are generally orthogonal (two ISAs might implement the same persistency model on top of different consistency models), but their interactions are generally tightly coupled — a persistency model might leverage the memory consistency model to induce orderings.

A growing body of research [20–23, 32, 35, 40, 41] explores ISAs and supporting micro-architectures to enforce these ordering constraints. Despite this previous work, scalability of persistence ordering support still remains an issue for NVMMs. Most previous work only considers the ordering of NVMM writes through one or two memory controllers [4, 20–23, 32, 40], but modern servers can include many memory controllers scattered across multiple sockets [15]. Enforcing ordering constraints between writes generated at many different cores and written into NVMM (that is, *persisted*) at many different memory controllers requires an efficient algorithm to capture and enforce these constraints.

In this paper, we propose a set of novel distributed algorithms for ordering writes to persistent memory on a large, shared-memory computer system. Our collection of algorithms, which we call Vector ORdered Persistence ALgorithms (Vorpal), uses a vector clock [12, 30] representation to (1) construct a partial order over the writes to NVMM and (2) efficiently enforce their order at multiple memory controllers.

In particular, this paper makes the following contributions:

- We describe a basic vector clock algorithm for enforcing write order to persistent memories and demonstrate that it can implement the acquire-release memory persistency (ARP) model, defined in Section 2.2.3.
- We address the scalability problems in vector clocks as a write ordering mechanism in cache-coherent, shared-memory

This work was supported in part by CRISP, one of six centers in JUMP, a Semiconductor Research Corporation (SRC) program sponsored by DARPA. We thank our shepherd, Marc Shapiro, for his valuable guidance in writing.

PODC '19, July 29-August 2, 2019, Toronto, ON, Canada

ACM ISBN 978-1-4503-6217-7/19/07...$15.00
https://doi.org/10.1145/3293611.3331598

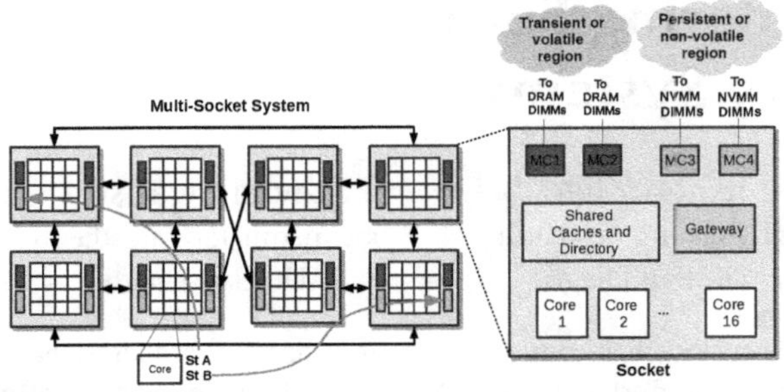

Figure 1: System overview Shows the expected memory system layout of a scale-up server with NVMM and DRAM. The left-hand side of the figure highlights the persistent write ordering problem where instructions 'Store A' and 'Store B' generate ordered writes. The right-hand side of the figure shows the participating entities of Vorpal inside a socket.

systems with a large number of memory controllers with other, more advanced, new vector clock algorithms.

- We provide safety and liveness proofs for each of the proposed algorithms.

2 BACKGROUND

This section describes the necessary architecture and theory background for situating the Vorpal algorithms, which use vector clocks to represent and enforce ordering across updates to persistent memory.

2.1 System Model

Future scale-up servers are expected to have tens of sockets, hundreds of cores, and tens of memory controllers controlling terabytes of memory [15]. In this work, we target a large, cache-coherent, shared-memory server that is divided into *sockets*, each of which has *cores* that execute programs and generate writes to persistent memory, *memory controllers* or *MCs* that persist the writes to NVMMs (see Figure 1), and a single *gateway* node used to manage asynchronous cross-socket communication (and used as a convenient point for processing outgoing messages from the socket). Without loss of generality, we assume single-threaded cores (e.g. hyperthreads can be considered two logically distinct cores). The components of this system are connected by an asynchronous, loss-less, FIFO, bounded-delay network (the memory bus) with no out-of-thin-air messages (every message received was sent and is not corrupted).

Given a write's physical address, there is exactly one controller that can persist it [19]. Note that successive ordered writes to persistent memory from a single core may be persisted at different memory controllers (see Figure 1, left-hand side).

2.2 Programming Model

2.2.1 Memory Regions. Our programming model assumes that a program's address space is divided into a *transient* and *persistent* region [36], both accessible via the traditional load/store (read/write) interface. For a given memory access, the hardware can determine whether it is persistent or not by its address. In the transient region, the program keeps state that it does not require to survive a crash, e.g., run-time variables that need not be persistent and can be regenerated at recovery such as locks, certain indexes, and (most likely) the stack. Since the transient region does not need to be usable in the wake of a crash, it is generally expected to be faster and might even reside in DRAM. Traditional programs without the use of NVMM can be viewed as programs that only contain a transient region. Figure 1 shows how the transient and the persistent regions are clearly separated between the DRAM and NVMM DIMMs, respectively.

In the persistent region, the program keeps state that it requires to survive a crash. This region resides in NVMM. The programmer must ensure that its state is updated in an order that allows it to be usable after a crash (For instance, in a linked-list insertion, the inserted node must be made persistent before the pointer to it, in order to avoid a dangling pointer in the event of a crash).

2.2.2 Memory Consistency. As with any parallel programming model on a shared-memory system (including those without persistent memory), our programming model uses a *memory consistency model.* A memory consistency model is a semantic model that describes the order in which an individual thread's memory updates become visible to other, concurrently running, threads. We chose the *release consistency* memory model [14] for this purpose. The release consistency model corresponds closely to that of the ARM v8 instruction set [3].

For single-threaded programs, release consistency is simple. A *store* instruction writes to a memory address, and a *load* instruction reads from a memory address. A load returns the value most recently written by a store to the address, where "recently" is with respect to the thread's executed program-order ($<_{PO}$).

In multi-threaded programs, release consistency also defines the order in which one thread's stores become visible to other threads (called the *release-acquire order* [1] and written as $<_{RA}$). A load returns the value of the most recent store within the release-acquire order, defined as follows. A program's (shared) memory is logically divided into two types of variables. *Data variables* are written-to, and read-from using normal load and store instructions. *Synchronization variables*, in contrast, are written-to and read-from exclusively using the special *load-acquire* and *store-release* instructions (abbreviated respectively as load-acq and store-rel), which define how one thread's writes propagate to another.

In more detail, the interaction between store-release and load-acquire on synchronization variables defines the release-acquire order (Figure 2), which in turn defines the order in which one thread's stores become visible to another's loads. When a thread uses a load-acquire to read a synchronization variable, it *synchronizes-with* the last thread that used a store-release to write to that location, and the load-acquire returns the store-release's written value. Therefore, when threads synchronize-with each other (e.g., by passing a lock or flag), the first thread's store-release *precedes* the second thread's load-acquire in release-acquire order (see Figure 2, where Thread 2 load-acquires x). Furthermore, any of the first thread's writes (to data or synchronization variables) that preceded the store-release in program order must now be visible to the second thread's reads that follow the load-acquire (see Figure 2, where Thread 2 loads a). The release-acquire order is also transitive — if the second thread

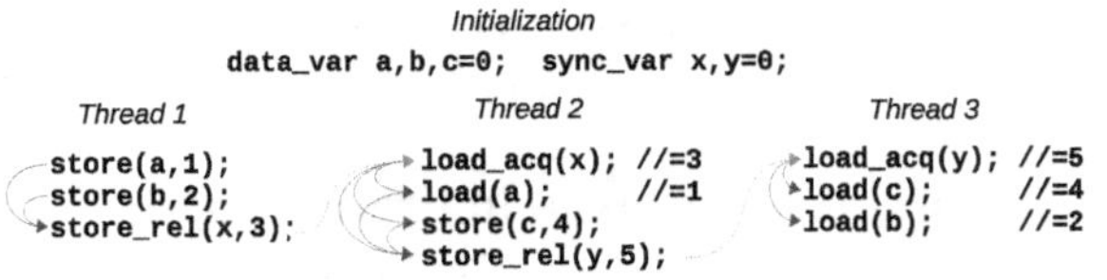

Figure 2: Memory Consistency Threads' updates become visible to other threads using the release-acquire order under the release consistency model. Arrows show the release-acquire relationships between instructions, and red arrows show those relationships that are also synchronize-with pairs.

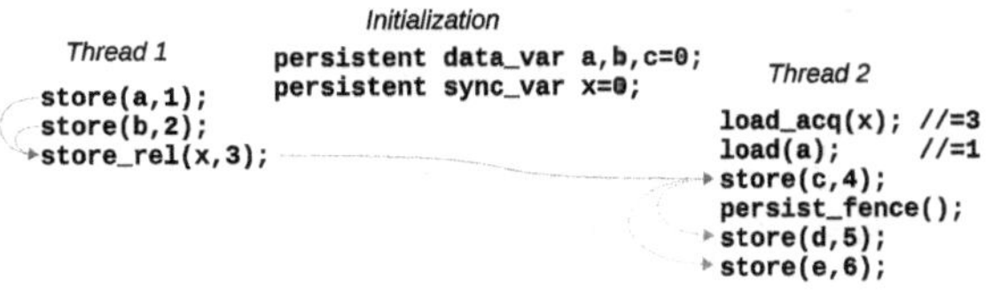

Figure 3: Memory Persistency Threads' updates are ordered into persist memory under the ARP memory persistency model. Arrows show the persist-before relationships between instructions. Purple, solid, arrows show those persist-before orderings derived from the release-acquire order. Green, dotted arrows show those orderings that are not release-acquire orderings but are persist-before orderings (ordered by the persist fence).

issues a subsequent store-release and a third thread synchronizes-with it using a load-acquire, the third thread will also see the first thread's writes (see Figure 2, where Thread 3 loads *b*).

For example, in a lock-based programming model under release consistency, every (data) memory location is associated with a specific lock. While a process holds a lock (a synchronization variable), i.e., between acquiring and releasing the lock, it has sole access to the associated memory locations (data variables), which it can read (load) or update (store). Before the first access to a memory location, the program must acquire the associated lock (load-acquire) and pull the current value of the location from the last writing process that has released the lock (via a store-release).

Note that the release-acquire order is a partial (not total) order across instructions, thereby allowing for aggressive optimization at the compiler and processor level. For instance, sequential stores to data variables by a thread can be reordered with no ill effects (they are not ordered by release-acquire and their effects are not guaranteed to be visible to other threads until the next store-release). It is important to also note that our memory consistency model relies on the *coherence* of synchronization variables — that is, all threads agree on the order of store-release and load-acquire's to a given synchronization variable and a load-acquire to that variable will give the most recent value stored by a store-release in this same order.

2.2.3 Memory Persistency. In persistent memory programming, not only must define a memory consistency model, but we also must define the *persists-before order*, that is, the order in which writes (i.e, stores) become persistent by leaving the cache hierarchy and entering NVMM [1]. The persist-before order (which we write as $<_{PB}$) is controlled using an ISA level *memory persistency model*, which is defined in addition to the memory consistency model. Like the release-acquire order, the persists-before order is a partial order, though, unlike release-acquire, persists-before only includes stores (and store-release's) to persistent memory addresses (as opposed to all memory accesses). In the event of a power failure, the programmer can expect that what will survive in NVMM is some consistent-cut across the persists-before order: given a store that was written to NVMM and survived a power failure, any prior store in persists-before order should also have been written and survived. Assuming the programmer used the persistency model correctly, this cut should be a state from which the program can recover its data. We chose a relatively relaxed persistency model called *acquire-release persistency* (ARP) [23] in order to demonstrate the flexibility of the Vorpal algorithms — with some work, Vorpal should support stricter persistency models as well.

As the name suggests, ARP is a persistency model that leverages the release consistency memory model to define the persists-before order. In ARP, all release-acquire orderings in the memory consistency model are *also* persists-before orderings in the memory persistency model; given two stores S_1 and S_2 to persistent addresses, $S_1 <_{RA} S_2 \implies S_1 <_{PB} S_2$. This rule means that if one thread updates persistent state, then synchronizes-with another thread, any of the second thread's later persistent writes will be ordered after the first thread's (in Figure 3, Thread 1's stores to a and b will become persistent before its store to x, and its store to x will become persistent before Thread 2's store to c). This rule simplifies reasoning for programs that are both concurrent and use persistence. However, this rule not sufficient. Writes to persistent memory might also need to be ordered within a single thread independent of synchronization. For instance, in a linked-list insertion, the inserted node must become persistent *before* the pointer to it, yet these two writes are unordered by the release-acquire order (as they are contained within a single thread). In order to solve this problem, ARP adds a *persist fence* instruction that ensures that stores that preceed the fence (in program order) persist-before those that follow the fence: given two stores S_1 and S_2 to persistent addresses and persist fence F, $S_1 <_{PO} F <_{PO} S_2 \implies S_1 <_{PB} S_2$). (in Figure 3, Thread 2 ensures the otherwise unordered stores to c and d become persistent in program order by putting a persist fence between them, otherwise, as is the case with stores a and b, the writes to persistent memory will be unordered). Like the release-acquire order, the persists-before order is transitive, that is, given three stores S_1, S_2, and S_3 to persistent addresses, ($S_1 <_{PB} S_2$ and $S_2 <_{PB} S_3$) $\implies S_1 <_{PB} S_3$. Thus, in Figure 3, Thread 1's store to a will become persistent before Thread 2's store to c).

2.3 Vector Clocks in Vorpal

We expect the hardware of our system to enforce the persists-before order ($<_{PB}$) across the many memory controllers in different sockets. For correctness, at any instant in (asynchronous) time, those stores persisted across all memory controllers must form a consistent-cut across the persists-before order. Our Vorpal algorithms represent this persists-before order using *vector clocks*.

Vector clocks [12, 30] are a well-known construct for representing logical time in a distributed system. If n is the number of nodes,

[1]Hereafter we write "store" or "load" to refer to a store or load instruction respectively. A store first enters the cache, then later becomes persistent once that cache-line is written back to NVMM.

a vector clock is an n-tuple of positive integers. Typically, each node maintains its own copy of a vector clock and every message between nodes is tagged with a copy of the sender's vector clock (we term this copy a *timestamp*). For a vector clock V, we note V_i the ith entry in the vector. Vector clocks are useful in that they represent time as a partial order: every node's vector clock acts as a local clock occasionally synchronized with remote clocks.

With vector clocks, a node can progress local time by *incrementing* the vector entry that corresponds to the local node by one. We express this operation as: V_i++, that is, an increment by 1 of the ith entry of V. When the local node receives a message from a remote node, it updates its local clock to include all remote clock times prior to the message's send time, that is, it *merges* its local clock with that of the message's send time. We express the merge of vector clocks U and V as $U \oplus V = Z$ where $\forall_i Z_i = \max(V_i, U_i)$. As vector clocks describe a partial order, we can compare clocks easily. Given clocks U and V, $V \leq U \iff \forall_i V_i \leq U_i$.

In Vorpal, we use vector clocks to represent and enforce the persist-before orderings. Every core has its own local clock stored in a vector clock register. The size of the vector clock register at any core is equal to the number of cores in the whole system. Cores tag the persistent store (and store-release) instructions they generate with a timestamp. When a core synchronizes-with another other (i.e., when one core load-acquires another's store-release), the acquiring core will merge its clock with the timestamp it receives (i.e, that timestamp attached to the store-release). In addition, each memory controller maintains its own vector clock register, of size again the same as the number of cores in the system, to track what stores (and their associated timestamps) have already been persisted. For our more advanced hierarchical Vorpal algorithm, clock registers at each socket gateway summarize clocks within the socket, which allows us to use smaller vector clocks (details in Section 6).

In general, we will discuss the metadata storage cost of vector clock registers and other costs as we procede through describing each of the algorithms below. Detailed analysis of the costs follows with results in Section 7.

3 OVERVIEW

Vorpal is a scalable, distributed mechanism for enforcing memory persistency models. [2] It uses vector clocks [12, 30] for encoding the persist-before orderings across stores and provides a scalable distributed algorithm for persisting stores at the memory controllers in accordance with this ordering.

Vorpal includes several variants, each of which is a refinement of previous versions. The simplest, Vorpal_0, is simple to implement but incurs extraneous orderings between persistent stores. Its refinement, Vorpal_{chunk}, operates on a group of mutually-unordered stores rather than single stores, thereby supporting a more relaxed persistent order (necessary for higher performance). However, neither Vorpal_0 nor Vorpal_{chunk} exploits the hierarchical nature of systems — and for systems with many processors, these algorithms will require very large vector clocks. To shrink the vector clocks, we introduce Vorpal_H, a variant that maintains smaller clocks by leveraging the hierarchical nature of modern systems [15]. For a brief summary of the metadata cost of each algorithm, see Table 1.

[2] We chose ARP for this work, though the Vorpal mechanism should extend to any stricter persistency model.

3.1 Vorpal Definitions and Preliminaries

Vorpal algorithms comprise two parts: *order construction* and *order enforcement*, each with its own requirements. We first explain both parts, then define correctness (both safety and liveness) for the entire class of Vorpal algorithms. Finally, we prove a theorem that shows if Vorpal algorithms satisfy the necessary requirements for both order construction and order enforcement, then they are safe. We leverage this theorem in proving each Vorpal variant.

Order Construction. In the order construction part, the Vorpal algorithm assigns vector timestamps to persistent stores (i.e., store instructions). The order built by these timestamps, termed the *clock order*, is designed to subsume the persists-before order.

In order to build the clock order, every single core maintains a vector clock register that will represent its local and monotonically-increasing logical time. We call this register the *core vector clock*. For simpler Vorpal algorithms, this vector clock contains as many entries as there are cores in the system (i.e., if there are N cores in the system, each core vector clock contains N entries). Our more advanced algorithm shrinks the register size for performance. Assuming the Vorpal algorithm works correctly, this clock represents the local core's view of the persist-before order, that is:

Definition 3.1 (Order Construction Requirement). A Vorpal algorithm satisfies the *order construction requirement* if and only if, given stores S and T with timestamps V^S and V^T, $S <_{PB} T \implies V^S < V^T$.

Order Enforcement. In the order enforcement part, memory controllers persist stores according to their clock order and, consequently, their persists-before order (given that the store's timestamps meet the Order Construction requirement). The controller persists new store if and only if *all* preceding stores in clock-order have been persisted, that is:

Definition 3.2 (Order Enforcement Requirement). Consider the set of persisted stores (with their timestamps) *Persisted* and some store S with vector timestamp V^S. A Vorpal memory controller that satisfies the *order enforcement requirement* will increase the set of persistent stores to $Persisted := Persisted \cup S$ if and only if $\forall_T V^T < V^S \implies T \in Persisted$.

To do order enforcement, each memory controller maintains a *progress vector clock* register to track the completion of stores. At any given time, the progress register P is equal to the merge of all persisted timestamps that the controller is aware of (i.e. it has either persisted them itself or it has received notification of their persistence from other controllers).

3.2 Correctness

As all Vorpal algorithms have a similar structure, we define our correctness criteria (safety and liveness) here. We also prove that if a Vorpal algorithm meets both the Order Construction and Order Enforcement requirements, it is safe. Subsequent proofs of correctness (following each variant description) will leverage this property to demonstrate our various Vorpal algorithms are correct.

```
1   // Core_i State and Events (Order Construction)
2   clock_register C;
3   On: Issue persistent store or persistent store−rel S to MCs Pending set
4     C_i ++; V^S := C;
5   On: Issue store−rel S (non−persistent)
6     V^S := C;
7   On: Issue load−acq A that synchronizes−with store−rel S
8     C := C ⊕ V^S;
9   // MC State and Events (Order Enforcement)
10  clock_register P;
11  On: Occasionally
12    if(∃_S S ∈ Pending ∧ S ∉ Persisted ∧immediately_succeeds(P, V^S))
13      {Persisted := Persisted ∪ S; P := P ⊕ V^S; }
14  On: Received broadcast clock B
15    P := P ⊕ B;
16  On: Occasionally
17    Broadcast P;
```

Figure 4: Vorpal$_0$: The pseudo-code for Vorpal$_0$, the baseline version of Vorpal. Actions of the cores and the memory controllers (MC) for order construction and enforcement, respectively, are shown.

Definition 3.3 (Safety). A Vorpal algorithm is safe if and only if, at any given point in time, the set of persisted stores is a consistent-cut across the persists-before order; that is, if a store is persisted, all of its predecessors in persists-before order are also persisted.

Theorem 3.4 (Safety). *Any Vorpal algorithm that meets both the Order Construction and Order Enforcement requirements is safe.*

Proof. By induction. **Base case.** $Persisted = \varnothing$. The empty set is a consistent-cut across any partial order. **Induction.** We induct across store persists. Assume $Persisted$ is a consistent-cut across the persist-before order and some controller adds a store S such that $Persisted' = Persisted \cup S$. By order enforcement, S is only persisted $\forall_T V^T < V^S \implies T \in Persisted$, and by order construction, $S \lessdot_{PB} T \implies V^S < V^T$. Therefore, store S is added to $Persisted$ only if $\forall_T T \lessdot S, T \in Persisted$. Since, for any partial order, the union of two consistent-cuts (both $Persisted$ and S and all its predecessors) is itself a consistent-cut, $Persisted'$ is a consistent-cut across the persists-before order. □

Definition 3.5 (Liveness). A Vorpal algorithm is live if and only if, given a long enough failure-free execution, a given persistent store will eventually become persisted.

4 VORPAL$_0$: BASELINE VORPAL

Having laid out the requirements for a Vorpal algorithm, we introduce Vorpal$_0$, a simple (though conservative) mechanism for meeting the two Vorpal requirements. Subsequent sections will refine the algorithm. Its code is shown in Figure 4 using an event-driven programming model. For simplicity, we assume any code block is executed atomically.

Order Construction. In Vorpal$_0$, as with all Vorpal algorithms, whenever a core issues a store, it tags the stores with a timestamp, setting it to the core's local vector clock. In Vorpal$_0$, the algorithm builds an over-constrained clock order using a timestamp that contains an entry for every core in the system. At every store, the issuing core increments its own clock for its own entry (line 3), and tags the store with the timestamp. At every load-acquire, the core merges the local clock with the timestamp value attached to the corresponding store-release (line 8).

Vorpal$_0$ meets the order construction requirement (the clock order across stores subsumes the persist-before order). To show this, we consider all possible ways two stores S_1 and S_2 to persistent addresses can be persist-before ordered under ARP. If S_1 and S_2 are issued by the same thread and persist-before ordered ($S_1 \lessdot_{PB} S_2$), they can only be persist-before ordered under ARP by some instruction X where X is a persist fence, store-release, or load-acquire, and $S_1 <_{PO} X <_{PO} S_2$. Since every store is assigned a timestamp issued in program order, this persist-before ordering is subsumed by the clock order. If S_1 and S_2 are issued by different threads and persist-before ordered, then $S_1 <_{RA} S_2$, consequently, there is a synchronizes-with event between them. Since, when issuing a load-acquire that synchronizes-with a store-release, a core merges its clock with the incoming store-release's timestamp, any subsequent stores it issues will be clock ordered after the incoming store-release — so the persist-before ordering is subsumed by the clock order.

Order Enforcement. Stores issued by the cores and those already assigned a timestamp (by Order Construction) arrive at their respective memory controllers and are placed in that controller's *Pending* set. Vorpal$_0$'s memory controllers enforce the ordering created by the processors using a simple rule that leverages its local progress vector clock (P), which, like the core vector clocks, contains an entry for every core. Whenever a controller persists a store (line 13), or discovers the store has been persisted at another controller (line 15), it merges the store's timestamp to its clock. In order to ensure all stores are eventually persisted, controllers occasionally broadcast their clocks to all other controllers (line 17). A controller who receives a broadcasted timestamp value will merge the timestamp into its own local progress clock.

To decide whether to persist a store, the memory controller uses a notion we term *immediate succession.* A timestamp B is the *immediate successor* of timestamp A if and only if $B_i \leq A_i$ for all vector entries i, except, for some vector entry j, $B_j = A_j + 1$. This is a useful concept because, if B is the immediate successor of A, then there cannot exist a timestamp X where $A < X < B$. Put another way, if X is a predecessor of B, it must be less than or equal to A. In code, we write the test of immediate succession as immediately_succeeds(A,B), checking if B immediately succeeds A.

In Vorpal$_0$, a memory controller persists a pending store S it has received with timestamp V^S if and only if the store's timestamp is the immediate successor to the current progress clock P. This ensures that, for any persisting store, all of its predecessors in clock order have already become persistent. The controller can persist several stores at once in a batch, assuming they are all immediate successors of its current progress clock. The ability to do so comes from the asynchronous nature of the system (see system description in Section 2.1), as well as, the usage of vector clocks by cores and memory controllers in concert (as described in 2.3).

We can show that Vorpal$_0$ meets the order enforcement requirement by induction on P, where our hypothesis is that any store with a clock $V \leq P$ is persisted. When a controller persists some store S, any preceding store $T \lessdot S$ must have a timestamp smaller than V^S

(by order construction), and, consequently, V^T must be less than or equal to P (by the immediate succession property). Therefore T is persistent (by induction).

Liveness. Vorpal$_0$ is not only safe (by order construction and enforcement), but also live. We reason by contradiction: suppose some store S cannot be persisted and has the smallest timestamp of any non-persisted store. Given a long enough failure-free execution, any persistent store (including S) will be issued to their controllers. Since S cannot be persisted, eventually all progress clocks will reach (or exceed) a timestamp value P such that $\forall_{T \in Persisted} V^T \leq P$, where, by safety, $P \leq S$. By our contradiction assumption, S cannot be the immediate successor to P since it cannot be persisted. Therefore, there exists some store $S' \notin Persisted$ where $P < S' < S$; yet the existence of S' violates our contradiction assumption that S has the smallest timestamp of any store that cannot be persisted.

5 VORPAL$_{chunk}$: CHUNK-GRANULARITY VECTOR CLOCK ORDERING

Vorpal$_0$ is correct but introduces many extraneous clock orderings. In particular, it assumes that all stores issued by a given thread must persist in program order, but this constraint is in fact not required by ARP. For instance, in Figure 3, stores to a and b would be persisted in program order by Vorpal$_0$, but this enforcement is unnecessary as they are not persist-before ordered — ARP assumes that a thread's stores are unordered into persistence unless constrained by a release-acquire ordering or persist fence.

```
18 // Core_i State and Events (Order Construction)
19 clock_register C; Integer ChunkCount; Set<Store> Chunk;
20 On: Issue persistent store or store−rel S
21   if (S switches controller ∨S is first store after load−acq
22     ∨S is first store after persist fence){
23       C_i ++; Issue Chunk w/ ChunkCount to MCs Pending Set;
24       ChunkCount:=0; Chunk:=∅;
25   }
26   Add S to Chunk; ChunkCount++; V^S := C;
27 On: Issue store−rel S (non−persistent)
28   V^S := C;
29 On: Issue load−acq A that synchronizes−with store−rel S
30   C := C ⊕ V^S;
31 On: Occasionally when ChunkCount≠0
32   C_i ++; Issue Chunk w/ ChunkCount to MCs Pending Set;
33   ChunkCount:=0; Chunk:=∅;
34 // MC State and Events (Order Enforcement)
35 clock_register P;
36 On: Occasionally
37   if(∃_Chunk Chunk ∈ Pending ∧Chunk ∉ Persisted
38     ∧immediately_succeeds(P, V^Chunk))
39       {Persisted := Persisted ∪ Chunk; P := P ⊕ V^Chunk;}
40 On: Received broadcast clock B
41   P := P ⊕ B;
42 On: Occasionally
43   Broadcast P;
```

Figure 5: Vorpal$_{chunk}$: The pseudo-code for Vorpal$_{chunk}$, a vector clock Vorpal algorithm that constructs and enforces ordering at a relaxed granularity of chunks. Actions of the cores and the memory controllers (MC) are shown.

5.1 Base Vorpal$_{chunk}$

In this subsection, we introduce a relaxed version of Vorpal$_0$, called Vorpal$_{chunk}$, which groups together stores that are unordered with respect to one another. These groups of unordered stores, or *chunks*, are those stores program-ordered between persist-before ordering instructions (store-release, load-acquire, or persist fences), issued from a single thread, and destined for a single memory controller (we relax this last restriction in Section 5.2). For instance, assuming all stores are destined for the same controller, Figure 3 contains four chunks (a,b; x; c; and d,e). All stores within a chunk are all assigned the same timestamp. Like all Vorpal algorithms, the clock order captured by Vorpal$_{chunk}$ ($\leq_C$) subsumes the persist-before order, that is: $\lessdot\ \subseteq \leq_C$, and, furthermore, the controller, in turn, completes the chunks following the generated vector clock order (corresponding to $\leq_C$). We show its code in Figure 5.

Order Construction. In Vorpal$_{chunk}$, a chunk is created by incrementing the local clock register — all stores in the chunk will receive the same timestamp (as with Vorpal$_0$, the timestamp has as many entries as there are cores in the system). A new chunk of stores is created on seeing new store following an earlier persist fence or load-acquire (lines 22 and 21 respectively). In addition to these instruction-triggered chunk boundaries, to simplify enforcement across memory controllers, Vorpal$_{chunk}$ creates a new chunk when the next store is issued to a different memory controller than the previous one (line 21). Cores also occasionally start new chunks to maintain liveness (line 32).

When a core starts a new chunk, the core sends the previous chunk, along with the count of stores inside the chunk, to the corresponding controller and resets the count of the number of stores (*ChunkCount*) inside a chunk (lines 23 and 32). Controllers use the *ChunkCount* for order enforcement: they must be sure all stores in any earlier chunk are persistent (by checking the number of stores tagged with the earlier chunk's timestamp) before it can persist any store in a subsequent chunk.

Vorpal$_{chunk}$'s clock-order subsumes the persist-before order (and therefore meets order construction). Instructions that induce a persist-before ordering (either a persist fence, store-release, or load-acquire) result in a chunk boundary the increment of the local clock register. The use of chunks is safe since stores in a chunk not persist-before ordered with respect to each other.

Order Enforcement. Vorpal$_{chunk}$ inherits its order enforcement code at the memory controller from the simpler Vorpal$_0$, but its code operates on chunks instead of stores. That is, if some pending chunk has yet to be persisted and is the immediate successor to the progress register P, then all component stores in the chunk can be persisted by the controller (line 36). Note that the count of stores inside the chunk is made known to its controller by the core at chunk dispatch time, hence it can safely complete the chunk's component stores in any order and then mark the chunk as complete (chunks can be sent piecemeal if necessary). As with Vorpal, the memory controller occasionally broadcasts its clock to allow for cross-controller progress (line 40).

For the correctness of order enforcement, the proof previously laid out for Vorpal$_0$'s enforcement can be reapplied verbatim, substituting "chunks" for "stores". This substitution is possible because an individual chunk is assigned a single timestamp, and stores that share a timestamp are unordered. Similarly, the Vorpal$_0$ proof of liveness applies, substituting in chunks for stores.

5.2 Vorpal$_{chunk+}$

Although Vorpal$_{chunk}$ has fewer extraneous orderings relative to Vorpal$_0$, the demarcation of chunks based on controller memory regions creates false orderings. Below we propose Vorpal$_{chunk+}$ which provides a way to remove these extraneous orderings through the use of *sub-chunks.*

In Vorpal$_{chunk+}$, cores do not create chunk boundaries between persistent stores issued to different memory controllers — a chunk spans all stores between two persist ordering instructions. Instead, in Vorpal$_{chunk+}$, within a chunk, cores create *sub-chunks* when they switch controllers. Sub-chunks of a given chunk all share a timestamp but are persisted at different memory controllers; thus a chunk is broken into a sequence of sub-chunks.

With regard to order creation, this modification is safe, as stores in different sub-chunks are still unordered with respect to each other in both clock-order and persists-before. However, enforcing the order becomes a problem as every component sub-chunk of some chunk C across all memory controllers needs to persist before any store of a subsequent chunk C' is persisted.

To solve this issue, we use a type of "chain notification": for a given chunk, every controller that persists a sub-chunk notifies the controller of the next sub-chunk when it finishes persisting but *does not* increment its local progress clock. The controller that persists the final sub-chunk in a chunk it increments its progress clock (eventually broadcasting this new timestamp to the other controllers). The effect of this chained notification is that the final memory controller effectively persisted all the entire chunk.

To implement this optimization, each sub-chunk contains a unique id, along with the ids of its successor and predecessor sub-chunks within the original chunk. Since chunks are issued by a single thread, sub-chunks can be ordered by the thread's executed program order. A single integer register, along with a unique core id, suffices for the id.

Vorpal$_{chunk+}$ also correctly achieves order enforcement: if two stores are clock-ordered, the first's chunk will entirely complete across all memory controllers before any progress clock is incremented, and, by the immediate successor property, the second's chunk must wait until the first's chunk completes; otherwise the proof of order enforcement is the same. Similarly, the liveness arguments of Vorpal$_{chunk}$ directly apply.

```
// Socket_p Gateway: State and Events (Order Construction)
clock_register L[N]; clock_register G;
typedef enum type = {LOCAL, GLOBAL}; type chunk_type = GLOBAL;
On: Received a first store event S after load–acq, persistent fence, or controller–switch
 from local core_i
  if(no remote stores or updates to G since this event fired last){L[i]_i ++;}
  else{G_p ++;}
  type new_chunk_type := (destination_socket(S)==p)?LOCAL:GLOBAL;
  if(chunk_type==LOCAL ∧new_chunk_type==GLOBAL)
    Notify core to dispatch chunk and mark as last local chunk
  else
    Notify core to dispatch chunk
  chunk_type:=new_chunk_type
On: Received a store–rel S from local core_i
  V_l^S := (L[i], G, p);
On: Received a load–acq A from local core_i that synchronizes–with local store–rel S
  L[i] := L[i] ⊕ V_l^S;
On: Received a load acq A from local core_i that synchronizes–with remote store–rel S
  G := G ⊕ V_g^S;
On: Received a clock request from local core_i to be assigned to a chunk
  Reply with clock (L[i], G, p);
// Core state and Events (Order Construction)
Integer ChunkCount; Set<Store> Chunk;
On: Any load–acquire, store–rel, persistent fence
 or when a persistent store switches controller or on a first store after load–acq
  Forward the event to the gateway
On: Received gateway notification to dispatch chunk (bool mark)
  (V_l, V_g) := RequestClocksFromGateway();
  if(mark){mark_as_last_local(Chunk);}
    {Issue Chunk w/ ChunkCount to MCs Pending Set;}
On: Issue persistent store S
  Add S to Chunk; ChunkCount++;
On: Occasionally
  Issue persist fence;
// MC State and Events (Order Enforcement)
clock_register P_g; clock_register P_l;
On: Occasionally complete chunks
  if(∃_Chunk Chunk ∈ Pending
   ∧ Chunk ∉ Persisted ∧immediately_succeeds(P_l, V_l^Chunk)
   ∧immediately_succeeds(P_g, V_g^Chunk) ∧is_from_local_socket(Chunk)){
    Persisted := Persisted ∪ Chunk; P_l := P_l ⊕ V_l^Chunk;
    if(is_last_local(Chunk))
      {Persisted := Persisted ∪ Chunk; P_g := P_g ⊕ V_g^Chunk;}
  }
  if(∃_Chunk Chunk ∈ Pending ∧Chunk ∉ Persisted
   ∧immediately_succeeds(P_g, V_g^Chunk) ∧!is_from_local_socket(Chunk))
    Persisted := Persisted ∪ Chunk; P_g := P_g ⊕ V_g^Chunk;
On: Received broadcast clock B_l
  P_l := P_l ⊕ B_l;
On: Received broadcast clock B_g
  P_g := P_g ⊕ B_g;
On: Occasionally
  Broadcast both P_l and P_g;
```

Figure 6: Vorpal$_H$: The pseudo-code for Vorpal$_H$, a vector-clock hierarchy-based Vorpal algorithm designed for large multi-socket systems. Actions of the cores, gateways and the memory controllers are shown.

6 VORPAL$_H$: HIERARCHY-BASED VECTOR CLOCK ORDERING

The above Vorpal variants capture and enforce the persist-before order with few false orderings, however, they are unlikely to scale to a many-socket machine because clock and timestamp size grows in proportion to the number of cores in the system. Since the algorithms require a clock entry per core, the vector clocks can get quite large and, more problematically, they ignore the organizational structure of the machine (see Figure 1).

In this section, we introduce a hierarchical variant of Vorpal, Vorpal$_H$. Vorpal$_H$ uses a two-level clock hierarchy — a *global clock* across sockets and many socket-specific *local clocks* across the local cores. A global clock contains an entry for each socket in the system, while the clock size for the socket-specific local clock is the number of cores inside the socket. The global clock for the socket subsumes all local clocks in that same socket. Using hierarchy, Vorpal$_H$ achieves a reduction in vector clock sizes, a task necessary to scale persistence ordering to large-scale systems. As the algorithm needs to capture messages heading into and out of the socket, Vorpal$_H$ leverages the socket's single gateway for processing messages across the server's FIFO inter-socket network.

Order Construction. In Vorpal$_H$, each store is labeled using a *hierarchical vector clock* with a *hierarchical timestamp.* This more detailed timestamp consists of two vector clock times (the global and local clock), along with the store's socket of origin. We write the hierarchical timestamp U originating at socket p as the tuple (U_l, U_g, p). Hierarchical timestamps generate a *hierarchical clock order*, written $\leq_H$. Given two timestamps $U = (U_l, U_g, p)$ and $V = (V_l, V_g, q)$, the order ($\leq_H$) between the timestamps can be stated as follows: $(U_l, U_g) \leq_H (V_l, V_g) \iff (U_g < V_g)$ *or* $(U_g = V_g$ *and* $U_l < V_l$ *and* $p = q)$. Vorpal$_H$ uses the per-socket gateway to assign global and local timestamps to store instructions of that socket. The gateway monitors the traffic into and out of its socket and is, therefore, a useful location for managing the clocks: the gateway contains a clock register (G) for the global clock and local clock registers ($L[N]$) for every one of the N cores of the socket.

The overall structure of Vorpal$_H$ is similar to the non-hierarchical variants. However, in Vorpal$_H$, cores do not keep their own clocks locally, but instead have a clock on the gateway – the gateway serves as a serializing point for all chunks within the socket. A Vorpal$_H$ core queries its gateway for copies of the global and its local clock. Upon receiving the clocks, a core sends the chunks it generates to the corresponding controllers along with their timestamps. The controllers then persist the chunks respecting the $\leq_H$ order, as specified by the hierarchical vector order.

Figure 6 shows the Vorpal$_H$ algorithm. Like Vorpal$_{chunk}$, Vorpal$_H$ groups together unordered stores into chunks, that all have the same timestamp. Like Vorpal$_{chunk}$, the boundaries between chunks are created at memory controller switches, persist fences, or load-acquire synchronization events. Vorpal$_H$ further differentiates between *local chunks*, whose stores are persisted by a memory controller in the local socket, and *global chunks*, that are persisted by remote memory controllers.

As the socket's gateway participates in Vorpal$_H$ on behalf of the cores of that socket — cores must query the gateway for their clocks (line 71). The constructed order as captured in the local and global clock registers is used to make the local and global clock assignments to the chunks at the cores (line 64 and line 73) and to construct a per-socket total order across chunks. Vorpal$_H$ uses this total order to issue timestamps based on the adjacent chunk type. When two successive chunks (in the total order serialized by the socket's gateway) are local, the algorithm uses the local clock registers (lines 49, 58 and 60) to order them, thereby avoiding publishing the ordering beyond the socket. In contrast, for any two successive chunks (again, within the socket's total order) in which one chunk is global, the algorithm orders them by the global clock (lines 49, 58 and 62). These timestamp rules on successive chunks mean the gateway oscillates between issuing global chunks, each with increasing global timestamps, and local chunks, each with an increasing local timestamp but common global timestamp (line 46).

By reasoning about local and global chunks, we can demonstrate that Vorpal$_H$'s order construction is correct. Consider any two stores that are adjacent in persist-before. Their ordering is induced by either a persist fence or persist-before ordering induced through the release-acquire order. Their corresponding chunks are also either local or global. If both are local, the ordering instruction (the persist fence or load-acquire) will result in ordering by the local vector clocks in the gateway (line 49) before the second store. If either one is or both are global, the intervening ordering instruction will result in ordering by the global vector clock (line 50) before the second store. In either case, the stores are ordered by the clock order $\leq_H$.

Algorithms	At Core	At Memory Controller	At Gateway	Per store/store-rel or chunk
Vorpal$_0$	(C)	(C)	None	(C)
Vorpal$_{chunk}$	(C)	(C)	None	$(C + CT)$
Vorpal$_{chunk+}$	(C)	$(C + CI)$	None	$(C + CT + 3 * CI)$
Vorpal$_H$	None	$(C_{socket} + S)$	$(C_{socket} \times C_{socket} + S)$	$(S + MB)$ - inter-socket $(C_{socket} + S)$ - intra-socket

Table 1: Metadata sizes (clocks and timestamps). C is the number of cores in the system, S is the number of sockets, C_{socket} is the number of cores per socket, M is the number of memory controllers in the system, CT is the size of the "chunk count" variable required in Vorpal$_{chunk}$ and Vorpal$_{chunk+}$, CI is the size needed for the "chunk id" in Vorpal$_{chunk+}$, and MB is the mark bit whose size is 1 used by Vorpal$_H$.

Order Enforcement. Order enforcement in Vorpal$_H$ takes advantage of the fact that its clock-order is *nested*, that is, two or more local chunks may carry the same global clock but are ordered by their local clock.

For enforcement, Vorpal$_H$ maintains two progress registers at a controller, one for the local clock (P_l) and another for global clocks (P_g). The controller completes the global chunks in global clock order (line 89) and the local chunks nested within the global chunk in their local clock order (line 83), updating the global and local progress registers respectively. When persisting local chunks, we delay updating the global progress clock until all nested local chunks that share a global timestamp are persisted. We accomplish this tracking using a single bit to *mark* the final local chunk before a global one (lines 53, 72, and 85).

Reasoning about global and local chunks also demonstrates that Vorpal$_H$'s order enforcement is correct. Using the safety proof of Vorpal$_{chunk}$, global chunks (and their stores) are correctly persisted with respect to other global chunks. Similarly, local chunks (and their stores) are persisted in the correct order with respect to other local chunks. Furthermore, local chunks are ordered with respect to subsequent global chunks through the marking mechanism, which guarantees an earlier local chunk persists before any subsequent global chunk, and persists after earlier global chunks by the immediate succession check on the global progress clock.

Liveness. Like all other Vorpal algorithms, Vorpal$_H$ is live. The liveness proof of Vorpal$_0$ applies verbatim here, substituting "chunk" for "store", and running the proof twice: first to show that global chunks are live, then to show that local chunks are live.

7 RESULTS

Metadata cost analysis. Vorpal incurs a metadata cost both in the clock registers at cores memory controllers, and gateways, and also in the timestamp sizes for different messages. Table 1 summarizes the overall metadata costs for different Vorpal algorithms.

With regard to the metadata cost for stores and chunks, Vorpal$_H$ not only reduced the effective size of messages by a factor C (number of cores) to a factor S (number of sockets) compared to Vorpal$_0$, but also enables many of the Vorpal MC broadcasts to be restricted inside the socket. We observe a 56% average reduction in the number

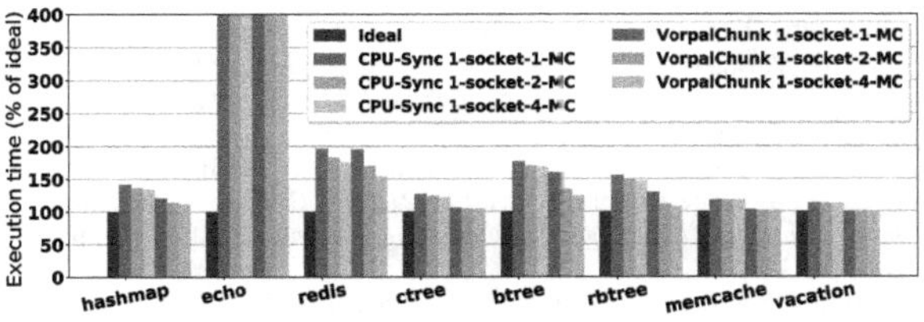

Figure 7: Scalability of Vorpal$_{chunk}$.

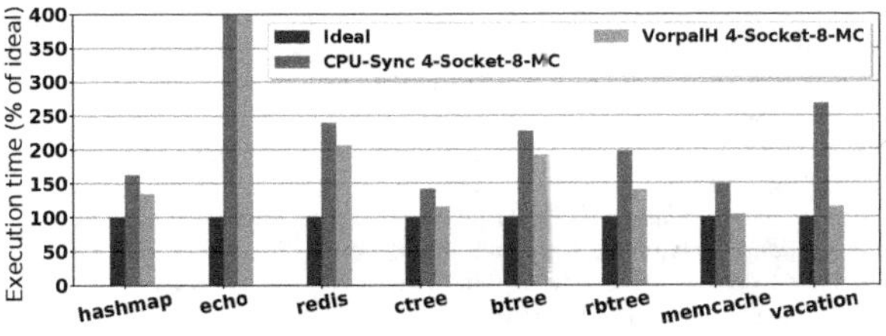

Figure 8: Scalability of Vorpal$_H$.

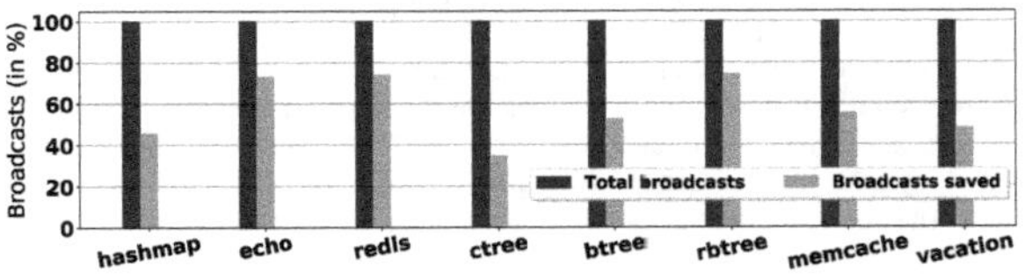

Figure 9: Broadcasts saved by Vorpal$_H$ versus Vorpal$_{chunk}$.

of broadcasts. Figure 9 shows the percentage broadcasts saved by the individual benchmarks (relative to the broadcasts in Vorpal$_{chunk}$).

Performance and scalability analysis. We implemented our algorithm as a shared memory system on top of the MARSSx86 [34] simulator to model our performance. The simulator models an out-of-order core running at 4GHZ. To test our solution, we use applications from the persistent memory Whisper suite for our evaluation [32].To model a non-volatile memory with slower write speed, we set the NVMM write latency to 600 cycles [11, 32]). and set the NVMM read and DRAM read/write latency to 150 cycles. Like ARM [4], our model does not assume that the memory controllers have access to residual power and will not be flushed to persistence on failure (in contrast to Intel's ADR [39] domain for Optane DC). For comparison, we modeled a non-distributed ordering implementation, where each core coordinates its own persistent ordering via synchronous messages with one memory controller at a time (similar to Kolli et al. [22]). We call it **CPU-Sync**, and we compare it against the Vorpal implementations. CPU-Sync requires synchronous messages between CPU and MC to enforce every ARP generated order. In contrast, we also implemented **Ideal**. Ideal witnesses no persistence-induced CPU stalls, i.e. the persistent stores are assumed to complete instantaneously. The Ideal baseline can be considered the best case scenario for persistence wherein the performance penalty of enforcing the order is zero. To evaluate the effect of controllers we vary the number of total number memory controllers as well as the number of sockets (e.g. **VorpalH 4-Socket-8-MC** has four sockets with two MCs each). We assume a 200 ns delay per inter-socket hop and topology with a single socket connected to at most two other sockets. Writes to the persistent memory generated by the stores of a given core are sent to the memory controllers at the granularity of a cache line. Each MC has a bounded length queue of 64 entries, each the size of a cache line. Each entry also stores the vector clock metadata for the line. We assume a 4 KB page size and spread consecutive pages across the controllers in a round robin fashion, as expected on interleaved NVMM [19]. All the figures show the average over eight runs — we did not notice any large variation.

Figure 7 Vorpal$_{chunk}$, compared to CPU-Sync and Ideal, varying the number of memory controllers. Vorpal's performance approaches that of Ideal with increasing controller count, by being able to exploit the parallelism offered by multiple memory controllers and deferred completion enabled by vector clocks, as opposed to the synchronous scheme. Most workloads benefit significantly from the proposed scheme (except for echo due to high store intensity).

In Figure 8 we show the results of Vorpal$_H$ for a multi-socket setting with additional hop latencies. Large slowdowns relative to Ideal are witnessed here for CPU-Sync. Compared to the slowdowns on a single socket system (Figure 7), the slowdowns witnessed are much higher, with slowdowns over 2×. Vorpal$_H$ due to its latency tolerance provides significant benefits in this setting.

8 RELATED WORK

Memory Persistency. In anticipation of the arrival of persistent memory devices, the research community has undertaken a significant effort in preparing various components of the system stack (from cores to caches to memory controllers) for their arrival [20, 22, 24]. Vorpal sits alongside a number of architectural solutions for enforcing the persists-before order. Most existing systems enforce persist orderings using synchronous communication [4, 20–23, 32, 35, 40, 41]. None of these systems scales to tens of MCs. Since ordering is enforced with some form of enqueue and acknowledgement messages, messages introduce slow serializing communication. Our design specifically deals with the challenge of scaling with multiple MCs through a distributed algorithm.

Alongside the architectural community, the theory community has explored what persistent memory means at the language level, investigating novel persistency models [35] for specifying the persists-before order, e.g. [17, 18, 37]. Other work has explored systems software, such as transactional memory-type abstractions [7, 16, 27, 45], file systems [47], and data structures [8, 13, 33, 44].

Vector Clocks. Vector clocks were introduced independently in 1988 by Mattern [30] and Fidge [12] as a method of ordering events in a distributed setting. In this manner, the clocks improved on the original scalar clocks of Lamport [26], which could not represent the partially ordered relationship between distributed events. Other methods of tracking logical time, including matrix time, have been proposed, for a summary of methods see [43]. The size of vector clocks has repeatedly been a concern, resulting in various methods of shrinking them [25, 42].

Causal Consistency. In a causal consistency model, observers cannot see a data item before they can see the data items that influenced its creation, a notion that shows some similarities with ARP. Causal consistency has drawn attention recently as it is the strongest consistency model available in the presence of partitions [29]. Causal memory [2] evolved from applying the notion of the causal ordering of events in a distributed system [26] to reads and writes. Enforcing causal consistency (for a summary, see [5]) in a distributed system has some similarities to our Vorpal algorithms enforcement of persist-before. Often, causal consistency is tracked using logical clocks (such as vector clocks) (e.g. [9, 10, 28]), and may even be hierarchical [6].

9 CONCLUSION

This paper addresses the problem of ensuring the ordering of stores on large-scale persistent memory systems. Previous solutions do not scale with core and memory controller count. In this paper, we proposed a distributed solution to the problem of persistent ordering using vector clocks. Our algorithms provide both scalability and performance (with an average speedup of 48%), while overcoming the limitations of applying vector clocks in this setting. We plan to explore even better algorithms and reflect on how the proposed implementations may impact persistent memory semantics as part of future work, for instance, leveraging other work in compressing vector clocks or combining the vector registers between cores.

REFERENCES

[1] Release-acquire ordering, 2017. https://en.cppreference.com/w/cpp/atomic/memory_order#Release-Acquire_ordering.

[2] M. Ahamad, G. Neiger, J. E. Burns, P. Kohli, and P. W. Hutto. Causal memory: definitions, implementation, and programming. *Distributed Computing*, 9(1): 37–49, Mar 1995.

[3] ARM. Armv8 reference manual, . https://developer.arm.com/docs/ddi0487/latest/arm-architecture-reference-manual-armv8-for-armv8-a-architecture-profile.

[4] ARM. ARMv8-A architecture evolution, persistent memory instructions, . https://community.arm.com/processors/b/blog/posts/armv8-a-architecture-evolution.

[5] M. Bravo, N. Diegues, J. Zeng, P. Romano, and L. Rodrigues. On the use of clocks to enforce consistency in the cloud. *Data Engineering*, p. 18, 2015.

[6] M. Bravo, L. Rodrigues, and P. Van Roy. Towards a scalable, distributed metadata service for causal consistency under partial geo-replication. In *Doctoral Symp. of the 16th Intl. Middleware Conf.*, Middleware Doct Symp. '15, pp. 5:1–5:4, Vancouver, BC, Canada, Dec. 2015.

[7] J. Coburn, A. M. Caulfield, A. Akel, L. M. Grupp, R. K. Gupta, R. Jhala, and S. Swanson. Nv-heaps: Making persistent objects fast and safe with next-generation, non-volatile memories. In *16th Intl. Conf. on Architectural Support for Programming Languages and Operating Systems*, ASPLOS XVI, pp. 105–118, Newport Beach, CA, Mar. 2011.

[8] N. Cohen, D. T. Aksun, and J. R. Larus. Object-oriented recovery for non-volatile memory. *ACM Program. Lang.*, 2(OOPSLA):153:1–153:22, Oct. 2018.

[9] J. Du, S. Elnikety, A. Roy, and W. Zwaenepoel. Orbe: Scalable causal consistency using dependency matrices and physical clocks. In *4th Ann. Symp. on Cloud Computing*, SOCC '13, pp. 11:1–11:14, Santa Clara, CA, Oct. 2013.

[10] J. Du, C. Iorgulescu, A. Roy, and W. Zwaenepoel. Gentlerain: Cheap and scalable causal consistency with physical clocks. In *ACM Symp. on Cloud Computing*, SOCC '14, pp. 4:1–4:13, Seattle, WA, Nov. 2014.

[11] S. R. Dulloor, A. Roy, Z. Zhao, N. Sundaram, N. Satish, R. Sankaran, J. Jackson, and K. Schwan. Data tiering in heterogeneous memory systems. In *11th European Conf. on Computer Systems*, EuroSys '16, pp. 15:1–15:16, London, UK, Apr. 2016.

[12] C. J. Fidge. Timestamps in message-passing systems that preserve the partial ordering. In *11th Australian Computer Science Conf.*, pp. 55–66, 1988.

[13] M. Friedman, M. Herlihy, V. Marathe, and E. Petrank. A persistent lock-free queue for non-volatile memory. In *23rd ACM SIGPLAN Symp. on Principles and Practice of Parallel Programming*, PPoPP '18, pp. 28–40, Vienna, Austria, Feb. 2018.

[14] K. Gharachorloo, D. Lenoski, J. Laudon, P. Gibbons, A. Gupta, and J. Hennessy. Memory consistency and event ordering in scalable shared-memory multiprocessors. In *17th Ann. Intl. Symp. on Computer Architecture*, ISCA '90, pp. 15–26, Seattle, WA, June 1990.

[15] Intel. Xeon servers, Intel, 2019. https://www.intel.com/content/www/us/en/processors/xeon/scalable/xeon-scalable-platform-brief.html.

[16] J. Izraelevitz, T. Kelly, and A. Kolli. Failure-atomic persistent memory updates via JUSTDO logging. In *21st Intl. Conf. on Architectural Support for Programming Languages and Operating Systems*, ASPLOS '16, pp. 427–442, Atlanta, GA, 2016.

[17] J. Izraelevitz, H. Mendes, and M. L. Scott. Linearizability of persistent memory objects under a full-system-crash failure model. In *30th Intl. Conf. on Distributed Computing*, DISC '16, pp. 313–327, Paris, France, Sept. 2016.

[18] J. Izraelevitz, H. Mendes, and M. L. Scott. Brief announcement: Preserving happens-before in persistent memory. In *28th ACM Symp. on Parallelism in Algorithms and Architectures*, SPAA'16, pp. 157–159, Asilomar Beach, CA, 2016.

[19] J. Izraelevitz, J. Yang, L. Zhang, J. Kim, X. Liu, A. Memaripour, Y. J. Soh, Z. Wang, Y. Xu, S. R. Dulloor, J. Zhao, and S. Swanson. Basic performance measurements of the Intel Optane DC persistent memory module, Apr. 2019.

[20] A. Joshi, V. Nagarajan, M. Cintra, and S. Viglas. Efficient persist barriers for multicores. In *48th Intl. Symp. on Microarchitecture*, MICRO-48, pp. 660–671, Waikiki, HI, Dec. 2015.

[21] A. Kolli, S. Pelley, A. Saidi, P. M. Chen, and T. F. Wenisch. High-performance transactions for persistent memories. In *21st Intl. Conf. on Architectural Support for Programming Languages and Operating Systems*, ASPLOS '16, pp. 399–411, Atlanta, GA, 2016.

[22] A. Kolli, J. Rosen, S. Diestelhorst, A. Saidi, S. Pelley, S. Liu, P. M. Chen, and T. F. Wenisch. Delegated persist ordering. In *49th Ann. IEEE/ACM Intl. Symp. on Microarchitecture (MICRO)*, pp. 1–13, Taipei, Taiwan, Oct 2016.

[23] A. Kolli, V. Gogte, A. Saidi, S. Diestelhorst, P. M. Chen, S. Narayanasamy, and T. F. Wenisch. Language-level persistency. In *44th Ann. Intl. Symp. on Computer Architecture*, ISCA '17, pp. 481–493, Toronto, ON, Canada, June 2017.

[24] K. Korgaonkar, I. Bhati, H. Liu, J. Gaur, S. Manipatruni, S. Subramoney, T. Karnik, S. Swanson, I. Young, and H. Wang. Density tradeoffs of non-volatile memory as a replacement for sram based last level cache. In *45th ACM/IEEE Ann. Intl. Symp. on Computer Architecture (ISCA)*, pp. 315–327, Los Angeles, CA, USA, June 2018.

[25] A. D. Kshemkalyani, A. Khokhar, and M. Shen. Encoded vector clock: Using primes to characterize causality in distributed systems. In *19th Intl. Conf. on Distributed Computing and Networking*, ICDCN '18, pp. 12:1–12:8, Varanasi, India, Jan. 2018.

[26] L. Lamport. Time, clocks, and the ordering of events in a distributed system. *Commun. ACM*, 21(7):558–565, July 1978.

[27] Q. Liu, J. Izraelevitz, S. K. Lee, M. L. Scott, S. H. Noh, and C. Jung. iDO: Compiler-directed failure atomicity for nonvolatile memory. In *51st Ann. IEEE/ACM Intl. Symp. on Microarchitecture (MICRO)*, pp. 258–270, Fukuoka City, Japan, Oct 2018.

[28] W. Lloyd, M. J. Freedman, M. Kaminsky, and D. G. Andersen. Don't settle for eventual: Scalable causal consistency for wide-area storage with COPS. In *23rd ACM Symp. on Operating Systems Principles*, SOSP '11, pp. 401–416, Cascais, Portugal, Oct. 2011.

[29] P. Mahajan, L. Alvisi, M. Dahlin, et al. Consistency, availability, and convergence.

[30] F. Mattern. Virtual time and global states of distributed systems. In *Parallel and Distributed Algorithms*, pp. 215–226, 1988.

[31] Micron. 3D XPoint Technology, 2017. http://www.micron.com/products/advanced-solutions/3d-xpoint-technology.

[32] S. Nalli, S. Haria, M. D. Hill, M. M. Swift, H. Volos, and K. Keeton. An analysis of persistent memory use with WHISPER. In *22nd Intl. Conf. on Architectural Support for Programming Languages and Operating Systems*, ASPLOS '17, pp. 135–148, Xi'an, China, Apr. 2017.

[33] F. Nawab, J. Izraelevitz, T. Kelly, C. B. M. III, D. R. Chakrabarti, and M. L. Scott. Dalí: A periodically persistent hash map. In *31st Intl. Symp. on Distributed Computing (DISC 2017)*, volume 91, pp. 37:1–37:16, Vienna, Austria, Oct. 2017.

[34] A. Patel, F. Afram, S. Chen, and K. Ghose. Marss: A full system simulator for multicore x86 CPUs. In *48th Design Automation Conf.*, DAC '11, pp. 1050–1055, San Diego, CA, 2011.

[35] S. Pelley, P. M. Chen, and T. F. Wenisch. Memory persistency. In *41st Ann. Intl. Symp. on Computer Architecture*, ISCA '14, pp. 265–276, Minneapolis, MN, 2014.

[36] pmem.io. Persistent Memory Development Kit, 2017. http://pmem.io/pmdk.

[37] A. Raad and V. Vafeiadis. Persistence semantics for weak memory: Integrating epoch persistency with the TSO memory model. *ACM Program. Lang.*, 2(OOPSLA): 137:1–137:27, Oct. 2018.

[38] S. Raoux, G. W. Burr, M. J. Breitwisch, C. T. Rettner, Y.-C. Chen, R. M. Shelby, M. Salinga, D. Krebs, S.-H. Chen, H.-L. Lung, and C. H. Lam. Phase-change random access memory: A scalable technology. *IBM J. Res. Dev.*, 52(4):465–479, July 2008.

[39] A. Rudoff. Deprecating the pcommit instruction, 2016. https://software.intel.com/en-us/blogs/2016/09/12/deprecate-pcommit-instruction. Accessed 04/18/2019.

[40] A. Rudolf. Processor support for NVM programming. http://www.snia.org/sites/default/files/AndyRudoff_Processor_Support_NVM.pdf.

[41] S. Shin, J. Tuck, and Y. Solihin. Hiding the long latency of persist barriers using speculative execution. In *44th Ann. Intl. Symp. on Computer Architecture*, ISCA '17, pp. 175–186, Toronto, ON, Canada, June 2017.

[42] M. Singhal and A. Kshemkalyani. An efficient implementation of vector clocks. *Information Processing Letters*, 43(1):47 – 52, 1992.

[43] M. Singhal and M. Raynal. Logical time: Capturing causality in distributed systems. *Computer*, 29:49–56, 02 1996.

[44] S. Venkataraman, N. Tolia, P. Ranganathan, and R. Campbell. Consistent and durable data structures for non-volatile byte-addressable memory. In *9th USENIX Conf. on File and Storage Technologies*, FAST '11, San Jose, CA, February 2011.

[45] H. Volos, A. J. Tack, and M. M. Swift. Mnemosyne: Lightweight persistent memory. In *16th Intl. Conf. on Architectural Support for Programming Languages and Operating Systems*, ASPLOS XVI, pp. 91–104, Newport Beach, CA, 2011.

[46] H. S. P. Wong, H. Y. Lee, S. Yu, Y. S. Chen, Y. Wu, P. S. Chen, B. Lee, F. T. Chen, and M. J. Tsai. Metal oxide RRAM. *IEEE*, 100(6):1951–1970, June 2012.

[47] J. Xu and S. Swanson. Nova: A log-structured file system for hybrid volatile/non-volatile main memories. In *14th USENIX Conf. on File and Storage Technologies (FAST 16)*, pp. 323–338, Santa Clara, CA, Feb. 2016.

On the Parallels between Paxos and Raft, and how to Port Optimizations

Zhaoguo Wang[†‡], Changgeng Zhao[*], Shuai Mu[◇], Haibo Chen[†‡], Jinyang Li[*]
† Shanghai Key Laboratory of Scalable Computing and Systems, Shanghai Jiao Tong University
‡ Institute of Parallel and Distributed Systems, Shanghai Jiao Tong University
* Department of Computer Science, New York University
◇ Department of Computer Science, Stony Brook University

ABSTRACT

In recent years, Raft has surpassed Paxos to become the more popular consensus protocol in the industry. While many researchers have observed the similarities between the two protocols, no one has shown how Raft and Paxos are formally related to each other. In this paper, we present a formal mapping between Raft and Paxos, and use this knowledge to port a certain class of optimizations from Paxos to Raft. In particular, our porting method can automatically generate an optimized protocol specification with guaranteed correctness. As case studies, we port and evaluate two optimizations, Mencius and Paxos Quorum Lease to Raft.

KEYWORDS

Paxos, Raft, optimization porting

ACM Reference Format:
Zhaoguo Wang, Changgeng Zhao, Shuai Mu, Haibo Chen, Jinyang Li. 2019. On the Parallels between Paxos and Raft, and how to Port Optimizations. In *2019 ACM Symposium on Principles of Distributed Computing (PODC'19), July 29–August 2, 2019, Toronto, ON, Canada.* ACM, New York, NY, USA, 10 pages. *https://doi.org/10.1145/3293611.3331595*

1 INTRODUCTION

Consensus protocols enable servers to reach agreement on the sequence of operations to execute despite the failure of some servers and arbitrary network delays. Classic Paxos [18] is one of the oldest and most well-studied consensus protocols. However, in recent years, Raft [31] has gradually overtaken Paxos as the consensus protocol of choice, esp. in the industry. Many researchers have observed that Raft and Paxos bear certain similarities. However, no one has shown how the two protocols are related in the formal sense. In fact, does such a formal relationship exist?

While it may seem like a pedantic endeavor, investigating a formal mapping between Raft and Paxos is meaningful for two reasons. First, making the connection between Raft and Paxos helps deepen our understanding of both protocols. In particular, it allows us to articulate what design decisions have made Raft more understandable or more efficient than Paxos. Second, Paxos is not an isolated protocol but consists of a large family of variants and optimizations as a result of almost two decades of research [16, 7, 25, 22, 29, 28]. These Paxos variants range from reducing latency for wide-area operation, balancing replica load, optimizing for mostly-conflict-free workload, to tolerating Byzantine faults. Knowing how Raft relates to Paxos allows one to port some of these optimizations to Raft without having to reinvent the wheel.

In this paper, we attempt to make a formal connection between Raft and Paxos using refinement mapping. We show that, beyond the broad stroke similarities between the two protocols, Raft differs from Paxos in several subtle details, such as allowing a follower to erase extra entries if its log is longer than the leader. Unfortunately, these differences between the two protocols prevent a direct refinement mapping between them. Therefore, we craft a variant of Raft, called Raft*, which is a refinement of Paxos by removing these superficial differences.

We use the refinement mapping between Raft* and Paxos to port existing ideas in the Paxos literature to the world of Raft. Specifically, we develop an automatic porting method which is able to port a certain class of Paxos optimizations to Raft*. The specific class of optimizations that can be ported automatically are those that do not mutate the original state in Paxos. For these optimizations, we derive the set of rules for applying them to Raft*, such that the resulting protocol automatically refines Raft* and the Paxos optimization, thus guaranteeing correctness. As Raft* is very similar to Raft, the derived protocol contains all Raft properties and is improved by the Paxos optimization. As case studies, we choose two published Paxos optimization, Mencius [25] and Paxos Quorum Lease [28], each of which improves one or more aspects of Paxos in terms of load-balancing and latency. We have ported these two protocols to Raft*.

We evaluate the performance benefits of our Raft* optimizations on Amazon AWS in a setup where data is replicated across several geographically separated data centers. For each optimization, we show that the Raft variant has similar benefits as its Paxos counterparts in the literature.

To summarize, we make the following contributions:

- We reveal the formal relationship between Raft and Paxos by showing a refinement mapping between Paxos and Raft*, a close variant of Raft (Section 3).
- We define the problem of porting optimizations across protocols and develop a methodology for automatically porting a

PODC '19, July 29-August 2, 2019, Toronto, ON, Canada

ACM ISBN 978-1-4503-6217-7/19/07...$15.00
https://doi.org/10.1145/3293611.3331595

restricted class of optimizations from one protocol to another (Section 4)
- We port Mencius and Quorum Lease from Paxos to Raft and provide experimental evaluation of the optimized versions of Raft protocols (Section 6)

Limitations. This paper represents a first attempt at automatically porting optimizations from one family of protocols to another related one. Our method has several limitations that limit its applicability. First, in order to port optimizations, we have to provide a refinement mapping between the two related protocols. As such, we can only automatically port optimizations from Paxos to Raft* instead of directly to Raft. Second, only a certain restricted class of optimizations can be automatically ported. Specifically, such optimizations must not mutate protocol state (Section 4.2). Last, optimization porting is done at the level of protocol specification, not implementation. Programmers still need to implement a derived protocol manually.

2 OVERVIEW

2.1 Background

Paxos [18]. Paxos solves the consensus problem using a bottom-up approach. First, single-decree Paxos is developed to let servers agree on a single value. Then, MultiPaxos builds upon single-decree Paxos to agree on a sequence of operations.

In single-decree Paxos, servers reach consensus via a two-phase protocol. In phase-1, a server picks a globally unique proposal number (called ballot) and sends a Prepare RPC to every server. A server receiving a Prepare replies success if it has not seen a higher ballot. In its reply, the server includes the highest ballot it has ever accepted, or *null* if it has never accepted any ballot. If the proposing server receives at least a majority of successful replies, it goes into the second phase, otherwise, it retries with a higher ballot.

In phase-2, the server picks the value for its ballot and sends it in an Accept RPC to every server. This can be any value (usually the operation the server wants to initiate) if the phase-1 replies do not contain any previously accepted value; Otherwise, it must be the value (an operation initiated by some other server) with the highest ballot in the replies. A server receiving the Accept RPC will accept this value and reply success if it has not seen a higher ballot. If the proposing server receives a majority of successful replies, it considers this value as chosen (or equivalently, *committed*). It could notify other servers of the committed operation immediately or piggyback this information with subsequent communication.

MultiPaxos builds upon single-decree Paxos to agree on a sequence of operations. In particular, MultiPaxos tries to agree on the operation for each position in the sequence using a separate instance of Paxos. MultiPaxos also optimizes performance by allowing concurrent instances and batching the phase-1 messages of these instances. Figure 1 gives the pseudocode of MultiPaxos. In the rest of the paper, Paxos refers to the multi-decree version of Paxos and single-decree Paxos refers to the single-decree version.

Raft [31]. Unlike Paxos' bottom-up approach, Raft solves the consensus problem in a top-down manner, by replicating a log of operations across servers without decomposing into single-decree consensus. The Raft protocol consists of two parts: electing a leader and replicating of log entries by the elected leader. Each server maintains a term number that monotonically increases. For leader election, a candidate server increments its term number and sends RequestVote RPCs to all servers to collect votes for itself to become a leader. Elections are ordered by their corresponding *term* numbers and a node rejects RequestVote if it has already processed a request with a higher term or the same term from a different candidate. Raft also adds another restriction to leader election: a node rejects RequestVote if its log is more recent than the sender's log. A candidate becomes the elected leader for this term if it receives a majority quorum of successful votes on its RequestVote RPCs.

The elected leader batches client operations and replicates them to all other servers (called followers) using the AppendEntries RPC. A server rejects the AppendEntries request if it has seen a higher term than the sender. The AppendEntries RPC also lets the receiver synchronize its log with the sender: the receiver catches up if it is missing entries, and it erases extraneous entries not found in the sender's log. The leader considers the operations in AppendEntries committed if a majority quorum of servers successfully replies. Figure 2 shows the pseudocode of Raft (ignoring the code in blue).

2.2 Our approach

At first glance, Raft bears many similarities to Paxos. Both protocols have two phases. Raft's RequestVote corresponds to Phase1a in Paxos. Both RequestVote and Phase1a are considered successful if a majority of ok replies are received. Afterward, Raft uses AppendEntries to replicate operations to other servers, similar to how Paxos uses Phase2a to disseminate an operation associated with a specific single-decree instance. In both protocols, a server rejects the AppendEntries/Accept request if it has seen a higher term/ballot and the operation is considered committed only when a majority of servers return ok.

Our work uses refinement mapping [1] to formally capture the connection between Paxos and Raft. Refinement mapping is commonly used to prove that a lower-level specification correctly implements a higher-level one. For example, existing work [36] has mapped Paxos, Viewstamp Replication and ZAB to a high-level abstract consensus algorithm instead of directly relating them to each other. By contrast, to shed the light on the relationship between Paxos and Raft, we attempt to provide a refinement mapping between the two protocols directly.

It turns out that there are subtle differences that make it impossible for Raft to have a direct refinement mapping to Paxos. Nevertheless, we can modify Raft slightly to remove these superficial differences and create a close variant protocol (called Raft*). By showing the refinement mapping from Raft* to Paxos, we illuminate the connection between Raft and Paxos.

Beyond providing a deeper understanding of protocols, can the refinement mapping between Raft* and Paxos be used for some practical purposes? Guided by this question, we proceed to explore how to migrate optimizations done for Paxos to work for Raft. Based on the refinement mapping, we develop a method to port certain Paxos optimizations to Raft* such that the resulting protocol's correctness is guaranteed. Specifically, some Paxos optimization only reads but does not mutate Paxos' state variables. The intuition is to port these optimizations by replacing Paxos variables with Raft* variables according to the refinement mapping. For example,

```
function Phase1a(s):
  s.ballot = s.ballot + 1
  unchosen = smallest unchosen instance id
  s sends <'prepare', s.ballot, unchosen> to all

function Phase1b(s):
  if s receives <'prepare', b, unchosen>
    && b > s.ballot
  then
    s.ballot = b
    s.phase1Succeeded = false
    reply <'prepareOK', s.ballot,
                      instances with id ≥ unchosen>

function Phase1Succeed(s):
  if s receives <'prepareOK', b, instances>
      from f + 1 acceptors with the same b
    && b == s.ballot
  then
    start = smallest unchosen instance id
    end = largest id of received instances
    for i in start ... end
      s.instances[i]= safeEntry(received
                          instances with id i)
    s.phase1Succeeded = true
```

(a) Phase 1

```
function Phase2a(s, i, v):
  if s.phase1Succeeded
    && (s.instances[i].val == v
          || s.instances[i] == Empty)
  then
    send <'accept', i, v, s.ballot> to all

function Phase2b(s):
  if s receives <'accept', i, v, b> && b ≥ s.ballot
  then
    if b > s.ballot
    then
      s.phase1Succeeded = false
      s.ballot = b
    s.instances[i].bal = b
    s.instances[i].val = v
    reply <'acceptOK', i, v, b>

function Learn(s):
    if s receives same <'acceptOK', i, v, b>
      from f + 1 acceptors
    then
      s.instances[i].val = v
      s.instances[i].bal = b
      add s.instances[i] to s.chosenSet
```

(b) Phase 2

Figure 1: MultiPaxos

considering an add-on checkpointing mechanism for Paxos which saves both system state and last applied instance id. According to the refinement mapping, the instance id is mapped to the log index. Thus, when porting the checkpoint mechanism to Raft*, we can replace the last applied instance id with the last applied index in the log with guaranteed correctness.

3 CONNECTING RAFT TO PAXOS

Refinement mapping. We use refinement mapping to describe the equivalence between two protocols. Intuitively, in order to show that a protocol $\mathcal{B}$ refines a protocol $\mathcal{A}$, we must show that how each state of in $\mathcal{B}$'s state space can be mapped to some state in $\mathcal{A}$'s state space such that any state transition sequence in $\mathcal{B}$ corresponds to a valid state transition sequence in $\mathcal{A}$ under the mapping. This intuitive definition of refinement mapping suffices for this section. In later sections (Section 4), we present a more formal definition of refinement mapping used for optimization porting.

Why Raft cannot be mapped to Paxos directly. Ideally, we should be able to directly refine Raft to Paxos. Unfortunately, this cannot be done for two reasons. First, Raft forces all servers that accept the leader's AppendEntries to match the leader's log. Therefore, if a follower's log is longer than that of the leader, the follower will erase the extra entries. When mapped to MultiPaxos, such an "erasing" step would correspond to a server deleting a previously accepted value for some Paxos instance, a state transition that would never happen in Paxos. Raft makes the erasing step safe by committing log indexes in order so that its phase-1 exchange ensures that the leader's log contains all potentially committed entries. By contrast, Paxos commits instances out of order. Thus Paxos' proposing server must fetch safe values for different uncommitted instances from other servers and never erase (but only overwrite) accepted values at other servers. Second, the term number in each log entry in Raft cannot be mapped to the accepted ballot number of each instance in Paxos. The reason is Raft's leader never modifies its existing log entries. As a result, a newly elected leader at term t would replicate a previously uncommitted log entry with term $t' < t$ without any change. Such a behavior has no equivalence in Paxos. The proposing server in Paxos always over-writes the accepted instance's ballot number with its current ballot number. Not changing the log entry's term number turns out to have subtle correctness implications such that the Raft paper ([31] Section 5.4.2) has to add an extra rule to prevent the loss of committed values.

Raft*. We modify Raft slightly to create a close variant, called Raft*, for which a refinement mapping to Paxos exists. Figure 2 shows the specification of Raft* in pseudocode (including code in blue). Raft* is identical to Raft, except for two introduced differences, based on the two reasons for why Raft cannot be shown to refine Paxos. First, when responding ok to a candidate's RequestVote, a server includes all the extra entries not present in the candidate's log in its reply (line 68-69). The leader chooses the safe values among its majority quorum of replies to extend its log (line 77-81). An acceptor rejects leader's append request if its log is longer than the leader's (line 110). Second, a ballot field is added to each entry. On appending a new entry, Raft* will change all entries' ballot to be the new entry's term (line 99-100).

Refining Paxos with Raft*. Figure 3 gives the refinement mapping between Raft* and Paxos. Most of them are straightforward. For example, the Raft's entries whose indexes are not greater than commitIndex (committed entries) are mapped to Paxos's instances in the chosenSet (chosen instances). We only explain the nuances mappings. First, most messages in Raft* do not have the same content with its counterparts in Paxos. For instance, requestVote includes lastIndex and lastTerm instead of the smallest id of unchosen instance. This is because, if two logs have the entries with the same

```
// s starts an election for the new leader
function RequestVote(s):
  s.currentTerm = s.currentTerm + 1
  s sends <'requestVote', s.currentTerm, s.lastIndex,
        s.log[s.lastIndex].term> to all

// s receives leader election request
function ReceiveVote(s):
  if s receives <'requestVote', term, lastIndex, lastTerm>
    && term > s.currentTerm
    && s.log[lastIndex].term < lastTerm
       || (s.log[lastIndex].term = lastTerm
          && s.lastIndex ≥ lastIndex)
  then
    s.currentTerm = term
    s.isLeader = false
    extraEnts = non-empty entries in s.log after lastIndex
    reply <'requestVoteOK', s.currentTerm, extraEnts>

// s becomes the new leader in the vote phase
function BecomeLeader(s):
  if s receives <'requestVoteOK', term, ents> from f + 1
    acceptors with same term && term == s.currentTerm
  then
    max = largest index of received entries
    for i in s.lastIndex + 1 ... max
      e = safeEntry(received entries of index i)
      s.log[i].bal = s.currentTerm
      s.log[i].term = s.currentTerm
      s.log[i].val = e.val
    s.isLeader = true
    s.lastIndex = max
```

(a) Phase 1

```
// s appends vals to the log from i and
// broadcasts all entries after prev to replicas
function AppendEntries(s, i, vals, prev):
  if s.isLeader && i == s.lastIndex + 1 then
    for each v in vals
      s.log[s.lastIndex+1].val = v
      s.log[s.lastIndex+1].term = s.currentTerm
      s.lastIndex = s.lastIndex + 1
    for i in prev + 1 ... lastIndex
      s.log[i].bal = s.currentTerm
    ents = s.log entries after prev
    pTerm = s.log[prev].term
    send <'append', s.currentTerm, prev, pTerm, ents,
         s.commitIndex> to all

// s receives append request from the leader
function ReceiveAppend(s):
  if s receives <'append', term, prev, pTerm, ents, commit>
    && term ≥ s.currentTerm
    && s.log[prev].term == pTerm
    && s.lastIndex ≤ prev + length(ents)
  then
    if term > s.currentTerm then
      s.isLeader = false
      s.currentTerm = term
    s.lastIndex = prev + length(ents)
    s.commitIndex = max(commit, s.commitIndex)
    replace entries after s.log[prev] with ents
    reply <'appendOK', s.currentTerm, s.lastIndex>

// the leader s learns the committed entries
function LeaderLearn(s):
  if s receives <'appendOK', term, index> from f acceptors with
       the same term
    && s.isLeader
    && term == s.currentTerm
  then
    minIndex = minimal received index
    s.commitIndex = max(s.commitIndex, minIndex)
```

(b) Phase 2

Figure 2: Raft*. The code in blue is introduced by Raft*

term at a given index, then these two logs are identical before the given index (log matching property). Furthermore, Raft is able to use the last entry's term (lastTerm) to detect if every entry in a log is more up-to-date. Second, Raft*'s leader directly appends entries into the log in AppendEntries and BecomeLeader. This can be considered as implicitly sending an append to itself, then receiving an appendOk from itself. Both explicit and implicit append/appendOk can imply accept/acceptOk. Last, a Raft*'s function may imply multiple functions in Paxos. For example, AppendEntries implies both Phase2a and Phase2b: the leader first implicitly accepts the entry, then sends it to others. The formal specification and the proof of the refinement mapping can be found in [37].

4 A METHOD FOR PORTING OPTIMIZATION

In this section, we show how to automatically port certain Paxos optimizations to Raft* by leveraging their refinement mapping. First, we define the problem of optimization porting formally (Section 4.1). We then characterize precisely which class of optimization is amicable to our method (Section 4.2). Lastly, we describe the algorithm to port the optimization such that the derived protocol specification is guaranteed to be correct (Section 4.3).

4.1 Problem definition

Specifying a protocol. To automatically port some optimization across protocols, we must describe a protocol and its optimization in a formal way. We specify a protocol as a state machine, which can be defined by its initial state and a set of allowed state transitions. We use the TLA$^+$ language [19] for specifying state machines.

In TLA$^+$, one specifies a protocol by describing the set of allowed state transitions called the *Next* action, represented as a collection of subactions $a_1 \lor a_2 \lor \ldots$ where $\lor$ is the or (disjunction) operator. Each subaction a_i is a formula in conjunctive form with one or more clauses; the clauses specify the state transition's enabling conditions and the next state value. As an example, we consider a key-value store supporting two operations Put(k, v) and Get(k). Figure 4a shows its TLA$^+$ specification. The key-value store's internal state is a hash table (table) where each entry corresponds to a set. Its next-state action (Next) consists of two subactions Put(k,v) and Get(k), for each potential key and value. In Figure 4a, the subaction Put(k, v) is defined to equal ($\triangleq$) to the boolean formula asserting that the hash table entry for key k must contain value v in the next state (line 2). In TLA$^+$, attaching the ' symbol with a variable represents its value in the new state. Hence the formula table'[k]={v} is true only when the hash table entry for key k in the next state equals to

		Raft*	**MultiPaxos**
variables	Constant	Quorums	Quorums
	per server	currentTerm isLeader entries with index ≤ commitIndex	ballot phase1succeeded chosenSet
	per instance	entry.index entry.val entry.bal	instance.id instance.val instance.bal
	messages	requestVote requestVoteOK (im/ex) append (im/ex) appendOK	prepare prepareOK accept acceptOK
functions		RequestVote	Phase1a
		ReceiveVote	Phase1b
		BecomeLeader	Phase1Succeed Phase2a Phase2b
		AppendEntries	Phase2a Phase2b
		ReceiveAppend	Phase2b
		LeaderLearn	Learn

Figure 3: Mapping between Raft* and MultiPaxos. "im" stands for implicit. "ex" stands for explicit

v. We use the output variable to represent value returned to users, thus `Get(k)` uses the clause output' = table[k] to assert the value of the output variable in the new state. In this example of $\mathcal{A}$, there is no subaction involving more than one clause in the conjunctive form because there is no enabling conditions for either Put or Get. We will see more sophisticated subactions in subsequent examples.

Refinement mapping with TLA$^+$. Using TLA$^+$ specifications, we can formally describe the refinement mapping. We use $\mathcal{B} \Rightarrow \mathcal{A}$ to refer that $\mathcal{B}$ has a refinement mapping to $\mathcal{A}$. (e.g., Raft* ⇒ Paxos). Let $Var_{\mathcal{A}}$ (or $Var_{\mathcal{B}}$) represent the state variables of $\mathcal{A}$ (or $\mathcal{B}$). To prove $\mathcal{B} \Rightarrow \mathcal{A}$, we need to find some function f that maps $\mathcal{B}$'s state space to $\mathcal{A}$'s, i.e., $Var_{\mathcal{A}} = f(Var_{\mathcal{B}})$. Suppose a_i is some subaction in $\mathcal{A}$, we use the term $\overline{a_i}$ to refer to the conjunctive formula when we substitute $Var_{\mathcal{A}}$ in a_i with $Var_{\mathcal{A}} = f(Var_{\mathcal{B}})$. If $\mathcal{B}$ refines $\mathcal{A}$ under f, then every subaction b_i in $\mathcal{B}$ implies some subaction a_j in $\mathcal{A}$ or a no-op step[1], i.e. $b_i \Rightarrow \overline{a_j} \vee f(Var'_{\mathcal{B}}) = f(Var_{\mathcal{B}})$, where $\Rightarrow$ is the boolean operator for implication.

Figure 4b shows an example protocol $\mathcal{B}$ which stores data in a log. Subaction Write(i, v) stores a value at the end of the log at index i. The conjunctive clause at line 2 ensures the invariant that values are stored in the log continuously. Subaction Read(i) reads the log entry i. Protocol $\mathcal{B}$ in Figure 4b refines protocol $\mathcal{A}$ in Figure 4a under the state mapping that maps the i-th entry of the log to the hash table entry with key $k = i$. The subaction Write in $\mathcal{B}$ implies Put in $\mathcal{A}$, and Read implies Get. The formal proof of the refinement between $\mathcal{A}$ and $\mathcal{B}$ can be found in [37].

Defining the problem of porting optimization. Informally, given two protocols $\mathcal{A}$ and $\mathcal{B}$, $\mathcal{B} \Rightarrow \mathcal{A}$, we would like to adapt some existing optimization on protocol $\mathcal{A}$ to also work for protocol $\mathcal{B}$. More importantly, we require the adaption to follow an algorithmic (instead of manual) procedure that can guarantee the correctness of the resulting protocol.

[1]The no-op step is commonly called a stuttering step [1, 23]

To state the task formally, we are given some protocol $\mathcal{A}$, its optimized version $\mathcal{A}^{\Delta}$, and another protocol $\mathcal{B}$ which refines $\mathcal{A}$, all specified in TLA$^+$. Furthermore, we assume that all three protocols $\mathcal{A}$, $\mathcal{A}^{\Delta}$, $\mathcal{B}$ have been proven correct. The problem of porting an optimization is to automatically derive the TLA$^+$ specification of protocol $\mathcal{B}^{\Delta}$ such that $\mathcal{B}^{\Delta}$ improves the performance of $\mathcal{B}$ and is guaranteed to be correct. We note that the goal is to derive the TLA$^+$ specification of an optimized protocol, not to automatically generate the implementation of the optimized protocol.

The optimization porting problem as stated above is quite general. In particular, we do not make any assumptions on the types of correctness proofs given for the protocols, nor on any formal relationships between $\mathcal{A}$ and $\mathcal{A}^{\Delta}$. However, in order to make the problem trackable, we devise a solution that only applies to a restricted class of optimization, which is described next.

4.2 Non-mutating optimization

Given protocol $\mathcal{A}$ and its optimized variant $\mathcal{A}^{\Delta}$, we consider the optimization to be the difference between the specification of $\mathcal{A}^{\Delta}$ and $\mathcal{A}$. In particular, the state variables of $\mathcal{A}^{\Delta}$ include all state variables of $\mathcal{A}$ and may contain additional variables introduced by the optimization. Each subaction of $\mathcal{A}^{\Delta}$ can be of three forms:

- *An added subaction.* This is a subaction that has no relationships to existing subactions in $\mathcal{A}$.
- *An unchanged subaction.* This is a subaction that is identical to an existing subaction in $\mathcal{A}$.
- *A modified subaction.* This is a subaction derived from an existing subaction in $\mathcal{A}$ by adding extra conjunctive clauses.[2]

Our proposed method for porting an optimization works for a restricted class of optimizations, which we refer to as *non-mutating optimization.* For an optimization $\mathcal{A}^{\Delta}$ to be considered as non-mutating, we require that none of its added subactions and none of the added clauses in its modified subactions mutate the state variables of $\mathcal{A}$ ($Var_{\mathcal{A}}$). The subactions are free to mutate the new state variables (Var_{Δ}) added by $\mathcal{A}^{\Delta}$.

Figure 4c shows protocol $\mathcal{A}^{\Delta}$, as an example of non-mutating optimization on the key-value store protocol $\mathcal{A}$. The optimized protocol $\mathcal{A}^{\Delta}$ adds a new state variable size that tracks how many values have been stored in the hash table. Comparing Figure 4c with Figure 4a, we can see that $\mathcal{A}^{\Delta}$ adds the new clause (line 4) to existing subaction Put and no new subactions. As the new clause does not modify $\mathcal{A}$'s state (table), $\mathcal{A}^{\Delta}$ is a non-mutating optimization.

Non-mutating optimization not only allows us to port optimization from $\mathcal{A}$ to $\mathcal{B}$ using the method in Section 4.3, it also has the added benefit that $\mathcal{A}^{\Delta}$ can be shown to refine $\mathcal{A}$ under the identical state mapping function that ignores the extra state. Therefore, non-mutating optimization always guarantees correctness. By contrast, state-mutating optimization may or may not have a refinement mapping to $\mathcal{A}$, and thus its correctness requires a separate proof.

```
VARIABLES table, output
Put(k, v) ≜ table'[k] = {v}
Get(k) ≜ output' = table[k]
Init ≜ ∀ k ∈ Nat: table[k] = {}
Next ≜ ∃ k ∈ Nat, v∈ Values: Put(k, v) ∨ Get(k)
```

(a) A key-value store ($\mathcal{A}$).

```
VARIABLES logs, output
Write(i, v) ≜ (i = 0 ∨ logs[i-1] ≠ {})
              ∧ logs'[i] = v
Read(i) ≜ output' = logs[i]
Init ≜ ∀ i ∈ Nat : logs[i] = {}
Next ≜ ∃ i ∈ Nat, v ∈ Values: Write(i, v) ∨ Read(i)
```

(b) The protocol $\mathcal{B}$ that stores data in a log. $\mathcal{B}$ refines the key-value store $\mathcal{A}$.

```
VARIABLES table, output, size
Put(k, v) ≜ table[k] = {}
            ∧ table'[k] = {v}
            ∧ size' = size + 1
Get(k) ≜ output' = table[k]
Init ≜ ∀ k ∈ Nat: table[k] = {} ∧ size = 0
Next ≜ ∃ k ∈ Nat, v ∈ Values: Put(k, v) ∨ Get(k)
```

(c) The optimized protocol $\mathcal{A}^\Delta$.

```
VARIABLES logs, output, size
Write(i, v) ≜ logs[i] = {}
              ∧ (i = 0 ∨ logs[i-1] ≠ {})
              ∧ logs'[i] = {v}
              ∧ size' = size + 1
Read(i) ≜ output' = logs[i]
Init ≜ ∀ k ∈ Nat: logs[i] = {} ∧ size = 0
Next ≜ ∃ i∈ Nat, v ∈ Values: Write(i, v) ∨ Read(i)
```

(d) The generated TLA$^+$ specification of $\mathcal{B}^\Delta$.

Figure 4: The TLA$^+$ specifications of the example.

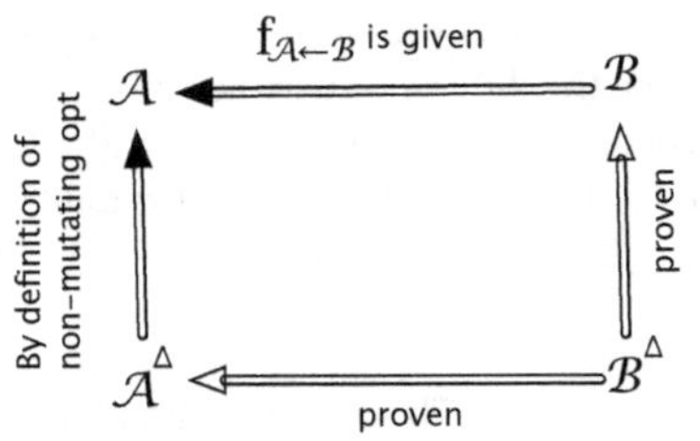

Figure 5: The refinement mappings among given protocols. $\mathcal{A}^\Delta$ is an optimized version of $\mathcal{A}$ using non-mutating optimization. $\mathcal{B}^\Delta$ is the optimized version of $\mathcal{B}$ generated by our method in Section 4.3.

4.3 How to port non-mutating optimization

We only consider the case of porting non-mutating optimizations. Additionally, if the optimization reads the parameters of protocol $\mathcal{A}$, our method also requires a *parameter mapping* from $\mathcal{B}$ to $\mathcal{A}$.

Parameter mapping. Let $P_\mathcal{A}$ and $P_\mathcal{B}$ be the parameter variables of $\mathcal{A}$ and $\mathcal{B}$, respectively. We say $\mathcal{B}$ has a parameter mapping to $\mathcal{A}$ if there exists a function f_{arg} that maps the arguments of subactions in $\mathcal{B}$ to the arguments of subactions in $\mathcal{A}$, i.e. $P_\mathcal{A} = f_{args}(P_\mathcal{B})$.[3] The extra clauses added in a modified subaction in $\mathcal{A}^\Delta$ may use parameter variables. Therefore, the parameter mapping is required in order to correctly translate those clauses to be used in a corresponding subaction in $\mathcal{B}^\Delta$.

Porting the optimization. We are now ready to describe how to transform the specification of $\mathcal{A}^\Delta$ to create $\mathcal{B}^\Delta$, thereby porting the optimization from $\mathcal{A}$ to $\mathcal{B}$. First, we obtain $\mathcal{B}^\Delta$'s state variables as $Var_{\mathcal{B}^\Delta} = Var_\mathcal{B} \cup Var_\Delta$. We also obtain $\mathcal{B}^\Delta$'s initial state ($Init_{\mathcal{B}^\Delta}$) from $Init_\mathcal{B}$ and $Init_{\mathcal{A}^\Delta}$ by replacing every state variable of $\mathcal{A}$ using the state mapping $Var_\mathcal{A} = f(Var_\mathcal{B})$. Next, we generate the subactions of $\mathcal{B}^\Delta$ from each subaction a_i^Δ of $\mathcal{A}^\Delta$ and the no-op step. There are three cases:

Case-1: a_i^Δ is an added subaction. We turn a_i^Δ into a corresponding added subaction b_i^Δ by substituting state variable Var_a with $f(Var_b)$ and keeping Var_Δ unchanged.

Case-2: a_i^Δ is an unchanged subaction which is equal to a^i in $\mathcal{A}$, or the no-op step. There is a set of subactions in $\mathcal{B}$ that imply a^i according to the refinement mapping $f_{\mathcal{B}\rightarrow\mathcal{A}}$. We directly add the set of subactions to $\mathcal{B}^\Delta$.

Case-3: a_i^Δ is a modified subaction of a^i in $\mathcal{A}$. Again, there is a set of subactions in $\mathcal{B}$ that imply a^i according to $f_{\mathcal{B}\rightarrow\mathcal{A}}$. Suppose b_j is a subaction in the set. We add b_j to $\mathcal{B}^\Delta$ if b_j is not already added (Case-2). Furthermore, we include the extra clauses added by a_i^Δ in b_j by substituting $Var_a = f(Var_b)$ and $P_a = f_{args}(P_b)$.

Correctness. We prove that the generated specification of $\mathcal{B}^\Delta$ is correct. The proof contains two parts. First, we need to show that $\mathcal{B}^\Delta$ correctly incorporates the optimization in $\mathcal{A}^\Delta$. This can be proven by demonstrating that $\mathcal{B}^\Delta$ refines $\mathcal{A}^\Delta$, thus $\mathcal{B}^\Delta$ preserves the invariants introduced by the optimization. Second, we also need to show that $\mathcal{B}^\Delta$ remains correct w.r.t. the original protocol $\mathcal{B}$. This can be proven by demonstrating that $\mathcal{B}^\Delta$ refines $\mathcal{B}$, thus $\mathcal{B}^\Delta$ preserves the invariants of the original protocol $\mathcal{B}$.

As a summary, Figure 5 illustrates the refinement mappings that exist among the four protocols, $\mathcal{A}$, $\mathcal{B}$, $\mathcal{A}^\Delta$, $\mathcal{B}^\Delta$. Next, we provide proof sketches for the refinement mappings of $\mathcal{B}^\Delta$.

First, we prove that $\mathcal{B}^\Delta$ refines $\mathcal{A}^\Delta$ using the state mapping function that maps the state variables of $\mathcal{B}$ to those of $\mathcal{A}$ according to f and leaves the variables introduced by optimization Δ unchanged. To prove the correctness of this refinement mapping, we must show that $\mathcal{B}^\Delta$'s initial state implies Init$_{\mathcal{A}^\Delta}$, and $\mathcal{B}^\Delta$'s next-state action (Next$_{\mathcal{B}^\Delta}$) implies Next$_{\mathcal{A}^\Delta}$. The former implication is relatively straightforward, so we focus the discussion on the latter.

[2] If the derivation deletes an existing conjunctive clause, then the resulting subaction of $\mathcal{A}^\Delta$ must be viewed as an added subaction instead of a modified one.

[3] To put it more formally, given parameter mapping $P_\mathcal{A} = f_{args}(P_\mathcal{B})$, we use $\overline{Next_\mathcal{A}}$ to refer to the formula after substituting state variables Var_a with $f(Var_b)$ and parameter variables $P_\mathcal{A}$ with $f_{args}(\mathcal{B})$. f_{args} is a valid parameter mapping if $Next_\mathcal{B} \Rightarrow \overline{Next_\mathcal{A}}$.

To show $\text{Next}_{\mathcal{B}^\Delta}$ implies $\text{Next}_{\mathcal{A}^\Delta}$, we show that each $\mathcal{B}^\Delta$'s subaction (b_i^Δ) implies some subaction of $\mathcal{A}^\Delta$ or a no-op step. According to our method, b_i^Δ can be added to $\mathcal{B}^\Delta$ in one of three cases. For case-1 and 2, it is easy to show that b_i^Δ implies a_i^Δ or the no-op step by construction. In case-3, b_i^Δ is constructed from b_i and a subaction a_j^Δ in $\mathcal{A}^\Delta$, such that $a_j^\Delta = a_j \wedge \Delta_{a_j}$, $b_i^\Delta = b_i \wedge \overline{\Delta_{a_j}}$. Δ_{a_j} is the set of extra conjunctive clauses added by the optimization to a_j to form a_j^Δ. $\overline{\Delta_{a_j}}$ is obtained from Δ_{a_j} by substituting variables $Var_a = f_{\mathcal{B}\rightarrow\mathcal{A}}(Var_b)$ and parameters P_a by $f_{args}(P_b)$. Because of $b_i \Rightarrow \overline{a_j}$, we have $b_i^\Delta \Rightarrow \overline{a_j} \wedge \overline{\Delta_{a_j}}$ which is equivalent to $b_i^\Delta \Rightarrow \overline{a_j^\Delta}$.

Next, we prove that $\mathcal{B}^\Delta$ refines $\mathcal{B}$, using the state mapping function that simply drops the new variables added by the optimization. To prove $\mathcal{B}^\Delta$ refines $\mathcal{B}$, we argue that $\mathcal{B}^\Delta$ is a non-mutating optimization by analyzing the three cases of our method. We leave the details to [37].

5 PORTING PAXOS OPTIMIZATION TO RAFT*.

The landscape of Paxos variants and optimization. We first study existing Paxos variants and optimizations using the lens of our method. Figure 6 shows the relationship between these protocols. Among them, six protocols belong to the class of non-mutating optimization for Paxos, shown in the double-lined box in Figure 6. Thus, these six optimizations can potentially be ported from Paxos to Raft* using our method. Flexible Paxos [11] relaxes the majority quorum restriction in Paxos to allow differently sized quorums as long as the quorums used in the two phases of Paxos exchange are guaranteed to intersect. As a result, Paxos refines Flexible Paxos but not the other way around. WPaxos [3] is a recently proposed non-mutating optimization on Flexible Paxos. Therefore, our method could also be used to port the optimization of WPaxos to Paxos.

As for the rest of the protocol variants (shown in the left-most box in Figure 6), their relationships to Paxos cannot be captured by refinement mapping. The reasons for the lack of refinement mapping are varied. For example, Fast Paxos changes the quorum size of Paxos to include a super-majority, which prevents a refinement mapping from Fast Paxos to Paxos. However, it also misses state transitions allowed in Paxos, which precludes a refinement mapping from Paxos to Fast Paxos.

Among the six candidate protocols, we choose to port two optimizations as case studies: Paxos Quorum Lease [28] and Mencius [25]. We explain what these optimizations are and how they are ported to Raft*. Our discussion uses pseudocode instead of TLA$^+$ for simplicity. A more formal description (including the refinement mapping, pseudocode, and TLA$^+$) can be found in the extended version of the paper [37].

Paxos Quorum Lease. In Paxos, a strongly consistent read operation is performed by persisting the operation into the log as if it were a write. Paxos Quorum Lease (PQL) [28] introduces an optimization that allows any replica to read locally if the replica holds leases from a quorum of replicas (*quorum-lease*).

Quorum-lease can co-exist perfectly with the quorum in Paxos. Any replica can grant a lease. A replica considers itself holding a quorum-lease if it holds leases from a quorum of replicas. Any lease-quorum must overlap with any Paxos quorum (usually both quorums are majorities of replicas). In Paxos any commit needs to collect from a quorum of acknowledgments, which will intersect with the lease quorum. Therefore, as long as we require every replica in a Paxos quorum to notify their granted lease holders before the replica commits any values, the system is safe—both read and write are consistent.

PQL is a non-mutating variant of Paxos, because all its added and modified subactions do not change the state variables in Paxos. Figure 7 shows the algorithmic changes introduced by PQL. The actions changed are Phase2b and Learn. In Phase2b, a server attaches all leases it granted with the "acceptOk" response (line 143). By collecting the granted leases from a quorum (line 146), a learner can find all servers who hold active leases (line 148), and commits an instance only if it receives "acceptOk" from these holders (line 150). The added actions are Read and LocalRead. When a client issues a "localRead" request, the server will return its local copy if it holds valid leases granted by a quorum, and all committed updates are in the chosen set (line 136-137).

Raft*-PQL. Figure 8 shows the algorithm after applying PQL to Raft*. The code in blue shows the changed part after porting the optimization to Raft*. For a replica to perform a local read, the replica needs to check if two conditions hold. First, the replica must be holding leases from at least $f + 1$ replicas (including itself). Second, the replica needs to wait until commitIndex is greater than the largest index of entries which modify the target record (line 156). This is transformed from PQL where all modifications must be in the chosenSet (line 137).

A replica attaches the lease holders granted by itself in appendOk message, which maps to the acceptOk message. In LeaderLearn, the leader needs to collect the holders of leases attached in the messages and granted by itself (line 165). This is because the f appendOk messages with one extra implicit appendOk message imply $f + 1$ acceptOk messages in Paxos. Thus, collecting leases attached in $f + 1$ messages (line 148) is transformed into collecting the leases from f messages and local granted (the implicit message).

Mencius. Paxos requires all clients requests to be sent to a leader for better throughput. This could lead to unbalanced load between the leader replica and other replicas. When replicas are located in different data centers, non-leader replicas will need at least two wide-area round-trips to commit any requests because requests need to be forwarded to the leader. To address these issues, Mencius [25] partitions the Paxos instances so that each replica serves as the default leader for a distinct subset of instances. With geo-replicas, a client can send its requests to the nearest replica. The replica can commit these requests using those Paxos instances for which it is the default leader. Thus, Mencius can balance the load among all replicas and also reduces wide-area round-trips.

Mencius partitions the instance (log) space in a round-robin way. For example, in a system with three replicas r_1, r_2, r_3, r_1 is the default leader for log entries $(0, 3, 6, ...)$, r_2 is the leader for $(1, 4, 7, ...)$, and r_3 for $(2, 5, 8, ...)$. Mencius separates the execution of a log entry from its commit. The log is executed sequentially. If some default leader has not received any user-submitted operations, it commits skip entries to keep log execution progressing forward. To prevent a crashed replica from delaying the system, the instances belong to that replica can be committed as no-op by other replicas.

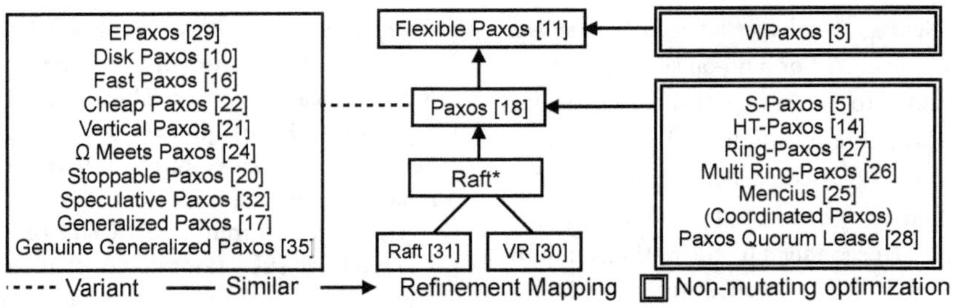

Figure 6: The relationship of different Paxos variants and optimization.

```
function Read(c, k):
  c sends <'localRead', k> to 1 server s
  if c receives <'ReadReply', v> from s
  then
    return v

function LocalRead(s):
  if s receives <'localRead', k>
    && s.validLeasesNum ≥ f + 1
    && all instances modified k are in chosenSet
  then
    s replies <'ReadReply', LocalCopy(k)>

function Phase2b(s):
    ...
    s replies <'acceptOk',..., leases granted by s>

function Learn(s):
  if s receives <'acceptOk', i, v, b, s, leases> from f + 1
       acceptors
  then
    holderSet = holders of received leases

  if s receives <'acceptOk', ... > from all holders in holderSet
  then
    ...
```

Figure 7: Paxos Quorum Lease

```
function LocalRead(s):
  if s receives <'localRead', k>
    && s.validLeasesNum ≥ f + 1
    && indexes of entries in s.log modified k ≤ s.commitIndex
  then
    ...

function LeaderLearn(s):
  if s receives <'appendOK', t, index, holders> from f acceptors
    && s.isLeader
    && s.currentTerm == t
  then
    holderSet = received holders ∪ holders of leases granted by
         the leader
  if s receives <'appendOK', ... > from all holders in holderSet
  then
    ...
```

Figure 8: Raft*-PQL

These optimizations help Mencius commit and execute requests within 1.5 round-trips on average.

Raft*-Mencius. The complete pseudocode of Raft*-Mencius is included in [37]. We describe some interesting details here. In addition to the Paxos state variables, each replica needs to keep an array of "skip-tags" to track those log entries that can be skipped. When a replica becomes the leader, it needs to collect not only values but also skip-tags from other replicas. Because Phase2b action in Paxos corresponds to many actions (AppendEntries, ReceiveAppend) in Raft*, whatever changes Mencius makes to Phase2b should be applied to these actions as well. As an example, if the newly appended entries are skip entries, they should be marked as executable.

Because Phase2b in Paxos is implied by multiple sub-actions in Raft*, it is possible that manual efforts for porting Mencius may miss some of the actions. For example, if the manual solution only applies changes on Phase2b in Paxos to ReceiveAppend in Raft* and miss AppendEntries, the solution could miss some optimization opportunities or even result in an incorrect protocol.

6 EVALUATION

This section shows that the generated algorithms achieve similar optimization effects with their Paxos counterparts [28, 25]. In particular, Raft*-PQL reduces the latency of read requests by performing local read. Raft*-Mencius improves the throughput by balancing the workload across all replicas. Our porting method guarantees the correctness of these derived algorithms. However, the extra effort is still needed for the implementation.

Testbed. The experiments were conducted on Amazon EC2 across 5 different geographical regions: Oregon, Ohio, Ireland, Canada and Seoul. In each region, two m4.xlarge instances are used for the client and server processes respectively. Each instance has 4 virtual CPUs, 16GB memory and one SSD with 750 Mbps bandwidth. The latency across sites varies from 25ms to 292ms.

Workload. Our evaluation uses closed-loop clients with a YCSB alike workload: each client issues get or put requests back-to-back. The system is initialized with 100K records. To simulate contention, each client accesses the same popular record at a configured rate (i.e., conflict rate). When not accessing the popular record, the key space is pre-partitioned among the datacenters evenly, and a key is selected from this partition with uniform probability. Raft*-PQL is evaluated with 90% read by default. For Raft*-Mencius, we use a workload with 100% writes. Each trial is run for 50 seconds with 10 seconds for both warm-up and cool-down. Each number reported is the median in 5 trials.

Implementation. The implementation of Raft* is based on a popular industrial Raft codebase—etcd (version c4fc8c09). Etcd has a few important optimizations. First, it has a customized network layer for efficient communication. Second, when a follower receives multiple requests from clients, it forwards them to the leader in a

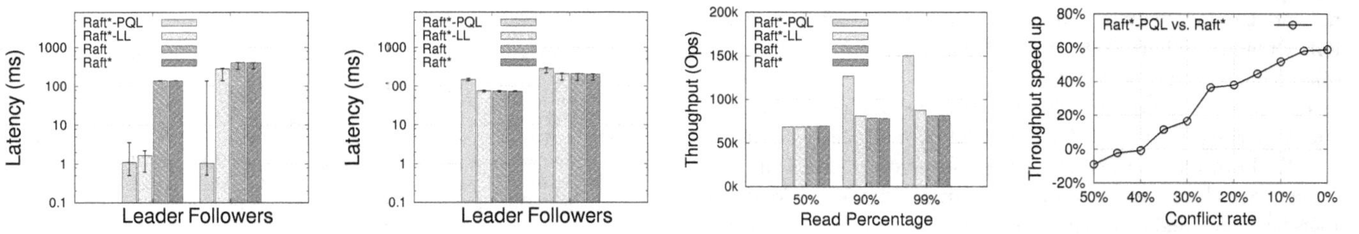

(a) Read latency (b) Write latency (c) Peak throughput (d) Speedup of Raft*-PQL over Raft

Figure 9: Raft*-PQL vs. LL vs. Raft. Each bar in (a) and (b) represents the 90th percentile latency of the requests with an error bar from the 50th to 99th percentiles. The y-axis is in log scale for (a) and (b).

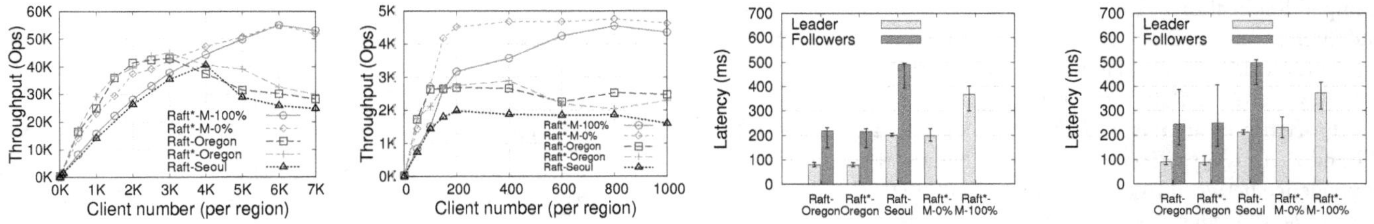

(a) Throughput - 8B (b) Throughput - 4KB (c) Latency - 8B (d) Latency - 4KB

Figure 10: Raft*-Mencius vs. Raft. Raft*-M-100% and Raft*-M-0% stand for Raft*-Mencius with workload under 100% and 0% conflict rate. Raft-Oregon and Raft-Seoul stand for the leader is in Oregon or Seoul. 8B and 4KB are the request size of the workload.

batch. Such techniques improve system throughput when follower servers accept client requests. In our tests, etcd is 2.4× better in throughput when these optimizations are turned on. We keep these optimizations on in our tests to give etcd extra advantages. Oregon is used as the leader site for etcd which gives it the best result since Oregon has the best network condition.

6.1 Raft*-PQL

We evaluate Raft*-PQL with the same lease parameters in [28]: the lease duration is 2 seconds, is renewed for every 0.5 seconds. We also compare Raft*-PQL with Leader Lease (LL). Here the leader has sole ownership of the lease, so only the leader can process a read request with its local copy. We use 90% read workload with 5% conflict rate by default.

Latency. First, we compare the latency with 50 clients per region. In Raft*-PQL, any server with an active lease is able to conduct local consistent reads, thus 90% of the read requests have only 1ms latency (Figure 9a). In comparison, for LL, only the leader can process read request with similar latency (1.6 ms). Raft*-PQL has 1% read requests have high latency (~137ms) on followers. This is because 5% contention in the workload: followers need to wait for conflicting write to commit before processing the read request. For write latency (Figure 9b) Raft*-PQL is a little bit higher than others, as it needs to wait for leaseholders' acknowledge to commit a write operation, while others can always choose the fastest majority.

Throughput. Figure 9c shows how is the peak throughput affected by reading percentage (50%, 90%, and 99%). Raft, Raft* and LL achieve almost the same peak throughput, as the leader's CPU is the bottleneck, and the saturated leader CPU has the same capability to handle requests for these algorithms. In contrast, Raft*-PQL achieves 1.6× and 1.9× speedup with 90% and 99% reads. The advantage is from conducting the read requests locally. Figure 9d shows how is the throughput speedup affected by the conflict rate. The figure does not show the speedup of Raft*-PQL over Raft*, as they are similar. The speedup increases with the decreasing of conflict rate since all followers can return read requests to the user immediately under a low conflict rate.

6.2 Raft*-Mencius

We use a 100% put workload to measure Raft*-Mencius with 0% and 100% contention, marked as Raft*-Mencius-0% and Raft*-Mencius-100% respectively. To make a fair comparison, we evaluate both the best and worst case scenarios for Raft in the wide area by placing the leader in the nearest (Oregon) and farthest (Seoul) servers to all other regions (Raft-Oregon and Raft-Seoul). We only evaluate Raft* with the leader at Oregon for reference.

Throughput. Figure 10a gives throughput when the system is bounded by the CPU. Raft*-Mencius can achieve a peak throughput of 55K operations per second (ops) since it balances the load among all replicas. In contrast, other systems can reach the peak throughput of 41K ops after their leaders' CPUs are saturated. Figure 10b gives throughput when the system is network bounded. Raft reaches the peak throughput after saturating leader's network bandwidth. Raft-Oregon has 30% higher throughput than Raft-Seoul as Oregon has higher bandwidth. Raft*-Mencius has 70% higher throughput than Raft-Oregon because it is able to utilize all replicas' network bandwidth. In both figures, with a small number of clients, Raft-Oregon and Raft*-Mencius-0% have better performance than others due to their lower latency.

Latency. Figure 10c and Figure 10d show the latency with 50 clients per region. The leader of Raft-Oregon processes requests with the lowest latency (79ms), as the quorum of Oregon, Ohio, and Canada are closest to each other. In comparison, Raft*-Mencius-100% has much higher 90% percentile latency, while Raft*-Mencius-0% has lower latency because of the different contention levels.

7 RELATED WORK

Elementary consensus protocols. In addition to Raft [31] and Paxos [18], there are many alternative protocols. For example, Viewstamped Replication (VR) [30] was published earlier than Paxos, and ZooKeeper [12] uses ZAB [13]. Our method is also suitable for these protocols. In particular, we can connect these protocols with Paxos by crafting a Raft* similar protocol.

Algorithm comparison. Renesse et al. [36] compared Paxos to VR and ZAB using *refinement mapping*. Lamport[15] discuss the equivalence between Byzantine Paxos and PBFT [7] is discussed. Song et al. [34] identified common traits in the Paxos, Chandra-Toueg [8], and Ben-Or [4] consensus algorithms. Abraham and Malkhi [2] discussed the connections between BFT consensus protocols and block-chain protocols. Compared to these works, we have two notable differences: we use a formal method TLA$^+$ [19] to model the refinement mappings [1]; we have mechanically exported the optimizations from one family of protocols to another.

Paxos variants and optimizations. Figure 6 has shown a number of Paxos variants. Among the non-mutating variants, WPaxos [3] partitions object and use flexible quorums for geo-replication [11]; HT-Paxos [14] and S-Paxos [5] assigns ordering tasks to multiple servers to remove bottlenecks. Ring Paxos [27] and Multi Ring-Paxos [26] partition the workload and achieve better performance. Among the mutating Paxos variants: Cheap Paxos [22] introduces auxiliary servers. Ω meets Paxos [24] elects a stable leader in a weak network environment. NetPaxos [9] adapts Paxos to SDN. Stoppable Paxos [20] is able to perform reconfiguration without slowing down. Additionally, Shraer et al. [33] and Vertical Paxos [21] discusses how to reconfigure a replicated state machine. Disk Paxos [10] achieves consensus in a disk cluster. Fast Paxos [16] and Multi-coordinated Paxos [6] introduce a fast quorum to reach consensus with a single round-trip. Generalized Paxos [17], Genuine Generalized Paxos [35] and EPaxos [29] resolve conflicts because execution. Speculative Paxos [32] introduces speculative execution when messages are delivered in order.

ACKNOWLEDGMENTS

We sincerely thank our anonymous reviewers for their insightful comments. We thank Lamont Nelson for his help and Aurojit Panda for his feedback on this work. This work is supported by the National Key Research & Development Program of China (No. 2016YFB1000104), NSF grant CNS-1409942 and CNS-1514422, and AFOSR FA9550-15-1-0302.

REFERENCES

[1] M. Abadi, AND L. Lamport The existence of refinement mappings. *Theoretical Computer Science* 82, 2 (1991).

[2] I. Abraham, D. Malkhi, K. Nayak, L. Ren, AND A. Spiegelman Solida: A cryptocurrency based on reconfigurable byzantine consensus. In *Proc. OPODIS*. 2017.

[3] A. Ailijiang, A. Charapko, M. Demirbas, AND T. Kosar WPaxos: Wide Area Network Flexible Consensus. *arXiv preprint arXiv:1703.08905* (2017).

[4] M. Ben-Or Another advantage of free choice (extended abstract): completely asynchronous agreement protocols. In *Proc. PODC*. Aug. 1983.

[5] M. Biely, Z. Milosevic, N. Santos, AND A. Schiper S-Paxos: offloading the leader for high throughput state machine replication. In *Proc. SRDS*. Oct. 2012.

[6] L. J. Camargos, R. M. Schmidt, AND F. Pedone Multicoordinated Paxos. In *Proc. PODC*. Aug. 2007.

[7] M. Castro, AND B. Liskov Practical byzantine fault tolerance. In *Proc. OSDI*. Feb. 1999.

[8] T. D. Chandra, AND S. Toueg Unreliable failure detectors for reliable distributed systems. *JACM* 43, 2 (Mar. 1996).

[9] H. T. Dang, D. Sciascia, M. Canini, F. Pedone, AND R. Soulé Netpaxos: Consensus at network speed. In *Proceedings of the 1st ACM SIGCOMM Symposium on Software Defined Networking Research*. 2015.

[10] E. Gafni, AND L. Lamport Disk paxos. *DC* (2003).

[11] H. Howard, D. Malkhi, AND A. Spiegelman Flexible paxos: Quorum intersection revisited. *arXiv preprint arXiv:1608.06696* (2016).

[12] P. Hunt, M. Konar, F. P. Junqueira, AND B. Reed ZooKeeper: wait-free coordination for internet-scale systems. In *Proc. USENIX ATC*. June 2010.

[13] F. P. Junqueira, B. C. Reed, AND M. Serafini Zab: high-performance broadcast for primary-backup systems. In *Proc. DSN*. June 2011.

[14] V. Kumar, AND A. Agarwal HT-Paxos: high throughput state-machine replication protocol for large clustered data centers. *The Scientific World Journal* (2015).

[15] L. Lamport Byzantizing Paxos by refinement. In *Proc. DISC*. July 2011.

[16] L. Lamport Fast Paxos. *DC* 19, 2 (Oct. 2006).

[17] L. Lamport *Generalized consensus and Paxos*. Tech. rep. MSR-TR-2005-33. Microsoft Research, 2005.

[18] L. Lamport Paxos made simple. *SIGACT* 32, 4 (2001).

[19] L. Lamport *Specifying systems: the TLA+ language and tools for hardware and software engineers*. Addison-Wesley Longman Publishing Co., Inc., 2002.

[20] L. Lamport, D. Malkhi, AND L. Zhou Reconfiguring a state machine. *ACM SIGACT News* (2010).

[21] L. Lamport, D. Malkhi, AND L. Zhou Vertical Paxos and primary-backup replication. In *Proc. PODC*. Aug. 2009.

[22] L. Lamport, AND M. Massa Cheap Paxos. In *Proc. DSN*. June 2004.

[23] L. Lamport, AND S. Merz Auxiliary variables in TLA+. *arXiv preprint arXiv:1703.05121* (2017).

[24] D. Malkhi, F. Oprea, AND L. Zhou Ω meets paxos: Leader election and stability without eventual timely links. In *Proc. DISC*. 2005.

[25] Y. Mao, F. P. Junqueira, AND K. Marzullo Mencius: building efficient replicated state machines for WANs. In *Proc. OSDI*. Dec. 2008.

[26] P. J. Marandi, M. Primi, AND F. Pedone Multi-ring paxos. In *Proc. DSN*. 2012.

[27] P. J. Marandi, M. Primi, N. Schiper, AND F. Pedone Ring Paxos: A high-throughput atomic broadcast protocol. In *Proc. DSN*. 2010.

[28] I. Moraru, D. G. Andersen, AND M. Kaminsky Paxos quorum leases: Fast reads without sacrificing writes. In *Proc. SoCC*. Nov. 2014.

[29] I. Moraru, D. G. Andersen, AND M. Kaminsky There is more consensus in egalitarian parliaments. In *Proc. SOSP*. Nov. 2013.

[30] B. M. Oki, AND B. H. Liskov Viewstamped replication: A new primary copy method to support highly-available distributed systems. In *Proc. PODC*. June 1988.

[31] D. Ongaro, AND J. K. Ousterhout In search of an understandable consensus algorithm. In *Proc. USENIX ATC*. June 2014.

[32] D. R. Ports, J. Li, V. Liu, N. K. Sharma, AND A. Krishnamurthy Designing distributed systems using approximate synchrony in data center networks. In *Proc. NSDI*. May 2015.

[33] A. Shraer, B. Reed, D. Malkhi, AND F. P. Junqueira Dynamic reconfiguration of primary/backup clusters. In *Proc. USENIX ATC*. June 2012.

[34] Y. J. Song, R. van Renesse, F. B. Schneider, AND D. Dolev The building blocks of consensus. In *IEEE ICDCN*. Jan. 2008.

[35] P. Sutra, AND M. Shapiro Fast genuine generalized consensus. In *Proc. SRDS*. Oct. 2011.

[36] R. Van Renesse, N. Schiper, AND F. B. Schneider Vive la différence: Paxos vs. viewstamped replication vs. zab. *IEEE Transactions on Dependable and Secure Computing* 12, 4 (July 2015).

[37] W. Zhaoguo, Z. Changgeng, M. Shuai, C. Haibo, AND L. Jinyang On the parallels between Paxos and Raft, and how to port optimizations (Extended Version). *arXiv preprint arXiv:1905.10786* (2019).

Brief Announcement: Linearizable State Machine Replication of State-Based CRDTs without Logs*

Jan Skrzypczak†
Zuse Institute Berlin
Berlin, Germany
skrzypczak@zib.de

Florian Schintke†
Zuse Institute Berlin
Berlin, Germany
schintke@zib.de

Thorsten Schütt†
Zuse Institute Berlin
Berlin, Germany
schuett@zib.de

ABSTRACT

General solutions of state machine replication have to ensure that all replicas apply the same commands in the same order, even in the presence of failures. Such strict ordering incurs high synchronization costs due to the use of distributed consensus or a leader.

This paper presents a protocol for *linearizable* state machine replication of conflict-free replicated data types (CRDTs) that neither requires consensus nor a leader. By leveraging the properties of state-based CRDTs—in particular the monotonic growth of a join semilattice—synchronization overhead is greatly reduced. In addition, updates just need a single round trip and modify the state 'in-place' without the need for a log. Furthermore, the message size overhead for coordination consists of a single counter per message. While reads in the presence of concurrent updates are not wait-free without a coordinator, we show that more than 97 % of reads can be handled in one or two round trips under highly concurrent accesses.

Our protocol achieves high throughput without auxiliary processes such as command log management or leader election. It is well suited for all practical scenarios that need linearizable access on CRDT data on a fine-granular scale.

CCS CONCEPTS

• **Theory of computation** → **Distributed algorithms**; • **Computer systems organization** → *Dependable and fault-tolerant systems and networks.*

KEYWORDS

state machine replication; conflict-free replicated data types; generalized lattice agreement; linearizability

ACM Reference Format:
Jan Skrzypczak, Florian Schintke, and Thorsten Schütt. 2019. Brief Announcement: Linearizable State Machine Replication of State-Based CRDTs without Logs. In *2019 ACM Symposium on Principles of Distributed Computing (PODC'19), July 29–August 2, 2019, Toronto, ON, Canada.* ACM, New York, NY, USA, 3 pages. https://doi.org/10.1145/3293611.3331568

*The full version of the paper is available at [13].

†This work was supported by the German Research Foundation (DFG) under grant RE 1389 as part of the DFG priority program SPP 2037 (Scalable Data Management for Future Hardware).

ACM ISBN 978-1-4503-6217-7/19/07.
https://doi.org/10.1145/3293611.3331568

1 INTRODUCTION

Replicated state machines (RSMs) enable fault-tolerant services. They allow clients to submit *update* commands that modify the state of the replicated object, or *read* commands that return (part of) the RSMs' state. To guarantee linearizable [5] RSM access, all commands have to be applied in the same order at all replicas. This is commonly achieved by using a consensus protocol such as Paxos [8]. However, distributed consensus often incurs high synchronization overhead. To achieve acceptable performance, most approaches use a leader and maintain a command log that has to be regularly truncated to prevent unbounded memory consumption. This often makes implementing RSMs correctly a challenging task.

Some approaches avoid these challenges by using weaker consistency models such as strong eventual consistency (SEC). SEC was defined by Shapiro et al. [12] with the introduction of conflict-free replicated data types (CRDTs), which are data structures whose mathematical properties ensure convergence of all replicas as long as all updates are propagated to them in arbitrary order. They do not require protocol-level conflict resolution mechanisms, as conflicting updates can be resolved computationally. This allows the conflict-free execution of both reads and updates in relaxed consistency models such as SEC. Possible data structures with CRDT properties include counters, sets, and certain types of graphs [12]. Numerous practical systems have employed CRDTs, such as Riak [2], SoundCloud [1], and Akka [7]. However, their usage is restricted to cases where relaxed consistency models are sufficient. This prevents their usage for atomic counters, for example, which are a ubiquitous primitive in distributed computing.

This paper introduces a protocol to implement a special class of replicated state machines that allows linearizable access on CRDTs. These RSMs support *update* operations that modify the state and *read* operations that return a value but do not modify the state. By exploiting mathematical properties of CRDTs, our protocol achieves high throughput even in the absence of a leader, thereby eliminating the need to implement leader election mechanisms and allowing for continuous availability as long as a majority of replicas is reachable. Our protocol does not replicate a log of commands, which is commonly the case for consensus protocols. Instead, we replicate the state directly. This results in a protocol with memory and message size overhead of a single counter per replica, which avoids the complexity associated with command log management.

Related Work. Our approach relies on solving *generalized lattice agreement* (GLA) [3]. Values proposed in GLA belong to a join semilattice—a partially ordered set that defines a join (least upper bound) for all element pairs. In contrast, such a join does not have to always exist in generalized consensus [9]. This makes GLA an easier problem to solve. Falerio et al. [3] propose a wait-free [4] protocol for solving GLA in $\mathcal{O}(N)$ message delays, where N is the number of proposers. However, it requires sending ever-increasing sets of all proposed values in the messages. Imbs et al. [6] solve lattice agreement by introducing an SCD broadcast primitive, which is built on top of FIFO broadcast. SCD broadcasting a message requires $\mathcal{O}(N^2)$ messages. In our approach, message sizes are bounded by the CRDT's state. Updates need two message delays with $\mathcal{O}(N)$ messages. Reads are not wait-free under concurrent updates, but our evaluation shows that more than 97 % of reads are handled within two round trips, with each round trip sending $\mathcal{O}(N)$ messages.

2 STATE-BASED CRDTS

In the eventual consistency model, updates are applied at some replica and at a later time propagated across the system. Eventually, all replicas receive all updates, possibly in different orders. However, concurrent updates may create conflicts. Resolving them often requires roll-backs and consensus decisions. The use of conflict-free replicated data types (CRDTs) [12] eliminates the need for roll-backs or consensus by leveraging mathematical properties preventing the emergence of conflicts. State-based CRDTs rely on the monotonicity in a join semilattice:

Definition 1 (Join Semilattice). *A join semilattice $\mathcal{S}$ is a set S equipped with a partial order $\sqsubseteq$ and a least upper bound (LUB) $\sqcup$ for all pairs of elements $x, y \in S$.*

The LUB of two elements $x, y \in S$ is the smallest element in S that is equal or larger than both x and y.

Definition 2 (Least Upper Bound). *$m = x \sqcup y$ is a LUB of $\{x, y\}$ under partial order $\sqsubseteq$ iff:*

$$\forall m' \in S,\ x \sqsubseteq m' \land y \sqsubseteq m' : \quad x \sqsubseteq m \ \land \ y \sqsubseteq m \ \land \ m \sqsubseteq m'$$

It follows that $\sqcup$ is idempotent, commutative, and associative.

Definition 3 (State-Based CRDT). *A state-based CRDT is a triple $(\mathcal{S}, Q, U)$, where $\mathcal{S}$ is a join semilattice defining the possible payload states S, Q is a set of query functions, and U is a set of monotonically non-decreasing update functions, i.e., $\forall u \in U, s \in S : s \sqsubseteq u(s)$.*

Payload states $s_1, s_2 \in S$ are *equivalent* ($s_1 \equiv s_2$) if all queries return the same result for both, i.e., $s_1 \sqsubseteq s_2 \land s_2 \sqsubseteq s_1 \implies s_1 \equiv s_2$. They are *comparable* if they can be ordered, i.e., $s_1 \sqsubseteq s_2 \lor s_2 \sqsubseteq s_1$.

3 PROBLEM STATEMENT

We consider a state-based CRDT $(\mathcal{S}, Q, U)$ replicated on N independent and asynchronous processes $\Pi = \{p_1, p_2, \ldots, p_N\}$, which communicate by message passing using unreliable communication links (messages can be lost, arrive out of order, or can be delayed). We assume over Π a fixed quorum system QS [14], i.e., a set of sets of processes with mutual overlap. Elements in QS are *quorums*. Processes can fail under the crash-recovery model without losing their internal state upon recovery. We assume that at least a quorum does not crash and is able to pairwise exchange messages.

Each process starts with an initial state $s_0 \in S$. Clients can submit update $u \in U$ or query $q \in Q$ commands to any process, and each process may receive an arbitrary number of commands. Updates modify the state of the CRDT but do not return its value, whereas queries return the latest value but do not modify the CRDT's state. As a prerequisite to achieving linearizability for query q that is submitted to process p, p must first *learn* state $s \in S$ by exchanging messages with the other processes before returning $q(s)$. We say that s is the state learned by query q at process p.

All learned values must satisfy the following safety conditions, which are based on Generalized Lattice Agreement [3]:

Validity Any learned state is equivalent to some set of submitted update functions applied on s_0.

Stability For any two states $s_1, s_2 \in S$ learned by *subsequent* queries q_1 and $q_2 \in Q$ at any two processes: $s_1 \sqsubseteq s_2$.

Consistency Any two states s_1 and s_2 learned at any two processes are comparable.

In addition to queries, the behavior of updates must be considered as well to provide linearizable access [3]. We say that a state s *includes* update u, if $s = u(s')$, $s = u'(s'')$ where s'' includes u, or $s = s_1 \sqcup s_2$ with s_1 and/or s_2 being a state that includes u.

Update Stability If the execution of update u_1 completes before update u_2 is submitted, then every learned state that includes u_2 also includes u_1.

Update Visibility If the execution of update u completes before query q is submitted, then the state learned of the query q includes u.

4 PROTOCOL OVERVIEW

Next, we give a brief overview of the protocol. More details and a proof of safety can be found in the full paper [13].

The protocol is described in terms of *proposers* that process incoming requests and *acceptors* that act as replicated CRDT storage. We assume that all processes implement both acceptor and proposer. The success path of the protocol is shown in Algorithm 1. Processes communicate by exchanging messages, which are tuples of elements prepended with a tag and denoted as $\langle TAG, e_0, \ldots, e_n \rangle$. Processes execute at most one action at a time if they have received enough messages with the corresponding

tag. If an action requires messages from a quorum, we aggregate them element-wise into multisets (e.g., see line 21 and 45).

Update and query commands are handled separately. Updates are processed in a single round trip by applying the received function f_u locally and sending the resulting state s' to all other acceptors. The update is completed once a quorum has acknowledged that it has merged s' into their local state (denoted as s).

Concurrent query commands are synchronized by a modified variant of the Paxos algorithm [8] in order to satisfy the safety conditions stated above. Thus, liveness is not guaranteed (without a leader). In the style of Paxos, *rounds* are used to order concurrent requests. Round r is a tuple $(number, ID)$, with r_{nr} and r_{id} providing access to r's round number and ID. Rounds can be totally ordered by first comparing their numbers and then their IDs. Acceptors store the highest round they have seen as r.

The query protocol consists of up to two phases. In the first phase, a proposer p chooses a round and sends *PREPARE* messages to all acceptors. The round can be chosen by letting acceptors increment their local round numbers (line 9) or by choosing a round number based on previous knowledge (line 19). An acceptor acknowledges

Algorithm 1 Linearizable state machine replication of state-based CRDTs

```
Proposer:
-------------- Update Commands --------------
1:  on receive ⟨UPDATE, f_u⟩ from client c:
2:      store c
3:      s' ← apply_update(f_u)
4:      send ⟨MERGE, s'⟩ to all remote acceptors
5:  on receive ⟨MERGED⟩ from some quorum:
6:      send ⟨UPDATE_DONE⟩ to c
-------------- Query Commands --------------
7:  on receive ⟨QUERY, f_q⟩ from client c:
8:      store c, f_q
9:      r ← (⊥, new_id())                         ▷ incremental prepare
10:     send ⟨PREPARE, r, s_0⟩ to all acceptors
11: on receive ⟨ACK, Ř, Š⟩ from some quorum:
12:     s' ← ⊔Š
13:     if ∀s_i ∈ Š : s_i ≡ s' then
14:         send ⟨QUERY_DONE, f_q(s')⟩ to c       ▷ s' learned by consistent states
15:     else if ∀r_i, r_j ∈ Ř : r_i = r_j then    ▷ consistent rounds
16:         send ⟨VOTE, any r ∈ Ř, s'⟩ to all acceptors
17:     else                        ▷ inconsistent rounds, retry with greater r
18:         r' ← max(Ř)
19:         r ← (r'_nr + 1, new_id())
20:         send ⟨PREPARE, r, s'⟩
21: on receive ⟨VOTED, {s, . . . , s}⟩ from some quorum:
22:     send ⟨QUERY_DONE, f_q(s)⟩ to c           ▷ s learned by unanimous vote

Acceptor:
23: on initialise:
24:     r ← (0, ⊥)
25:     s ← s_0
-------------- Update Commands --------------
26: function apply_update(f_u):
27:     s ← f_u(s)
28:     r_id ← write
29:     return s
30: on receive ⟨MERGE, s'⟩ from proposer p:
31:     s ← s ⊔ s'
32:     r_id ← write
33:     send ⟨MERGED⟩ to p
-------------- Query Commands --------------
34: on receive ⟨PREPARE, r', s'⟩ from proposer p:
35:     s ← s ⊔ s'       ▷ add s', (s_0 or a state seen in an acceptor)
36:     if r'_nr = ⊥ then
37:         r' ← (r_nr + 1, r'_id)
38:     if r'_nr > r_nr then
39:         r ← r'
40:         send ⟨ACK, r, s⟩
41: on receive ⟨VOTE, r', s'⟩ from proposer p:
42:     s ← s ⊔ s'       ▷ add s', a state seen in (another) acceptor
43:     if r' = r then
44:         r ← r'
45:         send ⟨VOTED, s'⟩
```

the *PREPARE* if it contains a round larger than r. The acceptor's replies also include their stored state. If p receives a quorum of replies with consistent states, it has immediately learned the current value (line 14). Otherwise, it proposes the LUB of the received values in the second phase. An acceptor accepts the proposal if it has not observed a higher round in the meantime.

The query protocol resembles a single-decree Paxos. We leverage the commutative property of state merges by including the currently known state in the protocol's messages. This accelerates convergence of the stored state. Once it converged, all queries are handled in a single round trip until a new update is issued.

5 EXPERIMENTAL RESULTS

We implemented our protocol in Erlang as part of the distributed key-value store Scalaris [11] and tested its correctness with a scheduler enforcing random message orderings.

We implemented a counter replicated on three nodes. The results in Figure 1 were achieved using a simple batching scheme (5 ms batches per node) with a workload of 90 % reads. More than 97 % of the reads are handled within two round trips. We also compare against leader based consensus algorithms Raft [10] and Paxos [8]. As we do not use a leader, the observed latencies remained stable during a node failure (not shown here). In addition, our implementation was able to handle about 150,000 requests per second in all tested workloads. For more details, see the full paper [13].

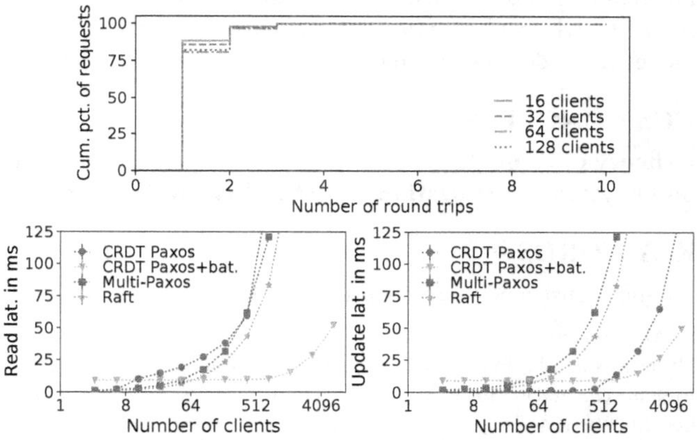

Figure 1: Round trips to process reads (top) and 95th pctl. latency comparison (bottom) (3 nodes, 90 % reads).

ACKNOWLEDGMENTS

We thank Alexander Reinefeld for dedicated comments and valuable discussions that helped to improve this manuscript.

REFERENCES

[1] P. Bourgon. 2014. Roshi:a CRDT system for timestamped events. http://developers.soundcloud.com/blog/roshi-a-crdt-system-for-timestamped-events. (2014).
[2] R. Brown et al. 2014. Riak DT map: a composable, convergent replicated dictionary. In *PaPEC@EuroSys 2014*. ACM.
[3] J. M. Falerio et al. 2012. Generalized lattice agreement. In *PODC*. ACM, 125–134.
[4] M. Herlihy. 1991. Wait-Free Synchronization. *ACM TOPLAS* 13, 1 (1991), 124–149.
[5] M. Herlihy and J. M. Wing. 1990. Linearizability: A Correctness Condition for Concurrent Objects. *ACM TOPLAS* 12, 3 (1990), 463–492.
[6] D. Imbs et al. 2018. Set-Constrained Delivery Broadcast: Definition, Abstraction Power, and Computability Limits. In *ICDCN 2018*. 7:1–7:10.
[7] Akka IO. 2019. Akka Distributed Data. https://doc.akka.io/docs/akka/current/typed/distributed-data.html. (2019). Accessed: 2019-05-17.
[8] L. Lamport. 2001. Paxos made simple. *ACM Sigact News* 32, 4 (2001), 18–25.
[9] L. Lamport. 2005. Generalized consensus and Paxos. *Technical Report MSR-TR-2005-33, Microsoft Research* (2005).
[10] I. Moraru, D. G. Andersen, and M. Kaminsky. 2013. There is more consensus in Egalitarian parliaments. In *SOSP 2013*. ACM, 358–372.
[11] T. Schütt, F. Schintke, and A. Reinefeld. 2008. Scalaris: reliable transactional P2P key/value store. In *SIGPLAN ERLANG workshop*. ACM, 41–48.
[12] M. Shapiro et al. 2011. Conflict-Free Replicated Data Types. In *SSS 2011*, Vol. 6976. Springer, 386–400.
[13] J. Skrzypczak, F. Schintke, and T. Schütt. 2019. Linearizable State Machine Replication of State-Based CRDTs without Logs. *CoRR* (2019). arXiv:1905.08733v1
[14] M. Vukolić. 2012. *Quorum Systems: With Applications to Storage and Consensus.* Morgan & Claypool Publishers.

Brief Announcement: On Mixing Eventual and Strong Consistency: Bayou Revisited*

Maciej Kokociński
Maciej.Kokocinski@cs.put.edu.pl

Tadeusz Kobus
Tadeusz.Kobus@cs.put.edu.pl

Paweł T. Wojciechowski
Pawel.T.Wojciechowski@cs.put.edu.pl

Institute of Computing Science
Poznan University of Technology
Poznań, Poland

ABSTRACT

In this paper we study the properties of eventually consistent distributed systems that feature arbitrarily complex semantics and mix eventual and strong consistency. These systems execute requests in a highly-available, weakly-consistent fashion, but also enable stronger guarantees through additional inter-replica synchronization mechanisms that require the ability to solve distributed consensus. We use the seminal Bayou system as a case study, and then generalize our findings to a whole class of systems. We show dubious and unintuitive behaviour exhibited by those systems and provide a theoretical framework for reasoning about their correctness. We also state an impossibility result that formally proves the inherent limitation of such systems, namely *temporary operation reordering*, which admits interim disagreement between replicas on the relative order in which the client requests were executed.

CCS CONCEPTS

• Theory of computation → Distributed algorithms; • Computer systems organization → Reliability; Availability;

KEYWORDS

eventual consistency, mixed consistency, fault-tolerance

ACM Reference Format:
Maciej Kokociński, Tadeusz Kobus, and Paweł T. Wojciechowski. 2019. Brief Announcement: On Mixing Eventual and Strong Consistency: Bayou Revisited. In *2019 ACM Symposium on Principles of Distributed Computing (PODC '19), July 29-August 2, 2019, Toronto, ON, Canada.* ACM, New York, NY, USA, 3 pages. https://doi.org/10.1145/3293611.3331583

1 INTRODUCTION

Modern replicated services running on the Internet are designed for high availability and low latency in serving client requests. These desirable traits come at the expense of weaker consistency guarantees, e.g., eventual or causal consistency [17]. Such weak consistency models are often sufficient and thus embraced by the widely employed NoSQL data stores. However, there are many use cases in which stronger guarantees are needed, in the form of, e.g., serializable transactions. This is why in recent years various NoSQL vendors started adding (quasi) transactional support to their systems [6] [7], albeit these add-on mechanisms are often very limited.[1]

In this paper we study the inherent limitations of replicated systems which mix eventual consistency with strong consistency, and at the same time retain rich transactional semantics. More precisely, we are interested in eventually consistent systems which facilitate serializable transactions that can operate on the same data as highly-available, weakly consistent operations. Weakly consistent operations are guaranteed to progress, and are handled in such a way that the processes eventually converge to the same state within each network partition, even when strongly consistent transactions cannot complete due to network and process faults. The full version of the paper is available in [11].

2 BAYOU – A CASE STUDY

In the past several mixed consistency systems have been proposed, most notably [16] [8] [4]. To showcase some of the problems which result from having multiple consistency models coexisting in a system we study the seminal Bayou system [16], one of the first always available, eventually consistent data stores.

Overview. Each Bayou server speculatively total-orders all received client requests using a simple timestamp-based mechanism and without prior agreement with other servers. This way a Bayou process (which we call a *replica*) can respond to a request even in the presence of network partitions in the system. In the background, Bayou replicas synchronize to enforce the final request execution order, as established by a primary replica (the primary periodically commits the operations it has received). When desired, a client may wait until the request *stabilizes*, i.e., it is processed according to the final execution order, so the response can never change. Logically, the state of each replica corresponds to the following list l of received requests: the prefix of l contains stabilized requests, arranged in the order established by the primary; other requests are kept further on l, arranged according to their timestamps. Stabilization of a request means that the request is moved from the second part of the list to the end of the first part of the list. Note that sometimes this operation might involve rolling back

*This work was supported by the Foundation for Polish Science, within the TEAM programme co-financed by the European Union under the European Regional Development Fund (grant No. POIR.04.04.00-00-5C5B/17-00). Kokociński and Kobus were also supported by the Polish National Science Centre (grant No. DEC-2012/07/B/ST6/01230) and partially by the internal funds of the Faculty of Computing, Poznan Univ. Techn.

PODC '19, July 29-August 2, 2019, Toronto, ON, Canada

ACM ISBN 978-1-4503-6217-7/19/07.
https://doi.org/10.1145/3293611.3331583

[1] For instance, Riak allows strongly consistent (serializable) operations to be performed only on distinct data [7], whereas using the so called light weight transactions in Apache Cassandra on data that are accessed also in the regular (eventually consistent) fashion leads to undefined behaviour [10].

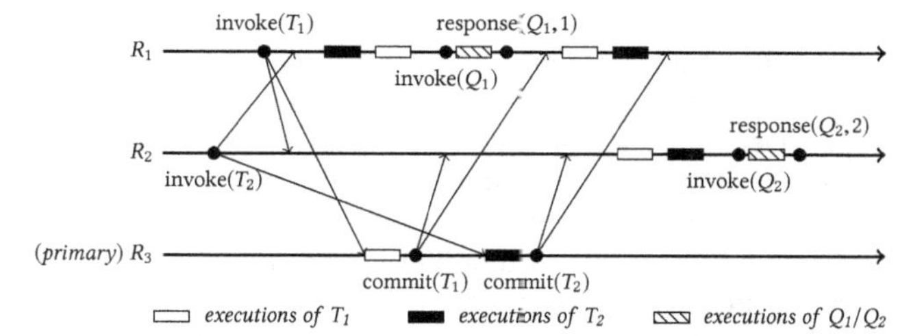


```
T1 {                T2 {                Q1/Q2 {
  x = 1               y = 1               return z
  if y = 1 then       if x = 1 then     }
    z = 1               z = 2
}                   }
```

Figure 1: Example execution of Bayou showing temporary operation reordering and circular causality. Initially, replica R_1 executes transactions T_1 and T_2 in order T_2, T_1, which corresponds to T_1's and T_2's timestamps. This transaction execution order is observed by the client who issues query Q_1. On the other hand, R_2 executes the transactions according to the final execution order (T_1, T_2), as established by the primary replica R_3. Hence, the client who issued query Q_2 observes a different execution order than the client who issued Q_1. The execution orders perceived by the clients form a circular dependency between T_1 and T_2: T_1 depends on T_2 as evidenced by Q_1's response, while T_2 depends on T_1 as evidenced by Q_2's response. Note that replicas execute the operations with a delay (e.g., caused by CPU being busy). Also, notice that R_1 reexecutes the operations once it gets to know the final order.

and reexecuting some of the requests. Intuitively, Bayou combines timestamp-based eventual consistency [17] and serializability [13].

For the purpose of our analysis we assume that requests in Bayou are arbitrary but deterministic *operations* that produce some response values. An operation might correspond to, e.g., a transaction specified in SQL. When a client is interested in the stable response, we say that the operation is *strong*. Otherwise it is *weak*, and the response is returned to the client before the final operation execution order is established. This way any weak operation is non-blocking (with respect to network communication), but its ultimate impact on the system's state might differ from what the client can infer from the response (if the final execution order differs from the tentative one). On the other hand, a strong operation returns a response only after the final execution order is established. Hence the guarantees on the execution order of strong operations are more stringent compared to the guarantees of weak operations. By abstracting a system described above, we obtain a model of a distributed system with arbitrarily complex semantics that mixes eventual and strong consistency. The semantics are formalized by a specification of a sequential data type exporting a set of operations available to the clients.

Anomalies. We demonstrate two phenomena present in Bayou that may come as dubious and unintuitive. Interestingly, they are never exhibited by popular NoSQL systems (which guarantee only eventual consistency), nor by strongly consistent solutions (e.g., DBMS). In the first phenomenon, which we call *temporary operation reordering*, the replicas may temporarily disagree on the relative order in which the requests (modeled as operations) submitted to the system were executed. The difference in operation execution order can be observed by the clients. The second phenomenon, *circular causality*, signifies a situation in which, by examining the return values of the operations processed by a system, one may discover a cycle in the causal dependency between the operations. Both of these anomalies are present in Bayou, because it features two incompatible ways of ordering operation executions (see Figure 1). Interestingly, circular causality can be avoided in Bayou [11], however, this is not the case with temporary operation reordering.

Correctness guarantees. Because of the phenomena described above, the guarantees provided by Bayou cannot be formalized using the correctness criteria used for contemporary eventually consistent systems. For example, *basic eventual consistency (BEC)* by Burckhardt [3] directly forbids circular causality. BEC also requires the relative order of any two operations, as perceived by the client, to be consistent and to never change. Similarly, *strong eventual consistency (SEC)* by Shapiro *et al.* requires any two replicas that delivered the same updates to have equivalent states. Obviously, Bayou neither satisfies BEC nor SEC. Bayou satisfies the operational specification in [8]. However, we aim to provide a declarative specification, similar in style to popular consistency criteria, such as *sequential consistency* [12], or *serializability* [13].

In order to formalize the guarantees of systems that, similarly to Bayou, admit temporary operation reordering, we introduce a new correctness criterion called *fluctuating eventual consistency (FEC)*, which can be viewed as a generalization of BEC. More precisely, BEC requires that the following three conditions are satisfied: EV, NCC, and RVAL($\mathcal{F}$). EV requires every operation to eventually become visible to all subsequent ones. NCC forbids circular causality. Finally, RVAL($\mathcal{F}$) requires the return values to be consistent with the replicated data type $\mathcal{F}$ specification,[2] i.e., for any given operation *op*, the value returned, and the value predicted by $\mathcal{F}$ (based on the set of operations visible to *op* and a single total order of all operations), have to match.

FEC retains EV and NCC but relaxes RVAL, so that different operations can perceive different operation orders. However, we require that the different perceived operation orders converge to one final execution order.

For strong operations Bayou provides more stringent guarantees, namely sequential consistency (SEQ). A response of a strong operation *op* always reflects the serial execution of all stabilized operations up to the point of *op*'s commit.

When weak and strong operations are mixed, we denote by FEC(*weak*, $\mathcal{F}$) $\land$ SEQ(*strong*, $\mathcal{F}$) the combination of guarantees including FEC for weak operations and sequential consistency for strong operations.

[2]A replicated data type specification is a generalization of a sequential data type specification, that is suitable for certain replicated data types such as MVRs [15]. Although this generalization is not necessary in case of Bayou, which always processes all operations sequentially, we adopt it for generality and compatibility with BEC.

Wait-freedom. Now we show that, unlike many existing eventually consistent data stores, Bayou does not guarantee bounded wait-free execution of operations, i.e., there does not exist a bound on the number of steps of the Bayou protocol that a replica takes before returning a response to the client [9]. Consider an infinite execution in which new operations are being invoked on each replica with a constant rate. Assume that one of the replicas is unable to keep up executing the operations at the same rate as it receives them over network. The replica starts lagging behind. Each new operation invoked at the replica will be executed only after the current stash of lagging requests is executed. Since the lag is increasing, so is the response time for the operations invoked on the replica. Thus no bound on response time exists. It is surprising, because the result holds also when the clients do not wait for the operations to stabilize.

Fault-tolerance. Bayou's reliance on the primary makes it not fault-tolerant (the primary is the single point of failure). Although the primary may recover, when it is down, operations do not stabilize, and thus no strong operation can complete. Alternatively, the primary could be replaced by a distributed commit protocol. If two-phase-commit (2PC) [1] is used, the phenomena illustrated in Figure 1 are not possible. However, in this approach, a failure of any replica blocks the execution of strong operations (in 2PC all the replicas need to be operational). On the other hand, if a *non-blocking* commit protocol is used, e.g., based on a *total order broadcast (TOB)* [14], the system may stabilize operations despite (a limited number of) failures. Any scheme which admits failures of at least one replica, and thus do not depend on synchronous communication with all the replicas, is necessarily prone to the phenomena described above.

3 IMPOSSIBILITY RESULT

Now we proceed to our central contribution. Informally, our result shows that it is impossible to devise a fault-tolerant system that mixes strong and weak consistency and implements arbitrary semantics (as defined by a specification of a replicated data type $\mathcal{F}$) but which never admits temporary operation reordering. Before we state our theorem, we discuss our approach to formulating it.

We are interested in the behaviour of systems, both in the fully asynchronous environment, when timing assumptions are consistently broken (e.g., because of prevalent network partitions), and in a stable one, when the minimal amount of synchrony is available so that consensus eventually terminates. Thus, we consider two kinds of *runs*: *asynchronous* and *stable*. Replicas are not aware which kind of a run they are currently executing. In the stable runs, we augment the system with the failure detector Ω, the weakest failure detector capable of solving distributed consensus in the presence of failures [5]. This way replicas can use, e.g., TOB for communication. In the asynchronous runs, a system which waits for TOB to complete may block forever.

We make some basic assumptions about the systems considered (we expressed the assumptions implicitly in Section 1). In case of weak operations the system needs to behave as a regular eventually consistent data store as defined by the *write-propagating data store* abstraction by Attiya *et al.* [2]. Intuitively, each replica processes weak operations as soon as possible, and eagerly synchronizes with other replicas, to ensure eventual consistency. The system cannot rely on a central coordinator for the propagation of the weak operations (as in [4]). In case of strong operations, we consider systems with *non-blocking strong operations*, which means that the execution of a strong operation never blocks on communication with all replicas. This assumption eliminates protocols such as 2PC for inter-replica synchronization required to complete strong operations; quorum-based mechanisms, such as TOB, are permitted.

If a mixed-consistency system could avoid temporary operation reordering, it would mean that it ensures BEC for weak operations and also provides at least sequential consistency (Seq) for strong operations. However, as we show, it is impossible.

Theorem 1. *Let $\mathcal{F}$ be an arbitrary replicated data type. If a system guarantees BEC(weak, $\mathcal{F}$) in asynchronous runs, then it does not guarantee BEC(weak, $\mathcal{F}$) $\wedge$ Seq(strong, $\mathcal{F}$) (neither in the asynchronous, nor in the stable runs).*

If we replaced BEC with FEC above, the theorem would not longer be true. In fact, in [11] we formally prove that a fault-tolerant version of Bayou that avoids circular causality guarantees FEC(*weak*, $\mathcal{F}$) in asynchonous runs and FEC(*weak*, $\mathcal{F}$)$\wedge$Seq(*strong*, $\mathcal{F}$) in stable runs. Thus our result shows that admitting temporary operation reordering is the inherent cost of mixing eventual and strong consistency when we make no assumptions about the semantics of $\mathcal{F}$. Naturally, for certain replicated data types achieving both BEC(*weak*, $\mathcal{F}$), and Seq(*strong*, $\mathcal{F}$) is possible (it is easy to show that it is the case for, e.g., a single distributed register).

REFERENCES

[1] Philip A., Bernstein, Vassco Hadzilacos, and Nathan Goodman. 1987. *Concurrency control and recovery in database systems.* Addison-Wesley.

[2] Hagit Attiya, Faith Ellen, and Adam Morrison. 2015. Limitations of Highly-Available Eventually-Consistent Data Stores. In *Proc. of PODC '15.*

[3] Sebastian Burckhardt. 2014. Principles of Eventual Consistency. *Foundations and Trends in Programming Languages* 1, 1-2 (Oct. 2014), 1–150.

[4] Sebastian Burckhardt, Daan Leijen, Jonathan Protzenko, and Manuel Fähndrich. 2015. Global Sequence Protocol: A Robust Abstraction for Replicated Shared State.. In *Proc. of ECOOP '15.*

[5] Tushar Deepak Chandra, Vassos Hadzilacos, and Sam Toueg. 1996. The Weakest Failure Detector for Solving Consensus. *J. ACM* 43, 4 (July 1996), 38.

[6] Apache Cassandra documentation. 2019. Light Weight Transactions in Cassandra. https://docs.datastax.com/en/cql/3.3/cql/cql_using/useInsertLWT.html.

[7] Basho documentation. 2019. Consistency levels in Riak. https://docs.basho.com/riak/kv/2.2.3/developing/app-guide/strong-consistency.

[8] Alan Fekete, David Gupta, Victor Luchangco, Nancy Lynch, and Alex Shvartsman. 1996. Eventually-serializable Data Services. In *Proc. of PODC '96.*

[9] Maurice Herlihy. 1991. Wait-free Synchronization. *ACM Transactions on Programming Languages and Systems (TOPLAS)* 13, 1 (Jan. 1991), 124–149.

[10] Apache Cassandra Issues (Jira). 2016. Mixing LWT and non-LWT operations can result in an LWT operation being acknowledged but not applied. https://jira.apache.org/jira/browse/CASSANDRA-11000.

[11] Maciej Kokociński, Tadeusz Kobus, and Paweł T. Wojciechowski. 2019. On mixing eventual and strong consistency: Bayou revisited. *ArXiv preprint arXiv:1905.11762 [cs.DC]* (2019). https://arxiv.org/abs/1905.11762

[12] L. Lamport. 1979. How to Make a Multiprocessor Computer That Correctly Executes Multiprocess Programs. *IEEE Trans. Comput.* C-28, 9 (Sept. 1979).

[13] Christos H. Papadimitriou. 1979. The Serializability of Concurrent Database Updates. *J. ACM* 26, 4 (1979).

[14] Fernando Pedone, Rachid Guerraoui, and André Schiper. 1998. Exploiting Atomic Broadcast in Replicated Databases. In *Proc. of Euro-Par '98.*

[15] Marc Shapiro, Nuno Preguiça, Carlos Baquero, and Marek Zawirski. 2011. Conflict-free Replicated Data Types. In *Proc. of SSS '11.*

[16] Douglas Terry, Marvin Theimer, Karin Petersen, Alan Demers, Mike Spreitzer, and Carl Hauser. 1995. Managing Update Conflicts in Bayou, a Weakly Connected Replicated Storage System. In *Proc. of SOSP '95.*

[17] Werner Vogels. 2009. Eventually Consistent. *Commun. ACM* 52, 1 (Jan. 2009), 5.

Massively Parallel Algorithms for Finding Well-Connected Components in Sparse Graphs*

Sepehr Assadi†
sassadi@princeton.edu
Princeton University
Princeton, NJ, USA

Xiaorui Sun
xiaorui@uic.edu
University of Illinois
Chicago, IL, USA

Omri Weinstein
omri@cs.columbia.edu
Columbia University
New York, NY, USA

Abstract

Massively parallel computation (MPC) algorithms for graph problems have witnessed a resurgence of interest in recent years. Despite major progress for numerous graph problems however, the complexity of the *sparse graph connectivity* problem in this model has remained elusive: While classical logarithmic-round PRAM algorithms for finding connected components in any n-vertex graph have been known for more than three decades (and imply the same bounds for MPC model), no $o(\log n)$-round MPC algorithms are known for this task with truly sublinear in n memory per machine (which is the only interesting regime for sparse graphs with $O(n)$ edges). It is conjectured that an $o(\log n)$-round algorithm for connectivity on general sparse graphs with $n^{1-\Omega(1)}$ per-machine memory may not exist, a conjecture that also forms the basis for multiple conditional hardness results on the round complexity of other problems in the MPC model.

We take an opportunistic approach towards the sparse graph connectivity problem by designing an algorithm with improved performance in terms of the connectivity structure of the input graph. Formally, we design an MPC algorithm that finds all connected components with *spectral gap* at least λ in a graph in $O(\log\log n + \log(1/\lambda))$ MPC rounds and n^{δ} memory per machine for any constant $\delta \in (0,1)$. While this algorithm still requires $\Theta(\log n)$ rounds in the worst-case, it achieves an exponential round reduction on "well-connected" components with $\lambda \geq 1/\text{polylog}(n)$ using only n^{δ} memory per machine and $\widetilde{O}(n)$ total memory, and still operates in $o(\log n)$ rounds even when $\lambda = 1/n^{o(1)}$.

En-route to our main result, we design a new distributed data structure for performing *independent random walks* from *all* vertices simultaneously, as well as a new leader-election algorithm with exponentially faster round complexity on *random* graphs.

*A full version of the paper is available on arXiv.

†Supported in part by the Simons Collaboration on Algorithms and Geometry. Majority of work done while the author was a graduate student at University of Pennsylvania.

PODC '19, July 29-August 2, 2019, Toronto, ON, Canada

ACM ISBN 978-1-4503-6217-7/19/07...$15.00
https://doi.org/10.1145/3293611.3331596

CCS Concepts

• **Theory of computation → Massively parallel algorithms**; *Design and analysis of algorithms; Graph algorithms analysis.*

Keywords

Sparse connectivity, spectral gap, random walk

ACM Reference Format:

Sepehr Assadi, Xiaorui Sun, and Omri Weinstein. 2019. Massively Parallel Algorithms for Finding Well-Connected Components in Sparse Graphs. In *2019 ACM Symposium on Principles of Distributed Computing (PODC '19), July 29-August 2, 2019, Toronto, ON, Canada.* ACM, New York, NY, USA, 10 pages. https://doi.org/10.1145/3293611.3331596

1 Introduction

Recent years have witnessed a resurgence of interest in the theory of parallel computation, motivated by the successful deployment of parallel computing platforms such as MapReduce, Hadoop and Spark [17, 46, 48]. The *massively parallel computation (MPC)* model [3, 9, 23, 28] is a theoretical abstraction which aims to capture the design principles and main distinguishing aspects of these platform over the classical PRAM model: more local computation power (in principle unbounded), and larger local memory per processor. Consequently, it is typically possible to simulate a PRAM algorithm in the MPC model with no asymptotic blowup in the number of rounds [23, 28]. However, these powerful features anticipate a potential for qualitatively smarter and dramatically faster parallel algorithms. A fundamental question on this front is then:

> *How can the additional power of the MPC model be leveraged to achieve faster algorithms compared to classical parallel models such as PRAM algorithms?*

The answer to this question turns out to be highly dependent on the type of problems at hand and the setting of parameters. For graph problems—the focus of this paper—the first improvement over PRAM algorithms was already achieved by Karloff *et al.* [28] who developed algorithms for graph connectivity and MST in $O(1)$ MPC rounds on machines with local memory $n^{1+\Omega(1)}$; here, n is the number of vertices in the graph. This is in contrast to the $\Omega(\log n)$ round needed in the standard PRAM model for these problems (see, e.g., [15, 18, 24, 27, 38, 40, 45]). Since then, numerous algorithms have been designed for various graph problems that achieve $O(1)$ round-complexity with local memory $n^{1+\Omega(1)}$ on each machine (see, e.g., [1, 8, 31, 33] and references therein).

The next set of improvements reduced the memory per machine to $\widetilde{O}(n)$. For example, an $O(1)$ round algorithm for MST and connectivity using only $O(n)$ memory per machine has been proposed in [26] building on previous work in [20, 25, 35] (see also [2, 10, 34] for related results). Another work is the recent $O(1)$ round algorithm of Assadi *et al.* [7] for $(\Delta+1)$-vertex coloring with $\widetilde{O}(n)$ memory per machine. A series of very recent papers [5, 6, 12, 16, 19, 30] have also achieved $O(\log\log n)$-round algorithms for different graph problems such as matching, vertex cover, and MIS in the MPC model, when the memory per machine is $O(n)$ or even $O(n/\text{polylog}(n))$.

Most recently, several algorithms were also designed for matching, vertex cover, MIS, and $(\Delta + 1)$ vertex coloring for the strongly sublinear memory regime, e.g. n^{δ} for any constant $\delta \in (0, 1)$ memory per machine. In particular, for maximal matching and MIS on machines with n^{δ} memory, Behnezhad *et al.* [11] and Brandt *et al.* [13] gave $O(\log\log n)$-round MPC algorithms on bounded arboricity graphs, and Ghaffari and Uitto [21] gave an $O(\sqrt{\log n})$ round algorithm on general graphs (see also [37] for an algorithm for approximate matching and vertex cover with the same guarantee). An $O(\sqrt{\log\log n})$ round algorithm for $(\Delta + 1)$ coloring in this regime was also given recently in [14].

Alas, this progress has came to a halt for the fundamental problem of *connectivity on (sparse) undirected graphs.* While classic $O(\log n)$-round PRAM algorithms for this problem have been known for more than three decades (see [18, 24, 27, 40, 45] and references therein), no faster MPC algorithm with truly sublinear $n^{1-\Omega(1)}$-memory per machine is known to date (see, e.g. [28, 29, 39]).

There are several substantial reasons for the lack of progress on this fascinating problem. On one hand, $\Omega(\log n)$ rounds are known to be necessary for a *restricted* class of (routing-style) MPC algorithms [9], and in fact it has been conjectured that this logarithmic barrier may be unavoidable for any MPC algorithm [3, 9, 39, 42]. This belief led to a series of recent results that used sparse connectivity as a hardness assumption for proving *conditional* lower bounds in the MPC model for other problems (see [3, 47] and references therein). On the other hand, it was observed by Roughgarden *et al.* [42] that proving *any* $\omega(1)$ lower bound on round complexity of connectivity would imply $\mathbf{NC}^1 \subsetneq \mathbf{P}$, a major breakthrough that is well beyond the reach of current techniques.

In this paper we take an *opportunistic* approach to the sparse connectivity problem, which exploits the connectivity structure of the underlying graph. In particular, we use *spectral gap* as a quantitative measure of connectedness of a graph and design an algorithm for connectivity with improved performance guarantee depending on the spectral gap of the connected components of the underlying graph. For example, when connected components of the graph have large spectral gap, say $\Omega(1)$ or even $\Omega(1/\text{polylog}(n))$ (as in expanders), our algorithm only requires $O(\log\log n)$ MPC rounds while using n^{δ} memory per machine for constant $\delta \in (0, 1)$ and $\widetilde{O}(n)$ total memory. We elaborate more on our results in Section 1.1.

Massively Parallel Computation Model. We adopt the most stringent model of modern parallel computation among [3, 9, 23, 28], the so-called *Massively Parallel Computation (MPC)* model of [9]. Let N be the input size. It is assumed that the local memory on each machine and the number of machine should be at most $N^{1-\delta}$ for some constant $\delta > 0$. Additionally, we are typically interested in algorithms with total memory $\widetilde{O}(N)$, i.e., proportional to the input size (within logarithmic factors) [3, 9], although total memories as large as $O(N^{2-2\delta})$ have been also considered in more relaxed variants [28]. The motivation behind these constraints is that the number of machines, and local memory of each machine should be much smaller than the input size to the problem since these frameworks are used to process large datasets.

In this model, computation proceeds in rounds. During a round each machine runs a local algorithm on the data assigned to the machine. No communication between machines is allowed during a round. Between rounds, machines are allowed to communicate so long as each machine send or receive a communication no more than its memory. Any data output from a machine must be computed locally from the data residing on the machine and initially the input data is distributed across machines adversarially. The final output also resides in a distributed fashion across the machines. The goal is to minimize the total number of rounds.

1.1 Our Results and Techniques

The *spectral gap* of a graph is defined to be the second eigenvalue of the normalized Laplacian associated with this graph. We use spectral gap as a measure of "connectedness" of a graph and design an *opportunistic* algorithm for connectivity with improved performance depending on the spectral gap of the underlying graph.

Theorem 1 (**Main Result**). *There exists an MPC algorithm that with high probability identifies all connected components of any given sparse undirected n-vertex graph $G(V, E)$ with $\widetilde{O}(n)$ edges and a lower bound of $\lambda \in (0, 1)$ on the spectral gap of its connected components.*

For constant $\delta > 0$, the algorithm can be implemented with $O(\frac{1}{\lambda^2} \cdot n^{1-\delta} \cdot \text{polylog}(n))$ machines each with $O(n^{\delta} \cdot \text{polylog}(n))$ memory, and in $O(\log\log n + \log(1/\lambda))$ MPC rounds.

We note that Theorem 1 can be extended to the case when the algorithm is *oblivious* to the value of λ and still manages to achieve an improved performance depending on λ (see full version). We should also remark that the dependence of $O(\log(1/\lambda))$ in Theorem 1 is best possible short of obtaining an $o(\log n)$-round algorithm for sparse connectivity in general graphs as $\lambda = 1/\text{poly}(n)$ in any undirected graph.

Our result is most interesting in the case when spectral gap of (each connected component) of the graph is lower bounded by a constant or even $1/\text{polylog}(n)$, i.e., for graphs with "well-connected" components. Examples of such graphs include random graphs and expanders (see also [22, 36] for real-life examples in social networks). In this case, we obtain an algorithm with $\widetilde{O}(n)$ total memory and n^{δ} per-machine memory for constant $\delta \in (0, 1)$ which can identify all connected components in only $O(\log\log n)$ rounds. Nevertheless, the algorithm in Theorem 1 still manages to achieve a non-trivial improvement even when the spectral gap is as small as $1/n^{o(1)}$. Even in this case, the algorithm requires $o(\log n)$ MPC rounds (and total memory which is larger than the input size by only an $n^{o(1)}$ factor).

We also prove an *unconditional* $\Omega(\log_s n)$-round lower bound for the promise problem of connectivity on sparse expanders on machines with memory s. This implies that the "full power" of the MPC model is indeed required to achieve our speedup, as with $s = \text{polylog}(n)$ memory, $\Omega(\log_s n) = \tilde{\Omega}(\log n)$ rounds are needed even on sparse expanders (this result us presented in Section 8).

Finally, we note that a simple application of the toolkit we develop in proving our main result in Theorem 1 also implies the following theorem.

Theorem 2. *There exists an MPC algorithm that given any arbitrary graph with high probability identifies all connected components in $O(\log\log n)$ rounds on machines of memory $O(n/\text{polylog}(n))$, or $O(\sqrt{\log n})$ rounds with $O(n/2^{O(\sqrt{\log n})})$ memory.*

Theorem 2 is reminiscent of the recent set of results in [5, 6, 12, 16, 19, 30] on achieving similar guarantees for other graph problems such as matching and vertex cover in the mildly sublinear in n per-machine memory regime. This result emphasizes the *truly sublinear* in n regime, i.e., $n^{1-\Omega(1)}$ per-machine memory, as the "real" barrier to obtaining efficient algorithms for sparse connectivity with improved performance compared to PRAM algorithms.

Techniques. The first main technical ingredient of this work is a distributed data structure for performing and processing short *independent random walks* (proportional to the *mixing time* of each component) from *all* vertices of the graph simultaneously, whose construction takes logarithmic number of rounds in length of the walk. While implementing random walks in distributed and parallel settings is a well-studied problem (see, e.g., [24, 27, 43, 44] and references therein), the guarantee of our algorithm in achieving *independent* random walks across all vertices in a small number of rounds and total memory, departs from previous work (independence is crucial in the context of our algorithm). Achieving this stronger guarantee requires different tools, in particular, a method for "regularizing" our graph using a parallel implementation of the replacement product operation (see, e.g. [41]) that we design .

The second main technical ingredient of this work is a novel leader-election based algorithm for finding a spanning tree of a *random graph.* The key feature of this algorithm that distinguishes it from previous MPC algorithms for sparse connectivity (see, e.g., [28, 29, 39]) is that on random graphs, it provably requires only $O(\log\log n)$ MPC rounds as opposed to $\Omega(\log n)$ (we point out that [29] also analyzed their algorithms on random graphs (see Lemma 9), but even on random graphs their algorithm requires $\Theta(\log^2 n)$ rounds). Our algorithm achieves this *exponential* speedup by contracting quadratically larger components to a single vertex in each step, while "preserving the randomness" in the resulting contracted graph to allow for recursion.

1.2 Recent Developments

Independently and concurrently to our work, Andoni *et al.* [4] and Lacki *et al.* [32] have also studied MPC algorithms for connectivity with the goal of achieving improved performance on graphs with "better connectivity" structure. Andoni *et al.* [4] considered graphs with *low diameter* and developed an algorithm with n^δ memory per machine and $O(\log D \cdot \log\log_{N/n}(n))$ rounds, where D is the largest diameter of any connected component and $N = \Omega(m)$ is the total memory. Lacki *et al.* [32] considered *random graphs* (where each edge independently appears w.p. $\Omega(\log n/n)$) and give an $O(\log\log n)$ round algorithm on such graphs with n^δ memory per machine.

While our results subsume that of [32], they are incomparable to the results by [4]: even though in any graph $D = O(\log n/\lambda)$, the number of rounds in [4] is $O(\log D \log\log n)$ for the main setting of interest when the total memory is within logarithmic factors of input size (the typical requirement of the MPC model[1] [3, 9]). As such, our algorithm achieves quadratically smaller round complexity when the spectral gap is large, i.e., is $\Omega(1)$ or even $\Omega(1/\text{polylog}(n))$ (as in random graphs and graphs with moderate expansion), while [4] achieve better performance on graphs with small spectral gap but not too-large diameter. We remark that our mildly-sublinear space algorithm for general graphs in Theorem 2 is entirely orthogonal to both [4] and [32]. We give a detailed comparison of our techniques with those of [4, 32] in the full version.

Organization. We start with some essential definitions in Section 2. Sections 3, 4, and 5 contain the three main steps of our algorithm and Section 6 show how to combine these results and prove Theorem 1. Our mildly sublinear space algorithm for general graphs and our lower bound result appear in, respectively, Section 7 and Section 8. Due to space limitations, most proofs are postponed to the full version of the paper.

2 Preliminaries

Notation. For a graph $G(V, E)$, we define $V(G) = V$ and $E(G) = E$, and let $n := |V(G)|$ and $m := |E(G)|$. For any vertex $v \in V$, we use d_v to denote the degree of v in G. Throughout the paper, we assume without loss of generality that $d_v \geq 1$ for all vertices $v \in G$ (i.e., G does not have isolated vertices). We say that a subset $C \subsetneq V(G)$ is a component of G if the induced subgraph of G on C is connected. We say that a partition $C = \{C_1, \ldots, C_k\}$ of $V(G)$ is a component-partition iff every C_i is a component of G.

For simplicity of exposition, we follow [16] in using the following concise notation for representing ranges: for a value x and parameter $\varepsilon \geq 0$, we use $[\![x \pm \varepsilon]\!]$ to denote the range $[x - \varepsilon, x + \varepsilon]$ and further extend this notation to include expressions, e.g. $[\![(x \pm \varepsilon)^2]\!]$.

Almost regular graphs. Let $\Delta \geq 1$ be an integer and $\varepsilon > 0$ be any parameter. We say that a graph $G(V, E)$ is $[\![(1 \pm \varepsilon)\Delta]\!]$-almost-regular iff degree of any vertex in $V(G)$ belongs to $[\![(1 \pm \varepsilon)\Delta]\!]$. We refer to ε as the *discrepancy factor* of the an almost-regular graph.

Spectral gap and mixing time. For an undirected graph $G(V, E)$ on n vertices, we use $\mathcal{L}$ to denote the *normalized Laplacian* matrix of G. The spectral gap of G is the second smallest eigenvalue of $\mathcal{L}$, denoted by $\lambda_2(G)$. It is well-known that a *lazy random walk* on a graph G takes $O(\log n/\lambda_2(G))$ steps to converge to its stationary distribution on a graph G (this number of steps is referred to as the

[1]Minimizing total memory is *critical* in this context as the straightforward algorithm that computes the transitive closure of the graph by matrix multiplication (see [28]) achieves $O(\log D)$ rounds, subsuming both our results and [4]. This algorithm however requires $\Omega(n^2)$ total memory and hence does not adhere to the restrictions of the MPC model.

mixing time). This is the main property of spectral gap that we use throughout the paper.

Random graphs. For any integers $n, d \geq 1$, we use $\mathbb{G}(n, d)$ to denote the distribution on random undirected graphs G on n vertices chosen by picking for each vertex $v \in V(G)$, $\lfloor d/2 \rfloor$ outgoing edges (u, v) for v chosen uniformly at random (with replacement) from $V(G)$ and then removing the direction of edges. Note that this notion of a random graph is related but no identical to the more familiar family of Erdos-Renyi random graphs.

3 Step 1: Regularization

In this section, we show how to "preprocess" our graph in order to prepare it for the main steps of our algorithm. Roughly speaking, this step takes the original graph G and turn it into a regular-graph without increasing its mixing time by much. Formally,

LEMMA 3.1. *There exists an MPC algorithm that given any graph $G(V, E)$ computes another graph H with the following properties with high probability:*

(1) $|V(H)| = 2m$ and H is Δ-regular for some absolute constant $\Delta = O(1)$.

(2) There is a one-to-one correspondence between the connected components of G and H.

(3) Let H_i be a connected component of H corresponding to the connected component G_i of graph G. For any $\gamma < 1$, $T_\gamma(H_i) = O\left(\frac{\log(n/\gamma)}{\lambda_2(G_i)}\right)$.

The algorithm can be implemented on $O(m^{1-\delta})$ machines each with $O(m^\delta)$ memory and in $O(\frac{1}{\delta})$ MPC rounds.

To prove Lemma 3.1, we use an approach based on the standard replacement product. Due to space limitations, we postpone this proof entirely to the full version of the paper.

4 Step 2: Randomization

We present the second step of our algorithm in this section. Roughly speaking, this step transforms each connected component of the graph into a "random graph" on the same set of vertices. Formally,

LEMMA 4.1. *Suppose $G(V, E)$ is any n-vertex Δ-regular graph such that $T_{\gamma^*}(G_i) \leq T$ for $\gamma^* := n^{-10}$ and for all connected component G_i of G. There exists an MPC algorithm that given G and integer T computes another graph H with the following properties with high probability:*

(1) $V(H) = V(G)$, $|E(H)| = O(n)$ and each connected component G_i of G corresponds to a connected component H_i of H on $V(H_i) = V(G_i)$.

(2) The connected component H_i of H is a random graph on $n_i = |V(H_i)|$ vertices sampled from the distribution $\mathbb{D}(H_i)$ such that $|\mathbb{D}(H_i) - \mathbb{G}(n_i, 100 \log n)|_{tvd} \leq n^{-8}$.

The algorithm can be implemented with $O(T^2 \cdot n^{1-\delta} \cdot \Delta \log^2 n)$ machines each with $O(n^\delta)$ memory and in $O(\frac{1}{\delta} \cdot (\log T + \log\log n))$ MPC rounds.

To prove Lemma 4.1, we design a general algorithm for performing *independent* random walks in the MPC model which can be of independent of interest. Let $G(V, E)$ be a Δ-regular graph and $W = \Delta^{-1} \cdot A$ be its random walk matrix (note that this is scalar product with Δ^{-1} as G is Δ-regular). For any vertex $u \in V$, and integer $t \geq 1$, the vector $W^t \cdot \boldsymbol{e}_u$ denotes the distribution of a random walk of length t starting from u where $\boldsymbol{e}_u$ is an n-dimensional vector which is all zero except for the entry u which is one. We use $\mathcal{D}_{\text{RW}}(u, t) = W^t \cdot \boldsymbol{e}_u$ to denote this distribution.

THEOREM 3. *There exists an MPC algorithm that given any Δ-regular graph $G(V, E)$ and integer $t \geq 1$, outputs a vector $(v_1, \ldots, v_n)$ such that:*

$$\left| \mathbb{D}(v_1, \ldots, v_n) - \bigotimes_{i=1}^{n} \mathcal{D}_{\text{RW}}(u_i, t) \right|_{tvd} \leq n^{-10},$$

where $\mathbb{D}(v_1, \ldots, v_n)$ denotes the distributions of the output vertices. The algorithm can be implemented with $O(t^2 \cdot n^{1-\delta} \cdot \Delta \log n)$ machines each with $O(n^\delta)$ memory and in $O(\frac{1}{\delta} \cdot (\log t + \log\log n))$ rounds.

Lemma 4.1 can be proven using Theorem 3. We postpone this proof to the full version and sketch the proof of Theorem 3 instead.

4.1 Proof Sketch of Theorem 3

We start by introducing a key data structure in our algorithm.

Layered Graph

A key component of our algorithm in Theorem 3 is the notion of a *layered graph* which we define in this section.

DEFINITION 1 (LAYERED GRAPH). *For a graph $G(V, E)$ and integer $t \geq 1$, the layered graph $\mathcal{G}(G, t)$ of G is defined as the following directed graph:*

*(1) **Vertex-set:** The vertex-set $\mathcal{V}$ of $\mathcal{G}$ is the set of all triples $(u, i, j) \in V \times [2t] \times [t + 1]$.*

*(2) **Edge-set:** There is a directed edge $(u, i, j) \rightarrow (v, \ell, k)$ in $\mathcal{G}$ whenever $(u, v) \in E$ and $k = j + 1$ for all choice of i and ℓ.*

For any vertex $\alpha = (u, i, j) \in \mathcal{V}$, we define $v(\alpha) = u \in V$. We partition the set of vertices $\mathcal{V}$ into $t + 1$ sets $\mathcal{V}_1, \ldots, \mathcal{V}_{t+1}$ where the j-th set consists of all vertices (u, i, j) for $u \in V$ and $i \in [2t]$. We refer to each set $\mathcal{V}_j$ as a *layer* of the graph $\mathcal{G}$. It is immediate to see that $\mathcal{G}$ consists of $t + 1$ layers and all edges in $\mathcal{G}$ are going from one layer to the next. Additionally, any vertex $u \in V$, contains $2t$ "copies" in every layer. As such, any edge in E is mapped to t directed bi-cliques on the $2 \cdot 2t$ copies of its endpoints between every two consecutive layers of $\mathcal{G}$.

Paths and walks in $\mathcal{G}$ and G: The key property of the layered graph $\mathcal{G}$ is that any path starting from $\mathcal{V}_1$ and ending in $\mathcal{V}_{t+1}$ in $\mathcal{G}$ corresponds to a walk of length t (but not necessarily a path) in G. More formally, consider a path $\mathcal{P}_\alpha = \alpha_1, \alpha_2, \ldots, \alpha_{t+1}$ where $\alpha = \alpha_1 \in \mathcal{V}_1$. We can associate to $\mathcal{P}_\alpha$ a walk of length t in G starting from the vertex $v = v(\alpha)$, denoted by $W(\mathcal{P}_\alpha)$, in a straightforward way by traversing the vertices $u_i = v(\alpha_i)$ for $\alpha_i \in \mathcal{P}_\alpha$.

Sampled layered graph. We work with a random subgraph of the layered graph defined as follows: For any vertex in $\mathcal{G}$ *independently*, we pick exactly one of its *outgoing* edges *uniformly at random* to form a subgraph $\mathcal{G}_S$, referred to as the *sampled layered graph*.

As the out-degree of any vertex in $\mathcal{G}_S$ is exactly one, starting from any vertex $\alpha \in \mathcal{V}_1$, there is a *unique* path $\mathcal{P}_\alpha$ of length t in $\mathcal{G}_S$ from α to some vertex $\beta \in \mathcal{V}_{t+1}$. It is easy see that a path $\mathcal{P}_\alpha$ in $\mathcal{G}_S$ corresponds to a *random* walk of length t in $\mathcal{G}$ starting from the vertex $v(\alpha)$ and ending in $v(\beta)$.

In the rest of this section, we show that a sampled layered graph contains $\Omega(n)$ *vertex disjoint paths* from the first layer to the last one with high probability. Intuitively, this allows us to "extract" $\Omega(n)$ *independent* random walks from a sampled layered graph. We then use this fact to design our algorithm for simulating independent random walks from all vertices in G.

Define $\mathcal{V}_1^* \subseteq \mathcal{V}_1$ as the set of all vertices $(v, 1, 1) \in \mathcal{V}_1$ for $v \in V$. The following lemma, whose proof is postponed to the full version, is key to our analysis.

Lemma 4.2. *For any vertex $\alpha \in \mathcal{V}_1^*$, $\mathcal{P}_\alpha$ in $\mathcal{G}_S$ is vertex disjoint from $\mathcal{P}_\beta$ for all $\beta \neq \alpha \in \mathcal{V}_1^*$, with probability at least 1/2.*

A Parallel Random Walk Algorithm

We start by presenting an algorithm with a weaker guarantee than our final random walk algorithm: in this algorithm only $\Omega(n)$ vertices are able to achieve a *truly* independent random walk destination; moreover, these vertices are unknown to the algorithm. We then present a subroutine for detecting these $\Omega(n)$ vertices. Finally, we combine these two subroutines to obtain our final algorithm.

Recall that for any vertex $u \in V(G)$ and integer $t \geq 1$, $\mathcal{D}_{\mathrm{RW}}(u, t)$ is the distribution of a random walk of length t from u. We present the following algorithm.

SimpleRandomWalk(G, t). An algorithm for performing a random walk of length t from every vertex in a given graph G.

Output: For any vertex $u_i \in V(G)$, a vertex $v_i \in V(G)$ such that $v_i \sim \mathcal{D}_{\mathrm{RW}}(u_i, t)$.

(1) Randomly sample a sampled subgraph $\mathcal{G}_S$ from the layered graph $\mathcal{G}(G, t)$.
   (a) Set $\mathcal{V} = V(G) \times [2t] \times [t+1]$, and distribute the vertices of $\mathcal{V}$ to all the machines such that each machine contains $O(n^\delta)$ vertices.
   (b) For every vertex $\alpha = (v, i, j) \in \mathcal{V}$ such that $j \leq t$ **in parallel** independently and uniformly sample a number n_α from $[\Delta]$ and i_α from $[2t]$.
   (c) Set $\mathcal{G}_S$ to be empty initially.
   (d) For every vertex $\alpha = (v, i, j) \in \mathcal{V}$ such that $j \leq t$ **in parallel** set v_α to be n_α-th neighbor of v in G, and add an edge from α to $(v_\alpha, i_\alpha, j+1)$ to $\mathcal{G}_S$.

(2) For any vertex $\alpha \in \mathcal{G}_S$, define $N_0(\alpha) = \beta$ where $(\alpha, \beta) \in \mathcal{G}_S$ is the (only) outgoing edge of α in $\mathcal{G}_S$ (define $\beta = \perp$ if α belongs to $\mathcal{V}_{t+1}$ and hence has no outgoing edge).

(3) For $i = 1$ to $\log t$ phases: For every $\alpha \in \mathcal{G}_S$ **in parallel** let $N_i(\alpha) = N_{i-1}(N_{i-1}(\alpha))$ (assuming $N_{i-1}(\perp) = \perp$).

(4) For any $\alpha \in \mathcal{V}_1^*$, return $v = v(N_{\log t}(\alpha))$ as the target of the vertex $u = v(\alpha)$ (recall that $\mathcal{V}_1^*$ is the set of all vertices $(u, 1, 1) \in \mathcal{V}$ for $u \in V(G)$).

We first have the following simple claim.

Claim 4.3. *For any vertex $\alpha \in \mathcal{V}_1^*$ of $\mathcal{G}_S$, $N_{\log t}(\alpha)$ is the endpoint of the path $\mathcal{P}_\alpha$ in $\mathcal{G}_S$.*

Proof. We prove by induction that $N_i(\alpha)$ is the vertex at distance 2^i from α in $\mathcal{P}_\alpha$. The base case for $i = 0$ is true as $N_0(\alpha) = \beta$ where β is the endpoint of the outgoing edge of α. For $i > 0$, by induction, $N_{i-1}(\alpha)$ is the vertex θ at distance 2^{i-1} from α and $N_{i-1}(\theta)$ is the vertex at distance 2^{i-1} from θ. Hence $N_i(\alpha) = N_{i-1}(N_{i-1}(\alpha))$ is at distance 2^i from α (as $\mathcal{G}_S$ is a directed acyclic graph with edges going only from one layer to the next). As such, $N_{\log t}(\alpha)$ is at distance t from α and hence is the endpoint of the path $\mathcal{P}_\alpha$. ∎

We say that SimpleRandomWalk(G, t) *finds* the vertex v for u if v is returned as the target vertex of u. Claim 4.3 combined with the construction of sampled layered graph already implies that for any vertex $u \in V(G)$, the vertex v found by SimpleRandomWalk is distributed according to $\mathcal{D}_{\mathrm{RW}}(u, t)$. We further have,

Lemma 4.4. *For any vertex $u \in G$, SimpleRandomWalk(G, t) finds a vertex $v \sim \mathcal{D}_{\mathrm{RW}}(u, t)$ such that with probability at least 1/2, v is* independent *of all other vertices found by* SimpleRandomWalk.

Proof. Follows immediately from Claim 4.3 and Lemma 4.2 and the fact that random bits used in vertex disjoint paths of $\mathcal{G}_S$ are independent of each other. ∎

By Lemma 4.4, we are able to find $\Omega(n)$ independent random walks in G with high probability. In the full version of the paper, we show that by running SimpleRandomWalk *in parallel* $O(\log n)$ times and combining them in $O(\log \log n)$ rounds, we can find a collection of independent random walks from *every* vertex of the graph with high probability.

5 Step 3: Connectivity on Random Graphs

In this section we present the final and paramount step of our algorithm, which involves finding connected components of a collection of disjoint random graphs chosen from $\mathbb{G}$.

Lemma 5.1. *Let $G(V, E)$ be a graph on n vertices such that any connected component G_i of G with $n_i = |V(G_i)|$ is sampled from $\mathbb{G}(n_i, 100 \log n)$. There exists an MPC algorithm which identifies all connected components of G with high probability (over the randomness of the algorithm and the distribution $\mathbb{G}$).*

For any $\delta > 0$, the algorithm can be implemented with $O(n^{1-\delta}) \cdot \mathrm{polylog}(n)$ machines each with $O(n^\delta) \cdot \mathrm{polylog}(n)$ memory and $O(\frac{1}{\delta} \cdot \log \log n)$ MPC rounds.

During the course of our exposition in this section, we need to set many parameters which we collect here for convenience.

- $\varepsilon := (100 \cdot \log n)^{-2}$: discrepancy of almost-regular graphs,
- $s := \frac{10^6 \cdot \log n}{\varepsilon^2}$: scaler for degree of almost-regular graphs,
- $\Delta := 100 \cdot s$: the degree of almost-regular graphs,
- $F := \arg\min_i \left\{\Delta^{2^i} \geq n^{1/100}\right\}$: number of phases.

Throughout this section, we define the degree of almost-regular graphs by multiplicative factors of s; this is needed to simplify many concentration bounds used in the proofs. We further point out that $F = O(\log\log n)$ and $\Delta^F \in [n^{1/100}, n^{1/50}]$ and hence $\Delta^{-F} = o(\varepsilon)$.

Preprocessing step. The first step in proving Lemma 5.1, is to make each connected component G_i of G "more random", i.e., turn it to a graph sampled from $\mathbb{G}$ with larger per-vertex degree. This can be easily done using Lemma 4.1 in previous section, as the graph $G_i \sim \mathbb{G}(n_i, 100\log n)$ has a small mixing time (see full version).

Now consider the following preprocessing process: For $(F \cdot \Delta \cdot s/(100\log n))$ steps in parallel, we run the algorithm in Lemma 4.1 on the original graph G. For each connected component G_i of G, this results us in having F graphs $\widetilde{G}_{i,1}, \ldots, \widetilde{G}_{i,F}$ which are (almost) sampled from the distribution $\mathbb{G}(n_i, \Delta \cdot s)$ (the distribution of these graphs is not exactly identical to this, but is rather close to this distribution in total variation distance which is sufficient for our purpose). As such, we now need to find the connected component of a graph $\widetilde{G}$ which is the union of all $\widetilde{G}_{i,j}$ for i ranging over all connected components of G and $j \in [F]$.

In the following lemma, we design an algorithm for this task. For simplicity of exposition, we state this lemma for the case of finding a spanning tree of one such connected component (i.e., assuming G itself is sampled from $\mathbb{G}$ as opposed to having its connected components sampled from this distribution); however, it would be evident that running this algorithm on the original input results in finding a spanning tree of each connected component separately.

Lemma 5.2. *Let $\widetilde{G}$ be a graph on n vertices such that $\widetilde{G} = \widetilde{G}_1 \cup \ldots \cup \widetilde{G}_F$ where $\widetilde{G}_i \sim \mathbb{G}(n, \Delta \cdot s)$. There exists an MPC algorithm that can find a spanning tree of $\widetilde{G}$ with high probability (over both the randomness of the algorithm and the distribution $\mathbb{G}$).*

For any $\delta > 0$, the algorithm can be implemented with $O(n^{1-\delta}) \cdot \text{polylog}(n)$ machines each with $O(n^{\delta}) \cdot \text{polylog}(n)$ memory, and in $O(\frac{1}{\delta} \cdot \log\log n)$ MPC rounds.

The rest of this section is devoted to the proof of Lemma 5.2. At the end of the section, we use this lemma to prove Lemma 5.1. In this section, n always refer to number of vertices in $\widetilde{G}$.

5.1 Proof of Lemma 5.2

We start with a simple definition.

Definition 2 (Contraction Graph). *For a graph $G(V, E)$ and a partition $C := \{C_1, \ldots, C_k\}$ of $V(G)$ (not necessarily a component-partition), we construct a* contraction graph *H of G with respect to C as the following graph:*

1. ***Vertex-set:** The vertex-set $V(H)$ of H is a collection of k vertices where $w_i \in V(H)$ is labeled with the component C_i of C, denoted by $C(w_i)$.*
2. ***Edge-set:** For any $w \neq z \in V(H)$, there exists an edge $(w, z) \in E(H)$ iff there exists vertices $u \in C(w)$ and $v \in C(z)$ where $(u, v) \in E(G)$ (H contains no parallel edges and no self-loops).*

In other words, H is obtained by "contracting" the vertices of G inside each set of C into a single vertex and removing parallel edges and self-loops.

Suppose C is a component-partition of G and H is a contraction graph of G with respect to H. Then it is immediate to see that we can construct a spanning tree (or forest) of G given only spanning trees of each component in C and a spanning tree of H.

Overview of the algorithm. The algorithm in Lemma 5.2 goes through F *phases*. In each phase $i \in [F]$, it only considers the edges in $\widetilde{G}_i$ and use them to "grow" the components of $\widetilde{G}$ found in the previous phases. This part is done using a new *leader-election* algorithm that we design in this paper. This algorithm takes the contraction graph of $\widetilde{G}_i$ with respect to the set of components found already, and merge these components further to build larger components. The novelty of this leader-election algorithm is that starting from an (almost) d-regular graph, it can grow each component by a factor of (almost) d (as opposed to typical leader-election algorithms that only increase size of each component by a constant factor).

Our main algorithm is then obtained by successively applying this leader election algorithm to contraction graph of $\widetilde{G}_i$ to build relatively large components of $\widetilde{G}_i$ and use them to refine the components found for G. The main step of our proof is to argue that if contraction graph of $\widetilde{G}_i$ was a *random* (almost) d-regular graph on n' vertices, then the contraction graph of $\widetilde{G}_{i+1}$ in this process would be another random (almost) d^2-regular graph on roughly n'/d vertices. Having achieved this, we can argue that each component of the graph G grows by a quadratic factor in each phase, and hence after only $O(\log\log n)$ phase, each component has size $n^{\Omega(1)}$ (due to technical reasons, one cannot continue this argument until just one connected component of size n remains). Finally, we prove that at this step, the diameter of the remaining graph, i.e., contraction of G on the found components is only $O(1)$. A simple broadcasting algorithm can then be used to found a spanning tree of the remaining graph in $O(1)$ rounds.

A Leader Election Algorithm

We introduce a leader election algorithm, called LeaderElection(H, d), which gets as an input an (almost) $(d \cdot s)$-regular graph and creates components of size (almost) d in this graph.

LeaderElection(H, d). A simple leader election algorithm for growing connected components on an (almost) $(d \cdot s)$-regular graph H.

1. Set $L = \emptyset$ initially.
2. For every vertex $v \in V(H)$ **in parallel** independently sample $p(v)$ from the Bernoulli distribution with probability $p := s/d$ and insert u to L iff $p(v) = 1$ (we refer to these vertices as *leaders*).
3. Let $R := V(H) \setminus L$.
4. For any vertex $v \in R$ **in parallel** set $N_L(v)$ be the set of neighbors of v in L in graph H.
5. For any vertex $v \in R$ **in parallel** let $M(v)$ be a vertex $u \in R$ chosen uniformly at random from $N_L(v)$ (we define $M(v) = \perp$ if $N_L(v) = \emptyset$).
6. Return $k := |L|$ sets $S_{v_1}, \ldots, S_{v_k}$ for $v_1, \ldots, v_k \in L$ such that $S_{v_i} = \{v_i\} \cup \{u \in R : M(u) = v_i\}$ (vertices with $M(u) = \perp$ are ignored).

We have the following simple claim (see full version for proof).

Claim 5.3. *Suppose in* LeaderElection *no vertex* $v \in R$ *has* $M(v) = \perp$. *Then, the collection* $S_1, \ldots, S_k$ *is a component-partition of* H.

The main property of LeaderElection is that when computed on almost regular graphs it results in a component-partition with *almost equal size components.* In other words, if H is a $[\![(1 \pm \varepsilon)d \cdot s]\!]$-almost-regular graph, then the resulting components are of size $[\![(1 \pm O(\varepsilon)) \cdot d]\!]$ each. The proof is deferred to the full version.

Lemma 5.4 (Equipartition Lemma). *Let* $\bar{\varepsilon} \in (\varepsilon, 1/100)$ *and* H *be a* $[\![(1 \pm \bar{\varepsilon})\, d \cdot s]\!]$*-almost-regular graph for* $d \geq s$. *Then, with probability* $1 - 1/n^{23}$, *for* $(S_1, \ldots, S_k) =$ LeaderElection(H, d):

(1) *For all* $i \in [k]$, $|S_i| \in [\![(1 \pm 3\bar{\varepsilon})\, d]\!]$.

(2) $(S_1, \ldots, S_k)$ *is a component-partition of* $V(H)$.

Growing Connected Components

We now use LeaderElection algorithm from the previous section to design our main algorithm which "grows" the size of connected components of G repeatedly over F phases.

GrowComponents$(\widetilde{G}, \Delta)$. An algorithm for "growing" connected components of size up to $n^{\Omega(1)}$ in a given graph $\widetilde{G} = \widetilde{G}_1 \cup \ldots \cup \widetilde{G}_F$ where $\widetilde{G}_i \sim \mathbb{G}(n, \Delta \cdot s)$.

(1) Let C_1 be a partition of $V(\widetilde{G})$ into singleton sets.
(2) For $i = 1$ to F phases:
  (a) Let $\Delta_i := \Delta^{2^{i-1}}$ and $p_i = \Delta_i^{-1} \cdot s$.
  (b) For every vertex $v \in V(\widetilde{G}_i)$ **in parallel** let $c_i(v) = j$ for $v \in C_j$.
  (c) Construct contraction graph H_i of $\widetilde{G}_i$ (*not* $\widetilde{G}$) with respect to C_i as follows:
    (i) Set H_i to be an empty set inititially.
    (ii) For every edge $(u, v) \in E(\widetilde{G}_i)$ **in parallel** add $(C_{c_i(u)}, C_{c_i(v)})$ to H_i.
  (d) Compute $(S_1, \ldots, S_k) =$ LeaderElection(H_i, Δ_i) (hence, each $S_j \subseteq V(H_i)$).
  (e) For each S_j **in parallel** let $C_{i+1,j} = \bigcup_{w \in S_j} C_i(w)$.
  (f) Let $C_{i+1} = \{C_{i+1,1}, \ldots, C_{i+1,k}\}$.
(3) Return the graph H_F.

We prove that for each phase $i \in [F]$, the contraction graph H_i constructed in this phase is an almost-regular graph with degree roughly $\Delta_i \cdot s$ and discrepancy factor $\varepsilon_i := (20^i \cdot \varepsilon)$. The following lemma is the heart of the proof.

Lemma 5.5. *In* GrowComponents$(\widetilde{G}, \Delta)$, *with high probability, for any* $i \in [F]$:

(I) C_i *is a component-partition of* $\widetilde{G}$ *with* $|C_{i,j}| \in [\![(1 \pm \varepsilon_i)\, \Delta_i/\Delta]\!]$ *for all* $C_{i,j} \in C_i$.

(II) H_i *is a* $[\![(1 \pm \varepsilon_i)\, \Delta_i \cdot s]\!]$*-almost-regular graph on*

$$n_i \in [\![(1 \pm \varepsilon_i) \cdot n\Delta/\Delta_i]\!]$$

vertices.

Proof. We prove this lemma inductively.

Base case: C_1 is clearly a component-partition of $\widetilde{G}$ as it only consists of singleton sets and $|C_{1,j}| = 1$ for all $C_{1,j} \in C_1$. Since $\Delta_1 = \Delta$, this proves the first part of the lemma in the base case. For the second part, as C_1 only consists of singleton sets, $H_1 = \widetilde{G}_1$ and hence $n_1 = n$. Finally, $H_1 = \widetilde{G}_1 \sim \mathbb{G}(n, \Delta \cdot s)$ and hence a simple Chernoff bound ensures that H_1 is a $[\![(1 \pm \varepsilon)\, \Delta \cdot s]\!]$-almost-regular graph, hence concluding the proof of the base case.

Induction step: Now suppose the lemma for $i > 1$ and we prove it for $i + 1$. By induction, we have that H_i is a $[\![(1 \pm \varepsilon_i)\, \Delta_i \cdot s]\!]$-almost-regular graph on $n_i \in [\![(1 \pm \varepsilon_i) \cdot n \cdot \Delta/\Delta_i]\!]$ vertices. In this phase, we compute $(S_1, \ldots, S_k) =$ LeaderElection(H_i, Δ_i). We can thus apply Lemma 5.4 with parameters $d = \Delta_i$, $p = p_i$, and $\bar{\varepsilon} = \varepsilon_i < 1/100$, and obtain that with high probability,

$$|S_i| \in [\![(1 \pm 3\bar{\varepsilon}) \cdot \Delta_i]\!] = [\![(1 \pm 3\varepsilon_i) \cdot \Delta_i]\!], \quad (1)$$

and $(S_1, \ldots, S_k)$ is a component-partition of H_i. In the following, we condition on this event.

Proof of part (I): Since C_i is a component-partition of $\widetilde{G}$ (by induction), we have that vertices in H_i correspond to components of $\widetilde{G}$, i.e., vertices in $C_i(w)$ for all $w \in V(H_i)$ are connected in $\widetilde{G}$. Moreover, by Lemma 5.4, $(S_1, \ldots, S_k)$ is a component-partition of H_i and hence vertices (of H_i) in each S_j for $j \in [k]$ are connected to each other (in H_i). As edges of H_i correspond to edges in $\widetilde{G}_i \subseteq \widetilde{G}$, any $C_{i+1,j} \in C_{i+1}$ is a component of $\widetilde{G}$, hence C_{i+1} is a component-partition of $\widetilde{G}$.

We now prove the bound on size of each $C_{i+1,j} \in C_{i+1}$. By definition,

$$|C_{i+1,j}| = \sum_{w \in S_j} |C_i(w)| \in [\![|S_j| \cdot (1 \pm \varepsilon_i)\, \Delta_i/\Delta]\!]$$

(by induction hypothesis on $C_i(w) \in C_i$)

$$\subseteq [\![((1 \pm 3\varepsilon_i) \cdot \Delta_i) \cdot ((1 \pm \varepsilon_i)\, \Delta_i/\Delta)]\!] \quad \text{(by Eq (1))}$$

$$\subseteq [\![(1 \pm 5\varepsilon_i) \cdot \Delta_i^2/\Delta]\!] = [\![(1 \pm 5\varepsilon_i) \cdot \Delta_{i+1}/\Delta]\!], \quad (2)$$

as $\Delta_i^2 = \Delta_{i+1}$. By the choice of $\varepsilon_{i+1} > 5\varepsilon_i$, this finalizes the proof of the first part. We now consider the second part.

Proof of part (II): Notice that $n_{i+1} = |C_{i+1}|$ as each set in C_{i+1} is contracted to a single vertex in H_{i+1}. Since C_{i+1} partitions $V(G)$, and as by Eq (2) each set in C_{i+1} has size in $[\![(1 \pm 5\varepsilon_i) \cdot \Delta_{i+1}/\Delta]\!]$, we have

$$n_{i+1} \in [\![\frac{n}{(1 \pm 5\varepsilon_i) \cdot \Delta_{i+1}/\Delta}]\!] \subseteq [\![(1 \pm 6\varepsilon_i)\, n \cdot \Delta/\Delta_{i+1}]\!]. \quad (3)$$

As $\varepsilon_{i+1} > 6\varepsilon_i$, this proves the bound on n_{i+1}. It remains to prove H_{i+1} is an $[\![(1 \pm \varepsilon_{i+1})\, \Delta_{i+1} \cdot s]\!]$-almost-regular graph. This is the main part of the argument.

Lemma 5.6. *For any vertex* $w \in V(H_{i+1})$, *degree of* w *in* H_{i+1} *is* $d_w \in [\![(1 \pm \varepsilon_{i+1})\, \Delta_{i+1} \cdot s]\!]$ *with high probability.*

Proof. Recall that H_{i+1} is a contraction graph of $\widetilde{G}_{i+1}$ with respect to the partition C_{i+1}. We define $C = C_{i+1}(w) \in C_{i+1}$. In H_{i+1}, w has an edge to another vertex $z \in V(H_{i+1})$ iff there exists a vertex $u \in C \subseteq V(\widetilde{G}_{i+1})$ such that u has an edge to some vertex $v \in C_{i+1}(z)$ in the graph $\widetilde{G}_{i+1}$. As such, degree of w is equal to the number of sets $C_{i+1,j} \subseteq V(\widetilde{G}_{i+1})$ such that there is an edge $(u,v) \in E(\widetilde{G}_{i+1})$ for $u \in C$ and $v \in C_{i+1,j}$.

Now consider the process of generating $\widetilde{G}_{i+1} \sim \mathbb{G}(n, \Delta \cdot s)$ and notice that the edges chosen in $\widetilde{G}_{i+1}$ are chosen independent of the choice of C_{i+1} as C_{i+1} is only a function of the graphs $\widetilde{G}_1, \ldots, \widetilde{G}_i$. Moreover, recall that in $\mathbb{G}(n, \Delta \cdot s)$ each vertex chooses $\Delta \cdot s/2$ other vertices uniformly at random to connect to (and then we remove the direction of edges). For any two sets $S, T \subseteq V(\widetilde{G}_{i+1})$, we say that S "hits" T if there exists a vertex in S which picks a directed edge to some vertex in T in the process of generating $\widetilde{G}_{i+1}$ (so it is possible that S hits T but T does not hit S). Let $K \subseteq [k]$ be such that for each $j \in K$, either C hits $C_{i+1,j}$ or vice versa. By the above argument $d_w \in [\![|K| \pm 1]\!]$ (to account for the fact that C hitting C does not change the degree of w as we have no self-loops in H_{i+1}). In the following two claims, we bound $|K|$. We postpone the proofs of these two claims to the full version.

Claim 5.7. *Let $K^+ \subseteq [k]$ be the set of all indices $j \in [k]$ such that C hits $C_{i+1,j}$. Then, with high probability, $|K^+| \in [\![(1 \pm \varepsilon_{i+1})\,\Delta_{i+1} \cdot s/2]\!]$.*

One interpretation of Claim 5.7 is that that distribution of H_{i+1} is similar to $\mathbb{G}(n_{i+1}, \Delta_{i+1} \cdot s)$ with the difference that the number of out-edges chosen in $\mathbb{G}$ is not exactly $\Delta_{i+1} \cdot s$ (but quite close to it for each vertex). As such, we would expect H_{i+1} to still behave similarly as $\mathbb{G}(n_{i+1}, \Delta_{i+1} \cdot s)$; in particular, be almost-regular with high probability.

Claim 5.8. *Let $K^- \subseteq [k]$ be the set of all indices $j \in [k] \setminus K^+$ such that $C_{i+1,j}$ hits C. Then, with high probability, $|K^-| \in [\![(1 \pm \varepsilon_{i+1})\,\Delta_{i+1} \cdot s/2]\!]$.*

Lemma 5.6 now follows from Claims 5.7 and 5.8. ∎ Lemma 5.6

To conclude the proof of Lemma 5.5, we simply take a union bound on all vertices $w \in V(H_{i+1})$ and by Lemma 5.6 obtain that with high probability $d_w \in [\![(1 \pm \varepsilon_{i+1})\,\Delta_{i+1} \cdot s]\!]$. This implies that H_{i+1} is a $[\![(1 \pm \varepsilon_{i+1})\,\Delta_{i+1} \cdot s]\!]$-almost regular graph, proving the induction step. ∎ Lemma 5.5

Finally, we claim that GrowComponents can also find a spanning tree of components in C_F.

Claim 5.9. *Let T be the set of edges chosen in* LeaderElection *(in defining $M(\cdot)$ for each non-leader vertex) in the course of execution of* GrowComponents$(\widetilde{G}, \Delta)$. *With high probability, the induced subgraph of T on each component in C_F is a spanning tree.*

Building the Spanning Tree

Recall that by the choice of F, $\Delta_F \in [n^{1/100}, n^{1/50}]$. By running GrowComponents$(\widetilde{G}, \Delta)$, we obtain a graph H_F which consists of $n_F \in [\![(1 \pm o(1)) \cdot n \cdot \Delta/\Delta_F]\!]$ vertices. Additionally, by Claim 5.7, with high probability, H_F is a "random" graph (in spirit of $\mathbb{G}$) with $[\![(1 \pm o(1))\,\Delta_F]\!]$ "out-degree" before removing the direction of edges. We use this to bound the diameter of H_F.

Claim 5.10. *Diameter of H_F is $D = O(1)$ with high probability.*

We use the above claim to design a very simple algorithm to build a spanning tree of H_F. We then combine this algorithm with GrowComponents to prove Lemma 5.2.

Claim 5.11. *Let H be any graph with m edges, n vertices, and diameter D. A spanning tree of H can be found in $O(D/\delta)$ MPC rounds with $O(m^{1-\delta})$ machines with memory $O(m^{\delta})$ for any $\delta > 0$.*

We are now ready to conclude the proof of Lemma 5.2.

Proof of Lemma 5.2. By Claim 5.9, we can find a spanning tree of every component of $\widetilde{G}$ in C_F. This step requires $O(\log\log n/\delta)$ MPC rounds on $\widetilde{O}(n^{1-\delta})$ machines of memory $\widetilde{O}(n^{\delta})$ (as $|E(\widetilde{G})| = \widetilde{O}(n)$ by construction). Note that the components in C_F correspond to vertices of H_F and hence by finding a spanning tree of H_F we obtain a spanning tree of $\widetilde{G}$.

By Claim 5.10, diameter of H_F is only $O(1)$. Hence, by the algorithm in Claim 5.11, we can find a spanning tree of H_F in only $O(1/\delta)$ rounds on machines of memory $O(n^{\delta})$. Combining these trees, we obtain a spanning tree of $\widetilde{G}$, finalizing the proof. ∎

6 Putting Everything Together

We now put all components of our algorithms in the previous three sections together and prove the following theorem which formalize Theorem 1 in the introduction.

Theorem 4. *There exists a randomized MPC algorithm that with high probability identifies all connected components of any given undirected n-vertex graph $G(V,E)$ with m edges and a lower bound of $\lambda \in (0,1)$ on the spectral gap of any of its connected components. For any $\delta > 0$, the algorithm can be implemented with $O(\frac{1}{\lambda^2} \cdot m^{1-\delta} \cdot \text{polylog}(n))$ machines each with $O(m^{\delta} \cdot \text{polylog}(n))$ memory, and in $O(\frac{1}{\delta} \cdot (\log\log n + \log(1/\lambda)))$ MPC rounds.*

Proof. We prove this theorem by applying the transformation steps in the previous sections to graph G.

<u>*Step 1.*</u> Let $G_1 := G$ with $n_1 := |V(G_1)|$ and $m_1 := |E(G_1)|$. We apply Lemma 3.1 to G_1 to obtain a Δ-regular graph G_2 with the following properties (with high probability): there is a one-to-one correspondence between connected components of G_1 and G_2, and each connected component of G_2 has mixing time $T_{\gamma^*} = O(\log n/\lambda)$ with $\gamma^* = n^{-10}$. Moreover, $n_2 := |V(G_2)| = O(m_1)$ and $\Delta = O(1)$. By identifying connected components of G_2, we immediately identify connected components of G_1.

This step can be implemented in $O(m^{1-\delta})$ machines with $O(m^{\delta})$ memory in $O(1/\delta)$ MPC rounds by Lemma 3.1 (as $m_1 = m$).

<u>*Step 2.*</u> We apply Lemma 4.1 to G_2 with $T = T_{\gamma^*}$ to (with high probability) obtain a graph G_3 such that $V(G_2) = V(G_3)$ and for any connected component $G_{2,i}$ on $n_{2,i}$ vertices, the induced subgraph of G_3 on vertices $V(G_{2,i})$, denoted by $G_{3,i}$, is a connected component of G_3 with distribution $\mathbb{D}(G_{3,i})$ where

$$\left|\mathbb{D}(G_{3,i}) - \mathbb{G}(n_{2,i}, 100\log n)\right|_{tvd} \leq n^{-10}.$$

Identifying connected components of G_2 is equivalent to identifying connected components of G_3.

This step can be implemented with $\widetilde{O}(n_2^{1-\delta})$ machines with $\widetilde{O}(n_2^{\delta})$ memory in $O((\log T + \log\log n)/\delta)$ rounds by Lemma 4.1. Plugging in the value of these parameters, we obtain that this step is implementable with $\widetilde{O}(m^{1-\delta})$ machines with $\widetilde{O}(m^{\delta})$ memory in $O(\frac{1}{\delta}(\log\log n + \log(1/\lambda)))$ MPC rounds.

Step 3. Let $n_3 = n_2$ be the number of vertices in G_3. We apply Lemma 5.1 to G_3 to identify the connected components of G. The distribution of each connected component $G_{3,i}$ of G_3 is (n^{-8})-close in total variation distance to $\mathbb{G}(n_{2,i}, 100\log n)$ $(n_{2,i} = |V(G_{3,i})|)$. Hence, by the guarantee of Lemma 5.1 with high probability we are able to identify connected components of the graph G_3. This allows us to identify connected components of G_2 and $G_1 = G$.

This step can be implemented in $\widetilde{O}(n_3^{1-\delta})$ machines with $\widetilde{O}(n_3^{\delta})$ memory in $O(\log\log n_3/\delta)$ rounds by Lemma 5.1. Plugging in the value of these parameters, we obtain that this step is implementable with $\widetilde{O}(m^{1-\delta})$ machines with $\widetilde{O}(m^{\delta})$ memory in $O(\log\log n/\delta)$ MPC rounds.

This concludes the proof of the theorem. ∎

7 A Mildly Sublinear Space Algorithm for Connectivity

In this section, we present a simple algorithm for solving the sparse connectivity problem (in general, e.g., with no assumption on spectral gap, etc.) using $o(n)$ memory per-machine, proving Theorem 2 from introduction.

The algorithm in Theorem 2 is a simple application of the toolkit we developed for proving our main result in Theorem 4, combined with the linear-sketching algorithm of Ahn *et al.* [2] for graph connectivity. In particular, we use the following result from [2].

Proposition 7.1 ([2]). *Let H be any graph partitioned between $|V(H)|$ players such that each player receives all edges incident on a unique vertex in $V(H)$ (hence each edge is received by exactly two players). There exists a randomized algorithm in which every player sends a message of size $O(\log^3|V(H)|)$ bits to a central coordinator who can output all connected components of H using only these messages with high probability. The algorithm requires players to have access to* polylog$(|V(H)|)$ shared random bits.

We are now ready to present the algorithm in Theorem 2.

SublinearConn(G). A mildly sublinear space algorithm for connectivity on a given graph G.

(1) Set $d := \frac{n\cdot(\log n)^4}{s}$ and $t := (d^3 \cdot 100\log n)$, and run SimpleRandomWalk(G, t).
(2) Create a graph $\widetilde{G}$ from G by connecting every vertex $v \in V(G)$ to all *distinct* vertices visited in the random walk starting from v computed in the previous step.
(3) Run LeaderElection$(\widetilde{G}, d)$ and let H be the graph obtained by contracting any component found by LeaderElection to a single vertex.
(4) Remove self-loops and duplicate edges from H and run the algorithm in Proposition 7.1 on H by using a dedicated machine to simulate a single player.

Theorem 2 can then be proven using SublinearConn algorithm as we show in the full version of the paper.

8 An Unconditional Lower Bound

We prove an *unconditional* lower bound on the number of MPC rounds required to solve the connectivity problem on *sparse* undirected graphs with a *constant spectral gap*. More formally, we henceforth denote by ExpanderConn$_n$ the decision *promise* problem of determining connectivity on n-vertex graphs G, where in both cases (each connected component of) G is guaranteed to be a sparse expander ($|E(G)| = O(n)$ and the spectral gap of each component is $\lambda_2 = \Omega(1)$).

Theorem 5 (Lower bound for expander connectivity). *Every MPC algorithm for* ExpanderConn$_n$ *with s space per machine (and an* arbitrary *number of machines) requires $r = \Omega(\log_s n)$ rounds of computation. This holds even against randomized MPC protocols with constant error probability.*

Proof of Theorem 5 uses a characterization result of [42] for MPC algorithms and appears in the full version of the paper.

We remark that Theorem 5 suggests that any MPC algorithm with polylog(n) memory per machine for connectivity even on union of expander graphs requires $\Omega(\log n/\log\log n)$ MPC rounds. In Remark 8.1, we further show a similar situation for (EREW) PRAM algorithms. Moreover, by a result of [42], the lower bound in Theorem 5 is asymptotically the best possible unconditional lower bound short of proving that $\mathrm{NC}^1 \subsetneq \mathrm{P}$ which would be a major breakthrough in complexity theory.

Remark 8.1 (Extension to the PRAM model). In Theorem 5 we proved the lower bound for ExpanderConn$_n$ in the MPC model as our main focus in this paper is on this model after all. However, our proof of Theorem 5 implies that ExpanderConn$_n$ requires $\Omega(\log n)$ rounds in the (EREW) PRAM model as well. The reason is that our proof implies ExpanderConn$_n$ is a *critical* function of $\Omega(n/\log n)$ variables: its output depends on the existence or non-existence of the $k = \Omega(n/\log n)$ expanders graphs $B_1, \ldots, B_k$ (think of ExpanderConn$_n$ as OR function of k bits, each denoting whether the i-th expander B_i is present in G or not). By results of [15, 38] this requires $\Omega(\log n)$ rounds in the (EREW) PRAM model.

Acknowledgments

We thank Alex Andoni, Michael Kapralov, Sanjeev Khanna, and Krzysztof Onak for helpful discussions. We are particularly grateful to Krzysztof Onak for pointing out a flaw in our original argument on the correctness of our random walk data structure that is fixed in the current version.

References

[1] Kook Jin Ahn and Sudipto Guha. 2015. Access to Data and Number of Iterations: Dual Primal Algorithms for Maximum Matching under Resource Constraints. In *Proceedings of the 27th ACM on Symposium on Parallelism in Algorithms and Architectures, SPAA 2015, Portland, OR, USA, June 13-15, 2015.* 202–211.
[2] Kook Jin Ahn, Sudipto Guha, and Andrew McGregor. 2012. Analyzing Graph Structure via Linear Measurements. In *Proceedings of the Twenty-third Annual ACM-SIAM Symposium on Discrete Algorithms (SODA '12).* SIAM, 459–467. http://dl.acm.org/citation.cfm?id=2095116.2095156
[3] Alexandr Andoni, Aleksandar Nikolov, Krzysztof Onak, and Grigory Yaroslavtsev. 2014. Parallel algorithms for geometric graph problems. In *Symposium on Theory of Computing, STOC 2014, New York, NY, USA, May 31 - June 03, 2014.* 574–583.
[4] Alexandr Andoni, Zhao Song, Clifford Stein, Zhengyu Wang, and Peilin Zhong. 2018. Parallel Graph Connectivity in Log Diameter Rounds. In *59th IEEE Annual*

Symposium on Foundations of Computer Science, FOCS 2018, Paris, France, October 7-9, 2018. 674–685.

[5] Sepehr Assadi. 2017. Simple Round Compression for Parallel Vertex Cover. *CoRR* abs/1709.04599 (2017).

[6] Sepehr Assadi, MohammadHossein Bateni, Aaron Bernstein, Vahab S. Mirrokni, and Cliff Stein. 2019. Coresets Meet EDCS: Algorithms for Matching and Vertex Cover on Massive Graphs. In *Proceedings of the Thirtieth Annual ACM-SIAM Symposium on Discrete Algorithms, SODA 2019, San Diego, California, USA, January 6-9, 2019.* 1616–1635.

[7] Sepehr Assadi, Yu Chen, and Sanjeev Khanna. 2019. Sublinear Algorithms for (Δ + 1) Vertex Coloring. In *Proceedings of the Thirtieth Annual ACM-SIAM Symposium on Discrete Algorithms, SODA 2019, San Diego, California, USA, January 6-9, 2019.* 767–786.

[8] Sepehr Assadi and Sanjeev Khanna. 2017. Randomized Composable Coresets for Matching and Vertex Cover. In *Proceedings of the 29th ACM Symposium on Parallelism in Algorithms and Architectures, SPAA 2017, Washington DC, USA, July 24-26, 2017.* 3–12.

[9] Paul Beame, Paraschos Koutris, and Dan Suciu. 2013. Communication steps for parallel query processing. In *Proceedings of the 32nd ACM SIGMOD-SIGACT-SIGART Symposium on Principles of Database Systems, PODS 2013, New York, NY, USA - June 22 - 27, 2013.* 273–284.

[10] Soheil Behnezhad, Mahsa Derakhshan, and MohammadTaghi Hajiaghayi. 2018. Brief Announcement: Semi-MapReduce Meets Congested Clique. *CoRR* abs/1802.10297 (2018).

[11] Soheil Behnezhad, Mahsa Derakhshan, MohammadTaghi Hajiaghayi, and Richard M. Karp. 2018. Massively Parallel Symmetry Breaking on Sparse Graphs: MIS and Maximal Matching. *CoRR* abs/1807.06701 (2018).

[12] Soheil Behnezhad, MohammadTaghi Hajiaghayi, and David G. Harris. 2019. Exponentially Faster Massively Parallel Maximal Matching. *CoRR* abs/1901.03744 (2019).

[13] Sebastian Brandt, Manuela Fischer, and Jara Uitto. 2018. Matching and MIS for Uniformly Sparse Graphs in the Low-Memory MPC Model. *CoRR* abs/1807.05374 (2018).

[14] Yi-Jun Chang, Manuela Fischer, Mohsen Ghaffari, Jara Uitto, and Yufan Zheng. 2018. The Complexity of (Delta+1) Coloring inCongested Clique, Massively Parallel Computation, and Centralized Local Computation. *arXiv preprint arXiv:1808.08419* (2018).

[15] Stephen A. Cook, Cynthia Dwork, and Rüdiger Reischuk. 1986. Upper and Lower Time Bounds for Parallel Random Access Machines without Simultaneous Writes. *SIAM J. Comput.* 15, 1 (1986), 87–97.

[16] Artur Czumaj, Jakub Lacki, Aleksander Madry, Slobodan Mitrovic, Krzysztof Onak, and Piotr Sankowski. 2018. Round compression for parallel matching algorithms. In *Proceedings of the 50th Annual ACM SIGACT Symposium on Theory of Computing, STOC 2018, Los Angeles, CA, USA, June 25-29, 2018.* 471–484.

[17] Jeffrey Dean and Sanjay Ghemawat. 2004. MapReduce: Simplified Data Processing on Large Clusters. In *Proceedings of the 6th Conference on Symposium on Opearting Systems Design & Implementation - Volume 6 (OSDI'04).* USENIX Association, Berkeley, CA, USA, 10–10. http://dl.acm.org/citation.cfm?id=1251254.1251264

[18] Hillel Gazit. 1986. An optimal randomized parallel algorithm for finding connected components in a graph. In *Foundations of Computer Science, 1986., 27th Annual Symposium on.* IEEE, 492–501.

[19] Mohsen Ghaffari, Themis Gouleakis, Slobodan Mitrovic, and Ronitt Rubinfeld. 2018. Improved Massively Parallel Computation Algorithms for MIS, Matching, and Vertex Cover. *CoRR* abs/1802.08237 (2018).

[20] Mohsen Ghaffari and Merav Parter. 2016. MST in Log-Star Rounds of Congested Clique. In *Proceedings of the 2016 ACM Symposium on Principles of Distributed Computing, PODC 2016, Chicago, IL, USA, July 25-28, 2016.* 19–28.

[21] Mohsen Ghaffari and Jara Uitto. 2019. Sparsifying Distributed Algorithms with Ramifications in Massively Parallel Computation and Centralized Local Computation. In *Proceedings of the Thirtieth Annual ACM-SIAM Symposium on Discrete Algorithms, SODA 2019, San Diego, California, USA, January 6-9, 2019.* 1636–1653.

[22] Christos Gkantsidis, Milena Mihail, and Amin Saberi. 2003. Conductance and congestion in power law graphs. In *Proceedings of the International Conference on Measurements and Modeling of Computer Systems, SIGMETRICS 2003, June 9-14, 2003, San Diego, CA, USA.* 148–159.

[23] Michael T. Goodrich, Nodari Sitchinava, and Qin Zhang. 2011. Sorting, Searching, and Simulation in the MapReduce Framework. In *Algorithms and Computation - 22nd International Symposium, ISAAC 2011, Yokohama, Japan, December 5-8, 2011. Proceedings.* 374–383.

[24] Shay Halperin and Uri Zwick. 1994. An Optimal Randomized Logarithmic Time Connectivity algorithm for the EREW PRAM (Extended Abstract). In *SPAA.* 1–10.

[25] James W. Hegeman, Gopal Pandurangan, Sriram V. Pemmaraju, Vivek B. Sardeshmukh, and Michele Scquizzato. 2015. Toward Optimal Bounds in the Congested Clique: Graph Connectivity and MST. In *Proceedings of the 2015 ACM Symposium on Principles of Distributed Computing, PODC 2015, Donostia-San Sebastián, Spain, July 21 - 23, 2015.* 91–100.

[26] Tomasz Jurdzinski and Krzysztof Nowicki. 2018. MST in $O(1)$ Rounds of Congested Clique. In *Proceedings of the Twenty-Ninth Annual ACM-SIAM Symposium on Discrete Algorithms, SODA 2018, New Orleans, LA, USA, January 7-10, 2018.* 2620–2632.

[27] David R. Karger, Noam Nisan, and Michal Parnas. 1992. Fast Connected Components Algorithms for the EREW PRAM. In *Proceedings of the Fourth Annual ACM Symposium on Parallel Algorithms and Architectures (SPAA '92).* ACM, New York, NY, USA, 373–381. https://doi.org/10.1145/140901.141920

[28] Howard J. Karloff, Siddharth Suri, and Sergei Vassilvitskii. 2010. A Model of Computation for MapReduce. In *Proceedings of the Twenty-First Annual ACM-SIAM Symposium on Discrete Algorithms, SODA 2010, Austin, Texas, USA, January 17-19, 2010.* 938–948.

[29] Raimondas Kiveris, Silvio Lattanzi, Vahab S. Mirrokni, Vibhor Rastogi, and Sergei Vassilvitskii. 2014. Connected Components in MapReduce and Beyond. In *Proceedings of the ACM Symposium on Cloud Computing, Seattle, WA, USA, November 03 - 05, 2014.* 18:1–18:13.

[30] Christian Konrad. 2018. MIS in the Congested Clique Model in O(log log Δ) Rounds. *CoRR* abs/1802.07647 (2018).

[31] Ravi Kumar, Benjamin Moseley, Sergei Vassilvitskii, and Andrea Vattani. 2013. Fast greedy algorithms in mapreduce and streaming. In *25th ACM Symposium on Parallelism in Algorithms and Architectures, SPAA '13, Montreal, QC, Canada - July 23 - 25, 2013.* 1–10.

[32] Jakub Lacki, Vahab S. Mirrokni, and Michal Wlodarczyk. 2018. Connected Components at Scale via Local Contractions. *CoRR* abs/1807.10727 (2018).

[33] Silvio Lattanzi, Benjamin Moseley, Siddharth Suri, and Sergei Vassilvitskii. 2011. Filtering: a method for solving graph problems in MapReduce. In *SPAA 2011: Proceedings of the 23rd Annual ACM Symposium on Parallelism in Algorithms and Architectures, San Jose, CA, USA, June 4-6, 2011 (Co-located with FCRC 2011).* 85–94. https://doi.org/10.1145/1989493.1989505

[34] Christoph Lenzen. 2013. Optimal deterministic routing and sorting on the congested clique. In *ACM Symposium on Principles of Distributed Computing, PODC '13, Montreal, QC, Canada, July 22-24, 2013.* 42–50.

[35] Zvi Lotker, Elan Pavlov, Boaz Patt-Shamir, and David Peleg. 2003. MST construction in O(log log n) communication rounds. In *SPAA 2003: Proceedings of the Fifteenth Annual ACM Symposium on Parallelism in Algorithms and Architectures, June 7-9, 2003, San Diego, California, USA (part of FCRC 2003).* 94–100.

[36] Fragkiskos D. Malliaros and Vasileios Megalooikonomou. 2011. Expansion Properties of Large Social Graphs. In *Database Systems for Adanced Applications - 16th International Conference, DASFAA 2011, International Workshops: GDB, SIM3, FlashDB, SNSMW, DaMEN, DQIS, Hong Kong, China, April 22-25, 2011. Proceedings.* 311–322.

[37] Krzysztof Onak. 2018. Round Compression for Parallel Graph Algorithms in Strongly Sublinear Space. *CoRR* abs/1807.08745 (2018).

[38] Ian Parberry and Pei Yuan Yan. 1991. Improved Upper and Lower Time Bounds for Parallel Random Access Machines Without Simultaneous Writes. *SIAM J. Comput.* 20, 1 (1991), 88–99.

[39] Vibhor Rastogi, Ashwin Machanavajjhala, Laukik Chitnis, and Anish Das Sarma. 2013. Finding connected components in map-reduce in logarithmic rounds. In *29th IEEE International Conference on Data Engineering, ICDE 2013, Brisbane, Australia, April 8-12, 2013.* 50–61.

[40] JH Reif. 1985. *Optimal parallel algorithms for interger sorting and graph connectivity. Technical report.* Technical Report. Harvard Univ., Cambridge, MA (USA). Aiken Computation Lab.

[41] Omer Reingold, Salil P. Vadhan, and Avi Wigderson. 2000. Entropy Waves, the Zig-Zag Graph Product, and New Constant-Degree Expanders and Extractors. In *41st Annual Symposium on Foundations of Computer Science, FOCS 2000, 12-14 November 2000, Redondo Beach, California, USA.* 3–13.

[42] Tim Roughgarden, Sergei Vassilvitskii, and Joshua R. Wang. 2016. Shuffles and Circuits: (On Lower Bounds for Modern Parallel Computation). In *Proceedings of the 28th ACM Symposium on Parallelism in Algorithms and Architectures, SPAA 2016, Asilomar State Beach/Pacific Grove, CA, USA, July 11-13, 2016.* 1–12.

[43] Atish Das Sarma, Sreenivas Gollapudi, and Rina Panigrahy. 2011. Estimating PageRank on graph streams. *J. ACM* 58, 3 (2011), 13:1–13:19.

[44] Atish Das Sarma, Danupon Nanongkai, Gopal Pandurangan, and Prasad Tetali. 2013. Distributed Random Walks. *J. ACM* 60, 1 (2013), 2:1–2:31.

[45] Yossi Shiloach and Uzi Vishkin. 1982. An O (logn) parallel connectivity algorithm. *Journal of Algorithms* 3, 1 (1982), 57–67.

[46] Tom White. 2009. *Hadoop: The Definitive Guide* (1st ed.). O'Reilly Media, Inc.

[47] Grigory Yaroslavtsev and Adithya Vadapalli. 2017. Massively Parallel Algorithms and Hardness for Single-Linkage Clustering Under ℓ_p-Distances. *arXiv preprint arXiv:1710.01431* (2017).

[48] Matei Zaharia, Mosharaf Chowdhury, Michael J. Franklin, Scott Shenker, and Ion Stoica. 2010. Spark: Cluster Computing with Working Sets. In *Proceedings of the 2Nd USENIX Conference on Hot Topics in Cloud Computing (HotCloud'10).* USENIX Association, Berkeley, CA, USA, 10–10. http://dl.acm.org/citation.cfm?id=1863103.1863113

The Complexity of $(\Delta + 1)$ Coloring in Congested Clique, Massively Parallel Computation, and Centralized Local Computation*

Yi-Jun Chang†
University of Michigan
cyijun@umich.edu

Manuela Fischer
ETH Zurich
manuela.fischer@inf.ethz.ch

Mohsen Ghaffari
ETH Zurich
ghaffari@inf.ethz.ch

Jara Uitto
ETH Zurich & University of Freiburg
jara.uitto@inf.ethz.ch

Yufan Zheng
University of Michigan
lwins.lights@gmail.com

ABSTRACT

In this paper, we present new randomized algorithms that improve the complexity of the classic $(\Delta + 1)$-coloring problem, and its generalization $(\Delta + 1)$-list-coloring, in three well-studied models of distributed, parallel, and centralized computation:

Distributed Congested Clique: We present an $O(1)$-round randomized algorithm for $(\Delta + 1)$-list-coloring in the congested clique model of distributed computing. This settles the asymptotic complexity of this problem. It moreover improves upon the $O(\log^* \Delta)$-round randomized algorithms of Parter and Su [DISC'18] and $O((\log \log \Delta) \cdot \log^* \Delta)$-round randomized algorithm of Parter [ICALP'18].

Massively Parallel Computation: We present a randomized $(\Delta + 1)$-list-coloring algorithm with round complexity $O(\sqrt{\log \log n})$ in the Massively Parallel Computation (MPC) model with strongly sublinear memory per machine. This algorithm uses a memory of $O(n^{\alpha})$ per machine, for any desirable constant $\alpha > 0$, and a total memory of $\widetilde{O}(m)$, where m is the number of edges in the graph. Notably, this is the first coloring algorithm with sublogarithmic round complexity, in the sublinear memory regime of MPC. For the quasilinear memory regime of MPC, an $O(1)$-round algorithm was given very recently by Assadi et al. [SODA'19].

Centralized Local Computation: We show that $(\Delta + 1)$-list-coloring can be solved by a randomized algorithm with query complexity $\Delta^{O(1)} \cdot O(\log n)$, in the centralized local computation model. The previous state of the art for $(\Delta + 1)$-list-coloring in the centralized local computation model are based on simulation of known LOCAL algorithms. The deterministic $O(\sqrt{\Delta}\text{poly} \log \Delta + \log^* n)$-round LOCAL algorithm of Fraigniaud et al. [FOCS'16] can be implemented in the centralized local computation model with query complexity $\Delta^{O(\sqrt{\Delta}\text{poly} \log \Delta)} \cdot O(\log^* n)$; the randomized $O(\log^* \Delta) + 2^{O(\sqrt{\log \log n})}$-round LOCAL algorithm of Chang et al. [STOC'18] can be implemented in the centralized local computation model with query complexity $\Delta^{O(\log^* \Delta)} \cdot O(\log n)$.

*The full version of the paper is available at arXiv [20].
†Supported by NSF grants CCF-1514383, CCF-1637546, and CCF-1815316.

PODC '19, July 29-August 2, 2019, Toronto, ON, Canada

ACM ISBN 978-1-4503-6217-7/19/07...$15.00
https://doi.org/10.1145/3293611.3331607

CCS CONCEPTS

• **Theory of computation → Distributed algorithms.**

KEYWORDS

coloring, congested clique, centralized local computation, massively parallel computation

ACM Reference Format:
Yi-Jun Chang, Manuela Fischer, Mohsen Ghaffari, Jara Uitto, and Yufan Zheng. 2019. The Complexity of $(\Delta + 1)$ Coloring in Congested Clique, Massively Parallel Computation, and Centralized Local Computation. In *2019 ACM Symposium on Principles of Distributed Computing (PODC '19), July 29-August 2, 2019, Toronto, ON, Canada.* ACM, New York, NY, USA, 10 pages. https://doi.org/10.1145/3293611.3331607

1 INTRODUCTION

In this paper, we present improved randomized algorithms for vertex coloring in three models of distributed, parallel, and centralized computation: the *congested clique* model of distributed computing, the *massively parallel computation* model, and the *centralized local computation* model. We next overview these results in three different subsections, while putting them in the context of the state of the art. The next section provides a technical overview of the known algorithmic tools as well as the novel ingredients that lead to our results.

$(\Delta + 1)$-coloring and $(\Delta + 1)$-list Coloring. Our focus is on the standard $(\Delta + 1)$ vertex coloring problem, where Δ denotes the maximum degree in the graph. All our results work for the generalization of the problem to $(\Delta + 1)$-list coloring problem, defined as follows: each vertex v in the graph $G = (V, E)$ is initially equipped with a set of colors $\Psi(v)$ such that $|\Psi(v)| = \Delta + 1$. The goal is to

find a proper vertex coloring where each vertex $v \in V$ is assigned a color in $\Psi(v)$ such that no two adjacent vertices are colored the same.

1.1 Congested Clique Model of Distributed Computing

Models of Distributed Computation. There are three major models for distributed graph algorithms, namely LOCAL, CONGEST, and CONGESTED-CLIQUE. In the LOCAL model [48, 56], the input graph $G = (V, E)$ is identical to the communication network and each $v \in V$ hosts a processor that initially knows $\deg(v)$, a unique $\Theta(\log n)$-bit $\mathrm{ID}(v)$, and global graph parameters $n = |V|$ and $\Delta = \max_{v \in V} \deg(v)$. Each processor is allowed unbounded computation and has access to a stream of private random bits. *Time* is partitioned into synchronized *rounds* of communication, in which each processor sends one unbounded message to each neighbor. At the end of the algorithm, each v declares its output label, e.g., its own color. The CONGEST model [56] is a variant of LOCAL where there is an $O(\log n)$-bit message size constraint. The CONGESTED-CLIQUE model, introduced in [49], is a variant of CONGEST that allows all-to-all communication: Each vertex initially knows its adjacent edges of the input graph $G = (V, E)$. In each round, each vertex is allowed to transmit $n - 1$ many $O(\log n)$-bit messages, one addressed to each other vertex.

In this paper, our new distributed result is an improvement for coloring in CONGESTED-CLIQUE. It is worth noting that the CONGESTED-CLIQUE model has been receiving extensive attention recently, see e.g., [11, 14, 15, 18, 19, 24, 25, 28–31, 36, 37, 39, 45, 50, 53–55].

State of the Art for Coloring in LOCAL *and* CONGEST. Most prior works on distributed coloring focus on the LOCAL model. The current state-of-the-art randomized upper bound for the $(\Delta + 1)$-list coloring problem is $O(\log^* \Delta) + O(\mathrm{Det}_d(\mathrm{poly}\log n)) = O(\mathrm{Det}_d(\mathrm{poly}\log n))$ of [21] (which builds upon the techniques of [34]), where $\mathrm{Det}_d(n') = 2^{O(\sqrt{\log\log n'})}$ is the deterministic complexity of $(\deg +1)$-list coloring on n'-vertex graphs [51]. In the $(\deg +1)$-list coloring problem, each v has a palette of size $\deg(v)+1$. This algorithm follows the *graph shattering* framework [10, 29]. The pre-shattering phase takes $O(\log^* \Delta)$ rounds. After that, the remaining uncolored vertices form connected components of size $O(\mathrm{poly}\log n)$. The post-shattering phase then applies a $(\deg +1)$-list coloring deterministic algorithm to color all these vertices.

State of the Art for Coloring in CONGESTED-CLIQUE. Hegeman and Pemmaraju [37] gave algorithms for $O(\Delta)$-coloring in the CONGESTED-CLIQUE model, which run in $O(1)$ rounds if $\Delta \geq \Theta(\log^4 n)$ and in $O(\log\log n)$ rounds otherwise. It is worth noting that $O(\Delta)$-coloring is a significantly more relaxed problem in comparison to $(\Delta + 1)$-coloring. For instance, we have long known a very simple $O(\Delta)$-coloring algorithm in LOCAL-model algorithm with round complexity $2^{O(\sqrt{\log\log n})}$ [10], but only recently such a round complexity was achieved for $(\Delta + 1)$ coloring [21, 34].

Our focus is on the much more stringent-$(\Delta + 1)$ coloring problem. For this problem, the LOCAL model algorithms of [21, 34] need messages of $O(\Delta^2 \log n)$ bits, and thus do not extend to CONGEST or CONGESTED-CLIQUE. For CONGESTED-CLIQUE model, the main challenge is when $\Delta > \sqrt{n}$, as otherwise, one can simulate the algorithm of [21] by leveraging the all-to-all communication in CONGESTED-CLIQUE which means each vertex in each round is capable of communicating $O(n \log n)$ bits of information. Parter [53] designed the first sublogarithmic-time $(\Delta+1)$ coloring algorithm for CONGESTED-CLIQUE, which runs in $O(\log\log \Delta \log^* \Delta)$ rounds. The algorithm of [53] is able to reduce the maximum degree to $O(\sqrt{n})$ in $O(\log\log \Delta)$ iterations, and each iteration invokes the algorithm of [21] on instances of maximum degree $O(\sqrt{n})$. Once the maximum degree is $O(\sqrt{n})$, the algorithm of [21] can be implemented in $O(\log^* \Delta)$ rounds in CONGESTED-CLIQUE. Subsequent to [53], the upper bound was improved to $O(\log^* \Delta)$ in [54]. Parter and Su [54] observed that the algorithm of [53] only takes $O(1)$ iterations if we only need to reduce the degree to $n^{1/2+\epsilon}$, for some constant $\epsilon > 0$, and they achieved this by modifying the internal details of [21] to reduce the required message size to $O(\Delta^{8/5} \log n)$.

Our Result. For the CONGESTED-CLIQUE model, we present a new algorithm for $(\Delta + 1)$-list coloring in the randomized congested clique model running in $O(1)$ rounds. This improves on the previous best known $O(\log^* \Delta)$-round algorithm of Parter and Su [54] and settles the asymptotic complexity of the problem.

Theorem 1.1. *There is an $O(1)$-round algorithm that solves the $(\Delta + 1)$-list coloring problem in* CONGESTED-CLIQUE, *with success probability* $1 - 1/\mathrm{poly}(n)$.

The proof is presented in two parts: If $\Delta \geq \log^{4.1} n$, the algorithm of Theorem 3.2 solves the $(\Delta + 1)$-list coloring problem in $O(1)$ rounds; the algorithm for the small degree case is omitted (see the full version of the paper [20]).

1.2 Massively Parallel Computation

Model. The Massively Parallel Computation (MPC) model was introduced by Karloff, Suri, and Vassilvitskii [43], as a theoretical abstraction for practical large-scale parallel processing settings such as MapReduce [23], Hadoop [60], Spark [61], and Dryad [41], and it has been receiving increasing attention over the past few years [1, 3–6, 8, 12, 13, 16, 17, 22, 31, 33, 35, 37, 40, 43, 44, 57]. In the MPC model, the system consists of a number of machines, each with S bits of memory, which can communicate with each other in synchronous rounds through a complete communication network. Per round, each machine can send or receive at most S bits in total. Moreover, it can perform some $\mathrm{poly}(S)$ computation, given the information that it has. In the case of graph problems, we assume that the graph G is partitioned among the machines using a simple and globally known hash function such that each machine holds at most S bits, and moreover, for each vertex or potential edge of the graph, the hash function determines which machines hold that vertex or edge.[1] Thus, the number of machines is $\Omega(m/S)$ and ideally not too much higher, where m denotes the number of edges. At the end, each machine should know the output of the vertices that it holds, e.g., their color.

[1] If $S = o(\Delta \log n)$, then we cannot afford to store all edges incident to a vertex v in a single machine. However, in this case we still need to have a machine holding v that is responsible for storing the output of v (e.g., the color of v for the $(\Delta + 1)$-coloring problem).

State of the Art for Coloring. The CONGESTED-CLIQUE algorithms discussed above can be used to obtain MPC algorithms with the same asymptotic round complexity if machines have memory of $S = \Omega(n \log n)$ bits. In particular, the work of Parter and Su [54] leads to an $O(\log^* \Delta)$-round MPC algorithm for machines with $S = \Omega(n \log n)$ bits. However, this MPC algorithm would have two drawbacks: (A) it uses $\Omega(n^2 \log n)$ global memory, and thus would require $(n^2 \log n)/S$ machines, which may be significantly larger than $\tilde{O}(m)/S$. This is basically because the algorithm makes each vertex of the graph learn some $\widetilde{\Theta}(n)$ bits of information. (B) It is limited to machines with $S = \Omega(n \log n)$ memory, and it does not extend to the machines with strongly sublinear memory, which is gaining more attention recently due to the increase in the size of graphs. We note that for the regime of machines with superlinear memory, very recently, Assadi, Chen, and Khanna [7] gave an $O(1)$-round algorithm which uses only $O(n \log^3 n)$ global memory.[2] However, this algorithm also relies heavily on $S = \Omega(n \log^3 n)$ memory per machine and cannot be run with weaker machines that have strongly sublinear memory.

Our Result. We provide the first sublogarithmic-time algorithm for $(\Delta + 1)$-coloring and $(\Delta + 1)$-list coloring in the MPC model with strongly sublinear memory per machine:

THEOREM 1.2. *For any constant $\alpha > 0$, there is an* MPC *algorithm that, in $O(\log^* \Delta + \sqrt{\log \log n}) = O(\sqrt{\log \log n})$ rounds, w.h.p. computes a $(\Delta + 1)$-list coloring of an n-vertex graph with m edges and maximum degree Δ and that uses $O(n^\alpha)$ memory per machine, as well as a total memory of $\widetilde{O}(m)$.*

The proof is presented in Section 3.3.

1.3 Centralized LOCAL Computation

Model. The Local Computation Algorithms (LCA) model is a centralized model of computation that was introduced in [58]; an algorithm in this model is usually called an LCA. In this model, there is a graph $G = (V, E)$, and the algorithm is allowed to make the following queries:

Degree Query: Given $\mathrm{ID}(v)$, the oracle returns $\deg(v)$.

Neighbor Query: Given $\mathrm{ID}(v)$ and an index $i \in [1, \Delta]$, if $\deg(v) \le i$, the oracle returns $\mathrm{ID}(u)$, where u is the ith neighbor of v; otherwise, the oracle returns $\perp$.

It is sometimes convenient to assume that there is a query that returns the list of all neighbors of v. This query can be implemented using (i) Δ neighbor queries or (ii) one degree query and $\deg(v)$ neighbor queries. For randomized algorithms, we assume that there is an oracle that given $\mathrm{ID}(v)$ returns an infinite-length random sequence associated with the vertex v. Similarly, for problems with input labels (e.g., the color lists in the list coloring problem), the input label of a vertex v can be accessed given $\mathrm{ID}(v)$. Given a graph problem $\mathcal{P}$, an LCA $\mathcal{A}$ accomplishes the following. Given $\mathrm{ID}(v)$, the algorithm $\mathcal{A}$ returns $\mathcal{A}(v)$ = the output of v, after making a small number of queries. It is required that the output of $\mathcal{A}$ at different vertices are consistent with one legal solution of $\mathcal{P}$.

We emphasize that the outcome $\mathcal{A}(v)$ cannot depend on the results of previous invocations of $\mathcal{A}$. For example, if we invoke $\mathcal{A}$ on $v_1, v_2, \ldots, v_k$ sequentially, the outcome $\mathcal{A}(v_i)$ cannot depend on the previous answers $\mathcal{A}(v_j)$, $1 \le j < i$.

The complexity measure for an LCA is the number of queries. A well-known technique for obtaining efficient LCA is simulation of known LOCAL algorithms [52]. That is, any τ-round LOCAL algorithm $\mathcal{A}$ can be transformed into an LCA $\mathcal{A}'$ with query complexity Δ^τ. The LCA $\mathcal{A}'$ simply simulates the LOCAL algorithm $\mathcal{A}$ by querying all radius-τ neighborhood of the given vertex v. This is also known as the Parnas-Ron reduction. See [47] for a recent survey of the state of the art in the centralized local model.

State of the Art LCA *for Coloring.* The previous state-of-the-art for $(\Delta + 1)$-list coloring in the centralized local computation model are based on simulation of known LOCAL algorithms. The deterministic $O(\sqrt{\Delta}\text{poly}\log \Delta + \log^* n)$-round LOCAL algorithm of [9, 27][3] can be implemented in the centralized local computation model with query complexity $\Delta^{O(\sqrt{\Delta}\text{poly}\log \Delta)} \cdot O(\log^* n)$; the randomized $O(\log^* \Delta) + 2^{O(\sqrt{\log \log n})}$-round LOCAL algorithm of [21] can be implemented in the centralized local computation model with query complexity $\Delta^{O(\log^* \Delta)} \cdot O(\log n)$.

Our Result. We show that $(\Delta + 1)$-list coloring can be solved with $\Delta^{O(1)} \cdot O(\log n)$ query complexity. Note that $\Delta^{O(1)} \cdot O(\log n)$ matches a "natural barrier" for randomized algorithms based on the graph shattering framework, as each connected component in the post-shattering phase has this size $\Delta^{O(1)} \cdot O(\log n)$.

THEOREM 1.3. *There is a centralized local computation algorithm that solves the $(\Delta + 1)$-list coloring problem with query complexity $\Delta^{O(1)} \cdot O(\log n)$, with success probability $1 - 1/\text{poly}(n)$.*

The proof is omitted (see the full version of the paper [20]).

2 TECHNICAL OVERVIEW: TOOLS AND NEW INGREDIENTS

In this section, we first review some of the known technical tools that we will use in our algorithms, and then we overview the two new technical ingredients that lead to our improved results (in combination with the known tools).

Notes and Notations. When talking about randomized algorithms, we require the algorithm to succeed *with high probability (w.h.p.)*, i.e., to have success probability at least $1 - 1/\text{poly}(n)$. For each vertex v, we write $N(v)$ to denote the set of neighbors of v. If there is an edge orientation, $N^{\text{out}}(v)$ refers to the set of out-neighbors of v. We write $N^k(v) = \{u \in V \mid \text{dist}(u, v) \le k\}$. We use subscript to indicate the graph G under consideration, e.g., $N_G(v)$ or $N_G^{\text{out}}(v)$. In the course of our algorithms, we slightly abuse the notation to also use $\Psi(v)$ to denote the set of *available colors* of v. i.e., the subset of $\Psi(v)$ that excludes the colors already taken by its neighbors in $N(v)$. The number of *excess colors* at a vertex is the number of available colors minus the number of uncolored neighbors. Moreover, we make an assumption that each color can be represented using $O(\log n)$ bits. This is without loss of generality (in all of the models

[2]Here "global memory" refers to the memory used for communication. Of course we still need $\tilde{O}(m)$ memory to store the graph.

[3]Precisely, the complexity is $O(\sqrt{\Delta} \log^{2.5} \Delta + \log^* n)$ in [27], and this has been later improved to $O(\sqrt{\Delta \log \Delta} \log^* \Delta + \log^* n)$ in [9].

under consideration in our paper), since otherwise we can hash the colors down to this magnitude, as we allow a failure probability of $1/\text{poly}(n)$ for randomized algorithms.

2.1 Tools

Lenzen's Routing. The routing algorithm of Lenzen [45] for CONGESTED-CLIQUE allows us to deliver all messages in $O(1)$ rounds, as long as each vertex v is the source and the destination of at most $O(n)$ messages. This is a very useful (and frequently used) communication primitive for designing CONGESTED-CLIQUE algorithms.

Lemma 2.1 (Lenzen's Routing). *Consider a graph $G = (V, E)$ and a set of point-to-point routing requests, each given by the IDs of the corresponding source-destination pair. As long as each vertex v is the source and the destination of at most $O(n)$ messages, namely $O(n \log n)$ bits of information, we can deliver all messages in $O(1)$ rounds in the* CONGESTED-CLIQUE *model.*

The Shattering Framework. Our algorithm follows the *graph shattering* framework [10], which first performs some randomized process (known as *pre-shattering*) to solve "most" of the problem, and then performs some clean-up steps (known as *post-shattering*) to solve the remaining part of the problem. Typically, the remaining graph is simpler in the sense of having small components and having a small number of edges. Roughly speaking, at each step of the algorithm, we specify an invariant that all vertices must satisfy in order to continue to participate. Those *bad vertices* that violate the invariant are removed from consideration, and postponed to the post-shattering phase. We argue that the bad vertices form connected components of size $\Delta^{O(1)} \cdot O(\log n)$ with probability $1 - 1/\text{poly}(n)$; we use this in designing LCA. Also, the total number of edges induced by the bad vertices is $O(n)$. Therefore, using Lenzen's routing, in CONGESTED-CLIQUE we can gather all information about the bad vertices to one distinguished vertex $v^\star$, and then $v^\star$ can color them locally. More precisely, we have the following lemma [10, 26].

Lemma 2.2 (The Shattering Lemma). *Let $c \geq 1$. Consider a randomized procedure that generates a subset of vertices $B \subseteq V$. Suppose that for each $v \in V$, we have $\Pr[v \in B] \leq \Delta^{-3c}$, and this holds even if the random bits not in $N^c(v)$ are determined adversarially. Then, the following is true.*

1. *With probability $1 - n^{-\Omega(c')}$, each connected component in the graph induced by B has size at most $(c'/c)\Delta^{2c} \log_\Delta n$.*
2. *With probability $1 - O(\Delta^c) \cdot \exp(-\Omega(n\Delta^{-c}))$, the number of edges induced by B is $O(n)$.*

Round Compression in CONGESTED-CLIQUE *and* MPC *by Information Gathering.* Suppose we are given a τ-round LOCAL algorithm $\mathcal{A}$ on a graph of maximum degree Δ. A direct simulation of $\mathcal{A}$ on CONGESTED-CLIQUE costs also τ rounds. However, if each vertex v already knows all information in its radius-τ neighborhood, then v can locally compute its output in zero rounds. In general, this amount of information can be as high as $\Theta(n^2)$, since there could be $\Theta(n^2)$ edges in the radius-τ neighborhood of v. For the case of $\Delta^\tau = O(n)$, it is possible to achieve an exponential speed-up in the round complexity in the CONGESTED-CLIQUE, compared to that of LOCAL. In particular, in this case, each vertex v can learn its radius-τ neighborhood in just $O(\log \tau)$ rounds in CONGESTED-CLIQUE. Roughly speaking, after k rounds, we are able to simulate the product graph G^{2^k}, which is the graph where any two vertices with distance at most 2^k in graph G are adjacent. This method is known as *graph exponentiation* [46], and it has been applied before in the design of algorithms in CONGESTED-CLIQUE and MPC models, see e.g., [4, 30, 32, 53, 54].

Round Compression via Opportunistic Information Gathering. Our goal is to achieve the $O(1)$ round complexity in CONGESTED-CLIQUE, so an exponential speed-up compared to the LOCAL model will not be enough. Consider the following "opportunisitc" way of simulating a LOCAL algorithm $\mathcal{A}$ in the CONGESTED-CLIQUE model. Each vertex u sends its local information (which has $O(\Delta \log n)$ bits) to each vertex $v \in V$ with some fixed probability $p = O(1/\Delta)$, independently, and it hopes that there exists a vertex $v \in V$ that gathers all the required information to calculate the outcome of $\mathcal{A}$ at u. To ensure that for each u, there exists such a vertex v w.h.p., it suffices that $p^{\Delta^\tau} \gg \frac{\log n}{n}$. We note that a somewhat similar idea was key to the $O(1)$-round MST algorithm of [42] for CONGESTED-CLIQUE.

Lemma 2.3, presented below, summarizes the criteria for this method to work; see the full version of the paper [20] for the proof of the lemma. Denote ℓ_{in} as the number of bits needed to represent the random bits and the input for executing $\mathcal{A}$ at a vertex. Denote ℓ_{out} as the number of bits needed to represent the output of $\mathcal{A}$ at a vertex. We assume that each vertex v initially knows a set $N_*(v) \subseteq N(v)$ such that throughout the algorithm $\mathcal{A}$, each vertex v only receives information from vertices in $N_*(v)$. We write $\Delta_* = \max_{v \in v} |N_*(v)|$.

Lemma 2.3 (Opportunistic Speed-up). *Let $\mathcal{A}$ be a τ-round* LOCAL *algorithm on $G = (V, E)$. There is an $O(1)$-round simulation of $\mathcal{A}$ in* CONGESTED-CLIQUE, *given that (i) $\Delta_*^\tau \log(\Delta_* + \ell_{\text{in}}/\log n) = O(\log n)$, (ii) $\ell_{\text{in}} = O(n)$, and (iii) $\ell_{\text{out}} = O(\log n)$.*

2.2 Our New Technical Ingredients, In a Nutshell

The results in our paper are based on the following two novel technical ingredients, which are used in combination with the known tools mentioned above: (i) a new graph partitioning algorithm for coloring and (ii) a sparsification of the CLP coloring algorithm [21]. We note that the first ingredient suffices for our CONGESTED-CLIQUE result for graphs with maximum degree at least $\text{poly}(\log n)$, and also for our MPC result. This ingredient is presented in Section 3. The second ingredient, which is also more involved technically, is used for extending our CONGESTED-CLIQUE result to graphs with smaller maximum degree, as well as for our LCA result. This ingredient is presented in the full version of the paper [20]. Here, we provide a brief overview of these ingredients and how they get used in our results.

Ingredient 1 — Graph Partitioning for Coloring. We provide a simple random partitioning that significantly simplifies and extends the one in [53, 54]. The main change will be that, besides partitioning the vertices randomly, we also partition the colors randomly. In particular, this new procedure partitions the vertices and colors in a way that allows us to easily apply CLP in a black box manner.

Concretely, our partitioning breaks the graph as well as the respective palettes randomly into many subgraphs $B_1, \ldots, B_k$ of maximum degree $O(\sqrt{n})$ and size $O(\sqrt{n})$, while ensuring that each vertex in these subgraphs receives a random part of its palette with size close to the maximum degree of the subgraph. The palettes for each part are disjoint, which allows us to color all parts in parallel. There will be one left-over subgraph L, with maximum degree $\tilde{O}(\Delta^{3/4})$, as well as sufficiently large remaining palettes for each vertex in this left-over subgraph.

Application in CONGESTED-CLIQUE: Since each subgraph has $O(n)$ edges, all of $B_1, \ldots, B_k$ can be colored, in parallel, in $O(1)$ rounds, using Lenzen's routing (Lemma 2.1). The left-over part L is handled by recursion. We show that when $\Delta > \log^{4.1} n$, we are done after $O(1)$ levels of recursion.

Application in Low-memory MPC: We perform recursive calls not only on L but also on $B_1, \ldots, B_k$. After $O(1)$ levels of recursion, the maximum degree can be made $O(n^{\beta})$, for any given constant $\beta > 0$, which enables us to run the CLP algorithm on a low memory MPC.

We note that the previous partitioning approach [53, 54] is unable to reduce the maximum degree to below $\sqrt{n}$; this is a significant limitation that our partitioning overcomes. We also note that the CONGESTED-CLIQUE or MPC coloring algorithms of [35, 38] also use the approach of randomly partitioning the palette. However, their algorithms needs a palette of size that is much higher than $\Delta + 1$ to ensure that the set of colors associated with each vertex set B_i is higher than its maximum degree. We avoid the use of extra colors by having a sufficiently large left-over part L and recursively applying the partitioning algorithm on L.

Ingredient 2 — Sparsification of the CLP Algorithm. In general, to calculate the output of a vertex v in a τ-round LOCAL algorithm $\mathcal{A}$, the output may depend on all of the τ-hop neighborhood of v. In particular, if we transform $\mathcal{A}$ into an LCA, the query complexity can be as high as Δ^{τ}. To efficiently simulate $\mathcal{A}$ in CONGESTED-CLIQUE or to transform $\mathcal{A}$ to an LCA, a strategy is to "sparsify" the algorithm $\mathcal{A}$ so that the number of vertices a vertex has to explore to decide its output is sufficiently small. This notion of sparsification is a key idea behind some recent algorithms [30, 32]. In the present paper, a key technical ingredient is providing such a sparsification for the $(\Delta + 1)$ coloring algorithm of CLP [21].

The pre-shattering phase of the CLP algorithm [21] consists of three parts: (i) initial coloring, (ii) dense coloring, and (iii) color bidding. Parts (i) and (ii) take $O(1)$ rounds;[4] part (iii) takes $\tau = O(\log^* \Delta)$ rounds. In this paper, we sparsify the color bidding part of the CLP algorithm. We let each vertex v sample $O(\text{poly} \log \Delta)$ colors from its palette at the beginning of this procedure, and we show that with probability $1 - 1/\text{poly}(\Delta)$, these colors are enough for v to correctly execute the algorithm. Based on the sampled colors, we can do an $O(1)$-round pre-processing step to let each vertex v identify a subset of neighbors $N_*(v) \subseteq N(v)$ of size $\Delta_* = O(\text{poly} \log \Delta)$ neighbors $N_*(v) \subseteq N(v)$, and v only needs to receive messages from neighbors in $N_*(v)$ in the subsequent steps of the algorithm.

[4] In the preliminary versions (arXiv:1711.01361v1 and STOC'18) of [21], dense coloring takes $O(\log^* \Delta)$ time. This time complexity has been later improved to $O(1)$ in a revised full version of [21].

Application in CONGESTED-CLIQUE: For the case $\Delta = O(\text{poly} \log n)$, the parameters $\tau = O(\log^* \Delta)$ and $\Delta_* = O(\text{poly} \log \Delta) = O(\text{poly}(\log \log n))$ satisfy the condition for applying the opportunistic speedup lemma (Lemma 2.3), and so the pre-shattering phase of the CLP algorithm can be simulated in $O(1)$ rounds in CONGESTED-CLIQUE.

Application in Centralized Local Computation: With sparsification, the pre-shattering phase of the CLP algorithm can be transformed into an LCA with $\Delta^{O(1)} \cdot \Delta_*^{\tau} = \Delta^{O(1)}$ queries.

The recent work [7] on $(\Delta + 1)$-coloring in MPC is also based on some form of palette sparsification, as follows. They showed that if each vertex samples $O(\log n)$ colors uniformly at random, then w.h.p., the graph still admits a proper coloring using the sampled colors. Since we only need to consider the edges $\{u, v\}$ where u and v share a sampled color, this effectively reduces the degree to $O(\log^2 n)$. For an MPC algorithm with $\tilde{O}(n)$ memory per processor, the entire sparsified graph can be sent to one processor, and a coloring can be computed there, using any coloring algorithm, local or not. This sparsification is not applicable for our setting. In particular, in our sparsified CLP algorithm, we need to ensure that the coloring can be computed by a LOCAL algorithm with a small locality volume; this is because the final coloring is constructed distributedly via the opportunistic speedup lemma (Lemma 2.3).

3 COLORING OF HIGH-DEGREE GRAPHS VIA GRAPH PARTITIONING

In this section, we describe our graph partitioning algorithm, which is the first new technical ingredient in our results. As mentioned in Section 2.2, this ingredient on its own leads to our CONGESTED-CLIQUE result for graphs with $\Delta = \Omega(\text{poly}(\log n))$ and also our MPC result, as we will explain in Section 3.2 and Section 3.3, respectively. The algorithm will be applied recursively, but it is required that the failure probability is at most $1 - 1/\text{poly}(n)$ in all recursive calls, where n is the number of vertices in the original graph.

In this section, the parameter n refers to the number of vertices in the original graph, not the number of vertices in the current subgraph $G = (V, E)$ under consideration.

3.1 Graph Partitioning

We consider a graph partitioning algorithm parameterized by two constants γ and λ satisfying $\gamma \geq 2$ and $\lambda = \frac{1}{2} + \frac{2}{3\gamma+2}$. Consider a graph $G = (V, E)$ with maximum degree Δ. Recall that in this section G is assumed to be a subgraph of the n-vertex original graph, and so $n \geq |V|$. Each vertex $v \in V$ has a palette $\Psi(v)$ of size $|\Psi(v)| \geq \max\{\deg_G(v), \Delta'\} + 1$, where $\Delta' = \Delta - \Delta^{\lambda}$. Denote $G[S]$ as the subgraph induced by the vertices $S \subseteq V$. For each vertex $v \in V$, denote $\deg_S(v)$ as $|N(v) \cap S|$. The algorithm is as follows, where we set $k = \sqrt{\Delta}$.

Vertex Set: The partition $V = B_1 \cup \cdots \cup B_k \cup L$ is defined by the following procedure. Including each $v \in V$ to the set L with probability $q = \Theta\left(\frac{\sqrt{\log n}}{\Delta^{1/4}}\right)$. Each remaining vertex joins one of $B_1, \ldots, B_k$ uniformly at random. Note that $\Pr[v \in B_i] = p(1-q)$, where $p = 1/k = 1/\sqrt{\Delta}$.

Palette: Denote $C = \bigcup_{v \in V} \Psi(v)$ as the set of all colors. The partition $C = C_1 \cup \cdots \cup C_k$ is defined by having each color $c \in C$ join one of $C_1, \ldots, C_k$ uniformly at random. Note that $\Pr[c \in C_i] = p = 1/k$.

We require that with probability $1 - 1/\text{poly}(n)$, the output of the partitioning algorithm satisfies the following properties, assuming that $\Delta = \omega(\log^{\gamma} n)$.

i) Size of Each Part: It is required that $|E(G[B_i])| = O(|V|)$, for each $i \in [k]$. Also, it is required that $|L| = O(q|V|) = O(\frac{\sqrt{\log n}}{\Delta^{1/4}}) \cdot |V|$.

ii) Available Colors in B_i: For each $i \in \{1, \ldots, k\}$ and $v \in B_i$, the number of available colors in v in the subgraph B_i is $g_i(v) := |\Psi(v) \cap C_i|$. It is required that $g_i(v) \geq \max\{\deg_{B_i}(v), \Delta_i - \Delta_i^{\lambda}\} + 1$, where $\Delta_i := \max_{v \in B_i} \deg_{B_i}(v)$.

iii) Available Colors in L: For each $v \in L$, define $g_L(v) := |\Psi(v)| - (\deg_G(v) - \deg_L(v))$. It is required that $g_L(v) \geq \max\{\deg_L(v), \Delta_L - \Delta_L^{\lambda}\} + 1$ for each $v \in L$, where $\Delta_L := \max_{v \in L} \deg_L(v)$. Note that $g_L(v)$ represents a lower bound on the number of available colors in v *after* all of $B_1, \ldots, B_k$ have been colored.

iv) Remaining Degrees: The maximum degrees of B_i and L are $\max_{v \in B_i} \deg_{B_i}(v) \leq \Delta_i = O(\sqrt{\Delta})$ and $\max_{v \in L} \deg_L(v) \leq \Delta_L = O(q\Delta) = O(\frac{\sqrt{\log n}}{\Delta^{1/4}}) \cdot \Delta$. For each vertex v, we have $\deg_{B_i}(v) \leq \max\{O(\log n), O(1/\sqrt{\Delta}) \cdot \deg(v)\}$ if $v \in B_i$, and $\deg_L(v) \leq \max\{O(\log n), O(q) \cdot \deg(v)\}$ if $v \in L$.

Intuitively, we will use this graph partitioning in the following way. First compute the decomposition of the vertex set and the palette, and then color each B_i using colors in C_i. Since $|E(G[B_i])| = O(|V|) = O(n)$, in the CONGESTED-CLIQUE model we are able to send the entire graph $G[B_i]$ to a single distinguished vertex $v_i^{\star}$ using Lenzen's routing (Lemma 2.1), and then $v_i^{\star}$ can compute a proper coloring of $G[B_i]$ locally. This procedure can be done in parallel for all i. If $|E(G[L])| = O(n)$, then similarly we can let a vertex compute a proper coloring of $G[L]$; otherwise we apply the graph partitioning recursively on $G[L]$, with the *same* parameter n. Later we will see that it suffices to set the recursion depth *constant*. This graph partitioning will be used as well in our MPC algorithm in the similar way.

Lemma 3.1. *Suppose $|\Psi(v)| \geq \max\{\deg_G(v), \Delta'\} + 1$ with $\Delta' = \Delta - \Delta^{\lambda}$, and $|V| > \Delta = \omega(\log^{\gamma} n)$, where γ and λ are two constants satisfying $\gamma \geq 2$ and $\lambda = \frac{1}{2} + \frac{2}{3\gamma+2}$. The two partitions $V = B_1 \cup \cdots \cup B_k \cup L$ and $C = \bigcup_{v \in V} \Psi(v) = C_1 \cup \cdots \cup C_k$ satisfy the required properties, with probability $1 - 1/\text{poly}(n)$.*

Proof. We prove that the properties i), ii), iii), and iv) hold with high probability.

i) Size of Each Part: We first show that $|E(G[B_i])| = O(|V|)$, for each $i \in [k]$, with probability $1 - 1/\text{poly}(n)$. To have $|E(G[B_i])| = O(|V|)$, it suffices to have $\deg_{B_i}(v) = O(p\Delta)$ for each v, and $|B_i| = O(p|V|)$, since $p = 1/\sqrt{\Delta}$. Note that we already have $\mathrm{E}[\deg_{B_i}(v)] \leq (1-q)p\Delta < p\Delta$ and $\mathrm{E}[|B_i|] = (1-q)p|V| < p|V|$, so we only need to show that these parameters concentrate at their expected values with high probability. This can be established by a Chernoff bound, as follows. Note that we have $\epsilon_1 < 1$ and $\epsilon_2 < 1$ in the following calculation. In particular, the inequality $\epsilon_1 < 1$ holds because of the assumption $\Delta = \omega(\log^{\gamma} n) \geq \omega(\log^2 n)$.

$$\Pr[\deg_{B_i}(v) \leq (1+\epsilon_1)(1-q)p\Delta]$$
$$= 1 - \exp(-\Omega(\epsilon_1^2(1-q)p\Delta)) = 1 - O(1/\text{poly}(n)),$$
$$\text{where } \epsilon_1 = \Theta\left(\sqrt{\frac{\log n}{(1-q)p\Delta}}\right) = \Theta\left(\sqrt{\frac{\log n}{p\Delta}}\right).$$

$$\Pr[|B_i| \leq (1+\epsilon_2)(1-q)p|V|]$$
$$= 1 - \exp(-\Omega(\epsilon_2^2(1-q)p|V|)) = 1 - O(1/\text{poly}(n)),$$
$$\text{where } \epsilon_2 = \Theta\left(\sqrt{\frac{\log n}{(1-q)p|V|}}\right) = \Theta\left(\sqrt{\frac{\log n}{p|V|}}\right).$$

Next, we show the analogous results for L, i.e., with probability $1 - 1/\text{poly}(n)$, both $|L|/|V|$ and Δ_L/Δ are $O(q) = O\left(\frac{\sqrt{\log n}}{\Delta^{1/4}}\right)$, where $\Delta_L = \max_{v \in L} \deg_L(v)$. Similarly, we already have $\mathrm{E}[\deg_L(v)] \leq q\Delta$ and $\mathrm{E}[|L|] = q|V|$, and remember that $q = O(\frac{\sqrt{\log n}}{\Delta^{1/4}})$, so we only need to show that these parameters concentrate at their expected values with high probability, by a Chernoff bound.

$$\Pr[\deg_L(v) \leq (1+\epsilon_3)q\Delta]$$
$$= 1 - \exp(-\Omega(\epsilon_3^2 q\Delta)) = 1 - O(1/\text{poly}(n)),$$
$$\text{where } \epsilon_3 = \Theta\left(\sqrt{\frac{\log n}{q\Delta}}\right).$$

$$\Pr[|L| \leq (1+\epsilon_4)q|V|]$$
$$= 1 - \exp(-\Omega(\epsilon_4^2 q|V|)) = 1 - O(1/\text{poly}(n)),$$
$$\text{where } \epsilon_4 = \Theta\left(\sqrt{\frac{\log n}{q|V|}}\right).$$

Similarly, we have $\epsilon_3 < 1$ and $\epsilon_4 < 1$. In particular, $\epsilon_3 < 1$ because $\Delta = \omega(\log^{\gamma} n) \geq \omega(\log^2 n)$.

ii) Available Colors in B_i: Now we analyze the number of available color for each set B_i. Recall that for each $v \in B_i$, the number of available colors in v in the subgraph B_i is $g_i(v) := |\Psi(v) \cap C_i|$. We need to prove the following holds with probability $1 - 1/\text{poly}(n)$: (i) $|\Psi(v) \cap C_i| \geq \deg_{B_i}(v) + 1$, and (ii) $|\Psi(v) \cap C_i| \geq \Delta_i - \Delta_i^{\lambda} + 1$, where $\Delta_i := \max_{v \in B_i} \deg_{B_i}(v)$. We will show that with probability $1 - 1/\text{poly}(n)$, we have $|\Psi(v) \cap C_i| \geq \Delta_i + 1$ for each B_i and each $v \in B_i$, and this implies the above (i) and (ii).

Recall that $\Delta' = \Delta\left(1 - \Delta^{-(1-\lambda)}\right)$, $q = \Theta\left(\frac{\sqrt{\log n}}{\Delta^{1/4}}\right) \gg \Delta^{-(1-\lambda)}$,[5] and $\epsilon_1 = \Theta\left(\frac{\sqrt{\log n}}{\Delta^{1/4}}\right)$. By selecting $q \geq 3\epsilon_1 = \Theta\left(\frac{\sqrt{\log n}}{\Delta^{1/4}}\right)$, we have

$$(1-\epsilon_1)p\Delta' = (1-\epsilon_1)\left(1 - \Delta^{-(1-\lambda)}\right)p\Delta \geq (1+\epsilon_1)(1-q)p\Delta + 1.$$

[5] The assumptions $\gamma \geq 2$ and $\lambda = \frac{1}{2} + \frac{2}{3\gamma+2}$ imply that $\lambda \in (1/2, 3/4]$, and so $\Delta^{-(1-\lambda)} \leq \Delta^{-1/4} \ll q$.

We already know that $\Delta_i \leq (1+\epsilon_1)(1-q)p\Delta$ with probability $1-1/\text{poly}(n)$. In order to have $|\Psi(v) \cap C_i| \geq \Delta_i + 1$, we only need to show that $|\Psi(v) \cap C_i| \geq (1-\epsilon_1)p\Delta'$ with probability $1-1/\text{poly}(n)$. For the expected value, we know that $\mathrm{E}[|\Psi(v) \cap C_i|] = p|\Psi(v)| \geq p\Delta'$. By a Chernoff bound, we have

$$\begin{aligned}\Pr[|\Psi(v) \cap C_i| \geq (1-\epsilon_1)p\Delta'] &= 1 - \exp(-\Omega(\epsilon_1^2 p\Delta')) \\ &= 1 - O(1/\text{poly}(n)).\end{aligned}$$

iii) Available Colors in L: Next, we consider the number of available colors in L. We show that with probability $1-1/\text{poly}(n)$, for each $v \in L$, we have $g_L(v) \geq \max\{\deg_L(v), \Delta_L - \Delta_L^\lambda\} + 1$, where $g_L(v) = |\Psi(v)| - (\deg_G(v) - \deg_L(v))$. It is straightforward to see that $g_L(v) \geq \deg_L(v) + 1$, since $g_L(v) = (|\Psi(v)| - \deg_G(v)) + \deg_L(v) \geq 1 + \deg_L(v)$. Thus, we only need to show that $g_L(v) \geq \Delta_L - \Delta_L^\lambda + 1$.

We first calculate the expected value of g_L. In the last inequality we use the assumption that $\deg_G(v) \leq |\Psi(v)| - 1$ and $\Delta' \leq |\Psi(v)| - 1$.

$$\begin{aligned}\mathrm{E}[g_L] &= (|\Psi(v)| - \deg_G(v)) + \mathrm{E}[\deg_L(v)] \\ &= (|\Psi(v)| - \deg_G(v)) + q\deg_G(v) \\ &= |\Psi(v)| - (1-q)\deg_G(v) \\ &\geq q\Delta'.\end{aligned}$$

We prove that $g_L(v) \geq (1-\epsilon_3)q\Delta'$ with probability $1-1/\text{poly}(n)$. Here we use the following variant of a Chernoff bound. If it is known that $\mathrm{E}[X] \leq \beta$, then the probability that X deviates from $\mathrm{E}[X]$ by an additive term of more than $\epsilon\beta$ is $\exp(-\Omega(\epsilon^2\beta))$. We set $X = \deg_L(v)$, $\epsilon = \epsilon_3(\Delta'/\Delta) = \Theta(\epsilon_3)$, and $\beta = q\Delta \geq \mathrm{E}[\deg_L(v)]$.

$$\begin{aligned}\Pr[g_L(v) \geq (1-\epsilon_3)q\Delta'] &= \Pr[\deg_L(v) \geq q\deg_G(v) - \epsilon_3 q\Delta'] \\ &= 1 - \exp(-\Omega(\epsilon_3^2 q\Delta')) \\ &= 1 - O(1/\text{poly}(n))\end{aligned}$$

Remember that $\epsilon_3 = \Theta\left(\sqrt{\frac{\log n}{q\Delta}}\right) = \Theta\left(\sqrt{\frac{\log n}{q\Delta'}}\right)$, and we already know that $\epsilon_3 < 1$. Using the above concentration bound, we infer that $g_L(v) \geq q\Delta - q\Delta^\lambda - O\left(\sqrt{q\Delta\log n}\right)$ holds with probability $1-1/\text{poly}(n)$.

$$\begin{aligned}g_L(v) &\geq (1-\epsilon_3)q\Delta' \\ &\geq q\Delta' - O\left(\sqrt{q\Delta'\log n}\right) \\ &\geq q\Delta - q\Delta^\lambda - O\left(\sqrt{q\Delta\log n}\right).\end{aligned}$$

Combining this with $\Delta_L \leq (1+\epsilon_3)q\Delta = q\Delta + O(\sqrt{q\Delta\log n})$, we obtain $g_L(v) \geq \Delta_L - q\Delta^\lambda - O(\sqrt{q\Delta\log n})$. Note that $q\Delta^\lambda + O(\sqrt{q\Delta\log n}) = o\left((q\Delta)^\lambda\right) = o\left(\Delta_L^\lambda\right)$,[6] and so we finally obtain $g_L(v) \geq \Delta_L - \Delta_L^\lambda + 1$.

iv) Remaining Degrees: The degree upper bounds of Δ_i and Δ_L follow immediately from the concentration bounds on $\deg_{B_i}(v)$ and $\deg_L(v)$ calculated in the proof of i). The bounds $\deg_{B_i}(v) \leq \max\{O(\log n), O(1/\sqrt{\Delta}) \cdot \deg(v)\}$ and $\deg_L(v) \leq \max\{O(\log n), O(q) \cdot \deg(v)\}$ can be derived by a straightforward application of Chernoff bound. □

3.2 Congested Clique Algorithm for High-Degree Graphs

In this section, we show that the $(\Delta+1)$-list coloring problem can be solved in $O(1)$ rounds in the CONGESTED-CLIQUE model when the degrees are assumed to be sufficiently high. The formal statement is captured in Theorem 3.2. First, we show that the partitioning algorithm can indeed be implemented in the CONGESTED-CLIQUE model. Then, we show how to color the parts resulting from the graph partitioning efficiently. The proof of Theorem 3.2 is completed by showing that only $O(1)$ recursive applications of the partitioning are required.

Implementation of the Graph Partitioning. The partitions can be computed in $O(1)$ rounds on CONGESTED-CLIQUE. Partitioning the vertex set V is straightforward, as every vertex can make the decision independently and locally, whereas it is not obvious how to partition C to make all vertices agree on the same partition. Note that we can assume $|C| \leq (\Delta+1)|V|$; if $|C|$ is greater than $(\Delta+1)|V|$ initially, then we can let each vertex decrease its palette size to $\Delta+1$ by removing some colors in its palette, and we will have $|C| \leq (\Delta+1)|V|$ after removing these colors.

A straightforward way of partitioning C is to generate $\Theta(|C|\log n)$ random bits at a vertex v locally, and then v broadcasts this information to all other vertices. Note that it takes $O(\log k) = O(\log|V|) = O(\log n)$ bits to encode which part of $C_1 \cup \cdots \cup C_k$ each $c \in C$ is in. A direct implementation of the approach cannot be done in $O(1)$ rounds, due to the message size constraint of CONGESTED-CLIQUE, as each vertex can send at most $\Theta(n\log n)$ bits in each round.

To solve this issue, observe that it is not necessary to use total independent random bits for each $c \in C$, and $\Theta(\log n)$-wise independence suffices. More precisely, suppose X is the summation of n K-wise independent 0-1 random variables with mean p, and so $\mu = \mathrm{E}[X] = np$. A Chernoff bound with K-wise Independence [59] guarantees that

$$\Pr[X \geq (1+q)\mu] \leq \exp\left(-\min\{K, q^2\mu\}\right).$$

In order to guarantee a failure probability of $1/\text{poly}(n)$ in all applications of Chernoff bound in Lemma 3.1, it suffices that $K = \Theta(\log n)$. Therefore, to compute the decomposition $C = C_1 \cup \cdots \cup C_k$ with K-wise independent random bits, we only need $O(K \cdot \log(|C|\log k)) = O(\log^2 n)$ total independent random bits.[7] Broadcasting $O(\log^2 n)$ bits of information to all vertices can be done in $O(1)$ rounds via Lenzen's routing (Lemma 2.1).

The Algorithm of $(\Delta+1)$-list coloring on High-degree Graphs. We next present our CONGESTED-CLIQUE-model coloring algorithm for high-degree graphs, using the partitioning explained above.

[6]The bound $\sqrt{q\Delta\log n} \ll (q\Delta)^\lambda$ can be derived from the assumptions $\lambda = \frac{1}{2} + \frac{2}{3\gamma+2}$ and $\Delta = \omega(\log^\gamma n)$, as follows: $q\Delta = \Theta(\Delta^{\frac{3}{4}}\log^{\frac{1}{2}} n) = \omega(\log^{\frac{3}{4}\gamma+\frac{1}{2}} n) \implies \sqrt{q\Delta\log n} = (q\Delta)^{\frac{1}{2}}\log^{1/2} n \ll (q\Delta)^{\frac{1}{2}}(q\Delta)^{\frac{1}{2}\left(\frac{3}{4}\gamma+\frac{1}{2}\right)^{-1}} = (q\Delta)^\lambda$.

[7]It is well-known that n Bernoulli random variables with $p = 1/2$ with d-wise independence can be constructed from $O(d\log n)$ Bernoulli random variables with $p = 1/2$ with total independence [2, Section 16.2].

Theorem 3.2. *Suppose $\Delta = \Omega(\log^{4+\epsilon} n)$ for some constant $\epsilon > 0$. There is an algorithm that solves $(\Delta + 1)$-list coloring in* CONGESTED-CLIQUE *in $O(1)$ rounds.*

Proof. We show that a constant-depth recursive applications of Lemma 3.1 suffices to give an $O(1)$-round CONGESTED-CLIQUE $(\Delta + 1)$-list coloring algorithm for graphs with $\Delta = \Omega(\log^{4+\epsilon} n)$, for any constant $\epsilon > 0$. Consider the graph $G = (V, E)$. First, we apply the graph partitioning algorithm of Lemma 3.1 to partition vertices V into subsets $B_1, \ldots, B_k, L$ with parameter $n = |V|$, and $k = \sqrt{\Delta}$. After that, let arbitrary $k = \sqrt{\Delta}$ vertices to be responsible for coloring each $G[B_i]$. Each of these k vertices, in parallel, gathers all information of $G[B_i]$ from vertices B_i, and then computes a proper coloring of $G[B_i]$, where each vertex $v \in B_i$ uses only the palette $\Psi(v) \cap C_i$. The existence of such a proper coloring is guaranteed by Property (ii). Using this approach, we can color all vertices in $V \setminus L$ in $O(1)$ rounds using Lenzen's routing. Note that Property (i) guarantees that $|E(G[B_i])| = O(n)$. Finally, each vertex $v \in L$ removes the colors that have been taken by its neighbors in $V \setminus L$ from its palette $\Psi(v)$. In view of Property (iii), after this operation, the number of available colors for each $v \in L$ is at least $g_L(v) \geq \max\{\deg_L(v), \Delta_L - \Delta_L^{\lambda}\} + 1$. Now the subgraph $G[L]$ satisfies all conditions required to apply Lemma 3.1, so long as $\Delta_L = \omega(\log^{\gamma} n)$. We will see that this condition is always met in our application.

We then recursively apply the algorithm of the lemma on the subgraph induced by vertices L *with the same parameter n*. The recursion stops once we reach a point that $|E(G[L])| = O(n)$, and so we can apply Lenzen's routing to let one vertex v gather all information of $G[L]$ and compute its proper coloring.

Now we analyze the number of iterations needed to reach a point that $|E(G[L])| = O(n)$. Here we use $\gamma = 2$ and $\lambda = 3/4$.[8] Define $V_1 = V$ and $\Delta_1 = \Delta$ as the vertex set and the maximum degree for the first iteration. Let $V = B_1 \cup \cdots \cup B_k \cup L$ be the outcome of the first iteration, and define $V_2 = L$ and $\Delta_2 = \Delta_L$. Similarly, for $i > 2$, we define V_i and Δ_i based on the set L in the outcome of the graph partitioning algorithm for the $(i - 1)$th iteration. We have the following formulas.

$$\Delta_1 = \Delta$$

$$\Delta_i = \Delta_{i-1} \cdot O\left(\frac{\sqrt{\log n}}{\Delta_{i-1}^{1/4}}\right) \quad \text{by Property iv)}$$

$$|V_1| = n$$

$$|V_i| = |V_{i-1}| \cdot O\left(\frac{\sqrt{\log n}}{\Delta_{i-1}^{1/4}}\right) \quad \text{by Property i)}$$

Let $\alpha > 0$ be chosen such that $\Delta = \Delta_1 = (\log n)^{2+\alpha}$, and assume $\alpha = \Omega(1)$ and $i = O(1)$. We can calculate the value of Δ_i and $|V_i|$ as follows.

$$\Delta_i = O\left((\log n)^{2+\alpha\cdot(3/4)^{i-1}}\right)$$

$$|V_i| = O(n/\Delta) \cdot \Delta_i = n \cdot O\left((\log n)^{\alpha((3/4)^{i-1}-1)}\right)$$

[8] We choose $\gamma = 2$ (the smallest possible) to minimize the degree requirement in Theorem 3.2.

Thus, given that $\alpha = \Omega(1)$ and $i = O(1)$, the condition of $\Delta_i = \omega(\log^{\gamma} n) = \omega(\log^2 n)$ for applying Lemma 3.1 must be met.

Next, we analyze the number of iterations it takes to make $\Delta_i|V_i|$ sufficiently small. In the CONGESTED-CLIQUE model, if $\Delta_i|V_i| = O(n)$, then we are able to compute a proper coloring of V_i in $O(1)$ rounds by information gathering. Let us write $\Delta = \log^{2+\alpha} n$, where $\alpha = 2 + \beta$. The lemma statement implies that $\beta = \Omega(1)$. Note that the condition for $\Delta_i|V_i| = O(n)$ can be re-written as

$$(2 - \alpha) + 2\alpha(3/4)^{i-1} \leq 0.$$

Combining this with $\alpha = 2 + \beta$, we obtain the formula $-\beta + 2(2 + \beta)(3/4)^{i-1} \leq 0$, and this can be re-written as $(4/3)^{i-1} \geq \frac{2(2+\beta)}{\beta}$. Now we can calculate the minimum i needed so that the condition for $\Delta_i|V_i| = O(n)$ is met:

$$i \geq 1 + \log_{4/3} 2(2 + \beta)/\beta.$$

Since $\beta = \Omega(1)$, we have $1 + \log_{4/3} 2(2 + \beta)/\beta = O(1)$, and so our algorithm takes only $O(1)$ iterations. In particular, when $\beta \geq 10.8$, i.e., $\Delta = \Omega(\log^{12.8} n)$, we have $i \geq 1 + \log_{4/3} 2(2 + \beta)/\beta$ for $i \geq 4$. Therefore, $\Delta_4|V_4| = O(n)$, and so 3 iterations suffice. Since each iteration can be implemented in CONGESTED-CLIQUE in $O(1)$ rounds, overall we get an algorithm with round complexity $O(1)$. □

Similar to the proof of Theorem 3.2, the graph partitioning algorithm also leads to an $O(1)$-round MPC coloring algorithm with $S = \tilde{O}(n)$ memory per processor and $\tilde{O}(m)$ total memory. This gives a simple alternate proof of a result of [7] that $(\Delta+1)$-coloring can be solved with $S = \tilde{O}(n)$ memory per processor. However, the coloring algorithm of [7] takes only one round of communication, and it uses only $\tilde{O}(n)$ bits in total.

3.3 Massively Parallel Computation with Strongly Sublinear Memory

We now show how to apply Lemma 3.1 as well as the CLP algorithm of [21], as summarized in the following lemma, to prove Theorem 1.2.

Lemma 3.3 ([21, 53]). *Let G be an n-vertex graph with m edges and maximum degree Δ. Suppose any vertex v has a palette $|\Psi(v)|$ that satisfies $|\Psi(v)| \geq \max\left\{\deg_G(v) + 1, \Delta - \Delta^{3/5}\right\}$. Then the list-coloring problem can be solved w.h.p. in $O(\sqrt{\log\log n})$ rounds of low-memory* MPC *with local memory $O(n^{\alpha})$ for an arbitrary constant $\alpha \in (0, 1)$ and total memory $\tilde{O}\left(\sum_v \deg_G(v)^2\right)$ if $\Delta^2 = O(n^{\alpha})$.*

The proof of Lemma 3.3 almost immediately follows from [21, 53]; there are only few changes that have to be made in order to turn their CONGESTED-CLIQUE algorithm into a low-memory MPC algorithm. The details are deferred to the full version of the paper [20].

Proof of Theorem 1.2. We present a recursive algorithm based on the randomized partitioning algorithm of Lemma 3.1. If $\Delta = \mathrm{poly}(\log n)$ then the conditions of Lemma 3.3 are satisfied trivially; we can solve the problem in $O(\log^* \Delta + \sqrt{\log\log n}) = O(\sqrt{\log\log n})$ rounds of low-memory MPC with total memory $\tilde{O}(n \cdot \Delta^2) = \tilde{O}(m)$. Otherwise, we execute the following algorithm.

Randomized Partitioning: Let G be the graph that we want to color. We apply the randomized partitioning algorithm of Lemma 3.1 to G, which gives us sets $B_1, \dots, B_k$ and L, as well as color sets $C_1, \dots, C_k$. The goal is now to first color $B_1, \dots, B_k$ with colors from $C_1, \dots, C_k$, respectively. Since the colors in the sets C_i are disjoint, this gives a proper coloring of $B := \bigcup_{i=1}^{k} B_i$. Then, for every vertex in L, we remove all colors already used by neighbors in B from the palettes, leaving us with a list-coloring problem of the graph induced by L with maximum degree Δ_L.

In the following, we first describe how to color each set B_i with colors in C_i, and then how to solve the remaining list-coloring problem in L. For the parameters in Lemma 3.1, we use $\gamma = 6$ and $\lambda = 3/5$.[9]

List-Coloring Problem in B_i: If the maximum degree Δ_i in B_i satisfies $\Delta_i^2 = O(n^\alpha)$, then, by Lemma 3.1 ii), B_i satisfies the conditions of Lemma 3.3 We thus can apply the algorithm of Lemma 3.3 to B_i. Otherwise, we recurse on B_i. Note that this is possible since, by Lemma 3.1 ii) applied to G, B_i satisfies the conditions of Lemma 3.1.

List-Coloring Problem in L: If the maximum degree Δ_L in L satisfies $\Delta_L^2 = O(n^\alpha)$, then, by Lemma 3.1 iii) applied to G, L satisfies the conditions of Lemma 3.3. We thus can apply the algorithm of Lemma 3.3 to L. Otherwise, we recurse on L. Note that this is possible since by Lemma 3.1 iii), L satisfies the conditions of Lemma 3.1.

Number of Iterations: Since the maximum degree in L reduces by a polynomial factor in every step, after at most $O(1/\alpha)$ steps, the resulting graph has maximum degree at most $O(n^{\alpha/2})$, where we satisfy the conditions of Lemma 3.3, and hence do not recurse further. Note that when recursing on sets B_i, the degree drop is even larger, and hence the same reasoning applies to bound the number of iterations.

Memory Requirements: It is obvious that the recursive partitioning of the input graph G does not incur any asymptotic overhead in the memory, neither local nor global. Now, let $\mathcal{H}$ be the set of all graphs H on which we apply the algorithm of Lemma 3.3. As we only apply this algorithm when the maximum degree Δ_H of H is $O(n^{\alpha/2})$ or poly($\log n$), we clearly have $\Delta_H^2 = O(n^\alpha)$, so the algorithm Lemma 3.3 is guaranteed to run with local memory $O(n^\alpha)$.

It remains to show how to guarantee the total memory requirement of $\widetilde{O}(m)$, where m is the number of edges in the input graph G, as promised in Theorem 1.2. First, observe that due to the specifications of Lemma 3.3, we can write the total memory requirement as $\sum_{H \in \mathcal{H}} \sum_{v \in H} (\deg_H(v))^2$. First, assume that the graph G has been partitioned at least three times to get to H. By Lemma 3.1 iv), the degree of any vertex v in H is either $\tilde{O}(1)$ or at most

$$\deg_G(v) \cdot \tilde{O}\left(\Delta^{-\frac{1}{4}}\right) \cdot \tilde{O}\left(\Delta^{-\frac{1}{4}\cdot\frac{3}{4}}\right) \cdot \tilde{O}\left(\Delta^{-\frac{1}{4}\cdot(\frac{3}{4})^2}\right)$$
$$= \deg_G(v) \cdot \tilde{O}\left(\Delta^{-37/64}\right) < \tilde{O}\left(\sqrt{\deg_G(v)}\right).$$

Note that in the above calculation we assume v always goes to the left-over part L in all three iterations. If v goes to B_i, then the degree shrinks faster. Remember that we set $q = \tilde{O}(\Delta^{-1/4})$. Hence, we require a total memory of

$$\widetilde{O}\left(\sum_{H \in \mathcal{H}} \sum_{v \in H} (\deg_H(v))^2\right) = \widetilde{O}\left(\sum_{H \in \mathcal{H}} \sum_{v \in H} \deg_G(v)\right)$$
$$= \widetilde{O}\left(\sum_{v \in G} \deg_G(v)\right) = \widetilde{O}(m).$$

Note that the algorithm can be easily adapted to always perform at least three partitioning steps if Δ_H is bounded from below by a sufficiently large poly($\log n$), because then the conditions of Lemma 3.1 are satisfied. On the other hand, if Δ_H = poly($\log n$), it is follows immediately that $\widetilde{O}\left(\sum_v (\deg_H(v))^2\right) = \text{poly}(\log n) = \widetilde{O}(1)$. Put together, we have $\sum_{H \in \mathcal{H}} \sum_{v \in H} (\deg_H(v))^2 = \widetilde{O}(m)$. □

[9] The choice $\lambda = 3/5$ is to ensure that the number of available colors for each vertex in each subgraph meets the palette size constraint specified in Lemma 3.3.

REFERENCES

[1] Kook Jin Ahn and Sudipto Guha. 2015. Access to Data and Number of Iterations: Dual Primal Algorithms for Maximum Matching Under Resource Constraints. In *Proc. SPAA*. 202–211.

[2] Noga Alon and Joel H. Spencer. 2016. *The Probabilistic Method* (4th ed.). Wiley Publishing.

[3] Alexandr Andoni, Aleksandar Nikolov, Krzysztof Onak, and Grigory Yaroslavtsev. 2014. Parallel Algorithms for Geometric Graph Problems. In *Proc. Symposium on Theory of Computation (STOC)*. 574–583.

[4] Alexandr Andoni, Clifford Stein, Zhao Song, Zhengyu Wang, and Peilin Zhong. 2018. Parallel Graph Connectivity in Log Diameter Rounds. In *Proceedings 59th IEEE Symposium on Foundations of Computer Science (FOCS)*. 674–685.

[5] Sepehr Assadi. 2017. Simple round compression for parallel vertex cover. *arXiv preprint arXiv:1709.04599* (2017).

[6] Sepehr Assadi, MohammadHossein Bateni, Aaron Bernstein, Vahab Mirrokni, and Cliff Stein. 2019. Coresets meet EDCS: algorithms for matching and vertex cover on massive graphs. In *Proceedings 30th Annual ACM-SIAM Symposium on Discrete Algorithms (SODA)*.

[7] Sepehr Assadi, Yu Chen, and Sanjeev Khanna. 2019. Sublinear Algorithms for (Δ + 1) Vertex Coloring. In *Proceedings 30th Annual ACM-SIAM Symposium on Discrete Algorithms (SODA)*.

[8] Sepehr Assadi, Xiaorui Sun, and Omri Weinstein. 2018. Massively Parallel Algorithms for Finding Well-Connected Components in Sparse Graphs. *arXiv preprint arXiv:1805.02974* (2018).

[9] Leonid Barenboim, Michael Elkin, and Uri Goldenberg. 2018. Locally-Iterative Distributed (Δ + 1)-Coloring below Szegedy-Vishwanathan Barrier, and Applications to Self-Stabilization and to Restricted-Bandwidth Models. In *Proceedings of the 2018 ACM Symposium on Principles of Distributed Computing (PODC)*. ACM, 437–446.

[10] Leonid Barenboim, Michael Elkin, Seth Pettie, and Johannes Schneider. 2016. The Locality of Distributed Symmetry Breaking. *J. ACM* 63, 3, Article 20 (2016), 20:1–20:45 pages.

[11] Leonid Barenboim and Victor Khazanov. 2018. Distributed Symmetry-Breaking Algorithms for Congested Cliques. In *Computer Science - Theory and Applications - 13th International Computer Science Symposium in Russia, CSR 2018, Moscow, Russia, June 6-10, 2018, Proceedings.* 41–52.

[12] Paul Beame, Paraschos Koutris, and Dan Suciu. 2013. Communication Steps for Parallel Query Processing. In *Proceedings of the 32Nd ACM SIGMOD-SIGACT-SIGAI Symposium on Principles of Database Systems (PODS)*. 273–284.

[13] Paul Beame, Paraschos Koutris, and Dan Suciu. 2014. Skew in Parallel Query Processing. In *Proceedings of the 33rd ACM SIGMOD-SIGACT-SIGART Symposium on Principles of Database Systems (PODS)*. 212–223.

[14] Ruben Becker, Andreas Karrenbauer, Sebastian Krinninger, and Christoph Lenzen. 2017. Near-Optimal Approximate Shortest Paths and Transshipment in Distributed and Streaming Models. In *31st International Symposium on Distributed Computing (DISC 2017) (Leibniz International Proceedings in Informatics (LIPIcs))*, Andréa W. Richa (Ed.), Vol. 91. Schloss Dagstuhl–Leibniz-Zentrum fuer Informatik, 7:1–7:16.

[15] Andrew Berns, James Hegeman, and Sriram V Pemmaraju. 2012. Super-fast distributed algorithms for metric facility location. In *Automata, Languages, and Programming*. Springer, 428–439.

[16] Mahdi Boroujeni, Soheil Ehsani, Mohammad Ghodsi, MohammadTaghi Haji-Aghayi, and Saeed Seddighin. 2018. Approximating edit distance in truly subquadratic time: quantum and MapReduce. In *Proc. Symposium on Discrete Algorithms (SODA)*. 1170–1189.

[17] Sebastian Brandt, Manuela Fischer, and Jara Uitto. 2018. Breaking the Linear-Memory Barrier in MPC: Fast MIS on Trees with n^ϵ Memory per Machine. *arXiv preprint arXiv:1802.06748* (2018).

[18] Keren Censor-Hillel, Petteri Kaski, Janne H. Korhonen, Christoph Lenzen, Ami Paz, and Jukka Suomela. 2016. Algebraic methods in the congested clique. *Distributed Computing* (2016). https://doi.org/10.1007/s00446-016-0270-2

[19] Keren Censor-Hillel, Dean Leitersdorf, and Elia Turner. 2018. Sparse Matrix Multiplication with Bandwidth Restricted All-to-All Communication. *CoRR* abs/1802.04789 (2018).

[20] Yi-Jun Chang, Manuela Fischer, Mohsen Ghaffari, Jara Uitto, and Yufan Zheng. 2018. The Complexity of $(\Delta+1)$ Coloring in Congested Clique, Massively Parallel Computation, and Centralized Local Computation. *CoRR* abs/1808.08419 (2018). arXiv:1808.08419 http://arxiv.org/abs/1808.08419

[21] Yi-Jun Chang, Wenzheng Li, and Seth Pettie. 2018. An Optimal Distributed $(\Delta + 1)$-coloring Algorithm?. In *Proceedings of the 50th Annual ACM SIGACT Symposium on Theory of Computing (STOC 2018)*. ACM, New York, NY, USA, 445–456. https://doi.org/10.1145/3188745.3188964

[22] Artur Czumaj, Jakub Lacki, Aleksander Madry, Slobodan Mitrovic, Krzysztof Onak, and Piotr Sankowski. 2018. Round Compression for Parallel Matching Algorithms. In *Proc. Symposium on Theory of Computation (STOC)*. 471–484.

[23] Jeffrey Dean and Sanjay Ghemawat. 2004. MapReduce: Simplified Data Processing on Large Clusters. In *Proceedings of the 6th Conference on Symposium on Operating Systems Design & Implementation (OSDI)*. USENIX Association, Berkeley, CA, USA, 10–10. http://dl.acm.org/citation.cfm?id=1251254.1251264

[24] Danny Dolev, Christoph Lenzen, and Shir Peled. 2012. "Tri, Tri Again": Finding Triangles and Small Subgraphs in a Distributed Setting. In *Distributed Computing*. Springer, 195–209.

[25] Andrew Drucker, Fabian Kuhn, and Rotem Oshman. 2014. On the Power of the Congested Clique Model. In *Proc. Principles of Distributed Computing (PODC)*. ACM, 367–376.

[26] Manuela Fischer and Mohsen Ghaffari. 2017. Sublogarithmic Distributed Algorithms for Lovász Local Lemma with Implications on Complexity Hierarchies. In *Proceedings 31st International Symposium on Distributed Computing (DISC)*. 18:1–18:16.

[27] Pierre Fraigniaud, Marc Heinrich, and Adrian Kosowski. 2016. Local conflict coloring. In *Proceedings 57th Annual IEEE Symposium on Foundations of Computer Science (FOCS)*. 625–634.

[28] Francois Le Gall. 2016. Further Algebraic Algorithms in the Congested Clique Model and Applications to Graph-Theoretic Problems. In *DISC*.

[29] Mohsen Ghaffari. 2016. An improved distributed algorithm for maximal independent set. In *Proceedings 27th Annual ACM-SIAM Symposium on Discrete Algorithms (SODA)*. 270–277.

[30] Mohsen Ghaffari. 2017. Distributed MIS via All-to-All Communication. In *Proc. Principles of Distributed Computing (PODC)*. 141–149.

[31] Mohsen Ghaffari, Themis Gouleakis, Christian Konrad, Slobodan Mitrović, and Ronitt Rubinfeld. 2018. Improved massively parallel computation algorithms for mis, matching, and vertex cover. In *Proc. Principles of Distributed Computing (PODC)*. arXiv:1802.08237.

[32] Mohsen Ghaffari and Jara Uitto. 2019. Sparsifying Distributed Algorithms with Ramifications in Massively Parallel Computation and Centralized Local Computation. In *Proceedings 30th Annual ACM-SIAM Symposium on Discrete Algorithms (SODA)*.

[33] Michael T. Goodrich, Nodari Sitchinava, and Qin Zhang. 2011. Sorting, searching, and simulation in the MapReduce framework. In *Proc. ISAAC*. Springer, 374–383.

[34] David G Harris, Johannes Schneider, and Hsin-Hao Su. 2018. Distributed $(\Delta + 1)$-Coloring in Sublogarithmic Rounds. *J. ACM* 65, 4 (2018), 19:1–19:21. https://doi.org/10.1145/3178120

[35] Nicholas J. A. Harvey, Christopher Liaw, and Paul Liu. 2018. Greedy and Local Ratio Algorithms in the MapReduce Model. In *Proceedings of the 30th on Symposium on Parallelism in Algorithms and Architectures (SPAA)*. ACM, New York, NY, USA, 43–52. https://doi.org/10.1145/3210377.3210386

[36] James W. Hegeman, Gopal Pandurangan, Sriram V. Pemmaraju, Vivek B. Sardeshmukh, and Michele Scquizzato. 2015. Toward Optimal Bounds in the Congested Clique: Graph Connectivity and MST. In *Proc. Principles of Distributed Computing (PODC)*. ACM, 91–100.

[37] James W Hegeman and Sriram V Pemmaraju. 2015. Lessons from the congested clique applied to MapReduce. *Theoretical Computer Science* 608 (2015), 268–281.

[38] James W. Hegeman and Sriram V. Pemmaraju. 2015. Lessons from the Congested Clique Applied to MapReduce. *Theor. Comput. Sci.* 608, P3 (Dec. 2015), 268–281. https://doi.org/10.1016/j.tcs.2015.09.029

[39] James W Hegeman, Sriram V Pemmaraju, and Vivek B Sardeshmukh. 2014. Near-constant-time distributed algorithms on a congested clique. In *Distributed Computing*. Springer, 514–530.

[40] Sungjin Im, Benjamin Moseley, and Xiaorui Sun. 2017. Efficient Massively Parallel Methods for Dynamic Programming. In *Proc. Symposium on Theory of Computation (STOC)*. 798–811.

[41] Michael Isard, Mihai Budiu, Yuan Yu, Andrew Birrell, and Dennis Fetterly. 2007. Dryad: Distributed Data-parallel Programs from Sequential Building Blocks. *SIGOPS Operating Systems Review* 41, 3 (2007), 59–72. https://doi.org/10.1145/1272998.1273005

[42] Tomasz Jurdzinski and Krzysztof Nowicki. 2018. MST in $O(1)$ Rounds of Congested Clique. In *Proceedings of the Twenty-Ninth Annual ACM-SIAM Symposium on Discrete Algorithms, SODA 2018, New Orleans, LA, USA, January 7-10, 2018*. 2620–2632.

[43] Howard J. Karloff, Siddharth Suri, and Sergei Vassilvitskii. 2010. A Model of Computation for MapReduce. In *Proc. Symposium on Discrete Algorithms (SODA)*. 938–948.

[44] Silvio Lattanzi, Benjamin Moseley, Siddharth Suri, and Sergei Vassilvitskii. 2011. Filtering: a method for solving graph problems in MapReduce. In *Proc. SPAA*. 85–94.

[45] Christoph Lenzen. 2013. Optimal Deterministic Routing and Sorting on the Congested Clique. In *Proceedings 33rd ACM Symposium on Principles of Distributed Computing (PODC)*. 42–50. https://doi.org/10.1145/2484239.2501983

[46] Christoph Lenzen and Roger Wattenhofer. 2010. Brief Announcement: Exponential Speed-up of Local Algorithms Using Non-local Communication. In *Proceedings of the 29th ACM SIGACT-SIGOPS Symposium on Principles of Distributed Computing (PODC)*. ACM, 295–296. https://doi.org/10.1145/1835698.1835772

[47] Reut Levi and Moti Medina. 2017. A (centralized) local guide. *Bulletin of EATCS* 2, 122 (2017).

[48] Nathan Linial. 1992. Locality in Distributed Graph Algorithms. *SIAM J. Comput.* 21, 1 (1992), 193–201.

[49] Zvi Lotker, Boaz Patt-Shamir, Elan Pavlov, and David Peleg. 2005. Minimum-weight spanning tree construction in O(log log n) communication rounds. *SIAM J. Comput.* 35, 1 (2005), 120–131.

[50] Danupon Nanongkai. 2014. Distributed Approximation Algorithms for Weighted Shortest Paths. In *Proc. Symposium on Theory of Computation (STOC)*.

[51] Alessandro Panconesi and Aravind Srinivasan. 1996. On the Complexity of Distributed Network Decomposition. *J. Algor.* 20, 2 (1996), 356–374.

[52] Michal Parnas and Dana Ron. 2007. Approximating the minimum vertex cover in sublinear time and a connection to distributed algorithms. *Theoretical Computer Science* 381, 1 (2007), 183 – 196. https://doi.org/10.1016/j.tcs.2007.04.040

[53] Merav Parter. 2018. $(\Delta + 1)$ coloring in the congested clique model.. In *Proceedings of the International Colloquium on Automata, Languages and Programming (ICALP)*. 160:1–160:14.

[54] Merav Parter and Hsin-Hao Su. 2018. Randomized $(\Delta + 1)$ coloring in $O(\log^* \Delta)$ congested clique rounds. In *Proceedings of the International Symposium on Distributed Computing (DISC)*. 39:1–39:18.

[55] Boaz Patt-Shamir and Marat Teplitsky. 2011. The round complexity of distributed sorting. In *Proc. Principles of Distributed Computing (PODC)*. 249–256.

[56] David Peleg. 2000. *Distributed Computing: A Locality-Sensitive Approach.* SIAM.

[57] Tim Roughgarden, Sergei Vassilvitskii, and Joshua R. Wang. 2016. Shuffles and Circuits: (On Lower Bounds for Modern Parallel Computation). In *Proc. SPAA*. 1–12.

[58] Ronitt Rubinfeld, Gil Tamir, Shai Vardi, and Ning Xie. 2011. Fast Local Computation Algorithms. In *Proceedings of the First Symposium on Innovations in Computer Science (ICS)*. 223–238. See also *CoRR* abs/1104.1377.

[59] Jeanette P. Schmidt, Alan Siegel, and Aravind Srinivasan. 1995. Chernoff-Hoeffding Bounds for Applications with Limited Independence. *SIAM Journal on Discrete Mathematics* 8, 2 (1995), 223–250.

[60] Tom White. 2012. *Hadoop: The Definitive Guide.* O'Reilly Media, Inc.

[61] Matei Zaharia, Mosharaf Chowdhury, Michael J. Franklin, Scott Shenker, and Ion Stoica. 2010. Spark: Cluster Computing with Working Sets. In *2nd USENIX Workshop on Hot Topics in Cloud Computing (HotCloud)*. https://www.usenix.org/conference/hotcloud-10/spark-cluster-computing-working-sets

Massively Parallel Computation of Matching and MIS in Sparse Graphs

Soheil Behnezhad*
University of Maryland
soheil@cs.umd.edu

Sebastian Brandt
ETH Zurich
brandts@ethz.ch

Mahsa Derakhshan*
University of Maryland
mahsa@cs.umd.edu

Manuela Fischer
ETH Zurich
manuela.fischer@inf.ethz.ch

MohammadTaghi Hajiaghayi*
University of Maryland
hajiagha@cs.umd.edu

Richard M. Karp
UC Berkeley
karp@cs.berkeley.edu

Jara Uitto†
ETH Zurich & University of Freiburg
jara.uitto@inf.ethz.ch

ABSTRACT

The *Massively Parallel Computation* (MPC) model serves as a common abstraction of many modern large-scale parallel computation frameworks and has recently gained a lot of importance, especially in the context of classic graph problems. In this work, we mainly consider *maximal matching* and *maximal independent set* problems in the MPC model.

These problems are known to admit efficient MPC algorithms if the space available per machine is near-linear in the number n of nodes. This is not only often significantly more than what we can afford, but also allows for easy if not trivial solutions for sparse graphs—which are common in real-world large-scale graphs. We are, therefore, interested in the *low-memory* MPC model, where the space per machine is restricted to be strongly sublinear, that is, n^δ for any constant $0 < \delta < 1$.

We parametrize our algorithms by the *arboricity* λ of the input graph. Our key ingredient is a degree reduction technique that reduces these problems in graphs with arboricity λ to the corresponding problems in graphs with maximum degree $\mathrm{poly}(\lambda, \log n)$ in $O(\log^2 \log n)$ rounds, giving rise to $O(\sqrt{\log \lambda} \cdot \log \log \lambda + \log^2 \log n)$-round algorithms.

Our result is particularly interesting for graphs with $\mathrm{poly}\log n$ arboricity as for such graphs, we get $O(\log^2 \log n)$-round algorithms. This covers most natural families of sparse graphs and almost exponentially improves over previous algorithms that all required $\log^{\Omega(1)} n$ rounds in this regime of MPC.

Finally, our maximal matching algorithm can be employed to obtain a $(1 + \varepsilon)$-approximate *maximum cardinality matching*, a $(2 + \varepsilon)$-approximate *maximum weighted matching*, as well as a 2-approximate *minimum vertex cover* in essentially the same number of rounds.

CCS CONCEPTS

• **Theory of computation → Parallel algorithms; Massively parallel algorithms.**

ACM Reference Format:
Soheil Behnezhad, Sebastian Brandt, Mahsa Derakhshan, Manuela Fischer, MohammadTaghi Hajiaghayi, Richard M. Karp, and Jara Uitto. 2019. Massively Parallel Computation of Matching and MIS in Sparse Graphs. In *2019 ACM Symposium on Principles of Distributed Computing (PODC '19), July 29-August 2, 2019, Toronto, ON, Canada.* ACM, New York, NY, USA, 10 pages. https://doi.org/10.1145/3293611.3331609

1 INTRODUCTION

Due to the prevalence of huge networks, scalable algorithms for fundamental graph problems have gained a lot of importance in the area of parallel computing. The *Massively Parallel Computation* (MPC) model [1, 6, 7, 10, 17, 20] constitutes a common abstraction of several popular large-scale computation frameworks—such as MapReduce [11], Dryad [19], Spark [33], and Hadoop [32]—and thus serves as the basis for the systematic study of massively parallel algorithms.

Most classic parallel or distributed algorithms can be simulated directly in the MPC model in the same number of rounds (often polylogarithmic) [17, 20]. The additional power of MPC, however, in free local computation (compared to PRAM) or of global all-to-all communication (compared to LOCAL) could potentially be exploited to obtain faster MPC algorithms. Achieving such improvements has been the main theme of research over the past few years in the study of this model.

Surprisingly, for *maximal matching* (MM) and *maximal independent set* (MIS) problems, which have been studied from the very early days of the area in 1980s, we are still far from understanding the full power of MPC. A remarkable series of recent results[2, 10, 14] show how the local memory can be reduced to

*Supported in part by NSF grants CCF:SPX 1822738, IIS:BIGDATA 1546108, DARPA grant SI3CMD, UMD Year of Data Science Program Grant, and Northrop Grumman Faculty Award.
†Supported by ERC Grant No. 336495 (ACDC).

PODC '19, July 29-August 2, 2019, Toronto, ON, Canada

ACM ISBN 978-1-4503-6217-7/19/07...$15.00
https://doi.org/10.1145/3293611.3331609

be $\widetilde{O}(n)$ while still having poly(log log n)-round algorithms. Yet, all these algorithms fail to go (substantially) below linear space without an (almost) exponential blow-up in the round complexity. Even more severely, for maximal matching, the only subpolylogarithmic algorithm by Lattanzi, Moseley, Suri, and Vassilvitskii [22] requires the memory per machine to be substantially superlinear in the number n of nodes in the graph.

The space requirement of the aforementioned algorithms is not only prohibitively large, but also allows an easy or even trivial solution for sparse graphs. This is unfortunate, since sparse large-scale graphs indeed appear quite a lot in practice [5, 10, 20]. For this, we study the *low-memory* MPC model with strongly sublinear space. It is natural to ask:

> *Can we take advantage of the graphs' sparsity to design sub-polylogarithmic, and ideally,* poly(log log n)*-round algorithms in the truly sublinear regime of the* MPC *model?*

We make a step towards answering this question by parametrizing our algorithms by *arboricity*[1] of the input graph. Arboricity is a well-received measure of sparsity that does not impose strict structural constraints such as planarity, bounds on maximum degree, or the like [3, 4, 9, 12, 18]. The family of graphs with arboricity poly(log n)—often called *uniformly sparse* graphs, and also known as *sparse everywhere* graphs—includes but is not restricted to graphs with maximum degree poly(log n), minor-closed graphs (e.g., planar graphs and graphs with bounded treewidth), as well as preferential attachment graphs, and thus arguably contains most sparse graphs of practical relevance [16, 29]. We show that:

Main Result. *There exist low-memory* MPC *algorithms that with high probability compute a maximal matching and maximal independent set of any given n-vertex graph of arboricity up to λ, in $O(\sqrt{\log \lambda} \cdot \log\log \lambda + \log^2 \log n)$ rounds.*

For all graphs with arboricity up to poly(log n), our algorithms take only $O(\log^2 \log n)$ rounds to find maximal matching or maximal independent set. This is almost exponentially faster than the previous algorithms in the low-memory MPC model, which we overview soon.

1.1 Low-Memory MPC Model for Graph Problems

We have M machines with local memory of $S = O(n^{\delta})$ words each, for some $0 < \delta \leq 1$[2]. A graph with n nodes, m edges, and maximum degree Δ is distributed arbitrarily across the machines. We assume the total memory in the system to be (nearly) linear in the input, i.e., $M \cdot S = \widetilde{\Theta}(m)$. The computation proceeds in rounds consisting of *local computation* in all machines in parallel, followed by *global communication* between the machines. We require that the total size of sent and received messages of a machine in every communication phase does not exceed its local memory capacity. The main interest lies in minimizing the number of rounds, aiming for poly(log log n).

1.2 Our Contribution

The main technicality of our approach lies in a degree reduction technique that reduces the problems of maximal matching and maximal independent set in a graph with arboricity λ to the corresponding problems in graphs with maximum degree poly(λ) in $O(\log^2 \log n)$ rounds.

Theorem 1.1. *There is an $O(\log\log_{\Delta} n \cdot \log\log_{\lambda} \Delta)$-round low-memory* MPC *algorithm that w.h.p.*[3] *reduces maximal matching and maximal independent set in graphs with arboricity $\lambda = n^{o(1)}$ to the respective problems in graphs with maximum degree $O(\lambda^{20} + \log^{20} n)$.*[4]

This improves over the degree reduction algorithm by Barenboim, Elkin, Pettie, and Schneider [4, Theorem 7.2], which runs in $O(\log_{\lambda} n)$ rounds in the LOCAL model and can be straightforwardly implemented in the low-memory MPC model.

Our degree reduction technique, combined with the state-of-the-art algorithms for maximal matching and maximal independent set by Ghaffari and Uitto [15] applied as a black box, gives rise to a number of low-memory MPC algorithms, as overviewed next.

Theorem 1.2. *There is an $O(\sqrt{\log \lambda} \cdot \log\log \lambda + \log\log n \cdot \log\log \Delta)$-round low-memory* MPC *algorithm that w.h.p. computes a maximal matching in a graph with arboricity λ.*

This improves over the $O(\log \lambda + \sqrt{\log n})$-round LOCAL algorithm by [4] and the $\widetilde{O}(\sqrt{\log \Delta})$-round algorithm by [15]. The only previous subpolylogarithmic round maximal matching algorithm due to Lattanzi et al. [22], requires space per machine of $n^{1+\Omega(1)}$.

We also note that the round complexity of all previous poly(log log n)-round MPC matching approximation algorithms for general graphs (even if we allow linear memory) [2, 10, 14] blows up by an $\Omega(\log n)$ overhead for the case of maximal matching. In fact, the problem of finding a maximal matching seems to be much more difficult than finding a $(1+\varepsilon)$-approximate maximum matching. Indeed, currently, an $O(1)$-approximation can be found almost exponentially faster than a maximal matching, and the approximation ratio can be easily improved from any constant to $1 + \varepsilon$ using a reduction of McGregor [26].

Theorem 1.3. *There is an $O(\sqrt{\log \lambda} \cdot \log\log \lambda + \log\log n \cdot \log\log \Delta)$-round low-memory* MPC *algorithm that w.h.p. computes a maximal independent set in a graph with arboricity λ.*

This algorithm improves over the $O\left(\log \lambda + \sqrt{\log n}\right)$-round algorithm that is obtained by simulating the LOCAL algorithm of [4, 13] and over the $\widetilde{O}\left(\sqrt{\log \Delta}\right)$-round algorithm of Ghaffari and Uitto [15]. It also improves over another $O(\log^3 \log n)$ round algorithm for MIS on trees by Brandt, Fischer and Uitto [8].

[1] The arboricity of a graph is the minimum number of forests into which its edges can be partitioned. Equivalently, Nash-Williams [28] showed that it can be defined as the average degree within the graph's densest subgraph.

[2] Note that we do not require δ to be a constant. For the sake of simplicity of presentation, we decided to omit the δ-dependency, which is a multiplicative factor of $O(\frac{1}{\delta})$, in the analysis of the running time of our algorithms.

[3] As usual, w.h.p. stands for *with high probability,* and means with probability at least $1 - n^{-c}$ for any constant $c \geq 1$.

[4] The purpose of the choice of all the constants in this work is merely to simplify presentation.

As a maximal matching automatically provides 2-approximations for maximum matching and minimum vertex cover, Theorem 1.2 directly implies the following result.

Corollary 1.4. *There is an $O(\sqrt{\log\lambda}\cdot\log\log\lambda+\log\log n\cdot\log\log\Delta)$-round low-memory* MPC *algorithm that w.h.p. computes a 2-approximate maximum matching and a 2-approximate minimum vertex cover in a graph with arboricity λ.*

McGregor's reduction [26] allows us to further improve the approximation to $1+\varepsilon$.

Corollary 1.5. *There is an $O((\frac{1}{\varepsilon})^{O(1/\varepsilon)}\cdot(\sqrt{\log\lambda}\cdot\log\log\lambda+\log\log n\cdot\log\log\Delta))$-round low-memory* MPC *algorithm that w.h.p. computes a $(1+\varepsilon)$-approximate maximum matching, for any $\varepsilon>0$.*

Due to a reduction by to Lotker, Patt-Shamir, and Pettie [25], our constant-approximate matching algorithm can also be employed to find a $(2+\varepsilon)$-approximate maximum weighted matching.

Corollary 1.6. *There is an $O(\log(\frac{1}{\varepsilon})\cdot(\sqrt{\log\lambda}\cdot\log\log\lambda+\log\log n\cdot\log\log\Delta))$-round low-memory* MPC *algorithm that w.h.p. computes a $(2+\varepsilon)$-approximate maximum weighted matching, for any $\varepsilon>0$.*

2 ALGORITHM OUTLINE AND ROADMAP

In the low-memory setting, one is inevitably confronted with the challenge of locality: as the space of a machine is strongly sublinear, it will never be able to see a significant fraction of the nodes, regardless of how sparse the graph is. Further building on the ideas by [8], we cope with this imposed locality by adopting local techniques—mainly inspired by the LOCAL model [24]—and enhancing them with the additional power of global communication, in order to achieve an improvement in the round complexity compared to the LOCAL algorithms while still being able to guarantee applicability in the presence of strongly sublinear memory.

The main observation behind our algorithms is the following: If the maximum degree in the graph is small, LOCAL algorithms can be simulated efficiently in the low-memory MPC model. Our method thus basically boils down to reducing the maximum degree of the input graph, as described in Theorem 1.1, and correspondingly consists of two parts: a *degree reduction* part followed by a LOCAL *simulation* part. In the degree reduction part, which constitutes the key ingredient of our algorithm, we want to find a partial solution (that is, either a matching or an independent set) so that the *remainder graph*—i.e., the graph after the removal of this partial solution (that is, after removing all matched nodes or after removing the independent set nodes along with all their neighbors)—has smaller degree.

Lemma 2.1. *There are $O(\log\log n\cdot\log\log\Delta)$-round low-memory* MPC *algorithms that compute a matching and an independent set in a graph with arboricity $\lambda=n^{o(1)}$ so that the remainder graph w.h.p. has maximum degree $O\left((\max\{\lambda,\log n\})^{20}\right)$.*

Note that this directly implies Theorem 1.1. Next, we show how Theorems 1.2 and 1.3 follow from Lemma 2.1 as well as from an efficient simulation of LOCAL algorithms due to [15].

Proof of Theorems 1.2 and 1.3. If λ, and hence Δ, is at least polynomial in n, we directly apply the algorithm by [15], which runs in $O(\sqrt{\log\Delta}\cdot\log\log\Delta+\sqrt{\log\log n})=O(\sqrt{\log n}\cdot\log\log n)$ rounds. Otherwise, we first apply the algorithm of Lemma 2.1 to obtain a partial solution that reduces the degree in the remainder graph to $\Delta'=O(\lambda^{20})$ if $\lambda\geq\log n$, or to $\Delta'=O(\log^{20}n)$ if $\lambda\leq\log n$. It runs in $O(\log\log n\cdot\log\log\Delta)$ rounds. We then apply the algorithm by [15] on the remainder graph. This takes $O(\sqrt{\log\Delta'}\cdot\log\log\Delta'+\sqrt{\log\log n})=O(\sqrt{\log\lambda}\cdot\log\log\lambda+\sqrt{\log\log n})$ rounds. □

Our degree reduction algorithm in Lemma 2.1 consists of several phases, each reducing the maximum degree by a polynomial factor, as long as the degree is still large enough.

Lemma 2.2. *There are $O(\log\log n)$-round low-memory* MPC *algorithms that compute a matching and an independent set, respectively, in a graph with arboricity $\lambda=o(\text{poly}(n))$ and maximum degree $\Delta=\Omega\left((\max\{\lambda,\log n\})^{20}\right)$ so that the remainder graph w.h.p. has maximum degree $O(\Delta^{0.4})$.*

We first show that indeed iterated applications of this polynomial degree reduction lead to the desired degree reduction in Lemma 2.1.

Proof of Lemma 2.1. We iteratively apply the polynomial degree reduction from Lemma 2.2, observing that as long as the maximum degree is still in $\Omega(\lambda^{20})$ and $\Omega(\log^{20}n)$, we reduce the maximum degree by a polynomial factor from Δ to $O(\Delta^{0.4})$ in each phase, resulting in at most $O(\log\log\Delta)$ phases. □

It remains to show that such a polynomial degree reduction, as claimed in Lemma 2.2, indeed is possible. This is done in two parts. First, in Section 3, we provide a centralized algorithm for a polynomial degree reduction, and then, in Section 4, we show how to implement this centralized algorithm efficiently in the low-memory MPC model. Several of the techniques we use throughout the paper can also be applied in a wider context. To provide some algorithmic tools for future work, we introduce generalized versions of a selection of our techniques in Section 5.

Remark 2.3. *While our algorithms, at first sight, seem to need to know λ, we can easily get rid of this assumption by employing the standard technique [21] of running the algorithm with doubly-exponentially increasing estimates for λ. Roughly speaking, the idea is as follows. We run $O(\log\log\Delta)$ copies, one for every estimate of λ, of the algorithm in parallel and pick (one of) the correct solution(s), which is easy to find in* MPC.

3 A CENTRALIZED DEGREE REDUCTION ALGORITHM

In this section, we present a centralized algorithm for the polynomial degree reduction as stated in Lemma 2.2. For details on how this algorithm can be implemented in the low-memory MPC model, we refer to Section 4. In Section 3.1, we give a formal description of the (centralized) algorithm. Then, in Section 3.2, we prove that this algorithm indeed leads to a polynomial degree reduction.

3.1 Algorithm Description

In the following, we set $d=\Delta^{1/10}$, and observe that $d=\Omega(\lambda^2)$ as well as $d=\Omega(\log^2 n)$, due to the assumptions on Δ in the lemma statement. We present an algorithm that reduces the maximum degree to $O(d^4)$. This algorithm consists of three phases: a *partition* phase, in which the nodes are partitioned into layers so that every node has at most d neighbors in higher-index layers, a *mark-and-propose* phase in which a random set of candidates is proposed independently in every layer, and a *selection* phase in which a valid subset of the candidate set is selected as partial solution by resolving potential conflicts across layers.

Partition Phase: We compute an H-partition, that is, a partition of the nodes into layers so that every node has at most d neighbors in layers with higher (or equal) index [3, 27, 28].

Definition 3.1 (H-Partition). *An H-partition with out-degree d, defined for any $d > 2\lambda$, is a partition of the nodes into ℓ layers $L_1, \ldots, L_\ell$ with the property that a node $v \in L_i$ has at most d neighbors in $\bigcup_{j=i}^{\ell} L_j$. We call i the* layer index *of v if $v \in L_i$. For neighbors $u \in L_i$ and $v \in L_j$ for $i < j$, we call v a* parent *of u and u a* child *of v. If we think of the edges as being directed from children to parents, this gives rise to a partial orientation of the edges, with no orientation of the edges connecting nodes in the same layer.*

Note that, for $d > 2\lambda$, such a partition can be computed easily by the following sequential greedy algorithm, also known as *peeling* algorithm: Iteratively, for $i \geq 1$, put all remaining nodes with remaining degree at most d into layer i, and remove them from the graph. Due to the well-known fact that the average degree of a graph with arboricity λ is 2λ, in every iteration a constant fraction of the nodes will be removed.

Mark-and-Propose Phase: We first mark a random set of candidates (either edges or nodes) and then propose a subset of these marked candidates for the partial solution as follows.

In the case of maximal matching, every node first marks an outgoing edge chosen uniformly at random and then proposes one of its incoming marked edges, if any, uniformly at random.

In the case of maximal independent set, every node marks itself independently with probability $p = d^{-2}$. Then, if a node is marked and none of its neighbors in the same layer is marked, this node is proposed. Note that whether a marked node gets proposed only depends on nodes in the same layer, thus on neighbors with respect to unoriented edges.

Selection Phase: The set of proposed candidates might not be a valid solution, meaning that it might have some conflicts (i.e., two incident edges or two neighboring nodes). In the selection phase, possible conflicts are resolved (deterministically) by picking an appropriate subset of the proposed candidates, as follows. Iteratively, for $i = \ell, \ldots, 1$, all (remaining) proposed candidates in layer i are added to the partial solution and then removed from the graph.

In the case of maximal matching, we add all (remaining) proposed edges directed to a node in layer i to the matching and remove both their endpoints from the graph.

In the case of maximal independent set, we add all (remaining) proposed nodes in layer i to the independent set and remove them along with their neighbors from the graph.

3.2 Proof of Correctness

It is easy to see that the selected solution is a valid partial solution, that is, that there are no conflicts. It remains to be shown that the

Figure 1: Illustration of the mark-and-propose and the selection phase for matching in (a) and independent set in (b). Blue indicates marked but not proposed, green stands for (marked and) proposed but not selected, and red means (marked and proposed and) selected. Note that we omitted all (but a few) irrelevant edges from the figure; the partition into layers thus might not correspond to a valid H-partition.

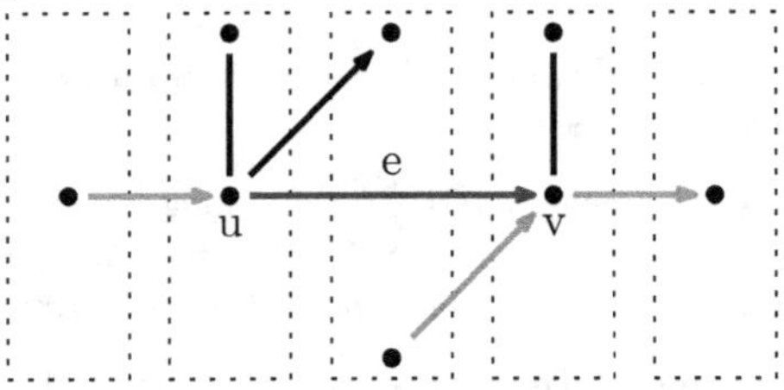

(a) An (oriented) edge $e = (u, v)$ that is selected to be added to the matching cannot have an incident edge that is also selected: an unoriented incident edge cannot be marked as only oriented edges are marked; an oriented edge with the same starting point u cannot be marked as u marks only one outgoing edge; an oriented edge with the same endpoint v cannot be proposed as v proposes only one incoming edge; all other oriented edges f are either processed before (in the case of an outgoing edge from v) or after (in the case of an incoming edge to u) edge e in the selection phase. In the former case, the selection of f would lead to the removal of e before e is processed; e thus would not be selected. In the latter case, the edge f is removed immediately after e is selected (and thus before f is processed), and thus cannot be selected.

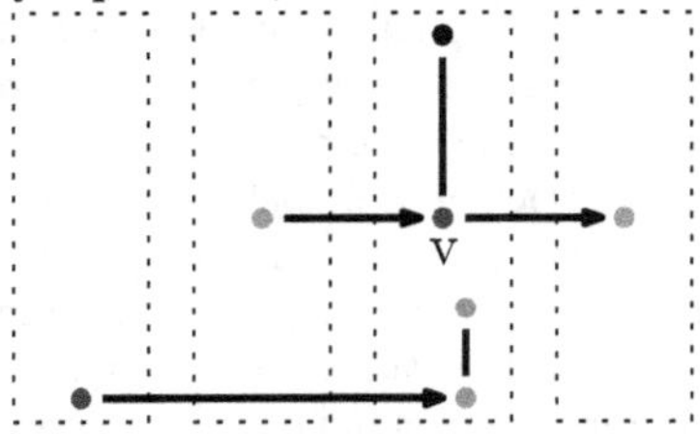

(b) If two neighboring nodes are marked, none of them will be proposed, and consequently, none of them will be selected. A node v that is selected to be added to the independent set cannot have a neighbor that is also selected: a neighbor in the same layer cannot be marked as otherwise v would not be proposed; a neighbor in a lower-index layer is removed from the graph when v joins the independent set, and hence before it potentially could be selected; a selected neighbor in a higher-index layer would lead to v's immediate removal from the graph; when v's layer is processed, v is not part of the graph anymore, and thus could not be selected.

degree indeed drops to $O(d^4)$. As the out-degree is bounded by d, it is enough to show the following.

Lemma 3.2. *Every node with in-degree at least d^4 gets removed or all but d^4 of its incoming edges get removed, with high probability.*

Proof of Lemma 3.2 for matching. Let v be a node with degree at least d^4. First, observe that if at least one incoming edge of v is proposed, then an edge incident to v (not necessarily incoming) will be selected to be added to the matching. This is because the only reason why v would not select a proposed incoming edge is that v has already been removed from the graph, and this happens only if its proposed edge has been selected to be added to the matching in a previous step. It thus remains to show that every node v with in-degree at least d^4 with high probability will have at least one incoming edge that has been proposed by the respective child. As every incoming edge of v is marked independently with probability at least $1/d$, the probability of v not having a marked, and hence not having a proposed incoming edge is at most $(1-1/d)^{d^4} \leq e^{-d^3} = e^{-\Omega(\log^6 n)} = o\left(\frac{1}{\text{poly}(n)}\right)$. A union bound over all nodes with degree at least d^4 concludes the proof. □

Proof of Lemma 3.2 for independent set. Let v be a node in layer i that is still in the graph and has at least d^4 children after all layers with index $\geq i$ have been processed. We show that then at least one of these children will be selected to join the independent set with high probability. Note that this then concludes the proof, as in all the cases either v will be removed from the graph or will not have a high in-degree anymore. Moreover, observe that such a child u of v (that is still there after having processed layers $\geq i$) will be selected to join the independent set iff it is proposed. This is because if it did not join even though it is proposed, then a parent of u would had been selected to join the independent set, in which case u would not have been part of the graph anymore, at latest after i has been processed, thus would not count towards v's high degree at that point.

Every such child u of v is marked independently with probability $p = d^{-2}$. The probability of u being proposed and hence joining the independent set is at least $p(1-p)^d$, as it has at most d neighbors in its layer, and it is proposed iff it is marked and none of its neighbors in the same layer is marked. Node v thus in expectation has at least $\mu := d^4 p(1-p)^d \geq d^2 e^{-2/d} = \Omega(d^2)$ children that join the independent set.

Since whether a node u proposes and hence joins the independent set depends on at most d other nodes (namely u's neighbors in the same layer), it thus follows from a variant of the Chernoff bounds for bounded dependence, e.g., from Theorem 2.1 in [31], that the probability of v having, say, 0.5μ neighbors that join the independent set is at most $e^{-\Omega(\mu/d)} = e^{-\Omega(d)} \leq e^{-\Omega(\log^2 n)} = o\left(\frac{1}{\text{poly}(n)}\right)$. A union bound over all nodes v with degree at least d^4 concludes the proof. □

4 IMPLEMENTATION OF THE DEGREE REDUCTION ALGORITHM IN MPC

The degree reduction algorithm described in Section 3 can be implemented in the LOCAL model in a relatively straightforward way in poly(log n) rounds. Due to the nature of LOCAL, this implies that every node/edge in the input graph can decide on its output by learning the topology of its poly(log n)-hop neighborhood. Given the additional power of the global all-to-all communication in the MPC model, however, one could hope for much faster algorithms than in the LOCAL model.

Graph Exponentiation: A very natural and intuitive approach for a speed-up in the all-to-all communication setting is the well-known *graph exponentiation* technique [23], which can be summarized as follows: Suppose that every node knows its 2^{i-1}-hop neighborhood in iteration $i-1$. Then, in iteration i, each node can inform the nodes in its 2^{i-1}-hop neighborhood of the topology of its 2^{i-1}-hop neighborhood. Hence, every node can learn of its 2^i-hop neighborhood in iteration i, allowing it to simulate any 2^i-round LOCAL algorithm in 0 rounds. Using this exponentiation technique, in principle, it is conceivable that every t-round LOCAL algorithm can be simulated in $O(\log t)$ MPC rounds. However, the memory restrictions in the truly sublinear regime of MPC impose the following two fundamental barriers for such an approach:

Local memory barrier. For any $t \geq 1$, the t-hop neighborhood of a node may be as large as $\Omega(m)$, exceeding the local memory of a machine. Even the 1-hop neighborhood of a node with degree higher than $\omega(n^\delta)$ cannot be stored on a single machine.

Global memory barrier. Storing the neighborhood of each node on its corresponding machine leads to storing overlapping neighborhoods, and hence redundant copies of nodes/edges, and thus a total aggregated memory that is significantly larger than the input size m.

In order to deal with these issues, the key observation is that a large fraction of the nodes in the graph are contained in the first layers of the H-partition. In particular, we show that if we focus on the graph remaining after $\ell/2$ iterations of peeling, we can perform roughly $\log \ell$ exponentiation steps without violating the memory constraints. Hence, we can perform 2^i steps of the degree reduction process in roughly i communication rounds. Before going into the details of the simulation, we note that the simulation approach introduced in this section is tailor-made for the MIS and MM problems. In Section 5.3, we show that the ideas used in the simulation generalize beyond MIS and MM. However, our generalization comes with a slight cost in the global memory requirement.

4.1 Distributed Simulation of the Centralized Degree Reduction

In this section, we show how to simulate the centralized degree reduction algorithm from Section 3 in the low-memory MPC model. In Section 4.2, we show how to implement the partition phase efficiently in the low-memory MPC model. Then, in Section 4.3, we describe how to perform the simulation of the mark-and-propose as well as the selection phase. Together with the correctness proof established in Section 3.2, this will conclude the proof of Lemma 2.2.

Throughout our algorithm, we often have to compute functions that depend on all the neighbors of some node v, such as the degree of v. The problem with computing such functions is that the degree of a vertex might be larger than the memory per machine.

We define a special class of such functions, which we call *separable*[5], that can be parallelized very efficiently. Due to their verbosity, we defer the formal lemma statements and their proofs to Section 5.2. For the rest of the section, we simply assume that any separable function can be computed in constant time.

Definition 4.1. *Let $f : 2^{\mathbb{R}} \to \mathbb{R}$ denote a set function. The function f is* separable *iff for any set of reals A and for any $B \subseteq A$, we have $f(A) = f(f(B), f(A \setminus B))$.*

Remark 4.2. *Notice that for the peeling, we need to compute the degree of every remaining node in every iteration. Here, we can use the*

[5] We note that the definition is almost the same of a $\mathcal{MRC}$*-parallelizeable* function by Karloff et al. [20]. Ours is slightly cleaner and yet sufficient for our purposes.

fact that computing the degree is separable, and thus avoid problems in the case where the degree of a node is too large to fit the local memory of a single machine.

4.2 Partition Phase

We first prove some properties of the H-partition constructed by the greedy peeling algorithm that will be useful for an efficient implementation in the low-memory MPC model.

Lemma 4.3. *The H-partition with out-degree d, constructed by the greedy peeling algorithm, satisfies the following properties.*

(i) *For all $0 \le i \le \ell$, the number $\left|\bigcup_{j=i}^{\ell} L_j\right|$ of nodes in layers with index $\ge i$ is at most $n\left(\frac{2\lambda}{d}\right)^{i-1}$. In other words, if we remove all nodes in layer i from the set of nodes in layers $\ge i$, then the number of nodes drops by a factor of $\frac{2\lambda}{d}$, i.e., $\left|\bigcup_{j=i+1}^{\ell} L_j\right| \le \frac{2\lambda}{d}\left|\bigcup_{j=i}^{\ell} L_j\right|$ for all $0 \le i \le \ell$.*

(ii) *There are at most $\ell = O\left(\log_{\frac{d}{\lambda}} n\right)$ layers.*

Proof. We prove (i) by induction, thus assume that there are $n_i \le n\left(\frac{2\lambda}{d}\right)^{i-1}$ nodes in the graph H_i induced by nodes in layers $\ge i$. Towards a contradiction, suppose that there are $n_{i+1} > n\left(\frac{2\lambda}{d}\right)^{i}$ nodes in layers $\ge i+1$. By construction, all these nodes must have had degree larger than d in H_i, as otherwise they would have been added to layer i. This results in an average degree of more than $\frac{n_{i+1}d}{n_i} = 2\lambda$ in H_i, which contradicts the well-known upper bound of 2λ on the average degree in a graph that has arboricty at most λ. Note that (ii) is a direct consequence of (i). □

In the following, we describe how to compute the H-partition with parameter $d = \Delta^{1/10}$ in the low-memory MPC model. Throughout this section, we assume that $\Delta \ge (2\lambda)^{20}$, i.e., that $d \ge (2\lambda)^2$. Observe that if $\Delta^2 > n^\delta$, then the H-partition with parameter $d = \Delta^{1/10}$ consists of $O(\log_{d/\lambda} n) = O(\log_\Delta n) = O(1/\delta)$ layers, in which case the arguments in this section imply that going through the layers one by one will easily yield at least as good runtimes as for the more difficult case of $\Delta^2 \le n^\delta$. Hence, throughout this section, we assume that $\Delta^2 \le n^\delta$.

The goal of the algorithm for computing the H-partition is that each node (or, more formally, the machine storing the node) knows in which layer of the H-partition it is contained. The algorithm proceeds in iterations, where each iteration consists of two parts: first, the output, i.e., the layer index, is determined for a large fraction of the nodes, and second, these nodes are removed for the remainder of the computation. The latter ensures that the remaining small fraction of nodes can use essentially all of the total available memory in the next iteration, resulting in a larger memory budget per node. However, there is a caveat: When the memory budget per node exceeds $\Theta(n^\delta)$, i.e., the memory capacity of a single machine, then it is not sufficient anymore to merely argue that the used memory of all nodes together does not exceed the total memory of all machines together[6]. We circumvent this issue by starting the above process repeatedly from anew (in the remaining graph) each time the memory requirement per node reaches the memory capacity of a single machine. As we will see, the number of repetitions, called *phases*, is bounded by $O(1/\delta)$.

In the following, we examine the phases and iterations in more detail.

Algorithm Details: Let k be the largest integer s.t. $\Delta^{2^k+1} \le n^\delta$ (which implies that $k \ge 0$). The algorithm consists of phases and each phase consists of $k+1$ iterations. Next, we describe our implementation of the graph exponentiation in more detail.

- In each iteration $i = 0, 1, \ldots, k$, we do the following.
  - Let $G_i = G_i^{(0)}$ be the graph at the beginning of iteration i. Each node connects its current 1-hop neighborhood to a clique by adding virtual edges to G_i; if $i = 0$, omit this step. Perform 20 repetitions of the following process if $i \ge 1$, and 60 repetitions if $i = 0$:
    - In repetition $0 \le j \le 19$ (resp. $0 \le j \le 59$), each node computes its layer index in the H-partition of $G_i^{(j)}$ (with parameter d) or determines that its layer index is strictly larger than 2^i, upon which all nodes in layer at most 2^i (and all its incident edges) are removed from the graph, resulting in a graph $G_i^{(j+1)}$.

    Set $G_{i+1} = G_i^{(20)}$ (resp. $G_{i+1} = G_i^{(60)}$ if $i = 0$).

  At the end of the phase remove all added edges.

The algorithm terminates when each node knows its layer.

Note that each time a node is removed from the graph, the whole layer that contains this node is removed, and each time such a layer is removed, all layers with smaller index are removed at the same time or before. By the definition of the H-partition, if we remove the ℓ layers with smallest index from a graph, then there is a 1-to-1 correspondence between the layers of the resulting graph and the layers with layer index at least $\ell + 1$ of the original graph. More specifically, layer ℓ' of the resulting graph contains exactly the same nodes as layer $\ell + \ell'$ of the original graph. Hence, if a node knows its layer index in some $G_i^{(j)}$, it can easily compute its layer index in our original input graph G, by keeping track of the number of deleted layers, which is uniquely defined by i, j and the number of the phase. We implicitly assume that each node performs this computation upon determining its layer index in some $G_i^{(j)}$ and in the following only consider how to determine the layer index in the current graph.

Implementation in the MPC Model: Let us take a look at one iteration. Connecting the 1-hop neighborhoods to cliques is done by adding the edges that are missing. Edges that are added by multiple nodes are only added once (since the edge in question is stored by the machines that contain an endpoint of the edge, this is straightforward to realize). Note that during a phase, the 1-hop neighborhoods of the nodes grow in each iteration (if not too many close-by nodes are removed from the graph); more specifically, after i iterations of connecting 1-hop neighborhoods to cliques, the new

[6]Furthermore, in the "shuffle" step of every MPC round [20], we assume that the nodes are stored in the machines in a balanced way, i.e., as long as a single node fits onto a single machine and the total memory is not exceeded, the underlying system takes care of load-balancing.

1-hop neighborhood of a node contains exactly the nodes that were contained in its 2^i-hop neighborhood at the beginning of the phase (and were not removed so far).

In iteration i, the layer of a node is computed as follows: First each node locally gathers the topology of its 2^i-hop neighborhood (without any added edges)[7]. Since this step is performed after connecting the 2^{i-1}-hop neighborhood of each node to a clique (by repeatedly connecting 1-hop neighborhoods to cliques), i.e., after connecting each node to any other node in its 2^i-hop neighborhood, only 1 round of communication is required for gathering the topology. Moreover, since a node that knows the topology of its 2^i-hop neighborhood can simulate any $(2^i - 1)$-round distributed process locally, it follows from the definition of the H-partition, that knowledge of the topology of the 2^i-hop neighborhood is sufficient for a node to determine whether its layer index is at most 2^i and, if this is the case, in exactly which layer it is contained. Thus, the only tasks remaining are to bound the runtime of our algorithm and to show that the memory restrictions of our model are not violated by the algorithm.

Runtime: It is easy to see that every iteration takes $O(1)$ rounds. Thus, in order to bound the runtime of our algorithm, it is sufficient to bound the number of iterations by $O((1/\delta) \cdot \log\log n)$. By Lemma 4.3 (ii) the number of layers in the H-partition of our original input graph G is $O(\log_{d/\lambda} n)$, which is $O(\log_\Delta n)$ since $d/(2\lambda) \geq \sqrt{d} = \Delta^{1/20}$. Consider an arbitrary phase. According to the algorithm description, in iteration $i \geq 1$, all nodes in the $20 \cdot 2^i$ lowest layers are removed from the current graph. Hence, ignoring iteration 0, the number of removed layers doubles in each iteration, and we obtain that the number of layers removed in the $k+1$ iterations of our phase is $\Omega(2^k)$. By the definition of k, we have $\Delta^{2^{k+1}+1} > n^\delta$, which implies $2^k > 1/3 \cdot \delta \cdot \log_\Delta n$.

Combining this inequality with the observations about the total number of layers and the number of layers removed per phase, we see that the algorithm terminates after $O(1/\delta)$ phases. Since there are $k+1 = O(\log\log n)$ iterations per phase, the bound on the number of iterations follows.

Memory Footprint: As during the course of the algorithm edges are added and nodes collect the topology of certain neighborhoods, we have to show that adding these edges and collecting these neighborhoods does not violate our memory constraints of $O(n^\delta)$ per machine. As a first step towards this end, the following lemma bounds the number of nodes contained in graph G_i.

Lemma 4.4. *Consider an arbitrary phase. Graph G_i from that phase contains at most $n'/(\Delta^{2^i})$ nodes, for all $i \geq 1$, where $n' = n/\Delta$.*

Proof. By Lemma 4.3 (i), removing the nodes in the layer with smallest index from the current graph decreases the number of nodes by a factor of at least $d/(2\lambda) \geq d^{1/2} = \Delta^{1/20}$. We show the lemma statement by induction. Since in iteration 0 the nodes in the 60 layers with smallest index are removed, we know that G_1 contains at most $n/(\Delta^3) = n'/(\Delta^{2^1})$ nodes. Now assume that G_i contains at most $n'/(\Delta^{2^i})$ nodes, for an arbitrary $i \geq 1$. According to the design of our algorithm, G_{i+1} is obtained from G_i by removing the nodes in the $20 \cdot 2^i$ layers with smallest index. Combining this fact with our observation about the decrease in the number of nodes per removed layer, we obtain that G_{i+1} contains at most $n'/(\Delta^{2^i}) \cdot 1/(\Delta^{2^i}) = n'/(\Delta^{2^{i+1}})$ nodes. □

Using Lemma 4.4, we now show that the memory constraints of the low-memory MPC model are not violated by our algorithm. Consider an arbitrary phase and an arbitrary iteration i during that phase. If $i = 0$, then no edges are added and each node already knows the topology of its 2^i-hop neighborhood, so no additional memory is required. Hence, assume that $i \geq 1$.

Due to Lemma 4.4, the number of nodes considered in iteration i is at most $n'/(\Delta^{2^i})$, where, again, $n' = n/\Delta$. After the initial step of connecting 1-hop neighborhoods to cliques in iteration i, each remaining node is connected to all nodes that were contained in its 2^i-hop neighborhood in the original graph G (and were not removed so far). Hence, each remaining node is connected to at most $O(\Delta^{2^i})$ other nodes, resulting in a memory requirement of $O(\Delta^{2^i})$ per node, or $O(n/\Delta)$ in total. Similarly, when collecting the topology of its 2^i-hop neighborhood, each node has to store $O(\Delta^{2^i} \cdot \Delta)$ edges, which requires at most $O(\Delta^{2^i} \cdot \Delta)$ memory, resulting in a total memory requirement of $O(n)$. Hence, the described algorithm does not exceed the total memory available in the low-memory MPC model. Moreover, due to the choice of k, the memory requirement of each single node does not exceed the memory capacity of a single machine.

4.3 Simulation of the Mark-and-Propose and Selection Phase

For the simulation of the mark-and-propose and selection phase, we rely heavily on the approach of Section 4.2. Recall that nodes were removed in *chunks* consisting of several consecutive layers and that before a node v was removed, v was directly connected to all nodes contained in a large neighborhood around v by adding the respective edges. For the simulation, we go through these chunks in the reverse order in which they were removed. Note that in which chunk a node is contained is uniquely determined by the layer index of the node. As each node computes its layer index during the construction of the H-partition, each node can easily determine in which part of the simulation it will actively participate.

However, there is a problem we need to address: For communication, we would like the edges that we added during the construction of the H-partition to be available also for the simulation. Unfortunately, during the course of the construction, we removed added edges again to free memory for the adding of other edges. Fortunately, there is a conceptually simple way to circumvent this problem: in the construction of the H-partition, add a preprocessing step in the beginning, in which we remove the lowest $c \cdot \log((1/\delta) \cdot \log\log n)$ layers (where c is a sufficiently large constant) one by one in $\log((1/\delta) \cdot \log\log n)$ rounds, which increases the available memory (compared to the number of (remaining) nodes) by a factor of $\Omega((1/\delta) \cdot \log\log n)$, by Lemma 4.3. Since the algorithm for constructing the H-partition consist of $O((1/\delta) \cdot \log\log n)$ iterations, this implies that we can store all edges that we add during the further course of the construction simultaneously without violating

[7]Note that it is easy to keep track of which edges are original and which are added, incurring only a small constant memory overhead; later we will also argue why storing the added edges does not violate our memory constraints.

the memory restriction, by an argument similar to the analogous statement for the old construction of the H-partition. Similarly, also the number of added edges incident to one particular node does not exceed the memory capacity of a single machine. In the following, we assume that this pre-processing step took place and all edges added during the construction of the H-partition are also available for the simulation.

Matching Algorithm: As mentioned above, we process the chunks one by one, in decreasing order w.r.t. the indices of the contained layers. After processing a chunk, we want each node contained in the chunk to know the output of all incident edges according to the centralized matching algorithm. In the following, we describe how to process a chunk, after some preliminary "global" steps.

The mark-and-propose phase of the algorithm is straightforward to implement in the low-memory MPC model: each node (in each chunk at the same time) performs the marking of an outgoing edge as specified in the algorithm description.[8] The proposing is performed for all nodes before going through the chunks sequentially: each node proposes one of its marked incoming edges (it there is at least one) uniformly at random. Note that proposes an edge does not necessarily indicate that this edge will be added to the matching; more specifically, an edge proposed by some node v will be added to the matching iff the edge that v marked is not selected to be added to the matching.[9]

After this mark-and-propose phase, the processing of the chunks begins. Consider an arbitrary chunk. Let i be the iteration (in some phase) in which this chunk was removed in the construction of the H-partition, i.e., the chunk consists of 2^i layers. Each node in the chunk collects the topology of its 2^i-hop neighborhood in the chunk including the information contained therein about proposed edges. Due to the edges added during the construction of the H-partition, this can be achieved in a constant number of rounds, and by an analogous argument to the one at the end of Section 4.2, collecting the indicated information does not violate the memory restrictions of our model. Lemma 4.5 shows that the information contained in the 2^i-hop neighborhood of a node is sufficient for the node to determine the output for each incident edge in the centralized matching algorithm.

Lemma 4.5. *The information about which edges are proposed in the 2^i-hop neighborhood of a node v uniquely determines the output of all edges incident to v according to the centralized matching algorithm.*

PROOF. From the design of the centralized matching algorithm, it follows that an edge is part of the matching iff 1) the edge is proposed and 2) either the higher-layer endpoint of the edge has no outgoing edges or the outgoing edge marked by the higher-layer endpoint is not part of the matching. Hence, in order to check whether an incident edge is in the matching, node v only has to consider the unique directed chain of proposed edges (in the chunk) starting in v. Clearly, the information which of the edges in this chain are proposed uniquely defines the output of the first edge in the chain, from which v can infer the output of all other incident edges. Since the number of edges in the chain is bounded by $2^i - 1$ as the chain is directed, the lemma statement follows. □

It thus follows from the bound on the number of iterations that the simulation of the selection phase for the matching algorithm can be performed in $O(1/\delta \cdot \log\log n)$ rounds of communication.

Independent Set Algorithm: The simulation of the independent set algorithm proceeds analogously to the case of the matching algorithm. First, each node performs the marking and proposing in a distributed fashion in a constant number of rounds. Then, the chunks are processed one by one, as above, where during the processing of a chunk removed in iteration i, each node contained in the chunk collects its 2^i-hop neighborhood, including the information about which nodes are proposed, and then computes its own output locally. By analogous arguments to the ones presented in the case of the matching algorithm, the algorithm adheres to the memory constraints of our model and the total number of communication rounds is $O(1/\delta \cdot \log\log n)$. The only part of the argumentation where a bit of care is required is the analogue of Lemma 4.5: In the case of the independent set algorithm the output of a node v may depend on *each* of its parents since each of those could be part of the independent set, which would prevent v from joining the independent set. However, *all* nodes in the chunk that can be reached from v via a directed chain of edges are contained in v's 2^i-hop neighborhood; therefore, collecting the own 2^i-hop neighborhood is sufficient for determining one's output. Note that at the end of processing a chunk, if we follow the above implementation, we have to spend an extra round for removing the neighbors of all selected independent set nodes since these may be contained in another chunk.

5 GENERAL ALGORITHMIC TOOLS FOR LOW-MEMORY MPC

In this section, we introduce a set of algorithmic tools that yield convenient basic primitives in the low-memory MPC model. Some variant of each of the tools is used in our work and hence, we believe that the more generic versions provided below may prove helpful in the future work in the area. We note that our variants have some problem-specific fine-tuning and hence, the guarantees given in the statements that follow are slightly weaker than the ones proven for our MIS and MM algorithms.

5.1 Graph Exponentiation via All-to-All Communication

The goal of the *graph exponentiation* technique is to collect the t-hop of every node in $O(\log t)$ rounds, i.e., create the t-th power G^t of the input graph G [23]. The approach is to inductively collect the 2^i-hop of every node by round i so long as we are guaranteed that the size of each of them is sufficiently small.

Lemma 5.1. *Given that for any node v, size of its t-hop is bounded by n^β for any $\beta \leq \delta/2$, there exists an algorithm that gathers the t-hop of every node in at least one machine within at most $O(\log t)$*

[8] Note that, formally, the algorithm for construction the H-partition only returns the layer index for each node; however, from this information each node can easily determine which edges are outgoing, unoriented, or incoming according to the partial orientation induced by the H-partition.

[9] In other words, only proposed edges can go into the matching and whether such an edge indeed goes into the matching can be determined by going through the layers in decreasing order and only adding a proposed edge if there is no conflict.

rounds of MPC *using* $O(n^{\delta})$ *space per machine and* $O(n^{1+2\beta})$ *total space.*

5.2 Load Balancing

This section addresses one of the technical details faced by low-memory MPC graph algorithms. Assume that we are given a separable function (cf. Definition 4.1) which we need to compute for all the nodes in the graph. For any node v the value of this function is based on its neighbors. The complication here arises from the fact that the degree of the nodes can be larger than the memory of the machines. Therefore, we are not able to simply gather neighbors of v in one machine and compute the given function. Examples of such functions are as follows.

- Finding the degree of the nodes.
- For any node in the graph find the neighbor with the minimum label. One usage of this is in the Luby's algorithm when each node picks a random number and we need to find the nodes who have the minimum number among their neighbors.
- Some nodes of the graph are chosen to be in the MIS and each node needs to know whether it is adjacent to any such node or not.

It is easy to verify that all of the functions above are separable. In Lemma 5.2 we prove that there is an algorithm that takes $O(1/\delta)$ rounds of MPC using $O(n^{\delta})$ space per machine and $\widetilde{O}(m)$ total space. For space limits, we omit the proof.

Lemma 5.2. *Fix an arbitrary n-vertex graph and suppose that we have a number x_v for any vertex v stored in some arbitrary machine. Given an arbitrary separable function f, there is an* MPC *algorithm that outputs, for every vertex v, the value of $f(\{x_{u_1}, \ldots, x_{u_d}\})$ where $u_1, \ldots, u_d$ are the vertices adjacent to v. If the space per machine is $O(n^{\delta})$, the algorithm takes $O(1/\delta)$ rounds and uses $\widetilde{O}(m)$ total space.*

5.3 Blind Coordination

The goal of this section is to highlight the simple but powerful concept of *blind coordination.* We apply this technique to compress multiple rounds of a large class of LOCAL algorithms, which we call *state-congested* local algorithms. Roughly speaking, in a state-congested local algorithm, we can maintain *states* on the nodes/edges over the rounds of the algorithm, but we restrict these states to be of size $O(\log n)$ bits and depend (loosely speaking) only on the states of the 1-hop of every node/edge at the previous round.

Definition 5.3. *A distributed* LOCAL *algorithm is* state-congested *if:*

1. *By the end of each round r, on any node v (and respectively on any edge e), the algorithm stores a state $s_r(v)$ (resp. $s_r(e)$) of size $O(\log n)$ bits. The initial state $s_0(v)$ of each node v is its ID and the initial state $s_0(e)$ of each edge e is the IDs of its two endpoints.*
2. *The state $s_r(v)$ of each node v by the end of any round r, depends only on its state $s_{r-1}(v)$ in the previous round, the states of its incident edges $\{s_{r-1}(e) \mid e \ni v\}$ in the previous round, and its tape $\rho(v)$ of* poly log *n random bits. Furthermore, the state $s_r(e)$ of each edge $e = (u, v)$ by the end of round r is only a function of $s_{r-1}(u)$, $s_{r-1}(v)$ and $s_{r-1}(e)$.*
3. *The states of the nodes/edges at the last round of the algorithm are sufficient in determining, collectively, the output of the algorithm.*

The key property of state-congested local algorithms is that the intermediate states of the algorithm are also small. This is in contrast, for example, with algorithms in which each node v first collects its, say, $O(\log n)$-hop and then makes its final decision in one shot. We note that state-congested local algorithms are similar to, but more restrictive, than a variant of LOCAL algorithms called CONGEST (see [30]) where the messages over the links are restricted to have $O(\log n)$ bits. Before describing the main result of this section, we need another definition.

Definition 5.4. *We call a state-congested local algorithm* low-memory, *if updating the state each node v can be done in a space of size $O(\deg(v) \cdot \text{poly} \log n)$ bits and updating the state of each edge e requires a space of size $O(\text{poly} \log n)$ bits.*

The definition above is required to ensure, e.g., that once we have the states and random tapes of all neighbors of a node v, we can update the state of v without using any extra space. This is almost always satisfied. We are now ready to formalize the main lemma of this section which results in compressing r rounds of a state-congested local algorithm into much fewer rounds of a low-memory MPC algorithm if the maximum degree Δ of the graph is small. The main theorem is as follows:

Lemma 5.5. *For any graph with n nodes, m edges, and maximum degree $\Delta \leq n^{\delta}$, where δ is a desirably small constant number in $(0, 1)$, one can compress r rounds of any low-memory state-congested local algorithm in $O(\frac{r}{\log_{\Delta} n} + \log \log_{\Delta} n)$ rounds of* MPC *using $O(n^{\delta})$ space per machine and $\widetilde{O}(m + n^{1+2\delta/3})$ total memory.*

Proof. Suppose that our goal is to compress r rounds of a low-memory state-congested local algorithm $\mathcal{A}$. Initially, each node will be assigned to a machine that will be responsible for keeping track of its state. Note that since the total space is at least $n^{1+2\delta/3}$, and memory per machine is $O(n^{\delta})$, we have at least $\Omega(n^{1-\delta/3})$ machines. It suffices to make each machine responsible for $n^{2\delta/3}$ nodes. This assignment can easily be done based on, say, the nodes' IDs. Let $t := \lfloor \frac{\delta}{3} \log_{\Delta} n \rfloor$. We first collect the t-hop neighborhood of each node in the machine that is responsible for it. Note that t is chosen to be small enough that the t-hop neighborhood of every node has at most $\Delta^t \leq n^{\delta/3}$ edges which is substantially smaller than the memory per machine. Therefore, we can use the graph exponentiation algorithm of Lemma 5.1 to collect the t-hop of every node in the machine responsible for it in only $O(\log t) = O(\log \log_{\Delta} n)$ rounds using a total memory of size $\widetilde{O}(m + n^{1+2\delta/3})$.

After collecting the neighborhoods, on each machine, we run t rounds of $\mathcal{A}$ on the subgraph that is stored in it. This can be done in only one round of MPC since no communication between the machines is required. The main intuition behind the *blind-coordination* idea is that the final state of a node v in the machine that is responsible for it is exactly the same as that of v after t rounds of the original algorithm $\mathcal{A}$. We emphasize that a node v may also be stored in machines not responsible for v, and in fact, the states computed for v in those machines might be completely different from its *correct* state by the end of round t of $\mathcal{A}$. However, crucially, the state of each node matches its correct state in the machine responsible for it. Formally, let us denote by $s_i(.)$ the state of a node or an edge by the end of round i of algorithm $\mathcal{A}$ and denote by $\hat{s}_{\mu,i}(.)$, for any $i \leq t$, the state of a node or an edge after simulating i rounds of $\mathcal{A}$ on the subgraph stored in machine μ; we have:

Observation 5.6. *Let v denote an arbitrary node whose i-hop neighborhood is stored in machine μ and let β be an arbitrary non-negative integer. If for any node or edge x in the i-hop neighborhood of v we have its correct state by round β, i.e., $\hat{s}_{\mu,\beta}(x) = s_\beta(x)$, then we compute the correct state of v after $\beta + i$ rounds in machine μ, i.e., $\hat{s}_{\mu,\beta+i}(v) = s_{\beta+i}(v)$ without any rounds of communication. Similarly, for any edge e incident to v, we have $\hat{s}_{\mu,\beta+i}(e) = s_{\beta+i}(e)$.*

Recall that our goal was to compress r rounds of a low-memory state-congested algorithm $\mathcal{A}$ into few rounds of a low-memory MPC algorithm. By the discussion above, after collecting the t-hop neighborhood of every node in $O(\log \log_\Delta n)$ rounds, if $r < t$, then the simulation takes only $O(1)$ extra rounds to complete. For most applications, however, r is much larger than t. In such cases, we cannot afford to collect the r-hop neighborhood of a node in one machine as its size may exceed the space per machine. The idea, here, is to compress every t rounds of $\mathcal{A}$ into $O(1)$ rounds of our low-memory MPC algorithm. To do this, with the above-mentioned approach we can access the state of each node and edge after t rounds. The idea, then, is that each machine shares the states of the nodes/edges that it is responsible for with other machines. Once collected this information, each machine then runs $\mathcal{A}$ for another t rounds with respect to the now updated states. By the end of this round, we are aware of the state $s_{2t}(.)$ of each node/edge on its responsible machine. We can continue this process for r/t rounds to complete compression of r rounds of $\mathcal{A}$. Overall it takes only $O(\frac{r}{t} + \log t) = O\left(\frac{r}{\epsilon \log_\Delta n} + \log \log_\Delta n\right)$ rounds to have the states of all nodes/edges by the end of round r. □

REFERENCES

[1] Alexandr Andoni, Aleksandar Nikolov, Krzysztof Onak, and Grigory Yaroslavtsev. 2014. Parallel Algorithms for Geometric Graph Problems. In *Proceedings of the Symposium on Theory of Computing (STOC)*. 574–583.

[2] Sepehr Assadi, MohammadHossein Bateni, Aaron Bernstein, Vahab Mirrokni, and Cliff Stein. 2017. Coresets Meet EDCS: Algorithms for Matching and Vertex Cover on Massive Graphs. *arXiv preprint: 1711.03076* (2017).

[3] Leonid Barenboim and Michael Elkin. 2010. Sublogarithmic Distributed MIS Algorithm for Sparse Graphs Using Nash-Williams Decomposition. *Distributed Computing* 22, 5-6 (2010), 363–379.

[4] Leonid Barenboim, Michael Elkin, Seth Pettie, and Johannes Schneider. 2016. The Locality of Distributed Symmetry Breaking. *Journal of the ACM (JACM)* 63, 3 (2016), 20.

[5] MohammadHossein Bateni, Soheil Behnezhad, Mahsa Derakhshan, Mohammad-Taghi Hajiaghayi, Raimondas Kiveris, Silvio Lattanzi, and Vahab Mirrokni. 2017. Affinity Clustering: Hierarchical Clustering at Scale. In *the Proceedings of the Conference on Neural Information Processing Systems (NIPS)*. 6867–6877. http://papers.nips.cc/paper/7262-affinity-clustering-hierarchical-clustering-at-scale.pdf

[6] Paul Beame, Paraschos Koutris, and Dan Suciu. 2014. Skew in Parallel Query Processing. In *the Proceedings of the 33rd ACM SIGMOD-SIGACT-SIGART Symposium on Principles of Database Systems (PODS)*. 212–223.

[7] Paul Beame, Paraschos Koutris, and Dan Suciu. 2017. Communication Steps for Parallel Query Processing. *Journal of the ACM (JACM)* 64, 6 (2017), 40.

[8] Sebastian Brandt, Manuela Fischer, and Jara Uitto. 2019. Breaking The Linear-Memory Barrier in MPC: Fast MIS on Trees with Strongly Sublinear Memory. In *the Proceedings of the International Colloquium on Structural Information and Communication Complexity (SIROCCO)*. to appear.

[9] Graham Cormode, Hossein Jowhari, Morteza Monemizadeh, and S. Muthukrishnan. 2017. The Sparse Awakens: Streaming Algorithms for Matching Size Estimation in Sparse Graphs. In *the Proceedings of the Annual European Symposium on Algorithms (ESA)*. 29:1–29:15.

[10] Artur Czumaj, Jakub Łącki, Aleksander Mądry, Slobodan Mitrović, Krzysztof Onak, and Piotr Sankowski. 2018. Round Compression for Parallel Matching Algorithms. In *Proceedings of the Symposium on Theory of Computing (STOC)*. 471–484.

[11] Jeffrey Dean and Sanjay Ghemawat. 2008. MapReduce: Simplified Data Processing on Large Clusters. *Commun. ACM* 51, 1 (2008), 107–113.

[12] Hossein Esfandiari, Mohammad Taghi Hajiaghayi, Vahid Liaghat, Morteza Monemizadeh, and Krzysztof Onak. 2015. Streaming Algorithms for Estimating the Matching Size in Planar Graphs and Beyond. In *the Proceedings of ACM-SIAM Symposium on Discrete Algorithms (SODA)*. 1217–1233.

[13] Mohsen Ghaffari. 2016. An Improved Distributed Algorithm for Maximal Independent Set. In *the Proceedings of ACM-SIAM Symposium on Discrete Algorithms (SODA)*. 270–277.

[14] Mohsen Ghaffari, Themis Gouleakis, Christian Konrad, Slobodan Mitrović, and Ronitt Rubinfeld. 2018. Improved Massively Parallel Computation Algorithms for MIS, Matching, and Vertex Cover. In *Proceedings of the International Symposium on Principles of Distributed Computing (PODC)*. 129–138.

[15] Mohsen Ghaffari and Jara Uitto. 2019. Sparsifying Distributed Algorithms with Ramifications in Massively Parallel Computation and Centralized Local Computation. In *the Proceedings of ACM-SIAM Symposium on Discrete Algorithms (SODA)*.

[16] Gaurav Goel and Jens Gustedt. 2006. Bounded Arboricity to Determine the Local Structure of Sparse Graphs. In *International Workshop on Graph-Theoretic Concepts in Computer Science*. Springer, 159–167.

[17] Michael T. Goodrich, Nodari Sitchinava, and Qin Zhang. 2011. Sorting, Searching, and Simulation in the MapReduce Framework. 374–383.

[18] Elena Grigorescu, Morteza Monemizadeh, and Samson Zhou. 2016. Estimating Weighted Matchings in o(n) Space. *CoRR* abs/1604.07467 (2016). arXiv:1604.07467 http://arxiv.org/abs/1604.07467

[19] Michael Isard, Mihai Budiu, Yuan Yu, Andrew Birrell, and Dennis Fetterly. 2007. Dryad: Distributed Data-Parallel Programs from Sequential Building Blocks, Vol. 41. 59–72.

[20] Howard Karloff, Siddharth Suri, and Sergei Vassilvitskii. 2010. A Model of Computation for MapReduce. In *the Proceedings of ACM-SIAM Symposium on Discrete Algorithms (SODA)*. 938–948.

[21] Amos Korman, Jean-Sébastien Sereni, and Laurent Viennot. 2013. Toward More Localized Local Algorithms: Removing Assumptions Concerning Global Knowledge. *Distributed Computing* 26, 5-6 (2013), 289–308.

[22] Silvio Lattanzi, Benjamin Moseley, Siddharth Suri, and Sergei Vassilvitskii. 2011. Filtering: a Method for Solving Graph Problems in MapReduce. In *the Proceedings of the Symposium on Parallel Algorithms and Architectures (SPAA)*. 85–94.

[23] Christoph Lenzen and Roger Wattenhofer. 2010. Brief Announcement: Exponential Speed-Up of Local Algorithms Using Non-Local Communication. In *Proceedings of the International Symposium on Principles of Distributed Computing (PODC)*. 295–296.

[24] Nathan Linial. 1992. Locality in Distributed Graph Algorithms. *SIAM J. Comput.* 21, 1 (1992), 193–201.

[25] Zvi Lotker, Boaz Patt-Shamir, and Seth Pettie. 2015. Improved Distributed Approximate Matching. *Journal of the ACM (JACM)* 62, 5 (2015).

[26] Andrew McGregor. 2005. Finding Graph Matchings in Data Streams. In *Approximation, Randomization and Combinatorial Optimization. Algorithms and Techniques*. Springer, 170–181.

[27] Crispin St. J. Nash-Williams. 1961. Edge-Disjoint Spanning Trees of Finite Graphs. *Journal of the London Mathematical Society* 1, 1 (1961), 445–450.

[28] Crispin St. J. Nash-Williams. 1964. Decomposition of Finite Graphs into Forests. *Journal of the London Mathematical Society* 1, 1 (1964), 12–12.

[29] Krzysztof Onak, Baruch Schieber, Shay Solomon, and Nicole Wein. 2018. Fully Dynamic MIS in Uniformly Sparse Graphs. In *the Proceedings of the International Colloquium on Automata, Languages and Programming (ICALP)*. 92:1–92:14.

[30] David Peleg. 2000. *Distributed Computing: A Locality-Sensitive Approach*. Society for Industrial and Applied Mathematics.

[31] Sriram V. Pemmaraju. 2001. Equitable Coloring Extends Chernoff-Hoeffding Bounds. In *Approximation, Randomization, and Combinatorial Optimization: Algorithms and Techniques*. Springer, 285–296.

[32] Tom White. 2012. *Hadoop: The Definitive Guide*.

[33] Matei Zaharia, Mosharaf Chowdhury, Michael J. Franklin, Scott Shenker, and Ion Stoica. 2010. Spark: Cluster Computing with Working Sets. *HotCloud* 10 (2010), 95.

Weighted Matchings via Unweighted Augmentations

Buddhima Gamlath
buddhima.gamlath@epfl.ch
EPFL

Sagar Kale
sagar.kale@epfl.ch
EPFL

Slobodan Mitrović
slobo@mit.edu
MIT

Ola Svensson
ola.svensson@epfl.ch
EPFL

ABSTRACT

We design a generic method to reduce the task of finding weighted matchings to that of finding short augmenting paths in *unweighted* graphs. This method enables us to provide efficient implementations for approximating weighted matchings in the massively parallel computation (MPC) model and in the streaming model.

For the MPC and the multi-pass streaming model, we show that *any* algorithm computing a $(1-\delta)$-approximate unweighted matching in bipartite graphs can be translated into an algorithm that computes a $(1-\varepsilon(\delta))$-approximate maximum weighted matching. Furthermore, this translation incurs only a constant factor (that depends on $\varepsilon > 0$) overhead in the complexity. Instantiating this with the current best MPC algorithm for unweighted matching yields a $(1-\varepsilon)$-approximation algorithm for maximum weighted matching that uses $O_\varepsilon(\log\log n)$ rounds, $O(m/n)$ machines per round, and $O_\varepsilon(n\,\mathrm{poly}(\log n))$ memory per machine. This improves upon the previous best approximation guarantee of $(1/2-\varepsilon)$ for weighted graphs. In the context of single-pass streaming with random edge arrivals, our techniques yield a $(1/2+c)$-approximation algorithm thus breaking the natural barrier of $1/2$.

CCS CONCEPTS

• **Theory of computation → Massively parallel algorithms; Streaming models; Vector / streaming algorithms.**

KEYWORDS

Weighted matching, Parallel algorithms, MPC, Semi-streaming

ACM Reference Format:

Buddhima Gamlath, Sagar Kale, Slobodan Mitrović, and Ola Svensson. 2019. Weighted Matchings via Unweighted Augmentations. In *2019 ACM Symposium on Principles of Distributed Computing (PODC '19), July 29-August 2, 2019, Toronto, ON, Canada.* ACM, New York, NY, USA, 10 pages. https://doi.org/10.1145/3293611.3331603

1 INTRODUCTION

The maximum matching problem is a classic problem in combinatorial optimization. For polynomial-time computation, efficient algorithms exist both for the unweighted (cardinality) version and the weighted version. However, in other models of computation, the weighted version turns out to be significantly harder, and better algorithms are known in the unweighted case. In fact, in some settings such as online algorithms, the weighted version is *provably* much harder than the unweighted case. In other models, such as massively parallel computation (MPC) and streaming, no such results are known. Instead the performance gap in the algorithms for unweighted and weighted matchings seems to arise due to a lack of techniques. The goal of this paper is to address this by developing new techniques for weighted matchings.

The MPC model encompasses many of today's most successful parallel computing paradigms such as MapReduce [16], Hadoop [44], Spark [45], and Dryad [27]. It is motivated by the need for devising efficient algorithms for large problem instances. As data and the size of instances keep growing, this becomes ever more relevant and a large body of recent work has been devoted to designing algorithms in this model.

While our main result is for parallel computation, it is instructive to consider first semi-streaming, that is another popular model for handling large data. As we will see, a simpler version of our techniques adapted to semi-streaming already improves the state-of-the-art. In this model the edges of a graph arrive one-by-one and the algorithm is restricted to use memory that is almost linear in the number of vertices. For unweighted graphs, the very basic greedy algorithm guarantees to return a $(1/2)$-approximate maximum matching. It is a major open problem to improve upon this factor when the order of the stream is adversarial. In the random-edge-arrival setting — where the edges of the stream are presented in a random order — algorithms that are more advanced than the greedy algorithm overcome this barrier [33]. In contrast, for weighted graphs a $(1/2-\varepsilon)$-approximation algorithm was given only recently for adversarial streams [22, 43], and here we give the first algorithm that breaks the natural "greedy" barrier of $1/2$ for random-edge-arrival streams:

THEOREM 1.1. *There is a $(1/2+c)$-approximation algorithm for finding weighted matchings in the streaming model with one pass over random-edge-arrivals, where $c > 0$ is an absolute constant.*

As we elaborate later, the result is achieved via a general approach that reduces the task of finding weighted matchings to that of finding (short) *unweighted* augmenting paths. This allows us to incorporate some of the ideas present in the streaming algorithms for unweighted matchings to achieve our result. Our techniques,

PODC '19, July 29-August 2, 2019, Toronto, ON, Canada

ACM ISBN 978-1-4503-6217-7/19/07...$15.00
https://doi.org/10.1145/3293611.3331603

perhaps surprisingly, also simplify the previous algorithms for finding unweighted matchings, and give an improved guarantee for general graphs.

The idea to reduce to the problem of finding unweighted augmenting paths is rather versatile, and we use it to obtain a general reduction from weighted matchings to unweighted matchings as our main result. We give implementations of this reduction in the models of MPC and multi-pass streaming that incur only a constant factor overhead in the complexity. In MPC, parallel computation is modeled by parallel machines with sublinear memory (in the input size) and data can be transferred between machines only between two rounds of computation (see Section 2 for a precise definition). The complexity of an algorithm in the MPC model, also referred to as the round complexity, is then measured as the number of (communication) rounds used. In multi-pass streaming, the algorithm is (as for single-pass) restricted to use memory that is almost linear in the number of vertices and the complexity is measured in terms of the number of passes that the algorithm requires over the data stream.

For the matching problem, McGregor [40] gave the first randomized streaming algorithm for approximating unweighted matchings within a factor $(1 - \varepsilon)$ that runs in a constant number of passes (depending only on ε); the dependency on ε was more recently improved for bipartite graphs [1, 17]. McGregor's techniques for unweighted matchings have been very influential. In particular, his general reduction technique can be used to transform any $O(1)$-approximation unweighted matching algorithm that uses R MPC rounds into a $(1 - \varepsilon)$ approximation unweighted matching algorithm that uses $O_\varepsilon(R)$ rounds in the MPC model. This together with a sequence of recent papers [6, 11, 15, 20], that give constant-factor approximation algorithms for unweighted matchings with improved round complexity, culminated in algorithms that find $(1 - \varepsilon)$-approximate maximum unweighted matchings in $O_\varepsilon(\log\log n)$ rounds. However, as McGregor's techniques apply to only unweighted matchings, it was not known how to achieve an analogous result in the presence of weights. In fact, McGregor raised as an open question whether his result can be generalized to weighted graphs. Our result answers this in the affirmative and gives a reduction that is *lossless* with respect to the approximation guarantee while only increasing the complexity by a constant factor. Moreover, our reduction is to bipartite graphs. Instantiating this with the aforementioned streaming and MPC algorithms for unweighted matchings yields the following[1]:

THEOREM 1.2. *There exists an algorithm that in expectation finds a $(1 - \varepsilon)$-approximate weighted matching that can be implemented*

1. *in $O_\varepsilon(U_M)$ rounds, $O(m/n)$ machines per round, and $O_\varepsilon(n\,\mathrm{poly}(\log n))$ memory per machine, where U_M is the number of rounds used by a $(1-\delta)$-approximation algorithm for* bipartite *unweighted matching using $O(m/n)$ machines per round and $O_\delta(n\,\mathrm{poly}(\log n))$ memory per machine in the MPC model, and*
2. *in $O_\varepsilon(U_S)$ passes and $O_\varepsilon(n\,\mathrm{poly}(\log n))$ memory, where U_S is the number of passes used by a $(1-\delta)$-approximation algorithm for* bipartite *unweighted matching using $O_\delta(n\,\mathrm{poly}(\log n))$ memory, in the multi-pass streaming model,*

where $\delta = \varepsilon^{28+900/\varepsilon^2}$. Using the algorithm of Ghaffari et al. [20] or that of Assadi et al. [6], we get that $U_M = O_\varepsilon(\log\log n)$, and using the algorithm of Ahn and Guha [1], we get that $U_S = O_\varepsilon(1)$.

Prior to this, the best known results for computing a $(1 - \varepsilon)$-approximate *weighted* matching required $\Omega(\log n)$ rounds [2] in the MPC model. We remark that if we allow for memory $\tilde{\Theta}(n^{1+1/p})$ per machine in the MPC model, then [2] gave an algorithm that uses only a constant number of rounds (depending on p and ε). Achieving a similar result with near linear memory per machine is a major open question in the MPC literature; our results show that it is sufficient to concentrate on unweighted graphs as any progress on such graphs gives analogous progress in the weighted setting.

Comparison of the MPC and other models. In addition to developing an algorithmic toolbox for MPC, a number of papers explored the proximity of the MPC and other models of computation. For instance, a line of work, e.g., [4, 5, 7, 15, 26, 31], was motivated by the question of whether it is possible to solve problems faster (in terms of parallel-round complexity) in MPC than in PRAM. In the context of comparing MPC to CONGESTED-CLIQUE, that is a well-studied model of distributed computation introduced by Lotker et al. [37], [20, 25] noted that a certain regime of MPC has similar power as CONGESTED-CLIQUE. This connection was explored in greater detail in [9]. Recent progress on computing maximal matchings in MPC [11, 21, 42] was in part inspired by local computation algorithms (LCA). In particular, [21, 42] show how to combine a degree-based graph sparsification and the graph exponentiation technique [35] to obtain an MPC algorithm whose round complexity is quadratically smaller than the so-called query-radius of its LCA counterpart.

Organization of the paper. We start with formalizing the semi-streaming and MPC models in Section 2 and give a brief review of the related work in Section 3. In Section 4, we lay out the basic outline of our reduction from finding weighted augmentations to unweighted ones, and in Section 5, we describe how this approach yields a single-pass streaming algorithm for weighted matching under random edge arrivals. In Section 6, we explain how our techniques can be further generalized to obtain a $(1 - \varepsilon)$-approximation algorithm for weighted matching in MPC and multi-pass streaming settings. We conclude with Section 6.1, which provides a brief technical outline of the MPC implementation. We invite the interested readers to read the full version [19] for a comprehensive description of our algorithms and formal proofs of all our results.

2 PRELIMINARIES

We formalize the streaming and the MPC model now.

The semi-streaming model. The semi-streaming model for graph problems was introduced by Feigenbaum et al. [18]. In this model, the edges of the input graph arrive one-by-one in the stream, and the algorithm is allowed to use $O(n\,\mathrm{poly}\log(n))$ memory at any time and may go over the stream one (single-pass) or more (multi-pass) times. Note that $\Omega(n \log n)$ memory is needed just to store a valid matching.

[1] Throughout the paper, we denote by n the number of vertices and by m the number of edges.

The MPC model. The MPC model is a theoretical abstraction of MapReduce [16], Hadoop [44], Spark [45], and Dryad [27]. It was introduced in [31] and refined in subsequent work [4, 8, 23]. In this model, the computation is performed by Γ machines, each machine having S bits of memory. Initially, data, e.g., the edges of a graph, is partitioned arbitrarily across the machines. Then, the computation proceeds in synchronous rounds. In each round, each machine first processes its data locally. After the local computation on all the machines is over, the machines exchange messages. Each machine can send messages to any other machine, with the constraint that at most S bits are sent and received by each machine.

In our work, we assume that $S \cdot \Gamma \in \tilde{O}(m)$, i.e., the total memory across all the machines is only a poly log n factor larger than the size of the input graph. We consider the regime in which the memory per machine is nearly-linear in the number of vertices, i.e., $S \in \tilde{\Theta}(n)$.

In a given regime of Γ and S, the complexity in the MPC model is measured by the number of rounds needed to execute a given algorithm. Although the computational complexity is de-emphasized in the MPC model, we note that our algorithms run in nearly-linear time.

3 RELATED WORK

There is a large body of work devoted to semi-streaming algorithms for the maximum matching problem. For unweighted graphs, the basic greedy approach yields a (1/2)-approximation, and for weighted graphs [43] recently gave a $(1/2 - \varepsilon)$-approximation based on the local ratio technique. These are the best known algorithms that take a single pass over an adversarially ordered stream. Better algorithms are known if the stream is randomly ordered or if the algorithm can take multiple passes through the stream. In the random-edge-arrival case, [33] first improved upon the approximation guarantee of 1/2 in the unweighted case. Our results give better guarantees in that setting and also applies to the weighted setting. The following discussion applies to unweighted matching. If the algorithm is allowed to use $\tilde{O}(n^{3/2})$ memory, as opposed to only $\tilde{O}(n)$, then [6] show how to compute a $(2/3-\varepsilon)$-approximation in randomly ordered streams. When considering multi-pass algorithms, [40] gave a $(1-\varepsilon)$-approximation algorithm using $(1/\varepsilon)^{O(1/\varepsilon)}$ passes. Complementing this, [1] gave a deterministic $(1-\varepsilon)$-approximation algorithm using $O(\log(n)\,\mathrm{poly}(1/\varepsilon))$ passes. Also, a $(1-\varepsilon)$-approximation can be obtained in p/ε passes and $O(n^{1+1/p})$ space [2]; setting $p = (\log n)/\log\log n$ gives a semi-streaming algorithm that uses $(\log n)/(\varepsilon \log\log n)$ passes. As for hardness results, [30] showed that no algorithm can achieve a better approximation guarantee than $(1 - 1/e)$ in the adversarial single pass streaming setting.

A simple and general technique of reducing weighted to unweighted was given in [14] to obtain both streaming and MPC algorithms. The reduction is non-adaptive (instead of iterative) and worsens the approximation by a factor of $1/2 - \varepsilon$, i.e., using an α-approximation algorithm for the unweighted case, they give a $(1/2 - \varepsilon)\alpha$-approximation for the weighted case.

The study of algorithms for matchings in the models of parallel computation dates back to the eighties. A seminal work of Luby [39] shows how to construct a maximal independent set in $O(\log n)$ PRAM rounds. When this algorithm is applied to the line graph of G, it outputs a maximal matching of G. Similar results, also in the context of PRAM, were obtained in [3, 28, 29].

Perfect maximum matchings were also a subject of study in the context of PRAM. In [38] it is shown that the decision variant is in RNC. That implies that there is a PRAM algorithm that in poly log n rounds decides whether a graph has a perfect matching or not. [32] were the first to prove that constructing perfect matchings is also in RNC. In [41] the same result was proved, and they also introduced the isolation lemma that had a great impact on many other problems.

In [23, 31] it was shown that it is often possible to simulate one PRAM round in $O(1)$ MPC rounds with $O(n^{\alpha})$ memory per machine, for any constant $\alpha > 0$. This implies that the aforementioned PRAM results lead to $O(\log n)$ MPC round complexity algorithms for computing maximal matchings. [34] developed an algorithm that computes (unweighted) maximal matchings in the MPC model in $O(1/\delta)$ rounds when the memory per machine is $S \in \Omega(n^{1+\delta})$, for any constant $\delta > 0$. When $S \in \tilde{O}(n)$, the algorithm given in [34] requires $\tilde{O}(\log n)$ MPC rounds of computation. In the context of maximum weighted matchings, [24] designed an algorithm for computing a 1/2 approximation in $O(1/\delta)$ and $O(\log n)$ rounds when $S \in \Omega(n^{1+\delta})$ and $S \in \tilde{O}(n)$, respectively.

Another line of work focused on improving $O(\log n)$ MPC round complexity in the regime $S \in \tilde{O}(n)$. [15] and [6, 11, 20] show how to compute a constant-factor approximation of maximum unweighted matching in $O((\log\log n)^2)$ and $O(\log\log n)$ MPC rounds, respectively, when the memory per machine is $\tilde{O}(n)$. As noted in [15], any $\Theta(1)$-approximation algorithm for maximum unweighted matchings can be turned into a $(1/2 - \varepsilon)$-approximation algorithm for weighted matchings by using the approach described in Section 4 of [36]. This transformation increases the round complexity by $O(1/\varepsilon)$.

In the regime of n^{δ} memory per machine, for any constant $\delta \in (0, 1)$, recent works [10, 12] show how to find maximal matchings in $O((\log\log n)^2)$ rounds for graphs of arboricity poly$(\log n)$. Also in this regime, [21] and [42] provide algorithms for constructing maximal matchings for general graphs in $\tilde{O}(\sqrt{\log n})$ MPC rounds. The algorithm of [21] requires $O(m)$ and the algorithm of [42] requires $O(m + n^{1+o(1)})$ total memory.

We now give an outline of our approach.

4 OUTLINE OF OUR APPROACH

Let M be a matching in a graph $G = (V, E)$ with edge-weights $w : E \to \mathbb{R}$. Recall that an alternating path P is a path in G that alternates between edges in M and in $E \setminus M$. If the endpoints of P are unmatched vertices or incident to edges in $M \cap P$, then removing the M-edges in P and adding the other edges of P gives a new matching. In other words, $M \Delta P = (M \setminus (P \cap M)) \cup P \setminus M$ is a new matching. We say that we updated M using the alternating path P, and we further say that P is augmenting if $w(M \Delta P) > w(M)$ where we used the notation $w(F) = \sum_{e \in F} w(e)$ for a subset of edges $F \subseteq E$. Also recall that an alternating cycle C is a cycle that alternates between edges in M and in $E \setminus M$, and $M \Delta C$ is also a matching. We say that C is augmenting if $w(M \Delta C) > w(M)$. Now a well-known structural result regarding approximate matchings is the following:

Fact 4.1. *For any $\ell \in \mathbb{N}$, if there is no augmenting path or cycle of length at most $2\ell - 1$, then M is a $(1 - 1/\ell)$-approximate matching.*

In particular, this says that in order to find a $(1 - \varepsilon)$-approximate matching it is sufficient to find augmenting paths or cycles of length $O(1/\varepsilon)$. This is indeed the most common route used to design efficient algorithms for finding approximate matchings: in the streaming model with random-edge-arrivals, [33] finds augmenting paths of length at most 3 and the MPC algorithms [6, 15] find augmenting paths of length $O(1/\varepsilon)$. However, those approaches work only for unweighted graphs. The high level reason being that it is easy to characterize the augmenting paths in the unweighted setting: they simply must start and end in unmatched vertices. Such a simple classification of augmenting paths is not available in the weighted setting and the techniques of those papers do not apply. Nevertheless, we propose a general framework to overcome this obstacle that allows us to tap into the results and techniques developed for unweighted matchings. Informally, we reduce the problem of finding augmenting paths in the weighted setting to the unweighted setting.

The high level idea is simple: Consider the example depicted on the left in Fig. 1. The current matching M consists of a single edge $\{c, d\}$ that is depicted by a solid line. The weights are written next to the edges and so $w(M) = 5$ (the edges $E \setminus M$ are dashed). The maximum matching consists of $\{a, c\}, \{d, f\}$ and has weight 8. Furthermore, there are several alternating paths of length 3 that are also augmenting. However, it is important to note that we cannot simply apply an algorithm for finding unweighted augmenting paths. Such an algorithm may find the alternating path $P = b, c, d, e$ which is augmenting in the unweighted sense but $w(M \Delta P) < w(M)$. To overcome this, we apply a *filtering* technique that we now explain in our simple example: First "guess" lower bounds on the weights of the edges incident to c and d in an augmenting path. Let τ_c and τ_d be those lower bounds. We then look for augmenting paths in the unweighted graph that keeps only those unmatched edges incident to c and d whose weights are above the guessed thresholds. Then to guarantee that an unweighted augmenting path that an algorithm finds is also an augmenting path in the weighted sense, we always set τ_c and τ_d such that $\tau_c + \tau_d > w(\{c, d\})$. In the center and right part of Fig. 1 we depict two *unweighted* graphs obtained for different values of τ_c and τ_d (in the center with $\tau_c = \tau_d = 3$ and to the right with $\tau_c = 2, \tau_d = 4$). Note that in both examples any unweighted augmenting path is also augmenting with respect to the weights.

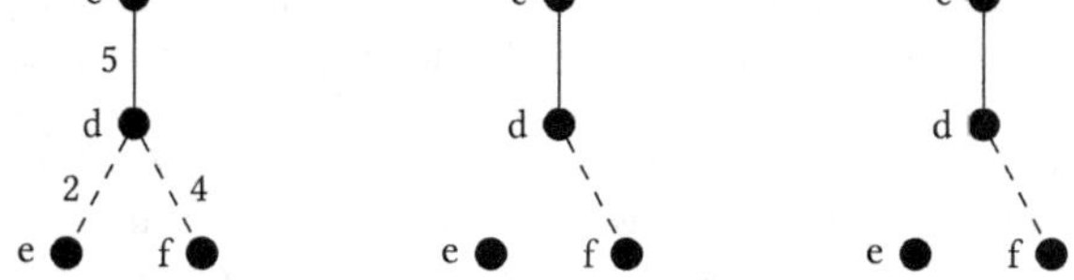

Figure 1: A simple illustration of the filtering technique.

While the implementation of the basic idea is simple in the above case, there are several challenges in general. Perhaps the most obvious one is that, for weighted matchings, M may be a perfect matching but still far from optimal. And a perfect matching obviously has no unweighted augmenting paths! On a very high level, we overcome this issue by dropping edges in M while making sure to set the guessed lower bounds (the τ's) so as to guarantee that any unweighted augmenting path is also a weighted augmenting path (even when taking the dropped edges into account).

In what follows, we describe in more detail the implementation of the above basic idea. We start with the simpler case, single-pass streaming with random edge arrivals, where we look only for augmenting paths of length 3. We then describe the technically more involved multi-pass streaming and MPC algorithms that consider long augmenting paths and cycles.

5 SINGLE-PASS STREAMING WITH RANDOM EDGE ARRIVALS

In contrast to unweighted graphs where the basic greedy algorithm gives a $(1/2)$-approximation, it was only very recently that a $(1/2-\varepsilon)$-approximation streaming algorithm was given for weighted matchings [43]. The algorithm of Paz and Schwartzman is based on the local ratio technique, which we now describe[2]. On an input graph $G = (V, E)$ with edge-weights $w : E \to \mathbb{R}$, the following simple local-ratio algorithm is known to return a $(1/2)$-approximate weighted matching: Initially, let $S = \emptyset$ and $\alpha_v = 0$ for all $v \in V$. For each $e = \{u, v\} \in E$ in an *arbitrary* order:

- if $\alpha_u + \alpha_v < w(e)$, add e to S and increase α_u and α_v by $w(e) - \alpha_u - \alpha_v$.

Finally, obtain a matching M by running the basic greedy algorithm on the edges in S in the reverse order (i.e., by starting with the edge last added to S).

Since the above algorithm returns a $(1/2)$-approximate matching irrespective of the order in which the edges are considered (in the for loop), it may appear immediate to use it in the streaming setting. The issue is that, if the edges arrive in an adversarial order, we may add *all* the edges to S. For dense graphs, this would lead to a memory consumption of $\Omega(n^2)$ instead of the wanted memory usage $O(n \operatorname{poly}(\log n))$ which is (roughly) linear in the output size. The main technical challenge in [43] is to limit the number of edges added to S; this is why that algorithm obtains a $(1/2 - \varepsilon)$-approximation, for any $\varepsilon > 0$, instead of a $(1/2)$-approximation.

McGregor and Vorotnikova observed that the technical issue in [43] disappears if we assume that edges arrive in a uniformly random order[3]. Indeed, we can then use basic probabilistic techniques (see, e.g., the "hiring problem" in [13]) to show that the expected (over the random arrival order) number of edges added to S is $O(n \log n)$. Even better, here we show that, with high probability, the following adaptation still adds only $O(n \log n)$ edges to S: update the vertex potentials (the α_v's) only for, say, 1% of the stream and then, in the remaining 99% of the stream, add *all* edges

[2]The description of the local-ratio technique is adapted from a recent grant proposal submitted to the Swiss National Science Foundation by the last author.

[3]Sofya Vorotnikova presented this result in the workshop "Communication Complexity and Applications, II (17w5147)" at the Banff International Research Station held in March 2017.

$\{u, v\}$ for which $\alpha_u + \alpha_v < w(\{u, v\})$ to S (without updating the vertex potentials). This adaptation allows us to prove the following structural result:

> In a random-edge-arrival stream, either the local-ratio algorithm already obtains a (close) to (1/2)-approximate matching M after seeing a small fraction of the stream (think 1%), or the set S (in the adaptation that freezes vertex potentials) contains a better than (1/2)-approximation in the end of the stream.

The above allows us to concentrate on the case when we have a (close) to (1/2)-approximate matching M_0 after seeing only 1% of the stream. We can thus use the remaining 99% to find enough augmenting paths to improve upon the initial (1/2)-approximation. It is here that our *filtering* technique is used to reduce the task of finding weighted augmenting paths to unweighted ones. By Fact 4.1, it is sufficient to consider very short augmentations to improve upon an approximation guarantee of 1/2. Specifically, the considered augmentations are of two types:

(1) Those consisting of a single edge $\{u, v\}$ to add satisfying $w(\{u, v\}) > w(M_0(u)) + w(M_0(v))$, where $w(M_0(x))$ denotes the weight of the edge of M_0 incident to vertex x (and 0 if no such edge exists)[4].
(2) Those consisting of two new edges o_1 and o_2 that form a path or a cycle $(e_1, o_1, e_2, o_2, e_3)$ with at most three edges $e_1, e_2, e_3 \in M_0$ and $w(o_1) + w(o_2) > w(e_1) + w(e_2) + w(e_3)$, i.e., adding o_1, o_2 and removing e_1, e_2, e_3 increases the weight of the matching.

For concreteness, consider the graph in Fig. 2. The edges in M_0 are solid and dashed edges are yet to arrive in the stream. An example of the first type of augmentations is to add $\{e, h\}$ (and remove $\{e, f\}$ and $\{g, h\}$) which results in a gain because $w(\{e, h\}) = 2 > 1 + 0 = w(M_0(e)) + w(M_0(h))$. Two examples of the second type of augmentations are the path $(\{b, a\}, \{a, d\}, \{d, c\}, \{c, f\}, \{f, e\})$ and the cycle $(\{e, f\}, \{f, h\}, \{h, g\}, \{g, e\})$.

The augmentations of the first type are easy to find in a greedy manner. For the second type, we now describe how to use our filtering technique to reduce the problem to that of finding length three *unweighted* augmenting paths. Let Unw-3-Aug-Paths be a streaming algorithm for finding such unweighted augmenting paths. We first initialize Unw-3-Aug-Paths with a (random) matching M'_0 obtained by including each edge in M_0 with probability 1/2. As we explain shortly, M'_0 corresponds to the edges e_2 from the second type of augmenting paths. Then, at the arrival of an edge $\{u, v\}$, it is forwarded as an unweighted edge to Unw-3-Aug-Paths if $w(\{u, v\}) > \tau_u + \tau_v$, where

$$\tau_x = \begin{cases} w(M_0(x))/2 & \text{if } x \text{ is incident to an edge in } M'_0, \\ w(M_0(x)) & \text{otherwise.} \end{cases}$$

For an example of the forwarded edges for a specific M'_0, see the right part of Fig. 2.

Note that the τ-values are set so that any augmenting path found by Unw-3-Aug-Paths will also improve the matching in

[4]To make sure that the weight of the matching increases significantly by an augmentation, the strict inequality needs to be satisfied with a slack. We avoid this technicality in the overview.

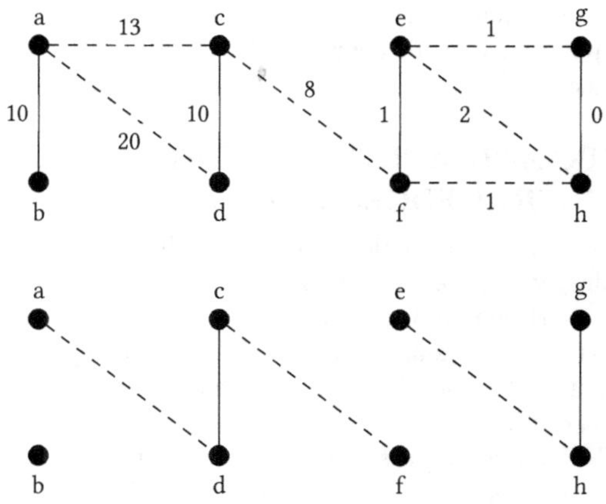

Figure 2: On the top, an example of a weighted graph with matching M_0 (solid edges) is shown. On the bottom, the unweighted graph obtained in the filtering step with $M'_0 = \{\{c, d\}, \{g, h\}\}$ is shown.

the weighted graph[5] . Indeed, suppose that Unw-3-Aug-Paths finds the length three augmenting path $\{o_1, e_2, o_2\}$ where $e_2 \in M'_0$. Let e_1 and e_3 be the other edges in M_0 incident to o_1 and o_2 (if they exist). Then, by the selection of the τ-values, we have

$$\begin{aligned} w(o_1) + w(o_2) &> (w(e_1) + w(e_2)/2) + (w(e_2)/2) + w(e_3)) \\ &= w(e_1) + w(e_2) + w(e_3), \end{aligned}$$

as required. Hence, the τ-values are set so as to guarantee that the augmenting paths will improve the weighted matching if applied.

The reason for the random selection of M'_0 is to make sure that any such beneficial weighted augmenting path $\{e_1, o_1, e_2, o_2, e_3\}$ is present as an unweighted augmenting path $\{o_1, e_2, o_2\}$ in the graph given to Unw-3-Aug-Paths with probability at least 1/8. This guarantees that there will be (in expectation) many length three unweighted augmenting paths corresponding to weighted augmentations (assuming the initial matching M_0 is no better than (1/2)-approximate).

This completes the high level description of our single-pass streaming algorithm except for the following omission: although all unweighted augmenting paths are equally beneficial, their weighted contributions can vary drastically. This may result in a situation where Unw-3-Aug-Paths returns a constant-fraction of the unweighted augmenting paths that have little value in the weighted graph. The solution is simple: we partition M'_0 into weight classes by geometric grouping, run Unw-3-Aug-Paths for each weight class in parallel, and then select vertex-disjoint augmenting paths in a greedy fashion starting with the augmenting paths in the largest weight class. This ensures that many unweighted augmenting paths also translates into a significant improvement of the

[5]We remark that there may be short augmentations that are beneficial in the weighted sense that are never present in the graph forwarded to Unw-3-Aug-Paths regardless of the choice of M'_0. An example would be $\{e_1, o_1, e_2, o_2, e_3\}$ with $w(e_1) = w(e_2) = w(e_3) = 10$ and $w(o_1) = 20$, $w(o_2) = 14$. In this case, o_2 is not forwarded to Unw-3-Aug-Paths due to the filtering if $e_2 \in M'_0$, $e_1, e_3 \notin M'_0$; and, in the other choices of M'_0, $\{o_1, e_2, o_2\}$ is not a length three unweighted augmenting path. However, as we prove in the full version [19], those augmentations are safe to ignore in our goal to beat the approximation guarantee of 1/2.

weighted matching. The formal and complete description of these techniques which yields the proof of Theorem 1.1 appears in the full version [19].

6 MPC AND MULTI-PASS STREAMING WITH GENERAL EDGE ARRIVALS

To achieve an approximation ratio greater than 1/2 for single-pass streaming, we reduce the problem via a crucial step to that of finding short (length-3) augmenting paths for a matching that is already (close) to 1/2-approximate. The crucial step involves an algorithm for the case when initial matching is far away from being 1/2-approximate.

In MPC and multi-pass streaming, the setting is somewhat different. On the one hand, the difficulty of handling the case when initial matching is small disappears because we can repeatedly find augmentations. In fact, we can even start with the empty matching. On the other hand, we now aim for the much stronger approximation guarantee of $(1-\varepsilon)$ for any fixed $\varepsilon > 0$. This results in a more complex filtering step as we now need to find augmenting paths and cycles of arbitrary length (depending on ε). We remark that the challenge of finding long augmenting cycles is one of the difficulties that appears in the weighted case where previous techniques do not apply [1, 40]. We overcome this and other challenges by giving a general reduction to the unweighted matching problem, which can be informally stated as follows:

Let M be the current matching and $M^\star$ be an optimal matching of maximum weight. If $w(M) < (1-\varepsilon)w(M^\star)$ then an $(1-\delta(\varepsilon))$-approximation algorithm for the unweighted matching problem on bipartite graphs can be used to find a collection of vertex-disjoint augmentations that in expectation increases the weight of M by $\Omega_\varepsilon(w(M^\star))$.

The reduction itself is efficient and can easily be implemented both in the multi-pass streaming and MPC models by incurring only a constant overhead in the complexity. Using the best-known approximation algorithms for the unweighted matching problem on bipartite graphs in these models then yields Theorem 1.2 by repeating the above $f(\varepsilon)$ times after starting with the empty matching $M = \emptyset$.

We now present the main ideas of our reduction. We start with a structural statement for weighted matchings similar to Fact 4.1:

Suppose the current matching M satisfies $w(M) \leqslant (1-\varepsilon)w(M^\star)$. Then there must exist a collection $\mathcal{C}$ of short (each consisting of $O(1/\varepsilon)$ edges) vertex-disjoint augmenting paths and cycles with total gain $\Omega(\varepsilon^2)\cdot w(M^\star)$. Moreover, each augmentation $C \in \mathcal{C}$ has gain at least $\Omega(\varepsilon^2 w(C))$, i.e., proportional to its total weight.

Our goal now is to find a large fraction of these short weighted augmentations. For this, we first reduce the problem to that of finding such augmentations C with $w(C) \approx W$ for some fixed W. This corresponds to what we call *augmentation classes*. Note that, by standard geometric grouping, we can reduce the number of choices of W to be at most logarithmic. We can thus afford to run our algorithm for all choices of W in parallel and then greedily select the augmentations starting with those of the highest weight augmentation class.

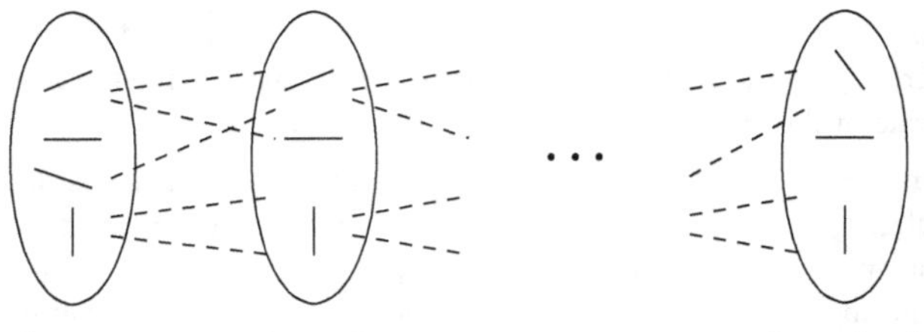

Figure 3: The layered graph consisting of $k+1$ layers. The solid edges inside the layers are subsets of M and the dashed edges between layers are subsets of $E \setminus M$.

Now, for each augmentation class (i.e., for each choice of W), we give a reduction from finding weighted augmentations to finding unweighted ones by constructing a set of tailored graphs. This construction resembles some of the ideas used in the construction of [40], but they are not the same. The intuition behind our construction is as follows. Suppose that, for a fixed W, we aim to find augmenting paths of length $2k+1$ in the input graph $G = (V, E)$. Then, as depicted in Fig. 3, we construct a new layered graph $\mathcal{L}$ consisting of $k+1$ layers of vertices, (each layer is a copy of V), where the edge set of each layer consists of a subset of the edges in the current matching M and the edges between layers are subsets of $E \setminus M$. The construction of $\mathcal{L}$ is so that if we consider an alternating path $C = (e_1, o_1, e_2, o_2, \ldots, e_k, o_k, e_{k+1})$ in $\mathcal{L}$ where $e_i \in M$ is an edge in layer i and o_i is an edge between layer i and $i+1$, then, assuming they all correspond to distinct edges in G, we can augment M with C to obtain the new matching $M\Delta C$. Moreover, the augmentation improves the matching, i.e., satisfies $w(M\Delta C) > w(M)$, if

$$\sum_{i=1}^{k} w(o_i) > \sum_{i=1}^{k+1} w(e_i)\,. \tag{1}$$

To ensure that any alternating path in the unweighted graph $\mathcal{L}$ satisfies (1) we use our filtering technique. For each layer $i = 1, \ldots, k+1$, we have a parameter τ_i^A that filters the edges in that layer: we keep an edge $e \in M$ in layer i only if $w(e)$ rounded up to the closest multiple of $\varepsilon^{12}W$ equals $\tau_i^A W$. Similarly, we have a parameter τ_i^B for each $i = 1, \ldots, k$, and we keep an edge $e \in E \setminus M$ between layer i and $i+1$ only if $w(e)$ rounded down to the closest multiple of $\varepsilon^{12}W$ equals $\tau_i^B W$. Now by considering only those τ-values satisfying $\sum \tau_i^B > \sum \tau_i^A$, we ensure that any augmenting path that is found improves the matching, i.e., (1) holds. Moreover, the rounding of edge-weights in the filtering step still keeps large (by weight) fraction of the augmentations in the original graph as the rounding error, which is less than $\varepsilon^{12}W$ for each edge, is very small compared to the length and total gain of the structural augmentations that we are looking for. It is thus enough to find the augmentations corresponding to each fixation of k and τ-values. To bound the number of choices, note that we may assume that each τ-value is such that $\tau \cdot W$ is a multiple of $\varepsilon^{12}W$ between 0 and W. Hence, as we need to consider augmentations of length $O(1/\varepsilon)$ only, we have, for a fixed $\varepsilon > 0$ and W, that the total number of choices of k and τ-values is a constant. They can thus all be considered in parallel. For each of these choices, we use the approximation algorithm for unweighted matchings to find a $(1-\delta(\varepsilon))$-approximate maximum unweighted matching in the corresponding layered graph and take the symmetric difference with the initial matched edges to find the desired unweighted augmentations. These augmentations are then translated back to weighted augmentations in the original graph.

Note that, unlike McGregor's layered graphs, our layered graphs allow edges (both matched and unmatched) to be repeated in different layers, which is crucial in identifying weighted augmenting cycles. Furthermore, edges in each layer are filtered with respect to a given edge-weight arrangement, that ensures that the augmenting paths in our layered graphs correspond to weighted augmentations with positive gain. These differences result from the different purposes of the two constructions: McGregor's construction aims to find unweighted augmenting paths efficiently, whereas our purpose is to reduce weighted augmentations to unweighted ones.

While, on a high level, this completes the description of our reduction, there are many interesting technical challenges to overcome. In the remaining part of this overview, we highlight two of these challenges.

Translating augmenting paths in layered graph to the original graph. From our high level description of the layered graph $\mathcal{L}$, there is no guarantee that an augmenting path in it corresponds to an augmentation with a positive gain in the original graph G. First, there is no reason that an augmenting path in $\mathcal{L}$ visits the layers from left-to-right as intended. In the formal definition of layered graphs (see the full version [19]), we take care of this and make sure[6] that any unweighted augmenting path in $\mathcal{L}$ corresponds to an alternating path of the form $(e_1, o_1, e_2, o_2, \ldots, e_k, o_k, e_{k+1})$, where $e_i \in M$ is an edge in layer i and o_i is an edge between layer i and $i+1$. Intuitively, such an alternating path can be made an unweighted augmenting path by discarding the matching edges of the first and last layers. However, a second and more challenging issue is that such an alternating path (going from the left to the right layer) may contain repeated edges and thus do not correspond to an augmentation in G. An example of this phenomena is shown in Fig. 4.

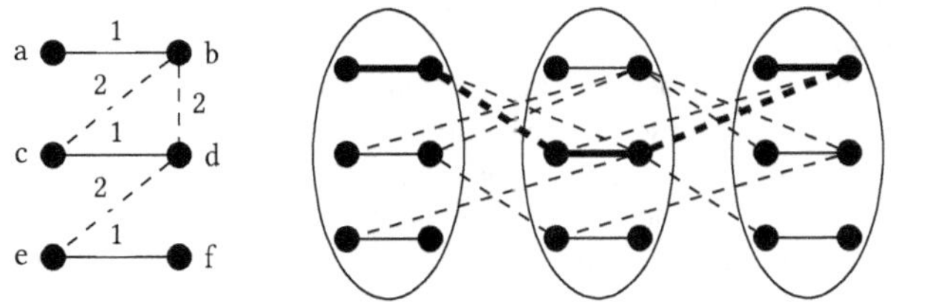

Figure 4: An example of an "incorrect" layered graph.

It depicts a weighted graph on the left and an "incorrect" layered graph on the right with $\tau_1^A W = \tau_2^A W = \tau_3^A W = 1$ and $\tau_B^1 W = \tau_B^2 W = 2$. The weighted graph has an augmentation that adds $\{b,c\}, \{d,e\}$ and removes $\{a,b\}, \{c,d\}, \{e,f\}$ and improves the weight of the matching by one. This augmentation is also present in the layered graph. However, an equally good augmentation in that graph from an unweighted perspective corresponds to the alternating path depicted in bold. In the original graph the bold edge set corresponds to the non-simple path $a-b-c-d-b-a$. Such a non-simple path clearly does not correspond to an augmentation and, even worse, there is no augmentation with a positive gain in the support $\{a,b\}, \{b,c\}, \{c,d\}, \{d,b\}$ of the considered path.

Our main idea to overcome this issue is as follows. We first select a random bipartition L and R of the vertex set of G. Then between two layers i and $i+1$, we keep only those edges that go from an R-vertex in layer i to an L-vertex in layer $i+1$. We emphasize that the edges going from an L-vertex to an R-vertex between two layers are not kept. For example, if we let $L = \{a, c, e\}$ and $R = \{b, d, f\}$ in the example considered in Fig. 4, then the layered graph (with the same τ-values) is the one given in Fig. 5.

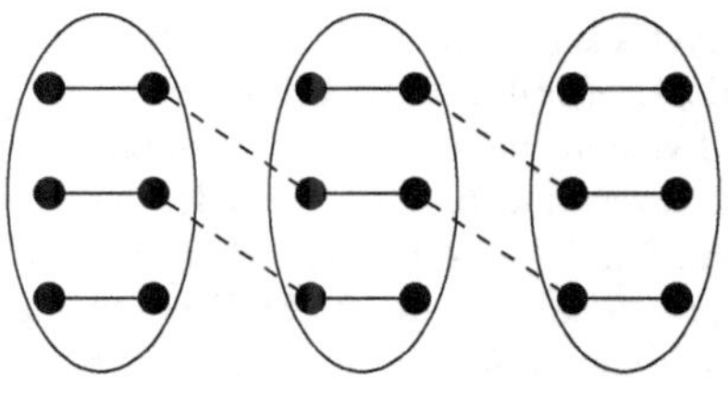

Figure 5: An example of a correct layered graph.

In this example, the remaining alternating path that visits all layers (in the formal proof we further refine the layered graph to make sure that these are the only paths that are considered) corresponds to the augmentation in G. However, in general, an alternating path may still not correspond to a simple path and an augmentation in G since it may contain repetitions. However, the bipartition and the refinement of the layered graph can be seen to introduce an "orientation" of the edges in G. This together with standard Eulerian techniques of directed graphs allow us to prove that any alternating path in the layered graph can be decomposed into a collection of alternating even-length cycles and an alternating path in G, one of which is also augmenting. Finally, let us remark that the idea to consider a bipartition L and R of the vertex set of G and to allow only those edges that are from an R-vertex to an L-vertex between consecutive layers has the additional benefit that the layered graph becomes bipartite. This is the reason that our reduction is from weighted matchings in general graphs to unweighted matchings in bipartite graphs.

Finding augmenting cycles. In the unweighted setting, matching algorithms do not have to consider cycles because alternating cycles cannot augment an existing matching. In contrast, algorithms for the weighted setting (at least the ones that try to iteratively improve an initial matching) have to somehow deal with augmenting cycles; weighted graphs can have perfect (unweighted) matchings whose weights are not close to the optimal and that can be improved only through augmenting cycles. For example, consider a 4-cycle with edge weights $(3,4,3,4)$, where the edges of weight 3 form an initial perfect matching of weight 6, but the optimal matching consists of edges of weight 4 and has a total weight of 8. The only way to augment the weight here is to consider the whole cycle. The

[6] To be completely accurate, the edges e_1 and e_{k+1} may not appear in the alternating path: e_1 does not appear if the vertex incident to o_1 in the first layer is not incident to a filtered edge in M; the case of e_{k+1} is analogous.

crucial property of our reduction is its ability to transform not only weighted augmenting paths, but also weighted augmenting *cycles* of the original graph into augmenting paths in the layered graphs.

Before explaining our solution, let us take a closer look at the above 4-cycle example. Let the edges of the 4-cycle be (e_1, o_1, e_2, o_2) where $\{e_1, e_2\}$ is the current matching. Note that the cycle can be represented as an alternating path $(e_1, o_1, e_2, o_2, e_1)$ in the layered graph using three layers (consisting of the three edges of the matching with e_1 repeated once). However, such a representation of the augmenting cycle cannot be captured by our filtering technique due to the constraint $\sum_i \tau_i^B > \sum_i \tau_i^A$ which ensures that any alternating path in the layered graph can be translated into a weighted augmentation. The reason being that for $(e_1, o_1, e_2, o_2, e_1)$ to be present in the layered graph we would need $\tau_i^A W = 3$ for $i = 1, 2, 3$, and $\tau_i^B W = 4$ for $i = 1, 2$ which would contradict the above inequality. This approach is therefore not sufficient to find augmenting cycles and achieve a $(1 - \varepsilon)$ approximation guarantee. Specifically, the issue is due to the fact that we account for the edge weight of e_1 twice in the filtering process, once for o_1 and once more for o_2. To overcome this issue, consider the 4-cycle with more general weights $2, 2 + \varepsilon, 2, 2 + \varepsilon$, where taking o_1, o_2 in place of e_1, e_2 gives an $\varepsilon/2$ fractional gain in weight. What we need is to make sure that, even if we account for the same edge e_1 (or e_2) twice, the alternating path we get in the layered graph ("corresponding" to the cycle) is still gainful. For this, we blow-up the cycle length by repeating the same cycle $O(1/\varepsilon)$ times. I.e., we consider the cycle

$$\underbrace{e_1, o_1, e_2, o_2}_{\text{instance } 1}, \underbrace{e_1, o_1, e_2, o_2}_{\text{instance } 2}, \ldots, \underbrace{e_1, o_1, e_2, o_2}_{\text{instance } c/\varepsilon}, e_1.$$

Since we have repeated the o_i edges many times, their gains add up so that it can account for the weight of considering e_1 one additional time. The considered cycle of length 4 is thus present as a "repeated" alternating path in the layered graph (with the appropriate τ-values and bipartition) consisting of $O(1/\varepsilon)$ layers. In general, to make sure that we can find augmenting cycles of length $O(1/\varepsilon)$ we will consider the layered graph with up to $O(1/\varepsilon^2)$ layers.

6.1 Description of the MPC Algorithm

We now briefly describe the algorithm and present some MPC-implementation details. In doing so, we first formally define augmentation classes and state some intermediate results.

Augmentation classes collections of augmentations with comparable gain and individual edge-weights. For a weight W and matching M (to be thought of as current matching of the algorithm), by the *augmentation class* of W we refer to the collection of all augmentations C having the following properties:

(1) The weight of each edge of C is between $\varepsilon^{12}W$ and $2W$.
(2) The gain $w^+(C)$ of C is at most $2W$.
(3) After appropriate rounding of weights to the nearest integer multiple of $\varepsilon^{12}W$, $w^+(C) \geqslant \varepsilon^{12}W$.
(4) The augmentation C consists of at most $64/\varepsilon^2 + 1$ vertices.

The following theorem says that it is sufficient to focus on augmentations that lie in some augmentation class. This is a simple adaptation of the fact that a matching far from optimum has many short augmentations.

THEOREM 6.1. *Let M be a matching such that $w(M) < (1 - \varepsilon)w(M^\star)$. Then, there exists a collection C of vertex-disjoint augmentations such that each $C \in C$ is in the augmentation class of $(1+\varepsilon^4)^i \leqslant w(C)$ for some $i \leqslant \lceil \log_{1+\varepsilon^4}((64/\varepsilon^2 + 1) \cdot \max\{w(e) : e \in E\}) \rceil$, and for the total gain of C it holds $w^+(C) \geqslant \varepsilon^2 w(M^\star)/200$.*

Using our filtering technique, earlier in this section we described a reduction to unweighted bipartite matching for each augmentation class. The reduction is formalized as follows.

THEOREM 6.2 (SINGLE AUGMENTATION CLASS). *Let M be the current matching. Let $w(M) < w(M^\star)/(1+\varepsilon)$. Let C_W denote a collection of vertex-disjoint augmentations belonging to the augmentation class of W. Define $w(M_W)$ to be the total weight of the edges of M with weights in $[\varepsilon^{12}W, 2W]$. Then there is an algorithm that, given W, outputs a collection $\mathcal{A}_W$ of vertex-disjoint augmentations ($\mathcal{A}_W$ is not necessarily a subset of C_W) having the following properties:*

(A) $\mathcal{A}_W$ is a subset of the augmentation class of W.
(B) In expectation, $w^+(\mathcal{A}_W) \geqslant \varepsilon^{c/\varepsilon^2}(w^+(C_W) - \varepsilon^{10}w(M_W))$, for some constant c.

This algorithm can be implemented in U_M MPC rounds with $O_\varepsilon(n \log n)$ memory per machine, where U_M is the MPC round complexity of unweighted bipartite matching and is $O_\varepsilon(\log\log n)$.

Our main algorithm for the MPC result of Theorem 1.2 is then just running the above algorithm in parallel for logarithmic choices of W and then do a greedy conflict resolution; we describe it in Algorithm 2 for completeness. We next describe the algorithm for single augmentation class.

Recall that we used thresholds τ_i^A and τ_i^B for edges within and between layers in our layered graph. Formally, we call a pair (τ_i^A, τ_i^B) a *good* pair if: in total, it has at most $64/\varepsilon^2 + 1$ entries; each entry is a non-negative integer multiple of ε^{12}; each of the entries except those corresponding to the first and the last layer is at least $2\varepsilon^{12}$; $\sum_i \tau_i^B \leqslant 1 + \varepsilon^4$; and $\sum_i \tau_i^B - \sum_i \tau_i^A \geqslant \varepsilon^{12}$. Note that the last condition effectively allows us to obtain a good gain from an augmentation. See Algorithm 1 for the complete pseudocode.

We now discuss how some steps of the algorithm can be implemented in MPC. For generating a random bipartition, collect all the vertices on one machine, call that machine μ, which randomly assigns them to L and R. Then, the edge-set is distributed across machines, and the vertex sets L and R are sent to each of those machines as follows: μ locally splits $L \cup R$ into Γ (i.e., the number of machines) sets, which it sends to the Γ machines — one set per machine; each machine then sends its set to each of the other machines. In a similar way, we make sure that each machine knows the current matching M.

Then all (τ^A, τ^B) pairs that give rise to the layered graphs are generated by each machine. For constant ε, there are at most $O(1)$ many such pairs. For each (τ^A, τ^B), each machine can then generate its part of the layered graph using M and the bipartition (L, R).

For each such layered graph, the unweighted bipartite matching algorithm UNW-BIP-MATCHING is called, which uses U_M MPC rounds and $O_\varepsilon(n)$ memory per machine. Irrespective of how this algorithm stores its output, the collection of augmenting paths in a layered graph (which contains repeated edges) can be collected on a fixed machine. That machine then translates them to the weighted augmenting paths in the original graph and redistributes the output.

Partition the vertex set into L and R by assigning each vertex to one of the sets uniformly at random and independently.
Let $\mathcal{T}$ be the set of all good (τ^A, τ^B) pairs.
for *each* $(\tau^A, \tau^B) \in \mathcal{T}$ *in parallel* **do**
  Define $\mathcal{L}'$ to be $\mathcal{L}(\tau^A, \tau^B, W)$ with the edges from the first and the last layer removed.
  Let $M' = $ UNW-BIP-MATCHING$(\mathcal{L}', \delta)$ be the matching returned by a $(1 - \delta)$-approximation bipartite unweighted matching algorithm (recall that $\mathcal{L}'$ is bipartite).
  Let $M_{\mathcal{L}'}$ be the matching M restricted to $\mathcal{L}'$.
  Let $\mathcal{P}$ be the collection of augmentations in $M' \cup M_{\mathcal{L}'}$.
  Let $\mathcal{A}^{(\tau^A, \tau^B)}$ be a set of augmentation in G. Initially, $\mathcal{A}^{(\tau^A, \tau^B)}$ is the empty set.
  for *each* $P \in \mathcal{P}$ **do**
    Using Eulerian techniques decompose P into a union of even-length cycles and a simple path in G. Let C be that decomposition.
    Choose an augmentation $C \in C$ that has the largest gain among the elements of C.
    If C does not intersect any element of $\mathcal{A}^{(\tau^A, \tau^B)}$, add C to $\mathcal{A}^{(\tau^A, \tau^B)}$.
Let $\mathcal{A}_W$ be a $\mathcal{A}^{(\tau^A, \tau^B)}$ set that maximizes gain over all (τ^A, τ^B) pairs.
return $\mathcal{A}_W$

Algorithm 1: Algorithm for single augmentation class.

$i_{\max} \leftarrow \lceil \log_{1+\varepsilon^4}\left((64/\varepsilon^2 + 1) \cdot \max\{w(e) : e \in E\}\right)\rceil$.
/* One MPC round can be spent to compute $\max\{w(e) : e \in E\}$. */
$\mathcal{W} \leftarrow \{(1 + \varepsilon^4)^i : i = 0, 1, \ldots, i_{\max}\}$
for *each* $W \in \mathcal{W}$ *in parallel* **do**
  Let $\mathcal{A}_W$ be the set of augmentations that Algorithm 1 outputs for the augmentation class W.
$\hat{\mathcal{A}} \leftarrow \emptyset$
for *each* $W \in \mathcal{W}$ *in decreasing order* **do**
  for *each augmentation* C *in* $\mathcal{A}_W$ **do**
    Add C to $\hat{\mathcal{A}}$ if C does not conflict with any other augmentation in $\hat{\mathcal{A}}$.
return the matching obtained after applying the augmentations in $\hat{\mathcal{A}}$ to M.

Algorithm 2: Main algorithm.

We note that the formal proofs of Theorem 6.1 and Theorem 6.2 appear in the full version [19], including the multi-pass streaming version of Theorem 6.2. The full version also contains more detailed explanations of the algorithms along with their implementation details in both MPC and multi-pass streaming models.

ACKNOWLEDGMENTS

B. Gamlath, S. Kale and O. Svensson were supported by ERC Starting grant 335288-OptApprox. S. Mitrović was supported in part by the Swiss NSF grant P2ELP2_181772 and MIT-IBM Watson AI Lab. This work was initiated while S. Mitrović was at EPFL and part of it was carried out while he was visiting ETH.

REFERENCES

[1] Kook Jin Ahn and Sudipto Guha. 2013. Linear Programming in the Semi-streaming Model with Application to the Maximum Matching Problem. *Inf. Comput.* 222 (Jan. 2013), 59–79. https://doi.org/10.1016/j.ic.2012.10.006

[2] Kook Jin Ahn and Sudipto Guha. 2018. Access to data and number of iterations: Dual primal algorithms for maximum matching under resource constraints. *ACM Transactions on Parallel Computing (TOPC)* 4, 4 (2018), 17.

[3] Noga Alon, László Babai, and Alon Itai. 1986. A Fast and Simple Randomized Parallel Algorithm for the Maximal Independent Set Problem. *Journal of Algorithms* 7, 4 (1986), 567–583. https://doi.org/10.1016/0196-6774(86)90019-2

[4] Alexandr Andoni, Aleksandar Nikolov, Krzysztof Onak, and Grigory Yaroslavtsev. 2014. Parallel algorithms for geometric graph problems. In *Proceedings of the 46th ACM Symposium on Theory of Computing, STOC 2014, New York, NY, USA, May 31–June 3, 2014.* 574–583. https://doi.org/10.1145/2591796.2591805

[5] Alexandr Andoni, Zhao Song, Clifford Stein, Zhengyu Wang, and Peilin Zhong. 2018. Parallel graph connectivity in log diameter rounds. In *2018 IEEE 59th Annual Symposium on Foundations of Computer Science (FOCS).* IEEE, 674–685.

[6] Sepehr Assadi, MohammadHossein Bateni, Aaron Bernstein, Vahab Mirrokni, and Cliff Stein. 2019. Coresets Meet EDCS: Algorithms for Matching and Vertex Cover on Massive Graphs. In *Proceedings of the 30th Annual ACM-SIAM Symposium on Discrete Algorithms.* SIAM.

[7] Sepehr Assadi, Xiaorui Sun, and Omri Weinstein. 2018. Massively parallel algorithms for finding well-connected components in sparse graphs. *arXiv preprint arXiv:1805.02974* (2018).

[8] Paul Beame, Paraschos Koutris, and Dan Suciu. 2013. Communication steps for parallel query processing. In *Proceedings of the 32nd ACM SIGMOD-SIGACT-SIGART Symposium on Principles of Database Systems, PODS 2013, New York, NY, USA, June 22–27, 2013.* 273–284. https://doi.org/10.1145/2463664.2465224

[9] Soheil Behnezhad, Mahsa Derakhshan, and MohammadTaghi Hajiaghayi. 2018. Brief Announcement: Semi-MapReduce Meets Congested Clique. *arXiv preprint arXiv:1802.10297* (2018).

[10] Soheil Behnezhad, Mahsa Derakhshan, MohammadTaghi Hajiaghayi, and Richard M Karp. 2018. Massively parallel symmetry breaking on sparse graphs: MIS and maximal matching. *arXiv preprint arXiv:1807.06701* (2018).

[11] Soheil Behnezhad, MohammadTaghi Hajiaghayi, and David G Harris. 2019. Exponentially Faster Massively Parallel Maximal Matching. *arXiv preprint arXiv:1901.03744* (2019).

[12] Sebastian Brandt, Manuela Fischer, and Jara Uitto. 2018. Matching and MIS for Uniformly Sparse Graphs in the Low-Memory MPC Model. *arXiv preprint arXiv:1807.05374* (2018).

[13] Thomas H. Cormen, Charles E. Leiserson, Ronald L. Rivest, and Clifford Stein. 2009. *Introduction to Algorithms, Third Edition* (3rd ed.). The MIT Press.

[14] Michael Crouch and Daniel M. Stubbs. 2014. Improved Streaming Algorithms for Weighted Matching, via Unweighted Matching. In *Approximation, Randomization, and Combinatorial Optimization. Algorithms and Techniques (APPROX/RANDOM 2014) (Leibniz International Proceedings in Informatics (LIPIcs)),* Vol. 28. 96–104.

[15] Artur Czumaj, Jakub Łącki, Aleksander Mądry, Slobodan Mitrović, Krzysztof Onak, and Piotr Sankowski. 2018. Round compression for parallel matching algorithms. In *Proceedings of the 50th Annual ACM SIGACT Symposium on Theory of Computing.* ACM, 471–484.

[16] Jeffrey Dean and Sanjay Ghemawat. 2004. MapReduce: Simplified Data Processing on Large Clusters. In *Proceedings of the 6th Conference on Symposium on Opearting Systems Design & Implementation, Volume 6 (OSDI'04).* USENIX Association, Berkeley, CA, USA, 10–10. http://dl.acm.org/citation.cfm?id=1251254.1251264

[17] Sebastian Eggert, Lasse Kliemann, Peter Munstermann, and Anand Srivastav. 2012. Bipartite Matching in the Semi-streaming Model. *Algorithmica* 63, 1 (2012), 490–508.

[18] Joan Feigenbaum, Sampath Kannan, Andrew McGregor, Siddharth Suri, and Jian Zhang. 2005. On graph problems in a semi-streaming model. *Theor. Comput. Sci.* 348, 2 (Dec. 2005), 207–216.

[19] Buddhima Gamlath, Sagar Kale, Slobodan Mitrovic, and Ola Svensson. 2018. Weighted Matchings via Unweighted Augmentations. *CoRR* abs/1811.02760 (2018). arXiv:1811.02760 http://arxiv.org/abs/1811.02760

[20] Mohsen Ghaffari, Themis Gouleakis, Christian Konrad, Slobodan Mitrović, and Ronitt Rubinfeld. 2018. Improved Massively Parallel Computation Algorithms for MIS, Matching, and Vertex Cover. In *Proceedings of the 2018 ACM Symposium on Principles of Distributed Computing.* ACM, 129–138.

[21] Mohsen Ghaffari and Jara Uitto. 2019. Sparsifying distributed algorithms with ramifications in massively parallel computation and centralized local computation. In *Proceedings of the 30th Annual ACM-SIAM Symposium on Discrete Algorithms*. SIAM.

[22] Mohsen Ghaffari and David Wajc. 2019. Simplified and Space-Optimal Semi-Streaming $(2 + \varepsilon)$-Approximate Matching. In *2nd Symposium on Simplicity in Algorithms*. arXiv:1701.03730

[23] Michael T. Goodrich, Nodari Sitchinava, and Qin Zhang. 2011. Sorting, searching, and simulation in the MapReduce framework. In *International Symposium on Algorithms and Computation*. Springer, 374–383.

[24] Nicholas JA Harvey, Christopher Liaw, and Paul Liu. 2018. Greedy and Local Ratio Algorithms in the MapReduce Model. *arXiv preprint arXiv:1806.06421* (2018).

[25] James W Hegeman and Sriram V Pemmaraju. 2015. Lessons from the congested clique applied to MapReduce. *Theoretical Computer Science* 608 (2015), 268–281.

[26] Sungjin Im, Benjamin Moseley, and Xiaorui Sun. 2017. Efficient massively parallel methods for dynamic programming. In *Proceedings of the 49th Annual ACM SIGACT Symposium on Theory of Computing*. ACM, 798–811.

[27] Michael Isard, Mihai Budiu, Yuan Yu, Andrew Birrell, and Dennis Fetterly. 2007. Dryad: Distributed Data-parallel Programs from Sequential Building Blocks. *SIGOPS Operating Systems Review* 41, 3 (March 2007), 59–72. https://doi.org/10.1145/1272998.1273005

[28] Amos Israeli and Alon Itai. 1986. A Fast and Simple Randomized Parallel Algorithm for Maximal Matching. *Inform. Process. Lett.* 22, 2 (1986), 77–80. https://doi.org/10.1016/0020-0190(86)90144-4

[29] Amos Israeli and Yossi Shiloach. 1986. An Improved Parallel Algorithm for Maximal Matching. *Inform. Process. Lett.* 22, 2 (1986), 57–60. https://doi.org/10.1016/0020-0190(86)90141-9

[30] Michael Kapralov. 2013. Better Bounds for Matchings in the Streaming Model. In *Proceedings of the Twenty-fourth Annual ACM-SIAM Symposium on Discrete Algorithms (SODA)*. 1679–1697.

[31] Howard J. Karloff, Siddharth Suri, and Sergei Vassilvitskii. 2010. A Model of Computation for MapReduce. In *Proceedings of the 21st Annual ACM-SIAM Symposium on Discrete Algorithms, SODA 2010, Austin, Texas, USA, January 17–19, 2010*. 938–948. https://doi.org/10.1137/1.9781611973075.76

[32] Richard M Karp, Eli Upfal, and Avi Wigderson. 1986. Constructing a perfect matching is in random NC. *Combinatorica* 6, 1 (1986), 35–48.

[33] Christian Konrad, Frédéric Magniez, and Claire Mathieu. 2012. Maximum Matching in Semi-Streaming with Few Passes. In *Approximation, Randomization, and Combinatorial Optimization. Algorithms and Techniques*, Vol. 7408. Springer, 231. http://arxiv.org/abs/1112.0184

[34] Silvio Lattanzi, Benjamin Moseley, Siddharth Suri, and Sergei Vassilvitskii. 2011. Filtering: a method for solving graph problems in MapReduce. In *Proceedings of the 23rd Annual ACM Symposium on Parallelism in Algorithms and Architectures, SPAA 2011, San Jose, CA, USA, June 4–6, 2011*. 85–94. https://doi.org/10.1145/1989493.1989505

[35] Christoph Lenzen and Roger Wattenhofer. 2010. Brief announcement: Exponential speed-up of local algorithms using non-local communication. In *Proceedings of the 29th ACM SIGACT-SIGOPS symposium on Principles of distributed computing*. ACM, 295–296.

[36] Zvi Lotker, Boaz Patt-Shamir, and Seth Pettie. 2015. Improved Distributed Approximate Matching. *J. ACM* 62, 5, Article 38 (Nov. 2015), 17 pages. https://doi.org/10.1145/2786753

[37] Zvi Lotker, Elan Pavlov, Boaz Patt-Shamir, and David Peleg. 2003. MST construction in O(log log n) communication rounds. ACM, 94–100.

[38] László Lovász. 1979. On determinants, matchings, and random algorithms.. In *FCT*, Vol. 79. 565–574.

[39] Michael Luby. 1986. A Simple Parallel Algorithm for the Maximal Independent Set Problem. *SIAM J. Comput.* 15, 4 (1986), 1036–1053. https://doi.org/10.1137/0215074

[40] Andrew McGregor. 2005. Finding graph matchings in data streams. In *Approximation, Randomization and Combinatorial Optimization. Algorithms and Techniques*. Springer, 170–181.

[41] Ketan Mulmuley, Umesh V Vazirani, and Vijay V Vazirani. 1987. Matching is as easy as matrix inversion. In *Proceedings of the nineteenth annual ACM symposium on Theory of computing*. ACM, 345–354.

[42] Krzysztof Onak. 2018. Round Compression for Parallel Graph Algorithms in Strongly Sublinear Space. *arXiv preprint arXiv:1807.08745* (2018).

[43] Ami Paz and Gregory Schwartzman. 2017. A $(2 + \varepsilon)$-Approximation for Maximum Weight Matching in the Semi-Streaming Model. In *Proceedings of the 28th Annual ACM-SIAM Symposium on Discrete Algorithms*. 2153–2161. https://doi.org/10.1137/1.9781611974782.140 arXiv:http://epubs.siam.org/doi/pdf/10.1137/1.9781611974782.140

[44] Tom White. 2012. *Hadoop: The Definitive Guide*. O'Reilly Media, Inc.

[45] Matei Zaharia, Mosharaf Chowdhury, Michael J. Franklin, Scott Shenker, and Ion Stoica. 2010. Spark: Cluster Computing with Working Sets. In *2nd USENIX Workshop on Hot Topics in Cloud Computing, HotCloud'10, Boston, MA, USA, June 22*. https://www.usenix.org/conference/hotcloud-10/spark-cluster-computing-working-sets

Implementing Mediators with Asynchronous Cheap Talk

Ittai Abraham
ittaia@cs.huji.ac.il
VMWARE

Danny Dolev*
dolev@cs.huji.ac.il
The Hebrew University of Jerusalem
Jerusalem, Israel

Ivan Geffner†
ieg8@cornell.edu
Cornell University

Joseph Y. Halpern‡
halpern@cs.cornell.edu
Cornell University

ABSTRACT

A mediator can help non-cooperative agents obtain an equilibrium that may otherwise not be possible. We study the ability of players to obtain the same equilibrium without a mediator, using only *cheap talk*, that is, nonbinding pre-play communication. Previous work has considered this problem in a synchronous setting. Here we consider the effect of asynchrony on the problem, and provide upper bounds for implementing mediators. Considering asynchronous environments introduces new subtleties, including exactly what solution concept is most appropriate and determining what move is played if the cheap talk goes on forever. Different results are obtained depending on whether the move after such "infinite play" is under the control of the players or part of the description of the game.

CCS CONCEPTS

• **Security and privacy → Formal security models**; *Distributed systems security*; • **Theory of computation → Algorithmic mechanism design**; **Solution concepts in game theory**; • **Networks** → *Network security*;

KEYWORDS

distributed computing, game theory, security

ACM Reference Format:
Ittai Abraham, Danny Dolev, Ivan Geffner, and Joseph Y. Halpern. 2019. Implementing Mediators with Asynchronous Cheap Talk. In *2019 ACM Symposium on Principles of Distributed Computing (PODC '19), July 29-August 2, 2019, Toronto, ON, Canada.* ACM, New York, NY, USA, 10 pages. https://doi.org/10.1145/3293611.3331623

*Supported by The Federmann Cyber Security Center in conjunction with the Israel National Cyber Directorate.
†Supported in part by NSF grant IIS-1703846.
‡Supported in part by NSF grants IIS-1703846 and IIS-1718108, ARO grant W911NF-17-1-0592, and a grant from Open Philanthropy.

PODC '19, July 29-August 2, 2019, Toronto, ON, Canada

ACM ISBN 978-1-4503-6217-7/19/07...$15.00
https://doi.org/10.1145/3293611.3331623

1 INTRODUCTION

Having a trusted mediator often makes solving a problem much easier. For example, a problem such as Byzantine agreement becomes trivial with a mediator: agents can just send their initial input to the mediator, and the mediator sends the majority value back to all the agents, which they then output. Not surprisingly, the question of whether a problem in a multiagent system that can be solved with a trusted mediator can be solved by just the agents in the system, without the mediator, has attracted a great deal of attention in both computer science (particularly in the cryptography community) and game theory. In cryptography, the focus has been on *secure multiparty computation* [12, 15]. Here it is assumed that each agent i has some private information x_i. Fix functions $f_1, \dots, f_n$. The goal is to have agent i learn $f_i(x_1, \dots, x_n)$ without learning anything about x_j for $j \neq i$ beyond what is revealed by the value of $f_i(x_1, \dots, x_n)$. With a trusted mediator, this is trivial: each agent i just gives the mediator its private value x_i; the mediator then sends each agent i the value $f_i(x_1, \dots, x_n)$. Work on multiparty computation provides conditions under which this can be done in a synchronous system [7, 12, 14, 15] and in an asynchronous system [6, 8]. In game theory, the focus has been on whether an equilibrium in a game with a mediator can be implemented using what is called *cheap talk*—that is, just by players communicating among themselves.

In the computer science literature, the interest has been in performing multiparty computation in the presence of possibly malicious adversaries, who do everything they can to subvert the computation. In contrast, in the game theory literature, the assumption is that players have preferences and seek to maximize their utility; thus, they will subvert the computation iff it is in their best interests to do so. In [2, 3] (denoted ADGH and ADH, respectively, in the rest of the paper), it was argued that it is important to consider deviations by both rational players, who have preferences and try to maximize them, and players that we can view as malicious, although it is perhaps better to think of them as rational players whose utilities are not known by the mechanism designer (or other players). ADGH and ADH considered equilibria that are (k, t)-*robust*; roughly speaking, this means that the equilibrium tolerates deviations by up to k rational players, whose utilities are presumed known, and up to t players with unknown utilities. Tight bounds were proved on the ability to implement a (k, t)-robust equilibrium in the game with a mediator using cheap talk in synchronous systems. These bounds depend on, among other things,

(a) the relationship between k, t and n, the total number of players in the system; (b) whether players know the exact utilities of the rational players; and (c) whether the game has a *punishment strategy*, where an m-punishment strategy is a strategy profile that, if used by all but at most m players, guarantees that every player gets a worse outcome than they do with the equilibrium strategy. The following is a high-level overview of results proved in the synchronous setting that will be of most relevance here. For these results, we assume that the communication with the mediator is bounded, it lasts for at most N rounds, and that the mediator can be represented by an arithmetic circuit of depth c.

R1. If $n > 3k + 3t$, then a mediator can be implemented using cheap talk; no punishment strategy is required, no knowledge of other agents' utilities is required, and the cheap-talk protocol has bounded running time $O(nNc)$, independent of the utilities.

R2. If $n > 2k + 3t$, then a mediator can be implemented using cheap talk if there is a $(k + t)$-punishment strategy and the utilities of the rational players are known; the cheap-talk protocol has expected running time $O(nNc)$. (In R2, unlike R1, the cheap-talk protocol may be unbounded, although it has finite expected running time.)

In ADH, lower bounds are presented that match the upper bounds above. Thus, for example, it is shown that $n > 3k+3t$ is necessary in R1; if $n \leq 3k+3t$, then we cannot implement a mediator in general if we do not have a punishment strategy or if the utilities are unknown. The proofs of the upper bounds make heavy use of the fact that the setting is synchronous. Here we consider the impact of asynchrony on these results. Once we introduce asynchrony, we must revisit the question of what it even means to implement an equilibrium using cheap talk. Notions like (Bayesian) Nash equilibrium implicitly assume that all uncertainty is described probabilistically. Having a probability is necessary to talk about an agent's expected utility, given that a certain strategy profile is played. If we were willing to put a distribution on how long messages take to arrive and on when agents are scheduled to move, then we could apply notions like Nash equilibrium without difficulty. However, it is notoriously difficult to quantify this uncertainty. The typical approach used to analyze algorithms in the presence of uncertainty that is not quantified probabilistically is to assume that all the non-probabilistic uncertainty is resolved by the environment according to some strategy. Thus, the environment uses some strategy to decide when each agent will be allowed to play and how long each message takes to be delivered. The algorithm is then proved correct no matter what strategy the environment is following in some class of strategies. For example, we might restrict the environment's strategy to being *fair*, so that every agent eventually gets a chance to move. (See [13] for a discussion of this approach and further references.)

We follow this approach in the context of games. Note that once we fix the environment's strategy, we have an ordinary game, where uncertainty is quantified by probability. In this setting, we consider *ex post equilibrium*. A strategy is an ex post equilibrium if it is an equilibrium no matter what strategy the environment uses. Ex post equilibrium is a strong notion, but, as we show by example, it can often be attained with the help of a mediator. It is arguably the closest analogue to Nash equilibrium in an asynchronous setting.

Another issue that plays a major role in an asynchronous setting is what happens if the strategies of players result in some players being *livelocked*, talking indefinitely without making a move in the underlying game, or in some players being *deadlocked*, waiting indefinitely without moving in the underlying game. We consider two approaches for dealing with this problem. One is called the *default-move approach*. In this approach, as part of the description of the game, there is a default move for each player which is imposed if that player fails to explicitly make a move in the cheap-talk phase. Aumann and Hart [5] considered a different approach, which we henceforth call the *AH approach*, where a player's strategy in the underlying game is a function of the (possibly infinite) history of the player in the cheap-talk phase. We can think of this almost as if the player writes a will, describing what he would like to have done (as a function of the history) if the game ends before he has had a chance to move.

We believe that both the AH approach and the default-move approach are reasonable in different contexts. The AH approach makes sense if the agent can leave instructions that will be carried out by an "executor" if the cheap-talk game deadlocks. But if we consider a game-theoretic variant of Byzantine agreement, it seems more reasonable to say that if a malicious agent can prevent an agent from making a move in finite time, the agent should not get a chance to make a move after the cheap-talk phase has ended.

Our results show that, in the worst case, the cost of asynchrony is an extra $k + t$ in the bounds on n, but we can sometimes save k or even $k + t$ if there is a punishment strategy or if we are willing to tolerate an ϵ "error". For example, with both the AH approach and the default-move approach, if the utilities are not known, we can implement a mediator using asynchronous cheap talk if $n > 4k + 4t$. Thus, compared to R1, we need an extra $k + t$. However, if we are willing to accept a small probability of error, so that rather than implementing the mediator we get only an ϵ-implementation, and are also willing to accept ϵ-(k,t)-robustness (which, roughly speaking, means that players get within ϵ of the best they could get), then we can do this if $n > 3k + 3t$, again, using both the AH approach and the default-move approach.

Just as in the synchronous case, we can do better if we assume that there is a punishment strategy and utilities are known (as in R2). Specifically, with the AH approach, we can implement a mediator if $n > 3k + 4t$ (compared to $n > 2k + 3t$ in the synchronous case), and can ϵ-implement a mediator if $n > 2k + 3t$. We use the punishment to deal with deadlock. If a good player is waiting for a message that never arrives, then the waiting player instructs his executor to carry out a punishment in his will. Having a punishment does not seem to help in the default-move approach unless the default move is a punishment; if it is, then we can get the same results as with the AH approach.

If there is a punishment strategy, these results significantly improve those of Even, Goldreich, and Lempel [10]. They provide a protocol with similar properties, but the expected number of messages sent is $O(1/\epsilon)$; with a punishment strategy, we show that a bounded number of messages can be sent, with the bound being independent of ϵ.

2 DEFINITIONS

Asynchronous games, mediator games, and cheap talk: We are interested in implementing mediators. Formally, this means we need to consider three games: an *underlying game* Γ, an extension Γ_d of Γ with a mediator, and an extension Γ_{CT} of Γ with (asynchronous) cheap talk. We assume that Γ is a *normal-form Bayesian game*: each player has a type t taken from some type space $\mathcal{T}_i$, such that there is a commonly known distribution on $\mathcal{T} \subseteq \mathcal{T}_1 \times \cdots \times \mathcal{T}_n$, the set of types; each player i chooses an action $a \in A_i$, the set of actions of agent i; player i's utility u_i is determined by the type profile of the players and the actions they take. A strategy for player i in the Bayesian game is just a function T_i to A_i, which tells player i what to do, given his type. If $A = A_1 \times \cdots \times A_n$, then a strategy profile $\vec{\sigma} = (\sigma_1, \ldots, \sigma_n)$ can be viewed as a function $\vec{\sigma} : \mathcal{T} \to \Delta(A)$ (where, as usual, $\Delta(X)$ denotes the set of probability distributions on X).

The basic notions of a game with a mediator, a cheap-talk game, and implementation are standard in the game-theory literature. However, since we consider them in an asynchronous setting, we must modify the definitions somewhat.

We first define *asynchronous games*. In an asynchronous game, we assume that players alternate making moves with the environment—first the environment moves, then a player moves, then the environment moves, and so on. The environment's move consists of choosing a player i to move next and a set of messages in transit to i that will be delivered just before i moves (so that i's move can depend on the messages i receives). The environment is subject to two constraints: all messages sent must eventually be delivered and, for all times m and players i, if i is still playing the game at time m, then there must be some time $m' \geq m$ that i is chosen to move. We can describe an asynchronous game by a game tree. Associated with each non-leaf node or history is either a player—the player whose move it is at that node—or the environment (note that both the players and the environment can use probabilistic strategies). The nodes where a player i moves are further partitioned into *information sets*; intuitively, these are nodes that player i cannot tell apart. We assume that the environment has complete information, so that the environment's information sets just consist of the singletons. A *strategy* for player i is a (possibly randomized) function from i's information sets to actions; we can similarly define a strategy for the environment. We can essentially view the environment strategy as defining a scheduler (and thus we sometimes refer to an environment strategy as a scheduler).

For our results, we start with an n-player Bayesian game Γ in normal form (called the *underlying game*), with $\{1, \ldots, n\}$ being the set of players, and then consider two games that *extend* Γ. A game Γ' extends Γ if the players have initial types from the same type space as Γ, with the same distribution over types; moreover, in each path of the game tree for Γ', the players send and receive messages, and perform at most one action from Γ. In a history where each player makes a move from Γ, each player gets the same utility as in Γ (where the utility is a function of the moves made and the types). That leaves open the question of what happens in a complete history of Γ' where some players do not make a move in Γ. As we suggested in the introduction, we consider two approaches to dealing with this. In the first approach, we assume that the description of Γ' includes a function M_i for each player i that maps player i's type to a move in Γ. In an infinite history h where i has type t and does not make a move in Γ, i is viewed as having made move $M_i(t)$. We can then define each player's utility in h as above. This is the *default-move approach*. In the AH approach, we extend the notion of strategy so that i's strategy in Γ' also describes what move i makes in the underlying game Γ in any infinite history h where i has not made a move in Γ. In the AH approach, i's move in h is under i's control; in the default-move approach, it is not.

Given an underlying Bayesian game Γ (which we assume is synchronous—the players move simultaneously), we will be interested in two types of extensions. A *mediator game* extending Γ is an asynchronous game where players can send messages to and receive messages from a mediator (who can be viewed as a trusted third party) as well as making a move in Γ; "good" or "honest" players do not send messages to each other, but "bad" players (i.e., one of the k rational deviating players or one of the t "malicious" players with unknown utilities) may send messages to each other as well as to the mediator. We assume that the space of possible messages that can be sent in a mediator game is fixed and finite.

In an asynchronous cheap-talk game extending Γ, there is no mediator. Players send messages to each other via asynchronous channels, as well as making a move in Γ. We assume that each pair of agents communicates over an *asynchronous authenticated private channel*, so the adversary cannot eavesdrop on conversations between the players, and players can identify the sender of each message. Finally, we assume that in both the mediator game and the cheap-talk game, when a player is first scheduled, it gets a signal that the game has started (either an external signal from the environment, or a game-related message from another player or the mediator).

Implementation: In the synchronous setting, a strategy profile $\vec{\sigma}'$ in a cheap-talk game Γ_{CT} extending an underlying game Γ *implements* a strategy $\vec{\sigma}$ in a mediator game Γ_d extending Γ if $\vec{\sigma}$ and $\vec{\sigma}'$ correspond to the same strategy in Γ; that is, they induce the same function from $\mathcal{T}$ to $\Delta(A)$. The notion of implementation is more complicated in an asynchronous setting, because the probability on action profiles also depends on the environment strategy. Because Γ_{CT} and Γ_d are quite different games, the environment's strategies in Γ_{CT} are quite different from those in Γ_d. So we now say that $\vec{\sigma}'$ implements $\vec{\sigma}$ if the set of distributions on actions profiles in Γ induced by $\vec{\sigma}$ and all possible choices of environment strategy is the same as that induced by $\vec{\sigma}'$ and all possible choices of environment strategy. More precisely, let $\mathcal{S}_{\Gamma',e}$ and $\mathcal{S}_{\Gamma'',e}$ denote the the set of environment strategies in Γ' and Γ'', respectively. A strategy $\sigma_e \in \mathcal{S}_{\Gamma',e}$ and a strategy profile $\vec{\sigma}$ for the players in Γ' together induce a function $(\vec{\sigma}, \sigma_e)$ from $\mathcal{T}$ to $\Delta(A)$. A strategy profile $\vec{\sigma}'$ in Γ' *implements* a strategy profile $\vec{\sigma}''$ in Γ'' if $\{(\vec{\sigma}', \sigma'_e) : \sigma'_e \in \mathcal{S}_{\Gamma',e}\} = \{(\vec{\sigma}'', \sigma''_e) : \sigma''_e \in \mathcal{S}_{\Gamma'',e}\}$. Since the outcome that arises if the players use a particular strategy may depend on what the environment does, this says that the set of outcomes that can result if the players use $\vec{\sigma}'$ is the same as the set of outcomes that can result if the players use $\vec{\sigma}''$.

For some of our results, we cannot get an exact implementation; there may be some error. Given two discrete distributions π and π' on some space S, the *distance* between π and π', denoted $dist(\pi, \pi')$, is at most ϵ if $\sum_{s \in S} |\pi(s) - \pi'(s)| \leq \epsilon$. As we observed earlier, in the mediator game and the cheap-talk game, a strategy profile $\vec{\sigma}$ for the players and a strategy σ_e for the environment together induce a mapping from type profiles to $\Delta(A)$. We lift the notion of distance to such function by defining $dist((\vec{\sigma}, \sigma_e)), (\vec{\sigma}', \sigma_e')) = \max_{\vec{x} \in \mathcal{T}} dist((\vec{\sigma}, \sigma_e)(\vec{x}), (\vec{\sigma}', \sigma_e')(\vec{x}))$. Say that $\vec{\sigma}'$ *ϵ-implements* $\vec{\sigma}''$ if

- for all $\sigma_e' \in \mathcal{S}_{\Gamma',e}$ there exists $\sigma_e'' \in \mathcal{S}_{\Gamma'',e}$ such that $dist((\vec{\sigma}', \sigma_e'), (\vec{\sigma}'', \sigma_e'')) \leq \epsilon$; and
- for all $\sigma_e'' \in \mathcal{S}_{\Gamma'',e}$ there exists $\sigma_e' \in \mathcal{S}_{\Gamma',e}$ such that $dist((\vec{\sigma}'', \sigma_e''), (\vec{\sigma}', \sigma_e')) \leq \epsilon$.

Note that $\vec{\sigma}'$ implements $\vec{\sigma}''$ iff $\vec{\sigma}'$ 0-implements $\vec{\sigma}''$.

The notion of implementation is quite strong. For example, if $\vec{\sigma}'$ involves fewer rounds of communication than $\vec{\sigma}''$, there may be far fewer distinct schedulers in the game involving $\vec{\sigma}'$ than in the game involving $\vec{\sigma}''$. Thus, we may not be able to recover the effect of all possible schedulers. (Indeed, for some of our results the implementation needs to be quite long precisely in order to capture all possible schedulers.) This suggests the following notion: a strategy profile $\vec{\sigma}'$ in Γ' *weakly implements* a strategy profile $\vec{\sigma}''$ in Γ'' if $\{(\vec{\sigma}', \sigma_e') : \sigma_e' \in \mathcal{S}_{\Gamma',e}\} \subseteq \{(\vec{\sigma}'', \sigma_e'') : \sigma_e'' \in \mathcal{S}_{\Gamma'',e}\}$. Thus, if $\vec{\sigma}'$ weakly implements $\vec{\sigma}''$, then every outcome of $\vec{\sigma}'$ is one that could also have arisen with $\vec{\sigma}''$, but the converse may not be true. Specifically, there may be some behaviors of the environment with $\vec{\sigma}''$ that cannot be simulated by $\vec{\sigma}'$. As we shall see, this may actually be a feature: we can sometimes simulate the effect of only "good" schedulers. In any case, note that in the synchronous setting, implementation and weak implementation coincide. We can also define a notion of weak ϵ-implementation in the obvious way; we leave the details to the reader.

Termination: We will be interested in asynchronous games where, almost surely, the honest players stop sending messages and make a move in the underlying game. In the mediator games that we consider, this happens after only a bounded number of messages have been sent. But even with this bound, there may not be a point in a history when players know that they can stop sending messages; although a player i may have moved in the underlying game, i may still need to keep checking for incoming message, and may need to respond to them, to ensure that other players can make the appropriate move.

For some of our results, we must assume that, in the mediator game, there comes a point when all honest players know that they have terminated the protocol; they will not get further messages from the mediator and can stop sending messages to the mediator, and should make a move in the underlying game if they have not done so yet. For simplicity, for these results, we restrict the honest players and the mediator to using strategy profiles that have the following *canonical form*: Using a canonical strategy, player i may send a message to the mediator whenever it is scheduled, as long as i has not received a message from the mediator containing "STOP". If player i gets a message from the mediator that includes "STOP", then i makes a move in the underlying game and halts. We assume that, as long as the honest players and mediator follow their part of the canonical strategy profile, there is a constant r such that, no matter what strategy the rational and malicious players and the environment use, the mediator sends each player i at most r messages in each history, and the final message includes "STOP". We conjecture that the assumption that players and mediator are using a strategy in canonical form in the mediator game is without loss of generality; that is, a (k,t)-robust strategy profile in a mediator game Γ_d can be implemented by a (k,t)-robust strategy profile in Γ_d that is in canonical form.

3 SOLUTION CONCEPTS

In this section, we review the solution concepts introduced in ADGH and extend them to asynchronous settings.

Note that in an asynchronous game Γ, the utility of a player i can depend not only on the strategies of the agents, but on what the environment does. Since we consider an underlying game, a mediator game, and a cheap-talk game, it is useful to include explicitly in the utility function which game is being considered. Thus, we write $u_i(\Gamma, \vec{\sigma}, \sigma_d, \sigma_e, \vec{x})$ to denote the expected utility of player i in game Γ when players play strategy profile $\vec{\sigma}$, the mediator plays σ_d, the environment plays σ_e, and the type profile is $\vec{x}$. We typically say "input profile" rather than "type profile", since in our setting, the type of player i is just i's initial input. Note that if Γ is the underlying game, the σ_e component is unnecessary, since the underlying game is assumed to be synchronous. We occasionally omit the mediator strategy σ_d when it is clear from context.

Given a type space $\mathcal{T}$, a set K of players, and $\vec{x} \in \mathcal{T}$, let $\mathcal{T}(\vec{x}_K) = \{\vec{x}' : \vec{x}'_K = \vec{x}_K\}$. If Γ is a Bayesian game over type space $\mathcal{T}$, $\vec{\sigma}$ is a strategy profile in Γ, and Pr is the probability on the type space $\mathcal{T}$, let

$$u_i(\Gamma, \vec{\sigma}, \sigma_e, \vec{x}_K) = \sum_{\vec{x}' \in \mathcal{T}(\vec{x}_K)} \Pr(\vec{x}' \mid \mathcal{T}(\vec{x}_K))\, u_i(\Gamma, \vec{\sigma}, \sigma_e, \vec{x}').$$

Thus, $u_i(\Gamma, \vec{\sigma}, \sigma_e, \vec{x}_K)$ is i's expected payoff if everyone uses strategy $\vec{\sigma}$ and type profiles are in $\mathcal{T}(\vec{x}_K)$.

k-resilient equilibrium: In a standard game, a strategy profile is a Nash equilibrium if no player can gain any advantage by using a different strategy, given that all the other players do not change their strategies. The notion of k-resilient equilibrium extends Nash equilibrium to allow for coalitions.

Definition 3.1. *$\vec{\sigma}$ is a k-*resilient equilibrium *(resp.,* strongly k-resilient equilibrium*) in an asynchronous game Γ if, for all subsets K of players with $1 \leq |K| \leq k$, all strategy profiles $\vec{\tau}_K$ for the players in K, all type profiles $\vec{x} \in \mathcal{T}$, and all strategies σ_e of the environment, $u_i(\Gamma, (\vec{\sigma}_{-K}, \vec{\tau}_K), \sigma_e, \vec{x}_K) \leq u_i(\Gamma, \vec{\sigma}, \sigma_e, \vec{x}_K)$ for some (resp., all) $i \in K$.*[1]

Thus, $\vec{\sigma}$ is k-resilient if, no matter what the environment does, no subset K of at most k players can all do better by deviating, even if they share their type information (so that if the true type is $\vec{x}$, the players in K know $\vec{x}_K$). It is strongly k-resilient if not even one of the players in K can do better if all the players in K deviate.

For some of our results we will be interested in equilibria that are "almost" k-resilient, in the sense that no player in a coalition can do more than ϵ better if the coalition deviates from the protocol, for some small ϵ.

Definition 3.2. *For $\epsilon > 0$, $\vec{\sigma}$ is an ϵ-k-*resilient equilibrium *(resp.,* strongly ϵ-k-resilient equilibrium*) if, for all subsets K of players, all*

[1] As usual, in the strategy profile $(\vec{\sigma}_{-K}, \vec{\tau}_K)$, each player $i \in K$ plays τ_i and each player $i \notin K$ plays σ_i.

strategy profiles $\vec{\tau}_K$ for the players in K, all type profiles $\vec{x} \in \mathcal{T}$, and all strategies σ_e of the environment, we have $u_i(\Gamma, (\vec{\sigma}_{-K}, \vec{\tau}_K), \sigma_e, \vec{x}_K) < u_i(\Gamma, \vec{\sigma}, \sigma_e, \vec{x}_K) + \epsilon$ for some (resp., for all) $i \in K$.

Note that we have "$< u_i(\Gamma, \vec{\sigma}, \sigma_e, \vec{x}_K) + \epsilon$" here, not "$\leq$"; this means that a 0-$k$-resilient equilibrium is not a k-resilient equilibrium. However, an equilibrium is k-resilient iff it is ϵ-k-resilient for all $\epsilon > 0$. We have used this slightly nonstandard definition to make the statements of our theorems cleaner.

Robustness: A standard assumption in game theory is that utilities are (commonly) known; when we are given a game we are also given each player's utility. When players make decision, they can take other players' utilities into account. However, in large systems, it seems almost invariably the case that there will be some fraction of users who do not respond to incentives the way we expect. For example, in a peer-to-peer network like Kazaa or Gnutella, it would seem that no rational agent should share files. Whether or not you can get a file depends only on whether other people share files; on the other hand, it seems that there are disincentives for sharing (the possibility of lawsuits, use of bandwidth, etc.). Nevertheless, people do share files. However, studies of the Gnutella network have shown almost 70 percent of users share no files and nearly 50 percent of responses are from the top 1 percent of sharing hosts [4]. It seems important to design protocols that tolerate such unanticipated behaviors, so that the payoffs of the users who follow the recommended strategy are not affected by players who deviate, provided that not too many deviate.

Definition 3.3. *A strategy profile $\vec{\sigma}$ is* t-immune *in a game Γ if, for all subsets T of players with $|T| \leq t$, all strategy profiles $\vec{\tau}$, all $i \notin T$, all type profiles $\vec{x} \in \mathcal{T}$, and all strategies σ_e of the environment, we have $u_i(\Gamma, (\vec{\sigma}_{-T}, \vec{\tau}_T), \sigma_e, \vec{x}_T) \geq u_i(\Gamma, \vec{\sigma}, \sigma_e, \vec{x}_T)$.*

Intuitively, $\vec{\sigma}$ is t-immune if there is nothing that players in a set T of size at most t can do to give the players not in T a worse payoff, even if the players in T share their type information.

The notion of t-immunity and k-resilience address different concerns. For t-immunity, we consider the payoffs of the players not in K; for k-resilience, we consider the payoffs of players in K. It is natural to combine both notions. Given a strategy profile $\vec{\tau}$, let $\Gamma^T_{\vec{\tau}}$ be the game which is identical to Γ except that the players in T are fixed to playing strategy $\vec{\tau}_T$.

Definition 3.4. *$\vec{\sigma}$ is a* (strongly) (k,t)-robust *equilibrium in a game Γ if $\vec{\sigma}$ is t-immune and, for all subsets T of players with $|T| \leq t$ and all strategy profiles $\vec{\tau}$, $(\vec{\sigma}_{-T}, \vec{\tau}_T)$ is a (strongly) k-resilient equilibrium of $\Gamma^T_{\vec{\tau}}$.*

We can define "approximate" notions of t-immunity and (k,t)-robustness analogous to Definition 3.2:

Definition 3.5. *For $\epsilon > 0$, a strategy profile $\vec{\sigma}$ is* ϵ-t-immune *in Γ if, for all subsets T of players with $|T| \leq t$, all strategy profiles $\vec{\tau}$, all $i \notin T$, all type profiles $\vec{x} \in \mathcal{T}$, and all strategies σ_e of the environment, we have $u_i(\Gamma, (\vec{\sigma}_{-T}, \vec{\tau}_T), \sigma_e, \vec{x}_T) > u_i(\Gamma, \vec{\sigma}, \sigma_e, \vec{x}_T) - \epsilon$.*

Definition 3.6. *For $\epsilon \geq 0$, $\vec{\sigma}$ is a* (strongly) ϵ-(k,t)-robust *equilibrium in Γ if $\vec{\sigma}$ is ϵ-t-immune and, for all subsets T of players with $|T| \leq t$ and strategy profiles $\vec{\tau}_T$, $(\vec{\sigma}_{-T}, \vec{\tau}_T)$ is a (strongly) ϵ-k-resilient equilibrium of $\Gamma^T_{\vec{\tau}}$.*

4 MAIN THEOREMS: FORMAL STATEMENTS

In this section, we state our results formally. We begin with a result that is an analogue of R1 in the asynchronous setting. We say that a game Γ' is a utility variant of a game Γ if Γ' and Γ have the same game tree, but the utilities of the players may be different in Γ and Γ'. We use the notation $\Gamma(\vec{u})$ if we want to emphasize that $\vec{u}$ is the utility function in game Γ. We then take $\Gamma(\vec{u}')$ to be the utility variant of Γ with utility function $\vec{u}'$.

Two more technical comments before stating the theorems: in the mediator game we can also view the mediator as a player (albeit one without a utility function) that is following a strategy. Thus, when we talk about a strategy profile that is a (k,t)-robust equilibrium in the mediator game, we must give the mediator's strategy as well as the players' strategies. We sometimes write $\vec{\sigma} + \sigma_d$ if we want to distinguish the players' strategy profile $\vec{\sigma}$ from the mediator's strategy σ_d. We occasionally abuse notation and drop the σ_d if it is clear from context, and just talk about $\vec{\sigma}$ being a (k,t)-robust equilibrium.

In general, we do not have a bound on the number of messages sent in our implementation. However, we can get a polynomial bound if we restrict the mediator to using what we call a *responsive* strategy. Roughly speaking, a responsive strategy is one where (1) the mediator sends messages only initially or in response to receiving a message since the last time it moved; (2) if it has received a message since the last time it was scheduled, it acts just as it would have acted if the message had been received immediately after the last time it acted (rather than possibly being received after a number of times that the mediator was scheduled without receiving a new message); and (3) there is a bound C such that the mediator uses at most C random bits in each run. see [11] for the formal definition.

Theorem 4.1. *If Γ is a normal-form Bayesian game with n players, $\vec{\sigma} + \sigma_d$ is a strategy profile for the players and the mediator in an asynchronous mediator game Γ_d that extends Γ, and $n > 4k + 4t$, then with both the default-move approach and the AH approach, there exists a strategy profile $\vec{\sigma}_{CT}$ that implements $\vec{\sigma} + \sigma_d$ in the asynchronous cheap-talk game Γ_{CT} such that for all utility variants $\Gamma_d(\vec{u}')$ of Γ_d, if $\vec{\sigma} + \sigma_d$ is a (strongly) (k,t)-robust equilibrium in $\Gamma_d(\vec{u}')$, then $\vec{\sigma}_{CT}$ is a (strongly) (k,t)-robust equilibrium in $\Gamma_{CT}(\vec{u}')$. If σ_d is responsive, the number of messages sent in a history of $\vec{\sigma}_{CT}$ is polynomial in n and N, linear in c, and independent of $\vec{u}'$.*

The proof of Theorem 4.1 uses ideas from the multiparty computation protocol of Ben-Or, Canetti, and Goldreich [6] (BCG from now on). Our construction actually needs stronger properties than these provided by BCG; we show that we can get protocols with these stronger properties in a companion paper [11]; see Section 5 for further discussion.

We can obtain better bounds if we are willing to accept ϵ-equilibrium, using ideas due to Ben-Or, Kelmer, and Rabin [8].

Theorem 4.2. *If Γ is a normal-form Bayesian game with n players, $\vec{\sigma} + \sigma_d$ is a strategy profile for the players and mediator in an asynchronous mediator game Γ_d that extends Γ, $M > 0$, and $n > 3k + 3t$, then with both the default-move approach and the AH approach, for all $\epsilon > 0$, there exists a strategy profile $\vec{\sigma}_{CT}$ in the asynchronous cheap-talk game Γ_{CT} that ϵ-implements $\vec{\sigma}$ such that for all utility variants $\Gamma_d(\vec{u}')$ of Γ_d bounded by $M/2$ (i.e., where the range of u_i'*

is contained in $[-M/2, M/2]$), if $\vec{\sigma} + \sigma_d$ is a (strongly) (k,t)-robust equilibrium in $\Gamma_d(\vec{u}')$, then $\vec{\sigma}_{CT}$ is a (strongly) ϵ-(k,t)-robust equilibrium in $\Gamma_{CT}(\vec{u}')$. If σ_d is responsive, the number of messages sent in a history of $\vec{\sigma}_{CT}$ is polynomial in n and N, linear in c, and independent of $\vec{u}'$.

If we have a punishment strategy and utilities are known, we can do better with the AH approach. To make this precise, we need the definition of an m-punishment strategy [2] (which generalizes the notion of punishment strategy defined by Ben Porath [9]). Before defining this carefully, note that in an asynchronous setting (i.e., in the mediator game and the cheap-talk game, but not in the underlying game), the utility of players depends on the environment's strategy as well as the players' strategy profile and the players' type profile.

DEFINITION 4.3. *If Γ' is an extension of an underlying game Γ, a strategy profile $\vec{\rho}$ in Γ is a k-*punishment strategy *with respect to a strategy profile $\vec{\sigma}'$ in Γ' if for all subsets K of players with $1 \leq |K| \leq k$, all strategy profiles $\vec{\sigma}$ in Γ, all strategies σ_e for the environment, all type profiles $\vec{x} \in \mathcal{T}$, and all players $i \in K$, we have*

$$u_i(\Gamma', \vec{\sigma}', \sigma_e, \vec{x}_K) > u_i(\Gamma, (\vec{\sigma}_K, \vec{\rho}_{-K}), \vec{x}_K).$$

Thus, if $\vec{\rho}$ is a k-punishment strategy with respect to $\vec{\sigma}'$ and all but k players play their part of $\vec{\rho}$ in the underlying tame, then all of the remaining players will be worse off than they would be in Γ' if everyone had played $\vec{\sigma}'$, no matter what they do in the underlying game.

THEOREM 4.4. *If Γ is a normal-form Bayesian game with n players, $\vec{\sigma} + \sigma_d$ is a strategy profile in canonical form for the players and mediator in an asynchronous mediator game Γ_d that extends Γ, there is a $(k+t)$-punishment strategy with respect to $\vec{\sigma}+\sigma_d$, and $n > 3k+4t$, then with the AH approach, there exists a strategy profile $\vec{\sigma}_{CT}$ that implements $\vec{\sigma} + \sigma_d$ in the asynchronous cheap-talk game Γ_{CT}, and if $\vec{\sigma} + \sigma_d$ is a (strongly) (k,t)-robust equilibrium in Γ_d, then $\vec{\sigma}_{CT}$ is a (strongly) (k,t)-robust equilibrium in Γ_{CT}. If we require only that $\vec{\sigma}_{CT}$ is a weak implementation, then the number of messages in a history of $\vec{\sigma}_{CT}$ is polynomial in n and linear in c.*

Note that in Theorem 4.4, the running time of the algorithm is significantly affected by whether we want $\vec{\sigma}_{CT}$ to implement $\vec{\sigma}$ or whether a weak implementation suffices.

If we assume both that there is a $(2k+2t)$-punishment strategy and that utilities are known, we can get an analogue to R2, but with an ϵ error.

THEOREM 4.5. *If Γ is a normal-form Bayesian game with n players, $\vec{\sigma} + \sigma_d$ is a strategy profile in canonical form for the players and mediator in an asynchronous mediator game Γ_d that extends Γ, there is a $(2k+2t)$-punishment strategy with respect to $\vec{\sigma}+\sigma_d$, and $n > 2k+3t$, then with the AH approach, for all $\epsilon > 0$ there is a strategy $\vec{\sigma}_{CT}$ that ϵ-implements $\vec{\sigma}$ in the asynchronous cheap-talk game Γ_{CT} such that if $\vec{\sigma} + \sigma_d$ is a (strongly) (k,t)-robust equilibrium in Γ_d, then $\vec{\sigma}_{CT}$ is a (strongly) ϵ-(k,t)-robust equilibrium in Γ_{CT}. If we require only that $\vec{\sigma}_{CT}$ is a weak implementation, then the number of messages in a history of $\vec{\sigma}_{CT}$ is polynomial in n and linear in c.*

We prove these results using ideas in the spirit of ADGH, but much more care must be taken to deal with asynchrony. Among other things, we need stronger security guarantees than are traditionally provided for multiparty communication; see Section 5 for details.

5 BISIMULATION AND COTERMINATION

Ben-Or, Goldwasser, and Wigderson [7] (BGW from now on) and Ben-Or, Canetti, and Goldreich [6] (BCG from now on) show that if a function f of n inputs provided by n players can be computed using a mediator, then it can be computed by the players without the mediator and without revealing any information beyond the function value, even when some of the players are malicious. BGW deal with the synchronous case and provide a protocol that tolerates up to $n/3$ malicious players; BCG deal with the asynchronous case and provide a protocol that tolerates up to $n/4$. The notion of not revealing any information is made precise by defining a set of *ideal* distributions over possible values of the function, and ensuring that the *real* distribution is identically distributed to one of those (see BGW and BCG for formal definitions and details).

We can view a mediator game as computing an action profile in the underlying game; the ideal distributions are the possible distributions over action profiles when the honest players play their component of the (k,t)-robust equilibrium strategy profile in the mediator game. BCG's protocol then essentially gives us a strategy in the cheap-talk game. However, the BCG protocol is not sufficient for our purposes for two reasons: it does not guarantee that the real protocol is an implementation of the ideal protocol in the sense of the definition in Section 2 (although it does suffice for *weak* implementation), nor does it guarantee that the protocol is a (k,t)-robust equilibrium. To prove these stronger results, we show that $\vec{\sigma}_{CT}$ can be constructed so as to satisfy some additional security properties, which we now define. For some of these definitions, it will be useful to introduce the notion of *adversary*. An adversary A is a tuple $(T, \vec{\tau}_T, \sigma_e)$ consisting of a set T of malicious players, a strategy $\vec{\tau}_T$ for players in T, and a strategy σ_e for the scheduler. To keep the notation as simple as possible, we omit the set T when it is clear from context, just writing A as the pair $(\vec{\tau}_T, \sigma_e)$. (Note that $\vec{\tau}_T$ is just a tuple of $|T|$ strategies. We write this tuple as $\vec{\tau}_T$ only because we view it as the strategies played by the players in T in the profile $\vec{\tau}$.)

DEFINITION 5.1 (t-BISIMULATION). *Let $\vec{\pi}(\vec{x}, A)$ be the distribution over outputs when running strategy $\vec{\pi}$ with adversary $A = (\tau_T, \sigma_e)$. Protocol $\vec{\pi}'$ t-*bisimulates *$\vec{\pi} + \pi_d$ if, for all T with $|T| \leq t$ and inputs $\vec{x}$:*

- *for all adversaries $A = (\vec{\tau}_T, \sigma_e)$, there exists an adversary $A' = (\vec{\tau}_T', \sigma_e')$ such that $\vec{\pi}(\vec{x}, A)$ and $\vec{\pi}'(\vec{x}, A')$ identically distributed;*
- *for all adversaries $A' = (\vec{\tau}_T', \sigma_e')$, there exists an adversary $A = (\vec{\tau}_T, \sigma_e)$ such that $\vec{\pi}(\vec{x}, A)$ and $\vec{\pi}'(\vec{x}, A')$ are identically distributed.*

Note that 0-bisimulation is equivalent to implementation. While implementation considers only what happens when there is no malicious behaviour, t-bisimulation generalizes this notion by taking malicious behavior into account. For some of our results (specifically, Theorems 4.1 and 4.2), we use this notion, and show that it is achievable under the conditions of these theorems.

We have required schedulers to eventually deliver each message that is sent. Because we assume that protocols in the mediator game are bounded, all protocols in the mediator game must terminate. This means that we can't hope to simulate a protocol in the cheap-talk game that deadlocks. (We assume that if the protocol deadlocks, it has a special output that we denote $\perp$. Given our constraints, we can never get an output of $\perp$ in the mediator game.) To deal with this situation, we relax this requirement on schedulers somewhat, but only in the mediator game. We take a *relaxed scheduler* to be one that may never deliver some messages. There is no requirement on messages sent by the players. We can define *relaxed t-bisimulation* just as we defined t-bisimulation, except that we allow the schedulers σ_e' and σ_e to be relaxed schedulers. Finally, we define *(t, t')-bisimulation* just as we defined relaxed t-bisimulation except that σ_e' and σ_e must be standard if $|T| \leq t'$ (note that t' must be smaller than t).

We need a further property to deal with protocols that involve punishment strategies. For a punishment strategy to be effective, all the honest players have to play it. In our protocols, the punishment strategy is played when there is a deadlock (so some players never terminate); that is, the punishment strategy is in the honest players' "wills". Thus, we want it to be the case that either none of the honest players terminate (in which case the punishment strategy will be effective) or all of them do; we do not want it to be the case that only some of the honest players terminate.

Definition 5.2 ((t, t')-cotermination). *A protocol $\vec{\pi}$ (t, t')-coterminates if, for all schedulers σ_e, all subsets T of at most t players, and all strategy profiles $\vec{\tau}_T$ for the players in T, in all histories of the protocol $(\vec{\pi}_{-T}, \vec{\tau}_T, \sigma_e)$, either all the players not in T terminate, or at most t' players not in T do. We say that $\vec{\pi}$ t-coterminates if it $(t, 0)$-coterminates.*

For some of our results, we need "approximate" versions of t-bisimulation, relaxed t-bisimulation, (t, t') bisimulation, t-cotermination and (t, t')-cotermination, that allow an ϵ probability of error. For t-bisimulation, relaxed t-bisimulation, and (t, t') bisimulation, this means that the distance between the distribution over outputs in the cheap-talk game and the distribution over outputs in the mediator game is at most ϵ (where the notion of distance is that used in the definition of ϵ-implementation in Section 2), while for t-cotermination and (t, t')-cotermination it means that the property holds with probability $1 - \epsilon$. We call these properties *ϵ-t-bisimulation, relaxed ϵ-t-bisimulation, ϵ-(t, t')-bisimulation, ϵ-t-cotermination,* and *ϵ-(t, t')-cotermination* respectively. In our companion paper [11], we prove the following results:

Theorem 5.3. *Given a mediator game Γ_d extending Γ and a strategy profile $\vec{\sigma} + \sigma_d$ in Γ_d in canonical form, there exists a strategy profile $\vec{\sigma}_{CT}$ for Γ_{CT} such that $\vec{\sigma}_{CT}$ $(t, 2t+1)$-coterminates and t-bisimulates (resp., (t, t')-bisimulates) $\vec{\sigma} + \sigma_d$ if $t < n/3$ and $t < n/4$ (resp., $3t + t' < n$) respectively. If σ_d is responsive, the number of messages sent in a history of $\vec{\sigma}_{CT}$ is polynomial in n and N, linear in c, and independent of $\vec{u}'$.*

Theorem 5.4. *Given a mediator game Γ_d extending Γ, a strategy profile $\vec{\sigma} + \sigma_d$ in Γ_d in canonical form, and a real number $\epsilon \in (0, 1]$, there exists a strategy profile $\vec{\sigma}_{CT}$ in Γ_{CT} such that $\vec{\sigma}_{CT}$ ϵ-$(t, t+1)$-coterminates and ϵ-t-bisimulates (resp., ϵ-(t, t')-bisimulates) $\vec{\sigma} + \sigma_d$ if $t < n/2$ and $t < n/3$ (resp., $2t + t' < n$) respectively. If σ_d is responsive, the number of messages sent in a history of $\vec{\sigma}_{CT}$ is polynomial in n and N, linear in c, and independent of $\vec{u}'$.*

We use the constructions provided by Theorems 5.3 and 5.4 to prove Theorems 4.1, 4.2, 4.4, and 4.5. For Theorems 4.1 and 4.2, we show that these constructions already satisfy all the desired properties. For Theorems 4.4 and 4.5, $(t + k, t)$-bisimulation and ϵ-$(t + k, t)$-bisimulation guarantee that that the only way in which rational and malicious players can make the outcome of the cheap-talk game different from that of the mediator game is by preventing the honest players from terminating. However, it is not in the interest of rational players that too many honest players end in deadlock, since if enough honest players do not terminate, they play the punishment strategy according to their wills.

We then show that the construction for Theorems 5.3 and 5.4 can be easily modified so that $\vec{\sigma}_{CT}$ terminate or none does. It would then seem that to always be in the interest of rational players that all honest players terminate. Unfortunately, a punishment strategy payoff is worse for rational players than the equilibrium payoff only in expectation, and thus, depending on the information rational players receive throughout the game, there might be some situations in which they might actually want to be punished (we provide a concrete example in the full paper). We deal with this issue by showing that all mediator games can be reduced to a mediator game where the mediator uses a *minimally-informative strategy*, so that players receive no information about the outcome until the very end. This makes the punishment strategy a persistent threat for rational players. The proof of Theorem 4.1 is given in Section 6.3, while the proofs of Theorems 4.2, 4.4 and 4.5 can be found in the full paper.

6 PROOFS OF THE MAIN THEOREMS

In this section, we sketch the proof of the main theorems. The details can be found in the full paper [1].

6.1 Coordination between the environment and malicious players

Before proving the main results, it is useful to understand some of the implication of (k, t)-robustness, particularly when it comes to the interactions between the environment and the malicious and rational players. The definition of (k, t)-robustness requires that rational players have no profitable deviation, no matter what the malicious players and the environment do. It may seem *a priori* that the malicious players, the rational players, and the environment all act independently, but in fact, we can assume without loss of generality that they are all under the control of a single adversary. Clearly rational players can coordinate by sending messages to each other. The malicious and rational players can also coordinate with the environment so that, for example, the malicious and rational players can act knowing who will be scheduled when and the environment can schedule rational and malicious players based on their inputs. This follows from the fact that (k, t)-robustness must hold for all schedulers.

To see that a player i can communicate with the environment, recall that we have assumed that the message space is finite, say

$\{m_0, \ldots, m_M\}$. Immediately after sending m_j, i sends j empty messages to itself. So, even though the environment cannot read the messages, it will know that i sent message m_j.[2] (Clearly the environment will also know who sent the message, since the environment delivered the message.) Thus, we can assume without loss of generality that the rational and malicious players know the environment's protocol (and thus know when a message that is sent will be delivered), hence it suffices for the environment to tell the non-honest players when the kth message is sent, who sent it, and who the intended recipient is. All the non-honest players i initially send themselves $(n+1)^2$ empty messages. If the first message was sent by player j_1 to player j_2 (treating the mediator as player 0 in the mediator game), then the environment delivers $(n+1)j_1 + j_2$ of these empty messages. Then player i sends another $(n+1)^2$ empty messages, allowing the environment to encode the sender and receiver of the next message, if there is one.

The fact that the environment and the malicious players can communicate allows us to prove a tighter correspondence between deviations in the cheap-talk game and deviations in the mediator game than the one given by t-bisimulation.

PROPOSITION 6.1. *Given two protocols $\vec{\pi}$ and $\vec{\pi}'$ and a scheduler σ_e, if $\vec{\pi}'$ t-bisimulates $\vec{\pi}$, there exists a function H_{σ_e} from strategies to strategies such that $H_{\sigma_e}(\vec{\pi}_i) = \vec{\pi}_i'$ for all i, and for all adversaries $A = (\vec{\tau}_T, \sigma_e)$ with $|T| \leq t$, there exists a scheduler σ_e' such that for all inputs $\vec{x}$, $\vec{\pi}(\vec{x}, A)$ and $\vec{\pi}'(\vec{x}, (H_{\sigma_e}(\vec{\tau}_T), \sigma_e'))$ are identically distributed (where we extend H_{σ_e} to strategy profiles by taking $H_{\sigma_e}(\tau_1, \ldots, \tau_m) = (H_{\sigma_e}(\tau_1), \ldots, H_{\sigma_e}(\tau_m))$).*

PROOF. Since $\vec{\pi}'$ t-bisimulates $\vec{\pi} + \pi_d$, for each adversary $A = (\vec{\tau}_T, \sigma_e)$, there exists an adversary $A' = (\vec{\tau}_T', \sigma_e')$ such that $\vec{\pi}(\vec{x}, A)$ and $\vec{\pi}'(\vec{x}, A')$ are identically distributed for all inputs $\vec{x}$. This means that, fixing σ_e, there exists a well-defined function $H_{\sigma_e}^{adv}$ from strategy profiles to adversaries such that for all subsets T with $|T| \leq t$ and all strategies $\vec{\tau}_T$ for players in T, there exists a scheduler σ_e' such that $(\vec{\pi} + \pi_d)(\vec{x}, (\vec{\tau}_T, \sigma_e))$ and $\vec{\pi}'(\vec{x}, H_{\sigma_e}^{adv}(\vec{\tau}_T))$ for all inputs $\vec{x}$. Given an adversary $A = (\vec{\tau}_T, \sigma_e)$, consider the following adversary $A' = (\vec{\tau}_T', \sigma_e')$:

(1) The scheduler begins the game by scheduling all players in T once.
(2) Each player $i \in T$ sends the description of the strategy $\vec{\tau}_i$ to the scheduler σ_e' the first time it is scheduled.
(3) After receiving the strategies of the players in T, the scheduler computes $H_{\sigma_e}^{adv}(\vec{\tau}_T)$ and sends each player $i \in T$ the (description of) strategy $H_{\sigma_e}^{adv}(\vec{\tau}_T)_i$, and then switches to using $H_{\sigma_e}^{adv}(\vec{\tau}_T)_e$.
(4) Each player $i \in T$ switches to the strategy sent by the scheduler after receiving it.

Consider the function H_{σ_e} that maps τ_i to τ_i' if $\tau_i \neq \pi_i$ and maps π_i to π_i' (note that H_{σ_e} is well defined, since τ_i' does not depend on the strategy of other players in T) and a scheduler σ_e'' that acts like σ_e' except that at step 1, it schedules only the players i in T such that $\tau_i \neq \pi_i$. We have by construction that $\vec{\pi}(\vec{x}, A) = \vec{\pi}'(\vec{x}, H_{\sigma_e}^{adv}(\vec{\tau}_T))$ and therefore that $\vec{\pi}(\vec{x}, A) = \vec{\pi}'(\vec{x}, (H_{\sigma_e}(\vec{\tau}_T), \sigma_e''))$, as desired. □

[2]We can encode m_j using using fewer messages by having i send message to other agents as well as itself. Our goal here is not to minimize the number of messages, but to show that communication with the environment is possible.

Proposition 6.1 implies that we can assume without loss of generality that individual deviations in the mediator game correspond to individual deviations in the cheap-talk game and vice-versa. An analogous result holds for ϵ-t-bisimulation:

PROPOSITION 6.2. *Given two protocols $\vec{\pi}$ and $\vec{\pi}'$ and a scheduler σ_e, if $\vec{\pi}'$ ϵ-t-bisimulates $\vec{\pi}$, there exists a function H_{σ_e} from strategies to strategies such that $H_{\sigma_e}(\vec{\pi}_i) = \vec{\pi}_i'$ for all i, and for all adversaries $A = (\vec{\tau}_T, \sigma_e)$ with $|T| \leq t$, there exists a scheduler σ_e' such that for all inputs $\vec{x}$, the distance between the distributions $\vec{\pi}(\vec{x}, A)$ and $\vec{\pi}'(\vec{x}, (H_{\sigma_e}(\vec{\tau}_T), \sigma_e'))$ is at most ϵ (where the notion of distance is that used in the definition of ϵ-implementation in Section 2).*

As we show next, since the scheduler can collude with malicious players, t-immune strategy profiles satisfy an even stronger condition: deviations by players in a set T with $|T| \leq t$ do not make things worse for the non-deviating players even if the environment colludes with the players in T.

PROPOSITION 6.3. *If $\vec{\sigma}$ is t-immune, then for all sets T of players with $|T| \leq t$, strategies σ_e and σ_e' for the environment, strategy profiles $\vec{\tau}_T$ for the players in T, input profiles $\vec{x}$ and $\vec{x}'$, and players $i \notin T$, we have*

$$u_i(\Gamma_d, (\vec{\sigma}_{-T}, \vec{\tau}_T), \sigma_e', \vec{x}_T') \geq u_i(\Gamma_d, \vec{\sigma}, \sigma_e, \vec{x}_T). \quad (1)$$

PROOF. Clearly, if (1) holds for all σ_e, σ_e', $\vec{x}$, and $\vec{x}'$, then $\vec{\sigma}$ is t-immune. For the converse, suppose by way of contradiction that $\vec{\sigma}$ is t-immunte but for some T, $\vec{\tau}$, σ_e, σ_e', and $i \notin T$, (1) does not hold. Consider a scheduler σ_e'' that acts just like σ_e, except that if some player i sends a message to itself it acts like σ_e'. Then players in T can effectively decrease i's payoff with scheduler σ_e'' by sending a message to themselves and playing as if they had input $\vec{x}_T'$; that is, there is a strategy $\vec{\tau}_T'$ such that

$$\begin{array}{rl} & u_i(\Gamma_d, (\vec{\sigma}_{-T}, \vec{\tau}_T'), \sigma_e'', \vec{x}_T) \\ = & u_i(\Gamma_d, (\vec{\sigma}_{-T}, \vec{\tau}_T), \sigma_e', \vec{x}_T') \\ < & u_i(\Gamma_d, \vec{\sigma}, \sigma_e, \vec{x}_T) \\ = & u_i(\Gamma_d, \vec{\sigma}, \sigma_e'', \vec{x}_T), \end{array}$$

contradicting the assumption that $\vec{\sigma}$ is t-immune. □

A similar argument shows that (k,t)-robust strategy profiles satisfy a correspondingly stronger condition, made precise in the following proposition:

PROPOSITION 6.4. *A strategy profile $\vec{\sigma}$ is (k,t)-robust (resp., strongly (k,t)-robust) if and only if it is t-immune and for all disjoint sets K and T with $1 \leq |K| \leq k$ and $|T| \leq t$, all strategy profiles $\vec{\tau}_K$, $\vec{\tau}_T$, and $\vec{\tau}_T'$ for the players in K and T, respectively, all environment strategies σ_e and σ_e', and all input profiles $\vec{x}$ and $\vec{x}'$, we have that*

$$\begin{array}{rl} & u_i(\Gamma_d, (\vec{\sigma}_{-(K\cup T)}, \vec{\tau}_K, \vec{\tau}_T'), \sigma_e', \vec{x}_{(K\cup T)}') \\ \leq & u_i(\Gamma_d, (\vec{\sigma}_{-(K\cup T)}, \vec{\tau}_K, \vec{\tau}_T'), \sigma_e', \vec{x}_{(K\cup T)}') \end{array} \quad (2)$$

for some $i \in K$ (resp., for all $i \in K$).

PROOF. Again, it is clear that if (2) holds for all K and T with $1 \leq |K| \leq k$ and $|T| \leq t$, all $\vec{\tau}_K$, $\vec{\tau}_T$, $\vec{\tau}_T'$, $\vec{x}$, and $\vec{x}'$, and some (resp., all) $i \in K$, then $\vec{\sigma}$ is (k,t)-robust (resp., strongly (k,t)-robust).

For the converse, assume by way of contradiction that $\vec{\sigma}$ is (k,t)-robust, but for some disjoint sets K and T with $1 \leq |K| \leq k$ and $|T| \leq t$, $\vec{\tau}_K$, $\vec{\tau}_T$, $\vec{\tau}_T'$, $\vec{x}$, and $\vec{x}'$, and all $i \in K$, (2) does not hold. Again, we use the fact that the rational players can effectively communicate with malicious players and with the scheduler. Consider a scheduler σ_e'' that acts like σ_e unless some player sends a message to itself, in which case it acts like σ_e', and a strategy profile $\vec{\tau}_T''$ in which each player $i \in T$ acts as if it was using strategy $(\tau_T)_i$, except that it switches to $(\tau_T')_i$ and acts as if it has input x_i' if it receives a message from a rational player (i.e., a player in K) asking it to do so. Then, given input profile $\vec{x}$, strategy profile $\vec{\tau}_T''$ for T, and scheduler σ_e'', player i can gain by sending a message to itself and sending a message to players in T asking them to follow $\vec{\tau}_T'$ and to act is if they have input $\vec{x}_T'$, and by having players in K play $\vec{\tau}_K$ as if they had input $\vec{x}_K'$, rather than playing $\vec{\sigma}$. This contradicts the assumption that $\vec{\sigma}$ is (k, t)-robust. The argument for strong (k, t)-robustness is analogous. □

Another property interesting in its own right that follows from this argument is that (k, t)-robust strategies must be *scheduler-proof*: the expected payoff for all players is the same regardless of the scheduler:

COROLLARY 6.5. *If $\vec{\sigma}$ is (k, t)-robust for some $k \geq 1$, then for all sets T with $|T| \leq t$, strategy profiles $\vec{\tau}_T$ for the players in T, environment strategies σ_e and σ_e', input profiles $\vec{x}$, and players $i \notin T$, we have $u_i(\Gamma, (\vec{\sigma}_{-T}, \vec{\tau}_T), \sigma_e, \vec{x}_T) = u_i(\Gamma, (\vec{\sigma}_{-T}, \vec{\tau}_T), \sigma_e', \vec{x}_T)$.*

We have analogous strengthenings of ϵ-t-immunity and ϵ-(k, t)-robustness, which are stated next. The proofs are essentially identical to that of Proposition 6.3 and 6.4 respectively, so we omit them here.

PROPOSITION 6.6. *If $\epsilon > 0$ and $\vec{\sigma}$ is ϵ-t-immune in game Γ, then for all sets T of players with $|T| \leq t$, strategy profiles τ_T for the players in T, environment strategies σ_e and σ_e', input profiles $\vec{x}$ and $\vec{x}'$, and players $i \notin T$, we have that*

$$u_i(\Gamma, (\vec{\sigma}_{-T}, \vec{\tau}_T), \sigma_e', \vec{x}_T') > u_i(\Gamma, \vec{\sigma}, \sigma_e, \vec{x}_T) - \epsilon.$$

PROPOSITION 6.7. *A strategy profile $\vec{\sigma}$ is ϵ-(k, t)-robust (resp., strongly ϵ-(k, t)-robust) in game Γ if and only if it is ϵ-t-immune and, for all disjoint sets K and T of players with $1 \leq |K| \leq k$ and $|T| \leq t$, all strategy profiles $\vec{\tau}_K$, $\vec{\tau}_T'$, and $\vec{\tau}_T$ for players in K and T, respectively, all environment strategies σ_e and σ_e', and all input profiles $\vec{x}$ and $\vec{x}'$, we have that*

$$u_i(\Gamma, (\vec{\sigma}_{-(K\cup T)}, \vec{\tau}_K, \vec{\tau}_T'), \sigma_e', \vec{x}_{(K\cup T)}') < u_i(\Gamma, (\vec{\sigma}_{-T}, \vec{\tau}_T), \sigma_e, \vec{x}_T) + \epsilon$$

for some $i \in K$ (resp., for all $i \in K$).

It will be useful for our later results that we can actually improve on the bound of ϵ in Propositions 6.6 and 6.7.

PROPOSITION 6.8. *If $\vec{\sigma}$ is an ϵ-t-immune strategy in a finite game Γ, then there exists ϵ_0 with $0 < \epsilon_0 < \epsilon$ such that for all sets of players T with $|T| \leq t$, strategy profiles $\vec{\tau}_T$ for the players in T, environment strategies σ_e and σ_e', input profiles $\vec{x}$ and $\vec{x}'$, and players $i \notin T$, we have that*

$$u_i(\Gamma, (\vec{\sigma}_{-T}, \vec{\tau}_T), \sigma_e', \vec{x}_T') > u_i(\Gamma, \vec{\sigma}, \sigma_e, \vec{x}_T) - \epsilon_0.$$

PROOF. Since, by Proposition 6.6, for each choice of $\vec{\tau}_T$, σ_e, and σ_e', we have

$$u_i(\Gamma, \vec{\sigma}, \sigma_e, \vec{x}_T) - u_i(\Gamma, (\vec{\sigma}_{-T}, \vec{\tau}_T), \sigma_e', \vec{x}_T') < \epsilon,$$

and the space of player strategy profiles, environment strategies, and input value profiles is compact, if we take the sup of the left-hand side over all choices of strategy profiles $\vec{\tau}_T$, environment strategies σ_e and σ_e', and input profiles $\vec{x}$ and $\vec{x}'$, it takes on some maximum value $\epsilon_1 < \epsilon_0$. We can then take $\epsilon_0 = (\epsilon + \epsilon_1)/2$. □

Using Proposition 6.7, we get a similar result for ϵ-(k, t)-robustness. The proof is analogous to that of Proposition 6.8.

PROPOSITION 6.9. *If Γ is a finite game and $\vec{\sigma}$ is a ϵ-(k, t)-robust strategy (resp., strongly ϵ- (k, t)-robust strategy) in Γ_d, then there exists ϵ_0 with $0 < \epsilon_0 < \epsilon$ such that for all disjoint sets K and T of players with $1 \leq |K| \leq k$ and $|T| \leq t$, all strategy profiles $\vec{\tau}_K$, $\vec{\tau}_T$ and $\vec{\tau}_T'$ for players in K and T, respectively, all environment strategies σ_e and σ_e', and all input profiles $\vec{x}$ and $\vec{x}'$, we have that*

$$u_i(\Gamma, (\vec{\sigma}_{-(K\cup T)}, \vec{\tau}_K, \vec{\tau}_T), \sigma_e, \vec{x}_{(K\cup T)}') < u_i(\Gamma, (\vec{\sigma}_{-T}, \vec{\tau}_T'), \sigma_e', \vec{x}_T) + \epsilon_0$$

for some $i \in K$ (resp., all $i \in K$).

6.2 Constructing a protocol that t-coterminates

If $t < n/3$ we can get an an analogue of Theorems 5.3 and 5.4 by replacing $(t, 2t + 1)$-cotermination by t-cotermination and ϵ-$(t, t + 1)$-cotermination by ϵ-t-cotermination respectively. We sketch the construction for t-cotermination; an analogous construction achieves ϵ-t-cotermination.

Consider a protocol $\vec{\sigma}_{CT}'$ in which players play just as in $\vec{\sigma}_{CT}$ except that, whenever an honest player i terminates in $\vec{\sigma}_{CT}$, it instead broadcasts an 'OK' message to all players and waits until it receives $3t+1$ 'OK' messages before it terminates in $\vec{\sigma}_{CT}'$. Note that if an honest player terminates in $\vec{\sigma}_{CT}'$, then at least $3t + 1$ players must have broadcast an 'OK' message in this history of $\vec{\sigma}_{CT}'$, of which at least $2t + 1$ are honest. Thus, at least $2t + 1$ players terminate in the corresponding history of $\vec{\sigma}_{CT}$. Since $\vec{\sigma}_{CT}$ $(t, 2t + 1)$-coterminates, it follows that all players not in T must terminate with $\vec{\sigma}_{CT}$, and hence all players not in T send an 'OK' message (and terminate) with $\vec{\sigma}_{CT}'$.

It remains to show that $\vec{\sigma}_{CT}'$ still (t, t')-bisimulates $\vec{\sigma} + \sigma_d$ if $3t + t' < n$. Clearly, it still relaxed t-bisimulates $\vec{\sigma} + \sigma_d$, so we just have to show that all players are guaranteed to terminate in the presence of at most t' malicious players. However, in this case, by assumption, all honest players are guaranteed to terminate in $\vec{\sigma}_{CT}$, and thus all honest players are guaranteed to eventually send an 'OK' broadcast in $\vec{\sigma}_{CT}'$. Since $n - t' > 3t + 1$, this guarantees that there will be at least $3t + 1$ 'OK' broadcasts and all honest players will eventually terminate, as desired.

Note that this construction requires players a reliable broadcast protocol, and thus can be done only if $n > 3(t + k)$. To prove Theorem 4.5 we require different techniques.

6.3 Proof of Theorem 4.1

By Theorem 5.3, if $n > 4k + 4t$, there exists a strategy profile $\vec{\sigma}_{CT}$ that $(k + t)$-bisimulates $\vec{\sigma} + \sigma_d$. It is immediate from the definition of $(k + t)$-bisimulation that $\vec{\sigma}_{CT}$ implements $\vec{\sigma} + \sigma_d$. Since the probability of deadlock is 0, what the players do in case of deadlock is irrelevant, so this approach works both in the case of the AH approach and the default-move approach. It remains to show that, for each utility variant $\Gamma_d(\vec{u}')$ of Γ_d, if $\vec{\sigma} + \sigma_d$ is a (strongly) (k,t)-robust equilibrium in $\Gamma_d(\vec{u}')$, then $\vec{\sigma}_{CT}$ is a (strongly) (k,t)-robust equilibrium in $\Gamma_{CT}(\vec{u}')$. We start by showing that $\vec{\sigma}_{CT}$ is t-resilient in $\Gamma_{CT}(\vec{u}')$.

Given T with $|T| \leq t$, $\vec{\tau}_T$, and σ_e, by Theorem 5.3 and Proposition 6.1, there exists a function H_{σ_e} from strategies to strategies and a scheduler σ_e' such that for all input profiles $\vec{x}$,

$$\begin{array}{ll} & u_i'(\Gamma_{CT}(\vec{u}'), ((\vec{\sigma}_{CT})_{-T}, \tau_T), \sigma_e, \vec{x}) \\ = & u_i'(\Gamma_d(\vec{u}'), (\vec{\sigma}_{-T}, H_{\sigma_e}(\vec{\tau}_T)), \sigma_e', \vec{x}) \end{array}$$

for all players i. There also exists a scheduler σ_e'' such that

$$u_i'(\Gamma_{CT}(\vec{u}'), \vec{\sigma}_{CT}, \sigma_e', \vec{x}) = u_i'(\Gamma_d(\vec{u}'), \vec{\sigma}, \sigma_e'', \vec{x}).$$

Since $\vec{\sigma}$ is t-immune, for all $i \notin T$ we have that

$$\begin{array}{lll} & u_i'(\Gamma_{CT}(\vec{u}'), ((\vec{\sigma}_{CT})_{-T}, \vec{\tau}_T), \sigma_e, \vec{x}_T) & \\ = & u_i'(\Gamma_d(\vec{u}'), (\vec{\sigma}_{-T}, H_{\sigma_e}(\vec{\tau}_T)), \sigma_e', \vec{x}_T) & \\ \geq & u_i'(\Gamma_d(\vec{u}'), \vec{\sigma}, \sigma_e'', \vec{x}_T) & \text{[by Lemma 6.3]} \\ = & u_i'(\Gamma_{CT}(\vec{u}'), \vec{\sigma}_{CT}, \sigma_e', \vec{x}_T). & \end{array}$$

Therefore, $\vec{\sigma}_{CT}$ is t-immune.

To show (strong) (k,t)-robustness, taking $\vec{\tau}_T$, σ_e, and σ_e' as above, suppose that K is a set of players disjoint from T such that $|K| \leq k$, and the players in K play $\vec{\tau}_K$. By Theorem 5.3 and Proposition 6.1, there exists σ_e^* and H_{σ_e} such that

$$\begin{array}{ll} & u_i'(\Gamma_{CT}(\vec{u}'), ((\vec{\sigma}_{CT})_{-(K\cup T)}, \vec{\tau}_K, \vec{\tau}_T), \sigma_e, \vec{x}) \\ = & u_i'(\Gamma_d(\vec{u}'), (\vec{\sigma}_{-(K\cup T)}, H_{\sigma_e}(\vec{\tau}_K), H_{\sigma_e}(\vec{\tau}_T)), \sigma_e^*, \vec{x}_{(K\cup T)}) \end{array}$$

for all players i. By Corollary 6.4, if $\vec{\sigma} + \sigma_d$ is (k,t)-robust (resp., strongly (k,t)-robust) in $\Gamma_d(\vec{u}')$, then

$$\begin{array}{ll} & u_i'(\Gamma_d(\vec{u}'), (\vec{\sigma}_{-(K\cup T)}, H_{\sigma_e}(\vec{\tau}_K), H_{\sigma_e}(\vec{\tau}_T)), \sigma_e^*, \vec{x}_{(K\cup T)}) \\ \leq & u_i'(\Gamma_d(\vec{u}'), (\vec{\sigma}_{-T}, H_{\sigma_e}(\vec{\tau}_T)), \sigma_e', \vec{x}_T) \end{array}$$

for some (resp., all) $i \in K$. For those $i \in K$ for which this inequality holds, we have

$$\begin{array}{ll} & u_i'(\Gamma_{CT}(\vec{u}'), ((\vec{\sigma}_{CT})_{-(K\cup T)}, \tau_K, \tau_T), \sigma_e, \vec{x}_{(K\cup T)}) \\ = & u_i'(\Gamma_d(\vec{u}'), (\vec{\sigma}_{-(K\cup T)}, H_{\sigma_e}(\vec{\tau}_K), H_{\sigma_e}(\vec{\tau}_T)), \sigma_e^*, \vec{x}_{(K\cup T)}) \\ \leq & u_i'(\Gamma_d(\vec{u}'), (\vec{\sigma}_{-T}, H_{\sigma_e}(\vec{\tau}_T)), \sigma_e', \vec{x}_T) \\ = & u_i'(\Gamma_{CT}(\vec{u}'), ((\vec{\sigma}_{CT})_{-T}, \sigma_e, \vec{x}_T). \end{array}$$

It follows that $\vec{\sigma}_{CT}$ is (strongly) (k,t)-robust in $\Gamma_{CT}(\vec{u}')$.

7 CONCLUSION

We have extended the results of ADGH on implementing mediators to the asynchronous setting. This setting raises a number of new subtleties, particularly regarding how to define utilities in a game where players do not terminate. Since many real-world applications are asynchronous, and thinking in terms of mediators in this setting provides much simpler approach to designing efficient mechanisms, having a "compiler" that can translate solutions with a mediator to one without a mediator can be quite useful in principle.

There are still a number of questions that remain open. The most obvious ones involve lower bounds. Lower bounds that match the upper bounds of ADGH in the synchronous setting were proved by Abraham, Dolev, and Halpern [3]. Can we provide analogous lower bounds here? In addition, we have considered only non-cryptographic setting; ADGH also provided bounds for the setting where players were polynomially-bounded and could use cyrptographic tools. To what extent do things change in this setting in the asynchronous case?

REFERENCES

[1] I. Abraham, D. Dolev, I. Geffner, and J. Y. Halpern. 2019. Implementing mediators with asynchronous cheap talk. (2019). Available at http://arxiv.org/abs/1806.01214.
[2] I. Abraham, D. Dolev, R. Gonen, and J. Y. Halpern. 2006. Distributed computing meets game theory: robust mechanisms for rational secret sharing and multiparty computation. In *Proc. 25th ACM Symposium on Principles of Distributed Computing*. 53–62.
[3] I. Abraham, D. Dolev, and J. Y. Halpern. 2008. Lower bounds on implementing robust and resilient mediators. In *Fifth Theory of Cryptography Conference*. 302–319.
[4] E. Adar and B. Huberman. 2000. Free riding on Gnutella. *First Monday* 5, 10 (2000).
[5] R. J. Aumann and S. Hart. 2003. Long cheap talk. *Econometrica* 71, 6 (2003), 1619–1660.
[6] M. Ben-Or, R. Canetti, and O. Goldreich. 1993. Asynchronous secure computation. In *STOC '93: Proceedings of the 25 Annual ACM Symposium on Theory of Computing*. 52–61.
[7] M. Ben-Or, S. Goldwasser, and A. Wigderson. 1988. Completeness theorems for non-cryptographic fault-tolerant distributed computation. In *Proc. 20th ACM Symp. Theory of Computing*. 1–10.
[8] M. Ben-Or, B. Kelmer, and T. Rabin. 1994. Asynchronous secure computations with optimal resilience (extended abstract). In *Proc. 13th ACM Symp. Principles of Distributed Computing*. 183–192.
[9] E. Ben-Porath. 2003. Cheap talk in games with incomplete information. *Journal of Economic Theory* 108, 1 (2003), 45–71.
[10] S. Even, O. Goldreich, and A. Lempel. 1985. A randomized protocol for signing contracts. *Commun. ACM* 28, 6 (1985), 637–647. https://doi.org/10.1145/3812.3818
[11] I. Geffner and J. Y. Halpern. 2018. Stronger security guarantees for multiparty computation. (2018). Available at http://arxiv.org.
[12] O. Goldreich, S. Micali, and A. Wigderson. 1987. How to play any mental game. In *Proc. 19th ACM Symp. Theory of Computing*. 218–229.
[13] J. Y. Halpern and M. R. Tuttle. 1993. Knowledge, probability, and adversaries. 40, 4 (1993), 917–962.
[14] A. Shamir, R. L. Rivest, and L. Adelman. 1981. Mental poker. In *The Mathematical Gardner*, D. A. Klarner (Ed.). Prindle, Weber, and Schmidt, Boston, MA, 37–43.
[15] A. Yao. 1982. Protocols for secure computation (extended abstract). In *Proc. 23rd IEEE Symp. Foundations of Computer Science*. 160–164.

Distributed Minimum Degree Spanning Trees

Michael Dinitz
Johns Hopkins University
Baltimore, Maryland
mdinitz@cs.jhu.edu

Magnús M. Halldórsson
Reykjavik University
Reykjavik, Iceland
mmh@ru.is

Taisuke Izumi
Nagoya Institute of Technology
Nagoya, Japan
t-izumi@nitech.ac.jp

Calvin Newport
Georgetown University
Washington, D.C.
cnewport@cs.georgetown.edu

ABSTRACT

The *minimum degree spanning tree* (MDST) problem requires the construction of a spanning tree T for graph G, such that the maximum degree of T is the smallest among all spanning trees of G. Let d be this MDST degree for a given graph. In this paper, we present a randomized distributed approximation algorithm for the MDST problem that constructs a spanning tree with maximum degree in $O(d + \log n)$. With high probability in n, the algorithm runs in $O((D + \sqrt{n}) \log^4 n)$ rounds, in the broadcast-CONGEST model, where D is the graph diameter and n is the graph size. We then show how to derandomize this algorithm, obtaining the same asymptotic guarantees on degree and time complexity, but now requiring the standard CONGEST model. Although efficient approximation algorithms for the MDST problem have been known in the sequential setting since the 1990's (finding an exact solution is NP-hard), our algorithms are the first efficient distributed solutions. We conclude by proving a lower bound that establishes that any randomized MDST algorithm that guarantees a maximum degree in $\tilde{\Omega}(d)$ requires $\tilde{\Omega}(n^{1/3})$ rounds, and any deterministic solution requires $\tilde{\Omega}(n^{1/2})$ rounds. These bounds proves our deterministic algorithm to be asymptotically optimal, and eliminates the possibility of significantly more efficient randomized solutions.

CCS CONCEPTS

• **Theory of computation → Distributed algorithms**; *Graph algorithms analysis.*

KEYWORDS

CONGEST, spanning tree, minimum degree

ACM Reference Format:
Michael Dinitz, Magnús M. Halldórsson, Taisuke Izumi, and Calvin Newport. 2019. Distributed Minimum Degree Spanning Trees. In *2019 ACM Symposium on Principles of Distributed Computing (PODC '19), July 29-August 2, 2019, Toronto, ON, Canada.* ACM, New York, NY, USA, 10 pages. https://doi.org/10.1145/3293611.3331604

ACM ISBN 978-1-4503-6217-7/19/07...$15.00
https://doi.org/10.1145/3293611.3331604

1 INTRODUCTION

We present a distributed approximation algorithms for the *minimum degree spanning tree* (MDST) problem. In this problem, we are given a graph $G = (V, E)$, and are asked to construct a spanning tree T of V such that the maximum degree of T is the smallest among all spanning trees of G.

As argued in [14, 15], in addition to their theoretical interest, these trees are particularly useful in network communication scenarios in which low-degree backbones reduce overhead. In designing optical networks, for example, high-degree switches are expensive, prioritizing the identification of low-degree spanning structures. These trees can also be used to maximize throughput in network settings in which devices can only transmit or receive messages along a single link at a time, such as when aggregating data in a sensor network, or flooding information in peer-to-peer scenarios where devices connect in a pairwise manner.

In the *centralized* setting, the problem is easily shown to be NP-hard by reduction from the Hamiltonian path problem. The best known approximation is due to Fürer and Raghavachari [15], who provide a polynomial-time algorithm that constructs a spanning tree with maximum degree $d + 1$, where d is the minimum maximum degree over all spanning trees in the graph. As we elaborate below, to the best of our knowledge, there exists no efficient *distributed* approximation algorithm for the MDST problem, despite its importance to network communication. This paper addresses this gap.

1.1 Results

We assume the CONGEST model of distributed computation. In this model, the network is described as an n-node graph $G = (V, E)$, with a computational process assigned to each node, and the edges representing communication channels. Time proceeds in synchronous rounds. In each round, each node can send a $O(\log n)$-bit message to each of its neighbors in the graph. Many of our results (including our main algorithm) hold in the harder *broadcast* variation of the CONGEST model (broadcast-CONGEST) in which nodes must broadcast the *same* message to all of their neighbors in a given round, whereas our lower bounds hold for the easier standard CONGEST model.

In the statement of our results, we let d denote the degree of an MDST (i.e., OPT) and let D denote the graph diameter. Throughout this paper we omit some details due to space constraints, but all missing details can be found in the full version [9].

Main Algorithm. Our main result is the following.

THEOREM 1.1. *There exists a (randomized) distributed algorithm in the broadcast-CONGEST model that constructs a spanning tree of degree $O(d + \log n)$, running in time $O((D + \sqrt{n}) \log^4 n)$ (in expectation).*

A nice property of this solution is that it is an iterative improvement algorithm, meaning that it strictly improves the degree of the current spanning tree with each phase until terminating with a degree at most $O(d + \log n)$. This means the process can be stopped once the degree is sufficiently small for a given application, potentially saving time for applications with looser degree requirements.

The basic idea of this new algorithm is to parallelize a large number of the improvement steps used in one of the original sequential solutions [14]. This alone, however, is not enough, as the number of such improvements is bounded by $O(n^2)$ [14, 22], meaning that a straightforward parallel approach might still be too slow. Our method instead enables many nodes to simultaneously make *large* improvements to their degrees in a short period of time, progressively lowering the threshold for a viable improvement size.

Derandomization. We also show that it is possible to derandomize this algorithm, at the cost of working in the CONGEST model (rather than broadcast-CONGEST) and a slightly worse logarithmic factor. The main idea is to generalize the derandomization techniques of Fischer [11] from ordinary matchings to the more complicated versions of matchings that we use in our randomized algorithm. This allows us to prove the following theorem:

THEOREM 1.2. *There is a deterministic distributed algorithm in the CONGEST model that finds a spanning tree of degree $O(d + \log n)$, running in time $O((D + \sqrt{n}) \log^5 n)$.*

Lower Bound. We show that the polynomial term in the time complexity is necessary. Specifically, there exists a family of instances of diameter $O(\log n)$ which incurs $\tilde{\Omega}(n^{1/3})$ rounds for any (randomized) MDST algorithm achieving a *polylogarithmic multiplicative approximation.* That lower bound is improved to $\tilde{\Omega}(n^{1/2})$ rounds for any deterministic algorithm, and even the randomized bound can be made arbitrarily close to the bound of $\tilde{\Omega}(n^{1/2})$ rounds if we consider instances of larger diameters. We prove the following theorem:

THEOREM 1.3. *For any $\epsilon < 1/6$, there exists a family of instances of diameter $D = \Theta(n^{1/2-3\epsilon} + \log n)$ where any MDST algorithm with a polylogarithmic multiplicative approximation factor needs $\tilde{\Omega}(n^{1/2-\epsilon} + D)$ rounds. There also exists a family of the instances of diameter $D = O(\log n)$ where any deterministic MDST algorithm with a polylogarithmic multiplicative approximation factor needs $\tilde{\Omega}(n^{1/2})$ rounds.*

Note that a more precise version of the lower-bound theorem (Theorem 5.1) also includes the tradeoffs betweeen time and approximation factors.

1.2 Background & Related Work.

The construction of spanning trees with useful properties is a primary topic in distributed graph algorithms. The most well-studied problem in this area is the *minimum spanning tree* (MST) problem, which requires the construction of a spanning tree that minimizes the sum of edge weights. Gallager, Humblet, and Spira [17] helped instigate this area with a distributed algorithm that constructs an MST in $O(n \log n)$ rounds (similar ideas appeared in a 1926 paper by Boruvka [23] that was not translated into English until more recently). A series of follow up papers [2, 8, 16] improved this complexity to $O(n)$ rounds, which is worst-case optimal in the sense that $\Omega(n)$ rounds are required in certain graphs with diameter $D = \Theta(n)$.

Garay, Kutten and Peleg [18] isolated the graph diameter D as a distinct parameter, enabling further progress. They described a distributed MST algorithm that solves the problem in $O(D + n^{0.61})$ rounds, which is sub-linear for graphs with sub-linear diameters. This result was subsequently improved to $O(D + \sqrt{n} \log^* n)$ rounds [21]. A series of lower bound results [10, 24, 25] established that any non-trivial approximation of an MST requires $\Omega(D + \sqrt{n/\log n})$ rounds, even in graphs with small diameters.

Turning our attention from MST to MDST, we note that prior to this paper the MDST problem has been primarily studied in the context of sequential algorithms. In 1990, Fürer and Raghavachari [13] gave an *NC* algorithm (and thus a polynomial-time sequential algorithm) that constructs a tree with a maximum degree $O(d \log n)$ (recall that d is the maximum degree of the optimal tree). Agrawal, Klein and Ravi [1] subsequently generalized this result by providing a sequential polynomial time algorithm for the Steiner tree variation of the MDST problem. Fürer and Raghavachari improved both results by presenting sequential algorithms that guarantee a maximum degree of $d + 1$ for both the standard [14] and Steiner tree [15] versions of the problem. Given that finding a spanning tree with maximum degree exactly d is NP-hard, these approximations are likely the best possible that can be achieved in polynomial time.

The $(d + 1)$-approximation algorithm of [14] operates by performing repeated improvements on an arbitrary initial tree. Each improvement involves a recursive application, making any parallel or distributed implementation highly challenging, if not impossible. We refer to these recursive improvements as *semi-local.* In the same paper, Fürer and Raghavachari [14] also gave a simpler algorithm involving *local* improvements. They showed that this algorithm terminates with a tree of maximum degree $2d + \log n$. They proved an upper bound of $O(n^3)$ on the number of improvement steps, which implies polynomial time complexity. Our algorithm leverages these local improvements, but chooses them more selectively to enable more parallelism and to significantly reduce the total number of improvements needed. It remains a key open question whether an efficient distributed solution exists that can provide a tree with degree in $O(d)$. Given the difficulty of parallelizing the semi-local improvements of [14], resolving this question would likely require novel techniques.

To the best of our knowledge, the first discussion of the MDST problem in the distributed context was by Blin and Butelle [3, 4], who observed that the search for improvements in [14] can be implemented in distributed models using global broadcast and aggregations. The time complexity of their solution, however, is in

$\Omega(n^2)$, leaving open the problem of identifying efficient distributed approximation algorithms for the problem.

Followup work along these lines [5, 6] focus on self-stabilization and/or space complexity, which is important but orthogonal to time complexity considerations. Indeed, the time complexity claimed for these self-stabilizing MDST algorithms is $O(mn^2 \log n)$ [6] and polynomial [5]. Another direction is the more general problem of finding a *minimum* spanning tree whose maximum degree is minimized. Lavault and Valencia-Pabon [22] give an algorithm with time complexity $O(\Delta n^{2+1/\ln b})$ that outputs a tree of degree $bd + \log_b n$, for any $b > 1$. In summary, none of this existing work provides a distributed MDST algorithm running in time less than n^2 (which is the complexity boundary beyond which it is possible to simply gather the entire graph topology at each node and run a centralized algorithm locally), supporting our claim that our $\tilde{O}(D + \sqrt{n})$-time algorithm is the first efficient distributed solution for this problem.

2 ITERATIVE IMPROVEMENT ALGORITHM

We give an iterative improvement algorithm in broadcast-CONGEST (see Section 1 for model definitions) that produces a spanning tree of degree at most $4(1+\epsilon)d + O(\log n)$. Recall that d is the degree of an optimal MDST.

Overview. A natural approach for finding low-degree spanning trees is to incrementally reduce the number of high degree nodes in an arbitrary initial spanning tree T. Adding a graph edge $e = (u, v)$ to T introduces a cycle C, and removing any edge in C results again in a spanning tree. If C contains a degree-k vertex w while the degrees of both u and v are at most $k-2$, then replacing one of the incident edges on w with e reduces the number of nodes of degree k (or more) in the tree.

The first step towards a distributed algorithm is to *parallelize* the search for improvements. We then seek a set M of graph edges so that there is a subset M' of tree edges for which $(T - M') \cup M$ is again a tree. This can be a tricky process in full generality, both in identifying the edges M' to replace and in maximizing $|M|$, the number of parallel improvements. We tackle this by restricting the set of improvements that can be identified, without reducing significantly the extent of the improvements. In particular, we restrict the improvement set so that each *improving* edge in M has an easily identifiable corresponding *replaced* edge in T.

The other major issue is to find sufficiently significant improvements in each parallel phase. The $O(n^3)$ bound on the number of improvement steps derived by Fürer and Raghavachari [14] suggests that the basic improvements alone form an insufficient basis for a distributed algorithm. Instead, we want to replace edges to high degree nodes by edges between nodes of quite low degree. We also want to allow high degree nodes to shed multiple edges in a single parallel phase. As part of this, we develop a strategy of *progressive* improvements, where nodes initially reduce their degree rapidly, while in later stages the degrees decrease more slowly. By defining a sequence of potential functions, we can prove a polylogarithmic bound on the number of phases.

In the next subsection, we give a matching-based algorithm to find parallel improvements, and show that under appropriate assumptions, there will be many improvements. We apply this algorithm systematically in Section 2.2 to gradually apply all significant improvements in a polylogarithmic number of calls. Distributed and parallel implementations are given in Section 2.4, but the main technical difficulty, of finding "constrained" matchings, is deferred to Section 3.

2.1 Parallel Improvements

We argue in this subsection that many improvements can be made in parallel, under the right conditions. Let γ and q be numbers, and let $\gamma_0 = \gamma - 2q$. We aim to reduce the number of vertices of degree γ or more, but only by increasing the degrees of nodes of degree less than γ_0. As mentioned, we need to be careful about how we define and find the possible parallel improvements.

Definitions. Let T be the current spanning tree and let $d_T(v)$ denote the degree of node v in T. Let X_t denote the set of nodes of degree at least t, for integer t. Removing the nodes in X_γ from T results in a collection of subtrees that we call *branches*. A branch is a *leaf branch* if only one edge in T has a single endpoint in the branch (i.e., the other endpoint has degree γ or more). The *head* of a leaf branch is the node in the branch that is incident on the edge from T that was removed. The *parent* of a leaf branch is the unique node outside the branch that is adjacent to its head. Leaf branches with the same parent are collectively called a *bundle*.

An edge in $G \setminus T$ is *good* if its endpoints are: of degree less than γ_0, in different branches, and with at least one in a leaf branch.

Definition 2.1. The *imp graph* $H = H_{T,\gamma,q}$ is a structured bipartite graph $H = (U, \mathcal{U}, Q, E')$ with sides U and Q, where U is the set of leaf branches, Q consists of the low-degree nodes, and $\mathcal{U}$ is the partition of U into bundles. There is an edge uq in E', for $q \in Q$, if the leaf branch $u \in U$ contains a node w such that wq is a good edge (in G). If both endpoints of a good edge are in leaf branches, then the edge contributes two edges to H.

Consider Figure 1 for illustration on a single bundle (with f as parent). There are four leaf branches given by $U = \{c, e, g, h\}$, while node i is in a non-leaf branch. All the nodes except f are of low degree (defined here as less than 4). The corresponding imp graph on the right has U on the left, and the low degree nodes (excluding the zero-degree nodes a, c) on the right. The edge hi is the only good edge that appears only once in H; for instance, the good edge gd in G leads to the edges **gd** and **eg** in H.

Notice that we overload notation by speaking of edges of G being contained in H; formally speaking, of course, they have a natural correspondence to edges in H.

Definition 2.2. A *constrained q-matching* M is a subgraph of H such that each bundle in $\mathcal{U}$ is incident on at most q edges in M. Namely, M satisfies: a) Each node in U is incident on at most one edge in M, b) Each node of Q is incident on at most q edges in M, and c) Each bundle $U_i \in \mathcal{U}$ is incident on at most q edges in M.

The corresponding optimization problem is to maximize the number of edges in the constrained matching found. In Section 3, we describe and analyze a distributed algorithm that efficiently approximates a constrained q-matching. This algorithm is a key subroutine in the MDST algorithm described and analyzed here. Formally, in Section 3 we prove:

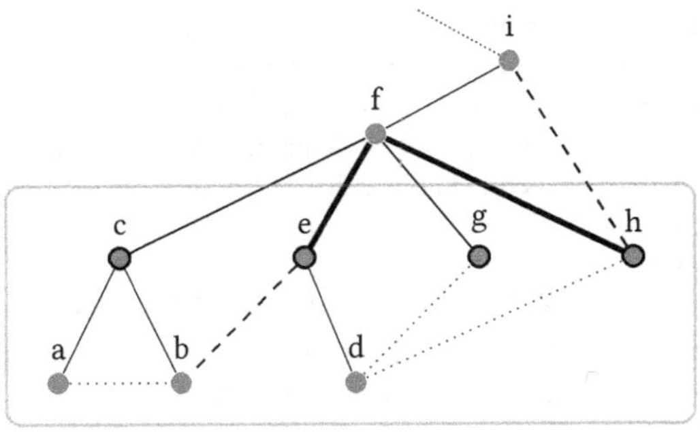

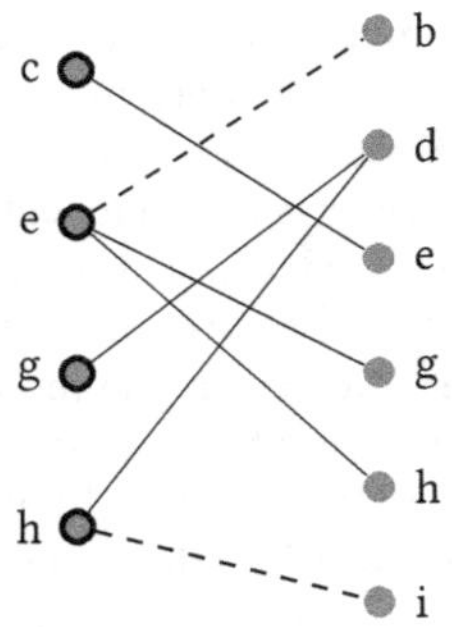

Figure 1: On left, a graph fragment with two parallel improvements is identified, formatted such that: tree edges are solid, replaced edges are bold, improvement edges are dashed, and other non-tree graph edges are dotted. The heads of the four leaf branches (within rectangle) are emphasized with a black border. On right, the corresponding imp graph, with zero-degree nodes (a, c) omitted. The dashed edge form a maximal 1-constrained matching.

THEOREM 2.3. *There exists a distributed algorithm that finds a c-approximate constrained q-matching in expected $O((D + \sqrt{n}) \log n)$ rounds in the broadcast-CONGEST mode, for some $c \leq 128$.*

We now continue with describing and analyzing the MDST algorithm that leverages the above theorem. We begin with some useful definitions and observations.

We say that an edge e *departs* a leaf branch B if the node in U corresponding to B is incident on e, and an edge *enters* a branch B if some node in Q contained in the branch B is incident on e. Our MDST algorithm transforms constrained matchings into those with the following useful property:

Definition 2.4. An *improvement subgraph* is a constrained q-matching with additional property that no leaf branch has both departing and entering edges.

Given an improvement subgraph $\bar{M}$, we can readily identify the edges $R_{\bar{M}}$ that it replaces. For *improving* edge e in $\bar{M}$, let B_e be the leaf branch that e departs from and let $e(B_e)$ denote the edge between the head and the parent of B_e, separating B_e from the rest of the tree $(T - B_e)$. Then, the *replaced* edges of T are given by $R_{\bar{M}} = \{e(B_e) : e \in \bar{M}\}$.

OBSERVATION 1. *If $\bar{M}$ is an improvement subgraph (of T), then $T_{\bar{M}} = (T \setminus R_{\bar{M}}) \cup \bar{M}$ is a (spanning) tree.*

PROOF. Let $\hat{T} = T - \cup_{e \in \bar{M}} B_e$ be the subtree obtained by removing all the vertices and incident edges of all leaf branches B_e from which an edge $e \in \bar{M}$ departs. Observe that each $e \in \bar{M}$ enters (a branch in) $\hat{T}$, since no branch has edges both entering and departing. To restate, each edge $e \in \bar{M}$ has one endpoint in a distinct leaf branch B_e and the other in $\hat{T}$. Each edge $e(B_e) \in R_{\bar{M}}$ also has one endpoint in B_e and the other in $\hat{T}$. □

The resulting degrees in $T_{\bar{M}}$ should also be "better" than before, but not too much better (in order for our analysis to work), and the nodes which are worse are not too much worse.

OBSERVATION 2. *For each edge e of an improvement subgraph $\bar{M}$ it holds that: a) the endpoints of $e = (u, v)$ are not too much worse off: $d_{T_{\bar{M}}}(u), d_{T_{\bar{M}}}(v) < \gamma_0 + q$, and b) the parent p of $e(B_e)$ is not improved too much: $d_{T_{\bar{M}}}(p) \geq \gamma - q$.*

Intuitively, decreasing the degree of a higher degree vertex should be more valuable than the increase in the degree of two lower degree nodes.

2.1.1 Improvement Algorithm. We encode our observations in an algorithm IMPROVE with parameters γ and q, which takes the tree T, finds an improvement subgraph $\bar{M}$, and produces a modified tree $T_{\bar{M}} = (T \setminus R_{\bar{M}}) \cup \bar{M}$.

The algorithm first computes an approximate *constrained q-matching* M in the imp graph H with the procedure CONSTRAINED-MATCHING presented and analyzed in Section 3. The algorithm then identifies an improvement subgraph $\bar{M} \subseteq M$ of size at least $\bar{M} \geq M/8$ using the following randomized selection procedure: Independently flip an unbiased coin for each leaf branch B to either mark its departing edge or its entering edges. If the set $\bar{M}$ of unmarked edges contains fewer than $|M|/8$ edges, redo the random marking step until $|\bar{M}| \geq |M|/8$.

Analysis. We first argue that every maximal constrained q-matching must have many edges. We first need an accounting of the adjacencies of nodes in X_γ that do not contribute to that count.

LEMMA 2.5. *$2(|X_\gamma| - 1)$ adjacencies of nodes in X_γ are to non-leaf branches or to other nodes in X_γ. More formally, for each vertex $v \in X_\gamma$, let $d'(v)$ denote the number of neighbors of v in T (or G) that are either in X_γ or in a non-leaf branch of T. Then, $\sum_{v \in X_\gamma} d'(v) = 2(|X_\gamma| - 1)$.*

PROOF. Form a tree T' on the nodes of X_γ as follows. Starting with T, remove all leaf branches and incident edges and contract every non-leaf branch into one of its adjacent nodes in X_γ. The adjacencies of nodes in X_γ, other than those to leaf branches, are unchanged. Since the tree T' has $X_\gamma - 1$ edges, it has $2(X_\gamma - 1)$ adjacencies. □

LEMMA 2.6. *H contains a constrained q-matching with at least $\frac{q}{\gamma}((\gamma - 2)|X_\gamma| - d|X_{\gamma_0}|)$ edges.*

PROOF. We restrict our attention to a certain subgraph of H. From each bundle with s leaf branches, retain an arbitrary set of $\min(s, \gamma)$ leaf branches, and let L denote the resulting combined set of leaf branches. As each leaf branch has exactly one adjacent node in X_γ, the set contributes exactly L to the adjacencies of nodes in X_γ. By Lemma 2.5, then, $|L| \geq \sum_{v \in X_\gamma} \min(d_T(v), \gamma) - 2(|X_\gamma| - 1) = (\gamma - 2)|X_\gamma| + 2$.

Let T^* be a spanning tree of maximum degree d. T^* must connect the branches of L to the rest of the graph. Root T^* at some vertex in a non-leaf branch and direct the edges towards the root. Select an arbitrary edge entering each leaf branch in L, to form a set R of edges. Note that R corresponds to a subgraph of H with one edge incident on each node of $U \cap L$. At most $d|X_{\gamma_0}|$ edges in R have one or more endpoints in X_{γ_0}, since T^* has maximum degree d. Let $R' \subseteq R$ be the subset of good edges, i.e., those with both endpoints of degree less than γ_0 in T. Then,

$$|R'| \geq |R| - d|X_{\gamma_0}| \geq (\gamma - 2)|X_\gamma| - d|X_{\gamma_0}| .$$

Now form the bipartite graph $H' = (\mathcal{U}, Q, R')$ on the edge set R' but with nodes on one side now representing the bundles (rather than the leaf branches). Observe that the maximum degree of H' is at most γ (since we constrained L to involve at most γ leaf branches from each bundle), each leaf branch is incident on at most one edge in R, and each node in Q is of degree less than γ in G. Since H' is bipartite, its edges can be colored with γ colors [20]. Let M be the union of the q largest color classes, whose size is then at least $q|R'|/\gamma$. We claim that M is a q-constrained matching of H. Namely, by design, each bundle and each node of Q is incident on at most one edge of each color, and thus at most q edges of M; and since $M \subseteq R$, each node in U is incident on at most one edge in M. □

The following is key to finding large parallel improvements. It is conditional on the parameter γ being large enough (roughly $> 4d$) and that there are not too many more intermediate degree nodes (between γ_0 and γ) than high degree nodes ($> \gamma$). Let c be the approximation factor of the Constrained-Matching algorithm.

Theorem 2.7. *Let $\delta > 0$, $\tau = 2/(1-\delta)$, $h = h_\delta = (d\tau^2+2)/(1-\delta)$, and $\Pi = \Pi_{\gamma,q,\delta} = \delta q|X_\gamma|/(8c)$. Suppose $\gamma \geq h$ and $|X_{\gamma_0}| \leq \tau^2 \cdot |X_\gamma|$. Then, Improve (γ, q) finds an improvement subgraph with at least Π edges.*

Proof. By Lemma 2.6, the hypothesis, and the assumed lower bound on γ, we have that H contains a constrained q-matching M^* with at least $q((1 - 2/\gamma)|X_\gamma| - d|X_{\gamma_0}|/\gamma) \geq q|X_\gamma|\left(1 - \frac{2+d\tau^2}{\gamma}\right) \geq \delta q|X_\gamma|$ edges. Thus, the improvement subgraph $\bar{M}$ output satisfies $|\bar{M}| \geq |M^*|/(8c) \geq \delta q|X_\gamma|/(8c) = \Pi$. □

2.2 Progressive Improvements

Theorem 2.7 allows us to find large improvements under certain assumptions (that $|X_{\gamma_0}| \leq \tau^2 \cdot |X_\gamma|$ and the lower bound on γ). We now want to show how to repeatedly find improvements in a smart way, so as to make significant progress on decreasing the degrees in the tree.

Notation. Our algorithm Prog takes a parameter q that specifies the "extent" of the improvements found, i.e., the required separation between the degrees of nodes that have their degrees increased/decreased. Recall also the parameter $\delta > 0$.

Let $k = \Delta(T)$ be the maximum degree spanning tree T at the start of Prog. Recall the notation $\tau = 2/(1-\delta)$, $h = h_\delta = (d\tau^2+2)/(1-\delta)$, X_γ, $\Pi = \Pi_{\gamma,q,\delta} = \delta q|X_\gamma|/(8c)$. Let $b_j = k+1-j \cdot q$, for $j \geq 0$; these will play the role of the parameter γ. Let $C_j = X_{b_j}$ denote the set of nodes of degree at least b_j, for $j \geq 0$, and note that $C_0 = \emptyset$. We refer to each non-empty set $C_j \setminus C_{j-1}$ as a *block*.

The algorithms also maintain a persistent variable $\hat{h}$ (which we later shows satisfies $\hat{h} \leq h$). Let t be the smallest value such that $b_{t-1} \geq \hat{h}$ at the start of Prog. The analysis of this subsection will be in terms of the parameters $\hat{h}, t, \tau$, which will be instantiated in the following subsection.

We say that a call to Improve (b_j, q) *fails* if the size of the improvement subgraph found is less than $\Pi_{b_j,q,\delta}$.

Algorithm 1 Prog (q)

```
Let t be the smallest number s.t. b_{t-1} ≥ ĥ
repeat
    j := arg max_{s=1}^{t} |C_s| τ^s
    Improve (b_j, q).
    if the call to Improve failed then
        ĥ = max(ĥ, b_j)
until b_j ≤ ĥ
```

We argue the termination of the algorithm using a potential function Φ. Define the potential $\Phi(v)$ of a node $v \in C_j \setminus C_{j-1}$, for $j \geq 1$ as

$$\begin{aligned}\Phi(v) &= (d_T(v) - b_j)\tau^{-j} + \sum_{s=j+1}^{t} (b_{s-1} - b_s)\tau^{-s} \\ &= (d_T(v) - b_j)\tau^{-j} + q \sum_{s=j+1}^{t} \tau^{-s}.\end{aligned}$$

Each adjacency of v contributes a term to the potential, with the terms increasing by a factor of τ as we move past each threshold b_s. Observe that if nodes v and v' are in $C_j \setminus C_{j+1}$, then $\Phi(v) = \Theta(\Phi(v')) = \Theta(q\tau^j) = \Theta(q \sum_{s=0}^{j} \tau^s)$. The potential of the whole tree T is $\Phi(T) = \sum_{v \in V} \Phi(j)$.

Lemma 2.8. *Each call by Prog to Improve, except the last one, reduces the potential of the tree by an $\Omega(1/(\tau t))$-factor.*

Proof. Since the call was not the last one, it neither failed nor was $j \geq t$.

We first claim that each edge $e = (u, u')$ of the subgraph $\bar{M}$ contributes a drop of $\Omega(\tau^j)$ in the total potential. Namely, it decreased the degree of a node in C_j, but its degree did not drop below b_{j+1}. Thus, it decreased the potential by at least $1/\tau^{j+1}$, while the nodes u and u' that increased in degree experienced a potential increase of at most $2/\tau^{j+2}$. The net decrease is then $1/t^{j+1} - 2/\tau^{j+2} = \delta/\tau^{j+1}$. Since $\bar{M}$ contained at least Π edges, the total decrease in potential, $\Phi(T) - \Phi(T_{\bar{M}})$, is then at least $\Omega(\Pi/\tau^{j+1}) = \Omega(q|C_j|\tau^{-j-1})$.

Observe that

$$\begin{aligned}\Phi(T) &= \sum_v \Phi(v) = \Theta\left(\sum_{j'} (|C_{j'}| - |C_{j'-1}|) \cdot q \sum_{s=j'}^{t} \tau^{-s}\right) \\ &= \Theta\left(\sum_{j'} |C_{j'}| \cdot q\tau^{-j'}\right).\end{aligned}$$

Since j maximized $|C_{j'}|/\tau^{j'}$, it follows that $\Phi(T) \leq t \cdot (|C_j|q\tau^{-j})$. Thus, the call to Improve decreases the potential by $\Phi(T) - \Phi(T_{\bar{M}}) = \Omega(\Phi(T)/(\tau t))$. □

This now lets us bound the number of improvements required.

Lemma 2.9. *Prog runs in $O(\tau t(\log n + t \log \tau))$ phases (or calls to Improve).*

Proof. Consider here only phases (or calls to Improve) that exclude the last one. The initial potential of each vertex (when running Prog) is at most $q \sum_{s=0} \tau^{-s} = O(q)$. Thus, the initial potential of the tree is $O(qn) = O(n^2)$. Since $C_t \neq \emptyset$ (before the last phase), the potential of the tree is at least τ^{-t}. Each phase reduces the potential by a fraction $\Omega(1/(\tau t))$, by Lemma 2.8. Hence, there are at most $O(\tau t \log(n^2 \tau^t)) = O(\tau t(\log n + t \log \tau))$ phases. □

We bound the degree of the tree in terms of our variable $\hat{h}$.

Lemma 2.10. *When Prog terminates, the degree k of the resulting tree is less than $\hat{h} + q(1 + \lfloor \log_\tau n \rfloor)$.*

Proof. When Prog terminates, $\hat{h} \geq b_j$. Since the initial degree of the tree was $b_0 - 1$, it follows that $k < b_0 = b_j + jq \leq \hat{h} + jq$. The claim then follows when $j \leq \tau' := 1 + \lfloor \log_\tau n \rfloor$.

Suppose then that $j > \tau'$. Since j maximized $|C_s|/\tau^s$, we have that $|C_j|/\tau^j \geq |C_{j-\tau'}|/\tau^{j-\tau'}$, or $n \geq |C_j| \geq |C_{j-\tau'}|\tau^{\tau'} > |C_{j-\tau'}|n$. Namely, $|C_{j-\tau'}| < 1$, and hence it cannot contain any node. Thus, the largest degree in the current tree is less than $b_{j-\tau'} = b_j + \tau' q \leq \hat{h} + \tau' q$. □

2.3 Main algorithm

Our top-level algorithm calls the Prog algorithm with progressively finer block-sizes.

Algorithm 2 Mds

```
q_0 := 2^{⌊lg Δ⌋-2}
ĥ := 1
i := 0
while q_i ≥ 1 do
    Prog(q_i)
    i := i + 1
    q_i := q_{i-1}/2
```

The variable $\hat{h}$ is a proper lower bound on h, so indirectly on the optimum degree, d.

Lemma 2.11. *The invariant $\hat{h} \leq h_\delta$ is maintained.*

Proof. The claim holds initially, since $d \geq 1$. Consider a call to Prog where $\hat{h}$ is increased. Then the call to Improve (b_j, q) failed to find an improvement subgraph with at least $\Pi_{\gamma,q,\delta}$ edges. Since j was maximized over $|C_s|/\tau^s$, it follows that $|X_{b_j}| = |C_j| \geq |C_{j+2}|/\tau^2 = |X_{b_{j+2}}|/\tau^2$. The contrapositive of Theorem 2.7 (where $\gamma = b_j$ and $\gamma_0 = b_{j+2}$) then implies that $b_j < h_\delta$. Since $\hat{h}$ was increased, it was assigned the value b_j. Thus, $\hat{h} \leq b_j < h_\delta$, maintaining the invariant. □

We are led to our main result.

Theorem 2.12. *For any given $\epsilon > 0$, Mds outputs a spanning tree of degree $4d(1+\epsilon) + O(\log n)$. The number of phases is $O(\log \Delta \log^2 n)$.*

Proof. In the final iteration of Mds, $q_i = 1$. By Lemma 2.10, $X_{b_j} = \emptyset$ for $b_j \geq \log_\tau n + 1 \geq \lg n + 1$. Setting $\tau = 2/(1-\delta)$, we have by Lemmas 2.10 and 2.11 that the degree of the spanning tree T is at most $\hat{h} + \lg_\tau n \leq h + \lg n = 4d/(1-\delta)^3 + 2/(1-\delta) + \lg n$. Choosing $\delta = 1 - 1/(1+\epsilon)^{1/3}$ yields the degree bound.

It follows by induction and Lemma 2.10 that the number of nonempty blocks is bounded by $t \leq 2 \log_\tau n$. The bound on the number of phases then follows from Lemma 2.9. □

If we want a purely multiplicative guarantee, we can obtain a bound that is slightly stronger than the $O(\log n)$ which is immediate from the previous theorem. However, note that for $d \geq \log \log n$, our mixed approximation gives a stronger bound.

Theorem 2.13. *There is a δ such that Mds outputs a spanning tree of degree $O(d \cdot \log n / \log \log n)$.*

Proof. Set $\delta = 1 - 1/(\log n)^{1/4}$ so $\tau = (\log n)^{1/4}$ and $h = O((\log n)^{3/4} d)$. Then, by Lemmas 2.11 and 2.10, the maximum degree of the resulting tree is at most $\hat{h} + \log_\tau n = O((\log n)^{3/4} d + \log n / \log \log n) = O(d \log n / \log \log n)$. □

2.4 Distributed Implementation

Up to this point, the Mds algorithm (and its constituent subroutines) has largely been described and analyzed as a centralized graph algorithm, with the exception being the construction of constrained matchings, for which we assumed from the beginning a distributed solution exists (see Section 3.1). Here we obtain a final time complexity by accounting for the time required to implement the centralized operations previously discussed in a distributed manner in the broadcast-CONGEST model.

There are three different types of standard distributed coordination strategies required for this implementation. The first type of strategies require a given value to be aggregated and/or disseminated globally in the network. For example, when Prog aggregates the total count of edges in the improvement subgraph produced by the preceding call to Improve. These global operations are easily implemented in $O(D)$ rounds using a global BFS tree initialized at the beginning of the algorithm execution.

The second type of strategies require the aggregation and/or dissemination of information within well-defined connected components (that is, components in which all nodes in the same component share the same component id). For example, when the nodes in Improve agree on a random coin flip for their component, and then count the total number of remaining unmarked edges. It is straightforward to implement these internal component aggregations and dissemination in $O(D + \sqrt{n})$ rounds (see [9] for details).[1]

[1]The standard trick here, which we summarize for the sake of completeness, and which we elaborate in [9], is to treat small components (less than $\sqrt{n}$ nodes) and large components (at least $\sqrt{n}$ nodes) differently. Communication within small components can be implemented with BFS trees in order of the component diameter time, which is no more than $\sqrt{n}$. Because there are at most $\sqrt{n}$ total large components, the aggregation/dissemination values for all components can be pipelined through a global BFS tree in $O(D + \sqrt{n})$ rounds.

The third type of distributed coordination strategies require nodes to discover the name of the component in which they now belong after edges are removed from a spanning tree. In our algorithm, this occurs at the beginning of IMPROVE where in order to construct the improvement graph needed by the constrained matching, nodes first remove high degree nodes from T, creating a forest T', and then agree upon names for the components in T'.

Consider the following strategy to accomplish this goal. First, each node marks itself with probability $\log n/\sqrt{n}$. Marked nodes initiate a flood of their id within T' up to distance $\alpha\sqrt{n}$, for a sufficiently large constant α. A node only accepts and passes on such a token if it has not accepted and broadcast an id token previously.

With high probability, there are $O(\sqrt{n}\log n)$ marked nodes and their floods cover all n nodes in the graph. In this case, consider the component graph that results where we treat for each marked node u, the set of nodes that accepted u's token as a component that we call u's *flood component*. It is not hard to show that the component graph defined over these flood components contains $O(\sqrt{n}\log n)$ total edges.[2] We can therefore broadcast the full topology of this component graph to the whole network in $O(D + \sqrt{n}\log n)$ rounds by pipelining these edges through the global BFS tree.

At this point, every node v knows its flood component and the full flood component graph. This allows v to determine the set of flood components that cover its tree in forest T'. Each such flood component is described by its marked node's id, so v can choose the largest such id as the name for its T' tree. All nodes in this same tree will choose the same name.

We now combine these distributed coordination strategies with our preceding results on the number of calls to the MDS subroutines to obtain the following bound. We defer the proof to the full version [9].

THEOREM 2.14. *There exists a distributed implementation of MDS that outputs a spanning tree of degree $O(a+\log n)$ in $O((D+\sqrt{n})\log^4 n)$ rounds, in expectation, in the broadcast-CONGEST model.*

3 ALGORITHM FOR CONSTRAINED MATCHINGS

We now prove Theorem 2.3 by designing a randomized distributed algorithm (in the broadcast-CONGEST model) for finding near-maximum constrained q-matchings, which runs in $O((D+\sqrt{n})\log n)$ rounds. The algorithm, which we call CONSTRAINED-MATCHING, is based on finding approximate flow in a shallow network.

What distinguishes constrained matchings from other variations of bipartite matching is the constraint on the bundles, which is a constraint on *sets* of vertices rather than just on individual vertices. It appears to preclude a simple reduction to a standard matching computation. To overcome this extra difficulty, we extend in the obvious way the standard relationships between bipartite matchings and flows on 4-layer graphs (a source s, the two layers of the bipartite graph, and the sink t) to add in a fifth layer which will constrain the bundles appropriately. We then find maximal flows in this graph in $O(\log n)$ phases, and show that these flows give an $O(1)$-approximation to the maximum constrained q-matching. At a high level, CONSTRAINED-MATCHING computes a maximal *fractional* solution and then rounds this fractional solution (all in a distributed fashion).

There is one additional difficulty, which is that one side of the bipartite graph we are working in (the imp graph H) consists of leaf branches, not just nodes. Fortunately, by using the communication primitives discussed in Section 2.4, each phase of the algorithm can be executed in $O(D + \sqrt{n})$ distributed rounds, thus giving a total running time of $O((D + \sqrt{n})\log n)$.

3.1 Algorithm

Constrained matchings correspond to flows in a related flow graph F. The vertices of the flow graph F consist of the set B of bundles, the extreme nodes s and t, as well as the sets U and Q from the graph H. There is a directed edge from s to each bundle node in B, from each bundle to its constituent leaf branches in U, from leaf branches to the nodes in Q they are adjacent to in H, and finally from each node in Q to t. Edges from s to bundles, and those from Q to t, are of capacity q, while the rest are of unit capacity.

Observe that there is a one-one correspondence between constrained q-matchings in H and integral flows in F. Moreover, each edge in H has a unique flow path in F and vice versa. Thus we may specify a flow in F by giving only the flow on edges in H.

For a flow f, let $f(e)$ denote the flow through edge e, $f(v)$ denote the flow going out of v, and $v(f) = f(s)$ be the *value* of the flow. The *size* of a constrained q-matching equals the value of the corresponding flow. We say that a node is *full* if it has incoming flow at least 1/8-th of its capacity (where the capacity of a vertex is the maximum of its total incoming and total outgoing capacities).

The algorithm initially assigns each flow path a flow of $1/m$, where m is the number of edges. In each phase, every non-full node in Q doubles the flow on its incident paths from non-full nodes in U (through its parents in B) by sending a "double the flow" message to its neighbors (full neighbors will ignore this message). It takes one round to send these "double" messages, and then in each leaf bundle we can use our intra-component aggregation primitive (the second type of strategy in Section 2.4) to make sure that in each leaf bundle C, every node knows how much flow goes through the node representing C in F before this doubling (so in particular knows if C is full already, and so should ignore the message) and after the doubling. After this knowledge has been disseminated, each node in a leaf bundle that is adjacent to at least one node in Q sends the new flow value to its neighbors in Q, which will then know which of its incident edges did actually double the flow. After at most $\log m$ doubling phases there will be no way of sending more flow using only non-full nodes (as we show in the next subsection), so we move to the next part of the algorithm, where we use randomized rounding to find a large constrained q-matching.

In particular, we would like to do the following (from a centralized perspective). First add each edge e in H to a set S independently with probability $f(e)$. Then any leaf branch in U with more than one incident edge in S removes all such edges from S, any bundle with more than q incident edges in S removes all such edges from S, and any node in Q with more than q incident edges in S removes all

[2] For the sake of analysis, orient all edges in T toward a common root before removing high degree nodes to create T'. In the resulting directed forest, each flood component has at most one *outgoing* edge from a node in the flood component to a parent outside the flood component. Each edge in the flood component graph is an outgoing edge for some component, so if there are $O(\sqrt{n}\log n)$ total components there are $O(\sqrt{n}\log n)$ total edges.

such edges from S. This would (by definition) result in a constrained q-matching, which we call S'.

In order to implement this in broadcast-CONGEST, we first have every vertex v in each leaf branch C in U make the appropriate randomized decisions for the edges from H that are incident on v, so every vertex v in each leaf branch known which edges of S are incident on it. Note that this results in the same S as in the centralized algorithm. Now if v added more than one incident edge to S, then it removes all of these edges from S and uses our intra-component communication primitive to send a message to all other nodes in C about this fact, which will then cause all other nodes in C to remove all of their incident edges from S (if there were any). Otherwise, if v added exactly one edge to S, it broadcasts the identity of this edge to all of its neighbors (and in particular the other endpoint of the added edge) as well as using our intra-component primitives to send the identity of the edge to the rest of the nodes in C. It is easy to see that if multiple such messages are being sent in some leaf branch, then we can detect that fact and send a "failure" message to all nodes in the branch so that they all remove their incident edges from S.

Now each leaf branch has either 0 or 1 incident edge in S, and all nodes in the branch know the identity of this edge (if it exists). The root of each leaf branch sends to its parent the identity of this edge. So now the root of each leaf *bundle* knows the edges incident on the bundle which are in S. If there are more than q such edges, then this bundle root removes them all by sending a message to all of the nodes in all of the leaf branches in the bundle (again using our primitives from Section 2.4). Similarly, each node in Q knows all of its incident edges that are in S, and if there are more than q of them then it removes all of them from S by broadcasting a failure message to its neighbors. The edges which survive this process are S', and it is easy to see that it is precisely the same set as would have been computed in the centralized version.

3.2 Analysis

We omit the proof of the following claim.

Lemma 3.1. *Constrained-Matching requires $O((D+\sqrt{n})\log n)$ rounds in broadcast-CONGEST.*

The flow f that the algorithm computed has the property that there is no way to send more flow using only non-full nodes (or else the algorithm would send more flow). Thus the value of f is at least $1/8$ of some *maximal* flow, which is where every $s-t$ path has some node that is *saturated*, i.e., whose flow is at full capacity. We now claim that any maximal flow is close to a maximum flow. The *depth* of a flow network is the length of the longest $s-t$ path, so in our flow network the depth is 4.

Lemma 3.2. *The value of a maximal flow in a depth-d flow network is at least $1/d$-fraction of the value of the maximum flow.*

Proof. The depth constraint implies that $v(f)\cdot d \geq \sum_{e\in F} f(e)$, for any flow f. Namely, since each flow path is of length at most d, each unit of flow is counted at most d times in the sum. Maximality means that there is an $s-t$ cut $(Z, V-Z)$ such that all edges in F that go from Z to $V-Z$ are at full capacity (in f). This implies that $\sum_{v\in Z} f(v) \geq cap(Z, V-Z)$, where $cap(Z, V-Z)$ is the sum of the edge capacities across the cut. Observe that $\sum_{v\in Z} f(v) \leq \sum_{v\in V\setminus\{t\}} f(v) = \sum_{e\in F} f(e)$. The capacity constraints imply that $cap(Z, V-Z) \geq v(f^*)$, where f^* is a maximum flow. Combined, we have that $v(f) \geq v(f^*)/d$. □

Corollary 3.3. *Let f be the flow computed by our algorithm. Then, $v(f) \geq \frac{1}{32}|M|$ for every constrained q-matching M of H.*

Proof. Since in f every $s-t$ path contains at least one full node, $v(f)$ is at least $1/8$ of the value of any maximal flow, and so by Lemma 3.2 we know that $v(f)$ is at least $1/32$ of the value of the maximum flow (which will be integral since alll capacities are integral). As discussed, there is a bijection between the integral flows in F and constrained q-matchings in H, so this implies that $v(f)$ is at least $1/32$ times the size of the maximum constrained q-matching in F. □

By construction S' is a feasible constrained q-matching, so we just need to show that it has large value.

Lemma 3.4. *Let f be the (fractional) flow and S' be the edge set computed by our algorithm. Then $\mathbb{E}[|S'|] \geq v(f)/4$.*

Proof. Consider an edge $e=(u,v)$ in H (i.e., from U to Q). Let A_e be the event that some other edge incident on u is added to S. Let B_e be the event that q or more edges are added that have endpoints in the same bundle as e but not u. Finally, let C_e be the event that q or more other edges incident on v were added to S. Observe that if e was added to S, then it will remain in S' if none of the three events (A_e, B_e and C_e) take place. Using that the flow is at most one-fourth of capacity,

$$\mathbb{P}[A_e] = 1 - \prod_{e'\ni u, e'\neq e} (1-f(e')) \leq \sum_{e'\ni u} f(e') \leq 1/4\,.$$

Let Y be the number of edges in S incident on the same bundle as e. Then, $\mathbb{E}[Y] \leq q/4$. So, by Markov's inequality, $\mathbb{P}[B_e] \leq \mathbb{P}[Y \geq 4\,\mathbb{E}[Y]] \leq 1/4$. Similarly, $\mathbb{P}[C_e] \leq 1/4$. By the union bound, the probability of a bad event is at most $\mathbb{P}[A_e \cup B_e \cup C_e] \leq 3/4$. Thus, the event X_e that edge e is contained in S' has probability

$$\mathbb{P}[X_e] \geq f(e)\cdot(1-\mathbb{P}[A_e\cup B_e\cup C_e]) = f(e)/4\,,$$

since the event of e being chosen in S is independent from the three bad events. Thus, by linearity of expectation,

$$\mathbb{E}[|S'|] = \sum_{e\in E(H)} \mathbb{P}[X_e] \geq \frac{1}{4}\sum_{e\in E(H)} f(e) = v(f)/4\,. \qquad \square$$

We can now combine these pieces to prove our main result regarding this algorithm (presented in Theorem 2.3):

Proof of Theorem 2.3. The running time is direct from Lemma 3.1. Lemma 3.4 and Corollary 3.3 imply that $\mathbb{E}[|S'|] \geq v(f)/4 \geq M^*/128$, where M^* is the size of an optimal q-constrained matching. So the algorithm returns a 128-approximation. □

4 DERANDOMIZATION

We sketch here how the algorithm can be derandomized in the CONGEST model.

The main effort is on constrained matching, for which adapt a method of Fischer [11] for deterministic matchings. We initially compute fractional matching deterministically with repeated doubling, and then round the flow values down to the nearest power of 2. The $O(\log \Delta)$ weight classes are then eliminated in sequence, starting with the lowest value. Each node has an number of incident edges with the lowest value and by arbitrarily coloring them, we obtain a partition into degree-2 subgraphs, i.e., paths and cycles. The idea is to shift the weight from even numbered edges on each path/cycle to the odd numbered edges, which obeys the capacity constraints while eliminating the lowest weight class.

The algorithm cannot be applied directly to the case of matching branches, since the communication paths involved may now induce heavy loads. We show that we can actually maintain unit load on the edges by leveraging the flexibility available in pairing the incident edges to a node, i.e., the edges that should belong to the same path/cycle. We still need to process the outgoing edges from each node in parallel, which limits the application to the the full CONGEST model. We refer to the full version for the complete details [9].

The other randomized step is in ensuring that a component does not both have an incoming and outgoing edges in improvement subgraph. This can be replaced by the following simple deterministic rule: A component with two or more incoming edges removes its outgoing edge. Then components with a single incoming and outgoing edges induce a degree-2 graph on which we compute a maximal matching.

5 LOWER BOUNDS

Our main lower bound is the following:

THEOREM 5.1. *For any $n \in \mathbb{N}$, $\alpha > 4$, and $h \geq 1$, there exist two families $\mathcal{G}^{\mathrm{Rand}}_{n,h,\alpha}$ and $\mathcal{G}^{\mathrm{Det}}_{n,\alpha}$ of $\Theta(n)$-node graphs, which have diameters $O(h + \log n)$ and $O(\log n)$ respectively and give the following lower bounds for the computation of $(\alpha - 4)$-additive or $\alpha/4$-multiplicative approximate MDSTs. 1) For graphs in $\mathcal{G}^{\mathrm{Rand}}_{n,h,\alpha}$ such that $h/\alpha = o(\sqrt{n}\log^2 n)$ holds, any randomized CONGEST algorithm with success probability at least $2/3$ requires $\tilde{\Omega}((nh/\alpha)^{1/3})$ rounds in the worst case. 2) For graphs in $\mathcal{G}^{\mathrm{Det}}_{n,h,\alpha}$, any deterministic CONGEST algorithm requires $\tilde{\Omega}(\sqrt{n}/\alpha)$ rounds in the worst case.*

Note that this theorem applies not only to broadcast-CONGEST but also to the standard CONGEST model.

Before discussing the proof of Theorem 5.1, we explain how this theorem matches our upper bound. Consider the randomized lower bound first. Let $h = \Theta(n^{1/2-3\epsilon})$ for an arbitrarily small positive constant $\epsilon < 1/6$, and α = polylog(n). Then the diameter D of the instances from $\mathcal{G}^{\mathrm{Rand}}_{n,h,\alpha}$ is $\Theta(n^{1/2-3\epsilon})$, and Theorem 5.1 yields a lower bound of $\tilde{\Omega}(n^{1/2-\epsilon}/\mathrm{polylog(n)})$ rounds. Since $D = o(n^{1/2-\epsilon}/\mathrm{polylog(n)})$ holds, it implies a $\tilde{\Omega}(n^{1/2-\epsilon} + D)$-round lower bound for any polylog(n)-multiplicative approximation algorithms. That is, our algorithm is round-optimal up to subpolynomial (i.e., $O(n^{o(1)})$) factors. The $\tilde{\Omega}(n^{1/3})$-round lower bound for the logarithmic diameter case is derived from choosing $h = O(\log n)$. In the deterministic case, we have $D = O(\log n)$. Then any $\tilde{O}(\sqrt{n} + D)$-round algorithm with polylog(n)-multiplicative approximation is round-optimal up to polylogarithmic factors. The deterministic lower bound also implies that there is no efficient deterministic algorithm with multiplicative dependency on D. That is, if there exists an algorithm running in $\tilde{O}(n^{1/3}D)$ rounds (the randomized lower bound does not exclude the possibility of such an algorithm), it must be randomized.

The proof of Theorem 5.1 follows the seminal framework by Das Sarma et al. [25] of reducing from two-party communication complexity. Due to space constraints, some details are deferred to the full version [9]. A key idea is to utilize the *gap-k disjointness* function $\mathrm{gdisj}_{N,k}$ [7, 12], which is a generalized version of the standard set-disjointness. In this problem, Alice has some vector $\boldsymbol{x} \in \{0,1\}^N$ and Bob has some vector $\boldsymbol{y} \in \{0,1\}^N$, and their goal is to determine whether $\boldsymbol{x} \cdot \boldsymbol{y} \geq k$ or $\boldsymbol{x} \cdot \boldsymbol{y} = 0$, where $\cdot$ is the (bitwise) inner product of two vectors. Clearly the case of $k = 1$ corresponds to the standard set-disjointness. We will use the following lower bound:

LEMMA 5.2 ([7, 12]). *The randomized communication complexity of $\mathrm{gdisj}_{N,k}$ with error probability at most $1/3$ is $\Omega(N/k)$, and the deterministic communication complexity of $\mathrm{gdisj}_{N,k}$ for $k \leq N/4\log N$ is $\Omega(N)$.*

The construction of the two families $\mathcal{G}^{\mathrm{Rand}}_{n,h,\alpha}$ and $\mathcal{G}^{\mathrm{Det}}_{n,\alpha}$ follows the reduction technique by Izumi [19] on top of the framework by Das Sarma et al. [25]. We first introduce a graph $\Gamma_{N,M,h}(\boldsymbol{a},\boldsymbol{b})$ associated with two parameters N and M, and a pair of two N-bit bianary vectors $(\boldsymbol{a},\boldsymbol{b})$. Each family is defined as the sets of $\Gamma_{N,M,h}(\boldsymbol{a},\boldsymbol{b})$ over all $(\boldsymbol{a},\boldsymbol{b})$ with an appropriate choice of N and M. For simplicity, we assume that N, M, and M/h are all integer values. The graph $\Gamma_{N,M,h}(\boldsymbol{a},\boldsymbol{b})$ is constructed as follows:

(1) We first create $4N + 1$ paths of length M, each of which is denoted by P_i $(0 \leq i \leq 4N)$.The nodes constituting P_i are identified by $v_{(i,0)}, v_{(i,1)}, \ldots, v_{(i,M-1)}$ from left to right.
(2) We then create a complete binary tree T with M leaves $u_0, u_1, \ldots u_{M-1}$. For every $i \in [0, M/h]$, the node u_{ih} is connected with all the nodes $v_{ih,j}$ for $j \in [0, 4N-1]$.
(3) For every $i \in [0, N-1]$, we add two edges $(v_{4i+1,0}, v_{4i+2+\boldsymbol{a}[i],0})$ and $(v_{4i+3-\boldsymbol{a}[i],0}, v_{4(i+1),0})$. Similarly, for every $i \in [0, N-1]$, we add two edges $(v_{4i,M-1}, v_{4i+1+\boldsymbol{b}[i],M-1})$ and $(v_{4i+2-\boldsymbol{b}[i],M-1}, v_{4i+3,M-1})$.

It is not difficult to check that $\Gamma_{N,M,h}(\boldsymbol{a},\boldsymbol{b})$ has diameter $O(h + \log n)$. Let $T_{\boldsymbol{a},\boldsymbol{b}}$ be the minimum-degree spanning tree of $\Gamma_{N,M,h}(\boldsymbol{a},\boldsymbol{b})$, and $\Delta(U)$ be the maximum degree of a spanning tree U. The key property of $\Gamma_{N,M,h}(\boldsymbol{a},\boldsymbol{b})$ is the following lemma:

LEMMA 5.3. *$\Delta(T_{\boldsymbol{a},\boldsymbol{b}}) \geq 1 + (\boldsymbol{a}\cdot\boldsymbol{b} + 1)h/M$ for every $(\boldsymbol{a},\boldsymbol{b}) \in (\{0,1\}^N)^2$. In addition, if $\boldsymbol{a}\cdot\boldsymbol{b} = 0$ then $d_{\boldsymbol{a},\boldsymbol{b}} \leq 3$.*

PROOF. Let Z_i be the subgraph of $\Gamma_{N,M,h}(\boldsymbol{a},\boldsymbol{b})$ induced by $\{v_{i,j} \mid k \in [4i, 4i+3], 0 \leq j \leq M-1\} \cup \{v_{4(i+1),0}\}$, and $Z = (\cup_i Z_i) \cup P_{4N}$. The graph Z_i forms a simple path Q_i from $v_{4i,0}$ to $v_{4(i+1),0}$ if $\boldsymbol{a}[i] \cdot \boldsymbol{b}[i] \neq 1$. Otherwise, it forms a simple path Q_i from $v_{4i,0}$ to $v_{4(i+1),0}$ and a cycle C_i disconnected in Z. The simple paths Q_i for all $i \in [0, N-1]$ and P_{4N} are concatenated into a long simple path, and the number of disconnected cycles is equal to $\boldsymbol{a}\cdot\boldsymbol{b}$. Consequently, Z consists of $\boldsymbol{a}\cdot\boldsymbol{b} + 1$ connected components, which must be connected in $T_{\boldsymbol{a},\boldsymbol{b}}$ using the edges incident to leaves of T. Since at most M/h nodes has those edges, at least one node must have a degree $(\boldsymbol{a}\cdot\boldsymbol{b} + 1)h/M$ or more. If $\boldsymbol{a}\cdot\boldsymbol{b} = 0$, Z forms a single path, and thus adding an edge $(u_0, v_{0,0})$ to $T \cup Z$ results in a spanning tree of the maximum degree three. □

The reduction utilizes the simulation theorem by Das Sarma et al., which allows Alice and Bob to simulate any $o(M)$-round CONGEST algorithm running on $\Gamma_{N,M,h}(\boldsymbol{a},\boldsymbol{b})$ with relatively few communication bits.

THEOREM 5.4 (DAS SARMA ET AL. [25]). *Assume that Alice and Bob respectively knows two N-bit strings $\boldsymbol{a}$ and $\boldsymbol{b}$. Let X be any CONGEST algorithm running in $\Gamma_{N,M,h}(\boldsymbol{a},\boldsymbol{b})$ within $r(n) = o(M)$ rounds. Then there exists a two-party protocol which uses $O(r(n)\log^2 n)$-bit communication and provides the outputs (i.e. the internal states at the beginning of round $r(n)+1$) of X at the nodes $v_{0,0}$ and $v_{0,M-1}$ respectively to Alice and Bob.*

Now we are ready to prove Theorem 5.1.

PROOF. We mainly consider the case of randomized algorithms. The deterministic case can be proved similarly with a different setting of N and M. We set $N = \left(\frac{\alpha n^2 \log^2 n}{h}\right)^{1/3}$ and $M = \left(\frac{hn}{\alpha \log^2 n}\right)^{1/3}$. We have already shown that $\mathcal{G}_{N,M,h}$ is the set of graphs of $\Theta(n)$ nodes and diameter $O(h + \log n)$. Suppose for contradiction a CONGEST algorithm X computing an α-approximate min-degree spanning tree, which runs in $o(M) = o\left(\frac{nh}{\alpha \log^2 n}\right)^{1/3}$ rounds for any instance $\Gamma_{N,M,h}(\boldsymbol{a},\boldsymbol{b}) \in \mathcal{G}_{n,h,\alpha}$. Without loss of generality, this algorithm informs all the nodes of the value $\Delta(U)$ for the constructed spanning tree U, which takes extra $O(h + \log n)$ rounds for the execution of X but does not affect the asymptotic time complexity of X. (recall that $\Omega(D) = \Omega(h + \log n)$ is the trivial lower bound). Let $k = \frac{\alpha M}{h} = \left(\frac{\alpha^2 n}{h^2 \log^2 n}\right)^{1/3}$. By Lemma 5.3, if $\boldsymbol{a}\cdot\boldsymbol{b} \geq k$, $\Delta(T_{\boldsymbol{a},\boldsymbol{b}})$ is at least $kh/M \geq \alpha$ and thus $\Delta(U) \geq \alpha$ holds. If $\boldsymbol{a}\cdot\boldsymbol{b} = 0$ holds, $\Delta(T\{\boldsymbol{a},\boldsymbol{b}\})$ is at most three, and thus $\Delta(U)$ is at most $3 + (\alpha - 4) \leq \alpha - 1$ in the additive approximation case, and is $3 \cdot \alpha/4 < \alpha$ in the multiplicative approximation case. In any case, the value of $gdistj_{N,k}(\boldsymbol{a},\boldsymbol{b})$ can be correctly decided from the output value of X. By Theorem 5.4, it yields a two-party protocol for the N-bit gap-k disjointness problem, which consumes $o(M\log^2 n)$-bit communication. Since $N/k = \left(\frac{hn\log^4 n}{\alpha}\right) = M\log^2 n$ holds, the communication complexity of that protocol is $o(M\log^2 n) = o(N/k)$ bits. It contradicts Theorem 5.2. For the proof of the deterministic case, we set $N = \left(\alpha n \log^2 n\right)^{1/2}$, $M = \left(\frac{n}{\alpha \log^2 n}\right)^{1/2}$, $h = 1$, and $k = \alpha M$. Then, the same argument results in a deterministic two-party protocol for $\mathrm{gdisj}_{N,k}$ consuming $o(M\log^2 n)$-bit communication. Since k satisfies $k \leq N/4\log N$ for sufficiently large n, the deterministic lower bound is $\Omega(N)$ bits by Lemma 5.2, but $M\log^2 N \geq N$ holds and thus we have a contradiction. □

ACKNOWLEDGMENTS

This work was supported in part by NSF Awards #7773087 and #1535887, JST SICORP, KAKENHI No.16H02878 and 19K11824, and Icelandic Research Fund grant 174484.

REFERENCES

[1] A. Agrawal, P. Klein, and R. Ravi. 1991. *How tough is the minimum-degree Steiner tree? A new approximate Min-Max equality.* Technical Report CS-91-94. Brown University.

[2] B. Awerbuch. 1987. Optimal distributed algorithms for minimum-weight spanning tree, counting, leader election and related problems. In *Proceedings of the Symposium on Theory of Computing.* 230–240.

[3] Lélia Blin and Franck Butelle. 2003. The first approximated distributed algorithm for the minimum degree spanning tree problem on general graphs. In *Proceedings of the International Parallel and Distributed Processing Symposium.*

[4] Lélia Blin and Franck Butelle. 2004. The First Approximated Distributed Algorithm For The Minimum Degree Spanning Tree Problem On General Graphs. *Int. J. Found. Comput. Sci.* 15, 3 (2004), 507–516.

[5] Lélia Blin and Pierre Fraigniaud. 2015. Space-Optimal Time-Efficient Silent Self-Stabilizing Constructions of Constrained Spanning Trees. In *35th IEEE International Conference on Distributed Computing Systems, ICDCS 2015, Columbus, OH, USA, June 29 - July 2, 2015.* 589–598.

[6] Lélia Blin, Maria Gradinariu Potop-Butucaru, and Stephane Rovedakis. 2011. Self-stabilizing minimum degree spanning tree within one from the optimal degree. *J. Parallel Distrib. Comput.* 71, 3 (2011), 438–449.

[7] Keren Censor-Hillel and Michal Dory. 2018. Distributed Spanner Approximation. In *Proc. of the 2018 ACM Symposium on Principles of Distributed Computing (PODC).* 139–148.

[8] F. Chin and H.F. Ting. 1985. An almost linear time and $O(n \log n + E)$ message distributed algorithm for minimum-weight spanning trees. In *Proceedings of the Symposium on Foundations of Computer Science.* 257–266.

[9] Michael Dinitz, Magnús M Halldórsson, Taisuke Izumi, and Calvin Newport. 2018. Distributed Algorithms for Minimum Degree Spanning Trees. *arXiv preprint arXiv:1806.03365* (2018).

[10] M. Elkin. 2004. Unconditional lower bounds on the time-approximation trade-offs for the distributed minimum spanning tree problem. In *Proceedings of the Symposium on Theory of Computing.* 331–340.

[11] Manuela Fischer. 2018. Improved deterministic distributed matching via rounding. *Distributed Computing* (2018).

[12] Orr Fischer, Tzlil Gonen, and Rotem Oshman. 2017. Distributed Property Testing for Subgraph-Freeness Revisited. *CoRR* abs/1705.04033 (2017).

[13] Martin Fürer and Balaji Raghavachari. 1990. An NC approximation for the minimum degree spanning tree problem. In *Proceedings of the Annual Allerton Conference on Communication, Control and Computing.* 274–281.

[14] Martin Fürer and Balaji Raghavachari. 1992. Approximating the minimum degree spanning tree to within one from the optimal degree. In *Proceedings of the Symposium on Discrete Algorithms.* 317–324.

[15] Martin Fürer and Balaji Raghavachari. 1994. Approximating the Minimum-Degree Steiner Tree to within One of Optimal. *Journal of Algorithms* 17, 3 (1994), 409 – 423.

[16] E. Gafni. 1985. Improvements in the time complexity of two message-optimal election algorithms. In *Proceedings of the Symposium on the Principles of Distributed Computation.* 175–185.

[17] R. G. Gallager, P. A. Humblet, and P. M. Spira. 1983. A distributed algorithm for minimum-weight spanning trees. *ACM Transactions on Programming Languages and Systems* 5, 1 (1983), 66–77.

[18] J. Garay, S. Kutten, and D. Peleg. 1998. A sub-linear time distributed algorithm for minimum-weight spanning trees. *SIAM Journal of Computing* 27 (1998), 302–316.

[19] Taisuke Izumi. 2014. Randomized Lower Bound for Distributed Spanning-Tree Verification. In *Proc. of the 21st International Colloquium on Structural Information and Communication Complexity (SIROCCO).* 137–148.

[20] Dénes König. 1916. Über graphen und ihre anwendung auf determinantentheorie und mengenlehre. *Math. Ann.* 77, 4 (1916), 453–465.

[21] S. Kutten and D. Peleg. 1995. Fast distributed construction of k-dominating sets and applications. In *Proceedings of the Symposium on the Principles of Distributed Computation.* 238–251.

[22] Christian Lavault and Mario Valencia-Pabon. 2008. A distributed approximation algorithm for the minimum degree minimum weight spanning trees. *J. Parallel and Distrib. Comput.* 68, 2 (2008), 200–208.

[23] J. Nešetřil, E. Milková, and H. Nešetřilová. 2001. Otakar Boruvka on minimum spanning tree problem. Translation of both the 1926 papers, comments, history. *Discrete Mathematics* 233, 1 (2001), 3–36.

[24] D. Peleg and V. Rubinovich. 2001. A near-tight lower bound on the time complexity of distributed MST construction. *SIAM Journal of Computing* 30, 5 (2001), 1427–1442.

[25] A. Sarma, S. Holzer, L. Kor, A. Korman, D. Nanongkai, G. Pandurangan, D. Peleg, and R. Wattenhofer. 2012. Distributed Verification and Hardness of Distributed Approximation. *SIAM J. Comput.* 41, 5 (2012), 1235–1265.

Improved Distributed Approximations for Minimum-Weight Two-Edge-Connected Spanning Subgraph*

Michal Dory
Technion, Israel
smichald@cs.technion.ac.il

Mohsen Ghaffari
ETH Zurich, Switzerland
ghaffari@inf.ethz.ch

ABSTRACT

The minimum-weight 2-edge-connected spanning subgraph (2-ECSS) problem is a natural generalization of the well-studied minimum-weight spanning tree (MST) problem, and it has received considerable attention in the area of network design. The latter problem asks for a minimum-weight subgraph with an edge connectivity of 1 between each pair of vertices while the former strengthens this edge-connectivity requirement to 2. Despite this resemblance, the 2-ECSS problem is considerably more complex than MST. While MST admits a linear-time centralized exact algorithm, 2-ECSS is NP-hard and the best known centralized approximation algorithm for it (that runs in polynomial time) gives a 2-approximation.

In this paper, we give a *deterministic* distributed algorithm with round complexity of $\widetilde{O}(D+\sqrt{n})$ that computes a $(9+\epsilon)$-approximation of 2-ECSS, for any constant $\epsilon > 0$. Up to logarithmic factors, this complexity matches the $\widetilde{\Omega}(D + \sqrt{n})$ lower bound that can be derived from the technique of Das Sarma et al. [STOC'11], as shown by Censor-Hillel and Dory [OPODIS'17]. Our result is the first distributed *constant* approximation for 2-ECSS in the nearly optimal time and it improves on a recent randomized algorithm of Dory [PODC'18], which achieved an $O(\log n)$-approximation in $\widetilde{O}(D + \sqrt{n})$ rounds.

We also present an alternative algorithm for $O(\log n)$-approximation, whose round complexity is linear in the *low-congestion shortcut* parameter of the network—following a framework introduced by Ghaffari and Haeupler [SODA'16]. This algorithm has round complexity $\widetilde{O}(D + \sqrt{n})$ in worst-case networks but it provably runs much faster in many well-behaved graph families of interest. For instance, it runs in $\widetilde{O}(D)$ time in planar networks and those with bounded genus, bounded path-width or bounded tree-width.

CCS CONCEPTS

• **Theory of computation → Graph algorithms analysis; Approximation algorithms analysis; Distributed algorithms.**

KEYWORDS

distributed graph algorithms, approximation algorithms, distributed network design, k-edge-connectivity

ACM Reference Format:
Michal Dory and Mohsen Ghaffari. 2019. Improved Distributed Approximations for Minimum-Weight Two-Edge-Connected Spanning Subgraph. In *2019 ACM Symposium on Principles of Distributed Computing (PODC '19), July 29-August 2, 2019, Toronto, ON, Canada.* ACM, New York, NY, USA, 10 pages. https://doi.org/10.1145/3293611.3331617

1 INTRODUCTION AND RELATED WORK

There is a large body of deep and beautiful work on developing centralized (approximation) algorithms for various *network design* problems. These are typically in the format of finding a minimum-weight subgraph H of a graph/network G, given certain weights for the network elements (edges or vertices), such that H satisfies some desired properties, e.g., certain connectivity requirements. The motivation is simple and practical: suppose that using each communication link of G has some cost (e.g., in monetary terms, to be paid to the provider). Which links should we use to minimize our costs while still meeting all of our connectivity requirements? Unlike the extensive amount of attention and progress on centralized algorithms for network design problems, developments on the distributed side have been much more scarce. Even for many of the basic problems of the area, we do not have satisfactory distributed algorithms. There are only few exceptions.

One prominent exception is the case of the minimum-weight spanning tree (MST) problem. This is the minimum-weight subgraph that ensures that all vertices are connected to each other. MST has been one of the central problems in the developments of distributed graph algorithms, starting from the pioneering work of Gallager et al. [10]. By now we have a relatively good understanding of the complexity of this problem: It can be solved in $O(D + \sqrt{n}\log^* n)$ rounds [24], in synchronous message-passing rounds with $O(\log n)$-bit messages (i.e., the CONGEST model [27]), where D denotes the network diameter and n denotes the number of vertices. Moreover, this bound almost matches an $\Omega(D + \sqrt{\frac{n}{\log n}})$ lower bound, developed in the line of work of [6, 8, 28].

As soon as we take just one step beyond the basic MST problem, in the realm of network design questions, we soon reach a problem for which we do not have a satisfactory algorithmic answer, yet. This is the minimum-weight 2-edge-connected spanning subgraph (2-ECSS) problem, where instead of asking all vertices to be connected, we ask them to be 2-edge-connected. That is, we want that the subgraph has some minimal resilience to edge failures and even if one of the links breaks, still all vertices are connected (without us having to recompute the subgraph). This is again a natural and practical property to desire in networking, given the prevalence and

*A full version of this paper is available at https://arxiv.org/abs/1905.10833.

PODC '19, July 29-August 2, 2019, Toronto, ON, Canada

ACM ISBN 978-1-4503-6217-7/19/07...$15.00
https://doi.org/10.1145/3293611.3331617

frequency of link failures. Although there has been recent progress on the distributed complexity of this problem, the answers are still not satisfactory, and that is where the contribution of this paper comes in. But before delving into our contribution, let us take a closer look at what is known about 2-ECSS.

The problem of computing a minimum 2-ECSS is known to be NP-hard, by a reduction from the Hamiltonian cycle problem [4]. This already shows that 2-ECSS is much harder than the closely related problem of MST, which admits a linear-time (randomized) centralized exact algorithm [20]. The best known centralized (polynomial-time) approximation algorithms for 2-ECSS give a 2-approximation [19, 22]. These algorithms also give a 2-approximation for the more general minimum-weight k-edge-connected spanning subgraph (k-ECSS). If all edge-weights are equal (i.e., in the unweighted case), then the best known approximation factor for 2-ECSS is 4/3 [30] and for k-ECSS is $1 + \frac{1}{2k} + O(\frac{1}{k^2})$ [9].

1.1 Our Contributions, in the Context of the Distributed State-of-the-Art

1.1.1 *First Contribution — Better Approximation.*

Distributed state-of-the-art: Censor-Hillel and Dory [3] provided an algorithm that runs in $O(h_{MST} + \sqrt{n}\log^* n)$ rounds and gives a 3-approximation of the min-weight 2-ECSS. Here, h_{MST} denotes the height of the minimum spanning tree; note that this can be as large as $\Theta(n)$, even in networks with small diameter D. Thus, this round complexity can be much higher than the lower bound of $\widetilde{\Omega}(D + \sqrt{n})$ [3, 6]. Dory [7] provided a randomized algorithm that runs in the near-optimal run time of $\widetilde{O}(D + \sqrt{n})$ and provides an $O(\log n)$-approximation.

Two comments are in order. First, for general k, one can obtain an $O(\log k)$-approximation but in round complexity of $O(knD)$ [16, 31], and an $O(k \log n)$-approximation in $O(k(D\log^3 n + n))$ rounds [7]. Both of these complexities are at least linear in the network size and well-above our target round complexity. Second, let us discuss the special case where all the weights are equal, i.e., when the problem is unweighted. This case is much easier and one can obtain a constant approximation locally in $(k \log^{1+o(1)} n)$ rounds [26]. The reason is that we can build k disjoint ultra-sparse spanners, one after the other, each in the graph remaining after the removal of previous ones. An ultra-sparse spanner is one with $O(n)$ edges. Hence, our total number of edges will be $O(nk)$, which is within a constant factor of the smallest number of edges needed for being k-edge-connected, namely $kn/2$. Pettie [29] shows a CONGEST model algorithm with round complexity $O(\log^{1+o(1)} n)$ that builds an ultra-sparse spanner with stretch $\widetilde{O}(\log n)$. Additionally, if we are interested in better approximations for *unweighted* 2-ECSS, there is an $O(D)$-round 2-approximation [3] and an $O(n)$-round 3/2-approximation [23].

Our First Result: Above we mentioned a 3-approximation with suboptimal time [3] and an optimal time with suboptimal approximation of $O(\log n)$ [7]. Our first main result is to provide an algorithm that gets the best of these two worlds (using a different technique), namely near-optimal time and constant approximation. More concretely, we show the following result:

THEOREM 1.1. *There is a deterministic $(9 + \epsilon)$-approximation algorithm for weighted 2-ECSS in the* CONGEST *model that takes* $O((D + \sqrt{n})\frac{\log^2 n}{\epsilon})$ *rounds.*

We think that achieving a constant approximation in the near-optimal time is the main strength of this result. Another advantage of our approach is that is gives a *deterministic* algorithm, while the $O(\log n)$-approximation algorithm of [7] was randomized. Very recently we were able to show that a variant of the algorithm we show here actually obtains a $(5 + \epsilon)$-approximation, for details see the full version.

1.1.2 *Second Contribution — Faster Algorithm in Well-Behaved Networks.*

Our second contribution is in a different direction. Instead of setting the $\widetilde{\Omega}(D + \sqrt{n})$ lower-bound as our target round complexity for all network topologies, we would like to have an algorithm that runs no slower than this in the worst-case, but also ideally much faster in less pathological network instances, e.g., in graph families which are more relevant in practical networking settings.

In this regard, we build on a framework set forth by Ghaffari and Haeupler [11], known as *low-congestion shortcuts.* This framework was first used to give $\widetilde{O}(D)$ round distributed algorithms for problems such as minimum spanning tree and minimum cut, in planar networks. Notice that this can be much faster than the $\widetilde{O}(D + \sqrt{n})$ bound. By now, it is known that the same concept can be applied to a wider range of graph families. We mention just a sampling here: in networks with bounded genus, bounded path-width, and bounded tree-width, one can also obtain an $\widetilde{O}(D)$ round MST algorithm [11, 17]. In the much more general family of excluded minor graphs, one can obtain an $\widetilde{O}(D^2)$ round MST algorithm [18]. Finally, in Erdos-Renyi random graphs $G_{n,p}$ with $p = \Omega(\log n/n)$, one can obtain an MST algorithm with complexity $2^{O(\sqrt{\log n})}$ [13, 14].

These different round complexities come from the quality of the *shortcuts* that can be obtained in the given graph family, and the time needed to construct them. Given a graph $G = (V, E)$, we say it admits α-congestion β-dilation shortcuts with construction time γ, if the following is satisfied: for any partitioning of V into vertex-disjoint parts $V_1, V_2, \ldots, V_N$, each of which induced a connected subgraph $G[V_i]$, in γ rounds, we can construct subgraphs $H_1, \ldots H_N$ such that (A) $\forall i \in \{1, 2, \ldots, N\}$, the subgraph $G[V_i] + H_i$ has diameter at most β and moreover, (B) each edge $e \in E$ appears in at most α many of the graphs $G[V_i] + H_i$. It was shown by Ghaffari and Haeupler [11] that MST and $(1+\varepsilon)$-approximation of minimum cut can be solved in $\widetilde{O}(\alpha+\beta+\gamma)$ time. It is notable that this *shortcut complexity* $SC(G) = \alpha + \beta + \gamma$ is in the worst-case $O(D + \sqrt{n})$, as shown by Ghaffari and Haeupler [11], but it can be much better: for instance, as listed above, we have $SC(G) = \widetilde{O}(D)$ for any network that is planar, bounded genus, bounded path-width, or bounded tree-width [11, 17]. Moreover, we have $SC(G) = \widetilde{O}(D^2)$ in any excluded minor graph [18], and $SC(G) = 2^{O(\sqrt{\log n})} \ll n^{o(1)}$ in any Erdos-Renyi graphs above the connectivity threshold [13, 14]. Hence, to summarize, the framework of shortcuts and the parameter $SC(G) = \alpha + \beta + \gamma$ provide a convenient way to develop algorithms that are in the worst-case as bad as the lower bound $\widetilde{\Omega}(D + \sqrt{n})$, but can also run much faster, in a provable way, in many graph families of interest.

Our Second Result: Our second contribution is a distributed algorithm with such a graceful complexity for $O(\log n)$-approximation of the minimum weight 2-ECSS problem.

THEOREM 1.2. *There is a randomized distributed algorithm that computes an $O(\log n)$-approximation of weighted 2-ECSS in the CONGEST model and runs in $\widetilde{O}(\text{SC} + D) = \widetilde{O}(\alpha + \beta + \gamma + D)$ rounds, in any network G with diameter D where for any partition we can build an α-congestion β-dilation shortcut, in γ rounds.*

Theorem 1.2 gives an algorithm that always runs in at most $\widetilde{O}(D + \sqrt{n})$ rounds, but it runs provably much faster in many graph families of interest. In particular, it implies that we can obtain an $O(\log n)$-approximation in $\widetilde{O}(D)$ rounds in any network that is planar, bounded genus, bounded path-width, or bounded tree-width, in $\widetilde{O}(D^2)$ rounds in any network that is excluded minor, and in $2^{O(\sqrt{\log n})}$ rounds in Erdos-Renyi random graphs $G_{n,p}$ with $p = \Omega(\log n/n)$.

1.2 Technical overview

2-ECSS Approximation Boils Down to Tree Augmentation: Let T be the MST of $G = (V, E)$. To obtain the minimum weight 2-ECSS, we would like to compute a minimum weight set of non-tree edges $A \subseteq E$ that *covers* all the tree edges of T, according to the following definition: We say that a non-tree edge $e \in E$ covers a tree edge $t \in T$ if $(T \cup \{e\}) \setminus \{t\}$ is connected. We say that a set of non-tree edges A covers the tree edge $t \in T$ if A contains an edge that covers t. Note that A covers all the tree edges iff $T \cup A$ is 2-edge-connected. The problem of computing the minimum cost set of edges A such that $T \cup A$ is 2-edge-connected is known as the *tree augmentation problem* (TAP) and it can be seen that any α-approximation for it, along with the MST, T, gives an $\alpha + 1$ approximation of 2-ECSS (See Section 2 for a formal statement). This follows from the following. First, the MST is no more costly than the optimal 2-ECSS, as the latter contains a spanning tree in it. Second, the optimal 2-ECSS also covers all the edges of the MST and thus its size is an upper bound on the size of the optimal tree augmentation. Therefore, our objective boils down to providing an approximation for TAP.

Tree Augmentation Can be Seen as a Set Cover Problem: TAP is a special case of the well-studied *minimum-cost set cover* problem, where we want to choose a minimum-cost collection of *sets* which cover all the *elements* [32]; in our case this is choosing a minimum-cost collection of non-tree edges $A \subseteq E$ which cover all the tree edges. Of course, in the distributed setting, this special case comes with its own difficulties, because the sets (in our case, non-tree edges) are not directly connected to their elements (in our case, tree edges), which means we cannot resort to standard distributed set cover algorithms in a naive way. However, distributed and parallel algorithms for set cover can still form a basis for a distributed algorithm for TAP.

Previous Approaches and the Challenge: The connection between TAP and set cover is used in [7], where it is shown that using a certain decomposition of the graph it is possible to solve TAP by simulating a distributed greedy algorithm for set cover. This results in a randomized $O((D + \sqrt{n}) \log^2 n)$-round $O(\log n)$-approximation for weighted TAP and weighted 2-ECSS. However, since the approximation ratio of the greedy algorithm for set cover is $O(\log n)$, we cannot obtain a better approximation by simulating a general algorithm for set cover. Another option is to design a specific algorithm that exploits the properties of TAP. This is done in [3], where it is shown how to obtain a 2-approximation for weighted TAP and a 3-approximation for weighted 2-ECSS in $O(h)$ rounds, where h is the height of the tree we augment. However, in the worst case, h can be linear, and the algorithm from [3] relies heavily on the fact that we need to scan the whole tree.

Our Approach: To overcome the above obstacles, we suggest a new algorithm for weighted TAP. As in [7], our algorithm simulates an algorithm for set cover, however, we simulate an algorithm that exploits the specific structure of the set cover problem we solve, which allows to get a *constant* approximation. A crucial ingredient in the algorithm is a certain layering of the graph, that allows to implement the algorithm efficiently, and results in a *deterministic* algorithm that is near-optimal both in terms of the round complexity and in the approximation ratio obtained. In more detail, our algorithm is inspired by a parallel algorithm for set cover instances with *small neighbourhood covers* [1], and we next give the high-level intuition of this property in our case. As a first step, we start by replacing the input graph G by a related virtual graph G', having the additional property that all the non-tree edges in G' are between ancestors to descendants. This is useful, because now the set cover problem we solve has an additional structure. Consider a path P with a root r, from all the non-tree edges that cover a tree edge $t \in P$ we can choose only *two* non-tree edges that cover exactly the same tree edges in P. This is done by taking the edges that cover t and go to the highest ancestor, or to the lowest descendant. If our tree is not a path, we can decompose it in a certain way to $O(\log n)$ layers, each one is composed of disjoint paths, and a similar property now holds for all the tree edges with respect to these paths. A generalization of this property called the *small neighbourhood cover* property is studied in [1], where the authors show an efficient parallel algorithm that obtains a constant approximation for set cover instances having this property. Our general approach is to simulate the algorithm from [1] on the virtual graph G'. A major difference in our setting is that the set cover graph is not given as an input, and in particular tree edges cannot communicate directly with non-tree edges that cover them. We next explain how we overcome this.

Distributed Implementation: The algorithm from [1] is a primal-dual algorithm that is composed of two main phases, the forward phase and the reverse-delete phase. For implementing the forward phase, we show that the only communication pattern between tree edges and non-tree edges in the algorithm is computation of *aggregate* functions. To implement such computations, we bring to our construction a decomposition of the tree into segments used in [7, 15]. While similar computations are done in [7], the main obstacle in our case is that our algorithm works with a virtual graph G' and we explain how to extend the algorithm to this case. The reverse-delete phase creates new obstacles, as it requires computation of a maximal independent set (MIS) in a *completely virtual* graph G_i. In G_i, the vertices are some of the tree edges, and two tree edges are connected by an edge if there is a non-tree edge that covers them. We present a specific algorithm to solve this task, which relies heavily on the structure of the decomposition and the layering. The high-level idea is first to compute an MIS of an induced subgraph of G_i that has only a carefully chosen set of $O(\sqrt{n})$ tree edges. We show that it is enough to let vertices learn about these edges and a constant number of non-tree edges that cover each of them, to simulate an MIS computation on the induced subgraph. Then, we let all the vertices simulate a local algorithm inside each segment, to add additional uncovered tree edges to the MIS. Finally, we prove that although we work on different segments at the same time, all the edges added to the MIS by different segments really form an MIS in the virtual graph G_i. Based on these ideas, we show that we can implement the whole algorithm in $\widetilde{O}(D + \sqrt{n})$ rounds. This algorithm obtains a $(4 + \epsilon)$-approximation for weighted TAP in the virtual graph G'. This translates to a $(8+\epsilon)$-approximation for weighted TAP in the original graph G, which results in a $(9 + \epsilon)$-approximation for weighted 2-ECSS.

A bird's eye view of our second algorithm: Due to space limitations, our second algorithm which proves Theorem 1.2 and obtains an $O(\log n)$-approximation in time proportional to the shortcut complexity of the network, appears in the full version. Here, we provide a very brief summary and comment on the novel components.

On the outer layer, this second algorithm also works by first computing an MST, T, and then finding an approximately minimum-weight augmentation for it. Also, we again view this tree augmentation as a set cover problem, where we would like to find a minimum-cost collection of non-tree edges, which cover all the tree edges of T. We follow a standard parallelization of the sequential greedy algorithm for set cover [2], which gives an $O(\log n)$-approximation. We gradually add more and more of the most cost-effective non-tree edges to the solution, while ensuring that they cover mostly different tree edges. Cost-effectiveness refers to how many tree edges we can cover, per unit of weight. We refer the reader to the full version for more detailed outline, and also to [7]. The main novelty in our algorithm is in how to perform each iteration of the parallel set cover, in time proportional to the shortcut complexity of the graph. Concretely, we will need two subroutines: (A) Given a collection of non-tree edges, any tree edge should know whether it is covered by this collection or not. (B) Each non-tree edge should know the number of tree edges that it can cover. To solve these two subroutines, we build two algorithmic tools, in the framework of shortcuts [11]. A tool that allows each node to know the summation of the values of all of its ancestors, in an arbitrary given tree, and a tool that allows us to compute the *heavy-light* decomposition of any tree. These would be trivial to do in time proportional to the height of the tree, but we want the complexity to be proportional to the shortcut complexity of the network. The problems solved by our tools are very basic and frequently used computations about a tree. Thus, we hope that these tools will find applications beyond our work.

1.3 Additional Related Work

Small Neighborhood Covers: Our algorithm is inspired by a parallel algorithm for set cover problems with the small neighborhood cover property (SNC) [1]. This class includes central problems such as vertex cover, interval cover and bag cover. The approximation obtained depends on a parameter τ that is related to the size of the neighborhood cover, and the time complexity depends on a certain layering of the problem.

The SNC property. We next give an intuition for the SNC property, for a formal definition see [1]. In a set cover problem, the goal is to cover a universe of elements by a minimum cost collection of sets. Two elements in the universe are *neighbors* if there is a set that covers both of them, and the *neigborhood* of an element includes all its neighbors. The τ-SNC property says that each collection of sets that cover some element u can be replaced by only τ sets that cover u and all its neighbors from certain layers. In our case, where we want to solve weighted TAP on the virtual graph G', the parameter $\tau = 2$, the elements are tree edges, and the sets correpond to non-tree edges. Two tree edges are neighbors if there is a non-tree edge that covers both of them. The SNC property is related to the following: if you look at a tree edge t and a set of non-tree edges that cover it, you can replace them by only $\tau = 2$ edges that cover t and all its neighbours that are at the layer of t or above it.

The approximation obtained. In [1], they show general sequential and parallel algorithms that obtain τ and $(2 + \epsilon)\tau^2$ approximations respectively for set cover problems with the τ-SNC property, and leave as an open question whether an efficient parallel algorithm can obtain a τ-approximation as the sequential one. Following the algorithm from [1], allows obtaining a $(2+\epsilon)\tau^2 = (2+\epsilon)4$-approximation for weighted TAP in the virtual graph G'. Changing slightly the forward phase leads to a $(1+\epsilon)4$-approximation, which leads to our $(9 + \epsilon)$-approximation for weighted 2-ECSS. Very recently we were able to get an improved approximation algorithm that obtains an approximation of $(\tau + \epsilon) = (2 + \epsilon)$ for weighted TAP in the virtual graph G', almost matching the approximation obtained by the sequential algorithm in [1]. This leads to a $(5 + \epsilon)$-approximation for weighted 2-ECSS.

There are a number of other problems which have been studied in distributed graph algorithms, and have some resemblance to 2-ECSS. To the best of our understanding, none of these are too directly related to the problem that we tackle in this paper or to our method.

Minimum Cut: One problem is that, given a network G, we wish to compute or approximate the edge-connectivity of G or, in the more general case of edge-weighted graphs, the minimum cut size of the graph. Ghaffari and Kuhn [12] gave a $2 + \varepsilon$ approximation algorithm that runs in $\widetilde{O}(D + \sqrt{n})$ rounds, for any constant $\varepsilon > 0$. Nanongkai and Su [25] gave a $1 + \varepsilon$ approximation algorithm that runs in $\widetilde{O}(D + \sqrt{n})$ rounds, and an exact algorithm for edge connectivity with round complexity of $\widetilde{O}((D + \sqrt{n})k^4)$, in graphs with edge-connectivity k. As mentioned above, a work of Ghafffari and Haeupler shows how to obtain a $(1 + \varepsilon)$ approximation in $\widetilde{O}(SC(G))$ time, where $SC(G)$ denotes the shortcut complexity of the graph. Finally, very recently, Daga et al. [5] have shown the first sublinear time algorithm for edge-connectivity for general k.

Fault-Tolerant MST:. Another related problem is that of computing a fault-tolerant minimum spanning tree, defined as follows: for each edge e in the minimum spanning tree T of G, we should know a minimum weight edge e' such that $(T \cup \{e'\}) \setminus \{e\}$ is a minimum spanning tree of $G \setminus \{e\}$. We note that despite the partial resemblance in the motivations, we do not see any real connection between this problem and 2-ECSS and an fault-tolerant MST may be far more heavy in weight than the minimum-weight 2-edge connected subgraph; in the former the goal is to have an MST in the graph remaining after the failure, in the latter the goal is to have a minimum-weight graph that can survive a link failure. Ghaffari and Parter [15] showed an algorithm that computes fault-tolerant minimum spanning tree sturcutres, in the above sense, in $\widetilde{O}(D+\sqrt{n})$ rounds.

2 PRELIMINARIES

Model: Throughout, we work with the standard CONGEST model of distributed computing [27]: The network is abstracted as an undirected graph $G = (V, E)$ and communication happens in synchronous rounds. Per round, each vertex can send $O(\log n)$ bits to each of its neighbors. In the distributed setting the input and output are local. At the beginning, each vertex knows the ids of its neighbours and the weights of the edges adjacent to it, and at the end, each vertex should know only a local part of the output. For example, when we compute a 2-edge-connected subgraph, each vertex should know which edges adjacent to it are taken to the solution.

Definitions: We say that an undirected graph G is *2-edge-connected* if it remains connected after the removal of any single edge. In the minimum weight 2-edge-connected spanning subgraph problem (2-ECSS), the goal is to find the minimum weight spanning subgraph that is 2-edge-connected. Given a tree T, we denote by $P_{u,v}$ the unique tree path between u and v, and by $p(v)$ the parent of v in the tree. It is easy to see that $e = \{u, v\}$ covers a tree edge t iff $t \in P_{u,v}$.

As explained in Section 1.2, a natural approach for solving 2-ECSS is to start by computing a minimum spanning tree (MST), and then add to it a minimum weight set of edges that augments its connectivity to 2. This motivates the *tree augmentation problem (TAP)*. In TAP, the input is a 2-edge-connected graph G and a spanning tree T, and the goal is to find a minimum weight set of edges A such that $T \cup A$ is 2-edge-connected. The following claim shows the connection between TAP and 2-ECSS.

Claim 2.1. *An α-approximation algorithm Alg for TAP gives an $(\alpha+1)$-approximation algorithm for 2-ECSS, with complexity $O(T_n + D + \sqrt{n}\log^* n)$ rounds, where T_n is the complexity of Alg.*

Proof. Computing an MST, T, and then augmenting its connectivity using the approximation algorithm for TAP results in a solution of weight $w(T) + \alpha \cdot w(A^*)$, where $w(T)$ is the weight of the MST, and $w(A^*)$ is the weight of an optimal augmentation for T. An optimal solution OPT for 2-ECSS is clearly of weight at least $w(T)$ and at least $w(A^*)$, since OPT is a valid augmentation. Hence, the approximation obtained for 2-ECSS is at most $(\alpha + 1)$. Computing an MST takes $O(D + \sqrt{n}\log^* n)$ rounds using the algorithm of Kutten and Peleg [24], and computing the augmentation takes $O(T_n)$ rounds, which completes the proof. □

Roadmap: Section 3 contains high-level overview of our first algorithm, full details and proofs appear in the full version. Our Second algorithm appears in the full version.

3 OVERVIEW OF OUR FIRST ALGORITHM

As explained in Section 1.2, our approach is to simulate a parallel algorithm for set cover to approximate weighted TAP on a related virtual graph G', which translates to an approximate solution for weighted 2-ECSS in the input graph G. We next provide a high-level overview of the algorithm. Full details and proofs appear in the full version.

3.1 Working with virtual edges

As a first step, we replace our input graph G by a virtual graph G' described in [3, 21], such that all the non-tree edges in the graph are between ancestors and descendants. This is done by replacing any non-tree edge $e = \{u, v\}$ that is not between an ancestor to its descendant, by the two edges $\{u, w\}, \{v, w\}$ where w is the lowest common ancestor (LCA) of u and v in the tree. As the tree path $P_{u,v}$ is composed of the two paths $P_{u,w}, P_{w,v}$, the new virtual edges cover together exactly the same edges covered by e. Working with the virtual graph instead of the original graph turns out to be very useful for the algorithm, as we explain later. As shown in [3], finding an α-approximation for weighted TAP in the virtual graph G', gives a 2α-approximation for weighted TAP in G, where the extra 2 factor comes from the duplication of edges, summarized as follows.

Lemma 3.1. *Let A' be an α-approximation augmentation in G', and let A be the corresponding augmentation in G where any edge in A' is replaced by a corresponding edge in A. Then, A is a 2α-approximation augmentation in G.*

To build the virtual graph, and work with the virtual edges during the algorithm we use LCA labels. These are labels of $O(\log n)$ bits per vertex, such that given the labels of two vertices u, v we can infer $LCA(u, v)$. Our whole algorithm works with the LCA labels of vertices instead of their ids, which turns out to be useful for many tasks. For example, the labels allow to check whether a vertex u is an ancestor of v, whether a non-tree edge e covers a tree edge t, and more. As shown in [3], it is possible to compute the LCA labels and build the virtual graph G' in $O(D + \sqrt{n}\log^* n)$ rounds. To simulate a distributed algorithm in G', for each virtual edge we have a vertex, which is the descendant of the virtual edge, that simulates it during the algorithm. For simplicity of presentation, in the description of the algorithm we say that edges do some computations. When we say this, we mean that the vertices that simulate the edges do the computations. For full details and proofs about the virtual edges see the full version.

3.2 Decomposing the tree into layers

Our algorithm works in a graph where all the non-tree edges are between ancestors to descendants. We next explain how we exploit this structure. Intuitively, this allows us to replace all the non-tree edges that cover a tree edge by only two edges that cover roughly the same tree edges. This property is called in [1] the *small neighbourhood cover* property. A key component in the algorithm is a

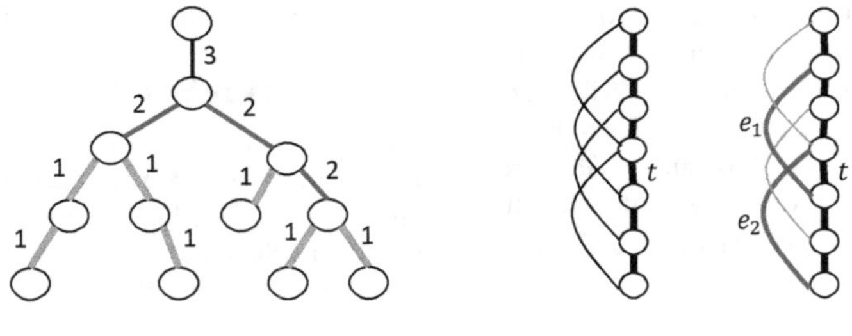

Figure 1: An illustration of the layering. On the left, there is a tree decomposed into layers. On the right, there is a tree (the path with bold edges) and non-tree edges that cover it, with an example of a tree edge t and its two petals e_1, e_2.

certain layering of the tree, we describe next. We say that a vertex is a *junction* if it has more than one child in the tree. Each layer is composed of disjoint paths in the tree, as follows. The first layer consists of all the tree paths between a leaf to its first ancestor that is a junction. To define the second layer, we first contract all the paths of the first layer, and get a new tree T_2. Note that several paths with the same ancestor can be contracted to the same vertex. The second layer is composed of all the tree paths between leaves in T_2 to their first ancestors that are junctions in T_2. We continue in the same manner, to define all the layers. See Figure 1 for an illustration. Since a leaf in layer i is a junction in layer $i-1$, which has at least two leaves in the subtree rooted at it in T_{i-1}, it follows that the number of layers is $O(\log n)$.

The petals of a tree edge. We say that two tree edges t_1, t_2 are *neighbours* with respect to a subset of non-tree edges X, if there is an edge $e \in X$ that covers both t_1 and t_2. The layering is useful in our algorithm for the following reason. If we look at a tree edge t in layer i and a subset of non-tree edges X, we can choose only two non-tree edges from X that cover t and all its neighbours in layers j for $j \geq i$. These edges are called the *petals* of t with respect to X. If t is an edge in the first layer, its petals are the two non-tree edges from X that cover e and get to the highest ancestor or the lowest descendant possible. See Figure 1 for an illustration. For a tree edge t in layer $i > 1$, the definition is slightly more involved. The first petal is again the non-tree edge that covers t and gets to the highest ancestor, but the second petal cannot be defined just as the non-tree edge that covers t and gets to the lowest descendant, because t may be in different leaf to root paths, and we cannot compare edges that cover different paths directly. To define the second petal, we denote by P the tree path in layer i that t belongs to, and compare edges with respect to P. The second petal is defined to be a non-tree edge that covers t and maximum number of edges in P below t. For a formal definition see the full version.

Computing the layers. In the full version, we show how to construct the layering in $O((D + \sqrt{n}) \log n)$ rounds, such that at the end all the tree edges know their layer number and some additional information about the layering. The high-level idea is to use a decomposition from [7, 15] we describe in the full version, and break the computation into several aggregate functions on trees we can compute in $O(D + \sqrt{n})$ rounds using the decomposition. Later, we show that in $O(D + \sqrt{n})$ rounds all the tree edges in layer i can learn their petals with respect to a subset of non-tree edges X. To compute the higher petal we need to compute the edge that gets to the highest ancestor from the edges that cover a tree edge. This is an aggregate function of the non-tree edges that cover a tree edge, and we show how to compute such functions efficiently in the full version. Computing the lower petal is more involved, and we show how certain information about the layers and the LCA labels allow to compute it as well. For full details and proofs about the layering see the full version.

3.3 The parallel set cover algorithm

We follow a parallel algorithm for set cover instances with the *small neighbourhood cover* property [1]. It is easy to implement the algorithm in a setting where the complete set cover graph is known: where sets can communicate directly with the elements they cover, and vice verse. In our case, the main obstacle is to show how to simulate an algorithm in our setting, where tree edges cannot communicate directly with non-tree edges that cover them and vice verse (these edges may be far from them in the graph, and they do not even know the identity of these edges). To overcome this, the main ingredient is a certain decomposition of the tree into segments from [7, 15]. We show in the full version, how all the non-tree edges can compute aggregate functions of the tree edges they cover, and how tree edges can compute aggregate functions of the non-tree edges that cover them efficiently using the decomposition. In addition, we show that many of the computations in the algorithm are based on such aggregate functions. Similar computations are done in [7], and the main challenge in our case is to show that the algorithm extends also to the case of working with virtual edges. We mention that in [1], the authors describe also a distributed algorithm, but it is only for the setting that the set cover graph is known and also requires very large messages, and hence is not suitable for the CONGEST model.

The algorithm. The algorithm is a primal-dual algorithm that processes the graph according to the layers. The primal LP has a variable $x(e)$ for each non-tree edge, which indicates whether e is added to the augmentation A, and its goal is to add a minimum weight set of edges to A while covering all tree edges. For a non-tree edge e, we denote by S_e all the tree edges covered by e. The primal and dual LPs are formulated as follows.

Primal LP	**Dual LP**
$\min \sum_{e\in E\setminus T} x(e)\cdot w(e)$	$\max \sum_{t\in T} y(t)$
$\forall t\in T,\ \sum_{e:t\in S_e} x(e)\geq 1$	$\forall e\in E\setminus T,\ \sum_{t\in S_e} y(t)\leq w(e)$
$x(e)\geq 0$	$y(t)\geq 0$

The algorithm is composed of two parts, a forward phase and a reverse-delete phase. The goal of the forward phase is to cover all the tree edges while making sure that all the dual constraints hold up to $(1+\epsilon')$ factor, and for all the edges added to the augmentation A it holds that $\sum_{t\in S_e} y(t)\geq w(e)$. Intuitively, $y(t)$ can be seen as a price an edge t can pay for the non-tree edges that cover it, and we add a non-tree edge e to the augmentation only if the tree edges in S_e pay at least $w(e)$ in total. In some sense, this guarantees that we do not add edges that are too expensive to A, if there is an alternative option to cover the same tree edges. However, there is no bound on the number of edges we add to A in this phase. In the reverse-delete phase the goal is to remove some of the edges from A, such that all the tree edges are covered and any tree edge t where $y(t)>0$ is covered at most c times for a constant c, in our algorithm $c=4$. This guarantees a $(c+\epsilon)$-approximation, as follows.

Lemma 3.2. *If each tree edge with $y(t)>0$ is covered at most c times, the algorithm guarantees a $(c+\epsilon)$-approximation.*

Proof. Let $B\subseteq A$ be the final cover obtained by the end of the reverse-delete phase. Since all the edges added to A satisfy $w(e)\leq\sum_{t\in S_e} y(t)$ and all the edges with $y(t)>0$ are covered at most c times by B, we get

$$w(B)=\sum_{e\in B} w(e)\leq\sum_{e\in B}\sum_{t\in S_e} y(t)\leq c\sum_{t\in T} y(t)$$

$$=c(1+\epsilon')\sum_{t\in T}\frac{y(t)}{(1+\epsilon')}\leq c(1+\epsilon')OPT,$$

The last inequality follows from the fact that all the dual constraints hold up to a $(1+\epsilon')$ factor, which shows that dividing the values of y by $(1+\epsilon')$ give a feasible dual solution, and from the weak duality theorem, as follows. By the weak duality theorem any feasible solution to the dual problem has value smaller or equal to the value of a feasible primal solution. Since the optimal augmentation is a set of edges that cover all the tree edges it is a feasible primal solution, and the inequality follows. Choosing $\epsilon'=\frac{\epsilon}{c}$ gives a $(c+\epsilon)$-approximation. □

We next explain the two phases of the algorithm.

3.4 The forward phase

The goal of the forward phase is to cover all the tree edges while making sure that all the dual constraints hold up to $(1+\epsilon)$ factor, and for all the edges added to the augmentation A it holds that $\sum_{t\in S_e} y(t)\geq w(e)$. We process the layers one by one according to their order, where in epoch k we make sure that all the tree edges of layer k are covered. Epoch k works as follows. Let R_k be all the tree edges of layer k that are still not covered, they are the only edges which increase their dual variables in epoch k. For a non-tree edge e, let $s(e)=\sum_{t\in S_e} y(t)$ be the current value of the dual constraint, and let S_e^k be the tree edges in $R_k\cap S_e$, if each one of these tree edges t sets $y(t)=\frac{w(e)-s(e)}{|S_e^k|}$, then the dual constraint becomes tight. Since we want to maintain feasibility of the dual, each tree edge $t\in R_k$ sets its dual variable to be $\min_{t\in S_e}\frac{w(e)-s(e)}{|S_e^k|}$. After this, we add to A edges e if their dual constraint becomes tight. In the next iteration, each tree edge in R_k that is still not covered by A, increases its dual variable by a multiplicative factor of $(1+\epsilon)$, and again we add edges to A if their dual constraint becomes tight, we continue in the same manner until all the edges in R_k are covered. This concludes the description of the forward phase.

Our algorithm differs slightly from the algorithm in [1], where they maintained the feasibility of the dual solution. Our approach allows us to get an improved approximation of $(1+\epsilon)4$, compared to the $(2+\epsilon)4$-approximation obtained by the approach in [1].

Correctness. From the above description, it follows that at the end all the tree edges are covered by A, and for each $e\in A$, its dual constraint becomes tight. For all the dual constraints it holds that $\sum_{t\in S_e} y(t)\leq(1+\epsilon)w(e)$, since we increase the value of $\sum_{t\in S_e} y(t)$ at most by $(1+\epsilon)$ factor at each iteration, and e is added to A once $\sum_{t\in S_e} y(t)\geq w(e)$. At this point, all the edges in S_e are covered and do not increase their dual variables anymore.

Implementation details. In the full version, we explain how to implement each iteration of the forward phase in $O(D+\sqrt{n})$ rounds. As already mentioned, the main building blocks we use are algorithms for computing aggregate functions of tree edges or non-tree edges. We show that all the computations in the forward phase are based on such functions. For example, non-tree edges should compute the value $\sum_{t\in S_e} y(t)$ which is an aggregate function of the tree edges they cover. Tree edges should learn if they are covered by A, which happens iff there is at least one edge that covers them that is added to A, this is an aggregate function of the tree edges that cover them, etc. Since there are $O(\log n)$ layers, there are $O(\log n)$ epochs. We show that each of them consists of $O(\frac{\log n}{\epsilon})$ iterations, based on the fact that uncovered tree edges increase their dual variable by a $(1+\epsilon)$ factor in each iteration. This results in a time complexity of $O((D+\sqrt{n})\frac{\log^2 n}{\epsilon})$ rounds for the whole phase. Full details and proofs appear in the full version.

3.5 The reverse-delete phase

In the reverse-delete phase we choose a subset $B\subseteq A$ with the following properties.

(1) B covers all the tree edges.
(2) Any $t\in T$ with $y(t)>0$ is covered at most 4 times by B.

The dual variables are not changed during the process. Recall that R_k are all the tree edges in layer k that are not covered before epoch k. From the description of the forward phase, the only tree edges with $y(t)>0$ are in R_k for some k. We need the following additional definitions. We denote by A_k the non-tree edges added to A in epoch k, and by F_k the tree edges that are first covered in epoch k. Note that F_k contains R_k and perhaps additional edges from higher layers. By the definition of R_k, edges in R_k are not covered by A_i for any $i < k$. This motivates going over the layers in the reverse direction. In the reverse-delete phase we go over the layers in the reverse direction, building B. Initially $B = \emptyset$ and we add to it edges from A during the algorithm. Our algorithm proceeds in epochs $k = L, ..., 1$, where L is the index of the last layer. We next describe epoch k.

Epoch k. In epoch k we make sure that the following holds.

(1) All the tree edges in F_i for $i \geq k$ are covered by B.
(2) All the edges in R_i for $i \geq k$ are covered at most 4 times.

Hence, at the end of epoch 1, B satisfies all the requirements. We next explain how we guarantee the above properties. At the beginning of epoch k, B already covers all the edges in F_i for $i > k$, and our goal is to add to it edges from A_k to cover F_k. We need to make sure that all the edges in R_i for $i \geq k$ are covered at most 4 times. Note that B already satisfies this for $i > k$, and by definition edges in A_k do not cover edges in R_i for $i > k$, so we need to take care only of edges in R_k. However, edges in R_k may already be covered by B, so we may need to remove edges from B, while making sure that all the edges in F_i for $i \geq k$ are covered. For doing so, we go over the layers $i = k, ..., L$ where L is the last layer. We need the following notation.

Let $X = B \cup A_k$, let $F = \cup_{i=k}^{L} F_i$, and let H_i be all the tree edges in F in layer i (note that F_i may contain also edges from layers higher than i). Notice that B covers F_i for $i > k$, and A_k covers F_k, hence X covers F. Let t be a tree edge in H_i, and let $p(t)$ be the set of non-tree edges in X that cover t. As explained in Section 3.2, we can replace $p(t)$ by two non-tree edges in $p(t)$ that cover all the tree edges covered by $p(t)$ in layers $i, ..., L$, which are called the *petals* of t in X. We next build a set $Y \subseteq X$ that covers F. We go over the layers in iterations $i = k, ..., L$, as follows.

Iteration i. In iteration i we make sure that the edges in H_i are covered. Let $\widetilde{H_i}$ be all the tree edges in H_i that are not covered by Y at the beginning of iteration i. We build a virtual graph G_i that its vertices are the tree edges in $\widetilde{H_i}$, and two vertices t_1, t_2 in G_i are connected if there is a non-tree edge in X that covers t_1, t_2. We find a maximal independent set (MIS), M_i, in the graph G_i. We call the elements in M_i anchors and add all their petals (with respect to X) to Y. Intuitively, the computation of the MIS, M_i, allows us to cover simultaneously all the edges in $\widetilde{H_i}$, while making sure that we do not cover edges too many times.

After going over all the layers $i = k, ..., L$, we set $B = Y$. This completes the description of epoch k.

Correctness proof. The correctness proof follows [1], we include it for completeness.

Lemma 3.3. *At the end of epoch k:*

(1) All the tree edges in $F = \cup_{i=k}^{L} F_i$ are covered by B.
(2) All the edges in R_i for $i \geq k$ are covered at most 4 times.

Proof. The proof is by induction on k. In the base case, $k = L+1$ and $B = \emptyset$, hence the claim clearly holds. We start by proving 1. From the description of iteration i, at the end of iteration i, Y covers H_i: All the edges in $H_i \setminus \widetilde{H_i}$ are already covered at the beginning of the iteration. All the edges in $\widetilde{H_i}$ are either anchors or have a neighbouring anchor $t \in M_i$, and then they are covered by the petals of t. Hence, after all the iterations, $B = Y$ covers $\cup_{i=k}^{L} H_i = F$.

We next prove 2. We start with a simple observation: all the anchors in all the layers, $\cup_{i=k}^{L} M_i$, are independent in the following sense. If we take any two anchors t_1, t_2, there is no edge in X that covers both of them. In the same layer, it follows from computing an MIS. In different layers $i < j$, it follows since the graph G_j contains only tree edges that are not yet covered, and we add the petals of all the anchors in M_i at the end of iteration i.

We next show that any tree edge $t \in R_i$ for $i \geq k$ is covered at most 4 times by Y. As explained earlier, for $i > k$ this already follows from previous epochs. This holds since $Y \subseteq X$, and $X = B \cup A_k$ (with the set B at the end of the previous epoch). Now, at the end of epoch $k+1$, all the edges in R_i for $i > k$ are covered at most 4 times by B from the induction hypothesis. Also, from the definition of the sets, A_k does not cover any edge in R_i for $i > k$. Hence, any set $Y \subseteq X$ we choose covers all the edges in R_i for $i > k$ at most 4 times.

We now show that any tree edge $t \in R_k$ is covered at most 4 times by Y. If t is an anchor, it is covered only by its petals, since the anchors are independent, and hence it is covered at most twice. Otherwise, we show that t has at most two neighbouring anchors. Since t is in layer k, and all the anchors are at layers at least k, the 2 petals of t cover all its anchors. Hence, if there are more than two anchors, at least two of them are covered by the same petal, which contradicts the fact that the anchors are independent. Hence, t is covered at most twice by the petals of each of its neighbouring anchors, and at most 4 times in total. This completes the proof. □

From Lemma 3.3 with respect to $k = 1$, we get that at the end of the reverse-delete phase B covers all tree edges, and for each $1 \leq i \leq L$, all the tree edges in R_i are covered at most 4 times, as needed. The algorithm has L epochs, each of them consists of at most L iterations, which sums up to $O(L^2) = O(\log^2 n)$ iterations. In the full version, we show how to implement each iteration in $O(D+\sqrt{n})$ rounds, which results in a complexity of $O((D+\sqrt{n})\log^2 n)$ rounds for the whole phase.

Implementation details. In the full version, we explain how we implement the reverse-delete phase. The main task we need to solve is to build an MIS in the virtual graph G_i in each iteration. This is a completely virtual graph, and we design a specific algorithm to solve this task which relies heavily on the structure of the decomposition of the tree into segments and the layering. The MIS, M_i, is a set of tree edges in $\widetilde{H_i}$ such that for any two tree edges $t, t' \in M_i$, there is no edge in X that covers both of them. Our algorithm is composed of a global part where all the vertices locally compute a global MIS that includes some of the tree edges. Then, it includes a local part, where we work on each segment separately, and add additional edges to the MIS by scanning the segment. To implement the global part, first, all the vertices in the graph learn $O(\log n)$ information about each segment: two of its tree edges and their petals. Let T' be all the tree edges learned. From the information, all the vertices can compute locally an MIS, M', of the tree edges T'. This is based on showing that the petals and LCA labels allow all vertices to compute the relevant virtual graph induced on all these edges (this is a subgraph of the virtual graph G_i). We add all the petals of edges in M' to the cover Y. Next, we work on each segment separately with the goal of covering all the edges in $\widetilde{H}_i$ that are not already covered by edges added to Y. This is done by scanning all the subpaths in layer i that are contained in a segment. We scan each subpath from its descendant to its ancestor, where each time we reach a tree edge t that is not already covered by edges added to Y by vertices below it on the segment, or before the local part, we add t to the MIS.

Since our algorithm works in different segments in parallel, we need to show that all the edges added to the MIS really form an MIS. In the global part it is clear, since we compute an MIS. Also, since at the end of the global part we add all the petals of edges in M' to Y, all the edges that have a neighbour in M' are already covered. The main challenge is showing that two edges t_1, t_2 that are added to the MIS in the local part of different segments are independent. For this, we exploit the structure of the decomposition, and show that there must be an edge $t \in T'$ in the tree path between t_1 and t_2. If $t \in M'$, we show that t_1, t_2 are already covered by the petals of t and therefore cannot be added to the MIS. Otherwise, t has a neighbour in M', and we show that its petals must cover at least one of t_1, t_2, which gives a contradiction. Full details and proofs appear in the full version.

Conclusion. Based on these ingredients we get a $(4+\epsilon)$-approximation for weighted TAP in the virtual graph G', which translates to a $(8+\epsilon)$-approximation for weighted TAP in the input graph G by Lemma 3.1. This gives a $(9+\epsilon)$-approximation for weighted 2-ECSS in G by Claim 2.1. The complexity of the whole algorithm is $O((D+\sqrt{n})\frac{\log^2 n}{\epsilon})$ rounds.

4 DISCUSSION

In this paper, we show a deterministic $(9+\epsilon)$-approximation algorithm for weighted 2-ECSS in near-optimal time. Very recently we were able to show that a variant of the algorithm actually obtians a $(5+\epsilon)$-approximation. To obtain this approximation, we change some elements in the algorithm. At a high-level, the analysis that gives a $(4+\epsilon)$-approximation for weighted TAP in the virtual graph G' is based on showing that we cover certain edges in the tree at most 4 times, by changing several elements in the algorithm and using a careful case analysis we can get an algorithm that covers these edges only 2 times, which improves the approximation of the whole algorithm. For full details see the full version. The techniques we use do not seem to allow improving the approximation below $(5+\epsilon)$. However, it would be interesting to study whether different approaches can get an approximation closer to 2 in near-optimal time.

A key ingredient that allowed us obtaining a constant approximation in near-optimal time is a parallel algorithm for set cover problems with small neighborhood covers [1]. In [1], the authors show many examples for additional problems having this property such as interval cover and bag cover. Therefore, we hope that the ideas we use here may be useful also for obtaining additional efficient distributed algorithms that give constant approximations for covering problems that have this structure.

This paper focuses on the weighted 2-ECSS problem. For $k > 2$ the weighted k-ECSS problem seems to be much more involved, and currently the best complexity for approximating it is at least linear [7]. An interesting question is whether *sublinear* algorithms exist for weighted k-ECSS also for larger values of k.

ACKNOWLEDGMENTS

We thank Merav Parter for bringing [26] to our attention. This project has received funding from the European Union's Horizon 2020 Research And Innovation Program under grant agreement no. 755839. Supported in part by the Israel Science Foundation (grant 1696/14) and by the Swiss National Foundation (SNF) under project number 200021_184735.

REFERENCES

[1] Archita Agarwal, Venkatesan T Chakaravarthy, Anamitra R Choudhury, Sambudha Roy, and Yogish Sabharwal. 2018. Set Cover Problems with Small Neighborhood Covers. *Theory of Computing Systems* (2018), 1–35.

[2] Bonnie Berger, John Rompel, and Peter W Shor. 1989. Efficient NC algorithms for set cover with applications to learning and geometry. In *Foundations of Computer Science, 1989., 30th Annual Symposium on.* IEEE, 54–59.

[3] Keren Censor-Hillel and Michal Dory. 2017. Fast Distributed Approximation for TAP and 2-Edge-Connectivity. In *21st International Conference on Principles of Distributed Systems, OPODIS 2017, Lisbon, Portugal, December 18-20, 2017.* 21:1–21:20. https://doi.org/10.4230/LIPIcs.OPODIS.2017.21

[4] Joseph Cheriyan, András Sebő, and Zoltán Szigeti. 1998. An improved approximation algorithm for minimum size 2-edge connected spanning subgraphs. In *International Conference on Integer Programming and Combinatorial Optimization.* Springer, 126–136.

[5] Mohit Daga, Monika Henzinger, Danupon Nanongkai, and Thatchaphol Saranurak. 2019. Distributed Edge Connectivity in Sublinear Time. In *Proceedings of the 51st annual ACM symposium on Theory of computing.* ACM, to appear.

[6] Atish Das Sarma, Stephan Holzer, Liah Kor, Amos Korman, Danupon Nanongkai, Gopal Pandurangan, David Peleg, and Roger Wattenhofer. 2011. Distributed verification and hardness of distributed approximation. In *Proceedings of the forty-third annual ACM symposium on Theory of computing.* ACM, 363–372.

[7] Michal Dory. 2018. Distributed Approximation of Minimum k-edge-connected Spanning Subgraphs. In *Proceedings of the 2018 ACM Symposium on Principles of Distributed Computing, PODC 2018, Egham, United Kingdom, July 23-27, 2018.* 149–158. https://doi.org/10.1145/3212734.3212760

[8] Michael Elkin. 2006. An unconditional lower bound on the time-approximation trade-off for the distributed minimum spanning tree problem. *SIAM J. Comput.* 36, 2 (2006), 433–456.

[9] Harold N Gabow and Suzanne R Gallagher. 2012. Iterated rounding algorithms for the smallest k-edge connected spanning subgraph. *SIAM J. Comput.* 41, 1 (2012), 61–103.

[10] Robert G. Gallager, Pierre A. Humblet, and Philip M. Spira. 1983. A distributed algorithm for minimum-weight spanning trees. *ACM Transactions on Programming Languages and systems (TOPLAS)* 5, 1 (1983), 66–77.

[11] Mohsen Ghaffari and Bernhard Haeupler. 2016. Distributed algorithms for planar networks ii: Low-congestion shortcuts, mst, and min-cut. In *Proceedings of the twenty-seventh annual ACM-SIAM symposium on Discrete algorithms.* SIAM, 202–219.

[12] Mohsen Ghaffari and Fabian Kuhn. 2013. Distributed minimum cut approximation. In *International Symposium on Distributed Computing.* Springer, 1–15.

[13] Mohsen Ghaffari, Fabian Kuhn, and Hsin-Hao Su. 2017. Distributed MST and routing in almost mixing time. In *Proceedings of the ACM Symposium on Principles of Distributed Computing.* ACM, 131–140.

[14] Mohsen Ghaffari and Jason Li. 2018. New Distributed Algorithms in Almost Mixing Time via Transformations from Parallel Algorithms. *arXiv preprint arXiv:1805.04764* (2018).

[15] Mohsen Ghaffari and Merav Parter. 2016. Near-optimal distributed algorithms for fault-tolerant tree structures. In *Proceedings of the 28th ACM Symposium on Parallelism in Algorithms and Architectures (SPAA).* ACM, 387–396.

[16] Michel X Goemans, Andrew V Goldberg, Serge A Plotkin, David B Shmoys, Eva Tardos, and David P Williamson. 1994. Improved Approximation Algorithms for Network Design Problems.. In *SODA*, Vol. 94. 223–232.

[17] Bernhard Haeupler, Taisuke Izumi, and Goran Zuzic. 2016. Low-congestion shortcuts without embedding. In *Proceedings of the 2016 ACM Symposium on Principles of Distributed Computing.* ACM, 451–460.

[18] Bernhard Haeupler, Jason Li, and Goran Zuzic. 2018. Minor excluded network families admit fast distributed algorithms. *arXiv preprint arXiv:1801.06237* (2018).

[19] Kamal Jain. 2001. A factor 2 approximation algorithm for the generalized Steiner network problem. *Combinatorica* 21, 1 (2001), 39–60.

[20] David R Karger, Philip N Klein, and Robert E Tarjan. 1995. A randomized linear-time algorithm to find minimum spanning trees. *Journal of the ACM (JACM)* 42, 2 (1995), 321–328.

[21] Samir Khuller and Ramakrishna Thurimella. 1993. Approximation algorithms for graph augmentation. *Journal of Algorithms* 14, 2 (1993), 214–225.

[22] Samir Khuller and Uzi Vishkin. 1994. Biconnectivity approximations and graph carvings. *Journal of the ACM (JACM)* 41, 2 (1994), 214–235.

[23] Sven O Krumke, Peter Merz, Tim Nonner, and Katharina Rupp. 2007. Distributed approximation algorithms for finding 2-edge-connected subgraphs. In *International Conference On Principles Of Distributed Systems (OPODIS)*. Springer, 159–173.

[24] Shay Kutten and David Peleg. 1998. Fast distributed construction of smallk-dominating sets and applications. *Journal of Algorithms* 28, 1 (1998), 40–66.

[25] Danupon Nanongkai and Hsin-Hao Su. 2014. Almost-tight distributed minimum cut algorithms. In *International Symposium on Distributed Computing*. Springer, 439–453.

[26] Merav Parter. 2019. Small Cuts and Connectivity Certificates: A Fault Tolerant Approach. *Manuscript* (2019).

[27] David Peleg. 2000. Distributed computing. *SIAM Monographs on discrete mathematics and applications* 5 (2000).

[28] David Peleg and Vitaly Rubinovich. 2000. A near-tight lower bound on the time complexity of distributed minimum-weight spanning tree construction. *SIAM J. Comput.* 30, 5 (2000), 1427–1442.

[29] Seth Pettie. 2008. Distributed algorithms for ultrasparse spanners and linear size skeletons. In *Proceedings of the twenty-seventh ACM symposium on Principles of distributed computing*. ACM, 253–262.

[30] András Sebö and Jens Vygen. 2014. Shorter tours by nicer ears: 7/5-Approximation for the graph-TSP, 3/2 for the path version, and 4/3 for two-edge-connected subgraphs. *Combinatorica* 34, 5 (2014), 597–629. https://doi.org/10.1007/s00493-014-2960-3

[31] Amir Shadeh. 2009. *Distributed primal-dual approximation algorithms for network design problems*. Open University of Israel.

[32] Vijay V Vazirani. 2013. *Approximation algorithms*. Springer Science & Business Media.

Near-Additive Spanners In Low Polynomial Deterministic CONGEST Time

Michael Elkin
Department of Computer Science, Ben-Gurion University of the Negev
Beer Sheva, Israel
elkinm@cs.bgu.ac.il

Shaked Matar
Department of Computer Science, Ben-Gurion University of the Negev
Beer Sheva, Israel
matars@post.bgu.ac.il

Abstract

Given a pair of parameters $\alpha \geq 1, \beta \geq 0$, a subgraph $G' = (V, H)$ of an n-vertex unweighted undirected graph $G = (V, E)$ is called an (α, β)-*spanner* if for every pair $u, v \in V$ of vertices, we have $d_{G'}(u, v) \leq \alpha d_G(u, v) + \beta$. If $\beta = 0$ the spanner is called a *multiplicative* α-spanner, and if $\alpha = 1 + \epsilon$, for an arbitrarily small $\epsilon > 0$, the spanner is said to be *near-additive*

Graph spanners [5, 36] are a fundamental and extremely well-studied combinatorial construct, with a multitude of applications in distributed computing and in other areas. Near-additive spanners, introduced in [27], preserve large distances much more faithfully than the more traditional multiplicative spanners. Also, recent lower bounds [1] ruled out the existence of arbitrarily sparse purely additive spanners (i.e., spanners with $\alpha = 1$), and therefore showed that essentially near-additive spanners provide the best approximation of distances that one can hope for.

Numerous distributed algorithms, for constructing sparse near-additive spanners, were devised in [17, 20, 25, 28, 40]. In particular, there are now known efficient randomized algorithms in the CONGEST model that construct such spanners [25], and also there are efficient deterministic algorithms in the LOCAL model [17]. However, the only known deterministic CONGEST-model algorithm for the problem [20] requires super-linear time in n. In this paper, we remedy the situation and devise an efficient deterministic CONGEST-model algorithm for constructing arbitrarily sparse near-additive spanners.

The running time of our algorithm is *low polynomial*, i.e., roughly $O(\beta \cdot n^{\rho})$, where $\rho > 0$ is an arbitrarily small positive constant that affects the additive term β. In general, the parameters of our new algorithm and of the resulting spanner are at the same ballpark as the respective parameters of the state-of-the-art randomized algorithm due to [25].

CCS Concepts

• **Theory of computation** → **Distributed computing models**;

This research was supported by the ISF grant No. (724/15) and the Frankel center for CS at BGU..

ACM ISBN 978-1-4503-6217-7/19/07...$15.00
https://doi.org/10.1145/3293611.3331635

Keywords

Spanners, Deterministic, CONGEST

ACM Reference Format:
Michael Elkin and Shaked Matar. 2019. Near-Additive Spanners In Low Polynomial Deterministic CONGEST Time. In *2019 ACM Symposium on Principles of Distributed Computing (PODC '19), July 29-August 2, 2019, Toronto, ON, Canada.* ACM, New York, NY, USA, 10 pages. https://doi.org/10.1145/3293611.3331635

1 Introduction

Graph *spanners* were introduced in the context of distributed algorithms by Awerbuch, Peleg and their co-authors [5, 8, 36–38] in the end of the eighties, and were extensively studied since then. See, e.g., [1, 2, 10, 11, 17, 25, 27, 30, 31], and the references therein. Numerous applications of spanners in Distributed Algorithms and other related areas were discovered in [3, 5, 19, 21, 27, 28, 32, 37, 41, 43, 44]. Also, spanners are a fundamental combinatorial construct, and their existential properties are being extensively explored [1, 2, 4, 10, 25–27, 36, 39, 45].

In this paper, we focus on *unweighted*, undirected graphs. Given a graph $G = (V, E)$, a subgraph $G' = (V, H)$, $H \subseteq E$, is said to be a (multiplicative) t-*spanner* of G, if for every pair $u, v \in V$ of vertices, we have $d_{G'}(u, v) \leq t \cdot d_G(u, v)$, for a parameter $t \geq 1$, where d_G (respectively, $d_{G'}$) stands for the distance in the graph G (respectively, in the subgraph G').

A fundamental tradeoff for multiplicative spanners is that for any $\kappa = 1, 2, \ldots$, and any n-vertex graph $G = (V, E)$, there exists a $(2\kappa - 1)$-spanner with $O(n^{1+1/\kappa})$ edges [4, 36]. Assuming Erdős-Simonovits girth conjecture (see e.g., [29]), this tradeoff is optimal. Efficient distributed algorithms for constructing multiplicative spanners that (nearly) realize this tradeoff were given in [6, 11, 13, 16, 18, 22, 25, 25, 30, 31].

A different variety of spanners, called *near-additive spanners*, was presented by Elkin and Peleg in [27]. They showed that for every $\epsilon > 0$ and $\kappa = 1, 2, \ldots$, there exists $\beta = \beta(\epsilon, \kappa)$, such that for every n-vertex graph $G = (V, E)$ there exists a $(1 + \epsilon, \beta)$-spanner $G' = (V, E)$, $H \subseteq E$, with $O_{\epsilon,\kappa}(n^{1+1/\kappa})$ edges. (The subgraph G' is called a $(1 + \epsilon, \beta)$-*spanner* of G if for every pair $u, v \in V$ of vertices, it holds that $d_{G'}(u, v) \leq (1 + \epsilon)d_G(u, v) + \beta$.)

In [27], the additive error β is given by $\beta_{EP} = \left(\frac{\log \kappa}{\epsilon}\right)^{\log \kappa - 1}$, and it remains the state-of-the-art. These spanners approximate large distances much more faithfully than multiplicative spanners. Recent lower bounds of Abboud and Bodwin [1], based on previous results of Coppersmith and Elkin [14], showed that this type of spanners is essentially the best one can hope for, as in general arbitrarily sparse purely additive spanners (i.e., with $\epsilon = 0$) do not exist. Abboud et al. [2] showed that the dependence on ϵ in [27] is nearly tight. Specifically, they showed a lower bound of $\beta = \Omega\left(\frac{1}{\epsilon \log k}\right)^{\log \kappa - 1}$.

Near-additive spanners were extensively studied in the past two decades [1, 2, 15, 17, 21, 25, 27, 28, 39, 40, 45], both in the context of distributed algorithms and in other settings. (In particular, they were used in the streaming setting [25, 28], and for dynamic algorithms [12, 32].) Efficient distributed deterministic constructions of such spanners using large messages (the so-called LOCAL model; see Section 1.3.1 for relevant definitions) were given by Derbel et al. [17]. They devised two constructions. In the first one, the running time is $O(\beta)$, and the additive term β is is roughly $\epsilon^{-(\kappa-2)}$, i.e., exponentially larger than β_{EP}. In the second construction of [17], the running time is $O(\beta \cdot 2^{O(\sqrt{\log n})})$, and β is roughly the same as in [27], i.e., $\beta \approx \beta_{EP}$.

Derbel et al. [17] explicitly raised the question of bulding $(1+\epsilon, \beta)$-spanners in the distributed CONGEST model (i.e., using short messages; see Section 1.3.1 for the definition), and this question remained open since their work. Efficient distributed randomized algorithms (in the CONGEST model) for constructing near-additive spanners were given in [25, 28, 40]. The state-of-the-art algorithm is due to [25]. They devised a randomized algorithm that constructs $(1+\epsilon, \beta)$-spanners with $O_{\epsilon,\kappa,\rho}(n^{1+1/\kappa})$ edges, with a *low polynomial* running time, that is, running time $O_{\epsilon,\kappa,\rho}(n^{\rho})$, for arbitrarily small $\epsilon, \rho, 1/\kappa > 0, 1/\kappa \leq \rho$, where $\beta_{EN} = \beta(\epsilon, \kappa, \rho) = O\left(\frac{\log \kappa\rho + \rho^{-1}}{\epsilon}\right)^{\log \kappa\rho + \rho^{-1} + O(1)}$. Note that the additive term β_{EN} of [25] is at the same ballpark as the existential bound β_{EP} of [27].

The importance of devising deterministic distributed algorithms that work in the CONGEST model for constructing spanners was recently articulated by Barenboim et al. [9], Grossman and Parter [31] and Ghaffari and Kuhn [30]. All these authors devised algorithms for constructing multiplicative spanners. The only deterministic CONGEST-model algorithm for building $(1+\epsilon, \beta)$-spanners with $\tilde{O}_{\epsilon,\kappa,\rho}(n^{1+1/\kappa})$ edges is due to [21]. That algorithm suffers however from a superlinear in n running time, $O(n^{1+\frac{1}{2\kappa}})$, and from additive term $\beta_E = (\frac{\kappa}{\epsilon})^{\log \kappa} \cdot (\rho^{-1})^{\rho^{-1}}$, which is significantly larger than β_{EN} (the additive term of [25]). Also, the number of edges in the resulting spanner is by a *polylog(n)* factor larger than the desired bound of $O_{\epsilon,\kappa,\rho}(n^{1+1/\kappa})$ (see [2, 25, 27, 40]).

In the current paper we devise a distributed *deterministic* algorithm that works in the CONGEST model, and for any $\epsilon > 0, \kappa = 1, 2, \ldots$ and $\rho > 1/\kappa$, and for any n-vertex graph, it constructs a $(1+\epsilon, \beta)$-spanner with $O_{\epsilon,\kappa,\rho}(n^{1+1/\kappa})$ edges in low polynomial, specifically $O_{\epsilon,\kappa,\rho}(n^{\rho})$ time, and its additive term β is at the same ballpark as β_{EN}. Specifically, our additive term satisfies:

$$\beta = \left(\frac{O\left(\log \kappa\rho + \rho^{-1}\right)}{\rho \cdot \epsilon}\right)^{\log \kappa\rho + \rho^{-1} + O(1)}. \quad (1)$$

See Table 1 for a concise overview of distributed algorithms, both deterministic and randomized, in both LOCAL and CONGEST models, for computing near-additive spanners. Observe that the algorithm in [21] is the only previously known deterministic construction of a near-additive spanner in the CONGEST model.

1.1 Technical Overview and Related Work

Our algorithm builds upon Elkin-Peleg's superclustering and interconnection approach (see [24, 25, 27] for an elaborate discussion of this technique). Its randomized distributed implementation by Elkin and Neiman [25] relies on random sampling of clusters. Those sampled clusters join nearby unsampled clusters to create superclusters, and this is iteratively repeated.

Our basic idea is to replace the random sampling by constructing ruling sets (see Section 1.3.2 for definition) using a deterministic procedure by Schneider et al. [42]. Recently, Ghaffari and Kuhn [30] used network decompositions for derandomizing algorithms that construct multiplicative spanners, hitting and dominating sets. All existing deterministic constructions of network decompositions [7, 9, 34] employ ruling sets. On the other hand, our approach avoids constructing network decomposition, but rather *directly* uses ruling sets for derandomization.

1.2 Outline

Section 1.3 provides necessary definitions for understanding this paper. Section 2 contains our spanner construction along with an analysis of the running time of the construction, and of the size and stretch of the spanner. Due to lack of space, some proofs and figures are omitted. For the full version of this paper, see [23].

1.3 Preliminaries

1.3.1 The Computational Model. In the distributed model [35] we have processors residing in vertices of the graph. The processors communicate with their graph neighbors in synchronous rounds. In the CONGEST model, messages are limited to $O(1)$ words, i.e., $O(1)$ edge weights[1] or ID numbers. In the LOCAL model, the length of messages is unbounded. The running time of an algorithm in the distributed model is the worst case number of communication rounds that the algorithm requires. Throughout this paper, we assume that all vertices have unique IDs such that for all v, $v.ID \in [n]$, and all vertices know their ID. Moreover, we assume that all vertices know the number of vertices n. In fact, our results apply even if vertices know an estimate $\tilde{n}$ for n, where $n \leq \tilde{n} \leq poly(n)$, and have distinct ID numbers in the range $[1, \tilde{n}]$.

1.3.2 Ruling Sets. Given a graph $G = (V, E)$, a set of vertices $W \subseteq V$ and parameters $\zeta, \eta \geq 0$, a set of vertices $A \subseteq W$ is said to be a *(ζ, η)-ruling set* for W if for every pair of vertices $u, v \in A$, the distance between them in G is at least ζ, and for every $u \in W$ there exists a representative $v \in A$ such that the distance between u, v is at most η.

2 A Deterministic Distributed Construction of Near-Additive Spanners

2.1 Overview

Let $G = (V, E)$ be an unweighted, undirected graph on n vertices, and let $\epsilon > 0$, $\kappa = 1, 2, \ldots$ and $1/\kappa \leq \rho < 1/2$. The algorithm constructs a sparse $(1+\epsilon, \beta)$ – *spanner* $H = (V, E_H)$ of G where $\beta(\epsilon, \kappa, \rho)$ is a function of the parameters ϵ, κ, ρ, given by eq. (1), and $|H| = O(\beta n^{1+1/\kappa})$, in deterministic time $O_{\epsilon,\kappa,\rho}(n^{\rho})$ in the CONGEST model.

[1] In our case, the graph is unweighted.

Table 1: Previous results for near-additive spanners

authors	model	stretch	size	running time
[27]	centralized, det	$(1+\epsilon, 4)$ $(1+\epsilon, \beta)$ $\beta = \left(\frac{\log\kappa}{\epsilon}\right)\kappa^{\log\kappa}$ $(1+\epsilon, \beta')$ $\beta' = \max\{\left(\frac{\log\kappa}{\epsilon}\right)\kappa^{\log\kappa}, \kappa^{-\log\rho}\}$	$O(\epsilon^{-1}n^{4/3})$ $O\left(\beta n^{1+1/\kappa}\right)$ $O\left(\beta' n^{1+1/\kappa}\right)$	$O(mn^{\frac{2}{3}})$ $\tilde{O}(m \cdot n)$ $\tilde{O}(n^{2+\rho})$
[21]	CONGEST, det	$(1+\epsilon, \beta_E)$ $\beta_E = (\frac{\kappa}{\epsilon})^{O(\log\kappa)} \cdot (\rho^{-1})^{\rho^{-1}}$ $\frac{1}{2\kappa} < \rho < \frac{1}{2\kappa} + \frac{1}{3}$	$\tilde{O}(\beta_E n^{1+1/\kappa})$	$O(n^{1+\frac{1}{2\kappa}})$
[28]	CONGEST, rand	$(1+\epsilon, \beta)$, $\beta = (\frac{\kappa}{\epsilon})^{O(\log\kappa)} \cdot (\rho^{-1})^{\rho^{-1}}$ Or $\beta = \left(\frac{\kappa\log\kappa}{\epsilon}\right)^{O(\log\kappa)} \cdot (\rho^{-1})^{\rho^{-1}}$ $\frac{1}{2\kappa} < \rho < \frac{1}{2\kappa} + \frac{1}{3}$	$O(n^{1+1/\kappa})$	$O(n^{\rho})$
[45]	centralized, rand	$(1+\epsilon, (O(1)/\epsilon)^{\kappa})$	$O(n^{1+\frac{1}{\kappa}})$	$O(mn^{1/\kappa})$
[15]	LOCAL, det	$(1+\epsilon, 8\log n)$	$O(n^{\frac{3}{2}})$	$O(\frac{1}{\epsilon}\log n)$
[16]	LOCAL, det	$(1+\epsilon, 2)$	$O(\epsilon^{-1}n^{3/2})$	$O(\epsilon^{-1})$
[17]	LOCAL, det	$(1+\epsilon, O(1/\epsilon)^{\kappa-2})$ $(1+\epsilon, \beta)$, $\beta = \left(\frac{\log\kappa}{\epsilon}\right)^{O(\log\kappa)}$ $(1+\epsilon, \beta)$, $\beta = \left(\frac{\log n}{\epsilon}\right)^{O(\log\log n)}$	$O(\epsilon^{-\kappa+1}n^{1+1/\kappa})$ $O(\beta n^{1+1/\kappa})$ $O(\beta n)$	$O(1)$ $O(\beta \cdot 2^{O(\sqrt{\log n})})$ $O(\beta \cdot \log n)$
[39]	centralized, rand	$\left(1+\epsilon, O\left(\epsilon^{-1} \cdot \log\log n\right)^{\log\log n}\right)$	$O\left(n\log\log(\epsilon^{-1}\log\log n)\right)$	NA
[40]	CONGEST, rand	$\left(1+\epsilon, O\left(\frac{\log\kappa+\rho^{-1}}{\epsilon}\right)^{\log_{\phi}\kappa+\rho^{-1}}\right)$	$O\left(n^{1+1/\kappa}\left(\frac{\log\kappa}{\epsilon}\right)^{\phi}\right)$, $\phi = \frac{1+\sqrt{5}}{2}$	$\tilde{O}(n^{\rho})$
[2]	centralized, rand	$(1+\epsilon, O(\frac{\log\kappa}{\epsilon})^{\log\kappa-1})$	$O((\frac{\log\kappa}{\epsilon})^{h_\kappa}\log\kappa n^{1+\frac{1}{\kappa}})$, $h_\kappa < \frac{3}{4}$	NA
[25]	CONGEST, rand	$(1+\epsilon, \beta)$ $\beta = O\left(\frac{\log\kappa\rho+\rho^{-1}}{\epsilon}\right)^{\log(\kappa\rho)+\rho^{-1}}$	$O(n^{1+1/\kappa})$, $\kappa \leq \frac{\log n}{\log(1/\epsilon)+\log\log n}$	$O(n^{\rho} \cdot \rho^{-1} \cdot \beta \cdot \log n)$
New	CONGEST, det	$(1+\epsilon, \beta)$ $\beta = \left(\frac{O(\log\kappa\rho+\rho^{-1})}{\rho\cdot\epsilon}\right)^{\log\kappa\rho+\rho^{-1}+O(1)}$	$O\left(\beta \cdot n^{1+1/\kappa}\right)$	$O\left(\beta \cdot n^{\rho} \cdot \rho^{-1}\right)$

The overall structure of our algorithm is reminiscent of that in [25]. However, unlike the algorithm of [25], the current algorithm does not use any randomization. We first provide a high-level overview of the algorithm.

The algorithm begins by initializing the edge set E_H of the spanner as an empty set, and proceeds in phases. It begins by partitioning V into singletons clusters $P_0 = \{\{v\} \mid v \in V\}$. Each phase i, for $i = 0, \ldots, \ell$, receives as input a collection of clusters P_i, and distance and degree threshold parameters δ_i, $\deg_i$. The parameters δ_i and deg_i will be specified later. We set the maximum index of a phase ℓ by $\ell = \lfloor\log\kappa\rho\rfloor + \lceil\frac{\kappa+1}{\kappa\rho}\rceil - 1$, as in [25].

Each of the clusters constructed by our algorithm will have a designated *center* vertex. Throughout the algorithm, we denote by r_C the center of the cluster C and say that C is *centered around* r_C. For a cluster C, define $Rad(C) = max\{d_H(r_C, v) \mid v \in C\}$. Note that the distance is measured in the spanner H, that the algorithm constructs. For a set of clusters P_i, define $Rad(P_i) = max\{Rad(C) \mid C \in P_i\}$. For a collection P_i, we denote by S_i the set of centers of P_i, i.e., $S_i = \{r_C \mid C \in P_i\}$.

Intuitively, in each phase we wish to add paths between pairs of cluster centers that are close to one another. However, if a center has many centers close to it, i.e., it is *popular*, this can add too many edges to the spanner. Two cluster centers $r_C, r_{C'}$ are said to be *close*, if $d_G(r_C, r_{C'}) \leq \delta_i$. A cluster C and its center r_C are said to be *popular* if r_C has at least deg_i cluster centers that are close to it. In order to avoid adding too many edges to the spanner, each phase consists of two steps, the *superclustering* step and the *interconnection* step.

The *superclustering* step of phase i detects popular clusters and builds larger clusters around them. For each new cluster C, a BFS tree of the cluster C is added to the spanner H. The collection of new clusters is the input for phase $i+1$. This allows us to defer the work on highly dense areas in the graph to later phases of the algorithm.

In the *interconnection* step of phase i, clusters that have not been superclustered in this phase (denoted by U_i) are connected to one another. For each center r_C that is not superclustered in this phase, paths are added to all centers of clusters that are close to it. As r_C is not superclustered, it is not *popular*, and so we will not add too many paths to the resulting spanner H.

In the last phase ℓ, the superclustering step is skipped and we move directly to the interconnection step. We will show that the number of clusters in the final collection of clusters P_ℓ is small. Specifically, we show that even if every pair of clusters in P_ℓ is interconnected by a path, the number of added edges will still be relatively small. Thus the superclustering step of phase ℓ can be safely skipped. This concludes the high-level overview of the algorithm.

The distance parameters are defined as follows. Define

$$R_0 = 0 \ \ and \ \ R_{i+1} = 2\epsilon^{-i}/\rho + (5/\rho)R_i. \tag{2}$$

We will show (see Lemma 2.3 below) that R_i is an upper bound on the radius of clusters in P_i, that is, $Rad(P_i) \leq R_i$ for all $0 \leq i \leq \ell$. Also, the distance threshold parameter δ_i is given by:

$$\delta_i = \epsilon^{-i} + 2R_i. \tag{3}$$

The degree threshold deg_i affects the number of clusters in each phase, and thus the number of phases of the algorithm. It also affects the number of edges added to the spanner by the interconnection step. Ideally, we would like to set $deg_i = n^{\frac{2^i}{\kappa}}$ for all i. However, the algorithm requires $\Omega(deg_i)$ time to execute phase i. Thus, we must keep $deg_i \leq n^\rho$ for all phases, as we aim at running time of roughly $O(n^\rho)$.

For this reason, we partition phases $0, 1, \ldots, \ell-1$ into two stages, the *exponential growth stage* and the *fixed growth stage*. In the *exponential growth stage*, that consists of phases $0, \ldots, i_0 = \lfloor \log(\kappa\rho) \rfloor$, we set $deg_i = n^{2^i/\kappa}$. In the *fixed growth stage*, which consists of phases $i_0 + 1, \ldots, i_1 = i_0 + \lceil \frac{\kappa+1}{\kappa\rho} \rceil - 2 = \ell - 1$, we set $deg_i = n^\rho$. Observe that for every index i, we have $deg_i \leq n^\rho$. The concluding phase ℓ is not a part of either these stages, as the number of clusters in P_ℓ is at most n^ρ. For notational purposes, we define $deg_\ell = n^\rho$. However, we note that as there are at most n^ρ clusters in P_ℓ, there are no popular clusters in this phase.

We will now discuss the differences between the current algorithm and the algorithm of [25]. In [25], the superclustering step uses a randomized selection of vertices to cover the popular cluster centers. The current algorithm replaces this selection with a deterministic procedure that computes a ruling set that covers these centers. For this aim, we use the algorithm of [33, 42] that computes ruling sets efficiently in the CONGEST model. As a result of the deterministic procedure, the distance parameter (and consequently, the radii of clusters) for each phase in the current algorithm is larger than in [25]. For this reason, the additive term that the current algorithm provides is slightly inferior to the additive term of [25]. The number of phases and the degree parameter sequence remain as in [25].

The deterministic detection of popular clusters' centers requires vertices to acquire information regarding their δ_i-neighborhood. This information is later utilized by our algorithm in the interconnection step as well. Thus, while in the algorithm of [25] the interconnection step executes Bellman-Ford explorations, the current algorithm relies on already acquired information. Therefore, the current execution of the interconnection step is simpler than the execution of the respective interconnection step in [25].

2.2 Superclustering

This section provides details of the execution of the superclustering steps for all phases $i \in [0, i_1 = \ell - 1]$, i.e., all phases other than the (concluding) phase ℓ on which there is no superclustering step. Recall that for the exponential growth stage, we have $deg_i = n^{2^i/\kappa}$. For the fixed growth stage, we have $deg_i = n^\rho$. The input to phase i is a set of clusters P_i. The phase begins by detecting popular clusters. To do so, we employ Algorithm 1 with the input $(G, P_i, \deg_i, \delta_i)$. The algorithm is a modification of the Bellman-Ford algorithm tailored to our needs. The following theorem summarizes the properties of the returned vertex set W_i. For its proof, see the full version of the paper [23].

Algorithm 1 Detecting Popular Clusters

```
Input: graph G = (V, E), a set of clusters P_i, parameters deg_i, δ_i
Output: a set W_i.
Each vertex v ∈ V initializes a list of centers it learned about
    and their distance from it as an empty list.
Each r_C ∈ S_i sends ⟨r_C.ID, 0⟩
for j = 1 to δ_i do
    for deg_i rounds do
        if v received at most deg_i messages ⟨r_C, j − 1⟩ then
            For each received messages ⟨r_C, j−1⟩, v sends ⟨r_C, j⟩
        if v received more than deg_i messages ⟨r_C, j − 1⟩ then
            For arbitrary deg_i received messages ⟨r_C, j − 1⟩, v
    sends ⟨r_C, j⟩
Each r_C ∈ S_i that has learned about at least deg_i other centers
    joins W_i.
```

Theorem 2.1. *Given a graph $G = (V, E)$, a collection of clusters P_i centered around cluster centers S_i and parameters δ_i, $\deg_i$, Algorithm 1 returns a set W_i in $O(deg_i \cdot \delta_i)$ time such that:*

(1) W_i is the set of all centers of popular clusters from P_i.

(2) Every cluster center $r_C \in S_i$ that did not join W_i knows the identities of all the centers $r_{C'} \in S_i$ such that $d_G(r_C, r_{C'}) \leq \delta_i$. Furthermore, for each pair of such centers $r_C, r_{C'}$, there is a shortest path π between them such that all vertices on π know their distance from $r_{C'}$.

Next, we wish to select a subset of vertices from W_i to grow large clusters around them. On the one hand, the number of clusters in P_{i+1} must be significantly smaller than the number of clusters in P_i. On the other hand, all cluster centers in W_i must be superclustered. In the centralized version of this algorithm, Elkin and Peleg [27] run multiple consecutive scans to detect popular clusters and build superclusters around them. In the distributed model of computation, this requires too much time. In the distributed randomized version of this algorithm, Elkin and Neiman [25] randomly select centers to grow superclusters around. In this deterministic distributed version, we select vertices by constructing a *ruling set* for the set W_i. We use the algorithm given in [33, 42], on the set W_i with parameters $q =$

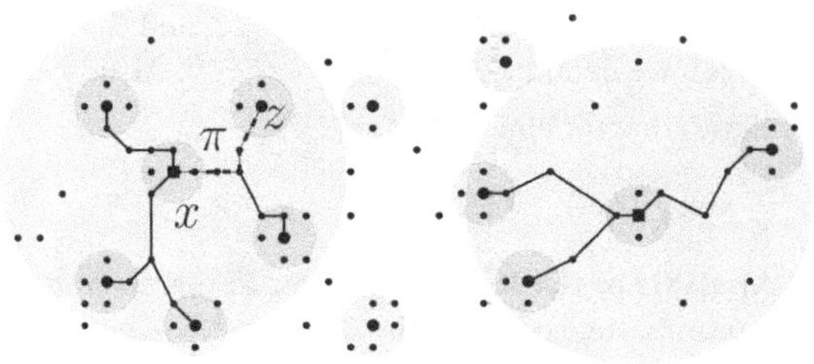

Figure 1: For every $r_{C'}$ that is spanned by the tree in F_i rooted at r_C, the path in F_i from r_C to $r_{C'}$ is added to the spanner H. For example, in the figure, the $x-z$ path π depicted by a thick dashed line is added to H.

$2\delta_i, c = \rho^{-1}$. The following theorem summarizes the properties of the returned ruling set.

Theorem 2.2. *Given a graph $G = (V, E)$, a set of vertices $W_i \subseteq V$ and parameters $q \in \{1, 2, \dots\}, c > 1$, one can compute a $(q+1, cq)$-ruling subset RS_i for W_i in $O(q \cdot c \cdot n^{\frac{1}{c}})$ deterministic time, in the* CONGEST *model.*

By Theorem 2.2, the returned subset RS_i is a $(2\delta_i + 1, (2/\rho) \cdot \delta_i)$-*ruling set* for the set W_i.

The ruling set RS_i is $(2\delta_i + 1)$-separated. This is done in order to guarantee that the sets of vertices in radius δ_i around each vertex in RS_i are pairwise disjoint. This allows us to bound the size of the ruling set RS_i, and eventually the size of the collection P_{i+1}.

We are now ready to create large *superclusters.* A BFS exploration rooted at the set RS_i is executed to depth $(2/\rho) \cdot \delta_i$ in G. This constructs a forest F_i, rooted at vertices of RS_i.

For a cluster center $r_{C'} \in S_i \backslash RS_i$ that is spanned by F_i, let r_C be the root of the forest tree of F_i to which $r_{C'}$ belongs. The cluster C' now becomes *superclustered* in the cluster $\widehat{C}$ centered around the cluster C.

The center r_C of C becomes the new cluster center of $\widehat{C}$, i.e., $r_{\widehat{C}} \leftarrow r_C$. The vertex set of the new supercluster $\widehat{C}$ is the union of the vertex set of the original cluster C, with the vertex sets of all clusters C' which are superclustered into $\widehat{C}$. We denote by $V(C)$ the vertex set of a cluster C.

For every cluster center $r_{C'}$ that is spanned by the tree in F_i rooted at r_C, the path in F_i from r_C to $r_{C'}$ is added to the spanner H (see Figure 1). Note that the path itself is *not* added to the cluster $\widehat{C}$. Recall that H is initialized as an empty set.

We define $\widehat{P_i}$ as the set of new superclusters, $\widehat{C}$, that were built by the superclustering step of phase i. We set $P_{i+1} = \widehat{P_i}$. Note that the set S_{i+1} of cluster centers of P_{i+1} is given by $S_{i+1} = RS_i$.

Next we show that R_i is an upper bound on $Rad(P_i)$, the radius of clusters in phase i.

Lemma 2.3. *For all integer $0 \le i \le \ell$, we have $Rad(P_i) \le R_i$.*

Proof. We will prove the lemma by induction on the index of the phase i. For $i = 0$, observe that $Rad(P_0) = 0$, and $R_0 = 0$ by definition. Thus the induction base case holds. For the inductive step, recall that by definition

$$R_{i+1} = 2\epsilon^{-i}/\rho + (5/\rho)R_i.$$

For analyzing $Rad(\widehat{P_i})$, consider a vertex $u \in \widehat{C}$. If $u \in C$, by the induction hypothesis, we have $d_H(r_C, u) \le R_i$, and since $\rho < 1$ we have that $R_i \le R_{i+1}$. Otherwise, $u \in C'$ for some $C' \in P_i$ such that C' is clustered into $\widehat{C}$ in the superclustering step of phase i. By the induction hypothesis, we have $d_H(r_{C'}, u) \le R_i$. Since C' is clustered into $\widehat{C}$, we have $d_G(r_C, r_{C'}) \le \frac{2}{\rho}\delta_i$. Moreover, a shortest $r_C - r_{C'}$ path was added to H, and by eq. (3), we have $d_H(r_C, r_{C'}) \le \frac{2}{\rho}\delta_i = \rho^{-1}\left[2\epsilon^{-i} + 4R_i\right]$. Since $\rho < 1$, we have $d_H(r_C, u) \le R_{i+1}$. Therefore, $Rad(P_{i+1}) = Rad(\widehat{P_i}) \le R_{i+1}$. □

Lemma 2.4. *All popular clusters in phase i are superclustered into clusters of $\widehat{P_i}$.*

Proof. Let C' be a popular cluster. Then, $r_{C'}$ belongs to the set W_i returned by Algorithm 1. There is a vertex r_C in the ruling subset RS_i computed for the set W_i, such that $d_G(r_C, r_{C'}) \le \frac{2}{\rho}\delta_i$. Hence the BFS exploration that is executed from the set RS_i to depth $\frac{2}{\rho}\delta_i$ reaches $r_{C'}$. Thus $r_{C'}$ is spanned by the forest F_i, and thus the cluster C' is superclustered into some supercluster in $\widehat{P_i}$. □

This concludes the analysis of the superclustering step of phase i.

2.3 Interconnection Next we provide the details of the execution of the interconnection step. Let $i \in [0, \ell]$. Denote by U_i the set of clusters of P_i which were not superclustered into clusters of $\widehat{P_i}$. For phase ℓ, the superclustering step is skipped. Therefore, we set $U_\ell = P_\ell$.

In the interconnection step for $i \ge 0$, we wish to connect clusters $C \in U_i$ to all the clusters $C' \in P_i$ that are close to them, i.e., such that $d_G(r_C, r_{C'}) \le \delta_i$. Note that we will connect a cluster $C \in U_i$ to all clusters $C' \in P_i$ that are close to it. This is regardless of whether C' has been superclustered in this phase or not (see Figure 2). However, by Lemma 2.4, every cluster in U_i is not popular. As $C \in U_i$, it has at most deg_i clusters close to it. Thus we can connect it to these other nearby clusters without adding too many edges to the spanner. By Theorem 2.1, the center r_C of each such cluster C knows all other centers $r_{C'}$ such that $C' \in P_i$ and $d_G(r_C, r_{C'}) \le \delta_i$, and the distances to them. Thus, each center r_C of a cluster $C \in U_i$ already knows which are the clusters it needs to connect to. For each $C' \in P_i$ such that $d_G(r_C, r_{C'}) \le \delta_i$, the center r_C traces back the message that informed r_C regarding $r_{C'}$ (see Theorem 2.1), and a shortest path between r_C and $r_{C'}$ is added to the spanner H.

The interconnection of the concluding phase ℓ is slightly different. As the superclustering step of this phase is skipped, we employ Algorithm 1 with the input $(G, P_\ell, deg_\ell, \delta_\ell)$. The output set W_i is an empty set[2], but the execution of the algorithm allows vertices to acquire the required information for the interconnection step. This completes the description of the interconnection step.

Denote by $U^{(i)}$ the union of all sets $U_0, U_1, \dots, U_i$, i.e., $U^{(i)} = \bigcup_{j=0}^{i} U_j$. In the full version we prove the following lemma:

Lemma 2.5. *The set $U^{(\ell)}$ defined by $U^{(\ell)} = \bigcup_{i=0}^{\ell} U_i$ is a partition of V.*

[2] Algorithm 1 does not explicitly *return* the set W_i. Rather each vertex $v \in V$ knows whether it belongs to the output W_i or not. In the execution of Algorithm 1 in phase ℓ, all vertices know that they do not belong to the output W_i.

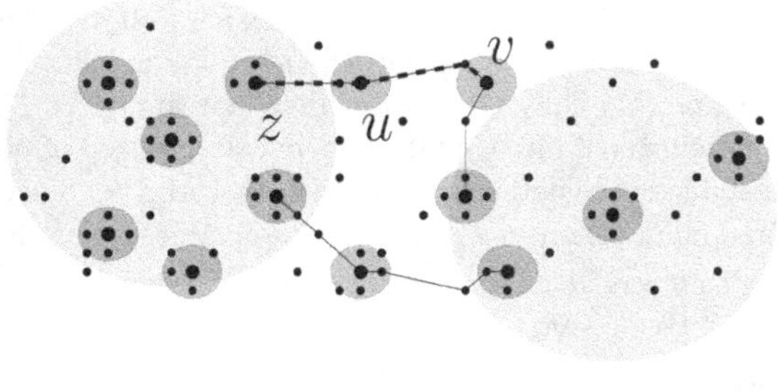

Figure 2: Each cluster center r_C such that $C \in U_i$ is connected to all cluster centers $r_{C'}$, such that $C' \in P_i$ that are close to it. For example, in the figure, the paths $u-v, u-z$ depicted by a thick dashed line are added to H.

2.4 Analysis of the Construction

In this section, we analyze the running time of the construction and the size and stretch of the resulting spanner. We begin by analyzing the radii of clusters' collections P_i for $i \in [\ell]$. By Lemma 2.3, these radii are upper bounded by R_i's. In the next lemma, we derive an explicit expression for these upper bounds. This upper bound is later used to bound δ_i, which is used in Sections 2.4.1, 2.4.2 and 2.4.3 to analyze the running time of the construction and the size and stretch of the spanner, respectively. Finally, in Section 2.4.4, we rescale ϵ to derive our ultimate result.

Lemma 2.6. *For $i \in [\ell]$, we have*

$$R_i = \sum_{j=0}^{i-1} 2/\rho \cdot \epsilon^{-j} \cdot (5/\rho)^{i-1-j}.$$

Proof. The proof is by induction on the index i.
Recall that $R_0 = 0$ and R_i is given by (see eq. (2))

$$R_{i+1} = \frac{2}{\rho}\epsilon^{-i} + (5/\rho)R_i.$$

For $i = 1$, it is easy to verify that $\sum_{j=0}^{i-1} 2/\rho \cdot \epsilon^{-j} \cdot (5/\rho)^{i-1-j} = 2/\rho$ and also $\frac{2}{\rho}\epsilon^{-0} + (5/\rho)R_0 = 2/\rho$. So the base case holds. For the induction step, by the induction hypothesis we have:

$$\begin{aligned} R_{i+1} &= (2/\rho)\cdot\epsilon^{-i} + (5/\rho)\sum_{j=0}^{i-1}\frac{2}{\rho}\left(\frac{1}{\epsilon}\right)^j(5/\rho)^{i-1-j} \\ &= \sum_{j=0}^{i}\frac{2}{\rho}\left(\frac{1}{\epsilon}\right)^j(5/\rho)^{i-j}. \end{aligned}$$

□

Assume that $\rho \geq 10\epsilon$. (This assumption will not affect our ultimate result. See Section 2.4.4.) Observe that Lemma 2.6 implies that $R_i \leq \frac{2}{\rho-5\epsilon}\cdot\epsilon^{-(i-1)} \leq \frac{4}{\rho}\cdot\epsilon^{-(i-1)}$. It follows that:

$$R_i \leq \frac{4}{\rho}\cdot\epsilon^{-(i-1)}. \tag{4}$$

Recall that $P_i = \widehat{P}_{i-1}$. Hence $Rad(P_i) = Rad(\widehat{P}_{i-1})$. By Lemma 2.3, we have for all $i \in [0,\ell]$, (assuming $\rho \geq 10\epsilon$),

$$Rad(P_i) = Rad(\widehat{P}_{i-1}) \leq R_i \leq \frac{4}{\rho}\cdot\epsilon^{-(i-1)}. \tag{5}$$

Recall that $\delta_i = \epsilon^{-i} + 2R_i$, and that $R_0 = 0$, and $\delta_0 = 1$. For $i \in [\ell]$, by eq. (4), we obtain: $\delta_i \leq \epsilon^{-i} + \frac{8}{\rho}\cdot\epsilon^{-(i-1)}$. Also, $\frac{8}{\rho}\epsilon^{-(i-1)} \leq \epsilon^{-i}$. It follows that for all $i \in [0,\ell]$:

$$\delta_i \leq O\left((1/\epsilon)^i\right). \tag{6}$$

2.4.1 Analysis of the Running Time.

In this section, we analyze the running time of the entire algorithm. We begin with the following lemma which analyses the running time of a single phase of the algorithm.

Lemma 2.7. *For all $i \in [0,\ell]$, the running time of phase i is $O(\rho^{-1}\cdot\delta_i\cdot n^\rho)$.*

Proof. The superclustering step consists of running Algorithm 1, which requires $O(deg_i\cdot\delta_i)$ time (see Theorem 2.1). Constructing a $(2\delta_i+1, \frac{2}{\rho}\delta_i)$-ruling set requires $O(\rho^{-1}\cdot\delta_i\cdot n^\rho)$ time (see Theorem 2.2). The BFS exploration to depth $\frac{2}{\rho}\delta_i$ that builds superclusters requires $O(\rho^{-1}\delta_i)$ time. (Note that no congestion occurs on this step.) In total, the superclustering step of phase i requires $O(deg_i\cdot\delta_i + \rho^{-1}\delta_i\cdot n^\rho + \rho^{-1}\delta_i)$ time. Since for all i, $deg_i \leq n^\rho$, it follows that the superclustering step of phase i requires $O(\rho^{-1}\cdot\delta_i\cdot n^\rho)$ time.

As for the interconnection step, note that each cluster that needs to add a path to the spanner H in the interconnection step of phase i knows all the clusters it needs to add a path to. Moreover, by Theorem 2.1, each cluster center r_C, $C \in U_i$, can trace back the shortest path that a message regarding a nearby cluster center $r_{C'}$ took to reach r_C, and add the edges along this route to H. By Theorem 2.1, this requires $O(deg_i\cdot\delta_i)$ time. Thus the running time of the interconnection step of a given phase is dominated by the running time of the superclustering step of this phase. An exception to that is the concluding phase, in which there is no superclustering step. In this phase, we execute Algorithm 1 with parameters n^ρ, δ_ℓ. By Theorem 2.1 this requires $O(n^\rho\cdot\delta_\ell)$ time. We then trace back the shortest paths in $O(n^\rho\cdot\delta_\ell)$ time. Thus the running time of the interconnection step of each phase $i \geq 0$ is dominated by $O(\rho^{-1}\cdot\delta_i\cdot n^\rho)$, and so the running time of a single phase of the algorithm is $O(\rho^{-1}\cdot\delta_i\cdot n^\rho)$. □

By Lemma 2.7 and eq. (6), the running time of the entire algorithm is bounded by:

$$\begin{aligned} \sum_{i=0}^{\ell} O(\rho^{-1}\cdot\delta_i\cdot n^\rho) &\leq n^\rho\cdot\rho^{-1}\sum_{i=0}^{\ell} O(\epsilon^{-i}) \\ &\leq O\left(n^\rho\cdot\rho^{-1}\cdot\epsilon^{-\ell}\right). \end{aligned} \tag{7}$$

Corollary 2.8. *The running time of the algorithm is bounded by $O\left(n^\rho\rho^{-1}\epsilon^{-\ell}\right)$.*

2.4.2 Analysis of the Number of Edges.

In this section, we analyze the number of edges added to the spanner H. First, observe that in the superclustering step of phase i, the edges that are added to H are a subset of the BFS forest F_i. Thus in each phase $O(n)$ edges are added to H by the superclustering step.

We will now analyze the number of edges added by the interconnection step. In the interconnection step of phase i, a path is added to the spanner from each cluster C in U_i to clusters in P_i that are close to it. As C belongs to U_i, it is not popular. Thus it has at most

deg_i other clusters in P_i that are close to it. To bound the size of U_i, we bound the size of P_i, as $U_i \subseteq P_i$.

The next two lemmas, provide an upper bound on the size of the cluster collection P_i in the exponential growth and the fixed growth stages.

LEMMA 2.9. *For* $i \in [0, i_0 + 1 = \lfloor \log(\kappa\rho) \rfloor + 1]$, *we have* $|P_i| \leq n^{1-\frac{2^i-1}{\kappa}}$.

PROOF. We will prove the lemma by induction on the index of the phase i.

For $i = 0$, the right-hand side is $n^{1-\frac{2^0-1}{\kappa}} = n$. Thus the claim is trivial.

Recall that for each index i, the set RS_i is the ruling set computed in phase i, and that S_i is the set of centers of clusters in P_i. Since for each phase $i \geq 1$, the clusters of the collection P_i are centered around vertices of RS_{i-1}, for $i \geq 1$, we have $S_i = RS_{i-1}$. The set RS_i is a $(2\delta_i + 1, \frac{2}{\rho}\delta_i)$-ruling set for W_i. By Theorem 2.1, all vertices in W_i are popular cluster centers. Thus, for every $r_C \in W_i$, it holds that $|\Gamma^{(\delta_i)}(r_C) \cap S_i| \geq deg_i$.

By Theorem 2.2, the set RS_i is $(2\delta_i + 1)$-separated, i.e., for every pair of distinct cluster centers $r_C, r_{C'} \in RS_i$, we have $d_G(r_C, r_{C'}) \geq 2\delta_i + 1$. Thus, for every pair of distinct centers $r_C, r_{C'} \in RS_i$, their δ_i-neighborhoods are disjoint, i.e., $\Gamma^{(\delta_i)}(r_C) \cap \Gamma^{(\delta_i)}(r_{C'}) = \emptyset$.

Together with the induction hypothesis, and since for i, $0 \leq i \leq i_0$, $deg_i = n^{\frac{2^i}{\kappa}}$, this implies that $|\widehat{P}_i| \leq \frac{|P_i|}{deg_i} \leq n^{1-\frac{2^i-1}{\kappa}}/n^{\frac{2^i}{\kappa}} = n^{1-\frac{2^{i+1}-1}{\kappa}}$.

As $P_{i+1} = \widehat{P}_i$, we conclude that $|P_{i+1}| \leq n^{1-\frac{2^{i+1}-1}{\kappa}}$. □

In the full version, we prove the following lemma. (The proof is similar to the proof of Lemma 2.9.)

LEMMA 2.10. *For* $i_0 + 1 \leq i \leq \ell$, *it holds that*

$$|P_i| \quad \leq \quad n^{1+\frac{1}{\kappa}-(i-i_0)\rho}.$$

The next lemma, provides an upper bound on the number of edges added to the spanner by each phase $i \in [0, \ell]$.

LEMMA 2.11. *For all* $i \in [0, \ell]$, *in each phase i*, $O(n^{1+1/\kappa} \cdot \delta_i)$ *edges are added to the spanner H.*

PROOF. Let $i \in [0, i_1]$ be an index (recall that $i_1 = i_0 + \lceil \frac{\kappa+1}{\kappa\rho} \rceil - 2 = \ell - 1$). Each cluster center r_C, such that $C \in U_i$, initiates a BFS exploration to depth δ_i. For each cluster center $r_{C'}$, $C' \in P_i$, that is discovered by this exploration, a shortest $r_C - r_{C'}$ path is added to the spanner H. Since $C \in U_i$, the cluster center r_C has at most deg_i other cluster centers $r_{C'} \in S_i$ within distance δ_i from it. So, the number of paths that are added to the spanner in the interconnection step of phase i is at most: $|U_i| \cdot deg_i \leq |P_i| \cdot deg_i$.

For $i \in [0, i_0 = \lfloor \log(\kappa\rho) \rfloor]$, by Lemma 2.9, we have $|P_i| \cdot deg_i \leq n^{1-\frac{2^i-1}{\kappa}} \cdot n^{\frac{2^i}{\kappa}} = n^{1+\frac{1}{\kappa}}$.

For $i \in [i_0+1, i_1]$, by Lemma 2.10, we have $|P_i| \cdot deg_i \leq n^{1+\frac{1}{\kappa}-(i-i_0)\rho} \cdot n^{\rho} \leq n^{1+\frac{1}{\kappa}}$.

So in each phase $i \in [0, i_1]$, the number of edges added to the spanner H by the interconnection step is $O(n^{1+\frac{1}{\kappa}} \cdot \delta_i)$, and the total number of edges added to H by the superclustering and the interconnection steps of phase i is:

$$O(n + n^{1+1/\kappa} \cdot \delta_i).$$

We will now discuss the number of edges added to H by phase ℓ, i.e., by the concluding phase. In this phase, we skip the superclustering step and execute the interconnection step. We set $U_\ell = P_\ell$. Note that by Lemma 2.10, for the last ($\ell = i_0 + \lceil \frac{\kappa+1}{\kappa\rho} \rceil - 1$) phase, the size of the input collection P_ℓ is bounded by $|P_\ell| \leq n^{1+\frac{1}{\kappa}-(\ell-i_0)\rho} = n^{1+\frac{1}{\kappa}-(i_0+\lceil \frac{\kappa+1}{\kappa\rho} \rceil-1-i_0)\rho} \leq n^{1+\frac{1}{\kappa}-(\frac{\kappa+1}{\kappa}-\rho)} \leq n^{\rho}$.

Therefore, even if every pair of clusters in P_ℓ is connected by the interconnection step of phase ℓ, at most $O(n^{2\rho} \cdot \delta_\ell)$ edges are added to H by the concluding phase. As we set $\rho \leq \frac{1}{2}$, the concluding phase adds at most $O(n \cdot \delta_\ell)$ edges to the spanner H.

Hence, the total number of edges added to the spanner H by a phase $i \in [0, \ell]$ is $O(n^{1+1/\kappa} \cdot \delta_i)$.

□

By Lemma 2.11 and eq. (6), the number of edges added to the spanner H by all phases of the algorithm is bounded by:

$$\begin{aligned} \Sigma_{i=0}^{\ell} O\left(n^{1+1/\kappa} \cdot \delta_i\right) &\leq \Sigma_{i=0}^{\ell} O\left(n^{1+1/\kappa} \cdot \epsilon^{-i}\right) \\ &\leq O\left(n^{1+1/\kappa} \cdot \epsilon^{-\ell}\right) \end{aligned} \quad (8)$$

COROLLARY 2.12. *The size of the spanner H is bounded by* $|E_H| = O\left(n^{1+1/\kappa} \cdot \epsilon^{-\ell}\right)$.

2.4.3 Analysis of the Stretch.

In this section, we analyze the stretch of the spanner H. The following two lemmas, provide necessary tools for Lemma 2.15, in which we analyze the stretch of the spanner H.

LEMMA 2.13. *For all* $i \in [0, \ell]$, *for every pair of clusters* $C \in U_i$, $C' \in P_i$ *at distance at most* $\left(\frac{1}{\epsilon}\right)^i$ *from one another, a shortest path between the clusters centers* $r_C, r_{C'}$ *was added to the spanner H.*

PROOF. Let $i \in [0, \ell]$, and let $C \in U_i$, $C' \in P_i$ a pair of clusters at distance at most $\left(\frac{1}{\epsilon}\right)^i$ from one another. Since R_i is an upper bound on $Rad(P_i)$ (see Lemma 2.3), we have that $d_G(r_C, r_{C'}) \leq 2R_i + \epsilon^{-i} = \delta_i$. Recall that by Lemma 2.4, all popular clusters in phase i are superclustered into clusters of P_{i+1}. Thus they do not belong to U_i. It follows that centers of clusters of U_i do not belong to W_i. Thus, since $C \in U_i$, by Theorem 2.1, in the interconnection step of phase i the center r_C of C knows the distance to $r_{C'}$. So r_C adds a shortest $r_C - r_{C'}$ path to the spanner H. □

We now provide an upper bound on the distance in H between neighboring clusters in G.

LEMMA 2.14. *Consider a pair of indices* $0 \leq j < i \leq \ell$, *and a pair of neighboring clusters* $C \in U_j$ *and* $C' \in U_i$. *Let w be some vertex in C, and let* $r_{C'}$ *be the center of the cluster* C'. *Let* $\rho < 1$. *Then, there is a path in H between w and* $r_{C'}$ *of length at most* $3R_j + 1 + R_i$.

PROOF. Let $(z', z) \in E$ be an edge such that $z \in C$ and $z' \in C'$ (see Figure 3 for an illustration). We will first consider phase j. Let $C'' \in P_j$ be the cluster such that $z' \in C''$, that is, C'' is the cluster of z' in the jth phase. Observe that $C \in U_j$, and $d_G(C, C'') = 1$. Then by Lemma 2.3, we have $d_G(r_C, r_{C''}) \leq 2R_j + 1$. Note that $2R_j + 1 \leq \epsilon^{-j} + 2R_j = \delta_j$, for all $j \in [0, \ell]$. Thus, a shortest $r_C - r_{C''}$ path was

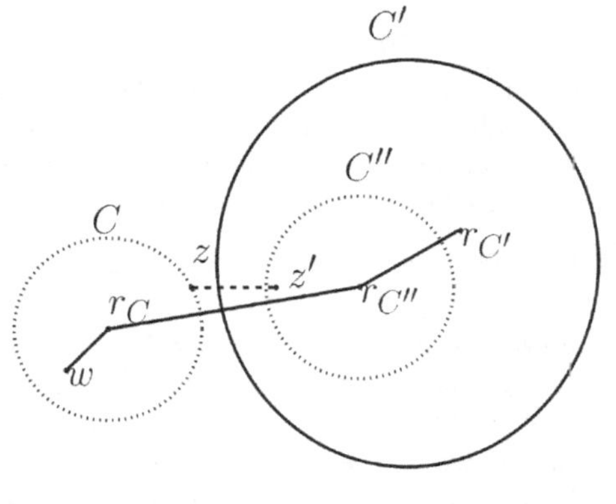

Figure 3: The path in the spanner H from w to $R_{C'}$. In the figure, the dotted ovals represent clusters in U_j, and the large oval represents a cluster in U_i. The dashed line represents an edge in G, and the solid lines represent the path in the spanner H.

added to H in the interconnection step of phase j. By Lemma 2.3, there is a path from w to r_C in H of length at most R_j, and there is a path from $r_{C''}$ to $r_{C'}$ of length at most R_i. Note also that $\epsilon^{-j} \leq R_j$. Thus, $d_H(w, r_{C'}) \leq d_H(w, r_C) + d_H(r_C, r_{C''}) + d_H(r_{C''}, r_{C'}) \leq 3R_j + 1 + R_i$.

□

Since $R_{i+1} = \frac{2}{\rho}\epsilon^{-i} + (5/\rho)R_i$, and since $\rho < 1$ and $j < i$, we have $3R_j \leq R_i$. It follows that:

$$d_H(w, r_{C'}) \leq 3R_j + 1 + R_i \leq 2R_i + 1. \quad (9)$$

We are now ready to analyze the stretch of our spanner. Recall that for every index i, the set $U^{(i)}$ is the union of all sets $U_0, U_1, \ldots, U_i$.

Lemma 2.15. *Assume $\epsilon \leq \frac{1}{10}$ and $\rho \geq 10\epsilon$. Consider a pair of vertices $u, v \in V$. Fix a shortest path $\pi(u, v)$ between them in G, and suppose that for some $i \leq \ell$ all the vertices of $\pi(u, v)$ are all clustered in the set $U^{(i)}$. Then,*

$$d_H(u, v) = \left(1 + (30 \cdot \epsilon \cdot i)\rho^{-1}\right) d_G(u, v) + 6\sum_{j=0}^{i} R_j \cdot 2^{i-j} \quad (10)$$

Proof. The proof is by induction on i. For the base case, $i = 0$, all the vertices on $\pi(u, v)$ are U_0-clustered, and so all the edges of the path are in the spanner, and $d_G(u, v) = d_H(u, v)$.

For the induction step, we first consider a pair of vertices x, y such that there is a path $\pi(x, y)$ in G of length at most ϵ^{-i}, and such that all the vertices on the path are clustered in the set $U^{(i)}$.

For each such segment x, y, we consider two cases.

Case 1: All vertices on the path $\pi(x, y)$ are $U^{(i-1)}$ clustered. Thus the induction hypothesis is applicable to x, y, and therefore by the induction hypothesis:

$$d_H(x, y) = \left(1 + (30\epsilon(i-1)) \cdot \rho^{-1}\right) d_G(x, y) + 6\sum_{j=0}^{i-1} R_j \cdot 2^{i-1-j} \quad (11)$$

Case 2: There exists a U_i clustered vertex in $\pi(x, y)$. To simplify presentation, we will imagine that the vertices of $\pi(x, y)$ appear

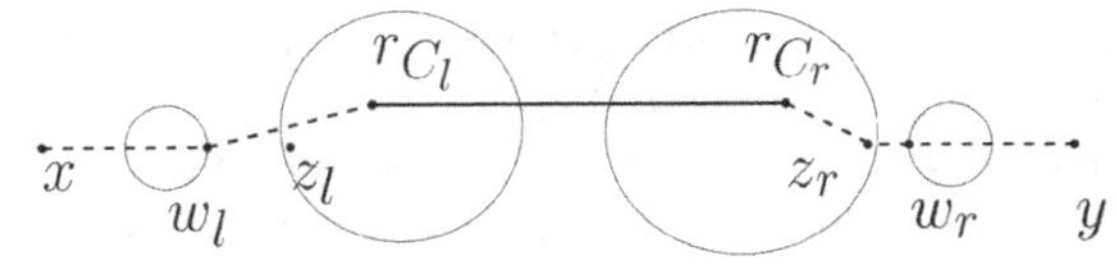

Figure 4: The path in the spanner H from x to y. In the figure, the dashed lines represent the path in the spanner H that is not necessarily a shortest path in G. The solid line represents the path in H, that is also a shortest path in G.

from left to right (see Figure 4 for an illustration), where x (respectively, y) is the leftmost (respectively, rightmost) vertex of the path. Let z_l, z_r be the leftmost and rightmost U_i-clustered vertices on $\pi(x, y)$, respectively, and let C_l, C_r (r_{C_l}, r_{C_r}) be their respective clusters (cluster centers).

Note that it is possible that z_l, z_r belong to the same cluster, i.e, $C_l = C_r$. However, this case is simpler, as in the analysis the path between the cluster centers r_{C_l}, r_{C_r} will simply be an empty path. Let w_l (respectively, w_r) be the neighbor of z_l (respectively, z_r) on the sub-path $\pi(x, z_l)$ (respectively, $\pi(z_r, y)$). Observe that w_l, w_r are $U^{(i-1)}$ clustered. By eq. (9), $d_H(w_l, r_{C_l}) \leq 2R_i + 1$ and $d_H(r_{C_r}, w_r) \leq 2R_i + 1$.

Note that as $|\pi(x, y)| \leq \epsilon^{-i}$, we have:

$$\begin{aligned} d_G(r_{C_l}, r_{C_r}) &\leq d_G(r_{C_l}, z_l) + d_G(z_l, z_r) + d_G(z_r, r_{C_r}) \\ &\leq d_G(z_l, z_r) + 2R_i \\ &\leq \epsilon^{-i} + 2R_i = \delta_i. \end{aligned}$$

From this and from the fact that $C_l, C_r \in U_i$, it follows that a shortest path between r_{C_l}, r_{C_r} was added to the spanner H in the interconnection step of phase i. Thus $d_G(r_{C_l}, r_{C_r}) = d_H(r_{C_l}, r_{C_r})$, and $d_H(r_{C_l}, r_{C_r}) \leq d_G(z_l, z_r) + 2R_i$.

As all the vertices in the sub-paths $\pi(x, w_l), \pi(w_r, y)$ are $U^{(i-1)}$ clustered, the induction hypothesis applies to them. Hence

$$\begin{aligned} d_H(x, w_l) &\leq \left(1 + (30\epsilon(i-1)) \cdot \rho^{-1}\right) \cdot d_G(x, w_l) \\ &\quad +6\textstyle\sum_{j=1}^{i-1} R_j \cdot 2^{i-1-j} \\ d_H(w_r, y) &\leq \left(1 + (30\epsilon(i-1)) \cdot \rho^{-1}\right) \cdot d_G(w_r, y) \\ &\quad +6\textstyle\sum_{j=1}^{i-1} R_j \cdot 2^{i-1-j}. \end{aligned}$$

Therefore $d_H(x, y)$ is bounded by:

$$\begin{aligned} d_H(x, y) &\leq d_H(x, w_l) + d_H(w_l, r_{C_l}) + d_H(r_{C_l}, r_{C_r}) \\ &\quad + d_H(r_{C_r}, w_r) + d_H(w_r, y) \\ &\leq d_H(x, w_l) + 2R_i + 1 + d_G(z_l, z_r) + 2R_i + 2R_i \\ &\quad + 1 + d_H(w_r, y) \\ &\leq \left(1 + (30\epsilon(i-1)) \cdot \rho^{-1}\right) d_H(x, y) + 6R_i \\ &\quad + 2 \cdot 6\textstyle\sum_{j=1}^{i-1} R_j \cdot 2^{i-1-j} \\ &= \left(1 + (30\epsilon(i-1)) \cdot \rho^{-1}\right) d_H(x, y) + 6\sum_{j=1}^{i} R_j \cdot 2^{i-j}. \end{aligned} \quad (12)$$

By eqs. (11) and (12) It follows that in both cases:

$$d_H(x, y) \leq \left(1 + (30\epsilon(i-1)) \cdot \rho^{-1}\right) d_H(x, y) + 6\sum_{j=1}^{i} R_j \cdot 2^{i-j}. \quad (13)$$

Now, consider a pair $u, v \in V$ such that all vertices of $\pi(u, v)$ are $U^{(i)}$ clustered, but $\pi(u, v)$ may be of an arbitrarily large length.

We divide the path into segments of length exactly ϵ^{-i}, except for maybe one segment that can be shorter. By eq. (13):

$$\begin{aligned} d_H(u,v) &\leq \left(1+\frac{30\epsilon(i-1)}{\rho}\right) d_G(u,v) \\ &+ \left\lfloor \frac{d_G(u,v)}{\epsilon^{-i}} \right\rfloor 6 \sum_{j=1}^{i} R_j \cdot 2^{i-j} + 6\sum_{j=1}^{i} R_j \cdot 2^{i-j} \\ &\leq d_G(u,v)\left[\left(1+\frac{30\epsilon(i-1)}{\rho}\right) + 6\epsilon^i \cdot \sum_{j=1}^{i} R_j \cdot 2^{i-j}\right] \\ &+ 6\sum_{j=1}^{i} R_j \cdot 2^{i-j}. \end{aligned} \tag{14}$$

It is left to show that $6\epsilon^i \cdot \sum_{j=1}^{i} R_j \cdot 2^{i-j} \leq \frac{30\epsilon}{\rho}$.

First, we will provide an upper bound on $6\sum_{j=1}^{i} R_j \cdot 2^{i-j}$. Recall that by eq. (5), $R_i \leq (4/\rho)\cdot\epsilon^{-(i-1)}$. It follows that $6\sum_{j=1}^{i} R_j \cdot 2^{i-j} \leq 6\sum_{j=1}^{i}(4/\rho)\cdot\epsilon^{-(j-1)}\cdot 2^{i-j} = 24/(\rho\cdot\epsilon^{i-1}\cdot(1-2\epsilon))$. Recall that $\epsilon < \frac{1}{10}$. Thus

$$6\sum_{j=1}^{i} R_j \cdot 2^{i-j} \leq \frac{24}{\rho\cdot\epsilon^{i-1}\cdot(1-2\epsilon)} \leq \frac{30}{\rho\cdot\epsilon^{i-1}}. \tag{15}$$

This yields: $6\epsilon^i \cdot \sum_{j=1}^{i} R_j \cdot 2^{i-j} \leq \epsilon^i \cdot 30/(\rho\cdot\epsilon^{i-1}) = (30\epsilon)/\rho$. To conclude,

$$\begin{aligned} d_H(u,v) &\leq d_G(u,v)\left[1+\frac{30\cdot\epsilon\cdot(i-1)}{\rho}+\frac{30\epsilon}{\rho}\right] + 6\sum_{j=1}^{i} R_j 2^{i-j} \\ &\leq d_G(u,v)\left(1+\frac{30\cdot\epsilon\cdot i}{\rho}\right) + 6\sum_{j=1}^{i} R_j 2^{i-j}. \end{aligned}$$

□

Recall that by Lemma 2.5, all vertices in V are $U^{(\ell)}$-clustered. Thus for any pair of vertices, the condition of Lemma 2.15 holds for $i = \ell$. By Lemma 2.15 and eq. (15),

Corollary 2.16. *For every pair $u, v \in V$, for $\rho \geq 10\epsilon$, $d_H(u,v) \leq \left(1+\frac{30\cdot\epsilon\cdot\ell}{\rho}\right)\cdot d_G(u,v) + \frac{30}{\rho\cdot\epsilon^{\ell-1}}$.*

2.4.4 Rescaling. In this section, we rescale ϵ to obtain a $(1+\epsilon,\beta)$-spanner. Set $\epsilon' = (30\cdot\epsilon\cdot\ell)/\rho$.

The condition $\epsilon < \frac{1}{10}$ now translates to $(\epsilon'\cdot\rho)/(30\ell) < 1/10$, i.e, $\epsilon' < \frac{3\ell}{\rho}$. We replace it with a much stronger condition, $\epsilon' < 1$. The condition $\rho \geq 10\epsilon$ translates to $\rho = (30\cdot\epsilon\cdot\ell)/\epsilon' > 10\epsilon$, i.e., $\epsilon' < 3\ell$, which holds trivially for $\epsilon' < 1$ and $\ell \geq 1$.

The additive term of the stretch now translates to $\frac{30}{\rho\cdot\epsilon^{\ell-1}} \leq \left(\frac{30\cdot\ell}{\rho\cdot\epsilon'}\right)^{\ell}$.

Denote $\beta = ((30\cdot\ell)/(\rho\cdot\epsilon'))^{\ell}$. Observe that

$$\beta = ((30\cdot\ell)/(\rho\cdot\epsilon'))^{\ell} = \epsilon^{-\ell}. \tag{16}$$

Thus we obtain stretch $\left(1+\epsilon', ((30\cdot\ell)(\rho\cdot\epsilon'))^{\ell}\right)$.

Recall that $\ell = \lfloor\log\kappa\rho\rfloor + \lceil\frac{\kappa+1}{\kappa\rho}\rceil - 1 \leq \log\kappa\rho + \rho^{-1} + O(1)$. It follows that:

$$\beta = \left(\frac{30\cdot\ell}{\rho\cdot\epsilon'}\right)^{\ell} = \left(\frac{30\cdot(\log\kappa\rho+\rho^{-1}+O(1))}{\rho\cdot\epsilon'}\right)^{\log\kappa\rho+\rho^{-1}+O(1)}.$$

By Corollary 2.12 and eq. (16), the number of edges in the spanner H is:

$$|H| = O(n^{1+1/\kappa}\cdot\epsilon^{-\ell}) = O(\beta\cdot n^{1+1/\kappa}).$$

By Corollary 2.8 and eq. (16), the time required to construct the spanner H is:

$$O\left(n^{\rho}\cdot\rho^{-1}\epsilon^{-\ell}\right) = O\left(\beta\cdot n^{\rho}\cdot\rho^{-1}\right).$$

Denote now $\epsilon = \epsilon'$.

Corollary 2.17. *For any parameters $0 < \epsilon \leq 1, \kappa \geq 2$, and $1/\kappa \leq \rho < 1/2$, and any n-vertex graph $G = (V,E)$, our algorithm constructs a $(1+\epsilon,\beta)$ – spanner with $O(\beta\cdot n^{1+1/\kappa})$ edges, in $O\left(\beta\cdot n^{\rho}\cdot\rho^{-1}\right)$ deterministic time in the CONGEST model, where*

$$\beta = \left(\frac{O\left(\log\kappa\rho+\rho^{-1}\right)}{\rho\cdot\epsilon}\right)^{\log\kappa\rho+\rho^{-1}+O(1)}. \tag{17}$$

3 Acknowledgments

The second-named author would like to thank Ohad Ben-Baruch and Michael Frank for helpful discussions.

References

[1] Abboud, A., and Bodwin, G. The 4/3 additive spanner exponent is tight. *CoRR abs/1511.00700* (2015).

[2] Abboud, A., Bodwin, G., and Pettie, S. A hierarchy of lower bounds for sublinear additive spanners. In *Proceedings of the Twenty-Eighth Annual ACM-SIAM Symposium on Discrete Algorithms, SODA 2017, Barcelona, Spain, Hotel Porta Fira, January 16-19* (2017), pp. 568–576.

[3] Aingworth, D., Chekuri, C., Indyk, P., and Motwani, R. Fast estimation of diameter and shortest paths (without matrix multiplication). *SIAM J. Comput. 28*, 4 (1999), 1167–1181.

[4] Althöfer, I., Das, G., Dobkin, D. P., Joseph, D., and Soares, J. On sparse spanners of weighted graphs. *Discrete & Computational Geometry 9* (1993), 81–100.

[5] Awerbuch, B. Complexity of network synchronization. *J. ACM 32*, 4 (1985), 804–823.

[6] Awerbuch, B., Berger, B., Cowen, L., and Peleg, D. Near-linear cost sequential and distribured constructions of sparse neighborhood covers. In *34th Annual Symposium on Foundations of Computer Science, Palo Alto, California, USA, 3-5 November 1993* (1993), pp. 638–647.

[7] Awerbuch, B., Goldberg, A. V., Luby, M., and Plotkin, S. A. Network decomposition and locality in distributed computation. In *30th Annual Symposium on Foundations of Computer Science, Research Triangle Park, North Carolina, USA, 30 October - 1 November 1989* (1989), pp. 364–369.

[8] Awerbuch, B., and Peleg, D. Sparse partitions (extended abstract). In *31st Annual Symposium on Foundations of Computer Science, St. Louis, Missouri, USA, October 22-24, 1990, Volume II* (1990), pp. 503–513.

[9] Barenboim, L., Elkin, M., and Gavoille, C. A fast network-decomposition algorithm and its applications to constant-time distributed computation - (extended abstract). In *Structural Information and Communication Complexity - 22nd International Colloquium, SIROCCO 2015, Montserrat, Spain, July 14-16, 2015, Post-Proceedings* (2015), pp. 209–223.

[10] Baswana, S., Kavitha, T., Mehlhorn, K., and Pettie, S. Additive spanners and (alpha, beta)-spanners. *ACM Trans. Algorithms 7*, 1 (2010), 5:1–5:26.

[11] Baswana, S., and Sen, S. A simple and linear time randomized algorithm for computing sparse spanners in weighted graphs. *Random Struct. Algorithms 30*, 4 (2007), 532–563.

[12] Bernstein, A., and Roditty, L. Improved dynamic algorithms for maintaining approximate shortest paths under deletions. In *Proceedings of the Twenty-Second Annual ACM-SIAM Symposium on Discrete Algorithms, SODA 2011, San Francisco, California, USA, January 23-25, 2011* (2011), pp. 1355–1365.

[13] Cohen, E. Fast algorithms for constructing t-spanners and paths with stretch t. *SIAM J. Comput. 28*, 1 (1998), 210–236.

[14] Coppersmith, D., and Elkin, M. Sparse source-wise and pair-wise distance preservers. In *Proceedings of the Sixteenth Annual ACM-SIAM Symposium on Discrete Algorithms, SODA 2005, Vancouver, British Columbia, Canada, January 23-25, 2005* (2005), pp. 660–669.

[15] Derbel, B., Gavoille, C., and Peleg, D. Deterministic distributed construction of linear stretch spanners in polylogarithmic time. In *Distributed Computing, 21st International Symposium, DISC 2007, Lemesos, Cyprus, September 24-26, 2007, Proceedings* (2007), pp. 179–192.

[16] Derbel, B., Gavoille, C., Peleg, D., and Viennot, L. On the locality of distributed sparse spanner construction. In *Proceedings of the Twenty-Seventh Annual ACM Symposium on Principles of Distributed Computing, PODC 2008, Toronto, Canada, August 18-21, 2008* (2008), pp. 273–282.

[17] Derbel, B., Gavoille, C., Peleg, D., and Viennot, L. Local computation of nearly additive spanners. In *Distributed Computing, 23rd International Symposium, DISC 2009, Elche, Spain, September 23-25, 2009. Proceedings* (2009), pp. 176–190.

[18] Derbel, B., Mosbah, M., and Zemmari, A. Sublinear fully distributed partition with applications. *Theory Comput. Syst. 47*, 2 (2010), 368–404.

[19] Dor, D., Halperin, S., and Zwick, U. All-pairs almost shortest paths. *SIAM J. Comput. 29*, 5 (2000), 1740–1759.

[20] Elkin, M. Computing almost shortest paths. In *Proceedings of the Twentieth Annual ACM Symposium on Principles of Distributed Computing, PODC 2001, Newport, Rhode Island, USA, August 26-29, 2001* (2001), pp. 53–62.

[21] Elkin, M. Computing almost shortest paths. *ACM Trans. Algorithms 1*, 2 (2005), 283–323.

[22] Elkin, M. A near-optimal distributed fully dynamic algorithm for maintaining sparse spanners. In *Proceedings of the Twenty-Sixth Annual ACM Symposium on Principles of Distributed Computing, PODC 2007, Portland, Oregon, USA, August 12-15, 2007* (2007), pp. 185–194.

[23] Elkin, M., and Matar, S. Near-additive spanners in low polynomial deterministic CONGEST time. *CoRR abs/1903.00872* (2019).

[24] Elkin, M., and Neiman, O. Hopsets with constant hopbound, and applications to approximate shortest paths. In *IEEE 57th Annual Symposium on Foundations of Computer Science, FOCS 2016, 9-11 October 2016, Hyatt Regency, New Brunswick, New Jersey, USA* (2016), pp. 128–137.

[25] Elkin, M., and Neiman, O. Efficient algorithms for constructing very sparse spanners and emulators. In *Proceedings of the Twenty-Eighth Annual ACM-SIAM Symposium on Discrete Algorithms, SODA 2017, Barcelona, Spain, Hotel Porta Fira, January 16-19* (2017), pp. 652–669.

[26] Elkin, M., Neiman, O., and Solomon, S. Light spanners. *SIAM J. Discrete Math. 29*, 3 (2015), 1312–1321.

[27] Elkin, M., and Peleg, D. (1+epsilon, beta)-spanner constructions for general graphs. In *Proceedings on 33rd Annual ACM Symposium on Theory of Computing, July 6-8, 2001, Heraklion, Crete, Greece* (2001), pp. 173–182.

[28] Elkin, M., and Zhang, J. Efficient algorithms for constructing (1+epsilon, beta)-spanners in the distributed and streaming models. *Distributed Computing 18*, 5 (2006), 375–385.

[29] Erdős, P., and Simonovits, M. Compactness results in extremal graph theory. *Combinatorica 2*, 3 (1982), 275–288.

[30] Ghaffari, M., and Kuhn, F. Derandomizing distributed algorithms with small messages: Spanners and dominating set. In *32nd International Symposium on Distributed Computing, DISC 2018, New Orleans, LA, USA, October 15-19, 2018* (2018), pp. 29:1–29:17.

[31] Grossman, O., and Parter, M. Improved deterministic distributed construction of spanners. In *31st International Symposium on Distributed Computing, DISC 2017, October 16-20, 2017, Vienna, Austria* (2017), pp. 24:1–24:16.

[32] Henzinger, M., Krinninger, S., and Nanongkai, D. A deterministic almost-tight distributed algorithm for approximating single-source shortest paths. In *Proceedings of the 48th Annual ACM SIGACT Symposium on Theory of Computing, STOC 2016, Cambridge, MA, USA, June 18-21, 2016* (2016), pp. 489–498.

[33] Kuhn, F., Maus, Y., and Weidner, S. Deterministic distributed ruling sets of line graphs. In *Structural Information and Communication Complexity - 25th International Colloquium, SIROCCO 2018, Ma'ale HaHamisha, Israel, June 18-21, 2018, Revised Selected Papers* (2018), pp. 193–208.

[34] Panconesi, A., and Srinivasan, A. On the complexity of distributed network decomposition. *J. Algorithms 20*, 2 (1996), 356–374.

[35] Peleg, D. Distributed computing: A locality-sensitive approach.

[36] Peleg, D., and Schäffer, A. A. Graph spanners. *Journal of Graph Theory 13*, 1 (1989), 99–116.

[37] Peleg, D., and Ullman, J. D. An optimal synchronizer for the hypercube. In *Proceedings of the Sixth Annual ACM Symposium on Principles of Distributed Computing, Vancouver, British Columbia, Canada, August 10-12, 1987* (1987), pp. 77–85.

[38] Peleg, D., and Upfal, E. A trade-off between space and efficiency for routing tables. *J. ACM 36*, 3 (1989), 510–530.

[39] Pettie, S. Low distortion spanners. *ACM Trans. Algorithms 6*, 1 (2009), 7:1–7:22.

[40] Pettie, S. Distributed algorithms for ultrasparse spanners and linear size skeletons. *Distributed Computing 22*, 3 (2010), 147–166.

[41] Roditty, L., Thorup, M., and Zwick, U. Deterministic constructions of approximate distance oracles and spanners. In *Automata, Languages and Programming, 32nd International Colloquium, ICALP 2005, Lisbon, Portugal, July 11-15, 2005, Proceedings* (2005), pp. 261–272.

[42] Schneider, J., Elkin, M., and Wattenhofer, R. Symmetry breaking depending on the chromatic number or the neighborhood growth. *Theor. Comput. Sci. 509* (2013), 40–50.

[43] Shi, H., and Spencer, T. H. Time-work tradeoffs of the single-source shortest paths problem. *J. Algorithms 30*, 1 (1999), 19–32.

[44] Thorup, M., and Zwick, U. Approximate distance oracles. In *Proceedings on 33rd Annual ACM Symposium on Theory of Computing, July 6-8, 2001, Heraklion, Crete, Greece* (2001), pp. 183–192.

[45] Thorup, M., and Zwick, U. Spanners and emulators with sublinear distance errors. In *Proceedings of the Seventeenth Annual ACM-SIAM Symposium on Discrete Algorithms, SODA 2006, Miami, Florida, USA, January 22-26, 2006* (2006), pp. 802–809.

A Trivial Yet Optimal Solution to Vertex Fault Tolerant Spanners

Greg Bodwin
gbodwin6@cc.gatech.edu
Georgia Institute of Technology
Atlanta, Georgia

Shyamal Patel
shyamalpatelb@gmail.com
Georgia Institute of Technology
Atlanta, Georgia

ABSTRACT

We give a short and easy upper bound on the worst-case size of fault tolerant spanners, which improves on all prior work and is fully optimal at least in the setting of vertex faults.

CCS CONCEPTS

• **Theory of computation** → **Sparsification and spanners**; • **Mathematics of computing** → *Combinatorics*; *Extremal graph theory*.

KEYWORDS

Fault-tolerant spanners, Greedy algorithms

ACM Reference Format:
Greg Bodwin and Shyamal Patel. 2019. A Trivial Yet Optimal Solution to Vertex Fault Tolerant Spanners. In *2019 ACM Symposium on Principles of Distributed Computing (PODC '19), July 29-August 2, 2019, Toronto, ON, Canada.* ACM, New York, NY, USA, 3 pages. https://doi.org/10.1145/3293611.3331588

1 INTRODUCTION

This paper concerns *spanners*, a fundamental primitive used in graph sketching.

Definition 1 (Spanners). *A k-spanner of a graph $G = (V, E, w)$ is a subgraph $H = (V, E' \subseteq E, w)$ for which $dist_H(s, t) \leq k \cdot dist_G(s, t)$ for all $s, t \in V$.*

Spanners have been intensively studied since the mid-80s [1–4, 6, 11, 18, 19, 21, 27–29]. A staple in the literature is the *greedy construction algorithm* of Althöfer et al [4], which works as follows: initialize H to be an empty graph, and then for each edge (u, v) in the input graph G in order of increasing weight, add (u, v) to H if currently $\text{dist}_H(u, v) > kw_{(u,v)}$. Besides its simplicity and obvious correctness, the greedy algorithm is popular because there is a simple proof that it is *existentially optimal* [4, 21], meaning that the number of edges in H never exceeds the worst-case number of edges needed for a k-spanner over all possible input graphs on as many nodes as G.

In practice, spanners are often applied to systems whose parts are prone to sporadic failures. A spanner for such a system must be robust to these failures, giving rise to the notion of *fault tolerance*:

PODC '19, July 29-August 2, 2019, Toronto, ON, Canada

ACM ISBN 978-1-4503-6217-7/19/07...$15.00
https://doi.org/10.1145/3293611.3331588

Definition 2 (Fault Tolerant Spanners). *Given a graph G, a subgraph H is an f* Vertex Fault Tolerant (VFT), resp. Edge Fault Tolerant (EFT), *k-spanner of G if for any set of F vertices (resp. edges) in G of size $|F| \leq f$, $H \setminus F$ is a k-spanner of $G \setminus F$.*

To construct FT spanners, it is natural to consider the obvious adaptation of the greedy algorithm:

Algorithm 1 The VFT (EFT) Greedy Algorithm

```
function FT-GREEDY(G = (V, E, w), k, f)
    H ← (V, ∅, w)
    for (u, v) ∈ E in order of increasing weight do
        if there exists a set F of |F| ≤ f vertices (edges) such that
dist_{H\F}(u, v) > k · w(u, v) then
            add (u, v) to H
    return H
```

Correctness is again obvious, but unfortunately the analyses used in the non-faulty setting all seem to break for the FT greedy algorithm. Most prior work on FT spanners has thus abandoned the greedy approach in favor of more involved constructions [5, 13, 14, 16, 23] (see also [7, 8, 10, 12, 15, 17, 22, 24–26, 30]); an analysis of the FT greedy algorithm was only obtained recently via fairly complex arguments [9]. In contrast, our main result is a simple analysis of the FT greedy algorithm which improves on all of these previous bounds.

Theorem 1 (Main Result). *Let $b(n, k)$ be the maximum possible number of edges in a graph on n nodes and girth $> k$. Then any graph H on n nodes returned by the VFT or EFT Greedy Algorithm with parameters f, k satisfies*

$$|E(H)| = O\left(f^2 \cdot b\left(\frac{n}{f}, k+1\right)\right).$$

This upper bound is best possible in the VFT setting, for any construction algorithm, due to a simple lower bound construction in [9] (meaning that any asymptotic tradeoff between $n, f, k, |E(H)|$ not promised by this theorem does not exist in general). In the EFT setting, the bound of Theorem 1 was already known to be the best possible tradeoff when $k < 5$ [9], but for larger k it is still conceivable to improve the upper bound as far as

$$|E(H)| \stackrel{?}{=} O\left(f \cdot b\left(\frac{n}{\sqrt{f}}, k+1\right) + nf\right).$$

It remains a major open question to asymptotically determine $b(n, k)$; the only known upper bound is the folklore *Moore bounds* which state $b(n, k) = O\left(n^{1+1/\lfloor k/2 \rfloor}\right)$. Plugging this into Theorem 1 yields:

Corollary 2. *For any graph H on n nodes returned by the VFT or EFT Greedy Algorithm with parameters $f, 2k-1$, we have*

$$|E(H)| = O\left(n^{1+1/k} f^{1-1/k}\right).$$

This corollary improves over the previous best upper bound in [9] by a factor of $\exp(k)$. The famous *Erdös girth conjecture* [20] posits that the Moore Bounds are tight, which would then imply that this corollary is best possible, at least for VFT spanners.

An open question left by this work is to improve the runtime of the FT greedy algorithm: in a naive implementation it is exponential in f. It would be interesting to improve this dependence, or perhaps to find a different fast algorithm achieving the existential size bounds proved in this paper. We note that [16] gives a construction with polynomial runtime dependence on f, at the price of somewhat suboptimal spanner size.

2 PROOF OF MAIN RESULT

We will state the proof in the VFT setting here; the proof in the EFT setting is essentially identical.

Definition 3 (Blocking Set). *Given a graph $G = (V, E)$, a k-blocking set for G is a set $B \subseteq V \times E$ such that (1) every $(v, e) \in B$ has $v \notin e$, and (2) for every cycle C in G on $\leq k$ edges, there exists $(v, e) \in B$ such that $v, e \in C$.*

Lemma 3. *Any graph H returned by the VFT greedy algorithm with parameters k, f has a $(k+1)$-blocking set of size at most $f|E(H)|$.*

Proof. For each edge $e = (u, v) \in H$, let F_e be the set of nodes such that $\text{dist}_{H \setminus F_e}(u, v) > kw_e$ when e is added to H. Let

$$B := \{(x, e) \mid e \in E(H), x \in F_e\};$$

since $|F_e| \leq f$ for all e, we have $|B| \leq f|E(H)|$. We now show that B is a $(k+1)$-blocking set. Let C be any cycle on $\leq k+1$ edges in the final graph H and let $e = (u, v)$ be the last edge in C considered by the greedy algorithm. By construction there is a $u \rightsquigarrow v$ path (through C) of total weight $\leq kw_{(u,v)}$ when e is added to H, and so some node $x \in C \setminus \{u, v\}$ must be included in F_e. Thus $(x, e) \in B$. □

Lemma 4. *Let H be any graph on n nodes and m edges, let $f = o(n)$ be a parameter, and suppose H has a $(k+1)$-blocking set B of size $|B| \leq f|E(H)|$. Then H has a subgraph on $O(n/f)$ nodes, $\Omega(m/f^2)$ edges, and girth $> k+1$.*

Proof. Let H' be an induced subgraph of H on a uniformly random subset of exactly $\lceil n/(2f) \rceil$ vertices, let $B' := B \cap (V(H') \times E(H'))$, and let H'' be obtained from H' by deleting every edge contained in any pair in B'. The graph H'' has girth $> k+1$, since by definition of blocking sets we have now deleted at least one node or edge from every cycle in H on $\leq k+1$ edges. Additionally:

- Each edge in $E(H)$ survives in $E(H')$ iff both of its endpoints survive in $V(H')$, which happens with probability

$$\frac{\lceil n/(2f) \rceil}{n} \cdot \frac{\lceil n/(2f) \rceil - 1}{n-1} = (1+o(1))\frac{1}{4f^2}.$$

- Each pair $(x, (u, v)) \in B$ survives in B' iff all of x, u, v survive in $V(H')$, which happens with probability

$$\frac{\lceil n/(2f) \rceil}{n} \cdot \frac{\lceil n/(2f) \rceil - 1}{n-1} \cdot \frac{\lceil n/(2f) \rceil - 2}{n-2} = (1+o(1))\frac{1}{8f^3}$$

We may now compute

$$\begin{aligned} \mathbb{E}\left[|E(H'')|\right] &\geq \mathbb{E}\left[|E(H')| - |B'|\right] \\ &= (1+o(1))\left(\frac{|E(H)|}{4f^2} - \frac{|B|}{8f^3}\right) \\ &\geq (1+o(1))\left(\frac{m}{4f^2} - \frac{m}{8f^2}\right) \\ &= \Omega\left(\frac{m}{f^2}\right). \end{aligned}$$

There exists a possible setting of H'' which matches or exceeds this expectation, which thus has $\Omega(m/f^2)$ edges and satisfies the lemma. □

Proof of Theorem 1. If $f = \Omega(n)$, then Theorem 1 holds trivially since it states $|E(H)| = O(n^2)$. Otherwise, let H be an output graph of the FT Greedy algorithm on n edges and m nodes. By Lemmas 3 and 4, H has a subgraph of girth $> k+1$ on $O(n/f)$ nodes and $\Omega(m/f^2)$ edges, and hence

$$b(O(n/f), k+1) = \Omega\left(\frac{m}{f^2}\right)$$

$$m = O\left(f^2 \cdot b(n/f, k+1)\right). \quad \square$$

We conclude by remarking on a limitation of our approach. Our definition of blocking sets is very VFT-centric; since a gap remains in the EFT setting, it is tempting to try to adapt this definition to the EFT setting in search of better upper bounds. In particular, let us say that an *edge k-blocking set* is a set of distinct edge pairs such that every $(\leq k)$-cycle C has $e_1, e_2 \in C$ for some $(e_1, e_2) \in B$. It is easy to show that any graph H returned by the EFT greedy algorithm with parameters f, k admits an edge $(k+1)$-blocking set of size $\leq f|E(H)|$ (the analog of Lemma 3). We would then need an *improved* analog of Lemma 4 in order to get improved upper bounds on EFT spanners for $k \geq 5$. However, no such improvement is possible: for any k we can show a graph H on $\Omega(f^2 \cdot b(n/f, k+1))$ edges that has an edge $(k+1)$-blocking set of size $\leq f|E(H)|$, and so our analog of Lemma 3 alone is not powerful enough to get improved upper bounds in the EFT setting. Specifically, this H is the same as the VFT lower bound graph of [9]: it is the Cartesian product of an arbitrary graph of girth $> k+1$ with a biclique on $\lfloor f/2 \rfloor$ nodes; the blocking set is then all pairs of edges that share an endpoint in the product graph and which correspond to the same edge in the initial high-girth graph. Hence any improvement to our EFT upper bounds (if possible) will need to exploit stronger properties of H than just the existence of a small edge blocking set.

REFERENCES

[1] Amir Abboud and Greg Bodwin. 2016. The 4/3 Additive Spanner Exponent is Tight. In *Proceedings of the 48th Annual ACM SIGACT Symposium on Theory of Computing (STOC)*. ACM Special Interest Group on Algorithms and Computation Theory, 351–361.

[2] Amir Abboud, Greg Bodwin, and Seth Pettie. 2017. A hierarchy of lower bounds for sublinear additive spanners. In *Proceedings of the 28th Annual ACM-SIAM Symposium on Discrete Algorithms (SODA)*. Society for Industrial and Applied Mathematics, 568–576.

[3] Donald Aingworth, Chandra Chekuri, Piotr Indyk, and Rajeev Motwani. 1999. Fast estimation of diameter and shortest paths (without matrix multiplication). *SIAM J. Comput.* 28, 4 (1999), 1167–1181.

[4] Ingo Althöfer, Gautam Das, David Dobkin, Deborah Joseph, and José Soares. 1993. On sparse spanners of weighted graphs. *Discrete & Computational Geometry* 9, 1 (1993), 81–100.

[5] Giorgio Ausiello, Paolo G Franciosa, Giuseppe F Italiano, and Andrea Ribichini. 2010. Computing graph spanners in small memory: fault-tolerance and streaming. *Discrete Mathematics, Algorithms and Applications* 2, 04 (2010), 591–605.

[6] Surender Baswana, Telikepalli Kavitha, Kurt Mehlhorn, and Seth Pettie. 2010. Additive spanners and (α, β)-spanners. *ACM Transactions on Algorithms (TALG)* 7, 1 (2010), 5.

[7] Aaron Bernstein and David Karger. 2008. Improved distance sensitivity oracles via random sampling. In *Proceedings of the nineteenth annual ACM-SIAM symposium on Discrete algorithms*. Society for Industrial and Applied Mathematics, 34–43.

[8] Davide Bilo, Luciano Guala, Stefano Leucci, and Guido Proietti. 2016. Compact and Fast Sensitivity Oracles for Single-Source Distances. In *24th Annual European Symposium on Algorithms (ESA 2016) (Leibniz International Proceedings in Informatics (LIPIcs))*, Piotr Sankowski and Christos Zaroliagis (Eds.), Vol. 57. Schloss Dagstuhl–Leibniz-Zentrum fuer Informatik, Dagstuhl, Germany, 13:1–13:14. http://drops.dagstuhl.de/opus/volltexte/2016/6364

[9] Greg Bodwin, Michael Dinitz, Merav Parter, and Virginia Vassilevska Williams. 2018. Optimal Vertex Fault Tolerant Spanners (for fixed stretch). In *Proceedings of the 29th Annual ACM-SIAM Symposium on Discrete Algorithms (SODA)*. Society for Industrial and Applied Mathematics, 1884–1900.

[10] Greg Bodwin, Fabrizio Grandoni, Merav Parter, and Virginia Vassilevska Williams. 2017. Preserving Distances in Very Faulty Graphs. In *Proceedings of the 44th International Colloquium on Automata, Languages, and Programming (ICALP)*. European Association for Theoretical Computer Science, 73:1–73:14.

[11] Shiri Chechik. 2013. New additive spanners. In *Proceedings of the 24th Annual ACM-SIAM Symposium on Discrete Algorithms (SODA)*. SIAM, 498–512.

[12] Shiri Chechik, Sarel Cohen, Amos Fiat, and Haim Kaplan. 2017. $(1+\epsilon)$-approximate f-sensitive distance oracles. In *Proceedings of the Twenty-Eighth Annual ACM-SIAM Symposium on Discrete Algorithms*. Society for Industrial and Applied Mathematics, 1479–1496.

[13] Shiri Chechik, Michael Langberg, David Peleg, and Liam Roditty. 2010. Fault tolerant spanners for general graphs. *SIAM J. Comput.* 39, 7 (2010), 3403–3423.

[14] Artur Czumaj and Hairong Zhao. 2004. Fault-tolerant geometric spanners. *Discrete & Computational Geometry* 32, 2 (2004), 207–230.

[15] Camil Demetrescu, Mikkel Thorup, Rezaul Alam Chowdhury, and Vijaya Ramachandran. 2008. Oracles for distances avoiding a failed node or link. *SIAM J. Comput.* 37, 5 (2008), 1299–1318.

[16] Michael Dinitz and Robert Krauthgamer. 2011. Fault-tolerant spanners: better and simpler. In *Proceedings of the 30th annual ACM SIGACT-SIGOPS symposium on Principles of distributed computing*. ACM, 169–178.

[17] Michael Dinitz and Zeyu Zhang. 2016. Approximating low-stretch spanners. In *Proceedings of the twenty-seventh annual ACM-SIAM symposium on Discrete algorithms*. Society for Industrial and Applied Mathematics, 821–840.

[18] Dorit Dor, Shay Halperin, and Uri Zwick. 2000. All-Pairs Almost Shortest Paths. *Siam Journal on Computing (SICOMP)* 29, 5 (2000), 1740–1759.

[19] Michael Elkin and David Peleg. 2004. $(1+\varepsilon,\beta)$-spanner constructions for general graphs. *SIAM J. Comput.* 33, 3 (2004), 608–631.

[20] Paul Erdős. 1963. Extremal problems in graph theory. In *Proceedings of the Symposium on Theory of Graphs and its Applications*. 2936.

[21] Arnold Filtser and Shay Solomon. 2016. The greedy spanner is existentially optimal. In *Proceedings of the 2016 ACM Symposium on Principles of Distributed Computing*. ACM, 9–17.

[22] Fabrizio Grandoni and Virginia Vassilevska Williams. 2012. Improved distance sensitivity oracles via fast single-source replacement paths. In *Foundations of Computer Science (FOCS), 2012 IEEE 53rd Annual Symposium on*. IEEE, 748–757.

[23] Christos Levcopoulos, Giri Narasimhan, and Michiel Smid. 1998. Efficient algorithms for constructing fault-tolerant geometric spanners. In *Proceedings of the thirtieth annual ACM symposium on Theory of computing*. ACM, 186–195.

[24] Merav Parter. 2015. Dual failure resilient BFS structure. In *Proceedings of the 2015 ACM Symposium on Principles of Distributed Computing*. ACM, 481–490.

[25] Merav Parter and David Peleg. 2013. Sparse fault-tolerant BFS trees. In *European Symposium on Algorithms*. Springer, 779–790.

[26] Merav Parter and David Peleg. 2018. Fault-Tolerant Approximate BFS Structures. *ACM Transactions on Algorithms (TALG)* 14, 1 (2018), 10.

[27] David Peleg and Jeffrey Ullman. 1989. An Optimal Synchronizer for the Hypercube. *SIAM Journal on Computing (SICOMP)* 18, 4 (1989), 740âĂŞ747.

[28] David Peleg and Eli Upfal. 1989. A trade-off between space and efficiency for routing tables. *Journal of the ACM (JACM)* 36, 3 (1989), 510–530.

[29] Mikkel Thorup and Uri Zwick. 2006. Spanners and emulators with sublinear distance errors. In *Proceedings of the 17th Annual ACM-SIAM Symposium on Discrete Algorithms (SODA)*. Society for Industrial and Applied Mathematics, 802–809.

[30] Oren Weimann and Raphael Yuster. 2013. Replacement paths and distance sensitivity oracles via fast matrix multiplication. *ACM Transactions on Algorithms (TALG)* 9, 2 (2013), 14.

From Classical to Blockchain Consensus: What Are the Exact Algorithms?

Yanhong A. Liu
Stony Brook University
liu@cs.stonybrook.edu

Scott D. Stoller
Stony Brook University
stoller@cs.stonybrook.edu

ABSTRACT

This tutorial describes well-known algorithms for distributed consensus problems, from classical consensus to blockchain consensus, and discusses exact algorithms that are high-level as in pseudocode and directly executable at the same time. The tutorial consists of five parts:

(1) A introduction to different distributed consensus problems, from classical consensus and Byzantine consensus to blockchain consensus.
(2) An overview of well-known algorithms, from Paxos for classical consensus to the Bitcoin algorithm for blockchain consensus, including important variants such as Viewstamped Replication and Virtual Synchrony, as well as Proof-of-Stake vs. Proof-of-Work.
(3) An overview of a method and language, DistAlgo, for expressing distributed algorithms precisely at a high-level as pseudocode and having them be directly executable at the same time.
(4) A study of exact algorithms expressed at a high level for the most extensively studied algorithm variants, including Lamport's Paxos for classical consensus and Nakamoto's Bitcoin algorithm for blockchain consensus.
(5) A demo of the direct execution of these exact algorithms by distributed processes.

CCS CONCEPTS

• **Computing methodologies** → **Distributed algorithms**; **Distributed programming languages**; • **Networks** → **Formal specifications**; • **Software and its engineering** → **Very high level languages**; **Concurrent programming structures**; **Specification languages**; • **Theory of computation** → *Distributed computing models*.

KEYWORDS

Distributed consensus, blockchain consensus, Paxos algorithm, Bitcoin algorithm, synchronization conditions, high-level queries

ACM Reference Format:
Yanhong A. Liu and Scott D. Stoller. 2019. From Classical to Blockchain Consensus: What Are the Exact Algorithms?. In *2019 ACM Symposium on Principles of Distributed Computing (PODC '19), July 29-August 2, 2019, Toronto, ON, Canada.* ACM, New York, NY, USA, 2 pages. https://doi.org/10.1145/3293611.3338022

ACM ISBN 978-1-4503-6217-7/19/07.
https://doi.org/10.1145/3293611.3338022

Distributed consensus

Distributed consensus is the problem of having a set of distributed processes, or agents, agree on a single value or a continuing sequence of values in the presence of faulty processes.

- Classical consensus considers failures where processes may crash and may later recover, and where messages may be lost, delayed, reordered, and duplicated.
- Byzantine consensus considers arbitrary failures, which may result from malicious actions, such as sending arbitrary messages.
- Blockchain consensus further considers Sybil attacks where a system is subverted by forging process identities.

Distributed consensus is at the core of distributed systems and services, which are increasingly indispensable in daily life.

- There is an increasing interest in algorithms for both classical consensus and blockchain consensus, especially the exact algorithms for deeper understanding and possible improvements by researchers, practitioners, and students.
- Especially desired are also languages and methods for expressing distributed algorithms and protocols precisely at a very high level, to facilitate the design and implementation, as well as analysis and verification, of these algorithms and protocols.

DistAlgo language

For expressing distributed algorithms at a high level, DistAlgo supports four main concepts:

(1) distributed processes that can send messages,
(2) high-level control flows for handling received messages, both synchronously and asynchronously,
(3) high-level queries for synchronization conditions, and
(4) declarative configuration for setting up and running.

DistAlgo minimally extends the Python programming language to support these concepts.

- DistAlgo has been used to express a wide variety of important distributed algorithms, including over a dozen well-known algorithms and variants for classical consensus and blockchain consensus.
- DistAlgo has been used by hundreds of students in graduate and undergraduate courses in dozens of different course projects, implementing the core of network protocols, distributed graph algorithms, distributed coordination services, distributed hash tables, distributed file systems, distributed

databases, parallel processing platforms, security protocols, and more.

- The algorithms and systems can be programmed much more easily and clearly compared to using conventional programming languages, e.g., in 30 lines instead of 300 lines, not to mention 3000 lines or more.

Tutorial materials

The tutorial materials are based on our studies of distributed algorithms, e.g., [1, 2], as well as many more algorithms studied in our ongoing research project, From Clarity to Efficiency for Distributed Algorithms, e.g., [3–5], after a dedicated workshop, Languages for Distributed Algorithms, organized by Black and Liu (http://sites.google.com/site/ladameeting)

(1) Y. A. Liu, S. Chand, and S. D. Stoller. Moderately Complex Paxos Made Simple: High-Level Executable Specification of Distributed Consensus Algorithm. arXiv:1704.00082 [cs.DC], revised Jan. 2019.
https://arxiv.org/pdf/1704.00082v3.pdf

(2) Y. A. Liu, Logical Clocks Are Not Fair: What Is Fair? A Case Study of High-level Language and Optimization. In *Proceedings of the Workshop on Advanced Tools, Programming Languages, and Platforms for Implementing and Evaluating Algorithms for Distributed Systems (APPLIED)*, pages 21–27, Jul. 2018. ACM Press.
http://www.cs.stonybrook.edu/~liu/papers/LclockUnfair-APPLIED18.pdf

(3) Y. A. Liu, S. D. Stoller, B. Lin, and M. Gorbovitski. From Clarity to Efficiency for Distributed Algorithms. In *Proceedings of 27th ACM SIGPLAN Conference on Object-Oriented Programming, Systems, Languages and Applications (OOPSLA)*, pages 395–410, Oct. 2012.
http://www.cs.stonybrook.edu/~liu/papers/DistPL-OOPSLA12.pdf

- Extended description of DistAlgo language and method appears in *ACM Transactions on Programming Languages and Systems (TOPLAS)*, Volume 39, Number 3, May 2017.
https://arxiv.org/pdf/1412.8461v3.pdf
- Open-source implementation is available on github and sourceforge, version 1.0 released Nov. 2016.
https://sites.google.com/site/distalgo

(4) Y. A. Liu, S. D. Stoller, and B. Lin. High-Level Executable Specifications of Distributed Algorithms. In *Proceedings of the 14th International Symposium on Stabilization, Safety, and Security of Distributed Systems (SSS)*, volume 7596 of LNCS, pages 95–110, Oct. 2012.
http://www.cs.stonybrook.edu/~liu/papers/DistSpec-SSS12.pdf

- This paper received the Best Student Paper Award.

Additional information and materials for the workshop will be made available at http://darlab.cs.stonybrook.edu/consensus, including presentation slides and executable specifications/programs in DistAlgo.

Biographies

Y. Annie Liu is a Professor of Computer Science at Stony Brook University. She received her BS from Peking University, MEng from Tsinghua University, and PhD from Cornell University. Her primary research is in languages and algorithms, and focuses specially on systematic methods for design and optimizations. The methods are centered around incrementalization, the discrete counterpart of differentiation in calculus. She has published in many prestigious venues, taught in a wide range of Computer Science areas, and presented over 100 conference and invited talks worldwide. Her awards include a State University of New York Chancellor's Award for Excellence in Scholarship and Creative Activities.

Scott D. Stoller is a Professor of Computer Science at Stony Brook University. He received his BS in Physics, summa cum laude, from Princeton University and his PhD in Computer Science from Cornell University. His primary research interests are design, analysis, optimization, testing, and verification of software, with focuses on computer security, concurrency, and incremental computation. He received an NSF CAREER Award, an ONR Young Investigator Award, a NASA Turning Goals Into Reality Award for Engineering Innovation, Best Paper Awards at Haifa Verification 2005, Runtime Verification 2011, and Data and Applications Security and Privacy 2016, and a SUNY Chancellor's Award for Excellence in Scholarship and Creative Activities.

Acknowledgments

We thank Leslie Lamport, Robbert van Renesse, Yair Amir, and Ken Birman for their clear explanations and helpful discussions about various consensus algorithms. We thank Bo Lin for his robust DistAlgo compiler with excellent support. We thank hundreds of students in distributed algorithms and distributed systems courses and projects for extending, developing variants of, testing, evaluating, and model checking our executable specifications, including running them on distributed machines, in the cloud, etc.

This material is based upon work supported in part by the National Science Foundation under Grants CCF 1414078, CCF 1248184, and CNS 1421893, and Office of Naval Research under Grant N000141512208. Any opinions, findings and conclusions or recommendations expressed in this material are those of the authors and do not necessarily reflect the views of the funding agencies.

REFERENCES

[1] Yanhong A. Liu, Saksham Chand, and Scott D. Stoller. 2019. Moderately Complex Paxos Made Simple: High-Level Executable Specification of Distributed Algorithm. *Computing Research Repository* arXiv:1704.00082 [cs.DC] (Jan. 2019), 24.

[2] Yanhong A. Liu. 2018. Logical Clocks Are Not Fair: What Is Fair? A Case Study of High-level Language and Optimization. In *Proceedings of the Workshop on Advanced Tools, Programming Languages, and Platforms for Implementing and Evaluating Algorithms for Distributed Systems*. ACM Press, 21–27.

[3] Yanhong A. Liu, Scott D. Stoller, Bo Lin, and Michael Gorbovitski. 2012. From Clarity to Efficiency for Distributed Algorithms. In *Proceedings of the 27th ACM SIGPLAN Conference on Object-Oriented Programming, Systems, Languages and Applications*. ACM Press, 395–410.

[4] Yanhong A. Liu, Scott D. Stoller, and Bo Lin. 2012. High-Level Executable Specifications of Distributed Algorithms. In *Proceedings of the 14th International Symposium on Stabilization, Safety, and Security of Distributed Systems*. Springer, 95–110.

[5] Yanhong A. Liu, Scott D. Stoller, and Bo Lin. 2017. From Clarity to Efficiency for Distributed Algorithms. *ACM Transactions on Programming Languages and Systems* 39, 3 (May 2017), 12:1–12:41.

Byzantine Fault Tolerant State Machine Replication in Any Programming Language

Ethan Buchman
Interchain Foundation
ethan@interchain.io

ABSTRACT

State machine replication is a fundamental primitive in fault tolerant distributed computing, but few production tools exist to support the replication of arbitrary state machines. The tools that do exist, like Apache Zookeeper, CoreOS's etcd, and Hashicorp's Consul, include an implementation of a consensus algorithm (eg. ZAB or Raft) for replication, and a service-discovery oriented key-value store as the state machine. While these tools can tolerate crash failures, they cannot tolerate malicious or adversarial ("Byzantine") faults.

We present Tendermint, a production-grade Byzantine Fault Tolerant State Machine Replication engine written in Go. Tendermint supports replication for state machines written in any language by using a socket protocol to communicate between the state machine and the replication engine. Tendermint is being used on the public internet today to secure upwards of $1 Billion USD in value, with deployments supporting hundreds of nodes. In this workshop, we provide an overview of the Tendermint system and demonstrate how to build Byzantine Fault Tolerant applications in Go and Javascript. We will also introduce the Cosmos Hub, an advanced Proof-of-Stake cryptocurrency system built on Tendermint.

CCS CONCEPTS

• **Computer systems organization** → **Reliability**; *Availability*; *Fault-tolerant network topologies*; • **Networks** → *Peer-to-peer networks*.

KEYWORDS

Byzantine Fault Tolerance, Replicated State Machine, Blockchain

ACM Reference Format:
Ethan Buchman. 2019. Byzantine Fault Tolerant State Machine Replication in Any Programming Language . In *2019 ACM Symposium on Principles of Distributed Computing (PODC '19), July 29-August 2, 2019, Toronto, ON, Canada.* ACM, New York, NY, USA, 1 page. https://doi.org/10.1145/3293611.3338023

PODC '19, July 29-August 2, 2019, Toronto, ON, Canada

ACM ISBN 978-1-4503-6217-7/19/07.
https://doi.org/10.1145/3293611.3338023

BIO

Ethan Buchman is an Internet Biophysicist. He received a BSc in Physical Science and a MASc in Engineering Systems and Computing, both from the University of Guelph. With background in cell biology, neuroscience, mathematics, machine learning, and distributed computing, his goal is to build tools that encourage humans to self-organize into functional systems, much like molecules managed to self-organize into Life. Ethan is a co-founder of the Tendermint and Cosmos projects, and currently serves as Technical Director of the Interchain Foundation, a non-profit with a mission to research, develop, and promote open, decentralized networks. He is focused primarily on building general purpose technology to support inter-operable replicated state machine on the public internet, and in proving their correctness. He also runs CoinCulture CryptoConsulting, which offers in-depth courses on blockchain technology for both non-technical and technical audiences.

Central Control over Distributed Asynchronous Systems: A Tutorial on Software-Defined Networks and Consistent Network Updates

Klaus-Tycho Foerster
klaus-tycho.foerster@univie.ac.at
Faculty of Computer Science, University of Vienna
Vienna, Austria

ABSTRACT

This tutorial will give an introduction to a topic that lies at the intersection of distributed computing and networking, and combines asynchronous distributed systems with central control, namely consistent updates in Software-Defined Networks (SDNs). We will give an overview on current models and algorithms, but also selected related topics, in particular those of potential interest to the PODC community, showcasing avenues for further research.

In more detail, SDNs have been an intensively studied topic in networking over the last years, but much of its focus has been on (logical) central control, abstracting away most of its underlying foundation, namely that a network is still a distributed asynchronous system at its core. Summarized in a simplified way, SDNs come with the promise that the network state can be optimized and updated from a global point of view. However, such a simplification becomes especially problematic when consistency guarantees have to maintained. In asynchronous distributed systems, it is not possible to simultaneously change the state of all nodes, such a naive approach will lead to an inconsistent mix of old and new states, introducing e.g. forwarding loops. Notwithstanding, most approaches tackle these issues from the viewpoints of the networking/systems communities, and we believe could henceforth greatly benefit from connections to and ideas from the PODC community.

CCS CONCEPTS

• Networks → Network management; • Theory of computation → Design and analysis of algorithms; • Computing methodologies → Distributed computing methodologies.

KEYWORDS

Software-Defined Networks, Asynchrony, Consistency, Congestion, Loops, Blackholes, Middleboxes, Migration, Updates

ACM Reference Format:

Klaus-Tycho Foerster. 2019. Central Control over Distributed Asynchronous Systems: A Tutorial on Software-Defined Networks and Consistent Network Updates. In *2019 ACM Symposium on Principles of Distributed Computing (PODC '19), July 29-August 2, 2019, Toronto, ON, Canada.* ACM, New York, NY, USA, 2 pages. https://doi.org/10.1145/3293611.3338024

PODC '19, July 29-August 2, 2019, Toronto, ON, Canada

ACM ISBN 978-1-4503-6217-7/19/07.
https://doi.org/10.1145/3293611.3338024

MATERIAL AND LITERATURE

The tutorial will be based on self-contained slides, please contact the author to obtain a copy or see http://www.foerster.me. While not all aspects of the tutorial are covered in the literature, a recent survey with an algorithmic focus can be found in [11]. Regarding consistency, we will follow the taxonomy introduced by Mahajan and Wattenhofer [8, 17], covering, e.g., 2-phase commits [20], loop freedom [2, 6, 13, 16], and congestion freedom [1, 3, 4, 14]. We will briefly note that even with perfectly timed synchrony [18], consistent updates are not trivial [5, 12, 22, 23]. Moreover, we will also showcase connections to topics such as proof labeling schemes [7, 15, 19, 21] and distributed control planes [9, 10, 21].

BIO

As of 2018, Klaus-Tycho Foerster is a postdoctoral researcher at the University of Vienna, Austria, working with Stefan Schmid. In 2017 he was a postdoc at Aalborg University, Denmark. He was a visiting researcher at Microsoft Research, Redmond, USA, working with Ratul Mahajan for Fall 2016. He received his PhD degree from ETH Zurich in September 2016, supervised by Roger Wattenhofer in the Distributed Computing Group, supported by Microsoft Research. He received best paper awards at IFIP Networking 2019 and at ICDCN 2016. His research interests revolve around algorithms and complexity for networked and distributed systems.

ACKNOWLEDGMENTS

The author would like to thank the PODC Workshop and Tutorial Chair Avery Miller for his support.

REFERENCES

[1] Saeed Akhoondian Amiri, Szymon Dudycz, Stefan Schmid, and Sebastian Wiederrecht. 2018. Congestion-Free Rerouting of Flows on DAGs. In *ICALP (LIPIcs)*, Vol. 107. Schloss Dagstuhl - Leibniz-Zentrum fuer Informatik, 143:1–143:13. https://doi.org/10.4230/LIPIcs.ICALP.2018.143

[2] Saeed Akhoondian Amiri, Arne Ludwig, Jan Marcinkowski, and Stefan Schmid. 2016. Transiently Consistent SDN Updates: Being Greedy is Hard. In *SIROCCO (Lecture Notes in Computer Science)*, Vol. 9988. 391–406. https://doi.org/10.1007/978-3-319-48314-6_25

[3] Sebastian Brandt, Klaus-Tycho Foerster, and Roger Wattenhofer. 2016. On consistent migration of flows in SDNs. In *INFOCOM*. IEEE, 1–9. https://doi.org/10.1109/INFOCOM.2016.7524332

[4] Klaus-Tycho Foerster. 2017. On the consistent migration of unsplittable flows: Upper and lower complexity bounds. In *NCA*. IEEE, 153–156. https://doi.org/10.1109/NCA.2017.8171348

[5] Klaus-Tycho Foerster. 2018. On the Consistent Migration of Splittable Flows: Latency-Awareness and Complexities. In *NCA*. IEEE, 1–4. https://doi.org/10.1109/NCA.2018.8548339

[6] Klaus-Tycho Foerster, Arne Ludwig, Jan Marcinkowski, and Stefan Schmid. 2018. Loop-Free Route Updates for Software-Defined Networks. *IEEE/ACM Trans. Netw.* 26, 1 (2018), 328–341. https://doi.org/10.1109/TNET.2017.2778426

[7] Klaus-Tycho Foerster, Thomas Luedi, Jochen Seidel, and Roger Wattenhofer. 2018. Local checkability, no strings attached: (A)cyclicity, reachability, loop free updates in SDNs. *Theor. Comput. Sci.* 709 (2018), 48–63. https://doi.org/10.1016/j.tcs.2016.11.018

[8] Klaus-Tycho Foerster, Ratul Mahajan, and Roger Wattenhofer. 2016. Consistent updates in software defined networks: On dependencies, loop freedom, and blackholes. In *Networking*. IEEE Computer Society, 1–9. https://doi.org/10.1109/IFIPNetworking.2016.7497232

[9] Klaus-Tycho Foerster, Juho Hirvonen, Stefan Schmid, and Jukka Suomela. 2019. On the Power of Preprocessing in Decentralized Network Optimization. In *INFOCOM*. IEEE.

[10] Klaus-Tycho Foerster, Janne H. Korhonen, Joel Rybicki, and Stefan Schmid. 2019. Brief Announcement: Does Preprocessing Help under Congestion?. In *PODC*.

[11] Klaus-Tycho Foerster, Stefan Schmid, and Stefano Vissicchio. 2019. Survey of Consistent Software-Defined Network Updates. *IEEE Communications Surveys Tutorials* (2019). https://doi.org/10.1109/COMST.2018.2876749

[12] Klaus-Tycho Foerster, Laurent Vanbever, and Roger Wattenhofer. 2019. Latency and Consistent Flow Migration: Relax for Lossless Updates. In *IFIP Networking*.

[13] Klaus-Tycho Förster and Roger Wattenhofer. 2016. The Power of Two in Consistent Network Updates: Hard Loop Freedom, Easy Flow Migration. In *ICCCN*. IEEE, 1–9. https://doi.org/10.1109/ICCCN.2016.7568583

[14] Chi-Yao Hong, Srikanth Kandula, Ratul Mahajan, Ming Zhang, Vijay Gill, Mohan Nanduri, and Roger Wattenhofer. 2013. Achieving high utilization with software-driven WAN. In *SIGCOMM*. ACM, 15–26. https://doi.org/10.1145/2486001.2486012

[15] Amos Korman, Shay Kutten, and David Peleg. 2005. Proof labeling schemes. In *PODC*. ACM, 9–18. https://doi.org/10.1145/1073814.1073817

[16] Arne Ludwig, Jan Marcinkowski, and Stefan Schmid. 2015. Scheduling Loop-free Network Updates: It's Good to Relax!. In *PODC*. ACM, 13–22. https://doi.org/10.1145/2767386.2767412

[17] Ratul Mahajan and Roger Wattenhofer. 2013. On consistent updates in software defined networks. In *HotNets*. ACM, 20:1–20:7. https://doi.org/10.1145/2535771.2535791

[18] Tal Mizrahi, Efi Saat, and Yoram Moses. 2016. Timed Consistent Network Updates in Software-Defined Networks. *IEEE/ACM Trans. Netw.* 24, 6 (2016), 3412–3425. https://doi.org/10.1109/TNET.2016.2529058

[19] Thanh Dang Nguyen, Marco Chiesa, and Marco Canini. 2017. Decentralized Consistent Updates in SDN. In *SOSR*. ACM, 21–33. https://doi.org/10.1145/3050220.3050224

[20] Mark Reitblatt, Nate Foster, Jennifer Rexford, Cole Schlesinger, and David Walker. 2012. Abstractions for network update. In *SIGCOMM*. ACM, 323–334. https://doi.org/10.1145/2342356.2342427

[21] Stefan Schmid and Jukka Suomela. 2013. Exploiting locality in distributed SDN control. In *HotSDN*. ACM, 121–126. https://doi.org/10.1145/2491185.2491198

[22] Jiaqi Zheng, Guihai Chen, Stefan Schmid, Haipeng Dai, Jie Wu, and Qiang Ni. 2017. Scheduling Congestion- and Loop-Free Network Update in Timed SDNs. *IEEE Journal on Selected Areas in Communications* 35, 11 (2017), 2542–2552. https://doi.org/10.1109/JSAC.2017.2760146

[23] Jiaqi Zheng, Bo Li, Chen Tian, Klaus-Tycho Foerster, Stefan Schmid, Guihai Chen, Jie Wu, and Rui Li. 2019. Congestion-Free Rerouting of Multiple Flows in Timed SDNs. *IEEE Journal on Selected Areas in Communications* 37, 5 (2019), 968–981. https://doi.org/10.1109/JSAC.2019.2906741

Tutorial: Specifying, Implementing, and Verifying Algorithms for Persistent Memory

Diego Cepeda
University of Waterloo
Electrical and Computer Engineering
Waterloo, Ontario, Canada
dcepeda@uwaterloo.ca

Sakib Chowdhury
University of Waterloo
Electrical and Computer Engineering
Waterloo, Ontario, Canada
sm6chowd@uwaterloo.ca

Wojciech Golab
University of Waterloo
Electrical and Computer Engineering
Waterloo, Ontario, Canada
wgolab@uwaterloo.ca

ABSTRACT

High-density byte-addressable non-volatile memory became a reality earlier this year when Intel launched the long-awaited Optane™ persistent memory module. This tutorial is intended for researchers interested in using persistent memory to construct fault-tolerant data structures that can maintain state consistently across power outages and system crashes without relying on conventional secondary storage. A number of practical and theoretical topics will be covered including hardware purchasing considerations, operating system and programming language support for persistent memory, definitions of correctness properties for fault-tolerant data structures, techniques for implementing fault-tolerant concurrency control and memory management, as well as verification of correctness.

CCS CONCEPTS

• **Theory of computation → Shared memory algorithms.**

KEYWORDS

concurrency; shared memory; persistent memory; fault tolerance

ACM Reference Format:
Diego Cepeda, Sakib Chowdhury, and Wojciech Golab. 2019. Tutorial: Specifying, Implementing, and Verifying Algorithms for Persistent Memory. In *2019 ACM Symposium on Principles of Distributed Computing (PODC '19), July 29-August 2, 2019, Toronto, ON, Canada.* ACM, New York, NY, USA, 1 page. https://doi.org/10.1145/3293611.3338025

PODC '19, July 29-August 2, 2019, Toronto, ON, Canada

ACM ISBN 978-1-4503-6217-7/19/07.
https://doi.org/10.1145/3293611.3338025

AUTHOR BIOGRAPHIES

Diego Cepeda graduated from the University of Monterrey in 2016 with a degree in Electronics Technologies and Robotics Engineering. During his undergraduate studies, he visited Tokyo University of Technology as an exchange student, and worked on an autonomous quadcopter vision system. After graduation, he spent two years working in industry as an Embedded Software Engineer. He is currently pursuing a Master of Applied Science degree in Electrical and Computer Engineering at the University of Waterloo.

Sakib Chowdhury graduated from the University of Windsor in 2018 with a degree in Electrical Engineering. During his undergraduate studies, he developed a myoelectrically-controlled robotic arm that could be remotely operated over the Internet as his Capstone project. He joined the University of Waterloo in 2018, and is pursuing a Master of Applied Science degree in Electrical and Computer Engineering. His research interests include analyzing linearizability in shared objects for persistent memory.

Wojciech Golab received his PhD degree in computer science from the University of Toronto in 2010. After a post-doctoral fellowship at the University of Calgary, he spent two years as a research scientist at Hewlett-Packard Labs in Palo Alto, and then joined the University of Waterloo in 2012. He is presently an Associate Professor in the Department of Electrical and Computer Engineering. His research focuses on algorithmic problems in distributed computing with applications to storage and processing of large data sets. His theoretical work on shared memory algorithms won the best paper award at DISC 2008 (shared with Robert Danek), and was distinguished by the ACM Computing Reviews as one of 91 "notable computing items published in 2012". Dr. Golab's research on software techniques for persistent memory is sponsored in part by an Ontario Early Researcher Award, and by a Google Faculty Research Award.

Author Index

NOTES

www.ingramcontent.com/pod-product-compliance
Lightning Source LLC
LaVergne TN
LVHW082016200926
848481LV00010B/2869
9781450362177